RANDOM HOUSE
WEBSTER'S

Quotationary

RANDOM HOUSE
WEBSTER'S
QUOTATIONARY

Leonard Roy Frank
Editor

Random House
New York

Random House Webster's Quotationary

This book is available for special purchases in bulk by organizations and institutions,
not for resale, at special discounts. Please direct your inquiries to the Random House
Special Sales Department, toll-free 888-591-1200 or fax 212-572-4961.

Please address inquiries about electronic licensing of this division's products, for use
on a network or in software or on CD-ROM, to the Subsidiary Rights Department,
Random House Reference & Information Publishing, fax 212-940-7370.

Visit the Random House Web site at www.randomhouse.com

Typeset and printed in the United States of America.

Random House Webster's quotationary: the authoritative source for over 20,000 quotations / [edited] by Leonard Roy Frank.
       p.   cm.
Includes bibliographical references and index.
ISBN 0-679-44850-0 (alk. paper)
1. Quotations, English. I. Frank, Leonard Roy.
PN6081.R29   1998
082—dc211   98-30433
                                                             CIP

First Edition
0 9 8 7 6 5 4 3 2 1
November 1998

ISBN 0-679-44850-0

New York Toronto London Sydney Auckland

❦ CONTENTS ❦

❧ ACKNOWLEDGMENTS ❧

I am indebted to many people for their important contributions to the *Quotationary*. For many years, my friend Wade Hudson has been a constant source of insight and strength. Mike Larsen and Elizabeth Pomada, my literary agents, generously gave of their time when I sought their advice and support. With the patient assistance of Robert Arbegast I was able to unravel the mysteries of the computer. Max Millard was helpful with editing suggestions. A number of librarians provided me with valuable research assistance: these included Cecil White (St. Patrick's Seminary Library, Menlo Park), Victor Fischer (University of California's Mark Twain Project, Berkeley), and Sally Fernandez, Van Luong, Ron Romano, Linda Suzuki, Gary Wong, and Erik Zea (San Francisco Public Library's Interlibrary Service). At Random House I had the good fortune to work with several outstanding people: including Charles Levine, Sol Steinmetz, Andy Ambraziejus, and Megan Schade. David Seham, Gregory Orpilla, and associates of KP Company, pitched in wholeheartedly during the book's final production phase. To each of them I wish to express my deep appreciation.

❦ INTRODUCTION ❦

Books like the *Quotationary* can transmit and shape culture. They contain what their editors regard as the best examples of the wit and wisdom accumulated up through their own time. The material is often familiar; but, what is unfamiliar may, owing to its inclusion in a quotation book, become familiar throughout a community, or even society at large, reappearing in other writings or popularized through word of mouth. Thus, the publication of a quotation book is a cultural event, with the potential to initiate, hasten, slow, stop, or reverse changes in the thinking of those who are exposed to its contents.

The *Random House Webster's Quotationary* consists of more than 20,000 quotations, aphorisms, observations, factual statements, song lyrics, sayings, slogans, titles (of books, plays, stories, etc.), and phrases organized in more than 1,000 subject categories. Combining the words quotation and dictionary, I coined the term "quotationary" to designate a book of quotations arranged alphabetically by subject. What words are to a dictionary, ideas are to the *Quotationary*.

My overall purpose in compiling the *Quotationary* has been to set down in a single volume the most interesting, well-phrased thoughts and observations that I have discovered over a course of study and reading that began nearly 40 years ago. I wanted the *Quotationary* to be: (1) a readable source for inspiring, challenging, instructive, and amusing information and knowledge; (2) a reliable, easy-to-use reference work for finding the precise wording, authors, and sources of quotations; (3) a storehouse of ideas in cross-referenced categories to stimulate thought and imagination; (4) a catalyst for creative personal and social change; and (5) a history of ideas, an overview of culture, a way to introduce oneself with relative ease to the wit, wisdom, knowledge, and ignorance of the ages.

Toward these ends, I used the following criteria in the selection of individual entries: (1) truth, wisdom, beauty, or a popular belief or opinion, (2) significance, (3) originality in content or form, (4) articulateness and terseness, (5) wit, humor, and irony, (6) comprehensibility independent of context, (7) category suitability, (8) a guide to conduct and growth, (9) a counterpoint to a truth, popular belief, or opinion, and (10) an expression of the author's (or the subject's) personality, character, or place in the social consciousness.

My studies, which laid the groundwork for the *Quotationary,* began in 1959 soon after taking stock of myself at age 27 and finding that my education had been entirely too narrow. Rather than return to school, I decided to undertake a course of self-education. I began reading mostly non-fiction books. Operating on the principle that a book worth reading was worth owning,* I accumulated an extensive library. Owning the books enabled me to mark and annotate them. With the more important books, I would review the marked portions, and record the best materials in loose-leaf notebooks, often making double entries by subject and author. In this way I fixed and organized the ideas in my mind. Memory

---

*See John Ruskin in "Books," p. 68.

of them was further strengthened when in reviewing the notebooks periodically I would redo particular sections that had become cumbersome and disorganized.

For many years, I continued this course of self-education for my own benefit, with no plan to compile the material for publication. This changed in 1986, when I bought my first personal computer. Since then, the *Quotationary* has almost fully occupied my attention.

I immediately began transferring the best entries from the notebooks to the computer, organizing them in categories. I soon realized, however, that some entries were inaccurate or incomplete, or lacking in citation information. This compelled me to return to the original sources, most of which remained in my personal library.

It was not long before I started reviewing the marked portions of all my books without regard to what had been previously recorded in the notebooks. I would then enter the most quoteworthy thoughts, a tiny part of all the marked material, directly into the computer according to their appropriate categories. The number of categories expanded organically as I went along. A bulky category seemingly announced its need to be divided; for example, the original category "Belief" eventually broke down into the categories "Belief," "Faith," and "Faith and Reason."

While engaged in this work, I continued my studies with newly purchased books and books borrowed from libraries. Selections from these works and from non-book sources, including newspapers, magazines, songs, films, television, and letters and conversation with friends and acquaintances have also been included in the *Quotationary*.

Previously published collections of quotations and proverbs were another rich source of material. When I found entries suitable for my collection I would attempt to track down the original sources to verify the wording and/or to find specific citation information. Of special importance was locating the chapter, section, act, etc., in which the quote appeared when this information, as was often the case, was missing in the secondary source. It was sometimes necessary to scour large portions of books to find an item. However, I never regretted this time-consuming activity because citation specifics would allow readers to check the context of particular entries. Moreover, conducting these searches led to my discovering many other quotations that were eventually placed in the book.

For any mistakes in the text, I take full responsibility. Readers are invited to send corrections and additional citation information to Random House at the address on the copyright page. While I have striven for diversity, readers will note that certain subjects, cultural groups, and authors are either neglected or underrepresented. It is hoped that later editions of the *Quotationary* will reflect my own growing knowledge and awareness, or that of future editors. To paraphrase Michelangelo, we are all still learning.*

---

*See Michelangelo, in "Learning (Process)," p. 449

❦ USING THE QUOTATIONARY ❦

Because the subject categories in the *Quotationary* are clearly organized and arranged alphabetically, readers will be able to go directly to the appropriate category for specific quotations and subjects. A quotation's key word, or a variant of that word, is often the same as the category heading.

To further assist readers in searching for quotations a comprehensive Index by Author or Source is provided toward the end of the book. The entries of this index comprise an alphabetical listing of all the authors included in the *Quotationary*. Under each author's name is an alphabetical listing of categories containing quotes from that author as well as the page number on which a quote or quotes, where there is more than one quote in a category by the same author, appear.

The alphabetically arranged Index of Subject Categories following the Index of Authors provides readers with quick access to the *Quotationary's* full range of subjects.

Another tool to aid research is extensive cross-referencing, which is explained with examples in the section immediately below. Many quotations could have been placed in two or more categories. Rather than repeating such quotations, the most suitable category was chosen.

CROSS-REFERENCING

One of the first things that readers will notice when using the *Quotationary*, which sets it apart from other such reference sources, is the use of extensive cross-referencing. Related categories and quotations are cross-referenced immediately beneath each category heading. For example:

AUTOBIOGRAPHY

See also • Biography ○ Books ○ Fiction: Alberto Moravia ○ Journals ○ Memoirs: [especially] Gore Vidal ○ Writing

Where an author's name immediately follows a colon (for example: "Fiction: Alberto Moravia"), the cross-reference is to that author's quotation and not to the category generally. Where an author's name immediately follows the word "especially" in brackets (for example: "Memoirs: [especially] Gore Vidal"), the cross-reference is to that author's quotation and to the category generally. Other related quotations, especially those similar in content or form, are cross-referenced immediately beneath individual entries.

Cross-Referencing Related Quotations Similar in Content:

If men and women are in chains anywhere in the world, then freedom is endangered everywhere.
> JOHN F. KENNEDY (1917-1963). Campaign statement, Washington, 2 October 1960
> See Injustice: Martin Luther King, Jr.

Injustice anywhere is a threat to justice everywhere.
> MARTIN LUTHER KING, JR. (1929-1968). "Letter from Birmingham City Jail," 16 April 1963
> See Slavery: John F. Kennedy

Cross-Referencing Related Quotations Similar in Form:

Nothing succeeds like success.
> ALEXANDRE DUMAS (1802-1870). *Ange Pitou*, 1.7, 1853
> See Excess: Oscar Wilde

Nothing succeeds like excess.
> OSCAR WILDE (1854-1900). *A Woman of No Importance*, 3, 1894
> See Success: Alexandre Dumas

ENTRIES

The entries in each category are alphabetically arranged by author. Multiple entries by an author in a category are arranged chronologically. We have departed from tradition by placing "anonymous" entries, sayings, and slogans toward the end of each category — giving more prominence to identified authors.

Spelling, punctuation, and hyphenation are Americanized, except for titles in the citations where the original English spelling is kept. For example:

> LORD BYRON (1788-1824). *Childe Harold's Pilgrimage*, 4.178, 1812-1818

Original spelling is kept when its uniqueness is integral to the author's style, as in the writings of Josh Billings, Finley Peter Dunne [Mr. Dooley], Artemus Ward, and Walt Whitman. For example:

> Natur dont put on enny airs.
> > JOSH BILLINGS (1818-1885). "Bred and Butter," *Everybody's Friend, or; Josh Billing's Encyclopedia and Proverbial Philosophy of Wit and Humor*, 1874

Where an entry consists of a dialogue between two parties, the formatting is often adapted (and is so indicated in the citation). For example, the first entry below appears in the original source; the second is its adaptation in the *Quotationary,*

> Léon Delbecque came to him in great distress. "General," he lamented, "all of my friends say you are deserting us. They want me to get you to change your Algerian policy. What should I do?" De Gaulle snapped back, "Change your friends."

> *Léon Delbecque* (in great distress): General, all of my friends say you are deserting us. They want me to get you to change your Algerian policy. What should I do?
> *De Gaulle* (snapping back): Change your friends.
> > CHARLES de GAULLE (1890-1970). Format adapted. In David Schoenbrun, *The Three Lives of Charles de Gaulle*, 4, 1968

Where a quotation is popularly known in words different from those in an original source, both versions are included:

> When they are at Rome, they do there as they see done.
> > ROBERT BURTON (1577-1640). *The Anatomy of Melancholy*, 3.4.2.1, 1621-1651 (Popular version: When in Rome, do as the Romans do.)

CITATIONS

Page numbers are included when chapters, sections, etc. are not used in the cited source:

Page Number

> ALBERT CAMUS (1913-1960). *The Fall,* (p. 58,) tr. Justin O'Brien, 1956

Otherwise chapter, section, act, stanza, line, etc., are included to make it easy for readers to refer directly to the original sources for context:

Chapter

> LEWIS CARROLL (1832-1898). *Through the Looking-Glass and What Alice Found There,* (4,) 1872

Chapter and Section

> DANIEL J. BOORSTIN (1914-). *The Image: A Guide to Pseudo-Events in America,* (5.4,) 1961

Act, Scene, Line

> SHAKESPEARE (1564-1616). *King Henry VIII,* (3.2.379,) 1612

Entry Number

> LA ROCHEFOUCAULD (1613-1680). *Maxims,* (271,) 1665, tr. Louis Kronenberger, 1959

Book and Line

> JOHN MILTON (1608-1674). *Paradise Lost,* (8.561,) 1667

Volume and Page

> ARNOLD J. TOYNBEE (1889-1975). *A Study of History,* (12.135,) 1961

For entries drawn from newspapers and magazines, the title of the article, and the day, month and year are generally included:

> MAUREEN DOWD (1952-). ("Camelot 144," *New York Times,* 25 April 1996)

An author's ethnicity and profession (or just his or her profession in the case of Americans) are included in the citation where such information adds significance and/or authenticity to an entry:

> A President's authority is not as great as his responsibility.
> > THEODORE C. SORENSEN (1928-). (Presidential assistant to John F. Kennedy.) *Decision-Making in the White House: The Olive Branch or the Arrows*, 3, 1963

If a quotation does not stand on its own, contextual information is provided in the citation:

It always appeared a most iniquitous scheme to me—to fight ourselves for what we are daily robbing and plundering from those who have as good a right to freedom as we have.
ABIGAIL ADAMS (1744-1818). On slavery and the struggle for American independence from England, letter to her husband John, 24 September 1774

Useful supplemental information is supplied for many entries: (1) Wherever possible, the author or speaker of a *Bible* quotation is given in the citation along with book, chapter, and verse. (2) Each Shakespeare quotation, in addition to being fully cited, is preceded by the name of the character who spoke it. Characters are sometimes identified in specific entries from the writings of other authors as well.

Entries drawn from edited books are dealt with in two different ways:

If the book contains only the author's writings, the editor's name appears after the title:

THOMAS MERTON (1915-1968). "Creative Silence," *Love and Living*, ed. Naomi Burton Stone, 1985

If the book has multiple authors, the editor's name appears before the title:

OCTAVIA WALDO (1929-). "Roman Spring." In Don Wolfe, ed., *American Scene*, 1963

Entries translated into English generally include the translator's name:

There is only one morality... just as there is only one geometry.
VOLTAIRE (1694-1778). "Morality," *Philosophical Dictionary*, 1764, tr. Theodore Besterman, 1971

A NOTE ON SOURCES

Unless otherwise indicated (as in the example below), *Bible* entries are taken from *The Holy Bible: Revised Standard Version*, 1952 (1881-1885):

How long halt ye between two opinions?
ELIJAH (9th cent. B.C.). *1 Kings* 18:21 (King James Version)

Entries from the journals and notebooks of Ralph Waldo Emerson are taken from the edition published by The Belknap Press of The Harvard University Press, *The Journal and Miscellaneous Notebooks of Ralph Waldo Emerson* (16 volumes), edited by William H. Gilman, 1960-1982.

Entries from the letters and speeches of Abraham Lincoln are generally taken from The Library of America's *Abraham Lincoln: Speeches and Writings* (two volumes), 1989.

Entries from the plays and poems of William Shakespeare are taken from *The Complete Works of Shakespeare* (one volume), edited by Hardin Craig, 1961, based on the Globe edition of Shakespeare's works, edited by William George Clark and William Aldis Wright, 1864.

Entries from the journals of Henry David Thoreau are taken from Dover Publications' *The Journal of Henry D. Thoreau* (two volumes), edited by Bradford Torrey and Francis H. Allen, 1962.

Entries from the writings of Oscar Wilde are taken from Dorset Press's *The Complete Works of Oscar Wilde* (one volume), undated.

ABBREVIATIONS

abr. (abridged)

comp. (compiler)

comps. (compilers)

ed. (editor)

eds. (editors)

p. (page)

rec. (recorder)

rev. (revised)

rev. ed. (revised edition)

tr. (translator)

ABILITY

See also • Excellence ○ Genius ○ Genius & Talent ○ Skill ○ Talent ○ Trade (Occupation)

He can fit his sails to every wind.
> JOHN CLARKE (1596–1658). Comp., *Proverbs: English and Latine,* p. 282, 1639

Efficiency is concerned with doing things right. Effectiveness is doing the right things.
> PETER F. DRUCKER (1909–). *Management: Tasks, Responsibilities, Practices,* 2, 1974, abr., 1977

I like people who can do things.
> RALPH WALDO EMERSON (1803–1882). Journal, 1846, undated

The acquisition of one sort of ability often makes that of another unlikely, if not impossible. . . . To take the gifts one does have, to concentrate one's strength upon their development, to disallow distractions—none of these is an easy task.
> JOSEPH EPSTEIN (1928–). *Ambition: The Secret Passion,* 7, 1980

There are many rare Abilities in the World, which Fortune never brings to Light.
> THOMAS FULLER (1654–1734). Comp., *Gnomologia: Adages and Proverbs,* 4855, 1732

The winds and the waves are always on the side of the ablest navigators.
> EDWARD GIBBON (1737–1794). *The Decline and Fall of the Roman Empire,* 68, 1776–1788

Men are in numberless instances qualified for certain things, for no other reason than because they are qualified for nothing else.
> WILLIAM HAZLITT (1778–1830). "On the Qualifications Necessary to Success in Life," *Table Talk,* 1822

A special ability means a heavy expenditure of energy in a particular direction, with a consequent drain from some other side of life.
> CARL G. JUNG (1875–1961). *Modern Man in Search of a Soul,* 8.2, tr. W. S. Dell and Cary F. Baynes, 1933

The workman is known by his work.
> LA FONTAINE (1621–1695). *Fables,* 1.21, 1668-1679

The implements to him who can handle them.
> NAPOLEON (1769–1821). In Thomas Carlyle, "The Hero as King," *On Heroes, Hero-Worship, and the Heroic in History,* 1841
> See Leaders & Staff: John Clarke

An able bad Man is an ill Instrument, and to be shunned as the Plague.
> WILLIAM PENN (1644–1718). *Some Fruits of Solitude,* 257, 1693

If you can do anything better than anybody else, this old country is so constituted they want to see you get all you can out of it.
> WILL ROGERS (1879–1935). Weekly column, 6 December 1925, *The Will Rogers Book,* 1.12, comp., Paula McSpadden Love, 1961

Every man loves what he is good at.
> THOMAS SHADWELL (1642–1692). *A True Widow,* 5.1, 1679

❦

Ability without ambition is like kindling wood without the spark.
> ANONYMOUS

He is not a mason who refuses a stone.
> SAYING (FRENCH)

ABORTION

See also • Birth Control ○ Conservatives & Liberals/Radicals: N. Sally Hass ○ Fathers ○ Killing ○ Mothers ○ Parents ○ Sex

This right of privacy, whether it be founded in the Fourteenth Amendment's concept of personal liberty and restrictions upon state action, as we feel it is, or, as the District Court determined, in the Ninth Amendment's reservation of rights to the people, is broad enough to encompass a woman's decision whether or not to terminate her pregnancy.
> HARRY A. BLACKMUN (1908–). *Roe v. Wade,* 1973

A woman's right to choose an abortion is] something central to a woman's life, to her dignity. . . . And when government controls that decision for her, she's being treated as less than a full adult human being responsible for her own choices.
> RUTH BADER GINSBURG (1933–). In Clare Cushman, ed., *The Supreme Court Justices: Illustrated Biographies, 1789-1995,* p. 535, 1995

The cemetery of the victims of human cruelty in our century is extended to include yet another vast cemetery, that of the unborn.
> POPE JOHN PAUL II (1920–). In *Observer* (British newspaper), 9 June 1991

If men could get pregnant, abortion would be a sacrament.
> FLORYNCE R. KENNEDY (1916–). In Gloria Steinem, "The Verbal Karate of Florynce R. Kennedy, Esq.," *Ms.,* March 1973

The preservation of life seems to be rather a slogan than a genuine goal of the anti-abortion forces; what they want is control. Control over behavior: power over women. Women in the anti-choice movement want to share in male power over women, and do so by denying their own womanhood, their own rights and responsibilities.
> URSULA K. LE GUIN (1929–). "The Princess," address before National Abortion Rights Action League, Portland (Maine), January 1982

I've noticed that everybody that is for abortion has already been born.
> RONALD REAGAN (1911–). Televised presidential campaign debate, Baltimore, 21 September 1980

❦

How can a moral wrong be a civil right?
> SLOGAN (AMERICAN). Anti-abortion position, 1990s

ABSTINENCE

See also • Asceticism ○ Chastity ○ Desire ○ Disease: Benjamin Franklin (2) ○ Excess ○ Hunger ○ Lust ○ Moderation ○ Passion ○ Pleasure ○ Prudery ○ Puritanism ○ Self-Control ○ Self-Denial ○ Self-Discipline ○ Sex

The way to avoid evil is not by maiming our passions, but by compelling them to yield their vigor to our moral nature. Thus they become, as in the ancient fable, the harnessed steeds which bear the chariot of the sun.

> HENRY WARD BEECHER (1813–1887). *Life Thoughts*, p. 76, rec. Edna Dean Proctor, 1858

Abstainer, *n.* A weak person who yields to the temptation of denying himself a pleasure.

> AMBROSE BIERCE (1842–1914). *The Devil's Dictionary*, p. 9, 1911, Dover edition, 1958

He who desires but acts not breeds pestilence.

> WILLIAM BLAKE (1757–1827). "Proverbs of Hell," *The Marriage of Heaven and Hell*, 7.5, 1790-1793?

Abstinence sows sand all over
The ruddy limbs and flaming hair,
But Desire Gratified
Plants fruits of life and beauty there.

> WILLIAM BLAKE (1757–1827). "Poems and Fragments from the Note-Book," 40, 1793?, *The Complete Writings of William Blake*, ed. Geoffrey Keynes, 1966

We did the proper thing but lost love.

> JOHN BOORMAN (1933–). *Hope and Glory* (film), 1987

I know a man who gave up smoking, drinking, sex, and rich food. He was healthy right up to the time he killed himself.

> JOHNNY CARSON (1925–). Television entertainment-program host. *The Tonight Show*, NBC, 20 November 1984

To abstain completely from all enjoyments may be easy. Yet to enjoy life and retain spiritual integrity—there is the challenge.

> ABRAHAM JOSHUA HESCHEL (1907–1972), *A Passion for Truth*, 4, 1973

Disuse is misuse.

> ELBERT HUBBARD (1856–1915). *A Thousand and One Epigrams*, p. 162, 1911

Abstinence is as easy to me as *temperance* would be difficult.

> SAMUEL JOHNSON (1709–1784). In William Roberts, *Memoirs of the Life and Correspondence of Mrs. Hannah More*, p. 249, 1834

The first thing men do when they have renounced pleasure, through decency, lassitude, or for the sake of health, is to condemn it in others. Such conduct denotes a kind of latent affection for the very things they left off; they would like no one to enjoy a pleasure they can no longer indulge in; and thus they show their feelings of jealousy.

> LA BRUYÈRE (1645–1696). "Of Mankind" (112), *The Characters*, 1688, tr. Henri van Laun, 1929

Abstinence is the beginning of saintliness.

> M. H. LUZZATTO (1707–1747). Jewish cabalist. *Mesillat Yesharim*, 13, 1740

This detachment (poverty, chastity, etc.) must not be mere amputation; everything which is shaken off must be simultaneously found again at a higher level.

> GABRIEL MARCEL (1889–1973). In Victor Gollancz, comp., *Man and God: Passages Chosen and Arranged to Express a Mood About the Human and Divine*, 5.1.3, 1951

When either a man or a woman makes a special vow, the vow of a Nazarite, to separate himself to the Lord, he shall separate himself from wine and strong drink.

> MOSES (14th cent. B.C.). *Numbers* 6:2-3

Abstinence is the best medicine.

> PETER PERCIVAL. Comp., *Tamil Proverbs with Their English Translations*, 1074, 1842

A life which goes excessively against natural impulse is . . . likely to involve effects of strain that may be quite as bad as indulgence in forbidden impulses would have been. People who live a life which is unnatural beyond a point are likely to be filled with envy, malice and uncharitableness.

> BERTRAND RUSSELL (1872–1970). *Authority and the Individual*, 1, 1949
> See Puritanism: Russell (1)

Refrain tonight,
And that shall lend a kind of easiness
To the next abstinence.

> SHAKESPEARE (1564–1616). *Hamlet*, 3.4.165, 1600

The stoical scheme of supplying our wants by lopping off our desires, is like cutting off our feet when we want shoes.

> JONATHAN SWIFT (1667–1745). "Thoughts on Various Subjects" (expanded from a version published in 1711), *Miscellanies in Prose and Verse* (published with Alexander Pope), vol. 1, 1727

One who causes himself pain by abstinence from something he desires is called a sinner.

> TALMUD (A.D. 1st–6th cent.). Rabbinical writings. In Louis I. Newman, comp., *The Talmudic Anthology*, 1, 1945

We are punished for our refusals. Every impulse that we strive to strangle broods in the mind, and poisons us. The body sins once, and has done with its sin, for action is a mode of purification. Nothing remains then but the recollection of a pleasure, or the luxury of a regret.

> OSCAR WILDE (1854–1900). *The Picture of Dorian Gray*, 2, 1891

❧

If you resolve to give up smoking, drinking and loving, you don't actually live longer, it just seems longer.

> ANONYMOUS. Quoted by Clement Freud. In *Observer*, 27 December 1964

Abstinence is a good thing, but it should always be practiced in moderation.

> ANONYMOUS

Abstinence signifies higher purpose, moral scruples, lack of opportunity, lack of satisfaction, fear of punishment, or incapacity.

> ANONYMOUS

He begins to die who quits his desires.

> SAYING (ENGLISH)

When in doubt, do without.

> SAYING (VERMONT). In Wolfgang Mieder, comp., "Money and Thriftiness," *Talk Less and Say More: Vermont Proverbs*, 1986

ACCIDENT

See also • Chance

Men's accidents are God's purposes.
> SOPHIA A. HAWTHORNE (1810?–1871). In Nathaniel Hawthorne, 1 June 1842, *The American Notebooks*, ed. Claude M. Simpson, 1932

Accident is the name one gives to the coincidence of events, of which one does not know the causation. . . . Accidents only exist in our heads, in our limited perceptions.
> FRANZ KAFKA (1883–1924). In Gustav Janouch, *Conversations with Kafka*, p. 55, tr. Goronwy Rees, 1953

Accident is something relative. It appears only at the point of intersection of *inevitable* processes.
> GEORGE PLEKHANOV (1856–1918). *The Role of the Individual in History*, 6, 1898

Accident is the mother of invention.
> SAYING (AMERICAN)
> See Invention: Gerald Brenan ○ Necessity: Plato (2)

ACHIEVEMENT

See also • Dignity: Arnold J. Toynbee ○ Enthusiasm: Samuel Taylor Coleridge ○ Envy: Helmut Schoeck ○ Excellence ○ Greatness ○ Success

I have no faith in act of parliament reform. All the great—the permanently great—things that have been achieved in the world have been so achieved by individuals, working from the instinct of genius or of goodness.
> SAMUEL TAYLOR COLERIDGE (1772–1834). 24 July 1832, *Table Talk*, 1835

None of us will ever accomplish anything excellent or commanding except when he listens to this whisper which is heard by him alone.
> RALPH WALDO EMERSON (1803–1882). "Greatness," *Letters and Social Aims*, 1876

His momentous achievements are rarely the result of a clean forward thrust but rather of a soul intensity generated in front of an apparently insurmountable obstacle which bars his way to a cherished goal.
> ERIC HOFFER (1902–1983). *The Ordeal of Change*, 15.5, 1964

There are some things one can only achieve by a deliberate leap in the opposite direction.
> FRANZ KAFKA (1883–1924). In Gustav Janouch, *Conversations with Kafka*, p. 107, tr. Goronwy Rees, 1953

All truly great achievements in history resulted from the actualization of principles, not from the clever evaluation of political conditions.
> HENRY A. KISSINGER. (1923–). "The Meaning of History: Reflections on Spengler, Toynbee and Kant" (unpublished undergraduate thesis), 1950

ACTING

See also • Actors ○ Art ○ Directors ○ Films ○ Theater

Acting is an empty and useless profession.
> MARLON BRANDO (1924–)

The most important thing in acting is honesty: if you can fake that, you've got it made.
> GEORGE BURNS (1896–1996). In news reports, 31 December 1984

An actor lends more force to a tragic character the more careful he is not to exaggerate it.
> ALBERT CAMUS (1913–1960). "Appendix: Franz Kafka," *The Myth of Sisyphus*, 1942, tr. Justin O'Brien, 1955

You never caught him acting.
> FRANK CAPRA (1897–1991). Director. On James Stewart, recalled on Stewart's death, 2 July 1997

Learn the lines and don't bump into the furniture.
> NOEL COWARD (1899–1973). Attributed. Advice to actors

An actor's most notable effects depend upon his skill in producing the appearance of emotion when he is keeping strong control of himself.
> CHARLES de GAULLE (1890–1970). "Of Prestige" (2), *The Edge of the Sword*, 1934, tr. Gerald Hopkins, 1960

The best actor sits inside his own performance as a cool spectator of the effects he is creating in an audience.
> DIDEROT (1713–1784). French philosopher. As paraphrased by Garry Wills, "What Makes a Good Leader?" *Atlantic*, April 1994

If you look back through history, the people who've been the strongest in film were people who could express a lot by holding certain things in reserve so the audience is curious to find out what the reserve is.
> CLINT EASTWOOD (1930–1979)

Whatever happens, look as if it were intended.
> FIRST RULE OF ACTING. In Arthur Bloch, comp., "Socio-Murphology," *Murphy's Law: Book Three*, 1982

I pretended to be somebody I wanted to be until finally I became that person. Or he became me.
> CARY GRANT (1904–1986). On shaping his personality as a young actor. In *Parade*, 22 September 1985

The whole essence of learning lines is to forget them so you can make them sound like you thought of them that instant.
> GLENDA JACKSON (1936–). In *Sunday Telegraph* (British newspaper), 26 July 1992

I created the character and then let her play herself through me.
> SHIRLEY MacLAINE (1934–). On her role as *Madame Sousatzka* (film), 1988, radio interview, KGO, San Francisco, 19 April 1989

Reporter: What kind of governor will you be?
Reagan: I don't know; I've never played a governor.
> RONALD REAGAN (1911–). Format adapted. On being elected governor of California. In news reports, November 1967

Acting is merely the art of keeping a large group of people from coughing.

> RALPH RICHARDSON (1902–1983). In *New York Herald Tribune*, 19 May 1946

Hamlet: To hold, as 'twere, the mirror up to nature.

> SHAKESPEARE (1564–1616). *Hamlet*, 3.2.23, 1600

I figured I needed a gimmick, so I dreamed up the drawl, the squint, and a way of moving which meant to suggest that I wasn't looking for trouble but would just as soon throw a bottle at your head as not.

> JOHN WAYNE (1907–1979). 1962

Talk low, talk slow, and don't say too much.

> JOHN WAYNE (1907–1979). On acting

ACTION

See also • Action & Inaction ○ Action & Talk ○ Action & Thought ○ Activity ○ Crises ○ Decisiveness ○ Deeds ○ Delay ○ Energy ○ Inaction ○ Indifference ○ Knowledge: Thomas Fuller ○ Life: Oliver Wendell Holmes, Jr. (1) ○ Morality ○ Motives ○ Paradoxes: Mohandas K. Gandhi ○ Patience ○ Procrastination ○ Self-Realization (Being) ○ Service ○ Speed ○ Time

To act is to be committed, and to be committed is to be in danger.

> JAMES BALDWIN (1924–1987). "My Dungeon Shook: Letter to My Nephew on the One Hundredth Anniversary of the Emancipation," *The Fire Next Time*, 1963

Action on the move creates its own route, creates to a very great extent the conditions under which it is to be fulfilled, and thus baffles all calculation.

> HENRI BERGSON (1859–1941). "Final Remarks," *The Two Sources of Morality and Religion*, 1932, tr. R. Ashley Audra and Cloudesley Brereton, 1935

"Be sure yu are rite then go ahed;" but in kase ov doubt go ahed enny wa.

> JOSH BILLINGS (1818–1885). *His Sayings*, 39, 1867

Great actions are sometimes historically barren; smallest actions have taken root in the moral soil and grown like banana forests to cover whole quarters of the world.

> THOMAS CARLYLE (1795–1881). Journal, 9 September 1830. In James Anthony Froude, *Thomas Carlyle: A History of the First Forty Years, 1795–1835*, 2.4, 1882

I like things to happen; and if they don't happen, I like to make them happen.

> WINSTON CHURCHILL (1874–1965). In Christopher Hassall, *Edward Marsh, Patron of the Arts: A Biography*, 1959

Act quickly and well because people are dying!

> DANILO DOLCI (1924–1997). Sicilian human rights activist

Action and becoming are one.

> MEISTER ECKHART (A.D. 1260?–1328?). "Sermons" (18), *Meister Eckhart: A Modern Translation*, tr. R. B. Blakney, 1941

Right action is freedom
From past and future also.

> T. S. ELIOT (1888–1965). "The Dry Salvages" (5), *Four Quartets*, 1943

Reward of an act is to have done it.

> RALPH WALDO EMERSON (1803–1882). "Notebook F No. 1," 1836–1840

In our era, the road to holiness necessarily passes through the world of action.

> DAG HAMMARSKJÖLD (1905–1961). 1955, *Markings*, tr. Leif Sjöberg and W. H. Auden, 1964
> See Self-Realization (Becoming): Swami Prabhavananda

Never confuse movement with action.

> ERNEST HEMINGWAY (1899–1961). Remark to Marlene Dietrich. In A. E. Hotchner, *Papa Hemingway: A Personal Memoir*, 1, 1967

By inwardness alone we do not come close to God. The purest intentions, the finest sense of devotion, the noblest spiritual aspirations are fatuous when not realized in action.

> ABRAHAM JOSHUA HESCHEL (1907–1972). *God in Search of Man: A Philosophy of Judaism*, 33, 1955

Action is basically a reaction against loss of balance—a flailing of the arms to regain one's balance. To dispose a soul to action we must upset its equilibrium.

> ERIC HOFFER (1902–1983). *The Ordeal of Change*, 5, 1964

To act is to affirm the worth of an end.

> OLIVER WENDELL HOLMES, JR. (1841–1935). "The Class of '61," speech at the Fiftieth Anniversary of Graduation from Harvard University, 28 June 1911

It is not book learning young men need, nor instruction about this and that, but a stiffening of the vertebrae which will cause them to be loyal to a trust, to act promptly, concentrate their energies, do a thing—"carry a message to Garcia."

> ELBERT HUBBARD (1856–1915). Referring to a diplomatic message carried by 1st Lt. Andrew S. Rowan (1857–1943), an American army officer disguised as an English sportsman, to Gen. Calixto García y Iñiguez, commander of Cuban forces fighting the Spanish during the Spanish-American War. In "A Message to Garcia," *The Philistine* (magazine), March 1899

Action follows conviction, not knowledge.

> PIERRE LECOMTE du NOÜY (1883–1947). *Human Destiny*, 11, 1947

Only those who themselves go into action now can make appeals for action.

> LENIN (1870–1924). *What Is To Be Done? Burning Questions of Our Movement*, 3.C, 1902, International Publishers edition, 1929

Let every action aim solely at the common good.

> MARCUS AURELIUS (A.D. 121–180). *Meditations*, 12.20, tr. Maxwell Staniforth, 1964
> See Purpose: *Bhagavad Gita*

We are born to act.

> MONTAIGNE (1533–1592). "That to Philosophize Is to Learn to Die," *Essays*, 1588, tr. Donald M. Frame, 1958

Actions will be judged according to intentions.

> MUHAMMAD (A.D. 570?–632). *The Sayings of Muhammad,* 1, tr. Abdullah Al-Suhrawardy, 1941

For us is the life of action, of strenuous performance of duty; let us live in the harness, striving mightily; let us rather run the risk of wearing out than rusting out.

> THEODORE ROOSEVELT (1858–1919). "Duties of a Great Nation," speech, New York City, 5 October 1898

Get action, do things; be sane; don't fritter away your time; create, act, take a place wherever you are and be somebody: get action.

> THEODORE ROOSEVELT (1858–1919). In Richard Hofstadter, *The American Political Tradition: And the Men Who Made It,* 9.1, 1948

Moral action is the meeting-place between the human and divine.

> LEON ROTH. *Jewish Thought as a Factor in Civilization,* 1954

Our intentions tend to be much more real to us than our actions, and this can lead to a great deal of misunderstanding with other people, to whom our actions tend to be much more real than our intentions.

> E. F. SCHUMACHER (1911–1977). *A Guide for the Perplexed,* 8, 1977

Action does not come to a stop in its structures, it remains in action. In other words, there is more in bodies, things and events than is contained in their structures or material forms. All things overflow their own structural limits. The inner Action transcends the outer structure, and there is thus a trend in things beyond themselves.

> JAN CHRISTIAN SMUTS (1870–1950). *Holism and Evolution,* 12, 1926

Every act alters the soul of the doer.

> OSWALD SPENGLER (1880–1936). "Cities and Peoples," *The Decline of the West,* 1918–1922, tr. Charles Francis Atkinson, 1962

Action from principle, the perception and performance of right, changes things and relations; it is essentially revolutionary, and does not consist wholly with anything which was. It not only divides states and churches, it divides families; ay, it divides the *individual,* separating the diabolical in him from the divine.

> HENRY DAVID THOREAU (1817–1862). "Civil Disobedience," 1849

No being can be what he is unless he is putting his essence into action in his field.

> ARNOLD J. TOYNBEE (1889–1975). *A Study of History,* 3.235, 1934

Human actions are not the mechanical effects of causes; they are purposive executions of decisions between alternative possible choices.

> ARNOLD J. TOYNBEE (1889–1975). *A Study of History,* 12.259, 1961

[Action] is the last resource of those who know not how to dream.

> OSCAR WILDE (1854–1900). "The Critic as Artist" (1), *Intentions,* 1891

❦

It was only after the first Hebrew jumped into the water that the Red Sea parted.

> ANONYMOUS (HEBREW)

We do as we are; we become as we do.

> SAYING

ACTION & INACTION

See also • Action ○ Inaction ○ Sin: *The Book of the Golden Precepts*

He who sees the inaction that is in action, and the action that is in inaction, is wise indeed.

> *BHAGAVAD GITA* (6th cent. B.C.). 4, tr. Swami Prabhavananda and Christopher Isherwood, 1954

Both action and inaction may find room in thee.

> *THE BOOK OF THE GOLDEN PRECEPTS.* Ancient Buddhist writing. 2.12, tr. Helena Petrovna Blavatsky, 1889

It is vain to say human beings ought to be satisfied with tranquillity: they must have action; and they will make it if they cannot find it.

> CHARLOTTE BRONTË (1816–1855). *Jane Eyre,* 12, 1847

Drastic action may be costly, but it can be less expensive than continuing inaction.

> RICHARD E. NEUSTADT (1919–). *Presidential Power: The Politics of Leadership,* 2.4, 1960

[Caesar] slept generally in his chariots or litters, employing even his rest in pursuit of action.

> PLUTARCH (A.D. 46?–119?). "Caesar," *Parallel Lives,* Dryden edition, 1693

Hard to rouse and hard to restrain: that had been a constant trait in my character.

> ROUSSEAU (1712–1778). *Confessions,* 1 (1723–1728), 1781, tr. J. M. Cohen, 1953

❦

All mankind is divided into three classes—the immovable, the movable, and those who move.

> SAYING (ARAB)

ACTION & TALK

See also • Action ○ Deeds: John Ray ○ Idealism: Herbert Hoover ○ Judging Others: Frederick II ○ Speaking ○ Talking ○ Virtue: William Godwin

I hold it to be of the highest importance for our interests that we should think rather of what we shall do than what we shall say. When we have decided upon that, it will be easy to accommodate our words to our acts.

> ANNIUS (1432–1502). Roman magistrate. In Machiavelli, *The Discourses,* 2.15, 1517, tr. Christian E. Detmold, 1940

He made no answer; but he took the city.

> LORD BYRON (1788–1824). *Don Juan,* 7.53, 1819–1824

Speech that leads not to action, still more that hinders it, is a nuisance on the earth.

> THOMAS CARLYLE (1795–1881). Letter to Jane Welsh (his future wife), 4 November 1825

The superior man is modest in his speech, but exceeds in his actions.
> CONFUCIUS (551–479 B.C.). *Confucian Analects,* 14.29, tr. James Legge, 1930

Speech is the shadow of action.
> DEMOCRITUS (460?–370? B.C.). In Diogenes Laertius (A.D. 3rd cent.), *Lives of Eminent Philosophers,* 9.7, tr. R. D. Hicks, 1925

The only speech will at last be Action such as Confucius describes the Speech of God.
> RALPH WALDO EMERSON (1803–1882). Journal, 11 October 1838

No sooner said than done, so acts your man of worth.
> ENNIUS (239–169 B.C.). Fragment 315

Great Talkers, little Doers.
> BENJAMIN FRANKLIN (1706–1790). *Poor Richard's Almanack,* April 1733

Well done is better than well said.
> BENJAMIN FRANKLIN (1706–1790). *Poor Richard's Almanack,* May 1737

Speak little, do much.
> BENJAMIN FRANKLIN (1706–1790). *Poor Richard's Almanack,* January 1755

Content yourself with doing, leave the talking to others.
> BALTASAR GRACIÁN (1601–1658). *The Art of Worldly Wisdom,* 295, 1647, tr. Joseph Jacobs, 1943

Saying and doing are two things.
> JOHN HEYWOOD (1497–1580). Comp., *A Dialogue Containing the Number of the Effectual Proverbs in the English Tongue,* 2.5, 1562

NEVER EXPLAIN WHAT YOU ARE DOING. This wastes a good deal of time and rarely gets through. Show them through your action, if they don't understand it, fuck 'em, maybe you'll hook them with the next action.
> ABBIE HOFFMAN (1936–1989). *Revolution for the Hell of It,* 7, 1968

When your work speaks for itself, don't interrupt.
> HENRY J. KAISER (1882–1967). Industrialist

Twaddle, rubbish, and gossip is what people want, not action. . . . The secret of life is to chatter freely about all one wishes to do and how one is always being prevented—and then do nothing.
> SÓREN KIERKEGAARD (1813–1855). Journal, 9 March 1846, tr. Alexander Dru, 1938

We talk on principle, but we act on interest.
> WALTER SAVAGE LANDOR (1775–1864). "Lopez Baños and Romero Alpuente," *Imaginary Conversations,* 1824-1853

Watch what we do, not what we say.
> JOHN N. MITCHELL (1913–1988). Attorney general. In Ralph Blumenfeld et al., *Henry Kissinger: The Private and Public Story,* 19, 1974

Some things are easier said than done.
> PLAUTUS (254–184 B.C.). *Asinaria,* 1.3

I have always had a horror of words that are not translated into deeds, of speech that does not result in action—in other words,

I believe in realizable ideals and in realizing them, in preaching what can be practiced and then in practicing it.
> THEODORE ROOSEVELT (1858–1919). *An Autobiography,* 6, 1913

First Murderer: Talkers are no good doers: be assured
We come to use our hands and not our tongues.
> SHAKESPEARE (1564–1616). *Richard III,* 1.3.352, 1592

Hamlet: Suit the action to the word, the word to the action.
> SHAKESPEARE (1564–1616). *Hamlet,* 3.2.19, 1600

Speech is a kind of action.
> SOCRATES (470?–399 B.C.). In Plato (427?-347 B.C.), *Cratylus,* 387, tr. Benjamin Jowett, 1894
> See Words: Aesop

His words and actions flowed from him as smoothly, as inevitably and spontaneously as fragrance exhales from a flower. He could not understand the value or significance of any word or deed taken separately.
> LEO TOLSTOY (1828–1910). On the fictional character Platon Karatayev, *War and Peace,* 4.1.13, 1863-1869, tr. Rosemary Edmonds, 1957

If a picture is worth a thousand words, one act is worth a thousand pictures.
> TOM WARSON. "Warson's Truth." In Paul Dickson, comp., *The New Official Rules,* p. 217, 1989
> See Photography: Fred R. Barnard ○ Quotations: Diogenes ○ Sayings: Saying

With me, it has always been a maxim rather to let my designs appear from my works than by my expressions.
> GEORGE WASHINGTON (1732–1799). In Geoffrey C. Ward, "Who Was Washington?" *American Heritage,* February-March 1993

Not retreat from the world, but engagement, commitment. If ultimately the aim of spirit is to gain power over matter, then it must face the responsibility of action, and not spend its time complaining that the world is out of joint.
> COLIN WILSON (1931–). *Religion and the Rebel,* 2.8, 1957

❧

After all is said and done, more is said than done.
> ANONYMOUS.

Actions speak louder than words.
> SAYING (ENGLISH)

His bark is worse than his bite.
> SAYING (ENGLISH)

Some things are easier done than said.
> SAYING

ACTION & THOUGHT

See also • Action ○ Deeds: Anonymous ○ Ideas ○ Liberation: Paulo Freire ○ Thinking ○ Thoughts

Plato for thought,
Christ for action.

> BRONSON ALCOTT (1799–1888). Journal, 23 March 1869, ed. Odell
> Shepard, 1938

Action limits us; whereas in the state of contemplation we are endlessly expansive.

> HENRI AMIEL (1821–1881). Journal, 8 March 1868, tr. Mrs. Humphrey
> Ward, 1887

Thought is sad without action, and action is sad without thought.

> HENRI AMIEL (1821–1881). In Cesare Lombroso, *The Man of Genius,*
> 1.3, 1888, ed. Havelock Ellis, 1896

It is best for men, when they take counsel, to be timorous, and imagine all possible calamities, but when the time for action comes, then to deal boldly.

> ARTABANUS (5th cent. B.C.). Persian minister. In Herodotus (484?–420?
> B.C.), *The Persian Wars,* 7.49, tr. George Rawlinson, 1942

The world can only be grasped by action, not by contemplation . . . . The hand is the cutting edge of the mind.

> JACOB BRONOWSKI (1795–1881). *The Ascent of Man,* 3, 1973

The end of Man is an Action, and not a Thought, though it were the noblest.

> THOMAS CARLYLE (1795–1881). *Sartor Resartus: The Life and Opinions
> of Herr Teufelsdröckh,* 2.6, 1835

"Think Globally, But Act Locally."

> RENÉ DUBOS (1901–1982). Chapter title, *Celebrations of Life,* 3, 1981

Thought is the seed of action.

> RALPH WALDO EMERSON (1803–1882). "Art," *Society and Solitude,* 1870

Idea and execution are not often entrusted to the same head.

> RALPH WALDO EMERSON (1803–1882). Title essay, *Natural History of
> Intellect and Other Papers,* 1893

Thought is behavior in rehearsal.

> SIGMUND FREUD (1856–1939). Early 1930s. In Joseph Wortis, "Retrospect
> and Conclusion," *Fragments of an Analysis with Freud,* 1954

It is much easier to think right without doing right than to do right without thinking right.

> J. C. HARE and A. W. HARE (1792–1834). *Guesses at Truth: Second
> Series,* 1848

Before he acts, he will pause to weigh the effects of his act in the scales of God.

> ABRAHAM JOSHUA HESCHEL (1907–1972). *Man Is Not Alone:
> A Philosophy of Religion,* 26, 1951

Sooner or later, false thinking brings wrong conduct.

> JULIAN HUXLEY (1887–1975). *Essays of a Biologist,* 6, 1923

Thought is a prelude to, and not an alternative to action.

> ANTONY JAY (1930–). *Management and Machiavelli: An Inquiry into the
> Politics of Corporate Life,* 17, 1967

It is easier to behave your way into a new way of thinking than to think your way into a new way of behaving.

KEGLEY'S PRINCIPLE OF CHANGE. In John Peers, comp., *1,001 Logical
Laws,* p. 177, 1979

The actions of men [are] the best interpreters of their thoughts.

> JOHN LOCKE (1632–1704). *An Essay Concerning Human Understanding,*
> 1.2.3, 1690, ed. Alexander Campbell Fraser, 1894

All the beautiful sentiments in the world weigh less than a single lovely action.

> JAMES RUSSELL LOWELL (1819–1891). "Rousseau and the
> Sentimentalists," 1867, *Among My Books,* 1870

The test of real and vigorous thinking, the thinking which ascertains truths instead of dreaming dreams, is successful application to practice.

> JOHN STUART MILL (1806–1873). *Considerations on Representative
> Government,* 3, 1861

The man of thought who will not act is ineffective; the man of action who will not think is dangerous.

> RICHARD M. NIXON (1913–1994). Speech, 1966. In William Safire,
> *Before the Fall: An Inside View of the Pre-Watergate White House,*
> 3.5, 1975

Think before you act.

> PYTHAGORAS (580?–500? B.C.)

Who reflects too much will accomplish little.

> FRIEDRICH von SCHILLER (1759–1805). *William Tell,* 3.1, 1804

We know what a person thinks not when he tells us what he thinks, but by his actions.

> ISAAC BASHEVIS SINGER (1904–1991). Richard Burgin interview, "Isaac
> Bashevis Singer Talks . . . About Everything," *New York Times
> Magazine,* 26 November 1978

Action taken on any plane will be in danger of going wrong if it is not taken in the light of the truth and of nothing but the truth; but it will be in equal danger of getting nowhere if it is not also taken in the light of no more of the truth than the minimum that is relevant to the particular piece of action that is on the current agenda.

> ARNOLD J. TOYNBEE (1867–1975). *A Study of History,* 10.227, 1954

An ounce of application is worth a ton of abstraction.

> BOOKER T. WASHINGTON (1856–1915). Headline in Continental Bank
> ad. In *Fortune,* October 1975

❦

Act quickly, think slowly.

> SAYING (GREEK). In Aristotle (384–322 B.C.). *Nicomachean Ethics,* 6.9,
> tr. J. A. K. Thomson, 1953
> See Prudence–Rules: C. C. Colton

ACTIVITY

See also • Action ○ Contemplation: Aristotle ○ Industry

A capacity for self-recollection—for withdrawal from the outward to the inward—is in fact the condition of all noble and useful activity.

> HENRI AMIEL (1821–1881). Journal, 7 January 1866, tr. Mrs. Humphrey
> Ward, 1887

'Tis good always to be doing something.

> JOHN CLARKE (1596–1658). Comp., *Proverbs: English and Latine*, p. 235, 1639

Activity in War is movement in a resistant medium.

> KARL von CLAUSEWITZ (1780–1831). *On War*, 1.7, 1832, tr. J. J. Graham, 1873

Activity is contagious.

> RALPH WALDO EMERSON (1803–1882). "Uses of Great Men," *Representative Men*, 1850

Be doing always something, that the Devil catch thee not at leisure.

> THOMAS FULLER (1654–1734). Comp., *Introductio ad Prudentiam*, 436, 1731

Some are very busy, and yet do nothing.

> THOMAS FULLER (1654–1734). Comp., *Gnomologia: Adages and Proverbs*, 4211, 1732

The superficiality of the American is the result of his hustling. It needs leisure to think things out; it needs leisure to mature. People in a hurry cannot think, cannot grow.

> ERIC HOFFER (1902–1983). *The Passionate State of Mind: And Other Aphorisms*, 172, 1954

[The weaker side] must make up in activity what it lacks in strength.

> THOMAS JONATHAN "STONEWALL" JACKSON (1824–1863). Letter, April 1863

I multiplied myself by my activity.

> NAPOLEON (1769–1821). *Talks of Napoleon at St. Helena* (with Gen. Gaspard Gourgaud), 8, tr. Elizabeth Wormeley Latimer, 1904

Happiness [is] an effect and knowledge a mere instrument of successful activity.

> BERTRAND RUSSELL (1872–1970). *A History of Western Philosophy*, 3.2.28, 1946

Motion universally takes place along the line of least resistance.

> HERBERT SPENCER (1820–1903). "The Filiation of Ideas," 1899. In David Duncan, *Life and Letters of Herbert Spencer*, Appendix B, 1908

Nowadays, people don't ask you how you are, they say, "Are you busy?," meaning "Are you *well*?" If someone actually does ask you how you are, the most cheerful answer, of course, is a robust "Busy!" to which the person will reply, "Good!" "Busy" used to be a negative sort of word. It meant having no time for yourself, no leisure. "No, I can't come out this weekend, I'm too busy." Sorry about that, you poor stiff. Now, though, busyness is bullish. Conspicuous industriousness is the rule.

> RICHARD STENGEL (1955–). "The Talk of the Town: Forty Winks Dept.," *New Yorker*, 25 August 1997

There is nothing, not even crime, more opposed to poetry, to philosophy, ay, to life itself, than this incessant business.

> HENRY DAVID THOREAU (1817–1862). "Life Without Principle," *Atlantic*, October 1863

[Apart from God] every activity is merely a passing whiff of insignificance.

> ALFRED NORTH WHITEHEAD (1861–1947). "Immortality," *The Philosophy of Alfred North Whitehead*, ed. Paul A. Schilpp, 1941

It's wonderful what we can do if we're always doing.

> GEORGE WASHINGTON (1732–1799). Quoted by Richard Norton Smith, Brian Lamb television interview, C-SPAN, 22 February 1993

❦

Before my opponent moves, I already am moving.

> SAYING (CHINESE)

ACTORS

See also • Acting ○ Critics: Examples ○ Directors ○ Films ○ Theater

An actor is a sculptor who carves in snow.

> LAWRENCE BARRETT (1838–1891). Attributed

For an actress to be a success, she must have the face of a Venus, the brains of a Minerva, the grace of Terpsichore, the memory of a Macaulay, the figure of Juno, and the hide of a rhinoceros.

> ETHEL BARRYMORE (1879–1959). In George Jean Nathan, "The State of the Theatre: Appendix," *The Theatre in the Fifties*, 1953

There are five stages to an actor's career. First, "Who's Robby Benson?" Then, "Get me Robby Benson." "Get me a Robby Benson type," that's three. "Get me a young Robby Benson," four. And five? "Who's Robby Benson?"

> ROBBY BENSON (1955–). In "Chatter," *People*, 23 November 1981

I'd love to redo [*The Private Lives of Elizabeth and Essex*] one more time. I would feel more comfortable as the older queen. Since I am *an* older . . . queen. [Ellipsis points in original.]

> BETTE DAVIS (1908–1989). Referring to the 1939 film in which she played Queen Elizabeth, 1974

Whenever you step outside, you're on, brother, you're on.

> SAMMY DAVIS, JR. (1925–1990). In Orrin E. Klapp, *Symbolic Leaders*, 1, 1964

You're only as good as your last picture.

> MARIE DRESSLER (1869–1934)

The only reason they come to see me is that I know life is great—and they know I know it.

> CLARK GABLE (1901–1960)

[An actor is] the kind of guy who if you ain't talking about him ain't listening.

> GEORGE GLASS. Film publicist. In Bob Thomas, *Marlon: Portrait of the Rebel as an Artist*, 7, 1973. This quote is often attributed to Marlon Brando.

An actress's life is so transitory—suddenly you're a building.

> HELEN HAYES (1900–1993). On having a theater in New York City named after her. In news reports, November 1955

Actors are cattle.

> ALFRED HITCHCOCK (1899–1980). Responding to protests from the acting community, Hitchcock modified his remark: "I didn't say actors are cattle. What I said was, actors should be *treated* like cattle."

Players, Sir! I look on them as no better than creatures set upon tables and joint-stools to make faces and produce laughter, like dancing dogs.

> SAMUEL JOHNSON (1709–1784). Quoted by Samuel Foote, 1775. In James Boswell, *The Life of Samuel Johnson,* 1791

It's nice to be included in people's fantasies, but you also like to be accepted for your own sake.

> MARILYN MONROE (1926–1962). Richard Meryman interview, *Life,* 3 August 1962

It is a great help for a man to be in love with himself, but for an actor it is absolutely essential.

> ROBERT MORLEY (1908–1992). In "No Turn Unstoned" (editorial), *Times* (London), 8 August 1995

An actor is not quite a human being—but then, who is?

> GEORGE SANDERS (1906–1972)

ADDICTION

See also • Alcohol ○ Coffee ○ Drugs, Illegal: [especially] Thomas S. Szasz ○ Drugs, Medical ○ Drugs, Psychiatric ○ Habit ○ Mental Illness ○ Tobacco

Addiction is the number one disease in our civilization.

> DEEPAK CHOPRA (1946–). Michael Toms radio interview, KALW, San Francisco, 7 July 1997

Crime is stupid, delinquency is stupid and the use of narcotics is stupid. What Synanon is dealing with is addiction to stupidity.

> CHARLES E. DEDERICH (1913–1997). In Lawrence Van Gelder, "Charles Dederich, 83, Synanon Founder, Dies," *New York Times,* 4 March 1997

Addiction is the disease of our age. It is cunning and powerful. It proceeds from our chronic spiritual hunger and is nourished by our focus on getting and spending, and on news and gossip outside ourselves. Everything we need is happening within us. The focus on reports of others is only a distraction from the needs of our own spirit. Addiction grows fat from our chronic quashing of the inner life. We believe the spiritual does not exist because we have made insufficient space for it to manifest in our lives. A self-fulfilling tautology.

> ERICA JONG (1942–). *Fear of Fifty: A Midlife Memoir,* 10, 1994

ADJUSTMENT

See also • Conformity ○ Normality ○ School: Robert Lindner

The "adjusted" person who does not live by the truth and who does not love is protected only from manifest conflicts. If he is not engrossed in work, he has to use the many avenues of escape which our culture offers in order to be protected from the frightening experience of being alone with himself and looking into the abyss of his own impotence and human impoverishment.

> ERICH FROMM (1900–1980). *Psychoanalysis and Religion,* 4, 1950

Only by the most outrageous violation of ourselves have we achieved our capacity to live in relative adjustment to a civiliza-tion apparently driven to its own destruction.

> R. D. LAING (1927–1989). *The Politics of Experience,* 3, 1967

"The Eleventh Commandment" . . . has become . . . You Must Adjust! Adjustment, that synonym for conformity . . . , is the theme of our swan song, the piper's tune to which we dance on the brink of the abyss, the siren's melody that destroys our senses and paralyzes our wills.

> ROBERT LINDNER (1914–1956). Title essay (3), *Must You Conform?* 1956

The supple, well-adjusted man is the one who has learned to hop into the meatgrinder while humming a hit-parade tune.

> MARSHALL McLUHAN (1911–1980). "Education," *The Mechanical Bride,* 1951

The adjusted are those who reflect their society, or their class within the society, with the least distortion.

> DAVID RIESMAN (1909–) (with NATHAN GLAZER and REUEL DENNEY). *The Lonely Crowd: A Study of the Changing American Character,* 12.1, 1950, abr., 1953

The use of religion, psychoanalysis, or the mass media, as instruments by which people are helped to adjust to a dehumanizing social order without being challenged to change it, is essentially a betrayal of man.

> RICHARD SHAULL (1919–). *Containment and Change: Two Dissenting Views of American Foreign Policy,* 11, 1967

ADOLESCENCE

See also • Age ○ Age & Youth ○ Children ○ Lust: St. Augustine (2) ○ Middle Age ○ Parents: [especially] Margaret Blair ○ Sex: J. D. Salinger ○ Sincerity: Debbi Goglio ○ Youth

One of the main tasks of adolescence is to achieve an identity—not necessarily a knowledge of who we are, but a clarification of the range of what we might become, a set of self-references by which we can make sense of our responses, and justify our decisions and goals.

> TERRI APTER (1949–). British psychologist. *Altered Loves: Mothers and Daughters During Adolescence,* 4, 1990

The conflict between the need to belong to a group and the need to be seen as unique and individual is the dominant struggle of adolescence.

> JEANNE ELIUM (1947–) and DON ELIUM (1954–). *Raising a Daughter: Parents and the Awakening of a Healthy Woman,* 11, 1994

The age of puberty is a crisis. . . . It is the passage from the Unconscious to the Conscious; from the sleep of the Passions to their rage; from careless receiving to cunning providing.

> RALPH WALDO EMERSON (1803–1882). Journal, 2 December 1834

Adolescence begins when children stop asking questions—because they know all the answers.

> EVAN ESAR (1899–1995). Comp., *20,000 Quips and Quotes,* p. 12, 1968

Perhaps a modern society can remain stable only by eliminating adolescence, by giving its young, from the age of ten, the skills, responsibilities, and rewards of grownups, and opportunities for action in all spheres of life.

> ERIC HOFFER (1902–1983). *Reflections on the Human Condition,* 58, 1973

During adolescence imagination is boundless. The urge toward self-perfection is at it peak. And with all their self-absorption and personalized dreams of glory, youth are in pursuit of something larger than personal passions, some values or ideals to which they might attach their imagination.

> LOUISE J. KAPLAN (1929–). *Adolescence: The Farewell to Childhood,* 9, 1984

Teen-agers have no monopoly on [adolescent behavior], except in so far as we are in fact a teen-age society—a society that likes to play "chicken" not with fast cars, but with ballistic missiles.

> THOMAS MERTON (1915–1968). "Events and Pseudo-Events: Letter to a Southern Churchman," *Katallagete,* Summer 1966

Let your child be the teenager he or she wants to be, not the adolescent you were or wish you had been.

> LAURENCE STEINBERG (1952–) and ANN LEVINE (10th cent.). *You and Your Adolescent: A Parent's Guide for Ages 10 to 20,* 1, 1990

What causes adolescents to rebel is not the assertion of authority but the *arbitrary* use of power, with little explanation of the rules and no involvement in the decision-making.

> LAURENCE STEINBERG (1952–) and ANN LEVINE. *You and Your Adolescent: A Parent's Guide for Ages 10 to 20,* 1, 1990

❦

[Adolescence:] a stage between infancy and adultery.

> ANONYMOUS

Teenagers are people who express a burning desire to be different by dressing exactly alike.

> ANONYMOUS

ADULTERY

See also • Divorce ○ Judging Others: Jesus (2) ○ Marriage ○ Sex

My sensuality . . . was so real that even for a ten-minute adventure I'd have disowned father and mother. . . . I had principles, to be sure, such as that the wife of a friend is sacred. But I simply ceased quite sincerely, a few days before, to feel any friendship for the husband.

> ALBERT CAMUS (1913–1960). *The Fall,* p. 58, tr. Justin O'Brien, 1956

There were three of us in this marriage, so it was a bit crowded.

> PRINCESS DIANA (1961–1997). In Max Frankel, "No Pix, No Di," *New York Times Magazine,* 21 September 1997

Where there's Marriage without Love, there will be Love without Marriage.

> BENJAMIN FRANKLIN (1706–1790). *Poor Richard's Almanack,* May 1734

Call your Husband Cuckold in Jest, and he will ne'er suspect you.

> THOMAS FULLER (1654–1734). Comp., *Gnomologia: Adages and Proverbs,* 1048, 1732

You have heard that it was said, "You shall not commit adultery." But I say to you that every one who looks at a woman lustfully has already committed adultery with her in his heart.

> JESUS (A.D. 1st cent.). *Matthew* 5:27–28
> See Divorce: Jesus ○ Lust: Jimmy Carter

The effort we make to remain faithful to someone we love is little better than infidelity.

> LA ROCHEFOUCAULD (1613–1680). *Maxims,* 381, 1665, tr. Leonard Tancock, 1959

When a husband's story is believed, he begins to suspect his wife.

> H. L. MENCKEN (1880–1956). *A Little Book in C Major,* 6.25, 1916

Adultery. Democracy applied to love.

> H. L. MENCKEN (1880–1956). *A Book of Burlesques,* 11, 1920

You shall not commit adultery.

> MOSES (14th cent. B.C.). The Seventh Commandment, *Exodus* 20:14
> See Lust: Jesus

If a man commits adultery with the wife of his neighbor, both the adulterer and the adulteress shall be put to death.

> MOSES (14th cent. B.C.). *Leviticus* 20:10

[I am] not a Don Juan. . . . I'm a very faithful man. I'm faithful to my wife. I'm faithful to my mistress.

> BARBET SCHROEDER (1941–). Swiss-German film director. In Ben Brantley, "Barbet's Feast," *Vanity Fair,* September 1992

Young men want to be faithful, and are not: old men want to be faithless and cannot.

> OSCAR WILDE (1854–1900). *The Picture of Dorian Gray,* 2, 1891

Let marriage be held in honor by all, and let the marriage bed be undefiled; for God will judge the immoral and adulterous.

> ANONYMOUS (*BIBLE*). *Hebrews* 13:4

ADVERSITY

See also • Burdens ○ Difficulty ○ Misfortune ○ Poverty ○ Prosperity ○ Prosperity & Adversity ○ Struggle ○ Unhappiness

Adversity stretcheth our days.

> SIR THOMAS BROWNE (1605–1682). *Hydriotaphia: Urn Burial,* 5, 1658, ed. John Addington Symonds, 1886

Adversity is the first path to truth.

> LORD BYRON (1785–1824). *Don Juan,* 12.50, 1819-1824

Look at a man in the midst of doubt and danger, and you will learn in his hour of adversity what he really is. It is then that true utterances are wrung from the recesses of his breast. The mask is torn off; the reality remains.

> LUCRETIUS (99–55 B.C.). *On the Nature of Things,* 2.55, tr. R. E. Latham, 1951

Adversity is the midwife of genius.

> NAPOLEON (1769–1821). *Napoleon in His Own Words,* 2, comp. Jules Bertaut, 1916

Duke: Sweet are the uses of adversity,
Which, like the toad, ugly and venomous,
Wears yet a precious jewel in his head.

> SHAKESPEARE (1564–1616). *As You Like It,* 2.1.12, 1599

By trying we can easily learn to endure adversity. Another man's, I mean.

> MARK TWAIN (1835–1910). *Following the Equator: A Journey Around the World,* 39 (epigraph), 1897
>
> See Grief: Shakespeare (3) ○ Misfortune: Alexander Pope ○ Prosperity: Twain ○ Trouble: La Rochefoucauld

Adversity in immunological doses has its uses; more than that crushes.

> JOHN UPDIKE (1932–). "On One's Own Oeuvre," *Hugging the Shore,* 1983

❦

Adversity reveals and shapes character.

> ANONYMOUS

Adversity weakens the weak and strengthens the strong.

> ANONYMOUS

Only with cutting is jade shaped to use; only with adversity does one achieve the Way.

> SAYING (CHINESE)

Adversity makes strange bedfellows.

> SAYING (ENGLISH)
>
> See Misery: Shakespeare ○ Politics: Charles Dudley Warner

ADVERTISING

See also • Advertising Copy & Slogans ○ Deception ○ Indoctrination ○ Media: [especially] Ferdinand Lundberg ○ Merchants & Customers ○ Motives ○ Propaganda ○ Publicity ○ Public Relations ○ Trees: Ogden Nash

[Advertising is] the first, second, and third elements of "success."

> P. T. BARNUM (1810–1891). In Michael Zuckerman, "And in the Center Ring. . . ," *Pennsylvania Gazette,* May 1993

The deeper problems connected with advertising come less from the unscrupulousness of our "deceivers" than from our pleasure in being deceived, less from the desire to seduce than from the desire to be seduced.

> DANIEL J. BOORSTIN. (1914–). *The Image: A Guide to Pseudo-Events in America,* 5.3, 1961

The successful advertiser is the master of a new art: the art of making things true by saying they are so. He is a devotee of the technique of the self-fulfilling prophecy.

> DANIEL J. BOORSTIN. (1914–). *The Image: A Guide to Pseudo-Events in America,* 5.4, 1961

When the gods wish to punish us, they make us believe our own advertising.

> DANIEL J. BOORSTIN. (1914–). *The Image: A Guide to Pseudo-Events in America,* 6 (introduction), 1961

It is pretty obvious that the debasement of the human mind caused by a constant flow of fraudulent advertising is no trivial thing. There is more than one way to conquer a country.

> RAYMOND CHANDLER (1888–1959). Letter to Carl Brandt, 15 November 1951, *Raymond Chandler Speaking,* ed. Dorothy Gardiner and Kathrine Sorley Walker, 1962

One of the main jobs of the advertiser in this conflict between pleasure and guilt is not so much to sell the product as to give moral permission to have fun without guilt.

> ERNEST DICHTER (1907–1991). Motivational researcher. In Vance Packard, *The Hidden Persuaders,* 6 (epigraph), 1957

Individuals project themselves into products. In buying a car they actually buy an extension of their own personality. When they are "loyal" to a commercial brand, they are loyal to themselves.

> ERNEST DICHTER (1907–1991). Motivational researcher. *The Strategy of Desire,* 5, 1960

You can tell the ideals of a nation by its advertisements.

> NORMAN DOUGLAS (1868–1952). *South Wind,* 7, 1917

Television, that great enforcer of emulation, brings the most decrepit ghetto dwelling intimate glimpses into the "lifestyles of the rich and famous," not to mention the merely affluent. Studying the televised array of products and comforts available, seemingly, to everyone else, the poor become more dangerous. There are no models, in the mainstream media, suggesting that anything less than middle-class affluence might be an honorable and dignified condition, nor is there any reason why corporate advertisers should promote such a subversive possibility.

> BARBARA EHRENREICH (1941–). *Fear of Falling: The Inner Life of the Middle Class,* 6, 1990

To keep people buying, you need first to make them dissatisfied with what they have. . . . Advertising is nothing more than a technique to keep people in a state of perpetual dissatisfaction with what they possess and in a permanent state of itchy acquisitiveness.

> FELIX GREENE (1909–1985). "The Face of Capitalism," *The Enemy: What Every American Should Know About Imperialism,* 1970

Playboy linked sex with upward mobility. If you can make people feel it's OK to enjoy themselves, you've got a winning product—whatever it is.

> HUGH HEFNER (1926–). In Merla Zellerbach "Revealing Secrets of Their Success," *San Francisco Chronicle,* 11 July 1979

The popular philosophy . . . is now molded by the writers of advertising copy, whose one idea is to persuade everybody to be as extroverted and uninhibitedly greedy as possible, since of course it is only the possessive, the restless, the distracted, who spend money on the things that advertisers want to sell.

> ALDOUS HUXLEY (1894–1963). *The Perennial Philosophy,* 8, 1946

Promise, large promise, is the soul of an advertisement.

> SAMUEL JOHNSON (1709–1784). In *The Idler* (English journal), 40, 20 January 1759

[Advertising] legitimizes the idealized, stereotyped roles of woman as temptress, wife, mother, and sex object, and portrays women as less intelligent and more dependent than men. It makes women

believe that their chief role is to please men and that their fulfillment will be as wives, mothers, and homemakers. It makes
women feel unfeminine if they are not pretty enough and guilty
if they do not spend most of their time in desperate attempts to
imitate gourmet cooks and eighteenth-century scullery maids. It
makes women believe that their own lives, talents, and interests
ought to be secondary to the needs of their husbands, and families and that they are almost totally defined by these relationships.

> LUCY KOMISAR (1942–). "The Image of Woman in Advertising." In
> Vivian Gornick and Barbara K. Moran, eds., *Woman in Sexist Society,*
> 1971

The advertising industry . . . encourages the pseudo-emancipation
of women, flattering them with its insinuating reminder, "You've
come a long way, baby" [the ad slogan of Virginia Slims ciga-
rettes], and disguising the freedom to consume as genuine autonomy.

> CHRISTOPHER LASCH (1932–1994). *The Culture of Narcissism: American
> Life in an Age of Diminishing Expectations,* 4, 1979

Advertising may be described as the science of arresting human
intelligence long enough to get money from it.

> STEPHEN LEACOCK (1869–1944). "The Perfect Salesman," *The Garden
> of Folly,* 1924

Half the money I spend on advertising is wasted, and the trouble
is I don't know which half.

> LORD LEVERHULME (1851–1925). English soap manufacturer and
> founder of Lever Bros. In David Ogilvy, *Confessions of an Advertising
> Man,* 3, 1963

[The highly masculine figures and the tattoo symbols set Marlboro
cigarettes] right in the heart of some core meanings of smoking:
masculinity, adulthood, vigor, and potency. Quite obviously these
meanings cannot be expressed openly. The consumer would
reject them quite violently. The difference between a top-flight
creative man and the hack is this ability to express powerful
meanings indirectly.

> PIERRE MARTINEAU (1905–1964). Motivational researcher. In Vance
> Packard, *The Hidden Persuaders,* 8, 1957

Who are these advertising men kidding? . . . Between the tired,
sad, gentle faces of the subway riders and the grinning Holy
Families of the Ad-Mass, there exists no possibility of even a wish-
ful identification.

> MARY McCARTHY (1912–). "America the Beautiful," *On the Contrary,*
> 1961

The best ad is a good product.

> ALAN H. MEYER

The [advertiser's] formula is: to make people ashamed of last
year's model; to hook up self-esteem itself with the purchasing of
this year's; to create a panic for status, and hence a panic of self-
evaluation, and to connect its relief with the consumption of specified commodities.

> C. WRIGHT MILLS (1916–1962). 1958, *Power, Politics and People:
> The Collected Essays of C. Wright Mills,* 3.10.5, ed. Irving Louis
> Horowitz, 1963

Whenever my agency is asked to advertise a politician or a political party, we refuse the invitation. . . . The use of advertising to
sell statesmen is the ultimate vulgarity.

> DAVID OGILVY (1911–). *Confessions of an Advertising Man,* 11, 1963

When I write an ad, I don't want you to tell me that you find it
"creative." I want you to find it so persuasive that you buy the
product—or buy it more often.

> DAVID OGILVY (1911–). In "David Ogilvy's Hard Advice," *New York
> Times,* 30 October 1991

We are selling perception as much as reality. We want to fill a
need in the consumer's mind, and it really doesn't matter if the
need is real or imagined.

> KEVIN O'MALLEY. Faberware general manager. On his company's intro-
> duction of Microbrew, a microwave coffee maker. In Douglas C.
> McGill, "Hunting for a Better Cup of Coffee," *New York Times,* 27 May
> 1989

Psychological obsolescence [is created] by the double-barreled
strategy of (1) making the public style-conscious, and then (2)
switching styles.

> VANCE PACKARD (1914–). *The Hidden Persuaders,* 16, 1957

By encouraging people constantly to pursue the emblems of success, and by causing them to equate possessions with status, what
are we doing to their emotions and their sense of values?

> VANCE PACKARD (1914–). Referring to advertising and marketing pres-
> sures, *The Status Seekers: An Exploration of Class Behavior in America
> and the Hidden Barriers that Affect You, Your Community, Your
> Future. A "View of Contemporary Pride and Prejudice,"* 21, 1959

Creative people are like a wet towel. You wring them out and pick
up another one.

> CHARLES REVSON (1906–1975). Revlon, Inc. founder and chairman.
> After changing advertising agencies seven times in three years. In
> Milton Moskowitz, Michael Katz, and Robert Levering, eds. *Everybody's
> Business,* p. 208, 1980

Let advertisers spend the same amount of money improving their
product that they do on advertising, and they wouldn't have to
advertise it.

> WILL ROGERS (1879–1935)

Advertising is the false spirituality of materialism, promising what
it can never deliver. Even the slogans of advertising sound religious, using the language of ultimate concern: "Buick, Something
to Believe In"; "Miller Beer—It Doesn't Get Any Better Than This";
"G.E., We Bring Good Things to Life." Television images of young,
beautiful, sexy, successful people enjoying the best of life surround
almost every product—and you can be just like them, suggest the
ads. If you just drink this beer, use this toothpaste, drive this car,
wear this perfume, or buy these jeans, this can be your life, too. Is
this not the essence of idolatry—a misdirected form of worship?

> JIM WALLIS (1948–). *The Soul of Politics: A Practical and Prophetic
> Vision for Change,* 7, 1994

✽

Merchants of discontent.

> ANONYMOUS (AMERICAN). On advertising executives. In Vance
> Packard, *The Hidden Persuaders,* 2, 1957

It pays to advertise.

> SAYING (AMERICAN)

A satisfied customer is the best advertisement.

> SAYING (AMERICAN)

ADVERTISING COPY & SLOGANS

See also • Advertising

Cigarettes, they're killers.

> AMERICAN CANCER SOCIETY. Slogan, 1960s

A complete set of instructions for the first-time smoker. [Headline in medium sized letters at the top of the page.]
Don't. [Sole word in small letters in the center of the page.]

> AMERICAN HEART ASSOCIATION. Sole ad content. In *National Geographic,* October 1986

"Light a Lucky and you'll never miss sweets that make you fat."

> AMERICAN TOBACCO CO. Ad headline quoting "Charming Motion Picture Star" Constance Talmadge, 1929

20,000 Physicians say Luckies are less irritating. [Headline.]
Toasting removes dangerous irritants that cause throat irritation and coughing. [Subheadline.]

> AMERICAN TOBACCO CO. Ad copy for Lucky Strike cigarettes, "It's toasted," 1930

So round, so firm, so fully packed, so free and easy on the draw.

> AMERICAN TOBACCO CO. Ad slogan for Lucky Strike cigarettes, 1940s

Looking Younger Is the Best Revenge.

> CHANEL. "Presenting the world's most luxurious, highly effective treatment for over-40 skin," ad headline for The No. 1 Collection. In *Connoisseur,* September 1989

the evidence: GRAY HAIR . . . the verdict: OLD! [Headline; ellipsis points in original.]
Clairol swiftly, secretly, beautifully ends the heartaches of gray or graying hair! [Subheadline.]

> CLAIROL, INC. Ad copy for "The original shampoo tint." In *Life,* 8 December 1943

A diamond is forever.

> DE BEERS CONSOLIDATED MINES, LTD. Corporate motto

Show her she's the reason it's never been lonely at the top.

> DE BEERS CONSOLIDATED MINES, LTD. Headline above the photograph of a beautiful, smiling woman wearing diamonds. In *Foreign Affairs,* Fall 1983

Better things for better living through chemistry.

> DUPONT CORP. Corporate motto, 1950s

There's a Ford in your future!

> FORD MOTOR CO. Ad slogan, 1928

Give her a *real* thrill this Christmas! [Headline.]
With a gift of a Frigidaire [Subheadline.]

> GENERAL MOTORS CORP. Frigidaire subsidiary. Ad copy. In *National Geographic,* December 1927

See the USA in your Chevrolet!

> GENERAL MOTORS CORP. Singing commercial (sung most famously by Dinah Shore), 1950s

Any car that is this responsive, obedient and satisfying to drive simply has no right to be this good looking.

> GENERAL MOTORS CORP. Ad copy for Pontiac. In *Life,* 5 February 1965

When you care enough to send the very best!

> JOYCE HALL (1891–1982). Hallmark Cards founder. Corporate motto, 1940s

You've bundled them off to school and office. Now you can relax with a second cup of coffee and the full-bodied flavor only one cigarette delivers . . .
THIS . . . IS THE L&M MOMENT. [Ellipsis points in original.]

> LIGGETT & MYERS, INC. Ad copy under the photograph of a woman looking relaxed at her kitchen table holding a lit cigarette in one hand as she mixes a cup of coffee with a spoon in the other. In *Life,* 19 May 1976

If you've got it, flaunt it.

> GEORGE LOIS (1937–). Advertising executive. Ad slogan for Braniff Airlines, 1977

We're number two. We try harder.

> NORTON-SIMON, INC. Ad slogan for Avis car rentals (Hertz was number one), 1960s

At Sixty Miles an Hour the Loudest Noise in the New Rolls-Royce comes from the electric clock.

> DAVID OGILVY (1911–). "The best [ad] headline I ever wrote contained *eighteen* words," *Confessions of an Advertising Man,* 6.1, 1963

Say it with flowers.

> PATRICK O'KEEFE. Advertising executive. Motto for the Society of American Florists. In *Florists' Exchange,* 15 December 1917

Honor thy father
give him our best.

> OLD GRAND-DAD DISTILLERY CO. Sole ad copy for Old Grand-Dad bourbon whiskey. In *New York Times,* 12 June 1965

Eminent doctors proved Philip Morris far less irritating to the nose and throat. [Headline.]
    When smokers changed to Philip Morris, every case of irritation of nose or throat—due to smoking—either cleared up completely or definitely improved!
    That is from the findings of distinguished doctors in clinical tests of actual smokers—reported in an authoritative medical journal.
    We claim no curative powers for Philip Morris—but that evidence *proves them less irritating* to the nose and throat.

> PHILIP MORRIS, INC. Ad for "America's FINEST Cigarette." In *Life,* 8 December 1943

You've come a long way, baby.

> PHILIP MORRIS, INC. Ad slogan for Virginia Slims cigarettes aimed at women, 1970s

Eat a chocolate. Light an Old Gold. And enjoy both! Two fine and healthful treats!

> P. LORILLARD CO. Ad copy, 1929

If you want a treat instead of a treatment, smoke Old Golds.

> P. LORILLARD CO. Ad slogan, 1940s

Scare claims fool no one, so . . .
Trust OLD GOLD for
a Treat instead of a Treatment! [Ellipsis points in original.]

> P. LORILLARD CO. Sole ad copy. In *Look,* 6 October 1953

"The misery of an old man is of interest to nobody." [Medium-size print.]
Life Insurance will help you in your old age—if you keep your policy in force. [Boxed in small letters below a drawing of a shabbily dressed, old, white-bearded man, walking alone assisted by two canes.]

> THE PRUDENTIAL INSURANCE COMPANY OF AMERICA. Sole ad copy. In *National Geographic,* July 1931

Watch the Game with a Friend
Seagram's 7 Crown.

> SEAGRAM COMPANY, LTD. Sole copy above the photograph of a football. In *TV Guide,* 1970s

We make money the old-fashioned way! We earn it!

> SMITH-BARNEY. Investment brokerage house. Motto, 1979

Honor thy self.

> SOMERSET IMPORTERS, LTD. Sole ad copy for Johnnie Walker Black Label Scotch. In *Saturday Review,* 20 March 1971

Joy to thyself.

> SOMERSET IMPORTERS, LTD. Sole ad copy at Christmas time for Johnnie Walker Black Label Scotch. In *U.S. News & World Report,* 10 December 1973

The priceless ingredient of every product is the honor and integrity of its maker.

> E. R. SQUIBB & SONS. Pharmaceutical manufacturer. Corporate motto. In *Life,* 19 February 1965

ADVICE

See also • Common Sense ○ Decision-Making ○ Wisdom: [especially] Saying (2) ○ Words: Kin Hubbard, Terence

Distrust interested advice.

> AESOP (6th cent. B.C.). "The Fox without a Tail," *Fables,* tr. Joseph Jacobs, 1894

Beware of unsolicited advice.

> AKIBA (A.D. 40?–135?). In *Talmud* (A.D. 1st–6th cent.). Rabbinical writings

Moste ov the advise we reseave from others, iz not so mutch an evidense ov their affeckshun for us, az it iz an evidense ov their affeckshun for themselves.

> JOSH BILLINGS (1818–1885). *His Sayings,* 13, 1867

People are always willing to follow advice when it accords with their own wishes.

> LADY BLESSINGTON (1789–1849). *The Confessions of an Elderly Lady,* p. 161, 1838

I wish to God that you had as much pleasure in following my advice, as I have in giving it [to] you.

> LORD CHESTERFIELD (1694–1773). Letter to his son, 5 February 1750

In those days Mr. Baldwin was wiser than he is now; he used frequently to take my advice.

> WINSTON CHURCHILL (1874–1965). House of Commons speech, 22 May 1935

Advice is generally judged by results, not by intentions.

> CICERO (106–43 B.C.). *Ad Atticum,* 9.7.a, tr. E. O. Winstedt, 1913

We ask advice, but we mean approbation.

> C. C. COLTON (1780–1832). *Lacon: or, Many Things in Few Words; Addressed to Those Who Think,* 1.189, 1823

And now *Monsieur le President* and *cher ami,* I say this. Listen only to yourself.

> CHARLES de GAULLE (1890–1970). Remark to Pres. John F. Kennedy. In "Le Bourgeois Gentilhomme," *Time,* 7 December 1962

How can they advise, if they see but a Part?

> BENJAMIN FRANKLIN (1706–1790). *Poor Richard's Almanack,* July 1748

Despise not Counsel. A Man is never nearer to Ruin than when he trusts too much to his own Wisdom.

> THOMAS FULLER (1654–1734). Comp., *Introductio ad Prudentiam,* 795, 1731

Counsel is irksome when the Matter is past Remedy.

> THOMAS FULLER (1654–1734). Comp., *Gnomologia: Adages and Proverbs,* 1181, 1732

He needs little Advice that is lucky.

> THOMAS FULLER (1654–1734). Comp., *Gnomologia: Adages and Proverbs,* 1996, 1732

If the Counsel be good, no Matter who gave it.

> THOMAS FULLER (1654–1734). Comp., *Gnomologia: Adages and Proverbs,* 2704, 1732

It is with advice as with taxation: we can endure very little of either, if they come to us in the direct way.

> SIR ARTHUR HELPS (1817–1875). "Advice," *Essays and Aphorisms,* 1893

We're all mighty unselfish when it comes t' handin' out advice we could use ourselves.

> KIN HUBBARD (1868–1930). *Abe Martin's Back Country Sayings,* unpaged, 1917

If you want to get rid of somebody, just tell him something for his own good.

> KIN HUBBARD (1868–1930)

Advice . . . always gives a temporary appearance of superiority.

> SAMUEL JOHNSON (1709–1784). In *The Rambler* (English journal), 87, 15 January 1751

Until thy feet have trod the Road
Advise not wayside folk.

> RUDYARD KIPLING (1865–1936). Opening lines, "The Comforters," 1890

With nothing are we so generous as advice.
> LA ROCHEFOUCAULD (1613–1680). *Maxims,* 110, 1665, tr. Louis Kronenberger, 1959

Ask counsel of him who governs himself well.
> LEONARDO da VINCI (1452–1519). *Note-books,* 1, tr. Edward McCurdy, 1908

Glory . . . is acquired by having been one against many in counseling an enterprise which success has justified.
> MACHIAVELLI (1469–1527). *The Discourses,* 3.35, 1517, tr. Christian E. Detmold, 1940

Phil Donahue: Where do you go for advice?
MacLaine: Inside.
> SHIRLEY MacLAINE (1934–). Appearing on *Donahue,* television talk program, September 1985

I can hardly blame anyone but myself for my mistakes or misfortunes, for I seldom ask the advice of others—except out of politeness or when I need information. . . . Though I set little value on my opinions, I set no more on the opinions of others.
> MONTAIGNE (1533–1592). *The Autobiography of Michel de Montaigne,* 16, ed. and tr. Marvin Lowenthal, 1935

When we are confronted with problems, the counsel of someone who has mastered similar problems can be a great help.
> PATANJALI (2nd cent. B.C.). Indian yogi. *Patanjali's Yogasutras: An Introduction,* 1.37, tr. T. K. V. Desikachar, 1987

It's a foolish *sheep* that makes the wolf his counselor.
> JOHN RAY (1628–1705). Comp., *A Collection of English Proverbs,* p. 23, 1678

I have sometimes doubted whether [Abraham Lincoln] ever asked anybody's advice about anything. He would hear everybody; but he rarely, if ever, asked for opinions.
> LEONARD SWETT (1825–1889). Letter to the author, 17 January 1866. In William H. Herndon and Jesse W. Weik, *Herndon's Lincoln: The True Story of a Great Life,* 18, 1889, Premier Books edition, 1961

There are few men who do not love better to give advice than to give assistance.
> HENRY DAVID THOREAU (1817–1862). Journal, 4 June 1850

Why should we ever go abroad, even across the way, to ask a neighbor's advice? There is a nearer neighbor within us incessantly telling us how we should behave. But we wait for the neighbor without to tell us of some false, easier way.
> HENRY DAVID THOREAU (1817–1862). Letter to Harrison Blake, 19 December 1854

I have found the best way to give advice to your children is to find out what they want, and then advise them to do it.
> HARRY S. TRUMAN (1884–1972). Edward R. Morrow television interview, *Person to Person,* CBS, 27 May 1955

If you can distinguish between good advice and bad advice, then you don't need advice.
> VAN ROY'S SECOND LAW. In Arthur Bloch, comp., "Expertsmanship", *Murphy's Law: Book Three,* 1982

Give not Advice without being Ask'd, and when desired, do it briefly.
> GEORGE WASHINGTON (1732–1799). Copybook, 1748 (at age 16), *Rules of Civility & Decent Behaviour in Company and Conversation,* #68. The rules were an amended version of Francis Hawkins's 1640 translation of *Decency of Conversation Among Men* (French Jesuit writing, 1595)

It is always a silly thing to give advice, but to give good advice is absolutely fatal.
> OSCAR WILDE (1854–1900). In Hesketh Pearson, *Oscar Wilde: His Life and Wit,* 12, 1946
> See Sincerity: Wilde

✺

Without counsel plans go wrong,
  but with many advisers they succeed.
> SAYING (*BIBLE*). *Proverbs* 15:22

Advice is least heeded when most needed.
> SAYING (ENGLISH)

Write down the advice of someone who loves you, though you don't like it at the time.
> SAYING (ENGLISH)

Bread is the best advice to the hungry.
> SAYING (RUSSIAN)

Be slow to give advice and quick to receive it.
> SAYING

Consult with your pillow.
> SAYING

AFRICAN AMERICANS

See also • Brotherhood: Martin Luther King, Jr. ○ Democracy: Langston Hughes ○ Ghettos: James Baldwin (1) ○ Prejudice ○ Racism ○ Racist Statements ○ Slavery ○ Sports: Melvin Rogers

Stamps, Arkansas, was Chitlin' Switch, Georgia; Hang 'Em High, Alabama; Don't Let the Sun Set on You Here, Nigger, Mississippi; or any other name just as descriptive. People in Stamps used to say that the whites in our town were so prejudiced that a Negro couldn't buy vanilla ice cream. Except on July Fourth. Other days he had to be satisfied with chocolate.
> MAYA ANGELOU (1928–). *I Know Why the Caged Bird Sings,* 8 (opening paragraph), 1970

All over Harlem, Negro boys and girls are growing into stunted maturity, trying desperately to find a place to stand; and the wonder is not that so many are ruined but that so many survive.
> JAMES BALDWIN (1924–1987). "The Harlem Ghetto," 1948, *Notes of a Native Son,* 1955

White people cannot, in the generality, be taken as models of how to live. Rather, the white man is himself in sore need of new standards, which will release him from his confusion and place him once again in fruitful communion with the depths of his own being.

JAMES BALDWIN (1924–1987). "Down at the Cross: Letter from a Region in My Mind," *The Fire Next Time,* 1963

It comes as a great shock to see Gary Cooper killing off the Indians and, although you are rooting for Gary Cooper, that the Indians are you.

JAMES BALDWIN (1924–1987). Recalling his youth, speech at the Cambridge Union, Cambridge University (England), 17 February 1965

To be black and conscious in America is to be in a constant state of rage.

JAMES BALDWIN (1924–1987). In "Negro Leaders on Violence," *Time,* 20 August 1965

"Say It Loud: 'I'm Black and I'm Proud.'"

JAMES BROWN (1934–). Song title, 1968

I am an invisible man. . . . I am a man of substance, of flesh and bone, fiber and liquids—and I might even be said to possess a mind. I am invisible, understand, simply because people refuse to see me.

RALPH ELLISON (1914–1994). Prologue to *The Invisible Man,* 1952

Black men built the railroads, not blue eyes.

RALPH WALDO EMERSON (1803–1882). Journal, 1845, undated

Black and White is not color no more, it's an attitude. . . . Every day more people wake up black than went to bed black.

DICK GREGORY (1932–). In Landon Gerald Dowdey, ed., "The Kingdom: A Free Community," *Journey to Freedom,* 1969

I always said if I lived to get grown and had a chance, I was going to try to get something for my mother and I was going to do something for the black man of the South [even] if it would cost my life; I was determined to see that things were changed.

FANNIE LOU HAMER (1917–1977). Mississippi human rights leader. In *Freedomways,* second quarter, 1965

What happens to a dream deferred?

Does it dry up
like a raisin in the sun?
Or fester like a sore—
And then run?
Does it stink like rotten meat?
Or crust and sugar over—
like a syrupy sweet?

Maybe it just sags
like a heavy load.

Or does it explode?

LANGSTON HUGHES (1902–1967). "Harlem [2]" (complete poem), 1959, *The Collected Poems of Langston Hughes,* ed. Arnold Rampersad and David Roessel, 1994

Dreams kick asunder,
Why not go under?

There's a world to gain.

But suppose I don't want it,
Why take it?

To remake it.

LANGSTON HUGHES (1902–1967). "Question and Answer," 1966, *The Collected Poems of Langston Hughes,* ed. Arnold Rampersad and David Roessel, 1994

Wear it
Like a banner
For the proud—
Not like a shroud.
Wear it
Like a song
Soaring high—
Not moan or cry.

LANGSTON HUGHES (1902–1967). "Color" (complete poem), 1967, *The Collected Poems of Langston Hughes,* ed. Arnold Rampersad and David Roessel, 1994

I have a dream that one day on the red hills of Georgia, sons of former slaves and sons of former slave-owners will be able to sit down together at the table of brotherhood.

I have a dream that one day, even the state of Mississippi, a state sweltering with the heat of injustice, sweltering with the heat of oppression, will be transformed into a oasis of freedom and justice.

I have a dream my four little children will one day live in a nation where they will not be judged by the color of their skin but by content of their character. I have a dream today!

MARTIN LUTHER KING, JR. (1929–1968). "I Have a Dream," keynote address of the Civil Rights March at the Lincoln Memorial, Washington, 28 August 1963

I never will forget a moment in Birmingham when a white policeman accosted a little Negro girl seven or eight years old, who was walking in a demonstration with her mother. "What do you want?" the policemen asked her gruffly, and the little girl looked him straight in the eye and answered, "Fee-dom." She couldn't even pronounce it, but she knew. It was beautiful! Many times when I have been in sorely trying situations, the memory of that little one has come into my mind, and has buoyed me.

MARTIN LUTHER KING, JR. (1929–1968). Alex Haley interview, *Playboy,* January 1965

We are not fighting for integration, nor are we fighting for separation. We are fighting for recognition as human beings.

MALCOLM X (1925–1965). Speech, New York City, 1964

Our objective is complete freedom, complete justice, complete equality, by any means necessary.

MALCOLM X (1925–1965). "I Don't Mean Bananas," *Malcolm X Speaks,* 1965

I had no idea when I refused to give up my seat on that Montgomery bus that my small action would help put an end to the segregation laws in the south. I only knew that I was tired of being pushed around. I was a regular person, just as good as anybody else. There had been a few times in my life when I was treated by white people like a regular person, so I knew what that felt like. It was time. It was time that other white people started treating me that way.

ROSA PARKS (1913–). *Rosa Parks: My Story,* 1, 1992

My feets is tired, but my soul is rested.

> SISTER POLLARD. Elderly Montgomery bus-boycotter, December 1955. In Martin Luther King, Jr., *Strength to Love,* 14.3, 1963

In one generation we have moved from denying a black man service at a lunch counter to elevating one to the highest military office in the nation, and to being a serious contender for the presidency.

This is a magnificent country and I am proud to be one of its sons.

> COLIN L. POWELL (1937–). Announcing his decision not to seek the presidential nomination, news conference, Alexandria (Virginia), 8 November 1995

The poor white man and the poor black man is sittin' in the same saddle today.

> NATE SHAW (1885–1973). *All God's Dangers: The Life of Nate Shaw,* ed. Theodore Rosengarten, 1974. In Wendell Berry, "A Remarkable Man" (2), 1975, *What Are People For?: Essays,* 1990

Caucasian-American combat soldier: "And what would you do with Hitler?"

African-American combat soldier: "I would have made him a Negro and dropped him somewhere in the USA."

> ARTHUR SZYK (1894–1951). Cartoon caption, 1944. In Pierce Butler, "Artistic Champion of Freedom: Portrait of a Master Illustrator," *Perceptions,* May-June 1996

Oppression has, at one stroke, deprived the descendants of the Africans of almost all the privile ges of humanity. The Negro of the United States has lost even the remembrance of his country; the language which his forefathers spoke is never heard around him; he abjured their religion and forgot their customs when he ceased to belong to Africa without acquiring any claim to European privileges.

> ALEXIS de TOCQUEVILLE (1805–1859). *Democracy in America,* 1.18, 1835, tr. Henry Reeve and Francis Bowen, 1862

I believe it is the duty of the Negro—as the greater part of the race is already doing—to deport himself modestly in regard to political claims, depending upon the slow but sure influences that proceed from the possession of property, intelligence, and high character for the full recognition of his political rights.

> BOOKER T. WASHINGTON (1856–1915). Atlanta Exposition address, 18 September 1895, *Up from Slavery: An Autobiography,* 14, 1901

It has been a matter of deep interest to me to note the number of people who have come to shake hands with me after an address, who say that this is the first time they have ever called a Negro "Mister."

> BOOKER T. WASHINGTON (1856–1915). *Up from Slavery: An Autobiography,* 15, 1901

Goddammit, look! We live here and they live there. We black and they white. They got things and we ain't. They do things and we can't. It's just like living in jail.

> RICHARD WRIGHT (1908–1960). *Native Son,* 1, 1940

❧

Ninety-nine percent of the boys I grew up with are dead, in jail or on drugs—it's a miracle I'm alive.

ANONYMOUS (AFRICAN-AMERICAN). Ghetto dweller. In "Tapping the Resources of the Ghetto," *Look,* 9 July 1968

We shall overcome, we shall overcome,
We shall overcome some day.
Oh, deep in my heart I do believe,
We shall overcome some day.

> ANONYMOUS. "We Shall Overcome" (civil rights song), 1946

I know one thing we did right
Was the day we started to fight,
Keep your eye on the prize,
Hold, hold on!

> ANONYMOUS. "Keep Your Eye on the Prize" (civil rights song), 1960s

Just like a tree that's standing by the water,
We shall not be moved.

> ANONYMOUS. "We Shall Not Be Moved" (civil rights song), adapted from a hymn

Black is beautiful.

> SLOGAN (AFRICAN-AMERICAN). 1960s

AGE

See also • Adolescence ○ Age & Youth ○ Avarice: Lord Byron ○ Death ○ Longevity ○ Middle Age ○ Youth

As we grow old, the beauty steals inward.

> BRONSON ALCOTT (1799–1888). In Ralph Waldo Emerson, journal, 1845, undated

The older I get, the greater power I seem to have to help the world; I am like a snowball—the further I am rolled, the more I gain.

> SUSAN B. ANTHONY (1820–1906). In Ida Husted Harper, *The Life and Work of Susan B. Anthony,* 46, 1898

The older I get, the faster I was.

> CHARLES BARKLEY (1963–). Basketball player. Bob Costa television interview, NBC, 22 January 1995

To me, old age is always fifteen years older than I am.

> BERNARD M. BARUCH (1870–1965). Remark made on his 85th birthday. In "Newsmakers," *Newsweek,* 29 August 1955

There is only one solution if old age is not to be an absurd parody of our former life, and that is to go on pursuing ends that give our existence a meaning—devotion to individuals, to groups or to causes, social, political, intellectual or creative work.

> SIMONE de BEAUVOIR (1908–1986). Conclusion to *The Coming of Age,* 1970, tr. Frank O'Brian, 1973

The [character] of a country can be seen simply in how it treats its old people.

> THE BRATZLAVER (1770–1811)

Old age takes away from us what we have inherited and gives us what we have earned.

> GERALD BRENAN (1894–1987). "Life," *Thoughts in a Dry Season: A Miscellany,* 1978

Grow old along with me!
The best is yet to be,
The last of life, for which the first was made.
> ROBERT BROWNING (1812–1889). Opening lines, "Rabbi Ben Ezra," *Dramatis Personae*, 1864

It's nice to be here. When you're 99 years old, it's nice to be any-place.
> GEORGE BURNS (1896–1996)

There's many a good tune played on an old fiddle.
> SAMUEL BUTLER (1835–1902). *The Way of All Flesh*, 61, 1903

To grow old is to move from passion to compassion.
> ALBERT CAMUS (1913–1960). April 1950, *Notebooks: 1942—1951*, tr. Justin O'Brien, 1966

One part of him is old and another is still unborn.
> ELIAS CANETTI (1905–1994). 1976, *The Secret Heart of the Clock: Notes, Aphorisms, Fragments: 1973–1985*, tr. Joel Agee, 1989

Considering the alternative, it's not too bad at all.
> MAURICE CHEVALIER (1888–1972). When asked on his seventy-second birthday how he felt about becoming elderly. In Michael Freedland, *Maurice Chevalier*, 20, 1981

Eighty years old! No eyes left, no ears, no teeth, no legs, no wind! And when all is said and done, how astonishingly well one does without them!
> PAUL CLAUDEL (1868–1955). French poet. In Malcolm Cowley, "Vices and Pleasures," *The View from 80*, 1980

I am old enough to tell the truth. It is one of the privileges of age.
> GEORGES CLEMENCEAU (1841–1929). Interview with the author at age 87. In George Sylvester Viereck, "The Tiger Looks at the Post-War World," *Glimpses of the Great*, 1930

Reporter: What do you think you'd hit if you were playing today?
Cobb: About .320.
Reporter: Why so low?
Cobb: You have to remember, I'm sixty-two years old.
> TY COBB (1886–1961). Baseball player. In David James Duncan, *The Brothers K*, 5.7.4, 1992

When you win, you're an old pro. When you lose, you're an old man.
> CHARLEY CONERLY (1921–). Football player. In Bob Green, "How Never to Be at a Loss for Words," *San Francisco Sunday Examiner & Chronicle*, 8 July 1979

Whilst I was young and strong I was capable of very warm attachments, but of late years, though I still have very friendly feelings towards many persons, I have lost the power of becoming deeply attached to anyone, not even so deeply to my good and dear friends Hooker and Huxley, as I should formerly have been. . . . The loss of these tastes is a loss of happiness, and may possibly be injurious to the intellect, and more probably to the moral character, by enfeebling the emotional part of our nature.
> CHARLES DARWIN (1809–1882). *Autobiography*. In Donald Fleming, "Charles Darwin, the Anaesthetic Man," *Victorian Studies*, March 1961

Getting old ain't for sissies.
> BETTE DAVIS (1908–1989). Quoted by Paul Newman, James Lipton television interview, *Inside the Actors Studio*, BVO, 31 May 1995

After the age of eighty, all contemporaries are friends.
> MADAME de DINO

Old man, exhausted by ordeal, detached from human deeds, feeling the approach of the eternal cold, but always watching in the shadows for the gleam of hope!
> CHARLES de GAULLE (1890–1970). Closing paragraph, *The Complete War Memoirs of Charles de Gaulle*, 1959, tr. Richard Howard, 1998

It is time to be old,
To take in sail.
> RALPH WALDO EMERSON (1803–1882). Opening lines, "Terminus," *May-Day and Other Poems*, 1867

My new book [*Society and Solitude*] sells faster, it appears, than either of its foregoers. This is not for its merit, but only shows that old age is a good advertisement. Your name has been seen so often that your book must be worth buying.
> RALPH WALDO EMERSON (1803–1882). Journal, 15 March 1870

It is nonsense for you to talk of old age so long as you outrun young men in the race for service and in the midst of anxious times fill rooms with your laughter and inspire youth with hope when they are on the brink of despair.
> MOHANDAS K. GANDHI (1869–1948). 22 May 1932. In Mahadev Desai, *The Diary of Mahadev Desai*, 1953

You know you're growing old when [almost] everything hurts, and what doesn't hurt doesn't work.
> HY GARDNER (1908–1989)

Joe McCarthy (baseball manager): Lefty, I don't think you're throwing as hard as you used to.
Gomez (pitcher): You're wrong, Joe. I'm throwing twice as hard, but the ball isn't going as fast.
> VERNON "LEFTY" GOMEZ (1909–1989). In Joseph Durso, "Vernon (Lefty) Gomez, 80, Dies; Starred as Pitcher for the Yankees," *New York Times*, 18 February 1989

Time goes by: reputation increases, ability declines.
> DAG HAMMARSKJÖLD (1905–1961). 1950, *Markings*, tr. Leif Sjöberg and W. H. Auden, 1964

I'm now at the age where I've got to prove that I'm just as good as I never was.
> REX HARRISON (1908–1990). Attributed

You will recognize, my boy, the first sign of old age: It is when you go out into the streets of London and realize for the first time how young the policemen look.
> SIR SEYMOUR HICKS (1871–1949). In C. R. D. Pulling, *They Were Singing*, 7, 1952

The best part of the art of living is to know how to grow old gracefully.
> ERIC HOFFER (1902–1983). *The Passionate State of Mind: And Other Aphorisms*, 235, 1954

Sensuality reconciles us with the human race. The misanthropy of the old is due in large part to the fading of the magic glow of desire.

> ERIC HOFFER (1902–1983). *Reflections on the Human Condition,* 138, 1973

Oh to be seventy again.

> OLIVER WENDELL HOLMES, JR. (1841–1935). Upon seeing an attractive woman on his 90th birthday, 1931

You know you're getting old when the candles cost more than the cake.

> BOB HOPE (1903–)

Love, the last defense against old age—the last, and for those whose good fortune it is to have some one person to care for, or who have learned the infinitely difficult art of loving all their neighbors, the best.

> ALDOUS HUXLEY (1894–1963). "Old Age," *Texts and Pretexts: An Anthology of Poetry with Commentaries,* 1933

That happy age when a man can be idle with impunity.

> WASHINGTON IRVING (1783–1859). "Rip Van Winkle," *The Sketch Book,* 1820

Whenever a man's friends begin to compliment him about looking young, he may be sure that they think he is growing old.

> WASHINGTON IRVING (1783–1859). "Bachelors," *Bracebridge Hall,* 1822

We treat old people like we treat animals. Just put them in a cage somewhere until they die.

> LYNDON B. JOHNSON (1908–1973). Referring to nursing homes. In Merle Miller, *Lyndon: An Oral Biography,* 6 ("The Private Citizen"), 1980

My diseases are an asthma and a dropsy, and what is less curable, seventy-five.

> SAMUEL JOHNSON (1709–1784). Letter to William Gerard Hamilton, 20 October 1784

Old people are fond of giving good advice; it consoles them for no longer being capable of setting a bad example.

> LA ROCHEFOUCAULD (1613–1680). *Maxims,* 93, 1665, tr. Leonard Tancock, 1959

"Oh to be old again," said a young corpse.

> STANISLAW J. LEC (1909–1966). *Unkempt Thoughts,* p. 81, tr. Jacek Galazka, 1962

When I get older, losing my hair,
  many years from now.
Will you still be sending me a valentine,
Birthday greetings, bottle of wine?
If I'd been out till quarter to three,
  would you lock the door?
Will you still need me,
  will you still feed me,
When I'm sixty-four?

> JOHN LENNON (1940–1980) and PAUL McCARTNEY (1942–). "When I'm Sixty-Four" (song), 1967

Age is opportunity no less
Than youth itself, though in another dress,
And as the evening twilight fades away
The sky is filled with stars, invisible by day.

> HENRY WADSWORTH LONGFELLOW (1807–1882). Closing lines, "Morituri Salutamus" (Poem for the Fiftieth Anniversary of the Class of 1825 in Bowdoin College), 1875

Nobody grows old by merely living a number of years. People grow old by deserting their ideals. Years may wrinkle the skin, but to give up interest wrinkles the soul. . . . You are as young as your faith, as old as your doubt; as young as your self-confidence, as old as your fear; as young as your hope, as old as your despair.

> DOUGLAS MacARTHUR (1880–1964). "War Is No Longer a Medium of Practical Settlement of International Differences," address at an American Legion dinner honoring him, Ambassador Hotel, Los Angeles, 26 January 1955

Old age is far more than white hair, wrinkles, the feeling that it is too late and the game finished, that the stage belongs to the rising generations. The true evil is not the weakening of the body, but the indifference of the soul.

> ANDRÉ MAUROIS (1885–1967). *The Art of Living,* 8, 1940, tr. James Whitall, 1959

The older I grow, the more I distrust the familiar doctrine that age brings wisdom.

> H. L. MENCKEN (1880–1956). "Advice to Young Men: The Venerable Examined," *Prejudices: Third Series,* 1922

You shall rise up before the hoary head, and honor the face of an old man.

> MOSES (14th cent. B.C.). *Leviticus* 19:32

To honor an old man is showing respect to God.

> MUHAMMAD (A.D. 570?–632). *The Sayings of Muhammad,* 19, tr. Abdullah Al-Suhrawardy, 1941

How confusing the beams from memory's lamp are;
One day a bachelor, the next a grampa.
What is the secret of the trick?
How did I get so old so quick?

> OGDEN NASH (1902–1971). "Preface to the Past," *You Can't Get There from Here,* 1957

One can savor sights and sounds more deeply when one gets really old. It may be the last time you see a sunset, a tree, the snow, or know winter. The sea, a lake, all become as in childhood, magical and a great wonder: then seen for the first time, now perhaps for the last. Music, bird songs, the wind, the waves: One listens to tones with deeper delight and appreciation—"loving well," to borrow from Shakespeare's seventy-third sonnet, "that which I must leave ere long."

> HELEN NEARING (1904–1990). "Twilight and Evening Star," *Loving and Leaving the Good Life,* 1992

A person is not old until regrets take the place of hopes and plans.

> SCOTT NEARING (1883–1985). In Helen Nearing, "Twilight and Evening Star," *Loving and Leaving the Good Life,* 1992

The older you get the stronger the wind gets—and it's always in your face.

JACK NICKLAUS (1940–). Golfer. In *International Herald Tribune* (Paris), February 1990

Age is mind over matter. If you don't mind, it doesn't matter.

LEROY "SATCHEL" PAIGE (1906–1982). Recalled on his death, 8 June 1982

How old would you be if you didn't know how old you was?

LEROY "SATCHEL" PAIGE (1906–1982). In Morrie Goldfischer, "Ruminations Inspired by a Medicare Card," *New York Times,* 8 June 1984

When men grow virtuous in their old age, they only make a sacrifice to God of the devil's leavings.

ALEXANDER POPE (1688–1744). "Thoughts on Various Subjects," *Miscellanies in Prose and Verse* (published with Jonathan Swift), vol. 2, 1727

Nothing is more beautiful than cheerfulness in an old face.

JEAN PAUL FRIEDRICH RICHTER (1763–1825). *Titan,* 1803

The whiter my hair becomes, the more ready people are to believe what I say.

BERTRAND RUSSELL (1872–1970). Woodrow Wyatt television interview, BBC, London, 1959, *Bertrand Russell Speaks His Mind,* 7, 1960

Old men are dangerous; it doesn't matter to them what is going to happen to the world.

GEORGE BERNARD SHAW (1856–1950). *Heartbreak House: A Fantasia in the Russian Manner on English Themes,* 2, 1919

Most people are dead at my age, anyway. You could look it up.

CASEY STENGEL (1890?–1975). Baseball manager

The older we get the more we seem to think that everything was better in the past.

JUNICHIRO TANIZAKI (1886–1965). "In Praise of Shadows," tr. Thomas J. Harper and Edward G. Seidensticker. In Phillip Lopate, ed., *The Art of the Personal Essay,* 1994

I have lived some thirty years on this planet, and I have yet to hear the first syllable of valuable or even earnest advice from my seniors.

HENRY DAVID THOREAU (1817–1862). "Economy," *Walden; or Life in the Woods,* 1854

Wrinkles should merely indicate where the smiles have been.

MARK TWAIN (1835–1910). *Following the Equator: A Journey Around the World,* 52 (epigraph), 1897

I'm Not as Old as I Used to Be.

FRANCES WEAVER. Book title, 1997

I this day enter on my eighty-fifth year; . . . How little have I suffered yet by "the rush of numerous years!" It is true, I am not so agile as I was in times past. I do not run or walk so fast as I did.

JOHN WESLEY (1703–1791). English evangelist and founder of Methodism. Journal, 28 June 1788. Wesley attributed his good health "to the power of God," "my constant exercise and change of air," "my having constantly, for about sixty years, risen at four in the morning," and "my constant preaching at five in the morning, for above fifty years."

All of a sudden, I'm older than my parents were when I thought *they* were old.

LOIS WYSE (1928–). "Age-Old Conversations," *Funny, You Don't Look Like a Grandmother,* 1990

An aged man is but a paltry thing,
A tattered coat upon a stick.

WILLIAM BUTLER YEATS (1865–1939). "Sailing to Byzantium" (2), *The Tower,* 1928

It's a sign of age if you feel like the morning after the night before and you haven't been anywhere.

ANONYMOUS

Growing old is mandatory; growing up is optional.

SAYING (AMERICAN). Bumper sticker. In Herb Caen column (on his 80th birthday), *San Francisco Chronicle,* 3 April 1996

The family with an old person in it possesses a jewel.

SAYING (CHINESE)

There's no fool like an old fool.

SAYING (ENGLISH)

There's no knave like an old knave.

SAYING (ENGLISH)

You can't teach an old dog new tricks.

SAYING (ENGLISH)

You're never too old to learn.

SAYING (ENGLISH)
See Repentance: John Ray

An old man loved is winter with flowers.

SAYING (GERMAN)

An old man in a house is a good sign.

SAYING (HEBREW)

AGE & YOUTH

See also • Adultery: Oscar Wilde ○ Age ○ Parents ○ Youth

Young men, in the conduct and manage[ment] of actions, embrace more than they can hold; stir more than they can quiet; fly to the end without consideration of the means and degrees. . . .

Men of age object too much, consult too long, adventure too little, repent too soon, and seldom drive business home to the full period, but content themselves with a mediocrity of success.

FRANCIS BACON (1561–1626). "Of Youth and Age," *Essays,* 1625

In youth we run into difficultys, in old age, diffikultys runs into us.

JOSH BILLINGS (1818–1885). "Jews Harps," *Everybody's Friend, or; Josh Billing's Encyclopedia and Proverbial Philosophy of Wit and Humor,* 1874

When we are young, we are courageous, but it is only in old age that prudence is at its height.

BION (325?–255? B.C.). In Diogenes Laertius (A.D. 3rd cent.), *Lives of Eminent Philosophers,* 4.7, tr. R. D. Hicks, 1925

Therefore I summon age
To grant youth's heritage.
> ROBERT BROWNING (1812–1889). "Rabbi Ben Ezra" (13), *Dramatis Personae*, 1864

The dominant thought of youth is the bigness of the world, of age its smallness.
> JOHN BUCHAN (1875–1940). "The Other Side of the Hill" (4), *Pilgrim's Way: An Essay in Recollection*, 1940

Youth is a blunder; manhood, a struggle; old age, a regret.
> BENJAMIN DISRAELI (1804–1881). *Coningsby: Or, The New Generation*, 3.1, 1844

In youth we learn, in old age we understand.
> MARIE von EBNER-ESCHENBACH (1830–1916). *Aphorisms*, p. 25, 1880–1905, tr. David Scrase and Wolfgang Mieder, 1994

In youth our judgments are obscured by our hopes; in age, by our regrets.
> PAUL ELDRIDGE (1888–1982). *Maxims for a Modern Man*, 144, 1965

In old age the root of virtue is fatigue; in youth, fear.
> PAUL ELDRIDGE (1888–1982). *Maxims for a Modern Man*, 258, 1965

I find it a great and fatal difference whether I court the Muse, or the Muse courts me: That is the ugly disparity between age and youth.
> RALPH WALDO EMERSON (1803–1882). Journal, July 1866

If youth but knew; if old age could!
> HENRI ÉSTIENNE (1531–1598). *Les Prémices*, 4.4, 1594

Old Boys have their Playthings as well as young Ones; the Difference is only in the Price.
> BENJAMIN FRANKLIN (1706–1790). *Poor Richard's Almanack*, August 1752
> See Possessions: Malcolm S. Forbes

There is a general moral deterioration in old age. The old saying that youth has no virtue is just the opposite of the truth: *only* in youth does one find virtue. The older you get, the worse you become.
> SIGMUND FREUD (1856–1939). Remark to the author, 18 January 1935. In Joseph Wortis, *Fragments of an Analysis with Freud*, 1954

Young men wish: love, money, and health. One day, they'll say: health, money, and love.
> PAUL GÉRALDY (1885–1983)

Whereas in my youth I succeeded daily and under all circumstances, I now succeed only periodically and under favorable conditions.
> GOETHE (1749–1832). On his literary productivity at age 79, 11 March 1828. In Peter Eckermann, *Conversations with Goethe*, 1836–1848, tr. John Oxenford, 1850

Pleasure is the business of the young, business the pleasure of the old.
> FULKE GREVILLE (1558–1628). *Maxims, Characters, and Reflections*, p. 10, 1756

The old man pays regard to riches, and the youth reverences virtue. The old man deifies prudence; the youth commits himself to magnanimity and chance. . . . Age looks with anger on the temerity of youth, and youth with contempt on the scrupulosity of age.
> SAMUEL JOHNSON (1709–1784). *Rasselas: The Prince of Abyssinia*, 26, 1759

If a young or middle—aged man, when leaving a company, does not recollect where he laid his hat, it is nothing; but if the same inattention is discovered in an old man, people will shrug up their shoulders, and say, "His memory is going."
> SAMUEL JOHNSON (1709–1784). Recorded in 1783. In James Boswell, *The Life of Samuel Johnson*, 1791

What youth found and must find outside, the man of life's afternoon must find within himself.
> CARL G. JUNG (1875–1961). "On the Psychology of the Unconscious" (5), 1917, *Two Essays on Analytical Psychology*, tr. R. F. C. Hull, 1953

Well, didn't we all
Behave like that as young men?
> JUVENAL (A.D. 60?–127?). *Satires*, 8.163, tr. Peter Green, 1967

Ageism is any discrimination against people on the basis of chronological age—whether old or young. It's responsible for an enormous neglect of social resources.
> MAGGIE KUHN (1905–1995). In Carol Offen, "Profile of a Gray Panther," *Retirement Living*, December 1972

From the earliest times the old have rubbed it into the young that they are wiser than they, and before the young had discovered what nonsense this was they were old too, and it profited them to carry on the imposture.
> W. SOMERSET MAUGHAM (1874–1965). *Cakes and Ale*, 11, 1930

There was no respect for youth when I was young, and now that I am old there is no respect for age—I missed it coming and going.
> J. B. PRIESTLY (1894–1984)

They who would be young when they are old must be old when they are young.
> JOHN RAY (1628–1705). Comp., *A Collection of English Proverbs*, p. 34, 1678

I will not make age an issue. . . . I am not going to exploit for political purposes my opponent's youth and inexperience.
> RONALD REAGAN (1911–). At age 73, on his 56-year-old opponent, Walter F. Mondale, televised presidential campaign debate, 21 October 1984

The young have aspirations that never come to pass, the old have reminiscences of what never happened.
> SAKI (1870–1916). "Reginald at the Carlton," *Reginald*, 1904

The main difference between youth and age will always be that youth looks forward to life, and old age to death: and that while the one has a short past and a long future before it, the case is just the opposite with the other.
> ARTHUR SCHOPENHAUER (1788–1860). "Counsels and Maxims" (5), *Essays of Arthur Schopenhauer*, tr. T. Bailey Saunders, 1851

Falstaff: A man can no more separate age and covetousness than 'a can part young limbs and lechery.
> SHAKESPEARE (1564–1616). *Henry IV,* Part II, 1.2.256, 1597

Crabbed age and youth cannot live together:
Youth is full of pleasance, age is full of care;
Youth like summer morn, age like winter weather;
Youth like summer brave, age like winter bare.
Youth is full of sport, age's breath is short;
    Youth is nimble, age is lame;
Youth is hot and bold, age is weak and cold;
    Youth is wild, and age is tame,
Age, I do abhor thee; youth, I do adore thee.
> SHAKESPEARE (1564–1616). *The Passionate Pilgrim,* 12, 1599

The denunciation of the young is a necessary part of the hygiene of older people, and greatly assists the circulation of their blood.
> LOGAN PEARSALL SMITH (1865–1946). "Last Words," *More Trivia,* 1934

Old and young, we are all on our last cruise.
> ROBERT LOUIS STEVENSON (1850–1894). "Crabbed Age and Youth," *Virginibus Puerisque,* 1881

The first half of life consists of the capacity to enjoy without the chance; the last half consists of the chance without the capacity.
> MARK TWAIN (1835–1910). Letter to Edward L. Dimmitt, 19 July 1901

Age demands respect; youth, love.
> MARY WOLLSTONECRAFT (1759–1797). *A Vindication of the Rights of Men,* p. 141, 1790

❧

Young folk, silly folk; old folk, cold folk.
> SAYING (DUTCH)

A new broom sweeps clean, but an old one knows the corners.
> SAYING (ENGLISH)

The old forget; the young don't know.
> SAYING (JAPANESE)

Young trees bend, old trees break.
> SAYING (YIDDISH)

The young are slaves to novelty; the old, to custom.
> SAYING

AGNOSTICISM

See also • Atheism ○ God

I do not consider it an insult, but rather a compliment to be called an agnostic. I do not pretend to know where many ignorant men are sure—that is all that agnosticism means.
> CLARENCE DARROW (1857–1938). Defending John Thomas Scopes who was being tried for teaching Darwinism in a public school, speech, Dayton (Tennessee), 13 July 1925

In my most extreme fluctuations I have never been an Atheist in the sense of denying the existence of a God. I think that generally (and more and more as I grow older), but not always, that an Agnostic would be the more correct description of my state of mind.
> CHARLES DARWIN (1809–1882). Letter, 1879, *The Autobiography of Charles Darwin and Selected Letters,* 3, ed. Francis Darwin, 1892

O God, if there is a God, have pity on my soul, if there is a soul.
> FREDERICK II (1712–1786). In Margaret Goldsmith, *Frederick the Great,* 4, 1929

Fix reason firmly in her seat, and call to her tribunal every fact, every opinion. Question with boldness even the existence of a god; because, if there be one, he must more approve of the homage of reason, than that of blindfolded fear.
> THOMAS JEFFERSON (1743–1826). Letter to his nephew Peter Carr, 10 August 1787

Well, I tell you, if I have been wrong in my agnosticism, when I die I'll walk up to God in a manly way and say, Sir, I made an honest mistake.
> H. L. MENCKEN (1880–1956). Quoted by John Kenneth Galbraith, interview with the author. In Naim Attallah, *Singular Encounters,* 1990

Which is it? Is man only God's mistake or God only man's mistake?
> FRIEDRICH NIETZSCHE (1844–1900). "Maxims and Arrows" (7), *Twilight of the Idols,* 1889, tr. R. J. Hollingdale, 1968

The very scale of the universe—more than a hundred billion galaxies, each containing more than a hundred billion stars—speaks to us of the inconsequentiality of human events in the cosmic context. We see a universe simultaneously very beautiful and very violent. We see a universe that does not exclude a traditional Western or Eastern god, but that does not require one either.
> CARL SAGAN (1934–1996). *Broca's Brain: Reflections on the Romance of Science,* 23, 1979

AGRICULTURE

See also • Farming

Of all the occupations by which gain is secured, none is better than agriculture, none more profitable, none more delightful, none more becoming to a free man.
> CICERO (106–43 B.C.). *De officiis,* 1.52, tr. Walter Miller, 1913

The agricultural human's pull historically has been toward the monoculture of annuals. Nature's pull is toward a polyculture of perennials.
> WES JACKSON. *New Roots for Agriculture.* In Wendell Berry, "A Practical Harmony," 1988, *What Are People For?: Essays,* 1990

No other human occupation opens so wide a field for the profitable and agreeable combination of labor with cultivated thought as agriculture.
> ABRAHAM LINCOLN (1809–1865). Address before the Wisconsin State Agricultural Society, Milwaukee, 30 September 1859

Agriculture is the earliest and most honorable of arts.
> ROUSSEAU (1712–1778). *Emile; or, Treatise on Education,* 3, 1762, tr. Barbara Foxley, 1911

With the introduction of agriculture mankind entered upon a long period of meanness, misery, and madness, from which they are only now being freed by the beneficent operation of the machine. . . . Companionship and cooperation are essential elements in the happiness of the average man, and these are to be obtained in industry far more fully than in agriculture.

> BERTRAND RUSSELL (1872–1970). *The Conquest of Happiness,* 10, 1930

Blessed be agriculture! if one does not have too much of it.

> CHARLES DUDLEY WARNER (1829–1900). "Preliminary," *My Summer in a Garden,* 1871
> See Farming: Warner

I know of no pursuit in which more real and important services can be rendered to any country than by improving its agriculture, its breed of useful animals, and other branches of a husbandman's cares.

> GEORGE WASHINGTON (1732–1799). Letter to John Sinclair, 20 July 1794

AIDS

See also • Homosexuality ○ Sexuality

When a person has sex, they're not just having it with that partner, they're having it with everybody that partner has had it with for the past ten years.

> OTIS RAY BOWEN (1918–). Statement on AIDS, 1987

Has America become a country where classroom discussion of the Ten Commandments is impermissible, but teacher instructions in safe sodomy are to be mandatory?

> PATRICK BUCHANAN (1938–). On AIDS health education. In *Conservative Digest,* August 1988

From the point of view of the pharmaceutical industry, the AIDS problem has already been solved. After all, we already have a drug which can be sold at the incredible price of $8,000 an annual dose, and which has the added virtue of not diminishing the market by actually curing anyone.

> BARBARA EHRENREICH (1941–). "Phallic Science," 1988, *The Worst Years of Our Lives: Irreverent Notes from a Decade of Greed,* 1990

Over and over, these men cry out against the weight of so many losses—not just a lover dead, but friends and friends of friends, dozens of them, until it seems that AIDS is all there is and all there ever will be.

> JANE GROSS. "AIDS: The Next Phase," *New York Times,* 16 March 1987

Sometimes I have a terrible feeling that I am dying not from the [AIDS] virus, but from being untouchable.

> AMANDA HEGGS. In *Guardian* (British newspaper), 12 June 1989

If you have a monogamous relationship, keep it. If you don't have one, get it.

> C. EVERETT KOOP (1916–). Surgeon general. On protecting yourself from AIDS. In "Currents," *U.S. News & World Report,* 4 May 1987

I have learned more about love, selflessness and human understanding in this great adventure in the world of AIDS than I ever did in the cutthroat, competitive world in which I spent my life.

> ANTHONY PERKINS (1932–1992). Actor. Posthumously published statement. In *Independent* (British newspaper), 20 September 1992

AIDS obliges people to think of sex as having, possibly, the direst consequences: suicide. Or murder.

> SUSAN SONTAG (1933–). *AIDS and Its Metaphors,* 7, 1989

⚜

Silence = Death.

> SLOGAN (AMERICAN). ACT UP (an AIDS activist group), 1990

AIRPLANES

See also • Machines ○ Misjudgments: Ralph Waldo Emerson ○ Religion & Science: Charles A. Lindbergh

On April 25, 1974, the *Toronto Star* reported the deaths of Mr. Todd Missfield and Ms. Bonnie Johnson who died when their Cessna 150 airplane crashed into a billboard. The message on the billboard read: "Learn to Fly."

> DON ATYEO (1950–) and JONATHON GREEN. Comps,. *Don't Quote Me,* 19, 1981

If I had to choose, I would rather have birds than airplanes.

> CHARLES A. LINDBERGH (1902–1974). Recalled on his death, 26 August 1974

Flight by machines heavier than air is unpractical and insignificant, if not utterly impossible.

> SIMON NEWCOMB (1835–1909). Eighteen months before the Wright brothers' flight at Kitty Hawk (North Carolina) in 1903. In Stephen Pile, *The Book of Heroic Failures,* 11, 1979

ALCOHOL

See also • Addiction ○ Advertising Copy & Slogans ○ Coffee ○ Drugs, Illegal ○ Lying: Tennessee Williams ○ Tobacco

R-E-M-O-R-S-E!
Those dry Martinis did the work for me;
Last night at twelve I felt immense,
Today I feel like thirty cents.
My eyes are bleared, my coppers hot,
I'll try to eat, but I cannot.
It is no time for mirth and laughter,
The cold, gray dawn of the morning after.

> GEORGE ADE (1866–1944). *The Sultan of Sulu,* 2, 1903

When you stop drinking, you have to deal with this marvelous personality that started you drinking in the first place.

> JIMMY BRESLIN (1930–). *Table Money,* 11, 1986

In the new study, the researchers found that women who were relatively heavy drinkers, consuming two to five alcoholic drinks each day, were 41 percent more likely to develop breast cancer than nondrinkers. But for moderate drinkers who consumed three-fourths to one drink, or 10 grams of alcohol a day, the risk was only 9 percent higher than among nondrinkers.

> JANE E. BRODY (1941–). Summarizing findings in a study published in the *Journal of the American Medical Association* (Stephanie Smith-Warner, lead author), "Studies Confirm Relationship of Alcohol to Breast Cancer," *New York Times,* 18 February 1998

Alcohol is nicissary f'r a man so that now an' thin he can have a good opinion iv himsilf, ondisturbed by th' facts.

> FINLEY PETER DUNNE (1867–1936). "Mr. Dooley on Alcohol," *Chicago Tribune,* 26 April 1914

First you take a drink, then the drink takes a drink, then the drink takes you.

> F. SCOTT FITZGERALD (1896–1940). In Jules Feiffer, 1964 (May 7), *Ackroyd,* 1977

Nothing more like a Fool than a drunken Man.

> BENJAMIN FRANKLIN (1706–1790). *Poor Richard's Almanack,* November 1733

Wine hath drowned more Men than the Sea.

> THOMAS FULLER (1654–1734). Comp., *Gnomologia: Adages and Proverbs,* 5744, 1732

Brandy . . . is a kind of slow poison.

> WILLIAM HAZLITT (1778–1830). "The Main Chance," *Table Talk,* 1822

Take that liquor away; I never touch strong drink. I like it too well to fool with it.

> THOMAS JONATHAN "STONEWALL" JACKSON (1820–1863). In George E. Pickett, letter to his wife, 3 June 1864

The sway of alcohol over mankind is unquestionably due to its power to stimulate the mystical faculties of human nature, usually crushed to earth by the cold facts and dry criticisms of the sober hour.

> WILLIAM JAMES (1842–1910). *The Varieties of Religious Experience: A Study in Human Nature,* 16 and 17, 1902

We drink [to] one another's health and spoil our own.

> JEROME K. JEROME (1859–1927). "On Eating and Drinking," *The Idle Thoughts of an Idle Fellow; A Book for an Idle Holiday,* 1892

I drink eternally. Drink always and ye shall never die. Keep running after a dog, and he will never bite you; drink always before the thirst, and it will never come upon you.

> JACK KEROUAC (1922–1969). Letter to Allen Ginsberg, 14 July 1955. In Joyce Carol Oates, "Down the Road," *New Yorker,* 27 March 1995

Candy
Is dandy
But liquor
Is quicker.

> OGDEN NASH (1902–1971). "Reflections on Ice-Breaking," *Hard Lines,* 1931

In the matter of drink, the only result of a century of "temperance" agitation has been a slight increase in hypocrisy.

> GEORGE ORWELL (1903–1950). "The English People" ("The Moral Outlook of the English People"), May 1947, *The Collected Essays, Journalism and Letters of George Orwell,* vol. 3, ed. Sonia Orwell and Ian Angus, 1968

Do not get drunk with wine, for that is debauchery; but be filled with the Spirit.

> PAUL (A.D. 1st cent.). *Ephesians* 5:18

Adam: Though I look old, yet I am strong and lusty;
For in my youth I never did apply
Hot and rebellious liquors in my blood.

> SHAKESPEARE (1564–1616). *As You Like It,* 2.3.47, 1599

Cassio: O God, that men should put an enemy in their mouths to steal away their brains! That we should, with joy, pleasance, revel and applause, transform ourselves into beasts!

> SHAKESPEARE (1564–1616). On drinking. *Othello,* 2.3.290, 1604

Porter: It provokes and unprovokes; it provokes the desire, but it takes away the performance: therefore, much drink may be said to be an equivocator with lechery: it makes him, and it mars him; it sets him on, and it takes him off.

> SHAKESPEARE (1564–1616). *Macbeth,* 2.3.32, 1605

I am a beer teetotaler, not a champagne teetotaler. I don't like beer.

> GEORGE BERNARD SHAW (1856–1950). *Candida,* 3, 1893

Alcohol produces artificial happiness, artificial courage, artificial gaiety, artificial self-satisfaction, thus making life bearable for millions who would otherwise be unable to endure their condition. To them alcohol is a blessing. Unfortunately, as it acts by destroying conscience, self-control, and the normal functioning of the body, it produces crime, disease, and degradation.

> GEORGE BERNARD SHAW (1856–1950). *The Intelligent Woman's Guide to Socialism, Capitalism, Sovietism and Fascism,* 79, 1928

Winston Churchill: Do you really never drink any wine at all?
Shaw: I am hard enough to keep in order as it is.

> GEORGE BERNARD SHAW (1856–1950). Format adapted. In Winston Churchill, "George Bernard Shaw," *Great Contemporaries,* 1937

Water taken in moderation cannot hurt anybody.

> MARK TWAIN (1835–1910). 12 March 1866, *Mark Twain's Notebook,* ed. Albert Bigelow Paine, 1935

Work is the curse of the drinking classes.

> OSCAR WILDE (1854–1900). In Hesketh Pearson, *The Life of Oscar Wilde,* 12, 1946

I read about the evils of drinking so I gave up reading.

> HENNY YOUNGMAN (1906–1998). In Michael Larsen, *Literary Agents: What They Do, How They Do It, and How to Find and Work with the Right One for You,* rev. ed., 13.16, 1996

❦

Drink is the curse of the working class.

> SAYING

Thought when sober, said when drunk.

> SAYING

ALIENATION

See also • Loneliness ○ Strangers

Affluence without authority breeds alienation.

> E. DIGBY BALTZELL (1915–1996). *The Protestant Establishment: Aristocracy & Caste in America,* 1, 1964

There's a scheme of evasion that has gotten into everybody. It's as though people were to say: "I get home dog tired after a terrible day out in that jungle, and then I don't want to think about it. Enough! I want to be brainwashed. I'm going to have my dinner and drink some beer, and I'm going to sit watching TV until I pass out—because that's how I feel." That means people are not putting up a struggle for the human part of themselves.

> SAUL BELLOW (1915–). "'Matters Have Gotten Out of Hand,' in a Violent Society," *U.S. News & World Report,* 28 June 1982

Another circumstance tormented me in those days: that no one resembled me and that I resembled no one else. "I am alone and they are *every one,*" I thought—and pondered.

> FYODOR DOSTOYEVSKY (1821–1881). *Notes from Underground,* 2.1, 1864, tr. Ralph E. Matlaw, 1960

When you don't feel yourself anything, I mean any part of anything, that's when you get scared.

> LILLIAN HELLMAN (1905–1984). *Days to Come,* 2.2, 1936

Estrangement from the self . . . is a precondition for both plasticity and conversion.

> ERIC HOFFER (1902–1983). *The True Believer: Thoughts on the Nature of Mass Movements,* 60, 1951

There is no alienation that a little power will not cure.

> ERIC HOFFER (1902–1983). *Reflections on the Human Condition,* 41, 1973

The more uncertain I have felt about myself, the more there has grown up in me a feeling of kinship with all things. In fact, it seems to me as if that alienation which so long separated me from the world has become transferred into my own inner world, and has revealed to me an unexpected unfamiliarity with myself.

> CARL G. JUNG (1875–1961). Closing words, *Memories, Dreams, Reflections,* ed. Aniela Jaffé, 1962

The distance to my fellow man is for me a very long one.

> FRANZ KAFKA (1883–1924). 1918, "The Eight Octavo Notebooks," *Dearest Father: Stories and Other Writings,* tr. Ernst Kaiser and Eithne Wilkins, 1954

Alienation is a form of living death. It is the acid of despair that dissolves society.

> MARTIN LUTHER KING, JR. (1929–1968). *The Trumpet of Conscience,* 3, 1967

We are born into a world where alienation awaits us. . . . Alienation as our present destiny is achieved only by outrageous violence perpetuated by human beings on human beings.

> R. D. LAING (1927–1989). Introduction to *The Politics of Experience,* 1967
>
> See Normality: Laing

The less you are, the more you have; the less you express your own life, the greater is your externalized life—the greater is your alienation.

> KARL MARX (1818–1883). *Economic and Philosophical Manuscripts,* 1844

There is no one among the living or the dead with whom I feel the slightest affinity.

> FRIEDRICH NIETZSCHE (1844–1900). In Henry Thomas and Dana Lee Thomas, "Friedrich Wilhelm Nietzsche" (6), *Living Biographies of Great Philosophers,* 1941

ALLIANCES

See also • Appeasement ○ Diplomacy ○ International Relations ○ Negotiation ○ Neutrality ○ Treaties

Alliance, *n.* In international politics, the union of two thieves who have their hands so deeply inserted in each other's pockets that they cannot separately plunder a third.

> AMBROSE BIERCE (1842–1914). *The Devil's Dictionary,* p. 11, 1911, Dover edition, 1958

For heaven's sake no sentimental alliances in which the consciousness of having performed a good deed furnishes the sole reward for our sacrifice.

> OTTO von BISMARCK (1815–1898). In Henry A. Kissinger, "The White Revolutionary: Reflections on Bismarck," *Daedalus,* Summer 1968

Never be ashamed of making alliances, and of being yourself the only party that draws advantage from them. Do not commit that stupid fault of not abandoning them whenever it is your interest so to do.

> FREDERICK II (1712–1786). "Morning the Fourth," *The Confessions of Frederick the Great,* ed. Douglas Sladen, 1915
>
> See Promises: Napoleon

Peace, commerce, and honest friendship with all nations, entangling alliances with none.

> THOMAS JEFFERSON (1734–1826). *First Inaugural Address,* 4 March 1801.

It is not the fact of alliance which deters aggression but the application it can be given in any concrete case.

> HENRY A. KISSINGER (1923–). "Reflections on American Diplomacy" (4), *Foreign Affairs,* October 1956

It is not wise to form an alliance with a prince that has more reputation than power.

> MACHIAVELLI (1469–1527). *The Discourses,* 2.11, 1517, tr. Christian E. Detmold, 1940

Our greatest advantage in coping with tribes so powerful is that they do not act in concert. Seldom is it that two or three states meet together to ward off a common danger. Thus, while they fight singly, all are conquered.

> TACITUS (A.D. 56?–120?). *The Life of Cnaeus Julius Agricola,* 30, tr. Alfred J. Church and William J. Brodribb, 1942

The only sure basis of an alliance is for each party to be equally afraid of the other.

> THUCYDIDES (460?–400? B.C.). *The Peloponnesian War,* 3.11, tr. Richard Crawley and rev. T. E. Wick, 1982

It is our true policy to steer clear of permanent alliances with any portion of the foreign world.

> GEORGE WASHINGTON (1732–1799). *Farewell Address,* 17 September 1796

AMBASSADORS

See also • Diplomacy ○ Diplomats ○ International Relations ○ Statesmen

A man-of-war is the best ambassador.

> OLIVER CROMWELL (1599–1658)

Do you know why everybody wants to be an ambassador? It's because when an ambassador walks down the corridor of his embassy, *everybody* kisses his ass.

> PHILIP HABIB (1920–1992). Undersecretary of state. In Martin Mayer, *The Diplomats,* 2 (epigraph), 1983

Ambassadors are, in the full meaning of the term, titled spies.

> NAPOLEON (1769–1821). Letter to his stepson Prince Eugène Beauharnais, 5 June 1805, *The Mind of Napoleon: A Selection from His Written and Spoken Words,* 220, ed. J. Christopher Herold, 1955

My point it that anybody that wants to be an ambassador wants to pay at least $250,000. . . . I want him to be bled for a quarter of a million, too.

> RICHARD M. NIXON (1913–1994). Referring to Gulf & Western Industries chairman Charles Bluhdorn, 23 June 1971 (secret White House tapes). In Associated Press, "Tapes Show More Dirt in Nixon's Presidency: He Sold Envoy Jobs, Had [Edward] Kennedy Tailed," *San Francisco Chronicle,* 1 November 1997

One cannot be too severe in punishing those [ambassadors] who exceed their authority.

> CARDINAL RICHELIEU (1585–1642). *Political Testament,* 2.6, tr. Henry Bertram Hill, 1961

An Ambassador is an honest man sent to lie abroad for the good of his Country.

> SIR HENRY WOTTON (1568–1639). In Isaak Walton, "The Life of Sir Henry Wotton, Late Provost of Eaton College," *The Life of John Donne, Sir Henry Wotton, Richard Hooker, George Herbert and Robert Sanderson,* 1765

AMBITION

See also • Ability: Anonymous ○ Power ○ Self-Interest ○ Success ○ Wealth

Ah, but a man's reach should exceed his grasp,
Or what's a Heaven for?

> ROBERT BROWNING (1812–1889). "Andrea del Sarto," l. 97, *Men and Women,* 1855

I'm going to be up there someday.

> GEORGE BUSH (1924–). While watching "a long-ago convention nominate someone for president," quoted by his sister. In Christopher Matthews, "The Rectitude of George Bush," *San Francisco Sunday Examiner & Chronicle,* 12 October 1997

Do you not think I have not just cause to weep, when I consider that Alexander at my age had conquered so many nations, and I have all this time done nothing that is memorable?

> JULIUS CAESAR (100–44 B.C.). Remark to his friends who, during a military campaign in Spain, were surprised to see him burst into tears after reading about Alexander's exploits. In Plutarch (A.D 46?–119?), "Caesar," *Parallel Lives,* Dryden edition, 1693

Ambition, the desire of shining and outshining, was the beginning of sin in this world.

> THOMAS CARLYLE (1795–1881). "Memoirs of the Life of Scott," 1838, *Critical and Miscellaneous Essays,* Carey & Hart edition, 1849

Ambition makes the same mistake concerning power that avarice makes concerning wealth: she begins by accumulating power as a means to happiness, and she finishes by continuing to accumulate it as an end. Ambition is, in fact, the avarice of power.

> C. C. COLTON (1780–1832). *Lacon: or, Many Things in Few Words; Addressed to Those Who Think,* 1.148, 1823

All ambitions are lawful except those which climb upwards on the miseries or credulities of mankind.

> JOSEPH CONRAD (1857–1924). "A Familiar Preface," *A Personal Record,* 1923

In friendship false, implacable in hate;
Resolv'd to ruin or to rule the State.

> JOHN DRYDEN (1631–1700). *Absalom and Achitophel,* 1.173, 1681

If I had not had so much ambition and had not tried to do so many things, I probably would have been happier, but less useful.

> THOMAS ALVA EDISON (1847–1931). 1930, *The Diary and Sundry Observations of Thomas Alva Edison,* 2.1.5, ed. Dagobert D. Runes, 1948

He who aims high must dread an easy home and popular manners.

> RALPH WALDO EMERSON (1803–1882). "Culture," *The Conduct of Life,* 1860

With [Henry David Thoreau's] great energy and practical ability he seemed born for great enterprise and for command; and I so much regret the loss of his rare powers of action, that I cannot help counting it a fault in him that he had no ambition. Wanting this, instead of engineering for all America, he was the captain of a huckleberry party.

> RALPH WALDO EMERSON (1803–1882). "Thoreau," *Lectures and Biographical Sketches,* 1883

Ambition [is] the fuel of achievement.

> JOSEPH EPSTEIN (1928–). Introduction to *Ambition: The Secret Passion,* 1980

Ambition is best not naked.

> MALCOLM S. FORBES (1919–1990). "Fact and Comment," *Forbes,* 3 October 1988

Nothing humbler than Ambition, when it is about to climb.

> BENJAMIN FRANKLIN (1706–1790). *Poor Richard's Almanack,* November 1753

I am actually not at all a man of science, not an observer, not an experimenter, not a thinker. I am by temperament nothing but a conquistador—an adventurer, if you want it translated—with all the curiosity, daring, and tenacity characteristic of a man of this sort.

> SIGMUND FREUD (1856–1939). Letter to Wilhelm Fliess, 1 February 1900, tr. Jeffrey Moussaieff Masson, 1985

I am not, so far as I know, ambitious.

> SIGMUND FREUD (1856–1939). *The Interpretation of Dreams,* 4, 1900, tr. A. A. Brill, 1938

The psychoanalysis of neurotics has taught us to recognize the intimate connection between wetting the bed and the character trait of ambition.

> SIGMUND FREUD (1856–1939). *The Interpretation of Dreams,* 5.B.4, 1900, tr. A. A. Brill, 1938

Ambition is not a reprehensible quality, nor are ambitious men to be censured, if they seek glory through honorable and honest means. In fact, it is they who produce great and excellent works. Those who lack this passion are cold spirits, inclined toward laziness than activity. But ambition is pernicious and detestable when it has as its sole end power.

> FRANCESCO GUICCIARDINI (1483–1540). *Remembrances,* C.32, 1530, tr. Mario Domandi, 1965

The incentive to ambition is the love of power.

> WILLIAM HAZLITT (1778–1830). "On Thought and Action," *Table Talk,* 1822

That man who thinks [Abraham] Lincoln calmly gathered his robes about him, waiting for the people to call him, has a very erroneous knowledge of Lincoln. He was always calculating, and always planning ahead. His ambition was a little engine that knew no rest.

> WILLIAM H. HERNDON (1818–1891) and JESSE W. WEIK (1857–1930). *Herndon's Lincoln: The True Story of a Great Life,* 12, 1888, ed. Paul M. Angle, 1930

One globe seemed all too small for the youthful Alexander.

> JUVENAL (A.D. 60?–127?). *Satires,* 10.169, tr. Peter Green, 1967

Once you say you're going to settle for second, that's what happens to you in life.

> JOHN F. KENNEDY (1917–1963). On the Vice Presidency, 1960. In Theodore C. Sorensen, *Kennedy,* 1, 1965

Nothing ever engaged him so completely that he would bring to it the sacrifice of personal advancement.

> HENRY A. KISSINGER (1923–). On Talleyrand (French minister of foreign affairs, 1754–1838), *A World Restored: Metternich, Castlereagh and the Problems of Peace 1812–1822,* 8.1, 1957

Love often leads on to ambition, but seldom does one return from ambition to love.

> LA ROCHEFOUCAULD (1613–1690). *Maxims,* 490, 1665, tr. Leonard Tancock, 1959

Every man is said to have his peculiar ambition. Whether it be true or not, I can say for one that I have no other so great as that of being truly esteemed of my fellow men, by rendering myself worthy of their esteem.

> ABRAHAM LINCOLN (1809–1865). At 23 as a candidate for the state legislature, "To the People of Sangamo County" (Illinois), 9 March 1832

Some day I shall be President.

> ABRAHAM LINCOLN (1809–1865). A frequent remark heard by many of his friends while he was still unknown. In Francis Fisher Browne, *The Every-Day Life of Abraham Lincoln,* 1.3, 1887

You are ambitious, which, within reasonable bounds, does good rather than harm.

> ABRAHAM LINCOLN (1809–1865). Letter to Gen. Joseph Hooker, 26 January 1863

If you would hit the mark, you must aim a little above it.

> HENRY WADSWORTH LONGFELLOW (1807–1882). "Elegiac Verse" (11), *In the Harbor,* 1882

Men rise from one ambition to another: First, they seek to secure themselves against attack, and then they attack others.

> MACHIAVELLI (1469–1527). *The Discourses,* 1.46, 1517, tr. Christian E. Detmold, 1940

I have the same goal I've had ever since I was a girl. I want to rule the world.

> MADONNA (1959–). In "The Ten Who Count the Most," *People,* 27 July 1992

Everybody is ambitious. The question is whether he is ambitious to be or ambitious to do.

> JEAN MONNET (1888–1979). French economist and statesman. In Henry A. Kissinger, *Years of Upheaval,* 5, 1982

Ambition never is in a greater hurry than I; it merely keeps pace with circumstances and with my general way of thinking.

> NAPOLEON (1769–1821) Remark to Pierre Roederer, 1804, *The Mind of Napoleon: A Selection from His Written and Spoken Words,* 62, ed. J. Christopher Herold, 1955

I have always hoped that as the result of a great war I would secure supreme command and such fame that after the war I would be able to become president or dictator by the ballot or by force. In that case we would not have needed a house for we would have persuaded a grateful people to build us a marble Palace at the flag pole at Fort Myer. However, as I approach [the age of] 41 and there is no war I almost doubt the Palace and fear that I shall live to retire a useless soldier.

> GEORGE S. PATTON, JR. (1885–1945). Letter to his wife Beatrice, 2 November 1926. In Martin Blumenson, *The Patton Papers, 1885–1940,* 39, 1972. Ft. Myer is located across the Potomac River from Washington, D.C.

The tallest Trees are most in the Power of the Winds, and Ambitious Men of the Blasts of Fortune.

> WILLIAM PENN (1644–1718). *More Fruits of Solitude,* 97, 1693

The same ambition can destroy or save,
And make a patriot as it makes a knave.

> ALEXANDER POPE (1688–1744). *An Essay on Man,* 2.201, 1734

Antony: When that the poor have cried, Caesar hath wept:
Ambition should be made of sterner stuff.

> SHAKESPEARE (1564–1616). *Julius Caesar,* 3.2.96, 1599

Ambition, if it feeds at all, does so on the ambition of others.

> SUSAN SONTAG (1933–). *The Benefactor,* 1, 1983

He that strives to touch the stars,
Oft stumbles at a straw.

> EDMUND SPENSER (1552–1599). "July," *The Shepherd's Calendar,* 1579

Ambition is the immoderate desire [for] power.

> BARUCH SPINOZA (1632–1677). "Byways of Emotions," *Ethics,* 1677, tr. Dagobert D. Runes, 1957

Where there are large powers with little ambition . . . , nature may be said to have fallen short of her purposes.

> HENRY TAYLOR (1800–1886). *The Statesman,* 19, 1836

The greatest evil which fortune can inflict on men is to endow them with small talents and great ambition.

> VAUVENARGUES (1715–1747). *Reflections and Maxims,* 562, 1746, tr. F. G. Stevens, 1940

Adam Maxwell, age twenty-four, husband to Ruth. A boy who wants to go to the top. As if the world had a top.

> OCTAVIA WALDO (1929–). "Roman Spring," in Don Wolfe, ed., *American Scene,* 1963

I have no other view than to promote the public good, and am unambitious of honors not founded in the approbation of my Country.

> GEORGE WASHINGTON (1732–1799). Letter to Henry Laurens, President of the Continental Congress, 31 January 1778

There is always room at the top.

> DANIEL WEBSTER (1782–1852). Attributed. When advised as a young man not to become a lawyer because the profession was overcrowded. John Braine titled his 1957 novel *Room at the Top.*

Ambition is the last refuge of the failure.

> OSCAR WILDE (1854–1900). "Phrases and Philosophies for the Use of the Young," *Cameleon* (British journal), December 1894
>
> See Patriotism: Samuel Johnson

If you strive for the moon, maybe you'll get over the fence.

> JAMES WOOD (1947–). Actor. Larry King television interview, CNN, 29 April 1991

Ambition! powerful source of good and ill!

> EDWARD YOUNG (1683–1765). *The Complaint: or, Night Thoughts on Life, Death, and Immortality,* 6.399, 1742–1745

Too low they build, who build beneath the stars.

> EDWARD YOUNG (1683–1765). *The Complaint: or, Night Thoughts on Life, Death, and Immortality,* 8.216, 1742–1745

Here a mound suffices for one for whom the world was not large enough.

> ANONYMOUS. Proposed epitaph for Alexander (356–323 B.C.)

If you would be Pope, you must think of nothing else.

> SAYING (SPANISH)

AMERICA

See also • American Foreign Policy ○ Civil War: [especially] Abraham Lincoln (3–5) ○ Country: John F. Kennedy ○ Democracy: Florence King ○ Destiny: Franklin D. Roosevelt ○ Dissent: Dwight D. Eisenhower ○ Freedom: Thomas Jefferson (1) ○ Individualism: Herbert Hoover ○ Nations ○ Revolutionary War: [especially] Abraham Lincoln ○ Values: J. William Fulbright, Ronald Reagan

America, America!
God shed His grace on thee

And crown thy good with brotherhood
From sea to shining sea!

> KATHERINE LEE BATES (1859–1929). "American the Beautiful" (song), 1893

God bless America,
Land that I love;
Stand beside her and guide her
Through the night with a light from above.

> IRVING BERLIN (1888–1989). "God Bless America" (song), 1938

The most important lesson of American history is the promise of the unexpected. None of our ancestors would have imagined settling way over here on this unknown continent. So we must continue to have a society that is hospitable to the unexpected, which allows possibilities to develop beyond our own imaginings.

> DANIEL J. BOORSTIN (1914–). In Tad Szulc, "The Greatest Danger We Face," *Parade,* 25 July 1993

America is never wholly herself unless she is engaged in high moral principle. We as a people have such a purpose today. It is to make kinder the face of the nation and gentler the face of the world.

> GEORGE BUSH (1924–). *Inaugural Address,* 20 January 1989

America is the only nation in history which miraculously has gone directly from barbarism to degeneration without the usual interval of civilization.

> GEORGES CLEMENCEAU (1841–1929). Attributed. In Hans Bendix, "Merry Christmas, America!" *Saturday Review,* 1 December 1945

After all, the chief business of the American people is business.

> CALVIN COOLIDGE (1872–1933). Speech before the American Society of Newspaper Editors, Washington, 17 January 1925

God and the politicians willing, the United States can declare peace upon the world, and win it.

> ELY CULBERTSON (1891–1955). *Must We Fight Russia?* 5, 1946

This will remain the land of the free only so long as it is the home of the brave.

> ELMER DAVIS (1890–1958). *But We Were Born Free,* 1, 1954

Whatever America hopes to bring to pass in the world must first come to pass in the heart of America.

> DWIGHT D. EISENHOWER (1890–1969). *First Inaugural Address,* 20 January 1953

Remarkable trait in the American Character is the union, not very infrequent, of Yankee cleverness with spiritualism.

> RALPH WALDO EMERSON (1803–1882). Journal, 1847, undated

Nothing is impracticable to this nation, which it shall set itself to do. Were ever men so endowed, so placed, so weaponed? Their power of territory seconded by a genius equal to every work. By new arts the earth is subdued, roaded, tunnelled, telegraphed, gas-lighted. . . . We are on the brink of more wonders.

> RALPH WALDO EMERSON (1803–1882). "The Fugitive Slave Law," address, Concord (Massachusetts), 3 May 1851

America means opportunity, freedom, power.

> RALPH WALDO EMERSON (1803–1882). "Public and Private Education,"
> *Unpublished Lectures*, 1932

My country tears of thee.

> LAWRENCE FERLINGHETTI (1919–). "Junkman's Obbligato" (poem),
> *A Coney Island of the Mind*, 1958

America is a mistake, a giant mistake.

> SIGMUND FREUD (1856–1939). Remark to the author sometime after
> Freud's visit to America in 1909. In Ernest Jones, *The Life and Work of
> Sigmund Freud*, 18, 1953–1957, abr. 1961

This land is your land, this land is my land,
From California to the New York Island.
From the redwood forest to the Gulf Stream waters,
This land was made for you and me.

> WOODY GUTHRIE (1912–1967). "This Land Is Your Land" (song), 1956

I believe that, for the rest of the world, contemporary America is
an almost symbolic concentration of all the best and the worst of
our civilization. On the one hand, there are its profound commitment to enhancing civil liberty and to maintaining the strength of
its democratic institutions, and the fantastic developments in science and technology which have contributed so much to our
well-being; on the other, there is the blind worship of perpetual
economic growth and consumption, regardless of their destructive
impact on the environment, or how subject they are to the dictates of materialism and consumerism, or how they, through the
omnipresence of television and advertising, promote uniformity,
and banality instead of a respect for human uniqueness.

> VÁCLAV HAVEL (1936–). Czech president. Address (after being awarded
> the Fulbright Prize), Washington, 3 October 1997, "The Charms of
> NATO," *New York Review of Books*, 15 January 1998

If I had a hammer, I'd hammer in the morning,
I'd hammer in the evening all over this land;
I'd hammer out danger, I'd hammer out warning,
I'd hammer out love between my brothers and my sisters,
All over this land.

> LEE HAYES (1933–) (lyrics) and PETE SEEGER (1919–) (music).
> "The Hammer Song," 1958

And for the support of this declaration, with a firm reliance on the
protection of Divine Providence, we mutually pledge to each
other our lives, our fortunes, and our sacred honor.

> THOMAS JEFFERSON (1743–1826). Closing words, Declaration of
> Independence, 4 July 1776

I tremble for my country when I reflect that God is just; that his
justice cannot sleep forever.

> THOMAS JEFFERSON (1743–1826). Referring to the slavery issue,
> *Notes on the State of Virginia*, 18, 1785

Sir, [the American colonists] are a race of convicts, and ought to
be thankful for anything we allow them short of hanging.

> SAMUEL JOHNSON (1709–1784). 1769. Quoted by John Campbell,
> 21 March 1775. In James Boswell, *The Life of Samuel Johnson*, 1791

With a good conscience our only sure reward, with history the
final judge of our deeds, let us go forth to lead the land we love,
asking His blessing and His help, but knowing that here on earth
God's work must truly be our own.

> JOHN F. KENNEDY (1917–1963). *Inaugural Address*, 20 January 1961

Oh, say, does that star-spangled banner yet wave
O'er the land of the free, and the home of the brave.

> FRANCIS SCOTT KEY (1779–1843). "The Star-Spangled Banner" (national
> anthem), 13-14 September 1814

What charms me [in America] is that all citizens are brethren.

> MARQUIS de LAFAYETTE (1757–1834). Letter to his wife, 20 June 1777

Give me your tired, your poor,
Your huddled masses yearning to breathe free.
The wretched refuse of your teeming shore,
Send these, the homeless, tempest-tossed, to me:
I lift my lamp beside the golden door.

> EMMA LAZARUS (1849–1887). Inscription on the Statue of Liberty,
> "The New Colossus," 1883

If destruction be our lot, we must ourselves be its author and fin-
isher. As a nation of freemen, we must live through all time, or
die by suicide.

> ABRAHAM LINCOLN (1809–1865). "The Perpetuation of Our Political
> Institutions," address before the Young Men's Lyceum of Springfield
> (Illinois), 27 January 1838
> See Nations: Richard Cobden

[The American people] will ever do well if well done by.

> ABRAHAM LINCOLN (1809–1865). Speech, Bloomington (Illinois),
> 21 November 1860

We, unhappily, are living in the hiatus between two dreams. We
have waked from one and not yet started the other. . . . Is it not,
perhaps, America's mission to find "the dream that is coming to
birth."

> ANNE MORROW LINDBERGH (1907–). *The Wave of the Future:
> A Confession of Faith*, p. 40, 1940

There is a growing belief that Johnson's America is no longer the
historic America, that it is a bastard empire which relies on superior force to achieve its purposes, and is no longer providing an
example of the wisdom and humanity of a free society.

> WALTER LIPPMANN (1889–1974). "The American Promise," *Newsweek*,
> 9 October 1967

The world of the 20th Century, if it is to come to life in any nobility of health and vigor, must be to a significant degree an
American Century.

> HENRY R. LUCE (1898–1967). "The American Century," *Life*, 17 February
> 1941

The greatest honor history can bestow is the title of peacemaker.
This honor now beckons America—the chance to help lead the
world at last out of the valley of the turmoil and on to that high
ground of peace that man has dreamed of since the dawn of civilization.

> RICHARD M. NIXON (1913–1994). *First Inaugural Address*, 20 January
> 1969. The first sentence of this excerpt is inscribed on Pres. Nixon's
> gravestone.
> See Peace: Jesus

America is a great nation today not because of what government did for people but because of what people did for themselves and for one another.

RICHARD M. NIXON (1913–1994). *Beyond Peace,* 1, 1994

If we look to the answer as to why for so many years we achieved so much, prospered as no other people on earth, it was because here in this land we unleashed the energy and individual genius of man to a greater extent than has ever been done before. Freedom and the dignity of the individual have been more available and assured here than in any other place on earth.

RONALD REAGAN (1911–). *First Inaugural Address,* 20 January 1981

All great change in America begins at the dinner table.

RONALD REAGAN (1911–). Farewell address, 11 January 1989

This is . . . a trait no other nation seems to possess in quite the same degree that we do—namely, a feeling of almost childish injury and resentment unless the world as a whole recognizes how innocent we are of anything but the most generous and harmless intentions.

ELEANOR ROOSEVELT (1884–1962). In Joseph P. Lash, *Eleanor: The Years Alone,* 4, 1972

What I do object to about America is the herd thinking. There is no room for individuals in your country—and yet you are dedicated to saving the world for individualism.

BERTRAND RUSSELL (1872–1970). Tommy Robbins interview, *Redbook,* September 1964

America is a "happy-ending" nation.

DORE SCHARY (1905–1980). Film studio executive. Speech before the Harvard Club of Los Angeles. In Louis Kronenberger, epigraph, *Company Manners: A Cultural Inquiry into American Life,* 1954

I like to be in America!
O.K. by me in America!
Ev'rything free in America
For a small fee in America!

STEPHEN SONDHEIM (1930–). "America" (song). In the musical *West Side Story,* 1957

It is probably true in America that if you work hard and play by the rules you will make more money than if you don't. But what are the rules? Are they the rules of Moses or P. T. Barnum, of William Bennett or Willie Sutton?

HERBERT STEIN (1916–). "The American Dream," *Wall Street Journal,* 24 December 1996

The American people taken in main is not only the most enlightened in the world, but—which I put much higher than that advantage—is the one whose practical political education is the most advanced.

ALEXIS de TOCQUEVILLE (1805–1859). Notebook, 13 January 1832, *Journey to America,* 6, tr. George Lawrence, 1971

America is a land of wonders, in which everything is in constant motion and every change seems an improvement. The idea of novelty is there indissolubly connected with the idea of amelioration. No natural boundary seems to be set to the efforts of man;

and in his eyes what is not yet done is only what he has not yet attempted to do.

ALEXIS de TOCQUEVILLE (1805–1859). *Democracy in America,* 1.18, 1835, tr. Henry Reeve and Francis Bowen, 1862

Although the desire of acquiring the good things of this world is the prevailing passion of the American people, certain momentary outbreaks occur when their souls seem suddenly to burst the bonds of matter by which they are restrained and to soar impetuously towards heaven.

ALEXIS de TOCQUEVILLE (1805–1859). *Democracy in America,* 2.2.12, 1840, tr. Henry Reeve and Francis Bowen, 1862

If I were asked . . . to what the singular prosperity and growing strength of that people ought mainly to be attributed, I should reply: To the superiority of their women.

ALEXIS de TOCQUEVILLE (1805–1859). *Democracy in America,* 2.3.12, 1840, tr. Henry Reeve and Francis Bowen, 1862

The strength of our Nation must continue to be used in the interest of all our people rather than a privileged few. It must continue to be used unselfishly in the struggle for world peace and the betterment of mankind.

HARRY S. TRUMAN (1884–1972). State of the Union Message, 5 January 1949

It is by the goodness of God that in our country we have those three unspeakably precious things: freedom of speech, freedom of conscience, and the prudence never to practice either of them.

MARK TWAIN (1835–1910). *Following the Equator: A Journey Around the World,* 20 (epigraph), 1897

I pledge allegiance to the flag of the United States of America and to the republic for which it stands, one nation under God, indivisible, with liberty and justice for all.

JAMES B. UPHAM (1845–1905) and FRANCIS BELLAMY (19th cent.). "The Pledge of Allegiance to the Flag," 1892. Since 1892 the pledge has been revised twice; in 1954 an act of Congress added "under God."

It will be worthy of a free, enlightened, and, at no distant period, a great nation, to give to mankind the magnanimous and too novel example of a People always guided by an exalted justice and benevolence.

GEORGE WASHINGTON (1732–1799). *Farewell Address,* 17 September 1796

The genius of the United States is not best or most in its executives or legislatures, nor in its ambassadors or authors or colleges, or churches, or parlors, nor even in its newspapers or inventors, but always most in the common people.

WALT WHITMAN (1819–1892). Preface (1855) to *Leaves of Grass,* 1855–1992

Fresh come, to a new world indeed, yet long prepared,
I see the genius of the modern, child of the real and ideal,
Clearing the ground for broad humanity, the true America, heir of the past so grand,
To build a grander future.

WALT WHITMAN (1819–1892). Closing lines, "Song of the Redwood-Tree," 1874, *Leaves of Grass,* 1855–1892

The crowning growth of the United States is to be spiritual and heroic.

> WALT WHITMAN (1819–1892). Preface to *November Boughs,* 1888

The business of America is not business. Neither is it war. The business of America is justice, and securing the blessings of liberty.

> GEORGE F. WILL (1941–). Closing words, "A Land Fit for Heroes," *Time,* 11 March 1991

❧

Don't sell America short.

> SAYING. Early 20th cent.

AMERICAN FOREIGN POLICY

See also • Alliances: Thomas Jefferson, George Washington ○ America ○ International Relations

In foreign affairs I will continue our policy of peace through strength.

> GEORGE BUSH (1924–). Presidential nomination acceptance speech, New Orleans, 18 August 1988

Human rights is the soul of our foreign policy because human rights is the very soul of our sense of nationhood.

> JIMMY CARTER (1924–). Speech at a ceremony commemorating the thirtieth anniversary of the United Nations' Universal Declaration of Human Rights, White House, 6 December 1978

America cannot and must not be the world's policeman. We cannot stop all war for all time. But we can stop some wars. We cannot save all women and all children. But we can save many of them. We can't do everything. But we must do what we can do. There are times and places where our leadership can mean the difference between peace and war.

> BILL CLINTON (1946–). Calling for public support for the stationing of U.S. peacekeeping troops in Bosnia, television broadcast, 27 November 1995

The broad principles that should govern our international conduct are not obscure. They grow out of the practice by the nations of the simple things Christ taught.

> JOHN FOSTER DULLES (1888–1959). 1943? In Arthur M. Schlesinger, Jr., "In the National Interest," *Worldview,* December 1984

If there be one principle more deeply rooted than any other in the mind of every American, it is, that we should have nothing to do with conquest.

> THOMAS JEFFERSON (1743–1826). Letter to William Short, 28 July 1791

We are firmly convinced . . . that with nations, as with individuals, our interests soundly calculated, will ever be found inseparable from our moral duties.

> THOMAS JEFFERSON (1743–1826). Referring to "foreign affairs," *Second Inaugural Address,* 4 March 1805

Don't forget, there are two hundred million of us in a world of three billion. They want what we've got—*and we're not going to give it to them!*

> LYNDON B. JOHNSON (1908–1973). Speech to American troops, Camp Stanley, South Korea, early 1950s. In Felix Greene, *The Enemy,* 2.11, 1970

Domestic policy can only lose elections. Foreign policy can kill us all.

> JOHN F. KENNEDY (1917–1963). In Arthur M. Schlesinger, Jr., *The Imperial Presidency,* 11.7, 1973

Before we engage ourselves, we must know what we are doing; and once we have engaged ourselves, we must prevail, or the impact will be catastrophic.

> HENRY A. KISSINGER (1923–). Remark at the Davos Symposium 1980 of the European Management Forum, 31 January 1980, *For the Record: Selected Statements, 1977–1980,* 1981

Our policy is directed not against any country or doctrine, but against hunger, poverty, desperation and chaos. Its purpose should be the revival of a working economy in the world so as to permit the emergence of political and social conditions in which free institutions can exist.

> GEORGE C. MARSHALL (1880–1959). Secretary of state. On the Marshall Plan, which helped rehabilitate Western Europe after World War II, speech, Harvard University, Cambridge (Massachusetts), 5 June 1947

The American continents . . . are henceforth not to be considered as subjects for future colonization by any European powers. . . . We owe it . . . to candor, and to the amicable relations existing between the United States and those powers, to declare that we should consider any attempt on their part to extend their system to any portion of this hemisphere as dangerous to our peace and safety. With the existing colonies or dependencies of any European power we have not interfered and shall not interfere.

> JAMES MONROE (1758–1831). Annual message to Congress, 2 December 1823. In this message, Pres. Monroe announced what became known in the 1850s as the Monroe Doctrine.

We must devote ourselves to the cause of peace and freedom in the world, but maintaining the will and the capability to employ force remains indispensable toward that end. Our readiness to resort to force to defend our security and interests deters those who would use force for aggressive purposes.

> RICHARD M. NIXON (1913–1994). *In the Arena: A Memoir of Victory, Defeat and Renewal,* 38, 1990

In the field of world policy I would dedicate this nation to the policy of the good neighbor.

> FRANKLIN D. ROOSEVELT (1882–1945). *First Inaugural Address,* 4 March 1933

ANARCHISM

See also • Government ○ Nations ○ Politics

If there is a State, there must necessarily be domination, and therefore slavery: a State without slavery, overt or concealed, is unthinkable—and that is why we are enemies of the State.

> MIKHAIL BAKUNIN (1814–1876). *State and Anarchism,* 1873. In *The Political Philosophy of Bakunin: Scientific Anarchism,* 3.4, ed. G. P. Maximoff, 1953

[The Marxists say that the] State yoke—the dictator [of the proletariat]—is a necessary transitional means in order to attain the emancipation of the people. . . .

[We Anarchists answer]: No dictatorship can have any other aim but that of self-perpetuation.

> MIKHAIL BAKUNIN (1814–1876). *State and Anarchism,* 1873. In *The Political Philosophy of Bakunin: Scientific Anarchism,* 3.4, ed. G. P. Maximoff, 1953
>
> See Class: Karl Marx (1) ○ Revolutionaries: Bakunin

We started off trying to set up a small anarchist community, but people wouldn't obey the rules.

> ALAN BENNETT. *Getting On,* 1, 1972

Anarchism: The philosophy of a new social order based on liberty unrestricted by man-made law; the theory that all forms of government rest on violence, and are therefore wrong and harmful, as well as unnecessary.

> EMMA GOLDMAN (1869–1940). "Anarchism: What It Really Stands For," *Anarchism and Other Essays,* 3rd rev. ed., 1917 (1910)

Anarchism is [not] synonymous with chaos. Translated from the Greek, anarchism means the absence of rulers, or orders—not of rules or order. Order emanates naturally from the free cooperation of persons in community.

> MICHAEL KANE (1869–1940). "Revolution, The Old Man and the Land," *Catholic Worker,* May 1990

Anarchism (from the Greek . . . contrary to authority), the name given to a principle or theory of life and conduct under which society is conceived without government—Harmony in such a society not being obtained by submission to law, or by obedience to any authority, but by free agreements concluded between the various groups, territorial and professional, freely constituted for the sake of production and consumption, as also for the satisfaction of the infinite variety of needs and aspirations of a civilized being. In a society developed on these lines, the voluntary associations which already now begin to cover all the fields of human activity would take a still greater extension so as to substitute themselves for the state in all its functions.

> PETER KROPOTKIN (1842–1921). "Anarchism," *The Encyclopedia Brittanica,* 11th ed., 1.914, 1911

So long as the state exists there is no freedom. When there is freedom, there will be no state.

> LENIN (1870–1924). *The State and Revolution,* 5.4, 1917, International Publishers edition, 1971

We anarchists do not want to *emancipate* the people; we want the people to *emancipate themselves.*

> ERRICO MALATESTA (1853–1932). In *L'Agitazione,* 18 June 1897

Whoever lays his hand on me to govern me is a usurper and a tyrant; I declare him to be my enemy. . . . Government of man by man is slavery [and its laws are] cobwebs for the rich and chains of steel for the poor. [Ellipsis points in original.]

> PIERRE-JOSEPH PROUDHON (1809–1865). In Barbara W. Tuchman, "The Anarchists," *Atlantic,* May 1963

❧

There's No Government like *No* Government.

> SLOGAN (AMERICAN). Button, 1980s

ANGELS

See also • Devil ○ Saints ○ Strangers: Anonymous (*Bible*) ○ Sympathy: Arthur Schopenhauer

Every man hath a good and a bad angel attending on him in particular all his life long.

> ROBERT BURTON (1577–1640). *The Anatomy of Melancholy,* 1.2.1.2, 1621–1651

Angels can fly because they take themselves lightly.

> G. K. CHESTERTON (1874–1936). *Orthodoxy,* 7, 1909

As there is much beast and some devil in man, so is there some angel and some God in him.

> SAMUEL TAYLOR COLERIDGE (1772–1834). 1 August 1831, *Table Talk,* 1835

If a man is not rising upwards to be an angel, depend upon it, he is sinking downwards to be a devil.

> SAMUEL TAYLOR COLERIDGE (1772–1834). 30 August 1833, *Table Talk,* 1835

My God sent his angel and shut the lions' mouths and they have not hurt me, because I was found blameless before him.

> DANIEL (8th cent. B.C.). Explaining his survival to King Darius, who had thrown him into the lions' den. *Daniel* 6:22

I am a little world made cunningly
Of elements and an angelic sprite.

> JOHN DONNE (1572–1631). *Holy Sonnets,* 5.1, 1635, ed. Roger E. Bennett, 1942

The angel of light and the angel of darkness are to wrestle on the bridge of the abyss. Which of the two shall hurl down the other?

> VICTOR HUGO (1802–1885). "Saint Denis" (15.1), *Les Misérables,* tr. Charles E. Wilbour, 1862

Look homeward Angel now and melt with ruth [i.e., compassion].

> JOHN MILTON (1608–1674). *Lycidas,* l. 163, 1638

In heaven an angel is nobody in particular.

> GEORGE BERNARD SHAW (1856–1950). "Maxims for Revolutionists: Greatness," *Man and Superman,* 1903

Around our pillows golden ladders rise,
And up and down the skies,
With winged sandals shod,
The angels come, and go, the Messengers of God,

> RICHARD HENRY STODDARD (1825–1903). "Hymn to the Beautiful"
>
> See Dreams–Examples: Jacob

Sometimes a man,
    In serving God,
Can
    only
  do
As
        angels
do,
    and
wing it.

GARRY TRUDEAU (1948–). "Service" (complete poem), "The Fireside Carter," *New York Times,* 2 October 1994

We were made men and not angels in order that we might seek our happiness through the medium of this life.

MIGUEL de UNAMUNO (1864–1936). *Tragic Sense of Life,* 11, 1913, tr. J. E. Crawford Flitch, 1921

✻

For thou hast made him a little lower than the angels, and hast crowned him with glory and honor.

ANONYMOUS (*BIBLE*). *Psalms* 8:5 (King James Version)

ANGER

See also • Anxiety ○ Depression ○ Moral Indignation ○ Self-Righteousness

It is easy to fly into a passion—anybody can do that—but to be angry with the right person and to the right extent and at the right time and with the right object and in the right way—that is not easy, and it is not everyone who can do it.

ARISTOTLE (384–322 B.C.). *Nicomachean Ethics,* 2.9, tr. J. A. K. Thomson, 1953

The voice of honest indignation is the voice of God.

WILLIAM BLAKE (1757–1827). "A Memorable Fancy," *The Marriage of Heaven and Hell,* 12–13, 1790–1793

I was angry with my friend:
I told my wrath, my wrath did end.
I was angry with my foe:
I told it not, my wrath did grow.

WILLIAM BLAKE (1757–1827). "A Poison Tree," *Songs of Experience,* 1794

Bonaparte's temper was bad, but his fits of ill humor passed away like a cloud and spent themselves in words. His violent language and bitter imprecations were frequently premeditated.

LOUIS de BOURRIENNE (1769–1834). *Memoirs of Napoleon Bonaparte,* 1.28, ed. R. W. Phipps, 1892

Never lose your temper, except intentionally.

DWIGHT D. EISENHOWER (1890–1969). A favorite maxim. In Sherman Adams, *Firsthand Report: The Story of the Eisenhower Administration,* 2, 1961

Anger is never without a Reason,
but seldom with a good One.

BENJAMIN FRANKLIN (1706–1790). *Poor Richard's Almanack,* July 1753

When angry, count ten before you speak; if very angry, an hundred.

THOMAS JEFFERSON (1743–1826). "A Decalogue of Canons for Observation in Practical Life," #10, letter to Thomas Jefferson Smith, 21 February 1825

Requite anger with virtue.

LAO-TZU (6th cent. B.C.). *The Way of Life,* 63, tr. R. B. Blakney, 1955

Our anger and annoyance are more detrimental to us than the things themselves which anger or annoy us.

MARCUS AURELIUS (A.D. 121–180). *Meditations,* 11.17, tr. Maxwell Staniforth, 1964

"Don't Get Mad; Don't Get Even; Get Ahead."

CHRISTOPHER MATTHEWS (1945–). Chapter title, *Hardball: How Politics Is Played—Told by One Who Knows the Game,* 6, 1988

Don't lose your temper; use it.

DOLLY PARTON (1946–). Joan River television interview, 26 November 1993

Be angry but do not sin; do not let the sun go down on your anger.

PAUL (A.D. lst cent.). *Ephesians* 4:26

Angry Young Man.

LESLIE PAUL (1905–1985). Book title, 1951. John Osborne helped popularize the term in his 1956 play, *Look Back in Anger.*

Anger dieth quickly with a good man.

JOHN RAY (1628–1705). Comp., *A Collection of English Proverbs,* p. 1, 1678

I always throw my golf club in the direction I'm going.

RONALD REAGAN (1911–). In Christopher Matthews, *Hardball: How Politics Is Played—Told by One Who Knows the Game,* 6, 1988

Better to be pissed off than pissed on.

MICHEL PAUL RICHARD (1933–). In "First Principles," *Thoughts For All Seasons: The Magazine of Epigrams,* vol. 4, 1992

Horatio: A countenance more in sorrow than in anger.

SHAKESPEARE (1564–1616). *Hamlet,* 1.2.231, 1600

When angry, count four; when very angry, swear.

MARK TWAIN (1835–1910). *The Tragedy of Pudd'nhead Wilson,* 10 (epigraph), 1894

✻

A soft answer turns away wrath,
but a harsh word stirs up anger.

SAYING (*BIBLE*). *Proverbs* 15:1

ANIMALS

See also • Birds ○ Cats ○ Dogs ○ Fish ○ Hunting ○ Insects ○ Nature ○ Snakes ○ Teachers: Job

If man was what he ought to be, he would be adored by the animals.

HENRI AMIEL (1812–1881). Journal, 6 October 1866, tr. Mrs. Humphrey Ward, 1887

The question is not, Can they *reason?* nor, Can they *talk?* but, Can they *suffer?*

JEREMY BENTHAM (1748–1842). "Notes" (330), *An Introduction to the Principles of Morals and Legislation,* 1789–1823

The animals were mingling with the people like relatives.

BLACK ELK (1862–1950). Vision. In John Brown Childs, "The Religious Left," *Nation,* 7 November 1994

Sympathy beyond the confines of man, that is, humanity to the lower animals, seems to be one of the latest moral acquisitions. . . . This virtue, one of the noblest with which man is endowed, seems to arise incidentally from our sympathies becoming more tender and more widely diffused, until they are extended to all sentient beings. As soon as this virtue is honored and practiced by some few men, it spreads through instruction and example to the young, and eventually becomes incorporated in public opinion.

> CHARLES DARWIN (1809–1882). *The Descent of Man and Selection in Relation to Sex*, 2nd ed., 4, 1874

We are as much strangers in nature as we are aliens from God. We do not understand the notes of birds. The fox and the deer run away from us.

> RALPH WALDO EMERSON (1803–1882). "Spirit," *Nature*, 1836

The charm which Henry T uses for bird and frog and mink, is patience. They will not come to him, or show him aright, until he becomes a log among logs, sitting still for hours in the same place; then they come around him and to him, and show themselves at home.

> RALPH WALDO EMERSON (1803–1882). Referring to Henry David Thoreau, journal, 11 May 1858

If you have men who will exclude any of God's creatures from the shelter of compassion and pity, you will have men who will deal likewise with their fellow men.

> ST. FRANCIS OF ASSISI (A.D. 1181?–1226)

The lower animals are our brethren. I include among them the lion and the tiger. We do not know how to live with these carnivorous beasts and poisonous reptiles because of our ignorance. When man learns better, he will learn to befriend even these. Today he does not even know how to befriend a man of a different religion or from a different country.

> MOHANDAS K. GANDHI (1869–1948). Quoted by Erik H. Erikson, "On the Nature of Psychohistorical Evidence: In Search of Gandhi." In Robert Jay Lifton, ed., *Explorations in Psychohistory*, 1974

Whenever . . . wild beasts clutch their living prey, the deadly horror which an agitated melancholiac feels is the literally right reaction on the situation.

> WILLIAM JAMES (1842–1910). *The Varieties of Religious Experience: A Study in Human Nature*, 6 and 7, 1902

The time will come when men . . . will look on the murder of animals as they now look on the murder of men.

> LEONARDO da VINCI (1452–1519). In Alice Herrington, testimony before the House Merchant Marine and Fisheries Subcommittee, 9 September 1971

The higher animals are in a sense drawn into Man when he loves them and makes them (as he does) much more nearly human than they would otherwise be.

> C. S. LEWIS (1898–1963). *Mere Christianity*, rev. ed., 8, 1952

It should not be believed that all beings exist for the sake of man. On the contrary, all the other beings too have been intended for their own sakes and not for the sake of something else.

> MOSES MAIMONIDES (A.D. 1135–1204). *The Guide for the Perplexed*, A.D. 1190

human wandering through the zoo
what do your cousins think of you?

> DON MARQUIS (1878–1937). "archy at the zoo," *archy and mehitabel*, 1927

In nothing does man, with his grand notions of heaven and charity, show forth his innate, low-bred, wild animalism more clearly than in his treatment of his brother beasts. From the shepherd with his lambs to the red-handed hunter, it is the same; no recognition of rights—only murder in one form or another.

> JOHN MUIR (1838–1914). 23 July 1881, *The Cruise of the Corwin*, 12, 1917

Nothing can be more obvious than that all animals were created solely and exclusively for the use of man.

> THOMAS LOVE PEACOCK (1785–1866). *Headlong Hall*, 2, 1816

It can truly be said: Men are the devils of the earth, and the animals are the tormented souls.

> ARTHUR SCHOPENHAUER (1788–1860). "On Religion" (3), 1851, *Essays and Aphorisms*, tr. R. J. Hollingdale, 1970.

The eternal being . . . , as it lives in us, also lives in every animal.

> ARTHUR SCHOPENHAUER (1788–1860). "On Religion" (3), 1851, *Essays and Aphorisms*, tr. R. J. Hollingdale, 1970.

I never go to a menagerie because I cannot endure the sight of the misery of the captive animals. The exhibiting of trained animals I abhor. What an amount of suffering and cruel punishment the poor creatures have to endure in order to give a few moments' pleasure to men devoid of all thought and feeling for them!

> ALBERT SCHWEITZER (1875–1965). *Memoirs of Childhood and Youth*, 2, 1925, tr. C. T. Campion, 1949

The behavior of men to the lower animals, and their behavior to each other, bear a constant relationship.

> HERBERT SPENCER (1820–1903). *Social Statics*, 4.30.2, 1851

The basis of all animal rights should be the Golden Rule: we should treat *them* as we would wish them to treat us, were any other species in our dominant position.

> CHRISTINE STEVENS. In Michael Fox, *Returning to Eden*, 1980

A man is forbidden to eat anything until he has fed his beast.

> TALMUD (A.D. 1st–6th cent.). Rabbinical writings. In Lewis Browne, ed., *The Wisdom of Israel*, rev. ed., p. 178, 1955 (1948)

No civilization is complete which does not include the dumb and defenseless of God's creatures within the sphere of charity and mercy.

> VICTORIA (1819–1901). British queen. In Elbert Hubbard, comp., *Elbert Hubbard's Scrap Book*, p. 20, 1923

He that *wrongs* any Creature sins against God, the Creator.

> BENJAMIN WHICHCOTE (1609–1683). *Moral and Religious Aphorisms*, 1053, 1753

ANSWERS

See Questions & Answers

ANTI-SEMITIC STATEMENTS

See also • Holocaust ○ Judaism ○ Prejudice ○ Racism ○ Racist Statements

The rats are underneath the piles.
The Jew is underneath the lot.

> T. S. ELIOT (1888–1955). "Burbank with a Baedeker: Bleistein with a Cigar," *Poems,* 1920

Was there any form of filth or profligacy, particularly in cultural life, without at least one Jew involved in it?
    If you cut even cautiously into such an abscess, you found, like a maggot in a rotting body, often dazzled by the sudden light—a kike.

> ADOLF HITLER (1889–1945). *Mein Kampf,* 1.2, 1924, tr. Ralph Manheim, 1943

I set the Aryan and the Jew over against each other; and if I call one of them a human being I must call the other something else. The two are as widely separated as man and beast. Not that I would call the Jew a beast. . . . He is a creature outside nature and alien to nature.

> ADOLF HITLER (1889–1945). Table talk, 1932–1934. In Hermann Rauschning, *The Voice of Destruction,* 16, 1940

The Jew, who is something of a nomad, has never yet created a cultural form of his own and as far as we can see never will, since all his instincts and talents require a more or less civilized nation to act as host for their development.

> CARL G. JUNG (1875–1961). "The State of Psychotherapy Today," 1934, *Civilization in Transition,* tr. R. F. C. Hull, 1964

There are sorcerers among the Jews, who delight in tormenting Christians, for they hold us as dogs.

> MARTIN LUTHER (1483–1546). *Table Talk,* 862, 1566, tr. William Hazlitt, 1857

What is the profane basis of Judaism? *Practical* need, *self-interest.* What is the worldly cult of the Jew? *Huckstering.* What is his worldly god? *Money.*

> KARL MARX (1818–1883). "On the Jewish Question" (2), 1844, *The Marx-Engels Reader,* 2nd ed., ed. Robert C. Tucker, 1978

The Jews of Poland are the smeariest of all races.

> KARL MARX (1818–1883). In *Neue Rheinische Zeitung,* 29 April 1849

Please get me the names of the Jews. You know, the big Jewish contributors of the Democrats. . . . Could we please investigate some of these c——suckers??

> RICHARD M. NIXON (1913–1994). Remark to H. R. Haldeman, 13 September 1971. In "And Now, 'Tricky Dick,'" *Newsweek,* 3 November 1997

My Jew boy.

> RICHARD M. NIXON (1913–1994). Referring to Henry A. Kissinger (an often-used phrase). In Walter Isaacson, *Kissinger: A Biography,* 24, 1992

Harrison and his ilk believe that the Displaced Person is a human being, which he is not, and this applies particularly to the Jews who are lower than animals.

> GEORGE S. PATTON, JR. (1885–1945). Diary, 15 September 1945. In Martin Blumenson, *The Patton Papers, 1940–1945,* 40, 1974

The Jews, who killed both the Lord Jesus and the prophets, and drove us out, and displease God and oppose all men by hindering us from speaking to the Gentiles that they may be saved.

> PAUL (A.D. 1st cent.). *1 Thessalonians* 2:14–16

If you compel Time to give money in advance, you will have to pay a rate of interest more ruinous than any Jew would require.

> ARTHUR SCHOPENHAUER (1788–1860). "Counsels and Maxims" (4.49), *Essays of Arthur Schopenhauer,* tr. T. Bailey Saunders, 1851

On the Day of Judgment the gravest crime standing to the German National Socialists' account might be, not that they had exterminated a majority of Western Jews, but that they had caused the surviving remnant of Jewry to stumble.

> ARNOLD J. TOYNBEE (1889–1975). Referring to the post–World War II treatment of the Palestinians by Israeli Jews, *A Study of History,* 8.290–291, 1954

In my eyes the West is a perpetual aggressor. I trace the West's arrogance back to the Jewish notion of a "Chosen People."

> ARNOLD J. TOYNBEE (1889–1975). *A Study of History,* 12.627, 1961

ANTI-SEMITISM

See also • Christianity: Eli Wiesel ○ Holocaust ○ Judaism ○ Prejudice ○ Racism ○ Racist Statements

[The Jews] have been the untouchables of Christianity. The parallel between their treatment by Christians and the treatment of untouchables by Hindus is very close. Religious sanction has been invoked in both cases for the justification of the inhuman treatment meted out to them.

> MOHANDAS K. GANDHI (1869–1948). In *Harijan,* 1 September 1946

For over a thousand years, the ruling classes of Europe used anti-Semitism against the Jews to divert attention from themselves as the cause of the people's poverty.

> FELIX GREENE (1909–1985). *The Enemy: What Every American Should Know About Imperialism,* 5.4, 1970

Anti-Semitism is . . . a movement in which we, as Christians, cannot have any part whatever. . . . Spiritually, we are Semites.

> POPE PIUS XI (1857–1939). Remarks to a group of Belgian pilgrims, September 1938

The worst mistake I made was that stupid suburban prejudice of anti-Semitism.

> EZRA POUND (1885–1972). Allen Ginsberg interview, *Evergreen Review,* June 1968

ANXIETY

See also • Anger ○ Depression ○ Fear ○ Guilt ○ Unhappiness ○ Worry

Anonymous: Who suffers most from anxiety?
Bion: He who is ambitious of the greatest prosperity.

BION (325?–255? B.C.). Format adapted. In Diogenes Laertius (A.D. 3rd cent.), *Lives of Eminent Philosophers*, 4.7, tr. R. D. Hicks, 1925

Anxiety leads to a narrowing of the field of attention, the so-called tunnel vision, and when people are anxious they are unable to attend to the total situation as is necessary to enable them to act rationally, but impulsively do the first thing that comes into their heads which is usually determined by what others are doing at the same time.

> J. A. C. BROWN (1911–1964). *Techniques of Persuasion: From Propaganda to Brainwashing*, 9, 1963

There's nought, no doubt, so much the spirit calms
  As rum and true religion.

> LORD BYRON (1788–1824). *Don Juan*, 2.34, 1819–1824

People wish to be settled; only as far as they are unsettled is there is any hope for them.

> RALPH WALDO EMERSON (1803–1882). "Circles," *Essays: First Series*, 1841

Anxiety is the reaction to danger.

> SIGMUND FREUD (1856–1939). *The Problem of Anxiety*, 10, 1926, tr. Henry Alden Bunker, 1936

Stupidity is without anxiety.

> GOETHE (1749–1832). 16 August 1824. In Peter Eckermann, *Conversations with Goethe*, 1836–1848, tr. John Oxenford, 1850

Bless your uneasiness as a sign that there is still life in you.

> DAG HAMMARSKJÖLD (1905–1961). 26 August 1956, *Markings*, tr. Leif Sjöberg and W. H. Auden, 1964

Failure to understand what is demanded of us is the source of anxiety.

> ABRAHAM JOSHUA HESCHEL (1907–1972). *Who Is Man?* 6, 1965

Do not be anxious about tomorrow, for tomorrow will be anxious for itself. Let the day's own trouble be sufficient for the day.

> JESUS (A.D. 1st cent.). *Matthew* 6:34

In political life as in individual life, anxieties which can be expressed are far less important than those which cannot.

> GUSTAVE LE BON (1841–1931). *Aphorisms of Present Times*, 4.7, 1913, tr. Alice Widener, 1979

Nerves provide me with energy. They work for me. It's when I don't have them, when I feel at ease, that I get worried.

> MIKE NICHOLS (1931–). In Lewish Funke, "Always in the Wings—the Shakes," *New York Times Magazine*, 17 May 1964

Both are foes to tranquillity— . . . the inability to change and the inability to endure.

> SENECA THE YOUNGER (5? B.C.–A.D. 65). "On Tranquillity of Mind" (14.1), *Moral Essays*, tr. John W. Basore, 1932

❦

A hundred cartloads of anxiety will not pay an ounce of debt.
SAYING (ITALIAN)

APHORISMS

See also • Axioms ○ Epigrams ○ Maxims ○ Proverbs ○ Quotations ○ Sayings

A genuine aphorism iz truth done up in a small package.

> JOSH BILLINGS (1818–1885). "Koarse Shot," *Everybody's Friend, or; Josh Billing's Encyclopedia and Proverbial Philosophy of Wit and Humor*, 1874

The great writers of aphorisms read as if they had all known each other very well.

> ELIAS CANETTI (1905–1994). 1943, *The Human Province*, tr. Joachim Neugroschel, 1978

An aphorism is the last link in a long chain of thought.

> MARIE von EBNER-ESCHENBACH (1830–1916). *Aphorisms*, p. 19, 1880–1905, tr. David Scrase and Wolfgang Mieder, 1994

Aphorisms tend to be distinctly more subversive [than maxims]; indeed, it is often a maxim that they set out to subvert.

> JOHN GROSS (1935–). Comp., introduction to *The Oxford Book of Aphorisms*, 1983

[An aphorism] bears the stamp and style of the mind which created it; its message is universal.

> JOHN GROSS (1935–). Comp., introduction to *The Oxford Book of Aphorisms*, 1983

Anxious to distance himself from the platitude, the aphorist is drawn towards the unsettling paradox.

> JOHN GROSS (1935–). Comp., introduction to *The Oxford Book of Aphorisms*, 1983

The excellence of aphorisms consists not so much in the expression of some rare and abstruse sentiment, as in the comprehension of some obvious and useful truths in a few words. We frequently fall into error and folly, not because the true principles of actions are not known, but because, for a time, they are not remembered; and he may, therefore, be justly numbered among the benefactors of mankind, who contracts the great rules of life into short sentences, that may be easily impressed on the memory, and taught by frequent recollection to recur habitually to the mind.

> SAMUEL JOHNSON (1709–1784). In *The Rambler* (English journal), 175, 19 November 1751

I fancy mankind may come in time to write all aphoristically, except in narrative; grow weary of preparation and connection and illustration and all those arts by which a big book is made.

> SAMUEL JOHNSON (1709–1784). 16 August 1773. In James Boswell, *The Journal of a Tour to the Hebrides, with Samuel Johnson, L.L.D.*, 1786

An aphorism can never be the whole truth; it is either a half-truth or a truth-and-a-half.

> KARL KRAUS (1874–1936). 1909. In Thomas S. Szasz, *Karl Kraus and the Soul-Doctors: A Pioneer Critic and His Criticism of Psychiatry and Psychoanalysis*, 8, 1976
>
> See Maxims: William Mathews

Someone who can write aphorisms should not fritter away his time writing essays.

> KARL KRAUS (1876–1936). "Riddles out of Solutions," *Half-Truths & One-and-a-Half Truths: Selected Aphorisms*, ed. Harry Zohn, 1976

Why do I write these short aphorisms? Because words fail me!

> STANISLAW J. LEC (1909–1966). *Unkempt Thoughts*, p. 110, tr. Jacek Galazka, 1962

[Aphorisms] are the guiding oracles which man has found out for himself in that great business of ours, of learning how to be, to do, to do without, and to depart.

> JOHN MORLEY (1838–1923). "Aphorisms," 1887, *Studies in Literature,* 1890

APPEARANCES

See also • Clothes ○ Deception ○ Fashion ○ Hypocrisy ○ Illusion ○ Reality

[Preoccupation with self-image] is a terrible weakness. It makes one look at oneself instead of at the problem. How will I look fielding this hot line drive to shortstop? This is a good way to miss the ball altogether.

> DEAN ACHESON (1893–1971). Referring to the Kennedy administration, letter to Pres. Harry S. Truman, early 1960s. In Alan Brinkley, "'Work Hard, Trust in God, Have No Fear,'" *New York Times Book Review,* 21 June 1992

Beware lest you lose the substance by grasping at the shadow.

> AESOP (6th cent. B.C.). "The Dog and the Shadow," *Fables,* tr. Joseph Jacobs, 1894

Outside show is a poor substitute for inner worth.

> AESOP (6th cent. B.C.). "The Fox and the Mask," *Fables,* tr. Joseph Jacobs, 1894

Appearances are deceptive.

> AESOP (6th cent. B.C.), "The Wolf in Sheep's Clothing," *Fables,* tr. Joseph Jacobs, 1894

It iz an actewal fackt that most ov us work harder, tew seem happy, than we should have to, to be happy.

> JOSH BILLINGS (1818–1885). "Josh Settles Up with His Correspondents Summarily," *Everybody's Friend, or; Josh Billing's Encyclopedia and Proverbial Philosophy of Wit and Humor,* 1874

In competition for prestige it seems only sensible to try to perfect our image rather than ourselves. That seems the most economical, direct way to produce the desired result. Accustomed to live in a world of pseudo-events, celebrities, dissolving forms, and shadowy but overshadowing images, we mistake our shadows for ourselves. To us they seem more real than the reality. Why should they not seem so to others?

> DANIEL J. BOORSTIN (1914–). *The Image: A Guide to Pseudo-Events in America,* 6.2, 1961

He was the mildest manner'd man
That ever scuttled ship or cut a throat.

> LORD BYRON (1788–1824). *Don Juan,* 3.41, 1819–1824

How we clutch at shadows as if they were substances; and sleep deepest while fancying ourselves most awake!

> THOMAS CARLYLE (1795–1881). *Sartor Resartus: The Life and Opinions of Herr Teufelsdröckh,* 1.8, 1835

Happy the man who never puts on a face, but receives every visitor with that countenance he has on.

> RALPH WALDO EMERSON (1803–1882). Journal, 28 July 1833

Against all appearances the nature of things works for truth and right forever.

> RALPH WALDO EMERSON (1803–1882). "Worship," *The Conduct of Life,* 1860

The lie is in the surrender of the man to his appearance; as if a man should neglect himself and treat his shadow on the wall with marks of infinite respect.

> RALPH WALDO EMERSON (1803–1882). "The Comic," *Letters and Social Aims,* 1876

It is a million times better to *appear* untrue before the world than to *be* untrue to ourselves.

> MOHANDAS K. GANDHI (1869–1948). In *Young India,* 16 February 1922

Pay no attention to *appearing. Being* is alone important.

> ANDRÉ GIDE (1869–1951). "Rule of Conduct," journal, November 1890, tr. Justin O'Brien, 1948

No man, for any considerable period, can wear one face to himself, and another to the multitude, without finally getting bewildered as to which may be the true.

> NATHANIEL HAWTHORNE (1804–1864). *The Scarlet Letter,* 20, 1850

All is not gold that glitters.

> JOHN HEYWOOD (1497?–1580). Comp., *A Dialogue Containing the Number of the Effectual Proverbs in the English Tongue,* 1.10, 1562 (Popular version: All that glitters is not gold.)

Things are not what they seem; or, to be more accurate, they are not only what they seem, but very much else besides.

> ALDOUS HUXLEY (1894–1963). "Man and Reality." In Christopher Isherwood, ed., *Vedanta for the Western World,* 1945

Now you Pharisees cleanse the outside of the cup and of the dish, but inside you are full of extortion and wickedness.

> JESUS (A.D. 1st cent.). *Luke* 11:39

Do not judge by appearances, but judge with right judgment.

> JESUS (A.D. 1st cent.). *John* 7:24

Above all, do not appear to others what you are not.

> ROBERT E. LEE (1807–1870). Letter to his son, 1860. Quoted by David McCullough, "The Unexpected Harry Truman." In William Zinsser, ed., *Extraordinary Lives: The Art and Craft of American Biography,* 1988

The great majority of mankind are satisfied with appearances, as though they were realities, and are often even more influenced by the things that seem than by those that are.

> MACHIAVELLI (1469–1527). *The Discourses,* 1.25, 1517, tr. Christian E. Detmold, 1940

He wears a mask, and his face grows to fit it.

> GEORGE ORWELL (1903–1950). "Shooting an Elephant," autumn 1936, *The Collected Essays, Journalism and Letters of George Orwell,* vol. 1, ed. Sonia Orwell and Ian Angus, 1968

The visible is a shadow cast by the invisible.

> PLATO (427?–347 B.C.). In Martin Luther King, Jr., *Strength to Love,* 9.3, 1963

But the Lord said to Samuel: "Do not look on his appearance or on the height of his stature, because I have rejected him; for the Lord sees not as man sees; man looks on the outward appearance, but the Lord looks on the heart."

> SAMUEL (11th? cent. B.C.). *1 Samuel* 16:7

Masks, wigs, cowls, and stays are too troublesome; if you are not always on the watch, the beastly things will fall off.

> GEORGE SANTAYANA (1863–1952). "Masks," *Soliloquies in England and Later Soliloquies*, 1922

No one shows himself as he is, but wears his mask and plays his part. Indeed, the whole of our social arrangements may be likened to a perpetual comedy; and this is why a man who is worth anything finds society so insipid, while a blockhead is quite at home in it.

> ARTHUR SCHOPENHAUER (1788–1860). "Studies in Pessimism: Further Psychological Observations," *Essays of Arthur Schopenhauer,* tr. T. Bailey Saunders, 1851

What is *actually* happening is often less important than what *appears* to be happening.

> WILLIAM V. SHANNON. "The Amazing Myth of George McGovern," *Dallas Morning News,* 2 July 1972

What you are you do not see, what you see is your shadow.

> RABINDRANATH TAGORE (1861–1941). *Stray Birds,* 18, 1914

❦

If it walks like a duck, and quacks like a duck, then it probably is a duck.

> ANONYMOUS (AMERICAN)

Many a rosy apple is rotten to the core.

> SAYING (AMERICAN)

APPEASEMENT

See also • Alliances ○ Diplomacy ○ International Relations ○ Negotiation ○ Treaties ○ World War II: Neville Chamberlain (1,2)

An infallible method of conciliating a tiger is to allow oneself to be swallowed.

> KONRAD ADENAUER (1876–1967). In Paul Dickson, comp., *The Official Explanations,* p. 2, 1980

An appeaser is one who feeds a crocodile—hoping it will eat him last.

> WINSTON CHURCHILL (1874–1965). Referring to Prime Minister Chamberlain and the Munich Pact, House of Commons speech, 2 October 1938

If you let a bully come into your front yard, he'll be on your porch the next day, and the day after that he'll rape your wife in your own bed.

> LYNDON B. JOHNSON (1908–1973). In Walter Isaacson and Evan Thomas, *The Wise Men: Six Friends and the World They Made,* 22, 1986

No appeasement will avoid necessary battles. It only makes them more costly and lengthy.

> GUSTAVE LE BON (1841–1931). *Aphorisms of Present Times,* 4.8, 1913, tr. Alice Widener, 1979

Appeasement does not always lead to war; sometimes it leads to surrender.

> WILLIAM SAFIRE (1929–). "Giving War a Chance," *New York Times,* 2 November 1989

❦

Appeasement invites aggression; reconciliation invites peace.

> ANONYMOUS

Appeasing a tyrant is like hand-feeding a shark.

> ANONYMOUS

APPLAUSE

See also • Popularity ○ Praise

He too serves a certain purpose who only stands and cheers.

> HENRY ADAMS (1838–1918). *The Education of Henry Adams,* 24, 1907

When the million applaud you, seriously ask yourself what harm you have done; when they censure you, what good!

> C. C. COLTON (1780–1832). *Lacon: or, Many Things in Few Words; Addressed to Those Who Think,* 1.193, 1823

Applause is the spur of noble minds, the end and aim of weak ones.

> C. C. COLTON (1780–1832). *Lacon: or, Many Things in Few Words; Addressed to Those Who Think,* 1.424, 1823

Some people have built-in filters that screen out the boos and amplify the hurrahs. Those are the people who never know when they're in trouble.

> TOMMY DAVIS (1939–). Baseball player. In Roger von Oech, "The Judge," *A Kick in the Seat of the Pants,* 1986

The highest applause is silence.

> ELBERT HUBBARD (1856–1915). In Alice Hubbard, comp., *An American Bible,* p. 147, 1946

Nobody kicks on bein' interrupted if it's by applause.

> KIN HUBBARD (1856–1915). *Abe Martin: Hoss Sense and Nonsense,* p. 126, 1926

I had rather be hissed for a good verse than applauded for a bad one.

> VICTOR HUGO (1802–1885)

Fans don't boo nobodies.

> REGGIE JACKSON (1946–). "Jackson's Observation on Fame." In Paul Dickson, comp., *The Official Explanations,* p. 99, 1980

To receive applause for works which do not demand all our powers hinders our advance towards a perfecting of our spirit. It usually means that thereafter we stand still.

> GEORG CHRISTOPH LICHTENBERG (1742–1799). *Aphorisms,* K.42, 1806, tr. R. J. Hollingdale, 1990

When I hear a man applauded by the mob, I always feel a pang of pity for him. All he has to do to be hissed is to live long enough.

> H. L. MENCKEN (1880–1956). *Minority Report: H. L. Mencken's Notebooks,* 351, 1956

I have not sought the applause of the Parisians; I am not an operatic performer.

> NAPOLEON (1769–1821). Letter to his brother Joseph Bonaparte, 12 March 1814, *The Corsican: A Diary of Napoleon's Life in His Own Words,* ed. R. M. Johnston, 1911

They named it *ovation*, from the Latin *ovis* [a sheep].

> PLUTARCH (A.D. 46?–119?). "Marcellus," *Parallel Lives*, Dryden edition, 1693

ARCHITECTURE

See also • Art ○ Cities ○ Creativity

The multi-use stadium is the civic icon of the late twentieth century. It's the equivalent of a cathedral, proof in the citizens' minds that they're world-class cities.

> PHILIP BESS. Chicago architect. In Hal Lancaster, "Stadium Projects Are Proliferating Amid Debate Over Benefit to Cities," *Wall Street Journal*, 20 March 1987

A building is not something you finish. A building is something you start.

> STEWART BRAND (1939–). *How Buildings Learn: What Happens After They're Built*, 1994. In Harold Gilliam, "Flexible Architecture," *San Francisco Chronicle Review*, 17 July 1994

We shape our buildings; thereafter they shape us.

> WINSTON CHURCHILL (1874–1965). In "Schools of Tomorrow" (epigraph), *Time*, 12 September 1960

[Radio City Music Hall] is the theater God would have built if He had the money.

> HENRY GELDZAHLER. New York City cultural commissioner. Calling for the theater's designation as a landmark (successfully as it turned out) in testimony before the Landmarks Preservation Commission. In "Ideas & Trends," *New York Times*, 2 April 1978

I have found a paper of mine among some others, in which I call architecture "petrified music."

> GOETHE (1749–1832). 23 March 1829. In Peter Eckermann, *Conversations with Goethe*, 1836–1848, tr. John Oxenford, 1850

Ev'rythin's up to date in Kansas City.
they've gone about as fur as they c'n go!
They went and built a skyscraper seven stories high,
about as high as a buildin' orta grow.

> OSCAR HAMMERSTEIN II (1895–1960). "Kansas City" (song). In the musical *Oklahoma*, 1943

The architectural profession gave the public 50 years of modern architecture, and the public's response has been 10 years of the greatest wave of historical preservation in the history of man.

> GEORGE E. HARTMAN. Architect. In Barbara Gamarekian, "New Game in Town: Facademanship," *New York Times*, 31 August 1983

If cities were built by the sound of music, then some edifices would appear to be constructed by grave, solemn tunes—others to have danced forth to light, fantastic airs.

> NATHANIEL HAWTHORNE (1804–1864). 4 January 1839, *The American Notebooks*, ed. Claude M. Simpson, 1932

The most magnificent edifices, most beautiful temples and monuments of worldly glory are repulsive to [the pious man] when they are built by the sweat and tears of suffering slaves, or erected through injustice and fraud.

> ABRAHAM JOSHUA HESCHEL (1907–1972). *Man Is Not Alone: A Philosophy of Religion*, 26, 1951

The architecture of despair.

> MARGARET MORTON. Photographer and Cooper Union School of Art associate professor. On the shanties of the homeless in New York City. In Patricia Lee Broun, "The Architecture of Those Called Homeless," *New York Times*, 28 March 1993

A modern plan is successful only when it embraces every human need appropriate to the structure without waste of space, duplication, clumsy and inefficient circulation.

> LEWIS MUMFORD (1895–1990). *The Culture of Cities*, 7.2, 1938

The Port of New York Authority's World Trade Center, 110 stories high, is a characteristic example of the purposeless giantism and technological exhibitionism that are now eviscerating the living tissue of every great city.

> LEWIS MUMFORD (1895–1990). *The Pentagon of Power: The Myth of the Machine*, Graphic Section 2.20, 1970

Thy arts of building from the bee receive.

> ALEXANDER POPE (1688–1744). *An Essay on Man*, 3.175, 1734

They're all made out of ticky-tacky,
And they all look just the same.

> MALVINA REYNOLDS. On the tract houses in the hills south of San Francisco, "Little Boxes" (song), 1963

"Form follows profit" is the aesthetic principle of our times.

> RICHARD ROGERS. British architect. In *Times* (London), 13 February 1991

When we build, let us think that we build forever.

> JOHN RUSKIN (1819–1900). *The Seven Lamps of Architecture*, 6.10, 1849

A house is not in its prime until it is five hundred years old.

> JOHN RUSKIN (1819–1900). In Ralph Waldo Emerson, "Immortality," *Letters and Social Aims*, 1876

Form ever follows function.

> LOUIS HENRI SULLIVAN (1854–1900). "The Tall Office Building Artistically Considered," *Lippincott's Magazine*, March 1896
>
> See Ideology: Anonymous (2)

The ancient Romans built their greatest masterpieces of architecture, the amphitheaters, for wild beasts to fight in.

> VOLTAIRE (1694–1778). Letter to the police commissioner of Paris, 20 June 1733

If Nature had been comfortable, mankind would never have invented architecture.

> OSCAR WILDE (1854–1900). "The Decay of Lying," *Intentions*, 1891

Architecture aims at Eternity.

> CHRISTOPHER WREN (1632–1723). "Of Architecture." In Christopher Wren (his son), ed., *Parentalia; or Memoirs of the Family of the Wrens*, 1750

The physician can bury his mistakes, but the architect can only advise his client to plant vines.

> FRANK LLOYD WRIGHT (1867–1959). "Frank Lloyd Wright Talks of His Art," *New York Times Magazine*, 4 October 1953

What the American people have to learn is that architecture is the great mother-art, the art behind which all the others are related. Until the time comes that when we speak of Art we think of buildings, we will have no culture of our own.

> FRANK LLOYD WRIGHT (1867–1959). "Frank Lloyd Wright Talks of His Art," *New York Times Magazine,* 4 October 1953

Form and function are one.

> FRANK LLOYD WRIGHT (1867–1959). In Clifton Fadiman, comp., *An American Treasury, 1455–1955,* p. 838, 1955

The skyscraper is responsible for the congestion, and is making the city of today impossible to use. The skyscraper piles the crowd up high, dumps it on the street, stuffs it in again, and the streets are not nearly wide enough.

> FRANK LLOYD WRIGHT (1867–1959). Henry Brandon interview, *Sunday Times* (London), 3 November 1957. In Christopher Silvester, ed., *The Norton Book of Interviews: An Anthology from 1859 to the Present Day,* 1996

If you seek his monument, look around you.

> ANONYMOUS. Inscription on the gravestone of the English architect Christopher Wren (1632–1723)

ARGUMENT

See also • Conversation ○ International Relations ○ Logic ○ Negotiation ○ Persuasion ○ Pubic Speaking ○ Quarrels ○ Reason ○ Tact ○ Words

We ought in fairness to fight our case with no help beyond the bare facts: nothing, therefore, should matter except the proof of these facts.

> ARISTOTLE (384–322 B.C.). *Rhetoric,* 3.1, tr. W. Rhys Roberts, 1954

For every why he had a wherefore.

> SAMUEL BUTLER (1612–1680). *Hudibras,* 1.1.132, 1663-1678, ed. John Wilders, 1967

It is not he who gains the exact point in dispute who scores most in controversy—but he who has shown the better temper.

> SAMUEL BUTLER (1612–1680). *The Note-Books of Samuel Butler,* 20, ed. Henry Festing Jones, 1907

In answering an opponent, arrange your ideas, but not your words.

> C. C. COLTON (1780–1832). *Lacon: or, Many Things in Few Words; Addressed to Those Who Think,* 1.119, 1823

There are two sides to every argument, unless a person is personally involved, in which case there is only one.

> CUTLER WEBSTER'S LAW. In Paul Dickson, comp., *The Official Rules,* p. 58, 1978

Not to put too fine a point on it.

> CHARLES DICKENS (1812–1870). *Bleak House,* 11, 1853

If I know your sect, I anticipate your argument.

> RALPH WALDO EMERSON (1803–1882). "Self-Reliance," *Essays: First Series,* 1841

It is only when they cannot answer your reasons that they wish to knock you down.

> RALPH WALDO EMERSON (1803–1882). "The Assault upon Mr. Sumner," speech, Town Hall, Concord (Massachusetts), 26 May 1856

The best argument is not the accosting in front the hostile premises, but the *flanking* them by a new generalization which incidentally disposes of them.

> RALPH WALDO EMERSON (1803–1882). Journal, 1864?, undated

Put the argument into a concrete shape, into an image—some hard phrase, round and solid as a ball, which they can see and handle and carry home with them—and the cause is half won.

> RALPH WALDO EMERSON (1803–1882). "Eloquence," *Society and Solitude,* 1870

Many times what cannot be refuted by arguments can be parried by laughter.

> DESIDERIUS ERASMUS (1466–1536). *The Praise of Folly,* 25, 1509, tr. Hoyt Hopewell Hudson, 1941

Those whose cause is just will never lack good arguments.

> EURIPIDES (485?–406 B.C.). *Hecuba,* l. 1235, tr. William Arrowsmith, 1956

"For your own good" is a persuasive argument that will eventually make a man agree to his own destruction.

> JANET FRAME (1924–). *Faces in the Water,* 4, 1961

These disputing, contradicting, and confuting People are generally unfortunate in their Affairs. They get Victory sometimes, but they never get Good Will, which would be of more use to them.

> BENJAMIN FRANKLIN (1706–1790). In Peter Baida, *Poor Richard's Legacy: American Business Valves from Benjamin Franklin to Michael Milken,* 1, 1990

Argument seldom convinces anyone contrary to his Inclinations.

> THOMAS FULLER (1654–1734). Comp., *Gnomologia: Adages and Proverbs,* 812, 1732

He that hath the worst Cause makes the most Noise.

> THOMAS FULLER (1654–1734). Comp., *Gnomologia: Adages and Proverbs,* 2153, 1732

Soft Words are hard Arguments.

> THOMAS FULLER (1654–1734). Comp., *Gnomologia: Adages and Proverbs,* 4203, 1732

There is no arguing with Johnson; for when his pistol misses fire, he knocks you down with the butt end of it.

> OLIVER GOLDSMITH (1728–1774). 26 October 1769. In James Boswell, *The Life of Samuel Johnson,* 1791

The advocate can make no greater mistake than to ignore or attempt to conceal the weak points in his case. The most effective strategy is at an early stage of the argument to invite attention to your weakest point before the court has discovered it, then to meet it with the best answers at your disposal, to deal with all the remaining points with equal candor and to end with as powerful a presentation of your strongest point as you are capable of making.

> ROBERT H. JACKSON (1892–1954). Supreme Court associate justice. In Eugene C. Gerhart, *America's Advocate: Robert H. Jackson,* 24, 1958

Treating your adversary with respect is giving him an advantage to which he is not entitled. The greatest part of men cannot judge of reasoning, and are impressed by character; so that, if you allow your adversary a respectable character, they will think, that though you differ from him, you may be wrong. Sir, treating your adversary with respect is striking soft in a battle.

> SAMUEL JOHNSON (1709–1784). 15 August 1773. In James Boswell, *The Journal of a Tour to the Hebrides, with Samuel Johnson, L.L.D.,* 1786

The end of argument or discussion should be, not victory, but enlightenment.

> JOSEPH JOUBERT (1754–1824). *Pensées,* 1838, tr. H. P. Collins, 1928
>
> See Conversation: Ralph Waldo Emerson (1)

The strongest always has the best argument.

> LA FONTAINE (1621–1695). *Fables,* 1.10, 1668–1679

There is no good in arguing with the inevitable. The only argument available with an east wind is to put on your overcoat.

> JAMES RUSSELL LOWELL (1819–1891). "Democracy," address at Town Hall, Birmingham (England), 6 October 1884

Never argue with a man whose job depends on not being convinced.

> H. L. MENCKEN (1880–1956). In Christopher Matthews, *Hardball: How Politics Is Played—Told by One Who Knows the Game,* 2, 1988

He who knows only his own side of the case knows little of that.

> JOHN STUART MILL (1806–1873). *On Liberty,* 2, 1859

So long as an opinion is strongly rooted in the feelings, it gains rather than loses in stability by having a preponderating weight of arguments against it.

> JOHN STUART MILL (1806–1873). *The Subjection of Women,* 1, 1869

He who imposes his argument by bravado and command shows that it is weak in reason.

> MONTAIGNE (1533–1592). "Of Cripples," *Essays,* 1588, tr. Donald M. Frame, 1958

When someone opposes me, he arouses my attention, not my anger. I go to meet a man who contradicts me, who instructs me. The cause of truth should be the common cause for both.

> MONTAIGNE (1533–1592). "Of the Art of Discussion," *Essays,* 1588, tr. Donald M. Frame, 1958

In the Conseil d'Etat there were men far more eloquent than I, but I regularly defeated them with this simple argument: Two and two is four.

> NAPOLEON (1769–1821). Deathbed statement, 17 April 1821, *The Mind of Napoleon: A Selection from His Written and Spoken Words,* 324, ed. J. Christopher Herold, 1955

Anyone who can set the terms of a debate can win it.

> GEORGE E. REEDY (1917–). *The Twilight of the Presidency,* 3, 1970

You mustn't exaggerate, young man. That's always a sign that your argument is weak.

> BERTRAND RUSSELL (1872–1956). Tommy Robbins interview, *Redbook,* September 1964

The truth is always the strongest argument.

> SOPHOCLES (496?–406 B.C.)

[Abraham Lincoln] always resolved every question into its primary elements, and gave up every point on his own side that did not seem to be invulnerable. One would think, to hear him present his case in the court, he was giving his case away. He would concede point after point to his adversary. But he always reserved a point upon which he claimed a decision in his favor, and his concession magnified the strength of his claim.

> JOSHUA F. SPEED (19th cent.). In Francis Fisher Browne, *The Every-Day Life of Abraham Lincoln,* 2.6, 1887

When a debater's point is not impressive, he brings forth many arguments.

> TALMUD (A.D. 1st–6th cent.). Rabbinical writings. In Louis I. Newman, comp., *The Talmudic Anthology,* 15, 1945

People do not always argue because they misunderstand one another; they argue because they hold different goals.

> WILLIAM H. WHYTE, JR. (1917–). "Groupthink," *Fortune,* March 1952

I dislike arguments of any kind. They are always vulgar, and often convincing.

> OSCAR WILDE (1854–1900). *The Importance of Being Earnest,* 3, 1895

⚜

There are three sides to every argument: your side, my side, and the truth.

> SAYING (AMERICAN)

When your argument is weak, pound the table.

> SAYING

ARISTOCRACY

See also • Class ○ Nature: Ralph Waldo Emerson (13) ○ Nobility

There is a rabble even amongst the gentry.

> SIR THOMAS BROWNE (1605–1682). *Religio Medici,* 2.1, 1642, ed. John Addington Symonds, 1886

An aristocracy and a despotism differ but in name.

> EDMUND BURKE (1729–1797). *A Vindication of Natural Society,* p. 48, M. Cooper edition, 1756
>
> See Nobility: Burke

Aristocracy of Feudal Parchment has passed away with a mighty rushing; and now, by a natural course, we arrive at Aristocracy of the Moneybag. It is the course through which all European Societies are, at this hour, traveling. Apparently a still baser sort of Aristocracy? An infinitely baser [one]; the basest yet known.

> THOMAS CARLYLE (1795–1881). *The French Revolution: A History,* 2.7.7, 1837

There are no wise few. Every aristocracy that has ever existed has behaved, in all essential points, exactly like a small mob.

> G. K. CHESTERTON (1874–1936). *Heretics,* 12, 1905

Democracy means government by the uneducated, while aristocracy . . . means government by the badly educated.

> G. K. CHESTERTON (1874–1936). "Mr. Chesterton Looks Us Over," *New York Times Magazine,* 1 February 1931

I know it was the fashion in Victorian times to say that England was represented by its great middle class and not by its aristocracy. That was the artfulness of its aristocracy. Never did a governing class govern so completely, by saying it did not govern at all.

> G. K. CHESTERTON (1874–1936). In "Thoughts on the Business of Life," *Forbes*, 4 March 1991

An aristocracy is a combination of many powerful men, for the purpose of maintaining and advancing their own particular interests.

> JAMES FENIMORE COOPER (1789–1851). "On the Advantages of an Aristocracy," *The American Democrat*, 1838

A social life which worships money and pursues social distinction as its aim is, in spirit and in fact, an aristocracy.

> JOSIAH GILBERT HOLLAND (1819–1881). "Self-Help," *Plain Talks on Familiar Subjects*, 1866

I agree with you that there is a natural aristocracy among men. The grounds of this are virtue and talents. . . . There is also an artificial aristocracy founded on wealth and birth, without either virtue or talents. . . . The artificial aristocracy is a mischievous ingredient in government, and provision should be made to prevent it's ascendancy.

> THOMAS JEFFERSON (1743–1826). Letter to John Adams, 28 October 1813

A decent oligarchy—call it aristocracy if you like—is the most ideal form of government. It depends on the quality of a nation whether they evolve a decent oligarchy or not. . . .

Without the aristocratic ideal there is no stability. You in England owe it to the "gentlemen" that you possess the world.

> CARL G. JUNG (1875–1961). Interview, *Observer* (British newspaper), 18 October 1936, "The Psychology of Dictatorship," *C. G. Jung Speaking: Interviews and Encounters*, ed. William McGuire and R. F. C. Hull, 1977

An aristocracy was . . . by definition a class of both obligation and privilege, the one validating the other.

> JOHN KEEGAN (1934–). *The Mask of Command*, 3, 1987

Social distinctions in the final analysis depend upon money. The great English lords of the eighteenth century were not treated by their inferiors with the obsequiousness which now turns our stomachs because of their titles, but because of their wealth, which, with the influence it gave them, enabled them to grant favors to their friends and dependents.

> W. SOMERSET MAUGHAM (1874–1965). 1941, *A Writer's Notebook*, 1949

It is the instinct of a true aristocracy, not to punish eccentricity by expulsion, but to throw a mantle of protection about it—to safeguard it from the suspicions and resentments of the lower orders.

> H. L. MENCKEN (1880–1956). "The National Letters: The Cultural Background," *Prejudices: Second Series*, 1920

Plutocracy, in a democratic state, tends to take the place of the missing aristocracy, and even to be mistaken for it. It is, of course, something quite different. It lacks all the essential characters of a true aristocracy: a clean tradition, culture, public spirit, honesty, honor, courage—above all, courage.

> H. L. MENCKEN (1880–1956). *Notes on Democracy*, 4.1, 1926

At the head of the Privileged, or in other words, the Satisfied Classes, must be placed the landed interest. They have the strongest reason for being satisfied with the government; they *are* the government.

> JOHN STUART MILL (1806–1873). "Reorganization of the Reform Party," *The London and Westminster Review* (English journal), April 1839

In an aristocratic society, the elevated class, though small in number, sets the fashion in opinion and feeling.

> JOHN STUART MILL (1806–1873). "M. de Tocqueville on Democracy in America" (vol. 2), *The Edinburgh Review* (Scotland), October 1840
>
> See Class: Karl Marx and Friedrich Engels (1) ○ Public Opinion: John Kenneth Galbraith

An aristocracy, when put to the proof, has in general shown wonderful facility in enduring the loss of riches and of physical comforts. The very pride, nourished by the elevation which they owed to wealth, supports them under the privation of it. But to those who have chased riches laboriously for half their lives, to lose it is the loss of all; *une vie manquée* [an unsuccessful life].

> JOHN STUART MILL (1806–1873). "M. de Tocqueville on Democracy in America" (vol. 2), *The Edinburgh Review* (Scotland), October 1840

I am an aristocrat. I love liberty; I hate equality.

> JOHN RANDOLPH (1773–1833). Virginia congressman

There is something to be said for government by a great aristocracy which has furnished leaders to the nation in peace and war for generations; even a democrat like myself must admit this.

> THEODORE ROOSEVELT (1858–1919). Letter to Edward Grey, 15 November 1913

To abolish aristocracy, in the sense of social privilege and sanctified authority, would be to cut off the source from which all culture has hitherto flowed.

> GEORGE SANTAYANA (1863–1952). *The Life of Reason or The Phases of Human Progress*, 2.5, 1905–1906

Aristocracies are of three kinds: (1) of birth and rank; (2) of wealth; and (3) of intellect. The last is really the most distinguished of the three.

> ARTHUR SCHOPENHAUER (1788–1860). "Counsels and Maxims" (2.10), *Essays of Arthur Schopenhauer*, tr. T. Bailey Saunders, 1851

The picture of American society has . . . a surface covering of democracy, beneath which the old aristocratic colors sometimes peep out.

> ALEXIS de TOCQUEVILLE (1805–1859). *Democracy in America*, 1.2, 1835, tr. Henry Reeve and Francis Bowen, 1862

Aristocratic institutions cannot exist without laying down the inequality of men as a fundamental principle.

> ALEXIS de TOCQUEVILLE (1805–1859). *Democracy in America*, 1.18, 1835, tr. Henry Reeve and Francis Bowen, 1862

The master and the workman have . . . here no similarity, and their differences increase every day. They are connected only like the two rings at the extremities of a long chain. Each of them fills the station which is made for him, and which he does not leave; the one is continually closely, and necessarily dependent upon the other and seems as much born to obey as that other is to command. What is this but aristocracy?

ALEXIS de TOCQUEVILLE (1805–1859). *Democracy in America*, 2.2.20, 1840, tr. Henry Reeve and Francis Bowen, 1862

🌿

Even workhouses have their aristocracy.
SAYING (ENGLISH)

ARMY

See also • Commanders ○ Militarism ○ Navy ○ Soldiers ○ War ○ War & Preparedness

The only way to form an army to be confided in, was a systematic discipline, by which means all men may be made heroes.
JOHN ADAMS (1735–1826). In Ralph Waldo Emerson, journal, August 1851

Just as the ethos of an upper-class Victorian family totally forbade any show of aggression by the child towards its parents, but encouraged organized aggression towards contemporaries in such school pursuits as boxing and sanctioned bullying, so in the Army the slightest hint of insubordination (i.e., aggression directed towards a superior) is severely punished, while aggression towards the enemy is encouraged and rewarded.
NORMAN F. DIXON (1922–). *On the Psychology of Military Incompetence*, 15, 1976

A standing army is of more danger to the state it protects than to that which it threatens.
RALPH WALDO EMERSON (1803–1882). Journal, January 1826

An army, like a serpent, travels on its belly.
FREDERICK II (1712–1786). Attributed
See Statesmen: B. H. Liddell Hart (2)

The third part of an army must be destroyed before a good one can be made out of it.
MARQUIS OF HALIFAX (1633–1695). "Of Money," *Political, Moral and Miscellaneous Reflections*, 1750

An army is the creation of its commander, not the sum of its units.
NIGEL HAMILTON (1944–). *Mon*•: *The Making of a General, 1887–1942*, 4.2, 1981

A cherished cause and a general who inspires confidence by previous success are powerful means of electrifying an army.
HENRI de JOMINI (1779–1869). *Summary of the Art of War*, 2, 1807, ed. J. D. Hittle, 1947

Death should be regarded as preferable to dishonor. It is easier to replace a defeated army than to recover honor.
CONRAD H. LANZA (1978–?). Annotator, *Napoleon and Modern War*, 57, 1943

Training distinguishes an army from an armed mob.
DOUGLAS MacARTHUR (1880–1964). "Annual Report of the Chief of Staff," 30 June 1934

An army ought to be ready every moment to offer all the resistance of which it is capable.
NAPOLEON (1769–1821). *Napoleon in His Own Words*, 8, comp. Jules Bertaut, 1916

The force of any army, like momentum in mechanics, is represented by the mass multiplied by the rate of movement.
NAPOLEON (1769–1821). *Napoleon in His Own Words*, 8, comp. Jules Bertaut, 1916

It is not the big armies that win battles; it is the good ones.
MAURICE de SAXE (1696–1750). *My Reveries on the Art of War*, 1732. In Thomas R. Phillips, ed., *Roots of Strategy*, p. 200, 1940

An army is efficient for action and motion exactly in the inverse ratio of its *impedimenta*.
WILLIAM TECUMSEH SHERMAN (1820–1891). *Memoirs of Gen. W. T. Sherman*, 4th ed., 25, 1891 (1875)

Terrible as an army with banners.
SOLOMON (10th cent. B.C.). *Song of Solomon* 6:10

It is generally supposed that governments increase their armies only to defend the state from other governments—oblivious of the fact that armies are needed by governments first of all for their defense against their oppressed and enslaved subjects.
LEO TOLSTOY (1828–1910). *The Kingdom of God Is Within You*, 7, 1893, tr. Aylmer Maude, 1936

An army is strengthened by labor and enervated by idleness.
VEGETIUS (A.D. 4th cent.). *De Re Militari*, A.D. 378. In Thomas R. Phillips, ed., *Roots of Strategy*, p. 172, 1940

An army is a nation within a nation; it is one of the vices of our age.
ALFRED de VIGNY (1797–1863). *Servitude et grandeur militaire*, 1.2, 1835

🌿

Join the army. Visit strange and exotic places. Meet fascinating people. And kill them.
SAYING (AMERICAN). 1960s

ART

See also • Acting ○ Architecture ○ Artists ○ Beauty ○ Books ○ Creativity ○ Creativity: First Person ○ Dance ○ Films ○ Media ○ Music ○ Nature ○ Painting ○ Photography ○ Poetry ○ Propaganda ○ Radio ○ Sculpture ○ Simplicity ○ Style ○ Television ○ Theater ○ Vision ○ Writing

Every great work of art has two faces, one toward its own time and one toward the future, toward eternity.
DANIEL BARENBOIM. In *International Herald Tribune* (Paris), 20 January 1989

Art has something to do with the achievement of stillness in the midst of chaos. A stillness which characterizes prayer, too, and the eye of the storm. . . . an arrest of attention in the midst of distraction.
SAUL BELLOW (1915–). Gordon Lloyd Harper interview, 1965. In George Plimpton, ed., *Writers at Work: Third Series*, 1967

Art is not a mirror held up to reality, but a hammer with which to shape it.
BERTOLT BRECHT (1898–1956). In Michael Larsen, *Literary Agents: What They Do, How They Do It, and How to Find and Work with the Right One for You*, rev. ed., 16.6, 1996

Without freedom, no art; art lives only on the restraints it imposes on itself, and dies of all others.

> ALBERT CAMUS (1913–1960). "Socialism of the Gallows," 1957,
> *Resistance, Rebellion, and Death,* tr. Justin O'Brien, 1961

There is not a single true work of art that has not in the end added to the inner freedom of each person who has known and loved it.

> ALBERT CAMUS (1913–1960). "The Wager of Our Generation," 1957,
> *Resistance, Rebellion, and Death,* tr. Justin O'Brien, 1961

Art . . . should simplify. That, indeed, is very nearly the whole of the higher artistic process; finding what conventions of form and what detail one can do without and yet preserve the spirit of the whole.

> WILLA CATHER (1873–1947). "On the Art of Fiction," 1920

This most valuable of arts, the art of living.

> CICERO (106–43 B.C.). In Montaigne, "Of the Education of Children,"
> *Essays,* 1588, tr. Donald M. Frame, 1958

The truth of art consists in its power to break the monopoly that those in power exercise by defining what is real. The supreme merit of art is that it contradicts the version of reality that obtains in social and economic life.

> DENIS DONOGHUE. *The Old Moderns: Essays on Literature and
> Theory,* 1994. In Kenneth Baker, "In Defense of Modernism,"
> *San Francisco Chronicle Review,* 29 May 1994

Art attracts us only by what it reveals of our most secret self.

> JEAN-LUC GODARD (1930–). "What Is Cinema?" *Godard on Godard:
> Critical Writings,* ed. Jean Narboni and Tom Milne, 1972

The highest art . . . sets down its creations and trusts in their magic, without fear of not being understood.

> HERMANN HESSE (1877–1962). *Reflections,* 516, ed. Volker Michels, 1974

The function of art is to do more than tell it like it is—it's to imagine what is *possible.*

> BELL HOOKS (1952–). *Outlaw Culture: Resisting Representation,* 29,
> 1994

Money and art
are far apart.

> LANGSTON HUGHES (1902–1967). "Plaint" (complete poem), 1955,
> *The Collected Poems of Langston Hughes,* ed. Arnold Rampersad and
> David Roessel, 1994

The finest works of art are precious, among other reasons, because they make it possible for us to know, if only imperfectly and for a little while, what it actually feels like to think subtly and feel nobly.

> ALDOUS HUXLEY (1894–1965). "Education," *Ends and Means:
> An Inquiry into the Nature of Ideals and into the Methods Employed
> for Their Realization,* 1937

To be great, art has to point somewhere.

> ANNE LAMOTT (1954–). *Bird by Bird: Some Instructions on Writing and
> Life,* 4 ("Giving"), 1995

Art, unless it leads to right action, is no more than the opium of an intelligentsia.

> W. SOMERSET MAUGHAM (1874–1965). 1949, *A Writer's Notebook,* 1949
> See Religion, Anti-: Karl Marx

Art is not an end in itself. It introduces the soul into a higher spiritual order, which it expresses and in some sense explains. Music and art and poetry attune the soul to God because they induce a kind of contact with the Creator and Ruler of the Universe.

> THOMAS MERTON (1915–1968). *No Man Is an Island,* 3.7, 1955

The more perfect the approximation to truth, the more perfect is art.

> MARIA MONTESSORI (1870–1952). *Spontaneous Activity in Education,* 9,
> tr. Florence Simmonds, 1917

The timelessness of art is its capacity to represent the transformation of endless becoming into being.

> LEWIS MUMFORD (1895–1990). *The Conduct of Life,* 5.4, 1951

Art is the sex of the imagination.

> GEORGE JEAN NATHAN (1882–1958). "Art," *American Mercury,* July 1926

The great end of art is to strike the imagination with the power of a soul that refuses to admit defeat even in the midst of a collapsing world.

> FRIEDRICH NIETZSCHE (1844–1900). *My Sister and I,* 2.2, tr. Oscar Levy,
> 1951

All art is propaganda. . . . On the other hand, not all propaganda is art.

> GEORGE ORWELL (1903–1950). "Charles Dickens" (5), 1940,
> *The Collected Essays, Journalism and Letters of George Orwell,*
> vol. 1, ed. Sonia Orwell and Ian Angus, 1968

Art's most effective
When concealed.

> OVID (43 B.C.–A.D. 17?). *The Art of Love,* 2.314, tr. Peter Green, 1982

All great, genuine art resembles and continues the Revelation of St. John.

> BORIS PASTERNAK (1890–1960). *Doctor Zhivago,* 3.17, 1957,
> tr. Max Hayward and Manya Harari, 1958

Art comes to you proposing frankly to give nothing but the highest quality to your moments as they pass.

> WALTER PATER (1839–1894). "Conclusion," *Studies in the History of the
> Renaissance,* 1873

All art is subversive.

> PABLO PICASSO (1881–1973). In Gerald Brenan, "Writing," *Thoughts in a
> Dry Season: A Miscellany,* 1978

Art: to nudge truth along a little.

> JULES RENARD (1864–1910). Journal, September 1908, tr. Louise Bogan
> and Elizabeth Roget, 1964

Only conservatives believe that subversion is still being carried on in the arts and that society is being shaken by it. . . . Advanced art today is no longer a cause—it contains no moral imperative. There is no virtue in clinging to principles and standards, no vice in selling or in selling out.

> HAROLD ROSENBERG (1906–1978). "The Cultural Situation Today,"
> *Partisan Review,* Summer 1972

True art is the intermediary between man's ordinary nature and his higher potentialities.

> E. F. SCHUMACHER (1911–1977). *A Guide for the Perplexed,* 10.2, 1977

All art is but imitation of nature.

> SENECA THE YOUNGER (5? B.C.–A.D. 65). "On the First Cause," *Moral Letters to Lucilius,* 65.3, tr. Richard M. Gummere, 1918

True art, art that comes from the center of a people, from their very core, is inherently political. The stuff you see on Sixth Avenue in New York is dead art, art that the patriarchy wants to buy, a terrible self-indulgence and insidious.

> BEVERLY SMITH. Linda Bellos interview, *Spare Rib,* August 1982

Art cannot be above the battle.

> HOWARD TAUBMAN (1907–1996). Drama critic. In Fredric Wertham, *A Sign for Cain: An Exploration of Human Violence,* 14, 1966

All great art . . . creates in the beholder not self-satisfaction but wonder and awe. Its great liberation is to lift us out of ourselves.

> DOROTHY THOMPSON (1894–1961). "The Twelve-foot Ceiling," *The Courage to Be Happy,* 1957

The highest condition of art is artlessness.

> HENRY DAVID THOREAU (1817–1862). Journal, 26 June 1840

Writing is the action of thinking, just as drawing is the action of seeing and composing music is the action of hearing.

> BRENDA UELAND (1891–1985). *Me,* 8, 1939

Great art is more than a transient refreshment. It is something which adds to the permanent richness of the soul's self-attainment. It justifies itself both by its immediate enjoyment, and also by its discipline of the inmost being. Its discipline is not distinct from enjoyment but by reason of it. It transforms the soul into the permanent realization of values extending beyond its former self.

> ALFRED NORTH WHITEHEAD (1861–1947). *Science and the Modern World,* 13, 1925

Life has been your art. You have set yourself to music. Your days are your sonnets.

> OSCAR WILDE (1854–1900). *The Picture of Dorian Gray,* 19, 1891

It is Art, and Art only, that reveals us to ourselves.

> OSCAR WILDE (1854–1900). In "Noted with Pleasure," *New York Times Book Review,* 12 January 1992

ARTISTS

See also • Art ○ Creativity: [especially] Garry Wills ○ Creativity: First Person ○ Poets ○ Writers

No one has ever written or painted, sculpted, modeled, built, invented, except to get out of hell.

> ANTONIN ARTAUD (1896–1948). "Van Gogh: The Man Suicided by Society," 1947, *Antonin Artaud Anthology,* ed. Jack Hirschman, 1965

The artist is extremely lucky who is presented with the worst possible ordeal which will not actually kill him. At that point, he's in business.

> JOHN BERRYMAN (1914–1972). Peter A. Stitt interview, 1970. In George Plimpton, ed., *Writers at Work: Fourth Series,* 1976

Works of Art can only be produc'd in Perfection where the Man is either in Affluence or is Above the Care of it.

> WILLIAM BLAKE (1757–1827). "A Vision of the Last Judgment," pp. 82–84, 1810, *The Complete Writings of William Blake,* ed. Geoffrey Keynes, 1966

Art advances between two chasms, which are frivolity and propaganda. On the ridge where the great artist moves forward, every step is an adventure, an extreme risk. In that risk, however, and only there, lies the freedom of art.

> ALBERT CAMUS (1913–1960). "Create Dangerously" (3), 1957, *Resistance, Rebellion, and Death,* tr. Justin O'Brien, 1961

The artist's struggle to transcend his pain can become the seed for many others' hope, transforming a personal journey into a vision for us all.

> DIANE COLE. *After Great Pain: A New Life Emerges,* 7, 1992

That is what the title of artist means: one who perceives more than his fellows, and who records more than he has seen.

> EDWARD G. CRAIG. "On the Art of the Theatre," 1905

The great artist is one whom constraint exalts, for whom the obstacle is a springboard.

> ANDRÉ GIDE (1869–1951). "The Evolution of the Theater," 1904, *Pretexts: Reflections on Literature and Morality,* ed. Justin O'Brien, 1959

The biographies of great artists make it abundantly clear that the creative urge is often so imperious that it battens on their humanity and yokes everything to the service of the work, even at the cost of health and ordinary human happiness. The unborn work in the psyche of the artist is a force of nature that achieves its end either with tyrannical might or with the subtle cunning of nature herself, quite regardless of the personal fate of the man who is its vehicle.

> CARL G. JUNG (1875–1961). "On the Relation of Analytical Psychology to Poetry," 1930, *The Spirit in Man, Art, and Literature,* tr. R. F. C. Hull, 1966
>
> See Creativity: First Person: Jung

In free society art is not a weapon. . . . Artists are not engineers of the soul.

> JOHN F. KENNEDY (1917–1963). Speech, Amherst College (Massachusetts), 26 October 1963
>
> See Indoctrination: Joseph Stalin

The artist's first responsibility is to educate him or herself. Then try to pass along some information or direction to their audience.

> LITTLE STEVEN. In Michael Albert, "Rockin' Radical," *Z Magazine,* October 1988

The artist is not a reporter, but a Great Teacher. It is not his business to depict the world as it is, but as it ought to be.

> H. L. MENCKEN (1880–1956). "Criticism of Criticism of Criticism," *Prejudices: First Series,* 1919

A bad artist almost always tries to conceal his incompetence by whooping up a new formula.

> H. L. MENCKEN (1880–1956). "The Greenwich Village Complex," *American Mercury,* June 1925

Nothing can come out of an artist that is not in the man.

> H. L. MENCKEN (1880–1956). "Beethoven," *Prejudices: Fifth Series,* 1926

An artist must have his measuring tools not in the hand, but in the eye.

MICHELANGELO (1475–1564). In Ralph Waldo Emerson, "Behavior," *The Conduct of Life,* 1860

An artist earns the right to call himself a creator only when he admits to himself that he is but an instrument.

HENRY MILLER (1891–1980). *The Time of the Assassins: A Study of Rimbaud,* 2, 1946

What is an artist? He's a man who has antennae, who knows how to hook up to the currents which are in atmosphere, in the cosmos.

HENRY MILLER (1891–1980). George Wickes interview, 1961. In George Plimpton, ed., *Writers at Work: Second Series,* 1963

Great artists have no country.

ALFRED de MUSSET (1810–1857). "L'Orfèvre," *Lorenzaccio,* 1834

See Class: Karl Marx and Friedrich Engels (2) ○ Merchants & Customers: Thomas Jefferson (2)

Is it not the artist who—like our dreams—dissolves the pretenses that hide us from ourselves, disclosing both our self-serving fantasies and our unsuspected potentialities?

DOROTHY NORMAN (1905–1997). *The Hero: Myth/Image/Symbol,* 18, 1969

Today, as you know, I am famous and very rich. But when I am alone with myself, I haven't the courage to consider myself an artist, in the great and ancient sense of that word. . . . I am only a public entertainer, who understands his age.

PABLO PICASSO (1881–1973). In Duncan Williams, *The Trousered Ape,* 2, 1971

He is the greatest artist who has embodied, in the sum of his works, the greatest number of the greatest ideas.

JOHN RUSKIN (1819–1900). *Modern Painters,* 1.1.2.9, 1843–1860, ed. Ernest Rhys, 1906

The true artist will let his wife starve, his children go barefoot, his mother drudge for his living at seventy, sooner than work at anything but his art.

GEORGE BERNARD SHAW (1856–1950). *Man and Superman,* 1, 1903

Poets, not otherwise than philosophers, painters, sculptors, and musicians, are, in one sense, the creators, and, in another, the creations, of their age.

PERCY BYSSHE SHELLEY (1792–1822). Preface to *Prometheus Unbound,* 1820

If you're an artist, you try to keep an ear to the ground and an ear to your heart.

BRUCE SPRINGSTEEN (1949–). Ed Bradley television interview, *60 Minutes,* CBS, 21 January 1996

Part of what we admire about a painting or a piece of music is the order which the artist has imposed upon what would otherwise have appeared disconnected or chaotic.

ANTHONY STORR (1920–). *Churchill's Black Dog, Kafka's Mice, and Other Phenomena of the Human Mind,* 7, 1988

Art postulates communion, and the artist has an imperative need to make others share the joy which he experiences himself.

IGOR STRAVINSKY (1882–1971). *An Autobiography,* 10, 1936

The more I become decomposed, the more sick and fragile I am, the more I become an artist.

VINCENT VAN GOGH (1853–1890). In Clemens E. Benda, "Illness and Artistic Creativity," *Atlantic,* July 1961

The romantic artist, off alone in his storm-battered castle, fuming whole worlds from his brain, reflects his culture's most persistent myth, of God creating from a primal loneliness.

GARRY WILLS (1934–). *Confessions of a Conservative,* 19, 1979

A work of art is the unique result of a unique temperament. Its beauty comes from the fact that the author is what he is. It has nothing to do with the fact that other people want what they want. Indeed, the moment that an artist takes notice of what other people want, and tries to supply the demand, he ceases to be an artist, and becomes a dull or an amusing craftsman, an honest or a dishonest tradesman.

OSCAR WILDE (1854–1900). "The Soul of Man Under Socialism," *Fortnightly Review* (British journal), February 1891

ASCETICISM

See also • Abstinence ○ Chastity ○ Self-Denial ○ Self-Discipline ○ Sex

The principle of asceticism never was, nor ever can be, consistently pursued by any living creature. Let but one tenth part of the inhabitants of this earth pursue it consistently, and in a day's time they will have turned it into a hell.

JEREMY BENTHAM (1748–1832). *An Introduction to the Principles of Morals and Legislation,* 2.10, 1789–1823

[Too often in Christianity] asceticism was considered as an end rather than a means, and so came to be anti-human, opposed to fullness of life and creativity.

NICOLAS BERDYAEV (1874–1948). *The Fate of Man in the Modern World,* tr. Donald A. Lowrie, 1935

Asceticism without a stench, what kind of asceticism is that?

ELIAS CANETTI, (1905–1994). 1966, *The Human Province,* tr. Joachim Neugroschel, 1978

The ascetic makes a necessity of virtue.

FRIEDRICH NIETZSCHE (1844–1900). *Human, All Too Human,* 76, 1878, tr. Marion Faber, 1984

Religions, which condemn the pleasures of sense, drive men to seek the pleasures of power. Throughout history power has been the vice of the ascetic.

BERTRAND RUSSELL (1872–1970). In *New York Herald Tribune Magazine,* 6 May 1938

ASSASSINATION

See also • Boxing: Jack Dempsey (1) ○ Crime ○ Death ○ Killing ○ Last Words: John F. Kennedy ○ Machiavellianism ○ Politics ○ Tyranny ○ Violence

Sic semper tyrannis! [Thus always to tyrants!] The South is avenged!

JOHN WILKES BOOTH (1839–1865). His shout from the stage of the Ford Theater in Washington after fatally shooting Pres. Abraham Lincoln, 14 April 1865. "Thus always to tyrants" is Virginia's motto. Although reported the next day in the *New York Times,* the second part of Booth's cry may be apocryphal.

Assassination has never changed the history of the world.

BENJAMIN DISRAELI (1804–1881). Referring to the assassination of Abraham Lincoln, House of Commons speech, 1 May 1865

Never strike a king unless you are sure you shall kill him.

RALPH WALDO EMERSON (1803–1882). Journal, August 1843

No person employed by or acting on behalf of the United States Government shall engage in, or conspire to engage in, assassination.

GERALD FORD (1913–). Presidential Executive Order No. 12333, 18 February 1976

Nobody wants to embarrass a President of the United States by discussing the assassination of foreign leaders in his presence. I just think we all had the feeling that we were hired . . . to keep those things out of the Oval Office.

RICHARD HELMS. Central Intelligence Agency director. Testimony before the Senate Select Committee on Intelligence, 13 June 1975

I shouted out, "Who killed the Kennedys?"
When after all, it was you and me.

MICK JAGGER (1943–) and KEITH RICHARDS (1943–). "Sympathy for the Devil" (song), 1968

Torby MacDonald: How would you choose to die?
Kennedy (pausing): Oh, a gun. You never know what's hit you. A gunshot is the perfect way.

JOHN F. KENNEDY (1917–1963). Format adapted. In Peter Collier and David Horowitz, *The Kennedys,* 3.3, 1984

I don't know what will happen now. We've got some difficult days ahead. But it doesn't matter with me now. Because I've been to the mountaintop. And I don't mind. Like anybody, I would like to live a long life. Longevity has its place. But I'm not concerned about that now. I just want to do God's will. And He's allowed me to go to the mountain. And I've looked over. And I've seen the promised land! I may not get there with you. But I want you to know tonight that we as a people will get to the promised land. And I'm not worried about anything. I'm not fearing any man. Mine eyes have seen the glory of the coming of the Lord.

MARTIN LUTHER KING, JR. (1929–1968). Closing paragraph of his last public address (on the eve of his assassination), [Bishop Charles] Mason Temple, Memphis (Tennessee), 3 April 1968

There seemed to be deathlike stillness about me. Then I heard subdued sobs, as if a number of people were weeping. I thought I left my bed and wandered downstairs. There the silence was broken by the same pitiful sobbing, but the mourners were invisible. I went from room to room; no living person was in sight, but the same mournful sounds of distress met me as I passed along. It was light in all the rooms; every object was familiar to me, but where were all the people who were grieving as if their hearts would break? I was puzzled and alarmed. What could be the meaning of all this? Determined to find the cause of a state of things so mysterious and so shocking, I kept on until I arrived at the East Room, which I entered. Before me was a catafalque on which was a form wrapped in funeral vestments. Around it were stationed soldiers who were acting as guards; there was a throng of people, some gazing mournfully upon the catafalque, others weeping pitifully. "Who is dead in the White House?" I demanded of one of the soldiers. "The President," was the answer. "He was killed by an assassin." There came a loud burst of grief from the crowd which woke me from my dream.

ABRAHAM LINCOLN (1809–1865). Recounting a recent dream to a group of friends shortly before being assassinated, 1865. In Emanuel Hertz, ed., "Father Abraham," *Lincoln Talks: A Biography in Anecdote,* 1939

A piece of each of us died at that moment.

MIKE MANSFIELD (1903–). Montana senator. Soon after the assassination of Pres. John F. Kennedy, November 1963

Against attempts on my life, I trust in my luck, my good genius, and my guards.

NAPOLEON (1769–1821). In Emil Ludwig, *Napoleon,* 2.3, 1925, tr. Eden and Cedar Paul, 1926

If I could find a way to get him out of there, even putting out a contract on him, if the CIA still did that sort of thing, assuming it ever did, I would be for it.

RICHARD M. NIXON (1913–1994). Referring to Saddam Hussein, appearing on *60 Minutes,* television magazine program, CBS, 14 April 1991

As the play progressed, guard John Parker left his post in the hallway leading to the state box [where Abraham Lincoln and his party were seated], and either sat down out in the gallery to watch the play or went outside for a drink.

STEPHEN B. OATES (1936–). Describing an occurrence shortly before John Wilkes Booth entered the box through the hallway and shot the President. *With Malice Toward None: The Life of Abraham Lincoln,* 11, 1977

I hope you're all Republicans.

RONALD REAGAN (1911–). Remark to physicians who were about to operate on him after being shot in an assassination attempt by John W. Hinckley, Jr., Washington, 30 March 1981

No soldier is obliged to obey an order counter to the law of God. No one has to comply with an immoral law. It is time now that you recover your conscience and obey its dictates rather than the command of sin.

ARCHBISHOP OSCAR ROMERO (1917–1980). Sermon addressed to his country's soldiers and police begging and commanding them to stop killing their "brother peasants," San Salvador, 23 March 1980 (the day before he was assassinated). In *Sojourners,* May 1980

I do not believe there is any danger of . . . an assault upon my life. . . . And if there were, it would be simple nonsense to try to prevent it, for, as Lincoln said, though it would be safer for a President to live in a cage, it would interfere with his business.

THEODORE ROOSEVELT (1858–1919). Letter to Henry Cabot Lodge, 6 August 1906

[Casca first, then the other conspirators and Brutus stab Caesar.]
Caesar: Et tu, Brute! Then fall, Caesar!
Cinna: Liberty! Freedom! Tyranny is dead!

Run hence, proclaim, cry it about the streets!
> SHAKESPEARE (1564–1616). *Julius Caesar,* 3.1.79, 1599

Antony (addressing the Romans): Brutus, as you know, was Caesar's angel;
Judge, O you gods, how dearly Caesar loved him!
This was the unkindest cut of all.
> SHAKESPEARE (1564–1616). *Julius Caesar,* 3.2.185, 1599

It is always your moralist who makes assassination a duty.
> GEORGE BERNARD SHAW (1856–1950). Notes ("Julius Caesar") to *Caesar and Cleopatra,* 1899

Assassination on the scaffold is the worst form of assassination because there it is invested with the approval of society.
> GEORGE BERNARD SHAW (1856–1950). "Maxims for Revolutionists: Crime and Punishment," *Man and Superman,* 1903

Assassination is the extreme form of censorship.
> GEORGE BERNARD SHAW (1856–1950). "The Rejected Statement—Part I" ("The Limits to Toleration"), *The Shewing-Up of Blanco Posnet,* 1911

It shows how dangerous it is to be too good.
> GEORGE BERNARD SHAW (1856–1950). On the assassination of Mohandas K. Gandhi in 1948. In Michael Holroyd, *Bernard Shaw: The Lure of Fantasy, 1918–1950,* 4.3, 1991

Now he belongs to the ages.
> EDWIN STANTON (1814–1869). Secretary of war. At the deathbed of Abraham Lincoln, 15 April 1865. In Ida M. Tarbell, *The Life of Abraham Lincoln,* 2.30, 1900. During the 1850s Stanton and Lincoln were co-counsels in a case tried in Cincinnati. The two men had a falling out, Stanton at one point angrily referring to Lincoln as "that giraffe." In spite of the insult, Lincoln appointed Stanton to his cabinet as secretary of war in 1862. (In Francis Fisher Browne, *The Every-Day Life of Abraham Lincoln,* 2.8, 1887)

A misreading of the law or misplaced moral squeamishness should not stop the president from talking about assassination. He should order up the options and see if it's possible. If we *can* kill Saddam [Hussein], we should.
> GEORGE STEPHANOPOULOUS (1961–). Former presidential aide to Bill Clinton. Closing paragraph, "Why We Should Kill Saddam," *Newsweek,* 1 December 1997

Assassins!
> ARTURO TOSCANINI (1867–1957). Scolding his entire orchestra during a rehearsal, recalled on his death, 16 January 1957

Rome had Caesar, a man of remarkable governing talents, although it must be said that a ruler who arouses opponents to resort to assassination is probably not as smart as he ought to be.
> BARBARA W. TUCHMAN (1912–1989). "An Inquiry into the Persistence of Unwisdom in Government," *Esquire,* 1980

The conspiracy theory of assassination—it's historical, particularly with Europeans. Most of their assassinations grew out of palace guard defections and things of that kind. It's the same in South America. Here, on the contrary, practically all of our assassins have just been demented people.
> EARL WARREN (1891–1974). In Merle Miller, *Lyndon: An Oral Biography,* 4 ("The Warren Commission"), 1980

I require no guard but the affections of the people.
> GEORGE WASHINGTON (1732–1799). April 1789, *Maxims of Washington,* comp. John Frederick Schroeder, p. 227, 1942
> See King: John Clarke

Operation Mongoose was the secret effort approved by President [John F.] Kennedy, and spurred by Attorney General Robert F. Kennedy, to make Fidel Castro disappear. The Kennedys were "operating a damned Murder Inc. in the Caribbean," in the indelicate words of President Lyndon B. Johnson.
> TIM WIENER. "The Trouble with Assassinations," *New York Times,* 23 November 1997

❦

Every country has its own constitution; ours is absolutism moderated by assassination.
> ANONYMOUS (RUSSIAN). On the assassination of Czar Paul I in 1801, remark to Georg Münster, Hanoverian diplomat, 1868.

ATHEISM

See also • Agnosticism ○ God ○ Idolatry ○ Religion, Anti- ○ Religion & Science

How can I believe in God when just last week I got my tongue caught in the roller of an electric typewriter?
> WOODY ALLEN (1935–). "Selections from the Allen Notebooks," *Without Feathers,* 1975

If God really existed, it would be necessary to abolish him.
> MIKHAIL BAKUNIN (1814–1876). *God and the State,* 1871. In *The Political Philosophy of Bakunin: Scientific Anarchism,* 1.2, ed. G. P. Maximoff, 1953

It was easier for me to think of a world without a creator than of a creator loaded with all the contradictions of the world.
> SIMONE de BEAUVOIR (1908–1986). In "Toward a Hidden God," *Time,* 8 April 1966

Atheism [is] the natural denial of God because of the pain and misery of the world. Atheism as the cry of the indignant human heart can only be conquered by a suffering God Who shares the fate of the world.
> NICOLAS BERDYAEV (1874–1948). *The Destiny of Man,* 2.2.1, 1931, tr. Natalie Duddington, 1955

Now that it has come of age, the world is more godless, and perhaps it is for that very reason nearer to God than ever before.
> DIETRICH BONHOEFFER (1906–1945). German theologian executed by the Nazis in 1945. 18 July 1944, *Letters and Papers from Prison,* 1951, tr. Eberhard Bethge, 1971

There is nothing in the world that breeds Atheism like Hypocrisy.
> SAMUEL BUTLER (1612–1680). "Religion," *Prose Observations,* ed. Hugh de Quehen, 1979

There can be no Creator, simply because his grief at the fate of his creation would be inconceivable and unendurable.
> ELIAS CANETTI (1905–1994). 1952, *The Human Province,* tr. Joachim Neugroschel, 1978

The most difficult thing for one who does not believe in God: that he has no one to give thanks to.

> ELIAS CANETTI (1905–1994). 1982, *The Secret Heart of the Clock: Notes, Aphorisms, Fragments: 1973–1985*, tr. Joel Agee, 1989

That all Godhood should vanish out of men's conception of this Universe seems to me precisely the most brutal error. . . . A man who thinks so will think *wrong* about all things in the world.

> THOMAS CARLYLE (1795–1881). "The Hero as Man of Letters," *On Heroes, Hero-Worship, and the Heroic in History*, 1841

There are no atheists in the foxholes.

> WILLIAM THOMAS CUMMINGS. Sermon to American troops on Bataan in the Philippines, March 1942. In Carlos P. Romulo, *I Saw the Fall of the Philippines*, 15, 1943

I don't believe in God because I don't believe in Mother Goose.

> CLARENCE DARROW (1857–1938). Speech, Toronto, 1930

Bishop Tihon: Outright atheism is more to be respected than world indifference. . . .

The complete atheist stands on the penultimate step to most perfect faith.

> FYODOR DOSTOYEVSKY (1821–1881). "Supplement: At Tihon's. Stavrogin's Confession," *The Possessed*, 1871, tr. Constance Garnett, 1936

If there were no God, he would have to be invented.

> FYODOR DOSTOYEVSKY (1821–1881). *The Brothers Karamazov*, 5.3, 1880, tr. Constance Garnett, 1912

If God is dead, everything is allowed.

> FYODOR DOSTOYEVSKY (1821–1881). In Erich Fromm, *Man for Himself: An Inquiry into the Psychology of Ethics*, 5, 1947

The death of a child is the greatest reason to doubt the existence of God.

> FYODOR DOSTOYEVSKY (1821–1881). As paraphrased by Mary Gordon, "What They Think about God," *New York Times*, 25 November 1990

Psychoanalytic investigation of the individual teaches with especial emphasis that god is in every case modeled after the father . . . and that god at bottom is nothing but an exalted father.

> SIGMUND FREUD (1856–1939). *Totem and Taboo*, 4.6, 1913, tr. A. A. Brill, 1938

In the nineteenth century the problem was that *God is dead;* in the twentieth century the problem is that *man is dead.*

> ERICH FROMM (1900–1980). *The Sane Society*, 9, 1976

God, equally with gods, angels, demons, spirits, and other small spiritual fry, is a human product, arising inevitably from a certain kind of ignorance and a certain degree of helplessness with respect to man's external environment.

> JULIAN HUXLEY (1887–1975). "Religion as an Objective Problem," *Man Stands Alone*, 1941

There are two kinds of atheism: one tends to dispense with the idea of God, and the other to deny His intervention in human affairs.

> JOSEPH JOUBERT (1754–1824). *Pensées*, 1838, tr. H. P. Collins, 1928

[A majority of people] are not theoretical atheists; they are practical atheists. They do not deny the existence of God with their lips, but they are continually denying his existence with their lives.

> MARTIN LUTHER KING, JR. (1929–1968). *Strength to Love*, 9.3, 1963

Every advocacy or justification of the idea of god, even the most subtle, even the best intentioned, is a justification of reaction.

> LENIN (1870–1924). Letter to Maxim Gorky, December 1913, *The Lenin Reader*, 1.9, ed. Stefan T. Possony, 1966

There is Auschwitz, and so there cannot be God.

> PRIMO LEVI (1920–1987). Auschwitz survivor. In Ferdinando Camon, closing words, *Conversations with Primo Levi*, tr. John Shepley, 1989. In reviewing the transcript of his conversation, Levi penciled in, "I don't find a solution to this dilemma. I keep looking, but I don't find it." A year after the interview, while undergoing psychiatric treatment for depression, Levi committed suicide.

It is not reasonable to deny the power of an infinite being because we cannot comprehend its operations.

> JOHN LOCKE (1632–1704). *An Essay Concerning Human Understanding*, 4.10.19, 1690, ed. Alexander Campbell Fraser, 1894

When we claim that "God does not exist," we mean to deny by this declaration the personal God of theology, the God worshipped in various ways and diverse modes by believers the world over, that God who from nothing created the universe, from chaos matter, that God of absurd attributes who is an affront to human reason.

> BENITO MUSSOLINI (1883–1945). Speech, Lausanne (Switzerland), July 1904

God is dead. God remains dead. And we have killed him.

> FRIEDRICH NIETZSCHE (1844–1900). *The Gay Science*, 125, 1882, tr. Walter Kaufmann, 1974
>
> See Revelation: Ralph Waldo Emerson (1)

If there were gods, how could I endure not to be a god? *Therefore* there are no gods.

> FRIEDRICH NIETZSCHE (1844–1900). "On the Blissful Islands," *Thus Spoke Zarathustra*, 1892, tr. R. J. Hollingdale, 1961

But what if God lives, and I have doomed myself to destruction because I have separated myself from Him?

> FRIEDRICH NIETZSCHE (1844–1900). *My Sister and I*, 11.31, tr. Oscar Levy, 1951

He was an embittered atheist (the sort of atheist who does not so much disbelieve in God as personally dislike Him).

> GEORGE ORWELL (1903–1950). *Down and Out in Paris and London*, 30, 1933

Outside man there is nothing.

> GEORGE ORWELL (1903–1950). Expressing a core Party belief in his futuristic dystopia, *Nineteen Eighty-Four*, 3.3, 1949

There are two things which make it impossible to believe that this world is the successful work of an all-wise, all-good, and at the same time, all-powerful being; firstly, the misery which abounds in it everywhere; and secondly, the obvious imperfection of its highest product, man, who is a burlesque of what he should be.

ARTHUR SCHOPENHAUER (1788–1860). "Studies in Pessimism: On the Sufferings of the World," *Essays of Arthur Schopenhauer,* tr. T. Bailey Saunders, 1851

Fervid atheism is usually a screen for repressed religion.

WILHELM STEKEL (1868–1940). *The Autobiography of Wilhelm Stekel: The Life Story of a Pioneer Psychoanalyst,* 5, ed. Emil A. Gutheil, 1950

God's only excuse is that He does not exist.

STENDHAL (1783–1842). In Friedrich Nietzsche, "Why I Am So Clever" (3), *Ecce Homo,* 1908, tr. Clifton Fadiman, 1927

[At the Potsdam Conference in Germany after World War II] I invited Stalin to come to Washington, and he said, "God willing, I will come." Well, I haven't met anybody yet who believes me, but that is what he said to me. [Laughter]

HARRY S. TRUMAN (1884–1972). Speech at a special conference with editors of business and trade publications, Washington, 23 April 1948

The fool says in his heart, "There is no God."

ANONYMOUS (*BIBLE*). *Psalms* 14:1

I am an atheist, thank God!

ANONYMOUS. In Samuel Butler, *The Note-Books of Samuel Butler,* 20, ed. Henry Festing Jones, 1907

God is dead—Nietzsche
Nietzsche is dead—God.

ANONYMOUS. Graffito. In Robert Reisner, "Collector's Choice: Religion," *Graffito: Two Thousand Years of Wall Writing,* 1971

What is the difference between God and Santa Claus?
Answer: There is a Santa Claus.

ANONYMOUS. Graffito. In Robert Reisner, "Collector's Choice: Religion," *Graffiti: Two Thousand Years of Wall Writing,* 1971

AUTHORITY

See also • Charisma ○ Dreams: D. Simpson ○ Experts ○ Leaders ○ Power: [especially] Jacques Maritain ○ Prestige: [especially] Gustave Le Bon, C. Wright Mills (3) ○ Professionals ○ Progress: T. H. Huxley ○ Religion: Ralph Waldo Emerson (1) ○ Science: Claude Bernard (2), Philip Wylie ○ Silence & Speech: Charles de Gaulle ○ Status ○ Truth: J. A. C. Brown

Nothing destroyeth authority so much as the unequal and untimely interchange of power pressed too far, and relaxed too much.

FRANCIS BACON (1561–1626). "Of Empire," *Essays,* 1625

Authority . . . [is] legitimated power.

JAMES MacGREGOR BURNS (1918–). *Leadership,* 1, 1978

Distrust of authority should be the first civic duty.

NORMAN DOUGLAS (1868–1952). 7 October, *An Almanac,* 1945

I hold it blasphemy to say that a man ought not to fight against authority: there is no great religion and no great freedom that has not done it, in the beginning.

GEORGE ELIOT (1819–1880). *Felix Holt, the Radical,* 1866

When the Lord sent me forth into the world, He forbade me to put off my hat to any, high or low; and I was required to Thee and Thou all men and women, without any respect to rich or poor, great or small. . . . Neither might I bow or scrape with my leg to anyone; and this made the sects and professions to rage.

GEORGE FOX (1624–1691). 1649, *The Journal of George Fox,* 1694, rev. Norman Penney, 1924

[Thomas Carlyle] taught like one that had authority—a tone which men naturally resent, and must resent, till the teacher has made his pretensions good.

JAMES ANTHONY FROUDE (1818–1894). *Thomas Carlyle: A History of the First Forty Years, 1795–1835,* 2.5, 1882

I had the greatest respect for the authorities of my day—until I studied things for myself, and came to my own conclusions.

SIGMUND FREUD (1856–1939). Remark to the author, 24 December 1934. In Joseph Wortis, *Fragments of an Analysis with Freud,* 1954

Calling me a genius is the latest way people have of starting their criticism of me. . . . If they thought I was a genius, one should think they would not question my authority.

SIGMUND FREUD (1856–1939). Remark to the author, 16 January 1935. In Joseph Wortis, *Fragments of an Analysis with Freud,* 1954

Power on the one side, fear on the other, are always the buttresses on which irrational authority is built.

ERICH FROMM (1900–1980). *Man for Himself: An Inquiry into the Psychology of Ethics,* 2.1, 1947

The prime offense in the authoritarian situation is rebellion against the authority's rule. Thus disobedience becomes the "cardinal sin"; obedience, the cardinal virtue. Obedience implies the recognition of the authority's superior power and wisdom; his right to command, to reward, and to punish according to his own fiats. The authority demands submission not only because of the fear of its power but out of the conviction of its moral superiority and right. The respect due the authority carries with it the taboo on questioning it.

ERICH FROMM (1900–1980). *Man for Himself: An Inquiry into the Psychology of Ethics,* 4.2.A, 1947

If there's anything mean in a feller, a little authority will bring it out.

KIN HUBBARD (1856–1915). *Abe Martin's Back Country Sayings,* unpaged, 1917

The importance of an authority figure in a field is inversely proportional to the amount that is known about the subject.

DON JONES. "Jones's Law of Authority." In Paul Dickson, comp., *The Official Explanations,* p. 107, 1980

Freud had a dream—I would not think it right to air the problem it involved. I interpreted it as best I could, but added that a great deal more could be said about it if he would supply me with some additional details from his private life. Freud's response to these words was a curious look—a look of the utmost suspicion. Then he said, "But I cannot risk my authority!" At that moment he lost it altogether. That sentence burned itself into my memory; and in it the end of our relationship was already foreshadowed. Freud was placing personal authority above truth.

CARL G. JUNG (1875–1961). During a visit to America in 1909 (the Freud/Jung split came in 1913), *Memories, Dreams, Reflections,* 5, ed. Aniela Jaffé, 1962

Weight of authority varies with the prestige of the authorities.

HAROLD D. LASSWELL (1902–1978) and ABRAHAM KAPLAN. *Power and Society: A Framework for Political Inquiry,* 6.5, 1950

To despise legitimate authority, no matter in whom it is invested, is unlawful; it is rebellion against God's will.

POPE LEO XIII (1810–1903). *Immortale Dei (On the Christian Constitution of States),* 1 November 1885

Authority has every reason to fear the skeptic, for authority can rarely survive in the face of doubt. Consequently, it puts a premium on faith and pays it the highest homage possible: faith is the source of its power.

ROBERT LINDNER (1914–1956). "Education for Maturity," *Must You Conform?* 1956

Most men, after a little freedom, have preferred authority with the consoling assurances and the economy of effort which it brings.

WALTER LIPPMANN (1889–1974). *A Preface to Morals,* 1.3, 1929

He who is firmly seated in authority soon learns to think security, and not progress, the highest lesson of statecraft.

JAMES RUSSELL LOWELL (1819–1891). "New England Two Countries Ago," *Among My Books,* 1870

When Jesus finished these sayings, the crowds were astonished at his teaching, for he taught them as one who had authority, and not as their scribes.

MATTHEW (A.D. 1st cent.). *Matthew* 7:28

If magistrates had true justice, and if physicians had the true art of healing, they would have no occasion for square caps.

BLAISE PASCAL (1623–1662). *Pensées,* 82, 1670, tr. William F. Trotter, 1931

Let every person be subject to the governing authorities. For there is no authority except from God, and those that exist have been instituted by God. Therefore he who resists the authorities resists what God has appointed, and those who resist will incur judgment.

PAUL (A.D. 1st cent.). *Romans* 13:1–2

See Struggle: Paul

Isabella: But man, proud man,
Drest in a little brief authority,
Most ignorant of what he's most assured,
His glassy essence, like an angry ape,
Plays such fantastic tricks before high heaven
As make the angels weep.

SHAKESPEARE (1564–1616). *Measure for Measure,* 2.2.117, 1604

Revolt against authority was, and remains to this day, the original sin, the classic crime, of the individual.

THOMAS S. SZASZ (1920–). *The Manufacture of Madness: A Comparative Study of the Inquisition and the Mental Health Movement,* 6, 1970

The man who submits to violence is debased by his compliance; but when he submits to that right of authority which he acknowl-

edges in a fellow creature, he rises in some measure above the person who gives the command.

ALEXIS de TOCQUEVILLE (1805–1859). *Democracy in America,* 1.14, 1835, tr. Henry Reeve and Francis Bowen, 1862

It is dangerous to be right in matters on which the established authorities are wrong.

VOLTAIRE (1694–1778). In J. R. Solly, comp., *A Cynic's Breviary,* 1925

I like to convince people rather than stand on mere authority.

DUKE OF WELLINGTON (1769–1852). In John Keegan, *The Mask of Command,* 2, 1987

I have . . . taken off my hat to nothing known or unknown.

WALT WHITMAN (1819–1892). "By Blue Ontario's Shore" (14), 1856, *Leaves of Grass,* 1855–1892

All authority is quite degrading. It degrades those who exercise it, and it degrades those over whom it is exercised.

OSCAR WILDE (1854–1900). "The Soul of Man Under Socialism," *Fortnightly Review* (British journal), February 1891

AUTOBIOGRAPHY

See also • Biography ○ Books ○ Fiction: Alberto Moravia ○ Journals ○ Memoirs: [especially] Gore Vidal ○ Writing

All fiction may be autobiographical, but all autobiography is of course fiction.

SHIRLEY ABBOT. In Mickey Pearlman, *Listen to Their Voices,* 12, 1993

Autobiography is an unrivaled vehicle for telling the truth about other people.

PHILIP GUEDALLA. British historian. In Hugh Leonard, "Can a Playwright Truly Depict Himself?" *New York Times,* 23 November 1980

A true autobiography is almost an impossibility; . . . man is bound to lie about himself.

FYODOR DOSTOYEVSKY (1821–1881). *Notes from Underground,* 1864. Quoted in Alfred Kazin, "The Self as History: Reflections on Autobiography" (epigraph). In Marc Pachter, ed., *Telling Lives: The Biographer's Art,* 1979

Autobiography is mostly alibiography.

CLARE BOOTHE LUCE (1903–1987). In Sylvia Jukes Morris, "On Meeting the Formidable Clare Boothe Luce," *At Random,* Spring-Summer, 1997

If you're going to write an autobiography, your duty is clear. You've got to open up them golden gates and let all the filth out, the full horror.

LAURENCE OLIVIER (1907–1989). In Charles Champlin, "Olivier on Olivier: A 'Confession,'" *Los Angeles Times,* 7 November 1982

Autobiography is only to be trusted when it reveals something disgraceful. A man who gives a good account of himself is probably lying, since any life when viewed from the inside is simply a series of defeats.

GEORGE ORWELL (1903–1950). Opening words, "Benefit of Clergy: Some Notes on Salvador Dali," 1944, *The Collected Essays, Journalism and Letters of George Orwell,* vol. 3, ed. Sonia Orwell and Ian Angus, 1968

Autobiographies are . . . only useful as the lives you read about and analyze may suggest to you something that you may find useful in your own journey through life.

ELEANOR ROOSEVELT (1884–1962). *This Is My Story,* 23, 1937

The true object of my confessions is to reveal my inner thoughts exactly in all the situations of my life. It is the history of my soul that I have promised to recount.

ROUSSEAU (1712–1778). *Confessions,* 7 (1741), 1781, tr. J. M. Cohen, 1953

Only when one has lost all curiosity about the future has one reached the age to write an autobiography.

EVELYN WAUGH (1903–1966). Opening words, *A Little Learning: An Autobiography,* 1964

AUTOMOBILES

See also • Advertising Copy and Slogans ○ Machines ○ Motorcycles

[There are] only two classes of pedestrians in these days of reckless motor traffic—the quick and the dead.

LORD DEWAR (1864–1930). British industrialist. In George Robey, *Looking Back on Life,* 28, 1933

Nothing ages your car as much as the sight of your neighbor's new one.

EVAN ESAR (1899–1995). Comp., *20,000 Quips and Quotes,* p. 113, 1968

Climbing into a hot car is like buckling on a pistol. It is the great equalizer.

HENRY GREGOR FELSEN. *To My Son—The Teen-Age Driver,* 9, 1964

Any customer can have a car painted any color that he wants so long as it is black.

HENRY FORD (1863–1947) (with SAMUEL CROWTHER). *My Life and Work,* 4, 1922

Here lies extinguished in his prime,
a victim of modernity:
but yesterday he hadn't time—
and now he has eternity.

PIET HEIN (1905–). "More Haste (inscription for a monument at the crossroads)," *Grooks,* 1966

As you move away from mass transit you become more dependent on the automobile, so you have to spread the housing out more to accommodate the cars.

SANDY HORNICK. Zoning director of New York's department of city planning. In "The City Low-Rise Side Stands Up," *New York Times,* 21 May 1989

What if we fail to stop the erosion of cities by automobiles? . . . In that case America will hardly need to ponder a mystery that has troubled men for millennia: What is the purpose of life? For us, the answer will be clear, established and for all practical purposes indisputable: The purpose of life is to produce and consume automobiles.

JANE JACOBS. *The Death and Life of Great American Cities,* 18, 1961

The automobile changed our dress, manners, social customs, vacation habits, the shape of our cities, consumer purchasing patterns, common tastes and positions in intercourse.

JOHN KEATS (1795–1821). *The Insolent Chariots,* 1, 1958

To George F. Babbitt, as to most prosperous citizens of Zenith, his motor car was poetry and tragedy, love and heroism. The office was his pirate ship but the car his perilous excursion ashore.

SINCLAIR LEWIS (1885–1951). *Babbitt,* 3.1, 1922

The Aquarium is gone. Everywhere,
giant finned cars nose forward like fish;
a savage servility
slides by on grease.

ROBERT LOWELL (1917–1977). Title poem, *For the Union Dead,* 1964

People on horses look better than they are. People in cars look worse than they are.

MARYA MANNES (1904–1990). *More in Anger,* 1.4, 1958

The car has become a secular sanctuary for the individual, his shrine to the self, his mobile Walden Pond.

EDWARD McDONAGH (1915–). California sociologist. In "Lincoln and Modern America: The Heritage of a Free Choice in an Organized Society," *Time,* 10 May 1963

The car has become an article of dress without which we feel uncertain, unclad, and incomplete in the urban compound.

MARSHALL McLUHAN (1911–1980). *Understanding Media: The Extensions of Man,* 22, 1964

They paved paradise
And put up a parking lot.

JONI MITCHELL (1943–). "Big Yellow Taxi" (song), 1969

Our national flower is the concrete cloverleaf.

LEWIS MUMFORD (1895–1990). *The Culture of Cities,* 1938

Unsafe at Any Speed.

RALPH NADER (1934–). On American-manufactured automobiles, report title, 1965

Beneath this slab
John Brown is stowed.
He watched the ads,
And not the road.

OGDEN NASH (1902–1971). "Lather As You Go," *Good Intentions,* 1942

Holden Caulfield: Take most people, they're crazy about cars. They worry if they get a little scratch on them, and they're always talking about how many miles they get to a gallon, and if they get a brand-new car already they start thinking about trading it in for one that's even newer. I don't even like *old* cars I mean they don't even interest me. I'd rather have a goddam horse. A horse is at least *human,* for God's sake.

J. D. SALINGER (1919–). *The Catcher in the Rye,* 17, 1951

Everything in life is somewhere else, and you get there in a car.

E. B. WHITE (1899–1985). "Fro-Joy," *One Man's Meat,* 1944

AVARICE

See also • Greed ○ Wrong: Cicero

So for a good old-gentlemanly vice,
I think I must take up with avarice.
> LORD BYRON (1788–1824). *Don Juan,* 1.216, 1819–1824

It is not Want, but rather Abundance, that makes Avarice
> THOMAS FULLER (1654–1734). Comp., *Gnomologia: Adages and Proverbs,* 3004, 1732

No Vice
Like Avarice.
> THOMAS FULLER (1654–1734). Comp., *Gnomologia: Adages and Proverbs,* 6171, 1732

Avarice is both knave and fool.
> FULKE GREVILLE (1554–1628). *Maxims, Characters, and Reflections,* p. 95, 1756

Avarice, the spur of industry.
> DAVID HUME (1711–1776). "Of Civil Liberty," *Essays, Moral and Political,* vol. 1, 1741

Poverty needs little; avarice, everything.
> PUBLIUS SYRUS (85–43 B.C.). *Moral Sayings,* 385, tr. Darius Lyman, Jr., 1862

Avarice hoards itself poor; charity gives itself rich.
> SAYING (GERMAN)

Avarice is the only passion that never ages.
> SAYING

AWE

See also • Miracles ○ Mystery: [especially] Jonathon Schell ○ Trees: John Steinbeck ○ Wonder

Things not only are what they are but also stand, however remotely, for something supreme. Awe is a sense for the transcendence, for the reference everywhere to mystery beyond all things. It enables us to perceive in the world intimations of the divine, to sense in small things the beginning of infinite significance, to sense the ultimate in the common and the simple; to feel in the rush of the passing the stillness of the eternal.
> ABRAHAM JOSHUA HESCHEL (1907–1972). *Who Is Man?* 5, 1965

Two things fill the mind with ever new and increasing admiration and awe the oftener and more steadily we reflect on them: *the starry heavens above me and the moral law within [me].*
> IMMANUEL KANT (1724–1804). Conclusion to *Critique of Practical Reason,* 1788, tr. Thomas Kingsmill Abbott, 1873

The highest point a man can attain is not Knowledge, or Virtue, or Goodness, or Victory, but something even greater, more heroic and more despairing: Sacred Awe!
> NIKOS KAZANTZAKIS (1885–1957). *Zorba the Greek,* 24, 1946, tr. Carl Wildman, 1953

The feeling of awe is frequently the beginning of religion.
> CHARLES FRANCIS POTTER (1885–1962). *The Great Religious Leaders,* 2, 1962

AXIOMS

See also • Aphorisms ○ Epigrams ○ Maxims ○ Proverbs ○ Quotations ○ Sayings

For every axiom there is an equal and opposite reaxiom.
> NICHOLAS FOSTER. "Foster's Revelation," In Paul Dickson, comp., *The New Official Rules,* p. 74, 1989

I've got no axiom to grind.
> ALLEN GINSBERG (1926–1997). In Jane Kramer, "Paterfamilias" (2), *New Yorker,* 24 August 1968

BABIES

See also • Children ○ Children's Learning ○ Fathers ○ Mothers ○ Parents

The toddler craves independence but . . . fears desertion.
> DOROTHY CORKVILLE BRIGGS. *Your Child's Self-Esteem,* 15, 1975

Every baby born into the world is a finer one than the last.
> CHARLES DICKENS (1812–1870). *The Life and Adventures of Nicholas Nickleby,* 36, 1839

The babe in arms is a channel through which the energies we call fate, love and reason visibly stream.
> RALPH WALDO EMERSON (1803–1882). "Considerations by the Way," *The Conduct of Life,* 1860

How pleasant it is to see a human countenance which cannot be insincere!
> SOPHIA A. HAWTHORNE (1810?–1871). Referring to her infant daughter Rose's smile. In Nathaniel Hawthorne, 13 October 1851, *The American Notebooks,* ed. Claude M. Simpson, 1932

Babies are such a nice way to start people.

DON HEROLD (1889–1966). In Laurence J. Peter, *The Peter Prescription: How to Make Things Go Right*, 12, 1972

It didn't take elaborate experiments to deduce that an infant would die from want of food. But it took centuries to figure out that infants can and do perish from want of love.

LOUISE J. KAPLAN (1929–). *No Voice Is Ever Wholly Lost*, 1, 1995

From how many years away does a baby come?

BOB KAUFMAN (1925–1986). "Jail Poems" (31), 1959, *Solitudes Crowded with Loneliness*, 1965

Each time a new baby is born there is a possibility of reprieve. Each child is a new being, a potential prophet, a new spiritual prince, a new spark of light precipitated into the outer darkness.

R. D. LAING (1927–1989). *The Politics of Experience*, 1, 1967

Physical punishment, such as spanking, teaches a toddler that might makes right and that it is fine to hit when one is stronger and can get away with it.

ALICIA F. LIEBERMAN. *The Emotional Life of the Toddler: Between One and Three Years*, 7, 1993

Disobedience is the infant's first step toward autonomy.

LEWIS MUMFORD (1895–1990). *The Pentagon of Power: The Myth of the Machine*, 13.6, 1970

Many recent letters [to *The New York Times*] have declared horror at the practice of infanticide in China and the unconscionable rates of infant morality in the country's orphanages. This was a principal mode of population control in Europe and the United States from 1750–1850, when the industrial revolution was in high gear. Our foundling hospitals, orphanages and parish workhouses served, correspondingly, to institutionalize and veil it from public concern. . . .

Of the 15,000 infants accepted at the London Foundling Hospital in the first four years after its founding in 1741, fewer than 5,000 lived to reach adolescence. Of 500,000 foundlings admitted to parish workhouses in England between 1728 and 1757, 60 percent had died by age 2. In Paris in 1818, nearly 70 percent died in their first year of life in the famous Hôspital des Enfants Trouvés founded by St. Vincent de Paul.

GERARD PIEL. *Scientific American* editor and publisher. In *New York Times*, 27 January 1996

A baby is God's opinion that life should go on.

CARL SANDBURG (1878–1967). *Remembrance Rock*, 2, 1948

I have been assured by a very knowing American of my acquaintance in London that a young healthy child well-nursed is at a year old a most delicious, nourishing, and wholesome food, whether stewed, roasted, baked, or boiled, and I make no doubt that it will equally serve in a fricassee, or a ragout.

JONATHAN SWIFT (1667–1745). *A Modest Proposal for Preventing the Children of Poor People in Ireland, from Being a Burden to Their Parents or Country; and for Making Them Beneficial to the Publick* (pamphlet), 1729

See Children: W. C. Fields (1)

A baby is an inestimable blessing and bother.

MARK TWAIN (1835–1910). Letter to Annie Webster, 1 September 1876

Heaven lies about us in our infancy!

WILLIAM WORDSWORTH (1770–1850). "Ode. Intimations of Immortality from Recollections of Early Childhood," 5, 1807

BACHELORHOOD

See Singlehood

BANKERS

See also • Banks

[There is a] perverse incentive that prompts bankers to lend money to virtually anybody during a boom and then, when things go bust, to shift the bill onto the taxpayers. Under the current system, the bankers are like suicide bombers, who must be appeased because they are threatening to blow everybody else up, too. Save us, they say, or the world economy goes down with us.

JOHN CASSIDY. "Paging J. P. Morgan: Who Should Pay Korea's Bills?" *New Yorker*, 19 January 1998

You are a den of vipers and thieves. I intend to rout you out, and by the eternal God, I will rout you out.

ANDREW JACKSON (1767–1845). Remark to a delegation of bankers, 1832.

A "sound" banker, alas! is not one who sees danger and avoids it, but one who, when he is ruined, is ruined in a conventional and orthodox way along with his fellows, so that no one can really blame him.

JOHN MAYNARD KEYNES (1883–1946). British economist. "The Consequences to the Banks of the Collapse of Money Values," August 1931, *Essays in Persuasion*, 1931

Most bankers dwell in marble halls,
Which they get to dwell in because they encourage deposits and discourage withdralls,
And particularly because they all observe one rule which woe betides the banker who fails to heed it,
Which is you must never lend any money to anybody unless they don't need it.

OGDEN NASH (1902–1971). "Bankers Are Just Like Anybody Else, Except Richer," *I'm a Stranger Here Myself*, 1938

A banker is a fellow who lends his umbrella when the sun is shining and wants it back the minute it begins to rain.

MARK TWAIN (1835–1910)

BANKS

See also • Bankers ○ Capitalism ○ Debt ○ Inflation: John Kenneth Galbraith ○ Money

What is robbing a bank compared with founding a bank?

BERTOLT BRECHT (1898–1956). *The Threepenny Opera*, 3.3, 1928

I sincerely believe . . . that banking establishments are more dangerous than standing armies.

THOMAS JEFFERSON (1743–1826). Letter to John Taylor, 28 May 1816

If you owe your bank a hundred pounds, you have a problem; but . . . if you owe [your bank] a million, it has.

> JOHN MAYNARD KEYNES (1883–1946). In "Down Communism's Sink," *Economist,* 13 February 1982

What's good for the bank is good for the country.

> DUDLEY NICHOLS. *Stagecoach* (film), 1939
>
> See Corporations: Charles E. Wilson

[This bill is] the most important legislation for financial institutions in 50 years. All in all, I think we've hit the jackpot.

> RONALD REAGAN (1911–). Remarks before a group of 200 guests, including savings and loan executives, bankers, congressmembers and journalists, who had been invited to witness his signing of the Garn-St. Germain Act, which loosened federal regulations for the savings and loan industry, Washington, 15 October 1982. In Stephen Pizzo, Mary Fricker, and Paul Muolo, introduction to *Inside Job—The Looting of America's Savings and Loans,* 1989

Private Banking: The process by which banks redistribute the national income, among themselves.

> LEO ROSTEN (1908–1997). "Political Lexicon," *New Republic,* 3 July 1935

Anonymous: Why do you rob banks?
Sutton: Because that's where the money is.

> WILLIE SUTTON. Attributed (he denied having said it). 1940s, *Where the Money Was,* p. 120, 1976

Was there ever such an autumn? And yet there was never such a panic and hard times in the commercial world. The merchants and banks are suspending and failing all the country over, but not the sandbanks, solid and warm, and streaked with bloody blackberry vines. You may run upon them as much as you please—even as the crickets do, and find their account in it. They are the stockholders in these banks, and I hear them creaking their content.

> HENRY DAVID THOREAU (1817–1862). Journal, 14 October 1857

BASEBALL

See also • Misjudgments: Chuck Dressen ○ Sports

Whoever wants to know the heart and mind of America had better learn baseball.

> JACQUES BARZUN (1907–). *God's Country and Mine: A Declaration of Love Spiced with a Few Harsh Words,* 8, 1954

You can observe a lot by watchin'.

> YOGI BERRA (1925–). On how he (as a player) prepared himself to be a manager. In Arthur Daley, "Casey's Little Helper," *New York Times,* 25 October 1963
>
> See Wit: Examples: Berra (all)

I guess the first thing I ought to say is that I thank everybody for making this day necessary.

> YOGI BERRA (1925–). Speech at the ceremony inducting him into the Baseball Hall of Fame, Cooperstown (New York). In Leonard Koppett, "Yogi in Hall; 'Hope I'll Put Something Back,'" *New York Times,* 8 August 1972

If the people don't want to come out to the park, nobody's gonna stop 'em.

> YOGI BERRA (1925–). Explaining a ball club's attendance problems. In Joe Garagiola, *It's Anybody's Ballgame,* 8, 1988

Ninety percent of the game is half mental.

> YOGI BERRA (1925–). *The Yogi Book: "I Really Didn't Say Everything I Said,"* p. 69, 1998

Slump? I ain't in no slump. I just ain't hitting.

> YOGI BERRA (1925–)

Boys, baseball is a game where you gotta have fun. You do that by winning. So let's have fun.

> DAVE BRISTOL (1933–). Remark to his players on becoming manager of the Cincinnati Reds. In "Baseball: All Odds & Ends," *Time,* 26 May 1967

To be good, you've gotta have a lot of little boy in you.

> ROY CAMPANELLA (1921–1993)

I lost 24 games my first year with the Mets. You've got to be a pretty good pitcher to lose that many. What manager is going to let you go out there that often?

> ROGER CRAIG (1931–). In "Scorecard," *Sports Illustrated,* 11 March 1968

A ball player's got to be kept hungry to become a big-leaguer. That's why no boy from a rich family every made the big leagues.

> JOE DiMAGGIO (1914–). In "Play Ball!" *New York Times Magazine,* 30 April 1961

I don't care where you are, but the fans only remember your last time at bat.

> MIKE DITKA (1939–). Football player and coach. Appearing on a television news program, ABC, 24 September 1989

Reporter: Why don't you be a nice guy for a change?
Durocher: Nice guys! Look over there [at the New York Giants' dugout]. Do you know a nicer guy than [Giants' manager] Mel Ott? Or any of the other Giants! Why they're the nicest guys in the world! And where are they? In seventh place. The nice guys are all over there. In seventh place.

> LEO DUROCHER (1906–1991). Format adapted. In Frank Graham, "Leo Doesn't Like Nice Guys," *New York Journal-American,* 6 July 1946 (Popular version: Nice guys finish last.)

I may have been given a bad break, but I have an awful lot to live for. With all this, I consider myself the luckiest man on the face of the earth.

> LOU GEHRIG (1903–1941). Remark on Gehrig Appreciation Day at New York's Yankee Stadium, 4 July 1939. In Frank Graham, *Lou Gehrig: A Quiet Hero,* 16, 1942. At the time, the future Hall of Famer knew he was afflicted with amyotrophic lateral sclerosis (now called Lou Gehrig's Disease), which caused his death two years later at 38.

Anyone with any real blood in his or her . . . veins cannot help being a fan. . . . Being a true American and being a fan are synonymous. [Ellipsis points in original.]

> LULU GLASER (1874–1958). In Gai Ingham Berlage, *Women in Baseball: The Forgotten History,* 1, 1994

Knowin' all 'bout baseball is jist 'bout as profitable as bein' a good whittler.

> KIN HUBBARD (1856–1915). *Abe Martin's Almanack,* 1911

Take me out to the ball game,
Take me out with the crowd.
Buy me some peanuts and cracker-jack,
I don't care if I never get back.

> JACK NORWORTH and ALBERT VON TILZER. "Take Me Out to the Ball Game" (song), 1908

The story of the curve ball is the story of the game itself. Some would say, of life itself.

> MARTIN QUIGLEY. *The Curve Ball in American Baseball History,* 1984

Why not, I had a better year than he did.

> GEORGE HERMAN "BABE" RUTH (1895–1948). Remark (during The Depression) to a reporter who had objected to Ruth's demanding $80,000 for the 1931 season, $5,000 more than Pres. Herbert Hoover's salary. In *Baseball,* television documentary series, PBS, September 1994

Who is this Baby Ruth and what does she do?

> GEORGE BERNARD SHAW (1856–1950). 1930s. In *Baseball,* television documentary series, PBS, September 1994

Baseball has the great advantage over cricket of being sooner ended.

> GEORGE BERNARD SHAW (1856–1950)

One year I hit .291 and had to take a salary cut. If you hit .291 today, you'd own the franchise.

> ENOS SLAUGHTER. (1915–)

[Babe] Ruth made a great mistake when he gave up pitching.

> TRIS SPEAKER (1888–1958). Baseball player. On Ruth's decision in 1921 to become an outfielder.

They didn't give him a cake. They were afraid he'd drop it.

> CASEY STENGEL (1890?–1975). Baseball manager. At a New York Mets team party celebrating the birthday of its notoriously weak-fielding first baseman Marv Throneberry. In *New York Daily News,* 23 April 1981

[Leroy "Satchel" Paige] threw the ball as far from the bat and as close to the plate as possible.

> CASEY STENGEL (1890?–1975). *The Gospel According to C•A•S•E•Y: Casey Stengel's Inimitable, Instructional, Historical Baseball Book,* ed. Ira Berkow and Jim Kaplan, 3, 1992

Good pitching will always stop good hitting and vice-versa.

> CASEY STENGEL (1890?–1975)

Most ball games are lost, not won.

> CASEY STENGEL (1890?–1975)

Williams: Postseason, perfect weather, great ball games—no place you'd rather be. We've got a saying going around here now, "Surrender yourself to the moment. Became a part of it."
Reporter: Just what does that mean, exactly?
Williams (laughing): I have no idea. It's way too heavy for me. But it's a kick in the pants, isn't it?

> MATT WILLIAMS (1965–). Cleveland Indians' ballplayer. Format adapted. Locker-room remarks following his team's victory in Game 4 of the American League Championship Series. In Bruce Jenkins, "Williams Has a Lot to Be Proud of," *San Francisco Chronicle,* 13 October 1997

BASKETBALL

See also • Sports

A coach's main job is to reawaken a spirit in which the players can blend together effortlessly.

> PHIL JACKSON (1945–). Basketball coach. Slightly modified. In Ira Berkow, "Rodman Big Surprise on Surprising Bulls," *New York Times,* 2 January 1995

Good teams become great ones when the members trust each other enough to surrender the "me" for the "we."

> PHIL JACKSON (1945–) (with HUGH DELEHANTY). *Sacred Hoops: Spiritual Lessons of a Hardwood Warrior,* 1, 1995

If the players were going to learn the offense, they would have to have the confidence to make decisions on their own. That would never happen if they were constantly searching for direction from me. I wanted them to *dis*connect themselves from me, so they could connect with their teammates—and the game.

> PHIL JACKSON (1945–) (with HUGH DELEHANTY). *Sacred Hoops: Spiritual Lessons of a Hardwood Warrior,* 6, 1995

There are two kinds of coaches—those who have been fired and those who will be fired.

> KEN LOEFFLER. Basketball coach. In Bob Broeg, "Sports Comment," *St. Louis Post-Dispatch,* 29 December 1964

Phil knows what he wants and he's direct, but he'll give you that little sarcastic smile that kind of takes the edge off it.

> DENNIS RODMAN (1961–). Basketball player. On coach Phil Jackson. In Ira Berkow, "Rodman Big Surprise on Surprising Bulls," *New York Times,* 2 January 1995

BEAT GENERATION

See also • Hippies

None of these people have anything interesting to say, and none of them can write, not even Mr. Kerouac. [What they do] isn't writing at all—*it's typing.*

> TRUMAN CAPOTE (1924–1984). On the Beat Generation writers. In Janet Winn, "Capote, Mailer and Miss Parker," *New Republic,* 9 February 1959

A man like Kerouac has talent. Certainly a man like Ginsberg has talent. He has the ability to arouse people, he has a rhetorical gift, but the beat movement was ridiculous. It attracted a lot of people who just wanted the chance to wear heavy eye shadow and play chess in coffee houses.

> HERBERT GOLD (1924–). Interview with the author, August 1963. In Roy Newquist, *Counterpoint,* 1964

We are beat, man. Beat means beatific, it means you get the beat.

> JACK KEROUAC (1922–1969). In Herb Gold, "The Beat Mystique," *Playboy,* February 1988

The worst feature of the 50s is that they were pregnant with the 60s.

> GEORGE F. WILL (1941–). "Daddy, Who Was Kerouac?" *Newsweek,* 4 July 1988

BEAUTY

See also • Art ○ Charm ○ Nature

Things are beautiful if you love them.

> JEAN ANOUILH (1910–1987). *Mademoiselle Colombe,* 2.2, 1950, tr. Louis Kronenberger, 1954

There is no excellent beauty that hath not some strangeness in the proportion.

> FRANCIS BACON (1561–1626). "Of Beauty," *Essays,* 1625

"A Pretty Girl Is Like a Melody."

> IRVING BERLIN (1888–1989). Song title. In the musical *Ziegfield Follies,* 1919

Character contributes to beauty. It fortifies a woman as her youth fades. A mode of conduct, a standard of courage, discipline, fortitude and integrity can do a great deal to make a woman beautiful.

> JACQUELINE BISSET (1946–). In Lydia Lane, "Actress with 3 Countries," *Los Angeles Times,* 16 May 1974

In certain situations, [being a black woman] helped me simply because I was mildly attractive, not because I was black or a woman. That gets you more mileage than anything else. . . . God help you if you're not an attractive woman.

> THERESA BROWN. Television newswoman. 3 April 1973. In Judith S. Gelfman, *Women in Television News,* 5, 1976

It has been said that a pretty face is a passport. But it's not, it's a visa, and it runs out fast.

> JULIE BURCHILL. "Kiss and Tell," 1988, *Sex and Sensibility,* 1992

It was a blonde. A blonde to make a bishop kick a hole in a stained-glass window.

> RAYMOND CHANDLER (1888–1959). *Farewell, My Lovely,* 13, 1940

Everything on earth [is] beautiful, everything, except what we ourselves think and do when we forget the higher purposes of life and our own human dignity.

> ANTON CHEKHOV (1860–1904). "The Lady with the Toy Dog," 1899, tr. S. S. Koteliansky and Gilbert Cannan, 1917

Beauty's but skin deep.

> JOHN DAVIES (1569–1626). *A Select Second Husband for Sir Thomas Overburie's Wife,* 6, 1616

The highest Beauty should be plain set.

> RALPH WALDO EMERSON (1803–1882). Journal, 24 September 1839
>
> See Virtue: Francis Bacon (2)

The line of beauty is the line of perfect economy.

> RALPH WALDO EMERSON (1803–1882). "Beauty," *The Conduct of Life,* 1860

All high beauty has a moral element in it.

> RALPH WALDO EMERSON (1803–1882). "Beauty," *The Conduct of Life,* 1860

Fair Faces need no Paint.

> THOMAS FULLER (1654–1734). Comp., *Gnomologia: Adages and Proverbs,* 1490, 1732

Beauty is life when life unveils her holy face,

> KAHLIL GIBRAN (1883–1931). "On Beauty," *The Prophet,* 1923

Beautiful is greater than Good, for it includes the Good.

> GOETHE (1749–1832). In John Stuart Mill, "On Education," inaugural address on being installed as rector, University of St. Andrews (Scotland), 1 February 1867

Beauty is no quality in things themselves: it exists merely in the mind which contemplates them.

> DAVID HUME (1711–1776). "Of the Standard of Taste," *Four Dissertations,* 1757

Beauty is in the eye of the beholder.

> MARGARET HUNGERFORD (1855?–1897). *Molly Bawn,* 1.12, 1878
>
> See Eyes: James MacGregor Burns

A thing of beauty is a joy forever.

> JOHN KEATS (1795–1821). Opening line, *Endymion,* 1818

"Beauty is truth, truth beauty"—that is all
Ye know on earth, and all ye need to know.

> JOHN KEATS (1795–1821). Closing lines, "Ode on a Grecian Urn," 1820

There are women who are not beautiful but only look that way.

> KARL KRAUS (1874–1936). *Aphorisms and More Aphorisms,* 1909

Some beautiful things are more impressive when left imperfect than when too highly finished.

> LA ROCHEFOUCAULD (1613–1680). *Maxims,* 627, 1665, tr. Leonard Tancock, 1959

The sublime and the ridiculous are often so nearly related that it is difficult to class them separately. One step above the sublime makes the ridiculous, and one step above the ridiculous makes the sublime again.

> THOMAS PAINE (1737–1809). *The Age of Reason: Being an Investigation of True and Fabulous Theology,* 2, 1796

The good is the beautiful.

> PLATO (427?–347 B.C.). *Lysis,* 216, tr. Benjamin Jowett, 1894

Beauty addresses itself chiefly to sight; but there is a beauty for the hearing too, as in certain combinations of words and in all kinds of music, for melodies and cadences are beautiful; and minds that lift themselves above the realm of sense to a higher order are aware of beauty in the conduct of life, in actions, in character, in the pursuits of the intellect; and there is the beauty of the virtues.

> PLOTINUS (A.D. 205–270). *The Enneads,* 1.6.1, tr. Stephen MacKenna and B. S. Page, 1952

Beauty is the flower of virtue.

> PLUTARCH (A.D. 46?–119?). "Of Love." In Ralph Waldo Emerson, "Encyclopedia," p. 143, 1824–1836

The horse that has thin flanks is thought handsomer than one of a different shape, and is also more swift. The athlete whose muscles have been developed by exercise is pleasing to the sight, and is so much the better prepared for the combat. True beauty is never separate from utility.

> QUINTILIAN (A.D. 35?–100?). *Institutio oratoria*, 8.3.10–11, tr. John Selby Watson, 1856

Remember that the most beautiful things in the world are the most useless; peacocks and lilies for instance.

> JOHN RUSKIN (1819–1900). *The Stones of Venice*, 1.2.17, 1851–1853

I always say beauty is only sin deep.

> SAKI (1870–1916). "Reginald's Choir Treat," *Reginald*, 1904

In each person I catch the fleeting suggestion of something beautiful and swear eternal friendship with that.

> GEORGE SANTAYANA (1863–1952). "The Middle Span," *Persons and Places*, 1944–1953

❦

Even Fuji is without beauty to one who is hungry and cold.

> SAYING (JAPANESE)

Beauty comes from within.

> SAYING

A joyful heart makes a fair face.

> SAYING

BEGGARS

See also • Compassion: Martin Luther King, Jr. ○ Homelessness ○ Patience: Philip Massinger ○ Poverty: [especially] R. H. Tawney ○ Rich & Poor: Shakespeare

Beggars must be no choosers.

> FRANCIS BEAUMONT (1584–1616) and JOHN FLETCHER (1579–1625). *The Scornful Ladie*, 3.1, 1617

Beggar, *n.* One who has relied on the assistance of his friends.

> AMBROSE BIERCE (1842–1914). *The Devil's Dictionary*, p. 17, 1911, Dover edition, 1958

Better die a Beggar than live a Beggar.

> THOMAS FULLER (1654–1734). Comp., *Gnomologia: Adages and Proverbs*, 888, 1732

Once I built a railroad, made it run,
Made it race against time.
Once I built a railroad, now it's done
Brother, can you spare a dime?

> E. Y. "YIP" HARBURG (1896–1981). "Brother, Can You Spare a Dime?" (song). In the musical *New Americana*, 1932

Maximum fine for begging without a permit in Orlando, Florida: $500
Minimum distance, in feet, that Orlando beggars must maintain from those they ask for money: 3.

> "HARPER'S INDEX." *Harper's*, April 1998

Beggars may sing before thieves.

> JAMES HOWELL (1593–1666). Comp., "English" (p. 5), *Paroimiographia: Proverbs, or Old Sayed Sawes & Adages in English . . . Italian, French and Spanish*, 1659

If you feel guilty, see a priest.

> EDWARD I. KOCH (1924–). New York mayor. Urging New Yorkers not to give to beggars, 10 August 1988.

There are people who can never forgive a beggar for their not having given him anything.

> KARL KRAUS (1874–1936). "Lord, Forgive Them . . . ," *Half-Truths & One-and-a-Half Truths: Selected Aphorisms*, ed. Harry Zohn, 1976

Beggars ought to be abolished: for one is vexed at giving to them and vexed at not giving to them.

> FRIEDRICH NIETZSCHE (1844–1900). *Daybreak*, 185, 1881, tr. R. J. Hollingdale, 1982

Why are beggars despised?—for they are despised, universally. I believe it is for the simple reason that they fail to earn a decent living. In practice nobody cares whether work is useful or useless, productive or parasitic; the sole thing demanded is that it shall be profitable. . . . Money has become the grand test of virtue. By this test beggars fail, and for this they are despised. If one could earn even ten pounds a week at begging, it would become a respectable profession immediately.

> GEORGE ORWELL (1903–1950). *Down and Out in Paris and London*, 31, 1933

The rain fell steadily, and the water flowed over the highways, for the culverts could not carry the water.

Then from the tents, from the crowded barns, groups of sodden men went out, their clothes slopping rags, their shoes muddy pulp. They splashed out through the water, to the towns, to the country stores, to the relief offices, to beg for food, to cringe and beg for food, to beg for relief, to try to steal, to lie. And under the begging, and under the cringing, a hopeless anger began to smolder. And in the little towns pity for the sodden men changed to anger, and anger at the hungry people changed to fear of them. Then sheriffs swore in deputies in droves, and orders were rushed for rifles, for tear gas, for ammunition.

> JOHN STEINBECK (1902–1968). On migrants in California during The Depression, *The Grapes of Wrath*, 29, 1939

❦

Better a live beggar than a dead emperor.

> SAYING (CHINESE)

Better beg than steal; better work than beg.

> SAYING (RUSSIAN)

BEGINNINGS & ENDINGS

See also • Progress

"Begin at the beginning," the King said, gravely, "and go till you come to the end; then stop."

> LEWIS CARROLL (1832–1898). *Alice's Adventures in Wonderland*, 12, 1865

Now this is not the end. It is not even the beginning of the end. But it is, perhaps, the end of the beginning.

> WINSTON CHURCHILL (1874–1965). On the British victory at El Alamein (Egypt), speech at the Lord Mayor's Day luncheon, Mansion House, London, 10 November 1942

An ill beginning hath an ill ending.
> JOHN CLARKE (1596–1658). Comp., *Proverbs: English and Latine,* p. 109, 1639

All's well that *ends* well.
> JOHN CLARKE (1596–1658). Comp., *Proverbs: English and Latine,* p. 117, 1639

Better never to begin than never to make an end.
> JOHN CLARKE (1596–1658). Comp., *Proverbs: English and Latine,* p. 247, 1639

In my beginning is my end.
> T. S. ELIOT (1888–1965). "East Coker" (1), *Four Quartets,* 1943

What we call the beginning is often the end
And to make an end is to make a beginning.
The end is where we start from.
> T. S. ELIOT (1888–1965). "Little Gidding" (5), *Four Quartets,* 1943

We shall not cease from exploration
And the end of all our exploring
Will be to arrive where we started
And know the place for the first time.
> T. S. ELIOT (1888–1965). "Little Gidding" (5), *Four Quartets,* 1943

A good beginning hath a good ending.
> JAMES HOWELL (1593–1666). Comp., "English" (p. 6), *Paroimiographia: Proverbs, or Old Sayed Sawes & Adages in English . . . Italian, French and Spanish,* 1659

A hard beginning hath a good ending.
> JAMES HOWELL (1593–1666). Comp., "English" (p. 7), *Paroimiographia: Proverbs, or Old Sayed Sawes & Adages in English . . . Italian, French and Spanish,* 1659

God provides thread for the work begun.
> JAMES HOWELL (1593–1666). Comp., "French" (p. 7), *Paroimiographia: Proverbs, or Old Sayed Sawes & Adages in English . . . Italian, French and Spanish,* 1659

There will come a time when you believe everything is finished. That will be the beginning.
> LOUIS L'AMOUR (1908–1988). Opening paragraph, *Lonely on the Mountain,* 1980

In my end is my beginning.
> MARY, QUEEN OF SCOTS (1542–1587). Motto

The beginning is the most important part of any work, especially in the case of a young and tender thing; for that is the time at which the character is being formed and the desired impression is more readily taken.
> PLATO (427?–347 B.C.). *The Republic,* 2.377, tr. Benjamin Jowett, 1894

Good to begin well, better to *end* well.
> JOHN RAY (1628–1705). Comp., *A Collection of English Proverbs,* p. 8, 1678

Something began me
and it had no beginning:
something will end me
and it has no end.
> CARL SANDBURG (1878–1967). *The People, Yes,* 91, 1936

Every exit [is] . . . an entrance somewhere else.
> TOM STOPPARD (1937–). *Rosencrantz and Guildenstern Are Dead,* 1, 1967

It is the beginning of the end.
> TALLEYRAND (1754–1838). Remark to Napoleon after the Battle of Leipzig, 18 October 1813

In the beginning God created the heavens and the earth.
> ANONYMOUS (*BIBLE*). Opening words, *Genesis*

A journey of a thousand miles must begin with a single step.
> SAYING (CHINESE). Pres. John F. Kennedy popularized this saying in a television broadcast from the White House announcing a treaty that banned the atmospheric testing of nuclear weapons, 26 July 1963.

Ninety miles is but halfway in a journey of a hundred miles.
> SAYING (CHINESE)

Don't start what you can't finish.
> SAYING (ENGLISH)

Sooner begun, sooner done.
> SAYING (ENGLISH)

A bad beginning may make a good ending.
> SAYING (GERMAN)

Who begins too much accomplishes little.
> SAYING (GERMAN)

Well begun is half done.
> SAYING (GREEK). In Aristotle (384–322 B.C.). *Politics,* 5.4, tr. Benjamin Jowett, 1885

Small beginnings are not to be despised.
> SAYING

The first and last steps are usually the hardest.
> SAYING

BELIEF

See also • Certainty ◦ Consistency ◦ Conviction ◦ Doubt ◦ Faith ◦ Faith & Reason ◦ Heresy ◦ Ideas ◦ Illusion ◦ Life: William James (2) ◦ Opinion ◦ Reason ◦ Religion ◦ Skepticism ◦ Superstition ◦ Trust

People everywhere enjoy believing things that they know are not true. It spares them the ordeal of thinking for themselves and taking responsibility for what they know.
> BROOKS ATKINSON (1894–1984). 2 February, *Once Around the Sun,* 1951

Believe that you may understand. (Crede ut intelligas.)
> ST. AUGUSTINE (A.D. 354–430). In E. F. Schumacher, *A Guide for the Perplexed,* 4, 1977

Believe in something larger than yourself.
> BARBARA BUSH (1925–). Commencement address at Wellesley College (Massachusetts), 1 June 1990

No iron chain, or outward force of any kind, could ever compel the soul of man to believe or disbelieve.

> THOMAS CARLYLE (1795–1881). "The Hero as Priest," *On Heroes, Hero-Worship, and the Heroic in History,* 1841

Seeing is believing all the world over.

> CERVANTES (1547–1616). *Don Quixote,* 2.3.10, 1615, tr. Peter Anthony Motteux and John Ozell, 1743

You do not believe; you only believe that you believe.

> SAMUEL TAYLOR COLERIDGE (1772–1834). In Thomas Carlyle, "The Hero as Priest," *On Heroes, Hero-Worship, and the Heroic in History,* 1841

I make it a rule only to believe what I understand.

> BENJAMIN DISRAELI (1808–1881). *The Infernal Marriage,* 1.4, 1834

The universal impulse to believe . . . is the principal fact in the history of the globe.

> RALPH WALDO EMERSON (1803–1882). "Experience," *Essays: Second Series,* 1844

He does not believe, that does not live according to his Belief.

> THOMAS FULLER (1654–1734). Comp., *Gnomologia: Adages and Proverbs,* 1838, 1732

Seeing's Believing, but Feeling's the Truth.

> THOMAS FULLER (1654–1734). Comp., *Gnomologia: Adages and Proverbs,* 4087, 1732

The fullest life is impossible without an immovable belief in a Living Law in obedience to which the whole universe moves.

> MOHANDAS K. GANDHI (1869–1948). In *Harijan,* 25 April 1936

The belief that becomes truth for me . . . is that which allows me the best use of my strength, the best means of putting my virtues into action.

> ANDRÉ GIDE (1869–1951). *The Counterfeiters,* 2.4, 1925, tr. Dorothy Bussy, 1951

We believe what we want to believe, what we like to believe, what suits our prejudices and fuels our passions.

> SYDNEY J. HARRIS (1917–1986). "Lies Are Not Easily Put to Rest," *Clearing the Ground,* 1986

Quick believers need broad shoulders.

> GEORGE HERBERT (1593–1633). Comp., *Outlandish Proverbs,* 39, 1640

Some things have to be believed to be seen.

> RALPH HODGSON (1871–1962)

All things are possible to him who believes.

> JESUS (A.D. 1st cent.). *Mark* 9:23

Blessed are those who have not seen and yet believe.

> JESUS (A.D. 1st cent.). *John* 20:29

Every man who attacks my belief diminishes in some degree my confidence in it, and therefore makes me uneasy; and I am angry with him who makes me uneasy.

> SAMUEL JOHNSON (1709–1784). 3 April 1776. In James Boswell, *The Life of Samuel Johnson,* 1791

Ah, the mysterious croak. Here today, gone tomorrow. It's the best reason I can think of to throw open the blinds and risk belief. Right now, this minute, time to move out into the grief and glory. High tide.

> BARBARA KINGSOLVER (1955–). Closing words, "Reprise," *High Tide in Tucson: Essays from Now or Never,* 1996

If you want to know what to believe, find out what is the current consensus and turn it upside down; that way you won't necessarily be right but at least you won't inevitably be wrong. If, in addition, you hope for a hint as to what is right, listen to those whom society stigmatizes as abnormal. They've got something.

> DAVID MARTIN. "R. D. Laing: Psychiatry & Apocalypse," *Dissent,* June 1971

You gotta believe.

> TUG McGRAW (1944–) Baseball player. Frequent saying as his team, the New York Mets, began its climb from 5th to 1st place late in the 1973 National League pennant race

Nothing is so firmly believed as what is least known.

> MONTAIGNE (1533–1592). "We Should Meddle Soberly with Judging Divine Ordinances," *Essays,* 1588, tr. Donald M. Frame, 1958

It is natural for the mind to believe, and for the will to love; so that, for want of true objects, they must attach themselves to false.

> BLAISE PASCAL (1623–1662). *Pensées,* 81, 1670, tr. William F. Trotter, 1931

Believe It or Not.

> ROBERT L. RIPLEY (1893–1949). Title of syndicated newspaper feature, 1918–1949

Conduct [is] the ultimate test of the worth of a belief.

> THEODORE ROOSEVELT (1858–1919). In Hermann Hagedorn and Sidney Wallach, "Signposts for Americans: Character and Conduct," *A Theodore Roosevelt Round-Up,* 1958

We believe, first and foremost, what makes us feel that we are fine fellows.

> BERTRAND RUSSELL (1872–1970). "An Outline of Intellectual Rubbish," *Unpopular Essays,* 1950

Belief in a Divine mission is one of the many forms of certainty that have afflicted the human race.

> BERTRAND RUSSELL (1872–1970). "Ideas That Have Harmed Mankind," *Unpopular Essays,* 1950

When a man tells you that something you've always believed was in fact not true, it gives you a frightful shock and you think, "Oh! I don't know where I am. When I think I'm planting my foot upon the ground, perhaps I'm not." And you get into a terror.

> BERTRAND RUSSELL (1872–1970). Woodrow Wyatt television interview, BBC, London, 1959, *Bertrand Russell Speaks His Mind,* 10, 1960

I confused things with their names: that is belief.

> JEAN-PAUL SARTRE (1905–1980). *The Words,* 2, 1964, tr. Bernard Frechtman, 1981

The statesman cannot govern without stability of belief, true or false.

GEORGE BERNARD SHAW (1856–1950). *Everybody's Political What's What?* 33, 1944

This poor, timid, unenlightened, thick-skinned creature, what *can* it believe? I am, of course, hopelessly ignorant and unbelieving until some divinity stirs within me. Ninety-nine one-hundredths of our lives we are mere hedgers and ditchers, but from time to time we meet with reminders of our destiny.

HENRY DAVID THOREAU (1817–1862). Journal, 13 January 1857

The courage to believe in nothing.

IVAN TURGENEV (1818–1883). *Fathers and Sons,* 14, 1862, tr. Constance Gernett, 1941

Between believing a thing and thinking you *know* is only a small step and quickly taken.

MARK TWAIN (1835–1910). Opening sentence, *3,000 Years Among the Microbes,* 1905, *Mark Twain's Which Was the Dream? And Other Symbolic Writings of the Later Years,* ed. John S. Tuckey, 1968

My own belief is not rule for another.

JOHN WESLEY (1703–1791). In Henry Thomas and Dana Lee Thomas, "John Wesley," *Living Biographies of Religious Leaders,* 1942

❦

I believe in the sun even when it is not shining.
I believe in love even when not feeling it.
I believe in God even when He is silent.

ANONYMOUS (JEWISH). Wall inscription in a cellar hideout, Cologne (Germany), 1942?

BERLIN

See also • Cities ○ Germany ○ World: Anonymous (American)

All free men, wherever they may live, are citizens of Berlin. And therefore, as a free man, I take pride in the words, "Ich bin ein Berliner."

JOHN F. KENNEDY (1917–1963). Speech before a huge crowd at West Berlin's City Hall, 26 June 1963. "Technically, Kennedy [blew] the line. '*Berliner*' means someone from Berlin. But '*ein Berliner*' describes a thing, specifically a pastry. Kennedy's line literally means 'I am a jelly doughnut.'" (Joel Achenback, "Let It Be Forgot That Once There Was a Spot: Clinton Should Drop His Fixation with JFK and Camelot," *Washington Post National Weekly Edition,* 1 August 1994)

BIBLE

See also • Dreams: Umberto Eco ○ God ○ Native Americans: Dan George ○ Religion ○ Scripture

I am halfway through *Genesis,* and quite appalled by the disgraceful behavior of all the characters involved, including God.

J. R. ACKERLEY (1896–1967). British writer. Letter to a friend. In Lance Morrow, "Evil" (essay), *Time,* 10 June 1991

Prosperity is the blessing of the Old Testament; adversity is the blessing of the New, which carrieth the greater benediction and the clearer revelation of God's favor.

FRANCIS BACON (1561–1626). "Of Adversity," *Essays,* 1625

There is not a single contradiction in the Bible from Genesis to Revelation.

HENRY WARD BEECHER (1813–1887). "The Bible," *Proverbs from Plymouth Pulpit,* ed. William Drysdale, 1887

[The Bible] is the history of God's disappointments.

MARTIN BUBER (1878–1965). "Biblical Leadership," *Israel and the World: Essays in a Time of Crisis,* 1948

The biblical point of view . . . proclaims that the way, the real way, from the creation to the kingdom is trod not on the surface of success, but in the depths of failure.

MARTIN BUBER (1878–1965). "Biblical Leadership," *Israel and the World: Essays in a Time of Crisis,* 1948

The Bible may be the truth, but it is not the whole truth, nor is it nothing but the truth.

SAMUEL BUTLER (1835–1902). *Further Extracts from the Note-Books of Samuel Butler,* 1, ed. A. T. Bartholomew, 1934

The Fall of Man, as the Bible recounts it, is in reality the Fall of God.

CYRIL CONNOLLY (1903–1974). "Ecce Gubernator," *The Unquiet Grave: A Word Cycle by Palinurus,* 1945

The bible is a sealed book to him who has not first heard its laws from his soul.

RALPH WALDO EMERSON (1803–1882). "Trust Yourself," sermon, Second Church of Boston, 3 December 1830

Make your own Bible. Select and collect all the words and sentences that in all your reading have been to you like the blast of trumpet out of Shakespeare, Seneca, Moses, John, and Paul.

RALPH WALDO EMERSON (1803–1882). Journal, 21 July 1836

I have spent a lot of time searching through the Bible for loopholes.

W. C. FIELDS (1880–1946). Attributed. Said during his last illness

It ain't necessarily so,
It ain't necessarily so,
De t'ings dat you li'ble
To read in de Bible
It ain't necessarily so.

IRA GERSHWIN (1896–1983). "It Ain't Necessarily So" (song). In the musical *Porgy and Bess,* 1935

What we all need to do is return to the Bible afresh—not going to it to prove a point, but seeing what it says as the Holy Spirit opens our eyes.

BILLY GRAHAM (1918–). Wes Michaelson and Jim Wallis interview, *Sojourners,* August 1979

The Bible points to a way of understanding the world from the point of view of God.

ABRAHAM JOSHUA HESCHEL (1907–1972). *God in Search of Man: A Philosophy of Judaism,* 1, 1955

In the midst of our applauding the feats of civilization, the Bible flings itself like a knife slashing our complacency, reminding us that God, too, has a voice in history.

ABRAHAM JOSHUA HESCHEL (1907–1972). *God in Search of Man: A Philosophy of Judaism,* 17, 1955

The incidents recorded in the Bible to the discerning eye are episodes of one great drama: the quest of God for man; His search for man and man's flight from Him.

> ABRAHAM JOSHUA HESCHEL (1907–1972). *God in Search of Man: A Philosophy of Judaism*, 20, 1955

The Bible is God's anthropology rather than man's theology.

> ABRAHAM JOSHUA HESCHEL (1907–1972). *God in Search of Man: A Philosophy of Judaism*, 41, 1955

The Bible is the record of man's efforts to find God and learn how to live in harmony with his laws.

> HELEN KELLER (1880–1968). *My Religion*, 4, 1927

There is nothing patent in the New Testament that is not latent in the Old.

> VINCENT STUCKEY LEAN (1820–1899). *Collectanea*, 4.153, 1904

Take all of this book upon reason that you can, and the balance, upon faith and you will live and die a better man.

> ABRAHAM LINCOLN (1809–1865). On the Bible, remark to Joshua F. Speed. In David Herman Donald, *Lincoln*, 18.3, 1995

When a biblical verse is contradicted by proof, we do not accept the Bible.

> MOSES MAIMONIDES (A.D. 1135–1204). *Responsa*, 3

The Book of Genesis, a farrago of nonsense so wholly absurd that even Sunday-school scholars have to be threatened with Hell to make them accept it.

> H. L. MENCKEN (1880–1956). "Forgotten Men," *American Mercury*, March 1928

The man who has not received the living witness of God knows really nothing about God, though he may have swallowed 100,000 Bibles.

> THOMAS MÜNSTER (1490?–1525). In Roland H. Bainton, *Here I Stand: A Life of Martin Luther*, 15, 1950

[The Bible] is a history of wickedness that has served to corrupt and brutalize mankind; and, for my part, I sincerely detest it as I detest everything that is cruel.

> THOMAS PAINE (1737–1809). *The Age of Reason: Being an Investigation of True and Fabulous Theology*, 1, 1794

There's a Bible on that shelf there. But I keep it next to Voltaire—poison and antidote.

> BERTRAND RUSSELL (1872–1970). Interview. In Kenneth Harris, *Kenneth Harris Talking to Maria Callas* [and others], 1971

At the center of the Old Testament is the pilgrimage of the people of Israel from Exodus and slavery to Promised Land and freedom. In the New, it is a movement from the first to the second Adam, from our present state to the new humanity.

> RICHARD SHAULL (1919–). *Containment and Change: Two Dissenting Views of American Foreign Policy*, 11, 1967

When the missionaries first came to Africa, they had the Bible and we had the land. They said "let us pray." We closed our eyes. When we opened them, we had the Bible and they had the land.

> BISHOP DESMOND TUTU (1931–). In *Observer* (British newspaper), 16 December 1984

It ain't those parts of the Bible that I can't understand that bother me, it is the parts that I do understand.

> MARK TWAIN (1835–1910). *The Wit and Wisdom of Mark Twain*, p. 24, ed. Alex Ayres, 1987

The Bible is like a once fearsome lion that, now toothless and declawed, can be petted and teased.

> JOHN UPDIKE (1932–). Opening words, "Stones Into Bread: Norman Mailer and the Temptations of Christ," *New Yorker*, 12 May 1997

We consider bibles and religions divine—I do not say they are not divine,
I say they have all grown out of you, and may grow out of you still,
It is not they who give the life, it is you who give the life.

> WALT WHITMAN (1819–1892). "A Song for Occupations" (3), 1855, *Leaves of Grass*, 1855–1892

I read the Bible to understand what is happening today.

> ELI WIESEL (1928–). National Press Club speech, Washington, 20 May 1997

BIGOTRY

See also • Prejudice

The mind of the bigot is like the pupil of the eye; the more light you pour upon it, the more it will contract.

> OLIVER WENDELL HOLMES, JR. (1841–1935)

My parents gave us a fantastic sense of security and worth. By the time the bigots got around to telling us we were nobody, we already *knew* we were somebody.

> FLORYNCE R. KENNEDY (1916–). In Gloria Steinem, "The Verbal Karate of Florynce R. Kennedy, Esq.," *Ms.*, March 1973

[Samuel Johnson] could discern clearly enough the folly and meanness of all bigotry but his own.

> THOMAS BABINGTON MACAULAY (1800–1859). "Samuel Johnson," *The Edinburgh Review* (Scotland), September 1831

Bigotry tries to keep truth safe in its hand with a grip that kills it.

> RABINDRANATH TAGORE (1861–1941). *Fireflies*, p. 29, 1928

Bigot: Someone who hates different people than I do.

> JERRY TUCKER (1941–). *The Experience of Politics: You and American Government*, p. 456, 1974

BIOGRAPHY

See also • Autobiography ○ Books ○ Historians ○ Journals ○ Memoirs ○ Writing

[Biography:] one of the new terrors of death.

> JOHN ARBUTHNOT (1667–1735). In Robert Carruthers, *The Poetical Works of Pope*, 1.3, 1853

I read biographies to see how other people handled problems like mine.

> JAMES CALLAGHAN (1912–). Kenneth Harris interview, *Observer* (British newspaper), 3 December 1976

A well-written life is almost as rare as a well-spent one.
> THOMAS CARLYLE (1795–1881). "John Paul Friedrich Richter," 1827, *Critical and Miscellaneous Essays,* Carey & Hart edition, 1849

Biography is the only history.
> THOMAS CARLYLE (1795–1881). Journal, 13 January 1832. In James Anthony Froude, *Thomas Carlyle,* 2.10, 1882
> See Greatness: Carlyle (2)

The labor of writing a biography, like the education of a child, involves a prolonged and strange mixture of love and critical distance, of commitment and restraint.
> BERNARD CRICK (1929–). Introduction to *George Orwell: A Life,* 1980

A key element of the biographer's art is knowing what to leave out.
> PETER FRANCE. "His Own Biggest Hero," *New York Times Book Review,* 15 February 1998

Whoever undertakes to write a biography binds himself to lying, to concealment, to hypocrisy, to flummery and even to hiding his own lack of understanding.
> SIGMUND FREUD (1856–1939). In Bruno Bettelheim, "Two Views of Freud" (1), 1958, *Freud's Vienna and Other Essays,* 1989

Good biography requires the psychologist's eye, the historian's nose, the novelist's feel for narrative. It is a form of highly organized gossip, and the more private corners the biographer can wriggle into—especially the dark ones—the better the resulting book.
> A. C. GRAYLING. "Philosophy With Warts," *New York Times Book Review,* 29 December 1996

Discretion is not the better part of biography.
> JUSTIN KAPLAN (1925–). "The Naked Self and Other Problems." In Marc Pachter, ed., *Telling Lives: The Biographer's Art,* 1979
> See Valor: Shakespeare

Biography . . . has become the revenge of little people on big people.
> EDMUND WHITE (1940–). In Susannah Hunnewell, "'The Sinner Is Closer to God'" [Edmund White], *New York Times,* 7 November 1993

❧

Biography is micro-history; history is macro-biography.
> ANONYMOUS

BIRDS

See also • Animals ○ Ideas: Joseph Joubert ○ Seasons: Rachel Carson ○ Woods: Henry David Thoreau

A Robin Red breast in a Cage
Puts all Heaven in a Rage.
> WILLIAM BLAKE (1757–1827). "Auguries of Innocence," l. 5, 1789

If I shouldn't be alive
When the Robins come,
Give the one in Red Cravat
A Memorial crumb.
> EMILY DICKINSON (1830–1886). "If I shouldn't be alive," 1860?

The red breast of the robin elicits aggressive behavior in another male, but sexual response in a female.
> NORMAN F. DIXON (1922–). *On the Psychology of Military Incompetence,* 16, 1976

Father Zossima: My brother asked the birds to forgiven him.
> FYODOR DOSTOYEVSKY (1821–1881). *The Brothers Karamazov,* 6.2(f), 1880, tr. Constance Garnett, 1912

A Nightingale cannot sing in a Cage.
> THOMAS FULLER (1654–1734). Comp., *Gnomologia: Adages and Proverbs,* 335, 1732

This is the reason for the lack of love
Twixt man and pigeons: while he likes the symbol
Of grace and peace, man, painting his own picture,
Resents all contributions from above.
> MARGARET LIEB. Biology professor. Letter to E. B. White, May 1957. In *Letters of E. B. White,* ed. Dorothy Lobrano Guth, 1976

I could not have slept if I had not restored those little birds to their mother.
> ABRAHAM LINCOLN (1809–1865). Remark to several colleagues he had been riding with after returning two fallen birdlings to their nest. In Francis Fisher Browne, *The Every-Day Life of Abraham Lincoln,* 2.2, 1887

The bluebird carries the sky on his back.
> HENRY DAVID THOREAU (1817–1862). Journal, 3 April 1852

In Boston yesterday an ornithologist said significantly, "If you held the bird in your hand—"; but I would rather hold it in my affections.
> HENRY DAVID THOREAU (1817–1862). Journal, 10 May 1854

I once had a sparrow alight upon my shoulder for a moment while I was hoeing in a village garden, and I felt that I was more distinguished by that circumstance that I should have been by any epaulette I could have worn.
> HENRY DAVID THOREAU (1817–1862). "Winter Animals," *Walden; or Life in the Woods,* 1854

What a delicious sound! It is not merely crow calling to crow, for it speaks to me too. I am part of one great creature with him.
> HENRY DAVID THOREAU (1817–1862). Journal, 12 January 1855

Princes and magistrates are often styled serene, but what is their turbid serenity to that ethereal serenity which the bluebird embodies? His Most Serene Birdship!
> HENRY DAVID THOREAU (1817–1862). Journal, 2 March 1859

We think caged birds sing, when indeed they cry.
> JOHN WEBSTER (1580–1625). *The White Devil,* 5.4, 1612

Ethereal minstrel! pilgrim of the sky!
> WILLIAM WORDSWORTH (1770–1850). Opening line, "To a Skylark," 1827

❧

Caged bird's stomach never empty,
Hungers only to be free.
> ANONYMOUS

Birds of prey do not sing.
    SAYING (GERMAN)

BIRTH CONTROL

See also • Abortion ○ Fathers ○ Mothers ○ Parents ○ Sex ○
Sterilization

Contraception is no problem—if you happen to be a camel.
    SARAH BOXER. Opening words, "Contraception Conundrum:
    It's Not Just Birth Control Anymore," *New York Times,*
    22 June 1997

The contraceptives that . . . guard against disease are the least reliable as birth control.
    SARAH BOXER. "Contraception Conundrum: It's Not Just Birth Control
    Anymore," *New York Times,* 22 June 1997

Whenever I hear people discussing birth control, I always remember that I was the fifth.
    CLARENCE DARROW (1857–1938).

Contraceptives should be used on every conceivable occasion.
    SPIKE MILLIGAN (1918–). Camden Theater, London, 30 April 1972,
    The Last Goon Show of Them All, 1972

No woman can call herself free who does not own and control
her own body. No woman can call herself free until she can
choose consciously whether she will or will not be a mother.
    MARGARET SANGER (1879–1966). *Woman and the New Race,* 8, 1920

BLAME

See also • Circumstances: George Bernard Shaw ○ Complaint ○
Criticism ○ Excuses ○ Guilt ○ Judging Others ○ Responsibility ○
Success: Thomas Fuller

People in our culture have a morbid tendency to avoid blame,
because they do not wish to take the trouble to change their conduct in any way: blame-avoidance and blame-transference are
therefore endemic amongst us. These are substitutes for repentance and renewal.
    BEHAVIOR RESEARCH PROJECT (Texas). In Lewis Mumford,
    The Conduct of Life, 6.3, 1951

We are all exceptional cases. We all want to appeal against something! Each of us insists on being innocent at all cost, even if he
has to accuse the whole human race and heaven itself.
    ALBERT CAMUS (1913–1960). *The Fall,* p. 81, tr. Justin O'Brien, 1956

Everyone threw the blame on me. I have noticed that they nearly
always do. I suppose it is because they think I shall be able to
bear it best.
    WINSTON CHURCHILL (1874–1965). *My Early Life: A Roving
    Commission,* 17, 1930

Blame is most readily averted by being so much like everybody
else that one passes unnoticed.
    JOHN DEWEY (1859–1952). *Introduction to Human Nature and Conduct:
    An Introduction to Social Psychology,* 1922

The apportioning of blame [is] the means by which society obtains
a modicum of revenge for the wrong it has suffered, expiates its
own guilt for such responsibility as it may have had for the event
in question, and finally seeks to prevent a repetition of the disaster.
    NORMAN F. DIXON (1922–). *On the Psychology of Military
    Incompetence,* 3, 1976

Authoritarian organizations are past masters at deflecting blame.
They do so by denial, by rationalization, by making scapegoats.
    NORMAN F. DIXON (1922–). *On the Psychology of Military
    Incompetence,* 3, 1976

"Oh, well," said Mr. Hennessy, "we are as th' Lord made us."
    "No," said Mr. Dooley, "lave us be fair. Lave us take some iv th'
blame oursilves."
    FINLEY PETER DUNNE (1867–1936). "Newport," *Observations by Mr.
    Dooley,* 1902

'Tis weak and vicious people who cast the blame on Fate.
    RALPH WALDO EMERSON (1803–1882). "Fate," *The Conduct of Life,*
    1860

It is the act of an ill-instructed man to blame others for his own
bad condition; it is the act of one who has begun to be instructed
to lay the blame on himself; and of one whose instruction is completed, neither to blame another nor himself.
    EPICTETUS (A.D. 55?–135?). *The Encheiridion,* 5, tr. George Long, 1890?

Accusing the Times is but excusing ourselves.
    THOMAS FULLER (1654–1734). Comp., *Gnomologia: Adages and
    Proverbs,* 759, 1732

Blame is like the lightning; it hits the highest.
    BALTASAR GRACIÁN (1601–1658). *The Art of Worldly Wisdom,* 83, 1647,
    tr. Joseph Jacobs, 1943

By accusing others of a crime we committed or are about to commit, we drain all force from any accusation which may by leveled
against us.
    ERIC HOFFER (1902–1983). *The Passionate State of Mind: And Other
    Aphorisms,* 192, 1954

What a lamentable thing it is that men should blame the gods . . .
as the source of their troubles, when it is their own wickedness that
brings them sufferings worse than any which Destiny allots them.
    HOMER (8th? cent. B.C.). *The Odyssey,* 1.32, tr. E. V. Rieu, 1946

The man who can smile when things go wrong has thought of
someone he can blame it on.
    JONES'S LAW. In Paul Dickson, comp., *The Official Rules,* p. 131, 1978

There are many scapegoats for our blunders, but the most popular one is Providence.
    MARK TWAIN (1835–1910). 4 July 1898, *Mark Twain's Notebook,* ed.
    Albert Bigelow Paine, 1935

When a man does all he can though it Succeeds not well, blame
not him that did it.
    GEORGE WASHINGTON (1732–1799). Copybook, 1748 (at age 16), *Rules
    of Civility & Decent Behaviour in Company and Conversation,* #44.
    The rules were an amended version of Francis Hawkins's 1640 transla-
    tion of *Decency of Conversation Among Men* (French Jesuit writing,
    1595)

✾

A worthless man blames his karma.
> SAYING (BURMESE)

He who cannot dance claims the floor is uneven.
> SAYING (HINDU)

A bad workman blames his tools.
> SAYING (SWAHILI)

BLESSINGS

See also • Curses

And so, as Tiny Tim observed, God Bless us Every One!
> CHARLES DICKENS (1812–1870). Closing words, *A Christmas Carol: A Ghost Story of Christmas*, 1843

An honest heart being the first blessing, a knowing head is the second.
> THOMAS JEFFERSON (1743–1826). Letter to Peter Carr, 19 August 1785

May the force be with you.
> GEORGE LUCAS (1944–). *Star Wars* (film), 1977

The Lord bless you and keep you:
The Lord make his face to shine upon you, and be gracious to you:
The Lord lift up his countenance upon you, and give you peace.
> MOSES (14th cent. B.C.). *Numbers* 6:24–26

May your happiest days of the past be your saddest days of your future.
> LAURENCE J. PETER (1919–1990). 29 September, *Peter's Almanac*, 1982
> See Curses: Saying (Chinese) (1)

May you live all the days of your life.
> JONATHAN SWIFT (1667–1745). *A Complete Collection of Polite and Ingenious Conversation*, 2, 1738

May God deny you peace, but give you glory!
> MIGUEL de UNAMUNO (1864–1936). Closing words, *Tragic Sense of Life*, 1913, tr. J. E. Crawford Flitch, 1921

Dieu et liberté! [God and liberty!]
> VOLTAIRE (1694–1778). The benediction given to Benjamin Franklin's grandson. In Samuel Arthur Bent, comp., *Familiar Short Sayings of Great Men*, 5th ed. rev., p. 553, 1887

✾

May your body leave your soul before your soul leaves your body.
> ANONYMOUS

God bless you.
> SAYING

BLUNDERS

See also • Errors ○ Failure: Elbert Hubbard ○ Mistakes

The man who never makes enny blunders seldum makes enny good hits.
> JOSH BILLINGS (1818–1885). "Kindling Wood," *Everybody's Friend, or; Josh Billing's Encyclopedia and Proverbial Philosophy of Wit and Humor*, 1874

They say [Woodrow] Wilson has blundered. Perhaps he has, but I notice he usually blunders forward.
> THOMAS ALVA EDISON (1847–1931). In John Dos Passos, *Mr. Wilson's War*, 2.4, 1963

It is worse than a crime. It is a blunder.
> JOSEPH FOUCHÉ (1759–1820). French police minister. Referring to the arrest and execution of the Duke of Enghien, whom Napoleon believed was conspiring against him, 21 March 1804. In Albert Carr, *Napoleon Speaks*, 8, 1941
> See Vietnam War: Dean Acheson

In placing civil disobedience before constructive work I was wrong, and I did not profit by the Himalayan blunder that I had committed.
> MOHANDAS K. GANDHI (1869–1948). *Gandhi on Non-Violence*, 5, ed. Thomas Merton, 1964

Great blunders are often made, like large ropes, of a multitude of fibers.
> VICTOR HUGO (1802–1885). "Cosette," *Les Misérables*, 5.10, 1862, tr. Charles E. Wilbour, 1987

Success covers a multitude of blunders.
> GEORGE BERNARD SHAW (1856–1950)
> See Success: William Napier

Human blunders usually do more to shape history than human wickedness.
> A. J. P. TAYLOR (1906–1990). *The Origins of the Second World War*, 10, 1961

BODY

See also • Emotion ○ Face ○ Health ○ Mind ○ Mind & Body ○ Passion ○ Sex ○ Soul ○ Soul & Body ○ Temptation

My navel is a button to push when I want inside out.
Am I not more than a mass of entrails and rough tissue?
> BOB KAUFMAN (1925–1986). "Jail Poems" (6), 1959, *Solitudes Crowded with Loneliness*, 1965

To delight in the human body without shame, to enjoy it without adulteration, is no simple human prerogative: it comes only at the summit of a high culture.
> LEWIS MUMFORD (1895–1990). *The Conduct of Life*, 7.2, 1951

Anatomy is destiny.
> NAPOLEON (1769–1821). In Sigmund Freud, "On the Universal Tendency to Debasement in the Sphere of Love" (3), 1912, tr. James Strachey, 1957
> See Character: Heraclitus ○ Temperament: Anonymous

There is but one temple in the universe and that is the body of man.
> NOVALIS (1772–1801). Quoted by Thomas Carlyle, journal, 7 September 1830. In James Anthony Froude, *Thomas Carlyle: A History of the First Forty Years, 1795–1835*, 2.4, 1882

No one is free who is a slave to the body.

> SENECA THE YOUNGER (5? B.C.–A.D. 65). "On the Happy Life," *Moral Letters to Lucilius*, 92.33, tr. Richard M. Gummere, 1918

We should conduct ourselves not as if we ought to live for the body, but as if we could not live without it.

> SENECA THE YOUNGER (5? B.C.–A.D. 65). "On the Reasons for Withdrawing from the World," *Moral Letters to Lucilius*, 14.2, tr. Richard M. Gummere, 1918

My body which my dungeon is,
And yet my parks and palaces.

> ROBERT LOUIS STEVENSON (1850–1894). "My Body Which My Dungeon Is," *Underwoods*, 1887

Every man is the builder of a temple, called his body, to the god he worships, after a style purely his own, nor can he get off by hammering marble instead. We are all sculptors and painters, and our material is our own flesh and blood and bones.

> HENRY DAVID THOREAU (1817–1862). "Higher Laws," *Walden; or Life in the Woods*, 1854

Napoleon: Our body is a machine for living.

> LEO TOLSTOY (1828–1910). *War and Peace*, 3.2.29, 1863–1869, tr. Rosemary Edmonds, 1957

"I Sing the Body Electric."

> WALT WHITMAN (1819–1892). Poem title, 1855, *Leaves of Grass*, 1855–1892

If anything is sacred, the human body is sacred.

> WALT WHITMAN (1819–1892). "I Sing the Body Electric" (8), 1855, *Leaves of Grass*, 1855–1892

❦

I will praise thee, for I am fearfully *and* wonderfully made.

> ANONYMOUS (*BIBLE*). *Psalms* 139:14 (King James Version)

BOLDNESS

See also • Commanders: Archibald Percival Wavell ○ Courage: [especially] Seneca the Younger ○ Defiance ○ Success: Xerxes ○ Winning: Lord Byron

[Boldness] is ill in counsel, good in execution. . . . For in counsel it is good to see dangers, and in execution not to see them, except they be very great.

> FRANCIS BACON (1561–1626). "Of Boldness," *Essays*, 1625

In battle the greatest danger always threatens those who show the greatest fear. Boldness is a bulwark.

> CATILINE (108?–62 B.C.). Speech to his troops before a battle. In Sallust (86?–34? B.C.). *The War with Catiline*, 58.19, tr. J. C. Rolfe, 1921

Boldness, directed by an overruling intelligence, is the stamp of the hero.

> KARL von CLAUSEWITZ (1780–1831). *On War*, 3.6, 1832, tr. J. J. Graham, 1873

Audacity, and again audacity, and always audacity, and France is saved.

> DANTON (1759–1794). Speech before the National Assembly, Paris, 2 September 1792

Conscious merit may be justly bold.

> JOHN DRYDEN (1631–1700). *The Hind and the Panther*, 3.1381, 1687

Where Necessity pinches, Boldness is Prudence.

> THOMAS FULLER (1654–1734). Comp., *Gnomologia: Adages and Proverbs*, 5650, 1732

Nought venture, nought have.

> JOHN HEYWOOD (1497–1580). Comp., *A Dialogue Containing the Number of the Effectual Proverbs in the English Tongue*, 1.11, 1562 (Popular version: Nothing ventured, nothing gained.)

In difficult and desperate situations, the boldest plans are safest.

> LUCIUS MARCIUS (3rd cent. B.C.). Roman commander. In Livy (59 B.C.–A.D. 17), *The History of Rome*, 25.38
> See Crises: Henry A. Kissinger (2) Daring: Karl von Clausewitz

[Caesar] took great risks in the adventures into which he was pushed by his boldness; his genius got him out of his difficulties.

> NAPOLEON (1769–1821). Remark to Gen. Gaspard Gourgaud, 1817, *The Mind of Napoleon: A Selection from His Written and Spoken Words*, 300, ed. J. Christopher Herold, 1955

Confront boldness by being still more bold.

> NAPOLEON (1769–1821). Slightly modified. 1815–1818, *Talks of Napoleon at St. Helena* (with Gen. Gaspard Gourgaud), 10, tr. Elizabeth Wormeley Latimer, 1904

The "fog of war" works both ways. The enemy is as much in the dark as you are. BE BOLD!!!!!

> GEORGE S. PATTON, JR. (1885–1945). Notebook, 1921–1922. In Martin Blumenson, *The Patton Papers, 1885–1940*, 1972

Take calculated risks. That is quite different from being rash.

> GEORGE S. PATTON, JR. (1885–1945)

Be bold, Be bold, and everywhere Be bold.

> EDMUND SPENSER (1553?–1599?). *The Faerie Queene*, 3.11.54, 1590–1596

❦

Always bold, sometimes foolish.
> SAYING

Boldness for getting; prudence for keeping.
> SAYING

Boldness sharpens the sword.
> SAYING

BOOKS

See also • Art ○ Autobiography ○ Biography ○ Children's Learning: Rousseau (3) ○ Conversation: Montaigne, Saying (Chinese) ○ Critics: Examples ○ Editors ○ Education ○ Freedom of the Press ○ Journals ○ Knowledge: [especially] John Wesley ○ Learning (Knowledge) ○ Libraries ○ Literature ○ Media ○ Memoirs ○ Publishers ○ Reading ○ Scholars ○ Study: Lord Chesterfield ○ Wisdom & Knowledge: Saying (Jewish) ○ Words ○ Writers ○ Writing

A real book is not one that's read, but one that reads us.
W. H. AUDEN (1907–1973). Recalled on his death, 28 September 1973

Some books are to be tasted, others to be swallowed, and some few to be chewed and digested.
FRANCIS BACON (1561–1626). "Of Studies," *Essays,* 1625

Some books . . . may be read by deputy, and extracts made of them by others.
FRANCIS BACON (1561–1626). "Of Studies," *Essays,* 1625

One may recollect generally that certain thoughts or facts are to be found in a certain book; but without a good index such a recollection may hardly be more available than that of the cabin boy, who knew where the ship's tea kettle was because he saw it fall overboard.
HORACE BINNEY (1780–1875). Letter to S. Austin Allibone, 20 February 1866

The oldest books are only just out to those who have not read them.
SAMUEL BUTLER (1835–1902). *Further Extracts from the Note-Books of Samuel Butler,* 5, ed. A. T. Bartholomew, 1934

In five minutes the earth would be a desert, and you cling to books.
ELIAS CANETTI (1905–1994). 1982, *The Secret Heart of the Clock: Notes, Aphorisms, Fragments: 1973–1985,* tr. Joel Agee, 1989

What one knows best is . . . what one has learned not from books but as a result of books, through the reflections to which they have given rise.
CHAMFORT (1741–1794). *Maxims and Thoughts,* 6, 1796, tr. W. S. Merwin, 1984

The diffusion of these silent teachers, books, through the whole community, is to work greater effects than artillery, machinery, and legislation. Its peaceful agency is to supersede stormy revolutions.
WILLIAM ELLERY CHANNING (1780–1842). "Self-Culture," address, Boston, September 1838

The easiest books are generally the best, for whatever author is obscure and difficult in his own language certainly does not think clearly.
LORD CHESTERFIELD (1694–1773). Letter to his son, 8 February 1750

The dearest ones of time, the strongest friends of the soul— BOOKS.
EMILY DICKINSON (1830–1886). Letter, quoted by Richard B. Sweall, "In Search of Emily Dickinson." In William Zinsser, ed., *Extraordinary Lives: The Art and Craft of American Biography,* 1988

Books are for the scholars' idle times. When he can read God directly, the hour is too precious to be wasted in other men's transcripts of their readings. But when the intervals of darkness come, as come they must—we repair to the lamps which were kindled by their ray, to guide our steps to the East again, where the dawn is.
RALPH WALDO EMERSON (1803–1882). "The American Scholar," address, Harvard University, Cambridge (Massachusetts), 31 August 1837

Let us answer a book of ink with a book of flesh and blood.
RALPH WALDO EMERSON (1803–1882). Journal, 1841, undated

In Roxbury, in 1825, I read Cotton's translation of Montaigne. It seemed to me as if I had written the book myself in some former life, so sincerely it spoke my thought and experience.
RALPH WALDO EMERSON (1803–1882). Journal, March 1843

Books are worth reading that sketch a principle, as lectures are. All others are tickings of a clock. And we have so much less time to live—the Robbers!
RALPH WALDO EMERSON (1803–1882). Journal, October 1848

[The best service of books is] that they set us free from themselves also. We read a line, a word, that lifts us; we rise into a succession of thoughts that is better than the book.
RALPH WALDO EMERSON (1803–1882). Journal, October 1874

Every book is good to read which sets the reader in a working mood.
RALPH WALDO EMERSON (1803–1882). "Greatness," *Letters and Social Aims,* 1876

I don't like to read books; they muss up my mind.
HENRY FORD (1863–1947). In Dixon Wecter, *The Hero in America: A Chronicle of Hero-Worship,* 16.1, 1941

One always tends to overpraise a long book, because one has got through it.
E. M. FORSTER (1879–1970). "T. E. Lawrence," *Abinger Harvest: A Miscellany,* 1927

The only books that influence us are those for which we are ready, and which have gone a little farther down our particular path than we have yet got ourselves.
E. M. FORSTER (1879–1970). "A Book That Influenced Me," *Two Cheers for Democracy,* 1951

Read much, but not many Books.
BENJAMIN FRANKLIN (1706–1790). *Poor Richard's Almanack,* February 1738

Learning hath gained most by those books . . . which the printers have lost.
THOMAS FULLER (1608–1661). *The Holy State and the Profane State,* 3.18.6, 1642, ed. James Nichols, 1841

Read not Books alone, but Man also; and chiefly thyself.
THOMAS FULLER (1654–1734). Comp., *Introductio ad Prudentiam,* 273, 1731

Out of the Books thou readest, extract what thou likest; and then single out some Particular from the rest for that Day's Meditation.
THOMAS FULLER (1654–1734). Comp., *Introductio ad Prudentiam,* 1640, 1731

All good books are alike in that they are truer than if they had really happened.
ERNEST HEMINGWAY (1899–1961). "Old Newsman Writes: A Letter from Cuba," *Esquire,* December 1934
See Truth: Ken Kesey

I always believed in life rather than in books.

> OLIVER WENDELL HOLMES, SR. (1809–1894). *The Autocrat of the Breakfast-Table,* 6, 1858
>
> See Reading: Logan Pearsall Smith

Life-transforming ideas have always come to me through books.

> BELL HOOKS (1952–). *Outlaw Culture: Resisting Representation,* 8, 1994

I do not read a book: I hold a conversation with the author.

> ELBERT HUBBARD (1856–1915). *A Thousand and One Epigrams,* p. 23, 1911

The best service a book can render you is not to impart truth, but to make you think it out for yourself.

> ELBERT HUBBARD (1856–1915). *The Note Book of Elbert Hubbard,* p. 158, comp. Elbert Hubbard II, 1927

Everything comes t' him who waits but a loaned book.

> KIN HUBBARD (1868–1930). *Abe Martin's Primer,* unpaged, 1914

Books worth reading are worth re-reading.

> HOLBROOK JACKSON (1874–1948). *Maxims of Books and Reading,* 3, 1934

If we are imprisoned in ourselves, books provide us with the means of escape. If we have run too far away from ourselves, books show us the way back.

> HOLBROOK JACKSON (1874–1948). *Maxims of Books and Reading,* 7, 1934

Great books conserve time.

> HOLBROOK JACKSON (1874–1948). Closing maxim, *Maxims of Books and Reading,* 1934

I cannot live without books.

> THOMAS JEFFERSON (1743–1826). Letter to John Adams, 10 June 1815

Some men are born only to suck out the poison of books.

> BEN JONSON (1572–1637). "Of Learning to Read Well, Speak Well, and Write Well" (4), *Timber: Or, Discoveries,* 1640, ed. Ralph S. Walker, 1953

A book must be the ax for the frozen sea within us.

> FRANZ KAFKA (1883–1924). Letter to Oskar Pollak, 27 January 1904

Books are a narcotic.

> FRANZ KAFKA (1883–1924). In Gustav Janouch, *Conversations with Kafka,* p. 36, tr. Goronwy Rees, 1953

Books which are no books. . . .
  I confess that it moves my spleen to see these *things in books' clothing.*

> CHARLES LAMB (1775–1834). "Detached Thoughts on Books and Reading," *The Last Essays of Elia,* 1833

When a book and a head collide and a hollow sound is heard, must it always have come from the book?

> GEORG CHRISTOPH LICHTENBERG (1742–1799). *Aphorisms,* D.66, 1806, tr. R. J. Hollingdale, 1990

A book is a mirror: if an ape looks into it, an apostle is unlikely to look out.

> GEORG CHRISTOPH LICHTENBERG (1742–1799). *Aphorisms,* F.17, 1806, tr. R. J. Hollingdale, 1990

People don't realize how a man's whole life can be changed by *one* book.

> MALCOLM X (1925–1965) (with ALEX HALEY). Epilogue to *The Autobiography of Malcolm X,* 1965

In the main, there are two sorts of books: those that no one reads and those that no one ought to read.

> H. L. MENCKEN (1880–1956). *A Little Book in C Major,* 7.5, 1916

Deep vers'd in books and shallow in himself.

> JOHN MILTON (1608–1674). *Paradise Regain'd,* 4.327, 1671

I have a low opinion of books; they are but piles of stones set up to show coming travelers where other minds have been. . . . One day's exposure to mountains is better than cartloads of books.

> JOHN MUIR (1838–1914). "The Philosophy of John Muir," *The Wilderness World of John Muir,* comp. Edwin Way Teale, 1954

To read a book early in the morning, at daybreak, in the vigor and dawn of one's strength—this is sheer viciousness!

> FRIEDRICH NIETZSCHE (1844–1900). "Why I Am So Clever" (8), *Ecce Homo,* 1908, tr. Clifton Fadiman, 1927

Most books are propaganda, direct or indirect.

> GEORGE ORWELL (1903–1950). Review of *The Civil War in Spain* by Frank Jellinek, 8 July 1938, *The Collected Essays, Journalism and Letters of George Orwell,* vol. 1, ed. Sonia Orwell and Ian Angus, 1968

The Bookful Blockhead.

> ALEXANDER POPE (1688–1744). *An Essay on Criticism,* l. 612, 1711
>
> See Scholars: Benjamin Franklin (1)

Do not read my book if you expect me to tell you everything.

> ROUSSEAU (1712–1778). *Emile; or, Treatise on Education,* 2, 1762, tr. Barbara Foxley, 1911

If a book is worth reading, it is worth buying.

> JOHN RUSKIN (1819–1900). "Of Kings' Treasuries," *Sesame and Lilies,* 1865

You can't tell a book by its movie.

> LOUIS A. SAFIAN. Comp., *The Book of Updated Proverbs,* 4, 1967

Holden Caulfield: What really knocks me out is a book that, when you're all done reading it, you wish the author that wrote it was a terrific friend of yours and you could call him up on the phone whenever you felt like it. That doesn't happen much though.

> J. D. SALINGER (1919–). *The Catcher in the Rye,* 3, 1951

Books, that paper memory of mankind.

> ARTHUR SCHOPENHAUER (1788–1860). "The Art of Literature: On Men of Learning," *Essays of Arthur Schopenhauer,* tr. T. Bailey Saunders, 1851

Whatever the quality of my works may be, read them as if I were still seeking, and were not aware of, the truth, and were seeking it obstinately, too.

> SENECA THE YOUNGER (5? B.C.–A.D. 65). "On Sophistical Argumentation," *Moral Letters to Lucilius,* 45.4, tr. Richard M. Gummere, 1918

People get nothing out of books but what they bring to them.

> GEORGE BERNARD SHAW (1856–1950). In Hesketh Pearson, "Grand Old Boy," *George Bernard Shaw: His Life and Personality,* 1963 (1942)

Books are good enough in their own way, but they are a mighty bloodless substitute for life.

> ROBERT LOUIS STEVENSON (1850–1894). "An Apology for Idlers," *Virginibus Puerisque,* 1881

One sure window into a person's soul is his reading list.

> MARY B. W. TABOR. "Book Notes," *New York Times,* 14 June 1995

An honest book's the noblest work of Man.

> HENRY DAVID THOREAU (1817–1862). Letter to his sister Helen Thoreau, 23 January 1840
> See Honesty: Alexander Pope

Books . . . which even make us dangerous to existing institutions—such call I good books.

> HENRY DAVID THOREAU (1817–1862). "Sunday," *A Week on the Concord and Merrimack Rivers,* 1849

Books are the treasured wealth of the world and the fit inheritance of generations and nations. . . . Their authors are a natural and irresistible aristocracy in every society, and more than kings or emperors, exert an influence on mankind.

> HENRY DAVID THOREAU (1817–1862). "Reading," *Walden; or Life in the Woods,* 1854

No one has stepped twice into the same river. But did anyone ever step twice into the same book?

> MARINA TSVETAEVA (1892–1941). *Pushkin and Pugachev,* 1937
> See Change: Heraclitus

Persons attempting to find a motive in this narrative will be prosecuted; persons attempting to find a moral in it will be banished; persons attempting to find a plot in it will be shot.

> MARK TWAIN (1835–1910). "Notice," *The Adventures of Huckleberry Finn,* 1884

"Classic." A book which people praise and don't read.

> MARK TWAIN (1835–1910). *Following the Equator: A Journey Around the World,* 25 (epigraph), 1897

Books are to be call'd for, and supplied, on the assumption that the process of reading is not a half sleep, but, in highest sense, an exercise, a gymnast's struggle; that the reader is to do something for himself, must be on the alert, must himself or herself construct indeed the poem, argument, history, metaphysical essay—the text furnishing the hints, the clue, the start or frame-work. Not the book needs so much to be the complete thing, but the reader of the book does. That were to make a nation of supple and athletic minds, well-train'd, intuitive, used to depend on themselves, and not on a few coteries of writers.

> WALT WHITMAN (1819–1892). *Democratic Vistas,* 1871, *Walt Whitman: Complete Poetry and Collected Prose,* ed. Justin Kaplan, p. 992–993, 1982

The books that the world calls immoral are books that show the world its own shame.

OSCAR WILDE (1854–1900). *The Picture of Dorian Gray,* 19, 1891

Enough of Science and of Art;
Close up those barren leaves;
Come forth, and bring with you a heart
That watches and receives.

> WILLIAM WORDSWORTH (1770–1850). Closing lines, "The Tables Turned," 1798

🌿

Of making many books there is no end, and much study is a weariness of the flesh.

> ANONYMOUS (*BIBLE*). *Ecclesiastes* 12:12

A book is a present you can open again and again.

> ANONYMOUS. Sign in the window of the Albatross Book Store, San Francisco, 1988

A book without an index is like a compass without a needle.

> ANONYMOUS

You can't judge a book by its cover.

> SAYING (AMERICAN)
> See Intelligence, Military: Anonymous

Beware of the man of one book.

> SAYING (ITALIAN)
> See Ideas: Alain

BOREDOM

See also • Idleness ○ Indifference ○ Life: H. L. Mencken ○ Work: Bertrand Russell (2)

Ennui has made more gamblers than avarice, more drunkards than thirst, and perhaps as many suicides as despair.

> C. C. COLTON (1780–1832). *Lacon: or, Many Things in Few Words; Addressed to Those Who Think,* 1.259, 1823
> See Suicide: George Sanders

Man is the only animal that can be *bored.*

> ERICH FROMM (1900–1980). *The Sane Society,* 3 ("The Human Situation"), 1955

Against boredom the gods themselves fight in vain.

> FRIEDRICH NIETZSCHE (1844–1900). *The Anti-Christ,* 48, 1895, tr. R. J. Hollingdale, 1968
> See Stupidity: Friedrich von Schiller

Wars, pogroms, and persecution have all been part of the flight from boredom. . . . Boredom is therefore a vital problem for the moralist, since at least half the sins of mankind are caused by the fear of it.

> BERTRAND RUSSELL (1872–1970). *The Conquest of Happiness,* 4, 1930

Hamlet: How weary, stale, flat and unprofitable
Seem to me all the uses of this world!

> SHAKESPEARE (1564–1616). *Hamlet,* 1.2.133, 1600

🌿

I am never bored when I am present.

ANONYMOUS. Quoted by Norman Parkinson. In Michael Gross, "A Photographer's 50 Years in Fashion: No Still Life," *New York Times,* 15 December 1987

BORES

See also • Classes, Two: Lord Byron ○ Manners ○ Politics: Richard M. Nixon (2)

Windbag: Have I bored you to death with my chatter?
Aristotle: Not really, for I was paying no attention to you.
> ARISTOTLE (384–322 B.C.). Format adapted. In Diogenes Laertius (A.D. 3rd cent.). *Lives of Eminent Philosophers,* 5.1, tr. R. D. Hicks, 1925

He's the kind of a bore who's here today and here tomorrow.
> BINNIE BARNES

Bore, *n.* A person who talks when you wish him to listen.
> AMBROSE BIERCE (1842–1914). *The Devil's Dictionary,* p. 18, 1911, Dover edition, 1958

He iz a man ov small *caliber,* but a good deal ov bore.
> JOSH BILLINGS (1818–1885). "Singular Beings" ("The Pompous Man"), *Everybody's Friend, or; Josh Billing's Encyclopedia and Proverbial Philosophy of Wit and Humor,* 1874

Everyone is a bore to someone. That is unimportant. The thing to avoid is being a bore to oneself.
> GERALD BRENAN (1894–1987). "Life," *Thoughts in a Dry Season: A Miscellany,* 1978

What's wrong with being a boring kind of guy?
> GEORGE BUSH (1924–). In *Daily Telegraph* (British newspaper), 28 April 1988

The man who lets himself be bored is even more contemptible than the bore.
> SAMUEL BUTLER (1835–1902). *The Fair Haven,* 3, 1873

As I usually do when I want to get rid of someone whose conversation bores me, I pretended to agree.
> ALBERT CAMUS (1913–1960). *The Stranger,* 2.1, 1942, tr. Stuart Gilbert, 1946

He is not only dull himself, but the cause of dullness in others.
> SAMUEL FOOTE (1720–1777). Quoted by Samuel Johnson under the date of 30 March 1783. In James Boswell, *The Life of Samuel Johnson,* 1791

> See Wit: Shakespeare (1)

It is the peculiarity of the bore that he is the last person to find himself out.
> OLIVER WENDELL HOLMES, SR. (1809–1894). *Over the Teacups,* 4, 1891

There is a certain weary look that appears on the faces of those who are bored. Look out for the weary look when you associate with people.
> E. W. HOWE (1853–1937). *Ventures in Common Sense,* 32.11, 1919

Some people can stay longer in an hour than others do in a week.
> WILLIAM DEAN HOWELLS (1837–1920)

Sir, he was dull in company, dull in his closet, dull everywhere. He was dull in a new way, and that made many people think him GREAT.
> SAMUEL JOHNSON (1709–1784). 28 March 1775. In James Boswell, *The Life of Samuel Johnson,* 1791

Sir, you have but two topics, yourself and me. I am sick of both.
> SAMUEL JOHNSON (1709–1784). Remark to a Mr. Levett who had been pestering him with questions, May 1776. In James Boswell, *The Life of Samuel Johnson,* 1791

We often forgive those who bore us, but we cannot forgive those who find us boring.
> LA ROCHEFOUCAULD (1613–1680). *Maxims,* 304, 1665, tr. Leonard Tancock, 1959

Only one person in a thousand is a bore, and he is interesting because he is one person in a thousand.
> HAROLD NICOLSON (1886–1968). Remark to his son. In Alden Whitman, "Sir Harold Nicolson Dead at 81; Chronicler of Politics in Britain," *New York Times,* 2 May 1968

A bore is a person not interested in you.
> MARY PETTIBONE POOLE. "Narcissus Was a Woman," *A Glass Eye at a Keyhole,* 1938

Dylan talked copiously, then stopped. "Somebody's boring me," he said, "I think it's me."
> DYLAN THOMAS (1914–1953). In Rayner Heppenstall, *Four Absentees,* 16, 1960

The secret of being a bore . . . is to tell everything.
> VOLTAIRE (1694–1778). "De la nature de l'homme" (l. 172), *Discours en Vers Sur l'Homme,* 1737

❦

A bore is a man who, when you ask him how he is, tells you.
> ANONYMOUS (AMERICAN). In Bert Leston Taylor, *The So-Called Human Race,* p. 163, 1922

Bores like to listen to themselves talk more than others do.
> ANONYMOUS

Bores never forgive those they bore.
> ANONYMOUS

BOSTON

See also • Cities

I have just returned from Boston. It is the only thing to do if you find yourself up there.
> FRED ALLEN (1894–1956). Letter to Groucho Marx, 12 June 1953

Where the Lowells talk to the Cabots,
And the Cabots talk only to God.
> JOHN COLLINS BOSSIDY (1860–1928). Toasting Boston, during a Holy Cross College alumni dinner at Harvard University, 1910

BOXING

See also • Sports

I am the greatest.

> MUHAMMAD ALI (1942–). Signature line. In Wilfrid Sheed, *Muhammad Ali,* 1976

Float like a butterfly,
Sting like a bee,
Your hands can't hit
What your eyes can't see!

> DREW "BUNDINI" BROWN. Muhammad Ali's trainer. Often attributed to Ali

Honey, I just forgot to duck.

> JACK DEMPSEY (1895–1983). Telephone remark to his wife Estelle after losing the world heavyweight title to Gene Tunney in Philadelphia, 23 September 1926. President Ronald Reagan jokingly said the same thing (without the "just") to his wife, Nancy, after being shot and severely wounded by John W. Hinckley, Jr., in Washington, 30 March 1981

A champion is one who gets up when he can't.

> JACK DEMPSEY (1895–1983). Summing up the fight game

Get me that Louis—I'll moider that bum!

> "TWO-TON" TONY GALENTO. Remark to his manager Joe Jacobs, early 1939 (on 28 June 1939, Joe Louis scored a fourth-round technical knock-out over Galento in their heavyweight title fight in New York City). In Joe Louis, *My Story,* 14, 1947

Reporter: [Billy] Conn is going to use plenty [of] footwork, and do lots of running.
Louis: He can run, but he can't hide.

> JOE LOUIS (1914–1981). Format adapted. Before defeating Conn in a heavyweight title fight in 1946. *My Life Story,* 21, 1947

I zigged when I should have zagged.

> JACK ROPER. Explaining why he was knocked out by Joe Louis in a heavyweight title fight, 17 April 1939

You don't understand. I coulda had class. I coulda been a contender. I coulda been somebody. Instead of a bum, which is what I am! Let's face it. It was you, Charley!

> BUDD SCHULBERG (1914–). *On the Waterfront* (film), 1954, spoken by Marlon Brando to his brother, Rod Steiger, who had pressured him into throwing an important prizefight years before

A powder-puff punch and a glass jaw—that's a great combination!

> BUDD SCHULBERG (1914–). *The Harder They Fall* (film), 1956, spoken by Humphrey Bogart (in the role of a cynical sportswriter)

✤

Hungry fighters win fights.

> SAYING. "The first maxim of the prizefight manager." In Norman Mailer, "The Third Presidential Paper—The Existential Hero," 1960, *The Presidential Papers,* 1963

BRAIN

See also • Brainwashing ○ Mind ○ Success: Herbert Spencer

My second favorite organ!

> WOODY ALLEN (1935–) and MARSHALL BRICKMAN (1941–). *Sleeper* (film), 1973

Brain, *n.* An apparatus with which we think that we think.

> AMBROSE BIERCE (1842–1914). *The Devil's Dictionary,* p. 19, 1911, Dover edition, 1958

The Brain—is wider than the Sky—
For—put them side by side—
The one the other will contain
With ease—and You—beside—

> EMILY DICKINSON (1830–1886). "The Brain—is wider than the sky," 1862?

The human brain is unique in that it is the only container of which it can be said that the more you put into it, the more it will hold.

> GLENN DOMAN. *How to Teach Your Baby to Read: The Gentle Revolution,* 2, 1964

The brain grows to the exact modes in which it has been exercised.

> WILLIAM JAMES (1842–1910). *The Principles of Psychology,* 22, 1890

The brain is viewed as an appendage of the genital glands.

> CARL G. JUNG (1875–1961). On Freud's theory of sexuality. In "The Wise Old Man," *Time,* 14 February 1955

There are three different kinds of brains: the one understands things unassisted, the other understands things when shown by others, the third understands neither alone nor with the explanations of others. The first kind is most excellent, the second also excellent, but the third useless.

> MACHIAVELLI (1469–1527). *The Prince,* 22, 1513, tr. Luigi Ricci, 1903

More brain, O Lord, more brain! Or we shall mar
Utterly this fair garden we might win.

> GEORGE MEREDITH (1828–1909). *Modern Love,* 48, 1862

The brain is nature's supreme achievement.

> FRIEDRICH NIETZSCHE (1844–1900). *Philosophy and Truth: Selections from Nietzsche's Notebooks of the Early 1870's,* 7.A.3, tr. Daniel Breazeale, 1979

Between my brain and me there is always a layer that I cannot penetrate.

> JULES RENARD (1864–1910). Journal, February 1910, tr. Louise Bogan and Elizabeth Roget, 1964

The brain is like a muscle. When it is in use, we feel very good. Understanding is joyous.

> CARL SAGAN (1934–1996). *Broca's Brain: Reflections on the Romance of Science,* 2, 1979

Many of the brain's remaining mysteries need for solution mere wiring diagrams; yet a metaphysical halo lingers about the mystery of self-consciousness. A computer, after all, of sufficient complexity could handle the stimuli and responses of living without any component that says "I." But within the human—and, dare we think, the cetacean and simian?—brain there is a watcher, who always recedes, and who answers every question with another question.

> JOHN UPDIKE (1932–). "Who Wants to Know," 1977, *Hugging the Shore: Essays and Criticism,* 1983

Our brains are no longer conditioned for reverence and awe. We cannot imagine a Second Coming that would not be cut down to size by the televised evening news, or a Last Judgment not subject to pages of holier-than-Thou second-guessing in the *The New York Review of Books.*

> JOHN UPDIKE (1932–). *Self-Consciousness: Memoirs*, 6, 1989

I not only use all the brains I have, but all I can borrow.

> WOODROW WILSON (1856–1924). 1914, "Woodrow Wilson in His Own Words," ed. Dorothy Fosdick, *New York Times Magazine*, 10 June 1956

BRAINWASHING

See also • Brain ○ Conversion ○ Cruelty ○ Dehumanization ○ Education ○ Freedom of Thought ○ Indoctrination ○ Manipulation ○ Propaganda ○ Punishment ○ Rights: Germaine Greer ○ Torture ○ Tyranny

The term "brainwashing" was first used by an American journalist, Edward Hunter, as a translation of the colloquialism *hsi nao* (literally "wash brain") which he quoted from Chinese informants who described its use after the Communist takeover [in 1949].

> J. A. C. BROWN (1911–1964). *Techniques of Persuasion: From Propaganda to Brainwashing*, 10, 1963

A few months in the solitary cell renders a prisoner strangely impressible. The chaplain can then make the brawny navvy cry like a child; he can work on his feelings in almost any way he pleases; he can, so to speak, photograph his thoughts, wishes and opinions on his patient's mind, and fill his mouth with his own phrases and language.

> W. L. CLAY (19th cent.). *The Prison Chaplain: Memoirs of the Rev. John Clay*, 1867. In Michael Ignatieff, *A Just Measure of Pain*, 7.4, 1978

The aim of brainwashing is to retrieve enemies and transform rather than eliminate them.

> JACQUES ELLUL (1912–1994). Appendix (2.3) to *Propaganda: The Formation of Men's Attitudes*, 1962, tr. Konrad Kellen and Jean Learner, 1965

What [the Pavlovian doctors] had learned from animals could be used to intrude into the mind and soul of man, to warp and change his brain. Brain-changing was the culmination of this whole evil process, when actual damage was done to a man's mind through drugs, hypnotism, or other means, so that a memory of what had actually happened would be wiped out of his mind and a new memory of what never happened inserted.

> EDWARD HUNTER (1902–1978). *Brainwashing: The Story of Men Who Defied It*, 2, 1956

Brainwashing was revealed as a political strategy for expansion and control made up of two processes. One is the conditioning, or softening-up, process primarily for control purposes. The other is an indoctrination or persuasion process for conversion purposes.

> EDWARD HUNTER (1902–1978). *Brainwashing: The Story of Men Who Defied It*, 8, 1956

If these emotions [i.e., fear, rage or anxiety] are kept at a high pitch of intensity for a long enough time, the brain goes "on strike." When this happens, new behavior patterns may be installed with the greatest of ease.

> ALDOUS HUXLEY (1894–1963). "Brainwashing," *Brave New World Revisited*, 1958

It seems to me perfectly in the cards that there will be within the next generation or so a pharmacological method of making people love their servitude, and producing . . . a kind of painless concentration camp for entire societies, so that people will in fact have their liberties taken away from them but will rather enjoy it, because they will be distracted from any desire to rebel by propaganda, brainwashing, or brainwashing enhanced by pharmacological methods.

> ALDOUS HUXLEY (1894–1963). 1959. In John Marks, *The Search for the "Manchurian Candidate": The CIA and Mind Control*, pt. 2 (epigraph), 1980

The only way to strengthen one's defenses against an organized attack on the mind and will is to understand better what the enemy is trying to do and to outwit him. Of course, one can vow to hold out until death, but even the relief of death is in the hands of the inquisitor. People can be brought to the threshold of death and then be stimulated into life again so that the torments can be renewed. Attempts at suicide are foreseen and can be forestalled.

In my opinion hardly anyone can resist such treatment. It all depends on the ego strength of the person and the exhaustive technique of the inquisitor.

> JOOST A. M. MEERLOO (1903–1976). *The Rape of the Mind: The Psychology of Thought Control, Menticide, and Brainwashing*, 1, 1956

Will you understand, Winston, that no one whom we bring to this place ever leaves our hands uncured? We are not interested in those stupid crimes that you have committed. The Party is not interested in the overt act: the thought is all we care about. We do not merely destroy our enemies; we change them.

> GEORGE ORWELL (1903–1950). *Nineteen Eighty-Four*, 3.2, 1949

We shall crush you down to the point from which there is no coming back. Things will happen to you from which you could not recover, if you lived a thousand years. Never again will you be capable of ordinary human feeling. Everything will be dead inside you. Never again will you be capable of love, or friendship, or joy of living, or laughter, or curiosity, or courage, or integrity. You will be hollow. We shall squeeze you empty, and then we shall fill you with ourselves.

> GEORGE ORWELL (1903–1950). *Nineteen Eighty-Four*, 3.2, 1949
> See Power: Orwell (4)

You must love Big Brother. It is not enough to obey him; you must love him.

> GEORGE ORWELL (1903–1950). *Nineteen Eighty-Four*, 3.4, 1949

The victim must prove that he has come round to the ideology which kills him, and that he has therefore agreed to his own crucifixion. That is why confession without apostasy is not enough. The accused, after admitting his crime, has also to show himself clear of past delusions. . . . To make apostasy durable, to give it the semblance of free action, a real transformation of personality is needed: free will and conscience must vanish, another will and another conscience have to be infused into the living corpse whose soul has been destroyed. The justice which tortured was nothing to what we have today: the justice which dements.

> JEAN ROLIN (1900–?). *Police Drugs*, 8.4, tr. Laurence J. Bendit, 1956

A study of the techniques of modern political brainwashing and the eliciting of confessions shows that the interrogators are always in search of topics on which the victim is sensitive; they play on these until they force him to confess or believe whatever is desired. If nothing can be found in his past life to arouse feelings of anxiety or guilt, then suitable situations or interpretations of situations have to be invented to create them—as some psychiatrists did during World War II, to cause states of excitement and collapse in their patients during drug abreactive treatment.

> WILLIAM SARGANT (1907–1988). British psychiatrist. *Battle for the Mind: A Physiology of Conversion and Brain-Washing,* 7, 1956

Brainwashing [is] the systematic, scientific and coercive elimination of the individuality of the mind of another.

> ALAN W. SCHEFLIN (1942–) and EDWARD M. OPTON, JR. (1936–). *The Mind Manipulators: A Non-Fiction Account,* 2, 1978

Obtaining *compliance* is relatively easy if one has total control over a prisoner. Almost everyone will confess and collaborate, at least to a degree, if enough pressure is applied. But forcible *conversion*—the more dramatic and popular image of brainwashing—is exceedingly difficult. The only way to distinguish between compliance and conversion is to release the prisoner into his or her former environment. The true convert is the one who, exposed to the pressures of his old life, does not backslide. Forcible conversion of that sort is very rare; not a single case occurred among the Korean [War] POWs.

> ALAN W. SCHEFLIN (1942–) and EDWARD M. OPTON, JR. (1936–). *The Mind Manipulators: A Non-Fiction Account,* 2, 1978

The influence process as exemplified in coercive persuasion is best thought of as a complex series of events occurring over a considerable period of time. These events can best be understood in terms of a model of change which includes three phases—unfreezing, changing, and refreezing. For influence to occur there must be induced a motive to change, there must be available some model or other information source which provides a direction of change, and there must be reward for and support of whatever change occurs.

> EDGAR H. SCHEIN (with INGE SCHNEIER and CURTIS H. BARKER). Conclusion to *Coercive Persuasion: A Socio-psychological Analysis of the "Brainwashing" of American Civilian Prisoners by the Chinese Communists,* 1961

There is a world of difference in the content of what is transmitted in religious orders, prisons, educational institutions, mental hospitals, and thought reform centers. But there are striking similarities in the manner in which the influence occurs.

> EDGAR H. SCHEIN (with INGE SCHNEIER and CURTIS H. BARKER). Conclusion to *Coercive Persuasion: A Socio-psychological Analysis of the "Brainwashing" of American Civilian Prisoners by the Chinese Communists,* 1961

Brainwashing: the forcible application of prolonged and intensive indoctrination sometimes including mental torture in an attempt to induce someone to give up basic political, social, or religious beliefs and attitudes and to accept contrasting regimented ideas.

> *WEBSTER'S THIRD NEW INTERNATIONAL DICTIONARY OF THE ENGLISH LANGUAGE UNABRIDGED,* ed. Philip Babcock Gove, p. 267, 1961

BRAVERY

See also • Courage: [especially] Tacitus ○ Courage, Moral ○ Fortune: Terence ○ Valor

It is easy to be brave from a safe distance.

> AESOP (6th cent. B.C.). "The Wolf and the Kid," *Fables,* tr. Joseph Jacobs, 1894

The coward calls the brave man rash, the rash man calls him a coward.

> ARISTOTLE (384–322 B.C.). *Nichomachean Ethics,* 2.8, tr. J. A. K. Thomson, 1953
> See Courage: Aristotle

The brave man is the man who faces or fears the right thing for the right purpose in the right manner at the right moment.

> ARISTOTLE (384–322 B.C.). *Nichomachean Ethics,* 3.7, tr. J. A. K. Thomson, 1953

Bravery is the capacity to perform properly even when scared half to death.

> OMAR N. BRADLEY (1893–1981)

The unreturning brave.

> LORD BYRON (1788–1824). *Childe Harold's Pilgrimage,* 3.27, 1812–1818

The truly brave are soft of heart and eyes,
And feel for what their duty bids them do.

> LORD BYRON (1788–1824). *Marino Faliero, Doge of Venice,* 2.2, 1821

None but the brave deserves the fair.

> JOHN DRYDEN (1631–1700). "Alexander's Feast," l. 15, 1697

A coward turns away but a brave man's choice
Is danger.

> EURIPIDES (485?–406 B.C.). *Iphigenia in Tauris,* l. 115, tr. Witter Bynner, 1956

Brave Actions never want a Trumpet.

> THOMAS FULLER (1654–1734). Comp., *Gnomologia: Adages and Proverbs,* 1016, 1732

Some have been thought brave because they were afraid to run away.

> THOMAS FULLER (1654–1734). Comp., *Gnomologia: Adages and Proverbs,* 4214, 1732

Cowards are cruel, but the brave
Love mercy, and delight to save.

> JOHN GAY (1685–1732). *Fables,* 1.1, 1727–1738

Even the poorest fighters turn into brave men when they stand side by side.

> HOMER (8th? cent. B.C.). *The Iliad,* 13.235, tr. E. V. Rieu, 1950

Bravery is knowledge of the cowardice in the enemy.

> E. W. HOWE (1853–1937). *Country Town Sayings: A Collection of Paragraphs from The Atchison Globe,* 1911

Today brave, tomorrow in the grave.

JAMES HOWELL (1593–1666). Comp., "French" (p. 4), *Paroimiographia: Proverbs, or Old Sayed Sawes & Adages in English . . . Italian, French and Spanish,* 1659

Few men are brave by nature, but good discipline and experience make many so.

MACHIAVELLI (1469–1527). *The Art of War,* 7, 1521, tr. Ellis Farneworth, 1762

Familiarity with danger makes a brave man braver, but less daring.

HERMAN MELVILLE (1819–1891). *White Jacket,* 23, 1850

Any fool can be brave on a battlefield when it's be brave or else be killed.

MARGARET MITCHELL (1900–1949). *Gone with the Wind,* 31, 1936

My lads, you must not fear death; when soldiers brave death, they drive him into the enemy's ranks.

NAPOLEON (1769–1821). Speech to one of his regiments before the Battle of Jena (Germany), 14 October 1806

There is often more bravery in containing oneself and passing by: *in order* to spare oneself for a worthier enemy!

FRIEDRICH NIETZSCHE (1844–1900). "Of Old and New Law-Tables" (21), *Thus Spoke Zarathustra,* 1892, tr. R. J. Hollingdale, 1961

That man is not truly brave who is afraid either to seem to be or to be, when it suits him, a coward.

EDGAR ALLAN POE (1809–1849). December 1846, *Marginalia,* University Press of Virginia edition, 1981

To brave the lake in all its wrath! 'Twas not
To put your trust in God! 'Twas tempting Him.

FRIEDRICH von SCHILLER (1759–1805). *William Tell,* 3.1, 1804, tr. Theodore Martin, 1894

Brave men earn the right to shape their own destiny.

ARTHUR M. SCHLESINGER, JR. (1917–). "The Decline of Greatness," *Saturday Evening Post,* 1 November 1958

There's a fine line between being brave and being stupid.

TOM SEAVER (1944–). Baseball announcer. Television broadcast, NBC, 5 August 1989

Sometimes it is an act of bravery even to live.

SENECA THE YOUNGER (5? B.C.–A.D. 65). "On the Healing Power of the Mind," *Moral Letters to Lucilius,* 78.2, tr. Richard M. Gummere, 1918

Bravery is half victory.

SNORRI STURLUSON (A.D. 1179–1241). *Heimskringla.* In Ralph Waldo Emerson, journal, October 1850

Where there is a brave man, there is the thickest of the fight, there the post of honor.

HENRY DAVID THOREAU (1817–1862). Journal, 2 December 1839

We should be ready for all issues, not daring to die but daring to live. To the brave even danger is an ally.

HENRY DAVID THOREAU (1817–1862). Journal, December 1839

They are surely to be esteemed the bravest spirits who, having the clearest sense of both the pains and pleasures of life, do not on that account shrink from danger.

THUCYDIDES (460?–400? B.C.). *History of the Peloponnesian War,* 2.40, tr. Benjamin Jowett, 1930

☙

The brave may know defeat but never despair.

ANONYMOUS

BRITAIN

See England

BROTHERHOOD

See also • African Americans: Martin Luther King, Jr. (1) ○ America: Katherine Lee Bates, Marquis de Lafayette ○ Community ○ Internationalism ○ Love ○ Unity

For a' that and a' that,
It's coming yet, for a' that;
That man to man the world o'er
Shall brothers be for a' that.

ROBERT BURNS (1759–1796). "For a' That and a' That," 5, 1795

Am I my brother's keeper?

CAIN. *Genesis* 4:9

A mystic bond of brotherhood makes all men one.

THOMAS CARLYLE (1795–1881). "Goethe's Works," 1832, *Critical and Miscellaneous Essays,* Carey & Hart edition, 1849

Be my brother, or I will kill thee.

CHAMFORT (1741–1794). Giving his own slant to the revolutionary slogan, "Fraternity or death." In Thomas Carlyle, *The French Revolution: A History,* 2.1.12, 1837

Brotherhood is not so wild a dream as those who profit by postponing it pretend.

NORMAN CORWIN (1910–). *On a Note of Triumph,* 1945. In Eric Sevareid, epigraph, *Not So Wild a Dream,* 1946

The heart and soul of all men being one, this bitterness of *His* and *Mine* ceases. His is mine. I am my brother, and my brother is me.

RALPH WALDO EMERSON (1803–1882). "Compensation," *Essays: First Series,* 1841

The brotherhood of men would be an empty dream without the fatherhood of God.

ABRAHAM JOSHUA HESCHEL (1907–1972). *Man Is Not Alone: A Philosophy of Religion,* 13, 1951

It is easier to love humanity as a whole than to love one's neighbor. . . . A low capacity for getting along with those near us often goes hand in hand with a high receptivity to the idea of the brotherhood of men.

ERIC HOFFER (1902–1983). *The Ordeal of Change,* 11, 1964

The world has narrowed to a neighborhood before it has broadened to a brotherhood.

LYNDON B. JOHNSON (1908–1973). Luncheon remark, United Nations, New York City, 17 December 1963

To see the earth as we now see it, small and blue and beautiful in that eternal silence where it floats, is to see ourselves as riders on the earth together, brothers in that bright loveliness in the unending night—brothers who *see* now they are truly brothers.

> ARCHIBOLD MacLEISH (1892–1982). Referring to photographs taken during the Appollo mission, showing the earth from beyond the moon, 1968, "Bubble of Blue Air," *Riders on the Earth: Essays and Recollections by Archibald MacLeish,* p. xiv (epigraph), 1978

There is a destiny that makes us brothers:
None goes his way alone:
All that we send into the lives of others
Comes back onto our own.

> EDWIN MARKHAM (1852–1940). "A Creed," 1900, *Poems,* ed. Charles L. Wallis, 1950

The brotherhood of Man presupposes the fatherhood of God.

> ARNOLD J. TOYNBEE (1889–1975). *A Study of History,* 1934–1939, abr. D. C. Somervell, 1.564, 1965

How good and pleasant it is
 when brothers dwell in unity!

> ANONYMOUS (*BIBLE*). *Psalms* 133:1

Let brotherly love continue.

> ANONYMOUS (*BIBLE*). *Hebrews* 11:2

As children of God, we are all brothers and sisters to one another.

> ANONYMOUS

BUDDHISM

See also • Compensation: Ralph Waldo Emerson (4) ○ Dogs: Gilbert Highet ○ Freedom: *The Book of the Golden Precepts* ○ Heart: The Buddha ○ Heaven: *The Book of the Golden Precepts* ○ Idolatry: Lewis Mumford ○ Inaction: *The Book of the Golden Precepts* ○ Knowledge: Pandit Usharbudh Arya ○ Religion ○ Religion & Science: Robert M. Pirsig ○ Self-Knowledge: *The Book of the Golden Precepts* ○ Self-Realization (Being): Amaro Bhikkhu, *The Dhammapada* ○ Zen

Thou canst not travel on the Path before thou hast become that Path itself.

> THE BOOK OF THE GOLDEN PRECEPTS. Ancient Buddhist writing. 1.32, tr. Helena Petrovna Blavatsky, 1889

Look inward: thou art Buddha.

> THE BOOK OF THE GOLDEN PRECEPTS. Ancient Buddhist writing. 2.8, tr. Helena Petrovna Blavatsky, 1889

Have patience, Candidate, as one who fears no failure, courts no success. Fix thy Soul's gaze upon the star whose ray thou art.

> THE BOOK OF THE GOLDEN PRECEPTS. Ancient Buddhist writing. 2.17, tr. Helena Petrovna Blavatsky, 1889

To live to benefit mankind is the first step.

> THE BOOK OF THE GOLDEN PRECEPTS. Ancient Buddhist writing. 2.23, tr. Helena Petrovna Blavatsky, 1889

Feel thyself abiding in all things, all things in SELF.

> THE BOOK OF THE GOLDEN PRECEPTS. Ancient Buddhist writing. 3.8, tr. Helena Petrovna Blavatsky, 1889

Now bend thy head and listen well, O Bodhisattva—Compassion speaks and saith: "Can there be bliss when all that lives must suffer? Shalt thou be saved and hear the whole world cry?"

> THE BOOK OF THE GOLDEN PRECEPTS. Ancient Buddhist writing. 3.35, tr. Helena Petrovna Blavatsky, 1889. In entry number 34 of the "Glossary to Part III," Madame Blavatsky explained the role of the bodhisattvas, those who renounce their own reward for the sake of others: "[They] refuse to pass into the Nirvanic state or . . . 'cross to the other shore,' as it would then become beyond their power to... contribute toward men's salvation by influencing them to follow the Good Law, i.e., lead them on the Path of Righteousness."
>
> See Heroism: Arnold J. Toynbee ○ Philosophers: Plato (3)

Right Belief
Right Intentions
Right Speech
Right Actions
Right Livelihood
Right Endeavoring
Right Mindfulness
Right Concentration.

> THE BUDDHA (6th cent. B.C.). "The Eightfold Path"

The followers of Buddha Gotama are awake . . . , and ever by night and by day they find joy in love for all beings.

> THE DHAMMAPADA: THE PATH OF PERFECTION (1st cent. B.C.). 300, tr. Juan Mascaró, 1973

BURDENS

See also • Adversity ○ Cooperation: Thomas à Kempis ○ Difficulty ○ Disability ○ Grief ○ Misfortune ○ Pain ○ Responsibility ○ Struggle ○ Unhappiness

Everyone has his burden; what counts is how you carry it.

> JOE BROWN and DAVID BROWN (MERLE MILLER, scriptwriter). *Kings Go Forth* (film), 1958, spoken by Natalie Wood

Only they who bear its burdens may rightfully enjoy the blessings of civilized society.

> EUGENE V. DEBS (1855–1926). Presidential nomination acceptance speech (Socialist Party), Indianapolis, May 1912

Heaven suits the back to the burden.

> CHARLES DICKENS (1812–1870). *The Life and Adventures of Nicholas Nickleby,* 18, 1839

Everyone thinks his sack heaviest.

> GEORGE HERBERT (1593–1633). Comp., *Outlandish Proverbs,* 748, 1640

Burdens shared are easier to bear.

> JESSE JACKSON (1941–). Democratic National Convention speech, Chicago, 26 August 1996

Let us remember that God burdens none of us with a heavier cross than he can bear.

> FRANZ JÄGERSTÄTTER (1907–1943). Austrian farmer. Letter to Franz Huber. In Gordon Zahn, *In Solitary Witness: The Life and Death of Franz Jägerstätter,* 9, 1964. Jägerstätter was beheaded for refusing to serve in the German army during World War II.

Allah tasketh not a soul beyond its scope.

> MUHAMMAD (A.D. 570?–632). *Quran,* 3.286, A.D. 670?, tr. Mohammed Marmaduke Pickthall, 1953

Bear one another's burdens, and so fulfill the law of Christ.

> PAUL (A.D. 1st cent.). *Galatians* 6:2

Each man will have to bear his own load.

> PAUL (A.D. 1st cent.). *Galatians* 6:5

Burdens will press less heavily upon those who bear them skillfully.

> SENECA THE YOUNGER (5? B.C.–A.D. 65). "On Tranquillity of Mind" (10.4), *Moral Essays,* tr. John W. Basore, 1932

People become attached to their burdens sometimes more than the burdens are attached to them.

> GEORGE BERNARD SHAW (1856–1950). "Family Affection," *Parents and Children,* 1914

Life has become a burden to me of late. I see that I have begun to understand too much.

> LEO TOLSTOY (1828–1910). *War and Peace,* 3.2.25, 1863–1869, tr. Rosemary Edmonds, 1957

☙

I saw a very small girl walking up a hill carrying an infant boy on her shoulders and said to her, "This boy is too heavy for you." "Not at all," replied the girl, "he's my brother."

> ANONYMOUS. Repeated by Mohandas K. Gandhi and others

Better to strengthen your back than lighten your burden.

> ANONYMOUS

Burdens well-borne weigh no less; they just seem to.

> ANONYMOUS

BUREAUCRACY

See also • Committees ○ Corporations ○ Decision-Making ○ Experts ○ Government ○ Institutions ○ Loyalty ○ Managers ○ Meetings ○ Organizations ○ Politicians ○ Politicians, Corrupt ○ Politics ○ Presidents & Staff

Bureaucracies are the same the world over—slow, complicated, timid, unimaginative, routine and inhuman. The perfect bureaucrat everywhere is the man who manages to make no decisions and escapes all responsibility.

> BROOKS ATKINSON (1894–1984). "September 9," *Once Around the Sun,* 1951

Loyalty is the supreme bureaucratic virtue.

> RICHARD J. BARNET (1929–). *Roots of War,* 3.3, 1971

"Boren's Guidelines" for bureaucrats: (1) When in charge, ponder. (2) When in trouble, delegate. (3) When in doubt, mumble.

> JAMES H. BOREN. National Association of Professional Bureaucrats president. In Benjamin Welles, "Bureaucrats Give Agnew the Bird (It's an Award)," *New York Times,* 8 November 1970

Bad news never flows up. The only times I saw anyone struggle to warn his superior of impending trouble . . . were on those occasions when the superior was sure to find out anyway. . . . When this is multiplied over dozens of departments and hundreds of thousands of employees, the result is a vast conspiracy of self-protection, benign in origin but devastating in effect.

> JAMES FALLOWS (1949–). On the "government's version of the law of gravity." In Bradley H. Patterson, Jr., *The Ring of Power: The White House Staff and Its Expanding Role in Government,* 4 (epigraph), 1988

You don't need a lot of bureaucrats looking over your shoulder and telling you how to run your life or how to run your business. We are a people who declared our independence 200 years ago, and we are not about to lose it now to paper shufflers and computers.

> GERALD R. FORD (1913–). On government bureaucrats, speech, Chicago, 25 August 1975

In a bureaucratic system, useless work drives out useful work.

> MILTON FRIEDMAN (1912–). "Gammon's 'Black Holes,'" *Newsweek,* 7 November 1977
>
> See Money: Sir Thomas Gresham

The tendency of bureaucracy [is] to find purpose in whatever it is doing.

> JOHN KENNETH GALBRAITH (1908–). "Foreign Policy: The Plain Lessons of a Bad Decade," *Foreign Policy,* December 1970

The official with good access to the press is respected, perhaps even feared. The one without such access, who avoids reporters and who is without voice on his own behalf, confesses to an insecurity or diffidence that others are invited to exploit.

> JOHN KENNETH GALBRAITH (1908–). "The canons of bureaucratic achievement" (2), *A Life in Our Times: Memoirs,* 26, 1981

Nothing so weakens the position of a senior public official as the knowledge that he so loves or is otherwise so committed to his job that he will always, in the end, come to terms.

> JOHN KENNETH GALBRAITH (1908–). "The canons of bureaucratic achievement" (8), *A Life in Our Times: Memoirs,* 26, 1981

Workers in the departments of government concerned with regulatory activity, tax collection and especially with welfare services have the fully negative reputation of bureaucracy; those so employed are, collectively, intrusive, incompetent and self-serving. In contrast, those in the military establishment, in lesser measure in the Department of State, the CIA and the other intelligence agencies, and notably also in the administration of social security are exempt from attack. The term *bureaucracy* is but rarely applied to them and almost never in a condemnatory tone. Those there serving are not bureaucrats and certainly not, in the common expression, "lousy bureaucrats." They are, generally, good and loyal public servants.

> JOHN KENNETH GALBRAITH (1908–). *The Culture of Contentment,* 6, 1992

Careerism and conformity have put a premium upon agreement and consensus at the cost of boldness and originality in the transmission of information and recommendation across and up the ranks. The dominant pattern is one of playing it safe and withdrawing from potential conflict before it occurs.

> ERWIN C. HARGROVE (1930–). *The Power of the Modern Presidency,* 8, 1974

The power of the bureaucracy is mainly passive, not active. It consists in the capacity to withhold needed services rather than in the capacity to oppose political superiors directly.

> HUGH HECLO (1943–). "Political Executives and the Washington Bureaucracy," *Political Science Quarterly,* Fall 1977

Running a government without the support of the bureaucracy is like running a train without an engine.

> STEPHEN HESS (1933–). Introduction to *Organizing the Presidency,* 1976

I used occasionally to say to him, "Father, just think..." He used immediately to interrupt me: "My son, I have no need to think, I'm an official."

> ADOLF HITLER (1889–1945). 1 January 1942. *Hitler's Secret Conversations, 1941–1944,* tr. Norman Cameron and R. H. Stevens, 1953

Bureaucracies . . . cannot be relied upon to defend existing regimes once they suspect that the victory of a new regime is probable.

> E. J. HOBSBAWM (1917–). *Revolutionaries: Contemporary Essays,* 19, 1973

Anonymous diplomat: How many persons work at the Vatican? *Pope John* (with a wink): Oh, no more than half of them!

> POPE JOHN XXIII (1881–1963). Format adapted. *Wit and Wisdom of Good Pope John,* 4, ed. Henri Fesquet and tr. Salvator Attanasio, 1964

The best way to kill a new idea is to put it in an old-line agency.

> LYNDON B. JOHNSON (1908–1973). In Rowland Evans, Jr., and Robert D. Novak, *Lyndon B. Johnson: The Exercise of Power, A Political Biography,* 1966

Any system which excludes the bureaucracy in formulating policy may not be able to count on the agencies to implement it.

> RICHARD TANNER JOHNSON (1927–). *Managing the White House: An Intimate Study of the Presidency,* 7, 1974

As a flood spreads wider and wider, the water becomes shallower and dirtier. The Revolution evaporates, leaving behind only the slime of a new bureaucracy. The chains of tormented mankind are made out of red tape.

> FRANZ KAFKA (1883–1924). In Gustav Janouch, *Conversations with Kafka,* p. 71, tr. Goronwy Rees, 1953

The growth of bureaucracy is largely self-engendered, in the sense that only a small part of it derives from the real requirements of the function to be served, the greater part being the product of tendencies and pressures arising within the bureaucratic process.

> GEORGE F. KENNAN (1904–). *Around the Cragged Hill: A Personal and Political Philosophy,* 7, 1993

The spirit of policy and that of bureaucracy are diametrically opposed. . . . The essence of bureaucracy is its quest for safety; its success is calculability. Profound policy thrives on perpetual creation, on a constant redefinition of goals. Good administration thrives on routine, the definition of relationships which can survive mediocrity. Policy involves an adjustment of risks; administration, an avoidance of deviation.

> HENRY A. KISSINGER (1923–). *A World Restored: Metternich, Castlereagh and the Problems of Peace 1812–1822,* 17.3, 1957

While the bureaucracy has been known to drag its feet in implementing directives with which it disagrees, its alacrity in carrying out instructions that it favors and that it fears may be changed is wonderful to behold.

> HENRY A. KISSINGER (1923–). *White House Years,* 10, 1979

The New York Department of Mental Hygiene produced and distributed a three-page illustrated memorandum on how to split an English muffin.

> ERWIN KNOLL (1931–1994). Ed., "Use Only As Directed," *No Comment,* 1984

[Franklin D.] Roosevelt triumphed over the established bureaucracy with its elephantine pace and resistance to change partly by ignoring it. He established his own bureaucracy to administer much of the New Deal.

> LOUIS W. KOENIG (1916–). *The Chief Executive,* 8, 1964

The weaker a government, the stronger its bureaucracy.

> GUSTAVE LE BON (1841–1931). *Aphorisms of Present Times,* 4.6, 1913, tr. Alice Widener, 1979

Consciousness of rank, knowing who is the peckee and who is the peckor, is the first stage in the evolution of a bureaucracy.

> THOMAS L. MARTIN, JR. *Malice in Blunderland: A Foolproof Guide for the Aspiring Bureaucrat,* 2, 1973

The only thing that saves us from the bureaucracy is [its] inefficiency. An efficient bureaucracy is the greatest threat to liberty.

> EUGENE McCARTHY (1916–). In "People," *Time,* 12 February 1979

Bureaucracy, the rule of no one, has become the modern form of despotism.

> MARY McCARTHY (1912–1989). "Philosophy at Work," *New Yorker,* 18 October 1958

Instilling attitudes of dignity and respect in the post office culture may be tough. It may be one of those long-term type of things.

The man [Marvin] Runyon replaced as postmaster general, Anthony M. Frank, says the attitude among many supervisors is: "I ate dirt for 20 years. Now it's your turn to eat dirt."

> PHIL McCOMBS. "Regulated to the Letter: Postal Employee Rules Create Unhappy Campers," *Washington Post National Weekly Edition,* 31 May 1993

The bureaucrat as such does not make policy; he provides information relevant to alternative policies and carries out the alternative that becomes official.

> C. WRIGHT MILLS (1916–1962). *The Power Elite,* 10.3, 1956

If an idea can survive a bureaucratic review and be implemented, it [isn't] worth doing.

> MOLLISON'S BUREAUCRACY HYPOTHESIS. In Arthur Bloch, comp., "Hierarchiology & Committology," *Murphy's Law: Book Two,* 1980

The effort expended by the bureaucracy in defending any error is in direct proportion to the size of the error.

> JOHN NIES. Washington lawyer. "Nies's Law." In Paul Dickson, comp., *The Official Rules,* p. 178, 1978

One of the most ridiculous practices in the bureaucracy is when promotions are based on how many people an individual supervises. The rule should be that those who can do the same job with fewer people get the promotions.

> RICHARD M. NIXON (1913–1994). *In the Arena: A Memoir of Victory, Defeat and Renewal,* 30, 1990

A classic administrative end–run: first, create a bureaucracy designed to duplicate that of an opposing agency; then eliminate the opposing bureaucracy in the name of efficiency.

> TIMOTHY NOAH. "Prisoners of Respectability," *Washington Monthly,* September 1983

Bureaucracy defends the status quo long past the time when the quo has lost its status.

> LAURENCE J. PETER (1919–1990). "Intimate Confessions of a Quotemonger," *San Francisco Sunday Examiner & Chronicle,* 29 January 1978

In a hierarchy every employee tends to rise to his level of incompetence.

> LAURENCE J. PETER (1919–1990) and RAYMOND HULL. "The Peter Principle," *The Peter Principle: Why Things Always Go Wrong,* 1, 1969

In most hierarchies, supercompetence is more objectionable than incompetence.

> LAURENCE J. PETER (1919–1990) and RAYMOND HULL. *The Peter Principle: Why Things Always Go Wrong,* 3, 1969

See that the Patron has *something to gain* by assisting you, or *something to lose* by not assisting you, to rise in the hierarchy.

> LAURENCE J. PETER (1919–1990) and RAYMOND HULL. *The Peter Principle: Why Things Always Go Wrong,* 4, 1969

No government ever voluntarily reduces itself in size. Government programs, once launched, never disappear. Actually, a government bureau is the nearest thing to eternal life we'll ever see on this earth!

> RONALD REAGAN (1911–). "A Time for Choosing," television broadcast, 27 October 1964, *Speaking My Mind,* 1989

The major problem facing bureaucracy is not the struggle for power but the evasion of responsibility; bureaucrats are very reluctant to take action.

> DEAN RUSK (1909–1994). *As I Saw It,* 33, 1990

The State is a collection of officials . . . drawing comfortable incomes so long as the *status quo* is preserved. The only alteration they are likely to desire in the *status quo* is an increase of bureaucracy and of the power of bureaucrats.

> BERTRAND RUSSELL (1872–1970). *Sceptical Essays,* 12, 1928

To beat the bureaucracy, make your problem their problem.

> MARSHALL L. SMITH. "Principle of Displaced Hassle." In Paul Dickson, comp., *The Official Rules,* p. 64, 1978

The less important you are on the table of organization, the more you'll be missed if you don't show up for work.

> BILL VAUGHAN. "Vaughan's Rule of Corporate Life." In Paul Dickson, comp., *The Official Explanations,* p. 228, 1980

❦

New people coming in can often get things done that others around a long time can't. People in the bureaucracy are telling

them it's impossible, but they don't know that something can't be done and they do it.

> ANONYMOUS (AMERICAN). In Hugh Heclo, *A Government of Strangers,* 6, 1977

If you sin, sin against God, not against the bureaucracy. God may forgive you. The bureaucracy never will.

> ANONYMOUS (AMERICAN). In Sam Roberts, "In Prison, a Fallen Leader Now Talks of Loftier Things," *New York Times,* 24 October 1988

Projects expand to accommodate funding: work diminishes as projects expand.

> ANONYMOUS

The bureaucracy [is] a fourth branch of government.

> SAYING (AMERICAN). In Henry A. Kissinger, *Diplomacy,* 17, 1994

BUSINESS (COMMERCE)

See also • America: Calvin Coolidge ○ Business (Occupation) ○ Capitalism ○ Corporations ○ Executives ○ Government ○ Merchants & Customers ○ Money ○ Morality: Henry Ford ○ Organizations ○ Price ○ Profit & Loss ○ Stock Market ○ Trade (Commerce) ○ Value ○ Wages ○ Work

The logical extension of business is murder.

> SIR CHARLES SPENCER "CHARLIE" CHAPLIN (1889–1977). *Monsieur Verdoux* (film), 1947, spoken by Chaplin

Without some dissimulation no business can be carried on at all.

> LORD CHESTERFIELD (1694–1773). Letter to his son, 22 May 1749

Went to Yarmouth Sunday 5; to Orleans Monday 6th; to Nauset Light on the back side of Cape Cod. Collins, the keeper, told us he found obstinate resistance on Cape Cod to the project of building a lighthouse on this coast, as it would injure the wrecking business.

> RALPH WALDO EMERSON (1803–1882). Journal, 5 September 1853

We mean to have less of government in business as well as more business in government.

> WARREN G. HARDING (1865–1923). Special address before Congress, 12 April 1921

American business is not a monster, but an expression of [the] God-given impulse to create, and the savior and guardian of our happiness.

> WARREN G. HARDING (1865–1923)

It is just as important that business keep out of government as that government keep out of business.

> HERBERT HOOVER (1874–1964). Speech, 22 October 1928

What we call Monopoly is Business at the end of its journey.

> HENRY DEMAREST LLOYD (1894–1903). *Wealth Against Commonwealth,* 1, 1894

Bad business practices, if left uncorrected, will drive out good business practices. A simple example is if an orange juice company adulterates its orange juice in ways that are really impossible to detect, it will disadvantage the orange juice company that doesn't—because it will have more money to spend to advertise against its competitors.

> RALPH NADER (1934–). Debra J. Saunders interview, "Public Citizen Number One," *San Francisco Sunday Examiner & Chronicle,* 13 October 1996
>
> See Money: Sir Thomas Gresham

The growth of a large business is merely the survival of the fittest. The American Beauty rose can be produced in the splendor and fragrance which bring cheer to its beholder only by sacrificing the early buds which grow up around it. This is not an evil tendency in business. It is merely the working-out of a law of nature and a law of God.

> JOHN D. ROCKEFELLER (1839–1937). In Richard Hofstadter, *Social Darwinism in American Thought,* rev. ed., 2.4, 1959 (1944)

Business must be profitable if it is to continue to succeed, but the glory of business is to make it so successful that it may do things that are great chiefly because they ought to be done.

> CHARLES M. SCHWAB (1937–). Charles M. Schwab & Co., Inc., chairman.

What recommends commerce to me is its enterprise and bravery.

> HENRY DAVID THOREAU (1817–1862). "Sounds," *Walden; or Life in the Woods,* 1854

It is not big business we have to fear. It is big government.

> WENDELL WILLKIE (1892–1944). Presidential nomination acceptance speech, Philadelphia, 26 June 1940
>
> See Corporations: Benjamin H. Hill

BUSINESS (OCCUPATION)

See also • Business (Commerce) ○ Merchants & Customers ○ Trade (Occupation) ○ Work

You had better take for business a man somewhat absurd than over-formal.

> FRANCIS BACON (1561–1626). "Ornamenta Rationalia; or, Elegant Sentences," *The Essays; or, Counsels, Civil and Moral,* A. L. Burt edition, 1883

Dispatch is the soul of business, and nothing contributes more to dispatch than method. Lay down a method for everything, and stick to it inviolably, as far as unexpected incidents may allow. Fix one certain hour and day in the week for your accounts, and keep them together in their proper order; by which means they will require very little time, and you can never be much cheated. Whatever letters and papers you keep, docket and tie them up in their respective classes, so that you may instantly have recourse to any one.

> LORD CHESTERFIELD (1694–1773). Letter to his son, 5 February 1750

Drive thy Business, or it will drive thee.

> BENJAMIN FRANKLIN (1706–1790). *Poor Richard's Almanack,* September 1744
>
> See Merchants & Customers: George Chapman

Do business, but be not a Slave to it.

> THOMAS FULLER (1654–1734). Comp., *Gnomologia: Adages and Proverbs,* 1304, 1732

With an honest and a good Man, Business is soon ended.

> THOMAS FULLER (1654–1734). Comp., *Gnomologia: Adages and Proverbs,* 5793, 1732

business business business
grind grind grind
what a life for a man
that might have been a poet.

> DON MARQUIS (1878–1937). "pete the parrot and shakespeare," *archy and mehitabel,* 1927

Perpetual devotion to what a man calls his business, is only to be sustained by perpetual neglect of many other things.

> ROBERT LOUIS STEVENSON (1850–1894). "An Apology for Idlers," *Virginibus Puerisque,* 1881

Most men are engaged in business the greater part of their lives because the soul abhors a vacuum, and they have not discovered any continuous employment for man's nobler faculties.

> HENRY DAVID THOREAU (1817–1862). Journal, 27 April 1854

Commerce is naturally adverse to all the violent passions; it loves to temporize, takes delight in compromise, and studiously avoids irritation. It is patient, insinuating, flexible, and never has recourse to extreme measures until obliged by the most absolute necessity. Commerce renders men independent of one another, gives them a lofty notion of their personal importance, leads them to seek to conduct their own affairs, and teaches how to conduct them well; it therefore prepares men for freedom, but preserves them from revolutions.

> ALEXIS de TOCQUEVILLE (1805–1859). *Democracy in America,* 2.3.21, 1840, tr. Henry Reeve and Francis Bowen, 1862

Business is like riding a bicycle. Either you keep moving or you fall down.

> JOHN DAVID WRIGHT (1909–1979). President of Thompson Products, Inc. In Gilbert Burck, "The Rush to Diversity," *Fortune,* September 1955

No one on his deathbed ever said, "I wish I had spent more time on my business."

> ARNOLD ZACK. Letter to his friend Sen. Paul Tsongas, 1984

❧

Never underpay or overcharge, and your business will thrive.

> SAYING

CALAMITY

See also • Crisis Leaders: C. C. Colton ○ Defeat ○ Disaster ○ Misfortune ○ Tragedy ○ Trouble

Calamities are of two kinds: misfortune to ourselves, and good fortune to others.

> AMBROSE BIERCE (1842–1914). *The Devil's Dictionary,* p. 19, 1911, Dover edition, 1958

Public calamity is a mighty leveller.

> EDMUND BURKE (1729–1797). "Conciliation with America," House of Commons speech, 22 March 1775

If [William Ewart] Gladstone fell into the Thames, that would be a misfortune; and if anybody pulled him out, that, I suppose, would be a calamity.

> BENJAMIN DISRAELI (1804–1881). When asked to distinguish between a misfortune and a calamity. In Leon A. Harris, *The Fine Art of Political Wit,* 4, 1966. Gladstone and Disraeli were political rivals.

Every calamity is a spur and valuable hint.

> RALPH WALDO EMERSON (1803–1882). "Fate," *The Conduct of Life,* 1860

Divine Providence sends the chiefest benefits under the mask of calamities.

> RALPH WALDO EMERSON (1803–1882). "The Fortune of the Republic," lecture, Old South Church, Boston, 30 March 1878

A collision at sea can ruin your entire day.

> W. B. "BILL" HAYLER. Naval officer. 1960. In Herb Caen, column, *San Francisco Chronicle,* 14 February 1971

Every now and then, in the course of great events, the elements of tradition and innovation ally themselves and each one's weakness supplements the other and together they achieve the perfect debacle.

> MURRAY KEMPTON (1917–1997). "The Genius of Mussolini" (3), *New York Review of Books,* 7 October 1982

The extent of the catastrophe that threatens gives the measure of the transformation that will be necessary in order to master it.

> LEWIS MUMFORD (1895–1990). *The Conduct of Life,* 4.6, 1951

Learn to see in another's calamity the ills which you should avoid.

> PUBLIUS SYRUS (85–43 B.C.). *Moral Sayings,* 120, tr. Darius Lyman, Jr., 1862

If catastrophe overtakes me at a certain point, work goes on at other points.

> ASA MEAD SIMPSON (1826–1891?). Sea captain. In "California Yankee Sea Captains in Those Good Ole Doghole Days: The Life of John Gage," *Californians,* January-February 1991

CALIFORNIA

See also • Hollywood ○ Los Angeles ○ San Francisco

California is a great place—if you happen to be an orange.

> FRED ALLEN (1894–1956)

The cumulative effect of Californians saying, year after year, "Have a nice day."

> CLARK BARRETT. Explaining the drought of 1991. In Herb Caen, column, *San Francisco Chronicle,* 27 December 1991

Whatever starts in California unfortunately has an inclination to spread.

> JIMMY CARTER (1924–). Remark at a cabinet meeting, 21 March 1977. In Robert Shogan, *Promises to Keep: Carter's First 100 Days,* 7, 1977

The attraction and superiority of California are in its days. It has better days, and more of them, than any other country.

> RALPH WALDO EMERSON (1803–1882). During a tour that included visits to San Francisco and Yosemite Valley, journal, May 1871

"California Here I Come."

> AL JOLSON (1886–1950), BUD DE SILVA, and JOSEPH MEYER. Song title, 1924

California reminds me of the popular American Protestant concept of heaven: there is always a reasonable flow of new arrivals; one meets many—not all—of one's friends; people spend a good deal of their time congratulating one another about the fact that they are there; discontent would be unthinkable; and the newcomer is slightly disconcerted to realize that now, the devil having been banished and virtue being triumphant, nothing terribly interesting can ever happen again.

> GEORGE F. KENNAN (1904–). 13 May 1956, *Sketches from a Life,* 1989

Ever'thing in California is owned. . . . An' them people that owns it is gonna hang on to it if they got ta kill ever'body in the worl' to do it. An' they're scairt, an' that makes 'em mad. You got to see it. You got to hear it. Purtiest goddamn country you ever seen, but they ain't nice to you, them folks. They're so scairt an' worried they ain't even nice to each other.

> JOHN STEINBECK (1902–1968). *The Grapes of Wrath,* 18, 1939

The destruction of California is a logical climax to the Westward Movement. The redwoods, the freeways, the dope laws, race riots, water pollution, smog, the FSM [i.e., Free Speech Movement], and now Governor Reagan—the whole thing is as logical as mathematics. California is the end, in every way, of Lincoln's idea that America was the "last best hope of man."

> HUNTER S. THOMPSON (1939–). Letter from San Francisco to Carey McWilliams, 18 June 1966, *The Proud Highway: Saga of a Desperate Southern Gentleman, 1955–1967,* ed. Douglas Brinkley, 1997

If you turned the country on its side, everything loose would fall into Southern California.

> FRANK LLOYD WRIGHT (1867–1959). Attributed. In Herb Caen, column, *San Francisco Chronicle,* 6 August 1978

❦

His great aim was to escape from civilization, and, as soon as he had money, he went to Southern California.

> ANONYMOUS. In Charles McCabe, "Insults," *San Francisco Chronicle,* 28 May 1980

CALUMNY

See also • Slander

Calumny is the offspring of Envy.

> LADY BLESSINGTON (1789–1849). *Night Thought Book* (unpublished), 1834, excerpted in Ernest J. Lovell, Jr. introduction to Lady Blessington, *Conversations of Lord Byron,* 1969

Calumnies are answer'd best with silence.

> BEN JONSON (1572–1637). *Volpone or The Foxe,* 2.1, 1607

Hamlet: Be thou as chaste as ice, as pure as snow, thou shalt not escape calumny.

> SHAKESPEARE (1564–1616). *Hamlet,* 3.1.139, 1600

To persevere in one's duty and be silent is the best answer to calumny.

> GEORGE WASHINGTON (1732–1799). Letter to Gov. William Livingston, 7 December 1779
>
> See Slander: Abraham Lincoln

CAMPAIGNS

See also • Campaign Slogans ○ Elections ○ Lobbies ○ Politics ○ Voting

I don't think you can find any evidence of the fact that I had changed government policy solely because of a [campaign] contribution.

> BILL CLINTON (1946–). Remark to reporters, March, 1997. In William Safire, "Bribes from Tribes," *New York Times,* 31 December 1997. Safire commented, "The careful qualifier *solely* was his intended escape hatch; reasons other than a payoff can always be dredged up. But in determining whether bribery took place, prosecutors need only prove that a policy decision was made *substantially* because of a heavy donation of his re-election."

You campaign in poetry. You govern in prose.

> MARIO CUOMO (1932–). In Fred Barnes, "Meet Mario the Moderate," *New Republic,* 8 April 1985

I was told that people did not like negative ads. So I didn't run any. I lost.

> ROBERT DOLE (1923–). Describing his race for the Republican presidential nomination against George Bush, appearing on *Nightline,* television news program, 10 November 1988

The way to win [an election] is to go on the offensive against your opponent early, distort positions to whatever degree you can get away with, play upon people's fears and prejudices—and never let up.

> ELIZABETH DREW (1935–). *Election Journal: Political Events of 1987–1988,* 15, 1989

Money buys access; access buys influence.

> ELIZABETH DREW. On campaign contributions, Michael Krasny radio interview, KQED, San Francisco, 15 May 1997

If I was runnin' fr office, I'd change me name, an' have printed on me cards: "Give him a chanst; he can't be worse."

> FINLEY PETER DUNNE (1867–1936). "Reform Administration," *Observations by Mr. Dooley,* 1902

There are now four essential ingredients to a professionally managed political campaign: political polls, data processing, imagery, and money. The polls discover what the voter already believes, and data processing interprets and analyzes the depth of voters' attitudes. After that, an image of the candidate is tailored to meet the voters' demands and desires, and the whole package is then sold by massive expenditures of money in the advertising media, particularly television.

> ZOLTON FERENCY. Chairman and gubernatorial candidate of the Democratic Party of Michigan. Speech, June 1970

PAC [Political Action Committee] money is destroying the electoral process. It feeds the growth of special interest groups created solely to channel money into political campaigns. It creates an impression that every candidate is bought and owned by the biggest givers.

> BARRY M. GOLDWATER (1909–1998). Testimony before the Senate Rules and Administration Committee, 29 September 1983

In *The Washington Post* a reporter who had been listening to recently released Nixon tapes from the archives quoted Nixon's reaction in 1972 to the news that his political rival George Wallace had been shot and severely wounded and that the gunman, about whom little was as yet known, had been apprehended. Nixon encouraged his aides to see if they could covertly break into the suspect's apartment and strew it with McGovern literature so it would look as if this would-be assassin were a Democratic partisan.

> MEG GREENFIELD (1930–). "Memorial Frenzy," *Newsweek,* 30 June 1997. Sen. George McGovern was Pres. Nixon's Democratic opponent in the 1972 presidential election

The methods now being used to merchandise the political candidate as though he were a deodorant positively guarantee the electorate against ever hearing the truth about anything.

> ALDOUS HUXLEY (1894–1963). *Brave New World Revisited,* 6, 1958

I have just received the following wire from my generous daddy. It says, "Dear Jack, don't buy a single vote more than is necessary. I'll be damned if I'm going to pay for a landslide."

> JOHN F. KENNEDY (1917–1963). After-dinner speech before the Gridiron Club, Washington, 15 March 1958. In John Henry Cutler, *Honey Fitz: Three Steps to the White House; The Life and Times of John F. (Honey Fitz) Fitzgerald,* 22, 1962

Never say anything in a national campaign that anyone might remember.

> EUGENE J. McCARTHY (1916–). "McCarthy's First Law of Politics." In John Leo, "Wit Is the Opiate of Politics," *U.S. News & World Report,* 26 November 1990

The only way to success in American public life lies in flattering and kowtowing to the mob. A candidate for office, even the highest, must either adopt its current manias *en bloc,* or convince it hypocritically that he has done so.

> H. L. MENCKEN (1880–1956). "On Being an American" (2), *Prejudices: Third Series,* 1922

At the conclusion of our port-mortem, I recognized the basic mistake I had made. I had concentrated too much on substance and not enough on appearance.

> RICHARD M. NIXON (1913–1994). On his performance in the first televised presidential-campaign debate with John F. Kennedy, 26 September 1960, *Six Crises,* 6, 1962

Which one of the three candidates would you want your daughter to marry?

> ROSS PEROT (1930–). Texas billionaire. While campaigning for the presidency against George Bush and Bill Clinton. In *International Herald Tribune* (Paris), 29 October 1992

Politics has got so expensive that it takes lots of money to even get beat with.

> WILL ROGERS (1879–1935). 28 June 1931, *The Autobiography of Will Rogers*, ed. Donald Day, 1949

The whole game is chemistry. It's what a voter gets in his gut.

> ED ROLLINS (1943–). Political consultant. In Maureen Dowd, "Finding Mr. Right: In Elections as in Romance, It's Often a Matter of Chemistry," *New York Times*, 8 March 1992

My hat is in the ring. The fight is on, and I'm stripped to the buff.

> THEODORE ROOSEVELT (1858–1919). Remark to a reporter, Cleveland, 1912. In William Safire, *Safire's New Political Dictionary: The Definitive Guide to the New Language of Politics*, p. 320, 1993 (1968)

Political campaigns tend to be exercises in progressive degeneration.

> ARTHUR M. SCHLESINGER, JR. (1917–). *The Age of Roosevelt: The Politics of Upheaval*, 33.8, 1960

Everyone was tired [of] the old-style politicians and their flowery rhetoric. I just told them there are tough times ahead, but that they would be less tough with me in charge.

> ANIBAL CAVACO SILVA (1939–). Portuguese premier. In *Independent* (British newspaper), 13 January 1992

In recent years members of Congress have legally raised campaign money from PACs [Political Actions Committees] or private individuals and kept what was left over for personal use. Year in and year out, strong incumbents who faced no opposition, or only token opposition, accumulated hundreds of thousands of dollars in cash. . . . The practice was so dubious that Congress passed a law in 1979 forbidding new members from building up personal funds this way, but those already in Congress were allowed to keep piling up personal fortunes.

> HEDRICK SMITH (1933–). *The Power Game: How Washington Works*, 9, 1988

When the print press examines a politician's performance, very few voters are interested in detail. The essence of the modern campaign is personality politics: the direct impressions that viewers form from thirty-second daily blips on the Boss Tube, preaching homilies and honing bumpers-sticker themes to stick in voters' memories.

> HEDRICK SMITH (1933–). *The Power Game: How Washington Works*, 19, 1988

The perfect candidate [is] a nice guy who would never challenge the conventional wisdom, and who would like to lead us if only we would be so kind as to tell him where we want to go.

> RONALD STEEL (1931–). Closing words. "Will He or Won't He?" *New York Times Magazine*, 17 September 1995

The idea that you can merchandise candidates for high office like breakfast cereal—that you can gather votes like box tops—is, I think, the ultimate indignity to the democratic process.

> ADLAI E. STEVENSON (1900–1965). Comment following his presidential nomination acceptance speech, Chicago, 18 August 1956

The hardest thing about any political campaign is how to win without proving that you are unworthy of winning.

> ADLAI E. STEVENSON (1900–1965). Speech, Fresno (California), 11 October 1956

Sen. Joseph I. Lieberman: Do you think you got your money's worth for the $300,000 you gave in campaign contributions to the Democratic Party?
Tamraz: I think next time I'll give $600,000.

> ROGER TAMRAZ. Format adapted. Testimony before the Senate Governmental Affairs Committee, 18 September 1997. In Edward Walsh, "Tamraz Defends Political Donations: Access to Top Officials Was 'Only Reason,' Pipeline Promoter Testifies," *Washington Post*, 19 September 1997

Anybody who runs for public office today has got to know his life or her life will be an open book. I've decided that if you want to run for public office you have to decide at the age of 5 and live accordingly.

> HELEN THOMAS (1920–). *Chronicle* staff interview, "Uncovering the White House," *San Francisco Sunday Examiner & Chronicle*, 29 January 1995

Political organization is basically a matter of list-keeping. You canvass a state by foot and by phone to find out who is for you, who is against you, and who is uncommitted. Once you have the list, you cross off the ones against you, barrage the uncommitted with pleas and information, and make sure your supporters get to the polls.

> HUNTER S. THOMPSON (1939–). "April," *Fear and Loathing: On the Campaign Trail '72*, 1973

I am going to make a common-sense, intellectually honest campaign. It will be a novelty and it will win.

> HARRY S. TRUMAN (1884–1972). Diary, 16 July 1948. In William Hillman, *Mr. President*, 3.2, 1952

I'm going to fight hard. I'm going to give them hell.

> HARRY S. TRUMAN (1884–1972). Commenting on his upcoming presidential reelection campaign, which to almost everybody's surprise he won, 17 September 1948
>
> See Truthfulness: Truman

The biggest bang for the buck comes from negative campaigning.

> GEORGE F. WILL (1941–). Commentator. *This Week with David Brinkley*, television news program, ABC, 28 October 1989

CAMPAIGN SLOGANS

See also • Campaigns ○ Elections

Instead of a NEW DEAL, we want a NEW DECK. The New Deal has never ripened. It is still a Raw Deal.

> W. C. FIELDS (1879–1946). *W. C. Fields By Himself: His Intended Autobiography*, 3, 1973

We stand today on the edge of a new frontier—the frontier of the 1960s, a frontier of unknown opportunities and paths, a frontier of unfulfilled hopes and threats. . . . The new frontier of which I speak is not a set of promises—it is a set of challenges. It sums up not what I intend to offer the American people, but what I intend to ask of them.

> JOHN F. KENNEDY (1917–1963). Presidential nomination acceptance speech, Los Angeles, 15 July 1960. Henry A. Wallace titled his 1934 book, *New Frontiers.* Alf Landon and Adlai E. Stevenson used the term *new frontier* in speeches during their presidential campaigns of 1936 and 1952, respectively.

I pledge you, I pledge myself, to a new deal for the American people. Let us all here assembled constitute ourselves prophets of a new order of competence and of courage. This is more than a political campaign; it is a call to arms. Give me your help, not to win votes alone, but to win in this crusade to restore America to its own people.

> FRANKLIN D. ROOSEVELT (1882–1945). Presidential nomination acceptance speech, Chicago, 2 July 1932. According to James David Barber (*The Presidential Character: Predicting Performance in the White House,* 7, 1972), Roosevelt took the term "new deal" from Mark Twain's *A Connecticut Yankee in King Arthur's Court* (1889).

If elected, I shall see to it that every man has a square deal, no less and no more.

> THEODORE ROOSEVELT (1858–1919). Presidential campaign speech, 4 November 1904

Every segment of our population and every individual has a right to expect from his government a fair deal.

> HARRY S. TRUMAN (1884–1972). State of the Union Message, 5 January 1949

Tippecanoe and Tyler, Too.

> SLOGAN (AMERICAN). Whig presidential campaign for William Henry Harrison, 1840

Fifty-Four Forty or Fight.

> SLOGAN (AMERICAN). Democratic presidential campaign for James K. Polk, 1844

Union and Liberty.

> SLOGAN (AMERICAN). Republican presidential campaign for Abraham Lincoln, 1860

Equal Rights to All; Special Privileges to None.

> SLOGAN (AMERICAN). Democratic presidential campaign for William Jennings Bryan, 1900

Stand Pat with McKinley.

> SLOGAN (AMERICAN). Republican presidential campaign for William McKinley, 1900

The New Freedom.

> SLOGAN (AMERICAN). Democratic presidential campaign for Woodrow Wilson, 1912. Also the title of his 1913 book, a collection of his speeches.

He Kept Us Out of War.

> SLOGAN (AMERICAN). Democratic presidential campaign for Woodrow Wilson, 1916

Back to Normalcy.

> SLOGAN (AMERICAN). Republican presidential campaign for Warren G. Harding, 1920

Convict No. 9653 for President.

> SLOGAN (AMERICAN). Socialist presidential campaign for Eugene V. Debs, 1920. Debs was in prison at the time for violation of the Espionage Act (1918).

Keep Cool with Coolidge.

> SLOGAN (AMERICAN). Republican presidential campaign for Calvin Coolidge, 1924

A Chicken in Every Pot; A Car in Every Garage.

> SLOGAN (AMERICAN). Republican presidential campaign for Herbert Hoover, 1928

You Never Had It So Good.

> SLOGAN (AMERICAN). Republican presidential campaign for Herbert Hoover, 1928

In Hoover We Trusted and Now We Are Busted.

> SLOGAN (AMERICAN). Democratic presidential campaign against Republican candidate Herbert Hoover, 1948

Prosperity Is Just Around the Corner.

> SLOGAN (AMERICAN). Republican presidential campaign for Herbert Hoover, 1932

Happy Days Are Here Again.

> SLOGAN (AMERICAN). Democratic presidential campaign for Franklin D. Roosevelt, 1932

One Good Term Deserves Another.

> SLOGAN (AMERICAN). Republican senatorial campaign (Michigan) for Arthur Vandenberg, 1934

Win with Willkie.

> SLOGAN (AMERICAN). Republican presidential campaign for Wendell Willkie, 1940

I'm Just Wild About Harry.

> SLOGAN (AMERICAN). Democratic presidential campaign for Harry S. Truman, 1948

I'm Just Mild About Harry.

> SLOGAN (AMERICAN). Republican presidential campaign against Democratic candidate Harry S. Truman, 1948

To Err Is Truman.

> SLOGAN (AMERICAN). Republican presidential campaign against Democratic candidate Harry S. Truman, 1948

Phooey on Dewey.

> SLOGAN (AMERICAN). Democratic presidential campaign against Republican candidate Thomas E. Dewey, 1948

I Like Ike.

> SLOGAN (AMERICAN). Republican presidential campaign for Dwight D. Eisenhower, 1952

I Still Like Ike.

> SLOGAN (AMERICAN). Republican presidential campaign for Dwight D. Eisenhower, 1956

We Need Adlai Badly.

> SLOGAN (AMERICAN). Democratic presidential campaign for Adlai E. Stevenson, 1956

All the Way with LBJ.

> SLOGAN (AMERICAN). Democratic presidential campaign for Lyndon B. Johnson, 1964

In Your Heart You Know He's Right.

> SLOGAN (AMERICAN). Republican presidential campaign for Barry M. Goldwater, 1964

In Your Guts You Know He's Nuts.

> SLOGAN (AMERICAN). Democratic presidential campaign against Republican candidate Barry M. Goldwater, 1964

The Politics of Joy.

> SLOGAN (AMERICAN). Democratic presidential campaign for Hubert H. Humphrey, 1968

Stand up for America.

> SLOGAN (AMERICAN). Independent presidential campaign for George C. Wallace, 1968

Nixon's the One.

> SLOGAN (AMERICAN). Republican presidential campaign for Richard M. Nixon, 1968

Come Home, America.

> SLOGAN (AMERICAN). Democratic presidential campaign for George S. McGovern, 1972

Why Not the Best?

> SLOGAN (AMERICAN). Democratic presidential campaign for Jimmy Carter, 1976. Also the title of his 1975 autobiography

Get the Government off Our Backs.

> SLOGAN (AMERICAN). Republican presidential campaign for Ronald Reagan, 1980

It's Morning Again in America.

> SLOGAN (AMERICAN). Republican presidential campaign for Ronald Reagan, 1984

Never Been Indicted.

> SLOGAN (AMERICAN). Campaign in Buffalo (New York), 1980s

It's the economy, stupid.

> SLOGAN (AMERICAN). Coined by James Carville, Democratic presidential campaign for Bill Clinton, 1992

A New Deal for Everyone.

> SLOGAN (BRITISH). Liberal prime ministerial campaign for David Lloyd George, 1919

What Britain Needs Is an Iron Lady.

> SLOGAN (BRITISH). Conservative prime ministerial campaign for Margaret Thatcher, 1979

CAMPING

See also • Nature ○ Wilderness

As I drifted over the dome-paved basin of Yosemite Creek . . . sunset found me only three miles back from the brow of El Capitan, near the head of a round smooth gap—the deepest groove in the El Capitan ridge. Here I lay down and thought of the time when the groove in which I rested was being ground away at the bottom of a vast ice-sheet that flowed over all the Sierra like a slow wind. . . . My huge camp fire glowed like a sun. . . . A happy brook sang confidingly, and by its side I made my bed of rich, spicy boughs, elastic and warm. Upon so luxurious a couch, in such a forest, and by such a fire and brook, sleep is gentle and pure. Wildwood sleep is always refreshing; and to those who receive the mountains into their souls, as well as into their sight—living with them clean and free—sleep is a beautiful death, from which we arise every dawn into a new-created world, to begin a new life in a new body. (Ellipsis points in original.)

> JOHN MUIR (1838–1914). November 1871. In William Frederic Badè, *The Life and Letters of John Muir,* 9.1, 1923

We camped at the southeast end of the lake on a sandy beach and made a grand fire. The sage was beautiful in the firelight. Grand tea and potatoes—the pomp of the kings ridiculous!

> JOHN MUIR (1838–1914). Journal, 2 July 1888. In *John of the Mountains: The Unpublished Journals of John Muir,* ed. Linnie Marsh Wolfe, 1938

CAPITALISM

See also • Banks ○ Business (Commerce) ○ Class ○ Communism ○ Corporations ○ Democracy ○ Economics ○ Executives ○ Fascism ○ Freedom ○ Inflation: John Maynard Keynes ○ Merchants & Customers ○ Profit & Loss ○ Socialism ○ Stock Market ○ Trade (Commerce) ○ Tyranny

Those who proclaim the faith that wars cease when capitalism is overthrown have left history and politics for religion.

> RICHARD J. BARNET (1929–). *Roots of War,* 8.1, 1971

Modern capitalism has been transformed by a widespread hedonism that has made mundane concerns, rather than transcendental ties, the center of people's lives. . . . Without the hedonism stimulated by mass consumption, the very structure of business enterprises would collapse.

> DANIEL BELL (1919–). "The New Class: A Muddled Concept." In B. Bruce-Briggs, ed., *The New Class?* 1979

Capitalism without bankruptcy is like Christianity without hell.

> FRANK BORMAN (1928–). Astronaut and Eastern Airlines chairman. In *Observer* (British newspaper), 6 March 1986

Laissez-faire, *n.* An economic doctrine which states that no act can be evil if it earns a profit.

> VICTOR L. CAHN (1948). *The Disrespectful Dictionary,* unpaged, 1974

The Socialist says we have too many capitalists. I say we have too few. The scattering of capital among a great many will solve the problem.

> G. K. CHESTERTON (1874–1936). *As I Was Saying: A Chesterton Reader,* 17, ed. Robert Knille, 1985

The inherent vice of capitalism is the unequal sharing of blessings. The inherent virtue of socialism is the equal sharing of miseries.

> WINSTON CHURCHILL (1874–1965). House of Commons speech, 22 October 1945

"Free enterprise" cannot be justified as being good for business. It can be justified only as being good for society.

PETER F. DRUCKER (1909–). *Management: Tasks, Responsibilities, Practices*, 2, 1974, abr., 1977

The basis of political economy is non-interference. The only safe rule is found in the self-adjusting meter of demand and supply.

RALPH WALDO EMERSON (1803–1882). "Wealth," *The Conduct of Life*, 1860

History suggests only that capitalism is a necessary condition for political freedom. Clearly it is not a sufficient condition.

MILTON FRIEDMAN (1912–). *Capitalism and Freedom*, 1, 1962

The Great Depression, like most other periods of severe unemployment, was produced by government mismanagement rather than by any inherent instability of the private economy.

MILTON FRIEDMAN (1912–). *Capitalism and Freedom*, 3, 1962

Under capitalism man exploits man. And under Communism it is just the reverse.

JOHN KENNETH GALBRAITH (1908–). *A Life in Our Times: Memoirs*, 22, 1981

The great dialectic in our time is not, as anciently and by some still supposed, between capital and labor; it is between economic enterprise and the state.

JOHN KENNETH GALBRAITH (1908–). *A History of Economics*, 21, 1987

Capitalism is an *economic* order marked by the private ownership of the means of production vested in a minority class called "capitalists," and by a market system that determines the incomes and distributes the outputs arising from its productive activity. It is a *social* order characterized by a "bourgeois" culture, among whose manifold aspects the drive for wealth is the most important.

ROBERT L. HEILBRONER (1919–). *An Inquiry into the Human Prospect*, 3, 1974

From the beginning, capitalism has been characterized by a tension between laissez-faire and intervention—laissez-faire representing the expression of its economic drive, intervention its democratic orientation. That tension continues today, a deeply imbedded part of the historic character of the capitalist system.

ROBERT L. HEILBRONER (1919–) and LESTER C. THUROW (1938–). *Economics Explained*, updated ed., 1, 1987 (1982)

Agriculture, manufactures, commerce, and navigation, the four pillars of our prosperity, are the most thriving when left to individual enterprise.

THOMAS JEFFERSON (1743–1826). *First Annual Message to Congress*, 8 December 1801

Everything is relative, everything is in chains. Capitalism is a condition both of the world and of the soul.

FRANZ KAFKA (1883–1924). In Gustav Janouch, *Conversations with Kafka*, p. 86, tr. Goronwy Rees, 1953

From one point of view capitalist society is a great confidence game, for it feeds on fantastic hopes. Millions throb with the prospect of fabulous riches in an economic system which is inherently destined to disappoint most of them.

HAROLD D. LASSWELL (1902–1978). *Politics: Who Gets What, When, How*, 4, 1936

Freedom in capitalist society always remains about the same as it was in the ancient Greek republics: freedom for the slave-owners.

LENIN (1870–1924). *The State and Revolution*, 5.2, 1917, International Publishers edition, 1971

These capitalists generally act harmoniously, and in concert, to fleece the people.

ABRAHAM LINCOLN (1809–1865). Speech on the state bank, Illinois legislature, 11 January 1837

You show me a capitalist, I'll show you a bloodsucker.

MALCOLM X (1925–1965). *Malcolm X Speaks*, 10, 1965

Not every problem someone has with his girlfriend is necessarily due to the capitalist mode of production.

HERBERT MARCUSE (1898–1979). In *Listener* (British magazine), 1978

Capitalism subjects any individual capitalist to the immanent laws of capitalist production, laws which are external and coercive. Without respite, competition forces him to extend his capital for the sake of maintaining it.

KARL MARX (1818–1883). *Capital: A Critique of Political Economy*, 1867–1894. In Karl R. Popper, *The Open Society and Its Enemies*, 2.16.1, 1945

The chief difference between free capitalism and State socialism seems to be this: that under the former a man pursues his own advantage openly, frankly and honestly, whereas under the latter he does so hypocritically and under false pretenses.

H. L. MENCKEN (1880–1956). *Minority Report: H. L. Mencken's Notebooks*, 397, 1956

The capitalists prohibit the utilization of new inventions, buying them up to avoid the loss of their investment in existing facilities. They are interested in increased productivity and in technical progress only as profits can thereby be maintained or increased.

C. WRIGHT MILLS (1916–1962). "Inventory of Marx's Ideas," *The Marxists*, 1962

The conflict between capitalism and democracy is inherent and continuous; it is often hidden by misleading propaganda and by the outward forms of democracy, such as parliaments and the sops that the owning classes throw to the other classes to keep them more or less contented.

JAWAHARLAL NEHRU (1889–1964). 7 August 1933, *Glimpses of World History*, rev. ed., 193, 1939

Capitalism works better than it sounds, while socialism sounds better than it works.

RICHARD M. NIXON (1913–1994). *Beyond Peace*, 3, 1994
See Criticism: Examples: Bill Nye

It can be said of capitalism what Winston Churchill once said of democracy—it is the worst possible system, except for all the others.

ROBERT J. SAMUELSON. Opening words, "Capitalism Under Siege," *Newsweek*, 6 May 1996
See Democracy: Winston Churchill

Capitalism justified itself and was adopted as an economic principle on the express ground that it provides selfish motives for doing good, and that human beings will do nothing except for selfish motives.

GEORGE BERNARD SHAW (1856–1950). *The Intelligent Woman's Guide to Socialism, Capitalism, Sovietism and Fascism*, 66, 1928

Under fully developed Capitalism civilization is always on the verge of revolution. We live as in a villa on Vesuvius.

GEORGE BERNARD SHAW (1856–1950). *The Intelligent Woman's Guide to Socialism, Capitalism, Sovietism and Fascism*, 66, 1928

Capitalism means the direction of industry by the owners of capital for their own pecuniary gain.

R. H. TAWNEY (1880–1962). *Religion and the Rise of Capitalism: A Historical Study*, 2.2, 1926

We need a free economy not only for the renewed material prosperity it will bring, but because it is indispensable to individual freedom, human dignity and to a more just, more honest society.

MARGARET THATCHER (1925–). Speech before the Zurich Economic Society, University of Zurich, 14 March 1977

Ideology produced the great macrosystems of capitalism and communism. The latter rose in response to the abuses and injustices of the former, and communism finally collapsed under the weight of its own hypocrisy, repression, and failure.

JIM WALLIS (1948–). *The Soul of Politics: A Practical and Prophetic Vision for Change*, 2, 1994

A kind of capitalism in which profits are private and losses are socialized.

GEORGE F. WILL (1941–). Commentator. Referring to the U.S. government's bailout of the savings and loan banking system, *This Week with David Brinkley*, television news program, ABC, 26 November 1989

The truth is, we are all caught in a great economic system which is heartless.

WOODROW WILSON (1856–1924). *The New Freedom: A Call for the Emancipation of the Generous Energies of a People*, 1, 1913

CATS

See also • Animals

A Cat has nine Lives.

THOMAS FULLER (1654–1734). Comp., *Gnomologia: Adages and Proverbs*, 34, 1732

He marveled at the fact that cats had two holes cut in their fur at precisely the spot where their eyes were.

GEORG CHRISTOPH LICHTENBERG (1742–1799). *Aphorisms*, G.26, 1806, tr. R. J. Hollingdale, 1990

When I play with my cat, who knows if I am not a pastime to her more than she is to me.

MONTAIGNE (1533–1592). "Apology for Raymond Sebond," *Essays*, 1588, tr. Donald M. Frame, 1958

Life with a cat is in certain ways a one-sided proposition. Cats are not educable; humans are. Moreover, cats know this. If you're not willing to humor them, you might as well stick to dogs.

TERRY TEACHOUT. Biographer. "What's New Pussycat?" *Washington Post Book World*, 10 November 1991

CAUSE & EFFECT

See also • Chance ○ Children's Learning: Herbert Spencer (3) ○ Logic ○ Luck ○ Means & Ends ○ Morality ○ Motives ○ Reason ○ Success: Albert Schweitzer ○ Wisdom: Oliver Goldsmith

Every action must be due to one or other of seven causes: chance, nature, compulsion, habit, reasoning, anger, or appetite.

ARISTOTLE (384–322 B.C.). *Rhetoric*, 1.10, tr. W. Rhys Roberts, 1954

What is found in the effect was already in the cause.

HENRI BERGSON (1859–1941). *Creative Evolution*, 1, 1907

Cause and effect are two sides of one fact.

RALPH WALDO EMERSON (1803–1882). "Circles," *Essays: First Series*, 1841

Every chemical substance, every plant, every animal in its growth, teaches the unity of cause, the variety of appearance.

RALPH WALDO EMERSON (1803–1882). "History," *Essays: First Series*, 1841

Cause and Effect, the chancellors of God.

RALPH WALDO EMERSON (1803–1882). "Self-Reliance," *Essays: First Series*, 1841

Curiosity, or love of the knowledge of causes, draws a man from consideration of the effect to seek the cause; and again, the cause of that cause, till of necessity he must come to this thought at last, that there is some cause, whereof there is no former cause, but is eternal, which . . . men call God.

THOMAS HOBBES (1588–1679). *Leviathan*, 11, 1651

In the spiritual life, every cause is also an effect, and every effect is at the same time a cause.

ALDOUS HUXLEY (1894–1963). "Reflections on the Lord's Prayer—III." In Christopher Isherwood, ed., *Vedanta for the Western World*, 1945

To prevent an effect from occurring at all requires a force equal to the cause of that effect, but to give it a new direction often requires only something very trivial.

GEORG CHRISTOPH LICHTENBERG (1742–1799). *Aphorisms*, J.232, 1806, tr. R. J. Hollingdale, 1990

How can we be so willfully blind as to look for causes in nature when nature herself is an effect?

JOSEPH-MARIE de MAISTRE (1753–1851)

Direct causes operate only within certain limits; beyond them they produce the opposite effect.

BORIS PASTERNAK (1890–1960). *Doctor Zhivago*, 11.8, 1957, tr. Max Hayward and Manya Harari, 1958

All things and events are foreshown and brought into being by causes; but the causation is of two Kinds; there are results originating from the Soul and results due to . . . the environment.

PLOTINUS (A.D. 205–270). *The Enneads*, 3.1.10, tr. Stephen MacKenna and B. S. Page, 1952

Thou Great First Cause, least Understood!

ALEXANDER POPE (1688–1744). "The Universal Prayer," 2, 1738

Life is not a process of mere predictable cause and effect. Both cause and effect are aspects of something greater than either.

LAURENS van der POST (1906–1996). "Point of Total Return," *Jung and the Story of Our Time,* 1975

Between cause and its so-called effect there falls, as it were, a cosmic shadow and out of this shadow man can accomplish a transfiguration of his own, participating, however minutely, in an act of universal creation, and something effective that no cause all alone and purely out of itself could have produced.

LAURENS van der POST (1906–1996). "Point of Total Return," *Jung and the Story of Our Time,* 1975

CELEBRITY

See also • Charisma ○ Fame ○ Heroism ○ Hero-Worship: Daniel J. Boorstin ○ Media: Richard Rutowsky ○ Publicity ○ Public Relations ○ Stardom

The celebrity is a person who is known for his well-knownness.

DANIEL J. BOORSTIN (1914–). *The Image: A Guide to Pseudo-Events in America,* 2.3, 1961

These new-model "heroes" are receptacles into which we pour our own purposelessness. They are nothing but ourselves seen in a magnifying mirror.

DANIEL J. BOORSTIN (1914–). On celebrities, *The Image: A Guide to Pseudo-Events in America,* 2.3, 1961

The hero is made by folklore, sacred texts, and history books, but the celebrity is the creature of gossip, of public opinion, of magazines, newspapers, and the ephemeral images of movie and television screen. The passage of time, which creates and establishes the hero, destroys the celebrity. One is made, the other unmade, by repetition. The celebrity is born in the daily papers and never loses the mark of his fleeting origin.

DANIEL J. BOORSTIN (1914–). *The Image: A Guide to Pseudo-Events in America,* 2.4, 1961

A sign of a celebrity is often that his name is worth more than his services.

DANIEL J. BOORSTIN (1914–). *The Image: A Guide to Pseudo-Events in America,* 5.4, 1961

[Celebrities are] the "names" who, once made by news, now make news by themselves.

CELEBRITY REGISTER. Ad. In Daniel J. Boorstin, *The Image: A Guide to Pseudo-Events in America,* 2.3, 1961

Celebrity: the advantage of being known by those who do not know you.

CHAMFORT (1741–1794). *Maxims and Thoughts,* 2, 1796, tr. W. S. Merwin, 1984

Celebrity is the religion of our time.

MAUREEN DOWD. "Camelot 144," *New York Times,* 25 April 1996

The insane coverage of [Princess Diana's] death is of a piece with the insane coverage of her life. We can't stop. The photographers can't stop. The reporters can't stop. The producers can't stop. The editors can't stop. And the consumers can't stop. The celebrity culture has become a mass psychosis.

MAUREEN DOWD. "Death and the Maiden," *New York Times,* 3 September 1997

By seeming to anoint new celebrities and banish many of the old from the media spotlight, the public not only feels knowing, it gets the exhilaration of seeming to exercise power over the culture. The public giveth and the public taketh away. It is the only way we can redress the imbalance between the famous and ourselves.

NEAL GARBLER. "The Brief Half-Life of Celebrity," *New York Times,* 16 October 1994

What is . . . different about contemporary celebrities is their power to assemble floating "communities" of like-minded followers—an identity that people can attach to and call their own. Celebrities are trusted, celebrities stand for certain things, the ideas and values to which followers can express political allegiance. In a fragmented society when people drift in isolation, this seems a weak (and sometimes pathetic) substitute for a genuine community, but people do the best they can with what they've got.

WILLIAM GREIDER (1936–). *Who Will Tell the People: The Betrayal of American Democracy,* 14, 1992

The celebrity cult celebrates the triumph of ordinariness—charm without character, showmanship without ability, bodies without minds, information without wisdom.

ORRIN E. KLAPP (1915–). *Heroes, Villains, and Fools: The Changing American Character,* 6, 1962

I have a slight understanding of what it's like to be half a man and half something else, something larger. . . . Obviously, a celebrity is a long, long, long, long way from the celestial, but nonetheless it does mean you have two personalities you live with all the time. One is your simple self, so to speak, which is to some degree still like other people's, and then there's the opposite one, the media entity, which gives you power that you usually don't know how to use well.

NORMAN MAILER (1923–). Sean Abbott interview, "Mailer Goes to the Mountain," *At Random,* Spring-Summer 1997

A celebrity is one who is known to many persons he is glad he doesn't know.

H. L. MENCKEN (1880–1956). *A Little Book in C Major,* 5.5, 1916

The power elite is not so noticeable as the celebrities, and often does not want to be; the "power" of the professional celebrity is the power of distraction.

C. WRIGHT MILLS (1916–1962). *The Power Elite,* 15.3, 1956

The fundamental rule of the Age of Celebrity: "It doesn't matter what you are, it only matters what people think you are."

LANCE MORROW (1939–). "The Stylishness of Her Privacy," *Time,* 30 May 1994

In a country where there is no royalty and where, post-Watergate, politicians are held in almost universal contempt, celebrity is next to Godliness. Indeed, we want to believe in celebrities for the same reason we want to believe in God: their omnipotence and invincibility, however illusory, hold out the promise that we, too, have a crack at immortality.

FRANK RICH (1949–). "Addicted to O.J.," *New York Times,* 23 June 1994

The faster the rise, the steeper the fall.

> FRANK RICH (1949–). On the "instant obsolescence" of celebrities, "The Glamour Gap," *New York Times*, 31 March 1995

People believe what they want to believe about celebrities. Usually it makes them feel better to believe something negative. That's called human nature.

> LIZ SMITH (1923–). "Brooks Won't Go the Elvis Route," *San Francisco Chronicle*," 8 August 1997

Reverence for celebrities is the flip side of tacit contempt for "average" people. It can be an insidious process: As we focus on the famous, other people fade into our peripheral vision. By an unspoken and unconscious logic the world becomes populated with a few somebodies and a glut of near-nobodies.

> NORMAN SOLOMON (1951–) and JEFF COHEN (1951–). "Hidden Costs of America's Celebrity Obsession," *Wizards of Media Oz: Behind the Curtain of Mainstream News*, 1997

Celebrity is a mask that eats into the face. As soon as one is aware of being "somebody," to be watched and listened to with extra interest, input ceases, and the performer goes blind and deaf in his overanimation. One can either see or be seen.

> JOHN UPDIKE (1932–). *Self-Consciousness: Memoirs*, 6, 1989

CELIBACY

See also • Abstinence ○ Chastity ○ Marriage ○ Singlehood

It's about time that we accepted total celibates as no more deranged, inefficient, unhappy or unhealthy than any other section of the population.

> GERMAINE GREER (1939–). In Val Hennessy, "Germaine Greer," *A Little Light Friction*, 1989

Marriage has many pains, but celibacy has no pleasures.

> SAMUEL JOHNSON (1709–1784). *Rasselas: The Prince of Abyssinia*, 26, 1759

Celibacy [is] a worse failure than marriage.

> GEORGE BERNARD SHAW (1856–1950). Preface ("Jesus on Marriage and the Family") to *Androcles and the Lion*, 1912

CENSORSHIP

See also • Assassination: George Bernard Shaw (3) ○ Freedom of Speech ○ Freedom of the Press ○ Ideas: A. Whitney Griswold ○ Media ○ The Press

We don't need a censorship of the press. We have a censorship by the press.

> G. K. CHESTERTON (1874–1936). *Orthodoxy*, 7, 1909

Where there is official censorship, it is a sign that speech is serious. Where there is none, it is pretty certain that the official spokesmen have all the loudspeakers.

> PAUL GOODMAN (1911–1972). *Growing Up Absurd: Problems of Youth in the Organized Society*, 2.2, 1956

Censorship is largely self-censorship by reporters and commentators who adjust to the realities of source and media organizational requirements, and by people at higher levels within media organizations who are chosen to implement, and have usually internalized, the constraints imposed by proprietary and other market and government centers of power.

> EDWARD S. HERMAN (1925–) and NOAM CHOMSKY (1928–). Preface to *Manufacturing Consent: The Political Economy of the Mass Media*, 1988

No totalitarian censor can approach the implacability of the censor who controls the line of communication between the outer world and our consciousness. Nothing is allowed to reach us which might weaken our confidence and lower our morale.

> ERIC HOFFER (1902–1983). *The Passionate State of Mind: And Other Aphorisms*, 59, 1954

No government ought to be without censors; and where the press is free, no [government] ever will.

> THOMAS JEFFERSON (1743–1826). Letter to George Washington, 9 September 1792

The first thing will be to establish a censorship of the writers of fiction, and let the censors receive any tale of fiction which is good, and reject the bad; and we will desire mothers and nurses to tell their children the authorized ones only.

> PLATO (427?–347 B.C.). *The Republic*, 2.377, tr. Benjamin Jowett, 1894

The weapon of the dictator is not so much propaganda as censorship.

> TERENCE H. QUALTER (1925–). Introduction to *Propaganda and Psychological Warfare*, 1962

All censorships exist to prevent anyone from challenging current conceptions and existing institutions. All progress is initiated by challenging current conceptions, and executed by supplanting existing institutions. Consequently, the first condition of progress is the removal of censorships. There is the whole case against censorships in a nutshell.

> GEORGE BERNARD SHAW (1856–1950). Preface to *Mrs. Warren's Profession*, 1893

History in the making is always censored.

> GRANT SINGLETON (1890–?). Letter

Censorship reflects a society's lack of confidence in itself.

> POTTER STEWART (1915–1985)

If there had been a censorship of the press in Rome, we should have had today neither Horace nor Juvenal, nor the philosophical writings of Cicero.

> VOLTAIRE (1694–1778). Letter to the Commissioner of Police of Paris, 20 June 1733

Self-censorship silences as effectively as a government decree.

> TOM WICKER (1926–). *On Press*, 12, 1978

I can imagine no greater disservice to the country than to establish a system of censorship that would deny to the people of a free republic like our own their indisputable right to criticize their own public officials. While exercising the great powers of the office I hold, I would regret in a crisis like the one through which we are now passing to lose the benefit of patriotic and intelligent criticism.

> WOODROW WILSON (1856–1924). Letter to Arthur Brisbane, 25 April 1917, three weeks after the United States entered World War I

CENSURE

See also • Criticism ○ Criticism: Examples ○ Praise

A man's first care should be to avoid the reproaches of his own heart; his next, to escape the censures of the world.

> JOSEPH ADDISON (1672–1719). In *The Spectator* (English essay series), 122, 20 July 1711

The silence of a friend commonly amounts to treachery. His not daring to say anything in our behalf implies a tacit censure.

> WILLIAM HAZLITT (1778–1830). *Characteristics in the Manner of Rochefoucault's Maxims*, 15, 1823

Mankind is in general more easily disposed to censure than to admiration.

> SAMUEL JOHNSON (1709–1784). In *The Adventurer* (English journal), 131, 5 February 1754

All censure of a man's self is oblique praise. It is in order to show how much he can spare.

> SAMUEL JOHNSON (1709–1784). 25 April 1778. In James Boswell, *The Life of Samuel Johnson*, 1791

They have a Right to censure that have a Heart to help: The rest is Cruelty, not Justice.

> WILLIAM PENN (1644–1718). *Some Fruits of Solitude*, 46, 1693

The dread of censure is the death of genius.

> WILLIAM G. SIMMS (1806–1870). In Peter Potter, "Criticism," *All About Success*, 1988

Censure is the tax a man pays to the public for being eminent.

> JONATHAN SWIFT (1667–1745). "Thoughts on Various Subjects" (expanded from a version published in 1711), *Miscellanies in Prose and Verse* (published with Alexander Pope), vol. 1, 1727
>
> See Envy: Ralph Waldo Emerson

Why should I expect to be exempt from censure, the unfailing lot of an elevated station?

> GEORGE WASHINGTON (1732–1799). Letter to Henry Laurens, President of the Continental Congress, 31 January 1778

❧

Look first at home, then censure me.

> SAYING
>
> See Criticism: John Greenleaf Whittier

CERTAINTY

See also • Belief ○ Conviction ○ Doubt ○ Faith ○ Morality: John Locke ○ Skepticism

If we begin with certainties, we shall end in doubts; but if we begin with doubts, and are patient in them, we shall end in certainties.

> FRANCIS BACON (1561–1626). *Advancement of Learning*, 1, 1605, Willey Book edition, 1944

Positive, *adj.* Mistaken at the top of one's voice.

> AMBROSE BIERCE (1842–1914). *The Devil's Dictionary*, p. 102, 1911, Dover edition, 1958

Sure things seldom are.

> MALCOLM S. FORBES (1919–1990). "More Definitions," *The Sayings of Chairman Malcolm: The Capitalist's Handbook*, 1978

Our Constitution is in actual operation; everything appears to promise that it will last; but nothing in this world is certain except death and taxes.

> BENJAMIN FRANKLIN (1706–1790). Letter to Jean-Baptiste Leroy, 13 November 1789

We are never so certain of our knowledge as when we're dead wrong.

> ADAIR LARA (1952–). "A Lot of Knowledge Is Dangerous Too," *San Francisco Chronicle*, 9 October 1997

I wish I was as cocksure of anything as Tom Macaulay is of everything.

> LORD MELBOURNE (1779–1848). British prime minister. Preface to *Lord Melbourne's Papers*, ed. Earl Cowper, 1889

It is a dull man who is always sure, and the sure man who is always dull.

> H. L. MENCKEN (1880–1956). "The National Letters: Epilogue," *Prejudices: Second Series*, 1920

To be absolutely certain about something, one must know everything or nothing about it.

> OLIN MILLER

Most of the greatest evils that man has inflicted upon man have come through people feeling quite certain about something which, in fact, was false.

> BERTRAND RUSSELL (1872–1970)
>
> See Evil: Russell

The certainties of one age are the problems of the next.

> R. H. TAWNEY (1880–1962). *Religion and the Rise of Capitalism: A Historical Study*, 5, 1926

Doubt is not a pleasant condition, but certainty is an absurd one.

> VOLTAIRE (1694–1778). Letter to Frederick II, 6 April 1767

CHANCE

See also • Accident ○ Cause & Effect ○ Destiny ○ Fate ○ Fortune ○ Luck ○ Misfortune ○ Necessity ○ Opportunity

Chances rule men, and not men chances.

> ARTABANUS (5th cent. B.C.). Persian minister. Remark to King Xerxes. In Herodotus (484?–420? B.C.). *The Persian Wars*, 7.49, tr. George Benjamin Disraeli Rawlinson, 1942
>
> See Circumstances: Benjamin Disraeli

Chance is necessity hidden behind a veil.

> MARIE von EBNER-ESCHENBACH (1830–1916). *Aphorisms*, p. 20, 1880–1905, tr. David Scrase and Wolfgang Mieder, 1994

Chance is perhaps God's pseudonym when He does not want to sign.

> ANATOLE FRANCE (1844–1924). *Le Jardin d'Épicure*, 1894

A wise man turns Chance into good Fortune.

> THOMAS FULLER (1654–1734). Comp., *Gnomologia: Adages and Proverbs*, 475, 1732

The laws of probability, so true in general, so fallacious in particular.

> EDWARD GIBBON (1737–1794). *Memoirs of My Life and Writings*, p. 112, 1796, Alexander Murray edition, 1869

Chance reveals virtues and vices as light reveals objects.

> LA ROCHEFOUCAULD (1613–1680). *Maxims*, 380, 1665, tr. Leonard Tancock, 1959

Chance governs all.

> JOHN MILTON (1608–1674). *Paradise Lost*, 2.910, 1667

No victor believes in chance.

> FRIEDRICH NIETZSCHE (1844–1900). *The Gay Science*, 258, 1882, tr. Walter Kaufmann, 1974

There's no such thing as chance;
And what to us seems merest accident
Springs from the deepest source of destiny.

> FRIEDRICH von SCHILLER (1759–1805). *The Death of Wallenstein*, 2.3, 1799, tr. Samuel T. Coleridge, 1800

His Sacred Majesty, Chance, decides everything.

> VOLTAIRE (1694–1778)

CHANGE

See also • Change & Changelessness ○ Changelessness ○ Constitutions: Thomas Jefferson ○ Conversion ○ Crises ○ Day of Judgment: Paul (1) ○ Evolution ○ History ○ The Individual: Lyndon B. Johnson ○ Opinion ○ Parents: Bob Dylan ○ Personality: Allen Wheelis ○ Progress ○ Reform ○ Self-Realization (Becoming) ○ Transformation ○ World: Anonymous

All appears to change when we change.

> HENRI AMIEL (1821–1881). Journal, 5 February 1853, tr. Mrs. Humphrey Ward, 1887

The people who are crazy enough to think they can change the world are the ones who do.

> APPLE COMPUTER, INC. Television ad, CNN, 15 December 1997

It is a secret, both in nature and state, that it is safer to change many things than one.

> FRANCIS BACON (1561–1626). "Of Regiment of Health," *Essays*, 1625

Any real change implies the breakup of the world as one has always known it, the loss of all that gave one an identity, the end of safety.

> JAMES BALDWIN (1924–1987). In Adrienne Rich, title essay, 1984, *Blood, Bread, and Poetry: Selected Prose 1979–1985*, 1986

No one who hopes for improvement should fail to see and respect the signs that we may be approaching some sort of historical waterfall, past which we will not, by changing our minds, be able to change anything else. We know that at any time an ecological or a technological or a political event that we will have allowed may remove from us the power to make change and leave us with the mere necessity to submit to it.

> WENDELL BERRY (1934–). "The Work of Local Culture," 1988, *What Are People For?: Essays*, 1990

Never underestimate your power to change yourself; never overestimate your power to change others.

> H. JACKSON BROWN, JR. (1940–). *Life's Little Instruction Book*, 1.284–285, 1991

As you come to know the seriousness of our situation—the war, the racism, the poverty in the world—you come to realize it is not going to be changed just by words or demonstrations. It's a question of living your life in a drastically different way.

> DOROTHY DAY (1897–1980)

No scheme for a change of society can be made to appear immediately palatable, except by falsehood, until society has become so desperate that it will accept any change.

> T. S. ELIOT (1888–1965). "The Idea of a Christian Society," 1939

All is change; all yields its place and goes.

> EURIPIDES (485?–406 B.C.). *Heracles*, l. 100, tr. William Arrowsmith, 1956

To a man who prospers and is blessed,
all change is grief.

> EURIPIDES (485?–406 B.C.). *Heracles*, l. 1290, tr. William Arrowsmith, 1956

All changes, even the most longed for, have their melancholy; for what we leave behind us is a part of ourselves; we must die to one life before we can enter into another!

> ANATOLE FRANCE (1844–1924). *The Crime of Sylvestre Bonnard*, 2.4 (September 20), 1881, tr. Lafcadio Hearn, 1890

Most of the change we think we see in life
Is due to truths being in and out of favor.

> ROBERT FROST (1874–1963). "The Black Cottage," *North of Boston*, 1914

Great changes can best be brought about under old forms.

> HENRY GEORGE (1839–1897). *Progress and Poverty: An Inquiry into the Cause of Industrial Depressions and of Increase of Want with Increase of Wealth*, 8.2, 1879

Everything is connected . . . no one thing can change by itself.

> PAUL HAWKEN (1946–). Allan Hunt Badiner interview, "Natural Capitalism," *Yoga Journal*, September-October 1994

Change, according to Hegel, was the rule of life. Every idea, every force, irrepressibly bred its opposite, and the two merged into a "unity" that in turn produced its own contradiction. And history, said Hegel, was nothing but the expression of this flux of conflicting and resolving ideas and forces.

> ROBERT L. HEILBRONER (1919–). Explaination of Hegel's dialectic process (thesis, antithesis and synthesis), *The Worldly Philosophers: The Lives, Times, and Ideas of the Great Economic Thinkers*, 5th ed., 6, 1980 (1953)

All things are in motion and nothing is at rest. . . . You cannot go into the same [river] twice.

HERACLITUS (540?–480? B.C.). As paraphrased by Socrates in Plato
(427?–327 B.C.), *Cratylus,* 402, tr. Benjamin Jowett, 1894

See Books: Marina Tsvetaeva

Every radical adjustment is a crisis in self-esteem: we undergo a
test; we have to prove ourselves. It needs inordinate self-confidence to face drastic change without inner trembling.

ERIC HOFFER (1902–1983). *The Ordeal of Change,* 1, 1964

Change is not made without inconvenience, even from worse to
better.

RICHARD HOOKER (1554?–1600). In Samuel Johnson, preface to *A
Dictionary of the English Language,* 1755

There is a certain relief in change, even though it be from bad to
worse; as I have found in traveling in a stage coach, that it is often
a comfort to shift one's position and be bruised in a new place.

WASHINGTON IRVING (1783–1859). "To the Reader," *Tales of a
Traveler,* 1824

As any change must begin somewhere, it is the single individual
who will experience it and carry it through. The change must
indeed begin with an individual; it might be any one of us.
Nobody can afford to look round and to wait for somebody else
to do what he is loath to do himself.

CARL G. JUNG (1875–1961). Ed., "Approaching the Unconscious:
Healing the Split," *Man and His Symbols,* 1964

The forces of change facing the world could be so far-reaching,
complex, and interactive that they call for nothing less than the
reeducation of humankind.

PAUL KENNEDY (1945–). *Preparing for the Twenty-First Century,*
14, 1993

Great change dominates the world, and unless we move with
change we will become its victims.

ROBERT F. KENNEDY (1925–1968). Farewell statement, news conference, Warsaw, 1 July 1964

Material Poverty provides the incentive to change precisely in situations where there is little margin for experiments. Material
Prosperity removes the incentive just when it might be safe to take
a chance.

JOHN MAYNARD KEYNES (1883–1946). *The End of Laissez-Faire,*
5, 1926

The prime condition of national survival has been timely adaptation to changing conditions.

B. H. LIDDELL HART (1895–1970). "Adaptability Is the Condition of
Survival," 15 February 1941, *This Expanding War,* 1942

When I speak of change, I do not mean a simple switch of positions or a temporary lessening of tensions, nor the ability to smile
or feel good. I am speaking of a basic and radical alteration in all
those assumptions underlining our lives.

AUDRE LORDE. "The Uses of Anger," *Women's Studies Quarterly,* Fall
1981

The wind of change is blowing through this continent, and,
whether we like it or not, this growth of national consciousness is
a political fact.

HAROLD MACMILLAN (1894–1986). British prime minister. Parliament
speech, Cape Town (South Africa), 3 February 1960

Observe how all things are continually being born of change. . . .
Whatever is, is in some sense the seed of what is to emerge
from it.

MARCUS AURELIUS (A.D. 121–180). *Meditations,* 4.36, tr. Maxwell
Staniforth, 1964

Control over change would seem to consist in moving not with it
but ahead of it.

MARSHALL McLUHAN (1911–1980). *Understanding Media:
The Extensions of Man,* 20, 1964

Change occurs when there is a confluence of both changing values and economic necessity, not before.

JOHN NAISBITT (1929–). *Megatrends: Ten New Directions Transforming
Our Lives,* 7, 1984

It is not possible for any thinking person to live in such a society
as our own without wanting to change it.

GEORGE ORWELL (1903–1950). "Why I Joined the Independent Labour
Party," 24 June 1938, *The Collected Essays, Journalism and Letters of
George Orwell,* vol. 1, ed. Sonia Orwell and Ian Angus, 1968

All things change, but nothing dies.

OVID (43 B.C.–A.D. 17). *Metamorphoses,* 15.162, tr. Mary M. Innes, 1955

Only the most absolute sincerity under heaven can affect any
change.

EZRA POUND (1885–1972). Summing up the teachings of Confucius. In
Robert Giroux, "The Poet in the Asylum," *Atlantic,* August 1988

All big changes in human history have been arrived at slowly and
through many compromises.

ELEANOR ROOSEVELT (1884–1962). In Joseph P. Lash, *Eleanor and
Franklin: The Story of Their Relationship,* 27, 1971

My contemplation of life and human nature in that secluded place
[in prison] had taught me that he who cannot change the very fabric of his thought will never be able to change reality, and will
never, therefore, make any progress. The fact that change is a prerequisite of progress may be axiomatic; but the fact that change
should take place first at a deeper and perhaps subtler level than
the conscious level was one I had established as a basis of action
ever since I discovered my real self in Cell 54.

ANWAR el-SADAT (1918–1981). *In Search of Identity: An Autobiography,*
10:13, 1978

The *participation hypothesis*— . . . Significant changes in human
behavior can be brought about rapidly only if the persons who
are expected to change participate in deciding what the change
shall be and how it shall be made.

HERBERT A. SIMON (1916–). "Recent Advances in Organization Theory."
In *Research Frontiers in Politics and Government* (Brookings Lectures),
1955

Nothing ever is, but all things are becoming. . . . All things are the
offspring of flux and motion.

SOCRATES (470?–399 B.C.). In Plato (427?–347 B.C.), *Theaetetus,* 152,
tr. Benjamin Jowett, 1894

Change is the process by which the future invades our lives.

> ALVIN TOFFLER (1928–). Introduction to *Future Shock,* 1970
>
> See Evolution: Toffler

"Future shock" . . . [is] the shattering stress and disorientation that we induce in individuals by subjecting them to too much change in too short a time.

> ALVIN TOFFLER (1928–). Introduction to *Future Shock,* 1970

The responsibility for change . . . lies with us. We must begin with ourselves, teaching ourselves not to close our minds prematurely to the novel, the surprising, the seemingly radical. This means fighting off the idea-assassins who rush forward to kill any new suggestion on grounds of its impracticality, while defending whatever now exists as practical, no matter how absurd, oppressive, or unworkable it may be. It means fighting for freedom of expression—the right of people to voice their ideas, even if heretical.

Above all, it means starting this process of reconstruction now, before the further disintegration of existing political systems sends the forces of tyranny jackbooting through the streets, and makes impossible a peaceful transition to Twenty-first Century Democracy.

> ALVIN TOFFLER (1928–). *The Third Wave,* 28, 1980

We believe that the most basic of all changes in human social organization have been the result of three processes. Starting 8,000 to 10,000 years ago, agriculture was invented in the Middle East—probably by a woman. That's the First Wave. Roughly 250 years ago, the Industrial Revolution triggered a Second Wave of change. Brute-force technologies amplified human and animal muscle power and gave rise to an urban, factory-centered way of life. Sometime after World War II, a gigantic Third Wave began transforming the planet, based on tools that amplify mind rather than muscle. The Third Wave is bigger, deeper and faster than the other two. This is the civilization of the computer, the satellite and Internet.

> ALVIN TOFFLER (1928–). Claudia Dreifus interview with Toffler and Heidi Toffler, "Present Shock," *New York Times Magazine,* 11 June 1995

The greater the power that we have to change the World into something nearer to our ideal, the greater becomes our distress at our failing to perform those beneficent and useful acts of creation which we know to be within our power.

> ARNOLD J. TOYNBEE (1889–1975). *Surviving the Future,* 2, 1971

The world will not change until we do.

> JIM WALLIS (1948–). *The Soul of Politics: A Practical and Prophetic Vision for Change,* 3, 1994

It is personalities, not principles, that move the age.

> OSCAR WILDE (1854–1900). "Oscariana," *The Works of Oscar Wilde: Epigrams, Phrases and Philosophies for the Use of the Young,* Sunflower edition, 1909

If you want to make enemies, try to change something.

> WOODROW WILSON (1856–1924). Speech, 10 July 1916

If life becomes hard to bear, we think of a change in our circumstances. But the most important and effective change, a change in

our own attitude, hardly ever occurs to us, and the resolution to take such a step is very difficult for us.

> LUDWIG WITTGENSTEIN (1889–1951). 1946, *Culture and Value,* 1977, tr. Peter Winch, 1980

There can be change without progress, but not progress without change.

> ANONYMOUS

CHANGE & CHANGELESSNESS

See also • Change ∘ Changelessness ∘ Wisdom: Octavio Paz

Only the fairy tale equates changelessness with happiness. . . . Permanence means paralysis and death. Only in movement, with all its pain, is life.

> JACOB BURCKHARDT (1818–1897). "On Fortune and Misfortune in History," 1871, *Force and Freedom: An Interpretation of History,* ed. James H. Nichols, 1943

One never knows what will happen if things are suddenly changed. But do we know what will happen if they are *not* changed?

> ELIAS CANETTI (1905–1994). 1971, *The Human Province,* tr. Joachim Neugroschel, 1978

Nothing is stable. Nothing absolute. All is fluid and changeable. There is an endless "becoming."

> BENJAMIN N. CARDOZON (1870–1938). *The Nature of Judicial Process,* 1, 1921

Change is constant.

> BENJAMIN DISRAELI (1804–1881). Speech, Edinburgh, Scotland, 29 October 1867

Good old Watson! You are the one fixed point in a changing age.

> SIR ARTHUR CONAN DOYLE (1859–1930). Title story, *His Last Bow,* 1917

A capacity to change is indispensable. Equally indispensable is the capacity to hold fast to that which is good.

> JOHN FOSTER DULLES (1888–1959)

I do dimly perceive that while everything around me is ever changing, ever dying, there is underlying all that change a living power that is changeless, that holds all together, that creates, dissolves, and recreates. That informing power of spirit is God, and since nothing else that I see merely through the senses can or will persist, He alone is.

> MOHANDAS K. GANDHI (1869–1948). Recorded voice in "The Spirit of Gandhi," radio documentary, KPFA, Berkeley (California), 20 July 1989

Nothing endures but change.

> HERACLITUS (540?–480? B.C.). In Diogenes Laertius (A.D. 3rd cent.), *Lives of Eminent Philosophers,* 9.8, tr. R. D. Hicks, 1925

There was that law of life, so cruel and so just, which demanded that one must grow or else pay more for remaining the same.

> NORMAN MAILER (1923–). *The Deer Park,* 1955. In "The Sixth Presidential Paper—A Kennedy Miscellany," *The Presidential Papers,* 1963

Everybody continues in its state of rest, or of uniform motion in a right line, unless it is compelled to change that state by forces impressed upon it.

> SIR ISAAC NEWTON (1642–1727). The first law of motion. *Principia Mathematica*, 1687, tr. Andrew Motte, 1729

Variables won't, constants aren't.

> DON OSBORN. "Osborn's Law." In Paul Dickson, comp., *The Official Rules*, p. 184, 1978

The One remains, the many change and pass.

> PERCY BYSSHE SHELLEY (1792–1822). *Adonais: An Elegy on the Death of John Keats, Author of Endymion, Hyperion, Etc.*, l. 460, 1821

Let us suppose that there are two sorts of existences—one seen, the other unseen. . . .
  The seen is the changing, and the unseen is the unchanging.

> SOCRATES (470?–399 B.C.). In Plato (427?–347 B.C.), *Phaedo*, 79, tr. Benjamin Jowett, 1894

Go where we will, we discover infinite change in particulars only, not in generals.

> HENRY DAVID THOREAU (1817–1862). Journal, 5 July 1840

Things do not change; we change.

> HENRY DAVID THOREAU (1817–1862). "Conclusion," *Walden; or Life in the Woods*, 1854

The opposition of the [leisure] class to changes in the cultural scheme is instinctive, and does not rest primarily on an interested calculation of material advantages; it is an instinctive revulsion of any departure from the accepted way of doing and of looking at things—a revulsion common to all men and only to be overcome by stress of circumstances.

> THORSTEIN VEBLEN (1857–1929). *The Theory of the Leisure Class: An Economic Study of Institutions*, 8, 1899

CHANGELESSNESS

See also • Change ∘ Change & Changelessness ∘ Consistency ∘ Obstinacy

The stationary condition is the beginning of the end.

> HENRI AMIEL (1821–1881). Journal, 2 December 1851, tr. Mrs. Humphrey Ward, 1887

A state without the means of some change is without the means of its conservation.

> EDMUND BURKE (1729–1797). *Reflections on the Revolution in France*, p. 106, 1790, Pelican Books edition, 1968
> See Reform: Thomas Babington Macaulay

There are things that must never be changed, under any circumstances.

> ELIAS CANETTI (1905–1994). 1982, *The Secret Heart of the Clock: Notes, Aphorisms, Fragments: 1973–1985*, tr. Joel Agee, 1989

When it is not necessary to change, it is necessary not to change.

> LUCIUS CARY. House of Commons speech, 22 November 1641, *Discourse on the Infallibility of the Church of Rome*, 1660

Things are more like they are now than they have ever been before.

> DWIGHT D. EISENHOWER (1890–1969)

It's a long Lane that never turns.

> THOMAS FULLER (1654–1734). Comp., *Gnomologia: Adages and Proverbs*, 2863, 1732

Nothing . . . is unchangeable but the inherent and inalienable rights of man.

> THOMAS JEFFERSON (1743–1826). Letter to Maj. John Cartwright, 5 June 1824

Can the Ethiopian change his skin,
  or the leopard his spots?

> JEREMIAH (7th cent. B.C.). *Jeremiah* 13:23 (Popular version: Can the leopard change his spots?)
> See Man: Lewis Mumford (3)

I the Lord do not change.

> MALACHI. *Malachi* 3:6

❧

What has been is what will be,
and what has been done is what will be done;
and there is nothing new under the sun.

> ANONYMOUS (*BIBLE*). *Ecclesiastes* 1:9

CHARACTER

See also • Adversity: Anonymous (1) ∘ Dignity ∘ Habit: William James ∘ Honesty ∘ Integrity ∘ Morality ∘ Nations: Theodore Roosevelt ∘ Personality ∘ Responsibility ∘ Self-Discipline ∘ Self-Realization (Being) ∘ Self-Reliance ∘ Speaking: Menander ∘ Sports: Heywood Hale Broun ∘ Success & Failure: Theodore Roosevelt ∘ Virtue

We aim to develop physique, mentality and character in our students; but because the first two are menaces without the third, the greatest of these is character.

> JOSEPH DANA ALLEN. Headmaster. In William M. Williams, "A Letter to Grandparents from the Headmaster," *Poly Prep Magazine*, Brooklyn, Fall 1989

Character will draw after it condition.

> HENRY WARD BEECHER (1813–1887). "Character," *Proverbs from Plymouth Pulpit*, ed. William Drysdale, 1887

To be thoroughly good-natured, and yet avoid being imposed upon, shows great strength ov [sic] character.

> JOSH BILLINGS (1818–1885). "Hot Korn," *Everybody's Friend, or; Josh Billing's Encyclopedia and Proverbial Philosophy of Wit and Humor*, 1874

The great hope of society is individual character.

> WILLIAM ELLERY CHANNING (1780–1842). "Remarks on the Life and Character of Napoleon Bonaparte," 2, 1827-1828

Education, more than nature, is the cause of that great difference which we see in the characters of men.

> LORD CHESTERFIELD (1694–1773). Letter to his son, 3 November 1749

Character is a journey, not a destination.

> BILL CLINTON (1946–). Remark to his inner circle. In Joe Klein, "The Politics of Promiscuity," *Newsweek*, 9 May 1994

The order of things is as good as the character of the population permits.

> RALPH WALDO EMERSON (1803–1882). "The Conservative," lecture, Masonic Temple, Boston, 9 December 1841

Character is that which can do without success.

> RALPH WALDO EMERSON (1803–1882). "Character," *Essays: Second Series,* 1844

No change of circumstances can repair a defect of character.

> RALPH WALDO EMERSON (1803–1882). "Character," *Essays: Second Series,* 1844

Character calls forth character.

> GOETHE (1749–1832). *The Maxims and Reflections of Goethe,* 29, tr. T. Bailey Saunders, 1892

Fame is a vapor, popularity an accident, riches take wings, those who cheer today will curse tomorrow; only one thing endures—character.

> HORACE GREELEY (1811–1872). Quoted by Clark M. Clifford, "The Presidency As I Have Seen It" (A Special Section). In Emmet John Hughes, *The Living Presidency: The Resources and Dilemmas of the American Presidential Office,* 1972

Character is destiny.

> HERACLITUS (540?–480? B.C.). *On the Universe,* 121
> See Body: Napoleon ○ Temperament: Anonymous

Resistance, whether to one's appetites or to the ways of the world, is a chief factor in the shaping of character.

> ERIC HOFFER (1902–1983). *The Ordeal of Change,* 16, 1964

Character is what you do when nobody is looking.

> HENRY HUFFMAN. Mount Lebanon (Pennsylvania), assistant superintendent of schools. In Stephen Bates, "A Textbook of Virtues," *New York Times,* 8 January 1995

Nothing discloses real character like the use of power.

> ROBERT G. INGERSOLL (1833–1899). "Fragments," *The Philosophy of Ingersoll,* ed. Vere Goldthwaite, 1906
> See Power: Saying (Greek)

What is character but the determination of incident? What is incident but the illustration of character?

> HENRY JAMES (1843–1916). "The Art of Fiction," *Partial Portraits,* 1888

A man's character is determined by how hard he fights for what he believes in.

> ABEN KANDEL and WARREN DUFF. *The Iron Major* (film), 1943, spoken by Pat O'Brien (in the title role)

The fate of a people depends much more on their character than on their intelligence.

> GUSTAVE LE BON (1841–1931). *Aphorisms of Present Times,* 2.3, 1913, tr. Alice Widener, 1979

There is no better indication of a man's character than the company which he keeps.

> MACHIAVELLI (1469–1527). *The Discourses,* 3.34, 1517, tr. Christian E. Detmold, 1940

Character is what emerges from all the little things you were too busy to do yesterday, but did anyway.

> MIGNON McLAUGHLIN (1915–). *The Second Neurotic's Notebook,* 4, 1966

In the long-run, the best proof of a good character is good actions.

> JOHN STUART MILL (1806–1873). *Utilitarianism,* 2, 1863

No man can climb out beyond the limitations of his own character.

> JOHN MORLEY (1838–1923). "Robespierre" (2), *Critical Miscellanies,* vol. 1, 1886

Character is much easier kept than recovered.

> THOMAS PAINE (1737–1809). *The Crisis* (pamphlet), 13, 19 April 1783

Character is simply habit long continued.

> PLUTARCH (A.D. 46?–119?)

You can tell a lot about a fellow's character by the way he eats jellybeans.

> RONALD REAGAN (1911–). Slightly modified. In Robert Lindsey, "Halcyon Era for the Jellybean," *New York Times,* 15 January 1981

You can tell the character of every man when you see how he gives and receives praise.

> SENECA THE YOUNGER (5? B.C.–A.D. 65). "On Choosing Our Teachers," *Moral Letters to Lucilius,* 52.12, tr. Richard M. Gummere, 1918

Standing for right when it is unpopular is a true test of moral character.

> MARGARET CHASE SMITH (1897–1995). Maine senator. Speech, Westbrook Junior College, Portland, 7 June 1953

His character was of an average kind, rather free from vices than distinguished by virtues.

> TACITUS (A.D. 56?–120?). *The History,* 1.49, tr. Alfred J. Church and William J. Brodribb, 1942

The one great requisite is character.

> *TALMUD* (A.D. 1st–6th cent.). Rabbinical writings. In Louis I. Newman, comp., *The Talmudic Anthology,* 127, 1945

Character is formed by an interaction between a person's heredity and his response to his environment.

> ARNOLD J. TOYNBEE (1889–1975). *The Toynbee-Ikeda Dialogue: Man Himself Must Choose,* 4, 1976

Character is power.

> BOOKER WASHINGTON (1856–1915). Quoted on *Tony Brown's Journal,* television interview program, PBS, 22 August 1987
> See Knowledge: Francis Bacon (1)

We should seek to arrange the development of character along a path of natural activity, in itself pleasurable.

> ALFRED NORTH WHITEHEAD (1861–1947). *The Aims of Education and Other Essays,* 3, 1929

✹

Character and conduct shape each other.

> ANONYMOUS

Character is the pivot on which everything turns.

> ANONYMOUS

Character is to personality what content is to form.
ANONYMOUS

CHARISMA

See also • Authority ○ Celebrity ○ Greatness ○ Heroism ○ Leaders

Charisma is the result of effective leadership, not the other way around.
WARREN BENNIS (1925–) and BURT NANUS (1936–). "Taking Charge: Leadership and Empowerment," *Leaders: The Strategies for Taking Charge,* 1985

Charisma is the ability to inspire followers with devotion and enthusiasm to a cause. It encourages disciples rather than independent persons. It is a way of investing oneself with authority over others rather than vesting others with authority over themselves.
PETER R. BREGGIN (1936–). *The Heart of Being Helpful: Empathy and the Creation of a Healing Presence,* 1, 1997

The term [charisma] has taken on a number of different but overlapping meanings: leaders' magical qualities; an emotional bond between leader and led; dependence on a father figure by the masses; popular assumptions that a leader is powerful, omniscient, and virtuous; imputation of enormous supernatural power to leaders (secular power, or both); and simply popular support for a leader that verges on love.
JAMES MacGREGOR BURNS (1918–). *Leadership,* 9, 1978

The charismatic leader is the anti-leader, in the sense that he leads everyone into leadership.
DAVID COOPER (1931–). "The Two Faces of Revolution" (footnote 13), *The Death of the Family,* 1970

If no charismatic emerges, people may be truly bereft and lost in a sea of forces and pressures beyond their adaptive capacity. The society may die. If someone does emerge, the people may understandably attribute his rise to "divine grace." Indeed, if he exercises leadership, he may well save his community and help it to renew itself. First, he binds people together by powerfully articulating their values, hopes, and pains. Second, he weaves their hopes into some image of the future. And third, heprovides energy, strategy, and faith that the vision can berealized.
RONALD A. HEIFETZ. *Leadership Without Easy Answers,* 10, 1994

The essence of the indispensability of the charismatic Hero lies in the belief he arouses that he can control the forces of history and achieve its transcendent objective.
JOHN T. MARCUS. "Transcendence and Charisma," *Western Political Quarterly,* March 1961

It's the aura that surrounds the charismatic figure more than it is the figure itself, that draws the followers. [The presidential public relations team's] task is to build that aura.
RAYMOND K. PRICE. In Joe McGinniss, *The Selling of the President 1968,* 2, 1969

Charismatic authority is foreign to all *previous* rules which concern authority.
K. J. RATNAM. "Charisma and Political Leadership" (1), *Political Studies,* October 1964

The type of leader we generally call "charismatic" gets his support very largely from the issues he is associated with, the grievances he seeks to put right and the manner in which he proposes to do so, and the time he chooses for making these issues and grievances the passionate concern of those whom he thinks will be his followers.
K. J. RATNAM. "Charisma and Political Leadership" (1), *Political Studies,* October 1964

A single act of defiance . . . might easily establish a claim to charismatic authority.
DANKWART A. RUSTOW. "Ataturk as Founder of a State," *Daedalus,* Summer 1968

The ability to produce powerful results in the absence of apparent power is the true political miracle, the most common warrant for charismatic legitimacy.
DANKWART A. RUSTOW. "Ataturk as Founder of a State," *Daedalus,* Summer 1968

More than just possessing an attractive magnetism which draws people toward him or her, the charismatic person commands respect by representing contact with some higher order of existence: as if history is personified through the individual.
ALAN W. SCHEFLIN (1942–) and EDWARD M. OPTON, JR. (1936–). Referring to Max Weber's ideas on charisma, *The Mind Manipulators: A Non-Fiction Account,* 2, 1978

Charisma in the narrower and original sense is the state or quality of being, produced by receipt of the gifts of grace.
EDWARD SHILS. "Charisma, Order, and Status," *American Sociological Review,* April 1965

Marvelous is the power which can be exercised, almost unconsciously, over a company, or an individual, or even upon a crowd by one person gifted with good temper, good digestion, good intellect, and good looks.
ANTHONY TROLLOPE (1815–1882). *Rachel Ray,* 26, 1863

To speak of charismatic leaders is to speak of charismatic movements; the two phenomena are inseparable.
ROBERT C. TUCKER (1918–). "The Theory of Charismatic Leadership," *Daedalus,* Summer 1968

The charismatic leader is one in whom, by virtue of unusual personal qualities, the promise or hope of salvation—deliverance from distress—appears to be embodied. He is a leader who convincingly offers himself to a group of people in distress as one peculiarly qualified to lead them out of their predicament. He is in essence a savior, or one who is so perceived by his followers. Charismatic leadership is specifically salvationist or messianic in nature.
ROBERT C. TUCKER (1918–). "The Theory of Charismatic Leadership," *Daedalus,* Summer 1968

The same leader who is charismatic in the eyes of people in distress, for whom salvation lies in change, will be counter-charismatic in the eyes of those who see in change not salvation but ruination.
ROBERT C. TUCKER (1918–). "The Theory of Charismatic Leadership," *Daedalus,* Summer 1968

They show a stubborn self-confidence and faith in the movement's prospects of victory and success. This, indeed, may be the quality that most of all underlies their charisma and explains the extreme devotion and loyalty that they inspire in their followers.

> ROBERT C. TUCKER (1918–). "The Theory of Charismatic Leadership," *Daedalus,* Summer 1968

The media can create the false appearance of charisma in the absence of the genuine wide-scale adulation which would make it a reality. They can fabricate a pseudo-personality cult.

> ROBERT C. TUCKER (1918–). "Personality and Political Leadership," *Political Science Quarterly,* Fall 1977

In order to do justice to their mission, the holders of charisma, the master as well as his disciples and followers, must stand outside the ties of this world, outside routine occupations, as well as outside the routine obligations of family life.

> MAX WEBER (1864–1920). "The Sociology of Charismatic Authority" (1), 1922, *From Max Weber: Essays in Sociology,* tr. H. H. Gerth and C. Wright Mills, 1958

The charismatic leader gains and maintains authority solely by proving his strength in life. If he wants to be a prophet, he must perform miracles; if he wants to be a war lord, he must perform heroic deeds. Above all, however, his divine mission must "prove" itself in that those who faithfully surrender to him must fare well. If they do not fare well, he is obviously not the master sent by the gods.

> MAX WEBER (1864–1920). "The Sociology of Charismatic Authority" (2), 1922, *From Max Weber: Essays in Sociology,* tr. H. H. Gerth and C. Wright Mills, 1958

[The charismatic] attitude is revolutionary and transvalues everything; it makes a sovereign break with all traditional or rational norms: "It is written, but I say unto you."

> MAX WEBER (1864–1920). "The Sociology of Charismatic Authority" (2), 1922, *From Max Weber: Essays in Sociology,* tr. H. H. Gerth and C. Wright Mills, 1958

[Charismatic confidence excludes] the easy self-confidence, no matter how great, of someone bred and schooled to it from an elite background and thus expected by popular assumption to possess it. [It refers instead] to extreme confidence linked to determination and will in the face of seemingly impossible obstacles or the self-confidence linked to the conviction that one is destiny's child chosen to accomplish what others perceive as an impossible mission.

> ANN RUTH WILLNER (1924–). *The Spellbinders: Charismatic Political Leadership,* 6, 1984

[John F.] Kennedy meant to frighten people so that they would flock toward him. Since the charismatic leader's special powers grow from special dangers, the two feed on each other. For some crises to be overcome, they must first be created.

> GARRY WILLS (1934–). *The Kennedy Imprisonment: A Meditation on Power,* 13, 1981

CHARITY

See also • Compassion ◦ Day of Judgment: *Talmud* (2) ◦ Giving ◦ Poverty: R. H. Tawney ◦ Welfare

Charity from the heart brings joy.

> THE BRATZLAVER (1770–1811). In Louis I. Newman, comp., *The Hasidic Anthology,* 87.13.B.3, 1934

Too many people have decided to do without generosity in order to practice charity.

> ALBERT CAMUS (1913–1960). *The Fall,* p. 114, tr. Justin O'Brien, 1956

Those who would administer [their surplus wealth] wisely must, indeed, be wise, for one of the serious obstacles to the improvement of our race is indiscriminate charity. It were better for mankind that the millions of the rich were thrown into the sea than so spent as to encourage the slothful, the drunken, the unworthy.

> ANDREW CARNEGIE (1835–1919). "Wealth," *North American Review,* June 1889

Charity begins at home but should not end there.

> THOMAS FULLER (1654–1734). Comp., *Gnomologia: Adages and Proverbs,* 1085, 1732

Charity excuses not Cheating.

> THOMAS FULLER (1654–1734). Comp., *Gnomologia: Adages and Proverbs,* 1086, 1732

Charity is disinterested, seeking no reward, nor allowing itself to be diminished by any return of evil for its good.

> ALDOUS HUXLEY (1894–1963). *The Perennial Philosophy,* 5, 1946

The whole modern scientific organization of charity is a consequence of the failure of simply giving alms.

> WILLIAM JAMES (1842–1910). *The Varieties of Religious Experience: A Study in Human Nature,* 14 and 15, 1902

Philanthropy is commendable, but it must not cause the philanthropist to overlook the circumstances of economic injustice which make philanthropy necessary.

> MARTIN LUTHER KING, JR. (1929–1968). *Strength to Love,* 3.2, 1963

There are eight degrees in almsgiving. . . . Supreme above all is to give assistance to a fellow man who has fallen on evil times by presenting him with a gift or loan, or entering into a partnership with him, or procuring him work, thereby helping him to become self-supporting. Next best is giving alms in such a way that the giver and recipient are unknown to each other. This is, indeed, the performance of a commandment from disinterested motives.

> MOSES MAIMONIDES (A.D. 1135–1204). In Lewis Browne, ed., *The Wisdom of Israel,* p. 357, 1962

In the economy of divine charity we have only as much as give.

> THOMAS MERTON (1915–1968). *No Man Is an Island,* 9.1, 1955

Better is he who gives little to charity from money honestly earned than he who gives much from dishonestly gained wealth.

> *MIDRASH* (4th cent. B.C –A.D. 12th cent.). Rabbinical writings. In Louis I. Newman, comp., *The Talmudic Anthology,* 37, 1945

When you reap your harvest in your field, and have forgotten a sheaf in the field, you shall not go back to get it; it shall be for the sojourner, the fatherless, and the widow; that the Lord your God may bless you in all the work of your hands.

> MOSES (14 cent. B.C.). *Deuteronomy* 24:19

The most excellent of alms is that of a man of small property, which he has earned by labor, and from which he gives as much as he is able.

> MUHAMMAD (A.D. 570?–632). *The Sayings of Muhammad,* 27, tr. Abdullah Al-Suhrawardy, 1941

A man's first charity should be to his own family.

> MUHAMMAD (A.D. 570?–632). *The Sayings of Muhammad,* 29, tr. Abdullah Al-Suhrawardy, 1941

Charity knows neither race nor creed.

> *TALMUD* (A.D. 1st–6th cent.). Rabbinical writings. In Louis I. Newman, comp., *The Talmudic Anthology,* 37, 1945

The greatest charity is to enable the poor to earn a living.

> *TALMUD* (A.D. 1st–6th cent.). Rabbinical writings

Charity begins at home.

> TERENCE (190?–159 B.C.). *Andria,* l. 635, tr. John Sargeaunt, 1912
> See Liberty: James B. Conant ○ Peace: Franklin D. Roosevelt

Our charitable institutions are an insult to humanity. A charity which dispenses the crumbs that fall from its overloaded tables, which are left after its feasts.

> HENRY DAVID THOREAU (1817–1862). Journal, 28 January 1852

With one hand I take thousands of rubles from the poor, and with the other I hand back a few kopecks.

> LEO TOLSTOY (1828–1910). *What Then Must We Do?* 16, 1886

In all the ages, three-fourths of the support of the great charities has been conscience money.

> MARK TWAIN (1835–1910). "A Humane Word from Satan," *Harper's Weekly,* 8 April 1905

Charity [the poor] feel to be a ridiculously inadequate mode of partial restitution, or a sentimental dole, usually accompanied by some impertinent attempt on the part of the sentimentalist to tyrannize over their private lives.

> OSCAR WILDE (1854–1900). "The Soul of Man Under Socialism," *Fortnightly Review* (British journal), February 1891

It is justice, not charity, that is wanting in the world!

> MARY WOLLSTONECRAFT (1759–1797). *A Vindication of the Rights of Woman,* 4, 1792

❦

Damn your charity! We want jobs!

> SAYING (AMERICAN). Among slum dwellers. In Saul D. Alinsky, *Reveille for Radicals,* 4, 1969

CHARM

See also • Beauty ○ Popularity ○ Tact

Charm . . . it's a sort of bloom on a woman. If you have it, you don't need to have anything else; and if you don't have it, it doesn't much matter what else you have.

> J. M. BARRIE (1860–1937). *What Every Woman Knows,* 1, 1908

You must have this charm to reach the pinnacle. It is made of everything and of nothing, the striving will, the look, the walk, the proportions of the body, the sound of the voice, the ease of the gestures. It is not at all necessary to be handsome or to be pretty; all that is needful is charm.

> SARAH BERNHARDT (1844–1923). *The Art of the Theatre,* 2, 1924

You know what charm is: a way of getting the answer yes without having asked any clear question.

> ALBERT CAMUS (1913–1960). *The Fall,* p. 56, tr. Justin O'Brien, 1956

All charming people have something to conceal, usually their total dependence on the appreciation of others.

> CYRIL CONNOLLY (1903–1974). *Enemies of Promise,* 16, 1938

Charm is a woman's strength, just as strength is a man's charm.

> HAVELOCK ELLIS (1859–1939). *The Task of Social Hygiene,* 3, 1912

Some people are unpleasant though worthy, others pleasant despite their faults.

> LA ROCHEFOUCAULD (1613–1680). *Maxims,* 155, 1665, tr. Leonard Tancock, 1959

When good character adds adornment to natural charms, whoever comes near is doubly captivated.

> MENANDER (343?–291 B.C.). Fragment, 645, tr. Francis G. Allinson, 1921

Charms strike the Sight, but Merit wins the Soul.

> ALEXANDER POPE (1688–1744). *The Rape of the Lock,* 5.34, 1714

A beauty is a woman you notice; a charmer is one who notices you.

> ADLAI E. STEVENSON (1900–1965). Speech, Radcliffe College, Cambridge (Massachusetts), 1963

When [John F. Kennedy] flashed his smile, he could charm a bird off a tree.

> SEYMOUR ST. JOHN. Son of the Choate School's headmaster. In Doris Kearns Goodwin, *The Fitzgeralds and the Kennedys,* 27, 1987

[Abraham Lincoln] did not "put you at your ease" when you came into his presence. You felt at your ease without being put there.

> HORACE WHITE (19th cent.). Chicago Tribune. In Dixon Wecter, *The Hero in America: A Chronicle of Hero-Worship,* 10.5, 1941

CHASTITY

See also • Abstinence ○ Asceticism ○ Celibacy ○ Lust: St. Augustine (2) ○ Marriage ○ Sex

Chastity is like an isikel. If it onse melts that's the last ov it.

> JOSH BILLINGS (1818–1885). *His Sayings,* 53, 1867

Chastity is an insult to the Creator and an abomination to man and beast.

> NORMAN DOUGLAS (1868–1952). 15 October, *An Almanac,* 1945

Chastity more rarely follows fear, or a resolution, or a vow, than it is the mere effect of lack of appetite and, sometimes even, of distaste.

> ANDRÉ GIDE (1869–1951). Journal, 12 March 1938, tr. Justin O'Brien, 1951

Chastity—the most unnatural of all sexual perversions.

> ALDOUS HUXLEY (1894–1963). *Eyeless in Gaza,* 27, 1936

Chastity . . . means crucifixion of the flesh.

> A. S. NEILL (1883–1973). *Summerhill: A Radical Approach to Child Rearing*, 7, 1960

CHEATING

See also • Corruption ○ Cunning ○ Deception ○ Lying ○ Theft

It iz a getting so no-a-daze if a man kant cheat in sum way he aint happy.

> JOSH BILLINGS (1818–1885). *On Ice: and Other Things*, 63, 1868

Every man cheats in his own way, and he is only honest who is not discovered.

> SUSANNA CENTLIVRE (1667?–1723). *The Artifice*, 5, 1724

A thing worth having is worth cheating for.

> W. C. FIELDS (1879–1946). *Drat! being the encapsulated view of life by W. C. Fields in His Own Words*, p. 53, comp. Richard J. Anobile, 1975

The world is like a game in which there are honest and dishonest players, so that a prince who plays in this game must learn how to cheat, not in order to do it, but in order not to be the dupe of others.

> FREDERICK II (1712–1786). *Anti-Machiavel*, 18, 1740, tr. Paul Sonnino, 1981

Take heed: Most Men will cheat without Scruple where they can do it without Fear.

> THOMAS FULLER (1654–1734). Comp., *Introductio ad Prudentiam*, 525, 1731

He that's cheated twice by the same Man is an Accomplice with the Cheater.

> THOMAS FULLER (1654–1734). Comp., *Gnomologia: Adages and Proverbs*, 2281, 1732

❧

Who cheats in small things is a fool; in great things, a rogue.

> SAYING (ENGLISH)

CHILD ABUSE

See also • Children ○ Crime ○ Exploitation ○ Oppression ○ Parents ○ Rape ○ Sex ○ Sexual Repression: Sue Armstrong ○ Tobacco: Ralph Nader

Then there was the pain. A breaking and entering when even the senses are torn apart. The act of rape on an eight-year-old body is a matter of the needle giving because the camel can't. The child gives, because the body can, and the violator cannot.

> MAYA ANGELOU (1928–). Describing her own experience, *I Know Why the Caged Bird Sings*, 12, 1970

Childhood trauma and suffering does not provide us with an excuse for our problems. It explains the origins of our problems while in no way relieving us of the responsibility to understand and to improve ourselves. The point is not to blame the people in our past, but to use insight into our past to refocus on the good effects and to free ourselves from its harmful ones.

> PETER R. BREGGIN (1936–). *The Heart of Being Helpful: Empathy and the Creation of a Healing Presence*, 15, 1997

So long as little children are allowed to suffer, there is no true love in this world.

> ISADORA DUNCAN (1877–1927). "Memoirs," 1924, *This Quarter*, Autumn 1929

SHAME SECRET HURT
I already have an
abortion on my conscience
from when a member
of my own family raped me.
Don't worry I won't mention
    your name
Don't worry I won't mention
    your name.

> KAREN FINLEY (1956–). Painting inscription, photograph in *New York Times*, 22 July 1990

I am not sure how many "sins" I would recognize in the world. Some would surely be defused by changed circumstances. But I can imagine none that is more irredeemably sinful than the betrayal, the exploitation, of the young by those who should care for them.

> ELIZABETH JANEWAY. "Incest: A Rational Look at the Oldest Taboo," *Ms.*, November 1981

We want President [Theodore] Roosevelt to hear the wail of the children who never have a chance to go to school but work eleven or twelve hours a day in the textile mills of Pennsylvania; who weave the carpets that . . . you walk upon; and the lace curtains in your windows, and the clothes of your people. Fifty years ago there was a cry against slavery and men gave up their lives to stop the selling of black children on the block. Today the white child is sold for two dollars a week to the manufacturers. Fifty years ago black babies were sold C.O.D. Today the white baby is sold on the installment plan.

> MARY "MOTHER" JONES (1830–1930). Speech, Coney Island, Brooklyn, July 1903, *The Autobiography of Mother Jones*, 10, 1925

No social problem is as universal as the oppression of the child.

> MARIA MONTESSORI (1870–1952). *The Child in the Family*, 1, 1956, tr. Nancy Rockmore Cirillo, 1970

I dinna ken any wrong ye have done this day but I'll thrash ye the same for I hae no doot ye deserve it!

> DANIEL MUIR (19th cent.). Remark that sometimes accompanied regular beatings he administered to his son John Muir (1838–1914). In introduction to *The Wilderness World of John Muir*, comp. Edwin Way Teale, 1954

Parents set themselves to bend the will of their children to their own—to break their stubborn spirit, as they call it—with the ruthlessness of Grand Inquisitors. Cunning, unscrupulous children learn all the arts of the sneak in circumventing tyranny: children of better character are cruelly distressed and more or less lamed for life by it.

> GEORGE BERNARD SHAW (1856–1950). "The Demagogue's Opportunity," *Parents and Children*, 1914

Neglect and ill-usage of children died hard. The streets of the slums were still the only playground for the majority of city children, few of whom had schools to go to until 1870, and none of whom had Play Centers till the turn of the Century. The Society for the Prevention of Cruelty to Children was not founded till 1844; since that year it has dealt effectively with more than five million cases.

> G. M. TREVELYAN (1876–1962). *English Social History: A Survey of Six Centuries, Chaucer to Queen Victoria*, 17, 1942.

Iqbal Masih was an indentured servant in a carpet factory at age 4. He escaped six years later to become a crusader against child labor, closing down dozens of carpet factories in his native Pakistan and winning international acclaim for his work. Last week the 12-year-old, who wanted to be "the Abraham Lincoln of his people," was shot dead in his village. A local man was arrested for the crime, which some suspect was the work of the carpet industry.

> *U.S. NEWS & WORLD REPORT*. "Outlook," 1 May 1995

Lucien Price: Were you ever thrashed by your parents when you were a child?
Whitehead: No. When I needed to be punished, they would give me a dose of medicine and tell me they were sorry I wasn't feeling well.

> ALFRED NORTH WHITEHEAD (1861–1947). 13 January 1944, *Dialogues of Alfred North Whitehead*, rec. Price, 1954

CHILDREN

See also • Adolescence ○ Babies ○ Child Abuse ○ Children's Learning ○ Education ○ Family ○ Fathers ○ Grandparents ○ Home ○ Learning (Process) ○ Mothers ○ Parents ○ Teachers ○ Youth

Children have never been very good at listening to their elders, but they have never failed to imitate them.

> JAMES BALDWIN (1924–1987). *Nobody Knows My Name: More Notes of a Native Son*, 3, 1961

Ah! happy years! once more who would not be a boy?

> LORD BYRON (1788–1824). *Childe Harold's Pilgrimage*, 2.23, 1812–1818

Children are uncertain comforts but certain cares.

> JOHN CLARKE (1596–1658). Comp., *Proverbs: English and Latine*, p. 240, 1639

In the little world in which children have their existence, whosoever brings them up, there is nothing so finely perceived and so finely felt as injustice.

> CHARLES DICKENS (1812–1870). *Great Expectations*, 9, 1861

It takes a family to raise a child.

> BOB DOLE (1923–). Presidential nomination acceptance speech, San Diego, 15 August 1996

I like my boy with his endless sweet soliloquies and iterations and his utter inability to conceive why I should not leave all my nonsense, business, and writing and come to tie up his toy horse, as if there was or could be any end to nature beyond his horse. And he is wiser than we when [he] threatens his whole threat "I will not love you."

> RALPH WALDO EMERSON (1803–1882). Journal, 9 July 1839

It is so easy to give a naughty boy a slap, overpower him in an instant, and make him obey, that in this world of hurry and distraction, who can possibly spend time to wait for the slow return of his reason and the conquest of himself in the uncertainty too whether that will ever come.

> RALPH WALDO EMERSON (1803–1882). Journal, 9 November 1839

We find a delight in the beauty and happiness of children that makes the heart too big for the body.

> RALPH WALDO EMERSON (1803–1882). "Illusions," *The Conduct of Life*, 1860

What silent wonder is waked in the boy by blowing bubbles from soap and water with a pipe.

> RALPH WALDO EMERSON (1803–1882). Journal, 1871–1872, undated

Anonymous: Do you like children?
Fields: I do if they're properly cooked!

> W. C. FIELDS (1879–1946). Format adapted. In *Fields for President*, 7, 1940
> See Babies: Jonathan Swift

Children should neither be seen nor heard from—ever again.

> W. C. FIELDS (1879–1946). Attributed

How children survive being Brought Up amazes me.

> MALCOLM S. FORBES (1919–1990). "Passing Parade," *The Sayings of Chairman Malcolm: The Capitalist's Handbook*, 1978

It is not attention that the child is seeking but love.

> SIGMUND FREUD (1856–1939). 23 January 1930. In Smiley Blanton, *Diary of My Analysis with Sigmund Freud*, 1971

If children grew up according to early indications, we should have nothing but geniuses.

> GOETHE (1749–1832)

Never do for a child what he is capable of doing for himself.

> ELIZABETH G. HAINSTOCK. *Teaching Montessori in the Home*, 1, 1968

Nathaniel Hawthorne: Are you a good little boy?
Julian (his son at age three): Yes.
Nathaniel: [Why] are you good?
Julian: Because I love all people.

> JULIAN HAWTHORNE (19th cent.). Format adapted. In Nathaniel Hawthorne, 6 September 1849, *The American Notebooks*, ed. Claude M. Simpson, 1932

[Toward the end of a long buggy trip in the country now under a full moon] the little man behaved himself still like an old traveler; but sometimes he looked round at me from the front seat (where he sat between Herman Melville and Evert Duyckinck) and smiled at me with a peculiar expression, and put back his hand to touch me. It was a method of establishing a sympathy in what doubtless appeared to him the wildest and unprecedentedest series of adventures that had ever befallen mortal travelers.

> NATHANIEL HAWTHORNE (1804–1864). Referring to his 5-year-old son Julian, 8 August 1851, *The American Notebooks,* ed. Claude M. Simpson, 1932

Better a snotty child than his nose wip'd off.

> GEORGE HERBERT (1593–1633). Comp., *Outlandish Proverbs,* 828, 1640

Be patient with the boys—you are dealing with soul-stuff.

> ELBERT HUBBARD (1856–1915). *The Note Book of Elbert Hubbard,* p. 78, comp. Elbert Hubbard II, 1927

No day can be so sacred but that the laugh of a little child will make it holier still.

> ROBERT G. INGERSOLL (1833–1899). "Liberty of Man, Woman and Child," *The Lectures of Col. R. G. Ingersoll: Latest,* 1898

We are the world,
We are the children,
We are the ones
To make a better day.

> MICHAEL JACKSON (1958–) and LIONEL RICHIE (1949–). "We Are the World" (song), 1985

Let the children come to me, do not hinder them; for to such belongs the kingdom of God.

> JESUS (A.D. 1st cent.). *Mark* 10:14

Children are people.

> JOSEPH JOUBERT (1754–1824). 1805. *Pensées,* 1838, tr. Paul Auster, 1983

Children have more need of models than of critics.

> JOSEPH JOUBERT (1754–1824). *Pensées,* 261, 1838, tr. Henry Attwell, 1877

"It Takes a City to Raise a Child,"

> ADAIR LARA (1952–). Column headline. *San Francisco Chronicle,* 16 March 1995

To this hour I cannot really understand why little children are not just as constantly laughing as they are constantly crying.

> GEORG CHRISTOPH LICHTENBERG (1742–1799). *Aphorisms,* K.32, 1806, tr. R. J. Hollingdale, 1990

Ye are better than all the ballads
  That ever were sung or said;
For ye are living poems,
  And all the rest are dead.

> HENRY WADSWORTH LONGFELLOW (1807–1882). Closing stanza, "Children," *Birds of Passage,* 1858

Children are God's apostles, day by day
Sent forth to preach of love, and hope, and peace.

> JAMES RUSSELL LOWELL (1819–1891). "On the Death of a Friend's Child," 1844

The knowingness of little girls
Is hidden underneath their curls.

> PHYLLIS McGINLEY. "What Every Woman Knows," *Times Three,* 1960

The child is innocence and forgetfulness, a new beginning, a sport, a self-propelling wheel, a first motion, a sacred Yes.

> FRIEDRICH NIETZSCHE (1844–1900). "Of the Three Metamorphoses," *Thus Spoke Zarathustra,* 1892, tr. R. J. Hollingdale, 1961

Children's liberation is the next item on our civil rights shopping list.

> LETTY COTTIN POGREBIN. "Down with Sexist Upbringing." In Francine Klagsbrun, ed., *The First Ms. Reader,* 1972

One cardinal principle might be named, that of maximum reasonable autonomy: the child (or for that matter anyone) should be free to act unless harmful consequences can be clearly shown.

> JOHN RADFORD (1931–). *Child Prodigies and Exceptional Early Achievers,* 11, 1990

The roots of a child's ability to cope and thrive, regardless of circumstance, lie in that child's having had at least a small, safe place (an apartment? a room? a *lap?*) in which, in the companionship of a loving person, that child could discover that he or she was lovable and capable of loving in return.

> FRED ROGERS (1928–). *Mister Rogers Talks with Parents,* 1, 1983

When the orphan sets a-crying, the throne of the Almighty is rocked from side to side.

> SA'DI (A.D. 1213?–1292). In Ralph Waldo Emerson, "The Fugitive Slave Law," address, The Tabernacle, New York City, 7 March 1854

Every child has a right to its own bent. . . . It has a right to find its own way and go its own way, whether that way seems wise or foolish to others, exactly as an adult has. It has a right to privacy as to its own doings and its own affairs as much as if it were its own father.

> GEORGE BERNARD SHAW (1856–1950). "The Manufacture of Monsters," *Parents and Children,* 1914

If for only half an hour a day, a child should do something serviceable to the community.

> GEORGE BERNARD SHAW (1856–1950). "The Horror of the Perpetual Holiday," *Parents and Children,* 1914

"Wanted: A Child's Magna Charta."

> GEORGE BERNARD SHAW (1856–1950). Section heading, *Parents and Children,* 1914

Oh, a devil of a childhood, rich only in dreams; frightful and loveless in realities.

> GEORGE BERNARD SHAW (1856–1950). On himself, letter, *The Wit and Wisdom of Bernard Shaw,* 30, ed. Stephen Winsten, 1949

[My childhood was] a period of waiting for the moment when I could send everyone and everything connected with it to hell.

> IGOR STRAVINSKY (1882–1971). In "Igor Stravinsky: An 'Inventor of Music' Whose Works Created a Revolution," *New York Times,* 7 April 1971

Every child comes with the message that God is not yet discouraged of man.

> RABINDRANATH TAGORE (1861–1941). *Stray Birds,* 77, 1914

Remember the feeling as a child
when you woke up and morning smiled,
it's time you felt like that again.

TAJ MAHAL. "Take a Giant Step" (song), 1969

The wildest colts make the best horses.
> THEMISTOCLES (523?–458 B.C.). In Plutarch (A.D. 46?–119?),
> "Themistocles," *Parallel Lives,* Dryden edition, 1693

Growing up is a dialectical process that requires things that one can push against in order to become stronger. It takes limited war against worthy opponents; a child matures by testing himself against limits set by loving adults.
> *TIME.* "On Being an American Parent" (essay), 15 December 1967

There was a child went forth every day.
And the first object he looked upon and received with wonder or pity or love or dread, that object he became.
And that object became part of him for the day or a certain part of the day. . . . or for many years or stretching cycles of years. [Ellipsis points in original.]
> WALT WHITMAN (1819–1892). Opening lines, "There Was a Child Went
> Forth," 1855, *Leaves of Grass,* 1855-1892

The Child is father of the Man.
> WILLIAM WORDSWORTH (1770–1850). "My Heart Leaps Up When I
> Behold," l. 7, 1807

❧

Anonymous: What do you want to be?
Anonymous third-grader (in writing): I would like to be myself. I tried to be other things, but I always failed.
> ANONYMOUS. Format adapted. In R. Buckminster Fuller, *I Seem To Be a
> Verb,* p. 177, 1970

It takes a village to raise a child.
> SAYING (AFRICAN)

Children are love made visible.
> SAYING (NEW YORK)

CHILDREN'S LEARNING

See also • Babies ○ Children ○ Education ○ Fathers ○ Learning (Process): [especially] John Holt ○ Morality: Rousseau ○ Mothers ○ Parents ○ Self-Realization (Becoming) ○ Teachers

Reading to children at night, responding to their smiles with a smile, returning their vocalizations with one of your own, touching them, holding them—all of these further a child's brain development and future potential, even in the earliest months.

Research demonstrates that the early responsiveness of caring parents sets the tone for future self-esteem, trust, problem solving, ability to communicate successfully and motivation for future learning.
> T. BERRY BRAZELTON (1918–). Pediatrician. Summarizing some of the
> research findings presented at a April White House conference on
> early child development, "Don't Pressure Bright Children," *San
> Francisco Chronicle,* 9 June 1997

Dr. [Paula] Menyuk and her co-workers [at Boston University's School of Education] found that parents who supplied babies with a steady stream of information were not necessarily helpful. Rather, early, rich language skills were more likely to develop when parents provided lots of opportunities for their infants and toddlers to "talk" and when parents listened and responded to the babies' communications.
> JANE E. BRODY (1941–). "Talking to the Baby: Some Expert Advice,"
> *New York Times,* 5 May 1987

Tiny children want to learn to the degree that they are unable to distinguish learning from fun. They keep this attitude until we adults convince them that learning is *not* fun.
> GLENN DOMAN. *How to Teach Your Baby to Read: The Gentle
> Revolution,* 2, 1964

Those acquirements crammed by force into the minds of children simply clog and stifle intelligence. In order that knowledge be properly digested, it must be swallowed with a good appetite.
> ANATOLE FRANCE (1844–1924). *The Crime of Sylvestre Bonnard,* 2.4
> (June 6), 1881, tr. Lafcadio Hearn, 1890

Children love repetition, but not when it's overdone. They will lose interest if you progress too slowly, and if you go too quickly the materials will be beyond their comprehension.
> ELIZABETH G. HAINSTOCK. *Teaching Montessori in the Home,* 1, 1968

Children who are not spoken to by . . . responsive adults will not learn to speak properly. Children who are not answered will stop asking questions. They will become incurious. And children who are not told stories and who are not read to will have few reasons for wanting to learn to read.
> GAIL HALEY. 1971, Caldecott Medal acceptance speech. In Jim Trelease,
> *The New Read-Aloud Handbook,* 1 (epigraph), 1982

I remember a lot of talk and a lot of laughter. I must have talked a great deal because Martha used to say again and again, "You remember you said this, you said that. . . . " She remembered everything I said, and all my life I've had the feeling that what I think and what I say are worth remembering. She gave me that.
> ERIC HOFFER (1902–1983). On Martha Bauer, the woman who raised
> him after his mother died. In Calvin Tompkins, "Profiles: The Creative
> Situation," *New Yorker,* 7 January 1967

If we continually try to force a child to do what he is afraid to do, he will become more timid, and will use his brains and energy, not to explore the unknown, but to find ways to avoid the pressures we put on him. If, however, we are careful not to push a child beyond the limits of his courage, he is almost sure to get braver.
> JOHN HOLT (1923–1985). "Sports," *How Children Learn,* 1967

People who are skillful with words are able, most of the time, to encourage the growth of that skill in their children. Such children, when still babies, are encouraged to try to talk by hearing talk around them. When they begin real talking, they are further encouraged, because their parents (and other older people) are persistent and resourceful in trying to understand them. In a family with little verbal skill, a baby can be handicapped, not just because he hears so little talk, but also because, when he does try to talk, he is less often understood, and hence less often encouraged. If people do not try very hard to understand what he says, he may come to feel that most of the time there is not much point in saying anything.
> JOHN HOLT (1923–1985). "Talk," *How Children Learn,* 1967

Man is by nature a learning animal. Birds fly, fish swim; man thinks and learns. Therefore, we do not need to "motivate" children into learning, by wheedling, bribing, or bullying. We do not need to keep picking away at their minds to make sure they are learning. What we need to do, and all we need to do, is bring as much of the world as we can into the school and the classroom; give children as much help and guidance as they need and ask for; listen respectfully when they feel like talking; and then get out of the way. We can trust them to do the rest.

> JOHN HOLT (1923–1985). Closing words, *How Children Learn,* 1967

Accustom your children constantly to this; if a thing happened at one window and they, when relating it, say that it happened at another, do not let it pass, but instantly check them; you do not know where deviation from truth will end.

> SAMUEL JOHNSON (1709–1784). 31 March 1778. In James Boswell, *The Life of Samuel Johnson,* 1791

Little people [i.e., babies] should be encouraged always to tell whatever they hear particularly striking to some brother, sister, or servant, immediately before the impression is erased by the intervention of newer occurrences.

> SAMUEL JOHNSON (1709–1784). On developing memory. In Hester Lynch Piozzi, *Anecdotes of the Late Samuel Johnson, LL.D.,* p. 21, 1786, ed. S. C. Roberts, 1932

I can say this, that among my earliest recollections I remember how, when a mere child, I used to get irritated when anybody talked to me in a way I could not understand. . . . I can remember going to my little bedroom, after hearing the neighbors talk of an evening with my father, and spending no small part of the night walking up and down, and trying to make out what was the exact meaning of some of their, to me, dark sayings. I could not sleep, though I often tried to, when I got on such a hunt after an idea, until I had caught it; and when I thought I had got it, I was not satisfied until I had repeated it over and over, until I had put it in language plain enough, as I thought, for any boy I knew to comprehend.

> ABRAHAM LINCOLN (1809–1865). 1 September 1864. In F. B. Carpenter, *Six Months at the White House with Abraham Lincoln,* 77, 1866

Only by being permitted to experience the consequences of his actions will the child acquire a sense of responsibility; and within the limits marked by the demands of his safety this must be done. From such training we can expect many benefits to the person, one of which certainly will be the development of a natural rather than an imposed control over [himself].

> ROBERT LINDNER (1914–1956). *Prescription for Rebellion,* 9, 1952

One great Reason why many Children abandon themselves wholly to silly sports and trifle away all their time insipidly is because they have found their *Curiosity* baulk'd and their *Enquiries* neglected. But had they been treated with more Kindness and Respect and their *Questions* answered, as they should, to their Satisfaction, I doubt not but they would have taken more Pleasure in Learning and improving their Knowledge, wherein there would be still Newness and Variety, which is what they are delighted with, than in returning over and over to the same Play and Playthings.

> JOHN LOCKE (1632–1704). *Some Thoughts Concerning Education,* 118, 1693

[Learning] must never be imposed as a Task, nor made a Trouble to them. There may be Dice and Playthings with the Letters on them to teach Children the *Alphabet* by playing; and twenty other Ways may be found, suitable to their particular Tempers, to make this kind of *Learning a Sport* to them.

> JOHN LOCKE (1632–1704). *Some Thoughts Concerning Education,* 148, 1693

If those about him will talk to him often about the Stories he has read and hear him tell them, it will, besides other Advantages, add Encouragement and Delight to his *Reading,* when he finds there is some Use and Pleasure in it.

> JOHN LOCKE (1632–1704). *Some Thoughts Concerning Education,* 156, 1693

Your child is mainly interested in the process of doing things; he is not very concerned with the end result.

> TERRY MALLOY. *Montessori and Your Child: A Primer for Parents,* 1, 1974

Allow time for your child to complete each activity that she begins.

> TERRY MALLOY. *Montessori and Your Child: A Primer for Parents,* 3, 1974

We suppress the child's curiosity (for example, there are questions one should not ask), and then when he lacks a natural interest in learning he is offered special coaching for his scholastic difficulties.

> ALICE MILLER (1923–). *The Drama of the Gifted Child,* 3, 1979, tr. Ruth Ward, 1981

The most striking [way in which children respond to external influences] and one that is almost like a magic wand for opening the gate to the normal expression of a child's natural gifts is activity concentrated on some task that requires movement of the hands guided by the intellect.

> MARIA MONTESSORI (1870–1952). *The Secret of Childhood,* 20, 1938, tr. M. Joseph Costelloe, 1972

The number of different objects in the world is infinite, while the qualities they possess are limited. These qualities are therefore like the letters of the alphabet which can make up an indefinite number of words.

If we present the children with objects exhibiting each of these qualities separately [and "classified in an orderly way"], this is like giving them an alphabet for their explorations, a key to the doors of knowledge.

> MARIA MONTESSORI (1870–1952). *The Absorbent Mind,* 17, 1949, tr. Claude A. Claremont, 1969

At particular epochs of their life, [children] reveal an intense and extraordinary interest in certain objects and exercises, which one might look for in vain at a later age. . . . Such attention is not the result of mere curiosity; it is more like a burning passion. A keen emotion first rises from the depths of the unconscious, and sets in motion a marvelous creative activity in contact with the outside world, thus building up consciousness.

> MARIA MONTESSORI (1870–1952). On "sensitivity periods." In E. M. Standing, *Maria Montessori: Her Life and Work,* 7, 1957

It is easy to substitute our will for that of the child by means of suggestion or coercion; but when we have done this we have robbed him of his greatest right, the right to construct his own personality.

MARIA MONTESSORI (1870–1952). In E. M. Standing, *Maria Montessori: Her Life and Work*, 14, 1957

Children do not extract meaning from what they hear others saying; they try, instead, to relate what has been said to what is going on.

JUDITH M. NEWMAN. Ed., *Whole Language: Theory in Use*, 4, 1985

Children seem to learn to talk by inventing their own words and rules: by experimenting with language. Children make statements in their own language for meanings which are perfectly obvious to adults and then wait for adults to put the statements into adult language so they can make a comparison. . . . If the adult says nothing or simply continues the conversation, the child assumes his or her utterance is correct. When adults "correct"—that is, expand in adult language what children have said—they are providing feedback. The adult and the child are actually speaking different languages, but because they understand the situation, the child can compare their different ways of saying the same thing. . . . The process is one of successive approximations toward adult forms of expression.

JUDITH M. NEWMAN. Ed., *Whole Language: Theory in Use*, 4, 1985

The lines which are set for him for his imitation in writing should not contain useless sentences, but such as convey some moral instruction. The remembrance of such admonitions will attend him to old age, and will be of use even for the formation of his character.

QUINTILIAN (A.D. 35?–100?). *Institutio oratoria*, 1.1.35-36, tr. John Selby Watson, 1856

At the end of the visit, Diana reviews the events and the learning with the children. She asks the children their favorite event. "The alone walk," they all clamor. Walking all alone along the trail. Each one being brave, courageous. Discovering that they can find their own way.

LOIS ROBIN (1930–). Referring to a schoolchildren's outing with Diana Almendariz, a Native American cultural interpreter, a descendent of the Nisenan-Maidu tribe, "A Day with Diana," *News from Native California*, Berkeley (California), Fall 1991

It is not [a child's] hearing of the word, but its accompanying intonation that is understood.

ROUSSEAU (1712–1778). *Emile; or, Treatise on Education*, 1, 1762, tr. Barbara Foxley, 1911

I would have the first words he hears few in number, distinctly and often repeated, while the words themselves should be related to things which can first be shown to the child.

ROUSSEAU (1712–1778). *Emile; or, Treatise on Education*, 1, 1762, tr. Barbara Foxley, 1911

Since everything that comes into the human mind enters through the gates of sense, man's first reason is a reason of sense-experience. It is this that serves as a foundation for the reason of the intelligence; our first teachers in natural philosophy are our feet, hands, and eyes. To substitute books for them does not teach us to reason, it teaches us to use the reason of others rather than our own; it teaches us to believe much and know little.

ROUSSEAU (1712–1778). *Emile; or, Treatise on Education*, 2, 1762, tr. Barbara Foxley, 1911

Do not merely exercise the strength, exercise all the senses by which it is guided; make the best use of every one of them, and check the results of one by the other. Measure, count, weigh, compare. Do not use force till you have estimated the resistance; let the estimation of the effect always precede the application of the means. Get the child interested in avoiding insufficient or superfluous efforts. If in this way you train him to calculate the effects of all his movements, and to correct his mistakes by experience, is it not clear that the more he does the wiser he will become?

ROUSSEAU (1712–1778). *Emile; or, Treatise on Education*, 2, 1762, tr. Barbara Foxley, 1911

If a child is reading aloud to you and comes to a word she doesn't understand, don't immediately ask her to sound it out. Instead, say, "What makes sense here?" Then the child has to think about how that word fits in with what she's been reading.

MASHA KABAKOW RUDMAN. University of Massachusetts educator. In Lawrence Kutner, "Improved Reading Begins at Home, Where a Child Can See How Reading Fits in with Other Activities," *New York Times*, 17 December 1992

The essence of [Maria Montessori's] method consists in giving a choice of [activities], any one of which is interesting to most children, and all of which are instructive.

BERTRAND RUSSELL (1872–1970). *Principles of Social Reconstruction*, 5, 1916

Children learn at their own pace, and it is a mistake to try to force them. The great incentive to effort, all through life, is experience of success after initial difficulties. The difficulties must not be so great as to cause discouragement, or so small as not to stimulate effort. From birth to death, this is a fundamental principle. It is by what we do ourselves that we learn.

BERTRAND RUSSELL (1872–1970). *Education and the Good Life*, 3, 1926

The human intellect is said to be so constituted that general ideas arise by abstraction from particular observations, and therefore come after them in point of time. . . .

Contrarily, the artificial method is to hear what other people say, to learn and to read, and so to get your head crammed full of general ideas before you have any sort of extended acquaintance with the world as it is, and as you may see it for yourself.

ARTHUR SCHOPENHAUER (1788–1860). "Studies in Pessimism: On Education," *Essays of Arthur Schopenhauer*, tr. T. Bailey Saunders, 1851. In the next paragraph Schopenhauer commented that to acquire "general ideas" first and then make "particular observations" is like "putting the cart before the horse."

The Carnegie [Corporation] report [*Starting Points: Meeting the Needs of Our Youngest Children*, 1994] compares the brain of a newborn child to a tangled and unconnected mass of electronic circuitry. As a child begins to recognize things around him—"to make connections"—the circuitry becomes organized. . . .

Parents play a critical role in helping a baby organize this neural circuitry. When they talk or sing to a child or play with him, they are doing more than amusing the child; they are providing stimulation that is essential to the maturation of the child's brain. If they or someone else does not provide this stimulation, his development will be permanently impaired.

> ALBERT SHANKER (1928–1997). "The High Price of Neglect" (ad), *New York Times,* 27 November 1994

Each child's mind [should go] through a process like that which the mind of humanity at large has gone through. The truths of number, of form, of relationship in position, were all originally drawn from objects; and to present these truths to the child in the concrete is to let him learn them as the race learned them.

> HERBERT SPENCER (1820–1903). *Education: Intellectual, Moral, and Physical,* 2, 1860

Children should be led to make their own investigations and to draw their own inferences. They should be *told* as little as possible and induced to *discover* as much as possible. Humanity has progressed solely by self-instruction. . . . If the subjects be put before him in right order and right form, any pupil of ordinary capacity will surmount his successive difficulties with but little assistance.

> HERBERT SPENCER (1820–1903). *Education: Intellectual, Moral, and Physical,* 2, 1860

A constant question with [my father] was, "I wonder what is the cause of so-and-so"; or again putting it directly to me, "Can you tell the cause of this?" Always the tendency in himself, and the tendency strengthened in me, was to regard everything as naturally caused. . . . There was [thus] established a habit of seeking for causes, as well as a tacit belief in the universality of causation.

> HERBERT SPENCER (1820–1903). *An Autobiography,* 1.1.2, 1904

The adult works to perfect his environment, whereas the child works to perfect himself, using the environment as the means. . . . The child is a being in a constant state of transformation.

> E. M. STANDING (1887–?). *Maria Montessori: Her Life and Work,* 8, 1957

Concentration is the key that opens up to the child the latent treasures within him.

> E. M. STANDING (1887–?). *Maria Montessori: Her Life and Work,* 10, 1957

It is necessary in life to have acquired the habit of cheerfully undertaking imposed tasks. The conditions can be satisfied if the tasks correspond to the natural cravings of the pupil at his stage of progress, if they keep his powers at full stretch, and if they attain an obviously sensible result, and if reasonable freedom is allowed in the mode of execution.

> ALFRED NORTH WHITEHEAD (1861–1947). *The Aims of Education and Other Essays,* 3, 1929

❦

There is a greater advance from the infant to the speaking child than there is from the schoolboy to a Newton.

> ANONYMOUS (GERMAN). In E. M. Standing, *Maria Montessori: Her Life and Work,* 21, 1957

CHINA

See also • Nations ○ Values: Sun Yat-sen

Nothing and no one can destroy the Chinese people. They are relentless survivors. They are the oldest civilized people on earth. Their civilization passes through phases, but its basic characteristics remain the same. They yield, they bend to the wind, but they never break.

> PEARL S. BUCK (1892–1973). *China, Past and Present,* 1, 1972

Since they taught us a lesson in living, the Chinese, long before us, since the beginning of time, it is all the more painful to watch them now emulating us. When they have finally caught up with us, they will have lost all the lead they had over us.

> ELIAS CANETTI (1905–1994). 1985, *The Secret Heart of the Clock: Notes, Aphorisms, Fragments. 1973–1985,* 1989

Number of Avon ladies in China: 15,000.

> "HARPER'S INDEX." *Harper's,* May 1993

We don't talk about politics anymore. Why should we? Who is our leader now? Money is our leader.

> MR. ZHANG. A Beijing merchant. In Patrick E. Tyler, "Riches Tasted, China Hungers for Freedom," *New York Times,* 30 May 1997

CHRISTIANITY

See also • Church ○ Clergy ○ Evangelism ○ Freedom: Albert Luthuli ○ Judaism ○ Music: John Lennon (2) ○ Preachers ○ Priests ○ Religion ○ Revelations

The divine proved by its own excellence, is not this the whole of Christianity? God manifest in all men, is not this its true goal and consummation?

> HENRI AMIEL (1821–1881). Journal, 28 April 1866, tr. Mrs. Humphrey Ward, 1887

Should Christ be born a thousand times anew,
Despair, O man, unless he's born in you!

> ANGELUS SILESIUS (1624–1677)

The Christian revelation is, first and foremost, a message of the Kingdom of God.

> NICOLAS BERDYAEV (1874–1948). *The Destiny of Man,* 3.3, 1931, tr. Natalie Duddington, 1955

Christian, *n.* One who follows the teachings of Christ in so far as they are not inconsistent with a life of sin.

> AMBROSE BIERCE (1842–1914). *The Devil's Dictionary,* p. 22, 1911, Dover edition, 1958

The difference between Socrates and Jesus Christ! The great Conscious; the immeasurably great Unconscious.

> THOMAS CARLYLE (1795–1881). Journal, 28 October 1833. In James Anthony Froude, *Thomas Carlyle: A History of the First Forty Years, 1795–1835,* 2.16, 1882

If Jesus Christ were to come today, people would not even cruci-fy him. They would ask him to dinner, and hear what he had to say, and make fun of it.

> THOMAS CARLYLE (1795–1881). Remark, 12 January 1850. In David Alec Wilson, *Carlyle at His Zenith (1848–1853),* 10, 1927

We should live our lives as though Christ were coming this after-noon.

> JIMMY CARTER (1924–). Speech at a Bible class in Plains (Georgia), March 1976. In *Boston Sunday Herald Advertiser,* 11 April 1976

And Jesus was a sailor
When he walked upon the water
And he spent a long time watching
From a lonely wooden tower
And when he knew for certain
That only drowning men could see him,
He said, "All men shall be sailors, then,
Until the sea shall free them."

> LEONARD COHEN (1934–). "Suzanne" (song), 1966

When Jesus tells us about his Father, we distrust him. When he shows us his Home, we turn away, but when he confides to us that he is "acquainted with Grief," we listen, for that also is an Acquaintance of our own.

> EMILY DICKINSON (1830–1886). In Kathleen Norris, "The Difference: October 1," *The Cloister Walk,* 1996

Had there been a Lunatic Asylum in the suburbs of Jerusalem, Jesus Christ would infallibly have been shut up in it at the outset of his public career. That interview with Satan on a pinnacle of the Temple would alone have damned him, and everything that hap-pened after could but have confirmed the diagnosis. The whole religious complexion of the modern world is due to the absence from Jerusalem of a Lunatic Asylum.

> HAVELOCK ELLIS (1859–1939). English doctor. *Impressions and Comments,* 3, 1915

They will have Christ for a Lord and not for a Brother. Christ preaches the greatness of man, but we hear only the greatness of Christ.

> RALPH WALDO EMERSON (1803–1882). Journal, 5 March 1838

Our dead Christianity.

> RALPH WALDO EMERSON (1803–1882). Journal, 10 September 1848

He who shall introduce into public affairs the principles of primi-tive Christianity will change the face of the world.

> BENJAMIN FRANKLIN (1706–1790). Remark to the French ministry, March 1778

[Jesus could even have been] an ordinary deluded creature.

> SIGMUND FREUD (1856–1939). Remark to the author (the bracketed words being his). In Ernest Jones, *The Life and Work of Sigmund Freud,* 3.13, 1953–1957

If Christ came back today and started teaching, we would put him on the cross quicker than we did 2,000 years ago.

> BILLY GRAHAM (1918–). In N.A.N.A., "Billy Graham and the Great Society," *San Francisco Chronicle,* 25 December 1965

Everything that we know about [Jesus] conforms so perfectly to the clinical picture of paranoia that it is hardly conceivable that people can even question the accuracy of the diagnosis.

> WILLIAM HIRSCH (19th–20th cent.). *Conclusions of a Psychiatrist,* 1912. As paraphrased by Albert Schweitzer, *The Psychiatric Study of Jesus,* p. 40, 1913, tr. Charles R. Joy, 1948

The Papacy is no other than the Ghost of the deceased Roman Empire, sitting crowned upon the grave thereof.

> THOMAS HOBBES (1588–1679). *Leviathan,* 47, 1651

The church allows people to believe that they can be good Christians and yet draw dividends from armament factories, can be good Christians and yet imperil the well-being of their fellows by speculating in stocks and shares, can be good Christians and yet be imperialists, yet participate in war. All that is required of the good Christian is chastity and a modicum of charity in immediate per-sonal relations.

> ALDOUS HUXLEY (1894–1963). "Education," *Ends and Means: An Inquiry into the Nature of Ideals and into the Methods Employed for Their Realization,* 1937

Of all the systems of morality, ancient or modern, which have come under my observation, none appear to me so pure as that of Jesus.

> THOMAS JEFFERSON (1743–1826). Letter to William Canby, 18 September 1813

I came that they may have life, and have it abundantly.

> JESUS (A.D. 1st cent.). *John* 10:10

A new commandment I give to you, that you love one another; even as I have loved you, that you also love one another. By this all men will know that you are my disciples, if you have love for one another.

> JESUS (A.D. 1st cent.). *John* 13:34–35

I am the way, and the truth, and the life; no one comes to the Father, but by me.

> JESUS (A.D. 1st cent.). *John* 14:6

He who believes in me will also do the words that I do; and greater works than these will he do.

> JESUS (A.D. 1st cent.). *John* 14:12

For God so loved the world that he gave his only son, that who-ever believes in him should not perish but have eternal life.

> JOHN (A.D. 1st cent.). *John* 3:16

Christianity is the highest perfection of humanity.

> SAMUEL JOHNSON (1709–1784). Letter to William Drummond, 13 August 1766. In James Boswell, *The Life of Samuel Johnson,* 1791

Christian civilization has proved hollow to a terrifying degree: it is all veneer, but the inner man has remained untouched, and there-fore unchanged. His soul is out of key with his external beliefs; in his soul the Christian has not kept pace with external develop-ments. Yes, everything is to be found outside—in image and in word, in Church and Bible—but never inside. Inside reign the archaic gods, supreme as of old.

> CARL G. JUNG (1875–1961). *Psychology and Alchemy,* 1, 1944, tr. R. F. C. Hull, 1968

The Christian symbol is a living thing that carries in itself the seeds of further development.

CARL G. JUNG (1875–1961). *The Undiscovered Self,* 4, tr. R. F. C. Hull, 1957

There has been only one Christian, and he died on the Cross.

FRIEDRICH NIETZSCHE (1844–1900). *The Anti-Christ,* 39, 1895, tr. R. J. Hollingdale, 1968

If Christ has not been raised, then your faith is futile and you are still in your sins.

PAUL (A.D. 1st cent.). *1 Corinthians* 15:17

If any one is in Christ, he is a new creation; the old has passed away, behold, the new has come. All this is from God, who through Christ reconciled us to himself and gave us the ministry of reconciliation; that is, God was in Christ reconciling the world to himself, not counting their trespasses against them, and entrusting to us the message of reconciliation.

PAUL (A.D. 1st cent.). *2 Corinthians* 5:17–19

I doubt if there is in the world a single problem, whether social, political, or economic, which would not find ready solution if men and nations would rule their lives according to the plain teaching of the Sermon on the Mount.

FRANKLIN D. ROOSEVELT (1882–1945). In Arthur M. Schlesinger, Jr., *The Age of Roosevelt: The Coming of the New Deal,* 35.7, 1959

Jesus did not expect the end of the world in the sense of destruction of the cosmos. He expected a divine, transforming miracle.

E. P. SANDERS. *The Historical Figure of Jesus,* 11, 1991

If Jesus wanted to make it today, I thought He'd be a rock singer.

TOM SHALES (1944–). 1968

Here's to you, Mrs. Robinson,
Jesus loves you more than you will know.

PAUL SIMON (1941–). "Mrs. Robinson" (song). In the film *The Graduate,* 1967

Protestant: one who no longer protests.

PETE SKERIS. In "A Gadfly's Dictionary," *Thoughts For All Seasons: The Magazine of Epigrams,* vol. 4, 1992

Our true friend, Whom alone we can trust, is Jesus Christ. When I depend upon Him, I feel so strong that I think I could stand firm against the whole world.

ST. TERESA (1515–1582)

I don't preach a social gospel; I preach *the* Gospel, period. The gospel of our Lord Jesus Christ is concerned for the whole person. When people were hungry, Jesus didn't say, "Now is that political, or social?" He said. "I feed you." Because the good news to a hungry person is bread. . . . If people wish to say, "God's writ does not run in the political sphere," I want to ask, "Whose does?"

BISHOP DESMOND TUTU (1931–). Rafael Suarez, Jr., interview, *Worldview,* December 1984

If Christ were here now, there is one thing he would *not* be—a Christian.

MARK TWAIN (1835–1910). 2 January 1897, *Mark Twain's Notebook,* ed. Albert Bigelow Paine, 1935

Jesus is not a blue-eyed right-winger, as some have implied; nor is he a guilt-ridden liberal or compromising centrist. Jesus is the one who entered the world among the dispossessed and the outcasts to announce an entirely new way of thinking and living. The way of Jesus and the prophets isn't just a welfare program; it calls for a change of heart, a revolution of the spirit, a transformation of our consciousness.

JIM WALLIS (1948–). *The Soul of Politics: A Practical and Prophetic Vision for Change,* 8, 1994

As society is now constituted, a literal adherence to the moral precepts scattered throughout the Gospels would mean sudden death.

ALFRED NORTH WHITEHEAD (1861–1947). *Adventures of Ideas,* 2.4, 1933

Things fall apart; the center cannot hold;
Mere anarchy is loosed upon the world,
The blood-dimmed tide is loosed, and everywhere
The ceremony of innocence is drowned;
The best lack all conviction, while the worst
Are full of passionate intensity.
Surely some revelation is at hand;
Surely the Second Coming is at hand.

WILLIAM BUTLER YEATS (1865–1939). "The Second Coming," *Michael Robartes and the Dancer,* 1921

❧

Christianity had been tried and failed, the religion of Christ remained to be tried.

SAYING. 1700s. In John Morley, *Notes on Politics and History: A University Address,* 2, 1913

CHURCH

See also • Christianity ○ Clergy ○ God & the Devil: Martin Luther ○ Religion ○ Religion, Anti-

It is not my duty . . . to attend the churches. My own spirit preaches sounder doctrine than I there hear, and I must listen to its divine teachings.

BRONSON ALCOTT (1799–1888). Journal, 20 December 1835, ed. Odell Shepard, 1938

There is no salvation outside the Church.

ST. AUGUSTINE (A.D. 354–430). *On Baptism,* 4.17

The church represents for the people a kind of celestial tavern, just as the tavern represents a kind of heavenly church on earth. In church as in the tavern they forget their hunger, oppression, and humiliation, at least for a minute, and they try to dull the memory of their daily woes either with mindless faith or with wine. One intoxicant is as good as the others.

MIKHAIL BAKUNIN (1814–1876). *Statism and Anarchy,* 1873, tr. Marshall S. Shatz, 1971

Every day people are straying away from the church and going back to God.

LENNY BRUCE (1925–1966). "Religions Inc.; Catholicism; Christ and Moses; and the Lone Ranger," *The Essential Lenny Bruce,* ed. John Cohen, 1967

The test of a religion or philosophy is the number of things it can explain: so true it is. But the religion of our churches explains neither art not society nor history, but itself needs explanation.

> RALPH WALDO EMERSON (1803–1882). Journal, 27 November 1838

I like the silent church before the service begins, better than any preaching.

> RALPH WALDO EMERSON (1803–1882). "Self-Reliance," *Essays: First Series,* 1841

God builds his temple in the heart on the ruins of churches and religions.

> RALPH WALDO EMERSON (1803–1882). "Worship," *The Conduct of Life,* 1860

The nearer to the church, the farther from God.

> JOHN HEYWOOD (1497–1580). Comp., *A Dialogue Containing the Number of the Effectual Proverbs in the English Tongue,* 1.9, 1562

A Church is God between four walls.

> VICTOR HUGO (1802–1885). *Ninety-Three,* 3.3.2, 1879

And I tell you, you are Peter, and on this rock I will build my church, and the powers of death shall not prevail against it.

> JESUS (A.D. 1st cent.). *Matthew* 16:18

Yes, I see the church as the body of Christ. But, oh! How we have blemished and scarred that body through social neglect and through fear of being nonconformists.

> MARTIN LUTHER KING, JR. (1929–1968). "Letter from Birmingham City Jail," 16 April 1963

If the church does not recapture its prophetic zeal, it will become an irrelevant social club without moral or spiritual authority.

> MARTIN LUTHER KING, JR. (1929–1968). *Strength to Love,* 6.3, 1963

Any church that violates the "whosoever will, let him come" doctrine is a dead, cold church, and nothing but a little social club with a thin veneer of religiosity

> MARTIN LUTHER KING, JR. (1929–1968). "The Drum Major Instinct," sermon, Ebenezer Baptist Church, Atlanta, 4 February 1968

I do not believe in the creed professed by . . . any church that I know of. My own mind is my own church.

All national institutions of churches, whether Jewish, Christian or Turkish, appear to me no other than human inventions set up to terrify and enslave mankind, and monopolize power and profit.

> THOMAS PAINE (1737–1809). *The Age of Reason: Being an Investigation of True and Fabulous Theology,* 1, 1794

The 11 o'clock hour on Sunday is the most segregated hour in American life.

> BISHOP JAMES A. PIKE (1913–1969). Recalled on his death, 7 September 1969

Some to Church repair,
Not for the Doctrine, but the Music there.

> ALEXANDER POPE (1688–1744). *An Essay on Criticism,* l. 342, 1711

The Churches must learn humility as well as teach it.

> GEORGE BERNARD SHAW (1856–1950). Preface ("Catholicism Not Yet Catholic Enough") to *Saint Joan,* 1923

The church is a sort of hospital for men's souls, and as full of quackery as the hospital for their bodies.

> HENRY DAVID THOREAU (1817–1862). "Sunday," *A Week on the Concord and Merrimack Rivers,* 1849

The church! it is eminently the timid institution, and the heads and pillars of it are constitutionally and by principle the greatest cowards in the community.

> HENRY DAVID THOREAU (1817–1862). Journal, 16 November 1858

She say, Celie, tell the truth, have you ever found God in church? I never did. I just found a bunch of folks hoping for him to show. Any God I ever felt in church I brought in with me. And I think all the other folks did too. They come to church to *share* God, not find God.

> ALICE WALKER (1944–). *The Color Purple,* p. 176, 1982, Washington Square Press edition, 1983

"Put down enthusiasm." . . . The Church of England in a nutshell.

> MARY AUGUSTA WARD (1851–1920). *Robert Elsmer,* 2.16, 1888

How is one to explain that neither Hitler nor Himmler was ever excommunicated by the church?

> ELI WIESEL (1928–). "To Be a Jew," *A Jew Today,* tr. Marion Wiesel, 1978

❧

Too hot to go to Church? What about Hell?

> ANONYMOUS. Poster, Dayton (Ohio), undated

The church is an anvil that has worn out many hammers.

> SAYING (ENGLISH)

CINEMA

See Films

CIRCUMSTANCES

See also • Decision-Making ∘ Events ∘ Good & Evil: Plutarch ∘ History: Paul Kennedy ∘ History ∘ Opportunity ∘ Principles, Theoretical

Everything depends upon circumstances: you must sail according to the wind.

> PICONNERIE de la BUGEAUD (1784–1849). In Ferdinand Foch, *The Principles of War,* 1, 1903, tr. Hilaire Belloc, 1920

I am the very slave of circumstance.

> LORD BYRON (1788–1824). *Sardanapalus,* 4.1, 1821

Man is not the creature of circumstances, circumstances are the creatures of men. We are free agents, and man is more powerful than matter.

> BENJAMIN DISRAELI (1804–1881). *Vivian Grey,* 6.7, 1826
>
> See Chance: Artabanus

It always remains true that if we had been greater, circumstance would have been less strong against us.

> GEORGE ELIOT (1819–1880). *Middlemarch,* 5, 1871–1872

What is the matter with the world that it is so out of joint? Simply that men do not rule themselves but let circumstances rule them.

> RALPH WALDO EMERSON (1803–1882). Journal, 25 June 1828

The tyrannical Circumstance!

> RALPH WALDO EMERSON (1803–1882). "Fate," *The Conduct of Life*, 1860

Men think to mend their condition by a change of circumstances. They might as well hope to escape from their shadows.

> JAMES ANTHONY FROUDE (1818–1894). *Thomas Carlyle: A History of the First Forty Years, 1795–1835*, 1.20, 1882

Watch and profit by every circumstance.

> HENRI de JOMINI (1779–1869). *Summary of the Art of War*, 1, 1807, ed. J. D. Hittle, 1947

It seems to me . . . that external circumstances often serve as occasions for a new attitude to life and the world, long prepared in the unconscious, to become manifest.

> CARL G. JUNG (1875–1961). "The Psychological Foundations of Belief in Sprits," 1920, *The Structure and Dynamics of the Psyche*, tr. R. F. C. Hull, 1960

Circumstances reveal us to others and still more to ourselves.

> LA ROCHEFOUCAULD (1613–1680). *Maxims*, 345, 1665, tr. Leonard Tancock, 1959

In any given set of circumstances, the proper course of action is determined by subsequent events.

> McDONALD'S COROLLARY TO MURPHY'S LAW. In Arthur Bloch, comp., "Advanced Murphology," *Murphy's Law: Book Three*, 1982

To each circumstance its own law.

> NAPOLEON (1769–1821). Remark, April 1815, *The Mind of Napoleon: A Selection from His Written and Spoken Words*, 202, ed. J. Christopher Herold, 1955

I had few really definite ideas, and the reason for this was that, instead of obstinately seeking to control circumstances, I obeyed them, and they forced me to change my mind all the time.

> NAPOLEON (1769–1821). Remark to Emmanuel Las Cases, 20 July 1816, *The Mind of Napoleon: A Selection from His Written and Spoken Words*, 57, ed. J. Christopher Herold, 1955
>
> See Events: Abraham Lincoln

Man cannot . . . make circumstances for his purpose, but he always has it in his power to improve them when they occur.

> THOMAS PAINE (1737–1809). *The Rights of Man*, 1, 1791

If circumstances require it, [the commander] must be able to turn the whole structure of his thinking inside out.

> ERWIN ROMMEL (1891–1944). 1942, *The Rommel Papers*, 9, ed. B. H. Liddell Hart, 1953

There may be circumstances that alter the case, as when there is a sufficient ground of partiality.

> THOMAS RYMER (1643?–1713). *The Tragedies of the Last Age*, p. 177, 1678 (Popular version: Circumstances alter cases.)

People are always blaming their circumstances for what they are. I don't believe in circumstances. The people who get on in this world are the people who get up and look for the circumstances they want, and, if they don't find them, make them.

> GEORGE BERNARD SHAW (1856–1950). *Mrs. Warren's Profession*, 2, 1893
>
> See Opportunity: Francis Bacon

Circumstances make men, not man circumstances.

> MARK TWAIN (1835–1910). 30 December 1902, *Mark Twain's Notebook*, ed. Albert Bigelow Paine, 1935

Circumstances should never alter principles.

> OSCAR WILDE (1854–1900). *An Ideal Husband*, 1, 1895

The men who are made by circumstances are unmade by trifling misfortunes; while they who conquer circumstances snap their fingers at luck.

> ANONYMOUS. In C. Wright Mills, *White Collar*, 12.1, 1951

CITIES

See also • Architecture ∘ Berlin ∘ Boston ∘ Ghettos ∘ Hollywood ∘ London ∘ Los Angeles ∘ New York City ∘ Paris ∘ Rome ∘ San Francisco ∘ Slums ∘ Travel ∘ Washington

A city is [not] fortunate when its walls are standing, while its morals are in ruins.

> ST. AUGUSTINE (A.D. 354–430). *The City of God*, 1.33, A.D. 413-426, tr. Henry Bettenson, 1972

The Asphalt Jungle.

> R. BURNETT. Book title, 1949, and film title, 1950

The cities die, men hole up deeper.

> ELIAS CANETTI (1905–1994). 1946, *The Human Province*, tr. Joachim Neugroschel, 1978

No city should be too large for a man to walk out of in a morning.

> CYRIL CONNOLLY (1903–1974). "Ecce Gubernator," *The Unquiet Grave: A Word Cycle by Palinurus*, 1945

God made the country, and man made the town.

> WILLIAM COWPER (1731–1800). *The Task*, 1.749, 1785

Cities should be built on one side of the street.

> BOB KAUFMAN (1925–1986). "Jail Poems" (22), 1959, *Solitudes Crowded with Loneliness*, 1965

The need of the city is to accelerate growth; the pride of the small town is to retard it.

> NORMAN MAILER (1923–). "Superman Comes to the Supermart," *Esquire*, November 1960

The city is not a concrete jungle; it is a human zoo.

> DESMOND MORRIS (1928–). Introduction to *The Human Zoo*, 1969

The rise of the city has been the historic sign of a society on the march.

> HERBERT J. MULLER (1905–1982). *The Uses of the Past: Profiles of Former Societies*, 3.3, 1952

Sicinius: What is the city but the people?
> SHAKESPEARE (1564–1616). *Coriolanus,* 3.1.198, 1607

Ultimately, cities may exist only as joyous tribal gatherings and fairs, to dissolve after a few weeks.
> GARY SNYDER (1930–). "Four Changes" (4), *Turtle Island,* 1974

The Shame of the Cities.
> LINCOLN STEFFENS (1866–1936). Book title, 1904

The new American finds his challenge and his love in traffic-choked streets, skies nested in smog, choking with the acids of industry, the screech of rubber and houses leashed in against one another while the townlets wither a time and die. . . . As all pendulums reverse their swing, so eventually will the swollen cities rupture like dehiscent wombs and disperse their children back to the countryside.
> JOHN STEINBECK (1902–1968). *Travels with Charley: In Search of America,* 2, 1961

Each town should have a park, or rather a primitive forest, of five hundred or a thousand acres, where a stick should never be cut for fuel, a common possession forever, for instruction and recreation.
> HENRY DAVID THOREAU (1817–1862). Journal, 15 October 1859

City life: millions of people being lonesome together.
> HENRY DAVID THOREAU (1817–1862). In "Thoughts on the Business of Life," *Forbes,* 30 August 1993

A great city is that which has the greatest men and women, If it be a few ragged huts it is still the greatest city in the whole world.
> WALT WHITMAN (1819–1892). "Song of the Broad-Axe" (4), 1856, *Leaves of Grass,* 1855–1892

❧

It's a nice place to visit, but I wouldn't want to live there.
> ANONYMOUS (AMERICAN). Said of a number of cities

A great city is a great solitude.
> SAYING (GREEK)

CIVILIZATION

See also • Civilization, Modern ○ Culture ○ History ○ Man ○ Mankind ○ Morality ○ Progress ○ Purpose ○ Religion ○ Science ○ Society ○ Trees: Saying (Greek)

Civilization degrades the many to exalt the few.
> BRONSON ALCOTT (1799–1888). "Pursuits. Callings," *Table Talk,* 3, 1877

The whole history of civilization is strewn with creeds and institutions which were invaluable at first, and deadly afterward.
> WALTER BAGEHOT (1826–1877). *Physics and Politics, or Thoughts on the Application of the Principles of "Natural Selection" and "Inheritance" to Political Society,* 2.3, 1872

Civilization, in the best sense, merely means the full authority of the human spirit over all externals.
> G. K. CHESTERTON (1874–1936). "Humanitarianism and Strength," *All Things Considered,* 1908

Civilization and profits go hand in hand.
> CALVIN COOLIDGE (1872–1933). Speech, New York City, 27 November 1920

All civilization has from time to time become a thin crust over a volcano of revolution.
> HAVELOCK ELLIS (1859–1939). "The Individual and the Race" (3), *Little Essays of Love and Virtue,* 1922

Although society seems to be delivered over from the hands of one set of criminals into the hands of another set of criminals, as fast as the government is changed, and the march of civilization is a train of felonies, yet, general ends are somehow answered.
> RALPH WALDO EMERSON (1803–1882). "Montaigne; or, The Skeptic," *Representative Men,* 1850

Civilization is the fruit of renunciation of instinctual satisfaction.
> SIGMUND FREUD (1856–1939). "Reflections upon War and Death" (1), 1915, tr. E. Colburn Mayne, *Character and Culture,* 1963

A civilization is to be judged by its treatment of minorities.
> MOHANDAS K. GANDHI (1869–1948). July 1946. In Louis Fischer, *The Life of Mahatma Gandhi,* 43, 1950

An Englishman who was wrecked on a strange shore and wandering along the coast . . . came to a gallows with a victim hanging on it, and fell down on his knees and thanked God that he at last beheld a sign of civilization.
> JAMES A. GARFIELD (1831–1881). House of Representatives speech, 15 June 1870

That larger Inquisition which we call Civilization!
> OLIVER WENDELL HOLMES, SR. (1809–1894). *The Autocrat of the Breakfast-Table,* 12, 1858

A decent provision for the poor is the true test of civilization.
> SAMUEL JOHNSON (1709–1784). Quoted by Rev. Dr. Maxwell, 1770. In James Boswell, *The Life of Samuel Johnson,* 1791

To pass in pursuit of an ideal from the barbarous to the civilized state, and then, when this ideal has lost its [hold], to decline and die, such is the cycle of the life of a people.
> GUSTAVE LE BON (1841–1931). Closing words, *The Crowd: A Study of the Popular Mind,* 3.5, 1895, Viking Press edition, 1960

The next great advance in the evolution of civilization cannot take place until war is abolished.
> DOUGLAS MacARTHUR (1880–1964). "War Is No Longer a Medium of Practical Settlement of International Differences," address at an American Legion dinner honoring him, Ambassador Hotel, Los Angeles, 26 January 1955

The boons of civilization are so noisily cried up by sentimentalists that we are all apt to overlook its disadvantages. Intrinsically, it is a mere device for regimenting men. Its perfect symbol is the goose step.
> H. L. MENCKEN (1880–1956). *In Defense of Women,* 12, 1922

Has civilization a motto? Then certainly it must be "Not *thy* will, O Lord, but *ours,* be done!"
> H. L. MENCKEN (1880–1956). "On the Nature of Man: The Goal," *Prejudices: Fourth Series,* 1924

In the long run, it may turn out that rascality is necessary to human government, and even to civilization itself—that civilization, at bottom, is nothing but a colossal swindle.

H. L. MENCKEN (1880–1956). *Notes on Democracy,* 4.2, 1926

One of the effects of civilization (not to say one of the ingredients in it) is, that the spectacle, and even the very idea, of pain, is kept more and more out of the sight of those classes who enjoy in their fullness the benefits of civilization.

JOHN STUART MILL (1806–1873). "Civilization: Signs of the Times," 1836, *Dissertations and Discussions,* vol. 1, 1859–1875

Standing as I do on the mountainside and contemplating the various hives of industry among civilizations old and new, all looming on my vision, dim in the great sea-divided distances, I have this one big well-defined faith for humanity as a workman, that the time is coming when every "article of manufacture" will be as purely a work of God as are these mountains and pine trees and bonnie loving flowers.

JOHN MUIR (1838–1914). Letter to Kate N. Daggett, 20 December 1872. In William Frederic Badè, *The Life and Letters of John Muir,* 10, 1923

Civilization begins by a magnificent materialization of human purpose; it ends in a purposeless materialism. An empty triumph, which revolts even the self that created it.

LEWIS MUMFORD (1895–1990). *The Transformations of Man,* 3.7, 1956

The creation of the world—that is to say, the world of civilized order—is the victory of persuasion over force.

PLATO (427?–347 B.C.). As paraphrased by Alfred North Whitehead, *Adventures of Ideas,* 2.8, 1933

You can't say civilization don't advance . . . for in every war they kill you a new way.

WILL ROGERS (1879–1935). 22 December 1929, *The Autobiography of Will Rogers,* ed. Donald Day, 1949

Civilization can only revive when there shall come into being in a number of individuals a new tone of mind independent of the one prevalent among the crowd and in opposition to it, a tone of mind which will gradually win influence over the collective one, and in the end determine its character. It is only an ethical movement which can rescue us from the slough of barbarism, and the ethical comes into existence only in individuals.

ALBERT SCHWEITZER (1875–1965). *The Philosophy of Civilization: The Decay and Restoration of Civilization,* 4, 1923, tr. C. T. Campion, 1923

The spiritual and moral perfection of the individual . . . is the final end of civilization.

ALBERT SCHWEITZER (1875–1965). *The Philosophy of Civilization: The Decay and Restoration of Civilization,* 5, 1923, tr. C. T. Campion, 1923

A civilization which develops only on its material side, and not in corresponding measure in the sphere of the spirit, is like a ship with defective steering gear which gets out of control at a constantly accelerating pace, and thereby heads for catastrophe.

ALBERT SCHWEITZER (1875–1965). *The Philosophy of Civilization: Civilization and Ethics,* 1, 1923, tr. C. T. Campion and Mrs. Charles E. B. Russell, 1946

Civilizations decline when they stop believing in themselves; ours has thrived because we have never lost our conviction that our values are worth defending.

GEORGE P. SHULTZ (1920–). "American and the Struggle for Freedom," speech before the Commonwealth Club of California, San Francisco, 22 February 1985

Civilizations . . . come to birth and proceed to grow by successfully responding to successive challenges. They break down and go to pieces if and when a challenge confronts them which they fail to meet.

ARNOLD J. TOYNBEE (1889–1975). "The Graeco-Roman Civilization," 1930?, *Civilization on Trial,* 1948

It is the historical function of civilizations to serve, by their downfalls, as stepping stones to a progressive process of the revelation of always deeper religious insight, and the gift of ever more grace to act on this insight.

ARNOLD J. TOYNBEE (1889–1975). "Christianity and Civilization," 1947, *Civilization on Trial,* 1948

The Graeco-Roman offensive has spent its force; a counter-offensive is on its way; but this counter-movement is not yet recognized for what it is, because it is being launched on a different plane. The offensive has been military, political, and economic; the counter-offensive is religious.

ARNOLD J. TOYNBEE (1889–1975). On the clash of civilizations during the decline phase of the Roman Empire in the 2nd century preceding the rise of Christianity, "The World and the Greeks and Romans," 1952, *The World and the West,* 1953

Since the rise of civilization, war has been one of its two chief scandals and scourges—the other being the system of social and economic inequality and injustice which expresses itself in class distinctions and which finds its extreme form in the institution of slavery.

ARNOLD J. TOYNBEE (1889–1975). *A Study of History,* 12.610, 1961

Every civilization reaches a moment of crisis. . . . This crisis presents its challenge: Smash or go on to higher things. So far no civilization has ever met this challenge successfully. History is the study of the bones of civilizations that failed, as the pterodactyl and the dinosaur failed.

COLIN WILSON (1931–). *Religion and the Rebel,* 2.9, 1957

CIVILIZATION, MODERN

See also • Civilization

I'm optimistic about the future, but not about the future of this civilization. I'm optimistic about the civilization which will replace this one.

JAMES BALDWIN (1924–1987). John Hall interview, 1970. In Fred L. Standley and Louis H. Pratt, eds., *Conversations with James Baldwin,* 1989

Our humanity is at risk. It's too powerful a thing to just lie down and give up the ghost. But we have to face the fact it is in danger. It is at risk because the feeling that life is sacred has died away in this century.

SAUL BELLOW (1915–). "'Matters Have Gotten Out of Hand,' in a Violent Society," *U.S. News & World Report,* 28 June 1982

We have too many men of science, too few men of God. We have grasped the mystery of the atom and rejected the Sermon on the Mount. The world has achieved brilliance without wisdom, power without conscience. Ours is a world of nuclear giants and ethical midgets. We know more about war than we know of peace, more about killing than we know about living.

OMAR N. BRADLEY (1893–1981). General. Armistice Day address, Boston, 11 November 1948

Civilization is conspiracy. . . . Modern life is the silent compact of comfortable folk to keep up pretenses.

JOHN BUCHAN (1875–1940). *The Power-House,* 3, 1916

We live in that final time which offers humans the clearest choice in history: the kingdom or the holocaust.

JAMES W. DOUGLASS (1937–). *Lightning East to West,* 2, 1980

It is said to be the age of the first person singular.

RALPH WALDO EMERSON (1803–1882). "Peculiarities of the Present Age," #2, journal, January-February 1827

We think our civilization near its meridian, but we are yet only at the cock-crowing and the morning star. In our barbarous society the influence of character is in its infancy.

RALPH WALDO EMERSON (1803–1882). "Politics," *Essays: Second Series,* 1844

As long as our civilization is essentially one of property, of fences, of exclusiveness, it will be mocked by delusions. Our riches will leave us sick; there will be bitterness in our laughter; and our wine will burn our mouth. Only that good profits, which we can taste with all doors open, and which serves all men.

RALPH WALDO EMERSON (1803–1882). "Napoleon; or, The Man of the World," *Representative Men,* 1850

The age has an engine, but no engineer.

RALPH WALDO EMERSON (1803–1882). Journal, 1854, undated

The fundamental struggle of our time is not the struggle between socialistic regime and capitalism. [The fundamental struggle is to] rehabilitate mankind and make man victorious everywhere, once and for all.

FRANTZ FANON (1925–1961). In Horace Sutton, "Fanon," *Saturday Review,* 17 July 1971

Our ignorance of history makes us libel our own times. People have always been like this.

GUSTAVE FLAUBERT (1821–1880)

These are the days when men of all social disciplines and all political faiths seek the comfortable and the accepted; when the man of controversy is looked upon as a disturbing influence; when originality is taken to be a mark of instability; and when, in minor modification of the scriptural parable, the bland lead the bland.

JOHN KENNETH GALBRAITH (1908–). *The Affluent Society,* 1.3, 1958

Journalist: Mr. Gandhi, what do you think of Western civilization? *Gandhi:* That would be a good idea.

MOHANDAS K. GANDHI (1869–1948). Format adapted. While visiting England in 1930. In E. F. Schumacher, *Good Work,* 2, 1979

All of us, East and West, are moving toward a new type of civilization whether we realize it or not. And it is that which compels

me to think that our old stereotypes have now lost their meaning and should be radically re-examined.

MIKHAIL S. GORBACHEV (1931–). "No Time for Stereotypes," *New York Times,* 24 February 1992

The planetary civilization to which we all belong confronts us with global challenges. We stand helpless before them because our civilization has essentially globalized only the surface of our lives. But our inner self continues to have a life of its own. And the fewer answers the era of rational knowledge provides to the basic questions of human being, the more deeply it would seem that people, behind its back as it were, cling to the ancient certainties of their tribe.

VÁCLAV HAVEL (1936–). Czech president. "The New Measure of Men," *New York Times,* 8 July 1994

The problem is the spirit of our age: denial of transcendence, the vapidity of values, emptiness in the heart, the decreased sensitivity to the imponderable quality of the spirit, the collapse of communication between the realm of tradition and the inner world of the individual.

ABRAHAM JOSHUA HESCHEL (1907–1972). *The Insecurity of Freedom: Essays on Human Existence,* 3, 1967

As at the beginning of the Christian Era, so again today we are faced with the problem of the moral backwardness which has failed to keep pace with our scientific, technical and social developments.

CARL G. JUNG (1875–1961). *The Undiscovered Self,* 7, tr. R. F. C. Hull, 1957

We live in an age which is so possessed by demons, that soon we shall only be able to do goodness and justice in the deepest secrecy, as if it were a crime.

FRANZ KAFKA (1883–1924). In Gustav Janouch, "Conversations with Kafka," tr. Goronwy Rees, *Encounter,* August 1971

Even in a time of elephantine vanity and greed, one never has to look far to see the campfires of gentle people.

GARRISON KEILLOR (1942–). "The Meaning of Life," *We Are Still Married: Stories & Letters,* 1989

Never before has man had such capacity to control his own environment, to end thirst and hunger, to conquer poverty and disease, to banish illiteracy and massive human misery. We have the power to make this the best generation of mankind in the history of the world—or to make it the last.

JOHN F. KENNEDY (1917–1963). United Nations address, New York City, 20 September 1963

The destruction of the personality is the great evil of the time.

ELLEN KEY (1849–1926). "The Conventional Woman," *The Morality of Woman and Other Essays,* 1911

Perhaps in time the so-called Dark Ages will be thought of as including our own.

GEORG CHRISTOPH LICHTENBERG (1742–1799)

We are living through the closing chapters of the established and traditional way of life. We are in the early beginnings of a struggle to remake our civilization. It is not a good time for politicians. It is a time for prophets and leaders and explorers and inventors and pioneers, and for those who are willing to plant trees for their children to sit under.

> WALTER LIPPMANN (1889–1974). "The American Promise," *Newsweek,* 9 October 1967

We are close to dead. There are faces and bodies like gorged maggots on the dance floor, on the highway, in the city, in the stadium; they are a host of chemical machines who swallow the product of chemical factories, aspirin, preservatives, stimulant, relaxant, and breathe out their chemical wastes into a polluted air. The sense of a long last night over civilization is back again.

> NORMAL MAILER (1923–). *Cannibals and Christians,* 1, 1966

We are caught up in a civilization having immense drive but no direction, marvelous capacity to get there but no idea where it is going.

> P. W. MARTIN (1893–?). *Experiment in Depth: A Study of the Work of Jung, Eliot and Toynbee,* 1, 1955

I have always felt that concentration camps, though they're a phenomenon of totalitarian states, are also the logical conclusion of contemporary life.

> ARTHUR MILLER (1915–). Olga Carlisle and Rose Styron interview, 1966. In George Plimpton, ed., *Writers at Work: Third Series,* 1967

Far from certainly, yet very possibly, Western civilization may be on the verge of . . . a crucial transformation today. A singular moment, which may hold incalculable practical consequences, may actually be at hand.

> LEWIS MUMFORD (1895–1990). *The Conduct of Life,* 8.3, 1951

No outward tinkering will improve this overpowered civilization, now plainly in the final and fossilized stage of its materialization. Nothing will produce an effective change but the fresh transformation that has already begun in the human mind.

> LEWIS MUMFORD (1895–1990). "Epilogue: The Advancement of Life," *The Pentagon of Power: The Myth of the Machine,* 1970

We live at a time when man believes himself fabulously capable of creation, but he does not know what to create. Lord of all things, he is not lord of himself. He feels lost amid his own abundance. With more means at its disposal, more knowledge, more techniques than ever, it turns out that the world today goes the same way as the worst of worlds that have been; it simply drifts.

> JOSÉ ORTEGA y GASSET (1883–1955). *The Revolt of the Masses,* 4, 1930, tr. anon., 1932

This is the gravest danger that today threatens civilization: State intervention; the absorption of all spontaneous social effort by the State, that is to say, of spontaneous historical action, which in the long run sustains, nourishes and impels human destinies.

> JOSÉ ORTEGA y GASSET (1883–1955). *The Revolt of the Masses,* 13, 1930, tr. anon., 1932

We live in an age in which the autonomous individual is ceasing to exist—or perhaps one ought to say, in which the individual is ceasing to have the illusion of being autonomous.

> GEORGE ORWELL (1903–1950). "Literature and Totalitarianism" (BBC Overseas Service), June 1941, *The Collected Essays, Journalism and Letters of George Orwell,* vol. 2, ed. Sonia Orwell and Ian Angus, 1968

Each age is a dream that is dying,
Or one that is coming to birth.

> ARTHUR O'SHAUGHNESSY (1844–1881). "Ode," 1874

But good God, what an age is this, and what a world is this, that a man cannot live without playing the knave and dissimulation.

> SAMUEL PEPYS (1633–1703). Diary, 1 September 1661

Two perceptions cast their shadow over my existence. One consists in my realization that the world is inexplicably mysterious and full of suffering; the other, in the fact that I have been born into a period of spiritual decadence in mankind.

> ALBERT SCHWEITZER (1875–1965). *Out of My Life and Thought: An Autobiography,* 21, tr. C. T. Campion, 1933

My expectation is that the challenges presented to Western civilization in our time are going to arouse us to repent, to reform and to lead a new life.

> ARNOLD J. TOYNBEE (1889–1975). "Ten Basic Questions—and Answers," *New York Times Magazine,* 20 February 1955

Western Civilization stands for not technology, but the sacredness of the individual human personality.

> ARNOLD J. TOYNBEE (1889–1975). "Man Owes His Freedom to God," *Collier's,* 30 March 1956

Today's challenge is to enlarge, by lengthening, the cultural memory of our society. . . . It is time to retrace our cultural steps, and rethink what we think.

> GEORGE F. WILL (1941–). *Statecraft as Soulcraft: What Government Does,* 7, 1983
>
> See Self-Realization (Becoming): Elias Canetti ◦ Values: Friedrich Nietzsche

Our civilization cannot survive materially unless it be redeemed spiritually.

> WOODROW WILSON (1856–1924). "The Road Away from Revolution," *Atlantic,* August 1923

One day posterity will remember
This strange era, these strange times, when
Ordinary common honesty was called courage.

> YEVGENY YEVTUSHENKO (1933–). In John Hohenberg, "A Czech Newspaperman," *Saturday Review,* 8 November 1969

CIVIL WAR

See also • America ◦ Commanders: Abraham Lincoln (all) ◦ Navy: David Farragut ◦ War

No terms except an unconditional and immediate surrender can be accepted. I propose to move immediately upon your works.

> ULYSSES S. GRANT (1822–1885). Message to Gen. Simon Bolivar Buckner, Fort Donelson (Tennessee), 16 February 1862

When the officer reached me, I was still suffering with the sick headache; but the instant I saw the contents of the note I was cured.

> ULYSSES S. GRANT (1822–1885). Referring to Gen. Robert E. Lee's surrender note, 9 April 1865, *Personal Memoirs of U. S. Grant,* 67, 1886

The groans from thousands of wounded in our front crying in anguish and pain, some for death to relieve them, others for water. Oh, if I could only drown this terrible sound, and yet I may also lie thus ere tomorrow's sun crosses the heavens.

> ALVA GRIEST (19th cent.). 19 September 1863. In Peter Cozzens, *This Terrible Sound: The Battle of Chickamauga* [Georgia], 1992

I am loath to close. We are not enemies, but friends. We must not be enemies. Though passion may have strained, it must not break our bonds of affection. The mystic chords of memory, stretching from every battlefield and patriot grave, to every living heart and hearthstone, all over this broad land, will yet swell the chorus of the Union, when again touched, as surely they will be, by the better angels of our nature.

> ABRAHAM LINCOLN (1809–1865). Referring to the people of the North and South just before the Civil War began, closing paragraph, *First Inaugural Address*, 4 March 1861. Secretary of State William A. Seward, thinking Lincoln's original concluding words too militant, drafted the following statement which Lincoln used after modifying: "I close. We are not, we must not, be aliens or enemies but fellow countrymen and brethren. . . . The mystic chords which proceeding from so many battlefields and so many patriot graves pass through all the hearts and all the hearths in this broad continent of ours will yet again harmonize in their ancient music when breathed upon by the guardian angel of the nation." (In John Updike, "Such a Sucker as Me," *New Yorker*, 30 October 1995)

The struggle of today is not altogether for today—it is for a vast future also.

> ABRAHAM LINCOLN (1809–1865). *First Annual Message to Congress*, 3 December 1861

My paramount object in this struggle *is* to save the Union, and is *not* either to save or to destroy slavery. If I could save the Union without freeing *any* slave, I would do it; and if I could save it by freeing *all* the slaves, I would do it; and if I could save it by freeing some and leaving others alone, I would also do that. . . .

I have here stated my purpose according to my view of *official* duty; and I intend no modification of my oft-expressed *personal* wish that all men everywhere could be free.

> ABRAHAM LINCOLN (1809–1865). Letter to Horace Greeley, 22 August 1862

Fourscore and seven years ago our fathers brought forth upon this continent a new nation conceived in liberty and dedicated to the proposition that all men are created equal.

> ABRAHAM LINCOLN (1809–1865). Opening words, *Gettysburg Address*, Pennsylvania, 19 November 1863
>
> See Misjudgments: Lincoln

We here highly resolve that these dead shall not have died in vain—that this nation, under God, shall have a new birth of freedom—and that government of the people, by the people, for the people, shall not perish from the earth.

> ABRAHAM LINCOLN (1809–1865). Closing words, *Gettysburg Address*, Pennsylvania, 19 November 1863
>
> See Democracy: Theodore Parker ○ Democracy: Daniel Webster ○ Imperialism: Louis Fischer (1) ○ World: Anonymous (American)

With malice toward none; with charity for all; with firmness in the right, as God gives us to see the right, let us strive on to finish the work we are in; to bind up the nation's wounds; to care for him who shall have borne the battle, and for his widow, and his orphan—to do all which may achieve and cherish a just, and a lasting peace, among ourselves, and with all nations.

> ABRAHAM LINCOLN (1809–1865). *Second Inaugural Address*, 4 March 1865. Some of the language in this famous passage may have been derived from John Quincy Adams's letter to A. Bronson, 30 July 1838, responding to an invitation to celebrate slavery's abolition in the British West Indies: "In charity to all mankind, bearing no malice or ill will to any human being, and even compassionating those who hold in bondage their fellow men, not knowing what they do. . . ."
>
> See Malice: Lincoln

I begin to regard the death and mangling of a couple thousand men as a small affair, a kind of morning dash—and it may be well that we become so hardened.

> WILLIAM TECUMSEH SHERMAN (1820–1891). Letter to his wife Ellen, July 1864
>
> See War: Sherman

If the people raise a great howl against my barbarity and cruelty, I will answer that war is war, and not popularity-seeking. If they want peace, they and their relatives must stop the war.

> WILLIAM TECUMSEH SHERMAN (1820–1891). Letter to Gen. Henry W. Halleck, 4 September 1864, before Sherman's march through Georgia, *Memoirs of Gen. W. T. Sherman*, 4th ed., 19, 1891 (1875)
>
> See War: Sherman

The whole army is burning with an insatiable desire to wreak vengeance upon South Carolina. I almost tremble at her fate, but feel that she deserves all that seems in store for her.

> WILLIAM TECUMSEH SHERMAN (1820–1891). Letter to Gen. Henry W. Halleck, 24 December 1864, *Memoirs of Gen. W. T. Sherman*, 4th ed., 21, 1891 (1875)
>
> See War: Sherman

A rich man's war and a poor man's fight.

> SLOGAN (AMERICAN). Used during the conscription riots in New York City, July 1863. Any Northerner subject to the draft could avoid service by paying $300 to a volunteer for taking his place.

Praise the Lord and pass the ammunition!

> SLOGAN (AMERICAN). Civil War, 1860s. This slogan was also popular in America's armed forces during World War II.

CLASS

See also • Aristocracy ○ Capitalism ○ Classes, Two ○ Communism ○ Democracy ○ Economics ○ Exploitation ○ Fascism ○ History: [especially] Karl Marx and Friedrich Engels ○ Imperialism ○ International Relations ○ Money ○ Morality: Lenin ○ Nations ○ Oppression ○ Politics ○ Poverty ○ Power ○ Property ○ Revolution ○ Socialism ○ Tyranny ○ Unions ○ Wages ○ War ○ Wealth ○ Work

The bonds of class are stronger than those of nationality.

> LORD ACTON (1834–1902). "Political Causes of the American Revolution," 1861, *Essays on Freedom and Power*, ed. Gertrude Himmelfarb, 1949
>
> See Crises: Bertrand Russell

The danger is not that a particular class is unfit to govern. Every class is unfit to govern.

LORD ACTON (1834–1902). Letter to Mary Gladstone, 24 March 1881. In Gertrude Himmelfarb, ed., introduction to *Essays on Freedom and Power,* 1949

The best political community is formed by citizens of the middle class, and . . . those states are likely to be well-administered, in which the middle class is large, and stronger if possible than both the other classes, or at any rate than either singly; for the addition of the middle class turns the scale, and prevents either of the extremes from being dominant.

ARISTOTLE (384–322 B.C.). *Politics,* 4.11, tr. Benjamin Jowett, 1885

History is a graveyard of classes which have preferred caste privileges to leadership.

E. DIGBY BALTZELL (1915–1996). *The Protestant Establishment: Aristocracy & Caste in America,* 3, 1964

Brevity, simplicity and the avoidance of euphemisms are the chief hallmarks of the upper-class American vocabulary.

STEPHEN BIRMINGHAM. *America's Secret Aristocracy,* 1, 1987

We gain nothing by trading the tyranny of capital for the tyranny of labor.

LOUIS BRANDEIS (1856–1941). 17 October 1941

A mixture of the military virtues, of respect for established ways of thinking and behaving, and of willingness to compromise, and if necessary, to innovate, is probably an adequate rough approximation of the qualities of a successful ruling class.

CRANE BRINTON (1896–1968). *The Anatomy of Revolution,* 2.4, 1952

In a socially stable society it seems likely that the great masses of poor and middling folk, as also the obscure and unsuccessful people who by birth and training might seem to be in the ruling class, really accept the leadership of those at the top of the social pyramid, and dream rather of *joining* them than of *dislodging* them.

CRANE BRINTON (1896–1968). *The Anatomy of Revolution,* 2.4, 1952

If you attack the establishment long enough and hard enough, they will make you a member of it.

ART BUCHWALD (1925–). In *International Herald Tribune* (Paris), 24 May 1989

The class which has the power to rob upon a large scale has also the power to control the government and legalize their robbery.

EUGENE V. DEBS (1855–1926). Speech, Canton (Ohio), 16 June 1918

The distinctions separating the social classes are false; in the last analysis they rest on force.

ALBERT EINSTEIN (1879–1955). "My Credo," *Wisdom,* January 1956

At the bottom, people tend to believe that class is defined by the amount of money you have. In the middle, people grant that money has something to do with it, but think education and the kind of work you do almost equally important. Nearer the top, people perceive that taste, values, ideas, style, and behavior are indispensable criteria of class, regardless of money or occupation or education.

PAUL FUSSELL (1924–). *Class,* 1, 1983

All the world over, I will back the masses against the classes.

WILLIAM EWART GLADSTONE (1809–1898). Speech, Liverpool, 28 June 1886

All communities divide themselves into the few and the many. The first are the rich and wellborn, the other the mass of the people. . . . The people are turbulent and changing; they seldom judge or determine right. Give therefore to the first class a distinct, permanent share in the government. They will check the unsteadiness of the second, and as they cannot receive any advantage by a change, they therefore will ever maintain good government.

ALEXANDER HAMILTON (1757–1804). Constitutional Convention speech, Philadelphia, 18 June 1787
See Property: Samuel Johnson

What I always hated and detested and cursed above all things was this contentment, this healthiness and comfort, this carefully preserved optimism of the middle classes, this fat and prosperous brood of mediocrity.

HERMANN HESSE (1877–1962). "For Madmen Only," *Steppenwolf,* 1927

There is still a natural tendency for the people of one class to look down on people who they think are lower class—as if they are less than human.

KATHY KAHN. In Meridee Merzer, "Kathy Kahn: Voice of Poor White Women," *Viva,* April 1974

Ruling classes have always sought to instill in their subordinates the capacity to experience exploitation and material deprivation as guilt, while deceiving themselves that their own material interests coincide with those of mankind as a whole.

CHRISTOPHER LASCH (1932–1994). *The Culture of Narcissism: American Life in an Age of Diminishing Expectations,* 1, 1979

People always have been the foolish victims of deception and self-deception in politics, and they always will be until they have learned to seek out the *interests* of some class or other behind all moral, religious, political and social phrases, declarations and promises.

LENIN (1870–1924). "The Three Sources and Three Component Parts of Marxism" (3), March 1913, *V. I. Lenin: Selected Works,* International Publishers edition, 1971

The strongest bond of human sympathy, outside of the family relation, should be one uniting all working people, of all nations, and tongues, and kindreds. Nor should this lead to a war upon property, or the owners of property. Property is the fruit of labor—is a positive good in the world. That some should be rich, shows that others may become rich, and hence is just encouragement to industry and enterprise. Let not him who is homeless pull down the house of another, but let him work diligently and build one for himself, thus by example assuring that his own shall be safe from violence when built.

ABRAHAM LINCOLN (1809–1865). Remarks to a delegation from the New York Workingmen's Association, Washington, 21 March 1864

Class struggle necessarily leads to the dictatorship of the proletariat. . . . This dictatorship itself is only a transition to the abolition of all classes and to a classless society.

KARL MARX (1818–1883). Letter, 5 March 1852
See Anarchism: Mikhail Bakunin (2)

Capital is dead labor, that, vampire-like, only lives by sucking living labor, and lives the more, the more labor it sucks.

KARL MARX (1818–1883). *Capital: A Critique of Political Economy*, 10.1, 1867–1894, tr. Samuel Moore and Edward Aveling, 1906

The ideas of the ruling class are in every epoch the ruling ideas: i.e., the class which is the ruling *material* force of society, is at the same time its ruling *intellectual* force. . . . The individuals composing the ruling class . . . among other things rule also as thinkers, as producers of ideas, and regulate the production and distribution of the ideas of their age.

KARL MARX (1818–1883) and FRIEDRICH ENGELS (1820–1895). "Feurbach: Opposition of the Materialistic and Idealistic Outlook" (A.2), *The German Ideology*, pt. 1, 1846, *The Marx-Engels Reader*, 2nd ed., ed. Robert C. Tucker, 1978

See Aristocracy: John Stuart Mill (2) ∘ Public Opinion: John Kenneth Galbraith

The workingmen have no country.

KARL MARX (1818–1883) and FRIEDRICH ENGELS (1820–1895). *The Communist Manifesto*, 2, 1847, ed. Engels, 1888

See Art: Alfred de Musset ∘ Merchants & Customers: Thomas Jefferson (2)

Hardly anything now depends upon individuals, but all upon classes; and, among classes, mainly upon the middle class. That class is now the power in society, the arbiter of fortune and success.

JOHN STUART MILL (1806–1873). "M. de Tocqueville on Democracy in America," vol. 2, *The Edinburgh Review* (Scotland), October 1840

This business of petty inconvenience and indignity, of being kept waiting about, of having to do everything at other people's convenience, is inherent in working-class life. A thousand influences constantly press a workingman into a *passive* role. He does not act, he is acted upon.

GEORGE ORWELL (1903–1950). *The Road to Wigan Pier*, 3, 1937

Middle-class people are really graded according to their degree of resemblance to the aristocracy.

GEORGE ORWELL (1903–1950). "The English People" ("The English Class System"), May 1947, *The Collected Essays, Journalism and Letters of George Orwell*, vol. 3, ed. Sonia Orwell and Ian Angus, 1968

There are only four ways in which a ruling group can fall from power. Either it is conquered from without, or it governs so inefficiently that the masses are stirred to revolt, or it allows a strong and discontented Middle Group to come into being, or it loses its own self-confidence and willingness to govern. These causes do not operate singly, and as a rule all four of them are present in some degree. A ruling class which could guard against all of them would remain in power permanently. Ultimately the determining factor is the mental attitude of the ruling class itself.

GEORGE ORWELL (1903–1950). *Nineteen Eighty-Four*, 2.9, 1949

Social justice cannot be said to have been satisfied as long as workingmen are denied a salary that will enable them to secure proper sustenance for themselves and for their families; as long as they are denied the opportunity of acquiring a modest fortune and forestalling the plague of universal pauperism; as long as they cannot make suitable provision through public or private insurance for old age, for periods of illness and unemployment.

POPE PIUS XI (1857–1939). *Divini Redemptoris (On Atheistic Communism)*, 19 March 1937

There are three distinct classes, any meddling of one with another, or the change of one into another, is the greatest harm to the State, and may be most justly termed evil-doing.

PLATO (427?–347 B.C.). *The Republic*, 4.434, tr. Benjamin Jowett, 1894

[The common people] are less well informed than the members of the other orders in the state . . . and so if not preoccupied with the search for the necessities of existence, find it difficult to remain within the limits imposed by both common sense and the law. . . . One should compare them with mules, which being accustomed to work, suffer more when long idle than when kept busy.

CARDINAL RICHELIEU (1585–1642). *Political Testament*, 1.4, tr. Henry Bertram Hill, 1961

Our middle classes, who are comfortable and irresponsible at other people's expense . . . are neither ashamed of that condition nor even conscious of it.

GEORGE BERNARD SHAW (1856–1950). Preface ("A Void in the Elizabethan Drama") to *Saint Joan*, 1923

Is it a Utopian dream, that once in history a ruling class might be willing to make the great surrender, and permit social change to come about without hatred, turmoil, and waste of human life?

UPTON SINCLAIR (1878–1968)

While indignant Radicalism denounces "the vile aristocrats," these in their turn enlarge with horror on the brutality of the mob. Neither party sees its own sins. Neither party recognizes in the other itself in a different dress. . . . Yet a cool bystander finds nothing to choose between them; knows that these class recriminations are but the inflammatory symptoms of a uniformly diffused immorality. Label men how you please with titles of "upper" and "middle" and "lower," you cannot prevent them from being units of the same society, acted upon by the same spirit of the age, molded after the same type of character.

HERBERT SPENCER (1820–1903). *Social Statics*, 3.20.7, 1851

The fate of a nation depends not upon laws or constitutions, ideals and programs, not even upon moral principles or racial instincts; it depends first and foremost upon the capabilities of the ruling minority.

OSWALD SPENGLER (1880–1936). *Aphorisms*, 200, tr. Gisela Koch-Weser O'Brien, 1967

Whether the category is as specialized as "physicians" or as generalized as "white males," members of a powerful group are raised to believe (however illogically) that whatever affects it will also affect them. On the other hand, members of less powerful groups are raised to believe (however illogically) that each individual can escape the group's fate. Thus, cohesion is encouraged on the one hand, and disunity is fostered on the other.

GLORIA STEINEM (1934–). *Moving Beyond Words*, pt. 6, 1994

Working Man, awake!
Learn your own power,
All the wheels are still
If your strong arm so wishes it.

MAX STIRNER (1806–1856). German philosopher. Quoted by Barthélemy de Ligt, *The Conquest of Violence: An Essay on War and Revolution,* 1938. In Mulford Q. Sibley, ed., *The Quiet Battle,* 1963

The Establishment is enlightened, tolerant, even well-meaning. It has never been exclusive, rather drawing in recruits from outside as soon as they are ready to conform to its standards and become respectable. There is nothing more agreeable in life than to make peace with the Establishment—and nothing more corrupting.

A. J. P. TAYLOR (1906–1990). "William Cobbett," 1953, *Essays in English History,* 1976

Never speak disrespectfully of Society, Algernon. Only people who can't get into it do that.

OSCAR WILDE (1854–1900). *The Importance of Being Earnest,* 3, 1895

Privilege is not good or bad of itself. . . . It can be used well or ill. It is the sword given not for ornament but use. All those with privilege should turn it not merely to influence but also to service.

GARRY WILLS (1934–). *Confessions of a Conservative,* 11, 1979

As soon as a man opens his mouth everybody knows to which class he belongs. In England this is the primary criterion of class membership.

FERDYNAND ZWEIG. *The British Worker,* 21, 1952

❧

Class interests are best served when masked as national interests.

ANONYMOUS

CLASSES, TWO

See also • Class ○ Crime: Anonymous ○ Equality ○ Nations: Thomas Jefferson

There are two kinds of people in one's life: people whom one keeps waiting and the people for whom one waits.

S. N. BEHRMAN (1893–1973)

[There are two classes of people in the world:] those who constantly divide the people of the world into two classes, and those who do not.

ROBERT BENCHLEY (1889–1945). In Stefan Kanfer, "Proverbs or Aphorisms?" *Time,* 11 July 1983

Society is now one polish'd horde,
Form'd of two mighty tribes, the *Bores* and *Bored.*

LORD BYRON (1788–1824). *Don Juan,* 13.95, 1819–1824

Man has set man against man, washed against unwashed.

THOMAS CARLYLE (1795–1881). *The French Revolution: A History,* 1837

There [are] but two families in the world, Have-much and Have-little.

CERVANTES (1547–1616). *Don Quixote,* 2.3.20, 1615, tr. Peter Anthony Motteux and John Ozell, 1743 (Popular version: The haves and the have-nots.)

Society is made up of two great classes: those who have more dinners than appetite, and those who have more appetite than dinners.

CHAMFORT (1741–1794). *Maxims and Thoughts,* 3, 1796, tr. W. S. Merwin, 1984

There are only two kinds of people; those who accept dogmas and know it, and those who accept dogmas and don't know it.

G. K. CHESTERTON (1874–1936). *As I Was Saying: A Chesterton Reader,* 17, ed. Robert Knille, 1985

Two nations; between whom there is no intercourse and no sympathy; who are as ignorant of each other's habits, thoughts, and feelings, as if they were dwellers in different zones, or inhabitants of different planets; who are formed by a different breeding, are fed by a different food, are ordered by different manners, and are not governed by the same laws. . . . *the rich and the poor.*

BENJAMIN DISRAELI (1804–1881). *Sybil: Or, The Two Nations,* 2.5, 1845

There's them as i born t' own land, and them as is born to sweat on't.

GEORGE ELIOT (1819–1880). *Adam Bede,* 32, 1859

Mankind divides itself into two classes—benefactors and malefactors. The second class is vast, the first a handful.

RALPH WALDO EMERSON (1803–1882). "Considerations by the Way," *The Conduct of Life,* 1860

I always divide people into two groups. Those who live by what they know to be a lie, and those who live by what they believe, falsely, to be the truth.

CHRISTOPHER HAMPTON (1946–). *The Philanthropist,* 6, 1970

There are only two classes in society: those who get more than they earn, and those who earn more than they get.

HOLBROOK JACKSON (1874–1948)

There are two classes of people in this world: there are those who prey, and those who are preyed upon.

MR. JACQUES (19th cent.). English headmaster. Remark to the author. In Samuel Butler (1835–1902), *Further Extracts from the Note-Books of Samuel Butler,* 1, ed. A. T. Bartholomew, 1934

The human species . . . is composed of two distinct races: *the men who borrow* and *the men who lend.*

CHARLES LAMB (1775–1834). "The Two Races of Men," *The Essays of Elia,* 1823

Mankind is composed of two sorts of men—those who love and create, and those who hate and destroy.

JOSÉ MARTÍ (1853–1895). Letter to a Cuban farmer

Society as a whole is more and more splitting up into two great hostile camps, into two great classes directly facing each other: Bourgeoisie and Proletariat.

KARL MARX (1818–1883) and FRIEDRICH ENGELS (1820–1895). *The Communist Manifesto,* 1, 1847, ed. Engels, 1888

The world is divided into those who want to become someone and those who want to accomplish something.

JEAN MONNET (1888–1979). In "Father of a Larger Community: Jean Monnet: 1888–1979," *Time,* 26 March 1979

Any city, however small, is in fact divided into two, one the city of the poor, the other of the rich; these are at war with one another.

PLATO (427?–347 B.C.). *The Republic,* 4.422-423, tr. Benjamin Jowett, 1894

There are only two qualities in the world: efficiency and inefficiency, and only two sorts of people: the efficient and the inefficient.

> GEORGE BERNARD SHAW (1856–1950). *John Bull's Other Island,* 4, 1904

Society is divided into two classes, the fleecers and fleeced: it is better to belong to the fleecers.

> TALLEYRAND (1754–1838)

The human race consists of the damned and the ought-to-be-damned.

> MARK TWAIN (1835–1910). 4 July 1898, *Mark Twain's Notebook,* ed. Albert Bigelow Paine, 1935

It is impossible on our wretched globe for men living in society not to be divided into two classes, one of oppressors, the other of the oppressed.

> VOLTAIRE (1694–1778). "Equality," *Philosophical Dictionary,* 1764, tr. Theodore Besterman, 1971

The two kinds of people I mean
Are the people who lift and the people who lean.

> ELLA WHEELER WILCOX (1850–1919). "Lifting and Leaning." In Hazel Felleman, ed., *The Best Loved Poems of the American People,* 1936

It is absurd to divide people into good and bad. People are either charming or tedious.

> OSCAR WILDE (1854–1900). *Lady Windemere's Fan,* 1, 1892

CLERGY

See also • Christianity ○ Church ○ Evangelism ○ Preachers ○ Priests ○ Professionals ○ Prophets ○ Rabbis ○ Religion ○ Saints

The clergy have never been wanting in benedictions for any victorious enormity.

> HENRI AMIEL (1821–1881). Journal, 6 October 1866, tr. Mrs. Humphrey Ward, 1887

The clergy are as like as peas. I cannot tell them apart.

> RALPH WALDO EMERSON (1803–1882). "The Preacher," *Lectures and Biographical Sketches,* 1883

Truth from his lips prevail'd with double sway,
And fools, who came to scoff, remain'd to pray.

> OLIVER GOLDSMITH (1728–1774). *The Deserted Village,* l. 179, 1770

It often happens that I wake up at night and begin to think of a serious problem and decide that I must tell the Pope about it. Then I wake up completely and remember that *I am the Pope.*

> POPE JOHN XXIII (1881–1963). In "Thoughts on the Business of Life," *Forbes,* 29 December 1997

Father McKenzie, writing the words
  of a sermon that no one will hear.

> JOHN LENNON (1940–1980) and PAUL McCARTNEY (1942–). "Eleanor Rigby" (song), 1966

Archbishop: a Christian ecclesiastic of a rank superior to that attained by Christ.

> H. L. MENCKEN (1880–1956). *A Little Book in C Major,* 4.1, 1916

When the authorized teachers of religion propagate through the great body of the people doctrines subversive of the authority of the sovereign, it is by violence only, or by the force of a standing army, that [the sovereign] can maintain his authority.

> ADAM SMITH (1723–1790). *The Wealth of Nations,* 5.1.3.3, 1776

Anonymous vicar: Was there anything you'd like my sermon to be about.
Wellington: Yes, about 10 minutes.

> DUKE OF WELLINGTON (1769–1852). Attributed

To all things clergic
I am allergic.

> ALEXANDER WOOLLCOTT (1887–1943). In Samuel Hopkins Adams, *A. Woollcott: His Life and His World,* 29, 1945

There are three sexes—men, women, and clergymen.

> SAYING (FRENCH). In Lady Holland, *A Memoir of the Reverend Sydney Smith,* 5.1.9, 1855

CLEVERNESS

See also • Cunning ○ Intelligence ○ Wisdom: Baltasar Gracián (2)

Cleverness is serviceable for everything, sufficient for nothing.

> HENRI AMIEL (1821–1881). Journal, 16 February 1868, tr. Mrs. Humphrey Ward, 1887

Cleverness is to trickery what manual dexterity is to picking pockets.

> CHAMFORT (1741–1794). *Maxims and Thoughts,* 2, 1796, tr. W. S. Merwin, 1984

It is exceedingly clever to know how to hide your cleverness.

> LA ROCHEFOUCAULD (1613–1680). *Maxims,* 245, 1665, tr. Louis Kronenberger, 1959

Here's a good rule of thumb:
Too clever is dumb.

> OGDEN NASH (1902–1971). "Reflection on Ingenuity," *Many Long Years Ago,* 1945

[Alexander I of Russia] is subtle and clever. He may go far.

> NAPOLEON (1769–1821). Remark to Emmanuel Las Cases, 10–12 March 1816, *The Mind of Napoleon: A Selection from His Written and Spoken Words,* 226, ed. J. Christopher Herold, 1955

If all the good people were clever,
  And all clever people were good,
The world would be nicer than ever
  We thought that it possibly could.

> ELIZABETH WORDSWORTH (1840–1932). "The Clever and the Good," *St. Christopher and Other Poems,* 1890

CLOTHES

See also • Appearances ○ Dress ○ Fashion

Good Clothes open all Doors.

> THOMAS FULLER (1654–1734). Comp., *Gnomologia: Adages and Proverbs,* 1705, 1732

Ever since we wear clothes we know not one another.
> GEORGE HERBERT (1593–1633). Comp., *Outlandish Proverbs,* 168, 1640

Take off your ties, they are chains around your necks.
> ABBIE HOFFMAN (1936–1989). *Revolution for the Hell of It,* 2, 1968

Clothing, as an extension of the skin, can be seen both as a heat-control mechanism and as a means of defining the self socially.
> MARSHALL McLUHAN (1911–1980). *Understanding Media: The Extensions of Man,* 12, 1964

How the attitude of women varies with a man's clothes. When a badly dressed man passes them they shudder away from him with a quite frank movement of disgust, as though he were a dead cat.
> GEORGE ORWELL (1903–1950). *Down and Out in Paris and London,* 24, 1933

In olden days a glimpse of stocking
Was looked on as something shocking
But now, heaven knows,
Anything goes.
> COLE PORTER (1892–1964). Title song. In the musical *Anything Goes,* 1934

She wears her clothes as if they were thrown on her with a pitch-fork.
> JONATHAN SWIFT (1667–1745). *A Complete Collection of Genteel and Ingenious Conversation,* 1, 1738

It is an interesting question how far men would retain their relative rank if they were divested of their clothes.
> HENRY DAVID THOREAU (1817–1862). "Economy," *Walden; or Life in the Woods,* 1854

Beware of all enterprises that require new clothes, and not rather a new wearer of clothes.
> HENRY DAVID THOREAU (1817–1862). "Economy," *Walden; or Life in the Woods,* 1854

The greater part of the expenditure incurred by all classes for apparel is incurred for the sake of a respectable appearance rather than for the protection of the person.
> THORSTEIN VEBLEN (1857–1929). *The Theory of the Leisure Class: An Economic Study of Institutions,* 7 1899

Do not conceive that fine Clothes make fine Men, any more than fine feathers make fine Birds.
> GEORGE WASHINGTON (1732–1799). Letter to his nephew Bushrod Washington, 15 January 1783

With an evening coat and a white tie, anybody, even a stockbroker, can gain a reputation for being civilized.
> OSCAR WILDE (1854–1900). *The Picture of Dorian Gray,* 1, 1891

❧

A man is judged by his clothes, a horse by its saddle.
> SAYING (CHINESE)

Clothes make the man.
> SAYING (LATIN)
> See Manners: William Blake ○ Money: John Clarke

A monkey in silk is still a monkey.
> SAYING (SPANISH)

CLOUDS

See also • Nature ○ Sky

What sculpture in these hard clouds; what expression of immense amplitude in this dotted and rippled rack, here firm and continental, there vanishing into plumes and auroral gleams. No crowding; boundless, cheerful, and strong.
> RALPH WALDO EMERSON (1803–1882). Journal, 25 May 1843

Clouds. Think of the cooling shadows of summer which benevolent Nature spreads over her darling forests and gardens—summer shadows of wonderful depth and brilliancy like the wings of a mother bird over her young.
> JOHN MUIR (1838–1914). Journal, 1913? In *John of the Mountains: The Unpublished Journals of John Muir,* ed. Linnie Marsh Wolfe, 1938

The clouds are the dust of his feet.
> NAHUM (7th? cent B.C.). *Nahum* 1:3

Clarence: Every cloud engenders not a storm.
> SHAKESPEARE (1564–1616). *Henry VI,* Part III, 5.3.13, 1590

You must not blame me if I talk to the clouds.
> HENRY DAVID THOREAU (1817–1862). Letter to Lucy Brown, 2 March 1842

❧

Every cloud has a silver lining.
> SAYING (ENGLISH)

COFFEE

See also • Addiction ○ Alcohol ○ Drugs, Illegal ○ Tobacco

Drinking five or more cups of coffee a day appears to increase a person's chances of developing lung cancer, according to a researcher who says his study is the first to pinpoint coffee alone. . . .

Those who drank five or more cups a day were seven times more likely to have died from lung cancer than the men who drank no coffee at all.
> ASSOCIATED PRESS. The article was based on a study by Dr. Leonard Schuman, a University of Minnesota epidemiologist, who had tracked the dietary habits and death rates of 17,818 men, all 45 and older, over an 18-year period, "5-Cup Coffee Habit Tied to Lung Cancer," *San Francisco Chronicle,* 24 June 1985

A pregnant woman who drinks coffee exposes her developing fetus to the same concentration of caffeine as that in her own blood. The caffeine equivalent of five-to-six cups of coffee per day has been shown to increase the risk of birth defect in laboratory animals. Whether the same effect occurs in humans is not yet clear.

One study, published by the journal *Postgraduate Medicine* in 1977, showed that among pregnant women who exceeded 600 mg. of caffeine per day [5-to-6 cups of coffee], 15 out of 16 pregnancies ended in spontaneous abortion, stillbirth or premature birth.
> TOM FERGUSON. Physician. Pacific News Service release, San Francisco, June 1982

Coffee is not my cup of tea.

> SAMUEL GOLDWYN (1882–1974)

Way too much coffee. But if it weren't for the coffee, I'd have no identifiable personality whatsoever.

> DAVID LETTERMAN (1947–). Explaining the adrenaline-rush he experiences on his nightly television program. In Bill Zehme, "Letterman Lets His Guard Down," *Esquire,* December 1994

Dashing the hopes of a morning with a cup of warm coffee.

> HENRY DAVID THOREAU (1817–1862). "Higher Laws," *Walden; or Life in the Woods,* 1854

Experts now generally agree that there is no consistent scientific evidence to prove coffee is detrimental to your health. "The good news about coffee is that there *is* no news," says Stanley Segall, a professor of nutrition and food science at Drexel University who has studied coffee and its health effects for 40 years. "From a health standpoint, coffee is an innocuous substance," he adds.

A recent study at the University of California at Davis suggests coffee may even be good for you. Takayuki Shibamoto, a professor in the department of environmental toxicology, found that freshly brewed coffee contains antioxidant compounds that may carry as much power as vitamins C and E. In part, Shibamoto says, the seductive smell of brewed coffee is caused by these compounds.

> DENSIE WEBB. "Don't Drop the Foods You Love," *Parade Magazine,* 16 November 1997

❧

Look here, Steward, if this is coffee, I want tea; but if this is tea, then I wish for coffee.

> ANONYMOUS. In *Punch* (British humor magazine), vol. 144, p. 44, 1902

Coffee has two virtues: it's wet and warm.

> SAYING (DUTCH)

Coffee should be black as hell, strong as death and sweet as love.

> SAYING (TURKISH)

COLD WAR

See also • Cuban Missile Crisis ○ Crisis Leaders: John Foster Dulles ○ International Relations ○ Nuclear Weapons: John Foster Dulles ○ War

Like apples in a barrel infected by one rotten one, the corruption of Greece would infect Iran and all to the east. It would also carry infection to Africa through Asia Minor and Egypt, and to Europe through Italy and France, already threatened by the strongest domestic Communist parties in Western Europe.

> DEAN ACHESON (1893–1971). Supporting the Truman Doctrine, February 1947, *Present at the Creation: My Years in the State Department,* 24, 1969

Let us be not deceived—today we are in the midst of a cold war.

> BERNARD M. BARUCH (1870–1965). Introducing the term "cold war" which had been coined by his speech writer Herbert Bayard Swope, address at the unveiling of his portrait in the capitol building in Columbia, South Carolina, 16 April 1947

The biggest thing that has happened in the world in my life, in our lives, is this. By the grace of God America won the cold war. . . .

The cold war didn't end; it was won. And I think of those who won it, in places like Korea and Vietnam, and some of them didn't come back. Back then they were heroes, but this year they were victors.

> GEORGE BUSH (1924–). State of the Union Message, 28 January 1992

From Stettin in the Baltic to Trieste in the Adriatic, an iron curtain has descended across the Continent.

> WINSTON CHURCHILL (1874–1965). Referring to the western border of Soviet-occupied Europe at the end of World War II, "The Sinews of Peace," address, Westminster College, Fulton (Missouri), 5 March 1946. Churchill's first use of "iron curtain" was in a telegram to Pres. Harry S. Truman dated 12 May 1945.
>
> See World War I: Elizabeth

Freedom has many flaws and our democracy is imperfect, but we have never had to put up a wall to keep our people in.

> JOHN F. KENNEDY (1917–1963). Speech at West Berlin's City Hall, almost two years after the Berlin Wall had been built, 26 June 1963

The superpowers [i.e., the United States and the Soviet Union] often behave like two heavily armed blind men feeling their way around a room, each believing himself in mortal peril from the other, whom he assumes to have perfect vision. Each side should know that frequently uncertainty, compromise and incoherence are the essence of policy-making. Yet each tends to ascribe to the other side a consistency, foresight and coherence that its own experience belies. Of course, over time even two armed blind men in a room can do enormous damage to each other, not to speak of the room.

> HENRY A. KISSINGER (1923–). *White House Years,* 13, 1979

We may be likened to scorpions in a bottle, each capable of killing the other, but only at the risk of his own life.

> J. ROBERT OPPENHEIMER (1904–1967). "Atomic Weapons and American Policy," *Foreign Affairs,* July 1953

There is one sign the Soviets can make that would be unmistakable, that would advance dramatically the cause of freedom and peace. General Secretary Gorbachev, if you seek peace, if you seek prosperity for the Soviet Union and Eastern Europe, if you seek liberalization: Come here to this gate! Mr. Gorbachev, open this gate! Mr. Gorbachev, tear down this wall!

> RONALD REAGAN (1911–). Reference to the Berlin Wall, speech at the Brandenburg Gate, West Berlin, 12 June 1987

COLLEGE

See also • Education ○ Learning (Process) ○ School ○ University

You think, 'cause you been to college, you know better than anybody.

> RICHARD HENRY DANA, JR. (1815–1882). *Two Years Before the Mast,* 6, 1840

Colleges are like old-age homes, except for the fact that more people die in colleges.

> BOB DYLAN (1941–). Nat Hentoff interview, *Playboy,* March 1966

We are shut up in schools and college recitation rooms for ten or fifteen years, and come out at last with a bellyful of words and do not know a thing.

> RALPH WALDO EMERSON (1803–1882). Journal, 14 September 1839

Happy the natural college thus self-instituted around every natural teacher; the young men of Athens around Socrates.

> RALPH WALDO EMERSON (1803–1882). "Education," *Lectures and Biographical Sketches,* 1883

A pine bench, with Mark Hopkins at one end of it and me at the other, is a good enough college for me!

> JAMES A. GARFIELD (1831–1881). U.S. President. Address, Williams College alumni dinner, New York City, 28 December 1871. Hopkins had been the Williams president during Garfield's undergraduate years, and the two had struck up a close relationship.

A college education shows a man how little other people know.

> THOMAS CHANDLER HALIBURTON (1796–1865)

A College Degree is a Social Certificate, not a proof of competence.

> ELBERT HUBBARD (1856–1915). *A Thousand and One Epigrams,* p. 106, 1911

For the most part, colleges are places where pebbles are polished and diamonds are dimmed.

> ROBERT G. INGERSOLL (1833–1899). "Education," *The Philosophy of Ingersoll,* ed. Vere Goldthwaite, 1906

We have but one rule here and it is that every student must be a gentleman.

> ROBERT E. LEE (1807–1870). Remark to a student who asked for a copy of the rules at Washington College, now Washington and Lee University, Lexington (Virginia), where Gen. Lee served as president following the Civil War. In Dixon Wecter, *The Hero in America: A Chronicle of Hero-Worship,* 11.3, 1941

COLONIALISM

See also • Empire ○ Imperialism

What is madness to the mother country is sanity to the colony.

> ELDRIDGE CLEAVER (1935–1998). David Susskind television interview, 28 May 1968

The colonized races, those slaves of modern times, are impatient.

> FRANTZ FANON (1925–1961). "Concerning Violence," *The Wretched of the Earth,* 1961, tr. Constance Farrington, 1963

[The colonies are] a vast system of outdoor relief for the upper classes.

> JOHN STUART MILL (1806–1873). In Robert L. Heilbroner, *The Worldly Philosophers: The Lives, Times, and Ideas of the Great Economic Thinkers,* 5th ed., 7, 1980 (1953)

Colonialism only loosens its hold when the knife is at its throat.

> NATIONAL LIBERATION FRONT. Algeria. Leaflet, 1956. In Frantz Fanon, "Concerning Violence," *The Wretched of the Earth,* 1961, tr. Constance Farrington, 1963

The saddest thing in my life was when I discovered that people can get their freedom from colonial masters and find themselves unfree.

> JOSHUA NKOMO (1917–). Zimbabwean political leader. In *Observer* (British newspaper), 22 April 1984

With us [Europeans], to be a man is to be an accomplice of colonialism, since all of us without exception have profited by colonial exploitation.

> JEAN-PAUL SARTRE (1905–1980). Preface to Frantz Fanon, *The Wretched of the Earth,* 1961, tr. Constance Farrington, 1963

The real wealth of these [colonized] peoples would consist in their coming to produce for themselves by agriculture and handicrafts as far as possible all the necessities of their life. Instead of that they are exclusively bent on providing the materials which world trade requires, and for which it pays them good prices. With the money thus obtained they procure from it manufactured goods and prepared foodstuffs, thereby making home industry impossible, and often even endangering the stability of their own agriculture.

> ALBERT SCHWEITZER (1875–1965). *Out of My Life and Thought: An Autobiography,* 17, tr. C. T. Campion, 1933

All colonialism is fundamentally based on violence. Just as fascism can be seen as the application of colonial methods to one's own country, so colonialism can be looked at as the application of fascistic methods to a foreign country. In some respects, fascism is a kind of colonialism at home, while colonialism is fascism abroad.

> FREDRIC WERTHAM (1895–1981). *A Sign for Cain: An Exploration of Human Violence,* 5, 1966

COMEDY

See also • Funniness ○ Humor: [especially] Roger Rosenblatt ○ Humor ○ Jests ○ Jokes ○ Laughter ○ Satire ○ Tragedy ○ Wit ○ World: Horace Walpole

Woody Allen's comedy is nothing but a set of variations on the theme of the man who does not have a real "self" or "identity," and feels superior to the inauthentically self-satisfied people because he is conscious of his situation and at the same time inferior to them because they are "adjusted."

> ALLAN BLOOM (1930–1992). "The German Connection," *The Closing of the American Mind: How Higher Education Has Failed Democracy and Impoverished the Souls of Today's Students,* 1987

Tragedy is if I cut my finger. Comedy is if you walk into an open sewer and die.

> MEL BROOKS (1926–). In Kenneth Tynan, "Profiles: Frolics and Detours of a Short Hebrew Man," *New Yorker,* 30 October 1978

Comedy is tragedy that happens to *other* people.

> ANGELA CARTER (1940–1992). *Wise Children,* 4, 1991

All I need to make a comedy is a park, a policeman, and a pretty girl.

> SIR CHARLES SPENCER "CHARLIE" CHAPLIN (1889–1977). *My Autobiography,* 10, 1964

The sense of disproportion is comedy.

> RALPH WALDO EMERSON (1803–1882). "The Comic," *Letters and Social Aims,* 1876

When Carlini was convulsing Naples with laughter, a patient waited on a physician in that city, to obtain some remedy for excessive melancholy, which was rapidly consuming his life. The physician endeavored to cheer his spirits, and advised him to go to the theater and see Carlini. He replied, "I am Carlini."

> RALPH WALDO EMERSON (1803–1882). Closing words, "The Comic," *Letters and Social Aims,* 1876

The test of a real comedian is whether you laugh at him before he opens his mouth.

> GEORGE JEAN NATHAN (1882–1958). "Theatre" (72), *American Mercury,* September 1929

There is no credit to being a comedian, when you have the whole Government working for you. All you have to do is report the facts. I don't even have to exaggerate.

> WILL ROGERS (1879–1935). In P. J. O'Brien, *Will Rogers, Ambassador of Good Will, Prince of Wit and Wisdom,* 9, 1935

A comic says funny things; a comedian says things funny.

> ED WYNN (1885–1965). Quoted by Milton Berle, Larry King television interview, CNN, 20 November 1993

COMMANDERS

Includes • Generals

See also • Army ○ Commanders & Soldiers ○ Commanders & Staff ○ Decision-Making ○ Intelligence, Military ○ Korean War: Harry S. Truman (5) ○ Leaders ○ Navy ○ Planning ○ Power: Oliver Wendell Holmes, Jr. (2) ○ Presidents ○ Soldiers ○ Strategy, Military ○ Victory: Roger A. Beaumont and Bernard J. James ○ War ○ World War II: [especially] Dwight D. Eisenhower (1)

A general needs to show daring towards his opponents, good will towards his subordinates and a cool head in crises.

> AGESILAUS II (444?–360 B.C.). In Plutarch (A.D. 46?–119?), "Sayings of the Spartans: Agesilaus" (66), *Plutarch on Sparta,* tr. Richard J. A. Talbert, 1988

The blood of the soldier makes the glory of the general.

> HENRY G. BOHN (1796–1884). Comp., *A Hand-Book of Proverbs,* p. 499, 1860

The general must rely on his ability to control the situation to his advantage as opportunity dictates. He is not bound by established procedures.

> CHIA LIN (4th cent. B.C.). In Sun-tzu "The Nine Variables" (9), *The Art of War,* tr. Samuel B. Griffith, 1963

Battles are won by slaughter and maneuver. The greater the general, the more he contributes in maneuver, the less he demands in slaughter.

> WINSTON CHURCHILL (1874–1965). *The Great War,* 1.498, 1933

Let us not hear of Generals who conquer without bloodshed.

> KARL von CLAUSEWITZ (1780–1831). *On War,* 4.11, 1832, tr. J. J. Graham, 1873

The Commander should have in his eye the object [on] which every line must converge.

> KARL von CLAUSEWITZ (1780–1831). *On War,* 5.3.A, 1832, tr. J. J. Graham, 1873

War is much too serious a matter to be entrusted to generals.

> GEORGES CLEMENCEAU (1841–1929). French premier
> See Environment: Helmut Sihler ○ Politicians: Charles de Gaulle ○ Priests: Anonymous

[The commander] must be able to see the situation as a whole, attribute to each object its relative importance, grasp the connections between each factor in the situation, and recognize its limits. All this implies a gift of synthesis which, in itself, demands a high degree of intellectual capacity.

> CHARLES de GAULLE (1890–1970). "The Conduct of War" (1), *The Edge of the Sword,* 1934, tr. Gerald Hopkins, 1960

He must keep his mind always on the stretch.

> CHARLES de GAULLE (1890–1970). "Of Politics and the Soldier" (2), *The Edge of the Sword,* 1934, tr. Gerald Hopkins, 1960

In war, you must either trust your general or sack him.

> JOHN DILL (1881–1944). British Chief of the Imperial General Staff. Letter to Gen. Archibald Percival Wavell, who soon afterwards was sacked, 1941. In Ronald Lewin, *The Chief,* 5, 1980

The ideal senior commander may be viewed as a device for receiving, processing and transmitting information in a way which will yield the maximum gain for the minimum cost.

> NORMAN F. DIXON (1922–). *On the Psychology of Military Incompetence,* 2, 1976

[Napoleon] sees where the matter hinges, throws himself on the precise point of resistance, and slights all other considerations. He is strong in the right manner, namely, by insight. He never blundered into victory, but won his battles in his head before he won them on the field. His principle means are in himself. He asks counsel of no other.

> RALPH WALDO EMERSON (1803–1882). "Napoleon; or, The Man of the World," *Representative Men,* 1850

Having decided what was to be done, he did that with might and main. He put out all his strength. He risked everything, and spared nothing, neither ammunition, nor money, nor troops, nor generals, nor himself.

> RALPH WALDO EMERSON (1803–1882). "Napoleon; or, The Man of the World," *Representative Men,* 1850

Your greatness does not depend on the size of your command, but on the manner in which you exercise it.

> FERDINAND FOCH (1851–1929). In Charles Bugnet, "Results" (The Ascent to Command), *Foch Speaks,* tr. Russell Green, 1929

Mad, is he? Then I hope he will *bite* some of my other generals.

> GEORGE II (1683–1760). British king. Remark to the Duke of Newcastle, who had complained that Gen. James Wolfe, the successful commander of British forces in the American colonies, was insane. In Henry Beckles Willson, *The Life and Letters of James Wolfe,* 17, 1909

When you get in trouble, you send for the sonsabitches.

> ERNEST KING (1878–1956). Admiral. Attributed. In Harries-Clichy Peterson, Jr., "Fortuna et Virtu," *Proceedings,* U.S. Naval Institute, September 1978

A mighty conqueror does not give battle.

LAO-TZU (6th cent. B.C.). *The Way of Life*, 68, tr. R. B. Blakney, 1955

The greatest commander of men was he whose intuitions most nearly happened. Nine-tenths of tactics were certain enough to be teachable in schools; but the irrational tenth was like the kingfisher flashing across the pool, and in it lay the test of generals. It could be ensued only by instinct (sharpened by thought practicing the stroke) until at the crisis it came naturally, a reflex.

T. E. LAWRENCE (1888–1935). *Seven Pillars of Wisdom: A Triumph*, 33, 1926

Like a Roman emperor, once [Winston Churchill] lost confidence in a frontier general he found reason for suspicion in anything and everything.

RONALD LEWIN (1914–1984). *The Chief*, 2, 1980

A commander should have a profound understanding of human nature, the knack of smoothing out troubles, the power of winning affection while communicating energy, and the capacity for ruthless determination where required by circumstances. He needs to generate an electrifying current, and to keep a cool head in applying it.

B. H. LIDDELL HART (1895–1970). October 1933, *Thoughts on War*, 11, 1944

There are over two thousand years of experience to tell us that the only thing harder than getting a new idea into the military mind is to get an old one out.

B. H. LIDDELL HART (1895–1970). March 1936, *Thoughts on War*, 5.6, 1944

I can't afford to lose this man. He fights.

ABRAHAM LINCOLN (1809–1865). Responding to newspaper criticism of Gen. Ulysses S. Grant for drunkenness and inefficiency during the Battle of Shiloh (Tennessee), April 1862. In Dixon Wecter, *The Hero in America: A Chronicle of Hero-Worship*, 12.2, 1941

I have just read your dispatch about sore-tongued and fatigued horses. Will you pardon me for asking what the horses of your army have done since the battle of Antietam that fatigues anything?

ABRAHAM LINCOLN (1809–1865). Telegram to Gen. George B. McClellan whose reluctance to engage the enemy had long irked the President, 24 October 1862

I have heard, in such way as to believe it, of your recently saying that both the Army and the Government needed a Dictator. Of course it was not *for* this, but in spite of it, that I have given you the command. Only those generals who gain successes, can set up dictators. What I now ask of you is military success, and I will risk the dictatorship.

ABRAHAM LINCOLN (1809–1865). Letter to Gen. Joseph Hooker, 26 January 1863.

See Confidence: First Person: Joseph "Fighting Joe" Hooker

Well, I wish some of you would tell me the brand of whiskey that Grant drinks. I would like to send a barrel of it to my other generals.

ABRAHAM LINCOLN (1809–1865). Attributed (he denied having said it). Responding to reports of Gen. Ulysses S. Grant's drinking bouts. In *New York Herald*, 23 November 1863

How difficult it is to find a place for an officer of . . . high rank when there is no place seeking him.

ABRAHAM LINCOLN (1809–1865). Letter to Vice Pres. Andrew Johnson, 27 July 1864

The great thing about Grant, I take it, is his perfect coolness and persistency of purpose. I judge he is not easily excited—which is a great element in an officer—and he has the *grit* of a bulldog! Once let him get his "teeth" *in*, and nothing can shake him off.

ABRAHAM LINCOLN (1809–1865). Response when asked by the author what impressed him about Gen. Ulysses S. Grant, 1864. In F. B. Carpenter, *Six Months at the White House with Abraham Lincoln*, 68, 1866

I don't do much, except think a lot, scold a little, pat a man on the back now and then, and try to keep a perspective.

DOUGLAS MacARTHUR (1880–1964). In Edgar F. Puryear, Jr., *19 Stars: A Study in Military Character and Leadership*, 3, 1971

The acid test of an officer who aspires to high command is his ability to be able to grasp quickly the essentials of a military problem, to decide rapidly what he will do, to make it quite clear to all concerned what he intends to achieve and how he will do it, and then to see that his subordinate commanders get on with the job. Above all, he has got to rid himself of all irrelevant detail; he must concentrate on the essentials.

BERNARD LAW MONTGOMERY (1887–1976). *The Memoirs of Field-Marshal Montgomery*, 21, 1958

A [commander] of great armies in the field must have an inner conviction which, though founded closely on reason, transcends reason.

BERNARD LAW MONTGOMERY (1887–1976). *The Path to Leadership*, 3, 1961

Nothing is more important in war than unity of command.

NAPOLEON (1769–1821). *Maximes de Guerre*, 63, 1830–1874. In Conrad H. Lanza, annotator, *Napoleon and Modern War*, 1943

Any commander in chief who undertakes to execute a plan which he considers bad is guilty. He should give his reasons, insist that the plan be changed and finally resign rather than become the instrument of the ruin of his army. . . . A military order requires literal obedience only when it is given by a superior who is present in the theater of war at the time he gives it.

NAPOLEON (1769–1821). *Maximes de Guerre*, 72, 1830–1874. In Conrad H. Lanza, annotator, *Napoleon and Modern War*, 1943

See Princes: Confucius (1)

The first quality for a commander in chief is a cool head, which receives a correct impression of things. He should not allow himself to be confused by either good or bad news. The impressions which he receives successively or simultaneously in the course of a day should classify themselves in his mind in such a way as to occupy the place which they merit.

NAPOLEON (1769–1821). *Maximes de Guerre*, 73, 1830–1874. In Conrad H. Lanza, annotator, *Napoleon and Modern War*, 1943

The important actions of a great general are not the results of chance or destiny; they arise always from planning and from genius.

NAPOLEON (1769–1821). *Maximes de Guerre,* 82, 1830–1874. In Conrad H. Lanza, annotator, *Napoleon and Modern War,* 1943

I have not a thought on any subject separated from the immediate object of my command.

HORATIO NELSON (1758–1805)

Generals must never show doubt, discouragement, or fatigue.

GEORGE S. PATTON, JR. (1885–1945). *War As I Knew It,* 3.1.4, 1947

See Presidents: Rexford G. Tugwell

Caesar . . . above all men was gifted with the faculty of making the right use of everything in war, and most especially of seizing the right moment.

PLUTARCH (A.D. 46?–119?). "Caesar," *Parallel Lives,* Dryden edition, 1693

The only inexcusable offense in a commanding officer is to be surprised.

MATTHEW B. RIDGWAY (1895–1993). Motto pinned on the wall behind his desk. In Leonard Mosley, *Marshall: Hero for Our Times,* 28, 1982

Viewed as a whole, it was a great mistake for the British to be continually replacing their Commander in Chief, and thus forcing the new man to learn the same bitter lessons all over again.

ERWIN ROMMEL (1891–1944). Reference to the North African campaign in 1941, 1944, *The Rommel Papers,* 23, ed. B. H. Liddell Hart, 1953

The admirals are really something to cope with—and I should know. To change anything in the Na-a-vy is like punching a feather bed. You punch it with your right and you punch it with your left until you are finally exhausted, and then you find the damn bed just as it was before you started punching it.

FRANKLIN D. ROOSEVELT (1882–1945). Remark to the author. In Marriner S. Eccles, *Beckoning Frontiers,* 6.1, 1951

He should be able to penetrate the minds of other men, while remaining impenetrable himself.

MAURICE de SAXE (1696–1750). *My Reveries on the Art of War,* 1732. In Thomas R. Phillips, ed., *Roots of Strategy,* p. 294, 1940

I have seen very good colonels become very bad generals.

MAURICE de SAXE (1696–1750). *My Reveries on the Art of War,* 1732. In Thomas R. Phillips, ed., *Roots of Strategy,* p. 297, 1940

[Ulysses S. Grant] was the steadfast center about and on which everything else turned.

PHILIP H. SHERIDAN (1831–1888). In J. F. C. Fuller, *Grant and Lee: A Study in Personality and Generalship,* 2, 1957

He whose generals are able and not interfered with by the sovereign will be victorious.

SUN TZU (4th cent. B.C.). "Offensive Strategy" (29), *The Art of War,* tr. Samuel B. Griffith, 1963

Know the enemy, know yourself; in a hundred battles you will never be in peril.

SUN-TZU (4th cent. B.C.). "Offensive Strategy" (31), *The Art of War,* tr. Samuel B. Griffith, 1963

[The general] ponders the dangers inherent in the advantages and the advantages inherent in the dangers.

TS'AO TS'AO (A.D. 155–220). In Sun-tzu (4th cent. B.C.), "The Nine Variables" (12), *The Art of War,* tr. Samuel B. Griffith, 1963

As for being a General, well at the age of four with paper hats and wooden swords we're all Generals. Only some of us never grow out of it.

PETER USTINOV (1921–). *Romanoff and Juliet,* 1, 1956

In this country [England] it is a good thing to kill an admiral from time to time to encourage the others.

VOLTAIRE (1694–1778). *Candide,* 23, 1759, tr. Richard Aldington, 1929

A bold general may be lucky, but no general can be lucky unless he is bold.

ARCHIBALD PERCIVAL WAVELL (1883–1950). *Generals and Generalship* (1), 1941, *The Good Soldier,* 1948

The ultimate test of a general's ability is not success . . . but the capacity to use whatever resources he has to the best advantage.

W. E. WOODWARD (1874–1950). *Meet General Grant,* 22, 1928

✦

A general who is courageous and stupid is a calamity.

SAYING (CHINESE). In Barbara W. Tuchman, "Generalship," 1972, *Practicing History,* 1981

He who would learn to command well must first of all learn to obey.

SAYING (GREEK). In Aristotle (384–322 B.C.), *Politics,* 7.14, tr. Benjamin Jowett, 1885

Great generals must have good sense, good lieutenants, and, above all, good luck.

ANONYMOUS

COMMANDERS & SOLDIERS

See also • Commanders ○ Commanders & Staff ○ Leaders & People ○ Presidents & People ○ Soldiers

To rally a beaten army after a long retreat is a supreme test of leadership.

CORRELLI BARNETT (1927–). "Field-Marshal Sir Claude Auchinleck." In Michael Carver, ed., *The War Lords,* 1976

An army of deer led by a lion is more to be feared than an army of lions led by a deer.

CHABRIAS (410?–357? B.C.). Greek general

The more a General is in the habit of demanding from his troops, the surer he will be that his demands will be answered.

KARL von CLAUSEWITZ (1780–1831). *On War,* 3.5, 1832, tr. J. J. Graham, 1873

Humility must always be the portion of any man who receives acclaim earned in the blood of his followers and the sacrifices of his friends.

DWIGHT D. EISENHOWER (1890–1969). Address, Guildhall, London, 12 June 1945

One of the duties of a general is to determine the best investment of human lives. If he thinks expenditure of 10,000 lives in the current battle will save 20,000 lives later, it is up to him to do it.

DWIGHT D. EISENHOWER (1890–1969). Remark to his wartime aide Harry C. Butcher. In Anthony C. Brown, *Bodyguard of Lies,* 4.7, 1975

[The commander's] personality is valuable but not essential. Soldiers are most inspired by obvious signs of competence and by success: personality falls flat if it does not produce anything but more crosses in the cemeteries.

CYRIL FALLS (1888–1971). Introduction to *The Art of War: From the Age of Napoleon to the Present Day,* 1961

The dissimulation of the general consists of the important art of hiding his thoughts. He should be constantly on the stage and should appear most tranquil when he is most occupied, for the whole army speculates on his looks, on his gestures, and on his mood.

FREDERICK II (1740–1786). *The Instruction of Frederick the Great for His Generals,* 1747. In Thomas R. Phillips, ed., *Roots of Strategy,* p. 346, 1940

A brave colonel makes a brave battalion.

FREDERICK II (1712–1786). Quoted by R. R. Palmer, "Frederick the Great, Guibert, Bülow: From Dynastic to National War." In Edward Mead Earle, ed., *Makers of Modern Strategy,* 1943

An army is the creation of its commander, not the sum of its units.

NIGEL HAMILTON (1944–). *Monty: The Making of a General, 1887–1942,* 4.2, 1981

The first and greatest imperative of command is to be present in person. Those who impose risk must be seen to share it. . . . It is the spectacle of heroism, or its immediate report, that fires the blood.

JOHN KEEGAN (1934–). Conclusion to *The Mask of Command,* 1987

Troops grant their confidence to generals when their interests are his or his orders are followed by victories.

CONRAD H. LANZA (1878–?). Annotator. *Napoleon and Modern War,* 81, 1943

Rewarding the unworthy causes alienation; punishing the innocent causes resentment. Those whose appreciation or anger are unpredictable perish.

ZHUGE LIANG (A.D. 180?–234?). *Records of the Loyal Lord of Warriors.* In *Mastering the Art of War,* tr. Thomas Cleary, 1989

No other general was ever more familiar with his soldiers; [Valerius] cheerfully shared all the fatigues with the lowest of his men.

LIVY (59 B.C.–A.D. 17). In Machiavelli, *The Discourses,* 3.22, 1517, tr. Christian E. Detmold, 1940

In all battles, a moment occurs, when the bravest troops, after having made the greatest efforts, feel inclined to run. That terror proceeds from a want of confidence in their own courage; and it only requires a slight opportunity, a pretense, to restore confidence to them. The art is to give rise to the opportunity, and to invent the pretense. . . . When a man has been present in many actions, he distinguishes that moment without difficulty: it is as easy as casting up an addition.

NAPOLEON (1769–1821). In Ralph Waldo Emerson, "Napoleon; or, The Man of the World," *Representative Men,* 1850

The gesture of a beloved general is worth more than a clever speech.

NAPOLEON (1769–1821). *Napoleon in His Own Words,* 8, comp. Jules Bertaut, 1916

Whenever he wanted some job done promptly by his troops, he first got down to it personally in full view of everyone.

PLUTARCH (A.D. 46?–119?). On Agesilaus (Spartan king, 444?–360 B.C.). In "Sayings of the Spartans: Agesilaus" (32), *Plutarch on Sparta,* tr. Richard J. A. Talbert, 1988

Soldiers in any war will endure hardships with very little complaint if they sense that their commander cares what happens to them.

EDGAR F. PURYEAR, JR. *19 Stars: A Study in Military Character and Leadership,* 5, 1971

I intend to demand of myself the same as I expect from each of my officers and men.

ERWIN ROMMEL (1891–1944). Letter to his wife Lu, 26 May 1942, *The Rommel Papers,* 9, ed. B. H. Liddell Hart, 1953

One must never make a show of false emotions to one's men. The ordinary soldier has a surprisingly good nose for what is true and what false.

ERWIN ROMMEL (1891–1944). June 1942, *The Rommel Papers,* 9, ed. B. H. Liddell Hart, 1953

The personal example of the commander works wonders, especially if he has had the wit to create some sort of legend round himself.

ERWIN ROMMEL (1891–1944). June 1942, *The Rommel Papers,* 10, ed. B. H. Liddell Hart, 1953

The commander must try, above all, to establish personal and comradely contact with his men, but without giving away an inch of his authority.

ERWIN ROMMEL (1891–1944). 1944, *The Rommel Papers,* 23, ed. B. H. Liddell Hart, 1953

He must never court popularity. If he has their appreciation and respect, it is sufficient. Efficiency in a general, his soldiers have a right to expect; geniality they are usually right to suspect.

ARCHIBALD PERCIVAL WAVELL (1883–1950). *Generals and Generalship* (2), 1941, *The Good Soldier,* 1948

❧

Caesar: Will this day be fortunate for us?
Centurion: You will be victorious. As for me, whether I live or die, I shall, by tonight, have deserved praise from Caesar.

ANONYMOUS (ROMAN). Format adapted. In Charles de Gaulle, "Of Prestige" (2), *The Edge of the Sword,* 1934, tr. Gerald Hopkins, 1960

Good commanders look after their troops, and good troops look after their commanders.

ANONYMOUS

COMMANDERS & STAFF

Includes • Commanders & Subordinates

See also • Commanders ○ Commanders & Soldiers ○ Decision-Making ○ Leaders & Staff ○ Presidents & Staff

For stretches of time, [Gen. Ulysses S. Grant's] mind seemed torpid. Rawlins [his chief of staff] and the others would systematically talk their ideas into it, for weeks, not directly, but by discussion among themselves, in his presence. In the end, he would announce the idea as his own, without seeming conscious of the discussion; and would give the orders to carry it out with all the energy that belonged to his nature.

> HENRY ADAMS (1838–1918). *The Education of Henry Adams,* 17, 1907

Nimitz would never speak ill of a subordinate except to his face.

> HENRY H. ADAMS. "Fleet Admiral Chester W. Nimitz." In Michael
> Carver, ed., *The War Lords,* 1976

[Marshall] did not feel it necessary to praise others. A man knew that he had met the Chief of Staff's expectations when he received increased responsibility and the rank that went with it.

> STEPHEN E. AMBROSE (1936–). "George C. Marshall," *American History
> Illustrated,* February 1970

Certain persons outside the chain of command police the command channels to guard against abuses or attempted cover-ups.

> MARTIN BLUMENSON (1918–) and JAMES L. STOKESBURY (1934–).
> *Masters of the Art of Command,* 5 ("Relieved of Command"), 1975

Officers who are constantly looking over their shoulders to see whether the ax is about to fall are diverting attention and energy from the more important matters on the battlefield.

> MARTIN BLUMENSON (1918–) and JAMES L. STOKESBURY (1934–).
> *Masters of the Art of Command,* 5 ("Relieved of Command"), 1975

Throughout the war I deliberately avoided intervening in a subordinate's duties. When an officer performed as I expected him to, I gave him a free hand. When he hesitated, I tried to help him. And when he failed, I relieved him.

> OMAR N. BRADLEY (1893–1981). *A Soldier's Story,* 2, 1951

There is nothing more common than to hear of men losing their energy on being raised to a higher position, to which they do not feel themselves equal.

> KARL von CLAUSEWITZ (1780–1831). *On War,* 1.3, 1832, tr. J. J. Graham,
> 1873

You must not retain for one instant any man in a responsible position where you have become doubtful of his ability to do the job. . . . This matter frequently calls for more courage than any other thing you will have to do, but I expect you to be perfectly cold-blooded about it.

> DWIGHT D. EISENHOWER (1890–1969). To Gen. George S. Patton,
> 6 March 1943. In Stephen E. Ambrose, *Eisenhower: Soldier, General
> of the Army, President-Elect, 1890–1952,* 12, 1983

[Robert E. Lee's] aversion to personal confrontation . . . became his greatest weakness as a military commander.

> JOHN EISENHOWER (1922–). "The Commander," *New York Times Book
> Review,* 6 August 1995

When I find any officer that answers me with firmness, intelligence, and clearness, I set him down in my list for making use of his service on proper occasions.

> FREDERICK II (1740–1786). "Morning the Fourth," *The Confessions of
> Frederick the Great,* ed. Douglas Sladen, 1915

All information funnels through a chief of staff and the commanding officer expects his staff to present him with a recommended course of action, not simply the facts and the alternatives.

> RICHARD TANNER JOHNSON (1927–). On the military staff system,
> *Managing the White House: An Intimate Study of the Presidency,*
> 4, 1974

I don't like to keep any man on a job so long that his ideas and forethoughts go no further than mine.

> GEORGE C. MARSHALL (1880–1959). Remark to the author, 26 January
> 1943. In Harry C. Butcher, *My Three Years with Eisenhower,* 1946

Douglas MacArthur: My staff tells me . . .
Marshall (interrupting him): General, you don't have a staff; you have a court.

> GEORGE C. MARSHALL (1880–1959). Format adapted. During World War
> II. In Dean Acheson, *Present at the Creation: My Years in the State
> Department,* 45, 1969

Remember, gentlemen, an order that can be misunderstood will be misunderstood.

> HELMUTH von MOLTKE (1800–1891). Prussian general

One must never be drawn off the job in hand by gratuitous advice from those who are not fully in the operational picture, and who have no responsibility.

> BERNARD LAW MONTGOMERY (1887–1976). *The Memoirs of Field-
> Marshal Montgomery,* 10, 1958

The Chief of Staff must be anonymous and must never attempt to take unto himself the powers of his leader; on the other hand, he must be prepared to give decisions on all matters of detail. He must, therefore, be completely in the mind of his boss, nothing being hidden from him, and being trusted absolutely.

> BERNARD LAW MONTGOMERY (1887–1976). *The Path to Leadership,*
> 15, 1961

All generals . . . always want to have more troops. Generals see only their own mission, their own army. . . . The head of an army must calculate the needs of all his generals on the basis of their positions and circumstances and not let their requests [for troops and supplies] determine his decisions.

> NAPOLEON (1769–1821). Remark to Pierre Roederer, 1809, *The Mind
> of Napoleon: A Selection from His Written and Spoken Words,* 326,
> ed. J. Christopher Herold, 1955

[My generals] don't like me—but they fear me, and that's good enough for me. . . . I give them commands—but I also keep an eye on them.

> NAPOLEON (1769–1821). Remark, 1811?, *The Mind of Napoleon:
> A Selection from His Written and Spoken Words,* ed. J. Christopher
> Herold, 1955

Those people think they are indispensable; they don't know I have a hundred division commanders who can take their place.

> NAPOLEON (1769–1821). On his marshals, a repeated remark, *The Mind
> of Napoleon: A Selection from His Written and Spoken Words,* 286,
> ed. J. Christopher Herold, 1955

In case signals can neither be seen nor perfectly understood, no captain can do very wrong if he places his ship alongside that of an enemy.

LORD NELSON (1758–1805). Memorandum before the Battle of Trafalgar (off the southwest coast of Spain), 9 October 1805

Final decision . . . is for him alone and not to be taken by a vote of advisers like a club election. Clive said he had only called one council of war and fortunately had not abided by its decision.

GEORGE S. PATTON, JR. (1885–1945). "War As She Is" (4), 1919. In Martin Blumenson, *The Patton Papers, 1885–1940*, 33, 1972. Robert Clive (1725–1774) was a British soldier who played a key role in the colonization of India.

Some officers require urging, others require suggestions, very few have to be restrained.

GEORGE S. PATTON, JR. (1885–1945). *War As I Knew It*, 3.1.4, 1947

[Bernard Law Montgomery] always gave the impression that he had nothing in the world to do except the business at hand. There were never any papers on his desk, there were never any interruptions; one almost had the feeling that here was an idle man, and that but for one's own visit he would have been at a loss to fill up his time. Most remarkable of all, to myself, was that he actually listened to what I said.

GORONWY REES. British general. In Nigel Hamilton, *Monty: The Making of a General, 1887–1942*, 4.14, 1981

Always use the chain of command to issue orders, but if you use the chain of command for information, you're dead.

HYMAN G. RICKOVER (1900–1986). Admiral. In Bill Walsh, "Information, Please!" *Forbes ASAP*, 27 February 1995

Always be tactful and well-mannered and teach your subordinates to be the same. Avoid excessive sharpness or harshness of voice, which usually indicates the man who has shortcomings of his own to hide.

ERWIN ROMMEL (1891–1944). Lecture to a class of cadets, 1938, *The Rommel Papers*, 10 (footnote), ed. B. H. Liddell Hart, 1953

The officers of a panzer division must learn to think and act independently within the framework of the general plan and not wait until they receive orders.

ERWIN ROMMEL (1891–1944). May 1940, *The Rommel Papers*, 1, ed. B. H. Liddell Hart, 1953

A commander must accustom his staff to a high tempo from the outset and continually keep them up to it. If he once allows himself to be satisfied with norms, or anything less than an all-out effort, he gives up the race from the starting point.

ERWIN ROMMEL (1891–1944). 1941, *The Rommel Papers*, 5, ed. B. H. Liddell Hart, 1953

It is always a bad sign in an army when scapegoats are habitually sought out and brought to sacrifice for every conceivable mistake. It usually shows something very wrong in the highest command. It completely inhibits the willingness of junior commanders to take decisions, for they will always try to get chapter and verse for everything they do.

ERWIN ROMMEL (1891–1944). December 1942, *The Rommel Papers*, 18, ed. B. H. Liddell Hart, 1953

A bulky staff implies a division of responsibility, slowness of action, and indecision; whereas a small staff implies activity and concentration of purpose.

WILLIAM TECUMSEH SHERMAN (1820–1891). *Memoirs of Gen. W. T. Sherman*, 4th ed., 25, 1891

No man can properly command an army from the rear, he must be "at its front"; and when a detachment is made, the commander thereof should be informed of the object to be accomplished, and left as free as possible to execute it in his own way.

WILLIAM TECUMSEH SHERMAN (1820–1891). *Memoirs of Gen. W. T. Sherman*, 4th ed., 25, 1891

When I am really honest with myself, I have to admit I love that guy because he makes *me* feel powerful.

WALTER BEDELL SMITH (1895–1961). On Gen. Dwight D. Eisenhower whom he served as chief of staff during World Ward II. In Eric Sevareid, "The Final Troubled Hours of Adlai E. Stevenson," *Look*, 30 November 1965

That devil of a man exercises a fascination on me that I cannot explain even to myself, and in such a degree that, though I fear neither God nor devil, when I am in his presence I am ready to tremble like a child, and he could make me go through the eye of a needle to throw myself into the fire.

DOMINIQUE-JOSEPH VANDAMME (18th–19th cent.). French general. On Napoleon, remark to Marshal d'Arnano, 1815. In Gustave Le Bon, *The Crowd*, 2.3.3, 1895, Viking Press edition, 1960

When I reflect upon the characters and attainments of some of the general officers of this army . . . I tremble; and, as Lord Chesterfield said of the generals of his day, "I only hope that when the enemy reads the list of their names he trembles as I do."

DUKE OF WELLINGTON (1769–1852). Letter to Lt. Col. Henry Torrens, 29 August 1810 (Popular version: I don't know what effect these men will have on the enemy, but, by God, they frighten me.)

COMMERCE

See • Business (Commerce) ∘ Merchants & Customers ∘ Trade (Commerce)

COMMITTEES

See also • Bureaucracy ∘ Creativity: A. Whitney Griswold ∘ Decision-Making ∘ Meetings ∘ Organizations

Committee—a group of men who individually can do nothing but as a group decide that nothing can be done.

FRED ALLEN (1894–1956)

Nothing is impossible until it is sent to a committee.

JAMES H. BOREN. "Boren's Rule," in Laurence J. Peter, *Peter's People*, 8, 1979

[Committee:] a cul-de-sac down which ideas are lured, and then quietly strangled.

SIR BARNETT COCKS. House of Commons clerk. In Tam Dalyell, "Following the Queen," *New Scientist*, 8 November 1973

If a committee is allowed to discuss a bad idea long enough, it will inevitably vote to implement the idea simply because so much work has already been done on it.

KEN CRUICKSHANK. In *Florida Times-Union*, Jacksonville, 25 June 1978

What is a committee? A group of the unwilling, picked from the unfit, to do the unnecessary.

RICHARD HARKNESS (1907–). In New York *Herald Tribune,* 15 June 1960

The more amiability and esprit de corps among the members of a policy-making in-group, the greater is the danger that independent critical thinking will be replaced by groupthink, which is likely to result in irrational and dehumanizing actions directed against out-groups.

IRVING L. JANIS (1918–1990). Offered "in the spirit of Parkinson's Laws," introduction to *Victims of Groupthink: A Psychological Study of Foreign-Policy Decisions and Fiascoes,* 1972

See Conformity: William H. Whyte, Jr.

Members of a cohesive in-group suppress deviational points of view by putting social pressure on any member who begins to express a view that deviates from the dominant beliefs of the group.

IRVING L. JANIS (1918–1990). *Victims of Groupthink: A Psychological Study of Foreign-Policy Decisions and Fiascoes,* 2, 1972

The dissenter was made to feel at home, providing he lived up to two restrictions: first, that he did not voice his doubts to outsiders and thus play into the hands of the opposition; and second, that he kept his criticisms within the bounds of acceptable deviation, not challenging any of the fundamental assumptions of the group's prior commitments.

IRVING L. JANIS (1918–1990). On the "domesticated dissenter" whose apparent frankness enables other members of the group to see themselves as objective and democratic, *Victims of Groupthink: A Psychological Study of Foreign-Policy Decisions and Fiascoes,* 5, 1972

Committees are consumers and sometimes sterilizers of ideas, rarely creators of them.

HENRY A. KISSINGER (1923–). *The Necessity for Choice: Prospects of American Foreign Policy,* 8.1, 1961

The committee system, which is an attempt to reduce the inner insecurity of our top personnel, has the paradoxical consequence of institutionalizing it.

HENRY A. KISSINGER (1923–). *The Necessity for Choice: Prospects of American Foreign Policy,* 8.1, 1961

A committee is an animal with four back legs.

JOHN LE CARRÉ (1931–). *Tinker, Tailor, Soldier, Spy,* 34, 1974

A committee is a group that keeps minutes and wastes hours.

McFADDEN'S TRUISM

The world is proof that God is a committee.

BOB STOKES

Committee: A structured decision-making body in which the level of collective judgment is lower than that of any individual member.

JERRY TUCKER (1941–). *The Experience of Politics: You and American Government,* 7.3, 1974

A camel is a horse designed by a committee.

ANONYMOUS. In *Financial Times* (London), 31 January 1976

A committee of one gets things done.

ANONYMOUS

COMMON SENSE

See also • Advice ○ Intelligence ○ Judgment ○ Reason ○ Wisdom: [especially] Joseph Joubert

Common sense is most ginnerally dispised bi those who haint got it.

JOSH BILLINGS (1818–1885). *On Ice: and Other Things,* 24, 1868

Common sense . . . is very uncommon.

LORD CHESTERFIELD (1694–1773). Letter to his son, 27 September 1748

Common sense in an uncommon degree is what the world calls wisdom.

SAMUEL TAYLOR COLERIDGE (1772–1834)

Nothing astonishes men so much as common sense and plain dealing.

RALPH WALDO EMERSON (1803–1882). "Art," *Essays: First Series,* 1841

Good Sense is a Thing all need, few have,
    and none think they [lack].

BENJAMIN FRANKLIN (1706–1790). *Poor Richard's Almanack,* June 1746

Common sense appears to be only another name for the thoughtlessness of the unthinking. It is made of the prejudices of childhood, the idiosyncrasies of individual character and the opinion of the newspapers.

W. SOMERSET MAUGHAM (1874–1965). 1901, *A Writer's Notebook,* 1949

Every time I hear a man pound a table with his fist and loudly endorse common sense, I permit myself a large and long-range spit.

H. L. MENCKEN (1880–1956). "Clinical Notes," *American Mercury,* November 1924

Judging by common sense is merely another phrase for judging by first appearances; and everyone who has mixed among mankind with any capacity for observing them, knows that the men who place implicit faith in their own common sense, are, without any exception, the most wrong-headed and impracticable persons with whom he has ever had to deal.

JOHN STUART MILL (1806–1973). "The Spirit of the Age" (2), *The Examiner* (English journal), 6 May–29 May 1831

Uncommon sense, that sense which is common only to the wisest.

HENRY DAVID THOREAU (1817–1862). "Friday," *A Week on the Concord and Merrimack Rivers,* 1849

Common sense[:] . . . a quick perception of common truths.

MARY WOLLSTONECRAFT (1759–1797). *A Vindication of the Rights of Woman,* 8, 1792

A handful of common sense is worth a bushel of learning.

SAYING

COMMUNICATIONS

See also • Ideas ○ Inventions ○ Media ○ News ○ Science ○ Technology ○ Telephone

[The] mass communications industry [is] concerned in the main neither with the true nor the false, but with the unreal, the more or less totally irrelevant.

> ALDOUS HUXLEY (1894–1963). "Propaganda in a Democratic Society," *Brave New World Revisited,* 1958

"The new electronic interdependence recreates the world in the image of a global village."

> MARSHALL McLUHAN (1911–1980). "Chapter gloss" heading, *The Gutenberg Galaxy: The Making of Typographic Man,* 1962

With the further development in the twentieth century of the telephone and the radio—and ultimately television—all the inhabitants of the planet could theoretically be linked together for instantaneous communication as closely as the inhabitants of a village. Indeed, it is conceivable—though not at all probable—that the Sermon on the Mount could now be preached to the greater part of mankind at the moment it was uttered, provided such a notorious agitator as Jesus of Nazareth could be admitted to studios controlled mainly in the interests of commercial advertisers or totalitarian governments, and allowed to speak without submitting a prepared script.

> LEWIS MUMFORD (1895–1990). *The Conduct of Life,* 8.5, 1951
> See Television: Edward R. Murrow (3)

The speed of communications is wondrous to behold. It is also true that speed can multiply the distribution of information that we know to be untrue.

> EDWARD R. MURROW (1908–1965). Last public speech (after receiving the Family of Man Award from the Protestant Council of New York), October 1964. In Alexander Kendrick, *Prime Time: The Life of Edward R. Murrow,* 1, 1969

The more we elaborate our means of communication, the less we communicate.

> J. B. PRIESTLY (1894–1984). "Televiewing," *Thoughts in the Wilderness,* 1957

We are eager to tunnel under the Atlantic and bring the old world some weeks nearer to the new; but perchance the first news that will leak through into the broad, flapping American ear will be that the Princess Adelaide has the whooping cough.

> HENRY DAVID THOREAU (1817–1862). On the prospect of a transatlantic cable, "Economy," *Walden; or Life in the Woods,* 1854

Roads, sea routes, and their orderly maintenance serve others beside the Government, e.g., St. Paul's use of Roman roads [to spread Christianity]. Will the higher religions of the present day make similar use of the worldwide communications provided by modern technology?

> ARNOLD J. TOYNBEE (1889–1975). *A Study of History,* 1954, abr. D. C. Somervell, 2.415, 1965

COMMUNISM

See also • Capitalism ○ Class ○ Economics ○ Fascism ○ Freedom ○ Misjudgments: Nikita Khrushchev (1,2), Lenin (2), Lincoln Steffens ○ Socialism ○ Tyranny

The world would not be in such a snarl
If Marx had been Groucho instead of Karl.

> IRVING BERLIN (1888–1989). Birthday message to Groucho Marx on his birthday in 1966, in Groucho Marx, *The Groucho Phile,* 8, 1976

Communism is a religion, and none the less potent for being a secular one.

> J. F. C. FULLER (1878–1966). *The Conduct of War: 1789–1961,* 11.4, 1961

I am yet ignorant of what exactly Bolshevism is. . . . But I do know that in so far as it is based on violence and denial of God, it repels me. I do not believe in short—violent—cuts to success. . . . I am an uncompromising opponent of violent methods even to serve the noblest of causes.

> MOHANDAS K. GANDHI (1869–1948). In *Young India,* 11 December 1924

Communism was overthrown by life, by thought, by dignity.

> VÁCLAV HAVEL (1936–). "Politics, Morality, and Civility," *Summer Meditations,* 1991, tr. Paul Wilson, 1992

As an organized political group, the Communists have done nothing to damage our society a fraction as much as what their enemies have done in the name of defending us against subversion.

> MURRAY KEMPTON (1917–1997). "What Harvey Did," *America Comes of Middle Age,* 1963

Communism has never come to power in a country that was not disrupted by war or corruption, or both.

> JOHN F. KENNEDY (1917–1963). Speech before the North Atlantic Treaty Organization (NATO), Naples, 3 July 1963

Far from being a classless society, Communism is governed by an elite as steadfast in its determination to maintain its prerogatives as any oligarchy known to history.

> ROBERT F. KENNEDY (1925–1968). *The Pursuit of Justice,* 11, ed. Theodore J. Lowi, 1964

How can I accept the [Communist] doctrine, which sets up as its bible above and beyond criticism, an obsolete textbook which I know not only to be scientifically erroneous but without interest or application to the modern world? How can I adopt a creed which, preferring the mud to the fish, exalts the boorish proletariat above the bourgeoisie and the intelligentsia, who with all their faults, are the quality of life and surely carry the seeds of all human achievement?

> JOHN MAYNARD KEYNES (1883–1946). British economist. In Robert L. Heilbroner, *The Worldly Philosophers: The Lives, Times, and Ideas of the Great Economic Thinkers,* 5th ed., 9, 1980 (1953)

It doesn't matter a jot if three-fourths of mankind perish! The only thing that matters is that, in the end, the remaining fourth should become communist.

> LENIN (1870–1924). In René Fülöp-Miller, *Leaders, Dreamers, and Rebels,* 6.5, 1935

What [Marxism] has delivered on its promissory note to a world enslaved is chiefly an exchange of masters, a Roman peace wherein one set of gods is traded for another.

ROBERT LINDNER (1914–1956). *Prescription for Rebellion,* 1, 1952

[Communism is] the opiate of the intellectuals . . . but no cure, except as a guillotine might be called a cure for a case of dandruff.

CLAIRE BOOTHE LUCE (1903–1987). In "Madam Ambassador Claire Boothe Luce: Her Versatility," *Newsweek,* 24 January 1955
See Religion, Anti-: Karl Marx

Communism is not love. Communism is a hammer which we use to crush the enemy.

MAO TSE-TUNG (1893–1976). "United Nations: Petition to Peking," *Time,* 18 December 1950

If Karl, instead of writing a lot about Capital, made a lot of Capital, it would have been much better.

HENRIETTA MARX (19th cent.). On her son. In Alan Valentine, ed., "'What He Builds Today He Destroys Again Tomorrow,'" *Fathers to Sons,* 1963

All I know is that I am not a Marxist.

KARL MARX (1818–1883). In Friedrich Engels, letter to Conrad Schmidt, 3 August 1890

I hope the bourgeoisie, as long as they live, will have cause to remember my carbuncles.

KARL MARX (1818–1883). Referring to the painful boils he suffered from while writing *Das Capital* at the British Museum in London. In Robert L. Heilbroner, *The Worldly Philosophers: The Lives, Times, and Ideas of the Great Economic Thinkers,* 5th ed., 6, 1980 (1953)

The theory of the Communists may be summed up in the single sentence: Abolition of private property.

KARL MARX (1818–1883) and FRIEDRICH ENGELS (1820–1895). *The Communist Manifesto,* 2, 1847, ed. Engels, 1888

The Communists disdain to conceal their views and aims. They openly declare that their ends can be attained only by the forcible overthrow of all existing social conditions. Let the ruling classes tremble at a Communist revolution. The proletarians have nothing to lose but their chains. They have a world to win.
WORKINGMEN OF ALL COUNTRIES, UNITE!

KARL MARX (1818–1883) and FRIEDRICH ENGELS (1820–1895). Closing paragraphs, *The Communist Manifesto,* 4, 1847, ed. Engels, 1888 (Popular version: Workers of the world, unite! You have nothing to lose but your chains.)

Revolutionary Marxism is committed to even further perpetuation and perfection of the very industrial process which is destroying us all. It offers only to "redistribute" the results—the money, maybe—of this industrialization to a wider section of the population. It offers to take wealth from the capitalists and pass it around; but in order to do so, Marxism must maintain the industrial system.

RUSSELL MEANS (1939–). "Fighting Words on the Future of the Earth," *Mother Jones,* December 1980

Communism is like Prohibition, it's a good idea but it won't work.

WILL ROGERS (1879–1935). 6 November 1927, *The Autobiography of Will Rogers,* ed. Donald Day, 1949

We must conclude that it is not only a particular political ideology that has failed, but the idea that men and women could ever define themselves in terms that exclude their spiritual needs.

SALMAN RUSHDIE (1947–). On the fall of communism in Eastern Europe. In *Independent* (British newspaper), 7 February 1990

Many quite sensible people believe that the Marxian class war will be a war to end war. If it ever comes, they too will be disillusioned—if any of them survive.

BERTRAND RUSSELL (1872–1970). *Sceptical Essays,* 11, 1928

Communism is fascism with a human face.

SUSAN SONTAG (1933–). In Richard Lacayo, "Stand Aside, Sisyphus," *Time,* 24 October 1988

A red is any son-of-a-bitch who wants thirty cents when we're payin' twenty-five.

JOHN STEINBECK (1902–1968). *The Grapes of Wrath,* 22, 1939

In the long run, I believe that communism will fail to captivate mankind because . . . communism has very little spiritual help or guidance to offer to men and women in the personal trials and troubles of their individual lives.

ARNOLD J. TOYNBEE (1889–1975). "Ten Basic Questions—and Answers," *New York Times Magazine,* 20 February 1955

Whatever may be the circumstances of my death, I shall die with unshaken faith in the Communist future. The faith in man and in his future gives me even now such power of resistance as cannot be given by any religion.

LEON TROTSKY (1879–1940). Last testament (written five months before his assassination in Mexico), 3 March 1940

Communism terribly overestimated how much humanity could be changed from the top down through enforced social engineering, while it fatally underestimated the corruptibility of the self-appointed elites who would carry out the utopian task. Communism was fatally undermined by not taking seriously the reality that evil resides not only in structures, but also in the human heart.

JIM WALLIS (1948–). *The Soul of Politics: A Practical and Prophetic Vision for Change,* 2, 1994

❦

Workers of the world, forgive me.

ANONYMOUS (HUNGARIAN). Graffito on a bust of Karl Marx in Bucharest. In *Times* (London), 4 May 1990

COMMUNITY

See also • Brotherhood ∘ Freedom: D. H. Lawrence ∘ Heaven: Elbert Hubbard ∘ Leaders & People: Robert C. Tucker (2) ∘ Meditation: Gary Snyder ∘ Self-Realization (Becoming): Herbert J. Muller ∘ Unity

Everyone is aware of the vast difference between a number of men as a chance collection of individuals and the same number as an organized group or community. A community has purpose and plan, and there is in us an almost instinctive recognition of the connection between unity and strength.

J. GLENN GRAY (1913–1977). *The Warriors: Reflections on Men in Battle,* 2, 1959

The vision of a world community based on justice, not power, is the necessity of our age.

HENRY A. KISSINGER (1923–). *Years of Upheaval,* 10, 1982

To create organs for neighborly help and initiative, to meet face to face for personal assessment and vivid discussion, to take part in communal celebrations, not in vast anonymous masses, but in a circle of identifiable faces and persons, all these survivals of aboriginal village life are still necessary. They keep intact the close chain of sympathetic responses in which man first securely established himself as irrevocably human: these friendly eyes are the indispensable mirror in which the self beholds its own image.

LEWIS MUMFORD (1895–1990). *The Transformations of Man*, 8.4, 1956

Above all we need, particularly as children, the reassuring presence of a visible community, an intimate group that enfolds us with understanding and love, and that becomes an object of our spontaneous loyalty, as a criterion and point of reference for the rest of the human race.

LEWIS MUMFORD (1895–1990). *The Transformations of Man*, 8.4, 1956

Social cohesion demands a creed, or a code of behavior, or a prevailing sentiment, or, best, some combination of all three; without something of the kind, a community disintegrates, and becomes subject to a tyrant or a foreign conqueror.

BERTRAND RUSSELL (1872–1970). *Power: A New Social Analysis*, 10, 1938

COMPASSION

See also • Charity ○ Faith: Abraham Joshua Heschel (2) ○ Giving ○ Grief ○ Indifference ○ Kindness ○ Mercy ○ Nations: Martin Luther King, Jr. ○ Pain ○ Pity ○ Sentimentality ○ Service ○ Silence & Protest ○ Sympathy ○ Tears ○ Unhappiness

Compassion . . . abolishes the distance, the in-between which always exists in human intercourse; and if virtue will always be ready to assert that it is better to suffer wrong than to do wrong, compassion will transcend this by stating in complete and even naive sincerity that it is easier to suffer than to see others suffer.

HANNAH ARENDT (1906–1975). *On Revolution*, 2.3, 1963

To feel compassion is to feel that we are in some sort and to some extent responsible for the pain that is being inflicted, that we ought to do something about it.

ALDOUS HUXLEY (1894–1963). "Abstraction," *Texts and Pretexts: An Anthology of Poetry with Commentaries*, 1933

We are called to play the good Samaritan on life's roadside; but that will be only an initial act. One day the whole Jericho road must be transformed so that men and women will not be beaten and robbed as they make their journey through life. True compassion is more than flinging a coin to a beggar; it understands that an edifice that produces beggars needs restructuring.

MARTIN LUTHER KING, JR. (1929–1968). *Where Do We Go from Here: Chaos or Community?* 6.3, 1967

Compassion arms the people God would save!

LAO-TZU (6th cent. B.C.). *The Way of Life*, 67, tr. R. B. Blakney, 1955

What value has compassion that does not take its object in its arms?

ANTOINE de SAINT-EXUPÉRY (1900–1944). *The Wisdom of the Sands*, 26, 1948, tr. Stuart Gilbert, 1950

When a man has compassion for others, God has compassion for him.

TALMUD (A.D. 1st–6th cent.). Rabbinical writings

Compassion is the desire that moves the individual self to widen the scope of its self-concern to embrace the whole of the universal self.

ARNOLD J. TOYNBEE (1889–1975). *The Toynbee-Ikeda Dialogue: Man Himself Must Choose*, 12, 1976

It is the experience of touching the pain of others that is the key to change. . . .
    Compassion is a sign of transformation.

JIM WALLIS (1948–). *The Soul of Politics: A Practical and Prophetic Vision for Change*, 8, 1994

Worse than idle is compassion
If it end in tears and sighs.

WILLIAM WORDSWORTH (1770–1850). "The Armenian Lady's Love," 4, 1835

❧

The measure of love is compassion; the measure of compassion is kindness.

ANONYMOUS

COMPENSATION

See also • Decision-Making: Theodore C. Sorensen (3) ○ Nature: Ralph Waldo Emerson (8) ○ Opposites ○ Paradoxes

O death, where is thy jolly old sting? As Bertie Wooster said when his Aunt Agatha died leaving him a cool fifty thousand.

GERALD BRENAN (1894–1987). "Death," *Thoughts in a Dry Season: A Miscellany*, 1978

The rebound is proportioned to the blow.

JAMES FENIMORE COOPER (1789–1851). "On Publick Opinion," *The American Democrat*, 1838

All things are double one against another, said Solomon. The whole of what we know is a system of compensations. Every defect in one manner is made up in another. Every suffering is rewarded; every sacrifice is made up; every debt is paid.

RALPH WALDO EMERSON (1803–1882). Journal, 8 January 1826

If I gain any good, I must pay for it. If I lose any good, I gain some other.

RALPH WALDO EMERSON (1803–1882). "Compensation," *Essays: First Series*, 1841
See Nature: Emerson (8)

The belief of the Buddhist [is] that no seed will die. Work on, you cannot escape your wages.

RALPH WALDO EMERSON (1803–1882). Journal, 1845, undated

Nothing is given or had for nothing.

EPICTETUS (A.D. 55?–135?). *Discourses*, 4.10, tr. George Long, 1890?
See Price: Milton Friedman

Everything has its drawbacks, as the man said when his mother-in-law died, and they came down upon him for the funeral expenses.

JEROME K. JEROME (1859–1927). *Three Men in a Boat*, 3, 1889

Every Flow hath its Ebb.

JAMES KELLY (18th cent.). Comp., *A Complete Collection of Scottish Proverbs Explained and Made Intelligible to the English Reader*, E.44, 1721

When we see a blow struck, we go on and think no more about it: yet every blow aimed at the most distant of our fellow creatures is sure to come back, some time or other, to our families and descendants.

WALTER SAVAGE LANDOR (1775–1864). "Bishop Shipley and Benjamin Franklin," *Imaginary Conversations*, 1824–1853

What the ocean invades in one place it loses in another.

NAPOLEON (1769–1821). Remark to Emmanuel Las Cases, 11 November 1816, *The Mind of Napoleon: A Selection from His Written and Spoken Words*, 101, ed. J. Christopher Herold, 1955

To every action there is always opposed an equal reaction.

SIR ISAAC NEWTON (1642–1727). "The third law of motion," *Principia Mathematica*, 1687, tr. Andrew Motte, 1729

The excessive increase of anything often causes a reaction in the opposite direction.

PLATO (427?–347 B.C.). *The Republic*, 8.563-564, tr. Benjamin Jowett, 1894

No rose without a thorn.

JOHN RAY (1628–1705). Comp., *A Collection of English Proverbs*, p. 197, 1678

What goes around, comes around.

SAYING (AMERICAN)

No wheat without its chaff.

SAYING (ENGLISH)

The bigger the front, the bigger the back.

SAYING (ZEN)

Every ebb has its flow.

SAYING

Every light has its shadow.

SAYING

The greater the stretch, the greater the snapback.

SAYING

What's lost on the swing is gained on the roundabout.

SAYING

COMPETITION

See also • Business (Commerce) ○ Cooperation ○ Defeat ○ Equality ○ Evolution ○ Exploitation ○ Failure ○ Greed ○ Inequality ○ International Relations ○ Machiavellianism ○ Men: Immanuel Kant ○ Merchants & Customers ○ Motives ○ Organizations: Bertrand Russell (2) ○ Politics ○ Power ○ Prudence: Rules ○ Self-Interest ○ Sports ○ Struggle ○ Success ○ Trade (Commerce) ○ Tyranny ○ Victory ○ War

It is impossible not to notice how little the proponents of the ideal of competition have to say about honesty, which is the fundamental economic virtue, and how *very* little they have to say about community, compassion, and mutual help.

But what the ideal of competition most flagrantly and disastrously excludes is affection.

WENDELL BERRY (1934–). "Economy and Pleasure," 1988, *What Are People For?: Essays*, 1990

Sometimes it seems like that is the choice—either kick ass or kiss ass.

JAMES CAAN (1939–). Murray Fisher interview, *Playboy*, February 1976

No man lives without jostling and being jostled; in all ways he has to *elbow* himself through the world, giving and receiving offense. His very life is a battle.

THOMAS CARLYLE (1795–1881). "Memoirs of the Life of Scott," 1838, *Critical and Miscellaneous Essays*, Carey & Hart edition, 1849

While the law [of competition] may be sometimes hard for the individual, it is best for the race because it insures the survival of the fittest in every department. We accept and welcome, therefore, as conditions to which we must accommodate ourselves, great inequality of environment, the concentration of business, industrial and commercial, in the hands of a few, and the law of competition between these, as being not only beneficial, but essential for the future progress of the race.

ANDREW CARNEGIE (1835–1919). "Wealth," *North American Review*, June 1889

Planning in business and government is short-range; the long-term threats are someone else's concern. This is to be expected in a competitive society where those who do not devote themselves to short-term advantage are unlikely to be in the competition in the long run.

NOAM CHOMSKY (1928–). *Turning the Tide: U.S. Intervention in Central America and the Struggle for Peace*, 4.5, 1985

I don't have ulcers; I give them.

HARRY COHEN (1891–1958). Film executive

We must scrunch or be scrunched.

CHARLES DICKENS (1812–1870). *Our Mutual Friend*, 3.5, 1865

Here is great competition of rich and poor. We live in a market, where is only so much wheat, or wool, or land; and if I have so much more, every other must have so much less. I seem to have no good without breach of good manners. Nobody is glad in the gladness of another, and our system is one of war, of an injurious superiority. Every child of the Saxon race is educated to wish to be first. It is our system; and a man comes to measure his greatness by the regrets, envies, and hatreds of his competitors.

RALPH WALDO EMERSON (1803–1882). "Uses of Great Men," *Representative Men*, 1850

You must conquer and rule or lose and serve, triumph or suffer, be the hammer or the anvil.

GOETHE (1749–1832). *Der Gross-Cophta*, 2, 1791

Whatever begins to be tranquil is gobbled up by something that is not tranquil.

WILLIAM RANDOLPH HEARST (1863–1951). In Eric Hoffer, *The Ordeal of Change*, 9, 1964

Competition, the wringing of success from somebody's failure.

JULES HENRY. *Culture Against Man*, 8, 1963

This is what the art of archery means: a profound and far-reaching contest of the archer with himself.

EUGEN HERRIGEL (1885–1955*). The Art of Archery*, p. 92, 1953, tr. R. F. C. Hull, 1964

Competition [for] Riches, Honor, Command, or other power inclineth to Contention, Enmity, and War: Because the way of one Competitor to the attaining of his desire is to kill, subdue, supplant, or repel the other.

THOMAS HOBBES (1588–1679). *Leviathan*, 11 1651

During the time men live without a common Power to keep them all in awe, they are in that condition which is called War; and such a war, as is of every man, against every man.

THOMAS HOBBES (1588–1679). *Leviathan*, 13, 1651

The only competition worthy of a wise man is with himself.

ANNA JAMESON (1797–1860). "Washington Allston," *Memoirs and Essays Illustrative of Art, Literature, and Social Morals*, 1846

Now this is the Law of the Jungle—as old and as true as the sky;
And the Wolf that shall keep it may prosper, but the Wolf that shall break it must die.

RUDYARD KIPLING (1865–1936). Opening verse, "The Law of the Jungle," *The Second Jungle Book*, 1895

Because he is no competitor,
No one in all the world
Can compete with him.

LAO-TZU (6th cent. B.C.). *The Way of Life*, 22, tr. R. B. Blakney, 1955

The wages of work is cash.
The wages of cash is want more cash.
The wages of want more cash is vicious competition.
The wages of vicious competition is—the world we live in.

D. H. LAWRENCE (1885–1930). "Wages," *The Collected Poems of D. H. Lawrence*, 1929

If competition has its evils, it prevents greater evils. . . . It is the common error of Socialists to overlook the natural indolence of mankind; their tendency to be passive, to be the slaves of habit, to persist indefinitely in a course once chosen. Let them once attain any state of existence which they consider tolerable, and the danger to be apprehended is that they will thenceforth stagnate. . . . Competition may not be the best conceivable stimulus, but it is at present a necessary one, and no one can foresee the time when it will not be indispensable to progress.

JOHN STUART MILL (1806–1973). *Principles of Political Economy with Some of Their Applications to Social Philosophy*, 4.7.7, 1848

Race with one another for forgiveness from your Lord.

MUHAMMAD (A.D. 570?–632). *Quran*, 57.21, A.D. 670?, tr. Mohammed Marmaduke Pickthall, 1953

Don't look back. Something might be gaining on you.

LEROY "SATCHEL" PAIGE (1906–1982). In Richard Donovan, "'Time Ain't Gonna Mess with Me,'" *Collier's*, 13 June 1953

Like many businessmen of genius he learned that free competition was wasteful, monopoly efficient.

MARIO PUZO (1920–). *The Godfather*, 14, 1969

If you're not part of the steamroller, you're part of the road.

GREGORY RAWLINS. Computer science professor. In Sarah Lyall, "Are These Books, or What? CD-ROM and the Literary Industry," *New York Times Book Review*, 14 August 1994

I don't meet competition. I crush it.

CHARLES REVSON (1906–1975). Revlon, Inc. founder and chairman. In "The Pink Jungle," *Time*, 16 June 1958

He must walk warily and fearlessly, and while he should never brawl if he can avoid it, he must be ready to hit hard if the need arises. Let him remember . . . that the unforgivable crime is soft hitting. Do not hit at all if it can be avoided; but *never* hit softly.

THEODORE ROOSEVELT (1858–1919). *Autobiography*, 3, 1913
See Politics: Alf Landon ∘ Power: Roosevelt (1)

The breakfast of champions is not cereal, it's the opposition.

NICK SEITZ

3rd Fisherman: Master, I marvel how the fishes live in the sea.
1st Fisherman: Why, as men do a-land; the great ones eat up the little ones.

SHAKESPEARE (1564–1616). *Pericles*, 2.1.29, 1609

The presence of people who refuse to enter in the great handicap race for sixpenny pieces, is at once an insult and a disenchantment for those who do.

ROBERT LOUIS STEVENSON (1850–1895). "An Apology for Idlers," *Virginibus Puerisque*, 1881

We cannot go outside of this alternative: liberty, inequality, survival of the fittest; not-liberty, equality, survival of the unfittest. The former carries society forward and favors all its best members; the latter carries society downwards and favors all its worst members.

WILLIAM GRAHAM SUMNER (1840–1910). Title essay, *The Challenge of Facts and Other Essays*, ed. Albert Galloway Keller, 1914

The trouble with the rat race is that even if you win, you're still a rat.

LILY TOMLIN (1939–). "Thoughts on the Business of Life," *Forbes*, 4 March 1991

Competition: A contest conducted according to rules made by the defending champion.

JERRY TUCKER (1941–). *The Experience of Politics: You and American Government*, 8.3, 1974

Ferocity and cunning . . . are useful to the individual only because there is so large a proportion of the same traits actively present in the human environment to which he is exposed. Any individual who enters the competitive struggle without the due endowment of these traits is at a disadvantage, somewhat as a hornless steer would find himself at a disadvantage in a drove of horned cattle.

THORSTEIN VEBLEN (1857–1929). *The Theory of the Leisure Class: An Economic Study of Institutions*, 10, 1899

In this world we run the risk of having to choose between being either the anvil or the hammer.

> VOLTAIRE (1694–1778). "Tyranny," *Philosophical Dictionary,* 1764, tr. Wade Baskin, 1961

❧

What's mine is mine, and what's yours is up for grabs.

> SAYING (AMERICAN)

There is nothing noble in being superior to someone else. The true nobility is in being superior to your previous self.

> SAYING (HINDU)

Eat or be eaten.

> SAYING

COMPLAINT

See also • Blame ○ Regret ○ Unhappiness

The more deep and sober sort of politic persons, in their greatness, are ever bemoaning themselves what a life they lead. . . . Not that they feel it so, but only to abate the edge of envy.

> FRANCIS BACON (1561–1626). "Of Envy," *Essays,* 1625

We have first raised a dust and then complain we cannot see.

> GEORGE BERKELEY (1685–1753). Introduction (3) to *A Treatise Concerning the Principles of Human Knowledge,* 1710

I never complained that my birthday was overlooked; people were even surprised, with a touch of admiration, by my discretion on this subject. But the reason for my disinterestedness was even more discrete: I longed to be forgotten in order to be able to complain to myself.

> ALBERT CAMUS (1913–1960). *The Fall,* p. 85, tr. Justin O'Brien, 1956

Never complain and never explain.

> BENJAMIN DISRAELI (1804–1881). In John Morley, *The Life of William Ewart Gladstone,* 1.2.2.1, 1903
>
> See Prime Ministers: Disraeli

Don't complain. The people who will listen can't do anything about it, while the people who can do something about it won't listen.

> JOHN M. HEBERT. "Hebert's First and Only Law of Complaints." In Paul Dixon, "Getting a Handle on Life's Slippery Truths," *San Francisco Chronicle,* 24 December 1992

A grievance is most poignant when almost redressed.

> ERIC HOFFER (1902–1983). *The True Believer: Thoughts on the Nature of Mass Movements,* 22, 1951

To have a grievance is to have a purpose in life.

> ERIC HOFFER (1902–1983). *The Passionate State of Mind: And Other Aphorisms,* 166, 1954

Today also my complaint is bitter,
  his hand is heavy in spite of my groaning.
Oh, that I knew where I might find him,
  that I might come even to his seat!
I would lay my case before him
  and fill my mouth with arguments.

> JOB, *Job* 23:1–4

Depend on it that if a man *talks* of his misfortunes, there is something in them that is not disagreeable to him; for where there is nothing but pure misery, there never is any recourse to the mention of it.

> SAMUEL JOHNSON (1709–1784). Quoted by Bennet Langton, 1780. In James Boswell, *The Life of Samuel Johnson,* 1791

Before complaining to myself I consider not so much what is taken away from me as what I still keep safe, both within and without.

> MONTAIGNE (1533–1592). "Of Physiognomy," *Essays,* 1588, tr. Donald M. Frame, 1958

One ceases to be a child when one realizes that telling one's trouble does not make it any better.

> CEASARE PAVESE (1908–1950). In W. H. Auden, "Hic et Ille," *The Dyer's Hand and Other Essays,* 1962

I had no shoes and complained until I beheld a man who had no feet.

> SA'DI (A.D. 1213?–1292). *The Maxims of Sa'di,* 8, tr. Mehdi Nakosteen, 1977

You gave me wings to fly;
Then took away the sky.

> LEONARA SPEYER. *Fiddler's Farewell,* pt. 5 (introduction), 1926

Complaint is the largest tribute Heaven receives, and the sincerest part of our devotion.

> JONATHAN SWIFT (1667–1745). "Thoughts on Various Subjects" (expanded from a version published in 1711), *Miscellanies in Prose and Verse* (published with Alexander Pope), vol. 1, 1727

❧

Complaint is self-accusation.

> ANONYMOUS

Always complain and never explain.

> SAYING (AMERICAN). 1990s

COMPUTERS

See also • Change: Alvin Toffler (4) ○ Libraries: Paul M. Horn ○ Information: [especially] Charles Rubin ○ Knowledge ○ Machines: [especially] Howard Mumford Jones ○ Misjudgments: Thomas J. Watson ○ Plagiarism: John Seabrook ○ Science ○ Technology

Sometimes when I work with these [computerized] voices, I have the illusion that I'm in touch with another intelligence, a wacky new life form. This happens only on good days, when all the systems are working. On bad days—when everything crashes and all the voices disappear—I start yelling at my computer, and then I think: "Wait a second. I might as well be talking to my electric pencil sharpener."

> LAURIE ANDERSON. Performance artist. "Dazed and Bemused," *New York Times Magazine,* 28 September 1997

To me, the computer is just another tool. It's like a pen. You have to have a pen, and to know penmanship, but neither will write the book for you.

RED BURNS. Interactive Telecommunications Program chairwoman, New York University's Tisch School of the Arts. In Sabra Chartrand, "Computer Theory as Social Science," *New York Times,* 4 December 1995

The advance arithmetical machines of the future will be electrical in nature, and they will perform at 100 times present speeds, or more.

Moreover, they will be far more versatile than present commercial machines, so that they may readily be adapted for a wide variety of operations. They will be controlled by a control card or film; they will select their own data and manipulate it in accordance with the instructions thus inserted; they will perform complex arithmetical computations at exceedingly high speeds; and they will record results in such form as to be readily available for distribution or for later further manipulation. Such machines will have enormous appetites.

VANNEVAR BUSH (1890–1974). "As We May Think," *Atlantic,* July 1945

Generally, any device that can perform numerical calculations—even an adding machine, an abacus, or a slide rule—may be called a computer. Currently, however, the term usually refers to an electronic device that can use a list of instructions, called a program, to perform calculations or to store, manipulate, and retrieve information.

COMPTON'S INTERACTIVE ENCYCLOPEDIA. In L. R. Shannon, "Navigating Through Reference Works on Disk," *New York Times,* 3 August 1993

Television was the baby of radio. It was radio with pictures—it was better radio. In the say way, the car was the baby of the horse. Movies were the baby of theater. The telephone was the baby of the telegraph. So what's the P.C. [personal computer] the baby of? The P.C., I'm sorry to say, the P.C. is the baby of the mainframe computer.

NICHOLAS DONATIELLO, JR. Keynote address at the Agenda 97 Conference, Phoenix, 1997. In Ken Auletta, "The Microsoft Provocateur," *New Yorker,* 12 May 1997

How DO we know that the people we meet are not computers programmed to simulate people?

R. BUCKMINSTER FULLER (1895–1983). *I Seem To Be a Verb,* p. 167, 1970

E-mail is a unique communication vehicle for a lot of reasons. However e-mail is not a substitute for direct interaction.

BILL GATES (1955–). E-mail to John Seabrook, "Getting Wired: E-Mail from Bill," October 1993–January 1994. In David Colbert, ed., *Eyewitness to America: 500 Years of America in the Words of Those Who Saw It Happen,* 1997

Do not fold, bend, or mutilate.

INTERNATIONAL BUSINESS MACHINES, CORP. Computer card message, 1960s

The 88% rise in Microsoft stock in 1996 meant [Bill Gates] made on paper more than $10.9 billion, or about $30 million a day. That makes him the world's richest person, by far. But he's more than that. He has become the Edison and Ford of our age. A technologist turned entrepreneur, he embodies the digital era.

WALTER ISAACSON (1952–). "In Search of the Real Bill Gates," *Time,* 13 January 1997

See Prediction: Bill Gates

I think one of the things which warmed us most during this flight was the realization that however extraordinary computers may be, we are still ahead of them, and that man is still the most extraordinary computer of all.

JOHN F. KENNEDY (1917–1963). Speech welcoming the return of astronaut Gordon Cooper who had taken over the controls of his spaceship in order to make a safe landing, Washington, 21 May 1963

There are only two kinds of computer users: those who *have* lost data in a crash, and those who *will* lose data in a crash.

BOB LeVITUS. *Dr. Macintosh: Tips, Techniques, and Advice on Mastering the Macintosh,* 2, 1989

The Tarzan Principle: Don't let go of the first vine until the next one is firmly in your grasp.

PETER H. LEWIS. On replacing one's computer system, "When Reliability Is Most Important," *New York Times,* 16 July 1989

See Prudence—Rules: Arthur Schopenhauer

Like any tyrant, a word-processing program both threatens and comforts. Obey its arbitrary inflexible rules, and it rewards you with tireless service in rearranging, removing, even correcting your words. Disobey its rules, and it responds either by issuing a warning beep and a terse instruction or by dissolving months of labor into scattered electrons. In millions of offices, the computer fulfills the tyrant's dream: it forbids everything that it does not permit.

EDWARD MENDELSON. Professor of English and comparative literature. "The Corrupt Computer," *New Republic,* 22 February 1988

The computer is no better than its program.

ELTING E. MORISON. *Men, Machines, and Modern Times,* 4, 1966

In creating the thinking machine, man has made the last step in submission to mechanization; and his final abdication before this product of his own ingenuity has given him a new object of worship: a cybernetic god.

LEWIS MUMFORD (1895–1990). *The Transformations of Man,* 7.3, 1956

As an instrument for organizing large quantities of information, or performing extremely complex symbolic operations beyond human capabilities within a normal life span, the computer is an invaluable adjunct to the brain, though not a substitute for it.

LEWIS MUMFORD (1895–1990). *The Pentagon of Power: The Myth of the Machine,* Graphic Section 1.6, 1970

There is no reason for any individual to have a computer in their home.

KEN OLSEN (1926–). Digital Equipment Corp. president. Speech before the Convention of the World Future Society, Boston, 1977

Computers are useless. They can only give you answers.

PABLO PICASSO (1881–1973)

The electronic computer is to individual privacy what the machine gun was to the horse cavalry.

ALAN W. SCHEFLIN (1942–) and EDWARD M. OPTON, JR. (1936–). *The Mind Manipulators: A Non-Fiction Account,* 12, 1978

The exploding arsenal of electronics—cellular telephones, fax machines, VCRs, satellite dishes, computers with modems—

demonstrated a trend for technology to become more compact, portable, versatile and inexpensive. As such, the new machines seemed to be weapons the citizen could wield against the state as readily as the state could use them on the citizen.

> SCOTT SHANE. *Dismantling Utopia,* 1994. In Jonathan Kirsch, "How a *Real* 'Information Revolution' Doomed the USSR," *Los Angeles Times,* 11 May 1994

Terrified of being alone, yet afraid of intimacy, we experience widespread feelings of emptiness, of disconnection, of the unreality of self. And here the computer, a companion without emotional demands, offers a compromise. You can be a loner, but never alone. You can interact, but need never feel vulnerable to another person.

> SHERRY TURKLE. *The Second Self,* 9, 1984

❧

To err is human, but to really foul things up requires a computer.

> ANONYMOUS. In "Capsules of Wisdom," *Farmers' Almanac for 1978,* 1977
>
> See Errors: Alexander Pope (1)

The computer is down. I hope it's down with something serious.

> ANONYMOUS. In Stanton Delaplane, "Dealing with Sick Computers," *San Francisco Chronicle,* 11 July 1984

Garbage in, garbage out. (GIGO)

> SAYING (AMERICAN)

CONCEIT

See also • Egoism ○ Egotism ○ Egotism: First Person ○ Vanity

The smaller the mind the greater the conceit.

> AESOP (6th cent. B.C.). "The Gnat and the Bull," *Fables*

I've never any pity for conceited people, because I think they carry their comfort about with them.

> GEORGE ELIOT (1819–1880). *The Mill on the Floss,* 5.4, 1860

The number of conceited people is so great that it must subserve great uses in nature, like sexual passion.

> RALPH WALDO EMERSON (1803–1882). Journal, 1859, undated

Conceit is the finest armor a man can wear.

> JEROME K. JEROME (1859–1927). "On Being Shy," *The Idle Thoughts of an Idle Fellow; A Book for an Idle Holiday,* 1892

As for conceit, what man will do any good who is not conceited? Nobody holds a good opinion of a man who has a low opinion of himself.

> ANTHONY TROLLOPE (1815–1882). *Orley Farm,* 22, 1862

CONFESSION

See also • Evil ○ Forgiveness ○ God ○ Guilt ○ Innocence ○ Morality ○ Prayer ○ Redemption ○ Religion ○ Repentance ○ Salvation ○ Sin

Priest: What frightful act have you committed in the course of your life?

Antalcidas: If I have done any such thing, the gods will know of it themselves.

> ANTALCIDAS (4th cent. B.C.). Format adapted. In "Sayings of the Spartans: Antalcidas" (1), *Plutarch on Sparta,* tr. Richard J. A. Talbert, 1988

We have left undone those things which we ought to have done, and we have done those things we ought not to have done.

> THE BOOK OF COMMON PRAYER. "Morning Prayer" ("General Confession"), 1662

If thou confesseth thy Sins and amendest not, thou mocketh God.

> THOMAS FULLER (1654–1734). Comp., *Introductio ad Prudentiam,* 661, 1731

Brother, Brother—We are both in the wrong.

> JOHN GAY (1685–1732). *The Beggar's Opera,* 2.10, 1728

If we say we have no sin, we deceive ourselves, and the truth is not in us. If we confess our sins, he is faithful and just, and will forgive our sins and cleanse us from all unrighteousness.

> JOHN (A.D. 1st cent.) *1 John* 1:8–9

We own up to minor failings, but only so as to convince others that we have no major ones.

> LA ROCHEFOUCAULD (1613–1680). *Maxims,* 327, 1665, tr. Leonard Tancock, 1959

Confession of a fault half amends it.

> JOHN RAY (1628–1705). Comp., *A Collection of English Proverbs,* p. 5, 1678

It is the confession, not the priest, that gives us absolution.

> OSCAR WILDE (1854–1900). *The Picture of Dorian Gray,* 8, 1891

Confession is the first step to repentance.

> SAYING (ENGLISH)

CONFIDENCE

See also • Confidence: First Person ○ Coolness ○ Dignity ○ Egotism ○ Inferiority ○ Leaders: Henry A. Kissinger (3) ○ Pride ○ Self-Respect

Real confidence comes from knowing and accepting yourself— your strengths and your limitations—in contrast to depending on affirmation from others.

> JUDITH M. BARDWICK. *The Plateauing Trap,* 8, 1988

All history makes clear that an indispensable quality of any man or class that wishes to lead, to hold power and privilege in society, is boundless self-confidence.

> JAMES BURNHAM (1905–1987). *The Managerial Revolution: What Is Happening in the World,* 3, 1941

The self-confidence of people who *show* themselves from all sides.

> ELIAS CANETTI (1905–1994). 1957, *The Human Province,* tr. Joachim Neugroschel, 1978

One good measure of ego-strength and inner confidence is the degree to which a person can risk unpopularity when the occasion demands.

NORMAN F. DIXON (1922–). *On the Psychology of Military Incompetence*, 27, 1976

Whether you believe you can do a thing or not, you are right.

HENRY FORD (1863–1947)

Good swimmers are oftenest drowned.

THOMAS FULLER (1654–1734). Comp., *Gnomologia: Adages and Proverbs*, 1729, 1732

With self-confidence fulfilled,
You'll find that folk have confidence in you.

GOETHE (1749–1832). *Faust*, 1 ("Faust's Study," 3), 1808–1832, tr. Philip Wayne, 1959

See Friends: Thomas Fuller (3) ○ Self-Respect: Baltasar Gracián

To measure up to all that is demanded of him, a man must overestimate his capacities.

GOETHE (1749–1832)

Confidence gives a fool the advantage over a wise man.

WILLIAM HAZLITT (1778–1830). "On Manner," *The Round Table*, 1817

Nothing so bolsters our self-confidence and reconciles us with ourselves as the continuous ability to create; to see things grow and develop under our hand, day in, day out.

ERIC HOFFER (1902–1983). *The True Believer: Thoughts on the Nature of Mass Movements*, 30, 1951

It generally happens that assurance keeps an even pace with ability.

SAMUEL JOHNSON (1709–1784). In *The Rambler* (English journal), 159, 24 September 1751

Self-confidence is the first requisite to great undertakings.

SAMUEL JOHNSON (1709–1784). "Pope," *Lives of the English Poets*, 1781

Self-confidence is at the root of most of our confidence in others.

LA ROCHEFOUCAULD (1613–1680). *Maxims*, 624, 1665, tr. Leonard Tancock, 1959

Mistress Ford: A man may be too confident.

SHAKESPEARE (1564–1616). *The Merry Wives of Windsor*, 2.1.193, 1600

What gives you confidence [in face-to-face confrontations] is the sense there is a clear injustice. Trying to change that gives you a shared purpose with other people.

GLORIA STEINEM (1934–). In Gail Sheehy, *Pathfinders*, 17, 1981

He's a cocky sumbitch. That's what makes him such a great player.

LAWRENCE TAYLOR. Football player. On team-mate Phil Simms. In Eric Pooley, "True Blue: From Giants to Supermen," *New York Times*, 26 January 1987

Consciousness of our powers augments them.

VAUVENARGUES (1715–1747). *Reflections and Maxims*, 75, 1746, tr. F. G. Stevens, 1940

Fired by success—they could do it because they believed they could do it.

VIRGIL (70–19 B.C.). *Aeneid*, 5.231, tr. C. Day Lewis, 1952

Self-assurance reassures others.

GARRY WILLS (1934–). Introduction to *Reagan's America*, 1987

❧

Better too much confidence than too little.

ANONYMOUS

CONFIDENCE: FIRST PERSON

See also • Confidence ○ Egotism: First Person

God didn't put me on this earth to be a loser. I'm a winner.

SPARKY ANDERSON (1934–). Baseball manager. In Murray Chass, "Tigers Are Hearing the Right Words," *New York Times*, 17 August 1988. The next season, his team, the Detroit Tigers, had the worst won-loss record in the Major Leagues.

Go on, my friend, and fear nothing; you carry Caesar and his fortune in your boat.

JULIUS CAESAR (100–44 B.C.). Remark during a storm to a boatman who had ordered his crew to turn back. In Plutarch (A.D. 46?–119?), "Caesar," *Parallel Lives*, Dryden edition, 1693

As I went to bed at about 3 A.M., I was conscious of a profound sense of relief. At last I had the authority to give directions over the whole scene. I felt as if I were walking with Destiny, and that all my past life had been but a preparation for this hour and for this trial. . . . I thought I knew a good deal about it all, and I was sure I should not fail. Therefore, although impatient for the morning, I slept soundly and had no need for cheering dreams. Facts are better than dreams.

WINSTON CHURCHILL (1874–1965). After being appointed British prime minister early in World War II, 10 May 1940, closing words, *The Second World War: The Gathering Storm*, 1948

See Destiny: Churchill (1)

As an adolescent . . . I was convinced that France would have to go through gigantic trials, that the interest of life consisted in one day rendering her some signal service and that I would have the occasion to do so.

CHARLES de GAULLE (1890–1970). In Russell Watson, "Charles de Gaulle: 1890-1970," *Newsweek*, 23 November 1970

If I have lost confidence in myself, I have the Universe against me.

RALPH WALDO EMERSON (1803–1882). Journal, November 1843

My progress in the English world was in general left to my own efforts, and those efforts were languid and slow. I had not been endowed by art or nature with those happy gifts of confidence and address, which unlock every door and every bosom.

EDWARD GIBBON (1737–1794). *Memoirs of My Life and Writings*, p. 52, 1796, Alex. Murray edition, 1869

My plans are perfect, and when I start to carry them out, may God have mercy on General Lee, for I will have none.

JOSEPH "FIGHTING JOE" HOOKER (1814–1879). Remark to his staff after assuming command of the Army of the Potomac, winter 1863. In T. Harry Williams, *Lincoln and His Generals*, 9, 1967. A few months later, Hooker resigned his command soon after being roundly defeated by Gen. Robert E. Lee at the Battle of Chancellorsville (Virginia) in May 1863.

See Commanders: Abraham Lincoln (3)

I knew very well what I was undertaking, and very well how to do it, and have done it very well.

> SAMUEL JOHNSON (1709–1784). On his *Dictionary of the English Language,* 10 October 1779. In James Boswell, *The Life of Samuel Johnson,* 1791

I must, in candor, say I do not think myself fit for the Presidency.

> ABRAHAM LINCOLN (1809–1865). Letter to Thomas J. Pickett, 16 April 1859

Why don't you run me? I can be nominated, I can be elected, and I can run the Government.

> ABRAHAM LINCOLN (1809–1865). Remark to a small group of political friends who were discussing the presidential candidate they would support at the upcoming Republican Convention of 1860, as reported by Judge David Davis. In Emanuel Hertz, ed., "Politician," *Lincoln Talks: A Biography in Anecdote,* 1939

For all the faith I have in French valor, I have equal faith in my lucky star, or perhaps in myself, and as a result I never count positively on victory unless I myself am in command.

> NAPOLEON (1769–1821). Remark, 1803, *The Mind of Napoleon: A Selection from His Written and Spoken Words,* 290, ed. J. Christopher Herold, 1955

I can outfight that little fart, Monty, anytime.

> GEORGE S. PATTON, JR. (1885–1945). On his British counterpart Field Marshall Bernard Law Montgomery, diary, 1943. In Charles M. Province, *The Unknown Patton,* p. 175, 1983

I know that I can save this country and that no one else can.

> WILLIAM PITT THE ELDER (1708–1778). First Earl of Catham, British prime minister. November 1756

Nothing but my mood and my inclination toward perseveration will tell me whether something is possible for me; impossible is only what I no longer feel like doing.

> ARTHUR SCHOPENHAUER (1788–1860). In Alfred Hock, *Reason and Genius: Studies in Their Origin,* 2.2.3, 1960

It would have been presumptuous of me to have compared myself to Chatham. But if I am honest, I must admit that my exhilaration came from a similar inner conviction.

> MARGARET THATCHER (1925–). On becoming British prime minister in 1979, *The Downing Street Years,* 1993. In Alan Ryan, "Yes, Minister," *New York Review of Books,* 2 December 1993

❦

Look out world, here I come!

> SAYING

CONFORMITY

See also • Adjustment ○ Fashion ○ Freedom ○ Imitation ○ Independence ○ Individuality ○ Law: Henry Miller ○ Majorities ○ Mediocrity ○ Nonconformity ○ Nonconformity, Anti- ○ Nonconformity & Conformity ○ Normality ○ Pleasing Others ○ Popularity ○ Public Opinion ○ Respectability ○ Self-Reliance ○ Success: Sam Rayburn

The price of group membership is conformity to prevailing norms.

> JAMES MacGREGOR BURNS (1918–). *Leadership,* 4, 1978

When they are at Rome, they do there as they see done.

> ROBERT BURTON (1577–1640). *The Anatomy of Melancholy,* 3.4.2.1, 1621–1651 (Popular version: When in Rome, do as the Romans do.)
> See Custom: Sophocles

We are the hollow men
We are the stuffed men
Leaning together
Headpiece filled with straw. Alas!

> T. S. ELIOT (1888–1965). Opening lines, *The Hollow Men,* 1925

A man must consider what a rich realm he abdicates when he becomes a conformist.

> RALPH WALDO EMERSON (1803–1882). Journal, 22 March 1839

Conformity is the ape of harmony.

> RALPH WALDO EMERSON (1803–1882). Journal, 10 May 1840

No man on earth is truly free.
All are slaves of money or necessity.
Public opinion or fear of prosecution
forces each one, against his conscience,
to conform.

> EURIPIDES (485?–406 B.C.). *Hecuba,* l. 860, tr. William Arrowsmith, 1956

In our effort to escape from aloneness and powerlessness, we are ready to get rid of our individual self either by submission to new forms of authority or by a compulsive conforming to accepted patterns.

> ERICH FROMM (1900–1980). *Escape from Freedom,* 4, 1941

The individual in any given society represses the awareness of those feelings and fantasies which are incompatible with the thought patterns of his society. The force affecting this repression is the fear of being isolated and of becoming an outcast through having thoughts and feelings which nobody [will] share.

> ERICH FROMM (1900–1980). *Sigmund Freud's Mission: An Analysis of His Personality and Influence,* 10, 1959

Do as most do, and few will speak ill of thee.

> THOMAS FULLER (1654–1734). Comp., *Introductio ad Prudentiam,* 135, 1731

If one plays by the rules, he gets all the honors—such honors as a monkey might get for performing pirouettes. The condition that has been imposed is that one cannot try to escape from the invisible cage.

> ERNESTO "CHE" GUEVARA (1928–1967). "Notes on Man and Socialism in Cuba," 1965, *Che Guevara Speaks,* ed. George Lavan, 1967

The less satisfaction we derive from being ourselves, the greater is our desire to be like others.

> ERIC HOFFER (1902–1983). *The True Believer: Thoughts on the Nature of Mass Movements,* 78, 1951

Conformity is the jailer of freedom and the enemy of growth.

> JOHN F. KENNEDY (1917–1963). United Nations address, New York City, 25 September 1961

Success, recognition, and conformity are the bywords of the modern world where everyone seems to crave the anesthetizing security of being identified with the majority.

MARTIN LUTHER KING, JR. (1929–1968). *Strength to Love*, 2 (introduction), 1963

The family is, in the first place, the usual instrument for what is called socialization, that is, getting each new recruit to the human race to behave and experience in substantially the same way as those who have already got here. We are all fallen Sons of Prophecy, who have learned to die in the Spirit and be reborn in the flesh.

This is also known as selling one's birthright for a mess of pottage.

R. D. LAING (1927–1989). *The Politics of Experience*, 3, 1967

George F. Babbitt: I've never done a single thing I've wanted to do in my whole life! I don't know's I've accomplished anything except just get along.

SINCLAIR LEWIS (1885–1951). *Babbitt*, 34.6, 1922

When all think alike, no one thinks very much.

WALTER LIPPMANN (1889–1974). In Laurence J. Peter, *The Peter Prescription: How to Make Things Go Right*, 4, 1972

Do not do what others do not choose to do; do not desire what others do not desire.

MENCIUS (371?–289? B.C.). *Mencius*, 7.A.17, tr. D. C. Lau, 1970

May God prevent us from becoming "right-thinking men"—that is to say, men who agree perfectly with their own police.

THOMAS MERTON (1915–1968). In Israel Shenker, "Thomas Merton Is Dead at 53; Monk Wrote of Search for God," *New York Times*, 11 December 1968

There's nothing in this world more instinctively abhorrent to me than finding myself in agreement with my fellow humans.

MALCOLM MUGGERIDGE (1903–1990). Radio broadcast, 29 April 1955, "Mini-Mania," *Muggeridge through the Microphone*, 1967

The surest way of ruining a youth is to teach him to respect those who think as he does more highly than those who think differently from him.

FRIEDRICH NIETZSCHE (1884–1900). *Daybreak*, 297, 1881, tr. R. J. Hollingdale, 1982

You will become smaller and smaller, you small people! You will crumble away, you comfortable people! You will yet perish—through your many small virtues, through your many small omissions, through your many small submissions!

FRIEDRICH NIETZSCHE (1884–1900). "Of the Virtue That Makes Small" (3), *Thus Spoke Zarathustra*, 1892, tr. R. J. Hollingdale, 1961

The real lost souls don't wear their hair long and play guitars. They have crew cuts, trained minds, sign on for research in biological warfare, and don't give their parents a moment's worry.

J. B. PRIESTLY (1894–1984)

The society of incipient population decline develops in its typical members a social character whose conformity is insured by their tendency to be sensitized to the expectations and preferences of others.

DAVID RIESMAN (1909–) (with NATHAN GLAZER and REUEL DENNEY). *The Lonely Crowd: A Study of the Changing American Character*, 1.1, 1950, abr., 1953

What is common to all the other-directed people is that their contemporaries are the source of direction for the individual—either those known to him or those with whom he is indirectly acquainted, through friends and through the mass media. This source is of course "internalized" in the sense that dependence on it for guidance in life is implanted early.

DAVID RIESMAN (1909–) (with NATHAN GLAZER and REUEL DENNEY). *The Lonely Crowd: A Study of the Changing American Character*, 1.1, 1950, abr., 1953

Good qualities are easier to destroy than bad ones, and therefore uniformity is most easily achieved by lowering all standards.

BERTRAND RUSSELL (1872–1970). "Modern Homogeneity," *The Will to Doubt*, 1958

[Sigmund Freud] was so fond of smoking that he was somewhat irritated when men around him did not smoke. Consequently nearly all who formed the inner circle became more or less passionate cigar smokers.

HANS SACHS (1494–1576). *Freud: Master and Friend*, 4, 1944

"Togetherness" is the banner under which we march into the brave new world.

ARTHUR M. SCHLESINGER, JR. (1917–). "The Decline of Greatness," *Saturday Evening Post*, 1 November 1958

No man stands on truth. They are merely banded together as usual, one leaning on another and all together on nothing.

HENRY DAVID THOREAU (1817–1862). Journal, 4 May 1852

We are half-ruined by conformity, but we should be wholly ruined without it.

CHARLES DUDLEY WARNER (1829–1900). "Eighteenth Week," *My Summer in a Garden*, 1871

[Groupthink] is a *rationalized* conformity—an open, articulate philosophy which holds that group values are not only expedient but right and good as well.

WILLIAM H. WHYTE, JR. (1917–). "Groupthink," *Fortune*, March 1952

See Committees: Irving L. Janis (1)

A sense of "belonging," a sense of meaningful association with others, has never required that one sacrifice his individuality as part of the bargain. Why, then, do so many rush to embrace a philosophy that tells them it *is* necessary?

WILLIAM H. WHYTE, JR. (1917–). "Groupthink," *Fortune*, March 1952

To the claims of conformity, no man may yield and remain free.

OSCAR WILDE (1854–1900). "The Soul of Man Under Socialism," *Fortnightly Review* (British journal), February 1891

Once conform, once do what other people do because they do it, and a lethargy steals over all the finer nerves and faculties of the soul. She becomes all outer show and inward emptiness; dull, callous, and indifferent.

VIRGINIA WOOLF (1882–1941). "Montaigne," *The Common Reader* (First Series), 1925

❧

Never forget that only dead fish swim with the stream!

ANONYMOUS (ENGLISH). Quoted by Malcolm Muggeridge. In *Radio Times* (British magazine), 9 July 1964
See Nonconformity, Anti-: John Clarke

When in the country, do as the country people do.
SAYING (CHINESE)

Birds of a feather flock together.
SAYING (GREEK). In Plato (427?–347 B.C.), *Phaedrus,* 240, tr. Benjamin Jowett, 1894

Beaten paths lead nowhere.
SAYING

CONGRESS

See • Campaigns ○ Elections ○ Politicians ○ Politicians, Corrupt

CONSCIENCE

See also • Courage, Moral: Douglas MacArthur ○ Crime: Henri Amiel ○ Crises: Jacob Burckhardt (3) ○ Freedom of Conscience ○ Duty: Mohandas K. Gandhi ○ Happiness: Ogden Nash ○ Heart ○ Joy: Thomas à Kempis ○ Morality ○ Peace: Henry A. Kissinger (2) ○ Peace of Mind ○ Reason ○ Right: Robert E. Lee ○ Self ○ Soul ○ Spirit ○ The Unconscious

Conscience is the spiritual, supernatural principle in man, and it is not of social origin at all. It is rather the perversion and confusion of conscience that is of social origin.
NICOLAS BERDYAEV (1874–1948). *The Destiny of Man,* 2.4.3, 1931, tr. Natalie Duddington, 1955

I will stay in jail to the end of my days before I make a butchery of my conscience.
JOHN BUNYAN (1628–1688). In Martin Luther King, Jr., "Letter from Birmingham City Jail," 16 April 1963

Conscience is thoroughly well-bred and soon leaves off talking to those who do not wish to hear it.
SAMUEL BUTLER (1835–1902). *Further Extracts from the Note-Books of Samuel Butler,* 4, ed. A. T. Bartholomew, 1934

Man's conscience is the oracle of God.
LORD BYRON (1788–1824). *The Island,* 1.6, 1823

The only wise and safe course is to act from day to day in accordance with what one's own conscience seems to decree.
WINSTON CHURCHILL (1874–1965). *The Second World War: The Gathering Storm,* 1.12, 1948

Ultimately our moral sense or conscience becomes a highly complex sentiment—originating in the social instinct, largely guided by the approbation of our fellow men, ruled by reason, self-interest, and in later times by deep religious feelings, and confirmed by instruction and habit.
CHARLES DARWIN (1809–1882). *The Descent of Man and Selection in Relation to Sex,* 2nd ed., 5, 1874

Never do anything against conscience, even if the state demands it.

ALBERT EINSTEIN (1879–1955). Remark to Virgil G. Hinshaw, Jr., "Einstein's Social Philosophy." In Paul Arthur Schilpp, ed., *Albert Einstein: Philosopher-Scientist,* 1949

Let me consider this as a resolution by which I pledge myself to act in all variety of circumstances and to which I must recur often in times of carelessness and temptation—to measure my conduct by the rule of conscience.
RALPH WALDO EMERSON (1803–1882). Journal, 25 March 1821

The shield against the stingings of conscience is the universal practice of our contemporaries. Again, it is very easy to be as wise and good as your companions.
RALPH WALDO EMERSON (1803–1882). "Uses of Great Men," *Representative Men,* 1850

A good Conscience is a continual Christmas.
BENJAMIN FRANKLIN (1706–1790). *Poor Richard's Almanack,* December 1741

Keep Conscience clear,
Then never fear.
BENJAMIN FRANKLIN (1706–1790). *Poor Richard's Almanack,* November 1749

"Social anxiety" is the essence of what is called conscience.
SIGMUND FREUD (1856–1939). *Group Psychology and the Analysis of the Ego,* 2, 1921, tr. James Strachey, 1922`

God is conscience.
Mohandas K. Gandhi (1869–1948). In *Young India,* 5 March 1925

I should love to satisfy all, if I possibly can; but in trying to satisfy all, I may be able to satisfy none. I have, therefore, arrived at the conclusion that the best course is to satisfy one's own conscience and leave the world to form its own judgment, favorable or otherwise.
MOHANDAS K. GANDHI (1869–1948). In Chandrashanker Shukla, *Gandhi's View of Life,* 1952

I have no conscience. My conscience is Adolf Hitler.
HERMANN GOERING (1893–1946). German political leader. Table talk, 1933. In Hermann Rauschning, *The Voice of Destruction,* 6, 1940

Conscience . . . is the impulse to do right because it is right, regardless of personal ends.
MARGARET C. GRAHAM. "A Matter of Conscience," *Do They Really Respect Us? and Other Essays,* 1911

I cannot and will not cut my conscience to fit this year's fashions.
LILLIAN HELLMAN (1907–1984). Explanation of her refusal to answer questions regarding the political opinions and activities of anyone other than herself, letter to John S. Wood, chairman of the House Committee on Un-American Activities, 19 May 1952, appended to John Phillips and Anne Hollander interview. In George Plimpton, ed., *Writers at Work: Third Series,* 1967

The conscience is . . . a brake, not a guide; a fence, not a way. It raises its voice after a wrong deed has been committed, but often fails to give us direction in advance of our actions.
ABRAHAM JOSHUA HESCHEL (1907–1972). *God in Search of Man: A Philosophy of Judaism,* 29, 1955

Providence has ordained that I should be the greatest liberator of humanity. I am freeing men from the restraints of an intelligence that has taken charge; from the dirty and degrading self-mortifications of a chimera called conscience and morality.

ADOLF HITLER (1889–1945). Table talk, 1932–1934. In Hermann Rauschning, *The Voice of Destruction,* 16, 1940

A sensitive conscience is often a by-product of a decline in vigor.

ERIC HOFFER (1902–1983). *Reflections on the Human Condition,* 164, 1973

Never yet were the feelings and instincts of our nature violated with impunity; never yet was the voice of conscience silenced without retribution.

ANNA JAMESON (1797–1860)

Welcome, O Life! I go to encounter for the millionth time the reality of experience and to forge in the smithy of my soul the uncreated conscience of my race.

JAMES JOYCE (1882–1941). *A Portrait of the Artist as a Young Man,* 5, 1916

Deep down, below the surface of the average man's conscience, he hears a voice whispering, "There is something not right," no matter how much his rightness is supported by public opinion or by the moral code.

CARL G. JUNG (1875–1961). "Introduction to Wickes's *Analyse der Kinderseele,*" 1931, *The Development of Personality,* tr. R. F. C. Hull, 1954

Conscience itself [asserts] that it is a voice of God.

CARL G. JUNG (1875–1961). "A Psychological View of Conscience," 1958, *Civilization in Transition,* tr. R. F. C. Hull, 1964

Every one of us has a bad conscience, which he tries to escape by going to sleep as quickly as possible.

FRANZ KAFKA (1883–1924). In Gustav Janouch, *Conversations with Kafka,* p. 50, tr. Goronwy Rees, 1953

Vanity asks the question—is it popular? Conscience asks the question—is it right?

MARTIN LUTHER KING, JR. (1929–1968). Passion Sunday sermon at the National Cathedral, Washington, 31 March 1968

Inability of those in power to still the voices of their own consciences is the great force leading to desired changes.

KENNETH KAUNDA (1924–). Zambian president. In *Observer* (British newspaper), 27 July 1965

No client ever had enough to bribe my conscience or to stop its utterance against wrong and oppression.

ABRAHAM LINCOLN (1809–1865). Attributed. *Recollected Words of Abraham Lincoln,* ed. Don E. Fehrenbacher and Virginia Fehrenbacher, p. 242, 1996

See Integrity: Ralph Waldo Emerson (1)

I cannot and will not recant anything, for to go against conscience is neither right nor safe. Here I stand. I cannot do no other, so help me God. Amen.

MARTIN LUTHER (1483–1546). Speech before the Diet of Worms (Germany), 18 April 1521

The Anglo-Saxon conscience does not prevent the Anglo-Saxon from sinning. It merely prevents him from enjoying it.

SALVADOR de MADARIAGA (1886–1978). Spanish diplomat and writer. In David Frost and Antony Jay, *To England with Love,* 16, 1967

Conscience: the inner voice which warns us someone may be looking.

H. L. MENCKEN (1880–1956). *A Little Book in C Major,* 4.12, 1916

Conscience is a mother-in-law whose visit never ends.

H. L. MENCKEN (1880–1956). *A Mencken Chrestomathy,* 30 ("This and That"), 1949

It is in the depths of conscience that God speaks, and if we refuse to open up inside and look into those depths, we also refuse to confront the invisible God who is present within us.

THOMAS MERTON (1915–1968). "Creative Silence," *Love and Living,* ed. Naomi Burton Stone and Brother Patrick Hart, 1985

"Where id was," as Freud . . . put it, "there shall ego be"; and one may add, to correct Freud's hostility to the superego, where ego is there superego shall be.

LEWIS MUMFORD (1895–1990). *The Conduct of Life,* 9.1, 1951. "Superego" and "conscience" are roughly equivalent terms.

The bad conscience is an illness . . . but an illness as pregnancy is an illness.

FRIEDRICH NIETZSCHE (1844–1900). *Toward a Genealogy of Morals,* 2.19, 1887, tr. Walter Kaufmann and R. J. Hollingdale, 1966

Were the impulses of conscience clear, uniform, and irresistibly obeyed, man would need no other lawgiver; but that not being the case, he finds it necessary to surrender up a part of his property to furnish means for the protection of the rest.

THOMAS PAINE (1737–1809). "Of the Origin and Design of Government in General," *Common Sense,* 1776

Consult your conscience, rather than popular opinion.

PUBLIUS SYRUS (85–43 B.C.). *Moral Sayings,* 146 tr. Darius Lyman, Jr., 1862

To obey God means, in practice, to obey one's conscience.

BERTRAND RUSSELL (1872–1970). *Marriage and Morals,* 13, 1929

In the depths of his conscience, man detects a law which he does not impose upon himself, but which holds him to obedience. Always summoning him to love good and avoid evil, the voice of conscience can when necessary speak to his heart more specifically: do this, shun that. For man has in his heart a law written by God. To obey it is the very dignity of man. According to it he will be judged.

Conscience is the most secret core and sanctuary of a man. There he is alone with God whose voice echoes in his depths. In a wonderful manner conscience reveals that law which is fulfilled by love of God and neighbor.

THE SECOND VATICAN ECUMENICAL COUNCIL. "The Church Today" (16), *The Documents of Vatican II,* 1965

Nothing shall I ever do for the sake of [public] opinion, everything for the sake of my conscience.

SENECA THE YOUNGER (5? B.C.–A.D. 65). "On the Happy Life" (20.4), *Moral Essays,* tr. John W. Basore, 1932

I have the right to believe freely, to be a slave to no man's authority. If this be heresy, so be it. It is still the truth. To go against conscience is neither right nor safe. I will not recant. No man can command my conscience.

> BEN SHAHN (1898–1969). Lithuanian-born American artist. Drawing inscription

King Richard: Conscience is but a word that cowards use,
Devised at first to keep the strong in awe:
Our strong arms be our conscience, swords our law.

> SHAKESPEARE (1564–1616). *Richard III,* 5.3.309, 1592

Hamlet: Conscience does make cowards of us all.

> SHAKESPEARE (1564–1616). *Hamlet,* 3.1.83, 1600
>
> See Fatigue: George S. Patton, Jr.

Cardinal Wolsey: A peace above all earthly dignities,
A still and quiet conscience.

> SHAKESPEARE (1564–1616). *King Henry VIII,* 3.2.379, 1612

A world without conscience: that is the horror of our condition.

> GEORGE BERNARD SHAW (1856–1950). *Back to Methuselah: A Metabiological Pentateuch,* 2, 1921

Conscience warns us as a friend before it punishes as a judge.

> STANISLAW I (1677–1766). Polish king

Conscience is God's presence in man.

> EMMANUEL SWEDENBORG (1688–1772). *Arcana Coelestia,* vol. 1, 1856

Conscience is, in most men, an anticipation of the opinions of others.

> HENRY TAYLOR (1800–1886). *The Statesman,* 9, 1836

Your conscience is a nuisance. A conscience is like a child. If you pet it and play with it and let it have everything that it wants, it becomes spoiled and intrudes on all your amusements and most of your griefs. Treat your conscience as you would anything else. When it is rebellious, spank it—be severe with it, argue with it, prevent it from coming to play with you at all hours, and you will secure a good conscience; that is to say, a properly trained one. A spoiled one simply destroys all the pleasure in life. I think I have reduced mine to order. At least, I haven't heard from it for some time. Perhaps I have killed it from over-severity.

> MARK TWAIN (1835–1910). Interview with the author. In Rudyard Kipling, *From Sea to Sea,* 1889

Labor to keep alive in your Breast that little Spark of Celestial fire Called Conscience.

> GEORGE WASHINGTON (1732–1799). Copybook, 1748 (at age 16), *Rules of Civility & Decent Behaviour in Company and Conversation,* #110 (last entry). The rules were an amended version of Francis Hawkins's 1640 translation of *Decency of Conversation Among Men* (French Jesuit writing, 1595).

Conscience is God's Viceregent [i.e., deputy]; the God dwelling within us.

> BENJAMIN WHICHCOTE (1609–1683). *Moral and Religious Aphorisms,* 1058, 1753

A conscience which has been bought once will be bought twice.

> NORBERT WIENER (1894–1964). *The Human Use of Human Beings,* 7, 1954

Conscience and cowardice are really the same thing, Basil. Conscience is the trade name of the firm. That is all.

> OSCAR WILDE (1854–1900). *The Picture of Dorian Gray,* 1, 1891

Certainly it is correct to say: Conscience is the voice of God.

> LUDWIG WITTGENSTEIN (1889–1951). 8 July 1916, *Notebooks, 1914–1916,* ed. G. E. M. Anscombe, 1961

Above all, the victory is most sure
For him, who, seeking faith by virtue, strives
To yield entire submission to the law
Of conscience—conscience reverenced and obeyed
As God's most intimate presence in the soul,
And his most perfect image in the world.

> WILLIAM WORDSWORTH (1770–1850). *The Excursion,* 4.222, 1814

❧

Conscience can't be compromised without being imperiled.

> ANONYMOUS

A guilty conscience needs no accuser.

> SAYING (ENGLISH)

A good conscience makes a soft pillow.

> SAYING (GERMAN)

There is one thing alone
that stands the brunt of life throughout its course,
a quiet conscience.

> SAYING (GREEK). In Euripides (485?–406 B.C.), *Hippolytus,* l. 425, tr. David Grene, 1942

Let conscience be your guide.

> SAYING
>
> See Reason: Kahlil Gibran

CONSCIOUSNESS

See also • Mind ○ Nonviolence: Leo Tolstoy ○ Self ○ The Unconscious

The center of our consciousness is unconscious, as the kernel of the sun is dark.

> HENRI AMIEL (1821–1888). Journal, 27 October 1856, tr. Mrs. Humphrey Ward, 1887

I do not know the man so bold
He dare in lonely Place
That awful stranger Consciousness
Deliberately face—

> EMILY DICKINSON (1830–1886). "I never hear that one is dead," 1874?

I am firmly convinced not only that a great deal of consciousness, but that any consciousness is a disease.

> FYODOR DOSTOEVSKY (1821–1881). *Notes from Underground,* 1.2, 1864, tr. Ralph E. Matlaw, 1960

The private and the universal consciousness.

> RALPH WALDO EMERSON (1803–1882). Journal, April 1848

Mental processes are essentially unconscious, and . . . those which are conscious are merely isolated acts and part of the whole psychic entity.

> SIGMUND FREUD (1856–1939). *A General Introduction to Psychoanalysis*, 1, 1917, tr. Joan Riviere, 1952

I think consciousness has a place in the cosmic game, the atoms-and-universe game, the big game. I can't imagine that it's mindless—there's too much organization, and the organization is too incredible.

> JERRY GARCIA (1942–1996). *The Wisdom of Jerry Garcia*, unpaged, 1995

Without a global revolution in the sphere of human consciousness, nothing will change for the better in the sphere of our being as humans, and the catastrophe toward which this world is headed—be it ecological, social, demographic or a general breakdown of civilization—will be unavoidable.

> VÁCLAV HAVEL (1936–). Czech president. Congress address, Washington, 21 February 1990

Our normal waking consciousness, rational consciousness as we call it, is but one special type of consciousness, whilst all about it, parted from it by the filmiest of screens, there lie potential forms of consciousness entirely different. We may go through life without suspecting their existence; but apply the requisite stimulus, and at a touch they are there in their completeness, definite types of mentality which probably somewhere have their field of application and adaptation. No account of the universe in its totality can be final which leaves these other forms of consciousness quite disregarded.

> WILLIAM JAMES (1842–1910). *The Varieties of Religious Experience: A Study in Human Nature*, 16 and 17, 1902

There is a continuum of cosmic consciousness, against which our individuality builds but accidental fences, and into which our several minds plunge as into a mother-sea or reservoir.

> WILLIAM JAMES (1842–1910). *Memories and Studies*, 1911

Consciousness rises out of the depths of unconscious psychic life, at first like separate islands, which gradually unite to form a "continent," a continuous landmass of consciousness. Progressive mental development means, in effect, extension of consciousness.

> CARL G. JUNG (1875–1961). "Marriage as a Psychological Relationship," 1925, *The Development of Personality*, tr. R. F. C. Hull, 1954
>
> See Self: Jung

Nothing so promotes the growth of consciousness as [the] inner confrontation of opposites.

> CARL G. JUNG (1875–1961). *Memories, Dreams, Reflections*, 12.2, ed. Aniela Jaffé, 1962

The conscious life of the mind is of small importance in comparison with its unconscious life.

> GUSTAVE LE BON (1841–1931). *The Crowd: A Study of the Popular Mind*, 1.1, 1895, Viking Press edition, 1960

Consciousness is the perception of what passes in a man's own mind.

> JOHN LOCKE (1632–1704). *An Essay Concerning Human Understanding*, 2.1.19, 1690, ed. Alexander Campbell Fraser, 1894

The mode of production in material life conditions the social, political and intellectual life process in general. It is not the consciousness of men that determines their being, but, on the contrary, their social being determines their consciousness.

> KARL MARX (1818–1883). Preface to *A Contribution to the Critique of Political Economy*, 1859, *The Marx-Engels Reader*, 2nd ed., ed. Robert C. Tucker, 1978

The awakening of consciousness [is] a series of spaced flashes, with the intervals between them gradually diminishing until bright blocks of perception are formed, affording memory a slippery hold.

> VLADIMIR NABOKOV (1899–1977). *Speak, Memory*, 1, 1951

We flatter ourselves that the controlling or highest principle is in our consciousness.

> FRIEDRICH NIETZSCHE (1844–1900). In Lancelot Law Whyte, *The Unconscious Before Freud*, 8, 1960

Consciousness reigns but does not govern.

> PAUL VALÉRY (1871–1945)

Often do I seem
Two consciousnesses, conscious of myself
And of some other Being.

> WILLIAM WORDSWORTH (1770–1850). *The Prelude; or, Growth of a Poet's Mind; An Autobiographical Poem*, 2.31, 1850

CONSERVATIVES

See also • Business (Commerce) ○ Conservatives & Liberals/Radicals ○ Liberals ○ Reformers ○ Revolutionaries ○ Tyrants

Conservatism is the politics of reality.

> WILLIAM F. BUCKLEY, JR. (1925–). David Butler interview, *Playboy*, May 1970

Every public action which is not customary either is wrong, or, if it is right, is a dangerous precedent. It follows that nothing should ever be done for the first time.

> FRANCIS MACDONALD CORNFORD (1874–1943). *Microcosmographia Academica: Being a Guide for the Young Academic Politician*, p. 32, 1923

A conservative government is an organized hypocrisy.

> BENJAMIN DISRAELI (1804–1881). House of Commons speech, 17 March 1845

The philosophical conservative is someone willing to pay the price of other people's suffering for his principles.

> E. L. DOCTOROW (1931–). Commencement address at Brandeis University, Waltham (Massachusetts), 21 May 1989

Faced with the unknown future, the human mind seeks a refuge, and usually believes it has found it in what has already happened.

> CHARLES de GAULLE (1890–1970). *The Army of the Future*, 5.1, 1941

There is always a certain meanness in the argument of conservatism, joined with a certain superiority in its fact.

> RALPH WALDO EMERSON (1803–1882). "The Conservative," lecture, Masonic Temple, Boston, 9 December 1841

The modern conservative is engaged in one of man's oldest exercises in moral philosophy, that is the search for a superior moral justification for selfishness.

> JOHN KENNETH GALBRAITH (1908–)

I am exasperated by those who shout: "Don't move," when no one is yet in place.

> ANDRÉ GIDE (1869–1951). Journal, 13 July 1930, tr. Justin O'Brien, 1951

Persuasion that property and freedom are inseparably connected, and that economic leveling is not economic progress. Separate property from private possession, and liberty is erased.

> RUSSELL KIRK (1918–1994). His fourth canon of "conservative thought," The Conservative Mind: From Burke to Eliot, 3rd ed. rev., 1, 1960 (1953)

The problem of spiritual and moral regeneration; the restoration of the ethical system and the religious sanction upon which any life worth living is founded. This is conservatism at its highest.

> RUSSELL KIRK (1918–1994). The Conservative Mind: From Burke to Eliot, 3rd ed. rev., 13.3, 1960 (1953)

What is conservatism? Is it not adherence to the old and tried, against the new and untried?

> ABRAHAM LINCOLN (1809–1865). Address, Cooper Institute, New York City, 27 February 1860

The more men have to lose, the less willing are they to venture.

> THOMAS PAINE (1737–1809). "Of the Present Ability of America," Common Sense, 1776

Be not the first by whom the New are try'd,
Nor yet the last to lay the Old aside.

> ALEXANDER POPE (1688–1744). An Essay on Criticism, l. 335, 1711

The true conservative is he who insists that property shall be the servant and not master of the commonwealth.

> THEODORE ROOSEVELT (1858–1919). "The New Nationalism," speech, Osawatomie (Kansas), 31 August 1910

Our worst revolutionaries today are those reactionaries who do not see and will not admit that there is any need for change.

> THEODORE ROOSEVELT (1858–1919). An Autobiography, 13, 1913

The preference for liberty over equality lies at the root of the Conservative tradition.

> CLINTON ROSSITER (1917–1970). Conservatism in America: The Thankless Persuasion, 2nd ed. rev. 2, 1962 (1955)

The reactionaries hold that government policies should be designed for the special benefit of small groups of people who occupy positions of wealth and influence. Their theory seems to be that if these groups are prosperous, they will pass along some of their prosperity to the rest of us. This can be described as the "trickle down theory."

> HARRY S. TRUMAN (1884–1972). Speech, St. Paul, 3 November 1949

The only reactionaries are those who find themselves at home in the present.

> MIGUEL de UNAMUNO (1864–1936). Conclusion to Tragic Sense of Life, 1913, tr. J. E. Crawford Flitch, 1921

The abjectly poor, and all those persons whose energies are entirely absorbed by the struggle for daily sustenance, are conservative because they cannot afford the effort of taking thought for the day after tomorrow; just as the highly prosperous are conservative because they have small occasion to be discontented with the situation as it stands today.

> THORSTEIN VEBLEN (1857–1929). The Theory of the Leisure Class: An Economic Study of Institutions, 8, 1899

What is valuable is not new, and what is new is not valuable.

> DANIEL WEBSTER (1782–1852). Speech, Marshfield (Massachusetts), 1 September 1848

Traditional conservatism has not been, and proper conservatism cannot be, merely a defense of industrialism and individualist "free-market" economics. Conservatism is about the cultivation and conservation of certain values, or it is nothing.

> GEORGE F. WILL (1941–). Statecraft as Soulcraft: What Government Does, 5, 1983

One of the pleasures of being a conservative is that you are always more or less pleased. Conservatives are pessimists, so when things go badly they have the pleasure of having their beliefs confirmed, and when things go well they enjoy the pleasant surprise.

> GEORGE F. WILL (1941–). "You Shoulda Been Here Last Week," San Francisco Chronicle, 24 April 1986

CONSERVATIVES & LIBERALS/RADICALS

See also • Conservatives ○ History: Jules de Goncourt ○ Liberals ○ Political Parties ○ Revolutionaries

Conservative, n. A statesman who is enamored of existing evils, as distinguished from the Liberal, who wishes to replace them with others.

> AMBROSE BIERCE (1842–1914). The Devil's Dictionary, p. 24, 1911, Dover edition, 1958

I argy in this way, if a man is right he cant be too radikal, if he is rong he kant be too conservative.

> JOSH BILLINGS (1818–1885). "Remarks," Everybody's Friend, or; Josh Billing's Encyclopedia and Proverbial Philosophy of Wit and Humor, 1874

If you're not a liberal at 20, you have no heart, and if you're not a conservative at 40, you have no head.

> WINSTON CHURCHILL (1874–1965). In Marjorie Connelly, "A 'Conservative' Is (Fill in the Blank)," New York Times, 3 November 1996

There is no right wing
or no left wing . . .
there is only up wing
an' down wing. [Ellipsis points in original.]

> BOB DYLAN (1941–). "11 Outlined Epitaphs" (liner notes to "The Times They Are A-Changin'"), 1963

Conservatism stands on man's incontestable limitations; reform on his indisputable infinitude.

> RALPH WALDO EMERSON (1803–1882). "The Conservative," lecture, Masonic Temple, Boston, 9 December 1841

Men are conservatives when they are least vigorous, or when they are most luxurious. They are conservatives after dinner, or before taking their rest; when they are sick, or aged: in the morning, or when their intellect or their conscience have been aroused, when they hear music, or when they read poetry, they are radicals.

> RALPH WALDO EMERSON (1803–1882). "New England Reformers," *Essays: Second Series,* 1844

Liberals defend military spending and conservatives social spending—in their own districts.

> ROBERT A. HALL. "Hall's Law of Politics." In Paul Dickson, comp., *The New Official Rules,* p. 87, 1989

Liberals want to strike down the abortion laws, so that unwanted babies can be killed off before they are born. Conservatives want to strike down the welfare laws, so that unwanted babies can be starved to death after they are born.

> N. SALLY HASS

Any man who has the brains to think and the nerve to act for the benefit of the people of the country is considered a radical by those who are content with stagnation and willing to endure disaster.

> WILLIAM RANDOLPH HEARST (1863–1951). Interview, *Cleveland Plain Dealer,* 24 October 1932

Conservatives have historically seen people falling through the cracks in society and said that's the way things work, survival of the fittest. Liberals see people falling through the cracks and say we've got to do something about those people falling through the cracks so we need a strong government that can provide programs and assist those people. Populists say there shouldn't be any cracks, let's fix them.

> JIM HIGHTOWER (1943–). Joy Zimmerman interview, "Texas Talker," *Pacific Sun,* Mill Valley (California), 20 March 1992

People with a sense of fulfillment think it a good world and would like to conserve it as it is, while the frustrated favor radical change.

> ERIC HOFFER (1902–1983). *The True Believer: Thoughts on the Nature of Mass Movements,* 2, 1951

The differences between the conservative and the radical seem to spring mainly from their attitude toward the future. Fear of the future causes us to lean against and cling to the present, while faith in the future renders us receptive to change.

> ERIC HOFFER (1902–1983). *The True Believer: Thoughts on the Nature of Mass Movements,* 5, 1951

The reactionary and the radical have more in common than either has with the liberal or the conservative.

> ERIC HOFFER (1902–1983). *The True Believer: Thoughts on the Nature of Mass Movements,* 62, 1951

There is radicalism in all getting, and conservatism in all keeping.

> ERIC HOFFER (1902–1983). *The Passionate State of Mind: And Other Aphorisms,* 21, 1954

Liberals want more government, and conservatives want less.

> RICHARD M. NIXON (1913–1994). *In the Arena: A Memoir of Victory, Defeat and Renewal,* 30, 1990

Both sides agree that we need change. The question is, change what? What needs fixing? The left says, "Fix the country." The right says, "Fix the government."

> GROVER NORQUIST. Conservative activist. As paraphrased by James P. Pinkerton, "The Emptiness in the 'Politics of Meaning,'" *Los Angeles Times,* 24 June 1993

A liberal calls it share-the-wealth—a conservative calls it soak-the-rich.

> LAURENCE J. PETER (1919–). 27 September, *Peter's Almanac,* 1982

I am reminded of four definitions. A radical is a man with both feet firmly planted—in the air; a conservative is a man with two perfectly good legs who, however, has never learned to walk; a reactionary is a somnambulist walking backwards; a liberal is a man who uses his legs and his hands at the behest of his head.

> FRANKLIN D. ROOSEVELT (1882–1945). Radio broadcast, 26 October 1939

The liberal have no money.
The wealthy have no liberality.

> SA'DI (A.D. 1213?–1292). *The Gulistan, or Rose Garden,* 7 (Story 20), A.D. 1258, tr. Edward Rehatsek, 1964

Liberals feel unworthy of their possessions. Conservatives feel they deserve everything they've stolen.

> MORT SAHL (1927–)

Conservatism defends those coercive arrangements which a still-lingering savageness makes requisite. Radicalism endeavors to realize a state more in harmony with the character of the ideal man.

> HERBERT SPENCER (1820–1903). *Social Statics,* 4.31.5, 1851

A radical is one of whom people say, "He goes too far." A conservative, on the other hand, is one who "doesn't go far enough." Then there is the reactionary, "one who doesn't go at all." All these terms are more or less objectionable, wherefore we have coined the term "progressive." I should say that a progressive is one who insists upon recognizing new facts as they present themselves—one who adjusts legislation to these new facts.

> WOODROW WILSON (1856–1924). Speech before the Kansas Society of New York, New York City, 29 January 1911

❦

A reactionary is an extreme conservative; a conservative is a moderate reactionary. A liberal is a moderate radical; a radical is an extreme liberal.

> ANONYMOUS

Liberals have more questions than answers; conservatives have more answers than questions.

> ANONYMOUS

CONSISTENCY

See also • Belief ○ Changelessness ○ Ideas ○ Obstinacy ○ Opinion

Predicament, *n.* The wage of consistency.

> AMBROSE BIERCE (1842–1914). *The Devil's Dictionary,* p. 102, 1911, Dover edition, 1958

The man who never alters his opinion is like standing water, and breeds reptiles of the mind.

> WILLIAM BLAKE (1757–1827). "A Memorable Fancy," *The Marriage of Heaven and Hell,* 17–20, 1790–1793?

Opinions are made to be changed—or how is truth to be got at?

> LORD BYRON (1788–1824). Letter to John Murray, 9 May 1817

True consistency, that of the prudent and the wise, is to act in conformity with circumstances.

> JOHN C. CALHOUN (1782–1850). Senate speech, 16 March 1848

I'd rather be right than consistent.

> AL DAVIS (1929–). Football-team owner. Bob Costas television interview, NBC, 24 December 1989

Consistency in regard to opinions is the slow poison of intellectual life.

> SIR HUMPHREY DAVY (1778–1829). English chemist. In Lord Acton, appendix (71) to *Essays on Freedom and Power,* ed. Gertrude Himmelfarb, 1949

We cannot remain consistent with the world save by growing inconsistent with our past selves.

> HAVELOCK ELLIS (1859–1939). Preface to *The Dance of Life,* 1923

My page about "Consistency" would be better written thus: Damn Consistency!

> RALPH WALDO EMERSON (1803–1882). Journal, 24 October 1840

A foolish consistency is the hobgoblin of little minds. . . . Speak what you think now in hard words; and tomorrow speak what tomorrow thinks in hard words again, though it contradict everything you said today.

> RALPH WALDO EMERSON (1803–1882). "Self-Reliance," *Essays: First Series,* 1841

At the time of writing I never think of what I have said before. My aim is not to be consistent with my previous statements on a given question, but to be consistent with truth as it may present itself to me [at the] given moment. The result has been that I have grown from truth to truth.

> MOHANDAS K. GANDHI (1869–1948). In *Harijan,* 30 September 1939

Anonymous: How readily you change your mind!
Leotychidas: Yes, but in accordance with the circumstances and not, like you people, because of a weak character.

> LEOTYCHIDAS (7th cent. B.C.). Spartan king. Format adapted. In Plutarch (A.D. 46?–119?), "Sayings of the Spartans: Leotychidas" (1), *Plutarch on Sparta,* tr. Richard J. A. Talbert, 1988

Holding it a sound maxim that it is better to be only sometimes right than at all times wrong, so soon as I discover my opinions to be erroneous I shall be ready to renounce them.

> ABRAHAM LINCOLN (1809–1865). Campaign statement at age 23 (as a candidate for the state legislature), "To the People of Sangamo County," Illinois, 9 March 1832

A large part of the mischief and folly of the world comes from rushing in, taking a position, and then not knowing how to retreat. There is something about making a speech or writing an article which perverts the human mind. When the utterance is published, the Rubicon has been crossed and the bridges have been burned. It seems to end the inquiry, and after that we almost cease to be interested in the truth, being so preoccupied to prove that we already possess it.

> WALTER LIPPMANN (1889–1974). Untitled column, *New York Herald Tribune,* 10 October 1933

The foolish and the dead alone never their change their opinion.

> JAMES RUSSELL LOWELL (1819–1891). "Abraham Lincoln," 1864, *My Study Windows,* 1871

I don't intend to let anybody make my mind become so set on anything that I can't change it according to the circumstances and conditions that I happen to find myself in.

> MALCOLM X (1925–1965). Claude Lewis interview, December 1964, *National Leader* (Special Report), 2 June 1983

'Tis quite another Thing to be stiff than steady in an Opinion.

> WILLIAM PENN (1644–1718). *More Fruits of Solitude,* 155, 1693

A man should never be ashamed to own he has been in the wrong, which is but saying, in other words, that he is wiser today than he was yesterday.

> ALEXANDER POPE (1688–1744). "Thoughts on Various Subjects," *Miscellanies in Prose and Verse* (published with Jonathan Swift), vol. 2, 1727

With regards to essentials, I have never had occasion to change my mind.

> HENRY DAVID THOREAU (1817–1862). Letter to Harrison Blake, 18 August 1857

Do I contradict myself?
Very well then I contradict myself,
(I am large, I contain multitudes.)

> WALT WHITMAN (1819–1892). "Song of Myself" (51), 1855, *Leaves of Grass,* 1855–1892

Consistency is the last refuge of the unimaginative.

> OSCAR WILDE (1854–1900). *The Wit and Humor of Oscar Wilde,* 40, ed. Alvin Redman, 1959
> See Patriotism: Samuel Johnson

CONSTITUTIONS

See also • Certainty: Benjamin Franklin ○ Freedom ○ Government ○ Justice ○ Law ○ Liberty: Learned Hand (1) ○ Rights: Ronald Reagan

We, the people of the United States, in order to form a more perfect union, establish justice, insure domestic tranquility, provide for the common defense, promote the general welfare, and secure the blessings of liberty to ourselves and our posterity, do ordain and establish this Constitution for the United States of America.

> CONSTITUTION OF THE UNITED STATES. Preamble, 17 September 1787

The American Constitution is, so far as I can see, the most wonderful work ever struck off at a given time by the brain and purpose of man.

WILLIAM EWART GLADSTONE (1809–1898). "Kin Beyond Sea," *The North American Review,* September-October 1878

It has been frequently remarked that it seems to have been reserved to the people of this country, by their conduct and example, to decide the important question, whether societies of men are really capable or not of establishing good government from reflection and choice, or whether they are forever destined to depend for their political constitutions on accident and force.

ALEXANDER HAMILTON (1757–1804). From the opening paragraph. In *The Federalist Papers* (essay series), 1, 1787, undated

The aim of every political constitution is, or ought to be, first to obtain for rulers men who possess most wisdom to discern, and most virtue to pursue, the common good of the society; and in the next place, to take the most effectual precautions for keeping them virtuous whilst they continue to hold their public trust.

ALEXANDER HAMILTON (1757–1804) or JAMES MADISON (1751–1836). In *The Federalist Papers* (essay series), 57, 19 February 1788

Our Constitution is color-blind, and neither knows nor tolerates classes among citizens. In respect of civil rights, all citizens are equal before the law. The humblest is the peer of the most powerful.

JOHN MARSHALL HARLAN (1833–1911). *Plessy v. Ferguson,* 1896

We are under a Constitution, but the Constitution is what the judges say it is, and the judiciary is the safeguard of our liberty and of our property under the Constitution.

CHARLES EVANS HUGHES (1862–1948). Address, Elmira (New York), 3 May 1907

Some men look at constitutions with sanctimonious reverence, and deem them like the ark of the covenant, too sacred to be touched. They ascribe to the men of the preceding age a wisdom more than human, and suppose what they did to be beyond amendment. . . . I am certainly not an advocate for frequent and untried changes in laws and constitutions. I think moderate imperfections had better be borne with; because, when once known, we accommodate ourselves to them, and find practical means of correcting their ill effects. But I know also that laws and institutions must go hand in hand with the progress of the human mind. As that becomes more developed, more enlightened, as new discoveries are made, new truths disclosed, and manners and opinions change with the change of circumstances, institutions must advance also, and keep pace with the times. We might as well require a man to wear still the coat which fitted him when a boy, as civilized society to remain ever under the regimen of their barbarous ancestors.

THOMAS JEFFERSON (1743–1826). Letter to Samuel Kercheval, 12 July 1816

All government and all private institutions must be designed to promote and protect . . . the integrity and the dignity of the individual. And that is the essential meaning of the Constitution and the Bill of Rights.

DAVID E. LILIENTHAL (1899–1981). Atomic Energy Commission chairman. Congressional testimony, 4 February 1947

Was it possible to lose the nation and yet preserve the constitution? By general law, life *and* limb must be protected, yet often a limb must be amputated to save a life; but a life is never wisely given to save a limb. I felt that measures, otherwise unconstitutional, might become lawful by becoming indispensable to the preservation of the constitution through the preservation of the nation. Right or wrong, I assumed this ground, and now avow it.

ABRAHAM LINCOLN (1809–1865). Letter to Albert G. Hodges, 4 April 1864 See Law: Thomas Jefferson (2) o Prudence: Rules: Cicero

Anonymous: What kind of constitution do you favor? *Lysander:* Whichever gives brave men and cowards their due.

LYSANDER (5th cent. B.C.). Spartan commander. Format adapted. In Plutarch (A.D. 46?-119?), "Sayings of the Spartans: Lysander" (11), *Plutarch on Sparta,* tr. Richard J. A. Talbert, 1988

Your constitution is all sail and no anchor.

THOMAS BABINGTON MACAULAY (1800–1859). On the U.S. Constitution, letter to Henry Stephens Randall, 23 May 1857

The people made the constitution, and the people can unmake it. It is the creature of their own will, and lives only by their will.

JOHN MARSHALL (1755–1835). *Cohens v. Virginia,* 1821

A Constitution is a thing *antecedent* to a Government, and a Government is only the creature of a Constitution. The Constitution of a country is not the act of its Government, but of the people constituting a Government.

THOMAS PAINE (1737–1809). *The Rights of Man,* 1, 1791

There is a higher law than the Constitution.

WILLIAM H. SEWARD (1801–1872). Senate speech, 11 March 1850

Frame constitutions of government with what wisdom and foresight we may, they must be imperfect, and leave something to discretion, and much to public virtue.

JOSEPH STORY (1779–1845). Address to the Suffolk Bar (New York), 4 September 1821

Arbitrary power and the rule of the Constitution cannot both exist. They are antagonistic and incompatible forces; and one or the other must of necessity perish whenever they are brought in conflict.

GEORGE SUTHERLAND. *Jones v. Securities & Exchange Commission,* 1936

Constitutions are checks upon the hasty action of the majority. They are the self-imposed restraints of a whole people upon a majority of them to secure sober action and a respect for the rights of the minority.

WILLIAM HOWARD TAFT (1857–1930). In vetoing the Arizona Enabling Act, 22 August 1911

I have never been more struck by the good sense and the practical judgment of the Americans than in the manner in which they elude the numberless difficulties resulting from their Federal Constitution.

ALEXIS de TOCQUEVILLE (1805–1859). *Democracy in America,* 1.8, 1835, tr. Henry Reeve and Francis Bowen, 1862

The basis of our political systems is the right of the people to make and alter their constitutions of government. But the constitution which at any time exists, until changed by an explicit and authentic act of the whole people, is sacredly obligatory upon all.

GEORGE WASHINGTON (1732–1799). *Farewell Address,* 17 September 1796

CONSUMERISM

See also • Materialism ○ Merchants & Customers ○ Possessions ○ Property ○ Values ○ Wealth

In a consumer society there are inevitably two kinds of slaves: the prisoners of addiction and the prisoners of envy.
> IVAN ILLICH (1926–). *Tools for Conviviality,* 3, 1973

The world has the wealth and resources to provide everyone the opportunity to live a decent life. We consume too much when market relationships displace the bonds of community, compassion, culture, and place. We consume too much when consumption becomes an end in itself and makes us lose affection and reverence for the natural world.
> MARK SAGOFF. Closing paragraph, "Do We Consume Too Much?" *Atlantic,* June 1997

The issue [of consumerism] is deeper than greed and selfishness. Material consumption—buying and possessing things—has become the primary way of belonging in America and around the world. If we can't buy, if we can't consume, we simply can't belong.
> JIM WALLIS (1948–). *The Soul of Politics: A Practical and Prophetic Vision for Change,* 7, 1994

The world is too much with us; late and soon,
Getting and spending, we lay waste our powers.
> WILLIAM WORDSWORTH (1770–1850). Opening lines, "The World Is Too Much with Us; Late and Soon," 1807

❦

I Shop, Therefore I Am.
> ANONYMOUS (AMERICAN). Bumper sticker. In Jim Wallis, *The Soul of Politics: A Practical and Prophetic Vision for Change,* 1, 1994
> See Resistance: James W. Douglass ○ Thinking: Descartes

CONTEMPLATION

See also • Action & Thought: Henri Amiel (1) ○ Exploitation: Henry David Thoreau ○ Meditation ○ Mysticism ○ Reflection ○ Spirituality ○ Thinking ○ Yoga ○ Zen

Contemplation is the highest form of activity.
> ARISTOTLE (384–322 B.C.), *Nicomachean Ethics,* 10.7, tr. J. A. K. Thomson, 1953

Contemplation is that condition of alert passivity in which the soul lays itself open to the divine Ground within and without, the immanent and transcendent Godhead.
> ALDOUS HUXLEY (1894–1963). *The Perennial Philosophy,* 16, 1946

Right action is the means by which the mind is prepared for contemplation.
> ALDOUS HUXLEY (1894–1963). *The Perennial Philosophy,* 27, 1946

No man who ignores the rights and needs of others can hope to walk in the light of contemplation because his way has turned aside from truth, from compassion, and therefore from God.
> THOMAS MERTON (1915–1968). *New Seeds of Contemplation,* 3, 1961

The poet enters into himself in order to create; the contemplative enters into God in order to be created.
> THOMAS MERTON (1915–1968). *New Seeds of Contemplation,* 13, 1961

Through contemplation, we realize that our own power proves inadequate, and we learn to trust a power that is beyond ourselves.
> JIM WALLIS (1948–). *The Soul of Politics: A Practical and Prophetic Vision for Change,* 8, 1994

CONTEMPT

See also • Hate

Contempt is the sharpest reproof.
> HENRY G. BOHN (1796–1886). Comp., *A Hand-Book of Proverbs,* p. 339, 1860

Contempt is not a thing to be despised.
> EDMUND BURKE (1729–1797). *Letters on a Regicide Peace,* 3, 1795–1797

There is nothing that people bear more impatiently, or forgive less, than contempt; and an injury is much sooner forgotten than an insult.
> LORD CHESTERFIELD (1694–1773). Letter to his son, 9 October 1746

Many can bear Adversity but few Contempt.
> THOMAS FULLER (1654–1734). Comp., *Gnomologia: Adages and Proverbs,* 3340, 1732

Contempt is a dangerous luxury. A man may be a very poor creature, and still have a faculty for mischief.
> JOHN MORLEY (1838–1923). "Robespierre" (2), *Critical Miscellanies,* vol. 1, 1886

Hatred comes from the heart; contempt, from the head.
> ARTHUR SCHOPENHAUER (1788–1860). "Studies in Pessimism: Further Psychological Observations," *Essays of Arthur Schopenhauer,* tr. T. Bailey Saunders, 1851

Contempt is not incompatible with indulgent and kindly treatment, and for the sake of one's own peace and safety, this should not be omitted. . . . But if this pure, cold, sincere contempt ever shows itself, it will be met with the most truculent hatred.
> ARTHUR SCHOPENHAUER (1788–1860). "Studies in Pessimism: Further Psychological Observations," *Essays of Arthur Schopenhauer,* tr. T. Bailey Saunders, 1851

Hatred . . . requires respect for one's opponent; acknowledgment of equal rank is a part of it. One despises beings of lower rank.
> OSWALD SPENGLER (1880–1936). *Aphorisms,* 108, tr. Gisela Koch-Weser O'Brien, 1967

❦

Better feared than despised.
> SAYING

CONVERSATION

See also • Argument ○ Books: Elbert Hubbard (1) ○ Bores: Albert Camus ○ Gossip: Henry David Thoreau ○ Manners: Rules ○ Repartee ○ Silence & Speech ○ Speaking ○ Talking

For parlor use, the vague generality is a life-saver.

GEORGE ADE (1866–1944). "The Wise Piker," *Forty Modern Fables*, 1901

Young Roosevelt is very promising, but I should think he'd wear himself out in the promiscuous and extended contacts he maintains with people. But as I observe him, he seems to clarify his ideas and teach himself as he goes along by that very conversational method.

NEWTON D. BAKER (1871–1937). Secretary of war. On Assistant Secretary of the Navy Franklin D. Roosevelt, 1913–1920. In James MacGregor Burns, *Roosevelt: The Lion and the Fox*, 3, 1956

Conversashun should be enlivened with wit, not compozed ov it.

JOSH BILLINGS (1818–1885). "Sollum Thoughts," *Everybody's Friend, or; Josh Billing's Encyclopedia and Proverbial Philosophy of Wit and Humor*, 1874

See Wit: William Hazlitt

Must we always talk for victory, and never once for truth, for comfort, and joy?

RALPH WALDO EMERSON (1803–1882). Referring to the scrappy conversational style of his friend Henry David Thoreau, journal, 29 February 1856

See Argument: Joseph Joubert

Conversation is the laboratory and workshop of the student.

RALPH WALDO EMERSON (1803–1882). "Clubs," *Society and Solitude*, 1870

In good conversation parties don't speak to the words, but to the meanings of each other.

RALPH WALDO EMERSON (1803–1882). "Social Aims," *Letters and Social Aims*, 1876

The chief ends of conversation are to *inform* or to be *informed*, to *please* or to *persuade*.

BENJAMIN FRANKLIN (1706–1790). 1771, *Autobiography*, 1798

Speak not but what may benefit others or yourself; avoid trifling conversation.

BENJAMIN FRANKLIN (1706–1790). Virtue #2 ("Silence"), 1784, *Autobiography*, 1798

[Albert Einstein] is cheerful, sure of himself and agreeable. He understands as much about psychology as I do about physics, so we had a very pleasant talk.

SIGMUND FREUD (1856–1939). 1926. In Ernest Jones, *The Life and Work of Sigmund Freud*, 29, 1953–1957, abr. 1961

Sir Arthur Conan Doyle is said to have once left a dinner party raving about [Oscar Wilde's] gift as a conversationalist. "But you did all the talking," his companion pointed out. "Exactly!" Conan Doyle said.

STEPHEN FRY. "Playing Oscar," *New Yorker*, 16 June 1997

Believe not all thou hearest, nor speak all thou believest.

THOMAS FULLER (1654–1734). Comp., *Introductio ad Prudentiam*, 323, 1731

Talk little, and Hear much. Reflect alone upon what passed in Company.

THOMAS FULLER (1654–1734). Comp., *Introductio ad Prudentiam*, 1492, 1731

Our companions please us less from the charms we find in their conversation than from those they find in ours.

FULKE GREVILLE (1554–1628). *Maxims, Characters, and Reflections*, p. 40, 1756

The best kind of conversation is that which may be called *thinking aloud*.

WILLIAM HAZLITT (1778–1830). *Characteristics in the Manner of Rochefoucault's Maxims*, 180, 1823

See Friends: Ralph Waldo Emerson (3)

Th' only way t' entertain some folks is t' listen t' em.

KIN HUBBARD (1868–1930). *Abe Martin: Hoss Sense and Nonsense*, p. 76, 1926

Be quick to hear, slow to speak.

JAMES (A.D. 1st cent.). *James* 1:19

When you're talkin', you ain't learnin' nothin'!

SAM JOHNSON (1709–1784). A favorite motto that his son Lyndon later framed and hung on his office wall. In James David Barber, *The Presidential Character: Predicting Performance in the White House*, 4, 1972

That is the happiest conversation where there is no competition, no vanity, but a calm quiet interchange of sentiments.

SAMUEL JOHNSON (1709–1784). 14 April 1775. In James Boswell, *The Life of Samuel Johnson*, 1791

A gossip is one who talks to you about others; a bore is one who talks to you about himself; and a brilliant conversationalist is one who talks to you about yourself.

LISA KIRK (1925–). In *New York Journal American*, 9 March 1954

The true spirit of conversation consists more in bringing out the cleverness of others than in showing a great deal of it yourself.

LA BRUYÈRE (1645–1696). "Of Society and of Conversation" (16), *The Characters*, 1688, tr. Henri van Laun, 1929

One of the reasons why so few people are to be found who seem sensible and pleasant in conversation is that almost everybody is thinking about what he wants to say himself rather than about answering clearly what is being said to him.

LA ROCHEFOUCAULD (1613–1680). *Maxims*, 139, 1665, tr. Leonard Tancock, 1959

Self-confidence adds more to conversation than wit.

LA ROCHEFOUCAULD (1613–1680). *Maxims*, 421, 1665, tr. Louis Kronenberger, 1959

Polite conversation is rarely either.

FRAN LEBOWITZ (1951–). *Social Studies*, 1, 1981

He that knows how to make those he converses with easy, without debasing himself to low and servile Flattery, has found the true Art of living in the World, and being both welcome and valued everywhere.

JOHN LOCKE (1632–1704). *Some Thoughts Concerning Education*, 143, 1693

The study of books is a languishing and feeble activity that gives no heat, whereas discussion teaches and exercises us at the same time.

MONTAIGNE (1533–1592). "Of the Art of Discussion," *Essays*, 1588, tr. Donald M. Frame, 1958

In a conversation, keep in mind that you're more interested in what you have to say than anyone else is.

ANDREW S. ROONE (1919–). "A Penny Saved Is a Waste of Time," *Pieces of My Mind*, 1984

In conversation remember two principles: Think before speak; stop talking before they say, "Enough."

SA'DI (A.D. 1213?–1292). *The Maxims of Sa'di*, 1, tr. Mehdi Nakosteen, 1977

When you fall into a man's conversation, the first thing you should consider is, whether he has a greater inclination to hear you, or that you should hear him.

RICHARD STEELE (1672–1729). In *The Spectator* (English essay series), 49, 26 April 1711

The reason why we have two ears and only one mouth is that we may listen the more and talk the less.

ZENO (335?–263? B.C.). Remark to a jabbering pupil, in Diogenes Laertius (A.D. 3rd cent.), *Lives of Eminent Philosophers*, 7.1, tr. R. D. Hicks, 1925

An ounce of dialogue is worth a pound of monologue.

ANONYMOUS

A single conversation across the table with a wise man is better than ten years' study of books.

SAYING (CHINESE). In Henry Wadsworth Longfellow, *Hyperion*, 1.7, 1839

Who speaks, sows; who listens, reaps.

SAYING (FRENCH)

From listening comes wisdom; from speaking, repentance.

SAYING (ITALIAN)

CONVERSION

See also • Alienation: Eric Hoffer (1) ○ Change ○ Evangelism ○ God ○ Persuasion ○ Redemption ○ Religion ○ Salvation ○ Self-Realization (Becoming)

Sex and the sense of guilt associated with it play a very large part in conversion and religious phenomena generally.

J. A. C. BROWN (1911–1964). *Techniques of Persuasion: From Propaganda to Brainwashing*, 9, 1963

Conversion is likely to have been preceded by some sort of mental conflict since those who are satisfied with themselves are less likely to be converted.

J. A. C. BROWN (1911–1964). *Techniques of Persuasion: From Propaganda to Brainwashing*, 9, 1963

A reciprocal action is . . . required between the conversion of the individual and the reform of the structures.

OSCAR CULLMANN (1902–?). *Jesus and the Revolutionaries*, p. 55, tr. Gareth Putnam, 1970

Is there a spiritual reality, inconceivable to us today, which corresponds in history to the physical reality which Einstein discovered and which led to the atomic bomb? Einstein discovered a law of physical change: the way to convert a single particle of matter into enormous physical energy. Might there not also be, as Gandhi suggested, an equally incredible and [as yet] undiscovered law of spiritual change, whereby a single person or small community of persons could be converted into an enormous spiritual energy capable of transforming a society and a world?

I believe that there is, that there must be, a spiritual reality corresponding to $E=mc^2$ because from the standpoint of creative harmony, the universe is incomplete without it, and because, from the standpoint of moral freedom, humankind is sentenced to extinction without it.

JAMES W. DOUGLASS (1937–). *Lightning East to West*, 1, 1980
See History: Abraham Joshua Heschel (1)

When we come to Christ, he doesn't just patch us up. He renews us. He doesn't just reform us. He transforms us by his power. Conversion is a deep work. It goes throughout our entire beings, throughout our minds, throughout our bodies, throughout our lives—our social lives, our business lives, our family lives, our neighborhood lives. We become partakers of God's nature.

BILLY GRAHAM (1918–). "Are You Sure You Are Converted?" *Decision*, April 1991

When the fruit is ripe, a touch will make it fall.

WILLIAM JAMES (1842–1910). On the conversion process, *The Varieties of Religious Experience: A Study in Human Nature*, 8, 1902

To be converted, to be regenerated, to receive grace, to experience religion, to gain an assurance, are so many phrases which denote the process, gradual or sudden, by which a self hitherto divided, and consciously wrong inferior and unhappy, becomes unified and consciously right superior and happy, in consequence of its firmer hold upon religious realities. This at least is what conversion signifies in general terms, whether or not we believe that a direct divine operation is needed to bring such a moral change about.

WILLIAM JAMES (1842–1910). *The Varieties of Religious Experience: A Study in Human Nature*, 9, 1902

The most characteristic of all the elements of the conversion crisis . . . is the ecstasy of happiness produced.

WILLIAM JAMES (1842–1910). *The Varieties of Religious Experience: A Study in Human Nature*, 10, 1902

Conversion is conversion from a self-centered person to a God-centered person.

E. STANLEY JONES (1884–1973). *Conversion*, 3, 1959

We should not think of conversion as the acceptance of a particular creed, but as a change of heart.

HELEN KELLER (1880–1968). *My Religion*, 6, 1927

The man is changed, no longer himself nor self-belonging; he is merged with the Supreme, sunken into it, one with it: center coincides with center, for on this higher plane things that touch at all are one.

PLOTINUS (A.D. 205–270). *The Enneads*, 6.9.10, tr. Stephen MacKenna and B. S. Page, 1952

The first aspect of conversions: the person emerges from a smaller, limited world of existence into a larger world of being.

> EDWIN DILLER STARBUCK (1866–1947). *The Psychology of Religion: An Empirical Study of the Growth of Religious Consciousness,* 12, 1899

Waking up is a spiritual metaphor for conversion.

> JIM WALLIS (1948–). *The Soul of Politics: A Practical and Prophetic Vision for Change,* 2, 1994

When you get converted, you still have the same personality. You merely exercise it in terms of a different set of values.

> ROBERT PENN WARREN (1905–1989). *All the King's Men,* 8, 1946

I went to America, to convert the Indians; but oh! who shall convert me?

> JOHN WESLEY (1703–1791). English religious leader and founder of Methodism. While returning to England after a two-year stay, journal, 24 January 1738

It is so easy to convert others. It is so difficult to convert oneself.

> OSCAR WILDE (1854–1900). "The Critic as Artist" (2), *Intentions,* 1891

Now as [Saul] journeyed, he approached Damascus, and suddenly a light from heaven flashed about him. And he fell to the ground and heard a voice saying to him, "Saul, Saul, why do you persecute me?" And he said, "Who are you, Lord?" And he said, "I am Jesus, whom you are persecuting; but rise and enter the city, and you will be told what you are to do."

> ANONYMOUS (*BIBLE*). On the conversion of Saul (afterwards known as Paul), *Acts* 9:3–6

Power coerces, knowledge persuades, love converts.

> ANONYMOUS

CONVICTION

See also • Belief ○ Certainty ○ Doubt ○ Faith ○ Fanatics ○ Ideas ○ Ideology: Harold D. Lasswell ○ Presidents: Sidney Warren ○ Skepticism

Conviction . . . is worthless till it convert itself into Conduct.

> THOMAS CARLYLE (1795–1881). *Sartor Resartus: The Life and Opinions of Herr Teufelsdröckh,* 2.9, 1835

The best way to teach that one should be suspicious of everything one holds dear is through the study of brilliant people of the past, who by modern standards are so wrong, and where it is easy to see that their errors were the result of cultural biases of their day.

> STEPHEN JAY GOULD (1941–). In Charles Petit, "A Thinker Who Delights in Discredited Theories," *San Francisco Sunday Examiner & Chronicle,* 14 February 1993

While opinions were arguable, convictions needed shooting to be cured.

> T. E. LAWRENCE (1988–1935). *Seven Pillars of Wisdom: A Triumph,* 33, 1926

The convictions of the mass of mankind run hand in hand with their interests or with their class feelings.

> JOHN STUART MILL (1806–1873). "Reorganization of the Reform Party," *The London and Westminster Review* (English journal), April 1839

Convictions are more dangerous enemies of truth than lies.

> FRIEDRICH NIETZSCHE (1844–1900). *Human, All Too Human,* 483, 1878, tr. Marion Faber, 1984

Our convictions on important matters are not the result of knowledge or critical thought, nor, it may be added, are they often dictated by supposed self-interest. Most of them are *pure prejudices* in the proper sense of that word. We do not form them ourselves. They are the whisperings of "the voice of the herd."

> JAMES HARVEY ROBINSON (1863–1936). *The Mind in the Making: The Relation of Intelligence to Social Reform,* 2, 1921

Human beings are perhaps never more frightening than when they are convinced beyond doubt that they are right.

> LAURENS van der POST (1906–1996). *The Lost World of the Kalahari,* 3, 1958

The strength or weakness of our conviction depends more on our courage than on our intelligence.

> VAUVENARGUES (1715–1747). *Reflections and Maxims,* 318, 1746, tr. F. G. Stevens, 1940

Conviction that yields to fact is not conviction.

> ANONYMOUS

COOLNESS

See also • Confidence ○ Courage ○ Preparedness: Richard M. Nixon ○ Universe: Walt Whitman (2)

The quality that distinguished [Billy the Kid's] courage from that of other brave men lay in a nerveless imperturbability. Nothing excited him. He had nerve but no nerves.

> WALTER N. BURNS. *The Saga of Billy the Kid,* 5, 1926

A man who does not possess himself enough to hear disagreeable things without visible marks of anger and change of countenance, or agreeable ones without sudden bursts of joy and expansion of countenance is at the mercy of every artful knave or pert coxcomb.

> LORD CHESTERFIELD (1694–1773). Letter to his son, 22 May 1749

A strong mind is one which does not lose its balance even under the most violent excitement.

> KARL von CLAUSEWITZ (1780–1831). *On War,* 1.3, 1832, tr. J. J. Graham, 1873

Keep cool: it will be all one a hundred years hence.

> RALPH WALDO EMERSON (1803–1882). "Montaigne; or, The Skeptic," *Representative Men,* 1850

We like cool people, who neither hope nor fear too much, but seem to have many strings to their bow, and can survive the blow well enough if stock should rise or fall, if parties should be broken up, if their money or their family should be dispersed; who can stand a slander very well; indeed on whom events make little or no impression, and who can face death with firmness.

> RALPH WALDO EMERSON (1803–1882). "Aristocracy," *Lectures and Biographical Sketches,* 1883

To bear all naked truths,
And to envisage circumstance, all calm,
That is the top of sovereignty. Mark well!

> JOHN KEATS (1795–1821). "Hyperion: A Fragment," 2.203, 1820

If you can keep your head when all about you are losing theirs, it's just possible you haven't grasped the situation.

> JEAN KERR (1923–). Introduction to *Please Don't Eat the Daisies,* 1957

If you can keep your head when all about you
    Are losing theirs and blaming it on you. . . .

> RUDYARD KIPLING (1865–1936). "If—," *Rewards and Fairies,* 1910

He who doesn't lose his wits over certain things has no wits to lose.

> GOTTHOLD EPHRAIM LESSING (1729–1781). *Emilia Golotti,* 4.7, 1772

It is by presence of mind in untried emergencies that the native metal of a man is tested.

> JAMES RUSSELL LOWELL (1819–1891) "Abraham Lincoln," 1864, *My Study Windows,* 1871

The world belongs to the enthusiast who keeps cool.

> WILLIAM McFEE (1881–1966). *Casuals of the Sea,* 1, 1916

I started high school in 1950. Cool was invented in this period. . . . You never let on what bothered you.

> JACK NICHOLSON (1937–). Fred Schruers interview, *Rolling Stone,* 14 August 1986

The tougher it gets, the cooler I get.

> RICHARD M. NIXON (1913–1994). News conference, Washington, 26 October 1973

[While Edgar Bergen and his puppet Charlie McCarthy were taping a skit for the television program *Laugh-In,* part] of the set fell down behind him. . . . Bergen was so cool, he didn't even turn around to see what had happened. But *Charlie* did turn around! What a genius!

> LILY TOMLIN (1939–). In Liz Smith, "Lily's Ringing Endorsement of Candice," *San Francisco Chronicle,* 26 July 1996

He's as cool as the other side of the pillow.

> WAYNE WALKER. Describing San Francisco 49er quarterback Joe Montana as he ducked an Indianapolis blitz and threw a long touchdown pass to end Jerry Rice, football game radio broadcast, KGO, San Francisco, 10 September 1989. In Herb Caen, column, *San Francisco Chronicle,* 15 September 1989

O to be self-balanced for contingencies,
To confront night, storms, hunger, ridicule, accidents, rebuffs, as the trees and animals do.

> WALT WHITMAN (1819–1892). "Me Imperturbe," 1860, *Leaves of Grass,* 1855–1892

ᵂ

Keep cool, but don't freeze.

> ANONYMOUS

COOPERATION

See also • Competition ○ Self-Interest ○ Service ○ Sharing ○ Success

One hand washes the other; give and take.

> EPICHARMUS (530?–440? B.C.)

One good Turn deserves another.

> THOMAS FULLER (1654–1734). Comp., *Gnomologia: Adages and Proverbs,* 3754, 1732

Cooperation: Doing what I tell you to do, and doing it quick.

> ELBERT HUBBARD (1856–1915). *The Roycroft Dictionary Concocted by Ali Baba and the Bunch on Rainy Days,* p. 31, 1914

Stand with anybody that stands *right.* Stand with him while he is right and *part* with him when he goes wrong.

> ABRAHAM LINCOLN (1809–1865). Speech on the Kansas-Nebraska Act, Peoria (Illinois), 16 October 1854

My brother . . . and I were born to work together, like a man's two hands, feet, or eyelids, or like the upper and lower rows of his teeth.

> MARCUS AURELIUS (A.D. 121–180). *Meditations,* 2.1, tr. Maxwell Staniforth, 1964

Cooperation, like other difficult things, can be learned only by practice: and to be capable of it in great things, a people must be gradually trained to it in small. Now, the whole course of advancing civilization is a series of such training.

> JOHN STUART MILL (1806–1873). "Civilization: Signs of the Times," 1836, *Dissertations and Discussions,* vol. 1, 1859–1875

What prodigious power a large body of men can put forth when they all work at the same task and are greatly interested in it. They begin by the same process, but the process differentiates and improves in their hands. Each gains skill and dexterity. They learn from each other, and the product is multiplied.

> WILLIAM GRAHAM SUMNER (1840–1910). *Folkways: A Study of the Sociological Importance of Usages, Manners, Customs, Mores, and Morals,* 134, 1907

God has . . . ordered things that we may learn to bear one another's burdens; for there is no man without his faults, none without his burden. None is sufficient in himself; none is wise in himself; therefore, we must support one another, comfort, help, teach, and advise one another.

> THOMAS à KEMPIS (1380–1471), *The Imitation of Christ,* 1.16, tr. Leo Sherley-Price, 1952

ᵂ

You scratch my back, and I'll scratch yours.

> SAYING (ENGLISH)

Many hands make light work.

> SAYING (GREEK)

Permit a man to light his fire from yours.

> SAYING (LATIN). In Cicero (106–43 B.C.), *De officiis,* 1.16, tr. Harry G. Edinger, 1974

CORPORATIONS

See also • Bureaucracy ○ Business (Commerce) ○ Capitalism ○ Executives ○ Government ○ Managers ○ Organizations ○ Stock Market ○ Trade (Commerce) ○ Unions

Corporation, *n.* An ingenious device for obtaining individual profit without individual responsibility.

> AMBROSE BIERCE (1842–1914). *The Devil's Dictionary,* p. 25, 1911, Dover edition, 1958

"Corpocracy" [refers] to large-scale corporate America's tendency to be like the government bureaucracy that corporate executives love to malign: bloated, risk-averse, inefficient and unimaginative.

> RICHARD G. DARMAN (1943–). Deputy secretary of the treasury. In Peter T. Kilborn, "Treasury Official Assails 'Inefficient' Big Business," *New York Times,* 8 November 1986

People just starting their careers may think a job is just a job. But when they choose a company, they often choose a way of life.

> TERRENCE E. DEAL and ALLAN A. KENNEDY. *Corporate Cultures: The Rites and Rituals of Corporate Life,* 1, 1982

When all is said and done, a company, its chief executive, and his whole management team are judged by one criterion alone—performance. . . .

Performance is not limited to one quarter's or a year's earning statement. Performance is something that is built into a company for the long haul.

> HAROLD GENEEN (1910–1997) (with ALVIN MOSCOW). *Managing,* 2, 1984
>
> See Managers: Peter F. Drucker (1)

But, sir, I have said I do not dread these corporations as instruments of power to destroy this country, because there are a thousand agencies which can regulate, restrain and control them; but there is a corporation we may all well dread. That corporation is the Federal Government.

> BENJAMIN H. HILL (19th cent.). Georgia senator. Senate speech on the Pacific Railroad funding bill, 27 March 1878
>
> See Business: Wendell Willkie

A corporation does things for one reason—profit.

> DWIGHT JOYCE. Glidden Co. chairman. Quoted in John McDonald, "How Executives Make Decisions." In *Fortune* Editors, eds., *The Executive Life,* 1956

"Simple Form, Lean Staff."

> THOMAS J. PETERS and ROBERT H. WATERMAN, JR. Chapter title, *In Search of Excellence: Lessons from America's Best-Run Companies,* 11, 1982

Concentration of economic power in all-embracing corporations . . . represents private enterprise become a kind of private government which is a power unto itself—a regimentation of other people's money and other people's lives.

> FRANKLIN D. ROOSEVELT (1882–1945). Presidential nomination acceptance speech, Chicago, 27 June 1936

There can be no effective control of corporations while their political activity remains.

> THEODORE ROOSEVELT (1858–1919). "The New Nationalism," speech, Osawatomie (Kansas), 31 August 1910

I cannot believe that our factory system is the best mode by which men may get clothing. The condition of the operatives is becoming every day more like that of the English; and it cannot be wondered at, since, as far as I have heard or observed, the principal object is, not that mankind may be well and honestly clad, but, unquestionably, that the corporations may be enriched.

> HENRY DAVID THOREAU (1817–1862). "Economy," *Walden; or Life in the Woods,* 1854

The public be damned! I'm working for my stockholders.

> WILLIAM HENRY VANDERBILT (1821–1885). Financier. When asked by reporter Clarence Dresser why the public should not be consulted about luxury trains. In *Chicago Daily News,* 8 October 1882

For years I thought that what was good for our country was good for General Motors, and vice versa. The difference does not exist. Our company is too big. It goes with the welfare of the country.

> CHARLES E. WILSON (1890–1961). General Motors president and secretary of defense. Confirmation hearing before the Senate Armed Services Committee, Washington, 15 January 1953 (Popular version: What's good for General Motors is good for the country.)
>
> See Banks: Dudley Nichols

❦

A corporation is just like any natural person, except that it has no pants to kick or soul to damn, and, by God, it ought to have both!

> ANONYMOUS (AMERICAN)

CORRUPTION

See also • Cheating ○ Crime ○ Evil ○ Government ○ Honesty ○ Integrity ○ Knaves ○ Lying ○ Machiavellianism ○ Morality ○ Politicians, Corrupt ○ Politics ○ Theft

Everybody's negotiable.

> MUHAMMAD ALI (1942–)

To preserve liberty by new laws and new schemes of government, whilst the corruption of a people continues and grows, is absolutely impossible.

> LORD BOLINGBROKE (1678–1751). *The Idea of a Patriot King,* p. 38, 1749, ed. Sydney W. Jackman, 1965

Among a people generally corrupt, liberty cannot long exist.

> EDMUND BURKE (1729–1797). Letter to the sheriffs of Bristol (England), 3 April 1777

Corruption is like a ball of snow, when once set a rolling it must increase.

> C. C. COLTON (1780–1832). *Lacon: or, Many Things in Few Words; Addressed to Those Who Think,* 2.6, 1824

Sell not virtue to purchase wealth, nor Liberty to purchase power.

> BENJAMIN FRANKLIN (1706–1790). *Poor Richard's Almanack,* May 1738

In this age, when it is said of a man, "He knows how to live," it may be implied he is not very honest.

> MARQUESS OF HALIFAX (1633–1695). "Of Cunning and Knavery," *Political, Moral and Miscellaneous Reflections,* 1750

From the least to the greatest of them,
    everyone is greedy for unjust gain;
and from prophet to priest,
    everyone deals falsely.

JEREMIAH (7th cent. B.C.). *Jeremiah* 6:13-15

Praise [and] money, the two powerful corrupters of mankind.

> SAMUEL JOHNSON (1709–1784). Letter to Mrs. Thale, autumn 1783. In James Boswell, *The Life of Samuel Johnson*, 1791

Corruption comes by degrees.

> JUVENAL (A.D. 60?–127?). *Satires*, 2.84, tr. Peter Green, 1967

People who don't want anything worry me. The price isn't right.

> HAROLD L. LINDSAY and RUSSEL CROUSE. *The State of the Union* (film), 1948, spoken by Adolphe Menjou

An evil-disposed citizen cannot affect any changes for the worse in a republic, unless it be already corrupt.

> MACHIAVELLI (1469–1527). *The Discourses*, 3.8, 1517, tr. Christian E. Detmold, 1940

Corruption is never an individual act. It always involves groups of people bound by one fundamental rule of association: an exchange of favors. This collective corruption is founded on traditional morality, well-established friendships and the opportunity at hand. It allows crimes to be practiced with impunity and is characterized by an intolerable arrogance.

> ROBERTO da MATTA. "Is Brazil Hopelessly Corrupt?" *New York Times*, 13 December 1993

All those men have their price.

> SIR ROBERT WALPOLE (1676–1745). In William Coxe, *Memoirs of the Life and Administration of Sir Robert Walpole, Earl of Orford*, 64, 1798
>
> See Integrity: Carl Sandburg

Few men have [enough] virtue to withstand the highest bidder.

> GEORGE WASHINGTON (1732–1799). Letter to Maj. Gen. Robert Howe, 17 August 1799

COUNTRY

See also • Corporations: Charles E. Wilson ○ Nations ○ Patriotism ○ States

What pity is it
That we can die but once to serve our country!

> JOSEPH ADDISON (1672–1719). *Cato*, 4.4, 1713

There is no greater sign of a general decay of virtue in a nation than a want of zeal in its inhabitants for the good of their country.

> JOSEPH ADDISON (1672–1719). *The Freeholder*, 5, 1716

What rascals we should be if we did for ourselves what we do for our country.

> CONTE CAMILLO BENSO di CAVOUR (1810–1861). Italian statesman

"My country, right or wrong" is a thing that no patriot would think of saying, except in a desperate case. It is like saying "My mother, drunk or sober."

> G. K. CHESTERTON (1874–1936). "Defence of Patriotism," *The Defendant*, 1901

Our country: in her intercourse with foreign nations, may she always be in the right; but our country, right or wrong!

> STEPHEN DECATUR (1779–1820). A dinner toast to America, Norfolk (Virginia), April 1816. In Alexander Slidell Mackenzie, *Life of Stephen Decatur: A Commodore in the Navy of the United States*, 14, 1848

There has never been any country at every moment so virtuous and so wise that it has not sometimes needed to be saved from itself.

> HAVELOCK ELLIS (1859–1939). *The Task of Social Hygiene*, 10, 1913

I only regret that I have but one life to lose for my country.

> NATHAN HALE (1755–1776). Attributed last words before being hanged by the British as a spy during the Revolutionary War, 22 September 1776
>
> See San Francisco: Herb Caen (2)

In every country the sun rises in the morning.

> GEORGE HERBERT (1593–1633). Comp., *Outlandish Proverbs*, 621, 1640

It is now the moment when by common consent we pause to become conscious of our national life and to rejoice in it, to recall what our country has done for each of us, and to ask ourselves what we can do for our country in return.

> OLIVER WENDELL HOLMES, JR. (1841–1935). Memorial Day address, Keene, New Hampshire, 30 May 1884

If any of you meets his fate and stops an arrow or a spear, well, let him die. He will have fallen for his country, and that is no dishonorable death.

> HOMER (8th? cent. B.C.). *The Iliad*, 15.495, tr. E. V. Rieu, 1950

For country 'tis a sweet and seemly thing
To die.

> HORACE (65–8 B.C.). *Odes*, 3.2, *The Complete Works of Horace*, ed. Casper J. Kraemer, Jr., 1936

And so, my fellow Americans: ask not what your country can do for you—ask what you can do for your country.
  My fellow citizens of the world: ask not what America will do for you, but what together we can do for the freedom of man.

> JOHN F. KENNEDY (1917–1963). *Inaugural Address*, 20 January 1961
>
> See School: George St. John

How hard, oh, how hard it is to die and leave one's country no better than if one had never lived for it!

> ABRAHAM LINCOLN (1809–1865). Remark to the writer. Quoted in William H. Herndon, letter to Ward H. Lamon, 6 March 1866. In Emanuel Hertz, ed., *The Hidden Lincoln: From the Letters and Papers of William H. Herndon*, 1.2, 1940

Where the very safety of the country depends upon the resolution to be taken, no considerations of justice or injustice, humanity or cruelty, nor of glory or of shame, should be allowed to prevail. But putting all other considerations aside, the only question should be, "What course will save the life and liberty of the country?"

> MACHIAVELLI (1469–1527). *The Discourses*, 3.41, 1517, tr. Christian E. Detmold, 1940
>
> See Nations: Murray Kempton

Whenever you hear a man speak of his love for his country, it is a sign that he expects to be paid for it.

> H. L. MENCKEN (1880–1956). *A Mencken Chrestomathy*, 30 ("The Mind of Man"), 1949

Our country is wherever we are well off.

> JOHN MILTON (1608–1674). Letter to P. Heinbach, 15 August 1666

The love of country is the highest virtue of civilized man.

> NAPOLEON (1769–1821). 14 July 1812, *The Corsican: A Diary of Napoleon's Life in His Own Words*, ed. R. M. Johnston, 1911

To love one's country above all others is in no way incompatible with respecting and wishing well to all others.

> THEODORE ROOSEVELT (1858–1919). "The Two Americas," 20 May 1901, *The Strenuous Life: Essays and Addresses*, 1905
>
> See Patriotism: Albert Schweitzer

Our country, right or wrong; if right, to be kept right; and if wrong, to be set right!

> CARL SCHURZ (1829–1906). Senate speech, 29 February 1872

Breathes there the man, with soul so dead,
Who never to himself hath said,
This is my own, my native land!

> SIR WALTER SCOTT (1771–1832). *The Lay of the Last Minstrel*, 6.1, 1805

Brutus: Who is here so vile that will not love his country?

> SHAKESPEARE (1564–1616). *Julius Caesar*, 3.2.35, 1599

Where liberty is, there is my country.

> ALGERNON SIDNEY (1622–1683)

COURAGE

See also • Boldness ○ Bravery ○ Coolness ○ Courage, Moral ○ Cowardice ○ Danger ○ Daring ○ Defiance ○ Resistance ○ Resolution ○ Self-Realization (Becoming): Carl G. Jung (2) ○ Self-Trust: Anonymous ○ Soldiers: Karl von Clausewitz ○ Valor ○ Victory: Plutarch ○ Victory & Defeat: Scipio Africanus ○ World War II: Chester W. Nimitz ○ Wound: Stephen Crane

The coward has too much fear and too little courage, the rash man too much courage and too little fear.

> ARISTOTLE (384–322 B.C.). *Nichomachean Ethics*, 3.7, tr. J. A. K. Thomson, 1953
>
> See Bravery: Aristotle (1)

The Courage we desire and prize is not the Courage to die decently, but to live manfully.

> THOMAS CARLYLE (1795–1881). "Boswell's Life of Johnson," 1832, *Critical and Miscellaneous Essays*, Carey & Hart edition, 1849

The paradox of courage is that a man must be a little careless of his life even in order to keep it.

> G. K. CHESTERTON (1874–1936). "The Methuselahite," *All Things Considered*, 1908

Courage is rightly esteemed the first of human qualities because, as has been said, it is the quality which guarantees all others.

> WINSTON CHURCHILL (1874–1965). "Alfonso XIII," *Great Contemporaries*, 1937
>
> See Humility: St. Augustine ○ Prudence: Edmund Burke ○ Self-Discipline: Adam Smith (2) ○ Self-Respect: John Herschel

The best measure of courage is the fear that is overcome.

> NORMAN F. DIXON (1922–). *On the Psychology of Military Incompetence*, 21, 1976

Courage is the price that Life exacts for granting peace.

> AMELIA EARHART (1897–1937). "Courage." In Mary S. Lovell, *The Sound of Wings: The Life of Amelia Earhart*, l, 1989

Courage charms us because it indicates that a man loves an idea better than all things in the world, that he is thinking neither of his bed, nor his dinner, nor his money, but will venture all to put in act the invisible thought of his mind.

> RALPH WALDO EMERSON (1803–1882). Journal, fall 1859

A great part of courage is the courage of having done the thing before.

> RALPH WALDO EMERSON (1803–1882). "Culture," *The Conduct of Life*, 1860

What a new face courage puts on everything!

> RALPH WALDO EMERSON (1803–1882). "Resources," *Letters and Social Aims*, 1876

To persevere, trusting in what hopes he has,
is courage in a man. The coward despairs.

> EURIPIDES (485?–406 B.C.). *Heracles*, l. 100, tr. William Arrowsmith, 1956

Courage: to bear unflinchingly what heaven sends.

> EURIPIDES (485?–406 B.C.). Slightly modified. *Heracles*, l. 1225, tr. William Arrowsmith, 1956

Courage is a virtue only so far as it is directed by prudence.

> FÉNELON (1651–1715). *Aventures de Télémaque*, bk. 10, 1699

Here comes Courage! that seiz'd the lion absent,
and [ran] away from the present mouse.

> BENJAMIN FRANKLIN (1706–1790). *Poor Richard's Almanack*, May 1736

Fearlessness is the first requisite of spirituality. Cowards can never be moral.

> MOHANDAS K. GANDHI (1869–1948). In *Young India*, 13 October 1921

Courage is contagious. When a brave man takes a stand, the spines of others are often stiffened.

> BILLY GRAHAM (1918–). "A Time for Moral Courage," *Reader's Digest*, July 1964

Few persons have courage to appear as good as they really are.

> J. C. HARE (1795–1855) and A. W. HARE (1792–1834). *Guesses at Truth: Second Series*, p. 491, 1848, Macmillan edition, 1867

Dorothy Parker: Exactly what do you mean by "guts"?
Hemingway: I mean grace under pressure.

> ERNEST HEMINGWAY (1899–1961). Format adapted. In Parker, "The Artist's Reward," *New Yorker*, 30 November 1929

Courage has need of reason, but it is not reason's child; it springs from deeper strata.

> HERMANN HESSE (1877–1962). *Reflections*, 129, ed. Volker Michels, 1974

The greatest test of courage is to bear defeat without losing heart.

> ROBERT G. INGERSOLL (1833–1899). "The Declaration of Independence," lecture

Courage is reckoned the greatest of all virtues; because, unless a man has that virtue, he has no security for preserving any other.

> SAMUEL JOHNSON (1709–1784). 5 April 1775. In James Boswell, *The Life of Samuel Johnson,* 1791

Whatever enlarges hope will exalt courage.

> SAMUEL JOHNSON (1709–1784). "Inch Kenneth," *A Journey to the Western Islands,* 1775

To face despair and not give in to it, that's courage.

> TED KOPPEL (1940–). Charlie Rose television interview, PBS, 29 February 1996

Courage is a sort of endurance of the soul.

> LACHES (475?–418 B.C.). Greek general. In Plato (427?–347 B.C.), *Laches,* 192, tr. Benjamin Jowett, 1894

No man can answer for his courage if he has never been in peril.

> LA ROCHEFOUCAULD (1613–1680). *Maxims,* 616, 1665, tr. Leonard Tancock, 1959

The courage of desperation.

> B. H. LIDDELL HART (1895–1970). "The Illusion of Victory," *Why Don't We Learn from History?* 1944

Because courage consists in transcending normal fears, the highest kind of courage is cold courage; that is to say, courage in which the danger has been fully realized and there is no emotional excitement to conceal the danger.

> WALTER LIPPMANN (1889–1974). *A Preface to Morals,* 11.3, 1929

Fortitude is the Guard and Support of the other Virtues; and without Courage a Man will scarce keep steady to his Duty, and fill up the Character of a truly worthy Man.

> JOHN LOCKE (1632–1704). *Some Thoughts Concerning Education,* 115, 1693

Courage is the ladder on which all the other virtues mount.

> CLARE BOOTHE LUCE (1903–1987). In "Quotable Quotes," *Reader's Digest,* May 1979

There were . . . plenty of toughs in the Army, whose peace of mind came from a certain vacancy which had always passed for courage; in them freedom from fear was the outcome of the slow working of their minds, the torpor of their imagination.

> LORD MORAN. 23 August 1944, *Churchill: Taken from the Diaries of Lord Moran,* 19, 1966

A courageous effort consecrates an unhappy end.

> LEWIS MUMFORD (1895–1990). *The Conduct of Life,* 9.10, 1951

Life shrinks or expands in proportion to one's courage.

> ANAÏS NIN (1903–1977). June 1941, *The Diary of Anaïs Nin,* 1966

Courage [is] a mean between cowardice and rashness, of which the former is a [deficiency], the latter an excess, of the spirited part of the soul.

> PLUTARCH (A.D. 46?–119?). "On Moral Virtue" (6), *Moralia,* 6, tr. W. C. Helmbold, 1939
>
> See Valor: Cervantes

He has more *guts* than brains.

> JOHN RAY (1628–1705). Comp., *A Collection of English Proverbs,* p. 249, 1678

He learned too late that courage and discipline are good things but only if they serve a good cause.

> MANFRED ROMMEL (1929–). Stuttgart mayor. On his father Erwin, one of Germany's best-known World War II generals, appearing on a television news program, NBC, 3 May 1985
>
> See Valor: Shakespeare (2) o Valor: Saying

I know of nothing so potent in its effect on my feelings as an act of courage performed at the right moment on behalf of the weak, unjustly oppressed.

> ROUSSEAU (1712–1778). *Confessions,* 12 (1765), 1781, tr. J. M. Cohen, 1953

Who, full himself of courage, kindles [mine].

> FRIEDRICH von SCHILLER (1759–1805). *The Death of Wallenstein,* 1.4, 1799, tr. Samuel T. Coleridge, 1800

No courage is so bold as that forced by utter desperation.

> SENECA THE YOUNGER (5? B.C.–A.D. 65). "On Mercy" (1.12.5), *Moral Essays,* tr. John W. Basore, 1928

Austria: Courage mounteth with occasion.

> SHAKESPEARE (1546–1616). *King John,* 2.1.82, 1596

I would define true courage to be a perfect sensibility of the measure of danger, and a mental willingness to incur it.

> WILLIAM TECUMSEH SHERMAN (1820–1891). *Memoirs of Gen. W. T. Sherman,* 4th ed., 25, 1891 (1875)

When one professes [courage] too openly, by words or bearing, there is reason to mistrust it.

> WILLIAM TECUMSEH SHERMAN (1820–1891). *Memoirs of Gen. W. T. Sherman,* 4th ed., 25, 1891 (1875)

To be courageous means to be afraid but to go a little step forward anyway.

> BEVERLY SMITH. In Jill Clark, "Becoming Visible: Black Lesbian Conference in New York," *Off Our Backs,* March 1981

What is more mortifying than to feel that you have missed the plum for want of courage to shake the tree?

> LOGAN PEARSALL SMITH (1865–1946). *Afterthoughts,* 1, 1931

Keep your fears to yourself, but share your courage.

> ROBERT LOUIS STEVENSON (1850–1894)

Courage is the peculiar excellence of man, and the Gods help the braver side.

> TACITUS (A.D. 56?–120?). *The History,* 4.17, tr. Alfred J. Church and William J. Brodribb, 1942
>
> See Fortune: Terence o God & Man: Bussy-Rabutin

Courage is resistance to fear, mastery of fear—not absence of fear.

> MARK TWAIN (1835–1910). *The Tragedy of Pudd'nhead Wilson,* 12 (epigraph), 1894

Grow
in your new courage, child; o son of gods
and ancestor of gods, this is the way to scale the stars.

> VIRGIL (70–19 B.C.). *Aeneid,* 9.641, tr. Allen Mandelbaum, 1961

❦

The courageous conquer fear by transcending it.
ANONYMOUS

Without courage the dream dies aborning.
ANONYMOUS

Wealth lost, something lost; honor lost, much lost; courage lost, all lost.
SAYING (GERMAN)

COURAGE, MORAL

See also • Bravery ○ Courage ○ Defiance ○ Mexico: Ulysses S. Grant ○ Valor

Courage is of two kinds: first, physical courage, or courage in the presence of danger to the person; and next, moral courage, or courage before responsibility, whether it be before the judgment seat of external authority, or of the inner power, the conscience.
KARL von CLAUSEWITZ (1780–1831). *On War,* 1.3, 1832, tr. J. J. Graham, 1873

Common experience shows how much rarer is moral courage than physical bravery. A thousand men will march to the mouth of the cannon where one man will dare espouse an unpopular cause.
CLARENCE DARROW (1857–1938). *Resist Not Evil,* 16, 1903

They are trying to send us to prison for speaking our minds. Very well, let them. I tell you that if it had not been for men and women who in the past have had the moral courage to go to prison, we would still be in the jungles.
EUGENE V. DEBS (1855–1926). In Charles A. Madison, "Eugene Victor Debs: Evangelical Socialist," *Critics & Crusaders,* 1948

The rarest and most admirable quality of public life, moral courage.
BENJAMIN DISRAELI (1804–1881). *Coningsby: Or, The New Generation,* 2.4, 1844

Few are willing to brave the disapproval of their fellows, the censure of their colleagues, the wrath of their society. Moral courage is a rarer commodity than bravery in battle or great intelligence. Yet it is the one essential vital quality for those who seek to change a world that yields most painfully to change.
ROBERT F. KENNEDY (1925–1968). In Jeanne Larson and Madge Micheels-Cyrus, comps., *Seeds of Peace,* p. 213, 1986

Moral courage, the courage of one's convictions, the courage to see things through. The world is in a constant conspiracy against the brave. It's the age-old struggle—the roar of the crowd on one side and the voice of your conscience on the other.
DOUGLAS MacARTHUR (1880–1964). On one of the "many things, some of them not within the covers of books written by any man," that he was taught at the United States Military Academy, West Point (New York), public statement, on his 84th and last birthday, 26 January 1964.

Moral courage—not afraid to say or do what you believe to be right.
BERNARD LAW MONTGOMERY (1887–1976). *The Memoirs of Field-Marshal Montgomery,* 33, 1958

As to moral courage, I have rarely met with the two-o'clock-in-the-morning kind: I mean unprepared courage, that which is necessary on an unexpected occasion; and which, in spite of the most unforeseen events, leaves full freedom of judgment and decision.
NAPOLEON (1769–1821). Remark to Emmanuel Las Cases, 1815. In Ralph Waldo Emerson, "Napoleon; or, The Man of the World," *Representative Men,* 1850

COURTESY

See also • Manners

If a man be gracious and courteous to strangers, it shows he is a citizen of the world, and that his heart is no island cut off from other lands, but a continent that joins to them.
FRANCIS BACON (1561–1626). "Of Goodness, and Goodness of Nature," *Essays,* 1625

Every courtesy to an opponent, even to the gallows.
OTTO von BISMARCK (1815–1898). In Albert Carr, *Juggernaut: The Path of Dictatorship,* 4, 1939

Full of courtesy, and full of craft.
JOHN CLARKE (1596–1658). Comp., *Proverbs: English and Latine,* p. 13, 1639

The first point of courtesy must always be truth.
RALPH WALDO EMERSON (1803–1882). "Manners," *Essays: Second Series,* 1844

Life is not so short but that there is always time enough for courtesy.
RALPH WALDO EMERSON (1803–1882). "Social Aims," *Letters and Social Aims,* 1876

Pluck not a Courtesy in the Bud before it is ripe.
THOMAS FULLER (1654–1734). Comp., *Gnomologia: Adages and Proverbs,* 3889, 1732

The greater man the greater courtesy.
ALFRED, LORD TENNYSON (1809–1892). "The Last Tournament" (l. 628), *The Idylls of the King,* 1859-1885

❦

Too much courtesy is discourtesy.
SAYING (JAPANESE)

The small courtesies sweeten life; the greater, ennoble it.
SAYING (MINNESOTA)

COWARDICE

See also • Courage ○ Excuses: George Bernard Shaw ○ Fear ○ Violence: Mohandas K. Gandhi (1)

Coward, *n.* One who in a perilous emergency thinks with his legs.
AMBROSE BIERCE (1842–1914). *The Devil's Dictionary,* p. 25, 1911, Dover edition, 1958

To stay is no wise action, when there's more reason to fear than to hope.

CERVANTES (1547–1616). *Don Quixote,* 1.3.9, 1615, tr. Peter Anthony Motteux and John Ozell, 1743

To see what is right and not to do it is want of courage.

CONFUCIUS (551–479 B.C.). *Confucian Analects,* 2.24, tr. James Legge, 1930

Everything is in our own hands; only through sheer cowardice will it slip through our fingers.

FYODOR DOSTOYEVSKI (1821–1881). *Crime and Punishment,* 1.1, 1866

God will not have his work made manifest by cowards.

RALPH WALDO EMERSON (1803–1882). Journal, 13 January 1833
See Revelation: Emerson (2)

Many would be Cowards if they had Courage enough.

THOMAS FULLER (1654–1734). Comp., *Gnomologia: Adages and Proverbs,* 3366, 1732

He was just a coward and that was the worst luck any man could have.

ERNEST HEMINGWAY (1899–1961). *For Whom the Bell Tolls,* 30, 1940

Cowardice . . . is almost always simply a lack of ability to suspend the functioning of the imagination.

ERNEST HEMINGWAY (1899–1961). Introduction to *Men at War,* 1942

I [would not be] in the least afraid of committing an act of cowardice if it were useful to me.

NAPOLEON (1769–1821). Remark to Talleyrand, 1813, *The Mind of Napoleon: A Selection from His Written and Spoken Words,* 202, ed. J. Christopher Herold, 1955

All men are afraid in battle. The coward is the one who lets his fear overcome his sense of duty.

GEORGE S. PATTON, JR. (1885–1945). In Charles M. Province, *The Unknown Patton,* p. 168, 1983

The timid man sees dangers that do not exist.

PUBLIUS SYRUS (85–43 B.C.). *Moral Sayings,* 668, tr. Darius Lyman, Jr., 1862

Cowardice is the unpardonable sin.

THEODORE ROOSEVELT (1858–1919). Quoted in *The American Experience,* television documentary series, PBS, fall 1996

Falstaff: A plague [on] all cowards.

SHAKESPEARE (1546–1616). *Henry IV,* Part I, 2.4.172, 1597

The human race is a race of cowards; and I am not only marching in that procession but carrying a banner.

MARK TWAIN (1835–1910). Epigraph, *Mark Twain in Eruption: Hitherto Unpublished Pages about Men and Events,* ed. Bernard DeVoto, 1940

❦

Man with heart of chicken must have legs of cheetah.

ANONYMOUS

I'd rather have them say "There he goes" than "Here he lies."

SAYING (AMERICAN)

Better a coward for a minute than dead for the rest of your life.

SAYING (IRISH)

The coward is always in danger.

SAYING (PORTUGUESE)

CREATIVITY

See also • Architecture ○ Art ○ Artists ○ Creativity: First Person ○ Dance ○ Discovery ○ Dreams ○ Films ○ Genius ○ Ideas ○ Imagination ○ Inspiration ○ Intuition: Arthur Koestler ○ Intuition ○ Invention ○ Inventions ○ Media ○ Music ○ Nonconformity ○ Originality ○ Painting ○ Plagiarism ○ Poetry ○ Poets ○ Progress ○ Revelation ○ Science ○ Sculpture ○ Spirituality ○ Success: Henry A. Kissinger ○ Technology: [especially] Alvin Toffler ○ Television ○ Thinking ○ Thoughts ○ Truth ○ Vision ○ Writers ○ Writing

Creativity is work that goes some place: it is sustained effort toward an ideal.

MICHAEL DRURY. "Of Course You're Creative!" *Glamour,* August 1963

After you have pumped your brains for thoughts and verses, there is a better poetry hinted in whistling a tune on your walk.

RALPH WALDO EMERSON (1803–1882). Journal, 1859, undated

What has been best done in the world—the works of genius—cost nothing. There is no painful effort, but it is the spontaneous flowing of the thought. Shakespeare made his Hamlet as a bird weaves its nest.

RALPH WALDO EMERSON (1803–1882). "Work and Days," *Society and Solitude,* 1870

The delicate muses lose their head if their attention is once diverted. Perhaps if you were successful abroad in talking and dealing with men, you would not come back to your bookshelf and your task. When the spirit chooses you for its scribe to publish some commandment, it makes you odious to men and men odious to you, and you shall accept that loathsomeness with joy. The moth must fly to the lamp, and you must solve those questions though you die.

RALPH WALDO EMERSON (1803–1882). "Inspiration," *Letters and Social Aims,* 1876

The capacity to be puzzled is . . . the premise of all creation, be it in art or in science.

ERICH FROMM (1900–1980). "The Creative Attitude." In Harold H. Anderson, ed., *Creativity and Its Cultivation,* 1959

The Muses love the Morning.

THOMAS FULLER (1654–1734). Comp., *Gnomologia: Adages and Proverbs,* 4681, 1732

When Alexander the Great visited Diogenes and asked whether he could do anything for the famed teacher, Diogenes replied: "Only stand out of my light." Perhaps some day we shall know how to heighten creativity. Until then, one of the best things we can do for creative men and women is to stand out of their light.

JOHN W. GARDNER (1912–)

My counsel is, to force nothing, and rather to trifle and sleep away all unproductive days and hours, than on such days to compose something that will afterwards give no pleasure.

GOETHE (1749–1832). 11 March 1828. In Peter Eckermann,
Conversations with Goethe, 1836–1848, tr. John Oxenford, 1850

If you have a great work in your head, nothing else thrives near it; all other thoughts are repelled, and the pleasure of life itself is for the time lost.

GOETHE (1749–1832). 18 February 1831. In Peter Eckermann,
Conversations with Goethe, 1836–1848, tr. John Oxenford, 1850

Could Hamlet have been written by a committee, or the Mona Lisa painted by a club? Could the New Testament have been composed as a conference report? Creative ideas do not spring from groups. They spring from individuals. The divine spark leaps from the finger of God to the finger of Adam, whether it takes ultimate shape in a law of physics or a law of the land, a poem or a policy, a sonata or a mechanical computer.

A. WHITNEY GRISWOLD (1906–1963). Baccalaureate address, Yale University, New Haven (Connecticut), 9 June 1957

Proximity to the crowd, to the majority view, spells the death of creativity. For a soul can create only when alone, and some are chosen for the flowering that takes place in the dark avenues of the night.

ABRAHAM JOSHUA HESCHEL (1907–1972). *A Passion for Truth*, 6, 1973

Creative achievements make such enormous claims upon the working power of the individual that any waste of that power on work that is easily obtainable from other sources would constitute a danger to the achievements of the individual. It is quite unnecessary that we should hew every stone with our own hands, or carve the beam we need ourselves; in short, that we should insist on producing everything out of our own resources. Nor is there any need for us to sit and wait, inactively, until an unexpected lucky coincidence presents us with a fruitful thought. Indeed, we can—by our conscious efforts—prepare its appearance.

ALFRED HOCK (1869?–). Closing words, *Reason and Genius: Studies in Their Origin*, 1960

Discontent is at the root of the creative process: . . . the most gifted members of the human species are at their creative best when they cannot have their way, and must compensate for what they miss by realizing and cultivating their capacities and talents.

ERIC HOFFER (1902–1983). *The Ordeal of Change*, 6, 1964

See Discontent: Hoffer

In animals, action follows on perception mechanically with almost chemical swiftness and certainty, but in man there is an interval of faltering and groping; and this interval is the seedbed of the images, ideas, dreams, aspirations, irritations, longings, and forebodings which are the warp and woof of the creative process.

ERIC HOFFER (1902–1983). *The Ordeal of Change*, 15.6, 1964

To be fertile in hypotheses is the first requisite [of creativity], and to be willing to throw them away the moment experience contradicts them is the next.

WILLIAM JAMES (1842–1910). "Great Men and Their Environment," 1880, *Will to Believe: And Other Essays in Popular Philosophy*, 1897

See Theories: Charles Darwin

The primordial experience is the source of [creativity]. . . . In itself it offers no words or images, for it is a vision seen "as in a glass,

darkly." It is merely a deep presentiment that strives to find expression. It is like a whirlwind that seizes everything within reach and, by carrying it aloft, assume a visible shape.

CARL G. JUNG (1875–1961). *Modern Man in Search of a Soul*, 8.1, tr. W. S. Dell and Cary F. Baynes, 1933

True creativity is characterized by a succession of acts each dependent on the one before and suggesting the one after.

EDWIN H. LAND (1909–1991). Inventor and founder of the Polaroid Corp.

It often happens that things come into the mind in a more finished form than could have been achieved after much study.

LA ROCHEFOUCAULD (1613–1680). *Maxims*, 101, 1665, tr. Leonard Tancock, 1959

The creative process takes its own course. If it did otherwise, it would not be creative.

P. W. MARTIN (1893–?). *Experiment in Depth: A Study of the Work of Jung, Eliot and Toynbee*, 12, 1955

The best work is done with the heart breaking, or overflowing.

MIGNON McLAUGHLIN (1915–). *The Neurotic's Notebook*, 4, 1963

Arts and sciences are not cast in a mold, but are formed and perfected by degrees, by others handling and polishing, as bears leisurely lick their cubs into form.

MONTAIGNE (1533–1592). *Essays*, 1588

One must have chaos in one, to give birth to a dancing star.

FRIEDRICH NIETZSCHE (1844–1900). "Zarathustra's Prologue" (5), *Thus Spoke Zarathustra*, 1892, tr. R. J. Hollingdale, 1961

Poets deal largely in simile and metaphor, those seemingly unlikely verbal analogies that can express a truth deeper than the words themselves. Paradigm shifts that spark scientific revolutions start with someone making a connection between ideas that the intellectual establishment supposes to be unrelated. Of course, creativity is not just making any old "unlikely" analogy. The trick lies in recognizing just the *right* analogy out of the multitude of potential analogies. How the mind does that is the true mystery.

WILLIAM POUNSTONE. "Welcome to the Digital Ant Farm," *New York Times Book Review*, 12 March 1995

Knowing a lot . . . is a springboard to creativity.

CHARLIE ROSE. Television interviewer. *The Charlie Rose Show*, PBS, 4 August 1994

Mentally, fallow is as important as seedtime. Even bodies can be exhausted by overcultivation.

GEORGE BERNARD SHAW (1856–1950). *The Intelligent Woman's Guide to Socialism, Capitalism, Sovietism and Fascism*, 81, 1928

The motive force which impels a man or woman to embark upon the hazardous, often unrewarding task of endeavoring to make coherence out of the external world or out of their own inner selves often originates from alienation and despair.

ANTHONY STORR (1920–). *Churchill's Black Dog, Kafka's Mice, and Other Phenomena of the Human Mind*, 12, 1988

In order to create there must be a dynamic force, and what force is more potent than love?

IGOR STRAVINSKY (1882–1971). *An Autobiography*, 5, 1936

[The] first stage [of the creative process] is *Preparation,* in which the subject is consciously pondered and studied from every angle. The second stage is *Incubation,* in which conscious thought is abandoned, but during which some scanning and sorting process is going on unconsciously from which the new solution will emerge. The third stage is *Illumination,* in which the new solution appears. The fourth stage is *Verification,* in which the new solution is subjected to rigorous examination and, where possible, objective testing and replication by others.

> GRAHAM WALLAS (1858–1932). As summarized by Anthony Storr, *Feet of Clay: Saints, Sinners, and Madmen: A Study of Gurus,* 9, 1996

Periods of tranquillity are seldom prolific of creative achievement. Mankind has to be stirred up.

> ALFRED NORTH WHITEHEAD (1861–1947). 2 November 1940, *Dialogues of Alfred North Whitehead,* rec. Lucien Price, 1954

Creativity advances through works that bring about the artist's continuing self-creation.

> GARRY WILLS (1934–). *Confessions of a Conservative,* 19, 1979

❦

The freedom to make mistakes provides the best environment for creativity.

> ANONYMOUS

CREATIVITY: FIRST PERSON

See also • Artists ○ Creativity ○ Dreams: Examples ○ Poets ○ Revelations ○ Science ○ Spirituality: First Person ○ Writers

Young admirer: Papa Bach, how do you manage to think of all these new tunes?
Bach: My dear fellow, I have no need to think of them. I have the greatest difficulty not to step on them when I get out of bed in the morning and start moving around my room.

> JOHANN SEBASTIAN BACH (1685–1750). Format adapted. In Laurens van der Post, "The Vigil and the Summons," *Jung and the Story of Our Time,* 1975

I have written this Poem from immediate Dictation, twelve or sometimes twenty or thirty lines at a time, without Premeditation and even against my Will; the Time it has taken in writing was thus render'd Non Existent, and an immense Poem Exists which seems to be the Labor of a long life, all produc'd without Labor or Study.

> WILLIAM BLAKE (1757–1827). Letter to his patron Thomas Butts, 25 April 1803

I may praise [the Poem], since I dare not pretend to be any other than the Secretary; the Authors are in Eternity.

> WILLIAM BLAKE (1757–1827). Letter to his patron Thomas Butts, 25 April 1803

The idea is like the seed corn; it grows imperceptibly in secret. When I have invented or discovered the beginning of a song . . . , I shut up the book and go for a walk or take up something else; I think no more of it for perhaps half a year. Nothing is lost, though. When I come back to it again, it has unconsciously taken a new shape, and is ready for me to begin working at it.

> JOHANNES BRAHMS (1833–1897). German composer. In Anthony Storr, *Churchill's Black Dog, Kafka's Mice, and Other Phenomena of the Human Mind,* 12, 1988

I know that creation is an intellectual and bodily discipline, a school of energy. I have never achieved anything in anarchy or physical slackness.

> ALBERT CAMUS (1913–1960). "Three Interviews" (3), 1959, *Lyrical and Critical Essays,* tr. Ellen Conroy Kennedy, 1968

At no time am I a quick thinker or writer: whatever I have done in science has solely been by long pondering, patience and industry.

> CHARLES DARWIN (1809–1882). Letter to Dr. F. E. Abbott, 16 November 1871. In *The Autobiography of Charles Darwin and Selected Letters,* 3, ed. Francis Darwin, 1892

I keep from thirty to forty large portfolios, in cabinets with labeled shelves, into which I can at once put a detached reference or memorandum. I have bought many books, and at their ends I make an index of all the facts that concern my work; or, if the book is not my own, write out a separate abstract, and of such abstracts I have a large drawer full. Before beginning on any subject I look to all the short indexes and make a general and classified index, and by taking the one or more proper portfolios I have all the information collected during my life ready to use.

> CHARLES DARWIN (1809–1882). 1 May 1881, *The Autobiography of Charles Darwin and Selected Letters,* 2, ed. Francis Darwin, 1892

May I not be forgiven for thinking it is a wonderful testimony to my being made for art, that when in the midst of this trouble and pain I sit down to my book, some beneficent power shows it all to me and tempts me to be interested, and I don't invent it—really do not—but *see it* and write it down?

> CHARLES DICKENS (1812–1870). Letter to his biographer John Forster. In J. F. Nisbet, *The Insanity of Genius,* 10, 1893

I don't even consider that I wrote it when I got done. . . . The song was there before me, before I came along. I just sorta came down and just sorta took it down with a pencil, but it was all there before I came around.

> BOB DYLAN (1941–)

M. A. Rosanoff: Mr. Edison, please tell me what laboratory rules you want me to observe.
Edison: Hell! there *ain't* no rules around here! We're trying to accomplish somep'n!

> THOMAS ALVA EDISON (1847–1931). In Rosanoff, "Edison in His Laboratory" (1), *Harper's,* September 1932

If there is such a thing as luck, then *I* must be the most unlucky fellow in the world. I've never once made a lucky strike in all my life. When I get after something that I need, I start finding everything in the world that I *don't* need—one damn thing after another. I find ninety-nine things that I don't need, and then comes number one hundred, and that—at the very last—turns out to be just what I had been looking for.

> THOMAS ALVA EDISON (1847–1931). Remarks to the author. In M. A. Rosanoff, "Edison in His Laboratory" (4), *Harper's,* September 1932

Give me bareness and poverty, so that I know them as the sure signs of the coming muse. . . . The solitude of the body is the populousness of the soul.

RALPH WALDO EMERSON (1803–1882). Journal, 1845, undated

Finally, two days ago I succeeded, not on account of my painful efforts, but by the Grace of God. Like a sudden flash of lightning, the riddle happened to be solved. I myself cannot say what was the conducting thread which connected what I previously knew with what made my success possible.

> CARL FRIEDRICH GAUSS (1777–1855). German mathematician and astronomer. Referring to a long-standing problem he had just solved. In Anthony Storr, *Churchill's Black Dog, Kafka's Mice, and Other Phenomena of the Human Mind*, 12, 1988

My work is hardly getting ahead at all, and will not progress any better so long as I am not convinced that I am writing a masterpiece.

> ANDRÉ GIDE (1869–1951). Journal, 8 August 1905, tr. Justin O'Brien, 1948

It has often happened that I have had a sheet of paper before me all aslant, and I have not discovered it till all has been written, or I have found no room to write anymore. [I have written] this little work almost unconsciously, like a sleepwalker.

> GOETHE (1749–1832). On writing The Sorrows of Young Werther (1774), *Dichtung und Wahrheit*, 1822

Nothing will change the fact that I cannot produce the least thing without absolute solitude.

> GOETHE (1749–1832). In Alfred Hock, *Reason and Genius: Studies in Their Origin*, 2.3.1, 1960

When my work does not advance, I return into the oratory with my rosary, say an *Ave;* immediately ideas come to me.

> FRANZ JOSEPH HAYDN (1732–1809). Austrian composer. In Cesare Lombroso, *The Man of Genius*, 1.2, 1888, ed. Havelock Ellis, 1896

Out of my own great woe
I make my little songs.

> HEINRICH HEINE (1797–1856). German poet. "Out of My Own Great Woe"

When I compose I sit down to the piano, shut my eyes, and play what I hear.

> ERNST THEODOR AMADEUS HOFFMANN (1776–1822). German composer. In Cesare Lombroso, *The Man of Genius*, 1.2, 1888, ed. Havelock Ellis. 1896

As I went along, thinking of nothing in particular, only looking at things around me and following the progress of the seasons, there would flow into my mind, with sudden and unaccountable emotion, sometimes a line or two of verse, sometimes a whole stanza at once, accompanied, not preceded, by a vague notion of the poem which they were destined to form part of. Then there would usually be a lull of an hour or so, then perhaps the spring would bubble up again.

> A. E. HOUSMAN (1859–1936). Lecture, University of Cambridge (England), 9 March 1933, *The Name and Nature of Poetry*, pp. 48–49, 1933

When walking along the street, thinking of the blue sky or the fine spring weather, I may either smile at some preposterously grotesque whim which occurs to me, or I may suddenly catch an intuition of the solution of a long-unsolved problem, which at that moment was far from my thoughts. Both notions are shaken out of the same reservoir. . . . The grotesque conceit perishes in a moment, and is forgotten. The scientific hypothesis arouses in me a fever of desire for verification. I read, write, experiment, consult experts. Everything corroborates my notion, which being then published in a book spreads from review to review and from mouth to mouth, till at last there is no doubt I am enshrined in the Pantheon of great diviners of nature's ways. The environment *preserves* the conception which it was unable to *produce* in any brain less idiosyncratic than my own.

> WILLIAM JAMES (1842–1910). "Great Men and Their Environment," 1880, *Will to Believe: And Other Essays in Popular Philosophy,* 1897

Chance furnishes me what I need. I am like a man who stumbles along; my foot strikes something, I bend over and it is exactly what I want.

> JAMES JOYCE (1882–1941)

All my writings may be considered tasks imposed from within, their source was a fateful compulsion. What I wrote were things that assailed me from within myself. I permitted the spirit that moved me to speak out.

> CARL G. JUNG (1875–1961). *Memories, Dreams, Reflections,* 7, ed. Aniela Jaffé, 1962
>
> See Artists: Jung

Far from all disturbances, suffering too a little from melancholy, I throw myself into my work on a tremendous scale.

> SÓREN KIERKEGAARD (1813–1855). Journal, 1848, tr. Alexander Dru, 1938

Part of my function as a writer is to dream awake. And that usually happens. If I sit down to write in the morning, in the beginning of that writing session and the ending of that session, I'm aware that I'm writing. I'm aware of my surroundings. It's like shallow sleep on both ends, when you go to bed and when you wake up. But in the middle, the world is gone and I'm able to see better.

> STEPHEN KING (1947–). "Stephen King." In Naomi Epel, ed., *Writers Dreaming,* 1993

Everything vanishes around me, and works are born as if out of the void. Ripe, graphic fruits fall off. My hand has become the obedient instrument of a remote will.

> PAUL KLEE (1879–1940). Swiss artist. Diary, January–February 1918, ed. Felix Klee, 1964

Songwriting is about getting the demon out of me. It's like being possessed. You try to go to sleep, but the song won't let you. So you have to get up and make it into something, and then you're allowed to sleep. It's always in the middle of the bloody night, or when you're half-awake or tired, when your critical faculties are switched off. So letting go is what the whole game is.

> JOHN LENNON (1940–1980)

Often an idea would occur to me which seemed to have force. . . . I never let one of those ideas escape me, but wrote it on a scrap of paper and put it in that drawer. In that way I saved my best thoughts on the subject, and, you know, such things often come in a kind of intuitive way more clearly than if one were to sit down and deliberately reason them out. To save the results of such mental action is true intellectual economy. . . . Of course, in this instance, I had to arrange the material at hand and adapt it to the particular case presented.

ABRAHAM LINCOLN (1809–1865). Remarks to James F. Wilson, June 1862. In George Iles, ed., *Autobiography, Greatest Americans,* 1924

When the evening comes, I return to the house and go into my study; and at the door I take off my country clothes, all caked with mud and slime, and put on court dress; and, when I am thus decently re-clad I enter into the ancient mansions of the men of ancient days. And there I am received by my hosts with all lovingkindness, and I feast myself on that food which alone is my true nourishment, and which I was born for. And here I am not abashed to speak with these Ancients and to question them on the reasons for their actions. And they, in their humanity, deign to answer me. And so, for four hours long, I feel no gêne, I forget every worry, I have no fear of poverty, I am not appalled by the thought of death: I sink my identity in that of my Ancient mentors. And since Dante says that there can be no science without some retention of that which Thought has once comprehended, I have made notes of the mental capital that I have acquired from their conversation, and have composed an essay *De Principatibus* [i.e., *The Prince*].

MACHIAVELLI (1469–1527). Letter to Francesco Vettori, 10 December 1513. In Arnold J. Toynbee, *A Study of History,* 3.308, 1934

I've been no more than a medium, as it were.

HENRI MATISSE (1869–1954) French artist. In Theodore F. Wolff, "The Drawings of Henri Matisse," *Christian Science Monitor,* 25 March 1985

Like every writer, I am asked where my work originates, and if I knew I would go there more often to find more.

ARTHUR MILLER (1915–). In Bernard Levin, "Honest as her creator's life is long." In *Times* (London), 12 October 1995

I didn't have to think up so much as a comma or a semicolon; it was all given, straight from the celestial recording room. Weary, I would beg for a break, an intermission, time enough, let's say, to go to the toilet or take a breath of fresh air on the balcony. Nothing doing!

HENRY MILLER (1891–1980). On writing *Tropic of Capricorn* (1939), "A Fortune in Francs," *Big Sur and the Oranges of Hieronymous Bosch,* 1957

Philip Roth: How do [you] account for this ability to reconstruct with such passionate exactitude an Irish world you haven't fully lived in for decades. How does your memory keep it alive, why won't this vanished world leave you alone?
O'Brien: At certain times I am sucked back there, and the ordinary world and the present time recede. This recollection, or whatever it is, invades me. It is not something that I can summon up; it simply comes, and I am the servant of it. My hand does the work, and I don't have to think; in fact, were I to think, it would stop the flow. It's like a dam in the brain that bursts.

EDNA O'BRIEN (1931–). Roth interview, "A Conversation with Edna O'Brien: 'The Body Contains the Life Story,'" *New York Times Book Review,* 18 November 1984

It appeared that after first contemplating a book on some subject, and after giving serious preliminary attention to it, I needed a peri-

od of subconscious incubation which could not be hurried and was if anything impeded by deliberate thinking. . . . Having, by a time of very intense concentration, planted the problem in my subconsciousness, it would germinate underground until, suddenly, the solution emerged with blinding clarity, so that it only remained to write down what had appeared as if in a revelation.

BERTRAND RUSSELL (1872–1970). "How I Write," *Portraits from Memory, and Other Essays,* 1956

All I dreamed about Dr. Jekyll was that one man was being pressed into a cabinet, when he swallowed a drug and changed into another being. I awoke and said at once that I had found the missing link for which I had been looking so long, and before I again went to sleep almost every detail of the story, as it stands, was clear to me. Of course, writing it was another thing.

ROBERT LOUIS STEVENSON (1850–1894). Referring to *The Strange Case of Dr Jekyll and Mr Hyde,* interview, New York Herald, 8 September 1887. In Christopher Silvester, ed., *The Norton Book of Interviews: An Anthology from 1859 to the Present Day,* 1996

I did not write it. God wrote it. I merely did his dictation.

HARRIET BEECHER STOWE (1811–1896). Attributed. Referring to *Uncle Tom's Cabin* (1852)

I have been surprised at the observations made by some of my characters. It seems as if an occult Power was moving the pen. The personage does or says something, and I ask, how the dickens did he come to think of that?

WILLIAM MAKEPEACE THACKERAY (1811–1863). In Anthony Storr, *Solitude: A Return to the Self,* 12, 1988

For once you are going to hear a dream, a dream that I have made sound. . . . I dreamt all this: never could my poor head have invented such a thing purposely.

RICHARD WAGNER (1813–1883). Referring to his opera *Tristan und Isolde,* letter to Mathilde Wesendonk. In Alfred Hock, *Reason and Genius: Studies in Their Origin,* 2.1.1, 1960

A master needs quiet. Calm and quiet are his most imperative needs. Isolation and complete loneliness are my only consolation, and my salvation.

RICHARD WAGNER (1813–1883). In Alfred Hock, *Reason and Genius: Studies in Their Origin,* 2.3.1, 1960

When I find myself in this state of inner unrest, no picture, no piece of plastic art has any effect on me. . . . I remain indifferent to all these things; in truth, I am dead to everything that is outside me, I see nothing but my inner visions, and they are crying out for sound, nothing but sound. All I am striving for is to be allowed to follow my inner creative urge, which is as lively as ever.

RICHARD WAGNER (1813–1883). Letter to Mathilde Wesendonk. In Alfred Hock, *Reason and Genius: Studies in Their Origin,* 2.3.1, 1960

CREED

See also • Doctrine ○ Dogma ○ Doubt: Alfred, Lord Tennyson ○ Faith: Abraham Joshua Heschel (1) ○ Ideas ○ Ideology ○ Orthodoxy ○ Principles, Moral ○ Systems ○ Theories

A creed is the shell of a lie.

AMY LOWELL (1874–1925). "Evelyn Ray," *What's O'Clock,* 1925

Creeds, parties, programs of every description have simply flopped, one after another. The only "ism" that has justified itself is pessimism.

GEORGE ORWELL (1903–1950). "The Limit to Pessimism," 25 April 1940, *The Collected Essays, Journalism and Letters of George Orwell,* vol. 1, ed. Sonia Orwell and Ian Angus, 1968

A creed never has force at its command to begin with, and the first steps in the production of a widespread opinion must be taken by means of persuasion alone.

We have thus a kind of seesaw: first, pure persuasion leading to the conversion of a minority; then force exerted to secure that the rest of the community shall be exposed to the right propaganda; and finally a genuine belief on the part of the great majority, which makes the use of force again unnecessary.

BERTRAND RUSSELL (1872–1970). *Power: A New Social Analysis,* 9, 1938

Creeds are at once the outcome of speculation and efforts to curb speculation.

ALFRED NORTH WHITEHEAD (1861–1947). *Adventures of Ideas,* 4.3, 1933

Wherever there is a creed, there is a heretic round the corner or in his grave.

ALFRED NORTH WHITEHEAD (1861–1947). *Adventures of Ideas,* 4.3, 1933

◆

The seed of deed is creed; the seed of creed is need.

ANONYMOUS

CRIME

See also • Assassination ○ Child Abuse ○ Corruption ○ Cruelty ○ Dehumanization ○ Evil ○ Guilt ○ Justice ○ Killing ○ Law ○ Murder ○ Police ○ Prison ○ Punishment ○ Rape ○ Revenge ○ Theft ○ Torture ○ Trials ○ Violence

Before crime is committed, conscience must be corrupted.

HENRI AMIEL (1821–1881). Journal, 30 May 1865, tr. Mrs. Humphrey Ward, 1887

The greatest crimes are caused by excess and not by necessity.

ARISTOTLE (384–322 B.C.). *Politics,* 2.7, tr. Benjamin Jowett, 1885

It is deliberate purpose that constitutes wickedness and criminal guilt.

ARISTOTLE (384–322 B.C.). *Rhetoric,* 1.13, tr. W. Rhys Roberts, 1954 (Popular version: The intention makes the crime.)

Crime is contagious. If the government becomes a lawbreaker, it breeds contempt for law; it invites every man to become a law unto himself; it invites anarchy. To declare that in the administration of the criminal law the end justifies the means—to declare that the government may commit crimes in order to secure the conviction of a private criminal—would bring terrible retribution.

LOUIS D. BRANDEIS (1856–1941). Supreme Court associate justice. In Edward Bennett Williams, *One Man's Freedom,* 7, 1962

How many crimes committed merely because their authors could not endure being wrong!

ALBERT CAMUS (1913–1960). *The Fall,* p. 18, tr. Justin O'Brien, 1956

Everybody calls me a racketeer. I call myself a businessman.

AL CAPONE (1899–1947). In Lewis H. Lapham, *Money and Class in America: Notes and Observations on the Civil Religion,* 4.1, 1988

Great is the mischief of a legal crime.

RALPH WALDO EMERSON (1803–1882). "The Fugitive Slave Law," address, Concord (Massachusetts), 3 May 1851

The Multitude of Offenders is their Protection.

THOMAS FULLER (1654–1734). Comp., *Gnomologia: Adages and Proverbs,* 4680, 1732

Possession of power and riches is a crime under an unjust Government.

MOHANDAS K. GANDHI (1869–1948). In *Young India,* 16 June 1920

The time for the State to protect itself against the criminal is before the criminal is made.

Most criminals are not born; they are MADE. . . .

What the State really punishes in a criminal is its own neglect, its own failure to do its duty to the citizen.

WILLIAM RANDOLPH HEARST (1863–1951). Editorial, *San Francisco Examiner,* 8 April 1926

The repetition of a crime is sometimes part of a device of justification: we do it again and again to convince ourselves and others that it is a common thing and not an enormity.

ERIC HOFFER (1902–1983). *The Passionate State of Mind: And Other Aphorisms,* 117, 1954

The duty to disclose knowledge of crime rests upon all citizens.

ROBERT H. JACKSON (1892–1954). *Stein v. New York,* 1952-1953

One of the biggest lies in the world is that crime doesn't pay. Of course, crime pays.

G. GORDON LIDDY (1930–). In David S. Broder, "Making Moral Judgments Stick," *Washington Post National Weekly Edition,* 10 April 1989

The study of crime begins with the knowledge of oneself.

HENRY MILLER (1891–1980). "The Soul of Anaesthesia," *The Air-Conditioned Nightmare,* 1945

The hero of Kafka's novel, *The Trial,* has no clear idea what he is accused of, or why. All he knows is that he is guilty, of the only crime there is, the essence of all criminality at all times and in all circumstances—being on the losing side.

MALCOLM MUGGERIDGE (1903–1990). *Jesus, The Man Who Lives,* 3, 1975

If crimes and misdemeanors increase, this is proof that misery is on the rise and that society is badly governed.

NAPOLEON (1769–1821). Deathbed statement, 17 April 1821, *The Mind of Napoleon: A Selection from His Written and Spoken Words,* 324, ed. J. Christopher Herold, 1955

San Franciscan Ocie McClure apparently wants to disprove the adage that crime does not pay. He has filed a $5-million suit against a cabdriver who, in May 1989, saw him struggle with a Japanese tourist and run off with her purse. The cabbie, Charles Hollom, chased McClure for several blocks in his car before pinning him against a building, breaking his leg in the process. McClure later negotiated a plea of guilty to second-degree robbery.

> MONICA POWELL. In "That's Outrageous!" ("spotlighting absurdities in our society is the first step toward eliminating them"), *Reader's Digest,* June 1991

A criminal is a person with predatory instincts who has not sufficient capital to form a corporation.

> HOWARD SCOTT

Successful crime goes by the name of virtue.

> SENECA THE YOUNGER (5? B.C.–A.D. 65). *Hercules Furens,* l. 250, tr. Frank Justus Miller, 1917

King Claudius: O, my offense is rank, it smells to heaven.

> SHAKESPEARE (1546–1616). *Hamlet,* 3.3.36, 1600

Anonymous: How could crime be reduced?
Solon: If it caused as much resentment in those who are not its victims as in those who are.

> SOLON (630?–560? B.C.). Format adapted. In Diogenes Laertius (A.D. 3rd cent.), *Lives of Eminent Philosophers,* 1.2, tr. R. D. Hicks, 1925

Starvation, and not sin, is the parent of modern crime.

> OSCAR WILDE (1854–1900). "The Soul of Man Under Socialism," *Fortnightly Review* (British journal), February 1891

Crime doesn't pay—as well as politics.

> ANONYMOUS (AMERICAN). In Sam Roberts, "In Prison, a Fallen Leader Now Talks of Loftier Things," *New York Times,* 24 October 1988

There are only two kinds of criminals: those who get caught and the rest of us.

> ANONYMOUS

It is the same thing to do a thing as not to prohibit it when in your power.

> SAYING (LATIN)

The instigator of a crime is worse than its perpetrator.

> SAYING (LATIN)

Crime unpunished is crime multiplied.

> SAYING

CRISES

See also • Action ∘ Change ∘ Crisis Leaders ∘ Crowds ∘ Cuban Missile Crisis ∘ Danger ∘ Decision-Making ∘ Evolution: [especially] Maria Montessori (1) ∘ Evolution ∘ Fanatics ∘ Greatness ∘ Heroism ∘ History ∘ International Relations ∘ Mass Movements ∘ Mobs ∘ Opportunity ∘ Progress ∘ Revolution ∘ Revolutionary War: Tom Paine (all) ∘ Self-Realization (Becoming): [especially] Henry David Thoreau (1) ∘ Society: T. H. Tawney ∘ Timing ∘ War

Man's extremity is God's opportunity.

> THOMAS ADAMS (16th cent.). *The Works of Thomas Adams,* p. 619, 1629

[Crises are] the accelerations of the historical process.

> JACOB BURCKHARDT (1818–1897). "The Crises of History," 1869. *Force and Freedom: An Interpretation of History,* ed. James H. Nichols, 1943

When the hour and the real cause has come, the infection flashes like an electric spark over hundreds of miles. . . . The message goes through the air, and, in the one thing that counts all men are suddenly of one mind even if only in a blind conviction: *Things must change.*

> JACOB BURCKHARDT (1818–1897). "The Crises of History," 1869, *Force and Freedom: An Interpretation of History,* ed. James H. Nichols, 1943

Every kind of iniquity had its representatives, simple honesty was derided and vanished, and the prevailing tone was one of crude physical violence. . . .
   Men find a sop for their consciences in the realization that the adversary would do the same if he could.

> JACOB BURCKHARDT (1818–1897). "The Crises of History." 1869, *Force and Freedom: An Interpretation of History,* ed. James H. Nichols, 1943

The crisis itself is an expedient of nature, like a fever, and the fanaticisms are signs that there still exist for men things they prize more than life and property.

> JACOB BURCKHARDT (1818–1897). "The Crises of History," 1869, *Force and Freedom: An Interpretation of History,* ed. James H. Nichols, 1943

All spiritual growth takes place by leaps and bounds, both in the individual and, as here, in the community. The crisis is to be regarded as a nexus of growth.

> JACOB BURCKHARDT (1818–1897). "The Crises of History," 1869, *Force and Freedom: An Interpretation of History,* ed. James H. Nichols, 1943

The great liner is sinking in a calm sea. One bulkhead after another gives way; one compartment after another is bilged, the list increases; she is sinking, but the captain and the crew are all in the saloon dancing to the jazz band. But wait till the passengers find out what is their position!

> WINSTON CHURCHILL (1874–1965). House of Commons speech, 26 January 1931

When great causes are on the move in the world, stirring all men's souls, drawing them from their firesides, casting aside comfort, wealth and the pursuit of happiness in response to impulses at once awe-striking and irresistible, we learn that we are spirits, not animals.

> WINSTON CHURCHILL (1874–1965). Radio broadcast, BBC, London, 16 June 1941

Routine becomes of no avail under the swift change of conditions; conventions fall away like dry husks.

> ALBERT EINSTEIN (1879–1955). Speech, Albert Hall, London, October 1933, *Out of My Later Years,* rev. ed., 24, 1956 (1950)

Only through perils and upheavals can Nations be brought to further developments. May the present upheavals lead to a better world.

> ALBERT EINSTEIN (1879–1955). Speech, Albert Hall, London, October 1933, *Out of My Later Years,* rev. ed., 24, 1956 (1950)

All social disturbances and upheavals have their roots in crises of individual self-esteem, and the great endeavor in which the masses most readily unite is basically a search for pride.

ERIC HOFFER (1902–1983). *The Passionate State of Mind: And Other Aphorisms,* 29, 1954

It is only in the depths of crisis and despair that the fear of losing one's personality breeds millennial hopes of rescue: otherwise, complacency prevails.

STANLEY HOFFMANN and INGE HOFFMANN. "The Will to Grandeur: de Gaulle as Political Artist," *Daedalus,* Summer 1968

The amelioration of the world cannot be achieved by sacrifices in moments of crisis; it depends on the efforts made and constantly repeated during the humdrum, uninspiring periods, which separate one crisis from another, and of which normal lives mainly consist.

ALDOUS HUXLEY (1894–1963). "Politics and Religion," *Grey Eminence: A Study in Religion and Politics,* 1941

Permanent crisis justifies permanent control of everybody and everything by the agencies of central government.

ALDOUS HUXLEY (1694–1963). "Over-Population," *Brave New World Revisited,* 1958

Great emergencies and crises show us how much greater our vital resources are than we had supposed.

WILLIAM JAMES (1842–1910). Letter to W. Lutoslawski, 6 May 1906

The nation will listen only if it is a moment of great urgency.

JOHN F. KENNEDY (1917–1963) 1961. In Arthur M. Schlesinger, Jr., *A Thousand Days: John F. Kennedy in the White House,* 27.2, 1965

Every crisis has both its dangers and its opportunities. Each can spell either salvation or doom.

MARTIN LUTHER KING, JR. (1929–1968). *Stride Toward Freedom,* 11, 1958

There cannot be a crisis next week. My schedule is already full.

HENRY A. KISSINGER (1923–). Tongue-in-cheek remark. In Patrick Anderson, "The Only Power Kissinger Has Is the Confidence of the President," *New York Times Magazine,* 1 June 1969

In crises the most daring course is often the safest. The riskiest course in my experience has been gradual escalation that the opponent matches step by step, inevitably reaching a higher level of violence and often an inextricable stalemate.

HENRY A. KISSINGER (1923–). *Years of Upheaval,* 8, 1982

See Boldness: Lucius Marcius o Daring: Karl von Clausewitz

Crisis demands dictatorship, centralization, concentration, obedience, and bias. Intercrisis permits concessions toward democracy, decentralization, dispersion, originality, and objectivity.

HAROLD D. LASSWELL (1902–1978). *Politics: Who Gets What, When, How,* 5, 1936

The dogmas of the quiet past are inadequate to the stormy present. The occasion is piled high with difficulty, and we must rise with the occasion. As our case is new, so we must think anew and act anew. We must disenthrall ourselves, and then we shall save our country.

ABRAHAM LINCOLN (1809–1865). *Second Annual Message to Congress,* 1 December 1862

Where the masses of people must cooperate in an uncertain and eruptive environment, it is usually necessary to secure unity and flexibility without real consent. The symbol does that. . . . It enormously sharpens the intention of the group and welds that group, as nothing else in a crisis can weld it, to purposeful action.

WALTER LIPPMANN (1889–1974). *Public Opinion,* 15.1, 1922

In really hard times the rules of the game are altered. The inchoate mass begins to stir. It becomes potent, and when it strikes . . . it strikes with incredible emphasis. Those are the rare occasions when a national will emerges from the scattered, specialized, or indifferent blocs of voters who ordinarily elect the politicians. Those are for good or evil the great occasions in a nation's history.

WALTER LIPPMAN (1889–1974). "The New Congress," *New York Herald Tribune,* 8 December 1931

It is only a step from victory to disaster. My experience is that, in a crisis, some detail always decides the issue.

NAPOLEON (1769–1821). Letter to Talleyrand, 7 October 1797, *Napoleon's Letters,* tr. J. M. Thompson, 1934

Panics, in some cases, have their uses; they produce as much good as hurt. Their duration is always short; the mind soon grows through them and acquires a firmer habit than before. But their peculiar advantage is that they are the touchstone of sincerity and hypocrisy, and bring things and men to light, which might otherwise have lain forever undiscovered.

THOMAS PAINE (1737–1809). *The Crisis* (pamphlet), 1, 23 December 1776

The nearer any disease approaches to a crisis, the nearer it is to a cure. Danger and deliverance make their advances together, and it is only the last push that one or the other takes the lead.

THOMAS PAINE (1737–1809). *The Crisis* (pamphlet), 4, 12 September 1777

A distracted people, busy with the fierce competitions of modern life, must be addressed while they are paying attention, which is usually at the moment of some great national or international event.

JAMES RESTON (1909–1995). In Joseph Kraft, "Washington's Most Powerful Reporter," *Esquire,* November 1958

Most people, at a crisis, feel more loyalty to their nation than to their class.

BERTRAND RUSSELL (1872–1970). *Power: A New Social Analysis,* 8, 1938

See Class: Lord Acton (1)

Passengers on a ship who are eating, sunning themselves, playing shuffleboard, and engaging in all the usual shipboard activities appear perfectly normal as long as their ship is sailing safely in quiet seas, but these same passengers doing these same things appear deranged if in full view of them all their ship is caught in a vortex that may shortly drag it and them to destruction. Then their placidity has the appearance of an unnatural loss of normal human responses—of a pathetic and sickening acquiescence in their own slaughter.

JONATHAN SCHELL (1943–). *The Fate of the Earth,* 2, 1982

We set our course by the ways in which we think—or decline to think—about in the weeks and months and years prior to the moment of supreme crisis, and by the little decisions we make in preparation for it.

> MICHAEL SHERRY (1945–). "The Slide to Total Air War," *New Republic,* 16 December 1981

Mankind does not reflect upon questions of economic and social organization until compelled to do so by the sharp pressure of some practical emergency.

> R. H. TAWNEY (1880–1962). *Religion and the Rise of Capitalism: A Historical Study,* 2 (introduction), 1926

Times of trouble best discover the true worth of a man.

> THOMAS à KEMPIS (1380–1471). *The Imitation of Christ,* 1.16, tr. Leo Sherley-Price, 1952

Reckless audacity came to be considered the courage of a loyal ally; prudent hesitation, specious cowardice; moderation was held to be a cloak for unmanliness: ability to see all sides of a question, inaptness to act on any.

> THUCYDIDES (460?–400? B.C.). *The Peloponnesian War,* 3.82, tr. Richard Crawley and rev. T. E. Wick, 1982

Blood became a weaker tie than party.

> THUCYDIDES (460?–400? B.C.) *The Peloponnesian War,* 3.82, tr. Richard Crawley and rev. T. E. Wick, 1982

The cause of all these evils was the lust for power arising from greed and ambition; and from these passions proceeded the violence of parties once engaged in contention.

> THUCYDIDES (460?–400? B.C.). *The Peloponnesian War,* 3.82, tr. Richard Crawley and rev. T. E. Wick, 1982

Religion was in honor with neither party; but the use of fair phrases to arrive at guilty ends was in high reputation.

> THUCYDIDES (460?–400? B.C.). *The Peloponnesian War,* 3.82, tr. Richard Crawley and rev. T. E. Wick, 1982

Within us all there are wells of thought and dynamos of energy which are not suspected until emergencies arise.

> THOMAS J. WATSON (1914–). In "Thoughts on the Business of Life," *Forbes,* 11 October 1982

❧

The crisis delivers or destroys according to the response it engenders.

> ANONYMOUS

CRISIS LEADERS

See also • Charisma: Garry Wills ○ Crisis ○ Decision-Making: [especially] Walter Lippmann ○ Leaders ○ Leaders & People ○ Revolutionaries ○ Statesmen ○ Tyrants

No leader can safely mumble at moments of crisis.

> BROCK BREWER. "Where Have All the Leaders Gone?" *Life,* 8 October 1971

In times of complete calm . . . mere talents push their way into the front rank. . . .

Great originality, shouted down at such times, has to wait for times of tempest.

> JACOB BURCKHARDT (1818–1897). "The Crises of History," 1869, *Force and Freedom: An Interpretation of History,* ed. James H. Nichols, 1943

The political function of the crisis-man [e.g., Napoleon, Mussolini, Hitler] . . . is to suspend the democratic constitution, replacing it with dictatorship in the interests of the ruling class.

> ALBERT CARR (1902–1971). "The Path of Dictatorship" (1), *Juggernaut: The Path of Dictatorship,* 1939

Times of general calamity and confusion have ever been productive of the greatest minds. The purest ore is produced from the hottest furnace, and the brightest thunderbolt is elicited from the darkest storm.

> C. C. COLTON (1780–1832). *Lacon: or, Many Things in Few Words; Addressed to Those Who Think,* 1.28, 1823

In war, as in other situations of mortal threat, there is an understandable urge to clutch at straws—the good aspects of a leader are seized upon, the less good conveniently denied.

> NORMAN F. DIXON (1922–). *On the Psychology of Military Incompetence,* 20, 1976

The ability to get to the verge without getting into war is the necessary art. If you cannot master it, you inevitably get into war. If you try to run away from it, if you are scared to go to the brink, you are lost.

> JOHN FOSTER DULLES (1888–1959). Secretary of state. Citing the 1953 Korean peace-talk crisis and the 1954 threats of major war over Formosa and Indochina ("We walked to the brink and looked it in the face."). In James Shepley, "How Dulles Averted War," *Life,* 16 January 1956. Adlai E. Stevenson coined the term brinksmanship in a Hartford (Connecticut) speech, 25 February 1956: "We hear the Secretary of State boasting of his brinkmanship—the art of bringing us to the edge of the abyss."

For a man of sensitivity and compassion to exercise great powers in a time of crisis is a grim and agonizing thing.

> RICHARD HOFSTADTER (1916–1970). Referring to Abraham Lincoln and the Civil War, *The American Political Tradition: And the Men Who Made It,* 5.7, 1948

The archetypal image of the wise man, the savior or redeemer, lies buried and dormant in man's unconscious since the dawn of culture; it is awakened whenever the times are out of joint and a human society is committed to a serious error.

> CARL G. JUNG (1875–1961). *Modern Man in Search of a Soul,* 8.2, tr. W. S. Dell and Cary F. Baynes, 1933

If you act creatively, you should be able to use crises to move the world towards the structural solutions that are necessary. In fact, very often the crises themselves are a symptom of the need for a structural rearrangement.

> HENRY A. KISSINGER (1923–). James Reston interview, "With Kissinger on the State of the World," *New York Times,* 13 October 1974

When one is on a tightrope, the most dangerous course is to stop.

> HENRY A. KISSINGER (1923–). *White House Years,* 32, 1979

A crisis does not always appear to a policy-maker as a series of dramatic events. Usually it imposes itself as an exhausting agenda of petty chores demanding both concentration and endurance. One is forced to react to scraps of information in very limited spans of time; longing for full knowledge, one must chart a route through the murk of unknowing.

HENRY A. KISSINGER (1923–). *Years of Upheaval*, 11, 1982

The public does not in the long run respect leaders who mirror its own insecurities or see only the symptoms of crises rather than the long-term trends. The role of the leader is to assume the burden of acting on the basis of a confidence in his own assessment of the direction of events and how they can be influenced. Failing that, crises will multiply, which is another way of saying that a leader has lost control over events.

HENRY A. KISSINGER (1923–). *Diplomacy*, 5, 1994

Every democrat feels in his bones that dangerous crises are incompatible with democracy because he knows how the inertia of the masses is such that to act quickly a very few must decide and the rest follow rather blindly.

WALTER LIPPMANN (1889–1974). *Public Opinion*, 17.4, 1922

Poverty never was allowed to stand in the way of the achievement of any rank or honor: . . . virtue and merit were sought for under whatever roof they dwelt. . . . [In 458 B.C. under siege by the Equeans, the Romans] resorted to the creation of a Dictator, their last remedy in times of difficulty. They appointed L. Quintius Cincinnatus, who at the time was on his little farm, which he cultivated with his own hands.

MACHIAVELLI (1469–1527). *The Discourses*, 3.25, 1517, tr. Christian E. Detmold, 1940. After successfully defending Rome, Cincinnatus returned to his farm.

In times of anarchy one may seem a despot in order to be a savior.

MIRABEAU (1749–1791). French revolutionary leader

At moments of crisis, where the roads to disintegration or to development separate, as on a watershed, a single decisive personality, or a small group of informed and purposeful men, may by a slight push determine the direction and movement of an otherwise uncontrollable mass of conflicting social forces, At such moments not a single institution or group, but a whole society, will be involved in a change far beyond its ordinary capacities for adaptation: yet the dynamic agent in this transformation, the "spark which kindles the great forest," will be the individual human person; for it is he who precipitates the change in the social order by first initiating a profound regrouping of forces and ideal goals within himself. At such a moment the human integer represents the whole and in turn has an effect on the whole. Only within the compass of the person can a total change be affected within the span of a single generation, sufficient to produce the necessary effect on civilization at large: like the seed crystal, he passes on to the whole the new order of the part.

LEWIS MUMFORD (1895–1990). *The Conduct of Life*, 8.3, 1951

A leader or a man of action in a crisis almost always acts subconsciously and then thinks of the reasons for his action.

JAWAHARLAL NEHRU (1889–1964)

In a crisis, the man worth his salt is the man who meets the needs of the situation in whatever way is necessary.

THEODORE ROOSEVELT (1858–1919). *An Autobiography*, 7, 1913

In desperate affairs, some determined man seizes a standard, he will render the whole century as brave as himself because it will follow him.

MAURICE de SAXE (1696–1750). *My Reveries on the Art of War*, 1732. In Thomas R. Phillips, ed., *Roots of War*, p. 242, 1940

In a crisis, like a shipwreck, when no one knows what to do, one, by acting, may lead them all through imitative suggestibility. People who are very suggestible can be led into states of mind which preclude criticism or reflection. Anyone who acquires skill in the primary processes of association, analogy, reiteration, and continuity, can play on others by stimulating these processes and then giving them selected data to work upon.

WILLIAM GRAHAM SUMNER (1840–1910). *Folkways: A Study of the Sociological Importance of Usages, Manners, Customs, Mores, and Morals*, 24, 1907

If the world's present emergency were to make a temporary world dictatorship the only alternative to the self-imposed extinction of mankind, . . . our attitude ought to be that of travelers who submit to a captain's dictation while they are *en voyage,* but, as a matter of course, resume their personal freedom of action as soon as their perilous journey is over.

ARNOLD J. TOYNBEE (1889–1975). *The Toynbee-Ikeda Dialogue: Man Himself Must Choose*, 8, 1976

CRITICISM

See also • Blame ○ Censure ○ Contempt: Henry G. Bohn ○ Criticism: Examples ○ Critics ○ Critics: Examples ○ Faults: Marquis of Halifax ○ Gossip ○ Insult ○ Judging Others ○ Praise: [especially] Saying (3) ○ Ridicule ○ Satire ○ Slander ○ Words

So long as I am acting from duty and conviction, I am indifferent to taunts and jeers. I think they will probably do me more good than harm.

WINSTON CHURCHILL (1874–1965). House of Commons speech, 6 December 1946

It is much easier to be critical than to be correct.

BENJAMIN DISRAELI (1804–1881). House of Commons speech, 24 January 1860

Bitter is the criticism from which, with the best of wills, we can derive no benefit.

MARIE von EBNER-ESCHENBACH (1830–1916). *Aphorisms*, p. 71, 1880-1905, tr. David Scrase and Wolfgang Mieder, 1994

Let me never fall into the vulgar mistake of dreaming that I am persecuted whenever I am contradicted.

RALPH WALDO EMERSON (1803–1882). Journal, 8 November 1838

The Sting of a Reproach is the Truth of it.

THOMAS FULLER (1654–1734). Comp., *Gnomologia: Adages and Proverbs*, 4769, 1732

See Slander: Marquis of Halifax

People seldom speak ill of themselves, but when they have a good chance of being contradicted.

FULKE GREVILLE (1554–1628). *Maxims, Characters, and Reflections*, p. 17, 1756

To avoid criticism, do nothing, say nothing, be nothing.
 ELBERT HUBBARD (1856–1915)

We often stand in need of hearing what we know full well.
 WALTER SAVAGE LANDOR (1775–1864). "Lord Bacon and Richard
 Hooker," *Imaginary Conversations,* 1824–1853

Second-rate minds usually condemn everything beyond their grasp.
 LA ROCHEFOUCAULD (1613–1680). *Maxims,* 375, 1665, tr. Louis
 Kronenberger, 1959

If both factions, or neither, shall abuse you, you will probably be about right. Beware of being assailed by one and praised by the other.
 ABRAHAM LINCOLN (1809–1865). Letter to Gen. John M. Schofield,
 27 May 1863

Most people believe that if any shot goes unanswered it must be true.
 CHRISTOPHER MATTHEWS (1945–). *Hardball: How Politics Is Played—
 Told by One Who Knows the Game,* 7, 1988

They who have put out the people's eyes, reproach them of their blindness.
 JOHN MILTON (1608–1674). *An Apology against a Pamphlet call'd
 A Modest Confutation of the Animadversions upon the Remonstrant
 against Smectymnuus* (pamphlet), 1642

Your self-condemnation is always accredited, your self-praise discredited.
 MONTAIGNE (1533–1592). "Of the Art of Discussion," *Essays,* 1588,
 tr. Donald M. Frame, 1958

He that corrects out of Passion raises Revenge sooner than Repentance.
 WILLIAM PENN (1644–1718). *Some Fruits of Solitude,* 290, 1693

When we speak evil of others, we generally condemn ourselves.
 PUBLIUS SYRUS (85–43 B.C.). *Moral Sayings,* 1058, tr. Darius Lyman, Jr.,
 1862

Criticism . . . makes very little dent upon me, unless I think there is some real justification and something should be done.
 ELEANOR ROOSEVELT (1884–1962). Letter to Carrie Chapman, 18 April
 1936. In Joseph P. Lash, *Eleanor and Franklin: The Story of Their
 Relationship,* 39, 1971

Correction by correction I follow the path that leads to God.
 ANTOINE de SAINT-EXUPÉRY (1900–1944). *The Wisdom of the Sands,*
 81, 1948, tr. Stuart Gilbert, 1950

Mistress Page: Better a little chiding than a great deal of heartbreak.
 SHAKESPEARE (1564–1616). *The Merry Wives of Windsor,* 5.3.10, 1600

When someone was knocking him, [Pres. Kennedy] always let him know that *he* knew.
 THEODORE C. SORENSEN (1928–). Presidential assistant to John F.
 Kennedy. In Christopher Matthews, *Hardball: How Politics Is Played—
 Told by One Who Knows the Game,* 5, 1988

What Paul says about Peter tells us more about Paul than about Peter.

BARUCH SPINOZA (1632–1677). In Erich Fromm, *Psychoanalysis and
 Religion,* 3, 1950

In reproving show no signs of choler [i.e., anger].
 GEORGE WASHINGTON (1732–1799). Copybook, 1748 (at age 16),
 Rules of Civility & Decent Behaviour in Company and Conversation,
 #45. The rules were an amended version of Francis Hawkins's 1640
 translation of *Decency of Conversation Among Men* (French Jesuit
 writing, 1595).

Be thou, in rebuking evil,
Conscious of thine own.
 JOHN GREENLEAF WHITTIER (1807–1892). "What the Voice Said,"
 15, 1847
 See Censure: Saying

❧

The dogs bark, but the caravan moves on.
 SAYING (ARAB)

The Lord reproves him whom he loves,
 as a father the son in whom he delights.
 SAYING (*BIBLE*). Proverbs 3:12

Do not reprove a scoffer, or he will hate you;
 reprove a wise man, and he will love you.
 SAYING (*BIBLE*). Proverbs 9:8

When criticized, consider the source.
 SAYING

CRITICISM: EXAMPLES

See also • Censure ○ Criticism ○ Critics: Examples ○ Insult ○
 Misjudgments ○ Praise ○ Praise: Examples ○ Repartee: Examples
 ○ Wit: Examples

It's a beautiful, well-constructed facade, but without central heating.
 RAYMOND BRET-KOCH. French artist. On Clare Boothe Luce
 (1903–1987). In Sylvia Jukes Morris, *Rage for Fame: The Ascent of
 Clare Boothe,* 18, 1997

Following Mrs. [Eleanor] Roosevelt in search of irrationality is like following a burning fuse in search of an explosive; one never has to wait very long.
 WILLIAM F. BUCKLEY, JR. (1925–). "The Liberal" (1), *Up from
 Liberalism,* 1959

He is a man of his most recent word.
 WILLIAM F. BUCKLEY, JR. (1925–). On Pres. Lyndon B. Johnson, "The
 Week," *National Review,* 24 August 1965

It was very good of God to let [Thomas] Carlyle and Mrs. Carlyle marry one another and so make only two people miserable instead of four.
 SAMUEL BUTLER (1835–1902). Letter to Miss Savage, 21 November 1884

It is . . . alarming and also nauseating to see Mr. Gandhi, a seditious Middle Temple lawyer, now posing as a fakir [i.e., a beggar] of a type well known in the East, striding half-naked up the steps of the Viceregal Palace, while he is still organizing and conducting a defiant campaign of civil disobedience, to parley on equal terms with the representative of the King-Emperor.

> WINSTON CHURCHILL (1874–1965). Speech, Epping (England), 23 February 1931

I have only one purpose, the destruction of Hitler, and my life is much simplified thereby. If Hitler invaded Hell, I would make at least a favorable reference to the Devil in the House of Commons.

> WINSTON CHURCHILL (1874–1965). Referring to Hitler's imminent invasion of the Soviet Union, remark to his private secretary John Colville, 21 June 1941 (the next day, Hitler launched the invasion), *The Second World War: The Grand Alliance,* 1.20, 1950

Hitler is a monster of wickedness, insatiable in his lust for blood and plunder. Not content with having all Europe under his heel . . . now this bloodthirsty guttersnipe must launch his mechanized armies upon new fields of slaughter, pillage and devastation.

> WINSTON CHURCHILL (1874–1965). On the German invasion of the Soviet Union, radio broadcast, BBC, London, 22 June 1941

A modest man who has a good deal to be modest about.

> WINSTON CHURCHILL (1874–1965). On Clement Attlee. Attributed (he denied having said it). In *Chicago Sunday Tribune Magazine of Books,* 27 June 1954

[A] sheep in sheep's clothing.

> WINSTON CHURCHILL (1874–1965). On Clement Attlee. In Lord Home, *The Way the Wind Blows,* 6, 1976.

An empty taxi arrived at 10 Downing Street, and when the door was opened [Clement] Attlee got out.

> WINSTON CHURCHILL (1874–1965). Attributed (he denied having said it). In Kenneth Harris, *Attlee,* 6, 1982.

[An] amiable dunce.

> CLARK CLIFFORD (1906–). An assumed off-the-record remark on Ronald Reagan. In Hugh Sidey, "Before It's Too Late," *Time,* 23 November 1981

He'd make a lovely corpse.

> CHARLES DICKENS (1812–1870). *The Life and Adventures of Martin Chuzzlewit,* 25, 1844

A born loser.

> DWIGHT D. EISENHOWER (1890–1969). On Vice Pres. Richard M. Nixon. In Emmet John Hughes, *The Living Presidency: The Resources and Dilemmas of the American Presidential Office,* 1.2, 1972

Anonymous: Have you ever met Douglas MacArthur?
Eisenhower: Not only have I met him, ma'am; I studied dramatics under him for five years in Washington and for four years in the Philippines.

> DWIGHT D. EISENHOWER (1890–1969). Format adapted. In William Manchester, *American Caesar: Douglas MacArthur: 1880–1964,* 4, 1978

[I have] nothing to say again' him, on'y it was a pity he couldna be hatched o'er again, an' hatched different.

> GEORGE ELIOT (1819–1880). *Adam Bede,* 18, 1859

Here was an experiment, under the most favorable conditions, of the powers of intellect without conscience. Never was such a leader so endowed, and so weaponed. . . . And what was the result of this vast talent and power, of these immense armies, burned cities, squandered treasures, immolated millions of men, of this demoralized Europe? It came to no result. All passed away, like the smoke of his artillery, and left no trace. He left France smaller, poorer, feebler, than he found it; and the whole contest for freedom was to be begun again. The attempt was, in principle, suicidal.

> RALPH WALDO EMERSON (1803–1882). On Napoleon, "Napoleon; or, The Man of the World," *Representative Men,* 1850

Stettinius was . . . one of those far from exceptional people who give everyone else a glow of satisfaction from feelings of undeniable superiority.

> JOHN KENNETH GALBRAITH (1908–). On Edward R. Stettinius, Jr., chairman of the War Resources Board (where Galbraith worked in 1940), who later became secretary of state, *A Life in Our Times: Memoirs,* 8, 1981

Who'd have thought that we were fighting this war against a bunch of jerks.

> JOHN KENNETH GALBRAITH (1908–). On seeing the Nazi war criminals en masse at the Nuremberg trials, 1946. In Alex Ross, "Watching for a Judgment of Real Evil," *New York Times,* 12 November 1995

[Richard M. Nixon] was the most dishonest individual I ever met in my life.
President Nixon lied to his wife, his family, his friends, longtime colleagues in the U.S. Congress, lifetime members of his own political party, the American people and the world.

> BARRY M. GOLDWATER (1909–1998) (with JACK CASSERLY). *Goldwater,* 9, 1988
>
> See Watergate: Richard M. Nixon (1)

Churchill is the very type of corrupt journalist. There's not a worse prostitute in politics.
He himself has written that it's unimaginable what can be done in war with the help of lies.
He's an utterly amoral, repulsive creature.

> ADOLF HITLER (1889–1945). 18 February 1942, *Hitler's Secret Conversations, 1941–1944,* tr. Norman Cameron and R. H. Stevens, 1953

I don't know what people have got against Jimmy Carter. He's done nothing.

> BOB HOPE (1903–). Remark during the Carter/Ronald Reagan presidential campaign, 2 November 1980

Jerry Ford is so dumb he can't fart and chew gum at the same time.

> LYNDON B. JOHNSON (1908–1973). In Richard Reeves, *A Ford, Not a Lincoln,* 2, 1975. In early press accounts, the comment read, ". . . *walk* and chew gum at the same time."

The most important thing for Americans to know about Ross Perot is that the country would probably not self-destruct under his leadership.

> BARBARA JORDAN (1936–1996). On the presidential candidate, appearing on *Peter Jennings Reporting,* television documentary, 29 June 1992

The tyrannical demagogue Moses.

> CARL G. JUNG (1875–1961). "'Ulysses': A Monologue," 1932, *The Spirit in Man, Art, and Literature,* tr. R. F. C. Hull, 1966

The man is, of course, a disaster. Now the Republican Party is a disaster. Fortunately, he can't be elected—or the whole country would be a disaster area.

> HENRY A. KISSINGER (1923–). On Richard M. Nixon who had just become the Republican nominee for President, 1968. In Ralph Blumenfeld et al., *Henry Kissinger: The Private and Public Story*, 13, 1974

Haig was an honorable man according to his lights—but his lights were dim.

> B. H. LIDDELL HART (1895–1970). On Field Marshal Douglas Haig, commander of British forces in France during World War I. In "The Evasion of Truth," *Why Don't We Learn from History?* 1944. Haig was denounced for his attrition strategy, which led to huge casualties.

[Franklin D. Roosevelt is] a very impressionable person without a firm grasp of public affairs and without very strong convictions. . . . He is an amiable man with many philanthropic impulses, but he is not the dangerous enemy of anything. . . . [He is] a pleasant man who, without any important qualifications for the office, would like to be President.

> WALTER LIPPMANN (1889–1974). In *New York Herald Tribune*, 8 January 1932

So [Franklin D.] Roosevelt is dead: a man who would never tell the truth when a lie would serve him just as well.

> DOUGLAS MacARTHUR (1880–1964). 1945. In Richard M. Nixon, *Leaders*, 4, 1982

The disease of power was coursing through [Harry S. Truman's] veins.

> DOUGLAS MacARTHUR (1880–1964). "Text of MacArthur's Statement in Reply to Charges Made by Truman in Memoirs," *New York Times*, 9 February 1956
>
> See Korean War: Harry S. Truman (5)

Best clerk I ever had.

> DOUGLAS MacARTHUR (1880–1964). On Dwight D. Eisenhower, his chief of staff in the Philippines during the 1930s. In William Manchester, *American Caesar: Douglas MacArthur: 1880–1964*, 4, 1978

The more I read about [Socrates], the less I wonder that they poisoned him.

> THOMAS BABINGTON MACAULAY (1800–1859). Letter to T. F. Ellis, 29 May 1835

There, but for the grace of God, goes God.

> HERMAN J. MANKIEWICZ (1897–1953). On the self-assured Orson Welles who at the time was filming *Citizen Kane*, which Mankiewicz had scripted, 1940.

[Abraham Lincoln] is nothing more than a well-meaning baboon. . . . I went to the White House where I found "the original Gorilla" about as intelligent as ever. What a specimen to be at the head of our affairs now!

> GEORGE B. McCLELLAN (1826–1885). Sacked commander of the Army of the Potomac. 1864

No man ever came to market with less seductive goods, and no man ever got a better price for what he had to offer.

> H. L. MENCKEN (1880–1956). On Pres. Calvin Coolidge, "The Coolidge Mystery," *Baltimore Evening Sun*, 30 January 1933

[Franklin D.] Roosevelt is a fraud from snout to tail.

> H. L. MENCKEN (1880–1956). Diary, 6 October 1939

Nice chap; no general.

> BERNARD LAW MONTGOMERY (1887–1976). On Gen. Dwight D. Eisenhower, Field Marshal Montgomery's chief during the Battle of France (1944). In Norman Gelb, *Ike and Monty*, 1, 1994

One may say that this man is immorality personified.

> NAPOLEON (1769–1821). On Talleyrand, the French minister of foreign affairs, remark to Gen. Gaspard Gourgaud, 1817, *The Mind of Napoleon: A Selection from His Written and Spoken Words*, 231, ed. J. Christopher Herold, 1955

Lenin . . . is one of those politicians who win an undeserved reputation by dying prematurely.

> GEORGE ORWELL (1903–1950). "James Burnham and the Managerial Revolution," May 1946, *The Collected Essays, Journalism and Letters of George Orwell*, vol. 4, ed. Sonia Orwell and Ian Angus, 1968

As to you, sir, treacherous to private friendship (for so you have been to me, and that in the day of danger) and a hypocrite in public life, the world will be puzzled to decide whether you are an apostate or an impostor, whether you have abandoned good principles or whether you every had any.

> THOMAS PAINE (1737–1809). Letter to George Washington (written in the belief that the President had abandoned him to imprisonment in France during the Reign of Terror), 30 July 1796

[If Bill Clinton came looking for work,] you wouldn't consider giving him a job anywhere above middle management.

> ROSS PEROT (1930–). Television interview. In "The Week," *Time*, 7 June 1993

This mad dog of the Middle East.

> RONALD REAGAN (1911–). On Col. Moammar Gadhafi of Libya, news conference, Washington, 9 April 1986

As a human being, [Lyndon Johnson] was a miserable person—a bully, sadist, lout, and egotist. He had no sense of loyalty. . . . He seemed to take a special delight in humiliating those who had cast in their lot with him.

> GEORGE E. REEDY (1917–). *Lyndon B. Johnson: A Memoir*, 16, 1982

The real [John F.] Kennedy—as opposed to the celebrated hero espoused by the Kennedy family, the media, and the Camelot School—lacked greatness in large part because he lacked the qualities inherent in good character. While he had ample courage and at times showed considerable prudence, he was deficient in integrity, compassion and temperance.

> THOMAS C. REEVES. *A Question of Character: A Life of John F. Kennedy*, 18, 1991
>
> See Praise: Examples: John Kenneth Galbraith

They looked like two little boys playing soldier. They seemed to be having a wonderful time, too wonderful in fact. It made me a little sad somehow.

> ELEANOR ROOSEVELT (1884–1962). On Franklin D. Roosevelt and Winston Churchill whom she had observed in animated conversation about the war in the White House's map room during the latter's visit soon after the attack on Pearl Harbor in December 1941. In Doris Kearns Goodwin, *No Ordinary Time: Franklin and Eleanor Roosevelt: The Home Front in World War II*, 12, 1994

[William McKinley] has no more backbone than a chocolate éclair.

> THEODORE ROOSEVELT (1858–1919). He was irked by the President's reluctance to declare war on Spain in 1898. In Bill Adler, comp., *Presidential Wit: From Washington to Johnson,* p. 90, 1966

[A] filthy little atheist.

> THEODORE ROOSEVELT (1858–1919). On Thomas Paine, quoted by Crane Brinton, "Paine, Thomas." In Dumas Malone, ed., *Dictionary of American Biography,* 14.166, 1934

Americans of all political persuasions are coming to the sad realization that our First Lady—a woman of undoubted talents who was a role model for many in her generation—is a congenital liar.

> WILLIAM SAFIRE (1929–). On Hillary Rodham Clinton and her defense against charges of dishonesty, opening paragraph, "Blizzard of Lies," *New York Times,* 8 January 1996

He's just like a Teflon frying pan: nothing sticks to him.

> PAT SCHROEDER (1940–). Colorado congresswoman. On Pres. Ronald Reagan. In *Boston Globe,* 24 October 1984

Henry [A. Kissinger] does not lie because it is in his interest. He lies because it is in his nature.

> HELMUT SONNENFELDT (1926–). A long-time Kissinger associate. Remark to Daniel Patrick Moynihan. In Walter Isaacson, *Kissinger: A Biography,* 29, 1992

[Adolf Hitler] was devoid of all feelings of empathy and tenderness. He was an inhuman being.

> ALBERT SPEER (1905–1980). German minister of armaments. Eric Norden interview, *Playboy,* June 1971

[Richard M.] Nixon is the kind of politician who would cut down a redwood tree, then mount the stump for a speech on conservation.

> ADLAI E. STEVENSON (1900–1965). In Leon A. Harris, *The Fine Art of Political Wit,* 11, 1964

You really have to get to know Dewey to dislike him.

> ROBERT A. TAFT (1889–1953). Ohio senator. On Thomas E. Dewey, the two-time Republican presidential nominee and New York governor, recalled on Taft's death, 31 July 1953

[Bertrand Russell] may be a genius in mathematics—as to that I'm no judge; but about politics he is a perfect goose.

> G. M. TREVELYAN (1876–1962). In A. L. Rowse, *Glimpses of the Great,* 1, 1985

The leader and prophet of this bourgeoisie [in India] is Gandhi. A fake leader and a false prophet!

> LEON TROTSKY (1879–1940). Open letter to the workers of India, July 1939

[Richard M.] Nixon is a shifty-eyed, goddamn liar, and people know it. . . . He's one of the few in the history of this country to run for high office talking out of both sides of his mouth at the same time and lying out of both sides.

> HARRY S. TRUMAN (1884–1972). Interview with the author, 1961–1962. In Merle Miller, *Plain Speaking: An Oral Biography of Harry S. Truman,* 14, 1974
>
> See Watergate: Richard M. Nixon (1)

The figure [Napoleon] makes in history is one of almost incredible self-conceit, of vanity, greed, and cunning, of callous contempt and disregard of all who trusted him, and a grandiose aping of Caesar, Alexander, and Charlemagne which would be purely comic if it were not caked over with human blood.

> H. G. WELLS (1866–1946). *The Outline of History,* 37.3, 1920

An excellent man; he has no enemies; and none of his friends like him.

> OSCAR WILDE (1854–1900). Tongue-in-cheek remark on George Bernard Shaw, in Shaw, letter to Ellen Terry, 25 September 1896

Being attacked on ethics by Al D'Amato is like being called ugly by a frog.

> DAVID WILHELM (1956–). Referring the New York senator. In John Leo, "An Aphorism a Day . . . ," *U.S. News & World Report,* 9 January 1995

⚜

Among President [Harry S.] Truman's many weaknesses was his utter inability to discriminate between history and histrionics.

> ANONYMOUS ("one of Truman's most prominent critics"). In Douglas MacArthur, *Reminiscences,* 9, 1964

Though I yield to no one in my admiration for Mr. [Calvin] Coolidge, I do wish he did not look as if he had been weaned on a pickle.

> ANONYMOUS. In Alice Roosevelt Longworth, *Crowded Hours,* 21, 1933

CRITICS

See also • Criticism ○ Critics: Examples ○ Media

The best authors are always the severest critics of their own works.

> LORD CHESTERFIELD (1694–1773). Letter to his son, 6 May 1751

Be gentle with one another's efforts. Always remember that it's just as hard to write a bad book as it is to write a good book.

> MALCOLM COWLEY (1898–1989). Literary critic. Suggestion to student writers, early 1960s. In Ken Kesey, "Remember This: Write What You Don't Know," *New York Times Book Review,* 31 December 1989

You know who the critics are? The men who have failed in literature and art.

> BENJAMIN DISRAELI (1804–1881). *Lothair,* 35, 1870

Don't pay any attention to the critics—don't even ignore them!

> SAMUEL GOLDWYN (1882–1974)

Asking a working writer what he thinks about critics is like asking a lamppost how it feels about dogs.

> CHRISTOPHER HAMPTON (1946–). In *Sunday Times* (London), 16 October 1977

[The critics'] profession has one recommendation peculiar to itself, that it gives vent to malignity without real mischief.

> SAMUEL JOHNSON (1709—1784). In *The Idler* (English journal), 60, 9 June 1759

I think I have not been attacked enough for it. Attack is the reaction; I never think I have hit hard unless it rebounds.

SAMUEL JOHNSON (1709–1784). Referring to his pamphlet *Taxation No Tyranny*, 2 April 1775. In James Boswell, *The Life of Samuel Johnson*, 1791

See Publicity: Johnson (2)

An author places himself uncalled before the tribunal of criticism and solicits fame at the hazard of disgrace.

SAMUEL JOHNSON (1709–1784). "Pope," *Lives of the English Poets*, 1781

When the reviews are bad, I tell my staff that they can join me as I cry all the way to the bank.

LIBERACE (1919–1987). *Liberace: An Autobiography*, 2, 1973

A wise skepticism is the first attribute of a good critic.

JAMES RUSSELL LOWELL (1819–1891). "Shakespeare Once More," *Among My Books*, 1870

I have a critic who is more exacting than you: it is my other self.

JEAN MEISONIER (1815–1891). French painter. In Alice Hubbard, comp., *An American Bible*, p. 192, 1946

The critical worth of a play reviewer may be determined in inverse ratio to the number of times he is quoted in the newspaper theatrical advertisements.

GEORGE JEAN NATHAN (1882–1958). "The Musical State: Appendix," *The Theatre in the Fifties*, 1953

Anonymous: What do you think of critics?
O'Neill: I love every bone in their heads.

EUGENE O'NEILL (1888–1953). Format adapted. In John Corry, "Brooks Atkinson Honored by O'Neill Committee," *New York Times*, 1 December 1980

You can spot a bad critic when he starts by discussing the poet and not the poem.

EZRA POUND (1885–1972). In Naomi Rachel, letter to *New Yorker*, 25 December 1995

I don't pay much attention to critics. The world is divided into two kinds of people: those who can, and those who criticize.

RONALD REAGAN (1911–). In Michael Korda, "Prompting the President," *New Yorker*, 6 October 1997

Every good poet includes a critic; the reverse will not hold.

WILLIAM SHENSTONE (1714–1763). "On Writing and Books," *Men & Manners*, ed., Havelock Ellis, 1927

I never read a book before reviewing it; it prejudices a man so.

SYDNEY SMITH (1771–1845). In Hesketh Pearson, *The Smith of Smiths: Being the Life, Wit, and Humour of Sydney Smith*, 3, 1934

The important thing is that neither the favorable nor the unfavorable critics move into your head and take part in the composition of your next work.

THORNTON WILDER (1897–1975). Richard H. Goldstone interview, 1956. In Malcolm Cowley, ed., *Writers at Work: First Series*, 1958

Writers are such appalling egotists for the most part that it won't do them very much harm to be told occasionally their book's no bloody good. If you know somebody is going to be awfully annoyed by something you write, that's obviously very satisfying, and if they howl with rage or cry, that's honey.

A. N. WILSON (1950–). Interview with the author. In Naim Attallah, *Singular Encounters*, 1990

CRITICS: EXAMPLES

See also • Actors ○ Beat Generation: Truman Capote ○ Books ○ Criticism: Examples ○ Critics ○ Films ○ Insult ○ Misjudgments ○ Praise: Examples ○ Theater ○ Wit: Examples ○ Writers

What a poor ignorant, malicious, short-sighted, crapulous mass, is Tom Paine's *Common Sense*.

JOHN ADAMS (1735–1826). Letter to Thomas Jefferson, 22 June 1819

Several tons of dynamite are set off in this picture—none of it under the right people.

JAMES AGEE (1909–1955). On *Tycoon* (film) 1947, *Agee on Film*, 1958–1960

There is less in this than meets the eye.

TALLULAH BANKHEAD (1902–1968). On the revival of Maurice Maeterlinck's *Aglavaine and Selysette* (play). In Alexander Woollcott, *Shouts and Murmurs*, 4, 1922

The covers of this book are too far apart.

AMBROSE BIERCE (1842–1914). A one-sentence review. In C. H. Grattan, *Bitter Bierce*, 1929

I am astonish'd how such Contemptible Knavery and Folly as this Book contains can ever have been call'd Wisdom by Men of Sense, but perhaps this never was the Case and all Men of Sense have despised the Book as Much as I do.

WILLIAM BLAKE (1757–1827). "Annotations to Bacon's 'Essays'" (editor's preface), 1798?, *The Complete Writings of William Blake*, ed. Geoffrey Keynes, 1966

In answer to queries, I'm pleased to report that historic John's Grill on Ellis, reopened after a disastrous fire, is unchanged from the original. The food is no worse than it ever was.

HERB CAEN (1916–1997). Column, *San Francisco Chronicle*, 28 September 1983

A little granite book you can lean on.

EMILY DICKINSON (1830–1886). On Ralph Waldo Emerson's *Representative Men* (1850). In Michael Dirda, "Journey Into the Self," *Washington Post National Weekly Edition*, 24 April 1995

Many thanks; I shall lose no time in reading it.

BENJAMIN DISRAELI (1808–1881). Acknowledging receipt of an unsolicited manuscript. In Wilfrid Meynell, *The Man Disraeli*, 1927

Dear Sir,
    I am not blind to the worth of the wonderful gift of "Leaves of Grass." I find it the most extraordinary piece of wit and wisdom that America has yet contributed. . . . I find incomparable things said incomparably well, as they must be. I find the courage of treatment, which so delights us, and which large perception only can inspire. I greet you at the beginning of a great career. . . .

RALPH WALDO EMERSON (1803–1882). Letter to Walt Whitman, 21 July 1855

Mr. Presley has no discernible singing ability. His specialty is rhythm songs which he renders in an undistinguished whine; his phrasing, if it can be called that, consists of the stereotyped variations that go with a beginner's aria in a bathtub. For the ear he is an unutterable bore.

JACK GOULD (1919–1993). "TV: New Phenomenon," *New York Times,* 6 June 1956

The remarkable thing about Shakespeare is that he is really very good—in spite of all the people who say he is very good.

ROBERT GRAVES (1895–1985). In *Observer* (British newspaper), 6 December 1964

I have read your book and much like it.

MOSES HADAS (1900–1966)

The sequence of ideas is commonplace to the point of banality, the ordinary coin of funereal oratory.

JAMES HURT. Literary critic. On Abraham Lincoln's *Gettysburg Address.* In Garry Wills, "The Words That Remade America: Lincoln at Gettysburg," *Atlantic,* June 1992

The perfection of rottenness.

WILLIAM JAMES (1842–1910). On Santayana's doctoral thesis. In Bertrand Russell, "George Santayana," *Portraits from Memory,* 1956

[Lord Chesterfield's letters to his son] teach the morals of a whore, and the manners of a dancing master.

SAMUEL JOHNSON (1709–1784). 1754. In James Boswell, *The Life of Samuel Johnson,* 1791

Corneille is to Shakespeare as a clipped hedge is to a forest.

SAMUEL JOHNSON (1709–1784). In Hester Lynch Piozzi, *Anecdotes of the Late Samuel Johnson, LL.D.,* p. 41, 1786, S. C. Roberts, ed., 1932

Batman Forever almost lives up to its title. I thought it would never end.

STANLEY KAUFFMANN (1916–). A two-sentence film review, "Cry Havoc," *New Republic,* 17 July 1995

I saw the play under the worst circumstances: the curtain was up.

GEORGE S. KAUFMAN (1899–1961)

Me no Leica.

WALTER KERR (1913–1996). On John Van Druten's *I Am a Camera* (play). In *New York Herald Tribune,* 31 December 1951

I will not say that "Portofino" is the worst musical *ever* produced, because I've only been seeing musicals since 1919.

WALTER KERR (1913–1996). Closing sentence of his review. In *New York Herald Tribune,* 1956, quoted in Frank Rich, "The Drama Critic Who Made the Pulse Race," *New York Times,* 20 October 1996

This book contains much that is good and new: pity that the good is not new, and the new is not good.

GOTTHOLD EPHRAIM LESSING (1729–1781)

I played myself. I was miscast.

OSCAR LEVANT (1906–1972). On his performance in *The Band Wagon* (film), 1953. In Joan Peyser, "Oscar Levant Might Have Said Life Miscast Him," *New York Times,* 6 October 1991

For people who like that sort of thing, that is about the sort of a thing they would like.

ABRAHAM LINCOLN (1809–1865). To a young poet who had asked him what he thought of his newly published poems. In Emanuel Hertz, ed., "Father Abraham," *Lincoln Talks: A Biography in Anecdote,* 1939

We do not go to hear what Emerson says so much as to hear Emerson.

JAMES RUSSELL LOWELL (1819–1891). "Emerson the Lecturer," *My Study Windows,* 1871

His imagination resembled the wings of an ostrich; it enabled him to run, though not to soar. When he attempted the highest flights, he became ridiculous; but while he remained in a lower region, he outstripped all competitors.

THOMAS BABINGTON MACAULAY (1800–1859). "John Dryden," *The Edinburgh Review* (Scotland), January 1828

The crudest of the great movies, but a great movie.

NORMAN MAILER (1923–). On Oliver Stone's *JFK,* "The Foothills in the Crypt," *Vanity Fair,* February 1992

Never in my life have I met anyone who did not agree that [Ralph Waldo] Emerson is an inspiring writer. One may not accept his thoughts in toto, but one comes away from a reading of him purified, so to say, and exalted. He takes you to the heights, he gives you wings. He is daring, very daring. In our day he would be muzzled, I am certain.

HENRY MILLER (1891–1980). *The Books in My Life,* 11, 1952

A symptom disguised as a system.

LEWIS MUMFORD (1895–1990). On Jean-Paul Sartre's *Existentialism* (1947), bibliography (Sartre) in *The Conduct of Life,* 1951

What [Marshall] McLuhan understands has long been familiar to students of technics: it is his singular gift for *mis*understanding both technology and man that marks his truly original contributions.

LEWIS MUMFORD (1895–1990). Bibliography (McLuhan) in *The Pentagon of Power: The Myth of the Machine,* 1970

I welcome Freud's "Woodrow Wilson" not only because of its comic appeal, which is great, but because that surely must be the last rusty nail in the Viennese Quack's coffin.

VLADIMIR NABOKOV (1899–1977). On Sigmund Freud and William C. Bullitt's *Thomas Woodrow Wilson: A Psychological Study,* complete letter to *Encounter,* February 1967

The best German book there is.

FRIEDRICH NIETZSCHE (1844–1900). On Peter Eckermann's *Conversations with Goethe,* 1836–1848. In Havelock Ellis, introduction to the Everyman edition, 1930

It was the worst inaugural address of our lifetime, and I think the only controversy will be between those who say it was completely and utterly banal and those who say, "Well, not completely and utterly."

PEGGY NOONAN (1950–). On Pres. Bill Clinton's 1997 inaugural address. In Jerry Pfarr, "The Unquotable President: Bill Clinton," *San Francisco Sunday Examiner & Chronicle,* 6 April 1997

I have been told that [Richard] Wagner's music is better than it sounds.

BILL NYE (1850–1896). In Mark Twain, 17 January 1906, *Mark Twain's Autobiography*, 1.338, ed., Albert Bigelow Paine, 1924

See Capitalism: Richard M. Nixon

I think Sartre is a bag of wind.

GEORGE ORWELL (1903–1950). Letter to F. J. Warburg, 22 October 1948, *The Collected Essays, Journalism and Letters of George Orwell*, vol. 4, eds., Sonia Orwell and Ian Angus, 1968

The House Beautiful is the play lousy.

DOROTHY PARKER (1893–1967). On Channing Pollack's play, 1933. In Alexander Woollcott, "Our Mrs. Parker," *While Rome Burns*, 1934

She runs the gamut of emotions from A to B.

DOROTHY PARKER (1893–1967). On Katharine Hepburn's performance in *The Lake* (play), 1933. In "Obituary Notes," *Publisher's Weekly*, 19 June 1967

The play is one big piece of Swiss cheese, minus the cheese.

FRANK RICH (1949–). In "Critics' Corner," *Reader's Digest*, January 1989

One of the dullest memoirs ever to lay waste to a forest.

FRANK RICH (1949–). On *Barbara Bush: A Memoir*, "That Nice Mrs. Bush," *New York Times*, 15 September 1994

[Eric] Hoffer, our resident Peasant Philosopher, is an example of articulate ignorance.

JOHN SEELYE (1931–)

I cannot express to you the pleasure it gives me to find that by the universal assent of every man of taste and learning whom I either know or correspond with, [*The Decline and Fall of the Roman Empire*] sets you at the very head of the whole literary tribe at present existing in Europe.

ADAM SMITH (1723–1790). Letter to Edward Gibbon, 10 December 1788

[Walt] Whitman . . . wanted to be in our hip pockets and night stands. In this he is clearly still a failure.

The loss is ours. Go outside and read aloud. Adventure waits. You may also find a piece of yourself you didn't know was missing.

JOEL L. SWERDLOW. Referring to *Leaves of Grass* (1855–1892). Closing words, "America's Poet: Walt Whitman," *National Geographic*, December 1994

I confess it difficult for me to read certain passages of Jefferson and Paine . . . without being brought to the edge of tears by their beauty and meaning.

ALVIN TOFFLER (1928–). *The Third Wave*, 28, 1980

Conjuring with the twenty-one "civilizations," and helping out his conjuring tricks with imperfect light, distracting noises and a certain amount of intellectual hanky-panky, he pretends that he has proved what he has merely stated. This seems to me, in so learned a man, a terrible perversion of history.

H. R. TREVOR-ROPER (1914–). On Arnold J. Toynbee's *A Study of History*, closing words, "Testing the Toynbee System," 1954. In Ashley Montagu, ed., *Toynbee and History: Critical Essays and Reviews*, 1956

I have just read your lousy review buried in the back pages. You sound like a frustrated old man who never made a success, an eight-ulcer man on a four-ulcer job, and all four ulcers working. I have never met you, but if I do you'll need a new nose and plen-

ty of beefsteak and perhaps a supporter below. Westbrook Pegler, a guttersnipe, is a gentleman compared to you. You can take that as more of an insult than as a reflection on your ancestry.

HARRY S. TRUMAN (1884–1972). Referring Paul Hume's unfavorable review of his daughter Margaret Truman's concert. Letter to Hume (*Washington Post* music critic), 6 December 1950

This is not at all bad, except as prose.

GORE VIDAL (1925–). On Herman Wouk's novel *Winds of War* (1973). In Paul Gray, "Gone with the Winds of War," *Time*, 21 May 1984

A lack of talent is not enough.

GORE VIDAL (1925–). On the Cockettes (San Francisco drag performers). In Herb Caen, column, *San Francisco Chronicle*, 10 June 1996

Critic: Your picture is not up to your mark; it is not good this time. *Whistler:* You shouldn't say it is not good. You should say you do not like it; and then, you know, you're perfectly safe. Now come and have something you do like—have some whiskey.

JAMES ABBOTT McNEILL WHISTLER (1834–1903). Painter. Format adapted. In Don C. Seitz, *Whistler Stories*, p. 35, 1913

[The] *French Revolution* is one of the most fascinating historical novels ever written.

OSCAR WILDE (1854–1900). On Thomas Carlyle's 1837 history, "The Decay of Lying," *Intentions*, 1891

The cruelest thing that has happened to Lincoln since he was shot by Booth has been to fall into the hands of Carl Sandburg.

EDMUND WILSON (1895–1972). On Sandburg's six-volume biography of Lincoln (1926–1939), letter to John Dos Passos, 30 April 1953

Anyone foolish enough to buy it deserves the excruciating experience of reading it.

JONATHAN YARDLEY (1939–). On Joe McGinniss's *The Last Brother: The Rise and Fall of Teddy Kennedy*, "'A Genuinely, Unrelievedly Rotten Book,'" *Washington Post National Weekly Edition*, 9 August 1993

❧

I don't know if Mr. Kissinger is a great writer, but anyone finishing his book is a great reader.

ANONYMOUS. On Henry A. Kissinger's *Nuclear Weapons and Foreign Policy*, 1957. In Ralph Blumenfeld et al., *Henry Kissinger: The Private and Public Story*, 10, 1974

CROWDS

See also • Crises ○ Fanatics ○ History ○ Leaders ○ Man ○ Mankind ○ The Masses ○ Mass Movements ○ Mobs ○ People ○ Propaganda ○ Revolution ○ Society ○ Tyranny ○ War

The usually isolated individual enjoys the sensation of freedom from conventional restraints and the awareness of powerwhich participation in a crowd gives him, and he may express views or commit acts of which he would otherwise be ashamed.

J. A. C. BROWN (1911–1964). *Techniques of Persuasion: From Propaganda to Brainwashing*, 4, 1963

The first point to emphasize is that the crowd never feels saturated. It remains hungry as long as there is one human being it has not reached.

ELIAS CANETTI (1905–1994). "The Crowd: The Eruption," *Crowds and Power*, tr. Carol Stewart, 1962

If it has to choose who is to be crucified, the crowd will always save Barabbas.

JEAN COCTEAU (1889–1963). "Le Coq et l'Arlequin," *Le Rappel à l'ordre*, 1926

It is necessary to join the crowd, or get out of their way, in order not to be trampled to death by them.

WILLIAM HAZLITT (1778–1830). *Characteristics in the Manner of Rochefoucault's Maxims*, 239, 1823

To be a member of a crowd is an experience closely akin to alcoholic intoxication. Most human beings feel a craving to escape from the cramping limitations of their ego, to take periodical holidays from their all too familiar, all too squalid little selves. As they do not know how to travel upwards from personality into a region of super-personality and as they are unwilling, even if they do know, to fulfill the ethical, psychological and physiological conditions of self-transcendence, they turn naturally to the descending road, the road that leads down from personality to the darkness of subhuman emotionalism and panic animality.

ALDOUS HUXLEY (1894–1963). "Decentralization and Self-Government," *Ends and Means: An Inquiry into the Nature of Ideals and into the Methods Employed for Their Realization*, 1937

See Self-Realization (Being): Huxley

Without a doubt criminal crowds exist, but virtuous and heroic crowds, and crowds of many other kinds, are also to be met with. The crimes of crowds only constitute a particular phase of their psychology.

GUSTAVE LE BON (1841–1931). Introduction to *The Crowd: A Study of the Popular Mind*, 1895, Viking Press edition, 1960

Thousands of isolated individuals may acquire at certain moments, and under the influence of certain violent emotions—such, for example, as a great national event—the characteristics of a psychological crowd. . . . An entire nation, though they may be no visible agglomeration, may become a crowd under the action of certain influences.

GUSTAVE LE BON (1841–1931). *The Crowd: A Study of the Popular Mind*, 1.1, 1895, Viking Press edition, 1960

In a crowd every sentiment and act is contagious, and contagious to such a degree that an individual readily sacrifices his personal interest to the collective interest.

GUSTAVE LE BON (1841–1931). *The Crowd: A Study of the Popular Mind*, 1.1, 1895, Viking Press edition, 1960

A happy expression, an image opportunely evoked, have occasionally deterred crowds from the most bloodthirsty acts.

GUSTAVE LE BON (1841–1931). *The Crowd: A Study of the Popular Mind*, 1.1, 1895, Viking Press edition, 1960

By the mere fact that he forms part of an organized crowd, a man descends several rungs in the ladder of civilization.

GUSTAVE LE BON (1841–1931). *The Crowd: A Study of the Popular Mind*, 1.1, 1895, Viking Press edition, 1960

The crowd, according to circumstances, may be better or worse than the individual. All depends on the nature of the suggestion to which it is exposed.

GUSTAVE LE BON (1841–1931). *The Crowd: A Study of the Popular Mind*, 1.1, 1895, Viking Press edition, 1960

A crowd may easily enact the part of an executioner, but not less easily that of a martyr.

GUSTAVE LE BON (1841–1931). *The Crowd: A Study of the Popular Mind*, 1.2.1, 1895, Viking Press edition, 1960

Whatever be the ideas suggested to crowds, they can only exercise effective influence on condition that they assume a very absolute, uncompromising, and simple shape.

GUSTAVE LE BON (1841–1931). *The Crowd: A Study of the Popular Mind*, 1.3.1, 1895, Viking Press edition, 1960

To know the art of impressing the imagination of crowds is to know at the same time the art of governing them.

GUSTAVE LE BON (1841–1931). *The Crowd: A Study of the Popular Mind*, 1.3.3, 1895, Viking Press edition, 1960

The crowd demands a god before everything else.

GUSTAVE LE BON (1841–1931). *The Crowd: A Study of the Popular Mind*, 1.4, 1895, Viking Press edition, 1960

A crowd is a servile flock that is incapable of [doing anything] without a master.

GUSTAVE LE BON (1841–1931). *The Crowd: A Study of the Popular Mind*, 2.3.1, 1895, Viking Press edition, 1960

The arousing of faith—whether religious, political, or social, whether faith in a work, in a person, or an idea—has always been the function of the great leaders of crowds. . . . To endow a man with faith is to multiply his strength tenfold.

GUSTAVE LE BON (1841–1931). *The Crowd: A Study of the Popular Mind*, 2.3.1, 1895, Viking Press edition, 1960

The leader [of a crowd] has most often started as one of the led. He has himself been hypnotized by the idea, whose apostle he has now become. . . . They are especially recruited from the ranks of those morbidly nervous, excitable, half-deranged persons who are bordering on madness.

GUSTAVE LE BON (1841–1931). *The Crowd: A Study of the Popular Mind*, 2.3.1, 1895, Viking Press edition, 1960

The intensity of their faith gives great power of suggestion to their words. The multitude is always ready to listen to the strong-willed man, who knows how to impose himself upon it. Men gathered in a crowd lose all force of will, and turn instinctively to the person who possesses the quality they lack.

GUSTAVE LE BON (1841–1931). *The Crowd: A Study of the Popular Mind*, 2.3.1, 1895, Viking Press edition, 1960

It is by examples not by arguments that crowds are guided.

GUSTAVE LE BON (1841–1931). *The Crowd: A Study of the Popular Mind*, 2.3.2, 1895, Viking Press edition, 1960

The crowd worships its heroes fanatically while they are in fashion, but it likes to turn about and roll them in the mud of satire, in order to teach them who made them and how easily it can unmake them.

WILLIAM GRAHAM SUMNER (1840–1910). *Folkways: A Study of the Sociological Importance of Usages, Manners, Customs, Mores, and Morals*, 1907

Otho did not fail to play his part; he stretched out his arms and bowed to the crowd . . . and altogether acted the slave to make himself the master.

TACITUS (A.D. 56?–120?). *The History*, 1.36, tr. Alfred J. Church and William J. Brodribb, 1942

CRUELTY

See also • Brainwashing ○ Crime ○ Dehumanization: [especially] George Orwell (1) ○ Holocaust: [especially] Adolf Eichmann (2) ○ Terrorism ○ Torture ○ Violence ○ War: [especially] Tacitus ○ World War I: Wilhelm II ○ World War II: Burke Davis

There was one little child, probably three years old, just big enough to walk through the sand. The Indians had gone ahead, and this little child was behind, following after them. The little fellow was perfectly naked, traveling in the sand. I saw one man get off his horse at a distance of about 75 yards and draw up his rifle and fire. He missed the child. Another man came up and said, "Let me try the son of a b——. I can hit him." He got down off his horse, kneeled down, and fired at the little child, but he missed him. A third man came up, and made a similar remark, and fired, and the little fellow dropped.

MAJ. ANTHONY (1820–1891). Testimony before a Congressional committee investigating "The Sand Creek Massacre" carried out by the U.S. First Colorado Cavalry Regiment in November 1864. In Helen Hunt Jackson, *A Century of Dishonor: A Sketch of the United States Government's Dealings with Some of the Indian Tribes*, 1881

Caesar saw that his work in Gaul could never be brought to a successful conclusion if similar revolts were allowed to break out constantly in different parts of the country; and his clemency was so well known that no one would think him a cruel man if for once he took severe measures. So he decided to deter all others by making an example of the defenders of Uxellodunum. All who had borne arms had their hands cut off and were then let go, so that everyone might see what punishment was meted out to evildoers.

JULIUS CAESAR (100–44 B.C.). *Commentaries on the Gallic Wars*, 8.2, tr. S. A. Handford, 1951

Do not receive overtures of peace or submission. . . . Kill every male Indian over twelve years of age.

PATRICK E. CONNOR (1820–1891). General. Order to his troops, Platte River campaign, 1865.

All the different forms of sadism which we can observe go back to one essential impulse; namely, to have complete mastery over another person, to make of him a helpless object of our will, to become the absolute ruler over him, to become his God, to do with him as one pleases. To humiliate him, to enslave him, are means toward this end, and the most radical aim is to make him suffer, since there is no greater power over another person than that of inflicting pain on him, to force him to undergo suffering without his being able to defend himself. The pleasure in the complete domination over another person (or other animate objects) is the very essence of the sadistic drive.

ERICH FROMM (1900–1980). *Escape from Freedom*, 5.1, 1941

A man of Cruelty is God's enemy.

THOMAS FULLER (1654–1734). Comp., *Gnomologia: Adages and Proverbs*, 303, 1732

Our sense of power is more vivid when we break a man's spirit than when we win his heart. For we can win a man's heart one day and lose it the next. But when we break a proud spirit, we achieve something that is final and absolute.

ERIC HOFFER (1902–1983). *The Passionate State of Mind: And Other Aphorisms*, 90, 1954

No one can understand the soul of those [Arab] beasts, those roaches. We shall either cut their throats or throw them out. I only say what you think. . . .

In two years time, [the Arabs] will turn on the radio and hear that Kahane has been named Minister of Defense. Then they will come to me, bow to me, lick my feet, and I will be merciful and will allow them to leave. Whoever does not leave will be slaughtered.

MEIR KAHANE (1932–1990). Speech, Haifa (Israel), 28 June 1985. In Robert I. Friedman, "The Sayings of Rabbi Kahane," *New York Review of Books*, 13 February 1986

Israeli soldiers have used new and highly toxic gases against Palestinian demonstrators in the Gaza Strip and West Bank, says a United Nations doctor who recently returned from the occupied region. . . .

In one incident, [Dr. John Hiddlestone, health director of the U.N. Relief and Works Agency] said, two young men were beaten and put into a room and an aerosol spray was sprayed into the room. "The room was the shut and after an hour or so two dead bodies were removed."

JAN KRCMAR. "U.N. Doctor Says Israelis Using Toxic Gas on Arabs," *San Francisco Examiner*, 14 April 1988
See Holocaust: Rudolf Hoess (2)

Moses was angry with the officers . . . who had come from service in the war. Moses said to them, "Have you let all the women live? Behold, these caused the people of Israel, by the counsel of Balaam, to act treacherously against the Lord in the matter of Pe'or, and so the plague came among the congregation of the Lord. Now therefore, kill every male among the little ones, and kill every woman who has known man by lying with him. But all the young girls who have not known man by lying with him, keep alive for yourselves.

MOSES (14th cent. B.C.). Following his army's victory over the Midianites, *Numbers* 31:14–18

There will be no loyalty, except loyalty toward the Party. There will be no love, except the love of Big Brother. There will be no laughter, except the laugh of triumph over a defeated enemy. . . . Always, at every moment, there will be the thrill of victory, the sensation of trampling on an enemy who is helpless. If you want a picture of the future, imagine a boot stamping on a human face—forever.

GEORGE ORWELL (1903–1950). *Nineteen Eighty-Four*, 3.3, 1949
See Revolutionaries: Jack London

All ferocity is born from weakness.

> SENECA THE YOUNGER (5? B.C.–A.D. 65). "On the Happy Life" (3.4), *Moral Essays*, tr. John W. Basore, 1932

I shall show you a king from the very bosom of Aristotle, even Alexander, who in the midst of a feast with his own hand stabbed Clitus, his dearest friend, with whom he had grown up, because he withheld his flattery and was reluctant to transform himself from a Macedonian and a free man into a slave. Lysimachus, like-wise a familiar friend, he threw to a lion.

> SENECA THE YOUNGER (5? B.C.–A.D. 65). "On Anger" (3.17.1), *Moral Essays*, tr. John W. Basore, 1928. Aristotle had been one of Alexander's teachers.

No body of men can be induced to do another man's killing for him unless he can convince them that they may honorably do so. The percentage of blackguards and sadists who enjoy cruelty for its own sake have to pretend that they are patriots and ministers of justice to secure the toleration of their fellow citizens.

> GEORGE BERNARD SHAW (1856–1950). *Everybody's Political What's What*, 16, 1944

The people must be left with nothing but their eyes to weep with over the war.

> PHILIP H. SHERIDAN (1831–1888). General. Urging stiff reprisals against French resistance fighters following the Franco-Prussian War, remark to Prussian Chancellor Otto von Bismarck. In Caleb Carr, "Should War Be Left to the Generals?" *New York Times Book Review*, 5 July 1992

We must act with vindictive earnestness against the Sioux, even to their extermination, men, women, and children. Nothing less will reach the root of the case.

> WILLIAM TECUMSEH SHERMAN (1820–1891). Dispatch to Gen. Ulysses S. Grant, 28 December 1866

Cruelty . . . is the conscious inflicting of pain.

> OSWALD SPENGLER (1880–1936). *Aphorisms*, 105, tr. Gisela Koch-Weser O'Brien, 1967

CUBAN MISSILE CRISIS

See also • Cold War ○ Crises ○ Decision-Making ○ International Relations ○ Lying: Arthur Sylvester ○ Nuclear Weapons ○ War

It is not hyperbolic to say, as many have, that the Cuban missile crisis was the single most dangerous episode in the history of mankind.

> BARRY GEWEN. Reviewing *The Kennedy Tapes: Inside the White House During the Cuban Missile Crisis*, "Profile in Caution," *New York Times Book Review*, 19 October 1997

We might . . . ask what would have happened if Khrushchev had not accepted within twenty-four hours Kennedy's reply/ultimatum of Saturday the 27th. At the time it seemed as if the U.S. had no fallback position and would have had to begin air strikes and an invasion [of Cuba] the following week. . . . In fact, as we have only learned in recent years, Kennedy did have a secret reserve position. He would, *in extremis*, have authorized Dean Rusk to encourage U Thant, the UN Secretary General, to propose a *public* missile swap [U.S. missiles in Turkey for Soviet missiles in Cuba] which the US would then have accepted.

> TONY JUDT (1948–). Citing Dean Rusk's *As I Saw It*, pp. 240–241, 1990, "On the Brink" (3), *New York Review of Books*, 15 January 1998

The Kennedy Tapes reveal a remarkable coolness in John Kennedy, a willingness and a capacity to listen, question, absorb, weigh, and finally adjudicate in extraordinary circumstances. At each turn in the proceedings, Kennedy chose the most moderate available option, sometimes against the specialized advice pressing in upon him.

> TONY JUDT (1948–). "On the Brink" (3), *New York Review of Books*, 15 January 1998. *The Kennedy Tapes: Inside the White House During the Cuban Missile Crisis* (Ernest R. May and Philip D. Zelikow, eds., 1997) consisted of transcripts of meetings during the crisis, which only the Kennedy brothers knew were being recorded.

I guess I'd better earn my salary this week.

> JOHN F. KENNEDY (1917–1963). Parting words in a private meeting with the writer, 18 October 1962. In Dean Acheson, "Dean Acheson's Version of Robert Kennedy's Version of the Cuban Missile Affair," *Esquire*, February 1969

If they want this job, fuck 'em. They can have it. It's no great joy to me.

> JOHN F. KENNEDY (1917–1963). After a meeting with Congressional leaders, which capped a week of intense sessions with his national security advisers, shortly before his television broadcast on the Cuban Missile Crisis, remark to his speech writer Theodore Sorensen, early evening, 22 October 1962. In Michael R. Beschloss, *The Crisis Years: Kennedy and Khrushchev, 1960–1963*, 17, 1991. Beschloss reported (p. 768 of endnotes) that his source for the quotation was Sorensen's draft of his memoir covering his years with Kennedy. The published version quoted Kennedy as saying, "If they want this job, they can have it—it's no great joy to me." (In Sorensen, *Kennedy*, 24, 1965)

This secret, swift, and extraordinary build-up of Communist missiles—in an area well known to have a special and historical relationship to the United States and the nations of the Western Hemisphere, in violation of Soviet assurances and in defiance of American and Hemispheric policy—this sudden, clandestine decision to station strategic weapons for the first time outside of Soviet soil—is a deliberately provocative and unjustified change in the status quo which cannot be accepted by this country, if our courage and our commitments are ever to be trusted again by either friend or foe.

> JOHN F. KENNEDY (1917–1963). Announcing a quarantine on all offensive military shipments to Cuba and calling upon Khrushchev to "halt and eliminate this clandestine, reckless and provocative threat to world peace," television broadcast (from the White House), 22 October 1962

If Khrushchev wants to rub my nose in the dirt, it's all over.

> JOHN F. KENNEDY (1917–1963). Remark to journalist James Wechsler. In Garry Wills, *The Kennedy Imprisonment: A Meditation on Power*, 22 (epigraph), 1981

You would agree to remove [Soviet] missiles from Cuba. . . . We, on our part, would agree . . . (a) to remove promptly the quarantine measures now in effect and (b) to give assurances against an invasion of Cuba.

> JOHN F. KENNEDY (1917–1963). Substantially agreeing to Nikita Khrushchev's proposals for ending the crisis in his letter of 26 October, letter to Khrushchev, 27 October 1962

One member of the Joint Chiefs of Staff . . . argued that we could use nuclear weapons, on the basis that our adversaries would use theirs against us in an attack. I thought, as I listened, of the many times that I had heard the military take positions which, if wrong, had the advantage that no one would be around at the end to know.

> ROBERT F. KENNEDY (1925–1968). Commenting on White House discussions during the Cuban Missile Crisis, October 1962, "Thirteen Days: The Story about How the World Almost Ended," *McCall's*, November 1968

[Soviet Ambassador Anatoly Dobrynin] raised the question of our removing [U.S.] missiles from Turkey [in return for the Soviets withdrawing their missiles from Cuba]. I said that there could be no quid pro quo or any arrangement made under this kind of threat or pressure. . . . However, I said, President Kennedy had been anxious to remove [U.S.] missiles from Turkey and Italy for a long period of time. He had ordered their removal some time ago, and it was our judgment that, within a short time after this crisis was over, those missiles would be gone.

> ROBERT F. KENNEDY (1925–1968). Recounting his conversation with Dobrynin during the evening of 27 October 1962, "Thirteen Days: The Story about How the World Almost Ended," *McCall's*, November 1968. The next day, Khrushchev, in a radio broadcast from Moscow, announced that Soviet missiles would be removed from Cuba under United Nations supervision.

While I was on an official visit to Bulgaria [in 1962] . . . one thought kept hammering away at my brain: what will happen if we lose Cuba? I knew it would have been a terrible blow to Marxism-Leninism. It would gravely diminish our stature throughout the world, but especially in Latin America. . . . We had to think up some way of confronting America with more than words. We had to establish a tangible and effective deterrent to American interference in the Caribbean. But what exactly? The logical answer was missiles.

> NIKITA KHRUSHCHEV (1894–1971). *Khrushchev Remembers*, tr. Strobe Talbott, 20, 1970

My thinking went like this: if we installed the missiles secretly and then if the United States discovered the missiles were there after they were already poised and ready to strike, the Americans would think twice before trying to liquidate our installations by military means. I knew that the United States could knock out some of our installations, but not all of them. If a quarter or even a tenth of our missiles survived—even if only one or two big ones were left—we could still hit New York, and there wouldn't be much of New York left. . . . The main thing was that the installation of our missiles in Cuba would, I thought, restrain the United States from precipitous military action against Castro's government. In addition to protecting Cuba, our missiles would have equalized what the West likes to call "the balance of power." The Americans had surrounded our country with military bases and threatened us with nuclear weapons, and now they would learn just what it feels like to have enemy missiles pointing at you; we'd be doing nothing more than giving them a little of their own medicine.

> NIKITA KHRUSHCHEV (1894–1971). *Khrushchev Remembers*, tr. Strobe Talbott, 20, 1970

If we don't do anything to Cuba, then they're going to push on Berlin, and push *real hard* because they've got us *on the run* . . . . This blockade and political action, I see leading into war. . . . this is almost as bad as the appeasement at Munich. . . . I just don't see any other solution except direct military action *right now*. [Ellipsis points in original.]

> CURTIS LeMAY (1906–1990). Air force general. Recommending an air attack on Cuba, on the fourth day of White House discussions during the Cuban Missile Crisis, 19 October 1962. In Tim Weiner, ed., "When Kennedy Faced Armageddon, and His Own Scornful Generals," *New York Times*, 5 October 1997

We are eyeball to eyeball, and the other fellow just blinked.

> DEAN RUSK (1909–1994). Secretary of state. Remark to his colleagues at the White House during the Cuban Missile Crisis soon after being informed that several Soviet ships believed to be carrying missiles to Cuba had turned back, 25 October 1962, *As I Saw It*, 13, 1990

The aftermath of the missile crisis was most interesting. Dean Acheson [former secretary of state] had opposed the quarantine strategy; he wanted an immediate air strike on Cuba. After the quarantine had proven successful, he said, "It was just plain dumb luck." Of course it was dumb luck. We were lucky; the Russians were lucky; the whole world was lucky. But I would hasten to add, you can give yourself a chance to be lucky. Acheson overlooked that.

> DEAN RUSK (1909–1994). Secretary of state. *As I Saw It*, 13, 1990

The gravest risk in this crisis was not that either head of government desired to initiate a major escalation but that events would produce actions, reactions, or miscalculations carrying the conflict beyond the control of one or the other or both.

> DEAN RUSK (1909–1994) and ROBERT M. McNAMARA (1916–) et al. "The Lessons of the Cuban Missile Crisis" (essay), *Time*, 27 September 1982. The two-page essay summarized a joint statement prepared by a number of Pres. Kennedy's key advisors on the twentieth anniversary of the crisis.

The odds that the Soviets would go all the way to war, [Pres. John F. Kennedy] later said, seemed to him then, "somewhere between one out of three and even."

> THEODORE C. SORENSEN (1928–). *Kennedy*, 24, 1965

CULTS

See also • Brainwashing ○ Evangelism ○ Heresy ○ Indoctrination ○ Religion ○ Religion, Anti- ○ Systems: Anthony Storr

The hostility expressed toward the new religions ventilates the anxieties and frustration endemic to our bureaucratized society. Offbeat groups are obvious targets because they offer an alternative to the status quo. In the present period of rapid cultural change, even solid citizens are ambivalent about conventional values. The specter of their children repudiating American traditions may make them feel even more beleaguered. Their hope is that eliminating these new movements may return us all to a more tranquil period.

> DICK ANTHONY (1939–) and THOMAS ROBBINS. "A Demonology of Cults," *Inquiry*, 1 September 1980

The difference between a religion and a cult is chiefly a matter of size. Forty-eight people donning plastic bags and shooting themselves in the head is a "cult," while a hundred million people bowing before a flesh-hating elderly celibate is obviously a world-class religion.

> BARBARA EHRENREICH (1941–). "Fun with Cults," 1994, *The Snarling Citizen: Essays*, 1995

In a time of recession and turmoil, the cults are a growth industry, their leaders successful entrepreneurs of salvation for the young. None of these new psychoreligious cults threatens to sweep the country, and probably none commands more than 5,000 full-time members. But in a country in which many of the young have recently tripped out on drugs and radical politics, the cults have become a new opiate for the youth of the '70s.

> BERKELEY RICE (1937–). "Honor Thy Father Moon," *Psychology Today*, January 1976

> See Religion, Anti-: Karl Marx

What makes a cult a cult is not its religion, whatever it is, but the practice of mind-control techniques, usually by a charismatic leader, that robs its members of their "independence of thought."

> FRANK RICH (1949–). "Heaven's Gate-gate," *New York Times*, 17 April 1997

The substitute-family function of charismatic cults . . . is the most important factor in attracting converts and holding them.

> ALAN W. SCHEFLIN (1942–) and EDWARD M. OPTON, JR. (1936–). *The Mind Manipulators: A Non-Fiction Account*, 2, 1978

For what is a cult but a collection of believers, like the early Christians, who have not yet achieved dominant status?

> RONALD STEEL (1931–). "The Hard Questions: Ordinary People," *New Republic*, 21 April 1997

Here and there in the midst of American society you meet with men full of a fanatical and almost wild spiritualism, which hardly exists in Europe. From time to time strange sects arise which endeavor to strike out extraordinary paths to eternal happiness. Religious insanity is very common in the United States.

> ALEXIS de TOCQUEVILLE (1805–1859). *Democracy in America*, 2.2.12, 1840, tr. Henry Reeve and Francis Bowen, 1862

There are too many nuts running around anyway, right? It's a good way to get rid of a few nuts, you know, you gotta look at it that way.

> TED TURNER (1938–). Expressing his opinion on the mass suicide by 39 members of the Heaven's Gate organization. In "Perspectives," *Newsweek*, 14 April 1997

A cult is a religion with no power.

> TOM WOLFE (1931–). *In Our Time*, 2, 1980

CULTURE

See also • Civilization ◦ Education ◦ History ◦ Man ◦ Mankind ◦ Values

Human culture is the art of revealing to a man the true idea of his being, his endowments, his possessions, and of fitting him to use these for the growth, renewal, and perfection of his spirit. It is the art of completing a man.

> BRONSON ALCOTT (1799–1888). "The Doctrine and Discipline of Human Culture," 1836. In George Hochfield, ed., *Selected Writings of the American Transcendentalists*, 1966

Culture, the acquainting ourselves with the best that has been known and said in the world, and thus with the history of the human spirit.

> MATTHEW ARNOLD (1822–1888). Preface to *Literature and Dogma*, 1873

People are joined to the land by work. Land, work, people, and community are all comprehended in the idea of culture.

> WENDELL BERRY (1934–). "People, Land, and Community," *Sierra*, September-October 1983

The great law of culture is: Let each become all that he was created capable of being; expand, if possible, to his full growth; resisting all impediments, casting off all foreign, especially all noxious adhesions; and show himself at length in his own shape and stature, be these what they may.

> THOMAS CARLYLE (1795–1881). "John Paul Friedrich Richter," 1827, *Critical and Miscellaneous Essays,* Carey & Hart edition, 1849

Culture may even be described simply as that which makes life worth living.

> T. S. ELIOT (1888–1965). *Notes Towards a Definition of Culture*, 1, 1948

End [i.e., purpose] of Culture, Self-creation.

> RALPH WALDO EMERSON (1803–1882). Journal, 1851, undated

One gets the impression that culture is something which was imposed on a resisting majority by a minority that understood how to possess itself of the means of power and coercion.

> SIGMUND FREUD (1856–1939). *The Future of an Illusion*, 1, 1927, tr. W. D. Robson-Scott, 1953

Storm trooper: Whenever I hear the word culture . . . I release the safety catch of my Browning [pistol]!

> HANNS JOHST (1890–1978). German playwright. *Schlageter*, 1.1, 1933 (Popular version: When I hear the word culture, I reach for my revolver.)

> See Honor: Ralph Waldo Emerson

The value of culture is its effect on character. It avails nothing unless it ennobles and strengthens that. Its use if for life. Its aim is not beauty but goodness.

> W. SOMERSET MAUGHAM (1874–1965). *The Summing Up*, 24, 1938

In achieving culture, man's first steps were doubtless the hardest, like the first pennies that lay the foundation for a fortune.

> LEWIS MUMFORD (1895–1990). *The Transformations of Man*, 1.1, 1956

The Making of a Counter Culture.

> THEODORE ROSZAK (1933–). Book title, 1969

The culture of distraction.

> ANDREI SAKHAROV (1921–1989). Referring to "mass culture" and "the degrading influence of television," Jean-Pierre Barou interview, *New York Review of Books*, 2 March 1989

Every historic culture-pattern is an organic whole in which all the parts are interdependent.

> ARNOLD J. TOYNBEE (1889–1975). "The Psychology of Encounters," *The World and the West*, 1953

CUNNING

See also • Cheating ○ Cleverness ○ Deception ○ Intelligence ○ Lying ○ Machiavellianism

Cunning often outwits itself.
> AESOP (6th cent. B.C.). "The Fox, the Cock, and the Dog," *Fables,* tr. Joseph Jacobs, 1894

Nothing doth more hurt in a State than that cunning men pass for wise.
> FRANCIS BACON (1561–1626). "Of Cunning," *Essays,* 1625

The weak in courage is strong in cunning.
> WILLIAM BLAKE (1757–1827). "Proverbs of Hell," *The Marriage of Heaven and Hell,* 9.10, 1790–1793?

Cunning proceeds from Want of Capacity.
> BENJAMIN FRANKLIN (1706–1790). *Poor Richard's Almanack,* November 1751
> See Deception: La Rochefoucauld (2)

We should do by our cunning as we do by our courage, always have it ready to defend ourselves, never to offend others.
> FULKE GREVILLE (1554–1628). *Maxims, Characters, and Reflections,* p. 173, 1756

Cunning is the art of concealing our own defects, and discovering other people's weaknesses.
> WILLIAM HAZLITT (1778–1830). *Characteristics in the Manner of Rochefoucault's Maxims,* 101, 1823

Cunning . . . is the sense of our weakness, and an attempt to affect by concealment when we cannot do openly and by force.
> WILLIAM HAZLITT (1778–1830). *Characteristics in the Manner of Rochefoucault's Maxims,* 220, 1823

✇

The greatest cunning is to have none.
> SAYING (FRENCH)

Cunning surpasses strength.
> SAYING (GERMAN)

CURIOSITY

See also • Children's Learning: John Locke (1), Alice Miller ○ Discovery ○ Intelligence ○ Knowledge ○ Wonder

When curiosity turns to serious matters, it's called research.
> MARIE von EBNER-ESCHENBACH (1830–1916). *Aphorisms,* p. 26, 1880–1905, tr. David Scrase and Wolfgang Mieder, 1994

Take heed of a gluttonous curiosity to feed on many things, lest the greediness of the appetite of thy memory spoil the digestion thereof.
> THOMAS FULLER (1608–1661). "Of Memory," *The Holy State and the Profane State,* 1642

Curiosity is ill Manners in another's House.
> THOMAS FULLER (1654–1734). Comp., *Gnomologia: Adages and Proverbs,* 1220, 1732

Curiosity is the thirst of the soul.
> SAMUEL JOHNSON (1709–1784). In *The Rambler* (English journal), 103, 12 March 1751

Curiosity is one of the most permanent and certain characteristics of a vigorous intellect.
> SAMUEL JOHNSON (1709–1784). In *The Rambler* (English journal), 103, 12 March 1751

Curiosity . . . is but an Appetite after Knowledge.
> JOHN LOCKE (1632–1704). *Some Thoughts Concerning Education,* 118, 1693

The spiritual reality behind the phenomena is . . . the ultimate objective of all curiosity. It is in virtue of this that curiosity has something divine in it.
> ARNOLD J. TOYNBEE (1889–1975). *Experiences,* 1.6.1, 1969

The public have an insatiable curiosity to know everything, except what is worth knowing.
> OSCAR WILDE (1854–1900). "The Soul of Man Under Socialism," *Fortnightly Review* (British journal), February 1891

✇

Curiosity killed the cat. Satisfaction brought it back.
> SAYING (AMERICAN)

CURSES

See also • Blessings

"You scoundrel, you have wronged me," hissed the philosopher. "May you live forever!"
> AMBROSE BIERCE (1842–1914). *Collected Works,* vol. 8, 1911

May he be cursed by day and by night. . . . May God never forgive him. We order that no one have commerce with him by speech or in writing, that no one ever give him the least sign of friendship, or approach him or live under the same roof as he, that no one read a work written or composed by him.
> PORTUGUESE SYNAGOGUE OF AMSTERDAM. Excommunication decree against the philosopher Baruch Spinoza, 2 July 1656. In André Gide, journal, summer 1948, tr. Justin O'Brien, 1951

Mercutio: A plague o' both your houses!
> SHAKESPEARE (1564–1616). *Romeo and Juliet,* 3.1.111, 1594

✇

May the worst day of your past be the best day of your future.
> SAYING (CHINESE)
> See Blessings: Laurence J. Peter

May you live in interesting times.
> SAYING (CHINESE)

May your every wish be granted.
> SAYING (CHINESE)

May all your teeth fall out, save one; and may it have a permanent tooth ache.
> SAYING (JEWISH)

May God send a fool to help you.
SAYING (JEWISH)

God damn you.
SAYING

CUSTOM

See also • Habit ○ Law ○ Past ○ Tradition

The slaves of custom are the sport of time.
FRANCIS BACON (1561–1626). *Advancement of Learning,*
6.3 (Innovation), 1605, Willey Book edition, 1944

If custom be prudently and skillfully introduced, it really becomes a second nature.
FRANCIS BACON (1561–1626). *Advancement of Learning,* 7.3, 1605,
Willey Book edition, 1944

Custom is most perfect when it beginneth in young years; this we call education.
FRANCIS BACON (1561–1626). "Of Custom," *Essays,* 1625

What is evident is not the difficulty of getting a fixed law, but getting out of a fixed law; not cementing . . . a cake of custom, but of breaking the cake of custom; not of making the first preservative habit, but of breaking through it, and reaching something better.
WALTER BAGEHOT (1826–1877). *Physics and Politics, or Thoughts
on the Application of the Principles of "Natural Selection" and
"Inheritance" to Political Society,* 2.2, 1872

Custom reconciles us to everything.
EDMUND BURKE (1729–1797). *A Philosophical Inquiry into the
Origin of Our Ideas of the Sublime and the Beautiful,* 4.18,
1756

No written law has even been more binding than unwritten custom supported by popular opinion.
CARRIE CHAPMAN CATT (1859–1947). "For the Sake of Liberty," speech
on women's suffrage at a Senate hearing, 13 February 1900

To follow foolish precedents, and wink
With both our eyes, is easier than to think.
WILLIAM COWPER (1731–1800). "Tirocinium: Or, a Review of Schools,"
l. 255, 1785

The opium of custom, whereof all drink and many go mad.
RALPH WALDO EMERSON (1803–1880). "Education," *Lectures and
Biographical Sketches,* 1883
See Religion, Anti-: Karl Marx

Nothing is so ridiculous that usage may not make it pass.
DESIDERIUS ERASMUS (1466?–1536). In William Graham Sumner,
*Folkways: A Study of the Sociological Importance of Usages, Manners,
Customs, Mores, and Morals,* 190, 1907

Bad Customs are better [broken] than kept up.
THOMAS FULLER (1654–1734). Comp., *Gnomologia: Adages and
Proverbs,* 832, 1732
See Promises: Abraham Lincoln (2)

Custom is the Guide of the Ignorant.
THOMAS FULLER (1654–1734). Comp., *Gnomologia: Adages and
Proverbs,* 1223, 1732

Custom makes all Things easy.
THOMAS FULLER (1654–1734). Comp., *Gnomologia: Adages and
Proverbs,* 1225, 1732

Custom conquers fear and shame.
JOHN GAY (1685–1732). *Fables,* 1.13, 1727–1738

Custom . . . is the great guide of human life.
DAVID HUME (1711–1776). *An Enquiry Concerning Human
Understanding,* 5.1, 1748

Every custom was once an eccentricity.
HOLBROOK JACKSON (1874–1948)

Custom is the crystallization of the whole of a society's habits. A people among whom custom is altogether sovereign endures the despotism of the dead.
BERTRAND de JOUVENEL (1903–1987). *On Power: Its Nature and the
History of Its Growth,* 11.6, 1945, tr. J. F. Huntington,
1948

The effect of custom, in preventing any misgiving respecting the rules of conduct which mankind impose on one another, is all the more complete because the subject is one on which it is not generally considered necessary that reasons should be given, either by one person to others or by each to himself.
JOHN STUART MILL (1806–1873). *On Liberty,* 1, 1859

The despotism of custom is everywhere the standing hindrance to human advancement.
JOHN STUART MILL (1806–1873). *On Liberty,* 3, 1859

Customs are made for customary circumstances and customary characters.
JOHN STUART MILL (1806–1873). *On Liberty,* 3, 1859

Social life is so immersed in an atmosphere of false conventions that society would be thrown into a turmoil if an attempt were made to correct them.
MARIA MONTESSORI (1870–1952). *The Secret of Childhood,* 23, 1938,
tr. M. Joseph Costelloe, 1972

Hamlet: It is a custom
More honor'd in the breach than the observance.
SHAKESPEARE (1564–1616). *Hamlet,* 1.4.16, 1600

Othello: The tyrant custom.
SHAKESPEARE (1564–1616). *Othello,* 1.3.230, 1604

Caesar. He is a barbarian, and thinks that the customs of his tribe and island are the laws of nature.
GEORGE BERNARD SHAW (1856–1950). *Caesar and Cleopatra,* 2, 1899

'Tis best, wherever we are, to follow still
The customs of the country.
SOPHOCLES (496?–406 B.C.). "Fragments" (674), *Sophocles: Tragedies
and Fragments,* 1, tr. E. H. Plumptre, 1865
See Conformity: Robert Burton

Custom adapts itself to expediency.

> TACITUS (A.D. 56?–120?). *The Annals,* 12.6, tr. Alfred J. Church and William J. Brodribb, 1942

Often, the less there is to justify a traditional custom, the harder it is to get rid of it.

> MARK TWAIN (1835–1910). *The Adventures of Tom Sawyer,* 5, 1876

Laws are sand, customs are rock. Laws can be evaded and punishment escaped, but an openly transgressed custom brings sure punishment.

> MARK TWAIN (1835–1910). "The Gorky Incident," 1906, *Letters from the Earth,* ed. Bernard DeVoto, 1962

Custom lie [*sic*] upon thee with a weight,
Heavy as frost, and deep almost as life!

> WILLIAM WORDSWORTH (1770–1850). "Ode: Intimations of Immortality from Recollections of Early Childhood," 8, 1807

🌿

Convention is like the shell to the chick, a protection till he is strong enough to break it through.

> ANONYMOUS. In Learned Hand, "The Preservation of Personality," commencement address at Bryn Mawr College (Pennsylvania), 2 June 1927

Custom is stronger than law, but necessity is stronger custom.

> ANONYMOUS

Follow the customs or flee the country.

> SAYING (ZULU)

CYNICISM

See also • Doubt ○ Faith ○ Idealism: Irving Layton ○ Pessimism: Mary Pettibone Poole ○ Sentimentality: Oscar Wilde ○ Skepticism

A cynic is just a man who found out when he was about ten that there wasn't any Santa Claus, and he's still upset.

> JAMES GOULD COZZENS (1903–1978)

Scratch a cynic and underneath, as often as not, you will find a dead idealist.

> JOSEPH EPSTEIN (1928–). "Our Favorite Cynic," *New Yorker,* 25 March 1996

A cynic is not merely one who reads bitter lessons from the past, he is one who is prematurely disappointed in the future.

> SYDNEY J. HARRIS (1917–1986). *On the Contrary,* 7, 1962

Cynicism is an unpleasant way of saying the truth.

> LILLIAN HELLMAN (1905–1984). *The Little Foxes,* 1, 1939

As more and more people find themselves working at jobs that are in fact beneath their abilities, as leisure and sociability themselves take on the qualities of work, the posture of cynical detachment becomes the dominant style of everyday intercourse.

> CHRISTOPHER LASCH (1932–1994). *The Culture of Narcissism: American Life in an Age of Diminishing Expectations,* 4, 1979

Cynics are only happy in making the world as barren for others as they have made it for themselves.

> GEORGE MEREDITH (1828–1909)

How do you keep commitment once you *know?* How do you not get cynical?

> JOHN SAYLES (1950–). Film maker. Claudia Dreifus interview, *Progressive,* November 1991

No matter how cynical you become, it's never enough to keep up.

> JANE WAGNER (1935–). *The Search for Signs of Intelligent Life in the Universe* (comedy show), 1985, performed by Lily Tomlin

Cecil Graham: What is a cynic?
Lord Darlington: A man who knows the price of everything and the value of nothing.

> OSCAR WILDE (1854–1900). *Lady Windermere's Fan,* 3, 1892

Cynicism is merely the art of seeing things as they are instead of as they ought to be.

> OSCAR WILDE (1854–1900). "Sebastian Melmoth," *The Works of Oscar Wilde: Epigrams, Phrases and Philosophies for the Use of the Young,* Sunflower edition, 1909

🌿

Cynicism is the last refuge of the indifferent.

> ANONYMOUS
>
> See Patriotism: Samuel Johnson

Cynics are always the last to change their spots.

> ANONYMOUS

DANCE

See also • Art ○ Creativity ○ Music

I just put my feet in the air and move them around.

> FRED ASTAIR (1899–1987)

Dancing is the body made poetic.

> ERNST BACON. *Notes on the Piano,* 14, 1963

Heaven,
I'm in heaven
And my heart beats so that
I can hardly speak,
And I seem to find
The happiness I seek
When we're out together dancing
Cheek to cheek.

IRVING BERLIN (1888–1989). "Cheek to Cheek" (song). In the musical film *Top Hat*, 1935

The truest expression of a people is in its dances and its music. Bodies never lie.

AGNES DE MILLE (1905–1993). "Do I Hear A Waltz?" *New York Times Magazine*, 11 May 1975

Movements are as eloquent as words.

ISADORA DUNCAN (1878–1927). Inscription on a plaque marking her birthplace on Taylor Street in San Francisco, 1973

Dancing is the loftiest, the most moving, the most beautiful of the arts, because it is no mere translation or abstraction from life; it is life itself.

HAVELOCK ELLIS (1859–1939). *The Dance of Life*, 2.5, 1923

"I Could Have Danced All Night."

ALAN JAY LERNER (1918–1986). Song title. In the musical *My Fair Lady*, 1956

Since nothing appears to me to give Children so much becoming Confidence and Behavior, and so raise them to the Conversation of those above their Age, as *Dancing*, I think they should be taught to dance as soon as they are capable of learning it.

JOHN LOCKE (1632–1704). *Some Thoughts Concerning Education*, 67, 1693

Always the question for dancers is: Can we fly?

JEAN-CHRISTOPHE MAILLOT. Ballet choreographer. In Jennifer Dunning, "The Return of a Dancer, Abstract and Stories," *New York Times*, 4 November 1997

Let that day be lost to us on which we did not dance once!

FRIEDRICH NIETZSCHE (1844–1900). "Of Old and New Law-Tables" (23), *Thus Spoke Zarathustra*, 1892, tr. R. J. Hollingdale, 1961

Those move easiest who have learn'd to dance.

ALEXANDER POPE (1688–1744). *An Essay on Criticism*, l. 363, 1711

[Dancing is] a perpendicular expression of a horizontal desire.

GEORGE BERNARD SHAW (1854–1950). In *New Statesman* (British magazine), 23 March 1962

DANGER

See also • Courage ○ Crises ○ Dehumanization: Erich Fromm ○ Desperation ○ Fear ○ Opportunity ○ Prudence: Rules ○ Safety ○ Speed ○ Suspicion

Mankind [is] naturally divided into three sorts; one third of them are animated at the first appearance of danger, and will press forward to meet and examine it; another third are alarmed by it, but will neither advance nor retreat, till they know the nature of it, but stand to meet it. The remaining third will run or fly upon the first thought of it.

JOHN ADAMS (1735–1826). In Ralph Waldo Emerson, journal, August 1851

A common danger unites even the bitterest enemies.

ARISTOTLE (384–322 B.C.). *Politics*, 5.5, tr. Benjamin Jowett, 1885

Perils commonly ask to be paid in pleasures.

FRANCIS BACON (1909–1992). "Of Love," *Essays*, 1625

Nothing in life is so exhilarating as to be shot at without result.

WINSTON CHURCHILL (1874–1965). *The Story of the Malakand Field Force*, 10, 1898

The greater the risk, the sweeter the fruit.

PIERRE CORNEILLE (1606–1684). *Cinna*, 1.1, 1639, tr. Noel Clark, 1993

A Danger foreseen is half avoided.

THOMAS FULLER (1654–1734). Comp., *Gnomologia: Adages and Proverbs*, 67, 1732

See Preparedness: Cervantes

Danger past, God is forgotten.

THOMAS FULLER (1654–1734). Comp., *Gnomologia: Adages and Proverbs*, 1234, 1732

Think of thy Deliverance, as well as of thy Danger.

THOMAS FULLER (1654–1734). Comp., *Gnomologia: Adages and Proverbs*, 4995, 1732

I wish to have no Connection with any Ship that does not sail *fast*, for I intend to go *in harm's way*.

JOHN PAUL JONES (1747–1792). Naval captain. Letter to le Ray de Chaumont, 16 November 1778

"You are out of danger," he said. I laughed, I guess, and said, "How can I be—I don't feel dead yet."

MARGARET LAURENCE (1926–1987). *A Jest of God*, 11, 1966

When we have just gotten out of the way of a vehicle, we are most in danger of being run over.

FRIEDRICH NIETZSCHE (1844–1900). *Human, All Too Human*, 564, 1878, tr. Marion Faber, 1984

What is essential . . . is not so much "bravery" in the face of [physical] danger as the ability to think "selflessly"—to blank out any thought of personal fear by concentrating completely on how to meet the danger.

RICHARD M. NIXON (1913–1994). *Six Crises*, 4 (epigraph), 1962

In a moment of extreme danger things can be done which have previously been thought impossible. Mortal danger is an effective antidote for fixed ideas.

ERWIN ROMMEL (1891–1944). 1942, *The Rommel Papers*, 11, ed. B. H. Liddell Hart, 1953

King Henry: 'Tis true that we are in great danger;
The greater therefore should our courage be.

SHAKESPEARE (1564–1616). *Henry V*, 4.1.1, 1598

Frogs will permit themselves to be boiled to death. If the temperature of the water in which the frog is sitting is slowly raised, the frog does not become aware of its danger until it is too late to do anything about it.

ROBERT THEOBALD. "What New Directions for Society?" *Los Angeles Times*, 24 May 1970

Fear creates danger, and courage dispels it.

HENRY DAVID THOREAU (1817–1862). Journal, 12 November 1859

I heard bullets whistle, and, believe me, there is something charming in the sound.

> GEORGE WASHINGTON (1732–1799). Following a skirmish near Great Meadow (Pennsylvania) during the French and Indian War. Letter to his brother John Augustine Washington, 31 May 1754

DARING

See also • Boldness ○ Bravery: Herman Melville ○ Courage

There are cases in which the greatest daring is the greatest wisdom.

> KARL von CLAUSEWITZ (1780–1831). *On War,* 2.5, 1832, tr. J. J. Graham, 1873
>
> See Boldness: Lucius Marcius ○ Crises: Henry A. Kissinger (2)

A daring pilot in extremity;
Pleas'd with the danger, when the waves went high,
He sought the storms; but, for a calm unfit,
Would steer too nigh the sands, to boast his wit.

> JOHN DRYDEN (1631–1700). *Absalom and Achitophel,* 1.159, 1681

Dare to be yourself.

> ANDRÉ GIDE (1869–1951). Journal, 10 June 1891, tr. Justin O'Brien, 1948

A daring beginning is halfway to winning.

> HEINRICH HEINE (1797–1856). "To the Young," *Romancero,* 1851

Over-daring is as great a vice as over-fearing.

> BEN JONSON (1573–1637). *The New Inn,* 4.3, 1629

Great daring often conceals great fear.

> LUCAN (A.D. 39–65). *Pharsalia,* 4.702

Dare to think and dare to do.

> MAO TSE-TUNG (1893–1976). Slogan. In Edgar Snow, *Red China Today,* 20, 1970

I have but dared too much.

> NAPOLEON (1769–1821). Remark to his brother Lucien Bonaparte after being defeated at Waterloo, 1815, *The Mind of Napoleon: A Selection from His Written and Spoken Words,* 59, ed. J. Christopher Herold, 1955

❧

Who dares, wins.

> SAYING

DAY OF JUDGMENT

See also • God ○ God & Man ○ Redemption ○ Religion ○ Salvation

So, I think, God hides some souls away,
Sweetly to surprise us, the last day.

> MARY BRANCH (1840–1922). "The Petrified Fern"

[God] might begin the Day of Judgment, but he would probably find himself in the dock long before it was over.

> SAMUEL BUTLER (1835–1902). *Further Extracts from the Note-Books of Samuel Butler,* 3, ed. A. T. Bartholomew, 1934

I'll tell you a big secret, *mon cher.* Don't wait for the Last Judgment. It takes place every day.

> ALBERT CAMUS (1913–1960). *The Fall,* p. 111, tr. Justin O'Brien, 1956

The resurrected suddenly begin accusing God in all languages: the true Last Judgment.

> ELIAS CANETTI (1905–1994). 1947, *The Human Province,* tr. Joachim Neugroschel, 1978

But see how many now cry out "Christ! Christ?"
who shall be farther from him at the Judgment
than many who, on earth, did not know Christ.

> DANTE (A.D. 1265–1321). "Paradise" (19.106), *The Divine Comedy,* 1321, tr. John Ciardi, 1954

The Day of Judgment is either approaching or it is not. If it is not, there is no cause for adjournment. If it is, I choose to be found doing my duty. I wish, therefore, that candles be brought.

> COL. DAVENPORT (18th cent.). Speaker of the Connecticut House of Representatives. Responding to his colleagues' clamor for adjournment because of their fear that the darkened skies at midday signaled the end of the world, 19 May 1790. In Alistair Cooke, "Getting Away from It All," *One Man's America,* 1952
>
> See Death: Montaigne (2)

Man's willingness to turn to history rather than to God for final judgment reveals how truly secular our culture and society have become. . . . This recourse to historical judgment is more natural among Marxists who have a faith in the course of history which others do not share. Leaders in the Western democracies, nevertheless, make a similar appeal to history, hoping that subsequent events will prove that their decisions were the right ones in both moral and practical terms.

> PETER W. DICKSON. *Kissinger and the Meaning of History,* 1, 1978

No man has learned anything until he knows that every day is the Judgment Day.

> RALPH WALDO EMERSON (1803–1882). Journal, May 1849

At the Day of Judgment, we shall not be asked what Proficiency we have made in Languages or Philosophy; but whether we have liv'd virtuously and piously.

> BENJAMIN FRANKLIN (1706–1790). *Poor Richard's Almanack,* December 1757

The haughtiness of man shall be humbled,
and the pride of men shall be brought low;
and the Lord alone will be exalted in that day.

> ISAIAH (8th cent. B.C.). *Isaiah* 2:17

If we are soon to die, or if we believe a day of judgment to be near at hand, how quickly do we put our moral house in order.

> WILLIAM JAMES (1842–1910). *The Varieties of Religious Experience: A Study in Human Nature,* 11, 12, and 13, 1902

You will hear of wars and rumors of wars.

> JESUS (A.D. 1st cent.). *Matthew* 24:6

This gospel of the kingdom will be preached throughout the whole world, as a testimony to all nations; and then the end will come.

JESUS (A.D. 1st cent.). *Matthew* 24:14

See Evangelism: Jesus

Of that day or that hour no one knows, not even the angels in heaven, nor the Son, but only the Father. Take heed, watch; for you do not know when the time will come. It is like a man going on a journey, when he leaves home and puts his servants in charge, each with his work, and commands the doorkeeper to be on the watch. Watch therefore—for you do not know when the master of the house will come, in the evening, or at midnight, or at cockcrow, or in the morning—lest he come suddenly and find you asleep. And what I say to you I say to all: Watch.

JESUS (A.D. 1st cent.). *Mark* 13:32–37

Only our concept of Time makes it possible for us to speak of the Day of Judgment by that name; in reality it is a summary court in perpetual session.

FRANZ KAFKA (1883–1924). "Reflections on Sin, Pain, Hope, and the True Way" (38), 1917–1920, *The Great Wall of China*, 1931, tr. Willa and Edwin Muir, 1946

In a sense, every day is judgment day, and we, through our deeds and words, our silence and speech, are constantly writing in the Book of Life.

MARTIN LUTHER KING, JR. (1929–1968). *Strength to Love*, 9.2, 1963

Oh, East is East, and West is West, and never the twain shall
  meet,
Till Earth and Sky stand presently at God's great Judgment Seat.

RUDYARD KIPLING (1865–1939). Opening lines, "The Ballad of East and West," 1889

To gladden the heart of the weary, to remove the suffering of the afflicted, has its own reward. In the day of trouble, the memory of the action comes like a rush of the torrent and takes our burden away.

MUHAMMAD (A.D. 570?–632). *The Sayings of Muhammad*, 247, tr. Abdullah Al-Suhrawardy, 1941

Lo! I tell you a mystery. We shall not all sleep, but we shall be changed, in a moment, in the twinkling of an eye, at the last trumpet. For the trumpet will sound, and the dead will be raised imperishable, and we shall be changed.

PAUL (A.D. 1st cent.). *1 Corinthians* 15:51–52

The day of the Lord will come like a thief in the night.

PAUL (A.D. 1st cent.). *1 Thessalonians* 5:2

When man appears before the Throne of Judgment, the first question he is asked is not: "Have you believed in God?" or "Have you prayed and observed the ritual?" He is asked: "Have you dealt honorably and faithfully in all your dealings with your fellow man?"

TALMUD. (A.D. 1st–6th cent.). Rabbinical writings. In Lewis Browne, ed., *The Wisdom of Israel*, rev. ed., pp. 186–187, 1955 (1948)

Charity and lovingkindness are powerful defenses on the Day of Judgment.

TALMUD (A.D. 1st–6th cent.). Rabbinical writings. In Louis I. Newman, comp., *The Talmudic Anthology*, 111, 1945

O wretched and foolish sinner, who tremble before the anger of man, how will you answer to God, who knows all your wickedness? Why do you not prepare yourself against the Day of Judgment, when no advocate can defend or excuse you, but each man will be hard put to answer for himself?

THOMAS à KEMPIS (1380–1471). *The Imitation of Christ*, 1.24, tr. Leo Sherley-Price, 1952

And the Lord will become king over all the earth; on that day the Lord will be one and his name one.

ZECHARIAH (6th cent. B.C.). *Zechariah* 14:9

DAYS

See also • Dance: Friedrich Nietzsche ○ Months ○ Morning ○ Present ○ Seasons ○ Time

Think that day lost whose descending sun
Views from thy hand no noble action done.

JACOB BOBART (17th cent.). *Virtus sua Gloria*. In David Krieg's autograph album (signed by the author and dated 1697), British Museum, London

The day, if well employed, is long enough for everything.

LORD CHESTERFIELD (1694–1773). Letter to his son, 8 January 1751

Today is the first day of the rest of your life.

CHARLES DEDERICH (1913–1997). Synanon founder. Attributed. Speech, 1969

A Day is a miniature Eternity.

RALPH WALDO EMERSON (1803–1882). Journal, 17 March 1836

Yesterday the best day of the year we spent in the afternoon on the river. A sky of Calcutta, light, air, clouds, water, banks, birds, grass, pads, lilies, were in perfection, and it was delicious to live.

RALPH WALDO EMERSON (1803–1882). Journal, 28 July 1857

Some days are for living. Others are for getting through.

MALCOLM S. FORBES (1919–1990). "You Don't Say?" *The Sayings of Chairman Malcolm: The Capitalist's Handbook*, 1978

One Today is worth two Tomorrows.

BENJAMIN FRANKLIN (1706–1790). *Poor Richard's Almanack*, April 1757

Praise not the Day before Night.

THOMAS FULLER (1654–1734). Comp., *Gnomologia: Adages and Proverbs*, 3919, 1732

What a Day may bring a Day may take away.

THOMAS FULLER (1654–1734). Comp., *Gnomologia: Adages and Proverbs*, 5475, 1732

Yesterday is but today's memory and tomorrow is today's dream.

KAHLIL GIBRAN (1883–1931). "On Time," *The Prophet*, 1923

Seize the day, put no trust in tomorrow. [Carpe diem.]

HORACE (65–8 B.C.). *Odes*, 1.11

Remember the weekday, to keep it holy.

ELBERT HUBBARD (1856–1915). *The Note Book of Elbert Hubbard*, p. 26, comp. Elbert Hubbard II, 1927

On a Clear Day You Can See Forever.
> ALAN JAY LERNER (1918–1986). Musical title, 1965

Each day the world is born anew
For him who takes it rightly.
> JAMES RUSSELL LOWELL (1819–1891). "Gold Egg: A Dream-Fantasy,"
> *Under the Willows and Other Poems,* 1868

So many deeds cry out to be done, and always urgently. The world rolls on. Time passes. Ten thousand years are too long. Seize the day, seize the hour.
> MAO TSE-TUNG (1893–1976). Quoted by Richard M. Nixon, dinner
> toast, Peking, February 1972. In Henry A. Kissinger, *White House
> Years,* 24, 1979

Remember the sabbath day, to keep it holy.
> MOSES (14th cen.t B.C.). The Fourth Commandment, *Exodus* 20:8

With the Lord one day is as a thousand years, and a thousand years as one day.
> PETER (A.D. 1st cent.). *Peter* 3:8

Every day should be passed as if it were to be our last.
> PUBLIUS SYRUS (85–43 B.C.). *Moral Sayings,* 633, tr. Darius Lyman, Jr.,
> 1862

Each day is a little life; every waking and rising a little birth, every fresh morning a little youth, every going to rest and sleep a little death.
> ARTHUR SCHOPENHAUER (1788–1860). "Counsels and Maxims" (2.13),
> *Essays of Arthur Schopenhauer,* tr. T. Bailey Saunders, 1851

Every evening we are poorer by a day.
> ARTHUR SCHOPENHAUER (1788–1860). "Studies in Pessimism:
> The Vanity of Existence," *Essays of Arthur Schopenhauer,* tr. T. Bailey
> Saunders, 1851

Only that day dawns to which we are awake.
> HENRY DAVID THOREAU (1817–1862). "Conclusion," *Walden; or Life in
> the Woods,* 1854

I find the best way to spend my days—at least did long ago—is the free way: not to make plans, but to go this path or that as the mood dictates.
> WALT WHITMAN (1819–1892). Remark to the author, 29 July 1888.
> In Horace Traubel, *Walt Whitman's Camden Conversations,* ed. Walter
> Teller, 1973

One of those heavenly days that cannot die.
> WILLIAM WORDSWORTH (1770–1850). "Nutting," l. 3, 1800

❦

Every day is a once-in-a-lifetime day.
> ANONYMOUS

One day at a time.
> SAYING

THE DEAD

See also • Death ○ Tradition: G. K. Chesterton

[Let] nothing but good be said of the dead.
> CHILON (6th cent. B.C.). One of the Seven Sages of Greece

The dead know only one thing: It is better to be alive.
> ELROY FLECKER (1884–1915). In Colin Wilson, *The Outsider,* 3, 1956
> See Epitaphs: W. C. Fields

When We Dead Awaken.
> HENRIK IBSEN (1828–1906). Play title, 1900

The earth belongs to the living, not to the dead.
> THOMAS JEFFERSON (1743–1826). Letter to John W. Eppes, 24 June
> 1813

Follow me; and let the dead bury their dead.
> JESUS (A.D. 1st cent.). Remark to a disciple who wanted to bury his
> father, *Matthew* 8:22 (King James Version)
> See Past: Henry Wadsworth Longfellow

When we are dead, we are praised by those who survive us, though we frequently have no other merit than that of being no longer alive.
> LA BRUYÈRE (1645–1696). "Of Opinions" (78), *The Characters,* 1688,
> tr. Henri van Laun, 1929

DEATH

See also • Age ○ Assassination ○ The Dead ○ Disease: Saying (Persian) ○ Epitaphs ○ Funerals ○ Grief ○ Immortality ○ Killing ○ Last Words ○ Life ○ Longevity ○ Murder ○ Punishment, Capital ○ Suicide ○ Timing: Anonymous (*Bible*) ○ Violence

It's not that I'm afraid to die. I just don't want to be there when it happens.
> WOODY ALLEN (1935–). "Death (A Play)," *Without Feathers,*
> 1975

Horror at the sight of death turns into satisfaction that it is someone else who is dead.
> ELIAS CANETTI (1905–1994). "The Survivor: The Survivor," *Crowds and
> Power,* tr. Carol Stewart, 1962

There's a remedy for all things but death, which will be sure to lay us flat one time or other.
> CERVANTES (1547–1616). *Don Quixote,* 2.3.10, 1615, tr. Peter Anthony
> Motteux and John Ozell, 1743

A woman of ninety said to M. de Fontenelle, then ninety-five, "Death has forgotten us." "Shh," said M. de Fontenelle, putting his finger to his lips.
> CHAMFORT (1741–1794). *Characters and Anecdotes,* 1796,
> tr. W. S. Merwin, 1984

Philip Marlow: You were dead, you were sleeping the big sleep.
> RAYMOND CHANDLER (1888–1959) *The Big Sleep,* 32, 1939

I, fed with judgment, in a fleshly tomb, am
Buried above ground.
> WILLIAM COWPER (1731–1800). "Lines Written during a Period of
> Insanity," l. 19, 1816
> See Unhappiness: Sophocles

Old Marley was as dead as a doornail.

> CHARLES DICKENS (1812–1870). *A Christmas Carol,* 1, 1843

First—Chill—then Stupor—then the letting go—

> EMILY DICKINSON (1830–1886). "After great pain, a formal feeling comes," 1862?

No man is an Island, entire of itself; every man is a piece of the Continent, a part of the main; if a clod be washed away by the sea, Europe is the less, as well as if a promontory were, as well as if a manor of thy friends or of thine own were; any man's death diminishes me because I am involved in Mankind; And therefore never send to know for whom the bell tolls; it tolls for thee.

> JOHN DONNE (1572–1631). *Devotions upon Emergent Occasions,* 17, 1624
>
> See Unity: Mohandas K. Gandhi

Death be not proud, though some have called thee
Mighty and dreadful, for thou art not so;
For those whom thou think'st thou dost overthrow
Die not, poor Death, nor yet canst thou kill me.

> JOHN DONNE (1572–1631). *Holy Sonnets,* 10.1, 1633, ed. Roger E. Bennett, 1942

How many deaths will it take till he knows
That too many people have died?
The answer, my friend, is blowin' in the wind,
The answer is blowin' in the wind.

> BOB DYLAN (1941–). "Blowin' in the Wind" (song), 1962

Perhaps the gods are kind to us, by making life more disagreeable as we grow older. In the end, death seems less intolerable than the manifold burdens we carry.

> SIGMUND FREUD (1856–1939). At age 74, interview with the author. In George Sylvester Viereck, "Sigmund Freud Confronts the Sphinx," *Glimpses of the Great,* 1930

To die is poignantly bitter, but the idea of having to die without having lived is unbearable.

> ERICH FROMM (1900–1980). *Man for Himself: An Inquiry into the Psychology of Ethics,* 4.2.B, 1947

Tired of living,
And scared of dying.

> OSCAR HAMMERSTEIN II (1895–1960). "Ol' Man River" (song). In the musical *Show Boat,* 1927

Death takes no bribes.

> JAMES HOWELL (1593–1666). Comp., "Spanish" (p. 15), *Paroimiographia: Proverbs, or Old Sayed Sawes & Adages in English . . . Italian, French and Spanish,* 1659

Godammit! He beat me to it.

> JANIS JOPLIN (1943–1970). Rock singer. On the death—shortly before her own—of rock musician Jimi Hendrix (both deaths were ascribed to drug abuse

But this *long run* is a misleading guide to current affairs. In the *long run,* we are all dead.

> JOHN MAYNARD KEYNES (1883–1946). *A Tract on Monetary Reform,* 3, 1923

Ishmael: Death is only a launching into the region of the strange Untried; it is but the first salutation to the possibilities of the immense Remote, the Wild, the Watery, the Unshored.

> HERMAN MELVILLE (1819–1891). *Moby-Dick; or, The Whale,* 112, 1851, ed. Harold Beaver, 1972

To live a life half dead, a living death.

> JOHN MILTON (1609–1674). *Samson Agonistes,* l. 100, 1671

We die only once, and for such a long time!

> MOLIÈRE (1622–1673). *Le Dépit amoureux,* 5.3, 1656

Death often weighs heavier on us by its weight on others, and pains us by their pain almost as much as by our own, and sometimes even more.

> MONTAIGNE (1533–1592). "On Vanity," *Essays,* 1588, tr. Donald M. Frame, 1958

I want death to find me planting my cabbages.

> MONTAIGNE (1533–1592). "That to Philosophize Is to Learn to Die," *Essays,* 1588, tr. Donald M. Frame, 1958
>
> See Day of Judgment: Col. Davenport

Slowly, gradually, he detached himself, breathing less and less, fainter and fainter; then was he off and free, like a dry leaf from the tree, floating down and away.

> HELEN NEARING (1904–1995). Recalling the death of her husband Scott soon after his one-hundredth birthday, "Twilight and Evening Star," *Loving and Leaving the Good Life,* 1992

How could they tell?

> DOROTHY PARKER (1893–1967). When informed of Pres. Calvin Coolidge's death, 1933. In John Keats, *You Might as Well Live,* 1970. Coolidge was notoriously sluggish.

When a man lies dying, he does not die from disease alone. He dies from his whole life.

> CHARLES PÉGUY (1873–1914). "Basic Verities: The Search for Truth," *Basic Verities: Prose and Poetry,* tr. Ann and Julian Green, 1943

Years foll'wing Years, steal something ev'ry day,
At last they steal us from our selves away.

> ALEXANDER POPE (1688–1744). *Imitations of Horace,* 2.2(Epistle).72, 1733–1738

Already, I am developing a taste for walking in cemeteries.

> JULES RENARD (1864–1910). A few months before his death, journal, December 1909, tr. Louise Bogan and Elizabeth Roget, 1964

I don't mind having to die. I've had my good time . . . and I don't mind having to pay for it. But to think that those swine will say that I'm out of the game. [Ellipsis points in original.]

> THEODORE ROOSEVELT (1858–1919). Referring to his political enemies in a remark to a friend who had found him in agony in a New York hotel room, February 1918 (a year before his death). In William Henry Harbaugh, *Power and Responsibility: The Life and Times of Theodore Roosevelt,* rev. ed., 31, 1975 (1963)

The worst evil of all is to leave the ranks of the living before one dies.

> SENECA THE YOUNGER (5? B.C.–A.D. 65). "Of Peace of Mind" (5), *Minor Dialogues,* tr. Aubrey Stewart, 1889

On him does death lie heavily, who, but too well-known to all,
dies to himself unknown.

> SENECA THE YOUNGER (5? B.C.–A.D. 65) *Thyestes*, l. 400,
> tr. Frank Justus Miller, 1917

Hamlet: The dread of something after death,
The undiscover'd country from whose bourn [i.e., boundary]
No traveler returns, puzzles the will
And makes us rather bear those ills we have
Than fly to others that we know not of?

> SHAKESPEARE (1564–1616). *Hamlet*, 3.1.78, 1600

Neither in war nor yet at law ought I or any man to use every way
of escaping death. . . . The difficulty, my friends, is not to avoid
death, but to avoid unrighteousness.

> SOCRATES (470?–399 B.C.). In Plato (427?–347 B.C.), *Apology*, 38,
> tr. Benjamin Jowett, 1894

It was not frightening to die *sometime*, it was frightening to die
right now.

> ALEKSANDR SOLZHENITSYN (1918–). *Cancer Ward*, 19, tr. Rebecca
> Frank, 1968

Do not go gentle into that good night,
Old age should burn and rave at close of day;
Rage, rage against the dying of the light.

> DYLAN THOMAS (1914–1953). As his father lay dying, opening verse,
> "Do Not Go Gentle into That Good Night," 1952

The report of my death was an exaggeration.

> MARK TWAIN 1835–1910). Note to the *Journal's* correspondent in
> London. In "Mark Twain Amused," *New York Journal*, 2 June 1897.
> Earlier, while Twain was visiting London, New York newspapers had
> reported his death.

Death plucks my ears and says, "Live—I am coming."

> VIRGIL (70–19 B.C.). In Oliver Wendell Holmes, Jr., on his ninetieth
> birthday, closing words of a radio address, 8 March 1931

I saw him now going the way of all flesh.

> JOHN WEBSTER (1580–1625) and THOMAS DEKKER (1572–1632).
> *Westward Hoe*, 2.2, 1607

❧

It's nature's way of telling you to slow down.

> ANONYMOUS (AMERICAN). Cited as "Madison Avenue's latest definition
> of death." In "Brainstorms," *Newsweek*, 25 April 1960

Let us eat and drink, for tomorrow we die.

> SAYING (*BIBLE*). Isaiah 22:13 (Popular version: Eat, drink, and be merry,
> for tomorrow we may die.)

Death always comes too early or too late.

> SAYING (ENGLISH)

Death keeps no calendar.

> SAYING (ENGLISH)

After the game, the king and pawn go into the same box.

> SAYING (ITALIAN)
> See Equality: Cervantes

DEBT

See also • Banks ○ Economics ○ Last Words: Socrates ○ Money ○
Prayers: Jesus ○ Words: Shakespeare (3)

They that go a-borrowing go a a-sorrowing.

> JOHN CLARKE (1596–1658). Comp., *Proverbs: English and Latine*,
> p. 111, 1639

Our expense is almost all for conformity. It is for cake that we run
in debt; 'tis not the intellect, not the heart, not beauty, not worship, that costs so much.

> RALPH WALDO EMERSON (1803–1882). "Man the Reformer," lecture,
> Masonic Temple, Boston, 25 January 1841

One great wrong must soon disappear: this right to burden the
unborn with state loans.

> RALPH WALDO EMERSON (1803–1882). Journal, May–June 1843

Pay as you go is the only safe rule of private affairs.

> RALPH WALDO EMERSON (1803–1882). Journal, 1864, undated

If there's anyone listening to whom I owe *money*, I'm prepared
to forget it if you are.

> ERROL FLYNN (1909–1959). Spoken jovially in a radio broadcast to
> Australia where he had accumulated a number of debts before leaving
> for Hollywood in the 1930s

Creditors have better memories than debtors.

> BENJAMIN FRANKLIN (1706–1790). *Poor Richard's Almanack,* September
> 1736

Rather go to Bed supperless than rise in Debt.

> BENJAMIN FRANKLIN (1706–1790). "The Way to Wealth," 7 July 1757

Think what you do when you run in Debt; *You give to another
Power over your Liberty.*

> BENJAMIN FRANKLIN (1706–1790). "The Way to Wealth," 7 July 1757

A national debt, if it is not excessive, will be to us a national
blessing.

> ALEXANDER HAMILTON (1755–1804). Letter to Robert Morris, 30 April
> 1781

There can be no doubt that it is a rule of borrowing and lending
that *to him that hath shall be lent.*

> SIR JOHN RICHARD HICKS (1904–1989). *The Social Framework*, 3.9, 1942

We all run in debt for things we wouldna' think o' payin' perfectly good money for.

> KIN HUBBARD (1868–1930). *Abe Martin's Primer*, unpaged, 1914

Ther's few things in this life that equal th' sensation o' bein' paid
up.

> KIN HUBBARD (1868–1930). *Abe Martin's Back Country Sayings,*
> unpaged, 1917

I sincerely believe . . . and that the principle of spending money
to be paid by posterity, under the name of funding, is but swin-
dling futurity on a large scale.

> THOMAS JEFFERSON (1743–1826). Letter to Virginia Sen. John Taylor,
> 28 May 1816

Never spend your money before you have it.

> THOMAS JEFFERSON (1743–1826). "A Decalogue of Canons for Observation in Practical Life," #3, letter to Thomas Jefferson Smith, 21 February 1825

Beyond Our Means: How America's Long Years of Debt, Deficits and Reckless Borrowing Now Threaten to Overwhelm Us.

> ALFRED L. MALABRE, JR. Book title, 1988

The big question is this: How can the world maintain the fear of failure to deter dangerous loans while not letting the system collapse when such loans go bad?

There is no easy answer. But it is a question than can no longer be ignored.

> FLOYD NORRIS. Referring to the Asian financial crisis, closing paragraphs, "Korean Crisis: Blame the Lenders," *New York Times*, 14 December 1997

A small loan makes a debtor; a great one, an enemy.

> PUBLIUS SYRUS (85–43 B.C.). *Moral Sayings*, 12, tr. Darius Lyman, Jr., 1862

It's not politics that is worrying this Country; it's the Second Payment.

> WILL ROGERS (1879–1935). 6 January 1924, *The Autobiography of Will Rogers*, ed. Donald Day, 1949

Polonius: Neither a borrower, nor a lender be.
For loan oft loses both itself and friend,
And borrowing dulls the edge of husbandry.

> SHAKESPEARE (1564–1616). *Hamlet*, 1.3.74, 1600

Timon: Creditors? devils!

> SHAKESPEARE (1564–1616). *Timon of Athens*, 3.4.105, 1600

You load sixteen tons, and what do you get?
Another day older and deeper in debt.
Saint Peter, don't you call me 'cause I can't go,
I owe my soul to the company sto'.

> MERLE TRAVIS. "Sixteen Tons" (song), 1947

Let us all be happy and live within our means, even if we have to borrer [*sic*] the money to do it with.

> ARTEMUS WARD (1834–1867). "Science and Natural History," *The Complete Works of Artemus Ward*, 1898

ᴗ

To have one's credit cards canceled is now akin to being excommunicated by the medieval church.

> ANONYMOUS (AMERICAN). In Nancy Sheperdson, "How the Credit Card Captured America," *Reader's Digest*, September 1993

I owe I owe—it's off to work I go.

> SAYING (AMERICAN). Bumper sticker, In Alex Raksin, "Money May Not Be the Great Motivator, After All," *Los Angeles Times*, 20 December 1993

Make a small loan and get a debtor. Make a big one and get a partner.

> SAYING (AMERICAN). In Floyd Norris, "Korean Crisis: Blame the Lenders," *New York Times*, 14 December 1997

The borrower is the slave of the lender.

> SAYING (*BIBLE*). Proverbs 22:7

DECEPTION

See also • Advertising ○ Appearances ○ Cheating ○ Cunning ○ Delusion ○ Fools: Anonymous (1) ○ Hypocrisy ○ Illusion ○ Indoctrination ○ Intelligence, Military ○ Lying ○ Machiavellianism ○ Propaganda ○ Secrets ○ Self-Deception ○ Sentimentality ○ Strategy, Military ○ Truthfulness

Deceit gets itself a credit in small things that it may practice to more advantage in larger.

> FRANCIS BACON (1561–1626). *Advancement of Learning*, 8.2, 1605, Willey Book edition, 1944

Of all the hard things to bear and grin,
The hardest is being taken in.

> PHOEBE CARY (1824–1871)

We are oftener deceived by being told some truth than no truth.

> FULKE GREVILLE (1554–1628). *Maxims, Characters, and Reflections*, p. 31, 1756

Few men would be deceived if their conceit of themselves did not help the skill of those that go about it.

> MARQUIS OF HALIFAX (1633–1695). "Cheats," *Political, Moral and Miscellaneous Reflections*, 1750

A man that hath the patience to go by steps may deceive one much wiser than himself.

> MARQUIS OF HALIFAX (1633–1695). "Wicked Ministers," *Political, Moral and Miscellaneous Reflections*, 1750

He that once deceives is ever suspected.

> GEORGE HERBERT (1593–1633). Comp., *Outlandish Proverbs*, 417, 1640

Fair words make me look to my purse.

> GEORGE HERBERT (1593–1633). Comp., *Outlandish Proverbs*, 548, 1640

Th' feller that agrees with ever'thing you say is either a fool er he is gettin' ready t' skin you.

> KIN HUBBARD (1868–1930). *Abe Martin's Sayings and Wisecracks, Abe's Neighbors, His Almanack, Comic Drawings*, 1, ed. David S. Hawes, 1984

[To] withhold information and even allow a listener to be misled . . . comes close to the definition of deceit.

> WALTER ISAACSON (1952–). *Kissinger: A Biography*, 24, 1992

O Lord, thou has deceived me,
and I was deceived.

> JEREMIAH (7th cent. B.C.). *Jeremiah* 20:7

Social life would not last long if men were not taken in by each other.

> LA ROCHEFOUCAULD (1613–1680). *Maxims*, 87, 1665, tr. Leonard Tancock, 1959

Tricks and treachery are merely proof of lack of skill.

> LA ROCHEFOUCAULD (1613–1680). *Maxims*, 126, 1665, tr. Louis Kronenberger, 1959
> See Cunning: Benjamin Franklin

You can fool all the people some of the time and some of the people all the time, but you cannot fool all the people all of the time.

> ABRAHAM LINCOLN (1809–1865). Attributed. First published in
> Alexander K. McClure, *"Abe" Lincoln's Yarns and Stories*, 1904
> See Fools: Laurence J. Peter

The essence of [the "con game"] consists of an approach to a formally respectable person with an offer of great gain to be made by engaging in an operation that is safe but frankly shady. In the end the person being "conned" is tricked through his own illicit greed.

> FERDINAND LUNDBERG (1902–1995). *The Rich and the Super-Rich:
> A Study in the Power of Money Today,* 9, 1968

Men are so simple and so ready to obey present necessities, that one who deceives will always find those who allow themselves to be deceived.

> MACHIAVELLI (1469–1527). *The Prince,* 18, 1513, tr. Luigi Ricci, 1903

You don't have to fool all the people all the time—just the right people some of the time.

> MILLARD'S CONCLUSION. In John Peers, comp., *1,001 Logical Laws,*
> p. 108, 1979

People can be induced to swallow anything, provided it is sufficiently seasoned with praise.

> MOLIÈRE (1622–1673). *L'Avare,* 1, 1668, tr. John Wood, 1959

It is easier to deceive than to undeceive.

> NAPOLEON (1769–1821). *In the Words of Napoleon,* p. 20, tr. Daniel
> Savage Gray, 1977

O, what a tangled web we weave,
When first we practice to deceive!

> SIR WALTER SCOTT (1771–1832). *Marmion,* 6.17, 1808

With ease the gods deceive the minds of men.

> SIMONIDES (556?–468? B.C.). Greek poet. Fragment

Some trickery is here. Trojans, do not
trust in the horse. Whatever it may be,
I fear the Greeks, even when they bring gifts.

> VIRGIL (70–19 B.C.). Referring to the large warrior-carrying, wooden
> horse the Greeks used as a ruse to capture the city of Troy, *Aeneid,*
> 2.49, tr. Allen Mandelbaum, 1961

❧

There are three kinds of deceivers: *fools,* those who deceive themselves but not others; *knaves,* those who deceive others but not themselves, and *philosophers,* those who deceive both themselves and others.

> ANONYMOUS

Fool me once, shame on you. Fool me twice, shame on me.

> SAYING (AMERICAN)
> See Wisdom: Saying (German)

Some lick before they bite.

> SAYING

DECISION-MAKING

See also • Advice ○ Bureaucracy ○ Circumstances ○ Commanders ○ Commanders & Staff ○ Committees ○ Crises ○ Crisis Leaders ○ Cuban Missile Crisis ○ Details ○ Events ○ Executives: [especially] John McDonald ○ Information ○ Intelligence, Military ○ International Relations ○ Leaders ○ Leaders & Staff ○ Meetings ○ Planning ○ Policy ○ Politicians ○ Presidents ○ Presidents & Staff ○ Problems & Solutions ○ Statesmen ○ Strategy, Military

The chief must from time to time familiarize himself with the whole record; he must consider opposing views, put forward as ably as possible. He must examine the proponents vigorously and convince them that he knows the record, is intolerant of superficiality or of favor-seeking, and not only welcomes but demands criticism.

> DEAN ACHESON (1893–1971). On "the great importance of interplay
> between head and staff at all stages in the development of decisions,"
> "Thoughts about Thought in High Places," *New York Times Magazine,*
> 11 October 1959

[Franklin D. Roosevelt] learned to seek solutions which would not so much compromise among competing interests as transcend them, include them, give each at least something and the hope of more. He selected among alternatives not by choosing and eliminating, but by emphasizing and ignoring.

> JAMES DAVID BARBER (1939–). *The Presidential Character: Predicting
> Performance in the White House,* 7, 1972

Because it is the job of decision-makers to decide, they cannot react to ambiguity by deferring judgment. When the problem is an environment that lacks clarity, an overload of conflicting data, and lack of time for rigorous assessment of sources and validity, ambiguity abets instinct and allows intuition to drive analysis. . . . The greater the ambiguity, the greater the impact of preconceptions.

> RICHARD K. BETTS (1947–). "Analysis, War, and Decision: Why
> Intelligence Failures Are Inevitable" (2), *World Politics,* October 1978

There is always a latent tension between what facilitates timely decision and what promotes thoroughness and accuracy in assessment.

> RICHARD K. BETTS (1947–). "Analysis, War, and Decision: Why
> Intelligence Failures Are Inevitable" (3), *World Politics,* October 1978

It is child's play deciding what should be done as compared with getting it done.

> ALAN BROOKE (1883–1963). British general. Letter to Bernard Law
> Montgomery, 29 September 1943. In Nigel Hamilton, *Monty: Master of
> the Battlefield, 1942–1944,* 2.6, 1983

A problem is defined and isolated; information is gathered; alternatives are set forth; an end is established; means are created to achieve that end; a choice is made.

> JAMES MacGREGOR BURNS (1918–). On the decision-making process,
> *Leadership,* 14, 1978

I did not suffer from any desire to be relieved of my responsibilities. All I wanted was compliance with my wishes after reasonable discussion.

> WINSTON CHURCHILL (1874–1965). *The Second World War: The Hinge
> of Fate,* 1.5, 1950

In any decision situation, the amount of relevant information available is inversely proportional to the importance of the decision.

> COOKE'S LAW. In Paul Dickson, comp., *The Official Rules*, p. 56, 1978

Presidents must take care lest their tentative suggestions close off discussion or be disseminated after the meetings as clear presidential preferences.

> I. M. DESTLER. "National Security Advice to U.S. Presidents: Some Lessons from Thirty Years," *World Politics*, January 1977

No decision has been made unless carrying it out in specific steps has become someone's work assignment and responsibility.

> PETER F. DRUCKER (1909–). *The Effective Executive*, 4.2.4, 1967

The first question the effective decision-maker asks is: "Is this a generic situation or an exception? Is this something that underlies a great many occurrences? Or is the occurrence a unique event that needs to be dealt with as such?" The generic always has to be answered through a rule, a principle. The exceptional can only be handled as such and as it comes.

> PETER F. DRUCKER (1909–). *The Effective Executive*, 6.2.1, 1967

Disagreement alone can provide alternatives to a decision. And a decision without an alternative is a desperate gambler's throw, no matter how carefully thought through it might be. There is always a high possibility that the decision will prove wrong—either because it was wrong to begin with or because a change in circumstances makes it wrong. If one has thought through alternatives during the decision-making process, one has something to fall back on.

> PETER F. DRUCKER (1909–). *The Effective Executive*, 7.1, 1967

The understanding that underlies the right decision grows out of the clash and conflict of opinions and out of the serious consideration of competing alternatives.

> PETER F. DRUCKER (1909–). *Management: Tasks, Responsibilities, Practices*, 29, 1974, abr., 1977

Feedback has to be built into the decision to provide continuous testing, against actual events, of the expectations that underlie the decision.

> PETER F. DRUCKER (1909–). *Management: Tasks, Responsibilities, Practices*, 29, 1974, abr., 1977

There are no easy matters that will come to you as President. If they are easy, they will be settled at a lower level.

> DWIGHT D. EISENHOWER (1890–1969). Remark to John F. Kennedy. In Theodore C. Sorensen, *Decision-Making in the White House: The Olive Branch or the Arrows*, 2, 1963

A President who doesn't know how to decentralize will be weighed down with details and won't have time to deal with the big issues.

> DWIGHT D. EISENHOWER (1890–1969). In James David Barber, *The Presidential Character: Predicting Performance in the White House*, 5, 1972

The truth is that only by entering deeply into detail is the President likely to gain sufficient understanding of the facts and the alternatives open to him.

> HERMAN FINER (1898–1969). *The Presidency: Crisis and Regeneration*, 3, 1960

To choose, it is first necessary to know.

> HERMAN FINER (1898–1969). *The Presidency: Crisis and Regeneration*, 5, 1960

A prince who will not undergo the difficulty of understanding must undergo the danger of trusting.

> MARQUIS OF HALIFAX (1633–1695). "Of Princes," *Political, Moral and Miscellaneous Reflections*, 1750

Rather than letting a paper process grind slowly toward you, you might find it better to have an early meeting of key, trusted players, listen to the debate, even if it is somewhat unformed, and then provide initial guidance by raising the questions and concerns that occur to you.

> BEN W. HEINEMAN, JR. and CURTIS A. HESSLER. *Memorandum for the President: A Strategic Approach to Domestic Affairs in the 1980s*, 3.F.8, 1980

Procedure is only as good as the people administering it and the quality of their relationships.

> ROBERT E. HUNTER. *Presidential Control of Foreign Policy: Management or Mishap?* 2, 1982

Most important decisions in corporate life are made by individuals, not by committees. My policy has always been to be democratic all the way to the point of decision. Then I become the ruthless commander. "Okay, I've heard everybody," I say. "Now here's what we're going to do."

> LEE IACOCCA (1924–). *Iacocca: An Autobiography*, 5, 1984

I have accustomed myself to receive with respect the opinions of others but always take the responsibility of deciding for myself.

> ANDREW JACKSON (1767–1845). In John F. Kennedy, foreword to Theodore C. Sorensen, *Decision-Making in the White House: The Olive Branch or the Arrows*, 1963

When you're in the presidency, and when you've got a major decision to make, you just put everything out of your mind and focus on that decision like a laser beam and when the decision is finally made you just put everything else out of your mind because there's another one right behind it and then you've got to focus on that.

> LYNDON B. JOHNSON (1908–1973). In Merle Miller, *Lyndon: An Oral Biography*, 4 ("Hyperbole and the Dominican Republic"), 1980

Truman's machinery was geared as an aggressive apparatus for acquiring and conveying information to the top; in contrast, Eisenhower arrayed his staff machinery like a shield. Truman wanted alternatives to choose from. Eisenhower wanted a recommendation to ratify.

> RICHARD TANNER JOHNSON (1927–). *Managing the White House: An Intimate Study of the Presidency*, 4, 1974

Both FDR and JFK had a [high] tolerance of interpersonal conflict. Both immersed themselves in the information process and derived satisfaction from reaching down and *shaping* the options—not just selecting from among those presented to them. The price they paid was that the personal demands on their time and attention were enormous.

RICHARD TANNER JOHNSON (1927–). *Managing the White House: An Intimate Study of the Presidency*, 8, 1974

The later a President interjects himself into the decision process, the more he limits the breadth of information available to him. The President's options are correspondingly reduced. . . .

There is no effective substitute for the President's involvement.

RICHARD TANNER JOHNSON (1927–). *Managing the White House: An Intimate Study of the Presidency*, 8, 1974

The essence of ultimate decision remains impenetrable to the observer—often, indeed, to the decider himself.

JOHN F. KENNEDY (1917–1963). Foreword to Theodore C. Sorensen, *Decision-Making in the White House: The Olive Branch or the Arrows*, 1963

The "ordinary" event can be dealt with by routine—a procedure established in advance of a given eventuality. Energies are freed for dealing with the unexpected or for creative acts.

HENRY A. KISSINGER (1923–). *The Necessity for Choice: Prospects of American Foreign Policy*, 8.3, 1961

To be helpful to the President the machinery for making decisions must . . . meet several criteria. It must be compatible with his personality and style. It must lead to action; desultory talk without operational content produces paralysis. Above all, it must be sensitive to the psychological relationship between the President and his close advisers: it must enable the president's associates to strengthen his self-confidence and yet give him real choices, to supply perspective and yet not turn every issue into a test of wills.

HENRY A. KISSINGER (1923–). *White House Years*, 2, 1979

Today's business environment clearly demands a new process of decision-making. In a rapidly moving world, individuals and weak committees rarely have the information needed to make good nonroutine decisions. Nor do they seem to have the creditability or the time required to convince others to make the personal sacrifices called for on implementing changes. Only teams with the right composition and sufficient trust among members can be highly effective under these new circumstances.

JOHN P. KOTTER (1947–). Harvard Business School professor of leadership. *Leading Change*, 4, 1996

At the top crust of Washington policy-making, it is the impact of decisive personalities—not that of impressive intellect—which ultimately spurs the winning recommendations and gives them decisive force.

DAVID LANDAU (1908–1968). "The Rise of Henry Kissinger," *Ramparts*, December 1971

The art of practical decision, the art of determining which of several ends to pursue, which of many means to employ, when to strike and when to recoil, comes from intuitions that are more unconscious than the analytical judgment. In great emergencies the man of affairs feels his conclusions first, and understands them later.

WALTER LIPPMANN (1889–1974). "The Scholar in a Troubled World," *Atlantic*, August 1932

When it is not necessary to make a decision, it is necessary not to make a decision.

LORD FALKLAND'S RULE (1610–1643). In Thomas L. Martin, Jr., *Malice in Blunderland: A Foolproof Guide for the Aspiring Bureaucrat*, 3, 1973

The decision-maker must not be distracted by problems his subordinates should resolve for themselves.

GEORGE C. MARSHALL (1880–1959). The "first organizing principle of leadership," quoted by Robert Williams, "The President and the Executive Branch." In Malcolm Shaw, ed., *The Modern Presidency: From Roosevelt to Reagan*, 1987

When you're debating fundamental policies, the consequences of which are profound, you should press your debating opponents to the very limit of their reasoning faculties. . . . If you are good friends with them, you are less inclined, in a debating sense, to drive your opponent to the wall and you very often permit a viewpoint to be expressed and to go unchallenged except in a peripheral way.

BILL MOYERS (1934–). Hugh Sidey interview, "The White House Staff vs. the Cabinet," *Washington Monthly*, February 1969

The more urgent the need for a decision, the less apparent becomes the identity of the decision-maker.

MURPHY'S EIGHTEENTH LAW. In Laurence J. Peter, *Peter's People*, 8, 1979

Most decisions are seat-of-the pants judgments. You can create a rationale for anything. In the end, most decisions are based on intuition and faith.

NATHAN MYHRVOLD. Microsoft Corp. computer scientist. In Ken Auletta, "The Microsoft Provocateur," *New Yorker*, 12 May 1997

People whose lives are affected by a decision must be part of the process of arriving at that decision.

JOHN NAISBITT (1929–). *Megatrends: Ten New Directions Transforming Our Lives*, 7, 1984

What presidents do every day is make decisions that are mostly thrust upon them, the deadlines all too often outside their control, on options mostly framed by others, about issues crammed with technical complexities and uncertain outcomes.

RICHARD E. NEUSTADT (1919–). "An Introduction: Reflections on Johnson and Nixon" (5), *Presidential Power: The Politics of Leadership*, 1976 (1960)

In decision-making one should not commit himself irrevocably to a course of action until he absolutely has to do so.

RICHARD M. NIXON (1913–1994). *Six Crises*, 4, 1962

President [Dwight D.] Eisenhower once told me that during his military career he insisted that all major problems be brought to his attention. But he also insisted that when a staff member informed him of a problem, he should at the same time make recommendations for solving it.

RICHARD M. NIXON (1913–1994). *In the Arena: A Memoir of Victory, Defeat and Renewal*, 30, 1990

The quality of the president's decisions improves when he provides for the participation of those responsible for ultimately implementing policies. Those responsible for implementing a program are sensitive to potential administrative difficulties that can prove crucial in evaluating various alternatives.

ROGER B. PORTER (1946–). Appendix to *Presidential Decision Making: The Economic Policy Board*, 1980

The decision-making machinery supporting American foreign policy is too well-organized. President [Jimmy] Carter has described his job as like taking a multiple-choice exam.

THOMAS POWERS (1940–). Introduction to *The Man Who Kept the Secrets: Richard Helms and the CIA*, 1981

A decision is the action an executive must take when he has information so incomplete that the answer does not suggest itself.

ARTHUR W. RADFORD (1896–1973). Admiral. In "Man Behind the Power," *Time*, 25 February 1957

Crisis conditions narrow and harden his area of choice.

NELSON ROCKEFELLER (1908–1979). "The Presidency As I Have Seen It" (A Special Section). In Emmet John Hughes, *The Living Presidency: The Resources and Dilemmas of the American Presidential Office*, 1972

Success in administration obviously stands or falls on skill in execution. Execution means, above all, the right people—it means having men and women capable of providing the information and carrying out the decision.

ARTHUR M. SCHLESINGER, JR. (1917–). *The Age of Roosevelt: The Coming of the New Deal*, 33.1, 1959

The worst error a president can make is to assume the automatic implementation of his own decisions.

ARTHUR M. SCHLESINGER, JR. (1917–). *The Age of Roosevelt: The Coming of the New Deal*, 33.3, 1959

[John F. Kennedy's] mind was forever critical; but his thinking always retained the cutting edge of decision. When he was told something, he wanted to know what he could do about it. He was pragmatic in the sense that he tested the meaning of a proposition by its consequences.

ARTHUR M. SCHLESINGER, JR. (1917–). *A Thousand Days: John F. Kennedy in the White House*, 4.7, 1965

A President's decision may vary according to how the question is formulated and even by who presents it.

THEODORE C. SORENSEN (1928–). *Decision-Making in the White House: The Olive Branch or the Arrows*, 2, 1963

The "lonely isolation" of the presidency refers to the solitude of his responsibility—not to insulating him from all the pressures, paper work, and discussions which are essential to his perspective.

THEODORE C. SORENSEN (1928–). *Decision-Making in the White House: The Olive Branch or the Arrows*, 3, 1963

It is a law of life that every gain incurs a cost—and the most efficient decision, therefore, is theoretically the one which produces the greatest margin of gain over cost.

THEODORE C. SORENSEN (1928–). *Decision-Making in the White House: The Olive Branch or the Arrows*, 3, 1963

Decisions are partially made whenever the president selects an appointee with a known position and reputation.

THEODORE C. SORENSEN (1928–). *Decision-Making in the White House: The Olive Branch or the Arrows*, 6, 1963

Consistently wise decisions can only be made by those whose wisdom is constantly challenged.

THEODORE C. SORENSEN (1928–). *Decision-Making in the White House: The Olive Branch or the Arrows*, 7, 1963

To govern is not to write resolutions and distribute directives; to govern is to control the implementation of the directives.

JOSEPH STALIN (1879–1953). In Neil McInnes, *The Communist Parties of Western Europe*, 3, 1975

Advisers advise, and ministers decide.

MARGARET THATCHER (1925–). British prime minister. House of Commons debate. In Craig R. Whitney, "British Cabinet in a Flurry; Minister and Rival Out," *New York Times*, 27 October 1989

A political system must not only be able to make and enforce decisions; it must operate on the right scale, it must be able to integrate disparate policies, it must be able to make decisions at the right speed; and it must both reflect and respond to the diversity of society. If it fails on any of these points, it courts disaster. Our problems are no longer a matter of "left-wing" or "right-wing," "strong leadership" or "weak." The decision system itself has become a disaster.

ALVIN TOFFLER (1928–). *The Third Wave*, 27, 1980

When the decision is up before you—and on my desk I have a motto which says, "The buck stops here"—the decision has to be made.

HARRY S. TRUMAN (1884–1972). Speech, National War College, Washington, 19 December 1952

To be President of the United States is to be lonely, very lonely at times of great decisions.

HARRY S. TRUMAN (1884–1972). Preface to *Memoirs: Year of Decisions*, 1955

Unless they mull over a wide range of possibilities, they cannot come up with the imaginative combinations of ideas which characterize their work.

H. EDWARD WRAPP. "Good Managers Don't Make Policy Decisions," *Harvard Business Review*, September-October 1967

Objectives get communicated only over time by a consistency or pattern in operating decisions.

H. EDWARD WRAPP. "Good Managers Don't Make Policy Decisions," *Harvard Business Review*, September–October 1967

DECISIVENESS

See also • Action ○ Indecision ○ Resolution ○ Speed

He showed the true stamp of leadership by instantly divining the right thing to be done, and doing it without the loss of a moment.

C. J. BRITTON. *New Chronicles of the Life of Lord Nelson*, 11, 1946

Napoleon knew his business. Here was a man who, in each moment and emergency, knew what to do next. It is an immense comfort and refreshment to the spirits, not only of kings, but of citizens. Few men have any next.

RALPH WALDO EMERSON (1803–1882). "Napoleon; or, The Man of the World," *Representative Men*, 1850

In our flowing affairs a decision must be made—the best, if you can, but any is better than none. There are twenty ways of going to a point, and one is the shortest; but set out at once on one. A man who has that presence of mind which can bring to him on the instant all he knows, is worth for action a dozen men who know as much but can only bring it to light slowly.

> RALPH WALDO EMERSON (1803–1882). "Power," *The Conduct of Life,* 1860

When a firm, decisive spirit is recognized, it is curious to see how the space clears around a man and leaves him room and freedom.

> JOHN WATSON FOSTER (1856–1915). In Elbert Hubbard, comp., *Elbert Hubbard's Scrap Book,* p. 107, 1923

I like a person who knows his own mind and sticks to it; who sees at once what is to be done in given circumstances and does it. He does not beat about the bush for difficulties or excuses, but goes the shortest and most effectual way to work to attain his own ends, or to accomplish a useful object.

> WILLIAM HAZLITT (1778–1830). "On Effeminacy of Character," *Table Talk,* 1822

My actions were as prompt as my thoughts.

> NAPOLEON (1769–1821). Letter to the Directory, 1796. In Ralph Waldo Emerson, "Napoleon; or, The Man of the World," *Representative Men,* 1850

Act swiftly and vigorously, without "buts" and "ifs". . . . I shall sanction everything that is vigorous, spirited, and politic.

> NAPOLEON (1769–1821). Letter to Marshal Bessiéres, 20 November 1809, *New Letters of Napoleon I,* tr. Lady Mary Loyd, 1898

The open mind never acts: when we have done our utmost to arrive at a reasonable conclusion, we still . . . must close our minds for the moment with a snap, and act dogmatically on our conclusions.

> GEORGE BERNARD SHAW (1856–1950). Preface ("Christianity and the Empire") to *Androcles and the Lion,* 1912

DEEDS

See also • Action ○ Action & Talk: Theodore Roosevelt ○ Creed: Anonymous ○ Defiance: Walt Whitman ○ Diplomats: Joseph Stalin ○ Friends: Saying ○ Good ○ Heaven & Hell: Anonymous ○ Morality: Herbert Spencer (1) ○ Motives: La Rochefoucauld ○ Motives: Oscar Wilde ○ Prayer: Anonymous, Saying (Mexican) ○ Repentance: *Talmud* ○ Self-Knowledge: *The Book of the Golden Precepts* ○ Sin: *Midrash* ○ Virtue

Our deeds determine us . . . as much as we determine our deeds.

> GEORGE ELIOT (1819–1880). *Adam Bede,* 29, 1859
>
> See Personality: Allen Wheelis ○ Thinking: Mohandas K. Gandhi

Good deeds misplaced . . . are evil deeds.

> ENNIUS (239–169 B.C.). In Cicero (106–43 B.C.), *De officiis,* 2.18, tr. Walter Miller, 1913

The spirit comes to guide me in my need,
I write, "In the beginning was the Deed."

> GOETHE (1749–1832). *Faust,* 1 ("Faust's Study," 2), 1808–1832, tr. Philip Wayne, 1959
>
> See Words: John

Commonplace deeds are adventures in the domain of the spiritual.

> ABRAHAM JOSHUA HESCHEL (1907–1972). *Man Is Not Alone: A Philosophy of Religion,* 26, 1951

It is not enough to do a good deed. One must be involved in it wholeheartedly. Each action should be performed with life and soul, with every limb, with all one's vitality.

> ABRAHAM JOSHUA HESCHEL (1907–1972). *A Passion for Truth,* 1, 1973

It is only our deeds that reveal who we are.

> CARL G. JUNG (1875–1961). Title essay, 1934, *The Development of Personality,* tr. R. F. C. Hull, 1954

We are only the actors, we are never wholly the authors of our own deeds or works. *It* is the author, the unknown inside us or outside us. The best we can do is to try to hold ourselves in unison with the deeps which are inside us.

> D. H. LAWRENCE (1885–1930). *Studies in Classic American Literature,* 2, 1923

Good deeds annul ill deeds.

> MUHAMMAD (A.D. 570?–632). *Quran,* 4.79, A.D. 670?, tr. Mohammed Marmaduke Pickthall, 1953

❧

Good thoughts elevate deeds; good deeds elevate thoughts.

> ANONYMOUS

One good deed is better than three days of fasting at a shrine.

> SAYING (JAPANESE)

We are the children of our deeds.

> SAYING (SPANISH)

DEFEAT

See also • Calamity ○ Competition ○ Courage: Robert G. Ingersoll ○ Delay ○ Disaster ○ Errors ○ Failure ○ Losing ○ Misfortune ○ Mistakes ○ Profit & Loss ○ Sports ○ Strategy, Military ○ Success ○ Tragedy ○ Trouble ○ Victory ○ Victory & Defeat ○ War ○ Winning

Woe to the vanquished!

> BRENNUS (4th cent. B.C.). Gallic chieftain. In Livy (59 B.C.–A.D. 17), *The History of Rome,* 5.48 tr. Aubrey de Sélincourt, 1960

Defeat is one thing; disgrace is another.

> WINSTON CHURCHILL (1874–1965). On the surrender of British forces at Tobruk (Libya), June 1942, *The Second World War: The Hinge of Fate,* 1.22, 1950

To overextend yourself is to invite defeat.

> G. WILLIAM DOMHOFF (1936–). *The Higher Circles: The Governing Class in America,* 8, 1970

Who are only undefeated
Because we have gone on trying.

> T. S. ELIOT (1888–1965). "The Dry Salvages" (5), *Four Quartets,* 1943

A man ain't whipped until he quits.

> THOMAS E. GADDIS (?–1984) (GAY TROSPER, scriptwriter). *Birdman of Alcatraz* (film), 1962, spoken by Burt Lancaster

Man is not made for defeat. A man can be destroyed but not defeated.

> ERNEST HEMINGWAY (1899–1961). *The Old Man and the Sea*, p. 103, 1952
>
> See Spirit: Seneca the Younger

It is the unique glory of the human species that its rejected do not fall by the wayside but become the building stones of the new, and that those who cannot fit into the present should become the shapers of the future.

> ERIC HOFFER (1902–1983). *The Ordeal of Change*, 15.5, 1964
>
> See Weakness: Hoffer (1)

There is no defeat except from within.

> ELBERT HUBBARD (1856–1915). *The Note Book of Elbert Hubbard*, p. 13, comp. Elbert Hubbard II, 1927

Defeat is simply a signal to press onward.

> HELEN KELLER (1880–1968). "Faith Arms the Soul," *Let Us Have Faith*, 1940

The sudden defeat of a state may lead to a wave of suicides among its humiliated leaders, and to such internalized collective behavior as religious revivalism.

> HAROLD D. LASSWELL (1902–1978). *Politics: Who Gets What, When, How*, 9, 1936

Napoleon's severest comment on his beaten enemies—that they "saw too many things at once."

> B. H. LIDDELL HART (1895–1970). March 1928, *Thoughts on War*, 5.6, 1944

A man is not finished when he's defeated, he's finished when he quits.

> RICHARD M. NIXON (1913–1994). 1969. In William Safire, epilogue to *Before the Fall: An Inside View of the Pre-Watergate White House*, 1975

YOU ARE NOT BEATEN UNTIL YOU ADMIT IT, Hence DON'T.

> GEORGE S. PATTON, JR. (1885–1945). Notebook, 1921–1922. In Martin Blumenson, *The Patton Papers, 1885–1940*, 37, 1972

"Pyrrhic defeat," one that accomplishes more than most victories.

> GARRY WILLS (1934–). "The Hostage," *New York Review of Books*, 13 August 1992
>
> See Victory: Pyrrhus

DEFECTS

See also • Faults ○ Judging Others ○ Weaknesses

Their own defect, invisible to them,
Seen in another, they at once condemn.

> WILLIAM COWPER (1731–1800). "Conversation," l. 155, 1782

Our very defects are . . . shadows of our virtues.

> RALPH WALDO EMERSON (1803–1882). Journal, 1831, undated

Bear patiently with the Defects of others, and labor to amend thy own.

> THOMAS FULLER (1654–1734). Comp., *Introductio ad Prudentiam*, 389, 1731

When the defects of others are perceived with too much clarity, it is because one possesses them oneself.

> JULES RENARD (1864–1910). Journal, October 1908

DEFIANCE

See also • Boldness ○ Conscience: John Bunyan, Lillian Hellman, Martin Luther, Ben Shahn ○ Courage ○ Courage, Moral ○ Dissent ○ Heresy ○ Liberty: Harriet Tubman ○ Native Americans: Tecumseh (2) ○ Nonconformity ○ Resistance ○ Resolution ○ Revolutionary War: Patrick Henry ○ Silence & Protest: [especially] William Lloyd Garrison, Socrates ○ Slavery: George Sand ○ Standing Alone ○ Struggle ○ World War I: Ferdinand Foch, Robert-Georges Nivelle ○ World War II: Anthony McAuliffe

I give thee sixpence! I will see thee damned first.

> GEORGE CANNING (1770–1827). British prime minister. "The Friend of Humanity and the Knife-Grinder" (9), *The Anti-Jacobin*, 11, 1797

I'm mad as hell, and I'm not going to take it anymore.

> PADDY CHAYEFSKY (1923–1981). *Network* (film), 1976, spoken by Peter Finch (in the role of Howard Beal)

As sure as the sun will shine
I'm going to get it, what's mine
And then the harder they come
The harder they fall,
One and all.

> JIMMY CLIFF (1948–). "The Harder They Come" (song), 1972
>
> See Quantity: Bob Fitzsimmons

I know what you're thinking. Did he fire six shots or only five? Well, to tell you the truth, in all this excitement I've kinda lost track myself. But being this is a .44 Magnum, the most powerful handgun in the world, and would blow your head clear off, you've gotta ask yourself one question: Do I feel lucky? Well, do ya, punk?

> HARRY JULIAN FINK, RITA M. FINK, and DEAN RIESNER. *Dirty Harry* (film), 1971, spoken by Clint Eastwood (in the role of "Dirty" Harry Callaghan, a San Francisco police detective) as he pointed his gun at a downed robber whose own gun was lying within reach. In the 1983 film *Sudden Impact*, Eastwood said, "Go ahead, make my day!" to another trapped gunman. (Popular version: Go ahead, punk, make my day!)

Xerxes (in a message): Deliver up your arms!
Leonidas (in response): Come and take them!

> LEONIDAS (5th cent. B.C.). Spartan commander and king. Format adapted. While defending the pass at Thermopylae where he and all his soldiers were later killed, 480 B.C. In Plutarch (A.D. 46?–119?). "Sayings of the Spartans: Leonidas Son of Anaxandridas" (11), *Plutarch on Sparta*, tr. Richard J. A. Talbert, 1988

Millions for defense, but not a cent for tribute!

> CHARLES COTESWORTH PINCKNEY (18th cent.). Attributed (he denied having said it). Responding to French Minister of Foreign Affairs Talleyrand's demand for a bribe to call off attacks on American shipping, October 1797

Gangster fixer: What makes you think you can get away with this?
Charlie Davis (right after winning a championship fight he was

supposed to have thrown): What are you gonna do? Kill me? Everybody dies.

> ABRAHAM POLONSKY (1910–). *Body and Soul* (film), 1947, spoken by John Garfield

Anonymous: You can't win: They'll fight you forever.
Willie Boy: Maybe, but they'll know I've been here.

> ABRAHAM POLONSKY (1910–). *Tell Them Willie Boy Is Here!* (film), 1969, spoken by Robert Blake

The man who seeks to do what is good and genuine, must avoid what is bad and be ready to defy the opinions of the mob, nay, even to despise it and its misleaders.

> ARTHUR SCHOPENHAUER (1788–1860). "The Wisdom of Life" (4.5), *Essays of Arthur Schopenhauer*, tr. T. Bailey Saunders, 1851

When one man says, "No, I won't," Rome begins to fear.

> DALTON TRUMBO. *Spartacus* (film), 1960, spoken by Kirk Douglas (in the title role)

They may take our lives, but they'll never take our freedom.

> RANDALL WALLACE. *Braveheart* (film), 1995, spoken by Mel Gibson (in the role of the Scottish rebel warrior William Wallace) to his troops before a battle

How beggarly appear arguments before a defiant deed!

> WALT WHITMAN (1819–1892). "Song of the Broad-Axe" (6), 1856, *Leaves of Grass*, 1855–1892

DEHUMANIZATION

See also • Brainwashing ○ Crime ○ Cruelty ○ Indoctrination ○ Personality ○ Prejudice ○ Prison ○ Propaganda ○ Slavery ○ Terrorism ○ Torture ○ Tyranny ○ Violence ○ War ○ War & Psychology

Every despotism has a specially keen and hostile instinct for whatever keeps up human dignity and independence. . . . To crush what is spiritual, moral, human so to speak, in man, by specializing him; to form mere wheels of the great social machine, instead of perfect individuals; to make society and not conscience the center of life, to enslave the soul to things, to depersonalize man, this is the dominant drift of our epoch.

> HENRI AMIEL (1821–1881). Journal, 17 June 1852, tr. Mrs. Humphrey Ward, 1887

It is a terrible, an inexorable, law that one cannot deny the humanity of another without diminishing one's own: in the face of one's victim, one sees oneself.

> JAMES BALDWIN (1924–1987). *Nobody Knows My Name*, 3, 1961

Treat men as pawns and ninepins, and you shall suffer as well as they. If you leave out their heart, you shall lose your own.

> RALPH WALDO EMERSON (1803–1882). "Compensation," *Essays: First Series*, 1841

The danger of the past was that men became slaves. The danger of the future is that men may become robots.

> ERICH FROMM (1900–1980). *The Sane Society*, 9, 1955

"Former People: Creatures That Once Were Men."

> MAXIM GORKY (1868–1936). Short story title, 1897

Just as death is the liquidation of being, dehumanization is the liquidation of being human.

> ABRAHAM JOSHUA HESCHEL (1907–1972). *Who Is Man?* 2, 1965

The most effective way to silence our guilty conscience is to convince ourselves and others that those we have sinned against are indeed depraved creatures, deserving every punishment, even extermination. We cannot pity those we have wronged, nor can we be indifferent toward them. We must hate and persecute them or else leave the door open to self-contempt.

> ERIC HOFFER (1902–1983). *The True Believer: Thoughts on the Nature of Mass Movements*, 71, 1951

Nationalism, Socialism, Communism, Fascism, militarism, cartelization and unionization, propaganda and advertising are all aspects of a general relentless drive to manipulate men and neutralize the unpredictability of human nature.

> ERIC HOFFER (1902–1983). *The Ordeal of Change*, 15.4, 1964

Wherever justice is uncertain and police spying and terror are at work, human beings fall into isolation, which, of course, is the aim and purpose of the dictator State, since it is based on the greatest possible accumulation of depotentiated social units.

> CARL G. JUNG (1875–1961). *The Undiscovered Self*, 6, tr. R. F. C. Hull, 1957

As Gregor Samsa awoke one morning from uneasy dreams he found himself transformed in his bed into a gigantic insect.

> FRANZ KAFKA (1883–1924). Opening words, "The Metamorphosis," 1915, *The Penal Colony*, tr. Willa and Edwin Muir, 1948

Human beings have so brutalized themselves, have become so banal and stultified, that they are unaware of their own debasement.

> R. D. LAING (1927–1989). *The Politics of Experience*, 3, 1967

It is a shameful and inhuman thing to treat men as mere chattels for profit, or to regard them as simply so much muscle power.

> POPE LEO XIII (1810–1903). *De Rerum Novarum (On the Condition of Workers)*, 15 May 1891

Before dying the victim must be degraded, so that the murderer will be less burdened by guilt. This is an explanation not devoid of logic, but it shouts to heaven.

> PRIMO LEVI (1919–1987). Auschwitz survivor. *The Drowned and the Saved*, 5, 1986, tr. Raymond Rosenthal, 1988

The decay of decency in the modern age, the rebellion against law and good faith, the treatment of human beings as things, as the mere instruments of power and ambition, is without a doubt the consequence of the decay of the belief in man as something more than an animal animated by highly conditioned reflexes and chemical reactions. For, unless man is something more than that, he has no rights that anyone is bound to respect, and there are no limitations upon his conduct which he is bound to obey.

> WALTER LIPPMANN (1889–1974): "The Forgotten Foundation," *New York Herald Tribune*, 17 December 1938

The practices originally brought in by capitalism, machine technics, the physical sciences, bureaucratic administration, and totalitarian government . . . [may] unite to form a more complete and watertight system, governed by a deliberately depersonalized intelligence. With this, of course, would go a corresponding neglect or suppression of older human traits and institutions, associated with the earlier transformations of man. Under these conditions all human purposes would be swallowed up in a mechanical process immune to any human desire that diverged from it. With that a new creature, post-historic man, would come into existence.

> LEWIS MUMFORD (1895–1990). *The Transformations of Man*, 7.1, 1956. Roderick Seidenberg coined the term *post-historic man* and used it as the title of his 1950 book.

In time, the human beings necessary to run post-historic culture will be provided at birth with built-in responses, subject solely to external controls: a more economic alternative to the wasteful methods now applied by the political commissar and the commercial advertiser. Under post-historic incentives, frontal lobotomy may be as widely performed on children, to ensure docility and discourage autonomy, as tonsillectomy now is.

> LEWIS MUMFORD (1895–1990). *The Transformations of Man*, 7.2, 1956

I thought of a rather cruel trick I once played on a wasp. He was sucking jam on my plate, and I cut him in half. He paid no attention, merely went on with his meal, while a tiny stream of jam trickled out of his severed esophagus. Only when he tried to fly away did he grasp the dreadful thing that had happened to him. It is the same with modern man. The thing that has been cut away is his soul.

> GEORGE ORWELL (1903–1950). "Notes on the Way," 6 April 1940, *The Collected Essays, Journalism and Letters of George Orwell*, vol. 2, ed. Sonia Orwell and Ian Angus, 1968

Syme was not only dead, he was abolished, an unperson.

> GEORGE ORWELL (1903–1950). *Nineteen Eighty-Four*, 2.5, 1949

One day Larisa Feodorovna went out and did not come back. She must have been arrested in the street at that time. She vanished without a trace and probably died somewhere, forgotten as a nameless number on a list that afterwards got mislaid in one of the innumerable mixed or women's concentration camps in the north.

> BORIS PASTERNAK (1890–1960). *Doctor Zhivago*, 15.17, 1957, tr. Max Hayward and Manya Harari, 1958

Wherever there is lost the consciousness that every man is an object of concern for us just because he is a man, civilization and morals are shaken, and the advance to fully developed inhumanity is only a question of time.

> ALBERT SCHWEITZER (1875–1965). *The Philosophy of Civilization: The Decay and Restoration of Civilization*, 1923, tr. C. T. Campion, 1923

DELAY

See also • Action ○ Defeat ○ Hesitation ○ Indecision ○ Irresolution ○ Opportunity ○ Patience ○ Procrastination ○ Slowness ○ Speed ○ Time

Delay always breeds danger; to protract a great design is often to ruin it.

> CERVANTES (1547–1616). *Don Quixote*, 1.4.2, 1615, tr. Peter Anthony Motteux and John Ozell, 1743

You may delay, but *Time* will not.

> BENJAMIN FRANKLIN (1706–1790). *Poor Richard's Almanack*, April 1758

Do not delay:
Do not delay; the golden moments fly!

> HENRY WADSWORTH LONGFELLOW (1807–1882). *The Masque of Pandora*, 7, 1875

Tardy measures are most dangerous when the occasion requires prompt action.

> MACHIAVELLI (1469–1527). *The Discourses*, 1:34, 1517, tr. Christian E. Detmold, 1940

Delay is itself a decision.

> THEODORE C. SORENSEN (1928–). *Decision-Making in the White House: The Olive Branch or the Arrows*, 3, 1963

❦

A delay is better than a disaster.

> SAYING

DELUSION

See also • Deception ○ Illusion ○ Liberty: Edmund Burke (1) ○ Mental Illness ○ Paranoia: [especially] Sigmund Freud (1) ○ Self-Deception ○ Systems: Anthony Storr

We swim, day by day, on a river of delusions. . . . But life is a sincerity. In lucid intervals we say, "Let there be an entrance for me into realities; I have worn the fool's cap too long."

> RALPH WALDO EMERSON (1803–1882). "Uses of Great Men," *Representative Men*, 1850

The more ways a man is deluded, the happier he is.

> DESIDERIUS ERASMUS (1466?–1536). *The Praise of Folly*, 19, 1509, tr. Hoyt Hopewell Hudson, 1941

The delusional formation, which we take to be the pathological product, is in reality an attempt at recovery, a process of reconstruction.

> SIGMUND FREUD (1856–1939). *Psychoanalytic Notes on an Autobiographical Account of a Case of Paranoia (Dementia Paranoides)*, 3, 1911, tr. James Strachey, 1958

Dazzled by the brilliant achievements of the intellect in science and technique, we have been deluded into believing that we are the masters of the earth and our will the ultimate criterion of what is right and wrong.

> ABRAHAM JOSHUA HESCHEL (1907–1972). *Man Is Not Alone: A Philosophy of Religion*, 5, 1951

The house of delusions is cheap to build but drafty to live in.

> A. E. HOUSMAN (1859–1936). Lecture before the Faculties of Arts and Laws and of Science, University College, London, 3 October 1892

One of the most interesting and harmful delusions to which men and nations can be subjected is that of imagining themselves special instruments of the Divine Will.

> BERTRAND RUSSELL (1872–1970). "Ideas That Have Harmed Mankind," *Unpopular Essays*, 1950

> See God & Man—First Person: Mohandas K. Gandhi (2), Abraham Lincoln (2), Napoleon

The most delusional fantasies can be made to masquerade as sanity if you've got the political power to reinforce them.

> PENNY SKILLMAN. "It's a Mad, Mad World," *San Francisco Chronicle Review,* 3 July 1988

Delusion: belief said to be false by someone who does not share it.

> THOMAS S. SZASZ (1920–). "Mental Illness," *Heresies,* 1976

Shams and delusions are esteemed for soundest truths. . . . By closing the eyes and slumbering, and consenting to be deceived by shows, men establish and confirm their daily life of routine and habit everywhere, which still is built on purely illusory foundations.

> HENRY DAVID THOREAU (1817–1862). "Where I Lived, and What I Lived For," *Walden; or Life in the Woods,* 1854

DEMOCRACY

See also • Capitalism ○ Democracy, Anti- ○ Elections ○ Equality ○ Freedom ○ Freedom of Speech: Pericles ○ Government ○ Majorities ○ The People ○ Politics ○ Presidents ○ Public Opinion ○ Tyranny ○ World War I: Woodrow Wilson (1)

No one pretends that democracy is perfect or all-wise. Indeed, it has been said that democracy is the worst form of government except all those other forms that have been tried from time to time.

> WINSTON CHURCHILL (1874–1965). House of Commons speech, 11 November 1947
>
> See Capitalism: Robert J. Samuelson

The central tenet of every democracy in the end is trust.

> BILL CLINTON (1946–). In Gwen Ifill, "Bill & Al's Traveling Medicine Show," *New York Times,* 9 September 1993

We, the people, elect leaders not to rule but to serve.

> DWIGHT D. EISENHOWER (1890–1969). *First Inaugural Address,* 20 January 1953

Western democracy, as it functions today, is diluted Nazism or Fascism. At best it is merely a cloak to hide the Nazi and Fascist tendencies of imperialism.

> MOHANDAS K. GANDHI (1869–1948). In *Harijan,* 18 May 1940

When we can make democracy work, we won't have to force it down other people's throats. If it really is such a good idea, and if they can see it working, they'll steal it.

> DICK GREGORY (1932–). In "A Separate Path to Equality," *Life,* 13 December 1968

When occasions present themselves, in which the interests of the people are at variance with their inclinations, it is the duty of the persons whom they have appointed to be the guardians of those interests, to withstand the temporary delusion, in order to give them time and opportunity for more cool and sedate reflection.

> ALEXANDER HAMILTON (1755–1804). In *The Federalist Papers* (essay series), 71, 18 March 1788

If democracy is not only to survive but to expand successfully . . . , it must rediscover and renew its own transcendental origins.

> VÁCLAV HAVEL (1936–). Czech president. Address, Stanford University (California), 29 September 1994. In Bill Workman, "Havel Says Democracy Lacks 'Spiritual' Side," *San Francisco Chronicle,* 30 September 1994

I swear to the Lord
I still can't see
Why Democracy means
Everybody but me.

> LANGSTON HUGHES (1902–1967). "The Black Man Speaks," 1943, *The Collected Poems of Langston Hughes,* ed. Arnold Rampersad and David Roessel, 1994

A monarchy requires a virtuous king; a democracy requires a virtuous people.

> HENRY HYDE. Illinois congressman. Remark during a House Judiciary Committee meeting, 7 May 1992

Democracy is a form of government which may be rationally defended, not as being good, but as being less bad than any other.

> DEAN WILLIAM RALPH INGE (1860–1954). "Our Present Discontents," *Outspoken Essays: First Series,* 1919

I know no safe depository of the ultimate powers of the society but the people themselves; and if we think them not enlightened enough to exercise their control with a wholesome discretion, the remedy is not to take it from them, but to inform their discretion by education.

> THOMAS JEFFERSON (1743–1826). Letter to William C. Jarvis, 28 September 1820

The true democracy, living and growing and inspiring, puts its faith in the people—faith that the people will not simply elect men who will represent their views ably and faithfully, but also elect men who will exercise their conscientious judgment—faith that the people will not condemn those whose devotion to principle leads them to unpopular courses, but will reward courage, respect honor and ultimately recognize right.

> JOHN F. KENNEDY (1917–1963). *Profiles in Courage,* 11, 1956

Chinks in America's egalitarian armor are not hard to find. Democracy is the fig leaf of elitism.

> FLORENCE KING. "Democracy," *Reflections in a Jaundiced Eye,* 1989

No man is good enough to govern another man, *without that other's consent.*

> ABRAHAM LINCOLN (1809–1865). Calling this principle "the sheet anchor of American republicanism," speech on the Kansas-Nebraska Act, Peoria (Illinois), 16 October 1854
>
> See Government: Thomas Jefferson (1) ○ Slavery: Jonathan Swift

As I would not be a *slave,* so I would not be a *master.* This expresses my idea of democracy. Whatever differs from this, to the extent of the difference, is no democracy.

> ABRAHAM LINCOLN (1809–1865). "On Slavery and Democracy" (fragment), 1858?, *Abraham Lincoln: Speeches and Writings, 1832–1858,* Library of America edition, 1989
>
> See Slavery: Epictetus ○ Slavery: Lincoln (3)

To support the Ins when things are going well; to support the Outs when [things] seem to be going badly, this, in spite of all that has been said about tweedledum and tweedledee, is the essence of popular government.

> WALTER LIPPMANN (1889–1974). *The Phantom Public: A Sequel to "Public Opinion,"* 12.1, 1930 (1925)

The evils of popular government appear greater than they are; there is compensation for them in the spirit and energy it awakens.

> MACHIAVELLI (1469–1527). In Ralph Waldo Emerson, journal, February 1847

A pure democracy [refers to] . . . a society consisting of a small number of citizens, who assemble and administer the government in person.

> JAMES MADISON (1751–1836). In *The Federalist Papers* (essay series), 10, 23 November 1787

The two great points of difference between a democracy and a republic are: first, the delegation of the government, in the latter, to a small number of citizens elected by the rest; secondly, the greater number of citizens, and greater sphere of country, over which the latter may be extended.

> JAMES MADISON (1751–1836). In *The Federalist Papers* (essay series), 10, 23 November 1787

A popular government without popular information, or the means of acquiring it, is but a prologue to a farce or a tragedy; or, perhaps both. Knowledge will forever govern ignorance. And a people who mean to be their own governors must arm themselves with the power which knowledge gives.

> JAMES MADISON (1751–1836). Letter to W. T. Barry, 4 August 1822

Ishmael: This august dignity I treat of, is not the dignity of kings and robes, but that abounding dignity which has no robed investiture. Thou shalt see it shining in the arm that wields a pick or drives a spike; that democratic dignity which, on all hands, radiates without end from God; Himself! The great God absolute! The center and circumference of all democracy! His omnipresence, our divine equality!

> HERMAN MELVILLE (1819–1891). *Moby-Dick; or, The Whale,* 26, 1851, ed. Harold Beaver, 1972

The three elements of democratic activity—timely information, the technology to communicate with one another, and then mobilization for action and results.

> RALPH NADER (1934–). "How Clinton Can Build Democracy," *Nation,* 30 November 1992

Man's capacity for justice makes democracy possible, but man's inclination to injustice makes democracy necessary.

> REINHOLD NIEBUHR (1892–1971). Foreword to *The Children of Light and the Children of Darkness: A Vindication of Democracy and a Critique of Its Traditional Defense,* 1944

Democracy is direct self-government, over all the people, for all the people, by all the people.

> THEODORE PARKER (1810–1860). "The Effect of Slavery on the American People," sermon, Music Hall, Boston, 4 July 1858
>
> See Civil War: Abraham Lincoln (5)

If we look to the laws, they afford equal justice to all in their private differences; if to social standing, advancement in public life falls to reputation for capacity, class considerations not being allowed to interfere with merit; nor again does poverty bar the way; if a man is able to serve the state, he is not hindered by the obscurity of his condition.

> PERICLES (495?–429 B.C.). On Athens' democratic ideal, funeral oration, 431 B.C. In Thucydides (460?–400? B.C.). *The Peloponnesian War,* 2.37, tr. Richard Crawley and rev. T. E. Wick, 1982

[Democracy] makes possible the reform of institutions without using violence.

> KARL R. POPPER (1902–1994). *The Open Society and Its Enemies,* 1.7.3, 1945

A democracy cannot flourish half rich and half poor, any more than it can flourish half free and half slave.

> FELIX G. ROHATYN. Financier. "Ethics in America's Money Culture," *New York Times,* 3 June 1987

The liberty of a democracy is not safe if the people tolerate the growth of private power to a point where it becomes stronger than their democratic state itself. That, in its essence, is fascism—ownership of government by an individual, by a group, or by any other controlling private power.

> FRANKLIN D. ROOSEVELT (1882–1945). Message to Congress, 29 April 1938

The people, being subject to the laws, ought to be their author: the conditions of the society ought to be regulated solely by those who come together to form it.

> ROUSSEAU (1712–1778). *The Social Contract,* 2.6, 1762, tr. G. D. H. Cole, 1950

Were there a people of gods, their government would be democratic.

> ROUSSEAU (1712–1778). *The Social Contract,* 3.5, 1762, tr. G. D. H. Cole, 1950

Democracy, as conceived by politicians, is a form of *government,* that is to say, it is a method of making people do what their leaders wish under the impression that they are doing what they themselves wish.

> BERTRAND RUSSELL (1872–1970). *Sceptical Essays,* 14, 1928

The first rule of democracy is to distrust all leaders who begin to believe their own publicity.

> ARTHUR M. SCHLESINGER, JR. (1917–). "On Heroic Leadership," *Encounter,* December 1960

All the ills of democracy can be cured by more democracy.

> AL SMITH (1973–1944). Speech, Albany (New York), 27 June 1933

Be sure that a democracy will be attained whenever the people are good enough for one.

> HERBERT SPENCER (1820–1903). *Social Statics,* 3.20.13, 1851

Self-criticism is the secret weapon of democracy.

> ADLAI E. STEVENSON (1900–1965). Presidential nomination acceptance speech, Chicago, 21 July, 1952

The foundation of democracy is the sense of spiritual independence which nerves the individual to stand alone against the powers of this world.

R. H. TAWNEY (1880–1962). *Religion and the Rise of Capitalism: A Historical Study,* 4.4, 1926

Is a democracy, such as we know it, the last improvement possible in government? Is it not possible to take a step further towards recognizing and organizing the rights of man?

HENRY DAVID THOREAU (1817–1862). "Civil Disobedience," 1849

Democracy does not give the people the most skillful government, but it produces what the ablest governments are frequently unable to create: namely, an all-pervading and restless activity, a superabundant force, and an energy which is inseparable from it and which may, however unfavorable circumstances may be, produce wonders.

ALEXIS de TOCQUEVILLE (1805–1859). *Democracy in America,* 1.14, 1835, tr. Henry Reeve and Francis Bowen, 1862

The very idea of the power and the right of the People to establish Government presupposes the duty of every Individual to obey the established Government.

GEORGE WASHINGTON (1732–1799). *Farewell Address,* 17 September 1796

It is, sir, the people's Constitution, the people's government, made for the people, made by the people, and answerable to the people.

DANIEL WEBSTER (1782–1852). In a Senate debate with Robert Young Hayne on Constitutional principles and governmental authority, 26 January 1830

See Civil War: Abraham Lincoln (5)

Democracy is the recurrent suspicion that more than half of the people are right more than half of the time.

E. B. WHITE (1899–1985). "Talk of the Town," *New Yorker,* 3 July 1943

The task of democracy is to relieve mass misery and yet preserve the freedom of the individual.

ALFRED NORTH WHITEHEAD (1861–1947). 17 March 1938, *Dialogues of Alfred North Whitehead,* rec. Lucien Price, 1954

I speak the password primeval, I give the sign of democracy,
By God! I will accept nothing which all cannot have their counterpart of on the same terms.

WALT WHITMAN (1819–1892). "Song of Myself" (24), 1855, *Leaves of Grass,* 1855–1892

See Sharing: Mohandas K. Gandhi

[Democracy] is a great word, whose history, I suppose, remains unwritten, because that history has yet to be enacted.

WALT WHITMAN (1819–1892). *Democratic Vistas,* 1871, *Walt Whitman: Complete Poetry and Collected Prose,* ed. Justin Kaplan, p. 960, 1982

DEMOCRACY, ANTI-

See also • Democracy

Remember, democracy never lasts long. It soon wastes, exhausts, and murders itself. There never was a democracy yet that did not commit suicide.

JOHN ADAMS (1735–1826). Letter to John Taylor, 15 April 1814

Democracy: in which you say what you like and do what you're told.

GERALD BARRY (1899–1968). English journalist

Universal suffrage is the government of a house by its nursery.

OTTO von BISMARCK (1815–1898)

In a democracy, the majority of the citizens is capable of exercising the most cruel oppressions upon the minority.

EDMUND BURKE (1729–1797). *Reflections on the Revolution in France,* p. 229, 1790, Pelican Books edition, 1968

The tendency of democracies is, in all things, to mediocrity.

JAMES FENIMORE COOPER (1789–1851). "On the Disadvantages of Democracy," *The American Democrat,* 1838

It is a besetting vice of democracies to substitute public opinion for law. This is the usual form in which masses of men exhibit their tyranny.

JAMES FENIMORE COOPER (1789–1851). "On the Disadvantages of Democracy," *The American Democrat,* 1838

Democracy stands between two tyrannies: the one which it has overthrown and the one into which it will develop.

PAUL ELDRIDGE (1888–1982). *Maxims for a Modern Man,* 642, 1965

Democracy is the theory that the common people know what they want, and deserve to get it good and hard.

H. L. MENCKEN (1880–1856). *A Little Book in C Major,* 2.1, 1916

Democracy is . . . a form of religion. It is the worship of jackals by jackasses.

H. L. MENCKEN (1880–1956). *A Little Book in C Major,* 4.16, 1916

Democracy is the art and science of running the circus from the monkey cage.

H. L. MENCKEN (1880–1956). *A Mencken Chrestomathy,* 30 ("The Citizen and the State"), 1949

Democracy substitutes selection by the incompetent many for appointment by the corrupt few.

GEORGE BERNARD SHAW (1856–1950). "Maxims for Revolutionists: Democracy," *Man and Superman,* 1903

On the soil of a democracy constitutional rights signify nothing without money and everything with it.

OSWALD SPENGLER (1880–1936). "Philosophy of Politics," *The Decline of the West,* 1918–1922, tr. Charles Francis Atkinson, 1962

The will-to-power operating under a pure democratic disguise has accomplished its task so well that the object's sense of freedom is actually flattered by the most thoroughgoing enslavement that has ever existed.

OSWALD SPENGLER (1880–1936). "Philosophy of Politics," *The Decline of the West,* 1918–1922, tr. Charles Francis Atkinson, 1962

[Democratic government] covers the surface of society with a network of small complicated rules, minute and uniform, through which the most original minds and the most energetic characters cannot penetrate to rise above the crowd. The will of man is not shattered but softened, bent, and guided; men are seldom forced by it to act, but they are constantly restrained from acting. Such a power does not destroy, but it prevents existence; it does not tyrannize, but it compresses, enervates, extinguishes, and stupefies a people, till each nation is reduced to nothing better than a flock of timid and industrious animals, of which the government is the shepherd.

> ALEXIS de TOCQUEVILLE (1805–1859). *Democracy in America,* 2.4.6, 1840, tr. Henry Reeve and Francis Bowen, 1862

Apparently, a democracy is a place where numerous elections are held at great cost without issues and with interchangeable candidates.

> GORE VIDAL (1925–). "Gods and Greens," 1989, *A View from the Diner's Club,* 1991

Democracy means simply the bludgeoning of the people by the people for the people.

> OSCAR WILDE (1854–1900). "The Soul of Man Under Socialism," *Fortnightly Review* (British journal), February 1891

DENMARK

See also • Nations

Marcellus: Something is rotten in the state of Denmark.

> SHAKESPEARE (1564–1616). *Hamlet,* 1.4.90, 1600

DEPRESSION

See also • Anger ○ Anxiety ○ Despair ○ Melancholy ○ Mental Illness ○ Suicide: Peter D. Kramer ○ Suicide ○ Unhappiness

A gloomy morning. On all sides a depressing outlook, and within, disgust with self.

> HENRI AMIEL (1821–1881). Journal, 26 April 1868, tr. Mrs. Humphrey Ward, 1887

What a creature of strange moods [Winston Churchill] is—always at the top of the wheel of confidence or at the bottom of an intense depression.

> LORD BEAVERBROOK (1879–1964). *Politicians and the War: 1914–1916,* 1.9, 1928
>
> See Enthusiasm: André Gide ○ Feelings: George Ade

No power in society, no hardship in your condition can depress you, keep you down, in knowledge, power, virtue, influence, but by your own consent.

> WILLIAM ELLERY CHANNING (1780–1842). "Self-Culture," address, Boston, September 1838
>
> See Inferiority: Eleanor Roosevelt

Black Dog.

> WINSTON CHURCHILL (1874–1965). His term for "the prolonged fits of depression from which he suffered" (Moran), 14 August 1944 (footnote). In Lord Moran, *Churchill: Taken from the Diaries of Lord Moran,* 19, 1966
>
> See Suicide: Churchill

By virtue of depression, we recall those misdeeds we buried in the depths of our memory. Depression exhumes our shames.

> E. M. CIORAN (1911–1995). *Anathemas and Admirations,* 11, 1986, tr. Richard Howard, 1991

The acute phase of Lincoln's depressive attack in January, 1841, lasted for more than a week. . . . His inability to attend the legislative session, and the fears of his colleagues that he would attempt suicide, would in modern times prompt most psychiatrists to arrange for inpatient hospitalization and treatment. I would insist on hospitalization, observation for suicidal intent, antidepressant drugs, and later administration of lithium as the treatment of choice for such a condition.

> RONALD R. FIEVE (1930–). Psychiatrist. *Moodswing: The Third Revolution in Psychiatry,* 7, 1973

Wherever there is distress which one cannot remove, one must fast and pray.

> MOHANDAS K. GANDHI (1869–1948). In *Young India,* 18 September 1924
>
> See Weeping: Nehemiah

The depression this evening is as black as yesterday. I must face the fact that the chief reason for the depression is that I cannot compose.

> ERIC HOFFER (1902–1983). 15 August 1958, *Working and Thinking on the Waterfront: A Journal,* 1969

Perhaps depression in women is an unacknowledged passion for rebirth. Something is pressing to appear. It is not the baby; it can only be the mother.

> ERICA JONG (1942–). *Fear of Fifty: A Midlife Memoir,* 10, 1994

Depression . . . is caused by the loss of hope.

> RONALD LEIFER (1932–). In Seth Farber, *Madness, Heresy, and the Rumor of Angels: The Revolt Against the Mental Health System,* 12, 1993

Black care rarely sits beside the rider whose pace is fast enough.

> THEODORE ROOSEVELT (1858–1919). On "fighting off personal depression." In James David Barber, *The Presidential Character: Predicting Performance in the White House,* 7, 1972

The key to the prison of depression is simply to become truly your own best friend.

> DOROTHY ROWE. Closing words, "The Wrong Sort of Depression," *Guardian Weekend* (British newspaper), 25 March 1995 ❦

Noble deeds and hot baths are the best cures for depression.

> DODIE SMITH (1896–?). *I Capture the Castle,* 1.3, 1949

Although a specific attack of depression may be relieved by physical methods of treatment, the tendency to become severely depressed cannot be understood without taking the whole personality into account.

> ANTHONY STORR (1920–). *Churchill's Black Dog, Kafka's Mice, and Other Phenomena of the Human Mind,* 10, 1988

In my experience, at least *of late years,* all that depresses a man's spirits is the sense of remissness—duties neglected, unfaithfulness—or shamming, impurity, falsehood, selfishness, inhumanity, and the like.

> HENRY DAVID THOREAU (1817–1862). Journal, 28 August 1854

The best way to cheer yourself is to try to cheer somebody else up.

MARK TWAIN (1835–1910). 26 November 1896, *Mark Twain's Notebook,* ed. Albert Bigelow Paine, 1935

Why are you cast down, O my soul,
    and why are you disquieted within me?
Hope in God; for I shall again praise him,
    my help and my God.

ANONYMOUS (*BIBLE*). *Psalms* 43:5

DESIRE

See also • Abstinence ◦ Lust ◦ Passion ◦ Self-Discipline ◦ Sex ◦ Tragedy: George Bernard Shaw (1)

Heaven always favors good desires.

CERVANTES (1547–1616). *Don Quixote,* 2.4.43, 1615, tr. Peter Anthony Motteux and John Ozell, 1743

Father Zossima: What follows from this right of multiplication of desires? In the rich, isolation and spiritual suicide: in the poor, envy and murder.

FYODOR DOSTOYEVSKY (1821–1881). *The Brothers Karamazov,* 6.2(e), 1880, tr. Constance Garnett, 1912

'Tis easier to suppress the first Desire than to satisfy all that follow it.

BENJAMIN FRANKLIN (1706–1790). "The Way to Wealth," 7 July 1757

Our desires always increase with our possessions; the knowledge that something remains yet unenjoyed, impairs our enjoyment of the good before us.

SAMUEL JOHNSON (1709–1784). In *The Adventurer* (English journal), 67, 26 June 1753

There is nothing better for the nurturing of the heart than to reduce the number of one's desires.

MENCIUS (371?–289? B.C.). *Mencius,* 7.B.35, tr. D. C. Lau, 1970

Desire for gain and fear of loss burn like fire.

DOROTHY NORMAN (1905–1997). *The Hero: Myth/Image/Symbol,* 20, 1969

First deserve, then desire.

SAYING (ENGLISH)

See Pleasure: Thomas Fuller

DESPAIR

See also • Bravery: Anonymous ◦ Courage: Ted Koppel ◦ Depression ◦ Desperation ◦ Failure ◦ Faith ◦ Heresy: Abraham Joshua Heschel ◦ Hope ◦ Optimism: Examples ◦ Pessimism ◦ Pessimism: Examples ◦ Self-Realization (Becoming) ◦ Struggle ◦ Suicide ◦ Tears: Alfred, Lord Tennyson ◦ Unhappiness

All despair is a kind of reproaching the deity.

FRANCIS BACON (1561–1626). *Advancement of Learning,* 9, 1605, Willey Book edition, 1944

There is one cardinal rule for the British nation . . . "Never despair."

WINSTON CHURCHILL (1874–1965). "Never Despair," speech, 1951, *Winston Churchill: His Complete Speeches 1897–1963,* vol. 8, ed. Robert R. James, 1974

One has no right to despair because one has been deceived in one's expectations; one must revise them.

SIGMUND FREUD (1856–1939). In Lucy Freeman and Marvin Small, *The Story of Psychoanalysis,* 6, 1960

And nothing to look backward to with pride,
And nothing to look forward to with hope.

ROBERT FROST (1874–1963). "The Death of the Hired Man," *North of Boston,* 1914

Do not turn away, through cowardice, from despair. Go through it. . . . Pass beyond. On the other side of the tunnel you will find light again.

ANDRÉ GIDE (1869–1951). Journal, 1928 ("detached pages"), tr. Justin O'Brien, 1951

Despair is due not to failures but to the inability to hear deeply and personally the challenge that confronts us.

ABRAHAM JOSHUA HESCHEL (1907–1972). *Who Is Man?* 6, 1965

God does not send us despair in order to kill us; he sends it in order to awaken us to new life.

HERMANN HESSE (1877–1962). *Reflections,* 192, ed. Volker Michels, 1974

Despair is a greater sin than any of the sins which provoke it.

C. S. LEWIS (1890–1960). *The Screwtape Letters,* rev. ed., 29, 1982 (1942)

It is not impossibilities which fill us with the deepest despair, but possibilities which we have failed to realize.

ROBERT MALLET (1915–). *Apostilles,* 1972

Despair, surely the least aggressive of sins, is dangerous to the totalitarian temperament because it is a state of intense inwardness, thus independence. The despairing soul is a rebel.

JOYCE CAROL OATES (1938–). "The One Unforgivable Sin," *New York Times Book Review,* 25 July 1993

[Despair is] the worst betrayal, the coldest seduction: to believe at last that the enemy will prevail.

MARGE PIERCY (1936–). Quoted by Peggy Kornegger, "Anarchism: The Feminist Connection." In Howard J. Ehrlich et al., eds., *Reinventing Anarchy,* 1979

Human life begins on the other side of despair.

JEAN-PAUL SARTRE (1905–1980). *The Flies,* 3.3, 1943

He who hears the rippling of rivers in these degenerate days will not utterly despair.

HENRY DAVID THOREAU (1817–1862). "Friday," *A Week on the Concord and Merrimack Rivers,* 1849

A stereotyped but unconscious despair is concealed even under what are the games and amusements of mankind.

HENRY DAVID THOREAU (1817–1862). "Economy," *Walden; or Life in the Woods,* 1854

Despair is a greater deceiver than hope.

VAUVENARGUES (1715–1747). *Reflections and Maxims,* 455, 1746, tr. F. G. Stevens, 1940

DESPERATION

See also • Courage: B. H. Liddell Hart, Seneca the Younger ○
Danger ○ Despair ○ Misery: Abraham Lincoln ○ Pain ○ Self-
Realization (Becoming) ○ Suicide ○ Unhappiness

Wandering between two worlds, one dead,
The other powerless to be born.
With nowhere yet to rest my head,
Like these, on earth I wait forlorn.

> MATTHEW ARNOLD (1822–1888). "Stanzas from the Grande Chartreuse,"
> l. 85, 1855

Desperation is the raw material of drastic change. Only those who
can leave behind everything they have ever believed in can hope
to escape.

> WILLIAM S. BURROUGHS (1914–1997). *The Western Lands*, 5, 1987

It is only those who know neither an inner call nor an outer doctrine whose plight truly is desperate.

> JOSEPH CAMPBELL (1904–1987). Prologue (1) to *The Hero with a
> Thousand Faces*, 1949

In the depth of winter, I finally learned that within me there lay
an invincible summer.

> ALBERT CAMUS (1913–1960). "Return to Tipasa," *Summer*, 1954
> See Misfortune: Ho Chi Minh ○ Seasons: Percy Bysshe Shelley

In a real dark night of the soul it is always three o'clock in the
morning, day after day.

> F. SCOTT FITZGERALD (1896–1940). "Handle with Care," *Esquire*, March
> 1936

The dark night, through which the soul passes, on its way to the
divine light of the perfect union of the love of God.

> ST. JOHN OF THE CROSS (1542–1591). Prologue (opening words) to
> *The Ascent of Mount Carmel*, tr. David Lewis, 1906

My life has been brought to an *impasse*, I loathe existence. . . .
Who am I? How did I come into the world? Why was I not con-
sulted?

> SÓREN KIERKEGAARD (1813–1855). "Repetition: An Essay in
> Experimental Psychology," tr. Walter Lowrie, 1941

I am utterly weary of life. I pray the Lord will come forthwith and
carry me hence. Let him come, above all, with his last Judgment:
I will stretch out my neck, the thunder will burst forth, and I shall
be at rest. O God, grant that it may come without delay.

> MARTIN LUTHER (1483–1546). Late in life. In William James,
> *The Varieties of Religious Experience: A Study in Human Nature*,
> 6 and 7, 1902

Three words were in the captain's heart. He shaped them sound-
lessly with his trembling lips, as he had not breath to spare for a
whisper, "I am lost." And having given up life, the captain suddenly began to live.

> CARSON McCULLERS (1917–1967). *Reflections in a Golden Eye*, 3, 1941

I frequently asked myself, if I could, or if I was bound to go on
living. . . . I generally answered to myself, that I did not think I
could possibly bear it beyond a year. When, however, not more
than half that duration of time had elapsed, a small ray of light
broke in upon my gloom. I was reading, accidentally, Marmontel's
"Mémoires," and came to the passage which relates his father's
death, the distressed position of the family, and the sudden inspiration by which he, then a mere boy, felt and made them feel that
he would be everything to them—would supply the place of all
that they had lost. A vivid conception of the scene and its feelings
came over me, and I was moved to tears. From this moment my
burden grew lighter. The oppression of the thought that all feeling was dead within me, was gone. I was no longer hopeless: I
was not a stock or a stone. I had still, it seemed, some of the material out of which all worth of character and all capacity for happiness are made.

> JOHN STUART MILL (1806–1873). *Autobiography*, 5, 1873

One day you will no longer see what is exalted in you; and what
is base in you, you will see all too closely. . . . One day you will
cry: "Everything is false!"

> FRIEDRICH NIETZSCHE (1844–1900). "Of the Way of the Creator,"
> *Thus Spoke Zarathustra*, 1892, tr. R. J. Hollingdale, 1961

To live is to feel oneself lost—he who accepts this has already
begun to find himself, to be on firm ground. Instinctively, as do
the shipwrecked, he will look round for something to which to
cling, and that tragic, ruthless glance, absolutely sincere, because
it is a question of his salvation, will cause him to bring order into
the chaos of his life. These are the only genuine ideas; the ideas
of the shipwrecked. All the rest is rhetoric, posturing, farce.

> JOSÉ ORTEGA y GASSET (1883–1955). *The Revolt of the Masses*, 14.7,
> 1930, tr. anon., 1932

Romeo: Tempt not a desperate man.

> SHAKESPEARE (1564–1616). *Romeo and Juliet*, 5.3.59, 1594

The mass of men lead lives of quiet desperation. What is called
resignation is confirmed desperation.

> HENRY DAVID THOREAU (1817–1862). "Economy," *Walden; or Life in
> the Woods*, 1854

Nowadays most men lead lives of noisy desperation.

> JAMES THURBER (1894–1961). "The Grizzly and the Gadgets,"
> *Further Fables for Our Time*, 1956

When you're at the bottom, you've got no place to go but up.

> HARRY S. TRUMAN (1884–1972). A repeated remark. In James David
> Barber, *The Presidential Character: Predicting Performance in the White
> House*, 8, 1972

❦

Any port in a storm.

> SAYING (ENGLISH)

DESPOTS

See also • Dehumanization: Henri Amiel ○ Dictators ○
Individuality: John Stuart Mill (3) ○ Tyranny: [especially] Voltaire
○ Tyrants

If it is a despot you would dethrone, see first that his throne erected within you is destroyed.

> KAHLIL GIBRAN (1883–1931). "On Freedom," *The Prophet*, 1923

It is the old practice of despots to use a part of the people to keep the rest in order.

> THOMAS JEFFERSON (1743–1826). Letter to John Taylor, 1 June 1798

Nobody can compel me to be happy in his own way. Paternalism is the greatest despotism imaginable.

> IMMANUEL KANT (1770–1804). In Isaiah Berlin, *Two Concepts of Liberty*, 3, 1958

[Despots] ultimately make war on other states as a means of diverting attention from internal conditions, and allowing discontent to explode outwards.

> B. H. LIDDELL HART (1895–1970). "The Standard Historical Pattern of Self-Made Despotic Rulers," *Why Don't We Learn from History?* 1944

People complain of the despotism of princes; they ought to complain of the despotism of *man*.

> JOSEPH-MARIE de MAISTRE (1753–1851). *The Study of Sovereignty*, 2.2, 1884

More than one emperor or despot discovered that permissiveness in the form of sensual inducements and enticements might be even more effective than coercion in securing compliance. Once established, the parasite identifies himself with his host and seeks to further the host's prosperity.

> LEWIS MUMFORD (1895–1990). *The Pentagon of Power: The Myth of the Machine*, 12.5, 1970

Let me tell you that in order to govern well one needs absolute unity of power. I won't shout this from the rooftops, since I mustn't frighten a lot of people who would raise loud cries of despotism.

> NAPOLEON (1769–1821). Remark to his brother Joseph Bonaparte, 1803, *The Mind of Napoleon: A Selection from His Written and Spoken Words*, 111, ed. J. Christopher Herold, 1955

[It is] not true that those who bear universal sway and seem able to do as they please can really do so. They limit their own freedom in limiting that of others; their despotism recoils and puts them also in bondage. We read, for instance, that the Roman emperors were the puppets of their soldiers. "In the Byzantine palace," says [Edward] Gibbon, "the emperor was the first slave of the ceremonies he imposed."

> HERBERT SPENCER (1820–1903). *Social Statics*, 4.30.14, 1851

For administrative efficiency, autocratic power is the best. . . . If you would have society actively regulated by staffs of State-agents; then by all means choose that system of complete centralization which we call despotism.

> HERBERT SPENCER (1820–1903). "Representative Government—What Is It Good For?" *The Westminster Review* (English journal), October 1857

With family governments, as with political ones, a harsh despotism itself generates a great part of the crimes it has to repress.

> HERBERT SPENCER (1820–1903). *Education: Intellectual, Moral, and Physical*, 3, 1860

The more complete the despotism, the more smoothly all things move on the surface.

> ELIZABETH CADY STANTON (1815–1902), SUSAN B. ANTHONY (1820–1906), and MATHILDA GAGE (1826–1898). *A History of Woman Suffrage*, 1881

A despot easily forgives his subjects for not loving him, provided they do not love one another. He does not ask them to assist him in governing the state; it is enough that they do not aspire to govern it themselves. He stigmatizes as turbulent and unruly spirits those who would combine their exertions to promote the prosperity of the community; and, perverting the natural meaning of words, he applauds as good citizens those who have no sympathy for any but themselves.

> ALEXIS de TOCQUEVILLE (1805–1859). *Democracy in America*, 2.2.4, 1840, tr. Henry Reeve and Francis Bowen, 1862

The aggressiveness of governments grows in proportion to the increase of their internal despotism.

> LEO TOLSTOY (1828–1910). *The Kingdom of God Is Within You*, 7, 1893, tr. Aylmer Maude, 1936

There are three kinds of despots. There is the despot who tyrannizes over the body. There is the despot who tyrannizes over the soul. There is the despot who tyrannizes over the soul and body alike. The first is called the Prince. The second is called the Pope. The third is called the People.

> OSCAR WILDE (1854–1900). "The Soul of Man Under Socialism," *Fortnightly Review* (British journal), February 1891

Despotism . . . kills virtue and genius in the bud.

> MARY WOLLSTONECRAFT (1759–1797). *A Vindication of the Rights of Woman*, 3, 1792

DESTINY

See also • Body: Napoleon ○ Chance ○ Character: Heraclitus ○ Fate ○ Fortune ○ Luck ○ Necessity ○ Opportunity ○ Problems & Solutions: John F. Kennedy ○ Unity: George D. Herron ○ Will, Free

Destiny, *n*. A tyrant's excuse for crime and a fool's excuse for failure.

> AMBROSE BIERCE (1842–1914). *The Devil's Dictionary*, p. 31, 1911, Dover edition, 1958

Destiny is not a matter of chance, it is a matter of choice; it is not a thing to be waited for, it is a thing to be achieved.

> WILLIAM JENNINGS BRYAN (1860–1925). Speech, Washington, 22 February 1899

"It is destiny"—phrase of the weak human heart; dark apology for every error. The strong and the virtuous admit no destiny.

> EDWARD GEORGE BULWER-LYTTON (1803–1873). *The Last of the Barons*, 8.6, 1843

This cannot be accident; it must be design. I was kept for this job.

> WINSTON CHURCHILL (1874–1965). On being British prime minister during World War II. Remark to the diarist. In Lord Moran, *Churchill: Taken from the Diaries of Lord Moran*, 71, 1966
> See Confidence: Churchill

The glory of human nature lies in our seeming capacity to exercise conscious control of our own destiny.

> WINSTON CHURCHILL (1874–1965). In C. E. M. Joad, "Churchill the Philosopher." In Charles Eade, ed., *Churchill by His Contemporaries*, 1953

The implacable destiny of which we are the victims—and the tools.
> JOSEPH CONRAD (1857–1924). *Lord Jim*, 34, 1900

Hanging and marriage . . . go by Destiny.
> GEORGE FARQUHAR (1678–1707). *The Recruiting Officer*, 3.23, 1706

No one should believe so fully in his star that he abandons himself to it blindly.
> FREDERICK II (1712–1786). *The Instruction of Frederick the Great for His Generals*, 1747. In Thomas R. Phillips, ed., *Roots of Strategy*, p. 394, 1940

Destiny leads the willing but drags the unwilling.
> THOMAS FULLER (1654–1734). Comp., *Gnomologia: Adages and Proverbs*, 1274, 1732

We are not permitted to choose the frame of our destiny. But what we put into it is ours.
> DAG HAMMARSKJÖLD (1905–1961). 1950, *Markings*, tr. Leif Sjöberg and W. H. Auden, 1964
>
> See Freedom: Martin Luther King, Jr.

Destiny is carried out, fate is suffered.
> J. CHRISTOPHER HEROLD. Introduction to *The Mind of Napoleon: A Selection from His Written and Spoken Words*, 1955

What extraordinary vehicles destiny selects to accomplish its design.
> HENRY A. KISSINGER (1923–). *White House Years*, 34, 1979

All my life I have sacrificed everything—comfort, self-interest, happiness—to my destiny.
> NAPOLEON (1769–1821). Letter to Josephine, 27 March 1807, *The Mind of Napoleon: A Selection from His Written and Spoken Words*, 54, ed. J. Christopher Herold, 1955

Our destiny commands us, even when we do not yet know what it is; it is the future which guides the rule to our present.
> FRIEDRICH NIETZSCHE (1844–1900). Preface (7) to *Human, All Too Human*, 1878, tr. Marion Faber, 1984

We are not launched into existence like a shot from a gun, with its trajectory absolutely predetermined. The destiny under which we fall when we come into this world . . . consists in the exact contrary. Instead of imposing on us one trajectory, it imposes several, and consequently forces us to choose. . . . To live is to feel ourselves *fatally* obliged to exercise our *liberty*, to decide what we are going to be in this world. Not for a single moment is our activity of decision allowed to rest. Even when in desperation we abandon ourselves to whatever may happen, we have decided not to decide.
> JOSÉ ORTEGA y GASSET (1883–1955). *The Revolt of the Masses*, 5, 1930, 5tr. anon., 1932

This generation of Americans has a rendezvous with destiny.
> FRANKLIN D. ROOSEVELT (1882–1945). Presidential nomination acceptance speech, Philadelphia, 27 June 1936

Within the limits of the physical laws of nature, we are still masters of our individual and collective destiny, for good or ill.
> E. F. SCHUMACHER (1911–1977). *Small Is Beautiful: Economics as if People Mattered*, 4.1, 1973

Alas! we are the sport of destiny.
> WILLIAM MAKEPEACE THACKERAY (1811–1863). *Barry Lyndon*, 3, 1844

Control Your Destiny or Someone Else Will.
> NOEL M. TICHY and STRATFORD SHERMAN. Book title, 1993

DETAILS

See also • Decision-Making ○ Failure: Henri Amiel ○ Failure ○ Planning ○ Success ○ Trifles

A man's accomplishments in life are the cumulative effect of his attention to detail.
> JOHN FOSTER DULLES (1888–1959). In Leonard Mosley, *Dulles: A Biography of Eleanor, Allen, and John Foster Dulles and Their Family Network*, 25, 1978

The world can never be learned by learning all its details.
> RALPH WALDO EMERSON (1803–1882). Journal, 28 October 1839

Don't drown yourself in details. Look at the whole.
> FERDINAND FOCH (1851–1929). In Charles Bugnet, "Power" ("The Power to Get Things Done . . . "), *Foch Speaks*, tr. Russell Green, 1929

[Theodore Roosevelt] seldom allowed himself to become immersed in details. He simply sampled.
> ERWIN C. HARGROVE (1930–). *Presidential Leadership: Personality and Political Style*, 1, 1966

The details vanish in the bird's-eye view; but so does the bird's-eye view vanish in the details.
> WILLIAM JAMES (1842–1910). "The Importance of Individuals," *The Will to Believe: And Other Essays in Popular Philosophy*, 1897

The smallest details of this world derive infinite significance from their relation to an unseen divine order.
> WILLIAM JAMES (1842–1910). *The Varieties of Religious Experience: A Study in Human Nature*, 14 and 15, 1902

Now, my man, go away, go away! I cannot meddle in your case. I could as easily bail out the Potomac River with a teaspoon as attend to all the details of the army.
> ABRAHAM LINCOLN (1809–1865). Remark to a soldier who in trying to have his grievance with the army redressed had overstretched Lincoln's patience. Quoted by James B. Fry, untitled essay. In Allen T. Rice, ed., *Reminiscences of Abraham Lincoln*, 1885

The details of this job are killing me.
> FRANKLIN D. ROOSEVELT (1882–1945). Remark to Sen. Harley M. Kilgore, 1944. In Alfred Steinberg, *The Man from Missouri*, 24, 1962. Among Pres. Roosevelt's duties during World War II, forty-seven war agencies reported directly to him.
>
> See Presidents & Staff: James K. Polk

❧

God is in the details.
> SAYING

The devil is in the details.
> SAYING

DEVIL

See also • Angels ○ God & the Devil ○ Scripture: Shakespeare

The heart of man is the place the devils dwell in; I feel sometimes a hell within myself; Lucifer keeps his court in my breast.

> SIR THOMAS BROWNE (1605–1682). *Religio Medici,* 1.51, 1642, ed. John Addington Symonds, 1886

The devil's most devilish when respectable.

> ELIZABETH BARRETT BROWNING (1806–1861). *Aurora Leigh,* 7.105, 1857

The devil is always that particular thing, institution, or party which restrains the free action of the soul and confines it to a prescribed formula, whether of religion, politics, or morals, or whatever would subject the soul to any law or authority distinguishable from itself.

> ORESTES A. BROWNSON (1803–1876). "Transcendentalism," 1846. In George Hochfield, ed., *Selected Writings of the American Transcendentalists,* 1966

Bodily Labor is the most useful for the driving away of the Devil.

> THOMAS FULLER (1654–1734). Comp., *Introductio ad Prudentiam,* 1206, 1731

Please allow me to introduce myself
I'm a man of wealth and taste.
I've been around for a long, long year,
Stole many a man's soul and faith.
And I was round when Jesus Christ
Had his moments of doubt and pain,
Made damn sure that Pilate
Washed his hands and sealed his fate.
Pleased to meet you, hope you guess my name,
But what's puzzling you
Is the nature of my game.

> MICK JAGGER (1943–) and KEITH RICHARDS (1943–). "Sympathy for the Devil" (song), 1968

Always behind what we imagine are our best deeds stands the devil, patting us paternally on the shoulder and whispering, "Well done!"

> CARL G. JUNG (1875–1961). "A Psychological View of Conscience," 1958, *Civilization in Transition,* tr. R. F. C. Hull, 1964

The afterthoughts with which you justify your accommodation of the Evil One are not yours but those of the Evil One.

> FRANZ KAFKA (1883–1924). "Reflections on Sin, Pain, Hope, and the True Way" (26), 1917–1920, *The Great Wall of China,* 1931, tr. Willa and Edwin Muir, 1946

Better keep the Devil at the Door than turn him out [of] the House.

> JAMES KELLY (18th cent.). Comp., *A Complete Collection of Scottish Proverbs Explained and Made Intelligible to the English Reader,* B.39, 1721

The devil is an optimist if he thinks he can make people worse than they are.

> KARL KRAUS (1874–1936). 1909. In Thomas S. Szasz, *Karl Kraus and the Soul-Doctors: A Pioneer Critic and His Criticism of Psychiatry and Psychoanalysis,* 8, 1976

Idiots, the lame, the blind, the dumb, are men in whom devils have established themselves—and all the physicians who heal those infirmities, as though they proceeded from natural causes, are ignorant blockheads, who know nothing about the power of the demon.

> MARTIN LUTHER (1483–1546). In Theo. B. Hyslop, *The Great Abnormals,* 4, 1925

That there is a Devil is a thing doubted by none but such as are under the influences of the Devil.

> COTTON MATHER (1663–1728). "A Discourse on the Wonders of the Invisible World," sermon, 4 August 1692

Without Satan, no Christ.

> DOROTHY NORMAN (1905–1997). *The Hero: Myth/Image/Symbol,* 24, 1969

Edgar: The prince of darkness is a gentleman.

> SHAKESPEARE (1564–1616). *King Lear,* 3.4.148, 1605

Don Juan (to the Devil): It is the success with which you have diverted the attention of men from their real purpose . . . that has earned you the name of The Tempter.

> GEORGE BERNARD SHAW (1856–1950). *Man and Superman,* 3, 1903

There was an anchorite who was able to banish the demons; and he asked them, "What makes you go away? Is it fasting?" They replied, "We do not eat or drink." "Is it vigils?" They replied, "We do not sleep." "Is it separation from the world?" "We live in the deserts." "What power sends you away then?" They said, "Nothing can overcome us, but only humility."

> THEODORA (A.D. 10th cent.). In "Theta: Theodora" (6), *The Sayings of the Desert Fathers: The Alphabetical Collection,* tr. Benedicta Ward, 1975

Everyone has a devil in him that is capable of any crime in the long run.

> HENRY DAVID THOREAU (1817–1862). "Wednesday," *A Week on the Concord and Merrimack Rivers,* 1849

But who prays for Satan? Who, in eighteen centuries, has had the common humanity to pray for the one sinner that needed it most.

> MARK TWAIN (1835–1910). *The Autobiography of Mark Twain,* 7, ed. Charles Neider, 1959

We don't deal the deck down here; we just play the percentages.

> JOHN UPDIKE (1932–) (MICHAEL CRISTOFER, scriptwriter). *The Witches of Eastwick* (film), 1987, spoken by Jack Nicholson (in the role of the devil)

❧

Better the devil you know than the devil you don't know.

> SAYING

DIARIES

See also • Journals ○ Notebooks ○ Writing

Keep a Diary of all thy considerable Actions, and of the most memorable Passages thou hearest and meetest with.

> THOMAS FULLER (1654–1734). Comp., *Introductio ad Prudentiam,* 692, 1731

A man loves to review his own mind. That is the use of a diary, or journal.

> SAMUEL JOHNSON (1709–1784). 30 March 1778. In James Boswell, *The Life of Samuel Johnson,* 1791

I am just scribbling to keep from biting the radiator.

> JOSEPH STILWELL (1883–1946). On keeping a diary. In Barbara W. Tuchman, forward to *Stilwell and the American Experience in China, 1911–1945,* 1970

I never travel without my diary. One should always have something sensational to read in the train.

> OSCAR WILDE (1854–1900). *The Importance of Being Earnest,* 2, 1895

DICTATORS

See also • Despots ○ Tyranny ○ Tyrants

When the true type of the dictator emerges into the stream of history, it is as if a strong hand has seized the helm of a distressed ship; for better or worse, the craft begins to move on a definite course.

> ALBERT CARR (1902–1971). "The Path of Dictatorship" (2), *Juggernaut: The Path of Dictatorship,* 1939

Dictators ride to and fro upon tigers from which they dare not dismount. And the tigers are getting hungry.

> WINSTON CHURCHILL (1874–1965). "Armistice—Or Peace?" 11 November 1937, *Step by Step,* 1939

A modern dictator with the resources of science at his disposal can easily lead the public on from day to day, destroying all persistency of thought and aim, so that memory is blurred by the multiplicity of daily news and judgment baffled by its perversion.

> WINSTON CHURCHILL (1874–1965). *The Second World War,* 1948–1953. In Douglass Cater, *The Fourth Branch of Government,* 10 (epigraph), 1959

The history of all these [nineteenth-century dictatorships] reveals the same evolution: material prosperity and power, soulless mediocrity, disaster.

> ALBERT L. GUERARD (1880–1959). "Last Reflections: Hero of the Will," *Reflections on the Napoleonic Legend,* 3, 1924

Dictators are the popes of nationalism.

> ALDOUS HUXLEY (1894–1963). "Writers and Readers," *The Olive Tree and Other Essays,* 1936

Dictatorships are ready to forgive cowardice, but never conviction.

> COUNT MICHAEL KAROLGI (1875–1955)

My dictatorship was indispensable, and the proof of this is that I was always offered more power than I wanted.

> NAPOLEON (1769–1821). In Emil Ludwig, *Napoleon,* 5.18, 1925, tr. Eden and Cedar Paul, 1926

The technique of acquiring dictatorship over what has been a democracy . . . always involves the same mixture of bribery, propaganda and violence.

> BERTRAND RUSSELL (1872–1970). *Power: A New Social Analysis,* 11, 1938

I am painted as the greatest little dictator, which is ridiculous—you always take some consultations.

> MARGARET THATCHER (1925–). English prime minister. Tongue-and-cheek remark. In *Times* (London), 1987

DIFFICULTY

See also • Adversity ○ Burdens ○ Disability: Georg Christoph Lichtenberg ○ Grief ○ Happiness: Samuel Johnson (2) ○ Martyrdom ○ Misfortune ○ Obstacles ○ Optimism: Examples: U.S. Army Corps of Engineers ○ Pain ○ Problems & Solutions ○ Responsibility ○ Struggle ○ Trouble ○ Unhappiness

Almost anything is easier to get into than to get out of.

> AGNES ALLEN. "Agnes Allen's Law." In Scot Morris, "You Make the Laws," *Omni,* May 1979

Difficulties are meant to rouse, not discourage. The human spirit is to grow strong by conflict.

> WILLIAM ELLERY CHANNING (1780–1842). "Self-Culture," address, Boston, September 1838

Most people prefer nuts in their shells, as they then have the pleasure of overcoming a small difficulty.

> RALPH WALDO EMERSON (1803–1882). Journal, February? 1856

It is difficulties which show what men are.

> EPICTETUS (A.D. 55?–135?). *Discourses,* 1.24, tr. George Long, 1890?

All things are difficult before they are easy.

> THOMAS FULLER (1654–1734). Comp., *Gnomologia: Adages and Proverbs,* 560, 1732

The worse the Passage, the more welcome the Port.

> THOMAS FULLER (1654–1734). Comp., *Gnomologia: Adages and Proverbs,* 4848, 1732

It is not always by plugging away at a difficulty and sticking at it that one overcomes it; but, rather, often by working on the one next to it. Certain people and certain things require to be approached on an angle.

> ANDRÉ GIDE (1869–1951). Journal, 26 October 1924, tr. Justin O'Brien, 1951

When the captain of a ship has put out from Singapore bound for Boston, we have only one question to ask. And this question does not refer to typhoons, hurricanes, pirates, shoals, shallows or icebergs. The one question we ask is, "Did you bring the ship into port?"

> ELBERT HUBBARD (1856–1915). *The Note Book of Elbert Hubbard,* p. 36, comp. Elbert Hubbard II, 1927

When the going gets tough, the tough get going.

> JOSEPH P. KENNEDY (1888–1969). A frequent remark to his children when he wanted to "bear down on them." In John Henry Cutler, *Honey Fitz: Three Steps to the White House; The Life and Times of John F. (Honey Fitz) Fitzgerald,* 20, 1962

To overcome difficulties is to experience the full delight of existence.

> ARTHUR SCHOPENHAUER (1788–1860). "Counsels and Maxims" (2.17), *Essays of Arthur Schopenhauer,* tr. T. Bailey Saunders, 1851

[Good men] should not shrink from hardships and difficulties, nor complain against fate; they should take in good part whatever happens, and should turn it to good. Not what you endure, but how you endure, is important.

> SENECA THE YOUNGER (5? B.C.–A.D. 65). "On Providence" (2.4), *Moral Essays*, tr. John W. Basore, 1928

No tree becomes rooted and sturdy unless many a wind assails it. For by its very tossing it tightens its grip and plants its roots more securely; the fragile trees are those that have grown in a sunny valley.

> SENECA THE YOUNGER (5? B.C.–A.D. 65). "On Providence" (4.16), *Moral Essays*, tr. John W. Basore, 1928

Nothing is so easy but it is difficult when you do it [reluctantly].

> TERENCE (190?–159 B.C.). *Heuton timoroumenos*, l. 806, tr. John Sergeaunt, 1912

The most stimulating challenge is one of mean degree between an excess of severity and a deficiency of it, since a deficient challenge may fail to stimulate the challenged party at all, while an excessive challenge may break his spirit.

> ARNOLD J. TOYNBEE (1889–1975). *A Study of History*, 1934–1939, abr. D. C. Somervell, 1.223, 1965

Nothing in the world is difficult for one who sets his mind to it.

> SAYING (CHINESE)

The harder the nut, the sweeter the kernel.

> SAYING

DIGNITY

See also • Character ○ Confidence ○ Democracy: Herman Melville ○ Honesty ○ Honor ○ Integrity ○ Morality ○ Peace: Pope John Paul II ○ Pride ○ Responsibility ○ Right to Silence: William O. Douglas ○ Self-Love ○ Self-Realization (Being) ○ Self-Reliance ○ Self-Respect ○ Virtue ○ Work: Booker T. Washington

Tru dignity is the effeck ov the conscious possession ov ability and vartue.

> JOSH BILLINGS (1818–1885). *His Sayings*, 56, 1867

Dignity [is] achieved only through work and struggle.

> FYODOR DOSTOYEVSKY (1821–1881). *A Diary of a Writer*, 3, 1873

Dignity is not negotiable.

> VARTAN GREGORIAN (1934–). Recalling his grandmother's saying. In Philip Hamburger, "Searching for Gregorian," *New Yorker*, 14 April 1986

The only kind of dignity which is genuine is that which is not diminished by the indifference of others.

> DAG HAMMARSKJÖLD (1905–1961). 1955, *Markings*, tr. Leif Sjöberg and W. H. Auden, 1964

Every man is to be respected as an absolute end in himself; and it is a crime against the dignity that belongs to him to use him as mere means to some external purpose.

> IMMANUEL KANT (1724–1804). In Cyril Connolly, "Ecce Gubernator," *The Unquiet Grave: A Word Cycle by Palinurus*, 1945

Never bend your head! Always hold it high! Look the world straight in the face!

> HELEN KELLER (1880–1968). To a five-year-old child, recalled on her death, 1 June 1968

A sense of one's own dignity is as admirable when kept to oneself as it is ridiculous when displayed to others.

> LA ROCHEFOUCAULD (1613–1680). *Maxims,* 307, 1665, tr. Leonard Tancock, 1959

Human dignity . . . is derived from a sense of independence.

> MARIA MONTESSORI (1870–1952). *The Child in the Family*, 6, 1956, tr. Nancy Rockmore Cirillo, 1970

Achieving dignity and individuality is always a personal affair. It can be facilitated or hindered; but, in the end, each person must do it for himself.

> THOMAS S. SZASZ (1920–). Epilogue to *Law, Liberty, and Psychiatry: An Inquiry into the Social Uses of Mental Health Practices*, 1963

Human dignity . . . can be achieved only in the field of ethics, and ethical achievement is measured by the degree in which our actions are governed by compassion and love, not by greed and aggressiveness.

> ARNOLD J. TOYNBEE (1889–1975). Closing words, *The Toynbee-Ikeda Dialogue: Man Himself Must Choose*, 1976

[Man's] true destiny as co-creator in the universe is his dignity and his grandeur.

> ALFRED NORTH WHITEHEAD (1861–1947). Closing words, 11 November 1947, *Dialogues of Alfred North Whitehead*, rec. Lucien Price, 1954

True dignity abides with him alone
Who, in the silent hour of inward thought,
Can still suspect, and still revere himself,
In lowliness of heart.

> WILLIAM WORDSWORTH (1770–1850). Closing lines, "Lines Left upon a Seat in a Yew-tree," 1798

DIPLOMACY

See also • Alliances ○ Ambassadors ○ Appeasement ○ Diplomats ○ International Relations ○ Machiavellianism ○ Negotiation ○ Politics ○ Statesmen ○ Tact ○ Treaties

To achieve [enduring good relations between states], the conduct of diplomacy should conform to the same moral and ethical principles which inspire trust and confidence when followed by and between individuals.

> DEAN ACHESON (1893–1971). Address, Amherst College (Massachusetts), 9 December 1964

Politics drives diplomacy, not vice versa.

> JAMES A. BAKER (1930) (with THOMAS M. DeFRANK). *The Politics of Diplomacy: Revolution, War and Peace, 1989–1992*, 2, 1995

The heart of the art of diplomacy is to grant graciously what you no longer have the power to withhold.

> EDMUND BURKE (1729–1797). In Glen Frankel, "Whether War Comes or Not, An Ancient Art Will Endure," *Washington Post National Weekly Edition*, 31 December 1990

All diplomacy is a continuation of war by other means.

> CHOU EN-LAI (1898–1976). Edgar Snow interview, *Saturday Evening Post*, 27 March 1954
>
> See War: Karl von Clausewitz (3)

Diplomacy is essentially the struggle to stay ahead of events by anticipating the movement of history.

> PETER W. DICKSON. *Kissinger and the Meaning of History*, 1, 1978

Diplomacy without arms is music without instruments.

> FREDERICK II (1712–1786)

There are few ironclad rules of diplomacy but to one there is no exception. When an official reports that talks were useful, it can safely be concluded that nothing was accomplished.

> JOHN KENNETH GALBRAITH (1908–). "The American Ambassador," *Foreign Service Journal*, June 1969

Diplomacy based on moral idealism or international law is easy to wage openly; but a realist approach involving ambiguous compromises and power ploys lends itself to covert acts and deception, since it is likely to arouse popular disapproval if publicly articulated.

> WALTER ISAACSON (1952–). *Kissinger: A Biography*, 34, 1992

Diplomacy and defense are not substitutes for one another. Either alone would fail.

> JOHN F. KENNEDY (1917–1963). Speech, University of Washington, Seattle, 16 November 1961

Diplomacy, the art of relating states to each other by agreement rather than by the exercise of force.

> HENRY A. KISSINGER (1923–). *A World Restored: Metternich, Castlereagh and the Problems of Peace 1812–1822*, 17.3, 1957

Ambiguity . . . is the stuff of diplomacy.

> HENRY A. KISSINGER (1923–). *White House Years*, 10, 1979

In a society of sovereign states, an agreement will be maintained only if all partners consider it in their interest. They must have a sense of participation in the result. The art of diplomacy is not to outsmart the other side but to convince it either of common interests or of penalties if an impasse continues.

> HENRY A. KISSINGER (1923–). *Years of Upheaval*, 6, 1982

The stronger one's real position, the less one needs to rub in the other side's discomfiture. It is rarely wise to inflame a setback with an insult. An important aspect of the art of diplomacy consists of doing what is necessary without producing extraneous motives for retaliation, leaving open the option of later cooperation on others issues.

> HENRY A. KISSINGER (1923–). *Years of Upheaval*, 21, 1982

Diplomacy [is] the continuation of business by other means.

> CHARLES KRAUTHAMMER (1950–). Closing words, "Right They Aren't," *New Republic*, 16 May 1981
>
> See War: Karl von Clausewitz (3) ○ War & Economics: Anonymous

The function of diplomacy is the management of the relations between independent States by processes of negotiation.

> HAROLD NICOLSON (1886–1968). *Diplomacy*, 4.1, 1939

The principle of give and take is the principle of diplomacy—give one and take ten.

> MARK TWAIN (1835–1910)

Keeping as many channels open as possible is the diplomatic imperative.

> GARRY WILLS (1934–). *Certain Trumpets: The Call of Leaders*, 4, 1994

❧

Politics drives diplomacy, and economics drives politics.

> ANONYMOUS

DIPLOMATS

See also • Ambassadors ○ Diplomacy ○ International Relations ○ Statesmen

Consul, *n.* In American politics, a person who having failed to secure an office from the people is given one by the administration on condition that he leave the country.

> AMBROSE BIERCE (1842–1914). *The Devil's Dictionary*, p. 24, 1911, Dover edition, 1958

The most persuasive method at the disposal of a government is the word of an honest man.

> JULES CAMBON (1845–1935). French diplomat. In Harold Nicolson, *Diplomacy*, 3.1, 1939

The good diplomat must have . . . . a sound judgment which takes the measure of things as they are and which goes straight to the goal by the shortest and most natural paths without wandering into meaningless refinements and sublets.

> FRANÇOIS de CALLIÈRES (1645–1717). *De la manière de négocier avec les souverains*, 1716

The negotiator . . . should study history and memoirs, be acquainted with foreign institutions and habits, and be able to tell where, in any foreign country, the real sovereignty lies.

> FRANÇOIS de CALLIÈRES (1645–1717). *De la manière de négocier avec les souverains*, 1716

I have found out the art of deceiving diplomatists: I speak the truth, and I am certain they will not believe me.

> CONTE CAMILLO BENSO di CAVOUR (1810–1861). Italian statesman

Diplomats are useful only in fair weather. As soon as it rains they drown in every drop.

> CHARLES de GAULLE (1890–1970). In "'Gaullism? Never Heard of It,'" *Newsweek*, 1 October 1962

How is the world ruled and led to war? Diplomats lie to journalists and believe these lies when they see them in print.

> KARL KRAUS (1876–1936). "In This War We Are Dealing . . . ," *Half-Truths & One-and-a-Half Truths: Selected Aphorisms*, ed. Harry Zohn, 1976

You must be aware that making confidences is a part of diplomacy and that Count Cobenzl . . . never confides anything except what he wants known.

NAPOLEON (1769–1821). Letter to his brother Joseph Bonaparte, who was representing the French in peace negotiations with the Austrians, 11 November 1800, *The Mind of Napoleon: A Selection from His Written and Spoken Words,* 220, ed. J. Christopher Herold, 1955

The first qualification of a diplomat is the ability to keep silent.

NAPOLEON (1769–1821). Letter to Talleyrand, 4 July 1802, *The Mind of Napoleon: A Selection from His Written and Spoken Words,* 220, ed. J. Christopher Herold, 1955

He must be imperturbable, able to receive bad news without manifesting displeasure, or to hear himself maligned and misquoted without the slightest twinge of irritation.

HAROLD NICOLSON (1886–1968). *The Evolution of Diplomacy,* 2.4, 1954

The basic quality for the diplomat is not intelligence but loyalty.

C. NORTHCOTE PARKINSON (1909–1993). "Mr. Upton-Cumming, of 'The Establishment'" *New York Times Magazine,* 20 August 1961

Words are one thing—deeds something entirely different. Fine words are a mask to cover shady deeds. A sincere diplomat is like dry water or wooden iron.

JOSEPH STALIN (1879–1953). In Morris Kominsky, *The Hoaxers: Plain Liars, Fancy Liars, and Damned Liars,* 9, 1970

Protocol, alcohol, and Geritol.

ADLAI E. STEVENSON (1900–1965). Defining the social life of a diplomat. In "People," *Time,* 24 July 1964

A diplomat . . . is a person who can tell you to go to hell in such a way that you actually look forward to the trip.

CASKIE STINNETT. *Out of the Red,* 4, 1960

When the enemy's envoys speak in humble terms, but he continues his preparations, he will advance.

SUN-TZU (4th cent. B.C.). "Marches" (25), *The Art of War,* tr. Samuel B. Griffith, 1963

Above all, gentlemen, not the slightest zeal.

TALLEYRAND (1754–1838). Advice to diplomats. In P. Chasles, *Voyages d'un critique à travers la vie et les livres,* 2.407, 1868

See Zeal: George Washington

DIRECTORS

See also • Acting ○ Actors ○ Films

In a close-up or a shot taken over the shoulder—give him nine bad takes, blow your lines, give a weak performance and wear him down. Then, finally, when you know he's tired and frustrated, you give him the one take in which you do it the way it should be done.

MARLON BRANDO (1924–). On dominating indecisive film directors. In Geoffrey O'Brien, "Pro and Con," *New Republic,* 5 December 1994

That's the way with these directors, they're always biting the hand that lays the golden egg.

SAM GOLDWYN (1882–1974). In Alva Johnston, *The Great Goldwyn,* 1, 1937

One doesn't direct Cary Grant; one simply puts him in front of a camera.

ALFRED HITCHCOCK (1899–1980). 1960s

Ninety percent of directing is casting.

MARTIN LANDAU (1934–). James Lipton television interview, *Inside the Actors Studio,* BVO, 27 November 1996

If you get an impulse in a scene, no matter how wrong it seems, follow the impulse. Because we're not on a stage. It might be something, and if it ain't—take 2. I try to tell [the actors] where the freedom lies, rather than the restraint. This is where unpredictability comes from. This is where the fortunate accident comes from.

JACK NICHOLSON (1937–). On directing films. Fred Schruers interview, *Rolling Stone,* 14 August 1986

The difference between being a director and being an actor is the difference between being the carpenter banging the nails into the wood, and being the piece of wood the nails are being banged into.

SEAN PENN (1960–). In *Guardian* (British newspaper), 28 November 1991

DISABILITY

See also • Burdens ○ Disease ○ Misfortune

He who knows he is infirm, and would climb, does not think of the summit which he believes to be beyond his reach but climbs slowly onwards, taking very short steps, looking below as often as he likes but not above him, never trying his powers, but seldom stopping, and then, sometimes, behold! he is on the top.

SAMUEL BUTLER (1835–1902). *The Note-Books of Samuel Butler,* 7, ed. Henry Festing Jones, 1907

He which hath but one eye see[s] the better for't.

JOHN CLARKE (1596–1658). Comp., *Proverbs: English and Latine,* p. 44, 1639

You who are strong and swift, see that you do not limp before the lame, deeming it kindness.

KAHLIL GIBRAN (1883–1931). "On Good and Evil," *The Prophet,* 1923

Damaged people are dangerous. They know they can survive.

JOSEPHINE HART. *Damage,* 12, 1991

All about me may be silence and darkness, yet within me, in the spirit, is music and brightness, and color flashes through all my thoughts.

HELEN KELLER (1880–1968). *The Open Door,* p. 39, 1957. Keller was speech-, sight-, and hearing-disabled.

The accomplishments of those born blind are a sure proof of how much the spirit can achieve when difficulties are placed in its way.

GEORG CHRISTOPH LICHTENBERG (1742–1799). *Aphorisms,* D.50, 1806, tr. R. J. Hollingdale, 1990

What has influenced my life more than any other single thing has been my stammer. Had I not stammered I would probably . . . have gone to Cambridge as my brothers did, perhaps have become a don and every now and then published a dreary book about French literature.

W. SOMERSET MAUGHAM (1874–1965). In "Newsmakers," *Newsweek*, 23 May 1960

His inarticulate and stammering pronunciation [Demosthenes] overcame and rendered more distinct by speaking with pebbles in his mouth; his voice he disciplined by declaiming and reciting speeches or verses when he was out of breath, while running or going up steep places.

PLUTARCH (A.D. 46?–119?). "Demosthenes" (384?–322 B.C.), *Parallel Lives,* Dryden edition, 1693

Anything can happen to anybody. I remember the last movie I did I played a paraplegic in a movie called *Above Suspicion,* and I went to a rehab center and I worked with the people there so I could simulate being a paraplegic. And every day I would get in my car and drive away and go, "Thank God, that's not me," and seven months later I was in this condition. And I remember in a way the smugness of that, as if I was privileged in a way. The point is we are all one great big family and any one of us can get hurt at any moment. So that taught me a really big lesson about complacency. We should never walk by somebody who's in a wheelchair and be afraid of them or think of them as a stranger. It could be us—in fact, it is us.

CHRISTOPHER REEVE (1952–). Oprah Winfrey television interview, ABC, 4 May 1998. Reeve became a paraplegic in 1995 after being thrown by a horse. His autobiography, *Still Me,* was published in 1998.

King Lear: No eyes in your head, nor no money in your purse? . . . Yet you see how this world goes.
Gloucester: I see it feelingly.

SHAKESPEARE (1564–1616). *King Lear,* 4.6.148, 1605

As they say of the blind,
Sounds are the things I see.

SOPHOCLES (496?–406 B.C.). *Oedipus at Colonus,* l. 138, tr. Robert Fitzgerald, 1941

There are two kinds of "disabled" persons: Those who dwell on what they have lost and those who concentrate on what they have left.

THOMAS S. SZASZ (1920–). "Personal Conduct," *The Untamed Tongue: A Dissenting Dictionary,* 1990

❦

In the Dalebura tribe a woman, a cripple from birth, was carried about by the tribes people in turn until her death at the age of sixty-six. . . . They never desert the sick.

ANONYMOUS (ABORIGINAL AUSTRALIAN). In C. S. Lewis, appendix (7) to *The Abolition of Man,* 1947

DISASTER

See also • Calamity ○ Defeat ○ Misfortune ○ Tragedy ○ Trouble ○ Victory & Defeat: Rudyard Kipling

Noble souls, through dust and heat,
Rise from disaster and defeat
    The stronger.

HENRY WADSWORTH LONGFELLOW (1807–1882). "The Sifting of Peter," *Ultima Thule,* 1880

See Strength: Ernest Hemingway, Friedrich Nietzsche

The only ultimate disaster that can befall us . . . is to feel ourselves to be at home here on earth.

MALCOLM MUGGERIDGE (1903–1990). *Jesus Rediscovered,* 2, 1969

Disaster is Virtue's opportunity.

SENECA THE YOUNGER (5? B.C.–A.D. 65). "On Providence" (4.6), *Moral Essays,* tr. John W. Basore, 1928

DISCONTENT

See also • Dissatisfaction ○ Misery ○ Unhappiness

Discontent is the first necessity of progress.

THOMAS ALVA EDISON (1847–1931). *The Diary and Sundry Observations of Thomas Alva Edison,* 2.4.16, ed. Dagobert D. Runes, 1948

There is probably nothing more sublime than discontent transmuted into a work of art, a scientific discovery, and so on.

ERIC HOFFER (1902–1983). 8 November 1958, *Working and Thinking on the Waterfront: A Journal,* 1969

See Creativity: Hoffer (1)

Duke of Gloucester: Now is the winter of our discontent
Made glorious summer by this sun of York.

SHAKESPEARE (1564–1616). *Richard III,* 1.1.1, 1592

DISCOVERY

See also • Creativity ○ Curiosity ○ Humility—First Person: Sir Isaac Newton ○ Ideas ○ Imagination ○ Inspiration ○ Intuition ○ Invention ○ Originality ○ Revelation ○ Science ○ Sea: Kahlil Gibran, Henry Wadsworth Longfellow ○ Solitude (Being Alone): Sigmund Freud ○ Spirituality ○ Truth

[They] are indolent discoverers, who seeing nothing but sea and sky, absolutely deny there can be any land beyond them.

FRANCIS BACON (1561–1626). *Advancement of Learning,* 3.4, 1605, Willey Book edition, 1944

The greatest obstacle to discovery is not ignorance—it is the illusion of knowledge.

DANIEL J. BOORSTIN (1914–). In Carol Krucoff, "The 6 O'Clock Scholar," *Washington Post,* 29 January 1984

What I have a passion for is the idea of discovery. People keep asking what's the next thing on the horizon, and I keep saying it's not there yet.

RED BURNS. Interactive Telecommunications Program chairwoman, New York University's Tisch School of the Arts. In John Markoff and Tim Race, "Wizards, Wonders, and Wonks," *New York Times Magazine,* 28 September 1997

Of all the discoveries which men need to make, the most important, at the present moment, is that of the self-forming power treasured up in themselves.

WILLIAM ELLERY CHANNING (1780–1842). "Self-Culture," address, Boston, September 1838

Very often it happens that a discovery is made whilst working upon quite another problem.

THOMAS ALVA EDISON (1847–1931). 1922, *The Diary and Sundry Observations of Thomas Alva Edison,* 2.3.10, ed. Dagobert D. Runes, 1948

One can organize to apply a discovery already made, but not to make one. Only a free individual can make a discovery. . . . Can you imagine an organization of scientists making the discoveries of Charles Darwin?

ALBERT EINSTEIN (1879–1955). Raymond Swing interview, "Einstein on the Atomic Bomb," *Atlantic,* November 1945

No great discovery was ever made in science except by one who lifted his nose above the grindstone of details and ventured on a more comprehensive vision.

ALBERT EINSTEIN (1879—1955). In Morris R. Cohen, *The Meaning of Human History,* 6.4(3), 1947

The intellect has little to do on the road to discovery. There comes a leap in consciousness, call it intuition or what you will, and the solution comes to you and you don't know how or why.

ALBERT EINSTEIN (1879–1955)

No productiveness of the highest kind, no remarkable discovery . . . is in the power of anyone; such things are above earthly control. Man must consider them as an unexpected gift from above, as pure children of God which he must receive and venerate with joyful thanks. . . . In such cases, man may often be considered an instrument in a higher government of the world—a vessel worthy to contain a divine influence.

GOETHE (1749–1832). 11 March 1828. In Peter Eckermann, *Conversations with Goethe,* 1836–1848, tr. John Oxenford, 1850

People who have read a good deal rarely make great discoveries. I do not say this in excuse of laziness, but because invention presupposes an extensive independent contemplation of things.

GEORG CHRISTOPH LICHTENBERG (1742–1799). In J. P. Stern, "Further Excerpts from Lichtenberg's Notebooks" (4), *Lichtenberg: A Doctrine of Scattered Occasions,* 1959

The great discoveries of science have all been achieved by the solitary research of some individual, whose mind is able to investigate unfettered by the mental grooves characteristic of all types of corporate institutions.

B. H. LIDDELL HART (1895–1970). *The Remaking of Modern Armies,* 11, 1928

The secret of all those who make discoveries is that they regard nothing as impossible.

JUSTUS LIEBIG (1803–1873). German chemist. In Ralph Waldo Emerson, journal, 1873–1874, undated

The envious nature of men, so prompt to blame and so slow to praise, makes the discovery and introduction of any new principles and systems as dangerous almost as the exploration of unknown seas and continents.

MACHIAVELLI (1469–1527). Introduction to the First Book, *The Discourses,* 1517, tr. Christian E. Detmold, 1940

Anonymous: How did you discover the law of gravitation?
Newton: By thinking about it all the time.

SIR ISAAC NEWTON (1642–1727). Format adapted. Quoted by Ernest Dimnet. In *Great Lives, Great Deeds,* publ. Reader's Digest Association, p. 418, 1964

Every great work is the fruit of patience, perseverance, and concentration—during months and years—upon one specific subject. He who wants to discover a new truth must be capable of the strictest abstinence and renunciation. The ideal case would be that of a scientist who, during this period of mental incubation, would pay no heed to any thought that is extraneous to his problem, like the somnambulist who listens only to the words of the hypnotizer. If he possesses this capacity to remain incessantly absorbed by one subject, he will be able to multiply his strength.

SANTIAGO RAMÓN y CAJAL (1852–1934). Spanish physician. In Alfred Hock, *Reason and Genius: Studies in Their Origin,* 2.4.2, 1960

Discovery consists of seeing what everybody has seen and thinking what nobody has thought.

ALBERT von SZENT-GYÖRGYI. In Irving John Good, ed., *The Scientist Speculates,* 1962

The process of discovery is very simple. An unwearied and systematic application of known laws to nature causes the unknown to reveal themselves.

HENRY DAVID THOREAU (1817–1862). "Friday," *A Week on the Concord and Merrimack Rivers,* 1849

DISEASE

See also • Disability ○ Doctors: [especially] Betty Fussell ○ Food ○ Gluttony: [especially] Moses Maimonides ○ Healing ○ Health ○ Physicians: [especially] Hippocrates ○ Vegetarianism: John Locke

Disease is the retribution of outraged nature.

HOSEA BALLOU (1771–1852)

When the aged see a younger Abkhasian who is even a little overweight, they inquire about his health.

SULA BENET. "Why They Live to Be 100, or Even Older, in Abkhasia," *New York Times,* 26 December 1971

Like any other major experience, illness actually changes us. How? Well, for one thing we are temporarily relieved from the pressure of meeting the world head-on. . . . We enter a realm of introspection and self-analysis. We think soberly, perhaps for the first time, about our past and future. . . . Illness gives us that rarest thing in the world—a *second chance,* not only at health but at life itself!

LOUIS E. BISCH. Physician. "Turn Your Sickness into an Asset," *Reader's Digest,* November 1937

Illness is a convent which has its rule, its austerity, its silences, and its inspirations.

ALBERT CAMUS (1913–1960). November 1942, *Notebooks: 1942–1951,* tr. Justin O'Brien, 1966

I am neither well nor ill, but *unwell.*

LORD CHESTERFIELD (1694–1773). Letter to his son, 17 October 1768

The chamber of sickness is the chapel of Devotion.

JOHN CLARKE (1596–1658). Comp., *Proverbs: English and Latine,* p. 273, 1639

We forget ourselves and our destinies in health, and the chief use of temporary sickness is to remind us of these concerns.

> RALPH WALDO EMERSON (1803–1882). Journal, 25 March 1821

Many dishes, many diseases. Many medicines, few cures.

> BENJAMIN FRANKLIN (1706–1790). *Poor Richard's Almanack,* January 1734

Against Diseases here, the strongest Fence,
Is the defensive Virtue, Abstinence.

> BENJAMIN FRANKLIN (1706–1790). *Poor Richard's Almanack,* October 1742

Diseases are the Price of ill Pleasures.

> THOMAS FULLER (1654–1734). Comp., *Gnomologia: Adages and Proverbs,* 1297, 1732

He is in great Danger, who being sick, thinks himself well.

> THOMAS FULLER (1654–1734). Comp., *Gnomologia: Adages and Proverbs,* 1921, 1732

Study Sickness while you are well.

> THOMAS FULLER (1654–1734). Comp., *Gnomologia: Adages and Proverbs,* 4269, 1732

A bodily disease, which we look upon as whole and entire within itself, may, after all, be but a symptom of some ailment in the spiritual part.

> NATHANIEL HAWTHORNE (1804–1864). *The Scarlet Letter,* 10, 1850

Most diseases are the result of medication which has been prescribed to relieve and take away a beneficent and warning symptom on the part of Nature.

> ELBERT HUBBARD (1856–1915). *The Note Book of Elbert Hubbard,* p. 18, comp. Elbert Hubbard II, 1927

It is more important to know what kind of patient has the disease than what kind of disease the patient has.

> SIR WILLIAM OSLER (1849–1919). Canadian physician. In *Psychiatric Annals,* October 1983

Acute illnesses are, with a few exceptions, nothing other than curative processes instituted by nature itself to remedy some disorder in the organism.

> ARTHUR SCHOPENHAUER (1788–1860). "On Various Subjects" (1.F), 1851, *Essays and Aphorisms,* tr. R. J. Hollingdale, 1970

Those who think they have not time for bodily exercise will sooner or later have to find time for illness.

> EDWARD STANLEY (1826–1893). Address, Liverpool College (England), 20 December 1873

For fourteen years I have not had a day's real health. I have wakened sick and gone to bed weary.

> ROBERT LOUIS STEVENSON (1850–1894). Letter to George Meredith, 1893. In Jack Hodges, *The Genius of Writers: The Lives of English Writers Compared,* 24, 1992. Stevenson died a year later at age 44.

Diseases and sins—these are the same as motion and heat: One passes into the other.

> LEO TOLSTOY (1828–1910). *Thoughts and Aphorisms,* 5.10, 1886–1893, tr. Leo Wiener, 1905

The symptoms of disease are marked by purpose, and the purpose is beneficent. The processes of disease aim not at the destruction of life, but at the saving of it.

> FREDERICK TREVES (19th cent.). Address, Edinburgh Philosophical Institution, Scotland, 31 October 1905

✌

Diseases enter by the mouth.

> SAYING (CHINESE)

Disease will have its course.

> SAYING (ENGLISH)

What can't be cured must be endured.

> SAYING (ENGLISH)

Every disease is a doctor.

> SAYING (IRISH)

Show him death, and he'll be content with fever.

> SAYING (PERSIAN)

DISLOYALTY

See also • Dissent: Edward R. Murrow ○ Loyalty

Mistakes, even occasional incompetence, could be understood and forgiven, but not disloyalty.

> JOSEPH A. CALIFANO, JR. (1931–). On presidential aides, *A Presidential Nation,* 9, 1975
> See Presidents & Staff: Califano (1,2)

It is a bad bird that defileth his own nest.

> JOHN CLARKE (1596–1658). Comp., *Proverbs: English and Latine,* p. 200, 1639

If I had to choose between betraying my *country* and betraying my *friend,* I hope I should have the guts to betray my *country.*

> E. M. FORSTER (1879–1970). "What I Believe," *Two Cheers for Democracy,* 1951

The most trifling disloyalty to ourselves does people far more harm in our eyes than the greatest they commit to others.

> LA ROCHEFOUCAULD (1613–1680). *Maxims,* 89, 1665, tr. Leonard Tancock, 1959

The first thing I want to teach is *disloyalty.* . . . This will beget independence—which is loyalty to one's best self and principles, and this is often disloyalty to the general idols and fetishes.

> MARK TWAIN (1835–1910). *Mark Twain's Notebook,* ed. Albert Bigelow Paine, 1935

✌

Don't bite the hand that feeds you.

> SAYING

Don't wash your dirty linen in public.

> SAYING

DISSATISFACTION

See also • Discontent ○ Unhappiness

We are less dissatisfied when we lack many things than when we seem to lack but one thing.

> ERIC HOFFER (1902–1983). *The True Believer: Thoughts on the Nature of Mass Movements,* 23, 1951

Be always restless, unsatisfied, unconforming. Whenever a habit becomes convenient, smash it! The greatest sin of all is satisfaction.

> NIKOS KAZANTZAKIS (1885–1957). "The March: First Step" (17), *The Saviors of God: Spiritual Exercises,* 1927, tr. Kimon Friar, 1960

It is better to be a human being dissatisfied than a pig satisfied; better to be Socrates dissatisfied than a fool satisfied.

> JOHN STUART MILL (1806–1873). *Utilitarianism,* 2, 1863

Dissatisfaction is a sign of people who are walking on the road and not standing still.

> LEO TOLSTOY (1828–1910). *Thoughts and Aphorisms,* 8.1, 1886–1893, tr. Leo Wiener, 1905

DISSENT

See also • Courage, Moral: Clarence Darrow ○ Defiance ○ Freedom of Speech ○ Heresy ○ Ideas ○ Ideology ○ Martyrdom ○ Nonconformity ○ Resistance ○ Tolerance

Here in America we are descended in blood and in spirit from revolutionaries and rebels—men and women who dared to dissent from accepted doctrine. As their heirs, may we never confuse honest dissent with disloyal subversion.

> DWIGHT D. EISENHOWER (1890–1969). Speech, Columbia University Bicentennial Dinner, New York City, 31 May 1954

I like the sayers of No better than the sayers of yes.

> RALPH WALDO EMERSON (1803–1882). Journal, 18 May 1833

To dissent from others' views is regarded as an insult because it is their condemnation.

> BALTASAR GRACIÁN (1601–1658). *The Art of Worldly Wisdom,* 43, 1647, tr. Joseph Jacobs, 1950

A dissenter is to the absoluteness of power what an exception is to the validity of a formulated scientific rule—both must be dealt with and somehow eliminated.

> ERIC HOFFER (1902–1983). Expressing with disapproval the tyrant's view, *Ordeal of Change,* 15.4, 1964

Those who begin coercive elimination of dissent soon find themselves exterminating dissenters.

> ROBERT H. JACKSON (1892–1954). *West Virginia State Board of Education v. Barnette,* 1943

Dissident minorities say whatever they please within a system loaded in favor of the most powerful elites. The dissidents let off steam; the controllers keep power.

> ANDREW KOPKIND (1935–1994). "Are We in the Middle of a Revolution?" *New York Times Magazine,* 10 November 1968

The dissenter is every human being at those moments of his life when he resigns momentarily from the herd and thinks for himself.

> ARCHIBALD MacLEISH (1892–1982). "In Praise of Dissent," *New York Times Book Review,* 16 December 1956

We must not confuse dissent with disloyalty.

> EDWARD R. MURROW (1908–1965). Report on Sen. Joseph R. McCarthy, *See It Now,* television series, CBS, 7 March 1954

Persecution of a dissenter is always popular in the group which he has abandoned. Toleration of dissent is no sentiment of the masses.

> WILLIAM GRAHAM SUMNER (1840–1910). *Folkways: A Study of the Sociological Importance of Usages, Manners, Customs, Mores, and Morals,* 100, 1907

He who resists a mania may be trodden under foot like any other heretic. There occur cases, however, in which he wins by dissent. If he can outlive the mania, he will probably gain at a later time, when its folly is proved to all.

> WILLIAM GRAHAM SUMNER (1840–1910). *Folkways: A Study of the Sociological Importance of Usages, Manners, Customs, Mores, and Morals,* 222, 1907

One thing about Thoreau keeps him very near to me. I refer to his lawlessness—his dissent—his going his absolute own road, let hell blaze all it chooses.

> WALT WHITMAN (1819–1892). In Richard Drinnon, "Thoreau's Politics of the Upright Man," *Massachusetts Review,* Autumn 1962

DISTRUST

See also • Fear ○ Paranoia ○ Prudence: Rules ○ Suspicion ○ Trust

Never trust a friend who deserts you [in] a pinch.

> AESOP (6th cent. B.C.). "The Two Fellows and the Bear," *Fables,* tr. Joseph Jacobs, 1894

"Never Trust Anyone under 80."

> CAROL BRIGHTMAN. Article title, *Nation,* 17 January 1994

He who knows himself trusts no one.

> PAUL ELDRIDGE (1888–1982). *Maxims for a Modern Man,* 2246, 1965

Never trust the man who hath reason to suspect that you know he hath injured you.

> HENRY FIELDING (1707–1754). *The History of the Life of the Late Mr Jonathan Wild the Great,* 3.4, 1743

Trust him no further than you can throw him.

> THOMAS FULLER (1654–1734). Comp., *Gnomologia: Adages and Proverbs,* 5286, 1732

Trust no one who doesn't trust you.

> WADE HUDSON (1944–). Personal communication, 1987
>
> See Prudence: Rules: Gerald Wilson

It is better . . . to be sometimes cheated than not to trust.

> SAMUEL JOHNSON (1709–1784). In *The Rambler* (English journal), 79, 18 December 1750

He who never puts his trust in any man will never be deceived.

> LEONARDO da VINCI (1452–1519). *Note-books,* 1, tr. Edward McCurdy, 1908

Trust that man in nothing who has not a conscience in everything.

> LAURENCE STERNE (1713–1768). *Tristram Shandy,* 2.17, 1759–1767

We have a saying in the movement that you can't trust anybody over thirty.

> JACK WEINBERG. Free speech movement leader, University of California, Berkeley. In James Benet, "Growing Pains at UC," *San Francisco Chronicle*, 15 November 1964 (Popular version: Never trust anyone over thirty.)
>
> See Middle Age: George Bernard Shaw

We have to distrust each other. It's our only defense against betrayal.

> TENNESSEE WILLIAMS (1911–1983). *Camino Real*, 10, 1953

❧

Put not your trust in princes,
  in a son of man, in whom there is no help.

> ANONYMOUS (*BIBLE*). *Psalms* 146:3

Never trust anyone who says, "Trust me."

> ANONYMOUS

Where there is no trust, there is no love.

> SAYING

DIVORCE

See also • Adultery ○ Marriage

A man may divorce his wife if he finds another woman more beautiful.

> AKIBA (A.D. 40?–135?). In *Talmud* (A.D. 1st–6th cent.). Rabbinical writings

A wife lasts only for the length of the marriage, but an ex-wife is there for the rest of your life.

> WOODY ALLEN (1935–). In "Celebrity Attitudes to Marriage," *San Francisco Chronicle*, 18 April 1990

Many a man owes his success to his first wife and his second wife to his success.

> JIM BACKUS (1924–1970)

Divorce is the psychological equivalent of a triple coronary bypass.

> MARY KAY BLAKELY. *American Mom: Motherhood, Politics, and Humble Pie*, 6, 1994

I have at last done the best office that can be done for most married people; that is, I have fixed the separation between my brother and his wife; and the definitive treaty of peace will be proclaimed in about a fortnight; for the only solid and lasting peace, between a man and his wife, is, doubtless, a separation.

> LORD CHESTERFIELD (1694–1773). Letter to his son, 1 September 1763

Some couples divorce because of a misunderstanding; others, because they understand each other too well.

> EVAN ESAR (1899–1995). Comp., *20,000 Quips and Quotes*, p. 237, 1968

Just another of our many disagreements. He wants a no-fault divorce, whereas I would prefer to have the bastard crucified.

> J. B. HANDELSMAN. Woman to her lawyer. Cartoon caption, *New Yorker*, 25 August 1997

Many married couples separate because they quarrel incessantly; but just as many separate because they were never honest enough or courageous enough to quarrel when they should have.

> SYDNEY J. HARRIS (1917–1986). Syndicated column, *Chicago Daily News*, 1965

There are already certain American cities in which the number of divorces is equal to the number of marriages. In a few years, no doubt, marriage licenses will be sold like dog licenses, good for a period of twelve months, with no law against changing dogs or keeping more than one animal at a time.

> ALDOUS HUXLEY (1894–1963). Foreword (1946) to *Brave New World*, 1932

What . . . God has joined together, let no man put asunder. . . . Whoever divorces his wife, except for unchastity and marries another, commits adultery.

> JESUS (A.D. 1st cent.). *Matthew* 19:6,9
>
> See Adultery: Jesus

Divorce is my generations' coming of age ceremony—a ritual scarring that makes anything that happens afterward seem bearable.

> ERICA JONG (1942–). *Fear of Fifty: A Midlife Memoir*, 10, 1994

Being divorced is like being hit by a Mack track. If you live through it, you start looking very carefully to the right and to the left.

> JEAN KERR (1923–). *Mary, Mary*, 1, 1960

The thing which is lawful, but disliked by God, is divorce.

> MUHAMMAD (A.D. 570?–632). *The Sayings of Muhammad*, 126, tr. Abdullah Al-Suhrawardy, 1941

Half of all marriages end in divorce—and then there are the really unhappy ones.

> JOAN RIVERS (1937–). In Liz Smith, "Rivers Shows She's Good at Comebacks," *San Francisco Chronicle*, 27 February 1997

There are many things children accept as "grown-up things" over which they have no control and for which they have no responsibility—for instance, weddings, having babies, buying houses, and driving cars. Parents who are separating really need to help their children put divorce on that grown-up list, so that children do not see themselves as the cause of their parents' decision to live apart.

> FRED ROGERS (1928–). *Mr. Rogers Talks with Parents*, 10, 1983

A lot of people have asked me how short I am. Since my last divorce, I think I'm about $100,000 short.

> MICKEY ROONEY (1920–). In *Chicago Sun-Times*, 22 June 1978

Divorces are made in heaven.

> OSCAR WILDE (1854–1900). *The Importance of Being Earnest*, 1, 1895
>
> See Marriage: John Lyly

DOCTORS

See also • Disease ○ Drugs, Medical ○ Gluttony: Saying ○ Healing ○ Health ○ Last Words: R. D. Laing ○ Physicians ○ Professionals ○ Psychiatrists ○ Psychiatry ○ Surgeons

The best doctors in the world are Doctor Diet, Doctor Quiet, and Doctor Merryman.

> WILLIAM BULLEIN (16th cent.). *Government of Health,* 50, 1558

Healer of others, full of sores himself.

> EURIPIDES (485?–406 B.C.). Fragment, 262. In Plutarch (A.D. 46?–119?). "On Brotherly Love" (6), *Moralia,* vol. 6, tr. W. C. Helmbold, 1939
> See Physicians: Jesus

God heals, and the Doctor takes the Fees.

> BENJAMIN FRANKLIN (1706–1790). *Poor Richard's Almanack,* November 1736

A quack is anyone who undertakes a treatment without possessing the knowledge and capacities necessary for it.

> SIGMUND FREUD (1856–1939). *The Question of Lay Analysis,* 6, 1925, tr. James Strachey, 1959

The medical establishment, focusing on pathology and chemical treatment by drugs, has long equated diet with what's put on hospital trays. Even today, when five of America's major health problems—heart, liver, cancer, diabetes and cerebrovascular diseases—have been proved to be related to diet, just 23 percent of American medical schools require a course in nutrition, and many offer none.

> BETTY FUSSELL. "A Mystery on Every Plate," *New York Times,* 23 December 1993

He cures most in whom most have faith.

> GALEN (A.D. 129?–199). Greek physician

One doctor makes work for another.

> VINCENT STUCKEY LEAN (1820–1899). *Lean's Collectanea,* 4.73, 1904

I often say a great doctor kills more people than a great general.

> GOTTFRIED LEIBNITZ (1646–1716). German philosopher. In *Bulletin of the New York Academy of Medicine,* vol. 5, p. 152, 1929

"I haven't got time to be sick!" he said. "People need me." For he was a country doctor, and he did not know what it was to spare himself.

> DON MARQUIS (1878–1937)

The reason doctors are so dangerous is that they believe in what they're doing.

> ROBERT S. MENDELSOHN (1927–1988). Physician. Appearing on *People Are Talking,* television talk program, KPIX, San Francisco, January 1986

The sun shines on their successes, and the earth hides their failures.

> MONTAIGNE (1533–1592). "Of the Resemblance of Children to Fathers," *Essays,* 1588, tr. Donald M. Frame, 1958

This is my vow: To perfect my medical art and never to swerve from it as long as God grants me my office, and to oppose all false medicine and teachings. Then to love the sick, each and all of them more than if my own body were at stake. Not to judge anything superficially but by symptoms, nor to administer any medicine without understanding, nor to collect any money without earning it. Not to trust any apothecary, nor to do violence to any child. Not to guess, but to know.

> PARACELSUS (1493–1541). "Credo," *Paracelsus: Selected Writings,* ed. Jolande Jacobi and tr. Norbert Guterman, 1988

Mrs. Mease told me when dying that among other things she had to repent of one was too much confidence in my remedies.

> BENJAMIN RUSH (1745–1813). Commonplace book, 27 July 1796

Time, Nature's great healer.

> SENECA THE YOUNGER (5? B.C.–A.D. 65). "On Consolation to Marcius" (1.6), *Moral Essays,* tr. John W. Basore, 1932
> *See* Drugs, Medical: Saying

Of all the anti-social vested interests the worst is the vested interest in ill-health.

> GEORGE BERNARD SHAW (1856–1950). Preface ("Latest Theories") to *The Doctor's Dilemma,* 1906

The doctor learns that if he gets ahead of the superstitions of his patients he is a ruined man; and the result is that he instinctively takes care not to get ahead of them.

> GEORGE BERNARD SHAW (1856–1950). Preface ("The Reforms Also Come from the Laity") to *The Doctor's Dilemma,* 1906

The generations which no longer believe in God transfer all their credulity to medical practice. . . . The consecrated wafer from the communion table may be wholesomer than the pill from the apothecary's shop.

> GEORGE BERNARD SHAW (1856–1950). *Everybody's Political What's What,* 24, 1944

Be enthusiastic. Remember the placebo effect—30% of medicine is show biz.

> RONALD SPARK. Advising his medical colleagues. In *Medical World News,* 16 February 1981

To return medicine to the service of the individual, nothing less will suffice than an extension of the protections of the First Amendment to the healing arts, guaranteeing that "Congress shall make no law respecting an establishment of medicine, or prohibiting the free exercise thereof."

> THOMAS S. SZASZ (1920–). "Therapeutic State," *The Second Sin,* 1973

Since half the human beings who apply to a doctor for care arrive in the waiting room with a psychological cause for their physical complaint, it is necessary only to convince them that the treatment is going to succeed for it to do so.

> PHILIP WYLIE (1902–1971). *Generation of Vipers,* 10, 1942

✹

Doctors will get off their pedestals when patients get off their knees.

> ANONYMOUS

Ask the patient, not the doctor.

> SAYING
> See Quality: Saying (Greek)

He who is his own doctor has a fool for a patient.

> SAYING
> See Healing: Saying ○ Teachers: Benjamin Franklin

DOCTRINE

See also • Creed ○ Dogma ○ Ideas ○ Ideology ○ Orthodoxy ○
Principles, Moral ○ Systems ○ Theories

What makes all Doctrines Plain and Clear?
About two Hundred Pounds a Year.
And that which was prov'd true before,
Prove false again? Two Hundred more.

> SAMUEL BUTLER (1612–1680). *Hudibras*, 3.1.1277, 1663–1678, ed. John
> Wilders, 1967

Once a doctrine, however irrational, has gained power in a society, millions of people will believe in it rather than feel ostracized
and isolated.

> ERICH FROMM (1900–1980). *Psychoanalysis and Religion*, 3, 1950

The effectiveness of a doctrine should not be judged by its profundity, sublimity or the validity of the truths it embodies, but by
how thoroughly it insulates the individual from his self and the
world as it is.

> ERIC HOFFER (1902–1983). *The True Believer: Thoughts on the Nature
> of Mass Movements*, 56, 1951

To be effective a doctrine must not be understood, but has to be
believed in. We can be absolutely certain only about things we do
not understand. A doctrine that is understood is shorn of it
strength.

> ERIC HOFFER (1902–1983). *The True Believer: Thoughts on the Nature
> of Mass Movements*, 57, 1951

The stability of a regime requires the allegiance of the intellectuals, and it is to win them rather than to foster self-sacrifice in the
masses that a doctrine is made intelligible.

> ERIC HOFFER (1902–1983). *The True Believer: Thoughts on the Nature
> of Mass Movements*, 57, 1951

All new doctrine goes through three stages. It is attacked and
declared absurd; then it is admitted as true and obvious but
insignificant. Finally, its true importance is recognized and its
adversaries claim the honor of having discovered it.

> WILLIAM JAMES (1842–1910)

Doctrines are the most fearful tyrants to which men ever are subject because doctrines get inside of a man's own reason and
betray him against himself.

> WILLIAM GRAHAM SUMNER (1840–1910). Title essay, *War and Other
> Essays*, 1911

Our ethical and philosophical doctrines in general . . . are merely the justification *a posteriori* [i.e., after the fact] of our conduct,
. . . the means we seek in order to explain and justify to others
and to ourselves our own mode of action.

> MIGUEL de UNAMUNO (1864–1936). *Tragic Sense of Life*, 11, 1913, tr.
> J. E. Crawford Flitch, 1921
>
> See Names: Ralph Waldo Emerson

A clash of doctrines is not a disaster—it is an opportunity.

> ALFRED NORTH WHITEHEAD (1861–1947). *Science and the Modern
> World*, 12, 1925

DOGMA

See also • Creed ○ Doctrine ○ Ideas ○ Ideals: Israel Zangwill ○
Ideology ○ Orthodoxy ○ Philosophy: Alfred North Whitehead
(1) ○ Systems ○ Theories

The modern world . . . holds certain dogmas so strongly that it
does not know that they are dogmas.

> G. K. CHESTERTON (1874–1936). *Heretics*, 20, 1905

Any theory and set of practices is dogmatic which is not based
upon critical examination of its own underlying principles.

> JOHN DEWEY (1859–1952). *Experience and Education*, 1, 1938

Dogma: A hard substance which forms in a soft brain.

> ELBERT HUBBARD (1856–1915). *The Roycroft Dictionary Concocted by
> Ali Baba and the Bunch on Rainy Days*, p. 36, 1914

A dogma, . . . an indisputable confession of faith, is set up only
when the aim is to suppress doubts once and for all. But that no
longer has anything to do with scientific judgment; only with a
personal power drive.

> CARL G. JUNG (1875–1961). *Memories, Dreams, Reflections*, 5, ed.
> Aniela Jaffé, 1962

Dogma is more useless than cow dung.

> MAO TSE-TUNG (1893–1976). In Edgar Snow, *Red China Today*,
> 19, 1970

The greater the ignorance, the greater the dogmatism.

> SIR WILLIAM OSLER (1849–1914). In *Montreal Medical Journal*,
> September 1902

You can't teach an old dogma new tricks.

> DOROTHY PARKER (1893–1967). In Robert E. Drennan, ed., "Dorothy
> Parker," *The Algonquin Wits*, 1968

If there is ever to be peace in the world, governments will have
to agree either to inculcate no dogmas, or all to inculcate the
same.

> BERTRAND RUSSELL (1872–1970). "An Outline of Intellectual Rubbish,"
> *Unpopular Essays*, 1950

Thinking for oneself is always arduous and is sometimes painful.
The temptation to stop thinking and to take dogma on faith is
strong. Yet, since the intellect does possess the capacity to think
for itself, it also has the impulse and feels the obligation. We may
therefore feel sure that the intellect will always refuse, sooner or
later, to take traditional doctrines on trust.

> ARNOLD J. TOYNBEE (1889–1975). *Change and Habit: The Challenge of
> Our Time*, 9, 1966

Dogmatism is the anti-Christ of learning.

> ALFRED NORTH WHITEHEAD (1861–1947). *Modes of Thought*,
> 1.3, 1938

Nothing is more curious than the self-satisfied dogmatism with
which mankind at each period of its history cherishes the delusion
of the finality of its existing modes of knowledge.

> ALFRED NORTH WHITEHEAD (1861–1947). "John Dewey and His
> Influence" (1). In Paul Arthur Schilpp, ed., *The Philosophy of John
> Dewey*, 1939

☙

Dogma is like a bitter pill: if you chew it, you will never be able to swallow it.

ANONYMOUS. Quoted by Chamfort (1741–1794). In Norman Lockridge, comp., *World's Wit and Wisdom*, p. 122, 1936

DOGS

See also • Animals ○ Happines: Charles Schulz

Mark what a generosity and courage [a dog] will put on when he finds himself maintained by a man, who to him is instead of a God.

FRANCIS BACON (1561–1626). "Of Atheism," *Essays*, 1625

I agree with Agassiz that dogs possess something very like a conscience.
Dogs possess some power of self-command, and this does not appear to be wholly the result of fear.

CHARLES DARWIN (1809–1882). Referring to Louis Agassiz, the Swiss-born American naturalist, *The Descent of Man and Selection in Relation to Sex*, 2nd ed., 4, 1874

The better I get to know men, the more I find myself loving dogs.

CHARLES de GAULLE (1890–1970). In "Some General Comments, *Entre Nous* . . . ," *Time*, 8 December 1967

The dog, to gain some private ends,
Went mad and bit the man. . . .
The man recover'd of the bite
The dog it was that died.

OLIVER GOLDSMITH (1728–1774). "An Elegy on the Death of a Mad Dog," *The Vicar of Wakefield*, 17, 1766

My favorite story is about the monk who said to a Master, "Has a dog Buddha-nature too?" The Master replied, "Wu"—which is what the dog himself would have said.

GILBERT HIGHET (1906–). "The Mystery of Zen," *Talents and Geniuses*, 1957. In Arthur M. Eastman, ed., *The Norton Reader*, 1965

At night, when all was quiet about the campfire, [Stickeen] would come to me and rest his head on my knee with a look of devotion as if I were his god.

JOHN MUIR (1838–1914). *Stickeen*, p. 44, 1897, Heyday Books edition, 1981

These Republican leaders have not been content with attacks on me, or on my wife, or on my sons. No, not content with that, they now include my little dog, Fala. Well, of course, I don't resent attacks, and my family doesn't resent attacks, but Fala [pause] Fala *does* resent them.
You know, you know, Fala's Scotch, and being a Scottie, as soon as he learned that the Republican fiction writers in Congress and out had concocted a story that I had left him behind on an Aleutian Island and had sent a destroyer back to find him—at a cost to the taxpayers of two or three, or eight or twenty million dollars—his Scotch soul was furious. He has not been the same dog since.

FRANKLIN D. ROOSEVELT (1882–1945). Delivered with mock-seriousness during an after-dinner speech, Hotel Statler, Washington, 23 September 1944

The dog . . . commends himself to our favor by affording play to our propensity for mastery.

THORSTEIN VEBLEN (1857–1929). *The Theory of the Leisure Class: An Economic Study of Institutions*, 6, 1899

☙

Love me, love my *dog*.

SAYING (LATIN)

A dog is man's best friend.

SAYING

Like master, like dog.

SAYING

DOUBT

See also • Belief ○ Certainty ○ Conviction ○ Cynicism ○ Faith: [especially] Hermann Hesse ○ Ideology ○ Skepticism

If the Sun and Moon should doubt,
They'd immediately Go out.

WILLIAM BLAKE (1757–1827). "Auguries of Innocence," l. 109, 1789

Doubt is the vestibule which *all* must pass before they can enter into the temple of wisdom.

C. C. COLTON (1780–1832). *Lacon: or, Many Things in Few Words; Addressed to Those Who Think*, 1.251, 1823

The deplorable mania of doubt exhausts me. I doubt about everything, even about my doubts.

GUSTAVE FLAUBERT (1821–1880). In Cesare Lombroso, *The Man of Genius*, 1.3, 1888, ed. Havelock Ellis, 1896

Doubt everything at least once, [even that] 2 times 2 is 4.

GEORG CHRISTOPH LICHTENBERG (1742–1799). In Jeremy Adler, "Lover of Crooked Lines," *Times Literary Supplement* (London), 25 September 1992

I respect faith, but doubt is what gets you an education.

WILSON MIZNER (1876–1933). In Alva Johnston, *The Legendary Mizners*, 4, 1953

Lucio: Our doubts are traitors
And make us lose the good we oft might win
By fearing to attempt.

SHAKESPEARE (1564–1616). *Measure for Measure*, 1.4.77, 1604

There lives more faith in honest doubt,
Believe me, than in half the creeds.

ALFRED, LORD TENNYSON (1809–1892). *In Memoriam A. H. H.*, 96, 1850

In the present age doubt has become immune to faith and faith has dissociated itself from doubt.

GABRIEL VAHANIAN. *The Death of God*, 1, 1962

DREAMS

See also • Creativity ○ Dreams: Examples ○ Inspiration ○ Prediction ○ Prophets ○ Revelation ○ Spirituality ○ The Unconscious ○ Vision

Dreams reflect current and future unsolved problems and rehearse their possible solutions.

> ALFRED ADLER (1870–1937). As paraphrased by Geoffrey A. Dudley, *How to Understand Your Dreams,* 10, 1963

I have encountered few truly prophetic dreams in my practice [as a psychotherapist], but I have seen many that seemed to say to the dreamer: If you continue along this particular path, it will probably give rise to such and such outcome.

> WILLIAM ALEX. *Dreams, the Unconscious and Analytical Therapy* (pamphlet), 1973

Most dreams with an unpleasant conflict are dreams in which the motivating force is not a repressed wish, but a guilty conscience.

> FRANZ G. ALEXANDER (1891–1964). *Fundamentals of Psychoanalysis,* 1948. In J. A. Hadfield, *Dreams and Nightmares,* 2, 1954

We are somewhat more than ourselves in our sleeps; and the slumber of the body seems to be but the waking of the soul.

> SIR THOMAS BROWNE (1605–1682). *Religio Medici,* 2.11, 1642, ed. John Addington Symonds, 1886

And dreams in their development have breath,
And tears, and tortures, and the touch of joy;
They leave a weight upon our waking thoughts,
They take a weight from off our waking toils,
They do divide our being; they become
A portion of ourselves as of our time
And look like heralds of eternity.

> LORD BYRON (1788–1824). "The Dream," 1, 1816

I am a worse man in my dreams than when awake—do cowardly acts, dream of being tried for a crime. I long ago came to the conclusion that my dreams are of no importance to me whatever.

> THOMAS CARLYLE (1795–1881). In William Allingham, diary, 7 February 1868

I do not understand the capricious lewdness of the sleeping mind.

> JOHN CHEEVER (1912–1982). Journal, 1955, ed., Robert Gottlieb, 1991

Now whence arises this distinction between true dreams and false ones? and if true dreams come from God, from whence come the false ones?

> CICERO (106–43 B.C.). *De divinatione,* 2.42, tr. C. D. Yonge, 1902

A dream is a scripture, and many scriptures are nothing but dreams.

> UMBERTO ECO (1929–). "Sixth Day: After Terce," *The Name of the Rose,* 1980, tr. William Weaver, 1983

Dreams wherein often we see ourselves in masquerade.

> RALPH WALDO EMERSON (1803–1882). "The Over-Soul," *Essays: First Series,* 1841

I have very joyful dreams which I cannot bring to paper, much less to any approach to practice, and I blame myself not at all for my reveries, but that they have not yet got possession of my house and barn.

> RALPH WALDO EMERSON (1803–1882). Letter to Thomas Carlyle, 29 February 1844

In dreams we are true poets.

> RALPH WALDO EMERSON (1803–1882). "Poetry and the Imagination," *Letters and Social Aims,* 1876

[Dreams] pique us by independence of us, yet we know ourselves in this mad crowd, and owe to dreams a kind of divination and wisdom. My dreams are not me; they are not Nature, or the Not-me: they are both. They have a double consciousness, at once sub- and ob-jective. We call the phantoms that rise, the creation of our fancy, but they act like mutineers, and fire on their commander; showing that every act, every thought, every cause, is bipolar, and in the act is contained the counteraction. If I strike, I am struck; if I chase, I am pursued.

> RALPH WALDO EMERSON (1803–1882). "Demonology," 1877, *Lectures and Biographical Sketches,* 1883

A skillful man reads his dreams for his self-knowledge; yet not the details, but the quality.

> RALPH WALDO EMERSON (1803–1882). "Demonology," 1877, *Lectures and Biographical Sketches,* 1883

The soul contains in itself the event that shall presently befall it, for the event is only the actualizing of its thoughts. It is no wonder that particular dreams and presentiments should fall out and be prophetic.

> RALPH WALDO EMERSON (1803–1882). "Demonology," 1877, *Lectures and Biographical Sketches,* 1883

People have recurrent dreams because they haven't got the message.

> NAOMI EPEL. Slightly modified. Tom Snyder television interview, CNBC, 21 July 1993

There were three sorts of dreams: multitude of business sometimes caused dreams; and there were whisperings of Satan in man in the night-season; and there were speakings of God to man in dreams.

> GEORGE FOX (1624–1691). 1647, *The Journal of George Fox,* 1694, rev. Norman Penney, 1924

The dream is the (disguised) fulfillment of a (suppressed, repressed) wish.

> SIGMUND FREUD (1856–1939). *The Interpretation of Dreams,* 4, 1900, tr. A. A. Brill, 1938

For the purposes of interpretation every element of the dream may represent its opposite, as well as itself. One can never tell beforehand which is to be posited; only the context can decide this point.

> SIGMUND FREUD (1856–1939). *The Interpretation of Dreams,* 6.H, 1900, tr. A. A. Brill, 1938

The interpretation of dreams is the via regia [i.e., royal road] to a knowledge of the unconscious element in our psychic life.

> SIGMUND FREUD (1856–1939). *The Interpretation of Dreams,* 7.E, 1900, tr. A. A. Brill, 1938
>
> See The Unconscious: Freud (1)

An overwhelming majority of symbols in dreams are sexual symbols.

> SIGMUND FREUD (1856–1939). *A General Introduction to Psychoanalysis,* 10, 1917, tr. Joan Riviere, 1952

Dreams bring to light material which cannot have originated either from the dreamer's adult life or from his forgotten childhood. We are obliged to regard it as part of the *archaic heritage* which a child brings with him into the world, before any experience of his own, influenced by the experiences of his ancestors. We have the counterpart of this phylogenetic material in the human legends and in surviving customs. Thus dreams constitute a source of human prehistory which is not to be despised.

SIGMUND FREUD (1856–1939). *An Outline of Psychoanalysis*, 5, 1940, tr. James Strachey, 1969

A dream . . . is a psychosis, with all the absurdities, delusions and illusions of a psychosis.

SIGMUND FREUD (1856–1939). *An Outline of Psychoanalysis*, 6, 1940, tr. James Strachey, 1969

Rather than be confronted with an overwhelming proof of the limitations of our understanding, we accuse the dreams of not making sense.

ERICH FROMM (1900–1980). Introduction to *The Forgotten Language: An Introduction to the Understanding of Dreams, Fairy Tales and Myths*, 1951

The paradoxical fact [is] that we are not only less reasonable and less decent in our dreams but that we are also more intelligent, wiser, and capable of better judgment when we are asleep than when we are awake.

ERICH FROMM (1900–1980). *The Forgotten Language: An Introduction to the Understanding of Dreams, Fairy Tales and Myths*, 3, 1951

Trust the dreams, for in them is hidden the gate to eternity.

KAHLIL GIBRAN (1883–1931). "On Death," *The Prophet*, 1923

Human nature possesses wonderful powers and has something good in readiness for when we least hope for it. There have been times in my life when I have fallen asleep in tears; but in my dreams the most charming forms have come to console and to cheer me, and I have risen the next morning fresh and joyful.

GOETHE (1749–1832). 12 March 1828. In Peter Eckermann, *Conversations with Goethe*, 1836–1848, tr. John Oxenford, 1850

If you compare dreams of olden times with those of our time, you will note that the basic problems have remained the same, although objects pictured are often peculiar to the immediate environment.

EMIL A. GUTHEIL (1899–1959). *What Your Dreams Mean*, 1, 1957

[A] remarkably close relation . . . exists between humanity's dreams and humanity's religions.

EMIL A. GUTHEIL (1899–1959). *What Your Dreams Mean*, 3, 1957

Would we say . . . that the function of the dream is to express something or to hide something? It is both at once.

J. A. HADFIELD (1882–1967). *Dreams and Nightmares*, 6, 1954

We are not hypocrites in our sleep. The curb is taken off from our passions, and our imagination wanders at will. When awake, we check these rising thoughts, and fancy we have them not. In dreams, when we are off our guard, they return securely and unbidden.

WILLIAM HAZLITT (1778–1830). "On Dreams," *Table Talk*, 1822

Dreams . . . are sent by Zeus.

HOMER (8th? cent. B.C.). *The Iliad*, 1.62, tr. E. V. Rieu, 1950

God speaks in one way,
and in two, though man does not
perceive it.
In a dream, in a vision of the night,
when deep sleep falls upon men,
while they slumber on their beds,
then he opens the ears of men,
and terrifies them with warnings,
that he may turn man aside from
his deed,
and cut off pride from man.

JOB. *Job* 33:14–17

Within each one of us there is another whom we do not know. He speaks to us in dreams and tells us how differently he sees us from how we see ourselves. When, therefore, we find ourselves in a difficult situation, to which there is no solution, he can sometimes kindle a light that radically alters our attitude, the very attitude that led us into the difficult situation.

CARL G. JUNG (1875–1961). "The Meaning of Psychology for Modern Man," 1934, *Civilization in Transition*, tr. R. F. C. Hull, 1964

The dream may either repudiate the dreamer in a most painful way, or bolster him up morally. The first is likely to happen to people who . . . have too good an opinion of themselves; the second to those whose self-valuation is too low.

CARL G. JUNG (1875–1961). "On the Nature of Dreams," 1945, *The Structure and Dynamics of the Psyche*, tr. R. F. C. Hull, 1960

Not all dreams are of equal importance. Even primitives distinguish between "little" and "big" dreams. . . . "Little" dreams are the nightly fragments of fantasy coming from the subjective and personal sphere, and their meaning is limited to the affairs of everyday. That is why such dreams are easily forgotten, just because their validity extends no further than the day-to-day fluctuations of the psychic balance. Significant dreams, on the other hand, are often remembered for a lifetime, and not infrequently prove to be the richest jewel in the treasure house of psychic experience.

CARL G. JUNG (1875–1961). "On the Nature of Dreams," 1945, *The Structure and Dynamics of the Psyche*, tr. R. F. C. Hull, 1960. Jung believed that "little" dreams come from the "personal unconscious" and "big" ones from the "collective unconscious."

See The Unconscious: Jung (5)

The two fundamental points in dealing with dreams are these: First, the dream should be treated as a fact, about which one must make no previous assumption except that it somehow makes sense; and second, the dream is a specific expression of the unconscious.

CARL G. JUNG (1875–1961). "Approaching the Unconscious: Past and Future in the Unconscious." In Jung, ed., *Man and His Symbols*, 1964

We have forgotten the age-old fact that God speaks chiefly through dreams and visions.

CARL G. JUNG (1875–1961). "Approaching the Unconscious: Healing the Split." In Jung, ed., *Man and His Symbols*, 1964

I can never decide whether my dreams are the result of my thoughts, or my thoughts the result of my dreams.

> D. H. LAWRENCE (1875–1961). Letter to Edward Garnett, 29 January 1912

Dreams or illusions, call them what you will,
They lift us from the commonplace of life
To better things.

> HENRY WADSWORTH LONGFELLOW (1807–1882). *Michael Angelo*, 1.1, 1883

Freud has popularized the theory that dreams give expression to our wishes. No doubt this is true of a percentage of dreams, but I think dreams are just as apt to give expression to our fears.

> BERTRAND RUSSELL (1872–1970). *Human Society in Ethics and Politics*, 2.4, 1962

Nothing could be madder, more irresponsible, more dangerous than this guidance of men by dreams.

> GEORGE SANTAYANA (1863–1952). "Imagination," *Soliloquies in England and Later Soliloquies*, 1922

Hamlet: Oh God, I could be bounded in a nutshell and count myself a king of infinite space, were it not that I have bad dreams.

> SHAKESPEARE (1564–1616). *Hamlet*, 2.2.260, 1600

Some say that gleams of a remoter world
Visit the soul in sleep.

> PERCY BYSSHE SHELLEY (1792–1822). "Mont Blanc," 3, 1816

Dreams of great consequence in the government of the world. Of equal authority with the Bible.

> D. SIMPSON (18th cent.). English clergyman. *Discourse on Dreams and Night Visions*, 1791. In Lancelot Law Whyte, *The Unconscious Before Freud*, 6, 1960

A dream that is not interpreted is like a letter that is unread.

> TALMUD (A.D. 1st–6th cent.). Rabbinical writings. In Louis I. Newman, comp., *The Talmudic Anthology*, 66, 1945

A dream is a prophecy in miniature.

> TALMUD (A.D. 1st–6th cent.). Rabbinical writings. In Louis I. Newman, comp., *The Talmudic Anthology*, 66, 1945

Dreams are the touchstones of our characters. . . . In dreams we see ourselves naked and acting out our real characters, even more clearly than we see others awake.

> HENRY DAVID THOREAU (1817–1862). "Wednesday," *A Week on the Concord and Merrimack Rivers*, 1849

Our truest life is when we are in dreams awake.

> HENRY DAVID THOREAU (1817–1862). "Wednesday," *A Week on the Concord and Merrimack Rivers*, 1849
>
> See Vision: Carl G. Jung

The intimations of the night are divine, methinks. Men might meet in the morning and report the news of the night—what divine suggestions have been made to them. I find that I carry with me into the day often some such hint derived from the gods—such impulses to purity, to heroism, to literary effort even, as are never day-born. . . .
 I rejoice when in a dream I have loved virtue and nobleness.

> HENRY DAVID THOREAU (1817–1862). Journal, 7 July 1851

There is . . . one difference between our ancestors and ourselves: they used to examine dreams in order to predict the future, while it is the past that intrigues us.

> ELI WIESEL (1928–). "Jews, Myth, and Modern Life," *Parabala*, February 1987

Ne'er fear it, dreams go by the contraries.

> WILLIAM WYCHERLEY (1640–1716). *The Gentleman Dancing-Master*, 4.1, 1673

❧

[Seeing their brother Joseph approach from a distance], they said to one another, "Here comes this dreamer. Come now, let us kill him and throw him into one of the pits; then we shall say that a wild beast devoured him, and we shall see what will become of his dreams."

> ANONYMOUS (*BIBLE*). *Genesis* 37:19–20
>
> See Dreams: Examples: Anonymous (*Bible*)

As wishes may inspire dreams, so dreams may inspire wishes.

> ANONYMOUS

Our waking hours form the text of our lives; our dreams, the commentary.

> ANONYMOUS

DREAMS: EXAMPLES

See also • Assassination: Abraham Lincoln ○ Creativity: First Person: [especially] Robert Louis Stevenson, Richard Wagner (1) ○ Dreams ○ Revelations ○ Spirituality: First Person

One night during the (1944 presidential) campaign (vice presidential candidate Harry S. Truman) woke up in a cold sweat from a dream that the president had died and he was called to assume the office.

> JAMES DAVID BARBER (1939–). *The Presidential Character: Predicting Performance in the White House*, 8, 1972

[In a dream a voice identified as Scipio's said:] The spirit is the true self, not that physical figure which can be pointed out by the finger. Know, then, that you are a god . . . which rules, governs, and moves the body over which it is set, just as the supreme God above us rules this universe.

> CICERO (106–43 B.C.). "The Dream of Scipio," *De republica*, 6.24, tr. Clinton Walker Keyes, 1928

I dreamed that I floated at will in the great Ether, and I saw this world floating also not far off, but diminished to the size of an apple. Then an angel took it in his hand and brought it to me and said, "This must thou eat." And I ate the world.

> RALPH WALDO EMERSON (1803–1882). Journal, 25 October 1840

I woke this morn with a dream which perchance was true that I was living in the morning of history amidst barbarians, that right and truth had yet no voice, no letters, no law, everyone did what he would and grasped what he could.

> RALPH WALDO EMERSON (1803–1882). Journal, 1845, undated

In dreams last night, a certain instructive racehorse was quite elaborately shown off, which seemed marvelously constructed for violent running, and so mighty to go that he stood up continually on his hind feet in impatience and triumphant power. . . . Then I noticed, for the first time, that he was a show horse, and had wasted all the time in this rearing on the hind legs, and had not run forward at all. I hope they did not mean to be personal.

RALPH WALDO EMERSON (1803–1882). Journal, September 1849

People who dream often, and with great enjoyment, of *swimming,* cleaving the waves, etc., have usually been bed-wetters.

SIGMUND FREUD (1856–1939). *The Interpretation of Dreams,* 6.E, 1900, tr. A. A. Brill, 1938

A dream, the other night, that the world had become dissatisfied with the inaccurate manner in which facts are reported and had employed me, with a salary of a thousand dollars, to relate things of public importance exactly as they happen.

NATHANIEL HAWTHORNE (1804–1864). 1 June 1842, *The American Notebooks,* ed. Claude M. Simpson, 1932

President [Abraham Lincoln] last night had a dream. He was in a party of plain people and as it became known who he was they began to comment on his appearance. One of them said, "He is a very common-looking man." The President replied, "Common looking people are the best in the world: that is the reason the Lord makes so many of them."

Waking, he remembered it, and told it as rather a neat thing.

JOHN HAY (1838–1905). Diary, 23 December 1863, *Lincoln and the Civil War in the Diaries and Letters of John Hay,* ed. Tyler Dennett, 1939 (Popular version: God must love the common people; He's made so many of them.)

He dreamed that there was a ladder set up on the earth, and the top of it reached to heaven; and behold, the angels of God were ascending and descending on it! And behold, the Lord stood above it and said, "I am the Lord, the God of Abraham your father and the God of Isaac; the land on which you lie I will give to you and to your descendants; and your descendants shall be like the dust of the earth, and you shall spread abroad to the west and to the east and to the north and to the south; and by you and your descendants shall all the families of the earth bless themselves. Behold, I am with you and will keep you wherever you go, and will bring you back to this land; for I will not leave you until I have done that of which I have spoken to you." Then Jacob awoke from his sleep and said, "Surely the Lord is in this place; and I did not know it."

JACOB. *Genesis* 28:12–16

See Angels: Richard Henry Stoddard

All of a sudden I saw a beautiful shining railroad train that circled around a mountain. Streams of children—and adults as well—rushed toward the train and could not be held back. . . . Then I heard a voice say to me: "This train is going to hell." Immediately it seemed as if someone took me by the hand, and the same voice said, "Now we will go to purgatory." And oh! so frightful was the suffering I saw and felt, I could only have thought that I was in hell itself if the voice had not told me we were going to purgatory. Probably no more than a few seconds passed while I saw all this. Then I heard a sigh and saw a light—and all was gone. . . .

[Interpretation:] I believe God has shown me most clearly through this dream, or revelation, and has convinced me in my heart how I must answer the question: should I be National Socialist—or Catholic? I would like to call out to everyone who is riding on this train: "Jump out before the train reaches its destination, even if it costs you your life?"

FRANZ JÄGERSTÄTTER (1907–1943). Austrian farmer and conscientious objector, executed 9 August 1943. As related by his widow to the author. In Gordon C. Zahn, *In Solitary Witness: The Life and Death of Franz Jägerstätter,* 6, 1964

[One of my patients] dreamed that she was commanded to descend into "a pit filled with hot stuff." This she did, till only one shoulder was sticking out of the pit. Then Jung came along, pushed her right down into the hot stuff, exclaiming "Not out but through!"

CARL G. JUNG (1875–1961). As paraphrased from his privately multigraphed 1938 paper by Aniela Jaffé, *From the Life and Work of C. G. Jung,* 4, 1968, tr. R. F. C. Hull, 1971

I dreamed that I was climbing a mountain. I had my crook across my shoulders in the manner of Cretan shepherds, and I was singing. . . .

Suddenly an old man darted out of a cave. His sleeves were tucked up, his hands covered with clay. Placing his finger on his lips to silence me, he commanded in a stern voice. "Stop singing! I want quiet! Can't you see I'm working?" (Here he indicated his hands.)

"What are you making?" I asked him.

"Can't you see for yourself? Inside this cave I am fashioning the Redeemed."

"The Redeemed? Who is redeemed?" I cried, and the old wounds began to flow again inside me.

"He who perceives, loves, and lives the totality!" replied the old man hurriedly burrowing again into his cave.

NIKOS KAZANTZAKIS (1885–1957). *Report to Greco,* 25, 1961, tr. P. A. Bien, 1965

Last night I dreamt there was a snake in the house. I picked up a stick and hit him, but he only crawled under the couch. I was nervous in the dream. I knew I should not hit snakes, but I felt compelled to do so. At breakfast I talked about the dream to my friend, and she suggested I should feed the snake and make friends with him if he should appear again in a dream.

SAM KEEN (1931–). *Beginnings Without End,* 4, 1975

The thirsty look in their sleep
On the whole world as a spring of water.

SA'DI (A.D. 1213?–1292). *The Gulistan, or Rose Garden,* 7 (Story 20), A.D. 1258, tr. Edward Rehatsek, 1964

Many a man hath seen himself in dreams
His mother's mate, but he who pays no heed
To suchlike matters bears the easier fate.

SOPHOCLES (496?–406 B.C.). *Oedipus Rex.* In Sigmund Freud, *The Interpretation of Dreams,* 5.D.b, 1900, tr. A. A. Brill, 1938

See Parents: Sigmund Freud

In the summer of A.D. 1936, in a time of physical sickness and spiritual travail, he dreamed, during a spell of sleep in a wakeful night, that he was clasping the foot of the crucifix hanging over the high altar of the Abbey of Ampleforth and was hearing a voice saying to him *Amplexus expecta* ("Cling and wait").

> ARNOLD J. TOYNBEE (1889–1975). Referring to himself in the third person, *A Study of History*, 9.634–635, 1954

The recurrent dream. Mine is appearing before lecture audiences in my shirttail. A most disagreeable dream.

> MARK TWAIN (1835–1910). 23 August 1895, *Mark Twain's Notebook*, ed. Albert Bigelow Paine, 1935

❦

Now Joseph had a dream, and when he told it to his brothers they only hated him the more. He said to them, "Hear this dream which I have dreamed: behold, we were binding sheaves in the field, and lo, my sheaf arose and stood upright; and behold, your sheaves gathered round it, and bowed down to my sheaf." His brothers said to him, "Are you indeed to reign over us? Or are you indeed to have dominion over us?" So they hated him yet more for his dreams and for his words.

> ANONYMOUS (*BIBLE*). *Genesis* 37:5–8
>
> See Dreams: Anonymous (*Bible*)

I am about to cross a river. I look for a bridge, but there is none. I am small, perhaps five or six. I cannot swim. Then I see a tall, dark man who makes a sign that he can carry me over in his arms. (The river is only about five feet deep.) I am glad for the moment and let him take me. While he holds me and starts walking, I am suddenly seized by panic. I know that if I don't get away I shall die. We are already in the river, but I muster all my courage and jump from the man's arms into the water. At first I think I'll be drowned. But then I start swimming, and soon reach the other shore. The man has disappeared.

> ANONYMOUS. In Erich Fromm, *The Forgotten Language: An Introduction to the Understanding of Dreams, Fairy Tales and Myths*, 6, 1951

DRESS

See also • Clothes ○ Fashion

Any affectation whatsoever in dress implies . . . a flaw in the understanding.

> LORD CHESTERFIELD (1694–1773). Letter to his son, 30 December 1748

The sense of being well-dressed gives a feeling of inward tranquillity which religion is powerless to bestow.

> MISS C. F. FORBES (1817–1911). English writer

Anonymous: Why do you never change your attire of black suit, black socks, black tie, and white shirt?
Kirstein: I long ago worked out that I would save a great deal of time if I forewent the particular choice of dress.

> LINCOLN KIRSTEIN. New York City Ballet founder. Format adapted. In Warren Bennis and Burt Nanus, "Leading Others, Managing Yourself," *Leaders: The Strategies for Taking Charge*, 1985

That's quite a dress you almost have on.

> ALAN JAY LERNER (1918–1986). *An American in Paris* (film), 1951, spoken by Gene Kelly to Nine Foch in a bare-shoulder gown

Dress for Success.

> JOHN T. MOLLOY. Book title, 1975

I hold that gentleman to be the best dressed whose dress no one observes.

> ANTHONY TROLLOPE (1815–1882). *Thackeray*, 9, 1879

Be careless in your dress if you must, but keep a tidy soul.

> MARK TWAIN (1835–1910). *Following the Equator: A Journey Around the World*, 23 (epigraph), 1897

❦

Why is it that the dress you don't like always lasts the longest?

> ANONYMOUS

DRUGS, ILLEGAL

See also • Addiction ○ Alcohol ○ Coffee ○ Death: Janis Joplin ○ Drugs, Medical ○ Drugs, Psychiatric ○ Healing ○ Tobacco

When I was in England [as a Rhodes scholar], I experimented with marijuana a time or two, and I didn't like it, and I didn't inhale, and I never tried it again.

> BILL CLINTON (1946–). Television appearance, CBS, 29 March 1992

Drug misuse is not a disease, it is a decision, like the decision to step out in front of a moving car. You would call that not a disease but an error of judgment.

> PHILIP K. DICK. "Author's Note," *A Scanner Darkly*, 1977

My appearance was immaculate. . . . I had bought myself a new shirt and white gloves, as the washable pair are no longer very nice; I had my hair set and my rather wild beard trimmed in the French style; altogether I spent fourteen francs on the evening. As a result I looked very fine and made a favorable impression on myself. We drove there in a carriage the expenses of which we shared. R. was terribly nervous, I quite calm with the help of a small dose of cocaine.

> SIGMUND FREUD (1856–1939). Recounting his preparations for a dinner engagement at the home of French neurologist Jean Martin Charcot with whom he studied in Paris, letter to his fiancé Martha Bernays, 20 January 1886, tr. Tania and James Stern, 1960. Cocaine was not an illegal drug at that time.

Early in use, all of the positive things that are said about cocaine are true. As use continues, all the negative things become true.

> FRANK GAWIN. Cocaine treatment program director, Yale University School of Medicine. In Peter Kerr, "Anatomy of the Drug Issue: How, After Years, It Erupted," *New York Times*, 17 November 1986

I saw the best minds of my generation destroyed by madness, starving hysterical naked,
dragging themselves through the negro streets at dawn looking for an angry fix.

> ALLEN GINSBERG (1926–1997). Opening lines, title poem, *Howl and Other Poems*, 1956

If they took all the drugs, nicotine, alcohol, caffeine off the market for six days, they'd have to bring out the tanks to control you.

> DICK GREGORY (1932–). Speech, Berkeley (California), 5 May 1981

Then I always manage to get
    my weekly check on Monday,
Pay my rent, get my laundry
    out, always have enough
Junk to last a coupla days

Have to buy a couple needles
    tomorrow, feels like
Shovin a nail in me.

    Just like shovin a nail in me
Goddamn—(Cough)—
        JACK KEROUAC (1922–1969). "59 Chorus," *Mexico City Blues,* 1959

If you take the game of life seriously, if you take your nervous system seriously, if you take your sense organs seriously, if you take the energy process seriously, you must turn on, tune in and drop out.
        TIMOTHY LEARY (1920–1996). Lecture, 1966, *The Politics of Ecstasy,* 21, 1968 (Popular version: Turn on, tune in, and drop out!)

Samuel L. Jackson: That shit is going to rob you of our ambition. *Bridget Fonda* (his pot-smoking layabout girlfriend): Not if your ambition is to get high and watch TV.
        ELMORE LEONARD. (QUENTIN TARANTINO, scriptwriter). *Jackie Brown* (film), 1997

What happens to the guy who smokes pot all the time? I don't know. But I do know something is being mortgaged; something is being drawn out of the future.
        NORMAN MAILER (1923–). Paul Carroll interview, *Playboy,* January 1968

No drug, not even alcohol, causes the fundamental ills of society. If we're looking for the sources of our troubles, we shouldn't test people for drugs, we should test them for stupidity, ignorance, greed and love of power.
        P. J. O'ROURKE (1947–). "Studying for Our Drug Test," *Give War a Chance,* 1992

Treating addiction to heroin with methadone is like treating addiction to scotch with bourbon.
        THOMAS S. SZASZ (1920–). "Drugs," *The Second Sin,* 1973

I prefer the natural sky to an opium eater's heaven.
        HENRY DAVID THOREAU (1817–1862). "Higher Laws," *Walden; or Life in the Woods,* 1854

Speed will turn you into your parents.
        FRANK ZAPPA (1940–1993)

                                    ✺

Just say no to drugs.
        SLOGAN. 1980s. Popularized by First Lady Nancy Reagan

DRUGS, MEDICAL

See also • Addiction ○ Disease: Elbert Hubbard ○ Doctors: [especially] George Bernard Shaw (3) ○ Drugs, Illegal ○ Drugs, Psychiatric ○ Epitaphs: Anonymous (English) ○ Healing ○ Physicians: [especially] Benjamin Franklin, Napoleon

Physic, for the most part, is nothing else but the substitute of exercise or temperance.
        JOSEPH ADDISON (1672–1719). In *The Spectator* (English essay series), 1711–1714

Apothecary, *n.* The physician's accomplice, undertaker's benefactor and grave worm's providers.
        AMBROSE BIERCE (1842–1914). *The Devil's Dictionary,* p. 12, 1911, Dover edition, 1958

Thare ain't mutch phun in phisick, but thare iz a good deal ov physick in phun.
        JOSH BILLINGS (1818–1885). "Koarse Shot," *Everybody's Friend, or; Josh Billing's Encyclopedia and Proverbial Philosophy of Wit and Humor,* 1874

Those two great medicines: Diet and Self-Control.
        MAX BIRCHER. Swiss physician. In Gordon Young, *Doctors Without Drugs,* 3, 1962

I read once of a man who was cured of a dangerous illness by eating his doctor's prescription which he understood was the medicine itself.
        SAMUEL BUTLER (1835–1902). *The Note-Books of Samuel Butler,* 20, ed. Henry Festing Jones, 1907

Pharmacomania: uncontrollable desire to take or to administer medicines.
        DORLAND'S ILLUSTRATED MEDICAL DICTIONARY. 25th ed., p. 1175, 1974

I firmly believe that if the whole *materia medica,* as now used, could be sunk to the bottom of the sea, it would be better for mankind—and all the worse for the fishes.
        OLIVER WENDELL HOLMES, SR. (1809–1894). Address before the Massachusetts Medical Society, Boston, 30 May 1860

Medicine in the hand of a fool was ever poison and death.
        CARL G. JUNG (1875–1961). "The Theory of Psychoanalysis" (8), 1913, *Freud and Psychoanalysis,* tr. R. F. C. Hull, 1961

We chat together: he gives me his prescriptions; I never follow them, and so I get well.
        MOLIÈRE (1622–1673)

The desire to take medicine is one feature which distinguishes man, the animal, from his fellow creatures. It is really one of the most serious difficulties with which we have to contend. Even in minor ailments, which would yield to dieting or to simple home remedies, the doctor's visit is not thought to be complete without the prescription.
        SIR WILLIAM OSLER (1849–1919). "Teaching and Thinking" (2). Remarks at the opening of the Medical Faculty building, McGill College, Montreal, 8 January 1895, *A Way of Life and Selected Writings of Sir William Osler,* 1951
        See Physicians: Osler

Poison is in everything, and no thing is without poison. The dosage makes it either a poison or a remedy.
        PARACELSUS (1493–1541). In "Checking the Additives," *Time,* 9 March 1959

Learn from the beasts the physic of the field.
        ALEXANDER POPE (1688–1744). *An Essay on Man,* 3.174, 1734

It is found easier by the shortsighted victims of disease, to palliate their torments by medicine, than to prevent them by regimen.

> PERCY BYSSHE SHELLEY (1792–1822). "Notes" (8.109), *Queen Mab: A Philosophical Poem: With Notes*, 1813

Faulty prescribing creates . . . a round robin of profits: The drug companies get theirs, as do the [doctors], and so finally do the hospitals. Recent studies show that in a typical year more than 650,000 older Americans are hospitalized because of toxic reactions to the drugs they are taking.

> ROBERT SHERRILL. "The Madness of the Market: The Drug Companies," *Nation*, 9 January 1995

❧

Moderation is medicine.

> SAYING (BURMESE)

The best medicine is tincture of time.

> SAYING
>
> See Doctors: Seneca the Younger

DRUGS, PSYCHIATRIC

See also • Depression: Ronald R. Fieve ○ Drugs, Illegal ○ Drugs, Medical ○ Psychiatric Treatment ○ Psychiatry

No one should fear taking a psychiatric medication if he is she has received a complete medical and physical examination and is properly monitored for both the medicine's benefit and side effects. Not only do psychiatric medications offer relief from the terror, loneliness, and sorrow that accompany untreated mental illnesses, but they enable people to take advantage of the psychotherapy (which psychiatrists usually prescribe in tandem with medication), self-help groups, and supportive services available through their psychiatrist. Better, these medications and the other services available through mental health care enable people who have mental illness to enjoy their lives, their families and their work.

> AMERICAN PSYCHIATRIC ASSOCIATION. Closing paragraph, *Let's Talk Facts about Psychiatric Medications* (pamphlet), 1993

Psychiatry has unleashed an epidemic of neurologic disease on the world. Even if tardive dyskinesia [a condition marked by rhythmical, involuntary movements of the mouth, tongue, jaw, and/or extremities] were the only permanent disability produced by these drugs [i.e., antipsychotic drugs, major tranquilizers, phenothiazines, or neuroleptics, including Haldol, Prolixin, and Thorazine], by itself, this would be among the worst medically induced disasters in history.

> PETER R. BREGGIN (1936–). Psychiatrist. *Psychiatric Drugs: Hazards to the Brain*, 6, 1983. Antipsychotic drugs are widely used in the treatment of psychosis and schizophrenia.

Were Moses to go up Mt. Sinai today, the two tablets he'd bring down with him would be aspirin and Prozac.

> JOSEPH A. CALIFANO, JR. (1931–). Slightly modified. Charlie Rose television interview, PBS, 16 January 1995

Drugs, the major method of [institutional psychiatric] treatment, are known as "major tranquilizers" or "antipsychotic agents." Their main effect is to slow down both thinking and motor activity, and

they are responsible for what is widely perceived as a "revolution" in mental hospitals since the early 1950s, when they came into widespread use. Mental institutions *are* quieter than they used to be, but the slurred speech and stiffly held bodies of the patients reveal the cost of that quiet.

> JUDI CHAMBERLIN (1944–). *On Our Own: Patient-Controlled Alternatives to the Mental Health System*, 1, 1978

Tranquilizers are used not only in mental hospitals but in many kinds of institutions where large numbers of people are supervised by underpaid, poorly trained staff members: institutions for the retarded, nursing homes, juvenile detention centers, and prisons. The purpose is clearly institutional management.

> JUDI CHAMBERLIN (1944–). *On Our Own: Patient-Controlled Alternatives to the Mental Health System*, 1, 1978

Lithium is "clearly" a human teratogen, and the patient who becomes pregnant while taking the drug needs to be so informed, Dr. Kenneth L. Jones said at a symposium sponsored by the Northern California Chapter, March of Dimes Birth Defects Foundation. In a worldwide lithium birth registry, 13 of 143 mothers who took it in pregnancy had malformed children. Nine were born with cardiovascular defects.

> CLINICAL PSYCHIATRY NEWS. "Lithium Said to Clearly Be a Human Teratogen," March 1984. Lithium is widely used in the treatment of manic depression (bipolar disorder).

[Being on the antidepressant Prozac] is not at all like being on cruise control. It's more like driving a car with an unreliable fuel gauge on a long trip on an unfamiliar highway with no signs to indicate the distance to the next gas station or rest stop—and not minding.

> SALLY HALPRIN. "Life with Prozac," *San Francisco Sunday Examiner & Chronicle*, 15 August 1993. Antidepressants are widely used in the treatment of moderate and severe depression.

One injection [of the long-acting neuroleptic Prolixin] every week or two and you have a nation of zombies, easily controlled. My entire body felt like it was being twisted up in contortions inside by some unseen wringer.

> WADE HUDSON (1944–). Testifying before a Senate judiciary subcommittee investigating "The Abuse and Misuse of Controlled Drugs in Institutions." In "Patients Made into 'Zombies,'" *San Francisco Chronicle*, 19 August 1975

The daily soma ration was an insurance against personal maladjustment, social unrest and the spread of subversive ideas. Religion, Karl Marx declared, is the opium of the people. In the Brave New World, this situation was reversed. Opium, or rather soma, was the people's religion.

> ALDOUS HUXLEY (1894–1963). "Chemical Persuasion," *Brave New World Revisited*, 1958. Soma was the euphoria-producing drug used in Huxley's pseudo-utopian *Brave New World* (1932).
>
> See Religion, Anti-: Karl Marx

The antidepressants are basically speed.

> RONALD LEIFER (1932–). Psychiatrist. In Seth Farber, *Madness, Heresy, and the Rumor of Angels: The Revolt Against the Mental Health System*, 12, 1993

Tamed by *Miltown*, we lie on Mother's bed.

> ROBERT LOWELL (1917–1997). "Man and Wife," 1959

[Prozac is] a quintessentially American drug. It does not enhance pleasure or bring happiness, but promotes adroit competitiveness. It is not a street drug that brings a quick high, it is an office drug that enhances the social skills necessary in a postindustrial, service-oriented economy.

> DAVID J. ROTHMAN. Columbia University professor of social medicine and history. "Shiny Happy People: The Problem with Cosmetic Psychopharmacology,'" *New Republic,* 14 February 1994.

Pre-menstrual dysphoric disorder . . . afflicts some women as a severe form of pre-menstrual stress and "cripples them emotionally," according to a study published last week in the Journal of the American Medical Association. The study, which said sufferers can be significantly aided by taking an antidepressant, was financed by Pfizer Inc., which makes the antidepressant Zoloft.

> JOE SHARKEY. "You're Not Bad, You're Sick. It's in the Book," *New York Times,* 28 September 1997

The blunting of consciousness, motivation, and the ability to solve problems under the influence of chlorpromazine [generic name for the neuroleptic Thorazine] resembles nothing so much as the effects of frontal lobotomy. The lobotomy syndrome was familiar to psychiatrists in 1943 because so many lobotomized patients had accumulated in mental hospitals. Research has suggested that lobotomies and chemicals like chlorpromazine may cause their effects in the same way, by disrupting the activity of the neurochemical, dopamine. At any rate, a psychiatrist would be hard-put to distinguish a lobotomized patient from one treated with chlorpromazine.

> PETER STERLING (1940–). University of Pennsylvania neuroanatomist. "Psychiatry's Drug Addiction," *New Republic,* 9 December 1979

DUTY

See also • Freedom ○ Happiness: George Washington ○ Morality ○ Responsibility ○ Silence & Protest

What is threatened today is moral liberty, conscience, respect for the soul, the very nobility of man. To defend the soul, its interests, its rights, its dignity, is the most pressing duty for whoever sees the danger.

> HENRI AMIEL (1812–1881). Journal, 17 June 1852, tr. Mrs. Humphrey Ward, 1887

The celebration of duty is an effective way to disguise the lust for power from oneself as much as from the outside world.

> RICHARD J. BARNET (1929–). *Roots of War,* 3.5, 1971
> See Idealism: Charles de Gaulle, Aldous Huxley

It is better to do your own duty, however imperfectly, than to assume the duties of another person, however successfully.

> *BHAGAVAD GITA* (6th cent. B.C.). 3, tr. Swami Prabhavananda and Christopher Isherwood, 1954

Duty, *n.* That which sternly impels us in the direction of profit, along the line of desire.

> AMBROSE BIERCE (1842–1914). *The Devil's Dictionary,* p. 33, 1911, Dover edition, 1958

Duty, faithfully performed, opens the mind to truth, both being of one family, alike immutable, universal, and everlasting.

> WILLIAM ELLERY CHANNING (1780–1842). "Self-Culture," address, Boston, September 1838

The reward of one duty is the power to fulfill another.

> GEORGE ELIOT (1819–1880). *Daniel Deronda,* 46, 1876

You will always find those who think they know what is your duty better than you know it.

> RALPH WALDO EMERSON (1803–1882). "Self-Reliance," *Essays: First Series,* 1841

To live without duties is obscene.

> RALPH WALDO EMERSON (1803–1882). "Aristocracy," *Lectures and Biographical Sketches,* 1883

This is your duty, to act well the part that is given to you.

> EPICTETUS (A.D. 55?–135?). *The Encheiridion,* 17, tr. George Long, 1890?

Nor is a Duty beneficial because it is commanded,
  but it is commanded because it's beneficial.

> BENJAMIN FRANKLIN (1706–1790). *Poor Richard's Almanack,* November 1739

It is not necessary that I live, but it is necessary that I perform my duty.

> FREDERICK II (1712–1786). In John Keegan, "The Awful Fate of Frederick the Great," *New York Review of Books,* 13 February 1986
> See Purpose: Lord Chesterfield

The still small voice within you must always be the final arbiter when there is a conflict of duty.

> MOHANDAS K. GANDHI (1869–1948). In *Young India,* 4 August 1920

There are two complementary parts of our cosmic duty—one to ourselves, to be fulfilled in the realization and enjoyment of our capacities; the other to others, to be fulfilled in service to the community and in promoting the welfare of the generations to come and the advancement of our species as a whole.

> JULIAN HUXLEY (1887–1975). "Transhumanism," *New Bottles for New Wine,* 1957

"Learn what is true in order to do what is right" is the summing up of the whole of duty of man.

> T. H. HUXLEY (1825–1895). "The Coming of Age of *The Origin of Species,*" *Science and Culture and Other Essays,* 1881

Helmer: So you'll run out like this on your most sacred vows.
Nora: What do you think are my most sacred vows?
Helmer: And I have to tell you that! Aren't they your duties to your husband and children?
Nora: I have other duties equally sacred.
Helmer: That isn't true. What duties are they?
Nora: Duties to myself.

> HENRIK IBSEN (1828–1926). *A Doll's House,* 3, 1879, tr. Rolf Fjelde, 1965

What's a man's first duty? The answer's brief: To be himself.

> HENRIK IBSEN (1828–1926). *Peer Gynt,* 4.1, 1867, Airmont Publishing edition, 1967

Duty is ours, consequences are God's.

> THOMAS JONATHAN "STONEWALL" JACKSON (1820–1863)

Duty, then is the sublimest word in our language. Do your duty in all things. . . . You cannot do more. You should never wish to do less.

ROBERT E. LEE (1807–1870). Attributed. Inscription under his bust, Hall of Fame for Great Americans, New York University, New York City

England expects that every man will do his duty.

HORATIO NELSON (1758–1805). His last signal to the fleet before the Battle of Trafalgar (off the southwest coast of Spain). In Robert Southey, *The Life of Nelson*, 9, 1813

A succession of small duties always faithfully done demands no less than do heroic actions.

ROUSSEAU (1712–1778). *Confessions*, 3 (1712–1778). 1781, tr. J. M. Cohen, 1953

A sense of duty is useful in work, but offensive in personal relations. People wish to be liked, not endured with patient resignation.

BERTRAND RUSSELL (1872–1970). *The Conquest of Happiness*, 10, 1930

Pursue the nearest duty.

FRIEDRICH von SCHILLER (1759–1805). *The Death of Wallenstein*, 3.18, 1799, tr. Samuel T. Coleridge, 1800

To obey the will of the Deity is the first rule of duty.

ADAM SMITH (1723–1790). *The Theory of Moral Sentiments*, 3.4, 1759

If it be a duty to respect other men's claims, so also is it a duty to maintain our own.

HERBERT SPENCER (1820–1903). *Social Statics*, 3.21.8, 1851

It is easier to do one's duty to others than to one's self. If you do your duty to others, you are considered reliable. If you do your duty to yourself, you are considered selfish.

THOMAS S. SZASZ (1920–). "Personal Conduct," *The Second Sin*, 1973

It is a duty to say what should be heard, and a duty not to say what should not be heard.

TALMUD (A.D. 1st–6th cent.). Rabbinical writings

Everyone has duties to the community in which alone the free and full development of his personality is possible.

UNIVERSAL DECLARATION OF HUMAN RIGHTS. United Nations, Article 29, 10 December 1948

The highest of all duties, the duty that one owes to one's self.

OSCAR WILDE (1854–1900). *The Picture of Dorian Gray*, 2, 1891

EARTH

See also • The Dead: Thomas Jefferson ○ Environment ○ God & Nature: Isaiah ○ Heaven ○ Nature ○ Perfection: Walt Whitman ○ Trees: Henry David Thoreau ○ Unity: Walt Whitman ○ World

The new earth, freshly torn from its parent sun, was a ball of whirling gases, intensely hot, rushing through the black spaces of the universe on a path and at a speed controlled by immense forces. Gradually the ball of flaming gases cooled. The gases began to liquefy, and Earth became a molten mass. The materials of this mass eventually became sorted out in a definite pattern: the heaviest in the center, the less heavy surrounding them, and the least heavy forming the outer rim.

RACHEL CARSON (1907–1964). *The Sea Around Us*, rev. ed., 1 ("The Gray Beginnings"), 1961

This earth—sin of the Creator!

E. M. CIORAN (1911–1995). *A Short History of Decay*, 1 ("In One of the Earth's Attics"), 1949, tr. Richard Howard, 1975

Old Earth, worn by the ages, wracked by rain and storm, exhausted yet every ready to produce what life must have to go on!

CHARLES de GAULLE (1890–1970). *The Complete War Memoirs of Charles de Gaulle*, 3.7, 1959, tr. Richard Howard, 1998

Right now I am a passenger on the Space Vehicle Earth zooming about the Sun at 60,000 miles per hour somewhere in the solar system.

R. BUCKMINSTER FULLER (1895–1983). Introduction to Gene Youngblood, *Expanded Cinema*, 1970

The most important fact about Spaceship Earth: An instruction book didn't come with it.

R. BUCKMINSTER FULLER (1895–1983). *I Seem To Be a Verb*, p. 6, 1970

Roll on, thou ball, roll on!
Through pathless realms of Space
    Roll on!

W. S. GILBERT (1836–1911). "To the Terrestrial Globe," *The "Bab" Ballads*, 1866–1871

Our earthly ball a peopled garden.

GOETHE (1749–1832). *Wilhelm Meister's Apprenticeship*, 7.5, 1796

Thus says the Lord: "Heaven is my throne
    and the earth is my footstool."

ISAIAH (8th cent. B.C.). *Isaiah* 66:1

[The] Earth is a single huge organism intentionally creating an optimum environment for itself.

RICHARD A. KERR. Defining James E. Lovelock's Gaia Hypothesis, "No Longer Willful, Gaia Becomes Respectable," *Science*, 22 April 1988

This vast ball, the Earth.
Was molded out of clay, and baked in fire.

HENRY WADSWORTH LONGFELLOW (1807–1882). *Michael Angelo*, 3.5, 1883

On Spaceship Earth there are no passengers; everybody is a member of the crew. We have moved into an age in which everybody's activities affect everybody else.

MARSHALL McLUHAN (1911–1980). In Barbara K. Rodes and Rice Odell, comps., *A Dictionary of Environmental Quotations,* p. 51, 1992

With high woods the hills were crown'd,
With tufts the valleys and each fountain side,
With borders long Rivers. That Earth now
Seem'd like to Heav'n, a seat where Gods might dwell.

JOHN MILTON (1608–1674). *Paradise Lost,* 7.326, 1667

Leontes: It is a bawdy planet.

SHAKESPEARE (1564–1616). *The Winter's Tale,* 1.1.201, 1610

What is the use of a house if you haven't got a tolerable planet to put it on?

HENRY DAVID THOREAU (1817–1862). Letter to Harrison Blake, 20 May 1860

I believe more and more that God must not be judged on this earth. It is one of His sketches that has turned out badly.

VINCENT VAN GOGH (1853–1890). In Albert Camus, "Rebellion and Art," *The Rebel: An Essay on Man in Revolt,* 1951, tr. Anthony Bower, 1956

In this broad earth of ours,
Amid the measureless grossness and the slag,
Enclosed and safe within its central heart,
Nestles the seed perfection.

WALT WHITMAN (1819–1892). "Song of the Universal" (1), 1874, *Leaves of Grass,* 1855–1892

✴

What's an earth for, but to make a heaven of.

ANONYMOUS

EARTHQUAKES

See also • Nature

It takes an earthquake to remind us that we walk on the crust of an unfinished planet.

CHARLES KURALT (1934–1997). Television magazine program host, *Sunday Morning,* CBS, 23 January 1994

✴

"If You Build Your House on a Crack in the Earth, It's Your Own Fault."

ANONYMOUS. Title of a scientific paper on earthquakes. In Laurence J. Peter, *Peter's People,* 5, 1979

ECCENTRICITY

See also • Madness: Anonymous ○ Nonconformity

Eccentricity, *n.* A method of distinction so cheap that fools employ it to accentuate their incapacity.

AMBROSE BIERCE (1842–1914). *The Devil's Dictionary,* p. 34, 1911, Dover edition, 1958

We might define an eccentric as a man who is a law unto himself, and a crank as one who, having determined what the law is, insists on laying it down to others.

LOUIS KRONENBERGER (1904–1980). *Company Manners: A Cultural Inquiry into American Life,* 3.3, 1954

I have an independent mind, you are eccentric, he is round the twist.

JONATHAN LYNN (1943–) and SIR ANTHONY JAY (1930–). "The Bishop's Gambit," *The Complete Yes Minister: The Diaries of a Cabinet Minister by the Right Honorable James Hacker MP,* 1984

There is one virtue, always to shun the eccentric.

MENANDER (343?–291 B.C.). Fragment, 203, tr. Francis G. Allinson, 1921

Eccentricity has always abounded when and where strength of character has abounded; and the amount of eccentricity in a society has generally been proportional to the amount of genius, mental vigor, and moral courage it contained. That so few dare to be eccentric marks the chief danger of the time.

JOHN STUART MILL (1806–1873). *On Liberty,* 3, 1859

Eccentricity is *not,* as dull people would have us believe, a form of madness. It is often a kind of innocent pride, and the man of genius and the aristocrat are frequently regarded as eccentrics because genius and aristocrat are entirely unafraid of and uninfluenced by the opinions and vagaries of the crowd.

EDITH SITWELL (1887–1964). *Taken Care Of: An Autobiography,* 15, 1965

There is all the difference in the world between departure from recognized rules by one who has learned to obey them, and neglect of them through want of training or want of skill or want of understanding. Before you can be eccentric you must know where the circle is.

ELLEN TERRY (1848–1928). British actress. *Ellen Terry's Memoirs,* 2nd ed., 5, 1932

ECONOMICS

See also • Business (Commerce) ○ Capitalism ○ Communism ○ Debt ○ Diplomacy: Anonymous ○ Economists ○ Fascism ○ Freedom: Milton Friedman (2) ○ Inflation ○ Machines: Henry Hazlitt ○ Money ○ Poverty ○ Price ○ Profit & Loss ○ Prosperity ○ Socialism ○ Taxes ○ Thrift ○ Trade (Commerce) ○ Value ○ Wages ○ War & Economics ○ Wealth ○ Work

What's good economics is bad politics; what's bad economics is good politics.

EUGENE W. BAER. "Baer's Quartet." In Paul Dickson, comp., *The Official Rules,* p. 27, 1978

If we wish to make the best use of people, places, and things, then we are going to have to deal with a law that reads about like this: as the quality of use increases, the scale of use (that is, the size of operations) will decline, the tools will become simpler, and the methods and the skills will become more complex.

WENDELL BERRY (1934–). "An Argument for Diversity," 1988, *What Are People For?: Essays,* 1990

If we are serious about reducing the size of government and its burdens, then we need to return economic self-determination to the people. . . . We must do it by fostering economic democracy. We must do everything possible to assure ordinary citizens the possibility of owning a small, usable share of the country.

WENDELL BERRY (1934–). "Decolonizing Rural America," *Audubon*,
March–April 1993

There are three basic types of human transactions: (1) the threat
system—"Give it to me or I'll kill you" or today's more sophisticated version: "How much will you pay me to stop harming or annoying you?" . . . (2) the exchange system, that narrow waveband of
market transactions with which economics concerns itself, and (3)
the integrative system, i.e., the transactions based on the love, sharing, and altruism of which human beings are capable in spite of the
denial of these phenomena in economic theory.

KENNETH BOULDING. *The Economics of the Coming Spaceship Earth*,
1966. As paraphrased by Hazel Henderson, *The Politics of the Solar
Age: Alternatives to Economics*, 7, 1981

As the economy gets better, everything else gets worse.

ART BUCHWALD (1925–). Citing as an example, "The more cars that are
sold, the bigger the pollution and traffic problems you have."
In "Buchwald's Law," *Time*, 31 January 1972

Our future prosperity depends more on capital spending than
spending in the capitol.

THE CIT GROUP. Headline in ad. In *New York Times*, 15 September
1993

Economics is the science of phenomena due to one love and one
aversion—gain and labor.

JOHN DEWEY (1859–1952). *Human Nature and Conduct:
An Introduction to Social Psychology*, 2.5, 1922

Production is not the application of tools to materials. It is the
application of logic to work.

PETER F. DRUCKER (1909–). *Management: Tasks, Responsibilities,
Practices*, 15, 1974, abr., 1977

Fundamentally, there are only two ways of coordinating the economic activities of millions. One is central direction involving the
use of coercion—the technique of the army and of the modern
totalitarian state. The other is voluntary cooperation of individuals—the technique of the market place.

MILTON FRIEDMAN (1912–). *Capitalism and Freedom*, 1, 1962

In economics, as in anatomy, the whole is much more than the
sum of the parts.

JOHN KENNETH GALBRAITH (1908–). Foreword (1) to *Economics and
the Public Purpose*, 1973

Economics is not primarily an expository science; it also serves the
controlling economic interest.

JOHN KENNETH GALBRAITH (1908–). Foreword (2) to *Economics and
the Public Purpose*, 1973

It is not mass production but only production by the masses that
can do the trick.

MOHANDAS K. GANDHI (1869–1948). Quoted by E. F. Schumacher, "
A Culture of Poverty." In Dom Moraes, ed., *Voices for Life: Reflections
on the Human Condition*, 1975

The most basic law of economics, namely that one cannot get
something for nothing.

R. F. HARROD (1900–1978). *Towards a Dynamic Economics: Some
Recent Developments of Economic Theory and Their Application to
Policy*, 2, 1948

Economics is our contemporary theology, regardless of how we
spend Sunday.

JAMES HILLMAN. "Opening the Book," *Kinds of Power: A Guide to Its
Intelligent Uses*, 1995

[I am not] suggesting scrapping our unjust, sacrilegious, undemo-
cratic, unfair economic system. What bothers me is that I still think
it's the best of all possible systems.

ARTHUR HOPPE (1925–). Closing words, "O. J.—Rush to Injustice,"
San Francisco Chronicle, 2 October 1995

Economics: The science of the production, distribution and use of
wealth, best understood by college professors on half rations.

ELBERT HUBBARD (1856–1915). *The Roycroft Dictionary Concocted by
Ali Baba and the Bunch on Rainy Days*, p. 46, 1914

Men at large still live as they always have lived, under a pain-and-
fear economy—for those of us who live in an ease-economy are
but an island in the stormy ocean.

WILLIAM JAMES (1842–1910). *The Moral Equivalent of War* (pamphlet),
1910

[The Depression] is not a crisis of poverty, but a crisis of abundance. It is not the harshness and the niggardliness of nature
which are oppressing us, but our own incompetence and wrong-
headedness which hinder us from making use of the bountifulness
of inventive science and cause us to be overwhelmed by its generous fruits.

JOHN MAYNARD KEYNES (1883–1946). "The World's Economic
Outlook" (5), *Atlantic*, May 1932

Not wholesale mechanization for the sake of power, profit, productivity, or prestige, but a mechanization measured by human
need and limited by vital norms . . . will dictate the nature of economic and social enterprises [in a One World culture]. This means
a general change from a money economy to a life economy.

LEWIS MUMFORD (1895–1990). *The Transformations of Man*, 8.6, 1956

A predominantly megatechnic economy can be kept in profitable
operation only by systematic and constant expansion. Instead of a
balanced economy, dedicated to the enhancement of life, mega-
technics demands limitless expansion on a colossal scale: a feat
that only war or mock-war—rocket building and space exploration—can supply.

LEWIS MUMFORD (1895–1990). *The Pentagon of Power: The Myth of
the Machine*, 13.1, 1970

Full employment is the foundation of a just economy. The most
urgent priority for domestic economic policy is the creation of
new jobs with adequate pay and decent working conditions. We
must make it possible as a nation for every one who is seeking a
job to find employment within a reasonable amount of time. Our
emphasis on this goal is based on the conviction that human work
has a special dignity and is a key to achieving justice in society.

NATIONAL CONFERENCE OF CATHOLIC BISHOPS. *Economic Justice for
All: Pastoral Letter on Catholic Social Teaching and the U.S. Economy*,
136, 1986

All economics is micro.

PEGGY NOONAN (1950–). *What I Saw at the Revolution: A Political Life
in the Reagan Era*, 6, 1990
See Politics: Thomas P. "Tip" O'Neill, Jr.

Expenditure rises to meet income.

> C. NORTHCOTE PARKINSON (1909–1993). Opening words, *The Law and the Profits,* 1960

New Deal: The wedding of good intentions to bad economics.

> LEO ROSTEN (1908–1997). "Political Lexicon," *New Republic,* 3 July 1935

Call a thing immoral or ugly, soul-destroying or a degradation of man, a peril to the peace of the world or to the well-being of future generations; as long as you have not shown it to be "uneconomic" you have not really questioned its right to exist, grow, and prosper.

> E. F. SCHUMACHER (1911–1977). *Small Is Beautiful: Economics as if People Mattered,* 1.3, 1973

Economic systems are not value-free columns of numbers based on rules of reason, but ways of expressing what varying societies believe is important.

> GLORIA STEINEM (1934–). "Revaluing Economics," *Moving Beyond Words,* 1994

A reasonable estimate of economic organization must allow for the fact that, unless industry is to be paralyzed by recurrent revolts on the part of outraged human nature, it must satisfy criteria which are not purely economic.

> R. H. TAWNEY (1880–1962). *Religion and the Rise of Capitalism: A Historical Study,* 5, 1926

Confidence and spending are handmaidens of an expanding economy.

> TIDE. Marketing trade journal. In Vance Packard, *The Hidden Persuaders,* 20, 1957

ECONOMISTS

See also • Business ○ Economics ○ Professionals

The big bull market is . . . going to go on forever.

Unless, of course, it doesn't. Often in economics, things that ought to go on forever, such as stock market hounds getting fatter by the day, stop going on forever. Afterward, economists tell you why; for predicting, though, they are not that great.

> RUSSELL BAKER (1925–). "Another Loophole Bananza," *New York Times,* 29 July 1997

Economists have the least influence on policy where they know the most and are most agreed; they have the most influence on policy where they know the least and disagree most vehemently.

> ALAN S. BLINDER (1945–). "Murphy's Law of Economic Policy." Introduction to *Hard Head, Soft Hearts: Tough-Minded Economics for a Just Society,* 1987

Respectable Professors of the Dismal Science.

> THOMAS CARLYLE (1795–1881). On political economists, "The Present Time," *Latter-Day Pamphlets,* 1850

The economists who are most highly regarded in their own time have almost always been those who confined themselves to abstract speculation unmarred by social purpose.

> JOHN KENNETH GALBRAITH (1908–). *A Life in Our Times: Memoirs,* 2, 1981

The experience of being disastrously wrong is salutary; no economist should be denied it, and not many are.

> JOHN KENNETH GALBRAITH (1908–). *A Life in Our Times: Memoirs,* 11, 1981

An economist is an expert who will know tomorrow why the things he predicted yesterday didn't happen today.

> LAURENCE J. PETER (1919–1990)

Economic forecasters exist to make astrologers look good.

> ROBERT B. REICH (1946–). Speech before the World Affairs Council, San Francisco, 3 April 1991

The purpose of studying economics is not to acquire a set of ready-made answers to economic questions, but to learn how to avoid being deceived by economists.

> JOAN ROBINSON (1903–1983). In John Kenneth Galbraith, *Economics and the Public Purpose,* 2 (epigraph), 1973

I don't care who writes a nation's laws—or crafts its advanced treaties—if I can write its economics textbooks.

> PAUL A. SAMUELSON (1915–). Author of *Economics: An Introductory Analysis,* 1948, the largest selling economics textbook in history. In Sylvia Nasar, "Hard Act to Follow? Here Goes" (epigraph), *New York Times,* 14 March 1995
>
> See Music: Andrew Fletcher of Saltoun ○ Superstition: Mark Twain

Economists are about as useful as astrologers in predicting the future (and, like astrologers, they never let failure on one occasion diminish certitude on the next).

> ARTHUR M. SCHLESINGER, JR. (1917–). "A Report Clinton Card, So Far," *New York Times,* 11 April 1993

If all economists were laid end to end, they would not reach a conclusion.

> GEORGE BERNARD SHAW (1856–1950). Attributed

I was in search of a one-armed economist so that the guy could never make a statement and then say, "On the other hand. . . ."

> HARRY S. TRUMAN (1884–1972). In John Greenwald, "Knitting New Notions," *Time,* 30 January 1989

EDITORS

See also • Books ○ Journalists ○ Media ○ News ○ Newspapers ○ Publishers: [especially] Mark Twain ○ Writers

Most editors are failed writers—but so are most writers.

> T. S. ELIOT (1888–1965). In Robert Giroux, *The Education of an Editor,* p. 22, 1982

The discovery of new talent is the greatest reward that can come from [publishing house] editorial work.

It is, in the end, the best reason for being an editor.

> ROBERT GIROUX. Closing words, *The Education of an Editor,* 1982

Editor: A person employed on a newspaper, whose business it is to separate the wheat from the chaff, and to see that the chaff is printed.

> ELBERT HUBBARD (1856–1915). *The Roycroft Dictionary Concocted by Ali Baba and the Bunch on Rainy Days,* p. 46, 1914

Perhaps an editor might begin a reformation in some such way as this. Divide his paper into 4 chapters, heading the 1st, Truths. 2d, Probabilities. 3d, Possibilities. 4th, Lies.

THOMAS JEFFERSON (1743–1826). Letter to John Norvell, 14 June 1807

Writing is adding; editing is subtracting.

MICHAEL LARSEN (1941–). Personal communication, 11 August 1994

There is no such thing in America as an independent press, unless it is in the country towns. . . .

I am paid $150 a week for keeping my honest opinions out of the paper I am connected with—others of you are paid similar salaries for similar things—and any of you who would be so foolish as to write his honest opinions would be out on the streets looking for another job. . . .

We are the tools and vassals of the rich men behind the scenes. We are the jumping jacks; they pull the strings and we dance. Our talents, our possibilities and our lives are all the property of other men. We are intellectual prostitutes.

JOHN SWINTON (1829–1901). *New York Sun* editor. Remarks at a dinner given in his honor by colleagues, 12 April 1893. In Upton Sinclair, ed., *The Cry for Justice: An Anthology of the Literature of Social Protest,* 15, 1915

Probably no country was ever ruled by so mean a class of tyrants as, with a few noble exceptions, are the editors of the periodical press in this country. And as they live and rule only by their servility, and appealing to the worse, and not the better, nature of man, the people who read them are in the condition of the dog that returns to his vomit.

HENRY DAVID THOREAU (1817–1862). "Slavery in Massachusetts," speech, Farmingham, 4 July 1854

An editor is a person who knows more about writing than writers do but who has escaped the terrible desire to write.

E. B. WHITE (1899–1985). Letter to Shirley Wiley, 30 March 1954. In *Letters of E. B. White,* ed. Dorothy Lobrano Guth, 1976

EDUCATION

See also • Books ○ Brainwashing ○ Children ○ Children's Learning ○ College ○ Culture ○ Doubt: Wilson Mizner ○ Genius: Benjamin Franklin ○ History ○ Indoctrination ○ Learning (Process) ○ Parents ○ Propaganda ○ Reading ○ Scholars ○ School: [especially] Earl Warren ○ Self-Realization (Becoming) ○ Teachers ○ University ○ Values

Nothing in education is so astonishing as the amount of ignorance it accumulates in the form of inert facts.

HENRY ADAMS (1838–1913). *The Education of Henry Adams,* 25, 1907

Education, *n.* That which discloses to the wise and disguises from the foolish their lack of understanding.

AMBROSE BIERCE (1842–1914). *The Devil's Dictionary,* p. 34, 1911, Dover edition, 1958

If you think education is expensive, try ignorance!

DEREK BOK (1930–). Harvard University president. In Ann Landers, syndicated column, 26 March 1978

Education is learning what you didn't even know you didn't know.

DANIEL J. BOORSTIN (1914–). "A Case of Hypochondria," *Newsweek,* 6 July 1970

Education should be constructed on two bases: morality and prudence. Morality in order to assist virtue, and prudence in order to defend you against the vices of others. In tipping the scales toward morality, you merely produce dupes and martyrs. In tipping it the other way, you produce egotistical schemers.

CHAMFORT (1741–1794). *Maxims and Thoughts,* 5, 1796, tr. W. S. Merwin, 1984

The main failure of education is that it has not prepared people to comprehend matters concerning human destiny.

NORMAN COUSINS (1912–1990). "Editor's Odyssey: Gleanings from Articles and Editorials by N.C.," ed. Susan Schiefelbein, *Saturday Review,* 15 April 1978

Children have to be educated, but they have also to be left to educate themselves.

ERNEST DIMNET. *The Art of Thinking,* 2.5, 1928

Wherever is found what is called a paternal government was found a State education. It had been discovered that the best way to insure implicit obedience [is] to commence tyranny in the nursery.

BENJAMIN DISRAELI (1804–1881). House of Commons speech, 15 June 1874

How is it that little children are so intelligent and men so stupid? It must be education that does it.

ALEXANDRE DUMAS (1824–1895). In L. Treich, *L'Esprit Francais,* 1947

Education is the drawing out [of] the Soul.

RALPH WALDO EMERSON (1803–1882). Journal, 13 September 1831

The alternations of speaking and hearing make our education.

RALPH WALDO EMERSON (1803–1882). Journal, 20 October 1835

Education is the ability to listen to almost anything without losing your temper or your self-confidence.

ROBERT FROST (1874–1963). In "Quotable Quotes," *Reader's Digest,* April 1960

In education the life of the mind proceeds gradually from scientific experiments to intellectual theories, to spiritual feeling, and then to God.

KAHLIL GIBRAN (1883–1931). "Sayings," *Spiritual Sayings of Kahlil Gibran,* tr. Anthony R. Ferris, 1962

Anyone who has passed through the regular gradations of a classical education, and is not made a fool by it, may consider himself as having had a very narrow escape.

WILLIAM HAZLITT (1778–1830). "On the Ignorance of the Learned," *Table Talk,* 1822

We need education in the obvious more than investigation of the obscure.

OLIVER WENDELL HOLMES, JR. (1841–1935). "Law and the Court," speech at a dinner of the Harvard Law School Association of New York, 15 February 1913

There is no end to education. We are all in the Kindergarten of God.

ELBERT HUBBARD (1856–1915). *The Note Book of Elbert Hubbard,* p. 194, comp. Elbert Hubbard II, 1927

The aim of education is the knowledge not of facts but of values.

> DEAN WILLIAM RALPH INGE (1860–1954). "The Training of the
> Reason." In A. C. Benson, ed., *Cambridge Essays on Education,* 1918

Education begins by teaching children to read and ends by making most of them hate reading.

> HOLBROOK JACKSON (1874–1948). *Maxims of Books and Reading,*
> 11, 1934

Education should be a lifelong process, the formal period serving as a foundation on which life's structure may rest and rise.

> ROBERT H. JACKSON (1892–954). Supreme Court associate justice. In
> Eugene C. Gerhart, *America's Advocate: Robert H. Jackson,* 24, 1958

Education should be gentle and stern, not cold and lax.

> JOSEPH JOUBERT (1754–1824). *Pensées,* 1838, tr. H. P. Collins, 1928

At present we educate people only up to the point where they can earn a living and marry; then education ceases altogether, as though a complete mental outfit had been acquired. . . . Vast numbers of men and women thus spend their entire lives in complete ignorance of the most important things.

> CARL G. JUNG (1875–1961). "Child Development and Education," 1923,
> *The Development of Personality,* tr. R. F. C. Hull, 1954

Intelligence plus character—that is the goal of true education.

> MARTIN LUTHER KING, JR. (1929–1968). Speech, Washington, 26 March
> 1964

Nine Parts of ten are what they are, good or evil, useful or not, by their Education.

> JOHN LOCKE (1632–1704). *Some Thoughts Concerning Education,*
> 1, 1693

Virtue . . . is the hard and valuable Part to be aim'd at in Education.

> JOHN LOCKE (1632–1704). *Some Thoughts Concerning Education,* |
> 70, 1693

The task of education is to make the individual so firm and sure that, as a whole being, he can no longer be diverted from his path.

> FRIEDRICH NIETZSCHE (1844–1900). *Human, All Too Human,* 224, 1878,
> tr. Marion Faber, 1984

Education must conform to the natural process of mental evolution—that there is a certain sequence in which the faculties spontaneously develop, and a certain kind of knowledge which each requires during its development.

> JOHANN HEINRICH PESTALOZZI (1746–1827). As paraphrased by
> Herbert Spencer, *Education: Intellectual, Moral, and Physical,* 2, 1860

Not art, not books, but life itself is the true basis of . . . education.

> JOHANN HEINRICH PESTALOZZI (1746–1827). *The Education of Man:
> Aphorisms,* 4, tr. Heinz and Ruth Norden, 1951

Do not use compulsion, but let early education be rather a sort of amusement.

> PLATO (427?–347 B.C.). *The Republic,* 7.536-537, tr. Benjamin Jowett, 1894

'Tis Education forms the common mind,
Just as the Twig is bent, the Tree's inclin'd.

> ALEXANDER POPE (1688–1744). *Moral Essays,* 1.101, 1731–1735

To educate a person in mind and not in morals is to educate a menace to society.

> THEODORE ROOSEVELT (1858–1919). In Stephen Bates, "A Textbook of
> Virtues," *New York Times,* 8 January 1995

Almost all education has a political motive: It aims at strengthening some group, national or religious or even social, in the competition with other groups. It is this motive, in the main, which determines the subjects taught, the knowledge offered and the knowledge withheld, and also decides what mental habits the pupils are expected to acquire. Hardly anything is done to foster the inward growth of mind and spirit; in fact, those who have had most education are very often atrophied in their mental and spiritual life.

> BERTRAND RUSSELL (1872–1970). *Principles of Social Reconstruction,*
> 5, 1916

If the object [of education] were to make pupils think, rather than to make them accept certain conclusions, education would be conducted quite differently; there would be less . . . instruction and more discussion.

> BERTRAND RUSSELL (1872–1970). *Principles of Social Reconstruction,*
> 5, 1916

Education should have two objects: first, to give definite knowledge, reading and writing, language and mathematics, and so on; secondly, to create those mental habits which will enable people to acquire knowledge and form sound judgments for themselves.

> BERTRAND RUSSELL (1872–1970). *Sceptical Essays,* 12, 1928

Education cannot be *for* students in any authentic way, if it is not *of* and *by* them.

> WILLIAM H. SCHUBERT (1944–). John Dewey Society president. "The
> Activist Library: A Symposium," *Nation,* 21 September 1992

My own education operated by a succession of eye-openers each involving the repudiation of some previously held belief.

> GEORGE BERNARD SHAW (1856–1950). *Everybody's Political What's
> What?* 19, 1944

To me, education is a leading out of what is already there in the pupil's soul. To Miss Mackay, it is a putting in of something that is not there, and that is not what I call education, I call it intrusion.

> MURIEL SPARK (1918–). *The Prime of Miss Jean Brodie,* 2, 1961

Education . . . is closely associated with change, is its pioneer, is the never-sleeping agent of revolution, is always fitting men for higher things and unfitting them for things as they are. Therefore, between institutions whose very existence depends upon man continuing what he is and true education, which is one of the instruments for making him something other than he is, there must always be enmity.

> HERBERT SPENCER (1820–1903). *Social Statics,* 3.26.7, 1851

[Education of the individual shall] progress from the simple to the complex, from the concrete to the abstract, from the empirical to the rational, . . . shall be as much as possible a process of self-evolution, and . . . shall be pleasurable.

> HERBERT SPENCER (1820–1903). *Education: Intellectual, Moral, and
> Physical,* 2, 1860

Life seems to take a zigzag course, instead of following a direct line toward what appears to be its goal. Growth too often proceeds by a series of maladjustments and corrections, by groping in the dark rather than by moving straight onward. The highest function of education is to conserve the life forces, to produce the best results with the least expenditure of energy.

> EDWIN DILLER STARBUCK (1866–1947). *The Psychology of Religion: An Empirical Study of the Growth of Religious Consciousness,* 31, 1899

Skill in education consists in taking off the newness of the next step in growth, by drawing those instincts into activity in an earlier stage, which are to function more strongly in a later [one].

> EDWIN DILLER STARBUCK (1866–1947). *The Psychology of Religion: An Empirical Study of the Growth of Religious Consciousness,* 31, 1899

There is going to be a race between mass self-education and mass self-destruction.

> ARNOLD J. TOYNBEE (1889–1975). "Conditions of Survival," *Saturday Review,* 29 August 1964
>
> See History: H. G. Wells (2)

The aim of all education is, or should be, to teach people to educate themselves.

> ARNOLD J. TOYNBEE (1889–1975). *Surviving the Future,* 5, 1971
>
> See University: John Updike

Lifelong part-time education is the surest way of raising the intellectual and moral level of the masses.

> ARNOLD J. TOYNBEE (1889–1975). *The Toynbee-Ikeda Dialogue: Man Himself Must Choose,* 3, 1976

Education consists mainly in what we have unlearned.

> MARK TWAIN (1835–1910). 4 July 1898, *Mark Twain's Notebook,* ed. Albert Bigelow Paine, 1935

Education is the acquisition of the art of the utilization of knowledge.

> ALFRED NORTH WHITEHEAD (1861–1947). *The Aims of Education and Other Essays,* 1, 1929

The secret of success [in education] is pace, and the secret of pace is concentration. But, in respect to precise knowledge, the watchword is pace, pace, pace. Get your knowledge quickly, and then use it. If you can use it, you will retain it.

> ALFRED NORTH WHITEHEAD (1861–1947). *The Aims of Education and Other Essays,* 3, 1929

Education is the guidance of the individual towards a comprehension of the art of life; and by the art of life I mean the most complete achievement of varied activity expressing the potentialities of that living creature in the face of its actual environment.

> ALFRED NORTH WHITEHEAD (1861–1947). *The Aims of Education and Other Essays,* 3, 1929

✦

Education should consist of a series of enchantments, each raising the individual to a higher level of awareness, understanding, and kinship with all living things.

> ANONYMOUS

EFFECT

See • Cause & Effect

EFFORT

See also • Children's Learning: Bertrand Russell ∘ Courage: Lewis Mumford ∘ Excellence ∘ Industry ∘ Paradoxes: Aldous Huxley (2) ∘ Persistence ∘ Presidents: Lyndon B. Johnson (2), Harry S. Truman (2) ∘ Prudence: Rules ∘ Resolution ∘ Struggle ∘ Success: [especially] T. H. Palmer, Anonymous (2) ∘ Work

[John Wooden] taught us that doing the best you are capable of is victory enough.

> KAREEM ABDUL-JABBAR (1947–) (with MIGNON McCARTHY). Referring to his basketball coach at the University of California, Los Angeles (UCLA), "Saturday December 3" (1988), *Kareem,* 3, 1990

As in a game ov cards, so in the game ov life, we must play what is dealt tew us, and the glory consists, not so mutch in winning, as in playing a poor hand well.

> JOSH BILLINGS (1818–1885). "Ods and Ens," *Everybody's Friend, or; Josh Billing's Encyclopedia and Proverbial Philosophy of Wit and Humor,* 1874

The greatest secret of good work whether in music, literature or painting lies in not attempting too much.

> SAMUEL BUTLER (1835–1902). *The Note-Books of Samuel Butler,* 7, ed. Henry Festing Jones, 1907

Whenever we do what we can, we immediately can do more.

> JAMES FREEMAN CLARKE (1810–1888). *Self-Culture: Physical, Intellectual, Moral,* and Spiritual, 21, 1880

Do not think of the fruit of action.
Fare forward.

> T. S. ELIOT (1888–1965). "The Dry Salvages" (3), *Four Quartets,* 1943
>
> See Progress: Eliot

For us, there is only the trying. The rest is not our business.

> T. S. ELIOT (1888–1965). "East Coker" (5), *Four Quartets,* 1943

He that will have the Kernel must crack the Shell.

> THOMAS FULLER (1654–1734). Comp., *Gnomologia: Adages and Proverbs,* 2348, 1732

He that would have the Fruit must climb the Tree.

> THOMAS FULLER (1654–1734). Comp., *Gnomologia: Adages and Proverbs,* 2366, 1732

Satisfaction lies in the effort, not in the attainment. Full effort is full victory.

> MOHANDAS K. GANDHI (1869–1948). In *Young India,* 9 March 1922

Do not undertake anything beyond your capacity and at the same time do not harbor the wish to do less than you can. One who takes up tasks beyond his powers is proud and attached. On the other hand, one who does less than he can is a thief.

> MOHANDAS K. GANDHI (1869–1948). Letter to Narandas Gandhi, 10 July 1932

Do thou thy best, and leave to God the rest.

> JAMES HOWELL (1593–1666). Comp., "Divers Centuries of New Sayings" (p. 3), *Paroimiographia: Proverbs, or Old Sayed Sawes & Adages in English . . . Italian, French and Spanish,* 1659

Nothing but your best is good enough.

ELBERT HUBBARD (1856–1915). *The Note Book of Elbert Hubbard,* p. 127, comp. Elbert Hubbard II, 1927

Every occupation, of whatever nature, is more efficiently performed if pursued for its own sake alone, rather than for the results to which it leads.

WILHELM von HUMBOLDT (1767–1835). *The Limits of State Action,* 3, 1854, ed. J. W. Burrow, 1969

You can't always get what you want.
But if you try sometimes,
You just might find
You get what you need.

MICK JAGGER (1943–) and KEITH RICHARDS (1943–). "You Can't Always Get What You Want" (song), 1969

Caesar was so energetic that he thought nothing done while anything remained to be done.

LUCAN (A.D. 39–65). *Pharsalia,* 2.657, tr. Robert Graves, 1956

The harder a man tries, the better he must hide it.

JOE McGINNISS. *The Selling of the President* 1968, 2, 1969

Rowing harder doesn't help if the boat is headed in the wrong direction.

KENICHI OHMAE. "Companyism and Do More Better," *Harvard Business Review,* January-February 1989

When it becomes necessary to do a thing, the whole heart and soul should go into the measure, or not attempt it.

THOMAS PAINE (1737–1809). *The Rights of Man,* 1, 1791

A man must live by his lights and do what little he can and do it as best he can. In this world goodness is destined to be defeated. But a man must go down fighting. That is the victory. To do anything less is to be less than a man.

WALKER PERCY (1916–1990). *The Moviegoer,* 1.5, 1961

For when the one Great Scorer comes
    To write against your name,
He marks—not that you won or lost—
    But how you played the game.

GRANTLAND RICE (1880–1954). "Alumnus Football," 1925

Do what you can, with what you have, where you are.

THEODORE ROOSEVELT (1858–1919). A favorite saying
See Good: John Wesley ○ Kindness: Scott Nearing

Play every game . . . as if your job depended on it. It just might.

CASEY STENGEL (1890?–1975). Baseball manager. *The Gospel According to C•A•S•E•Y: Casey Stengel's Inimitable, Instructional, Historical Baseball Book,* ed. Ira Berkow and Jim Kaplan, 7, 1992

I know of no more encouraging fact than the unquestionable ability of man to elevate his life by a conscious endeavor.

HENRY DAVID THOREAU (1817–1862). "Where I Lived, and What I Lived For," *Walden; or Life in the Woods,* 1854

When a man does all he can though it succeeds not well blame not him that did it.

GEORGE WASHINGTON (1732–1799). Copybook, 1748 (at age 16), *Rules of Civility & Decent Behaviour in Company and Conversation,*

#44. The rules were an amended version of Francis Hawkins's 1640 translation of *Decency of Conversation Among Men* (French Jesuit writing, 1595).

To trust altogether in the justice of our cause, without our own utmost exertions, would be tempting Providence.

GEORGE WASHINGTON (1732–1799). Letter to Gov. Jonathan Trumbull, 7 August 1776

We try often, though we fall back often. A brave delight, fit for freedom's athletes, fills these arenas, and fully satisfies, out of the action in them, irrespective of success.

WALT WHITMAN (1819–1892). *Democratic Vistas,* 1871, *Walt Whitman: Complete Poetry and Collected Prose,* ed. Justin Kaplan, p. 952, 1982

If a task once begun
Never leave it till it's done.
Be the labor great or small,
Do it well or not at all.

ANONYMOUS. "Always Finish" (complete poem). In Hazel Felleman, ed., *The Best Loved Poems of the American People,* 1936

You never know what you can do till you try.

SAYING (ENGLISH)

Every moment of every day
We do our best in every way.

SAYING

Never ask more or less of yourself than your best.

SAYING

EGOISM

See also • Conceit ○ Egotism ○ Self-Interest ○ Selfishness ○ Self-Love

That favorite subject. Myself.

JAMES BOSWELL (1740–1795). Letter to W. Johnstone Temple, 26 July 1763

He was like a cock who thought the sun had risen to hear him crow.

GEORGE ELIOT (1819–1880). *Adam Bede,* 33, 1859

All the thoughts of a turtle are turtle.

RALPH WALDO EMERSON (1803–1882). Journal, 5 September 1855

The worst egoist is the person to whom the thought has never occurred that he might be one.

SIGMUND FREUD (1856–1939). "Notebook of aphorisms," 1871 (at age 15). As cited without quotation marks by Alice Miller, foreword to *The Drama of the Gifted Child,* 1979, tr. Ruth Ward, 1981

General Peckem liked listening to himself talk, liked most of all listening to himself talk about himself.

JOSEPH HELLER (1923–). *Catch-22,* 29, 1961

Man must have something higher than himself
To think of.

HENRY WADSWORTH LONGFELLOW (1807–1882). *Michael Angelo,* 2.3, 1883

It is of great advantage that man should know his station, and not erroneously imagine that the whole Universe exists only for him.

> MOSES MAIMONIDES (A.D. 1135–1204). *The Guide for the Perplexed*, 3.12, A.D. 1190, tr. M. Friedländer, 1904

We are interested in others, when they are interested in us.

> PUBLIUS SYRUS (85–43 B.C.). *Moral Sayings*, 16, tr. Darius Lyman, Jr., 1862

Each man is the most important thing in the world to himself.

> ALEXANDER SMITH (1830–1867). *Dreamthorp*, 8, 1863

Nothing is more to me than myself!

> MAX STIRNER (1806–1856). Preface (closing words) to *The Ego and His Own*, tr. Stephen T. Byington, 1907, and ed. John Carroll, 1971

I should not talk so much about myself if there were anybody else whom I knew as well.

> HENRY DAVID THOREAU (1817–1862). "Economy," *Walden; or Life in the Woods*, 1854

The whole theory of the universe is directed unerringly to one single individual—namely to You.

> WALT WHITMAN (1819–1892). "By Blue Ontario's Shore" (15), 1856, *Leaves of Grass*, 1855–1892

People wrapped up in themselves make very small packages.

> ANONYMOUS

EGOMANIA: FIRST PERSON

See also • Egotism ○ Egotism: First Person ○ Humility: First Person ○ Paranoia

I was born in this Iron Age to restore the Age of Gold. I am the man for whom Heaven has reserved the most dangerous and glorious adventures.

> CERVANTES (1547–1616). *Don Quixote*, 1.3.6, 1615, tr. Peter Anthony Motteux and John Ozell, 1743

When I want to know what France thinks, I ask myself.

> CHARLES de GAULLE (1890–1970). In "France: Down from Olympus," *Time*, 17 December 1965

I alone have confounded twenty centuries of political imbecility; and it is to me alone that present and future generations will look for the origin of their immense happiness.

> CHARLES FOURIER (1772–1837). French reformer. In Robert L. Heilbroner, *The Worldly Philosophers: The Lives, Times, and Ideas of the Great Economic Thinkers*, 5th ed., 5, 1980 (1953)

We are certainly getting ahead; if I am Moses, then you are Joshua and will take possession of the promised land of psychiatry, which I shall only be able to glimpse from afar.

> SIGMUND FREUD (1856–1939). Letter to Carl G. Jung, 17 January 1909, tr. Ralph Manheim, 1974

I may say with Christ that not only do I teach truth, but that I am myself truth.

> GEORG HEGEL (1770–1831). Opening words of a lecture. In Carl von Seidlitz, *Dr. Arthur Schopenhauer*, 1872

I have achieved everything that I set out to do, and have thus become perhaps the greatest German in history.

> ADOLF HITLER (1889–1945). Immediately before Germany's annexation of Austria, 11 February 1938. In Alan Bullock, *Hitler: A Study in Tyranny*, rev. ed., 8.3, 1960 (1953)

Air Force corporal (pointing to the presidential helicopter): This is your helicopter, sir.
Johnson: They're all my helicopters, son.

> LYNDON B. JOHNSON (1908–1973). Format adapted. In David Halberstam, *The Best and the Brightest*, 20, 1972

Ludwig Erhard (German chancellor, during a visit to the LBJ Ranch in Texas): I understand you were born in a log cabin.
Johnson: No, no, no! You have me confused with Abe Lincoln. I was born in a manger.

> LYNDON B. JOHNSON (1908–1973). Attributed. Format adapted. In Robert Dallek, *Lyndon Baines Johnson*, televised lecture series on recent American Presidents, C-SPAN, 16 April 1995

I am the State!

> LOUIS XIV (1643–1715). French king. Attributed, 1655

You may also dispense with comparing me to God. I am willing to believe that you wrote this without thinking; the phrase is so singularly lacking in respect to me.

> NAPOLEON (1769–1821). Letter to Adm. Decrès, 22 May 1808, *The Mind of Napoleon: A Selection from His Written and Spoken Words*, 330, ed. J. Christopher Herold, 1955

Since the old God is abolished, I am prepared *to rule the world*—

> FRIEDRICH NIETZSCHE, (1844–1900). Appendix ("Variants from Nietzsche's Drafts") to *Ecce Homo, 1908*, tr. Walter Kaufmann, 1969

The representative of the people—that is Me. For I, I alone, am right.

> PIERRE-JOSEPH PROUDHON (1809–1865). In Hal Draper, "A Note on the Father of Anarchism," *New Politics*, Winter 1969

I have resolved on an enterprise which has no precedent, and which, once complete, will have no imitator. My purpose is to display to my kind a portrait in every way true to nature, and the man I shall portray will be myself.

> ROUSSEAU (1712–1778). Opening words, *Confessions*, 1 (1712–1719), 1781, tr. J. M. Cohen, 1953

With the single exception of Homer, there is no eminent writer, not even Sir Walter Scott, whom I can despise so entirely as I despise Shakespeare when I measure my mind against his.

> GEORGE BERNARD SHAW (1856–1950). "Blaming the Bard," 1896, *Dramatic Opinions and Essays*, vol. 2, 1907

Isn't egomania always the precondition of all creative work? I have found little to dispel that notion.

> TENNESSEE WILLIAMS (1911–1983). *Memoirs*, 9, 1975

Why has Jesus Christ so far not succeeded in inducing the world to follow His teachings in [matters of world peace]? It is because He taught the ideal without devising any practical means of attaining it. That is why I am proposing a practical scheme to carry out His aims.

WOODROW WILSON (1856–1924). On his own proposals for the League of Nations, 1919. In David Lloyd George, *Memoirs of the Peace Conference,* 1.4, 1939

EGOTISM

See also • Conceit ○ Confidence ○ Egoism ○ Egomania: First Person ○ Egotism: First Person ○ Envy ○ Humility ○ Malice ○ Modesty ○ Pride ○ Self-Love ○ Vanity

That's it, baby, when you got it, flaunt it.

MEL BROOKS (1926–). *The Producers* (film), 1968

It ain't bragging if you can do it.

DIZZY DEAN (1911–1974). Baseball player

Take egotism out, and you would castrate the benefactors.

RALPH WALDO EMERSON (1803–1882). Journal, June 1863

Those who have it don't need to flaunt it.

MALCOLM S. FORBES (1919–1990). "Simple Truths," *The Sayings of Chairman Malcolm,* 1978

Egotism: the art of seeing in yourself what others cannot see.

GEORGE HIGGINS (1939–). Clergyman. In *Suburban People News,* 2 March 1986

We credit ourselves for our successes; we blame others for our faults.

ELBERT HUBBARD (1856–1915). *The Philosophy of Elbert Hubbard,* p. 150, comp. Elbert Hubbard II, 1930

If others could only see us as we think we are.

KIN HUBBARD (1868–1930). *Abe Martin's Back Country Sayings,* unpaged, 1917

Ther's one thing we ought t' let folks find out for 'emselves, and that's how great we are.

KIN HUBBARD (1868–1930). *Abe Martin: Hoss Sense and Nonsense,* p. 77, 1926

There's a world of difference between a strong ego which is essential, and a large ego—which can be destructive. The guy with a strong ego knows his own strength. He's confident. . . .

But the guy with a large ego is always looking for recognition. He constantly needs to be patted on the back.

LEE IACOCCA (1924–). *Iacocca: An Autobiography,* 5, 1984

[Lyndon B. Johnson] handed out plastic busts of himself to world leaders in three sizes (small, medium, and large), depending on their stature.

WALTER ISAACSON (1952–) and EVAN THOMAS (1951–). *The Wise Men: Six Friends and the World They Made,* 22, 1986

The more the ego is allowed to expand, the more powerful the temptation to reach for even larger expansion.

GEORGE F. KENNAN (1904–). *Around the Cragged Hill: A Personal and Political Philosophy,* 1, 1993

Whenever the world throws rose petals at you, which thrill and seduce the ego, beware.

ANNE LAMOTT (1954–). *Bird by Bird: Some Instructions on Writing and Life,* 4 ("Publication"), 1995

Your boasting will mean that you have failed.

LAO-TZU (6th cent. B.C.). *The Way of Life,* 24, tr. R. B. Blakney, 1955

We always like those who admire us, but not always those we admire.

LA ROCHEFOUCAULD (1613–1680). *Maxims,* 294, 1665, tr. Leonard Tancock, 1959

Perhaps the most valuable asset that any man can have in this world is a naturally superior air, a talent for sniffishness and reserve. The generality of men are always greatly impressed by it, and accept it freely as a proof of genuine merit. One need but disdain them to gain their respect.

H. L. MENCKEN (1880–1956). "Types of Men: The King," *Prejudices: Third Series,* 1922

There are two kinds of egotists: Those who admit it and the rest of us.

LAURENCE J. PETER (1919–1990). Comp., *Peter's Quotations: Ideas for Our Time,* p. 166, 1977

None so Empty as those who are Full of *themselves.*

BENJAMIN WHICHCOTE (1609–1683). *Moral and Religious Aphorisms,* 987, 1753

EGOTISM: FIRST PERSON

See also • Conceit ○ Confidence: First Person ○ Egomania: First Person ○ Egotism ○ Humility: First Person

My only regret in the theater is that I could never sit out front and watch me.

JOHN BARRYMORE (1882–1942). In Eddie Cantor, *The Way I See It,* 2, 1959

O fortunate Roman State, born in my great Consulate.

CICERO (106–43 B.C.). In Juvenal (A.D. 60?–127?). *Satires,* 10.123, tr. Peter Green, 1967

I have never done anything mean or malicious and cannot trace any temptation to do so, so I am not in the least proud of it. . . .

Why I—and incidentally my six adult children also—have to be thoroughly decent human beings is quite incomprehensible to me.

SIGMUND FREUD (1856–1939). Letter to James Putnam, 1915. In Ernest Jones, *The Life and Work of Sigmund Freud,* 25, 1953–1957, abr. 1961

Perhaps no human being was ever more perfectly exempt from the taint of malevolence, vanity, or falsehood.

EDWARD GIBBON (1737–1794). On himself, *Memoirs of My Life and Writings,* p. 102, 1796, Alex. Murray edition, 1869

You've no idea what a poor opinion I have of myself — and how little I deserve it.

W. S. GILBERT (1836–1911). *Ruddigore* (opera), 1, 1887

My great virtue is that I have no vanity. People criticize me, but when they meet me nobody can help liking me.

LIBERACE (1919–1987). In Dorothy Kilgallen, *New York Journal-American,* 19 June 1956

I looked around at the little fishes present and said, "I'm the Kingfish."

HUEY LONG (1893–1935). Louisiana governor. In Arthur M. Schlesinger, Jr., *The Age of Roosevelt: The Politics of Upheaval,* 4.5, 1960

When I was a child, my mother said to me, "If you become a soldier, you'll be a general. If you become a monk, you'll end up as the Pope." Instead, I became a painter and wound up as Picasso.

PABLO PICASSO (1881–1973)

I would have been bored silly if I hadn't been there myself.

GEORGE BERNARD SHAW (1856–1950). On a social event he had attended. In Herb Caen, column, *San Francisco Chronicle,* 10 June 1993

My mother brought me up to a genius, and she was one of the most successful women I've ever known.

PRESTON STURGES (1898–1959). Film maker. 1940s

If I only had a little humility, I would be perfect.

TED TURNER (1938–). Tongue-in-cheek remark. In Steve Cady, "A Brash Captain Courageous," *New York Times,* 19 September 1977

It was a damned nice thing. I do believe if I had not been there, we should not have won.

DUKE OF WELLINGTON (1769–1852). Referring to the Battle of Waterloo (Belgium). In Bertrand Russell, "How to Read and Understand History," *Understanding History, And Other Essays,* 1957

Early in life I had to choose between honest arrogance and hypocritical humility. I chose honest arrogance and have seen no occasion to change.

FRANK LLOYD WRIGHT (1867–1959). Recalled on his death, 9 April 1959

ELECTIONS

See also • Campaigns ○ Campaign Slogans ○ Democracy ○ Democracy, Anti-: Gore Vidal ○ Lobbies ○ Politics ○ Presidents ○ Public Opinion Polls: Anonymous (3) ○ Voting

Our people are slow to learn the wisdom of sending character instead of talent to Congress.

RALPH WALDO EMERSON (1803–1882). Journal, 8 May 1844

The salvation of America and of the human race depends on the next Election, if we believe the newspapers.

RALPH WALDO EMERSON (1803–1882). Journal, October 1848

Elections give the illusion of freedom but are in fact a game among the powers that be—this is why we talk of "formal democracy": instead of drawing forth the best energies of a people, this legal institution hands actual control to very different forces, turning democracy into another form of oligarchy and dictatorship.

KARL JASPERS (1883–1969). *The Future of Mankind,* 17, 1958, tr. E. B. Ashton, 1961

While the President is a million votes ahead in the popular vote, when the country vote comes in Mr. Truman will be defeated by an overwhelming majority.

H. V. KALTENBORN (1878–1965). Radio news newscaster. Reporting early presidential election returns (the next morning Pres. Truman's victory was announced), NBC, 2 November 1948. In Harry S. Truman, after-dinner remarks to presidential electors, 19 January 1949

The Many can elect after the Few have nominated.

WALTER LIPPMANN (1889–1974). *Public Opinion,* 14.6, 1922

One might say that a nation is politically stable when nothing of radical consequence is determined by its elections.

WALTER LIPPMANN (1889–1974). *The Phantom Public: A Sequel to "Public Opinion,"* 12.1, 1930 (1925)

More men have been elected between Sundown and Sunup than ever were elected between Sunup and Sundown.

WILL ROGERS (1879–1935). "Mr. Ford and Other Political Self-Starters," *The Illiterate Digest,* 1924

Whose side is God on in the 1992 presidential race? His side.

WILLIAM SAFIRE (1929–). "God Bless Us," *New York Times,* 27 August 1992

In New Zealand [1972], the vacuity of mainstream politics prompted one protester to change his name to Mickey Mouse and enter himself as a candidate. So many others did likewise—adopting names like Alice in Wonderland—that Parliament rushed through a law banning anyone from running for office if he or she had legally changed a name within six months prior to an election.

ALVIN TOFFLER (1928–). *The Third Wave,* 27, 1980

Says [Theodore] Becker, "Between 50 and 60 percent of the American Congress should be chosen at random from the American people in much the same way they are pressed into military service through drafts when they are deemed necessary." Startling as the suggestion is at first blush, it forces us to consider seriously whether randomly chosen representatives would (or could) do worse than those chosen through today's methods.

ALVIN TOFFLER (1928–). *The Third Wave,* 28, 1980

The people have spoken—the bastards!

DICK TUCK. After losing his campaign for the California state legislature. In *Playboy,* February 1974

I know nothing grander, better exercise, better digestion, more positive proof of the past, the triumphant result of faith in human kind, than a well-contested American national election.

WALT WHITMAN (1819–1892). *Democratic Vistas,* 1871, *Walt Whitman: Complete Poetry and Collected Prose,* ed. Justin Kaplan, p. 954, 1982

The only thing you can say about the 1970 elections is that the Democrats picked up nine seats in the House and the Republicans one and a half senators. If you wonder how there can be a half-senator, you haven't met some of those fellows.

TOM WICKER (1926–). "The Politics Before Us," *New York Review of Books,* 11 February 1971

ELOQUENCE

See also • Oratory: [especially] Publius Syrus ○ Public Speaking ○ Speaking ○ Talking ○ Words

Eloquence may exist without a proportionable degree of wisdom.

EDMUND BURKE (1729–1797). *Reflections on the Revolution in France,* p. 278, 1790, Pelican Books edition, 1968

I grow intoxicated with my own eloquence.

BENJAMIN DISRAELI (1804–1881). *Contarini Fleming: A Psychological Autobiography,* 1.7, 1832

Eloquence is the power to translate a truth into language perfectly intelligible to the person to whom you speak.

RALPH WALDO EMERSON (1803–1882). "Eloquence," *Letters and Social Aims,* 1876

Tone of voice, look, and manner can prove no less eloquent than choice of words.

LA ROCHEFOUCAULD (1613–1680). *Maxims,* 249, 1665, tr. Louis Kronenberger, 1959

The finest eloquence is that which gets things done and the worst is that which delays them.

DAVID LLOYD GEORGE (1863–1945). Speech at the Paris Peace Conference, 18 January 1919

Simple speech is the best and truest eloquence.

MARTIN LUTHER (1483–1546). *Table Talk,* 1566, tr. Preserved Smith and Herbert P. Gallinger, 1915

The eloquence that diverts us to itself harms its content.

MONTAIGNE (1533–1592). "Of the Education of Children," *Essays,* 1588, tr. Donald M. Frame, 1958

Eloquence was never so prized as when it had ceased to serve any real need, merely concealing the fact that great public issues were no longer being debated.

HERBERT J. MULLER (1890–1967). On ancient Rome, *The Uses of the Past: Profiles of Former Societies,* 7.2, 1952

Continuous eloquence wearies.

BLAISE PASCAL (1623–1662). *Pensées,* 355, 1670, tr. William F. Trotter, 1931

You are eloquent enough if truth speaks through you.

PUBLIUS SYRUS (85–43 B.C.). *Moral Sayings,* 861, tr. Darius Lyman, Jr., 1862

It is strength of feeling combined with energy of intellect that renders us eloquent.

QUINTILIAN (A.D. 35?–100?). *Institutio oratoria,* 10.7.15, tr. John Selby Watson, 1856

True eloquence . . . comes, if it come at all, like the outbreaking of a fountain from the earth, or the bursting forth of volcanic fires, with spontaneous, original, native force.

DANIEL WEBSTER (1782–1852). Speech, Boston, 2 August 1826

EMOTION

See also • Body ○ Enthusiasm ○ Feelings ○ Heart ○ Mysticism: Albert Einstein ○ Passion ○ Reason & Passion ○ Spirituality: Abraham Joshua Heschel ○ Spirituality: First Person: Carl G. Jung ○ Sports: Jane O'Reilly ○ Tears ○ Temperament

It is the emotion which drives the intelligence forward in spite of obstacles.

HENRI BERGSON (1859–1941). "Moral Obligation," *The Two Sources of Morality and Religion,* 1932, tr. R. Ashley Audra and Cloudesley Brereton, 1935

Emotion is the moment when steel meets flint and a spark is struck forth, for emotion is the chief source of consciousness. There is no change from darkness to light or from inertia to movement without emotion.

CARL G. JUNG (1875–1961). "Psychological Aspects of the Mother Archetype" (4.2), 1938, *The Archetypes and the Collective Unconscious,* tr. R. F. C. Hull, 1959

"Negative" emotions ["fear, anxiety, despair"] are much like repressed and dispossessed peoples in the body politic. They cease to be destructive when they are invited into full participation in the commonwealth. Repress them and there will be insurrection rather than resurrection.

SAM KEEN (1931–). *Beginnings Without End,* 1, 1975

The energy that actually shapes the world springs from emotions.

GEORGE ORWELL (1903–1950). In B. H. Liddell Hart, "The Dilemma of the 'Intellectual,'" *Why Don't We Learn from History?* 1944

An emotion can only be restrained by an emotion stronger than and contrary to itself.

BARUCH SPINOZA (1632–1677). "Reason and Virtue," *Ethics,* 1677, tr. Dagobert D. Runes, 1957

Emotion: The human spirit experienced in the flesh.

JERRY TUCKER (1941–). *The Experience of Politics: You and American Government,* 2.3, 1974

Ninety percent of our lives is governed by emotion. Our brains merely register and act upon what is telegraphed to them by our bodily experience. Intellect is to emotion as our clothes are to our bodies: we could not very well have civilized life without clothes, but we would be in a poor way if we had only clothes without bodies.

ALFRED NORTH WHITEHEAD (1861–1947). 10 June 1943, *Dialogues of Alfred North Whitehead,* rec. Lucien Price, 1954

EMPIRE

See also • Colonialism ○ Imperialism

All Empires have been cemented in blood.

EDMUND BURKE (1729–1797). *A Vindication of Natural Society,* M. Cooper edition, p. 37, 1756

Empire is neither built nor maintained without some strokes of hard policy and with the generation of deep resentments. And if we are sometimes exasperated by officialdom even at home, can we imagine what must be the reaction of awakening minds in regions where the officialdom represents the foreigner, and the foreigner is in the country also to exploit it?

SIR HERBERT BUTTERFIELD (1900–1979). English historian. *Christianity, Diplomacy and War,* 8, 1953

The loss of India would mark and consummate the downfall of the British Empire. That great organism would pass at a stroke out of life into history. From such a catastrophe there could be no recovery.

WINSTON CHURCHILL (1874–1965). Speech before the Indian Empire Society, London, 12 December 1930

The empires of the future are the empires of the mind.

WINSTON CHURCHILL (1874–1965). Speech, Harvard University, Cambridge (Massachusetts), 6 September 1942

Let me . . . make this clear, in case there should be any mistake about it in any quarter. We mean to hold our own. I have not become the King's First Minister in order to preside over the liquidation of the British Empire.

WINSTON CHURCHILL (1874–1965). Speech at the Lord Mayor's Day luncheon, Mansion House, London, 10 November 1942

The maxim of Lord Beaconsfield [Benjamin Disraeli], *Imperium et Libertas,* is still our guide. This truth has already been proved abundantly since those words were spoken. Without freedom there is no foundation for our Empire; without Empire there is no safeguard for our freedom.

WINSTON CHURCHILL (1874–1965). "Imperium et Libertas," speech, 1945, *Winston Churchill: His Complete Speeches 1897–1963,* vol. 7, ed. Robert R. James, 1974. Disraeli had said in a speech at Guildhall, London (9 November 1879), "One of the greatest of Romans, when asked what was his politics, replied, 'Imperium et libertas.' That would not make a bad program for a British ministry." (In Samuel Arthur Bent, comp., *Familiar Short Sayings of Great Men,* 5th ed. rev., p. 48, 1887)

The highest ambition of our magistrates and generals was to defend our provinces and allies with justice and honor. And so our government could be called more accurately a protectorate of the world than a dominion.

CICERO (106–43 B.C.). On the Roman Empire, *De officiis,* 2.8, tr. Walter Miller, 1913

We assert that no nation can long endure half republic and half empire, and we warn the American people that imperialism abroad will lead quickly and inevitably to despotism at home.

DEMOCRATIC NATIONAL PLATFORM. 1900

All empire is no more than pow'r in trust.

JOHN DRYDEN (1631–1700). *Absalom and Achitophel,* 1.411, 1681

See Politicians: Henry Clay ○ Power: Edmund Burke (3) ○ Riches: Ralph Waldo Emerson (1)

To robbery, slaughter, plunder, [the Romans] give the lying name of empire; they make a solitude and call it peace.

GALGACUS (A.D. 1st cent.). Caledonian chief. Speech to his army before the Battle of the Grampians (Britain), where he was defeated by the Romans, A.D. 86. In Tacitus (A.D. 56?–120?). *The Life of Cnaeus Julius Agricola,* 30, tr. Alfred J. Church and William J. Brodribb, 1942 (Popular version: They make a desert and call it peace.)

The process of empire building brought with it prosperity for the empire builders. No small part of the gain in working-class amenities . . . was the result of sweated labor overseas: the colonies were now the proletariat's proletariat. No wonder imperialism was a popular policy.

ROBERT L. HEILBRONER (1919–). Referring to late nineteenth-century British imperialism, *The Worldly Philosophers: The Lives, Times, and Ideas of the Great Economic Thinkers,* 5th ed., 7, 1980 (1953)

Empires have no interest in operating within an international system; they aspire to *be* the international system.

HENRY A. KISSINGER (1923–). *Diplomacy,* 1, 1994

An empire founded by war has to maintain itself by war.

MONTESQUIEU (1689–1755). *Considérations sur les causes de la grandeur des Romaines et de leur décadence,* 8, 1734

Great empires die of indigestion.

NAPOLEON (1769–1821). Attributed. In J. A. Hobson, *Imperialism: A Study,* 2.4.1, 1902

The sun never sets upon my empire.

PHILIP II (1527–1598). Spanish king

See England: Lord Palmerston

Would you have a great empire? Rule over yourself.

PUBLIUS SYRUS (85–43 B.C.). *Moral Sayings,* 345, tr. Darius Lyman, Jr., 1862

I contend that we are the first race in the world, and that the more of the world we inhabit, the better it is for the human race. I contend that every acre added to our territory provides for the birth of more of the English race, who otherwise would not be brought into existence. Added to which the absorption of the greater portion of the world under our rule simply means the end of all wars.

[I will work] for the furtherance of the British Empire, for the bringing of the civilized world under British rule, for the recovery of the United States, for the making of the Anglo-Saxon race into one Empire. What a dream! But yet it is probable! It is possible!

CECIL RHODES (1853–1902). British colonial administrator. 1877, at age 24, personal statement given to his friend W. T. Stead with instructions that the envelope which contained it was not to be opened until after his death. In Sarah Gertrude Millin, *Rhodes,* 4.3, 1952

With a hero at head and a nation
Well gagged and well drilled and well cowed
And a gospel of war and damnation
Has not Empire a right to be proud!

ALGERNON SWINBURNE (1837–1909)

The expansion of one's rim of power diffuses internal resources, stretches the thin periphery even further out, so that a small concentration of hostile force can burst the bubble of empire.

GARRY WILLS (1934–). *The Kennedy Imprisonment: A Meditation on Power,* 23, 1981

ENDINGS

See • Beginnings & Endings

ENDS

See • Means & Ends

ENEMIES

See also • Friends ○ Friends & Enemies ○ Liberty: Thomas Paine ○ Truthfulness: Paul, Plato

He that wrestles with us strengthens our nerves and sharpens our skill. Our antagonist is our helper.

EDMUND BURKE (1729–1797). *Reflections on the Revolution in France,* p. 278, 1790, Pelican Books edition, 1968

The enmity of one's kindred is far more bitter than the enmity of strangers.

> DEMOCRITUS (460?–370? B.C.). In T. V. Smith, ed., "The Golden Sayings of Democritus" (90), *From Thales to Plato*, 4, 1934

The cruelest foe is a masked benefactor.

> RALPH WALDO EMERSON (1803–1882). "The Sovereignty of Ethics," *Lectures and Biographical Sketches*, 1883

There is no little enemy.

> BENJAMIN FRANKLIN (1706–1790). *Poor Richard's Almanack*, September 1733

Love your Enemies, for they tell you your Faults.

> BENJAMIN FRANKLIN (1706–1790). *Poor Richard's Almanack*, March 1756

Pray for thy enemy; for if thou beest a good Man thyself, thou canst not but rejoice to see thy worst Enemy become a good Man too.

> THOMAS FULLER (1654–1734). Comp., *Introductio ad Prudentiam*, 878, 1731

The real existence of an enemy upon whom one can foist off everything evil is an enormous relief to one's conscience. You can then at least say, without hesitation, who the devil is; you are quite certain that the cause of your misfortune is outside, and not in your own attitude.

> CARL G. JUNG (1875–1961). "General Aspects of Dream Psychology," 1916, *The Structure and Dynamics of the Psyche*, tr. R. F. C. Hull, 1960
>
> See Peace: Jung

We has met the enemy, and he is us.

> WALT KELLY (1913–1973). Comic strip balloon, *Pogo*, Earth Day, 22 April 1971, *The Best of Pogo*, ed. Mrs. Walt Kelly and Bill Crouch, Jr., 1982

The face of the enemy frightens me only when I see how much it resembles mine.

> STANISLAW J. LEC (1909–1966). *Unkempt Thoughts*, p. 87, tr. Jacek Galazka, 1962

The best way to destroy an enemy is to make him a friend.

> ABRAHAM LINCOLN (1809–1865)

Whoever lives for the sake of combating an enemy has an interest in the enemy's staying alive.

> FRIEDRICH NIETZSCHE (1844–1900). *Human, All Too Human*, 531, 1878, tr. Marion Faber, 1984

Cruellest enemy—
Yourself!

> FRIEDRICH NIETZSCHE (1844–1900). "The Sorcerer," *Thus Spoke Zarathustra*, 1892, tr. R. J. Hollingdale, 1961

As the aphorism has it, our enemy is by tradition our savior, in preventing us from superficiality.

> JOYCE CAROL OATES (1938–). "Master Race," *Partisan Review* (Fiftieth Anniversary issue), 1984

The most formidable enemy lies hid in one's own heart.

> PUBLIUS SYRUS (85–43 B.C.). *Moral Sayings*, 300, tr. Darius Lyman, Jr., 1862

Love your enemies, and you will have none.

> PAUL RICHARD (1874–1967). *The Scourge of Christ*, 5.2, 1929, ed. Michel Paul Richard, 1987

Judge me by the enemies I've made.

> FRANKLIN D. ROOSEVELT (1882–1945). In Arthur M. Schlesinger, Jr., "The Ultimate Approval Rating," *New York Times Magazine*, 15 December 1996

Who despises an insignificant enemy resembles him who is careless about fire.

> SA'DI (A.D. 1213?–1292). *The Gulistan, or Rose Garden*, 8 (Admonition 4), A.D. 1258, tr. Edward Rehatsek, 1964

Know your enemies: avoid them, if you can; intimidate them, if you can't; subdue them, if you must.

> THOMAS S. SZASZ (1920–). "Ethics," *The Untamed Tongue: A Dissenting Dictionary*, 1990

If two men claim thy help, and one is thy enemy, help him first.

> TALMUD (A.D. 1st–6th cent.). Rabbinical writings. In Louis I. Newman, comp., *The Talmudic Anthology*, 136, 1945

My enemy is dead, a man divine as myself is dead.

> WALT WHITMAN (1819–1892). "Reconciliation," 1865, *Leaves of Grass*, 1855–1892

✹

Do not rejoice when your enemy falls,
    and let not your heart be glad when he stumbles.

> SAYING (*BIBLE*). Proverbs 24:17

ENERGY

See also • Action ○ Passion

Energy is Eternal Delight.

> WILLIAM BLAKE (1757–1827). "The Voice of the Devil," *The Marriage of Heaven and Hell*, 4, 1790–1793?

The worshipper of energy is too physically energetic to see that he cannot explore certain higher fields until he is still.

> CLARENCE DAY (1874–1935). *This Simian World*, 5, 1920

$E = mc2$ (Energy equals mass times the speed of light squared).

> ALBERT EINSTEIN (1879–1955). *Annalen der Physik*, 1904

The greater the tension, the greater is the potential. Great energy springs from a correspondingly great tension of opposites.

> CARL G. JUNG (1875–1961). "Paracelsus as a Spiritual Phenomenon" (1 [introduction]), 1942, *Alchemical Studies*, tr. R. F. C. Hull, 1967

I suppose if you had to choose just one quality to have that would be it: vitality.

> JOHN F. KENNEDY (1917–1963). In Arthur M. Schlesinger, Jr., *A Thousand Days: John F. Kennedy in the White House*, 25.2, 1965

Energy and matter are two aspects of the same thing.

> GUSTAVE LE BON (1841–1931). *Aphorisms of Present Times*, 3.6, 1913, tr. Alice Widener, 1979

More energy! More energy!

NAPOLEON (1769–1821). Letter to his brother Louis Bonaparte, king of Holland, 15 December 1806, *The Mind of Napoleon: A Selection from His Written and Spoken Words*, 215, ed. J. Christopher Herold, 1955

This world belongs to the energetical.

ALEXIS de TOCQUEVILLE (1805–1859). In Ralph Waldo Emerson, journal, 1862, undated

Hungering, hungering, hungering, for primal energies and Nature's dauntlessness.

WALT WHITMAN (1819–1892). "Rise O Days from Your Fathomless Deeps" (3), 1865, *Leaves of Grass*, 1855–1892

ENGLAND

Includes • Britain

See also • London ○ Nations

I will not cease from Mental Fight,
Nor shall my Sword sleep in my hand
Till we have built Jerusalem
In England's green and pleasant Land.

WILLIAM BLAKE (1757–1827). Preface to *Milton: A Poem*, 1.13, 1804–1808

Be England what she will,
With all her faults, she is my country still.

CHARLES CHURCHILL (1731–1764). *The Farewell*, l. 27, 1764

What General Weygand called the "Battle of France" is over. I expect that the Battle of Britain is about to begin. Upon this battle depends the survival of Christian civilization. Upon it depends our own British life, and the long continuity of our institutions and our Empire. . . . Let us therefore brace ourselves to our duties, and so bear ourselves that, if the British Empire and its Commonwealth last for a thousand years, men will say, "This was their finest hour."

WINSTON CHURCHILL (1874–1965). After the evacuation at Dunkirk. House of Commons speech, 18 June 1940, *The Second World War, Their Finest Hour*, 1.11, 1949

Slaves cannot breathe in England; if their lungs
Receive our air, that moment they are free;
They touch our country, and their shackles fall.

WILLIAM COWPER (1731–1800). *The Task*, 2.40, 1785

You have only got to look at the pages of British imperial history to hide your head in shame that you are British.

SIR STAFFORD CRIPPS (1889–1952). In John Gunther, *Inside Europe*, rev. ed., 19, 1937 (1936)

The English nation is never so great as in adversity.

BENJAMIN DISRAELI (1804–1881). House of Commons speech, 11 August 1857

English are they who do not stop until they have reached their aim.

RALPH WALDO EMERSON (1803–1882). Journal, 1853, undated

Every Englishman expects to kick all those below him, and to be kicked by all those above him.

RALPH WALDO EMERSON (1803–1882). Journal, 1856, undated

For six days a week the Englishman worships at the Bank of England, and on the seventh day at the Church of England.

JOHN GUNTHER (1901–1970). *Inside Europe*, rev. ed., 16, 1937 (1936)

What is our task? To make Britain a fit country for heroes to live in.

DAVID LLOYD GEORGE (18633–1945). Speech, Wolverhampton, 24 November 1918

We know no spectacle so ridiculous as the British public in one of its periodical fits of morality.

THOMAS BABINGTON MACAULAY (1800–1859). "Moore's Life of Lord Byron," *The Edinburgh Review* (Scotland), June 1831

England is the most class-ridden country under the sun. It is a land of snobbery and privilege, ruled largely by the old and silly. But in any calculation about it one has got to take into account its emotional unity, the tendency of nearly all its inhabitants to feel alike and act together in moments of supreme crisis.

GEORGE ORWELL (1903–1950). "The Lion and the Unicorn" (1.3), 19 February 1941, *The Collected Essays, Journalism and Letters of George Orwell*, vol. 2, ed. Sonia Orwell and Ian Angus, 1968

A family with the wrong members in control—that, perhaps, is as near as one can come to describing England in a phrase.

GEORGE ORWELL (1903–1950). "The Lion and the Unicorn" (1.3), 19 February 1941, *The Collected Essays, Journalism and Letters of George Orwell*, vol. 2, ed. Sonia Orwell and Ian Angus, 1968

The sun never sets upon the interests of this country.

LORD PALMERSTON (1784–1865). House of Commons speech, 1 March 1843

See Empire: Philip II

"There'll Always Be an England."

ROSS PARKER and HUGH CHARLES. Song title, 1939

Gaunt: This other Eden, demi-paradise. . . .
This blessed plot, this earth, this realm, this England. . . .
This land of such dear souls, this dear dear land.

SHAKESPEARE (1564–1616). *Richard II*, 2.1.42, 1595

We were not fairly beaten, my lord. No Englishman is ever fairly beaten.

GEORGE BERNARD SHAW (1856–1950). *Saint Joan*, 4, 1923

To found a great empire for the sole purpose of raising up a people of customers, may at first sight appear a project fit only for a nation of shopkeepers.

ADAM SMITH (1723–1790). *The Wealth of Nations*, 4.7.3, 1776

I know why the sun never sets on the British Empire—God wouldn't trust an Englishman in the dark.

DUNCAN SPAETH

It is a commonplace that the characteristic virtue of Englishmen is their power of sustained practical activity, and their characteristic vice a reluctance to test the quality of that activity by reference to principles.

R. H. TAWNEY (1880–1962). Opening words, *The Acquisitive Society*, 1920

We must be free or die, who speak the tongue
That Shakespeare spake; the faith and morals hold
Which Milton held.

> WILLIAM WORDSWORTH (1770–1850). Untitled (l. 11). In *Morning Post*,
> 16 April 1803

ENLIGHTENMENT

See also • America: George Washington ○ Meditation: Sogyal Rinpoche (1) ○ Myths: Anonymous ○ Self-Knowledge: Lao-tzu ○ Self-Realization (Becoming) ○ Self-Realization (Being)

The seers renounce the fruits of their actions, and so reach enlightenment.

> *BHAGAVAD GITA* (6th cent. B.C.). 2, tr. Swami Prabhavananda and
> Christopher Isherwood, 1954

So irresistible is the transformative power of enlightenment that your life seems to be shifted into a new dimension, opened to new and unsuspected possibilities.

> EUGEN HERRIGEL (1885–1955). "Enlightenment, Rebirth, Buddha
> Nature," *The Method of Zen*, 1960, ed. Hermann Tausend and tr.
> R. F. C. Hull, 1964

The enlightened ones are neither attached to nor detached from their senses and thoughts.

> HUANG-PO. Adapted. In Aldous Huxley, *The Perennial Philosophy*,
> 4, 1946
>
> See Self-Realization (Being): The Kotzker

[Enlightenment is] becoming conscious of the Unconscious.

> D. T. SUZUKI (1870–1966). Japanese Zen master. In Aldous Huxley,
> "The Education of an Amphibian," *Tomorrow and Tomorrow and
> Tomorrow*, 1956
>
> See The Unconscious: Friedrich Nietzsche

The action of the creative individual may be described as a twofold motion of withdrawal-and-return: withdrawal for the purpose of his personal enlightenment, return for the task of enlightening his fellow men.

> ARNOLD J. TOYNBEE (1889–1975). *A Study of History*, 1934–1939, abr.
> D. C. Somervell, 2.400, 1965

Lovingkindness is the path to enlightenment.

> ANONYMOUS

The enlightened are involved without being attached.

> ANONYMOUS

Before enlightenment, chop wood, carry water. After enlightenment, chop wood, carry water.

> SAYING (ZEN). In Jon Carroll, "Doing Nothing: An Expert Speaks," *San
> Francisco Chronicle*, 8 February 1995

ENTHUSIASM

See also • Emotion ○ Fanatics ○ Passion ○ Psychotherapy: Carl G. Jung (3) ○ Zeal

Enthusiasm is the glory and hope of the world.

> BRONSON ALCOTT (1799–1888). "Orphic Sayings" (2), *The Dial* (New
> England journal), July 1840

Nothing great was ever achieved without enthusiasm.

> SAMUEL TAYLOR COLERIDGE (1772–1834). *The Statesman's Manual;
> The Bible the Best Guide to Political Skill and Foresight: A Lay Sermon
> Addressed to the Higher Classes of Society*, p. 24, 1816

I was still full of fervor just a few days ago; it seemed to me that I could move mountains; today I am crushed.

> ANDRÉ GIDE (1869–1951). Journal, 14 June 1926, tr. Justin O'Brien, 1951
>
> See Depression: Lord Beaverbrook ○ Feelings: George Ade

Enthusiasm is of the greatest value, so long as we are not carried away by it.

> GOETHE (1749–1832). *The Maxims and Reflections of Goethe*, 211, tr.
> T. Bailey Saunders, 1892

Some kind of widespread enthusiasm or excitement is apparently needed for the realization of vast and rapid change.

> ERIC HOFFER (1902–1983). *The True Believer: Thoughts on the Nature
> of Mass Movements*, 1, 1951

Enthusiasm is the great hill-climber.

> ELBERT HUBBARD (1856–1915). *A Thousand and One Epigrams*,
> p. 159, 1911

Enthusiasm begets enthusiasm.

> HENRY WADSWORTH LONGFELLOW (1807–1882). *Hyperion:
> A Romance*, 4.7, 1839

The remedy for exuberance is easy, but barrenness is incurable by any labor.

> QUINTILIAN (A.D. 35?– 100?). *Institutio oratoria*, 2.4.6, tr. John Selby
> Watson, 1856, and ed. James J. Murphy, 1965

Opposition may inflame the enthusiast but never converts him.

> FRIEDRICH von SCHILLER (1759–1805). *Love and Intrigue*, 3.1, 1784

The sense of this word among the Greeks affords the noblest definition of it: enthusiasm signifies God in us.

> MADAME de STAËL (1766–1817). *De l'Allemagne*, 4.10, 1810

In enthusiasm we undulate to the divine spiritus—as the lake to the wind.

> HENRY DAVID THOREAU (1817–1862). Journal, 16 December 1840

It is enthusiasm that flings the minds of men out of the beaten track and affects the great revolutions of the intellect as well as the great revolutions of the political world.

> ALEXIS de TOCQUEVILLE (1805–1859). *Democracy in America*, 2.3.21,
> 1840, tr. Henry Reeve and Francis Bowen, 1862

Man never rises to great truths without enthusiasm.

> VAUVENARGUES (1715–1747). *Reflections and Maxims*, 335, 1746, tr.
> F. G. Stevens, 1940

If we're not enthusiastic, we can't get things done. If we're over-enthusiastic, we run into the danger of being fanatical.

> WOODROW WYATT (1918–). Television interview with Bertrand Russell,
> London, 1959, *Bertrand Russell Speaks His Mind*, 11, 1960

ENVIRONMENT

See also • Earth ○ Evolution ○ Farming ○ Nature ○ Nuclear Energy
○ Pollution ○ Wilderness

We are far more concerned about the desecration of the flag than
we are about the desecration of our land.

> WENDELL BERRY (1934–). "Feminism, the Body, and the Machine,"
> 1989, *What Are People For?: Essays*, 1990

How would you describe the difference between modern war and
modern industry—between, say, bombing and strip mining, or
between chemical warfare and chemical manufacturing? The difference seems to be only that in war the victimization of humans is
directly intentional and in industry it is "accepted" as a "tradeoff."

> WENDELL BERRY (1934–). "Word and Flesh," 1989, *What Are People
> For?: Essays*, 1990

Soil is not usually lost in slabs or heaps of magnificent tonnage. It
is lost a little at a time over millions of acres by the careless acts of
millions of people. It cannot be saved by heroic feats of gigantic
technology, but only by millions of small acts and restraints, conditioned by small fidelities, skills, and desires. Soil loss is ultimately a
cultural problem; it will be corrected only by cultural solutions.

> WENDELL BERRY (1934–). "Decolonizing Rural America," *Audubon*,
> March–April 1993

All going, to make way for more and more devalued human stock,
with less and less of the wild spark, the priceless ingredient—
energy into matter. A vast mudslide of soulless sludge.

> WILLIAM S. BURROUGHS (1914–1997). In Richard Severo, "William S.
> Burroughs, The Beat Writer Who Distilled His Raw Nightmare Life,
> Dies at 83," *New York Times*, 4 August 1997

The history of life on earth has been a history of interaction
between living things and their surroundings. To a large extent,
the physical form and the habits of the earth's vegetation and its
animal life have been molded by the environment. Considering
the whole span of earthly time, the opposite effect, in which life
actually modifies its surroundings, has been relatively slight. Only
within the moment of time represented by the present century has
one species—acquired significant power to alter the nature of his
world.

> RACHEL CARSON (1907–1964). *Silent Spring*, 2, 1962
>
> See Evolution: Julian Huxley (1)

I believe natural beauty has a necessary place in the spiritual
development of any individual or any society. I believe that whenever we destroy beauty, or whenever we substitute something
man-made and artificial for a natural feature of the earth, we have
retarded some part of man's spiritual growth.

> RACHEL CARSON (1907–1964). In Terry Tempest Williams, "The Spirit of
> Rachel Carson," *Audubon*, July–August 1992

Man has been endowed with reason and creative powers to
increase what has been given him, but so far he has not created but
destroyed. There are fewer and fewer forests, the rivers are drying
up, the game birds are becoming extinct, the climate is ruined, and
every day the earth is becoming poorer and more hideous.

> ANTON CHEKHOV (1860–1904). *Uncle Vanya*, 1, 1897, tr. David
> Magarshack, 1950

We have become so preoccupied with power and control over
nature that we have lost an important dimension of our being, the
disposition of thankfulness, of commemoration, of perceiving and
enjoying something for its own sake. Instead of viewing these immediate objects of our environment in terms of their own being, we
have come to regard them solely in terms of what they are for us.
And to such an exploitative mentality, nature's own voice becomes
mute. Approached as material merely, to be worked up and pressed
into the service of a self-styled lord of creation, she contains no revelation and no blessing.

> J. GLENN GRAY (1913–1977). "Conclusion," *The Warriors: Reflections on
> Men in Battle*, 1959

In the relations of man with the animals, with the flowers, with the
objects of creation, there is a great ethic, scarcely perceived as yet,
which will at length break forth into light.

> VICTOR HUGO (1802–1885). In Douglas H. Chadwick, "Dead or Alive:
> The Endangered Species Act," *National Geographic*, March 1995

The earth we abuse and the living things we kill will, in the end,
take their revenge; for in exploiting their presence we are diminishing our future.

> MARYA MANNES (1904–1990). *More in Anger*, 1.5, 1958

I am I plus my surroundings; and if I do not preserve the latter, I
do not preserve myself.

> JOSÉ ORTEGA y GASSET (1883–1955). "To the Reader," *Meditations on
> Quixote*, 1914

The nation that destroys its soil destroys itself.

> FRANKLIN D. ROOSEVELT (1882–1945). Letter to state governors urging
> uniform soil conservation laws, 26 February 1937

The environment is too important to be left to the environmentalists.

> HELMUT SIHLER. German chemical company president. 1990
>
> See Commanders: Georges Clemenceau ○ Politicians: Charles de Gaulle ○
> Priests: Anonymous

"From the masses to the masses" the most
Revolutionary consciousness is to be found
Among the most ruthlessly exploited classes:
Animals, trees, water, air, grasses.

> GARY SNYDER (1930–). "Revolution in the Revolution in the Revolution."
> In Stephanie Mills, "Householding," *Whatever Happened to Ecology?*
> 1989

There is a unity of the body with the environment, as well as a
unity of the body and soul into one person.

> ALFRED NORTH WHITEHEAD (1861–1947). *Modes of Thought*, 3.8, 1938

It is one of the paradoxes of the human race and possibly its last
paradox, that the people who control the fortunes of our community should at the same time be wildly radical in matters that concern our own change of our environment, and rigidly conservative
in the social matters that determine our adaptation to it.

> NORBERT WIENER (1894–1964). Massachusetts Institute of Technology
> mathematician. *The Human Use of Human Beings: Cybernetics and
> Society*, 2, 1950

☙

What a man can be is born with him; what he becomes is a result
of his environment.

SAYING (NORTH DAKOTA). In Wolfgang Mieder, ed., *A Dictionary of American Proverbs,* p. 182, 1992

ENVY

See also • Egotism ∘ Hate: [especially] C. C. Colton ∘ Jealousy ∘ Malice ∘ Moral Indignation ∘ Pride ∘ Self-Righteousness ∘ Unhappiness: Montaigne ∘ Vanity

How rare, men with the character to praise
a friend's success without a trace of envy.

AESCHYLUS (525–456 B.C.). *Agamemnon,* l. 818, tr. Robert Fagles, 1975

All wise men, to decline the envy of their own virtues, . . . ascribe them to Providence and Fortune.

FRANCIS BACON (1561–1626). "Of Fortune," *Essays,* 1625

He that standeth [still] when others rise can hardly avoid motions of envy.

FRANCIS BACON (1561–1626). "Of Nobility," *Essays,* 1625

The dullard's envy of brilliant men is always assuaged by the suspicion that they will come to a bad end.

SIR MAX BEERBOHM (1872–1956). *Zuleika Dobson,* 4, 1911

Envy we must overcome by generosity and nobleness of soul.

CERVANTES (1547–1616). *Don Quixote,* 2.3.8, 1615, tr. Peter Anthony Motteux and John Ozell, 1743

He sicken'd at all triumphs but his own.

CHARLES CHURCHILL (1731–1764). *The Rosciad,* l. 64, 1761

Envy is the sincerest form of flattery.

JOHN CHURTON COLLINS (1848–1908). *Aphorisms,* 1904?
See Flattery: Saying (English)

Envy is the tax which all distinction must pay.

RALPH WALDO EMERSON (1803–1882). Journal, 10 January 1824
See Censure: Jonathan Swift

Pity cureth Envy.

THOMAS FULLER (1654–1734). Comp., *Gnomologia: Adages and Proverbs,* 3876, 1732

When another is vastly superior to you, there is no remedy but to love him.

GOETHE (1749–1832). "From Ottilie's Journal," *Elective Affinities,* 2.5, 1809, tr. R. J. Hollingdale, 1971

Envy . . . desires not so much its own happiness as another's misery.

SAMUEL JOHNSON (1709–1784). In *The Rambler* (English journal), 183, December 1751

Envy is so . . . shameful that we never dare confess it.

LA ROCHEFOUCAULD (1613–1680). *Maxims,* 27, 1665, tr. Louis Kronenberger, 1959

You shall not covet your neighbor's house; you shall not covet your neighbor's wife, or his manservant, or his maidservant, or his ox, or his ass, or anything that is your neighbor's.

MOSES (14th cent. B.C.). The Tenth Commandment, *Exodus* 20:17

Better . . . to be envied than pitied.

PERIANDER (625?–585 B.C.). One of the Seven Sages of Greece. In Herodotus (484?–420? B.C.), *The Persian Wars,* 3.52, tr. George Rawlinson, 1942

To withstand the assaults of envy, you must be either a hero or a saint.

PUBLIUS SYRUS (85–43 B.C.). *Moral Sayings,* 392, tr. Darius Lyman, Jr., 1862

The vice of envy is . . . always a confession of inferiority.

THEODORE ROOSEVELT (1858–1919). "Christian Citizenship," 30 December 1900, *The Strenuous Life: Essays and Addresses,* 1905

The only activity that liberates from envy is that which fills us with new, different impulses, feelings and thoughts which, to be of help, have to be value-asserting, dynamic and forward-looking. To many, the desire to overcome their envy may have been a genuine incentive for positive achievement, and hence have led to satisfaction in a sense of achievement.

HELMUT SCHOECK (1922–). *Envy: A Theory of Social Behaviour,* 22, 1966

Iago: The green-ey'd monster.

SHAKESPEARE (1564–1616). *Othello,* 3.3.166, 1604

To an envious man nothing is more delightful than another's misfortune, and nothing more painful than another's success.

BARUCH SPINOZA (1632–1677). "Man's Loves and Hates," *Ethics,* 1677, tr. Dagobert D. Runes, 1957

Man will do many things to get himself loved; he will do all things to get himself envied.

MARK TWAIN (1835–1910). *Following the Equator: A Journey Around the World,* 21 (epigraph), 1897

Every time a friend succeeds, I die a little.

GORE VIDAL (1925–). In Wilfrid Sheed, "Writer as Wretch and Rat," *New York Times Book Review,* 4 February 1973

❧

The grass is always greener on the other side of the fence.

SAYING (DUTCH)

Envy is stronger than greed.

SAYING (FRENCH)

Where there is envy, there is malice.

SAYING (GREEK)

Virtue conquers envy.

SAYING (LATIN)

EPIGRAMS

See also • Aphorisms ∘ Axioms ∘ Maxims ∘ Proverbs ∘ Quotations ∘ Sayings

Anyone can tell the truth, but only very few of us can make epigrams.

W. SOMERSET MAUGHAM (1874–1965). 1896, *A Writer's Notebook,* 1949

I trust that those who do not find my epigrams amusing will at least find them offensive.

MICHEL PAUL RICHARD. In "Dear Editor," *Thoughts For All Seasons: The Magazine of Epigrams*, vol. 4, 1992

✹

Put your thought into an epigram, spice it with ill nature, and it will keep longer than any plain and pleasant truth. And thousands who are yet unborn will quote you as an endorser of their sins; perhaps thank you for a pretext to avoid their self-contempt.

ANONYMOUS (AMERICAN). "Influence of Proverbs," *New York Times*, 29 April 1877

EPITAPHS

See also • Death ○ Homosexuality: Leonard Matlovich ○ Last Words ○ Politicians, Corrupt: George Washington Plunkett ○ World War II: Anonymous (American) (1)

Here lies my wife: here let her lie!
Now she's at rest, and so am I.

JOHN DRYDEN (1631–1700)

Here lies W. C. Fields. I would rather be living in Philadelphia.

W. C. FIELDS (1880–1946). Proposed epitaph for himself. In *Vanity Fair*, 1925. The epitaph on the vault holding his ashes reads, "W. C. Fields, 1880–1946."

See The Dead: Elroy Flecker

> The body of
> B. Franklin
> Printer
> Like the cover of an old book,
> its contents torn out,
> and stripped of its lettering and gilding,
> lies here, food for worms.
> But the work shall not be wholly lost;
> for it will, as he believed, appear once more,
> in a new and more perfect edition
> corrected and amended
> by the Author.
> He was born Jan. 7 1706
> Died   17

BENJAMIN FRANKLIN (1706–1790). Proposed epitaph for himself

And were an epitaph to be my story
I'd have a short one ready for my own.
I would have written of me on my stone:
I had a lover's quarrel with the world.

ROBERT FROST (1874–1963). Read before the Phi Beta Kappa Society, Harvard University, Cambridge (Massachusetts), 20 June 1941, "The Lesson for Today," *A Witness Tree*, 1942

Here lies one whose name was writ in water.

JOHN KEATS (1795–1821). Proposed epitaph for himself

This is the epitaph I want on my tomb: "Here lies one of the most intelligent animals who ever appeared on the face of the earth."

BENITO MUSSOLINI (1883–1945). 1941. In Galeazzo Ciano, *Hidden Diary*, 1953

This is on me.

DOROTHY PARKER (1893–1967). Proposed epitaph for herself. In Robert E. Drennan, ed., "Dorothy Parker," *The Algonquin Wits*, 1968

Nature, and Nature's Laws lay hid in Night.
God said, *Let Newton be!* and All was *Light*.

ALEXANDER POPE (1688–1744). "Epitaph. Intended for Sir Isaac Newton, In Westminster-Abbey," 1730

When I die, my epitaph or whatever you call those signs on gravestones is going to read: "I joked about every prominent man of my time, but I never met a man I dident like." I am so proud of that I can hardly wait to die so it can be carved.

WILL ROGERS (1879–1935). Talk at a Boston church, June 1930. In Ben Yagoda, *Will Rogers: A Biography*, 10 (footnote), 1993

Here lies Will Rogers. Politicians turned honest and he starved to death.

WILL ROGERS (1879–1935). One of at least 20 he proposed for himself. In Homer Croy, *Our Will Rogers*, 26, 1953

Jonathan Swift lies here, where savage indignation can no longer tear the heart.

JONATHAN SWIFT (1667–1745). Proposed epitaph for himself. "Jonathan Swift." In Houston Peterson, ed. *Great Essays*, 1954

✹

I was well, I wished to be better; here I am.

ANONYMOUS (ENGLISH). "Inscription upon the tombstone of the man who had endeavored to mend a tolerable constitution by taking physic." In Adam Smith, *The Theory of Moral Sentiments*, 3.3, 1759

EQUALITY

See also • Campaign Slogans: Slogan (American) (4) ○ Civil War: Abraham Lincoln (4) ○ Classes, Two ○ Competition ○ Democracy: [especially] Pericles ○ Feminism: Equal Rights Amendment, Elizabeth Cady Stanton, Walt Whitman ○ Freedom: [especially] Anonymous (2) ○ Rights: [especially] Thomas Jefferson ○ Unity

It is not the possessions but the desires of mankind which require to be equalized.

ARISTOTLE (384–322 B.C.). *Politics*, 2.7, tr. Benjamin Jowett, 1885

Death and sleep make us all alike, rich and poor, high and low.

CERVANTES (1547–1616). *Don Quixote*, 2.4.43, 1615, tr. Peter Anthony Motteux and John Ozell, 1743

See Death: Saying (Italian)

There is One Mind, and . . . all the powers and privileges which lie in any, lie in all.

RALPH WALDO EMERSON (1803–1882). "Thoughts on Modern Literature," *Natural History of Intellect and Other Papers*, 1893

A society that puts equality—in the sense of equality of outcome—ahead of freedom will end up with neither equality nor freedom. The use of force to achieve equality will destroy freedom, and the force, introduced for good purposes, will end up in the hands of people who use it to promote their own interests.

MILTON FRIEDMAN (1912–) and ROSE FRIEDMAN. *Free to Choose: A Personal Statement*, 5 ("Conclusion"), 1979

We are all children of one and the same God and, therefore, absolutely equal.

MOHANDAS K. GANDHI (1869–1948). In *Harijan*, 2 February 1934

Given the opportunity, every human being has the same possibility for spiritual growth.

MOHANDAS K. GANDHI (1869–1948). In *Harijan,* 11 November 1946

The ideal social state is not that in which each gets an equal amount of wealth, but in which each gets in proportion to his contribution to the general stock.

HENRY GEORGE (1839–1897). *Social Problems,* 6, 1883

There can be no truer principle than this—that every individual of the community at large has an equal right to the protection of government.

ALEXANDER HAMILTON (1757–1804). Constitutional Convention speech, Philadelphia, 29 June 1787

It is . . . the essence of the demand for equality before the law that people should be treated alike in spite of the fact that they are different.

FRIEDRICH HAYEK (1899–1992). *The Constitution of Liberty,* 6.1, 1960

The most propitious environment for equality is constituted by a society where the means of production are owned cooperatively, where power is decentralized, and where the community is organized in a multiplicity of small, interrelated but, as far as may be, self-governing groups of mutually responsible men and women.

ALDOUS HUXLEY (1894–1963). "Inequality," *Ends and Means: An Inquiry into the Nature of Ideals and into the Methods Employed for Their Realization,* 1937

Every attempt at social leveling ends with leveling to the bottom, never to the top.

GEORGE F. KENNAN (1904–). *Around the Cragged Hill: A Personal and Political Philosophy,* 6, 1993

All of us do not have equal talent, but all of us should have an equal opportunity to develop our talents.

JOHN F. KENNEDY (1917–1963). Address, San Diego State College, 6 June 1963

The true virtue of human beings is fitness to live together as equals; claiming nothing for themselves but what they as freely concede to everyone else; regarding command of any kind as an exceptional necessity, and in all cases a temporary one; and preferring, whenever possible, the society of those with whom leading and following can be alternate and reciprocal. To these virtues, nothing in life as at present constituted gives cultivation by exercise.

JOHN STUART MILL (1806–1973). *The Subjection of Women,* 2, 1869

ALL ANIMALS ARE EQUAL
BUT SOME ANIMALS ARE MORE
EQUAL THAN OTHERS

GEORGE ORWELL (1903–1950). The farm's "single Commandment," *Animal Farm: A Fairy Story,* 10, 1945

The system of equality . . . must result from, rather than precede, the moral improvement of humankind.

PERCY BYSSHE SHELLEY (1792–1822). "Essay on Christianity," 1817

There is . . . a manly and lawful passion for equality that incites men to wish all to be powerful and honored. This passion tends to elevate the humble to the rank of the great; but there exists also in the human heart a depraved taste for equality, which impels the weak to attempt to lower the powerful to their own level and reduces men to prefer equality in slavery to inequality with freedom.

ALEXIS de TOCQUEVILLE (1805–1859). *Democracy in America,* 1.3, 1835, tr. Henry Reeve and Francis Bowen, 1862

In order to combat the evils which equality may produce, there is only one effectual remedy: namely, political freedom.

ALEXIS de TOCQUEVILLE (1805–1859). *Democracy in America,* 2.2.4, 1840, tr. Henry Reeve and Francis Bowen, 1862

Men are born equal and . . . violence and ability made the first masters. The present ones have been made by laws.

VOLTAIRE (1694–1778). "Master," *Philosophical Dictionary,* 1764, tr. Wade Baskin, 1961

What one is, why may not millions be?

WILLIAM WORDSWORTH (1770–1850). In Ralph Waldo Emerson, "Progress of Culture," *Letters and Social Aims,* 1876

All peoples are created equal.

ANONYMOUS

ERRORS

See also • Blunders ○ Defeat ○ Failure ○ Falsehood ○ Faults ○ Mistakes ○ Truth ○ Truth & Untruth

An error is the more dangerous in proportion to the degree of truth which it contains.

HENRI AMIEL (1821–1881). Journal, 26 December 1852, tr. Mrs. Humphrey Ward, 1885
See Lying: Marie von Ebner-Eschenbach

Any man is liable to err, but only a fool persists in error.

CICERO (106–43 B.C.). *Philippics,* 12.2

Error is always in Haste.

THOMAS FULLER (1654–1734). Comp., *Gnomologia: Adages and Proverbs,* 1382, 1732

For man must strive, and striving he must err.

GOETHE (1749–1832). *Faust,* 1 ("Prologue in Heaven"), 1808–1832, tr. Philip Wayne, 1959

Admitting Error clears the Score
And proves you Wiser than before.

ARTHUR GUITERMAN (1871–1943). "Of Apology," *A Poet's Proverbs: Being Mirthful, Sober, and Fanciful Epigrams on the Universe, With Certain Old Irish Proverbs, All in Rhymed Couplets,* 1924

We believe that to err is human. To blame it on someone else is politics.

HUBERT H. HUMPHREY (1911–1978). In Hugh Sidey, "Will These Mud Crawlers Learn to Fly" (epigraph), *Time,* 7 November 1988

The most dangerous error is failure to recognize our own tendency to error.

B. H. LIDDELL HART (1895–1970). "Blindfolded Authority," *Why Don't We Learn from History?* 1944

All men are liable to error; and most men are in many points, by passion or interest, under temptation to it.

> JOHN LOCKE (1632–1704). *An Essay Concerning Human Understanding,* 4.20.17, 1690, ed. Alexander Campbell Fraser, 1894

The little I have seen of the world . . . teaches me to look upon the errors of others in sorrow, not in anger.

> HENRY WADSWORTH LONGFELLOW (1807–1882). *Hyperion: A Romance,* 4.3, 1839

The most powerful cause of error is the war existing between the senses and reason.

> BLAISE PASCAL (1623–1662). *Pensées,* 82, 1670, tr. William F. Trotter, 1931

To Err is Human; to Forgive, Divine.

> ALEXANDER POPE (1688–1744). *An Essay on Criticism,* l. 525, 1711
>
> See Computers: Anonymous (1) ○ Mistakes: Elbert Hubbard (2) ○ Pity: Horace Mann

With Pleasure own your Errors past,
And make each Day a Critic on the last.

> ALEXANDER POPE (1688–1744). *An Essay on Criticism,* l. 570, 1711

ESTEEM

See also • Respect ○ Self-Esteem ○ Self-Respect

The rewards . . . in this life are *esteem* and *admiration* of others— the punishments are *neglect* and *contempt.* . . . The desire of the esteem of others is as real a want of nature as hunger—and the neglect and contempt of the world as severe a pain as the gout or stone.

> JOHN ADAMS (1735–1826). 1805. In Paul Fussell, *Class,* 1, 1983

Esteem and knowledge of a person are generally as the two sides of a seesaw: when one rises, the other falls.

> PAUL ELDRIDGE (1888–1982). *Maxims for a Modern Man,* 1296, 1965

Men . . . measure their esteem of each other by what each has, not by what each is.

> RALPH WALDO EMERSON (1803–1882). "Self-Reliance," *Essays: First Series,* 1841
>
> See Knaves: Samuel Butler (2) ○ Possessions: Henri Amiel

Esteem established, good will follows, which at times reaches affection. It persuades without words and obtains without earning.

> BALTASAR GRACIÁN (1601–1658). *The Art of Worldly Wisdom,* 44, 1647, tr. Joseph Jacobs, 1943

I have always found that so-called bad people gain in one's estimation when one gets to know them better, and good people decline.

> GEORG CHRISTOPH LICHTENBERG (1742–1799). *Aphorisms,* G.25, 1806, tr. R. J. Hollingdale, 1990

Even a nod from a person who is esteemed is of more force than a thousand arguments or studied sentences from others.

> PLUTARCH (A.D. 46?–119?). In Harold D. Lasswell and Abraham Kaplan, *Power and Society: A Framework for Political Inquiry,* 6.5, 1950

Those who stand highest in the esteem of men are most exposed to grievous peril, since they often have too great a confidence in themselves.

> THOMAS à KEMPIS (1380–1471). *The Imitation of Christ,* 1.20, tr. Leo Sherley-Price, 1952

ETERNITY

See also • Immortality ○ Silence & Speech: Thomas Carlyle ○ Time

Eternity looks grander and kinder if Time grow[s] meaner and more hostile.

> THOMAS CARLYLE (1795–1881). Letter to John Carlyle, 29 March 1833

What, to eternity, is a thousand years? Not so much as the blinking of an eye to the turning of the slowest of the spheres.

> DANTE (A.D. 1265–1321). "Purgatory" (11.106), *The Divine Comedy,* 1321, tr. John Ciardi, 1954

As eternity
is reckoned,
there's a lifetime
in a second.

> PIET HEIN (1905–) "A Moment's Thought," *Grooks,* 1966

What looks absurd within the limits of time may be luminous within the scope of eternity.

> ABRAHAM JOSHUA HESCHEL (1907–1972). *A Passion for Truth,* 9, 1973

The eternity of every moment.

> HERMANN HESSE (1877–1962). *Siddhartha,* 2 ("The Ferryman"), 1922, tr. Hilda Rosner, 1951

Gentleman-rankers out on the spree,
Damned from here to Eternity

> RUDYARD KIPLING (1865–1936). "Gentleman-Rankers," 1892. James Jones titled his 1951 novel *From Here to Eternity.*

The things that are unseen are eternal.

> PAUL (A.D. 1st cent.). *1 Corinthians* 4:16

Eternity's a terrible thought. I mean, where's it all going to end?

> TOM STOPPARD (1937–). *Rosencrantz and Guildenstern Are Dead,* 2, 1967

The soul awakes . . . between two dim eternities—the eternal past, the eternal future.

> HARRIET BEECHER STOWE (1811–1896). *Uncle Tom's Cabin,* 22, 1852

As if you could kill time without injuring eternity.

> HENRY DAVID THOREAU (1817–1862). "Economy," *Walden; or Life in the Woods,* 1854

The clock indicates the moment—but what does eternity indicate?

> WALT WHITMAN (1819–1892). "Song of Myself" (44), 1855, *Leaves of Grass,* 1855–1892

Many times man lives and dies
Between his two eternities.

> WILLIAM BUTLER YEATS (1865–1939). "Under Ben Bulben," *Last Poems,* 1939

ETHICS

See also • Good ○ Morality ○ Right & Wrong: Bertolt Brecht

To [the revolutionary] whatever aids the triumph of the revolution is ethical; whatever hinders it is unethical and criminal.
> MIKHAIL BAKUNIN (1814–1876). *Catechism of the Revolutionist,* 1960

Ethics judges not only man, but God also.
> NICOLAS BERDYAEV (1874–1948). *The Destiny of Man,* 1.2.1, 1931, tr. Natalie Duddington, 1955

Good comes into being at the same time as evil and disappears together with it. This is the fundamental paradox of ethics.
> NICOLAS BERDYAEV (1874–1948). *The Destiny of Man,* 1.2.2, 1931, tr. Natalie Duddington, 1955

Without ethics, everything happens as if we were all five billion passengers on a big machinery and nobody is driving the machinery. And it's going faster and faster, but we don't know where.
> JACQUES COUSTEAU (1910–1997). Ted Turner television interview, CNN, 24 February 1989

There is only one ethics, one set of rules of morality, one code: That of individual behavior in which the same rules apply to everyone alike.
> PETER F. DRUCKER (1909–). In Edward J. Conry, "The Indivisibility of Ethics," *New York Times,* 3 March 1991

I consider ethics to be an exclusively human concern with no superhuman authority behind it.
> ALBERT EINSTEIN (1879–1955). Letter to a Baptist pastor, 17 July 1953

Ethics is . . . to be regarded as a therapeutic attempt—as an endeavor to achieve, by means of a command of the superego, something which has so far not been achieved by means of any other cultural activities. As we already know, the problem before us is how to get rid of the greatest hindrance to civilization—namely, the constitutional inclination of human beings to be aggressive towards one another.
> SIGMUND FREUD (1856–1939). *Civilization and Its Discontents,* 4, 1930, tr. James Strachey, 1961

I regard utility as the ultimate appeal on all ethical questions; but it must be utility in the largest sense, grounded on the permanent interests of man as a progressive being. Those interests, I contend, authorize the subjection of individual spontaneity to external control only in respect to those actions of each which concern the interest of other people.
> JOHN STUART MILL (1806–1973). *On Liberty,* 1, 1859

All ethics begins when the individual is taken to be of *infinite importance*—in contrast to nature, which behaves cruelly and playfully toward the individual.
> FRIEDRICH NIETZSCHE (1844–1900). *Philosophy and Truth: Selections from Nietzsche's Notebooks of the Early 1870's,* 1.52, tr. Daniel Breazeale, 1979

Without doubt half the ethical rules they din into our ears are designed to keep us at work.
> LLEWELYN POWYS (1884–1939). *The Book of Days of Llewelyn Powys,* 1937

Ethical life and service are an aid, but they are not an end in themselves. The end is to be one with God.
> SWAMI PRABHAVANANDA (1893–1976). "Self-Surrender." In Christopher Isherwood, ed., *Vedanta for the Western World,* 1945

Ethics is in origin the art of recommending to others the sacrifices required for cooperation with oneself.
> BERTRAND RUSSELL (1872–1970). "On Scientific Method in Philosophy," *Mysticism and Logic,* 1918

Ethics is the activity of man directed to secure the inner perfection of his own personality. . . .
By its means man is to become capable of acting among men and in the world as a higher and purer force, and thus to do his part towards the actualization of the ideal of general progress.
> ALBERT SCHWEITZER (1875–1965). *The Philosophy of Civilization: The Decay and Restoration of Civilization,* 5, 1923, tr. C. T. Campion, 1923

The view of Reverence for Life is ethical mysticism. It allows union with the Infinite to be realized [through] ethical action.
> ALBERT SCHWEITZER (1875–1965). *Out of My Life and Thought: An Autobiography,* 21, tr. C. T. Campion, 1933
> See Zen: Eugen Herrigel

The ethic of Reverence for Life is the ethic of Love widened into universality.
> ALBERT SCHWEITZER (1875–1965). *Out of My Life and Thought: An Autobiography,* 21, tr. C. T. Campion, 1933

Slowly in our European thought comes the notion that ethics has not only to do with mankind but with the animal creation as well. This begins with St. Francis of Assisi. . . . Ethics is reverence for *all* life.
> ALBERT SCHWEITZER (1875–1965). "Religion and Modern Civilization" (pt. 2), *Christian Century,* 28 November 1934
> See Love: Elbert Hubbard

Let me give you a definition of ethics: It is good to maintain and further life; it is bad to damage and destroy life.
> ALBERT SCHWEITZER (1875–1965). "Religion and Modern Civilization" (pt. 2), *Christian Century,* 28 November 1934

EUTHANASIA

See also • Physicians: Christoph Hufeland ○ Holocaust ○ Killing ○ Sterilization ○ Violence

As to the exposure and rearing of children, let there by a law that no deformed child shall live.
> ARISTOTLE (384–322 B.C.). *Politics,* 7.13, tr. Benjamin Jowett, 1885

Euthanasia is a long, smooth-sounding word, and it conceals its danger as long-smooth words do, but the danger is there, nonetheless.
> PEARL S. BUCK (1892–1973) *The Child Who Never Grew,* 2, 1950

Those who have murdered, robbed while armed with automatic pistol or machine gun, kidnapped children, despoiled the poor of their savings, misled the public in important matters, should be humanely and economically disposed of in small euthanasic institutions supplied with proper gases. A similar treatment could be advantageously applied to the insane, guilty of criminal acts. Modern society should not hesitate to organize itself with reference to the normal individual. Philosophical systems and sentimental prejudices must give way before such a necessity. The development of human personality is the ultimate purpose of civilization.

> ALEXIS CARREL (1873–1944). French physician and winner of the 1912 Nobel Prize in physiology or medicine. *Man, the Unknown,* 8.12, 1935

The militarists may be cheered to think that even when war is totally abolished, there is still a place in morality for killing, and an infinitely more humane place than that occupied by murder in war, that is to say by killing the unfit, not by killing the fit. Only so can we be true to the instincts that have created Man.

It is the aim of eugenics to eliminate, so far as possible the unfit stocks, which by their constitutional defects lower the level of human achievement and increase the difficulties of life.

> HAVELOCK ELLIS (1859–1939). "The Control of Population," *More Essays of Love and Virtue,* 1931

It is one of the unfortunate results of Christianity among us today—amid other results more fortunate—that we were led to reject infanticide, and that we still feel compelled to our own pain and trouble, to the injury of the race, and to the misery of the victims of our supposed "humanitarianism," to keep alive even the most hopelessly maimed and defective of newborn infants. We know in the back of our minds that we only do it out of quaint superstition.

> HAVELOCK ELLIS (1859–1939). "The Control of Population," *More Essays of Love and Virtue,* 1931

My specialty is death.

> JACK KEVORKIAN (1928–). "Assisted suicide" physician. In Nancy Gibbs, "Rx for Death," *Time,* 31 May 1993

This is the sort of medicine and this is the sort of law, which you will sanction in your state. They will minister to better natures, giving health both of soul and of body; but those who are diseased in their bodies they will leave to die, and the corrupt and incurable souls they will put an end to themselves. That is clearly the best thing both for the patients and for the State.

> PLATO (427?–347 B.C.). *The Republic,* 3.410, tr. Benjamin Jowett, 1894

I think very soon the right to die will become the duty to die.

> CECILY SAUNDERS (1918–). Physician. Expressing with disapproval a modern trend, appearing on *60 Minutes,* television magazine program, CBS, 24 July 1983

As soon as life becomes a burden to the community, the State must be unsentimental and dispose of its lunatics, its criminals, and its misfits. The means, however, must be humane.

> GEORGE BERNARD SHAW (1856–1950). Remark to the author, 1940s. In Stephen Winsten, *Days with Bernard Shaw,* 19, 1949

Patients will be afraid that their doctor may be a great believer in death with dignity when all they need is their asthma medicine.

> MARK SIEGLER. Center for Clinical Medical Ethics director, University of Chicago. In Isabel Wilkerson, "Essay on Mercy Killing Reflects Conflict on Ethics for Physicians and Journalists," *New York Times,* 23 February 1988

The mass killing of mental patients [in Nazi Germany] was a large project. It was organized as well as any modern community psychiatric project, and better than most. . . . The organization comprised a whole chain of mental hospitals and institutions, university professors of psychiatry and directors and staff members of mental hospitals.

> FREDRIC WERTHAM (1895–1981). German-born American psychiatrist. On the murder of "at least 275,000" individuals identified as "useless eaters," "persons devoid of value," "worthless people," "superfluous people," "misfits," "undesirables," "cripples," "schizophrenics," "idiots," et al. in more than 30 German psychiatric facilities with "special departments" set up for that purpose, *A Sign for Cain: An Exploration of Human Violence,* 9, 1966

In 1941 the psychiatric institution Hadamar celebrated the cremation of the ten thousandth mental patient in a special ceremony. Psychiatrists, nurses, attendants, and secretaries all participated. Everybody received a bottle of beer for the occasion.

> FREDRIC WERTHAM (1895–1981). *A Sign for Cain: An Exploration of Human Violence,* 9, 1966

Technical experience [with gassing and cremation] first gained with killing psychiatric patients was utilized later for the destruction of millions. The psychiatric murders came first.

> FREDRIC WERTHAM (1895–1981). *A Sign for Cain: An Exploration of Human Violence,* 9, 1966

EVANGELISM

See also • Christianity ○ Clergy ○ Conversion ○ Cults ○ God ○ Persuasion ○ Propaganda ○ Redemption ○ Religion ○ Salvation

If I waz a-going tew civilize a parcel of heathen on sum distant ile by the job, i should debate sum time in mi mind which tew send, dancing-masters or missionarys.

> JOSH BILLINGS (1818–1885). "Hard Tack," *Everybody's Friend, or; Josh Billing's Encyclopedia and Proverbial Philosophy of Wit and Humor,* 1874

The essential thing in any effective evangelistic work is the ringing summons to individual men and women to come to terms with their ultimate loyalties.

> ANTON T. BOISEN (1876–1965). *The Exploration of the Inner World: A Study of Mental Disorder and Religious Experience,* 12, 1936

The first vital step in saving outcasts consists in making them feel that some decent human being cares enough for them to take an interest in the question whether they are to rise or sink.

> WILLIAM BOOTH (1829–1912). English religious leader and founder of the Salvation Army. As paraphrased by William James, *The Varieties of Religious Experience: A Study in Human Nature,* 9, 1902

Father Zossima: If the people around you are spiteful and callous and will not hear you, fall down before them and beg their forgiveness; for in truth you are to blame for their not wanting to hear you. And if you cannot speak to them in their bitterness, serve them in silence, and in humility, never losing hope.

> FYODOR DOSTOYEVSKY (1821–1881). *The Brothers Karamazov,* 6.2(h), 1880, tr. Constance Garnett, 1912

To aim to convert a man by miracles is a profanation of the soul.

> RALPH WALDO EMERSON (1803–1882). "The Divinity School Address," Cambridge (Massachusetts), 15 July 1838

Be not magisterial in thy Dictates, nor pertinaciously contentious in ordinary discourse for thy Opinion . . . Thou art not bound to convert all the World to Truth.

> THOMAS FULLER (1654–1734). Comp., *Introductio ad Prudentiam,* 1557, 1731

That was one of the things she held against missionaries: How they stressed Christ's submission to humiliation, and so had conditioned the people of Africa to humiliation by the white man.

> NADINE GORDIMER (1923–). Title story, *Not for Publication,* 1965

Proselytizing is more a passionate search for something not yet found than a desire to bestow upon the world something we already have. It is a search for a final and irrefutable demonstration that our absolute truth is indeed the one and only truth. The proselytizing fanatic strengthens his own faith by converting others.

> ERIC HOFFER (1902–1983). *The True Believer: Thoughts on the Nature of Mass Movements,* 88, 1951

Revivalism has always assumed that only its own type of religious experience can be perfect; you must first be nailed on the cross of natural despair and agony, and then in the twinkling of an eye be miraculously released.

> WILLIAM JAMES (1842–1910). *The Varieties of Religious Experience: A Study in Human Nature,* 10, 1902

Go into all the world and preach the gospel to the whole creation. He who believes and is baptized will be saved; but he who does not believe will be condemned.

> JESUS (A.D. 1st cent.). *Mark* 16:15–16
> See Day of Judgment: Jesus (2) ○ Salvation: Jesus

Learn a little of anything, and you're ready to proselytize.

> MIGNON McLAUGHLIN (1915–). *The Neurotic's Notebook,* 7, 1963

When an apostle seeks to win a soul to religion, . . . he appeals to understanding, not to imagination, for he knows that his task is not to create something, but to call aloud to that which is slumbering in the depths of the heart.

> MARIA MONTESSORI (1870–1952). *Spontaneous Activity in Education,* 9, tr. Florence Simmonds, 1917

The nations to which [Muhammad] addressed himself were savage and poor. They lacked everything and were extremely ignorant. If he had spoken to their minds, he would not have been heard.

> NAPOLEON (1767–1821). Dictation, St. Helena, 1817?, *The Mind of Napoleon: A Selection from His Written and Spoken Words,* 73, ed. J. Christopher Herold, 1955

If I preach the gospel, that gives me no ground for boasting. For necessity is laid upon me. Woe to me if I do not preach the gospel!

> PAUL (A.D. 1st cent.). *1 Corinthians* 9:16

Like George Fox, one must often be prepared not to act, but to "stand still in the light," confident that only such a stillness possesses the eloquence to draw men away from lives we must believe they inwardly loathe, but which misplaced pride will goad

them to defend under aggressive pressure to the very death—their death and ours.

> THEODORE ROSZAK (1933–). *The Making of the Counter Culture: Reflections on the Technocratic Society and Its Youthful Opposition,* 8, 1969

An informal survey of individuals who came forward and converted when [Rev. Billy] Graham called for converts [during a crusade in New York City] indicated that only those individuals who were subsequently integrated into local churches maintained their faith. For the others the conversion was merely a temporary response which was neither integrated into the rest of their personality nor received support from significant others.

> EDGAR H. SCHEIN (1928–) (with INGE SCHNEIER and CURTIS H. BARKER). *Coercive Persuasion: A Socio-psychological Analysis of the "Brainwashing" of American Civilian Prisoners by the Chinese Communists,* 11, 1961

I look upon all the world as my parish; thus far I mean, that, in whatever part of it I am, I judge it meet, right, and my bounden duty to declare unto all that are willing to hear, the glad tidings of salvation.

> JOHN WESLEY (1703–1791). Journal, 11 June 1739

EVENTS

See also • Circumstances ○ Decision-Making ○ Fortune ○ History ○ Opportunity ○ Optimism—Examples: Voltaire ○ Principles, Theoretical

Events always take much longer to develop than expected, but once they begin, they occur much faster and go much farther than anticipated.

> BARTON M. BIGGS. Financier. In Jonathan Fuerbringer, "Discounting a Short Mideast War," *New York Times,* 13 January 1991

[Pseudo-events or] counterfeit happenings tend to drive spontaneous happenings out of circulation.

> DANIEL J. BOORSTIN (1914–). *The Image: A Guide to Pseudo-Events in America,* 1.5, 1961

From time to time a great event, ardently desired, does not take place because some future time will fulfill it in greater perfection.

> JACOB BURCKHARDT (1818–1897). "On Fortune and Misfortune in History," 1871, *Force and Freedom: An Interpretation of History,* ed. James H. Nichols, 1943

It was one of those events which are incredible until they happen.

> WINSTON CHURCHILL (1974–1965). On the return of British forces to the European mainland in World War I, "Sir John French," *Great Contemporaries,* 1937

There were great decisions [during World War II], of course, but I was swept along by events.

> WINSTON CHURCHILL (1874–1965). Remark to the diarist, 8 November 1951. In Lord Moran, *Churchill: Taken from the Diaries of Lord Moran,* 34, 1966

I have no political system, and I have abandoned all political principles. I am a man dealing with events as they come in the light of my experience.

GEORGES CLEMENCEAU (1841–1929). Remark to the author. In Winston Churchill, "Clemenceau," *Great Contemporaries*, 1937

See Policy: Abraham Lincoln (2)

Events have made me great, more than my talents or my forces.

FREDERICK II (1712–1786). "Morning the Sixth," *The Confessions of Frederick the Great*, ed. Douglas Sladen, 1915

The enemy of conventional wisdom is not ideas but the march of events.

JOHN KENNETH GALBRAITH (1908–). *The Affluent Society*, 2.4, 1958

To shape events, an action must be performed not only in an unstable environment, but also by an actor who is strategically placed in that environment.

FRED I. GREENSTEIN. "The Impact of Personality on Politics: An Attempt to Clear Away Underbrush," *American Political Science Review*, September 1967

All events are secretly interrelated; . . . the sweep of all we are doing reaches beyond the horizon of our comprehension.

ABRAHAM JOSHUA HESCHEL (1907–1972). *Man Is Not Alone: A Philosophy of Religion*, 25, 1951

Not the great historical events, but the personal incidents that call up single sharp pictures of some human being in its pang or struggle, reach us most nearly.

OLIVER WENDELL HOLMES, SR. (1809–1894). *The Autocrat of the Breakfast-Table*, 12, 1858

Phenomena are best understood when placed within their series, studied in their germ and in their over-ripe decay.

WILLIAM JAMES (1842–1910). *The Varieties of Religious Experience: A Study in Human Nature*, 16 & 17, 1902

In retrospect all events seem inevitable.

HENRY A. KISSINGER (1923–). *White House Years*, 27, 1979

A statesman who cannot shape events will soon be engulfed by them.

HENRY A. KISSINGER (1923–). *Years of Upheaval*, 24, 1982

See International Relations: Napoleon ○ Presidents: Harry S. Truman (3)

I claim not to have controlled events, but confess plainly that events have controlled me.

ABRAHAM LINCOLN (1809–1865). Letter to Albert G. Hodges, 4 April 1864

[Freud discovered] that single events—traumas or injuries— that took place in earliest childhood, might leave traces on the human personality that would outweigh in their effect a lifetime of habit. . . . Such events, both in childhood and much later, may profoundly reshape the personality. Not only a trauma but a benign occurrence may have such a disproportionate effect—a sentence casually dropped by a teacher in the midst of a lesson, a single act of heroism or generosity or sacrifice, may even without visibly standing out in memory operate under the surface and determine a score of later events.

LEWIS MUMFORD (1895–1990). *The Conduct of Life*, 8.3, 1951

All great events hang by a single thread. The clever man takes advantage of everything, neglects nothing that may give him some added opportunity; the less clever man, by neglecting one thing, sometimes misses everything.

NAPOLEON (1769–1821). Letter to Talleyrand, 26 September 1797, *The Mind of Napoleon: A Selection from His Written and Spoken Words*, 55, ed. J. Christopher Herold, 1955

Believe me, friend Infernal-racket! The greatest events—they are not our noisiest but our stillest hours.

The world revolves, not around the inventors of new noises, but around the inventors of new values; it revolves *inaudibly*.

FRIEDRICH NIETZSCHE (1844–1900). "Of Great Events," *Thus Spoke Zarathustra*, 1892, tr. R. J. Hollingdale, 1961

Nearly every historical event is simultaneously an act of "securing" by somebody of the already ripened fruit of preceding development and a link in the chain of events which are preparing the fruits of the future.

GEORGE PLEKHANOV (1856–1918?). *The Role of the Individual in History*, 4, 1898

So often do the spirits
Of great events stride on before the events,
And in today already walks tomorrow.

FRIEDRICH von SCHILLER (1759–1805). *The Death of Wallenstein*, 5.3, 1799, tr. Samuel T. Coleridge, 1800

All events that occur within nations and within mankind can be traced to spiritual causes contained in the prevailing attitudes toward life.

ALBERT SCHWEITZER (1875–1965). *Out of My Life and Thought: An Autobiography*, 13, tr. C. T. Campion, 1933

It is one thing to be moved by events; it is another to be mastered by them.

RALPH W. SOCKMAN (1889–1970). *Bulletin of the Fourth Presbyterian Church, Chicago*, 17 November 1957

[Abraham Lincoln] believed from the first, I think, that the agitation of slavery would produce its overthrow, and he acted upon the result as though it was present from the beginning. His tactics were to get himself in the right place and remain there still, until events would find him in that place.

LEONARD SWETT (1825–1889). Letter to the author, 17 January 1866. In William H. Herndon and Jesse W. Weik, *Herndon's Lincoln: The True Story of a Great Life*, 18, 1889, Premier Books edition, 1961

The things that make good headlines attract our attention because they are on the surface of the stream of life, and they distract our attention from the slower, impalpable, imponderable movements that work below the surface and penetrate to the depths. But, of course, it is really these deeper, slower movements that, in the end, make history, and it is they that stand out huge in retrospect, when the sensational passing events have dwindled, in perspective, to their true proportions.

ARNOLD J. TOYNBEE (1889–1975). "Encounters Between Civilizations" (1), 1947, *Civilization on Trial*, 1948

Historical events are not inevitable; it's only in retrospect that they seem so.

ARNOLD J. TOYNBEE (1889–1975). Conversation with his son Philip Toynbee, *Comparing Notes: A Dialogue Across a Generation*, p. 64, 1963

The events which we see, and which look like freaks of chance, are only the last steps in long lines of causation.

> ALFRED NORTH WHITEHEAD (1861–1947). 5 May 1943, *Dialogues of Alfred North Whitehead*, rec. Lucien Price, 1954

It is by observing the flow of events in a large time frame that we are sometimes able to discern their direction.

> ANONYMOUS

Those who do nothing while awaiting events are likely to be engulfed by them.

> ANONYMOUS

A strong imagination creates the event.

> SAYING. In Montaigne, "Of the Power of the Imagination," *Essays*, 1588, tr. Donald M. Frame, 1958

EVIL

See also • Corruption ○ Crime ○ Good ○ Good & Evil ○ Guilt ○ Inaction ○ Morality: Edmund Burke ○ Remorse: John Milton ○ Repentance ○ Sin ○ Vice ○ Wicked ○ Wrong

Eichmann in Jerusalem, A Report on the Banality of Evil.

> HANNAH ARENDT (1906–1975). Book title, 1963

A belief in a supernatural source of evil is not necessary; men alone are quite capable of every wickedness.

> JOSEPH CONRAD (1857–1924). *Under Western Eyes*, 2.4, 1911

Much less evil would be done on earth if evil could not be done in the name of good.

> MARIE von EBNER-ESCHENBACH (1830–1916). *Aphorisms*, p. 29, 1880–1905, tr. David Scrase and Wolfgang Mieder, 1994

What we call evil is simply ignorance bumping its head in the dark.

> HENRY FORD (1863–1947). In *Observer* (British newspaper), 16 March 1930

The man who does evil to another does evil to himself.

> HESIOD (8th cent. B.C.). *Works and Days*, l. 265, tr. Richmond Lattimore, 1959

Everyone who does evil hates the light, and does not come to the light, lest his deeds should be exposed.

> JESUS (A.D. 1st cent.). *John* 3:20

What we call evil is only a necessary moment in our endless development.

> FRANZ KAFKA (1883–1924 "Reflections on Sin, Pain, Hope, and the True Way" (52), 1917–1920, *The Great Wall of China*, 1931, tr. Willa and Edwin Muir, 1946

To ignore evil is to become an accomplice to it.

> MARTIN LUTHER KING, JR. (1929–1968). *Where Do We Go from Here: Chaos or Community?* 3.2, 1967

The evil of our time is the loss of consciousness of evil.

> KRISHNAMURTI (1895–1986). In Stephanie Salter, "Evil's Shadow Falls Across a Killer's Sanity Trial" (epigraph), *San Francisco Sunday Examiner & Chronicle*, 9 February 1992

Few men are sufficiently discerning to appreciate all the evil they do.

> LA ROCHEFOUCAULD (1613–1680). *Maxims*, 269, 1665, tr. Leonard Tancock, 1959

Evil, what is evil?
There is only one evil, to deny life.

> D. H. LAWRENCE (1885–1930). "Cypresses," *The Collected Poems of D. H. Lawrence*, 1929

The greatest evil is not done in those sordid dens of evil that Dickens loved to paint . . . but is conceived and ordered (moved, seconded, carried and minuted) in clear, carpeted, warmed, well-lighted offices, by quiet men with white collars and cut fingernails and smooth-shaven cheeks who do not need to raise their voices.

> C. S. LEWIS (1898–1963). Introduction to *The Screwtape Letters*, rev. ed., 1982 (1942)

You find out the strength of a wind by trying to walk against it, not by lying down. . . . You never find out the strength of the evil impulse inside us until we try to fight it.

> C. S. LEWIS (1898–1963). *Mere Christianity*, rev. ed., 3.11, 1952

I would consent to any *great* evil, to avoid a *greater* one.

> ABRAHAM LINCOLN (1809–1865). Speech on the Kansas–Nebraska Act, Peoria (Illinois), 16 October 1854
> See Good & Evil: Baruch Spinoza

Blessed . . . is he who has it in his power to do evil, yet does it not.

> MARGARET OF NAVARRE (1492–1549). *The Heptameron, or Novels of the Queen of Navarre*, 43.5, 1558

Ishmael: All evil, to crazy Ahab, [was] visibly personified, and made visibly personified, and made practically assailable in Moby Dick. He piled upon the whale's white hump the sum of all the general rage and hate felt by his whole race from Adam down; and then, as if his chest had been a mortar, he burst his hot heart's shell upon it.

> HERMAN MELVILLE (1819–1891). *Moby-Dick; or, The Whale*, 41, 1851, ed. Harold Beaver, 1972

It is a sin to believe evil of others, but it is seldom a mistake.

> H. L. MENCKEN (1880–1956). *A Little Book in C Major*, 5.23, 1916

Whatever may be said of evil turning into good, the general tendency of evil is toward further evil.

> JOHN STUART MILL (1806–1873). "Nature," *Three Essays on Religion*, 1874

Do not be overcome by evil, but overcome evil with good.

> PAUL (A.D. 1st cent.). *Romans* 12:21
> See Good & Evil: Anonymous (Bible) ○ Heaven: Alfred North Whitehead

We should consider it a lesser evil to suffer great wrongs and outrages than to do them.

> PLATO (427?–347 B.C.). *Epistles*, 7.335.a, tr. John Harward, 1932

When a man is compelled to choose one of two evils, no one will choose the greater when he may have the less[er].

> PLATO (427?–347 B.C.). *Protagoras*, 358, tr. Benjamin Jowett, 1894
> See Good & Evil: Baruch Spinoza

To deny Evil a place among realities is necessarily to do away with the Good as well.

> PLOTINUS (A.D. 205–270). *The Enneads*, 1.8.12, tr. Stephen MacKenna and B. S. Page, 1952

Evil by definition is a falling short in good.

> PLOTINUS (A.D. 205–270). *The Enneads*, 3.2.5, tr. Stephen MacKenna and B. S. Page, 1952

What is the worst thing the Evil Urge can achieve? To make man forget that he is the son of a king.

> SHELOMO OF KARLIN. In Martin Buber, "Shelomo of Karlin," *Tales of the Hasidim: The Early Masters*, tr. Olga Marx, 1947

Of two evils, always choose the lesser.

> THOMAS à KEMPIS (1380–1471). *The Imitation of Christ*, 3.12, tr. Leo Sherley-Price, 1952

There are a thousand hacking at the branches of evil to one who is striking at the root.

> HENRY DAVID THOREAU (1817–1862). "Economy," *Walden; or Life in the Woods*, 1854

It is easier . . . to prevent an evil than to rectify mistakes.

> GEORGE WASHINGTON (1732–1799). In P. M. Zall, ed., "Aphorisms on People and Politics," *George Washington Laughing: Humorous Anecdotes by and About Our First President from Original Sources*, 1989

Evil is the brute motive force of fragmentary purpose, disregarding the eternal vision.

> ALFRED NORTH WHITEHEAD (1861–1947). *Science and the Modern World*, 12, 1925

❧

Do no evil—either to an enemy or for a friend.

> ANONYMOUS

Evil: too much, too little, or the wrong kind of a good thing.

> ANONYMOUS

Indifference to evil is complicity with evil.

> ANONYMOUS

Evil conduct is the root of all misery.

> SAYING (CHINESE)

Submitting to one evil brings on another.

> SAYING (LATIN)
> See Nonviolence: Jesus (1)

EVOLUTION

See also • Change & Changelessness ○ Competition ○ Crises ○ Environment ○ Faith: Jimmy Carter ○ God & History ○ God & Man: Seth Farber ○ History ○ Life ○ Man ○ Mankind ○ Nature ○ Personality: Julian Huxley ○ Progress ○ Revolution ○ Self-Realization (Becoming) ○ Self-Realization (Being) ○ World

A decision is imperative. Mankind lies groaning, half crushed beneath the weight of its own progress. Men do not sufficiently realize that their future is in their own hands. Theirs is the task of determining first of all whether they want to go on living or not. Theirs the responsibility, then, for deciding if they want merely to live, or intend to make just the extra effort required for fulfilling, even on this refractory planet, the essential function of the universe, which is a machine for the making of gods.

> HENRI BERGSON (1859–1941). Closing words, *The Two Sources of Morality and Religion*, 1932, tr. R. Ashley Audra and Cloudesley Brereton, 1935
> See God & the World: Henry Ward Beecher

Some call it Evolution,
And others call it God.

> WILLIAM HERBERT CARRUTH (1841–1920). "Each in His Own Tongue"

I have called this principle, by which each slight variation, if useful, is preserved, by the term of Natural Selection.

> CHARLES DARWIN (1809–1882). *On the Origin of Species by Means of Natural Selection, or the Preservation of Favoured Races in the Struggle for Life*, 3, 1859, ed. J. W. Burrow, 1968

I use the term Struggle for Existence in a large and metaphorical sense, including dependence of one being on another, and including (which is more important) not only the life of the individual, but success in leaving progeny.

> CHARLES DARWIN (1809–1882). *On the Origin of Species by Means of Natural Selection, or the Preservation of Favoured Races in the Struggle for Life*, 3, 1859, ed. J. W. Burrow, 1968

As natural selection works solely by and for the good of each being, all corporeal and mental endowments will tend to progress towards perfection.

> CHARLES DARWIN (1809–1882). *On the Origin of Species by Means of Natural Selection, or the Preservation of Favoured Races in the Struggle for Life*, 14, 1859, ed. J. W. Burrow, 1968

From the war of nature, from famine and death, the most exalted object which we are capable of conceiving, namely, the production of the higher animals, directly follows. There is grandeur in this view of life, with its several powers, having been originally breathed into a few forms or into one; and that, whilst this planet has gone cycling on according to the fixed law of gravity, from so simple a beginning endless forms most beautiful and most wonderful have been, and are being evolved.

> CHARLES DARWIN (1809–1882). Closing words, *On the Origin of Species by Means of Natural Selection, or the Preservation of Favoured Races in the Struggle for Life*, 1859, ed. J. W. Burrow, 1968

Man is descended from a hairy, tailed quadruped, probably arboreal in its habits.

> CHARLES DARWIN (1809–1882). *The Descent of Man and Selection in Relation to Sex*, 2nd ed., 21, 1874

Is man an ape or an angel? I, my lord, I am on the side of the angels. I repudiate with indignation and abhorrence those new-fangled theories.

> BENJAMIN DISRAELI (1804–1881). On Charles Darwin's theory of evolution, speech before the Oxford Diocesan Conference (England), 25 November 1864

It's more comfortable to feel that we're a slight improvement on a monkey thin such a fallin' off fr'm th' angels.

FINLEY PETER DUNNE (1867–1936). "On the Descent of Man," *Mr. Dooley on Making a Will and Other Necessary Evils,* 1919

There comes now and then a bolder spirit, I should rather say, a more surrendered soul, more informed and led by God, which is much in advance of the rest, quite beyond their sympathy, but predicts what shall soon be the general fullness; as when we stand by the seashore, whilst the tide is coming in, a wave comes up the beach far higher than any foregoing one, and recedes; and for a long while none comes up to that mark; but after some time the whole sea is there and beyond it.

RALPH WALDO EMERSON (1803–1882). "Lecture on the Times," Masonic Temple, Boston, 2 December 1841

That point of imperfection which we occupy—is it on the way *up* or *down*?

RALPH WALDO EMERSON (1803–1882). Journal, March? 1843

I suppose you could never prove to the mind of the most ingenious mollusk that such a creature as a whale was possible.

RALPH WALDO EMERSON (1803–1882). Journal, April-May 1848

I am not a thing, a noun.
I seem to be a verb,
an evolutionary process—
an integral function of the universe.

R. BUCKMINSTER FULLER (1895–1983). Epigraph, *I Seem To Be a Verb,* 1970

An epoch will come when people will disclaim kinship with us as we disclaim kinship with the monkeys.

KAHLIL GIBRAN (1883–1931). "Sayings," *Spiritual Sayings of Kahlil Gibran,* tr. Anthony R. Ferris, 1962

All mankind in its present condition, its evolution uncompleted, is suspended between the aboriginal chaos, above which it has risen some way, and a higher order of which it still perceives only glimmers.

LOUIS J. HALE. "The Language of Statesman," *Saturday Review,* 16 October 1971

What is the nature of the evolutionary change we are going through? Are we trapped by culture and design? What is the role of memory in terms of control, imagination, invention? Is there another relationship to matter that is important for us to know about now? Is the next physical horizon the divinization of the flesh?

JOAN HALIFAX. Anthropologist. In "Currents," *Utne Reader,* May–June 1995

The predicament of contemporary man is grave. We seem to be destined either for a new mutation or for destruction.

ABRAHAM JOSHUA HESCHEL (1907–1972). *A Passion for Truth,* 10, 1973

I think it not improbable that man, like the grub that prepares a chamber for the winged thing it never has seen but is to be—that man may have cosmic destinies that he does not understand. And so beyond the vision of battling races and an impoverished earth, I catch a dreaming glimpse of peace.

OLIVER WENDELL HOLMES, JR. (1841–1935). "Law and the Court," speech at a dinner of the Harvard Law School Association of New York, 15 February 1913

The process of evolution can only be described as the gradual insertion of more and more freedom into matter.

T. E. HULME (1883–1917). "The Philosophy of Intensive Manifolds," *Speculations: Essays on Humanism and the Philosophy of Art,* 1924

Man's responsibility and destiny [is] to be an agent for the rest of the world in the job of realizing its inherent potentialities as fully as possible.

It is as if man had been suddenly appointed managing director of the biggest business of all, the business of evolution—appointed without being asked if he wanted it, and without proper warning and preparation. What is more, he can't refuse the job. Whether he wants to or not, whether he is conscious of what he is doing or not, he *is* in point of fact determining the future direction of evolution on this earth. That is his inescapable destiny, and the sooner he realizes it and starts believing in it, the better for all concerned.

JULIAN HUXLEY (1887–1975). "Transhumanism," *New Bottles for New Wine,* 1957

See Environment: Rachel Carson (1)

The human species can, if it wishes, transcend itself—not just sporadically, an individual here in one way, an individual there in another way, but in its entirety, as humanity.

"I believe in transhumanism": once there are enough people who can truly say that, the human species will be on the threshold of a new kind of existence, as different from ours as ours is from that of Peking man. It will at last be consciously fulfilling its real destiny.

JULIAN HUXLEY (1887–1975) Closing words, "Transhumanism," *New Bottles for New Wine,* 1957

Man as we know him is a poor creature; but he is halfway between an ape and a god, and he is traveling in the right direction.

DEAN WILLIAM RALPH INGE (1860–1954). "Confessio Fidei," *Outspoken Essays: Second Series,* 1922

The fermentative influence of geniuses *must* be admitted as . . . one factor in the changes that constitute social evolution. The community *may* evolve in many ways. The accidental presence of this or that ferment decides in which way it *shall* evolve.

WILLIAM JAMES (1842–1910). "Great Men and Their Environment," 1880, *Will to Believe: And Other Essays in Popular Philosophy,* 1897

Social evolution is a resultant of the interaction of two wholly distinct factors: the individual . . . bearing all the power of initiative and origination in his hands; and, second, the social environment, with its power of adopting or rejecting both him and his gifts. Both factors are essential to change. The community stagnates without the impulse of the individual. The impulse dies away without the sympathy of the community.

WILLIAM JAMES (1842–1910). "Great Men and Their Environment," 1880, *Will to Believe: And Other Essays in Popular Philosophy,* 1897

Lord Monboddo, the Scotch judge, has lately written a strange book about the origin of language, in which he traces monkeys up to men, and says that in some countries the human species have tails like other beasts.

SAMUEL JOHNSON (1709–1784). Letter to Hester Lynch Piozzi (Mrs. Thrale), 25 August 1773

Like all evolution in nature, the slow evolution of society is followed from time to time by periods of accelerated evolution which are called revolutions.

> PETER KROPOTKIN (1842–1921). "Anarchism," *Encyclopedia Brittanica,*
> 11th ed., 1910–1911

There are said to be creative pauses,
pauses that are as good as death, empty and dead as death itself.
And in these awful pauses the evolutionary change takes place.
Perhaps it is so.
the tragedy is over, it has ceased to be tragic, the last pause is upon us.
Pause, brethren, pause!

> D. H. LAWRENCE (1885–1930). "Nullus," *The Collected Poems of
> D. H. Lawrence,* 1929

[The] transformation of man into an active, responsible individual is the new event which, more than any other, characterizes man. Of course the ancient mechanism of evolution, natural selection, will again enter into play. But, instead of depending as formerly on the slow action of biological laws and of chance, natural selection now depends on *conscience,* a manifestation of cerebral activity based on freedom which becomes, in each of us, the means put at our disposal to advance.

> PIERRE LECOMTE du NOÜY. *Human Destiny,* 16, 1947

The conversion of one species into another takes place by a leap.

> TROFIM LYSENKO (1898–1976). *The Science of Biology,* 1948

If men cease to believe that they will one day become gods then they will surely become worms.

> HENRY MILLER (1891–1980). *The Colossus of Maroussi,* 3, 1941

The crisis we are witnessing is not one of those that mark the passage from one era to another; it can only be compared to the opening of a new biological or geological epoch, when new beings come on the scene, more evolved and more perfect, whilst on earth are realized conditions of life which have never existed before.

> MARIA MONTESSORI (1870–1952). Lecture on education and peace
> before the League of Nations, Geneva, 1926. In E. M. Standing, *Maria
> Montessori: Her Life and Work,* 4, 1957

The greatest step forward in human evolution was made when society began to help the weak and the poor, instead of oppressing and despising them.

> MARIA MONTESSORI (1870–1952). *The Absorbent Mind,* 22, 1949, tr.
> Claude A. Claremont, 1969

A vital force is active in every individual and leads it towards its own evolution.

> MARIA MONTESSORI (1870–1952). In E. M. Standing, *Maria Montessori:
> Her Life and Work,* 12, 1957

Such a being is man, who has flowed down through other forms of being and absorbed and assimilated portions of them into himself, thus becoming a microcosm most richly Divine because most richly terrestrial, just as a river becomes rich by flowing on and on through varied climes and rocks, through many mountains and vales, constantly appropriating portions to itself, rising higher in the scale of rivers as it grows rich in the absorption of the soils and smaller streams.

> JOHN MUIR (1838–1914). Journal, 15 March 1873. In *John of the
> Mountains: The Unpublished Journals of John Muir,* ed. Linnie Marsh
> Wolfe, 1938

The birth of a universal personality is the equivalent, if not more than the equivalent, of the sudden appearance of a new species in nature.

> LEWIS MUMFORD (1895–1990). *The Conduct of Life,* 4.2, 1951

I teach you the Superman. Man is something that should be overcome. What have you done to overcome him?

> FRIEDRICH NIETZSCHE (1844–1900). "Zarathustra's Prologue" (3), *Thus
> Spoke Zarathustra,* 1892, tr. R. J. Hollingdale, 1961

Man is a rope stretched between the animal and the Superman—a rope over an abyss.

> FRIEDRICH NIETZSCHE (1844–1900). "Zarathustra's Prologue" (4), *Thus
> Spoke Zarathustra,* 1891, tr. Thomas Common, 1898

The whole process of evolution, for the Spirit, is an awakening to the truths, and the means of implementation of those truths, that are eternally present in itself.

> N. SRI RAM (1889–?). *Thoughts for Aspirants,* 1, 1972

There is no reason why, in the ages to come, the sort of man who is now exceptional should not become usual, and if that were to happen, the exceptional man in that new world would rise as far above Shakespeare as Shakespeare now rises above the common man.

> BERTRAND RUSSELL (1872–1970). *Human Society in Ethics and Politics,*
> 2.10, 1962

I am paying attention to what seems to be the largest change of all, a wholesale abandonment of industrial-age structures and models in favor of new, biologically based metaphors. It is a century-scale change, and possibly something even larger. I find myself drawn to Nietzsche's observation "Nearly two thousand years, and no new god." Perhaps something much bigger is lurking just over the horizon.

> PAUL SAFFO. Futurist. In "Currents," *Utne Reader,* May–June
> 1995

The need for freedom of evolution is the sole basis of toleration, the sole valid argument against Inquisitions and Censorships, the sole reason for not burning heretics and sending every eccentric person to the madhouse.

> GEORGE BERNARD SHAW (1856–1950). "The Lesson of the Plays," *The
> Quintessence of Ibsenism,* 1891

One of two things must happen. Either out of that darkness some new creation will come to supplant us as we have supplanted the animals, or the heavens will fall in thunder and destroy us.

> GEORGE BERNARD SHAW (1856–1950). *Heartbreak House: A Fantasia
> in the Russian Manner on English Themes,* 3, 1919

Greater power and greater knowledge: These are what we are all pursuing even at the risk of our lives and the sacrifice of our pleasures. Evolution is that pursuit and nothing else. It is the path to godhead. A man differs from a microbe only in being further on the path.

> GEORGE BERNARD SHAW (1856–1950). *Back to Methuselah:
> A Metabiological Pentateuch,* 2, 1921

Man is not God's last word: God can still create. If you cannot do His work, He will produce some being who can.

GEORGE BERNARD SHAW (1856–1950). *Back to Methuselah: A Metabiological Pentateuch,* 2, 1921

The ultimate objective of social futurism [is] not merely the transcendence of technocracy and the substitution of more humane, more far-sighted, more democratic planning, but the subjection of the process of evolution itself to conscious human guidance. For this is the supreme instant, the turning point in history at which man either vanquishes the processes of change or vanishes, at which, from being the unconscious puppet of evolution he becomes either its victim or its master.

ALVIN TOFFLER (1928–). *Future Shock,* 20, 1970

Man will become immeasurably stronger, wiser, and subtler; his body will become more harmonized; his movements more rhythmic, his voice more musical. The forms of life will become dynamically dramatic. The average human type will rise to the heights of an Aristotle, a Goethe, or a Marx. And above this ridge new peaks will rise.

LEON TROTSKY (1879–1940). Closing words, *Literature and Revolution,* 1925, tr. Rose Strunsky, 1960

The evolution of society is substantially a process of mental adaptation on the part of individuals under the stress of circumstances which will no longer tolerate habits of thought formed under and conforming to a different set of circumstances in the past.

THORSTEIN VEBLEN (1857–1929). *The Theory of the Leisure Class: An Economic Study of Institutions,* 8, 1899

It is possible to believe that all the past is but the beginning of a beginning, and that all that is and has been is but the twilight of the dawn. It is possible to believe that all that the human mind has ever accomplished is but the dream before the awakening . . . . We are creatures of the twilight. . . .

All this world is heavy with the promise of greater things, and a day will come in the unending succession of days when beings, beings who are now latent in our thoughts and hidden in our loins shall stand upon this earth as one stands upon a footstool, and shall laugh and reach out their hands amid the stars.

H. G. WELLS (1866–1946). Closing words, *The Discovery of the Future,* 1913

A world primal again, vistas of glory incessant and branching,
A new race dominating previous ones and grander far, with new contests,
New politics, new literatures and religions, new inventions and arts.
These, my voice announcing—I will sleep no more but arise,
You oceans that have been calm within me! how I feel you, fathomless, stirring, preparing unprecedented waves and storms.

WALT WHITMAN (1819–1892). "Starting from Paumanok" (17), 1860, *Leaves of Grass,* 1855–1892

In the center of all, and object of all, stands the Human Being, towards whose heroic and spiritual evolution poems and everything directly or indirectly tend, Old World or New.

WALT WHITMAN (1819–1892). Preface to *November Boughs,* 1888

❧

Evolution has been canceled.

ANONYMOUS. Sign on classroom door, Parsons School of Design. In Ron Alexander, "Metropolitan Diary," *New York Times,* 26 November 1989

Evolution, not revolution.

SAYING. 19th cent. In Crane Brinton, introduction (1) to *The Anatomy of Revolution,* 1952

EXAMPLE

See also • Crowds: Gustave Le Bon (4) ○ Experience ○ Imitation ○ Leaders & People: Saying (Chinese)

Example is the best precept.

AESOP (6th cent. B.C.). "The Two Crabs," *Fables,* tr. Joseph Jacobs, 1894

Every life is a profession of faith, and exercises an inevitable and silent propaganda. As far as lies in its power, it tends to transform the universe and humanity into its own image.

HENRI AMIEL (1821–1881). Journal, 2 May 1852, tr. Mrs. Humphrey Ward, 1887

Human models are more vivid and more persuasive than explicit moral commands.

DANIEL J. BOORSTIN (1914–). *The Image: A Guide to Pseudo-Events in America,* 2 (introduction), 1961

Setting too good an Example is a Kind of Slander seldom forgiven.

BENJAMIN FRANKLIN (1706–1790). *Poor Richard's Almanack,* February 1753

Nothing is so contagious as example, and our every really good or bad action inspires a similar one.

LA ROCHEFOUCAULD (1613–1680). *Maxims,* 230, 1665, tr. Leonard Tancock, 1959

Be noble! and the nobleness that lies
In other men, sleeping, but never dead,
Will rise in majesty to meet thine own.

JAMES RUSSELL LOWELL (1819–1891). "Sonnet 4," 1840

Example, the surest method of instruction.

PLINY THE YOUNGER (A.D. 62?–113?). *Letters,* 8.14, tr. Betty Radice, 1963

Few things are harder to put up with than the annoyance of a good example.

MARK TWAIN (1835–1910). *The Tragedy of Pudd'nhead Wilson,* 19 (epigraph), 1894

We live. We die. The best we can do is leave a worthwhile example for those who come after us.

ADAM WALINSKY. Referring to Robert F. Kennedy. In Christopher Matthews, "Of Kennedy and King," *San Francisco Sunday Examiner and Chronicle,* 6 June 1993

❧

The example of good men is visible philosophy.

SAYING (ENGLISH)

Words move, but examples draw.

> SAYING. In Pope John XXIII, 29 November 1940, *Journal of a Soul*, 1964, tr. Dorothy White, 1965

EXCELLENCE

See also • Ability ○ Achievement ○ Effort ○ Faults: Oliver Goldsmith (2) ○ Genius ○ Happiness: John F. Kennedy ○ Judging Others: Henry Ward Beecher ○ Leisure: André Gide ○ Perfection ○ Quality

I would rather excel others in the knowledge of what is excellent than in the extent of my power and dominion.

> ALEXANDER (356–323 B.C.). Congratulatory letter from Asia to his teacher Aristotle whose writings had just been published. In Plutarch (A.D. 46?–119?). "Alexander," *Plutarch's Lives*, Dryden edition, 1693
> See Poets: James Wolfe

The sad truth is that excellence makes people nervous.

> SHANA ALEXANDER (1925–). "Neglected Kids—the Bright Ones," 1966, *The Feminist Eye*, 1970

Anyone who has achieved excellence in any form knows that it comes as a result of ceaseless concentration.

> LOUISE BROOKS. "The Other Face of W. C. Fields," *Lulu in Hollywood*, 1982

Strive for excellence, not perfection.

> H. JACKSON BROWN, JR. (1940–). *Life's Little Instruction Book*, 1.156, 1991

If a man write a better book, preach a better sermon, or make a better mousetrap than his neighbor, though he build his house in the woods, the world will make a beaten path to his door.

> RALPH WALDO EMERSON (1803–1882). As recorded by Mrs. Sarah S. B. Yule during a lecture he gave in Oakland (California), 18 May 1871

Excellence is lost sight of in the hunger for sudden performance and praise.

> RALPH WALDO EMERSON (1803–1882). "Success," *Society and Solitude*, 1870

Men of genius do not excel in any profession because they labor in it, but they labor in it because they excel.

> WILLIAM HAZLITT (1778–1830). *Characteristics in the Manner of Rochefoucault's Maxims*, 416, 1823

We never do anything well till we cease to think about the manner of doing it.

> WILLIAM HAZLITT (1778–1830). "On Prejudice," *Sketches and Essays*, 1839

Those who attain any excellence, commonly spend life in one pursuit; for excellence is not often gained upon easier terms.

> SAMUEL JOHNSON (1709–1784). "Pope," *Lives of the English Poets*, 1781

Excellence . . . exposes him to a great many risks, the chief of which is an exaggerated self-confidence.

> CARL G. JUNG (1875–1961). "The Gifted Child," 1942, *The Development of Personality*, tr. R. F. C. Hull, 1954

If people knew how hard I have had to work to gain my mastery, it wouldn't seem so wonderful.

> MICHELANGELO (1475–1564)
> See Writers: Walt Whitman (3)

One of the greatest satisfactions one can ever have, comes from the knowledge that he can do some one thing superlatively well.

> HORTENSE ODLUM. *A Woman's Place: The Autobiography of Hortense Odlum*, 17, 1939

Nature . . . has ordained that difficulty should precede every work of excellence.

> QUINTILIAN (A.D. 35?–100?). *Institutio oratoria*, 10.3.4, tr. John Selby Watson, 1856

Albany: Striving to better, oft we mar what's well.

> SHAKESPEARE (1564–1616). *King Lear*, 1.4.369, 1605

Our whole life is taxed for the least thing well done.

> HENRY DAVID THOREAU (1817–1862). Journal, 28 February 1841

There is nothing more debasing than the work of those who do well what is not worth doing at all.

> GORE VIDAL (1925–). In Jack Kroll, "Lost Weekend," *Newsweek*, 25 March 1968

We never do anything well, unless we love it for its own sake.

> SAYING. In Mary Wollstonecraft, *A Vindication of the Rights of Woman*, 6, 1792

Anything worth doing is worth doing well.

> SAYING

EXCESS

See also • Abstinence ○ Fanatics ○ Gluttony ○ Moderation ○ Passion ○ Self-Discipline ○ Thrift ○ Wealth & Poverty: André Gide

Can we ever have too much of a good thing?

> CERVANTES (1547–1616). *Don Quixote*, 1.1.6, 1615, tr. Peter Anthony Motteux and John Ozell, 1743

To go beyond is as wrong as to fall short.

> CONFUCIUS (551–479 B.C.). *Confucian Analects*, 11.15, tr. James Legge, 1930

More than enough is too much.

> THOMAS FULLER (1654–1734). Comp., *Gnomologia: Adages and Proverbs*, 3461, 1732

Other people's appetites easily appear excessive when one doesn't share them.

> ANDRÉ GIDE (1869–1951). *The Counterfeiters*, 3.1, 1925, tr. Dorothy Bussy, 1951

A man hath too little heat, or wit, or courage, if he hath not sometimes more than he should.

> MARQUESS OF HALIFAX (1633–1695). "Youth," *Political, Moral and Miscellaneous Reflections*, 1750

Too much is seldom enough.

> J. C. HARE (1795–1855) and A. W. HARE (1792–1834). *Guesses at Truth: Second Series*, p. 370, 1848, Macmillan edition, 1867

You can never get enough of what you don't really want.

> ERIC HOFFER (1902–1983). In James Hillman and Michael Ventura, *We've Had a Hundred Years of Psychotherapy—And the World's Getting Worse*, 2, 1992.

One cannot have too much sense or money.

> JAMES HOWELL (1593–1666). Comp., "French" (p. 11), *Paroimiographia: Proverbs, or Old Sayed Sawes & Adages in English . . . Italian, French and Spanish*, 1659

It is only through extremes that men can arrive at the middle path of wisdom and virtue.

> WILHELM von HUMBOLDT (1767–1835). *The Limits of State Action*, 8, 1854, ed. J. W. Burrow, 1969
>
> See Wisdom: William Blake

Anything worth doing is worth doing to excess.

> EDWIN H. LAND (1909–1991). Tongue-in-cheek remark on the importance of concentration and hard work. In Eric Pace, "Edwin H. Land Is Dead at 81; Inventor of Polaroid Camera," *New York Times*, 2 March 1991

Excess on occasion is exhilarating. It prevents moderation from acquiring the deadening effect of habit.

> W. SOMERSET MAUGHAM (1874–1965). *The Summing Up*, 15, 1938

Better moderate excess than excessive moderation.

> ROBERT F. MORGAN (1941–). Personal communication, 15 January 1992

I am not afraid of letting my affection carry me too far; there is no danger of excess where there ought to be no limits.

> PLINY THE YOUNGER (A.D. 62?–113?). *Letters*, 8.24, tr. Betty Radice, 1963

Intemperance is the physician's provider.

> PUBLIUS SYRUS (85–43 B.C.). *Moral Sayings*, 483, tr. Darius Lyman, Jr., 1862

Too much of a good thing can be wonderful.

> MAE WEST (1893–1980). "Misc. West," *The Wit and Wisdom of Mae West*, ed. Joseph Weintraub, 1967

Nothing succeeds like excess.

> OSCAR WILDE (1854–1900). *A Woman of No Importance*, 3, 1894
>
> See Success: Alexandre Dumas

❦

With some things, only too much is enough; with other things, even a little is too much.

> ANONYMOUS

Where there is too much, something is missing.

> SAYING (JEWISH)

EXCUSES

See also • Blame ◦ Destiny: Ambrose Bierce ◦ Responsibility

Any excuse will serve a tyrant.

> AESOP (6th cent. B.C.). "The Wolf and the Lamb," *Fables*, tr. Joseph Jacobs, 1894

The boy who is good at excuses is generally good for nothing else.

> SAMUEL FOOTE (1720–1777). *The Table-Talk and Bon-Mots of Samuel Foote*, p. 212, ed. William Cooke, 1889

Accuse not others to excuse thyself.

> THOMAS FULLER (1654–1734). Comp., *Introductio ad Prudentiam*, 1048, 1731

Don't make excuses—make good!

> ELBERT HUBBARD (1856–1915). *A Thousand and One Epigrams*, p. 135, 1911

Never explain: your friends don't require it, and your enemies won't believe you anyway.

> ELBERT HUBBARD (1856–1915). *A Thousand and One Epigrams*, p. 145, 1911

Several excuses are always less convincing than one.

> ALDOUS HUXLEY (1894–1963). *Point Counter Point*, 1, 1928

I've come to the conclusion that "burnout" is a concept which was invented to hide the fact that the job was probably over one's head in the first place.

> BILL JOHNSON (1930–). "Thoughts about Things in General," *Au Contraire*, August 1983

I wasn't kissing her. I was whispering in her mouth.

> CHICO MARX (1891–1961). When his wife caught him kissing a chorus girl. In Groucho Marx and Richard J. Anobile, *Marx Brothers Scrapbook*, 24, 1973

The plea of ignorance will never take away our responsibilities.

> JOHN RUSKIN (1911–). *Lectures on Architecture and Painting*, 2, 1854

Man gives every reason for his conduct save one, every excuse for his crimes save one, every plea for his safety save one; and that one is his cowardice.

> GEORGE BERNARD SHAW (1856–1950). *Man and Superman*, 3, 1903

Like so many generals when plans have gone wrong, I could find plenty of excuses, but only one reason—myself.

> WILLIAM SLIM (1891–1970). British general. On his decision to evacuate Gallabat (Sudan) in 1940 after having "taken counsel of [his] fears." In Norman F. Dixon, *On The Psychology of Military Incompetence*, 27, 1976

It is better to offer no excuse than a bad one.

> GEORGE WASHINGTON (1732–1799). Letter to his niece Harriet Washington, 30 October 1791

EXECUTIVES

See also • Business (Commerce) ◦ Capitalism ◦ Corporations ◦ Decision-Making ◦ Failure: William Smithburg ◦ Leaders ◦ Managers ◦ Merchants & Customers ◦ Professionals ◦ Stock Market: Peter Lynch ◦ Success

Champions are pioneers, and pioneers get shot at. The companies that get the most from champions, therefore, are those that have rich support networks so their pioneers will flourish. . . . No support systems, no champions. No champions, no innovations.

JONATHAN ALTER. "Precarious Prosperity: The Siren Song of the Service Sector," *Washington Monthly,* December 1982

In general, business executives feel about [government] regulation the way children feel about rules that limit their consumption of ice cream.

PETER BAIDA (1950–). "Men Who Made the Rules," *American Heritage,* February 1989

The Leaders of Industry, if Industry is ever to be led, are virtually the Captains of the World. . . . Captains of Industry are the true Fighters, henceforth recognizable as the only true ones.

THOMAS CARLYLE (1795–1881). *Past and Present,* 4.4, 1843

It is the duty of the executive to remove ruthlessly anyone . . . who consistently fails to perform with high distinction. To let such a man stay on corrupts the others.

PETER F. DRUCKER (1909–). *The Effective Executive,* 4.1.4, 1967

It requires building on strength to make weaknesses irrelevant. Few things make an executive as effective as building on the strength of his superior.

PETER F. DRUCKER (1909–). *The Effective Executive,* 4.2, 1967

Never hire someone who knows less than you do about what he's (or she's) hired to do.

MALCOLM S. FORBES (1919–1990). "Arrived," *The Sayings of Chairman Malcolm: The Capitalist's Handbook,* 1978

Few trends could so thoroughly undermine the very foundations of our free society as the acceptance by corporate officials of a social responsibility other than to make as much money for their stockholders as possible.

MILTON FRIEDMAN (1912–). In "The Intellectual Provocateur," *Time,* 19 December 1969

These men of the technostructure are the new and universal priesthood. Their religion is business success; their test of virtue is growth and profit. Their bible is the computer printout; their communion bench is the committee room.

JOHN KENNETH GALBRAITH (1908–). *The Age of Uncertainty,* 9, 1977

The salary of the chief executive of the large corporation is not a market award for achievement. It is frequently in the nature of a warm personal gesture by the individual to himself.

JOHN KENNETH GALBRAITH (1908–). *Annals of an Abiding Liberal,* 6, 1979

True delegation of authority . . . involves a thoughtful decision on the part of an executive to divest himself of certain tasks while retaining, even if only at the highest level, a supervisory interest.

ALEXANDER L. GEORGE and JULIETTE L. GEORGE. *Woodrow Wilson and Colonel House: A Personality Study,* 7, 1956

My father always told me that all businessmen were sons of bitches, but I never believed it till now!

JOHN F. KENNEDY (1917–1963). Remark to several of his advisers after United States Steel Board Chairman Roger Blough announced a large increase in steel prices on the heels of a noninflationary labor-contract settlement Pres. Kennedy had helped negotiate, 10 April 1962. In Wallace Carroll, "Steel: A 72-Hour Drama With an All-Star Cast," *New York Times,* 23 April 1962. Three weeks later, Pres. Kennedy told Ben Bradlee, "I said sons of bitches, or bastards, or pricks. I don't know which. But I never said anything about *all* businessmen." Bradlee paraphrased Kennedy as then saying, "that it was bankers and steelmen that [my] father hated, not all businessmen." In Ben Bradlee, 15 May 1962, *Conversations with Kennedy,* pp. 81–82, 1975

Corporations that do a better-than-average job of developing leaders put an emphasis on creating challenging opportunities for relatively young employees. In many businesses, decentralization is the key. By definition, it pushes responsibility lower in an organization and in the process creates more challenging jobs at lower levels.

JOHN P. KOTTER (1947–). "What Leaders Really Do," *Harvard Business Review,* May–June 1990

"You're fired!"

No other words can so easily and succinctly reduce a confident, self-assured executive to an insecure, groveling shred of his former self.

FRANK LOUCHHEIM. Chairman of Right Associates, a "reemployment consulting firm." "The Art of Getting Fired," *Wall Street Journal,* 16 July 1984

The business executive is by profession a decision-maker. Uncertainty is his opponent. Overcoming it is his mission. Whether the outcome is a consequence of luck or of wisdom, the moment of decision is without doubt the most creative and critical event in the life of the executive.

JOHN McDONALD. "How Executives Make Decisions." In *Fortune* Editors, *The Executive Life,* 1956

A good executive is one who makes people contentedly settle for less than they meant to get, in return for more than they meant to give.

MIGNON McLAUGHLIN (1915–). *The Neurotic's Notebook,* 9, 1963

The person who knows "how" will always have a job. The person who knows "why" will always be his boss.

DIANE RAVITCH (1938–). Educator. "The Law of Selective Advancement." In "New Prospect, Old Values," *Time,* 17 June 1985

Latest fashion among Japanese businessmen is the study of classical military strategy and tactics in order to apply them to business operations.

REUTERS. British news service. "Business Is a Battlefield," 13 December 1962. In Marshall McLuhan, *Understanding Media: The Extensions of Man,* 24, 1964

Entrust a business to an intelligent man
Although it may not be his occupation.

SA'DI (A.D. 1213?–1292). *The Gulistan, or Rose Garden,* 8 (Maxim 5), A.D. 1258, tr. Edward Rehatsek, 1964

The Man in the Gray Flannel Suit.

SLOAN WILSON (1920–). Book title, 1955

Nothing is illegal if one hundred businessmen decide to do it.

ANDREW YOUNG (1932–). In Bob Green, "How Never to Be at a Loss for Words," *San Francisco Sunday Examiner & Chronicle,* 8 July 1979

❦

Don't do yourself anything you can get others to do as well. Confine your efforts to the impossible things.

> ANONYMOUS (AMERICAN). Advice from a life insurance company chief executive to Adolph S. Ochs on the eve of his becoming publisher of *The New York Times*, August 1896. In Jean Strouse, "Adolph S. Ochs of The Times, in the First Person Singular," *New York Times,* 26 June 1996

When I hear artists or authors making fun of businessmen, I think of a regiment in which the band makes fun of the cooks.

> ANONYMOUS (AMERICAN)

Hire people smarter than you are and get out of their way.

> SAYING (AMERICAN). Quoted by Howard Schultz (Starbucks Corp. chief executive officer). In "The Starbucks Enterprise Shifts into Warp Speed," *Business Week,* 14 October 1994

EXERCISE

See also • Disease: Edward Stanley ○ Health ○ Sports

Use legs and have legs.

> JOHN CLARKE (1596–1658). Comp., *Proverbs: English and Latine,* p. 107, 1639

Exercise is the yuppie version of bulimia.

> BARBARA EHRENREICH (1941–). "Food Worship," 1985, *The Worst Years of Our Lives: Irreverent Notes from a Decade of Greed,* 1990

If fitness was consumption, it was also penance, a continual balancing of calories ingested with calories expended, a social acceptable equivalent of bulimia. . . . Fitness literature emphasized that regular, strenuous exercise made for a more manageable appetite and efficient metabolism. In a very real sense, eating was what one got in shape *for.*

> BARBARA EHRENREICH (1941–). On the fitness craze in the 1980s, *Fear of Falling: The Inner Life of the Middle Class,* 5, 1990

Some people exercise by jumping to conclusions, some by sidestepping their responsibilities, but most people get it by running down their friends.

> EVAN ESAR (1899–1995). Comp., *20,000 Quips and Quotes,* p. 282, 1968

Some people would never get any exercise at all if they didn't have to walk to their cars.

> EVAN ESAR (1899–1995). Comp., *20,000 Quips and Quotes,* p. 282, 1968

Give about two [hours], every day, to exercise; for health must not be sacrificed to learning. A strong body makes the mind strong.

> THOMAS JEFFERSON (1743–1826). Letter to Peter Carr, 19 August 1785

Walking is the best possible exercise.

> THOMAS JEFFERSON (1743–1826). Letter to Peter Carr, 19 August 1785

It is remarkable how one's wits are sharpened by physical exercise.

> PLINY THE YOUNGER (A.D. 62?–113?). *Letters,* 1.6, tr. Betty Radice, 1963

Walking is an excellent exercise. At 65, my grandmother began walking five miles a day. She's now 100—and we have no idea where she is.

ROBERT B. REICH (1946–). Repeating an old joke, speech at the U.S. Conference of Mayors, 27 January 1994

Without a proper amount of daily exercise no one can remain healthy.

> ARTHUR SCHOPENHAUER (1788–1860). "The Wisdom of Life" (2), *Essays of Arthur Schopenhauer,* tr. T. Bailey Saunders, 1851

An early morning walk is a blessing for the whole day.

> HENRY DAVID THOREAU (1817–1862). Journal, 20 April 1840

❦

Whenever I feel an urge to exercise I lie down until it goes away.

> ANONYMOUS. Attributed to Mark Twain, W. C. Fields, and others

EXPECTATION

See also • Hope

Blessed is he that expecteth nothing, for he shall be gloriously surprised.

> G. K. CHESTERTON (1874–1936). *Heretics,* 4, 1905

Great Expectations.

> CHARLES DICKENS (1812–1870). Book title, 1861

"Blessed is the man who expects nothing, for he shall never be disappointed" was the ninth beatitude which a man of wit . . . added to the eighth.

> ALEXANDER POPE (1688–1744). Letter to William Fortescue, 23 September 1725

I have no expectation of making a hit every time I come to bat. What I seek is the highest possible batting average.

> FRANKLIN D. ROOSEVELT (1882–1945). In James David Barber, *The Presidential Character: Predicting Performance in the White House,* 7, 1972

Helena: Oft expectation fails and most oft there
Where most it promises, and oft it hits
Where hope is coldest and despair most fits.

> SHAKESPEARE (1564–1616). *All's Well that Ends Well,* 2.1.145, 1602

We should expect the best and the worst from mankind, as from the weather.

> VAUVENARGUES (1715–1747). *Reflections and Maxims,* 102, 1746, tr. F. G. Stevens, 1940

❦

Expectations tend to be self-fulfilling.

> ANONYMOUS

EXPERIENCE

See also • Example ○ Learning (Process): [especially] Robert Ascham ○ Luck ○ Misfortune ○ Study: Francis Bacon (1) ○ Thinking: Arthur Schopenhauer ○ Truth: Albert Einstein ○ Wisdom: Samuel Richardson

"Experience iz a good schoolmaster," but reason iz a better one.

> JOSH BILLINGS (1818–1885). "Ink Brats," *Everybody's Friend, or; Josh Billing's Encyclopedia and Proverbial Philosophy of Wit and Humor,* 1874

The Law of Primacy . . . states that the earlier an experience the more potent its effect since it influences how later experiences will be interpreted.

> J. A. C. BROWN (1911–1964). *Techniques of Persuasion: From Propaganda to Brainwashing,* 2, 1963

We learn geology the morning after the earthquake.

> RALPH WALDO EMERSON (1803–1882). "Considerations by the Way," *The Conduct of Life,* 1860

Experience keeps a dear school, yet Fools will learn in no other.

> BENJAMIN FRANKLIN (1706–1790). *Poor Richard's Almanack,* December 1743

A moment's insight is sometimes worth a life's experience.

> OLIVER WENDELL HOLMES, SR. (1809–1894). *The Professor at the Breakfast-Table,* 10, 1860

Experience . . . has ways of *boiling over,* and making us correct our present formulas.

> WILLIAM JAMES (1842–1910). *Pragmatism,* 6, 1907

Events seen and participated in leave disproportionate impressions. Furthermore . . . the lessons drawn from firsthand experiences are overgeneralized. So if people do not learn enough from what happens to others, they learn too much from what happens to themselves.

> ROBERT JERVIS. *Perception and Misperception in International Politics,* 6, 1976

Experience enables you to recognize a mistake when you make it again.

> FRANKLIN P. JONES (1881–1960)

As we experience the world, so we act.

> R. D. LAING (1927–1989). *The Politics of Experience,* 6, 1967

Experience is a hard teacher because she gives the test first, the lesson afterward.

> VERNON LAW. Baseball player. In "How to Be a Winner," *This Week,* 14 August 1960

The world doesn't fear a new idea. It can pigeonhole any idea. But it can't pigeonhole a real new experience.

> D. H. LAWRENCE (1885–1930). *Studies in Classic American Literature,* 1, 1923

a man who is so dull
that he can learn only by personal experience
is too dull to learn
anything important by experience.

> DON MARQUIS (1878–1937). "archy on this and that," *archy does his part,* 1935

We can learn from experience if we are ready to adapt that experience to changed conditions.

> J. C. MASTERMAN (1891–1977). *The Double-Cross System in the War of 1939 to 1945,* 1, 1972

If it be knowledge or wisdom one is seeking, then one had better go direct to the source. And the source is not the scholar or philosopher, not the master, saint, or teacher, but life itself—direct experience of life.

> HENRY MILLER (1891–1980). Preface to *The Books in My Life,* 1952

We must not study ourselves while having an experience.

> FRIEDRICH NIETZSCHE (1844–1900)

I like to think of my behavior in the sixties as a "learning experience." Then again, I like to think of anything stupid I've done as a "learning experience." It makes me feel less stupid.

> P. J. O'ROURKE (1947–). "Second Thoughts about the Sixties," speech before the Second Thoughts Conference, Washington, October 1987, *Give War a Chance,* 1992

The best of all teachers, experience.

> PLINY THE YOUNGER (A.D. 62?–113?). *Letters,* 1.20, tr. Betty Radice, 1963

She had some experience of the world, and the capacity for reflection that makes such experience profitable.

> ROUSSEAU (1712–1778). *Confessions,* 3 (1731–1732). 1781, tr. J. M. Cohen, 1953

Our experience is composed rather of illusions lost than of wisdom acquired.

> JOSEPH ROUX (1834–1886). *Meditations of a Parish Priest,* 4.28, tr. Isabel F. Hapgood, 1886

Experience of the world may be looked upon as a kind of text, to which reflection and knowledge form the commentary.

> ARTHUR SCHOPENHAUER (1788–1860). "Counsels and Maxims" (2.8), *Essays of Arthur Schopenhauer,* tr. T. Bailey Saunders, 1851

We learn from experience that men never learn anything from experience.

> GEORGE BERNARD SHAW (1856–1950). Letter, *The Wit and Wisdom of Bernard Shaw,* 30, ed. Stephen Winsten, 1949

❦

When a man with money meets a man with experience, the man with the experience ends up with the money and the man with the money ends up with the experience.

> ANONYMOUS (AMERICAN). "59-year-old's discovery." In "Thoughts on the Business of Life," *Forbes,* 21 November 1994

There's no educational value in the second kick of a mule.

> SAYING (AMERICAN)

If you would know the road ahead, ask someone who has traveled it.

> SAYING (CHINESE)

Once burned, twice shy.

> SAYING (ENGLISH)

EXPERTS

See also • Authority ○ Bureaucracy ○ Intellectuals ○ Organizations ○ Philosophers ○ Professionals ○ Science ○ Specialists ○ Status ○ Technology

An expert is a man who has made all the mistakes, which can be made, in a very narrow field.

> NIELS BOHR (1885–1962). Danish nuclear physicist

Too bad all the people who know how to run the country are too busy driving taxicabs or cutting hair.

GEORGE BURNS (1896–1996). In James Ainsworth, "America's Cup," *Punch* (British humor magazine), 25 September 1985

The function of the expert is not to be more right than others, but to be wrong for more sophisticated reasons.

DAVID BUTLER (1924–). British psephologist. In *Observer* (British newspaper), 1969

Everyone is a reactionary on the subject he is expert about.

CONQUEST'S LAW. In John O'Sullivan, "1861 and All That," *National Review*, 14 May 1990

A man who knows no one thing intimately has no views worth hearing on things in general.

CHARLES HORTON COOLEY (1864–1929). *Human Nature and the Social Order*, rev. ed., 4, 1922 (1902)

If you consult enough experts, you can confirm any opinion.

HIRAM'S LAW. In Arthur Bloch, comp., "Expertsmanship," *Murphy's Law: Book Three*, 1982

All my life I've known better than to depend on the experts. How could I have been so stupid, to let them go ahead?

JOHN F. KENNEDY (1917–1963). On the Bay of Pigs reversal, 20 April 1961. In Theodore C. Sorensen, *Kennedy*, 11, 1965

The expert has his constituency—those who have a vested interest in commonly held opinions; elaborating and defining its consensus at a high level has, after all, made him an expert.

HENRY A. KISSINGER (1923–). *American Foreign Policy*, 1.3, 1969

There is a tradition of men becoming experts simply by being put in positions that require expertise.

MICHAEL LEWIS. "Beyond Economics, Beyond Politics, Beyond Accountability," *Worth*, May 1995

We have not overthrown the divine right of kings to fall down for the divine right of experts.

HAROLD MACMILLAN (1907–1991). British prime minister. Speech, Strasbourg (France), 16 August 1950

Expertise can always be hired.

GEORGE E. REEDY (1917–). *The Twilight of the Presidency*, 4, 1970

The distinctive feature of the regime of experts lies in the fact that, while possessing ample power to coerce, it prefers to charm conformity from us by exploiting our deep-seated commitment to the scientific world-view and by manipulating the securities and creature comforts of the industrial affluence which science has given us.

THEODORE ROSZAK (1933–). *The Making of the Counter Culture: Reflections on the Technocratic Society and Its Youthful Opposition*, 1, 1969

Parties and governments may come and go, but the experts stay on forever. Because without them, the system does not work. The machine stops. And *then* where are we?

THEODORE ROSZAK (1933–). *The Making of the Counter Culture: Reflections on the Technocratic Society and Its Youthful Opposition*, 1, 1969

Centralized bigness breeds the regime of expertise, whether the big system is based on privatized or socialized economics.

THEODORE ROSZAK (1933–). *The Making of the Counter Culture: Reflections on the Technocratic Society and Its Youthful Opposition*, 7, 1969

Expert, *n.* A modern seer, often self-styled, whose pronouncements are received as if emanating from an oracle. A "recognized expert" is one whose pronouncements are closest to conventional wisdom.

EDMUND H. VOLKART (1919–). *The Angel's Dictionary: A Modern Tribute to Ambrose Bierce*, p. 75, 1986

More and more the specialized knowledge of the expert became the foundation for the power position of the officeholder. Hence a concern of the ruler was how to exploit the special knowledge of experts without having to abdicate in their favor . . . his dominant position.

MAX WEBER (1864–1920). "Bureaucracy" (13), 1922, *From Max Weber: Essays in Sociology*, tr. H. H. Gerth and C. Wright Mills, 1958

An expert is a man who has stopped thinking—he knows.

FRANK LLOYD WRIGHT (1867–1959). In Laurence J. Peter, *The Peter Prescription: How to Make Things Go Right*, 3, 1972

Experts are never right or wrong; they win or lose. Right and wrong are decided by proof; winning and losing are decided by who is doing the talking or talks the loudest, has the last, latest, or only word, and is quoted by reporters.

M. A. ZEIDNER. "Experts: A Definition," *Quarterly Review of Doublespeak*, October 1988

❧

The more the experts agree among themselves, the less likely they are to be right.

ANONYMOUS

EXPLOITATION

See also • Child Abuse: [especially] Mary "Mother" Jones, *U.S. News & World Report* ○ Class ○ Competition ○ Dehumanization ○ Environment: Gary Snyder ○ Greed ○ Imperialism ○ Inequality ○ Injustice ○ Machiavellianism ○ Nonviolence: Mohandas K. Gandhi (8) ○ Oppression ○ Poverty ○ Power ○ Self-Interest ○ Slavery ○ Tyranny ○ Values: William Greider ○ Wages ○ Wealth ○ Wealth & Poverty

Almost all of our relationships begin and most of them continue as forms of mutual exploitation, a mental or physical barter, to be terminated when one or both parties run out of goods.

W. H. AUDEN (1907–1973). "Hic et Ille," *The Dyer's Hand and Other Essays*, 1962

Those whom we cannot exploit we denounce a selfish.

PAUL ELDRIDGE (1888–1982). *Maxims for a Modern Man*, 2226, 1965

In the Feejee [sic] islands, it appears, cannibalism is now familiar. They eat their own wives and children. We only devour widows' houses, and great merchants outwit and absorb the substance of small ones and every man feeds on his neighbor's labor if he can. It is a milder form of cannibalism.

RALPH WALDO EMERSON (1803–1882). Journal, 12 February 1841

The human race cannot forever exist half-exploiter and half-exploited

> HENRY FORD (1863–1947) (with SAMUEL CROWTHER). *My Life and Work,* 17, 1922

Exploitation is the essence of violence.

> MOHANDAS K. GANDHI (1869–1948). In *Harijan,* 4 November 1939

As a rule, those who know how to exploit are endowed with the skill to justify their acts, while those who are easily exploited possess no skill in pleading their own cause.

> ABRAHAM JOSHUA HESCHEL (1907–1972). *The Prophets,* 11, 1962

The Lord enters into judgment
   with the elders and princes of his people:
"It is you who have devoured the vineyard,
   the spoil of the poor is in your houses.
What do you mean by crushing my people,
   by grinding the face of the poor?"
   says the Lord God of hosts.

> ISAIAH (8th cent. B.C.). *Isaiah* 3:14–15

[I] never would believe that Providence had sent a few men into the world, ready booted and spurred to ride, and millions ready saddled and bridled to be ridden.

> RICHARD RUMBOLD (1622–1685). Scaffold speech (before being hanged for sedition), Edinburgh (Scotland). In Thomas Babington Macaulay, *The History of England,* 1.5, 1849–1861

Poverty and slavery are . . . only two forms of—one might almost say two words for—the same thing, the essence of which is that a man's energies are expended for the most part not on his own behalf but on that of others; the outcome being partly that he is overloaded with work, partly that his needs are very inadequately met.

> ARTHUR SCHOPENHAUER (1788–1860). "On Law and Politics" (5), 1851, *Essays and Aphorisms,* tr. R. J. Hollingdale, 1970

Remember, Drucker, if you don't feel exploited, you're not working hard enough

> MIKE SHAPIRO. Manager to employee, cartoon caption, *Barron's,* 25 August 1997

No elaboration of physical or moral accomplishment can atone for the sin of parasitism.

> GEORGE BERNARD SHAW (1856–1950). "Maxims for Revolutionists: The Perfect Gentleman," *Man and Superman,* 1903

To exploit a person is to make money out of her without giving her an equivalent return.

> GEORGE BERNARD SHAW (1856–1950). *The Intelligent Woman's Guide to Socialism, Capitalism, Sovietism and Fascism,* 31, 1928

The exploitation of the weak by the powerful, organized for the purposes of economic gain, buttressed by imposing systems of law, and screened by decorous draperies of virtuous sentiment and resounding rhetoric, has been a permanent feature in the life of most communities that the world has yet seen.

> R. H. TAWNEY (1880–1962). *Religion and the Rise of Capitalism: A Historical Study,* 5, 1926

If I devote myself to other pursuits and contemplation, I must first see, at least, that I do not pursue them sitting upon another man's shoulders.

> HENRY DAVID THOREAU (1817–1862). "Civil Disobedience," 1849

❦

Blood oils the machinery of exploitation.

> ANONYMOUS

Exploitation is to war what robbery is to murder.

> ANONYMOUS

One sows and another reaps.

> SAYING (*BIBLE*). Quoted by Jesus. In *John* 4:37

EYES

See also • Perception ○ Seeing

It needs no dictionary of quotations to remind me that the eyes are the windows of the soul.

> MAX BEERBOHM (1872–1956). *Zuleika Dobson,* 4, 1911

This Life's dim windows of the Soul
Distorts the Heavens from Pole to Pole
And leads you to Believe a Lie
When you see with, not thro', the Eye.

> WILLIAM BLAKE (1757–1827). "The Everlasting Gospel," d.103, 1818

The eye of the beholder may govern what is seen.

> JAMES MacGREGOR BURNS (1918–). *Leadership,* 4, 1978
> See Beauty: Margaret Hungerford

Eyes can speak and eyes can understand.

> GEORGE CHAPMAN (1559?–1634). *The Gentleman Usher,* 2.1, 1595

So shall we come to look at the world with new eyes.

> RALPH WALDO EMERSON (1803–1882). "Prospects," *Nature,* 1836

Eyes so transparent,
That through them one sees the soul.

> THÉOPHILE GAUTIER (1811–1872). "The Two Beautiful Eyes"

The eyes have one language everywhere.

> GEORGE HERBERT (1593–1633). Comp., *Outlandish Proverbs,* 959, 1640
> See Smiles: Saying

Close your eyes, and you will see.

> JOSEPH JOUBERT (1754–1824). 1801, *Pensées,* 1838, tr. Paul Auster, 1983

"Would You Wear My Eyes?"

> BOB KAUFMAN (1925–1986). Poem title, *Solitudes Crowded with Loneliness,* 1965

Picture yourself in a boat on a river,
With tangerine trees and marmalade skies,
Somebody calls you, you answer quite slowly,
A girl with kaleidoscope eyes.

> JOHN LENNON (1940–1980) and PAUL McCARTNEY (1942–). "Lucy in the Sky with Diamonds" (song), 1967

He kept him as the apple of his eye.

> MOSES (14th cent. B.C.). *Deuteronomy* 32:10

All looks yellow to the Jaundic'd Eye.

> ALEXANDER POPE (1688–1744). *An Essay on Criticism,* l. 559, 1711

In a dark time, the eye begins to see.

> THEODORE ROETHKE (1908–1963). *In a Dark Time,* 1, 1964

Bassanio: Sometimes from her eyes
I did receive fair speechless messages.

> SHAKESPEARE (1564–1616). *The Merchant of Venice,* 1.1.163, 1596

They have eyes, but they see not.

> ANONYMOUS (*BIBLE*). *Psalms* 135:16

FACE

See also • Body

A good face is a letter of recommendation.

> JOSEPH ADDISON (1672–1719). In *The Spectator* (English essay series), 221, 13 November 1711

Alas, after a certain age every man is responsible for his face.

> ALBERT CAMUS (1913–1960). *The Fall,* p. 57, tr. Justin O'Brien, 1956

Every man finds room in his face for all his ancestors.

> RALPH WALDO EMERSON (1803–1882). Journal, 1850, undated

There are some faces that have no more expression in them than any other part of the body—the hand of one person may express more than the face of another.

> NATHANIEL HAWTHORNE (1804–1864). 27 July 1844, *The American Notebooks,* ed. Claude M. Simpson, 1932

Was this the face that launch'd a thousand ships?

> CHRISTOPHER MARLOWE (1564–1593). *The Tragicall History of Doctor Faustus,* 13, 1604

At 50, everyone has the face he deserves.

> GEORGE ORWELL (1903–1950). "Extracts from a Manuscript Notebook," 17 April 1949, *The Collected Essays, Journalism and Letters of George Orwell,* vol. 4, ed. Sonia Orwell and Ian Angus, 1968

A face which is always serene possesses a mysterious and powerful attraction; sad hearts come to it as to the sun to warm themselves.

> JOSEPH ROUX (1834–1886). *Meditations of a Parish Priest,* 9.10, tr. Isabel F. Hapgood, 1886

King Henry: In thy face I see
The map of honor, truth, and loyalty.

> SHAKESPEARE (1564–1616). *Henry VI,* Part II, 3.1.202, 1590

Macbeth: False face must hide what the false heart doth know.

> SHAKESPEARE (1564–1616). *Macbeth,* 1.7.82, 1605

In the faces of men and women I see God, and in my own face in the glass.

> WALT WHITMAN (1819–1892). "Song of Myself" (48), 1855, *Leaves of Grass,* 1855–1892
>
> See People: Whitman

The face is the index of the mind.

> SAYING (LATIN)

FACTS

See also • Confidence—First Person: Winston Churchill ○ Faith: William James, Albert Schweitzer ○ Ideas ○ Imagination: John Burroughs, Alfred North Whitehead ○ Information ○ Intelligence, Military ○ Knowledge ○ Logic ○ Reality: [especially] Ronald Steel ○ Science: Henri Poincaré ○ Statistics ○ Theories: Mark Twain ○ Truth

Facts are facts and flinch not.

> ROBERT BROWNING (1812–1889). *The Ring and the Book,* 2.1049, 1869

Generally the theories we believe we call facts, and the facts we disbelieve we call theories.

> FELIX COHEN

The facts speak for themselves.

> DEMOSTHENES (384–322 B.C.). *De falsa legatione,* 81

Now, what I want is, Facts. . . . Facts alone are wanted in life.

> CHARLES DICKENS (1812–1870). *Hard Times,* 1.1, 1854

An unexpected fact is less readily absorbed than one which was expected.

> NORMAN F. DIXON (1922–). *On the Psychology of Military Incompetence,* 2, 1976

[Everyone is prone to] look for the facts that fit the conclusion they have already reached.

> PETER F. DRUCKER (1909–). *The Effective Executive,* 7.1, 1967

Every fact depends for its value on how much we already know.

> RALPH WALDO EMERSON (1803–1882). Journal, 18 May 1831

No facts are to me sacred; none are profane; I simply experiment, an endless seeker, with no Past at my back.

> RALPH WALDO EMERSON (1803–1882). "Circles," *Essays: First Series,* 1841

Always the thought is prior to the fact; all the facts of history pre-exist in the mind as laws.

RALPH WALDO EMERSON (1803–1882). "History," *Essays: First Series,* 1841

A fact is an Epiphany of God.

RALPH WALDO EMERSON (1803–1882). "Education," *Lectures and Biographical Sketches,* 1883

A little fact is worth a whole limbo of dreams.

RALPH WALDO EMERSON (1803–1882). "The Superlative," *Lectures and Biographical Sketches,* 1883

The reliability of the person giving you the facts is as important as the facts themselves. Keep in mind that facts are seldom facts, but what people think are facts, heavily tinged with assumptions.

HAROLD GENEEN (1910–1997) (with ALVIN MOSCOW). *Managing,* 13, 1984

A wise man recognizes the convenience of a general statement, but he bows to the authority of a particular fact.

OLIVER WENDELL HOLMES, SR. (1809–1894). *The Poet at the Breakfast-Table,* 10, 1872

Facts do not cease to exist because they are ignored.

ALDOUS HUXLEY (1894–1963). "A Note on Dogma: Paradox," *Proper Studies,* 1927

Truly it has been said, that to a clear eye the smallest fact is a window through which the Infinite may be seen.

T. H. HUXLEY (1825–1895). "The Study of Zoology," *Discourses, Biological and Geological Essays,* 1896

A fact which can[not] be scientifically verified . . . finds no place in an official view of the world.

CARL G. JUNG (1875–1961). *Memories, Dreams, Reflections,* 9.5, ed. Aniela Jaffé, 1962

Facts: Words treated as statements of actuality by those who agree with them.

CHERIS KRAMARAE (1938–) and PAULA A. TREICHLER. Comps., *A Feminist Dictionary: In Our Own Words,* p. 148, 1985

Facts are stubborn things.

ALAIN-RENÉ LESAGE (1668–1747). *L'Histoire de Gil Blas de Santillane,* 10.1, 1715–1735

Bullets—the hardest of facts.

B. H. LIDDELL HART (1895–1970). *The Ghost of Napoleon,* 3.3, 1933

The facts we see depend on where we are placed, and the habits of our eyes.

WALTER LIPPMANN (1889–1974). *Public Opinion,* 6.1, 1922

If the facts do not conform to the theory, they must be disposed of.

MAIER'S LAW. In Arthur Bloch, comp., "Researchmanship," *Murphy's Law: And Other Reasons Why Things Go gnorW,* 1979

My master is the hard fact, how things are.

NAPOLEON (1769–1821). Letter to Josephine, 3 December 1806. In Maurice Hutt, ed., *Napoleon,* 4, 1972

Facts are stupid things, uh, stubborn things, I should say.

RONALD REAGAN (1911–). Slip-of-the-tongue in his farewell address to the Republican National Convention, Chicago, 20 August 1988

Data will arrange themselves to fit preconceived conclusions.

GEORGE E. REEDY (1917–). *Lyndon B. Johnson: A Memoir,* 15, 1982

Every fact means something beyond itself.

ODELL SHEPARD. Preface to *The Heart of Thoreau's Journals,* 1927

"Oh, don't tell me of facts—I never believe facts; you know Canning said nothing was so fallacious as facts, except figures.

SYDNEY SMITH (1771–1845). "Rev. Sydney Smith." In James Thornton, ed., *Table Talk from Ben Jonson to Leigh Hunt,* 1934

Facts, or what a man believes to be facts, are always delightful. . . . Get your facts first, and then you can distort 'em as much as you please.

MARK TWAIN (1835–1910). Interview with Rudyard Kipling, *From Sea to Sea,* 1889. In Christopher Silvester, ed., *The Norton Book of Interviews: An Anthology from 1859 to the Present Day,* 1996

It is the spirit of the age to believe that any fact, no matter how suspect, is superior to any imaginative exercise, no matter how true.

GORE VIDAL (1925–). "French Letters: Theories of the New Novel," *Encounter,* December 1967

Just the facts, ma'am.

JACK WEBB (1920–1982). In the role of Sgt. Friday, his signature line, *Dragnet,* television police series, 1952–1959

We want the facts to fit the preconceptions. When they don't, it is easier to ignore the facts than to change the preconceptions.

JESSAMYN WEST (1902–1984). Ed., introduction to *The Quaker Reader,* 1962

Our monstrous worship of facts.

OSCAR WILDE (1854–1900). "The Decay of Lying," *Intentions,* 1891

❦

A fact merely marks the point where we have agreed to let investigation cease.

ANONYMOUS. "On Having Known a Poet," *Atlantic,* May 1966

If the facts are against me, so much the worse for the facts.

SAYING (AMERICAN)

FAILURE

See also • Bible: Martin Buber ○ Competition ○ Defeat ○ Details ○ Errors ○ Faults ○ Indecision: John F. Kennedy ○ Loneliness: Eric Hoffer ○ Mistakes ○ Success ○ Success & Failure ○ Trifles ○ Weakness

Hurtful timidity, unprofitable conscientiousness, fatal slavery to detail!

HENRI AMIEL (1821–1881). Journal, 1 September 1875, tr. Mrs. Humphrey Ward, 1887

Failure is impossible.

SUSAN B. ANTHONY (1820–1906). On her 86th birthday, one month before her death in 1906. In Lynn Sherr, *Failure Is Impossible: Susan B. Anthony in Her Own Words,* 1995

There are only two kinds of people who fail: Those who listen to nobody, and . . . those who listen to everybody.

THOMAS M. BESHERE, JR. "Beshere's Formula for Failure," in Paul Dickson, comp., *The Official Explanations,* p. 14, 1980

When a feller gits a goin down hil, it dus seem as tho evry thing had bin greased for the okashun.

> JOSH BILLINGS (1818–1885). *His Sayings,* 28, 1867

To dry one's eyes and laugh at a fall,
And baffled, get up and begin again.

> ROBERT BROWNING (1812–1889). "Life in a Love," l. 13

He that is down needs fear no fall.

> JOHN BUNYAN (1628–1688). *The Pilgrim's Progress,* 2.6, 1678–1684

Pregnant failures are not unknown in history. History recognizes what I may call "delayed achievement": The apparent failures of today may turn out to have made a vital contribution to the achievement of tomorrow—prophets born before their time.

> EDWARD HALLETT CARR. *What Is History?* 5, 1961

If a man once fall, all will tread on him.

> JOHN CLARKE (1596–1658). Comp., *Proverbs: English and Latine,* p. 68, 1639

Ty Cobb (timidly to his father on the phone)*:* There's a job open with a team over in Anniston.
Cobb: Go after it. And I want to tell you one other thing—don't come home a failure.

> WILLIAM H. COBB. At the outset of his son's baseball career, 1904. In Ty Cobb (with Al Stump), *My Life in Baseball: The True Record,* 3, 1961

Failure after long perseverance is much grander than never to have a striving good enough to be a called a failure.

> GEORGE ELIOT (1819–1880). *Middlemarch,* 22, 1871–1872

There are no second acts in American lives.

> F. SCOTT FITZGERALD (1896–1940). "Hollywood, Etc." (Notes), *The Last Tycoon,* ed. Edmund Wilson, 1941

A Stumble may prevent a Fall.

> THOMAS FULLER (1654–1734). Comp., *Gnomologia: Adages and Proverbs,* 424, 1732

In Life as in Football
Fall Forward when you fall.

> ARTHUR GUITERMAN (1871–1943). "Of Sport," *A Poet's Proverbs: Being Mirthful, Sober, and Fanciful Epigrams on the Universe, With Certain Old Irish Proverbs, All in Rhymed Couplets,* 1924

Half the failures in life arise from pulling in one's horse as he is leaping.

> J. C. HARE (1795–1855) and A. W. HARE (1792–1834). *Guesses at Truth: First Series,* p. 156, 1827, Macmillan edition, 1867

More undertakings fail for want of spirit than for want of sense.

> WILLIAM HAZLITT (1778–1830). "On Manner," *The Round Table,* 1817

Failure: A man who has blundered but is not able to cash in on the experience.

> ELBERT HUBBARD (1856–1915). *The Roycroft Dictionary Concocted by Ali Baba and the Bunch on Rainy Days,* p. 53, 1914

People are constantly spoiling a project when it lacks only a step to completion.

> LAO-TZU (6th cent. B.C.). *The Way of Life,* 64, tr. R. B. Blakney, 1955

Failure is the path of least persistence.

> MICHAEL LARSEN (1941–). *Literary Agents: What They Do, How They Do It, and How to Find and Work with the Right One for You,* rev. ed., 15.7, 1996

Failure seldom stops you; what stops you is the fear of failure.

> JACK LEMMON (1925–). Appearing on *Signature,* television interview series, 1987?

Not failure, but low aim is crime.

> JAMES RUSSELL LOWELL (1819–1891). "For an Autograph," *Under the Willows and Other Poems,* 1868

The history of failure in war can be summed up in two words: Too Late.

> DOUGLAS MacARTHUR (1880–1964). Letter to William Allen White. In William Manchester, *American Caesar: Douglas MacArthur: 1880–1964,* 4, 1978

I wanted too much. . . . I strung the bow too tightly, and trusted too much in my good fortune.

> NAPOLEON (1769–1821). Explaining his fall, St. Helena, after 1815. In Emil Ludwig, *Napoleon,* 5.15, 1925, tr. Eden and Cedar Paul, 1926

To do two things at once is to do neither.

> PUBLIUS SYRUS (85–43 B.C.). *Moral Sayings,* 7, tr. Darius Lyman, Jr., 1862

When I was young, I observed that nine out of every ten things I did were failures, so I did ten times more work.

> GEORGE BERNARD SHAW (1856–1950)

There isn't one senior manager in this company who hasn't been associated with a product that flopped. That includes me. It's like learning to ski. If you're not falling down, you're not learning.

> WILLIAM SMITHBURG. Quaker Oats chairman. In Warren Bennis and Burt Nanus, "Leading Others, Managing Yourself," *Leaders: The Strategies for Taking Charge,* 1985

I cannot give you the formula for success, but I can give you the formula for failure, which is: Try to please everybody.

> HERBERT BAYARD SWOPE (1882–1958). Speech, St. Louis, 20 December 1950

Dear George:—
Remember <u>no</u> man is a failure who has <u>friends</u>.
Thanks for the wings!
  Love
  Clarence

> PHILIP VAN DOREN STERN (1897–1991) (FRANK CAPRA, FRANCES GOODRICH, ALBERT HACKETT, and JO SWERLING, scriptwriters). Note from the angel Clarence (played by Henry Travers) to George Bailey (played by James Stewart), final scene, *It's a Wonderful Life* (film), 1946

❦

Failure teaches success.

> SAYING (JAPANESE)

If you're falling, dive.

> SAYING

FAITH

See also • Belief ○ Certainty ○ Conviction ○ Doubt ○ Faith &
Reason ○ Healing: Jesus ○ Heaven: Muhammad ○ Hope ○ Reason
○ Religion ○ Self-Realization (Becoming) ○ Skepticism ○ Trust ○
Truth: Kahlil Gibran

Mystery on all sides! And faith the only star in this darkness and
uncertainty!

> HENRI AMIEL (1821–1881). Journal, 11 January 1867, tr. Mrs. Humphrey
> Ward, 1887

I am one of those who would rather sink with faith than swim without it.

> STANLEY BALDWIN (1867–1947). Speech, Leeds (England), 12 October
> 1923

Faith is not being sure where you're going but going anyway.

> FREDERICK BUECHNER. "Faith," Wishful Thinking: A Theological ABC,
> 1973

You can do very little with faith, but you can do nothing without it.

> SAMUEL BUTLER (1835–1902). The Note-Books of Samuel Butler, 21, ed.
> Henry Festing Jones, 1907

Who created the singularity that later became the entire universe!
How did this happen! Human beings can't comprehend it. Human
consciousness can't encompass this. That strengthens my faith in a
great and incomprehensible Creator, rather than causing me to
doubt the creation just because I don't think it happened in six days
or because I believe in evolution.

> JIMMY CARTER (1924–). Don Lattin interview, "A Statesman and a Man of
> Faith," San Francisco Sunday Examiner & Chronicle, 12 January 1997

To lose one's faith—surpass
The loss of an Estate—
Because Estates can be
Replenished—faith cannot—

> EMILY DICKINSON (1830–1886). "To lose one's faith—surpass," 1862?

Faith is a commitment to the world's transformation through God
to a kingdom of justice and peace.

> JAMES W. DOUGLASS (1937–). Lightning East to West, 5, 1980

Learning takes us through many states of life, but it fails utterly in
the hour of danger and temptation. Then faith alone saves.

> MOHANDAS K. GANDHI (1869–1948). In Young India, 22 January 1925

Faith is nothing but a living, wide-awake consciousness of God
within.

> MOHANDAS K. GANDHI (1869–1948). In Young India, 24 September
> 1925

Faith does not admit of telling. It has to be lived and then it
becomes self-propagating.

> MOHANDAS K. GANDHI (1869–1948). In Young India, 20 October 1927

My faith is brightest in the midst of impenetrable darkness.

> MOHANDAS K. GANDHI (1869–1948). 6 February 1939. In Louis Fischer,
> The Life of Mahatma Gandhi, 36, 1950

Real works are the natural products of faith taking its next step.

> PAUL GOODMAN (1911–1972). Growing Up Absurd: Problems of Youth
> in the Organized Society, 7.3, 1956

There are many creeds, but only one universal faith. . . . A minimum of creed and a maximum of faith is the ideal synthesis.

> ABRAHAM JOSHUA HESCHEL (1907–1972). Man Is Not Alone:
> A Philosophy of Religion, 17, 1951

Faith is the beginning of compassion, of compassion for God.

> ABRAHAM JOSHUA HESCHEL (1907–1972). A Passion for Truth, 9, 1973

Faith and doubt go hand in hand, they are complementaries. One
who never doubts will never truly believe.

> HERMANN HESSE (1877–1962). Reflections, 291, ed. Volker Michels,
> 1974

True faith is belief in the reality of absolute values.

> DEAN WILLIAM RALPH INGE (1860–1954). "Confessio Fidei," Outspoken
> Essays: Second Series, 1922

What does it profit, my brethren, if a man says he has faith but has
not works? Can his faith save him? If a brother or sister is ill-clad
and in lack of daily food, and one of you says to them, "Go in
peace, be warmed and filled," without giving them the things
needed for the body, what does it profit? So faith by itself, if it has
no works, is dead.

> JAMES (A.D. 1st cent.). James 2:14–17

A fact [may] not come at all unless a preliminary faith exists in its
coming. . . . Faith in a fact can help create the fact.

> WILLIAM JAMES (1842–1910). Title essay (9), The Will to Believe:
> And Other Essays in Popular Philosophy, 1897

How can we profess faith in God's word and then refuse to let it
inspire and direct our thinking, our activity, our decisions, and our
responsibilities toward one another?

> POPE JOHN PAUL II (1920–). Homily delivered at Camden Yards,
> Baltimore, 8 October 1995

Faith leads us beyond ourselves. It leads us directly to God.

> POPE JOHN PAUL II (1920–). Homily delivered at Camden Yards,
> Baltimore, 8 October 1995

Faith cannot be made: it is in the truest sense a gift of grace.

> CARL G. JUNG (1875–1961). Modern Man in Search of a Soul, 6, tr.
> W. S. Dell and Cary F. Baynes, 1933

Man cannot live without an enduring faith in something inde-
structible within him.

> FRANZ KAFKA (1883–1924). In Max Brod, introduction to Gustav
> Janouch, Conversations with Kafka, tr. Goronwy Rees, 1953

Faith is the strength by which a shattered world shall emerge into
the light.

> HELEN KELLER (1880–1968)

Faith is the opening of all sides and at every level of one's life to
the divine inflow.

> MARTIN LUTHER KING, JR. (1929–1968). Strength to Love, 15.3, 1963

Little faith is put in them
Whose faith is small.

> LAO-TZU (6th cent. B.C.). The Way of Life, 23, tr. R. B. Blakney, 1955

Let us have faith that right makes might, and in that faith, let us,
to the end, dare to do our duty as we understand it.

ABRAHAM LINCOLN (1809–1865). Closing words, address, Cooper Institute, New York City, 27 February 1860

Men with faith can face martyrdom while men without it feel stricken when they are not invited to dinner.

WALTER LIPPMANN (1889–1974). Address before the American Catholic Philosophical Association, Philadelphia, 29 December 1941

True faith is never merely a source of spiritual comfort. It may indeed bring peace, but before it does so it must involve us in struggle. A "faith" that avoids this struggle is really a temptation against true faith.

THOMAS MERTON (1915–1968). *New Seeds of Contemplation,* 15, 1961

Kindness is the mark of faith; and whoever has not kindness has not faith.

MUHAMMAD (A.D. 570?–632). *The Sayings of Muhammad,* 254, tr. Abdullah Al-Suhrawardy, 1941

Much of what passes for religious faith today amounts to a side bet, covering a vague belief that "there must be something" or that man needs to believe (especially when in foxholes).

HERBERT J. MULLER (1890–1967). *The Uses of the Past: Profiles of Former Societies,* 11.2, 1952

"Faith" has been at all times . . . only a cloak, a pretext, a *screen,* behind which the instincts played their game.

FRIEDRICH NIETZSCHE (1844–1900). *The Anti-Christ,* 39, 1895, tr. R. J. Hollingdale, 1968

Faith . . . tells what the senses do not tell, but not the contrary of what they see. It is above them and not contrary to them.

BLAISE PASCAL (1623–1662). *Pensées,* 265, 1670, tr. William F. Trotter, 1931

If I have all faith, so as to remove mountains, but have not love, I am nothing.

PAUL (A.D. 1st cent.). *1 Corinthians* 13:2
See Love: Paul (1) o Love: George Sand

Faith which refuses to face indisputable facts is but little faith.

ALBERT SCHWEITZER (1875–1965). "The Conception of the Kingdom of God in the Transformation of Eschatology," epilogue to E. N. Mozley, *The Theology of Albert Schweitzer for Christian Inquirers,* p. 115, 1951

Faith is the bird that feels the light
and sings when the dawn is still dark.

RABINDRANATH TAGORE (1861–1941). *Fireflies,* p. 205, 1928

❦

Faith is believing what you know ain't so.

ANONYMOUS (AMERICAN). A schoolboy. In Mark Twain, 2 February 1894, *Mark Twain's Notebook,* ed. Albert Bigelow Paine, 1935

By faith we understand that the world was created by the word of God, so that what is seen was made out of things which do not appear.

ANONYMOUS (*BIBLE*). *Hebrews* 11:3

Better works without faith than faith without works.

ANONYMOUS

FAITH & REASON

See also • Belief o Faith o Reason

Reason is our soul's left hand, faith her right;
By these we reach divinity.

JOHN DONNE (1572–1631). Letter to the Countess of Bedford, 1610

Faith does not contradict reason but transcends it.

MOHANDAS K. GANDHI (1869–1948). In D. G. Tendulkar, *Mahatma, Life of Mohandas Karamchand Gandhi,* 1954

Without reason we would not know how to apply the insights of faith to the concrete issues of living. . . . The rejection of reason is cowardice and betrays a lack of faith.

ABRAHAM JOSHUA HESCHEL (1907–1972). *God in Search of Man: A Philosophy of Judaism,* 1, 1955

Reason, devoid of [the] purifying power of faith, can never free itself from distortions and rationalizations.

MARTIN LUTHER KING, JR. (1929–1968). "Pilgrimage to Nonviolence" (1), *Christian Century,* 13 April 1960

Reason is the greatest enemy that faith has: it never comes to the aid of spiritual things, but—more frequently than not—struggles against the Divine Word, treating with contempt all that emanates from God.

MARTIN LUTHER (1483–1546). *Table Talk,* 353, 1566, tr. William Hazlitt, 1857

❦

Faith without reason leads to superstition: Reason without faith leads to cynicism.

ANONYMOUS

Their faith is small who sacrifice reason to it.

ANONYMOUS

FALSEHOOD

See also • Errors o Lying: [especially] William Shenstone o Truth o Truth & Untruth

The beginning of all is to have done with falsity—to eschew falsity as death eternal.

THOMAS CARLYLE (1795–1881). Journal, 23 June 1870

Falsehood is invariably the child of fear in one form or another.

ALEISTER CROWLEY (1875–1947). *The Confessions of Aleister Crowley,* 49, 1929

So let us not talk falsely now, the hour is getting late.

BOB DYLAN (1941–). "All Along the Watchtower" (song), 1968

The united voice of millions cannot lend the smallest foundation to falsehood.

OLIVER GOLDSMITH (1728–1774). *The Vicar of Wakefield,* 8, 1766

You shall not bear false witness against your neighbor.

MOSES (14th cent. B.C.). The 9th Commandment, *Exodus* 20:16

Antonio: O, what a good outside falsehood hath!

SHAKESPEARE (1564–1616). *The Merchant of Venice,* 1.3.103, 1596

Falsehood is a scorpion that will sting itself to death.

PERCY BYSSHE SHELLEY (1792–1822). *A Declaration of Rights,* 12, 1812

❧

One falsehood spoils a thousand truths.

SAYING (ASHANTI)

See Lying: Baltasar Gracián

False as a bulletin!

SAYING (FRENCH). Referring to Napoleon's communiqués. In Thomas Carlyle, "The Hero as King," *On Heroes, Hero-Worship, and the Heroic in History,* 1841

False in one thing; false in everything.

SAYING (LATIN)

FAME

See also • Celebrity ○ Glory ○ Honor ○ Popularity ○ Prestige ○ Publicity ○ Public Relations ○ Stardom ○ Status ○ Success ○ Vanity: George Santayana

Those who taste the joys and sorrows of fame when they have passed forty know how to look after themselves. They know what is concealed beneath the flowers, and what the gossip, the calumnies, and the praise are worth. But as for those who win fame when they are twenty, they know nothing and are caught up in the whirlpool.

SARAH BERNHARDT (1844–1923). French actress. *The Art of the Theatre,* 3, 1924

Famous, *adj.* Conspicuous miserable.

AMBROSE BIERCE (1842–1914). *The Devil's Dictionary,* p. 40, 1911, Dover edition, 1958

Fame, which flees the man who seeks it, overtakes the man who is heedless of it.

JACOB BURCKHARDT (1818–1897). "The Great Men of History," 1870, *Force and Freedom: An Interpretation of History,* ed. James H. Nichols, 1943

Passion for fame; A passion which is the instinct of all great souls.

EDMUND BURKE (1729–1797). "American Taxation," House of Commons speech, 19 April 1774

I awoke one morning and found myself famous.

LORD BYRON (1788–1824). Memorandum written after publication in 1812 of the first two cantos of *Childe Harold's Pilgrimage.* In Thomas More, *The Life of Lord Byron,* 16, 1830

The philosophers themselves, even in those books in which they tell us to despise fame, inscribe their names.

CICERO (106–43 B.C.). *Pro archia poeta,* 11

See Hypocrisy: Ralph Waldo Emerson

A man should say, . . . I am not concerned that I am not known, I seek to be worthy to be known.

CONFUCIUS (551–479 B.C.). *Confucian Analects,* 4.14, tr. James Legge, 1930

Fame is a bee
  It has a song—

It has a sting—
  Ah, too, it has a wing.

EMILY DICKINSON (1830–1886). "Fame is a bee" (complete poem), undated

If you you'd not be forgotten
As soon as you are dead and rotten,
Either write things worth reading,
or do things worth the writing.

BENJAMIN FRANKLIN (1706–1790). *Poor Richard's Almanack,* May 1738

Fame is a powerful aphrodisiac.

GRAHAM GREENE (1904–1991). In *Radio Times* (British magazine), 10 September 1964

See Power: Henry A. Kissinger, Napoleon

Fame usually comes to those who are thinking of something else.

OLIVER WENDELL HOLMES, SR. (1809–1894). *The Autocrat of the Breakfast-Table,* 12, 1858

Make your best bow to her and bid adieu,
Then, if she likes it, she will follow you.

JOHN KEATS (1795–1821). "Two Sonnets on Fame," l. 13

The more I had won that year, the less it meant . . . and the more tired and sad I became. And the more I won, the more people wanted a part of me. I will tell you King's First Law of Recognition: You never get it when you want it, and then when it comes, you get too much.

BILLIE JEAN KING (1943–). Tennis champion. *Billie Jean,* 3, 1982

I can't believe the recognition I get. All over the world. I was in Israel, at the Wailing Wall, and this old rabbi is there praying. He looks up at me and says, "So what's with Perot?" I have a nice franchise here, and I totally enjoy it. I feel like I'm part of history.

LARRY KING (1933–). His CNN television interview program, *Larry King Live* is seen six days per week via satellite in more than 200 countries. Quoted in *Total TV* (magazine). In Leah Garchik, "Personals," *San Francisco Chronicle,* 6 June 1995

In order to be known and admired, they must have great virtues, or perhaps great vices.

LA BRUYÈRE (1645–1696). "Of Opinions" (112), *The Characters,* 1688, tr. Henri van Laun, 1929

The famous . . . substitute for the national lack of a historical consciousness. Desperate cultural efforts have been made to "enshrine" individual accomplishment in halls of fame. Pantheons for strippers, baseball players, statesmen . . .—nearly 750 halls of fame have been established . . . in a crude attempt to fix points of reference and cultural values.

JOHN LAHR (1941–). "Notes on Fame," *Harper's,* January 1978

At first you can stand the spotlight in your eyes. Then it blinds you. Others can see you, but you cannot see them.

CHARLES A. LINDBERGH (1902–1974). In Lewis H. Lapham, "Fatted Calf," *Harper's,* November 1997

If cash comes with fame, come fame; if cash comes without fame, come cash.

JACK LONDON (1876–1916). Letter to Cloudesley Johns, 1 November 1899

When you're famous, you kind of run into human nature in a raw kind of way. It stirs up envy, fame does. People you run into feel that, well, who is she—who does she think she is, Marilyn Monroe? They feel fame gives them some kind of privilege to walk up to you and say anything to you, you know, of any kind of nature—and it won't hurt your feelings—like it's happening to your clothing. One time here I am looking for a home to buy and I stopped at this place. A man came out and was very pleasant, very cheerful, and said, "Oh, just a moment, I want my wife to meet you." Well, she came out and said, "Will you please get off the premises?"

> MARILYN MONROE (1926–1962). Richard Meryman interview, *Life*, 3 August 1962

Fame will go by and, so long, I've had you, fame. If it goes by, I've always known it was fickle. So at least it's something I experienced, but that's not where I live.

> MARILYN MONROE (1926–1962). Closing words of an interview given shortly before her death on 5 August 1962, Richard Meryman interview, *Life*, 3 August 1962

Those whom the gods wish to destroy, they first make famous.

> JOYCE CAROL OATES (1938–). Opening words, "Down the Road," *New Yorker*, 27 March 1995
>
> See Madness: Euripides

The fortunate man . . . is he to whom the gods have granted the power either to do something which is worth recording or to write what is worth reading, and most fortunate of all is the man who can do both.

> PLINY THE YOUNGER (A.D. 62?–113?). *Letters*, 6.16, tr. Betty Radice, 1963

Nor Fame I slight, nor for her Favors call;
She comes unlook'd for, if she comes at all.

> ALEXANDER POPE (1688–1744). *The Temple of Fame*, l. 513, 1715

Oh grant an honest Fame, or grant me none!

> ALEXANDER POPE (1688–1744). Closing line, *The Temple of Fame*, 1715

Posthumous fame is often bought at the expense of contemporary praise, and vice versa.

> ARTHUR SCHOPENHAUER (1788–1860). "Religion and Other Essays: On Books and Reading," *Essays of Arthur Schopenhauer*, tr. T. Bailey Saunders, 1851

Hamlet: There's hope a great man's memory may outlive his life half a year.

> SHAKESPEARE (1564–1616). *Hamlet*, 3.2.139, 1600

I would rather be remembered by a song than by a victory.

> ALEXANDER SMITH (1830–1867). *Dreamthorp*, 7, 1863

A plague on eminence! I hardly dare cross the street anymore without a convoy.

> IGOR STRAVINSKY (1882–1971). "Stravinsky on the Musical Scene and Other Matters," *New York Review of Books*, 12 May 1966

Little presses write to me for manuscripts and when I write back that I haven't any, they write to ask if they can print the letter saying I haven't any.

> JOHN STEINBECK (1902–1968). Soon after publication of *The Grapes of Wrath*, letter to Elizabeth Otis, July 1939. In George Plimpton, ed., *Writers at Work: Fourth Series*, 1976

Blessed is he whose fame does not outshine his truth.

> RABINDRANATH TAGORE (1861–1941). *Stray Birds*, 296, 1914

Men often mistake notoriety for fame, and would rather be remarked for their vices and follies than not be noticed at all!

> HARRY S. TRUMAN (1884–1972). In William Hillman, *Mr. President*, 5.5, 1952

Fame is a vapor; popularity an accident; the only earthly certainty is oblivion.

> MARK TWAIN (1835–1910). 1868, *Mark Twain's Notebook*, ed. Albert Bigelow Paine, 1935

In the future everybody will be world famous for fifteen minutes.

> ANDY WARHOL (1927–1987). "Warhol in His Own Words," ed. Neil Printz. In Kynaston McShine, *Andy Warhol: A Retrospective*, 1986

I'm bored with that line. I never use it anymore. My new line is, "In 15 minutes, everybody will be famous."

> ANDY WARHOL (1927–1987). In Paul Richard, "Mirror of the Glitterati, High Judge of Pop Society," *Washington Post*, 15 November 1979

If I can use whatever prominence may have come to me as an instrument with which to do good, I am content to have it.

> BOOKER T. WASHINGTON (1856–1915). *Up from Slavery: An Autobiography*, 17, 1901
>
> See Glory: Plutarch ○ Popularity: Theodore Roosevelt

I exist as I am, that is enough,
If no other in the world be aware I sit content,
And if each and all be aware I sit content.

> WALT WHITMAN (1819–1892). "Song of Myself" (20), 1855, *Leaves of Grass*, 1855–1892

What rage for fame attends both great and small!
Better be damn'd than mentioned not at all!

> JOHN WOLCOT (1738–1819). *Lyric Odes, To the Royal Academicians: A Distant Relation to the Poet of Thebes*, 9, 1784

FAMILIARITY

See also • Manners

Familiarity breeds contempt.

> AESOP (6th cent. B.C.). "The Fox and the Lion," *Fables*
>
> See Prestige: Charles de Gaulle

Bernard Law Montgomery: They say that familiarity breeds contempt.
Churchill: I would like to remind you that without a degree of familiarity we could not breed anything.

> WINSTON CHURCHILL (1874–1965). After suggesting to Field Marshal Montgomery before the Battle of El Alamein (Egypt) that he study logistics, 1942. In William Manchester, "Preamble: The Lion at Bay," *The Last Lion: Winston Spencer Churchill, Visions of Glory, 1874–1932*, 1983

Though familiarity may not breed contempt, it takes off the edge of admiration; and the shining points of character are not those we chiefly wish to dwell upon.

> WILLIAM HAZLITT (1778–1830). *Characteristics in the Manner of Rochefoucault's Maxims*, 2, 1823
>
> See Heroism: Anne-Marie de Cornuel

Familiarity breeds consent.

> LAZARUS' OBSERVATION. In John Peers, comp., *1,001 Logical Laws*, p. 150, 1979

Familiarity breeds.

> MARY PETTIBONE POOLE. "Beggars Can't Be Losers," *A Glass Eye at a Keyhole*, 1938

Familiarity breeds content.

> ANNA QUINDLEN (1953–). "Welcome to the Club," *New York Times*, 27 January 1993

Familiarity breeds acquiescence as well as contempt.

> ARNOLD J. TOYNBEE (1889–1975). *A Study of History*, 3.370, 1934

Familiarity breeds contempt—and children.

> MARK TWAIN (1835–1910). 2 February 1894, *Mark Twain's Notebook*, ed. Albert Bigelow Paine, 1935

❦

Familiarity breeds attempt.

> ANONYMOUS (AMERICAN). Graffito. In T. F. Palmer, comp., *Off the Wall: Graffito of San Francisco*, 1982

Familiarity breeds contempt; distance breeds respect.

> SAYING (NIGERIEN)

Familiarity breeds indifference.

> SAYING

FAMILY

See also • Children ○ Fathers ○ Grandparents ○ Home ○ Marriage ○ Mothers ○ Parents

The stronger and more numerous a man's connections in the way of sympathy are, the stronger is the hold which the law has upon him. A wife and children are so many pledges a man gives to the world for his good behavior.

> JEREMY BENTHAM (1748–1832). "Notes" (43), *An Introduction to the Principles of Morals and Legislation*, 1789-1823

The family requires the most delicate mixture of nature and convention, of human and divine, to subsist and perform its function. Its base is merely bodily reproduction, but its purpose is the formation of civilized human beings.

> ALLAN BLOOM (1930–1992). "The Clean Slate," *The Closing of the American Mind: How Higher Education Has Failed Democracy and Impoverished the Souls of Today's Students*, 1987

To us, family means putting your arms around each other and being there.

> BARBARA BUSH (1925–). Republic National Convention speech, Houston, 19 August 1992

More unhappiness comes from this source than from any other— I mean from the attempt to prolong family connection unduly and to make people hang together artificially who would never naturally do so.

> SAMUEL BUTLER (1835–1902). *The Note-Books of Samuel Butler*, 2, ed. Henry Festing Jones, 1907

Many men can make a fortune, but very few can build a Family.

> J. S. BRYAN. In Joseph Epstein, *Ambition: The Secret Passion*, 5, 1980

Domestic happiness, thou only bliss
Of Paradise that has surviv'd the fall!

> WILLIAM COWPER (1731–1800). *The Task*, 3.41, 1785

When . . . the larger culture aggrandizes wife beaters, degrades women, or nods approvingly at child slappers, the family gets a little more dangerous for everyone, and so, inevitably, does the larger world.

> BARBARA EHRENREICH (1941–). Closing words, "Oh, Those Family Values," 1994, *The Snarling Citizen: Essays*, 1995

Blood's thicker than water, and when one's in trouble
Best to seek out a relative's open arms.

> EURIPIDES (485?–406 B.C.). *Andromache*, l. 985, tr. John Frederick Nims, 1956

No better relation than a prudent and faithful Friend.

> BENJAMIN FRANKLIN (1706–1790). *Poor Richard's Almanack*, May 1737

Families break up when people take hints you don't intend and miss hints you do intend.

> ROBERT FROST (1874–1963). Richard Poirier interview. In George Plimpton, ed., *Writers at Work: Second Series*, 1963

Distant relatives er th' best kind, an' th' further th' better.

> KIN HUBBARD (1868–1930). "February," *Abe Martin's Almanack*, 1908

Th' richer a relative is, th' less he bothers you.

> KIN HUBBARD (1868–1930). *Abe Martin's Primer*, unpaged, 1914

The happiest moments of my life have been the few which I have passed at home in the bosom of my family.

> THOMAS JEFFERSON (1743–1826). Letter to Francis Willis, Jr., 18 April 1790

The whole world is my family.

> POPE JOHN XXIII (1881–1963). 29 November–5 December 1959, *Journal of a Soul*, 1964, tr. Dorothy White, 1965

Every family should extend First Amendment rights to all its members, but this freedom is particularly essential for our kids. Children must be able to say what they think, openly express their feelings, and ask for what they want and need if they are ever able to develop an integrated sense of self.

> STEPHANIE MARSTON. Psychotherapist. *The Magic of Encouragement: Nurturing Your Child's Self-Esteem*, 1, 1990

Patriarchy's chief institution is the family. It is both a mirror of and a connection with the larger society; a patriarchal unit within a patriarchal whole. Mediating between the individual and the social structure, the family affects control and conformity where political and other authorities are insufficient. . . . Serving as an agent of the larger society, the family not only encourages its own members to adjust and conform, but acts as a unit in the government of the patriarchal state which rules its citizens through its family heads.

> KATE MILLET (1934–). *Sexual Politics*, 2.3, 1969

One would be in less danger
From the wiles of the stranger

If one's own kin and kith
Were more fun to be with.

> OGDEN NASH (1902–1971). "Family Court," *Many Long Years Ago,* 1945

If anyone does not provide for his relatives, and especially for his own family, he has disowned the faith and is worse than an unbeliever.

> PAUL (A.D. 1st cent.). *1 Timothy* 5:8

Like many another romance, the romance of the family turns sour when the money runs out. If we really cared about families, we would not let "born again" patriarchs send up moral abstractions as a smokescreen for the scandal of American family economics.

> LETTY COTTIN POGREBIN (1939–). *Family Politics: Love and Power on an Intimate Frontier,* 4, 1983

In a democratic family, those with superior knowledge and resources (i.e., power) use them to strengthen others in the family. In an authoritarian family, power is used to "tame" and control others.

> LETTY COTTIN POGREBIN (1939–). *Family Politics: Love and Power on an Intimate Frontier,* 5, 1983

Happy families are all alike; every unhappy family is unhappy in its own way.

> LEO TOLSTOY (1828–1910). Opening words, *Anna Karenina,* 1873–1876, tr. Constance Garnett, 1930

❦

In time of test, family is best.

> SAYING (BURMESE)

A large family, quick help.

> SAYING (SERBIAN)

An ounce of blood is worth more than a pound of friendship.

> SAYING (SPANISH)

A family divided against itself will perish together.

> SAYING (TAMIL)

FANATICS

See also • Conviction ○ Crises ○ Crowds ○ Enthusiasm ○ Excess ○ Idealism: F. A. Hayek ○ Mass Movements ○ Mobs ○ Opposites: Friedrich Nietzsche ○ Passion ○ Prejudice ○ Terrorism: Eric Hoffer ○ Zeal

If we can destroy all of the demons in the world, it will eliminate those within me without my having to recognize that they have been there.

> J. A. C. BROWN (1911–1964). Expressing with disapproval the attitude of fanatics, *Techniques of Persuasion: From Propaganda to Brainwashing,* 11, 196

The fanatic cannot be weaned away from his cause by an appeal to his reason or moral sense. . . . He cannot be convinced, but only converted.

> ERIC HOFFER (1902–1983). *The True Believer: Thoughts on the Nature of Mass Movements,* 61, 1951

There is a close connection between lack of confidence and the passionate state of mind, and . . . passionate intensity may serve as a substitute for confidence.

> ERIC HOFFER (1902–1983). *The Ordeal of Change,* 1, 1964

[To fanatics] all thought is divinely classified into two kinds—that which is their own and that which is false and dangerous.

> ROBERT H. JACKSON (1892–1954). *American Communications Association v. Douds,* 1950

His uncertainty forces the enthusiast to puff up his truths, of which he feels none too sure, and to win proselytes to his side in order that his followers may prove to himself the value and trustworthiness of his own convictions. . . . Only when convincing someone else does he feel safe from gnawing doubts.

> CARL G. JUNG (1875–1961). "The Relations between the Ego and the Unconscious" (1.2), 1928, *Two Essays on Analytical Psychology,* tr. R. F. C. Hull, 1953

Fanatics have their dreams, wherewith they weave
A paradise for a sect.

> JOHN KEATS (1795–1821). "The Fall of Hyperion: A Dream," 1.1, 1856

In the history of mankind, fanaticism has caused more harm than vice.

> LOUIS KRONENBERGER (1904–1980). "Aphorisms," *Vogue,* 1 March 1964

In every age of transition men are never so firmly bound to one way of life as when they are about to abandon it, so that fanaticism and intolerance reach their most intense forms just before tolerance and mutual acceptance come to be the natural order of things.

> BERNARD LEVIN (1928–). *The Pendulum Years: Britain and the Sixties,* 4, 1970

When people are fanatically dedicated to political or religious faiths or any other kind of dogmas or goals, it's always because these dogmas or goals are in doubt.

> ROBERT M. PIRSIG (1928–). *Zen and the Art of Motorcycle Maintenance,* 13, 1974

Fanatics fear liberty more than they fear persecution.

> ERNEST RENAN (1823–1892). Preface to *The Hibbert Lectures,* 1880

Fanaticism consists in redoubling your effort when you have forgotten your aim.

> GEORGE SANTAYANA (1863–1952). Introduction to *The Life of Reason or The Phases of Human Progress,* vol. 1, 1905–1906

We are dominated by the fanatic, whose worst vice is his sincerity.

> OSCAR WILDE (1854–1900). "The Critic as Artist" (2), *Intentions,* 1891

The best lack all conviction, while the worst are full of passionate intensity.

> WILLIAM BUTLER YEATS (1865–1939). "The Second Coming," *Michael Robartes and the Dancer,* 1921

❦

Fanaticism is both parent and child of persecution.

> ANONYMOUS

FARMING

See also • Agriculture ○ Environment: [especially] Franklin D. Roosevelt ○ Gardening ○ Nature ○ Pessimism—Examples: Peter Walker ○ Work

Farming, if it is to pay, is a pursuit of small economies.

> AUGUSTINE BIRRELL (1850–1933). "Edmund Burke," *Obiter Dicta: Second Series,* 1887

The corn is as high as an elephant's eye,
An' it looks like it's climbin' clear up to the sky.

> OSCAR HAMMERSTEIN II (1895–1960). "Oh, What a Beautiful Mornin'," song. In the musical *Oklahoma,* 1943

One hears a lot about the rules of good husbandry; there is only one—leave the land far better than you found it.

> GEORGE HENDERSON. *The Farming Ladder,* 1944

The main characteristic of Nature's farming can . . . be summed up in a few words. Mother earth never attempts to farm without livestock; she always raises mixed crops; great pains are taken to preserve the soil and to prevent erosion; the mixed vegetable and animal wastes are converted into humus; there is no waste; the processes of growth and the processes of decay balance one another; ample provision is made to maintain large reserves of fertility; the greatest care is taken to store the rainfall; both plants and animals are left to protect themselves against disease.

> ALBERT HOWARD. Explaining the methods of Nature, "The Supreme Farmer," *An Agricultural Testament,* 1940. In Wendell Berry, "A Practical Harmony," 1988, *What Are People For?: Essays,* 1990

To plow is to pray; to plant is to prophesy; and the harvest answers and fulfills.

> ROBERT G. INGERSOLL (1833–1899). "Fragments," *The Philosophy of Ingersoll,* ed. Vere Goldthwaite, 1906

Wherever there are in any country uncultivated lands and unemployed poor, it is clear that the laws of property have been extended as to violate natural right. The earth is given as a common stock for man to labor and live on.

> THOMAS JEFFERSON (1743–1826). Letter to James Madison, 28 October 1785

Those who labor in the earth are the chosen people of God, if ever he had a chosen people, whose breasts he has made his peculiar deposit for substantial and genuine virtue. It is the focus in which he keeps alive that sacred fire, which otherwise might escape from the face of the earth.

> THOMAS JEFFERSON (1743–1826). *Notes on the State of Virginia,* 19, 1785

Have you become a farmer? Is it not pleasanter than to be shut up within four walls and delving eternally with the pen?

> THOMAS JEFFERSON (1743–1826). Letter to Henry Knox, 1795

K. planted melons and many other things. Last night it showered a little. The opinion among intelligent people is that the general cultivation of the soil is fast changing this climate.

> GEORGIANA BRUCE KIRBY (1818–1887). 3 May 1853, *Journal of Georgiana Kirby* (unpublished). In Ida Rae Egli, ed., *No Rooms of Their Own: Women Writers of Early California,* 1992

Bowed by the weight of centuries he leans
Upon his hoe and gazes on the ground,
The emptiness of ages in his face,
And on his back the burden of the world.

> EDWIN MARKHAM (1852–1940). "The Man with a Hoe," 1899, *Poems,* ed. Charles L. Wallis, 1950

The bourgeoisie has subjected the country to the rule of the towns. It has created enormous cities, has greatly increased the urban population as compared with the rural, and has thus rescued a considerable part of the population from the idiocy of rural life.

> KARL MARX (1818–1883) and FRIEDRICH ENGELS (1820–1895). *The Communist Manifesto,* 1, 1847, ed. Engels, 1888

Consult the Genius of the Place in all;
That tells the Waters or to rise, or fall, . . .
Now breaks or now directs, th' intending Lines;
Paints as you plant, and, as you work, designs.

> ALEXANDER POPE (1688–1744). *Epistle IV. To Richard Boyle, Earl of Burlington,* l. 57, 1731

"How are crops this year?"
"Not so good for a good year
but not so bad for a bad year."

> CARL SANDBURG (1878–1967). *The People, Yes,* 48, 1936

"How do you do, my farmer friend?"
"Howdy."
"Nice looking country you have here."
"Fer them that likes it."
"Live here all your life?"
"Not yit."

> CARL SANDBURG (1878–1967). *The People, Yes,* 60, 1936

I see a million hills green with crop-yielding trees and a million neat farm homes snuggled in the hills. These beautiful tree farms hold the hills from Boston to Austin, from Atlanta to Des Moines. The hills of my vision have farming that fits them and replaces the poor pasture, the gullies, and the abandoned lands that characterize today so large a part of these hills.

> J. RUSSELL SMITH (1874–1966). *Tree Crops,* 1929.

Whoever could make two ears of corn, or two blades of grass to grow upon a spot of ground where only one grew before, would deserve better of mankind, and do more essential service to his country, than the whole race of politicians put together.

> JONATHAN SWIFT (1667–1745). *Gulliver's Travels,* 2.7, 1726

To own a bit of ground, to scratch it with a hoe, to plant seeds, and watch their renewal of life—this is the commonest delight of the race, the most satisfactory thing a man can do.

> CHARLES DUDLEY WARNER (1829–1900). "Preliminary," *My Summer in a Garden,* 1871
>
> See Agriculture: Warner

When tillage begins, other arts follow. The farmers, therefore, are the founders of human civilization.

> DANIEL WEBSTER (1782–1852). "Remarks on the Agriculture of England," speech, Boston, 13 January 1840

A good farmer is nothing more nor less than a handy man with a sense of humus.

> E. B. WHITE (1899–1985). "The Practical Farmer," *One Man's Meat,* 1944

FASCISM

See also • Capitalism ○ Class ○ Colonialism: Frederic Wertham ○ Communism ○ Economics ○ Freedom ○ The Individual: Erich Fromm, Alfredo Rocco ○ Nationalism ○ Socialism ○ Tyranny

The morale of the people requires a new demonstration of power from time to time to justify the sacrifices made for the army. Hitler must conquer here or there, somewhere, once or twice a year. Otherwise, docile as Germans are under tyranny, he will risk a rapid crumbling of internal credit and morale.

> ALBERT CARR. *Juggernaut: The Path of Dictatorship,* 17, 1939

Doctrines and "ideas" shall no longer govern your existence. The Fuehrer himself, and only he, is the current and future reality of Germany, and his word is your law.

> MARTIN HEIDEGGER (1889–1976). German philosopher. Open letter to the students of the University of Freiburg, 3 November 1933.

Those who see in National Socialism nothing more than a political movement know scarcely anything about it. It is more even than a religion: it is the will to create mankind anew.

> ADOLF HITLER (1889–1945). Table talk, 1932–1934. In Hermann Rauschning, *The Voice of Destruction,* 17, 1940

All for the State; nothing outside the State; nothing against the State.

> BENITO MUSSOLINI (1883–1945). In José Ortega y Gasset, *The Revolt of the Masses,* 13, 1930, tr. anon., 1932

Fascism denies that the majority, by the simple fact that it is a majority, can direct human society; it denies that numbers alone can govern by means of a periodical consultation, and it affirms the immutable, beneficial, and fruitful inequality of mankind.

> BENITO MUSSOLINI (1883–1945). "The Political and Social Doctrine of Fascism," *International Conciliation,* December 1935

For Fascism, the growth of empire, that is to say the expansion of the nation, is an essential manifestation of vitality, and its opposite a sign of decadence. Peoples which are rising, or rising again after a period of decadence, are always imperialist; any renunciation is a sign of decay and of death.

> BENITO MUSSOLINI (1883–1945). "The Political and Social Doctrine of Fascism," *International Conciliation,* December 1935

In Soviet Russia the state owns industry; in Germany and Italy, on the contrary, industry owns the state.

> GEORGE SELDES (1890–1995). *Iron, Blood and Profits: An Exposure of the World-Wide Munitions Racket,* 18, 1934

Capitalist Dictatorship (Fascism).

> GEORGE BERNARD SHAW (1856–1950). *The Intelligent Woman's Guide to Socialism, Capitalism, Sovietism and Fascism,* 65, 1928

The best safeguard against fascism is to establish social justice to the maximum possible extent.

> ARNOLD J. TOYNBEE (1889–1975). *The Toynbee-Ikeda Dialogue: Man Himself Must Choose,* 8, 1976

Fascism is government by the few and for the few.

> UNITED STATES ARMY, Orientation Fact Sheet 64, 1945

Fascism—or state capitalism—will always be neighbor–raping.
    The economic system of theft has one immense advantage: it works. But it also has one great disadvantage: it works only while there is something to steal.

> PHILIP WYLIE (1902–1971). *Generation of Vipers,* 1, 1942

❧

Hitler over Germany. Germany over the world.

> SLOGAN (GERMAN). Nazi Party, 1930s

Today Germany, tomorrow the world.

> SLOGAN (GERMAN). Nazi Party, 1930s

Order, hierarchy, discipline.

> SLOGAN (ITALIAN). Fascist Party, 1930s

Long live death! Down with intelligence!

> SLOGAN (SPANISH). Fascist Party (The Falange), 1936

FASHION

See also • Appearances ○ Clothes ○ Conformity ○ Dress ○ Style

Fashion, *n.* A despot whom the wise ridicule and obey.

> AMBROSE BIERCE (1842–1914). *The Devil's Dictionary,* p. 40, 1911, Dover edition, 1958

Fashion matters considerably more than horoscopes, rather more than dog shows and slightly more than hockey.

> ROY BLOUNT, JR. (1941–). In Eric P. Nash, ed., "Does Fashion Matter?" *New York Times Magazine,* 24 October 1993

Does fashion matter? Only if you're out of it.

> KIM CAMPBELL (1947–). Canadian prime minister. In Eric P. Nash, ed., "Does Fashion Matter?" *New York Times Magazine,* 24 October 1993

As soon as a fashion has caught on, it has outlived itself.

> MARIE von EBNER-ESCHENBACH (1830–1916). *Aphorisms,* p. 52, 1880–1905, tr. David Scrase and Wolfgang Mieder, 1994

Be neither too early in the Fashion, nor too long out of it, nor at any time too precisely in it.

> THOMAS FULLER (1654–1734). Comp., *Introductio ad Prudentiam,* 498, 1731

Fashion can beget and hallow
Even what's unnatural.

> GOETHE (1749–1832). *Faust,* 2.1 ("Spacious Hall"), 1808–1832, tr. Philip Wayne, 1959

What is called fashion is the tradition of the moment.

> GOETHE (1749–1832). *The Maxims and Reflections of Goethe,* 392, tr. T. Bailey Saunders, 1892

You must . . . be a *little* out of the fashion to be *well* in it.

> FULKE GREVILLE (1554–1628). *Maxims, Characters, and Reflections,* p. 262, 1756

Yesterday's avant–garde experiment is today's chic and tomorrow's cliché.

RICHARD HOFSTADTER (1916–1970). *Anti-Intellectualism in American Life,* 15.6, 1962

Understand something. When it comes to today's fashion, lads—*there are no rules!*

SIMON LeBON (1958–). British rock musician, member of Duran Duran. In Gerri Hirshey, "The Snooty Dame at the Block Party," *New York Times Magazine,* 24 October 1993

Trends, like horses, are easier to ride in the direction they are already going.

JOHN NAISBITT (1929–). Introduction to *Megatrends: Ten New Directions Transforming Our Lives,* 1984

Fashion is something barbarous, for it produces innovation without reason and imitation without benefit.

GEORGE SANTAYANA (1863–1952). *The Life of Reason or The Phases of Human Progress,* 3.7, 1905–1906

Mercutio: These fashion–mongers.

SHAKESPEARE (1564–1616). *Romeo and Juliet,* 2.4.33, 1594

Fashions, after all, are only induced epidemics.

GEORGE BERNARD SHAW (1856–1950). Preface ("Fashions and Epidemics"), to *The Doctor's Dilemma,* 1906

Let us know and conform only to the fashions of eternity.

HENRY DAVID THOREAU (1817–1862). Journal, 1 September 1841

We worship . . . Fashion. She spins and weaves and cuts with full authority. The head monkey at Paris puts on a traveler's cap, and all the monkeys in America do the same.

HENRY DAVID THOREAU (1817–1862). "Economy," *Walden; or Life in the Woods,* 1854

The more rapidly the styles succeed and displace one another, the more offensive they are to sound taste.

THORSTEIN VEBLEN (1857–1929). *The Theory of the Leisure Class: An Economic Study of Institutions,* 7, 1899

❦

The difference between a fad and a trend is that a trend has an underlying economic basis.

ANONYMOUS. In Michael Larsen, *How to Write a Book Proposal,* 1, 1985

FATE

See also • Chance ○ Destiny ○ Fortune ○ Luck ○ Misfortune ○ Necessity ○ Opportunity ○ Will, Free

I want to seize fate by the throat.

LUDWIG von BEETHOVEN (1770–1827). Letter to Franz Wegeler, 16 November 1801

As long as I am weak, I shall talk of Fate; whenever the God fills me with his fullness, I shall see the disappearance of Fate.

RALPH WALDO EMERSON (1803–1882). Journal, April 1842

If you please to plant yourself on the side of Fate, and say, Fate is all; then we say, a part of Fate is the freedom of man. Forever wells up the impulse of choosing and acting in the soul.

RALPH WALDO EMERSON (1803–1882). "Fate," *The Conduct of Life,* 1860

I gather heart to risk the world's encounter,
To bear my human fate as fate's surmounter.

GOETHE (1749–1832) (1808–1832). *Faust,* 1 ("Night. Faust's Study," 1), tr. Philip Wayne, 1959

One cannot escape oneself. That is fate. The only possibility is to look on and forget that a game is being played with us.

FRANZ KAFKA (1883–1924). In Gustav Janouch, *Conversations with Kafka,* p. 99, tr. Goronwy Rees, 1953

History is often cruel, and rarely logical, and yet the wisest of realists are those who recognize that fate can indeed be shaped by human faith and courage.

HENRY A. KISSINGER (1923–). "Golda Meir: An Appreciation," 13 November 1977. *For the Record: Selected Statements, 1977–1980,* 1981

Fate and temperament are two words for one and the same concept.

NOVALIS (1772–1801). German poet. In Hermann Hesse, *Demian,* 4, 1919, tr. Michael Roloff and Michael Lebeck, 1965

Through kindness, you can change your fate.

NGUYEN T. NGUYEN (1918–). Repeating a favorite saying of his parents, personal communication, 7 August 1992

Let us stand valiantly for what is decent and right; let us strike hard, and take with unshaken front whatever comes, whether it be good or ill. Then the fates must decide what the outcome will be.

THEODORE ROOSEVELT (1858–1919). Letter. In James MacGregor Burns, *Presidential Government,* 2, 1965

The great appeal of fatalism . . . is as a refuge from the terror of responsibility.

ARTHUR M. SCHLESINGER, JR. (1917–). "The Decline of Greatness," *Saturday Evening Post,* 1 November 1958

Cassius: Men at some time are masters of their fates:
The fault, dear Brutus, is not in our stars,
But in ourselves, that we are underlings.

SHAKESPEARE (1564–1616). *Julius Caesar,* 1.2.139, 1599

Fate has terrible power.
You cannot escape it by wealth or war.
No fort will keep it out, no ships outrun it.

SOPHOCLES (496?–406 B.C.). *Antigone,* l. 950, tr. Elizabeth Wyckoff, 1954

Man is man and master of his fate.

ALFRED, LORD TENNYSON (1809–1892). "The Marriage of Geraint" (l. 355), *The Idylls of the King,* 1859–1885

Every human being is the artificer of his own fate. . . . Events, circumstances, etc., have their origin in ourselves. They spring from seeds which we have sown.

HENRY DAVID THOREAU (1817–1862). Journal, 27 April 1854

Around every man a fatal circle is traced beyond which he cannot pass; but within the wide verge of that circle he is powerful and free; as it is with man, so with communities.

ALEXIS de TOCQUEVILLE (1805–1859). *Democracy in America,* 2.4.8, 1840, tr. Henry Reeve and Francis Bowen, 1862

FATHERS

See also • Babies ○ Children ○ Children's Learning ○ Family ○ Grandparents ○ Mothers ○ Parents

Anonymous father: My son has forsaken God. What, Rabbi, shall I do?
The Baal Shem Tov: Love him more than ever.
> THE BAAL SHEM TOV (1690?–1760)

One who adopts an orphan is like unto him who begot him.
> THE BRATZLAVER (1770–1811)

While you were a child, I endeavored to form your heart habitually to virtue and honor, before your understanding was capable of showing you their beauty and utility.
> LORD CHESTERFIELD (1694–1773). Letter to his son, 3 November 1749

Blessed indeed is the man who hears many gentle voices call him father!
> LYDIA M. CHILD (1802–1880). *Philothea: A Romance,* 19, 1836

That was and still is the great disaster of my life—that lovely, lovely little boy. . . . There's no tragedy in life like the death of a child. Things never get back to the way they were.
> DWIGHT D. EISENHOWER (1890–1969). On the death of his first son Doud Dwight ("Icky") at age three. In *Ike,* television documentary, PBS, 15 October 1986

My son, a perfect little boy of five years and three months, had ended his earthly life. You can never sympathize with me; you can never know how much of me such a young child can take away. A few weeks ago I accounted myself a very rich man, and now the poorest of all.
> RALPH WALDO EMERSON (1803–1882). Soon after his son Waldo's death from scarlet fever, letter to Thomas Carlyle, 28 February 1842

Obey thy Natural Father, but thy Spiritual more.
> JAMES HOWELL (1593–1666)

When I was a kid, my father told me every day, "You're the most wonderful boy in the world, and you can do anything you want to."
> JAN HUTCHINS (1949–). Radio talk-program host. KGO, San Francisco, 17 May 1988

Take more pleasure in giving what is best to another than in having it yourself, and then all the world will love you, and I more than all the world.
> THOMAS JEFFERSON (1743–1826). Letter to his daughter Maria, 11 April 1790

Get up, Lyndon. Every boy in the county's got a two-hour start on you.
> SAM JOHNSON (1877–1937). Words used in routing his young son out of bed in the morning. In James David Barber, *The Presidential Character: Predicting Performance in the White House,* 4, 1972

There must always be a struggle between a father and son, while one aims at power and the other at independence.
> SAMUEL JOHNSON (1709–1784). 14 July 1763. In James Boswell, *The Life of Samuel Johnson,* 1791

Many people have asked "Has writing this book made you feel closer to your father?" to which I could only answer: "My relationship with him has greatly improved since his death."
> ADRIAN LAING. Referring to his newly published book *R. D. Laing: A Biography* and his relationship with the Scottish psychiatrist, "In the Shadow of a Sixties Messiah," *Independent* (British newspaper), 21 August 1994

Are you lost daddy, I asked tenderly.
Shut up, he explained.
> RING LARDNER (1885–1933). *The Young Immigrants,* 10, 1920

I learned [as a youth] that when I defended my rights by open rebellion my father relented, but when I remained meek and submissive he only cursed and beat me the more.
> MAO TSE-TUNG (1893–1976). In Edgar Snow, *Red Star Over China,* rev. ed., 4.1, 1961

Biff Loman (on his father Willy): He threw me out of this house, remember that.
Linda Loman (Biff's mother): Why did he do that? I never knew why.
Biff: Because I know he's a fake and he doesn't like anybody around who knows!
> ARTHUR MILLER (1915–). *Death of a Salesman,* 1, 1949

It is much easier to become a father than to be one.
> KENT NERBURN (1946–). Theologian. *Letters to My Son: Reflections on Becoming a Man,* 25, 1994

What the father kept silent the son speaks out.
> FRIEDRICH NIETZSCHE (1844–1900). "Of the Tarantulas," *Thus Spoke Zarathustra,* 1892, tr. R. J. Hollingdale, 1961

There's a stake in your fat black heart
And the villagers never liked you.
They are dancing and stamping on you.
They always *knew* it was you.
Daddy, daddy, you bastard, I'm through.
> SYLVIA PLATH (1932–1963). Last stanza, "Daddy," 12 October 1962, *The Collected Poems,* ed. Ted Hughes, 1981

We think our Fathers Fools, so wise we grow;
Our wiser Sons, no doubt, will think us so.
> ALEXANDER POPE (1688–1744). *An Essay on Criticism,* l. 438, 1711

I cheat my boys every chance I get. I want to make 'em sharp. I trade with the boys and skin 'em and I just beat 'em every time I can.
> WILLIAM A. ROCKEFELLER (1810–1908?). Father of John D. Rockefeller. In John K. Winkler, *John D: A Portrait in Oils,* 1, 1929

This is my father, Mrs. Baines. Try what you can do with him. He won't listen to me because he remembers what a fool I was when I was a baby.
> GEORGE BERNARD SHAW (1856–1950). *Major Barbara,* 2, 1905

He who does not teach his son an occupation is as one who has taught his son to rob.
> TALMUD (A.D. 1st–6th cent.). Rabbinical writings

The only time a son should disobey his father is if the father orders him to commit a sin.

TALMUD (A.D. 1st–6th cent.). Rabbinical writings

As long as I have been in the White House, I can't help waking at 5 a.m. and hearing the old man at the foot of the stairs calling and telling me to get out and milk the cows.

HARRY S. TRUMAN (1884–1972). Remark to Sen. George D. Aiken, 1945. In Robert J. Donovan, *Conflict and Crisis: The Presidency of Harry S. Truman, 1945–1948*, 15, 1977

Always obey your parents, when they are present.

MARK TWAIN (1835–1910). "Advice to Youth," speech before the Saturday Morning Club, Boston, 15 April 1882

When I was a boy of 14, my father was so ignorant I could hardly stand to have the old man around. But when I got to be 21, I was astonished at how much the old man had learned in seven years.

MARK TWAIN (1835–1910). In "Bringing Up Father," p. 22, *Reader's Digest*, September 1937. Although often attributed to Twain, this well-known observation has not been found in his writings. Twain was 11 years old when his father died.

The fathers have eaten sour grapes, and the children's teeth are set on edge.

SAYING (*BIBLE*). *Jeremiah* 31:29

One father can support ten children, but ten children can't support one father.

SAYING (SPANISH)

Father knows best.

SAYING

FATIGUE

See also • Sleep

The test of a people is what they can do when they're tired.

WINSTON CHURCHILL (1874–1965)

Our greatest weariness comes from work not done.

ERIC HOFFER (1902–1983). *Reflections on the Human Condition*, 178, 1973

I suppose it is good for the body. But the tired part of me is *inside* and out of reach.

ABRAHAM LINCOLN (1809–1865). Replying (during his Presidency) to a friend's suggestion that he rest. In Richard Hofstadter, *The American Political Tradition: And the Men Who Made It*, 5.7, 1948

When we are tired, we are attacked by ideas we conquered long ago.

FRIEDRICH NIETZSCHE (1844–1900)

Fatigue makes cowards of us all.

GEORGE S. PATTON, JR. (1883–1945). "Letter of Instruction Number 1," 6 March 1944, appendix (D) to *War As I Knew It*, 1947

See Conscience: Shakespeare (2)

FAULTS

See also • Defects ◦ Errors ◦ Failure ◦ Judging Others ◦ Mistakes ◦ Perfection: Oscar Wilde ◦ Self-Esteem: Kahlil Gibran ◦ Weaknesses ◦ Women & Men: Anonymous

Faultless to a fault.

ROBERT BROWNING (1812–1889). *The Ring and the Book*, 9.1175, 1869

The greatest of faults . . . is to be conscious of none.

THOMAS CARLYLE (1795–1891). "The Hero as Prophet," *On Heroes, Hero-Worship, and the Heroic in History*, 1841

Our own self-love draws a thick veil between us and our faults.

LORD CHESTERFIELD (1694–1773). Letter to his son, 21 June 1748

It is a trait of fools to perceive the faults of others but not their own.

CICERO (106–43 B.C.). *Tusculanae disputationes*, 3.30

Wink at small faults.

JOHN CLARKE (1596–1658). Comp., *Proverbs: English and Latine*, p. 108, 1639

To have faults and not to reform them—this, indeed, should be pronounced having faults.

CONFUCIUS (551–479 B.C.). *Confucian Analects*, 15.29, tr. James Legge, 1930

Look upon the man who tells thee thy faults as if he told thee of a hidden treasure.

THE DHAMMAPADA: THE PATH OF PERFECTION (1st cent. B.C.). 76, tr. Juan Mascaró 1973

The faults of others console us in our own.

PAUL ELDRIDGE (1888–1982). *Maxims for a Modern Man*, 2178, 1965

J.L.S. has this fatal fault that he is too easily pleased.

RALPH WALDO EMERSON (1803–1882). Journal, 29 June 1840

There is none without his foible. I verily believe if an angel should come to ravish [him] with the melodies of the moral law in speech sweeter and richer than Shakespeare's, he would eat too much gingerbread, or be moody when he was alone, or keep a capital lookout for number one, as the children say, or have some one or other pitiful hole in his coat.

RALPH WALDO EMERSON (1803–1882). Journal, 23 April 1841

Tell me my Faults, and mend your own.

BENJAMIN FRANKLIN (1706–1790). *Poor Richard's Almanack*, December 1756

A perfect character might be attended with the inconvenience of being envied and hated; . . . a benevolent man should allow a few faults in himself, to keep his friends in countenance.

BENJAMIN FRANKLIN (1706–1790). 1784, *Autobiography*, 1798

Happy is the Man who sees his Faults in his Youth.

THOMAS FULLER (1654–1734). Comp., *Gnomologia: Adages and Proverbs*, 1792, 1732

Your main Fault is, you are good for nothing.

THOMAS FULLER (1654–1734). Comp., *Gnomologia: Adages and Proverbs*, 6054, 1732

I am very imperfect. Before you are gone you will have discovered a hundred of my faults, and if you don't, I will help you to see them.

> MOHANDAS K. GANDHI (1869–1948). Remark to the author during his week–long visit with Gandhi in 1942. In Louis Fischer, *The Life of Mahatma Gandhi*, 38, 1950

All his faults were such that one loves him still the better for them.

> OLIVER GOLDSMITH (1728–1774). *The Good-Natur'd Man*, 1, 1768

There are some faults so nearly allied to excellence that we can scarce weed out the vice without eradicating the virtue.

> OLIVER GOLDSMITH (1728–1774). *The Good-Natur'd Man*, 1, 1768

The lower sort of men must be indulged the consolation of finding fault with those above them; without that, they would be so melancholy that it would be dangerous, considering their numbers.

> MARQUIS of HALIFAX (1633–1695). "Of the People," *Political, Moral and Miscellaneous Reflections*, 1750

Edward Bennett Williams (Washington lawyer): Jimmy, there's no point in arguing: you're wrong.
Hoffa: Damn it, damn it! I may have faults, but being wrong ain't one of them.

> JIMMY HOFFA (1913–1975). International Brotherhood of Teamsters president. In A. H. Raskin, "Was Jimmy Hoffa a Hood? Or Was He Robin Hood?" *New York Times*, 20 December 1992

The awareness of their individual blemishes and shortcomings inclines the frustrated to detect ill will and meanness in their fellow men. Self-contempt, however vague, sharpens our eyes for the imperfections of others. We usually strive to reveal in others the blemishes we hide in ourselves.

> ERIC HOFFER (1902–1983). *The True Believer: Thoughts on the Nature of Mass Movements*, 100, 1951
>
> See Judging Others: Carl G. Jung

Faults are thick where love is thin.

> JAMES HOWELL (1593–1666). Comp., *Paroimiographia. Proverbs, or Old Sayed Sawes & Adages in English . . . Italian, French and Spanish*, 1659

A person's faults are largely what make him or her likable.

> ANNE LAMOTT (1954–). *Bird by Bird: Some Instructions on Writing and Life*, 1 ("Character"), 1995

Some people's faults are becoming, other people's virtues prove drawbacks.

> LA ROCHEFOUCAULD (1613–1680). *Maxims*, 251, 1665, tr. Louis Kronenberger, 1959

We try to make virtues out of the faults we have no wish to correct.

> LA ROCHEFOUCAULD (1613–1680). *Maxims*, 442, 1665, tr. Leonard Tancock, 1959

It is always well to accept your own shortcomings with candor but to regard those of our friends with polite incredulity.

> RUSSELL LYNES (1910–1991). "The Art of Accepting," *Vogue*, 1 September 1952

He whose faults are not told him
Ignorantly thinks his defects are virtues.

> SA'DI (A.D. 1213?–1292). *The Gulistan, or Rose Garden*, 4 (Story 12), A.D. 1258, tr. Edward Rehatsek, 1964

We hate those faults most in others which we are guilty of ourselves.

> WILLIAM SHENSTONE (1714–1763). "Of Men and Manners," *Men & Manners*, ed. Havelock Ellis, 1927

Bear with the faults and frailties of others, for you, too, have many faults which others have to bear. If you cannot mold yourself as you would wish, how can you expect other people to be entirely to your liking? For we require other people to be perfect, but do not correct our own faults.

> THOMAS à KEMPIS (1380–1471). *The Imitation of Christ*, 1.16, tr. Leo Sherley-Price, 1952

❦

Faultless, *adj.* Friendless.

> ANONYMOUS

Faults are more easily forgiven than virtues.

> ANONYMOUS

Even the sun has its spots.

> SAYING (HUNGARIAN)

FEAR

See also • Anxiety ○ Courage: Norman F. Dixon, Robert Louis Stevenson, Mark Twain, Anonymous (1) ○ Cowardice ○ Danger ○ Distrust ○ Faith ○ Hate ○ Love: John (2), Marianne Williamson ○ Paranoia ○ Safety ○ Sea: M. Synge ○ Self-Realization (Being): Edward Weeks ○ Suspicion ○ War & Psychology: Thomas Merton ○ Worry

The habit of doing one's duty drives out fear.

> CHARLES BAUDELAIRE (1821–1867). *Intimate Journals*, 116, 1887, tr. Christopher Isherwood, 1957

I am not afraid of pain, nor of sorrow. But this loneliness, this futility, this emptiness—I dare not face them.

> RUTH BENEDICT (1887–1948). Journal, October 1912, *An Anthropologist at Work: Writings of Ruth Benedict*, pt. 2, 1959

It iz a disgrace tew enny man tew be feared.

> JOSH BILLINGS (1818–1885)

No passion so effectually robs the mind of all its powers of acting and reasoning as fear.

> EDMUND BURKE (1890–1958). *A Philosophical Inquiry into the Origin of Our Ideas of the Sublime and the Beautiful*, 2.2, 1756

The first and great commandment is, Don't let them scare you.

> ELMER DAVIS (1890–1958). *But We Were Born Free*, 1, 1954

Those who fear what they should not fear, and who do not fear what they should fear . . . go the downward path.

> THE DHAMMAPADA: THE PATH OF PERFECTION (1st cent. B.C.). 317, tr. Juan Mascaro, 1973

[What people fear most is] taking a new step or uttering a new word.

> FYODOR DOSTOYEVSKI (1821–1881). *Crime and Punishment*, 1.1, 1866, tr. David Magarshack, 1951

I knew a man scared by the rustle of his own hatband.
> RALPH WALDO EMERSON (1803–1882). Journal, 2 August 1837

We are afraid of truth, afraid of fortune, afraid of death, and afraid of each other.
> RALPH WALDO EMERSON (1803–1882). "Self-Reliance," *Essays: First Series,* 1841

The basest of all things is to be afraid.
> WILLIAM FAULKNER (1897–1962). Acceptance address for Nobel Prize in literature, Stockholm, 10 December 1950

Those who love to be feared fear to be loved.
> ST. FRANCES de SALES (1567–1622). In Jean-Pierre Camus, *The Spirit of Saint Frances de Sales,* 7.3, 1952

Better hazard once than always be in fear.
> THOMAS FULLER (1654–1734). Comp., *Gnomologia: Adages and Proverbs,* 906, 1732

A degree of fear sharpeneth, the excess of it stupifieth.
> MARQUIS OF HALIFAX (1633–1695). "Fear," *Political, Moral and Miscellaneous Reflections,* 1750

Whenever I feel afraid
I hold my head erect
And whistle a happy tune
So no one will suspect
I'm afraid. . . .
The result of this deception
Is very strange to tell,
For when I fool the people I fear
I fool myself as well!
> OSCAR HAMMERSTEIN II (1895–1960). "I Whistle a Happy Tune" (song). In the musical *The King and I,* 1951

You can discover what your enemy fears most by observing the means he uses to frighten you.
> ERIC HOFFER (1902–1983). *The Passionate State of Mind: And Other Aphorisms,* 222, 1954

Fear: A club used by priests, presidents, kings and policemen to keep the people from recovering stolen goods.
> ELBERT HUBBARD (1856–1915). *The Roycroft Dictionary Concocted by Ali Baba and the Bunch on Rainy Days,* p. 54, 1914

Never take counsel of your fears.
> THOMAS JONATHAN "STONEWALL" JACKSON (1824–1863). Remark to Maj. Jedekiah Hotchkiss, June 1862. In Douglas Southall Freeman, *Lee's Lieutenants: A Study in Command,* 1.28, 1942–1944

Anonymous friend (referring to a Mexican War engagement during which Lieut. Jackson had bravely performed): Were you scared? *Jackson:* No, the only anxiety of which I was conscious during the engagements was a fear lest I should not meet danger enough to make my conduct conspicuous.
> THOMAS JONATHAN "STONEWALL" JACKSON (1824–1863). Format adapted, 1847? In Douglas Southall Freeman, appendix (2) to vol. 1, *Lee's Lieutenants: A Study in Command,* 1942–1944

No greater hell than to be slave to fear.
> BEN JONSON (1572–1637). *Every Man in His Humour,* 3.2, 1598

Our problem is not to be rid of fear but rather to harness and master it.
> MARTIN LUTHER KING, JR. (1929–1968). *Strength to Love,* 14 (introduction), 1963

Many he must fear whom many fear.
> LABERIUS (115?–43 B.C.). In Seneca the Younger (5? B.C.–A.D. 65). "On Anger" (2.11.3), *Moral Essays,* tr. John W. Basore, 1928

Fear has the largest eyes of all.
> BORIS PASTERNAK (1890–1960). "Hoarfrost," *The Poetry of Boris Pasternak: 1917–1959,* tr. George Reavey, 1959

Cry, the beloved country, for the unborn child that is the inheritor of our fear.
> ALAN PATON (1903–1988). *Cry, the Beloved Country,* 12, 1948

This is preeminently the time to speak the truth, the whole truth, frankly and boldly. Nor need we shrink from honestly facing conditions in our country today. This great nation will endure as it has endured, will revive and will prosper. So, first of all, let me assert my firm belief that the only thing we have to fear is fear itself— nameless, unreasoning, unjustified terror which paralyzes needed efforts to convert retreat into advance.
> FRANKLIN D. ROOSEVELT (1882–1945). *First Inaugural Address,* 4 March 1933

There were all kinds of things of which I was afraid at first, from grizzly bears to "mean" horses and gunfighters; but by acting as if I was not afraid I gradually ceased to be afraid.
> THEODORE ROOSEVELT (1858–1919). *An Autobiography,* 2, 1913

An irrational fear should never be simply let alone, but should be gradually overcome by familiarity with its fainter forms.
> BERTRAND RUSSELL (1872–1970). *Education and the Good Life,* 4, 1926

The slave of fear: the worst of slaveries.
> GEORGE BERNARD SHAW (1856–1950). *Misalliance,* p. 59, 1910

Keep your fears to yourself but share your courage.
> ROBERT LOUIS STEVENSON (1850–1894)

Nothing is so much to be feared as fear.
> HENRY DAVID THOREAU (1817–1862). Journal, 7 September 1851

It's what people know about themselves inside that makes them afraid.
> ERNEST TIDYMAN (1928–1984). *High Plains Drifter* (film), 1973, spoken by Clint Eastwood

I'm more afraid of being nothing than of being hurt.
> ROBERT TOWNE (1936–). *Days of Thunder* (film), 1990, spoken by Tom Cruise (in the role of a victory-driven race-car driver)

❧

The Lord is my light and my salvation;
whom shall I fear?
> ANONYMOUS (*BIBLE*). Psalms 27:1

The rule for overcoming fear is to head right into it.
> ANONYMOUS

Fear not only anticipates misfortunes that never happen, it also precipitates some that would not otherwise have happened.

ANONYMOUS

FEELING

See also • Emotion ∘ Temperament ∘ Thinking: Vauvenargues

Last night at twelve I felt immense,
But now I feel like thirty cents.

GEORGE ADE (1866–1944). "Remorse," *The Sultan of Sulu,* 1902

See Depression: Lord Beaverbrook ∘ Enthusiasm: André Gide

There are some feelings Time cannot benumb.

LORD BYRON (1788–1824). *Childe Harold's Pilgrimage,* 4.19, 1812–1818

The thoughts they had were the parents of the actions they did; their feelings were parents of their thoughts.

THOMAS CARLYLE (1795–1881). "The Hero as Divinity," *On Heroes, Hero-Worship, and the Heroic in History,* 1841

See Opinion: Herbert Spencer

The ability to feel is indivisible. Repress awareness of any one feeling, and all feelings are dulled. . . . The same nerve endings are required for weeping and dancing, fear and ecstasy.

SAM KEEN (1931–). *Fire in the Belly: On Being a Man,* p. 139, 1991

One feeling may be opposed by another feeling, but never by reason.

GUSTAVE LE BON (1841–1931). *The Psychology of the Great War,* 1.1.2, tr. E. Andrews, 1916

The roots of reason are embedded in feelings—feelings that have formed and accumulated and developed over a lifetime of personality-shaping. These feelings are not a source of weakness but a resource of strength. They are not there for occasional using but are inescapable. To know what we think, we must know how we feel. It is feeling that shapes belief and forms opinion. It is feeling that directs the strategy of argument. It is our feelings, then, with which we must come to honorable terms.

JAMES E. MILLER, JR. *Word, Self, Reality: The Rhetoric of Imagination,* 2, 1972

FEMINISM

See also • Misogynous Statements ∘ Rights: Peter Finley Dunne ∘ Sex ∘ Sexism ∘ Sexist Statements ∘ Sexual Revolution ∘ Women ∘ Women & Men

Do not put such unlimited power into the hands of the Husbands. Remember all Men would be tyrants if they could. If particular care and attention is not paid to the Ladies, we are determined to foment a Rebellion, and will not hold ourselves bound by any Laws in which we have no voice, or Representation.

ABIGAIL ADAMS (1744–1818) Letter to her husband John, 31 March 1776

The true republic: men, their rights and nothing more; women, their rights and nothing less.

SUSAN B. ANTHONY (1820–1906). Motto of *Revolution* (feminist newspaper), 1868

Join the union, girls, and together "Equal Pay for Equal Work."

SUSAN B. ANTHONY (1820–1906). In *Revolution* (feminist newspaper), 18 March 1869

No passing of legal enactments can set free a woman with a slave mind.

TERESA BILLINGTON-GREIG (1877–1964). *The Militant Suffrage Movement: Emancipation in a Hurry,* 9, 1911

Feminism is an entire world view or gestalt, not just a laundry list of women's issues.

CHARLOTTE BUNCH (1944–). "Understanding Feminist Theory," *New Directions for Women,* September-October 1981

The right of citizens of the United States to vote shall not be denied or abridged by the United States or by any State on account of sex.

CONSTITUTION OF THE UNITED STATES. Nineteenth Amendment, 26 August 1920

Men who want to support women in our struggle for freedom and justice should understand that it is not terrifically important to us that they learn to cry; it is important to us that they stop the crimes of violence against us.

ANDREA DWORKIN (1946–). "The Rape Atrocity and the Boy Next Door," speech, 1 March 1975, *Our Blood,* 4, 1976

Mr. Craig: I like a cleverish woman—a woman o' sperrit—a managing woman.

GEORGE ELIOT (1819–1880). *Adam Bede,* 53, 1859

Let the laws be purged of every barbarous remainder, every barbarous impediment to women.

RALPH WALDO EMERSON (1803–1882). "Woman," Woman's Rights Convention speech, Boston, 20 September 1855

Section 1. Equality of rights under the law shall not be denied or abridged by the United States or by any state on account of sex.

EQUAL RIGHTS AMENDMENT. Proposed constitutional amendment defeated in 1982

[The 1980s] has seen a power counterassault on women's rights, a backlash, an attempt to retract the handful of small and hard-won victories that the feminist movement did manage to win for women. This counterassault is largely insidious: in a kind of pop-culture version of the Big Lie, it stands the truth boldly on its head and proclaims that the very steps that elevated women's position have actually led to their downfall.

SUSAN FALUDI (1959–). Introduction to *Backlash: The Undeclared War Against American Women,* 1991

I am more than a hole.

KAREN FINLEY (1956–). In Marcelle Clements, "Karen Finley's Rage, Pain, Hate and Hope," *New York Times,* 22 July 1990

It is easier to live through someone else than to complete yourself. The freedom to lead and plan your own life is frightening if you have never faced it before. It is frightening when a woman finally realizes that there is no answer to the question "who am I" except the voice inside herself.

BETTY FRIEDAN (1921–). *The Feminine Mystique,* 14, 1963

When she stopped conforming to the conventional picture of femininity, she finally began to enjoy being a woman.

> BETTY FRIEDAN (1921–). *The Feminine Mystique,* 14, 1963

The time is at hand when the voices of the feminine mystique can no longer drown out the inner voice that is driving women on to become complete.

> BETTY FRIEDAN (1921–). Closing words, *The Feminine Mystique,* 1963

True emancipation begins neither at the polls nor in courts. It begins in woman's soul.

> EMMA GOLDMAN (1869–1940). "The Tragedy of Women's Emancipation," *Anarchism and Other Essays,* 3rd rev. ed., 1917 (1910)

Woman is born free and her rights are the same as those of a man. . . . All citizens, be they men or women, being equal in [the state's] eyes, must be equally eligible for all public offices, positions and jobs, according to their capacity and without any other criteria than those of their virtues and talents.

> OLYMPE de GOUGES (1748–1793). French writer and revolutionary. Referring to The Declaration of the Rights of Man and the Citizen (1789), which states in Article 1 that "Men are born free and equal in rights." *Déclaration des droits de la femme et la citoyenne,* 1791

I became a feminist as an alternative to becoming a masochist.

> SALLY KEMPTON (1943–). "Cutting Loose," *Esquire,* July 1970

Women's liberation is the liberation of the feminine in the man and the masculine in the woman.

> CORITA KENT (1918–1986). In Lucie Kay Scheuer, "A Time of Transition for Corita Kent," *Los Angeles Times,* 11 July 1974

Scarlett O'Hara: I'm tired of saying, "How wonderful you are!" to fool men who haven't got one-half the sense I've got, and I'm tired of pretending I don't know anything, so men can tell me things and feel important while they're doing it.

> MARGARET MITCHELL (1900–1949). *Gone with the Wind,* 5, 1936

It was the usual masculine disillusionment in discovering that a woman has a brain.

> MARGARET MITCHELL (1900–1949). *Gone with the Wind,* 36, 1936

Sisterhood Is Powerful.

> ROBIN MORGAN (1941–). Ed., book title, 1970

For me, to be a feminist is to answer the question: "Are women human?" with a yes. It is not about whether women are better than, worse than or identical with men. It's certainly not about trading personal liberty—abortion, divorce, sexual self–expression—for social protection as wives and mothers, as pro-life feminists propose. It's about justice, fairness and access to the broad range of human experience. It's about women consulting their own well-being and being judged as individuals rather than as members of a class with one personality, one social function, one road to happiness. It's about women having intrinsic value as persons rather than contingent value as a means to an end for others: fetuses, children, "the family," men.

> KATHA POLLITT (1949–). Introduction to *Reasonable Creatures: Essays on Women and Feminism,* 1994

We're half the people; we should be half the Congress.

> JEANNETTE RANKIN (1880–1973). Montana congresswoman and first woman member of the House of Representatives, 1917. In "Where Are They Now," *Newsweek,* 14 February 1966

[Responsibility to yourself] means that you refuse to sell your talents and aspirations short, simply to avoid conflict and confrontation. And this, in turn, means resisting the forces in society which say that women should be nice, play safe, have low professional expectations, drown in love and forget about work, live through others, and stay in the places assigned to us. It means that we insist on a life of meaningful work, insist that work be as meaningful as love and friendship in our lives. It means, therefore, the courage to be "different"; not to be continuously available to others when we need time for ourselves and our work; to be able to demand of others— parents, friends, roommates, teachers, lovers, husbands, children— that they respect our sense of purpose and our integrity as persons.

> ADRIENNE RICH (1929–). "Claiming and Education," 1977, *On Lies, Secrets, and Silence: Selected Prose 1966–1978,* 1979

The connections between and among women are the most feared, the most problematic, and the most potentially transforming force on the planet.

> ADRIENNE RICH (1929–). "Disloyal to Civilization: Feminism, Racism, Gynophobia," *Chrysalis,* 1979

Woman must not accept; she must challenge. She must not be awed by that which has been built up around her; she must reverence that within her which struggles for expression. Her eyes must be less upon what is and more clearly upon what should be. She must listen only with a frankly questioning attitude to the dogmatized opinions of man–made society. When she chooses the new, free course of action, it must be in the light of her own opinion—of her own intuition. Only so can she give play to the feminine spirit. Only thus can she free her mate from the bondage which he wrought for himself when he wrought hers. Only thus can she restore to him that of which he robbed himself in restricting her. Only thus can she remake the world.

> MARGARET SANGER (1883–1966). *Woman and the New Race,* 8, 1920

Woman, if she dares face the fact that she is being [sexually used], must either loathe herself or else rebel.

> GEORGE BERNARD SHAW (1856–1950). "The Womanly Woman," *The Quintessence of Ibsenism,* 1891

Can man be free if woman be a slave?

> PERCY BYSSHE SHELLEY (1792–1822). *The Revolt of Islam,* 2.43, 1817

We hold these truths to be self-evident: that all men and women are created equal. . . .

The history of mankind is a history of repeated injuries and usurpations on the part of man toward woman, having in direct object the establishment of an absolute tyranny over her.

> ELIZABETH CADY STANTON (1815–1902). Declaration of Sentiments. First Woman's Rights Convention, Seneca Falls, New York, 19 July 1848
>
> See Rights: Thomas Jefferson

All the truth telling and the creation of alternate institutions have begun to delineate and give value to a *women's culture,* a set of perspectives that differs from the more traditional, masculine ones. We need to learn, but so do men. Together, we can create a shared culture that includes the most useful and creative features of each.

Power is also being redefined. Women often explain with care that we mean power to control our lives but not to dominate others.

> GLORIA STEINEM (1935–). "Words and Change," *Outrageous Acts and Everyday Rebellions,* 1983

If you say, "I'm for equal pay," that's a reform. But if you say, "I'm a feminist," that's . . . a transformation of society.

> GLORIA STEINEM (1935–). In "How to Survive a Revolution," *Time,* 9 March 1992

Dat man ober dar say that women needs to be helped into carriages, and lifted ober ditches, and to have de best place every whar. Nobody ever help me into carriages, or ober mud puddles, or gives me any best places . . . and ar'nt I a woman? Look at me! Look at my arm! . . . I have plowed, and planted, and gathered into barns, and no man could head me—and ar'nt I a woman? I could work as much as a man (when I could get it), and bear de lash as well—and ar'nt I a woman? I have borne five chilern and I seen 'em mos' all sold off into slavery, and when I cried out with a mother's grief, none but Jesus heard—and arn't I a woman?

> SOJOURNER TRUTH (1797?–1883). Quoted by Frances M. Beal, "Double Jeopardy: To Be Black and Female," 1969. In Robin Morgan, ed., *Sisterhood Is Powerful: An Anthology of Writings from the Women's Liberation Movement,* 1970

If women want any rights more'n they got, why don't they just *take 'em,* and not be talkin' about it.

> SOJOURNER TRUTH (1797?–1883)

I myself have never been able to find out precisely what feminism is: I only know that people call me a feminist whenever I express sentiments that differentiate me from a doormat.

> REBECCA WEST (1892–1983). In *The Clarion,* 14 November 1913

I will show of male and female that either is but the equal of the other.

> WALT WHITMAN (1819–1892). "Starting from Paumanok" (12), 1860, *Leaves of Grass,* 1855–1892

Weakness may excite tenderness and gratify the arrogant pride of man; but the lordly caresses of a protector will not gratify a noble mind that pants for and deserves to be respected.

> MARY WOLLSTONECRAFT (1759–1797). *A Vindication of the Rights of Woman,* 2, 1792

❦

A woman's place is in the House—and in the Senate.

> SAYING (AMERICAN)

See Misogynous Statements: James Howell ○ Sexist Statements: Saying

FICTION

See also • Novels ○ Truth: Lord Byron, Mark Twain (1,2) ○ Writing

Fiction never exceeds the reach of the writer's courage.

> DOROTHY ALLISON. *Skin: Talking About Sex, Class & Literature,* 22, 1994

That is what we are supposed to do when we are at our best—make it all up—but make it up so truly that later it will happen that way.

> ERNEST HEMINGWAY (1899–1961). Letter to F. Scott Fitzgerald, 28 May 1934

You can't be a serious writer of fiction unless you believe the story you are telling.

> NORMAN MAILER (1923–). Sean Abbott interview. "Mailer Goes to the Mountain," *At Random,* Spring-Summer 1997

Fiction is higher autobiography.

> ALBERTO MORAVIA (1907–1990). In James Atlas, "'The Busy, *Busy* Wasp,'" *New York Times Magazine,* 18 October 1992

In [writing] fiction, every sentence is its own reward.

> AMY TAM (1952–). Wendy Tokuda conversation, radio rebroadcast, KQED, San Francisco, 27 January 1996

Fiction reveals truths that reality obscures.

> JESSAMYN WEST (1902–1984). *To See the Dream,* pt. 1, 1956

The good end happily, and the bad unhappily. That is what Fiction means.

> OSCAR WILDE (1854–1900). *The Importance of Being Earnest,* 2, 1895

All fiction for me is a kind of magic and trickery—a confidence trick, trying to make people believe something is true that isn't.

> ANGUS WILSON (1913–1991). Michael Millgate interview. In Malcolm Cowley, ed., *Writers at Work: First Series,* 1958

FIGURES

See also • Facts: Sydney Smith ○ Mathematics ○ Numbers ○ Statistics

[The War Office kept three sets of figures:] one to mislead the public, another to mislead the Cabinet, and the third to mislead itself.

> HERBERT ASQUITH (1852–1928). British prime minister. In Alistair Horne, *The Price of Glory: Verdun 1916,* 2, 1962

A witty statesman said, you might prove anything by figures.

> THOMAS CARLYLE (1795–1881). *Chartism,* 2, 1840

In any collection of data, the figure most obviously correct, beyond all need of checking, is the mistake.

> FINAGLE'S THIRD LAW. In Arthur Bloch, comp., "Murphology," *Murphy's Law: And Other Reasons Why Things Go gnorW,* 1979

❦

Figures don't lie, but liars figure.

> ANONYMOUS

Figures are not always facts.

> SAYING (AMERICAN)

Liars figure and figures lie.

> SAYING

FILMS

See also • Books: Louis A. Safian ○ Critics: Examples ○ Acting ○ Actors ○ Art ○ Creativity ○ Directors ○ Hollywood ○ Los Angeles ○ Media ○ Misjudgments: Gary Cooper, Auguste Lumière, Irving Thalberg, Harry Warner ○ Television ○ Theater

I love Mickey Mouse more than any woman I've known.

> WALT DISNEY (1901–1966). In "Air Hercules Joins Disney's Pantheon of Pitchmen," *New York Times,* 22 June 1997

When you're making a movie, you can't think anybody will ever see it. You've just got to make a movie for the values it has. The greatest films were made because someone really wanted to make them. And, hopefully, the audience will show up, too.

> CLINT EASTWOOD (1930–). In Bernard Weinraub, "Fistful of Praise and Clips for Clint Eastwood Tribute," *New York Times,* 6 May 1996

A movie should have a beginning, a middle and an end, though not necessarily in that order.

> JEAN-LUC GODARD (1930–). In Phillip Lopate, "Brilliance and Bardot, All in One," *New York Times,* 22 June 1997

Pictures are for entertainment; messages should be delivered by Western Union.

> SAMUEL GOLDWYN (1882–1974). On preachy films. In Arthur Marx, *Goldwyn: The Man behind the Myth,* 15, 1976

For me the cinema is not a slice of life, but a piece of cake.

> ALFRED HITCHCOCK (1899–1980). In *Sunday Times* (London), 6 March 1977

In a good movie, the sound could go off, and the audience would still have a perfectly clear idea of what was going on.

> ALFRED HITCHCOCK (1899–1980)

A good trailer doesn't guarantee a hit, but a hit must have a good trailer.

> WADE HUDSON (1944–). Personal communication, 29 December 1997

At the present time, the cinema acts far more effectively as the opium of the people than does religion.

> ALDOUS HUXLEY (1894–1963). "Writers and Readers," *The Olive Tree and Other Essays,* 1936
>
> See Religion, Anti-: Karl Marx

Good movies make you care, make you believe in possibilities again.

> PAULINE KAEL (1919–). *Going Steady,* 2.1, 1968

The words "Kiss Kiss Bang Bang," which I saw on an Italian movie poster, are perhaps the briefest statement imaginable of the basic appeal of movies. This appeal is what attracts us, and ultimately what makes us despair when we begin to understand how seldom movies are more than this.

> PAULINE KAEL (1919–). "A Note on the Title," *Kiss Kiss Bang Bang,* 1968

Life in the movie business is like the beginning of a new love affair: it's full of surprises and you're constantly getting fucked.

> DAVID MAMET (1947–). *Speed-the-Plow: A Play,* 1, 1987

Movies in America have not developed advertising intervals simply because the movie itself is the greatest of all forms of advertisement for consumer goods.

> MARSHALL McLUHAN (1911–1980). *Understanding Media: The Extensions of Man,* 21, 1964

In the evenings I usually watch television or go to the movies. . . . Our neighborhood theater in Gentilly has permanent lettering on the front of the marquee reading: Where Happiness Costs So Little.

> WALKER PERCY (1916–1990). *The Moviegoer,* 1.1, 1961

What's really magical about films is [an actor's] being inappropriate, or being irresponsible, by letting it go, by not caring. And that way the film captures magic. And a film is only as good as a collection of the best magic moments, the best lucky accidents that they happen to catch on film.

> CHRISTOPHER REEVE (1952–). James Lipton television interview, *Inside the Actors Studio* ("A Fifty Year Celebration"), BVO, 27 November 1996

It's the only business where you can sit out front and applaud yourself.

> WILL ROGERS (1879–1935). The last of "fourteen points on the moving picture business," 1919, *The Autobiography of Will Rogers,* ed. Donald Day, 1949

Samuel Goldwyn (referring to a Shaw play he wanted to bring to the screen): I'll make it a great piece of art.
Shaw: That's the trouble. All you think of is art, and all I think of is money.

> GEORGE BERNARD SHAW (1856–1950). Format adapted. In D.W.C., "Memo: From G.B.S. to S.G.," *New York Times,* 27 September 1936

In good films, there is always a directness that entirely frees us from the itch to interpret.

> SUSAN SONTAG (1933–). "Against Interpretation" (7), *Evergreen Review,* December 1964

I've got this preoccupation with ordinary people pursued by large forces.

> STEVEN SPIELBERG (1947–). 1978?

I like to be able to remember the movie longer than the time it takes to get to my car.

> SYLVESTER STALLONE (1946–). On his own recent films. In Trip Gabriel, "Stallone Seeks a Serious Turn for the Better," *New York Times,* 10 August 1997

I grew a beard for Nero, in *Quo Vadis,* but Metro–Goldwyn–Mayer thought it didn't look real, so I had to wear a false one.

> PETER USTINOV (1921–)

The biggest electric train set any boy ever had.

> ORSON WELLES (1915–1985). On the RKO studios. In Peter Noble, *The Fabulous Orson Welles,* 7, 1956

They shoot too many pictures and not enough actors.

> WALTER WINCHELL (1897–1972)

FISH

See also • Animals

And the Lord appointed a great fish to swallow up Jonah; and Jonah was in the belly of the fish three days and three nights.

> JONAH. *Jonah* 1:17

Captain Ahab: There she blows!—there she blows! A hump like a snow hill! It is Moby Dick.

HERMAN MELVILLE (1819–1891). *Moby-Dick; or, The Whale,* 133, 1851, ed. Harold Beaver, 1972

Who hears the fishes when they cry? It will not be forgotten by some memory that we were contemporaries.

HENRY DAVID THOREAU (1817–1862). "Saturday," *A Week on the Concord and Merrimack Rivers,* 1849

FLATTERY

See also • Insult ○ Praise

Do not trust flatterers.

AESOP (6th cent. B.C.). "The Fox and the Crow," *Fables,* tr. Joseph Jacobs, 1894

Man would not succumb so easily to flattery if he did not begin by flattering himself.

IRVING BABBITT (1865–1933). *Democracy and Leadership,* 7, 1924

There is no such flatterer as is a man's self.

FRANCIS BACON (1561–1626). "Of Friendship," *Essays,* 1625

Thare is no such thing as flattery—if commendashun is deserved, it is no flattery but truth, and if commendashun is underserved, it is not flattery but slander.

JOSH BILLINGS (1818–1885). *On Ice: and Other Things,* 60, 1868

Deference iz silent flattery.

JOSH BILLINGS (1818–1885). "Embers on the Harth," *Everybody's Friend, or; Josh Billing's Encyclopedia and Proverbial Philosophy of Wit and Humor,* 1874

Flattery is so necessary to all of us that we flatter one another just to be flattered in return.

MARJORIE BOWEN (1888–1952). "The Art of Flattery," *World's Wonder and Other Essays,* 1938

When they were about to depart [from the Delectable Mountains to the Celestial City], one of the shepherds gave them a note. . . . Another of them bid them beware of the Flatterer.

JOHN BUNYAN (1628–1688). *The Pilgrim's Progress,* 1.8, 1678–1684

Flattery corrupts both the receiver and the giver.

EDMUND BURKE (1729–1797). *Reflections on the Revolution in France,* p. 90, 1790, Pelican Books edition, 1968

Some who affect to dislike flattery may yet be flattered indirectly by a well-seasoned abuse and ridicule of their rivals.

C. C. COLTON (1780–1832). *Lacon: or, Many Things in Few Words; Addressed to Those Who Think,* 1.83, 1823

It is one of the sad aspects about great flatterers like Lyndon Johnson that among the few things they are vulnerable to is flattery.

DAVID HALBERSTAM (1934–). *The Best and the Brightest,* 20, 1972

Flattery won't hurt you if you don't swaller it.

KIN HUBBARD (1868–1930). *Abe Martin: Hoss Sense and Nonsense,* p. 124, 1926

The mischief of flattery is not that it persuades any man that he is what he is not, but that it suppresses the influence of honest ambition, by raising an opinion that honor may be gained without the toil of merit.

SAMUEL JOHNSON (1709–1784). In *The Rambler* (English journal), 155, 10 September 1751

Flattery is counterfeit money which, but for vanity, would have no circulation.

LA ROCHEFOUCAULD (1613–1680). *Maxims,* 158, 1665, tr. Louis Kronenberger, 1959

I was not very much accustomed to flattery, and it came the sweeter to me. I was rather like the Hoosier, with the gingerbread, when he said he reckoned he loved it better than any other man and got less of it.

ABRAHAM LINCOLN (1809–1865). Lincoln–Douglas debate, Ottawa (Illinois), 21 August 1858

Whoever has flattered his friend successfully must at once think himself a knave, and his friend a fool.

ALEXANDER POPE (1688–1865). "Thoughts on Various Subjects," *Miscellanies in Prose and Verse* (published with Jonathan Swift), vol. 2, 1727

Great Lords by reason of their flatterers are the first that know their own virtues and the last that know their own vices.

JOHN SELDEN (1584–1654). "Lords before the Parliament" (1), *Table Talk,* 1689, ed. Frederick Pollock, 1927

'Tis the most pleasing flattery to like what others like.

JOHN SELDEN (1564–1654). "Pleasure" (2), *Table Talk,* 1689, ed. Frederick Pollock, 1927

Celia: Well said; that was laid on with a trowel.

SHAKESPEARE (1564–1616). *As You Like It,* 1.2.112, 1599

Decius: But, when I tell [Caesar], he hates flatterers,
He says he does, being then most flattered.

SHAKESPEARE (1564–1616). *Julius Caesar,* 2.1.207, 1599

What really flatters a man is that you think him worth flattering.

GEORGE BERNARD SHAW (1856–1950). *John Bull's Other Island,* 4, 1904

Baloney is flattery so thick it cannot be true; blarney is flattery so thin we like it.

BISHOP FULTON J. SHEEN (1895–1979)

Puff: I am, Sir, a Practitioner in Panegyric, or to speak more plainly—a Professor of the Art of Puffing, at your service—or anybody else's.

RICHARD SHERIDAN (1751–1816). *The Critic,* 1.2, 1779

I suppose flattery hurts no one, that is, if he doesn't inhale.

ADLAI E. STEVENSON (1900–1965). Speech, 30 March 1952

The mode of flattery . . . best adapted to the purposes of a statesman is the flattery of *listening.*

HENRY TAYLOR (1800–1886). *The Statesman,* 31, 1836

Face–flatterer and backbiter are the same.

ALFRED, LORD TENNYSON (1809–1892). "Merlin and Vivien" (l. 822), *The Idylls of the King,* 1859–1885

❦

Flattery is the lowest form of insincerity.

ANONYMOUS

See Imitation: Saying (English)

Who flatters me to my face will speak ill of me behind my back.

SAYING

FLOWERS

See also • Nature ○ Paradoxes: Henry David Thoreau (3)

The modest rose puts forth a thorn,
The humble Sheep a threat'ning horn;
While the Lilly white shall in Love delight,
Nor a thorn, nor a threat, stain her beauty bright.

WILLIAM BLAKE (1757–1827). "The Lilly," *Songs of Experience,* 1794

Earth laughs in flowers.

RALPH WALDO EMERSON (1803–1882). "Hamatreya" (l. 13), *Poems,* 1847

How cunningly nature hides every wrinkle of her inconceivable antiquity under roses and violets and morning dew!

RALPH WALDO EMERSON (1803–1882). "Progress of Culture," *Letters and Social Aims,* 1876

A gush of violets along a wood path.

NATHANIEL HAWTHORNE (1804–1864). 23 January 1842, *The American Notebooks,* ed. Claude M. Simpson, 1932

There are crowds who trample a flower into the dust without once thinking that they have one of the sweetest thoughts of God under their heel.

JOSIAH GILBERT HOLLAND (1819–1881). "Patience" *Gold–Foil, Hammered from Popular Proverbs,* 1860

The Amen! of Nature is always a flower.

OLIVER WENDELL HOLMES, SR. (1809–1896). *The Autocrat of the Breakfast–Table,* 10, 1858

Consider the lilies of the field, how they grow; they neither toil nor spin; yet I tell you, even Solomon in all his glory was not arrayed like one of these.

JESUS (A.D. 1st cent.). *Matthew* 6:28

All for each. The winds wander, the snow and rain and dew fall, the earth whirls—all but to prosper a poor lush violet.

JOHN MUIR (1838–1914). Journal, 1913. In *John of the Mountains: The Unpublished Journals of John Muir,* ed. Linnie Marsh Wolfe, 1938

Beautiful, tender flowers grow upon the lava lips of Mono craters, pines ascend their ashy slopes, and it is just where the glaciers have crushed heaviest that the greatest quantity of beautiful life appears.

JOHN MUIR (1838–1914). Journal, 1873. In *John of the Mountains: The Unpublished Journals of John Muir,* ed. Linnie Marsh Wolfe, 1938

Every flower is a soul blossoming in Nature.

GÉRARD de NERVAL (1808–1855). "Vers Doré," *L'Artiste,* 16 March 1845

"Where Have All the Flowers Gone?"

PETE SEEGER (1919–). Song title, 1961

Where is the fountain that throws up these flowers in a ceaseless outbreak of ecstasy?

RABINDRANATH TAGORE (1803–1882). *Stray Birds,* 70, 1914

"Are you too proud to kiss me?" the morning light asks the buttercup.

RABINDRANATH TAGORE (1803–1882). *Stray Birds,* 246, 1914

"How may I sing to thee and worship, O Sun?" asks the little flower. "By the simple silence of thy purity," answers the sun.

RABINDRANATH TAGORE (1803–1882). *Stray Birds,* 247, 1914

Thou canst not stir a flower
Without troubling a star.

FRANCIS THOMPSON (1859–1907). "The Mistress of Vision," 1897

'Tis my faith that every flower
Enjoys the air it breathes.

WILLIAM WORDSWORTH (1770–1850). "Lines Written in Early Spring," l. 11, 1798

I wandered lonely as a cloud
That floats on high o'er vales and hills,
When all at once I saw a crowd,
A host, of golden daffodils;
Beside the lake, beneath the trees,
Fluttering and dancing in the breeze. . . .

For oft, when on my couch I lie
In vacant or in pensive mood,
they flash upon that inward eye
Which is the bliss of solitude;
And then my heart with pleasure fills,
And dances with the daffodils.

WILLIAM WORDSWORTH (1770–1850). First and last stanzas of a four–stanza poem, "I Wandered Lonely as a Cloud," 1807

To me the meanest flower that blows can give
Thoughts that do often lie too deep for tears.

WILLIAM WORDSWORTH (1770–1850). Closing lines, "Ode: Intimations of Immortality from Recollections of Early Childhood," 11, 1807. Ralph Waldo Emerson, described this poem as "the high-water mark which the intellect has reached in this age." ("Personal," *English Traits,* 1856)

FOG

See also • Nature ○ Weather

The fog comes
on little cat feet.
It sits looking
over harbor and city
on silent haunches
and then moves on.

CARL SANDBURG (1878–1967). "Fog." *Chicago Poems,* 1916

FOOD

See also • Body ○ Disease: [especially] Saying (Chinese) ○ Gluttony ○ Healing ○ Health ○ Hunger ○ Longevity ○ Moderation ○ Vegetarianism

Tell me what you eat, and I will tell you what you are.

> ANTHELME BRILLAT–SAVARIN (1755–1826). "Aphorismes pour servir de
> prolégomènes" (4), *Physiologie du goût*, 1825 (Popular version: You
> are what you eat.)
>
> See Reading: Mark Crispin Miller ○ Writing: Michael Wood

Man does not live by bread alone, but he also does not live long without it.

> FREDERICK BUECHNER. "Bread," *Wishful Thinking: A Theological ABC*,
> 1973

My mother made me eat broccoli. I hate broccoli. I am the President of the United States. I will not eat any more broccoli.

> GEORGE BUSH (1924–). March 1990

82: Percentage of people who know that a poor diet can increase their risk of cancer.
15: Percentage who have changed their diet to lower that risk.

> *HIPPOCRATES* (magazine). "Vital Statistics," January–February 1989

Feed sparingly and defy the Physician.

> JAMES HOWELL (1593–1666). Comp., "English" (p. 14), *Paroimiographia:
> Proverbs, or Old Sayed Sawes & Adages in English . . . Italian, French
> and Spanish*, 1659

The longer it takes you t' select a cantaloupe th' worse it is.

> KIN HUBBARD (1856–1915). *Abe Martin's Primer*, unpaged, 1914

Indigestion is charged by God with enforcing morality on the stomach.

> VICTOR HUGO (1802–1885). "Fantine" (3.7), *Les Misérables*, tr. Charles
> E. Wilbour, 1862

We never repent of having eaten too little.

> THOMAS JEFFERSON (1743–1824). "A Decalogue of Canons for
> Observation in Practical Life," #6, letter to Thomas Jefferson Smith,
> 21 February 1825

A cucumber should be well sliced, and dressed with pepper and vinegar, and then thrown out as good for nothing.

> SAMUEL JOHNSON (1709–1784). 5 October 1773. In James Boswell, *The
> Journal of a Tour to the Hebrides, with Samuel Johnson, L.L.D.*, 1786

To safeguard one's health at the cost of too strict a diet is a tiresome illness indeed.

> LA ROCHEFOUCAULD (1613–1680). *Maxims*, 633, 1665, tr. Leonard
> Tancock, 1959

If you wish to grow thinner, diminish your dinner.

> HENRY SAMBROOKE LEIGH. "A Day for Wishing," *Carols of Cockayne*,
> 1869

Man does not live by bread alone.

> MOSES (14th cent. B.C.). *Deuteronomy* 8:3
>
> See Technology: Arnold J. Toynbee (2) ○ Words: Adlai E. Stevenson,
> Robert Louis Stevenson (1)

We may find in the long run that tinned food is a deadlier weapon than the machine gun.

> GEORGE ORWELL (1903–1950). *The Road to Wigam Pier*, 6, 1937

Strange to see how a good dinner and feasting reconciles everybody.

> SAMUEL PEPYS (1633–1703). Diary, 9 November 1665

The proselyte to a pure diet must be warned to expect a temporary diminution of muscular strength. The subtraction of a powerful stimulus will suffice to account for this event. But it is only temporary, and is succeeded by an equable capability for exertion far surpassing his former various and fluctuating strength.

> PERCY BYSSHE SHELLEY (1792–1822). "Notes" (8.109), *Queen Mab:
> A Philosophical Poem: With Notes*, 1813

The rest of the world lives to eat, while I eat to live.

> SOCRATES (470?–399 B.C.). Adapted. In Diogenes Laertius (A.D. 3rd cent.),
> *Lives of Eminent Philosophers*, 2.5, tr. R. D. Hicks, 1925

Mother: It's broccoli, dear.
Daughter: I say it's spinach, and I say the hell with it.

> E. B. WHITE (1899–1985). Cartoon caption, *New Yorker*, p, 27,
> 8 December 1928

A headache is a message from the stomach to the brain saying, "Don't send down any more garbage!"

> PHILIP YORDAN. *Anna Lucasta* (film), 1956

Regard thy table as the table before the Lord. Chew well, and hurry not.

> ZOHAR (A.D. 13th cent). Jewish mystical writings

🌿

An apple a day keeps the doctor away; an onion a day keeps everyone away.

> SAYING (AMERICAN)

Skinny Cooks Can't Be Trusted.

> SAYING (AMERICAN). Button in photograph. In "Home Cooking," *Life*,
> July 1987

You shall eat the fruit of the labor of your hands;
   you shall be happy, and it shall be well with you.

> ANONYMOUS (*BIBLE*). *Psalms* 128:2

FOOLS

See also • Ignorance ○ Illusion ○ Stupidity ○ Suckers ○ Wisdom ○ The Wise & the Foolish

Make not a fool of yourself to make others merry.

> ROBERT BURTON (1577–1640). *The Anatomy of Melancholy*, 1621–1651

Any fool can criticize, condemn and complain—and most do.

> DALE CARNEGIE (1888–1955). *How to Win Friends and Influence
> People*, rev. ed., 1.1, 1981 (1936)

"Tis hard if all is false that I advance
A fool must now and then be right, by chance.

> WILLIAM COWPER (1731–1800). "Conversation," l. 95, 1782

Beware of taking any one thing out of its connections, for that way folly lies.

> RALPH WALDO EMERSON (1803–1882). Journal, September 1848

Sloth and Silence are a Fool's Virtues.

> BENJAMIN FRANKLIN (1706–1790). *Poor Richard's Almanack*, July 1735

There are no fools so troublesome as those that have wit.

BENJAMIN FRANKLIN (1706–1790). *Poor Richard's Almanack,* November 1741

Most fools think they are only ignorant.

BENJAMIN FRANKLIN (1706–1790). *Poor Richard's Almanack,* October 1748

He that makes an Ass of himself must not take it ill if Men ride him.

THOMAS FULLER (1654–1734). Comp., *Gnomologia: Adages and Proverbs,* 2232, 1732

The Fool is busy in everyone's Business but his own.

THOMAS FULLER (1654–1734). Comp., *Gnomologia: Adages and Proverbs,* 4537, 1732

A fool is so unreasonably raised by his hopes that he is half dead by disappointment.

MARQUIS OF HALIFAX (1633–1695). "Of Hope," *Political, Moral and Miscellaneous Reflections,* 1750

He must be a thorough fool, who can learn nothing from his own folly.

J. C. HARE (1795–1855) and A. W. HARE (1792–1834). *Guesses at Truth: First Series,* 1827

None is a fool always, everyone sometimes.

GEORGE HERBERT (1593–1633). Comp., *Outlandish Proverbs,* 163, 1640

Self–satisfaction is the opiate of fools.

ABRAHAM JOSHUA HESCHEL (1907–1972). *Who Is Man?* 5, 1965
See Religion, Anti-: Karl Marx

A fool and his money are soon parted.

JAMES HOWELL (1593–1666). Comp. "English" (p. 2.). *Paroimiographia: Proverbs, or Old Sayed Sawes & Adages in English . . . Italian, French and Spanish,* 1959

A fool and his money are soon spotted.

KIN HUBBARD (1856–1915). "July," *Abe Martin's Almanack,* 1908

Anybody who feels at ease in the world today is a fool.

ROBERT M. HUTCHINS (1899–1977). Address, New York City, 21 January 1959

There are two kinds of fools: one says, "This is old, therefore it is good"; the other says, "This is new, therefore it is better."

DEAN WILLIAM RALPH INGE (1860–1954)

There are fools with wit, but never any with judgment.

LA ROCHEFOUCAULD (1613–1680). *Maxims,* 456, 1665, tr. Louis Kronenberger, 1959

A man may be a fool and not know it—but not if he is married.

H. L. MENCKEN (1880–1956). *A Little Book in C Major,* 6.44, 1916

The fool thinks everyone else is a fool.

MIDRASH (4th cent. B.C.–A.D. 12th cent.). Rabbinical writings
See Madness: Publius Syrus

If one man says to thee, "Thou art a donkey," do not mind; if two speak thus, purchase a saddle for thyself.

MIDRASH (4th cent. B.C.–A.D. 12th cent.). Rabbinical writings

A fellow who is always declaring he's no fool usually has his suspicions.

WILSON MIZNER (1876–1933)

I suffer fools gladly, for I have always been on good terms with myself.

CHRISTOPHER MORLEY (1890–1957). *Inward Ho!* 13, 1923

Not only did [Dean Acheson] not suffer fools gladly; he did not suffer them at all.

LESTER B. PEARSON (1897–1972). Canadian prime minister. On the American secretary of state. In "The Diplomat Who Did Not Want to Be Liked," *Time,* 25 October 1971

You can fool some of the people all of the time and all of the people some of the time, but you can make a damn fool of yourself any old time.

LAURENCE J. PETER (1910–1990). 3 December, *Peter's Almanac,* 1982
See Deception: Abraham Lincoln

Fools rush in where Angels fear to tread.

ALEXANDER POPE (1688–1744). *An Essay on Criticism,* l. 625, 1711

Puck: Lord, what fools these mortals be!

SHAKESPEARE (1564–1616). *A Midsummer Night's Dream,* 3.2.115, 1595

Folly is the direct pursuit of Happiness and Beauty.

GEORGE BERNARD SHAW (1856–1950). "Maxims for Revolutionists: Beauty and Happiness, Art and Riches," *Man and Superman,* 1903
See Happiness: Aldous Huxley

Fools are more dangerous than rogues.

GEORGE BERNARD SHAW (1856–1950). The Intelligent Woman's Guide to Socialism, Capitalism, Sovietism and Fascism, 84, 1928

A fool and his words are soon parted.

WILLIAM SHENSTONE (1714–1763). "On Reserve," *Men & Manners,* ed. Havelock Ellis, 1927

The ultimate result of shielding men from the effects of folly is to fill the world with fools.

HERBERT SPENCER (1820–1903). "State-tamperings with Money and Banks," *Essays: Moral, Political and Aesthetic,* 1866

Hain't we got all the fools in town on our side? And ain't that a big enough majority in any town?

MARK TWAIN (1835–1910). *The Adventures of Huckleberry Finn,* 26, 1884

Let us be thankful for the fools. But for them the rest of us could not succeed.

MARK TWAIN (1835–1910). *Following the Equator: A Journey Around the World,* 28 (epigraph), 1897

There is probably no man living, though ever so great a fool, that cannot do *something* or other well.

SAMUEL WARREN (1807–1877). *Ten Thousand a Year,* 28, 1841

The wisest thing to do with a fool is to encourage him to hire a hall and discourse to his fellow citizens. Nothing chills nonsense like exposure to the air.

WOODROW WILSON (1856–1924). *Constitutional Government in the United States,* 2, 1908

❦

A fool would rather be deceived than disturbed.

ANONYMOUS

The fool mistakes power for virtue, acclaim for merit, nonconformity for dangerousness, conviction for truth, revenge for justice, license for liberty, and kindness for weakness.

ANONYMOUS

FOOTBALL

See also • Sports ○ Winning: Vince Lombardi (1,2)

If a man watches three football games in a row, he should be declared legally dead.

ERMA BOMBECK (1927–1996). Appearing on *Donahue,* television talk program, 22 May 1986

Football is . . . a wonderful way to get rid of aggressions without going to jail for it.

HEYWOOD HALE BROUN (1888–1939). *Tumultuous Merriment,* 5, 1979

Bill, Thanks for giving me the opportunity and teaching me how to take advantage of it.

DWIGHT CLARK (1957–). Inscription on a photograph he had given to his football coach Bill Walsh. In Lowell Cohn, "Walsh's Life Without a Team," *San Francisco Chronicle,* 22 September 1989

I give so much of myself on Sunday. I drain all the life out of myself out there. I get paid to play, to win, to give the city pride, so maybe everybody can forget for a little while how hard life is.

RANDALL CUNNINGHAM (1963–). In Ron Thomas, "How Will the 49ers Defend Cunningham?" *San Francisco Chronicle,* 23 September 1989. The Philadelphia Eagles reportedly paid quarterback Cunningham $3,000,000 in 1989.

Pro football is like nuclear warfare. There are no winners, only survivors.

FRANK GIFFORD (1930–). Football player and television sports broadcaster. In "Scorecard," *Sports Illustrated,* 4 July 1960

Sometime, Rock, when the team's up against it, when things are going wrong and the breaks are beating the boys, tell them to go in there with all they've got and win just one for the Gipper. I don't know where I'll be then, Rock, but I'll know about it, and I'll be happy.

GEORGE GIPP (1895–1920). Football player. Whispered remark to his coach Knute Rockne as he lay dying from a viral throat infection two weeks after being named to the All-America team, December 1920. In Red Smith, "One for the Gipper," *New York Times,* 21 January 1981

The way you motivate a football team is to eliminate the unmotivated ones.

LOU HOLTZ (1937–). Notre Dame football coach. Reported on a television news program, NBC, 29 December 1988

He's fair. He treats us all the same—like dogs.

HENRY JORDAN. On his hard-driving football coach Vince Lombardi, affectionately recalled on his death, 3 September 1970

Football isn't a contact sport; it's a collision sport. Dancing is a contact sport.

VINCE LOMBARDI (1913–1970). Football coach. In James A. Michener, *Sports in America,* 13, 1976

To play this game you must have fire in you, and there is nothing that stokes fire like hate.

VINCE LOMBARDI (1913–1970). Football coach. In James A. Michener, *Sports in America,* 13, 1976

You can only really yell at the players you trust.

BILL PARCELLS (1941–). Football coach. In Eric Pooley, "True Blue: From Giants to Supermen," *New York Times,* 26 January 1987

A successful coach is one who is still coaching.

BEN SCHWARTZWALDER (1909–1993). Football coach. Speech before a group of coaches, San Francisco, 19 December 1963

Football combines the two worst features of American life. It is violence punctuated by committee meetings.

GEORGE F. WILL (1941–). In Joseph A. Cincotti, "It Started with the Cubs," *New York Times Book Review,* 1 April 1990

FORCE

See also • Power ○ Violence

Force and right are the governors of this world; force till right is ready.

MATTHEW ARNOLD (1822–1888). *Essays in Criticism: First Series,* 1, 1865

The use of force alone is but *temporary.* It may subdue for a moment; but it does not remove the necessity of subduing again: and a nation is not governed, which is perpetually to be conquered.

EDMUND BURKE (1729–1797). "Conciliation with America," House of Commons speech, 22 March 1775

[Force] is the prerequisite of movement and the midwife of progress.

CHARLES de GAULLE (1890–1970). Foreword to *The Edge of the Sword,* 1934, tr. Gerald Hopkins, 1960

A leader's fundamental choice is whether to approve the use of force. If he decides to do so, his only vindication is to succeed. His doubts provide no justification for failure; restraint in execution is a boon to the other side; there are no awards for those who lose with moderation. Once the decision to use force has been made, the President has no choice but to pursue it with total determination—and to convey the same spirit to all those implementing it. Nations must not undertake military enterprises or major diplomatic initiatives that they are not willing to see through.

HENRY A. KISSINGER (1923–). *White House Years,* 23, 1979

Force is the midwife of every old society pregnant with a new one.

KARL MARX (1880–1883). *Capital: A Critique of Political Economy,* 31, tr. Samuel Moore and Edward Aveling, 1906

Who overcomes
By force, hath overcome but half his foe.

JOHN MILTON (1608–1674). *Paradise Lost,* 1.648, 1667

Do you know, Fontanes, what most amazes me in the world? The inability of force to maintain anything at all. There are only two powers in the world: the sword and the mind. In the long run, the sword is always defeated by the mind.

NAPOLEON (1769–1821). In Albert Camus, November 1939, *Notebooks: 1935–1942*, tr. Philip Thody, 1963

See Violence: Napoleon

I was not born to be forced. I will breathe after my own fashion. . . . They only can force me who obey a higher law than I.

HENRY DAVID THOREAU (1817–1862). "Civil Disobedience," 1849

The recourse to force, however unavoidable, is a disclosure of the failure of civilization.

ALFRED NORTH WHITEHEAD (1861–1947). *Adventures of Ideas*, 5.6, 1933

See Violence: Charles E. Merriam

FOREIGN AFFAIRS

See • International Relations

FORESTS

See also • Nature ○ Trees ○ Wilderness ○ Woods

Among the scenes which are deeply impressed on my mind, none exceed in sublimity the primeval forests undefaced by the hand of man. No one can stand in these solitudes unmoved, and not feel that there is more in man than the mere breath of his body.

CHARLES DARWIN (1809–1882). *Journal of Researches into the Geology and Natural History of the Various Countries Visited by H.M.S. Beagle*, 21, 1839

This is the forest primeval. The murmuring pines and the hemlocks,
Bearded with moss, and in garments green, indistinct in the twilight,
Stand like Druids of old, with voices sad and prophetic.

HENRY WADSWORTH LONGFELLOW (1807–1882). *Evangeline: A Tale of Acadie*, 1847

america was once a paradise
of timberland and stream
but it is dying because of the greed
and money lust of a thousand little kings
who slashed the timber all to hell
and would not be controlled
and changed the climate
and stole the rainfall from posterity.

DON MARQUIS (1878–1937). "what the ants are saying," *archy does his part*, 1935

It appears likely that no fewer than 1.2 million species, at least a quarter of the biological diversity existing in the mid-1980s, will vanish during this quarter-century or soon thereafter . . . as the remaining forest refuges are decimated.

PETER H. RAVEN. Missouri Botanical Garden director. In William S. Ellis, "Brazil's Imperiled Rain Forest" (epigraph), *National Geographic*, December 1988

Ashes are the work of a moment, a forest the work of centuries.

SENECA THE YOUNGER (5? B.C.–A.D. 65). *Physical Investigations*, 3.27.2

If I were a Brazilian without land or money or the means to feed my children, I would be burning the rain forest too.

STING (1951–). British rock musician. In *International Herald Tribune'* Paris, 14 April 1989

A people who would begin by burning the fences and let the forest stand!

HENRY DAVID THOREAU (1817–1862). Journal. 11 November 1850

The paper for the 5.2 million copies of *Time*'s "Planet of the Year" issue printed in the U.S. came from about 16,000 trees.

TIME (letters section). In its special *Planet* issue focusing on environmental issues including deforestation, 30 January 1989

ℳ

Forest preceded man, desert follows him.

ANONYMOUS (FRENCH). Graffito, student revolt, 1968

FORGIVENESS

See also • Confession ○ Evil ○ Faults: Anonymous (2) ○ God ○ Grace ○ Guilt ○ Innocence ○ Judging Others ○ Morality ○ Prayer ○ Redemption ○ Religion ○ Repentance ○ Revenge ○ Salvation ○ Sin: [especially] Waldo Frank

Forgiving our enemys haz the same refreshing effekt upon our souls az it duz tew confess our sins.

JOSH BILLINGS (1818–1885). "Gnats," *Everybody's Friend, or; Josh Billing's Encyclopedia and Proverbial Philosophy of Wit and Humor*, 1874

Forgiveness. The experience of reconciliation following upon some breach of trust, marked on the one side by the acknowledgment of wrongdoing and the desire to make amends and on the other side by the capacity to understand and the willingness to resume friendly relations.

ANTON T. BOISEN (1876–1965). Appendix to *The Exploration of the Inner World: A Study of Mental Disorder and Religious Experience*, 1936

Men never forgive those in whom there is nothing to pardon.

EDWARD GEORGE BULWER–LYTTON (1803–1873). "Thoughts'" (30), *Weeds and Wildflowers*, 1826

To understand is to forgive, even oneself.

ALEXANDER CHASE. *Perspectives*, 1966

Who pardons easily invites offense.

PIERRE CORNEILLE (1606–1684). *Cinna*, 4.1, 1639, tr. Noel Clark, 1993

Of God we ask one favor,
That we may be forgiven—
For what, he is presumed to know—
The Crime, from us, is hidden—

EMILY DICKINSON (1830–1886). "Of God we ask one favor," 1884?

Father Zossima: There is no sin and there can be no sin on all the earth, which the Lord will not forgive to the truly repentant! Man cannot commit a sin so great as to exhaust the infinite love of God.

FYODOR DOSTOYEVSKY (1821–1881). *The Brothers Karamazov*, 2.3, 1880, tr. Constance Garnett, 1912

Absolve you to yourself, and you shall have the suffrage of the world.

> RALPH WALDO EMERSON (1803–1882). "Self–Reliance," *Essays: First Series*, 1841

It is in pardoning that we are pardoned.

> ST. FRANCIS OF ASSISI (A.D. 1181?–1226). "The Prayer of St. Francis," attributed, tr. Leo Sherley-Price

God will forgive me; it's His trade.

> HEINRICH HEINE (1797–1856). Among his last words, 17 February 1856. In Alfred Meissner, *Heinrich Heine. Erinnerungen*, 5, 1856

Ministers ask: Is it possible for God to forgive Man? And when I think of what has been suffered—of the centuries of agony and tears, I ask: Is it possible for Man to forgive God?

> ROBERT G. INGERSOLL (1833–1899). "The Foundations of Faith"

If you forgive men their trespasses, your heavenly Father also will forgive you; but if you do not forgive men their trespasses, neither will your Father forgive your trespasses.

> JESUS (A.D. 1st cent.). *Matthew* 6:14–15

If your brother sins, rebuke him, and if he repents, forgive him; and if he sins against you seven times in the day, and turns to you seven times, and says, "I repent," you must forgive him.

> JESUS (A.D. 1st cent.). *Luke* 17:3–4

Father, forgive them; for they know not what they do.

> JESUS (A.D. 1st cent.). *Luke* 23:34
>
> See Ignorance: Shakespeare (1)

We forgive to the extent that we love.

> LA ROCHEFOUCAULD (1613–1680). *Maxims*, 330, 1665, tr. Louis Kronenberger, 1959

I think if God forgives us we must forgive ourselves. Otherwise it is almost like setting up ourselves as a higher tribunal than Him.

> C. S. LEWIS (1898–1963). Letter to Miss Breckenridge, 19 April 1951, *Letters of C. S. Lewis*, ed. W. H. Lewis and Walter Hooper, 1993

I am a patient man—always willing to forgive on the Christian terms of repentance, and also to give ample *time* for repentance.

> ABRAHAM LINCOLN (1809–1865). Letter to Reverdy Johnson, 26 July 1862

To understand is not only to pardon, but in the end to love.

> WALTER LIPPMANN (1889–1974). *A Preface to Morals*, 15.3, 1929

People will sometimes forgive you the good you have done them, but seldom the harm they have done you.

> W. SOMERSET MAUGHAM (1874–1965). 1933, *A Writer's Notebook*, 1949

God forgives, but [not without] repentance.

> MUHAMMAD (A.D. 570?–632). *The Sayings of Muhammad*, 209, tr. Abdullah Al–Suhrawardy, 1941

The folly which we might have ourselves committed is the one which we are least ready to pardon in another.

> JOSEPH ROUX (1834–1886). *Meditations of a Parish Priest*, 4.84, tr. Isabel F. Hapgood, 1886

You saw his weakness; that he'll ne'er forgive.

> FRIEDRICH von SCHILLER (1759–1805). *William Tell*, 3.1, 1804, tr. Theodore Martin, 1894

If I do not forgive everyone, I shall be untrue to myself.

> ALBERT SCHWEITZER (1875–1965). "Your Second Job," *Reader's Digest*, October 1949

King Claudius: "Forgive me my foul murder?"
That cannot be: since I am still possess'd
Of those effects for which I did the murder.

> SHAKESPEARE (1564–1616). *Hamlet*, 3.3.52, 1600

I am content to follow to its source
Every event in action or in thought;
Measure the lot; forgive myself the lot!
When such as I cast out remorse
So great a sweetness flows into the breast
We must laugh and we must sing,
We are blest by everything,
Everything we look upon is blest.

> WILLIAM BUTLER YEATS (1865–1939). Closing stanza, "A Dialogue of Self and Soul," *The Winding Stair and Other Poems*, 1933

Lead us not into the temptation of believing that we have truly forgiven, while rancor lingers.

> KATHERINE ZELL. "Den Psalmen Misere," 1558

FORTUNE

See also • Cause & Effect ○ Chance ○ Circumstances ○ Destiny ○ Events ○ Fate ○ God ○ Luck ○ Misfortune ○ Necessity ○ Opportunity ○ Prosperity ○ Success: Horace ○ Virtue: Seneca the Younger (1)

Fortune never takes enny boddy by the hand, but she often allows them to take her by the hand.

> JOSH BILLINGS (1818–1885). "Plum Pits," *Everybody's Friend, or; Josh Billing's Encyclopedia and Proverbial Philosophy of Wit and Humor*, 1874

Fortune, in order to come to me, must conform to certain conditions imposed on her by my character.

> CHAMFORT (1741–1794). *Maxims and Thoughts*, 5, 1796, tr. W. S. Merwin, 1984

When Fortune smiles, embrace her.

> THOMAS FULLER (1654–1734). Comp., *Gnomologia: Adages and Proverbs*, 5553, 1732

The day of fortune is like a harvest day,
We must be busy when the corn is ripe.

> GOETHE (1749–1832). *Torquato Tasso*, 4.4, 1790

Complaint against fortune is often a mask'd apology for indolence.

> FULKE GREVILLE (1554–1628). *Maxims, Characters, and Reflections*, p. 35, 1756

Fortune often delights to dignify what nature has neglected, and that renown which cannot be claimed by intrinsic excellence is sometimes derived from unexpected accident.

SAMUEL JOHNSON (1709–1784). *Thoughts on the Late Transactions Respecting Falkland's Islands* (pamphlet), 1771

Fortune is the ruler in half our actions, but . . . she allows the other half or thereabouts to be governed by us.

MACHIAVELLI (1469–1527). *The Prince*, 25, 1513, tr. Luigi Ricci, 1903

Fortune . . . shows her power where no measures have been taken to resist her.

MACHIAVELLI (1469–1527). *The Prince*, 25, 1513, tr. Luigi Ricci, 1903

Men may second Fortune but cannot oppose her; they may develop her designs but cannot defeat them. But men should never despair on that account; for, not knowing the aims of Fortune, which she pursues by dark and devious ways, men should always be hopeful and never yield to despair, whatever troubles or ill fortune may befall them.

MACHIAVELLI (1469–1527). *The Discourses*, 2.29, 1517, tr. Christian E. Detmold, 1940

Fortune makes a fool of him whom she favors too much.

PUBLIUS SYRUS (85–43 B.C.). *Moral Sayings*, 271, tr. Darius Lyman, Jr., 1862

Industry is fortune's right hand, and frugality her left.

JOHN RAY (1628–1705). Comp., *A Collection of English Proverbs*, p. 14, 1678
See Wealth: Benjamin Franklin

When fortune closes one door, it opens another.

SA'DI (A.D. 1213?–1292). *The Maxims of Sa'di*, 1, tr. Mehdi Nakosteen, 1977

Fortune can neither give to any man honesty, diligence, and other good qualities, nor can she take them away.

SALLUST (86?–34? B.C.). *The War with Jugurtha*, 1.3, tr. J. C. Rolfe, 1921

No man is crushed by hostile Fortune who is not first deceived by her smiles.

SENECA THE YOUNGER (5? B.C.–A.D. 65). "On Consolation to Helvia." 5.5, *Moral Essays*, tr. John W. Basore, 1932

Pandulph: When Fortune means to men most good,
She looks upon them with a threatening eye.

SHAKESPEARE (1564–1616). *King John*, 3.4.119, 1596

Pisanio: Fortune brings in some boats that are not steer'd.

SHAKESPEARE (1564–1616). *Cymbeline*, 4.3.46, 1609

The power of fortune is confessed only by the miserable, for the happy impute all their success to prudence or merit.

JONATHAN SWIFT (1667–1745). "Thoughts on Various Subjects" (expanded from a version published in 1711). *Miscellanies in Prose and Verse* (published with Alexander Pope), vol. 1, 1727

Fortune favors the brave.

TERENCE (190?–159 B.C.). *Phormio*, l. 203, tr. John Sergeaunt, 1912
See Courage: Tacitus o God & Man: Bussy-Rabutin

O Fortune—Fortune—thou art a bitch.

JOHN VANBRUGH (1664–1726). *The Relapse; or Virtue in Danger*, 1.2, 1697

❧

Fortune favors the foolish.

SAYING (ENGLISH)

Whom fortune favors, the world favors.

SAYING (GERMAN)

Fortune is like a wall that falls on those who lean on it.

SAYING (MEXICAN)

Fortune favors the clever.

SAYING (RUSSIAN)

Fortune favors those she can't intimidate.

SAYING

Fortune favors those who are quick to follow her, but not too quick.

SAYING

Fortune favors those who make themselves worthy to her.

SAYING

FOUNTAINS

See also • Nature

No fountain so small but that Heaven may be imaged in its bosom.

NATHANIEL HAWTHORNE (1804–1864). 25 October 1836, *The American Notebooks*, ed. Claude M. Simpson, 1932

FRANCE

See also • Nations o Paris

France: a country in which it is often useful to display one's vices, and always dangerous to show one's virtues.

CHAMFORT (1741–1794). *Maxims and Thoughts*, 8, 1796, tr. W. S. Merwin, 1984

How can you be expected to govern a country that has 246 kinds of cheese.

CHARLES de GAULLE (1890–1970). In "Gaullism? Never Heard of It,'" *Newsweek*, 1 October 1962

France cannot be France without greatness.

CHARLES de GAULLE (1890–1970). *Memoirs of Hope: Renewal and Endeavor*, 1971

France is the thriftiest of all nations; to a Frenchman sex provides the most economical way to have fun. The French are a logical race.

ANITA LOOS (1893–1991). *Kiss Hollywood Goodbye*, 1, 1974

The Frenchman is first and foremost a *man*. He is likable often just because of his weaknesses, which are always thoroughly human, even if despicable.

HENRY MILLER (1891–1980). "Raimu," *The Wisdom of the Heart*, 1941

The French people can be killed but [not] intimidated!

NAPOLEON (1769–1821). Remark to Lord Whitworth at a diplomatic reception, 13 March 1803, *The Corsican: A Diary of Napoleon's Life in His Own Words*, ed. R. M. Johnston, 1911

When I learn that a nation can live without bread, then I will believe that the French people can live without glory.

> NAPOLEON (1769–1821). *Napoleon in His Own Words,* 9, comp. Jules Bertaut, 1916

France fell because there was corruption without indignation.

> ROMAIN ROLLAND (1866–1944). French writer. 1940

France has neither winter nor summer nor morals—apart from these drawbacks it is a fine country.

> MARK TWAIN (1835–1910). 7 May 1879, *Mark Twain's Notebook,* ed. Albert Bigelow Paine, 1935

Your nation is divided into two species: the one of idle monkeys, who mock at everything; and the other of tigers, who tear.

> VOLTAIRE (1694–1778). Letter to Madame du Deffand, 21 November 1766

FREE WILL

See • Will, Free

FREEDOM

See also • Capitalism ○ Civil War: Abraham Lincoln (5) ○ Communism ○ Conformity ○ Constitutions ○ Democracy ○ Duty ○ Equality: [especially] Hazel Scott ○ Fascism ○ Feminism: Percy Bysshe Shelley ○ Freedom of Conscience ○ Freedom of Religion ○ Freedom of Speech ○ Freedom of the Press ○ Freedom of Thought ○ Government ○ Independence ○ Justice ○ Korean War: Anonymous ○ Liberation ○ Liberty ○ Nonconformity ○ Nonviolence: Herbert Spencer ○ Paradoxes: Ralph Waldo Emerson (4) ○ Responsibility ○ Revolutionary War: Patrick Henry ○ Rights: [especially] John G. Diefenbaker ○ Right to Privacy ○ Right to Silence ○ Self–Realization (Being) ○ Self-Reliance ○ Slavery ○ Socialism ○ Truth: Jesus, Anonymous (4) ○ Tyranny ○ Unity ○ Will, Free ○ World: Anonymous (American)

Only through human freedom and responsibility are history and salvation able to fulfill themselves.

> LEO BAECK (1873–1956). "Faith in Man: In Mankind," *The Essence of Judaism,* 1936, ed. Irving Howe, 1948

The freedom of all is essential to my freedom.

> MIKHAIL BAKUNIN (1814–1876). 1871, *The Political Philosophy of Bakunin: Scientific Anarchism,* 3.13, ed. G. P. Maximoff, 1953
>
> See Unity: Herbert Spencer

The way to final freedom is within thy SELF.

> *THE BOOK OF THE GOLDEN PRECEPTS.* Ancient Buddhist writing. 2.28, tr. Helena Petrovna Blavatsky, 1889

None who have always been free can understand the terrible fascinating power of the hope of freedom to those who are not free.

> PEARL S. BUCK (1892–1973). *What America Means to Me,* 4, 1943

Freedom is not a gift received from a State or a leader but a possession to be won every day by the effort of each and the union of all.

> ALBERT CAMUS (1913–1960). "Bread and Freedom," 1957, *Resistance, Rebellion, and Death,* tr. Justin O'Brien, 1961

Freedom is participation in power.

CICERO (106–43 B.C.). In Martin Luther King, Jr., *Where Do We Go from Here: Chaos or Community?* 2.3, 1967

The instinct of nearly all societies is to lock up anybody who is truly free. First, society begins by trying to beat you up. If this fails, they try to poison you. If this fails too, they finish by loading honors on your head.

> JEAN COCTEAU (1889–1963). In Landon Gerald Dowdey, ed., "Struggle: Participation in the Journey," *Journey to Freedom,* 1969

There is no such thing as a little freedom. Either you are all free, or you are not free.

> WALTER CRONKITE (1916–). Oriana Fallaci interview, "What Does Walter Cronkite Really Think?" *Look,* 17 November, 1970

Freedom stretches as far as your self-control.

> MARIE von EBNER–ESCHENBACH (1830–1916)

Talkin' about [freedom] and bein' it, that's two different things. I mean it's real hard to be free when you're bought 'n sold in the market place. But don' ever tell anybody that they're not free, 'cause then they gonna get to killin' and maimin' to prove to ya that they are. Oh yea, they gonna talk to ya an' talk to ya an' talk to ya an' talk to ya about individual freedom, but if they see a free individual, it's gonna scare 'em.

> PETER FONDA (1939–), DENNIS HOPPER (1936–), and DENNIS SOUTHERN. *Easy Rider* (film), 1969, spoken by Jack Nicholson

The great threat to freedom is the concentration of power.

> MILTON FRIEDMAN (1912–). Introduction to *Capitalism and Freedom,* 1962

Economic freedom is a necessary but not sufficient condition for political freedom. . . . Political freedom in turn is a necessary condition for the long-term maintenance of economic freedom.

> MILTON FRIEDMAN (1912–). Closing paragraph, "Free Markets and the Generals," 25 January 1982, *Bright Promises, Dismal Performance: An Economist's Protest,* ed. William R. Allen, 1983

I want freedom for the full expression of my personality.

> MOHANDAS K. GANDHI (1869–1948). Remark to Louis Fischer, July 1946. In K. G. Mashruwala, appendix (3) to *Gandhi and Marx,* 1951

Freedom to cut down world's oldest trees
Freedom to make Indians get down on their knees
And pray to your God and obey your FBI
And freedom to protest if you're not too scared to die.

> ALLEN GINSBERG (1926–). "Industrial Wave," 20, *White Shroud: Poems, 1980–1985,* 1986

The superior virtue is not to be free but to fight for freedom.

> NIKOS KAZANTZAKIS (1883–1957). "The Action: The Relationship between Man and Man" (71), *The Saviors of God: Spiritual Exercises,* 1927, tr. Kimon Friar, 1960

Freedom is always within the framework of destiny.

> MARTIN LUTHER KING, JR. (1929–1968). *Strength to Love,* 10.1, 1963
>
> See Destiny: Dag Hammarskjöld

Freedom's just another word for nothin' left to lose.

> KRIS KRISTOFFERSON (1936–) and FRED FOSTER. "Me and Bobby McGee" (song), 1969

Men are free when they are obeying some deep, inward voice of religious belief. Obeying from within. Men are free when they belong to a living, organic, *believing* community, active in fulfilling some unfulfilled . . . purpose.

D. H. LAWRENCE (1885–1930). *Studies in Classic American Literature,* 1, 1923

By "freedom" the capitalists have always meant the freedom of the rich to accumulate profits, and the freedom of the worker to die of starvation.

LENIN (1870–1924). "Thesis and Report on Bourgeois Democracy and the Dictatorship of the Proletariat," 4 March 1919, *The Lenin Reader,* 4.2, ed. Stefan T. Possony, 1966

True freedom is to share
All the chains our brothers wear,
And, with heart and hand, to be
Earnest to make others free!

JAMES RUSSELL LOWELL (1819–1891). "Stanzas on Freedom," 1843

"The Road to Freedom Is Via the Cross."

ALBERT LUTHULI (1898–1967). Zulu chief. Essay title. In Mulford Q. Sibley, ed., *The Quiet Battle,* 19, 1963

There are more instances of the abridgment of the freedom of the people by gradual and silent encroachments of those in power than by violent and sudden usurpations.

JAMES MADISON (1751–1836). Speech to Virginia Convention, Richmond, 6 June 1788

The only freedom which deserves the name is that of pursuing our own good in our own way, so long as we do not attempt to deprive others of theirs, or impede their efforts to obtain it.

JOHN STUART MILL (1806–1873). *On Liberty,* 1, 1859

The [free] individual is not accountable to society for his actions in so far as these concern the interests of no person but himself. Advice, instruction, persuasion, and avoidance by other people, if thought necessary by them for their own good, are the only measures by which society can justifiably express its dislike or disapprobation of his conduct.

JOHN STUART MILL (1806–1873). *On Liberty,* 5, 1859
See Liberty: Mill

How is freedom measured, in individuals as in nations? By the resistance which has to be overcome.

FRIEDRICH NIETZSCHE (1844–1900). "Expeditions of an Untimely Man" (38), *Twilight of the Idols,* 1889, tr. R. J. Hollingdale, 1968

Where the Spirit of the Lord is present, there is freedom.

PAUL (A.D. 1st cent.). *2 Corinthians* 3:17

In the truest sense freedom cannot be bestowed; it must be achieved.

FRANKLIN D. ROOSEVELT (1882–1945). Message on the 74th anniversary of the Emancipation Proclamation, 22 September 1936

In the future days, which we seek to make secure, we look forward to a world founded upon four essential human freedoms.

The first is freedom of speech and expression—everywhere in the world.

The second is freedom of every person to worship God in his own way—everywhere in the world.

The third is freedom from want—which, translated into world terms, means economic understandings which will secure to every nation a healthy peacetime life for its inhabitants—everywhere in the world.

The fourth is freedom from fear—which, translated into world terms, means a worldwide reduction of armaments to such a point and in such a thorough fashion that no nation will be in a position to commit an act of physical aggression against any neighbor—anywhere in the world.

That is no vision of a distant millennium. It is a definite basis for a kind of world attainable in our own time and generation.

FRANKLIN D. ROOSEVELT (1882–1962). "Four Freedoms" speech, joint session of Congress, 6 January 1941

True individual freedom cannot exist without economic security and independence. "Necessitous men are not free men." People who are hungry and out of a job are the stuff of which dictatorships are made.

In our day these economic truths have become accepted as self-evident. We have accepted, so to speak, a second Bill of Rights under which a new basis of security and prosperity can be established for all—regardless of station, race or creed.

Among these are:

The right to a useful and remunerative job in the industries or shops or farms or mines of the nation;

The right to earn enough to provide adequate food and clothing and recreation.

FRANKLIN D. ROOSEVELT (1882–1962). "The Economic Bill of Rights," annual message to Congress, 11 January 1944
See Hunger: Marat

Freedom is not a gift which can be enjoyed save by those who show themselves worthy of it.

THEODORE ROOSEVELT (1858–1919). In Hermann Hagedorn and Sidney Wallach, "Signposts for Americans: The American Heritage," *A Theodore Roosevelt Round–Up,* 1958

Those who would be free must be virtuous.

CLINTON ROSSITER (1917–1970). *Conservatism in America: The Thankless Persuasion,* 2nd ed. rev. 2, 1962 (1955)

Economic freedom cannot exist without political freedom.

WILLIAM SAFIRE (1929–). "Gravy Trains Don't Run on Time," *New York Times,* 19 January 1998

[Nowadays] a great shout of triumph goes up whenever anybody has found some further evidence—in physiology or psychology or sociology or economics or politics—of unfreedom, some further indication that people cannot help being what they are and doing what they are doing, no matter how inhuman their actions might be. The denial of freedom, of course, is a denial of responsibility: there are no acts, but only events; everything simply happens.

E. F. SCHUMACHER (1911–1977). *Small Is Beautiful: Economics as if People Mattered,* 4.1, 1973

Who ever walked behind anyone to freedom? If we can't go hand in hand, I don't want to go.

HAZEL SCOTT (1920–). In Margo Jefferson, "Great (Hazel) Scott!" *Ms.,* November 1974

To obey God is freedom.
> SENECA THE YOUNGER (5? B.C.–A.D. 65). "On the Happy Life" (15.7),
> *Moral Essays,* tr. John W. Basore, 1932

My definition of a free society is a society where it is safe to be unpopular.
> ADLAI E. STEVENSON (1900–1965). Speech, Masonic Temple, Detroit,
> 7 October 1952

[Autonomy] is freedom to develop one's self—to increase one's knowledge, improve one's skills, and achieve responsibility for one's conduct. And it is freedom to lead one's own life, to choose among alternative courses of action so long as no injury to others results.
> THOMAS S. SZASZ (1920–). *The Ethics of Psychoanalysis: The Theory
> and Method of Autonomous Psychotherapy,* 1, 1965

Those who prize freedom only for the material benefits it offers have never kept it for long.
> ALEXIS de TOCQUEVILLE (1805–1859). *The Old Regime and the French
> Revolution,* 3.3, 1856, tr. Stuart Gilbert, 1955

When I found I had crossed dat *line* [to freedom], I looked at my hands to see if I was de same pusson. There was such a glory ober ebery ting; de sun came like gold through the trees, and ober the fields, and I felt like I was in Heaben.
> HARRIET TUBMAN (1820–1913). In Sara H. Bradford, *Scenes in the Life
> of Harriet Tubman,* p. 19, 1869

All human beings are born free and equal in dignity and rights. They are endowed with reason and conscience and should act towards one another in a spirit of brotherhood.
> UNIVERSAL DECLARATION OF HUMAN RIGHTS. United Nations, Article
> 1, 10 December 1948

Freedom is not only the absence of external restraints. It also is the absence of irresistible internal compulsions, unmanageable passions and uncensorable appetites. From the need to resist, manage and censor the passions there flows the need to do so in the interest of some ends rather than others. Hence freedom requires reflective choice about the ends of life.
> GEORGE F. WILL (1941–). *Statecraft as Soulcraft: What Government
> Does,* 4, 1983

Sometimes naked, sometimes mad, now wise, now foolish, thus they appear on earth, the free ones.
> ANONYMOUS (HINDU)

I hope for nothing, I fear nothing, I am free.
> ANONYMOUS. Inscription on the grave of Nikos Kazantzakis (Greek
> writer, 1885–1956) at Iraklion, Crete

Being hungry and free is no more possible than being ignorant and free.
> ANONYMOUS
> See Hunger: Marat

Better freedom without equality than equality without freedom.
> ANONYMOUS

Freedom is a gift that must be earned.
> ANONYMOUS

No freedom without responsibility; no responsibility without freedom.
> ANONYMOUS

There are masters, there are slaves—and then there are the free.
> ANONYMOUS

Till all are free, no one is free; one bound, all bound.
> ANONYMOUS

Live free or die.
> SLOGAN (NEW HAMPSHIRE). State motto

FREEDOM OF CONSCIENCE

See also • Conscience ○ Freedom ○ Rights

Conscience can't be compelled.
> THOMAS FULLER (1654–1734). Comp., *Gnomologia: Adages and
> Proverbs,* 1144, 1732

In matters of conscience, the law of [the] majority has no place.
> MOHANDAS K. GANDHI (1869–1948). In *Young India,* 4 August 1920

Whilst . . . [conscience] is a good guide for individual conduct, imposition of that conduct upon all [would] be an insufferable interference with everybody's freedom of conscience.
> MOHANDAS K. GANDHI (1869–1948). In *Young India,* 23 September
> 1926

Freedom of conscience is a natural right, both antecedent and superior to all human laws and institutions whatever: a right which laws never gave and which laws never take away.
> JOHN GOODWIN (17th cent.). *Might and Right Well Met,* 1648

No one should interfere in matters of the individual's conscience.
> MIKHAIL S. GORBACHEV (1931–). In Clyde Haberman, "Gorbachev
> Lauds Religion on Eve of Meeting Pope," *New York Times,*
> 1 December 1989

Any attempt to replace the personal conscience by a collective conscience does violence to the individual and is the first step toward totalitarianism.
> HERMANN HESSE (1877–1962). *Reflections,* 32, ed. Volker Michels, 1974

It behooves every man who values liberty of conscience for himself, to resist invasions of it in the case of others.
> THOMAS JEFFERSON (1743–1826). Letter to Benjamin Rush, 21 April 1803

The one thing that doesn't abide by majority rule is a person's conscience.
> HARPER LEE (1926–). *To Kill a Mockingbird,* 11, 1960

My dominion ends where that of conscience begins.
> NAPOLEON (1769–1821). In Ainsworth Rand Spofford, *The Higher Law
> Tried by Reason and Authority,* 1851

No power on earth has a right to stand between God and the conscience.
> PHILIP SCHAFF (1819–1893). "The American System Compared with
> Other Systems," *Church and State in the United States,* 1888

While we are contending for our own Liberty, we should be very cautious of violating the Rights of Conscience in others, ever considering that God alone is the Judge of the Hearts of Men, and to him only in this Case, they are answerable.

> GEORGE WASHINGTON (1732–1799). Letter to Col. Benedict Arnold, 14 September 1775

[Forcing of conscience is] soul-rape.

> ROGER WILLIAMS (1603?–1683). *The Bloudy Tenent of Persecution for Cause of Conscience Discussed,* 80, 1644, ed. Edward Bean Underhill, 1848

FREEDOM OF RELIGION

See also • Freedom ○ Religion ○ Rights

If any man or woman, after legal conviction, shall have or worship any other God but the Lord God, he shall be put to death.

> BLUE LAWS (Puritan). 1672. In Samuel Peter, *General History of Connecticut,* 1781

Congress shall make no law respecting an establishment of religion, or prohibiting the free exercise thereof.

> CONSTITUTION OF THE UNITED STATES. Bill of Rights, First Amendment, 15 December 1791

Men may believe what they cannot prove. They may not be put to the proof of their religious doctrines or beliefs. Religious experiences which are as real as life to some may be incomprehensible to others.

> WILLIAM O. DOUGLAS (1898–1980). *United States v. Ballard,* 1944

If nowhere else, in the relation between Church and State, "good fences make good neighbors."

> FELIX FRANKFURTER (1882–1965). *McCollum v. Board of Education,* 1948

All religions must be tolerated . . . ; for in this country every man must get to heaven his own way.

> FREDERICK II (1740–1786). Marginalia on a report by the Board of Religion, 22 June 1740.

The day that this country ceases to be free for irreligion, it will cease to be free for religion—except for the sect that can win political power.

> ROBERT H. JACKSON (1892–1954). *Zorach v. Clauson,* 1952

I never will, by any word or act, bow to the shrine of intolerance, or admit a right of inquiry into the religious opinions of others. On the contrary, we are bound, you, I, and everyone, to make common cause, even with error itself, to maintain the common right of freedom of conscience.

> THOMAS JEFFERSON (1743–1826). Letter to Edward Dowse, 19 April 1803

So natural to mankind is intolerance in whatever they really care about, that religious freedom has hardly anywhere been practically realized, except where religious indifference, which dislikes to have its peace disturbed by theological quarrels, has added its weight to the scale.

> JOHN STUART MILL (1806–1873). *On Liberty,* 1, 1859

If your brother, the son of your mother, or your son, or your daughter, or the wife of your bosom, or your friend who is as your own soul, entices you secretly, saying, "Let us go and serve other gods," . . . you shall not yield to him or listen to him, nor shall your eye pity him, nor shall you spare him, nor shall you conceal him; but you shall kill him.

> MOSES (14th cent. B.C.). *Deuteronomy* 13:6–8

Of its very nature, the exercise of religion consists before all else in those internal, voluntary, and free acts whereby man sets the course of his life directly toward God. No merely human power can either command or prohibit acts of this kind.

> THE SECOND VATICAN ECUMENICAL COUNCIL. "Religious Freedom" (3), *The Documents of Vatican II,* 1965

[The affidavit] says that Socrates is a doer of evil, who corrupts the youth; and who does not believe in the gods of the state, but has other new divinities of his own.

> SOCRATES (470?–399 B.C.). Paraphrasing the charge of which he was found guilty and sentenced to death. In Plato (427?–347 B.C.). *Apology,* 24, tr. Benjamin Jowett, 1894

FREEDOM OF SPEECH

See also • Censorship ○ Dissent: [especially] Andrew Kopkind ○ Family: Stephanie Marston ○ Freedom ○ Media ○ Nonconformity ○ Propaganda ○ Public Speaking ○ Rights ○ Right to Silence ○ Speaking ○ Talking

You can cage the singer but not the song.

> HARRY BELAFONTE (1927–). On the arts in South Africa. In *International Herald Tribune,* 3 October 1988

Those who won our independence believed that the final end of the State was to make men free to develop their faculties. . . . They valued liberty both as an end and as a means. They believed liberty to be the secret of happiness and courage to be the secret of liberty. They believed that freedom to think as you will and to speak as you think are means indispensable to the discovery and spread of political truth; that without free speech and assembly discussion would be futile; that with them, discussion affords ordinarily adequate protection against the dissemination of noxious doctrine; that the greatest menace to freedom is an inert people; that public discussion is a political duty; and that this should be a fundamental principle of the American Government.

> LOUIS D. BRANDEIS (1855–1941). *Whitney v. California,* 1927

No danger flowing from speech can be deemed clear and present, unless the incidence of the evil apprehended is so imminent that it may befall before there is opportunity for full discussion. If there be time to expose through discussion the falsehood and fallacies, to avert the evil by the processes of education, the remedy to be applied is more speech, not enforced silence.

> LOUIS D. BRANDEIS (1855–1941). *Whitney v. California,* 1927

If there is a bedrock principle underlying the First Amendment, it is that the government may not prohibit the expression of an idea simply because society finds the idea itself offensive or disagreeable.

> WILLIAM J. BRENNAN, JR. (1906–1997). *Texas v. Johnson,* 1989

Congress shall make no law . . . abridging the freedom of speech.

> CONSTITUTION OF THE UNITED STATES. Bill of Rights, First
> Amendment, 15 December 1791

The Constitution is a delusion and a snare if the weakest and humblest man in the land cannot be defended in his right to speak and his right to think as much as the strongest in the land.

> CLARENCE DARROW (1857–1938). Defending the Communist Labor
> Party, 1920

My people and I have an agreement. They *say* whatever they like, and I *do* whatever I like.

> FREDERICK II (1712–1786). In Margaret Goldsmith, *Frederick the Great,*
> 4, 1929

If I went on the Ed Sullivan show tonight and spoke in favor of integrated marriages, nothing would happen to me. If Ed Sullivan spoke in favor of the same thing, he would lose his rating and his job. Who is free?

> DICK GREGORY (1932–). "The Shadow That Scares Me," *Black Scholar,*
> March 1970

The most stringent protection of free speech would not protect a man in falsely shouting fire in a theater, and causing a panic. . . . The question in every case is whether the words used are used in such circumstances and are of such a nature as to create a clear and present danger that they will bring about the substantive evils that Congress has a right to prevent.

> OLIVER WENDELL HOLMES, JR. (1841–1935). *Schenck v. United States,*
> 1919

The right to be heard does not automatically include the right to be taken seriously.

> HUBERT H. HUMPHREY (1911–1978). Speech before the National
> Student Association, University of Wisconsin, Madison, 23 August 1965

For God's sake, let us freely hear both sides!

> THOMAS JEFFERSON (1743–1826). Letter to Nicholas G. Dufief, 19 April
> 1814

Every man has a right to liberty of conscience, and with that the magistrate cannot interfere. People confound liberty of thinking with liberty of talking. . . . No member of a society has a right to *teach* any doctrine contrary to what the society holds to be true.

> SAMUEL JOHNSON, (1709–1784). 7 May 1773. In James Boswell, *The
> Life of Samuel Johnson,* 1791

Every man has a right to utter what he thinks truth, and every other man has a right to knock him down for it.

> SAMUEL JOHNSON (1709–1784). 1780. In James Boswell, *The Life of
> Samuel Johnson,* 1791

Under the impresss of Freud's personality I had, as far as possible, cast aside my own judgments and repressed my criticisms. That was the prerequisite for collaborating with him.

> CARL JUNG (1875–1961). *Memories, Dreams, Reflections,* 5, ed., Aniela
> Jaffé, 1962

The American's conviction that he must be able to look any man in the eye and tell him to go to hell is the very essence of the free man's way of life.

> WALTER LIPPMANN (1889–1974)

If all mankind minus one were of one opinion, mankind would be no more justified in silencing that one person than he, if he had the power, would be justified in silencing mankind.

> JOHN STUART MILL (1806–1873). *On Liberty,* 2, 1859

To refuse a hearing to an opinion because they are sure that it is false, is to assume that *their* certainty is the same thing as *absolute* certainty. All silencing of discussion is an assumption of infallibility.

> JOHN STUART MILL (1806–1873). *On Liberty,* 2, 1859

Though the silenced opinion be an error, it may, and very commonly does, contain a portion of truth; and since the general or prevailing opinion on any subject is rarely or never the whole truth, it is only by the collision of adverse opinions that the remainder of the truth has any chance of being supplied.

> JOHN STUART MILL (1806–1873). *On Liberty,* 2, 1859

Give me the liberty to know, to utter, and to argue freely according to conscience, above all liberties.

> JOHN MILTON (1608–1674). *Areopagitica* (A Speech for the Liberty of
> Unlicensed Printing), 1644

You have not converted a man because you have silenced him.

> JOHN MORLEY (1838–1923). *On Compromise,* 5, 1877

Freedom of speech was not designed to give everybody equal time on a soapbox but to make sure that nobody who wanted to speak was prevented from doing so by being hit over the head, locked up, tortured, or shot.

> G. WARREN NUTTER. "Income Redistribution." In *Income Redistribution,*
> ed., Colin D. Campbell, 1976

If liberty means anything at all, it means the right to tell people what they do not want to hear.

> GEORGE ORWELL (1903–1950). "The Freedom of the Press" (a previously
> unpublished essay written in 1945 as an introduction to *Animal Farm*),
> *New York Times Magazine,* 8 October 1972

Instead of looking on discussion as a stumbling block in the way of action, we think it an indispensable preliminary to any wise action at all.

> PERICLES (495?–429 B.C.). On Athens' democratic ideal, funeral oration,
> 431 B.C. In Thucydides (460?–400? B.C.), *The Peloponnesian War,* 2.40,
> tr. Richard Crawley and rev. T. E. Wick, 1982

The right to speak out is also the duty to speak out.

> VLADIMIR POZNER. Speech before the Commonwealth Club of
> California, San Francisco, 21 September 1990

Free speech has been preserved, but its effective existence is disastrously curtailed if the more important means of publicity are only open to opinions which have the sanction of orthodoxy.

> BERTRAND RUSSELL (1872–1970). "Symptoms of Orwell's *1984,*"
> *Portraits from Memory, and Other Essays,* 1956

Tamora: The eagle suffers little birds to sing.

> SHAKESPEARE (1564–1616). *Titus Andronicus,* 4.4.83, 1593

If you think that by killing men you can prevent someone from censuring your evil lives, you are mistaken. That is not a way of escape which is either possible or honorable. The easiest and noblest way is not to be disabling others, but to be improving yourselves.

SOCRATES (470?–399 B.C.). In Plato (427?–347 B.C.), *Apology,* 39, tr. Benjamin Jowett, 1894

When a man says he is Jesus or makes some other claim that seems to us outrageous, we call him psychotic and lock him up in the madhouse. Freedom of speech is only for normal people.

THOMAS S. SZASZ (1920–). "Schizophrenia," *The Untamed Tongue: A Dissenting Dictionary,* 1990

I disapprove of what you say, but I will defend to the death your right to say it.

VOLTAIRE (1694–1778). Attributed

❦

Kings and fools speak freely.

SAYING (DUTCH)

FREEDOM OF THE PRESS

See also • Books ○ Censorship ○ Critics—Examples: Henry Miller ○ Freedom ○ Media ○ Propaganda ○ Rights

With freedom of the press, nations are not sure of going toward justice and peace. But without it, they are sure of not going there.

ALBERT CAMUS (1913–1960). "Homage to an Exile," 1955, *Resistance, Rebellion, and Death,* tr. Justin O'Brien, 1961

Press criticism in the absence of a political party is ultimately only one hand clapping.

ALEXANDER COCKBURN (1941–). "The Gulf War and the Media," interview, 4 June 1991. In David Barsamian, ed., *Stenographers to Power,* 1992

Congress shall make no law . . . abridging the freedom . . . of the press.

CONSTITUTION OF THE UNITED STATES. Bill of Rights, First Amendment, 15 December 1791

What progress we are making. In the Middle Ages they would have burned me; nowadays they are content with burning my books.

SIGMUND FREUD (1856–1939). Soon after the Nazis came to power in Germany. In Ernest Jones, *The Life and Work of Sigmund Freud,* 29, 1953–1957, abr. 1961

Senator Joseph McCarthy: Mr. Hammett, if you were in our position, would you allow your book in the U.S.I.S. [United States Information Service] libraries?
Hammett: If I were you, Senator, I would not allow any libraries.

DASHIELL HAMMETT (1894–1961). Format adapted. Testifying before a Senate committee chaired by Senator McCarthy in the 1950s. Hammett's popular 1930 detective story, *The Maltese Falcon,* had been taken off I.S.I.S. library shelves. Quoted by Lillian Hellman during an interview with John Phillips and Anne Hollander. In George Plimpton, ed., *Writers at Work: Third Series,* 1967

Wherever books are burned, sooner or later men also are burned.

HEINRICH HEINE (1797–1856). *Almansor,* l. 245, 1823

To prohibit the reading of certain books is to declare the inhabitants to be either fools or slaves.

HELVÉTIUS (1715–1771). *De l'homme,* 1772

Our liberty depends on the freedom of the press, and that cannot be limited without being lost.

THOMAS JEFFERSON (1743–1826). Letter to James Currie, 18 January 1786

Were it left to me to decide whether we should have a government without newspapers, or newspapers without a government, I should not hesitate a moment to prefer the latter.

THOMAS JEFFERSON (1743–1826). Letter to Col. Edward Carrington, 16 January 1787

If a nation expects to be ignorant and free . . . it expects what never was and never will be. . . . Where the press is free, and every man able to read, all is safe.

THOMAS JEFFERSON (1743–1826). Letter to Col. Charles Yancey, 6 January 1816

If nothing may be published but what civil authority shall have previously approved, power must always be the standard of truth.

SAMUEL JOHNSON (1709–1784). "Milton," *Lives of the English Poets,* 1781

Freedom of the press is guaranteed only to those who own one.

A. J. LIEBLING (1904–1963). "The Wayward Press," *New Yorker,* 14 May 1960

A press monopoly is incompatible with a free press; and one can proceed with this principle: if there is a monopoly of the means of communications—of radio, television, magazines, books, public meetings—it follows that this society is by definition and in fact deprived of freedom.

WALTER LIPPMAN (1889–1974). Address before the International Press Institute, London, 27 May 1965

If you print that, Katie Graham's gonna get her tit caught in a big fat wringer.

JOHN N. MITCHELL (1913–1988). Attorney general. Referring Katharine Graham, *Washington Post* publisher, and the Watergate story, 1973?, remark to the author. In Carl Bernstein, "The Idiot Culture," *New Republic,* 8 June 1992

The press of Italy is free, freer than the press of any other country, so long as it supports the regime.

BENITO MUSSOLINI (1883–1945). In George Seldes, *Sawdust Caesar,* 27, 1935

I shall never tolerate the newspapers to say or do anything against my interests; they may publish a few little articles with just a little poison in them, but one fine morning somebody will shut their mouths.

NAPOLEON (1769–1821). Letter to his minister of police Joseph Fouché, 22 April 1805, *The Mind of Napoleon: A Selection from His Written and Spoken Words,* 160, ed. J. Christopher Herold, 1955

If I were to give liberty to the press, my power could not last three days.

NAPOLEON (1769–1821). In Ralph Waldo Emerson, "Napoleon; or, The Man of the World," *Representative Men,* 1850

Freedom of the press is to the machinery of the state what the safety valve is to the steam engine.

ARTHUR SCHOPENHAUER (1788–1860)

Woe to that nation whose literature is cut short by the intrusion of force. This is not merely interference with freedom of the press but the sealing up of a nation's heart, the excision of its memory.

ALEKSANDR SOLZHENITSYN (1918–). In "Solzhenitsyn: An Artist Becomes an Exile," *Time*, 25 February 1974

As for the modern press, the sentimentalist may beam with contentment when it is constitutionally "free"—but the realist merely asks at whose disposal it is.

OSWALD SPENGLER (1880–1936). "Philosophy of Politics," *The Decline of the West*, 1918-1922, tr. Charles Francis Atkinson, 1962

The rock–bottom foundation of a free press is the integrity of the people who run it.

ADLAI E. STEVENSON (1900–1965). Speech to journalists, Portland (Oregon), 8 September 1952

The last new journal thinks that it is very liberal, nay, bold. . . . If it had been published at the time of the famous dispute between Christ and the doctors, it would have published only the opinions of the doctors and suppressed Christ's. There is no need of a law to check the license of the press. It is law enough, and more than enough, to itself. Virtually, the community have come together and agreed what things shall be uttered, have agreed on a platform and to excommunicate him who departs from it, and not one in a thousand dares utter anything else. . . . [The journals] have been bribed to keep dark. They are in the service of hypocrisy.

HENRY DAVID THOREAU (1817–1862). Journal, 2 March 1858

Servitude cannot be complete if the press is free; the press is the chief democratic instrument of freedom.

ALEXIS de TOCQUEVILLE (1805–1859). *Democracy in America*, 2.4.7, 1840, tr. Henry Reeve and Francis Bowen, 1862

FREEDOM OF THOUGHT

Includes • Freedom of Mind ○ Freedom of Opinion

See also • Brainwashing ○ Freedom ○ Ideas ○ Indoctrination ○ Literature: George Orwell ○ Mind ○ Nonconformity ○ Opinion ○ Propaganda ○ Rights ○ Right to Privacy ○ Right to Silence ○ Thinking ○ Thoughts

Every man haz a perfekt right tew hiz opinyun, provided it agrees with ours.

JOSH BILLINGS (1818–1885). "Ramrods," *Everybody's Friend, or; Josh Billing's Encyclopedia and Proverbial Philosophy of Wit and Humor*, 1874

He that complies against his Will,
Is of his own opinion still.

SAMUEL BUTLER (1612–1680). *Hudibras*, 3.3.547, 1663–1678, ed. John Wilders, 1967

Freedom of speech and freedom of action are meaningless without freedom to think.

BERGEN EVANS (1904–1978). *The Natural History of Nonsense*, 19, 1946

Some who are too scrupulous to steal your possessions nevertheless see no wrong in tampering with your thoughts.

KAHLIL GIBRAN (1883–1931). "Sayings," *Spiritual Sayings of Kahlil Gibran*, tr. Anthony R. Ferris, 1962

Freedom of speech and expression, and the right of all men to disseminate ideas, popular or unpopular, are fundamental to ordered liberty. Government has no power or right to control men's minds, thoughts, and expressions. This is the command of the First Amendment. . . .
   If the First Amendment protects the freedom to express ideas, it necessarily follows that it must protect the freedom to generate ideas. Without the latter protection, the former is meaningless.

HORACE W. GILMORE, GEORGE E. BOWLES, and JOHN D. O'HAIR. In ruling that an involuntarily detained mental patient may not consent to experimental psychosurgery, *Kaimowitz v. Department of Mental Health for the State of Michigan*, 1973

If there is any principle of the Constitution that more imperatively calls for attachment than any other, it is the principle of free thought—not free thought for those who agree with us but freedom for the thought that we hate.

OLIVER WENDELL HOLMES, JR. (1841–1935). *United States v. Schwimmer*, 1929

The very aim and end of our institutions is just this: that we may think what we like and say what we think.

OLIVER WENDELL HOLMES, SR. (1809–1894). *The Professor at the Breakfast-Table*, 5, 1860

He who endeavors to control the mind by force is a tyrant, and he who submits is a slave.

ROBERT G. INGERSOLL (1833–1899). "Fragments," *The Philosophy of Ingersoll*, ed. Vere Goldthwaite, 1906

If there is any fixed star in our constitutional constellation, it is that no official, high or petty, can prescribe what shall be orthodox in politics, nationalism, religion, or other matters of opinion or force citizens to confess by word or act their faith therein.

ROBERT H. JACKSON (1892–1954). *West Virginia State Board of Education v. Barnette*, 1943

Intellectual freedom means the right to re-examine much that has been long taken for granted. A free man must be a reasoning man, and he must dare to doubt what a legislative or electoral majority may most passionately assert.

ROBERT H. JACKSON (1892–1954). *American Communications Association v. Douds*, 1950

Subject opinion to coercion: whom will you make your inquisitors? Fallible men; men governed by bad passions, by private as well as public reasons.

THOMAS JEFFERSON (1743–1826). *Notes on the State of Virginia*, 17, 1785

Almighty God hath created the mind free.

THOMAS JEFFERSON (1743–1826). *The Virginia Act for Religious Freedom*, 1786

The opinions of men are not the subject of civil government, nor under its jurisdiction.

THOMAS JEFFERSON (1743–1826). *The Virginia Act for Religious Freedom,* 1786

It is time enough for the rightful purposes of civil government for its officers to interfere when principles break out into overt acts against peace and good order.

THOMAS JEFFERSON (1743–1826). *The Virginia Act for Religious Freedom,* 1786

I have sworn upon the altar of God, eternal hostility against every form of tyranny over the mind of man.

THOMAS JEFFERSON (1743–1826). Letter to Benjamin Rush, 23 September 1800

It is hard to fight an enemy who has outposts in your head.

SALLY KEMPTON (1943–). "Cutting Loose," *Esquire,* July 1970

What opinions the masses hold, or do not hold, is looked on as a matter of indifference. They can be granted intellectual liberty because they have no intellect. In a Party member, on the other hand, not even the smallest deviation of opinion on the most unimportant subject can be tolerated.

GEORGE ORWELL (1903–1950). *Nineteen Eighty-Four,* 2.9, 1949

When opinions are free, either in matters of government or religion, truth will finally and powerfully prevail.

THOMAS PAINE (1737–1809). Closing words, *The Age of Reason: Being an Investigation of True and Fabulous Theology,* 1796

If there is anything that cannot bear free thought, let it crack.

WENDELL PHILLIPS (1811–1884). In Upton Sinclair, ed., *The Cry for Justice: An Anthology of the Literature of Social Protest,* 5, 1915

Thought is not free if the profession of certain opinions makes it impossible to earn a living. . . . Thought is not free if all the arguments on one side of a controversy are perpetually presented as attractively as possible, while the arguments on the other side can only be discovered by diligent search. . . .

Thought is free when it is exposed to free competition among beliefs, i.e., when all beliefs are able to state their case, and no legal or pecuniary advantages or disadvantages attach to beliefs.

BERTRAND RUSSELL (1872–1970). *Sceptical Essays,* 12, 1928

Government which attempts to control minds is accounted tyrannical, and it is considered an abuse of sovereignty and a usurpation of the rights of subjects to seek to prescribe what shall be accepted as true, or rejected as false, or what opinions should actuate men in their worship of God. All these questions fall within a man's natural right, which he cannot abdicate even with his own consent.

BARUCH SPINOZA (1632–1677). *Tractatus Theologico–Politicus,* 20, 1670, tr. R. H. M. Elwes, 1895

The mind is the expression of the soul, which belongs to God and must be let alone by government.

ADLAI E. STEVENSON (1900–1965). Speech, Mormon Tabernacle Temple, Salt Lake City, 14 October 1952

"To believe your own thought," observed Emerson, "to believe that what is true for you in your private heart is true for all men— that is genius." But to impose what you believe is true for you upon all men, indeed upon a single individual—that is despotism.

THOMAS S. SZASZ (1920–). "Control and Self–Control," *The Second Sin,* 1973

See Genius: Ralph Waldo Emerson (5)

In formal logic, a contradiction is the signal of a defeat: but in the evolution of real knowledge it marks the first step in progress towards a victory. This is one great reason for the utmost toleration of variety of opinion. Once and forever, this duty of toleration has been summed up in the words, "let both grow together until the harvest."

ALFRED NORTH WHITEHEAD (1861–1947). *Science and the Modern World,* 12, 1925

❦

No one deserves punishment for his thoughts.

SAYING (LATIN)

FRIENDS

See also • Enemies ○ Failure: Philip Van Doren Stern ○ Friends & Enemies ○ Loyalty: [especially] Theodore Roosevelt ○ Wounds: Zechariah

A friend in power is a friend lost.

HENRY ADAMS (1838–1918). *The Education of Henry Adams,* 7, 1907

A friend is a second self.

ARISTOTLE (384–322 B.C.). *Nicomachean Ethics,* 9.4, tr. J. A. K. Thomson, 1953

[Friendship] redoubleth joys and cutteth griefs in halves. For there is no man that imparteth his joys to his friend, but he joyeth the more; and no man that imparteth his griefs to his friend, but he grieveth the less.

FRANCIS BACON (1561–1626). "Of Friendship," *Essays,* 1625

See Sharing: Saying (English)

Friendships last when each friend thinks he has a slight superiority over the other.

BALZAC (1799–1850)

It is one of the severest tests of friendship to tell your friend of his faults. . . . To speak painful truth through loving words—that *is* friendship.

HENRY WARD BEECHER (1813–1887). *Life Thoughts,* p. 146, rec. Edna Dean Proctor, 1858

Friendless, *adj.* Having no favors to bestow. Destitute of fortune. Addicted to utterance of truth and common sense.

AMBROSE BIERCE (1842–1914). *The Devil's Dictionary,* p. 45, 1911, Dover edition, 1958

Friendship is a strong and habitual inclination in two persons to promote the good and happiness of one another.

EUSTACE BUDGELL (1686–1737). In *The Spectator* (English essay series), 385, 22 May 1712

Agreement in likes and dislikes—this, and this only, is what constitutes true friendship

CATILINE (108–62 B.C.). In Sallust (86?–34? B.C.). *The War with Catiline,* 20.4, tr. J. C. Rolfe, 1921

Two may talk together under the same roof for many years, yet never really meet; and two others at first speech are old friends.

> MARY CATHERWOOD (1847–1901). "Marianson," *Mackinac and Lake Stories,* 1899

Treat your friends as you do your pictures, and place them in their best light.

> JENNIE JEROME CHURCHILL (1854–1921). American–born British mother of Winston Churchill. "Friendship," *Small Talk on Big Subjects,* 1916

My foul–weather friend.

> WINSTON CHURCHILL (1874–1965). On Lord Beaverbrook (British newspaper publisher and political leader), quoted by James C. Humes, Brian Lamb television interview, C-SPAN, 22 June 1997

To bear each other's burdens, never to ask each other for anything inconsistent with virtue and rectitude, and not only to serve and love but also to respect each other.

> CICERO (106–43 B.C.). *De amicitia,* 22, tr. E. S. Shuckburgh, 1900

To give and receive advice—the former with freedom and yet without bitterness, the latter with patience and without irritation—is peculiarly appropriate to genuine friendship.

> CICERO (106–43 B.C.). *De amicitia,* 25, tr. E. S. Shuckburgh, 1900

What a delight it is to make friends with someone you have despised!

> COLETTE (1873–1954). "Sido and I," *Earthly Paradise: An Autobiography,* tr. Herma Briffault, 1966

Have no friends not equal to yourself.

> CONFUCIUS (551–479 B.C.). *Confucian Analects,* 1.8, tr. James Legge, 1930

Léon Delbecque (in great distress): General, all of my friends say you are deserting us. They want me to get you to change your Algerian policy. What should I do?
De Gaulle (snapping back): Change your friends.

> CHARLES de GAULLE (1890–1970). Format adapted. In David Schoenbrun, *The Three Lives of Charles de Gaulle,* 4, 1968

Similarity of outlook creates friendship.

> DEMOCRITUS (460–370 B.C.). In Kathleen Freeman, tr., *Ancilla to Pre–Socratic Philosophers: A Complete Translation of the Fragments in Diels,* Fragmente der Vorsokratiker, 68.186, 1983 (1948)

You got a lotta nerve
To say you are my friend
When I was down
You just stood there grinning

You got a lotta nerve
To say you gotta helping hand to lend
You just want to be on
The side that's winning

> BOB DYLAN (1941–). "Positively 4th Street" (song), 1965

There are very few honest friends—the demand is not particularly great.

> MARIE von EBNER-ESCHENBACH (1830–1916). *Aphorisms,* p. 71, 1880–1905, tr. David Scrase and Wolfgang Mieder, 1994

Best friend, my wellspring in the wilderness!

> GEORGE ELIOT (1819–1880). *The Spanish Gypsy,* bk. 3, 1868

One Mind. The ancients exchanged their names with their friends, signifying that in their friend they loved their own soul.

> RALPH WALDO EMERSON (1803–1882). Journal, 20 October 1838

We are never so fit for friendship as when we cease to seek for it, and take ourselves to friend.

> RALPH WALDO EMERSON (1803–1882). Journal, 1840, undated

A friend is a person with whom I may be sincere. Before him, I may think aloud.

> RALPH WALDO EMERSON (1803–1882). "Friendship," *Essays: First Series,* 1841
>
> See Conversation: William Hazlitt

Better be a nettle in the side of your friend than his echo.

> RALPH WALDO EMERSON (1803–1882). "Friendship," *Essays: First Series,* 1841

Friends are self-elected. Reverence is a great part of it.

> RALPH WALDO EMERSON (1803–1882). "Friendship," *Essays: First Series,* 1841

The only way to have a friend is to be one.

> RALPH WALDO EMERSON (1803–1882). "Friendship," *Essays: First Series,* 1841

When I see my friend after a long time, my first question is, Has anything become clear to you?

> RALPH WALDO EMERSON (1803–1882). Journal, May 1847

I found the friends I went to seek on the way to my door.

> RALPH WALDO EMERSON (1803–1882). Journal, 1859, undated

'Tis great Confidence in a Friend to tell him your Faults, greater to tell him his.

> BENJAMIN FRANKLIN (1706–1790). *Poor Richard's Almanack,* August 1751

A Brother may not be a Friend,
     but a Friend will always be a Brother.

> BENJAMIN FRANKLIN (1706–1790). *Poor Richard's Almanack,* May 1752

To keep up and improve Friendship, thou must be willing to receive a Kindness, as well as to do one.

> THOMAS FULLER (1654–1734). Comp., *Introductio ad Prudentiam,* 1186, 1731

Virtue is the only firm Ground for [Friendship] to stand upon.

> THOMAS FULLER (1654–1734). Comp., *Introductio ad Prudentiam,* 1349, 1731

Be a Friend to thyself, and others will be so too.

> THOMAS FULLER (1654–1734). Comp., *Gnomologia: Adages and Proverbs,* 847, 1732
>
> See Confidence: Goethe (1) ○ Self-Respect: Baltasar Gracián

Friendships multiply Joys and divide Griefs.

> THOMAS FULLER (1654–1734). Comp., *Gnomologia: Adages and Proverbs,* 1622, 1732

True friendship comes when silence between two people is comfortable.

> DAVE TYSON GENTRY

Our most intimate friend is not he to whom we show the worst, but the best, of our nature.

> NATHANIEL HAWTHORNE (1804–1864). 11 October 1845, *The American Notebooks,* ed. Claude M. Simpson, 1932

We appreciate *what we share,* we do not appreciate *what we receive.* Friendship, affection is not acquired by giving presents. Friendship, affection comes about by two people sharing a significant moment, by having an experience in common.

> ABRAHAM JOSHUA HESCHEL (1907–1972). *The Insecurity of Freedom: Essays on Human Existence,* 5.3, 1967

He can hardly be a true friend to another, who is an enemy to himself.

> JAMES HOWELL (1593–1666). Comp., "French" (p. 3), *Paroimiographia: Proverbs, or Old Sayed Sawes & Adages in English . . . Italian, French and Spanish,* 1659

Your friend is the man who knows all about you, and still likes you.

> ELBERT HUBBARD (1859–1915). *A Thousand and One Epigrams,* p. 88, 1911

A friend thet hain't in need is a friend indeed.

> KIN HUBBARD (1868–1930). *Abe Martin's Sayings and Wisecracks, Abe's Neighbors, His Almanack, Comic Drawings,* 2 ("Abe Martin's Almanack," December), ed. David S. Hawes, 1984

Friendship is seldom lasting but between equals, or where the superiority on one side is reduced by some equivalent advantage on the other.

> SAMUEL JOHNSON (1709–1784). In *The Rambler* (English journal), 64, 27 October 1750

Friendship may well deserve the sacrifice of pleasure, though not of conscience.

> SAMUEL JOHNSON (1709–1784). In *The Rambler* (English journal), 64, 27 October 1750

Winter, spring, summer or fall
All you have to do is call
And I'll be there,
You've got a friend.

> CAROLE KING (1942–). "You've Got a Friend" (song), 1971

The friend who holds your hand and says the wrong thing is made of dearer stuff than the one who stays away.

> BARBARA KINGSOLVER (1955–). "Stone Soup, 1995, *High Tide in Tucson: Essays from Now or Never,* 1996

What men call friendship is just an arrangement for mutual gain and an exchange of favors.

> LA ROCHEFOUCAULD (1613–1680). *Maxims,* 83, 1665, tr. Louis Kronenberger, 1959

Never do a wrong thing to make a friend or keep one.

> ROBERT E. LEE (1807–1870). Letter to his son, 1860, quoted by David McCullough, "The Unexpected Harry Truman." In William Zinsser, ed., *Extraordinary Lives: The Art and Craft of American Biography,* 1988

Oh I get by with a little help from my friends.
Mmm, I get high with a little help from my friends.

> JOHN LENNON (1940–1980) and PAUL McCARTNEY (1942–). "With a Little Help from My Friends" (song), 1967

How miserably things seem to be arranged in this world! If we have no friends, we have no pleasure; and if we have them, we are sure to lose them, and be doubly pained by the loss.

> ABRAHAM LINCOLN (1809–1865). Letter to Joshua F. Speed, 25 February 1842

I desire so to conduct the affairs of this administration that if at the end, when I come to lay down the reins of power, I have lost every other friend on earth, I shall at least have one friend left, and that friend shall be down inside of me.

> ABRAHAM LINCOLN (1809–1865). Reply to the Missouri Committee of Seventy, 30 September 1864
> See Integrity: George Washington

May God preserve me from the love of a friend who will never dare to rebuke me.

> THOMAS MERTON (1915–1968). *No Man Is an Island,* 1.9, 1955

The best way to keep your friends is not to give them away.

> WILSON MIZNER (1876–1933)

Friendship is equality.

> PYTHAGORAS (580?–500? B.C.). In Diogenes Laertius (A.D. 3rd cent.), *Lives of Eminent Philosophers,* 8.10, tr. R. D. Hicks, 1925

In time of prosperity *friends* will be plenty.
In time of adversity not one among twenty.

> JOHN RAY (1628–1705). Comp., *A Collection of English Proverbs,* p. 11, 1678

A *friend* in need is a friend indeed.

> JOHN RAY (1628–1705). Comp., *A Collection of English Proverbs,* p. 142, 1678

Old friends are best: King James used to call for his old shoes, they were easiest to his feet.

> JOHN SELDEN (1584–1654). "Friends," *Table Talk,* 1689, ed. Frederick Pollock, 1927

[Hecato wrote:] "What progress, you ask, have I made? I have begun to be a friend to myself." That was indeed a great benefit; such a person can never be alone. You may be sure that such a man is a friend to all mankind.

> SENECA THE YOUNGER (5? B.C.–A.D. 65). "On Sharing Knowledge," *Moral Letters to Lucilius,* 6.7, tr. Richard M. Gummere, 1918

He that is thy friend indeed
He will help thee in thy need.

> SHAKESPEARE (1564–1616). *The Passionate Pilgrim,* 21, 1599

Among true and real friends, all is common; and were ignorance and envy and superstition banished from the world, all mankind would be friends.

> PERCY BYSSHE SHELLEY (1792–1822). "Essay on Christianity," 1817

I am for frank explanations with friends in cases of affronts. They sometimes save a perishing friendship, and even place it on a firmer basis than at first; but secret discontent must always end badly.

> SYDNEY SMITH (1771–1845). *The Wit and Wisdom of Sydney Smith,* p. 374, undated

The more someone disliked him, the harder he'd try to be his friend.

> CLAYTON STRIBLING. On Lyndon B. Johnson (1908–1973). In Robert A. Caro, *The Path to Power*, 7, 1982

We are so fond of each other because our ailments are the same.

> JONATHAN SWIFT (1667–1745). 1 February 1711, *The Journal to Stella*, 1766–1768

What is a friend? For some, a partner for playing *folie à deux;* for others, a sympathetic but incorruptible judge of one's judgments.

> THOMAS S. SZASZ (1920–). "Social Relations," *Heresies*, 1976

Friends will not only live in harmony, but in melody.

> HENRY DAVID THOREAU (1817–1862). Sole entry, journal, 3 April 1841

A Friend is one who incessantly pays us the compliment of expecting from us all the virtues, and who can appreciate them in us.

> HENRY DAVID THOREAU (1817–1862). "Wednesday," *A Week on the Concord and Merrimack Rivers*, 1849

They cherish each other's hopes. They are kind to each other's dreams.

> HENRY DAVID THOREAU (1817–1862). "Wednesday," *A Week on the Concord and Merrimack Rivers*, 1849

Friendship is . . . a relation of perfect equality. . . . Not that the parties to it are in all respects equal, but they are equal in all that respects or affects their Friendship.

> HENRY DAVID THOREAU (1817–1862). "Wednesday," *A Week on the Concord and Merrimack Rivers*, 1849

My friend is one . . . who takes me for what I am.

> HENRY DAVID THOREAU (1817–1862). Journal, 23 October 1852

A slender acquaintance with the world must convince every man that actions, not words, are the true [criteria] of the attachment of his friends.

> GEORGE WASHINGTON (1732–1799). Letter to John Sullivan, 15 December 1779

Be courteous to all, but intimate with few; and let those few be well tried before you give them your confidence. True friendship is a plant of slow growth, and must undergo and withstand the shocks of adversity before it is entitled to the appellation.

> GEORGE WASHINGTON (1732–1799). Letter to his nephew Bushrod Washington, 15 January 1783

❦

A man dies as often as he loses his friends.

> ANONYMOUS. In Francis Bacon (1561–1626). "Ornamenta Rationalia; or, Elegant Sentences," *The Essays; or, Counsels, Civil and Moral*, A. L. Burt edition, 1883

A real friend never gets in your way—unless you happen to be on your way down.

> ANONYMOUS

Fair–weather friends abound;
foul–weather friends never around.

> ANONYMOUS

Friends feel each others' joys and sorrows as their own.

> ANONYMOUS

The road to a friend's house is never long.

> SAYING (DANISH)

We are known by our friends.

> SAYING

A friend is easier lost than found.

> SAYING

A friend in deed is a friend indeed.

> SAYING

FRIENDS & ENEMIES

See also • Enemies ○ Friends ○ Judging Others: Joseph Conrad ○ Reconciliation

It is easier to guard against an enemy than against a friend.

> ALCMAEON (6th cent. B.C.). In Kathleen Freeman, tr., *Ancilla to Pre-Socratic Philosophers: A Complete Translation of the Fragments in Diels,* Fragmente der Vorsokratiker, 24.5, 1983 (1948)

Some men are better served by their bitter–tongued enemies than by their sweet–smiling friends; because the former often tell the truth, the latter, never.

> CATO THE YOUNGER (95–46 B.C.). In Cicero (106–43 B.C.), *De amicitia,* 34, tr. William Armstead Falconer, 1923

We should render a service to a friend to bind him closer to us, and to an enemy in order to make a friend of him.

> CLEOBULUS (6th cent. B.C.). As paraphrased by Diogenes Laertius (A.D. 3rd cent.), *Lives of Eminent Philosophers*, 1.6, tr. R. D. Hicks, 1925

He who has a thousand friends has not one friend to spare,
And he who has one enemy will meet him everywhere.

> RALPH WALDO EMERSON (1803–1882). Journal, 1855, undated

Do good to thy Friend to keep him,
to thy enemy to gain him.

> BENJAMIN FRANKLIN (1706–1790). *Poor Richard's Almanack*, July 1734

An intimate friend and a hated enemy have always been indispensable to my emotional life; I have always been able to create them anew, and not infrequently my childish ideal has been so closely approached that friend and enemy have coincided in the same person.

> SIGMUND FREUD (1856–1939). *The Interpretation of Dreams*, 6.H, 1900, tr. A. A. Brill, 1938

Make God thy Friend, and then it's no matter who is thy Enemy.

> THOMAS FULLER (1654–1734). Comp., *Introductio ad Prudentiam*, 324, 1731

Those will be thy worst Enemies not to whom thou hast done evil, but who had done evil to thee. And those will be thy best Friends not to whom thou hast done good, but who have done good to thee.

> THOMAS FULLER (1654–1734). Comp., *Introductio ad Prudentiam*, 1262, 1731

An open foe may prove a curse,
But a pretended friend is worse.

> JOHN GAY (1685–1732). *Fables,* 1.17, 1727–1738

God guard me from my friends, for I shall guard myself from my enemies.

> JAMES HOWELL (1593–1666). Comp., "Italian" (p. 11), *Paroimiographia: Proverbs, or Old Sayed Sawes & Adages in English . . . Italian, French and Spanish,* 1659

Friends come and go, but enemies accumulate.

> JONES'S MOTTO. In John Peers, comp., *1,001 Logical Laws,* p. 142, 1979

Show me somebody who can't tell his friends from his enemies, and I'll show you somebody who's going to end up with no friends.

> JIM LEHRER (1934–). *A Bus of My Own,* 1992. In William Safire, "Wedges and Bounces," *New York Times Magazine,* 20 September 1992

Keep your friends close, but keep your enemies closer.

> MARIO PUZO (1920–). Machiavellian advice from Don Corleone as recalled by his son Michael (played by Al Pacino), *The Godfather, Part II* (film), 1974

No friend ever served me, and no enemy ever wronged me, whom I have not repaid in full.

> SULLA (138–78 B.C.). Roman general. In Martin Blumenson and James L. Stokesbury, *Masters of the Art of Command,* 2 ("Sulla"), 1975

I call to the world to distrust the accounts of my friends, but listen to my enemies, as I myself do.

> WALT WHITMAN (1819–1892). "Myself and Mine," 1860, *Leaves of Grass,* 1855–1892

Enemies should be chosen as carefully as friends.

> ANONYMOUS

❧

Better a wise enemy than a foolish friend.

> SAYING (ARAB)

A hundred friends are too few; one enemy is too many.

> SAYING (GERMAN)

FUNERALS

See also • Death ○ Grief ○ Laughter: Charles Lamb ○ Motorcycles: Herb Caen

If you don't go to other men's funerals, they won't go to yours.

> CLARENCE DAY (1874–1935). "Father Plans to Get Out," *Life with Father,* 1935

Minister: We are gathered here today to honor the memory of Frederick P. Zoltin, who lived to the age of 89 years and never had a clue.

> JOHN GUMPERTZ. Cartoon caption, *Gumpertz, San Francisco Sunday Examiner & Chronicle,* 28 June 1992

If General—had known how big a funeral he would have had, he would have died years ago.

ABRAHAM LINCOLN (1809–1865). On a recently deceased politician whose merit was marred by great vanity, remark to Petroleum V. Nasby. In Emanuel Hertz, ed., "Father Abraham," *Lincoln Talks: A Biography in Anecdote,* 1939

Memorial services are the cocktail parties of the geriatric set.

> HAROLD MACMILLAN (1894–1986). In Alistair Horne, *Macmillan,* 2.20, 1989

❧

The only reason I might go to the funeral is to make absolutely sure that he's dead.

> ANONYMOUS (BRITISH). On Lord Beaverbrook. In Anthony Sampson, *Anatomy of Britain Today,* 9, 1965

FUNNINESS

See also • Comedy ○ Humor ○ Jests ○ Jokes

I think being funny is not anyone's first choice.

> WOODY ALLEN (1935–). In *The Guardian* (British newspaper), 23 March 1992

What do you mean, funny? Funny peculiar, or funny ha–ha?

> IAN HAY (1876–1952). *Housemaster,* 3, 1936

A thing is funny when—in some way that is not actually offensive or frightening—it upsets the established order. Every joke is a tiny revolution. . . . Whatever destroys dignity and brings down the mighty from their seats, preferably with a bump, is funny.

> GEORGE ORWELL (1903–1950). "Funny, But Not Vulgar," December 1944, *The Collected Essays, Journalism and Letters of George Orwell,* vol. 3, ed. Sonia Orwell and Ian Angus, 1968

Everything is funny as long as it is happening to somebody else.

> WILL ROGERS (1879–1935). "Warning to Jokers: Lay Off the Prince," *The Illiterate Digest,* 1924

When a thing is funny, search it for a hidden truth.

> GEORGE BERNARD SHAW (1856–1950). *Back to Methuselah: A Metabiological Pentateuch,* 5, 1921

FUTURE

See also • Cruelty: George Orwell ○ Destiny: Friedrich Nietzsche ○ Lobbies: Peter G. Peterson ○ Past ○ Prediction ○ Present ○ Time

Man is unique in nature and among animals in being able to conceive a future.

> CRANE BRINTON (1898–1968). *The Anatomy of Revolution,* 7.3, 1952

One faces the future with one's past.

> PEARL S. BUCK (1892–1973). "China Faces the Future," lecture, New York City, 13 October 1942

You can never plan the future by the past.

> EDMUND BURKE (1729–1797). Letter to a member of the French National Assembly, 1791

How paramount the future is to the present when one is surrounded by children.

CHARLES DARWIN (1809–1882). Letter to Rev. William Darwin Fox, 7 March 1852, *The Autobiography of Charles Darwin and Selected Letters*, 8, ed. Francis Darwin, 1892

I never think of the future. It comes soon enough.

ALBERT EINSTEIN (1879–1955). Interview, December 1930

Those who live for the future must always appear selfish to those who live for the present.

RALPH WALDO EMERSON (1803–1882). Journal, May–June 1843

All our hopes for the future depend on a sound understanding of the past.

FREDERIC HARRISON (1831–1923). *The Meaning of History*, 6, 1862

See Prediction: Patrick Henry

The only certain thing about the future is that it will surprise even those who have seen furthest into it.

E. J. HOBSBAWM (1917–). Closing words, *The Age of Empire: 1875–1914*, 1987

That man is in the right who is most closely in league with the future.

HENRIK IBSEN (1828–1906). Letter to Georg Brandes, 3 January 1882

A young man who doesn't believe in tomorrow morning is a traitor to himself.

FRANZ KAFKA (1883–1924). In Gustav Janouch, "Conversations with Kafka," tr. Goronwy Rees, *Encounter*, August 1971

My interest is in the future because I am going to spend the rest of my life there.

CHARLES F. KETTERING (1876–1958)

The future must be shaped or it will impose itself as catastrophe.

HENRY A. KISSINGER (1923–). *Years of Upheaval*, 16, 1982

The future . . . [is] something which everyone reaches at the rate of sixty minutes an hour, whatever he does, whoever he is.

C. S. LEWIS (1898–1963). *The Screwtape Letters*, rev. ed., 25, 1982 (1942)

The struggle of today is not altogether for today—it is for a vast future also. With a reliance on Providence, all the more firm and earnest, let us proceed in the great task which events have devolved upon us.

ABRAHAM LINCOLN (1809–1865). *First Annual Message to Congress*, 3 December 1861

The future belongs to those who fuse intelligence with faith, and who with courage and determination grope their way forward from chance to choice, from blind adaptation to creative evolution.

CHARLES E. MERRIAM (1876–1953). Closing words, *Political Power*, 1934

If you do the very best you can, the future will take care of itself.

GEORGE MITCHELL (1933–). Maine senator. Brian Lamb television interview, C-SPAN, 30 November 1994

From an Industrial Society to an Information Society
From Forced Technology to High Tech/High Touch
From a National Economy to a World Economy
From Short Term to Long Term
From Centralization to Decentralization
From Institutional Help to Self-Help
From Representative Democracy to Participatory Democracy
From Hierarchies to Networking
From North to South
From Either/Or to Multiple Option

JOHN NAISBITT (1929–). Chapter titles, *Megatrends: Ten New Directions Transforming Our Lives*, 1984

Fundamental thought: we must consider the future as decisive for all our evaluations—and not seek the laws of our action *behind* us!

FRIEDRICH NIETZSCHE (1844–1900). *The Will to Power* (notebooks, 1883–1888), 1000, 1911, tr. Walter Kaufmann and R. J. Hollingdale, 1967

Only the day after tomorrow belongs to me. Some are born posthumously.

FRIEDRICH NIETZSCHE (1844–1900). Foreword to *The Anti-Christ*, 1895, tr. R. J. Hollingdale, 1968

Who will answer for tomorrow?

CHARLES PÉGUY (1873–1914). "The Modern World: The Future," *Basic Verities: Prose and Poetry*, tr. Ann and Julian Green, 1943

The future has no lobby.

PETER G. PETERSON (1926–). "The Morning After," *Atlantic*, October 1987

Not one looks backward, onward still he goes,
Yet ne'er looks forward further than his nose.

ALEXANDER POPE (1688–1744). *An Essay on Man*, 4.223, 1734

The future is given shape by our faith, or condemned to drift and disaster by our indifference.

PAGE SMITH (1917–1995). *The Historian and History*, 14, 1964

Not even the future is what it used to be.

PAUL VALÉRY (1871–1945). In Joseph Epstein, introduction to *Ambition: The Secret Passion*, 1980

See Past: Anonymous (1)

The future is like a corridor into which we can see only by the light coming from behind.

EDWARD WEYER, JR. Introduction to *Primitive Peoples Today*, 1959

See Prediction: Patrick Henry

The future is big with every possibility of achievement and of tragedy.

ALFRED NORTH WHITEHEAD (1861–1947). *Modes of Thought*, 4.9, 1938

❦

Due to a lack of interest tomorrow has been canceled.

ANONYMOUS (AMERICAN). Graffito, 1980s

The future belongs to those who earn it.

ANONYMOUS (AMERICAN). In Smith Barney, Inc. (stock brokerage firm) ad, *New York Times*, 1 June 1994

GAMBLING

See also • Money ○ Stock Market

The less you bet, the more you lose when you win.
> BONETTI'S LAW. In John Peers, comp., *1,001 Logical Laws*, p. 147, 1979

Betting and such sports are only the stunted and twisted shapes of the original instinct of man for adventure and romance.
> G. K. CHESTERTON (1874–1936). *Orthodoxy*, 7, 1909

Th' only absolutely safe way t' double your money is t' fold it once an' put it in your hip pocket.
> KIN HUBBARD (1868–1930). *Abe Martin: Hoss Sense and Nonsense*, p. 108, 1926

Man is a gaming animal. He must be always trying to get the better in something or other.
> CHARLES LAMB (1775–1834). "Mrs. Battle's Opinions on Whist," *The Essays of Elia*, 1823

One of the worst things that can happen in life is to win a bet on a horse at an early age.
> DANNY McGOORTY (1901–1970)

There is no moral difference between gambling at cards or in lotteries or on the race track and gambling in the stock market. One method is just as pernicious to the body politic as the other kind.
> THEODORE ROOSEVELT (1858–1919). Message to Congress, 31 January 1908

If there was two birds setting on a fence, he would bet you which one would fly first.
> MARK TWAIN (1835–1910). "The Celebrated Jumping Frog of Calaveras County," *New York Saturday Press*, 18 November 1865

[Gaming] is the child of Avarice, the brother of Iniquity, and father of Mischief.
> GEORGE WASHINGTON (1732–1799). Letter to his nephew Bushrod Washington, 15 January 1783

One should always play fairly—when one has the winning cards.
> OSCAR WILDE (1854–1900). *An Ideal Husband*, 1, 1895

Nobody every bet enough on the winning horse.
> ANONYMOUS

The best throw of the dice is to throw them away.
> SAYING (ENGLISH)

Young gambler, old beggar.
> SAYING (GERMAN)

If I bet on the tide, it wouldn't come in.
> SAYING (IRISH)

GARDENING

See also • Farming ○ Nature ○ Work

Physical work is degrading [only] if the body is used as a slave or a machine—if, in other words, it is misused. But working in one's own garden does not misuse the body, nor does it dull or "brutalize" the mind. The work of gardening is not drudgery, but is the finest sort of challenge to intelligence. Gardening is not a discipline that can be learned once for all, but keeps presenting problems that must be directly dealt with. It is, in addition, an agricultural and ecological education, and that sort of education corrects the cheap–energy mind.
> WENDELL BERRY (1934–). "The Reactor and the Garden," *The Gift of Good Land: Further Essays Cultural and Agricultural*, 1981

A garden is the most direct way to recapture the issue of health, and to make it a private instead of a governmental responsibility.
> WENDELL BERRY (1934–). "The Reactor and the Garden," *The Gift of Good Land: Further Essays Cultural and Agricultural*, 1981

Train up a fig-tree in the way it should go, and when you are old sit under the shade [of] it.
> CHARLES DICKENS (1812–1870). *Dombey and Son*, 19, 1848

When I go into my garden with a spade and dig a bed, I feel such an exhilaration and health, that I discover that I have been defrauding myself all this time in letting others do for me what I should have done with my own hands. But not only health but education is in the work.
> RALPH WALDO EMERSON (1803–1882). "Man the Reformer," lecture, Masonic Temple, Boston, 25 January 1841

My garden is an honest place. Every tree and every vine are incapable of concealment, and tell after two or three months exactly what sort of treatment they have had. The sower may mistake and sow his peas crookedly: the peas make no mistake but come and show his line.
> RALPH WALDO EMERSON (1803–1882). Journal, 8 May 1843

All gardeners live in beautiful places because they make them so.
> JOSEPH JOUBERT (1754–1824). 1806, *Pensées*, 1838, tr. Paul Auster, 1983

All gardening is landscape painting.
> ALEXANDER POPE (1688–1744). In Joseph Spence, *Observations, Anecdotes, and Characters, of Books and Men Collected from the Conversation of Mr. Pope, and Other Eminent Persons of His Time*, 2nd ed., 4 (1734–1736), 1858

When I used to pick the berries for dinner on the East Quarter hills I did not eat one till I had done, for going a–berrying implies more things than eating the berries. They at home got only the pudding: I got the forenoon out of doors and the appetite for the pudding.
> HENRY DAVID THOREAU (1817–18862). Journal, 22 August 1860

GENERALS

See • Commanders

GENEROSITY

See also • Gifts ○ Giving

Not to do a magnanimous thing
Notwithstanding it never be known

Notwithstanding it cost us existence once
Is Rapture herself spurn—

>EMILY DICKINSON (1830–1886). "Not to do a magnanimous thing," undated

Liberality is not giving largely but giving wisely.

>THOMAS FULLER (1654–1734). Comp., *Gnomologia: Adages and Proverbs,* 3203, 1732

People who think they're generous to a fault usually think that's their only fault.

>SYDNEY J. HARRIS (1917–1986). *On the Contrary,* 7, 1962

We'd all like a reputation for generosity, and we'd all like to buy it cheap.

>MIGNON McMAUGHLIN (1915–). *The Neurotic's Notebook,* 9, 1963

The first essential is to be content with your own lot; the second, to support and assist those you know to be most in need, embracing them all within the circle of your friendship.

>PLINY THE YOUNGER (A.D. 62?–113?). On generosity, *Letters,* 9.30, tr. Betty Radice, 1963

He who gives money he has not earned is generous with other people's labor.

>GEORGE BERNARD SHAW (1856–1950). "Maxims for Revolutionists: Charity," *Man and Superman,* 1903

The truly beneficent never relapses into a creditor.

>HENRY DAVID THOREAU (1817–1862). Journal, 2 September 1841

Generosity gives assistance rather than advice.

>VAUVENARGUES (1715–1747). *Reflections and Maxims,* 491, 1746, tr. F. G. Stevens, 1940

GENIUS

See also • Ability ○ Censure: William G. Simms ○ Creativity ○ Excellence ○ Genius & Talent ○ Greatness ○ Heroism ○ Leaders ○ Madness ○ Memory: Hesketh Pearson ○ Nonconformity ○ Thinkers

Susceptibility to the highest forces is the highest genius.

>HENRY ADAMS (1838–1918). *The Education of Henry Adams,* 33, 1907

No great genius has ever existed without some touch of madness.

>ARISTOTLE (384–322 B.C.). *Problemata,* 30.1. In Seneca the Younger (5? B.C.–A.D. 65), "On Tranquillity of Mind" (17.10), *Moral Essays,* tr. John W. Basore, 1932
>
>See Madness: John Dryden (1)

I have known no man of genius who had not to pay, in some affliction or defect either physical or spiritual, for what the gods had given him.

>SIR MAX BEERBOHM (1872–1956). "No. 2, The Pines," *And Even Now,* 1920

Genius defies all anticipation.

>HENRI BERGSON (1859–1941). "Moral Obligation," *The Two Sources of Morality and Religion,* 1932, tr. R. Ashley Audra and Cloudesley Brereton, 1935

The inertia of humanity has never yielded, save under the impulsion of genius. In a word, science demands a twofold effort, that of a few men to find some new thing and that of all the others to adopt it and adapt themselves to it.

>HENRI BERGSON (1859–1941). "Static Religion," *The Two Sources of Morality and Religion,* 1932, tr. R. Ashley Audra and Cloudesley Brereton, 1935

Since when was genius found respectable?

>ELIZABETH BARRETT BROWNING (1806–1861). *Aurora Leigh,* 6.275, 1857

Genius . . . has been defined as a supreme capacity for taking trouble. . . . It might be more fitly described as a supreme capacity for getting its possessors into pains of all kinds, and keeping them therein so long as the genius remains.

>SAMUEL BUTLER (1835–1902). *The Note–Books of Samuel Butler,* 11, ed. Henry Festing Jones, 1907

[Genius is] a supreme capacity for saving other people from having to take pains.

>SAMUEL BUTLER (1835–1902). *The Note-Books of Samuel Butler,* 11, ed. Henry Festing Jones, 1907

[Genius knows] both love and hate, but not as we know them, for it will fly to help its bitterest foe or attack its dearest friend in the interests of the art it serves.

>SAMUEL BUTLER (1835–1902). *The Note–Books of Samuel Butler,* 11, ed. Henry Festing Jones, 1907

The good plan itself, this comes not of its own accord; it is the fruit of genius (which means transcendent capacity of taking trouble, first of all).

>THOMAS CARLYLE (1795–1881). *History of Frederick II of Prussia,* 4.3, 1865

The sum total of excellence is good sense and method. When these have passed into the instinctive readiness of habit, when the wheel revolves so rapidly that we cannot see it revolve at all, then we call the combination genius.

>SAMUEL TAYLOR COLERIDGE (1772–1834). In Lord Acton, appendix (70) to *Essays on Freedom and Power,* ed. Gertrude Himmelfarb, 1949

One is not born a genius: one becomes a genius.

>SIMONE de BEAUVOIR (1908–1986). *The Second Sex,* 8, 1950, tr. H. M. Parshley, 1952
>
>See Women: de Beauvoir

The individuals who seem to us most outstanding, who are honored with the name of genius, are those who have proposed to enact the fate of all humanity in their personal existences.

>SIMONE de BEAUVOIR (1908–1986). *The Second Sex,* 25, 1950, tr. H. M. Parshley, 1952

Time, place, and action, may with pains be wrought;
But genius must be born, and never can be taught.

>JOHN DRYDEN (1631–1700). "To My Dear Friend Mr. Congreve, On His Comedy Call'd the Double–Dealer," 1693?

You may have heard people repeat what I have said, "Genius is one percent inspiration, ninety-nine percent perspiration." Yes, sir, it's mostly *hard work*.

THOMAS ALVA EDISON (1847–1931). Remark to the author. In M. A. Rosanoff, "Edison in His Laboratory" (4), *Harper's*, September 1932

See Success: Elbert Hubbard (6)

The words of genius have a wider meaning than the thought that prompted them.

GEORGE ELIOT (1819–1880). *Adam Bede*, 33, 1859

Genius at first is little more than a great capacity for receiving discipline.

GEORGE ELIOT (1819–1880). *Daniel Deronda*, 23, 1876

Every man of genius sees the world at a different angle from his fellows, and there is his tragedy.

HAVELOCK ELLIS (1859–1939). *The Dance of Life*, 3.4, 1923

The man of genius inspires us with a boundless confidence in our own powers.

RALPH WALDO EMERSON (1803–1882). "Encyclopedia," p. 136, 1824–1836

Genius is the enemy of genius by overinfluence.

RALPH WALDO EMERSON (1803–1882). Journal, 29 July 1837

When nature has work to be done, she creates a genius to do it.

RALPH WALDO EMERSON (1803–1882). "The Method of Nature," address, Waterville (now Colby) College (Maine), 11 August 1841

In every work of genius we recognize our own rejected thoughts.

RALPH WALDO EMERSON (1803–1882). "Self-Reliance," *Essays: First Series*, 1841

To believe your own thought, to believe that what is true for you in your private heart is true for all men—that is genius.

RALPH WALDO EMERSON (1803–1882). "Self-Reliance," *Essays: First Series*, 1841

See Freedom of Thought: Thomas S. Szasz

The true romance which the world exists to realize, will be the transformation of genius into practical power.

RALPH WALDO EMERSON (1803–1882). Closing words, "Experience," *Essays: Second Series*, 1844

The secret of genius is . . . first, last, midst, and without end, to honor every truth by use.

RALPH WALDO EMERSON (1803–1882). Closing words, "Goethe; or, The Writer," *Representative Men*, 1850

Every soul is potentially Genius, if not arrested.

RALPH WALDO EMERSON (1803–1882). Journal, 1861, undated

Genius believes its faintest presentiment against the testimony of all history, for it knows that facts are not ultimates, but that a state of mind is the ancestor of everything.

RALPH WALDO EMERSON (1803–1882). "Quotation and Originality," *Letters and Social Aims*, 1876

Genius without Education is like Silver in the Mine.

BENJAMIN FRANKLIN (1706–1790). *Poor Richard's Almanack*, August 1750

High original genius is always ridiculed on its first appearance; most of all by those who have won themselves the highest repu-

tation in working on the established lines. Genius only commands recognition when it has created the taste which is to appreciate it.

JAMES ANTHONY FROUDE (1818–1894). *Thomas Carlyle: A History of the First Forty Years, 1795–1835*, 2.17, 1882

[The genius] is especially inspired with the good spirit of recognizing quickly what is useful to him.

GOETHE (1749–1832). *Wilhelm Meister's Travels*, 2.9, 1829, tr. Edward Bell, 1882

An occasional genius, by extremely dexterous and willful actions, may achieve a historical mutation.

CARL G. GUSTAVSON (1915–). *A Preface to History*, 10, 1955

Genius is an infinite capacity for giving pains.

DON HEROLD (1889–1966)

The "one–sidedness" and the monomaniac quality with which the genius pursues his object, and the idée fixe of the madman on the other hand can easily induce confused concepts, especially when the genius also produces hallucinations, a symptom frequently observed in the insane, or when the madman comes up with the inspirations of a genius. What distinguishes them decisively and fundamentally is the success of their efforts.

ALFRED HOCK (1869–?). *Reason and Genius: Studies in Their Origin*, 2.4.1, 1960

See Paranoia: Ernst Kretschmer

Genius only means an infinite capacity for taking pains.

JANE ELLICE HOPKINS (1836–1904). *Work Amongst Working Men*, 1870

Genius: The ability to act wisely without precedent—the power to do the right thing for the first time. A capacity for evading hard work.

ELBERT HUBBARD (1856–1915). *The Roycroft Dictionary Concocted by Ali Baba and the Bunch on Rainy Days*, p. 60, 1914

Constant effort and frequent mistakes are the stepping stones of genius.

ELBERT HUBBARD (1856–1915). *The Philosophy of Elbert Hubbard*, p. 109, comp. Elbert Hubbard II, 1930

Not every "man" fits every "hour." . . . A given genius may come either too early or too late. Peter the Hermit would now be sent to a lunatic asylum. John [Stuart] Mill in the tenth century would have lived and died unknown.

WILLIAM JAMES (1842–1910). "Great Men and Their Environment," 1880, *Will to Believe: And Other Essays in Popular Philosophy*, 1897

Geniuses are commonly believed to excel other men in their power of sustained attention. . . . *But it is their genius making them attentive, not their attention making geniuses of them.*

WILLIAM JAMES (1842–1910). *The Principles of Psychology*, 11, 1890

Genius . . . means little more than the faculty of perceiving in an unhabitual way.

WILLIAM JAMES (1842–1910). *The Principles of Psychology*, 19, 1890

A man of genius makes no mistakes. His errors are volitional and are the portals of discovery.

JAMES JOYCE (1882–1941). "Scylla and Charybdis," *Ulysses*, 1922

Is genius genius in spite of this psychopathic component, or because of it?

> ERNST KRETSCHMER (1888–1964). *The Psychology of Men of Genius*, 1, tr. R. B. Cattell, 1931

He must seem to us one capable of doing that which we ourselves cannot do.

> WILHELM LANGE–EICHBAUM (1875–1950). *The Problem of Genius*, 1.C.3, 1931, tr. Eden and Cedar Paul, 1932

We love most of all to see a genius wearing the martyr's crown.

> WILHELM LANGE–EICHBAUM (1875–1950). *The Problem of Genius*, 1.C.3, 1931, tr. Eden and Cedar Paul, 1932

Geniuses, it has been said, serve the human race. Often enough they do; but, first of all, the genius serves himself.

> WILHELM LANGE–EICHBAUM (1875–1950). *The Problem of Genius*, 5.C.2, 1931, tr. Eden and Cedar Paul, 1932

The man who early on regards himself as a genius is lost.

> GEORG CHRISTOPH LICHTENBERG (1742–1799). *Aphorisms*, J.197, 1806, tr. R. J. Hollingdale, 1990

Towering genius disdains a beaten path. It seeks regions hitherto unexplored. It sees *no distinction* in adding story to story, upon the monuments of fame, erected to the memory of others. It *denies* that it is glory enough to serve under any chief. It *scorns* to tread in the footsteps of *any* predecessor, however illustrious. It thirsts and burns for distinction; and, if possible, it will have it, whether at the expense of emancipating slaves, or enslaving freemen.

> ABRAHAM LINCOLN (1809–1865). "The Perpetuation of Our Political Institutions," address before the Young Men's Lyceum of Springfield (Illinois), 27 January 1838

Genius sees the dynamic purpose first, finds reasons afterward.

> WALTER LIPPMANN (1889–1974). *A Preface to Politics*, 7, 1914

Genius, being essentially original and a lover of originality, is the natural enemy of traditions and conservatism: he is the born revolutionary, the precursor and the most active pioneer of revolutions.

> CESARE LOMBROSO (1836–1909). *The Man of Genius*, 4.2, 1888, ed. Havelock Ellis, 1896

The inarticulate message of his contemporaries simply becomes articulate in someone, and behold a genius.

> EVERETT DEAN MARTIN (1880–1941). *The Behavior of Crowds: A Psychological Study*, 7, 1920

Genius, all over the world, stands hand in hand, and one shock of recognition runs the whole circle round.

> HERMAN MELVILLE (1819–1891). In James Atlas, "The Great Reminiscer," *New York Times Book Review*, 3 September 1995

Persons of genius . . . are, and are always likely to be, a small minority; but in order to have them, it is necessary to preserve the soil in which they grow. Genius can only breathe freely in an *atmosphere* of freedom. Persons of genius are, more individual than any other people—less capable, consequently, of fitting themselves, without hurtful compression, into any of the small number of molds which society provides in order to save its members the trouble of forming their own character.

> JOHN STUART MILL (1806–1873). *On Liberty*, 3, 1859

A people which is becoming conscious of its dangers produces a genius.

> FRIEDRICH NIETZSCHE (1844–1900). *Philosophy and Truth: Selections from Nietzsche's Notebooks of the Early 1870's*, 1.24, tr. Daniel Breazeale, 1979

Someone who has completely lost his way in a forest, but strives with uncommon energy to get out of it in whatever direction, sometimes discovers a new, unknown way: this is how geniuses come into being, who are then praised for their originality.

> FRIEDRICH NIETZSCHE (1844–1900). *Human, All Too Human*, 231, 1878, tr. Marion Faber, 1984

His mere personal life [is] something subordinate, serving only to advance ends higher than itself.

> ARTHUR SCHOPENHAUER (1788–1860). "The Art of Literature: On Genius," *Essays of Arthur Schopenhauer*, tr. T. Bailey Saunders, 1851

It is necessary for the welfare of society that genius should be privileged to utter sedition, to blaspheme, to outrage good taste, to corrupt the youthful mind, and, generally, to scandalize its uncles.

> GEORGE BERNARD SHAW (1856–1950). Preface (1908) to *The Sanity of Art*, 1895

When a true genius appears in the world, you may know him by this sign, that the dunces are all in confederacy against him.

> JONATHAN SWIFT (1667–1745). "Thoughts on Various Subjects" (expanded from a version published in 1711), *Miscellanies in Prose and Verse* (published with Alexander Pope), vol. 1, 1727

The persecution of genius fosters its influence.

> TACITUS (A.D. 56?–120?). *Annals*, 4.35, tr. Alfred J. Church and William J. Brodribb, 1964

The emergence of a superman or a great mystic or a genius or a superior personality inevitably precipitates a social conflict. The conflict will be more or less acute, according to the degree in which the creative individual happens to rise above the average level of his former kin and kind. But some conflict is inevitable, since the social equilibrium which the genius has upset by the mere fact of his personal emergence has eventually to be restored either by his social triumph or by his social defeat.

> ARNOLD J. TOYNBEE (1889–1975). *A Study of History*, 3.236, 1934

Thousands of geniuses live and die undiscovered—either by themselves or by others.

> MARK TWAIN (1835–1910). *The Autobiography of Mark Twain*, 27, ed. Charles Neider, 1959

[Genius] is another name for the perfection of human nature; for genius is not a fact, but an ideal. It is nothing less than the possession of all the powers and impulses of humanity, in their greatest possible strength and most harmonious combination.

> EDWIN PERCY WHIPPLE (1819–1886). "Genius," *Literature and Life*, 1849

I have nothing to declare but my genius.

> OSCAR WILDE (1854–1900). Remark to a New York City customs officer, January 1882. In Frank Harris, *Oscar Wilde*, 5, 1930

❧

Genius creates the conditions which assure its success.

> ANONYMOUS

Genius prepares with difficulty and executes with ease.

ANONYMOUS

Genius sharpens itself on the whetstone of struggle.

ANONYMOUS

GENIUS & TALENT

See also • Ability ○ Genius ○ Talent ○ Wisdom & Knowledge: [especially] Josh Billings (2)

To do easily what is difficult for others is the mark of talent. To do what is impossible for talent is the mark of genius.

HENRI AMIEL (1821–1881). Journal, 17 December 1856, tr. Mrs. Humphrey Ward, 1887

One man ov genius to 97 thousand four hundred and 42 men ov tallent iz just about the rite perporshun for aktual bizzness.

JOSH BILLINGS (1818–1885). "Shooting Stars," *Everybody's Friend, or; Josh Billing's Encyclopedia and Proverbial Philosophy of Wit and Humor,* 1874

Genius does what it must, and Talent does what it can.

EDWARD ROBERT BULWER–LYTTON (1831–1891). "Last Words of a Sensitive Second-Rate Poet," *Cornhill Magazine* (English magazine), November 1860

Genius must have talent as its complement and implement. . . . The higher intellectual powers can only act through a corresponding energy of the lower.

SAMUEL TAYLOR COLERIDGE (1772–1834). 20 August 1833, *Table Talk,* 1835

Genius points the way, talent takes it.

MARIE von EBNER-ESCHENBACH (1830–1916). *Aphorisms,* p. 52, 1880–1905, tr. David Scrase and Wolfgang Mieder, 1994

The difference between talent and genius is in the direction of the current: in genius, it is from within outward; in talent, from without inward.

RALPH WALDO EMERSON (1803–1882). Journal, 4 May 1841

How many young geniuses we have known, and none but ourselves will ever hear of them for want in them of a little talent!

RALPH WALDO EMERSON (1803–1882). "The Scholar," *Lectures and Biographical Sketches,* 1883

GENIUS, like a planet, takes a wide circuit through the pure expanse of nature, and visits not regions only but whole worlds SENSE does not know to exist.

FULKE GREVILLE (1554–1628). *Maxims, Characters, and Reflections,* p. 267, 1756

The world is always ready to receive talent with open arms. Very often it does not know what to do with genius. Talent is a docile creature. It bows its head meekly while the world slips the collar over it. . . . It draws its load cheerfully, and is patient of the bit and of the whip. But genius is always impatient of its harness; its wild blood makes it hard to train.

OLIVER WENDELL HOLMES, SR. (1809–1894). *The Professor at the Breakfast-Table,* 10, 1860

Talent is a very common family trait; genius belongs rather to individuals—just as you find one giant or one dwarf in a family, but rarely a whole brood of either. Talent is often to be envied, and genius very commonly to be pitied. It stands twice the chance of the other of dying in a hospital, in jail, in debt, in bad repute. It is a perpetual insult to mediocrity; its every word is a trespass against somebody's vested ideas.

OLIVER WENDELL HOLMES, SR. (1809–1894). *The Professor at the Breakfast–Table,* 10, 1860

Talent is that which is in a man's power; genius is that in whose power a man is.

JAMES RUSSELL LOWELL (1819–1891). "Rousseau and the Sentimentalists," 1867, *Among My Books,* 1870

Genius is not talent brought to a very high degree, nor even to its limit, but it is of another order than talent.

CHARLES PÉGUY (1873–1914). "Basic Verities: The Search for Truth," *Basic Verities: Prose and Poetry,* tr. Ann and Julian Green, 1943

Talent repeats; Genius creates. Talent is a cistern; Genius, a fountain. . . . Talent accumulates knowledge, and has it packed up in the memory; Genius assimilates it with its own substance, grows with every new accession, and converts knowledge into *power.* Talent gives out what it has taken in; Genius, what has risen from its unsounded wells of living thought. Talent, in difficult situations, tries to untie knots, which Genius instantly cuts with one swift decision. Talent is full of thoughts; Genius, of thought.

EDWIN PERCY WHIPPLE (1819–1886). "Genius," *Literature and Life,* 1849

GENTLEMEN

See also • Manners

[A gentleman] never suspects that he is either slighted or laughed at, unless he is conscious that he deserves it.

LORD CHESTERFIELD (1694–1773). Letter to his son, 27 September 1749

A gentleman . . . is the natural defender and raiser of the weak and oppressed.

RALPH WALDO EMERSON (1803–1882). Journal, February? 1858

Repose and cheerfulness are the badge of the gentleman—repose in energy.

RALPH WALDO EMERSON (1803–1882). "Culture," *The Conduct of Life,* 1860

Manners and Money make a Gentleman.

THOMAS FULLER (1654–1734). Comp., *Gnomologia: Adages and Proverbs,* 3333, 1732

A gentleman is one who never hurts anyone's feelings unintentionally.

OLIVER HERFORD (1865–1935)

Reticence, sensitivity, unselfseeking, personal discipline and sobriety in dress, conduct and speech, all married to total self–assurance.

JOHN KEEGAN (1934–). Defining the English "gentlemanly ideal" embodied by the Duke of Wellington, *The Mask of Command,* 2, 1987

To be a gentleman is to be oneself, all of a seam, on camera and off.

> MURRAY KEMPTON (1917–1997). "The Party's Over," *America Comes of Middle Age*, 1963

The forbearing use of power . . . is a test of a true gentleman.

> ROBERT E. LEE (1807–1870). In Dixon Wecter, *The Hero in America: A Chronicle of Hero–Worship*, 11.1, 1941

Anonymous aide (on seeing Abraham Lincoln doff his hat to a Negro who had just greeted him on a Washington street with the same courtesy): Mr. President, [why] would you take off your hat to a ragged old rapscallion like that?
Lincoln (with a smile): My friend, I allow no man to be a greater gentleman than I am.

> ABRAHAM LINCOLN (1809–1865). Format adapted. In Brant House, comp., "1862," *Lincoln's Wit*, 1958

A gentleman is one who never strikes a woman without provocation.

> H. L. MENCKEN (1880–1956). *A Little Book in C Major*, 6.13, 1916

It is almost a definition of a gentleman to say he is one who never inflicts pain.

> CARDINAL JOHN HENRY NEWMAN (1801–1890). *The Idea of a University Defined and Illustrated*, 1.8.10, 1873

This is the final test of a gentleman: his respect for those who can be of no possible service to him.

> WILLIAM L. PHELPS (1865–1943)

Not a gentleman; dresses too well.

> BERTRAND RUSSELL (1872–1900). On Anthony Eden (British prime minister), in Alistair Cooke, *Six Men*, 5, 1977

Mendoza: I am a brigand: I live by robbing the rich.
Tanner: I am a gentleman: I live by robbing the poor.

> GEORGE BERNARD SHAW (1856–1950). *Man and Superman*, 3, 1903

To live like a drone on the labor and service of others is to be a lady or a gentleman.

> GEORGE BERNARD SHAW (1856–1950). *The Intelligent Woman's Guide to Socialism, Capitalism, Sovietism and Fascism*, 17, 1928

Every other inch a gentleman.

> REBECCA WEST (1892–1983). On Michael Arlen. In Victoria Glendinning, *Rebecca West*, 3.5, 1987

❦

A gentleman is a man who can disagree without being disagreeable.

> ANONYMOUS

GERMANY

See also • Berlin ○ Holocaust ○ Nations

We Germans fear God, but nothing else in the world.

> OTTO von BISMARCK (1815–1898). Reichstag speech, 6 February 1888.

[The Germans] combine in the most deadly manner the qualities of the warrior and the slave.

> WINSTON CHURCHILL (1874–1965). House of Commons speech, 21 September 1943

The Germans, if this [British] Government is returned [to office], are going to pay every penny; they are going to be squeezed as a lemon is squeezed—until the pips squeak. My only doubt is not whether we can squeeze hard enough, but whether there is enough juice.

> SIR ERIC GEDDES (1875–1937). British businessman and political leader. On German war reparations following in World War I, speech, Cambridge, 10 December 1918

It happens to be the destined lot of the German to emerge as the representative of all the citizens of the world.

> GOETHE (1749–1832). Letter to Büchler, 14 June 1820, tr. Hermann J. Weigand, 1949

The Germans must be set free from within. From without there is no help.

> HEINRICH HEINE (1797–1856). In Mina Curtiss, "Heinrich Heine: 1856–1956," *The Nation*, 11 February 1956

A sleep-walking people.

> ADOLF HITLER (1889–1945). On the Germans. In George Orwell, "The Lion and the Unicorn" (1.2), 19 February 1941, *The Collected Essays, Journalism and Letters of George Orwell*, vol. 2, ed. Sonia Orwell and Ian Angus, 1968

"Germany, Germany over all, over all the world!" ("Deutschland, Deutschland über Alles, über Alles in der Welt!")

> AUGUST HEINRICH HOFFMAN (1798–1874). Poem title which became the national anthem in 1922, *Das Lied der Deutschland*, 1841

In the face of death I confess that I despise the Germans for their unspeakable bestiality and am ashamed to belong to them.

> ARTHUR SCHOPENHAUER (1788–1860). In Theo. B. Hyslop, *The Great Abnormals*, 10, 1925

We know that a man can read Goethe or Rilke in the evening, that he can play Bach and Schubert, and go to his day's work at Auschwitz in the morning.

> GEORGE STEINER (1929–). French–born American writer. Preface to *Language and Silence*, 1967

High deeds, O Germans, are to come from you!

> WILLIAM WORDSWORTH (1770–1850). Opening line, "A Prophecy," 1807

GHETTOS

See also • Cities ○ Slums

All over Harlem, Negro boys and girls are growing into stunted maturity, trying desperately to find a place to stand; and the wonder is not that so many are ruined but that so many survive.

> JAMES BALDWIN (1924–1987). "The Harlem Ghetto," 1948, *Notes of a Native Son*, 1955

A ghetto can be improved in one way only: out of existence.

> JAMES BALDWIN (1924–1987). *Nobody Knows My Name: More Notes of a Native Son*, 3, 1961

So we stand here
On the edge of hell
In Harlem
And look out on the world
And wonder
What we're gonna do
In the face of what
We remember.

> LANGSTON HUGHES (1902–1967). "Harlem [1]," 1949, *The Collected Poems of Langston Hughes*, ed. Arnold Rampersad and David Roessel, 1994

The ghetto:
    kaleidoscope of shifting misery
    and shifting chance.
    Refuge of sorrows,
    dream and pawnshop:
    the stubborn penny profit,
    the moonbeam's radiance.

> ALFREDO ORTIZ-VARGAS. "El Ghetto," *Las Torres de Manhattan*, 1939

Within ghetto walls a new generation is growing along with new activities, ideologies, institutions and drugs. Crack sells briskly across the street from drug–treatment centers, and children walk past homeless shelters. An army of men strips cars, and hordes of scavengers push loaded shopping carts along the streets. Houses stand alone like fortresses, enclosed by fences. Dozens of cities are falling into ruin, and along their streets billboards beg people to stop killing one another.

> CAMILO JOSÉ VERGARA. "A Guide to the Ghettos," *Nation*, 15 March 1993

GHOSTS

you want to know
whether i believe in ghosts
of course i do not believe in them
if you had known
as many of them as i have
you would not
believe in them either.

> DON MARQUIS (1878–1937). "ghosts," *archy and mehitabel*, 1927

GIFTS

See also • Generosity ○ Giving ○ Possessions: Seneca the Younger (2)

A gift is pure when it is given from the heart to the right person at the right time and at the right place, and when we expect nothing in return.

> *BHAGAVAD GITA* (6th cent. B.C.). 17.20, tr. Juan Mascaró, 1962

God's gifts put man's best dreams to shame.

> ELIZABETH BARRETT BROWNING (1806–1861). *Sonnets from the Portuguese*, 1, 1850

The manner of giving is worth more than the gift.

> PIERRE CORNEILLE (1606–1684). *Le Menteur*, 1.1, 1642

A gift much expected is paid, not given.

> GEORGE HERBERT (1593–1633). Comp., *Outlandish Proverbs*, 574, 1640

No man ought to look a [gift]horse in the mouth.

> JOHN HEYWOOD (1497–1580). Comp., *A Dialogue Containing the Number of the Effectual Proverbs in the English Tongue*, 1.5, 1562

You never give a man a present when he's feeling good. You want to do it when he's down.

> LYNDON B. JOHNSON (1908–1973). In James Deakin, "The Dark Side of L.B.J.," *Esquire*, August 1967

Anything that has real and lasting value is always a gift from within.

> FRANZ KAFKA (1883–1924). In Gustav Janouch, "Conversations with Kafka," tr. Goronwy Rees, *Encounter*, August 1971

The greatest grace of a gift, perhaps, is that it anticipates and admits of no return.

> HENRY WADSWORTH LONGFELLOW (1807–1882). Letter to Mrs. James T. Fields, 28 February 1871

Gifts are like hooks.

> MARTIAL (A.D. 42?–102?). *Epigrams*, 5.18, tr. Walter C. A. Ker, 1919

A gift confers no rights.

> FRIEDRICH NIETZSCHE (1844–1900)

He lessens the favor conferred who waits to be asked.

> PUBLIUS SYRUS (85–43 B.C.). *Moral Sayings*, 754, tr. Darius Lyman, Jr., 1862

It is sometimes very dangerous to refuse presents from one's superiors.

> CARDINAL de RETZ (1613–1679). *Memoirs of Cardinal de Retz*, 2, Grolier Society edition, undated

The best aid to give is intellectual aid, a gift of useful knowledge. . . . Nothing becomes truly "one's own" except on the basis of some genuine effort or sacrifice. . . . The gift of material goods makes people dependent, but the gift of knowledge makes them free.

> E. F. SCHUMACHER (1911–1977). Referring to aid to people in poor countries, *Small Is Beautiful: Economics as if People Mattered*, 3.3, 1973

What then is a benefit? It is the act of a well–wisher who bestows joy and derives joy from the bestowal of it, and is inclined to do what he does from the prompting of his own will.

> SENECA THE YOUNGER (5? B.C.–A.D. 65). "On Benefits" (1.6.1), *Moral Essays*, tr. John W. Basore, 1935

Ophelia: Rich gifts wax poor when givers prove unkind.

> SHAKESPEARE (1564–1616). *Hamlet*, 3.1.101, 1600

The excellence of a gift lies in its appropriateness rather than in its value.

> CHARLES DUDLEY WARNER. (1829–1900). "Eleventh Study," *Backlog Studies*, 1873

❦

A benefit is not conferred upon one against his will.

> SAYING (LATIN)

GIVING

See also • Charity ○ Compassion ○ Generosity ○ Gifts ○ Golden Rule: [especially] Thomas Fuller ○ Good ○ Gratitude ○ Greed ○ Kindness ○ Indifference ○ Love ○ Mercy ○ Self-Interest ○ Self-Sacrifice ○ Service ○ Sharing

Nothing that I am able to give to you do I find worthy of you, and only in this way do I discover that I am a poor man. And so I give to you the only thing that I possess—myself.

> AESCHINES (5th cent. B.C.). Remark to his teacher Socrates who was receiving presents from his pupils. In Seneca the Younger (5? B.C.–A.D. 65). "On Benefits" (1.8.1), *Moral Essays,* tr. John W. Basore, 1935

The good man thinks it more blessed to give than to receive.

> ARISTOTLE (384–322 B.C.). *Nichomachean Ethics,* 4.1, tr. J. A. K. Thomson, 1953

Give to another human being without the expectation of a return.

> BILL BRADLEY (1943–). "Faith, Politics and Society." Speech at the Call to Renewal Conference, C–SPAN, September 1996

A man there was, though some did count him mad,
The more he cast away, the more he had.

> JOHN BUNYAN (1628–1688). *The Pilgrim's Progress,* 2.7, 1678–1684

He that gives quickly gives twice.

> CERVANTES (1547–1616). *Don Quixote,* 1.4.7, 1615, tr. Peter Anthony Motteux and John Ozell, 1743

We receive but what we give.

> SAMUEL TAYLOR COLERIDGE (1772–1834). "Dejection: An Ode," 4, 1802

It is in giving that we receive.

> ST. FRANCIS OF ASSISI (A.D. 1181?–1226). "The Prayer of St. Francis," attributed, tr. Leo Sherley-Price

Give freely to him that deserveth well, and asketh nothing; and that is a way of giving to thyself.

> THOMAS FULLER (1654–1734). Comp., *Introductio ad Prudentiam,* 505, 1731

There are those who give with joy, and that joy is their reward.

> KAHLIL GIBRAN (1883–1931). "On Giving," *The Prophet,* 1923

It is well to give when asked, but it is better to give unasked, through understanding.

> KAHLIL GIBRAN (1883–1931). "On Giving," *The Prophet,* 1923

We like to give but hate to lose.

> ERIC HOFFER (1902–1983). *The Passionate State of Mind: And Other Aphorisms,* 229, 1954

To give is to receive, but only if one does not give *in order* to receive.

> WADE HUDSON (1944–). Personal communication, 24 April 1998

When you give alms, do not let your left hand know what your right hand is doing, so that your alms may be in secret; and your Father who sees in secret will reward you.

> JESUS (A.D. 1st cent.). *Matthew* 6:3–4

It is more blessed to give than to receive.

> JESUS (A.D. 1st cent.). In Paul, *Acts* 20:35

Nothing that you have not given away will ever be really yours.

> C. S. LEWIS (1898–1963). *Mere Christianity,* rev. ed., 4.11, 1952

The one desire which grows more and more is to give. . . . Giving and receiving are at bottom one thing, dependent upon whether one lives open or closed. Living openly one becomes a medium, a transmitter; living thus, as a river, one experiences life to the full, flows along with the current of life, and dies in order to live again as an ocean.

> HENRY MILLER (1891–1980). *The Colossus of Maroussi,* 3, 1941

We attach ourselves more readily to those whom we have benefited than to our benefactors.

> NAPOLEON (1769–1821). Remark to Gaspard Gaspard, 1817, *The Mind of Napoleon: A Selection from His Written and Spoken Words,* 7, ed. J. Christopher Herold, 1955

God loves a cheerful giver.

> PAUL (A.D. 1st cent.). *2 Corinthians,* 9:7

Students (reproachfully): Why did you give your last coin to a man of evil reputation?
The Sassover: Shall I be more particular than God, who gave the coin to me?

> THE SASSOVER (1745–1807). Format adapted. In Louis I. Newman, comp., *The Hasidic Anthology,* 78.9, 1934

There is no greater joy in life than giving to worthy causes.

> TED TURNER (1938–). Remark to reporters the day after announcing his $1 billion gift to the United Nations, 19 September 1997. In Howard Fineman, "Why Ted Gave It Away," *Newsweek,* 29 September 1997

When I give I give myself.

> WALT WHITMAN (1819–1892). "Song of Myself" (40), 1855, *Leaves of Grass,* 1855–1892
>
> See Revelations: Thomas à Kempis

The habit of giving only enhances the desire to give.

> WALT WHITMAN (1819–1892). "Notes for Lectures on Religion," *Walt Whitman's Workshop: A Collection of Unpublished Manuscripts,* ed. Clifton Joseph Furness, 1964

❧

Give what thou hast, then shalt thou receive.

> ANONYMOUS. "Mystic injunction from . . . the so-called Mithras Liturgy." In Carl G. Jung, letter to Sigmund Freud, 31 August 1910, tr. R. F. C. Hull, 1974

Those who give cheerfully give twice—once to others, once to themselves.

> ANONYMOUS

One man gives freely, yet grows all the richer;
  another withholds what he should give, and only suffers want.

> SAYING (*BIBLE*). *Proverbs* 11:24

Give all, but without expectation or hope of recompense.

> SAYING. In Pope John XXIII (1881–1963). A favorite saying, *Wit and Wisdom of Good Pope John,* 6, ed. Henri Fesquet and tr. Salvator Attanasio, 1964

Receive no more than you need; give no less than you can.
SAYING

GLORY

See also • Dignity ∘ Fame ∘ God & Nature: Isaiah ∘ Honor ∘ Shame ∘ Tyranny: Thomas Paine

What Price Glory?
MAXWELL ANDERSON (1888–1959) and LAURENCE STALLINGS (1894–1968). Play title, 1924

Glory and honor are the spurs to virtue.
FRANCIS BACON (1561–1626). *Advancement of Learning,* 6.3 (Sophism 10), 1605, Willey Book edition, 1944

The greater the difficulty, the greater the glory.
CICERO (106–43 B.C.). *De officiis,* 1.19, tr. Walter Miller, 1913

Glory, built
On selfish principles, is shame and guilt.
WILLIAM COWPER (1731–1800). Opening lines, "Table Talk," 1782

My infant imagination was idolatrous of glory.
RALPH WALDO EMERSON (1803–1882). Journal, 13 May 1822

What is more glorious than a soul when it liberates itself?
ANDRÉ GIDE (1869–1951). Journal, 1916 (detached page), tr. Justin O'Brien, 1948

The glory's nought, the deed is all.
GOETHE (1749–1832). *Faust,* 2.4 ("Mountain Heights"), 1808–1832, tr. Philip Wayne, 1959

The paths of glory lead but to the grave.
THOMAS GRAY (1716–1771). "Elegy Written in a Country Churchyard," 9, 1750

Glory is largely a theatrical concept. There is no striving for glory without a vivid awareness of an audience—the knowledge that our mighty deeds will come to the ears of our contemporaries or "of those who are to be."
ERIC HOFFER (1902–1983). *The True Believer: Thoughts on the Nature of Mass Movements,* 47, 1951

The glory of great men must always be measured against the means they have used to acquire it.
LA ROCHEFOUCAULD (1613–1680). *Maxims,* 157, 1665, tr. Leonard Tancock, 1959

All that is in the heavens and the earth glorifieth Allah.
MUHAMMAD (A.D. 570?–632). *Quran,* 57.1, A.D. 670?, tr. Mohammed Marmaduke Pickthall, 1953

The man who is completely wise and virtuous has no need at all of glory, except so far as it disposes and eases his way of action the greater trust that it procures him.
PLUTARCH (A.D. 46?–119?). "Agis," *Parallel Lives,* Dryden edition, 1693
See Fame: Booker T. Washington ∘ Popularity: Theodore Roosevelt

The nearest way to glory . . . is to strive to be what you wish to be thought to be.
SOCRATES (470?–399 B.C.). In Cicero (106–43 B.C.), *De officiis,* 2.12, tr. Walter Miller, 1913

The desire of glory is the last infirmity cast off even by the wise.
TACITUS (A.D. 56?–120?). *The History,* 4.6, tr. Alfred J. Church and William J. Brodribb, 1942

The path of duty be the way to glory.
ALFRED, LORD TENNYSON (1809–1892). "Ode on the Death of the Duke of Wellington," 8, 1852

The glory of a good man is the witness of a good conscience.
THOMAS à KEMPIS (1380–1471). *The Imitation of Christ,* 2.6, tr. Leo–Sherley-Price, 1952

The heavens declare the glory of God; and the firmament sheweth his handiwork.
ANONYMOUS (*BIBLE*). *Psalms* 19:1 (King James Version)
See God & Nature: Isaiah

Glory is acquired, honor is inherited; glory is ours to win, honor is ours to lose.
ANONYMOUS

Glory seldom comes to those who dream of it, to fewer still who don't.
ANONYMOUS

No guts, no glory.
SAYING (AMERICAN)

GLUTTONY

See also • Disease: [especially] Benjamin Franklin (1) ∘ Excess ∘ Food ∘ Hunger

Gluttony is an emotional escape, a sign that something is eating us.
PETER DE VRIES (1910–1993). *Comfort Me with Apples,* 15, 1956

Intemperate eating kills more people than tobacco and alcohol, because it is the most widespread fault. . . . If people knew how to eat properly they would retain their youthful resiliency much longer.
HENRY FORD (1863–1947). Interview with the author. In George Sylvester Viereck, "The Metaphysics of Henry Ford" (1), *Glimpses of the Great,* 1930

A full Belly makes a dull Brain.
BENJAMIN FRANKLIN (1706–1790). *Poor Richard's Almanack,* August 1758

Gluttony kills more than the sword.
GEORGE HERBERT (1593–1633). Comp., *Outlandish Proverbs,* 503, 1640

I saw few die of hunger, of eating much a hundred thousand.
JAMES HOWELL (1594?–1666). Comp., "Spanish" (p. 11), *Paroimiographia: Proverbs, or Old Sayed Sawes & Adages in English . . . Italian, French and Spanish,* 1659

The Gluttons dig their own graves with their teeth.
JAMES HOWELL (1593–1666). Comp., "French" (p. 13), *Paroimiographia: Proverbs, or Old Sayed Sawes & Adages in English . . . Italian, French and Spanish,* 1659

Most illnesses which befall men arise either from bad food, or from immoderate indulgence in food, even of the wholesome kind.

> MOSES MAIMONIDES (A.D. 1135–1204). In Lewis Browne, ed., *The Wisdom of Israel,* p. 356, 1962

⚘

We live off half of what we eat, and the doctors live off the other half.

> SAYING

Take twice as long to eat half as much.

> SAYING

GOALS

See also • Ambition: Madonna ○ Means & Ends ○ Purpose

It is not enough to take steps which may some day lead to a goal; each step must be itself a goal and a step likewise.

> GOETHE (1749–1832). 18 September 1823. In Peter Eckermann, *Conversations with Goethe,* 1836–1848, tr. John Oxenford, 1850

Nobody knows what the goal is—we are sailing under sealed orders.

> ELBERT HUBBARD (1856–1915). In *The Philosophy of Elbert Hubbard,* p. 32, comp. Elbert Hubbard II, 1930

The going is the goal.

> HORACE KALLEN. In Herbert J. Muller, *The Uses of the Past: Profiles of Former Societies,* 11.3, 1952

Our goal is to create a beloved community, and this will require a qualitative change in our souls as well as a quantitative change in our lives.

> MARTIN LUTHER KING, JR. (1929–1968). "Nonviolence: The Only Road to Freedom," *Ebony,* October 1966

The final goal of human effort is man's self-transformation.

> LEWIS MUMFORD (1895–1990). *The Conduct of Life,* 9.1, 1951

By losing your goal—you have lost your way, too!

> FRIEDRICH NIETZSCHE (1844–1900). "The Shadow," *Thus Spoke Zarathustra,* 1892, tr. R. J. Hollingdale, 1961

The highest goal of mankind is the liberty of the individual.

> ERNEST RENAN (1823–1892). *Marcus Aurelius,* 1882. In Jacob Burckhardt, *Judgments on History and Historians,* 11, tr. Harry Zohn, 1958

The value of the goal lies in the goal itself; and therefore the goal cannot be attained unless it is pursued for its own sake.

> ARNOLD J. TOYNBEE (1889–1975). *A Study of History,* 12.563, 1961

GOD

See also • Agnosticism ○ Atheism ○ Bible ○ Confession ○ Conscience ○ Conversion ○ Day of Judgment ○ Devil ○ Evangelism ○ Faith ○ Forgiveness ○ Fortune ○ Freedom ○ God & History ○ God & Man ○ God & Man: First Person ○ God & Nature ○ God & the Devil ○ God & the World ○ Grace ○ Heaven ○ History ○ Idolatry ○ Man ○ Miracles ○ Morality ○ Mysticism ○ Nature ○ Prayer ○ Prayers ○ Purpose ○ Redemption ○ Religion ○ Repentance ○ Revelation ○ Revelations ○ Salvation ○ Scripture ○ Self-Realization (Becoming) ○ Self–Realization (Being) ○ Soul ○ Spirituality ○ Trust

If it turns out that there is a God, I don't think he's evil. But the worst thing that you can say about him is that basically he's an underachiever.

> WOODY ALLEN (1935–). *Love and Death* (film), 1975

The Oneness of many and the manifoldness of One.

> PANDIT USHARBUDH ARYA (1934–). "Maxims on Universal Laws," *Dawn,* vol. 6, no. 1, 1986

Who is He? I can think of no better answer than, He who is.

> ST. BERNARD (A.D. 1090–1153). Quoted by Aldous Huxley, "Reflections on the Lord's Prayer—I." In Christopher Isherwood, ed., *Vedanta for the Western World,* 1945

From him comes destruction, and from him comes creation.

> *BHAGAVAD GITA* (6th cent. B.C.). 13.16, tr. Juan Mascaró, 1962

If God is, whence come evil things? If He is not, whence come good.

> BOETHIUS (A.D. 480–524). *The Consolation of Philosophy,* 1, tr. W. V. Cooper, 1981

Almighty God, the fountain of all Goodness.

> THE BOOK OF COMMON PRAYER. "Morning Prayer," 1662

God is love, so loving that, whatever he can love he must love, whether he will or not.

> MEISTER ECKHART (A.D. 1260–1328). "Fragments" (32), *Meister Eckhart: A Modern Translation,* tr. R. B. Blakney, 1941

Our Father-Mother God, all-harmonious.

> MARY BAKER EDDY (1821–1910). *Science and Health with Key to the Scriptures,* p. 16, 1875

God is subtle, but he is not malicious.

> ALBERT EINSTEIN (1879–1955). Remark made during his first visit to Princeton University (New Jersey), in April 1921, later inscribed above the fireplace of the Common Room in Princeton's Fine Hall. In Ronald W. Clark, *Einstein,* 14, 1971

At any rate, I am convinced that *He* does not play dice.

> ALBERT EINSTEIN (1879–1955). Letter to Max Born, 4 December 1926 (Popular version: God doesn't play dice with the universe.)

Light is but his shadow dim.

> RALPH WALDO EMERSON (1803–1882). Journal, 6 July 1831

God is day and night, winter and summer, war and peace, satiety and hunger.

> HERACLITUS (540?–480? B.C.). In T. V. Smith, ed., "Heraclitus" (36), *From Thales to Plato,* 2, 1934

The grandeur and majesty of God do not come to expression in the display of ultimate sovereignty and power, but rather in rendering righteousness and mercy.

> ABRAHAM JOSHUA HESCHEL (1907–1972). *The Prophets,* 11, 1962

God's absence is an illusion.

> ABRAHAM JOSHUA HESCHEL (1907–1972). *A Passion for Truth,* 1, 1973

God is love.

> JOHN (A.D. 1st cent.). *1 John* 4:8
> See Love: Lew Wallace

Yahweh is both just and unjust, kindly and cruel, truthful and deceitful.

> CARL G. JUNG (1875–1961). "A Psychological View of Conscience," 1958, *Civilization in Transition,* tr. R. F. C. Hull, 1964

God's Way is gain that works no harm.

> LAO-TZU (6th cent. B.C.). *The Way of Life,* 81, tr. R. B. Blakney, 1955

The greatest of all perplexities in theology has been to reconcile the infinite goodness of God with his omnipotence.

> WALTER LIPPMANN (1889–1974)

Where is the God of justice?

> MALACHI. *Malachi* 2:17

Eternal King; thee Author of all being,
Fountain of Light, thy self invisible.

> JOHN MILTON (1608–1674). *Paradise Lost,* 3.374, 1667

Know therefore this day, and lay it to your heart, that the Lord is God in heaven above and on the earth beneath; there is no other.

> MOSES (14th cent. B.C.). *Deuteronomy* 4:39

God is one.

> MOSES (14th cent. B.C.). *Deuteronomy* 6:4
> See God & the World: Anonymous (2) ○ Unity: Xenophanes

God is gentle and loves gentleness.

> MUHAMMAD (A.D. 570?–632). *The Sayings of Muhammad,* 198, tr. Abdullah Al-Suhrawardy, 1941

It is incomprehensible that God should exist, and it is incomprehensible that He should not exist.

> BLAISE PASCAL (1623–1662). *Pensées,* 230, 1670, tr. William F. Trotter, 1931

No master but God.

> ERNEST RENAN (1823–1892). *The Life of Jesus,* 14, 1863, Modern Library edition, 1927

[God is] a circle whose center is everywhere and circumference nowhere.

> TIMAEUS OF LOCRIS (4th cent. B.C.). Greek Astronomer. In Voltaire, *Philosophical Dictionary,* 1764, tr. H. I. Woolf, 1924

God's love is unlimited but . . . his power is not.

> ARNOLD J. TOYNBEE (1889–1975). *Experiences,* 1.9.2, 1969

All things speak of God.

> EDWARD YOUNG (1683–1765). *The Complaint: or, Night Thoughts on Life, Death, and Immortality,* 9.774, 1742–1745

❦

Righteousness and justice are the foundation of thy throne; steadfast love and faithfulness go before thee.

> ANONYMOUS (*BIBLE*). *Psalms* 89:14

To an unknown god.

> ANONYMOUS (GREEK). Inscription on an Athenian altar. In Paul. In *Acts* 17:23

GOD & HISTORY

See also • Evolution ○ God ○ God & the World ○ History ○ Man ○ Progress ○ Purpose ○ World

The God of the universe is the God of history.

> MARTIN BUBER (1878–1965). In Maurice Friedman, "Martin Buber's Influence on Twentieth Century Religious Thought," *Judaism,* Fall 1985

The Judeo–Christian [system sees] history as a spiritual progression toward the Kingdom of God.

> PETER W. DICKSON. *Kissinger and the Meaning of History,* 2, 1978

God governs the world; the actual working of His government, the carrying out of His plan, is the history of the world.

> GEORG HEGEL (1770–1831). Introduction (3.2.2) to *Philosophy of History,* 1832, tr. John Sibree, 1900

It is as if a *divine cunning* operated in human history, using our instincts as pretexts for the attainment of goals which are universally valid, a scheme to harness man's lower forces in the service of higher ends.

> ABRAHAM JOSHUA HESCHEL (1907–1972). *Man Is Not Alone: A Philosophy of Religion,* 21, 1951
> See Purpose: Heschel

The purposes of the Almighty are perfect and must prevail, though we erring mortals may fail to accurately perceive them in advance. We hoped for a happy termination of this terrible war long before this, but God knows best and has ruled otherwise. We shall yet acknowledge His wisdom and our own error therein. Meanwhile we must work earnestly in the best light He gives us, trusting that so working still conduces to the great ends He ordains. Surely He intends some great good to follow this mighty convulsion, which no mortal could make, and no mortal could stay.

> ABRAHAM LINCOLN (1806–1865) Letter to Eliza P. Gurney, 4 September 1864

The Great Disposer of events.

> ABRAHAM LINCOLN (1806–1865). "Proclamation of Thanksgiving," 20 October 1864

God lives and is observable in the whole of history. Every deed bears witness of him, every moment proclaims his name but especially do we find it in the connecting line that runs through history.

> LEOPOLD von RANKE (1795–1886). German historian. Letter to his brother, 1826. In Pieter Geyl, *Debates with Historians,* rev. ed., 1, 1958 (1955)

History [is] the record of divine manifestations imperfectly understood.

> LEOPOLD von RANKE (1795–1886). German historian. In Page Smith, *The Historian and History,* 5, 1964

History is not a cyclic and not a mechanical process. It is the masterful and progressive execution, on the narrow stage of this world, of a divine plan.

ARNOLD J. TOYNBEE (1889–1975). "My View of History," 1947, *Civilization on Trial*, 1948

History [is] a vision of God's creation on the move.

ARNOLD J. TOYNBEE (1889–1975). *A Study of History*, 10.3, 1954

GOD & MAN

See also • Day of Judgment ○ Dreams: George Fox, Homer, Carl G. Jung (5), Anonymous (*Bible*) (2) ○ Fortune ○ God ○ God & Man: First Person ○ Good & Evil: Aldous Huxley (2) ○ Holocaust: Eli Wiesel (all) ○ Man ○ Mysticism ○ Progress ○ Purpose: [especially] Arnold J. Toynbee, *Westminster Shorter Catechism of the Presbyterian Church* ○ Redemption ○ Revelation ○ Salvation: [especially] Lewis Mumford, George Bernard Shaw ○ Self-Trust: Ralph Waldo Emerson (3) ○ Spirituality

People whose history and future were threatened each day by extinction considered that it was only by divine intervention that they were able to live at all. I find it interesting that the meanest life, the poorest existence, is attributed to God's will, but as human beings become more affluent, as their living standard and style begin to ascend the material scale, God descends the scale of responsibility at a commensurate speed.

MAYA ANGELOU (1928–). *I Know Why the Caged Bird Sings*, 18, 1970

If the concept of God has any validity or any use, it can only be to make us larger, freer, and more loving. If God cannot do this, then it is time we got rid of Him.

JAMES BALDWIN (1924–1987). "Down at the Cross: Letter from a Region in My Mind," *The Fire Next Time*, 1963

God needs us, just as we need God. Why should He need us unless it be to love us? . . . [In this view, Creation is] God undertaking to create creators, that He may have, besides Himself, beings worthy of His love.

HENRI BERGSON (1859–1941). "Dynamic Religion," *The Two Sources of Morality and Religion*, 1932, tr. R. Ashley Audra and Cloudesley Brereton, 1935

When a man sees that the God in himself is the same God in all that is, he hurts not himself by hurting others: then he goes indeed to the highest Path.

BHAGAVAD GITA (6th cent. B.C.). 13.28, tr. Juan Mascaró, 1962

The Lord lives in the heart of every creature.

BHAGAVAD GITA (6th cent. B.C.). 18, tr. Swami Prabhavananda and Christopher Isherwood, 1954

Sagredo: Where is God in your system of the universe?
Galileo: Within ourselves. Or—nowhere.

BERTOLT BRECHT (1898–1956). *Galileo*, 3, 1939, tr. Charles Laughton, 1961

God is usually on the side of the big squadrons against the small.

BUSSY-RABUTIN (1618–1693). Letter to Comte de Limoges, 18 October 1677

See Courage: Tacitus ○ Fortune: Terence

When the Lord himself answers Job out of the whirlwind, He makes no attempt to vindicate His work in ethical terms, but only magnifies His Presence, bidding Job do likewise on earth in human emulation of the way of heaven [*Job* 40:7–14].

JOSEPH CAMPBELL (1904–1987). *The Hero with a Thousand Faces*, 1.2.4, 1949

God expects but one thing of you, and that is that you . . . let God be God in you.

MEISTER ECKHART (A.D. 1260?–1328?). In Aldous Huxley, *The Perennial Philosophy*, 10, 1946

God can no more do without us than we can do without him.

MEISTER ECKHART (A.D. 1260?–1328?)

Man has access to the entire mind of the Creator, is himself the creator in the finite. This view . . . animates me to create my own world through the purification of my soul.

RALPH WALDO EMERSON (1803–1882). "Spirit," *Nature*, 1836

Think of God more frequently than you breathe.

EPICTETUS (A.D. 55?–135?). Fragment, 119, tr. George Long, 1890?

God is involved with humanity in a process of spiritual evolution.

SETH FARBER (1951–). "Overcoming Psychoanalysis: A Sketch of a Metaphysics of Faith," unpublished paper, 1987

The Lord showed me, so that I did see clearly, that He did not dwell in these temples which men had commanded and set up, but in people's hearts. . . . His people were His temple, and He dwelt in them.

GEORGE FOX (1624–1691). 1646, *The Journal of George Fox*, 1694, rev. Norman Penney, 1924

That there in one God, who made all things.
   That he governs the world by his providence.
   That he might be worshipped by adoration, prayer, and thanksgiving.
   But that the most acceptable service of God is doing good to man.
   That the soul is immortal.
   And that God will certainly reward virtue and punish vice, either here or hereafter.

BENJAMIN FRANKLIN (1706–1790). "An intended creed," 1730s, *Autobiography*, 1798

He who would be friends with God must remain alone or make the whole world his friend.

MOHANDAS K. GANDHI (1869–1948). *An Autobiography: The Story of My Experiments with Truth*, 1.6, 1929, tr. Mahadev Desai, 1940

The Eternal–Feminine
Draws us onward.

GOETHE (1749–1832). Closing lines, *Faust*, 1808–1832, tr. Charles E. Passage, 1965

"To Know God Is to Do Justice."

GUSTAVO GUTIÉRREZ. Section heading, *A Theology of Liberation: History, Politics and Salvation*, 10, 1971, tr. Caridad Inda and John Eagleson, 1973

Providence seldom [grants] to mortals any more than just that degree of encouragement which suffices to keep them at a reasonably full exertion of their powers.

NATHANIEL HAWTHORNE (1804–1864). *The House of Seven Gables,* 3, 1851

Our need of Him is but an echo of His need of us.

ABRAHAM JOSHUA HESCHEL (1907–1972). *Man Is Not Alone,* 23, 1951

The supreme imperative is not merely to believe in God but to do the will of God.

ABRAHAM JOSHUA HESCHEL (1907–1972). *God in Search of Man: A Philosophy of Judaism,* 29, 1955

God's dream is not to be alone, [but] to have mankind as a partner in the drama of continuous creation. By whatever we do, by every act we carry out, we either advance or obstruct the drama of redemption.

ABRAHAM JOSHUA HESCHEL (1907–1972). Closing words, *Who Is Man?* 1965

God comes at last when we think he is farthest off.

JAMES HOWELL (1593–1666). Comp., "Italian" (p. 6), *Paroimiographia: Proverbs, or Old Sayed Sawes & Adages in English . . . Italian, French and Spanish,* 1659

[God is equally] present in all creatures; but all creatures are not equally aware of the fact.

ALDOUS HUXLEY (1894–1963). "The Magical and the Spiritual." In Christopher Isherwood, ed., *Vedanta for the Western World,* 1945

It is only by becoming Godlike that we can know God—and to become Godlike is to identify ourselves with the divine element which in fact constitutes our essential nature, but of which, in our mainly voluntary ignorance, we choose to remain unaware.

ALDOUS HUXLEY (1894–1963). Paraphrasing Plato, *The Perennial Philosophy,* 1, 1946

The chessboard is the world; the pieces are the phenomena of the universe; the rules of the game are what we call the laws of Nature. The player on the other side is hidden from us. We know that his play is always fair, just, and patient. But also we know, to our cost, that he never overlooks a mistake, or makes the smallest allowance for ignorance.

T. H. HUXLEY (1825–1895). "A Liberal Education," *Lay Sermons, Addresses, and Reviews,* 1870

We are fellow workers with God in realizing His purposes in time.

DEAN WILLIAM RALPH INGE (1860–1954). "Confessio Fidei," *Outspoken Essays: Second Series,* 1922

Thou meetest him that joyfully works righteousness.

ISAIAH (8th cent. B.C.). *Isaiah* 64:5

We and God have business with each other; and in opening ourselves to his influence our deepest destiny is fulfilled. The universe . . . takes a turn genuinely for the worse or for the better in proportion as each one of us fulfills or evades God's demands.

WILLIAM JAMES (1842–1910). *The Varieties of Religious Experience: A Study in Human Nature,* 20, 1902

Man is the link between God and Nature. . . . As God has descended into man, so man must ascend to God.

JILI (1366–1428). Sufi metaphysician. In Whitall N. Perry, comp., *A Treasury of Traditional Wisdom,* p. 50, 1986

The word of God lives in you.

JOHN (A.D. 1st cent.). *1 John* 2:14

Just as man was once revealed out of God, so, when the circle closes, God may be revealed out of man.

CARL G. JUNG (1875–1961). "A Psychological Approach to the Dogma of the Trinity" (5.1), 1942, *Psychology and Religion: West and East,* tr. R. F. C. Hull, 1958

Man always has some mental reservation, even in the face of divine decrees. Otherwise, where would be his freedom? And what would be the use of that freedom if it could not threaten Him who threatens it?

CARL G. JUNG (1875–1961). *Memories, Dreams, Reflections,* 7, ed. Aniela Jaffé, 1962

God is imperiled. He is not almighty, that we may cross our hands, waiting for certain victory. He is not all-holy, that we may wait trustingly for him to pity and to save us.

Within the province of our ephemeral flesh all of God is imperiled. He cannot be saved unless we save him with our own struggles; nor can we be saved unless he is saved.

We are one.

NIKOS KAZANTZAKIS (1883–1957). "The Action: The Relationship between God and Man," 39–41, *The Saviors of God: Spiritual Exercises,* 1927, tr. Kimon Friar, 1960

Here on earth, God's work must surely be our own.

JOHN F. KENNEDY (1917–1963). *Inaugural Address,* 20 January 1961

Men forget to ask: "What will God think?" And so they live in fear because they tend to seek social approval on the horizontal plane rather than spiritual devotion on the vertical plane.

MARTIN LUTHER KING, JR. (1929–1968). *Stride Toward Freedom,* 11, 1958

Man has a dual citizenry. He lives both in time and in eternity; both in heaven and on earth. But he owes his ultimate allegiance to God.

MARTIN LUTHER KING, JR. (1929–1968). *Stride Toward Freedom,* 11, 1958

He who loves God above all things is at length the friend of God.

GOTTFRIED LEIBNITZ (1646–1716). "Ethical Definitions," 1697–1698, *The Philosophic Works of Leibnitz,* ed. George Martin Duncan, 1908

He who loves God loves all.

GOTTFRIED LEIBNITZ (1646–1716). "Ethical Definitions," 1697–1698, *The Philosophic Works of Leibnitz,* ed. George Martin Duncan, 1908

If there is a God, we're all it.

JOHN LENNON (1940–1980). Interview with Jann Wenner "Part One: The Working Class Hero," *Rolling Stone,* 7 January 1971

Man's love of God is identical with his knowledge of Him.

MOSES MAIMONIDES (A.D. 1135–1204). *The Guide for the Perplexed,* 3.51, A.D. 1190, tr. M. Friedländer, 1904

We were born to make manifest the glory of God that is within us. It's not just in some of us, it's in every one. And as we let our own light shine, we unconsciously give other people permission to do the same.

NELSON MANDELA (1918–). South African president. *Inaugural Address*, 10 May 1994

Even those who resist Him carry out His will without realizing that they are doing so.

THOMAS MERTON (1915–1968). *No Man Is an Island*, 4.2, 1955

We could not seek God unless He were seeking us.

THOMAS MERTON (1915–1968). *No Man Is an Island*, 13.2, 1955

To serve the God of Love one must be free, one must face the terrible responsibility of the decision to love *in spite of all unworthiness* whether in oneself or in one's neighbor.

THOMAS MERTON (1915–1968). *New Seeds of Contemplation*, 10, 1961

You will find [the Lord your God], if you search after him with all your heart and with all your soul.

MOSES (14th cent. B.C.). *Deuteronomy* 4:29

Be strong and of good courage, do not fear or be in dread of them: for it is the Lord your God who goes with you; he will not fail you or forsake you.

MOSES (14th cent. B.C.). *Deuteronomy* 31:6

In the name of Allah, the Beneficent, the Merciful.
1. Praise be to Allah, Lord of the Worlds,
2. Beneficent, the Merciful.
3. Owner of the Day of Judgment,
4. Thee (alone) we worship; Thee (alone) we ask for help.
5. Show us the straight path,
6. The path of those whom Thou has favored;
7. Not (the path) of those who earn Thine anger nor of those who go astray.

MUHAMMAD (A.D. 570?–632). Opening words, *Quran*, A.D. 670?, tr. Mohammed Marmaduke Pickthall, 1953

Allah changeth not the condition of a folk until they (first) change that which is in their hearts.

MUHAMMAD (A.D. 570?–632). *Quran*, 13.11, A.D. 70?, tr. Mohammed Marmaduke Pickthall, 1953

There is no God save Him. Unto Him is the journeying.

MUHAMMAD (A.D. 570?–632). *Quran*, 40.3, A.D. 670?, tr. Mohammed Marmaduke Pickthall, 1953

Trust in God: She will provide.

EMMELINE PANKHURST (1858–1928). English suffragist. In "The New Feminists: Revolt Against Sexism" (footnote), *Time*, 21 November 1969

Do you not know that you are God's temple and that God's spirit dwells in you?

PAUL (A.D. 1st cent.). *1 Corinthians* 3:16

It is only through love that we can attain to communion with God. All living knowledge of God rests upon this foundation: that we experience Him in our lives as Will–to–Love.

ALBERT SCHWEITZER (1875–1965). *Out of My Life and Thought: An Autobiography*, 21, tr. C. T. Campion, 1933

See Power: Friedrich Nietzsche (2)

We do not need to uplift our hands towards heaven, or to beg the keeper of a temple to let us approach his idol's ear, as if in this

way our prayers were more likely to be heard. God is near you, he is with you, he is within you.

SENECA THE YOUNGER (5? B.C.–A.D. 65). "On the God Within Us," *Moral Letters to Lucilius*, 41.1, tr. Richard M. Gummere, 1918

Hamlet: There's a divinity that shapes our ends,
Rough–hew them how we will.

SHAKESPEARE (1564–1616). *Hamlet*, 5.2.10, 1600

We are here to help God, to do His work, to remedy His old errors, to strive towards Godhead ourselves.

GEORGE BERNARD SHAW (1856–1950). Letter to Leo Tolstoy, 1909. In Michael Holroyd, *Bernard Shaw: The Pursuit of Power, 1898–1918*, 5.1, 1989

God, being unable to affect His purposes without hands and brains, has made us evolve our hands and brains to act and think for Him: in short, we are not in the hands of God; but God is in our hands.

GEORGE BERNARD SHAW (1856–1950). *Everybody's Political What's What*, 37, 1944

When you have succeeded in enshrining God within your heart, you will see Him everywhere.

SWAMI SHIVANANDA (1887–1963). "Spiritual Maxims." In Christopher Isherwood, ed., *Vedanta for the Western World*, 1945

God is truly on the side of the biggest bank accounts.

ADAM SMITH (1930–) (Pen name of GEORGE J. W. GOODMAN). *The Money Game*, 21, 1967

Such as men themselves are, such will God Himself seem to them to be.

JOHN SMITH THE PLATONIST (1618–1652). In Dorothy Norman, *The Hero: Myth/Image/Symbol*, 24, 1969

There is no mediator between God's children and God.

TALMUD (A.D. 1st–6th cent.). Rabbinical writings

Speak to Him, thou, for He hears,
    and Spirit with Spirit can meet—
Closer is He than breathing,
    and nearer than hands and feet.

ALFRED, LORD TENNYSON (1809–1892). "The Higher Pantheism" (6), *The Holy Grail and Other Poems*, 1869

God genuinely puts His created works in jeopardy . . . in order to win an opportunity for creating something new.

ARNOLD J. TOYNBEE (1889–1975). "My View of History," 1947, *Civilization on Trial*, 1948

God has created Man to be God's free partner in the work of creation.

ARNOLD J. TOYNBEE (1889–1975). "Man Owes His Freedom to God," *Collier's*, 30 March 1956

None of us can be as great as God, but any of us can be as good.

MARK TWAIN (1835–1910). 30 December 1902, *Mark Twain's Notebook*, ed. Albert Bigelow Paine, 1935

"If God did not exist, it would be necessary to invent him." I am rarely satisfied with my lines, but I own that I have a father's tenderness for that one.

VOLTAIRE (1694–1778). Letter to M. Saurin, 10 November 1770

The concept of "God" is the way in which we understand this incredible fact—that what cannot be, yet is.

> ALFRED NORTH WHITEHEAD (1861–1947). *Process and Reality: An Essay in Cosmology,* 5.2.6, 1929

❧

What is man that thou art mindful of him,
    and the son of man that thou dost care for him?
Yet thou has made him little less than God,
    and dost crown him with glory and honor.
Thou has given him dominion over the works of thy hands;
    thou has put all things under his feet.

> ANONYMOUS (*BIBLE*). Psalms 8:4–6

I say, "You are gods,
    sons of the Most High, all of you."

> ANONYMOUS (*BIBLE*). Psalms 82:6

He himself would be with them, whether invoked or uninvoked.

> ANONYMOUS (GREEK). In Thucydides (460?–400? B.C.), *The Peloponnesian War,* 2.42, tr. Richard Crawley and rev. T. E. Wick, 1982

In him we live and move and have our being.

> ANONYMOUS (GREEK?). Quoted by Paul, *Acts* 17:28

Called or not called, God will be present,

> ANONYMOUS (LATIN). An inscription in Latin over the door of Carl G. Jung's home, Switzerland, quoted by James C. Aylward, "Memory of an Immortal." In Ferne Jensen, ed., *C. G. Jung, Emma Jung and Toni Wolff: A Collection of Remembrances,* 1982

Because God is seeking us, we will eventually find Him.

> ANONYMOUS

Is God a figment of our imagination? Or are we a figment of His?

> ANONYMOUS

There are limits to God's power but not to Her love.

> ANONYMOUS

We are both the instruments and beneficiaries of God's mercy.

> ANONYMOUS

In all your ways acknowledge him,
    and he will make straight your paths.

> SAYING (*BIBLE*). Proverbs 3:6

GOD & MAN: FIRST PERSON

See also • God & Man ○ Prayers ○ Revelations ○ Spirituality: First Person ○ Truth: Meister Eckhart ○ World War I: Peter Vansittart

God in me, God without! Beyond compare!
A Being wholly here and wholly there!

> ANGELUS SILESIUS (1624–1677)

I fear God, yet am not afraid of Him.

> SIR THOMAS BROWNE (1605–1682). *Religio Medici,* 1.52, 1642, ed. John Addington Symonds, 1886

I am in a good mood: God is good; I am sullen: God is wicked; I am indifferent: He is neutral. My states confer upon Him corresponding attributes.

> E. M. CIORAN (1911–1995). *A Short History of Decay,* 4 ("Theology"), 1949, tr. Richard Howard, 1975

Of Course—I prayed—
And did God Care?
He cared as much as on the Air
A Bird—had stamped her foot—
And cried "Give Me"—
My Reason—Life—
I had not had—but for Yourself—

> EMILY DICKINSON (1830–1886). "Of Course—I prayed—," 1862?

God gave a Loaf to every Bird—
But just a Crumb—to Me—

> EMILY DICKINSON (1830–1886). "God gave a Loaf to every Bird," 1863?

I believe we shall in some manner be cherished by our Maker—that the One who gave us this remarkable earth has the power still farther to surprise that which He has caused. Beyond that all is silence.

> EMILY DICKINSON (1830–1886). Letter to her cousins, November 1882

We learn that God is; that he is in me; and that all things are shadows of him.

> RALPH WALDO EMERSON (1803–1882). "Circles," *Essays: First Series,* 1841

In the secret of my heart I am in perpetual quarrel with God that he should allow such things to go on.

> MOHANDAS K. GANDHI (1869–1948). Referring to the death and destruction he anticipated at the start of World War II, September 1939. In Louis Fischer, *The Life of Mahatma Gandhi,* 37, 1950

I am confident that God has made me the instrument of showing the better way.

> MOHANDAS K. GANDHI (1869–1948). In *Harijan,* 29 September 1940
> See Delusion: Bertrand Russell

If I could persuade myself that I should find Him in a Himalayan cave, I would proceed there immediately. But I know that I cannot find Him apart from humanity.

> MOHANDAS K. GANDHI (1869–1948). In James W. Douglass, *The Non–Violent Cross: A Theology of Revolution and Peace,* 2, 1969

It is as if I were the only man on the globe, and God, too were alone, waiting for me.

> ABRAHAM JOSHUA HESCHEL (1907–1972). *God in Search of Man: A Philosophy of Judaism,* 34, 1955

I go the way that Providence dictates with the assurance of a sleepwalker.

> ADOLF HITLER (1889–1945). Referring to the German Army's re–occupation of the Rhineland which he had ordered against the advice of his counselors, Speech, Munich, 14 March 1936

I myself believe that the evidence for God lies primarily in inner personal experiences.

> WILLIAM JAMES (1842–1910). *Pragmatism,* 3, 1907

Though he slay me, yet will I trust in him: but I will maintain mine own ways before him.

> JOB. *Job* 13:15 (King James Version)

I could not say I believe. I know! I have had the experience of being gripped by something stronger than myself, something that people call God.

> CARL G. JUNG (1875–1961). When asked if he believed in God. In "The Old Wise Man," *Time,* 14 February 1955

From the beginning I had a sense of destiny, as though my life was assigned to me by fate and had to be fulfilled. This gave me an inner security, and though I could never prove it to myself, it proved itself to me. *I* did not have this certainty, *it* had me. Nobody could rob me of the conviction that it was enjoined upon me to do what God wanted and not what I wanted. That gave me the strength to go my own way. Often I had the feeling that in all decisive matters I was no longer among men, but was alone with God.

> CARL G. JUNG (1875–1961). *Memories, Dreams, Reflections,* 2, ed. Aniela Jaffé, 1962

I know there is a God—and I see a storm coming; If he has a place for me, I believe that I am ready.

> JOHN F. KENNEDY (1917–1963). Words written on a slip of paper found by his secretary Evelyn Lincoln following a disappointing meeting with Soviet Premier Nikita Khrushchev in Vienna, June 1961. In Lincoln, *My Twelve Years with John F. Kennedy,* 25, 1965

The most excellent method which I found of going to God was that of *doing my common business* purely for the love of God.

> BROTHER LAWRENCE (17th cent.). In Rufus M. Jones, "The Mystic's Experience of God" (2), *Atlantic,* November 1921

What do I believe? I believe in God, if he exists.

> STANISLAW J. LEC (1909–1966). *Unkempt Thoughts,* p. 87, tr. Jacek Galazka, 1962

I have felt His hand upon me in great trials and submitted to His guidance, and I trust that as He shall further open the way, I will be ready to walk therein, relying on His help and trusting in His goodness and wisdom.

> ABRAHAM LINCOLN (1809–1865). Remark to a White House visitor, June 1862. In James F. Wilson, *North American Review,* December 1896

It is a momentous thing to be the instrument, under Providence, of the liberation of a race.

> ABRAHAM LINCOLN (1809–1865). Remark to Col. McKaye, 1863. In F. B. Carpenter, *Six Months at the White House with Abraham Lincoln,* 59, 1866
>
> See Delusion: Bertrand Russell

Clergyman: I *hope* the Lord is on our side.
Lincoln: I am not at all concerned about that, for I know that the Lord is *always* on the side of the *right.* But it is my constant anxiety and prayer that *I* and *this nation* should be on the Lord's *side.*

> ABRAHAM LINCOLN (1809–1865). 1864. Format adapted. In F. B. Carpenter, *Six Months at the White House with Abraham Lincoln,* 68, 1866

I have been many times driven to my knees by the overwhelming conviction that I had nowhere else to go. My own wisdom, and that of all about me, seemed insufficient for that day.

> ABRAHAM LINCOLN (1809–1865). Quoted by Noah Brooks, 1865. In William E. Barton, appendix (4) to *The Soul of Abraham Lincoln,* 1920

I have some obsession with how God exists. Is He an essential god or an existential god; is He all–powerful or is He, too, an embattled existential creature who may succeed or fail in His vision?

> NORMAN MAILER (1923–). Steven Marcus interview, 1963. In George Plimpton, ed., *Writers at Work: Third Series,* 1967

Believe me, there is a providence which guides all. I am merely its instrument.

> NAPOLEON (1769–1821). In Emil Ludwig, *Napoleon,* 5.9, 1925, tr. Eden and Cedar Paul, 1926
>
> See Delusion: Bertrand Russell

I would believe only in a God who could dance.

> FRIEDRICH NIETZSCHE (1844–1900). "On Reading and Writing," *Thus Spoke Zarathustra,* 1892, tr. Walter Kaufmann, 1954

God is in me. I am in God. I want Him, I seek Him. . . . I hope to improve myself. I do not know how to, but I feel that God will help all those who seek Him. I am a seeker, for I can feel God. God seeks me and therefore we will find each other.

> VASLAV NIJINSKY (1890–1950). Closing words, 27 February 1919, *The Diary of Vaslav Nijinsky,* 1936, ed. Romola Nijinsky, 1968

I believe in one God and no more; and I hope for happiness beyond this life.

> THOMAS PAINE (1737–1809). *The Age of Reason: Being an Investigation of True and Fabulous Theology,* 1, 1794

Antonio: This deity in my bosom.

> SHAKESPEARE (1564–1616). *The Tempest,* 2.1.278, 1611

God loves to see in me, not his servant,
but himself who serves all.

> RABINDRANATH TAGORE (1861–1941). *Fireflies,* p. 153, 1928

It is not when I am going to meet him, but when I am turning away and leaving him alone, that I discover that God is.

> HENRY DAVID THOREAU (1817–1862). Letter to Harrison Blake, 3 April 1850

God could not be unkind to me if he should try.

> HENRY DAVID THOREAU (1817–1862). Journal, 5 December 1856

I do not know whether the nature of the Ultimate Reality is personal or is supra-personal.

> ARNOLD J. TOYNBEE (1889–1975). Appendix ("Groping in the Dark," 2) to *An Historian's Approach to Religion,* 2nd ed., 1979 (1956)

In loving God in myself, . . . am I not loving myself in God?

> MIGUEL de UNAMUNO (1864–1936). *Tragic Sense of Life,* 10, 1913, tr. J. E. Crawford Flitch, 1921

By the miraculous care of Providence that protected me beyond all human expectation, I had four Bullets through my Coat and two Horses shot under me, and yet escaped unhurt.

> GEORGE WASHINGTON (1732–1799). Letter to his brother John during the French and Indian War, 18 July 1755

[Providence] has at times been my only dependence for all other resources seemed to have fail'd us.

GEORGE WASHINGTON (1732–1799). Referring generally to Revolutionary War crises in which he had participated. Letter to Rev. William Gordon, 9 March 1781

The finger of God was on me all day—nothing else could have saved me.

DUKE OF WELLINGTON (1769–1852). Remark to his sister-in-law a day after his victory over Napoleon at the Battle of Waterloo, June 1815. In John Keegan, *The Mask of Command*, 2, 1987

I have always believed in God, though I have my quarrels with Him. In the Jewish tradition, one may say no to God if it is on behalf of other people.

ELI WIESEL (1928–). In "One Must Not Forget," *U.S. News & World Reports*, 27 October 1986

GOD & NATURE

See also • God ∘ God & the World ∘ Nature

"What," it will be Question'd, "When the Sun rises, do you not see a round disk of fire somewhat like a Guinea?" O no, no, I see an Innumerable company of the Heavenly host crying, "Holy, Holy, Holy is the Lord God Almighty."

WILLIAM BLAKE (1757–1827). "A Vision of the Last Judgment," pp. 92–95, 1810, *The Complete Writings of William Blake*, ed. Geoffrey Keynes, 1966

All things are artificial, for nature is the art of God.

SIR THOMAS BROWNE (1605–1682). *Religio Medici*, 1.16, 1642, ed. John Addington Symonds, 1886

Earth's crammed with heaven,
And every common bush afire with God.

ELIZABETH BARRETT BROWNING (1806–1861). *Aurora Leigh*, 7.821, 1857

What I call God,
And fools call Nature.

ROBERT BROWNING (1812–1889). *The Ring and the Book*, 10.1072, 1869

Nature is but a name for an effect,
Whose cause is God.

WILLIAM COWPER (1731–1800). *The Task*, 6.223, 1785

Whether you like it or not, whether you know it or not, secretly all nature seeks God and works toward him. . . . Covertly, nature seeks, hunts, tries to ferret out the track on which God may be found.

MEISTER ECKHART (A.D. 1260?–1328?). "Sermons" (15), *Meister Eckhart: A Modern Translation*, tr. R. B. Blakney, 1941

The Use of Nature is to awaken the feeling of the Absolute. Nature is perpetual effect. It is the shadow pointing to an unseen Sun.

RALPH WALDO EMERSON (1803–1882). Journal, 7 June 1836

Nature is saturated with deity.

RALPH WALDO EMERSON (1803–1882). Journal, April 1847

When a god wishes to ride, any chip or pebble will bud and shoot out winged feet and serve him for a horse.

RALPH WALDO EMERSON (1803–1882). "Fate," *The Conduct of Life*, 1860

The grandeur of nature is only the beginning. *Beyond the grandeur is God.*

ABRAHAM JOSHUA HESCHEL (1907–1972). *God in Search of Man: A Philosophy of Judaism*, 9, 1955

Holy, holy, holy is the Lord of hosts;
the whole earth is full of his glory.

ISAIAH (8th cent. B.C.) *Isaiah* 6:3
See Glory: Anonymous (*Bible*)

Nature is a revelation of God; Art is a revelation of man.

HENRY WADSWORTH LONGFELLOW (1807–1882). *Hyperion: A Romance*, 3.5, 1839

There is not a flower that opens, not a seed that falls into the ground, and not an ear of wheat that nods on the end of its stalk in the wind that does not preach and proclaim the greatness and the mercy of God to the whole world.

THOMAS MERTON (1915–1968). *The Seven Storey Mountain*, 1.3.8, 1948

The radiance in some places is so great as to be fairly dazzling, keen lance rays of every color flashing, sparkling in glorious abundance, joining the plants in their fine, brave beauty-work—every crystal, every flower a window opening into heaven, a mirror reflecting the Creator.

JOHN MUIR (1838–1914). 26 July 1869, *My First Summer in the Sierra*, 6 ("Mount Hoffman and Lake Tenaya"), 1911

Rocks and waters, etc., are words of God and so are men. We all flow from one fountain Soul. All are expressions of one Love. God does not appear and flow out only from narrow chinks and round bored wells here and there in favored races and places, but He flows in grand undivided currents, shoreless and boundless over creeds and forms and all kinds of civilizations and peoples and beasts, saturating all and fountainizing all.

JOHN MUIR (1838–1914). Letter to Catharine Merrill, 9 June 1872. In William Frederic Badè, *The Life and Letters of John Muir*, 9.2, 1923

On the rim of the Yosemite I once heard a man say: "How was this tremendous old rocky gorge formed?" "Oh, stop your science," said another of the party. "Hush! stand still and behold the glory of God!"

JOHN MUIR (1838–1914). Journal, 1913?, *John of the Mountains: The Unpublished Journals of John Muir*, ed. Linnie Marsh Wolfe, 1938

Nature has some perfections to show that she is the image of God, and some defects to show that she is only His image.

BLAISE PASCAL (1623–1662). *Pensées*, 580, 1670, tr. William F. Trotter, 1931

All are but parts of one stupendous whole,
Whose body Nature is, and God the soul.

ALEXANDER POPE (1688–1744). *An Essay on Man*, 1.267, 1734

For what else is Nature but God and the Divine Reason that pervades the whole universe and all its parts.

SENECA THE YOUNGER (5? B.C.–A.D. 65). "On Benefits" (4.7.1), *Moral Essays*, tr. John W. Basore, 1935

Nature is the glass reflecting God.
> EDWARD YOUNG (1683–1765). *The Complaint: or, Night Thoughts on Life, Death, and Immortality,* 9.1007, 1742–1745

GOD & THE DEVIL

See also • Devil ○ God

Anyone unable to understand a god sees it as a devil and is thus defended from the approach.
> JOSEPH CAMPBELL (1904–1987). *The Hero with a Thousand Faces,* 1.1.5, 1949

It may be the devil or it may be the Lord
But you're gonna have to serve somebody.
> BOB DYLAN (1941–). "Gotta Serve Somebody" (song), 1979

Satan—God's scapegoat.
> PAUL ELDRIDGE (1888–1982). *Maxims for a Modern Man,* 2215, 1965

Our god is named Abraxas, and he is both god and the devil at the same time.
> HERMANN HESSE (1877–1962). In Miguel Serrano, "Abraxas," *C. G. Jung and Hermann Hesse,* tr. Frank MacShane, 1966

All gods and devils that have ever existed are within us.
> HERMANN HESSE (1877–1962). *Reflections,* 307, ed. Volker Michels, 1974
>
> See The Unconscious: Carl G. Jung (6)

The Devil is God's shadow.
> JAMES HOWELL (1593–1666). Comp., "Divers Centuries of New Sayings" (p. 1), *Paroimiographia: Proverbs, or Old Sayed Sawes & Adages in English . . . Italian, French and Spanish,* 1659

Resist the devil and he will flee from you. Draw near to God and he will draw near to you.
> JAMES (A.D. 1st cent.). *James* 4:7–8

[In] the Christian reformation of the Jewish concept of the Deity, the morally ambiguous Yahweh became an exclusively good God, while everything evil was united in the devil. . . . The moral splitting of the divinity into two halves.
> CARL G. JUNG (1875–1961). "Psychological Aspects of the Mother Archetype" (5), 1938, *The Archetypes and the Collective Unconscious,* tr. R. F. C. Hull, 1959

One night I demanded of God, "Lord, when are You going to pardon Lucifer?" and God answered, "When he pardons me."
> NIKOS KAZANTZAKIS (1883–1957). Epilogue to *Report to Greco,* 1961, tr. P. A. Bien, 1965

g(o)od and (d)evil.
> SAM KEEN (1931–). *Beginnings Without End,* 9, 1975

Where God built a church, there the Devil would also build a chapel.
> MARTIN LUTHER (1483–1546). *Table Talk,* 67, 1566, tr. William Hazlitt, 1857

The Devil is God in exile.
> NORMAN MAILER (1923–). Paul Carroll interview, *Playboy,* January 1968

The devil hath engrossed them and so hath caused them to forget remembrance of Allah.
> MUHAMMAD (A.D. 570?–632). *Quran,* 58.19, A.D. 670?, tr. Mohammed Marmaduke Pickthall, 1953

When the god in him is repressed, the half-gods and devils take possession of man.
> LEWIS MUMFORD (1895–1900). *The Conduct of Life,* 3.6, 1951

God seeks comrades and claims love,
the Devil seeks slaves and claims obedience.
> RABINDRANATH TAGORE (1861–1941). *Fireflies,* p. 31, 1928

GOD & THE WORLD

See also • God ○ God & History ○ God & Nature ○ History ○ Man ○ Progress ○ Universe: [especially] Miguel de Unamuno ○ World

As a house implies a builder, and a garment a weaver, and a door a carpenter, so does the existence of the Universe imply a Creator.
> AKIBA (A.D. 40?–135?). In *Midrash* (4th cent. B.C.–A.D. 12th cent.). Rabbinical writings

This world is God's workshop for making men in.
> HENRY WARD BEECHER (1813–1887). "Manhood," *Proverbs from Plymouth Pulpit,* ed. William Drysdale, 1887
>
> See Evolution: Henri Bergson

How many persons who shudder at the sound of this word ["Pantheism"] can tell the difference between that doctrine and their own professed belief in the omnipresence of the Deity.
> OLIVER WENDELL HOLMES, SR. (1809–1894). *Ralph Waldo Emerson,* 16, 1885

The whole of creation, with all its laws, is a revelation of God.
> DEAN WILLIAM RALPH INGE (1860–1954). "Confessio Fidei," *Outspoken Essays: Second Series,* 1922

Lift up your eyes on high and see;
  who created these?
> ISAIAH (8th cent. B.C.). *Isaiah* 40:25

And God stepped out on space,
And He looked around and said,
"I'm lonely—
I'll make me a world."
> JAMES WELDON JOHNSON (1871–1938). "The Creation," *God's Trombones,* 1927

If God wishes to be born as man and to unite mankind in the fellowship of the Holy Ghost, He suffers the terrible torment of having to bear the world in its reality. It is a crux, indeed, He Himself is His own cross. The world is God's suffering, and every individual human being who wishes even to approach his own wholeness knows very well that this means bearing his own cross. But the eternal promise for him who bears his own cross is the Paraclete.
> CARL G. JUNG (1875–1961). "A Psychological Approach to the Dogma of the Trinity" (5.1), 1942, *Psychological Reflections,* ed. Jolande Jacobi, 1953

The extent of the whole universe is but a point, an atom, compared to His immensity.

> LA BRUYÈRE (1645–1696). "Of Freethinkers" (47), *The Characters*, 1688, tr. Henri van Laun, 1929

God . . . has given us this world only as a place of exile, and not as our true country.

> POPE LEO XIII (1810–1903). *Rerum Novarum (On the Condition of Workers)*, 15 May 1891

This world is a great sculptor's shop. We are the statues and there is a rumor going round the shop that some of us are some day going to come to life.

> C. S. LEWIS (1898–1963). *Mere Christianity*, rev. ed., 4.1, 1952

The visible marks of extraordinary wisdom and power appear so plainly in all the works of the creation that a rational creature, who will but seriously reflect on them, cannot miss the discovery of a Deity.

> JOHN LOCKE (1632–1704). *An Essay Concerning Human Understanding*, 1.3.9, 1690, ed. Alexander Campbell Fraser, 1894

The material universe is . . . a message in code from God.

> MALCOLM MUGGERIDGE (1903–1990). *Jesus Rediscovered*, 1.1, 1969

The visible order of the universe proclaims a supreme intelligence.

> ROUSSEAU (1712–1778). *Emile; or, Treatise on Education*, 4 ("The Creed of a Savoyard Priest"), 1762, tr. Barbara Foxley, 1911

The universe is one of God's thoughts.

> FRIEDRICH von SCHILLER (1759–1805). "Theosophie des Julius," *Philosophische, Briefe*, 1786

In whatever direction you turn, you will see God coming to meet you; nothing is void of him, he himself fills all his work.

> SENECA THE YOUNGER (5? B.C.–A.D. 65). "On Benefits" (4.8.2), *Moral Essays*, tr. John W. Basore, 1935

We are told that when Jehovah created the world he saw that it was good. What would he say now?

> GEORGE BERNARD SHAW (1856–1950). "Maxims for Revolutionists: Stray Sayings," *Man and Superman*, 1903

God fills the universe just as the soul fills the body of man.

> TALMUD (A.D. 1st–6th cent.). Rabbinical writings

That God, which ever lives and loves,
One God, one law, one element,
And one far-off divine event,
To which the whole creation moves.

> ALFRED, LORD TENNYSON (1809–1892). Closing lines, *In Memoriam A.H.H.*, 1850

It is impossible to account for the creation of the universe without the agency of a Supreme Being.

> GEORGE WASHINGTON (1732–1799). In James K. Paulding, *The Life of Washington*, 22, 1848

❦

And God saw everything that he had made, and behold, it was very good.

> ANONYMOUS (*BIBLE*). Genesis 1:31

A watch without a watchmaker is less incredible than a creation without a Creator.

> ANONYMOUS

God is one in all; all are one in God.

> ANONYMOUS
> See God: Moses (2) ○ Unity: Xenophanes

In terms of greatness, the entire creation is to the Creator what a speck of dust is to the entire creation.

> ANONYMOUS

GOLD

See also • Money ○ Wealth

Gold is tried with the touchstone, and men with gold.

> CHILON (6th cent. B.C.). One of the Seven Sages of Greece

An Ass is but an Ass tho' laden with Gold.

> THOMAS FULLER (1654–1734). Comp., *Gnomologia: Adages and Proverbs*, 585, 1732

Fetters of Gold are still Fetters.

> THOMAS FULLER (1654–1734). Comp., *Gnomologia: Adages and Proverbs*, 1522, 1732
> See Slavery: Josh Billings

To have gold brings fear, to have none brings grief.

> JAMES HOWELL (1593–1666). Comp., "Italian" (p. 12), *Paroimiographia: Proverbs, or Old Sayed Sawes & Adages in English . . . Italian, French and Spanish*, 1659

I will make a man more precious than fine gold.

> ISAIAH (8th cent. B.C.). *Isaiah* 13:12 (King James Version)

Whoever has gold must have an army to guard it, or resign himself to losing it.

> H. L. MENCKEN (1880–1956). "Four Moral Causes: War," *Prejudices: Fifth Series*, 1926

"Gold Will Buy 'Most Anything But a True Girl's Heart."

> MONROE H. ROSENFELD. Song title, 1898

Lately in a wreck of a Californian ship, one of the passengers fastened a belt about him with two hundred pounds of gold in it, with which he was found afterwards at the bottom. Now, as he was sinking—had he the gold? or had the gold him?

> JOHN RUSKIN (1819–1900). *Unto This Last*, 4, 1860
> See Greed: Pliny the Younger

Romeo: Saint-seducing gold.

> SHAKESPEARE (1564–1616). *Romeo and Juliet*, 1.1.220, 1594

Gold is a living god, and rules in scorn
All earthly things but virtue.

> PERCY BYSSHE SHELLEY (1792–1822). *Queen Mab: A Philosophical Poem: With Notes*, 5, 1813

It is not enough to tell me that you worked hard to get your gold. So does the Devil work hard.

HENRY DAVID THOREAU (1817–1862). "Life Without Principle," *Atlantic*, October 1863

❧

A golden key opens every door except that of heaven.
SAYING (DANISH)

No gold without dross.
SAYING (ENGLISH)

GOLDEN RULE

See also • Giving ○ Good ○ Justice ○ Morality

Anonymous: How should we behave to friends?
Aristotle: As we should wish them to behave to us.
ARISTOTLE (384–322 B.C.). In Diogenes Laertius (A.D. 3rd cent.). *Lives of Eminent Philosophers*, 5.1, tr. R. D. Hicks, 1925

I'll be damned if I want most folk out there to do unto me what they do unto themselves.
TONI CADE BAMBARA. In Claudia Tate, *Black Women Writers at Work*, 2, 1983

He has observ'd the Golden Rule,
Till he's become the Golden Fool.
WILLIAM BLAKE (1757–1827). "Epigrams, Verses and Fragments from the Note-Book" (21), 1808–1811?, *The Complete Writings of William Blake*, ed. Geoffrey Keynes, 1966

Do as you would be done by.
LORD CHESTERFIELD (1694–1773). Letter to his son, 27 September 1748

Recompense injury with justice, and recompense kindness with kindness.
CONFUCIUS (551–479 B.C.). *Confucian Analects*, 14.36, tr. James Legge, 1930

What you do not want done to yourself do not do to others.
CONFUCIUS (551–479 B.C.). *Confucian Analects*, 15.23, tr. James Legge, 1930

"Do other men, for they would do you." That's the true business precept.
CHARLES DICKENS (1812–1870). *The Life and Adventures of Martin Chuzzlewit*, 11, 1844

Do unto others as you would expect them to do unto you.
ROBERT DOLE (1923–). Paraphrase of his advice to invading Croatian soldiers on their treatment of Serbs in the Krajina region of former Yugoslavia, television news program, 4 August 1995

Give as thou wouldest receive.
THOMAS FULLER (1654–1734). Comp., *Introductio ad Prudentiam*, 418, 1731

What is hateful to you don't do to another. This is the whole Torah [i.e., Law]; the rest is commentary.
HILLEL (A.D. 1st–6th cent.). Rabbinical writings

I do to others what they do to me, only worse.
JIMMY HOFFA (1913–1975). International Brotherhood of Teamsters president. Remark to the author, 19 March 1957. In Robert F. Kennedy, *The Enemy Within*, 3, 1960

Do unto others as though you were the others.
ELBERT HUBBARD (1856–1915). *The Note Book of Elbert Hubbard*, opposite p. 144, comp. Elbert Hubbard II, 1927

Whatever you wish that men would do to you, do so to them; for this is the law and the prophets.
JESUS (A.D. 1st cent.). *Matthew* 7:12 (Popular version: Do unto others as you would have them do unto you.)

Do unto yourself as you would have others do unto you.
SAM KEEN (1931–). *Beginnings Without End*, 7, 1975

Richard M. Nixon: My rule in international affairs is: do unto others as they would do unto you.
Kissinger: Plus ten percent.
HENRY A. KISSINGER (1923–). President Nixon's national security adviser. Format adapted. Basing his comment on "an experience with my chief extending over more than four years," 1 March 1973, *Years of Upheaval*, 6, 1982

To the good I would be good; to the not-good I would also be good, in order to make them good.
LAO-TZU (6th cent. B.C.). In Bertrand Russell, *Sceptical Essays*, 8, 1928

The great principle of morality, "To do as one would be done to," is more commended than practiced.
JOHN LOCKE (1632–1704). *An Essay Concerning Human Understanding*, 2.2.7, 1690, ed. Alexander Campbell Fraser, 1894

Necessity may force you to do unto the prince that which you see the prince about to do to you.
MACHIAVELLI (1469–1527). *The Discourses*, 3.6, 1517, tr. Christian E. Detmold, 1950

Stranger: Do to me as you would have me to do to you in the like case.
HERMAN MELVILLE (1819–1891). *Moby-Dick; or, The Whale*, 128, 1851, ed. Harold Beaver, 1972

Try your best to treat others as you wish to be treated yourself, and you will find that this is the shortest way to benevolence.
MENCIUS (371?–289? B.C.). *Mencius*, 7.A.4, tr. D. C. Lau, 1970

To do unto all men as you would wish to have done unto you, and to reject for others what you would reject for yourself.
MUHAMMAD (A.D. 570?–632). *The Sayings of Muhammad*, 138, tr. Abdullah Al-Suhrawardy, 1941

Neither urge another to that thou wouldst be unwilling to do thyself, nor do thyself what looks to thee unseemly and intemperate in another.
WILLIAM PENN (1644–1718). *Some Fruits of Solitude*, 71, 1693

To do good to wicked persons is like
Doing evil to good men.
SA'DI (A.D. 1213?–1292). *The Gulistan, or Rose Garden*, 1 (Story 4), A.D. 1258, tr. Edward Rehatsek, 1964

Do thou good as Allah had done unto thee.

> SA'DI (A.D. 1213?–1292). *The Gulistan, or Rose Garden,* 8 (Maxim 1), A.D. 1258, tr. Edward Rehatsek, 1964

Do it to him before he does it to you.

> BUDD SCHULBERG (1914–). *On the Waterfront* (film), 1954, spoken by Marlon Brando

Do not do unto others as you would they should do unto you. Their tastes may not be the same.

> GEORGE BERNARD SHAW (1856–1950). "Maxims for Revolutionists: The Golden Rule," *Man and Superman,* 1903

The golden rule is that there are no golden rules.

> GEORGE BERNARD SHAW (1856–1950). "Maxims for Revolutionists: The Golden Rule," *Man and Superman,* 1903

Doing evil in return for evil . . . is the morality of the many. . . .
   We ought not to retaliate or render evil for evil to anyone, whatever evil we may have suffered from him.

> SOCRATES (470?–399 B.C.). In Plato (427?–347 B.C.), *Crito,* 49, tr. Benjamin Jowett, 1894

The need to treat ourselves as well as we treat others. It's women's version of the Golden Rule.

> GLORIA STEINEM (1934–). "Doing Sixty," *Moving Beyond Words,* 1994

Do unto others as they want you to do unto them.

> THOMAS S. SZASZ (1920–). Defining "The Rule of Respect," "Ethics," *The Untamed Tongue: A Dissenting Dictionary,* 1990

Do unto others as you, in your superior wisdom, know ought to be done unto them in their own best interest.

> THOMAS S. SZASZ (1920–). Defining "The Rule of Paternalism," "Ethics," *The Untamed Tongue: A Dissenting Dictionary,* 1990

Do unto the other feller the way he'd like to do unto you, an' do it fust.

> EDWARD NOYES WESTCOTT (1847–1898). *David Harum: A Story of American Life,* 20, 1898

The Golden Rule: Whoever has the gold makes the rules.

> ANONYMOUS (AMERICAN)

Do others or they will do you.

> SAYING (AMERICAN)

Do not allow others to do unto you as you would not do unto them.

> SAYING

Do not do for others what they can do for themselves.

> SAYING

Do unto others as they would do unto you if they had the chance.

> SAYING

GOLF

See also • Sports

The pat on the back, the arm around the shoulder, the praise for what was done right and the sympathetic nod for what wasn't are as much a part of golf as life itself.

> GERALD R. FORD (1913–). Speech at the dedication of the World Golf Hall of Fame, Pinehurst (North Carolina), 12 September 1974

Touring pro: I'm having trouble with my long putts.
Hogan: Why don't you try hitting your irons closer to the pin?

> BEN HOGAN (1912–1997). Format adapted. In Dave Anderson, "Ben Hogan's Real Secret: That Dual Mystique," *New York Times,* 27 July 1997

The main idea in golf as in life, I suppose, is to learn to accept what cannot be altered, and to keep on doing one's own reasoned and resolute best whether the prospect be bleak or rosy.

> BOBBY JONES (1902–1971). In Jerry Tarde, "Bobby Jones's Reputation Still Growing," *New York Times,* 9 April 1990

If you think it's hard to meet new people, try picking up the wrong golf ball.

> JACK LEMMON (1925–). In "Scorecard," *Sports Illustrated,* 9 December 1985

Golf is the most fun you can have without taking your clothes off.

> CHI CHI RODRÍGUEZ

Golf is a good walk spoiled.

> MARK TWAIN (1835–1910). In "Quotable Quotes," *Reader's Digest,* December 1948

GOOD

See also • Assassination: George Bernard Shaw (4) ○ Deeds ○ Ethics ○ Evil ○ Giving ○ Golden Rule ○ Good & Evil ○ Morality: [especially] Somerset Maugham, Henry David Thoreau ○ Right ○ Right & Wrong ○ Service ○ Virtue

It is not always the same thing to be a good man and a good citizen.

> ARISTOTLE (384–322 B.C.). *Nichomachean Ethics,* 5.2, tr. J. A. K. Thomson, 1953

There can be no true goodness nor true love without the utmost clear-sightedness.

> ALBERT CAMUS (1913–1960). *The Plague,* 2, 1947, tr. Stuart Gilbert, 1948

To live according to nature is the highest good; that is, to lead a life regulated by conscience and conformed to virtue and temperance.

> CICERO (106–43 B.C.). *On the Laws,* 1.21, tr. C. D. Yonge, 1902

It is not enough to do good; one must do it in a good way.

> CONDORCET (1743–1794). In John Morley, *On Compromise,* 2, 1877

It must be a good thing to be good or ivrybody wudden't be pretendin' he was.

> FINLEY PETER DUNNE (1867–1936). "Hypocrisy," *Observations by Mr. Dooley,* 1902

All which liveth tendeth to good.

> RALPH WALDO EMERSON (1803–1882). Journal, 9 July 1839

What good shall I do today?
What good have I done today?

> BENJAMIN FRANKLIN (1706–1790). Questions he asked himself regularly (the first on awakening, the second before going to sleep). In Michael Zuckerman, "And in the Center Ring . . . ," *Pennsylvania Gazette,* May 1993

He who fasteth and doth no Good saveth his Bread but loseth his Soul.

> THOMAS FULLER (1654–1734). Comp., *Gnomologia: Adages and Proverbs,* 2382, 1732

To do good without ulterior motive is a generous and almost divine thing in itself.

> FRANCESCO GUICCIARDINI (1483–1540). *Remembrances,* C.11, 1530, tr. Mario Domandi, 1965

An act is not good because we feel obliged to do it; it is rather that we feel obliged to do it because it is good.

> ABRAHAM JOSHUA HESCHEL (1907–1972). *Man Is Not Alone: A Philosophy of Religion,* 13, 1951

Waste no more time arguing what a good man should be. Be one.

> MARCUS AURELIUS (A.D. 121–180). *Meditations,* 10.16, tr. Maxwell Staniforth, 1964

The world would be better off
  if people tried to become better.
And people would become better
  if they stopped trying to become
  better off.
For when everybody tries to become
  better off, nobody is better off.
But when everybody tries to become
  better, everybody is better off.

> PETER MAURIN (1877?–1947). Untitled. In *Catholic Worker,* March–April 1996

He has showed you, O man, what is good;
  and what does the Lord require of you
but to do justice, and to love kindness,
  and to walk humbly with your God?

> MICAH (8th cent. B.C.). *Micah* 6:8

There is a sort of gratification in doing good which makes us rejoice in ourselves.

> MONTAIGNE (1533–1592). "Of Repentance," *Essays,* 1588, tr. Donald M. Frame, 1958

All God's creatures are His family; and he is the most beloved of God who does most good to God's creatures.

> MUHAMMAD (A.D. 570?–632). *The Sayings of Muhammad,* 251, tr. Abdullah Al-Suhrawardy, 1941

By doing good we become good.

> ROUSSEAU (1712–1778). *Emile; or, Treatise on Education,* 4, 1762, tr. Barbara Foxley, 1911

"Good" is what helps me and others along on this journey of liberation.

> E. F. SCHUMACHER (1911–1977). *A Guide for the Perplexed,* 10.3, 1977

A man, to be greatly good, must imagine intensely and comprehensively; he must put himself in the place of another and of many others; the pains and pleasures of his species must become his own.

> PERCY BYSSHE SHELLEY (1792–1822). *A Defence of Poetry,* p. 14, 1821, ed. Albert S. Cook, 1890
>
> See Sympathy: *Bhagavad Gita*

If I knew for a certainty that a man was coming to my house with the conscious design of doing me good, I should run for my life.

> HENRY DAVID THOREAU (1817–1862). "Economy," *Walden; or Life in the Woods,* 1854

To be good is noble, but to show others how to be good is nobler and no trouble.

> MARK TWAIN (1835–1910). Epigraph. *Following the Equator: A Journey Around the World,* 1897

Do all the good you can,
By all the means you can,
In all the ways you can,
In all the places you can,
At all the times you can,
To all the people you can,
As long as ever you can.

> JOHN WESLEY (1703–1791). "Rule of Conduct"
>
> See Effort: Theodore Roosevelt ○ Kindness: Scott Nearing

To be good is to be in harmony with oneself.

> OSCAR WILDE (1854–1900). *The Picture of Dorian Gray,* 6, 1891

❦

Good that comes late is good for nothing.

> SAYING (ENGLISH)

One may be so good as to be good for nothing.

> SAYING (ITALIAN)

Better a doer of good than a do-gooder.

> SAYING

Never good through evil.

> SAYING

No one is so good that another may not be just as good.

> SAYING

GOOD & EVIL

See also • Ethics: Nicolas Berdyaev (2), Albert Schweitzer (5) ○ Evil ○ Good ○ Heaven & Hell ○ Judging Others: Anonymous ○ Knowledge: Anonymous (*Bible*) ○ Lying: Isaiah ○ Morality: [especially] Herbert Spencer (4) ○ Motives: John Locke ○ Religion ○ Right & Wrong ○ Strength & Weakness: Napoleon ○ Virtue & Vice ○ Wisdom: Socrates (2)

Only evil grows of itself, while for goodness we want effort and courage.

> HENRI AMIEL (1821–1881). Journal, 16 November 1864, tr. Mrs. Humphrey Ward, 1887

Good can imagine Evil, but Evil cannot imagine Good.

> W. H. AUDEN (1907–1973). "Imagination," *A Certain World: A Commonplace Book,* 1971

The good may prove to be a hidden form of evil. The evil may prove to be a new and not yet recognized form of the good.

> NICOLAS BERDYAEV (1874–1948). *The Destiny of Man,* 2.4.1, 1931, tr. Natalie Duddington, 1955

Good is Heaven. Evil is Hell.

> WILLIAM BLAKE (1757–1827). *The Marriage of Heaven and Hell,* 3, 1790–1793?

We may draw good out of evil; we must not do evil that good may come.

> MARIA WESTON CHAMPMAN (1806–1885). "How Can I Help to Abolish Slavery," speech, New York City, 1955

Good and bad men are each less so than they seem.

> SAMUEL TAYLOR COLERIDGE (1772–1834). 19 April 1830, *Table Talk,* 1835

The meaning of good and bad . . . is simply helping or hurting.

> RALPH WALDO EMERSON (1803–1882). Journal, 27 August 1838

The common interests
of states and individuals alike demand
that good and evil receive their just rewards.

> EURIPIDES (485?–406 B.C.). *Hecuba,* l. 900, tr. William Arrowsmith, 1956

I don't rack my brains much about the problem of good and evil, but on the whole I have not found much of the "good" in people. Most of them are in my experience riffraff, whether they proclaim themselves adherents of this or of that ethical doctrine, or of none at all.

> SIGMUND FREUD (1856–1939). Letter to Oskar Pfister, 9 October 1918. In Ernest Jones, *The Life and Work of Sigmund Freud,* 23, 1953–1957, abr., 1961

It's no great Commendation to just forbear doing ill: thou art bound moreover to do good to others.

> THOMAS FULLER (1654–1734). Comp., *Introductio ad Prudentiam,* 716, 1731

Nothing is good or bad but by Comparison.

> THOMAS FULLER (1654–1734). Comp., *Gnomologia: Adages and Proverbs,* 3666, 1732

Good is to evil as love is to fear.

> RICHARD M. GROSS (1944–). "Selected Aphorisms," *Personal Political Perplexing,* 1998

When "Do no Evil" has been understood,
Then learn the harder, braver rule, "Do Good."

> ARTHUR GUITERMAN (1871–1943). "Of Duty," *A Poet's Proverbs: Being Mirthful, Sober, and Fanciful Epigrams on the Universe, With Certain Old Irish Proverbs, All in Rhymed Couplets,* 1924

The good person loves people and uses things, while the bad person loves things and uses people.

> SYDNEY J. HARRIS (1917–1986). *Pieces of Eight,* 4, 1982

Bear with evil and expect good.

> GEORGE HERBERT (1593–1633). Comp., *Outlandish Proverbs,* 511, 1640

That action is best which procures the greatest happiness for the greatest numbers; and the worst, which, in like manner, occasions misery.

> FRANCIS HUTCHESON (1694–1746). Scottish philosopher. *An Inquiry into the Original of Our Ideas of Beauty and Virtue,* 2.3.8, 1725
>
> See Government: George Washington ○ Happiness: Jeremy Bentham ○ Right & Wrong: John Stuart Mill ○ States: Plato (2)

Good is that which makes for unity; Evil is that which makes for separateness.

> ALDOUS HUXLEY (1894–1963). "Ethics," *Ends and Means: An Inquiry into the Nature of Ideals and into the Methods Employed for Their Realization,* 1937

Thoughts and actions are good, when they make us, morally and spiritually, more capable of realizing the God who is *ours,* imminently in every soul and transcendently as that universal principle in which we live and move and have our being. They are bad when they tend to reinforce the barriers which stand between God and our souls, or the souls of other beings.

> ALDOUS HUXLEY (1894–1963). "Reflections on the Lord's Prayer—I." In Christopher Isherwood, ed., *Vedanta for the Western World,* 1945

If you derive pleasure from the good which you have performed and you grieve for the evil which you have committed, you are a true believer.

> MUHAMMAD (A.D. 570?–632). *The Sayings of Muhammad,* 67, tr. Abdullah Al-Suhrawardy, 1941

Every human being has two inclinations—one prompting him to good . . . and the other prompting him to evil . . . ; but Divine assistance is near, and he who asks the help of God in contending with the evil promptings of his own heart obtains it.

> MUHAMMAD (A.D. 570?–632). *The Sayings of Muhammad,* 361, tr. Abdullah Al-Suhrawardy, 1941

What is good? All that heightens the feeling of power, the will to power, power itself in man.
  What is bad? All that proceed from weakness.

> FRIEDRICH NIETZSCHE (1844–1900). *The Anti-Christ,* 2, 1895, tr. R. J. Hollingdale, 1968

It is circumstance and proper measure that give an action its character, and make it either good or bad.

> PLUTARCH (A.D. 46?–119?). "Agesilaus," *Parallel Lives,* Dryden edition, 1693

It is good to maintain and to encourage life; it is bad to destroy life or to obstruct it.

> ALBERT SCHWEITZER (1875–1965). *The Philosophy of Civilization: Civilization and Ethics,* 21, 1923, tr. C. T. Campion and Mrs. Charles E. B. Russell, 1946

Antony: The evil that men do lives after them;
The good is oft interred with their bones.

> SHAKESPEARE (1564–1616). *Julius Caesar,* 3.2.80, 1599

Hamlet: There is nothing either good or bad, but thinking makes it so.

> SHAKESPEARE (1564–1616). *Hamlet,* 2.2.254, 1600

Lady Macbeth: Whither should I fly?
I have done no harm. But I remember now
I am in this earthly world; where to do harm
Is often laudable, to do good sometime
Accounted dangerous folly.

> SHAKESPEARE (1564–1616). *Macbeth,* 4.2.74, 1605

There is only one good, that is, knowledge; and only one evil, that is, ignorance.

> SOCRATES (470?–399 B.C.). In Diogenes Laertius (A.D. 3rd cent.). *Lives of Eminent Philosophers,* 2.5, tr. R. D. Hicks, 1925

Under the guidance of reason we should pursue the greater of two goods and the lesser of two evils.

> BARUCH SPINOZA (1632–1677). "Reason and Desire," *Ethics,* 1677, tr. Dagobert D. Runes, 1957
>
> See Evil: Abraham Lincoln, Plato (2)

A human being may be defined as a personality with a will of its own capable of making moral choices between good and evil.

> ARNOLD J. TOYNBEE (1889–1975). *A Study of History,* 7.565, 1954

Everything that exalts and expands consciousness is good, while that which depresses and diminishes it is evil.

> MIGUEL de UNAMUNO (1864–1936). *Tragic Sense of Life,* 11, 1913, tr. J. E. Crawford Flitch, 1921

Nonresistance to evil implies resistance to good.

> MIGUEL de UNAMUNO (1864–1936). *Tragic Sense of Life,* 11, 1913, tr. J. E. Crawford Flitch, 1921

When I'm good, I'm very, very good, but when I'm bad, I'm better.

> MAE WEST (1893–1980). In *I'm No Angel* (film), 1933

✺

When I do good, I feel good, when I do bad, I feel bad, and that's my religion.

> ANONYMOUS (AMERICAN). Recalled by Abraham Lincoln from a talk given "an old man named Glenn" at a church meeting in Indiana, 1810s? In William H. Herndon and Jesse W. Weik, *Herndon's Lincoln: The True Story of a Great Life,* 14, 1889, Premier Books edition, 1961
>
> See Morality: Ernest Hemingway

Depart from evil, and do good.

> ANONYMOUS (*BIBLE*). *Psalms* 34:14
>
> See Evil: Paul

GOSSIP

See also • Criticism ∘ News ∘ Publicity ∘ Rumor ∘ Slander

Gossip? It's the mother's milk of journalism.

> HERB CAEN (1916–1997). In Jerry Carroll, "Psst! Heard the Latest?" *San Francisco Chronicle,* 10 April 1990
>
> See Money: Jesse Unruh

M.—— said, , "I heard something to the discredit of M. de——; I would have believed it six months ago, but we have been reconciled."

> CHAMFORT (1741–1794). Appendix (1) to *Characters and Anecdotes,* 1796, tr. W. S. Merwin, 1984

Were there no hearers, there would be no backbiters.

> GEORGE HERBERT (1593–1633). Comp., *Outlandish Proverbs,* 69, 1640

Men have always detested women's gossip because they suspect the truth: their measurements are being taken and compared.

> ERICA JONG (1942–). *Fear of Flying,* 6, 1973

Gossip is the opiate of the oppressed.

> ERICA JONG (1942–). *Fear of Flying,* 6, 1973
>
> See Religion, Anti-: Karl Marx

If you can't say something good about anyone, sit right here by me.

> ALICE ROOSEVELT LONGWORTH (1884–1980). Embroidery on a chair pillow. In Alden Whitman, "Alice Roosevelt Longworth Dies; She Reigned in Capital 80 Years," *New York Times,* 21 February 1980

Believe nothing against another but upon good Authority: Nor report what may hurt another, unless it be a greater hurt to others to conceal it.

> WILLIAM PENN (1644–1718). *Some Fruits of Solitude,* 145, 1693

Gossip is a guilty pleasure—the guilt, of course, making it all the more pleasurable.

> DIANA POSTLETHWAITE. Opening words, "Buffalo Harlots!" *Nation,* 11 May 1998

No one gossips about other people's secret virtues.

> BERTRAND RUSSELL (1872–1970). *On Education: Especially in Early Childhood,* 2, 1926

Tale Bearers are as bad as the Tale Makers—'tis an old observation and a very true one.

> RICHARD SHERIDAN (1751–1816). *The School for Scandal,* 1.1, 1777

When our life ceases to be inward and private, conversation degenerates into mere gossip.

> HENRY DAVID THOREAU (1817–1862). "Life Without Principle," *Atlantic,* October 1863

Speak not Evil of the absent for it is unjust.

> GEORGE WASHINGTON (1732–1799). Copybook, 1748, at age 16. *Rules of Civility & Decent Behaviour in Company and Conversation, #89.* The rules were an amended version of Francis Hawkins's 1640 translation of *Decency of Conversation Among Men* (French Jesuit writing, 1595)

✺

He who goes about gossiping reveals secrets;
  therefore do not associate with one who speaks foolishly.

> SAYING (*BIBLE*). *Proverbs* 20:19

Who chatters to you will chatter about you.

> SAYING (EGYPTIAN)

GOVERNMENT

See also • America: Richard M. Nixon (2) ∘ Anarchism ∘ Bureaucracy ∘ Business (Commerce) ∘ Constitutions ∘ Corporations ∘ Democracy ∘ Freedom ∘ Italy: Lord Byron ∘ Nations ∘ Organizations ∘ Politicians, Corrupt ∘ Politics ∘ Rights: The Declaration of the Rights of Man and the Citizen ∘ Tyranny ∘ Welfare

As the happiness of the people is the sole end of government, so the consent of the people is the only foundation of it, in reason, morality, and the natural fitness of things.

> JOHN ADAMS (1735–1826). Proclamation adopted by the Council of Massachusetts Bay, 1774

A government of laws, and not of men.

> JOHN ADAMS (1735–1826). "Novanglus" (his pen name) papers, *Boston Gazette*, 7, 1774 (later incorporated in the Massachusetts Constitution), 1780

Government is essentially organized and institutionalized power.

> HANNAH ARENDT (1906–1975). *On Violence*, 2, 1970

There are two parts of good government; one is the actual obedience of citizens to the laws, the other part is the goodness of the laws which they obey.

> ARISTOTLE (384–322 B.C.). *Politics*, 4.8, tr. Benjamin Jowett, 1885

No government can stand which is not founded upon justice.

> ARISTOTLE (384–322 B.C.). *Politics*, 7.14, tr. Benjamin Jowett, 1885

The art of government includes the political offices; viz., 1. the preservation; 2. the happiness; and 3. the enlargement of the state.

> FRANCIS BACON (1561–1626). *Advancement of Learning*, 8.3, 1605, Willey Book edition, 1944

The worst thing in the world, next to anarchy, is government.

> HENRY WARD BEECHER (1813–1887). "Political," *Proverbs from Plymouth Pulpit*, ed. William Drysdale, 1887

The business of government is to promote the happiness of the society, by punishing and rewarding.

> JEREMY BENTHAM (1748–1832). *An Introduction to the Principles of Morals and Legislation*, 7.1, 1789–1823

The political organization of the state rests both on force and on faith.

> NICOLAS BERDYAEV (1874–1948). *The Destiny of Man*, 2.4.6, 1931, tr. Natalie Duddington, 1955

The good of the people is the ultimate and true end of government. . . . Now, the greatest good of the people is their liberty.

> LORD BOLINGBROKE (1678–1751). *The Idea of a Patriot King*, p. 31, 1749, ed. Sydney W. Jackman, 1965

I have simplified my politics into an utter detestation of all existing governments. . . . The fact is, riches are power, and poverty is slavery all over the earth, and one sort of establishment is no better, or worse, for a *people* than another.

> LORD BYRON (1788–1824). Journal, 16 January 1814

A simple and a proper function of government is just to make it easy for us to do good and difficult for us to do wrong.

> JIMMY CARTER (1924–). Presidential nomination acceptance speech, New York City, 15 July 1976

In the long run every Government is the exact symbol of its People, with their wisdom and unwisdom; we have to say, Like People like Government.

> THOMAS CARLYLE (1795–1881). *Past and Present*, 4.4, 1843

Self-government is the natural government of man.

> HENRY CLAY (1777–1852). House of Representatives speech, 24 March 1818

Government is everywhere to a great extent controlled by powerful minorities, with an interest distinct from that of the mass of the people.

> GOLDSWORTHY LOWES DICKINSON (1862–1932). *The Choice Before Us*, 4, 1917

Any government is in itself an evil insofar as it carries within it the tendency to deteriorate into tyranny.

> ALBERT EINSTEIN (1879–1955). "A Reply to the Soviet Scientists," *Bulletin of the Atomic Scientists*, February 1948

The less government we have the better—the fewer laws, and the less confided power. The antidote to this abuse of formal Government is the influence of private character, the growth of the Individual. . . . To educate the wise man, the State exists; and with the appearance of the wise man, the State expires. The appearance of character makes the State unnecessary.

> RALPH WALDO EMERSON (1803–1882). "Politics," *Essays: Second Series*, 1844

Strange that our government, so stupid as it is, should never blunder into a good measure.

> RALPH WALDO EMERSON (1803–1882). Journal, 1859, undated

Government must not be a parish clerk, a justice of the peace. It has, of necessity, in any crisis of the state, the absolute powers of a Dictator.

> RALPH WALDO EMERSON (1803–1882). "American Civilization," lecture, Smithsonian Institute, Washington, 31 January 1862

The role of government [in a free society] . . . is to do something that the market cannot do for itself, namely, to determine, arbitrate, and enforce the rules of the game.

> MILTON FRIEDMAN (1912–). *Capitalism and Freedom*, 2, 1962

Regulatory bodies, like the people who comprise them, have a marked life cycle. In youth they are vigorous, aggressive, evangelistic, and even intolerant. Later they mellow, and in old age—after a matter of ten or fifteen years—they become, with some exceptions, either an arm of the industry they are regulating or senile.

> JOHN KENNETH GALBRAITH (1908–). *The Great Crash, 1929*, 9.7, 1954

Everything now seems to be under federal control except the national debt and the budget.

> BOB GODDARD

The best government is that which makes itself superfluous.

> GOETHE (1749–1832)

How small, of all that human hearts endure,
That part which laws or kings can cause or cure.
Still to ourselves in every place consign'd,
Our own felicity we make or find.

> OLIVER GOLDSMITH (1728–1774). *The Traveller: Or a Prospect of Society*, l. 429, 1764

A government that is big enough to give you all you want is big enough to take it all away.

BARRY M. GOLDWATER (1909–1998). Speech, West Chester (Pennsylvania), 21 October 1964

It is earnestly desired that each man should be wise enough to govern himself without the intervention of any compulsory restraint; and, since government, even in its best state, is an evil, the object principally to be aimed at is that we should have as little of it as the general peace of human society will permit.

WILLIAM GODWIN (1756–1836). *Enquiry Concerning Political Justice and Its Influence on Morals and Happiness,* 3.7, 1793

The science of government becomes simply a science of how to keep the people working and how to keep them quiet.

CARL G. GUSTAVSON (1915–). *A Preface to History,* 14, 1955

It is in a disorderly Government as in a river, the lightest things swim at the top.

MARQUIS OF HALIFAX (1633–1695). "Of Government," *Political, Moral and Miscellaneous Reflections,* 1750

If the government is in the hands of a few, they will tyrannize the many; if in the hands of the many, they will tyrannize over the few.

ALEXANDER HAMILTON (1757–1804). Letter to Robert Morris, 30 April 1781

Why has government been instituted at all? Because the passions of men will not conform to the dictates of reason and justice without constraint.

ALEXANDER HAMILTON (1757–1804). In *The Federalist Papers* (essay series), 15, December 1787

Happy it is when the interest which the government has in the preservation of its own power, coincides with a proper distribution of the public burdens, and tends to guard the least wealthy part of the community from oppression!

ALEXANDER HAMILTON (1757–1804). In *The Federalist Papers* (essay series), 36, 8 January 1788

Governments are instituted among men, deriving their just powers from the consent of the governed.

THOMAS JEFFERSON (1743–1826). Declaration of Independence, 4 July 1776

See Democracy: Abraham Lincoln (1) o Slavery: Jonathan Swift

The legitimate powers of government extend to such acts only as are injurious to others.

THOMAS JEFFERSON (1743–1826). *Notes on the State of Virginia,* 17, 1785

See Liberty: The Declaration of the Rights of Man and the Citizen

A wise and frugal Government, which shall restrain men from injuring one another, shall leave them otherwise free to regulate their own pursuits of industry and improvement, and shall not take from the mouth of labor the bread it has earned. This is the sum of good government.

THOMAS JEFFERSON (1743–1826). *First Inaugural Address,* 4 March 1801

That government is the strongest of which every man feels himself a part.

THOMAS JEFFERSON (1743–1826). Letter to H. D. Tiffin, 2 February 1807

I know no safe depository of the ultimate powers of society but the people themselves; and if we think them not enlightened enough to exercise their control with a wholesome discretion, the remedy is not to take it from them, but to inform their discretion by education.

THOMAS JEFFERSON (1743–1826). Letter to W. C. Jarvis, 28 September 1820

I would not give half a guinea to live under one form of government rather than another. It is of no moment to the happiness of an individual.

SAMUEL JOHNSON (1709–1784). 31 March 1772. In James Boswell, *The Life of Samuel Johnson,* 1791

Every increase of state authority must involve an immediate diminution of the liberty of each citizen.

BERTRAND de JOUVENEL (1903–1987). *On Power: Its Nature and the History of Its Growth,* 9 (introduction), 1945, tr. J. F. Huntington, 1948

Any system of government will work when everything is going well. It's the system that functions in the pinches that survives.

JOHN F. KENNEDY (1917–1963). Closing words, *Why England Slept,* 1940

My experience in government is that when things are noncontroversial, beautifully coordinated, and all the rest, it must be that not much is going on.

JOHN F. KENNEDY (1917–1963). In Arthur M. Schlesinger, Jr., *A Thousand Days: John F. Kennedy in the White House,* 25.3, 1965

I go for all sharing the privileges of the government, who assist in bearing its burdens.

ABRAHAM LINCOLN (1809–1865). Letter to *Sangamo Journal* (Illinois), 13 June 1836

To secure to each laborer the whole product of his labor, or as nearly as possible, is a most worthy object of any good government.

ABRAHAM LINCOLN (1809–1865). "Fragments on the Tariff," August 1846–December 1847, *Abraham Lincoln: Speeches and Writings, 1832–1858,* Library of America edition, 1989

If all men were just, there still would be *some,* though not *so much,* need of government.

ABRAHAM LINCOLN (1809–1865). "Fragments on Government," 1854?, *Abraham Lincoln: Speeches and Writings, 1832-1858,* Library of America edition, 1989

Must a government, of necessity, be too *strong* for the liberties of its own people, or too *weak* to maintain its own existence?

ABRAHAM LINCOLN (1809–1865). Message to Congress in special session, 4 July 1861

It is as much the duty of government to render prompt justice against itself, in favor of citizens, as it is to administer the same between private individuals.

ABRAHAM LINCOLN (1809–1865). *First Annual Message to Congress,* 3 December 1861

'Tis not without reason that [Man] seeks out and is willing to join in Society with others who are already united or have a mind to unite for the mutual *Preservation* of their Lives, Liberties and Estates, which I call by the general Name, *Property.*

The great and *chief end,* therefore, of Men's uniting into Commonwealths, and putting themselves under Government, *is the Preservation of their Property.*

> JOHN LOCKE (1632–1704). *Two Treatises of Government,* 2.123–124, 1690
>
> See Rights: Thomas Jefferson

That government is or ought to be instituted for the common benefit, protection, and security of the people, nation, or community; of all the various modes and forms of government, that is best which is capable of producing the greatest degree of happiness and safety, and is most effectually secured against the danger of mal-administration, and that whenever any government shall be found inadequate, or contrary to these purposes, a majority of the community hath an indubitable, unalienable, and indefeasible right to reform, alter or abolish it in such manner as shall be judged most conducive to the weal.

> GEORGE MASON (1725–1792). Virginia Bill of Rights, 12 June 1776
>
> See Revolution: Thomas Jefferson

The ideal government . . . is one which lets the individual alone— one which barely escapes being no government at all.

> H. L. MENCKEN (1880–1956). "Matters of State: Le Contrat Social," *Prejudices: Third Series,* 1922

The Bill of Rights was designed trustfully to prohibit forever two of the favorite crimes of all known governments: the seizure of private property without adequate compensation and the invasion of the citizen's liberty without justifiable cause and due process.

> H. L. MENCKEN (1880–1956). "On Government" (2), *Prejudices: Fourth Series,* 1924

All government, in its essence, is organized exploitation.

> H. L. MENCKEN (1880–1956). Opening words, "The Constitution," *Baltimore Evening Sun,* 19 August 1935

In all the more advanced communities the great majority of things are worse done by the intervention of government than the individuals most interested in the matter would do them, or cause them to be done, if left to themselves.

> JOHN STUART MILL (1806–1873). *Principles of Political Economy with Some of Their Applications to Social Philosophy,* 5.11.5, 1848

The best government is that which governs least.

> JOHN L. O'SULLIVAN (1813–1895). Introduction to *United States Magazine and Democratic Review,* October 1837

Society in every state is a blessing, but government, even in its best state, is but a necessary evil; in its worst state, an intolerable one.

> THOMAS PAINE (1737–1809). "Of the Origin and Design of Government in General," *Common Sense,* 1776

Government, like dress, is the badge of lost innocence.

> THOMAS PAINE (1737–1809). "Of the Origin and Design of Government in General," *Common Sense,* 1776

The necessity of establishing some form of government [is] to supply the defect of moral virtue.

> THOMAS PAINE (1737–1809). "Of the Origin and Design of Government in General," *Common Sense,* 1776

Today the nations of the world may be divided into two classes— the nations in which the government fears the people, and the nations in which the people fear the government.

> AMOS R. E. PINCHOT. Open letter, 16 April 1935

We may distinguish two main types of government. The first type consists of governments of which we can get rid without bloodshed—for example, by way of general elections. . . . The second type consists of governments which the ruled cannot get rid of except by way of a successful revolution—that is to say, in most cases, not at all.

> KARL R. POPPER (1902–1994). On "democracy" and "tyranny," *The Open Society and Its Enemies,* 1.7.2, 1945

In this [economic] crisis, government is not the solution to our problem. Government is the problem.

> RONALD REAGAN (1911–). Referring to unemployment and inflation, *First Inaugural Address,* 20 January 1981

I hope we have once again reminded people that man is not free unless government is limited. There's a clear cause and effect here that is as neat and predictable as a law of physics: as government expands, liberty contracts.

> RONALD REAGAN (1911–). Farewell address, 11 January 1989

Thank heavens we don't get all the government we pay for.

> WILL ROGERS (1879–1935). In *Will Rogers U.S.A.,* CBS-TV, 9 March 1972

The art of government is the organization of idolatry.

> GEORGE BERNARD SHAW (1856–1950). "Maxims for Revolutionists: Idolatry," *Man and Superman,* 1903

A government which robs Peter to pay Paul can always depend on the support of Paul.

> GEORGE BERNARD SHAW (1856–1950). *Everybody's Political What's What?* 30, 1944

Were all men virtuous, the institutes of religion and laws would be unnecessary.

> JOHN SHEBBEARE (1709–1788). *The History of the Excellence and Decline of the Constitution, Religion, Laws, Manners, and Genius of the Sumatrans*

What institution of government could tend so much to promote the happiness of mankind as the general prevalence of wisdom and virtue? All government is but an imperfect remedy for the deficiency of these.

> ADAM SMITH (1723–1790). *The Theory of Moral Sentiments,* 4.2, 1759

Civil government, so far as it is instituted for the security of property, is in reality instituted for the defense of the rich against the poor, or of those who have some property against those who have none at all.

> ADAM SMITH (1723–1790). *The Wealth of Nations,* 5.1.2, 1776

No apparatus of senators, judges, and police can compensate for the want of an internal governing sentiment. . . . No administrative sleight of hand can save us from ourselves.

> HERBERT SPENCER (1820–1903). *Social Statics,* 3.21.7, 1851

The original and essential office of a government is that of protecting its subjects against aggression external and internal.

> HERBERT SPENCER (1820–1903). "Representative Government—What Is It Good For?" *The Westminster Review* (English journal), October 1857

The object of government is not to change men from rational beings into beasts or puppets, but to enable them to develop their minds and bodies in security, and to employ their reason unshackled; neither showing hatred, anger or deceit, nor watched with the eyes of jealousy and injustice. In fact, the true aim of government is liberty.

> BARUCH SPINOZA (1632–1677). *Tractatus Theologico-Politicus,* 20, 1670, tr. R. H. M. Elwes, 1895

The government must be the trustee for the little man because no one else will be. The powerful can usually help themselves—and frequently do.

> ADLAI E. STEVENSON (1900–1965). In Laurence J. Peter, *Peter's People,* 5, 1979

It is the supreme test of a system of government whether its machinery is adequate for repressing the selfish undertakings of cliques formed on special interests and saving the public from raids of plunderers.

> WILLIAM GRAHAM SUMNER (1840–1910). *Folkways: A Study of the Sociological Importance of Usages, Manners, Customs, Mores, and Morals,* 167, 1907

Pray for the welfare of the government, for were it not for the fear of the government, a man would swallow up his neighbor alive.

> TALMUD (A.D. 1st–6th cent.). Rabbinical writings

I heartily accept the motto—"That government is best which governs least"; and I should like to see it acted up to more rapidly and systematically. Carried out, it finally amounts to this, which also I believe—"That government is best which governs not at all"; and when men are prepared for it, that will be the kind of government which they will have.

> HENRY DAVID THOREAU (1817–1862). Opening words, "Civil Disobedience," 1849

Why is [government] not more apt to anticipate and provide for reform? Why does it not cherish its wise minority? Why does it cry and resist before it is hurt? Why does it not encourage its citizens to be on the alert to point out faults. . . . Why does it always crucify Christ, and excommunicate Copernicus and Luther, and pronounce Washington and Franklin rebels?

> HENRY DAVID THOREAU (1817–1862). "Civil Disobedience," 1849

The effect of a good government is to make life more valuable; of a bad one, to make it less valuable.

> HENRY DAVID THOREAU (1817–1862). "Slavery in Massachusetts," address, Farmingham, 4 July 1854

The most important care of a good government should be to get people used little by little to managing without it.

> ALEXIS de TOCQUEVILLE (1805–1859). Notebook, 20 September 1831, *Journey to America,* 2, tr. George Lawrence, 1971

The art of government consists in taking as much money as possible from one class of citizens and giving it to the other.

> VOLTAIRE (1694–1778). "Money," *Philosophical Dictionary,* 1764

Many people consider the things which government does for them to be social progress, but they consider the things government does for others as socialism.

> EARL WARREN (1891–1974). Speech, Madison (Wisconsin), June 1955

The aggregate happiness of the society, which is best promoted by the practice of a virtuous policy, is, or ought to be, the end of all government.

> GEORGE WASHINGTON (1732–1799). Letter to Comte de Moustier, 1 November 1790
>
> See Good & Evil: Francis Hutcheson ○ Happiness: Jeremy Bentham ○ Right & Wrong: John Stuart Mill ○ States: Plato (2)

Benevolence never developed a man or a nation. We do not want a benevolent government. We want a free and a just government. Every one of the great schemes of social uplift which are now so much debated by noble people amongst us is based, when rightly conceived, upon justice, not upon benevolence.

> WOODROW WILSON (1856–1924). *The New Freedom: A Call for the Emancipation of the Generous Energies of a People,* 9, 1913

❧

The less government, the more freedom.

> SAYING

GOVERNMENT CORRUPTION

See • Politicians, Corrupt

GRACE

See also • Faith: [especially] Carl G. Jung ○ Forgiveness ○ God ○ Mysticism ○ Redemption ○ Religion ○ Revelation ○ Salvation: [especially] St. Bernard ○ Spirituality ○ Virtue: M. Esprit, Socrates

True liberation comes through grace and not through free will.

> NICOLAS BERDYAEV (1874–1948). *The Destiny of Man,* 1.3.5, 1931, tr. Natalie Duddington, 1955

The *Thou* meets me through grace—it is not found by seeking.

> MARTIN BUBER (1878–1965). *I and Thou,* 1, 1923, tr. Ronald Gregor Smith, 1958

It is the grace of God that helps those who do everything that lies within their power to achieve that which is beyond their power.

> ABRAHAM JOSHUA HESCHEL (1907–1972). *God in Search of Man: A Philosophy of Judaism,* 40, 1955

We need grace in order to be able to live in such a way as to qualify ourselves to receive grace.

> ALDOUS HUXLEY (1894–1963). "Reflections on the Lord's Prayer—II." In Christopher Isherwood, ed., *Vedanta for the Western World,* 1945

The daily bread of grace, without which nothing can be achieved, is given to the extent to which we ourselves give and forgive.

> ALDOUS HUXLEY (1894–1963). "Reflections on the Lord's Prayer—III." In Christopher Isherwood, ed., *Vedanta for the Western World,* 1945

Spiritual grace cannot be received continuously or in its fullness, except by those who have willed away their self-will to the point of being able truthfully to say, "Not I, but God in me."

> ALDOUS HUXLEY (1894–1963). *The Perennial Philosophy*, 10, 1946

In the contemporary idiom, grace is a happening rather than an achievement, a gift rather than a reward.

> SAM KEEN (1931–). *To a Dancing God*, 5, 1970

Amazing grace! how sweet the sound
That saved a wretch like me!
I once was lost, but now am found,
Was blind, but now I see.

> JOHN NEWTON (18th cent.) English clergyman. "Amazing Grace," *Olney Hymns*, 1779

By [free will] I can either enlarge or restrict my capacity for Thy grace.

> NICHOLAS OF CUSA (1401–1464). In Aldous Huxley, *The Perennial Philosophy*, 10, 1946

Man by grace is made like unto God, and a partaker in His divinity, and . . . without grace he is like unto the brute beasts.

> BLAISE PASCAL (1623–1662). *Pensées*, 434, 1670, tr. William F. Trotter, 1931

By grace you have been saved through faith; and this is not your own doing, it is the gift of God—not because of works, lest any man should boast.

> PAUL (A.D. 1st cent.). *Ephesians* 2:8–9

The breeze of God's grace is blowing continually. You have to set your sail to catch that breeze.

> SWAMI PRABHAVANANDA (1893–1976). "Divine Grace." In Christopher Isherwood, ed., *Vedanta for the Western World*, 1945
>
> See Opportunity: Thomas Fuller (1)

The state of love is the state of grace.

> N. SRI RAM (1899–?). *Thoughts for Aspirants*, 5, 1972

The sign of grace is luck.

> GARRY WILLS (1934–). *The Kennedy Imprisonment: A Meditation on Power*, 23, 1981

❦

God opposes the proud, but gives grace to the humble.

> ANONYMOUS (*BIBLE*). In James, *James* 4:6

God does not refuse grace to those who do what they can.

> SAYING (MEDIEVAL LATIN)

GRANDPARENTS

See also • Children ○ Family ○ Fathers ○ Mothers ○ Parents

Grandparents who want to be truly helpful will do well to keep their mouths shut and their opinions to themselves until these are requested. At that point, if their ideas can be discussed—not as formed opinions but as suggestions to be taken or disregarded—they can be helpful.

> T. TERRY BRAZELTON (1918–). *Touchpoints: Your Child's Emotional and Behavioral Development*, 44, 1992

Young people . . . have more compassion and tenderness toward the elderly than most middle-aged adults. Nothing—not avarice, not pride, not scrupulousness, not impulsiveness—so disillusions a youth about her parents as the seemingly inhumane way they treat her grandparents.

> LOUISE J. KAPLAN (1929–). *Adolescence: The Farewell to Childhood*, 12, 1984

The people whom the sons and daughters find it hardest to understand are the fathers and mothers, but young people can get on very well with the grandfathers and grandmothers.

> SIMEON STRUNSKY. *No Mean City*, 18, 1944

So if you have a grandma
Thank the Good Lord up above,
And give Grandmama hugs and kisses,
For grandmothers are to love.

> LOIS WYSE (1928–). Closing verse, "Grandmothers Are to Love," *Funny, You Don't Look Like a Grandmother*, 1989

GRASS

See also • Nature

Grass is the hair of the earth.

> THOMAS DEKKER (1570–1641). *The Gull's Handbook*, 3, 1609

Gonzalo: How lush and lusty the grass looks! how green!

> SHAKESPEARE (1564–1616). *The Tempest*, 2.1.52.109, 1611

A child said *What is the grass?* fetching it to me with full hands,
How could I answer the child? I do not know what it is any more than he.

> WALT WHITMAN (1819–1892). "Song of Myself" (6), 1855, *Leaves of Grass*, 1855–1892

I believe a leaf of grass is no less than the journey-work of the stars.

> WALT WHITMAN (1819–1892). "Song of Myself" (31), 1855, *Leaves of Grass*, 1855–1892

GRATITUDE

See also • Giving ○ Ingratitude

Gratitude is the sign of noble souls.

> AESOP (6th cent. B.C.). "Androcles," *Fables*, tr. Joseph Jacobs, 1894

Got no check books, got no banks.
Still I'd like to express my thanks—
I got the sun in the mornin'
And the moon at night.

> IRVING BERLIN (1888–1989). "I Got the Sun in the Mornin'" (song), 1946

Thank you for nothing.

> CERVANTES (1547–1616). *Don Quixote*, 1.3.1, 1615, tr. Peter Anthony Motteux and John Ozell, 1743

Maybe the only thing worse than having to give gratitude constantly all the time, is having to accept it.

WILLIAM FAULKNER (1897–1962). *Requiem for a Nun,* 2.1, 1951

Most People return small Favors, acknowledge middling ones, and repay great ones with Ingratitude.

BENJAMIN FRANKLIN (1706–1790). *Poor Richard's Almanack,* April 1751

If we meet someone who owes us a debt of gratitude, we remember the fact at once. How often we can meet someone to whom we owe a debt of gratitude without thinking about it at all!

GOETHE (1749–1832). "From Ottilie's Journal," *Elective Affinities,* 2.4, 1809, tr. R. J. Hollingdale, 1971

There is a built-in *sense of indebtedness in the consciousness of man,* an awareness of *owing gratitude,* of being *called upon* at certain moments to reciprocate, to answer, to live in a way which is compatible with the grandeur and mystery of living.

ABRAHAM JOSHUA HESCHEL (1907–1972). *Who Is Man?* 6, 1965

Nature seems to have implanted gratitude in all living creatures. . . . It appears to me that culture, which brings luxury and self-ishness with it, has a tendency rather to weaken than promote this affection.

SAMUEL JOHNSON (1709–1784). 20 September 1773. In James Boswell, *The Journal of a Tour to the Hebrides, with Samuel Johnson, L.L.D.,* 1786

Don't kneel to me, that is not right. You must kneel to God only, and thank Him for the liberty you will hereafter enjoy.

ABRAHAM LINCOLN (1809–1865). Remark to a newly freed slave in Richmond (Virginia), April 1864. In Francis Fisher Browne, *The Every-Day Life of Abraham Lincoln,* 3.16, 1887

No gratitude is felt for a benefit when it has lingered long in the hands of him who gives it, when the giver has seemed sorry to let it go, and has given it with the air of one who was robbing himself.

SENECA THE YOUNGER (5? B.C.–A.D. 65). "On Benefits" (2.1.2), *Moral Essays,* tr. John W. Basore, 1935

Men are more ready to repay an injury than a benefit because gratitude is a burden and revenge a pleasure.

TACITUS (A.D. 56?–120?). In Machiavelli, *The Discourses,* 1.29, 1517, tr. Christian E. Detmold, 1940

❧

O Lord my God, I will give thanks to thee forever.

ANONYMOUS (*BIBLE*). *Psalms* 30:12

GREATNESS

See also • Achievement ○ Charisma ○ Crisis Leaders: C. C. Colton ○ Genius ○ Heroism ○ Leaders: [especially] John Buchan ○ Madness: Shakespeare (3) ○ Nations: Adlai E. Stevenson ○ Power: Stewart L. Udall ○ Public Relations: Daniel J. Boorstin

It is not in the still calm of life, or in the repose of a pacific station that great characters are formed. . . . Great necessities call out great virtues.

ABIGAIL ADAMS (1744–1818). Letter to her son John Quincy Adams, 19 January 1780

All rising to great place is by a winding stair.

FRANCIS BACON (1561–1626). "Of Great Place," *Essays,* 1625

The great figures of world history appear as the champions of God.

LEO BAECK (1873–1956). "Faith in Man: In Mankind," *The Essence of Judaism,* 1936, ed. Irving Howe, 1948

The most characteristic mark of a great mind is to choose some one important object, and pursue it for life.

ANNA LETITIA BARBAULD (1743–1825). "Against Inconsistency in Our Expectations," *Miscellaneous Pieces in Prose,* 1773

Greatness lies not in being strong, but in the right use of strength; and strength is not used rightly when it only serves to carry a man above his fellows for his own solitary glory. He is greatest whose strength carries up the most hearts by the attraction of his own.

HENRY WARD BEECHER (1813–1887). *Life Thoughts,* p. 52, rec. Edna Dean Proctor, 1858

An article of the democratic faith is that greatness lies in each person.

BILL BRADLEY (1943–). New Jersey senator. Commencement address at Middlebury College (Connecticut), May 1989

The great man's faculties unfold naturally and completely, keeping pace with the growth of his self-confidence and the tasks before him. It is not only that he appears complete in every situation, but every situation at once seems to cramp him. He does not merely fill it. He may shatter it.

JACOB BURCKHARDT (1818–1897). "The Great Men of History," 1870, *Force and Freedom: An Interpretation of History,* ed. James H. Nichols, 1943

He looks at everything from the standpoint of its utilizable strength.

JACOB BURCKHARDT (1818–1897). "The Great Men of History," 1870, *Force and Freedom: An Interpretation of History,* ed. James H. Nichols, 1943

When he makes use of his power, he will appear alternately as the supreme embodiment of the corporate life or the deadly enemy of existing conditions, until one or the other succumbs.

JACOB BURCKHARDT (1818–1897). "The Great Men of History," 1870, *Force and Freedom: An Interpretation of History,* ed. James H. Nichols, 1943

Not every age finds its great man, and not every great endowment finds its time. There may now exist great men for things that do not exist. In any case, the dominating feeling of our age, the desire of the masses for a higher standard of living, cannot possibly become concentrated in one great figure. What we see before us is a general leveling down, and we might declare the rise of great individuals an impossibility if our prophetic souls did not warn us that the crisis may suddenly pass from the contemptible field of "property and gain" on to quite another and that then the "right man" may appear overnight—and all the world will follow in his train.

JACOB BURCKHARDT (1818–1897). "The Great Men of History," 1870, *Force and Freedom: An Interpretation of History,* ed. James H. Nichols, 1943

That which makes the difference between one man and another—between the weak and the powerful, the great and the insignificant—is energy, invincible determination, a purpose once formed and then death or victory.

> THOMAS FOWELL BUXTON (1786–1845). English abolitionist. In Elbert Hubbard, comp., *Elbert Hubbard's Scrap Book*, p. 72, 1923

He who ascends to mountain tops shall find
The loftiest peaks most wrapt in clouds and snow;
He who surpasses or subdues mankind,
Must look down on the hate of those below.

> LORD BYRON (1788–1824). *Childe Harold's Pilgrimage*, 3.45, 1812–1818

What millions died that Caesar might be great!

> THOMAS CAMPBELL (1777–1844). *The Pleasures of Hope*, 2.174, 1799

Great men are the Fire-pillars in this dark pilgrimage of mankind; they stand as heavenly Signs, ever-living witnesses of what has been, prophetic tokens of what may still be, the revealed, embodied Possibilities of human nature.

> THOMAS CARLYLE (1795–1881). "Schiller," 1831, *Critical and Miscellaneous Essays*, Carey & Hart edition, 1849

No great man lives in vain. The history of the world is but the biography of great men.

> THOMAS CARLYLE (1795–1881). "The Hero as Divinity," *On Heroes, Hero-Worship, and the Heroic in History*, 1841
>
> See Biography: Carlyle (2)

The great man [is] an outstanding individual who is at once a product and an agent of the historical process, at once the representative and the creator of social forces which change the shape of the world and the thoughts of men.

> EDWARD HALLETT CARR (1892–1982). *What Is History?* 2, 1961

The sign of a great man is that the closer you get, the greater he seems.

> CHOFETZ CHAIM (A.D. 9th cent.). Jewish sage. In Daphne Merkin, "Witness to the Holocaust," *New York Times Book Review*, 17 December 1995

They're only truly great who are truly good.

> GEORGE CHAPMAN (1559?–1634). *Revenge for Honour*, 5.2, 1654

The great leaders have always carefully stage-managed their effects.

> CHARLES de GAULLE (1890–1970). "Of Prestige" (2), *The Edge of the Sword*, 1934, tr. Gerald Hopkins, 1960

Every man of action has a strong dose of egotism, pride, hardness, and cunning. But all those things will be forgiven him, indeed, they will be regarded as high qualities, if he can make of them the means to achieve great ends.

> CHARLES de GAULLE (1890–1970). "Of Prestige" (2), *The Edge of the Sword*, 1934, tr. Gerald Hopkins, 1960

C. L. Sulzberger: Do you foresee a new age of political giants? *De Gaulle:* I suppose that depends on the world situation. When that situation is grave, the giants come nearer to a return.

> CHARLES de GAULLE (1890–1970). Format adapted. In Sulzberger, "The Last of the Giants," *New York Times*, 11 November 1970

The spirit of the age is the very thing that a great man changes.

> BENJAMIN DISRAELI (1804–1881). *Coningsby: Or, The New Generation*, 3.1, 1844

The defects of great men are the consolation of dunces.

> ISAAC D'ISRAELI (1766–1848). *Literary Character of Men of Genius, Drawn from Their Own Feelings and Confessions*, 7, 1795

The great man makes the great thing. Wherever Macdonald sits, there is the head of the table.

> RALPH WALDO EMERSON (1803–1882). "The American Scholar," address, Harvard University, Cambridge (Massachusetts), 31 August 1837

We are very near to greatness: one step and we are safe: can we not take the leap?

> RALPH WALDO EMERSON (1803–1882). Journal, 28 October 1841

It is easy in the world to live after the world's opinion; it is easy in solitude to live after our own; but the great man is he who, in the midst of the crowd, keeps with perfect sweetness the independence of solitude.

> RALPH WALDO EMERSON (1803–1882). "Self-Reliance," *Essays: First Series*, 1841

To be great is to be misunderstood.

> RALPH WALDO EMERSON (1803–1882). "Self-Reliance," *Essays: First Series*, 1841

A successful man is a good hit, a lucky adjustment to the men about him and their aims. . . . What is a great man, but the like felicity of adjustment on a higher platform?

> RALPH WALDO EMERSON (1803–1882). Journal, October 1848

Great men are they who see that spiritual is stronger than any material force, that thoughts rule the world.

> RALPH WALDO EMERSON (1803–1882). "Progress of Culture," *Letters and Social Aims*, 1876

The great always introduce us to facts; small men introduce us always to themselves.

> RALPH WALDO EMERSON (1803–1882). "Thoughts on Modern Literature," *Natural History of Intellect and Other Papers*, 1893

A great man and a great rogue are synonymous terms.

> HENRY FIELDING (1707–1754). *The History of the Life of the Late Mr Jonathan Wild the Great*, 4.15, 1743

I distrust Great Men. They produce a desert of uniformity around them and often a pool of blood too, and I always feel a little man's pleasure when they come a cropper.

> E. M. FORSTER (1879–1970). "What I Believe," *Two Cheers for Democracy*, 1951

I have always thought that one man of tolerable abilities may work great changes, and accomplish great affairs among mankind, if he first forms a good plan, and, cutting off all amusements or other employments that would divert his attention, makes the execution of that same plan his sole study and business.

> BENJAMIN FRANKLIN (1706–1790). 1788, *Autobiography*, 1798

Who bends his knee to the great ones of this world, he knows them not!

FREDERICK II (1712–1786). In Heinrich von Treitschke, *The Life of Frederick the Great*, p. 132, ed. Douglas Sladen, 1915

I have often felt as though I had inherited all the defiance and all the passions with which our ancestors defended their Temple and could gladly sacrifice my life for one great moment in history.

SIGMUND FREUD (1856–1939). Letter to his fiancé Martha Bernays, 2 February 1886, tr. Tania and James Stern, 1960

One of the immortal infantile wishes . . . the wish to become great.

SIGMUND FREUD (1856–1939). *The Interpretation of Dreams*, 7.C, 1900, tr. A. A. Brill, 1938

Few great men could pass Personnel.

PAUL GOODMAN (1911–1972). *Growing Up Absurd: Problems of Youth in the Organized Society*, 7.6, 1956

There are no great men, only great challenges that ordinary men are forced by circumstances to meet.

WILLIAM F. "BULL" HALSEY (1882–1959). American admiral. In Thomas A. Bailey, *Presidential Greatness: The Image and the Man from George Washington to the Present*, 19, 1966

[Abraham Lincoln] read very little. Scarcely ever looked into a newspaper unless I called his attention to an article on some special subject. He frequently said, "I know more about that than any of them." It is absurd to call him a modest man. No great man is ever modest.

JOHN HAY (1838–1905). Lincoln's private secretary during the Civil War and later secretary of state. Letter to William H. Herndon, 5 September 1866. In Emanuel Hertz, ed., *The Hidden Lincoln: From the Letters and Papers of William H. Herndon*, 2.1, 1940

That spirit which had taken this fresh step in history is the inmost soul of all individuals; but in a state of unconsciousness which the great men in question aroused. Their fellows, therefore, follow these soul-leaders; for they feel the irresistible power of their own inner spirit thus embodied.

GEORG HEGEL (1770–1831). Introduction (3.2.2) to *Philosophy of History*, 1832, tr. John Sibree, 1900

They are *great* men because they willed and accomplished something great; not a mere fancy, a mere intention, but that which met the case and fell in with the needs of the age.

GEORG HEGEL (1770–1831). Introduction (3.2.2) to *Philosophy of History*, 1832, tr. John Sibree, 1900

A great ship asks deep waters.

GEORGE HERBERT (1593–1633). Comp., *Outlandish Proverbs*, 449, 1640

Great men are rarely isolated mountain peaks; they are the summits of ranges.

THOMAS WENTWORTH HIGGINSON (1823–1911). "A Plea for Culture," *Atlantic Essays*, 1871

Great men do not ask permission to be born. Nor do they ask permission of democracies to lead them. They find their own way to the tasks they feel called to fulfill, unless crushed by a hostile environment or isolated by the tide of events. Democracies do not have to seek these heroes when it seeks leaders. For if they exist, they will make themselves heard.

SIDNEY HOOK (1902–1989). *The Hero in History: A Study in Limitation and Possibility*, 11, 1943

[T. E. Lawrence] is one of those great men for whom one feels intensely sorry because he was nothing but a great man.

ALDOUS HUXLEY (1894–1963). Letter to Victoria Ocampo, 12 December 1946

He who is greatest among you shall be your servant; whoever exalts himself will be humbled, and whoever humbles himself will be exalted.

JESUS (A.D. 1st cent.). *Matthew* 23:11–12

No man ever yet became great by imitation. [Whoever] hopes for the veneration of mankind must have invention in the design or the execution; either the effect must itself be new, or the means by which it is produced.

SAMUEL JOHNSON (1709–1784). In *The Rambler* (English journal), 154, 17 September 1751

[Thomas Gray] was dull in a new way, and that made many people think him *great*.

SAMUEL JOHNSON (1709–1784). 28 March 1775. In James Boswell, *The Life of Samuel Johnson*, 1791

Self-confidence is the first requisite to great undertakings.

SAMUEL JOHNSON (1709–1784). "Pope," *Lives of the English Poets*, 1781

Great crises produce great men, and great deeds of courage.

JOHN F. KENNEDY (1917–1963). *Profiles in Courage*, pt. 2 ("The Time and the Place"), 1956

That's your new definition of greatness. . . . It means that everybody can be great. Because everybody can serve. You don't have to have a college degree to serve. You don't have to make your subject and your verb agree to serve. . . . You don't have to know the second theory of thermodynamics in physics to serve. You only need a heart full of grace. A soul generated by love. And you can be that servant.

MARTIN LUTHER KING, JR. (1929–1968). "The Drum Major Instinct," sermon, Ebenezer Baptist Church, Atlanta, 4 February 1968

It may well be that, in the last analysis, history is made by scene-stealers—that this is what we mean by "great men."

ORRIN E. KLAPP (1915–). *Symbolic Leaders: Public Dramas and Public Men*, 8, 1964

World sovereignty can be
Committed to that man
Who loves all people
As he loves himself.

LAO-TZU (6th cent. B.C.). *The Way of Life*, 13, tr. R. B. Blakney, 1955

He is aloof, as if his talk
Were priced beyond the purchasing;
But once his project is contrived,
The folk will want to say of it:
"Of course! We did it by ourselves!"

LAO-TZU (6th cent. B.C.). *The Way of Life*, 17, tr. R. B. Blakney, 1955

Good boys who to their books apply
Will all be great men by and by.

> ABRAHAM LINCOLN (1809–1865). Doggerel penned as a youngster for
> his friend Joseph C. Richardson. In William H. Herndon and Jesse
> W. Weik, *Herndon's Lincoln: The True Story of a Great Life,* 2, 1889,
> Premier Books edition, 1961

This is the way of greatness. In the supreme moments of history, terms like duty, truth, justice, and mercy—which in our torpid hours are tired words—become the measure of decision. . . .
  The straight and righteous path is the shortest and the surest.

> WALTER LIPPMANN (1889–1974). "The Fascination of Greatness,"
> *New York Herald Tribune,* 7 September 1943

Lives of great men all remind us
  We can make our lives sublime,
And, departing, leave behind us
  Footprints on the sands of time.

> HENRY WADSWORTH LONGFELLOW (1807–1882). "A Psalm of Life"
> (7), *Voices of the Night,* 1839

Great men stand like solitary towers in the city of God.

> HENRY WADSWORTH LONGFELLOW (1807–1882). *Kavanagh,* 1, 1849

A great man is made up of qualities that meet or make great occasions.

> JAMES RUSSELL LOWELL (1819–1891). "James Garfield," *My Study
> Windows,* 1871

A truly great man is ever the same under all circumstances; and if his fortune varies, exalting him at one moment and oppressing him at another, he himself never varies, but always preserves a firm courage, which is so closely interwoven with his character that everyone can readily see that the fickleness of fortune has no power over him.

> MACHIAVELLI (1469–1527). *The Discourses,* 3.31, 1517, tr. Christian E.
> Detmold, 1940

Ishmael: All men tragically great are made so through a certain morbidness. Be sure of this, O young ambition, all mortal greatness is but disease.

> HERMAN MELVILLE (1819–1891). *Moby-Dick; or, The Whale,* 16, 1851,
> ed. Harold Beaver, 1972

The commanding man in a momentous day seems only to be the last accident in a series. . . . Comet, not great fixed star—the accident of a peculiar individuality coinciding with opportunity or demand.

> JOHN MORLEY (1838–1923). *Notes on Politics and History: A University
> Address,* 4, 1913

A consecutive series of great actions never is the result of chance and luck; it always is the product of planning and genius. . . . Is it because they are lucky that they become great? No, but being great, they have been able to master luck.

> NAPOLEON (1769–1821). Remarks to Emmanuel Las Cases,
> 14 November 1816, *The Mind of Napoleon: A Selection from His
> Written and Spoken Words,* 56, ed. J. Christopher Herold, 1955

Greatness means: to give a direction.

> FRIEDRICH NIETZSCHE (1844–1900). *Human, All Too Human,* 521,
> 1878, tr. Marion Faber, 1984

Great leaders make their own rules.

> RICHARD M. NIXON (1913–1994). *Leaders,* 9, 1982
> See Strength: F. Scott Fitzgerald

He who would do some great thing in this short life must apply himself to work with such a concentration of his forces as, to idle spectators who live only to amuse themselves, looks like insanity.

> FRANCIS PARKMAN (1823–1893). Historian. In Elbert Hubbard, *Elbert
> Hubbard's Scrap Book,* p. 47, 1923

While an eminent man wins our admiration through his great qualities, he can hold our love only from his human weaknesses, that make him one of ourselves.

> DONN PIATT (19th cent.). "Abraham Lincoln," *Memories of the Men
> Who Saved the Union,* 1887

Not a day passes over the earth but men and women of no note do great deeds, speak great words, and suffer noble sorrows.

> CHARLES READE (1814–1884). *The Cloister and the Hearth,* 1, 1861

Whether for good or for evil, the fact that each had not died at birth made a difference to everyone who lived after them. . . .
  Those mighty figures. . . seized history with both hands and gave it an imprint, even a direction, which it otherwise might not have had.

> ARTHUR M. SCHLESINGER, JR. (1888–1965). "The Decline of Greatness,"
> *Saturday Evening Post,* 1 November 1958
> See Heroism: Sidney Hook (1)

Great men enable us to rise to our own highest potentialities. They nerve lesser men to disregard the world and trust to their own deepest instinct. . . . Which one of us has not gained fortitude and faith from the incarnation of ideals in men, from the wisdom of Socrates, from the wondrous creativity of Shakespeare, from the strength of Washington, from the compassion of Lincoln, and above all, perhaps, from the life and the death of Jesus? "We feed on genius," said Emerson, "Great men exist that there may be greater men" ["Uses of Great Men," *Representative Men,* 1850].
  Yet this may be only the smaller part of their service. Great men have another and larger role—to affirm human freedom against the supposed inevitabilities of history.

> ARTHUR M. SCHLESINGER, JR. (1888–1965). "The Decline of Greatness,"
> *Saturday Evening Post,* 1 November 1958

Great minds are like eagles, and build their nest in some lofty solitude.

> ARTHUR SCHOPENHAUER (1788–1860). "Counsels and Maxims" (3.22),
> *Essays of Arthur Schopenhauer,* tr. T. Bailey Saunders, 1851

A great pilot can sail even if his canvas is rent.

> SENECA THE YOUNGER (5? B.C.–A.D. 65). "On Conquering the
> Conqueror," *Moral Letters to Lucilius,* 30.3, tr. Richard M. Gummere,
> 1918

Brutus: The abuse of greatness is, when it disjoins
Remorse from power.

> SHAKESPEARE (1564–1616). *Julius Caesar,* 2.1.18, 1599

Malvolio: Be not afraid of greatness: some are born great, some achieve greatness and some have greatness thrust upon 'em.

> SHAKESPEARE (1564–1616). *Twelfth Night,* 2.5.156, 1599
> See Mediocrity: Joseph Heller

[Pathfinders] can only come out of a society that is ready to risk a new path. It is their patience in explaining new realities with which they have wrestled in private periods of withdrawal and their passion for breathing new life into our oldest, shared beliefs and values, that permits them to help a confused society find its way back to a clarity of purpose. Let us hope we shall continue to know them when we see them.

> GAIL SHEEHY (1937–). Afterword to *Pathfinders,* 1981

There are moments . . . when the individual feels himself to be identical with Destiny, the center of the world, and his own personality seems to him almost as a covering in which the history of the future is about to clothe itself.

> OSWALD SPENGLER (1880–1936). "Philosophy of Politics," *The Decline of the West,* 1918–1922, tr. Charles Francis Atkinson, 1962

A Call to Greatness.

> ADLAI E. STEVENSON (1900–1965). Book title, 1954

Great crises come when great new forces are at work changing fundamental conditions, while powerful institutions and traditions still hold old systems intact. . . . It is in such crises that great men find their opportunity. The man and the age act on each other.

> WILLIAM GRAHAM SUMNER (1840–1910). *Folkways: A Study of the Sociological Importance of Usages, Manners, Customs, Mores, and Morals,* 121, 1907

There is no greatness where simplicity, goodness and truth are absent.

> LEO TOLSTOY (1828–1910). *War and Peace,* 4.3.18, 1863–1869, tr. Rosemary Edmonds, 1957

Keep away from people who try to belittle your ambitions. Small people always do that, but the really great make you feel that you, too, can become great.

> MARK TWAIN (1835–1910). In Gay MacLaren, *Morally We Roll Along,* 3.5, 1938

When great departures come in the lives of peoples, they are generally the result of two or more causes coming together; but although one man cannot initiate such great changes, once these changes are in motion, one man may be able to give them their direction, this way or that.

> ALFRED NORTH WHITEHEAD (1861–1892). 29 August 1944, *Dialogues of Alfred North Whitehead,* rec. Lucien Price, 1954

He or she is greatest who contributes the greatest original practical example.

> WALT WHITMAN (1819–1892). "By Blue Ontario's Shore" (13), 1856, *Leaves of Grass,* 1855–1892

❧

Men of destiny should not stand too long outside the door.

> ANONYMOUS. In John Gunther, *Inside Europe,* rev. ed., 11, 1937 (1936)

GREED

See also • Avarice ○ Competition ○ Exploitation ○ Giving ○ Misers ○ Money ○ Self-Interest ○ Selfishness ○ Thrift ○ Wealth

Greed oft o'erreaches itself.

> AESOP (6th cent. B.C.). "The Goose and the Golden Eggs," *Fables,* tr. Joseph Jacobs, 1894

Greed is all right. . . . Greed is healthy. You can be greedy and still feel good about yourself.

> IVAN BOESKY 1937–). Commencement address at the School of Business Administration, University of California, Berkeley, 18 May 1986

There is nothing so characteristic of narrowness and littleness of soul as the love of riches.

> CICERO (106–43 B.C.). *De officiis,* 1.20, tr. Walter Miller, 1913

Much would have more.

> JOHN CLARKE (1596–1658). Comp., *Proverbs: English and Latine,* p. 37, 1639

Nothing is enough to the man for whom enough is too little.

> EPICURUS (341–270 B.C.)

It is precisely the greed of the businessman, or, more appropriately, his profit-seeking, which is the unexcelled protector of the consumer.

> ALAN GREENSPAN (1926–). Essay, 1960s. In Michael Lewis, "Beyond Economics, Beyond Politics, Beyond Accountability," *Worth,* May 1995

Never in the history of the world have so many people been so rich; never in the history of the world have so many of those same people felt themselves so poor.

> LEWIS H. LAPHAM (1935–). Preamble to *Money and Class in America: Notes and Observations on the Civil Religion,* 1988

The love of money is the root of all evil.

> PAUL (A.D. 1st cent.). *1 Timothy* 6:10 (Kings James version) (Popular version: Money is the root of all evil.)
> See Idleness: George Farquhar ○ Money: Samuel Butler ○ Thrift: George Bernard Shaw (2)

The love of money is the mother of all evil.

> PHOCYLIDES (6th cent. B.C.)

Greed for ownership has taken such a hold of us that we seem to be possessed by wealth rather than to possess it.

> PLINY THE YOUNGER (A.D. 62?–113?). *Letters,* 9.30, tr. Betty Radice, 1963
> See Gold: John Ruskin

It has been demonstrated again and again, from Imperial Rome to Weimar Germany, that epidemic greed is a symptom not of reveling in present triumphs but of a fear that the game is winding down.

> LAURENCE SHAMES (1951–). "Wall Street's Greed Is Fueled by Fear," *New York Times,* 15 June 1989

We are told that the love of money is the root of all evil; but money itself is one of the most useful contrivances ever invented: it is not its fault that some people are foolish or miserly enough to be fonder of it than of their own souls.

> GEORGE BERNARD SHAW (1856–1950). *The Intelligent Woman's Guide to Socialism, Capitalism, Sovietism and Fascism,* 6, 1928

If all the rich men in the world divided up their money among themselves, there wouldn't be enough to go round.

> CHRISTINA STEAD (1902–1983). "Credo," *House of All Nations,* 1938

It is not the creation of wealth that is wrong, but love of money for its own sake.

> MARGARET THATCHER (1925–). Speech before the General Assembly of the Church of Scotland, Edinburgh, 21 May 1988

The point is you can't be too greedy.

> DONALD J. TRUMP (1946–) (with TONY SCHWARTZ). *Trump: The Art of the Deal*, 2, 1987

Greed is good. Greed is right. Greed works. Greed will save the U.S.A.

> STANLEY WEISER (1946–) and OLIVER STONE (1946–). Paraphrasing Ivan Boesky, *Wall Street* (film), 1987, spoken by Michael Douglas (in the role of Gordon Gekko)

❦

Greed is in: guilt is out.

> ANONYMOUS (AMERICAN). 1987

The love of unearned money is the root of all evil.

> SAYING (AMERICAN)

GRIEF

See also • Burdens ○ Compassion ○ Death: [especially] Montaigne (1) ○ Despair ○ Difficulty ○ Funerals ○ Joy ○ Misfortune ○ Pain ○ Sorrow ○ Tears ○ Unhappiness

Grief is itself a med'cine.

> WILLIAM COWPER (1731–1800). "Charity," l. 159, 1782

Endow the Living—with the Tears—
You squander on the Dead.

> EMILY DICKINSON (1830–1886). "Endow the Living—with the Tears—," 1862?

Oh to be a stone! To feel no grief!

> EURIPIDES (485?–406 B.C.). *Heracles*, l. 1395, tr. William Arrowsmith, 1956

Between grief and nothing I will take grief.

> WILLIAM FAULKNER (1897–1962). *The Wild Palms*, p. 324, Modern Library edition, 1939

What we call mourning for our dead is perhaps not so much grief at not being able to call them back as it is grief at not being able to want to do so.

> THOMAS MANN (1875–1955). "Highly Questionable", *The Magic Mountain*, 7, 1924, tr. H. T. Lowe-Porter, 1927]

When we saw [Socrates] drinking [the poison], and saw too that he had finished the draught, we could no longer forbear, and in spite of myself my own tears were flowing fast; so that I covered my face and wept, not for him, but at the thought of my own calamity in having to part from such a friend.

> PHAEDO (4th cent. B.C.). Disciple of Socrates. In Plato (427?–347 B.C.), *Phaedo*, 117, tr. Benjamin Jowett, 1894

The light has gone out of my life.

> THEODORE ROOSEVELT (1858–1919). On his wife Alice Lee, who died two days after the birth of their daughter, diary, 1884. In Peter Collier, "The Goodness of Badlands," *Audubon*, January–February 1993

Grief best is pleased with grief's society.

> SHAKESPEARE (1564–1616). *The Rape of Lucrece*, l. 1111, 1594
>
> See Misery: Saying (English)

Bolingbroke: Grief makes one hour ten.

> SHAKESPEARE (1564–1616). *Richard II*, 1.3.261, 1595

Benedick: Everyone can master a grief but he that has it.

> SHAKESPEARE (1564–1616). *Much Ado About Nothing*, 3.2.29, 1598
>
> See Adversity: Mark Twain ○ Misfortune: Alexander Pope ○ Trouble: La Rochefoucauld

Lafeu: Moderate lamentation is the right of the dead, excessive grief the enemy to the living.

> SHAKESPEARE (1564–1616). *All's Well that Ends Well*, 1.1.63, 1602

The bitterest tears shed over graves are for words left unsaid and deeds left undone.

> HARRIET BEECHER STOWE (1811–1896). *Little Foxes*, 3, 1865

God's inhumanity to man makes countless thousands mourn.

> MARK TWAIN (1835–1910). 4 July 1898, *Mark Twain's Notebook,* ed. Albert Bigelow Paine, 1935

My captain does not answer, his lips are pale and still,
My father does not feel my arm, he has no pulse nor will,
The ship is anchor'd safe and sound, its voyage closed and done,
From fearful trip the victor ship comes in with object won;
Exult O shores, and ring O bells!
  But I with mournful tread,
    Walk the deck my Captain lies,
      Fallen cold and dead.

> WALT WHITMAN (1819–1892). Eulogizing Abraham Lincoln, "O Captain! My Captain!" 1865, *Leaves of Grass*, 1855-1892

Have I not reason to lament
What man has made of man?

> WILLIAM WORDSWORTH (1770–1850). Closing lines, "Lines Written in Early Spring," 1798

GUERRILLA WARFARE

See also • Revolutionary War: Alexander Hamilton ○ Strategy, Military ○ Vietnam War ○ War

Rebels who can count on popular support can lose themselves in the population . . . , count on the population for secrecy (in wars in which intelligence is practically the whole art of defense), and reconstitute their forces by easy recruitment; if they can do all of these things, they can be practically certain of victory, short of a resort to genocide by the incumbents.

> HARRY ECKSTEIN. "On the Etiology of Internal Wars," *History and Theory*, vol. 4, no. 2, 1965

The essential thing about anti-guerrilla warfare—one must hammer this home to everybody—is that whatever succeeds is right. . . .
  Anything which assists in the annihilation of the guerrillas will be considered right and conversely anything which does not contribute to the annihilation of the guerrillas will be considered wrong.

> ADOLF HITLER (1889–1945). Table talk, 1 December 1942. In Walter Warlimont, *Inside Hitler's Headquarters: 1939–1945*, 5.2, 1962

In guerrilla war, superior mobility and fire power lose their old relevance. Guerrillas need only join battle where they enjoy local superiority, but the defenders must be strong everywhere in anticipation of the unexpected. No longer is the ability to occupy territory decisive, for the real target has become the morale of the population and the system of the civil administration. If these can be undermined through protracted struggle, the insurgents will prevail no matter how many battles the defending forces have won.

> HENRY A. KISSINGER (1923–). "Reflections on Power and Diplomacy" (4). In E. A. J. Johnson, *The Dimensions of Diplomacy*, 1964

The conventional army loses if it does not win. The guerrilla wins if he does not lose.

> HENRY A. KISSINGER (1923–). "The Vietnam Negotiations," *Foreign Affairs*, January 1969

Our tactics were always tip and run, not pushes, but strokes. We never tried to maintain or improve an advantage, but to move off and strike somewhere else. We used the smallest force, in the quickest time, at the farthest place.

> T. E. LAWRENCE (1888–1935). On the theory of guerrilla warfare he devised in leading Arab forces against the occupying Turkish Army in the Middle East during World War I, "The Evolution of a Revolt," *Army Quarterly* (England), October 1920

[We could go against the Turks] like an army with banners; but suppose we were (as we might be) an influence, an idea, a thing intangible, invulnerable, without front or back, drifting about like a gas? Armies were like plants, immobile, firm-rooted, nourished through long stems to the head. We might be a vapor, blowing where we listed.

> T. E. LAWRENCE (1888–1935). *Seven Pillars of Wisdom: A Triumph*, 33, 1926

In frontless war where there are no clear lines on the map to show victory and defeat, the only true measure of progress must be political and nonquantifiable: the impact on the enemy's will to continue the fight.

> EDWARD N. LUTTWAK (1942–). *The Pentagon and the Art of War: The Question of Military Reform*, 1 (footnote), 1985

By May 1928 . . . basic principles of guerrilla warfare, simple in nature and suited to the conditions of the time, had already been evolved, that is, the sixteen-character formula: "The enemy advances, we retreat; the enemy camps, we harass; the enemy tires, we attack; the enemy retreats, we pursue."

> MAO TSE-TUNG (1893–1976). "Problems of Strategy in China's Revolutionary War" (5.3), December 1936, *Selected Works of Mao Tse-tung*, Foreign Languages Press edition, vol. 1, 1965

Our strategy is "pit one against ten," and our tactics are "pit ten against one"—This is one of our fundamental principles for gaining mastery over the enemy.

> MAO TSE-TUNG (1893–1976). "Problems of Strategy in China's Revolutionary War" (5.6), December 1936, *Selected Works of Mao Tse-tung*, Foreign Languages Press edition, vol. 1, 1965

Many people think it impossible for guerrillas to exist for long in the enemy's rear. Such a belief reveals lack of comprehension of the relationship that should exist between the people and the troops. The former may be likened to water and the latter to the fish who inhabit it.

> MAO TSE-TUNG (1893–1976). *Guerrilla Warfare*, 6, 1937, tr. Samuel B. Griffith, 1940

Proper guerrilla policy will provide for unified strategy and independent activity.

> MAO TSE-TUNG (1893–1976). *Guerrilla Warfare*, 7, 1937, tr. Samuel B. Griffith, 1940

To wish for victory and yet neglect political mobilization is like wishing to "go south by driving the chariot north," and the result would inevitably be to forfeit victory.

> MAO TSE-TUNG (1893–1976). "On Protracted War" (66), May 1938, *Selected Works of Mao Tse-tung*, Foreign Languages Press edition, vol. 2, 1965

We must oppose "only retreat, never advance," which is flightism, and at the same time oppose "Only advance, never retreat," which is desperate recklessness.

> MAO TSE-TUNG (1893–1976). "On Protracted War" (92), May 1938, *Selected Works of Mao Tse-tung*, Foreign Languages Press edition, vol. 2, 1965
>
> See Strategy, Military: J. F. C. Fuller (3)

The flea bites, hops, and bites, again, nimbly avoiding the foot that would crush him. He does not seek to kill his enemy at a blow, but to bleed him and feed on him, to plague and bedevil him, to keep him from resting and to destroy his nerve and his morale.

> ROBERT TABER. Explaining the title of his book, *War of the Flea: A Study of Guerrilla Warfare Theory and Practice*, 4, 1965

❦

They approach like foxes, fight like lions, and fly away like birds.

> ANONYMOUS (JESUIT). On Iroquois military tactics, 17th cent.

GUILT

See also • Anxiety ○ Blame ○ Confession ○ Crime ○ Dehumanization: Primo Levi ○ Evil ○ Forgiveness ○ Indifference ○ Innocence ○ Judging Others ○ Morality ○ Punishment ○ Regret ○ Religion ○ Remorse ○ Repentance ○ Responsibility ○ Shame ○ Silence & Protest ○ Sin ○ Theft: Saying (German)

There are multitudes of men and women who . . . attempt to get rid of the sense of moral failure by identifying themselves with groups which condone or approve the indulgences which they are either unable or unwilling to give up.

> ANTON T. BOISEN (1876–1965). *The Exploration of the Inner World: A Study of Mental Disorder and Religious Experience*, 6, 1936

The guilty think all talk is of themselves.

> GEOFFREY CHAUCER (1343–1400). "The Canon's Yeoman's Prologue," *The Canterbury Tales*, 1390?, tr. Nevill Coghill, 1951

The root of the guilt problem lies in human nature itself, in our failure as human beings to live in accordance with our potentialities and our vision of the good.

> J. GLENN GRAY (1913–1977). *The Warriors: Reflections on Men in Battle*, 6, 1959

A great many people feel "guilty" about things they shouldn't feel guilty about, in order to shut out feelings of guilt about the things they should feel guilty about.

> SYDNEY J. HARRIS (1917–1986). Syndicated column, *Chicago Daily News*, 1971

The feeling that one may be guilty of wrongdoing can be heightened when the questionable act is followed by adversity. Conversely, it may be minimized by the successful execution of a venture.

> RICHARD HOFSTADTER (1916–1970). "Cuba, the Philippines, and Manifest Destiny" (5), 1952, *The Paranoid Style in American Politics and Other Essays,* 1967

Admit thy guilt and seek forgiveness, for the denial of guilt is two iniquities.

> SOLOMON IBN GABIROL (A.D. 1020?–1070). *Choice of Pearls,* 109, tr. A. Cohen, 1925

True guilt is guilt at the obligation one owes to oneself to be oneself. . . . False guilt is guilt felt at not being what other people feel one ought to be or assume that one is.

> R. D. LAING (1927–1989). *Self and Others,* 10, 1961

Since then, it seems to me, I should have been entirely happy but for the never-absent idea that there is *one* still unhappy whom I have contributed to make so. That kills my soul.

> ABRAHAM LINCOLN (1809–1865). Referring to "the fatal first of January, 1841" when he broke his engagement with Mary Todd whom he later married, letter to Joshua F. Speed, 27 March 1842

It really hurts me very much to suppose that I have wronged anybody on earth.

> ABRAHAM LINCOLN (1809–1865). Lincoln-Douglas debate, Quincy (Illinois), 13 October 1858

There is no man so good that if he placed all his actions and thoughts under the scrutiny of the laws, he would not deserve hanging ten times in his life.

> MONTAIGNE (1533–1592). "Of Vanity," *Essays,* 1588, tr. Donald M. Frame, 1958

If Allah took mankind to task by that which they deserve, He would not leave a living creature on the surface of the earth.

> MUHAMMAD (A.D. 570?–632). *Quran,* 35.45, A.D. 670?, tr. Mohammed Marmaduke Pickthall, 1953

> See Judging Others: Shakespeare ∘ Sin: Paul (1), Solomon

The Schofield Kid (a young gunfighter feeling guilt soon after his first killing): It don't seem real. I ain't never gonna breathe again, ever. Now he's dead and the other one too. All on account of pulling a trigger.
Will Munny: It's a helluva thing killing a man. You take away all he's got and all he's ever gonna have.
Kid: Well, I guess they had it coming.
Munny (pause): We all have it coming, kid.

> DAVID WEBB PEOPLES. *Unforgiven* (film), 1992, spoken by Clint Eastwood (in the role of Munny)

If we see cruelty or wrong that we have the power to stop, and do nothing, we make ourselves sharers in the guilt.

> ANNA SEWELL (1820–1878). *Black Beauty,* 3.38, 1877

Hamlet: Use every man after his desert, and who should 'scape whipping?

> SHAKESPEARE (1564–1616). *Hamlet,* 2.2.554, 1600

Lady Macbeth: Out, damned spot! out, I say!

> SHAKESPEARE (1564–1616). *Macbeth,* 5.1.39, 1605

Guilt *n.* The sense of sin as seen through your own eyes, as distinguished from shame, which is the same thing viewed through the eyes of others.

> EDMUND H. VOLKART (1919–). *The Angel's Dictionary: A Modern Tribute to Ambrose Bierce,* p. 92, 1986

❧

Guilt is private shame; shame is public guilt.

> ANONYMOUS

People generally bear guilt more easily than a sense of inferiority.

> ANONYMOUS

GULF WAR

See also • International Relations ∘ Strategy, Military: Colin L. Powell ∘ War

A line has been drawn in the sand.

> GEORGE BUSH (1924–). On his decision to send military forces to the Persian Gulf to protect Saudi Arabia from Iraq which had just invaded and annexed Kuwait, news conference, Washington, 8 August 1990

Our action in the Gulf is not about religion, greed, or cultural differences, as Iraq's leader would have us believe. What is at stake is truly vital. Our action in the Gulf is about fighting aggression and preserving the sovereignty of nations. It's about keeping our word, our solemn word of honor, and standing by old friends. . . . Our jobs, our way of life, our own freedom and the freedom of friendly countries around the world would all suffer if control of the world's great oil reserves fell into the hands of Saddam Hussein.

> GEORGE BUSH (1924–). Speech before Department of Defense employees at the Pentagon, Washington, 15 August 1990

The United States has no quarrel with the Iraqi people. Our quarrel is with Iraq's dictator, and with his aggression. Iraq will not be permitted to annex Kuwait. And that's not a threat, not a boast. It's just the way it's going to be.

> GEORGE BUSH (1924–). Congress speech, 11 September 1990

We have before us the opportunity to forge for ourselves and for future generations a new world order—a world where the rule of law, not the law of the jungle, governs the conduct of nations. When we are successful—and we will be—we have a real chance at this new world order, an order in which a credible United Nations can use its peacekeeping role to fulfill the promise and vision of the U.N.'s founders.

> GEORGE BUSH (1924–). Announcing allied military action (air attacks) in the Gulf War, television broadcast, 16 January 1998

> See Internationalism: Frederick Charles Hicks

We went halfway around the world to do what is moral and just and right. And we fought hard and, with others, we won the war [to lift] the yoke of tyranny and aggression from a small country that many Americans had never heard of.

> GEORGE BUSH (1924–). Congress speech, 6 March 1991

If the principal export of Kuwait was broccoli, we wouldn't be there.

> JANICE DECKER. San Francisco peace demonstrator, whose son was stationed in an armored division in Saudi Arabia. Referring to the American military build-up in the oil-rich Persian Gulf region and Pres. George Bush's well-known distaste for broccoli, letter to *San Francisco Chronicle,* 22 December 1990

[If the United States attacks Iraq,] there will be columns of dead bodies which may have a beginning but will have no end.

> SADDAM HUSSEIN (1937–). Broadcast to the Iraqi people, 25 August 1990, caption of photograph. In Elaine Sciolino, "In Saddam Hussein's Iraq, All Real Power Settles at the Top," *New York Times,* 26 August 1990

Our best hope is in American strength and will, unashamedly laying down the rules of world order and being prepared to enforce them.

> CHARLES KRAUTHAMMER (1950–). During the Gulf War. In "New World Order: What's New? Which World? Whose Orders?" *Economist,* 23 February 1991

If Saddam Hussein gains in any way from his aggression, despite our unprecedented commitment of economic, diplomatic, and military power, other aggressors will be encouraged to wage war against their neighbors and peace will be in jeopardy everywhere in the world. That is why our commitment in the gulf is a highly moral enterprise.

> RICHARD M. NIXON (1913–1994). Closing words, "Why," *New York Times,* 6 January 1991

As far as Saddam Hussein being a great military strategist, he is neither a strategist, nor is he schooled in the operational art, nor is he a tactician, nor is he a general, nor is he a soldier. Other than that, he's a great military man. I want you to know that.

> H. NORMAN SCHWARZKOPF (1934–). Commander of allied forces in the Gulf War, news conference, Riyadh (Saudi Arabia), 27 February 1991

About six million barrels of oil, weighing roughly a million tons, around 10 percent of the world's daily oil ration, are going up in smoke every day from the 500 Kuwait wells set afire by Iraqi occupiers. . . .

Joel S. Levine of NASA, an authority on biomass burning [said that] . . . the Kuwaiti well fires were "the most intense burning source, probably, in the history of the world."

> TOM WICKER (1926–). "Smoke Over Kuwait," *New York Times,* 3 March 1991

GUN CONTROL

See also • Crime ○ Violence ○ War

The right of the people to bear arms shall not be infringed.

> CONSTITUTION OF THE UNITED STATES. Bill of Rights, Second Amendment, 15 December 1791

It is America's first freedom, the one that protects all the others. Among freedom of speech, of the press, or religion, of assembly, of redress of grievances, it is the first among equals. It alone offers the absolute capacity to live without fear. The right to keep and bear arms is the one right that allows rights to exist at all.

> CHARLTON HESTON (1923–). National Rifle Association vice president, speech before the National Press Club, Washington, 11 September 1997

[A gun] is a recreational tool, like a golf club or a tennis racket. You can kill someone with a golf club, you know.

> MARTEL LOVELACE. National Rifle Association official. In Erwin Knoll, ed., "Fore," *No Comment,* 1984

GURUS

See also • Teachers

Disciple: The Scriptures speak of service to the *guru* as a necessary means for spiritual realization. Up to what point is this true? *Brahmânanda:* It is necessary in the preliminary stages. But after that it is your own spirit which plays the role of *guru.*

> SWAMI BRAHMÂNANDA (1863–1922). In Whitall N. Perry, comp., *A Treasury of Traditional Wisdom,* p. 295, 1986

Why do you bother about the Masters: The essential [thing] is that you should be free and strong, and you can never be free and strong if you are a pupil of another, if you have gurus, mediators, Masters over you.

> KRISHNAMURTI (1895–1986). In Henry Miller, *The Books in My Life,* 9, 1952

The *Guru* is a mediator. He brings man and God together.

> SRI RAMAKRISHNA (1836–1886)

Your own heart is your guru.

> SWAMI SHIVANANDA (1887–1963). Quoted by Allen Ginsberg, Thomas Clarke interview, 1965. In George Plimpton, ed., *Writers at Work: Third Series,* 1967

The teacher is he who knows the Eternal Wisdom. . . .

The syllable "gu" means darkness, the syllable "ru" means dispeller; he is therefore called a "guru" because he dispels darkness.

> UPANISHADS (10th?–6th? cent. B.C.). Hindu scriptures. In Whitall N. Perry, comp., *A Treasury of Traditional Wisdom,* p. 288, 1986

HABIT

See also • Addiction ○ Custom ○ Dissatisfaction: Nikos Kazantzakis

Habit with him was all the test of truth,
"It must be right: I've done it from my youth."
> GEORGE CRABBE (1754–1832). Letter 3, "The Vicar" (l. 138), *The Borough*, 1810

Habit is second nature.
> DIOGENES (410?–320? B.C.)

'Tis easier to prevent bad habits than to break them.
> BENJAMIN FRANKLIN (1706–1790). *Poor Richard's Almanack*, October 1745

Habit: The great economizer of energy.
> ELBERT HUBBARD (1856–1915). *The Roycroft Dictionary Concocted by Ali Baba and the Bunch on Rainy Days*, p. 65, 1914

Habit simplifies the movements required to achieve a given result, makes them more accurate and diminishes fatigue.
> WILLIAM JAMES (1842–1910). *The Principles of Psychology*, 4, 1890

To *make our nervous system our ally instead of our enemy . . . we must make automatic and habitual, as early as possible, as many useful actions as we can,* and guard against the growing into ways that are likely to be disadvantageous to us, as we should guard against the plague.
> WILLIAM JAMES (1842–1910). *The Principles of Psychology*, 4, 1890

Never suffer an exception to occur till the new habit is securely rooted in your life. Each lapse is like the letting fall of a ball of string which one is carefully winding up, a single slip undoes more than a great many turns will wind again. *Continuity* of training is the great means of making the nervous system act infallible right.
> WILLIAM JAMES (1842–1910). *The Principles of Psychology*, 4, 1890

The hell to be endured hereafter, of which theology tells, is no worse than the hell we make for ourselves in this world by habitually fashioning our characters in the wrong way. Could the young but realize how soon they will become mere walking bundles of habits, they would give more heed to their conduct while in the plastic state. We are spinning our own fates, good or evil.
> WILLIAM JAMES (1842–1910). *The Principles of Psychology*, 4, 1890

Habituation puts to sleep the eye of our judgment.
> MONTAIGNE (1533–1592). "Of Custom," *Essays*, 1588, tr. Donald M. Frame, 1958

Iron chain of silent habit.
> JOHN MORLEY (1838–1923). *Notes on Politics and History: A University Address*, 5, 1913

We love our habits more than our income, often more than our life.
> BERTRAND RUSSELL (1872–1970). *Sceptical Essays*, 11, 1928

One habit overcomes another.
> THOMAS à KEMPIS (1380–1471). *The Imitation of Christ*, 1.21, tr. Leo Sherley-Price, 1952

Unless we can extensively program our behavior, we waste tremendous amounts of information-processing capacity on trivia.

This is why we form habits. Watch a committee break for lunch and then return to the same room: almost invariably its members seek out the same seats they occupied earlier. . . . Choosing the same seat spares us the need to survey and evaluate other possibilities.
> ALVIN TOFFLER (1928–). *Future Shock*, 16, 1970

Habit is habit, and not to be flung out of the window by any man, but coaxed downstairs a step at a time.
> MARK TWAIN (1835–1910). *The Tragedy of Pudd'nhead Wilson*, 6 (epigraph), 1894

Habit a second nature! Habit is ten times nature.
> DUKE OF WELLINGTON (1769–1852). In William James, *The Principles of Psychology*, 4, 1890

❦

Habits are at first cobwebs; at last, chains.
> SAYING (ENGLISH)

Bad habits are easier to abandon today than tomorrow.
> SAYING (YIDDISH)

Old habits die hard.
> SAYING

HAPPINESS

See also • Activity: Bertrand Russell ○ Appearances: Ralph Waldo Emerson (1) ○ Grief ○ Health ○ Heaven: Arthur Schopenhauer ○ Joy ○ Laughter ○ Morality: Immanuel Kant (1), Herbert Spencer (4) ○ Motives: William James ○ Optimism—Examples: Jack Yellin ○ Pleasure ○ Politics: Thomas Carlyle ○ Purpose ○ Security: Henri Bergson ○ Self-Realization (Being) ○ Strength & Weakness: Henry Wadsworth Longfellow ○ Success ○ Tears ○ Unhappiness ○ Virtue ○ World: William Wordsworth

Happiness does not consist in pastimes and amusements but in virtuous activities.
> ARISTOTLE (384–322 B.C.). *Nicomachean Ethics*, 10.6, tr. J. A. K. Thomson, 1953

The life of the intellect is the best and pleasantest for man, because the intellect more than anything else *is* the man. Thus it will be the happiest life as well.
> ARISTOTLE (384–322 B.C.). *Nicomachean Ethics*, 10.7, tr. J. A. K. Thomson, 1953

Happiness [is] prosperity combined with virtue.
> ARISTOTLE (384–322 B.C.). *Rhetoric*, 1.5, tr. W. Rhys Roberts, 1954

No human being can *make* another one happy.
> W. H. AUDEN (1907–1973). "Postscript: The Frivolous & the Earnest," *The Dyer's Hand and Other Essays*, 1962

A large income is the best recipe for happiness I ever heard of.
> JANE AUSTEN (1775–1817). *Mansfield Park*, 22, 1816

The happiest excitement in life is to be convinced that one is fighting for all one is worth on behalf of some clearly seen and deeply felt good, and against some greatly scorned evil.

> RUTH BENEDICT (1887–1948). Journal, 1915–1934 (undated), *An Anthropologist at Work: Writings of Ruth Benedict*, pt. 2, 1959

The *greatest happiness* or *greatest felicity* principle: . . . The greatest happiness of all those whose interest is in question [is] the right and proper, and only right and proper and universally desirable, end of human action.

> JEREMY BENTHAM (1748–1832). "Notes" (4), *An Introduction to the Principles of Morals and Legislation*, 1789–1823
>
> See Good & Evil: Francis Hutcheson o Government: George Washington o Right & Wrong: John Stuart Mill o States: Plato (2)

Human happiness konsists in having what yu want, and wanting what yu hav.

> JOSH BILLINGS (1818–1885). "Plum Pits," *Everybody's Friend, or; Josh Billing's Encyclopedia and Proverbial Philosophy of Wit and Humor*, 1874

We are happy in this world just in proporshun as we make others happy.

> JOSH BILLINGS (1818–1885). "Parboils," *Everybody's Friend, or; Josh Billing's Encyclopedia and Proverbial Philosophy of Wit and Humor*, 1874

Happiness consists in the practice of virtue.

> SIMON BOLIVAR (1783–1830). Speech at the Second National Congress of Venezuela, Angostura, 15 February 1819

All happiness [is] . . . connected with the practice of virtue, which necessarily depends on the knowledge of truth.

> EDMUND BURKE (1729–1797). *A Vindication of Natural Society*, p. 7, M. Cooper edition, 1756

Doubtless they suspected me of living fully, given up completely to happiness; and that cannot be forgiven.

> ALBERT CAMUS (1913–1960). *The Fall*, p. 79, tr. Justin O'Brien, 1956

That is happiness; to be dissolved into something complete and great.

> WILLA CATHER (1876–1947). *My Ántonia*, 1.2, 1918

My greatest happiness consists precisely in doing nothing whatever that is calculated to obtain happiness.

> CHUANG-TZU (369–286 B.C.). As interpreted by Thomas Merton, "Perfect Joy," *The Way of Chuang Tzu*, 1965

Annual income twenty pounds, annual expenditure nineteen nineteen six, result happiness. Annual income twenty pounds, annual expenditure twenty pounds ought and six, result misery.

> CHARLES DICKENS (1812–1870). *David Copperfield*, 12, 1850

If all the griefs I am to have
Would only come today,
I am so happy I believe
They'd laugh and run away!

> EMILY DICKINSON (1830–1886). "If all the griefs I am to have," undated

The better part of happiness is to wish to be what you are.

> DESIDERIUS ERASMUS (1466–1536). *The Praise of Folly*, 10, 1509, tr. Hoyt Hopewell Hudson, 1941

Happiness depends more on the inward Disposition of Mind than on the outward Circumstances.

> BENJAMIN FRANKLIN (1706–1790). *Poor Richard's Almanack*, November 1757

One's true happiness depends more upon one's own judgment of one's self, or a consciousness of rectitude in action and intention, and the approbation of those few, who judge impartially, than upon the applause of the unthinking, undiscerning multitude, who are apt to cry *Hosanna* today, and tomorrow, *Crucify him*.

> BENJAMIN FRANKLIN (1706–1790). Letter to Mrs. Jane Mecom, 1 March 1766

Human felicity is produced not so much by great pieces of good fortune that seldom happen, as by little advantages that occur every day.

> BENJAMIN FRANKLIN (1706–1790). 1788, *Autobiography*, 1798

That is but a slippery Happiness which Fortune can give and can take away.

> THOMAS FULLER (1654–1734). Comp., *Introductio ad Prudentiam*, 1483, 1731

Comparison, more than Reality, makes Men happy or wretched.

> THOMAS FULLER (1654–1734). Comp., *Gnomologia: Adages and Proverbs*, 1133, 1732

The first and indispensable requisite of happiness is a clear conscience.

> EDWARD GIBBON (1737–1794). *Memoirs of My Life and Writings*, p. 110, 1796, Alex. Murray edition, 1869

My happiness is to increase other people's. To be happy myself I need the happiness of all.

> ANDRÉ GIDE (1869–1951). *More Fruits of the Earth*, 1.4, 1935

None but those who are happy in themselves can make other so.

> WILLIAM HAZLITT (1778–1830). "Common Places" (62), *Literary Examiner* (English journal), September–December 1823

Better to be happy than wise.

> JOHN HEYWOOD (1497–1580). Comp., *A Dialogue Containing the Number of the Effectual Proverbs in the English Tongue*, 2.6, 1562

The supreme happiness of life is the conviction that we are loved; loved for ourselves—say rather, loved in spite of ourselves.

> VICTOR HUGO (1802–1885). "Fantine" (5.4), *Les Misérables*, tr. Charles E. Wilbour, 1862

The ancients sought for happiness in virtue; the moderns have too long been endeavoring to develop the latter from the former.

> WILHELM von HUMBOLDT (1767–1835). *The Limits of State Action*, 1, 1854, ed. J. W. Burrow, 1969

Happiness is not achieved by the conscious pursuit of happiness; it is generally the by-product of other activities.

> ALDOUS HUXLEY (1894–1963). "Religion and Time." In Christopher Isherwood, ed., *Vedanta for the Western World*, 1945
>
> See Fools: George Bernard Shaw (1)

Happiness is positive cash flow.

> CARL C. ICAHN (1936–). Financier. Saying on a throw pillow in his office, photograph, *New York Times*, 10 February 1990

[I have never] been able to conceive how any rational being could propose happiness to himself from the exercise of power over others.

> THOMAS JEFFERSON (1743–1826). Letter to Destutt de Tracy, 26 January 1811

To receive and to communicate assistance, constitutes the happiness of human life: man may indeed preserve his existence in solitude, but can enjoy it only in society.

> SAMUEL JOHNSON (1709–1784). In *The Adventurer* (English journal), 67, 26 June 1753

That kind of life is most happy which affords us most opportunities of gaining our own esteem. . . .

To strive with difficulties, and to conquer them, is the highest human felicity.

> SAMUEL JOHNSON (1709–1784). In *The Adventurer* (English journal), 111, 27 November 1753

It is an element of all happiness to fancy that we deserve it.

> JOSEPH JOUBERT (1754–1824). *Pensées*, 1838, tr. H. P. Collins, 1928

Many persons have a wrong idea of what constitutes true happiness. It is not attained through self-gratification but through fidelity to a worthy purpose.

> HELEN KELLER (1880–1968). 10 December 1936, *Helen Keller's Journal, 1936–1937*, 1938

When one door of happiness closes, another opens; but often we look so long at the closed door that we do not see the one which has been opened for us.

> HELEN KELLER (1880–1968). *The Open Door*, p. 11, 1957

The ancient Greek definition of happiness was the full use of your powers along lines of excellence.

> JOHN F. KENNEDY (1917–1963). A favorite quotation. Remark to a group of foreign students, 8 May 1963

You're happiest while you're making the greatest contribution.

> ROBERT F. KENNEDY (1925–1968). In *Bobby Kennedy: In His Own Words*, television documentary, KCSM, San Mateo (California), 2 November 1997

Our happiness or unhappiness depends as much on our temperaments as on our luck.

> LA ROCHEFOUCAULD (1613–1680). *Maxims*, 61, 1665, tr. Louis Kronenberger, 1959

Happiness cannot be the reward of virtue; it must be the intelligible consequence of it.

> WALTER LIPPMANN (1889–1974). *A Preface to Morals*, 7.7, 1929

A happiness that is sought for ourselves alone can never be found: for a happiness that is diminished by being shared is not big enough to make us happy. . . .

True happiness is found in unselfish love, a love which increases in proportion as it is shared.

> THOMAS MERTON (1915–1968). Opening words, *No Man Is an Island*, 1955

True happiness is not found in any other reward than that of being united with God.

> THOMAS MERTON (1915–1968). *No Man Is an Island*, 4.3, 1955

Happiness is the test of all rules of conduct and the end of life. But . . . this end was only to be attained by not making it the direct end. Those only are happy, I thought, who have their minds fixed on some object other than their own happiness; on the happiness of others, on the improvement of mankind, even on some art or pursuit, followed not as a means, but as itself an ideal end. Aiming thus at something else, they find happiness by the way.

> JOHN STUART MILL (1806–1873). *Autobiography*, 5, 1873

There is only one way to achieve happiness
   on this terrestrial ball,
And that is to have either a clear conscience,
   or none at all.

> OGDEN NASH (1902–1971). "Interoffice Memorandum," *I'm a Stranger Here Myself*, 1938

The secret for harvesting from existence the greatest fruitfulness and the greatest enjoyment is—to *live dangerously*! Build your cities on the slopes of Vesuvius! Send your ships into uncharted seas!

> FRIEDRICH NIETZSCHE (1844–1900). *The Gay Science*, 283, 1882, tr. Walter Kaufmann, 1974

Formula of my happiness: a Yes, a No, a straight line, a *goal*.

> FRIEDRICH NIETZSCHE (1844–1900). "Maxims and Arrows" (44), *Twilight of the Idols*, 1889, tr. R. J. Hollingdale, 1968

Precisely the least, the softest, lightest, a lizard's rustling, a breath, a breeze, a moment's glance—it is *little* that makes the *best* happiness.

> FRIEDRICH NIETZSCHE (1844–1900). "At Noon," *Thus Spoke Zarathustra*, 1892, tr. Walter Kaufmann, 1954

I have learned, in whatever state I am, to be content. I know how to be abased, and I know how to abound; in any and all circumstances I have learned the secret of facing plenty and hunger, abundance and want.

> PAUL (A.D. 1st cent.). *Philippians* 4:11–12

There can be no happiness either for the community or for the individual man, unless he passes his life under the rule of righteousness with the guidance of wisdom.

> PLATO (427?–347 B.C.). *Epistles*, 7.335.d, tr. John Harward, 1932

It is not enough to be happy: It is also necessary that others not be.

> JULES RENARD (1864–1910). Journal, May 1894, tr. Louise Bogan and Elizabeth Roget, 1964
> See Malice: Gore Vidal

The happiness that is genuinely satisfying is accompanied by the fullest exercise of our faculties, and the fullest realization of the world in which we live.

> BERTRAND RUSSELL (1872–1970). *The Conquest of Happiness*, 7, 1930

True happiness for human beings is possible only to those who develop their godlike potentialities to the utmost.

> BERTRAND RUSSELL (1872–1970). *Human Society in Ethics and Politics*, 2.10, 1962

I believe four ingredients are necessary for happiness: health, warm personal relations, sufficient means to keep you from want, and successful work.

BERTRAND RUSSELL (1872–1970). Tommy Robbins interview, *Redbook*,
September 1964

There is only one happiness in life, to love and be loved.

GEORGE SAND (1804–1876). Letter to Lina Calamatta, 31 March 1862

How much our happiness depends upon our spirits, and these
again upon on our state of health, may be seen by comparing the
influence which the same external circumstances or events have
upon us when we are well and strong with the effect which they
have when we are depressed and troubled with ill health. It is not
what things are objectively and in themselves, but what they are
for us, in our way of looking at them, that makes us happy or the
reverse.

ARTHUR SCHOPENHAUER (1788–1860). "The Wisdom of Life" (2),
Essays of Arthur Schopenhauer, tr. T. Bailey Saunders, 1851

Happiness consists in a frequent repetition of pleasure.

ARTHUR SCHOPENHAUER (1788–1860). "The Wisdom of Life" (2),
Essays of Arthur Schopenhauer, tr. T. Bailey Saunders, 1851

Happiness Is a Warm Puppy.

CHARLES SCHULZ (1922–). Book title, 1962

True happiness is founded upon virtue.

SENECA THE YOUNGER (5? B.C.–A.D. 65). "On the Happy Life" (16.1),
Moral Essays, tr. John W. Basore, 1932

Claudio: I were but little happy, if I could say how much.

SHAKESPEARE (1564–1616). *Much Ado About Nothing*, 2.1.317, 1598

Give a man health and a course to steer; and he'll never stop to
trouble about whether he's happy or not.

GEORGE BERNARD SHAW (1856–1950). *Captain Brassbound's
Conversion*, 3, 1901

What can be added to the happiness of the man who is in health,
who is out of debt, and has a clear conscience?

ADAM SMITH (1723–1790). *The Theory of Moral Sentiments*, 1.3.1, 1759

What so great happiness as to be beloved, and to know that we
deserve to be beloved? What so great misery as to be hated, and
to know that we deserve to be hated?

ADAM SMITH (1723–1790). *The Theory of Moral Sentiments*, 3.1, 1759

Vigorous health and its accompanying high spirits are larger elements of happiness than any other things whatever.

HERBERT SPENCER (1820–1903). *Education: Intellectual, Moral, and
Physical*, 1, 1860

People find happiness both in wisdom and folly, virtue and vice.
Contentment is no index of true worth.

VAUVENARGUES (1715–1747). *Reflections and Maxims*, 69, 1746, tr.
F. G. Stevens, 1940

The body of an athlete and the soul of a sage—these are what we
require to be happy.

VOLTAIRE (1694–1778). Letter to Helvétius

See Mind & Body: Juvenal

Be virtuous and you'll be happy!

ARTEMUS WARD (1834–1867). Closing words, "Fourth of July Oration,"
Weathersfield (Connecticut), 1859, *The Complete Works of Artemus
Ward*, 1898

Those who are happiest are those who do the most for others.

BOOKER T. WASHINGTON (1856–1915). *Up from Slavery:
An Autobiography*, 4, 1901

Human happiness and moral duty are inseparably connected.

GEORGE WASHINGTON (1732–1799). Letter to the bishops, clergy, and
laity of the Protestant Episcopal Church, New York City, undated

Society can only be happy and free in proportion as it is virtuous.

MARY WOLLSTONECRAFT (1759–1797). *A Vindication of the Rights of
Woman*, 12, 1792

Happiness is neither virtue nor pleasure, nor this thing nor that,
but simply growth.

WILLIAM BUTLER YEATS (1865–1939). Letter, 1909. In Lewis Mumford,
The Conduct of Life, 5.5, 1951

⚘

Be happy while y'er leevin',
For y'er a lang time deid.

ANONYMOUS (SCOTTISH)

Success is getting what you want; happiness is wanting what you
get.

ANONYMOUS

HASTE

See also • Automobiles: Piet Hein ○ Slowness ○ Speed

I knew a wise man that had it for a byword, when he saw men
hasten to a conclusion, "Stay a little that we may make an end the
sooner."

FRANCIS BACON (1561–1626). "Of Dispatch," *Essays*, 1625

Hasty climbers have sudden falls.

JOHN CLARKE (1596–1658). Comp., *Proverbs: English and Latine*, p. 23,
1639

Without haste, but without rest.

GOETHE (1749–1832) and FRIEDRICH von SCHILLER (1759–1805).
Zahme Xenien, 2.6.281, 1796

Haste maketh waste.

JOHN HEYWOOD (1497–1580). Comp., *A Dialogue Containing the
Number of the Effectual Proverbs in the English Tongue*, 1.2, 1562

The more haste, the worse speed.

JAMES HOWELL (1593–1666). Comp., "Italian" (p. 3), *Paroimiographia:
Proverbs, or Old Sayed Sawes & Adages in English . . . Italian, French
and Spanish*, 1659

⚘

The hasty and the slow meet at the ferry.

SAYING (ARAB)

See Speed: Anonymous (English)

Hasten slowly.

SAYING (LATIN)

Hasty work, double work.

SAYING

Less haste, more speed.

SAYING

HATE

See also • Contempt ○ Envy ○ Fear ○ Indifference ○ Love ○ Malice ○ Prejudice ○ Racism ○ Revenge ○ Tolerance

There is only one way of not hating those who do us wrong, and that is by doing them good.

HENRI AMIEL (1821–1881). *Journal,* 22 November 1880, tr. Mrs. Humphrey Ward, 1887

Then farewell, Horace; whom I hated so,
Not for thy faults, but mine.

LORD BYRON (1788–1824). *Childe Harold's Pilgrimage,* 4.77, 1812–1818

People hate those who make them feel their own inferiority.

LORD CHESTERFIELD (1694–1773). Letter to his son, 30 April 1750

See Inferiority: Samuel Johnson

The price of hating other human beings is loving oneself less.

ELDRIDGE CLEAVER (1935–1998). "On Becoming," *Soul on Ice,* 1968

The hate, which we all bear with the most Christian patience, is the hate of those who envy us.

C. C. COLTON (1780–1832). *Lacon: or, Many Things in Few Words; Addressed to Those Who Think,* 1.216, 1823

No man who hates dogs and children can be all bad.

BYRON DARNTON. *New York Times* journalist. In Cedric Worth, "Dog Food for Thought," *Harper's,* November 1937

Hate is not conquered by hate: hate is conquered by love. This is a law eternal.

THE DHAMMAPADA: THE PATH OF PERFECTION (1st cent. B.C.). 5, tr. Juan Mascaró, 1973

The more cruel the wrong that men commit against an individual or a people, the deeper their hatred and contempt for their victim. Conceit and false pride on the part of a nation prevent the rise of remorse for its crime.

ALBERT EINSTEIN (1879–1955). Statement read at the unveiling of the Memorial for the Battle of the Warsaw Ghetto, Warsaw, 19 April 1948, *Out of My Later Years,* rev. ed., 31, 1956 (1950)

Hate at first sight.

RALPH WALDO EMERSON (1803–1882). "Work and Days," *Society and Solitude,* 1870

See Love, Romantic: Saying

That which I hate and fear is really in myself.

RALPH WALDO EMERSON (1803–1882). "Character," *Lectures and Biographical Sketches,* 1883

If you hate a person, you hate something in him that is part of yourself. What isn't part of ourselves doesn't disturb us.

HERMANN HESSE (1877–1962). *Demian: The Story of Emil Sinclair's Youth,* 6, 1919, tr. Michael Roloff and Michael Lebeck, 1965

That hatred springs more from self-contempt than from a legitimate grievance is seen in the intimate connection between hatred and a guilty conscience.

ERIC HOFFER (1902–1983). *The True Believer: Thoughts on the Nature of Mass Movements,* 69, 1951

He who says he is in the light and hates his brother is in the darkness still.

JOHN (A.D. 1st cent.). *1 John* 2:9

Hate is too great a burden to bear. It injures the hater more than it injures the hated.

CORETTA SCOTT KING (1927–). Speech before the First National Conference on the Black Family and Crack Cocaine, San Francisco, 14 April 1989

Woe to those who have more hate than enemies.

STANISLAW J. LEC (1909–1966). *More Unkempt Thoughts,* p. 49, tr. Jacek Galazka, 1968

Hatred is gained as much by good works as by evil.

MACHIAVELLI (1469–1527). *The Prince,* 19, 1513, tr. Luigi Ricci, 1903

Hatreds generally spring from fear or envy.

MACHIAVELLI (1469–1527). Introduction to the Second Book, *The Discourses,* 1517, tr. Christian E. Detmold, 1940

Hate for an outsider checks and deflects the hate and aggression each man feels toward his own group and toward himself. The more fear there is in a society, the more guilt each individual member of the society feels, the more need there is for internal scapegoats and external enemies. *Internal confusion looks for discharge in outside wars.*

JOOST A. M. MEERLOO (1903–1976). *The Rape of the Mind: The Psychology of Thought Control, Menticide, and Brainwashing,* 7, 1956

It is not only our hatred of others that is dangerous but also and above all our hatred of ourselves: particularly that hatred of ourselves which is too deep and too powerful to be consciously faced. For it is this which makes us see our own evil in others and unable to see it in ourselves.

THOMAS MERTON (1915–1968). *New Seeds of Contemplation,* 16, 1961

He who hates a man is as if he hated God.

MIDRASH (4th cent. B.C.–A.D. 12th cent.). Rabbinical writings. In Louis I. Newman, comp., *The Talmudic Anthology,* 136, 1945

Hatred is love frustrated.

ASHLEY MONTAGU (1905–). "The Natural Superiority of Women," *Saturday Review,* 1 March 1952

All hate is self-hate.

A. S. NEILL (1883–1973). *Summerhill: A Radical Approach to Child Rearing,* 7, 1960

Rather perish than hate and fear, and *twice rather perish than make oneself hated and feared*—this must someday become the highest maxim for every single commonwealth.

FRIEDRICH NIETZSCHE (1844–1900). *The Wanderer and His Shadow,* 1880. In J. Glenn Gray, conclusion to *The Warriors,* 1959

Always remember, others may hate you, but those who hate you don't win unless you hate them. And then you destroy yourself.

RICHARD M. NIXON (1913–1994). Speech to the members of his administration after resigning from the Presidency, 9 August 1974

Anger, yes, but not hatred. A man remains in ignorance as long as he hates. I hate what someone does, but I don't hate him.

> BUCK O'NEAL. Baseball player. Appearing on *Nightline,* television news program, ABC, 26 September 1994

Those whom they have injured they also hate.

> SENECA THE YOUNGER (5? B.C.–A.D. 65). "On Anger" (2.33.1), *Moral Essays,* tr. John W. Basore, 1928

They hate not only their enemies but everyone who does not share their hatred.

> GEORGE BERNARD SHAW (1856–1950). *Androcles and the Lion,* 2, 1912

Hatred . . . requires respect for one's opponent; acknowledgment of equal rank is a part of it. One despises beings of lower rank.

> OSWALD SPENGLER (1880–1936). *Aphorisms,* 108, tr. Gisela Koch-Weser O'Brien, 1967

Hatred is increased by being reciprocated and can, on the other hand, be destroyed by love.

> BARUCH SPINOZA (1632–1677). "Man's Loves and Hates," *Ethics,* 1677, tr. Dagobert D. Runes, 1957

Self-hatred leads to the need either to dominate or to be dominated.

> GLORIA STEINEM (1934–). "A Personal Preface," *Revolution from Within: A Book of Self-Esteem,* 1992

Let no man pull you so low as to make you hate him.

> BOOKER T. WASHINGTON (1856–1915). In Martin Luther King, Jr., *Stride Toward Freedom,* 6, 1958

❦

Who hates even one individual can love no other.

> ANONYMOUS

HAWAII

Hawaii is not a state of mind, but a state of grace.

> PAUL THEROUX (1941–). In *Observer* (British newspaper), 29 October 1989

HEALING

See also • Disease ○ Doctors ○ Drugs, Medical ○ Food ○ Health ○ Physicians ○ Psychiatry ○ Surgeons

There is no curing a sick man who believes himself in health.

> HENRI AMIEL (1821–1881). Journal, 6 February 1877, tr. Mrs. Humphrey Ward, 1887

The treatment is really a cooperative effort of a trinity—the patient, the doctor, and the "inner doctor."

> RALPH BIRCHER. Swiss physician. In Gordon Young, *Doctors Without Drugs,* 3, 1962

An attack on cancer that is concentrated wholly or even largely on therapeutic measures (even assuming a "cure" could be found), in Dr. [W. C.] Hueper's opinion, will fail because it leaves untouched the great reservoirs of carcinogenic agents which would continue to claim new victims faster than the as yet elusive "cure" could allay the disease.

> RACHEL CARSON (1907–1964). Referring to such chemical toxins as pesticides, *Silent Spring,* 14, 1962

'Tis an old Saying, That an Ounce of Prevention is worth a Pound of Cure.

> BENJAMIN FRANKLIN (1706–1790). Letter to Samuel Johnson, 13 September 1750

He that eats till he is sick must fast till he is well.

> THOMAS FULLER (1654–1734). Comp., *Gnomologia: Adages and Proverbs,* 2094, 1732

Remedies often make diseases worse. . . . It takes a wise doctor to know when not to prescribe.

> BALTASAR GRACIÁN (1601–1658). *The Art of Worldly Wisdom,* 138, 1647, tr. Joseph Jacobs, 1943

Desperate cases need the most desperate remedies.

> HIPPOCRATES (460–377 B.C.). *Aphorisms,* 1.6, tr. J. Chadwick and W. N. Mann, 1950 (Popular version: Extreme maladies require extreme remedies.)

Rest, as soon as there is pain, is a great restorative in all disturbances of the body.

> HIPPOCRATES (460–377 B.C.). *Aphorisms,* 2.48, tr. J. Chadwick and W. N. Mann, 1950

In cases where such treatment is advantageous, bleeding or purging is more efficacious in the spring.

> HIPPOCRATES (460–377 B.C.). *Aphorisms,* 6.47, tr. J. Chadwick and W. N. Mann, 1950

Rise and go your way; your faith has made you well.

> JESUS (A.D. 1st cent.). Remark to a Samaritan who after being healed had thrown himself at Jesus' feet and thanked him, *Luke* 17:19

Experience has proved the toad to be endowed with valuable qualities. If you run a stick through three toads, and, after having dried them in the sun, apply them to any pestilent tumor, they draw out all the poison, and the malady will disappear.

> MARTIN LUTHER (1483–1546). *Table Talk,* 780, 1566, tr. William Hazlitt, 1857

If you feed a cold, as is often done, you frequently have to starve a fever.

> BERNARR MACFADDEN (1868–1955). "When a Cold Is Needed," *Physical Culture,* February 1934

He who advises a sick man, whose manner of life is prejudicial to health, is clearly bound first of all to change his patient's manner of life.

> PLATO (427?–347 B.C.). *Epistles,* 7.330.c, tr. John Harward, 1932

There are some remedies worse than the disease.

> PUBLIUS SYRUS (85–43 B.C.). *Moral Sayings,* 301, tr. Darius Lyman, Jr., 1862

The wish for healing has ever been the half of health.

> SENECA THE YOUNGER (5? B.C.–A.D. 65). *Hippolytus,* l. 240, tr. Frank Justus Miller, 1917

Nothing . . . refreshes and aids a sick man so much as the affection of his friends.

SENECA THE YOUNGER (5? B.C.–A.D. 65). "On the Healing Power of the Mind," *Moral Letters to Lucilius,* 78.2, tr. Richard M. Gummere, 1918

But what is quackery? It is commonly an attempt to cure the diseases of a man by addressing his body alone.

HENRY DAVID THOREAU (1817–1862). "Wednesday," *A Week on the Concord and Merrimack Rivers,* 1849

The art of medicine consists of amusing the patient while nature cures the disease.

VOLTAIRE (1694–1778)

❦

Every sore has its salve.

SAYING (ENGLISH)

More die of the remedy than of the malady.

SAYING (FRENCH)

Patient, heal yourself.

SAYING

See Doctors: Saying (2) ○ Physicians: Saying (*Bible*)

HEALTH

See also • Body ○ Disease ○ Doctors ○ Exercise ○ Food ○ Happiness: Herbert Spencer ○ Healing ○ Longevity ○ Moderation ○ Physicians ○ Vegetarianism: Polly Strand

Health is the first of all liberties.

HENRI AMIEL (1821–1881). Journal, 3 April 1865, tr. Mrs. Humphrey Ward, 1887

From labor health, from health contentment springs.

JAMES BEATTIE (1735–1803). *The Minstrel; or, The Progress of Genius,* 8th ed., 13, 1784 (1771)

In health the flesh is graced, the holy enters the world.

WENDELL BERRY (1934–). "Healing" (1), 1977, *What Are People For?: Essays,* 1990

Health . . . is the first and greatest of all blessings.

LORD CHESTERFIELD (1694–1773). Letter to his son, 12 March 1768

The poorest man would not part with health for money, but . . . the richest would gladly part with all their money for health.

C. C. COLTON (1780–1832). *Lacon: or, Many Things in Few Words; Addressed to Those Who Think,* 1.225. 1823

Give me health and a day, and I will make the pomp of emperors ridiculous.

RALPH WALDO EMERSON (1803–1882). "Beauty," *Nature,* 1836

Health is not valued till Sickness comes.

THOMAS FULLER (1654–1734). Comp., *Gnomologia: Adages and Proverbs,* 2478, 1732

He that goes to bed thirsty riseth healthy.

GEORGE HERBERT (1593–1633). Comp., *Outlandish Proverbs,* 1003, 1640

Health without money is half a sickness.

JAMES HOWELL (1593–1666). Comp., "Italian" (p. 14), *Paroimiographia: Proverbs, or Old Sayed Sawes & Adages in English . . . Italian, French and Spanish,* 1659

In health we should continue to be the men we vowed to become when sickness prompted our words.

PLINY THE YOUNGER (A.D. 62?–113?). *Letters,* 7.26, tr. Betty Radice, 1963

Health is better than wealth.

JOHN RAY (1628–1705). Comp., *A Collection of English Proverbs,* p. 153, 1678

With health, everything is a source of pleasure; without it, nothing else, whatever it may be, is enjoyable. . . . Health is by far the most important element in human happiness.

ARTHUR SCHOPENHAUER (1788–1860). "The Wisdom of Life" (2), *Essays of Arthur Schopenhauer,* tr. T. Bailey Saunders, 1851

Having good health is very different from only being not sick.

SENECA THE YOUNGER (5? B.C.–A.D. 65). Preface (1.6) to *Natural Questions,* tr. Thomas A. Corcoran, 1921

Measure your health by your sympathy with morning and spring.

HENRY DAVID THOREAU (1817–1862). Journal, 25 February 1859

Who lacks health lacks everything.

SAYING (FRENCH)

HEART

See also • Conscience ○ Emotion ○ Heaven: Abraham Joshua Heschel ○ Mind ○ Peace: Anonymous (1) ○ Revelations: Ezekiel (2), Jeremiah (3), Moses, *Srimad Bhagavatam* (1) ○ Self ○ Soul ○ Thoughts: Vauvenargues ○ The Unconscious ○ Unity: John Muir

If the harte iz rite, the hed cant be very rong.

JOSH BILLINGS (1818–1885). *His Sayings,* 29, 1867

What is most needed is a loving heart.

THE BUDDHA (6th cent. B.C.). *The Three Baskets of Wisdom*

To live and move among men, the heart must break or harden.

CHAMFORT (1741–1794)

The human heart is vast enough to contain all the world.

JOSEPH CONRAD (1857–1924). *Lord Jim,* 34, 1900

The heart in thee is the Heart of all.

RALPH WALDO EMERSON (1803–1882). Journal, 11 October 1839

Speak to his heart, and the man becomes suddenly virtuous.

RALPH WALDO EMERSON (1803–1882). "The Over-Soul," *Essays: First Series,* 1841

Do not worry about what others are doing! Each of us should turn the searchlight inward and purify his or her own heart as much as possible.

MOHANDAS K. GANDHI (1869–1948). Radio broadcast, 16 January 1948. In Louis Fischer, *Gandhi: His Life and Message for the World,* 33, 1954

The tiny flame that lights up the human heart is like a blazing torch that comes down from heaven to light up the paths of mankind.

For in one soul are contained the hopes and feelings of all Mankind.

> KAHLIL GIBRAN (1883–1931). *The Voice of the Master,* 18, tr. Anthony R. Ferris, 1958

The heart of man is made to reconcile contradictions.

> DAVID HUME (1711–1776). "Of the Parties of Great Britain," *Essays, Moral and Political,* vol. 1, 1741

Blessed are the pure in heart, for they shall see God.

> JESUS (1st cent. A.D.). *Matthew* 5:8

Discouraged not by difficulties without, or the anguish of ages within, the heart listens to a secret voice that whispers: "Be not dismayed; in the future lies the Promised Land."

> HELEN KELLER (1880–1968). In Upton Sinclair, ed., *The Cry for Justice: An Anthology of the Literature of Social Protest,* 4, 1915

The heart of a good man is the sanctuary of God in this world.

> MADAME NECKER (1766–1841). Swiss writer. In Abel Stevens, *Madame de Staël,* 2, 1881

The heart has its reasons, which reason does not know.

> BLAISE PASCAL (1623–1662). *Pensées,* 277, 1670, tr. William F. Trotter, 1931

How frail the human heart must be—
a mirrored pool of thought. So deep
and tremulous an instrument
of glass that it can either sing,
or weep.

> SYLVIA PLATH (1932–1963). "I Thought That I Could Not Be Hurt," 1946. In introduction to *Letters Home: Correspondence 1950–1963,* ed. Amelia Schober Plath, 1975

Our heart is the sanctuary where the Lord of the universe . . . dwells in all His glory.

> SWAMI RAMDAS (1886–1963). In Whitall N. Perry, comp., *A Treasury of Traditional Wisdom,* p. 823, 1986

We distrust our heart too much, and our head not enough.

> JOSEPH ROUX (1834–1886). *Meditations of a Parish Priest,* 9.4, tr. Isabel F. Hapgood, 1886

Words may be false and full of art,
Sighs are the natural language of the heart.

> THOMAS SHADWELL (1642?–1692). *Psyche,* 3, 1675

Sit still my heart, do not raise your dust.
Let the world find its way to you.

> RABINDRANATH TAGORE (1861–1941). *Stray Birds,* 190, 1914

God desires the heart.

> *TALMUD* (A.D. 1st–6th cent.). Rabbinical writings. In Louis I. Newman, comp., *The Talmudic Anthology,* 137, 1945

Search thine own heart. What paineth thee
In others in thyself may be.

> JOHN GREENLEAF WHITTIER (1807–1892). "The Chapel of the Hermits," 85, 1851

❧

I bless the Lord who gives me counsel;
in the night also my heart instructs me.

> ANONYMOUS (*BIBLE*). *Psalms* 16:7

Keep your heart with all vigilance;
for from it flow the springs of life.

> SAYING (*BIBLE*). *Proverbs* 4:23

HEAVEN

See also • Earth ○ Heaven & Hell ○ Hell ○ Peace ○ Profit & Loss: Edwin H. Land ○ Redemption ○ Revelations: [especially] John ○ Salvation ○ Self-Realization (Being) ○ Unity ○ World

If thou would'st Nirvana reach . . . let not the fruit of action and inaction be thy motive.

> THE BOOK OF THE GOLDEN PRECEPTS. Ancient Buddhist writing. 2.33–34, tr. Helena Petrovna Blavatsky, 1889

All will love one another too much to desire to play the tyrant. Human nature will be reverenced too much not to be allowed to have free scope for the full and harmonious development of all its faculties.

> ORESTES A. BROWNSON (1803–1876). "New Views of Christianity, Society, and the Church," 1836. In George Hochfield, ed., *Selected Writings of The American Transcendentalists,* 1966

I've been walking through the middle of nowhere,
Trying to get to heaven before they close the door.

> BOB DYLAN (1941–). "Tryin' to Get to Heaven" (song), 1997

The Promised Land always lies on the other side of a wilderness.

> HAVELOCK ELLIS (1859–1939). *The Dance of Life,* 5.4, 1923

Crosses are Ladders to Heaven.

> THOMAS FULLER (1654–1734). Comp., *Gnomologia: Adages and Proverbs,* 1208, 1732

Heaven is a cheap Purchase, whatever [the] cost.

> THOMAS FULLER (1654–1734). Comp., *Gnomologia: Adages and Proverbs,* 2481, 1732

Ram Raj—The establishment of the Kingdom of Righteousness on earth.

> MOHANDAS K. GANDHI (1869–1948). In *Young India,* 4 May 1921

I looked, and beheld not poverty, neither did I see anything above what suffices. Rather did I meet brotherhood and equality.

I saw not any physician, for each morrow is a healer unto itself by the law of knowledge and experience.

Neither did I see a priest, for conscience was become the High Priest.

> KAHLIL GIBRAN (1883–1931). "A Glimpse into the Future," *A Tear and a Smile,* tr. H. M. Nahmad, 1950

Nothing is further than Earth from Heaven; nothing is nearer than Heaven to Earth.

> J. C. HARE (1795–1855) and A. W. HARE (1792–1834). *Guesses at Truth: Second Series,* p. 563, 1848, Macmillan edition, 1867

Love rules his kingdom without a sword.

> GEORGE HERBERT (1593–1633). Comp., *Outlandish Proverbs,* 541, 1640

The world to come is not only a hereafter but also a *herenow.*

> ABRAHAM JOSHUA HESCHEL (1907–1972). *Man Is Not Alone:*
> *A Philosophy of Religion,* 26, 1951

The heart of stone will be taken away, a heart of flesh will be given instead (*Ezekiel* 11:19). Even the nature of the beasts will change to match the glory of the age. The end of days will be the end of fear, the end of war; idolatry will disappear, knowledge of God will prevail.

> ABRAHAM JOSHUA HESCHEL (1907–1972). *The Prophets,* 9, 1962
>
> See Revelations: Ezekiel (2)

All the birds sing at once.
Men and animals rise up reborn.
What could be more natural?
After sorrow comes happiness.

> HO CHI MINH (1892–1969). Written while in prison, 1942–1943. "Good
> Days Coming," tr. Kenneth Rexroth, *Avant Garde* (magazine), 1968

In Heaven all desires turn to fruition.

> JAMES HOWELL (1593–1666). Comp., "Divers Centuries of New Sayings"
> (p. 4), *Paroimiographia: Proverbs, or Old Sayed Sawes & Adages in*
> *English . . . Italian, French and Spanish,* 1659

Heaven is always pictured as a community—never as made up of individuals who live in boxes, which they call homes, where they lock themselves in by locking others out.

> ELBERT HUBBARD (1856–1915). In Alice Hubbard, comp., *An American*
> *Bible,* p. 244, 1946

"Our kingdom go" is the necessary and unavoidable corollary of "Thy kingdom come."

> ALDOUS HUXLEY (1894–1963). *The Perennial Philosophy,* 6, 1946

The wolf shall dwell with the lamb,
  and the leopard shall lie down
    with the kid,
and the calf and the lion
    and the fatling together,
  and a little child shall lead them.
The cow and the bear shall feed;
  their young shall lie down together;
  and the lion shall eat straw
    like the ox.
The sucking child shall play over
    the hole of the asp,
  and the weaned child shall put
    his hand on the adder's den.
They shall not hurt or destroy
  in all my holy mountain;
for the earth shall be full of
  the knowledge of the Lord
    as the waters cover the sea.

> ISAIAH (8th cent. B.C.). *Isaiah* 11:6–9

The wilderness and the dry land shall be glad,
  the desert shall rejoice and blossom.

> ISAIAH (8th cent. B.C.). *Isaiah* 35:1

They shall build houses and inhabit them;
  they shall plant vineyards and eat their fruit.
They shall not build and another inhabit;
  they shall not plant and another eat.

> ISAIAH (8th cent. B.C.). *Isaiah* 65:21–22

Unless your righteousness exceeds that of the scribes and Pharisees, you will never enter the kingdom of heaven.

> JESUS (A.D. 1st cent.). *Matthew* 5:20

Not every one who says to me, "Lord, Lord," shall enter the kingdom of heaven, but he who does the will of my Father who is in heaven.

> JESUS (A.D. 1st cent.). *Matthew* 7:21

The kingdom of heaven is like a grain of mustard seed which a man took and sowed in his field; it is the smallest of all seeds, but when it has grown it is the greatest of shrubs and becomes a tree, so that the birds of the air come and make nests in its branches.

> JESUS (A.D. 1st cent.). *Matthew* 13:31–32

The kingdom of heaven is like treasure hidden in a field, which a man found and covered up, then in his joy he goes and sells all that he has and buys that field.

> JESUS (A.D. 1st cent.). *Matthew* 13:44

Unless you turn and become like children, you will never enter the kingdom of heaven.

> JESUS (A.D. 1st cent.). *Matthew* 18:3

It is easier for a camel to go through the eye of a needle than for a rich man to enter the kingdom of God.

> JESUS (A.D. 1st cent.). *Matthew* 19:24

The kingdom of God is within you.

> JESUS (A.D. 1st cent.). *Luke* 17:21 (King James Version)

Except a man be born again, he cannot see the kingdom of God.

> JESUS (A.D. 1st cent.). *John* 3:3 (King James Version)

And it shall come to pass afterward,
  that I will pour out my spirit on all flesh;
your sons and your daughters shall prophesy,
  your old men shall dream dreams,
  and your young men shall see visions.

> JOEL (6th cent. B.C.). *Joel* 2:28

Repent, for the kingdom of heaven is at hand.

> JOHN THE BAPTIST (A.D. 1st cent.). *Matthew* 3:2

The Kingdom of God is neither the thesis of individual enterprise nor the antithesis of collective enterprise, but a synthesis which reconciles the truths of both.

> MARTIN LUTHER KING, JR. (1929–1968). *Stride Toward Freedom,* 6, 1958

"Strawberry Fields Forever."

> JOHN LENNON (1940–1980) and PAUL McCARTNEY (1942–). Song title,
> 1967

Aim at Heaven and you will get earth "thrown in": aim at earth and you will get neither.

> C. S. LEWIS (1898–1963). *Mere Christianity,* rev. ed., 3.10, 1952

They shall beat their swords
    into plowshares,
  and their spears into
    pruning hooks;
nation shall not lift up sword
    against nation,
  neither shall they learn war
    any more;
but they shall sit every man
    under his vine and
    under his fig tree,
  and none shall make them afraid;
  for the mouth of the Lord of
    hosts has spoken.

> MICAH (8th cent. B.C.). *Micah* 4:3–4

A Heav'n on Earth.

> JOHN MILTON (1608–1674). *Paradise Lost,* 4.208, 1667

You will not enter Paradise until you have faith, and you will not complete your faith until you love one another.

> MUHAMMAD (A.D. 570?–632). *The Sayings of Muhammad,* 176, tr. Abdullah Al-Suhrawardy, 1941

[The Gospel] said: In that new way of living and new form of society, which is born of the heart, and which is called the Kingdom of Heaven, there are no nations, there are only individuals.

> BORIS PASTERNAK (1890–1960). *Doctor Zhivago,* 4.12, 1957, tr. Max Hayward and Manya Harari, 1958

The kingdom of God does not consist in talk but in power.

> PAUL (A.D. 1st cent.). *1 Corinthians* 4:20

All power renounced but that of love; the gentleness in all of us redeemed and exalted: the peaceable kingdom.

> THEODORE ROSZAK (1933–). "The Hard and the Soft." In Betty Roszak and T. Roszak, eds., *Masculine/Feminine: Readings in Sexual Mythology and the Liberation of Women,* 1969

This kingdom is not in our power to bring; but it is, to receive.

> JOHN RUSKIN (1819–1900). *Modern Painters,* 5.9.12, 1843–1860, ed. Ernest Rhys, 1906

We must . . . make the kingdom of God a reality in this world by works of love.

> ALBERT SCHWEITZER (1875–1965). "Religion and Modern Civilization," *Christian Century* (magazine), 1934

God has given us a world that nothing but our own folly keeps from being a paradise.

> GEORGE BERNARD SHAW (1856–1950). *Candida,* 1, 1893

When you go to heaven, Ann, you will be frightfully conscious of your wings for the first year or so. When you meet your relatives there, and they persist in treating you as if you were still a mortal, you will not be able to bear them. You will try to get into a circle which has never known you except as an angel.

> GEORGE BERNARD SHAW (1856–1950). *Man and Superman,* 1, 1903

If you go to heaven without being naturally qualified for it, you will not enjoy yourself there.

> GEORGE BERNARD SHAW (1856–1950). *Man and Superman,* 3, 1903

When man's maturer nature shall disdain
The playthings of its childhood; kingly glare
Will lose its power to dazzle; its authority
Will silently pass by; the gorgeous throne
Shall stand unnoticed in the regal hall,
Fast falling to decay; whilst falsehood's trade
Shall be as hateful and unprofitable
As that of truth is now.

> PERCY BYSSHE SHELLEY (1792–1822). *Queen Mab: A Philosophical Poem: With Notes,* 3, 1813

The lion now forgets to thirst for blood:
There might you see him sporting in the sun
Beside the dreadless kid; his claws are sheathed,
His teeth are harmless, custom's force has made
His nature as the nature of a lamb.

> PERCY BYSSHE SHELLEY (1792–1822). *Queen Mab: A Philosophical Poem: With Notes,* 8, 1813

Heaven must be in me before I can be in heaven.

> CHARLES STANFORD (1823–1886)

Be glad, you humble! Leap for joy, O poor! The Kingdom of God is yours if you will but live in the truth.

> THOMAS à KEMPIS (1380–1471). *The Imitation of Christ,* 3.58, tr. Leo Sherley-Price, 1952

When you travel to the Celestial City, carry no letter of introduction. When you knock, ask to see God—none of the servants. In what concerns you much, do not think that you have companions: know that you are alone in the world.

> HENRY DAVID THOREAU (1817–1862). Letter to Harrison Blake, 27 March 1848

Here or nowhere is our heaven.

> HENRY DAVID THOREAU (1817–1862). "Friday," *A Week on the Concord and Merrimack Rivers,* 1849

The kingdom of heaven is not the isolation of good from evil. It is the overcoming of evil by good.

> ALFRED NORTH WHITEHEAD (1861–1947). *Religion in the Making,* 4.4, 1926
>
> See Evil: Paul

There is a Temple in Heaven that is opened only through song.

> ZOHAR (A.D. 13th cent.). Jewish mystical writings. In Louis I. Newman, comp., *The Talmudic Anthology,* 229, 1945
>
> See Tears: Talmud

In the coming world, they will not ask me: "Why were you not Moses?" They will ask me: "Why were you not Zusya?"

> ZUSYA (?–1800). Before his death. In Martin Buber, "Zusya of Hanipol," *Tales of the Hasidim: The Early Masters,* tr. Olga Marx, 1947

❦

There ain't no kneeling in the land where I'm bound.

> ANONYMOUS (AFRICAN-AMERICAN). Hymn

Narrow is the road and wide is the gate that leads to heaven.

> ANONYMOUS

The Kingdom of God begins within you.
ANONYMOUS

HEAVEN & HELL

See also • Good & Evil: [especially] William Blake ∘ Heaven ∘ Hell ∘ Mind: John Milton

If it's heaven for climate, it's hell for company.
J. M. BARRIE (1860–1937). *The Little Minister,* 3, 1891

The way to heaven is as up a ladder, and the way to hell is as down a hill.
JOHN BUNYAN (1628–1688). *The Pilgrim's Progress,* 2.4, 1678–1684

Both heaven and hell are within us.
MOHANDAS K. GANDHI (1869–1948). In *Young India,* 25 October 1928

Paradise is nearer you than the thongs of your sandals; and the Fire likewise.
MUHAMMAD (A.D. 570?–632). *The Sayings of Muhammad,* 224, tr. Abdullah Al-Suhrawardy, 1941

I appeal as a human being to human beings: remember your humanity, and forget the rest. If you can do so, the way lies open to a new Paradise; if you cannot, nothing lies before but universal death.
BERTRAND RUSSELL (1872–1970). "Man's Duel with the Hydrogen Bomb," *Saturday Review,* 2 April 1955

Mankind today must either realize the Kingdom of God or perish.
ALBERT SCHWEITZER (1875–1965). "The Conception of the Kingdom of God in the Transformation of Eschatology," epilogue to E. N. Mozley, *The Theology of Albert Schweitzer for Christian Inquirers,* p. 115, 1951

There are only two countries: heaven and hell; but two conditions of men: salvation and damnation.
GEORGE BERNARD SHAW (1856–1950). *John Bull's Other Island,* 4, 1904

The road to Hell is paved with good intentions; the road to Heaven is paved with good deeds.
ANONYMOUS. In Gary W. Fenchuk, comp., "Developing Values," *Timeless Wisdom: Thoughts on Life . . . the Way It Should Be,* 1995

One road leads to heaven, but many lead to hell.
SAYING (HUNGARIAN)

Heaven and hell can be had in this world.
SAYING (YIDDISH)

HELL

See also • Heaven ∘ Heaven & Hell ∘ Holocaust: Hannah Arendt ∘ Nuclear Weapons: Richard M. Nixon ∘ War

Damnation is in the essence.
A damned person could be in the highest heaven:
He would still experience hell and its torments.
ANGELUS SILESIUS (1624–1677). In Whitall N. Perry, comp., *A Treasury of Traditional Wisdom,* p. 266, 1986

Hell is nothing other than complete separation from God.
NICOLAS BERDYAEV (1874–1948). *The Destiny of Man,* 3.2, 1931, tr. Natalie Duddington, 1955

Then I saw that there was a way to hell, even from the gates of heaven. . . .
So I awoke, and behold it was a dream.
JOHN BUNYAN (1628–1688). *The Pilgrim's Progress,* 1.11, 1678–1684

ABANDON ALL HOPE YE WHO ENTER HERE.
DANTE (A.D. 1265–1321). Inscription on the entrance gate to hell, "Inferno" (3.9), *The Divine Comedy,* 1321, tr. John Ciardi, 1954

What is hell? I maintain that it is the suffering of not being able to love.
FYODOR DOSTOYEVSKY (1821–1881). *The Brothers Karamazov,* 6.2(i), 1880, tr. Constance Garnett, 1912

All places shall be hell that are not heaven.
CHRISTOPHER MARLOWE (1564–1593). *The Tragicall History of Doctor Faustus,* 5, 1604

Hell is where no one has anything in common with anybody else except the fact that they all hate one another and cannot get away from one another and from themselves.
THOMAS MERTON (1915–1968). *New Seeds of Contemplation,* 17, 1961

Religion cannot compete with the political and military perils. What vision of hell compares with the realities we now confront?
C. WRIGHT MILLS (1916–1962). *The Causes of World War Three,* 23.2, 1958

The Hell within him.
JOHN MILTON (1608–1674). *Paradise Lost,* 4.20, 1667

All Hell broke loose.
JOHN MILTON (1608–1674). *Paradise Lost,* 4.918, 1667

The infliction of cruelty with a good conscience is a delight to moralists. That is why they invented Hell.
BERTRAND RUSSELL (1872–1970). *Sceptical Essays,* 1, 1928

Human imagination long ago pictured Hell, but it is only through recent skill that men have been able to give reality to what they had imagined.
BERTRAND RUSSELL (1872–1970). *Human Society in Ethics and Politics,* 2.10, 1962

❦

There is no redemption from hell.
SAYING (ENGLISH)

HELPING OTHERS

See also • Golden Rule: Saying (2) ∘ Nations: Ralph Waldo Emerson (2) ∘ Self-Reliance ∘ Service ∘ Unity: George Bernard Shaw

If I can stop one Heart from breaking
I shall not live in vain.
If I can ease one Life the Aching
Or cool one Pain

Or help one fainting Robin
Unto his Nest again
I shall not live in Vain.

> EMILY DICKINSON (1830–1886). "If I can stop one Heart from breaking"
> (complete poem), 1864?

You can't be of help to everybody! say the narrow-minded, and help nobody.

> MARIE von EBNER-ESCHENBACH (1830–1916). *Aphorisms,* p. 30,
> 1880–1905, tr. David Scrase and Wolfgang Mieder, 1994

People must help one another; it's nature's law.

> La FONTAINE (1621–1695). *Fables,* 8, 1668–1679

Every one helps his neighbor,
   and says to his brother, "Take courage!"

> ISAIAH (8th cent. B.C.). *Isaiah* 41:6

By helping yourself, you are helping mankind. By helping mankind, you are helping yourself. That's the law of all spiritual progress.

> CHRISTOPHER ISHERWOOD (1904–1986). Ed., introduction to *Vedanta
> for the Western World,* 1945

People have a right to their own lives, and if you can't help somebody, you ought to get out of their way.

> KATE MILLET (1934–). Andrea Freud Loewenstein interview, *Sojourners,*
> June 1987

[The] spirit of brotherhood recognizes of necessity both the need of self-help and also the need of helping others in the only way which ever ultimately does great good, that is, of helping them to help themselves.

> THEODORE ROOSEVELT (1858–1919). "Christian Citizenship,"
> 30 December 1900, *The Strenuous Life: Essays and Addresses,* 1905

If someone comes to you entreating aid, do not say in refusal: "Trust in God; He will help," but act as if there were no God, and none to help but you.

> THE SASSOVER (1745–1807). In Louis I. Newman, comp., *The Hasidic
> Anthology,* 186.1, 1934

Only those who have helped themselves know how to help others, and to respect their right to help themselves.

> GEORGE BERNARD SHAW (1856–1950). "The Womanly Woman," *The
> Quintessence of Ibsenism,* 1891

Not ignorant of trials,
I can now learn to help the miserable.

> VIRGIL (70–19 B.C.). *Aeneid,* 1.629, tr. Allen Mandelbaum, 1961

We are here to help each other get through this thing, whatever it is.

> MARK VONNEGUT. In Kurt Vonnegut, Jr., *Timequake,* 20, 1997

✿

If you're coming to help me, you are wasting your time. But if you have come because your liberation is bound up with mine, then let us work together.

> ANONYMOUS (ABORIGINAL AUSTRALIAN). Remark to the author by a
> woman who asked that her name not be used. In Jim Wallis, *The Soul
> of Politics: A Practical and Prophetic Vision for Change,* 8, 1994

People in the same boat should help each other.

> SAYING (CHINESE)

Every little bit helps.

> SAYING (ENGLISH)

HERESY

See also • Belief ○ Defiance ○ Dissent ○ Ideas ○ Ideology ○ Martyrdom ○ Nonconformity ○ Resistance ○ Standing Alone ○ Truth: Anonymous (4) ○ Wisdom: Henry David Thoreau (1) ○ Witchcraft

The greatest heresy is despair.

> ABRAHAM JOSHUA HESCHEL (1907–1972). In Taylor Branch, *Pillar of
> Fire: America in the King Years,* 2, 1998

Heresy is what the minority believe; it is the name given by the powerful to the doctrine of the weak.

> ROBERT G. INGERSOLL (1833–1899). "Heretics and Heresies," *Lectures
> of Col. R. G. Ingersoll: Latest,* 1898

In the history of the world, the man who is ahead has always been called a heretic.

> ROBERT G. INGERSOLL (1833–1899). "Liberty of Man, Woman and
> Child," *Lectures of Col. R. G. Ingersoll: Latest,* 1898

In corporation religions as in others, the heretic must be cast out not because of the probability that he is wrong but because of the possibility that he is right.

> ANTONY JAY (1930–). *Management and Machiavelli: An Inquiry into the
> Politics of Corporate Life,* 25, 1967

Whatever crime a man commits, if he acts without an error of his understanding he is not a heretic. For example, if a man commits fornication or adultery, although he is disobeying the command *Thou shalt not commit adultery,* yet he is not a heretic unless he holds the opinion that it is lawful to commit adultery.

> HEINRICH KRAMER (15th cent.) and JAMES SPRENGER (15th cent.).
> *Malleus Maleficarum,* 3 (introduction), 1486, tr. Montague Summers,
> 1928

The Catholic and the Communist are alike in assuming that an opponent cannot be both honest and intelligent. Each of them tacitly claims that "the truth" has already been revealed, and that the heretic, if he is not simply a fool, is secretly aware of "the truth" and merely resists it out of selfish motives.

> GEORGE ORWELL (1903–1950). "The Prevention of Literature," January
> 1946, *The Collected Essays, Journalism and Letters of George Orwell,*
> vol. 4, ed. Sonia Orwell and Ian Angus, 1968

The heresy of heresies was common sense. . . .
   The Party told you to reject the evidence of your eyes and ears. It was their final, most essential command.

> GEORGE ORWELL (1903–1950). *Nineteen Eighty-Four,* 1.7, 1949

The heresy of one age is the orthodox belief and "only infallible rule" of the next.

> THEODORE PARKER (1810–1860). "The Transient and Permanent in
> Christianity," 1841. In George Hochfield, ed., *Selected Writings of The
> American Transcendentalists,* 1966

The Inquisitor: Heresy begins with people who are to all appearances better than their neighbors. A gentle and pious girl or a young man, who has obeyed the command of our Lord by giving all his riches to the poor and putting on the garb of poverty, the life of austerity, and the rule of humility and charity, may be the founder of a heresy that will wreck both Church and Empire if not ruthlessly stamped out in time.

> GEORGE BERNARD SHAW (1856–1950). *Saint Joan,* 6, 1923

The thirteenth century bred in every heart such a sentiment in regard to heretics that inquisitors had no more misgivings in their proceedings than men would have now if they should attempt to exterminate rattlesnakes.

> WILLIAM GRAHAM SUMNER (1840–1910). *Folkways: A Study of the Sociological Importance of Usages, Manners, Customs, Mores, and Morals,* 232, 1907

The [Inquisition] which had destroyed honest thinkers and sincere churchmen had cultivated a class of smooth hypocrites and submissive cowards.

> WILLIAM GRAHAM SUMNER (1840–1910). *Folkways: A Study of the Sociological Importance of Usages, Manners, Customs, Mores, and Morals,* 263, 1907

HEROISM

See also • Boldness: Karl von Clausewitz ○ Celebrity ○ Genius ○ Greatness ○ Hero-Worship ○ Leaders ○ Myths ○ Pain: George Orwell ○ World: William James

How important it is for us to recognize and celebrate our heroes and she-roes!

> MAYA ANGELOU (1928–). In Chris Orr, "Moms and Whoopi: Pioneers of Black Theater," *Plexus,* November 1983

True heroism is remarkably sober, very undramatic. It is not the urge to surpass all others at whatever cost, but the urge to serve others at whatever cost.

> ARTHUR ASHE (1943–1993). In "Points to Ponder," *Reader's Digest,* August 1994

Heroism may be the only way to love. Now, heroism cannot be preached, it has only to show itself, and its mere presence may stir others to action. For heroism itself is a return to movement, and emanates from an emotion—infectious like all emotions—akin to the creative act.

> HENRI BERGSON (1859–1941). "Moral Obligation," *The Two Sources of Morality and Religion,* 1932, tr. R. Ashley Audra and Cloudesley Brereton, 1935

He whom prosperity humbles, and adversity strengthens, is the true hero.

> JOSH BILLINGS (1818–1885). "Stray Children," *Everybody's Friend, or; Josh Billing's Encyclopedia and Proverbial Philosophy of Wit and Humor,* 1874

The hero is known for achievements; the celebrity for well-knownness. The hero reveals the possibilities of human nature. The celebrity reveals the possibilities of the press and media. Celebrities are people who make news, but heroes are people who make history. Time makes heroes but dissolves celebrities.

> DANIEL J. BOORSTIN (1914–). In Ponchitta Pierce, "Who Are Our Heroes?" *Parade Magazine,* 6 August 1995
>
> See Celebrity: Boorstin (2)

Andrea: Unhappy is the land that breeds no hero.
Galileo: No, Andrea: Unhappy is the land that needs a hero.

> BERTOLT BRECHT (1898–1956). *Galileo,* 12, 1939, tr. Charles Laughton, 1961

Part of the magic of heroes and heroines has always been their ability to embody a vision of life that at the moment is not yet developed enough. . . . Heroes are not always just reflections of what has already happened but are also harbingers of what is to come.

> TODD BRENNAN. "Where Have All the Heroes Gone?" *The Critic,* Fall 1976

The heroes of all time have gone before us; the labyrinth is thoroughly known; we have only to follow the thread of the hero-path. And where we had thought to find an abomination, we shall find a god; . . . where we had thought to be alone, we shall be with all the world.

> JOSEPH CAMPBELL (1904–1987). Prologue (1) to *The Hero with a Thousand Faces,* 1949

The standard path of the mythological adventure of the hero is a magnification of the formula represented in the rites of passage: *separation—initiation—return:* which might be named the nuclear unit of the monomyth.

A hero ventures forth from the world of common day into a region of supernatural wonder: fabulous forces are there encountered and a decisive victory is won: the hero comes back from this mysterious adventure with the power to bestow boons on his fellow man.

> JOSEPH CAMPBELL (1904–1987). Prologue (3) to *The Hero with a Thousand Faces,* 1949

Having responded to his own call, and continuing to follow courageously as the consequences unfold, the hero finds all the forces of the unconscious at his side. Mother Nature herself supports the mighty task. And in so far as the hero's act coincides with that for which his society itself is ready, he seems to ride on the great rhythm of the historical process.

> JOSEPH CAMPBELL (1904–1987). *The Hero with a Thousand Faces,* 1.1.3, 1949

Alone in some little room . . . , the young world-apprentice learns the lesson of the seed powers, which reside just beyond the sphere of the measured and the named.

The myths agree that an extraordinary capacity is required to face and survive such experience.

> JOSEPH CAMPBELL (1904–1987). *The Hero with a Thousand Faces,* 2.3.2, 1949

The modern hero, the modern individual who dares to heed the call and seek the mansion of that presence with whom it is our whole destiny to be atoned, cannot, indeed must not, wait for his community to cast off its slough of pride, fear, rationalized avarice, and sanctified misunderstanding. "Live," Nietzsche says, "as though the day were here." It is not society that is to guide and save the creative hero, but precisely the reverse. And so every one of us shares the supreme ordeal—carries the cross of the redeemer—not in the bright moments of his tribe's great victories, but in the silences of his personal despair.

> JOSEPH CAMPBELL (1904–1987). Closing words, *The Hero with a Thousand Faces,* 1949

The hero of the book is condemned because he doesn't play the game. . . . If you ask yourself in what way Meursault doesn't play the game. The answer is simple. He refused to lie.

> ALBERT CAMUS (1913–1960). Preface to an American edition of *The Stranger* (1942). In Conor Cruise O'Brien, "The Fall," *New Republic,* 16 October 1995

In rebellious ages, when Kingship itself seems dead and abolished, Cromwell, Napoleon step forth again as Kings.

> THOMAS CARLYLE (1795–1881). "The Hero as King," *On Heroes, Hero-Worship, and the Heroic in History,* 1841

The hero saves us. Praise the hero! Now, who will save us from the hero?

> CATO THE ELDER (234–149 B.C.). Roman Senate speech. In David Schoenbrun, *The Three Lives of Charles de Gaulle,* pt. 2 (epigraph), 1968

No man is a hero to his valet.

> ANNE-MARIE de CORNUEL (1614–1694). *Lettres de Mlle Aïssé,* 12.13, 1728
> See Familiarity: William Hazlitt

When ye build yer triumphal arch to yer conquerin' hero, Hinnissey, build it out of bricks so the people will have somethin' convenient to throw at him as he passes through.

> FINLEY PETER DUNNE (1867–1936). "Fame"

I have regard to appearance still. So am I no hero.

> RALPH WALDO EMERSON (1803–1882). Journal, 6 April 1839

Every hero becomes a bore at last.

> RALPH WALDO EMERSON (1803–1882). "Uses of Great Men," *Representative Men,* 1850

In the grossly distorted individualism of today, we are incapable of imagining the selflessly disinterested hero. This may not matter; we may think we can do without him. But what it also means is that we are incapable of imagining the selflessly disinterested hero in ourselves who would give himself to a cause.

> HENRY FAIRLIE (1924–1990). "Too Rich for Heroes," *Harper's,* November 1978

Show me a hero, and I will write you a tragedy.

> F. SCOTT FITZGERALD (1896–1940). "The Note-Books" (E), *The Crack-Up,* ed. Edmund Wilson, 1945

A hero is a man who stands up manfully against his father and in the end victoriously overcomes him.

> SIGMUND FREUD (1856–1939). *Moses and Monotheism,* 1, 1939, tr. Katherine Jones, 1955

Whenever history is rising to supreme heights, she provides her heroes with the costumes, the limelight and the scenery of a great redemptionist drama.

> RENÉ FÜLÖP-MILLER. *Leaders, Dreamers, and Rebels: An Account of the Great Mass-Movements of History and of the Wish-Dreams That Inspired Them,* 2.3, 1935

No man, they say, is a hero to his valet. But that is merely because it takes a hero to appreciate a hero.

> GOETHE (1749–1832). "From Ottilie's Journal," *Elective Affinities,* 2.5, 1809, tr. R. J. Hollingdale, 1971

Heroism is active genius; genius, contemplative heroism. Heroism is the self-devotion of genius manifesting itself in action.

> J. C. HARE (1795–1855) and A. W. HARE (1792–1834). *Guesses at Truth: Second Series,* p. 302, 1848, Macmillan edition, 1867

The hero in history is the individual to whom we can justifiably attribute preponderant influence in determining an issue or event whose consequences would have been profoundly different if he had not acted as he did.

> SIDNEY HOOK (1902–1989). *The Hero in History: A Study in Limitation and Possibility,* 9, 1943
> See Greatness: Arthur M. Schlesinger, Jr. (1)

[The hero] finds a fork in the historical road, but he also helps, so to speak, to create it. He increases the odds of success for the alternative he chooses by virtue of the extraordinary qualities he brings to bear to realize it.

> SIDNEY HOOK (1902–1989). *The Hero in History: A Study in Limitation and Possibility,* 9, 1943

Life, misfortunes, isolation, abandonment, poverty, are battlefields which have their heroes; obscure heroes, sometimes greater than the illustrious heroes.

> VICTOR HUGO (1802–1885). "Marius" (5.1), *Les Misérables,* tr. Charles E. Wilbour, 1862

The hero type of leader acts as though possessed by a destiny that requires his being the center of attention, and having arrived there, he never willingly retires from the center until he feels no longer needed.

> EUGENE E. JENNINGS (1926–). *An Anatomy of Leadership: Princes, Heroes, and Supermen,* 6, 1960

The hero of the future will be that individual with the great mission to overcome the mass feeling of alienation and self-inadequacy. He will recognize that this struggle starts not with his community, nor even with his principal organization, but rather it starts with *himself.*

> EUGENE E. JENNINGS (1926–). *An Anatomy of Leadership: Princes, Heroes, and Supermen,* 11, 1960

Heroes are created by popular demand, sometimes out of the scantiest materials, or none at all.

> GERALD W. JOHNSON (1890–1980). *American Heroes and Hero-Worship,* 1, 1943

A hero is someone we can admire without apology.

> KITTY KELLEY (1942–). "An 80-Year Hitting Streak," *New York Times,* 25 February 1995

It was involuntary. They sank my boat.

> JOHN F. KENNEDY (1917–1963). When asked how he became a war hero. In Arthur M. Schlesinger, Jr., *A Thousand Days: John F. Kennedy in the White House,* 4.9, 1965

Heroes are such because of monomaniacal determination. They are rarely pleasant men; their rigidity approaches the fanatic.

> HENRY A. KISSINGER (1923–). *White House Years,* 12, 1979

The political leaders with whom we are familiar generally aspire to be superstars rather than heroes. The distinction is crucial. Superstars strive for approbation; heroes walk alone. Superstars crave consensus; heroes define themselves by the judgment of a future they see it as their task to bring about. Superstars seek success in a technique for eliciting support; heroes pursue success as the outgrowth of inner values.

> HENRY A. KISSINGER (1923–). "With Faint Praise," *New York Times Book Review,* 16 July 1995

One can "play the hero" a moment too soon or too late and be the biggest kind of fool. The successful hero steps into a situation at exactly the moment when audience expectation and the plot call for such a part; things have gotten as bad as possible for the victim, and the crisis has been properly developed; suspense and interest are at a maximum, so no one is tired of the situation; and the balance has become so precarious that it can easily be tipped in his favor.

> ORRIN E. KLAPP (1915–). *Symbolic Leaders: Public Dramas and Public Men,* 3, 1964

If a tiny force achieving a vast result makes a hero, a small result from a grandiose effort makes a fool.

> ORRIN E. KLAPP (1915–). *Symbolic Leaders: Public Dramas and Public Men,* 7 (footnote 32), 1964

Apart from great vanity, heroes are made like everybody else.

> LA ROCHEFOUCAULD (1613–1680). *Maxims,* 24, 1665, tr. Leonard Tancock, 1959

When you feel like the world is against you or you give up hope, you look at your heroes and say, "They were able to do it. They had hard times and a lot of opposition, but they got through it." Then you feel, "I can do it too."

> JOHN LEGUIZAMO (1965–). Columbian-born actor and playwright. In Ponchitta Pierce, "Who Are Our Heroes?" *Parade Magazine,* 6 August 1995

A hero . . . is not a hero until he is recognized as one. This means that the actualization of the hero is a two-way projection. First the hero must project by way of his deeds, his style, his character. When the projection registers, an imaginative process begins to remake the hero to fit as fully as possible the symbolic weight of his image. Legend and myth take over the historical personage, and through either an oral or a written tradition he is reborn in his heroic apotheosis.

> HAROLD LUBIN. Ed., "The Isolated Hero," *Heroes and Anti-Heroes,* 3, 1968

The asceticism, the scorn of material values, the search for transcendental experiences, the visionary fervor, all of these qualities so often characteristic of your rebel today are also common to religious mystics. Perhaps we are on the threshold of a new religious revival. If so, it will need and it will find new prophets and new saints—new heroes. . . . It would be ironic if this search ended in a new religious commitment to a God-ruled world.

> HAROLD LUBIN. Ed., "What's Past Is Prologue," *Heroes and Anti-Heroes,* 4, 1968

Stripped of all illusions, he must transcend nihilism and make of his rebellion against the absurdities of existence a god-like defense of human values.

> HAROLD LUBIN. Ed., "What's Past Is Prologue," *Heroes and Anti-Heroes,* 4, 1968

Only a hero can capture the secret imagination of a people, and so be good for the vitality of his nation; a hero embodies the fantasy and so allows each private mind the liberty to consider its fantasy and find a way to grow.

> NORMAN MAILER (1923–). "The Third Presidential Paper–The Existential Hero," 1960, *The Presidential Papers,* 1963

The chief business of the nation, as a nation, is the setting up of heroes, mainly bogus.

> H. L. MENCKEN (1880–1956). "On Being an American" (1), *Prejudices: Third Series,* 1922

They ask nothing of you except that you participate in their superabundant joy of living. They never inquire which side of the fence you are on because the world they inhabit has no fences. They make themselves invulnerable by habitually exposing themselves to every danger. They grow more heroic in the measure that they reveal their weaknesses.

> HENRY MILLER (1891–1980). *The Colossus of Maroussi,* 3, 1941

Heroes: Fanatics who succeed.

> DAVID A. MODELL. "A Modernist's Lexicon," *Smart Set,* September 1914

True heroism consists in rising superior to misfortune.

> NAPOLEON (1769–1821). *Napoleon in His Own Words,* 2, comp. Jules Bertaut, 1916

Within the Arab circle there is a role wandering aimlessly in search of a hero. . . . The role is to spark the tremendous latent strengths in the region surrounding us to create a great power, which will then rise up to a level of dignity and undertake a positive part in building the future of mankind.

> GAMAL ABDEL NASSER (1918–1970). *The Philosophy of the Revolution,* 3, 1954

To adopt the posture of the hero is the most unheroic of all acts.

> DOROTHY NORMAN (1905–1997). *The Hero: Myth/Image/Symbol,* 16, 1969

The high sentiments always win in the end, the leaders who offer blood, toil, tears and sweat always get more out of their followers than those who offer safety and a good time. When it comes to the pinch, human beings are heroic.

> GEORGE ORWELL (1903–1950). "The Art of Donald McGill," September 1941, *The Collected Essays, Journalism and Letters of George Orwell,* vol. 2, ed. Sonia Orwell and Ian Angus, 1968

Heroing is one of the shortest-lifed professions there is.

> WILL ROGERS (1879–1935). 17 February 1925, *The Autobiography of Will Rogers,* ed. Donald Day, 1949

Where have you gone, Joe DiMaggio?
A nation turns its lonely eyes to you.

> PAUL SIMON (1941–). "Mrs. Robinson" (song). In the film *The Graduate,* 1967

It is not heroes that make history, but history that makes heroes.

> JOSEPH STALIN (1879–1953)

Heroes come along when you need them.

> RONALD STEEL (1931–). Opening words, "Will He or Won't He?" *New York Times Book Review*, 17 September 1995

Who is a hero? He who turns his enemy into a friend.

> TALMUD (A.D. 1st–6th cent.), Rabbinical writings. In Louis I. Newman, comp., *The Talmudic Anthology*, 98, 1945

[Heroes] are famous or infamous because the progress of events has chosen to make them its steppingstones.

> HENRY DAVID THOREAU (1817–1862). Journal, 27 December 1837

What a hero one can be without moving a finger!

> HENRY DAVID THOREAU (1817–1862). Journal, 13 July 1838

The hero obeys his own law.

> HENRY DAVID THOREAU (1817–1862). Journal, 1 February 1852

Christ has emptied Himself of His divine power and glory to become incarnate as a man and to suffer death upon the cross for our sake. And for our sake likewise a bodhisattva who has reached the threshold of Nirvana has refrained from taking the last step into bliss. This heroic pathfinder has deliberately condemned himself to go on haunting the sorrowful treadmill of existence . . . ; and he has made this extreme sacrifice for the love of fellow sentient beings whose feet he can guide into the day of salvation so long as he pays the huge price of himself remaining sentient and suffering.

> ARNOLD J. TOYNBEE (1889–1975). "The World and the Greeks and Romans," 1952, *The World and the West*, 1953
>
> See Buddhism: *The Book of the Golden Precepts* (6) ○ Philosophers: Plato (3)

The greatest height of heroism to which an individual, like a people, can attain is to know how to face ridicule; better still, to know how to make oneself ridiculous and not to shrink from . . . ridicule.

> MIGUEL de UNAMUNO (1864–1936). Conclusion to *Tragic Sense of Life*, 1913, tr. J. E. Crawford Flitch, 1921

In modern movies, the hero may pull a fast one for the sake of his mother, or his girl friend, or some worthy ideal, but not for himself.

> DIXON WECTER. *The Hero in America: A Chronicle of Hero-Worship*, 18.2, 1941

The numberless unknown heroes equal to the greatest heroes known!

> WALT WHITMAN (1819–1892). "Song of Myself" (18), 1855, *Leaves of Grass*, 1855–1892

Is society debasing the idea of heroism by using it to describe anyone who makes people feel good about themselves?

> LENA WILLIAMS. "What It Takes to Make a Hero," *New York Times*, 18 June 1995

The Byronic hero is marked by deformity or defect in a way that drives him from the comforts of the prosaic world into the enforced solitude where genius creates an entirely new human vision, brilliant even if one-sided.

> GARRY WILLS (1934–). *Certain Trumpets: The Call of Leaders*, 1, 1994

No man is a hero to his valet or his relatives.

> ISRAEL ZANGWILL (1864–1926). *Dreamers of the Ghetto*, 1898

The cowards never started—and the weak died along the way.

> ANONYMOUS (AMERICAN). A settler who had made the trek across the Oregon Trail, 1845? In Bruce Catton, *This Week*, 11 March 1955

Heroism is endurance for one moment more.

> SAYING. Among Caucasian mountaineers. In George F. Kennan, letter to Henry Munroe Rogers, 25 July 1921

HERO-WORSHIP

See also • Heroism ○ Idolatry

Celebrity-worship and hero-worship should not be confused. Yet we confuse them every day, and by doing so we come dangerously close to depriving ourselves of all real models. We lose sight of the men and women who do not simply seem great because they are famous but who are famous because they are great.

> DANIEL J. BOORSTIN (1914–). *The Image: A Guide to Pseudo-Events in America*, 2 (introduction), 1961

The cult of the hero is the absolutely necessary complement of the massification of society. We see the automatic creation of this cult in connection with champion athletes [and] movie stars. . . . The individual who is prevented by circumstances from becoming a real person, who can no longer express himself through personal thought or action, who finds his aspirations frustrated, projects onto the hero all he would wish to be. He lives vicariously and experiences the athletic or amorous or military exploits of the god with whom he lives in spiritual symbiosis.

> JACQUES ELLUL (1912–1994). *Propaganda: The Formation of Men's Attitudes*, 4, 1962, tr. Konrad Kellen and Jean Learner, 1965

The youth, intoxicated with his admiration of a hero, fails to see, that it is only a projection of his own soul, which he admires.

> RALPH WALDO EMERSON (1803–1882). "Literary Ethics," address, Dartmouth College, Hanover (New Hampshire), 24 July 1838

A great style of hero draws equally all classes, all the extremes of society, till we say the very dogs believe in him.

> RALPH WALDO EMERSON (1803–1882). "Greatness," *Letters and Social Aims*, 1876

Anyone who idolizes you is going to hate you when he discovers that you are fallible. He never forgives. He has deceived himself, and he blames you for it.

> ELBERT HUBBARD (1856–1915). In Alice Hubbard, comp., *An American Bible*, p. 228, 1946

The same principles [that apply in polytheism] naturally deify mortals, superior in power, courage, or understanding, and produce *hero-worship*.

> DAVID HUME (1711–1776). Probable first use of the term hero-worship, *Four Dissertations*, 1757. In Dixon Wecter, *The Hero in America: A Chronicle of Hero-Worship*, 1.3, 1941

More books have been written about Napoleon than about any other human being. The fact is deeply and alarmingly significant. What must be the daydreams of people for whom the world's most agile social climber and ablest bandit is the hero they most desire to hear about? Duces and Fuehrers will cease to plague the world only when the majority of its inhabitants regard such adventurers with the same disgust as they now bestow on swindlers and pimps. So long as men worship the Caesars and Napoleons, Caesars and Napoleons will duly rise and make them miserable. The proper attitude toward the "hero" is not Carlyle's, but Bacon's. "He doth like the ape," wrote Bacon of the ambitious tyrant, " . . . the higher he climbs, the more he shows his arse." The hero's qualities are brilliant; but so is the mandrill's rump.

> ALDOUS HUXLEY (1894–1963). "Decentralization and Self-Government,"
> *Ends and Means: An Inquiry into the Nature of Ideals and into the
> Methods Employed for Their Realization,* 1937

It is part of the rational statesman's makeup to reject hero-worship—not only because he knows that he can be wrong but because such an attitude toward him on the people's part would destroy the very point of his political activity, the expansion of freedom.

> KARL JASPERS (1883–1969). *The Future of Mankind,* 14, 1958, tr. E. B.
> Ashton, 1961

Comrades! The cult of the individual acquired such monstrous size chiefly because Stalin himself, using all conceivable methods, supported the glorification of his own person.

> NIKITA KHRUSHCHEV (1894–1971). Speech at a closed session of the
> 20th Congress of the Communist Party, 23 February 1956

The initiation of all wise or noble things comes and must come from individuals; generally at first from some one individual. The honor and glory of the average man is that he is capable of following that initiative. . . . I am not countenancing the sort of "hero-worship" which applauds the strong man of genius for forcibly seizing on the government of the world and making it do his bidding in spite of itself. All he can claim is freedom to point out the way. The power of compelling others into it is not only inconsistent with the freedom and development of all the rest, but corrupting to the strong man himself.

> JOHN STUART MILL (1806–1873). *On Liberty,* 3, 1859

I have not the slightest faith in Carlyle. In ten years—possibly in five—he will be remembered only as a butt for sarcasm. . . . The book about "Hero-Worship"—is it possible that it ever excited a feeling beyond contempt? *No* hero-worshipper can possess anything within himself. That man is no man who stands in awe of his fellow-man.

> EDGAR ALLAN POE (1809–1849). Referring to Thomas Carlyle's *On
> Heroes, Hero-Worship, and the Heroic in History* (1841), April 1846,
> *Marginalia,* University Press of Virginia edition, 1981

To say that there is a case for heroes is not to say that there is a case for hero-worship. The surrender of decision, the unquestioning submission to leadership, the prostration of the average man before the Great Man—these are the diseases of heroism, and they are fatal to human dignity. . . . History amply shows that it is possible to have heroes without turning them into gods.

And history shows, too, that when a society, in flight from hero-worship, decides to do without great men at all, it gets into troubles of its own.

> ARTHUR M. SCHLESINGER, JR. (1917–). "The Decline of Greatness,"
> *Saturday Evening Post,* 1 November 1958

The power of the charlatan is dependent upon the fact that his clients consist, as it were, of passive charlatans. . . . Their worship of the heroic may be a substitute for action from which they are barred by circumstance, fear and convention.

> HANS SPEIER. "Risk, Security, and Modern Hero Worship," *Social Order
> and the Risks of War,* 1952

Hero-worship is strongest where there is least regard for human freedom.

> HERBERT SPENCER (1820–1903). *Social Statics,* 4.30.6, 1851

Bravery, honesty, strength of character are the stuff for hero-worship. At the boy's level, this worship gravitates toward the doer of spectacular deeds; on the average adult level, toward the wielder of power; and in the eyes of a more critical judgment, toward idealism and moral qualities.

> DIXON WECTER. *The Hero in America: A Chronicle of Hero-Worship,*
> 18.2, 1941

HESITATION

See also • Delay ◦ Indecision ◦ Presidents: Emmet John Hughes

It's all right to hesitate if you then go ahead!

> BERTOLT BRECHT (1898–1956). Prologue to *The Good Woman of
> Setzuan,* 1938-1940, tr. Eric Bentley, 1947

Hesitation increases in relation to risk in equal proportion to age.

> ERNEST HEMINGWAY (1899–1961). In A. E. Hotchner, *Papa Hemingway:
> A Personal Memoir,* 3, 1966

In crises boldness is the safest course. Hesitation encourages the adversary to persevere, maybe even to raise the ante.

> HENRY A. KISSINGER (1923–). *White House Years,* 9, 1979

He who hesitates is sometimes saved.

> JAMES THURBER (1894–1961). "The Glass in the Field," *The Thurber
> Carnival,* 1945

He who hesitates is last.

> MAE WEST (1893–1980). "Misc. West," *The Wit and Wisdom of Mae
> West,* ed. Joseph Weuntraub, 1967

❦

He who hesitates is bossed.

> SAYING (ENGLISH)

He who hesitates is lost.

> SAYING (ENGLISH)

HIPPIES

See also • Beat Generation

Do your thing. Be what you are. If you don't know what you are, find out.

Fuck leaders.

COMMUNICATION COMPANY (San Francisco). "A New Life Style" ("Sheep? Baa"), 6 April 1967. In Jerry Hopkins, ed., *The Hippie Papers: Notes from the Underground Press,* 1968

Abbie [Hoffman], you must understand, is pure Marxist-Lennonist—Harpo Marx and John Lennon.

JACK NEWFIELD. In Ethel Grodzins Romm, *The Open Conspiracy: What America's Angry Generation Is Saying,* 11, 1971

We Are the People Our Parents Warned Us Against.

NICHOLAS VON HOFFMAN. Book title, 1968

HISTORIANS

Includes • Written History

See also • Biography ○ History ○ Writers

History, real solemn history, I cannot be interested in. I read it a little as a duty; but it tells me nothing that does not either vex or weary me. The quarrels of popes and kings, with wars and pestilence in every page; the men so good for nothing, and hardly any women at all.

JANE AUSTEN (1775–1817). In "Thoughts on the Business of Life," *Forbes,* 7 July 1997

Any written history inevitably reflects the thought of the author in his time and cultural setting.

CHARLES A. BEARD (1874–1948). "Written History as an Act of Faith," *American Historical Review,* January 1934

Only three broad conceptions of all history as actuality are possible. History is chaos and every attempt to interpret it otherwise is an illusion. History moves around in a kind of cycle. History moves in a line, straight or spiral, and in some direction. The historian may seek to escape these issues by silence or by a confession of avoidance or he may face them boldly, aware of the intellectual and moral perils inherent in any decision—in his act of faith.

CHARLES A. BEARD (1874–1948). "Written History as an Act of Faith," *American Historical Review,* January 1934

History, *n.* An account mostly false, of events mostly unimportant, which are brought about by rulers mostly knaves, and soldiers mostly fools.

AMBROSE BIERCE (1842–?1914). *The Devil's Dictionary,* p. 57, 1911, Dover edition, 1958

The true historian, . . . seeking to compose a true picture of the thing acted must collect facts, select facts, and combine facts.

AUGUSTINE BIRRELL (1850–1933). "The Muse of History," *Obiter Dicta: Second Series,* 1887

What the metahistorian and the sociologist are trying to do is to clear away the confusion of facts and reveal the pattern, or establish the law, which lies beneath. But this is not the historian's purpose; what he wants to know is what happened. For him, general propositions are both necessary and illuminating, but they are not the essential purpose of his work.

ALAN BULLOCK (1914–). "The Historian's Purpose: History and Metahistory," *History Today,* February 1951

See Poets: Aristotle (1)

History is the record of what one age finds worthy of note in another.

JACOB BURCKHARDT (1818–1897). Introduction to *Judgments on History and Historians,* tr. Harry Zohn, 1958

The first accounts we have of mankind are but accounts of their butcheries. All empires have been cemented in blood.

EDMUND BURKE (1729–1797). *A Vindication of Natural Society,* p. 13, M. Cooper edition, 1756

The main work of the historian is not to record, but to evaluate; for, if he does not evaluate, how can he know what is worth recording?

EDWARD HALLETT CARR (1914–1997). *What Is History?* 1, 1961

What the historian is called on to investigate is what lies behind the act; and to this the conscious thought or motive of the individual actor may be quite irrelevant.

EDWARD HALLETT CARR (1914–1997). *What Is History?* 2, 1961

Progress in history is achieved through the interdependence and interaction of facts and values. The objective historian is the historian who penetrates most deeply into this reciprocal process.

EDWARD HALLETT CARR (1914–1997). *What Is History?* 5, 1961

Almost the whole of history is nothing but a series of horrors. . . . [Tyrants] seem willing to allow the crimes of their predecessors to be transmitted to posterity, to divert attention from the horror that they themselves inspire. In fact there is no longer any way of consoling the people except by teaching them that their forebears were as wretched as they are, or more so.

CHAMFORT (1741–1794). *Maxims and Thoughts,* 8, 1796, tr. W. S. Merwin, 1984

I am most anxious that nothing should be published which might seem to others to threaten our current relations in our public duties or impair the sympathy *and* understanding which exists between our two countries. I have therefore gone over the book [*The Second World War: Triumph and Tragedy,* the last volume of his six volume account] again in the last few months and have taken great pains to ensure that it contains nothing which might imply that there was in those days any controversy or lack of confidence between us.

WINSTON CHURCHILL (1874–1965). Letter to Pres. Dwight D. Eisenhower, 1953. In Timothy Garton Ash, "In The Churchill Museum," *New York Review of Books,* 7 May 1987

History will bear me out, particularly as I shall write that history myself.

WINSTON CHURCHILL (1874–1965). In Timothy Garton Ash, "In The Churchill Museum," *New York Review of Books,* 7 May 1987

I never [read history] for the story itself as a story. The only thing interesting to me was the principles to be evolved from, and illustrated by, the facts.

SAMUEL TAYLOR COLERIDGE (1772–1834). 13 July 1832, *Table Talk,* 1835

[Written] history is largely the glorification of the iniquities of the triumphant.

PAUL ELDRIDGE (1888–1982). *Maxims for a Modern Man,* 1023, 1965

Historians . . . are the guardians of mankind's collective memory.
> PIETER GEYL (1887–1966). *Debates with Historians*, rev. ed., 13, 1958 (1955)

History . . . is, indeed, little more than the register of the crimes, follies, and misfortunes of mankind.
> EDWARD GIBBON (1737–1794). *The Decline and Fall of the Roman Empire*, 3, 1776–1788

Truth, naked unblushing truth, the first virtue of more serious history.
> EDWARD GIBBON (1737–1794). *Memoirs of My Life and Writings*, p. 5, 1796, Alex. Murray edition, 1869

History repeats itself. Historians repeat each other.
> PHILIP GUEDALLA (1889–1944). "Some Historians," *Supers and Supermen*, 1920

We are human because, at a very early stage in the history of the species, our ancestors discovered a way of preserving and disseminating the results of experience.
> ALDOUS HUXLEY (1894–1963). "Knowledge and Understanding," *Tomorrow and Tomorrow and Tomorrow and Other Essays*, 1956

Events in the past may be roughly be divided into those which probably never happened and those which do not matter. This is what makes the trade of historian so attractive.
> DEAN WILLIAM RALPH INGE (1860–1954). "Prognostications," *Assessments and Anticipations*, 1929

What are all the records of history, but narratives of successive villainies, of treasons and usurpations, massacres and wars?
> SAMUEL JOHNSON (1709–1784). In *The Rambler* (English journal), 175, 19 November 1751

History is not contained in thick books but lives in our very blood.
> CARL G. JUNG (1875–1961). "Woman in Europe," 1927, *Civilization in Transition*, tr. R. F. C. Hull, 1964

A historian is often just a journalist looking backward.
> KARL KRAUS (1874–1936). 1910. In Thomas S. Szasz, *Karl Kraus and the Soul-Doctors: A Pioneer Critic and His Criticism of Psychiatry and Psychoanalysis*, 8, 1976

The time is not come for impartial history. If the truth were told just now, it would not be credited.
> ROBERT E. LEE (1807–1870). 1868. In David Macrae, *The Americans at Home*, 20, 1870

The search for truth for truth's sake is the mark of the historian.
> B. H. LIDDELL HART (1895–1970). "Blinding Loyalties," *Why Don't We Learn from History?* 1944

A sound rule of historical evidence is that while assertions should be treated with critical doubt, admissions are likely to be reliable.
> B. H. LIDDELL HART (1895–1970). "The Exploration of History," *Why Don't We Learn from History?* 1944

The vital influences are to be detected, not in the formal documents compiled by rulers, ministers and generals, but in their marginal notes and verbal asides.
> B. H. LIDDELL HART (1895–1970). "The Germs of War," *Why Don't We Learn from History?* 1944

History has its foreground and its background; and it is principally in the management of its perspective that one artist differs from another. Some events must be represented on a large scale, others diminished; the great majority will be lost in the dimness of the horizon; and a general idea of their joint effect will be given by a few slight touches.
> THOMAS BABINGTON MACAULAY (1895–1970). "History," *The Edinburgh Review* (Scotland), May 1828

The perfect historian is he in whose work the character and spirit of an age is exhibited in miniature.
> THOMAS BABINGTON MACAULAY (1800–1859). "History," *The Edinburgh Review* (Scotland), May 1828

The histories of mankind that we possess are histories only of the higher classes.
> THOMAS ROBERT MALTHUS (1766–1834). *An Essay on the Principle of Population, as it Affects the Future Improvement of Society*, 1.2, 1798

The challenge [in writing history] is to get the reader beyond thinking that things had to be way they turned out and to see the range of possibilities of how it could have been otherwise.
> DAVID McCULLOUGH (1933–). In Esther B. Fein, "Immersed in Facts, to Touch Truman's Life," *New York Times*, 14 August 1992

Few learn much from history who do not bring much with them to its study.
> JOHN STUART MILL (1806–1873). *The Subjection of Women*, 1, 1869

When the anonymous masses enter history, it is chiefly to be slaughtered in battle, to die of famine or privation—to illustrate the failures of their betters. . . . We have the mighty pyramids, but no firsthand account of the feelings of the wretches who built them.
> HERBERT J. MULLER (1905–1982). *Uses of the Past: Profiles of Former Societies*, 3.4, 1952

History is written by the winners.
> GEORGE ORWELL (1903–1950). "As I Please," 4 February 1944, *The Collected Essays, Journalism and Letters of George Orwell*, vol. 3, ed. Sonia Orwell and Ian Angus, 1968

If all records told the same tale—then the lie passed into history and became truth. "Who controls the past," ran the Party slogan, "controls the future: who controls the present controls the past." . . . All that was needed was an unending series of victories over your own memory. "Reality control," they called it; in Newspeak, "doublethink."
> GEORGE ORWELL (1903–1950). *Nineteen Eighty-Four*, 1.3, 1949

When one knew that any document was due for destruction, or even when one saw a scrap of waste paper lying about, it was an automatic action to lift the flap of the nearest *memory hole* and drop it in, whereupon it would be whirled away on a current of warm air to the enormous furnaces which were hidden somewhere in the recesses of the building. [Italics added.]
> GEORGE ORWELL (1903–1950). On the Ministry of Truth's destruction of evidence at variance with the current Party line, *Nineteen Eighty-Four*, 1.4, 1949

Fortune has caused nearly all events in the known world to point in one direction, and she has compelled everything to incline toward one and the same goal. It is therefore my duty to concentrate for the reader through my history, in one overall survey, the workings of Fortune through which she has fulfilled her general design. . . .

It is only by interconnecting and comparing each event with all others, and by noting similarities and differences, that one can gain the ability to observe the facts closely and to extract both pleasure and profit from history.

> POLYBIUS (208?–126? B.C.). *The Histories,* 1.4, tr. Mortimer Chambers, 1966

There is no history of mankind, there is only an indefinite number of histories of all kinds of aspects of human life. And one of these is the history of political power. This is elevated into the history of the world. But . . . *the history of power politics is nothing but the history of international crime and mass murder.* . . . This history is taught in schools, and some of the greatest criminals are extolled as its heroes.

> KARL POPPER (1902–1994). *The Open Society and Its Enemies,* 2.25.4, 1945

The easiest way to change history is to become a historian.

> REVISIONIST'S RULE. In Paul Dickson, comp., *The Official Explanations,* p. 191, 1980

The history of the world and its peoples
in three words— . . .
 "Born,
  troubled,
  died."

> CARL SANDBURG (1878–1967). *The People, Yes,* 49, 1936

"I shall arrange the facts and leave the interpretation to the reader," said the hopeful biographer to the somber historian. "The moment you begin to arrange you interpret," emitted the somber historian.

> CARL SANDBURG (1878–1967). *The People, Yes,* 67, 1936

Historians ought to stay out of the future.

> ARTHUR M. SCHLESINGER, JR. (1917–). Interview, *Playboy,* May 1966

The present, as historians well know, re-creates the past. This is partly because, once we know how things have come out, we tend to rewrite the past in terms of historical inevitability.

> ARTHUR M. SCHLESINGER, JR. (1917–). "The Historian as Participant," *Daedalus,* Spring 1971

The historian is a prophet looking backwards.

> FRIEDRICH von SCHLEGEL (1772–1829). "Selected Aphorisms from *The Athenaeum*" (80), *Dialogue on Poetry and Literary Aphorisms,* 1797-1800, tr. Ernst Behler and Roman Struc, 1968

The historian must recognize that history is not a scientific enterprise but a moral one. It is the study of human beings involved in an extraordinary drama, and its dramatic qualities are related to the moral values inherent in all life.

> PAGE SMITH (1917–1995). *The Historian and History,* 14, 1964

The continual rearrangement of the past to suit current prejudices is . . . the historian's work.

> RONALD STEEL (1931–). "Two Cheers for Ike," *New York Review of Books,* 24 September 1981

The absence of romance in my history will, I fear, detract somewhat from its interest; but if it be judged useful by those inquirers who desire an exact knowledge of the past as an aid to the interpretation of the future, which in the course of human things must resemble if it does not reflect it, I shall be content. In fine, I have written my work, not as an essay which is to win the applause of the moment, but as a possession for all time.

> THUCYDIDES (460?–400? B.C.). *The Peloponnesian War,* 1.22, tr. Richard Crawley and rev. T. E. Wick, 1982

The general historian looks for the cause of the event not in the power of any one individual but in the interaction of many persons connected with the event.

> LEO TOLSTOY (1828–1910). "Epilogue" (2.2), *War and Peace,* 1863–1869, tr. Rosemary Edmonds, 1957

The historian's elemental question[:] "How has this come out of that?"

> ARNOLD J. TOYNBEE (1889–1975). *A Study of History,* 10.91, 1954

The study of history would be meaningless if it did not have an ultimately religious significance and religious goal.

> ARNOLD J. TOYNBEE (1889–1975). *Surviving the Future,* 4, 1971

Selection [in writing history] is the task of distinguishing the significant from the insignificant. It must be honest, that is, true to the circumstances, and fair, that is, truly representative of the whole, never loaded. It can be used to reveal large meaning in a small sample.

> BARBARA W. TUCHMAN (1912–1989). "Problems in Writing the Biography of General Stilwell," 1971, *Practicing History: Selected Essays,* 1981

Although this work is a History, I believe it to be true.

> MARK TWAIN (1835–1910). Opening words, "3,000 Years Among the Microbes," 1905, *Mark Twain's Which Was the Dream? And Other Symbolic Writings of the Later Years,* ed. John S. Tuckey, 1968

Official history is a matter of believing murderers on their own word.

> SIMONE WEIL (1909–1943). In Thomas Merton, "The Death of God and the End of History," *Faith and Violence,* 1968

When I read history, I want to know where I am. The date should be at the top of each page.

> ALFRED NORTH WHITEHEAD (1861–1947). 14 November 1944, *Dialogues of Alfred North Whitehead,* rec. Lucien Price, 1954

As soon as histories are properly told, there is no more need of romances.

> WALT WHITMAN (1819–1892). Preface (1855) to *Leaves of Grass,* 1855–1892

HISTORY

See also • Blunders: A. J. P. Taylor ○ Change: [especially] Alvin Toffler (4) ○ Circumstances ○ Civilization ○ Class ○ Crises ○ Crowds ○ Culture ○ Education ○ Events ○ Evolution ○ Freedom: Leo Baeck ○ God & History ○ God & the World ○ Greatness: Thomas Carlyle (2) ○ Historians ○ Imperialism ○ International Relations ○ Man ○ Mankind ○ Mass Movements ○ Myths ○ Nonviolence ○ Past ○ Politics ○ Progress ○ Purpose ○ Reform ○ Religion ○ Revolution ○ Violence ○ War ○ World

1. Whom the gods destroy, they first make mad with power.
2. The mills of God grind slowly, yet they grind exceedingly small.
3. The bee fertilizes the flower it robs.
4. When it is dark enough, you can see all the stars.

> CHARLES A. BEARD (1874–1948). Historian. When asked if he could summarize the lessons of history in a short book, he said he could do it in four sentences, "Condensed History Lesson," *Reader's Digest*, February 1941

There is no obstacle which cannot be broken down by wills sufficiently keyed up, if they deal with it in time. There is thus no unescapable historic law.

> HENRI BERGSON (1859–1941). "Final Remarks," *The Two Sources of Morality and Religion*, 1932, tr. R. Ashley Audra and Cloudesley Brereton, 1935

We are all victims as well as agents of the historical process.

> SIR HERBERT BUTTERFIELD (1900–1979). "Marxist History" (1), *History and Human Relations*, 1952

There is the moral of all human tales,
'Tis but the same rehearsal of the past,
First Freedom, and then Glory—when that fails,
Wealth, vice, corruption—barbarism at last.

> LORD BYRON (1788–1824). *Childe Harold's Pilgrimage*, 4.108, 1812–1818

If men could learn from history, what lessons it might teach us! But passion and party blind our eyes, and the light which experience gives is a lantern on the stern, which shines only on the waves behind us!

> SAMUEL TAYLOR COLERIDGE (1772–1834). 18 December 1831, *Table Talk*, 1835

History is a vast early warning system.

> NORMAN COUSINS (1912–1990). "Editor's Odyssey: Gleanings from Articles and Editorials by N.C.," 1973, ed. Susan Schiefelbein, *Saturday Review*, 15 April 1978

History's biggest battles in the last analysis are fought in the hidden corners of our lives.

> PETER W. DICKSON. *Kissinger and the Meaning of History*, 5, 1978

History is philosophy teaching by examples.

> DIONYSIUS OF HALICARNASSUS (1st cent. B.C.). *The Antiquities of Rome*

Every observation of history inspires a confidence that we shall not go far wrong; that things will mend.

> RALPH WALDO EMERSON (1803–1882). "The Young American," lecture, Mercantile Library Association, Boston, 7 February 1844

Believe the faintest of your presentiments against the testimony of all sacred and profane history.

> RALPH WALDO EMERSON (1803–1882). Journal, 1859, undated

The first lesson of history is the good of evil.

> RALPH WALDO EMERSON (1803–1882). "Considerations by the Way," *The Conduct of Life*, 1860

The use of history is to give value to the present hour and its duty.

> RALPH WALDO EMERSON (1803–1882). "Work and Days," *Society and Solitude*, 1870

The history of man is a series of conspiracies to win from nature some advantage without paying for it.

> RALPH WALDO EMERSON (1803–1882). "Demonology," *Lectures and Biographical Sketches*, 1883

The history of mankind is the history of arrested growth.

> RALPH WALDO EMERSON (1803–1882). Title essay, *Natural History of Intellect and Other Papers*, 1893

History is more or less bunk. It's tradition. We don't want tradition. We want to live in the present, and the only history that is worth a tinker's dam is the history we make today.

> HENRY FORD (1863–1947). Charles N. Wheeler interview, *Chicago Tribune*, 25 May 1916 (Popular version: History is bunk.)

History is past politics, and politics present history.

> EDWARD AUGUSTUS FREEMAN (1823–1892). *The Methods of Historical Study*, 1, 1886

What we may be witnessing is not the end of the Cold War but the end of history as such; that is, the end point of man's ideological evolution and the universalization of Western liberal democracy.

> FRANCIS FUKUYAMA. In *National Interest*, Summer 1989

To believe that what has not occurred in history will not occur at all is to argue disbelief in the dignity of man.

> MOHANDAS K. GANDHI (1869–1948). In Louis Fischer, *The Life of Mahatma Gandhi*, 16, 1950

History is but the unrolled scroll of prophecy.

> JAMES A. GARFIELD (1831–1881). President. "The Province of History," *Williams Quarterly*, June 1856

Parallels in history, however indispensable and frequently instructive, are never wholly satisfactory, because each phenomenon is embedded in its own circumstances, never to be repeated, from which it cannot be completely detached.

> PIETER GEYL (1887–1966). "Toynbee's System of Civilizations" (7), 1948. In Geyl, Arnold J. Toynbee and Pitirim A. Sorokin, *The Pattern of the Past: Can We Determine It?* 1949

There are only two great currents in the history of mankind: the baseness which makes conservatives and the envy which makes revolutionaries.

> JULES de GONCOURT (1830–1870). Journal, 12 July 1867, tr. Robert Baldick, 1980

What experience and history teach is this—that peoples and governments never have learned anything from history, or acted on principles deduced from it.

> GEORG HEGEL (1770–1831). Introduction (2.2) to *Philosophy of History*, 1832, tr. John Sibree, 1900
> See Past: George Santayana

The history of the world is none other than the progress of the consciousness of freedom.

> GEORG HEGEL (1770–1831). Introduction (3.2.1) to *Philosophy of History*, 1832, tr. John Sibree, 1900

The march of world history stands outside virtue, vice and justice.

> GEORG HEGEL (1770–1831). In Isaiah Berlin, "The Question of
> Machiavelli," *New York Review of Books*, 4 November 1971

Unless history is a vagary of nonsense, there must be a counterpart to the immense power of man to destroy, there must be a voice that says NO to man, a voice not vague, faint and inward, like qualms of conscience, but equal in spiritual might to man's power to destroy.

> ABRAHAM JOSHUA HESCHEL (1907–1972). *God in Search of Man:*
> *A Philosophy of Judaism,* 17, 1955
>
> See Conversion: James W. Douglass

The darkness of history . . . conceals a light. Beyond the mystery is meaning. And the meaning is destined to be disclosed.

> ABRAHAM JOSHUA HESCHEL (1907–1972). *The Prophets,* 9, 1962
>
> See Mystery: Heschel

The "real movement" of history, it turns out, is fueled not by matter but by spirit, by the will to freedom.

> GERTRUDE HIMMELFARB (1922–). *On Looking into the Abyss,* 3, 1994

History is a bath of blood.

> WILLIAM JAMES (1842–1910). *The Moral Equivalent of War* (pamphlet),
> 1910

The drumbeat of history is quickening.

> LYNDON B. JOHNSON (1908–1973). Speech before the National
> Industrial Conference Board, Washington, 17 February 1965

History, Stephen said, is a nightmare from which I am trying to awake.

> JAMES JOYCE (1882–1941). *Ulysses,* 1, 1922

No one can make history who is not willing to risk everything for it, to carry the experiment with his own life through to the bitter end, and to declare that his life is not a continuation of the past but a new beginning.

> CARL G. JUNG (1875–1961). "Woman in Europe," 1927, *Civilization in*
> *Transition,* tr. R. F. C. Hull, 1964

History is made out of the failures and heroism of each insignificant moment. If one throws a stone into a river, it produces a succession of ripples. But most men live without being conscious of a responsibility which extends beyond themselves. And that—I think—is at the root of our misery.

> FRANZ KAFKA (1883–1924). In Gustav Janouch, *Conversations with*
> *Kafka,* p. 76, tr. Goronwy Rees, 1953

To have a sense of history one must consider *oneself* a piece of history.

> ALFRED KAZIN (1915–1998). "The Self as History: Reflections on
> Autobiography." In Marc Pachter, *Telling Lives: The Biographer's Art,*
> 1979

Men make their own history, but they . . . make it within a historical circumstance which can restrict (as well as open up) possibilities.

> PAUL KENNEDY (1945–). Introduction to *The Rise and Fall of the Great*
> *Powers: Economic Change and Military Conflict from 1500 to 2000,*
> 1987

The ultimate meaning of history—as of life—we can find only within ourselves.

> HENRY A. KISSINGER (1923–). "The Meaning of History: Reflections on
> Spengler, Toynbee and Kant" (unpublished undergraduate thesis),
> p. 23, 1950

As a professor, I tended to think of history as run by impersonal forces. But when you see it in practice, you see the difference personalities make.

> HENRY A. KISSINGER (1923–). Remark to reporters after his first Middle
> East shuttle visit, January 1974. In Walter Isaacson, introduction
> (epigraph) to *Kissinger: A Biography,* 1992

History is not, of course, a cookbook offering pretested recipes. It teaches by analogy, not by maxims.

> HENRY A. KISSINGER (1923–). *White House Years,* 3, 1979

The most persistent sound which reverberates through history is the beating of war drums.

> ARTHUR KOESTLER (1905–1983). Prologue to *Janus: A Summing Up,*
> 1978

The memorable events of history are the visible effects of invisible changes in human thought.

> GUSTAVE LE BON (1841–1931). Introduction to *The Crowd: A Study of*
> *the Popular Mind,* 1895, Viking Press edition, 1960

History does not move in a straight line, but by zigzags.

> LENIN (1870–1924). In Raymond L. Garthoff, *How Russia Makes War:*
> *Soviet Military Doctrine,* 10, 1954

The practical value of history is to throw the film of the past through the material projector of the present on to the screen of the future.

> B. H. LIDDELL HART (1895–1970). *The Remaking of Modern Armies,* 11,
> 1928

The history of mankind is the history of thought—of the gradual ascendancy of mind over matter.

> B. H. LIDDELL HART (1895–1970). September 1935, *Thoughts on War,*
> 1.1, 1944

History marches on the stomachs of statesmen.

> B. H. LIDDELL HART (1895–1970). "The Exploration of History,"
> *Why Don't We Learn from History?* 1944

The people, and the people alone, are the motive force in the making of world history.

> MAO TSE-TUNG (1893–1976). "On Coalition Government," 23 April
> 1945, *Selected Works of Mao Tse-tung,* Foreign Languages Press edi-
> tion, vol. 3, 1965

Men make their own history, but they do not make it just as they please; they do not make it under circumstances chosen by themselves but under circumstances directly encountered, given and transmitted from the past.

> KARL MARX (1818–1883). *The Eighteenth Brumaire of Louis Napoleon,*
> 1, 1852, *The Marx-Engels Reader,* 2nd ed., ed. Robert C. Tucker, 1978

The history of all hitherto existing society is the history of class struggles.

> KARL MARX (1818–1883) and FRIEDRICH ENGELS (1820–1895).
> Opening words, *The Communist Manifesto,* 1847, ed. Engels, 1888

A nation that forgets its past can function no better than an individual with amnesia.

> DAVID McCULLOUGH. In Digby Diehl, "Publishing Is the Big Winner at the 29th National Book Awards," *Los Angeles Times Book Review,* 23 April 1978

[History] is made up of the total effect of all our decisions and actions.

> THOMAS MERTON (1915–1968). "Is 'the World' a Problem?" *Katallagate,* Spring 1974

History is the myth, the true myth, of man's fall made manifest in time.

> HENRY MILLER (1891–1980). *Plexus,* 12, 1949

To be grounded in history is to expect of the future that which does not follow mechanistically but flows from large decisions not yet made.

> C. WRIGHT MILLS (1916–1962). *Power, Politics and People: The Collected Essays of C. Wright Mills,* 1.3.3, 1942, ed. Irving Louis Horowitz, 1963

America was discovered accidentally by a great seaman who was looking for something else. . . . History is like that, very chancy.

> SAMUEL ELIOT MORISON (1887–1976). *The Oxford History of the American People,* 2, 1965

History perfect and complete would be cosmic self-consciousness.

> FRIEDRICH NIETZSCHE (1844–1900). *Assorted Opinions and Maxims,* 185, 1879, tr. R. J. Hollingdale, 1977

History consists of a series of swindles, in which the masses are first lured into revolt by the promise of Utopia, and then, when they have done their job, enslaved over again by new masters.

> GEORGE ORWELL (1903–1950). Summarizing Burnham's view of history. "James Burnham and the Managerial Revolution," May 1946, *The Collected Essays, Journalism and Letters of George Orwell,* vol. 4, ed. Sonia Orwell and Ian Angus, 1968

History is simply the biography of the mind of man.

> SIR WILLIAM OSLER (1849–1919). "The Growth of Truth" (1), Harveian Oration, Royal College of Physicians, London, 18 October 1906, *A Way of Life and Selected Writings of Sir William Osler,* 1951

History teaches us the mistakes we are going to make.

> LAURENCE J. PETER (1919–1990). Comp., *Peter's Quotations: Ideas for Our Time,* p. 244, 1977
>
> See Past: George Santayana

History [is] . . . an exercise in political ironics—an intelligible story of how men's actions produce results other than those they intended.

> J. G. A. POCOCK. In Garry Wills, *The Kennedy Imprisonment: A Meditation on Power,* pt. 5 (epigraph), 1981

The knowledge gained from history is the truest education and training for political action.

> POLYBIUS (208?–126? B.C.). *The Histories,* 1.1, tr. Mortimer Chambers, 1966

History is invaluable in increasing our knowledge of human nature because it shows how people may be expected to behave in new situations. Many prominent men and women are completely ordinary in character, and only exceptional in their circumstances.

> BERTRAND RUSSELL (1872–1970). "How to Read and Understand History," *Understanding History, And Other Essays,* 1957

History . . . is for time what geography is for space.

> ARTHUR SCHOPENHAUER (1788–1860). "The Art of Literature: On Some Forms of Literature," *Essays of Arthur Schopenhauer,* tr. T. Bailey Saunders, 1851

One truth stands firm. All that happens in world history rests on something spiritual. If the spiritual is strong, it creates world history. If it is weak, it suffers world history. The question is, shall we make world history or only suffer it passively? Will our thinking again become ethical-religious? Shall we again win ideals that will have power over reality? This is the question before us today.

> ALBERT SCHWEITZER (1875–1965). "Religion in Modern Civilization" (pt. 1), *Christian Century,* 21 November 1934

History is not concerned with predicting: the ability to predict would mean a closed and determined universe or, perhaps worse, a managed one. And if we know anything from our observation of the drama of history, it is that history is open, full of extraordinary potential and inexplicable turns and changes.

> PAGE SMITH (1917–1995). *The Historian and History,* 14, 1964

All history is only one long story to this effect: men have struggled for power over their fellow-men in order that they might win the joys of earth at the expense of others, and might shift the burdens of life from their own shoulders upon those of others.

> WILLIAM GRAHAM SUMNER (1840–1910). Title essay, 1883, *The Forgotten Man and Other Essays,* 1918

Like most of those who study history, he learned from the mistakes of the past how to make new ones.

> A. J. P. TAYLOR (1906–1990). On Napoleon III (1808–1873), "Mistaken Lessons from the Past," *Listener,* 6 June 1963

All human history from the earliest times to our own day may be considered as a movement of consciousness both of individuals and of homogeneous groups from lower ideas to higher ones.

> LEO TOLSTOY (1828–1910). "Patriotism and Government," 2, 1900, tr. Aylmer Maude, 1936

After the Greeks and Romans had conquered the world by force of arms, the world took its conquerors captive by converting them to new religions which addressed their message to all human souls without discriminating between rulers and subjects or between Greeks, Orientals, and barbarians. Is something like this historic denouement of the Graeco-Roman story going to be written into the unfinished history of the world's encounter with the West? We cannot say, since we cannot foretell the future. We can only see that something which has actually happened once, in another episode of history, must at least be one of the possibilities that lie ahead of us.

> ARNOLD J. TOYNBEE (1889–1975). "The World and the Greeks and Romans," 1952, *The World and the West,* 1953

History is not merely what happened: it is what happened in the context of what might have happened.

> H. R. TREVOR-ROPER (1914–). Valedictory lecture, Oxford University (England), 20 May 1980. In Ronald Lewin, *The American Magic,* 3 (epigraph), 1982

The historic ascent of humanity, taken as a whole, may be summarized as a succession of victories of consciousness over blind forces—in nature, in society, in man himself.

> LEON TROTSKY (1879–1940). Conclusion to *The History of the Russian Revolution,* tr. Max Eastman, vol. 3, 1932

Men make history and not the other way 'round. In periods where there is no leadership, society stands still. Progress occurs when courageous, skillful leaders seize the opportunity to change things for the better.

> HARRY S. TRUMAN (1884–1972). In *This Week,* 22 February 1959

Man fails to profit from the lessons of history because his prejudgments prevent him from drawing the indicated conclusions and [because] history will often capriciously take a different direction from that in which her lessons point.

> BARBARA W. TUCHMAN (1912–1989). "Is History a Guide to the Future?" 1966, *Practicing History: Selected Essays,* 1981

The history of mankind is the history of the attainment of external power.

> H. G. WELLS (1866–1946). Opening words, *The World Set Free: A Story of Mankind,* 1914

Human history becomes more and more a race between education and catastrophe.

> H. G. WELLS (1866–1946). *The Outline of History,* 40.4, 1920
>
> See Education: Arnold J. Toynbee (1)

History can suggest to us alternatives that we would never otherwise consider. It can both warn and inspire. It can warn us that it is *possible* for a whole nation to be brainwashed, for "enlightened" and "educated" people to commit genocide, for a "democratic" country to maintain slavery, for oppressed to turn into oppressors, for "socialism" to be tyrannical and "liberalism" to be imperialist, for whole peoples to be led to war like sheep. It can also show us that apparently powerless underlings can defeat their rulers, that men (for at least moments of time) can live like brothers, that man can make incredible sacrifices on behalf of a cause.

> HOWARD ZINN (1922–). *The Politics of History,* 17, 1970

❧

It's too early to say.

> ANONYMOUS (CHINESE). Twentieth-century historian. When asked his opinion about the French Revolution

Every time history repeats itself the price goes up.

> ANONYMOUS. In "Thoughts on the Business of Life," *Forbes,* 7 July 1997

History is what pessimists suffer and optimists make.

> ANONYMOUS

HOLLYWOOD

See also • California ○ Cities ○ Films ○ Los Angeles

If my books had been any worse, I should not have been invited to Hollywood; and . . . if they had been any better, I should not have come.

RAYMOND CHANDLER (1888–1959). Detective-novel writer.
> On becoming a scriptwriter, letter to Charles Morton, 12 December 1945, *Selected Letters of Raymond Chandler,* ed. Frank MacShane, 1981

This is a town that doesn't just want you to fail, it wants you to die.

> DAVID GEFFEN (1943–). On Hollywood. In Peter J. Boyer, "Katzenberg's Seven-Year Itch," *Vanity Fair,* November 1991

The propaganda arm of the American Dream machine, Hollywood.

> MOLLY HASKELL (1939–). "The Big Lie," *From Reverence to Rape: The Treatment of Women in the Movies,* 2nd ed., 1987 (1974)

Our town worships success, the bitch goddess whose smile hides a taste for blood.

> HEDDA HOPPER (1890–1956). Journalist. On Hollywood (her beat)

Where is Hollywood located? Chiefly between the ears. In that part of the American brain lately vacated by God.

> ERICA JONG (1942–). "Hello to Hollywood . . . " (epigraph), *To Save Your Own Life,* 1977

Strip away the phony tinsel of Hollywood and you'll find the real tinsel underneath.

> OSCAR LEVANT (1906–1972)

[Hollywood's] a trip through a sewer in a glass-bottomed boat.

> WILSON MIZNER (1876–1933). In Alva Johnston, *The Legendary Mizners,* 4, 1953

Hollywood is high school with money.

> MARTIN MULL (1943–). Quoted by David Letterman, television entertainment-program host, *Late Show with David Letterman,* CBS, 6 April 1994

Hollywood money isn't money. It's congealed snow, melts in your hand, and there you are.

> DOROTHY PARKER (1893–1967). Marion Capron interview, 1956. In Malcolm Cowley, ed., *Writers at Work: First Series,* 1958

A town that has to be seen to be disbelieved.

> WALTER WINCHELL (1897–1972). Journalist. On Hollywood

HOLOCAUST

See also • Anti-Semitic Statements ○ Anti-Semitism ○ Cruelty ○ Euthanasia ○ Germany: [especially] George Steiner ○ Judaism ○ Killing ○ Prejudice ○ Racism ○ Slavery ○ Sterilization ○ Terrorism ○ Torture ○ Violence

Hell in the most literal sense was embodied by those types of camps perfected by the Nazis, in which the whole of life was thoroughly and systematically organized with a view to the greatest possible torment.

> HANNAH ARENDT (1906–1975). *The Origins of Totalitarianism,* 12.3, 1973 (1951)

If the Germans want to put the yellow Jewish star in Denmark, I and my whole family will wear it as a sign of the highest distinction.

> CHRISTIAN X (1870–1947). Danish king

Arriving at Auschwitz, Belzec, Chelmno, Majdanek, Sobiror, and Treblinka, the Jews encountered a standard procedure. At camps maintaining labor installations, like Auschwitz, 10 percent of the arrivals—those who looked fittest—were selected for work. The remainder were consigned to the gas chambers. They were instructed to undress; the women and girls had their hair cut. They were then marched between files of auxiliary police (Ukrainians usually) who hurried them along with whips, sticks, or guns, to the gas chambers. As in Operation T-4 [code name for the program that murdered tens of thousands of mental patients in German insane asylums], these were identified as shower rooms. The Jews were rammed in, one person per square foot. The gassing lasted from ten to thirty minutes, depending on the facilities and techniques used. In Belzec, according to an eyewitness, it took thirty-two minutes and "finally, all were dead," he wrote, "like pillars of basalt, still erect, not having any space to fall." To make room for the next load, the bodies were right away tossed out, "blue, wet with sweat and urine, the legs covered with feces and menstrual blood." Later the bodies were burned, either in the open air or in crematoria. . . . A worker at Auschwitz said that "the stench given off by the pyres contaminated the surrounding countryside. At night the red sky over Auschwitz could be seen for miles."

> LUCY S. DAWIDOWICZ (1915–). *The War Against the Jews: 1933–1945,* 7, 1975

Every individual attempt to stand up to the Germans [during deportations to the death camps] ended in death. The Jew who refused to budge when ordered, who spat at the German, who cursed him, who slapped his face, threw stones, or reached for a stick was shot on the spot. Thousands of such individual acts of resistance became nothing more than induced suicide.

> LUCY S. DAWIDOWICZ (1915–). *The War Against the Jews: 1933–1945,* 14, 1975. There was little organized Jewish resistance against the Germans, the most significant of which was the Warsaw ghetto uprising in April 1943. Thousands among the lightly "armed" Jews were killed; 16 German soldiers died.

My men had as one of their basic orders that all unnecessary harshness was to be avoided. This fundamental principle was also accepted by the Hungarian officials. In practice they may not have been adhered to it 100%. But that did not and could not interest me, because it was not my responsibility.

> ADOLF EICHMANN (1906–1962). While awaiting trial in Israel for his role in the murder of six million Jews during World War II, "Eichmann's Own Story: Part II," *Life,* 5 December 1960

I once saw a soldier beat a frail old Jew over the head with a rubber club. I spoke to the soldier, reported him to his commander and demanded he be punished and demoted. Himmler could not stand for that kind of thing. That is sadism.

> ADOLF EICHMANN (1906–1962). While awaiting trial in Israel for participating in the murder of six million Jews during World War II, "Eichmann's Own Story: Part II," *Life,* 5 December 1960

To sum it all up, I must say that I regret nothing. . . .
I will not humble myself or repent in any way.

> ADOLF EICHMANN (1906–1962). While awaiting trial in Israel for participating in the murder of six million Jews during World War II, "Eichmann's Own Story: Part II," *Life,* 5 December 1960

What was done was not of my doing. I had the feeling of a Pontius Pilate. I felt that it was not with me that the guilt lay.

> ADOLPH EICHMANN (1906–1962). In *New York Herald Tribune,* 27 June 1961

Since the fourth century after Christ, there have been three anti-Jewish policies: conversion, expulsion, and annihilation. The second appeared as an alternative to the first, and the third emerged as an alternative to the second.

> RAUL HILBERG (1926–). *The Destruction of the European Jews,* 1, 1961

The hard decision had to be taken—This People Must Disappear From The Face Of The Earth. For the organization which had to carry out this order it was the toughest of all the assignments it had ever had. It was carried out—I think I can say—without our men and our leaders suffering any damage to their spirit and their soul. The road between the two possibilities, either to become brutal and heartless and cease to have any regard for human life or to become soft, to lose one's mental balance and to end in nervous breakdown—the road between these Scylla and Charybdis is terribly narrow.

> HEINRICH HIMMLER (1900–1945). Speech, 6 October 1943. In Erich Goldhagen, "Albert Speer, Himmler, and the Secrecy of the Final Solution," *Midstream,* October 1971

I want today once again to make a prophecy: if the international Jewish financiers within and without Europe succeed once more in hurling the people into a world war, the result will be, not the Bolshevization of the world and with it a victory of Jewry, but the annihilation of the Jewish race in Europe.

> ADOLF HITLER (1889–1945). Reichstag speech, 30 January 1939

The "final solution" of the Jewish question meant the complete extermination of all Jews in Europe.

> RUDOLF HOESS (1900–1947). German commandant of Auschwitz. Nuremberg trial affidavit, 5 April 1946

It took from 3 to 15 minutes to kill the people in the death chamber depending upon climatic conditions. We knew when the people were dead because their screaming stopped.

> RUDOLF HOESS (1900–1947). German commandant of Auschwitz. Nuremberg trial affidavit, 5 April 1946
>
> See Cruelty: Jan Kromar

Another improvement that we made over Treblinka was that we built our gas-chambers to accommodate two thousand people at one time, whereas at Treblinka their 10 gas chambers only accommodated 200 people each.

> RUDOLF HOESS (1900–1947). German commandant of Auschwitz. Nuremberg trial affidavit, 5 April 1946

My wife's garden was a paradise of flowers. The prisoners never missed an opportunity for doing some little act of kindness to my wife or children and thus attracting their attention.

No former prisoner can ever say that he was in any way or at any time badly treated in our house. My wife's greatest pleasure would have been to give a present to every prisoner who was in any way connected with our household.

The children were perpetually begging me for cigarettes for the prisoners. They were particularly fond of the ones who worked in the garden.

RUDOLF HOESS (1900–1947). German commandant of Auschwitz. Nuremberg trial affidavit, 5 April 1946

What the hell are they putting out? My relatives are soap.

HENRY A. KISSINGER (1923–). After finding out that the Bonn government had announced that he might visit some of his relatives during a trip to his native-country Germany as Pres. Richard M. Nixon's national security adviser, remark to aides, 1970? In Walter Isaacson, *Kissinger: A Biography,* l, 1992

The evil of the Holocaust was realized through the exercise of a certain kind of power—coercive power. It was a power that sought to dominate and control. It was a power legitimated through law, buttressed by propaganda, augmented by terror, and affected through all the institutions of society.

MARY JO LEDDY (1946–). Catholic theologian. "A Different Power" (3). In Carol Rittner and John K. Roth, eds., *Different Voices: Women and the Holocaust,* 1993

Precisely because the Lager [i.e., camp] was a great machine to reduce us to beasts, we must not become beasts; that even in this place one can survive, and therefore one must want to survive, to tell the story, to bear witness; and that to survive we must force ourselves to save at least the skeleton, the scaffolding, the form of civilization. We are slaves, deprived of every right, exposed to every insult, condemned to certain death, but we still possess one power, and we must defend it with all our strength for it is the last—the power to refuse our consent.

PRIMO LEVI (1919–1987). Auschwitz survivor. "Initiation," *Survival in Auschwitz: The Nazi Assault on Humanity,* 1958, tr. Stuart Woolf, 1961

The crematoria ovens . . . were designed, built, assembled, and tested by a German company, Topf of Wiesbaden (it was still in operation in 1975, building crematoria for civilian use, and had not considered the advisability of changing its name).

PRIMO LEVI (1919–1987). Auschwitz survivor. Preface to *The Drowned and the Saved,* 1986, tr. Raymond Rosenthal, 1988

Up to the moment of this writing, and notwithstanding the horror of Hiroshima and Nagasaki, the shame of the Gulags, the useless and bloody Vietnam War, the Cambodian self-genocide, the *desaparecidos* of Argentina, and many atrocious and stupid wars we have seen since, the German concentration camp system still remains, a *unicum,* both in its extent and its quality. At no other place or time has one seen a phenomenon so unexpected and so complex: never have so many human lives been extinguished in so short a time, and with so lucid a combination of technological ingenuity, fanaticism, and cruelty.

PRIMO LEVI (1919–1987). Auschwitz survivor. Preface to *The Drowned and the Saved,* 1986, tr. Raymond Rosenthal, 1988

We, the survivors, are not the true witnesses.

PRIMO LEVI (1919–1987). Auschwitz survivor. *The Drowned and the Saved,* 3, 1986, tr. Raymond Rosenthal, 1988

[At the concentration camp at Buna thousands of inmates were assembled to watch the hanging of two men and a boy suspected of blowing up the camp's electric power station.] Then the march [past the gallows] began. The two adults were no longer alive. Their tongues hung swollen, blue-tinged. But the third rope was still moving; being so light, the child was still alive.

For more than half an hour he stayed there, struggling between life and death, dying in slow agony under our eyes. And we had to look him full in the face. He was still alive when I passed in front of him. His tongue was still red, his eyes not yet glazed. Behind me, I heard [a] man asking:

"Where is God now?"

And I heard a voice within me answer him:

"Where is He? Here He is—He is hanging here on this gallows."

ELIE WIESEL (1928–). Auschwitz survivor. *Night,* 4, 1958

Where was God in all this? Was this another test, one more? Or a punishment? And if so, for what sins? What crimes were being punished? Was there a misdeed that deserved so many mass graves? Would it ever again be possible to speak of justice, of truth, of divine charity, after the murder of one million Jewish children?

ELIE WIESEL (1928–). Auschwitz survivor. "To Be a Jew," *A Jew Today,* tr. Marion Wiesel, 1978

Although we know that God is merciful, please God, do not have mercy for those people who created this place.

ELIE WIESEL (1928–). Auschwitz survivor. Speech, marking the 50th anniversary of the liberation of the Auschwitz death camp, 26 January 1995

The barbed-wire kingdom will forever remain an immense question mark on the scale of both humanity and its Creator. Faced with unprecedented suffering and agony, He should have intervened, or at least expressed Himself, which side was He on? Isn't He the Father of us all?

ELIE WIESEL (1928–). Auschwitz survivor. *All Rivers Run to the Sea,* 1995. In Michiko Kakutani, "Remembering as a Duty of Those Who Survived," *New York Times,* December 1995

❦

It must never happen again—never again.

ANONYMOUS. Narrator's closing words in *Mein Kampf* (Swedish documentary film), 1961. In John F. Davenport, "Source of 'Never Again,' " letter to *New York Times,* 19 November 1990

HOME

See also • Children ○ Family ○ Housework ○ Marriage ○ Nations Saying (Ashanti) ○ Parents ○ Women & Men: Saying (American)

You are a king by your own fireside, as much as any monarch [on] his throne.

CERVANTES (1547–1616). Preface to *Don Quixote,* 1615, tr. Peter Anthony Motteux and John Ozell, 1743

Where could one settle more pleasantly than [in] one's home?

CICERO (106–43 B.C.). *Ad familiares,* 4.8, tr. W. Glynn Williams, 1927

When I can no longer bear to think of the victims of broken homes, I begin to think of the victims of intact ones.

PETER DE VRIES (1910–1993). *The Tunnel of Love,* 8, 1954

The ornament of a house is the friends who frequent it. There is no event greater in life than the appearance of new persons about our hearth, except it be the progress of the character which draws them.

RALPH WALDO EMERSON (1803–1882). "Domestic Life," *Society and Solitude,* 1870

Home is the place where, when you have to go there,
They have to take you in.

> ROBERT FROST (1874–1963). "The Death of the Hired Man," *North of
> Boston*, 1914

Better one's House be too little one day than too big all the Year
after.

> THOMAS FULLER (1654–1734). Comp., *Gnomologia: Adages and
> Proverbs*, 919, 1732

The most important thing a man can know is that, as he approaches his own door, someone on the other side is listening for the sound of his footsteps.

> CLARK GABLE (1901–1960). In Ronald Reagan, *Where's the Rest of Me?*
> 18, 1965

Home, home on the range,
Where the deer and the antelope play;
Where seldom is heard a discouraging word,
And the skies are not cloudy all day.

> BREWSTER HIGLEY (19th cent.). "Home on the Range" (song),
> 1873?

The difference between a house and a home is this: A house may fall down, but a home is broken up.

> ELBERT HUBBARD (1856–1915). *The Roycroft Dictionary Concocted by
> Ali Baba and the Bunch on Rainy Days*, p. 70, 1914

The fellow that owns his own home is always just coming out of a hardware store.

> KIN HUBBARD (1868–1930). In Charles McCabe, "The Fearless
> Spectator," *San Francisco Chronicle*, 23 September 1971

She's leaving home after living alone
For so many years. . . .
Something inside that was always denied
For so many years.

> JOHN LENNON (1940–1980) and PAUL McCARTNEY (1942–). "She's
> Leaving Home" (song), 1967

A home is not a mere transient shelter: its essence lies in its permanence, in its capacity for accretion and solidification, in its quality of representing, in all its details, the personalities of the people who live in it.

> H. L. MENCKEN (1880–1956). "On Living in Baltimore," *Prejudices: Fifth
> Series*, 1924

Mid pleasures and palaces though we may roam,
Be it ever so humble, there's no place like home.

> JOHN HOWARD PAYNE (1791–1852). "Home, Sweet Home" (song).
> In the opera *Clari, or The Maid of Milan*, 1.1, 1823

Home is where the heart is.

> PLINY THE YOUNGER (A.D. 62?–113?). Attributed

Home is the girl's prison and the woman's workhouse.

> GEORGE BERNARD SHAW (1856–1950). "Maxims for Revolutionists:
> Women in the Home," *Man and Superman*, 1903

East and West, Home is best.

> CHARLES HADDON SPURGEON (1834–1892). *John Ploughman's Talks*,
> 13, 1869

Everybody's always talking about people breaking into houses, ma'am; but there are more people in the world who want to break out of houses.

> THORNTON WILDER (1897–1975). *The Matchmaker*, 4, 1954

❦

He who troubles his household will inherit the wind.

> SAYING (*BIBLE*). *Proverbs* 11:29

Every bird loves its own nest.

> SAYING

HOMELESSNESS

See also • America: Emma Lazarus ○ Architecture: Margaret
Morton ○ Beggars ○ Poverty

How can you worship a homeless man on Sunday and ignore one on Monday?

> COALITION FOR THE HOMELESS. Large-type caption under
> a drawing of Jesus in a full-page ad, *New York Times*,
> 16 January 1994

How does it feel
To be without a home
Like a complete unknown
Like a rolling stone?

> BOB DYLAN (1941–). "Like a Rolling Stone" (song), 1965

Better to seek with never finding
Like the homeless, lost wind, ever-moving;
Than to find one's place of fulfillment of dreams
To be a success with screams inside.

> TIM MILLS. Closing stanza, untitled poem, 8 August 1990. In Michael A.
> Susko, ed., *Cry of the Invisible: Writings from the Homeless and
> Survivors of Psychiatric Hospitals*, 2, "Tim Mills' Story," 1991

What we have found in this country, and maybe we're more aware of it now, is one problem that we've had, even in the best of times, and that is the people who are sleeping on the grates, the homeless who are homeless, you might say, by choice.

> RONALD REAGAN (1911–). 31 January 1984. In Mark Green and Gail
> MacColl, "A Deficit of Economics," *Reagan's Reign of Error: The Instant
> Nostalgia Edition*, 1987

At least 117 homeless people . . . died in San Francisco in the past year, according to a preliminary report conducted for the San Francisco Department of Public Health. The study, based on coroner's records and death certificates, marked the seventh consecutive year in which more than 100 homeless people died on city streets, in alleys and in shelters.

> BRIAN SHOTT and JOSH BRANDON. "Report Says 117 S.F. Homeless
> Died This Year," *San Francisco Chronicle*, 21 December 1994

There can be no reasonable right to live on sidewalks. Society needs order, and hence has a right to a minimally civilized ambiance in public spaces. Regarding the homeless, this is not merely for aesthetic reasons because the anesthetic is not merely unappealing. It presents a spectacle of disorder and decay that becomes a contagion.

> GEORGE F. WILL (1941–). "Homelessness: Sign of Decay on Urban
> Streets," *Hartford Courant*, 19 November 1987

HOMOSEXUALITY

See also • AIDS ○ Sex

If homosexuality is inherited, shouldn't it have died out by now?

> GEORGE BOOTH (1926–). Cartoon caption, *New Yorker,* 16 August 1993

I don't care what people do, as long as they don't do it in the street and frighten the horses!

> MRS. PATRICK CAMPBELL (1865–1940). English actress. When told of a homosexual affair between two actors. In Michèle Brown and Ann O'Connor, comps., "Sex," *Hammer and Tongues: The Best of Women's Wit and Humor,* 1986

Naturally homosexuality is something pathological, it is an arrested development.

> SIGMUND FREUD (1856–1939). Remark to the author, 1 November 1934. In Joseph Wortis, *Fragments of an Analysis with Freud,* 1954

America I'm putting my queer shoulder to the wheel.

> ALLEN GINSBERG (1926–1997). Closing line, "America," 1956

Charlie had that defensive contempt for homosexuals which people often have when their own sexuality is an embarrassment to them.

> ERICA JONG (1942–). *Fear of Flying,* 13, 1973

When I was in the military they gave me a medal for killing two men and a discharge for loving one.

> LEONARD MATLOVICH (1943–1988). Air force sergeant. Inscription on the gravestone of the first active-duty soldier to acknowledge his homosexuality. In photograph, *Washington Post National Weekly,* 26 August 1991

If a man lies with a male as with a woman, both of them shall have committed an abomination; they shall be put to death, their blood is upon them.

> MOSES (14th cent. B.C.). *Leviticus* 20:13

HONESTY

See also • Character ○ Civilization, Modern: Yevgeny Yevtushenko ○ Corruption ○ Dignity ○ Honor ○ Lying ○ Morality ○ Promises ○ Responsibility ○ Truth ○ Truthfulness ○ Virtue

Our honesty iz az mutch the effekt ov interest as principle.

> JOSH BILLINGS (1818–1885). "Ramrods," *Everybody's Friend; or Josh Billing's Encyclopedia and Proverbial Philosophy of Wit and Humor,* 1874

An honest God's the noblest work of man.

> SAMUEL BUTLER (1835–1902). *Further Extracts from the Note-Books of Samuel Butler,* 1, ed. A. T. Bartholomew, 1934

Nobody can boast of Honesty till they are try'd.

> SUSANNA CENTLIVRE (1667?–1723). *The Perplex'd Lovers,* 3.1, 1712

He is only honest who is not discovered.

> SUSANNA CENTLIVRE (1667?– 1723). *The Artifice,* 5, 1724

Honesty's the best policy.

> CERVANTES (1547–1616). *Don Quixote,* 2.3.33, 1615, tr. Peter Anthony Motteux and John Ozell, 1743

Honesty is, in fact, the policy that pays the best.

> WINSTON CHURCHILL (1874–1965). "The Free Trade League," speech, 1904. In *Winston Churchill: His Complete Speeches 1897–1963,* vol. 7, ed. Robert R. James, 1974

An honest Man will receive neither *Money* nor *Praise,* that is not his Due.

> BENJAMIN FRANKLIN (1706–1790). *Poor Richard's Almanack,* December 1756

He that resolves to deal with none but honest Men must leave off dealing.

> THOMAS FULLER (1654–1734). Comp., *Gnomologia: Adages and Proverbs,* 2267, 1732

There is . . . more [intelligence] requisite to be an honest man than there is to be a knave.

> MARQUIS OF HALIFAX (1633–1695). "Of Cunning and Knavery," *Political, Moral and Miscellaneous Reflections,* 1750

If you are honest because you think that is the best policy, your honesty has already been corrupted.

> SYDNEY J. HARRIS (1917–1986)

Men are disposed to live honestly, if the means of doing so are open to them.

> THOMAS JEFFERSON (1743–1826). Letter to François de Marbois, 14 June 1817

Honesty's praised but honest men freeze.

> JUVENAL (A.D. 60?–127?). *Satires,* 1.74, tr. Peter Green, 1967 (Popular version: Honesty is praised but starves.)

Honesty is better than any policy.

> IMMANUEL KANT (1724–1804). Appendix (1) to "Perpetual Peace," 1795, *On History,* ed. Lewis White Beck, 1963

He that loseth his honesty hath nothing else to lose.

> JOHN LYLY (1554?–1606). "Euphues," *Euphues: The Anatomy of Wit,* 1579

honesty is a good
thing but
it is not profitable to
its possessor
unless it is
kept under control.

> DON MARQUIS (1878–1937). "archygrams," *archy s life of mehitabel,* 1933

An honest Man's the noblest work of God.

> ALEXANDER POPE (1688–1744). *An Essay on Man,* 4.248, 1734

> See Books: Henry David Thoreau (1) ○ God & Man: Samuel Butler

There are three kinds of "honest" people: those who are dishonest but whose dishonesty remains undetected; those who have stopped being dishonest because their fortunes are already made; and finally all those who would like to be dishonest, but who lack the courage or the opportunity.

> PAUL RICHARD (1874–1967). *The Scourge of Christ,* 8.4, 1929, ed. Michel Paul Richard, 1987

Hamlet: To be honest, as this world goes, is to be one man picked out of ten thousand.

> SHAKESPEARE (1564–1616). *Hamlet,* 2.2.179, 1600

Hamlet: What's the news?
Rosencrantz: None, my lord, but that the world's grown honest.
Hamlet: Then is doomsday near: but your news is not true.

> SHAKESPEARE (1564–1616). *Hamlet,* 2.2.240, 1600

Iago: O monstrous world! Take note, take note, O world,
To be direct and honest is not safe.

> SHAKESPEARE (1564–1616). *Othello,* 3.3.378, 1604

Autolycus: Though I am not naturally honest, I am so sometimes by chance.

> SHAKESPEARE (1564–1616). *The Winter's Tale,* 4.4.731, 1610

I am afraid we must make the world honest before we can honestly say to our children that honesty is the best policy.

> GEORGE BERNARD SHAW (1856–1950). Radio broadcast, 11 July 1932

Honesty in States, as well as Individuals, will ever be found the soundest policy.

> GEORGE WASHINGTON (1732–1799). Letter to David Stuart, 5 November 1787

I hope I shall always possess firmness and virtue enough to maintain (what I consider the most enviable of all titles) the character of *an honest man.*

> GEORGE WASHINGTON (1732–1799). Letter to Alexander Hamilton, 28 August 1788

HONOR

See also • America: Richard M. Nixon (1) ○ Dignity ○ Fame ○ Glory: [especially] Anonymous (1) ○ Honesty ○ Integrity ○ Nonviolence: Mohandas K. Gandhi (6) ○ Pride ○ Resistance: Antonin Artaud ○ Shame ○ Self-Respect

Nothing is lost except our honor.

> LORD BYRON (1788–1824). Letter to Thomas Moore, 14 May 1821

My honor is dearer to me than my life.

> CERVANTES (1547–1616). *Don Quixote,* 1.4.1., 1615, tr. Peter Anthony Motteux and John Ozell, 1743

Either live or die with honor.

> JOHN CLARKE (1596–1658). Comp., *Proverbs: English and Latine,* p. 324, 1639

"War," he sung, "is toil and trouble;
Honor, but an empty bubble."

> JOHN DRYDEN (1631–1700). "Alexander's Feast," l.99, 1697

The louder he talked of his honor, the faster we counted our spoons.

> RALPH WALDO EMERSON (1803–1882). "Worship," *The Conduct of Life,* 1860
>
> See Culture: Hanns Joust ○ Virtue & Vice: Samuel Johnson

Honor and profit lie not in one sack.

> GEORGE HERBERT (1593–1633). Comp., *Outlandish Proverbs,* 232, 1640

Honor? tut, a breath;
There's no such thing in nature: a mere term
Invented to awe fools.

> BEN JONSON (1572–1637). *Volpone or The Foxe,* 3.6, 1607

Who sows virtue reaps honor.

> LEONARDO da VINCI (1452–1519). *Note-books,* 1, tr. Edward McCurdy, 1908

Fellow citizens, *we* cannot escape history. We, of this Congress and this administration, will be remembered in spite of ourselves. No personal significance, or insignificance, can spare one or another of us. The fiery trial, through which we pass, will light us down in honor or dishonor, to the latest generation.

> ABRAHAM LINCOLN (1809–1865). *Second Annual Message to Congress,* 1 December 1862

He has honor if he holds himself to an ideal of conduct though it is inconvenient, unprofitable, or dangerous to do so.

> WALTER LIPPMANN (1889–1974). *A Preface to Morals,* 11.3, 1929

Honor puts us under an obligation as binding as necessity is for other people.

> PLINY THE YOUNGER (A.D. 62?–113?). *Letters,* 4.10, tr. Betty Radice, 1963

Honor and shame from no Condition rise;
Act well you part: there all the honor lies.

> ALEXANDER POPE (1688–1744). *An Essay on Man,* 4.193, 1734

He who violates another's honor loses his own.

> PUBLIUS SYRUS (85–43 B.C.), *Moral Sayings,* 718, tr. Darius Lyman, Jr., 1862

In their rules there was only one clause:
  DO WHAT YOU WILL
because people who are free, well-born, well-bred and easy in honest company have a natural spur and instinct which drives them to virtuous deeds and deflects them from vice; and this they called honor.

> RABELAIS (1483?–1553). *Gargantua and Pantagruel,* 1.57, 1532–1552, tr. J. M. Cohen, 1955

It is preferable to die with honor than to live in disgrace.

> SA'DI (A.D. 1213?–1292). *The Gulistan, or Rose Garden,* 3 (Story 11), A.D. 1258, tr. Edward Rehatsek, 1964

Antony: Brutus is an honorable man;
So are they all, all honorable men.

> SHAKESPEARE (1564–1616). *Julius Caesar,* 3.2.87, 1599

Antony: If I lose mine honor,
I lose myself.

> SHAKESPEARE (1564–1616). *Antony and Cleopatra,* 3.4.22, 1606

Let the honor of thy fellow be as dear to thee as thine own.

> TALMUD (A.D. 1st–6th cent.). Rabbinical writings

Say, what is Honor?—'Tis the finest sense
Of *justice* which the human mind can frame.

> WILLIAM WORDSWORTH (1770–1850). Untitled poem, 1815

❦

Better honor than honors.
SAYING (FLEMISH)

Better to deserve honor and not have it than to have honor and not deserve it.
SAYING (PORTUGUESE)
See Success: Joseph Addison

Honor is easier kept than recovered.
SAYING

HOPE

See also • Despair ○ Expectation ○ Faith ○ Optimism ○ Optimism: Examples ○ Patience

Hope is only the love of life. . . . Who knows? God may save us, may work a miracle.
HENRI AMIEL (1821–1881). Journal, 23 January 1881, tr. Mrs. Humphrey Ward, 1887

The politic and artificial nourishing and entertaining of hopes . . . is one of the best antidotes against the poison of discontentments. And it is a certain sign of a wise government . . . [that] it can hold men's hearts by hopes, when it cannot by satisfaction.
FRANCIS BACON (1561–1626). "Of Seditions and Troubles," Essays, 1625

The hope of the world lies in what one demands, not of others, but of oneself.
JAMES BALDWIN (1924–1987). "Malcolm and Martin," Esquire, April 1972

When hope is taken away from the people, moral degeneration follows swiftly after.
PEARL S. BUCK (1892–1973). Letter to New York Times, 14 November 1941

Those who have much to hope and nothing to lose will always be dangerous, more or less.
EDMUND BURKE (1729–1797). Letter to Charles J. Fox, 8 October 1777

Work without hope draws nectar in a sieve,
And hope without an object cannot live.
SAMUEL TAYLOR COLERIDGE (1772–1834). "Work Without Hope," 1828

Never was Cat or Cog drown'd that could but see the Shore.
THOMAS FULLER (1654–1734). Comp., Gnomologia: Adages and Proverbs, 3532, 1732

No condition so low but may have Hopes, none so high but may have Fears.
THOMAS FULLER (1654–1734). Comp., Gnomologia: Adages and Proverbs, 3555, 1732

Hope, the best comfort of our imperfect condition.
EDWARD GIBBON (1737–1794). The Decline and Fall of the Roman Empire, 2, 1776–1788

Hope, like the gleaming taper's light,
Adorns and cheers our way;

And still, as darker grows the night,
Emits a brighter ray.
OLIVER GOLDSMITH (1728–1774). The Captivity: An Oratorio, 2, 1764

Hope is the poor man's bread.
GEORGE HERBERT (1593–1633). Comp., Outlandish Proverbs, 477, 1640

It is the around-the-corner brand of hope that prompts people to action, while the distant hope acts as an opiate.
ERIC HOFFER (1902–1983). The Ordeal of Hope, 10, 1964

Who lives by hope dies fasting.
JAMES HOWELL (1593–1666). Comp., "Italian" (p. 13), Paroimiographia: Proverbs, or Old Sayed Sawes & Adages in English . . . Italian, French and Spanish, 1659

Keep hope alive!
JESSE JACKSON (1941–). Signature saying, 1980s

Where there is no hope, there can be no endeavor.
SAMUEL JOHNSON (1709–1784). In The Rambler (English journal), 110, 6 April 1751

Hope is the feeling you have that the feeling you have isn't permanent.
JEAN KERR (1923–). Finishing Touches, 3, 1974

Hope begins in the dark, the stubborn hope that if you just show up and try to do the right thing, the dawn will come. You wait and watch and work: you don't give up.
ANNE LAMOTT (1954–). Introduction to Bird by Bird: Some Instructions on Writing and Life, 1995

the only way boss
to keep hope in the world
is to keep changing its
population frequently.
DON MARQUIS (1878–1937). "archy and the old un," archy s life of mehitabel, 1933

When hope is hungry, everything feeds it.
MIGNON McLAUGHLIN (1915–). The Neurotic's Notebook, 4, 1963

Our final hope
Is flat despair.
JOHN MILTON (1608–1674). Paradise Lost, 2.142, 1667

Where no hope is left, is left no fear.
JOHN MILTON (1608–1674). Paradise Regain'd, 3.206, 1671

Man is a victim of dope
In the incurable form of hope.
OGDEN NASH (1902–1971). "Good-by, Old Year, You Oaf or Why Don't They Pay the Bonus?" The Primrose Path, 1935

Hope springs eternal in the human breast:
Man never Is, but always To be blest.
ALEXANDER POPE (1688–1744). An Essay on Man, 1.95, 1734

If it were not for hope the heart would break.
JOHN RAY (1628–1705). Comp., A Collection of English Proverbs, p. 156, 1678

Hope encourages men to endure and attempt everything; in depriving them of it, or in making it too distant, you deprive them of their very soul.

> MAURICE de SAXE (1696–1750). *My Reveries on the Art of War,* 1732. In Thomas R. Phillips, ed., *Roots of Strategy,* p. 200, 1940

Hope feeds the soul but leaves your belly rumbling.

> JOHN SAYLES (1950–). *Matewan* (film), 1987

To defy Power, which seems omnipotent;
To love, and bear; to hope till Hope creates
From its own wreck the thing it contemplates.

> PERCY BYSSHE SHELLEY (1792–1822). *Prometheus Unbound,* 4.572, 1820

While there's life, there's hope.

> TERENCE (190?–159 B.C.). *Heuton timoroumenos,* l. 981

The first hope in our inventory—the hope that includes and at the same time transcends all others—must be the hope that love is going to have the last word.

> ARNOLD J. TOYNBEE (1889–1975). "Conditions of Survival," *Saturday Review,* 29 August 1964

Hope unbelieved is always considered nonsense. But hope believed is history in the process of being changed.

> JIM WALLIS (1948–). *The Soul of Politics: A Practical and Prophetic Vision for Change,* 8, 1994

※

Hope deferred makes the heart sick.

> SAYING (*BIBLE*). Proverbs 13:12

Hope dies last.

> SAYING (MEXICAN)

HOUSEWORK

See also • Home

All work and no pay makes a housewife.

> EVAN ESAR (1899–1995). Comp., *20,000 Quips & Quotes,* p. 398, 1968

I personally am inclined to approach [housework] the way governments treat dissent: ignore it until it revolts.

> BARBARA KINGSOLVER (1955–). "The Household Zen," 1990, *High Tide in Tucson: Essays from Now or Never,* 1996

HUMANITY

See • Mankind

HUMAN NATURE

See also • Celebrity: Liz Smith ○ Change & Changelessness ○ Dehumanization: Eric Hoffer (2) ○ Destiny: Winston Churchill ○ Dreams: Goethe ○ Guilt: J. Glenn Gray ○ Heaven: Orestes A. Brownson ○ Man ○ Peace: Dalai Lama, Mohandas K. Gandhi ○ Revolution: George Orwell (1) ○ Rights: Alexander Hamilton ○ War & Psychology: Bertrand Russell (3)

There is in human nature generally more of the fool than of the wise.

> FRANCIS BACON (1561–1626). "Of Boldness," *Essays,* 1625

Scratch the surface, abolish everything we owe to an education which is perpetual and unceasing, and you will find in the depth of our nature primitive humanity, or something very near to it.

> HENRI BERGSON (1859–1941). "Static Religion," *The Two Sources of Morality and Religion,* 1932, tr. R. Ashley Audra and Cloudesley Brereton, 1935

Human nature is the image of God.

> WILLIAM BLAKE (1757–1827). "Annotations to Lavater's 'Aphorisms on Man'" (554), 1788?, *The Complete Writings of William Blake,* ed. Geoffrey Keynes, 1966

The double nature of man, as the being that is both brought forth from "below" and sent from "above," results in the duality of his basic characteristics.

> MARTIN BUBER (1878–1965). *Eclipse of God: Studies in the Relation between Religion and Philosophy,* 8, tr. Maurice S. Friedman, 1952

He who gave our nature to be perfected by our virtue willed also the necessary means of its perfection.

> EDMUND BURKE (1729–1797). *Reflections on the Revolution in France,* p. 197, 1790, Pelican Books edition, 1968

We are but fettered by chains of our own forging, and which ourselves also can rend asunder. This deep, paralyzed subjection to physical objects comes not from Nature, but from our own unwise mode of *viewing* Nature.

> THOMAS CARLYLE (1795–1881). "Signs of the Times," 1829, *Critical and Miscellaneous Essays,* Carey & Hart edition, 1849

Human nature is the same all over the world.

> LORD CHESTERFIELD (1694–1773). Letter to his son, 2 October 1747

Nothing is static. Human nature either goes up or goes down.

> MOHANDAS K. GANDHI (1869–1948). In *Harijan,* 8 June 1947

The greatest need in the world at this moment is the transformation of human nature.

> BILLY GRAHAM (1918–). "Focus on Hong Kong," television broadcast, 16 August 1997

Human beings have a strong tendency towards rationality and decency. (If they had not, they would not desire to legitimize their prejudices and their passions.)

> ALDOUS HUXLEY (1894–1963). "Writers and Readers," *The Olive Tree and Other Essays,* 1936

We have pretty well finished the geographical exploration of the earth; we have pushed the scientific exploration of nature, both lifeless and living, to a point at which its main outlines have become clear; but the exploration of human nature and its possibilities has scarcely begun. A vast New World of uncharted possibilities awaits its Columbus.

> JULIAN HUXLEY (1887–1975). "Transhumanism," *New Bottles for New Wine,* 1957

Morality, compassion, generosity are innate elements of the human constitution.

> THOMAS JEFFERSON (1743–1826). Letter to Pierre-Samuel Du Pont, 24 April 1816

I have an unshakable belief that mankind's higher nature is on the whole still dormant. The greatest souls reveal excellencies of mind and heart which their lesser fellows possess—hidden, it is true, but there all the same. The unborn goodness renders it possible for most people to recognize nobility when they see it, as the latent poet in a reader enables him to appreciate a fine poem.

> HELEN KELLER (1880–1968). "Faith Regenerates," *Let Us Have Faith*, 1940

Human nature must be accepted as it is.

> GUSTAVE LE BON (1841–1931). *The Psychology of Revolutions*, 1912, tr. Alice Widener, 1979

Within limits that we have not measured, human nature is malleable.

> WALTER LIPPMANN (1889–1974). *The Public Philosophy*, 8.1, 1955

Human nature is not a machine to be built after a model, and set to do exactly the work prescribed for it, but a tree, which requires to grow and develop itself on all sides, according to the tendency of the inward forces which make it a living thing.

> JOHN STUART MILL (1806–1873). *On Liberty*, 3, 1859

After the primary necessities of food and raiment, freedom is the first and strongest want of human nature.

> JOHN STUART MILL (1806–1873). *The Subjection of Women*, 4, 1869

It is a part of the essential nature of man to transcend the limits of his own biological nature, and to be ready if necessary to die in order to make such transcendence possible.

> LEWIS MUMFORD (1895–1990). "Epilogue: The Advancement of Life," *The Pentagon of Power: The Myth of the Machine*, 1970

If human nature never changes, why is it that we not only don't practice cannibalism any more, but don't even want to?

> GEORGE ORWELL (1903–1950). "As I Please," 21 July 1944, *The Collected Essays, Journalism and Letters of George Orwell*, vol. 3, ed. Sonia Orwell and Ian Angus, 1968

Man is by nature good. . . . Men are depraved and perverted by society.

> ROUSSEAU (1712–1778). *Emile; or, Treatise on Education*, 4, 1762, tr. Barbara Foxley, 1911

If human nature were unchangeable, as ignorant people still suppose it to be, the situation would indeed be hopeless.

> BERTRAND RUSSELL (1872–1970). *Sceptical Essays*, 17.4, 1928

What passes as "human nature" is at most one-tenth nature, the other nine-tenths being nurture.

> BERTRAND RUSSELL (1872–1970). *Sceptical Essays*, 17.4, 1928

In the twentieth century what astonishes many of us is not so much that human nature is fundamentally corrupt; we are astonished rather that it does not behave more wickedly than it obviously does.

> MORTON IRVING SEIDEN. *The Paradox of Hate: A Study in Ritual Murder*, 1, 1967

Man will return to his idols and his cupidities, in spite of all "movements" and all revolutions, until his nature is changed.

> GEORGE BERNARD SHAW (1856–1950). "The Revolutionist's Handbook" (7), *Man and Superman*, 1903

How selfish soever man may be supposed, there are evidently some principles in his nature, which interest him in the fortune of others, and render their happiness necessary to him, though he derives nothing from it, except the pleasure of seeing it.

> ADAM SMITH (1723–1790). Opening words, *The Theory of Moral Sentiments*, 1759

Surely it is but reasonable, before devising measures for the benefit of society, to ascertain what society is made of. Is human nature constant, or is it not? If so, why? If not, why not? Is it in essence always the same? Then what are its permanent characteristics? Is it changing? Then what is the nature of the change it is undergoing? What is it becoming, and why?

> HERBERT SPENCER (1820–1903). *Social Statics*, 4.31.3, 1851

That which the best human nature is capable of is within the reach of human nature at large.

> HERBERT SPENCER (1820–1903). *The Data of Ethics*, 14, 1879

Man's nature is generally so constituted that he takes pity on those who fare ill, and envies those who fare well.

> BARUCH SPINOZA (1632–1677). "Man's Loves and Hates," *Ethics*, 1677, tr. Dagobert D. Runes, 1957

There [are] two opposing drives in human nature: the drive toward closeness to other human beings, and the drive toward being independent and self-sufficient.

> ANTHONY STORR (1920–). *Solitude: A Return to the Self*, 5, 1988

The science of Human Nature has never been attempted, as the science of Nature has. The dry light has never shone on it. Neither physics nor metaphysics have touched it.

> HENRY DAVID THOREAU (1817–1862). Journal, 15 June 1840

The distinctive characteristics of human nature are the freedom of the human consciousness and the human will.

> ARNOLD J. TOYNBEE (1889–1975). *A Study of History*, 12.568, 1961

Human nature is the same everywhere: it deifies success, it has nothing but scorn for defeat.

> MARK TWAIN (1835–1910). *Personal Recollections of Joan of Arc*, 1.8, 1896

The tendency since the end of the war in 1945 has been for nations to solidify their nationalism, rather than build an interdependent world. The parochial streak in people is perhaps the strongest streak in human nature, and I have no idea how it can ever be eradicated sufficiently to allow a better state of affairs.

> E. B. WHITE (1899–1985). Letter to Robert S. Palmer, 4 December 1964, *Letters of E. B. White*, ed. Dorothy Lobrano Guth, 1976

Human nature loses its most precious quality when it is robbed of its sense of things beyond, unexplored and yet insistent.

> ALFRED NORTH WHITEHEAD (1861–1947). "Harvard: The Future" (4), *Atlantic*, September 1936

The systems that fail are those that rely on the permanency of human nature, and not on its growth and development.

> OSCAR WILDE (1854–1900). "The Soul of Man Under Socialism," *Fortnightly Review* (British journal), February 1891

A conception of human nature can be somewhat self-fulfilling.
> GEORGE F. WILL (1941). *Statecraft as Soulcraft: What Government Does,* 4, 1983

Human nature is not a set condition but an evolving process.
> ANONYMOUS

Human nature can't be changed.
> SAYING

HUMILITY

See also • Devil: Theodora ○ Dignity: William Wordsworth ○ Egotism ○ Good: Micah ○ Humility: First Person ○ Modesty ○ Nonviolence: Fyodor Dostoyevsky ○ Pride

Humility is the foundation of all the other virtues; hence, in the soul in which this virtue does not exist there cannot be any other virtue except in mere appearance.
> ST. AUGUSTINE (A.D. 354–430). In "Humility" (1), *Spiritual Diary: Selected Sayings and Examples of Saints,* 1775, St. Paul Editions, 1962
> See Courage: Winston Churchill ○ Prudence: Edmund Burke ○ Self-Discipline: Adam Smith (2) ○ Self-Respect: John Herschel

They are proud in humility; proud in that they are not proud.
> ROBERT BURTON (1577–1640). *The Anatomy of Melancholy,* 1.2.3.14, 1621–1651

Extremes meet, and there is no better example than the haughtiness of humility.
> RALPH WALDO EMERSON (1803–1882). "Greatness," *Letters and Social Aims,* 1876

This is the deepest degree of humility: to rejoice when one is humiliated and jeered at, just as the vain person takes pride in great honors; and to feel hurt when honored and esteemed, as the proud person suffers when taunted and ridiculed.
> ST. FRANCIS de SALES (1567–1622). In "Humility" (17), *Spiritual Diary: Selected Sayings and Examples of Saints,* 1775, St. Paul Editions, 1962

Humility is the first of the virtues—for other people.
> OLIVER WENDELL HOLMES, SR. (1809–1894). *The Professor at the Breakfast-Table,* 5, 1860

Humility: Pride getting ready for a Pounce.
> ELBERT HUBBARD (1856–1915). *The Roycroft Dictionary Concocted by Ali Baba and the Bunch on Rainy Days,* p. 69, 1914

Humility is a strange thing. The minute you think you've got it, you've lost it.
> E. D. HULSE

Blessed are the meek, for they shall inherit the earth.
> JESUS (A.D. 1st cent.). *Matthew* 5:5

Everyone who exalts himself will be humbled, and he who humbles himself will be exalted.
> JESUS (A.D. 1st cent.). *Luke* 14:11

Eminence without humility:
This is the death indeed of all our hope.
> LAO-TZU (6th cent. B.C.). *The Way of Life,* 67, tr. R. B. Blakney, 1955

Humility is often merely feigned submissiveness assumed in order to subject others, an artifice of pride which stoops to conquer.
> LA ROCHEFOUCAULD (1613–1680). *Maxims,* 254, 1665, tr. Leonard Tancock, 1959

The first step toward humility [is] to realize that one is proud.
> C. S. LEWIS (1898–1963). *Mere Christianity,* rev. ed., 3.11, 1952

When it is trodden on, a worm will curl up. That is prudent. It thereby reduces the chance of being trodden on again. In the language of morals: *humility.*
> FRIEDRICH NIETZSCHE (1844–1900). "Maxims and Arrows" (31), *Twilight of the Idols,* 1889, tr. R. J. Hollingdale, 1968

Never humble yourself before anyone but God.
> SWAMI PRABHAVANANDA (1893–1976). "The Sermon on the Mount—III." In Christopher Isherwood, ed., *Vedanta for the Western World,* 1945

Do not consider yourself to have made any spiritual progress, unless you account yourself the least of all men.
> THOMAS à KEMPIS (1380–1471). *The Imitation of Christ,* 2.2, tr. Leo Sherley-Price, 1952

Humility is the root of love.
Humility exerts an irresistible power upon God.
> SIMONE WEIL (1909–1943). *The Simone Weil Reader,* 5 ("The Father's Silence"), ed. George A. Panichas, 1977

Now the man Moses was very meek, more than all men that were on the face of the earth.
> ANONYMOUS (*BIBLE*). *Numbers* 12:3

Too much humility is pride.
> SAYING (GERMAN)

Too humble is half-proud.
> SAYING (YIDDISH)

HUMILITY: FIRST PERSON

See also • Egotism: First Person ○ Humility

I am tired of riding the high horse of this pretense. I am not yet even a human being.
> ELIAS CANETTI (1905–1994). *The Human Province,* 1967, tr. Joachim Neugroschel, 1978

In letters I am perhaps equal to other men, but the character of the superior man, carrying out in his conduct what he professes, is what I have not yet attained to.
> CONFUCIUS (551–479 B.C.). *Confucian Analects,* 7.32, tr. James Legge, 1930

With such moderate abilities as I possess, it is truly surprising that I should have influenced to a considerable extent the belief of scientific men on some important points.
> CHARLES DARWIN (1809–1882). 1 May 1881, *The Autobiography of Charles Darwin and Selected Letters,* 2, ed. Francis Darwin, 1892

I don't have anything but darkness to lose.
> BOB DYLAN (1941–)

Look next from the history of my intellect to the history of my heart. A blank, my lord. I have not the kind affections of a pigeon.

> RALPH WALDO EMERSON (1803–1882). Journal, 13 May 1822

I tell you,
Miss, I knows [sic] an undesirable character
When I see one; I've been one myself for years.

> CHRISTOPHER FRY (1907–). *Venus Observed*, 2.1, 1950

I have never heard of any crime which I might not have committed.

> GOETHE (1749–1832). In Ralph Waldo Emerson, "Goethe; or, The Writer," *Representative Men*, 1850

I am not a perfect servant. I am a public servant doing my best against the odds. As I develop and serve, be patient. God is not finished with me yet.

> JESSE JACKSON (1941–). Democratic National Convention speech, San Francisco, 17 July 1984

Anybody can be pope; the proof of this is that I have become one.

> POPE JOHN XXIII (1881–1963). Letter to a young boy

Whereas I formerly believed it to be my bounden duty to call other persons to order, I now admit that I need calling to order myself.

> CARL G. JUNG (1875–1961). *Modern Man in Search of a Soul*, 10, tr. W. S. Dell and Cary F. Baynes, 1933

I had nothing to offer anybody except my own confusion.

> JACK KEROUAC (1922–1926). *On the Road*, 2.3, 1957

All are clear, I alone am clouded.

> LAO-TZU (6th cent. B.C.). In Carl G. Jung (1875-1961), "Retrospect," *Memories, Dreams, Reflections*, ed. Aniela Jaffé, 1962

It's almost as if I, a small parish priest, had been asked to become the Pope.

> ARTHUR LEVITT (1930–). Financier. On being appointed chairman of the Securities and Exchange Commission, Lou Dobbs interview, *Moneyline*, CNN, 9 September 1993

He despises me because he does not know me, and I despise his accusations because I know myself.

> GEORG CHRISTOPH LICHTENBERG (1742–1799)

Abraham Lincoln,
  His hand and pen,
He will be good,
  But God knows when.

> ABRAHAM LINCOLN (1809–1865). Doggerel written as a youngster in his notebook. In William H. Herndon and Jesse W. Weik, *Herndon's Lincoln: The True Story of a Great Life*, 2, 1889, Premier Books edition, 1961

I have now come to the conclusion never again to think of marrying, and for this reason: I can never be satisfied with anyone who would be blockhead enough to have me.

> ABRAHAM LINCOLN (1809–1865). After Mary Owens had refused his marriage proposal (four years later they married), letter to Mrs. Orville H. Browning, 1 April 1838
>
> See Wit: Examples: Groucho Marx (2)

I have only been able to change a few places in the vicinity of Peking.

> MAO TSE-TUNG (1893–1976). Remark to Pres. Richard M. Nixon, February 1972. In Henry A. Kissinger, *White House Years*, 24, 1979

What I have learned bears no other fruit than to make me realize how much I still have to learn.

> MONTAIGNE (1533–1592). "Of Experience," *Essays*, 1588, tr. Donald M. Frame, 1958

I do not know what I may appear to the world, but to myself I seem to have been only like a boy playing on the seashore, and diverting myself in now and then finding a smoother pebble or a prettier shell than ordinary, whilst the great ocean of truth lay all undiscovered before me.

> SIR ISAAC NEWTON (1642–1727). *Memoirs of the Life, Writings, and Discoveries of Sir Isaac Newton*, 2.27, ed. David Brewster, 1855

I do not do the good I want, but the evil I do not want is what I do.

> PAUL (A.D. 1st cent.). *Romans* 7:19
>
> See Mankind: Ralph Waldo Emerson o Reason & Passion: Ovid

Antonio: This thing of darkness I
Acknowledge mine.

> SHAKESPEARE (1564–1616). *The Tempest*, 5.1.275, 1611

There is an idea abroad among moral people that they should make their neighbors good. One person I have to make good: myself.

> ROBERT LOUIS STEVENSON (1850–1894)

My writing days are over; for such things have been revealed to me that all I have written and taught seems of but small account to me.

> ST. THOMAS AQUINAS (A.D. 1225–1274). Following a mystical experience which led him to halt work on the last chapters of *Summa Theologica* (his magnum opus). In Joseph Campbell, *The Hero with a Thousand Faces*, 2.3.7, 1949

Now if there are any who think that I am vainglorious, that I set myself up above others and crow over their low estate, let me tell them that I could tell a pitiful story respecting myself as well as them, if my spirits held out to do it; . . . I could enumerate a list of as rank offenses as ever reached the nostrils of heaven; that I think worse of myself than they can possibly think of me, being better acquainted with the man. I put the best face on the matter.

> HENRY DAVID THOREAU (1817–1862). Journal, 10 February 1852

I have lain in prison for nearly two years. Out of my nature has come wild despair; an abandonment to grief that was piteous even to look at; terrible and impotent rage; bitterness and scorn; anguish that wept aloud; misery that could find no voice; sorrow that was dumb. . . . Now I find hidden somewhere away in my nature something that tells me that nothing in the whole world is meaningless, and suffering least of all. That something hidden away in my nature, like a treasure in a field, is humility.

It is the last thing left in me, and the best: the ultimate discovery at which I have arrived, the starting point for a fresh development.

> OSCAR WILDE (1854–1900). *De Profundis*, 1905

HUMOR

See also • Comedy ∘ Funniness ∘ Jests ∘ Jokes ∘ Laughter ∘ Satire ∘ Wit: [especially] Josh Billings

Humor is not merely the telling of funny stories. It recognizes the vast difference between life as we imagine it and life as we live it, and between the fanciful and imposing impressions we have of ourselves and what we actually are.

> BROOKS ATKINSON (1894–1984). 4 April, *Once Around the Sun,* 1951

People should be taught what is, not what should be. All my humor is based on destruction and despair. If the whole world were tranquil, without disease and violence, I'd be standing in the bread line—right back of J. Edgar Hoover.

> LENNY BRUCE (1925–1966). Epigraph, *The Essential Lenny Bruce,* ed. John Cohen, 1967

This is not an easy time for humorists because the government is far funnier than we are.

> ART BUCHWALD (1925–). Speech at an international meeting of satirists and cartoonists, 1987

[Humor:] a genial sympathy with the under side.

> THOMAS CARLYLE (1795–1881). In James Anthony Froude, *Thomas Carlyle: A History of the First Forty Years, 1795–1835,* 1.20, 1882

[The humorist] does not laugh so much at mankind as he invites mankind to laugh at itself.

> PETER DE VRIES (1910–1993). Interview with the author, March 1964. In Roy Newquist, *Counterpoint,* 1964

All higher humor begins with ceasing to take oneself seriously.

> HERMANN HESSE (1877–1962). *Reflections,* 588, ed. Volker Michels, 1974

A good half of the humor of the late Mark Twain consisted of admitting frankly the possession of vices and weaknesses that all of us have and few of us care to acknowledge. Practically all of the sagacity of George Bernard Shaw consists of bellowing vociferously what everyone knows.

> H. L. MENCKEN (1880–1956). "The Ulster Polonius," *Prejudices: First Series,* 1919

Humor is the shock absorber of life; it helps us take the blows.

> PEGGY NOONAN (1950–). *What I Saw at the Revolution: A Political Life in the Reagan Era,* 8, 1990

I'm learning the difference between humor and comedy, between the laugh that lasts forever and the one that evaporates as soon as it hits air. Humor is giving, and comedy is taking away. Humor is companionable, comedy cold. Humor is character, comedy personality.

> ROGER ROSENBLATT (1940–). "What Brand of Laughter Do You Use?" *New York Times,* 17 November 1991

When humor is meant to be taken seriously, it's no joke.

> LIONEL STRACHEY (1864–1927)

Humor: The ability to laugh at any mistake you survive.

> JERRY TUCKER (1941–). *The Experience of Politics: You and American Government,* 12.3, 1974

HUNGER

See also • Christianity: Bishop Desmond Tutu ∘ Food ∘ Gluttony ∘ Poverty

Hunger makes thief of any man.

> PEARL S. BUCK (1892–1973). *The Good Earth,* 15, 1931

He whose Belly is full believes not him whose [Belly] is empty.

> THOMAS FULLER (1654–1734). Comp., *Gnomologia: Adages and Proverbs,* 2399, 1732

Love and business and family and religion and art and patriotism are nothing but shadows of words when a man's starving.

> O. HENRY (1862–1910). "Cupid à la Carte," *Heart of the West,* 1907

Fear for one's daily bread destroys one's character.

> FRANZ KAFKA (1883–1924). In Gustav Janouch, "Conversations with Kafka," tr. Goronwy Rees, *Encounter,* August 1971

Of what use is political liberty to those who have no bread?

> MARAT (1743–1793). French revolutionary leader. Letter to Camille Desmoulins, 24 June 1790
>
> See Freedom: Franklin D. Roosevelt (3) ∘ Freedom: Anonymous (2)

In the last 24 hours about 40,000 children, most of them under five have died in the world. More than 80 percent of those deaths are from preventable diseases like tetanus, measles, whooping cough, acute respiratory infection and diarrhea. Such deaths are often associated with malnutrition.

> *NEW INTERNATIONALIST.* London, April 1989. In *In These Times,* 24 May 1989

We cannot exist as a little island of well-being in a world where two-thirds of the people go to bed hungry every night.

> ELEANOR ROOSEVELT (1884–1962). Speech at a Democratic Party dinner, 8 December 1959

No man was ever more than about nine meals away from crime or suicide.

> ERIC SEVAREID (1912–1992). "A New Kind of Leadership," speech before the Conference on Vision Care, Washington, D.C. 26 April 1974

Well, by God, I'm hungry. . . . My guts is yellin' bloody murder.

> JOHN STEINBECK (1902–1968). *The Grapes of Wrath,* 6, 1939

There is a crime here that goes beyond denunciation. There is a sorrow here that weeping cannot symbolize. There is a failure here that topples all our success. The fertile earth, the straight tree rows, the sturdy trunks, and the ripe fruit. And children dying of pellagra must die because a profit cannot be taken from an orange. And coroners must fill in the certificate—died of malnutrition—because the food must rot, must be forced to rot. . . .

In the eyes of the people there is the failure; and in the eyes of the hungry there is a growing wrath. In the souls of the people the grapes of wrath are filling and growing heavy, growing heavy for the vintage.

> JOHN STEINBECK (1902–1968). *The Grapes of Wrath,* 25, 1939

He that feeds the hungry feeds God also.

> *TALMUD* (A.D. 1st–6th cent.) Rabbinical writings

❧

The belly talks but doesn't listen.

ANONYMOUS

The hunger of one is the shame of all.

ANONYMOUS

HUNTING

See also • Animals

Though boys throw stones at frogs in sport, the frogs do not die in sport, but in earnest.

BION (325?–255? B.C.). In Plutarch (A.D. 46?–119?), "Which Are the Most Crafty, Water or Land Animals?"

Detested sport,
That owes its pleasures to another's pain;
That feeds upon the sobs and dying shrieks
Of harmless nature.

WILLIAM COWPER (1731–1800). *The Task*, 3.326, 1785

Wild animals never kill for sport. Man is the only one to whom the torture and death of his fellow creatures is amusing in itself.

JAMES ANTHONY FROUDE (1818–1894). *Oceana*, 5, 1886

A sportsman is a man who, every now and then, simply has to get out and kill something. Not that he's cruel. He wouldn't hurt a fly. It's not big enough.

STEPHEN LEACOCK (1869–1944). *My Remarkable Uncle, and Other Sketches*, p. 73, 1942

Hunting: the least honorable form of war on the weak.

PAUL RICHARD (1874–1967). *The Scourge of Christ*, 7.4, 1929, ed. Michel Paul Richard, 1987

When a man wants to murder a tiger, he calls it sport: when the tiger wants to kill him, he calls it ferocity.

GEORGE BERNARD SHAW (1856–1950). "Maxims for Revolutionists: Crime and Punishment," *Man and Superman*, 1903

❧

Dr. Saul Cohen, a Maine cardiologist who acts as a White House consultant, shot a 320-pound black bear and presented the pelt to Ronald Reagan "as a show of my admiration for him and as a demonstration of his concern for the environment."

ANONYMOUS. In "No Comment," *Progressive*, April 1985

HYPOCRISY

See also • Appearances ∘ Assassination: George Bernard Shaw (1) ∘ Deception ∘ Holocaust: Adolf Eichmann (1,2) ∘ Moral Indignation ∘ Morality: Bertrand Russell (1) ∘ Preachers: John Selden ∘ Puritanism ∘ Rabbis: Jesus (1) ∘ Self-Righteousness ∘ Self-Sacrifice ∘ Sentimentality ∘ Sincerity ∘ Truthfulness ∘ War: George Orwell (1)

It always appeared a most iniquitous scheme to me—to fight ourselves for what we are daily robbing and plundering from those who have as good a right to freedom as we have.

ABIGAIL ADAMS (1744–1818). On slavery and the struggle for American independence from England, letter to her husband John, 24 September 1774

The hypocrite's crime is that he bears false witness against himself.

HANNAH ARENDT (1906–1975). *On Revolution*, 2.5 1963

I have been a selfish being all my life, in practice, though not in principle.

JANE AUSTEN (1775–1817). *Pride and Prejudice*, 58, 1813

They say to me: Eat and drink! Be glad you have it!
But how can I eat and drink if I snatch what I eat
From the starving, and
My glass of water belongs to one dying of thirst!
And yet I eat and drink.

BERTOLT BRECHT (1898–1956). "To Those Born Later" (1), 1936–1938, *Poems: 1913–1956*, ed. John Willett and Ralph Manheim, 1976

They play one tune and dance [to] another.

JOHN CLARKE (1596–1658). Comp., *Proverbs: English and Latine*, p. 18, 1639

Plain dealing is praised more than practiced.

JOHN CLARKE (1596–1658). Comp., *Proverbs: English and Latine*, p. 138, 1639

To please a profligate superior, men have affected some vices to which they were not inclined, and thus have made *their* hypocrisy an homage paid by *virtue* to *vice*.

C. C. COLTON (1780–1832). *Lacon: or, Many Things in Few Words; Addressed to Those Who Think*, 1.586, 1823

I own I am shock'd at the purchase of slaves,
And fear those who buy them and sell them are knaves;
What I hear of their hardships, their tortures, and groans,
Is almost enough to draw pity from stones.
I pity them greatly, but I must be mum,
For how could we do without sugar and rum?
Especially sugar, so needful we see?
What? give up our desserts, our coffee, and tea!

WILLIAM COWPER (1731–1800). "Pity for Poor Africans," l. 1, 1800

He blam'd and protested, but join'd in the plan;
He shar'd in the plunder, but pitied the man.

WILLIAM COWPER (1731–1800). "Pity for Poor Africans," l. 43, 1800

The hater of property and of government takes care to have his warranty deed recorded, and the book written against Fame and learning has the author's name on the title page.

RALPH WALDO EMERSON (1803–1882). Journal, spring 1857

See Fame: Cicero

Mankind are very odd Creatures: One Half censure what they practice, the other half practice what they censure; the rest always say and do as they ought.

BENJAMIN FRANKLIN (1706–1790). *Poor Richard's Almanack*, June 1752

The true hypocrite is the one who ceases to perceive his deception, the one who lies with sincerity.

ANDRÉ GIDE (1869–1951). Journal, August 1921, tr. Justin O'Brien, 1951

The words of an Angel, the deeds of a Devil.

> JAMES HOWELL (1593–1666). Comp., "Italian" (p. 5), *Paroimiographia: Proverbs, or Old Sayed Sawes & Adages in English . . . Italian, French and Spanish*, 1659

Be not too hasty to trust or to admire the teachers of morality: they discourse like angels, but they live like men.

> SAMUEL JOHNSON (1709–1784). *Rasselas: The Prince of Abyssinia*, 18, 1759

I have, all my life long, been lying till noon; yet I tell all young men, and tell them with great sincerity, that nobody who does not rise early will ever do any good.

> SAMUEL JOHNSON (1709–1784). 14 September 1773. In James Boswell, *The Journal of a Tour to the Hebrides, with Samuel Johnson, LL.D.*, 1786

How is it that we hear the loudest *yelps* for liberty among the drivers of negroes?

> SAMUEL JOHNSON (1709–1784). On American demands for independence from England, *Taxation No Tyranny* (pamphlet), 1775

He had grown up in a country run by politicians who sent the pilots to man the bombers to kill the babies to make the world safer for children to grow up in.

> URSULA K. LE GUIN (1929–). *The Lathe of Heaven*, 6, 1971

I met men who invoked the name of the Prince of Peace in their diatribes against war, and who put rifles in the hands of Pinkertons with which to shoot down strikers in their own factories. I met men incoherent with indignation at the brutality of prizefighting, and who, at the same time, were parties to the adulteration of food that killed each year more babies than even redhanded Herod had killed.

> JACK LONDON (1876–1916). "What Life Means to Me" (essay), 1906

What is most strange is that some Western countries that have supported the most vicious dictators for decades are now . . . taking it upon themselves to lecture [Congo leader Laurent Kabila] on democracy.

> NELSON MANDELA (1918—). In "Notebook," *Time*, 2 June 1997

A Pharisee is a man who prays publicly and preys privately.

> DON MARQUIS (1878–1937). In Edward Anthony, *O Rare Don Marquis*, 11, 1962

What is most extraordinary . . . and I believe unparalleled in history is that I rose from being a private [individual] to the astonishing height of power I possess without having committed a single crime.

> NAPOLEON (1769–1821). Remark to Dr. Barry E. O'Meara, 5 December 1816. In Maurice Hutt, ed., *Napoleon*, 6, 1972

Jim Harnsberger, who has been married five times, owes $18,000 in child support and has been accused of threatening an ex-wife and former girlfriend, is the leader of a San Diego, California, family values group.

> *NEW REPUBLIC.* "Notebook," 14 August 1995

When they call themselves "the good and just," do not forget that nothing is lacking to make them into Pharisees except—power!

> FRIEDRICH NIETZSCHE (1844–1900). "Of the Tarantulas," *Thus Spoke Zarathustra*, 1892, tr. R. J. Hollingdale, 1961

All left-wing parties in the highly industrialized countries are at bottom a sham, because they make it their business to fight against something which they do not really wish to destroy. They have internationalist aims, and at the same time they struggle to keep up a standard of life with which those aims are incompatible. We all live by robbing Asiatic coolies, and those of us who are "enlightened" all maintain that those coolies ought to be set free; but our standard of living, and hence our "enlightenment," demands that the robbery shall continue. A humanitarian is always a hypocrite.

> GEORGE ORWELL (1903–1950). "Rudyard Kipling," February 1942, *The Collected Essays, Journalism and Letters of George Orwell*, vol. 2, ed. Sonia Orwell and Ian Angus, 1968

There should be no disagreement between our lives and our doctrines.

> PUBLIUS SYRUS (85–43 B.C.). *Moral Sayings*, 635. tr. Darius Lyman, Jr., 1862

We deplore injustice but fail to give up the benefits of an unjust system.

> CHARLES A. REICH (1928–). "The Party of the Withdrawn," *New York Times*, 23 July 1978]

Why do grown-ups always say, "Don't hit," and then they go and start a big war?

> BENJAMIN ROTTMAN. Letter to *Los Angeles Times*. In "The War Some Wanted," *Progressive*, March 1991

You talk one way, you live another.

> SENECA THE YOUNGER (5? B.C.–A.D. 65). "On the Happy Life" (18.1), *Moral Essays*, tr. John W. Basore, 1932

This world, sir, is very clearly a place of torment and penance, a place where the fool flourishes and the good and wise are hated and persecuted, a place where men and women torture one another in the name of love; where children are scourged and enslaved in the name of parental duty and education; where the weak in body are poisoned and mutilated in the name of healing.

> GEORGE BERNARD SHAW (1856–1950). *John Bull's Other Island*, 4, 1904

It is narrated of Colonel D'Oyley, the first governor of Jamaica, that within a few days after having issued an order "for the distribution to the army of 1,701 Bibles," he signed another order for the payment "of the sum of twenty pounds sterling, out of the impost money, to pay for fifteen dogs, brought by John Hoy, for the hunting of the Negroes."

> HERBERT SPENCER (1820–1903). *Social Statics*, 4.30.9, 1851

Prohibit not something to others which you permit to yourself.

> *TALMUD* (A.D. 1st–6th cent.). Rabbinical writings

I sit on a man's back, choking him and making him carry me, and yet assure myself and others that I am very sorry for him and wish to lighten his load by all possible means—except by getting off his back.

> LEO TOLSTOY (1828–1910). *What Then Must We Do?* 16, 1886, tr. Aylmer Maude, 1935

I hope you have not been leading a double life, pretending to be wicked and being really good all the time. That would be hypocrisy.

OSCAR WILDE (1854–1900). *The Importance of Being Earnest*, 2, 1895

When the fox preaches, look to your geese.

SAYING (GERMAN)

IDEALISM

See also • Ideals ○ Materialism

As was only human, [Franklin D. Roosevelt's] will to power clothed itself in idealism.

CHARLES de GAULLE (1890–1970). In Eric Larrabee, epilogue to *Commander in Chief: Franklin Delano Roosevelt, His Lieutenants, and Their War*, 1987

See Duty: Richard J. Barnet

Every materialist will be an idealist; but an idealist can never go backward to be a materialist.

RALPH WALDO EMERSON (1803–1882). "The Transcendentalist," lecture, Masonic Temple, Boston, December 1840

An idealist is a person who helps other people to be prosperous.

HENRY FORD (1863–1947). Testifying in his libel suit against the *Chicago Tribune*, Mt. Clemens, Michigan, July 1919. The *Tribune* had called the industrialist an "anarchist" and an "ignorant idealist." Ford won the suit and was awarded 6 cents.

Idealism increases in direct proportion to one's distance from the problem.

JOHN GALSWORTHY (1867–1933)

I am not a visionary. I claim to be a practical idealist.

MOHANDAS K. GANDHI (1869–1948). In *Young India*, 11 August 1920

From the saintly and single-minded idealist to the fanatic is often but a step.

F. A. HAYEK (1899–1992). *The Road to Serfdom*, 4, 1944

Words without actions are the assassins of idealism.

HERBERT HOOVER (1874–1964)

Our nature abhors a moral and intellectual vacuum. Passion and self-interest may be our chief motives, but we hate to admit the fact even to ourselves. We are not happy unless our acts of passion can be made to look as though they were dictated by reason, unless our self-interest can be explained and embellished so as to seem idealistic.

ALDOUS HUXLEY (1894–1963). "Writers and Readers," *The Olive Tree and Other Essays*, 1936

See Duty: Richard J. Barnet

An idealist without illusions.

JOHN F. KENNEDY (1917–1963). On himself, quoted by Arthur M. Schlesinger, Jr., appearing on *Meet the Press*, television news program, NBC, 28 November 1965

Idealist: a cynic in the making.

IRVING LAYTON (1912–). "Aphs," *The Whole Bloody Bird*, 1969

An idealist is one who, on noticing that a rose smells better than a cabbage, concludes that it is also more nourishing.

H. L. MENCKEN (1880–1956). *A Little Book in C Major*, 2.3, 1916

I am an idealist. I don't know where I'm going, but I'm on my way.

CHARLES SANDBURG (1878–1967). *Incidentals*, p. 8, 1907

Just as the water of the streams we see is small in amount compared to that which flows underground, so the idealism which becomes visible is small in amount compared with what men and women bear locked in their hearts, unreleased or scarcely released. To unbind what is bound, to bring the underground waters to the surface: mankind is waiting and longing for such as can do that.

ALBERT SCHWEITZER (1875–1965). *Out of My Life and Thought: An Autobiography*, 9, tr. C. T. Campion, 1933

I see plenty of good in the world working itself out as fast as the idealists will allow it.

GEORGE BERNARD SHAW (1856–1950). Preface to *Arms and the Man*, 1894

When they come downstairs from their Ivory Towers, idealists are apt to walk straight into the gutter.

LOGAN PEARSALL SMITH (1865–1946). *Afterthoughts*, 3, 1931

IDEALS

See also • Ideas ○ Idealism ○ Meaning ○ Principles, Moral ○ Purpose ○ Values

The image is made to order, tailored to us. An ideal, on the other hand, has a claim on us. It does not serve us; we serve it. If we have trouble striving toward it, we assume the matter is with us, and not with the ideal.

DANIEL J. BOORSTIN (1914–). *The Image: A Guide to Pseudo-Events in America*, 5.2, 1961

The ideals men die for often become the prejudices their descendants kill for.

PAUL ELDRIDGE (1888–1982). *Maxims for a Modern Man*, 1439, 1965

I see the world gradually being turned into a wilderness, I hear the ever approaching thunder, which will destroy us too. I can feel the sufferings of millions and yet, if I look up into the heavens, I think that it will all come right, that this cruelty too will end, and that peace and tranquillity will return again.

In the meantime, I must uphold my ideals, for perhaps the time will come when I shall be able to carry them out.

ANNE FRANK (1929–1945). 15 July 1944 (three weeks later she and her family were arrested at their hiding place in Amsterdam; she died in the death camp at Bergen-Belsen in March 1945 two months before Germany's surrender), *Anne Frank: The Diary of a Young Girl,* tr. B. M. Mooyart-Doubleday, 1952

See People: Frank

All genuine ideals have one thing in common: they express the desire for something which is not yet accomplished but which is desirable for the purposes of the growth and happiness of the individual.

ERICH FROMM (1900–1980). *Escape from Freedom,* 7.2, 1941

Anyone who repudiates the lust for life because he is caught in the lust for ideals has not advanced in the most fundamental sense.

EUGEN HERRIGEL (1885–1955). "Zen Priests," *The Method of Zen,* 1960, ed. Hermann Tausend and tr. R. F. C. Hull, 1964

Ideal: An excuse for murder, tyranny or for self-aggrandizement. Any theory that justifies our secret itch.

ELBERT HUBBARD (1856–1915). *The Roycroft Dictionary Concocted by Ali Baba and the Bunch on Rainy Days,* p. 73, 1914

It is from numberless diverse acts of courage and belief that human history is shaped. Each time a man stands up for an ideal, or acts to improve the lot of others, or strikes out against injustice, he sends forth a tiny ripple of hope, and crossing each other from a million different centers of energy and daring, those ripples can sweep down the mightiest walls of repression and resistance. Like it or not we live in interesting times, and everyone here will ultimately be judged, will ultimately judge himself, on the efforts he has contributed to building a new world society and the extent to which his ideals and goals have shaped that effect.

ROBERT F. KENNEDY (1925–1968). "Day of Affirmation," address, University of Capetown (South Africa), 6 June 1966. The first two sentences of this quotation are inscribed on the Robert F. Kennedy gravesite in Arlington National Cemetary (Virginia).

There is an ideal standard somewhere and only that matters: and I cannot find it. Hence this aimlessness.

T. E. LAWRENCE (1888–1935). Letter to Eric Kennington, 6 August 1934

Ideals are very often formed in the effort to escape from the hard task of dealing with facts.

WILLIAM GRAHAM SUMNER (1840–1910). *Folkways: A Study of the Sociological Importance of Usages, Manners, Customs, Mores, and Morals,* 203, 1907

Every dogma has its day, but ideals are eternal.

ISRAEL ZANGWILL (1864–1926). Address, 13 November 1892

IDEAS

See also • Action & Thought ○ Belief ○ Communications ○ Conviction ○ Creativity ○ Creed ○ Discovery ○ Doctrine ○ Dogma ○ Doubt ○ Dreams: D. H. Lawrence ○ Facts ○ Faith ○ Freedom of Thought ○ Heresy ○ Ideals ○ Ideology ○ Imagination ○ Indoctrination ○ Inspiration ○ Intuition ○ Invention ○ Mind: Anonymous (3) ○ Opinion ○ Originality ○ Orthodoxy ○ Philosophy ○ Principles, Moral ○ Principles, Theoretical ○ Propaganda ○ Public Opinion ○ Revelation ○ Skepticism ○ Spirituality ○ Systems ○ Theories ○ Thinking ○ Thoughts ○ Truth ○ Words

Nothing is more dangerous than an idea when it is the only one we have.

ALAIN (1868–1951). *Propos sur la religion,* 74, 1938
See Books: Sayings (Italian)

Concord. All day with Emerson and Ideas, the rain pouring outside also.

BRONSON ALCOTT (1799–1888). Journal, 7 December 1851, ed. Odell Shepard, 1938

A new idea is delicate. It can be killed by a sneer or a yawn; it can be stabbed to death by a quip and worried to death by a frown on the right man's brow.

CHARLES H. BROWER (1904–1984). In "What They're Saying," *Advertising Age,* 10 August 1959

If you want to get across an idea, wrap it up as a person.

RALPH J. BUNCHE (1904–1971). His favorite saying

Every new idea has something of the pain and peril of childbirth about it.

SAMUEL BUTLER (1835–1902). *The Note-Books of Samuel Butler,* 7, ed. Henry Festing Jones, 1907

Ideas or hypotheses are tested by the consequences which they produce when they are acted upon.

JOHN DEWEY (1859–1952). *Experience and Education,* 7, 1938

Father Zossima: How many ideas have there been in the history of man which were unthinkable ten years before they appeared?

FYODOR DOSTOYEVSKY (1821–1881). *The Brothers Karamazov,* 6.2(f), 1880, tr. Constance Garnett, 1912

Ideas come from God.

ALBERT EINSTEIN (1879–1955). Remark to the author. In Banesh Hoffman, "My Friend, Albert Einstein," *Reader's Digest,* January 1968

God screens us evermore from premature ideas.

RALPH WALDO EMERSON (1803–1882). "Spiritual Laws," *Essays: First Series,* 1841

Ideas must work through the brains and the arms of good and brave men, or they are no better than dreams.

RALPH WALDO EMERSON (1803–1882). "American Civilization," lecture, Smithsonian Institute, Washington, 31 January 1862

Ideas are inherently conservative. They yield not to the attack of other ideas but to the massive onslaught of circumstances with which they cannot contend.

JOHN KENNETH GALBRAITH (1908–). *The Affluent Society,* 2.4, 1958

Ideas won't go to jail. In the long run of history, the censor and the inquisitor have always lost. The only sure weapon against bad ideas is better ideas.

A. WHITNEY GRISWOLD (1906–1963). "A Little Learning," *Atlantic,* November 1952

You talk of our having an idea; we do not have an idea. The idea has us, and martyrs us, and scourges us, and drives us into the arena to fight and die for it, whether we want to or not.

HEINRICH HEINE (1797–1856). In Jacob de Haas, *Theodore Herzl,* 1927

There never was an idea started that woke up men out of their stupid indifference but its originator was spoken of as a crank.

OLIVER WENDELL HOLMES, SR. (1809–1894). *Over the Teacups,* 7, 1891

One can resist the invasion of armies; one cannot resist the invasion of ideas.

VICTOR HUGO (1802–1885). Conclusion to *Histoire d'un crime,* 1877 (Popular version: Nothing is so powerful as an idea whose time has come.)

The vast majority of human beings dislike and even actually dread all notions with which they are not familiar. . . . Hence it comes about that at their first appearance innovators have generally been persecuted and always derided as fools and madmen.

ALDOUS HUXLEY (1894–1963). "Varieties of Intelligence: Orthodoxy and Heresy," *Proper Studies,* 1927

An idea, to be suggestive, must come to the individual with the force of a revelation.

WILLIAM JAMES (1842–1910). *The Varieties of Religious Experience: A Study in Human Nature,* 4 and 5, 1902

In general, whether a given idea shall be a live idea depends more on the person into whose mind it is injected than on the idea itself.

WILLIAM JAMES (1842–1910). "The Energies of Men," address, 1906

That fellow seems to me to possess but one idea, and that is a wrong one.

SAMUEL JOHNSON (1709–1784). On a "dull, tiresome" acquaintance, quoted by Rev. Dr. Maxwell, 1770. In James Boswell, *The Life of Samuel Johnson,* 1791

But the idea of the nest in the bird's mind, where does it come from?

JOSEPH JOUBERT (1754–1824). 1800, *Pensées,* 1838, tr. Paul Auster, 1983

Ideas never lack for words. It is words that lack ideas.

JOSEPH JOUBERT (1754–1824). 1800, *Pensées,* 1838, tr. Paul Auster, 1983

[Ideas] gain favor when they enter the service of interests and instincts.

BERTRAND de JOUVENEL (1903–1987). *On Power: Its Nature and the History of Its Growth,* 13.1, 1945, tr. J. F. Huntington, 1948

The power of vested interests is vastly exaggerated compared with the gradual encroachment of ideas.

JOHN MAYNARD KEYNES (1883–1946). *The General Theory of Employment, Interest, and Money,* 24.5, 1935

For the spread and endurance of an idea the originator is dependent on the self-development of the receivers and transmitters.

B. H. LIDDELL HART (1895–1970). "Some Conclusions," *Why Don't We Learn from History?* 1944

Various fresh ideas gained acceptance . . . when they could be presented not as something radically new, but as the revival in modern terms of a time-honored principle or practice that had been forgotten.

B. H. LIDDELL HART (1895–1970). Preface to *Strategy,* 1954

The stock of ideas which mankind has to work with is very limited, like the alphabet, and can at best have an air of freshness given it by new arrangements and combinations, or by application to new times and circumstances.

JAMES RUSSELL LOWELL (1819–1891). "Carlyle," *My Study Windows,* 1871

We are most likely to get angry and excited in our opposition to some idea when we ourselves are not quite certain of our own position, and are inwardly tempted to take the other side.

THOMAS MANN (1875–1955). *Buddenbrooks,* 8.2, 1902, tr. H. T. Lowe-Porter, 1924

Where do correct ideas come from? Do they drop from the skies? No. Are they innate in the mind? No. They come from social practice, and from it alone.

MAO TSE-TUNG (1893–1976). "Where Do Correct Ideas Come From?" May 1963

An idea isn't responsible for the people who believe in it.

DON MARQUIS (1878–1937). "The Sun Dial" column, *New York Sun,* 1918

There are few minds in a century that can look upon a new idea without terror. Fortunately for the rest of us, there are very few new ideas about.

W. SOMERSET MAUGHAM (1874–1965). 1896, *A Writer's Notebook,* 1949

[Economic] and social changes, though among the greatest, are not the only forces which shape the course of our species. Ideas are not always the mere signs and effects of social circumstances: they are themselves a power in history.

JOHN STUART MILL (1806–1873). "M. de Tocqueville on Democracy in America" (vol. 2), *The Edinburgh Review* (Scotland), October 1840

Intellectual work is related to power in numerous ways, among them these: with ideas one can uphold or justify power, attempting to transform it into legitimate authority; with ideas one can also debunk authority, attempting to reduce it to mere power. . . . And with ideas of more hypnotic though frivolous shape, one can divert attention from problems of power and authority and social reality in general.

C. WRIGHT MILLS (1916–1962). 1955, *Power, Politics and People: The Collected Essays of C. Wright Mills,* 4.11.3, ed. Irving Louis Horowitz, 1963

Men become susceptible to ideas, not by discussion and argument, but by seeing them personified and by loving the person who so embodies them.

LEWIS MUMFORD (1895–1990). *The Conduct of Life,* 4.3, 1951

Many times I have found that my best ideas have come when I thought I could not work for another minute and when I literally had to drive myself to finish the task before a deadline.

RICHARD M. NIXON (1913–1994). *Six Crises,* 2, 1962

Ideas brush past fleeting and insubstantial as moths. But I let them go, I don't want them. What I want is a voice.

JOYCE CAROL OATES (1938–). "Selections from a Journal: January 1985–January 1988," 1985. In Daniel Halpern, ed., *Antaeus,* Autumn 1988

A powerful idea communicates some of its strength to him who challenges it.

> MARCEL PROUST (1871–1922). "Madame Swann at Home,"
> *Remembrance of Things Past: Within a Budding Grove,* 1913–1927,
> tr. C. K. Scott Moncrieff, 1930

The instinct of conventionality, horror of uncertainty, and vested interests, all militate against the acceptance of a new idea.

> BERTRAND RUSSELL (1872–1970). "Individual Liberty and Public
> Control" (2), *Atlantic,* July 1917

Ideas come in pairs and they contradict one another; their opposition is the principal engine of reflection.

> JEAN-PAUL SARTRE (1905–1980). "Ideology and Revolution," *Studies on
> the Left,* vol. 1, no. 3, 1960

We are not always able to form new ideas about our surroundings, or to command original thoughts; they come if they will, and when they will.

> ARTHUR SCHOPENHAUER (1788–1860). "Counsels and Maxims" (2.13),
> *Essays of Arthur Schopenhauer,* tr. T. Bailey Saunders, 1851

I do not believe that we can put into anyone ideas which are not in him already.

> ALBERT SCHWEITZER (1875–1965). *Memoirs of Childhood and Youth,*
> 5, 1925, tr. C. T. Campion, 1949

To enable it to do its work naturally, every new idea must be in some way embedded in what is old.

> ALBERT SCHWEITZER (1875–1965). "The Conception of the Kingdom of
> God in the Transformation of Eschatology," epilogue to E. N. Mozley,
> *The Theology of Albert Schweitzer for Christian Inquirers,* p. 114, 1951

This creature Man, who in his own selfish affairs is a coward to the backbone, will fight for an idea like a hero.

> GEORGE BERNARD SHAW (1856–1950). *Man and Superman,* 3, 1903

New ideas come into this world somewhat like falling meteors, with a flash and an explosion.

> HENRY DAVID THOREAU (1817–1862). Letter to Daniel Ricketson,
> 18 August 1857

The man with a new idea is a Crank until the idea succeeds.

> MARK TWAIN (1835–1910). *Following the Equator: A Journey Around
> the World,* 32 (epigraph), 1897

We use ideas merely to justify our evil, and speech merely to conceal our ideas.

> VOLTAIRE (1694–1778). *Le Chapon et la Poularde,* 14, 1766

There is nothing so powerful as an old idea whose time has come again.

> BEN WATTENBERG (1933–). Quoted by Hugh Sidey. In *Washington Star,*
> 6 May 1979

Ideas come when we do not expect them, and not when we are brooding and searching at our desks. Yet ideas would certainly not come to mind had we not brooded at our desks and searched for answers with passionate devotion.

> MAX WEBER (1864–1920). "Science as a Vocation," 1919, *From Max
> Weber: Essays in Sociology,* tr. H. H. Gerth and C. Wright Mills, 1958

Ideas won't keep. Something must be done about them.

> ALFRED NORTH WHITEHEAD (1861–1947). 28 April 1938, *Dialogues of
> Alfred North Whitehead,* rec. Lucien Price, 1954

A really new idea affronts current agreement—it wouldn't be a new idea if it didn't—and the group, impelled as it is to agreement, is instinctively hostile to that which is divisive.

> WILLIAM H. WHYTE, JR. (1917–). *The Organization Man,* 5, 1956

An idea that is not dangerous is unworthy of being called an idea at all.

> OSCAR WILDE (1854–1900). "The Critic as Artist" (2), *Intentions,* 1891

The value of an idea has nothing whatever to do with the sincerity of the man who expresses it.

> OSCAR WILDE (1854–1900). "Oscariana," *The Works of Oscar Wilde:
> Epigrams, Phrases and Philosophies for the Use of the Young,*
> Sunflower edition, 1909

Ideas that we do not know we have, have us.

> WILLIAM APPLEMAN WILLIAMS (1921–1986). "Empire as a Way of Life,"
> *Nation,* 2 August 1980

IDEOLOGY

See also • Creed ○ Dissent ○ Doctrine ○ Dogma ○ Heresy ○ Ideas ○ Idolatry: Carl G. Jung ○ Indoctrination ○ Nations: Arthur M. Schlesinger, Jr. ○ Orthodoxy ○ Philosophy ○ Propaganda ○ Revolution: Carl Leiden and Karl M. Schmitt ○ Systems ○ Theories

Ideologies are *administered* by bureaucracies that control their meaning. They develop systems, they decide what is right- and what is wrong-thinking, who is faithful and who is a heretic; in short, the manipulation of ideologies becomes one of the most important means for the control of people through the control of their thoughts.

> ERICH FROMM (1900–1980). *May Man Prevail? An Inquiry into the Facts
> and Fictions of Foreign Policy,* 4, 1961

Abuse of words, foundation of ideology.

> JOSEPH JOUBERT (1754–1824). 1808, *Pensées,* 1838, tr. Paul Auster,
> 1983

A well-established ideology perpetuates itself with little planned propaganda by those whom it benefits most. When thought is taken about ways and means of sowing conviction, conviction has already languished.

> HAROLD D. LASSWELL (1902–1978). *Politics: Who Gets What, When,
> How,* 2, 1936

As nearly as I can see, all the new isms—Socialism, Communism, Fascism, and especially the late but not lamented Technocracy— outdo even Capitalism itself in their preoccupation with one thing: The distribution of more machine-made commodities to more people. They all proceed on the theory that if we can all keep warm and full, and all own a Ford and a radio, the good life will follow. Their programs differ only in ways to mobilize machines to this end. Though they despise each other, they are all, in respect of this objective, as identically alike as peas in a pod. They are competitive apostles of a single creed: *salvation by machinery.*

ALDO LEOPOLD (1886–1948). "The Conservation Ethic," lecture, Southwestern Division, American Association for the Advancement of Science, Las Cruces (New Mexico), 1 May 1933

All the isms are daddies.

YOKO ONO (1933–). David Sheff interview with Ono and John Lennon, *Playboy,* January 1981

We are now again in an epoch of wars of religion, but a religion is now called an "ideology."

BERTRAND RUSSELL (1872–1970). "Philosophy and Politics," *Unpopular Essays,* 1950

By ideology I mean a body of systematic and rigid dogma by which people seek to understand the world—and to preserve or transform it.

ARTHUR M. SCHLESINGER, JR. (1917–). "The One Against the Many," epilogue to *Paths of American Thought,* ed. Schlesinger and Morton White, 1963

❦

Democracy + Private Ownership = Capitalism
Democracy + Public Ownership = Socialism
Dictatorship + Public Ownership = Communism
Dictatorship + Private Ownership = Fascism.

ANONYMOUS

Ideology follows interests.

ANONYMOUS

See Architecture: Louis Henri Sullivan

IDLENESS

See also • Boredom ○ Industry ○ Laziness ○ Leisure ○ Poverty: R. H. Tawney ○ Procrastination ○ Unemployment ○ Wages: Samuel Johnson ○ Work

In a society organized upon the principles of equality and justice . . . idleness and parasites will be impossible. Having become exceedingly rare exceptions, those cases of idleness shall be regarded as special maladies to be subjected to clinical treatment.

MIKHAIL BAKUNIN (1814–1876). 1871, *The Political Philosophy of Bakunin: Scientific Anarchism,* 3.13, ed. G. P. Maximoff, 1953

The laborer is worthy of his hire, and the idler of his also, namely, of starvation.

THOMAS CARLYLE (1795–1881). Journal, 28 October 1830. In James Anthony Froude, *Thomas Carlyle: A History of the First Forty Years, 1795–1835,* 2.4, 1882

Standing pools gather filth.

JOHN CLARKE (1596–1658). Comp., *Proverbs: English and Latine,* p. 144, 1639

We do not know whether today we are busy or idle. I have seemed to myself very indolent at times, when, as it afterwards appeared, much was accomplished in me.

RALPH WALDO EMERSON (1803–1882). Journal, 22 April 1842

Idleness is the root of all evil.

GEORGE FARQUHAR (1678–1707). *The Beaux's Stratagem,* 1.1, 1707

See Greed: Paul

Be always asham'd to catch yourself idle.

BENJAMIN FRANKLIN (1706–1790). *Poor Richard's Almanack,* May 1741

Idleness and pride tax with a heavier hand than kings and parliaments.

BENJAMIN FRANKLIN (1706–1790). On the Stamp Act, letter, 1 July 1765

Idle Men are dead all their Life long.

THOMAS FULLER (1654–1734). Comp., *Gnomologia: Adages and Proverbs,* 3055, 1732

To be employ'd in useless Things is half to be idle.

THOMAS FULLER (1654–1734). Comp., *Gnomologia: Adages and Proverbs,* 5134, 1732

[The] rule should be "No labor, no meal."

MOHANDAS K. GANDHI (1869–1948). In *Young India,* 13 August 1925

The tediousness of an idle life.

EDWARD GIBBON (1737–1794). *Memoirs of My Life and Writings,* p. 51, 1796, Alex. Murray edition, 1869

Without business, debauchery.

GEORGE HERBERT (1593–1633). Comp., *Outlandish Proverbs,* 1009, 1640

An Idle youth, a needy Age.

GEORGE HERBERT (1593–1633). Comp., *Jacula Prudentum,* 1042, 1651

A man is not idle because he is absorbed in thought. There is a visible labor and there is an invisible labor. . . .
Thales remained motionless for four years. He founded philosophy.

VICTOR HUGO (1802–1885). Referring to Thales (625?–547? B.C.), one of the Seven Sages of Greece, "Cosette" (7.8), *Les Misérables,* tr. Charles E. Wilbour, 1862

If you are idle, be not solitary; if you are solitary, be not idle.

SAMUEL JOHNSON (1709–1784). Letter to the author, 27 October 1779. In James Boswell, *The Life of Samuel Johnson,* 1791

Now do not misunderstand this letter. I do not write it in any unkindness. I write it in order, if possible, to get you to *face* the truth—which truth is, you are destitute because you have *idled* away all your time. Your thousand pretenses for not getting along better, are all nonsense—they deceive nobody but yourself. *Go to work* is the only cure for your case.

ABRAHAM LINCOLN (1809–1865). Letter to his stepbrother John D. Johnston, 4 November 1851

Toil is man's allotment; toil of brain, or toil of hands, or a grief that's more than either, the grief and sin of idleness.

HERMAN MELVILLE (1819–1891). *Mardi: And a Voyage Thither,* 63, 1849

If I do not labor, I shall not eat.

MIDRASH (4th cent. B.C.–12th cent. A.D.). Rabbinical writings. In Louis I. Newman, comp., *The Talmudic Anthology,* 179, 1945

If any one will not work, let him not eat.

PAUL (A.D. 1st cent.). *2 Thessalonians* 3:10

Better to be *idle* than not well occupied.

JOHN RAY (1628–1705). Comp., *A Collection of English Proverbs,* p. 161, 1678

Never be entirely idle, but be reading or writing, in prayer or in meditation, or else be engaged in some work for the common good.

> THOMAS à KEMPIS (1380–1471). *The Imitation of Christ,* 1.19, tr. Leo Sherley-Price, 1952

❦

Idleness is the parent of poverty.

> SAYING (ENGLISH)

Idleness is the devil's workshop.

> SAYING (GERMAN)

A lazy youth, a lousy age.

> SAYING

No bees, no honey; no work, no money.

> SAYING

Those with nothing to do never have time to do anything.

> SAYING

IDOLATRY

See also • Atheism ○ Computers: Lewis Mumford (1) ○ Facts: Lewis Mumford (1) ○ God ○ Hero-Worship ○ Institutions: Arnold J. Toynbee ○ Nationalism: C. Wright Mills ○ Respect: Albert Einstein ○ Science: Martin Luther King, Jr.

Mammon, *n.* The god of the world's leading religion.

> AMBROSE BIERCE (1842–1914). *The Devil's Dictionary,* p. 85, 1911, Dover edition, 1958

The amassing of wealth is one of the worst species of idolatry, no idol more debasing.

> ANDREW CARNEGIE (1835–1919). Memorandum, 1868

We boast our emancipation from many superstitions; but if we have broken any idols, it is through a transfer of idolatry.

> RALPH WALDO EMERSON (1803–1882). "Character," *Essays: Second Series,* 1844

Words can become idols, and machines can become idols; leaders, the state, power, and political groups may also serve. Science and the opinion of one's neighbors can become idols, and God has become an idol for many.

> ERICH FROMM (1900–1980). *Psychoanalysis and Religion,* 5, 1950

Just as love for one individual which excludes the love for others is not love, love for one's country which is not part of one's love for humanity is not love, but idolatrous worship.

> ERICH FROMM (1900–1980). *The Sane Society,* 3.C, 1955

Is there really as much difference as we think between the Aztec human sacrifices to their gods and the modern human sacrifices in war to the idols of nationalism and the sovereign state?

> ERICH FROMM (1900–1980). *You Shall Be as Gods: A Radical Interpretation of the Old Testament and Its Tradition,* 2, 1966

Attribution of omnipotence to reason is as bad a piece of idolatry as is worship of stock and stone, believing it to be God.

> MOHANDAS K. GANDHI (1869–1948). In *Young India,* 14 October 1926

The moralists cease to be realistic and commit idolatry inasmuch as they worship, not God, but their own ethical ideals, inasmuch as they treat virtue as an end in itself and not as the necessary condition of the knowledge and love of God—a knowledge and love without which that virtue will never be made perfect or even socially effective.

> ALDOUS HUXLEY (1894–1963). *The Perennial Philosophy,* 21, 1946

No one can serve two masters; for either he will hate the one and love the other, or he will be devoted to the one and despise the other. You cannot serve God and mammon.

> JESUS (A.D. 1st cent.). *Matthew* 6:24

Our fearsome gods have only changed their names: they now rhyme with—*ism.*

> CARL G. JUNG (1875–1961). "The Relations between the Ego and the Unconscious" (2.2), 1928, *Two Essays on Analytical Psychology,* tr. R. F. C. Hull, 1953

For at least another hundred years we must pretend to ourselves and to everyone that fair is foul and foul is fair; for foul is useful and fair is not. Avarice and usury and precaution must be our gods for a little longer still.

> JOHN MAYNARD KEYNES (1883–1946). British economist. "Economic Possibilities for Our Grandchildren" (2), 1930, *Essays in Persuasion,* 1931

And God spoke all these words, saying,
I am the Lord your God, who brought you out of the land of Egypt, out of the house of bondage.
You shall have no other gods before me.

> MOSES (14th cent. B.C.). The First Commandment, *Exodus* 20:1–3
> See Revelations: Isaiah (2)

The ignorant fools take stones and worship them. O Hindus, how shall the stone which itself sinketh carry you across.

> NANAK (1469–1539). Indian religious leader and founder of Sikhism. In Charles Francis Potter, *The Great Religious Leaders,* 14, 1962

My God was Power, and in my powerlessness I realize that I have built upon foundations of sand.

> FRIEDRICH NIETZSCHE (1844–1900). Written in an asylum, *My Sister and I,* 2.9, tr. Oscar Levy, 1951

Power-worship . . . is the new religion of Europe.

> GEORGE ORWELL (1903–1950). "The Lion and the Unicorn," 1.2, 19 February 1941, *The Collected Essays, Journalism and Letters of George Orwell,* vol. 2, ed. Sonia Orwell and Ian Angus, 1968
> See Power: Orwell (1)

Their god is the belly.

> PAUL (A.D. 1st cent.). *Philippians* 3:19

It is not God that is worshipped but the group or the authority that claims to speak in His name. Sin becomes disobedience to authority and not violation of integrity.

G. SARVAPALLI RADHAKRISHNAN (1888–1975). Indian philosopher. On organized religion. In J. A. C. Brown, *Techniques of Persuasion: From Propaganda to Brainwashing,* 11, 1963

Juliet (to Romeo): Thy gracious self,
Which is the god of my idolatry.
SHAKESPEARE (1564–1616). *Romeo and Juliet,* 2.2.114, 1594

The savage bows down to idols of wood and stone: the civilized man, to idols of flesh and blood.
GEORGE BERNARD SHAW (1856–1950). "Maxims for Revolutionists: Idolatry," *Man and Superman,* 1903

Those who set out to serve both God and Mammon soon discover that there is no God.
LOGAN PEARSALL SMITH (1865–1946). *Afterthoughts,* 3, 1931

The keynote of idolatry is contentment with the prevalent gods.
ALFRED NORTH WHITEHEAD (1861–1947). *Adventures of Ideas,* 2.1, 1933

❦

Idols need not be smashed; they crumble of themselves.
ANONYMOUS

No image-maker worships the gods—he knows what stuff they are made of.
SAYING (CHINESE). In Herbert J. Muller, *The Uses of the Past: Profiles of Former Societies,* 10.3, 1952

IGNORANCE

See also • Fools ○ Illusion ○ Knowledge ○ Stupidity

The ignorant man is dead while still alive.
'ALI (A.D. 600?–661). *Maxims of 'Ali,* tr. Maulana Akbar, undated. In Whitall N. Perry, comp., *A Treasury of Traditional Wisdom,* p. 767, 1986

There are some people that if they don't know, you can't tell 'em.
LOUIS "SATCHMO" ARMSTRONG (1900–1971). In Elmer Shabart, *Memoirs of a Barbed Wire Surgeon,* 19 (epigraph), 1997

It iz better tew know nothing than two know what ain't so.
JOSH BILLINGS (1818–1885). "Sollum Thoughts," *Everybody's Friend,* 1874

Ignorance is not innocence but sin.
ROBERT BROWNING (1812–1889). *The Inn Album,* 5, 1875

A seeming ignorance is very often a most necessary part of worldly knowledge.
LORD CHESTERFIELD (1694–1773). Letter to his son, 15 January 1753

I alone know that I know nothing.
DEMOCRITUS (460?–370 B.C.). In Kathleen Freeman, tr., *Ancilla to Pre-Socratic Philosophers: A Complete Translation of the Fragments in Diels, Fragmente der Vorsokratiker,* 68.304, 1983 (1948)

I seemed to have gained nothing in trying to educate myself unless it was to discover more and more fully how ignorant I was.
DESCARTES (1596–1650). *Discourse on Method,* 1, 1637, tr. Laurence J. Lafleur, 1964

To be conscious that you are ignorant is a great step to knowledge.
BENJAMIN DISRAELI (1804–1881). *Sybil: Or, The Two Nations,* 1.5, 1845
See Wisdom: N. Sri Ram (2)

Being ignorant is not so much a Shame,
as being unwilling to learn.
BENJAMIN FRANKLIN (1706–1790). *Poor Richard's Almanack,* October 1755

Nothing is more terrible than ignorance in action.
GOETHE (1749–1832). *The Maxims and Reflections of Goethe,* 231, tr. T. Bailey Saunders, 1892

Where ignorance is bliss,
'Tis folly to be wise.
THOMAS GRAY (1716–1771). Closing verse, *Ode on a Distant Prospect of Eton College,* 1747

Ignorance of the world leaves one at the mercy of its malice.
WILLIAM HAZLITT (1778–1830). "On the Disadvantages of Intellectual Superiority," *Table Talk,* 1822

Between true Science and erroneous Doctrines, Ignorance is in the middle.
THOMAS HOBBES (1588–1679). *Leviathan,* 4, 1651

We don't know because we don't want to know.
ALDOUS HUXLEY (1894–1963). "Beliefs," *Ends and Means: An Inquiry into the Nature of Ideals and into the Methods Employed for Their Realization,* 1937

There is no slavery but ignorance.
ROBERT G. INGERSOLL (1833–1899). "Fragments," *The Philosophy of Ingersoll,* ed. Vere Goldthwaite, 1906

My people go into exile for want of knowledge.
ISAIAH (8th cent. B.C.). *Isaiah* 5:13

Ignorance, when it is voluntary, is criminal.
SAMUEL JOHNSON (1709–1784). *Rasselas: The Prince of Abyssinia,* 30, 1759

Nothing in all the world is more dangerous than sincere ignorance and conscientious stupidity.
MARTIN LUTHER KING, JR. (1929–1968). *Strength to Love,* 4.3, 1963

A great part of mankind are . . . unavoidably given over to invincible ignorance.
JOHN LOCKE (1632–1704). *An Essay Concerning Human Understanding,* 4.20.2, 1690, ed. Alexander Campbell Fraser, 1894

The ignorant man always adores what he cannot understand.
CESARE LOMBROSO (1836–1909). *The Man of Genius,* 3.3, 1888, ed. Havelock Ellis, 1896

The know-nothings are, unfortunately, seldom the do-nothings.
MIGNON McLAUGHLIN (1915–). *The Neurotic's Notebook,* 5, 1963

Confusion is a word we have invented for an order which is not understood.
HENRY MILLER (1891–1980). "Interlude," *Tropic of Capricorn,* 1939

Herein is the evil of ignorance, that he who is neither good nor wise is nevertheless satisfied with himself: he has no desire for that of which he feels no want.

> PLATO (427?–347 B.C.). *Symposium,* 204, tr. Benjamin Jowett, 1894

Ignorance is not a simple lack of knowledge but an active aversion to knowledge, the refusal to know, issuing from cowardice, pride or laziness of mind.

> KARL POPPER (1902–1994). As paraphrased by Ryszard Kapuscinski, "The Philosopher as Giant-Slayer," *New York Times Magazine,* 1 January 1995

That life is most pleasant which is passed in ignorance.

> PUBLIUS SYRUS (85–43 B.C.). *Moral Sayings,* 263, tr. Darius Lyman, Jr., 1862

There are two kinds of people: those who don't know and those who don't know they don't know.

> ROBERT B. REICH (1946–). Television news program, NBC, 8 February 1995

You know, Percy, everybody is ignorant, only on different subjects.

> WILL ROGERS (1879–1935). "Defending My Soup Plate Position," *The Illiterate Digest,* 1924

The risk is not in what he does not know, but in what he thinks he knows.

> ROUSSEAU (1712–1778). *Emile; or, Treatise on Education,* 3, 1762, tr. Barbara Foxley, 1911

Claudio: O, what men dare do! what men may do! what men daily do, not knowing what they do!

> SHAKESPEARE (1564–1616). *Much Ado About Nothing,* 4.1.20, 1598
>
> See Forgiveness: Jesus (3)

Clown: There is no darkness but ignorance.

> SHAKESPEARE (1564–1616). *Twelfth Night,* 4.2.46, 1599

The more ignorant men are, the more convinced are they that their little parish and their little chapel is an apex to which civilization and philosophy has painfully struggled up the pyramid of time from a desert of savagery.

> GEORGE BERNARD SHAW (1856–1950). Notes ("Apparent Anachronisms") to *Caesar and Cleopatra,* 1899

Where there is no knowledge, ignorance calls itself knowledge.

> GEORGE BERNARD SHAW (1856–1950). "Maxims for Revolutionists: Stray Sayings," *Man and Superman,* 1903

Although I do not suppose that either of us knows anything really beautiful and good, I am better off than he is — for he knows nothing, and thinks that he knows; I neither know nor think that I know.

> SOCRATES (470?–399 B.C.). In Plato (427?–347 B.C.), *Apology,* 21, tr. Benjamin Jowett, 1894
>
> See Knowledge: *Upanishads*

I heard one boy say to another in the street today, "You don't know much more than a piece of putty."

> HENRY DAVID THOREAU (1817–1862). Journal, 28 October 1852

When [ignorance] does not know something, it says that what it does not know is stupid.

> LEO TOLSTOY (1828–1910). *A Confession,* 7, 1882, tr. Alylmer Maude, 1921

That is just the way with some people. They get down on a thing when they don't know nothing about it.

> MARK TWAIN (1835–1910). *The Adventures of Huckleberry Finn,* 1, 1884

It's not so much what folks don't know that causes problems, it's what they do know that ain't so.

> ARTEMUS WARD (1834–1867). In James F. Clarity and Warren Weaver, Jr., "Briefings," *New York Times,* 18 October 1984

It is better to light one candle than to curse the darkness.

> SAYING (CHINESE)

ILLUSION

See also • Appearances ◦ Belief ◦ Deception ◦ Delusion ◦ Fools ◦ Ignorance ◦ Lying ◦ Madness: Friedrich Nietzsche ◦ Mental Illness ◦ Truth ◦ Reality ◦ Self-Deception ◦ Self-Knowledge: Aldous Huxley ◦ Stupidity

Our greatest illusion is to believe that we are what we think ourselves to be.

> HENRI AMIEL (1821–1881). Journal, 10 February 1853, tr. Mrs. Humphrey Ward, 1887

People everywhere enjoy believing things that they know are not true. It spares them the ordeal of thinking for themselves and taking responsibility for what they know.

> BROOKS ATKINSON (1894–1984). February 2, *Once Around the Sun,* 1951

Nature intended illusions for the wise as well as for fools lest the former should be rendered too miserable by their wisdom.

> CHAMFORT (1741–1794). *Maxims and Thoughts,* 1, 1796, tr. W. S. Merwin, 1984

People are more persuaded than ever that they have perfect freedom.

> FYODOR DOSTOYEVSKY (1821–1881). *The Brothers Karamazov,* 5.5, 1880, tr. Constance Garnett, 1912

We do not like those who unmask our illusions.

> RALPH WALDO EMERSON (1803–1882). "Character," *Lectures and Biographical Sketches,* 1883

We are at full stop. We think we have arrived.

> HENRY FAIRLIE (1924–1990). "Too Rich for Heroes," *Harper's,* November 1978

My illusions—apart from the fact that no penalty is imposed for not sharing them—are not, like the religious ones, incapable of correction.

> SIGMUND FREUD (1856–1939). *The Future of an Illusion,* 10, 1927, tr. W. D. Robson-Scott, 1953

Modern man lives under the illusion that he knows what he wants, while he actually wants what he is *supposed* to want.

> ERICH FROMM (1900–1980). *Escape from Freedom,* 7.1, 1941

It is possible that people need to believe that they are unmanaged if they are to be managed effectively.

> JOHN KENNETH GALBRAITH (1908–). *The New Industrial State,* 19.5, 1967

Of all the illusions that beset mankind none is quite so curious as [the] tendency to suppose that we are mentally and morally superior to those who differ from us in opinion.

> ELBERT HUBBARD (1856–1915). In Laurence J. Peter, *Peter's People,* 1, 1979

Rob the average man of his life-illusion, and you rob him of his happiness as well.

> HENRIK IBSEN (1828–1906). *The Wild Duck,* 5, 1884

The more intelligent and cultured a man is, the more subtly he can humbug himself.

> CARL G. JUNG (1875–1961). "Analytical Psychology and Education," 1, 1924, *The Development of Personality,* tr. R. F. C. Hull, 1954

The masses have never thirsted after truth. They turn aside from evidence that is not to their taste, preferring to deify error, if error seduce[s] them. Whoever can supply them with illusions is easily their master; whoever attempts to destroy their illusions is always their victim.

> GUSTAVE LE BON (1841–1931). *The Crowd: A Study of the Popular Mind,* 2.2.2, 1895, Viking Press edition, 1960

Many men easily do without truth but none is strong enough to do without illusions.

> GUSTAVE LE BON (1841–1931)

And so we plow along, as the fly said to the ox.

> HENRY WADSWORTH LONGFELLOW (1807–1882). *The Spanish Student,* 3.6, 1840

In my youth I had illusions. I got rid of them fast.

> NAPOLEON (1769–1821). Deathbed statement, 17 April 1821, *The Mind of Napoleon: A Selection from His Written and Spoken Words,* 324, ed. J. Christopher Herold, 1955

Let the People think they Govern, and they will be Govern'd.

> WILLIAM PENN (1644–1718). *Some Fruits of Solitude,* 337, 1693

We, undisciplined in discernment of the inward, knowing nothing of it, run after the outer, never understanding that it is the inner which stirs us; we are [like] one who sees his own reflection but not realizing whence it comes goes in pursuit of it.

> PLOTINUS (A.D. 205–270). *The Enneads,* 5.7.2, tr. Stephen MacKenna and B. S. Page, 1952

They pray not only for their daily bread, but also for their daily illusion.

> GUSTAV STRESEMANN (1878–1929). German political leader. On the German people during the pre-Nazi period. In J. A. C. Brown, *Techniques of Persuasion: From Propaganda to Brainwashing,* 5, 1963

I stopped believing in Santa Claus when I was six. Mother took me to see him in a department store, and he asked for my autograph.

> SHIRLEY TEMPLE (1928–). In Herb Caen, column, *San Francisco Chronicle,* 20 December 1993

❧

Our illusions are like the blinders mill horses wear without which they wouldn't move.

> ANONYMOUS

IMAGINATION

See also • Creativity ○ Discovery ○ Ideas ○ Inspiration ○ Intelligence ○ Intuition ○ Invention ○ Originality ○ Mind ○ Reason ○ Revelation ○ Spirituality

What is now proved was once only imagin'd.

> WILLIAM BLAKE (1757–1827). "Proverbs of Hell," *The Marriage of Heaven and Hell,* 8.13, 1790–1793?

Use your imagination not to scare yourself to death but to inspire yourself to life.

> ADELE BROOKMAN (1946–). Personal communication, 1 February 1994

To treat your facts with imagination is one thing, to imagine your facts is another.

> JOHN BURROUGHS (1837–1921). 24 October 1907, *The Heart of Burroughs's Journals,* ed. Clara Barrus, 1928

Imagination depends mainly on memory, but there is a small percentage of creation of something out of nothing with it. We can invent a trifle more than can be got at by mere combination of remembered things.

> SAMUEL BUTLER (1835–1902). *The Note-Books of Samuel Butler,* 10, ed. Henry Festing Jones, 1907

To make a prairie it takes a clover and one bee,
One clover, and a bee,
And revery.
The revery alone will do,
If bees are few.

> EMILY DICKINSON (1830–1886). "To make a prairie it takes a clover and one bee," undated

Imagination is more important than knowledge. Knowledge is limited. Imagination encircles the world.

> ALBERT EINSTEIN (1879–1955). Interview with the author. In George Sylvester Viereck, "What Life Means to Einstein," *Glimpses of the Great,* 1930

Imagination is a very high sort of seeing.

> RALPH WALDO EMERSON (1803–1882). "The Poet," *Essays: Second Series,* 1844

What is the imagination? . . . Only the precursor of the reason.

> RALPH WALDO EMERSON (1803–1882). "Books," *Society and Solitude,* 1870

Imagination selects ideas from the treasures of remembrance, and produces novelty only by varied combinations.

> SAMUEL JOHNSON (1709–1784). In *The Idler* (English journal), 44, 17 February 1759

Fancy is always to act in subordination to Reason. We may take Fancy for a companion, but must follow Reason as our guide. We may allow Fancy to suggest certain ideas in certain places; but Reason must always be heard when she tells us that those ideas and those places have no natural or necessary relation.

> SAMUEL JOHNSON (1709–1784). Letter to the author, 15? March 1774. In James Boswell, *The Life of Samuel Johnson,* 1791

He who has imagination without learning has wings and no feet.

> JOSEPH JOUBERT (1754–1824). *Pensées,* 53, 1838, tr. Henry Attwell, 1877

Imaginative ideas are independent of the subject's will.

> WILHELM LANGE-EICHBAUM (1875–1950). *The Problem of Genius,* 3.E.3, 1931, tr. Eden and Cedar Paul, 1932

In happy hours, when the imagination
Wakes like a wind at midnight, and the soul
Trembles in all its leaves, it is a joy
To be uplifted on its wings, and listen
To the prophetic voices in the air
That call us onward.

> HENRY WADSWORTH LONGFELLOW (1807–1882). *Michael Angelo,* 1.1, 1883

Imagination is like the Danube: at it source, it can be crossed in a leap.

> NAPOLEON (1769–1821). Remark to Gen. Gaspard Gourgaud, 1817, *The Mind of Napoleon: A Selection from His Written and Spoken Words,* 60, ed. J. Christopher Herold, 1955

Imagination is built upon knowledge.

> ELIZABETH STUART PHELPS (1844–1911). *Chapters from a Life,* 11, 1897

The world of reality has its bounds, the world of imagination is boundless.

> ROUSSEAU (1712–1778). *Emile; or, Treatise on Education,* 2, 1762, tr. Barbara Foxley, 1911

If the imagination is to yield any real product, it must have received a great deal of material from the external world.

> ARTHUR SCHOPENHAUER (1788–1860). "Studies in Pessimism: Further Psychological Observations," *Essays of Arthur Schopenhauer,* tr. T. Bailey Saunders, 1851

Theseus: The lunatic, the lover and the poet
Are of imagination all compact.

> SHAKESPEARE (1564–1616). *A Midsummer Night's Dream,* 5.1.7, 1595

Reason is the enumeration of quantities already known; imagination is the perception of the value of those quantities, both separately and as a whole. Reason respects the differences, and imagination the similitudes of things. Reason is to imagination as the instrument to the agent, as the body to the spirit, as the shadow to the substance.

> PERCY BYSSHE SHELLEY (1792–1822). *A Defence of Poetry,* p. 1, 1821, ed. Albert S. Cook, 1890

Plato taught me, by example, not to be ashamed of using my imagination as well as my intellect. He taught me, when, in a mental voyage, I found myself at the upper limit of the atmos-phere accessible to the Reason, not to hesitate to let my imagination carry me on up into the stratosphere on the wings of a myth.

> ARNOLD J. TOYNBEE (1889–1975). *A Study of History,* 10.228, 1954

The imagination needs moodling—long, inefficient, happy idling, dawdling and puttering.

> BRENDA UELAND (1891–1985). *If You Want to Write,* 2nd ed., 4, 1987 (1938)

Imagination is not to be divorced from the facts: it is a way of illuminating the facts.

> ALFRED NORTH WHITEHEAD (1861–1947). *The Aims of Education and Other Essays,* 7.2, 1929

The imagination's power lies in its receptivity, not in any power to "invent."

> COLIN WILSON (1931–). *Religion and the Rebel,* 2.4, 1957

Imagination is something you do alone.

> STEVE WOZNIAK (1950–). Apple Computer co-founder. Speech before the Commonwealth Club of California, San Francisco, 27 February 1987

IMITATION

See also • Conformity ○ Example ○ Individuality: Clint Eastwood ○ Originality ○ Plagiarism ○ Writers: Chateaubriand

This unconscious imitation and encouragement of appreciated character, and this equally unconscious shrinking from and persecution of disliked character, is the main force which molds and fashions men in society.

> WALTER BAGEHOT (1826–1877). *Physics and Politics, or Thoughts on the Application of the Principles of "Natural Selection" and "Inheritance" to Political Society,* 3, 1872

Why doth one man's yawning make another yawn?

> ROBERT BURTON (1577–1640). *The Anatomy of Melancholy,* 1.2.3.2, 1621–1651

We are, in truth, more than half what we are by imitation. The great point is, to choose good models and to study them with care.

> LORD CHESTERFIELD (1694–1773). Letter to his son, 18 January 1750

Insist on yourself; never imitate.

> RALPH WALDO EMERSON (1803–1882). "Self-Reliance," *Essays: First Series,* 1841

There is much difference between imitating a good man and counterfeiting him.

> BENJAMIN FRANKLIN (1706–1790). *Poor Richard's Almanack,* November 1738

Imitate Jesus and Socrates.

> BENJAMIN FRANKLIN (1706–1790). Virtue #13 ("Humility"), 1784, *Autobiography,* 1798

In whatsoever Condition thou art, still ask thyself, What would my blessed Savior have thought, said, and done in this Case.

> THOMAS FULLER (1654–1734). Comp., *Introductio ad Prudentiam,* 693, 1731

Imitate what is good wheresoever thou findest it.

> THOMAS FULLER (1654–1734). Comp., *Introductio ad Prudentiam,* 780, 1731

Whomsoever you follow, howsoever great he might be, see to it that you follow the spirit of the master and not imitate him mechanically.
MOHANDAS K. GANDHI (1869–1948). In *Young India,* 9 February 1928

We copy when we lack the inclination, the ability, or the time to work out an independent solution.
ERIC HOFFER (1902–1983). *The True Believer: Thoughts on the Nature of Mass Movements,* 81, 1951

Imitation will be relatively free of resentment when it is possible for the imitators to identify themselves wholeheartedly with their model.
ERIC HOFFER (1902–1983). *The Ordeal of Change,* 4, 1964

O imitators, you slavish herd!
HORACE (65–8 B.C.). *Epistles,* 1.19

Imitation: The sincerest form of insult.
ELBERT HUBBARD (1856–1915). *The Roycroft Dictionary Concocted by Ali Baba and the Bunch on Rainy Days,* p. 74, 1914

To do the opposite of something is also a form of imitation, namely an imitation of its opposite.
GEORG CHRISTOPH LICHTENBERG (1742–1799). *Aphorisms,* D.96, 1806, tr. R. J. Hollingdale, 1990

Imitate the ways of God.
MOSES MAIMONIDES (1135–1204). *The Guide for the Perplexed,* 3.54, A.D. 1190, tr. M. Friedländer, 1904

He who wants to set a good example must add a grain of foolishness to his virtue; then others can imitate and, at the same time, rise above the one being imitated—something which people love.
FRIEDRICH NIETZSCHE (1844–1900). *Human, All Too Human,* 561, 1878, tr. Marion Faber, 1984

To model ourselves upon good men is to produce an image of an image: we have to fix our gaze above the image and attain Likeness to the Supreme Exemplar.
PLOTINUS (A.D. 205–270). *The Enneads,* 1.2.7, tr. Stephen MacKenna and B. S. Page, 1952

Being invited once to hear a man who admirably imitated the nightingale, [Agesilaus] declined, saying he had heard the nightingale itself.
PLUTARCH (A.D. 46?–119?). "Agesilaus" (485–401 B.C.), *Parallel Lives,* Dryden edition, 1693

How much more readily we imitate those whom we like can scarcely be expressed.
QUINTILIAN (A.D. 35?–100?). *Institutio oratoria,* 2.2.8, tr. John Selby Watson, 1856

A mere copier of nature can never produce anything great; can never raise and enlarge the conceptions, or warm the heart of the spectator.
SIR JOSHUA REYNOLDS (1723–1792). "Discourse Three," 14 December 1770, *Discourses on Art,* 1769–1790

Genius . . . is the child of imitation.
SIR JOSHUA REYNOLDS (1723–1792). "Discourse Three," 14 December 1770, *Discourses on Art,* 1769–1790

Only through imitation do we develop toward originality.
JOHN STEINBECK (1902–1968). *Travels with Charley: In Search of America,* 3, 1961

The Imitation of Christ.
THOMAS á KEMPIS (1380–1471). Book title

The problem of bringing the uncreative rank and file into line with the creative pioneers . . . cannot be solved in practice, on the social scale, without bringing into play the faculty of sheer mimesis [i.e., imitation]—one of the less exalted faculties of Human Nature which has more in it of drill than of inspiration.
ARNOLD J. TOYNBEE (1889–1975). *A Study of History,* 3.245, 1934

Aping but others, ye are but intelligent apes.
WALT WHITMAN (1819–1892). "Notes for Lectures on Literature," *Walt Whitman's Workshop: A Collection of Unpublished Manuscripts,* ed. Clifton Joseph Furness, 1964

[No one can] act wisely from imitation because in every circumstance of life there is a kind of individuality, which requires an exertion of judgment to modify general rules.
MARY WOLLSTONECRAFT (1759–1797). *A Vindication of the Rights of Woman,* 12, 1792

❧

Imitation is the sincerest form of flattery.
SAYING (ENGLISH)
See Envy: Churton Collins ○ Flattery: Anonymous ○ Television: Fred Allen (2)

Monkey see, monkey do.
SAYING

IMMORTALITY

See also • Death ○ Eternity ○ Longevity ○ Religion ○ Youth: William Hazlitt

I don't want to achieve immortality through my work. . . . I want to achieve it through not dying.
WOODY ALLEN (1935–). In Eric Lax, *Woody Allen and His Comedy,* 12, 1975

The voice of Nature loudly cries,
And many a message from the skies,
That something in us never dies.
ROBERT BURNS (1759–1796). "New Year's Day," 3, 1791

To live in the hearts we leave
Is not to die.
THOMAS CAMPBELL (1777–1844). "Hallowed Ground," 1825

If my bark sinks, 'tis to another sea.
WILLIAM ELLERY CHANNING (1780–1842). "A Poet's Hope," 1840?

Be the first to say something obvious and achieve immortality.
MARIE von EBNER-ESCHENBACH (1830–1916). *Aphorisms,* p. 19, 1880–1905, tr. David Scrase and Wolfgang Mieder, 1994

He had decided to live forever or die in the attempt.

> JOSEPH HELLER (1923–). *Catch-22*, 3, 1961

Not all of me shall die. For Death,
  Though he should still my beating heart,
Takes but a fragment with my breath
  And leaves untouched the greater part.

> HORACE (65–8 B.C.). *Odes*, 3.30, *The Complete Works of Horace*,
> ed. Casper J. Kraemer, Jr., 1936

He ne'er is crowned
With immortality, who fears to follow
Where airy voices lead.

> JOHN KEATS (1795–1821). *Endymion*, 2, 1817

Men are mortal, but ideas are immortal.

> WALTER LIPPMANN (1889–1974). *A Preface to Morals*, 3.2, 1929

Life is real! Life is earnest!
  And the grave is not its goal;
Dust thou art, to dust returnest,
  Was not spoken of the soul.

> HENRY WADSWORTH LONGFELLOW (1807–1882). "A Psalm of Life"
> (2), *Voices of the Night*, 1839

There is no Death! What seems so is transition.

> HENRY WADSWORTH LONGFELLOW (1807–1882). "Resignation" (5),
> *The Seaside and the Fireside*, 1850

As "Old soldiers never die," I promise to keep on living as though I expected to live forever.

> DOUGLAS MacARTHUR (1880–1964). "War Is No Longer a Medium
> of Practical Settlement of International Differences," address at an
> American Legion dinner honoring him, Ambassador Hotel,
> Los Angeles, 26 January 1955
>
> See Soldiers: MacArthur (1)

Death cannot kill what never dies.

> WILLIAM PENN (1644–1718). *More Fruits of Solitude*, 128, 1693

When I die, I die. I have never believed in personal survival. An eternity of G.B.S. or anyone else is unthinkable. Individuals perish, but creation goes on. I believe in Life Everlasting, not in Smith, Brown, Jones and Robinson everlasting.

> GEORGE BERNARD SHAW (1856–1950). In Hesketh Pearson,
> "Perambulating London," *George Bernard Shaw: His Life and
> Personality*, 1963 (1942)

Nurslings of immortality!

> PERCY BYSSHE SHELLEY (1792–1822). *Prometheus Unbound*, 1.749,
> 1820

One world at a time.

> HENRY DAVID THOREAU (1817–1862). His whispered response, a few
> weeks before dying, to his friend Parker Pillsbury who had wished to
> talk with him of "the next world," April 1862. In Henry Seidel Canby,
> *Thoreau*, 27.1, 1939

I think that Man is immortal, but not men.

> H. G. WELLS (1866–1946). In *Living Philosophies*, 6, AMS edition, 1979
> (1931)

❦

Millions long for immortality who don't know what to do with themselves on a rainy Sunday afternoon.

> ANONYMOUS. In Susan Ertz, *Anger in the Sky: A Novel*, 5, 1943

"Is There Life Before Death?"

> ANONYMOUS. Student newspaper headline. In Bertram Gross, *Friendly
> Fascism: The New Face of Power in America*, 4, 1980

IMPERIALISM

See also • Class ○ Colonialism ○ Democracy: Mohandas K. Gandhi ○ Empire ○ Exploitation ○ History ○ International Relations ○ Nations ○ Oppression ○ Politics ○ Tyranny ○ War ○ War & Economics ○ World War I: Lenin

The essence of imperialism, regardless of the economic system from which it proceeds, is the unjust bargain. Human beings are used to serve ends that are not their own and in the process they pay more than they receive.

> RICHARD J. BARNET (1929–). *Roots of War*, 8.6, 1971

Whatever happens, we have got
The Maxim Gun, and they have not.

> HILAIRE BELLOC (1870–1953). On British imperialism in Africa,
> *The Modern Traveller*, 6, 1898

Learn to think imperially.

> JOSEPH CHAMBERLAIN (1836–1914). British colonial secretary. Speech,
> Guildhall, London, 19 January 1904

The conquest of the earth, which mostly means the taking it away from those who have a different complexion or slightly flatter noses than ourselves, is not a pretty thing when you look into it.

> JOSEPH CHAMBERLAIN (1836–1914). British colonial secretary. Speech,
> Birmingham, 12 May 1904

Eleanor Roosevelt (haranguing Winston Churchill about British imperialism in India): The Indians have suffered for years under British oppression.
Churchill: Are we talking about the brown-skinned Indians in India who have multiplied under benevolent British rule, or are we speaking about the red-skinned Indians in America who, I understand, are now almost extinct?

> WINSTON CHURCHILL (1874–1965). Format adapted. During a World
> War II visit to the White House. In Richard Pearson, "Statesman,
> Soldier, Savior," *Washington Post National Weekly Edition*, 2 October
> 1995

The issue is not a mean one. It is whether you will be content to be a comfortable England, modeled and molded upon Continental principles and meeting in due course an inevitable fate, or whether you will be a great country—an imperial country—a country where your sons, when they rise, rise to paramount positions, and obtain not merely the esteem of their countrymen, but command the respect of the world.

> BENJAMIN DISRAELI (1804–1881). Speech, Crystal Palace, London, 24
> June 1872

George Faulkner: England has drained Ireland of fifty thousand pounds in specie annually for fifty years.

Samuel Johnson: How so, sir! you must have a very great trade?
Faulkner: No trade.
Johnson: Very rich mines?
Faulkner: No mines.
Johnson: From whence, then, does all this money come?
Faulkner: Come! why out of the blood and bowels of the poor people of Ireland!

> GEORGE FAULKNER. 16 August 1773. In James Boswell, *The Journal of a Tour to the Hebrides, with Samuel Johnson, L.L.D.*, 1786

The existence of Soviet imperialism calls into question the whole Marxist paradigm; if capitalism can be eliminated without eliminating imperialism, then there must be other than capitalist economic factors which contribute to imperialism.

> MANSOUR FARHANG (1936–). *U.S. Imperialism: The Spanish-American War to the Iranian Revolution*, 1, 1981

It seems to be in the nature of imperialism to fear everything that is not subject to its influence.

> MANSOUR FARHANG (1936–). *U.S. Imperialism: The Spanish-American War to the Iranian Revolution*, 2, 1981

Too many Third World leaders are the unconscious victims of imperialism. The perceptions which were imposed on their fathers by colonialism and imperialism have gradually become so internalized that they consider them to be the product of their own thinking. Cultural imperialism has penetrated the deepest levels of their psyches.

> MANSOUR FARHANG (1936–). *U.S. Imperialism: The Spanish-American War to the Iranian Revolution*, 7, 1981

Only a qualitative change in the values and priorities of imperialist societies can end imperialism.

> MANSOUR FARHANG (1936–). *U.S. Imperialism: The Spanish-American War to the Iranian Revolution*, 7, 1981

Imperialism, like dictatorship, sears the soul, degrades the spirit, and makes individuals small, the better to rule them. Fear and cowardice are its allies. Imperialism is government of other people, by other people, and for other people.

> LOUIS FISCHER (1896–1970). *The Life of Mahatma Gandhi*, 22, 1950
> See Civil War: Abraham Lincoln (5)

Imperialism is not a function or phase of capitalism. It antedated capitalism. It is a feature of any nation which is underdeveloped, yet strong militarily and dominated by a caste wedded to the exercise of autocracy abroad and at home.

> LOUIS FISCHER (1896–1970). *The Life of Lenin*, 5, 1964

Imperialism first makes its subject ill, and then it constructs the hospital in which the patient lies imprisoned and without any possibility of being cured.

> EDUARDO GALEANO (1940–). "Latin America and the Theory of Imperialism," *Monthly Review*, April 1970

We should keep [the Panama Canal]. After all, we stole it fair and square.

> S. I. HAYAKAWA (1906–1992). Semanticist and California senator. While negotiations between Panama and the U.S. over the Canal's future were underway, 1979. In Erwin Knoll, ed., "Language in Action," *No Comment*, 1984

The economic root of imperialism is the desire of strong organized industrial and financial interests to secure and develop, at the public expense and by the public force, markets for their surplus goods and their surplus capital. War, militarism and a "spirited foreign policy" are the necessary means to this end.

> J. A. HOBSON (1858–1940). *Imperialism: A Study*, 1.7, 1902

This genius of inconsistency, of holding conflicting ideas or feelings in the mind simultaneously, in watertight compartments, is perhaps peculiarly British. It is . . . not hypocrisy; a consciousness of inconsistency would spoil the play: it is a condition of the success of this conduct that it should be unconscious. For such inconsistency has its uses. Much of the brutality and injustice involved in "Imperialism" would be impossible without this capacity.

> A. HOBSON (1858–1940). *Imperialism: A Study*, 2.3.3, 1902
> See Newspeak: George Orwell (3)

Imperialism is based upon a persistent misrepresentation of facts and forces, chiefly through a most refined process of selection, exaggeration, and attenuation, directed by interested cliques and persons so as to distort the face of history.

The gravest peril of Imperialism lies in the state of mind of a nation which has become habituated to this deception and which has rendered itself incapable of self-criticism.

For this is the condition which Plato terms "the lie in the soul"— a lie which does not know itself to be a lie.

> J. A. HOBSON (1858–1940). *Imperialism: A Study*, 2.3.3, 1902

The rules of ordinary international morality imply reciprocity. But barbarians will not reciprocate. They cannot be depended on for observing any rules. Their minds are not capable of so great an effort, nor their will sufficiently under the influence of distant motives. In the next place, nations which are still barbarous have not got beyond the period during which it is likely to be for their benefit that they should be conquered and held in subjection by foreigners.

> JOHN STUART MILL (1806–1873). "A Few Words on Non-Intervention," *Fraser's Magazine* (England), December 1859

[The British government in India] was not only one of the purest in intention but one of the most beneficent in act every known among mankind.

> JOHN STUART MILL (1806–1873). In Reinhold Niebuhr, *Moral Man and Immoral Society*, 5, 1932

We have had imposed upon us by the unlucky prowess of our ancestors the task of ruling a vast number of millions of alien dependents. We undertake it with a disinterestedness, and execute it with a skill of administration, to which history supplies no parallel.

> JOHN MORLEY (1838–1923). English political leader and writer. *On Compromise*, 1, 1877

Imperialism is absolutely necessary to a people which desires spiritual as well as economic expansion.

> BENITO MUSSOLINI (1883–1945). Speech, Milan, 23 March 1919

We must expand or explode.

> BENITO MUSSOLINI (1883–1945). In George Seldes, *Sawdust Caesar*, 24, 1935

I listened to the wild speeches [at a meeting of London's unemployed], which were just a cry for "bread, bread!" and on my way home I pondered over the scene and became more than ever convinced of the importance of imperialism. . . . My cherished idea is a solution for the social problem, i.e., in order to save the 40,000,000 inhabitants of the United Kingdom from a bloody civil war, we colonial statesmen must acquire new lands to settle the surplus population, to provide new markets for the goods produced in the factories and mines. The Empire, as I have always said, is a bread and butter question. If you want to avoid civil war, you must become imperialists.

> CECIL RHODES (1853–1902). British colonial administrator. 1895.
> In James H. Mittelman, "America's Investment in Apartheid," *Nation*,
> 9 June 1979

I would annex the planets if I could.

> CECIL RHODES (1853–1902). British colonial administrator. 1895.
> In Hannah Arendt, *The Origins of Totalitarianism*, pt. 2 (epigraph),
> 1973 (1951)

The twentieth century looms before us big with the fate of many nations. If we stand idly by, if we seek merely swollen, slothful ease and ignoble peace, if we shrink from the hard contests where men must win at hazard of their lives and at the risk of all they hold dear, then the bolder and stronger peoples will pass us by, and will win for themselves the domination of the world.

> THEODORE ROOSEVELT (1858–1919). Title essay, 10 April 1899,
> *The Strenuous Life: Essays and Addresses*, 1905

Every expansion of a great civilized power means a victory for law, order and righteousness.

> THEODORE ROOSEVELT (1858–1919). "Expansion and Peace,"
> 21 December 1899, *The Strenuous Life: Essays and Addresses*, 1905

The English and Dutch administrators of Malaysia have done admirable work; but the profit to the Europeans in those States has always been one of the chief elements considered; whereas in the Philippines our whole attention was concentrated upon the welfare of the Filipinos themselves, if anything to the neglect of our own interests.

> THEODORE ROOSEVELT (1858–1919). *An Autobiography*, 14, 1913

Imperialism: The aims of your neighbor; opposite to your own aims, which is called Foreign Policy.

> LEO ROSTEN (1908–1997). "Political Lexicon," *New Republic*, 3 July
> 1935

Imperialism does not have to take the form of direct rule over the foreign population. In the twentieth century, the indirect form of "neoimperialism" has increasingly replaced the old-fashioned direct kind; it is more subtle and less visible but no less effective a form of imperialism. In this situation, the imperial State rules the foreign population through its effective control over native client-rulers.

> MURRAY N. ROTHBARD (1926–1995). *For a New Liberty:
> The Libertarian Manifesto*, rev. ed., 14, 1978

IMPOTENCE

See also • Sex ○ Sexual Dissatisfaction

Nothing is potent against love save only impotence.

> SAMUEL BUTLER (1835–1902). *Further Extracts from the Note-Books of
> Samuel Butler*, 5, ed. A. T. Bartholomew, 1934

A woman's a woman until the day she dies, but a man's only a man as long as he can.

> MOMS MABLEY (1894–1975). In *New York Daily News*, 1975

Poins: Is it not strange that desire should so many years outlive performance?

> SHAKESPEARE (1564–1616). *Henry IV*, Part II, 2.4.283, 1597

INACTION

See also • Action ○ Action & Inaction ○ Indecision ○ Indifference

Expect poison from the standing water.

> WILLIAM BLAKE (1757–1827). "Proverbs of Hell," *The Marriage of
> Heaven and Hell*, 9.6, 1790–1793?

The only thing necessary for evil to triumph is for good men to do nothing.

> EDMUND BURKE (1729–1797). Attributed

Inaction in a deed of mercy becomes an action in a deadly sin.

> *THE BOOK OF THE GOLDEN PRECEPTS*. Ancient Buddhist writing.
> 2.17, tr. Helena Petrovna Blavatsky, 1889
> See Sin: James

Every onlooker is either a coward or a traitor.

> FRANTZ FANON (1925–1961). "The Pitfalls of National Consciousness,"
> *The Wretched of the Earth*, 1961, tr. Constance Farrington, 1963

Inaction is only a gathering together of forces for the coming leap—the fallow years are just as natural, just as necessary, as the years of plenty.

> ELBERT HUBBARD (1856–1915). In Alice Hubbard, comp., *An American
> Bible*, p. 179, 1946

Bad men need nothing more to compass their ends than that good men should look on and do nothing.

> JOHN STUART MILL (1806–1873). "On Education," inaugural address
> on being installed as rector, University of St. Andrews (Scotland),
> 1 February 1867

Heaven never helps the men who will not act.

> SOPHOCLES (496?–406 B.C.). "Fragments," 288, *Sophocles: Tragedies
> and Fragments*, 1, tr. E. H. Plumptre, 1865

A life which does not go into action is a failure.

> ARNOLD J. TOYNBEE (1889–1975). *A Study of History*, 10.35, 1954

INDECISION

See also • Inaction ○ Decisiveness ○ Delay ○ Hesitation ○ Irresolution

Indecision has rendered all my faculties barren.

> HENRI AMIEL (1821–1881). Journal, 14 October 1872, tr. Mrs. Humphrey
> Ward, 1887

People say I'm indecisive, but I don't know about that.

> GEORGE BUSH (1924–). Tongue-in-cheek remark before the Gridiron Club, Washington, 1 April 1989

How long halt ye between two opinions?

> ELIJAH (9th cent. B.C.). *1 Kings* 18:21 (King James Version)

Reporter: Is it fair to say you are moving to the right?
Gorbachev: Actually, I'm going around in circles.

> MIKHAIL GORBACHEV (1931–). Soviet president. Format adapted. As the Soviet Union was breaking apart. In David Remnick, "'We are Already in a State of Chaos,'" *Washington Post,* 19 December 1990

There is no more miserable human being than one in whom nothing is habitual but indecision.

> WILLIAM JAMES (1842–1910). *The Principles of Psychology,* 4, 1890

No one who puts his hand to the plow and looks back is fit for the kingdom of God.

> JESUS (A.D. 1st cent.). *Luke* 9:62

I know from experience that failure is more destructive than an appearance of indecision.

> JOHN F. KENNEDY (1917–1963). Remark to Henry Cabot Lodge, 1963. In Thomas Powers, *The Man who Kept the Secrets: Richard Helms and the CIA,* 7 (note 15), 1979

What I have done, what I am doing, what I am going to do, puzzle me and bewilder me. Have you ever been a leaf and fallen from your tree in autumn and been really puzzled about it? That's the feeling.

> T. E. LAWRENCE (1888–1935). Letter to Eric Kennington, 1935. In William Pfaff, "The Fallen Hero," *New Yorker,* 8 May 1989

We have all heard the story of the animal standing in doubt between two stacks of hay and starving to death.

> ABRAHAM LINCOLN (1809–1865). In Brant House, comp., "Politics," *Lincoln's Wit,* 1958

In meeting a crisis in life, one must either fight or run away. But one must do something. Not knowing how to act or not being able to act is what tears your insides out.

> RICHARD M. NIXON (1913–1994). *Six Crises,* 3, 1962

If the bugle gives an indistinct sound, who will get ready for battle?

> PAUL (A.D. 1st cent.). *1 Corinthians* 14:8

The man I worry about is the one who hasn't taken any position.

> ROSS PEROT (1930–). In "Personality: The Odyssey of Ross Perot," *Time,* 12 January 1970

Timorous minds are much more inclined to deliberate than to resolve.

> CARDINAL de RETZ (1613–1679). "Political Maxims from Cardinal de Retz" (17). In Lord Chesterfield (1694–1773), *Letters, Sentences, and Maxims,* Chesterfield Society edition, undated

Isabella: I am
At war 'twixt will and will not.

> SHAKESPEARE (1564–1616). *Measure for Measure,* 2.2.32, 1604

I feel ripe for something, yet do nothing, can't discover what that thing is. I feel fertile merely. It is seedtime with me. I have lain fallow long enough.

> HENRY DAVID THOREAU (1817–1862). Journal, 16 November 1850

❦

But Lot's wife behind him looked back, and she became a pillar of salt.

> ANONYMOUS (*BIBLE*). *Genesis* 19:26

He who observes the wind will not sow;
  and he who regards the clouds will not reap.

> ANONYMOUS (*BIBLE*). *Ecclesiastes* 11:4

INDEPENDENCE

See also • Conformity ○ Dignity: Maria Montessori ○ Freedom ○ Individuality ○ Nonconformity ○ Nonconformity, Anti-: [especially] Ambrose Bierce ○ Nonconformity & Conformity ○ Resistance ○ Self-Reliance ○ Standing Alone

I've lived a life that's full,
  I've traveled each and ev'ry highway,
And more, much more than this,
  I did it my way.

> PAUL ANKA (1941–). "My Way," (song), 1969

It is in the nature of a group and its power to turn against independence, the property of individual strength.

> HANNAH ARENDT (1906–1975). *On Violence,* 2, 1970

No one can come near me but through my act.

> RALPH WALDO EMERSON (1803–1882). "Self-Reliance," *Essays: First Series,* 1841

When I was introduced to [Abraham Lincoln], he said, "Oh Mr. Emerson, I once heard you say in a lecture that a Kentuckian seems to say by his air and manners, '*Here I am; if you don't like me, the worse for you.*'"

> RALPH WALDO EMERSON (1803–1882). Referring to his recent meeting in Washington with the Kentucky-born President, who "impressed me more favorably than I had hoped," journal, 31 January 1862

Content to live, content to die unknown,
Lord of myself, accountable to none.

> BENJAMIN FRANKLIN (1706–1790). *Poor Richard's Almanack,* September 1742

The first of earthly blessings, independence.

> EDWARD GIBBON (1737–1794). *Memoirs of My Life and Writings,* p. 88, 1796, Alex. Murray edition, 1869

Independence: An achievement, not a bequest.

> ELBERT HUBBARD (1856–1915). *The Roycroft Dictionary Concocted by Ali Baba and the Bunch on Rainy Days,* p. 77, 1914

He sympathizes with every sect, but belongs to none.

> ELBERT HUBBARD (1856–1915). *The Note Book of Elbert Hubbard,* p. 110, comp. Elbert Hubbard II, 1927

Declaration of Independence.

> THOMAS JEFFERSON (1743–1826). 4 July 1776

I am a sect by myself, as far as I know.

> THOMAS JEFFERSON (1743–1826). Letter to Rev. Ezra Stiles, 25 June 1819

I'm tough, I'm ambitious, and I know exactly what I want. If that makes me a bitch, OK.

> MADONNA (1958–). In "The Ten Who Count the Most," *People,* 27 July 1992

The greatest thing in the world is to know how to belong to one-self.

> MONTAIGNE (1533–1592). "Of Solitude," *Essays,* 1588, tr. Donald M. Frame, 1958

Monsieur Lafayette . . . is a decent fellow. I wanted to make him a senator, and he refused. Well, so much the worse for him. I can manage without his vote.

> NAPOLEON (1769–1821). Remark to Louis de Bourrienne, 1802, *The Mind of Napoleon: A Selection from His Written and Spoken Words,* 91, ed. J. Christopher Herold, 1955

Now I know the things I know,
And do the things I do;
and if you do not like me so,
To hell, my love, with you!

> DOROTHY PARKER (1893–1967). "Indian Summer," *Enough Rope,* 1926

To conquer Fortune and everything else, begin by independence.

> ROUSSEAU (1712–1778). *Emile; or, Treatise on Education,* 3, 1762, tr. Barbara Foxley, 1911

Know all men by these presents, that I, Henry Thoreau, do not wish to be regarded as a member of any incorporated society which I have not joined.

> HENRY DAVID THOREAU (1817–1862). "Civil Disobedience," 1849

It is my living sentiment, and by the blessing of God it shall be my dying sentiment—independence now and independence for-ever.

> DANIEL WEBSTER (1782–1852). Eulogy for John Adams and Thomas Jefferson, Faneuil Hall, Boston, 2 August 1826

The beauty of independence, departure, actions that rely on themselves.

> WALT WHITMAN (1819–1892). "Song of the Broad-Axe" (3), 1856, *Leaves of Grass,* 1855–1892

What is independence? Freedom from all laws or bonds except those of one's own being, control'd by the universal ones.

> WALT WHITMAN (1819–1892). *Democratic Vistas,* 1871, *Walt Whitman: Complete Poetry and Collected Prose,* ed. Justin Kaplan, p. 978, 1982

I am a radical of radicals—but I don't belong to any school.

> WALT WHITMAN (1819–1892). Remark to the author, 27 May 1888. In Horace Traubel, *Walt Whitman's Camden Conversations,* ed. Walter Teller, 1973

❧

So lead your life that you can look any man in the eye and tell him to go to hell.

> ANONYMOUS (AMERICAN). Quoted by John D. Rockefeller, Jr. Speech at Dartmouth College, Hanover (New Hampshire)

I don't give a damn for any damned man that don't give a damn for me.

> SAYING (AMERICAN)

INDIFFERENCE

See also • Age: André Maurois ○ Boredom ○ Compassion ○ Cynicism: Anonymous (1) ○ Evil: [especially] Anonymous (3) ○ Guilt ○ Hate ○ Inaction ○ Morality ○ Poverty: R. H. Tawney ○ Resistance ○ Responsibility ○ Sentimentality ○ Silence & Protest ○ Universe: Albert Camus

Nothing matters very much, and few things matter at all.

> ARTHUR BALFOUR (1848–1930). British prime minister. "Balfour's Declaration." In John Peers, comp., *1,001 Logical Laws,* p. 93, 1979

Political indifference, that mainstay of the modern state.

> CRANE BRINTON (1898–1968). *The Anatomy of Revolution,* 7.1, 1952

The least pain in our little finger gives more concern and uneasi-ness than the destruction of millions of our fellow beings.

> WILLIAM HAZLITT (1778–1830). "American Literature—Dr. Channing," *The Edinburgh Review* (Scotland), October 1829

All that is left to us is our being horrified at the loss of our sense of horror.

> ABRAHAM JOSHUA HESCHEL (1907–1972). *God in Search of Man: A Philosophy of Judaism,* 36, 1955

Do I let the poor suffer, and consign them, as old Friedrich used to say, to statistics and the devil? Well, so does God.

> H. L. MENCKEN (1880–1956). Closing words, *Damn! A Book of Calumny,* 1918

To be politically indifferent is to see no political meaning in one's life or in the world in which one lives, to avoid any political dis-appointments or gratifications.

> C. WRIGHT MILLS (1916–1962). *White Collar: The American Middle Classes,* 15.1, 1951

Rhett Butler to Scarlett O'Hara: I wish I could care what you do or where you go but I can't. . . . My dear, I don't give a damn.

> MARGARET MITCHELL (1900–1949). *Gone with the Wind,* 57, 1936

We are the most unfair, not towards him whom we do not like, but towards him for whom we feel nothing at all.

> FRIEDRICH NIETZSCHE (1844–1900). "Of the Compassionate," *Thus Spoke Zarathustra,* 1892, tr. R. J. Hollingdale, 1961

The greatest tragedy is indifference.

> RED CROSS. Motto

People really care about nothing that does not affect them per-sonally.

> ARTHUR SCHOPENHAUER (1788–1860). "Counsels and Maxims," 3.26, *Essays of Arthur Schopenhauer,* tr. T. Bailey Saunders, 1851

What makes people hard-hearted is this, that each man has, or fancies he has, as much as he can bear in his own troubles.

ARTHUR SCHOPENHAUER (1788–1860). "Studies in Pessimism: Further Psychological Observations," *Essays of Arthur Schopenhauer*, tr. T. Bailey Saunders, 1851

The worst sin towards our fellow creatures is not to hate them, but to be indifferent to them: that's the essence of inhumanity.

GEORGE BERNARD SHAW (1856–1950). *The Devil's Disciple*, 2, 1897

I did not hate them; I was indifferent to them. My crime was far worse because I was *not* an anti-Semite. . . .

My conscience was progressively callused and blunted. Of course, one's conscience does not just cease to exist overnight; it is slowly eroded over the years, eaten away day by day, anesthetized by a multiplicity of little crimes. . . . As the Nazi environment enveloped us, its evils grew invisible—because we were part of them.

ALBERT SPEER (1905–1981). Eric Norden interview, *Playboy*, June 1971

Indifference, to me, is the epitome of evil. The opposite of love is not hate, it's indifference.

ELIE WIESEL (1928–). In "One Must Not Forget," *U.S. News & World Report*, 27 October 1986

❧

The know-nothings are less of a problem than the feel-nothings.

ANONYMOUS

THE INDIVIDUAL

See also • Achievement: Samuel Taylor Coleridge ○ Change: Carl G. Jung ○ Civilization: Albert Schweitzer (1,2) ○ Civilization, Modern: George Orwell ○ Creativity: A. Whitney Griswold ○ Crisis Leaders: Lewis Mumford ○ Individualism ○ Individuality ○ Nature: Ralph Waldo Emerson (7,10) ○ Nonconformity ○ Society: Albert Schweitzer ○ States: Max Stirner, Henry David Thoreau

Society cares about the individual only in so far as he is profitable.

SIMONE de BEAUVOIR (1908–1986). Conclusion to *The Coming of Age*, 1970, tr. Frank O'Brian, 1973

No individual can arrive even at the threshold of his potentialities without a culture in which he participates. Conversely, no civilization has in it any element which in the last analysis is not the contribution of an individual.

RUTH BENEDICT (1887–1948)

All that is valuable in human society depends upon the opportunity for development accorded to the individual.

ALBERT EINSTEIN (1879–1955). Public statement, England, 15 September 1933

We fancy men are individuals; so are pumpkins; but every pumpkin in the field goes through every point of pumpkin history.

RALPH WALDO EMERSON (1803–1882). "Nominalist and Realist," *Essays: Second Series*, 1844

The psychic development of the individual is a short repetition of the course of development of the race.

SIGMUND FREUD (1856–1939). *Leonardo da Vinci: A Study in Psychosexuality*, 3, 1916, tr. A. A. Brill, 1947

There is no greater mistake and no graver danger than not to see that in our own society we are faced with the same phenomenon that is fertile soil for the rise of Fascism anywhere: the insignificance and powerlessness of the individual.

ERICH FROMM (1900–1980). *Escape from Freedom*, 7.1, 1941

In a nation of millions and a world of billions, the individual is still the first and basic agent of change.

LYNDON B. JOHNSON (1908–1973)

See Individuality: Mohandas K. Gandhi

If humanity is to have a hopeful future, there is no escape from the preeminent involvement and responsibility of the single human soul, in all its loneliness and frailty.

GEORGE F. KENNAN (1904–). Epilogue to *Around the Cragged Hill: A Personal and Political Philosophy*, 1993

The life of an individual cannot be adequately understood without references to the institutions within which his biography is enacted.

C. WRIGHT MILLS (1916–1962). *The Sociological Imagination*, 8.5, 1959

The concept of the person, associated with creativity and divinity, was originally confined to a single individual, the supreme ruler of the land, identified and worshipped as a god. Now it has become the essential mark of human development, in which all men share.

LEWIS MUMFORD (1895–1990). *The Transformations of Man*, 9.5, 1956

For liberalism, the individual is the end, and society the means. For fascism, society is the end, individuals the means, and its whole life consists in using individuals as instruments for its social ends.

ALFREDO ROCCO (1875–1935). *The Political Doctrine of Fascism*, 1926

Whoever destroys a single life is as guilty as though he had destroyed the entire world; and whoever rescues a single life earns as much merit as though he had rescued the entire world.

TALMUD (A.D. 1st–6th cent.). Rabbinical writings

The whole theory of the universe is directed unerringly to one single individual—namely to You.

WALT WHITMAN (1819–1892). "By Blue Ontario's Shore" (15), 1856, *Leaves of Grass*, 1855–1892

INDIVIDUALISM

See also • America: Bertrand Russell ○ The Individual ○ Individuality: [especially] Page Smith ○ Nations: Henry David Thoreau ○ Nonconformity ○ Nonconformity, Anti-: George Orwell

While I can make no claim for having introduced the term "rugged individualism," I should be proud to have invented it. It has been used by American leaders for over a half-century in eulogy of those God-fearing men and women of honesty whose stamina and character and fearless assertion of rights led them to make their own way in life.

HERBERT HOOVER (1874–1964). *The Challenge to Liberty*, 5, 1934

See School: Marshall McLuhan

Individualism is rather like innocence; there must be something unconscious about it.

> LOUIS KRONENBERGER (1904–1980). *Company Manners: A Cultural Inquiry into American Life,* 3.3, 1954

I believe in individualism . . . up to the point where the individual starts to operate at the expense of society.

> FRANKLIN D. ROOSEVELT (1882–1945). Presidential nomination acceptance speech, Chicago, 27 June 1936

Unrestricted individualism spells ruin to the individual himself. But so does the elimination of individualism, whether by law or custom.

> THEODORE ROOSEVELT (1858–1919). *An Autobiography,* 5, 1913

Individualism is in one sense the only possible ideal; for whatever social order may be most valuable can be valuable only for its effect on conscious individuals.

> GEORGE SANTAYANA (1863–1952). *The Life of Reason or The Phases of Human Progress,* 2.2, 1905–1906

Individualism, at first, only saps the virtues of public life; but in the long run it attacks and destroys all others and is at length absorbed in downright selfishness.

> ALEXIS de TOCQUEVILLE (1805–1859). *Democracy in America,* 2.2.2, 1840, tr. Henry Reeve and Francis Bowen, 1862

INDIVIDUALITY

See also • Brainwashing: Alan W. Scheflin and Edward M. Opton, Jr. (1) ○ Conformity ○ Dignity: Thomas S. Szasz ○ Freedom ○ Imitation: [especially] Mary Wollstonecraft ○ Independence ○ The Individual ○ Individualism ○ Minorities ○ Nonconformity ○ Nonconformity, Anti-: [especially] J. A. C. Brown ○ Nonconformity & Conformity ○ Parents ○ Self-Reliance ○ Soldiers: Philip Wylie ○ Standing Alone

Nature made him and then broke the mold.

> LUDOVICO ARIOSTO (1474–1533). *Orlando Furioso,* 10.84, 1532

The absolutely banal—my sense of my own uniqueness.

> W. H. AUDEN (1907–1973). "Hic et Ille," *The Dyer's Hand and Other Essays,* 1962

What you do is thee. For that I gave you birth.
Be that. So be the only you that's truly you on earth.

> RAY BRADBURY (1920–). "What I Do Is Me—For That I Came," *Where Robot Mice and Robot Men Roam Round in Robot Towns: New Poems, Both Light and Dark,* 1977

Individuality is the aim of political liberty.

> JAMES FENIMORE COOPER (1789–1851). Opening words, "On Individuality," *The American Democrat,* 1838

All greatness of character is dependent on individuality. The man who has no other existence than that which he partakes in common with all around him will never have any other than an existence of mediocrity.

> JAMES FENIMORE COOPER (1789–1851). "On Individuality," *The American Democrat,* 1838

There's a rebel lying deep in my soul. Anytime anybody tells me the trend is such and such, I go in the opposite direction. I hate the idea of trends. I hate imitation; I have a reverence for individuality. I got where I am by coming off the wall.

> CLINT EASTWOOD (1930–). Gerald Lubenow interview, "'Rebel in My Soul,'" *Newsweek,* 22 July 1985

The more finished the character, the more striking is its individuality.

> RALPH WALDO EMERSON (1803–1882). "Trust Yourself," sermon, Second Church of Boston, 3 December 1830

Individuality . . . lies at the root of all progress.

> MOHANDAS K. GANDHI (1869–1948). In *The Modern Review,* October 1935
>
> See The Individual: Lyndon B. Johnson

A necessary quality for the attainment of individuality is the ability to tolerate some degree of loneliness in the sense of independent adherence to values that those around you will not support.

> D. W. HARDING (1906–). In J. A. C. Brown, *Techniques of Persuasion: From Propaganda to Brainwashing,* 12, 1963

If individuality has no play, society does not advance; if individuality breaks out of all bounds, society perishes.

> T. H. HUXLEY (1825–1895). "Administrative Nihilism," 1871

An unlearned carpenter of my acquaintance once said in my hearing: "There is very little difference between one man and another; but what little there is, *is very important.*" This distinction seems to me to go to the root of the matter. It is not only the size of the difference which concerns the philosopher, but also its place and its kind.

> WILLIAM JAMES (1842–1910). "The Importance of Individuals," *The Will to Believe: And Other Essays in Popular Philosophy,* 1897

Though all men be made of one metal, yet they be not cast all in one mold.

> JOHN LYLY (1554?–1606). "Euphues," *Euphues: The Anatomy of Wit,* 1579

Always remember that you are absolutely unique. Just like everyone else.

> MARGARET MEAD (1910–1978). "Meade's Maxim," in John Peers, comp., *1,001 Logical Laws,* p. 155, 1979

Society has now fairly got the better of individuality; and the danger which threatens human nature is not the excess, but the deficiency, of personal impulses and preferences.

> JOHN STUART MILL (1806–1873). *On Liberty,* 3, 1859

In proportion to the development of his individuality, each person becomes more valuable to himself, and is, therefore, capable of being more valuable to others.

> JOHN STUART MILL (1806–1873). *On Liberty,* 3, 1859

Whatever crushes individuality is despotism, by whatever name it may be called and whether it professes to be enforcing the will of God or the injunctions of men.

> JOHN STUART MILL (1806–1873). *On Liberty,* 3, 1859

The values involved in the cultural problem of individuality are conveniently embodied in all that is suggested by the ideal of The Renaissance Man. The threat to that ideal is the ascendancy among us of The Cheerful Robot.

C. WRIGHT MILLS (1916–1962). *The Sociological Imagination,* 9.4, 1959

There are no precedents: You are the first You that ever was.

CHRISTOPHER MORLEY (1890–1957). *Inward Ho!* 14, 1923

It's a good thing when a man is different from your image of him. It shows he isn't a type. If he were, it would be the end of him as a man. But if you can't place him in a category, it means that at least a part of him is what a human being ought to be. He has risen above himself, he has a grain of immortality.

BORIS PASTERNAK (1890–1960). *Doctor Zhivago,* 9.14, 1957, tr. Max Hayward and Manya Harari, 1958

Individualism, with its rapacious and exploitative attitude toward the world, is the antithesis of that individuality which is the authentic self realized within a genuine community.

PAGE SMITH (1917–1995). *The Historian and History,* 15, 1964

Pronounced individuality is necessarily more or less at variance with authority.

HERBERT SPENCER (1820–1903). "The Filiation of Ideas," 1899. In David Duncan, appendix (B) to *Life and Letters of Herbert Spencer,* 1908

Confidence that one is of value and significance as a unique individual is one of the most precious possessions which anyone can have.

ANTHONY STORR (1920–). *Solitude: A Return to the Self,* 7, 1988

INDOCTRINATION

See also • Advertising ○ Brainwashing ○ Deception ○ Dehumanization ○ Education ○ Freedom of Thought ○ Ideas ○ Ideology ○ Lying ○ Machiavellianism ○ Manipulation ○ Media ○ Newspeak ○ Politics ○ Propaganda ○ Publicity ○ Public Opinion ○ Public Relations: [especially] James R. Gaines ○ Tyranny

We first throw away the Tales along with the Rattles of our Nurses. Those of the Priest keep their hold a little longer; those of our Governors the longest of all.

EDMUND BURKE (1729–1797). *A Vindication of Natural Society,* p. 105, M. Cooper edition, 1756

All wise Princes have ever . . . instill[ed] into their People a Contempt and Hatred of Foreign Nations to render them the more united among themselves.

SAMUEL BUTLER (1612–1680). "Princes and Government," *Prose Observations,* ed. Hugh de Quehen, 1979

When I transfer my knowledge, I teach. But when I transfer my beliefs, I indoctrinate.

ARTHUR C. DANTO (1926–). *Analytical Philosophy of Knowledge,* 4.7, 1968

A belief constantly inculcated during the early years of life, while the brain is impressible, appears to acquire almost the nature of an instinct; and the very essence of an instinct is that it is followed independently of reason.

CHARLES DARWIN (1809–1882). *The Descent of Man and Selection in Relation to Sex,* 2nd ed., 4, 1874

Present-day tyranny differs from the old in that the new absolutism must control the mass production of ideas, the spiritual element, or else lose control of the situation. It differs not merely in increased quantity of police for purposes of repression, but also in the thorough "thought control" which reaches to the most intimate core of the personality.

CARL G. GUSTAVSON (1915–). *A Preface to History,* 14, 1955

A really efficient totalitarian state would be one in which the all-powerful executive of political bosses and their army of managers control a population of slaves who do not have to be coerced because they love their servitude. To make them love it is the task assigned, in present-day totalitarian states, to ministries of propaganda, newspaper editors and schoolteachers.

ALDOUS HUXLEY (1894–1963). Foreword (1946) to *Brave New World,* 1932

Thought control is a copyright of totalitarianism, and we have no claim to it. It is not the function of our government to keep the citizen from falling into error; it is the function of the citizen to keep the government from falling into error.

ROBERT H. JACKSON (1892–1954). *American Communications Association v. Douds,* 1950

Instead of the rich being irresistible exploiters . . . , as Marxists present them, the situation as a whole is much more like a sado-masochistic process with one small group internally programmed for command and the other, much larger, for gratifying submission. While the outcome of submission is not widely relished, the process of submission itself appears to be pleasing. In Barnum's words, they are born suckers. They like to salute.

FERDINAND LUNDBERG (1902–1995). *The Rich and the Super-Rich: A Study in the Power of Money Today,* 15, 1968

Freud looked upon all civilization as a process of necessary repression. Most of this repression is achieved by psychological means through the uptraining of children in certain ways by parents and parental substitutes. Where such training fails and overt rebels against the system of repression appear, the police and military stand ready. They carry out direct repression.

FERDINAND LUNDBERG (1902–1995). *The Rich and the Super-Rich: A Study in the Power of Money Today,* 15, 1968

Do we need conditioned adepts or free-thinking students? Scholastic fact-factories keep many a pupil too busy to think and educate him in progressive immaturity. Students are caught in a compulsive school regimentation which imprints on them dependency and awe of authority.

JOOST A. M. MEERLOO (1903–1976). "Pavolvian Strategy as a Weapon of Menticide," *American Journal of Psychiatry,* May 1954

Every method is used to prove to men that in given political, economic and social situations they are bound to be happy, and those who are unhappy are mad or criminals or monsters.

ALBERTO MORAVIA (1907–1990). Title essay, *Man As an End,* 1964, tr. Bernard Wall, 1965

Mass man: incapable of choice, incapable of spontaneous, self-directed activities: at best patient, docile, disciplined to monotonous work to an almost pathetic degree, but increasingly irresponsible as his choices become fewer and fewer: finally, a creature governed mainly by his conditioned reflexes—the ideal type desired, if never quite achieved, by the advertising agency and the sales organization of modern business, or by the propaganda office and the planning bureaus of totalitarian and quasi-totalitarian governments. The handsomest encomium for such creatures is: "They do not make trouble." Their highest virtue is: "They do not stick their necks out." Ultimately, such a society produces only two groups of men: the conditioners and the conditioned; the active and the passive barbarians. . . .

This mechanical chaos is plainly not self-perpetuating, for it affronts and humiliates the human spirit; and the tighter and more efficient it becomes as a mechanical system, the more stubborn will be the human reaction against it. Eventually, it must drive modern man to blind rebellion, to suicide, or to renewal: and so far it has worked in the first two ways.

> LEWIS MUMFORD (1895–1990). *The Conduct of Life,* 1.3, 1951

When you are trained to despise "just what you like" then, of course, you become a much more obedient servant of others—a *good* slave. When you learn not to do "just what you like" then the System loves you.

> ROBERT M. PIRSIG (1928–). *Zen and the Art of Motorcycle Maintenance: An Inquiry into Values,* 19, 1974

There is no absurdity so palpable but that it may be firmly planted in the human head if you only begin to inculcate it before the age of five, by constantly repeating it with an air of great solemnity.

> ARTHUR SCHOPENHAUER (1788–1860). "Studies in Pessimism: Further Psychological Observations," *Essays of Arthur Schopenhauer,* tr. T. Bailey Saunders, 1851

Without self-awareness . . . man acts, speaks, studies, reacts mechanically, like a machine: on the basis of "programs" acquired accidentally, unintentionally, mechanically. He is not aware that he is acting in accordance with programs; it is therefore not difficult to reprogram him—to make him think and do quite different things from those he had thought and done before—provided only [that] the new program does not wake him up. When he is awake, no one can program him: he programs himself.

> E. F. SCHUMACHER (1911–1977). *A Guide for the Perplexed,* 6, 1977

There is no belief, however grotesque and even villainous, that cannot be made a part of human nature if it is inculcated in childhood and not contradicted in the child's hearing.

> GEORGE BERNARD SHAW (1856–1950). *The Intelligent Woman's Guide to Socialism, Capitalism, Sovietism and Fascism,* 81, 1928

Naturally, the master in parliaments, in schools, and in newspapers makes the most desperate efforts to prevent us from realizing our slavery. From our earliest years we are taught that our country is the land of the free.

> GEORGE BERNARD SHAW (1856–1950). Speech, London (BBC and CBS broadcast), 18 June 1935, "Freedom and Government," *Nation,* 10 July 1935

To indoctrinate the child early with the prevailing world-view of the society and class in which he has been born, to enforce conformity in later life by the thunders of the priest and by the sword of the magistrate has been "the wisdom of our ancestors" at every stage in their progress from savagery to civilization.

> PRESERVED SMITH (1880–1941). *A History of Modern Culture,* 1.11.1, 1930–1934

The proletarian state must bring up thousands of excellent "mechanics of culture," "engineers of the soul."

> JOSEPH STALIN (1879–1953). Remark to the speaker, 26 October 1934, quoted by Maxim Gorky, speech before the Writers' Congress, 1934.
> See Artists: John F. Kennedy

Those who corrupt the public mind are just as evil as those who steal from the public purse.

> ADLAI E. STEVENSON (1900–1965). Speech, National Guard Armory, Albuquerque, 12 September 1952

The objective of "conditioning" is to deprive human beings permanently of their capacity to think and to will, and, since this is the capacity that makes us human, for good or for evil, "conditioning" is an attempt to destroy human nature itself. Perhaps we do not yet know enough about its results, up to date, to be able to tell whether or not its aim is actually attainable. We do know, however, that this has been the aim of its practitioners in our time; and we also know that the new science of psychology has equipped them with devilish devices which, in the past, were not at the drill sergeant's, priest's, or advertiser's disposal.

> ARNOLD J. TOYNBEE (1889–1975). *A Study of History,* 12.565–566, 1961

Organization domination, which calls for continuous administration, requires that human conduct be conditioned to obedience towards those masters who claim to be the bearers of legitimate power.

> MAX WEBER (1864–1920). "Politics as a Vocation," 1919, *From Max Weber: Essays in Sociology,* tr. H. H. Gerth and C. Wright Mills, 1958

If the first half of the century was the era of technical engineering, the second half will be the era of social engineering.

> WILLIAM H. WHYTE, JR. (1917–). "The Social Engineers," *Fortune,* January 1952

INDUSTRY

See also • Activity ○ Effort ○ Idleness ○ Laziness ○ Persistence ○ Success ○ Wealth ○ Work ○ Youth: Thomas Jefferson

Hard work never killed anybody, but why take the chance?

> EDGAR BERGEN (1903–1978). Ventriloquist. A favorite line of his dummy Charlie McCarthy

Heaven's help is better than early rising.

> CERVANTES (1547–1616). *Don Quixote,* 2.4.34, 1615, tr. Peter Anthony Motteux and John Ozell, 1743

There is no substitute for hard work.

> THOMAS ALVA EDISON (1847–1931). Interview, *Golden Book* (magazine), April 1931

Work too hard and you lose sight of what is important in life.

ENTERTAINMENT WEEKLY, INC. Sole copy in ad for its new magazine *Entertainment Weekly.* In *New York Times,* 12 February 1990

Industry need not wish.

BENJAMIN FRANKLIN (1706–1790). *Poor Richard's Almanack,* October 1739

Diligence overcomes Difficulties; Sloth makes them.

BENJAMIN FRANKLIN (1706–1790). *Poor Richard's Almanack,* November 1755

Plow deep, while Sluggards sleep.

BENJAMIN FRANKLIN (1706–1790). *Poor Richard's Almanack,* August 1756

Lose no time; be always employ'd in something useful; cut off all unnecessary actions.

BENJAMIN FRANKLIN (1706–1790). Virtue #6 ("Industry"), 1784, *Autobiography,* 1798

See Wealth: Franklin

I've met a few people in my time who were enthusiastic about hard work. And it was just my luck that all of them happened to be men I was working for at the time.

BILL GOLD

If you want work well done, select a busy man—the other kind has no time.

ELBERT HUBBARD (1856–1915). *A Thousand and One Epigrams,* p. 103, 1911

Where there is no Desire, there will be no Industry.

JOHN LOCKE (1632–1704). *Some Thoughts Concerning Education,* 126, 1693

If you have great talents, industry will improve them: if you have but moderate abilities, industry will supply their deficiency. Nothing is denied to well-directed labor: nothing is to be obtained without it.

SIR JOSHUA REYNOLDS (1723–1792). "Discourse Two," 11 December 1769, *Discourses on Art,* 1769-1790

Far and away the best prize that life offers is the chance to work hard at work worth doing.

THEODORE ROOSEVELT (1858–1919). Labor Day address, Syracuse (New York), 7 September 1903

The hope, and not the fact, of advancement is the spur to industry.

HENRY TAYLOR (1800–1886). *The Statesman,* 23, 1836

Nothing is so difficult that it may not be won by industry.

TERENCE (190?–159 B.C.). *Heauton Timoroumenos,* 4.2.8

It is not enough to be industrious, so are the ants. What are you industrious about?

HENRY DAVID THOREAU (1817–1862). Letter to Harrison Blake, 16 November 1857

Nothing ever comes to one, that is worth having, except as a result of hard work.

BOOKER T. WASHINGTON (1856–1915). *Up from Slavery: An Autobiography,* 12, 1901

We live in the age of the overworked and the under-educated; the age in which people are so industrious that they become absolutely stupid.

OSCAR WILDE (1854–1900). "The Critic as Artist" (2), *Intentions,* 1891

✿

God helps the early riser.

SAYING (SPANISH)

INEQUALITY

See also • Class ○ Classes, Two ○ Competition ○ Equality ○ Exploitation ○ Injustice ○ Life: John F. Kennedy ○ Oppression ○ Revolution: Aristotle ○ Rich & Poor: Adam Smith ○ Tyranny

There can be no rule of God in the present state of iniquitous inequalities in which a few roll in riches and the masses do not get enough to eat.

MOHANDAS K. GANDHI (1869–1948). In *Harijan,* 1 June 1947

So far is it from being true that men are naturally equal, that no two people can be half an hour together, but one shall acquire an evident superiority over the other.

SAMUEL JOHNSON (1709–1784). 15 February 1766. In James Boswell, *The Life of Samuel Johnson,* 1791

One-way first-name calling always means inequality—witness servants, children and dogs.

MARJORIE KARMEL. *Thank You, Dr. Lamaze,* 7, 1959

An earthly kingdom cannot exist without inequality of persons. Some must be free, some serfs, some rulers, some subjects.

MARTIN LUTHER (1483—1546)

See Leaders & People: Sigmund Freud ○ Slavery: Aristotle

The difference between the most dissimilar characters, between a philosopher and a common street porter . . . seems to arise not so much from nature, as from habit, custom, and education.

ADAM SMITH (1723–1790). *The Wealth of Nations,* 1.2, 1776

Inequalities of condition spring from inequalities of talent and courage.

VAUVENARGUES (1715–1747). *Reflections and Maxims,* 126, 1746, tr. F. G. Stevens, 1940

INFERIORITY

See also • Confidence ○ Envy: Theodore Roosevelt ○ Guilt: Anonymous (2) ○ Pleasing Others: Samuel Johnson (2) ○ Self-Respect ○ Weakness

Everyone . . . has a feeling of inferiority. But the feeling of inferiority is not a disease; it is rather a stimulant to health, normal striving and development. It becomes a pathological condition only when the sense of inadequacy overwhelms the individual and, far from stimulating him to useful activity, makes him depressed and incapable of development.

ALFRED ADLER (1870–1937). *The Individual Psychology of Alfred Adler: A Systematic Presentation in Selections from His Writings,* 9.D.2, 1929, ed. Heinz L. Ansbacher and Rowena R. Ansbacher, 1956

See Neurosis: Adler (2)

The inability to act spontaneously, to express what one genuinely feels and thinks, and the resulting necessity to present a pseudo-self to others and oneself, are the root of the feeling of inferiority and weakness.

> ERICH FROMM (1900–1980). *Escape from Freedom,* 7.2, 1941

No man will be fond of what forces him daily to feel himself inferior.

> SAMUEL JOHNSON (1709–1784). In Hester Lynch Piozzi, *Anecdotes of the Late Samuel Johnson, LL.D.,* p. 104, 1786, ed. S. C. Roberts, 1932
> See Hate: Lord Chesterfield

No one can make you feel inferior without your consent.

> ELEANOR ROOSEVELT (1884–1962). 1936, *The Wit and Wisdom of Eleanor Roosevelt,* p. 92, ed. Alex Ayres, 1996
> See Depression: William Ellery Channing

INFLATION

See also • Economics ○ Money ○ Nations: Ernest Hemingway

Inflation might almost be called legal counterfeiting.

> IRVING FISHER (1867–1947). *Stabilizing the Dollar,* 2, 1920

Inflation occurs when the quantity of money rises appreciably more rapidly than output, and the more rapid the rise in the quantity of money per unit of output, the greater the rate of inflation. There is probably no other proposition in economics that is as well established as this one.

> MILTON FRIEDMAN (1912–) and ROSE FRIEDMAN. *Free to Choose: A Personal Statement,* 9 ("The Proximate Cause of Inflation"), 1979

Inflation yields revenue to the government . . . by paying off—or repudiating, if you will—part of the government's debt. Government borrows in dollars and pays back in dollars. But thanks to inflation, the dollars it pays back can buy less than the dollars it borrowed.

> MILTON FRIEDMAN (1912–) and ROSE FRIEDMAN. *Free to Choose: A Personal Statement,* 9 ("Government Revenue from Inflation"), 1979

As it has become politically less attractive to vote higher taxes to pay for higher spending, legislators have resorted to financing spending through inflation, a hidden tax that can be imposed without having been voted, taxation without representation.

> MILTON FRIEDMAN (1912–) and ROSE FRIEDMAN. *Free to Choose: A Personal Statement,* 10 (introduction), 1979

To bring monetary policy to bear against inflation, the Federal Reserve [Board] discourages the lending of money by the banks. This it accomplishes by raising interest rates and by increasing the banks' reserve requirements—the cash they must hold in reserve—so that they have less money to lend.

> JOHN KENNETH GALBRAITH (1908–). *A Life in Our Times: Memoirs,* 22, 1981

Inflation is the opium of the people.

> HENRY HAZLITT (1894–1993). *Economics in One Lesson,* 22.5, 1946
> See Religion, Anti-: Karl Marx

Lenin is said to have declared that the best way to destroy the Capitalist System was to debauch the currency. By a continuing process of inflation, Governments can confiscate, secretly and unobserved, an important part of the wealth of their citizens.

> JOHN MAYNARD KEYNES (1883–1946). British economist. "Inflation," 1919, *Essays in Persuasion,* 1931

Inflation is like sin; every government denounces it and every government practices it.

> SIR FREDERICK LEITH-ROSS (1887–1968). In *Observer* (British newspaper), 30 June 1957

❦

Inflation occurs when too much money is chasing too few goods.

> ANONYMOUS

When prices are falling, better a full purse than a full cupboard; when prices are rising, better a full cupboard than a full purse.

> ANONYMOUS

INFORMATION

See also • Computers ○ Decision-Making ○ Facts ○ Intelligence, Military ○ Judgment: Arthur Hays Sulzberger ○ Knowledge ○ Learning (Knowledge) ○ Success: Lyndon B. Johnson ○ Wisdom & Knowledge: T. S. Eliot

Do not seek for information of which you cannot make use.

> ANNA C. BRACKETT (1836–1911). *The Technique of Rest,* 2, 1892

Book-burning fire captain: Chock them so damned full of "facts" they feel stuffed, but absolutely "brilliant" with information. Then they'll feel they're thinking, they'll get a sense of motion without moving.

> RAY BRADBURY (1920–). *Fahrenheit 451,* 1953. In Joel L. Swerdlow, "Information Revolution," *National Geographic,* October 1995

We are so made, we love to be pleased better than to be informed; information is, in a certain degree, mortifying, as it implies our previous ignorance; it must be sweetened to be palatable.

> LORD CHESTERFIELD (1694–1773). Letter to his son, 11 February 1751

Mal-information is more hopeless than non-information.

> C. C. COLTON (1780–1832). *Lacon: or, Many Things in Few Words; Addressed to Those Who Think,* 1.1, 1823

Information is, above all, a principle of economy. The fewer data needed, the better the information. And an overload of information leads to information blackout. It does not enrich, but impoverishes.

> PETER F. DRUCKER (1909–). *Management: Tasks, Responsibilities, Practices,* 30, 1974, abr., 1977

1. The information we have is not what we want.
2. The information we want is not what we need.
3. The information we need is not available.

> FINAGLE'S NEW LAWS OF INFORMATION. In John Peers, comp., *1,001 Logical Laws,* p. 188, 1979

One question: if this is the Information Age, how come nobody knows anything?

ROBERT MANKOFF. Woman to man at a party, cartoon caption, *New Yorker*, 20 April 1998

Information is the currency of democracy.
RALPH NADER (1934–). Speech, Washington, 25 March 1998

We are drowning in information but starved for knowledge.
JOHN NAISBITT (1929–). *Megatrends: Ten New Directions Transforming Our Lives*, 1, 1984

In every institution, information is blood.
BRADLEY H. PATTERSON, JR. (1921–). *The Ring of Power: The White House Staff and Its Expanding Role in Government*, 7.3, 1988

Information is the coin in the realm in cyberspace.
CHARLES RUBIN. Co-author of *Guerrilla Marketing Online: The Entrepreneur's Guide to Earning Profits on the Internet*. In Michael Larsen, *Literary Agents: What They Do, How They Do It, and How to Find and Work with the Right One for You*, rev. ed., 16.2, 1996

Analysts and policy makers alike tend to interpret information to support their own viewpoints.
DEAN RUSK (1909–1994). *As I Saw It*, 35, 1990

Everyone spoke of an information overload, but what there was in fact was a non-information overload.
RICHARD SAUL WURMAN (1935–). *What-If, Could-Be*, 1976

INGRATITUDE

See also • Gratitude ○ Politicians: Louis XIV

We set ourselves to bite the hand that feeds us.
EDMUND BURKE (1729–1797). *Thoughts on the Cause of the Present Discontents* (pamphlet), 23 April 1770

The hand that feeds should be heavily gloved.
PAUL ELDRIDGE (1888–1982). *Maxims for a Modern Man*, 408, 1965

Lucky to get off from those you have served without a slap.
RALPH WALDO EMERSON (1803–1882). "Notebook Phi," p. 118, 1838–1851?

When I'm not thank'd at all, I'm thank'd enough.
I've done my duty, and I've done no more.
HENRY FIELDING (1707–1754). *Tom Thumb*, 1.3, 1730

The ingratitude of the world can never deprive us of the conscious happiness of having acted with humanity ourselves.
OLIVER GOLDSMITH (1728–1774). *The Good-Natur'd Man*, 3, 1768

People who bite the hand that feeds them usually lick the boot that kicks them.
ERIC HOFFER (1902–1983). *Reflections on the Human Condition*, 141, 1973

How sharper than a serpent's tooth is a thankless parent!
ELBERT HUBBARD (1856–1915). *A Thousand and One Epigrams*, p. 62, 1911

Ingratitude is often disproportionate to the benefaction received.
KARL KRAUS (1874–1936). "Lord, Forgive Them . . . ," *Half-Truths & One-and-a-Half Truths: Selected Aphorisms*, ed. Harry Zohn, 1976

We find few guilty of ingratitude while we are still in a position to help them.
LA ROCHEFOUCAULD (1613–1680). *Maxims*, 306, 1665, tr. Leonard Tancock, 1959

There is much less ingratitude than we think because there is much less generosity than we imagine.
LOUIS XIV (1638–1715). In Voltaire, *The Century of Louis XIV*, 1751

Viola: I hate ingratitude more in a man
Than lying, vainness, babbling, drunkenness,
Or any taint of vice whose strong corruption,
Inhabits our frail blood.
SHAKESPEARE (1564–1616). *Twelfth Night*, 3.4.388, 1599

Lear: How sharper than a serpent's tooth it is
To have a thankless child!
SHAKESPEARE (1564–1616). *King Lear*, 1.4.310, 1605

If you pick up a starving dog and make him prosperous, he will not bite you. This is the principle difference between a dog and a man.
MARK TWAIN (1835–1910). *The Tragedy of Pudd'nhead Wilson*, 16 (epigraph), 1894

INJUSTICE

See also • Exploitation ○ Inequality ○ Justice ○ Oppression ○ Tyranny ○ Tyrants: Thomas Carlyle

Remove justice, and what are kingdoms but gangs of criminals on a large scale?
ST. AUGUSTINE (A.D. 354–430). *The City of God*, 4.4, A.D. 413–426, tr. Henry Bettenson, 1972

If I had to choose between justice and disorder on the one hand, and injustice and order on the other, I would always choose the latter.
GOETHE (1749–1832). Quoted by Henry A. Kissinger. In James Reston, *Deadline: A Memoir*, 44 (epigraph), 1991

An act of injustice is condemned, not because the law is broken, but because a person has been hurt.
ABRAHAM JOSHUA HESCHEL (1907–1972). *The Prophets*, 11, 1962

There is but one blasphemy, and that is injustice.
ROBERT G. INGERSOLL (1833–1899). Lecture, Chicago, 20 September 1880

Injustice anywhere is a threat to justice everywhere.
MARTIN LUTHER KING, JR. (1929–1968). "Letter from Birmingham Jail," 16 April 1963.
See Slavery: John F. Kennedy

Injustice is relatively easy to bear; what stings is justice.
H. L. MENCKEN (1880–1956). "Footnote on Criticism," *Prejudices: Third Series*, 1922

All men believe in their hearts that injustice is far more profitable to the individual than justice.
PLATO (427?–347 B.C.) *The Republic*, 2.360, tr. Benjamin Jowett, 1894

[Man] only blames injustice who, owing to cowardice or age or some weakness, has not the power of being unjust. And this is proved by the fact that when he obtains the power, he immediately becomes unjust as far as he can be.

> PLATO (427?–347 B.C.). *The Republic,* 2.366, tr. Benjamin Jowett, 1894

Extreme justice is often extreme injustice.

> TERENCE (190?–159 B.C.). *Heauton Timoroumenos,* l. 795

Whatever the human law may be, neither an individual nor a nation can ever commit the least act of injustice against the obscurest individual without having to pay the penalty for it.

> HENRY DAVID THOREAU (1817–1862). "Slavery in Massachusetts," Speech, Farmingham, 4 July 1854

INNOCENCE

See also • Forgiveness ○ Guilt ○ Judging Others ○ Religion ○ Sin

Innocent, *adj.* Undiscovered.

> VICTOR L. CAHN (1948–). *The Disrespectful Dictionary,* unpaged, 1974

This world where only the stones are innocent.

> ALBERT CAMUS (1913–1960). "Historical Rebellion: State Terrorism and Irrational Terror," *The Rebel: An Essay on Man in Revolt,* 1951, tr. Anthony Bower, 1956

Blameless people are always the most exasperating.

> GEORGE ELIOT (1819–1880). *Middlemarch,* 12, 1871–1872

Innocence itself sometimes hath need of a Mask.

> THOMAS FULLER (1654–1734). Comp., *Gnomologia: Adages and Proverbs,* 3101, 1732

Innocence is very far from finding as many defenders as crime.

> LA ROCHEFOUCAULD (1613–1680). *Maxims,* 465, 1665, tr. Leonard Tancock, 1959

To vice, innocence must always seem only a superior kind of chicanery.

> OUIDA (1839–1908). "Two Little Wooden Shoes," *Wisdom, Wit, and Pathos,* 1884

Through our own recovered innocence we discern the innocence of our neighbors.

> HENRY DAVID THOREAU (1817–1862). "Spring," *Walden; or Life in the Woods,* 1854

❦

I did nothing wrong, and I'll never do it again.

> SAYING (AMERICAN). 1980s

All the ways of a man are pure in his own eyes,
  but the Lord weighs the spirit.

> SAYING (*BIBLE*). Proverbs 16:2

No one is innocent, no one is guilty.

> ANONYMOUS

One is innocent 'til proven guilty.

> SAYING

INSANITY

See also • Madness ○ Mental Illness ○ Psychiatry

The man who cannot believe his senses and the man who cannot believe anything else, are both insane.

> G. K. CHESTERTON (1874–1936)

Insanity [is] disproportion between means and ends.

> RALPH WALDO EMERSON (1803–1882). Journal, fall 1859

The insane are but grown up children, children too, who have received false notions, and a wrong direction.

> JEAN ESQUIROL (1772–1840). *Mental Maladies: A Treatise on Insanity,* 1.5, 1838, tr. E. K. Hunt, 1845. In Thorne Shipley, ed., *Classics in Psychology,* 1961

Ordinarily he is insane, but he has lucid moments when he is only stupid.

> HEINRICH HEINE (1797–1856). On an ambassador, 1848

The behavior of the insane is merely sane behavior, a bit exaggerated and distorted.

> ALDOUS HUXLEY (1894–1963). "Beliefs," *Ends and Means: An Inquiry into the Nature of Ideals and into the Methods Employed for Their Realization,* 1937

Everything that the modern mind cannot define it regards as insane.

> CARL G. JUNG (1875–1961). *Psychology and Alchemy,* 1, 1944, tr. R. F. C. Hull, 1968

Insanity and *psychosis* can no longer be respected as meaningful definitions—but are used by limited individuals in positions of social power to describe ways of behaving and thinking that are alien, threatening, and *obscure* to them.

> SEYMOUR KRIM (1922–1989). "The Insanity Bit," *Views of a Nearsighted Cannoneer,* 1961

Insanity—a perfectly rational adjustment to the insane world.

> R. D. LAING (1927–1989). In *Guardian* (British newspaper), 1972

Insanity is hereditary—you get it from your children.

> SAM LEVENSON (1911–1980). Humorist. In *Diner's Club Magazine,* November 1963

Insanity? The mental processes of the man with whom one disagrees, are always wrong.

> JACK LONDON (1876–1916). *The Iron Heel,* 1907. In Thomas S. Szasz, ed., *The Age of Madness: The History of Involuntary Mental Hospitalization Presented in Selected Texts,* 2.7, 1973

We go by the major vote, and if the majority are insane, the sane must go to the hospital.

> HORACE MANN (1796–1859)

To pursue the unattainable is insanity.

> MARCUS AURELIUS (A.D. 121–180). *Meditations,* 5.17, tr. Maxwell Staniforth, 1964

Ishmael: Man's insanity is heaven's sense.

> HERMAN MELVILLE (1819–1891). *Moby-Dick; or, The Whale,* 93, 1851, ed. Harold Beaver, 1972

See The Wise & the Foolish: Paul

Sanity was statistical; it was merely a question of learning to think as they thought.

> GEORGE ORWELL (1903–1950). *Nineteen Eighty-Four*, 3.4, 1949

If I am insane, the whole world is crazy.

> JACK RUBY (1911–1967). While in detention following his assassination of Lee Harvey Oswald. In news reports, 1963

Sanity—an aptitude to judge of things like other men, and regular habits, etc. Insanity a departure from this.

> BENJAMIN RUSH (1745–1813). 5 November 1810, "Notes for Lectures," *The Autobiography of Benjamin Rush: His "Travels Through Life" together with his "Commonplace Book for 1789–1813,"* ed. George W. Corner, 1948

Greediness, ambition, and so forth are forms of insanity.

> BARUCH SPINOZA (1632–1677). *Ethics*, 1677. In Erich Fromm, "Individual and Social Origins of Neurosis," *American Sociological Review*, August 1944

We take our bearings, daily, from others. To be sane is, to a great extent, to be sociable.

> JOHN UPDIKE (1932–). In *Christian Science Monitor*, 5 March 1979

INSECTS

See also • Animals

His Labor is a Chant—
His Idleness—a Tune—
Oh, for a Bee's experience
Of Clovers, and of Noon!

> EMILY DICKINSON (1830–1886). "His Feet are shod with Gauze—," 1864?

The spiders have done their science studies, with particular emphasis on geometry.

> JULES RENARD (1864–1910). Journal, September 1904, tr. Louise Bogan and Elizabeth Roget, 1964

I have never been able to prevent myself from saving a fly caught in a spider's web.

> JULES RENARD (1864–1910). Journal, August 1908, tr. Louise Bogan and Elizabeth Roget, 1964

If he comes across an insect which has fallen into a puddle, he stops a moment in order to hold out a leaf or a stalk on which it can save itself.

> ALBERT SCHWEITZER (1875–1965). *The Philosophy of Civilization: Civilization and Ethics*, 21, 1923, tr. C. T. Campion and Mrs. Charles E. B. Russell, 1946

Toby (to a fly): Go, poor devil, get thee gone! Why should I hurt thee? This world surely is wide enough to hold both thee and me.

> LAURENCE STERNE (1713–1768). *Tristram Shandy*, 2.12, 1759–1767

In a bright day, during any of the summer months, your walk is through an atmosphere of butterflies, so gaudy in hue, and so varied in form, that I often thought they looked like flowers on the wing.

> FRANCES TROLLOPE (1780–1863). *Domestic Manners of the Americans*, 23, 1832

A divine power is at work in the sensation of the meanest insect as well as in the brain of a Newton.

> VOLTAIRE (1694–1778). "Sensation," *Philosophical Dictionary*, 1764, tr. Wade Baskin, 1961

INSPIRATION

See also • Creativity ○ Discovery ○ Dreams ○ Ideas ○ Imagination ○ Intuition ○ Invention ○ Originality ○ Revelation ○ Spirituality

I am one who, when Love inspires, attend, and according as he speaks within me, so I express myself.

> DANTE (A.D. 1265–1321). In Cesare Lombroso, *The Man of Genius*, 1.2, 1888, ed. Havelock Ellis, 1896

The most wonderful inspirations die with their subject, if he has no hand to paint them to the senses.

> RALPH WALDO EMERSON (1803–1882). "Intellect," *Essays: First Series*, 1841

It isn't like a big thing of, you know, you gotta take a thunderbolt and throw it at Zeus, except every once in a while, but that comes on its own. Zeusie and thunderbolts come on their own; you can't call them up. They're products of circumstance, and time, and history, and yourself, and your metabolism, and your love affairs, and your money, and your lack of money, and your food, and your drugs, and your shoes, and your Brooks Brothers, and your Empire State Building, and the winter snow, and your mother's living death, or something. So you can't combine all those things on your own. You have to wait for nature to throw up a great wave.

> ALLEN GINSBERG (1926–1997). Tom Vitale television interview, "Allen Ginsberg: When the Muse Calls, Answer," PBS, September 1990

Don't loaf and invite inspiration.
Light out after it with a club.

> JACK LONDON (1876–1916). In Douglas Brinkley, "Editor's Note" (epigraph) to Hunter S. Thompson, *The Proud Highway: Saga of a Desperate Southern Gentleman, 1955–1967*, 1997

Inspiration cannot be willed, although it can be wooed.

> ANTHONY STORR (1920–). *Churchill's Black Dog, Kafka's Mice, and Other Phenomena of the Human Mind*, 12, 1988

So-called "inspiration" is no more than an extreme example of a process which constantly goes on in the minds of all of us.

> ANTHONY STORR (1920–). *Churchill's Black Dog, Kafka's Mice, and Other Phenomena of the Human Mind*, 12, 1988

My affirmations or utterances come to me ready-made—not forethought—so that I occasionally awake in the night simply to let fall ripe a statement which I had never consciously considered before, and as surprising and novel and agreeable to me as anything can be. As if we only thought by sympathy with the universal mind, which thought while we were asleep. There is such a necessity [to] make a definite statement that our minds at length do it without our consciousness.

> HENRY DAVID THOREAU (1817–1862). Journal, 1 April 1860

INSTITUTIONS

See also • Bureaucracy ○ Information: Bradley H. Patterson, Jr. ○ Organizations

No outward institutions can supply the place of inward principle, of moral energy.

> WILLIAM ELLERY CHANNING (1780–1842). "Remarks on the Life and Character of Napoleon Bonaparte," 2, 1827–1828

Every institution goes through three stages—utility, privilege, and abuse.

> CHATEAUBRIAND (1768–1848). In Max Nordau, *The Interpretation of History*, 1, tr. M. A. Hamilton, 1911

An institution is the lengthened shadow of one man.

> RALPH WALDO EMERSON (1803–1882). "Self-Reliance," *Essays: First Series*, 1841

Progressive societies outgrow institutions as children outgrow clothes.

> HENRY GEORGE (1839–1897). *Social Problems*, 1, 1883

[An] institution is the lever . . . whereby the individual may transform his own personal will into social action.

> CARL G. GUSTAVSON (1915–). *A Preface to History*, 10, 1955

Of institutions we may judge by their effects.

> SAMUEL JOHNSON (1709–1784). "Milton," *Lives of the English Poets*, 1781

You tell me it's the institution.
Well, you know,
You better free your mind instead.

> JOHN LENNON (1940–1980) and PAUL McCARTNEY (1942–). "Revolution" (song), 1968

The safety and happiness of society are the objects at which all political institutions aim, and to which all such institutions must be sacrificed.

> JAMES MADISON (1751–1836). In *The Federalist Papers* (essay series), 43, 1787–1788

Our criteria for judging institutions should always include the quality of the men and women they develop and select.

> C. WRIGHT MILLS (1916–1962). *Power, Politics and People: The Collected Essays of C. Wright Mills*, 3.6.5, ed. Irving Louis Horowitz, 1963

To be celebrated, to be wealthy, to have power requires access to major institutions.

> C. WRIGHT MILLS (1916–1962). *The Power Elite*, 1.2, 1956

Without people nothing is possible; without institutions nothing is lasting.

> JEAN MONNET (1888–1979). French economist and statesman. In Ralph Nader, speech, Washington, 25 March 1998

What is any established institution but a Society for the Prevention of Change?

> LEWIS MUMFORD (1895–1990). *The Conduct of Life*, 4.3, 1951

The less a person knows about the workings of the social institutions of his society, the more he must trust those who wield power in it; and the more he trusts those who wield such power, the more vulnerable he makes himself to becoming their victim.

> THOMAS S. SZASZ (1920–). Foreword to Seth Farber, *Madness, Heresy, and the Rumor of Angels: The Revolt Against the Mental Health System*, 1993

One generic evil of an institution of any kind is that people who have identified themselves with it are prone to make an idol of it.

> ARNOLD J. TOYNBEE (1889–1975). *An Historian's Approach to Religion*, 2nd ed. 19, 1979 (1956)

I hear it was charged against me that I sought to destroy institutions,
But really I am neither for nor against institutions.
(What indeed have I in common with them? or what with the destruction of them?)
Only I will establish in the Mannahatta and in every city of these States inland and seaboard,
And in the fields and woods, and above every keel little or large that dents the water.
Without edifices or rules or trustees or any argument,
The institution of the dear love of comrades.

> WALT WHITMAN (1819–1892). "I Hear It Was Charged against Me" (complete poem), 1860, *Leaves of Grass*, 1855–1892

INSULT

See also • Contempt: Lord Chesterfield ○ Criticism ○ Criticism: Examples ○ Critics: Examples ○ Flattery ○ Praise ○ Repartee: Examples ○ Ridicule ○ Slander ○ Wit ○ Wounds: H. L. Mencken

Zingers should glow with intelligence as well as drip with contempt.

> MAUREEN DOWD (1952–). "Decline of the Insult," *New York Times*, 21 June 1997

Cashiered army officer (who had several times appealed unsuccessfully to Lincoln for reinstatement): Well, Mr. President, I see you are determined not to do me justice!
Lincoln (while seizing him by the collar and throwing him out of his office): Sir, I give you fair warning never to show yourself in this room again. I can bear censure, but not insult!

> ABRAHAM LINCOLN (1809–1865). Format adapted. 1864.
> In F. B. Carpenter, *Six Months at the White House with Abraham Lincoln*, 36, 1866

At ev'ry Trifle scorn to take Offense,
That always shows Great Pride, or Little Sense.

> ALEXANDER POPE (1688–1744). *An Essay on Criticism*, l. 386, 1711

A truly noble nature cannot be insulted.

> PUBLIUS SYRUS (85–43 B.C.). *Moral Sayings*, 369, tr. Darius Lyman, Jr., 1862

A man of courage never endures an insult; an honorable man never offers one.

> PUBLIUS SYRUS (85–43 B.C.). *Moral Sayings*, 997, tr. Darius Lyman, Jr., 1862

The success of an insult depends upon the sensitiveness and the indignation of the victim.

> SENECA THE YOUNGER (5? B.C.–A.D. 65). "On the Firmness of the Wise Man" (17.4), *Moral Essays*, tr. John W. Basore, 1928

Silence is the most perfect expression of scorn.

> GEORGE BERNARD SHAW (1856–1950). *Back to Methuselah: A Metabiological Pentateuch*, 5, 1921

The cruelest insult . . . which can be offered to the unfortunate, is to appear to make light of their calamities.

> ADAM SMITH (1723–1790). *The Theory of Moral Sentiments*, 1.1.2, 1759

No one dares to offend or insult a power of known superiority in action.

> VEGETIUS (A.D. 4th cent.) *De Re Militari*, (A.D. 378). In Thomas R. Phillips, ed., *Roots of Strategy*, p. 124, 1940

There are offenses given and offenses not given but taken.

> IZAAK WALTON (1593–1683). "Epistle to the Reader," *The Compleat Angler*, 1653

Who puts up with insult invites injury.

> SAYING

INTEGRITY

See also • Character ○ Conscience: Abraham Lincoln ○ Corruption ○ Dignity ○ Honesty ○ Honor ○ Lying ○ Morality ○ Promises ○ Responsibility ○ Self-Realization (Becoming) ○ Truthfulness ○ Virtue

As Shakespere says, be thrue to y'ersilf an' ye will not thin be false to ivry man.

> FINLEY PETER DUNNE (1867–1936). "Casual Observations," *Mr. Dooley's Philosophy*, 1900

Society has no bribe for me, neither in politics, nor church, nor college, nor city.

> RALPH WALDO EMERSON (1803–1882). Journal, 31 August 1838
> See Conscience: Abraham Lincoln

In failing circumstances no man can be relied on to keep his integrity.

> RALPH WALDO EMERSON (1803–1882). "Wealth," *The Conduct of Life*, 1860

Calamity and Prosperity are the Touchstones of Integrity.

> BENJAMIN FRANKLIN (1706–1790). *Poor Richard's Almanack*, March 1752

A man in a corrupted age must make a secret of his integrity, or else he will be looked upon as a common enemy. He must engage his friends not to speak of it; for he setteth himself for a mark to be ill used.

> MARQUIS OF HALIFAX (1633–1695). "Integrity," *Political, Moral and Miscellaneous Reflections*, 1750

I wanted to try to live in accord with the promptings which came from my true self. Why is that so difficult?

> HERMANN HESSE (1877–1962). *Demian: The Story of Emil Sinclair's Youth*, 3, 1919, tr. Michael Roloff and Michael Lebeck, 1965

Integrity without knowledge is weak and useless, and knowledge without integrity is dangerous and dreadful.

> SAMUEL JOHNSON (1709–1784). *Rasselas: The Prince of Abyssinia*, 41, 1759

You might as well praise a man for not robbing a bank.

> BOBBY JONES (1902–1971). On penalizing himself one stroke, the margin of his defeat, in a national championship golf match after driving his ball into the woods and, unseen, accidentally nudging it. In Alistair Cooke, *Alistair Cooke's America*, 11, 1973

Excuse me, sir; I cannot consent to receive pay for services I do not render.

> ROBERT E. LEE (1807–1870). Explaining his rejection of a $10,000-a-year salary to act as titular head of an insurance company after the Civil War. In Dixon Wecter, *The Hero in America: A Chronicle of Hero-Worship*, 11.3, 1941
> See Honesty: Benjamin Franklin

This old anvil laughs at many broken hammers.
    There are men who can't be bought.

> CARL SANDBURG (1878–1967). *The People, Yes*, 107, 1936
> See Corruption: Sir Robert Walpole

Polonius: This above all: to thine own self be true,
And it must follow, as the night the day,
Thou canst not then be false to any man.

> SHAKESPEARE (1564–1616). *Hamlet*, 1.3.78, 1600

First Bandit: There is no time so miserable but a man may be true.

> SHAKESPEARE (1564–1616). *Timon of Athens*, 4.3.461, 1607

The cadet will not lie, cheat or steal, nor tolerate those who do.

> UNITED STATES MILITARY ACADEMY. West Point (New York), Code of Honor

Integrity and firmness are all I can promise. These, be the voyage long or short, shall never forsake me, although I may be deserted by all men; for of the consolations, which are to be derived from these, under any circumstances, the world cannot deprive me.

> GEORGE WASHINGTON (1732–1799). Four weeks before assuming the Presidency, letter to Henry Knox, 1 April 1789
> See Friends: Abraham Lincoln (2)

Whatever happened to integrity?

> ANONYMOUS

INTELLECTUALS

See also • Doctrine: Eric Hoffer (3) ○ Experts ○ Philosophers ○ Professionals ○ Scholars ○ Statesmen: John R. Elting ○ Thinkers ○ Tyrants: Albert Camus

A spirit of national masochism prevails, encouraged by an effete corps of impudent snobs who characterize themselves as intellectuals.

> SPIRO T. AGNEW (1918–1996). Vice president. Referring to Vietnam War protesters at a Moratorium Day demonstration, after-dinner speech, New Orleans, 19 October 1969

[Intellectuals] have a preference for learning things rather than experiencing them.

> MARGARET ANDERSON (1886–1973). *The Fiery Fountains: The Autobiography, Continuation and Crisis to 1950*, 1 ("A Life for a Life"), 1951

An intellectual is someone whose mind watches itself.

> ALBERT CAMUS (1913–1960). June 1941, *Notebooks: 1935–1942*, tr. Philip Thody, 1963

You do not arrest Voltaire.

> CHARLES de GAULLE (1890–1970). Answering demands by nationalists to arrest Jean-Paul Sartre (France's preeminent intellectual) for denouncing the Algerian War, 1960?

Establishment-oriented intellectuals are not bought. Indeed, they are not even very well paid. They are merely patronized, flattered, and wittingly or unwittingly, used.

> G. WILLIAM DOMHOFF (1936–). *The Higher Circles: The Governing Class in America,* 7, 1970

An "intellectual" is a man who takes more words than he needs to say more than he knows.

> DWIGHT D. EISENHOWER (1890–1969)

Only those who know the supremacy of the intellectual life . . . can understand the grief of one who falls from that serene activity into the absorbing soul-wasting struggle with worldly annoyances.

> GEORGE ELIOT (1819–1880). *Middlemarch,* 73, 1871–1872

There's always something suspect about an intellectual on the winning side.

> VÁCLAV HAVEL (1936–). Czech dissident and later president. *Disturbing the Peace,* 5, 1986, tr. Paul Wilson, 1990

When the intellectual comes into his own, he becomes a pillar of stability and finds all kinds of lofty reasons for siding with the strong against the weak.

> ERIC HOFFER (1902–1983). *The Ordeal of Change,* 6, 1964

It appears . . . to be the fate of intellectuals either to berate their exclusion from wealth, success, and reputation, or to be seized by guilt when they overcome this exclusion. They are troubled, for example, when power disregards the counsels of intellect, but because they fear corruption they are even more troubled when power comes to intellect for counsel. . . . The intellectual is either shut out or sold out.

> RICHARD HOFSTADTER (1916–1970). *Anti-Intellectualism in American Life,* 15.6, 1962

An intellectual . . . [is] a person who has learned to establish relations between the different elements of his sum of knowledge, one who possesses a coherent system of relationships into which he can fit all such new items of information as he may pick up in the course of his life.

> ALDOUS HUXLEY (1894–1963). "Education," *Ends and Means: An Inquiry into the Nature of Ideals and into the Methods Employed for Their Realization,* 1937

The intellectual whose capital is his knowledge.

> HAROLD D. LASSWELL (1902–1978), DANIEL LERNER, and C. EASTON ROTHWELL. *The Comparative Study of Elites: An Introduction and Bibliography,* 2, 1952

Beating up on "intellectuals" is the last refuge of demagogues.

> ANTHONY LEWIS (1927–). "The Czar's New Clothes," *New York Times,* 14 December 1989

Ingenious fools too clever to be wise, though brilliant at inventing the most ingenious reasons for their fatuous beliefs. But, tire-some as intellectuals can be, even they are probably much less menacing and pernicious to the world than anti-intellectuals.

> F. L. LUCAS (1894–1967). "Johnson," *The Search for Good Sense: Four Eighteenth-Century Characters,* 1958

A highbrow is a person educated beyond his intelligence.

> BRANDER MATTHEWS (1852–1929)

No ruling class can endure without its intelligentsia.

> JOSEPH STALIN (1879–1953). In Eric Hoffer, *The Ordeal of Change,* 13.1, 1964

The way of the egghead is hard.

> ADLAI E. STEVENSON (1900–1965). Forward to *Call to Greatness,* 1954

[The Russian intelligentsia's] deception is not Machiavellian—not done with a consciousness of the deception they are producing—but for the most part with a naive conviction that they are doing something good and elevated.

> LEO TOLSTOY (1818–1910). "Christianity and Patriotism," 15, 1894, tr. Aylmer Maude, 1936

INTELLIGENCE

See also • Cleverness ◦ Common Sense ◦ Cunning ◦ Curiosity ◦ Imagination ◦ Knowledge ◦ Memory ◦ Mind ◦ Reason ◦ Stupidity ◦ Wisdom

You don't realize that you're intelligent until it gets you into trouble.

> JAMES BALDWIN (1924–1987). Julius Lester interview, April 1984, *Conversations with James Baldwin,* ed. Fred L. Standley and Louis H. Pratt, 1989

Of work comes knowledge, of knowledge comes fruitful work; of the union of knowledge and work comes the development of intelligence.

> VINOBA BHAVE (1895–1982). Prelude (2) to *Thoughts on Education,* tr. Marjorie Sykes, 1964

Intelligence is not something possessed once for all. It is in constant process of forming, and its retention requires constant alertness in observing consequences, an open-minded will to learn and courage in re-adjustment.

> JOHN DEWEY (1895–1952). *Reconstruction in Philosophy,* 4, 1920

Intelligence—yes, but of what kind and aim? There is the intelligence of Socrates, and the intelligence of a thief or a forger.

> RALPH WALDO EMERSON (1803–1882). Journal, 1868, undated

The test of a first-rate intelligence is the ability to hold two opposed ideas in the mind at the same time, and still retain the ability to function. One should, for example, be able to see that things are hopeless and yet be determined to make them otherwise.

> F. SCOTT FITZGERALD (1896–1940). "The Crack-Up," *Esquire,* February 1936, *The Crack-Up,* ed. Edmund Wilson, 1945

The test of intelligence [is] not how much we know how to do, but how we behave when we don't know what to do. Similarly, any situation, any activity, that puts before us real problems, that we have to solve for ourselves, problems for which there are no answers in any book, sharpens our intelligence.

> JOHN HOLT (1923–1985). "Art, Math, and Other Things," *How Children Learn,* 1967

Intelligent people are allus on th' unpop'lar side of anything.

> KIN HUBBARD (1868–1930). *Abe Martin: Hoss Sense and Nonsense,* p. 100, 1926

You can't beat brains.

> JOHN F. KENNEDY (1917–1963). A repeated remark. In Richard Reeves, *President Kennedy: Profile of Power,* 28, 1993

To be able to distinguish, classify, and catalogue external things on the basis of a secure order already established in the mind—this is at once intelligence and culture.

> MARIA MONTESSORI (1870–1952). *Spontaneous Activity in Education,* 8, tr. Florence Simmonds, 1917

To perceive exactly and to connect the things perceived logically is the work of the highest intelligence.

> MARIA MONTESSORI (1870–1952). *Spontaneous Activity in Education,* 8, tr. Florence Simmonds, 1917

One of the functions of intelligence is to take account of the dangers that come from trusting solely to the intelligence.

> LEWIS MUMFORD (1895–1990). *The Transformations of Man,* 7.1, 1956

The smarter the guy, the bigger the rascal.

> WILL ROGERS (1879–1935). Weekly column, 6 January 1929, *The Will Rogers Book,* 6.11, comp. Paula McSpadden Love, 1961

Intelligence is quickness in seeing things as they are.

> GEORGE SANTAYANA (1863–1952). "Against Prying Philosophers," *Little Essays,* 62, ed. Logan Pearsall Smith, 1920

Intelligence alone, without wisdom and empathy for suffering, is hollow.

> JOHN G. STOESSINGER (1927–). *Why Nations Go to War,* 3rd ed., 4, 1982 (1974)

The folly of intelligent people, clear-headed and narrow-visioned, has precipitated many catastrophes.

> ALFRED NORTH WHITEHEAD (1861–1947). *Adventures of Ideas,* 4.2, 1933

✷

The smarter you are, the smaller your strike zone.

> ANONYMOUS

If you're so smart, how come you ain't rich?

> SAYING (AMERICAN)

INTELLIGENCE, MILITARY

See also • Commanders ○ Deception ○ Decision-Making ○ Facts ○ Information ○ Knowledge ○ Planning ○ Secrets ○ Strategy, Military ○ War ○ World War II: W. Winterbotham

Under conditions of uncertainty, [military] officers have reason to overstate threats in order to hedge against failure but also to overstate results in operations in order to prove their own competence.

> RICHARD K. BETTS (1947–). *Soldiers, Statesmen, and Cold War Crises,* 10, 1977

An army without secret agents is exactly like a man without eyes or ears.

> CHIA LIN (4th cent. B.C.). In Sun-tzu, "Employment of Secret Agents," (23), *The Art of War,* tr. Samuel B. Griffith, 1963

In wartime, truth is so precious that she should always be attended by a bodyguard of lies.

> WINSTON CHURCHILL (1874–1965). Remark to Joseph Stalin at the Teheran Conference (Iran), 30 November 1943, *The Second World War: Closing the Ring,* 2.4, 1951
>
> See Lying: Machiavelli

[A] great part of the information obtained in War is contradictory, a still greater part is false, and by far the greatest part is of a doubtful character. What is required of an officer is a certain power of discrimination, which only knowledge of men and things and good judgment can give. The law of probability must be his guide.

> KARL von CLAUSEWITZ (1780–1831). *On War,* 1.6, 1832, tr. J. J. Graham, 1873

An ideal command system . . . should be able to gather information accurately, continuously, comprehensively, selectively, and fast. Reliable means must be developed to distinguish the true from the false, the relevant from the irrelevant, the material from the immaterial.

> MARTIN van CREVELD (1946–). *Command in War,* 1, 1985

The perfect deception plan is like a jigsaw puzzle. Pieces of information are allowed to reach the enemy in such a way as to convince him that he has discovered them by accident. If he puts them together himself, he is far more likely to believe that the intended picture is a true one.

> CHARLES CRUICKSHANK (1914–1989). Introduction to *Deception in World War II,* 1979

It was not the absence of intelligence which led us into trouble but our unwillingness to draw unpleasant conclusions from it.

> H. A. de WEERD. On the American decision in 1950 to call Communist China's bluff by continuing to advance above the 38th Parallel toward the Chinese border, "Strategic Surprise in the Korean War," *Orbis,* 1962

Having gradually (and perhaps painfully) accumulated information in support of a decision people become progressively more loath to accept contrary evidence.

> NORMAN F. DIXON (1922–). *On the Psychology of Military Incompetence,* 2, 1976

Hide what you have and reveal what you haven't.

> J. F. C. FULLER (1878–1966). *A Military History of the Western World,* 3.13, 1956

All too often . . . intelligence estimates tell us more about interests and foreign policy preferences of powerful groups in government than it does about what the other side's intentions and capabilities are.

> ROBERT JERVIS. "Intelligence and Foreign Policy," *International Security,* Winter 1986-1987

There are four means of obtaining information about the enemy's operations: espionage, reconnaissances, questioning prisoners, and signals.

> HENRI de JOMINI (1779–1869). Compressed. *Summary of the Art of War,* 6, 1807, ed. J. D. Hittle, 1947

[Central Intelligence Agency] analysts were only too aware that no one has ever been penalized for not having foreseen an opportunity, but that many careers have been blighted for not predicting a risk. Therefore the intelligence community has always been tempted to forecast dire consequences for any conceivable course of action, an attitude that encourages paralysis rather than adventurism.

> HENRY A. KISSINGER (1923–). *White House Years,* 2, 1979

The Spy Who Came in from the Cold.

> JOHN LE CARRÉ (1931–). Book title, 1963

Nearly always, the best deception trades on the enemy's own preconceptions. If he already believes what you want him to believe, you have merely to confirm his own ideas rather than to undertake the more difficult task of inserting new ones into his mind.

> RONALD LEWIN (?–1984). *Ultra Goes to War: The First Account of World War II's Greatest Secret Based on Official Documents,* 10, 1978

There was the negative intelligence so important in deception: to know what the enemy has *not* done can be as conclusive as some positive act.

> RONALD LEWIN (1914–1984). *Ultra Goes to War: The First Account of World War II's Greatest Secret Based on Official Documents,* 10, 1978

The practical value of intelligence depends on the attitude of mind of its recipients.

> RONALD LEWIN (1914–1984). *Ultra Goes to War: The First Account of World War II's Greatest Secret Based on Official Documents,* 12, 1978

In terms of . . . intelligence operations, noise is the buzz set up by competing information signals which prevents the essential message from being heard loud and clear.

> RONALD LEWIN (1914–1984). *The American Magic: Codes, Ciphers and the Defeat of Japan,* 3, 1982

Be very careful never to show your own bias to anyone who is giving you information, or passing it on to you. Once he sees that you have a particular inclination he will instinctively tend to tell you what he thinks will suit you, and enhance your opinion of him.

> B. H. LIDDELL HART (1895–1970). "Intelligence Problems," *This Expanding War,* 1942

A commander's most important function is to separate the five percent of intelligence he receives which is important from the 95 percent which is not important.

> DOUGLAS MacARTHUR (1880–1964). In Richard M. Nixon, *Leaders,* 4, 1982

Any manifest error on the part of an enemy should make us suspect some stratagem.

> MACHIAVELLI (1469–1527). *The Discourses,* 3.48, 1517, tr. Christian E. Detmold, 1940

A lie when it is needed will only be believed if it rests on a firm foundation of previous truth.

> J. C. MASTERMAN (1891–1977). *The Double-Cross System in the War of 1939 to 1945,* 1, 1972

A deception is often safer and more likely to be effective if it reaches the enemy in parts through a number of agents than if the whole of it rests upon the authority of a single agent.

> J. C. MASTERMAN (1891–1977). *The Double-Cross System in the War of 1939 to 1945,* 4, 1972

Go up into the Negeb yonder, and go up into the hill country, and see what the land is, and whether the people who dwell in it are strong or weak, whether they are few or many, and whether the land that they dwell in is good or bad, and whether the cities that they dwell in are camps or strongholds.

> MOSES (14th cent. B.C.). Remarks to his spies, *Numbers* 13:17–19

Bad Agents send in a great deal of news, and good ones very little.

> WALTER NICOLAI. "Espionage," 1920–1924. In Ladislas Farago, ed., *The Axis Grand Strategy,* 1942

In all branches of the intelligence service, the source of information determines its value.

> WALTER NICOLAI. "Espionage," 1920–1924. In Ladislas Farago, ed., *The Axis Grand Strategy,* 1942

Whereas spies are obsessed with the missing pieces, the analysts are devoted to patterns.

> THOMAS POWERS (1940–). *The Man Who Kept the Secrets: Richard Helms and the CIA,* 3, 1981

The day has eyes, the night has ears.

> JOHN RAY (1628–1705). Comp., *A Collection of English Proverbs,* p. 391, 1678

Analysts and policy makers alike tend to interpret information to support their own viewpoints.

> DEAN RUSK (1909–1994). *As I Saw It,* 35, 1990

Polonius: By indirections find directions out.

> SHAKESPEARE (1564–1616). *Hamlet,* 2.1.66, 1600

Do not swallow too much from a defector or an informer. Some of his revelations are probably true. But a considerable fraction consists of intentional exaggerations to please your ears, unintentional falsifications out of subconscious revenge, and unrepresentative sampling of data.

> R. G. H. SIU (1917–). *The Craft of Power,* 2.7, 1984

The bulk of intelligence activities does not involve . . . sleuthings but careful analyses and judgments of openly available data.

> R. G. H. SIU (1917–). *The Craft of Power,* 2.41, 1984

Gentlemen do not read other people's mail.

> HENRY L. STIMSON (1867–1930). Secretary of war. 1929. In Walter Isaacson, *Kissinger: A Biography,* 1, 1992

As living spies we must recruit men who are intelligent but appear to be stupid.

> TU MU (A.D. 803–852). In Sun-tzu (4th cent. B.C.). "Employment of Secret Agents," 11, *The Art of War,* tr. Samuel B. Griffith, 1963

All the business of war, and indeed all the business of life, is to endeavor to find out what you don't know from what you do; that's what I call "guessing at what is on the other side of the hill."

DUKE OF WELLINGTON (1769–1852). Letter, 3 September 1852

We failed to anticipate Pearl Harbor not for want of the relevant materials, but because of a plethora of irrelevant ones.

ROBERTA WOHLSTETTER (1912–). *Pearl Harbor: Warning and Decision,* 7, 1962

In both Honolulu and Washington, individual reactions to danger had been numbed, or at least dulled, by the continuous international tension.

ROBERTA WOHLSTETTER (1912–). *Pearl Harbor: Warning and Decision,* 7, 1962

The fact that intelligence predictions must be based on moves that are almost always reversible makes understandable the reluctance of the intelligence analyst to make bold assertions.

ROBERTA WOHLSTETTER (1912–). *Pearl Harbor: Warning and Decision,* 7, 1962

Military intelligence is a contradiction in terms.

ANONYMOUS

You can't judge a spy by his cover.

ANONYMOUS
See Books: Saying (American)

Fields have eyes and woods have ears.

SAYING (ENGLISH)

INTERNATIONALISM

See also • Brotherhood ○ International Relations ○ Nationalism ○ Nations ○ Patriotism ○ Unity: [especially] Walter Lippmann (1) ○ World

[The United Nations] must represent peoples, not just governments.

NORMAN COUSINS (1912–1990). 1976, "Editor's Odyssey: Gleanings from Articles and Editorials by N.C.," ed. Susan Schiefelbein, *Saturday Review,* 15 April 1978

The wise man belongs to all countries, for the home of a great soul is the whole world.

DEMOCRITUS (460?–370 B.C.). Attributed. In Karl R. Popper, *The Open Society and Its Enemies,* 1.10.4, 1945

To become a true Russian is to become the brother of all men, a universal man. . . . Our future lies in Universality, not won by violence, but by the strength derived from our great ideal—the reuniting of all mankind.

FYODOR DOSTOYEVSKY (1821–1881). Speech, 1880. In Henry Miller, *The Books in My Life,* 1 (footnote), 1952

Isolated independence is not the goal. It is voluntary interdependence.

MOHANDAS K. GANDHI (1869–1948). Describing his aim for India and England during a visit to England in 1931. In Louis Fischer, *The Life of Mahatma Gandhi,* 32, 1950

I believe that our Great Maker is preparing the world, in His own good time, to become one nation, speaking one language, and when armies and navies will no longer be required.

ULYSSES S. GRANT (1822–1855). *Second Inaugural Address,* 4 March 1873

New World Order: International Organization, International Law, International Cooperation.

FREDERICK CHARLES HICKS (1875–1956). Book title, 1920
See Gulf War: George Bush (4)

I represent a party which does not yet exist: the party of revolution, civilization.
    This party will make the twentieth century.
    There will come from it first the United States of Europe, then the United States of the World.

VICTOR HUGO (1802–1885). On the wall of the room in which he died, Place des Vosges, Paris.

Through war, through the taxing and never-ending accumulation of armament, through the want which any state, even in peacetime, must suffer internally, Nature forces [societies] to make at first inadequate and tentative attempts; finally, after devastations, revolutions, and even complete exhaustion, she brings them to that which reason could have told them at the beginning and with far less sad experience, to wit, to step from the lawless condition of savages into a league of nations.

IMMANUEL KANT (1724–1804). "Idea for a Universal History from a Cosmopolitan Point of View," 1784, *On History,* ed. Lewis White Beck, 1963

The world state is inherent in the United Nations as an oak tree is in an acorn.

WALTER LIPPMANN (1889–1974). *One World or None,* 13, 1946

I look upon all men as my compatriots, and embrace a Pole as a Frenchman, making less account of the national than of the universal and common bond.

MONTAIGNE (1533–1592). "Of Vanity," *Essays,* 1588, tr. Donald M. Frame, 1958

The most generous dreams of the past have now become immediate practical necessities: a worldwide cooperation of people, a more just distribution of all the goods of life; the use of knowledge and energy for the service of life, and the use of life itself for the extension of the human spirit to provinces where human values and purposes could not heretofore penetrate. If we awaken in time to overcome the automatisms and irrational compulsions that are now pushing the nations toward destruction, we shall create a universal community.

LEWIS MUMFORD (1895–1990). *The Conduct of Life,* 1.1, 1951

The political unification of mankind cannot be realistically conceived except as part of [the] effort at self-transformation.

LEWIS MUMFORD (1895–1990). *The Transformations of Man,* 8.1, 1956

I dislike frontiers. To me the earth is one single state.

VASLAV NIJINSKY (1890–1950). *The Diary of Vaslav Nijinsky,* 1, 1936, ed. Romola Nijinsky, 1968

My country is the world, and my religion is to do good.

> THOMAS PAINE (1737–1809). *The Rights of Man,* 2.5, 1792
> See Women: Mary Woolf

The whole world is my country.

> SENECA THE YOUNGER (5? B.C.–A.D. 65). "On the Happy Life" (20.5), *Moral Essays,* tr. John W. Basore, 1932

I am neither an Anthenian nor a Greek, but a citizen of the world.

> SOCRATES (470?–399 B.C.). Sightly modified. In Plutarch (A.D. 46?–119?), "On Banishment, or Flying One's Country," *Plutarch's Essays,* Little Brown edition, 1883

Man cannot endure indefinitely without evolving the institutional structure of a planetary society.

> ROBERT C. TUCKER (1918–). "Personality and Political Leadership," *Political Science Quarterly,* Fall 1977

INTERNATIONAL RELATIONS

Includes • Foreign Affairs

See also • Alliances ∘ Ambassadors ∘ American Foreign Policy ∘ Appeasement ∘ Argument ∘ Cold War ∘ Competition ∘ Crises ∘ Cuban Missile Crisis ∘ Deception ∘ Diplomacy ∘ Diplomats ∘ Gulf War ∘ Imperialism ∘ Internationalism ∘ Leaders ∘ Machiavellianism ∘ Nations: [especially] Jimmy Carter, Ralph Waldo Emerson ∘ Negotiation ∘ Neutrality ∘ Politics ∘ Power ∘ Presidents ∘ Revolution ∘ Revolutionary War ∘ Self-Interest ∘ Statesmen ∘ Tact ∘ Treaties ∘ Vietnam War ∘ Violence ∘ War ∘ World War I ∘ World War II

While small States are virtuous because of their feebleness, powerful States sustain themselves only through crime.

> MIKHAIL BAKUNIN (1814–1876). *Federalism, Socialism, and Anti-Theologism.* In *The Political Philosophy of Bakunin: Scientific Anarchism,* 1.14, ed. G. P. Maximoff, 1953

As [Egyptian Vice President Zaharia Mohieddin] once put it, in the game of nations "there are no winners, only losers. The objective of each player is not so much to win as to avoid loss." Problems do not get solved. They are managed. Success is achieved if disaster is averted or even postponed until the next administration. . . . [Secretary of State Dean] Rusk looked back on his eight years [1961–1969] with satisfaction because nuclear weapons had not been used.

> RICHARD J. BARNET (1929–). *Roots of War,* 5.1, 1971

Institutions like to continue doing what they have been doing, always on a grander scale, if possible. When old enemies disappear, mellow, or turn into allies, as frequently happens in international relations, new enemies must be found and new threats must be discovered. The failure to replenish the supply of enemies is the supreme threat facing any national security bureaucracy.

> RICHARD J. BARNET (1929–). On "bureaucratic inertia," *Roots of War,* 5.1, 1971

National security is primarily defined in terms of reputation for having more power than all other nations and a willingness to use it.

> RICHARD J. BARNET (1929–). *Roots of War,* 9.4, 1971

Easy availability of military options encourages authorities to use them in a crisis rather than to search energetically for diplomatic solutions.

> RICHARD K. BETTS (1947–). *Soldiers, Statesmen, and Cold War Crises,* 6, 1977

Positive experience—especially an intervention that proves unexpectedly easy—lessens fear when future interventions are considered.

> RICHARD K. BETTS (1947–). Referring to America's successful Dominican Republic intervention just before accelerating her combat involvement in Vietnam in 1965, *Soldiers, Statesmen, and Cold War Crises,* 9, 1977

"The law ov nashuns;" iron klad gun botes.

> JOSH BILLINGS (1818–1885). *His Sayings,* 45, 1867

Success achieved by force or fraud rests on an insecure foundation; conversely, success based on reciprocal advantage gives promise of even further success to come.

> FRANÇOIS de CALLIÈRES (1645–1717). *De la manière de négocier avec les souverains,* 1716

The best foreign policy is to live our daily lives in honesty, decency and integrity.

> DWIGHT D. EISENHOWER (1890–1969). In Norman Solomon, comp., *The Power of Babble,* p. 63, 1992

[The aim of foreign policy is] to preserve and enrich the state and enhance its power and influence at the expense of enemies either actual or potential.

> SAMUEL B. GRIFFITH (1906–1983). Introduction to Sun-tzu (4th cent. B.C.). *The Art of War,* 1963

There can be no greater error than to expect or calculate upon real favors from nation to nation. It is an illusion which experience must cure, which a just pride ought to discard.

> ALEXANDER HAMILTON (1757–1804). In Garry Wills, *Nixon Agonistes: The Crisis of the Self-Made Man,* 4.5, 1969

No consideration of foreign policy can proceed from any other criterion than this: *Does it benefit our nationality now or in the future, or will it be injurious to it?*

> ADOLF HITLER (1889–1945). *Mein Kampf,* 2.13, 1924, tr. Ralph Manheim, 1943

Mankind will never know what it was spared because of risks avoided or because of actions taken that averted awful consequences—if only because once thwarted the consequences can never be proved.

> HENRY A. KISSINGER (1923–). *White House Years,* 3, 1979

Throughout history the political influence of nations has been roughly correlative to their military power.

> HENRY A. KISSINGER (1923–). *White House Years,* 7, 1979

Serious students of international affairs know that common policies can endure only if both parties serve their own purposes.

> HENRY A. KISSINGER (1923–). *Years of Upheaval,* 5, 1982

In foreign policy one must do with what one has.

> HENRY A. KISSINGER (1923–). *Years of Upheaval,* 12, 1982

If crisis management requires cold and even brutal measures to show determination, it also imposes the need to show the opponent a way out. Grandstanding is good for the ego but bad for foreign policy. . . . Many wars have started because no line of retreat was left open. Superpowers have a special obligation not to humiliate each other.

> HENRY A. KISSINGER (1923–). *Years of Upheaval,* 12, 1982

The most perilous moment is often when an adversary is seemingly prepared to retreat and is then jolted into new defiance by an assault on his self-esteem.

> HENRY A. KISSINGER (1923–). *Years of Upheaval,* 12, 1982

Realpolitik—foreign policy based on calculations of power and the national interest.

> HENRY A. KISSINGER (1923–). *Diplomacy,* 6, 1994

Facing down a nonexistent threat is an easy way to enhance a nation's standing.

> HENRY A. KISSINGER (1923–). *Diplomacy,* 6, 1994

Law and justice play no role in the relations of peoples of unequal strength.

> GUSTAVE LE BON (1841–1931). *Aphorisms of Present Times,* 2.6, 1913, tr. Alice Widener, 1979

International relations are governed by interests, and not by moral principles

> B. H. LIDDELL HART (1895–1970). "The Illusion of Treaties," *Why Don't We Learn from History?* 1944

International incidents must not be allowed to shape foreign policy; foreign policy must shape the incidents.

> NAPOLEON (1769–1821). A repeated remark, *The Mind of Napoleon: A Selection from His Written and Spoken Words,* 220, ed. J. Christopher Herold, 1955
>
> See Events: Henry A. Kissinger (2) ∘ Presidents: Harry S. Truman (3)

The public is bored by foreign affairs until a crisis arises; and . . . then it is guided by feelings rather than by thoughts.

> HAROLD NICOLSON (1886–1968). British diplomat. *The Evolution of Diplomacy,* 4.3, 1954

The animosity which Nations reciprocally entertain is nothing more than what the policy of their Governments excites to keep up the spirit of the system. Each Government accuses the other of perfidy, intrigue, and ambition, as a means of heating the imagination of their respective Nations, and incensing them to hostilities. Man is not the enemy of Man, but through the medium of a false system of Government.

> THOMAS PAINE (1737–1809). *The Rights of Man,* 1 ("Conclusion"), 1791

We have no eternal allies, and we have no perpetual enemies. Our interests are eternal and perpetual, and these interests it is our duty to follow.

> LORD PALMERSTON (1784–1865). British foreign minister and later prime minister. House of Commons speech, 1 March 1848
>
> See States: Charles de Gaulle

Each side feels that defeat on its periphery is a threat to its center.

> THOMAS POWERS (1940–). "What Is It About?" *Atlantic,* January 1984

The world is a collection of states, each a law unto itself. The object of international politics is power. Power is gained and maintained by violence.

> ANATOL RAPOPORT (1911–). Summarizing Clausewitz's views, introduction (1968) to Karl von Clausewitz, *On War,* 1832

Without a central administrative focus, foreign policy turns into a series of unrelated decisions—crisis-oriented, *ad hoc* and after-the-fact in nature. We become prisoners of events.

> NELSON ROCKEFELLER (1908–1979). New York governor. Statement, 21 June 1968. In Henry A. Kissinger, *White House Years,* 2, 1979

Physicists and astronomers see their own implications in the world being round, but to me it means that only one-third of the world is asleep at any given time and the other two-thirds is up to something.

> DEAN RUSK (1909–1994). Speech before the American Bar Association, Atlanta, 22 October 1964. In *Atlanta Constitution,* 23 October 1964

Chief among the requisites for successful foreign policy is a credible military able to give weight and support to policy.

> BRENT SCOWCROFT (1925–) and RICHARD HAASS (1951–). "Foreign Policy Nears a Peril Point," *New York Times,* 5 January 1994

I asked Tom if countries always apologized when they had done wrong, and he says: "Yes; the little ones does."

> MARK TWAIN (1835–1910). *Tom Sawyer Abroad,* 12, 1894

A country cannot gain unless another loses.

> VOLTAIRE (1694–1778). "Fatherland," *Philosophical Dictionary,* 1764, tr. Theodore Besterman, 1971

It is a maxim founded on the universal experience of mankind that no nation is to be trusted farther than it is bound by its interest; and no prudent statesman or politician will venture to depart from it.

> GEORGE WASHINGTON (1732–1799). Letter to Henry Laurens, President of the Continental Congress, 14 November 1778

There can be no greater error than to expect or calculate upon real favors from Nation to Nation.

> GEORGE WASHINGTON (1732–1799). *Farewell Address,* 17 September 1796

What is called national prestige consists in behaving always in such a way as to demoralize other nations by giving them the impression that, if it comes to war, one would certainly defeat them.

> SIMONE WEIL (1909–1943). *The Simone Weil Reader,* 3 ("The Power of Words"), ed. George A. Panichas, 1977

INTOLERANCE

See also • Prejudice ∘ Tolerance

There is nothing that dies so hard and rallies so often as intolerance.

> WILLIAM E. BORAH (1865–1940). Senate speech, 24 April 1929

Religious intolerance . . . was inevitably born with the belief in one God.

SIGMUND FREUD (1856–1939). *Moses and Monotheism*, 2.2, 1939, tr. Katherine Jones, 1955

Intolerance betrays want of faith in one's cause.

MOHANDAS K. GANDHI (1869–1948). In *Young India*, 2 February 1921

No loss by flood and lightning, no destruction of cities and temples by the hostile forces of nature, has deprived man of so many noble lives and impulses as those which his intolerance has destroyed.

HELEN KELLER (1880–1968). *Optimism*, 2, 1903

I hate people who are intolerant.

LAURENCE J. PETER (1919–1990)

INTUITION

See also • Creativity ○ Discovery: [especially] Albert Einstein (3) ○ Ideas ○ Imagination ○ Inspiration ○ Invention ○ Originality ○ Reason: Karl R. Popper ○ Revelation ○ Spirituality

Intuition [is] perception via the unconscious.

CARL G. JUNG (1875–1961). "Conscious, Unconscious, and Individuation," 1939, *Archetypes and the Collective Unconscious*, tr. R. F. C. Hull, 1959

The moment of truth, the sudden emergence of a new insight, is an act of intuition. Such intuitions give the appearance of miraculous flashes, or short-circuits of reasoning. In fact they may be likened to an immersed chain, of which only the beginning and the end are visible above the surface of consciousness. The diver vanishes at one end of the chain and comes up at the other end, guided by invisible links.

ARTHUR KOESTLER (1905–1983). *The Act of Creation*, 1.2.8, 1964

You get your intuition back when you make space for it, when you stop the chattering of the rational mind.

ANNE LAMOTT (1954–). *Bird by Bird: Some Instructions on Writing and Life*, 2 ("Broccoli"), 1995

Nelson realized with such intensity the inmost secrets of his profession, that experience and study had in him been converted into intuition.

EDWIN PERCY WHIPPLE (1819–1896). On Horatio Nelson (1758–1795). "Character," 1857, *Character and Characteristic Men*, 1884

INVENTION

See also • Creativity ○ Creativity: First Person ○ Discovery: [especially] Georg Christoph Lichtenberg ○ Ideas ○ Imagination ○ Inspiration ○ Intuition ○ Inventions ○ Misjudgments: Charles H. Duell ○ Originality ○ Revelation ○ Spirituality

A bad memory is the mother of invention.

GERALD BRENAN (1894–1987). "Life," *Thoughts in a Dry Season: A Miscellany*, 1978

See Accident: Saying (American) ○ Necessity: Plato (2)

Want, the Mistress of Invention, still tempts me on.

SUSANNA CENTLIVRE (1667?–1723). *The Busy Body*, 1, 1709

I do not invent my best thoughts; I find them.

ALDOUS HUXLEY (1894–1963). "Knowledge and Understanding," *Tomorrow and Tomorrow and Tomorrow and Other Essays*, 1956

Inventing is a combination of brains and materials. The more brains you use, the less material you need.

CHARLES F. KETTERING (1876–1958). Electrical engineer and inventor

Invention presupposes an extensive contemplation of things on one's own account; one must see for oneself more than let oneself be told.

GEORG CHRISTOPH LICHTENBERG (1742–1799). *Aphorisms*, E.85, 1806, tr. R. J. Hollingdale, 1990

To be fruitful in invention, it is indispensable to have a *habit* of observation and reflection.

ABRAHAM LINCOLN (1809–1865). Lecture on discoveries and inventions, Jacksonville (Illinois), 11 February 1859

Invention, strictly speaking, is little more than a new combination of those images which have been previously gathered and deposited in the memory: nothing can come of nothing: he who has laid up no materials can produce no combinations.

SIR JOSHUA REYNOLDS (1723–1792). "Discourse Two," 11 December 1769, *Discourses on Art*, 1769–1790

Invention is one of the great marks of genius; but . . . it is by being conversant with the inventions of others that we learn to invent; as by reading the thoughts of others we learn to think.

SIR JOSHUA REYNOLDS (1723–1792). "Discourse Six," 10 December 1774, *Discourses on Art*, 1769–1790

I invent nothing. I rediscover.

AUGUSTE RODIN (1840–1917). French sculptor

INVENTIONS

See also • Communications ○ Creativity ○ Invention ○ Machines ○ Progress ○ Science ○ Technology

These three [inventions—printing, gunpowder, and the compass—] have changed the appearance and state of the whole world: first in literature, then in warfare, and lastly in navigation; and innumerable changes have been thence derived, so that no empire, sect, or star, appears to have exercised a greater power and influence on human affairs than these mechanical discoveries.

FRANCIS BACON (1561–1626). *Novum Organum*, 1.129, 1620, Willey Book edition, 1944

It is questionable if all the mechanical inventions yet made have lightened the day's toil of any human being. They have enabled a greater population to live the same life of drudgery and imprisonment, and an increased number of manufacturers and others to make fortunes. They have increased the comforts of the middle classes. But they have not yet begun to affect those great changes in human destiny, which it is in their nature and in their futurity to accomplish.

JOHN STUART MILL (1806–1873). *Principles of Political Economy with Some of Their Applications to Social Philosophy*, 4.6.2, 1848

What hath God wrought!

> SAMUEL S. B. MORSE (1791–1872). The first telegraph message, 24 May 1844. In Alvin Toffler, *Powershift: Knowledge, Wealth, and Violence at the Edge of the 21st Century,* 10, 1990

The improvements in transportation do not cut down traveling time but merely increase the area over which people have to travel.

> BERTRAND RUSSELL (1872–1970). As paraphrased by Daniel Bell, *The End of Ideology,* 12, 1960

The first wheel maker saw a wheel, carried
in his head a wheel, and one day found his
hand shaping a wheel, the first wheel.

> CARL SANDBURG (1878–1967). *The People, Yes,* 91, 1936

It is said to have been reported to one of the Roman emperors, as a piece of good news, that one of his subjects had invented a process for manufacturing unbreakable glass. The emperor gave orders that the inventor should be put to death and the records of his invention should be destroyed. If the invention had been put on the market, the manufacturers of ordinary glass would have been put out of business; there would have been unemployment that would have caused political unrest, and perhaps revolution.

> ARNOLD J. TOYNBEE (1889–1975). *Change and Habit: The Challenge of Our Time,* 7, 1966

All the modern inconveniences.

> MARK TWAIN (1835–1910). *Life on the Mississippi,* 43, 1883

If it hadn't been for Thomas Edison, we'd all be listening to the radio by candlelight.

> ANONYMOUS

IRELAND

See also • Imperialism: George Faulkner ○ Nations

"A Little Bit of Heaven, Sure They Call It Ireland."

> J. KEIRN BRENNAN. Song title, 1914

The Irish are a fair people—they never speak well of one another.

> SAMUEL JOHNSON (1709–1784). February 1775. In James Boswell, *The Life of Samuel Johnson,* 1791

Being Irish is to know the world was meant to break your heart.

> ANONYMOUS

IRRESOLUTION

See also • Delay ○ Indecision ○ Resolution ○ Will

God Almighty hates a quitter.

> SAMUEL FESSENDEN (1847–1908). Republican National Convention speech, St. Louis, June 1896

A half measure is a program sufficient to generate pressures but not to deal with them.

> HENRY A. KISSINGER (1923–). Karen Elliott House and Thomas J. Bray interview, *Wall Street Journal,* 21 January 1980

Want of firmness in the execution arises either from respect [for one's opponents] or from the innate cowardice of him who is to commit the act.

> MACHIAVELLI (1469–1527). *The Discourses,* 3.6, 1517, tr. Christian E. Detmold, 1950

The thing done only halfway had best not be attempted at all.

> S. L. A. MARSHALL (1900–1977). "Leaders and Leadership," 1975, *Military Leadership,* 2nd ed., ed. Robert L. Taylor and William E. Rosenbach, 1992

One does not govern a nation by half measures.

> NAPOLEON (1769–1821). *Napoleon in His Own Words,* 4, comp. Jules Bertaut, 1916

If you're coasting, you're going downhill.

> L. W. PIERSON. In Donald Rumsfeld, "Rumsfeld's Rules" (collected while serving at the White House and Pentagon), *Washingtonian,* February 1977

Lady Macbeth: Infirm of purpose!

> SHAKESPEARE (1564–1616). *Macbeth,* 2.2.53, 1605

Half measures can kill when on the brink of precipices, . . . we cannot jump halfway across.

> YEVGENY YEVTUSHENKO (1933–). "Half-Measures"

ITALY

See also • Nations ○ Rome

There is, in fact, no law or government at all [in Italy]; and it is wonderful how well things go on without them.

> LORD BYRON (1788–1824). Letter to Thomas Moore, 2 January 1821

A man who has not been in Italy is always conscious of an inferiority.

> SAMUEL JOHNSON (1709–1784). 11 April 1776. In James Boswell, *The Life of Samuel Johnson,* 1791

Italy . . . anarchy tempered by bureaucracy.

> GEORGE F. WILL (1941). Brian Lamb television interview, C-SPAN, 1 December 1997

JEALOUSY

See also • Envy

Jealousy is a terrible thing. It resembles love, only it is precisely love's contrary. Instead of wishing for the welfare of the object loved, it desires the dependence of that object upon itself, and its own triumph.

> HENRI AMIEL (1821–1881). Journal, 28 December 1880, tr. Mrs. Humphrey Ward, 1887

Jealousy dislikes the world to know it.

> LORD BYRON (1788–1824). Don Juan, 1.65, 1819–1824

Jealousy, the jaundice of the soul.

> JOHN DRYDEN (1631–1700). The Hind and the Panther, 3.1367, 1687

The kernel of all jealousy is lack of love.

> CARL G. JUNG (1875–1961). Memories, Dreams, Reflections, 4, ed. Aniela Jaffé, 1962

In jealousy there is more self-love than love.

> LA ROCHEFOUCAULD (1613–1680). Maxims, 324, 1665, tr. Leonard Tancock, 1959

It's matrimonial suicide to be jealous when you have a really good reason.

> CLARE BOOTH LUCE (1903–1987). The Women, 3, 1937

The Jealous are Troublesome to others, but a Torment to themselves.

> WILLIAM PENN (1644–1718). More Fruits of Solitude, 190, 1693

✺

Love expels jealousy.

> SAYING (FRENCH)

No jealousy, no love.

> SAYING (GERMAN)

JESTS

See also • Comedy ○ Funniness ○ Humor ○ Jokes ○ Laughter ○ Ridicule: Samuel Johnson

Clumsy jesting is no joke.

> AESOP (6th cent. B.C.). "The Ass and the Lapdog," Fables, tr. Joseph Jacobs, 1894

I expect that the jesters who played so invaluable a part in the Courts of the Middle Ages saved their skins from being flayed and their necks from being wrung by the impartiality with which their bladder-blows were bestowed in all directions, and upon all alike.

> WINSTON CHURCHILL (1874–1965). "George Bernard Shaw," Great Contemporaries, 1937

Better lose a Jest than a Friend.

> THOMAS FULLER (1654–1734). Comp., Gnomologia: Adages and Proverbs, 915, 1732

There is many a true Word spoken in jest.

> JAMES KELLY. (18th cent.) Comp., A Complete Collection of Scottish Proverbs Explained and Made Intelligible to the English Reader, T.32, 1721

Aside from laughing it off, the only real answer to a jest is a better jest.

> ORRIN E. KLAPP (1915–). Symbolic Leaders: Public Dramas and Public Men, 7, 1964

JOKES

See also • Comedy ○ Funniness ○ Humor ○ Jests ○ Laughter

There's no such thing as a new joke. All jokes are public domain. It's not the gag, it's how you deliver it.

> MILTON BERLE (1908–). In Clifton Fadiman, comp., An American Treasury, 1455–1955, p. 835, 1955

If it were not for these stories, jokes, jests, I should die; they give vent—are the vents—of my moods and gloom.

> ABRAHAM LINCOLN (1809–1865). Quoted by William H. Herndon, letter to Jesse W. Weik, 17 November 1885. In Emanuel Hertz, ed., The Hidden Lincoln: From the Letters and Papers of William H. Herndon, 1.3, 1940

Those who have no sense of humor run the risk of having jokes made at their expense.

> MICHEL PAUL RICHARD. In "First Principles," Thoughts For All Seasons: The Magazine of Epigrams, vol. 4, 1992

There are only a handful of possible jokes. The chief members of this joke band may be said to be: the fall of dignity [and] mistaken identity.

> MACK SENNETT (1880–1960)

All very serious revolutionary propositions begin as huge jokes. Otherwise they would be stamped out by the lynching of their first exponents.

> GEORGE BERNARD SHAW (1856–1950). "What Is the New Element in the Norwegian School?" The Quintessence of Ibsenism, 1891

My way of joking is to tell the truth. It's the funniest joke in the world.

> GEORGE BERNARD SHAW (1856–1950). John Bull's Other Island, 2, 1904
>
> See Truthfulness: Shaw (2)

JOURNALISM

See also • Gossip: Herb Caen ○ Journalists ○ Literature: Cyril Connolly, Oscar Wilde (1) ○ Media ○ News ○ Newspapers ○ The Press

There is a bias in television journalism. It is not against any particular party or point of view—it is against understanding.

> JOHN BIRT (1944–). English broadcasting executive. In Times (London), 28 February 1975

Success in the field [of journalism] comes from a fortuitous combination of luck and shoe leather.

> DOUGLASS CATER (1923–1995). The Fourth Branch of Government, 1, 1959

Journalism largely consists in saying "Lord Jones Dead" to people who never knew that Lord Jones was alive.

> G. K. CHESTERTON (1874–1936). "The Purple Wig," *The Wisdom of Father Brown,* 1914

What someone doesn't want you to publish is journalism; all else is publicity.

> PAUL FUSSELL (1924–). "'A Power of Facing Unpleasant Facts,'" (1981), *Thank God for the Atom Bomb and Other Essays,* 1988

I call "journalism" everything that will be less interesting tomorrow than today.

> ANDRÉ GIDE (1869–1951). Journal, 1921 (detached page), tr. Justin O'Brien, 1948

There can be no higher law in journalism than to tell the truth and shame the devil.

> WALTER LIPPMANN (1889–1974). "Journalism and the Higher Law," *Liberty and the News,* 1920

Journalism is the last refuge of the vaguely talented.

> WALTER LIPPMANN (1889–1974). Quoted by Charles McDowell, commentator, *Washington Week,* television news program, PBS, 4 March 1994
>
> See Patriotism: Samuel Johnson

[Modern journalism] justifies its own existence by the great Darwinian principle of the survival of the vulgarest.

> OSCAR WILDE (1854–1900). "The Critic as Artist" (1), *Intentions,* 1891

JOURNALISTS

See also • Editors ○ Journalism ○ Media ○ News ○ Newspapers ○ Publishers ○ Television ○ Writers

The punditocracy is a tiny group of highly visible political pontificators who make their living offering "inside political opinions and forecasts" in the elite national media. And it is their debate, rather than any semblance of a democratic one, that determines the parameters of political discourse in the nation today.

> ERIC ALTERMAN (1960–). Introduction to *Sound and Fury: The Washington Punditocracy and the Collapse of American Politics,* 1992

Walk fast, type fast, and never break a deadline.

> BEN H. BAGDIKIAN (1920–). Marty Moss-Coane radio interview, NPR, 7 August 1995

A correspondent indiscreet enough to use honest, intemperate language will lose "access" to officials, which is much like a surgeon losing his knife.

> RICHARD J. BARNET (1929–). On the Washington press corps, *Roots of War,* 10.8, 1971

Most stories come out of meetings or in story conferences. They go from ideas that aren't well formed—that haven't yet collided with facts—through editors to a reporter. It's up to the reporter to bring them to life. That's the earliest test of a good journalist—how those ideas get translated into stories. You've got to learn when to say, "That's enough, I'm going to write it now."

> BEN BRADLEE (1921–). Ken Adelman interview, *Washingtonian,* September 1991

[As a reporter] I like to keep in the middle and be disliked by both sides.

> JIMMY BRESLIN (1929–). In Associated Press, "Goetz Trial Testimony Ends with Feisty Breslin," *San Francisco Chronicle,* 18 April 1996

There were Three Estates in Parliament; but, in the Reporters' Gallery yonder, there sat a *Fourth Estate* more important far than they all.

> EDMUND BURKE (1729–1797). In Thomas Carlyle, "The Hero as Man of Letters," *On Heroes, Hero-Worship, and the Heroic in History,* 1841

The reporter [is] one who each twenty-four hours dictates a first draft of history.

> DOUGLASS CATER (1923–1995). *The Fourth Branch of Government,* 1, 1959

I have always felt that whatever the Divine Providence permitted to occur I was not too proud to report.

> CHARLES A. DANA (1819–1897). In Daniel J. Boorstin, *The Image: A Guide to Pseudo-Events in America,* 1 (introduction), 1961

A friendship between reporter and source lasts only until it is profitable for one to betray the other.

> MAUREEN DOWD (1952–). Stating the "Woodward-Darman law," "Thou Shalt Not Leave a Paper Trail," *New York Times Magazine,* 8 May 1994

Hey, I never knew that before; and hey, I never thought of that before.

> THOMAS L. FRIEDMAN (1953–). His personal criteria for judging a good column, Charlie Rose television interview, PBS, 30 July 1996

Television newsmen are breathless on how the game is being played, largely silent on what the game is all about.

> JOHN KENNETH GALBRAITH (1908–). *A Life in Our Times: Memoirs,* 3, 1981

Get it first but get it right.

> WILLIAM RANDOLPH HEARST (1863–1951). Publisher. A repeated remark to his reporters. In Herb Caen, column, *San Francisco Chronicle,* 11 January 1995. To which his deadline-pressed reporters responded, "Don't get it right, get it written."

Any politician worth his salt is going to be able to dodge a question once. But when you're on live television, it becomes quickly apparent if you dodge it twice or three times. The problem is that the reporters don't follow up each other's questions.

> MARK HERTSGAARD (1956–). "The Five O'Clock Follies" (interview). 15 March 1991. In David Barsamian, ed., *Stenographers to Power,* 1992

Reporters, especially those in Washington, face an old journalistic dilemma: because their stature tends to rise and fall with that of the people they cover, they thus have a stake in the successes of their subject.

> WALTER ISAACSON (1952–). *Kissinger: A Biography,* 25, 1992

With an air of slight indiscretion and personal trust, neither totally feigned, [Henry A.] Kissinger would share confidences and inside information [with journalists]. "You always have the feeling that he's told you ten percent more than he has to," said Barbara Walters.

> WALTER ISAACSON (1952–). *Kissinger: A Biography,* 25, 1992

The fact that a man is a newspaper reporter is evidence of some flaw in character.

> LYNDON B. JOHNSON (1908–1973). In "Lyndon Baines Johnson, an American Original," *People,* 2 February 1987

A news writer is a man without virtue who lies at home for his own profit. To these compositions is required neither genius nor knowledge, neither industry not sprightliness; but contempt of shame and indifference to truth are absolutely necessary.

> SAMUEL JOHNSON (1709–1784). In *The Idler* (English journal), 30, 11 November 1758

The task of editorial writers is to come down out of the hills after the battle is over to shoot the wounded.

> MURRAY KEMPTON (1917–1997). As paraphrased by Lance Morrow, "A Battle with No Victors," *Time,* 27 May 1996

Once every four days there was a voice on the other end of the phone: "Did you read what those pricks said today?" We'd all know who "they" were: *The New York Times* editorial writers. Not that the President of the United States used that kind of language.

> ROBERT F. KENNEDY (1925–1968). Anthony Lewis interview, "Civil Rights Activities, 1961-1962," *Robert Kennedy in His Own Words: The Unpublished Recollections of the Kennedy Years,* ed. Edwin O. Guthman and Jeffrey Shulman, 1988

The journalist has comparably interested motives in his contacts with the official. He must woo and flatter the official because without his goodwill he will be deprived of information. But he cannot let himself be seduced—the secret dream of most officials—or he will lose his objectivity.

> HENRY A. KISSINGER (1923–). *White House Years,* 2, 1979

Journalist: a person without any ideas but with an ability to express them; a writer whose skill is improved by a deadline: the more time he has, the worse he writes.

> KARL KRAUS (1874–1936). In Thomas S. Szasz, *Karl Kraus and the Soul-Doctors: A Pioneer Critic and His Criticism of Psychiatry and Psychoanalysis,* 8, 1976

Every journalist who is not too stupid or too full of himself to notice what is going on knows that what he does is morally indefensible. He is a kind of confidence man, preying on people's vanity, ignorance, or loneliness, gaining their trust, and betraying them without remorse.

> JANET MALCOLM (1934–). "The Journalist and the Murderer," *New Yorker,* March 1989

I have an old-fashioned belief that Americans like to make up their own minds on the basis of all available information. The conclusions you draw are your own affair. I have no desire to influence them, and shall leave such efforts to those who have more confidence in their own judgment than I have in mine.

> EDWARD R. MURROW (1908–1965). Radio broadcast to the United States, London, 1? September 1939. In Alexander Kendrick, *Prime Time: The Life of Edward R. Murrow,* 6, 1969

As I leave the press, all I can say is this: for sixteen years, ever since the Hiss case, you've had a lot of fun—a lot of fun—that you've had an opportunity to attack me, and I think I've given as good as I've taken.

I leave you gentlemen now and you will now write it. You will interpret it. That's your right. But as I leave you, I want you to know—just think how much you're going to be missing.

You won't have Nixon to kick around anymore, because, gentlemen, this is my last press conference.

> RICHARD M. NIXON (1913–1994). Remarks to reporters after being defeated in his California gubernatorial campaign, news conference, Beverly Hills, 7 November 1962

Robert C. Pierpoint: Mr. President, you have lambasted the television networks pretty well. Could I ask you, at the risk of reopening an obvious wound, you say after you have put on a lot of heat that you don't blame anyone. I find that a little puzzling. What is it about the television coverage of you in these past weeks and months that has so aroused your anger?
Nixon: Don't get the impression that you arouse my anger. [Laughter]
Pierpoint: I'm afraid, sir, that I have that impression. [Laughter]
Nixon: You see, one can only be angry with those he respects.

> RICHARD NIXON (1913–1994). Format adapted. News conference (during the Watergate scandal), Washington, 26 October 1973

If you spend your life as a hatchet man—and there's something to be said for that—then eventually you find that everybody's out to lunch when you call. You're left with only your own opinion. I wouldn't like that because my own opinions aren't that good.

> JAMES RESTON (1909–). In *New Republic,* 1980. Quoted in R. W. Apple, Jr., "James Reston, a Journalist Nonpareil, Dies at 86," *New York Times,* 8 December 1995

Journalists are, in the very nature of their calling, alarmists; and this is their way of giving interest to what they write. Herein they are like little dogs; if anything stirs, they immediately set up a shrill bark.

> ARTHUR SCHOPENHAUER (1788–1860). "The Art of Literature: On Some Forms of Literature," *Essays of Arthur Schopenhauer,* tr. T. Bailey Saunders, 1851

A true journalist is fact-proof.

> GEORGE BERNARD SHAW (1856–1950). "Echolalia," *The Sanity of Art,* 1895

Good! Now we'll have news from hell before breakfast.

> WILLIAM TECUMSEH SHERMAN (1820–1891). After being told that three members of the press had been killed by artillery-fire during the siege of Vicksburg, 1863. In Dixon Wecter, *The Hero in America: A Chronicle of Hero-Worship,* 12.3, 1941

Writing a column is easy. I just sit down at the typewriter, open a vein and bleed it out.

> WALTER "RED" SMITH (1905–1982). Sportswriter. In Pete Axthelm, "The Master's Touch," *Newsweek,* 17 May 1976

You're only as good as your last story.

> HELEN THOMAS (1920–). Complete acceptance speech on receiving the first Helen Thomas Lifetime Achievement Award, White House Correspondents Dinner, Washington, 25 April 1998

I always learned more about what was on the minds of the people from the reporters' questions than they could possibly learn from me.

> HARRY S. TRUMAN (1884–1972). "My View of the Presidency," *Look,* 11 November 1958

If I ever needed a brain transplant, I'd choose a sportswriter because I'd want a brain that had never been used.

> NORM VAN BROCKLIN (1916–1983). Football player

A newsman knows everything. He is aware not only of what goes on in the world today, but his brain is a repository of the accumulated wisdom of the ages. He is not only handsome, but he has the physical strength which enables him to perform great feats of energy. He can go for nights without sleep. He dresses well and he talks with charm. Men admire him, women adore him, tycoons and statesmen are willing to share their secrets with him. He hates lies and meanness and sham, but he keeps his temper. He is loyal to his paper, and when he dies a lot of people are sorry, and some of them remember him for several days.

> STANLEY WALKER. *New York Herald Tribune* city editor. 1930s. In Russell Baker, "Reading Without Pain," *New York Times,* 14 June 1997

Shakspeer rote good plase, but he wouldn't hav succeeded as a Washington correspondent of a New York daily paper. He lackt the rekesit fancy and imagginashun.

> ARTEMUS WARD (1834–1867). "On 'Forts,'" *The Complete Works of Artemus Ward,* 1898

When a reporter sits down at the typewriter, he's nobody's friend.

> THEODORE H. WHITE (1915–1986). In "The Hard-to-Cover Campaign," *Newsweek,* 23 October 1972

Nothing is ever finally off the record if it's said within the hearing of a reporter, no matter what the social circumstances.

> TOM WICKER (1926–). *On Press,* 7, 1978

Be neither *in* nor *out.*

> TOM WICKER (1926–). Referring to the journalist's news sources, his "Third Law of Journalism," *On Press,* 7, 1978

Newspaper people, whose stock in trade is information and the reputation for having it.

> TOM WICKER (1926–). *On Press,* 10, 1978

Follow the money.

> EDWARD BENNETT WILLIAMS (1920–1988). Early 1970s, quoted by Evan Thomas, commentator, *Inside Washington,* television news program, 14 June 1997. This saying, now proverbial among investigative reporters, was popularized by the 1976 film *All the President's Men.* It is not in the 1974 book about the Watergate scandal by *Washington Post* reporters Bob Woodward and Carl Bernstein on which the film was based.

You cannot hope
to bribe or twist,
thank God! the
British journalist.
But, seeing what
the man will do
unbribed, there's
no occasion to.

> HUMBERT WOLFE (1885–1940). "Over the Fire," *The Uncelestial City,* 1930

❧

Never let the truth stand in the way of a good story.

> SAYING (AMERICAN). Journalist's credo

JOURNALS

See also • Autobiography ○ Biography ○ Books ○ Diaries ○ Memoirs ○ Notebooks ○ Writing

These pages are not written to be read [by others]; they are written for my own consolation and warning.

> HENRI AMIEL (1821–1881). Journal, 3 March 1852, tr. Mrs. Humphrey Ward, 1887

Value of a Journal. A sentence now; a sentence last year; a sentence yesterday. Tomorrow a question comes that for the first time brings together these three and shows them to be the three fractions of [a] Unit.

> RALPH WALDO EMERSON (1803–1882). "Notebook Delta," 1837–1862, undated

The great thing to be recorded is the state of your own mind; and you should write down everything that you remember, for you cannot judge at first what is good or bad; and write immediately while the impression is fresh, for it will not be the same a week afterwards.

> SAMUEL JOHNSON (1709–1784). 11 April 1773. In James Boswell, *The Life of Samuel Johnson,* 1791

"What are you doing now?" [Ralph Waldo Emerson] asked. "Do you keep a journal?" So I make my first entry today.

> HENRY DAVID THOREAU (1817–1862). At age 20. Journal, 22 October 1837

My Journal is that of me which would else spill over and run to waste, gleanings from the field which in action I reap. I must not live for it, but in it for the gods. They are my correspondent[s], to whom daily I send off this sheet postpaid. I am clerk in their counting room, and at evening transfer the account from daybook to ledger.

> HENRY DAVID THOREAU (1817–1862). Journal, 8 February 1841

Associate reverently and as much as you can with your loftiest thoughts. Each thought that is welcomed and recorded is a nest egg, by the side of which more will be laid. Thoughts accidentally thrown together become a frame in which more may be developed and exhibited. Perhaps this is the main value of a habit of writing, of keeping a journal—that so we remember our best hours and stimulate ourselves. . . . Having by chance recorded a few disconnected thoughts and then brought them into juxtaposition, they suggest a whole new field in which it was possible to labor and to think. Thought begat thought.

> HENRY DAVID THOREAU (1817–1862). Journal, 22 January 1852

JOY

See also • Giving: Ted Turner ○ God & Man: Isaiah ○ Good: Montaigne ○ Grief ○ Happiness ○ Laughter ○ Love, Romantic: John Clarke ○ Pleasure ○ Prayers: Anonymous (*Bible*) (1) ○ Purpose: George Bernard Shaw (1) ○ Struggle: Germaine Greer ○ Suffering ○ Tears ○ Weeping: George Herbert, Shakespeare, Anonymous (*Bible*)

When large numbers of people share their joy in common, the happiness of each is greater because each adds fuel to the other's flame.

> ST. AUGUSTINE (354–430). *Confessions,* 8.4, tr. R. S. Pine-Coffin, 1961

Joy to the world,
All the boys and girls.
Joy to the fishes in the deep blue sea,
Joy to you and me.

> HOYT AXTON, "Joy to the World" (song), 1970

He who binds to himself a joy
Doth the winged life destroy;
But he who kisses the joy as it flies
Lives in eternity's sun rise.

> WILLIAM BLAKE (1757–1827). "Poems and Fragments from the Note-Book" ("Eternity"), 43, 1793?, *The Complete Writings of William Blake,* ed. Geoffrey Keynes, 1966

True ecstasy hails neither from spirit nor from nature, but from the union of these two.

> MARTIN BUBER (1878–1965). Introduction (4) to *Tales of the Hasidim: The Early Masters,* tr. Olga Marx, 1947

My bosom underwent a glorious glow,
   And my internal spirit cut a caper.

> LORD BYRON (1788–1824). *Don Juan,* 10.3, 1819–1824

Joy rises in me, like as a summer's morn.

> SAMUEL TAYLOR COLERIDGE (1772–1834). "A Christmas Carol," 8, 1799

The highest joy of man should be the growth of personality.

> GOETHE (1749–1832). In Carl G. Jung, "On Psychic Energy" (3.d), 1928, *The Structure and Dynamics of the Psyche,* 1960

Enjoyment is *not* a goal, it is a feeling that accompanies important ongoing activity.

> PAUL GOODMAN (1911–1972). *Growing Up Absurd,* 11.12, 1960

Love and Joy are twins, or born of each other.

> WILLIAM HAZLITT (1778–1830). "Common Places" (63), *Literary Examiner* (English journal), September–December 1823

To love and be loved—this
On earth is the highest bliss.

> HEINRICH HEINE (1797–1856). "Journey from Munich to Genoa" (16), *Italy,* 1828

The root of joy, as of duty, is to put all one's powers towards some great end.

> OLIVER WENDELL HOLMES, JR. (1841–1935). "The Class of '61," speech at the Fiftieth Anniversary of Graduation from Harvard University, 28 June 1911

Joy's smile is much closer to tears than laughter.

> VICTOR HUGO (1802–1885). *Hernani,* 5.3, 1830

Winning is important to me, but what brings me real joy is the experience of being fully engaged in whatever I'm doing.

> PHIL JACKSON (1945–) (with HUGH DELEHANTY). *Sacred Hoops: Spiritual Lessons of a Hardwood Warrior,* 11, 1995

He only has known the full joy of living who somewhere and at some time has struck a decisive blow for the freedom of the human spirit.

> WALTER LIPPMANN (1889–1974). "The South and the New Society," *Social Forces,* September 1927

Let your one delight and refreshment be to pass from one service to the community to another, with God ever in mind.

> MARCUS AURELIUS (A.D. 121–180). *Meditations,* 6.7, tr. Maxwell Staniforth, 1964

Bliss is the same in subject or in king.

> ALEXANDER POPE (1688–1744). *An Essay on Man,* 4.58, 1734

Never elated, while one man's oppress'd.

> ALEXANDER POPE (1688–1744). *An Essay on Man,* 4.323, 1734

Look toward the true good, and rejoice only in that which comes from "your own store" . . . from your very self, that which is the best part of you.

> SENECA THE YOUNGER (5? B.C.–A.D. 65). "On the True Joy Which Comes from Philosophy," *Moral Letters to Lucilius,* 23.6, tr. Richard M. Gummere, 1918

No man can safely rejoice, unless he possesses the testimony of a good conscience.

> THOMAS à KEMPIS (1380–1471). *The Imitation of Christ,* 1.20, tr. Leo Sherley-Price, 1952

Grief can take care of itself, but to get the full value of a joy you must have somebody to divide it with.

> MARK TWAIN (1835–1910). *Following the Equator: A Journey Around the World,* 48 (epigraph), 1897

Joy is not in things; it is in us.

> RICHARD WAGNER (1813–1883). In Elbert Hubbard, comp., *Elbert Hubbard's Scrap Book,* p. 164, 1923

Blessed are the joymakers.

> NATHANIEL PARKER WILLIS (1806–1867). In Elbert Hubbard, comp., *Elbert Hubbard's Scrap Book,* p. 91, 1923

JUDAISM

See also • Anti-Semitic Statements ○ Anti-Semitism ○ Christianity ○ Holocaust ○ Rabbis ○ Religion ○ Revelations

To be a Jew . . . means first of all to acknowledge and follow in practice those fundamentals in humaneness laid down in the Bible.

> ALBERT EINSTEIN (1879–1955). Address before the National Labor Committee for Palestine, Commodore Hotel, New York, 17 April 1938, *Out of My Later Years,* rev. ed., 52, 1956 (1950)

Christianity marked a progress in the history of religion: that is to say, in regard to the return of the repressed. From now on, the Jewish religion was, so to speak, a fossil.

> SIGMUND FREUD (1856–1939). *Moses and Monotheism,* 3.1.4, 1939, tr. Katherine Jones, 1955

To be a Jew is to affirm the world without being enslaved to it; to be a part of civilization and to go beyond it; to conquer space and to sanctify time. Judaism is *the art of surpassing civilization,* sanctification of time, sanctification of history.

> ABRAHAM JOSHUA HESCHEL (1907–1972). *God in Search of Man: A Philosophy of Judaism,* 42, 1955

We remember the beginning and believe in the end. We live between two historic poles: Sinai and the Kingdom of God.

> ABRAHAM JOSHUA HESCHEL (1907–1972). *God in Search of Man: A Philosophy of Judaism,* 43, 1955

Israel is under judgment; the covenant with God must not be taken as immunity from judgment.

> ABRAHAM JOSHUA HESCHEL (1907–1972). *The Prophets,* 9, 1962

And Moses went up to God, and the Lord called him out of the mountain, saying, "Thus you shall say to the house of Jacob, and tell the people of Israel: You have seen what I did to the Egyptians, and how I bore you on eagles' wings and brought you to myself. Now therefore, if you will obey my voice and keep my covenant, you shall be my own possession among all peoples; for all the earth is mine, and you shall be to me a kingdom of priests and a holy nation."

> MOSES (14th cent. B.C.). *Exodus* 19:3–5

And the Lord said to Moses, "I have seen this people, and behold, it is a stiff-necked people."

> MOSES (14th cent. B.C.). *Exodus* 32:9

Hear, O Israel: the Lord our God, the Lord is one. And thou shalt love the Lord thy God with all thy heart, and with all thy soul, and with all thy might.

> MOSES (14th cent. B.C.). *Deuteronomy* 6:4 (Masoretic Text)

I call heaven and earth to witness against you this day, that I have set before you life and death, blessing and curse; therefore choose life, that you and your descendants may live, loving the Lord your God, obeying his voice, and cleaving to him, for that means life to you and length of days, that you may dwell in the land which the Lord swore to your fathers, to Abraham, to Isaac, and to Jacob, to give them.

> MOSES (14th cent. B.C.). *Deuteronomy* 30:19–20

[Moses'] life seems actually to have been the historical bridge between animistic polytheism and ethical monotheism—that is practically to say, from superstition to religion.

> CHARLES FRANCIS POTTER (1885–1962). *The Great Religious Leaders,* 2, 1962

Shylock: I am a Jew. Hath not a Jew eyes? hath not a Jew hands, organs, dimensions, senses, affections, passions? fed with the same food, hurt with the same weapons, subject to the same diseases, healed by the same means, warmed and cooled by the same winter and summer, as a Christian is? If you prick us, do we not bleed? If you tickle us, do we not laugh? if you poison us, do we not die? and if you wrong us, shall we not revenge?

> SHAKESPEARE (1564–1616). *The Merchant of Venice,* 3.1.60, 1596

Jews are like everybody else, only more so.

> HOWLAND SPENCER (1820–1903)

Jewry, in the form in which it collided with Western Christendom, was certainly an exceptional social phenomenon, but it was also certainly not unique. Jewry was exceptional in being a fossilized relic of a civilization that was extinct in every other shape.

> ARNOLD J. TOYNBEE (1889–1975). *A Study of History,* 8.274, 1954

I marvel at the resilience of the Jewish people. Their best characteristic is their desire to remember. No other people has such an obsession with memory.

> ELI WIESEL (1928–). In *Daily Mail* (British newspaper), 15 July 1988

✹

By the waters of Babylon,
  there we sat down and wept,
  when we remembered Zion.

> ANONYMOUS (*BIBLE*). *Psalms* 137:1

JUDGES

See also • Justice ○ Law ○ Trials

The parts of a judge in hearing are four: to direct the evidence; to moderate length, repetition, or impertinency of speech; to recapitulate, select, and collate the material points of that which hath been said; and to give the rule or sentence.

> FRANCIS BACON (1561–1626). "Of Judicature," *Essays,* 1625

A judge rarely performs his functions adequately unless the case before him is adequately presented.

> LOUIS D. BRANDEIS (1856–1941). "The Living Law," *Illinois Law Review,* 1916

The magistrate is a speaking law, and the law a silent magistrate.

> CICERO (106–43 B.C.). *De legibus,* 3.1, tr. C. D. Yonge, 1902

I don't want to know what the law is, I want to know who the judge is.

> ROY COHEN (1927–1986). Lawyer. A favorite saying. In Tom Wolfe, "Dangerous Obsessions," *New York Times Book Review,* 3 April 1988

Father Zossima: You cannot be a judge of anyone. For no one can judge a criminal until he recognizes that he is just such a criminal as the man standing before him.

> FYODOR DOSTOYEVSKY (1821–1881). *The Brothers Karamazov,* 6.2(h), 1880, tr. Constance Garnett, 1912

It's very hard to judge or understand
A case like this until we've heard both sides.

> EURIPIDES (485?–406 B.C.). *The Heracleidae,* l. 175, tr. Ralph Gladstone, 1955

Oons, Sir! do you say that I am drunk? I say, Sir, that I am as sober as a judge.

> HENRY FIELDING (1707–1754). *Don Quixote in England,* 3.14, 1734

A good Judge conceives quickly, judges slowly.

> GEORGE HERBERT (1593–1633). Comp., *Outlandish Proverbs,* 599, 1640

We do not inquire what the legislature meant; we ask only what the statute means.

> OLIVER WENDELL HOLMES, JR. (1841–1935). "The Theory of Legal Interpretation," *Harvard Law Review,* 25 January 1899

Anonymous: What great principle has guided your judicial decisions?
Holmes: I have spent seventy years finding out that I am not God.

> OLIVER WENDELL HOLMES, JR. (1841–1935). Format adapted. In Adlai E. Stevenson, "What Is Their Purpose? And Ours?" *New York Times Magazine,* 4 November 1962

Woe to those who are wise in their own eyes,
  and shrewd in their own sight! . . .
who acquit the guilty for a bribe,
  and deprive the innocent of the right!

> ISAIAH (8th cent. B.C.). *Isaiah* 5:21–23

No man is allowed to be a judge in his own cause because his interest would certainly bias his judgment and, not improbably, corrupt his integrity.

> JAMES MADISON (1751–1836). In *The Federalist Papers* (essay series),
> 10, 23 November 1787

[San Francisco] Giants multimillionaire slugger Barry Bonds, pleading hardship in the wake of the baseball strike, has persuaded a San Mateo County judge to cut in half his spousal and child-support payments.
  The judge—Domestic Relations Commissioner George Taylor—then promptly turned around and asked Bonds for his autograph.

> PHILLIP MATIER (1953–) and ANDREW ROSS (1953–). "Barry Bonds
> Tells Starstruck Judge He's Strapped," *San Francisco Chronicle*, 20
> August 1994

A judge is . . . surrounded by people who keep telling him what a wonderful fellow he is. And if he once begins to believe it, he is a lost soul.

> HAROLD R. MEDINA (1888–1990). "Some Reflections on the Judicial
> Function: A Personal Viewpoint," *American Bar Association Journal*,
> February 1952

You shall do no injustice in judgment; you shall not be partial to the poor or defer to the great, but in righteousness shall you judge your neighbor.

> MOSES (14th cent. B.C.). *Leviticus* 19:15

The hungry Judges soon the Sentence sign,
And Wretches hang that Jurymen may Dine.

> ALEXANDER POPE (1688–1744). *The Rape of the Lock*, 3.21, 1712

The judge is condemned when the guilty is acquitted.

> PUBLIUS SYRUS (85–43 B.C.). *Moral Sayings*, 407, tr. Darius Lyman, Jr.,
> 1862

Angelo: Thieves for their robbery have authority
When judges steal themselves.

> SHAKESPEARE (1564–1616). *Measure for Measure*, 4.2.176, 1604

Judges are but men, and in all ages have shown a fair share of frailty. Alas! Alas! The worst crimes of history have been perpetrated under their sanction, the blood of martyrs and patriots, crying from the ground, summons them to judgment.

> CHARLES SUMNER (1811–1874). Massachusetts Republican Convention
> speech, 7 September 1854

Judges . . . are picked out from the most dexterous lawyers who are grown old or lazy: and having been biased all their lives against truth and equity, lie under such a fatal necessity of favoring fraud, perjury, and oppression, that I have known several of them refuse a large bribe from the side where justice lay, rather than injure the faculty by doing anything unbecoming their nature or their office.

> JONATHAN SWIFT (1667–1745). *Gulliver's Travels*, 4.5, 1726

The judge who renders a just decision is as though he had collaborated with God in the work of creation.

> *TALMUD* (A.D. 1st–6th cent.). Rabbinical writings. In Louis I. Newman,
> comp., *The Talmudic Anthology*, 110, 1945

A judge should not stand in judgment over a person whom he likes or dislikes.

> *TALMUD* (A.D. 1st–6th cent.). Rabbinical writings. In Louis I. Newman,
> comp., *The Talmudic Anthology*, 164, 1945

In ethics-conscious Washington, the judiciary is joining cabinet members and lawmakers on the suspect list. At issue are judges who ruled in favor of West Publishing Co.—a publisher of court rulings—after taking trips at its expense, sometimes staying at lavish hotels. Seven Supreme Court justices, including current Justices Antonin Scalia, Anthony Kennedy, Sandra Day O'Connor and John Paul Stevens, accepted West's hospitality during a decade in which the court refused to hear appeals of five cases decided by lower courts in West's favor. The *Minneapolis Star Tribune* reported that then Justice Lewis Powell, a member of a West-sponsored award committee, suggested it meet in the Virgin Islands—which it did just before the court declined to hear a case against West. Consumer advocate Ralph Nader will complain this week in the U.S. Judicial Conference about judges' roles in the West award.

> *U.S. NEWS & WORLD REPORT.* "Outlook," 27 March 1995

When the world is judged, the judges are brought to the Heavenly Tribunal first.

> *ZOHAR* (A.D. 14th cent.). Jewish mystical writings. In Louis I. Newman,
> comp., *The Talmudic Anthology*, 111, 1945

A judge [may not listen] to one litigant when the other is not present.

> *ZOHAR* (A.D. 14th cent.). Jewish mystical writings. In Louis I. Newman,
> comp., *The Talmudic Anthology*, 169, 1945

✒

The opinion of Parliament is the opinion of yesterday, and the opinion of judges is that of the day before yesterday.

> ANONYMOUS (ENGLISH). As paraphrased by John Morley, *Notes on
> Politics and History: A University Address*, 2, 1913

The judge answers questions of law; the jury answers questions of fact.

> SAYING (LATIN)

The judge does not consider trifles.

> SAYING (LATIN)

Fear the judge, not the law.

> SAYING (RUSSIAN)

Let the judge see no person, but only intent and results.

> SAYING

JUDGING OTHERS

See also • Blame ○ Criticism ○ Defects ○ Faults ○ Forgiveness ○ Guilt ○ Innocence ○ Justice ○ Nations: Woodrow Wilson ○ Praise

We ought not to judge men by their absolute excellence, but by the distance which they have traveled from the point at which they started.

> HENRY WARD BEECHER (1813–1887). *Life Thoughts,* p. 161, rec. Edna Dean Proctor, 1858

Men judge each other bi their suksess, not bi their undertakings; but the Lord judges bi the undertaking, not bi the suksess.

> JOSH BILLINGS (1818–1885). *On Ice: and Other Things,* 14, 1868

I hate judgments that only crush and don't transform.

> ELIAS CANETTI (1905–1994). 1973, *The Secret Heart of the Clock: Notes, Aphorisms, Fragments: 1973–1985,* tr. Joel Agee, 1989

You shall judge of a man by his foes as well as by his friends.

> JOSEPH CONRAD (1857–1924). *Lord Jim,* 34, 1900

Men are not judged by their words . . . but by their actions.

> FREDERICK II (1712–1786). *Anti-Machiavel,* 18, 1740, tr. Paul Sonnino, 1981

A man is most accurately judged by how he treats those who are not in a position either to retaliate or to reciprocate.

> PAUL ELDRIDGE (1888–1982). *Maxims for a Modern Man,* 1198, 1965

Weigh thy Neighbor in the same Balance with thyself.

> THOMAS FULLER (1654–1732). Comp., *Introductio ad Prudentiam,* 122, 1731

When thou seest any doing ill, presently ask thyself, Have not I done the like, or as bad?

> THOMAS FULLER (1654–1734). Comp., *Introductio ad Prudentiam,* 613, 1731

You cannot judge a Man till you know his whole Story.

> THOMAS FULLER (1654–1734). Comp., *Gnomologia: Adages and Proverbs,* 5876, 1732

Life teaches us to be less harsh with ourselves and with others.

> GOETHE (1749–1832). *Iphigenie auf Tauris,* 4.4, 1787

Judge not your neighbor till you've been in his place.

> HILLEL (1st cent. B.C.)
> See Understanding: Harper Lee

There is a tendency to judge a race, a nation or any distinct group by its least worthy members.

> ERIC HOFFER (1902–1983). *The True Believer: Thoughts on the Nature of Mass Movements,* 18, 1951

Judge not, that you be not judged. For with the judgment you pronounce you will be judged, and the measure you give will be the measure you get. Why do you see the speck that is in your brother's eye, but do not notice the log that is in your own eye?

> JESUS (A.D. 1st cent.). *Matthew* 7:1–3

He that is without sin among you, let him first cast a stone at her.

> JESUS (A.D. 1st cent.). Referring to "a woman taken in adultery," *John* 8:7 (King James Version)

As I know more of mankind, I expect less of them, and am ready now to call a man *a good man,* upon easier terms than I was formerly.

> SAMUEL JOHNSON (1709–1784). Near the end of his life, quoted by an unnamed friend, 1783. In James Boswell, *The Life of Samuel Johnson,* 1791

Everything that is unconscious in ourselves we discover in our neighbor, and we treat him accordingly. . . . What we combat in him is usually our own inferior side.

> CARL G. JUNG (1875–1961). *Modern Man in Search of a Soul,* 7, tr. W. S. Dell and Cary F. Baynes, 1933
> See Faults: Eric Hoffer

They judge lest they be judged.

> KARL KRAUS (1874–1936). "Lord, Forgive Them . . . ," *Half-Truths & One-and-a-Half Truths: Selected Aphorisms,* ed. Harry Zohn, 1976

Most people judge others simply by how prosperous or popular they are.

> LA ROCHEFOUCAULD (1613–1680). *Maxims,* 212, 1665, tr. Louis Kronenberger, 1959

The world is full of pots jeering at kettles.

> LA ROCHEFOUCAULD (1613–1680). *Maxims,* 507, 1665, tr. Leonard Tancock, 1959

I have never for one instant seen clearly within myself; how then would you have me judge the deeds of others.

> MAURICE MAETERLINCK (1862–1949). *Pelleas and Melisande,* 1.3, 1892

We are all inclined to judge ourselves by our ideals; others by their acts.

> HAROLD NICOLSON (1886–1968). Diary

Any man who has once declared the other man to be a fool, a bad fellow, is annoyed when that man ends by showing that he is not.

> FRIEDRICH NIETZSCHE (1844–1900). *Human, All Too Human,* 90, 1878, tr. Marion Faber, 1984

When a man points a finger at someone else, he should remember that four of his fingers are pointing at himself.

> LOUIS NIZER (1902–1994). Lawyer

All judgment is self-judgment.

> PAUL RICHARD (1874–1967). *The Scourge of Christ,* 5.5, 1929, ed. Michel Paul Richard, 1987

King Henry: Forbear to judge, for we are sinners all.

> SHAKESPEARE (1564–1616). *Henry VI,* Part II, 3.3.31, 1590
> See Guilt: Muhammad ○ Sin: Paul (1) ○ Sin: Solomon

There is no more mischievous absurdity than this judging of actions from the *outside* as they look to us, instead of from the *inside* as they look to the actors; nothing more irrational than to criticize deeds as though the doers of them had the same desires, hopes, fears, and restraints as ourselves.

> HERBERT SPENCER (1820–1903). *Social Statics,* 3.20.6, 1851

Judge every man in the most favorable light.

> *TALMUD* (A.D. 1st–6th cent.). Rabbinical writings. In Louis I. Newman, comp., *The Talmudic Anthology,* 166, 1945

❧

There is so much good in the worst of us,
And so much bad in the best of us,
That it hardly become any of us
To talk about the rest of us.

ANONYMOUS

People who live in glass houses shouldn't throw stones.

SAYING (ENGLISH)

He sees a louse as far away as China but not the elephant on his own nose.

SAYING (MALAY)

Before judging another, walk two moons in his moccasins.

SAYING (NATIVE AMERICAN)

See Understanding: Harper Lee

The sieve says to the needle, you have a hole in your tail.

SAYING

JUDGMENT

See also • Common Sense ○ Ideas ○ Intelligence ○ Memory: [especially] La Rochefoucauld ○ Mind ○ Reason ○ Thinking ○ Wisdom: [especially] Barbara W. Tuchman

Supreme judgment . . . is absolute and universal love that embraces everything and turns every antagonism into complementarity.

HERMAN AIHARA (1920–1998). "Supreme Judgment," 1985, *Kaleidoscope*, ed. Sandy Rothman, 1986

By a small sample we may judge of the whole piece.

CERVANTES (1547–1616). *Don Quixote*, 1.1.4, 1615, tr. Peter Anthony Motteux and John Ozell, 1743

Some to the fascination of a name
Surrender judgment hoodwink'd.

WILLIAM COWPER (1731–1800). *The Task*, 6.100, 1785

Distrust your judgment the moment you can discern the shadow of a personal motive in it.

MARIE von EBNER-ESCHENBACH (1830–1916). *Aphorisms*, p. 74, 1880–1905, tr. David Scrase and Wolfgang Mieder, 1994

Our judgments about things vary according to the time left us to live—that we think is left us to live.

ANDRÉ GIDE (1869–1951). Journal, 19 December 1930, tr. Justin O'Brien, 1951

The senses do not deceive; it is the judgment that deceives.

GOETHE (1749–1832). *The Maxims and Reflections of Goethe*, 346, tr. T. Bailey Saunders, 1892

A man should hear all parts ere he judge any.

JOHN HEYWOOD (1497?–1580?). Comp., *A Dialogue Containing the Number of the Effectual Proverbs in the English Tongue*, 1.13, 1562

Good judgment in our dealings with others consists not in seeing through deceptions and evil intentions but in being able to waken the decency dormant in every person.

ERIC HOFFER (1902–1983). *The Passionate State of Mind: And Other Aphorisms*, 141, 1954

Few things makes us feel finer than havin' our judgment vindicated.

KIN HUBBARD (1868–1930). *Abe Martin: Hoss Sense and Nonsense*, p. 106, 1926

A principle source of erroneous judgment [is] viewing things partially and only on *one side*.

SAMUEL JOHNSON (1709–1784). Quoted by Rev. Dr. Maxwell, 1770. In James Boswell, *The Life of Samuel Johnson*, 1791

Judgment, to estimate things at their true value.

SAMUEL JOHNSON (1709–1784). 16 April 1775. In James Boswell, *The Life of Samuel Johnson*, 1791

Only through the capacity to see all relevant factors, to weigh them fairly, and to place them in relation to each other, can we hope to reach an accurately balanced judgment.

B. H. LIDDELL HART (1895–1970). "The Scientific Approach," *Why Don't We Learn from History?* 1944

If we could know *where* we are, and *whither* we are tending, we could then better judge *what* to do, and *how* to do it.

ABRAHAM LINCOLN (1809–1865). Republican State Convention speech, Springfield (Illinois), 16 June 1858

Men only judge of matters by the result.

MACHIAVELLI (1469–1527). *The Discourses*, 3.35, 1517, tr. Christian E. Detmold, 1940]

To judge of great and lofty things we need a soul of the same caliber; otherwise we attribute to them the vice that is our own.

MONTAIGNE (1533–1592). "That the Taste of Good and Evil Depends in Large Part on the Opinion We Have of Them," *Essays*, 1588, tr. Donald M. Frame, 1958

Fear and Gain are great Perverters of Mankind, and where either prevails the Judgment is violated.

WILLIAM PENN (1644–1718). *Some Fruits of Solitude*, 127, 1693

Judgment is to be made of actions according to the times in which they were performed.

PLUTARCH (A.D. 46?–119?). "Poplicola and Colon Compared," *Parallel Lives*, Dryden edition, 1693

The number of those who go thro' the fatigue of judging for themselves is very small indeed!

RICHARD SHERIDAN (1751–1816). *The Critic*, 1.2, 1779

Judgment is the ability to think of many matters at once, in their interdependence, their related importance, and their consequences.

C. P. SNOW (1905–1980). In Barbara W. Tuchman, "Generalship," 1971, *Practicing History*, 1981

A man's judgment cannot be better than the information on which he has based it.

ARTHUR HAYS SULZBERGER (1891–1968). Speech before the New York State Publishers Association, 30 August 1948.

When god would change the course of a man's fortune, he corrupts his judgment.

VELLEIUS PATERCULUS (19? B.C.–A.D. 30?). *Historia Romana*, 2.118

❦

Judgment comes from experience, and great judgment comes from bad experience.

SAYING

JURIES

See also • Judges: Alexander Pope, Saying (Latin) (1) ○ Justice ○ Trials: [especially] Constitution of the United States

The court is obliged to submit the case fairly, but let the jury do the deciding, each according to its own judgment.

ANTON CHEKHOV (1860–1904). Letter to Alexei Suvorin, 27 October 1888, ed. Lillian Hellman, 1955

A jury consists of twelve persons chosen to decide who has the better lawyer.

ROBERT FROST (1874–1963)

A Fox should not be [on] the jury at a Goose's Trial.

THOMAS FULLER (1654–1734). Comp., *Gnomologia: Adages and Proverbs,* 116, 1732

I have not found juries specially inspired for the discovery of truth. . . . I have not found them freer from prejudice than an ordinary judge would be.

OLIVER WENDELL HOLMES, JR. (1841–1935). "Law in Science—Science in Law," *Collected Legal Papers,* 1921

It is better to toss up cross and pile [heads or tails] in a cause than to refer it to a judge whose mind is warped by any motive whatever, in that particular case. But the common sense of twelve honest men gives still a better chance of just decision than the hazard of cross and pile.

THOMAS JEFFERSON (1743–1826). *Notes on the State of Virginia,* 14, 1785

The jury system puts a ban upon intelligence and honesty, and a premium upon ignorance, stupidity and perjury.

MARK TWAIN (1835–1910). *Roughing It,* 48, 1872

JUSTICE

See also • Constitutions ○ Crime ○ Freedom ○ Golden Rule ○ Injustice ○ Judges ○ Judging Others ○ Juries ○ Law ○ Lawyers ○ Mercy ○ Morality ○ Peace: Anonymous (2) ○ Police ○ Prison ○ Punishment ○ Punishment, Capital ○ Revenge ○ Rights ○ Trials ○ Witnesses

The price of justice is eternal publicity.

ARNOLD BENNETT (1867–1931). "Secret Trials," *Things That Have Interested Me* (Second Series), 1923

See Liberty: John Philpot Curran

He who is only just is cruel; who
Upon the earth would live were all judged justly?

LORD BYRON (1788–1824). *Marino Faliero; Doge of Venice,* 5.1, 1821

Justice requires that everyone should have enough to eat. But it also requires that everyone should contribute to the production of food.

ELIAS CANETTI (1905–1994). "The Crowd in History: Distribution and Increase," *Crowds and Power,* tr. Carol Stewart, 1962

Justice which does not bear a sword beside its scales soon falls into ridicule.

CHARLES de GAULLE (1890–1970). *The Army of the Future,* 3.2, 1941

The greatest enemy of justice is privilege.

MARIE von EBNER-ESCHENBACH (1830–1916). *Aphorisms,* p. 45, 1880–1905, tr. David Scrase and Wolfgang Mieder, 1994

Wrong none by doing injuries, or omitting the benefits that are your duty.

BENJAMIN FRANKLIN (1706–1790). Virtue #8 ("Justice"), 1784, *Autobiography,* 1798

Those are ever the most ready to do justice to others, who feel that the world has done them justice.

WILLIAM HAZLITT (1778–1830). *Characteristics in the Manner of Rochefoucault's Maxims,* 12, 1823

They sow the wind,
  and they shall reap the whirlwind.

HOSEA (8th cent. B.C.). *Hosea* 8:7

Justice is indiscriminately due to all, without regard to numbers, wealth, or rank.

JOHN JAY (1745–1829). Supreme Court chief justice. *Georgia v. Brailsford,* 1794

The utmost excellence at which humanity can arrive is a constant and determinate pursuit of justice, without regard to present dangers or advantages; a continual reference of every action to the divine will.

SAMUEL JOHNSON (1709–1784). In *The Rambler,* English journal, 185, 24 December 1751

Justice is truth in action.

JOSEPH JOUBERT (1754–1824). *Pensées,* 203, 1838, tr. Henry Attwell, 1877

The best guarantee for justice in public dealings is the participation in their own government of the people most likely to suffer from injustice.

JOHN MORLEY (1838–1923). *On Compromise,* 3, 1877

Justice without might is helpless; might without justice is tyrannical.

BLAISE PASCAL (1623–1662). *Pensées,* 298, 1670, tr. William F. Trotter, 1931

Do not be deceived: God is not mocked, for whatever a man sows, that he will also reap.

PAUL (A.D. 1st cent.). *Galatians* 6:7

Of all the things of a man's soul which he has within him, justice is the greatest good and injustice the greatest evil.

PLATO (427?–347 B.C.). *The Republic,* 2.366–367, tr. Benjamin Jowett, 1894

We can best get justice by doing justice.

THEODORE ROOSEVELT (1858–1919). "National Duties," 2 September 1901, *The Strenuous Life: Essays and Addresses,* 1905

The first reward of justice is the consciousness that we are acting justly.

> ROUSSEAU (1712–1778). *Emile; or, Treatise on Education,* 4 ("The Creed of a Savoyard Priest"), 1762, tr. Barbara Foxley, 1911
>
> See Virtue: Pliny the Younger

That spirit of justice in every heart.

> ROUSSEAU (1712–1778). *Confessions,* 12 (1765), 1781, tr. J. M. Cohen, 1953

Do justice to your brother (you can do that, whether you love him or not), and you will come to love him. But do injustice to him because you don't love him, and you will come to hate him.

> JOHN RUSKIN (1819–1900). "Work," *The Crown of Wild Olive,* 1866

Anonymous: How can justice be secured in Athens?
Solon: If those who are not injured feel as indignant as those who are.

> SOLON (630?–560? B.C.). Format adapted. In Earl Warren, "The Law and the Future," *Fortune,* November 1955

Only the Wise are just.

> HENRY DAVID THOREAU (1817–1862). "Wednesday," *A Week on the Concord and Merrimack Rivers,* 1849

Everywhere there is one principle of justice, which is the interest of the stronger.

> THRASYMACHUS (4th cent. B.C.). In Plato (427?–347 B.C.). *The Republic,* 1.339, tr. Benjamin Jowett, 1894

Fairness, *n.* That impartiality and equity of treatment that everyone approves of, so long as their own interests are not threatened.

> EDMUND H. VOLKART (1919–). *The Angel's Dictionary: A Modern Tribute to Ambrose Bierce,* p. 78, 1986

Justice . . . will not be a powerful spring of action unless it extend[s] to the whole creation.

> MARY WOLLSTONECRAFT (1759–1797). *A Vindication of the Rights of Woman,* 12, 1792

There is no true justice unless mercy is part of it.

> ZOHAR (A.D. 13th cent.). Jewish mystical writings. In Louis I. Newman, comp., *The Talmudic Anthology,* 167, 1945
>
> See Mercy: Vauvenargues

Equal Justice Under Law.

> ANONYMOUS. Inscription on the West Portico of the Supreme Court Building, Washington

Justice in the life and conduct of the state is possible only as first resides in the hearts and souls of the citizens.

> ANONYMOUS. Inscription on the Department of Justice Building, Washington

Justice the Guardian of Liberty.

> ANONYMOUS. Inscription on the East Portico of the Supreme Court Building, Washington

Let your love of justice be exceeded only by your love of mercy.

> ANONYMOUS

One hour in the execution of justice is worth seventy years of prayer.

> SAYING (ISLAMIC). In John Ruskin, "Work," *The Crown of Wild Olive,* 1866

They who sow the wind shall reap the typhoon.

> SAYING (PHILIPPINE)

KILLING

See also • Abortion ○ Assassination ○ Crime ○ Death ○ Euthanasia ○ Guilt: David Webb Peoples ○ Holocaust ○ Murder ○ Suicide ○ Violence

Do not receive overtures of peace or submission. . . . Kill every male Indian over twelve years of age.

> PATRICK E. CONNOR (1820–1891). General. Order to his troops, Platte River campaign, 1865

Mike Wallace: You killed at least one man . . . How many more?
Cohen: Well, I have killed no man, in the first place, that didn't deserve killing.

> MICKEY COHEN. Gangster. Wallace television interview, 1957, excerpted in *Mike Wallace Remembers,* CBS, 11 September 1997

What no human soul desires there is no need to prohibit; it is automatically excluded. The very emphasis of the commandment, *Thou shalt not kill,* makes it certain that we spring from an endless ancestry of murderers, with whom the lust for killing was in the blood, as possibly it is to this day with ourselves.

> SIGMUND FREUD (1856–1939). "Reflections upon War and Death" (2), 1915, tr. E. Colburn Mayne, *Character and Culture,* 1963

There's no difference between one's killing and making decisions that will send others to kill. It's exactly the same thing, or even worse.

> GOLDA MEIR (1898–1978). Interview, 1974

We kill because we are afraid of our own shadow, afraid that if we used a little common sense we'd have to admit that our glorious principles were wrong.

HENRY MILLER (1891–1980). "The Alcoholic Veteran with the Washboard Cranium," *The Wisdom of the Heart,* 1941

You shall not kill.

MOSES (14th cent. B.C.). The Sixth Commandment, *Exodus* 20:13

Collot d'Herbois committed atrocities in Lyons. It is inconceivable how he could order the shooting of five or six thousand individuals: certainly, in a city like Lyons, the execution of fifty or sixty ringleaders would have been more than enough.

NAPOLEON (1769–1821). Remark to Gen. Gaspard Gourgaud, 1817, *The Mind of Napoleon: A Selection from His Written and Spoken Words,* 224, ed. J. Christopher Herold, 1955

No hatred! no, no hatred! Eliminate as a matter of principle!

PIERRE-JOSEPH PROUDHON (1809–1865). In Hal Draper, "A Note on the Father of Anarchism," *New Politics,* Winter 1969

When I put a question to [Lenin] about socialism in agriculture, he explained with glee how he had incited the poorer peasants against the richer ones, "and they soon hanged them from the nearest tree—ha! ha! ha!" His guffaw at the thought of those massacred made my blood run cold.

BERTRAND RUSSELL (1872–1970). Referring to a 1920 interview in Moscow, "Eminent Men I Have Known," *Unpopular Essays,* 1950

To take life is always to die a little.

JOHN WAIN (1925–1994). "A Song about Major Eatherly" (2), *Weep Before Gods,* 1961

KINDNESS

See also • Compassion ○ Enlightenment: Anonymous (1) ○ Faith: Muhammad ○ Fate: Nguyen T. Nguyen ○ Giving ○ Love: Robert Louis Stevenson ○ Mercy ○ Pity ○ Strangers: Tennessee Williams ○ Sympathy ○ Wisdom: *Talmud*

Shall we make a new rule of life from tonight: always to try to be a little kinder than is necessary?

J. M. BARRIE (1860–1937). *The Little White Bird,* 4, 1902

A great many people do many things that seem to be inspired more by a spirit of ostentation than by heartfelt kindness. . . . Such a pose is nearer akin to hypocrisy than to generosity or moral goodness.

CICERO (106–43 B.C.). *De officiis,* 1.14, tr. Walter Miller, 1913

If thou hast done a Man great Kindnesses, endeavor not therefore to insult him and govern him, for that would cancel all Courtesy.

THOMAS FULLER (1654–1734). Comp., *Introductio ad Prudentiam,* 765, 1731

A forced Kindness deserves no Thanks.

THOMAS FULLER (1654–1734). Comp., *Gnomologia: Adages and Proverbs,* 113, 1732

True kindness presupposes the faculty of imagining as one's own the sufferings and joy of others.

ANDRÉ GIDE (1869–1951). "Portraits and Aphorisms: An Unprejudiced Mind" (1), 1931, *Pretexts: Reflections on Literature and Morality,* ed. Justin O'Brien, 1959

Random Kindness and Senseless Acts of Beauty.

ANNE HERBERT and MARGARET PAVEL. Book title, 1993

If the instinctual and repressed kindness of mankind were suddenly let loose upon the earth, sooner than we think would we be members one of another, sitting around one family hearthstone, and singing the song of the new humanity.

GEORGE D. HERRON (1862–1925). In Upton Sinclair, ed., *The Cry for Justice: An Anthology of the Literature of Social Protest,* 16, 1915

Kindness can become its own motive. We are made kind by being kind.

ERIC HOFFER (1902–1983). *The Passionate State of Mind: And Other Aphorisms,* 123, 1954

In this world, you must be a bit too kind in order to be kind enough.

PIERRE MARIVAUX (1688–1763). *Le Jeu de l'amour et du hasard,* 1730

Whoever is kind to His creatures, God is kind to him.

MUHAMMAD (570?–A.D. 632). *The Sayings of Muhammad,* 252, tr. Abdullah Al-Suhrawardy, 1941

Do the thing you believe in. Do the best you can in the place where you are and be kind.

SCOTT NEARING (1883–1983). On Helen Nearing "Twilight and Evening Star," *Loving and Leaving the Good Life,* 1992

See Effort: Theodore Roosevelt ○ Good: John Wesley

What is it to practice benevolence? It is to imitate the Deity.

PUBLIUS SYRUS (85–43 B.C.). *Moral Sayings,* 784, tr. Darius Lyman, Jr., 1862

Deeds of kindness are equal in weight to all the commandments.

TALMUD (A.D. 1st–6th cent.). Rabbinical writings. In Louis I. Newman, comp., *The Talmudic Anthology,* 177, 1945

In hours of weariness, sensations sweet,
Felt in the blood, and felt along the heart;
And passing even into my purer mind,
With tranquil restoration—feelings too
Of unremembered pleasure: such, perhaps,
As have no slight or trivial influence
On that best portion of a good man's life,
His little, nameless, unremembered, acts
Of kindness and of love.

WILLIAM WORDSWORTH (1770–1850). "Lines Composed a Few Miles Above Tintern Abbey," l. 27, 1798

❦

Throughout this toilsome world, alas!
Once and only once I pass;
If a kindness I may show,
If a good deed I may do
To a suffering fellow man,
Let me do it while I can.
No delay, for it is plain
I shall not pass this way again.

ANONYMOUS. "I Shall Not Pass This Way Again" (complete poem). In Hazel Felleman, ed., *The Best Loved Poems of the American People,* 1936

Kindness expiates a multitude of sins.
> ANONYMOUS

Kindness begets kindness.
> SAYING (SWEDISH)

KINGS

See also • Assassination: Ralph Waldo Emerson ○ Leaders ○ Philosophers: Immanuel Kant, Plato (1) ○ Presidents ○ Princes ○ Rulers ○ Tyrants

I am,
indeed,
a king,
because I know how
to rule myself.
> PIETRO ARETINO (1492–1557). Letter to Agostino Ricchi, 10 May 1537

That the king can do no wrong is a necessary and fundamental principle of the English constitution.
> WILLIAM BLACKSTONE (1723–1780). *Commentaries on the Laws of England,* 3.17, 1765-1769
> See Presidents: Richard M. Nixon (3)

I'm king of the world.
> JAMES CAMERON (1954–). 1997 Academy Award (best director, for the film *Titanic*), acceptance speech, Los Angeles, 23 March 1998

The love of the subjects is the safety of the King.
> JOHN CLARKE (1596–1658). Comp., *Proverbs: English and Latine,* p. 279, 1639
> See Assassination: George Washington

How fatal 'tis to be too good a king!
> JOHN DRYDEN (1631–1700). *Absalom and Achitophel,* 1.812, 1681

I have found it impossible to carry the heavy burden of responsibility and to discharge my duties as King as I would wish to do without the help and support of the woman I love.
> EDWARD VIII (1894–1972). British king. Abdication speech, 11 December 1936

We should be all kings and all queens.
> RALPH WALDO EMERSON (1803–1882). Journal, 18 June 1839

In the country of the blind, the one-eyed man is king.
> DESIDERIUS ERASMUS (1466–1536). *Adagia,* 3.4.96, 1508

Weak kings are subject to flashes of temper
Ruled by their emotion. So are strong ones.
> GAVIN EWART. "The Law Allows Cruel Experiments on Friendly Animals," *The Pleasures of the Flesh,* 1966

In a few years there will be only five kings in the world—the king of England and the four kings in a pack of cards.
> FAROUK (1920–1965). In William H. Attwood, "The Problem King of Egypt," *Life,* 10 April 1950

Kings have no Power over Souls.
> THOMAS FULLER (1654–1734). Comp., *Gnomologia: Adages and Proverbs,* 3130, 1732

Sail, quoth the King; hold, saith the Wind.
> THOMAS FULLER (1654–1734). Comp., *Gnomologia: Adages and Proverbs,* 4064, 1732

Of the various forms of government which have prevailed in the world, an hereditary monarchy seems to present the fairest scope for ridicule.
> EDWARD GIBBON (1737–1794). *The Decline and Fall of the Roman Empire,* 7, 1776-1788

The greatest slave in a kingdom is generally the king of it.
> FULKE GREVILLE (1554–1628). *Maxims, Characters, and Reflections,* p. 175, 1756

The Royal Crown cures not the headache.
> GEORGE HERBERT (1593–1633). Comp., *Outlandish Proverbs,* 576, 1640

'Twixt kings and tyrants there's this difference known:
Kings seek their subjects' good, tyrants their own.
> ROBERT HERRICK (1591–1674). "Kings and Tyrants," *Hesperides: or Works Both Humane and Divine,* 1648

We cannot all be kings here; and mob rule is a bad thing. Let there be one commander only, one King, set over us by Zeus.
> HOMER (8th? cent. B.C.). *The Iliad,* 2.203, tr. E. V. Rieu, 1950

Kings are for nations in their swaddling clothes.
> VICTOR HUGO (1802–1885). French Constituent Assembly speech, 1848

There is no king, who, with a sufficient force, is not always ready to make himself absolute.
> THOMAS JEFFERSON (1743–1826). Letter to George Wythe, 13 August 1786

Kings are accountable for injustice permitted as well as done.
> SAMUEL JOHNSON (1709–1784). *Rasselas: The Prince of Abyssinia,* 8, 1759

You don't kill the king unless you've got an heir apparent.
> CHARLES KRAUTHAMMER (1950–). Commentator. *Inside Washington,* television news program, PBS, 22 June 1997

It is legal because I wish it.
> LOUIS XIV (1638–1546). French king
> See Presidents: Richard M. Nixon (3)

On the loftiest throne in the world we are still sitting only on our own rump.
> MONTAIGNE (1533–1592). "Of Experience," *Essays,* 1588, tr. Donald M. Frame, 1958

In China the sovereign is worshipped as a god. That I think is how it ought to be.
> NAPOLEON (1769–1821). *Talks of Napoleon at St. Helena* (with Gen. Gaspard Gourgaud), 5, tr. Elizabeth Wormeley Latimer, 1904

[Monarchy is] the gold filling in a mouth of decay.
> JOHN OSBORNE (1929–1994). In Bernard Levin, *The Pendulum Years: Britain and the Sixties,* 19, 1970

Of more worth is one honest man to society and in the sight of God than all the crowned ruffians that ever lived.

THOMAS PAINE (1737–1809). "Of Monarchy and Hereditary Succession,"
Common Sense, 1776

Tyranny is the wretchedest form of government and the rule of a king the happiest.

PLATO (427?–347 B.C.). *The Republic,* 9.576, tr. Benjamin Jowett, 1894

A king can stand people's fighting, but he can't last long if people start thinking.

WILL ROGERS (1879–1935). 30 September 1923, *The Autobiography of Will Rogers,* ed. Donald Day, 1949

The first art of kings [is] the power to suffer hatred.

SENECA THE YOUNGER (5? B.C.–A.D. 65). *Hercules Furens,* l. 350, tr. Frank Justus Miller, 1917

King Henry: Uneasy lies the head that wears a crown.

SHAKESPEARE (1564–1616). *Henry IV,* Part II, 3.1.31, 1597

Kings are not born: they are made by universal hallucination.

GEORGE BERNARD SHAW (1856–1950). "Maxims for Revolutionists: Royalty," *Man and Superman,* 1903

Vulgarity in a king flatters the majority of the nation.

GEORGE BERNARD SHAW (1856–1950). "Maxims for Revolutionists: Royalty," *Man and Superman,* 1903

Anonymous: Sparta is preserved because the kings are fitted to rule.
Theopompus: No, it is rather because the people are fitted to obey.

THEOPOMPUS (8th? cent. B.C.). Spartan king. Format adapted. In Plutarch (A.D. 46?–119?). "Precepts of Statecraft," 20, *Moralia,* vol. 10, tr. W. C. Helmbold, 1936

All kings is mostly rapscallions as fur as I can make out.

MARK TWAIN (1835–1910). *The Adventures of Huckleberry Finn,* 23, 1884

The institution of Royalty in any form is an insult to the human race.

MARK TWAIN (1835–1910). 12 September 1888, *Mark Twain's Notebook,* ed. Albert Bigelow Paine, 1935

The first king was a successful soldier.

VOLTAIRE (1694–1778). *Mérope,* 1.3, 1743

The king reigns but does not rule.

JAN ZAMOYSKI. On King Sigismund III, speech in Polish Parliament, 1605

☙

God is the king of all the earth.

ANONYMOUS (*BIBLE*). *Psalms* 47:7

Better a good king than an old law.

SAYING (DANISH)

Kings have long arms and many eyes and ears.

SAYING (ITALIAN)

If the king says at noonday, "It is night," the wise man says, "Behold the stars!"

SAYING (PERSIAN)

The greatest king must at last be put to bed with a shovel.

SAYING (RUSSIAN)

By the king's example the realm is ruled.

SAYING (SPANISH)

The king needs no unwilling subject.

SAYING

KISSING

See also • Films: Pauline Kael (2) ○ Sex ○ Youth: Shakespeare (1)

A long, long kiss, a kiss of youth, and love,
    And beauty, all concentrating like rays
Into one focus, kindled from above.
    Such kisses as belong to early days,
Where heart, and soul, and sense, in concert move,
    And the blood's lava, and the pulse ablaze,
Each kiss a heart-quake—for a kiss's strength,
I think it must be reckon'd by its length .

LORD BYRON (1788–1824). *Don Juan,* 2.186, 1819–1824

I never knew it could be like this. Nobody ever kissed me like this.

JAMES EARL JONES (1921–1977) (DANIEL TARADASH, scriptwriter). *From Here to Eternity* (film), 1953, spoken by Deborah Kerr to Burt Lancaster

The slowest kiss makes too much haste.

THOMAS MIDDLETON (1570?–1627). *A Chaste Maid in Cheapside,* 4, 1607

A kiss on the cheek may be quite continental,
But diamonds are a girl's best friend.

LEO ROBIN (1899–1984). "Diamonds Are a Girl's Best Friend" (song). In the musical *Gentleman Prefer Blonds,* 1949

There's a line between love and fascination
That's hard to see on an evening such as this,
For they both give the very same sensation
When you're lost in the magic of a kiss.

NED WASHINGTON (1901–1976). "My Foolish Heart" (song), 1949

KNAVES

See also • Corruption ○ Crime ○ Fools ○ Rogues ○ Scoundrels ○ Stupidity: Woodrow Wilson

A knave is one who disobeys the imperatives of conscience; a fool is one who cannot hear or understand them.

W. H. AUDEN (1907–1973). "Balaam and His Ass" (7), *The Dyer's Hand and Other Essays,* 1962

There are more Fools than Knaves in the World, Else the Knaves would not have enough to live upon.

SAMUEL BUTLER (1612–1680). "Sundry Thoughts," *Prose Observations,* ed. Hugh de Quehen, 1979

Great and Notorious Cheats, that do their business to the Purpose and grow rich by their frauds and Impostures, rather gain than lose Credit by it; for men are trusted and esteemed in the world [for] what they have, not what they are.

> SAMUEL BUTLER (1612–1680). "Unclassified Prose Observations from the Butler's Manuscript," *Prose Observations*, ed. Hugh de Quehen, 1979
>
> See Esteem: Ralph Waldo Emerson ○ Possessions: Henri Amiel

More knave than fool.

> CERVANTES (1547–1616). *Don Quixote*, 1.4.4, 1615, tr. Peter Anthony Motteux and John Ozell, 1743

No greater curse in life can be found than knavery that wears the mask of wisdom.

> CICERO (106–43 B.C.). *De officiis*, 3.17, tr. Walter Miller, 1913

Surely nobody would be a charlatan who could afford to be sincere.

> RALPH WALDO EMERSON (1803–1882). "Politics," *Essays: Second Series*, 1844

Knaves and Fools divide the World.

> THOMAS FULLER (1654–1734). Comp., *Gnomologia: Adages and Proverbs*, 3133, 1732

Knaves are in such Repute that honest Men are accounted Fools.

> THOMAS FULLER (1654–1734). Comp., *Gnomologia: Adages and Proverbs*, 3134, 1732

Knaves imagine nothing can be done without Knavery.

> THOMAS FULLER (1654–1734). Comp., *Gnomologia: Adages and Proverbs*, 3135, 1732

Who friendship with a knave has made
Is judg'd a partner in the trade.

> JOHN GAY (1685–1732). *Fables*, 1.23, 1727–1738

All men are frauds. The only difference between them is that some admit it. I myself deny it.

> H. L. MENCKEN (1880–1956). *A Little Book in C Major*, 2.16, 1916

I defy anyone to trick me. Men would have to be exceptional rascals to be as bad as I assume them to be.

> NAPOLEON (1769–1821). Remark to Gen. Gaspard Gourgaud, 1816, *The Mind of Napoleon: A Selection from His Written and Spoken Words*, 5, ed. J. Christopher Herold, 1955

You're a one-eyed jack 'roun here, Dad. I seen the other side of your face.

> CHARLES NEIDER (GUY TROSPER, and CALDER WILLINGHAM, scriptwriters). *One-Eyed Jacks* (film), 1961, spoken by Marlon Brando to Karl Malden

KNOWLEDGE

See also • Books ○ Computers ○ Creativity: Charlie Rose ○ Curiosity ○ Democracy: James Madison (3) ○ Education: [especially] Alfred North Whitehead (1) ○ Facts ○ Good & Evil: Socrates ○ Ignorance ○ Imagination: Albert Einstein ○ Information: [especially] John Naisbitt ○ Intellectuals ○ Intelligence ○ Intelligence, Military ○ Learning (Knowledge) ○ Learning (Process) ○ Paradoxes: *Upanishads* ○ Philosophy ○ Reading ○ Scholars ○ Self-Knowledge: [especially] Richard of Saint-Victor ○ Study ○ Teaching ○ Truth ○ The Unconscious: Friedrich Nietzsche ○ University ○ Wisdom ○ Wisdom & Knowledge

In the Buddhist scriptures there is [an] analogy. Take a mountain that is eight billion miles high. Suppose a bird takes a cloth made of the finest silk in its beak, and every 100,000 years flies over that mountain, allowing the silk cloth to brush the very tip of the mountain as it flies over. The amount of time it will take the bird to make the mountain disappear is how long it will take an individual to know all the knowledge there is to be known.

> PANDIT USHARBUDH ARYA (1934–). "Maxims on Universal Laws," *Dawn*, vol. 6, no. 1, 1986

Knowledge itself is power.

> FRANCIS BACON (1561–1626). "De Haeresibus," *Meditationes Sacrae*, 1597
>
> See Character: Booker T. Washington ○ Language: Adrienne Rich ○ Opinion: Thomas Jefferson (2) ○ Wealth: Henry David Thoreau

Some men covet knowledge out of a natural curiosity and inquisitive temper; some to entertain the mind with variety and delight; some for ornament and reputation; some for victory and contention; many for lucre and a livelihood; and but few for employing the Divine gift of reason to the use and benefit of mankind.

> FRANCIS BACON (1561–1626). *Advancement of Learning*, 1, 1605, Willey Book edition, 1944

Knowledge is like waters; some descend from the heavens, some spring from the earth. For all knowledge proceeds from a twofold source—either from divine inspiration or external sense.

> FRANCIS BACON (1561–1626). *Advancement of Learning*, 3.1, 1605, Willey Book edition, 1944

Knowledge of the universe would somehow be . . . defective were no practical results to follow.

> CICERO (106–43 B.C.). *De officiis*, 1.43, tr. Walter Miller, 1913

A strong argument that men's knowledge antedates their birth is the fact that mere children, in studying difficult subjects, so quickly lay hold upon innumerable things that they seem not to be . . . learning . . . for the first time, but to be recalling.

> CICERO (106–43 B.C.). *De senectute*, 21, tr. William Armstead Falconer, 1959

When you know a thing, to hold that you know it; and when you do not know a thing, to allow that you do not know it—this is knowledge.

> CONFUCIUS (551–479 B.C.). *Confucian Analects*, 2.17, tr. James Legge, 1930

Depend on it there comes a time when for every addition of knowledge you forget something that you knew before. It is of the highest importance, therefore, not to have useless facts elbowing out the useful ones.

> SIR ARTHUR CONAN DOYLE (1859–1930). *A Study in Scarlet*, 2, 1888

My name is Sherlock Holmes. It is my business to know what other people don't know.

> SIR ARTHUR CONAN DOYLE (1859–1930). "The Adventure of a Carbuncle," *The Adventures of Sherlock Holmes*, 1892

A man should keep his little brain attic stocked with all the furniture that he is likely to use, and the rest he can put away in the lumber room of his library, where he can get it if he wants it.

SIR ARTHUR CONAN DOYLE (1859–1930). "The Five Orange Pips," *The Adventures of Sherlock Holmes,* 1892

Now at midnight all the agents
And the superhuman crew
Come out and round up everyone
That knows more than they do.

BOB DYLAN (1941–). "Desolation Row" (song), 1965

You have first an instinct, then an opinion, then a knowledge, as the plant has root, bud, and fruit.

RALPH WALDO EMERSON (1803–1882). Journal, 21 July 1836

An Indian has his knowledge for use, and it only appears in use. Most white men that we know have theirs for talking purposes.

RALPH WALDO EMERSON (1803–1882). Journal, August 1857

There is no other source of knowledge but the intellectual manipulation of carefully verified observations—in fact, what is called research . . . and no knowledge can be obtained from revelation, intuition, or inspiration. [Ellipsis points in original.]

SIGMUND FREUD (1856–1939). *New Introductory Lectures on Psychoanalysis,* 35, 1933. In Helen Walker Puner, *Freud: His Life and His Mind,* 13, 1947
See Science: Freud (1)

Action is the proper Fruit of Knowledge.

THOMAS FULLER (1654–1734). Comp., *Gnomologia: Adages and Proverbs,* 760, 1732

What is word knowledge but a shadow of wordless knowledge?

KAHLIL GIBRAN (1883–1931). "The Farewell," *The Prophet,* 1923

Philosophy have I digested,
The whole of Law and Medicine,
From each its secrets I have wrested,
Theology, alas, thrown in.
Poor fool, with all this sweated lore,
I stand no wiser than I was before.

GOETHE (1749–1832). *Faust,* 1 ("Night. Faust's Study," 1), 1808–1832, tr. Philip Wayne, 1959

The condition of mankind is to be weary of what we do know and afraid of what we do not.

MARQUIS OF HALIFAX (1633–1695). "Of the World," *Political, Moral and Miscellaneous Reflections,* 1750

"Knowledge Is Money."

JOHN R. HAYES. Article title, *Forbes,* 13 February 1995

Knowledge is pleasure as well as power.

WILLIAM HAZLITT (1778–1830). "On Imitation," *The Round Table,* 1817

Wonder, rather than doubt, is the root of knowledge.

ABRAHAM JOSHUA HESCHEL (1907–1872). *Man Is Not Alone,* 2, 1951

Far more crucial than what we know or do not know is what we do not want to know.

ERIC HOFFER (1902–1983). *The Passionate State of Mind: And Other Aphorisms,* 38, 1954

It is not a question how much a man knows, but what use he can make of what he knows.

JOSIAH GILBERT HOLLAND (1819–1881). "Self-Help," *Plain Talks on Familiar Subjects,* 1866

In spiritual matters, knowledge is dependent upon being; as we are, so we know.

ALDOUS HUXLEY (1894–1963). "Words and Reality." In Christopher Isherwood, ed., *Vedanta for the Western World,* 1945

If a little knowledge is dangerous, where is the man who has so much as to be out of danger?

T. H. HUXLEY (1825–1895). "On Elementary Instruction in Physiology," 1877, *Collected Essays,* vol. 3, 1895

Knowledge is of two kinds. We know a subject ourselves, or we know where we can find information upon it.

SAMUEL JOHNSON (1709–1784). 18 April 1775. In James Boswell, *The Life of Samuel Johnson,* 1791

The acquisition of knowledge for which no use can be found is a sure method of driving a man to revolt.

GUSTAVE LE BON (1841–1931). *The Crowd,* 2.1.5, 1895, Viking Press edition, 1960

A complacent satisfaction with present knowledge is the chief bar to the pursuit of knowledge.

B. H. LIDDELL HART (1895–1970). *The Ghost of Napoleon,* 4.3, 1933

No man's knowledge here can go beyond his experience.

JOHN LOCKE (1632–1704). *An Essay Concerning Human Understanding,* 2.1.19, 1690 ed. Alexander Campbell Fraser, 1894

The only Fence against the World is a thorough Knowledge of it.

JOHN LOCKE (1632–1704). *Some Thoughts Concerning Education,* 94, 1693

Practice, knowledge, again practice, and again knowledge. This form repeats itself in endless cycles, and with each cycle the content of practice and knowledge rises to a higher level.

MAO TSE-TUNG (1893–1976). "On Practice," July 1937, *Selected Works of Mao Tse-tung,* Foreign Languages Press edition, vol. 1, 1965

As knowledge increases, wonder deepens.

CHARLES MORGAN (1894–1958). English writer

The acquisition of knowledge is a duty incumbent on every Muslim, male and female.

MUHAMMAD (A.D. 570?–632). *The Sayings of Muhammad,* 289, tr. Abdullah Al-Suhrawardy, 1941

Acquire knowledge. It enables its possessor to distinguish right from wrong; it lights the way to Heaven; it is our friend in the desert, our society in solitude, our companion when friendless; it guides us to happiness; it sustains us in misery; it is an ornament among friends and an armor against enemies.

MUHAMMAD (A.D. 570?–632). *The Sayings of Muhammad,* 290, tr. Abdullah Al-Suhrawardy, 1941

Most of our positive knowledge has passed through a filter devised to eliminate those aspects of experience that reveal autonomous and purposeful activities, not characteristic of purely physical systems.

> LEWIS MUMFORD (1895–1990). *The Transformations of Man,* 9.4, 1956

To arrive at knowledge slowly, by one's own experience, is better than to learn by rote, in a hurry, facts that other people know, and then, be glutted with words, to lose one's own free, observant and inquisitive ability to study.

> JOHANN HEINRICH PESTALOZZI (1746–1827). *The Education of Man: Aphorisms,* 4, tr. Heinz and Ruth Norden, 1951

Knowledge is the food of the soul.

> PLATO (427?–347 B.C.). *Protagoras,* 313, tr. Benjamin Jowett, 1894

Knowledge which is acquired under compulsion obtains no hold on the mind.

> PLATO (427?–347 B.C.). *The Republic,* 7.536, tr. Benjamin Jowett, 1894

Knowledge without conscience is but the ruin of the soul.

> RABELAIS (1493?–1553). *Gargantua and Pantagruel,* 2.8, 1532–1552, tr. J. M. Cohen, 1955

The pursuit of knowledge is, I think, mainly actuated by love of power.

> BERTRAND RUSSELL (1872–1970). *Human Society in Ethics and Politics,* 2.2, 1962

A library may be very large; but if it is in disorder, it is not so useful as one that is small but well arranged. In the same way, a man may have a great mass of knowledge, but if he has not worked it up by thinking it over for himself, it has much less value than a far smaller amount which he has thoroughly pondered.

> ARTHUR SCHOPENHAUER (1788–1860). "The Art of Literature: On Thinking for One's Self," *Essays of Arthur Schopenhauer,* tr. T. Bailey Saunders, 1851

Those who think they know it all are very annoying to those who do.

> SHEETZ'S RUMINATION. In John Peers, comp., *1,001 Logical Laws,* p. 119, 1979

Our knowledge is a little island in a great ocean of non-knowledge.

> ISAAC BASHEVIS SINGER (1904–1991). Richard Burgin interview, *New York Times Magazine,* 3 December 1978

Any piece of knowledge which the pupil has himself acquired, any problem which he has himself solved, becomes by virtue of the conquest much more thoroughly his than it could else be. The preliminary activity of mind which his success implies, the concentration of thought necessary to it, and the excitement consequent on his triumph, conspire to register all the facts in his memory in a way that no mere information heard from a teacher or read in a school book can be registered.

> HERBERT SPENCER (1820–1903). *Education: Intellectual, Moral, and Physical,* 2, 1860

When a man's knowledge is not in order, the more knowledge he has, the greater will be his confusion.

> HERBERT SPENCER (1820–1903). *The Principles of Sociology,* 1876–1896

Knowledge is seeing the oneness of the Self with God.

> SRIMAD BHAGAVATAM (5th? cent. B.C.). Hindu scriptures. In *The Wisdom of God,* tr. Swami Prabhavananda, 1943

If we value the pursuit of knowledge, we must be free to follow wherever that search may lead us.

> ADLAI E. STEVENSON (1900–1965). Speech, University of Wisconsin, Madison, 8 October 1952

Knowledge . . . serves as a wealth and force multiplier. It can be used to augment the available force or wealth, or alternately, to reduce the amount needed to achieve any given purpose. In either case, it increases efficiency, permitting one to spend fewer power "chips" in any showdown.

> ALVIN TOFFLER (1928–). *Powershift: Knowledge, Wealth, and Violence at the Edge of the 21st Century,* 2, 1990
> See Power: Toffler (2)

He knows who says: we do not know.

> UPANISHADS (10th?–6th? cent. B.C.). Hindu scriptures. In Vinoba Bhave, *Thoughts on Education,* 1, tr. Marjorie Sykes, 1964
> See Ignorance: Socrates

Beware you be not swallowed up in books: an ounce of love is worth a pound of knowledge.

> JOHN WESLEY (1703–1791). Letter to Joseph Benson, 7 November 1768

True knowledge leads to love.

> WILLIAM WORDSWORTH (1770–1850). "Lines Left upon a Seat in a Yew-tree," l. 60, 1798

❦

When you eat of [the fruit of the tree] your eyes will be opened, and you will be like God, knowing good and evil.

> ANONYMOUS (*BIBLE*). Referring to "the tree of the knowledge of good and evil" (*Genesis* 2:17), commonly known as "the tree of knowledge," *Genesis* 3:5

A loving heart is the beginning of all Knowledge.

> ANONYMOUS. In Thomas Carlyle, "Biography," 1832, *Critical and Miscellaneous Essays,* Carey & Hart edition, 1849

Knowledge leads either to reverence or arrogance.

> ANONYMOUS

You can never know too little of what is not worth knowing.

> ANONYMOUS

KOREAN WAR

See also • Intelligence, Military: H. A. de Weerd ○ International Relations ○ War

The wrong war, at the wrong place, at the wrong time, and with the wrong enemy.

> OMAR N. BRADLEY (1893–1981). On the Korean War, testimony before a Senate committee, 15 May 1951

The Korean War began in a way in which wars often begin: a potential aggressor miscalculated.

> JOHN FOSTER DULLES (1888–1959). Speech, St. Louis, 2 September 1953

I shall go to Korea and try to end the war.

> DWIGHT D. EISENHOWER (1890–1969). Speech, Detroit Masonic
> Auditorium, 24 October 1952. After winning the election, Pres.
> Eisenhower visited Korea (2–5 December 1952).

We shall land at Inchon, and I shall crush them.

> DOUGLAS MacARTHUR (1880–1964). To the Joint Chiefs of Staff, Tokyo,
> 23 August 1950

The boys will be home by Christmas.

> DOUGLAS MacARTHUR (1880–1964). November 1950. In Harry S.
> Truman, *Memoirs: Years of Trial and Hope,* 24, 1956
>
> See World War I: Wilhelm II (2)

I could have won the war in Korea in a maximum of ten days,
once the campaign was under way, and with considerably fewer
casualties than were suffered during the so-called truce period. It
would have altered the course of history.

The enemy's air [*sic*] would first have been taken out. I would
have dropped between thirty and fifty tactical atomic bombs on
his air bases and other depots strung across that neck of
Manchuria from just across the Yalu [River].

> DOUGLAS MacARTHUR (1880–1964). Part of his plan for ending the
> Korean War following the entry of Chinese forces in November 1951,
> remarks to the author, 26 January 1954. In Bob Considine, *General
> Douglas MacArthur,* p. 114, 1964

We want you to feel unhampered tactically and strategically to
proceed north of the 38th Parallel.

> GEORGE C. MARSHALL (1880–1959). Secretary of defense. This decision
> (following the Inchon landing and the expulsion of North Korean
> forces from South Korea) led to Chinese intervention and a prolonga-
> tion of the war. "Your-eyes-only" cable to Douglas MacArthur, late
> September 1950. In William Manchester, *American Caesar: Douglas
> MacArthur: 1880–1964,* 9, 1978. The 38th Parallel, halfway down the
> peninsula, separated the two Koreas.

The attack on [South] Korea makes it plain that beyond all doubt
communism has passed beyond the use of subversion to conquer
independent nations and will now use armed invasion and war.

> HARRY S. TRUMAN (1884–1972). Public statement on his orders commit-
> ting U.S. forces to the defense of South Korea against North Korea's
> invasion, 27 June 1950

With deep regret, I have concluded that General of the Army
Douglas MacArthur is unable to give his wholehearted support to
the policies of the United States Government and of the United
Nations in matters pertaining to his official duties.

> HARRY S. TRUMAN (1884–1972). Opening paragraph of his public
> statement relieving Gen. MacArthur of his command in the Far East,
> 11 April 1951

Just how sensitive and on edge the world had become [over the
possibility of the Korean War leading to a general war] was
demonstrated when the words "atomic bomb" were mentioned at
my press conference on November 30 [1951].

At the conference I made the remark that "we will take whatever steps are necessary to meet the military situation, just as we
always have."

"Will that include the atomic bomb?" one of the reporters asked.

"That includes every weapon we have," I replied.

"Mr. President," the questioner shot back, "you said 'every
weapon that we have.' Does that mean that there is active consideration of the use of the atomic bomb?"

"There has always been active consideration of its use," I told
him. "I don't want to see it used. It is a terrible weapon, and it
should not be used on innocent men, women, and children who
have nothing whatever to do with this military aggression. That
happens when it is used."

> HARRY S. TRUMAN (1884–1972). *Memoirs: Years of Trial and Hope,* 25,
> 1956. Soon after the press conference the White House issued a "clari-
> fying statement" indicating that use of the atom bomb had been con-
> sidered since the start of the Korean War, that "consideration of the
> use of any weapon is always implicit in the very possession of that
> weapon," and that the President's earlier remarks did "not represent
> any change in this situation."

This was the toughest decision I had to make as President. What
we faced in the attack on Korea was the ominous threat of a third
world war.

> HARRY S. TRUMAN (1884–1972). On his decision to commit
> U.S. forces on the Korean peninsula, *Memoirs: Years of Trial and
> Hope,* 28, 1956

I fired [Gen. Douglas MacArthur] because he wouldn't respect the
authority of the President. That's the answer to that. I didn't fire
him because he was a dumb son of a bitch, although he was, but
that's not against the law for generals. If it was, half to three quarters of them would be in jail.

> HARRY S. TRUMAN (1884–1972). Interview with the author, 1961–1962.
> In Merle Miller, *Plain Speaking: An Oral Biography of Harry S.
> Truman,* 24, 1974
>
> See Criticism: Examples: Douglas MacArthur (2)

❧

Freedom Is Not Free.

> ANONYMOUS. Inscription on the Korean War Veterans Memorial
> in Washington, dedicated 42 years after the war's end, 22 July
> 1995

❧

LANGUAGE

See also • Language, Political ○ Literature ○ Names ○ Newsspeak ○ Propaganda ○ Slang ○ Words ○ Writing

If you can describe clearly without a diagram the proper way of making this or that knot, then you are a master of the English language.

> HILAIRE BELLOC (1870–1953)

There seems to be a way possibly to show that a core part of language, the core part of the mechanisms that relate sound and meaning, are not only largely universal, but in fact even from a certain point of view virtually optimal. Meaning on very general considerations if you were to design a system, like if you were God designing a system, you would come close to doing it this way.

> NOAM CHOMSKY (1928–). "Looking Ahead," 20 December 1994, *Class Warfare: Interviews with David Barsamian,* 1996

By being so long in the lowest form [at Harrow] I gained an immense advantage over the cleverer boys. They all went on to learn Latin and Greek and splendid things like that. But I was taught English. We were considered such dunces that we could learn only English. . . . As I remained in the Third Fourth three times as long as anyone else, I had three times as much of it. I learned it thoroughly. Thus I got into my bones the essential structure of the ordinary British sentence—which is a noble thing.

> WINSTON CHURCHILL (1874–1965). *My Early Life: A Roving Commission,* 2, 1930

The corruption of man is followed by the corruption of language. . . . In due time, the fraud is manifest, and words lose all power to stimulate the understanding or the affections.

> RALPH WALDO EMERSON (1803–1882). "Language," *Nature,* 1836
> See Literature: Goethe

Language is fossil poetry.

> RALPH WALDO EMERSON (1803–1882). "The Poet," *Essays: Second Series,* 1844

How did language develop? In much the same way as an economic order develops through the market—out of the voluntary interaction of individuals, in this case seeking to trade ideas or information or gossip rather than goods and services with one another.

> MILTON FRIEDMAN (1912–) and ROSE FRIEDMAN. *Free to Choose: A Personal Statement,* 1 ("A Broader View"), 1979

Language is the house of Being. In its home man dwells.

> MARTIN HEIDEGGER (1889–1976). In Richard Rorty, "A Master from Germany," *New York Times Book Review,* 3 May 1998

There have been periods in the history of the various cultures, when the language of spirituality was clear, accurate and exhaustive. At the present time it is muddled, inadequate to the fact and dangerously equivocal. Lacking a proper vocabulary, people find it hard, not only to think about the most important issues of life, but even to realize that these issues exist.

> ALDOUS HUXLEY (1894–1963). "Words and Reality." In Christopher Isherwood, ed., *Vedanta for the Western World,* 1945

Language is the dress of thought.

> SAMUEL JOHNSON (1709–1784). "Cowley," *Lives of the English Poets,* 1781
> See Style: Seneca the Younger

He speaks English with the flawless imperfection of a New Yorker.

> GILBERT MILLSTEIN. On restaurateur André Surmain, "Lutèce: Lucullan Apogée," *Esquire,* January 1962

The use of language is all we have to pit against death and silence.

> JOYCE CAROL OATES (1938–). 1969 National Book Award (for fiction) acceptance address, 1970

If thought corrupts language, language can also corrupt thought.

> GEORGE ORWELL (1903–1950). "Politics and the English Language," April 1946, *The Collected Essays, Journalism and Letters of George Orwell,* vol. 4, ed. Sonia Orwell and Ian Angus, 1968

Language is power. . . . Language can be used as a means of changing reality.

> ADRIENNE RICH (1929–). "Teaching Language in Open Admissions," 1972, *On Lies, Secrets, and Silence: Selected Prose 1966–1978,* 1979
> See Knowledge: Francis Bacon (1)

Clarity in language depends on clarity in thought.

> ARTHUR M. SCHLESINGER, JR. (1917–). Brian Lamb television interview, C-SPAN, 10 May 1998

Casca: But, for mine own part, it was Greek to me.

> SHAKESPEARE (1564–1616). *Julius Caesar,* 1.2.286, 1599

England and America are two countries separated by the same language.

> GEORGE BERNARD SHAW (1856–1950). In "Picturesque Speech and Patter," *Reader's Digest,* November 1942

Perhaps of all the creations of man language is the most astonishing.

> LYTTON STRACHEY (1880–1932). Introduction to George H. W. Rylands, *Words and Poetry,* 1928

I never taught language for the purpose of teaching it; but invariably used language as a medium for the communication of thought; thus learning of language was coincident with the acquisition of knowledge.

> ANNE SULLIVAN (1866–1936). Educator and Helen Keller's tutor. Speech before the American Association to Promote the Teaching of Speech to the Deaf, July 1894

We have really everything in common with America nowadays, except, of course, language.

> OSCAR WILDE (1854–1900). *The Canterville Ghost,* 2, 1887

Language is not simply a reporting device for experience but a defining framework for it.

> BENJAMIN WHORF (1897–1941). "Thinking in Primitive Communities." In Eric H. Lenneberg, ed., *New Directions in the Study of Language,* 1964

🌿

Now the whole earth had one language and few words.

> ANONYMOUS (*BIBLE*). *Genesis* 11:1

It was Hebrew to me.

> SAYING (GREEK)

LANGUAGE, POLITICAL

See also • Language ○ Media ○ Newspeak ○ Newspeak: Examples ○ Propaganda

"Yes in principle" is often a synonym for "no."

> TIMOTHY GARTON ASH. On political–diplomatic negotiations. "In the Churchill Museum," *New York Review of Books,* 7 May 1987

One way for us to curtail the use of the language of oppression is for those who find themselves being defined into subjugation to rebel against such linguistic suppression. It isn't strange that those persons who insist on defining themselves, who insist on this elemental privilege of self-naming, self-definition, and self-identity encounter vigorous resistance. Predictably, the resistance usually comes from the oppressor or would-be oppressor and is a result of the fact that he or she does not want to relinquish the power which comes from the ability to define others.

> HAIG A. BOSMAJIAN. Introduction to *The Language of Oppression,* 1974

[A Minister's] perfect reply to an embarrassing question in the House of Commons is one that is brief, appears to answer the question completely, if challenged can be proved to be accurate in every word, gives no opening for awkward "supplementaries," and discloses really nothing.

> H. E. DALE. *The Higher Civil Service of Great Britain,* 4, 1941

Language has lost its meaning in the universal cant. *Representative Government* is really misrepresentative. . . . They call it Chivalry and Freedom; I call it the stealing [of] all the earnings of a poor man and the earnings of his little girl and boy, and the earnings of all that shall come from him, his children's children forever.

But this is Union, and this is Democracy; and our poor people, led by the nose by these fine words, dance and sing, ring bells and fire cannon, with every new link of the chain which is forged for their limbs by the plotters in the Capitol.

> RALPH WALDO EMERSON (1803–1882). Speech, Kansas Relief Meeting, Cambridge (Massachusetts), 10 September 1856

The business of obscuring language is a mask behind which stands out the much greater business of plunder. . . . Everything can be explained to the people, on the single condition that you really want them to understand.

> FRANTZ FANON (1925–1961). "The Pitfalls of National Consciousness," *The Wretched of the Earth,* 1961, tr. Constance Farrington, 1963

In any social movement, when changes are affected, the language sooner or later reflects the change. Our approach is different. Instead of *passively* noting the change, we are changing language patterns to *actively affect* the changes.

> WILMA SCOTT HEIDE. "Feminism: The Sine Qua Non for a Just Society," speech, University of Nebraska, Lincoln, 6 March 1972

[Pres. Richard M. Nixon] was a master of the philosophical explanation that explained nothing but created the impression that he was sharing a confidence with his interlocutor.

> HENRY A. KISSINGER (1923–). *Years of Upheaval,* 21, 1982

The first step toward freedom will be a new respect for the symbol, a purification and clarification of language itself, an abstention from unclean slogans and conditioned verbal reflexes. The death of the advertising agency and the propaganda bureau will be one of the surest signs of the birth of a new society.

> LEWIS MUMFORD (1895–1990). *The Conduct of Life,* 5.5, 1951

In our time, political speech and writing are largely the defense of the indefensible.

> GEORGE ORWELL (1903–1950). "Politics and the English Language," April 1946, *The Collected Essays, Journalism and Letters of George Orwell,* vol. 4, ed. Sonia Orwell and Ian Angus, 1968

Political language has to consist largely of euphemism, question-begging and sheer cloudy vagueness. Defenseless villages are bombarded from the air, the inhabitants driven out into the countryside, the huts set on fire with incendiary bullets: this is called *pacification.*

> GEORGE ORWELL (1903–1950). "Politics and the English Language," April 1946, *The Collected Essays, Journalism and Letters of George Orwell,* vol. 4, ed. Sonia Orwell and Ian Angus, 1968

Political language . . . is designed to make lies sound truthful and murder respectable, and to give the appearance of solidity to pure wind.

> GEORGE ORWELL (1903–1950). "Politics and the English Language," April 1946, *The Collected Essays, Journalism and Letters of George Orwell,* vol. 4, ed. Sonia Orwell and Ian Angus, 1968

Beauty, purity, respectability, religion, morality, art, patriotism, bravery and the rest. . . . are mere words, useful for duping barbarians into adopting civilization, or the civilized poor into submitting to be robbed and enslaved. This is the family secret of the governing class.

> GEORGE BERNARD SHAW (1856–1950). *Man and Superman,* 3, 1903

The reduction of political discourse to sound bites is one of the worst things that's happened in American political life.

> JOHN SILBER (1926–). Boston University president. In "Soundbites," *USA Today,* 1 October 1990

[Russian Gen. Aleksandr Ledbed] signed and published two completely contradictory economic programs during his [presidential] campaign this spring. One advocated free markets above all. The other called for strong state support of industry. When a panic-stricken campaign aide asked him how he hoped to explain the contradiction, Ledbed laughed and told him nobody would notice. He was right.

> MICHAEL SPECTOR. "The Wars of Aleksandr Ivanovich Ledbed," *New York Times Magazine,* 13 October 1996

Napoleon: What is all this about non-intervention?
Talleyrand: Sire, it means about the same as intervention.

> TALLEYRAND (1754–1838). Format adapted. In Ralph Waldo Emerson, journal, March? 1857

Politics has its own language, which is often so complex that it borders on being a code, and the main trick in political journalism is learning how to translate—to make sense of the partisan bullshit that even your friends will lay on you—without crippling your access to the kind of information that allows you to keep functioning.

> HUNTER S. THOMPSON (1939–). "Author's Note," *Fear and Loathing: On the Campaign Trail, '72,* 1973

LAST WORDS

See also • Assassination: Shakespeare (1) ○ Country: Nathan
Hale ○ Death ○ Epitaphs ○ Navy: James Lawrence ○ Self-
Sacrifice: Charles Dickens

Anonymous: Have you anything to say?
André (on the scaffold): Nothing but to request you to witness to
the world that I die like a brave man.

> MAJ. JOHN ANDRÉ (1751–1780). British army officer. Hanged as a spy
> during the Revolutionary War, 2 October 1780

Have I played my part in the farce of life creditably enough?
  If I have pleased you, kindly signify
  Appreciation with a warm goodbye [i.e. applause].

> CAESAR AUGUSTUS (63 B.C.–A.D. 14). To a group of friends he had
> summoned on the day of his death. In Suetonius (A.D. 69?–122), *The
> Twelve Caesars*, 2.99, tr. Robert Graves and rev. Michael Grant, 1979

Major, tell my father I died with my face to the enemy.

> I. E. AVERY. Confederate colonel. Battle of Gettysburg (Pennsylvania),
> 2 July 1863

It is in the nature of all things that take form to dissolve again.
Strive with your whole being to attain perfection.

> THE BUDDHA (563–483 B.C.). To a large group of his disciples in a for-
> est grove. In Sogyal Rinpoche, *The Tibetan Book of Living and Dying*,
> 22, 1992

I must sleep now.

> LORD BYRON (1788–1824)

I am not the least afraid to die.

> CHARLES DARWIN (1809–1882). 19 April 1882, *The Autobiography of
> Charles Darwin and Selected Letters*, 18, ed. Francis Darwin, 1892

Let us go in; the fog is rising.

> EMILY DICKINSON (1830–1886). Attributed

I want to go. God take me.

> DWIGHT D. EISENHOWER (1890–1969). Last words spoken softly to the
> author, his son. In John S. D. Eisenhower, *Strictly Personal*, 12,
> 1974

All my possessions for a moment of time.

> ELIZABETH I (1533–1603). English queen. Attributed. In Nancy Gibbs,
> "How America Has Run Out of Time," *Time*, 24 April 1989

I am tired of ruling over slaves.

> FREDERICK II (1712–1786). 1 April 1786

Open the second shutter, so that more light can come in.

> GOETHE (1749–1832). Attributed. (Popular version: More light!)

I have loved justice and hated iniquity; therefore, I die in exile.

> POPE GREGORY VII (A.D. 1020–1085). In John William Bowden,
> *The Life and Pontificate of Gregory the Seventh*, 2.3.20, 1840

Only one man ever understood me. . . . And he didn't understand
me.

> GEORG HEGEL (1770–1831)

Turn up the lights; I don't want to go home in the dark.

> O. HENRY (1862–1910). Quoting a 1907 song by Harry Williams.
> In C. Alphonso Smith, *O. Henry Biography*, 9, 1916

I am about to take my last voyage, a great leap in the dark.

> THOMAS HOBBES (1588–1679)

Let us cross over the river and rest under the trees.

> THOMAS JONATHAN "STONEWALL" JACKSON (1824–1863).
> Battle of Chancellorsville (Virginia), 10 May 1863. In Douglas
> Southall Freeman, *Lee's Lieutenants: A Study in Command*, 2.36,
> 1942–1944

My God, my God, why hast thou forsaken me?

> JESUS (A.D. 1st cent.). *Matthew* 27:46

Dear Professor, don't be disturbed. My bags are always packed.
When the moment to depart arrives, I won't lose any time.

> POPE JOHN XXIII (1881–1963). Remark to Professor Gasparrini, 1 June
> 1963 (two days before dying). *Wit and Wisdom of Good Pope John*, 24,
> ed. Henri Fesquet and tr. Salvator Attanasio, 1964

Then I will take no more physic, not even opiates, for I have prayed
that I may render my soul to God unclouded.

> SAMUEL JOHNSON (1709–1784). When told he was near death. In Peter
> Andrews, "Famous Last Apothegms," *Horizon*, January 1977

Nellie Connally: You sure can't say Dallas doesn't love you, Mr.
President.
Kennedy (smiling): No, you can't.

> JOHN F. KENNEDY (1917–1963). Format adapted. Apparently his last
> words spoken moments before being assassinated on 22 November
> 1963. In William Manchester, *The Death of a President: November
> 20–November 25, 1963*, 2, 1967. The wife of Texas Gov. John B.
> Connally, was commenting on the friendly Dallas crowd which had
> turned out to greet the President.

No bloody doctors.

> R. D. LAING (1927–1989). British psychiatrist. As he lay stricken with a
> fatal heart attack on a tennis court in southern France. In James Hillman
> and Michael Ventura, *We've Had a Hundred Years of Psychotherapy—
> And the World's Getting Worse*, 2 ("Mediocrity"), 1992

Let the tent be struck.

> ROBERT E. LEE (1807–1870). 12 October 1870

Mary Lincoln (placing her hand in Lincoln's and nestling close to
him): What will Miss Harris think of my hanging on to you so?"
Lincoln: She won't think anything about it.

> ABRAHAM LINCOLN (1809–1865). Format adapted. Moments before being
> assassinated by John Wilkes Booth at the Ford Theater in Washington,
> 14 April 1865. In Stephen B. Oates, *With Malice Toward None: The Life
> of Abraham Lincoln*, 11, 1977. Clara Harris and her fiancé, Maj. Henry R.
> Rathbone, were also seated in the presidential box.

Out of the shadows of night
The world rolls into light;
  It is daybreak everywhere.

> HENRY WADSWORTH LONGFELLOW (1807–1882). The last lines of his
> last poem, 15 March 1882 (nine days before dying), "The Bells of San
> Blas," *In the Harbor*, 1882

Take care of my dear Lady Hamilton [said repeatedly]. . . . Thank
God, I have done my duty.

HORATIO NELSON (1758–1805). In the painful hours after being mortally wounded during the Battle of Trafalgar (off the southwest coast of Spain), 21 October 1805. In Nigel Nicolson, "Once in Love with Emma," *New York Times Book Review*, 8 January 1995

Die, my dear doctor? That is the last thing I shall do.

LORD PALMERSTON (1784–1865). British prime minister. In Peter Andrews, "Famous Last Apothegms," *Horizon*, January 1977

Draw the curtain; the farce is ended.

RABELAIS (1483?–1553). In "Their Last Words," *Wisdom*, January 1956

So little done, so much to do.

CECIL RHODES (1853–1902). British colonialist. In Lewis Michell, *The Life and Times of the Right Honourable Cecil John Rhodes*, 2.39, 1910

I have a terrific pain in the back of my head.

FRANKLIN D. ROOSEVELT (1882–1945). To his sixth cousin Margaret Suckley, Warm Springs (Georgia), 12 April 1945. In R. W. B. Lewis, "Daisy and Franklin: The Newly Discovered Diaries of One of F.D.R.'s Female Friends," *New York Times Book Review*, 9 April 1995. After lunch of gruel and cream, Pres. Roosevelt suddenly fell forward. Suckley, stepping over him, asked, "Have you dropped your cigarette?" He then spoke his last words, lost consciousness, and died at 3:30 in the afternoon.

Everybody has got to die, but I always believed an exception would be made in my case. Now what?

WILLIAM SAROYAN (1908–1981). Telephone remark to an Associated Press reporter a few hours before his death, 13 May 1981

Crito, I owe a cock to Asclepius; will you remember to pay the debt?

SOCRATES (470?–399 B.C.). In Plato (427?–347 B.C.). *Phaedo*, 118, tr. Benjamin Jowett, 1894

Stein: What is the answer?
Toklas: [Silence.]
Stein: In that case, what is the question?

GERTRUDE STEIN (1874–1946). Format adapted. During the last phase of her terminal illness. In Alice B. Toklas, *What Is Remembered*, 12, 1963

It is well. I die hard, but am not afraid to go.

GEORGE WASHINGTON (1732–1799). 14 December 1799

I am ready.

WOODROW WILSON (1856–1924). 3 February 1924. In *Biography* television documentary series, A&E, 14 January 1998

LAUGHTER

See also • Comedy ○ Happiness ○ Humor ○ Jests ○ Jokes ○ Joy ○ Smiles ○ Tears ○ Wit

Pyroteknikally konsidered, [laffing] is the fire-works of the soul.

JOSH BILLINGS (1818–1885). "Laffing," *Everybody's Friend, or; Josh Billing's Encyclopedia and Proverbial Philosophy of Wit and Humor*, 1874

Laff every good chance ya kan git, but don't laff unless yu feal like it, for there ain't nothing in this world more harty than a good honest laff, nor nothing more hollow than a hartless one.

JOSH BILLINGS (1818–1885). "Laffing," *Everybody's Friend, or; Josh Billing's Encyclopedia and Proverbial Philosophy of Wit and Humor*, 1874

The man who laughs
Has simply not yet [heard]
The terrible news.

BERTOLT BRECHT (1898–1956). "To Those Born Later" (1), 1936–1938, *Poems: 1913–1956*, ed. John Willett and Ralph Manheim, 1976

And if I laugh at any mortal thing,
'Tis that I may not weep.

LORD BYRON (1788–1824). *Don Juan*, 4.4, 1819–1824

That of all days is the most completely wasted in which one did not once laugh.

CHAMFORT (1741–1794). *Maxims and Thoughts*, 1, 1796, tr. W. S. Merwin, 1984

In my mind, there is nothing so illiberal and so ill-bred, as audible laughter. . . . I am sure that since I have had the full use of my reason, no human being has ever heard me laugh.

LORD CHESTERFIELD (1694–1773). Letter to his son, 9 March 1748

The vulgar only laugh, but never smile; whereas well-bred people often smile, but seldom laugh.

LORD CHESTERFIELD (1694–1773). Letter to his son, 17 February 1954

Too much laughing argues lightness.

JOHN CLARKE (1596–1658). Comp., *Proverbs: English and Latine*, p. 274, 1639

We only laugh at those instances of moral absurdity to which we are conscious we ourselves are not liable.

OLIVER GOLDSMITH (1728–1774). *An Enquiry into the Present State of Polite Learning in Europe*, 11, 1759

Anything awful makes me laugh. I misbehaved once at a funeral.

CHARLES LAMB (1775–1834). Letter to Robert Southey, 9 August 1815

He laughs best whose laugh lasts.

LAURENCE J. PETER (1919–1990). 11 January, *Peter's Almanac*, 1982

To make other people laugh is no great feat so long as one does not mind whether they are laughing at our wit or at us ourselves.

GEORG CHRISTOPH LICHTENBERG (1742–1799)

His laughter . . . sparkled like a splash of water in sunlight.

JOSEPH LELYVELD. On V. S. Pritchard at age 85, "V. S. Pritchard, in Step With the Years, Writes On," *New York Times*, 16 December 1985

He who laughs, lasts!

MARY PETTIBONE POOLE. "Beggars Can't Be Losers," *A Glass Eye at a Keyhole*, 1938

Othello: They laugh that win.

SHAKESPEARE (1564–1616). *Othello*, 4.1.125, 1604

Iachimo: With his eyes in flood with laughter.

SHAKESPEARE (1564–1616). *Cymbeline*, 1.6.74, 1609

The only thing which provokes laughter is another's distress.

GEORGE BERNARD SHAW (1856–1950). Remark to the author, 1940s. In Stephen Winsten, *Days with Bernard Shaw*, 13, 1949

A good laugh is sunshine in a house.
> WILLIAM MAKEPEACE THACKERAY (1811–1863)

Never laugh at live dragons.
> J.R.R. TOLKIEN (1892–1973). *The Hobbit: or, There and Back Again*, 12, 1937

Against the assault of laughter nothing can stand.
> MARK TWAIN (1835–1910). "The Mysterious Stranger"

Laugh, and the world laughs with you;
> Weep, and you weep alone;
For the sad old earth must borrow its mirth,
> But has trouble enough of its own.
> ELLA WHEELER WILCOX (1855–1919). "Solitude," *New York World*, 3 February 1883

❦

He laughs best who laughs last.
> SAYING (ENGLISH)

The fool laughs at everything; the knave, at nothing.
> SAYING (SPANISH)

LAW

See also • Constitutions ○ Crime ○ Custom ○ Judges ○ Justice ○ Lawyers ○ Liberty: Walt Whitman (2) ○ Punishment ○ Trials

Written laws [are] like spiders' webs, and would catch . . . the weak and poor, but easily be broken by the mighty and rich.
> ANACHARSIS (6th? cent. B.C.). As paraphrased by Plutarch (A.D. 46?–119?), "Solon," *Parallel Lives*, Dryden edition, 1693 (Popular version: Laws are like cobwebs that entangle the weak but are broken by the strong.)

An unjust law is no law at all.
> ST. AUGUSTINE (A.D. 354–430). In Martin Luther King, Jr., "Letter from Birmingham City Jail," 16 April 1963
> See Nonviolence: Martin Luther King, Jr. (6)

There is far too much law for those who can afford it and far too little for those who cannot.
> DEREK BOK (1930–). "Report to the Board of Overseers," 21 April 1983

A good parson once said that where mystery begins religion ends. Cannot I say, as truly at least, of human laws, that where mystery begins justice ends?
> EDMUND BURKE (1729–1797). *A Vindication of Natural Society*, p. 87, M. Cooper edition, 1756

That great Law of Nature, Self-Preservation.
> SAMUEL BUTLER (1612–1680). "A Modern Politician," *The Genuine Remains in Verse and Prose of Mr. Samuel Butler, Author of Hudibras*, vol. 2, 1759 (Popular version: The first law of nature is self-preservation.)

I am ashamed the law is such an ass.
> GEORGE CHAPMAN (1559?–1634). *Revenge for Honour*, 3.2, 1654

The safety of the people shall be their highest law.
> CICERO (106–43 B.C.). *De legibus*, 3.3, tr. Clinton Walker Keyes, 1928. (Popular version: The good of the people is the highest law.)

When arms speak, the laws are silent.
> CICERO (106–43 B.C.). *Pro Milone*, 4, tr. N. H. Watts, 1931. (Popular version: In time of war, the laws are silent.)

Do what thou wilt shall be the whole of the law.
> ALEISTER CROWLEY (1875–1947). A favorite saying, preface to *The Confessions of Aleister Crowley*, 1929

The multitude of laws frequently furnishes an excuse for vice, and a state is better governed with a few laws which are strictly adhered to.
> DESCARTES (1596–1650). *Discourse on Method*, 2, 1637, tr. Laurence J. Lafleur, 1964

Is not the whole trend of our legislation a sustained effort to pamper the unfit at the expense of the fit?
> NORMAN DOUGLAS (1868–1952). 19 February, *An Almanac*, 1945

People say law, but they mean wealth.
> RALPH WALDO EMERSON (1803–1882). Journal, September–October 1841

No law can be sacred to me but that of my nature.
> RALPH WALDO EMERSON (1803–1882). "Self-Reliance," *Essays: First Series*, 1841

Every actual State is corrupt. Good men must not obey the laws too well.
> RALPH WALDO EMERSON (1803–1882). "Politics," *Essays: Second Series*, 1844

The law, in its majestic equality, forbids the rich as well as the poor to sleep under bridges, to beg in the streets, and to steal bread.
> ANATOLE FRANCE (1844–1924). *The Red Lily*, 7, 1894

Laws *too gentle* are seldom *obeyed*;
> *too severe*, seldom *executed*.
> BENJAMIN FRANKLIN (1706–1790). *Poor Richard's Almanack*, May 1756

Our human laws are but the copies, more or less imperfect, of the eternal laws, so far as we can read them.
> JAMES ANTHONY FROUDE (1818–1894). "Calvinism," *Short Studies on Great Subjects*, 1867–1883

Law cannot persuade where it cannot punish.
> THOMAS FULLER (1654–1734). Comp., *Gnomologia: Adages and Proverbs*, 3148, 1732

Unkindness has no Remedy at Law.
> THOMAS FULLER (1654–1734). Comp., *Gnomologia: Adages and Proverbs*, 5402, 1732

As in law so in war, the longest purse finally wins.
> MOHANDAS K. GANDHI (1869–1948). Address before the Bombay Provincial Cooperative Conference, 17 September 1917

Law not served by power is an illusion, but power not ruled by law is a menace.
> ARTHUR GOLDBERG (1908–1990). Speech, Catholic University of America, Washington. In "Universities," *Time*, 17 June 1966

Laws grind the poor, and rich men rule the law.
> OLIVER GOLDSMITH (1728–1774). *The Traveller: Or a Prospect of Society*, l. 386, 1764

No man is obliged to conform to any rule of conduct farther than the rule is consistent with justice.

> WILLIAM GODWIN (1756–1836). *Enquiry Concerning Political Justice and Its Influence on Morals and Happiness,* 2.6, 1793, ed. and abr. Raymond A. Preston, 1926

I am the law.

> FRANK HAGUE (1876–1956). In "'I Am the Law,' Mayor Hague Tells 1,000 in Speech on Jersey City [New Jersey] Government," *New York Times,* 11 November 1937

It will be of little avail to the people, that the laws are made by men of their own choice, if the laws be so voluminous that they cannot be read, or so incoherent that they cannot be understood; if they be repealed or revised before they are promulgated, or undergo such incessant changes that no man, who knows what the law is today, can guess what it will be tomorrow.

> ALEXANDER HAMILTON (1757–1804) or JAMES MADISON (1751–1836). In *The Federalist Papers* (essay series), 62, February? 1788

It is only rogues who feel the restraints of law.

> JOSIAH GILBERT HOLLAND (1819–1881). "Perfect Liberty," *Gold-Foil, Hammered from Popular Proverbs,* 1860

The law is the witness and external deposit of our moral life. Its history is the history of the moral development of the race.

> OLIVER WENDELL HOLMES, JR. (1841–1935). Speech, Boston, 8 January 1897

The great can protect themselves, but the poor and humble require the arm and shield of the law.

> ANDREW JACKSON (1767–1845). Letter to John Quincy Adams, 26 August 1821

The care of every man's soul belongs to himself. But what if he neglect[s] the care of it? Well what if he neglect[s] the care of his health or estate . . . ? Will the magistrate make a law that he shall not be poor or sick? Laws provide against injury from others, but not from ourselves. God himself will not save men against their wills.

> THOMAS JEFFERSON (1743–1826). Notes labeled "Scraps Early in the Revolution," October 1776?

A strict observance of the written laws is doubtless *one* of the high duties of a good citizen, but it is not *the highest.* The laws of necessity, of self-preservation, of saving our country when in danger, are of higher obligation. To lose our country by a scrupulous adherence to written law would be to lose the law itself, with life, liberty, property and all those who are enjoying them with us; thus absurdly sacrificing the end to the means.

> THOMAS JEFFERSON (1743–1826). Letter to John B. Colvin, 20 September 1810
>
> See Constitutions: Abraham Lincoln

If civil authorities pass laws or command anything opposed to the moral order and consequently contrary to the will of God, neither the laws made nor the authorization granted can be binding on the consciences of the citizen since God has more right to be obeyed than men.

> POPE JOHN XXIII (1881–1963). *Pacem in Terris (On Establishing Universal Peace in Truth, Justice, Charity and Liberty),* 11 April 1963

The law is the last result of human wisdom acting upon human experience for the benefit of the public.

> SAMUEL JOHNSON (1709–1784). In Hester Lynch Piozzi, *Anecdotes of the Late Samuel Johnson, LL.D.,* p. 73, 1786, ed. S. C. Roberts, 1932

The precepts of the law are these: to live honestly, to injure no one, and to give everyone his due.

> JUSTINIAN I (482?–565). *Justinian Code,* A.D. 533

We should never forget that everything Hitler did in Germany was "legal" and everything the Hungarian freedom fighters did in Hungary was "illegal."

> MARTIN LUTHER KING, JR. (1929–1968). "Letter from Birmingham City Jail," 16 April 1963

Morality cannot be legislated, but behavior can be regulated. Judicial decrees may not change the heart, but they can restrain the heartless.

> MARTIN LUTHER KING, JR. (1929–1968). *Strength to Love,* 3.3, 1963

Nine-tenths of human law is about possession.

> BARBARA KINGSOLVER (1923–). "Marking Peace," *High Tide in Tucson: Essays from Now or Never,* 1996

There are times when national interest is more important than the law.

> HENRY A. KISSINGER (1923–). In Leslie H. Gelb, "The Kissinger Legacy," *New York Times Magazine,* 31 October 1976

You must remember that some things that are *legally* right are not *morally* right

> ABRAHAM LINCOLN (1809–1865). Remark to a prospective client refusing to take his case (involving a $600 claim) against a widow with six children, 1840s? In Francis Fisher Browne, *The Every-Day Life of Abraham Lincoln,* 2.6, 1887

No law is stronger than is the public sentiment where it is to be enforced.

> ABRAHAM LINCOLN (1809–1865). Letter to John J. Crittenden, 22 December 1859
>
> See Pubic Opinion: George Orwell

Possession is nine-tenths of the law.

> LORD MANSFIELD (1705–1793?). *Corporation of Kingston-upon-Hull v. Horner,* 1774

The only law which is really lived up to wholeheartedly and with a vengeance is the law of conformity.

> HENRY MILLER (1891–1980). *The Time of the Assassins: A Study of Rimbaud,* 1, 1946

I have my own laws and court to judge me, and I address myself to them more than anywhere else.

> MONTAIGNE (1533–1592). "Of Repentance," *Essays,* 1588, tr. Donald M. Frame, 1958

The laws do not . . . punish any other than overt acts.

> MONTESQUIEU (1689–1755). *The Spirit of the Laws,* 12.11, 1748, tr. Thomas Nugent, 1750, Hafner Publishing edition, 1949

Useless laws debilitate . . . necessary ones.

> MONTESQUIEU (1689–1755). *The Spirit of the Laws,* 29.16, 1748, tr. Thomas Nugent, 1750, Hafner Publishing edition, 1949

There shall be one law for the native and for the stranger who sojourns among you.

> MOSES (14th cent. B.C.). *Exodus* 12:49

Mankind must have laws and conform to them, or their life would be as bad as that of the most savage beast.

> PLATO (427?–347 B.C.). *Laws,* 9.874, tr. Benjamin Jowett, 1894

They that make *laws* must not break them.

> JOHN RAY (1628–1705). Comp., *A Collection of English Proverbs,* p. 166, 1678

One of the greatest delusions in the world is the hope that the evils in this world are to be cured by legislation.

> THOMAS BRACKETT REED (1839–1902). House of Representatives speech, 1886

Laws unsupported by force soon fall into contempt.

> CARDINAL de RETZ (1613–1679). In Charles de Gaulle, forward to *The Edge of the Sword,* 1934, tr. Gerald Hopkins, 1960

Ignorance of the Law excuses no man, not that all men know the Law, but 'tis an excuse every man will plead and no man can tell how to confute him.

> JOHN SELDEN (1584–1654). "Law" (2), *Table Talk,* 1689, ed. Frederick Pollock, 1927

Accomodation: Did you give Athens the best laws?
Solon: No, but the best it would receive.

> SOLON (630?–560? B.C.). One of the Seven Sages of Greece. In Ralph Waldo Emerson, journal, October 1848

Laws were most numerous when the commonwealth was most corrupt.

> TACITUS (A.D. 56?–120?). *The Annals,* 3.27, tr. Alfred J. Church and William J. Brodribb, 1942

Must the citizen ever for a moment, or in the least degree, resign his conscience to the legislator? Why has every man a conscience then? I think that we should be men first, and subjects afterwards. It is not desirable to cultivate a respect for the law, so much as for the right. The only obligation which I have a right to assume is to do at any time what I think right.

> HENRY DAVID THOREAU (1817–1862). "Civil Disobedience," 1849

Let a man but realize that the purpose of his life is to fulfill the law of God, and that law will dominate him and supplant all other laws, and by its supreme dominion will in his eyes deprive all human laws of their right to command and restrict him.

> LEO TOLSTOY (1828–1910). *The Kingdom of God Is Within You,* 9, 1893, tr. Aylmer Maude, 1936

Law! What do I care about the law. Hain't I got the power?

> CORNELIUS VANDERBILT (1794–1877). Railroad magnate. In Robert L. Heilbroner, *The Worldly Philosophers: The Lives, Times, and Ideas of the Great Economic Thinkers,* 8, 1972

It is the spirit and not the form of law that keeps justice alive.

> EARL WARREN (1891–1974). "The Law and the Future," *Fortune,* November 1955

Our [legal] system faces no theoretical dilemma but a single continuous problem: how to apply to ever changing conditions the never changing principles of freedom.

> EARL WARREN (1891–1974). "The Law and the Future," *Fortune,* November 1955

The success of any legal system is measured by its fidelity to the universal ideal of justice.

> EARL WARREN (1891–1974). "The Law and the Future," *Fortune,* November 1955

Willie Stark: The law is always too short and too tight for growing humankind. The best you can do is do something and then make up some law to fit and by the time that law gets on the books you would have done something different.

> ROBERT PENN WARREN (1905–1989). *All the King's Men,* 3, 1946

There is plenty of law at the end of a stick.

> GROVER A. WHALEN (1886–1962) New York City police commissioner. Attributed

The law is not concerned with trifles.

> SAYING (LATIN)

The more laws, the less justice.

> SAYING (LATIN)

Where the law is uncertain, there is no law.

> SAYING (LATIN)

Where power, there law.

> SAYING (RUSSIAN)

LAWYERS

See also • Conscience: Abraham Lincoln ○ Justice ○ Law ○ Trials ○ Professionals

Lawyers with a weakness for seeing the merits of the other side end up being employed by neither.

> RICHARD J. BARNET (1929–). *Roots of War,* 3.3, 1971

Lawyer, *n.* One skilled in circumvention of the law.

> AMBROSE BIERCE (1842–1914). *The Devil's Dictionary,* p. 75, 1911, Dover edition, 1958

What the lawyer needs to redeem himself is not more ability, but more courage in the face of financial loss and personal ill will to stand for right and justice.

> LOUIS D. BRANDEIS (1856–1941). Address, 22 June 1907

In a good law office, the beginner, fresh out of law school, is first assigned to drafting the strongest possible case for the other lawyer's client.

> PETER F. DRUCKER (1909–). *The Effective Executive,* 7.1, 1967

God works wonders now and then;
Behold! a Lawyer, an honest Man!

> BENJAMIN FRANKLIN (1706–1790). *Poor Richard's Almanack,* December 1733

No workman without tools,
No Lawyer without Fools.

> BENJAMIN FRANKLIN (1706–1790). *Poor Richard's Almanack,* February 1742

If it were not for lawyers, we wouldn't need them.

A. K. GIFFIN. "Lawyer's Paradox." In Paul Dickson, comp., *The New Official Rules,* p. 126, 1989

There's no better way of exercising the imagination than the study of law. No poet ever interpreted nature as freely as a lawyer interprets truth.

JEAN GIRAUDOUX (1882–1944). *Tiger at the Gates,* 1, 1935, tr. Christopher Fry, 1955

Lawyers spend a great deal of their time shoveling smoke.

OLIVER WENDELL HOLMES, JR. (1841–1935)

Lawyers in making laws favor laws that make lawyers a necessity.

ELBERT HUBBARD (1856–1915). *The Note Book of Elbert Hubbard,* p. 193, comp. Elbert Hubbard II, 1927

His oral statement to be persuasive must at least be *clear.* . . . To clarity he must add *force;* for the court, if captured at all, must be taken by storm.

ROBERT H. JACKSON (1892–1954). Supreme Court associate justice. In Eugene C. Gerhart, *America's Advocate: Robert H. Jackson,* 24, 1958

I do not care to speak ill of any man behind his back, but I believe the gentleman is an *attorney.*

SAMUEL JOHNSON (1709–1784). Slightly modified. 1770. In James Boswell, *The Life of Samuel Johnson,* 1791

A lawyer has no business with the justice or injustice of the cause which he undertakes, unless his client asks his opinion, and then he is bound to give it honestly. The justice or injustice of the cause is to be decided by the judge.

SAMUEL JOHNSON (1709–1784). 15 August 1773. In James Boswell, *The Journal of a Tour to the Hebrides, with Samuel Johnson, L.L.D.,* 1786

A lawyer is not to tell what he knows to be a lie.

SAMUEL JOHNSON (1709–1784). 15 August 1773. In James Boswell, *The Journal of a Tour to the Hebrides, with Samuel Johnson, L.L.D.,* 1786

He is no lawyer who cannot take two sides.

CHARLES LAMB (1775–1834). Letter to Samuel Rogers, December 1833

When the law is against you, argue the facts. When the facts are against you, argue the law. When both are against you, call the other lawyer names.

LAWYER'S RULE. In Paul Dickson, comp., *The Official Rules,* p. 142, 1978

Discourage litigation. Persuade your neighbors to compromise whenever you can. Point out to them how the *nominal* winner is often a *real* loser—in fees, and expenses, and waste of time. As a peacemaker the lawyer has a superior opertunity [*sic*] of being a good man. There will still be business enough.

ABRAHAM LINCOLN (1809–1865). "Notes on the Practice of Law," 1850?, *Abraham Lincoln: Speeches and Writings, 1832–1858,* Library of America edition, 1989

There is a vague popular belief that lawyers are necessarily dishonest. . . . Let no young man, choosing the law for a calling, for a moment yield to this popular belief. Resolve to be honest at all events; and if, in your own judgment, you cannot be an honest lawyer, resolve to be honest without being a lawyer. Choose some other occupation, rather than one in the choosing of which you do, in advance, consent to be a knave.

ABRAHAM LINCOLN (1809–1865). Closing words, "Notes on the Practice of Law," 1850?, *Abraham Lincoln: Speeches and Writings, 1832–1858,* Library of America edition, 1989

Every defendant is entitled to a trial in which his interests are vigorously and conscientiously advocated by an able lawyer. A proceeding in which the defendant does not receive meaningful assistance in meeting the forces of the state does not in my opinion, constitute due process.

THURGOOD MARSHALL (1908–1993). *Strickland v. Washington,* 1984

Lawyers are like rhinoceroses: thick-skinned, short-sighted, and always ready to charge.

DAVID MELLOR (1949–). British political leader. Appearing on *Question Time,* BBC, London, 3 December 1992

[Lawyers are] specifically educated to discover legal excuses for dishonest, dishonorable and anti-social acts.

H. L. MENCKEN (1880–1956). "On Government" (2), *Prejudices: Fourth Series,* 1924

Until last December [J. Michael Liles] was serving as attorney in two suits in Missouri against Playtex for toxic-shock syndrome caused by its tampons. Liles then withdrew because he was hired by Playtex as a consultant to advise it in the defense of toxic-shock lawsuits. Playtex paid him $500,000.

CHARLES PETERS (1926–). "Tilting at Windmills," *Washington Monthly,* January 1990

Don Corleone: A lawyer with his briefcase can steal more than a hundred men with guns.

MARIO PUZO (1920–). *The Godfather,* 1, 1969

Why does a hearse horse snicker
Hauling a lawyer away?

CARL SANDBURG (1878–1967). "The Lawyers Know Too Much," *Smoke and Steel,* 1920

Dick the butcher: The first thing we do, let's kill all the lawyers.

SHAKESPEARE (1564–1616). *Henry VI,* Part II, 4.2.84, 1590

There was a society of men among us, bred up from their youth in the art of proving by words multiplied for that purpose, that white is black and black is white, according as they are paid.

JONATHAN SWIFT (1667–1745). On lawyers, *Gulliver's Travels,* 4.5, 1726

The lawyer's truth is not Truth, but consistency or a consistent expediency.

HENRY DAVID THOREAU (1817–1862). "Civil Disobedience," 1849

[A lawyer] can never excuse himself for accepting a defendant's confidence and then betraying it by a half-hearted defense.

EDWARD BENNETT WILLIAMS (1920–1988). *One Man's Freedom,* 2, 1962

Law practice is the exact opposite of sex: even when it's good, it's bad.

MORTIMER ZUCKERMAN (1937–). Publisher and non-practicing lawyer. Brian Lamb television interview, C-SPAN, 28 November 1993

❦

Why don't sharks eat lawyers? Professional courtesy.
ANONYMOUS

A lawyer and a wagon wheel must be well greased.
SAYING (GERMAN)

One lawyer makes work for another.
SAYING (SPANISH)

LAZINESS

See also • Idleness ○ Industry ○ Leisure ○ Procrastination ○ Sleep ○ Work

Up, Sluggard, and waste not life;
in the grave will be sleeping enough.
BENJAMIN FRANKLIN (1706–1790). *Poor Richard's Almanack,* September 1741

Sloth (like Rust) consumes faster than Labor wears:
the used Key is always bright.
BENJAMIN FRANKLIN (1706–1790). *Poor Richard's Almanack,* July 1744

He that never eats too much will never be lazy.
BENJAMIN FRANKLIN (1706–1790). *Poor Richard's Almanack,* October 1756

He that riseth late must trot all Day.
BENJAMIN FRANKLIN (1706–1790). "The Way to Wealth," 7 July 1757

Our greatest weariness comes from work not done.
ERIC HOFFER (1902–1983). "Thoughts of Eric Hoffer," *New York Times Magazine,* 25 April 1971

Ever' once in a while we meet a feller that's too proud t' beg, an' too honest t' steal, an' too lazy t' work.
KIN HUBBARD (1868–1930). *Abe Martin's Sayings and Wisecracks, Abe's Neighbors, His Almanack, Comic Drawings,* 2 ("Abe Martin's Almanack," April), ed. David S. Hawes, 1984

Our minds are lazier than our bodies.
LA ROCHEFOUCAULD (1613–1680). *Maxims,* 487, 1665, tr. Louis Kronenberger, 1959

Indolence never lacks excuse to avoid labor.
PUBLIUS SYRUS (85–43 B.C.). *Moral Sayings,* 339, tr. Darius Lyman, Jr., 1862

Laziness: the habit of resting before fatigue sets in.
JULES RENARD (1864–1910). Journal, May 1906, tr. Louise Bogan and Elizabeth Roget, 1964

❦

The sluggard says, "There is a lion outside!
I shall be slain in the streets!"
SAYING (*BIBLE*). Proverbs 22:13

Sloth is the parent of poverty.
SAYING (ENGLISH)

Laziness is sometimes mistaken for patience.
SAYING (FRENCH)

LEADERS

See also • Authority ○ Charisma ○ Commanders ○ Confidence: James Burnham ○ Crisis Leaders ○ Crowds ○ Decision-Making ○ Diplomats ○ Executives ○ Genius ○ Greatness ○ Heroism ○ Kings ○ Leaders & People ○ Leaders & Staff ○ Machiavellianism ○ Managers ○ Organizations ○ Politics ○ Politicians ○ Presidents ○ Prime Ministers ○ Princes ○ Reformers ○ Revolutionaries ○ Rulers ○ Statesmen ○ Tyrants

Leaders are people who do the right thing; managers are people who do things right. Both roles are crucial, but they differ profoundly. I often observe people in top positions doing the wrong thing well.
WARREN BENNIS (1925–). *Why Leaders Can't Lead: The Unconscious Conspiracy Continues,* 2, 1989

In the postbureaucratic world, the laurel will go to the leader who encourages healthy dissent and values those followers brave enough to say no. The successful leader will have, not the loudest voice, but the readiest ear. And his or her real genius may well lie, not in personal achievement, but in unleashing other people's talent.
WARREN BENNIS (1925–). Preface (closing words) to *Leaders on Leadership: Interviews with Top Executives,* 1992

Leadership is like the Abominable Snowman, whose footprints are everywhere but who is nowhere to be seen.
WARREN BENNIS (1925–) and BURT NANUS (1936–). "Leading Others, Managing Yourself," *Leaders: The Strategies for Taking Charge,* 1985

Intuitive judgment by the leader is essential, but it is effective only if it has been preceded by thorough analysis.
WARREN BENNIS (1925–) and BURT NANUS (1936–). "Strategy IV: The Deployment of Self," *Leaders: The Strategies for Taking Charge,* 1985

While we can elucidate as clearly as possible the principles we've been able to learn from our effective leaders, the process of internalizing them is a lifetime challenge.
WARREN BENNIS (1925–) and BURT NANUS (1936–). "Taking Charge: Leadership and Empowerment," *Leaders: The Strategies for Taking Charge,* 1985

The craving for political leadership is a pathologic urge marked by chronicity.
C. S. BLUEMEL (1884–?). Psychiatrist. *War, Politics, and Insanity,* 9, 1948

A potential leader can hardly afford to wait to become a legend in his own time; to satisfy us, he must almost become a legend *ahead* of his time.
BROCK BREWER. "Where Have All the Leaders Gone?" *Life,* 8 October 1971

Great leadership arises out of great conflict.
JAMES MacGREGOR BURNS (1918–). "More than Merely Power: II," *New York Times,* 17 November 1978

Leadership is fired in the forge of ambition and opportunity.
JAMES MacGREGOR BURNS (1918–). *Leadership,* 5, 1978

Leaders are not pale reflectors of major social conflicts; they play up some, play down others, ignore still others.

>JAMES MacGREGOR BURNS (1918–). *Leadership,* 8, 1978

Divorced from ethics, leadership is reduced to management and politics to mere technique.

>JAMES MacGREGOR BURNS (1918–). *Leadership,* 14, 1978

Woe to him that claims obedience when it is not due; woe to him that refuses it when it is.

>THOMAS CARLYLE (1795–1881). "The Hero as King," *On Heroes, Hero-Worship, and the Heroic in History,* 1841

The wise man, . . . when he must govern, knows how to do nothing. . . . In complete silence, his voice will be like thunder. His movements will be invisible, like those of a spirit, but the powers of heaven will go with them. Unconcerned, doing nothing, he will see all things grow ripe around him. Where will he find time to govern?

>CHUANG-TZU (369–286 B.C.). As interpreted by Thomas Merton, "Leaving Things Alone," *The Way of Chuang Tzu,* 1965

The Walsh Scale [of leadership] factors in the ability to put together an organization from scratch, to utilize talent to the max, and most important, to give the impression that you're a genius.

>LOWELL COHN (1945–). Referring to San Francisco 49ers football coach Bill Walsh. "The Men Who Turned Bay Teams Around," *San Francisco Chronicle,* 2 November 1989

He who exercises government by means of his virtue may be compared to the north polar star, which keeps its place and all the stars turn towards it.

>CONFUCIUS (551–479 B.C.). *Confucian Analects,* 2.1, tr. James Legge, 1930

Perhaps the most central characteristic of authentic leadership is the relinquishing of the impulse to dominate others.

>DAVID COOPER (1931–?). *Psychiatry and Anti-Psychiatry,* 5, 1967

Leadership is generally defined as the capacity to make things happen that would otherwise not happen.

>THOMAS E. CRONIN (1940–). *The State of the Presidency,* 2nd ed., 11, 1980

The prime role of a leader is to offer an example of courage and sacrifice.

>RÉGIS DEBRAY (1941–). *Revolution in the Revolution? Armed Struggle and Political Struggle in Latin America,* 1 ("The Party and the Guerrilla" 2), tr. Bobbye Ortiz, 1967

The task of the leader is always to weigh up the circumstances, to make decisions and to give orders and then, once the action has been launched, to reassess from time to time the system of the means at his disposal, which [is] continually being modified by circumstances.

>CHARLES de GAULLE (1890–1970). *The Army of the Future,* 6.1, 1941

One cannot govern with "buts."

>CHARLES de GAULLE (1890–1970)

The very exercise of leadership fosters capacity for it.

>CYRIL FALLS (1888–1971). *Ordeal by Battle,* 11, 1943

Leadership is particularly necessary to ensure ready acceptance of the unfamiliar and that which is contrary to tradition.

>CYRIL FALLS (1888–1971). *Ordeal by Battle,* 11, 1943

[Leaders] can express the values that hold the society together. Most important, they can conceive and articulate goals that lift people out of their petty preoccupations, carry them above the conflicts that tear a society apart, and unite them in the pursuit of objectives worthy of their best efforts.

>JOHN W. GARDNER (1912–). "The Antileadership Vaccine," *Annual Report of the Carnegie Corporation,* 1965

Leadership cannot really be taught. It can only be learned.

>HAROLD GENEEN (1910–1997) (with ALVIN MOSCOW). *Managing,* 6 (epigraph), 1984

Divide and rule, the politician cries;
Unite and lead, is watchword of the wise.

>GOETHE (1749–1832). *Sprüche in Prosa,* 1819
>See Machiavellianism: Saying (Latin)

Leadership has to be more than a moral posture: it must bring a payment in cash.

>STANLEY HOFFMANN and INGE HOFFMANN. "The Will to Grandeur: de Gaulle as Political Artist," *Daedalus,* Summer 1968

The time to be toughest is when things are going the best.

>DONALD E. KEOGH. Coca Cola president. In "Voices," *Working Woman,* March 1988

A leader does not deserve the name unless he is willing occasionally to stand alone.

>HENRY A. KISSINGER (1923–). *The Necessity for Choice: Prospects of American Foreign Policy,* 7.4, 1961

The convictions that leaders have formed before reaching high office are the intellectual capital they will consume as long as they continue in office. There is little time for leaders to reflect. They are locked in an endless battle in which the urgent constantly gains on the important. The public life of every political figure is a continual struggle to rescue an element of choice from the pressure of circumstance.

>HENRY A. KISSINGER (1923–). *White House Years,* 3, 1979

Leaders are responsible not for running public opinion polls but for the consequences of their actions.

>HENRY A. KISSINGER (1923–). *White House Years,* 8, 1979

Highly intelligent, superbly endowed physically, [John B. Connally] looked and acted as if he were born to lead. His build was matched by his ego—but those who aspire to the apex must not be criticized for that; they could never lead effectively without extraordinary self-confidence.

>HENRY A. KISSINGER (1923–). *White House Years,* 22, 1979

Leaders establish the vision for the future and set the strategy for getting there.

>JOHN P. KOTTER (1947–). Harvard Business School professor of organizational behavior. In "Missing in Action" (editorial), *Business Week,* 29 October 1990

You have to know one big thing and stick with it . . . The [leaders] who had one very big idea and one very big commitment. This permitted them to create something. Those are the ones who leave a legacy.

> IRVING KRISTOL (1920–). "Person of the Century," Charlie Rose television panel, PBS, 2 April 1998

Be the chief but never the lord.

> LAO-TZU (6th cent. B.C.). *The Way of Life,* 10, tr. R. B. Blakney, 1955

At times leaders must also be followers if they wish to remain leaders.

> CARL LEIDEN and KARL M. SCHMITT. *The Politics of Violence: Revolution in the Modern World,* 5, 1968

Some single mind must be master, else there will be no agreement in anything.

> ABRAHAM LINCOLN (1809–1865). Letter to William M. Fishback, 17 February 1864

I must run the machine as I find it.

> ABRAHAM LINCOLN (1809–1865). In Donn Piatt, "Abraham Lincoln," *Memories of the Men Who Saved the Union,* 1887
>
> See Politics: Richard M. Nixon (1)

It is loyalty to great ends, even though forced to combine the small and opposing motives of selfish men to accomplish them; it is the anchored cling to solid principles of duty and action, which knows how to swing with the tide, but is never carried away by it—that we demand in public men, and not sameness of policy, or a conscientious persistency in what is impracticable.

> JAMES RUSSELL LOWELL (1819–1891). "Abraham Lincoln," 1864, *My Study Windows,* 1871

The cardinal responsibility of leadership is to identify the dominant contradiction at each point of the historical process and to work out a central line to resolve it.

> MAO TSE-TUNG (1893–1976). As paraphrased by James MacGregor Burns, *Leadership,* 8, 1978

It is not difficult to govern. All one has to do is not to offend the noble families.

> MENCIUS (371?–289? B.C.). *Mencius,* 4.A.6, tr. D. C. Lau, 1970

It not infrequently happens that persons without any other special qualifications than the drama of their lives are precipitated into important political positions.

> CHARLES E. MERRIAM (1876–1953). *Political Power,* 1, 1934

If nothing is to be done in the given situation, he must invent plausible reasons for doing nothing; and if something must be done, he must suggest the something. The unpardonable sin is to propose nothing, when action is imperative.

> CHARLES E. MERRIAM (1876–1953). *Political Power,* 1, 1934

The real leader has no need to lead—he is content to point the way.

> HENRY MILLER (1891–1980). Title essay, *The Wisdom of the Heart,* 1941

The sublimity of administration consists in knowing the proper degree of power that should be exerted on different occasions.

> MONTESQUIEU (1689–1755). *The Spirit of the Laws,* 12.25, 1748, tr. Thomas Nugent, 1750, Hafner Publishing edition, 1949

No leader, however great, can long continue unless he wins victories.

> BERNARD LAW MONTGOMERY (1887–1976). *The Memoirs of Field-Marshal Montgomery,* 6, 1958

I am sometimes a fox and sometimes a lion. . . . The whole secret of government lies in knowing when to be the one or the other.

> NAPOLEON (1769–1821). Quoted by Louis Madelin, *The Consulate and the Empire, 1789–1815,* 1933. In Maurice Hutt, ed., *Napoleon,* 14, 1972
>
> See Princes: Machiavelli (5)

In order to govern, the question is not to follow out a more or less valid theory but to build with whatever materials are at hand. The inevitable must be accepted and turned to advantage.

> NAPOLEON (1769–1821). Deathbed statement, 17 April 1821, *The Mind of Napoleon: A Selection from His Written and Spoken Words,* 324, ed. J. Christopher Herold, 1955

A leader is a dealer in hope.

> NAPOLEON (1769–1821). *Napoleon in His Own Words,* 4, comp. Jules Bertaut, 1916

One should never forbid what one lacks the power to prevent.

> NAPOLEON (1769–1821). A repeated remark. *The Mind of Napoleon: A Selection from His Written and Spoken Words,* 115, ed. J. Christopher Herold, 1955

Leadership is more than technique, though techniques are necessary. In a sense, management is prose; leadership is poetry. . . . The manager thinks of today and tomorrow. The leader must think of the day after tomorrow. A manager represents a process. The leader represents a direction of history.

> RICHARD M. NIXON (1913–1994). *Leaders,* 1, 1982

[We find] the stuff of leadership . . . in a MacArthur and a Churchill—proud, vain, paradoxical, posing always, yet brilliant, insightful, with their eyes on the long view of history; driven men, driving others, whose views of their own destinies coincided more often than not with their views of their countries' destinies.

> RICHARD M. NIXON (1913–1994). *Leaders,* 9, 1982

The leader must be an actor. . . . But with him as with his bewigged counterpart he is unconvincing unless he lives his part.

> GEORGE S. PATTON, JR. (1885–1945). "The Secret of Victory," lecture, 26 March 1926. In Martin Blumenson, *The Patton Papers, 1885–1940,* 39, 1972

Lead, follow, or get out of the way.

> LAURENCE J. PETER (1919–1990). "Peter's Survival Principle," *Peter's People,* 8, 1979
>
> See Prudence: Rules: Saying (1)

Anyone can hold the helm when the sea is calm.

> PUBLIUS SYRUS (85–43 B.C.). *Moral Sayings,* 358, tr. Darius Lyman, Jr., 1862

Favor comes [to the political leader] because for a brief moment in the great space of human change and progress some general human purpose finds in him a satisfactory embodiment.

> FRANKLIN D. ROOSEVELT (1882–1945). Speech, Poughkeepsie (New York), 1932 (election eve). In James MacGregor Burns, *Roosevelt: The Lion and the Fox,* 8, 1956

I wouldn't make the slightest concession for moral leadership. It's much overrated.

> DEAN RUSK (1909–1994). Secretary of state. 1962. In David Halberstam, *The Best and the Brightest*, 16, 1972

They that govern most make [the] least noise.

> JOHN SELDEN (1584–1654). "Power: State" (2), *Table Talk*, 1689, ed. Frederick Pollock, 1927
>
> See Leaders & People: Napoleon

You learn to know a pilot in a storm.

> SENECA THE YOUNGER (5? B.C.–A.D. 65). "On Providence" (4.5), *Moral Essays*, tr. John W. Basore, 1928

One must steer, not talk.

> SENECA THE YOUNGER (5? B.C.–A.D. 65). "On the Approaches to Philosophy," *Moral Letters to Lucilius*, 108.37, tr. Richard M. Gummere, 1918

What you cannot enforce,
Do not command!

> SOPHOCLES (496?–406 B.C.). *Oedipus at Colonus*, l. 839, tr. Robert Fitzgerald, 1941

They command us, though they speak no words.

> SOPHOCLES (496?–406 B.C.). In Plutarch (A.D. 46?–119?), "Agis," *Parallel Lives*, Dryden edition, 1693

In the place where there is a leader, do not seek to become a leader. In the place where there is no leader, strive to become a leader.

> TALMUD (A.D. 1st–6th cent.). Rabbinical writings. In Louis I. Newman, comp., *The Talmudic Anthology*, 190, 1945

The Rabbis have said: "Be rather the tail of a lion than the head of a fox." The Romans, however, said: "Be rather the head of a fox than the tail of lion."

> TALMUD (A.D. 1st–6th cent.). Rabbinical writings. Slightly modified. In Louis I. Newman, comp., *The Talmudic Anthology*, 190, 1945

The nature of the group's situation at a given time predetermines what traits are likely to bring a certain individual to the fore as the leader and what traits will impede such an outcome in others.

> ROBERT C. TUCKER (1918–). "Personality and Political Leadership," *Political Science Quarterly*, Fall 1977

Leaders should lead as far as they can and then vanish. Their ashes should not choke the fire they have lit.

> H. G. WELLS (1866–1946). In John W. Gardner, *On Leadership*, 12, 1990

Learning to accede to smaller demands so as not to have to grant larger ones is part of the art of leadership. The difficulty is that narrow concessions may also spread into wide ones.

> AARON WILDAVSKY (1930–1993). *The Nursing Father: Moses as a Political Leader*, 2, 1984

Leadership is, among other things, the ability to inflict pain and get away with it—short-term pain for long-term gain.

> GEORGE F. WILL (1941–). *Statecraft as Soulcraft: What Government Does*, 7, 1983

Leadership—mobilization toward a common goal.

> GARRY WILLS (1934–). *Certain Trumpets: The Call of Leaders*, 7, 1994

Absolute identity with one's cause is the first and great condition of successful leadership.

> WOODROW WILSON (1856–1924). "John Bright," March 1880

❧

If you don't know what else to do, throw a fit—do something.

> ANONYMOUS. Football coach. Quoted by George S. Patton, Jr., "Cavalry in the Next War," 1929. In Martin Blumenson, *The Patton Papers, 1885–1940*, 41, 1972

The essence of superior leadership is the inspired application of principle to circumstance.

> ANONYMOUS

LEADERS & PEOPLE

See also • Commanders & Soldiers ○ Crisis Leaders ○ Leaders ○ Presidents & People ○ War & Peace: Thomas Jefferson

The task of leadership is not to put greatness into humanity, but to elicit it, for the greatness is already there.

> JOHN BUCHAN (1875–1940)

Your representative owes you, not his industry only, but his judgment; and he betrays instead of serving you if he sacrifices it to your opinion.

> EDMUND BURKE (1729–1797). Speech to the electors of Bristol, (England), 3 November 1774

Transactional leaders approach followers with an eye to exchanging one thing for another: jobs for votes, or subsidies for campaign contributions. . . . The *transforming* leader looks for potential motives in followers, seeks to satisfy higher needs, and engages the full person of the follower. The result of transforming leadership is a relationship of mutual stimulation and elevation that converts followers into leaders and may convert leaders into moral agents.

> JAMES MacGREGOR BURNS (1918–). Prologue to *Leadership*, 1978

The ultimate test of practical leadership is the realization of intended, real change that meets people's enduring needs.

> JAMES MacGREGOR BURNS (1918–). *Leadership*, 17, 1978

Woodrow Wilson called for leaders who, by boldly interpreting the nation's conscience, could lift a people out of their everyday selves. That people can be lifted *into* their better selves is the secret of transforming leadership.

> JAMES MacGREGOR BURNS (1918–). Closing words, *Leadership*, 1978

Surely of all the "rights of man," this right of the ignorant man to be guided by the wiser, to be, gently or forcibly, held in the true course by him, is the indisputablest.

> THOMAS CARLYLE (1795–1881). *Chartism*, 6, 1840

To govern mankind, one must not overrate them.

> LORD CHESTERFIELD (1694–1773). Letter to his son, 15 February 1754
>
> See People: H. L. Mencken

I was only the servant of my country and had I, at any moment, failed to express her unflinching resolve to fight and conquer, I should at once have been rightly cast aside.

> WINSTON CHURCHILL (1874–1965). After being introduced as the "architect of victory" in World War II, address, University of Copenhagen, 10 October 1950

Go before the people with your example, and be laborious in their affairs.

> CONFUCIUS (551–479 B.C.). *Confucian Analects*, 13.1, tr. James Legge, 1930

I am not a . . . leader. I don't want you to follow me or anything else. If you are looking for a Moses to lead you out of the . . . wilderness, you will stay right where you are. I would not lead you into this promised land if I could, because if I could lead you in, someone else could lead you out.

> EUGENE V. DEBS (1855–1926). Presidential campaign speech, 1912. In Emmet John Hughes, *The Ordeal of Power: A Political Memoir of the Eisenhower Years*, 10.4, 1963

You don't need a weatherman
To know which way the wind blows . . .
Don't follow leaders
Watch the parkin' meters.

> BOB DYLAN (1941–). "Subterranean Homesick Blues" (song), 1965

The national leader requires a foundation of good qualities; if he possesses these, the nation will endow him with the rest.

> CYRIL FALLS (1888–1971). *Ordeal by Battle*, 11, 1943

The trust of the people in the leaders reflects the confidence of the leaders in the people.

> PAULO FREIRE (1921–1997). *Pedagogy of the Oppressed*, 4, tr. Myra Bergman Ramos, 1968

One instance of the innate and ineradicable inequality of men is their tendency to fall into two classes of leaders and followers. The latter constitute the vast majority; they stand in need of an authority which will make decisions for them and to which they for the most part offer an unqualified submission. This suggests that more care should be taken than hitherto to educate an upper stratum of men with independent minds, not open to intimidation and eager in the pursuit of truth, whose business it would be to give direction to the dependent masses.

> SIGMUND FREUD (1856–1939). Letter to Albert Einstein, September 1932, tr. James Strachey, 1963
>
> See Inequality: Martin Luther o Slavery: Aristotle

All of the great leaders have had one characteristic in common: it was the willingness to confront unequivocally the major anxiety of their people in their time. This, and not much else, is the essence of leadership.

> JOHN KENNETH GALBRAITH (1908–). *The Age of Uncertainty*, 12, 1977

Let no one say that he is a follower of Gandhi. It is enough that I should be my own follower. I know what an inadequate follower I am of myself, for I cannot live up to the convictions I stand for. You are no followers but fellow students, fellow pilgrims, fellow seekers, fellow workers.

> MOHANDAS K. GANDHI (1869–1948). In *Harijan*, 2 March 1940

A true leader has to have a genuine open-door policy so that his people are not afraid to approach him for any reason.

> HAROLD GENEEN (1910–1997) (with ALVIN MOSCOW). *Managing*, 6, 1984

That is what leadership is all about: staking your ground ahead of where opinion is and convincing people, not simply following the popular opinion of the moment.

> DORIS KEARNS GOODWIN (1943–). In Anthony Lewis, "Leading from Behind," *New York Times*, 19 December 1994

Leaders are . . . characterized by constant activity, by an ability to understand and appreciate the position of another person, a self-disciplined personality, and willingness to fight for what they believe. Superior intelligence may be important, but if that intelligence is greatly superior to the group, such a person is apt to be suspect and hence not permitted to lead.

> CARL G. GUSTAVSON (1915–). *A Preface to History*, 10, 1955

Your position never gives you the right to command. It only imposes on you the duty of so living your life that others can receive your orders without being humiliated.

> DAG HAMMARSKJÖLD (1905–1961). 1955, *Markings*, tr. Leif Sjöberg and W. H. Auden, 1964

Those who cannot think or take responsibility for themselves need, and clamor for, a leader.

> HERMANN HESSE (1877–1962). *Reflections*, 106, ed. Volker Michels, 1974

A creative organizer creates an organization that can function well without him. When a creative leader has done his work, his followers will say, "We have done it ourselves," and feel that they can do great things without a leader. With the noncreative it is the other way around: in whatever they do, they arrange things so that they themselves become indispensable.

> ERIC HOFFER (1902–1983). *Reflections on the Human Condition*, 87, 1973

A genuine leader is not a searcher for consensus but a molder of consensus.

> MARTIN LUTHER KING, JR. (1929–1968). *Where Do We Go from Here: Chaos or Community?* 2.4, 1967

A leader who confines his role to his people's experience dooms himself to stagnation; a leader who outstrips his people's experience runs the risk of not being understood.

> HENRY A. KISSINGER (1923–). *Diplomacy*, 2, 1994

Leadership consists not in degrees of technique but in traits of character; it requires moral rather than athletic or intellectual effort, and it imposes on both leader and follower alike the burdens of self-restraint.

> LEWIS H. LAPHAM (1935–). *Money and Class in America: Notes and Observations on the Civil Religion*, 10, 1988

There go the people. I must follow them, for I am their leader.

> ALEXANDRE LEDRU-ROLLIN (1807–1864). French revolutionary leader. Attributed

It's quite possible to do anything, but not to put it on the leaders and the parking meters. Don't expect Jimmy Carter or Ronald Reagan or John Lennon or Yoko Ono or Bob Dylan or Jesus Christ to come and do it for you. You have to do it yourself.

> JOHN LENNON (1940–1980). David Sheff interview with Lennon and
> Yoko Ono, *Playboy,* January 1981

Much of [Winston Churchill's] strength as a war leader derived from this very habit of myth-making, of surrounding even the ordinary and the humdrum with enchantment. Like Shakespeare's Glendower, he could "call spirits from the vasty deep"—and the British believed in them.

> RONALD LEWIN (1914–1984). *Ultra Goes to War: The First Account of
> World War II's Greatest Secret Based on Official Documents,* 7, 1978
> See Spirituality: Shakespeare

Leadership, I think you must have that, particularly when a team's on the field, they look to you. In critical situations, they look into your eyes to see if you're there. If you're not there, they start quitting.

> DAN MARINO, SR. Father of Miami Dolphins' quarterback Dan Marino.
> 4 November 1984

The leader and led both define themselves, and find their selves, in the course of special circumstances and in a creative encounter. In the process, a selection is made from the available psychic repository, the shared culture. Ideology codifies and freezes this selection, but it is made real and alive to the led through the leader's image. The organization created by the leader allows for the personal development of the followers.

> BRUCE MAZLISH (1923–). "Leader and Led, Individual and Group,"
> 1981, *The Leader, the Led, and the Psyche: Essays in Psychohistory,*
> 1990

No man is great enough or wise enough for any of us to surrender our destiny to. The only way in which anyone can lead us is to restore to us the belief in our own guidance.

> HENRY MILLER (1891–1980). "The Alcoholic Veteran with the
> Washboard Cranium," *The Wisdom of the Heart,* 1941

The function of leadership is to produce more leaders, not more followers.

> RALPH NADER (1934–). In "Leadership: The Biggest Issue," *Time,* 8
> November 1976

Leadership involves finding a parade and getting in front of it.

> JOHN NAISBITT (1929–). *Megatrends: Ten New Directions Transforming
> Our Lives,* 7, 1984

Barère still believes that the masses must be stirred. On the contrary, they must be guided without their noticing it.

> NAPOLEON (1769–1821). Letter to Joseph Fouché, 9 September 1804,
> *The Mind of Napoleon: A Selection from His Written and Spoken
> Words,* 150, ed. J. Christopher Herold, 1955
> See Leaders: John Selden

The great principle of all is that no one of either sex should be without a commander; nor should the mind of anyone be accustomed to do anything, either in jest or earnest, of his own motion, but in war and in peace he should look to and follow his leader, even in the least things being under his guidance; for example, he should stand or move, or exercise, or wash, or take his meals, or get up in the night to keep guard and deliver messages when he is bidden; and in the hour of danger he should not pursue and not retreat except by order of his superior; and in a word, not teach the soul or accustom her to know or understand how to do anything apart from others. . . . And we ought in time of peace from youth upwards to practice this habit of commanding others, and of being commanded by others.

> PLATO (427?–347 B.C.). *Laws,* 12.942, tr. Benjamin Jowett, 1894

How should I be able to govern others when I don't know how to govern myself.

> RABELAIS (1483?–1553). *Gargantua and Pantagruel,* 1.52, 1532–1552, tr.
> J. M. Cohen, 1955

Maintaining a monopoly of authoritative answers is . . . the essence of leadership.

> GEORGE E. REEDY (1917–). *The Twilight of the Presidency,* 4, 1970

You've got to look inside; you can't expect some leader to take you anywhere.

> CHRISTOPHER REEVE (1952–). Larry King television interview, CNN,
> 17 April 1997

The leader holds his position purely because he is able to appeal to the conscience and to the reason of those who support him, and the boss holds his position because he appeals to fear of punishment and hope of reward.

The leader works in the open, and the boss in covert. The leader leads, and the boss drives.

> THEODORE ROOSEVELT (1858–1919). Speech, Binghamton (New York),
> 24 October 1910

One must often be prepared not to act, but to "stand still in the light" [George Fox], confident that only such a stillness possesses the eloquence to draw men away from lives we must believe they inwardly loathe.

> THEODORE ROSZAK (1933–). *The Making of the Counter Culture:
> Reflections on the Technocratic Society and Its Youthful Opposition,*
> 8, 1969

When men willingly follow a leader, they do so with a view to the acquisition of power by the group which he commands, and they feel that his triumphs are theirs.

> BERTRAND RUSSELL (1872–1970). *Power: A New Social Analysis,* 2, 1938

Leaders are people we as followers want to regard with awe as the fullest flowering of our own possibilities.

> GAIL SHEEHY (1937–). *Pathfinders,* 17, 1981

Leadership is a relation to which the leaders, the followers, and the requirements of the situation, including the traditions of the group, all contribute.

> SOCIAL SCIENCE RESEARCH COUNCIL'S COMMITTEE ON HISTORIOG-
> RAPHY. *Report,* 1954. In Arnold J. Toynbee, *A Study of History,*
> 12.126–127, 1961

Whenever [Pericles] saw them unseasonably and insolently elated, he would with a word reduce them to alarm; on the other hand, if they fell victims to a panic, he could at once restore them to confidence.

> THUCYDIDES (460?–400? B.C.). *The Peloponnesian War,* 2.65, tr. Richard
> Crawley and rev. T. E. Wick, 1982

You know what makes leadership? It is the ability to get men to do what they don't want to do and like it.

> HARRY S. TRUMAN (1884–1972). In "Leadership: The Biggest Issue," *Time,* 8 November 1976

The leader must foster understanding of the other group's plight and appeal to the generous instincts of those in comfortable circumstances, their capacity for acting according to the dictates of decency and of long-range self-interest.

> ROBERT C. TUCKER (1918–). "Personality and Political Leadership," *Political Science Quarterly,* Fall 1977

Can we foresee and foster the advent to power of leaders who will dedicate themselves to supranational goals that include the building of a universal community?

> ROBERT C. TUCKER (1918–). "Personality and Political Leadership," *Political Science Quarterly,* Fall 1977

A corrupt people is not responsive to virtuous leadership.

> GARRY WILLS (1934–). Introduction to *Certain Trumpets: The Call of Leaders,* 1994

I do not believe that any man can lead who does not act . . . under the impulse of a profound sympathy with those whom he leads.

> WOODROW WILSON (1856–1924). In Arthur M. Schlesinger, Jr., "The Ultimate Approval Rating," *New York Times Magazine,* 15 December 1996

First organize the inner, then organize the outer. . . . First organize the great, then organize the small. First organize yourself, then organize others.

> ZHUGE LIANG (A.D. 180?–234?). *Records of the Loyal Lord of Warriors.* In *Mastering the Art of War,* tr. Thomas Cleary, 1989

❦

Every one who was in distress, and every one who was in debt, and every one who was discontented, gathered to [David]; and he became captain over them. And there were with him about four hundred men.

> ANONYMOUS (*BIBLE*). *1 Samuel* 22:2

People judge a leader less by how he or she is doing than by how they are doing.

> ANONYMOUS

Not the cry, but the flight of the wild duck, leads the flock to fly and follow.

> SAYING (CHINESE)

We make our arches of brick so that, after the leader passes through, we have something to throw at him.

> SAYING. In Maureen Dowd, "Clinton as National Idol: Can the Honeymoon Last?" *New York Times,* 3 January 1993

LEADERS & STAFF

Includes • Leaders & Associates ○ Leaders & Subordinates

See also • Commanders & Staff ○ Decision-Making ○ Leaders ○ Presidents & Staff

History is filled with undistinguished leaders who succeeded because they had a flair for selecting sound counselors.

> GEORGE W. BALL (1909–1994). "Kennedy Up Close," *New York Review of Books,* 3 February 1994

If you turned Sam Rayburn down once, men learned, he would never ask you again—for anything.

> ROBERT A. CARO (1935–). On the Texas Speaker of the House of Representatives, *The Path to Power: The Years of Lyndon Johnson,* 18, 1982

Set the saddle on the right horse.

> JOHN CLARKE (1596–1658). Comp., *Proverbs: English and Latine,* p. 182, 1639
>
> See Ability: Napoleon

Always mistrust a subordinate who never finds fault with his superior!

> JOHN CHURTIN COLLINS (1848–1908)

Patience is a virtue with which [Winston Churchill] was totally unfamiliar. As soon as he had ordered something to be done he expected that it had been completed. Many was the time when he told me to do something and before I had time to get back to my telephone he had rung the bell to enquire [of] the result.

> JOHN COLVILLE (1915–). 12 May 1940, *The Fringes of Power: 10 Downing Street Diaries, 1939–1955,* 5, 1985

One rule of action more important than all others consists in never doing anything that someone else can do for you.

> CALVIN COOLIDGE (1872–1933). In James David Barber, *The Presidential Character: Predicting Performance in the White House,* 5, 1972

Let the Care of one business be committed but to one Person; for otherwise, besides Disagreement which may arise when Account is taken, everyone's Answer is, That he thought others had done it.

> THOMAS FULLER (1654–1734). Comp., *Introductio ad Prudentiam,* 1072, 1731
>
> See Presidents & Staff: Arthur M. Schlesinger, Jr. (1)

You can lead an organization through persuasion or formal edict. I have never found the arbitrary use of authority to control an organization either effective or, for that matter, personally interesting. If you cannot persuade your colleagues of the correctness of your position, it is probably worthwhile to rethink your own.

> ALAN GREENSPAN (1926–). In David E. Rosenbaum, "Federal Reserve's Chairman Blends Eye for Politics with Economic Skills," *New York Times,* 26 July 1990

A staff can be no better than the man it serves.

> DAVID HALBERSTAM (1934–). *The Best and the Brightest,* 10, 1972

The more you establish parameters and encourage people to take initiatives within those boundaries, the more you multiply your own effectiveness by the effectiveness of other people.

> ROBERT HASS. Levi Strauss & Co. executive. Robert Howard interview. In *Leaders on Leadership: Interviews with Top Executives* (Harvard Business Review Book), 1992

Get in a lot of youngsters who don't know it can't be done.
> WILLIAM RANDOLPH HEARST (1863–1951)

The uncanny powers of a leader manifest themselves not so much in the hold he has on the masses as in his ability to dominate and almost bewitch a small group of able men.
> ERIC HOFFER (1902–1983). *The True Believer: Thoughts on the Nature of Mass Movements,* 90, 1951

You can judge a leader by the size of the problem he tackles. . . . Other people can cope with the waves, it's his job to watch the tide.
> ANTONY JAY (1930–). *Management and Machiavelli: An Inquiry into the Politics of Corporate Life,* 17, 1967

Though we would probably have denied this hotly then, there is no doubt that [Winston Churchill's] taunts and exhortations and his criticism of every detail of our work, kept us continuously on our toes.
> JOHN KENNEDY. *The Business of War: The War Narrative of Major-General Sir John Kennedy,* 15, 1958

While I hold strong opinions, I have always felt it essential to test them against men and women of intelligence and character; those who stood up to me earned my respect and often became my closest associates.
> HENRY A. KISSINGER (1923–). *White House Years,* 2, 1979

If you did not need to know, you scrupulously did not seek to know.
> RONALD LEWIN (1914–1984). On the members of Winston Churchill's military staff, *Ultra Goes to War: The First Account of World War II's Greatest Secret Based on Official Documents,* 7, 1978

Unwilling executants do not make for good execution.
> B. H. LIDDELL HART (1895–1970). *The German Generals Talk,* 4, 1948

Ask your subordinates about matters you don't understand or don't know, and do not lightly express your approval or disapproval.
> MAO TSE-TUNG (1893–1976). "Methods of Work of Party Committees," March 1949, *Selected Works of Mao Tse-tung,* Foreign Languages Press edition, vol. 4, 1961

The final test of a leader is the feeling you have when you leave his presence after a conference or interview. Have you a feeling of uplift and confidence? Are you clear as to what is to be done, and what is your part of the task? Are you determined to pull your weight in achieving the object? Or is your feeling the reverse?
> BERNARD LAW MONTGOMERY (1887–1976). *The Path to Leadership,* 1, 1961

A certain ruthlessness is essential, particularly with inefficiency and also with those who would waste his time. People will accept this provided the leader is ruthless with himself.
> BERNARD LAW MONTGOMERY (1887–1976). *The Path to Leadership,* 15, 1961

Having decided on his policy, his objective, he must not be led off his target by the faint-hearted; he will do well to discard the faint-hearted once they are discovered.
> BERNARD LAW MONTGOMERY (1887–1976). *The Path to Leadership,* 15, 1961

When in doubt about honesty, trustfulness, and other moral qualities [of the candidate for a leadership position], a good test is to say to oneself, "Would I go in the jungle with that man?"
> BERNARD LAW MONTGOMERY (1887–1976). *The Path to Leadership,* 15, 1961

The art of choosing men is not nearly so difficult as the art of enabling those one has chosen to attain their full worth.
> NAPOLEON (1769–1821). Remark to François Mollien, 1802, *The Mind of Napoleon: A Selection from His Written and Spoken Words,* 219, ed. J. Christopher Herold, 1955

Work with your ministers twice a week—once with each of them separately and once with them all together in Council.
> NAPOLEON (1769–1821). Letter to his stepson Eugène Beauharnais, viceroy of Italy, 5 June 1805, *Napoleon's Letters,* tr. J. M. Thompson, 1934

The art consists in making others work rather than in wearing oneself out.
> NAPOLEON (1769–1821). Letter to his stepson Eugène Beauharnais, 27 February 1806, *The Mind of Napoleon: A Selection from His Written and Spoken Words,* 219, ed. J. Christopher Herold, 1955

When I give a minister an order, I leave it to him to find [the] means to carry it out.
> NAPOLEON (1769–1821). Letter to Adm. Decrès, 22 May 1808, *Napoleon's Letters,* tr. J. M. Thompson, 1934

I had no flatterers . . . in my train!
> NAPOLEON (1769–1821). Letter to his brother Jerome Bonaparte, 25 July 1809, *New Letters of Napoleon I,* tr. Lady Mary Loyd, 1898

To be successful, a leader must develop a core of loyal staff members who share his sense of mission, serve as his early warning system, possess acute political instincts, and have the competence to protect him from his own mistakes.
> RICHARD M. NIXON (1913–1994). *In the Arena: A Memoir of Victory, Defeat and Renewal,* 30 (opening words), 1990

A leader must give credit to a staffer for a job well done both personally and if possible publicly as well. The best rule: Be generous in sharing credit with subordinates when an initiative succeeds and be prepared to take the blame if it fails.
> RICHARD M. NIXON (1913–1994). *In the Arena: A Memoir of Victory, Defeat and Renewal,* 30 (closing words), 1990

I despise toadies who suck up to their bosses; they are generally the same people who bully their subordinates.
> DAVID OGILVY (1911–). *Confessions of an Advertising Man,* 1, 1963

I stay in the background if things get done.
> ROSS PEROT (1930–). Barbara Walters television interview, *20/20,* ABC, 29 May 1992

The leader must know, must know that he knows, and must be able to make it abundantly clear to those about him that he knows.
> CLARENCE B. RANDALL. *Making Good in Management: Reflections on the Challenges and Opportunities of a Business Career,* 8, 1964

If someone knows of a problem and conceals it from me, I get more upset from that than from the problem itself. I tell our people time and time again: Bad news first.

> DONALD T. REGAN (1918–). In Bernard Weinraub, "How Donald Regan Runs the White House," *New York Times Magazine*, 5 January 1986

If indulgence can at times tolerate some incapacity, it can never suffer malice.

> CARDINAL RICHELIEU (1585–1642). *Political Testament*, 2.7, tr. Henry Bertram Hill, 1961

A man in power must have men around him whom his awesome power does not intimidate.

> WILLIAM SAFIRE (1929–). *Before the Fall: An Inside View of the Pre-Watergate White House*, 4.6, 1975

Be on the constant lookout for capable lieutenants, especially capable individuals who fit well into your personal style of doing things.

> R. G. H. SIU (1917–). *The Craft of Power*, 2.32, 1984

❦

[When asked what Sergiu Comissioná, Houston Symphony conductor, was like, two of his musicians answered], Terrific. [When asked why, after hesitating, they said,] Because he doesn't waste our time.

> ANONYMOUS. In Warren Bennis and Burt Nanus, "Leading Others, Managing Yourself," *Leaders: The Strategies for Taking Charge*, 1985

Tasks must be delegated without responsibilities being abdicated.

> ANONYMOUS

LEARNING (KNOWLEDGE)

See also • Books ○ Faith: Mohandas K. Gandhi (1) ○ Imagination: Joseph Joubert ○ Information ○ Knowledge ○ Learning (Process) ○ Understanding: Heraclitus

It is through suffering that learning comes

> AESCHYLUS (525–456 B.C.). In Arnold J. Toynbee, "Christianity and Civilization," 1947, *Civilization on Trial*, 1948

The justest division of human learning is that derived from the three different faculties of the soul, the seat of learning; history being relative to the memory, poetry to the imagination, and philosophy to the reason.

> FRANCIS BACON (1561–1626). *Advancement of Learning*, 2.1, 1605, Willey Book edition, 1944

He that has less Learning than his Capacity is able to manage shall have more Use of it than he that has more than he can master. For no Man can have an active and ready Command of that which is too heavy for him.

> SAMUEL BUTLER (1612–1680). "Thoughts on Various Subjects," *The Genuine Remains in Verse and Prose of Mr. Samuel Butler, Author of Hudibras*, vol. 2, 1759

Learning makes a Man fit Company for himself.

> THOMAS FULLER (1654–1734). Comp., *Gnomologia: Adages and Proverbs*, 3163, 1732

A little learning misleadeth, and a great deal often stupifieth the understanding.

> MARQUIS OF HALIFAX (1633–1695). "False Learning," *Political, Moral and Miscellaneous Reflections*, 1750

A handful of good life is better than a bushel of learning.

> GEORGE HERBERT (1593–1633). Comp., *Outlandish Proverbs*, 3, 1640

Nothing has more retarded the advancement of learning than the disposition of vulgar minds to ridicule and vilify what they cannot comprehend.

> SAMUEL JOHNSON (1709–1784). In *The Rambler* (English journal), 117, 30 April 1751

A little learning is a dang'rous Thing;
Drink deep, or taste not the Pierian Spring:
There shallow Draughts intoxicate the Brain,
And drinking largely sobers us again.

> ALEXANDER POPE (1688–1744). *An Essay on Criticism*, l. 215, 1711

And the same age saw Learning fall, and Rome.

> ALEXANDER POPE (1688–1744). *An Essay on Criticism*, l. 686, 1711

It is only when we forget all our learning that we begin to know.

> HENRY DAVID THOREAU (1817–1862). Journal, 4 October 1859
> See Wisdom: James Russell Lowell

❦

Learning makes the wise wiser and the foolish more foolish.

> SAYING (ENGLISH)

Learning acquired in youth is inscribed on stone.

> SAYING (TAMIL)

LEARNING (PROCESS)

See also • Children ○ Children's Learning ○ College ○ Dogma: Alfred North Whitehead (1) ○ Education ○ Experience ○ Knowledge ○ Learning (Knowledge) ○ Scholars ○ School ○ Self-Realization (Becoming) ○ Study ○ Teachers ○ University

They know enough who know how to learn.

> HENRY ADAMS (1838–1918). *The Education of Henry Adams*, 21, 1907

I like to have a thing suggested rather than told in full. When every detail is given, the mind rests satisfied and the imagination loses the desire to use its own wings.

> THOMAS BAILEY ALDRICH (1836–1907)

What we learn to do, we learn by doing.

> ARISTOTLE (384–322 B.C.). *Nichomachean Ethics*, 2.1
> See Teacher: Rousseau (2) ○ Understanding: Saying (Chinese)

Learning teacheth more in one year than experience in twenty, and learning teacheth safely, when experience maketh more miserable than wise. . . . It is costly wisdom that is bought by experience.

> ROGER ASCHAM (1515–1568). *The Schoolmaster*, 1, 1570, ed. Lawrence V. Ryan, 1967

Learn from others what to pursue and what to avoid, and let your teachers be the lives of others.

DIONYSIUS CATO (A.D. 4th cent.). *Disticha de moribus ad filium*, 3.13

I am always ready to learn, although I do not always like being taught.

WINSTON CHURCHILL (1874–1965). House of Commons speech, 4 November 1952

Learn one thing well first.

JOHN CLARKE (1596–1658). Comp., *Proverbs: English and Latine*, p. 100, 1639

In ancient times, men learned with a view to their own improvement. Nowadays, men learn with a view to the approbation of others.

CONFUCIUS (551–479 B.C.). *Confucian Analects*, 14.25, tr. James Legge, 1930

A primary method of learning is to go from the familiar to the unfamiliar.

GLENN DOMAN. *How to Teach Your Baby to Read: The Gentle Revolution*, 7, 1964

What we have learned from others becomes our own by reflection.

RALPH WALDO EMERSON (1803–1882). "Blotting Book 1," p. 10, 1826–1827

You are as one who has a private door that leads him to the King's chamber. You have learned nothing rightly that you have not learned so.

RALPH WALDO EMERSON (1803–1882). Journal, 29 July 1831

Every soul has to learn the whole lesson for itself. It must go over the whole ground. What it does not see, what it does not live, it will not know.

RALPH WALDO EMERSON (1803–1882). Journal, 2 October 1837

It is impossible for a man to begin to learn what he thinks he knows.

EPICTETUS (A.D. 55?–135?). Slightly modified. *Discourses*, 2.17, tr. George Long, 1890?

'Tis harder to unlearn than learn.

THOMAS FULLER (1654–1734). Comp., *Gnomologia: Adages and Proverbs*, 5085, 1732

We learn only from those whom we love.

GOETHE (1749–1832). 12 May 1825. In Peter Eckermann, *Conversations with Goethe*, 1836–1848, tr. John Oxenford, 1850

You learn more from getting your butt kicked than from getting it kissed.

TOM HANKS (1957–). Larry King television interview, CNN, 30 June 1995

We learn to use language well, spoken or written, only when we use it for a purpose, our purpose, to say something we think is important, to people we want to say it to, or to make something happen that we want to happen.

JOHN HOLT (1923–1985). *Instead of Education: Ways to Help People Do Things Better*, 7, 1976

Most learning is not the result of instruction. It is rather the result of unhampered participation in a meaningful setting.

IVAN ILLICH (1926–). *Deschooling Society*, 3, 1970

Learn to do good.

ISAIAH (8th cent. B.C.). *Isaiah* 1:17

Be done with rote learning
And its attendant vexations.

LAO-TZU (6th cent. B.C.). *The Way of Life*, 20, tr. R. B. Blakney, 1955

[Robert F. Kennedy] was one of the few adults, one of the few politicians, who kept learning after they grew up. Most of us just build up our intellectual capital and then live off it.

FRANK MANKIEWICZ (1924–). In Christopher Matthews, "Of Kennedy and King," *San Francisco Sunday Examiner & Chronicle*, 6 June 1993

To learn is no easy matter and to apply what one has learned is even harder.

MAO TSE-TUNG (1893–1976). "Problems of Strategy in China's Revolutionary War" (1.4), December 1936, *Selected Works of Mao Tse-tung*, Foreign Languages Press edition, vol. 1, 1965

I am still learning.

MICHELANGELO (1475–1564). His favorite saying

Men are either learned or learning: the rest are blockheads.

MUHAMMAD (A.D. 570?–632). In Ralph Waldo Emerson, journal, 1845, undated

It is right to learn even from one's enemies.

OVID (43 B.C.–A.D. 17). *Metamorphoses*, 4.428, tr. Mary M. Innes, 1955

Each day grow older, and learn something new.

SOLON (630?–560? B.C.). One of the Seven Sages of Greece. In Plutarch (A.D. 46?–119?), "Solon," *Parallel Lives*, Dryden edition, 1693

Let us learn on earth those things whose knowledge might continue in heaven.

ST. PAUL'S SCHOOL. Concord, New Hampshire. Motto

I have learned throughout my life as a composer chiefly through my mistakes and pursuits of false assumptions, not by my exposure to founts of wisdom and knowledge.

IGOR STRAVINSKY (1882–1971). "Contingencies," *Themes and Episodes*, 1966

Every act of conscious learning requires the willingness to suffer an injury to one's self-esteem. That is why young children, before they are aware of their own self-importance, learn so easily; and why older persons, especially if vain or important, cannot learn at all.

THOMAS S. SZASZ (1920–). "Education," *The Second Sin*, 1973

Before making a practical beginning [on the job, the apprentice/student] has had an opportunity of following some general and summary course of instruction, so as to have a framework ready prepared in which to store the observations he is shortly to make. Furthermore he is able . . . to avail himself of sundry technical courses which he can follow in his leisure hours, so as to coordinate step by step the daily experience he is gathering.

HIPPOLYTE-ADOLPHE TAINE (1828–1893). French philosopher. In Gustave Le Bon, *The Crowd*, 2.1.5, 1895, Viking Press edition, 1960

Learn in order to teach and to practice.

> TALMUD (A.D. 1st–6th cent.). Rabbinical writings. In Louis I. Newman, comp., *The Talmudic Anthology*, 346, 1945

❧

Learn to teach yourself.

> ANONYMOUS (AFRICAN-AMERICAN). Graffito. In photograph, "Atlanta: Energy and Optimism in the New South," *National Geographic*, July 1988

We learn well and fast when we experience the consequences of what we do—and don't do.

> ANONYMOUS

Learning is like rowing upstream; not to advance is to drop back.

> SAYING (CHINESE)

LEISURE

See also • Idleness ○ Laziness ○ Travel ○ Wealth ○ Work: [especially] Percy Bysshe Shelley

In a society where labor has become for the overwhelming majority of people [an] alienating activity . . . the world of leisure has become the relatively free place where people attempt to realize *who they really are*. The space of "free time" is where the physical and emotional damage of work is repaired, the place where people relieve all the piled up unmet needs of rest, fun, creativity, critical thinking, and social connection. In sum, leisure is the location of a struggle to become more fully human.

> SANDY CARTER. "Pop Music and the Left," *Zeta Magazine*, October 1988

Leisure is Time for doing something useful; this Leisure the diligent Man will obtain but the lazy Man never.

> BENJAMIN FRANKLIN (1706–1790). "The Way to Wealth," 7 July 1757

A Life of Leisure and a Life of Laziness are two things.

> THOMAS FULLER (1654–1734). Comp., *Gnomologia: Adages and Proverbs*, 240, 1732

Nothing excellent can be done without leisure.

> ANDRÉ GIDE (1869–1951). Journal, 15 January 1946, tr. Justin O'Brien, 1951

Leisure is the mother of Philosophy.

> THOMAS HOBBES (1588–1679). *Leviathan*, 46, 1651

Your job today tells me nothing of your future—your use of your leisure today tells me just what your tomorrow will be.

> ROBERT H. JACKSON (1892–1954). Supreme Court associate justice. Dedicating the new Jamestown High School building (New York), 1935. In Eugene C. Gerhart, *America's Advocate: Robert H. Jackson*, 24, 1958

They talk of the dignity of work. Bosh. The dignity is in leisure.

> HERMAN MELVILLE (1819–1891)

To be able to fill leisure intelligently is the last product of civilization, and at present very few people have reached this level.

> BERTRAND RUSSELL (1872–1970). *The Conquest of Happiness*, 14, 1930

He enjoys true leisure who has time to improve his soul's estate.

> HENRY DAVID THOREAU (1817–1862). Journal, 11 February 1840

❧

Leisure is the reward of labor.

> SAYING (ENGLISH)

The busiest people have the most leisure time.

> SAYING (ENGLISH)

Leisure does body and soul good.

> SAYING (GERMAN)

LIBERALS

See also • Conservatives ○ Conservatives & Liberals/Radicals ○ Reformers ○ Revolutionaries

It is the duty of the liberal to protect and to extend the basic democratic freedoms. . . . But fundamentally, liberalism is an attitude. The chief characteristics of that attitude are human sympathy, a receptivity to change and a scientific willingness to follow reason rather than faith or any fixed set of ideas.

> CHESTER BOWLES (1901–1986). In Eric F. Goldman and Mary Paull, "Liberals on Liberalism," *New Republic*, 22 July 1946

A liberal is a man who leaves the room when the fight starts.

> HEYWOOD BROUN (1888–1939). In Robert E. Drennan, ed., "Heywood Broun," *The Algonquin Wits*, 1968

The true liberal is liberal in human relations and conservative in his economics. He seeks to conserve a capitalistic system characterized by free enterprise and the profit motive because it is essential to liberty.

> HARRY J. CARMAN. Letter to *St. Louis Post-Dispatch*, 10 August 1964

Liberalism to me is a philosophy that looks at people and says, "Gosh, you're hurting. What kind of government program can we set up to ease your pain?" Populism sees someone hurting and says, "What's causing that? How do we change the structure so that these people aren't hurt that way?"

> TOM HARKIN (1939–). Iowa senator. In Molly Ivins, "And They Call Themselves Populists!" *San Francisco Chronicle*, 7 February 1996

[Liberalism] regards man as improvable but not perfectable.

> WALTER LIPPMANN (1889–1974). Ronald Steel interview, "Walter Lippmann at 83," *Washington Post*, 25 March 1973

A major objective [of liberalism] is the protection of the economic weak and doing it within the framework of a private property economy.

> WAYNE MORSE (1900–1974). Oregon senator. In Eric F. Goldman and Mary Paull, "Liberals on Liberalism," *New Republic*, 22 July 1946

In a pinch the liberals can always be counted on to back up the principles of the established order.

> SCOTT NEARING (1883–1983). In *Modern Monthly*, July 1950

Those liberal bastards are fucking me again.

> RICHARD M. NIXON (1913–1994). In Joe McGinniss, *The Selling of the President 1968*, 4, 1969

The New Class [i.e., American liberals and radicals in the 1960s] covers its political campaigns . . . with an aura of morality so thick it would make the righteous Anglo-Saxons of a century ago envious. Because two of its chief causes—civil rights (including poverty) and resistance to the Indochinese war—are morally sound, it has been able to conceal its own lust for power and its own class interests, at least from itself.

> MICHAEL NOVAK (1933–). "Needing Niebuhr Again," *Commentary*, September 1972

We liberals must acknowledge this: that while the rights of the individual are precious, at some deep level individualism alone does not suffice. And the ability of the radical right to seize and exploit the terrain of the soul has been helped immeasurably by the failure of so many of the rest of us to even acknowledge the soul's existence.

> ANNA QUINDLEN (1953–). "America's Sleeping Sickness," *New York Times*, 17 October 1993

I can remember way back when a liberal was one who was generous with his own money.

> WILL ROGERS (1879–1935)

The essence of the Liberal outlook lies not in *what* opinions are held, but in *how* they are held: instead of being held dogmatically, they are held tentatively, and with a consciousness that new evidence may at any moment lead to their abandonment. This is the way in which opinions are held in science, as opposed to the way in which they are held in theology.

> BERTRAND RUSSELL (1872–1970). "Philosophy and Politics," *Unpopular Essays*, 1950

Liberals are variously described as limousine, double-domed, screaming, knee-jerk, professional, bleeding heart; also see pinko; parlor pink; committed; egghead.

> WILLIAM SAFIRE (1929–). *Safire's New Political Dictionary: The Definitive Guide to the New Language of Politics*, p. 408, 1993 (1968)

Limousine Liberal[:] one who takes up hunger as a cause but has never felt a pang; who will talk at length about the public school system but sends his children to private schools.

> WILLIAM SAFIRE (1929–). *Safire's New Political Dictionary: The Definitive Guide to the New Language of Politics*, p. 413, 1993 (1968)

A liberal will hang you from a lower branch.

> ADLAI E. STEVENSON (1900–1965). Quoted by Mort Sahl, Larry King television interview, CNN, 14 September 1996

The modern, liberal-scientific ethic: if it's bad for you, it should be prohibited; if it's good for you, it should be required.

> THOMAS S. SZASZ (1920–). "Ethics," *Heresies*, 1976

Liberals differ from revolutionaries primarily in their willingness to bear the indefinite continuance of unjust suffering. How can they rightfully do that except by sharing in that suffering?

> GLEN TINDER. "Liberals and Revolution," *New Republic*, 27 January 1979

Liberal: Someone who believes crime is the fault of Society—until he's robbed.

> JERRY TUCKER (1941–). *The Experience of Politics: You and American Government*, 4.3, 1974

✹

A liberal is a conservative who has been arrested.

> SAYING. In Tom Wolfe, *The Bonfire of the Vanities*, 24, 1987

LIBERATION

See also • Children: Letty Cottin Pogrebin ○ Freedom ○ Liberty ○ Nonviolence: Council of the War Resisters' International, Barbara Deming

The paradox of liberation is that in order to preserve freedom and to struggle for it, one must in a sense be already free, having freedom within oneself.

> NICOLAS BERDYAEV (1874–1948). *The Destiny of Man*, 2.3.3, 1931, tr. Natalie Duddington, 1955

Liberation is a praxis: the action and reflection of men upon their world in order to transform it.

> PAULO FREIRE (1921–1997). *Pedagogy of the Oppressed*, 2, tr. Myra Bergman Ramos, 1968

The price you must pay for your own liberation through another's sacrifice is that you in turn must be willing to liberate in the same way, irrespective of the consequences to yourself.

> DAG HAMMARSKJÖLD (1905–1961). Easter 1960, *Markings*, tr. Leif Sjöberg and W. H. Auden, 1964

Liberation is not deliverance.

> VICTOR HUGO (1802–1885). "Fantine" (2.9), *Les Misérables*, tr. Charles E. Wilbour, 1862

LIBERTY

See also • Freedom ○ Goals: Ernest Renan ○ Liberation ○ Money: Robert Louis Stevenson ○ Progress: Ralph Waldo Emerson ○ Revolutionary War: Patrick Henry ○ Rights ○ Self-Control: Edmund Burke ○ Virtue: Edmund Burke

A day, an hour of virtuous liberty
Is worth a whole eternity in bondage.

> JOSEPH ADDISON (1672–1719). *Cato*, 2, 1713

Our liberty, wisely understood, is but a voluntary obedience to the universal laws of life.

> HENRI AMIEL (1821–1881). Journal, 21 September 1868, tr. Mrs. Humphrey Ward 1887

Our liberty cannot be taken away unless the people are themselves accomplices.

> LORD BOLINGBROKE (1678–1751). *A Dissertation upon Parties*, 1735. In Sir Herbert Butterfield, *The Statecraft of Machiavelli*, 4, 1940

To practice justice is to practice liberty.

> SIMON BOLIVAR (1783–1830). Speech at the Second National Congress of Venezuela, Angostura, 15 February 1819

Experience should teach us to be most on our guard to protect liberty when the Government's purposes are beneficent. Men born to freedom are naturally alert to repel invasion of their liberty by evil-minded rulers. The greatest dangers to liberty lurk in insidious encroachment by men of zeal, well-meaning but without understanding.

> LOUIS D. BRANDEIS (1856–1941). *Olmstead v. United States*, 1928

The people never give up their liberties but under some delusion.

> EDMUND BURKE (1729–1797). Speech, Buckinghamshire (England), 1784

A brave people will certainly prefer liberty, accompanied with a virtuous poverty, to a depraved and wealthy servitude.

> EDMUND BURKE (1729–1797). *Reflections on the Revolution in France,* p. 239, 1790, Pelican Books edition, 1968

Liberty, like charity, must begin at home.

> JAMES B. CONANT (1893–1978). "Our Fighting Faith, Our Unique Heritage," address, Harvard College, Cambridge (Massachusetts), 30 June 1942
>
> See Charity: Terence ○ Peace: Franklin D. Roosevelt

The condition upon which God hath given liberty to man is eternal vigilance; which condition if he break[s], servitude is at once the consequence of his crime and the punishment of his guilt.

> JOHN PHILPOT CURRAN (1750–1817). On the right of election of the Lord Mayor of Dublin, speech before the Privy Council, Dublin (Ireland), 10 July 1790 (Popular version: Eternal vigilance is the price of liberty.)
>
> See Justice: Arnold Bennett

Liberty is the capacity to do anything that does no harm to others.

> THE DECLARATION OF THE RIGHTS OF MAN AND THE CITIZEN. France, Article 4, 26 August 1789
>
> See Government: Thomas Jefferson (2)

The history of liberty has largely been the history of the observance of procedural safeguards.

> FELIX FRANKFURTER (1882–1965). *McNabb v. United States,* 1943

Those who would give up essential Liberty, to purchase a little temporary Safety, deserve neither Liberty nor Safety.

> BENJAMIN FRANKLIN (1706–1790) et al. Pennsylvania Assembly committee. Reply to Gov. Robert Morris, 11 November 1755

Liberty lies in the hearts of men and women; when it dies there, no constitution, no law, no court can save it.

> LEARNED HAND (1872–1961). "The Spirit of Liberty," address at the "I Am an American Day" ceremony in New York City's Central Park, 21 May 1944, "We Seek Liberty," *Life,* 3 July 1944

The spirit of liberty is the spirit which is not too sure that it is right; the spirit of liberty is the spirit which seeks to understand the minds of other men and women; the spirit of liberty is the spirit which weighs their interests alongside its own without bias.

> LEARNED HAND (1872–1961). "The Spirit of Liberty," address at the "I Am an American Day" ceremony in New York City's Central Park, 21 May 1944, "We Seek Liberty," *Life,* 3 July 1944

Liberty not only means that the individual has both the opportunity and the burden of choice; it also means that he must bear the consequences of his actions. . . . Liberty and responsibility are inseparable.

> FRIEDRICH HAYEK (1899–1992). *The Constitution of Liberty,* 5.1, 1960

The love of liberty is the love of others; the love of power is the love of ourselves.

> WILLIAM HAZLITT (1778–1830). "*The Times* Newspaper," *Political Essays,* 1819

We are not to expect to be translated from despotism to liberty in a featherbed.

> THOMAS JEFFERSON (1743–1826). Letter to Marquis de Lafayette, 2 April 1790

I would rather be exposed to the inconveniencies attending too much liberty than those attending too small a degree of it.

> THOMAS JEFFERSON (1743–1826). Letter to Archibald Stuart, 23 December 1791

Timid men . . . prefer the calm of despotism to the boisterous sea of liberty.

> THOMAS JEFFERSON (1743–1826). Letter to Phillip Mazzei, 24 April 1796

Liberties enjoyed are in proportion to risks taken.

> BERTRAND de JOUVENEL (1903–1987). *On Power: Its Nature and the History of Its Growth,* 18.3, 1945, tr. J. F. Huntington, 1948

I believe any man who takes the liberty of another into his keeping is bound to become a tyrant, and that any man who yields up his liberty, in however slight the measure, is bound to become a slave.

> H. L. MENCKEN (1880–1956). "Why Liberty?" *Chicago Tribune,* 30 January 1927

I believe in only one thing: liberty; but I do not believe in liberty enough to want to force it upon anyone.

> H. L. MENCKEN (1880–1956)

The sole end for which mankind are warranted, individually or collectively, in interfering with the liberty of action of any of their number, is self-protection. That the only purpose for which power can be rightfully exercised over any member of a civilized community, against his will, is to prevent harm to others. His own good, either physical or moral, is not a sufficient warrant.

> JOHN STUART MILL (1806–1873). *On Liberty,* 1, 1859
>
> See Freedom: Mill (2)

License they mean, when they cry liberty,
For who loves that, must first be wise, and good.

> JOHN MILTON (1608–1674). "Sonnet 11," l. 11, 1645?

To none accountable, preferring
Hard Liberty before the easy yoke.

> JOHN MILTON (1608–1674). *Paradise Lost,* 2.255, 1667

Liberty is a right of doing whatever the laws permit. . . .

A government may be so constituted, as no man shall be compelled to do things to which the law does not oblige him, nor forced to abstain from things which the law permits.

> MONTESQUIEU (1689–1755). *The Spirit of the Laws,* 11.3–4, 1748, tr. Thomas Nugent, 1750, Hafner Publishing edition, 1949

Proclaim liberty throughout the land to all the inhabitants.

> MOSES (14th cent. B.C.). *Leviticus* 25:10

He that would make his own liberty secure must guard even his enemy from oppression.

> THOMAS PAINE (1737–1809). "Dissertation on First Principles of Government," 1795

Liberty is mere talk where people have lost their sensibilities, where their understanding has not been fed by knowledge, and their power of judgment has been neglected—most of all, however, where they are unmindful of their rights and duties as moral beings.

> JOHANN HEINRICH PESTALOZZI (1746–1827). *The Education of Man: Aphorisms*, 7, tr. Heinz and Ruth Norden, 1951

Oh liberty, oh liberty, what crimes are committed in thy name!

> MADAME MARIE-JEANNE ROLAND (1754–1793). Attributed. While passing a statue dedicated to liberty on her way to the guillotine site where she was executed during the French Revolution, 8 November 1793. In Thomas Babington Macaulay, "Mirabeau," *The Edinburgh Review* (Scotland), July 1832

True liberty shows itself to best advantage in protecting the rights of others, and especially of minorities.

> THEODORE ROOSEVELT (1858–1919). In Hermann Hagedorn and Sidney Wallach, "Signposts for Americans: The American Heritage," *A Theodore Roosevelt Round-Up*, 1958

To renounce liberty is to renounce being a man.

> ROUSSEAU (1712–1778). *The Social Contract*, 1.4, 1762, tr. G. D. H. Cole, 1913

It is of small importance to any of us whether we get liberty; but of the greatest that we deserve it. Whether we can win it, fate must determine; but that we will be worthy of it, we may ourselves determine; and the sorrowfullest fate, of all that we can suffer, is to have it, *without* deserving it.

> JOHN RUSKIN (1819–1900). *The Queen of the Air*, 3.150, 1869

Liberty means responsibility. That's why most men dread it.

> GEORGE BERNARD SHAW (1856–1950). "Maxims for Revolutionists: Liberty and Equality," *Man and Superman*, 1903

Liberty is the breath of life to nations; and liberty is the one thing that parents, schoolmasters, and rulers spend their lives in extirpating for the sake of an immediately quiet and finally disastrous life.

> GEORGE BERNARD SHAW (1856–1950). Closing words, "Government by Bullies," *Parents and Children*, 1914

A person should be deprived of his liberty only if he is proved guilty of breaking the law.

> THOMAS S. SZASZ (1920–). "Summary and Conclusions," *Law, Liberty, and Psychiatry: An Inquiry into the Social Uses of Mental Health Practices*, 1963

I had started with this idea in my head, "Dere's *two* things I've got a *right* to, and dese are, Death or Liberty—one or tother I mean to have. No one will take me back alive."

> HARRIET TUBMAN (1820–1913). In Sara H. Bradford, *Scenes in the Life of Harriet Tubman*, p. 21, 1869

Liberty, when it begins to take root, is a plant of rapid growth.

> GEORGE WASHINGTON (1732–1799). Letter to James Madison, 2 March 1788

God grants liberty only to those who love it, and are always ready to guard and defend it.

> DANIEL WEBSTER (1782–1852). Speech, 3 June 1834

Liberty exists in proportion to wholesome restraint; the more restraint on others to keep off from us, the more liberty we have.

> DANIEL WEBSTER (1782–1852). After-dinner speech before the Charleston Bar (South Carolina), 10 May 1847

Liberty is the only thing you cannot have unless you give it to others.

> WILLIAM ALLEN WHITE (1868–1944). "A Free Press in a Machine Age," speech, University of Pennsylvania, Philadelphia, 2 May 1938

Liberty relies upon itself, invites no one, promises nothing, sits in calmness and light, is positive and composed, and knows no discouragement.

> WALT WHITMAN (1819–1892). Preface (1855) to *Leaves of Grass*, 1855–1892

The shallow . . . consider liberty a release from all law, from every constraint. The wise see in it, on the contrary, the potent Law of Laws, namely, the fusion and combination of the conscious will, or partial individual law, with those universal, eternal, unconscious ones which run through all Time, pervade history, prove immortality, give moral purpose to the entire objective world, and the last dignity to human life.

> WALT WHITMAN (1819–1892). "Freedom," *Specimen Days and Collect*, 1882

The history of liberty is a history of resistance. The history of liberty is a history of the limitation of governmental power, not the increase of it.

> WOODROW WILSON (1856–1924). Speech before New York Press Club, 9 September 1912

The birthright of man . . . is such a degree of liberty, civil and religious, as is compatible with the liberty of every other individual with whom he is united in a social compact.

> MARY WOLLSTONECRAFT (1759–1797). *A Vindication of the Rights of Men*, p. 7, 1790

❧

Where liberty dwells, there is my country.

> SAYING (LATIN). In Benjamin Franklin, letter to B. Vaughan, 14 March 1783

LIBRARIES

See also • Books ○ Reading

The true University of these days is a Collection of Books.

> THOMAS CARLYLE (1795–1881). "The Hero as Man of Letters," *On Heroes, Hero-Worship, and the Heroic in History*, 1841

A few Books well chosen, and well made use of, will be more profitable to thee than a great confused *Alexandrian* Library.

> THOMAS FULLER (1654–1734). Comp., *Introductio ad Prudentiam*, 1606, 1731

Unlike a lot of other libraries, [the New York Society Library] still allows you to go to the shelves yourself. . . . I appreciate the serendipity of the stacks, looking for one book, but on occasion finding another, better one, which I did not even know existed.

DAVID HALBERSTAM (1934–). "Where the Third 'R' Stands for Repose," *New York Times*, 19 December 1997. The Society Library is New York City's oldest library.

Every library should try to be complete on something, if it were only the history of pinheads.

OLIVER WENDELL HOLMES, SR. (1809–1894). *The Poet of the Breakfast-Table*, 8, 1872

At some point in the future, it would theoretically be possible to store all 16 million volumes in the Library of Congress on a disk the size of a penny.

PAUL M. HORN. International Business Machines senior vice president for research. As paraphrased by William Grime, "Libraries Ponder Role in the Digital Age," *New York Times*, 29 April 1996

Your library is your portrait.

HOLBROOK JACKSON (1874–1948). *Maxims of Books and Reading*, 13, 1934

No place affords a more striking conviction of the vanity of human hopes than a public library.

SAMUEL JOHNSON (1709–1784). In *The Rambler* (English journal), 106, 23 March 1751

Man, lots of times I just wish I could start back in school, from about the sixth grade. Man, I'd be the last one out of that library every night.

MALCOLM X (1925–1965). 1963–1965. Quoted by Alex Haley, "Alex Haley Remembers," in David Gallen, *Malcolm X: As They Knew Him*, 1992

Artists dying in childbirth, wise-
women charred at the stake,
centuries of books unwritten piled
behind these shelves.

ADRIENNE RICH (1929–). *Twenty-One Love Poems*, 5.15, 1974–1976

Prospero: My library
Was dukedom large enough.

SHAKESPEARE (1564–1616). *The Tempest*, 1.2.109, 1611

I go into my library, and all history unrolls before me.

ALEXANDER SMITH (1830–1867). *Dreamthorp*, 11, 1863

It seems to me one cannot sit down in that place without a heart full of grateful reverence. I own to have said my grace at the table, and to have thanked Heaven for this my English birthright, freely to partake of these beautiful books, and speak the truth I find there.

WILLIAM MAKEPEACE THACKERAY (1811–1863). On the Round Reading Room of the British Museum, London, 1860. In Angeline Goreau, "The Round Room Comes to an End," *New York Times Book Review*, 9 November 1997

LIFE

See also • Courage: Anaïs Nin ○ Death ○ Ethics: Albert Schweitzer (4) ○ Evolution ○ Man ○ Meaning ○ Morality: Leo Tolstoy ○ Purpose ○ Simple Living

Knowledge, love, power—there is the complete life.

HENRI AMIEL (1821–1881). Journal, 7 April 1851, tr. Mrs. Humphrey Ward, 1887

Life is short and we have never too much time for gladdening the hearts of those who are traveling the dark journey with us. Oh, be swift to love, make haste to be kind!

HENRI AMIEL (1821–1881). Journal, 16 December 1868, tr. Mrs. Humphrey Ward, 1887

Life is but a daily oscillation between revolt and submission.

HENRI AMIEL (1821–1881). Journal, 16 April 1875, tr. Mrs. Humphrey Ward, 1887

There is a very fine line between loving life and being greedy for it.

MAYA ANGELOU (1928–). Robert Chrisman interview, *Black Scholar*, January-February 1977

I love to see a young girl go out and grab the world by the lapels. Life's a bitch. You've got to go out and kick ass.

MAYA ANGELOU (1928–). "Kicking Ass," 13 October 1986, *Conversations with Maya Angelou*, 1989

Trust life, and it will teach you, in joy and sorrow, all you need to know.

JAMES BALDWIN (1924–1987). "The White Man's Guilt," *Ebony*, August 1965

The trick in life is not in getting what you want but in wanting what you get after you get it.

WARREN BEATTY (1937–) and ROBERT TOWNE. *Love Affair* (film), 1994, spoken by Katharine Hepburn

Everything that lives is holy, life delights in life.

WILLIAM BLAKE (1757–1827). "America: A Prophecy," 8.13, 1793

Life . . . is a battle not between Bad and Good, but between Bad and Worse.

JOSEPH BRODSKY (1940–). "'A Writer Is a Lonely Traveler, and No One Is His Helper,'" *New York Times*, 1 October 1972

"Life Is Just a Bowl of Cherries."

LEW BROWN (1893–1958). Song title, 1931

Life is a pure flame, and we live by an invisible sun within us.

SIR THOMAS BROWNE (1605–1682). *Hydriotaphia: Urn Burial*, 5, 1658, ed. John Addington Symonds, 1886

I count life just a stuff
To try the soul's strength on.

ROBERT BROWNING (1812–1889). *In a Balcony, A Scene*, 1855

Life is the art of drawing sufficient conclusions from insufficient premises.

SAMUEL BUTLER (1835–1902). *The Note-Books of Samuel Butler*, 1, ed. Henry Festing Jones, 1907

To live is like to love—all reason is against it, and all healthy instinct for it.

SAMUEL BUTLER (1835–1902). *The Note-Books of Samuel Butler*, 14, ed. Henry Festing Jones, 1907

Life is like playing a violin solo in public and learning the instrument as one goes on.

SAMUEL BUTLER (1835–1902). *Further Extracts from the Note-Books of Samuel Butler,* 5, ed. A. T. Bartholomew, 1934

The sum of a life, less than its parts.

ELIAS CANETTI (1905–1994). 1985, *The Secret Heart of the Clock: Notes, Aphorisms, Fragments: 1973–1985,* tr. Joel Agee, 1989

Art is long and life is short; and of the three score and ten years allotted to the liver, how small a portion is spent in anything but vanity and vice, if not in wretchedness, and worse than unprofitable struggling with the adamantine law of fate!

THOMAS CARLYLE (1795–1881). Letter to his brother John, 15 March 1822. In James Anthony Froude, *Thomas Carlyle: A History of the First Forty Years, 1795–1835,* 1.9, 1882

One Life; a little gleam of Time between two Eternities; no second chance to us forevermore!

THOMAS CARLYLE (1795–1881). "The Hero as Man of Letters," *On Heroes, Hero-Worship, and the Heroic in History,* 1841

Life is a humbug.

THOMAS CARLYLE (1795–1881). In Ralph Waldo Emerson, "Carlyle," *Lectures and Biographical Sketches,* 1883

Life is like a beautiful flirt, whom we love and to whom, finally, we grant every condition she imposes as long as she doesn't leave us.

CASANOVA (1725–1798). Foreword to *The Story of My Escape from the Prisons of the Republic of Venice Called the Leads,* 1788, tr. John Friedberg, unpublished

Life is a continual search for real integrity, literally integration, trying to put your mind and your body and your spirit in the same place at the same time.

BILL CLINTON (1946–). In David Maraniss, "Clinton's Journey of the Spirit," *Washington Post National Weekly Edition,* 13 July 1992

Life is a maze in which we take the wrong turning before we have learnt to walk.

CYRIL CONNOLLY (1903–1974). "Ecce Gubernator," *The Unquiet Grave: A Word Cycle by Palinurus,* 1945

The essence of life is statistical improbability on a colossal scale.

RICHARD DAWKINS (1941–). English biologist. *The Blind Watchmaker,* 11, 1986

My life is one demd horrid grind.

CHARLES DICKENS (1812–1870). *The Life and Adventures of Nicholas Nickleby,* 64, 1839

"Where was it," thought Raskolnikov, "where was it I read about a man sentenced to death who, one hour before his execution, says or thinks that if he had to live on some high rock, on a cliff, on a ledge so narrow that there was only room enough for him to stand there, and if there were bottomless chasms all round, the ocean, eternal darkness, eternal solitude, and eternal gales, and if he had to spend all his life on that square yard of space—a thousand years, an eternity—he'd rather live like that than die at once! Oh, only to live, live, live! Live under any circumstances—only to live!"

FYODOR DOSTOYEVSKI (1821–1881). *Crime and Punishment,* 1.2, 1866, tr. David Magarshack, 2.6, 1951

The secret of man's being is not only to live but to have something to live for.

FYODOR DOSTOYEVSKY (1821–1881). *The Brothers Karamazov,* 5.5, 1880, tr. Constance Garnett, 1912

I believe in life after birth.

MAXIE DUNHAM. 1 July. In Esther Armstrong and Dale Stitt, comps., *Thoughts for the Journey,* 1996

Birth, and copulation, and death.
That's all the facts when you come to brass tacks:
I've been born, and once is enough.

T. S. ELIOT (1888–1965). "Fragment of an Agon," *Sweeney Agonistes,* 1932

Sad is this continual postponement of life.

RALPH WALDO EMERSON (1803–1882). Journal, 6 May 1837

The current of inward life . . . increases as it is spent.

RALPH WALDO EMERSON (1803–1882). "The Method of Nature," address, Waterville (later, Colby) College (Maine), 11 August 1841

Life is a progress, and not a station.

RALPH WALDO EMERSON (1803–1882). "Compensation," *Essays: First Series,* 1841

All life is an experiment. The more experiments you make the better. What if they are a little coarse, and you may get your coat soiled or torn? What if you do fail, and get fairly rolled in the dirt once or twice? Up again, you shall never be so afraid of a tumble.

RALPH WALDO EMERSON (1803–1882). Journal, 11 November 1842

Life must be lived on a higher platform, to which we are always invited to ascend; there, the whole aspect of things changes.

RALPH WALDO EMERSON (1803–1882). "Nominalist and Realist," *Essays: Second Series,* 1844

Our life is March weather, savage and serene in one hour.

RALPH WALDO EMERSON (1803–1882). "Montaigne; or, The Skeptic," *Representative Men,* 1850

Life is an ecstasy.

RALPH WALDO EMERSON (1803–1882). "Fate," *The Conduct of Life,* 1860

Life is a search after power.

RALPH WALDO EMERSON (1803–1882). "Power," *The Conduct of Life,* 1860

Life is a game played on us while we are playing other games.

EVAN ESAR (1899–1995). Comp., preface to *20,000 Quips and Quotes,* 1968

To love and to work. (Lieben und arbeiten.)

SIGMUND FREUD (1856–1939). In Erik H. Erikson, *Childhood and Society,* 7.6, 1950

Govern thy Life and Thoughts as if the whole World were to see the one, and read the other.

THOMAS FULLER (1654–1734). Comp., *Introductio ad Prudentiam,* 417, 1731

A Good life fears not Life nor Death.

> THOMAS FULLER (1654–1734). Comp., *Gnomologia: Adages and Proverbs*, 157, 1732

We are born crying, live complaining, and die disappointed.

> THOMAS FULLER (1654–1734). Comp., *Gnomologia: Adages and Proverbs*, 5427, 1732

Life is hardly more than a fraction of a second. Such a little time to prepare oneself for eternity!!!

> PAUL GAUGUIN (1848–1903). *Intimate Journals of Paul Gauguin*, p. 18, 1936, tr. Van Wyck Brooks, 1949

Never cease to be convinced that life might be better—your own and others'; not a future life that might console us for the present one and help us to accept its misery, but this one of ours.

> ANDRÉ GIDE (1869–1951). *More Fruits of the Earth*, 4.2, 1935

Life's not *linear*. It ebbs and flows. It's like Yang and Yin. It's contradictions, the Unnamable, the Inexplicable. People don't plot anymore; they just flow.

> GAIL GODWIN (1937–). *The Odd Woman*, 2, 1974

Life is mostly froth and bubble,
Two things stand like stone,
Kindness in another's trouble,
Courage in your own.

> ADAM LINDSAY GORDON (1833–1870). "Fytte 8," *Ye Wearie Wayfarer*, 1866

You're only here for a short visit. Don't hurry. Don't worry. And be sure to smell the flowers along the way.

> WALTER HAGEN (1892–1969). Golfer. *The Walter Hagen Story*, 1956

The art of life is to know how to enjoy a little and to endure much.

> WILLIAM HAZLITT (1778–1830). "Common Places" (1), *Literary Examiner* (English journal), September-December 1823

Living is
  a thing you do
now or never—
  which do you?

> PIET HEIN (1905–). "Living Is—," *Grooks*, 1966

Life without commitment is not worth living.

> ABRAHAM JOSHUA HESCHEL (1907–1972). *God in Search of Man*, 22, 1955

Our existence seesaws between animality and divinity, between that which is more and that which is less than humanity.

> ABRAHAM JOSHUA HESCHEL (1907–1972). *Who Is Man?* 6, 1965

Just to be is a blessing, just to live is holy.

> ABRAHAM JOSHUA HESCHEL (1907–1972). *The Insecurity of Freedom: Essays on Human Existence*, 5.3, 1967

To build a life as if it were a work of art.

> ABRAHAM JOSHUA HESCHEL (1907–1972). Television interview, *I Asked for Wonder*, ed. Samuel H. Dresner, 1988

Life is short, the art long, opportunity fleeting, experience treacherous, judgment difficult.

> HIPPOCRATES (460?–377? B.C.). *Aphorisms*, 1.1, tr. W. H. S. Jones, 1923

As life is action and passion, it is required of a man that he should share the passion and action of his time at peril of being judged not to have lived.

> OLIVER WENDELL HOLMES, JR. (1841–1935). Memorial Day address, Keene (New Hampshire), 30 May 1884

Life is a romantic business. It is painting a picture, not doing a sum—but you have to make romance. And it will come to the question how much fire you have in your belly.

> OLIVER WENDELL HOLMES, JR. (1841–1935). Letter to Oswald Ryan, 5 June 1911

Life is a roar of bargain and battle, but in the very heart of it there rises a mystic spiritual tone that gives meaning to the whole. It transmutes the dull details into romance. It reminds us that our only but wholly adequate significance is as parts of the unimaginable whole. It suggests that even while we think that we are egotists we are living to ends outside ourselves.

> OLIVER WENDELL HOLMES, JR. (1841–1935). "The Class of '61," speech at the Fiftieth Anniversary of Graduation from Harvard University, 28 June 1911

Life is 10 percent what happens to me and 90 percent how I react to it.

> LOU HOLTZ (1937–). Notre Dame football coach

Life is a compromise between fate and free will.

> ELBERT HUBBARD (1856–1915). *A Thousand and One Epigrams*, p. 36, 1911

Do not take life too seriously—you will never get out of it alive.

> ELBERT HUBBARD (1856–1915). *A Thousand and One Epigrams*, p. 74, 1911

True life lies in laughter, love and work.

> ELBERT HUBBARD (1856–1915). In Alice Hubbard, comp., *An American Bible*, p. 251, 1946

Folks, I'm telling you,
birthing is hard
and dying is mean—
so get yourself
a little loving
in between.

> LANGSTON HUGHES (1902–1967). "Advice" (complete poem), 1946, *The Collected Poems of Langston Hughes*, ed. Arnold Rampersad and David Roessel, 1994

Life is a voyage.

> VICTOR HUGO (1802–1885). *The Toilers of the Sea*, 3.1.1, 1866

Life is not so bad if you have plenty of luck, a good physique and not too much imagination.

> CHRISTOPHER ISHERWOOD (1904–1986). In Jon Winokur, comp., "Curmudgeon," *Funny Times*, October 1996

What is your life? For you are a mist that appears for a little time and then vanishes.

> JAMES (A.D. 1st cent.). *James* 4:14

If this life be not a real fight, in which something is eternally gained for the universe by success, it is no better than a game of private theatricals from which one may withdraw at will. But it *feels* like a real fight—as if there were something really wild in the universe which we, with all our idealities and faithfulnesses, are needed to redeem.

> WILLIAM JAMES (1842–1910). "Is Life Worth Living?" (4), *The Will to Believe: And Other Essays in Popular Philosophy,* 1897

Be not afraid of life. Believe that life *is* worth living, and your belief will help create the fact.

> WILLIAM JAMES (1842–1910). "Is Life Worth Living?" (4), *The Will to Believe: And Other Essays in Popular Philosophy,* 1897

My life is a hesitation before birth.

> FRANZ KAFKA (1883–1924). 24 January 1922, *The Diaries of Franz Kafka, 1910–1923,* 1949

Sing love and life and life and love
All that lives is Holy,
The unholiest, most holy all.

> BOB KAUFMAN (1925–1986). Closing lines, "Night Sung Sailor's Prayer," *Golden Sardine,* 1967

Life is a crusade in the service of God. Whether we wished to or not, we set out as crusaders to free . . . that God buried in matter and in our souls.

> NIKOS KAZANTZAKIS (1883–1957). "The Action: The Relationship between God and Man" (49), *The Saviors of God: Spiritual Exercises,* 1927, tr. Kimon Friar, 1960

There is always inequality in life. Some men are killed in a war and some men are wounded, and some men never leave the country and some men are stationed in the Antarctic and some in San Francisco. It is very hard in military or in personal life to assure complete equality. Life is unfair.

> JOHN F. KENNEDY (1917–1963). News conference, Washington, 21 March 1962

Life at its best is a creative synthesis of opposites in fruitful harmony.

> MARTIN LUTHER KING, JR. (1929–1968). *Strength to Love,* 1 (introduction), 1963

Life, like art, should be the celebration of a vision.

> MICHAEL LARSEN (1941–). *Literary Agents: What They Do, How They Do It, and How to Find and Work with the Right One for You,* rev. ed., 15.1, 1996

Life is what happens to you
While you're busy
Making other plans.

> JOHN LENNON (1940–1980). "Beautiful Boy" (song), 1981

Life is very short and there's no time
For fussing and fighting, my friend.

> JOHN LENNON (1940–1980) and PAUL McCARTNEY (1942–). "We Can Work It Out" (song), 1965

All life is a struggle in the dark.

> LUCRETIUS (99–55 B.C.). *On the Nature of Things,* 2.55, tr. R. E. Latham, 1951

We are always beginning to live, but we are never living.

> MARCUS MANILIUS (1st cent. B.C.). *Astronomica,* 4

A man lives not only his personal life, as an individual, but also, consciously or unconsciously, the life of his epoch and his contemporaries.

> THOMAS MANN (1875–1955). *The Magic Mountain,* 2 ("At Tienappels'"), 1924, tr. H. T. Lowe-Porter, 1927

There is no reason for life and life has no meaning.

> W. SOMERSET MAUGHAM (1874–1965). *The Summing Up,* 71, 1938

It is a funny thing about life, if you refuse to accept anything but the best, you very often get it: if you utterly decline to make do with what you get, then somehow or other you are very likely to get what you want.

> W. SOMERSET MAUGHAM (1874–1965). "The Treasure," *The Mixture as Before,* 1940

The basic fact about human existence is not that it is a tragedy, but that it is a bore. It is not so much a war as an endless standing in line.

> H. L. MENCKEN (1880–1956). "The Human Mind: On Suicide," *Prejudices: Sixth Series,* 1927

The law of our life can be summed up in the axiom "be what you are."

> THOMAS MERTON (1915–1968). *The New Man,* 152, 1961

It's not true that life is one damn thing after another—it is one damn thing over and over.

> EDNA ST. VINCENT MILLAY (1892–1950). Letter to A. R. MacDougall, 24 October 1930, *Letters of Edna St. Vincent Millay,* ed. Allan Ross MacDougall, 1952

Life . . . is for most of us one long postponement.

> HENRY MILLER (1891–1980). "The Enormous Womb," *The Wisdom of the Heart,* 1941

The partition separating life from death is so tenuous. The unbelievable fragility of our organism suggest a vision on a screen: a kind of mist condenses itself into a human shape, lasts a moment and scatters.

> CZESLAW MILOSZ (1911–). "Fragments from a Journal," 1987. In Daniel Halpern, ed., *Antaeus,* Autumn 1988

I've looked at life from both sides now
From win and lose, and still somehow
It's life's illusions I recall
I really don't know life at all.

> JONI MITCHELL (1943–). "Both Sides Now" (song), 1969

Life's under no obligation to give us what we expect. We take what we get and are thankful it's no worse than it is.

> MARGARET MITCHELL (1900–1949). *Gone with the Wind,* 53, 1936

Life's a tough proposition, and the first hundred years are the hardest.

> WILSON MIZNER (1876–1933). In Alva Johnston, *The Legendary Mizners,* 4, 1953

There are three ingredients in the good life: learning, earning, and yearning.

> CHRISTOPHER MORLEY (1890–1957). *Parnassus on Wheels,* 10, 1917

Life is one day at a time. And thank God! I couldn't take much more.

> DANIEL PATRICK MOYNIHAN (1927–). New York senator. Appearing on *Meet the Press,* television news program, NBC, 19 June 1994

This life is but a tillage for the next; do good [here] that you may reap there.

> MUHAMMAD (A.D. 570?–632). *The Sayings of Muhammad,* 149, tr. Abdullah Al-Suhrawardy, 1941

Life is a score that we play at sight, not merely before we have divined the intentions of the composer, but even before we have mastered our instruments: even worse, a large part of the score has been only roughly indicated, and we must improvise the music for our particular instrument, over long passages. On these terms, the whole operation seems one of endless difficulty and frustration; and indeed, were it not for the fact that some of the passages have been played so often by our predecessors that, when we come to them, we seem to recall some of the score and can anticipate the natural sequence of the notes, we might often give up in sheer despair. The wonder is not that so much cacophony appears in our actual individual lives, but that there is any appearance of harmony and progression.

> LEWIS MUMFORD (1895–1990). *The Conduct of Life,* 9.5, 1951

Life at its fullest and best is divine service.

> LEWIS MUMFORD (1895–1990). *The Transformations of Man,* 5.3, 1956

Our existence is but a brief crack of light between two eternities of darkness.

> VLADIMIR NABOKOV (1899–1977). *Speak, Memory,* 1, 1951

To absorb, to emit, to form new combinations—this is life.

> NAPOLEON (1769–1821). Remark to Dr. Francesco Antommarchi, 1819, *The Mind of Napoleon: A Selection from His Written and Spoken Words,* 44, ed. J. Christopher Herold, 1955

Life is a game—play to win.

> AL NEUHARTH (1924–). *USA Today* publisher. His signature line. In Alex Raksin, "Money May Not Be the Great Motivator, After All," *Los Angeles Times,* 20 December 1993

Life is one crisis after another.

> RICHARD M. NIXON (1913–1994). Interview, 1980. In Robert Sam Anson, *Exile: The Unquiet Oblivion of Richard M. Nixon,* 17, 1984

Most people get a fair amount of fun out of their lives, but on balance life is suffering, and only the very young or the very foolish imagine otherwise.

> GEORGE ORWELL (1903–1950). "Lear, Tolstoy and the Fool," March 1947, *The Collected Essays, Journalism and Letters of George Orwell,* vol. 4, ed. Sonia Orwell and Ian Angus, 1968

Man is born to live, not to prepare for life.

> BORIS PASTERNAK (1890–1960). *Doctor Zhivago,* 9.14, 1957, tr. Max Hayward and Manya Harari, 1958

This long Disease, my Life.

> ALEXANDER POPE (1688–1744). *An Epistle to Dr. Arbuthnot,* l. 132, 1735

Our life seems like a trial run.

> JULES RENARD (1864–1910). Journal, July 1899, tr. Louise Bogan and Elizabeth Roget, 1964

Life was meant to be lived. . . . One must never, for whatever reason, turn his back on life.

> ELEANOR ROOSEVELT (1884–1962). Preface (closing words) to *The Autobiography of Eleanor Roosevelt,* 1961

I long ago come to the conclusion that all life is 6 to 5 against.

> DAMON RUNYON (1884–1946). "A Nice Prize," *Money from Home,* 1935

Instinct, mind and spirit are all essential to a full life; each has its own excellence and its own corruption. Each can attain a spurious excellence at the expense of the others; each has a tendency to encroach upon the others; but in the life which is to be sought all three will be developed in coordination, and intimately blended in a single harmonious whole.

> BERTRAND RUSSELL (1872–1970). *Principles of Social Reconstruction,* 7, 1916

There is no cure for birth and death save to enjoy the interval.

> GEORGE SANTAYANA (1863–1952). "War Shrines," *Soliloquies in England and Later Soliloquies,* 1922

[Existence has] neither cause nor reason nor necessity.

> JEAN-PAUL SARTRE (1905–1980). In Edward Hallett Carr, *What Is History?* 4, 1961

Life is what happens to us while we are making other plans.

> ALLEN SAUNDERS. In "Quotable Quotes," *Reader's Digest,* January 1957

Human life must be some kind of mistake. . . . Existence has no real value in itself.

> ARTHUR SCHOPENHAUER (1788–1860). "Studies in Pessimism: The Vanity of Existence," *Essays of Arthur Schopenhauer,* tr. T. Bailey Saunders, 1851

The art of living is always to make a good thing out of a bad thing.

> E. F. SCHUMACHER (1911–1977). Epilogue to *A Guide for the Perplexed,* 1977

There must be more to life than having everything!

> MAURICE SENDAK (1928–). In John Kane, ed., *Moving Forward, Keeping Still: The Gateway to Eastern Wisdom,* p. 123, 1997

All life is slavery.

> SENECA THE YOUNGER (5? B.C.–A.D. 65). "Of Peace of Mind" (10), *Minor Dialogues,* tr. Aubrey Stewart, 1889

Life, Lucilius, is really a battle.

> SENECA THE YOUNGER (5? B.C.–A.D. 65). "On Facing Hardships," *Moral Letters to Lucilius,* 96.5, tr. Richard M. Gummere, 1918

Begin at once to live, and count each separate day as a separate life.

> SENECA THE YOUNGER (5? B.C.–A.D. 65). "On the Futility of Planning Ahead," *Moral Letters to Lucilius,* 101.10, tr. Richard M. Gummere, 1918

Macbeth: Life's but a walking shadow, a poor player
That struts and frets his hour upon the stage
And then is heard no more: it is a tale
Told by an idiot, full of sound and fury,
Signifying nothing.

> SHAKESPEARE (1564–1616). *Macbeth,* 5.5.24, 1605

Life is not meant to be easy, my child; but take courage: it can be delightful.

GEORGE BERNARD SHAW (1856–1950). *Back to Methuselah: A Metabiological Pentateuch,* 5, 1921

The unexamined life is not worth living.

SOCRATES (470?–399 B.C.). In Plato (427?–347 B.C.), *Apology,* 38, tr. Benjamin Jowett, 1894

The art of life isn't controlling what happens, which is impossible; it's using what happens.

GLORIA STEINEM (1934–). "Doing Sixty," *Moving Beyond Words,* 1994

The irresponsible life is not worth living.

THOMAS S. SZASZ (1920–). Closing words, *Law, Liberty, and Psychiatry: An Inquiry into the Social Uses of Mental Health Practices,* 1963

I slept and dreamt that life was joy.
I awoke and saw that life was duty.
I acted and behold, duty was joy.

RABINDRANATH TAGORE (1861–1941)

To live, let live, help live.

HENRY THOMAS and DANA LEE THOMAS. Summarizing Emerson's philosophy, "Ralph Waldo Emerson" (1), *Living Biographies of Great Philosophers,* 1941

My life is like a stroll upon the beach,
As near to the ocean's edge as I can go.

HENRY DAVID THOREAU (1817–1862). "Wednesday," *A Week on the Concord and Merrimack Rivers,* 1849

We live but a fraction of our life. Why do we not let on the flood, raise the gates, and set all our wheels in motion? He that hath ears to hear, let him hear. Employ your senses.

HENRY DAVID THOREAU (1817–1862). Journal, 13 June 1851

Here I am thirty-four years old, and yet my life is almost wholly unexpanded. How much is in the germ! There is such an interval between my ideal and the actual in many instances that I may say I am unborn.

HENRY DAVID THOREAU (1817–1862). Journal, 19 July 1851

Go not so far out of your way for a truer life; keep strictly onward in that path alone which your genius points out. Do the things which lie nearest to you, but which are difficult to do. Live a purer, a more thoughtful and laborious life, more true to your friends and neighbors, more noble and magnanimous.

HENRY DAVID THOREAU (1817–1862). Journal, 12 January 1852

All our life . . . is a persistent dreaming awake.

HENRY DAVID THOREAU (1817–1862). Journal, 27 August 1859

A man who lives by this life alone, who does not anticipate any other—this is a heavy sleep.

LEO TOLSTOY (1828–1910). *Thoughts and Aphorisms,* 13.15, 1886–1893, tr. Leo Wiener, 1905

One can live magnificently in this world, if one knows how to work and how to love, to work for the person one loves and to love one's work.

LEO TOLSTOY (1828–1910). In Henri Troyat, *Tolstoy,* 3, 1965, tr. Nancy Amphoux, 1967

Let us endeavor so to live that when we come to die even the undertaker will be sorry.

MARK TWAIN (1835–1910). *The Tragedy of Pudd'nhead Wilson,* 6 (epigraph), 1894

Good friends, good books and a sleepy conscience: this is the ideal life.

MARK TWAIN (1835–1910). "Written in the Archduchess's album," 4 July 1898, *Mark Twain's Notebook,* ed. Albert Bigelow Paine, 1935

Obscurity and a competence—that is the life that is best worth living.

MARK TWAIN (1835–1910). 5 November 1908, *Mark Twain's Notebook,* ed. Albert Bigelow Paine, 1935

If I wanted life to be easy, I should have gotten born [in] a different universe.

REBECCA WEST (1892–1983). "Goodness Doesn't Just Happen." In Edward P. Morgan, ed., *This I Believe,* 1952

What is life but an experiment? and mortality but an exercise? with reference to results beyond.

WALT WHITMAN (1819–1892). Preface (1872) to *Leaves of Grass,* 1855-1892

To live is the rarest thing in the world. Most people exist, that is all.

OSCAR WILDE (1854–1900). "The Soul of Man Under Socialism," *Fortnightly Review* (British journal), February 1891

All life weighed in the scales of my own life seems to me a preparation for something that never happens.

WILLIAM BUTLER YEATS (1865–1939). Closing words, *Reveries over Childhood and Youth,* 1916, *Autobiographies,* 1955

❧

Holmes, Sr.: Life is a great bundle of little things. . . . You smile, perhaps life seems to you a little bundle of great things?
Divinity student (starting another smile and then suddenly pulling it back): Life is a great bundle of great things.

ANONYMOUS (AMERICAN). Format adapted. In Oliver Wendell Holmes, Sr., *The Professor at the Breakfast-Table,* 1, 1860

Life's a bitch, and then you die.

SAYING (NORTH AMERICAN?)

It's loving and giving that make life worth living.

SAYING (ONTARIO)

LIKABILITY

See also • Faults: Anne Lamott ○ Popularity ○ Success: Arthur Miller

If yu would make yurself agreeable wherever yu go, listen tew the grivences ov others, but never relate yure own.

JOSH BILLINGS (1818–1885). *On Ice: and Other Things,* 24, 1868

In a Nutshell: Six Ways to Make People Like You—
    Principle 1: Become genuinely interested in other people.
    Principle 2: Smile.
    Principle 3: Remember that a person's name is to that person the sweetest and most important sound in any language.

Principle 4: Be a good listener. Encourage others to talk about themselves.

Principle 5: Talk in terms of the other person's interests.

Principle 6: Make the other person feel important—and do it sincerely.

> DALE CARNEGIE (1888–1955). *How to Win Friends and Influence People,* rev. ed., 2.6, 1981 (1936)

Great merit, or great failings, will make you be respected or despised; but trifles, little attentions, mere nothings, either done or neglected, will make you either liked or disliked, in the general run of the world.

> LORD CHESTERFIELD (1694–1773). Letter to his son, 20 July 1749
>
> See Popularity: Alexis de Tocqueville

Those whom you can make like themselves will, I promise you, like you very well.

> LORD CHESTERFIELD (1694–1773). Letter to his son, 6 August 1750

When the multitude hate a man, it is necessary to examine into the case. When the multitude like a man, it is necessary to examine into the case.

> CONFUCIUS (551–479 B.C.). *Confucian Analects* 15:27, tr. James Legge, 1930

Everybody hates me because I'm so universally liked.

> PETER DE VRIES (1910–1993). *The Vale of Laughter,* 1.1, 1967

"My idea of an agreeable person," said Hugo Bohun, "is a person who agrees with me."

> BENJAMIN DISRAELI (1804–1881). *Lothair,* 41, 1870

I can't deny the fact that you like me right now; you like me!

> SALLY FIELD (1946–). 1984 Academy Award acceptance speech, for Best actress, Los Angeles, 25 March 1985

If the world likes you at all, despise it, and it will like you a great deal.

> FULKE GREVILLE (1554–1628). *Maxims, Characters, and Reflections,* p. 209, 1756

Everyone liked Ike because Ike liked everyone. He radiated sunniness and optimism.

> ERWIN C. HARGROVE (1930–). On President Dwight D. Eisenhower, *Presidential Leadership: Personality and Political Style,* 6, 1966.

It was one of the rules which, above all others, made Doctor [Benjamin] Franklin the most amiable of men in society: never to contradict anybody.

> THOMAS JEFFERSON (1743–1826). In Dixon Wecter, *The Hero in America: A Chronicle of Hero-Worship,* 4.1, 1941

I have heard you mentioned as *a man whom everybody likes.* I think life has little more to give.

> SAMUEL JOHNSON (1709–1784). Letter to the author, 3 July 1778. In James Boswell, *The Life of Samuel Johnson,* 1791

How I like to be liked, and what I do to be liked!

> CHARLES LAMB (1775–1834). Letter to Dorothy Wordsworth, 8 January 1821

In daily life we are more often liked for our defects than for our qualities.

> LA ROCHEFOUCAULD (1613–1680). *Maxims,* 90, 1665, tr. Leonard Tancock, 1959

Some persons are likable in spite of their unswerving integrity.

> DON MARQUIS (1878–1937). In Edward Anthony, *O Rare Don Marquis,* 11, 1962

Likeness causes liking.

> SAYING (ENGLISH)

We like those who like us.

> SAYING

LITERATURE

See also • Books ○ Language ○ Poetry ○ Propaganda ○ Words ○ Writing

Literature in its most comprehensive sense is the autobiography of humanity.

> BERNARD BERENSON (1865–1959). Notebook, 11 December 1892. In *The Bernard Berenson Treasury,* ed. Hanna Kiel, 1962

Contemporary literature. Easier to shock than to convince.

> ALBERT CAMUS (1913–1960). 17 October 1947, *Notebooks: 1942–1951,* tr. Justin O'Brien, 1966

Literature is the art of writing something that will be read twice; journalism, what will be grasped at once.

> CYRIL CONNOLLY (1903–1974). *Enemies of Promise,* 3, 1938

Our literature is a substitute for religion, and so is our religion.

> T. S. ELIOT (1888–1965). "A Dialogue on Dramatic Poetry," 1928, *Selected Essays,* 1932

To provoke dreams of terror in the slumber of prosperity has become the moral duty of literature.

> ERNST FISCHER (1899–1972). *Art Against Ideology,* 1, 1966, tr. Anna Bostock, 1969

In an incarcerated society, free literature can exist only as denunciation and hope.

> EDUARDO GALEANO (1940–). "In Defense of the Word" (7), tr. Bobbye S. Ortiz, *Days and Nights of Love and War,* 1977, tr. Judith Brister, 1983

Literature decays only as men become more and more corrupt.

> GOETHE (1749–1832). *The Maxims and Reflections of Goethe,* 466, tr. T. Bailey Saunders, 1892
>
> See Language: Ralph Waldo Emerson (1)

It takes a great deal of history to produce a little literature.

> HENRY JAMES (1843–1916). *Hawthorne,* 1, 1879

National literature begins with fables and ends with novels.

> JOSEPH JOUBERT (1754–1824). *Pensées,* 383, 1838, tr. Henry Attwell, 1877

Literature is a form of permanent insurrection. Its mission is to arouse, to disturb, to alarm, to keep men in a constant state of dissatisfaction with themselves.

MARIO VARGAS LLOSA (1936–). "Literature Is Fire," 1967. In Jay Parini, "The Truth of Life," *New York Times Book Review,* 3 August 1997

Literature is mostly about having sex and not much about having children. Life is the other way round.

DAVID LODGE (1935–). *The British Museum Is Falling Down,* 4, 1965

A great literature is . . . chiefly the product of doubting and inquiring minds in revolt against the immovable certainties of the nation.

H. L. MENCKEN (1880–1956). "The Natural Letters: Epilogue," *Prejudices: Second Series,* 1920

Literature is doomed if liberty of thought perishes.

GEORGE ORWELL (1903–1950). "The Prevention of Literature," January 1946, *The Collected Essays, Journalism and Letters of George Orwell,* vol. 4, ed. Sonia Orwell and Ian Angus, 1968

Literature is both my joy and my comfort: it can add to every happiness and there is no sorrow it cannot console.

PLINY THE YOUNGER (A.D. 62?–113?). *Letters,* 8.19, tr. Betty Radice, 1963

Great literature is simply language charged with meaning to the utmost possible degree.

EZRA POUND (1885–1972). *ABC of Reading,* 1.2, 1934

To my mind that literature is best and most enduring which is characterized by a noble simplicity.

MARK TWAIN (1835–1910). Speech, Windsor Hotel, Montreal, 8 December 1881

Literature is mostly about having sex and not much about having children. Life is the other way around.

JOHN K. VAN de KAMP (1936–). California attorney general. In Richard Louv, *Childhood's Future,* pt. 1 (epigraph), 1981

Ernest: What is the difference between literature and journalism? *Gilbert:* Oh! journalism is unreadable, and literature is not read.

OSCAR WILDE (1854–1900). "The Critic as Artist" (1), *Intentions,* 1891

Literature always anticipates life. It does not copy it, but molds it to its purpose.

OSCAR WILDE (1854–1900). "Sebastian Melmoth," *The Works of Oscar Wilde: Epigrams, Phrases and Philosophies for the Use of the Young,* Sunflower edition, 1909

LOBBIES

See also • Campaigns ○ Elections ○ Politicians, Corrupt ○ Politics ○ Surgeons: American Society of Plastic Surgeons ○ Tobacco: Lance Williams

Lobbies exist to behave swinishly on behalf of people too delicate to behave swinishly for themselves. . . . Most lobbies are too worldly to whine when someone notices their snouts in the trough lapping up the slops.

RUSSELL BAKER (1925–). "Snouts in the Slops," *New York Times,* 21 October 1995

Our American system of government by lobbyist guarantees us a form of taxation with representation that the founding fathers did not foresee: special interests get the representation while the broad public gets the taxation.

ALAN S. BLINDER (1945–). *Hard Head, Soft Hearts: Tough-Minded Economics for a Just Society,* 1, 1987

All legislative bodies which control important pecuniary interests are as sure to have a lobby as an army to have camp followers. Where the body is, there will the vultures be gathered together.

JAMES BRYCE (1838–1922). Appendix (Note B to Chapter 16), *The American Commonwealth,* vol. 1, 1888

The future has no lobby.

PETER G. PETERSON (1926–). "The Morning After," *Atlantic,* October 1987

I don't want to leave the impression that there is something fundamentally foul about the familiar relationship between politics, campaign fund-raising, and lobbying. . . . Like anything else, within acceptable limits the relationship can be ethical and legitimate. Unfortunately, in today's Washington, those limits are long gone.

KENNETH SCHLOSSBERG. Public-relations firm president. "The Greening of Washington," *New York Times,* 14 May 1986

Reporter: Would you be against lobbyists who are working for your program? *Truman:* We probably wouldn't call those people lobbyists. We would call them citizens appearing in the public interest.

HARRY S. TRUMAN (1884–1972). Format adapted. 1948. In William Safire, *Safire's New Political Dictionary: The Definitive Guide to the New Language of Politics,* p. 418, 1993 (1968)

See Newspeak—Examples: James G. Watt

The President is the only lobbyist that 150 million Americans have. The other 20 million are able to employ people to represent them—and that's all right, it's the exercise of the right of petition—but someone has to look after the interests of the 150 million that are left.

HARRY S. TRUMAN (1884–1972). Speech before the Press and Union Club, San Francisco, 25 October 1956

Lobbiers [are among the] lousy combings and born freedom sellers of the earth.

WALT WHITMAN (1819–1892). In William Safire, *Safire's New Political Dictionary: The Definitive Guide to the New Language of Politics,* p. 418, 1993 (1968)

LOGIC

See also • Argument ○ Cause & Effect ○ Facts ○ Imagination ○ Judgment ○ Mind ○ Persuasion ○ Philosophy ○ Reason ○ Thinking

The logic of words should yield to the logic of realities.

LOUIS D. BRANDEIS (1856–1941). *Di Santo v. Pennsylvania,* 1927

No mistake is more common and more fatuous than appealing to logic in cases which are beyond her jurisdiction.

SAMUEL BUTLER (1835–1902). *Further Extracts from the Note-Books of Samuel Butler,* 5, ed. A. T. Bartholomew, 1934

"Contrariwise," continued Tweedledee, "if it was so, it might be; and if it were so, it would be: but as it isn't, it ain't. That's logic."

LEWIS CARROLL (1832–1898). *Through the Looking-Glass and What Alice Found There,* 4, 1872

No dusty logic can divine
The meaning of a sacred sign.

> GOETHE (1749–1832). *Faust,* 1 ("Night. Faust's Study," 1), 1808–1832, tr. Philip Wayne, 1959

Logic: An instrument for bolstering a prejudice.

> ELBERT HUBBARD (1856–1915). *A Thousand and One Epigrams,* p. 109, 1911

How it chanced that a man who reasoned on his premises so ably, should assume his premises so foolishly, is one of the great mysteries of human nature.

> THOMAS BABINGTON MACAULAY (1800–1859). "Samuel Johnson," *The Edinburgh Review* (Scotland), September 1831

Logic . . . lays down the general principles and laws of the search after truth.

> JOHN STUART MILL (1806–1873). "On Education," inaugural address on being installed as rector, University of St. Andrews (Scotland), 1 February 1867

Logic [enables people] to refrain from drawing conclusions which only *seem* to follow.

> BERTRAND RUSSELL (1872–1970). *Sceptical Essays,* 7, 1928

Since proofs need premises, it is impossible to prove anything unless some things are accepted without proof.

> BERTRAND RUSSELL (1872–1970). *The Faith of a Rationalist,* 1947

Pure logic is the ruin of the spirit.

> ANTOINE de SAINT-EXUPÉRY (1900–1944). *Flight to Arras,* 2, tr. Lewis Galantière, 1942

A mind all logic is like a knife all blade.
It makes the hand bleed that uses it.

> RABINDRANATH TAGORE (1861–1941). *Stray Birds,* 193, 1914

LONDON

See also • Cities ○ England

I wander thro' each dirty street,
Near where the dirty Thames does flow,
And mark in every face I meet
Marks of weakness, marks of woe.
In every cry of every man
In every infant's cry of fear
In every voice, in every ban
The mind forg'd manacles I hear.

> WILLIAM BLAKE (1757–1827). "Poems and Fragments from the Note-Book" ("London"), 19, 1793?, *The Complete Writings of William Blake,* ed. Geoffrey Keynes, 1966

London is a modern Babylon.

> BENJAMIN DISRAELI (1804–1881). *Tancred: Or, The New Crusade,* 5.5, 1847

It is not the walls that make the city, but the people who live within them. The walls of London may be battered, but the spirit of the Londoner stands resolute and undismayed.

> GEORGE VI (1895–1952). English king. During the German bombing blitz, radio broadcast, 23 September 1940

The noisy and extensive scene of crowds without company and dissipation without pleasure.

> EDWARD GIBBON (1737–1794). On London, *Memoirs of My Life and Writings,* p. 52, 1796, Alex. Murray edition, 1869

Prepare for death, if here at night you roam,
And sign your will before you sup from home.

> SAMUEL JOHNSON (1709–1784). "London: A Poem," l. 224, 1738

When a man is tired of London, he is tired of life; for there is in London all that life can afford.

> SAMUEL JOHNSON (1709–1784). 20 September 1777. In James Boswell, *The Life of Samuel Johnson,* 1791

Parks [are] the lungs of London.

> WILLIAM PITT THE ELDER (1708–1778). In William Windham, House of Commons speech, 30 June 1808

Dear, damn'd distracting, Town, farewell!

> ALEXANDER POPE (1688–1744). Opening line, "A Farewell to London," 1775

Hell is a city much like London—
  A populous and a smoky city;
There are all sorts of people undone,
And there is little or no fun done;
  Small justice shown, and still less pity.

> PERCY BYSSHE SHELLEY (1792–1822). *Peter Bell the Third,* 3.1, 1819

LONELINESS

See also • Alienation ○ Individuality: D. W. Harding ○ Solitude (Being Alone): [especially] Paul Tillich ○ Solitude (Living Alone)

[D. H. Lawrence] was the first modern novelist to realize that men and women cannot solve one another's loneliness.

> ANATOLE BROYARD (1920–1990). "The Combustible Lawrence, Still Smoldering," *New York Times Book Review,* 8 November 1987

[Loneliness is the] wretchedness of superior beings.

> ÉMILE FAGUET (1847–1916). In Charles de Gaulle, "Of Prestige" (2), *The Edge of the Sword,* 1934, tr. Gerald Hopkins, 1960

Loneliness is never more cruel than when it is felt in close propinquity with someone who has ceased to communicate.

> GERMAINE GREER (1939–). "Security," *The Female Eunuch,* 1970

Alone. But loneliness can be a communion.

> DAG HAMMARSKJÖLD (1905–1961). 1950, *Markings,* tr. Leif Sjöberg and W. H. Auden, 1964

We reach out towards the other. In vain—because we have never dared to give ourselves.

> DAG HAMMARSKJÖLD (1905–1961). 1950, *Markings,* tr. Leif Sjöberg and W. H. Auden, 1964

What makes loneliness an anguish
Is not that I have no one to share my burden,
But this:
I have only my own burden to bear.

> DAG HAMMARSKJÖLD (1905–1961). 1952, *Markings,* tr. Leif Sjöberg and W. H. Auden, 1964

Loneliness is the way by which destiny endeavors to lead man to himself.

> HERMANN HESSE (1877–1962). *Reflections,* 196, ed. Volker Michels, 1974

There is no loneliness greater than the loneliness of a failure.

> ERIC HOFFER (1902–1983). *The Passionate State of Mind: And Other Aphorisms,* 223, 1954

Sometimes when I'm lonely
Don't know why,
Keep thinkin' I won't be lonely
By and by.

> LANGSTON HUGHES (1902–1967). "Hope [1]" (complete poem), 1942, *The Collected Poems of Langston Hughes,* ed. Arnold Rampersad and David Roessel, 1994

My life is spent in a perpetual alternation between two rhythms, the rhythm of attracting people for fear I may be lonely and the rhythm of trying to get rid of them because I know that I am bored.

> C. E. M. JOAD (1891–1953). In *Observer* (British newspaper), 12 December 1948

It is . . . only in the state of complete abandonment and loneliness that we experience the helpful powers of our own natures.

> CARL G. JUNG (1875–1961). *Modern Man in Search of a Soul,* 11, tr. W. S. Dell and Cary F. Baynes, 1933

If a man knows more than others, he becomes lonely.

> CARL G. JUNG (1875–1961). "Retrospect," *Memories, Dreams, Reflections,* ed. Aniela Jaffé, 1962

All the lonely people,
where do they all come from?
All the lonely people,
where do they all belong?

> JOHN LENNON (1940–1980) and PAUL McCARTNEY (1942–). "Eleanor Rigby" (song), 1966

"Sergeant Pepper's Lonely Hearts Club Band."

> JOHN LENNON (1940–1980) and PAUL McCARTNEY (1942–). Song title, 1967

Whom the heart of man shuts out,
Sometimes the heart of God takes in.

> JAMES RUSSELL LOWELL (1819–1925). "The Forlorn," 1842

Loneliness. There perhaps are souls that never weary, that go always unhalting and glad, tuneful and songful as mountain water. Not so, weary, hungry me. In all God's mountain mansions, I find no human sympathy, and I hunger.

> JOHN MUIR (1838–1914). Journal, October 1872. In *John of the Mountains: The Unpublished Journals of John Muir,* ed. Linnie Marsh Wolfe, 1938

I lie here buried alive in my loneliness.

> FRIEDRICH NIETZSCHE (1844–1900). *My Sister and I,* 12.13, tr. Oscar Levy, 1951

Man's loneliness is but his fear of life!

> EUGENE O'NEIL (1888–1953). *Lazarus Laughed,* 3.2, 1927

Oh lonesome's a bad place
To get crowded into.

> KENNETH PATCHEN (1911–1972). "Lonesome Boy Blues," 1952

The moon has set, and the Pleiads; it is the middle of the night and time passes, time passes, and I lie alone.

> SAPPHO (610–580 B.C.). In Aldous Huxley, "Loneliness," *Texts and Pretexts,* 1933

The Loneliness of the Long-Distance Runner.

> ALAN SILLITOE (1928–). Book title, 1959

It would give me such joy to know that a friend had come to see me, and yet that pleasure I seldom if ever experience.

> HENRY DAVID THOREAU (1817–1862). Journal, 23 December 1851
>
> See Solitude (Being Alone): Thoreau

Loneliness is now so widespread it has become, paradoxically, a shared experience.

> ALVIN TOFFLER (1928–). *The Third Wave,* 25, 1980

Be good & you will be lonesome.

> MARK TWAIN (1835–1910). Holographed caption under frontispiece photograph of the author, *Following the Equator: A Journey Around the World,* 1897
>
> See Virtue: Josh Billings (2)

LONGEVITY

See also • Age ○ Death ○ Food ○ Health ○ Immortality ○ Moderation ○ Vegetarianism: George Bernard Shaw

If I'd known I was gonna live this long, I'd have taken better care of myself.

> EUBIE BLAKE (1883–1983). Musician. Remark made on his 100th birthday five days before his death. In *Observer,* British newspaper, 13 February 1983.

'Tis very certain the desire of life
Prolongs it.

> LORD BYRON (1788–1824). *Don Juan,* 2.64, 1819–1824

Red meat and gin.

> JULIA CHILD (1912–). When asked (at age 84) to what she credited her longevity. In *Minneapolis Star Tribune,* quoted in *Reader's Digest,* p. 96, January 1997

No one is so old as to think he cannot live one more year.

> CICERO (106–43 B.C.). *De senectute,* 7, tr. William Armstead Falconer, 1959

The length of our life is less important than its depth.

> MARY DAVID FISHER. Family AIDS Network founder. Keynote speech, Trinity College, Hartford (Connecticut), 23 May 1993. In "Commencements," *New York Times,* 24 May 1993

To lengthen thy Life, lessen thy Meals.

> BENJAMIN FRANKLIN (1706–1790). *Poor Richard's Almanack,* June 1733

If thou would'st live long, live well;
for Folly and Wickedness shorten Life.

> BENJAMIN FRANKLIN (1706–1790). *Poor Richard's Almanack,* February 1739

He lives longest that is awake most Hours.

> THOMAS FULLER (1654–1734). Comp., *Gnomologia: Adages and Proverbs,* 1967, 1732

If there is one single secret to long life, that secret is moderation.

> GEORGE GALLOP (1901–1984) and EVAN HILL. *The Secrets of Long Life,* 3, 1959

Measurement of life should be proportioned rather to the intensity of the experience than to its actual length.

> THOMAS HARDY (1840–1928). *A Pair of Blue Eyes,* 27, 1873

[The best way to ensure a long, productive life is to] have a chronic disease and take care of it.

> OLIVER WENDELL HOLMES, SR. (1809–1894). Physician. In Suzy Szasz, *Living with It: Why You Don't Have to Be Healthy to Be Happy,* 4, 1991

Whom the gods love die young no matter how long they live.

> ELBERT HUBBARD (1856–1915). In *The Philistine* (magazine), 1895–1915

No more shall there be in it
  an infant that lives but a few days
  or an old person who does not live out
    a lifetime;
for one who dies at a hundred years
  will be considered a youth,
  and one who falls short of a hundred
    will be considered accursed.

> ISAIAH (8th cent. B.C.). *Isaiah* 65:20 (New Revised Standard Version)

It is generally supposed that life is longer in places where there are few opportunities of luxury.

> SAMUEL JOHNSON (17609–1784). "Ostig in Sky," *A Journey to the Western Islands,* 1775

Burn a Candle at both ends, and it will not last long.

> JAMES KELLY (18th cent.). Comp., *A Complete Collection of Scottish Proverbs Explained and Made Intelligible to the English Reader,* B.124, 1721

They that live longest fetch wood farthest.

> JAMES KELLY (18th cent.). Comp., *A Complete Collection of Scottish Proverbs Explained and Made Intelligible to the English Reader,* T.60, 1721

The Electress Dowager: Doctor, I wish you may live forty years to come.
Luther: Madam, rather than live forty years more, I would give up my chance of Paradise.

> MARTIN LUTHER (1483–1546). In William James, *The Varieties of Religious Experience: A Study in Human Nature,* 6 and 7, 1902

The idea is to die young as late as possible.

> ASHLEY MONTAGU (1905–). In Paul Dickson, comp., *The Official Rules,* p. 162, 1978

A Lacedaemonian was asked what had made him live healthy so long. "Ignorance of medicine," he replied.

> MONTAIGNE (1533–1592). "Of the Resemblance of Children to Fathers," *Essays,* 1588, tr. Donald M. Frame, 1958

What have I done to achieve longevity? Woken up each morning and tried to remember not to wear my hearing aid in the bath.

> ROBERT MORLEY (1908–1992). British actor. In *London Review of Books,* 20 March 1986

How long is life to the wretched, how short for the happy!

> PUBLIUS SYRUS (85–43 B.C.). *Moral Sayings,* 621, tr. Darius Lyman, Jr., 1862

He *liveth* long that liveth well.

> JOHN RAY (1628–1705). Comp., *A Collection of English Proverbs,* p. 16, 1678

Katharine: A light heart lives long.

> SHAKESPEARE (1564–1616). *Love's Labour's Lost,* 5.2.18, 1594

A life spent worthily should be measured by a nobler line—by deeds—not years. . . . He prematurely falls, whose memory records no benefit conferred by him on man: They only have lived long who have lived virtuously.

> RICHARD SHERIDAN (1751–1816). *Pizarro,* 4.1, 1799

[What counts] is not the years in your life but the life in your years.

> ADLAI E. STEVENSON (1900–1965). "If I Were Twenty-One," *Coronet,* December 1955

It isn't time to die yet. I am needed by my children and grandchildren, and it isn't bad in this world—except that I can't turn the earth over, and it has become difficult to climb trees.

> AKHBA SULEIMAN. A 99-year-old man. In Sula Benet, "Why They Live to Be 100, or Even Older, in Abkhasia," *New York Times,* 26 December 1971

Every man desires to live long, but no man would be old.

> JONATHAN SWIFT (1667–1745). "Thoughts on Various Subjects" (expanded from a version published in 1711). *Miscellanies in Prose and Verse* (published with Alexander Pope), vol. 1, 1727

Pick the right grandparents, don't eat or drink too much, be circumspect in all things, and take a two-mile walk every morning before breakfast.

> HARRY S. TRUMAN (1884–1972). Prescription for reaching the age of 80, remark to reporters on his own eightieth birthday, Washington, 8 May 1964

✹

The days of Jacob, the years of his life, were a hundred and forty-seven years.

> ANONYMOUS (*BIBLE*). *Genesis* 47:28

A hoary head is a crown of glory;
  it is gained in a righteous life.

> SAYING (*BIBLE*). *Proverbs* 16:31

He who would live long must sometimes change his way of living.

> SAYING (ITALIAN)

A merry heart makes a long life.

> SAYING

Grow old early, if you would be old long.

> SAYING. In Oliver Wendell Holmes, Sr., *The Autocrat of the Breakfast-Table,* 7, 1858

LOS ANGELES

See also • California ○ Cities ○ Hollywood

A big hard-boiled city with no more personality than a paper cup.
> RAYMOND CHANDLER (1888–1959). On Los Angeles, *The Little Sister*, 26, 1949

The only town in the world where you can wake up in the morning and listen to the birds coughing in the trees.
> JOE FRISCO. On smoggy Los Angeles

A circus without a tent.
> CAREY McWILLIAMS (1905–1980). On Los Angeles, in *Southern California Country*, 1946

LOSING

See also • Defeat ○ Giving: Eric Hoffer ○ Victory ○ Winning

I hate to lose more than I like to win.
> LARRY BIRD (1956–). Basketball coach. In Associated Press, "Pitino's Celtics Stun Bulls; Bird Drops Coaching Debut," *San Francisco Chronicle*, 1 November 1997

They who lose today may win tomorrow.
> CERVANTES (1547–1616). *Don Quixote*, 1.1.7, 1615, tr. Peter Anthony Motteux and John Ozell, 1743

I have lost all and found myself.
> JOHN CLARKE (1596–1658). Comp., *Proverbs: English and Latine*, p. 198, 1639

Contrary to reports that I took the loss badly, I slept like a baby—every two hours I woke up and cried.
> ROBERT J. DOLE (1923–). On losing his bid for the Republican presidential nomination, 14 August 1988

When you think you've lost everything,
you find out you can always lose a little more.
> BOB DYLAN (1941–). "Tryin' to Get to Heaven" (song), 1997

I lost everything. And, you know, you *see* in those moments.
> KAREN FINLEY (1956–). In Marcelle Clements, "Karen Finley's Rage, Pain, Hate and Hope," *New York Times*, 22 July 1990

He is dangerous who has nothing to lose.
> GOETHE (1749–1832). *Die natürliche Tochter*, 1.3, 1804

He loseth nothing that loseth not God.
> GEORGE HERBERT (1593–1633). Comp., *Outlandish Proverbs*, 35, 1640

It's not what they take away from you that counts. It's what you do with what you have left. Never give up and never give in.
> HUBERT H. HUMPHREY (1911–1978). Remark to reporters after losing the presidential election, 10 November 1968

Good God, man, history is full of examples of battles being lost because units stopped on the near side of a river.
> GEORGE S. PATTON, JR. (1885–1945). Remark to Gen. Troy Middleton, who had just described his division's position, France, 2 August 1944. In Harry H. Semmes, *Portrait of Patton*, 10, 1964

There are two kinds of losers: (1) the good loser and (2) those who can't act.
> LAURENCE J. PETER (1919–1990). *Peter's People*, 8, 1979

Whatever you can lose, reckon of no account.
> PUBLIUS SYRUS (85–43 B.C.). *Moral Sayings*, 191, tr. Darius Lyman, Jr., 1862

He *loseth* nothing who keeps God for his friend.
> JOHN RAY (1628–1705). Comp., *A Collection of English Proverbs*, p. 16, 1678

There are fights which should be made even if a loss is certain.
> FRANK TOLLMAN. "Everybody's Friend—Nobody's Leader," *New Republic*, 9 August 1954

Sometimes it is too late to win. But it's never too late to lose.
> TOM WARSON. "Warson's Truth," in Paul Dickson, comp., *The New Official Rules*, p. 217, 1989

Show me a good loser and I'll show you a sure loser.
> SAYING (AMERICAN)

LOSS

See • Profit & Loss

LOVE

See also • Brotherhood ○ Ethics: Albert Schweitzer (3) ○ Forgiveness: La Rochefoucauld: Walter Lippmann ○ Happiness: Victor Hugo, George Sand ○ Hate ○ Justice: John Ruskin ○ Love, Romantic ○ Nonviolence: Mohandas K. Gandhi (7) ○ Salvation: Alice Walker ○ Self-Love ○ Self-Realization (Becoming): P. W. Martin (5) ○ Tragedy: W. Somerset Maugham ○ Wisdom: Charles Dickens, N. Sri Ram (1)

Love is, above all, the gift of oneself.
> JEAN ANOUILH (1910–1987). *Ardèle*, 2, 1948, tr. Lucienne Hill, 1951

We must love one another or die.
> W. H. AUDEN (1907–1973). "September 1, 1939" (poem), 8, 1940

Love, and do what you will!
> ST. AUGUSTINE (A.D. 354–430). *In Epist. Joannis ad Parthos*, 7.8

Love to faults is always blind,
Always is to joy inclin'd,
Lawless, wing'd, and unconfin'd,
And Breaks all chains from every mind.
> WILLIAM BLAKE (1757–1827). "Poems and Fragments from the Note-Book," 29, 1793?, *The Complete Writings of William Blake*, ed. Geoffrey Keynes, 1966

To wait an Hour—is long—
If Love be just beyond—
To wait Eternity—is short—
If Love reward the end—
> EMILY DICKINSON (1830–1886). "To wait an Hour—is long" (complete poem), 1863?

That Love is all there is,
Is all we know of Love.

> EMILY DICKINSON (1830–1886). "That Love is all there is," undated

Love either finds equality or makes it.

> JOHN DRYDEN (1631–1700). *Marriage à la Mode*, 3.1, 1673

When Love is suppressed, Hate takes its place.

> HAVELOCK ELLIS (1859–1939). "The Meaning of Purity" (3), *Little Essays on Love and Virtue*, 1922

Love would put a new face on this weary old world in which we dwell as pagans and enemies too long.

> RALPH WALDO EMERSON (1803–1882). "Man the Reformer," lecture, Mechanics' Apprentices' Library Association, Boston, 25 January 1841

All mankind love a lover.

> RALPH WALDO EMERSON (1803–1882). "Love," *Essays: First Series*, 1841 (Popular version: All the world loves a lover.)
>
> See Winning: Saying (American) (2)

Love has that temperance which asks for nothing which is not already [in] the moment granted.

> RALPH WALDO EMERSON (1803–1882). Journal, 1845, undated

The superiority that has no superior; the redeemer and instructor of souls, as it is their primal essence, is love.

> RALPH WALDO EMERSON (1803–1882). "Worship," *The Conduct of Life*, 1860

If you would be loved, love and be lovable.

> BENJAMIN FRANKLIN (1706–1790). *Poor Richard's Almanack*, February 1755

A love that does not discriminate seems to me to forfeit a part of its own value, by doing an injustice to its object; and secondly, not all men are worthy of love.

> SIGMUND FREUD (1856–1939). *Civilization and Its Discontents*, 4, 1930, tr. James Strachey, 1961

If this grandiose commandment [i.e., "Love thy neighbor as thyself"] had run "Love thy neighbor as thy neighbor loves thee," I should not take exception to it. And there is a second commandment, which seems to me even more incomprehensible and arouses still stronger opposition in me. It is "Love thine enemies."

> SIGMUND FREUD (1856–1939). *Civilization and Its Discontents*, 5, 1930, tr. James Strachey, 1961.
>
> See Religion: Mohandas K. Gandhi (3) ○ Self-Love: Moses

Exclusive love is a contradiction in itself.

> ERICH FROMM (1900–1980). *Escape from Freedom*, 4, 1941

Love is union with somebody, or something, outside oneself, *under the condition of retaining the separateness and integrity of one's own self*. It is an experience of sharing, of communing, which permits the full unfolding of one's own inner activity.

> ERICH FROMM (1900–1980). *The Sane Society*, 3.A, 1955

"Love, the Answer to the Problem of Human Existence."

> ERICH FROMM (1900–1980). *The Art of Loving*, 2.1 (section title), 1956

Love never claims, it ever gives.

> MOHANDAS K. GANDHI (1869–1948). In *Young India*, 9 July 1925

Love . . . is the Law of our Being.

> MOHANDAS K. GANDHI (1869–1948). In *Harijan*, 26 September 1936

When you love you should not say, "God is in my heart," but rather, "I am in the heart of God."
     And think not you can direct the course of love, for love, if it finds you worthy, directs your course.

> KAHLIL GIBRAN (1883–1931). "On Love," *The Prophet*, 1923

To love life and men as God loves them—for the sake of their infinite possibilities.

> DAG HAMMARSKJÖLD (1905–1961). 22 April 1956, *Markings*, tr. Leif Sjöberg and W. H. Auden, 1964

Tender Love, Tough love, which is better[?]

> NATHANIEL HAWTHORNE (1804–1864). 1 June 1842, *The American Notebooks*, ed. Claude M. Simpson, 1932

Love is that condition in which the happiness of another person is essential to your own.

> ROBERT A. HEINLEIN (1907–). *Stranger in a Strange Land*, 34, 1961

Love rules his kingdom without a sword.

> GEORGE HERBERT (1593–1633). Comp., *Outlandish Proverbs*, 541, 1640

Like all true values, love cannot be bought. Pleasure can be bought, but not love.

> HERMANN HESSE (1877–1962). *Reflections*, 629, ed. Volker Michels, 1974

Thou shalt love the stars, the ocean, the forest, and reverence all living things, recognizing that the source of life is one.

> ELBERT HUBBARD (1856–1915). *The Note Book of Elbert Hubbard*, p. 120, comp. Elbert Hubbard II, 1927
>
> See Ethics: Albert Schweitzer (4)

What a grand thing, to be loved! What a grander thing still, to love!

> VICTOR HUGO (1802–1885). "Saint Denis" (5.4), *Les Misérables*, tr. Charles E. Wilbour, 1862

That disinterested love of God which "asks nothing and refuses nothing."

> ALDOUS HUXLEY (1894–1963). *The Perennial Philosophy*, 5, 1946

Love blinds us to faults, hatred to virtues.

> MOSES IBN EZRA (A.D. 1070?–1138?)

You have heard that it was said, "You shall love your neighbor and hate your enemy." But I say to you, Love your enemies and pray for those who persecute you, so that you may be sons of your Father who is in heaven.

> JESUS (A.D. 1st cent.). *Matthew* 5:43–45
>
> See Religion: Mohandas K. Gandhi (3) ○ Self-Love: Moses

He who does not love does not know God; for God is love.

> JOHN (A.D. 1st cent.). *1 John* 4:8

There is no fear in love, but perfect love casts out fear.

> JOHN (A.D. 1st cent.). *I John* 4:18

Love doesn't make the world go 'round. Love is what makes the ride worthwhile.

> FRANKLIN P. JONES (1881–1960)

Where love reigns, there is no will to power; and where the will to power is paramount, love is lacking.

> CARL G. JUNG (1875–1961). "On the Psychology of the Unconscious" (4.1), 1917, *Two Essays on Analytical Psychology,* tr. R. F. C. Hull, 1953

Agape is disinterested love. . . . *Agape* does not begin by discriminating between worthy and unworthy people, or any qualities people possess. It begins by loving others *for their sakes.* . . . Therefore, *agape* makes no distinction between friend and enemy; it is directed toward both.

> MARTIN LUTHER KING, JR. (1929–1968). *Stride Toward Freedom,* 6, 1958

When I speak of love, I am speaking of that force which all the great religions have seen as the supreme unifying principle of life. Love is the key that unlocks the door which leads to ultimate reality.

> MARTIN LUTHER KING, JR. (1929–1968). *Where Do We Go from Here: Chaos or Community?* 6.3, 1967

Where love is, no disguise can hide it for long; where it is not, none can simulate it.

> LA ROCHEFOUCAULD (1613–1680). *Maxims,* 70, 1665, tr. Leonard Tancock, 1959

A disinterested love . . . is free from hope and from fear, and from regard for personal advantage.

> GOTTFRIED LEIBNITZ (1646–1716). "On the Notions of Right and Justice," 1693, *The Philosophic Works of Leibnitz,* ed. George Martin Duncan, 1908

To *love* is to take delight in the happiness of another, or, what amounts to the same thing, it is to account another's happiness one's own.

> GOTTFRIED LEIBNITZ (1646–1716). "On the Notions of Right and Justice," 1693, *The Philosophic Works of Leibnitz,* ed. George Martin Duncan, 1908

"All You Need Is Love."

> JOHN LENNON (1940–1980) and PAUL McCARTNEY (1942–). Song title, 1967

Do not waste time bothering whether you "love" your neighbor; act as if you did. As soon as we do this we find one of the great secrets. When you are behaving as if you loved someone, you will presently come to love him. If you injure someone you dislike, you will find yourself disliking him more. If you do him a good turn, you will find yourself disliking him less.

> C. S. LEWIS (1898–1963). *Mere Christianity,* rev. ed., 3.9, 1952

We do not only love ourselves in others but hate ourselves in others too.

> GEORG CHRISTOPH LICHTENBERG (1742–1799). *Aphorisms,* F.54, 1806, tr. R. J. Hollingdale, 1990

Him that I love, I wish to be
Free—
Even from me.

> ANNE MORROW LINDBERGH (1906–). "Even—," *The Unicorn and Other Poems, 1935–1955,* 1956

In all true love there is the love of the Infinite in the person or thing we love.

JUAN MASCARÓ (?–1987). Introduction to *Bhagavad Gita* (6th cent. B.C.), 1962

There is in the human will an innate tendency, an inborn capacity for disinterested love. This power to love another for his own sake is one of the things that makes us like God.

> THOMAS MERTON (1915–1968). *The Seven Storey Mountain* (from the unpublished, original manuscript, 1948), *A Thomas Merton Reader,* 5.1, ed. Thomas P. McDonnell, 1974

We are obliged to love one another. We are not strictly bound to "like" one another.

> THOMAS MERTON (1915–1968). *No Man Is an Island,* 9.6, 1955

[Love] both gives and receives, and in giving it receives.

> THOMAS MERTON (1915–1968). "The Good Samaritan," *A Thomas Merton Reader,* ed. Thomas P. McDonnell, 1974

The proof of true love is to be unsparing in criticism.

> MOLIÈRE (1622–1673). *Le Misanthrope,* 2, 1666, tr. John Wood, 1959

You shall love the Lord your God with all your heart, and with all your soul, and with all your might.

> MOSES (14th cent. B.C.). *Deuteronomy* 6:5

In the development of the person, love is actually the central element of integration: love as erotic desire and procreativeness, love as passion and aesthetic delight, lingering over images of beauty and shaping them anew, love as fellow feeling and neighborly helpfulness, bestowing its gifts on those who need them, love as parental solicitude and sacrifice, finally, love with its miraculous capacity for overvaluing its own object, thereby, glorifying it and transfiguring it, releasing for life something that only the lover at first can see. Without a positive concentration upon love in all its phases, we can hardly hope to rescue the earth and all the creatures that inhabit it from the insensate forces of hate, violence, and destruction that now threaten it.

> LEWIS MUMFORD (1895–1990). *The Transformations of Man,* 9.5, 1956

If I can't love Hitler, I can't love at all.

> A. J. MUSTE (1885–1967). In Milton Mayer, "'If You Keep Moving, They Can't Hit You,'" *Center Magazine,* July-August 1973

Whatever is done from love always occurs beyond good and evil.

> FRIEDRICH NIETZSCHE (1844–1900). *Beyond Good and Evil,* 153, 1886, tr. Walter Kaufmann, 1966

There is only one thing that has power, and that is love. Because when a man loves, he seeks no power, and therefore he has power.

> ALAN PATON (1903–1988). *Cry, the Beloved Country,* 7, 1948

If I speak in the tongues of men and of angels, but have not love, I am a noisy gong or a clanging cymbal.

> PAUL (A.D. 1st cent.). *1 Corinthians* 13:1
>
> See Faith: Paul

Love is patient and kind; love is not jealous or boastful; it is not arrogant or rude. Love does not insist on its own way; it is not irritable or resentful; it does not rejoice at wrong, but rejoices in the right. Love bears all things, believes all things, hopes all things.

> PAUL (A.D. 1st cent.). *1 Corinthians* 13:4–7

Love . . . binds everything together in perfect harmony.
> PAUL (A.D. 1st cent.). *Colossians* 3:14

Love . . . has the greatest power, and is the source of all our happiness and harmony, and makes us friends with the gods who are above us, and with one another.
> PLATO (427?–347 B.C.). *Symposium,* 188, tr. Benjamin Jowett, 1894

He whom Love touches not walks in darkness.
> PLATO (427?–347 B.C.). *Symposium,* 197, tr. Benjamin Jowett, 1894

Human nature is so constructed that it gives affection most readily to those who seem least to demand it.
> BERTRAND RUSSELL (1872–1970). *The Conquest of Happiness,* 12, 1930

It is love, not faith, that removes mountains.
> GEORGE SAND (1804–1876). 10 September 1832. *The Intimate Journal of George Sand,* ed. Marie Jenney Howe, 1977 (1929)
> See Faith: Paul

Love . . . includes fellowship in suffering, in joy, and in effort.
> ALBERT SCHWEITZER (1875–1965). *The Philosophy of Civilization: Civilization and Ethics,* 21, 1923, tr. C. T. Campion and Mrs. Charles E. B. Russell, 1946

Does my behavior in respect of love affect nothing? That is because there is not enough love in me.
> ALBERT SCHWEITZER (1875–1965). *Memoirs of Childhood and Youth,* 5, 1925, tr. C. T. Campion, 1949

Love means not ever having to say you're sorry.
> ERICH SEGAL (1937–). *Love Story,* 13, 1970

Brutus: Poor Brutus, with himself at war,
Forgets the shows of love to other men.
> SHAKESPEARE (1564–1616). *Julius Caesar,* 1.2.46, 1599

Brutus: When love begins to sicken and decay,
It useth an enforced ceremony.
> SHAKESPEARE (1564–1616). *Julius Caesar,* 4.2.20, 1599

Cleopatra: All people are strangers and enemies to us except those we love.
> GEORGE BERNARD SHAW (1856–1950). *Caesar and Cleopatra,* 4, 1899

Fate, Time, Occasion, Chance, and Change? To these
All things are subject but eternal Love.
> PERCY BYSSHE SHELLEY (1792–1822). *Prometheus Unbound,* 2.4.119, 1820

Love is but the discovery of ourselves in others, and the delight in the recognition.
> ALEXANDER SMITH (1830–1867). *Dreamthorp,* 8, 1863

The essence of love is kindness.
> ROBERT LOUIS STEVENSON (1850–1894). Title essay (3), *Virginibus Puerisque,* 1881

All the world loves a lover, and a lover loves all the world.
> ANTHONY STORR (1920–). *Solitude: A Return to the Self,* 12, 1988

Power said to the world, "You are mine."
The world kept it prisoner on her throne.

Love said to the world, "I am thine."
The world gave it the freedom of her house.
> RABINDRANATH TAGORE (1861–1941). *Stray Birds,* 93, 1914

Love's gift cannot be given,
it waits to be accepted.
> RABINDRANATH TAGORE (1861–1941). *Fireflies,* p. 271, 1928

Love is a mighty power, a great and complete good. Love alone lightens every burden, and makes the rough places smooth. . . . Nothing is sweeter than love, nothing stronger, nothing higher, nothing wider, nothing more pleasant, nothing fuller or better in heaven or earth; for love is born of God, and can rest only in God, above all created things.

Love flies, runs, and leaps for joy; it is free and unrestrained. Love gives all for all, resting in One who is highest above all things, from whom every good flows and proceeds. Love does not regard the gifts, but turns to the Giver of all good gifts.
> THOMAS à KEMPIS (1380–1471). *The Imitation of Christ,* 3.5, tr. Leo Sherley-Price, 1952

To love one's neighbors, to love one's enemies, to love everything—to love God in all His manifestations. Human love serves to love those dear to us but to love one's enemies we need divine love.
> LEO TOLSTOY (1828–1910). *War and Peace,* 3.3.32, 1863–1869, tr. Rosemary Edmonds, 1957

Love, like virtue, is its own reward.
> JOHN VANBRUGH (1664–1726). *The Provok'd Wife,* 2.1, 1692
> See Virtue: Ovid

Love is God.
> LEW WALLACE (1827–1905). *Ben-Hur: A Tale of the Christ,* 6.2, 1880
> See God: John

The aim of love is to love: no more, and no less.
> OSCAR WILDE (1854–1900). *De Profundis,* 1905

Love is what we were born with. Fear is what we learned here.
> MARIANNE WILLIAMSON (1953–). Introduction to *A Return to Love: Reflections on the Principles of a Course in Miracles,* 1992

✿

Love given away wholeheartedly, inclusively, and unconditionally is inexhaustible.
> ANONYMOUS

Why not give love a chance? We've tried everything else.
> ANONYMOUS

Love makes the world go round.
> SAYING (FRENCH). 17th cent.
> See Money: Publius Syrus

Love grows best in the soil of liberty.
> SAYING

Love your enemy as yourself.
> SAYING
> See Religion: Mohandas K. Gandhi (3) ○ Self-Love: Moses

LOVE, ROMANTIC

See also • Love ○ Marriage ○ Security: Shelley Winters ○ Sex ○ Women & Men ○ Youth: Beaumarchais

They say falling in love is wonderful,
It's wonderful, so they say.

> IRVING BERLIN (1888–1989). "Falling in Love" (song). In the musical, *Annie Get Your Gun*, 1946

Romantic love is sexually passionate love. Romance uses sexual intimacy to create or amplify closeness and mutual fulfillment.

> PETER R. BREGGIN (1936–). *The Heart of Being Helpful: Empathy and the Creation of a Healing Presence*, 10, 1997

Books, places, amusements, people—how meaningless they become when we suspect that the person we love loves someone else!

> GERALD BRENAN (1894–1987). "Love," *Thoughts in a Dry Season: A Miscellany*, 1978

How do I love thee? Let me count the ways.
I love thee to the depth and breadth and height
My soul can reach.

> ELIZABETH BARRETT BROWNING (1806–1861). *Sonnets from the Portuguese*, 43, 1850

And stood by the rose-wreathed gate. Alas,
    We loved, sir—used to meet:
How sad and bad and mad it was—
    But then, how it was sweet!

> ROBERT BROWNING (1812–1889). Closing stanza, "Confessions," *Dramatis Personae*, 1864

When we are not in love too much, we are not in love enough.

> BUSSY-RABUTIN (1618–1693). *Histoire amoureuse des Gaules: maximes d'amour*, 1700

Absence is to love what wind is to fire;
It extinguishes the small, it kindles the great.

> BUSSY-RABUTIN (1618–1693). *Histoire amoureuse des Gaules: maximes d'amour*, 1700

The ultimate experience of [sexual] love is a realization that beneath the illusion of two-ness dwells identity: "Each is both."

> JOSEPH CAMPBELL (1904–1987). *The Hero with a Thousand Faces*, 2.1.4, 1949

True love is the joy of life.

> JOHN CLARKE (1596–1658). Comp., *Proverbs: English and Latine*, p. 26, 1639

Love Laughs at Locksmiths.

> GEORGE COLMAN THE YOUNGER (1762–1836). Opera title, 1806

Love and murder will out.

> WILLIAM CONGREVE (1670–1729). *The Double Dealer*, 4.6, 1694
> See Nature: Aesop ○ Truth: John Lydgate

Love reckons hours for months, and days for years;
And every little absence is an age.

> JOHN DRYDEN (1631–1700). *Amphitryon*, 3.1, 1691

"Baby, You're the Only Dream I've Ever Had That's Come True."

> ROBERT DUVALL (1931–). Song title. In *Tender Mercies* (film), 1983

Stay, lady, stay, stay with your man awhile
Why wait any longer for the world to begin
You can have your cake and eat it too
Why wait any longer for the one you love
When he's standing in front of you.

> BOB DYLAN (1941–). "Lay, Lady, Lay" (song), 1969

Here's looking at you, kid.

> JULIUS J. EPSTEIN (1909–), PHILIP G. EPSTEIN, and HOWARD KOCH. *Casablanca* (film), 1942, farewell words spoken by Humphrey Bogart to Ingrid Bergman

Love is the strangest bird
that ever winged about the world.

> LAWRENCE FERLINGHETTI (1919–). Opening lines, "Song of Love & Desire," *Open Eye, Open Heart*, 1973

Love is a tyrant,
Resisted.

> JOHN FORD (1586?–1640?). *The Lover's Melancholy*, 1.3, 1629

In love the paradox occurs that two beings become one and yet remain two.

> ERICH FROMM (1900–1980). *The Art of Loving*, 2.1, 1956

Love one another, but make not a bond of love:
Let it rather be a moving sea between the shores of your souls.

> KAHLIL GIBRAN (1883–1931). "On Marriage," *The Prophet*, 1923

What love is, if thou wouldst be taught,
Thy heart must teach alone—
Two souls with but a single thought,
Two hearts that beat as one.

> FRIEDRICH HALM (1806–1871). *Ingomar, the Barbarian*, 2.1, tr. Maria Lovell, 1896

Fish gotta swim and birds gotta fly
I gotta love one man till I die,
Can't help lovin' dat man of mine.

> OSCAR HAMMERSTEIN II (1895–1960). "Can't Help Lovin' Dat Man of Mine" (song). In the musical *Showboat*, 1927

When I'm not near the girl I love,
I love the girl I'm near.

> E. Y. "YIP" HARBURG (1898–1981). "When I'm Not Near the Girl I Love" (song), 1947

A lover without indiscretion is no lover at all.

> THOMAS HARDY (1840–1928). *The Hand of Ethelberta*, 20, 1876

Just because I loves you—
That's de reason why
Ma soul is full of color
Like da wings of a butterfly.

Just because I loves you
That's de reason why
My heart's a fluttering aspen leaf
When you pass by.

> LANGSTON HUGHES (1902–1967). "Reasons Why" (complete poem), 1922, *The Collected Poems of Langston Hughes*, ed. Arnold Rampersad and David Roessel, 1994

De lady I work for
Told her husband
She wanted a
Robe o' love—
But de damn fool
Give her
A fur coat!

Yes,
He did!

> LANGSTON HUGHES (1902–1967). "Present" (complete poem), 1942,
> *The Collected Poems of Langston Hughes,* ed. Arnold Rampersad and
> David Roessel, 1994

When love has melted and mingled two beings into an angelic and sacred unity, the secret of life is found for them . . . they are then but the two wings of a single spirit. Love, soar!

> VICTOR HUGO (1802–1885). "Saint Denis" (5.4), *Les Misérables,* tr.
> Charles E. Wilbour, 1862

I am in the night. There is a being who has gone away and carried the heavens with her.

> VICTOR HUGO (1802–1885). "Saint Denis" (5.4), *Les Misérables,* tr.
> Charles E. Wilbour, 1862

I met in the street a very poor young man who was in love. His hat was old, his coat was threadbare—there were holes at his elbows; the water passed through his shoes and the stars through his soul.

> VICTOR HUGO (1802–1885). "Saint Denis" (5.4), *Les Misérables,* tr.
> Charles E. Wilbour, 1862

I love your hills, and I love your dales,
    And I love your flocks a-bleating—
But O, on the heather to lie together,
    With both our hearts a-beating!

> JOHN KEATS (1795–1821). "The Devon Maid," 3

True love is like seeing ghosts: we all talk about it, but few of us have ever seen one.

> LA ROCHEFOUCAULD (1613–1680). *Maxims,* 76, 1665, tr. Louis
> Kronenberger, 1959

He that can jest at love has never loved.

> JOHANN CASPAR LAVATER (1741–1801). *Aphorisms on Man,* 525, 1788
> See Wounds: Shakespeare (1)

Eight days a week I love you.

> JOHN LENNON (1940–1980) and PAUL McCARTNEY (1942–). "Eight
> Days a Week" (song), 1964

Come live with me, and be my love,
And we will all the pleasures prove
That valleys, groves, hills, and fields,
Woods, or steepy mountain yields.

> CHRISTOPHER MARLOWE (1564–1593). Opening stanza, "The
> Passionate Shepherd to His Love," *The Passionate Pilgrim,* 1599

What passes as love between man and woman can be many things. Promiscuity, possessiveness, misuse of sex for purposes of power, are all highly disintegrative. . . . But love between man and woman that is the relationship in depth, the "marriage of true minds," is a drawing to wholeness. Each calls up in the other the deep center, the seed of the Self. It is by such love that the "real being" grows and lives.

> P. W. MARTIN (1893–?). *Experiment in Depth: A Study of the Work of
> Jung, Eliot and Toynbee,* 10, 1955

Mutual love, the Crown of all our bliss.

> JOHN MILTON (1608–1674). *Paradise Lost,* 4:728, 1667

Our State cannot be severed, we are one,
One Flesh; to lose thee were to lose my self.

> JOHN MILTON (1608–1674). *Paradise Lost,* 9.958, 1667

Fame, wealth, and honor! what are you to Love?

> ALEXANDER POPE (1688–1744). "Eloisa to Abelard," l. 80, 1717

Night and day you are the one,
Only you beneath the moon and under the sun.

> COLE PORTER (1892–1964). "Night and Day" (song). In the musical
> *Gay* Divorce, 1932

Birds do it, bees do it,
Even educated fleas do it.
Let's do it, let's fall in love.

> COLE PORTER (1892–1964). "Let's Do It" (song), 1954 (words added to
> the original 1928 song)

Love me tender, love me sweet,
Never let me go.

> ELVIS PRESLEY (1935–1977) and VERA MATSON. "Love Me Tender"
> (song), 1956

Like everybody who is not in love, he imagined that one chose the person whom one loved after endless deliberations and on the strength of various qualities and advantages.

> MARCEL PROUST (1871–1922). *Remembrance of Things Past: Cities of
> the Plain,* 1, 1913–1927, tr. C. K. Scott Moncrieff, 1941

To fear love is to fear life, and those who fear life are already three parts dead.

> BERTRAND RUSSELL (1872–1970). *Marriage and Morals,* 19, 1929

In love, one and one are one.

> JEAN-PAUL SARTRE (1905–1980). In Eli Wiesel, "To a Young Jew of
> Today," *One Generation After,* tr. Lily Edelman and the author, 1965

Juliet: My bounty is as boundless as the sea,
My love as deep; the more I give to thee,
The more I have, for both are infinite.

> SHAKESPEARE (1564–1616). *Romeo and Juliet,* 2.2.133, 1594

The desire to give inspires no affection unless there is also the power to withhold; and the successful wooer, in both sexes alike, is the one who can stand out for honorable conditions, and, failing them, go without.

> GEORGE BERNARD SHAW (1856–1950). "The Womanly Woman," *The
> Quintessence of Ibsenism,* 1891

The fickleness of the women whom I love is only equaled by the infernal constancy of the women who love me.

> GEORGE BERNARD SHAW (1856–1950). *The Philanderer,* 2, 1893

[Being in love] is something like poetry. Certainly, you can analyze it and expound its various senses and intentions, but there is always something left over, mysteriously hovering between music and meaning.

> MURIEL SPARK (1918–). "On Love," *Partisan Review* (50th Anniversary issue), 1984

'Tis better to have loved and lost
Than never to have loved at all.

> ALFRED, LORD TENNYSON (1809–1892). *In Memoriam A. H. H.*, 27, 1850

We are most alive when we're in love.

> JOHN UPDIKE (1932–). Interview with the author. In Naim Attallah, *Singular Encounters*, 1990

To be in love is to surpass oneself.

> OSCAR WILDE (1854–1900). *The Picture of Dorian Gray*, 5, 1891

❧

It is impossible to love and be wise.

> ANONYMOUS. In Francis Bacon, "Of Love," *Essays*, 1625

Let your love be like the misty rain, coming softly, but flooding the river.

> SAYING (MADAGASCAN)

Love at first sight.

> SAYING
>
> See Hate: Ralph Waldo Emerson (1)

LOYALTY

See also • Bureaucracy ○ Country: Mohandas K. Gandhi ○ Diplomats: C. Northcote Parkinson ○ Disloyalty ○ Friends ○ Leaders: James Russell Lowell ○ Managers: Ferdinand Lundberg ○ Joseph A. Califano, Jr. (1,2) ○ Trust

Fidelity, *n.* A virtue peculiar to those who are about to be betrayed.

> AMBROSE BIERCE (1842–1914). *The Devil's Dictionary*, p. 42, 1911, Dover edition, 1958

Worthy Bertuccio, I have known you ever
Trusty and brave, with head and heart to plan
What I have still been prompt to execute.
For my own part, I seek no other chief;
What the rest will decide I know not, but
I am with you, as I have ever been.

> LORD BYRON (1788–1824). *Marino Faliero, Doge of Venice*, 2.2, 1821

An ounce of loyalty is worth a pound of cleverness.

> ELBERT HUBBARD (1856–1915). *A Thousand and One Epigrams*, p. 160, 1911

No one can serve two masters.

> JESUS (A.D. 1st cent.). *Matthew* 6:24

I don't want loyalty, I want *loyalty*. I want him to kiss my ass in Macy's window at high noon and tell me it smells like roses. I want his pecker in my pocket.

> LYNDON B. JOHNSON (1908–1973). On the importance of loyalty in the White House inner circle. In David Halberstam, *The Best and the Brightest*, 20, 1972
>
> See Vietnam War: Johnson (4)

Loyalty is in most people only a ruse used by self-interest to attract confidences.

> LA ROCHEFOUCAULD (1613–1680). *Maxims*, 246, 1665, tr. Louis Kronenberger, 1959

Loyalty is a noble quality, so long as it is not blind and does not exclude the higher loyalty to truth and decency.

> B. H. LIDDELL HART (1895–1970). "Blinding Loyalties," *Why Don't We Learn from History?* 1944

A servile loyalty [is] demeaning both to master and servant.

> B. H. LIDDELL HART (1895–1970). "Blinding Loyalties," *Why Don't We Learn from History?* 1944

I do not want to be considered either so affectionate or so loyal a servant as to be found fit to betray anyone.

> MONTAIGNE (1533–1592). "Of the Useful and the Honorable," *Essays*, 1588, tr. Donald M. Frame, 1958

Loyalty is reciprocal.

> RICHARD E. NEUSTADT (1919–). *Presidential Power: The Politics of Leadership*, 3.1, 1960

Certain loyalty comes only through dependency.

> RICHARD M. NIXON (1913–1994). *Leaders*, 7, 1982

I entirely appreciate loyalty to one's friends, but loyalty to the cause of justice and honor stands above it.

> THEODORE ROOSEVELT (1858–1919). In Hermann Hagedorn and Sidney Wallach, "Signposts for Americans: Random Thoughts," *A Theodore Roosevelt Round-Up*, 1958

Entreat me not to leave you or to return from following you; for where you go I will go, and where you lodge I will lodge; your people shall be my people, and your God my God; where you die I will die, and there will I be buried. May the Lord do so to me and more also if even death parts me from you.

> RUTH. Remarks to her mother-in-law Naomi (both widowed), *Ruth* 1:16-17

Cardinal Wolsey: Had I but served my God with half the zeal I served my King, He would not in mine age Have left me naked to mine enemies.

> SHAKESPEARE (1564–1616). *Henry VIII*, 3.2.455, 1612

I knew wherever I was that you thought of me, and if I got in a tight place you would come—if alive.

> WILLIAM TECUMSEH SHERMAN (1820–1891). Letter to Gen. Ulysses S. Grant, 10 March 1864, *Memoirs of Gen. W. T. Sherman*, 4th ed., 15, 1891 (1875)

❧

Loyalty down fosters loyalty up.

> ANONYMOUS

Whose bread I eat, his song I sing.

> SAYING (GERMAN)

LUCK

See also • Cause & Effect ○ Chance ○ Destiny ○ Experience ○ Fate ○ Fortune ○ Misfortune ○ Necessity ○ Opportunity

Luck to me [means] hard work—and realizing what is opportunity and what isn't.

> LUCILLE BALL (1911–1989). In Eleanor Harris, *The Real Story of Lucille Ball*, 1, 1954

Trusting to luck is only another name for *trusting to lazyness.*

> JOSH BILLINGS (1818–1885). "Plum Pits," *Everybody's Friend, or; Josh Billing's Encyclopedia and Proverbial Philosophy of Wit and Humor,* 1874

I'm lucky. . . . [but] I knew what to do with luck when it hit me.

> BEN BRADLEE (1921–). Michael Krasny radio interview, KQED, San Francisco, 17 October 1995

Luck is not chance—
It's Toil—
Fortune's expensive smile
Is earned—

> EMILY DICKINSON (1830–1886). "Luck is not chance," 1875?

Good luck is another name for tenacity of purpose.

> RALPH WALDO EMERSON (1803–1882). "Wealth," *The Conduct of Life,* 1860

In this world
the lucky person passes for a genius.

> EURIPIDES (485?–406 B.C.). *The Heracleidae,* l. 745, tr. Ralph Gladstone, 1955

Hard work and a proper frame of mind prepare you for the lucky breaks that finally come along—or don't.

> HARRISON FORD (1942–). In Glenn Plaskin, "The Real Harrison Ford," *San Francisco Chronicle,* 13 August 1990

A pound of pluck is worth a ton of luck.

> JAMES A. GARFIELD (1831–1881). In Thomas A. Bailey, *Presidential Greatness: The Image and the Man from George Washington to the Present,* 6 (epigraph), 1966

It is a great piece of skill to know how to guide your luck even while waiting for it.

> BALTASAR GRACIÁN (1601–1658). *The Art of Worldly Wisdom,* 36, 1647, tr. Joseph Jacobs, 1943

The only sure thing about luck is that it will change.

> BRET HARTE (1836–1902). "The Outcasts of Poker Flat," 1869, *The Luck of Roaring Camp and Other Sketches,* 1870

When a man has no reason to trust himself, he trusts in luck.

> E.W. HOWE (1853–1937)

Nature creates ability: luck endows it with opportunities.

> LA ROCHEFOUCAULD (1613–1680). *Maxims,* 153, 1665, tr. Louis Kronenberger, 1959

Fortunate people seldom mend their ways, for when good luck crowns their misdeeds with success they think it is because they are right.

> LA ROCHEFOUCAULD (1613–1680). *Maxims,* 227, 1665, tr. Leonard Tancock, 1959

I am a great believer in luck, and I find the harder I work the more I have of it.

> STEPHEN LEACOCK (1869–1944)

Luck is what happens when preparation meets opportunity.

> ELMER G. LETERMAN
>
> See Preparedness: Louis Pasteur

now and then
there is a person born
who is so unlucky
that he runs into accidents
which started out to happen
to somebody else.

> DON MARQUIS (1878–1937). "archy says," *archy's life of mehitabel,* 1933

Concentration of strength, activity, and a firm resolve to die gloriously . . . are the three principles of the military art which have disposed luck in my favor in all my operations.

> NAPOLEON (1769–1821). Letter to Gen. Lauriston, 12 December 1804, *The Mind of Napoleon: A Selection from His Written and Spoken Words,* 292, ed. J. Christopher Herold,

Give a man *luck,* and throw him into the sea.

> JOHN RAY (1628–1705). Comp., *A Collection of English Proverbs,* p. 172, 1678

Luck is the residue of design.

> BRANCH RICKEY (1881–1965). Baseball-team owner. In "The Mahatma," *Time,* 17 December 1965

We must believe in luck. For how else can we explain the success of those we don't like?

> ERIK SATIE (1866–1925). French composer

A man is never so on trial as in the moment of excessive good fortune.

> LEW WALLACE (1827–1905). *Ben-Hur: A Tale of the Christ,* 5.7, 1880

Of all axioms this shall win the prize—
'Tis better to be fortunate than wise.

> JOHN WEBSTER (1580?–1625?). *The White Devil,* 5.6, 1612

There is luck in sharing a thing.

> SAYING (IRISH)

LUST

See also ○ Abstinence ○ Desire ○ Marriage: Paul ○ Passion ○ Sex

My will was perverse and lust had grown from it, and when I gave in to lust habit was born, and when I did not resist the habit it became a necessity. These were the links which together formed what I have called my chain, and it held me fast in the duress of servitude.

> ST. AUGUSTINE (A.D. 354–430). *Confessions,* 8.5, A.D. 400?, tr. R. S. Pine-Coffin, 1961

As a youth I had been woefully at fault, particularly in early adolescence. I had prayed to you for chastity and said, "Give me
chastity and continence, but not yet." For I was afraid that you
would answer my prayer at once and cure me too soon of the disease of lust, which I wanted satisfied, not quelled.

> ST. AUGUSTINE (A.D. 354–430). *Confessions,* 8.7, A.D. 400?, tr. R. S.
> Pine-Coffin, 1961

The lust of the goat is the bounty of God.

> WILLIAM BLAKE (1757–1827). "Proverbs of Hell," *The Marriage of
> Heaven and Hell,* 8.3, 1790-1793?

I've looked on a lot of women with lust. I've committed adultery
in my heart many times. This is something that God recognizes I
will do—and I have done it—and God forgives me for it.

> JIMMY CARTER (1924–). Robert Scheer interview, *Playboy,* October 1976
> (one month before being elected President)
>
> See Adultery: Jesus

If my hands tremble with desire they tremble likewise when I
reach for the chalice on Sunday, and if lust makes me run and
caper it is no stronger a force than that which brings me to my
knees to say thanksgivings and litanies. What can this capricious
skin be but a blessing?

> JOHN CHEEVER (1912–1982). 1957, *The Journals of John Cheever,* ed.
> Robert Gottlieb, 1991

LUXURY

See also • Longevity: Samuel Johnson ○ Money ○ Possessions ○
Property ○ Wealth

Luxury, then, is a way of
being ignorant comfortably.

> IMAMU AMIRI BARAKA (LeROI JONES) (1934–). Opening lines,
> "Political Poem," 1964. In Richard Ellmann and Robert O'Clair, ed.,
> *The Norton Anthology of Modern Poetry,* 2nd ed., 1988 (1973)

Is not the hope of being one day able to purchase and enjoy luxuries a great spur to labor and industry? May not luxury, therefore,
produce more than it consumes, if without such a spur people
would be, as they are naturally enough inclined to be, lazy and
indolent?

> BENJAMIN FRANKLIN (1706–1790). Letter to Benjamin Vaughan, 26 July
> 1784

The lust for comfort, that stealthy thing that enters the house a
guest, and then becomes a host, and then a master.

> KAHLIL GIBRAN (1883–1931). "On Houses," *The Prophet,* 1923

Every state of society is as luxurious as it can be. Men always take
the best they can get.

> SAMUEL JOHNSON (1709–1784). 14 April 1778. In James Boswell, *The
> Life of Samuel Johnson,* 1791

The evils of too-long peace. Luxury, deadlier
Than any armed invader.

> JUVENAL (A.D. 60?–127?). *Satires,* 6.291, tr. Peter Green, 1967

Luxury either comes of riches or makes them necessary; it corrupts at once rich and poor, the rich by possession and the poor

by covetousness; it sells the country to softness and vanity, and
takes away from the State all its citizens, to make them slaves one
to another, and one and all to public opinion.

> ROUSSEAU (1712–1778). *The Social Contract,* 3.4, 1762, tr. G. D. H. Cole,
> 1950

Nature's needs are easily provided and ready to hand. It is the
superfluous things for which men sweat.

> SENECA THE YOUNGER (5? B.C.–A.D. 65). "On the Terrors of Death,"
> *Moral Letters to Lucilius,* 4.11, tr. Richard M. Gummere, 1918

Most of the luxuries, and many of the so-called comforts of life,
are not only not indispensable, but positive hindrances to the elevation of mankind.

> HENRY DAVID THOREAU (1817–1862). "Economy," *Walden; or Life in
> the Woods,* 1854

☙

The luxuries of the few are bought with the blood, sweat and
tears of the many.

> ANONYMOUS

LYING

See also • Cheating ○ Corruption ○ Cunning ○ Deception ○
Falsehood ○ Honesty ○ Illusion ○ Imperialism: J. A. Hobson (2)
○ Indoctrination ○ Integrity ○ Machiavellianism ○ Morality:
T. H. Huxley ○ Mothers: Austin O'Malley ○ Newspeak:
Examples: Alexander Haig ○ Propaganda ○ Sin: Oliver Wendell
Holmes, Sr. ○ Truth ○ Truth & Untruth ○ Truthfulness ○
Violence: Aleksandr Solzhenitsyn

A liar will not be believed, even when he speaks the truth.

> AESOP (6th cent. B.C.). "The Shepherd's Boy," *Fables,* tr. Joseph Jacobs,
> 1894

A deft administrator these days . . . must master "the technique of
denying the truth without actually lying."

> DANIEL J. BOORSTIN (1914–). *The Image: A Guide to Pseudo-Events in
> America,* 1.4, 1961

The best liar is he who makes the smallest amount of lying go the
longest way.

> SAMUEL BUTLER (1835–1902). *The Way of All Flesh,* 39, 1903

We pay a person the compliment of acknowledging his superiority whenever we lie to him.

> SAMUEL BUTLER (1835–1902). *The Note-Books of Samuel Butler,* 19, ed.
> Henry Festing Jones, 1907

I do not mind lying, but I hate inaccuracy.

> SAMUEL BUTLER (1835–1902). *The Note-Books of Samuel Butler,* 19, ed.
> Henry Festing Jones, 1907

One lies more to one's self than to anyone else.

> LORD BYRON (1788–1824). Journal, 6 December 1813

And, after all, what is a lie? 'Tis but
The truth in masquerade.

> LORD BYRON (1788–1824). *Don Juan,* 11.37, 1819–1824

A man whose *word* will not inform you at all what he means or will do, is not a man you can bargain with. You must get out of that man's way, or put him out of yours!

> THOMAS CARLYLE (1795–1881). "The Hero as King," *On Heroes, Hero-Worship, and the Heroic in History,* 1841

If I'm elected, at the end of four years or eight years I hope the people will say, "You know, Jimmy Carter made a lot of mistakes, but he never told a lie."

> JIMMY CARTER (1924–). Presidential campaign speech, 6 May 1976. In Peter Meyer, *James Earl Carter: The Man and the Myth,* 1 (epigraph), 1978

Show me a liar, and I'll show thee a thief.

> JOHN CLARKE (1596–1658). Comp., *Proverbs: English and Latine,* p. 148, 1639

I always make it a point of business ethics never to tell a lie unless I think I can get away with it.

> KENNETH COOK and KERRY COOK. *The Film-Makers,* 4, 1983

There are three kinds of lies: lies, damned lies, and statistics.

> BENJAMIN DISRAELI (1804–1881). Attributed. In Mark Twain, April 1904, *Mark Twain's Autobiography,* 1.246, ed. Albert Bigelow Paine, 1924

I think a lie with a purpose is wan iv th' worst kind an' th' mos' profitable.

> FINLEY PETER DUNNE (1867–1936). "On Lying," *Mr. Dooley's Opinions,* 1901

The little bit of truth contained in many a lie is what makes them so terrible.

> MARIE von EBNER-ESCHENBACH (1830–1916). *Aphorisms,* p. 42, 1880–1905, tr. David Scrase and Wolfgang Mieder, 1994
>
> See Errors: Henri Amiel

Little liars are makers of gossip; big liars, makers of history.

> PAUL ELDRIDGE (1888–1982). *Maxims for a Modern Man,* 2633, 1965

No one ever lies. People often do what they have to do to make their story sound right.

> WILLIAM H. GINSBURG. In Francis X. Clines, "Day of Facing the Nation, Meeting the Press, Etc." *New York Times,* 2 February 1998

A single lie destroys a whole reputation for integrity.

> BALTASAR GRACIÁN (1601–1658). *The Art of Worldly Wisdom,* 181, 1647, tr. Joseph Jacobs, 1943
>
> See Falsehood: Saying (Ashanti)

The more lies are told, the more important it becomes for the liars to justify themselves by deep moral commitments to high-sounding objectives that mask the pursuit of money and power.

> BERTRAM GROSS (1912–1997). *Friendly Fascism: The New Face of Power in America,* 9, 1980

Nothing gives such a blow to friendship as the detecting another in an untruth. It strikes at the root of our confidence ever after.

> WILLIAM HAZLITT (1778–1830). *Characteristics in the Manner of Rochefoucault's Maxims,* 199, 1823

There is no lie too improbable, no distortion too great, no smear campaign too dirty for the State Department and the media to embrace.

> JESSE HELMS (1921–). North Carolina senator. In "Overheard," *Newsweek,* 18 August 1986

Liar: one who tells an unpleasant truth.

> OLIVER HERFORD (1863–1935)

Why can't somebody give us a list of things that everybody thinks and nobody says, and another list of things that everybody says and nobody thinks?

> OLIVER WENDELL HOLMES, SR. (1809–1894). *The Professor at the Breakfast-Table,* 6, 1860

I loathe like Hell's Gates the man who thinks one thing and says another.

> HOMER (8th? cent. B.C.). *The Iliad,* 9.310, tr. E. V. Rieu, 1950

The punishment of the liar is that he eventually believes his own lies.

> ELBERT HUBBARD (1856–1915). *The Note Book of Elbert Hubbard,* p. 47, comp. Elbert Hubbard II, 1927
>
> See Propaganda: Garry Wills

We lie to ourselves, in order that we may still have the excuse of ignorance, the alibi of stupidity and incomprehension, possessing which we can continue with a good conscience to commit and tolerate the most monstrous crimes.

> ALDOUS HUXLEY (1894–1963). "Words and Behavior," *The Olive Tree and Other Essays,* 1936

Woe to those who call evil good and good evil.

> ISAIAH (8th cent. B.C.). *Isaiah* 5:20

Boys, I may not know much, but I know the difference between chicken shit and chicken salad.

> LYNDON B. JOHNSON (1908–1973). When asked (as Senate Majority Leader) if he took seriously a particular speech by Vice President Richard M. Nixon. In David Halberstam, *The Best and the Brightest,* 20, 1972

For a long time I have not said what I believed nor do I ever believe what I say, and if indeed sometimes I do happen to tell the truth, I hide it among so many lies that it is hard to find.

> MACHIAVELLI (1469–1527). Letter to Francesco Guicciardini. In Murray Kempton, "The Truth About Machiavelli," *New Republic,* 11 March 1967
>
> See Intelligence, Military: Winston Churchill

The great majority of us are required to live a life of constant, systematic duplicity. Your health is bound to be affected if, day after day, you say the opposite of what you feel, if you grovel before what you dislike and rejoice at what brings you nothing but misfortune. Our nervous system isn't just a fiction, it's a part of our physical body, and our soul exists in space and is inside us, like the teeth in our mouth. It can't be forever violated with impunity.

> BORIS PASTERNAK (1890–1960). *Doctor Zhivago,* 15.7, 1957, tr. Max Hayward and Manya Harari, 1958

If anyone at all is to have the privilege of lying, the rulers of the State should be the persons; and they, in their dealings either with enemies or with their own citizens, may be allowed to lie for the public good.

> PLATO (427?–347 B.C.). *The Republic,* 3.389, tr. Benjamin Jowett, 1894

If . . . the ruler catches anybody beside himself lying in the State . . . he will punish him for introducing a practice which is equally subversive and destructive of ship or State.

> PLATO (427?–347 B.C.). *The Republic*, 3.389, tr. Benjamin Jowett, 1894

There are three essential elements to a lie: the material must be untrue; it must be known to be untrue; and it must be told with the intention to deceive.

> TERENCE H. QUALTER (1925–). *Propaganda and Psychological Warfare*, 1, 1962

Lying is done with words, and also with silence.

> ADRIENNE RICH (1929–). "Women and Honor: Some Notes on Lying," 1975, *On Lies, Secrets, and Silence: Selected Prose 1966–1978*, 1979

You must not tell lies because if you do you will find yourself unable to believe anything that is told to you.

> GEORGE BERNARD SHAW (1856–1950). *The Intelligent Woman's Guide to Socialism, Capitalism, Sovietism and Fascism*, 74, 1928

A liar begins with making falsehood appear like truth and ends with making truth itself appear like falsehood.

> WILLIAM SHENSTONE (1714–1763). "Of Men and Manners," *Men & Manners*, ed. Havelock Ellis, 1927

The cruelest lies are often told in silence.

> ROBERT LOUIS STEVENSON (1850–1894). Title essay (4), *Virginibus Puerisque*, 1881

It would seem to be basic, all through history, that a government's right—and by government I mean a people . . . that it's inherent in that government's right, if necessary, to lie to save itself when it's going up into a nuclear war. This seems to me basic. (Ellipsis points in original.)

> ARTHUR SYLVESTER (1901–1979). Deputy secretary of defense for public affairs. Responding to a journalist's question about "half-truths which were told by various governmental officials during the Cuban missile crisis," following a speech before the Deadline Club, New York City, 6 December 1962. In "Sylvester Defends News Policy, Notes Government's 'Right to Lie,'" *Aviation Week and Space Technology*, 17 December 1962

You didn't tell a lie, you just left a big hole in the truth.

> HELEN THOMAS (1920–). Journalist. Phil Donahue-Vladimir Pozner television interview, CNBC, July 1993

You want to be very careful about lying; otherwise you are nearly sure to get caught.

> MARK TWAIN (1835–1910). "Advice to Youth," speech before the Saturday Morning Club, Boston, 15 April 1882

The principle differences between a cat and a lie is that the cat has only nine lives.

> MARK TWAIN (1835–1910). *Following the Equator: A Journey Around the World*, 68 (epigraph), 1897

Everyone realizes that one can believe little of what people say about each other. But it is not so widely realized that even less can one trust what people say about themselves.

> REBECCA WEST (1892–1983). In *Sunday Telegraph* (British newspaper), 1975, quoted in Victoria Glendinning, epigraph, *Rebecca West: A Life*, 1987

Brick: Mendacity is a system that we live in. Liquor is one way out, an' death's the other.

> TENNESSEE WILLIAMS (1911–1983). *Cat on a Hot Tin Roof*, 2, 1955

A man is justified in lying to protect the honor of a woman or to promote public policy.

> WOODROW WILSON (1856–1924). December 1912, remark to Col. Edward House. In Thomas A. Bailey, *Presidential, Greatness: The Image and the Man from George Washington to the Present*, 11, 1966

Those who will lie for you will lie against you.

> SAYING (BOSNIAN)

A little truth helps the lie go down.

> SAYING (ITALIAN)

A liar [should] have a good memory.

> SAYING (LATIN). In Quintilian (A.D. 35?–100?), *Institutio oratoria*, 4.2.91, tr. John Selby Watson, 1856
> See Truthfulness: Mark Twain

Big lies tailgate small ones.

> SAYING

Caught in one lie, always suspect.

> SAYING

MACHIAVELLIANISM

Let them hate, if only they fear.

> LUCIUS ACCIUS (170?–86 B.C.). In Cicero (106–43 B.C.), *De officiis*, 1.28, tr. Walter Miller, 1913

Machiavelli was writing advice for weak princes.

> DEAN ACHESON (1893–1971). *Present at the Creation: My Years in the State Department*, 76, 1969

The honor he should distribute himself, but the punishment should be inflicted by officers and courts of law.

> ARISTOTLE (384–322 B.C.). *Politics*, 5.11, tr. Benjamin Jowett, 1885

He must put to death men of spirit; he must not allow common meals, clubs, education, and the like; he must be upon his guard against anything which is likely to inspire either courage or confidence among his subjects; he must prohibit literary meetings or other meetings for discussion, and he must take every means to prevent people from knowing one another (for acquaintance begets mutual confidence).

ARISTOTLE (384–322 B.C.). *Politics,* 5.11, tr. Benjamin Jowett, 1885

Pompey . . . wholly bent himself, by numberless stratagems, to cover his desires and ambition, whilst he brought the state to confusion, that it might then of necessity submit to him.

FRANCIS BACON (1561–1626). *Advancement of Learning,* 8.2, 1605, Willey Book edition, 1944

Let this be one invariable rule of your conduct—Never to show the least symptom of resentment which you cannot to a certain degree gratify; but always to smile, where you cannot strike.

LORD CHESTERFIELD (1694–1773). Letter to his son, 26 March 1754

No book on earth is more necessary to the politician than Machiavelli.

KARL von CLAUSEWITZ (1780–1831). Notebook, 1807. In Peter Paret, *Clausewitz and the State,* 8.3, 1976

Their abilities matter less than their skill in pleasing, and promises are more effective than arguments. The statesman, therefore, must concentrate all his efforts on captivating men's minds. He must know when to dissemble, when to be frank. He must pose as the servant of the pubic in order to become its master.

CHARLES de GAULLE (1890–1970). "Of Politics and the Soldier" (1), *The Edge of the Sword,* 1934, tr. Gerald Hopkins, 1960

All that business of titles and sentimentalism is a very good cement, but there is something better; persuade four members of the circle to do [in] a fifth on the pretense that he is a traitor, and you'll tie them all together with the blood they've shed as though it were a knot. They'll be your slaves, they won't dare to rebel or call you to account.

FYODOR DOSTOYEVSKY (1821–1881). *The Possessed,* 1871, quoted by Franz Neumann, "Anxiety and Politics," 1957. In Eric and Mary Josephson, eds., *Man Alone: Alienation in Modern Society,* 1962

Machiavelli wrote only for petty princes.

FREDERICK II (1712–1786). *Anti-Machiavel,* 13, 1740, tr. Paul Sonnino, 1981

In everything I say, I affect the air of thinking of nothing but the happiness of my subjects.

FREDERICK II (1712–1786). "Morning the Fourth," *The Confessions of Frederick the Great,* ed. Douglas Sladen, 1915

It is good policy to be always attempting something, and to be perfectly persuaded that we have a right to everything that suits us.

FREDERICK II (1712–1786). "Morning the Fifth," *The Confessions of Frederick the Great,* ed. Douglas Sladen, 1915

To make oneself respected and feared by one's neighbors is the very summit of high policy. This end is to be achieved by two means: the first is to have a real force and effectual resources; the second is to make the most of the strength one has.

FREDERICK II (1712–1786). "Morning the Fifth," *The Confessions of Frederick the Great,* ed. Douglas Sladen, 1915

No ministers at home but clerks. No ambassadors abroad but spies. Formal alliances only to sow animosities. Kindle and prolong wars between neighbors. Always promise help and never send it.

FREDERICK II (1712–1786). Marginal notes in his copy of the historical writings of Tacitus (A.D. 56?–120?). In James A. Nathan, "The Heyday of the Balance of Power: Frederick The Great and the Decline of the Old Regime," *Naval War College Review,* July-August, 1980

[Pres. Lyndon B. Johnson] dominated other men, leaning on them, sensing that every man had his price or his breaking point.

DAVID HALBERSTAM (1934–). *The Best and the Brightest,* 20, 1972

My task is not to make men better but to make use of their weaknesses.

ADOLF HITLER (1889–1945). Remark to the author, 1932–1934. In Hermann Rauschning, *The Voice of Destruction,* 19, 1940

People don't support you because they like you. You can count on a person's support only when you can do something for him or something to him.

LYNDON B. JOHNSON (1908–1973). In Richard M. Nixon, *In the Arena: A Memoir of Victory, Defeat and Renewal,* 21, 1990

[Machiavelli's] thought was closed, formalistic, and committed to history as a lesson in repetition.

MURRAY KEMPTON (1917–1997). "The Truth About Machiavelli," *New Republic,* 11 March 1967

There is really very little of Machiavelli that can be accepted or used in the modern world.

HENRY A. KISSINGER (1923–). Interview with the author, 2 November 1972. In Oriana Fallaci, *Interview with History,* tr. John Shepley, 1976

I have always thought that Machiavelli derives his bad name from a too transparent honesty. Less direct minds would have found high-sounding ethical sanctions in which to conceal the real intent. . . .

Machiavelli's morals are not one bit worse than the practices of the men who rule the world today.

WALTER LIPPMANN (1889–1974). *A Preface to Politics,* 7, 1914

[Machiavelli] has a worse name and more disciples than any political thinker who ever lived.

WALTER LIPPMANN (1889–1974). *Public Opinion,* 17.2, 1922

Men must either be caressed or annihilated; they will revenge themselves for small injuries, but cannot do so for great ones; the injury therefore that we do to a man must be such that we need not fear his vengeance.

MACHIAVELLI (1469–1527). *The Prince,* 3, 1513, tr. Luigi Ricci, 1903

It is easy to persuade [the people] of a thing, but difficult to keep them in that persuasion. And so it is necessary to order things so that when they no longer believe, they can be made to believe by force.

MACHIAVELLI (1469–1527). *The Prince,* 6, 1513, tr. Luigi Ricci, 1903

One ought to be both feared and loved, but as it is difficult for the two to go together, it is much safer to be feared than loved, if one of the two has to be wanting. . . . Love is held by a chain of obligation, which men being selfish, is broken whenever it serves their purpose; but fear is maintained by a dread of punishment which never fails.

MACHIAVELLI (1469–1527). *The Prince,* 17, 1513, tr. Luigi Ricci, 1903

See Motives: Richard M. Nixon

It is well to seem merciful, faithful, humane, sincere, religious, and also to be so; but you must have the mind so disposed that when it is needful to be otherwise you may be able to change to the opposite qualities. . . . He must have a mind disposed to adapt itself according to the wind, and as the variations of fortune dictate, and, as I have said before, not deviate from what is good, if possible, but be able to do evil if [necessary].

MACHIAVELLI (1469–1527). *The Prince,* 18, 1513, tr. Luigi Ricci, 1903

He will always have good friends if he has good arms.

MACHIAVELLI (1469–1527). *The Prince,* 19, 1513, tr. Luigi Ricci, 1903

Whoever desires to found a state and give it laws must start with assuming that all men are bad and ever ready to display their vicious nature, whenever they may find occasion for it.

MACHIAVELLI (1469–1527). Introduction to First Book, *The Discourses,* 1517, tr. Christian E. Detmold, 1940

When the act accuses him, the result should excuse him.

MACHIAVELLI (1469–1527). *The Discourses,* 1.9, 1517, tr. Christian E. Detmold, 1940

See Means & Ends: Machiavelli

Government consists mainly in so keeping your subjects that they shall be neither able nor disposed to injure you; and this is done by depriving them of all means of injuring you, or by bestowing such benefits upon them that it would not be reasonable for them to desire any change of fortune.

MACHIAVELLI (1469–1527). *The Discourses,* 2.23, 1517, tr. Christian E. Detmold, 1940

Scipio, from the moment he entered Spain, gained the affection and respect of the people of that province by his humanity and benevolence. Hannibal, on the contrary, conducted himself in Italy with violence, cruelty, rapine, and every kind of perfidy. Yet he obtained the same success that Scipio had in Spain. . . .

It matters little whether a general adopts the one or the other course, provided he be possessed of . . . high ability.

MACHIAVELLI (1469–1527). *The Discourses,* 3.21, 1517, tr. Christian E. Detmold, 1940

Hardball is clean, aggressive Machiavellian politics. It is the discipline of gaining and holding power, useful to any profession or undertaking, but practiced most openly and unashamedly in the world of public affairs.

CHRISTOPHER MATTHEWS (1945–). Introduction to *Hardball: How Politics Is Played—Told by One Who Knows the Game,* 1988

Never fight fair with a stranger, boy. You'll never get out of the jungle that way.

ARTHUR MILLER (1915–). *Death of a Salesman,* 1, 1949

Like most of those who take pride in seeing human nature as it is, Machiavelli only saw half [of] it.

JOHN MORLEY (1838–1923). *Machiavelli: The Romanes Lecture,* p. 21, 1897

Peace has been completely restored in Cairo. . . . The rebels have lost a couple of thousand men. Every night we have about thirty heads cut off, including many of the leaders'. I think this will be a good lesson for them.

NAPOLEON (1769–1821). Letter to Gen. Reynier, 27 October 1798, *The Mind of Napoleon: A Selection from His Written and Spoken Words,* 224, ed. J. Christopher Herold, 1955

When it comes to conspiracy, everything is permissible.

NAPOLEON (1769–1821). 8 November 1799, *The Corsican: A Diary of Napoleon's Life in His Own Words,* ed. R. M. Johnston, 1911

I soon learned, on seating myself here [on the throne of Louis XVI] that I must beware of attempting to do all the good one might do. Opinion would outrun me.

NAPOLEON (1769–1821). Remark to Matthieu Dumas, February 1800. In Jacob Burckhardt, "The Great Men of History," 1870, *Force and Freedom: An Interpretation of History,* ed. James H. Nichols, 1943

Machiavelli is right: one always must live with one's friends [being aware] that they may turn into one's enemies. He should have said, with everybody.

NAPOLEON (1769–1821). Remark, 1803, *The Mind of Napoleon: A Selection from His Written and Spoken Words,* 7, ed. J. Christopher Herold, 1955

Nothing is more salutary than a terrible example given at the right time.

NAPOLEON (1769–1821). Letter to Gen. Andoche Junot, 4 February 1806, *The Mind of Napoleon: A Selection from His Written and Spoken Words,* 207, ed. J. Christopher Herold, 1955

They think I am stern, even hard-hearted. So much the better—this makes it unnecessary for me to justify my reputation.

NAPOLEON (1769–1821). Remark to Gen. Louis de Caulaincourt, December 1812, *The Mind of Napoleon: A Selection from His Written and Spoken Words,* 205, ed. J. Christopher Herold, 1955

If fifty thousand men were to die for the good of the State, I certainly would weep for them, but political necessity comes before everything else.

NAPOLEON (1769–1821). Remark to Gen. Gaspard Gourgaud, 1816, *The Mind of Napoleon: A Selection from His Written and Spoken Words,* 55, ed. J. Christopher Herold, 1955

When I need anyone, I don't make too fine a point of it; I would kiss his ___.

NAPOLEON (1769–1821). Remark. In Gen. Louis de Caulaincourt, *With Napoleon in Russia,* 2, ed. George Libaire, 1935

In evaluating a leader, the key question about his behavioral traits is not whether they are attractive or unattractive, but whether they are useful. Guile, vanity, dissembling—in other circumstances these might be unattractive habits, but to the leader they can be essential. He needs guile in order to hold together the shifting coalitions of often bitterly opposed interest groups that governing requires. He needs a certain measure of vanity in order to create the right kind of public impression. He sometimes has to dissemble in order to prevail on crucial issues.

RICHARD M. NIXON (1913–1994). *Leaders,* 9, 1982

Don Corleone: He's a businessman. I'll make him an offer he can't refuse.

> MARIO PUZO (1920–). *The Godfather,* 1, 1969

Strike the head of a serpent with the hand of a foe because one of two advantages will result. If the enemy succeeds, thou hast killed the snake and if the latter, thou hast been delivered from a foe.

> SA'DI (A.D. 1213?–1292). *The Gulistan, or Rose Garden,* 8 (Admonition 13), A.D. 1258, tr. Edward Rehatsek, 1964

If you injure your neighbor, better not do it by halves.

> GEORGE BERNARD SHAW (1856–1950). "Maxims for Revolutionists: Stray Sayings," *Man and Superman,* 1903

If Machiavelli had had a prince for [his] disciple, the first thing he would have recommended him to do would have been to write a book against Machiavell[ian]ism.

> VOLTAIRE (1694–1778). *Memoirs.* In Max Lerner, introduction (4) to Machiavelli, *The Prince* and *The Discourses,* 1950

If all the other doctrines of devils which have been committed to writing since letters were in the world, were collected together in one volume, it would fall short of ["the Works of Nicholas Machiavel"], and, that should a Prince form himself by this book, so calmly recommending hypocrisy, treachery, lying, robbery, oppression, adultery, whoredom and murder of all kinds, Domitian or Nero would be an angel of light, compared to that man.

> JOHN WESLEY (1703–1791). Journal, 1 January 1737

Machiavelli wrote rules for a short-term success.

> ALFRED NORTH WHITEHEAD (1861–1947). 18 July 1939, *Dialogues of Alfred North Whitehead,* rec. Lucien Price, 1954

❦

Divide and conquer.

> SAYING (LATIN)
> See Leaders: Goethe ○ Strategy: Saying (Soviet)

Silver or lead.

> SAYING (MEDELLIN DRUG CARTEL). 1989, meaning "bribes or bullets"

Divert and conquer.

> SAYING

MACHINES

See also • Agriculture: Bertrand Russell ○ Airplanes ○ Automobiles ○ Computers ○ Ideology: Aldo Leopold ○ Inventions ○ Motorcycles ○ Property ○ Science ○ Trains

The greatest task before civilization at present is to make machines what they ought to be, the slaves, instead of the masters of men.

> HAVELOCK ELLIS (1859–1939). *Little Essays of Love and Virtue,* 7, 1922

The civilized man has built a coach, but has lost the use of his feet. . . . His notebooks impair his memory; his libraries overload his wit; the insurance office increases the number of accidents; and it may be a question; whether machinery does not encumber.

> RALPH WALDO EMERSON (1803–1882). "Self-Reliance," *Essays: First Series,* 1841

The machine unmakes the man. Now that the machine is so perfect, the engineer is nobody. Every new step in improving the engine restricts one more act of the engineer—unteaches him. Once it took Archimedes; now it only needs a fireman, and a boy to know the coppers, to pull up the handles or mind the water tank. But when the engine breaks, they can do nothing.

> RALPH WALDO EMERSON (1803–1882). "Works and Days," *Society and Solitude,* 1860

Machinery is the new messiah.

> HENRY FORD (1863–1947). Quoted by Bill Moyers, *Walk through the Twentieth Century,* television documentary, 1988

What I object to is the "craze" for machinery, not machinery as such. . . . Today machinery merely helps a few to ride on the backs of millions.

> MOHANDAS K. GANDHI (1869–1948). In *Young India,* 13 November 1924

Among the most viable of all economic delusions is the belief that machines on net balance create unemployment.

> HENRY HAZLITT (1894–1993). *Economics in One Lesson,* 7.1, 1946

One machine can do the work of fifty ordinary men. No machine can do the work of one extraordinary man.

> ELBERT HUBBARD (1856–1915). *A Thousand and One Epigrams,* p. 151, 1911

Ours is the age which is proud of machines that think, and suspicious of men who try to.

> HOWARD MUMFORD JONES (1892–1980). In "Thoughts on the Business of Life," *Forbes,* 20 March 1989

Big machines are the cathedrals of the 20th century. They're awe-inspiring.

> DANIEL KLEPPNER. Physicist. In William J. Broad, "Developing 'Crisis' Seen in Costly Trend Toward Big Machines," *New York Times,* 11 June 1985

The vast material displacements the machine has made in our physical environment are perhaps in the long run less important than its spiritual contributions to our culture.

> LEWIS MUMFORD (1895–1990). "The Drama of the Machines," *Scribner's Magazine,* August 1930

The Machine, the genie that man has thoughtlessly let out of its bottle and cannot put back again.

> GEORGE ORWELL (1903–1950). 1941. In Lawrence Malkin, "Halfway to 1984," *Horizon* (magazine), 1970

Machines are worshipped because they are beautiful, and valued because they confer power; they are hated because they are hideous, and loathed because they impose slavery.

> BERTRAND RUSSELL (1872–1970). *Sceptical Essays,* 6, 1928

The great trouble with the machine, from the point of view of the emotions, is its *regularity.* And, of course, conversely, the great objection to the emotions, from the point of view of the machine, is their *irregularity.* As the machine dominates the thoughts of people who consider themselves "serious," the highest praise they can give to a man is to suggest that he has the qualities of a machine—that he is reliable, punctual, exact, etc. And an "irregular" life has come to be synonymous with a bad life.

BERTRAND RUSSELL (1872–1970). *Sceptical Essays,* 6, 1928

The machine yes the machine
never wastes anybody's time
never watches the foreman
never talks back
never talks what is right or wrong
never listens to others talking or if
   it does listen it doesn't hear
never says we've been thinking, or, our
   feeling is like this.

CARL SANDBURG (1878–1967). *The People, Yes,* 50, 1936

✤

The larger and more complex a machine, the more unforgiving it is when something goes wrong.

ANONYMOUS

MADNESS

See also • Change: Apple Computer, Inc. ○ Genius: Alfred Hock ○ Insanity ○ Means & Ends: Herman Melville ○ Mental Illness ○ Psychiatry ○ Suicide: Benjamin Rush

A time is coming when men will go mad, and when they see someone who is not mad, they will attack him, saying: "You are not mad, you are not like us."

ANTHONY THE GREAT (A.D. 250?–355)

And what is a genuine lunatic?
   He is a man who prefers to go mad, in the social sense of the word, rather than forfeit a certain higher idea of human honor.
   That's how society strangled all those it wanted to get rid of, or wanted to protect itself from, and put them in asylums, because they refused to be accomplices to a kind of lofty swill.
   For a lunatic is a man that society does not wish to hear, but wants to prevent from uttering certain unbearable truths.

ANTONIN ARTAUD (1896–1948). "Van Gogh: The Man Suicided by Society," 1947, *Antonin Artaud Anthology,* ed. Jack Hirschman, 1965

We are all born mad. Some remain so.

SAMUEL BECKETT (1906–1989). *Waiting for Godot,* 1, 1955

Mad, *adj.* Affected with a high degree of intellectual independence; not conforming to standards of thought, speech and action derived by the conform[ists] from study of themselves; at odds with the majority; in short, unusual.

AMBROSE BIERCE (1842–1914). *The Devil's Dictionary,* p. 83, 1911, Dover edition, 1958

This world is full of madmen, and he who would not wish to see one must not only shut himself up alone, but also break his looking glass.

NICOLAS BOILEAU (1636–1711)

I and the world happened to have a slight difference of opinion; the world said I was mad, and I said the world was mad. I was *outvoted,* and here I am.

RICHARD BROTHERS (1757–1824). British religious leader. When asked why he had been committed to Bedlam. In C. C. Colton, *Lacon: or,*

Many Things in Few Words; Addressed to Those Who Think, 1.130, 1823

Drapetomania is from [the Greek word] "drapetes," a runaway slave, and "mania," mad or crazy. It is unknown to our medical authorities, although its diagnostic symptom, the absconding from service, is well known to our planters and overseers, as it was to the ancient Greeks. . . . The cause, in the most of cases, that induces the negro to run away from service, is as much a disease of the mind as any other species of mental alienation, and much more curable, as a general rule.

SAMUEL A. CARTWRIGHT. "Report on the Diseases and Physical Peculiarities of the Negro Race," *New Orleans Medical and Surgical Journal,* vol. 7, 1851. In Thomas S. Szasz, "The Sane Slave," *American Journal of Psychotherapy,* April 1971

The men who really believe in themselves are all in lunatic asylums.

G. K. CHESTERTON (1874–1936). *Orthodoxy,* 2, 1909

It may be a question which is the worst delirium, that by which a man possessing some great truth has lost the use of his practical intellect, or that other widespread delirium, in which the mind is enslaved to the lowest cares and meanest aims, and all that is loftiest and greatest in the soul is stupefied and deadened in worldliness.

JAMES FREEMAN CLARKE (1810–1888). "Jones Very," 1839. In George Hochfield, ed., *Selected Writings of the American Transcendentalists,* 1966

If one has to go mad, the tactic to learn in our society is one of discretion.

DAVID COOPER (1931–?). *Psychiatry and Anti-Psychiatry,* 1, 1967

There is only one difference between a madman and me. I am not mad.

SALVADOR DALI (1904–1989). May 1952, *Diary of a Genius,* 1966

Much Madness is divinest Sense—
To a discerning Eye—
Much Sense—the starkest Madness—
'Tis the Majority
In this, as All, prevail—
Assent—and you are sane—
Demur—you're straightway dangerous—
And handled with a Chain—

EMILY DICKINSON (1830–1886). "Much Madness is divinest Sense" (complete poem), 1862?

Great wits are sure to madness near allied,
And thin partitions do their bounds divide.

JOHN DRYDEN (1631–1700). *Absalom and Achitophel,* 1.163, 1681
See Genius: Aristotle

There is a pleasure sure
In being mad, which none but madmen know!

JOHN DRYDEN (1631–1700). *The Spanish Friar,* 2.1, 1681

You think that I suffer from a morbid conscience,
From brooding over faults I might have forgotten.
You think I'm sickening, when I'm just recovering!

T. S. ELIOT (1888–1965). *The Elder Statesman,* 3, 1959

Those whom God wishes to destroy, he first makes mad.

> EURIPIDES (485?–406 B.C.). Fragment
>
> See Fame: Joyce Carol Oates

You are mad, Paul! Your great learning is driving you mad!

> FESTUS (A.D. 1st cent.). Roman procurator in Judea. To Paul, who was
> being held as a prisoner, *Acts* 26:24

To be only 25 percent ahead of one's time results in being regarded as a lunatic.

> JOHN FISHER (1841–1920). British admiral

For the nineteenth century, the initial model of madness would be to believe oneself to be God, while for the preceding centuries it had been to deny God.

> MICHEL FOUCAULT (1926–1984). *Madness and Civilization:
> A History of Insanity in the Age of Reason,* 9, 1961, tr. Richard
> Howard, 1965

In private life I have no patience with lunatics. I only see the harm they do.

> SIGMUND FREUD (1856–1939). In Colin Bingham, comp., *Men and
> Affairs: A Modern Miscellany,* p. 410, 1967

There was only one catch and that was Catch-22, which specified that a concern for one's own safety in the face of dangers that were real and immediate was the process of a rational mind. Orr was crazy and could be grounded. All he had to do was ask; and as soon as he did, he would no longer be crazy and would have to fly more [combat] missions. Orr would be crazy to fly more missions and sane if he didn't, but if he was sane he had to fly them. If he flew them he was crazy and didn't have to; but if he didn't want to he was sane and had to.

> JOSEPH HELLER (1923–). *Catch-22,* 5, 1961

Madness is man's desperate attempt to reach transcendence, to rise beyond himself.

> ABRAHAM JOSHUA HESCHEL (1907–1972). *The Prophets,* 23, 1962

A fixed idea ends in madness or heroism.

> VICTOR HUGO (1802–1885). *Ninety-Three,* 3.1.6, 1879

The lunatic's visions of horror are all drawn from the material of daily fact. Our civilization is founded on the shambles, and every individual existence goes out in a lonely spasm of helpless agony. If you protest, my friend, wait till you arrive there yourself.

> WILLIAM JAMES (1842–1910). *The Varieties of Religious Experience:
> A Study in Human Nature,* 6 and 7, 1902

Some particular train of ideas fixes the attention, all other intellectual gratifications are rejected; the mind, in weariness or leisure, recurs constantly to the favorite conception and feasts on the luscious falsehood whenever she is offended with the bitterness of truth. By degrees the reign of fancy is confirmed; she grows first imperious, and in time despotic. Then fictions begin to operate as realities, false opinions fasten upon the mind, and life passes in dreams of rapture or of anguish.

> SAMUEL JOHNSON (1709–1784). *Rasselas: The Prince of Abyssinia,* 44,
> 1759

Madness need not be all breakdown. It may also be a breakthrough. It is potentially liberation and renewal as well as enslavement and existential death.

> R. D. LAING (1927–1989). *The Politics of Experience,* 6, 1967

I look back upon ["my frenzy"] at times with a gloomy kind of envy; for, while it lasted, I had many, many hours of pure happiness. Dream not, Coleridge, of having tasted all the grandeur and wildness of fancy, till you have gone mad! All now seems to me vapid, comparatively so.

> CHARLES LAMB (1775–1834). Following his brief stay in an asylum, letter to Samuel Taylor Coleridge, 10 June 1796

Captain Ahab: They think me mad—Starbuck does; but I'm demoniac, I am madness maddened! That wild madness that's only calm to comprehend itself! The prophecy was that I should be dismembered; and—Aye! I lost this leg. I now prophesy that I will dismember my dismemberer.

> HERMAN MELVILLE (1819–1891). Ahab's vow of vengeance, *Moby-Dick;
> or, The Whale,* 37, 1851, ed. Harold Beaver, 1972

Manxman: One daft with strength, the other daft with weakness.

> HERMAN MELVILLE (1819–1891). *Moby-Dick; or, The Whale,* 125, 1851,
> ed. Harold Beaver, 1972

Having stripped myself of all illusions, I have gone mad.

> FRIEDRICH NIETZSCHE (1844–1900). Written in an asylum, *My Sister
> and I,* 5.12, tr. Oscar Levy, 1951

Being in a minority, even a minority of one, did not make you mad. There was truth and there was untruth, and if you clung to the truth even against the whole world, you were not mad.

> GEORGE ORWELL (1903–1950). *Nineteen Eighty-Four,* 2.9, 1949

Men are so necessarily mad, that not to be mad would amount to another form of madness.

> BLAISE PASCAL (1623–1662). *Pensées,* 414, 1670, tr. William F. Trotter,
> 1931

His marbles are a little flat on one side.

> CARROLL H. PONTIUS. In Herb Caen, column, *San Francisco Chronicle,*
> 15 February 1983

The madman thinks the rest of the world crazy.

> PUBLIUS SYRUS (85–43 B.C.). *Moral Sayings,* 386, tr. Darius Lyman, Jr.,
> 1862
>
> See Fools: *Midrash* (1)

What's madness, but nobility of soul
At odds with circumstance?

> THEODORE ROETHKE (1908–1963). In James Hillman and Michael
> Ventura, *We've Had a Hundred Years of Psychotherapy—And the
> World's Getting Worse,* 3, 1992

Women in consequence of the greater predisposition imparted to their bodies by menstruation, pregnancy, and parturition and to their minds, by living so much alone in their families, are more predisposed to madness than men.

> BENJAMIN RUSH (1745–1813). *Medical Inquiries and Observations Upon
> the Diseases of the Mind,* 2nd ed., 2, 1818 (1812)

A woman in our hospital was delivered many years ago of a fine child during her derangement, which was of a chronic and torpid nature. The affection, which was suddenly awakened for this child, removed her disease for several days. The child was taken from her breast, lest it should contract the seeds of madness from her milk. Her disease immediately returned, and she is now, and probably always will be, an incurable tenant of our hospital.

> BENJAMIN RUSH (1745–1813). *Medical Inquiries and Observations Upon the Diseases of the Mind,* 2nd ed., 8, 1818 (1812)

The Love Mania. All marriages, without a visible or probable means of subsistence, are founded in madness. All premature attachments between the sexes which obstruct the pursuits of business, are likewise the offspring of the love mania.

> BENJAMIN RUSH (1745–1813). "On the Different Species of Mania" (18), *The Selected Writings of Benjamin Rush,* ed. Dagobert D. Runes, 1947

The Doctor Phobia. This distemper . . . arises . . . from the dread of taking physic [i.e., purgative drugs], or of submitting to the remedies of bleeding and blistering.

> BENJAMIN RUSH (1745–1813). "On the Different Species of Phobia" (12), *The Selected Writings of Benjamin Rush,* ed. Dagobert D. Runes, 1947

The Home Phobia. This disease belongs to all those men who prefer tavern, to domestic society, and to all those women who spend the principal part of their time in morning, and afternoon visits, or in long evening parties, at the theater, or in tumultuous meetings of any kind.

> BENJAMIN RUSH (1745–1813). "On the Different Species of Phobia" (15), *The Selected Writings of Benjamin Rush,* ed. Dagobert D. Runes, 1947

Sure sign of madness, he rages against himself.

> SENECA THE YOUNGER (5? B.C.–A.D. 65). *Hercules Furens,* l. 1210, tr. Frank Justus Miller, 1917

Polonius: Your noble son is mad:
Mad call I it; for, to define true madness,
What is't but to be nothing else but mad?

> SHAKESPEARE (1564–1616). *Hamlet,* 2.2.92, 1600

Polonius: Though this be madness, yet there is method in't.

> SHAKESPEARE (1564–1616). *Hamlet,* 2.2.208, 1600

King Claudius: Madness in great ones must not unwatch'd go.

> SHAKESPEARE (1564–1616). *Hamlet,* 3.1.197, 1600

We always hesitate to treat a dangerously good man as a lunatic because he may turn out to be a prophet in the true sense: that is, a man of exceptional sanity who is in the right when we are in the wrong.

> GEORGE BERNARD SHAW (1856–1950). Preface ("The Gospel of Laodicea") to *Getting Married,* 1908

We want a few mad people now. See where the sane ones have landed us!

> GEORGE BERNARD SHAW (1856–1950). *Saint Joan,* 1, 1923

I have a sixth sense, but not the other five. If I wasn't making money, they'd put me away.

> RED SKELTON (1913–1997). In "Thoughts on the Business of Life," *Forbes,* 19 February 1990

Madness is a disease of the brain, which necessarily prevents a man from thinking and acting like other men.

> VOLTAIRE (1694–1778). "Madness," *Philosophical Dictionary,* 1764, tr. Wade Baskin, 1961

Madness is to think of too many things in succession too fast, or of one thing too exclusively.

> VOLTAIRE (1694–1778)

The difference between the lunatic and the sane person is only that the sane person prefers to get other people to cooperate in maintaining his delusions.

> COLIN WILSON (1931–). "An Autobiographical Introduction," *Religion and the Rebel,* 1957

Madness need not be regarded as an illness. Why shouldn't it be seen as a sudden—more or less sudden—change of character?

> LUDWIG WITTGENSTEIN (1889–1951). 1947, *Culture and Value,* 1977, tr. Peter Winch, 1980

Madness is moneyless eccentricity; eccentricity is moneyed madness.

> ANONYMOUS

Better mad with all the world than sane alone.

> SAYING (FRENCH)

Everyone's mad but me and thee, and sometimes I wonder about thee.

> SAYING

His pail doesn't reach to the bottom of the well.

> SAYING

MAGAZINES

See also • Media

Vanity Fair is for the thinking rich, and *Town & Country* is for the *stinking rich.*

> TINA BROWN (1953–). *Vanity Fair* editor. In Thomas Maier, *Newhouse: All the Glitter, Power, and Glory of America's Richest Media Empire and the Secretive Man Behind It,* 10, 1994

The basic structure of the *Time* formula is the extrapolation from insignificant detail to cosmic truth.

> ANDREW KOPKIND (1935–1994). "Serving Time," *New York Review of Books,* 12 September 1968

MAJORITIES

See also • Conformity ○ Democracy ○ Fools: Mark Twain (1) ○ Minorities ○ Public Opinion ○ Society

One with the law is a majority.

> CALVIN COOLIDGE (1872–1933). Vice-presidential nomination acceptance speech, Chicago, June 1920

Nor is the people's judgment always true:
The most may err as grossly as the few.

> JOHN DRYDEN (1631–1700). *Absalom and Achitophel,* 1.781, 1681

Majorities, the argument of fools, the strength of the weak.

> RALPH WALDO EMERSON (1803–1882). Journal, 1846, undated

To say . . . the majority are wicked means no malice, no bad heart in the observer, but simply that the majority are unripe and have not yet come to themselves.

> RALPH WALDO EMERSON (1803–1882). "Considerations by the Way," *The Conduct of Life,* 1860

Dr. Stockmann: The most insidious enemy of truth and freedom among us is the solid majority. Yes, the damned, solid, liberal majority.

> HENRIK IBSEN (1828–1906). Soon after speaking these words at a town meeting, Dr. Stockmann was declared "an enemy of the people," *An Enemy of the People,* 4, 1882, tr. Rolf Fjelde, 1965

All . . . will bear in mind this sacred principle, that though the will of the majority is in all cases to prevail, that will to be rightful must be reasonable; that the minority possess their equal rights, which equal law must protect, and to violate would be oppression.

> THOMAS JEFFERSON (1743–1826). *First Inaugural Address,* 4 March 1801

And so tonight—to you, the great silent majority of my fellow Americans—I ask for your support.

> RICHARD M. NIXON (1913–1994). Referring to his policy for ending the Vietnam War, television broadcast, 3 November 1969

One on God's side is a majority.

> WENDELL PHILLIPS (1811–1884). Speech, Brooklyn, 1 November 1859

The majority in a democracy has no more right to tyrannize over a minority than, under a different system, the latter would have to oppress the former.

> THEODORE ROOSEVELT (1858–1919). In Hermann Hagedorn and Sidney Wallach, "Signposts for Americans: The American Heritage," *A Theodore Roosevelt Round-Up,* 1958

Posterity forms the majority of the species.

> ARTHUR SCHOPENHAUER (1788–1860). "The Art of Literature: On Genius," *Essays of Arthur Schopenhauer,* tr. T. Bailey Saunders, 1851

The majority is always led by the nose by some ambitious schemer with the gift of the gab.

> GEORGE BERNARD SHAW (1856–1950). *Everybody's Political What's What,* 3, 1944

Any man more right than his neighbors constitutes a majority of one.

> HENRY DAVID THOREAU (1817–1862). "Civil Disobedience," 1849

"Tyranny of the Majority."

> ALEXIS de TOCQUEVILLE (1805–1859). Section heading, *Democracy in America,* 1.15, 1835, tr. Henry Reeve and Francis Bowen, 1862

Hain't we got all the fools in town on our side? And ain't that a big enough majority in any town?

> MARK TWAIN (1835–1910). *The Adventures of Huckleberry Finn,* 26, 1884

The majority is always in the wrong.

> Whenever you find that you are on the side of the majority, it's time to reform — (or pause and reflect).

> MARK TWAIN (1835–1910). 13 October 1904, *Mark Twain's Notebook,* ed. Albert Bigelow Paine, 1935

MALICE

See also • Envy ○ Hate ○ Revenge

Whoso is out of hope to attain another's virtue, will seek to come at even hand, by depressing another's fortune.

> FRANCIS BACON (1561–1626). "Of Envy," *Essays,* 1625

We have a degree of delight, and that no small one, in the real misfortunes and pains of others.

> EDMUND BURKE (1729–1797). *A Philosophical Inquiry into the Origin of Our Ideas of the Sublime and the Beautiful,* 1.14, 1756

No one likes to see those who are happier than himself.

> CHAMFORT (1741–1794). *Maxims and Thoughts,* 3, 1796, tr. W. S. Merwin, 1984

The sting of our pains is diminished by the assurance that they are *common to all;* but from feelings equally egotistical, it unfortunately happens that the zest and relish of our pleasures is heightened by the contrary consideration, namely, that they *are confined to ourselves.*

> C. C. COLTON (1780–1832). *Lacon: or, Many Things in Few Words; Addressed to Those Who Think,* 2.247, 1824

I have never killed a man, but I have read many obituaries with a lot of pleasure.

> CLARENCE DARROW (1857–1938)

I don't think we injye other people's sufferin', Hinnissy. It isn't acshally injyement. But we feel betther fr it.

> FINLEY PETER DUNNE (1867–1936). "Enjoyment" (complete entry), *Observations by Mr. Dooley,* 1902

There is pleasure in hardships heard about.

> EURIPIDES (485?–406 B.C.). *Helen,* l. 665, tr. Richmond Lattimore, 1956

We feel somewhat ashamed of being happy at the sight of certain miseries.

> LA BRUYÈRE (1645–1696). "Of Mankind" (82), *The Characters,* 1688, tr. Henri van Laun, 1929

A neighbor's ruin is relished by friends and enemies alike.

> LA ROCHEFOUCAULD (1613–1680). *Maxims,* 521, 1665, tr. Leonard Tancock, 1959

I shall do nothing in malice. What I deal with is too vast for malicious dealing.

> ABRAHAM LINCOLN (1809–1865). Letter to Cuthbert Bullitt, 28 July 1862
> See Civil War: Lincoln (6)

Malice sucks up the greater part of its own venom, and poisons itself with it.

> MONTAIGNE. "Of Repentance," *Essays,* 1588, tr. Donald M. Frame, 1958

The solace that comes from having company in misery smacks of ill will.

SENECA THE YOUNGER (5? B.C.–A.D. 65). "On Consolation to Marcius" (12.5), *Moral Essays,* tr. John W. Basore, 1932

See Misery: Saying (English)

It is not enough to succeed. Others must fail.

GORE VIDAL (1925–). In G. Irvine, "Antipanegeric for Tom Driberg," 8 December 1975

See Happiness: Jules Renard

The highlight of my baseball career came in Philadelphia's Connie Mack Stadium when I saw a fan fall out of the upper deck. When he got up and walked away, the crowd booed.

BOB UECKER (1935–). In "Quotes That Say It All About '92," *San Francisco Chronicle,* 30 December 1992

Show not yourself glad at the Misfortune of another though he were your enemy.

GEORGE WASHINGTON (1732–1799). Copybook, 1748 (at age 16), *Rules of Civility & Decent Behaviour in Company and Conversation,* #22. The rules were an amended version of Francis Hawkins's 1640 translation of *Decency of Conversation Among Men* (French Jesuit writing, 1595).

MAN

See also • Civilization ○ Community ○ Crowds ○ Culture ○ Epitaphs: Will Rogers (1) ○ Evolution: [especially] Friedrich Nietzsche (2) ○ Freedom ○ God & Man ○ History ○ Human Nature ○ Life ○ Mankind ○ The Masses ○ Men ○ People ○ The People ○ Population ○ Progress ○ The Public ○ Self-Realization (Being) ○ Society ○ Tools: Thomas Carlyle ○ Unity ○ Women ○ Women & Men ○ World

Man is nothing but contradiction: the less he knows it, the more dupe he is.

HENRI AMIEL (1821–1881). Journal, 3 May 1860, tr. Mrs. Humphrey Ward, 1887

Man is by nature a political animal.

ARISTOTLE (384–322 B.C.). *Politics,* 1.2, tr. Benjamin Jowett, 1885

It is a characteristic of man that he alone [among animals] has any sense of good and evil, of just and unjust.

ARISTOTLE (384–322 B.C.). *Politics,* 1.3, tr. Benjamin Jowett, 1885

Man is a history-making creature.

W. H. AUDEN (1907–1973). "D. H. Lawrence," *The Dyer's Hand and Other Essays,* 1962

Man . . . [is] a custom-making animal.

WALTER BAGEHOT (1826–1877). *Physics and Politics, or Thoughts on the Application of the Principles of "Natural Selection" and "Inheritance" to Political Society,* 3, 1872

Man is a creature who has received the order to become God.

ST. BASIL (A.D. 329–379)

Man is not a fragmentary part of the world but contains the whole riddle of the universe and the solution of it.

NICOLAS BERDYAEV (1874–1948). *The Destiny of Man,* 1.3.1, 1931, tr. Natalie Duddington, 1955

Man is a being who transcends himself and the world. He is a continual protest against reality.

NICOLAS BERDYAEV (1874–1948). *The Destiny of Man,* 1.3.1, 1931, tr. Natalie Duddington, 1955

If you eliminated from the man of today what has been deposited in him by unceasing education, he would be found to be identical, or nearly so, with his remotest ancestors.

HENRI BERGSON (1859–1941). "Final Remarks," *The Two Sources of Morality and Religion,* 1932, tr. R. Ashley Audra and Cloudesley Brereton, 1935

Man . . . is an animal, biped and reasoning.

BOETHIUS (A.D. 480–524). *The Consolation of Philosophy,* 5, tr. W. V. Cooper, 1981

Every animal leaves traces of what it was; man alone leaves traces of what he has created.

JACOB BRONOWSKI (1908–1974). *The Ascent of Man,* 1, 1973

Man is a noble animal.

SIR THOMAS BROWNE (1605–1682). *Hydriotaphia: Urn Burial,* 5, 1658, ed. John Addington Symonds, 1886

Man partly is and wholly hopes to be.

ROBERT BROWNING (1812–1889). "A Death in the Desert" (l. 586), *Dramatis Personae,* 1864

Man is by his constitution a religious animal.

EDMUND BURKE (1729–1797). *Reflections on the Revolution in France,* p. 187, 1790, Pelican Books edition, 1968

Man is to a great degree a creature of his own making and, when made as he ought to be made, is destined to hold no trivial place in the creation.

EDMUND BURKE (1729–1797). Slightly modified. *Reflections on the Revolution in France,* p. 189, 1790, Pelican Books edition, 1968

Man is God's highest present development. He is the latest thing in God.

SAMUEL BUTLER (1835–1902). *Further Extracts from the Note-Books of Samuel Butler,* 1, ed. A. T. Bartholomew, 1934

Man is in part divine,
A troubled stream from a pure source.

LORD BYRON (1788–1824). "Prometheus," 3, 1816

Admire, exult, despise, laugh, weep—for here
There is such matter for all feeling—Man!
Thou pendulum betwixt a smile and a tear.

LORD BYRON (1788–1824). *Childe Harold's Pilgrimage,* 4.109, 1812–1818

To the eye of vulgar Logic . . . what is man? An omnivorous Biped that wears Breeches. To the eye of Pure Reason, what is he? A Soul, a Spirit, and divine Apparition.

THOMAS CARLYLE (1795–1881). *Sartor Resartus: The Life and Opinions of Herr Teufelsdröckh,* 1.10, 1835

"Man," said M.——, "is a foolish animal, judging from myself."

CHAMFORT (1741–1794). *Characters and Anecdotes,* 1796, tr. W. S. Merwin, 1984

Man is an embodied paradox, a bundle of contradictions.

> C. C. COLTON (1780–1832). *Lacon: or, Many Things in Few Words; Addressed to Those Who Think*, 1.401, 1823

Man is a Universe in little.

> DEMOCRITUS (460–370 B.C.). In Kathleen Freeman, tr., *Ancilla to Pre-Socratic Philosophers: A Complete Translation of the Fragments in Diels*, Fragmente der Vorsokratiker, 68.34, 1983 (1948)

What is a man? Shall I say a rational animal? . . .

I am . . . a thinking being, that is to say, a mind, an understanding, or a reasoning being. . . .

A thing which thinks.

> DESCARTES (1596–1650). *Meditations on First Philosophy*, 2, 1641, tr. Laurence J. Lafleur, 1964

Man . . . is a being born to believe.

> BENJAMIN DISRAELI (1804–1881). Speech before the Oxford Diocesan Conference, 25 November 1864

The best definition of man is—a creature that walks on two legs and is ungrateful.

> FYODOR DOSTOYEVSKY (1821–1881). *Notes from Underground*, 1.8, 1864, tr. Ralph E. Matlaw, 1960

Man is, at one and the same time, a solitary being and a social being.

> ALBERT EINSTEIN (1879–1955). "Why Socialism?" *Monthly Review*, May 1949

Man is a Gate betwixt hell and heaven.

> RALPH WALDO EMERSON (1803–1882). Journal, May 1841

Every man is a divinity in disguise, a god playing the fool.

> RALPH WALDO EMERSON (1803–1882). "History," *Essays: First Series*, 1841

Man is a stream whose source is hidden. Our being is descending into us from we know not whence.

> RALPH WALDO EMERSON (1803–1882). "The Over-Soul," *Essays: First Series*, 1841

I think that a man should compare advantageously with a river, with an oak, with a mountain: endless flow, expansion, and grit.

> RALPH WALDO EMERSON (1803–1882). Journal, November 1851

I believe that man will not merely endure: he will prevail. He is immortal, not because he alone among creatures has an inexhaustible voice, but because he has a soul, a spirit capable of compassion and sacrifice and endurance.

> WILLIAM FAULKNER (1897–1962). Nobel Prize (in literature) acceptance address, Stockholm, 10 December 1950

Man is a tool-making animal.

> BENJAMIN FRANKLIN (1706–1790). 7 April 1778. In James Boswell, *The Life of Samuel Johnson*, 1791

Man . . . the cornerstone of creation.

> KAHLIL GIBRAN (1883–1931). "A Glimpse into the Future," *A Tear and a Smile*, tr. H. M. Nahmad, 1950

Man is in process of becoming.

> ANDRÉ GIDE (1869–1951). *More Fruits of the Earth*, 4.1, 1935

Man is very much a creature of habit.

> ALEXANDER HAMILTON (1757–1804). In *The Federalist Papers* (essay series), 27, 25 December 1787

Man—a reasoning rather than a reasonable animal.

> ALEXANDER HAMILTON (1757–1804)

Man is the only animal that laughs and weeps; for he is the only animal that is struck with the difference between what things are, and what they ought to be.

> WILLIAM HAZLITT (1778–1830). *Lectures on the English Comic Writers*, 1, 1819

Man is a fountain of immense meaning, not merely a drop in the ocean of being.

> ABRAHAM JOSHUA HESCHEL (1907–1972). *Man Is Not Alone: A Philosophy of Religion*, 20, 1951

The essence of man is not in what he is, but in what he is able to be.

> ABRAHAM JOSHUA HESCHEL (1907–1972). *Man Is Not Alone: A Philosophy of Religion*, 20, 1951

Man must live on the summit to avoid the abyss.

> ABRAHAM JOSHUA HESCHEL (1907–1972). *The Prophets*, 1, 1962

Man . . . is *a messenger who forgot the message*.

> ABRAHAM JOSHUA HESCHEL (1907–1972). *Who Is Man?* 6, 1965

In each individual, the spirit has become flesh, in each man the creation suffers, within each one is a redeemer nailed to the cross.

> HERMANN HESSE (1877–1962). Prologue to *Demian: The Story of Emil Sinclair's Youth*, 1919, tr. Michael Roloff and Michael Lebeck, 1965

Man is always something more than what he knows of himself. He is not what he is simply once for all, but is a process; he is not merely an extant life, but is, within that life, endowed with possibilities through the freedom he possesses to make of himself what he will by the activities on which he decides.

> KARL JASPERS (1883–1969). *Man in the Modern Age*, 4 (introduction), 1931, tr. Eden and Cedar Paul, 19570

Man is an imitative animal.

> THOMAS JEFFERSON (1743–1826). *Notes on the State of Virginia*, 18, 1785

I do not recollect in all the animal kingdom a single species but man which is eternally and systematically engaged in the destruction of its own species. . . . When we add to this [the destruction of] other species of animals, the lions and tigers are mere lambs compared with man as a destroyer.

> THOMAS JEFFERSON (1743–1826). Letter to James Madison, 1 January 1797

What a Bedlamite is man!

> THOMAS JEFFERSON (1743–1826). Letter to John Adams, 22 January 1821

Every man lives behind bars, which he carries within him.

> FRANZ KAFKA (1883–1924). In Gustav Janouch, "Conversations with Kafka," tr. Goronwy Rees, *Encounter*, August 1971

Man is neither villain nor hero; he is rather both villain and hero.

> MARTIN LUTHER KING, JR. (1929–1968). *Strength to Love,* 11 (introduction), 1963

Man is a moral animal.

> D. H. LAWRENCE (1885–1930). *Studies in Classic American Literature,* 2, 1923

Man is the animal who loves.

> ARCHIBALD MacLEISH (1892–1982). In Phoebe Pettingell, "The Gamut of A. MacLeish," *New Leader,* 1 June 1992

Man is the creature of circumstances.

> THOMAS ROBERT MALTHUS (1766–1834). In Robert L. Heilbroner, *The Worldly Philosophers: The Lives, Times, and Ideas of the Great Economic Thinkers,* 5th ed., 5, 1980 (1953)

Man is born for deeds of kindness.

> MARCUS AURELIUS (A.D. 121–180). *Meditations,* 9.42, tr. Maxwell Staniforth, 1964

Ishmael: Men may seem detestable as joint-stock companies and nations; knaves, fools, and murderers there may be; men may have mean and meager faces; but man, in the ideal, is so noble and so sparkling, such a grand and glowing creature, that over any ignominious blemish in him all his fellows should run to throw their costliest robes.

> HERMAN MELVILLE (1819–1891). *Moby-Dick; or, The Whale,* 26, 1851, ed. Harold Beaver, 1972

Man is the yokel *par excellence,* the booby unmatchable, the king dupe of the cosmos.

> H. L. MENCKEN (1880–1956). "Ad Imaginem Dei Creavit Illum: Meditation in Meditation," *Prejudices: Third Series,* 1922

Man
God's latest image.

> JOHN MILTON (1608–1674). *Paradise Lost,* 4.566, 1667

Man, I can assure you, is a nasty animal.

> MOLIÈRE (1622–1673). *Le Tartuffe,* 5, 1667

Man is first and foremost the self-fabricating animal.

> LEWIS MUMFORD (1895–1990). *The Conduct of Life,* 2.6, 1951

Nothing about his life is more strange to [man] or more unaccountable in purely mundane terms than the stirrings he finds in himself, usually fitful but sometimes overwhelming, to look beyond his animal existence and not be fully satisfied with its immediate substance. He lacks the complacency of the other animals: he is obsessed by pride and guilt, pride at being something more than a mere animal, guilt at falling perpetually short of the high aims he sets for himself.

> LEWIS MUMFORD (1895–1990). *The Conduct of Life,* 3.3, 1951

Man is... the leopard who knows how to change his spots.

> LEWIS MUMFORD (1895–1990). *The Conduct of Life,* 5.1, 1951
> See Changelessness: Jeremiah

Man [is] the transformer of nature.

> LEWIS MUMFORD (1895–1990). *The Conduct of Life,* 8.6, 1951

Man [is a] . . . self-transcending animal.

> LEWIS MUMFORD (1895–1990). Bibliography (Bertalanffy) in *The Pentagon of Power: The Myth of the Machine,* 1970

[Every man is a] revelation in the Flesh.

> NOVALIS (1772–1801). In Thomas Carlyle, "The Hero as King," *On Heroes, Hero-Worship, and the Heroic in History,* 1841

What is man in nature? A Nothing in comparison with the Infinite, an all in comparison with the Nothing, a mean between nothing and everything.

> BLAISE PASCAL (1623–1662). *Pensées,* 72, 1670, tr. William F. Trotter, 1931

Man is but a reed, the most feeble thing in nature; but he is a thinking reed.

> BLAISE PASCAL (1623–1662). *Pensées,* 347, 1670, tr. William F. Trotter, 1931

What a chimera then is man! What a novelty! What a monster, what a chaos, what a contradiction, what a prodigy! . . . The pride and refuse of the universe!

> BLAISE PASCAL (1623–1662). *Pensées,* 434, 1670, tr. William F. Trotter, 1931

Man is a wolf to man.

> PLAUTUS (254–184 B.C.). *Asinaria,* 2.4.88. In Sigmund Freud, *Civilization and Its Discontents,* 5, 1930, tr. James Strachey, 1961

Let us (since Life can little more supply
Than just to look about us and die)
Expatiate free o'er all this scene of Man;
A mighty maze! but not without a plan.

> ALEXANDER POPE (1688–1744). *An Essay on Man,* 1.3, 1734

Created half to rise, and half to fall;
Great lord of all things, yet a prey to all;
Sole judge of Truth, in endless Error hurl'd:
The glory, jest and riddle of the world!

> ALEXANDER POPE (1688–1744). *An Essay on Man,* 2.15, 1734

Man is the measure of all things.

> PROTAGORAS (490?–421 B.C.). In Plato (427?–347 B.C.), *Theaetetus,* 160, tr. Benjamin Jowett, 1894

Man is a rational animal—so at least I have been told. Throughout a long life, I have looked diligently for evidence in favor of this statement, but so far I have not had the good fortune to come across it.

> BERTRAND RUSSELL (1872–1970). "An Outline of Intellectual Rubbish," *Unpopular Essays,* 1950

Man, viewed morally, is a strange amalgam of angel and devil.

> BERTRAND RUSSELL (1872–1970). "Ideas That Have Helped Mankind," *Unpopular Essays,* 1950

Man is a useless passion.

> JEAN-PAUL SARTRE (1905–1980). *Being and Nothingness: A Phenomenological Essay on Ontology,* 4.2.3 (closing words), 1943, tr. Hazel E. Barnes, 1956

A man is what he wills himself to be.

> JEAN-PAUL SARTRE (1905–1980). *No Exit* (one-act play), 1944, tr. Stuart Gilbert, 1946

[As someone has said] a man is in fact three men—what *he* thinks he is—what *others* think he is—and what he *really* is. There is, I think, still a fourth identity—what he *tries* to be. My hunch is that what he tries to be fuses all the others and brings the true portrait of the man into focus.

> DORE SCHARY (1905–1980). Letter to Adlai E. Stevenson, 1956, *Heyday*, 30, 1980

Man is a metaphysical animal.

> ARTHUR SCHOPENHAUER (1788–1860). "Religion and Other Essays: A Dialogue," *Essays of Arthur Schopenhauer*, tr. T. Bailey Saunders, 1851

Apart from man, no being wonders at its own existence.

> ARTHUR SCHOPENHAUER (1788–1860)

Man is a contemptible thing unless he rises above his human concerns.

> SENECA THE YOUNGER (5? B.C.–A.D. 65). Preface (1.5) to *Natural Questions*, tr. Thomas A. Corcoran, 1921

Hamlet: What a piece of work is a man! how noble in reason! how infinite in faculty! in form and moving how express and admirable! in action how like an angel! in apprehension how like a god! the beauty of the world! the paragon of animals!

> SHAKESPEARE (1564–1616). *Hamlet*, 2.2.314, 1600

Man is of soul and body, formed for deeds
Of high resolve, on fancy's boldest wing
To soar unwearied.

> PERCY BYSSHE SHELLEY (1792–1822). *Queen Mab: A Philosophical Poem: With Notes*, 4, 1813

Man is but breath and shadow, nothing more.

> SOPHOCLES (496–406 B.C.). "Fragments" (13), *Sophocles: Tragedies and Fragments*, 1, tr. E. H. Plumptre, 1865

Man, unlike any other thing organic or inorganic in the universe, grows beyond his work, walks up the stairs of his concepts, emerges ahead of his accomplishments.

> JOHN STEINBECK (1902–1968). *The Grapes of Wrath*, 14, 1939

Man is a strange animal; he doesn't like to read the handwriting on the wall until his back is up against it.

> ADLAI E. STEVENSON (1900–1965). In James Reston, *Deadline: A Memoir*, 31 (epigraph), 1991

Man seems to be a problem-seeking as well as a problem-solving animal. We are programmed to change, develop, and meet new challenges until we die.

> ANTHONY STORR (1920–). *Churchill's Black Dog, Kafka's Mice, and Other Phenomena of the Human Mind*, 6, 1988

I hate and detest that animal called man; although I heartily love John, Peter, Thomas, and so forth.

> JONATHAN SWIFT (1667–1745). Letter to Alexander Pope, 29 September 1725

Man has been a dazzling success in the field of intellect and "know-how" and a dismal failure in the things of the spirit.

> ARNOLD J. TOYNBEE (1889–1975). "Christianity and Civilization," 1947, *Civilization on Trial*, 1948

Man is a spiritual being.

> ARNOLD J. TOYNBEE (1889–1975). *Surviving the Future*, 4, 1971

Man was made at the end of the week's work, when God was tired.

> MARK TWAIN (1835–1910). 23 May 1903, *Mark Twain's Notebook*, ed. Albert Bigelow Paine, 1935

❦

Man, *n.* God's crowning achievement, but still a work in progress.

> ANONYMOUS

MANAGERS

See also • Bureaucracy ○ Corporations ○ Executives ○ Failure: William Smithburg ○ Leaders: [especially] Warren Bennis (1), Richard M. Nixon (1) ○ Organizations ○ Success: Ferdinand Lundberg

Have three people do five jobs but pay them like four.

> ARNOLD W. DONALD. Monsanto Agricultural Co. division manager. In "Fortune People," *Fortune*, September 1991

The ultimate test of management is performance.

> PETER F. DRUCKER (1909–). *Management: Tasks, Responsibilities, Practices*, 1, 1974, abr., 1977
>
> See Corporations: Harold Geneen

A managerial job is defined by relationships—upwards, downwards, and sideways.

> PETER F. DRUCKER (1909–). *Management: Tasks, Responsibilities, Practices*, 24, 1974, abr., 1977

Integrity is the one absolute requirement of managers.

> PETER F. DRUCKER (1909–). *Management: Tasks, Responsibilities, Practices*, 28, 1974, abr., 1977

The synonyms for controls are measurements and information. The synonym for control is direction. . . . Controls deal with facts, that is, with events of the past. Control deals with expectations, that is, with the future. . . .
   In the task of a manager, controls are purely a means to an end. The end is control.

> PETER F. DRUCKER (1909–). *Management: Tasks, Responsibilities, Practices*, 31, 1974, abr., 1977

The top-management tasks require at least four different kinds of human being: the person of thought, the person of action, the "people person," and the "front man."

> PETER F. DRUCKER (1909–). *Management: Tasks, Responsibilities, Practices*, 38, 1974, abr., 1977

There should be a *top-management work plan* . . . that spells out in considerable detail who is responsible for what; what the objectives and goals are with respect to each task; and what the deadlines are.

> PETER F. DRUCKER (1909–). *Management: Tasks, Responsibilities, Practices*, 38, 1974, abr., 1977

The superior manager's record of success and his confidence in his ability give his high expectations credibility.

J. STERLING LIVINGSTON. "Pygmalion in Management." In *Classic Advice on Handling the Manager's Job (Harvard Business Review on Human Relations,* vol. 3), 1986

When the milk is watered, it is necessary to have a line of loyal managers, to have nobody present who is apt to blow the whistle and call in the police. To insure this one needs carefully screened people. People who are excluded are, then, not basically excluded on racial or religious grounds . . . but on grounds of reliability, real or supposed. Anyone about whom there is some doubt that his *primary* loyalty will be to the corporation must be left out.

FERDINAND LUNDBERG (1902–1995). *The Rich and the Super-Rich: A Study in the Power of Money Today,* 8, 1968

The sign of a good manager is his ability to give and take negative feedback.

RICHARD TANNER PASCALE (1938–). "Zen and the Art of Management." In Classic Advice on Handling the Manager's Job (Harvard Business Review on Human Relations, vol. 3), 1986

Second-rate people hire third-rate people.

LEO ROSTEN (1908–1997)

See Mediocrity: Henri de Jomini

[The good manager] has a high tolerance for ambiguity.

GARY STEINER. In H. Edward Wrapp, "Good Managers Don't Make Policy Decisions," *Harvard Business Review,* September-October 1967

Generally, management of many is the same as management of few. It is a matter of organization.

SUN-TZU (4th cent. B.C.). "Energy" (10), *The Art of War,* tr. Samuel B. Griffith, 1963

🌿

Making the most of other people's strengths and the least of their weaknesses is a surefire formula for managerial success.

ANONYMOUS

MANIPULATION

See also • Brainwashing ○ Indoctrination ○ Oppression ○ Propaganda

The conscious and intelligent manipulation of the organized habits and opinions of the masses is an important element in democratic society. Those who manipulate this unseen mechanism of society constitute an invisible government which is the true ruling power of our country.

EDWARD L. BERNAYS (1891–1995). Opening words, *Propaganda,* 1928

Never have so many been manipulated so much by so few.

ALDOUS HUXLEY (1894–1963). On media control by "the Power Elite," "Over-Organization," *Brave New World Revisited,* 1958

See World War II: Winston Churchill (5)

The victim of mind-manipulation does not know that he is a victim. To him, the walls of his prison are invisible, and he believes himself to be free.

ALDOUS HUXLEY (1894–1963). "What Can Be Done?" *Brave New World Revisited,* 1958

That the manufacture of consent is capable of great refinements no one, I think, denies. . . . The opportunities for manipulation open to anyone who understands the process are plain enough.

WALTER LIPPMANN (1889–1974). *Public Opinion,* 15.4, 1922

See Public Opinion: Ralph Waldo Emerson (2)

Manipulation is a secret or impersonal exercise of power; the one who is influenced is not explicitly told what to do but is nevertheless subject to the will of another.

C. WRIGHT MILLS (1916–1962). *White Collar: The American Middle Classes,* 5.6.3, 1951

Under the system of explicit authority, in the round, solid nineteenth century, the victim knew he was being victimized, the misery and discontent of the powerless were explicit. In the amorphous twentieth-century world, where manipulation replaces authority, the victim does not recognize his status. . . . Men internalize what the managerial cadres would have them do, without knowing their own motives, but nevertheless having them. Many whips are inside men, who do not know how they got there, or indeed that they are there.

C. WRIGHT MILLS (1916–1962). *White Collar: The American Middle Classes,* 5.6.3, 1951

MANKIND

Includes • Humanity

See also • Civilization ○ Crowds ○ Culture ○ Evolution ○ Expectations: Vauvenargues ○ History ○ Man ○ The Masses ○ Men ○ Optimism—Examples: Lewis Mumford ○ People ○ The People ○ Population ○ The Public ○ Society ○ Unity: Bertrand Russell ○ Women

More than any other time in history, mankind faces a crossroads. One path leads to despair and utter hopelessness. The other, to total extinction. Let us pray we have the wisdom to choose correctly.

WOODY ALLEN (1935–). "My Speech to the Graduates," *Side Effects,* 1981

It is one of the greatest impulses of mankind to arrive at something higher than a natural state.

JAMES BALDWIN (1924–1987). *Nobody Knows My Name: More Notes of a Native Son,* 10, 1961

We drink without being thirsty and make love at any time; that is all that distinguishes us from other animals.

BEAUMARCHAIS (1732–1799). *The Marriage of Figaro,* 2.21, 1784

The human species is forever in a state of change, forever becoming.

SIMONE de BEAUVOIR (1908–1986). *The Second Sex,* 1, 1950, tr. H. M. Parshley, 1952

What shadows we are, and what shadows we pursue.

EDMUND BURKE (1729–1797). Speech, Bristol (England), 9 September 1780

Nothing remains for us . . . but to be reborn or to die.

> ALBERT CAMU (1913–1960). "Historical Rebellion: Rebellion and Revolution," *The Rebel: An Essay on Man in Revolt*, 1951, tr. Anthony Bower, 1956

We are really God's lowest creature, that is to say, God's executioner in his world.

> ELIAS CANETTI (1905–1994). 1966, *The Human Province*, tr. Joachim Neugroschel, 1978

O poor mortals, how ye make this earth bitter for each other.

> THOMAS CARLYLE (1795–1881). *The French Revolution: A History*, 1.5.5., 1837

To despise our species is the price we must too often pay for our knowledge of it.

> C. C. COLTON (1780–1832). *Lacon: or, Many Things in Few Words; Addressed to Those Who Think*, 2.157, 1824

We are single cells in a body of three billion cells. The body is humankind.

> NORMAN COUSINS (1912–1990). 1975. "Editor's Odyssey: Gleanings from Articles and Editorials by N.C.," ed. Susan Schiefelbein, *Saturday Review*, 15 April 1978

"pity this busy monster, manunkind."

> E. E. CUMMINGS (1894–1962). Poem title, *1 x 1*, 1944

One is born into a herd of buffaloes and must be glad if one is not trampled underfoot before one's time.

> ALBERT EINSTEIN (1879–1955). Letter to Cornelius Lanczos, 9 July 1952

We know better than we do. We do not yet possess ourselves, and we know at the same time that we are much more.

> RALPH WALDO EMERSON (1883–1882). "The Over-Soul," *Essays: First Series*, 1841
>
> See Humility: First Person: Paul ○ Reason & Passion: Ovid

We are living at a time when humankind can face whatever threatens it only if we, by which I mean each of us, manage to revive, with new energy and a new ethos, a sense of responsibility for the rest of the world.

> VÁCLAV HAVEL (1936–). Czech president. Address (after being awarded the Fulbright Prize), Washington, 3 October 1997, "The Charms of NATO," *New York Review of Books*, 15 January 1998

Mankind are earthen jugs with spirit in them.

> NATHANIEL HAWTHORNE (1804–1864). 1 June 1842, *The American Notebooks*, ed. Claude M. Simpson, 1932

Mankind are a herd of knaves and fools.

> WILLIAM HAZLITT (1778–1830). *Characteristics in the Manner of Rochefoucault's Maxims*, 239, 1823

We are gods in the chrysalis.

> ELBERT HUBBARD (1856–1915). *The Note Book of Elbert Hubbard*, comp. Elbert Hubbard II, p. 51, 1927

We are human because, at a very early stage in the history of the species, our ancestors discovered a way of preserving and disseminating the results of experience. They learned to speak and were thus enabled to translate what they had perceived, what they had inferred from given fact and home-grown fantasy, into a set of concepts, which could be added to by each generation and bequeathed, a treasure of mingled sense and nonsense, to posterity.

> ALDOUS HUXLEY (1894–1963). "Knowledge and Understanding," *Tomorrow and Tomorrow and Tomorrow and Other Essays*, 1956

We are the manger in which the Lord is born.

> CARL G. JUNG (1875–1961). "A Psychological Approach to the Dogma of the Trinity" (5.1), 1942, *Psychology and Religion: West and East*, tr. R. F. C. Hull, 1958

We're all Christ, we're all Hitler.

> JOHN LENNON (1940–1980)
>
> See The Unconscious: Carl G. Jung (6)

We [are] hybrids molded from clay and spirit.

> PRIMO LEVI (1919–1987). *The Drowned and the Saved*, 2, 1986, tr. Raymond Rosenthal, 1988

Mankind [is] more prone to evil than to good.

> MACHIAVELLI (1469–1527). *The Discourses*, 1.9, 1517, tr. Christian E. Detmold, 1940

Homo boobians.

> H. L. MENCKEN (1880–1956). "Meditations in the Methodist Desert: Optimist vs. Optimist," *Prejudices: Fourth Series*, 1924

There are one hundred and ninety-three living species of monkeys and apes. One hundred and ninety-two of them are covered with hair. The exception is a naked ape self-named *Homo sapiens*.

> DESMOND MORRIS (1928–). Introduction to *The Naked Ape*, 1967

I have always despised mankind.

> NAPOLEON (1769–1821). Remark, St. Helena, after 1815. In Albert Carr, *Napoleon Speaks*, 14, 1941

There is a design for all humanity, which will be manifested only as humanity becomes a whole, a design which will make clear all that has gone before.

> N. SRI RAM (1899–?). *Thoughts for Aspirants*, 7, 1972

I love mankind—it's people I can't stand.

> CHARLES M. SCHULZ (1922–). Comic strip balloon, *Go Fly a Kite, Charlie Brown*, 1963

Mankind is constantly developing in the direction of progress.

> ALBERT SCHWEITZER (1875–1965). *Out of My Life and Thought: An Autobiography*, 13, tr. C. T. Campion, 1933

Prospero: We are such stuff
As dreams are made on, and our little life
Is rounded with a sleep.

> SHAKESPEARE (1564–1616). *The Tempest*, 4.1.156, 1611

We are the lamps in which the light of the world burns: . . . we are gods though we die like men.

> GEORGE BERNARD SHAW (1856–1950). Preface ("Jesus as Biologist") to *Androcles and the Lion*, 1912

We are the choices we have made.

> MERYL STREEP (1949–). Katie Couric television interview, *The Today Show*, NBC, 2 June 1995
>
> See Self-Realization (Becoming): Thomas S. Szasz

We are Ancients of the earth,
And in the morning of the times.
> ALFRED, LORD TENNYSON (1809–1892). "The Day-Dream," l. 231, 1842

How hard it is to be greatly related to mankind! They are only my uncles and aunts and cousins. I hear of some persons greatly related, but only he is so who has all mankind for his friend.
> HENRY DAVID THOREAU (1817–1862). Journal, 30 March 1842

We are still being born.
> HENRY DAVID THOREAU (1817–1862). "Friday," *A Week on the Concord and Merrimack Rivers*, 1849

The human race's prospects of survival were considerably better when we were defenseless against tigers than they are today when we have become defenseless against ourselves.
> ARNOLD J. TOYNBEE (1889–1975). In *Observer* (British newspaper), 1963

Can any plausible excuse be found for the crime of creating the human race?
> MARK TWAIN (1835–1910). Annotation in his copy of Charles Darwin's *Journal of Researches*. Quoted in "Business Digest," *San Francisco Chronicle*, 18 July 1997

What small potatoes we all are, compared with what we might be!
> CHARLES DUDLEY WARNER (1829–1900). "Fifteenth Week," *My Summer in a Garden*, 1871

We're all of us guinea pigs in the laboratory of God. Humanity is just a work in progress.
> TENNESSEE WILLIAMS (1911–1983). *Camino Real*, 12, 1953

Distinguish'd link in being's endless chain!
Midway from nothing to the Deity!
> EDWARD YOUNG (1683–1765). *The Complaint: or, Night Thoughts on Life, Death, and Immortality*, 1.74, 1742–1745

❧

We are a journey that has forgotten its destination.
> ANONYMOUS

MANNERS

See also • Bores ○ Courtesy ○ Familiarity ○ Gentlemen ○ Manners: Rules ○ Pleasing Others ○ Popularity ○ Tact

Manners make the Man, not Habits.
> WILLIAM BLAKE (1757–1827). "A Vision of the Last Judgment," p. 91, 1810, *The Complete Writings of William Blake*, ed. Geoffrey Keynes, 1966
> See Clothes: Saying (Latin) ○ Money: John Clarke

The greatest favors may be done so awkwardly and bunglingly as to offend; and disagreeable things may be done so agreeably as almost to oblige.
> LORD CHESTERFIELD (1694–1773). Letter to his son, 7 April 1751

Fools and low people . . . take civility and a little attention as a favor; remember and acknowledge it: this, in my mind, is buying them cheap; and therefore they are worth buying.
> LORD CHESTERFIELD (1694–1773). Letter to his son, 14 February 1752

Straightforwardness, without the rules of propriety, becomes rudeness.
> CONFUCIUS (551–479 B.C.). *Confucian Analects*, 8.2, tr. James Legge, 1930

The knock at the door tells the character of the visitor!
> T. K. V. DESIKACHAR. Tr. *Patanjali's Yogasutras: An Introduction*, 2.30, 1987

Manners have been somewhat cynically defined to be a contrivance of wise men to keep fools at a distance.
> RALPH WALDO EMERSON (1803–1882). "Behavior," *The Conduct of Life*, 1860

Politeness is the outward garment of good will. But many are the nutshells, in which, if you crack them, nothing like a kernel is to be found.
> J. C. HARE (1795–1855) and A. W. HARE (1792–1834). *Guesses at Truth: Second Series*, p. 539, 1848, Macmillan edition, 1867

I don't recall your name, but your manners are familiar.
> OLIVER HERFORD (1863–1935). Remark to a back-slapping boor who approached him with a confident, "You remember me?" In Cleveland Amory, *Who Killed Society?* pt. 3 (epigraph), 1960

Rudeness is the weak man's imitation of strength.
> ERIC HOFFER (1902–1983). *The Passionate State of Mind: And Other Aphorisms*, 241, 1954

Come uncalled, sit unserved.
> JAMES KELLY (18th cent.). Comp., *A Complete Collection of Scottish Proverbs Explained and Made Intelligible to the English Reader*, C.6, 1721

Ordinary politeness, including even a certain charitable reticence, can easily conceal feelings of quite a different nature. Outward deference, as everyone knows who has ever occupied a high executive position, easily slips over into unctuousness and flattery.
> GEORGE F. KENNAN (1904–). *Around the Cragged Hill: A Personal and Political Philosophy*, 1, 1993

Good manners are the technique of expressing consideration for the feelings of others.
> ALICE DUER MILLER (1874–1942). "I Like American Manners," *Saturday Evening Post*, 13 August 1932

The most useful of all social graces is the ability to yawn with your mouth closed.
> LAURENCE J. PETER (1919–1990)

True politeness consists in being easy one's self, and in making everyone about one as easy as one can.
> ALEXANDER POPE (1688–1744). "Thoughts on Various Subjects," *Miscellanies in Prose and Verse* (published with Jonathan Swift), vol. 2, 1727

Too civil by half.
> RICHARD SHERIDAN (1751–1816). *The Rivals*, 3.4, 1775

If a man makes me keep my distance, the comfort is, he keeps his at the same time.
> JONATHAN SWIFT (1667–1745). "Thoughts on Various Subjects" (expanded from a version published in 1711). *Miscellanies in Prose and Verse* (published with Alexander Pope), vol. 1, 1727

Good manners is the art of making those people easy with whom we converse.

> JONATHAN SWIFT (1667–1745). "A Treatise on Good Manners and Good Breeding"

Good breeding consists in concealing how much we think of ourselves and how little we think of the other person.

> MARK TWAIN (1835–1910). 4 July 1898, *Mark Twain's Notebook,* ed. Albert Bigelow Paine, 1935

In large part [manners] are an expression of the relation of status—a symbolic pantomime of mastery on the one hand and of subservience on the other.

> THORSTEIN VEBLEN (1857–1929). *The Theory of the Leisure Class: An Economic Study of Institutions,* 3, 1899

MANNERS: RULES

See also • Conversation ○ Manners

Acquire an easiness and versatility of manners, as well as of mind; and, like the chameleon, take the hue of the company you are with.

> LORD CHESTERFIELD (1694–1773). Letter to his son, 11 January 1750

To behave to every one as if you were receiving a great guest.

> CONFUCIUS (551–479 B.C.). *Confucian Analects,* 12.2, tr. James Legge, 1930

"After you" is good Manners.

> JAMES KELLY (18th cent.). Comp., *A Complete Collection of Scottish Proverbs Explained and Made Intelligible to the English Reader,* A.263, 1721

A man of sense knows when he pleases or is tiresome; he goes away the very minute before it might have been thought he stayed too long.

> LA BRUYÈRE (1645–1696). "Of Society and of Conversation" (2), *The Characters,* 1688, tr. Henri van Laun, 1929

Be merry but with modesty, be sober but not too sullen, be valiant but not venturous.

> JOHN LYLY (1554?–1606). "Euphues," *Euphues: The Anatomy of Wit,* 1579

To do *exactly as your neighbors* do is the only sensible rule.

> EMILY POST (1872–1960). *Etiquette,* 33, 1922

The prompter the refusal, the less the disappointment.

> PUBLIUS SYRUS (85–43 B.C.). *Moral Sayings,* 492, tr. Darius Lyman, Jr., 1862

Henry Higgins: The great secret, Eliza, is not having bad manners or good manners or any other particular sort of manners, but having the same manner for all human souls: in short, behaving as if you were in Heaven, where there are no third-class carriages, and one soul is as good as another.

> GEORGE BERNARD SHAW (1856–1950). *Pygmalion,* 5, 1912

I try to approach others carefully and to assess whether or not I'm welcome and whether or not they have the time to talk to me. And I would only ask the same of others.

> GARY SNYDER (1930–). "Tracking Down the Natural Man," *The Real Work,* ed. Wm. Scott McLean, 1980

A man should not enter a house suddenly, without . . . knocking.

> *TALMUD* (A.D. 1st–6th cent.). Rabbinical writings. In Louis I. Newman, comp., *The Talmudic Anthology,* 48, 1945

Do not trouble your guest with many questions about himself; he will tell you what he wishes you to know.

> WABASHA (1773?–1855?). "The Teachings of Wabasha." In Ernest T. Seton and Julia M. Seton, comps., *The Gospel of the Redman,* 1966

Never come between anyone and the fire.

> WABASHA (1773?–1855?). "The Teachings of Wabasha." In Ernest T. Seton and Julia M. Seton, comps., *The Gospel of the Redman,* 1966

Sleep not when others Speak.

> GEORGE WASHINGTON (1732–1799). Copybook, 1748 (at age 16), *Rules of Civility & Decent Behaviour in Company and Conversation,* #6. The rules were an amended version of Francis Hawkins's 1640 translation of *Decency of Conversation Among Men* (French Jesuit writing, 1595).

If any hesitate in his Words, help him not, nor Prompt him without [being asked]. Interrupt him not, nor Answer him till his Speech be ended.

> GEORGE WASHINGTON (1732–1799). Copybook, 1748 (at age 16). *Rules of Civility & Decent Behaviour in Company and Conversation,* #74. The rules were an amended version of Francis Hawkins's 1640 translation of *Decency of Conversation Among Men* (French Jesuit writing, 1595).

While you are talking, Point not with your Finger at him [to] Whom you Discourse nor Approach too near him to whom you talk, especially to his face.

> GEORGE WASHINGTON (1732–1799). Copybook. 1748 (at age 16), *Rules of Civility & Decent Behaviour in Company and Conversation,* #76. The rules were an amended version of Francis Hawkins's 1640 translation of *Decency of Conversation Among Men* (French Jesuit writing, 1595).

Whisper not in the Company of Others.

> GEORGE WASHINGTON (1732–1799). Copybook, 1748 (at age 16), *Rules of Civility & Decent Behaviour in Company and Conversation,* #77. The rules were an amended version of Francis Hawkins's 1640 translation of *Decency of Conversation Among Men* (French Jesuit writing, 1595).

Put not another bite into your Mouth till the former be Swallowed, let not your Morsels be not too big for the [mouth].

> GEORGE WASHINGTON (1732–1799). Copybook, 1748 (at age 16). *Rules of Civility & Decent Behaviour in Company and Conversation,* #97. The rules were an amended version of Francis Hawkins's 1640 translation of *Decency of Conversation Among Men* (French Jesuit writing, 1595).

Better a friendly refusal than an unwilling compliance.

> SAYING (GERMAN)

Treat your guest as a guest for two days; on the third day, give him a hoe.

> SAYING (SWAHILI)

MARRIAGE

See also • Adultery ○ Celibacy ○ Divorce ○ Family ○ Home ○
Love, Romantic ○ M.adness: Benjamin Rush (3) ○ Sex ○
Singlehood ○ Women & Men

When I was young, if a girl married poverty, she became a drudge;
if she married wealth, she became a doll.

> SUSAN B. ANTHONY (1820–1906). 1896. In Ida Husted Harper, *The Life
> and Work of Susan B. Anthony*, 46, 1898–1906

Women hope men will change after marriage but they don't; men
hope women won't change but they do.

> BETTINA ARNDT. *Private Lives*, 2, 1986

I married beneath me—all women do.

> NANCY ASTOR (1879–1964). Speech, Oldham, England, 1951

Wives are young men's mistresses, companions for middle age, and
old men's nurses.

> FRANCIS BACON (1561–1626). "Of Marriage and Single Life," *Essays*, 1625

Well-married, a man is winged; ill-matched, he is shackled.

> HENRY WARD BEECHER (1813–1887). "The Family," *Proverbs from
> Plymouth Pulpit*, ed. William Drysdale, 1887

Bride, *n.* A woman with a fine prospect of happiness behind her.

> AMBROSE BIERCE (1842–1914). *The Devil's Dictionary*, p. 19, 1911, Dover
> edition, 1958

I often hear affekshunate husbands kall their wifes "Mi Duck," i
wunder if this ain't a sli delusion tew their big bills?

> JOSH BILLINGS (1818–1885). *His Sayings*, 63, 1867

By marriage, the husband and wife are one person in law: that is,
the very being or legal existence of the woman is suspended during marriage, or at least incorporated and consolidated into that of
the husband. . . . But though our law in general considers man and
wife as one person, yet there are some instances in which she is
separately considered; as inferior to him, and acting by his compulsion.

> WILLIAM BLACKSTONE (1723–1780). *Commentaries on the Laws of
> England*, 1.14, 1765–1769

I *N.* take thee *M.* to my wedded husband, to have and to hold from
this day forward, for better for worse, for richer for poorer, in sickness and in health, to love, cherish and to obey, till death us do
part, according to God's holy ordinance; and thereto I give thee my
troth.

> THE BOOK OF COMMON PRAYER. "Solemnization of Matrimony," 1662.
> The husband's declaration omits the words "to obey."

One was never married, and that's his hell; another is, and that's his
plague.

> ROBERT BURTON (1577–1640). *The Anatomy of Melancholy*, 1.2.4.7,
> 1621–1651

It was very good of God to let [Thomas] Carlyle and Mrs. Carlyle
marry one another and so make only two people miserable instead
of four, besides being very amusing.

> SAMUEL BUTLER (1835–1902). Letter to Miss E. M. A. Savage, 21
> November 1884

Love and marriage, love and marriage,
Go together like a horse and carriage.

> SAMMY CAHN (1913–1993). "Love and Marriage" (song). In the musical
> *Our Town*, 1936

The dread of loneliness is greater than the fear of bondage, so we
get married.

> CYRIL CONNOLLY (1903–1974). "Ecce Gubernator," *The Unquiet Grave:
> A Word Cycle by Palinurus*, 1945

What is there in the vale of life
Half so delightful as a wife,
When friendship, love, and peace combine
To stamp the marriage bond divine?

> WILLIAM COWPER (1731–1800). Opening lines, "Love Abused," letter to
> Mary Unwin, 27 July 1780

Marriage probably originated as a straightforward food-for-sex
deal among foraging primates. Compatibility was not a big issue,
nor, or course, was there any tension over who would control the
remote.

> BARBARA EHRENREICH (1941–). "Burt, Loni, and Our Way of Life,"
> 1993, *The Snarling Citizen: Essays*, 1995

Marry above thy match, and thou'lt get a Master.

> BENJAMIN FRANKLIN (1706–1790). *Poor Richard's Almanack*, September
> 1740

A mother is only brought unlimited satisfaction by her relation to
a son. . . . Even a marriage is not made secure until the wife has
succeeded in making her husband her child as well and in acting
as a mother to him.

> SIGMUND FREUD (1856–1939). *New Introductory Lectures on
> Psychoanalysis*, 33, 1933, tr. James Strachey, 1965

The ideal that marriage aims at is that of spiritual union through
the physical. The human love that it incarnates is intended to
serve as a stepping stone to divine or universal love.

> MOHANDAS K. GANDHI (1869–1948). In *Young India*, 21 May 1931

You were born together, and together you shall be forevermore. . . .
   But let there be spaces in your togetherness,
   And let the winds of the heavens dance between you.

> KAHLIL GIBRAN (1883–1931). "On Marriage," *The Prophet*, 1923

How to Be Happy Though Married.

> REV. E. J. HARDY. Book title, 1910

It was the triumph of hope over experience.

> SAMUEL JOHNSON (1709–1784). On an acquaintance's remarriage soon
> after his first wife's death ended their unhappy marriage, quoted by Rev.
> Dr. Maxwell, 1770. In James Boswell, *The Life of Samuel Johnson*, 1791

Love is moral even without legal marriage, but marriage is
immoral without love.

> ELLEN KEY (1849–1926). Title essay, *The Morality of Woman and Other
> Essays*, 1911

There is no more lovely, friendly and charming relationship, communion or company than a good marriage.

> MARTIN LUTHER (1483–1546). *Table Talk*, 292, 1566, tr. William Hazlitt,
> 1857

Marriages are made in heaven and consummated on earth.

> JOHN LYLY (1554?–1606). *Mother Bombie*, 4.1, 1590
>
> See Divorce: Oscar Wilde

When a man is newly married, he shall not go out with the army or be charged with any business; he shall be free at home one year, to be happy with his wife whom he has taken.

> MOSES (14th cent. B.C.). *Deuteronomy* 24:5

A virtuous wife is a man's best treasure.

> MUHAMMAD (A.D. 570?–632). *The Sayings of Muhammad*, 418,
> tr. Abdullah Al-Suhrawardy, 1941

If they cannot contain, let them marry: for it is better to marry than to burn.

> PAUL (A.D. 1st cent.). *1 Corinthians* 7:9 (King James Version)

Saw a wedding in the church; and strange to see what delight we married people have to see these poor fools decoyed into our condition.

> SAMUEL PEPYS (1633–1703). Diary, 25 December 1665

Wedlock is a padlock.

> JOHN RAY (1628–1705). Comp., *A Collection of English Proverbs*, p. 56,
> 1678

A good marriage is that in which each appoints the other the guardian of his solitude.

> RAINER MARIA RILKE (1875–1926). Letter to Paula Modersohn Becker,
> 12 February 1902, tr. Jane Bannard Greene and M. D. Herter Norton,
> 1945

The horror of wedlock, the most appalling, the most loathsome of all the bonds humankind has devised for its own discomfort and degradation.

> MARQUIS de SADE (1740–1814). *L'Histoire de Juliette*, pt. 2, 1798

Marriage is the most licentious of human institutions. . . .
  That is the secret of its popularity.

> GEORGE BERNARD SHAW (1856–1950). *Man and Superman*, 3, 1903

Marriage is popular because it combines the maximum of temptation with the maximum of opportunity.

> GEORGE BERNARD SHAW (1856–1950). "Maxims for Revolutionists:
> Marriage," *Man and Superman*, 1903

My dear, my better half.

> SIR PHILIP SIDNEY (1554–1586). *The Arcadia*, 3, 1590–1593

Anonymous: Should I marry or not?
Socrates: Whichever you do you will repent it.

> SOCRATES (470?–399 B.C.). Format adapted. In Diogenes Laertius (A.D.
> 3rd cent.), *Lives of Eminent Philosophers*, 2.5, tr. R. D. Hicks, 1925
>
> See Women and Men: Aristophanes

A wife is the joy of a man's heart.

> *TALMUD* (A.D. 1st–6th cent.). Rabbinical writings. In Louis I. Newman,
> comp., *The Talmudic Anthology*, 399, 1945

Take it from me, marriage isn't a word. . . . It's a *sentence!*

> KING VIDOR (1894–1982). Screen caption, *The Crowd* (film), 1928

There is one thing worse than an absolutely loveless marriage: a marriage in which there is love, but on one side only.

> OSCAR WILDE (1854–1900). *An Ideal Husband*, 4, 1895

Therefore a man leaves his father and his mother and cleaves to his wife, and they become one flesh.

> ANONYMOUS (*BIBLE*). *Genesis*, 2:24

In joy and sorrow they share each other's tears.

> ANONYMOUS

The difference between war and marriage is that in marriage you sleep with the enemy.

> ANONYMOUS

Who marries for money earns it.

> SAYING (ENGLISH)

Early marriage, long love.

> SAYING (GERMAN)

Marry your like.

> SAYING

MARTYRDOM

See also • Defiance ∘ Difficulty ∘ Dissent ∘ Grief ∘ Heresy ∘ Nonconformity ∘ Nonconformity, Anti- ∘ Pain ∘ Prejudice ∘ Resistance ∘ Self-Sacrifice ∘ Struggle

The cross and the hemlock have been meted out not so much to those who have threatened our economic interests as to those who have threatened the moral self-respect of men.

> ANTON T. BOISEN (1876–1965). *The Exploration of the Inner World:
> A Study of Mental Disorder and Religious Experience*, 5, 1936

Martyrs . . . must choose between being forgotten, mocked, or made use of. As for being understood—never!

> ALBERT CAMUS (1913–1960). *The Fall*, p. 76, tr. Justin O'Brien, 1956

He that dies a martyr proves that he was not a knave, but by no means that he was not a fool.

> C. C. COLTON (1780–1832). *Lacon: or, Many Things in Few Words;
> Addressed to Those Who Think*, 1.410, 1823

Father Zossima: Men reject their prophets and slay them, but they love their martyrs and honor those whom they have slain.

> FYODOR DOSTOYEVSKY (1821–1881). *The Brothers Karamazov*, 6.2(h),
> 1880, tr. Constance Garnett, 1912

Let us all be brave enough to die the death of a martyr, but let no one lust for martyrdom.

> MOHANDAS K. GANDHI (1869–1948). In *Young India*, 13 January 1927

The Dutch tell of a German soldier [in Nazi-occupied Holland during World War II], who was a member of an execution squad ordered to shoot innocent hostages. Suddenly he stepped out of rank and refused to participate in the execution. On the spot he was charged with treason by the officer in charge and was placed with the hostages, where he was promptly executed by his comrades.

J. GLENN GRAY (1913–1977). *The Warriors: Reflections on Men in Battle*, 6, 1959

The martyr role must emerge from a seemingly voluntary choice for the good of the cause. One could not, for example, impose martyrdom on a fleeing victim, though if he turned and stood he might easily win the role.

ORRIN E. KLAPP (1915–). *Symbolic Leaders: Public Dramas and Public Men*, 3, 1964

The masses prefer martyrs, prefer those who in one way or another can be crucified, as their demigods, for otherwise the superiority of these is found intolerable.

WILHELM LANGE-EICHBAUM (1875–1950). *The Problem of Genius*, 5.C.2, 1931, tr. Eden and Cedar Paul, 1932

In this place there are no martyrdoms. . . . We do not allow the dead to rise up against us. . . . Nothing will remain of you: not a name in a register, not a memory in a living brain. You will be annihilated in the past, as well as in the future. You will never have existed.

GEORGE ORWELL (1903–1950). *Nineteen Eighty–Four*, 3.2, 1949

Everything will be done to try and prevent the martyr from standing out as a shining example . . . the torturers will do their utmost to deprive him of his power of irradiation.

JEAN ROLIN (1900–?). *Police Drugs*, 8.5, tr. Laurence J. Bendit, 1956

No man is worth his salt who is not ready at all times to risk his body, to risk his well-being, to risk his life, in a great cause.

THEODORE ROOSEVELT (1858–1919). In Elbert Hubbard, comp., *Elbert Hubbard's Scrap Book*, p. 137, 1923

A martyr . . . a victim by vocation.

JEAN-PAUL SARTRE (1905–1980). *No Exit* (one-act play), 1944, tr. Stuart Gilbert, 1946

Martyrdom, sir, is what these people like: it is the only way in which a man can become famous without ability.

GEORGE BERNARD SHAW (1856–1950). *The Devil's Disciple*, 3, 1897

If Savonarola only tells the ladies of Florence that they ought to tear off their jewels and finery and sacrifice them to God, they offer him a cardinal's hat, and praise him as a saint; but if he induces them to actually do it, they burn him as a public nuisance.

GEORGE BERNARD SHAW (1856–1950). Preface ("Worldliness of the Majority") to *Androcles and the Lion*, 1912

The believers and unbelievers who think for themselves will let themselves be burnt alive rather than conform to a creed imposed on them by any power except their own consciences.

GEORGE BERNARD SHAW (1856–1950). *The Intelligent Woman's Guide to Socialism, Capitalism, Sovietism and Fascism*, 82, 1928

Fear the time when Manself will not suffer and die for a concept, for this one quality is the foundation of Manself, and this one quality is man, distinctive in the universe.

JOHN STEINBECK (1902–1968). *The Grapes of Wrath*, 14, 1939

We multiply whenever we are [cut] down by you; the blood of Christians is seed.

TERTULLIAN (A.D. 160–220). *Apology*, 50.13, tr. T. R. Glover, 1931 (Popular version: The blood of the martyrs is the seed of the Church.)

'Tis not the dying for a faith that so hard, Master Harry—'tis the living up to it that is difficult.

WILLIAM MAKEPEACE THACKERAY (1811–1863). *The History of Henry Esmond*, 1.6, 1852

See Principles, Moral: Alfred Adler ○ Religion: Georg Christoph Lichtenberg (1)

A thing is not necessarily true because a man dies for it.

OSCAR WILDE (1854–1900). "The Portrait of Mr. W. H.," *Blackwood's Edinburgh Magazine* (Scotland), July 1889

❧

Vanity has made more martyrs than has truth.

ANONYMOUS

THE MASSES

See also • Crowds ○ Illusions: Gustave Le Bon ○ Man ○ Mankind ○ Mass Movements ○ Mobs ○ People ○ The People ○ The Public ○ Society

Leave this hypocritical prating about the masses. Masses are rude, lame, unmade, pernicious in their demands and influence, and need not to be flattered but to be schooled. I wish not to concede anything to them, but to tame, drill, divide and break them up, and draw individuals out of them.

RALPH WALDO EMERSON (1803–1882). "Considerations by the Way," *The Conduct of Life*, 1860

The masses are advancing. Without some new spiritual influence, our age, which is a revolutionary age, will produce a catastrophe.

GEORG HEGEL (1770–1831). In José Ortega y Gasset, *The Revolt of the Masses*, 6, 1930, tr. anon., 1932

The masses are governed more by impulse than conviction.

WENDELL PHILLIPS (1811–1884). "The Philosophy of the Abolition Movement," speech before the Massachusetts Anti-Slavery Society, Boston, 27 January 1853

MASS MOVEMENTS

See also • Crises ○ Crowds ○ Fanatics ○ Heroism ○ History ○ Leaders ○ The Masses ○ Mobs ○ Propaganda ○ Revolution ○ Tyranny ○ War

Communism and Fascism or Nazism although poles apart in their intellectual content are similar in this, that both have emotional appeal to the type of personality that takes pleasure in being submerged in a mass movement and submitting to superior authority.

J. A. C. BROWN (1911–1964). *Techniques of Persuasion: From Propaganda to Brainwashing*, 5, 1963

Although emotional and evangelical movements have frequently been initiated by individual members of the ruling or middle classes, their followers have ordinarily come from the toiling masses. In some cases, notably in the case of Wesley's Methodist movement, incipient political revolution on the part of the masses has been replaced by a religious one.

J. A. C. BROWN (1911–1964). *Techniques of Persuasion: From Propaganda to Brainwashing*, 9, 1963

A mass movement must develop at the earliest moment a compact corporate organization and a capacity to absorb and integrate all comers.

> ERIC HOFFER (1902–1983). *The True Believer: Thoughts on the Nature of Mass Movements,* 34, 1951

The vigor of a mass movement stems from the propensity of its followers for united action and self-sacrifice.

> ERIC HOFFER (1902–1983). *The True Believer: Thoughts on the Nature of Mass Movements,* 43, 1951

Mass movements can rise and spread without belief in a God, but never without belief in a devil.

> ERIC HOFFER (1902–1983). On the mass movement's need for hated enemies, or scapegoats, *The True Believer: Thoughts on the Nature of Mass Movements,* 65, 1951

The quality of ideas seems to play a minor role in mass-movement leadership. What counts is the arrogant gesture, the complete disregard of the opinion of others, the single-handed defiance of the world.

> ERIC HOFFER (1902–1983). *The True Believer: Thoughts on the Nature of Mass Movements,* 91, 1951

Mass movements do not usually rise until the prevailing order has been discredited.

> ERIC HOFFER (1902–1983). *The True Believer: Thoughts on the Nature of Mass Movements,* 104, 1951

A movement is pioneered by men of words, materialized by fanatics and consolidated by men of action.

> ERIC HOFFER (1902–1983). *The True Believer: Thoughts on the Nature of Mass Movements,* 113, 1951

The monarch or statesman who wishes to head off a popular movement can still do it infallibly by drawing a war across its path.

> GEORGE BERNARD SHAW (1856–1950). *Everybody's Political What's What?* 17, 1944

He who wishes to lead a movement must conduct a fight on two fronts—against those who lag behind and those who rush ahead.

> JOSEPH STALIN (1879–1953). In John Gunther, *Inside Europe,* rev. ed., 33 (epigraph), 1937 (1936)

A movement is only people moving.

> GLORIA STEINEM (19324–). In "How to Survive a Revolution," *Time,* 9 March 1992

A trifle might start a movement which the wisest could not explain nor the most powerful restrain.

> WILLIAM GRAHAM SUMNER (1840–1910). *Folkways: A Study of the Sociological Importance of Usages, Manners, Customs, Mores, and Morals,* 216, 1907

MASTURBATION

See also • Sex

Hey, don't knock masturbation! It's sex with someone I love.

> WOODY ALLEN (1935–) and MARSHALL BRICKMAN (1941–). *Annie Hall* (film), 1977

Six months ago, the surgeon general said we should teach masturbation in school. I said to myself, "Just my luck! Thirty years after I graduate, they think of something I could have made an A in."

> JAMES CARVILLE (1944–). In *Men's Journal.* Quoted in Leah Garchik, "Personals," *San Francisco Chronicle,* 20 November 1995

The one thing that it seems impossible to escape from, once the habit is formed, is masturbation. It goes on and on, on into old age, in spite of marriage or love affairs or anything else. And it always carries this secret feeling of futility and humiliation. And this is, perhaps, the deepest and most dangerous cancer of our civilization.

> D. H. LAWRENCE (1885–1930). "Pornography and Obscenity," 1930, *Phoenix: The Posthumous Papers of D. H. Lawrence,* ed. E. McDonald, 1936

Masturbation: the primary sexual activity of mankind. In the nineteenth century, it was a disease; in the twentieth, it's a cure.

> THOMAS S. SZASZ (1920–). "Sex," *The Second Sin,* 1973

✹

Onan knew that the offspring would not be his; so when he went in to his brother's wife he spilled the semen on the ground; lest he should give offspring to his brother. And what he did was displeasing in the sight of the Lord, and he slew him.

> ANONYMOUS (*BIBLE*). *Genesis* 38:9–10

MATERIALISM

See also • Consumerism ○ Idealism: [especially] Ralph Waldo Emerson ○ Possessions ○ Property ○ Success: Theodore Roosevelt ○ Values ○ Wealth

Materialism is decadent and degenerate only if the spirit of the nation has withered and if individual people are so unimaginative that they wallow in it.

> BROOKS ATKINSON (1894–1984). 22 January, *Once Around the Sun,* 1951

I would suggest to you that we are in the midst of what can only be called the climactic overthrow of the superstition of materialism.

> DEEPAK CHOPRA (1946–). Keynote address at the State of the World Forum, San Francisco, 28 September 1995

Materialism is the belief that if there are other things in life besides money, it takes money to buy them.

> EVAN ESAR (1899–1995). Comp., *20,000 Quips and Quotes,* p. 12, 1968

The cure for "materialism" is to have enough for everybody and to spare. When people are sure of having what they need they cease to think about it.

> HENRY FORD (1863–1947)

Our life on earth is, and ought to be, material and carnal. But we have not yet learned to manage our materialism and carnality properly; they are still entangled with the desire for ownership.

> E. M. FORSTER (1879–1970). "My Wood," *Abinger Harvest: A Miscellany,* 1927

Materialism as a doctrine emphasizes the primacy of material reality; economically, it emphasizes the motivating and controlling force of material production, goods, needs and profits.

CHERIS KRAMARAE (1938–) and PAULA A. TREICHLER. Comps., *A Feminist Dictionary: In Our Own Words,* p. 261, 1985

As against what we self-righteously condemn as the godless materialism of the Communists we seem to have dedicated ourselves to a godly materialism of our own.

ARTHUR M. SCHLESINGER, JR. (1917–). "The New Mood in Politics," 1960, *The Politics of Hope,* 1963

A way of life that bases itself on materialism, i.e., on permanent, limitless expansionism in a finite environment, cannot last long, and that its life expectation is the shorter the more successfully it pursues its expansionist objectives.

E. F. SCHUMACHER (1911–1977). *Small Is Beautiful: Economics as if People Mattered,* 4.5, 1973

The soul has wants which must be satisfied; and whatever pains are taken to divert it from itself, it soon grows weary, restless, and disquieted amid the enjoyments of sense. If ever the faculties of the great majority of mankind were exclusively bent on the pursuit of material objects, it might be anticipated than an amazing reaction would take place in the souls of some men. . . .

I should be surprised if mysticism did not soon make some advance among a people solely engaged in promoting their own worldly welfare.

ALEXIS de TOCQUEVILLE (1805–1859). *Democracy in America,* 2.2.12, 1840, tr. Henry Reeve and Francis Bowen, 1862

When we try in good faith to believe in materialism, in the exclusive reality of the physical, we are asking our selves to step aside; we are disavowing the very realm where we exist and where all things precious are kept—the realm of emotion and conscience; of memory and intention and sensation.

JOHN UPDIKE (1932–). *Self-Consciousness: Memoirs,* 6, 1989

MATHEMATICS

See also • Figures ∘ Numbers ∘ Science ∘ Statistics

If a man's wit be wandering, let him study the mathematics; for in demonstrations, if his wit be called away [ever] so little, he must begin again.

FRANCIS BACON (1561–1626). "Of Studies," *Essays,* 1625

Arithmetic is a certain and infallible Art.

THOMAS HOBBES (1588–1679). *Leviathan,* 5, 1651

From the intrinsic evidence of his creation, the Great Architect of the Universe now begins to appear as a pure mathematician.

SIR JAMES HOPWOOD JEANS (1877–1946). *The Mysterious Universe,* 5, 1930

Stand firm in your refusal to remain conscious during algebra. In real life, I assure you, there is no such thing as algebra.

FRAN LEBOWITZ (1951–). "Tips for Teens," *Social Studies,* 1981

I have hardly ever known a mathematician who was capable of reasoning.

PLATO (427?–347 B.C.). *The Republic,* 7.531, tr. Benjamin Jowett, 1894

Mathematics, rightly viewed, possesses not only truth, but supreme beauty—a beauty cold and austere, like that of sculpture, without appeal to any part of our weaker nature, without the gorgeous trappings of painting or music, yet sublimely pure, and capable of a stern perfection such as only the greatest art can show.

BERTRAND RUSSELL (1872–1970). "The Study of Mathematics," *Mysticism and Logic,* 1918

Mathematics is, I believe, the chief source of the belief in eternal and exact truth, as well as in a super-sensible intelligible world.

BERTRAND RUSSELL (1872–1970). *A History of Western Philosophy,* 1.1.3, 1946

The science of pure mathematics, in its modern developments, may claim to be the most original creation of the human spirit.

ALFRED NORTH WHITEHEAD (1861–1947). *Science and the Modern World,* 2, 1925

There is no sect in geometry.

VOLTAIRE (1694–1778). "Sect," *Philosophical Dictionary,* 1764, tr. Theodore Besterman, 1971

❧

Who knows not geometry, enter not here.

ANONYMOUS (GREEK). Inscription over the entrance to Plato's home. In Ralph Waldo Emerson, "Notebook Platoniana," p. 31, 1845–1848

MAXIMS

See also • Aphorisms ∘ Axioms ∘ Epigrams ∘ Principles, Moral ∘ Principles, Theoretical ∘ Proverbs ∘ Quotations ∘ Sayings ∘ Temperament: Benjamin Disraeli

A maxim [is] an equation in which the elements of the first term reappear in the second, but in a different order.

ALBERT CAMUS (1913–1960). "Chamfort," *Sewanee Review,* Winter 1948

[Chamfort's maxims] are sallies, flashes of insight, but not laws.

ALBERT CAMUS (1913–1960). "Chamfort," *Sewanee Review,* Winter 1948

We invent maxims to fill the holes in our own natures.

ALBERT CAMUS (1913–1960). Preface to *Lyrical and Critical Essays,* tr. Ellen Conroy Kennedy, 1968

Most maxim mongers have preferred the prettiness to the justness of a thought, and the turn to the truth.

LORD CHESTERFIELD (1694–1773). Letter to his son, 15 January 1753

It is far better for us to possess only a few maxims of philosophy that are nevertheless always at our command and in use than to acquire vast knowledge that notwithstanding serves no practical purpose.

DEMETRIUS (A.D. 1st cent.). As paraphrased by Seneca the Younger (5? B.C.–A.D. 65). "On Benefits" (7.1.3), *Moral Essays,* tr. John W. Basore, 1935

If we were perfectly enlightened, our moral books would contain only maxims, and our books on physics and spirituality would contain only axioms and facts. Everything else is clutter and shows no more than our gropings, our efforts, and our difficulties.

JOSEPH JOUBERT (1754–1824). 1796, *Pensées,* 1838, tr. Paul Auster, 1983

The reason for so much outcry against maxims that lay bare the human heart is that people are afraid of having their own laid bare.

LA ROCHEFOUCAULD (1613–1680). *Maxims,* 524, 1665, tr. Leonard Tancock, 1959

Every man who has seen the world knows that nothing is so useless as a general maxim.

THOMAS BABINGTON MACAULAY (1800–1859). "Machiavelli," *The Edinburgh Review* (Scotland), March 1827

All maxims have their antagonistic maxims; proverbs should be sold in pairs, a single one being but a half-truth.

WILLIAM MATHEWS

See Aphorisms: Karl Kraus (1)

These are the precepts that he must never let go, nay, must cling fast to, and make a part of himself, and by daily meditation reach the point where these wholesome maxims occur to him of their own accord, and are promptly at hand whenever they are desired, and the great distinction between base and honorable action presents itself without delay.

SENECA THE YOUNGER (5? B.C.–A.D. 65). "On Benefits" (7.2.1), *Moral Essays,* tr. John W. Basore, 1935

It is more trouble to make a maxim than it is to do right.

MARK TWAIN (1835–1910). *Following the Equator: A Journey Around the World,* 3 (epigraph), 1897

[Benjamin Franklin's] maxims were full of animosity toward boys. Nowadays a boy cannot follow out a single natural instinct without tumbling over some of those everlasting aphorisms and hearing from Franklin on the spot. . . . If he wants to spin his top when he has done work, his father quotes, "Procrastination is the thief of time." If he does a virtuous action, he never gets anything for it because "Virtue is its own reward." And that boy is hounded to death and robbed of his natural rest because Franklin said once, in one of his inspired flights of malignity:

Early to bed and early to rise
Makes a man healthy and wealthy and wise.

MARK TWAIN (1835–1910). "The Late Benjamin Franklin," *Sketches New and Old,* 1903

See Sleep: John Clarke

Men's maxims reveal their character.

VAUVENARGUES (1715–1747). *Reflections and Maxims,* 107, 1746, tr. F. G. Stevens, 1940

The maxims of the Gospel are exactly the opposite of those of the world.

ST. VINCENT de PAUL (1581–1660). In "Simplicity" (24), *Spiritual Diary: Selected Sayings and Examples of Saints,* 1775, St. Paul Editions, 1962

We are well enough aware that there are maxims to suit all tastes and tempers; that some affirm what others deny; that frequently they are direct contradictions. But this does not hinder us from adopting any one of them as a rule or motive or excuse for something we wish to do, or that we have done.

ANONYMOUS (AMERICAN). "Influence of Proverbs," *New York Times,* 29 April 1877

MEANING

See also • History: Abraham Joshua Heschel (2), Henry A. Kissinger (1) ○ Ideals ○ Life: [especially] Oliver Wendell Holmes, Jr. (3), W. Somerset Maugham ○ Principles, Moral ○ Purpose ○ Unity: Walter Lippmann (1) ○ Values

The world is not divine sport; it is divine destiny. There is divine meaning in the life of the world; of man, of human persons, of you and of me.

MARTIN BUBER (1878–1965). *I and Thou,* 3, 1923, tr. Ronald Gregor Smith, 1958

To look for a meaning in anything is less the act of a naif than of a masochist.

E. M. CIORAN (1911–1995). "Strangled Thoughts" (3), *The New Gods,* 1969, tr. Richard Howard, 1974

The moment a man questions the meaning and value of life, he is sick, since objectively neither has any existence.

SIGMUND FREUD (1856–1939). Letter to Marie Bonaparte, 13 August 1937, tr. Tania and James Stern, 1960

There is no meaning in life except the meaning man gives his life by the unfolding of his powers, by living productively. . . . Only constant vigilance, activity, and effort can keep us from failing in the one task that matters—the full development of our powers within the limitations set by the laws of our existence.

ERICH FROMM (1900–1980). *Man for Himself: An Inquiry into the Psychology of Ethics,* 3.1.B, 1947

If we do discover a complete [unified] theory [of the universe], it should in time be understandable in broad principle by everyone, not just a few scientists. Then we shall all, philosophers, scientists, and just ordinary people, be able to take part in the discussion of the question of why it is that we and the universe exist. If we find the answer to that, it would be the ultimate triumph of human reason—for then we should know the mind of God.

STEPHEN HAWKING (1942–). *A Brief History of Time: From the Big Bang to Black Holes,* 11, 1988

Life is not meaningful . . . unless it is serving an end beyond itself; unless it is of value to someone else.

ABRAHAM JOSHUA HESCHEL (1907–1972). *Man Is Not Alone: A Philosophy of Religion,* 19, 1951

To translate meaning into life . . . is to realize the Tao.

CARL G. JUNG (1875–1961). Appendix to *Commentary* to *The Secret of the Golden Flower,* 1929, tr. Cary F. Baynes, 1961

Life has to be given a meaning because of the obvious fact that it has no meaning.

HENRY MILLER (1891–1980). "Creative Death," *The Wisdom of the Heart,* 1941

Each life may have a significance which transcends the social process but not one which can be developed without reference to that process.

REINHOLD NIEBUHR (1892–1971). *Beyond Tragedy: Essays on the Christian Interpretation of History,* 15.2, 1938

Here we are in this wholly fantastic universe with scarcely a clue as to whether our existence has any real significance.

E. F. SCHUMACHER (1911–1977). *Small Is Beautiful: Economics as if People Mattered,* 2.1, 1973

The one possible way of giving meaning to [man's] existence is that of raising his natural relation to the world to a spiritual one.

ALBERT SCHWEITZER (1875–1965). *Out of My Life and Thought: An Autobiography,* 21, tr. C. T. Campion, 1933

The meaning of life consists in the love and service of God.

LEO TOLSTOY (1828–1910). *The Kingdom of God Is Within You,* 4, 1893, tr. Aylmer Maude, 1936

There is a land of the living and a land of the dead and the bridge is love, the only survival, the only meaning.

THORNTON WILDER (1897–1975). Closing words, *The Bridge of San Luis Rey,* 1927

To believe in God means to see that life has a meaning.

LUDWIG WITTGENSTEIN (1889–1951). 8 July 1916, *Notebooks, 1914–1916,* ed. G. E. M. Anscombe, 1961

MEANS & ENDS

See also • Cause & Effect ○ Goals ○ Insanity: Ralph Waldo Emerson ○ Morality ○ Purpose ○ Revolutionaries: Aldous Huxley, John Keep ○ Wisdom: Lord Bolingbroke, Francis Hutcheson

The history of all the world tells us that immoral means will ever intercept good ends.

SAMUEL TAYLOR COLERIDGE (1772–1834). 8 May 1830, *Table Talk,* 1835

Imagine that you are creating a fabric of human destiny with the object of making men happy in the end, giving them peace and rest at last. Imagine that you are doing this but that it is essential and inevitable to torture to death only one tiny creature . . . in order to found that edifice on its unavenged tears. Would you consent to be the architect on those conditions?

FYODOR DOSTOYEVSKY (1821–1881). *The Brothers Karamazov,* 5.4, 1880, tr. Constance Garnett, 1912

Perfection of means and confusion of goals seem—in my opinion—to characterize our age.

ALBERT EINSTEIN (1879–1955). Broadcast recording for the Science Conference, London, 28 September 1941, *Out of My Later Years,* rev. ed., 15, 1956 (1950)

Most of the great results of history are brought about by discreditable means.

RALPH WALDO EMERSON (1803–1882). "Considerations by the Way," *The Conduct of Life,* 1860

As the means, so the end.

MOHANDAS K. GANDHI (1869–19478). In *Young India,* 17 July 1924

If one takes care of the means, the end will take care of itself.

MOHANDAS K. GANDHI (1869–1948). In *Harijan,* 6 February 1939
See Thrift: Saying (English) (2)

Means and ends are convertible terms in my philosophy of life.

MOHANDAS K. GANDHI (1869–1948). In John Gunther, *Procession,* 9, 1965

Act so that you treat humanity, whether in your own person or in that of another, always as an end and never as a means only.

IMMANUEL KANT (1724–1804). *Foundations of the Metaphysics of Morals,* 2, 1797, tr. Lewis White Beck, 1969

I have tried to make it clear that it is wrong to use immoral means to attain moral ends. But now I must affirm that it is just as wrong, or even more so, to use moral means to preserve immoral ends.

MARTIN LUTHER KING, JR. (1929–1968). "Letter from Birmingham City Jail," 16 April 1963

Immoral means cannot bring moral ends, for the ends are pre-existent in the means.

MARTIN LUTHER KING, JR. (1929–1968). *Strength to Love,* 12.1, 1963

Let us diligently apply the means, never doubting that a just God, in his own good time, will give us the rightful result.

ABRAHAM LINCOLN (1809–1865). Closing words, letter to James C. Conkling, 26 August 1863

In the actions of men . . . the end justifies the means.

MACHIAVELLI (1469–1527). *The Prince,* 18, 1513, tr. Luigi Ricci, 1903
See Machiavellianism: Machiavelli (7)

Captain Ahab: All my means are sane, my motive and object mad.

HERMAN MELVILLE (1819–1891). *Moby-Dick; or, The Whale,* 41, 1851, ed. Harold Beaver, 1972

The evil means men use in our day to push themselves show clearly that the end is not worth much.

MONTAIGNE (1533–1592). "Of Solitude," *Essays,* 1588, tr. Donald M. Frame, 1958

The end in view selectively controls and orders the sequence that brings about its accomplishment; and the better that end is interpreted, the more direct the voyage is likely to be. Organic activities create their own occasions, instead of being entirely at the mercy of nature's offerings.

LEWIS MUMFORD (1895–1990). *The Transformations of Man,* 9.4, 1956

The ends and means are a seamless web.

GLORIA STEINEM (1934–). "Doing Sixty," *Moving Beyond Words,* 1994

Means have no merit, if our end amiss.
If wrong our hearts, our heads are right in vain.

EDWARD YOUNG (1683–1765). *The Complaint: or, Night Thoughts on Life, Death, and Immortality,* 6.280, 1742–1745

✻

When means can't be adjusted to ends, ends must be adjusted to means.

ANONYMOUS

If the wrong man uses the right means, the right means work in the wrong way.

SAYING (CHINESE). In Carl G. Jung, introduction (1) to *Commentary* to *The Secret of the Golden Flower,* 1929, tr. Cary F. Baynes, 1961

The means justifies the end.

SAYING

MEDIA

See also • Advertising ○ Art ○ Books ○ Censorship ○ Critics ○ Editors ○ Films ○ Freedom of Speech ○ Freedom of the Press ○ Indoctrination ○ Language, Political ○ Journalism ○ Journalists ○ Magazines ○ News ○ Newspapers ○ Newspeak ○ Photography ○ The Press ○ Propaganda ○ Public Opinion ○ Public Relations ○ Publishers ○ Radio ○ Right to Privacy ○ Television ○ Theater

The structure is the message.

> BEN H. BAGDIKIAN (1920–). Referring to ownership concentration in the media, appearing on *MacNeil/Lehrer Newshour,* television news program, PBS, 20 June 1989

There are good reasons why everybody should heed politicians' advice not to believe the media. One of the best is that the media report what politicians say.

> RUSSELL BAKER (1925–). Opening paragraph, "Mugged by Facts," *New York Times,* 25 August 1992

The media, while they won't admit it, are not in the news business; they're in entertainment. We tried to create the most entertaining, visually attractive scenes to fill that box, so that the networks would have to use it.

> MICHAEL DEAVER (1938–). Presidential assistant to Ronald Reagan. In Timothy J. Russert, "For '92, the Networks Have to Do Better," *New York Times,* 4 March 1990

The message of the media is the commercial.

> ALICE EMBREE. "Media Images I: Madison Avenue Brainwashing— The Facts." In Robin Morgan, ed., *Sisterhood Is Powerful: An Anthology of Writings from the Women's Liberation Movement,* 1970

The dependence upon corporate advertising of the mass media— newspapers, magazines, radio and television—makes them editorially subservient, without in any way being prompted, to points of view known or thought to be favored by the big property owners. . . . The willing subservience shows itself most generally, apart from specific acts of omission or commission, in an easy blandness on the part of the mass media toward serious social problems.

> FERDINAND LUNDBERG (1902–1995). *The Rich and the Super-Rich: A Study in the Power of Money Today,* 4, 1968

"The Medium Is the Message."

> MARSHALL McLUHAN (1911–1980). Chapter title, *Understanding Media: The Extensions of Man,* 1, 1964

The mass production of distraction is now as much a part of the American way of life as the mass production of automobiles.

> C. WRIGHT MILLS (1916–1962). 1953, *Power, Politics and People: The Collected Essays of C. Wright Mills,* 3.8.2, ed. Irving Louis Horowitz, 1963

The media make you into a god, and then they kill you.

> RICHARD RUTOWSKI. In Jaime Wolf, "Oliver Stone Doesn't Want to Start an Argument," *New York Times Magazine,* 21 September 1997

In the land of the media, whether it is movies, magazines or TV, Daddy always goes to the office, not to the factory.

> FLOYD SMITH. International Association of Machinists president. In "The Blue-Collar Worker's Low-Down Blues," *Time,* 9 November 1970

[The media's] selection and description of particular events—far more than their editorials—help to create or promote national issues, to shape the minds of the Congress and public, and to influence the President's agenda and timing.

> THEODORE C. SORENSEN (1928–). Presidential assistant to John F. Kennedy. *Decision-Making in the White House: The Olive Branch or the Arrows,* 4, 1963

Newspapers, magazines, colleges, and all forms of government and religion express the superficial activity of a few, the mass either conforming or not attending.

> HENRY DAVID THOREAU (1817–1862). Journal, 9 August 1858

The media celebrities who modestly claim only to report the news are clearly its arbiters now. Corporate conglomerates have taken over the news business. Television has taken over the role that party bosses once played in selecting political candidates and issues. Producers and their telegenic news superstars define the issues for the public and decide who does and does not get to speak to them. The commentators tell us what reasonable people should think about the issues, and then they take another poll to see what we think about what they have told us. Right on cue, the eager politicians, along with their own pollsters and "spin doctors," take the results and announce their positions on the major questions of our public life.

This closed system of media-oriented political entertainment continually preempts genuine public dialogue and debate about the issues that most affect people's lives and the character of the nation.

> JIM WALLIS (1948–). *The Soul of Politics: A Practical and Prophetic Vision for Change,* 1, 1994

MEDIOCRITY

See also • Conformity ○ Democracy, Anti-: James Fenimore Cooper (1) ○ Normality ○ Words: Arthur Schopenhauer

Mediocre people have an answer for everything and are astonished at nothing.

> EUGÈNE DELACROIX (1798–1863). Journal, 25 February 1852, tr. Walter Pach, 1937

Mediocrity knows nothing higher than itself.

> SIR ARTHUR CONAN DOYLE (1859–1930). *The Valley of Fear,* 1, 1915

The mediocre always feel as if they're fighting for their lives when confronted by the excellent.

> MARIE von EBNER-ESCHENBACH (1830–1916). *Aphorisms,* p. 83, 1880–1905, tr. David Scrase and Wolfgang Mieder, 1994

Mediocrity obtains more with application than superiority without it.

> BALTASAR GRACIÁN (1601–1658). *The Art of Worldly Wisdom,* 18, 1647, tr. Joseph Jacobs, 1943

Some men are born mediocre, some men achieve mediocrity, and some men have mediocrity thrust upon them. With Major Major it had been all three. Even among men lacking all distinction he inevitably stood out as a man lacking more distinction than all the rest, and people who met him were always impressed by how unimpressive he was.

> JOSEPH HELLER (1923–). *Catch-22*, 9, 1961
>
> See Greatness: Shakespeare (2)

Mediocre minds are always jealous and inclined to surround themselves with persons of little ability.

> HENRI de JOMINI (1779–1869). *Summary of the Art of War*, 2, 1807, ed. J. D. Hittle, 1947
>
> See Managers: Leo Rosten

Mediocrity is excellence to the mediocre.

> JOSEPH JOUBERT (1754–1824). *Pensées*, 1838, tr. H. P. Collins, 1928

So many have used their oppression as an excuse for mediocrity.

> MARTIN LUTHER KING, JR. (1929–1968). "The Rising Tide of Racial Consciousness," speech at the Golden Anniversary Conference of the National Urban League, *YWCA Magazine*, December 1960

Only a mediocre person is always at his best.

> W. SOMERSET MAUGHAM (1874–1965). In Laurence J. Peter, *The Peter Prescription: How to Make Things Go Right*, 3, 1972

Where unkind Nature . . . unequally yokes lofty objects in a man with a short mental reach, she stamps him with the very definition of mediocrity.

> JOHN MORLEY (1838–1923). "Robespierre" (2), *Critical Miscellanies*, vol. 1, 1886

Nothing is good but mediocrity. The majority has settled that, and finds fault with him who escapes it at whichever end. . . . To leave the mean is to abandon humanity.

> BLAISE PASCAL (1623–1662). *Pensées*, 378, 1670, tr. William F. Trotter, 1931

Gregariousness is always the refuge of mediocrities.

> BORIS PASTERNAK (1890–1960). *Doctor Zhivago*, 1.5, 1957, tr. Max Hayward and Manya Harari, 1958
>
> See Patriotism: Samuel Johnson

Indifference is the revenge the world take on mediocrities.

> OSCAR WILDE (1854–1900). *Vera, or The Nihilists*, 1883

Ernest Harrowden, one of those middle-aged mediocrities so common in London clubs who have no enemies, but are thoroughly disliked by their friends.

> OSCAR WILDE (1854–1900). *The Picture of Dorian Gray*, 14, 1891

✵

Mediocrity loves company.

> ANONYMOUS
>
> See Misery: Saying (English)

Mediocrity tends to draw downward what is up but not upward what is down.

> ANONYMOUS

MEDITATION

See also • Books: Thomas Fuller (2) ○ Contemplation ○ Mysticism ○ Religion ○ Self ○ Silence ○ Soul ○ Spirituality ○ Wisdom: Publius Syrus ○ Yoga ○ Zen

The art of meditation may be exercised at all hours and in all places; and men of genius, in their walks, at table, and amidst assemblies, turning the eye of the mind inwards, can form an artificial solitude; retired amidst a crowd, calm amidst distraction, and wise amidst folly.

> ISAAC D'ISRAELI (1766–1848). *Literary Character of Men of Genius, Drawn from Their Own Feelings and Confessions*, 11, 1795

To meditate is to observe simultaneously the formation of thought and breath, and then let it go, without complicating it, without formalizing it, without identifying with it, without rejecting it, letting it follow its own way.

> ALLEN GINSBERG (1926–1997). Jean-Jacques Lebel interview, *Le Monde*, 1 June 1979, quoted by Lawrence Ferlinghetti, Lebel interview, *The Populist Manifestos*, 1981

Zen meditation does not mean sitting and thinking. On the contrary, it means acting with as little thought as possible. The fencing master trained his pupil to guard against every attack with the same immediate, instinctive rapidity with which our eyelid closes over our eye when something threatens it. His work is aimed at breaking down the wall between thought and act, at completely fusing body and senses and mind so that they might all work together rapidly and effortlessly.

> GILBERT HIGHET (1906–). *Talents and Geniuses*, 1957

[Meditation is] the cultivation of resistance, of exclusive concentration on an idea of our choice. . . . Instead of creating resistance, why not go into each interest as it arises and not merely concentrate on one idea, one interest?

> KRISHNAMURTI (1895–1986). In Aldous Huxley, "The Education of an Amphibian," *Tomorrow and Tomorrow and Tomorrow*, 1956

Without laying the foundation of a righteous life, meditation becomes an escape and therefore has no value whatever.

> KRISHNAMURTI (1895–1986). *Meditations*, p. 6, 1979, Shambhala Publications edition, 1991
>
> See Mysticism: Aldous Huxley (2)

Meditation is the breeze that comes in when you leave the window open; but if you deliberately keep it open, deliberately invite it to come, it will never appear.

> KRISHNAMURTI (1895–1986). *Meditations*, p. 14, 1979, Shambhala Publications edition, 1991

Meditation is the action of silence.

> KRISHNAMURTI (1895–1986). *Meditations*, p. 75, 1979, Shambhala Publications edition, 1991

The gift of learning to meditate is the greatest gift you can give yourself in this life. For it is only through meditation that you can undertake the journey to discover your true nature, and so find the stability and confidence you will need to live, and die, well. Meditation is the road to enlightenment.

> SOGYAL RINPOCHE. *The Tibetan Book of Living and Dying*, 5, 1992

In the ancient meditation instructions, it is said that at the beginning thoughts will arrive one on top of another, uninterrupted, like a steep mountain waterfall. Gradually, as you perfect meditation, thoughts become like the water in a deep, narrow gorge, then a great river slowly winding its way down to the sea, and finally the mind becomes like a still and placid ocean, ruffled by only the occasional ripple or wave.

> SOGYAL RINPOCHE). *The Tibetan Book of Living and Dying*, 5, 1992

Everything can be used as an invitation to meditation. A smile, a face in the subway, the sight of a small flower growing in the crack of a cement pavement, a fall of rich cloth in a shop window, the way the sun lights up flower pots on a window sill. Be alert for any sign of beauty or grace. Offer up every joy, be awake at all moments, to "the news that is always arriving out of silence" (Rainer Maria Rilke).

> SOGYAL RINPOCHE. T*he Tibetan Book of Living and Dying*, 5, 1992

Wisdom is intuitive knowledge of the mind of love and clarity that lies beneath one's ego-driven anxieties and aggressions. Meditation is going into the mind to see this for yourself—over and over again, until it becomes the mind you live in. Morality is bringing it back out in the way you live, through personal example and responsible action, ultimately toward the true community (sangha) of "all beings."

> GARY SNYDER (1930–). "Buddhism and the Coming Revolution," *Earth House Hold: Technical Notes & Queries to Fellow Dharma Revolutionaries*, 1969

❧

Business before pleasure, pleasure before study, study before reflection, reflection before meditation.

> ANONYMOUS

MEETINGS

See also • Bureaucracy ○ Committees ○ Decision-Making ○ Organizations

Never let the other fellow set the agenda.

> JAMES BAKER (1930–). Secretary of state. In *Daily Telegraph*, British newspaper, 15 November 1988

Meetings are by definition a concession to deficient organization. For one either meets or one works. One cannot do both at the same time. In an ideally designed structure . . . there would be no meetings.

> PETER F. DRUCKER (1909–). *The Effective Executive*, 2.3.3, 1967

Too many meetings signify that work that should be in one job or in one component is spread over several jobs or several components.

> PETER F. DRUCKER (1909–). *The Effective Executive*, 2.3.3, 1967

The effective man always states at the outset of a meeting the specific purpose and contribution it is to achieve. . . . He always, at the end of his meetings, goes back to the opening statement and relates the final conclusions to the original intent.

> PETER F. DRUCKER (1909–). *The Effective Executive*, 3.4, 1967

[Meetings] are indispensable when you don't want to do anything.

> JOHN KENNETH GALBRAITH (1908–). 22 April 1961, *Ambassador's Journal: A Personal Account of the Kennedy Years*, 5, 1969

The efficiency of a committee meeting is inversely proportional to the number of participants and the time spent on deliberations.

> OLD AND KAHN'S LAW). In Arthur Bloch, comp., "Committology," *Murphy's Law: And Other Reasons Why Things Go gnorW*, 1979

The Law of Triviality . . . means that the time spent on any item of the agenda will be in inverse proportion to the sum [of money] involved.

> C. NORTHCOTE PARKINSON (1909–1993). *Parkinson's Law and Other Studies in Administration*, 3, 1957

Say as little as possible while appearing to be awake.

> WILLIAM P. ROGERS (1913–). Secretary of state. On attending meetings

International Conferences: Social functions at which statesmen who know that something is wrong agree that nothing can be done about it.

> LEO ROSTEN (1908–1997). "Political Lexicon," *New Republic*, 3 July 1935

The interaction of many minds is usually more illuminating than the intuition of one.

> THEODORE C. SORENSEN (1928–). Citing an important advantage of meetings. *Decision-Making in the White House: The Olive Branch or the Arrows*, 5, 1963

MELANCHOLY

See also • Depression ○ Mental Illness

I never knu a man trubbled with melankolly, who had plenty to dew, and did it.

> JOSH BILLINGS (1818–1885). "Puddin and Milk," *Everybody's Friend, or; Josh Billing's Encyclopedia and Proverbial Philosophy of Wit and Humor*, 1874

All other joys to this are folly,
None so sweet as melancholy. . . .
All my griefs to this are jolly,
None so damn'd as melancholy.

> ROBERT BURTON (1577–1640). "The Author's Abstract of Melancholy," *The Anatomy of Melancholy*, 1621–1651

I write of melancholy, by being busy to avoid melancholy. There is no greater cause of melancholy than idleness, "no better cure than business," as Rhasis holds.

> ROBERT BURTON (1577–1640). "Democritus to the Reader," *The Anatomy of Melancholy*, 1621–1651

If there be a hell upon earth, it is to be found in a melancholy man's heart.

> ROBERT BURTON (1577–1640). *The Anatomy of Melancholy*, 1.4.1, 1621–1651

He's a Fool that is not melancholy once a Day.

> THOMAS FULLER 1654–1734). Comp., *Gnomologia: Adages and Proverbs*, 2434, 1732

My character passes from extreme joy to extreme melancholy.
> GOETHE (1749–1832). In Cesare Lombroso, *The Man of Genius,* 1.3, 1888, ed. Havelock Ellis, 1896

Melancholy has ceased to be an individual phenomenon, an exception. It has become the class privilege of the wage earner, a mass state of mind that finds its cause wherever life is governed by production quotas.
> GÜNTHER GRASS (1927–). "On Stasis in Progress," *From the Diary of a Snail,* 1972

Riches beget riches, poverty poverty; melancholy reflection!
> FULKE GREVILLE (1554–1628). *Maxims, Characters, and Reflections,* p. 91, 1756

[A] chronic melancholy . . . is taking hold of the civilized races with the decline of belief in a beneficent power.
> THOMAS HARDY (1840–1928). *Tess of the D'Urbervilles,* 18, 1891

[Abraham Lincoln] was a sad-looking man; his melancholy dripped from him as he walked. His apparent gloom impressed his friends, and created sympathy for him—one means of his great success. He was gloomy, abstracted, and joyous—rather humorous—by turns; but I do not think he knew what real joy was for many years.
> WILLIAM H. HERNDON (1818–1891) and JESSE W. WEIK (1857–1930). *Herndon's Lincoln: The True Story of a Great Life,* 20, 1889, Premier Books edition, 1961

Melancholy, indeed, should be diverted by every means but drinking.
> SAMUEL JOHNSON (1709–1784). 28 March 1776. In James Boswell, *The Life of Samuel Johnson,* 1791

Employment, Sir, and hardships prevent melancholy.
> SAMUEL JOHNSON (1709–1784). 20 September 1777. In James Boswell, *The Life of Samuel Johnson,* 1791

But hail thou Goddess, sage and holy,
Hail divinest Melancholy.
> JOHN MILTON (1608–1674). "Il Penseroso," l. 11, 1631?

Go—you may call it madness, folly;
You shall not chase my gloom away.
There's such a charm in melancholy,
I would not, if I could, be gay.
> SAMUEL ROGERS (1763–1855). "To—, 1814"

Never give way to melancholy; resist it steadily, for the habit will encroach. I once gave a lady two-and-twenty recipes against melancholy: one was a bright fire; another, to remember all the pleasant things said to and of her; another, to keep a box of sugarplums on the chimney piece, and a kettle simmering on the hob.
> SYDNEY SMITH (1771–1845). *The Wit and Wisdom of Sydney Smith,* p. 396, undated

From the first
Having two natures in me, joy the one
The other melancholy.
> WILLIAM WORDSWORTH (1770–1850). *The Prelude; or, Growth of a Poet's Mind; An Autobiographical Poem* (1805–1806 version), 10.868, 1850

MEMOIRS

See also • Autobiography ○ Biography ○ Books ○ Journals ○ Writing

Men rarely write memoirs to make themselves contemptible in the eyes of posterity.
> CRANE BRINTON (1898–1968). *The Lives of Talleyrand,* 2, 1936

Memoirs are the most unreliable source of historical evidence. Events are always distorted by refraction through the writer's ego.
> FELIX FRANKFURTER (1882–1965). In Geoffrey C. Ward, "LBJ's Alter Ego," *American Heritage,* February 1989

A memoir is how one remembers one's own life, while an autobiography is history, requiring research, dates, facts double-checked.
> GORE VIDAL (1925–). *Palimpsest,* 1995. In Michael Wood, "Selective Memory," *New York Times Book Review,* 8 October 1995

MEMORY

See also • Age & Youth: Samuel Johnson ○ Intelligence ○ Judgment ○ Mind ○ Reason

In the memory everything is preserved separately, according to its category.
> ST. AUGUSTINE (A.D. 354–430). *Confessions,* 10.8, A.D. 400?, tr. R. S. Pine-Coffin, 1961

It isn't so astonishing, the number of things that I can remember, as the number of things I can remember that aren't so.
> JOSH BILLINGS (1818–1885). As paraphrased by Mark Twain. In Albert Bigelow Paine, *Mark Twain: A Biography,* 3.1269, 1912

Except by physical damage to the brain there is no evidence that any memory of any significance can be wholly destroyed, although it can be repressed.
> J. A. C. BROWN (1911–1964). *Techniques of Persuasion: From Propaganda to Brainwashing,* 10, 1963

Intelligence may be the pride—the towering distinction of man; emotion gives color and force to his actions; but memory is the bastion of his being. Without memory, there is no personal identity, there is no continuity to the days of his life. Memory provides the raw material for designs both small and great. Thus, governed and enriched by memory, all the enterprises of man go forward.
> D. EWEN CAMERON (1901–1967). "The Process of Remembering," *British Journal of Psychiatry,* May 1963

It is the sublime miracle of the human mind: memory.
> ELIAS CANETTI (1905–1994). 1984, *The Secret Heart of the Clock: Notes, Aphorisms, Fragments: 1973–1985,* tr. Joel Agee, 1989

I remember things the way they should have been.
> TRUMAN CAPOTE (1924–1984). Remark to Donald Windham. In Julie Baumgold, "Unanswered Prayers. Part II: The Magical Drape," *New York,* 26 November 1984

"It's a poor sort of memory that only works backwards," the Queen remarked.
> LEWIS CARROLL (1832–1898). *Through the Looking-Glass and What Alice Found There,* 5, 1872

After the manner of the Pythagoreans—to keep my memory in working order—I repeat in the evening whatever I have said, heard, or done in the course of each day.

> CICERO (106–43 B.C.). At age 84, *De senectute,* 11, tr. E. S. Shuckburgh, 1900

Vanity plays lurid tricks with our memory.

> JOSEPH CONRAD (1857–1924). *Lord Jim,* 41, 1900

Of all the million images that are imprinted, the very one we want reappears in the center of the plate in the moment when we want it.

> RALPH WALDO EMERSON (1803–1882). "Memory," *Natural History of Intellect and Other Papers,* 1893

We estimate a man by how much he remembers.

> RALPH WALDO EMERSON (1803–1882). "Memory," *Natural History of Intellect and Other Papers,* 1893

Method is mother of memory.

> THOMAS FULLER (1608–1661)

The memory of all that—
No, No! They can't take that away from me.

> IRA GERSHWIN (1896–1983). "The Can't Take That Away from Me" (song). In the musical *Shall We Dance?* 1937

O Memory! thou fond deceiver.

> OLIVER GOLDSMITH (1728–1774). *The Captivity: An Oratorio,* 1, 1764

We cannot afford to forget any experience, not even the most painful.

> DAG HAMMARSKJÖLD (1905–1961). 1951, *Markings,* tr. Leif Sjöberg and W. H. Auden, 1964

Memory is the primary and fundamental power, without which there could be no other intellectual operation.

> SAMUEL JOHNSON (1709–1784). In *The Idler* (English journal), 44, 17 February 1759

Everybody complains of his memory, but nobody of his judgment.

> LA ROCHEFOUCAULD (1613–1680). *Maxims,* 89, 1665, tr. Leonard Tancock, 1959

I have proved in my own case that it is of no small benefit on finding oneself in bed in the dark to go over again in the imagination the main outlines of the forms previously studied, or of other noteworthy things conceived by ingenious speculation; and this exercise is entirely to be commended, and it is useful in fixing things in the memory.

> LEONARDO da VINCI (1452–1519). *Note-books,* 3, tr. Edward McCurdy, 1908

I am slow to learn and slow to forget that which I have learned. My mind is like a piece of steel—very hard to scratch anything on it, and almost impossible after you get it there to rub it out.

> ABRAHAM LINCOLN (1809–1865). Quoted by Joshua F. Speed, letter to the author, 6 December 1866. In William H. Herndon (and Jesse W. Weik), *Herndon's Lincoln: The True Story of a Great Life,* 18, 1889, Premier Books edition, 1961

Memory is a wonderfully useful tool, and without it judgment does its work with difficulty.

> MONTAIGNE (1533–1592). "Of Presumption," *Essays,* 1588, tr. Donald M. Frame, 1958

Oft, in the stilly night
Ere Slumber's chain has bound me,
Fond Memory brings the light
Of other days around me.

> THOMAS MOORE (1779–1852). "Oft in the Stilly Night," *National Airs,* 1815

The advantage of a bad memory is that, several times over, one enjoys the same good things for the first time.

> FRIEDRICH NIETZSCHE (1844–1900). *Human, All Too Human,* 580, 1878, tr. Marion Faber, 1984

A good memory constitutes about seventy per cent of what commonly passes for genius.

> HESKETH PEARSON (1887–1964). *Oscar Wilde: His Life and Wit,* 13, 1946

A people's memory is history; and a man without a memory, like a people without a history, cannot grow wiser, better.

> ISAAC LEIBUSH PERETZ (1851–1915). Vegn Geshichte, 1890

Memory may be rendered duller or more retentive by the condition of the body.

> QUINTILIAN (A.D. 35?–100?). *Institutio oratoria,* 11.2.4, tr. John Selby Watson, 1856

Nothing is so much strengthened by practice, or weakened by neglect, as memory.

> QUINTILIAN (A.D. 35?–100?). *Institutio oratoria,* 11.2.40, tr. John Selby Watson, 1856

People tend to remember best the things they have felt most deeply.

> DAVID RIESMAN (1909–). "Books: Gunpowder of the Mind," *Atlantic,* December 1957

"Thanks for the Memory."

> LEO ROBIN (1899–1984) and RALPH RAINTER. Song title (Bob Hope's theme song), 1937

The truth is—and it's merciful—that in memory, humiliations and failures tend to vanish and successes are magnified.

> BERTRAND RUSSELL (1872–1970). Tommy Robbins interview, *Redbook,* September 1964

The memory of an old man gets clearer and clearer, the further it goes back.

> ARTHUR SCHOPENHAUER (1788–1860). "Religion and Other Essays: Psychological Observations," *Essays of Arthur Schopenhauer,* tr. T. Bailey Saunders, 1851

Our memories are independent of our wills. It is not so easy to forget.

> RICHARD SHERIDAN (1751–1816). *The Rivals,* 1.2, 1775

A man's real possession is his memory. In nothing else is he rich, in nothing else is he poor.

> ALEXANDER SMITH (1830–1867). *Dreamthorp,* 3, 1863

Memory, the mother of the Muses.

> SOCRATES (470?–399 B.C.). In Plato (427?–347 B.C.), *Theaetetus,* 191, tr. Benjamin Jowett, 1894

I sometimes worry about my short attention span, but not for very long.

> STRANGE de JIM. In Herb Caen, column, *San Francisco Chronicle,* 10 February 1974

It is so hard to forget what it is worse than useless to remember!

> HENRY DAVID THOREAU (1817–1862). "Life Without Principle," *Atlantic,* October 1863

If there is a single theme that dominates all my writings, all my obsessions, it is that of memory—because I fear forgetfulness as much as hatred and death.

> ELI WIESEL (1928–). Preface to *From the Kingdom of Memory: Reminiscences,* 1990

Memory . . . is the diary that we all carry about with us.

> OSCAR WILDE (1854–1900). *The Importance of Being Earnest,* 2, 1895

✹

Memory, *n.* The truest indicator of raw intelligence.

> ANONYMOUS

MEN

See also • Man ○ Mankind ○ Misogynous Statements ○ Sex ○ Sexism ○ Sexist Statements ○ Society ○ Women ○ Women & Men

Men may be known six different ways, viz.—1. by their countenances; 2. their words; 3. their actions; 4. their tempers; 5. their ends; and, 6. by the relation of others.

> FRANCIS BACON (1561–1626). *Advancement of Learning,* 8.2, 1605, Willey Book edition, 1944

There are more things in men to admire than to despise.

> ALBERT CAMUS (1913–1960). 9 March 1943, *Notebooks: 1942–1951,* tr. Justin O'Brien, 1966

The better I get to know men, the more I find myself loving dogs.

> CHARLES de GAULLE (1890–1970). "Some General Comments, *Entre Nous . . . ,*" *Time,* 8 December 1967

Men are but children of a larger growth;
Our appetites as apt to change as theirs,
And full as craving too, and full as vain.

> JOHN DRYDEN (1631–1700). *All for Love,* 4.1, 1678

Men are the poetry of God.

> RALPH WALDO EMERSON (1803–1882). "Notebook F No. 1," p. 43, 1836–1840

Men walk as prophecies of the next age.

> RALPH WALDO EMERSON (1803–1882). "Circles," *Essays: First Series,* 1841

Men are naturally benevolent as well as selfish.

> BENJAMIN FRANKLIN (1706–1790). In Michael Zuckerman, "And in the Center Ring . . . ," *Pennsylvania Gazette,* May 1993

The state of peace among men living side by side is not the natural state; the natural state is one of war.

> IMMANUEL KANT (1724–1804). "Perpetual Peace" (2), 1795, *On History,* ed. Lewis White Beck, 1963

Most men become men at the cost of a certain innate decency.

> NORMAN MAILER (1923–). "Norman Mailer: Stormin' No More," *San Francisco Sunday Examiner & Chronicle,* 24 November 1991

Men are like ciphers: they acquire their value merely from their position.

> NAPOLEON (1769–1821). Remark to L. F. J. de Bausset, 1800s. *The Mind of Napoleon: A Selection from His Written and Spoken Words,* 8, ed. J. Christopher Herold, 1955

There are three classes of men—lovers of wisdom, lovers of honor, lovers of gain.

> PLATO (427?–347 B.C.). *The Republic,* 9.581, tr. Benjamin Jowett, 1894

MEN & WOMEN

See • Women & Men

MENTAL HOSPITALS

See also • Psychiatry

Psychiatric hospitals, like prisons, are "total institutions," and share with the Chinese thought-reform centers a marked degree of milieu control and the basic assumption that the inmate is in the hospital because there is something wrong with his thinking and that change, in the direction desired by his attendants, is necessary.

> DANIEL BLAIN (1898–?) et al. In Sylvano Arieti, ed., *American Handbook of Psychiatry,* 3.393, 1966

[McLean Hospital is a] Bastille for the incarceration of some persons obnoxious to their relatives.

> *BOSTON TIMES MESSENGER.* 1865. In Norman Dain, *Concepts of Insanity in the United States, 1789–1865,* 1964

Modern mental hospitals, where every method of control has been euphemistically renamed, can be frightening places. The actions of every staff member—the aide who holds a patient down, the nurse who injects the medication, the doctor who prescribes it—all have been defined as benevolent. Patients who dare to utter the unauthorized reality—that they are prisoners and that their "helpers" are jailers—only provide further evidence that they are indeed ill. Succumbing to brainwashing, accepting reality as defined by one's captors, differs from a psychiatric "cure" only because in the latter case the accepted reality is the prevailing one. Holding a minority position makes a person a potential subject for psychiatric brainwashing.

> JUDI CHAMBERLIN (1944–). *On Our Own: Patient-Controlled Alternatives to the Mental Health System,* 5, 1978

The male "incontinent ward" [in Pennsylvania's Philadelphia State Hospital] was like a scene out of Dante's *Inferno.* Three hundred nude men stood, squatted and sprawled in this bare room amid shrieks, groans, and unearthly laughter. These represented the most deteriorated patients. Winter or summer, these creatures never were given any clothing at all. Some lay about on the floor in their own excreta. The filth-covered walls and floors were rotting away. Could a truly civilized community permit humans to be reduced to such animal-like level?

> ALBERT DEUTSCH (1905–1961). *The Shame of the States,* 4, 1948

All physicians who have habitually the cure of insane persons have recommended their seclusion [i.e., hospitalization] in almost every case as the most essential condition and one of the first measures to be adopted in their treatment. . . . As long as the disease continues, they are angry with those who have deprived them of their liberty; but as soon as they have recovered their reason, resentment is changed into gratitude.

> ÉTIENNE GEORGET (1795–1828). In James Cowles Prichard, *A Treatise on Insanity*, pp. 208–209, 1837

After being subjected to a degradation ceremonial known as psychiatric examination, [the patient] is bereft of his civil liberties in being imprisoned in a total institution known as a "mental" hospital. More completely, more radically than anywhere else in our society, he is invalidated as a human being.

> R. D. LAING (1927–1989). British psychiatrist. *The Politics of Experience*, 5, 1967

The best therapeutic approach is often to provide a supportive environment in which the patient's experiences are allowed to unfold. . . . Instead of mental hospitals, we need initiation ceremonies in which the person will be guided through inner space by people who have been there and back again.

> R. D. LAING (1927–1989). Slightly modified. Remarks to the author, April 1978. In Fritjof Capra, *Uncommon Wisdom: Conversations with Remarkable People*, 4, 1998

Most of the inmates of mental hospitals have been committed as the result of a petition by a family member. Psychiatric commitment is often the result of an acute or prolonged family disruption, which results in the exclusion and isolation of one member (usually the least powerful). Psychiatric commitment therefore serves to relieve intolerable family conflicts by removing one member from the group.

> RONALD LEIFER (1932–). Psychiatrist. *In the Name of Mental Health: The Social Functions of Psychiatry*, 5, 1969

By the threat of example as effective over the general population as detention centers in dictatorships, the image of the madhouse floats through every mind for the course of its lifetime.

> KATE MILLET (1934–). Conclusion to *The Loony-Bin Trip*, 1990

They only let me out [of the insane asylum] to move definitively among reasonable people when I agreed formally that I had been "sick," which made me lose much of my self-respect and even of my veracity. "Confess, confess," they called to me, as one did in the past to heretics and witches.

> GÉRARD de NERVAL (1808–1855). Letter to Madame Alexander Dumas, 9 November 1841. In Charles Rosen, "The Mad Poets," *New York Review of Books*, 22 October 1992

This house of violence.

> FRIEDRICH NIETZSCHE (1844–1900). Written in an asylum, *My Sister and I*, 10.31, tr. Oscar Levy, 1951

A heavy responsibility presses upon those who preside or officiate in the asylums of lunacy. Little is it known how much injustice is committed, and how much useless and wantonly inflicted misery is endured in those infirmaries for disordered, or rather cemeteries for deceased intellect. . . . Many of the depots for the captivity of intellectual invalids may be regarded only as nurseries for and manufactories of madness.

> JOHN REID (1776–1822). *Essays on Insanity, Hypochondriasis, and Other Nervous Affections*, 1816. In Richard Hunter and Ida Macalpine, eds., "John Reid," *Three Hundred Years of Psychiatry, 1535–1860*, 1963

Many evils arise from an indiscriminate intercourse of mad people with visitors, whether members of their own families or strangers. They often complain to them of the managers, officers, and physicians of the Hospital, and at times in so rational a manner as to induce a belief that their tales of injustice and oppression are true.

> BENJAMIN RUSH (1745–1813). Letter to the Managers of the Pennsylvania Hospital (Philadelphia), 24 September 1810

Mental hospitals are the POW camps of our undeclared and inarticulated civil wars.

> THOMAS S. SZASZ (1920–). Hungarian-born American psychiatrist. "Mental Hospitalization," *The Second Sin*, 1973

Voluntary patients *think* they can leave the hospital; involuntary patients *know* they cannot.

> THOMAS S. SZASZ (1920–). "Mental Hospitalization," *The Second Sin*, 1973

Mental hospitals: . . . Cemeteries for the living dead: dormitory beds are the gravesites; psychiatric diagnoses, the gravestones; psychiatrists, the gravediggers; patients, the corpses.

> THOMAS S. SZASZ (1920–). "Mental Hospital," *The Untamed Tongue: A Dissenting Dictionary*, 1990

MENTAL ILLNESS

See also • Addiction ○ Delusion ○ Depression ○ Illusion ○ Insanity ○ Madness ○ Melancholy ○ Neurosis ○ Neurosis & Psychosis ○ Paranoia ○ Psychiatry ○ Psychoanalysis ○ Psychotherapy ○ Schizophrenia

Mental illness is in the eye of the controller.

> PETER R. BREGGIN (1936–). Psychiatrist. Chris Welch radio interview, KPFA, Berkeley (California), 10 December 1992

The man who does not assent to his nothingness is mentally diseased.

> E. M. CIORAN (1911–1995). *A Short History of Decay*, 1 ("The Arrogance of Prayer"), 1949, tr. Richard Howard, 1975

I swear, gentlemen, that to be too conscious is an illness—a real thoroughgoing illness.

> FYODOR DOSTOYEVSKY (1821–1881). *Notes from Underground*, 1.2, 1864, tr. Constance Garnett

The dogma that "mental diseases are diseases of the brain" is a hangover from the materialism of the 1870s. It has become a prejudice which hinders all progress, with nothing to justify it.

> CARL G. JUNG (1875–1961). "General Aspects of Dream Psychology," 1916, *The Structure and Dynamics of the Psyche*, tr. R. F. C. Hull, 1960

In the entire catalogue of "mental" ills, perplexities, distresses, and organically unfounded discomfitures of the human organism—as well as acts considered strange or offensive—I cannot think of one which is not based, however remotely, upon the conflict between the rebellious urge and the adjustment imperative.

> ROBERT LINDNER (1914–1956). Psychoanalyst. *Prescription for Rebellion*, 4, 1952

Mental health problems do not affect three or four out of every five persons but one out of one.

> WILLIAM MENNINGER (1900–1966). Psychiatrist. In "Neglect Is Noted in Mental Health," *New York Times,* 22 November 1957

The main [symptom] of a psychiatric case is that the person is perfectly unaware that he is a psychiatric case.

> OLEG P. SHCHEPIN. Soviet deputy minister of health. In Felicity Barringer, "Soviet Psychiatry Is Willing to Change, Up to a Point," *New York Times,* 13 November 1988

In contemporary America [mental health] has come to mean conformity to the demands of society. According to the commonsense definition, mental health is the ability to play the game of social living, and to play it well. Conversely, mental illness is the refusal to play, or the inability to play well.

> THOMAS S. SZASZ (1920–). Hungarian-born American psychiatrist. *Law, Liberty, and Psychiatry: An Inquiry into the Social Uses of Mental Health Practices,* 17, 1963

Being considered or labeled mentally disordered—abnormal, crazy, mad, psychotic, sick, it matters not what variant is used—is the most profoundly discrediting classification that can be imposed on a person today. Mental illness casts the "patient" out of our social order just as surely as heresy cast the "witch" out of medieval society. That, indeed, is the very purpose of stigma terms.

> THOMAS S. SZASZ (1920–). *The Manufacture of Madness: A Comparative Study of the Inquisition and the Mental Health Movement,* 12, 1970

Mental illness is a myth, whose function is to disguise and thus render more palatable the bitter pill of moral conflicts in human relations.

> THOMAS S. SZASZ (1920–). "Myth of Mental Illness," *The Second Sin,* 1973

MERCHANTS & CUSTOMERS

See also • Advertising ○ Business (Commerce) ○ Business (Occupation) ○ Capitalism ○ Competition ○ Consumerism ○ Executives ○ Price ○ Profit & Loss ○ Trade (Commerce) ○ Trade (Occupation) ○ Value

For the merchant, even honesty is a financial speculation.

> CHARLES BAUDELAIRE (1821–1867). *Intimate Journals,* 97, 1887, tr. Christopher Isherwood, 1957

There is no such thing as "soft sell" and "hard sell." There is only "smart sell" and "stupid sell."

> CHARLES H. BROWER (1901–1984). Advertising executive. Comment to a national convention of sales executives, 20 May 1958

Keep thy shop, and thy shop will keep you.

> GEORGE CHAPMAN (1559?–1634), BEN JONSON (1572–1637), and JOHN MARSTON (1567–1634). *Eastward Hoe,* 1.1, 1605

A small Shop may have a good Trade.

> THOMAS FULLER (1654–1734). Comp., *Gnomologia: Adages and Proverbs,* 411, 1732

He who findeth Fault meaneth to buy.

> THOMAS FULLER (1654–1734). Comp., *Gnomologia: Adages and Proverbs,* 2383, 1732

Weigh right and sell dear.

> THOMAS FULLER (1654–1734). Comp., *Gnomologia: Adages and Proverbs,* 5467, 1732

Anonymous: What's two and two?
Grade: Buying or selling?

> LORD GRADE (1906–). British entertainment magnate. In *Observer* (British newspaper), 1962

The merchants will manage the better, the more they are left free to manage for themselves.

> THOMAS JEFFERSON (1743–1826). Letter to Gideon Granger, 13 August 1800

Merchants have no country. The mere spot they stand on does not constitute so strong an attachment as that from which they draw their gains.

> THOMAS JEFFERSON (1743–1826). Letter to Horatio Gates Spafford, 17 March 1814

> See Art: Alfred de Musset ○ Class: Karl Marx and Friedrich Engels (2)

You've got to let the monkey *have* the banana every once in a while.

> ED LAUR. "Laur's Advice to Negotiators and Traders." In Paul Dickson, comp., *The Official Explanations,* p. 120, 1980

Exchange is no robbery.

> JOHN RAY (1628–1705). Comp., *A Collection of English Proverbs,* p. 133, 1678

Pleasing ware is half sold.

> JOHN RAY (1628–1705). Comp., *A Collection of English Proverbs,* p. 190, 1678

Never underestimate the power of the irate customer.

> JOEL E. ROSS and MICHAEL J. KAMI. *Corporate Management in Crisis: Why the Mighty Fall,* 9, 1973

Autolycus: Let me have no lying: it becomes none but tradesmen.

> SHAKESPEARE (1564–1616). *The Winter's Tale,* 4.4.743, 1610

People of the same trade seldom meet together, even for merriment and diversion, but the conversation ends in a conspiracy against the public, or in some contrivance to raise prices.

> ADAM SMITH (1723–1790). *The Wealth of Nations,* 1.10.2, 1776

❦

No one without a smiling face should open a shop.

> SAYING (CHINESE)

When you go to buy, use your eyes, not your ears.

> SAYING (CZECH)

He is no merchant who always gains.

> SAYING (DUTCH)

Bad ware is never cheap.

> SAYING (FRENCH)

There are more foolish buyers than foolish sellers.

> SAYING (FRENCH)

Let the buyer beware. [Caveat emptor.]

> SAYING (LATIN)
> See Reading: Saying (Latin)

Beware of too great a bargain.
SAYING (NEW ENGLAND)

Be rich when you sell, poor when you buy.
SAYING (WELSH)

Buy cheap and sell dear.
SAYING

Make every bargain clear and plain
That none may afterwards complain.
SAYING

Sometimes the best purchase is the one you don't make.
SAYING

The customer is always right.
SAYING

MERCY

See also • Compassion ○ Giving ○ Justice ○ Kindness ○ Revenge

We hand folks over to God's mercy, and show none ourselves.
GEORGE ELIOT (1819–1880). *Adam Bede,* 42, 1859

In whom mercy lacketh . . . in him all other virtues be drowned.
SIR THOMAS ELYOT (1499–1546). *The Boke Named the Gouernour,* 3.7, 1531

The just is close to the people's heart, but the merciful is close to the heart of God.
KAHLIL GIBRAN (1883–1931). "Sayings," *Spiritual Sayings of Kahlil Gibran,* tr. Anthony R. Ferris, 1962

Blessed are the merciful: for they shall obtain mercy.
JESUS (A.D. 1st cent.). *Matthew* 5:7 (King James Version)

Yet I shall temper so
Justice with Mercy.
JOHN MILTON (1608–1674). *Paradise Lost,* 10.77, 1667

Tamora: Wilt thou draw near the nature of the gods?
Draw near them then in being merciful:
Sweet mercy is nobility's true badge.
SHAKESPEARE (1564–1616). *Titus Andronicus,* 1.1.117, 1593

Portia: The quality of mercy is not strain'd;
It droppeth as the gentle rain from heaven
Upon the place beneath: it is twice bless'd;
It blesseth him that gives and him that takes.
SHAKESPEARE (1564–1616). *The Merchant of Venice,* 4.1.186, 1596

Portia: [Mercy] is an attribute to God himself;
And earthly power doth then show likest God's
When mercy seasons justice.
SHAKESPEARE (1564–1616). *The Merchant of Venice,* 4.1.195, 1596

Mercy is better than justice.
VAUVENARGUES (1715–1747). *Reflections and Maxims,* 167, 1746, tr. F. G. Stevens, 1940

See Justice: *Zohar*

🖋

The merciful man doeth good to his own soul.
SAYING (*BIBLE*). *Proverbs* 11:17 (King James Version)

MEXICO

See also • Nations

Poor Mexico! So far from God and so close to the United States.
PORFIRIO DÍAZ (1830–1915). Mexican general and president. In John D. Eisenhower, epigraph, *So Far from God: The U.S. War with Mexico, 1846–1848,* 1989

I do not think there was ever a more wicked war than that waged by the United States on Mexico. I thought so at the time, when I was a youngster, only I had not moral courage enough to resign.
ULYSSES S. GRANT (1822–1885). In Dixon Wecter, *The Hero in America: A Chronicle of Hero-Worship,* 12.2, 1941. Grant participated in the Mexican War as an army supply officer several years after graduating from the United States Military Academy, West Point (New York).

The war has not been waged with a view to conquest.
JAMES K. POLK (1795–1849). On the Mexican War, message to Congress, 8 December 1846
See Newspeak—Examples: Polk

Mexico's tragedy is that she has no political idea of herself as rich as her blood.
RICHARD RODRIGUEZ (1944–). *Days of Obligation: An Argument with My Mexican Father,* 1, 1992

MIDDLE AGE

See also • Adolescence ○ Age ○ Age & Youth ○ Time: Garrison Keillor ○ Youth

When we hover between fool and sage.
LORD BYRON (1788–1824). On middle age, *Don Juan,* 12.1, 1819–1824

Our hair
Grows grizzled, and we are not what we were.
LORD BYRON (1788–1824). *Don Juan,* 12.1, 1819–1824

Forty—somber anniversary to the hedonist—in seekers after truth like Buddha, Muhammad, Mencius, St. Ignatius, the turning point of their lives.
CYRIL CONNOLLY (1903–1974). "Ecce Gubernator," *The Unquiet Grave: A Word Cycle by Palinurus,* 1945

Midway in our life's journey, I went astray from the straight road and woke to find myself alone in a dark wood.
DANTE (A.D. 1265–1321). Opening words, "Inferno," *The Divine Comedy,* 1321, tr. John Ciardi, 1954

I am forty years old now, and forty years, after all is a whole lifetime; after all, that is extremely old age. To live longer than forty years is bad manners; it is vulgar, immoral.
FYODOR DOSTOYEVSKY (1821–1881). *Notes from Underground,* 1.1, 1864, tr. Ralph E. Matlaw, 1960

The years between 50 and 70 are the hardest. . . . You are always being asked to do things, and yet you are not decrepit enough to turn them down.

> T. S. ELIOT (1888–1965). In "People," *Time,* 23 October 1950

After thirty a man is too sensible of the straight limitations which his physical constitution sets to his activity. The stream feels its banks, which it had forgotten in the run and overflow of the first meadows.

> RALPH WALDO EMERSON (1803–1882). Journal, 13 September 1838

It is in the thirties that we want friends. In the forties we know they won't save us any more than love did.

> F. SCOTT FITZGERALD (1896–1940). "The Note-Books" (O), *The Crack-Up,* ed. Edmund Wilson, 1945

She may very well pass for forty-three
In the dusk with a light behind her!

> W. S. GILBERT (1836–1911). *Trial by Jury* (opera), 1, 1875

Middle age is when your age starts to show around your middle.

> BOB HOPE (1903–). In news reports, 15 February 1954

Boys'll be boys, an' so'll a lot o' middle-aged men.

> KIN HUBBARD (1868–1930). *Abe Martin: Hoss Sense and Nonsense,* p. 52, 1926

I think middle age is the best time, if we can escape the fatty degeneration of the conscience which often sets in at about fifty.

> DEAN WILLIAM RALPH INGE (1860–1954). In *Observer* (British newspaper), 8 June 1930

The nearer we approach to the middle of life, and the better we have succeeded in entrenching ourselves in our personal attitudes and social positions, the more it appears as if we had discovered the right course and the right ideals and principles of behavior. For this reason we suppose them to be eternally valid, and make a virtue of unchangeably clinging to them.

> CARL G. JUNG (1875–1961). "The Stages of Life," 1931, *The Structure and Dynamics of Psyche,* tr. R. F. C. Hull, 1960

My energies are smaller but more concentrated, and I don't dissipate them on insignificant things. It is easier to say no and yes without qualification or apology.

> SAM KEEN (1931–). *Beginnings Without End,* 9, 1975

When you get to fifty-two, food becomes more important than sex.

> PRUE LEITH (1940–). British chef and writer. On his 52nd birthday. In *Guardian* (British newspaper), 11 November 1992

Middle age: the time when a man is always thinking that in a week or two he will feel just as good as ever.

> DON MARQUIS (1878–1937). In Edward Anthony, *O Rare Don Marquis,* 11, 1962

"After 30, Life Is All Reruns."

> STEPHEN McCAULEY (1955–). Article title, *New York Times Book Review,* 8 March 1992

I have been to a ball at Weimar. The Emperor Alexander dances, but I don't. Forty is forty.

> NAPOLEON (1769–1821). Letter to Josephine, 9 October 1808, *Napoleon's Letters,* tr. J. M. Thompson, 1934

At another year
I would not boggle,
Except that when I jog
I joggle.

> OGDEN NASH (1902–1971). "Birthday on the Beach," *You Can't Get There from Here,* 1957

I feel exactly the same as I've always felt: a lightly reined-in, voracious beast.

> JACK NICHOLSON (1937–). In Melinda Beck, "The New Middle Age," *Newsweek,* 7 December 1992

Middle age is when you stop criticizing the older generation and start criticizing the younger one.

> LAURENCE J. PETER (1919–1990). Comp., *Peter's Quotations: Ideas for Our Time,* p. 336, 1977

Middle age is when it takes longer to rest than to get tired.

> LAURENCE J. PETER (1919–1990). 3 May. *Peter's Almanac,* 1982

Middle age is when work is a lot less fun and fun is a lot more work.

> LAURENCE J. PETER (1919–1990). 4 May. *Peter's Almanac,* 1982

Life Begins at Forty.

> WALTER B. PITKIN (1878–1953). Book title, 1932

Every man over forty is a scoundrel.

> GEORGE BERNARD SHAW (1856–1950). "Maxims for Revolutionists: Stray Sayings," *Man and Superman,* 1903
>
> See Distrust: Jack Weinberg

The youth gets together his materials to build a bridge to the moon, or perchance a palace or temple on the earth, and at length the middle-aged man concludes to build a woodshed with them.

> HENRY DAVID THOREAU (1817–1862). Journal, 14 July 1852

He's in his 50s, and he doesn't realize what it's like now.

> ANONYMOUS. In R. Buckminster Fuller, *I Seem To Be a Verb,* p. 91, 1970

You've reached middle age when all you exercise is caution.

> ANONYMOUS

MILITARISM

See also • Army ○ Imperialism: J. A. Hobson (1) ○ Navy ○ War

Fortified towns, well-stored arsenals, noble breeds of war horses, armed chariots, elephants, engines, all kinds of artillery, arms, and the like, are nothing more than a sheep in a lion's skin, unless the nation itself be, from its origin and temper, stout and warlike.

> FRANCIS BACON (1561–1626). *Advancement of Learning,* 8.3 ("The Military Statesman"), 1605, Willey Book edition, 1944

Those very characteristics which are demanded by war—the ability to tolerate uncertainty, spontaneity of thought and action, having a mind open to the receipt of novel, and perhaps threatening, information—are the antitheses of those possessed by people attracted to the controls, and orderliness, of militarism.

> NORMAN F. DIXON (1922–). *On the Psychology of Military Incompetence,* 17, 1976

A warlike spirit, which alone can create and civilize a state, is absolutely essential to national defense and to national perpetuity.

> DOUGLAS MacARTHUR (1880–1964). In *Infantry Journal*, March 1927

A republic should make only partial peace. One must always have some little war in reserve, to keep up the military spirit.

> NAPOLEON (1769–1821). Remark, 1799. In Jean Savant, *Napoleon in His Time*, 1954

The security of every society must always depend, more or less, upon the martial spirit of the great body of the people.

> ADAM SMITH (1723–1790). *The Wealth of Nations*, 5.1.3.2, 1776

The aim and end of war is murder; the weapons employed in war are espionage, treachery and the encouragement of treachery, the ruining of a country, the plundering and robbing of its inhabitants for the maintenance of the army, and trickery and lying which all appear under the heading of the art of war. The military world is characterized by the absence of freedom—in other words, a rigorous discipline—enforced inactivity, ignorance, cruelty, debauchery, and drunkenness.

> LEO TOLSTOY (1828–1910). *War and Peace*, 3.2.25, 1863–1869, tr. Rosemary Edmonds, 1957

They will avoid the necessity of those overgrown Military establishments which, under any form of government, are inauspicious to liberty, and which are to be regarded as particularly hostile to Republican Liberty.

> GEORGE WASHINGTON (1732–1799). *Farewell Address*, 17 September 1796

> See War & Economics: Dwight D. Eisenhower

MIND

See also • Body ○ Brain ○ Consciousness ○ Freedom of Thought ○ Heart ○ Ideas ○ Imagination ○ Intelligence ○ Judgment ○ Memory ○ Mind & Body ○ Philosophy ○ Reason ○ Self ○ Soul ○ Soul & Body ○ Thinking ○ The Unconscious

The movement from unity to multiplicity, between 1200 and 1900, was unbroken in sequence, and rapid in acceleration. Prolonged one generation longer, it would require a new social mind. . . . Thus far, since five or ten thousand years, the mind had successfully reacted, and nothing yet proved that it would fail to react—but it would need to jump.

> HENRY ADAMS (1838–1918). *The Education of Henry Adams*, 33 ("A Law of Acceleration"), 1907

The mind . . . is a filter which permits passage only to those messages for which it is prepared unless reality is so pressing as to overwhelm it completely.

> J. A. C. BROWN (1911–1964). *Techniques of Persuasion: From Propaganda to Brainwashing*, 4, 1963

The march of the human mind is slow.

> EDMUND BURKE (1729–1797). "Conciliation with America," House of Commons speech, 22 March 1775

The ability to discriminate between that which is true and that which is false is one of the last attainments of the human mind.

> JAMES FENIMORE COOPER (1789–1851). "Rumour," *The American Democrat*, 1838

It is not enough to have a good mind: one must use it well.

> DESCARTES (1596–1650). *Discourse on Method*, 1, 1637, tr. Laurence J. Lafleur, 1964

Minds are like parachutes. They only function when they are open.

> SIR JAMES DEWAR (1842–1923). Attributed

My mind to me a kingdom is.
Such perfect joy therein I find
That it excels all other bliss
That world affords or grows by kind.

> SIR EDWARD DYER (1543–1607). "In Praise of a Contented Mind," 1588?

Observe the invincible tendency of the mind to unify. It is a law of our constitution that we should not contemplate things apart without the effort to arrange them in order with known facts and ascribe them to the same law.

> RALPH WALDO EMERSON (1803–1882). Journal, 13 October 1836

Let a man not resist the law of his own mind, and he will be filled with the divinity which flows through all things.

> RALPH WALDO EMERSON (1803–1882). Journal, May 1841

Nothing is at last sacred but the integrity of your own mind.

> RALPH WALDO EMERSON (1803–1882). "Self-Reliance," *Essays: First Series*, 1841

Memory, Imagination, [and] Reason are only modes of the same power.

> RALPH WALDO EMERSON (1803–1882). Journal, 1850, undated

Goodbye I'm going
I'm selling everything
and giving away the rest
to the Good Will Industries.
It will be dark out there
with the Salvation Army Band.
And the mind its own illumination.

> LAWRENCE FERLINGHETTI (1919–). "Junkman's Obbligato," *A Coney Island of the Mind*, 1958

We are only at the beginning. I am only a beginner. I was successful in digging up buried monuments from the substrata of the mind. But where I have discovered a few temples, others may discover a continent.

> SIGMUND FREUD (1856–1939). Interview with the author. In George Sylvester Viereck, "Sigmund Freud Confronts the Sphinx," *Glimpses of the Great*, 1930

The grand instrument for forwarding the improvement of the mind is the publication of truth.

> WILLIAM GODWIN (1756–1836). *Enquiry Concerning Political Justice and Its Influence on Morals and Happiness*, 3.7, 1793, ed. and abr. Raymond A. Preston, 1926

There are no chaste minds. Minds copulate wherever they meet.

> ERIC HOFFER (1902–1983). *Reflections on the Human Condition*, 142, 1973

Every now and then a man's mind is stretched by a new idea or sensation, and never shrinks back to its former dimensions.

OLIVER WENDELL HOLMES, SR. (1809–1894). *The Autocrat of the Breakfast-Table,* 11, 1858

My mind is like a beehive, for in the midst of buzz and apparent confusion there [is] great order, regularity of structure, and abundant food, collected with incessant industry from the choicest stores of nature.

JOHN HUNTER (1728–1793). British anatomist and surgeon. In Isaac D'Israeli, *Literary Character of Men of Genius,* 11, 1795

It is a man's own fault, it is from want of use, if his mind grows torpid in old age.

SAMUEL JOHNSON (1709–1784). 9 April 1778. In James Boswell, *The Life of Samuel Johnson,* 1791

A study of the history of opinion is a necessary preliminary to the emancipation of the mind.

JOHN MAYNARD KEYNES (1833–1946). *The End of Laissez-Faire,* 1, 1926

Too much gravity argues a shallow mind.

JOHN CASPAR LAVATER (1741–1801). *Aphorisms on Man,* 183, 1788

In the conquest of mind-space it is the inches, consolidated, that count.

B. H. LIDDELL HART (1895–1970). "Some Conclusions," *Why Don't We Learn from History?* 1944

The first capacity of human intellect is that the mind is fitted to receive the impressions made on it, either through the senses by outward objects, or by its own operations when it reflects on them.

JOHN LOCKE (1632–1704). *An Essay Concerning Human Understanding,* 2.1.24, 1690, ed. Alexander Campbell Fraser, 1894

A man's mind is known by the company it keeps.

JAMES RUSSELL LOWELL (1819–1891). "Pope," *My Study Windows,* 1871

The most incessant occupation of the human intellect throughout life is the ascertainment of truth.

JOHN STUART MILL (1806–1873). "On Education," inaugural address on being installed as rector, University of St. Andrews (Scotland), 1 February 1867

The human mind is sometimes impelled all the more violently in one direction by an overzealous and demonstrative attempt to drag it in the opposite.

JOHN STUART MILL (1806–1873). "On Education," inaugural address on being installed as rector, University of St. Andrews (Scotland), 1 February 1867

Everything external is but a reflection projected by the mind machine.

HENRY MILLER (1891–1980). "The Creative Life." In Leo Hamalian and Edmond L. Volpe, eds., *Essays of Our Time,* 1960

The mind is its own place, and in itself
Can make a Heav'n of Hell, a Hell of Heav'n.

JOHN MILTON (1608–1674). *Paradise Lost,* 1.254, 1667

See Propaganda: Adolf Hitler (4)

Is there no way out of the mind?

SYLVIA PLATH (1932–1963). "Apprehensions," 1971

The primary indication . . . of a well-ordered mind is a man's ability to remain in one place and linger in his own company.

SENECA THE YOUNGER (5? B.C.–A.D. 65). "On Discursiveness in Reading," *Moral Letters to Lucilius,* 2.1, tr. Richard M. Gummere, 1918

The more the mind receives, the more does it expand.

SENECA THE YOUNGER (5? B.C.–A.D. 65). "On the Approaches to Philosophy," *Moral Letters to Lucilius,* 101.10, tr. Richard M. Gummere, 1918

Hamlet: In my mind's eye, Horatio.

SHAKESPEARE (1564–1616). *Hamlet,* 1.2.186, 1600

The human mind is part of the infinite intellect of God.

BARUCH SPINOZA (1632–1677). "Ideas, Things, and the Human Mind," *Ethics,* 1677, tr. Dagobert D. Runes, 1957

The mind's highest good is the knowledge of God.

BARUCH SPINOZA (1632–1677). "Man Is to Man a God," *Ethics,* 1677, tr. Dagobert D. Runes, 1957

We should treat our minds, that is, ourselves, as innocent and ingenuous children, whose guardians we are, and be careful what objects and what subjects we thrust on their attention. Read not the Times. Read the Eternities.

HENRY DAVID THOREAU (1817–1862). "Life Without Principle," *Atlantic,* October 1863

The mind is the soul's eye.

VAUVENARGUES (1715–1747). *Reflections and Maxims,* 149, 1746, tr. F. G. Stevens, 1940

The unfed mind devours itself.

GORE VIDAL (1925–). In Arthur Lubow, "Gore's Lore," *Vanity Fair,* September 1992

Mind is the great lever of all things.

DANIEL WEBSTER (1782–1852). Address on laying the cornerstone of the Bunker Hill Monument, Charlestown (Massachusetts), 17 June 1825

Mind at the End of Its Tether.

H. G. WELLS (1866–1946). Book title, 1945

The divine light . . . readily enters into the eye of the mind that is prepared to receive it.

BENJAMIN WHICHCOTE (1609–1683). Sermon

The Mind of Man—
My haunt, and the main region of my song.

WILLIAM WORDSWORTH (1770–1850). Preface (l. 40) to *The Excursion,* 1814

❦

What is Matter?—Never mind.
What is Mind?—No matter.

ANONYMOUS. In *Punch* (British humor magazine), vol. 29, p. 19, 1855

A cluttered mind is little better than an empty one.

ANONYMOUS

As a field must be plowed before being sown, so a mind must be troubled before being introduced to a new idea.

ANONYMOUS

Mind is to soul what wave is to ocean.
ANONYMOUS

A concentrated mind will pierce a rock.
SAYING (JAPANESE)

A mind is a terrible thing to waste.
SAYING. Motto of the United Negro College Fund

Company broadens the mind; solitude deepens it.
SAYING

MIND & BODY

See also • Body ○ Mind ○ Soul & Body

We have rudiments of reverence for the human body, but we consider as nothing the rape of the human mind.
ERIC HOFFER (1902–1983). *The Passionate State of Mind: And Other Aphorisms,* 254, 1954

A sound mind in a sound body.
JUVENAL (A.D. 60?–127?). *Satires,* 10.357, tr. Peter Green, 1967
See Happiness: Voltaire

Simple grace is to the body what common sense is to the mind.
LA ROCHEFOUCAULD (1613–1680). *Maxims,* 67, 1665, tr. Leonard Tancock, 1959

The first great awakeners of the mind seem to be the wants of the body.
THOMAS ROBERT MALTHUS (1766–1834). *An Essay on the Principle of Population, as It Affects the Future Improvement of Society,* 1.18, 1798

To strengthen the mind you must harden the muscles.
MONTAIGNE (1533–1592). In Rousseau, *Emile; or, Treatise on Education,* 2, 1762, tr. Barbara Foxley, 1911

All the soarings of my mind begin in my blood.
RAINER MARIA RILKE (1875–1926). Letter to a young girl, July 1921, *Wartime Letters of Rainer Maria Rilke,* tr. M. D. Herter Norton, 1940

We employ the mind to rule, the body rather to serve.
SALLUST (86–34 B.C.). *The War with Catiline,* 1.2, tr. J. C. Rolfe, 1921

The principle of the mind does not differ from that of the body, which cannot be sustained without constant nourishment.
VAUVENARGUES (1715–1747). *Reflections and Maxims,* 194, 1746, tr. F. G. Stevens, 1940

Dominion strong is the body's; dominion stronger is the mind's.
WALT WHITMAN (1819–1892). *Democratic Vistas,* 1871, *Walt Whitman: Complete Poetry and Collected Prose,* ed. Justin Kaplan, p. 955, 1982

❦

The mind is host,
the body guest.
SAYING (JAPANESE). In John Kane, ed., *Moving Forward, Keeping Still: The Gateway to Eastern Wisdom,* p. 116, 1997

MINORITIES

See also • Civilization: Mohandas K. Gandhi ○ Madness: George Orwell ○ Majorities ○ Nonconformity ○ Standing Alone ○ Truth: Ralph Waldo Emerson (6)

The most certain test by which we judge whether a country is really free is the amount of security enjoyed by minorities.
LORD ACTON (1834–1902). "The History of Freedom in Antiquity," 1877, *The History of Freedom and Other Essays,* ed. J. N. Figgis and R. V. Laurence, 1907

All history is the record of the power of minorities, and of minorities of one.
RALPH WALDO EMERSON (1803–1882). "Progress of Culture," *Letters and Social Aims,* 1876

If a man is a minority of one, we lock him up.
OLIVER WENDELL HOLMES, JR. (1841–1935). "Law and the Court," speech at a dinner of the Harvard Law School Association of New York, 15 February 1913

The saving of our world from pending doom will come, not through the complacent adjustment of the conforming majority, but through the creative maladjustment of a nonconforming minority.
MARTIN LUTHER KING, JR. (1929–1968). *Strength to Love,* 2.3, 1963

Never doubt that a small group of thoughtful, committed citizens can change the world; indeed, it's the only thing that every has.
MARGARET MEAD (1901–1978). In David Helvarg, "Global Guardians" (epigraph), *San Francisco Focus,* April 1995

The finest fruits of human progress, like all of the nobler virtues of man, are the exclusive possession of small minorities, chiefly unpopular and disreputable.
H. L. MENCKEN (1880–1956). *Notes on Democracy,* 1.8, 1926

How a minority,
Reaching majority,
Seizing authority,
Hates a minority!
LEONARD H. ROBBINS (1877–1947). "Minorities"

A minority is powerless while it conforms to the majority; it is not even a minority then; but it is irresistible when it clogs by its whole weight.
HENRY DAVID THOREAU (1817–1862). "Civil Disobedience," 1849

MIRACLES

See also • Awe ○ God ○ Mystery ○ Religion ○ Wonder

This is also a miracle; not only to produce effects against or above nature, but before nature; and to create nature, as great a miracle as to contradict or transcend her. We do too narrowly define the power of God, restraining it to our capacities.
SIR THOMAS BROWNE (1605–1682). *Religio Medici,* 1.26, 1642, ed. John Addington Symonds, 1886

All the works of Nature are Miracles, and nothing makes them appear otherwise but our Familiarity with them.

SAMUEL BUTLER (1612–1680). "Nature," *Prose Observations,* ed. Hugh de Quehen, 1979

Where there is great love, there are always miracles.

WILLA CATHER (1876–1947). *Death Comes for the Archbishop,* 1.4, 1926

You want a miracle? You make a fish from scratch!

LARRY GELBART (1928–). *Oh God!* (film), 1977, spoken by George Burns (in the lead role)

To contrast the size of the oak with that of the parent acorn, as if the poor seed had paid all costs from its slender strongbox, may serve for a child's wonder; but the real miracle lies in that divine league which bound all the forces of nature to the service of the tiny germ in fulfilling its destiny.

JAMES RUSSELL LOWELL (1819–1891). "Abraham Lincoln," 1864, *My Study Windows,* 1871

That greatest miracle of all, the human being.

MARYA MANNES (1904–1990). *More in Anger,* 2.2, 1958

Miracles arise from our ignorance of nature, not from nature.

MONTAIGNE (1533–1592). "Of Custom," *Essays,* 1588, tr. Donald M. Frame, 1958

Most of the miracles we hear of are infinitely less wonderful than the commonest of natural phenomena, when fairly seen.

JOHN MUIR (1838–1914). 4 August 1869, *My First Summer in the Sierra,* 7 ("A Strange Experience"), 1911

The story of the whale swallowing Jonah, though a whale is large enough to do it, borders greatly on the marvelous; but it would have approached nearer to the idea of a miracle if Jonah had swallowed the whale.

THOMAS PAINE (1737–1809). *The Age of Reason: Being an Investigation of True and Fabulous Theology,* 1, 1796

Miracles are instantaneous; they cannot be summoned but come of themselves, usually at unlikely moments and to those who least expect them.

KATHERINE ANNE PORTER (1890–1980). *Ship of Fools,* 3, 1962

Miracles are for those who have little faith.

THE RIZINER (?–1850). In Martin Buber, "Israel of Rizhyn," *Tales of the Hasidim: The Later Masters,* tr. Olga Marx, 1948

Expect a miracle!

ORAL ROBERTS (1918–). His signature line

Miracles, in the sense of phenomena we cannot explain, surround us on every hand: life itself is the miracle of miracles.

GEORGE BERNARD SHAW (1856–1950). Preface ("Credibility of the Gospels") to *Androcles and the Lion,* 1912

Men talk about Bible miracles because there is no miracle in their lives. Cease to gnaw that crust. There is ripe fruit over your head.

HENRY DAVID THOREAU (1817–1862). Journal, 9 June 1850

Miracles do happen, but one has to work very hard for them.

CHAIM WEIZMANN (1874–1952)

All the things of the universe are perfect miracles, each as profound as any.

WALT WHITMAN (1819–1892). "Starting from Paumanok" (12), 1860, *Leaves of Grass,* 1855–1892

MISERS

See also • Greed: [especially] George Bernard Shaw ∘ Money ∘ Thrift ∘ Wealth: Bion

He who is frugal is the richest of men, and the miser is the poorest.

CHAMFORT (1741–1794). *Maxims and Thoughts,* 2, 1796, tr. W. S. Merwin, 1984

He will not part with the parings of his nails.

JOHN CLARKE (1596–1658). Comp., *Proverbs: English and Latine,* p. 37, 1639

The miser has lived poor to die rich; and if the prodigal quits life in debt to others, the miser quits it, still deeper in debt to himself.

C. C. COLTON (1780–1832). *Lacon: or, Many Things in Few Words; Addressed to Those Who Think,* 2.131, 1824

The Prodigal robs the Heir, the Miser himself.

THOMAS FULLER (1654–1734). Comp., *Gnomologia: Adages and Proverbs,* 4722, 1732

What greater evil could you wish a miser than long life?

PUBLIUS SYRUS (85–43 B.C.). *Moral Sayings,* 69, tr. Darius Lyman, Jr., 1862

His money comes from him like drops of blood.

JOHN RAY (1628–1705). Comp., *A Collection of English Proverbs,* p. 90, 1678

He makes money with his teeth, by keeping them idle.

CHARLES HADDON SPURGEON (1834–1892). *John Ploughman's Pictures,* 16, 1880

MISERY

See also • Evil: Saying (Chinese) ∘ History: Franz Kafka ∘ Pain ∘ Poverty: E. F. Schumacher (2) ∘ Unhappiness ∘ Wretchedness

To be weak is the true misery.

THOMAS CARLYLE (1795–1881). *Sartor Resartus: The Life and Opinions of Herr Teufelsdröckh,* 2.7, 1835

If it be true that men are miserable because they are wicked, it is likewise true that many are wicked because they are miserable.

SAMUEL TAYLOR COLERIDGE (1772–1834)

My external condition may to many seem comfortable, to some enviable, but I think that few men ever suffered (in degree not in amount) more genuine misery than I have suffered.

RALPH WALDO EMERSON (1803–1882). At age 22, journal, 16 March 1826

[The] great part of the miseries of mankind are brought upon them by the false estimates they have made of the value of things, and by their *giving too much for their whistles.*

BENJAMIN FRANKLIN (1706–1790). Referring to the time when at age 7 he was charmed by another boy's whistle which he bought with all the money he had, letter to Madame Brillon, 10 November 1779

The misery of being always under a mask.

> NATHANIEL HAWTHORNE (1804–1864). 25 October 1836, *The American Notebooks*, ed. Claude M. Simpson, 1932

Spent a miserable morning comparing myself with Raphael.

> BENJAMIN ROBERT HAYDON (1786–1846). English painter. Diary, quoted by Bertrand Russell. In Woodrow Wyatt television interview, *Bertrand Russell Speaks His Mind*, 7, 1960

I would consent to have a limb amputated to recover my spirits.

> SAMUEL JOHNSON (1709–1784). On "the misery which he felt." Quoted by Dr. W. Adams, spring 1764. In James Boswell, *The Life of Samuel Johnson*, 1791. Dr. Adams, who was visiting Johnson, found him "in a deplorable state, sighing, groaning, talking to himself, and restlessly walking from room to room."

The misery of man proceeds not from any single crush of overwhelming evil, but from small vexations continually repeated.

> SAMUEL JOHNSON (1709–1784). "Pope," *Lives of the English Poets*, 1781

I am now the most miserable man living. If what I feel were equally distributed to the whole human family, there would not be one cheerful face on the earth. Whether I shall ever be better I cannot tell; I awfully forebode I shall not. To remain as I am is impossible. I must die or be better, it appears to me.

> ABRAHAM LINCOLN (1809–1865). Referring to "the fatal first of January, 1841" when he broke his engagement with Mary Todd, whom he later married. Letter to John T. Stuart, 23 January 1841

It is difficult to make a man miserable while he feels he is worthy of himself and claims kindred to the great God who made him.

> ABRAHAM LINCOLN (1809–1865). "Address on Colonization to a Committee of Colored Men," 14 August 1862

Me miserable! which way shall I fly
Infinite wrath, and infinite despair?
Which way I fly is Hell, my self am Hell;
And in the lowest deep a lower deep
Still threatening to devour me opens wide,
To which the Hell I suffer seems a Heav'n.

> JOHN MILTON (1608–1674). *Paradise Lost*, 4.73, 1667

All these same miseries prove man's greatness. They are the miseries of a great lord, of a deposed king.

> BLAISE PASCAL (1623–1662). *Pensées*, 397, 1670, tr. William F. Trotter, 1931

The chief cause of our misery is less the violence of our passions than the feebleness of our virtues.

> JOSEPH ROUX (1834–1886). *Meditations of a Parish Priest*, 5.25, tr. Isabel F. Hapgood, 1886

If there is nothing to cause me misery, I am tormented by the thought that there must be something hidden from me.

> ARTHUR SCHOPENHAUER (1788–1860). In Theo. B. Hyslop, *The Great Abnormals*, 10, 1925

Trinculo: Misery acquaints a man with strange bedfellows.

> SHAKESPEARE (1564–1616). *The Tempest*, 2.2.41, 1611
> See Adversity: Saying (English) ◦ Politics: Charles Dudley Warner

The secret of being miserable is to have leisure to bother about whether you are happy or not.

> GEORGE BERNARD SHAW (1564–1616). "Children's Happiness," *Parents and Children*, 1914

If misery loves company, misery has company enough.

> HENRY DAVID THOREAU (1817–1862). Journal, 1 September 1851

❧

Misery loves company.

> SAYING (ENGLISH)
>
> See Grief: Shakespeare (1) ◦ Malice: Seneca the Younger ◦ Mediocrity: Anonymous (1) ◦ Wretchedness: Publius Syrus (2)

MISFORTUNE

See also • Adversity ◦ Burdens ◦ Calamity ◦ Chance ◦ Defeat ◦ Difficulty ◦ Disability ◦ Disaster ◦ Experience ◦ Fate ◦ Fortune ◦ Grief ◦ Luck ◦ Pain ◦ Struggle ◦ Tragedy ◦ Trouble ◦ Unhappiness

Misfortin and twins hardly ever cum singly.

> JOSH BILLINGS (1818–1885). *His Sayings*, 26, 1867
> See Sorrow: Shakespeare (2)

How soon the sunk spirits rise again, how quick the little wounds of fortune skin over and are forgotten.

> RALPH WALDO EMERSON (1803–1882). Journal, 5 October 1838

Misfortunes tell us what Fortune is.

> THOMAS FULLER (1654–1734). Comp., *Gnomologia: Adages and Proverbs*, 3420, 1732

We feel public misfortune only in so far as it affects our private interests.

> HANNIBAL (247–182 B.C.). In Livy (59 B.C.–A.D. 17), *The History of Rome*, 30.46, tr. Aubrey de Sélincourt, 1965

He that hath no ill fortune is troubled with good.

> GEORGE HERBERT (1593–1633). Comp., *Outlandish Proverbs*, 358, 1640

Without the cold and bleakness of winter
The warmth and splendor of spring there could never be.
Misfortunes have steeled and tempered me
And strengthened my resolve even further.

> HO CHI MINH (1892–1969). "Advice to Myself," *Prison Diary*, 5th ed., Foreign Languages Publishing House (Hanoi), 1972
> See Desperation: Albert Camus ◦ Seasons: Percy Bysshe Shelley

Little minds are tamed and subdued by misfortune, but great minds rise above it.

> WASHINGTON IRVING (1881–1966). "Philip of Pokanoket," *The Sketch Book*, 1820

When Bad Things Happen to Good People.

> HAROLD S. KUSHNER (1935–). Rabbi. Book title, 1981

No occurrences are so unfortunate that the shrewd cannot turn them to some advantage, nor so fortunate that the imprudent cannot turn them to their own disadvantage.

> LA ROCHEFOUCAULD (1613–1680). *Maxims*, 59, 1665, tr. Leonard Tancock, 1959

Here is a rule to remember in future, when anything tempts you to feel bitter: not, "This is a misfortune," but "To bear this worthily is good fortune."

> MARCUS AURELIUS (A.D. 121–180). *Meditations*, 4.49, tr. Maxwell Staniforth, 1964

People don't ever seem to realize that doing what's right's no guarantee against misfortune.

> WILLIAM McFEE (1881–1966). *Casuals of the Sea*, 2.1.6, 1916

The man who feels the hail coming down on his head thinks the entire hemisphere is swept by the storm.

> MONTAIGNE (1533–1592). *The Autobiography of Michel de Montaigne*, 28, ed. Marvin Lowenthal, 1935

Misfortune and experience are lost upon mankind when they produce neither reflection nor reformation.

> THOMAS PAINE (1737–1809). *The Crisis*, 7, 21 November 1778

To hope and to act, these are our duties in misfortune.

> BORIS PASTERNAK (1890–1960). *Doctor Zhivago*, 15.14, 1957, tr. Max Hayward and Manya Harari, 1958

I never knew any man in my life who could not bear another's misfortunes perfectly like a Christian.

> ALEXANDER POPE (1688–1744). "Thoughts on Various Subjects," *Miscellanies in Prose and Verse* (published with Jonathan Swift), vol. 2, 1727
>
> See Adversity: Mark Twain ○ Grief: Shakespeare (3) ○ Trouble: La Rochefoucauld

It is a source of consolation to look back upon those great misfortunes which never happened.

> ARTHUR SCHOPENHAUER (1788–1860). "Counsels and Maxims" (2.14), *Essays of Arthur Schopenhauer*, tr. T. Bailey Saunders, 1851

Constant misfortune brings this one blessing, that those whom it always assails, it at last fortifies.

> SENECA THE YOUNGER (5? B.C.–A.D. 65). "On Consolation to Helvia" (2.3), *Moral Essays*, tr. John W. Basore, 1932

Son: Ill blows the wind that profits nobody.

> SHAKESPEARE (1564–1616). *Henry VI*, Part III, 2.5.55, 1590

Some misfortunes we bring upon ourselves; others are completely beyond our control. But no matter what happens to us, we always have some control over what we do about it.

> SUZY SZASZ (1955–). *Living With It: Why You Don't Have to Be Healthy to Be Happy*, 4, 1991

Misfortunes one can endure—they come from outside, they are accidents. But to suffer for one's own faults—ah!—there is the sting of life.

> OSCAR WILDE (1854–1900). *Lady Windermere's Fan*, 1, 1892
>
> See Trouble: Sophocles

✹

Misfortune does not always come to injure.

> SAYING (ITALIAN)

Fortune and misfortune are like the twisted strands of a rope.

> SAYING (JAPANESE)

The heaviest rains fall on the leaky house.

> SAYING (JAPANESE)

From fortune to misfortune is a small step, but from misfortune to fortune is a big step.

> SAYING (YIDDISH)
>
> See Wealth & Poverty: Saying (Japanese)

MISJUDGMENTS

See also • Criticism: Examples ○ Critics: Examples ○ Korean War: Douglas MacArthur (2) ○ Praise: Examples ○ Prediction ○ Ships: Anonymous ○ World War I: Wilhelm II (2), Woodrow Wilson (3) ○ World War II: Neville Chamberlain (3), George Fielding Eliot, Hermann Goering, Adolf Hitler (1,2), Franklin D. Roosevelt (1,2)

Churchill? He's a busted flush!

> LORD BEAVERBROOK (1879–1964). Canadian-born British publisher. Explaining his unwillingness to hire Winston Churchill to write for one of his newspapers, 1932

To kill a man will be considered as disgusting [in the 20th century] as we in this day consider it disgusting to eat one.

> ANDREW CARNEGIE (1835–1919). In Paul Dickson, "It'll Never Fly, Orville," *Saturday Review*, December 1979

Iran under the great leadership of the Shah is an island of stability in one of the most troubled areas of the world. This is a great tribute to you, your Majesty, and to your leadership and to the respect, admiration, and love which your people give to you.

> JIMMY CARTER (1924–). Toasting the Shah a year before he was deposed, Teheran, 31 December 1977

In spite of the hardness and ruthlessness I thought I saw in [Adolf Hitler's] face, I got the impression that here was a man who could be relied upon when he had given his word.

> NEVILLE CHAMBERLAIN (1869–1940). British prime minister. Soon after returning from the Munich Conference, 1938. In Keith Feiling, *The Life of Neville Chamberlain*, 28, 1946

You'll never get anywhere with all those damned little short sentences.

> GREG CLARK. Remark to fellow *Toronto Star* reporter Ernest Hemingway early in his career, 1920s

Gone With the Wind is going to be the biggest flop in Hollywood history. I'm just glad it'll be Clark Gable who's falling flat on his face and not Gary Cooper.

> GARY COOPER (1901–1961). After Gable's acceptance of the Rhett Butler role he himself had turned down, 1938. In Larry Swindell, *The Last Hero: A Biography of Gary Cooper*, 7, 1980

[Man will never reach the moon] regardless of all future scientific advances.

> LEE DE FOREST (1873–1961). Audion tube inventor. 25 February 1957 (12 years before the moon-landing). In Timothy Dickinson, "Fearless Forecasts," *New York Times*, 31 December 1992

You ain't goin' nowhere with *that*, son. You ought to go back to drivin' a truck.

JIM DENNY. "Grand Ole Opry" booking agent. Remark to Elvis Presley after hearing his first Opry performance, Nashville, 1954. In Dee Presley et al. (as told to Martin Torgoff), *Elvis, We Love You Tender*, 2, 1979

The Giants is dead.

CHUCK DRESSEN (1898–1966). Baseball manager. Referring to the New York Giants who, late in the 1951 season, were far behind his league-leading Brooklyn Dodgers. The Giants then staged a comeback, winning the pennant in the last game of the season with a ninth-inning home run by Bobby Thompson.

Everything that can be invented has been invented.

CHARLES H. DUELL. U.S. Patent Office director. Urging Pres. William McKinley to abolish the Patent Office, 1899

The use of small quantities [of uranium], sufficient, say, to operate a car or an airplane, so far is impossible, and one cannot predict when it will be achieved. No doubt, it will be achieved, but nobody can say when.

ALBERT EINSTEIN (1879–1955). Raymond Swing interview, "Einstein on the Atomic Bomb," *Atlantic*, November 1945

I think we are not quite yet fit for Flying Machines and therefore there will be none.

RALPH WALDO EMERSON (1803–1882). Journal, May-June 1843

The British won't fight.

LEOPOLDO GALTIERI (1926–). Argentine president. Remark during the Falklands crisis to Secretary of State Alexander Haig, 10 April 1982

I do not consider Hitler as bad as he is depicted. He is showing an ability that is amazing, and he seems to be gaining his victories without much bloodshed.

MOHANDAS K. GANDHI (1869–1948). Remark, May 1940. In Robert Payne, *The Life and Death of Mahatma Gandhi*, 1969

In no nation are the fruits of accomplishment more secure. . . . I have no fears for the future of our country. It is bright with hope.

HERBERT HOOVER (1874–1964). *Inaugural Address*, 4 March 1929. Seven months later the stock market crashed, triggering the Great Depression.

Rembrandt is not to be compared in the painting of character with our extraordinary [sic] gifted English artist, Mr. Rippingille.

JOHN HUNT (1775–1848). In Stephen Pile, *The Book of Heroic Failures*, 11, 1979

Those who wait for that must wait until a shrimp learns to whistle.

NIKITA KHRUSHCHEV (1894–1971). Soviet premier. On the possibility of the Soviet Union rejecting Communism, speech, Moscow, 17 September 1955

Whether you like it or not, history is on our side. We will bury you.

NIKITA KHRUSHCHEV (1899–1971). Referring to his belief that Communism would replace capitalism, speech before Western diplomats at a Polish embassy reception for Wladyslaw Gomulka in Moscow following the signing of a Moscow-Warsaw joint declaration, 18 November 1956. At the National Press Club in Washington on 16 September 1959, Khrushchev, responding to a reporter's question, tried to clarify his famous remark: "The expression I used was distorted, and on purpose, because what was meant was not the physical burial of any people but the question of the historical force of development. . . . I said that looking at the matter from the historical point of view, socialism, communism, would take the place of capitalism and capitalism thereby would be, so to speak, buried."

There has been a little distress selling on the Stock Exchange.

THOMAS W. LAMONT. J. P. Morgan senior partner. Remark to reporters at noon, 24 October 1929, during one of the worst sell-offs in stock-market history. In Frederick Lewis Allen, *Only Yesterday: An Informal History of the Nineteen-Twenties*, 13.3, 1931

[I doubt whether] we, the old, [will] live to see the decisive battles of the coming revolution.

LENIN (1870–1924). January 1917, six weeks later the revolution broke out in Russia and seven months after that, in October, the communists seized power. In Edward Hallett Carr, *The Bolshevik Revolution, 1917–1923*, 1.1.3, 1953

Give me four years to teach the children, and the seed I have sown will never be uprooted.

LENIN (1870–1924). In John Gunther, *Inside Europe*, rev. ed., 35 (epigraph), 1937 (1936)

The world will little note nor long remember what we say here, but it can never forget what they did here.

ABRAHAM LINCOLN (1809–1865). Referring to the day's speeches honoring those who had fought and died during the Battle of Gettysburg, (Pennsylvania), *Gettysburg Address*, 19 November 1863

See Civil War: Lincoln (4)

Young man, you can be grateful that my invention is not for sale, for it would undoubtedly ruin you. It can be exploited for a certain time as a scientific curiosity, but apart from that it has no commercial value whatsoever.

AUGUSTE LUMIÈRE (1862–1954). French chemist. On the motion-picture camera he invented in 1895

In the future there will be more people, and there won't be enough grain, so men will have to get food from minerals.

MAO TSE-TUNG (1893–1976). "Talk on Questions of Philosophy," 18 August 1964, *Chairman Mao Talks to the People: Talks and Letters: 1956–1971*, tr. John Chinnery and Tieyun and ed. Stuart Schram, 1974

The energy produced by the atom is a very poor kind of thing. Anyone who expects a source of power from the transformation of these atoms is talking moonshine.

LORD ERNEST RUTHERFORD (1871–1937). British physicist and winner of the 1908 Nobel Prize in chemistry. September 1933, soon after the first experimental splitting of the atom

I do not hesitate to forecast that atomic batteries will be commonplace long before 1980.

DAVID SARNOFF (1891–1971). Inventor and Radio Corporation of America chairman. "The Fabulous Future," *Fortune*, January 1955

So you've been over into Russia?" said Bernard Baruch, and I answered very literally, "I have been over into the future, and it works."

LINCOLN STEFFENS (1866–1971). Soon after returning from the Soviet Union following the Russian Revolution, 1919, *Autobiography*, 18, 1931 (Popular version: I have seen the future, and it works.)

Louis, forget it. No Civil War picture ever made a nickel.

IRVING THALBERG (1899–1936). Film studio executive. Remark to Louis B. Mayer on hearing about plans to make *Gone With the Wind* (1939), 1930s.

[I am] convinced of [Hitler's] sincerity in desiring peace in Europe.

> ARNOLD J. TOYNBEE (1889–1975). After a long interview with Hitler in 1936. In H. R. Trevor-Roper, "Arnold Toynbee's Millennium," *Encounter,* June 1957

Who the hell wants to hear actors talk?

> HARRY WARNER (1881–1958). Warner Brothers Pictures president. Referring to the newly introduced "talkies," 1927?

I think there is a world market for maybe five computers.

> THOMAS J. WATSON (1874–1956). International Business Machines chairman. 1943. In Michael Krantz, "Cashing in on Tomorrow," *Time,* 15 July 1996

Video won't be able to hold onto any market it captures after the first six months. People will get tired of staring at a plywood box every night.

> DARRYL F. ZANUCK (1902–1979). 1940s

❧

Clearing and colder preceded by light snow.

> ANONYMOUS (AMERICAN). New York City weather forecast for 12 March 1888 (the day of "The Blizzard of '88")

Lean, thin hair, can't be photographed very well, not much personality, and so forth. Also dances.

> ANONYMOUS (AMERICAN). Metro-Goldwyn-Mayer film studio executive. Commenting on Fred Astaire after a 1928 screen test. Quoted by Conrad Nagel, "Conrad Nagel." In Bernard Rosenberg and Harry Silverstein, eds., *The Real Tinsel,* 1970 (Popular version: Can't act. Can't sing. Slightly bald. Can dance a little.)

We don't like their sound. Groups of guitars are on the way out.

> ANONYMOUS (AMERICAN). Decca Recording Company executive. Explaining why he turned down the Beatles, 1962

Reagan doesn't have the presidential look.

> ANONYMOUS (AMERICAN). United Artists studio executive. Rejecting the suggestion that he offer Ronald Reagan the role of President in the film *The Best Man,* 1964

MISOGYNOUS STATEMENTS

See also • Feminism ○ Men ○ Prejudice ○ Sex ○ Sexism ○ Sexist Statements ○ Witchcraft: [especially] Heinrich Kramer and James Sprenger (1) ○ Women ○ Women & Men

Man is the whole world and the breath of God; woman the rib and crooked piece of man.

> SIR THOMAS BROWNE (1605–1682). *Religio Medici,* 2.9, 1642, ed. John Addington Symonds, 1886

A woman is but an animal; and an animal not of the highest order.

> EDMUND BURKE (1729–1797). *Reflections on the Revolution in France,* p. 171, 1790, Pelican Books edition, 1968

I have endeavored to gain the hearts of twenty women, whose persons I would not have given a fig for.

> LORD CHESTERFIELD (1694–1773). In Mary Wollstonecraft, *A Vindication of the Rights of Woman,* 4, 1792

Certain women should be struck regularly, like gongs.

> NOEL COWARD (1899–1973). *Private Lives,* 3, 1930

Neither earth nor ocean
produces a creature as savage and monstrous
as woman.

> EURIPIDES (485?–406 B.C.). *Hecuba,* l. 1180, tr. William Arrowsmith, 1956

Success is feminine and like a woman; if you cringe before her, she will override you. So the way to treat her is to show her the back of your hand. Then maybe she will do the crawling.

> WILLIAM FAULKNER (1897–1962). Jean Stein vanden Heuvel interview, 1956. In Malcolm Cowley, ed., *Writers at Work: First Series,* 1958

You can usually scare a certain amount of brains into a woman but usually you can't make them stick.

> F. SCOTT FITZGERALD (1896–1940). "The Note-Books" (O), *The Crack-Up,* ed. Edmund Wilson, 1945

The fact that women must be regarded as having little sense of justice is no doubt related to the predominance of envy in their mental life. . . . We also regard women as weaker in their social interests and as having less capacity for sublimating their instincts than men.

> SIGMUND FREUD (1856–1939). *New Introductory Lectures on Psychoanalysis,* 33, 1933, tr. James Strachey, 1965

A woman, an ass, and a walnut tree,
Bring the more fruit the more beaten they be.

> STEFANO GUAZZO. *Civil Conversations,* 3.20, tr. George Pettie, 1581

Women in State affairs are like Monkeys in Glass shops.

> JAMES HOWELL (1593–1666). Comp., "English" (p. 12), *Paroimiographia: Proverbs, or Old Sayed Sawes & Adages in English . . . Italian, French and Spanish,* 1659
>
> See Feminism: Saying (American)

The female of the species is more deadly than the male.

> RUDYARD KIPLING (1865–1936). "The Female of the Species," 1, 1911

There is a large number of women whose brains are closer in size to the gorillas than to the most developed male brains. This inferiority is so obvious that no one can contest it for a moment; only its degree is worth discussion. All psychologists who have studied the intelligence of women . . . recognize today that they represent the most inferior forms of human evolution, and that they are closer to children and savages than to an adult, civilized man.

> GUSTAVE LE BON (1841–1931). In *Revue d'Anthropologie,* 1879

Woman is at once the serpent, the apple—and the bellyache.

> H. L. MENCKEN (1880–1956). *A Book of Burlesques,* 12.18, 1920

I expect that Woman will be the last thing civilized by Man.

> GEORGE MEREDITH (1828–1909). *The Ordeal of Richard Feverel,* 1, 1859

Are you visiting women? Do not forget your whip!

> FRIEDRICH NIETZSCHE (1844–1900). "Of Old and Young Women," *Thus Spoke Zarathustra,* 1892, tr. R. J. Hollingdale, 1961

A little woman, bent on revenge, would annihilate Destiny itself. Woman is unspeakably more wicked than man, and cleverer also. In a woman goodness is already a sign of *degeneration.*

> FRIEDRICH NIETZSCHE (1844–1900). "Why I Write Such Excellent Books" (5), *Ecce Homo,* 1908, tr. Clifton Fadiman, 1927

There are two kinds of women—goddesses and doormats.

> PABLO PICASSO (1881–1973). Attributed

Men, some to Bus'ness, some to Pleasure take;
But ev'ry Woman is at heart a Rake.

> ALEXANDER POPE (1688–1744). *Moral Essays,* 2.215, 1731–1735

The fundamental fault of the female character is that it has no sense of justice.

> ARTHUR SCHOPENHAUER (1788–1860). "Studies in Pessimism: On Women," *Essays of Arthur Schopenhauer,* tr. T. Bailey Saunders, 1851

They are dependent, not upon strength, but upon craft; and hence their instinctive capacity for cunning, and their ineradicable tendency to say what is not true. . . . Dissimulation is innate in woman.

> ARTHUR SCHOPENHAUER (1788–1860). "Studies in Pessimism: On Women," *Essays of Arthur Schopenhauer,* tr. T. Bailey Saunders, 1851

Praised be Thou . . . who hast not made me a woman.

> TALMUD (1st–6th cent. A.D.). Rabbinical writings

The tactic used against Professor [Anita] Hill is suggested in a Senate speech of Alan K. Simpson. He warned that she would be "injured and destroyed, and belittled and hounded and harassed—real harassment, different from the sexual kind, just plain old Washington-variety harassment."

The threat was borne out in the language used by her Senate questioners. [Arlen] Specter called Hill "a flat-out perjurer." Senator Orrin G. Hatch portrayed her as a "deviant." Senator Simpson, referring to her testimony, spoke of "this foul, foul stack of stench" and "a garbage stench of verbiage."

> WASHINGTON SPECTATOR. Referring to Judge Clarence Thomas's October 1991 Supreme Court confirmation hearings before the Senate Judiciary Committee during which Law Professor Hill charged him with sexual harassment when she worked in a government office he headed during the early 1980s. "For Politicians: A New, Stunning Issue," 1 January 1992

However degraded a man may be, he is immeasurably above the most superior woman, so much so that comparison and classification of the two are impossible.

> OTTO WEININGER (1880–1903). *Sex and Character,* 12, 1903, authorized translation from the sixth German edition, 1909

❦

Find 'em, feel 'em, fuck 'em, forget 'em.

> SAYING (AMERICAN). 4-F club motto, quoted by Margo St. James, "Afterword." In Claude Jaget, ed., *Prostitutes—Our Life,* 1980

A dog is wiser than a woman; it doesn't bark at its master.

> SAYING (RUSSIAN)

Beware of a bad woman and put no trust in a good one.

> SAYING (SPANISH)

MISTAKES

See also • Blunders ○ Defeat ○ Errors ○ Failure ○ Faults ○ Safety ○ Vietnam War: Dean Acheson ○ The Wise & the Foolish: Saying

If I had to live my life again, I'd make the same mistakes, only sooner.

> TALLULAH BANKHEAD (1903–1968)

Every great mistake has a halfway moment, a split second when it can be recalled and perhaps remedied.

> PEARL S. BUCK (1892–1973). *What America Means to Me,* 10, 1943

Only those who do nothing . . . make no mistakes.

> JOSEPH CONRAD (1857–1924). *An Outcast of the Islands,* 3.2, 1896

My brethren, by the bowels of Christ I beseech you, bethink you that you may be mistaken.

> OLIVER CROMWELL (1599–1658). Letter to the General Assembly of the Church of Scotland, 3 August 1650. In Alfred North Whitehead, *Science and the Modern World,* 1, 1925

Helen: Why don't you learn from my mistakes? It takes half your life to learn from your own.

> SHELAGH DELANEY (1939–). *A Taste of Honey,* 1.2, 1958

As she frequently remarked when she made any such mistake, it would be all the same a hundred years hence.

> CHARLES DICKENS (1812–1870). *The Life and Adventures of Martin Chuzzlewit,* 19, 1844

Repeating mistakes is more likely than profiting from them.

> MALCOLM S. FORBES (1919–1990). "Fact and Comment," *The Sayings of Chairman Malcolm: The Capitalist's Handbook,* 1978

The huge elementary mistake, the betrayal of that within me which is greater than I—in a complacent adjustment to alien demands.

> DAG HAMMARSKJÖLD (1905–1961). 1950, *Markings,* tr. Leif Sjöberg and W. H. Auden, 1964

The greatest mistake you can make in life is to be continually fearing you will make one.

> ELBERT HUBBARD (1856–1915). *The Note Book of Elbert Hubbard,* opposite p. 113, comp. Elbert Hubbard II, 1927

To make mistakes is human, but to profit by them is divine.

> ELBERT HUBBARD (1856–1915).
> See Errors: Alexander Pope (1)

When I make a mistake, it's a beaut!

> FIORELLO LA GUARDIA (1882–1947). New York mayor. Remark, 1936. In William Manners, *Patience and Fortitude: Fiorello La Guardia,* 21, 1976

What should happen when you make a mistake is this: you take your knocks, you learn your lessons, and then you move on.

> RONALD REAGAN (1911–). Television broadcast, 4 March 1987

We may make mistakes—but they must never be mistakes which result from faintness of heart or abandonment of moral principle.

> FRANKLIN D. ROOSEVELT (1882–1945). *Fourth Inaugural Address,* 20 January 1945

If we have made obvious mistakes, we should not try, as we generally do, to gloss them over, or to find something to excuse . . . them; we should admit to ourselves that we have committed faults, and open our eyes wide to all their enormity, in order that we may firmly resolve to avoid them in time to come.

ARTHUR SCHOPENHAUER (1788–1860). "Counsels and Maxims" (2.12), *Essays of Arthur Schopenhauer,* tr. T. Bailey Saunders, 1851

❧

Stupidity is the name we give to other people's mistakes; our own mistakes we chalk up to experience.

ANONYMOUS

See Sin: Ralph Waldo Emerson

The mistakes we aren't allowed to make in our youth, we make later on in life—at greater cost and with less benefit.

ANONYMOUS

Better a mistake at the beginning than at the end.

SAYING (AFRICAN)

MOBS

See also • Crises ○ Crowds ○ Fanatics ○ The Masses ○ Mass Movements ○ Revolution ○ War

It is an easy and vulgar thing to please the mob, . . . but . . . to improve them is a work fraught with difficulty and teeming with danger.

C. C. COLTON (1780–1832). *Lacon: or, Many Things in Few Words; Addressed to Those Who Think,* 1.452, 1823

"It's always best on these occasions to do what the mob do."
"But suppose there are two mobs?" suggested Mr. Snodgrass.
"Shout with the largest," replied Mr. Pickwick.

CHARLES DICKENS (1812–1870). *Pickwick Papers,* 13, 1837

The mob is man voluntarily descending to the nature of the beast.

RALPH WALDO EMERSON (1803–1882). "Compensation," *Essays: First Series,* 1841

In the hands of vicious men,
a mob will do anything.
But under good leaders
it's quite a different story.

EURIPIDES (485?–406 B.C.). *Orestes,* l. 770, tr. William Arrowsmith, 1958

A Mob's a Monster; Heads enough, but no Brains.

BENJAMIN FRANKLIN (1706–1790). *Poor Richard's Almanack,* November 1747

Beware, my dear sir, of magnifying a riot into an insurrection, by employing in the first instance an inadequate force. 'Tis better far to err on the other side. Whenever the government appears in arms, it ought to appear like a Hercules, and inspire respect by the display of strength.

ALEXANDER HAMILTON (1757–1804). *The Basic Ideas of Alexander Hamilton,* 1799, ed. Richard B. Morris, 1957

Assemble a mob of men and women previously conditioned by a daily reading of newspapers; treat them to amplified band music, bright lights, and the oratory of a demagogue who . . . is simultaneously the exploiter and the victim of herd intoxication, and in next to no time you can reduce them to a state of almost mindless sub-humanity. Never before have so few been in a position to make fools, maniacs, or criminals of so many.

ALDOUS HUXLEY (1894–1963). Appendix to *The Devils of Loudun,* 1952

There is no grievance that is a fit object of redress by mob law.

ABRAHAM LINCOLN (1809–1865). "The Perpetuation of Our Political Institutions," address before the Young Men's Lyceum of Springfield (Illinois), 27 January 1838

The mob is either a humble slave or a cruel master.

LIVY (59 B.C.–A.D. 17). *The History of Rome,* 24.25, tr. Aubrey de Sélincourt, 1965

Nothing is so apt to restrain an excited multitude as the reverence inspired by some grave and dignified man of authority who opposes them.

MACHIAVELLI (1469–1527). *The Discourses,* 1.54, 1517, tr. Christian E. Detmold, 1940

You shall not follow a multitude to do evil.

MOSES (14th cent. B.C.). *Exodus* 23:2

The wretches! They should have swept down five hundred with grapeshot, and the rest would have fled.

NAPOLEON (1769–1821). As a young artillery captain, after witnessing Louis XVI on his palace balcony at Tuileries donning a liberty cap in capitulation to the demand of a mob which had just broken onto the grounds, 20 June 1792.

With a mob, everything depends on the first impression made upon it.

NAPOLEON (1769–1821). Sanctioning severity, remark to Dr. Barry E. O'Meara, 1817, *The Mind of Napoleon: A Selection from His Written and Spoken Words,* 224, ed. J. Christopher Herold, 1955

One must never show fear in the face of a mob.

RICHARD M. NIXON (1913–1994). *Six Crises,* 4, 1962

If you must fire, do a good job—a few casualties become martyrs, a large number an object lesson.

GEORGE S. PATTON, JR. (1885–1945). "Federal Troops in Domestic Disturbances," November 1932. In Martin Blumenson, *The Patton Papers, 1885–1940,* 44, 1972

The nose of a mob is its imagination. By, at any time, it can be quietly led.

EDGAR ALLAN POE (1809–1849). *Marginalia,* June 1849, University Press of Virginia edition, 1981

Beware the mob! *Cave canem!*

ROMAIN ROLLAND (1866–1944). *Mahatma Gandhi: The Man Who Became One with the Universal Being,* 2.6, 1924

Mobs must be faced if civilization is to be saved.

GEORGE BERNARD SHAW (1856–1950). Preface ("The Alternative to Barabbas") to *Androcles and the Lion,* 1912

Our supreme governors, the mob.

HORACE WALPOLE (1675–1745). Letter to Sir Horace Mann, 7 September 1743

A mob is humanity going the wrong way.

FRANK LLOYD WRIGHT (1867–1959). Mike Wallace television interview, 1958

❧

The mob rides an emotional roller coaster and is always on the brink of shedding blood—or tears.

ANONYMOUS

MODERATION

See also • Abstinence ○ Excess ○ Food ○ Health ○ Longevity: [especially] George Gallop and Evan Hill ○ Passion ○ Self-Discipline ○ Self-Knowledge: Heraclitus ○ Slavery: William Lloyd Garrison ○ Thrift

The temperate . . . man is so constituted that the bodily pleasures never make him do anything against his principle[s].

ARISTOTLE (384–322 B.C.). *Nicomachean Ethics*, 7.9, tr. J. A. K. Thomson, 1953

You never know what is enough unless you know what is more than enough.

WILLIAM BLAKE (1757–1827). "Proverbs of Hell," *The Marriage of Heaven and Hell*, 9.7, 1790–1793?

Moderation in all things.

CLEOBULUS (6th cent. B.C.)

Moderation multiplies pleasures.

DEMOCRITUS (460–370 B.C.). In Kathleen Freeman, tr., *Ancilla to Pre-Socratic Philosophers: A Complete Translation of the Fragments in Diels*, Fragmente der Vorsokratiker, 68.211, 1983 (1948)

It is difficult . . . for a rich man to be moderate, or for a moderate man to be rich.

EPICTETUS (A.D. 55?–135?). Fragment, 21, tr. George Long, 1890?

I would remind you that extremism in the defense of liberty is no vice. And let me remind you also that moderation in the pursuit of justice is no virtue.

BARRY M. GOLDWATER (1909–1998). Presidential nomination acceptance speech, San Francisco, 16 July 1964

Enough is as good as a feast.

JOHN HEYWOOD (1497–1580). Comp. *A Dialogue Containing the Number of the Effectual Proverbs in the English Tongue*, 2.11, 1562

Moderation is a virtue only in those who are thought to have a choice.

HENRY A. KISSINGER (1923–). *White House Years*, 7, 1979

Damn temperance and he that first invented it!

CHARLES LAMB (1775–1834). Letter to Dorothy Wordsworth, autumn 1810

Moderation has been declared a virtue so as to curb the ambition of the great and console lesser folk for their lack of fortune and merit.

LA ROCHEFOUCAULD (1613–1680). *Maxims*, 308, 1665, tr. Leonard Tancock, 1959

The middle way is safest.

OVID (43 B.C.–A.D. 17). *Metamorphoses*, 2.135, tr. Mary M. Innes, 1955

Those words, "temperate and moderate," are words either of political cowardice, or of cunning, or seduction. A thing moderately good, is not so good as it ought to be. Moderation in temper is always a virtue, but moderation in principle is a species of vice.

THOMAS PAINE (1737–1809). "Letter addressed to the addressers on the late proclamation," 1792, undated

Whatever is enough is abundant in the eyes of virtue.

SENECA THE YOUNGER (5? B.C.–A.D. 65). "On Virtue as a Refuge from Worldly Distractions," *Moral Letters to Lucilius*, 74.12, tr. Richard M. Gummere, 1918

❧

Moderation in everything but virtue.

ANONYMOUS

MODESTY

See also • Egotism ○ Humility

Modesty is the only sure bait when you angle for praise.

LORD CHESTERFIELD (1694–1773). Letter to his son, 17 May 1750

[Clement Attlee is] a modest man with a lot to be modest about.

WINSTON CHURCHILL (1874–1965). Attributed (he denied having said it). In John Beavan, "Tales of Churchill," *New York Times Magazine*, 29 November 1959

The only thing worse than false modesty is no modesty at all.

JOSEPH EPSTEIN (1928–). "What Is Vulgar?" *The Middle of My Tether*, 1983

Tho' Modesty be a Virtue, yet Bashfulness is a Vice.

THOMAS FULLER (1654–1734). Comp. *Gnomologia: Adages and Proverbs*, 5006, 1732

Women commend a modest Man but like him not.

THOMAS FULLER (1654–1734). Comp. *Gnomologia: Adages and Proverbs*, 5805, 1732

Modesty is a vastly overrated virtue.

JOHN KENNETH GALBRAITH (1908–). *The Ambassador's Journal: A Personal Account of the Kennedy Years*, 2, 1969

True modesty does not consist in an ignorance of our merits but in a due estimate of them.

J. C. HARE (1795–1855) and A. W. HARE (1792–1834). *Guesses at Truth: First Series*, p. 6, 1827, Macmillan edition, 1867

A modest man is usually admired—if people ever hear of him.

E. W. HOWE (1853–1937). *Ventures in Common Sense*, 4.7, 1919

Modesty is the opiate of the mediocre.

MICHAEL O'HARRO. "O'Harro's Law." In Paul Dickson, comp., *The New Official Rules*, p. 159, 1989

Be modest! It is the kind of pride least likely to offend.

JULES RENARD (1864–1910). Journal, September 1895, tr. Louise Bogan and Elizabeth Roget, 1964

If there is something more unpleasant than pushiness, it is a display of modesty.

JULES RENARD (1864–1910). Journal, November 1909, tr. Louise Bogan and Elizabeth Roget, 1964

One is vain by nature, modest by necessity.

PIERRE REVERDY (1889–1960). French poet. En Vrac

[Modesty] was invented only as protection against envy.

ARTHUR SCHOPENHAUER (1788–1860). "The Art of Literature: On Reputation," Essays of Arthur Schopenhauer, tr. T. Bailey Saunders, 1851

With people of only moderate ability, modesty is mere honesty; but with those who possess great talent, it is hypocrisy.

ARTHUR SCHOPENHAUER (1788–1860). "Studies in Pessimism: Further Psychological Observations," Essays of Arthur Schopenhauer, tr. T. Bailey Saunders, 1851

❧

[Modesty is] the art of encouraging people to find out for themselves how wonderful you are.

ANONYMOUS

Too little or too much modesty loses respect.

ANONYMOUS

MONEY

See also • Banks ○ Business (Commerce) ○ Class ○ Debt ○ Economics ○ Gambling ○ Gold ○ Greed ○ Inflation ○ Luxury ○ Misers ○ Pay ○ Possessions ○ Poverty ○ Power ○ Price ○ Profit & Loss ○ Property ○ Prudence: Rules ○ Riches ○ Stock Market ○ Thrift ○ Time: Josh Billings, Benjamin Franklin (2) ○ Trade (Commerce) ○ Value ○ Wages ○ Wealth ○ Work ○ Worry: J. P. Donleavy

Money can't buy everything. For example: poverty.

NELSON ALGREN (1909–1981). A Walk on the Wild Side, 3, 1956

Money is like muck, not good except it be spread.

FRANCIS BACON (1561–1626). "Of Seditions and Troubles," Essays, 1625

Money, it turned out, was exactly like sex, you thought of nothing else if you didn't have it and thought of other things if you did.

JAMES BALDWIN (1924–1987). Nobody Knows My Name: More Notes of a Native Son, 13, 1961

Holdup Man: Your money or your life? Come on, hurry up!
Benny: I'm thinking it over!

JACK BENNY (1894–1974). Comedian and radio personality. His signature joke

Money has only one use—to give one independence from his enemies.

HUMPHREY BOGART (1899–1957)

Money is honey—my little sonny!
And a rich man's joke is [always] funny.

T. E. BROWN (1830–1897). The Doctor, 1887, The Collected Poems of T. E. Brown, 1909

It has been said that the love of money is the root of all evil. The want of money is so quite as truly.

SAMUEL BUTLER (1835–1902). Erewhon, 20, 1872
See Greed: Paul

Ready money is Aladdin's lamp.

LORD BYRON (1788–1824). Don Juan, 12.12, 1819–1824

The sinews of war, money in abundance.

CICERO (106–43 B.C.), Philippics, 5.2, tr. C. D. Yonge, 1903 (Popular version: Money is the sinews of war.)

Money makes a man.

JOHN CLARKE (1596–1658). Comp., Proverbs: English and Latine, p. 99, 1639
See Clothes: Saying (Latin) ○ Manners: William Blake

Show me the money!

CAMERON CROWE. Jerry Maguire (film), 1997, spoken by Cuba Gooding, Jr.

Money, Paul, can do anything.

CHARLES DICKENS (1812–1870). Dombey and Son, 8, 1848

A billion here, a billion there, and pretty soon you're talking about real money.

EVERETT DIRKSEN (1896–1969). Illinois senator. Off-the-cuff remark. Attributed to him by his friend John Kriegsman

Money is coined liberty.

FYODOR DOSTOYEVSKY (1821–1881). Notes from the House of the Dead, 1.1, 1862, tr. Constance Garnett, 1914

Let me ask you one question
Is your money that good
Will it buy you forgiveness
Do you think that it could
I think you will find
When your death takes its toll
All the money you made
Will never buy back your soul.

BOB DYLAN (1941–). "Masters of War" (song), 1963

Money doesn't talk, it swears.

BOB DYLAN (1941–). "It's Alright, Ma (I'm Only Bleeding)" (song), 1965

"Money does not bring happiness"—only the wherewithal, perhaps, to endure its absence.

BARBARA EHRENREICH (1941–). Fear of Falling: The Inner Life of the Middle Class, 6, 1990

Money often costs too much.

RALPH WALDO EMERSON (1803–1882). "Wealth," The Conduct of Life, 1860

Money helps, though not so much as you think when you don't have it.

LOUISE ERDRICH. "Insulation," The Bingo Palace, 1994

Money is the sinews of love, as of war.

GEORGE FARQUHAR (1678–1707). Love and a Bottle, 2.1, 1699

"Money isn't everything," according to those who have it.

MALCOLM S. FORBES (1919–1990). "Nobody's Capitalist Fool," The Sayings of Chairman Malcolm: The Capitalist's Handbook, 1978

Nothing but Money,
Is sweeter than Honey.
>   BENJAMIN FRANKLIN (1706–1790). *Poor Richard's Almanack,* June 1735

If you'd know the Value of Money, go and borrow some.
>   BENJAMIN FRANKLIN (1706–1790). *Poor Richard's Almanack,* April 1754

"After getting the first hundred pound[s], it is more easy to get the second," money itself being of a prolific nature.
>   BENJAMIN FRANKLIN (1706–1790). 1788, *Autobiography,* 1798

A light Purse makes a heavy Heart.
>   THOMAS FULLER (1654–1734). Comp., *Gnomologia: Adages and Proverbs,* 241, 1732

He that is without Money is a Bird without Wings.
>   THOMAS FULLER (1654–1734). Comp., *Gnomologia: Adages and Proverbs,* 2200, 1732

Money is the God of the World.
>   THOMAS FULLER (1654–1734). Comp., *Gnomologia: Adages and Proverbs,* 3440, 1732

Whoever controls the volume of money in any country is absolute master of all industry and commerce.
>   JAMES GARFIELD (1831–1881). President. Attributed

NEVER UNDERESTIMATE THE POWER OF CASH.
>   GEORGIA-PACIFIC CORP. Forest products producer. Sole copy on one page of a two-page ad. In *Forbes,* 23 July 1990

People who don't respect money don't have any.
>   J. PAUL GETTY (1892–1976). Oil magnate

Bad money drives out good money.
>   SIR THOMAS GRESHAM (1519–1579). English financier. Attributed
>   See Bureaucracy: Milton Friedman ○ Business (Commerce): Ralph Nader ○ Politics: Bertrand Russell (1) ○ The Press: Anthony Lewis ○ Talking: Doug "Leo" Hanbury

They who are of [the] opinion that money will do everything may very well be suspected to do everything for money.
>   MARQUIS OF HALIFAX (1633–1695). "Of Money," *Political, Moral and Miscellaneous Reflections,* 1750

Soon gotten, soon spent; ill gotten, ill spent.
>   JOHN HEYWOOD (1497–1580). Comp., *A Dialogue Containing the Number of the Effectual Proverbs in the English Tongue,* 2.6, 1562

Put not your trust in money, but put your money in trust.
>   OLIVER WENDELL HOLMES, SR. (1809–1894). *The Autocrat of the Breakfast-Table,* 2, 1858

Money is paper blood.
>   BOB HOPE (1903–). Attributed

Make money, fairly make it, if you may,
But, if not fairly, then in any way.
>   HORACE (65–8 B.C.). Expressing with disapproval a popular view, *Epistles,* 1.1, *The Complete Works of Horace,* ed. Casper J. Kraemer, Jr., 1936
>   See Profit & Loss: Hesiod ○ Victory & Defeat: Saying (Arab)

Money is the measure of power.
>   ELBERT HUBBARD (1856–1915). *The Note Book of Elbert Hubbard,* p. 134, comp. Elbert Hubbard II, 1927

When a feller says, "It hain't th' money, but th' principle o' th' thing," it's th' money.
>   KIN HUBBARD (1868–1930). *Abe Martin's Sayings and Wisecracks, Abe's Neighbors, His Almanack, Comic Drawings,* 1, ed. David S. Hawes, 1984

Not only does money speak; it also imposes silence.
>   ALDOUS HUXLEY (1894–1963). "Censorship and Spoken Literature," *Tomorrow and Tomorrow and Tomorrow,* 1956

The almighty dollar, that great object of universal devotion throughout our land.
>   WASHINGTON IRVING (1783–1859). "The Creole Village," *Wolfert's Roost and Miscellanies,* 1855

There are few ways in which a man can be more innocently employed than in getting money.
>   SAMUEL JOHNSON (1709–1784). 27 March 1775. In James Boswell, *The Life of Samuel Johnson,* 1791

Money always implies the promise of magic, but the effect is much magnified when, as now, people have lost faith in everything else.
>   LEWIS H. LAPHAM (1935–). *Money and Class in America: Notes and Observations on the Civil Religion,* 9, 1988

For I don't care too much for money,
For money can't buy me love.
>   JOHN LENNON (1940–1980) and PAUL McCARTNEY (1942–). "Can't Buy Me Love" (song), 1964

Money is the alienated essence of man's work and existence; this essence dominates him and he worships it.
>   KARL MARX (1818–1883). "On the Jewish Question" (2), 1844, *The Marx-Engels Reader,* 2nd ed., ed. Robert C. Tucker, 1978

The value of money is that with it we can tell any man to go to the devil. It is the sixth sense which enables you to enjoy the other five.
>   W. SOMERSET MAUGHAM (1874–1965). *Of Human Bondage,* 51, 1915

Money to get power, power to protect money.
>   MEDICI FAMILY (15th cent.). Motto. In Bertram Gross, *Friendly Fascism: The New Face of Power in America,* 10, 1980

It is pretty to see what money will do.
>   SAMUEL PEPYS (1633–1703). Diary, 21 March 1667

There, London's voice: "Get Money, Money still!
And then let Virtue follow, if she will."
>   ALEXANDER POPE (1688–1744). *Imitations of Horace,* 1.1(Epistle).79, 1733–1738

Money alone sets all the world in motion.
>   PUBLIUS SYRUS (85–43 B.C.). *Moral Sayings,* 656, tr. Darius Lyman, Jr., 1862
>   See Love: Saying (French)

A heavy purse makes a *light* heart.
>   JOHN RAY (1628–1705). Comp., *A Collection of English Proverbs,* p. 168, 1678

I know of nothing more despicable and pathetic than a man who devotes all the hours of the waking day to the making of money for money's sake.

> JOHN D. ROCKEFELLER, SR. (1839–1937). In Lewis H. Lapham, *Money and Class in America: Notes and Observations on the Civil Religion,* 8, 1988

"My boy," he says, "always try to rub up against money, for if you rub up against money long enough, some of it may rub off on you."

> DAMON RUNYON (1884–1946). "A Very Honourable Guy," *Cosmopolitan,* August 1929

There are more important things than money—the only trouble is they all cost money.

> LOUIS A. SAFIAN. Comp., *The Book of Updated Proverbs,* 7, 1967

Money is power, freedom, a cushion, the
  root of all evil, the sum of blessings.

> CARL SANDBURG (1878–1967). *The People, Yes,* 65, 1936

Money is human happiness in the abstract: he, then, who is no longer capable of enjoying human happiness in the concrete, devotes his heart entirely to money.

> ARTHUR SCHOPENHAUER (1788–1860). "Religion and Other Essays: Psychological Observations," *Essays of Arthur Schopenhauer,* | tr. T. Bailey Saunders, 1851

Money makes a man laugh.

> JOHN SELDEN (1584–1654). "Money" (1), *Table Talk,* 1689, ed. Frederick Pollock, 1927

Money comes from sacrilege and theft.

> SENECA THE YOUNGER (5? B.C.–A.D. 65). "Some Arguments in Favor of the Simple Life," *Moral Letters to Lucilius,* 87.22, tr. Richard M. Gummere, 1918
> See Property: Pierre-Joseph Proudhon

Ford: They say, if money go before, all ways do lie open.
Falstaff: Money is a good soldier, sir, and will on.

> SHAKESPEARE (1564–1616). *The Merry Wives of Windsor,* 2.2.175, 1600

That is the use of money: it enables us to get what we want instead of what other people think we want.

> GEORGE BERNARD SHAW (1856–1950). *The Intelligent Woman's Guide to Socialism, Capitalism, Sovietism and Fascism,* 6, 1928

Money is that dear thing which
  if you're not careful, you can
  squander
your whole life thinking of.

> MARY JO SLATER. "A Benediction," 6.1, 1994

Money, says the proverb, makes money. When you have got a little, it is often easy to get more. The great difficulty is to get that little.

> ADAM SMITH (1723–1790). *The Wealth of Nations,* 1.9, 1776

The price we have to pay for money is paid in liberty.

> ROBERT LOUIS STEVENSON (1850–1894). "Henry David Thoreau: His Character and Opinions" (2), *Familiar Studies of Men and Books,* 1882

No one would remember the Good Samaritan if he'd only had good intentions. He had money as well.

> MARGARET THATCHER (1925–). Television interview, 6 January 1986. In *Times* (London), 12 January 1986

I prefer a man without money to money without a man.

> THEMISTOCLES (523?–458? B.C.). When asked whether he would have his daughter marry someone who was poor and honest or rich and dishonest. In Cicero (106–43 B.C.), *De officiis,* 2.20, tr. Walter Miller, 1913

The more money, the less virtue.

> HENRY DAVID THOREAU (1817–1862). "Civil Disobedience," 1849
> See Riches: Plato (1)

Money is not required to buy one necess[ity] of the soul.

> HENRY DAVID THOREAU (1817–1862). "Conclusion," *Walden; or Life in the Woods,* 1854

Money begets money.

> GIOVANNI TORRIANO. Comp., *Select Italian Proverbs,* 1642

Money was never a big motivation for me, except as a way to keep score. The real excitement is playing the game.

> DONALD J. TRUMP (1946–) (with TONY SCHWARTZ). *Trump: The Art of the Deal,* 2, 1987
> See Wealth: Bertrand Russell

Get money. Get it quickly. Get it in abundance. Get it in prodigious abundance. Get it dishonestly if you can, honestly if you must.

> MARK TWAIN (1835–1910). In Bernard A. Weisberger, "The Wrongdoers," *American Heritage,* December 1989

Money is freedom.

> HORACE WALPOLE (1717–1797). "Horace Walpole." In James Thornton, ed., *Table Talk from Ben Johnson to Leigh Hunt,* 1934
> See Wealth: James Russell Lowell

There is only one class in the community that thinks more about money than the rich, and that is the poor. The poor can think of nothing else.

> OSCAR WILDE (1854–1900). "The Soul of Man Under Socialism," *Fortnightly Review* (British journal), February 1891

Lord Fermor: Young people, nowadays, imagine that money is everything.
Lord Henry: Yes, and when they grow older they know it.

> OSCAR WILDE (1854–1900). Format adapted. *The Picture of Dorian Gray,* 3, 1891

Money gave me exactly what I wanted, power over others.

> OSCAR WILDE (1854–1900). *An Ideal Husband,* 2, 1895
> See Riches: John Ruskin (2)

🌿

Most people are too busy earning a living to make any money.

> ANONYMOUS

Money isn't everything—as long as you have enough of it.

> ANONYMOUS

You can make money or you can make waves, but you can't make both.

> ANONYMOUS

Money doesn't grow on trees.
> SAYING (AMERICAN)

Money talks, but all it ever says is goodbye.
> SAYING (AMERICAN)

If a little money does not go, much money cannot come.
> SAYING (CHINESE and JAPANESE)

Money is a good servant but a bad master.
> SAYING (FRENCH)
> See Passion: Saying (English) ○ The Press: James Fenimore Cooper

Money is flat and meant to be piled.
> SAYING (NEW ENGLAND)

When money speaks, truth is silent.
> SAYING (RUSSIAN)

Money is God's lieutenant.
> SAYING (SPANISH)

Dirty hands make clean money.
> SAYING (VERMONT)

A full purse is not as good as an empty one is bad.
> SAYING (YIDDISH)

With money in your pocket, you are wise and handsome, and you sing well too.
> SAYING (YIDDISH)

Never throw good money after bad.
> SAYING

The more dollars, the less sense.
> SAYING

MONTANA

It seems to me that Montana is a great splash of grandeur. The scale is huge but not overpowering. The land is rich with grass and color, and the mountains are the kind I would create if mountains were ever put on my agenda.
> JOHN STEINBECK (1902–1968). *Travels with Charley: In Search of America*, 3, 1961

MONTHS

See also • Days ○ Nature ○ Seasons ○ Time ○ Weather

Oh, it's a long, long while
From May to December,
But the days grow short;
When you reach September.
> MAXWELL ANDERSON (1888–1959). "September Song." In the musical *Knickerbocker Holiday*, 1938

What sweeter words can fall on the human ear? It's going to be May all week long.
> RUSSELL BAKER (1925–). 22 May, *Poor Russell's Almanac*, 1972

Oh, to be in England
Now that April's there.
> ROBERT BROWNING (1812–1889). Opening lines, "Home-Thoughts from Abroad," 1847

April showers make May flowers.
> JOHN CLARKE (1596–1658). Comp., *Proverbs: English and Latine*, p. 307, 1639 (Popular version: April showers bring May flowers.)
> See Rain: B. G. DeSylva

April is the cruelest month, breeding
Lilacs out of the dead land, mixing
Memory and desire, stirring
Dull roots with spring rain.
> T. S. ELIOT (1888–1965). Opening lines, *The Waste Land*, 1922

In March many weathers. March always comes [even] if it do[es] not come till May. May generally does not come at all.
> RALPH WALDO EMERSON (1803–1882). Journal, 1 March 1841

Thirty days hath November,
April, June, and September,
February hath twenty-eight alone,
And all the rest have thirty-one.
> RICHARD GRAFTON (1513?–1573). *Chronicles of England*, 1562

"June Is Bustin' Out All Over."
> OSCAR HAMMERSTEIN II (1895–1960). Song title. In the musical *Carousel*, 1945

The most serious charge which can be brought against New England is not Puritanism but February.
> JOSEPH WOOD KRUTCH (1893–1970). "February," *Twelve Seasons*, 1949

And what is so rare as a day in June?
Then, if ever, come perfect days.
> JAMES RUSSELL LOWELL (1819–1891). *The Vision of Sir Launfal*, 1.5 (prelude), 1848

Every April God rewrites the Book of Genesis.
> AUSTIN O'MALLEY (1858–1932)

The merry month of May.
> JOHN RAY (1628–1705). Comp., *A Collection of English Proverbs*, p. 44, 1678

❧

May is crueler than April.
> ANONYMOUS. Graffito. In "Talk of the Town," *New Yorker*, 14 May 1960

Hooray, Hooray, the first of May,
Outdoor fucking begins today.
> SAYING (ENGLISH). 1960s?

March comes in like a lion and goes out like a lamb.
> SAYING (ENGLISH)

A cold wet May fills the barn with hay.
> SAYING (VERMONT)

MOON

See also • Nature ○ Space

See yonder fire! It is the moon
Slow rising o'er the eastern hill.
It glimmers on the forest tips,
And through the dewy foliage drips
In little rivulets of light,
And makes the heart in love with night.

> HENRY WADSWORTH LONGFELLOW (1807–1882). "The Golden
> Legend" (6), 1851, *Christus: A Mystery*, 1872

Perhaps the crescent moon smiles in doubt
at being told that it is a fragment
awaiting perfection.

> RABINDRANATH TAGORE (1861–1941). *Fireflies*, p. 179, 1928

MORAL INDIGNATION

See also • Anger ○ Envy ○ Hypocrisy ○ Morality: Bertrand Russell
(2) ○ Puritanism ○ Self-Righteousness

Moral indignation is in most cases 2 percent moral, 48 percent
indignation, and 50 percent envy.

> VITTORIO DE SICA (1901–1974). In *Observer* (British newspaper), 1961

Moral indignation is one of envy's stylish disguises.

> PAUL ELDRIDGE (1888–1982). *Maxims for a Modern Man*, 2743, 1965

There is perhaps no phenomenon which contains so much
destructive feeling as "moral indignation," which permits envy or
hate to be acted out under the guise of virtue. The "indignant"
person has for once the satisfaction of despising and treating a
creature as "inferior," coupled with the feeling of his own superiority and rightness.

> ERICH FROMM (1900–1980). *Man for Himself: An Inquiry into the
> Psychology of Ethics*, 4.5.C, 1947

Righteous Indignation: Your own wrath as opposed to the shocking bad temper of others.

> ELBERT HUBBARD (1856–1915). *The Roycroft Dictionary Concocted by
> Ali Baba and the Bunch on Rainy Days*, p. 129, 1914

To be able to destroy with good conscience, to be able to behave
badly and call your bad behavior "righteous indignation"—this is
the height of psychological luxury, the most delicious of moral
treats.

> ALDOUS HUXLEY (1894–1963). Recalled on his death, 22 November
> 1963

Moral indignation is jealousy with a halo.

> H. G. WELLS (1866–1946). *The Wife of Sir Isaac Harman*, 9.2, 1914

MORALITY

See also • Action ○ Cause & Effect ○ Character ○ Charity ○
Civilization ○ Conscience ○ Corruption ○ Crime ○ Dignity ○ Duty
○ Ethics ○ Evil ○ Forgiveness ○ Giving ○ God ○ Golden Rule ○
Good ○ Good & Evil ○ Guilt ○ Honesty ○ Indifference ○

Innocence ○ Integrity ○ Justice ○ Means & Ends ○ Policy:
Napoleon (1) ○ Politics: Adolf Hitler (2), Lenin (2), Karl R.
Popper, Rousseau ○ Principles, Moral ○ Punishment ○
Reform: T. H. Tawney ○ Religion: [especially] Henry Ward
Beecher ○ Resistance ○ Responsibility ○ Self-Realization
(Becoming) ○ Silence & Protest ○ Sin ○ Unity ○ Values ○ Vice ○
Virtue ○ Virtue & Vice ○ Will, Free: James Anthony Froude,
Immanuel Kant

Respect for the freedom of others is the highest duty of man. To
love this freedom and to serve it—such is the only virtue. That is
the basis of all morality; and there can be no other.

> MIKHAIL BAKUNIN (1814–1876). 1871, *The Political Philosophy of
> Bakunin: Scientific Anarchism*, 3.13, ed. G. P. Maximoff, 1953

Moral, *adj.* Conforming to a local and mutable standard of right.
Having the quality of general expediency.

> AMBROSE BIERCE (1842–1914). *The Devil's Dictionary*, p. 89, 1911,
> Dover edition, 1958

The money and morality ov this world are a good deal alike, the
principle never loses sight ov the interest.

> JOSH BILLINGS (1818–1885). "Jews Harps," *Everybody's Friend, or Josh
> Billing's Encyclopedia and Proverbial Philosophy of Wit and Humor*,
> 1874

Morality turns on whether the pleasure precedes or follows the
pain.

> SAMUEL BUTLER (1835–1902). *The Note-Books of Samuel Butler*, 2, ed.
> Henry Festing Jones, 1907
> See Pleasure: Benjamin Franklin

Morality is the custom of one's country and the current feeling of
one's peers. Cannibalism is moral in a cannibal country.

> SAMUEL BUTLER (1835–1902). *The Note-Books of Samuel Butler*, 2, ed.
> Henry Festing Jones, 1907

Enjoy and give pleasure, without doing harm to yourself or to
anyone else—that, I think, is the whole of morality.

> CHAMFORT (1741–1794). *Maxims and Thoughts*, 5, 1796,
> tr. W. S. Merwin, 1984

The moral sense perhaps affords the best and highest distinction
between man and the lower animals.

> CHARLES DARWIN (1809–1882). *The Descent of Man and Selection in
> Relation to Sex*, 2nd ed., 4, 1874

There is no moral principle, no rule of virtue whatever.

> DIDEROT (1713–1784). In Lewis Mumford, *The Conduct of Life*, 6.4, 1951

Caught in the relaxing interval between one moral code and the
next, an unmoored generation surrenders itself to luxury, corruption, and a restless disorder of family and morals.

> WILL DURANT (1885–1981) and ARIEL DURANT (1898–1981). In Lewis
> H. Lapham, "In the Garden of Tabloid Delight" (epigraph), *Harper's*,
> August 1997

The moral sentiment . . . is the drop that balances the sea.

> RALPH WALDO EMERSON (1803–1882). "Montaigne; or, The Skeptic,"
> *Representative Men*, 1850

Morality—the plain, practical development of life according to its nature.

The social effect of this morality finds expression in devoting business to the service of the whole people instead of to the service of the few.

> HENRY FORD (1863–1947) (with SAMUEL CROWTHER). *Today and Tomorrow,* 26, 1926

Freedom, the ability to preserve one's integrity against power, is the basic condition for morality.

> ERICH FROMM (1900–1980). *Man for Himself: An Inquiry into the Psychology of Ethics,* 5, 1947

True morality consists not in following the beaten track, but in finding out the true path for ourselves and fearlessly following it.

> MOHANDAS K. GANDHI (1869–1948). *Ethical Religion,* 2, 1930

Responsibility, not to a superior, but to one's conscience, the awareness of a duty not exacted by compulsion, the necessity to decide which of the things one values are to be sacrificed to others, and to bear the consequences of one's own decision, are the very essence of any morals which deserve the name.

> F. A. HAYEK (1899–1992). *The Road to Serfdom,* 14, 1944

I know only that what is moral is what you feel good after, and what is immoral is what you feel bad after.

> ERNEST HEMINGWAY (1899–1961). *Death in the Afternoon,* 1, 1932
> See Good & Evil: Anonymous (American)

The character of every act depends upon the circumstances in which it is done.

> OLIVER WENDELL HOLMES, JR. (1841–1935). *Schenck v. United States,* 1919

The moral law obliges us to regard every man as an end in himself.

> WILHELM von HUMBOLDT (1767–1835). *The Limits of State Action,* 8, 1854, ed. J. W. Burrow, 1969

The foundation of morality is to have done, once and for all, with lying.

> T. H. HUXLEY (1825–1895). "Science and Morals," 1886, *Essays Upon Some Controverted Questions,* 1893

Whenever you are to do a thing, though it can never be known but to yourself, ask yourself how you would act were the whole world looking at you, and act accordingly.

> THOMAS JEFFERSON (1743–1826). Letter to Peter Carr, 19 August 1785

I . . . never believed there was one code of morality for a public [man], and another for a private man.

> THOMAS JEFFERSON (1743–1826). Letter to Don Valentine de Feronda, 4 October 1809

The moral sense is as much a part of our constitution as that of feeling, seeing, or hearing.

> THOMAS JEFFERSON (1743–1826). Letter to John Adams, 14 October 1816

Morality is made up of customs and habits. Custom makes public morality, and habit individual morality.

> JOSEPH JOUBERT (1754–1824). *Pensées,* 1838, tr. H. P. Collins, 1928

Without freedom there can be no morality.

> CARL G. JUNG (1875–1961). "The Relations between the Ego and the Unconscious" (1.2), 1928, *Two Essays on Analytical Psychology,* tr. R. F. C. Hull, 1953

Morality is not properly the doctrine [of] how we should *make* ourselves happy, but how we should make ourselves *worthy* of happiness.

> IMMANUEL KANT (1724–1804). *Critique of Practical Reason,* 1.2.2.5, 1788, tr. Thomas Kingsmill Abbott, 1873

There is . . . only one categorical imperative. It is: Act only according to that maxim by which you can at the same time will that it should become a universal law.

> IMMANUEL KANT (1724–1804). *Foundations of the Metaphysics of Morals,* 2, 1797, tr. Lewis White Beck, 1969

The moral sense is a natural faculty in us like the sense of smell or of touch.

> PETER KROPOTKIN (1842–1921). *Anarchist Morality* (pamphlet, 6), 1909, *Kropotkin's Revolutionary Pamphlets,* ed. Roger N. Baldwin, 1927

Our morality is entirely subordinated to the interests of the proletariat's class struggle.

> LENIN (1870–1924). "The Tasks of the Youth Leagues," speech, 2 October 1920, *V. I. Lenin: Selected Works,* International Publishers edition, 1971

Children first conceive morality as rules for pleasing their parents—only with the fullness of time comes a grasp of the idea of conscientious choice.

> MICHAEL LEVIN. "Ethics Courses: Useless," *New York Times,* 25 November 1989

Moral knowledge is as capable of real certainty as mathematics.

> JOHN LOCKE (1632–1704). *An Essay Concerning Human Understanding,* 4.4.7, 1690, ed. Alexander Campbell Fraser, 1894

Man is so essentially, so necessarily, a moral being that, when he denies the existence of all morality, that very denial already becomes the foundation of a new morality.

> MAURICE MAETERLINCK (1862–1949). In Elbert Hubbard, comp., *Elbert Hubbard's Scrap Book,* p. 200, 1923

Failure or success in the struggle for existence is the sole moral standard. Good is what survives.

> W. SOMERSET MAUGHAM (1874–1965). 1901, *A Writer's Notebook,* 1949

Lifestyle and livelihood are pivotal moral issues.

> STEPHANIE MILLS (1948–). "Householding," *Whatever Happened to Ecology?* 1989

Morality is herd instinct in the individual.

> FRIEDRICH NIETZSCHE (1844–1900). *The Gay Science,* 116, 1882, tr. Walter Kaufmann, 1974

There are *master-morality* and *slave-morality*.

> FRIEDRICH NIETZSCHE (1844–1900). *Beyond Good and Evil,* 260, 1886, tr. Walter Kaufmann, 1966

Mankind can best be *led by the nose* with morality.

> FRIEDRICH NIETZSCHE (1844–1900). *The Anti-Christ,* 44, 1895, tr. R. J. Hollingdale, 1968

The only moral lesson which is suited for a child—the most important lesson for every time of life—is this, "Never hurt anybody."

ROUSSEAU (1712–1778)

We have . . . two kinds of morality side by side: one which we preach but do not practice, and another which we practice but seldom preach.

BERTRAND RUSSELL (1872–1970). *Sceptical Essays,* 8, 1928

A stern morality [enables] you to inflict suffering without a bad conscience.

BERTRAND RUSSELL (1872–1970). Woodrow Wyatt television interview, BBC, London, 1959, *Bertrand Russell Speaks His Mind,* 5, 1960

Pickering: Have you no morals, man?
Alfred Doolittle: Can't afford them, Governor. Neither could you if you was as poor as me.

GEORGE BERNARD SHAW (1856–1950). *Pygmalion,* 2, 1912

The so-called new morality is too often the old immorality condoned.

LORD SHAWCROSS (1902–). In *Observer* (British newspaper), 17 November 1963

The mechanical law that action and reaction are equal has its moral analogue. The deed of one man to another tends ultimately to produce a like effect upon both, be the deed good or bad.

HERBERT SPENCER (1820–1903). *Social Statics,* 3.20.7, 1851

Morality knows nothing of geographical boundaries or distinctions of race.

HERBERT SPENCER (1820–1903). *Social Statics,* 3.23.1, 1851

Social arrangements can be conformed to the moral law only in as far as the people are themselves moral.

HERBERT SPENCER (1820–1903). *Social Statics,* 4.31.5, 1851

All theories of morality agree in considering that conduct whose total results, immediate and remote, are beneficial, is good conduct; while conduct whose total results, immediate and remote, are injurious, is bad conduct. The happiness or misery caused by it are the *ultimate* standards by which all men judge of behavior.

HERBERT SPENCER (1820–1903). *Education: Intellectual, Moral, and Physical,* 3, 1860

A right rule of conduct must be one which may with advantage be adopted by all.

HERBERT SPENCER (1820–1903). *The Data of Ethics,* 13, 1879

The art of acting morally is behaving *as if everything we do matters.*

GLORIA STEINEM (1934–). "The Birth of Ms." *New York,* 19 April 1993

Do not be too moral. You may cheat yourself out of much life so. Aim above morality. Be not simply good, be good for something.

HENRY DAVID THOREAU (1817–1862). Letter to Harrison Blake, 27 March 1848

The recognition of the sanctity of the life of every man is the first and only basis of all morality.

LEO TOLSTOY (1828–1910). *The Kingdom of God Is Within You,* 12.3, 1893, tr. Aylmer Maude, 1936

As a family, we had a code, which was to do the right thing, do it the best we could, never complain and never take advantage.

MARGARET TRUMAN (1924–) (with MARGARET COUSINS). *Souvenir: Margaret Truman's Own Story,* 8, 1956

There is a Moral Sense, and there is an Immoral Sense. History shows us that the Moral Sense enables us to perceive morality and how to avoid it, and that the Immoral Sense enables us to perceive immorality and how to enjoy it.

MARK TWAIN (1835–1910). *Following the Equator: A Journey Around the World,* 16 (epigraph), 1897

There is only one morality . . . just as there is only one geometry.

VOLTAIRE (1694–1778). "Morality," *Philosophical Dictionary,* 1764, tr. Theodore Besterman, 1971

See Truth: Herbert Spencer

Reason and experience both forbid us to expect that national morality can prevail in exclusion of religious principle.

GEORGE WASHINGTON (1732–1799). *Farewell Address,* 17 September 1796

Modern morality consists in accepting the standard of one's age. I consider that for any man of culture to accept the standard of his age is a form of the grossest immorality.

OSCAR WILDE (1854–1900). *The Picture of Dorian Gray,* 6, 1891

MORNING

See also • Creativity: Thomas Fuller ○ Days

Waking up in the morning, to a virtuous man, iz the same thing az being born agin.

JOSH BILLINGS (1818–1885). "Slips of the Pen," *Everybody's Friend, or Josh Billing's Encyclopedia and Proverbial Philosophy of Wit and Humor,* 1874

To get up early, filled with energy and enthusiasm, wonderfully ready to commit some wretched nastiness.

E. M. CIORAN (1911–1995). "Strangled Thoughts" (3), *The New Gods,* 1969, tr. Richard Howard, 1974

Will there really be a "Morning"?
Is there such a thing as "Day"?
Could I see it from the mountains
If I were as tall as they?

Has it feet like Water lilies?
Has it feathers like a Bird?
Is it brought from famous countries
Of which I have never heard?

Oh some Scholar! Oh some Sailor!
Oh some Wise Man from the skies!
Please to tell a little Pilgrim
Where the place called "Morning" lies!

EMILY DICKINSON (1830–1886). "Will there really be a 'Morning?'" 1859?

This morn the air smells of vanilla and oranges.

RALPH WALDO EMERSON (1803–1882). Journal, 8 May 1844

Morning prospective: imagination.
Evening retrospective: memory.

> RALPH WALDO EMERSON (1803–1882). Journal, 1853, undated

Oh, what a beautiful mornin',
Oh, what a beautiful day.
I got a beautiful feelin'
Ev'rything's goin' my way.

> OSCAR HAMMERSTEIN II (1895–1960). "Oh, What a Beautiful Mornin'"
> (song). In the musical *Oklahoma,* 1943

It's completely usual for me to get up in the morning, take a look around, and laugh out loud.

> BARBARA KINGSOLVER (1955–). Title essay, *High Tide in Tucson:*
> *Essays from Now or Never,* 1996

Sweet is the breath of morn, her rising sweet,
With charm of earliest Birds; pleasant the Sun
When first on this delightful Land he spreads
His orient Beams, on herb, tree, fruit, and flow'r,
Glist'ring with dew.

> JOHN MILTON (1608–1674). *Paradise Lost,* 4.641, 1667

All memorable events . . . transpire in morning time and in a morning atmosphere.

> HENRY DAVID THOREAU (1817–1862). "Where I Lived, and What I
> Lived for," *Walden; or Life in the Woods,* 1854

Morning brings back the heroic ages.

> HENRY DAVID THOREAU (1817–1862). "Where I Lived, and What I
> Lived for," *Walden; or Life in the Woods,* 1854

Morning is when I am awake and there is a dawn in me.

> HENRY DAVID THOREAU (1817–1862). "Where I Lived, and What I
> Lived for," *Walden; or Life in the Woods,* 1854

❧

The morning is wiser than the evening.

> SAYING (RUSSIAN)

MOTHERS

See also • Abortion ○ Babies ○ Birth Control ○ Children ○ Children's Learning ○ Family ○ Fathers ○ Grandparents ○ Parents

The Kennedy home was a place of much action and laughter, a lively, brawling mob of children overseen by a mother who knew when to look the other way.

> JAMES DAVID BARBER (1939–). *The Presidential Character: Predicting*
> *Performance in the White House,* 9, 1972

[My mother] shone for me like the Evening Star. I loved here dearly—but at a distance. My nurse was my confidante. . . . It was to her I poured out my many troubles.

> WINSTON CHURCHILL (1874–1965). *My Early Life: A Roving*
> *Commission,* 1, 1930

I want a girl just like the girl
that married dear old dad.

> WILLIAM DILLON. "I Want a Girl" (song), 1911

There never was child so lovely but his mother was glad to get him asleep.

> RALPH WALDO EMERSON (1803–1882). Journal, 30 September 1837

"Mother Knows Best"

> EDNA FERBER (1887–1968). Short story title, 1927

The causes of conflict between mother and daughter arise when the daughter grows up and finds herself watched by her mother when she longs for real sexual freedom, while the mother is reminded by the budding beauty of her daughter that for her the time has come to renounce sexual claims.

> SIGMUND FREUD (1856–1939). *The Interpretation of Dreams,* 5.D.b,
> 1900, tr. A. A. Brill, 1938

A man who has been the indisputable favorite of his mother keeps for life the feeling of a conqueror, that confidence of success that often induces real success.

> SIGMUND FREUD (1856–1939). "A Childhood Recollection in *Dichtung*
> *und Warheit,"* 1917. In Ernest Jones, *The Life and Work of Sigmund*
> *Freud,* 1, 1953–1957, abr., 1961

Where yet was ever found a mother,
Who'd give her booby for another?

> JOHN GAY (1685–1732). *Fables,* 1.3, 1727–1738

I have a last thank-you. It is to my mother Celia Amster Bader, the bravest and strongest person I have known, who was taken from me much too soon. I pray that I may be all that she would have been had she lived in an age when women could aspire and achieve and daughters are cherished as much as sons.

> RUTH BADER GINSBURG (1933–). Supreme Court associate justice.
> Nomination acceptance speech, Washington, 14 June 1993

Bringing a child into the world is the greatest act of hope there is.

> LOUISE HART. "Postscript: On Nightmares," *The Winning Family:*
> *Increasing Self-Esteem in Your Children and Yourself,* 1987

Whenever I held my newborn baby in my arms, I used to think that what I said and did to him could have an influence not only on him but on all whom he met, not only for a day or a month or a year, but for all eternity—a very, very challenging and exciting thought for a mother.

> ROSE KENNEDY (1890–1995). In Gail Cameron, *Rose: A Biography of*
> *Rose Fitzgerald Kennedy,* 5, 1971

Lady Madonna, children at your feet,
Wonder how you manage to make ends meet.

> JOHN LENNON (1940–1980) and PAUL McCARTNEY (1942–). "Lady
> Madonna" (song), 1968

If a mother respects both herself and her child from his very first day onward, she will never need to teach him respect for others.

> ALICE MILLER (1923–). Foreword to *The Drama of the Gifted Child,*
> 1979, tr. Ruth Ward, 1981

Certainly I can say that my own childhood was unhappy. This was due to a clash of wills between my mother and myself. My early life was a series of fierce battles, from which my mother invariably emerged the victor. If I could not be seen anywhere, she would say—"Go and find out what Bernard is doing and tell him to stop it."

BERNARD LAW MONTGOMERY (1887–1976). *The Memoirs of Field-Marshal Montgomery,* 1, 1958

The perjurer's mother told white lies.

AUSTIN O'MALLEY (1858–1932)

No matter how old a mother is she watches her middle-aged children for signs of improvement.

FLORIDA SCOTT-MAXWELL (1884–1979). *The Measure of My Days,* 1968

"Working mother" is a misnomer. . . . It implies that any mother without a definite career is indolently not working, lolling around eating bon-bons, reading novels, and watching soap operas. But the word "mother" is already a synonym for some of the hardest, most demanding work ever shouldered by any human.

LIZ SMITH (1923–). "Work Work Work!" *The Mother Book,* 1978

It is the securely attached child who is most able to leave the mother's side in order to explore the environment and investigate the objects which it contains. Thus, the earliest manifestation of "interests" cannot be regarded as a substitute for affectional ties, but rather as bearing witness to their adequacy.

ANTHONY STORR (1920–). *Solitude: A Return to the Self,* 10, 1988

Happy he
With such a mother! faith in womankind
Beats with his blood, and truth in all things high
Comes easy to him.

ALFRED, LORD TENNYSON (1809–1892). *The Princess; A Medley,* 7.308, 1847

The hand that rocks the cradle
Is the hand that rules the world.

WILLIAM ROSS WALLACE (1819–1881). "What Rules the World," 1, 1865

❧

Q: What would have made combining a family and career easier for you?
A: Being born a man.

ANONYMOUS. Physician and mother of four. In Deborah J. Swiss and Judith P. Walker, *Women and the Work/Family Dilemma: How Today's Professional Women Are Finding Solutions,* 2 (epigraph), 1993

A mother understands what a child does not say.

SAYING

MOTIVES

See also • Action ○ Advertising ○ Cause & Effect ○ Heaven: *The Book of the Golden Precepts* ○ Idealism: Aldous Huxley ○ Passion ○ Passion, Ruling ○ Persuasion ○ Possessions: George Santayana ○ Purpose ○ Self-Interest ○ Service ○ Values ○ Virtue: Voltaire (1) ○ Will: Abraham Lincoln ○ Work: Arnold J. Toynbee

Never ascribe to an opponent motives meaner than your own.

J. M. BARRIE (1860–1937). Rectorial address, St. Andrew's University (Scotland), 3 May 1922

Nature has placed mankind under the governance of two sovereign masters, *pain* and *pleasure.* . . . They govern us in all we do, in all we say, in all we think.

JEREMY BENTHAM (1748–1832). *An Introduction to the Principles of Morals and Legislation,* 1.1, 1789–1823

Man acts from motives relative to his interests; and not on metaphysical speculations.

EDMUND BURKE (1729–1797). "Conciliation with America," House of Commons speech, 22 March 1775

Love draws me one [way], and glory the other.

CERVANTES (1547–1616). *Don Quixote,* 1.4.4, 1615, tr. Peter Anthony Motteux and John Ozell, 1743

M.—— said, "One must either entice men's cupidity or threaten their self-esteem. They are monkeys who never jump except for nuts on the one hand or the whip on the other."

CHAMFORT (1741–1794). *Characters and Anecdotes,* tr. W. S. Merwin, 1984

Give me virtuous actions, and I will not quibble . . . about the motives.

LORD CHESTERFIELD (1694–1773). Letter to his son, 5 September 1748

Studies based on analysis of several hundred biographies and life histories indicate that life can be divided into two large aspects. The satisfaction of desires is the dominant motivating force behind all our actions until the age of thirty-five. After that age the fulfillment of an assignment or a life task becomes more and more predominant.

ERNEST DICHTER (1907–1991). Appendix (2) to *The Strategy of Desire,* 1960

Two points of view in general regulate the conduct of men: honor and interest.

FREDERICK II (1712–1786). "Morning the Sixth," *The Confessions of Frederick the Great,* ed. Douglas Sladen, 1915

The desire of reward is one of the strongest incentives of human conduct; . . . the best security for the fidelity of mankind is to make their interest coincide with their duty.

ALEXANDER HAMILTON (1757–1804). In *The Federalist Papers* (essay series), 72, 21 March 1788

There are some persons who never decide from deliberate motives at all, but are the mere creatures of impulse.

WILLIAM HAZLITT (1778–1830). *Characteristics in the Manner of Rochefoucault's Maxims,* 210, 1823

The two great springs of life, Hope and Fear.

WILLIAM HAZLITT (1778–1830). "On the Conduct of Life," *Literary Remains,* 1836

Passions, private aims, and the satisfaction of selfish desires, are . . . most effective springs of action. Their power lies in the fact that they respect none of the limitations which justice and morality would impose on them; and [they] have a more direct influence over man than the artificial and tedious discipline that tends to order and self-restraint, law and morality.

GEORG HEGEL (1770–1831). Introduction (3.2.2) to *Philosophy of History,* 1832, tr. John Sibree, 1900

How to gain, how to keep, how to recover happiness is in fact for most men at all times the secret motive of all they do, and of all they are willing to endure.

WILLIAM JAMES (1842–1910). *The Varieties of Religious Experience: A Study in Human Nature,* 4 and 5, 1902

Sex and envy are the two greatest drives in life.

LYNDON B. JOHNSON (1908–1973). Quoted by Joseph A. Califano, Jr., Larry King television interview, CNN, 25 October 1992

Thanks be to Nature . . . for the incompatibility, for heartless competitive vanity, for the insatiable desire to possess and to rule! Without them, all the excellent natural capacities of humanity would forever sleep, undeveloped.

IMMANUEL KANT (1724–1804). "Idea for a Universal History from a Cosmopolitan Point of View," 1784, *On History,* ed. Lewis White Beck, 1963

We should often blush at our noblest deeds if the world were to see all their underlying motives.

LA ROCHEFOUCAULD (1613–1680). *Maxims,* 409, 1665, tr. Leonard Tancock, 1959

The greater part of our daily actions are the result of hidden motives which escape our observation.

GUSTAVE LE BON (1841–1931). *The Crowd: A Study of the Popular Mind,* 1.1, 1895, Viking Press edition, 1960

It is not by reason, but most often in spite of it, that are created those sentiments that are the mainsprings of all civilization—sentiments such as honor, self-sacrifice, religious faith, patriotism, and the love of glory.

GUSTAVE LE BON (1841–1931). *The Crowd: A Study of the Popular Mind,* 2.2.4, 1895, Viking Press edition, 1960

Good and Evil, *Reward* and *Punishment,* are the only Motives to a rational Creature: These are the Spur and Reins whereby all Mankind are set on Work and guided.

JOHN LOCKE (1632–1704). *Some Thoughts Concerning Education,* 54, 1693

There are secret aspects, beyond divining, in all we do— . . . aspects mute and invisible, unknown to their own possessors, brought forth only under the incitements of circumstance.

MONTAIGNE (15331–592). In Garry Wills, epilogue (epitaph) to *The Kennedy Imprisonment: A Meditation on Power,* 1981

A man always has two reasons for the things he does—a good one and the real one.

J. P. MORGAN (1837–1913). Remark to an associate. In Ron Chernow, *The House of Morgan: An American Banking Dynasty and the Rise of Modern Finance,* 6, 1990

There are two levers for moving men: interest and fear.

NAPOLEON (1769–1821). Remark to the author, 1800. In Louis de Bourrienne, *Memoirs of Napoleon Bonaparte,* 1.28, ed. R. W. Phipps, 1892

People react to fear, not love—they don't teach that in Sunday School, but it's true.

RICHARD M. NIXON (1913–1994). In William Safire, prologue to *Before the Fall: An Inside View of the Pre-Watergate White House,* 1975

See Machiavellianism: Machiavelli (3)

Even honorable motives of action, unless directed by judgment, are followed by disastrous results.

OTHO (A.D. 32–69). Roman emperor. In Tacitus (A.D. 56?–120?). *The History,* 1.83, tr. Alfred J. Church and William J. Brodribb, 1942

Self-love, the spring of motion.

ALEXANDER POPE (1688–1744). *An Essay on Man,* 2.59, 1734
See Self-Love: Pope (2)

This manifold restless motion is produced and kept up by the agency of two simple impulses—hunger and the sexual instinct; aided a little, perhaps, by the influence of boredom, but by nothing else.

ARTHUR SCHOPENHAUER (1788–1860). "Studies in Pessimism: The Vanity of Existence," *Essays of Arthur Schopenhauer,* tr. T. Bailey Saunders, 1851

What Makes Sammy Run?

BUDD SCHULBERG (1914–). Book title, 1941

If a messenger from heaven were on a sudden to annihilate the love of power, the love of wealth, and the love of esteem in the human heart, in half an hour's time the streets would be as empty, and as silent, as they are in the middle of the night.

SYDNEY SMITH (1771–1845). *The Wit and Wisdom of Sydney Smith,* p. 356, undated

Hunger, love, vanity, and fear. There are four great motives of human action.

WILLIAM GRAHAM SUMNER (1840–1910). *Folkways: A Study of the Sociological Importance of Usages, Manners, Customs, Mores, and Morals,* 22, 1907

We ignore and never mention the Sole Impulse which dictates and compels a man's every act: the imperious necessity of securing his own approval, in every emergency and at all costs.

MARK TWAIN (1835–1910). *What Is Man?* 2, 1906

What we believe to be the motives of our conduct are usually but the pretexts for it.

MIGUEL de UNAMUNO (1864–1936). *Tragic Sense of Life,* 11, 1913, tr. J. E. Crawford Flitch, 1921

Duty, Honor, Country.

UNITED STATES MILITARY ACADEMY. West Point (New York), motto

Had it been merely vanity that had made him do his one good deed? Or the desire for a new sensation? . . . Or that passion to act a part that sometimes makes us do things finer than we are ourselves?

OSCAR WILDE (1854–1900). *The Picture of Dorian Gray,* 20, 1891

MOTORCYCLES

See also • Automobiles ○ Machines

The true biker exults in laying down an onslaught of noise that loosens the wisdom teeth of passers-by and blows soup right out the bowl along the road.

RUSSELL BAKER (1925–). "Gone With the Side Car," *New York Times,* 23 June 1987

A strange and touching scene at Cypress Lawn Monday. A young man killed in a motorcycle accident was buried along with the

Harley-Davidson he was riding at the time of the crash. "It was his whole life," sobs his mother.

> HERB CAEN (1916–1997). Column, *San Francisco Chronicle,* 24 September 1970

I don't want a pickle,
Just want to ride on my motorsickle,
And I don't want a tickle,
'Cause I'd rather ride on my motorsickle
And I don't want to die,
Just want a ride on my motorsickle.

> ARLO GUTHRIE (1947–). "The Motorcycle Song" (song), 1967

If you're going to repair a motorcycle, an adequate supply of gumption is the first and most important tool. If you haven't got that you might as well gather up all the other tools and put them away, because they won't do you any good.

Gumption is the psychic gasoline that keeps the whole thing going. If you haven't got it there's no way the motorcycle can possibly be fixed. But if you *have* got it and know how to keep it there's absolutely no way in this whole world that motorcycle can *keep* from getting fixed.

> ROBERT M. PIRSIG (1928–). *Zen and the Art of Motorcycle Maintenance: An Inquiry into Values,* 26, 1974
> See Work: Pirsig

MOVEMENTS

See • Mass Movements

MOUNTAIN CLIMBING

See also • Mountains o Sports

Now, a cautious mountaineer seldom takes a step on unknown ground which seems at all dangerous that he cannot retrace in case he should be stopped by unseen obstacles ahead. This is the rule of mountaineers who live long.

> JOHN MUIR (1838–1914). *Stickeen,* p. 44, 1897, Heyday Books edition, 1981

The basic rules [in mountaineering] are: Push yourself all the way to the limit and then leave a margin for safety. There's a kind of mixture of boldness and prudence in that. It breeds self-discipline. And the next rule is: No whining!

> GARY SNYDER (1930–). In Burr Snider, "The Sage of the Sierra," *San Francisco Examiner,* 17 September 1989

MOUNTAINS

See also • Books: John Muir o Mountain Climbing o Nature o Wilderness

Welcome to the Delectable Mountains!

> JOHN BUNYAN (1628–1688). *The Pilgrim's Progress,* 1.8, 1678–1684

'Tis distance lends enchantment to the view,
And robes the mountain in its azure hue.

> THOMAS CAMPBELL (1777–1844). *The Pleasures of Hope,* 1.7, 1799

Monument Mountain, in the early sunshine; its base enveloped in mist, parts of which are floating in the sky; so that the great hill looks really as if it were founded on a cloud.

> NATHANIEL HAWTHORNE (1804–1864). 19 August 1850, *The American Notebooks,* ed. Claude M. Simpson, 1932

In all my lonely journeys among the most distant and difficult pathless mountains, I never wander, am never lost. Providence guides through every danger and takes me to all the truths which I need to learn, and some day I hope to show you my sheaves, my big bound pages of mountain gospel.

> JOHN MUIR (1838–1914). Letter to his mother Margaret Muir, 16 November 1871. In William Frederic Badè, *The Life and Letters of John Muir,* 9.1, 1923

Heaven knows that John Baptist was not more eager to get all his fellow sinners into the Jordan than I to baptize all of mine in the beauty of God's mountains.

> JOHN MUIR (1838–1914). Journal, 1872. In *John of the Mountains: The Unpublished Journals of John Muir,* ed. Linnie Marsh Wolfe, 1938

The higher we go in the mountains, the milkier becomes the Milky Way.

> JOHN MUIR (1838–1914). Journal, 16? August 1873. In *John of the Mountains: The Unpublished Journals of John Muir,* ed. Linnie Marsh Wolfe, 1938

Climb the mountains and get their good tidings. Nature's peace will flow into you as sunshine flows into trees. The winds will blow their own freshness into you, and the storms their energy, while cares will drop off like autumn leaves.

> JOHN MUIR (1838–1914). "The Philosophy of John Muir," *The Wilderness World of John Muir,* comp. Edwin Way Teale, 1954

The mountain remains unmoved at its seeming defeat by the mist.

> RABINDRANATH TAGORE (1861–1941). *Fireflies,* p. 116, 1928

MURDER

See also • Crime o Killing o Punishment, Capital o Suicide: [especially] Karl A. Menninger

The world is drenched in mutual slaughter. . . . Held to be a crime when committed by individuals, homicide is called a virtue when committed by the state.

> ST. CYPRIAN (A.D. 3rd cent.). *Letters.* He was beheaded for refusing to sacrifice to the gods of Rome.

One murder made a villain,
Millions, a hero. Princes were privileg'd
To kill, and numbers sanctified the crime.

> BEILBY PORTEUS (1731–1808). "Death," l.154, 1759
> See Statistics: Joseph Stalin

We are mad not only individually, but nationally. We check manslaughter and isolated murders; but what of war and the much-vaunted crime of slaughtering whole peoples? . . . Deeds that would be punished by loss of life when committed in secret are praised by us because uniformed generals have carried them out.

> SENECA THE YOUNGER (5? B.C.–A.D. 65). "On the Usefulness of Basic Principles," *Moral Letters to Lucilius,* 95.30, tr. Richard M. Gummere, 1918

Ghost: Murder most foul, as in the best it is;
But this most foul, strange and unnatural.

> SHAKESPEARE (1564–1616). *Hamlet,* 1.5.27, 1600

Caesar: To the end of history, murder shall breed murder, always in the name of right and honor and peace, until the gods are tired of blood and create a race that can understand.

> GEORGE BERNARD SHAW (1856–1950). *Caesar and Cleopatra,* 4, 1899

I didn't want to hurt the man. I thought he was a very nice gentleman. Soft-spoken. I thought so right up to the moment I cut his throat.

> PERRY SMITH. Confession. In Truman Capote, *In Cold Blood: A True Account of a Multiple Murder and Its Consequences,* 4, 1966

It is forbidden to kill; therefore all murderers are punished unless they kill in large numbers and to the sound of trumpets.

> VOLTAIRE (1694–1778). "War," *Philosophical Dictionary,* 1764

❧

Murder will out.

> SAYING (ENGLISH). In Geoffrey Chaucer, "The Nun's Priest's Tale," *The Canterbury Tales,* 1390?, tr. Nevill Coghill, 1951

MUSIC

See also • Art ○ Creativity ○ Creativity: First Person: [especially] Johann Sebastian Bach, Bob Dylan, Ernst Theodor Amadeus Hoffmann, John Lennon, Richard Wagner ○ Dance ○ Misjudgments: Jim Denny, Anonymous (American) (3) ○ Optimism: Examples: Walt Whitman ○ Perfection: Vladimir Horowitz

Music, the greatest good that mortals know,
And all of heaven we have below.

> JOSEPH ADDISON (1672–1719). "A Song for St. Cecilia's Day," l. 27, 1694

Before I got into rock 'n' roll, I was going to be a dentist.

> GREGG ALLMAN (1947–). Rock musician

Man, if you gotta ask, you'll never know.

> LOUIS "SATCHMO" ARMSTRONG (1900–1971). When asked to define jazz

[Rock music is] junk food for the soul.

> ALLAN BLOOM (1930–1992). "Music," *The Closing of the American Mind: How Higher Education Has Failed Democracy and Impoverished the Souls of Today's Students,* 1987

Who hears music, feels his solitude
Peopled at once.

> ROBERT BROWNING (1812–1889). *Balaustion's Adventure,* l.323, 1871

Songs without either words or music. That is what I want to write.

> SAMUEL BUTLER (1835–1902). *Further Extracts from the Note-Books of Samuel Butler,* 1, ed. A. T. Bartholomew, 1934

Canned music is like audible wallpaper.

> ALISTAIR COOKE (1908–). Attributed

Interviewer: Do you know what your songs are about?
Dylan: Yeah, some of them are about ten minutes long, others five or six.

> BOB DYLAN (1941–). 1965?

Music heard so deeply
That it is not heard at all, but you are the music
While the music lasts.

> T. S. ELIOT (1888–1965). "The Dry Salvages" (5), *Four Quartets,* 1943

The sweetest music is not in the oratorio, but in the human voice when it speaks from its instant life tones of tenderness, truth, or courage.

> RALPH WALDO EMERSON (1803–1882). "Art," *Essays: First Series,* 1841

Ilsa: Play it once, Sam, for old times' sake.
Sam: I don't know what you mean, Miss Ilsa.
Ilsa: Play it, Sam. Play "As Time Goes By."

> JULIUS J. EPSTEIN (1909–), PHILIP G. EPSTEIN, and HOWARD KOCH. *Casablanca* (film), 1942. Spoken by Ingrid Bergman and Dooley Wilson (Popular version: Play it again, Sam.)

I knew a very wise man who believed that if a man were permitted to make all the ballads, he need not care who should make the laws of a nation.

> ANDREW FLETCHER OF SALTOUN (1655–1716). Letter to the Marquis of Montrose, 1704
>
> See Economists: Paul A. Samuelson ○ Superstition: Mark Twain

Singin' in the rain, just singin' in the rain.
What a glorious feeling, I'm happy again.

> ARTHUR FREED (1894–1973). "Singin' in the Rain." In the musical film *Hollywood Revue of 1929,* 1929

Bach almost persuades me to be a Christian.

> ROGER FRY (1866–1934). In Virginia Woolf, *Roger Fry: A Biography,* 8, 1940

Most people get into bands for three very simple rock and roll reasons: to get laid, to get fame, and to get rich.

> BOB GELDOF (1954–). In *Melody Maker,* 27 August 1977

If I don't practice one day, I know it: two days, the critics know it: three days, the public knows it.

> JASCHA HEIFETZ (1901–1987). In "Jascha Heifetz Against Rock? It Ain't Necessarily So," *San Francisco Sunday Examiner & Chronicle,* 18 April 1971

Music helps not the toothache.

> GEORGE HERBERT (1593–1633). Comp. *Outlandish Proverbs,* 532, 1640

After silence that which comes nearest to expressing the inexpressible is music.

> ALDOUS HUXLEY (1894–1963)

Blues are the songs of despair, but gospel songs are the songs of hope.

> MAHALIA JACKSON (1911–1972) (with EVAN McLOUD WYLIE). *Movin' On Up,* 6, 1966

On stage, I make love to 25,000 different people, then I go home alone.

> JANIS JOPLIN (1943–1970)

Heard melodies are sweet, but those unheard
    Are sweeter.
> JOHN KEATS (1795–1821). "Ode on a Grecian Urn," 2, 1820

The sweetest music is the sound of the voice of the woman we love.
> LA BRUYÈRE (1645–1696). "Of Women" (10), *The Characters*, 1688, tr. Henri van Laun, 1929

You have always given me more than I gave to you. . . . You were the wings on which I soared. [Ellipsis points in original.]
> LOTTE LEHMANN (1888–1976). To farewell concert audience, photograph caption. In "Exit Crying: Lotte Lehmann Ends 41 Years of Singing," *Life*, 5 March 1951

Will the people in the cheaper seats clap your hands? All the rest of you, if you'll just rattle your jewelry.
> JOHN LENNON (1940–1980). At a Royal Variety Performance by the Beatles, London, 4 November 1963. In Ray Colman, *John Winston Lennon*, 1.11, 1984

Christianity will go. It will vanish and shrink. I needn't argue about that: I'm right, and I will be proved right. We're more popular than Jesus Christ now. I don't know which will go first—rock 'n' roll or Christianity.
> JOHN LENNON (1940–1980). On the Beatles, "According to John," *Time*, 12 August 1966

People think the Beatles know what's going on. We don't. We're just doing it.
> JOHN LENNON (1940–1980)

[The Beatles] were just a band that made it very big, that's all. Our best work was never recorded.
> JOHN LENNON (1940–1980)

Awop-bop-a-loo-mop alop-bam-boom!
> LITTLE RICHARD (RICHARD PENNIMAN) (1932–). "Tutti-Frutti" (song), 1955

A hundred years from now, people will listen to the music of the Beatles the same way we listen to Mozart.
> PAUL McCARTNEY (1942–). 1992. In Mark Hertsgaard, "Letting It Be," *New Yorker*, 24 January 1994

The violinist is that peculiarly human phenomenon distilled to a rare potency—half tiger, half poet.
> YEHUDI MENUHIN (1916–). "On Composers and Performances," *The Compleat Violinist: Thoughts, Exercises, Reflections of an Itinerant Violinist*, 1986

Don't play the saxophone. Let it play you.
> CHARLIE PARKER (1920–1955). In William Safire and Leonard Safir, comps., *Words of Wisdom: More Good Advice*, p. 79, 1989

All art constantly aspires towards the condition of music.
> WALTER PATER (1839–1894). "The School of Giorgione," *Studies in the History of the Renaissance*, 1873

Country music addresses the poignancy of past loves and the loss of innocence. One of the best descriptions of it is the title of the book *Country Music: White Man's Blues*, by John Grissim.
> JOHN REYNOLDS, JR. Letter to *Time*, 20 April 1992

Music is essentially useless, as life is.
> GEORGE SANTAYANA (1863–1952). *The Life of Reason or The Phases of Human Progress*, 4.4, 1905-1906

Forget the notes so that you can play them.
> JAN SARDI. *Shine* (film), 1996, spoken by John Gieldgud (in the role of David Helfgott's piano teacher)

The notes I handle no better than many pianists. But the pauses between the notes—ah, that is where the art resides!
> ARTUR SCHNABEL (1882–1951). In *Chicago Daily News*, 11 June 1958

I know two kinds of audiences only—one coughing, and one not coughing.
> ARTUR SCHNABEL (1882–1951). *My Life and Music*, 2.10, 1961

Is not music the food of love?
> RICHARD SHERIDAN (1751–1816). *The Rivals*, 2.1, 1775

Rock 'n' roll is the most brutal, ugly, vicious form of expression—sly, lewd, in plain fact, dirty . . . rancid smelling, aphrodisiac . . . the martial music of every delinquent on the face of the earth.
> FRANK SINATRA (1915–1998). 1957

Music was my way of keeping people from looking through and around me. I wanted the heavies to know I was around.
> BRUCE SPRINGSTEEN (1949–). On composing his own music. In "The Backstreet Phantom of Rock," *Time*, 27 October 1975

I think on a night when we're really good, you can come and hopefully you can see your relationships with your parents, brothers, sisters, your town, your country, your friends, everything—sexual, political, the whole social thing. It should be a combination of a circus, a political thing, and a spiritual event. And hopefully you'll come and your life will flash before your eyes.
> BRUCE SPRINGSTEEN (1949–). In Sandy Carter, "Pop Music and the Left," *Z Magazine*, October 1988

A musician may suddenly reach a point at which pleasure in the technique of the art entirely falls away, and in some moment of inspiration, he becomes the instrument through which music is played.
> EDWIN DILLER STARBUCK (1866–1947). *The Psychology of Religion: An Empirical Study of the Growth of Religious Consciousness*, 1899. In William James, *The Varieties of Religious Experience: A Study in Human Nature*, 9, 1902

A Steinway will never sound quite the same again.
> STEINWAY & SONS. Piano manufacturer. Sole copy in ad honoring the memory of Vladimir Horowitz who had just died, *New York Times*, 10 November 1989

Everywhere in the world, music enhances a hall, with one exception: Carnegie Hall enhances the music.
> ISAAC STERN (1920–). In John Rockwell, "Carnegie Hall to Close for 7 Months Next Year," *New York Times*, 17 May 1985

The trouble with music appreciation in general is that people are taught to have too much respect for music; they should be taught to love it instead.
> IGOR STRAVINSKY (1882–1971). In "Subject: Music," *New York Times Magazine*, 27 September 1964

Too many pieces of music finish too long after the end.

> IGOR STRAVINSKY (1882–1971). In *New York Times Book Review,* 1971

In a world of peace and love, music would be the universal language.

> HENRY DAVID THOREAU (1817–1862). *The Service,* 2, 1840, ed. F. B. Sanborn, 1902

I heard one evening a symphony of Beethoven's. I thereupon fell ill of a fever, and when I recovered I was—a musician.

> RICHARD WAGNER (1813–1883). Slightly modified. In Theo. B. Hyslop, *The Great Abnormals,* 11, 1925

Piano playing, a dance of human fingers.

> LUDWIG WITTGENSTEIN (1889–1951). 1939–1940, *Culture and Value,* 1977, tr. Peter Winch, 1980

The music in my heart I bore,
Long after it was heard no more.

> WILLIAM WORDSWORTH (1770–1850). Closing lines, "The Solitary Reaper," 1807

MYSTERY

See also • Awe ○ Faith: Henri Amiel ○ Miracles ○ Religion & Science: Olympia Brown ○ Wonder

The eternal mystery of the world is its comprehensibility.

> ALBERT EINSTEIN (1879–1955). "Physics and Reality," *Journal of the Franklin Institute,* March 1936

Beyond all mystery is the mercy of God.

> ABRAHAM JOSHUA HESCHEL (1907–1972). *God in Search of Man: A Philosophy of Judaism,* 16, 1955
> See History: Heschel (2)

If death is one mystery, life is another, greater one. . . . We can only feel awe before a mystery that both is what we are and surpasses our understanding.

> JONATHAN SCHELL (1943–). *The Fate of the Earth,* 2, 1982

The more unintelligent a man is, the less mysterious existence seems to him.

> ARTHUR SCHOPENHAUER (1788–1860)

Mystery is not the denial of reason but its honest confirmation: reason, indeed, leads inevitably to mystery . . . : mystery and reality are the two halves of the same sphere.

> WALT WHITMAN (1819–1892). Remark to the author, 14 July 1888. In Horace Traubel, *Walt Whitman's Camden Conversations,* ed. Walter Teller, 1973

The true mystery of the world is the visible, not the invisible.

> OSCAR WILDE (1854–1900). *The Picture of Dorian Gray,* 2, 1891

MYSTICISM

See also • Contemplation ○ Ethics: Albert Schweitzer (2) ○ God ○ God & Man ○ Grace ○ Meditation ○ Prophets ○ Religion & Science: Booth Tarkington ○ Revelation ○ Saints ○ Self ○ Soul ○ Spirituality ○ The Unconscious

What is religion without mysticism? A rose without perfume.

> HENRI AMIEL (1821–1881). Journal, 17 March 1861, tr. Mrs. Humphrey Ward, 1887

Ghent: Will future conceptions of God take on a more mystical cast? *Armstrong:* I don't think, in our kind of society, we'll be able to develop a full-blown mystical religion or concept of God because we seek instant gratification, fast food, endless talk and noise. The silence in mysticism is alien. People want to do a few courses in mysticism, rather like the way you do French before going on holiday, and emerge a mystic. Mysticism isn't like that.

> KAREN ARMSTRONG (1944–). Theologian. Format adapted. In Janet Silver Ghent, "Ex-Nun Challenges Major Religions to Reinvent God," *Jewish Bulletin of Northern California,* 28 October 1994

True mystics simply open their souls to the oncoming wave.

> HENRI BERGSON (1859–1941). "Moral Obligation," *The Two Sources of Morality and Religion,* 1932, tr. R. Ashley Audra and Cloudesley Brereton, 1935

If a word of a great mystic, or some one of his imitators, finds an echo in one or another of us, may it not be that there is a mystic dormant within us, merely waiting for an occasion to awake?

> HENRI BERGSON (1859–1941). "Moral Obligation," *The Two Sources of Morality and Religion,* 1932, tr. R. Ashley Audra and Cloudesley Brereton, 1935

Mysticism means nothing, absolutely nothing, to the man who has no experience of it.

> HENRI BERGSON (1859–1941). "Dynamic Religion," *The Two Sources of Morality and Religion,* 1932, tr. R. Ashley Audra and Cloudesley Brereton, 1935

The soul of the great mystic does not stop at ecstasy, as at the end of a journey. The ecstasy is indeed rest, if you like, but as though at a station, where the engine is still under steam, the onward movement becoming a vibration on one spot, until it is time to race forward again.

> HENRI BERGSON (1859–1941). "Dynamic Religion," *The Two Sources of Morality and Religion,* 1932, tr. R. Ashley Audra and Cloudesley Brereton, 1935

An innate knowledge, or rather an acquired ignorance, suggests to it straightaway the step to be taken, the decisive act, the unanswerable word. Yet effort remains indispensable, endurance and perseverance likewise. But they come of themselves, they develop of their own accord, in a soul acting and acted upon, whose liberty coincides with the divine activity.

> HENRI BERGSON (1859–1941). "Dynamic Religion," *The Two Sources of Morality and Religion,* 1932, tr. R. Ashley Audra and Cloudesley Brereton, 1935

Mysticism is undoubtedly at the origin of great moral transformations. And mankind seems to be as far away as ever from it. But who knows?

> HENRI BERGSON (1859–1941). "Final Remarks," *The Two Sources of Morality and Religion,* 1932, tr. R. Ashley Audra and Cloudesley Brereton, 1935

Among those who have passed through mystical experiences there are those who emerge with new insights and those in whom the net result is an emotional reinforcement of traditional beliefs.

ANTON T. BOISEN (1876–1965). *The Exploration of the Inner World: A Study of Mental Disorder and Religious Experience,* 7, 1936

The most beautiful emotion we can experience is the mystical. It is the power of all true art and science. He to whom this emotion is a stranger, who can no longer wonder and stand rapt in awe, is as good as dead. To know that what is impenetrable to us really exists, manifesting itself as the highest wisdom and the most radiant beauty, which our dull faculties can comprehend only in primitive form—this knowledge, this feeling, is at the center of true religiousness. In this sense, and in this sense only, I belong to the rank of devoutly religious men.

ALBERT EINSTEIN (1879–1955). In Philipp Frank, *Einstein: His Life and Times,* 12.5, 1947

In mysticism, . . . the attempt is given up to know God by thought, and it is replaced by the experience of union with God in which there is no more room—and no need—for knowledge *about* God.

ERICH FROMM (1900–1980). *The Art of Loving,* 2.1, 1956

The mystic would have so much to tell us, just because he has so much to keep silent about.

EUGEN HERRIGEL (1885–1955). "Higher Stages of Meditation," *The Method of Zen,* 1960, ed. Hermann Tausend and tr. R. F. C. Hull, 1964

Mystic: A person who is puzzled before the obvious, but who understands the nonexistent.

ELBERT HUBBARD (1856–1915). *The Roycroft Dictionary Concocted by Ali Baba and the Bunch on Rainy Days,* p. 101, 1914

Mystical experience . . . is a direct intuition of ultimate reality.

ALDOUS HUXLEY (1894–1963). "Beliefs," *Ends and Means: An Inquiry into the Nature of Ideals and into the Methods Employed for Their Realization,* 1937

Virtue is the essential preliminary to the mystical experience.

ALDOUS HUXLEY (1894–1963). "Beliefs," *Ends and Means: An Inquiry into the Nature of Ideals and into the Methods Employed for Their Realization,* 1937

See Meditation: Krishnamurti (2)

If a man would travel far along the mystic road, he must learn to desire God intensely but in stillness, passively and yet with all his heart and mind and strength.

ALDOUS HUXLEY (1894–1963). "Nothing Fails Like Success," *Grey Eminence: A Study in Religion and Politics,* 1941

Formless and vague and fleeting as it is, the mystical experience is the bedrock of religious faith. In it the soul, acting as a unity with all its faculties, rises above itself and becomes spirit; it asserts its claim to be a citizen of heaven.

DEAN WILLIAM RALPH INGE (1860–1954). "Confessio Fidei," *Outspoken Essays: Second Series,* 1922

No adequate report of [mysticism's] contents can be given in words. It follows from this that its quality must be directly experienced; it cannot be imparted or transferred to others. In this peculiarity mystical states are more like states of feeling than like states of intellect.

WILLIAM JAMES (1842–1910). *The Varieties of Religious Experience: A Study in Human Nature,* 16 and 17, 1902

When the characteristic sort of consciousness once has set in, the mystic feels as if his own will were in abeyance, and indeed sometimes as if he were grasped and held by a superior power.

WILLIAM JAMES (1842–1910). *The Varieties of Religious Experience: A Study in Human Nature,* 16 and 17, 1902

This incommunicableness of the transport is the keynote of all mysticism. Mystical truth exists for the individual who has the transport, but for no one else.

WILLIAM JAMES (1842–1910). *The Varieties of Religious Experience: A Study in Human Nature,* 16 and 17, 1902

We pass into mystical states from out of ordinary consciousness as from a less into a more, as from a smallness into a vastness, and at the same time as from an unrest to a rest. We feel them as reconciling, unifying states. They appeal to the yes-function more than to the no-function in us. In them the unlimited absorbs the limits and peacefully closes the account.

WILLIAM JAMES (1842–1910). *The Varieties of Religious Experience: A Study in Human Nature,* 16 and 17, 1902

This overcoming of all the usual barriers between the individual and the Absolute is the great mystic achievement. In mystic states we both become one with the Absolute, and we become aware of our oneness.

WILLIAM JAMES (1842–1910). *The Varieties of Religious Experience: A Study in Human Nature,* 16 and 17, 1902

A tremendous muchness is suddenly revealed.

WILLIAM JAMES (1842–1910). In Rufus M. Jones, "The Mystic's Experience of God" (3), *Atlantic,* November 1921

Mystical experience . . . is the awareness of a Presence, the consciousness of a Beyond.

The most striking effect of such experience is not new fact-knowledge, not new items of empirical information, but new moral energy, heightened conviction, increased caloric quality, enlarged spiritual vision, an unusual radiant power of life. In short, the whole personality, in the case of the constructive mystics, appears to be raised to a new level of life.

RUFUS M. JONES (1863–1948). "The Mystic's Experience of God" (3), *Atlantic,* November 1921

Mysticism and exaggeration go together. A mystic must not fear ridicule if he is to push all the way to the limits of humility or the limits of delight.

MILAN KUNDERA (1929–). Czech writer. *The Book of Laughter and Forgetting,* 3.2, 1978

Everything begins in mysticism and ends in politics.

CHARLES PÉGUY (1873–1914). "The Modern World: Politics and Mysticism," *Basic Verities: Prose and Poetry,* tr. Ann and Julian Green, 1943

When mystical activity is at its height, we find consciousness possessed by the sense of a being at once *excessive* and *identical* with the self: great enough to be God; interior enough to be *me.*

EDOUARD RÉCÉJAC. *Essai sur les fondements de la conscience mystique,* 1897. In William James, *The Varieties of Religious Experience: A Study in Human Nature,* 20, 1902

Mysticism is not a religion but a religious disease.

> GEORGE SANTAYANA (1863–1952). *Interpretations of Poetry and Religion*, 4, 1900

It is not the worldly ecclesiastics that kindle the fires of persecution, but mystics who think they hear the voice of God.

> GEORGE SANTAYANA (1863–1952). "The Alleged Catholic Danger," *New Republic*, 15 January 1916

"Mystical" . . . has acquired a somewhat "mystical" meaning, when in fact nothing other is involved than the attentive exploration of one's own inner life.

> E. F. SCHUMACHER (1911–1977). *A Guide for the Perplexed*, 6, 1977

The ultimate knowledge, in which man recognizes his own being as a part of the All, belongs, they say, to the realm of mysticism, by which is meant that he does not reach it by the method of ordinary reflection, but somehow or other lives himself into it.

> ALBERT SCHWEITZER (1875–1965). *The Philosophy of Civilization: The Decay and Restoration of Civilization*, 5, 1923, tr. C. T. Campion, 1923

There is an inevitable tension between mysticism and religious orthodoxy. . . . For the mystic, whatever his professed creed, final authority lies in his own experience.

> SIDNEY SPENCER (1888–?). *Mysticism in World Religion*, 9.4, 1963

Our normal everyday consciousness always has objects. They may be physical objects, or images, or even our own feelings or thoughts perceived introspectively. Suppose then that we [ignore] all objects physical or mental. When the self is not engaged in apprehending objects, it becomes aware of itself. The self itself emerges.

> W. T. STACE (1886–1967). *Mysticism and Philosophy*, 2.7, 1961

The mystic in man, that which knows without proof, and is beyond materialism.

> WALT WHITMAN (1819–1892). "Notes on Lecturing and Oratory," *Walt Whitman's Workshop: A Collection of Unpublished Manuscripts*, ed. Clifton Joseph Furness, 1964

What does mysticism really mean? It means the way to attain knowledge. It's close to philosophy, except in philosophy you go horizontally while in mysticism you go vertically.

> ELI WIESEL (1928–). John S. Friedman interview, 1978. In George Plimpton, ed., *Writers at Work: Eighth Series*, 1988

MYTHS

See also • Heroism ○ History ○ Religion

Mythology, *n.* The body of a primitive people's beliefs concerning its origin, early history, heroes, deities and so forth, as distinguished from the true accounts which it invents later.

> AMBROSE BIERCE (1842–1914). *The Devil's Dictionary*, p. 90, 1911, Dover edition, 1958

The goal of the myth is to . . . [affect] a reconciliation of the individual consciousness with the universal will.

> JOSEPH CAMPBELL (1904–1987). *The Hero with a Thousand Faces*, 1.3.6, 1949

The patterns and logic of fairy tale and myth correspond to those of dream.

> JOSEPH CAMPBELL (1904–1987). *The Hero with a Thousand Faces*, 2.1.1, 1949

Mythology is defeated when the mind rests solemnly with its favorite or traditional images, defending them as though they themselves were the message that they communicate. These images are to be regarded as no more than shadows from the unfathomable reach beyond.

> JOSEPH CAMPBELL (1904–1987). *The Hero with a Thousand Faces*, 2.1.3, 1949

I can find my biography in every fable that I read.

> RALPH WALDO EMERSON (1803–1882). Journal, 1866, undated

I find nothing in fables more astonishing than my experience in every hour. One moment of a man's life is a fact so stupendous as to take the luster out of all fiction.

> RALPH WALDO EMERSON (1803–1882). "Demonology," *Lectures and Biographical Sketches*, 1883

A myth is a religion in which no one any longer believes.

> JAMES K. FEIBLEMAN. *Understanding Philosophy: A Popular History of Ideas*, 3, 1973

[Myths are] projections of certain unconscious impulses otherwise confessed only in our dreams, but which once raised to the level of full consciousness serve as grids of perception through which we screen so-called "reality."

> LESLIE FIEDLER (1917–). "Pity and Fear," *Tyranny of the Normal: Essays on Bioethics, Theology & Myth*, 1996

Myths have their magic power because they cast on the screen of our imaginations, like the figures of the heavenly constellations, immense projections of our own hopes and capabilities.

> ROBERT L. HEILBRONER (1919–). *An Inquiry into the Human Prospect*, 5, 1974

Myth is the revelation of divine life in man. It is not we who invent myth, rather it speaks to us as a Word of God.

> CARL G. JUNG (1875–1961). *Memories, Dreams, Reflections*, 12.1, ed. Aniela Jaffé, 1962

True myth concerns itself centrally with the onward adventure of the integral soul.

> D. H. LAWRENCE (1885–1930). *Studies in Classic American Literature*, 5, 1923

What a myth never contains is the critical power to separate its truths from its errors.

> WALTER LIPPMANN (1889–1974). *Public Opinion*, 9.3, 1922

The greatest myths are never divorced from our deepest sense of reality—the primitive knowledge with which we are born. That kind of knowledge we are able to sense despite all the barriers of our modern development, and we can even sense how it motivates us without our conscious understanding or control—this primitive knowledge we can never quite name. Or tame.

> NORMAN MAILER (1923–). Sean Abbott interview, "Mailer Goes to the Mountain," *At Random*, Spring-Summer 1997

It is a sure sign that a culture has reached a dead end when it is no longer intrigued by its myths.

> GREIL MARCUS (1945–). Rock journalist. "Elvis Presley," *Mystery Train,* 1976

Myths of the heroes are cosmic creation myths in microcosm. They depict, in no matter how subtle variation, the eternal battle we wage to release the creative energies within ourselves and in the world.

> DOROTHY NORMAN (1905–1997). Opening words, *The Hero: Myth/Image/Symbol,* 1969

Myths which are believed in tend to become true.

> GEORGE ORWELL (1903–1950). "The English People" ("England at First Glance"), May 1947, *The Collected Essays, Journalism and Letters of George Orwell,* vol. 3, ed. Sonia Orwell and Ian Angus, 1968

Legend: A lie that has attained the dignity of age.

> LAURENCE J. PETER (1919–1990). Comp., *Peter's Quotations: Ideas for Our Times,* p. 313, 1997

A myth may itself contain contradictions. At the same time such complexity greatly aids the myth in diffusion by making it to a degree pass tender as all things to all men.

> GEORGE SAWYER PETTEE (1903–1950). *The Process of Revolution,* 1.5, 1938

The basic function of a myth is always to govern present action towards future hopes.

> GEORGE SAWYER PETTEE (1903–1950). *The Process of Revolution,* 1.5, 1938

Take the myth at its full value, and it reminds us of the task that has been laid upon us as nature's uniquely self-creating, self-

defining species: to discover the godlikeness in whose image we are said to have been cast.

> THEODORE ROSZAK (1933–). In Eugene Taylor, "Desperately Seeking Spirituality," *Psychology Today,* December 1994

The first of requirements . . . for the right reading of myths is the understanding of the nature of all true vision by noble persons; namely, that it is founded on constant laws common to all human nature; that it perceives, however darkly, things which are for all ages true; that we can only understand it so far as we have some perception of the same truth.

> JOHN RUSKIN (1819–1900). *The Queen of the Air,* 1.18, 1869

Mythology . . . is an intuitive form of apprehending and expressing universal truths.

> ARNOLD J. TOYNBEE (1889–1975). *A Study of History,* 3.259, 1934

Myths are unenlightening if they do not transcend experience, and unwarrantable if they contradict it.

> ARNOLD J. TOYNBEE (1889–1975). *A Study of History,* 12.562, 1961

The world of myth is always just behind us . . . we keep groping back with our foot for it like first basemen.

> C. K. WILLIAMS. "Journal," 1971–1972. In Daniel Halpern, ed., *Antaeus,* Autumn 1988

❦

The same myths that enable some people to accommodate themselves to the darkness serve others as stepping stones to enlightenment.

> ANONYMOUS

❦

NAMES

See also • Language ○ Reputation ○ Words

We have long since lost the true names for things. It is precisely because squandering the goods of others is called generosity, and recklessness in wrongdoing is called courage, that the republic is reduced to extremities.

> CATO THE YOUNGER (96–46 B.C.). Roman Senate speech. In Sallust (86?–34? B.C.), *The War with Catiline,* 52.11, tr. J. C. Rolfe, 1921

If names be not correct, language is not in accordance with the truth of things. If language be not in accordance with the truth of things, affairs cannot be carried on to success.

> CONFUCIUS (551–479 B.C.). *Confucian Analects,* 13.3, tr. James Legge, 1930

We do what we must, and call it by the best names we can.

> RALPH WALDO EMERSON (1883–1882). "Experience," *Essays: Second Series,* 1844
>
> See Doctrine: Miguel de Unamuno

What signifies knowing the Names,
  if you know not the Natures of Things.

> BENJAMIN FRANKLIN (1706–1790). *Poor Richard's Almanack,* November 1750

A man that should call everything by its right name would hardly pass the streets without being knocked down as a common enemy.

> MARQUIS OF HALIFAX (1633–1695). "Of Caution and Suspicion," *Political, Moral and Miscellaneous Reflections,* 1750

Men give different names to one and the same thing from the difference of their own passions. As they that approve a private opinion, call it Opinion; but they that mislike it, Heresy.

> THOMAS HOBBES (1588–1679). *Leviathan,* 11, 1651

The boy who, when asked how many legs his calf would have if he called its tail a leg, replied, "Five," to which the prompt response was made that *calling* the tail a leg would not *make* it one.

> ABRAHAM LINCOLN (1809–1865). Quoted by George W. Julian, untitled essay. In Allen T. Rice, ed., *Reminiscences of Abraham Lincoln,* 1885

The unnamed should not be mistaken for the nonexistent.

> CATHARINE A. MacKINNON (1946–). *The Sexual Harassment of Working Women: A Case of Sex Discrimination*, 3, 1979

I call a fig a fig, a spade a spade.

> MENANDER (343?–291 B.C.). Fragment, 545, tr. Francis G. Allinson, 1921

It always matters to name rubbish as rubbish; . . . to do otherwise is to legitimize it.

> SALMAN RUSHDIE (1947–). "Outside the Whale," *Imaginary Homelands: Essays and Criticism, 1981–1991*, 1991

Juliet: What's in a name? That which we call a rose
By any other name would smell as sweet.

> SHAKESPEARE (1564–1616). *Romeo and Juliet*, 2.2.43, 1594

Patriotism, public opinion, parental duty, discipline, religion, morality, are only fine names for intimidation.

> GEORGE BERNARD SHAW (1856–1950). "The Revolutionist's Handbook" (8), *Man and Superman*, 1903

Human pride
Is skillful to invent most serious names
To hide its ignorance.

> PERCY BYSSHE SHELLEY (1792–1822). *Queen Mab: A Philosophical Poem: With Notes*, 7, 1813

Many people liked this very license, but they screened it under respectable names.

> TACITUS (A.D. 56?–120?). *The Annals*, 14.21, tr. Alfred J. Church and William J. Brodribb, 1942

Let us make distinctions, call things by the right names.

> HENRY DAVID THOREAU (1817–1862). Journal, 28 November 1860

See Wisdom: Saying (Chinese) (1)

NATIONALISM

See also • Fascism ○ Idolatry: Erich Fromm (2,3) ○ Internationalism ○ Nations ○ Patriotism

I am waiting
for a way to be devised
to destroy all nationalisms
without killing anybody.

> LAWRENCE FERLINGHETTI (1919–). "I Am Waiting," *A Coney Island of the Mind*, 1958

The nationalist has a broad hatred and a narrow love.

> ANDRÉ GIDE (1869–1951). Journal, 1918 (detached page), tr. Justin O'Brien, 1948

Nationalism is today the world's idolatrous religion.

> C. WRIGHT MILLS (1916–1962). *The Causes of World War Three*, 23.1, 1958

Everyone sees the need of a new principle of life. But as always happens in similar crises—some people attempt to save the situation by an artificial intensification of the very principle which has led to decay. This is the meaning of the "nationalist" outburst of recent years. . . . The last flare, the longest; the last sigh, the deepest. On the very eve of their disappearance there is an intensification of frontiers—military and economic.

> JOSÉ ORTEGA y GASSET (1883–1955). *The Revolt of the Masses*, 14.9, 1930, tr. anon., 1932

By "nationalism" I mean first of all the habit of assuming that human beings can be classified like insects and that whole blocks of millions or tens of millions of people can be confidently labeled "good" or "bad." But secondly . . . I mean the habit of identifying oneself with a single nation or other unit, placing it beyond good and evil and recognizing no other duty than that of advancing its interests. Nationalism is not to be confused with patriotism. . . . By "patriotism" I mean devotion to a particular place and a particular way of life, which one believes to be the best in the world but has no wish to force upon other people. Patriotism is of its nature defensive, both militarily and culturally. Nationalism, on the other hand, is inseparable from the desire for power. The abiding purpose of every nationalist is to secure more power and more prestige, *not* for himself but for the nation or other unit in which he has chosen to sink his own individuality.

> GEORGE ORWELL (1903–1950). "Notes on Nationalism," May 1945, *The Collected Essays, Journalism and Letters of George Orwell*, vol. 3, ed. Sonia Orwell and Ian Angus, 1968

Nationalism appeals to our tribal instincts, to passion and to prejudice, and to our nostalgic desire to be relieved from the strain of individual responsibility which it attempts to replace by a collective or group responsibility.

> KARL R. POPPER (1902–1994). *The Open Society and Its Enemies*, 2.12.3, 1945

What is nationalism? It is an ignoble patriotism.

> ALBERT SCHWEITZER (1875–1965). *The Philosophy of Civilization: The Decay and Restoration of Civilization*, 3, 1923, tr. C. T. Campion, 1923

See Patriotism: Richard Aldington

⚜

I love my country too much to be a nationalist.

> ANONYMOUS. In Albert Camus, "Letters to a German Friend" (preface), *Resistance, Rebellion, and Death*, tr. Justin O'Brien, 1961

NATIONS

See also • America ○ Anarchism ○ China ○ Country ○ Denmark ○ England ○ France ○ Germany ○ Government ○ Imperialism ○ Internationalism ○ International Relations ○ Ireland ○ Italy ○ Mexico ○ Nationalism ○ Patriotism ○ Russia (Soviet Union) ○ Scotland ○ States ○ Switzerland ○ Travel

A strong nation, like a strong person, can afford to be gentle, firm, thoughtful, and restrained. It can afford to extend a helping hand to others. It's a weak nation, like a weak person, that must behave with bluster and boasting and rashness and other signs of insecurity.

> JIMMY CARTER (1924–). Speech, Liberty Party dinner, New York City, 14 October 1976

Every great nation fell by suicide.

> RICHARD COBDEN (1804–1865). English political leader. In Ralph Waldo Emerson, journal, 1853, undated

See America: Abraham Lincoln (1)

A nation is born Stoic, dies Epicurean.

> WILL DURANT (1885–1981). In "Teachers: The Essence of the Centuries," *Time*, 13 August 1965

An immoral nation invites its own ruin.

> DWIGHT D. EISENHOWER (1890–1969). "Some Thoughts on the Presidency," *Reader's Digest*, November 1968

We estimate the wisdom of nations by seeing what they did with their surplus capital.

> RALPH WALDO EMERSON (1803–1882). "Wealth," *English Traits*, 1856

Nations were made to help each other as much as families were.

> RALPH WALDO EMERSON (1803–1882). "The Fortune of the Republic," lecture, Old South Church, Boston, 30 March 1878

The problem is a world problem. No nation can find its own salvation by breaking away from others. We must all be saved or we must all perish together.

> MOHANDAS K. GANDHI (1869–1948). In *Young India*, 13 March 1921

The first panacea for a mismanaged nation is inflation of the currency; the second is war. Both bring a temporary prosperity; both bring a permanent ruin. Both are the refuge of political and economic opportunists.

> ERNEST HEMINGWAY (1899–1961). "Notes on the Next War," *Esquire*, September 1935

The nations are like a drop from a bucket,
   and are accounted as the dust on the scales.

> ISAIAH (8th cent. B.C.). *Isaiah* 40:15

Among [European governments], under pretense of governing, they have divided their nations into two classes, wolves and sheep.

> THOMAS JEFFERSON (1743–1826). Letter to Col. Edward Carrington, 16 January 1787

Nations love dangers, and when there are none to be found create them to fill the want.

> JOSEPH JOUBERT (1754–1824). *Pensées*, 1838, tr. H. P. Collins, 1928

There are things a man must not do even to save a nation.

> MURRAY KEMPTON (1917–1997). "To Save a Nation," *America Comes of Middle Age*, 1963
>
> See Country: Machiavelli

Ultimately a great nation is a compassionate nation.

> MARTIN LUTHER KING, JR. (1929–1968). Passion Sunday sermon at the National Cathedral, Washington, 31 March 1968

Nations rarely pay for services already rendered.

> HENRY A. KISSINGER (1923–). *Years of Upheaval*, 21, 1982

The great nations have always acted like gangsters, and the small nations like prostitutes.

> STANLEY KUBRICK (1928–). In *Guardian* (British newspaper), 5 June 1963

Can a nation be free if it oppresses other nations? It cannot.

> LENIN (1870–1924). In C. L. Sulzberger, "Khrushchev's Lenin: II—The Parrot's New Word," *New York Times*, 13 June 1956

There is no nation on earth so dangerous as a nation fully armed, and bankrupt at home.

> HENRY CABOT LODGE (1902–1985). Speech before the National Security League, Washington, 22 January 1916

A nation becomes a great power only on one condition: that its military establishment and resources are such that it could really threaten decisive warfare. . . . Military power determines the political standing of nations.

> C. WRIGHT MILLS (1916–1962). *The Power Elite*, 4.3, 1956

Nations, like men, have their various ages—infancy, maturity, old age.

> NAPOLEON (1769–1821). Dictation, St. Helena, after 1815, *The Mind of Napoleon: A Selection from His Written and Spoken Words*, 66, ed. J. Christopher Herold, 1955

No Nation has a monopoly on good things. Each one has something that the others could well afford to adopt.

> WILL ROGERS (1879–1935). Weekly column, 30 November 1930, *The Will Rogers Book*, 7.36, comp. Paula McSpadden Love, 1961

In the last analysis the all-important factor in national greatness is national character.

> THEODORE ROOSEVELT (1858–1919). In Hermann Hagedorn and Sidney Wallach, "Signposts for Americans: Our National Life," *A Theodore Roosevelt Round-Up*, 1958

Nations follow their historic interests rather more faithfully than they do their ideologies.

> ARTHUR M. SCHLESINGER, JR. (1917–). *The Bitter Heritage: Vietnam and American Democracy, 1941–1966*, 7, 1967

Every nation mocks at other nations, and all are right.

> ARTHUR SCHOPENHAUER (1788–1860). "The Wisdom of Life" (4.2), *Essays of Arthur Schopenhauer*, tr. T. Bailey Saunders, 1851

[Nations are] susceptible to all moral feelings, including—however painful a step it may be—repentance. . . . *Every* nation without exception, however persecuted, however cheated, however flawlessly righteous it feels itself to be today, has certainly at one time or another contributed its share of inhumanity.

> ALEKSANDR SOLZHENITSYN (1918–). In Lawrence A. Uzzell, "Solzhenitsyn the Centrist," *National Review*, 28 May 1990

We must never delude ourselves into thinking that physical power is a substitute for moral power, which is the true sign of national greatness.

> ADLAI E. STEVENSON (1900–1965). Speech, Hartford (Connecticut), 18 September 1952

Each nation *knowing* it has the only true religion and the only sane system of government, each despising all the others, each an ass and not suspecting it.

> MARK TWAIN (1835–1910). *What Is Man?* 6, 1906

Of all dangers to a nation, as things exist in our day, there can be no greater one than having certain portions of the people set off from the rest by a line drawn—they not privileged as others, but degraded, humiliated, made of no account.

> WALT WHITMAN (1819–1892). *Democratic Vistas*, 1871, *Walt Whitman: Complete Poetry and Collected Prose*, ed. Justin Kaplan, p. 949, 1982

No nation is fit to sit in judgment upon any other nation.

> WOODROW WILSON (1856–1924). Speech, New York City, 20 April 1915

The ruin of a nation begins in the homes of its people.

> SAYING (ASHANTI)

Righteousness exalts a nation,
  but sin is a reproach to any people.

> SAYING (*BIBLE*). Proverbs 14:34

NATIVE AMERICANS

See also • Cruelty: Maj. Anthony, Philip H. Sheridan, William Tecumseh Sherman ○ Imperialism: Winston Churchill ○ Killing: Patrick E. Connor ○ Knowledge: Ralph Waldo Emerson ○ Prejudice ○ Racism ○ Racist Statements: [especially] Christopher Columbus, Theodore Roosevelt (1) ○ Religion: Seattle

We told them [the white men] to let us alone, and keep away from us; but they followed on, and beset our paths, and they coiled themselves among us, like the snake. They poisoned us by their touch.

> BLACK HAWK (1767–1838). Native American chief. Speech, Prairie du Chien (Wisconsin), August 1835

The most Indian thing about the Indian is surely not his moccasins or his calumet, his wampum or his stone hatched, but traits of character and sagacity, skill, or passion.

> RALPH WALDO EMERSON (1803–1882). Journal, March-April 1842

If it be the design of Providence to extirpate these savages in order to make room for cultivators of the earth, it seems not improbable that rum may be the appointed means. It has already annihilated all the tribes who formerly inhabited the seacoast.

> BENJAMIN FRANKLIN (1706–1790). 1788, *Autobiography*, 1798

When the white man came, we had the land and they had the Bibles; now they have the land and we have the Bibles.

> DAN GEORGE (1899–1982). Native American. Attributed

Land of opportunity, land for the huddled masses—where would the opportunity have been without the genocide of those Old Guard, bristling Indian tribes?

> EDWARD HOAGLAND (1932–). "Lament the Real Wolf," *Sports Illustrated,* 14 January 1974

[There is] a mistaken belief that [the word *Indian*] refers somehow to the country, India. When Columbus washed up on the beach in the Caribbean, he was not looking for a country called India. Europeans were calling that country Hindustan in 1492. . . . Columbus called the tribal people he met "Indio," from the Italian *in dio,* meaning "in God."

> RUSSELL MEANS (1939–). "Fighting Words on the Future of the Earth," *Mother Jones,* December 1980

A government treaty gave Cherokees their land as long as the grass grows and the water flows, but when they discovered oil, they took it back because there was nuthin' in the treaty about oil.

> WILL ROGERS (1879–1935). In *Will Rogers U.S.A.,* CBS-TV, 9 March 1972

My forefathers didn't come over on the *Mayflower,* but they met the boat.

> WILL ROGERS (1879–1935). Part Native American. Attributed

One memorial stone reads:
"We, near whose bones you stand, were Iroquois.
The wide land which is now yours, was ours.
Friendly hands have given us back enough for a tomb."

> CARL SANDBURG (1878–1967). *The People, Yes,* 85, 1936

Once they were a happy race. Now they are made miserable by the white people, who are never contented but are always encroaching.

> TECUMSEH (1768?–1813). Native American chief. Replying to Gov. William Henry Harrison at the Council at Vincennes, Indiana Territory, 14 August 1810

These lands are ours. No one has a right to remove us because we were the first owners. The Great Spirit above has appointed this place for us, on which to light our fires, and here we will remain.

> TECUMSEH (1768?–1813). Native American chief. Message to Pres. James Madison, 1810

In the midst of this American society, so well policed, so sententious, so charitable, a cold selfishness and complete insensibility prevails when it is a question of the natives of the country. The Americans of the United States do not let their dogs hunt the Indians as do the Spaniards in Mexico, but at bottom it is the same pitiless feeling which here, as everywhere else, animates the European race. This world here belongs to us, they tell themselves every day: the Indian race is destined for final destruction which one cannot prevent and which it is not desirable to delay. Heaven has not made them to be become civilized; it is necessary that they die. Besides I do not at all want to get mixed up in it. I will not do anything against them: I will limit myself to providing everything that will hasten their ruin. In time I will have their lands and will be innocent of their death. Satisfied with his reasoning, the American goes to the church where he hears the minister of the gospel repeat every day that all men are brothers, and the Eternal Being who has made them all in like image, has given them all the duty to help one another.

> ALEXIS de TOCQUEVILLE (1805–1859). Notebook, 20 July 1831, *Journey to America,* 7, tr. George Lawrence, 1971

Walk tall as the trees; live strong as the mountains; be gentle as the spring winds; keep the warmth of summer in your heart, and the Great Spirit will always be with you.

> ANONYMOUS (NATIVE AMERICAN). Chant. In Helen Nearing, "Twilight and Evening Star," *Loving and Leaving the Good Life,* 1992

NATURE

See also • Animals ○ Camping ○ Clouds ○ Days ○ Earth ○ Earthquakes ○ Environment ○ Evolution ○ Farming ○ Flowers ○ Fog ○ Forests ○ Fountains ○ Gardening ○ God & Nature ○ Grass ○ Months ○ Moon ○ Mountains ○ Plants ○ Pollution ○ Ponds ○ Progress: Blaise Pascal ○ Rain ○ Rainbows ○ Rivers ○ Sea ○ Seasons ○ Sky ○ Stars ○ Sun ○ Time ○ Trees ○ Weather ○ Wilderness ○ Woods ○ World

Nature will out.

> AESOP (6th cent. B.C.). "The Cat-Maiden," *Fables,* tr. Joseph Jacobs, 1894
>
> See Love, Romantic: William Congreve ○ Truth: John Lydgate

Nature, Mr. Allnut, is what we are put into this world to rise above.

> JAMES AGEE (1909–1955). *The African Queen* (film), 1951, spoken by Katharine Hepburn

Nature . . . makes nothing in vain.

> ARISTOTLE (384–322 B.C.). *Politics,* 1.2, tr. Benjamin Jowett, 1885

Nature is only to be commanded by obeying her.

> FRANCIS BACON (1561–1626). *Novum Organum,* 1.129, 1620, Willey Book edition, 1944

Nature is often hidden, sometimes overcome, seldom extinguished. Force maketh nature more violent in the return.

> FRANCIS BACON (1561–1626). "Of Nature in Men," *Essays,* 1625

There is no forgiveness in nature.

> UGO BETTI (1892–1953). *Goat Island,* 1.4, 1946, ed. Gino Rizzo, 1966

Natur dont put on enny airs.

> JOSH BILLINGS (1818–1885). "Bred and Butter," *Everybody's Friend, or; Josh Billing's Encyclopedia and Proverbial Philosophy of Wit and Humor,* 1874

When we are happy, we love Nature. When we are dull and depressed, it says nothing to us. Our feeling for it would therefore seem to be a reflection of our moods.

> GERALD BRENAN (1894–1987). "Nature," *Thoughts in a Dry Season: A Miscellany,* 1978

Man masters nature not by force but by understanding.

> JACOB BRONOWSKY (1908–1974). "The Creative Mind," *Science and Human Values,* 1956

There is a pleasure in the pathless woods,
There is a rapture on the lonely shore,
There is society, where none intrudes,
By the deep Sea, and music in its roar;
I love not Man the less, but Nature more.

> LORD BYRON (1788–1824). *Childe Harold's Pilgrimage,* 4.178, 1812–1818

Truth and goodness and beauty are but different faces of the same All. But beauty in nature is not ultimate. It is the herald of inward and eternal beauty.

> RALPH WALDO EMERSON (1803–1882). "Beauty," *Nature,* 1836

In nature nothing is done but in the cheapest way.

> RALPH WALDO EMERSON (1803–1882). Journal, 7 February 1839

Nature is a mutable cloud, which is always and never the same.

> RALPH WALDO EMERSON (1803–1882). "History," *Essays: First Series,* 1841

Nature is an endless combination and repetition of a very few laws.

> RALPH WALDO EMERSON (1803–1882). "History," *Essays: First Series,* 1841

Power is in nature the essential measure of right. Nature suffers nothing to remain in her kingdoms which cannot help itself.

> RALPH WALDO EMERSON (1803–1882). "Self-Reliance," *Essays: First Series,* 1841

Nature, as we know her, is no saint.

> RALPH WALDO EMERSON (1803–1882). "Experience," *Essays: Second Series,* 1844

The oceanic working of Nature which accumulates a momentary individual as she forms a momentary wave in a running sea.

> RALPH WALDO EMERSON (1803–1882). Journal, 14 March 1848

Nature uniformly does one thing at a time: if she will have a perfect hand, she makes head and feet pay for it. So now, as she is making railroad and telegraph ages, she starves the *spirituel,* to stuff the *matériel* and *industriel.*

> RALPH WALDO EMERSON (1803–1882). Journal, October 1848

Nature is good, but intellect is better, as the law-giver is before the law-receiver.

> RALPH WALDO EMERSON (1803–1882). "Plato; or, The Philosopher," *Representative Men,* 1850

Nature is reckless of the individual. When she has points to carry, she carries them.

> RALPH WALDO EMERSON (1803–1882). "Culture," *The Conduct of Life,* 1860

Nature has her own mode of doing each thing, and she has somewhere told it plainly, if we will keep our eyes and ears open.

> RALPH WALDO EMERSON (1803–1882). "Wealth," *The Conduct of Life,* 1860

Nature works in immense time and spends individuals and races prodigally to prepare new individuals and races.

> RALPH WALDO EMERSON (1803–1882). "The Fortune of the Republic," lecture, Old South Church, Boston, 30 March 1878

The terrible aristocracy that is in nature.

> RALPH WALDO EMERSON (1803–1882). "Aristocracy," *Lectures and Biographical Sketches,* 1883

There is no unemployed force in Nature. All decomposition is recomposition.

> RALPH WALDO EMERSON (1803–1882). "The Man of Letters," *Lectures and Biographical Sketches,* 1883

Nature is always serious—does not jest with us.

> RALPH WALDO EMERSON (1803–1882). "The Superlative," *Lectures and Biographical Sketches,* 1883

Nature, in her indifference, makes no distinction between good and evil.

> ANATOLE FRANCE (1844–1924). *L'Affaire Crainquebille,* 1901

Nature provides exceptions to every rule.

> MARGARET FULLER (1810–1850). "The Great Lawsuit. Man versus Men. Woman verses Women," *The Dial* (New England journal), July 1843

[Nature] is crafty, but for a good end.

> GOETHE (1749–1832). "Nature: Aphorisms," *The Maxims and Reflections of Goethe,* tr. T. Bailey Saunders, 1892

[Nature] is whole and yet never finished.

> GOETHE (1749–1832). "Nature: Aphorisms," *The Maxims and Reflections of Goethe*, tr. T. Bailey Saunders, 1892

Nothing in nature is isolated. Nothing is without reference to something else. Nothing achieves meaning apart from that which neighbors it.

> GOETHE (1749–1832). Quoted by Richard B. Sweall, "In Search of Emily Dickinson." In William Zinsser, ed., *Extraordinary Lives: The Art and Craft of American Biography,* 1988

You may drive out Nature with a pitchfork, yet she still will hurry back.

> HORACE (65–8 B.C.). *Epistles,* 1.10

Nurture overcomes nature.

> JAMES HOWELL (1593–1666). Comp. "Italian," *Paroimiographia: Proverbs, or Old Sayed Sawes & Adages in English . . . Italian, French and Spanish,* p. 6, 1659

Like all compulsory legislation, that of Nature is harsh and wasteful in its operation. Ignorance is visited as sharply as willful disobedience—incapacity meets with the same punishment as crime. Nature's discipline is not even a word and a blow, and the blow first; but the blow without the word. It is left to you to find out why your ears are boxed.

> T. H. HUXLEY (1825–1895). "A Liberal Education," *Lay Sermons, Addresses, and Reviews,* 1870

In nature there are neither rewards nor punishments—there are consequences.

> ROBERT G. INGERSOLL (1833–1899). "Nature," *The Philosophy of Ingersoll,* ed. Vere Goldthwaite, 1906

Nature *must not* win the game, but she *cannot* lose.

> CARL G. JUNG (1875–1961). "Paracelsus as a Spiritual Phenomenon" (4.C), 1942, *Alchemical Studies,* tr. R. F. C. Hull, 1967

Contend with the powers of nature, force them to the yoke of superior purpose.

> NIKOS KAZANTZAKIS (1883–1957). "The Action: The Relationship between Man and Nature" (13), *The Saviors of God: Spiritual Exercises,* 1927, tr. Kimon Friar, 1960

Nothing takes place all at once . . . *nature never makes leaps.*

> GOTTFRIED LEIBNITZ (1649–1716). "New Essays on the Understanding: Preface," 1704, *The Philosophic Works of Leibnitz,* ed. George Martin Duncan, 1908

Nature never makes excellent things for mean or no uses.

> JOHN LOCKE (1632–1704). *An Essay Concerning Human Understanding,* 2.1.15, 1690, ed. Alexander Campbell Fraser, 1894

The End of Nature.

> BILL McKIBBEN. Referring to the "greenhouse effect." Book title, 1989

Accuse not Nature, she hath done her part;
Do thou but thine.

> JOHN MILTON (1608–1674). *Paradise Lost,* 8.561, 1667

With the tenderness of a mother, Nature has provided that our necessary actions should be pleasant. She invites us to them not only by reason but also by appetite, and it is ingratitude to break her laws.

> MONTAIGNE (1533–1592). *The Autobiography of Michel de Montaigne,* 34, ed. Marvin Lowenthal, 1935

Nature is ever at work building and pulling down, creating and destroying, keeping everything whirling and flowing, allowing no rest but in rhythmical motion, chasing everything in endless song out of one beautiful form into another.

> JOHN MUIR (1838–1914). *Our National Parks,* 3 (closing words), 1901

What nature has made one cannot be divided but only mutilated.

> NAPOLEON (1769–1821). Deathbed statement, 17 April 1821, *The Mind of Napoleon: A Selection from His Written and Spoken Words,* 324, ed. J. Christopher Herold, 1955

Nature often deceives us and does not subject herself to her own rules.

> BLAISE PASCAL (1623–1662). *Pensées,* 91, 1670, tr. William F. Trotter, 1931

Ulysses: One touch of nature makes the whole world kin.

> SHAKESPEARE (1564–1616). *Troilus and Cressida,* 3.3.175, 1601

King Lear: Nature's above art.

> SHAKESPEARE (1564–1616). *King Lear,* 4.6.86, 1605

There are many wonderful things in nature, but the most wonderful of all is man.

> SOPHOCLES (496–406 B.C.), *Antigone,* l.330

Nature's rules . . . have no exceptions.

> HERBERT SPENCER (1820–1903). Introduction ("Lemma II") to *Social Statics,* 1851

A stern discipline pervades all nature, which is a little cruel that it may be very kind.

> EDMUND SPENSER (1552?–1599).

Patterns and structure. Everywhere we look we see them. What appears random and chaotic also has order. And on Earth much of the order is linked to interrelationships that drive constant change. Cycles and rhythms. Pulses and flows. Changes in magnetic fields. Continental plates moving. Water cycles. Seasons changing. Life and death. Process and connection. Nature flows through webs of structure and shifting time: from ocean to cloud to rain to river to ocean. Natural rhythms.

> PAYSON R. STEVENS (1946–). "Natural Rhythms," *Embracing Earth: New Views of Our Changing Planet,* 1992

In nature, there is less death and destruction than death and transmutation.

> EDWIN WAY TEALE (1899–1980). "July 5," *Circle of the Seasons,* 1953

Nature, red in tooth and claw.

> ALFRED, LORD TENNYSON (1809–1892). *In Memoriam A. H. H.,* 56, 1850

Man tames Nature only that he may at last make her more free even than he found her.

> HENRY DAVID THOREAU (1817–1862). "Thursday," *A Week on the Concord and Merrimack Rivers,* 1849

Ah, dear nature, the mere remembrance, after a short forgetfulness, of the pine woods! I come to it as a hungry man to a crust
of bread.

> HENRY DAVID THOREAU (1817–1862). Journal, 12 December 1851

It is surprising how much room there is in nature—if a man will
follow his proper path.

> HENRY DAVID THOREAU (1817–1862). Journal, 26 January 1853

Nature is slow but sure; she works no faster than need be; she is
the tortoise that wins the race by her perseverance.

> HENRY DAVID THOREAU (1817–1862). Journal, 14 January 1861

People make the mistake of talking about "natural laws." There
are no natural laws. There are only temporary habits of nature.

> ALFRED NORTH WHITEHEAD (1861–1947). 11 November 1947,
> *Dialogues of Alfred North Whitehead*, rec. Lucien Price, 1954

We all look at Nature too much, and live with her too little.

> OSCAR WILDE (1854–1900). *De Profundis*, 1905

Nature never did betray
The heart that loved her.

> WILLIAM WORDSWORTH (1770–1850). "Lines Composed a Few Miles
> Above Tintern Abbey," l. 122, 1798

❦

Nature is a hanging judge.

> ANONYMOUS

Nature is no teacher of morality; she herself needs lessons.

> ANONYMOUS

Nature abhors a vacuum.

> SAYING (LATIN)

NAVY

See also • Army ○ Commanders ○ Commanders & Staff: Horatio
Nelson ○ Danger: John Paul Jones ○ Revolutionary War: John
Paul Jones ○ Militarism ○ Sea ○ Ships ○ World War II: William F.
"Bull" Halsey, Jr. ○ War

The only great qualification for being put at the head of the Navy
is that I am very much at sea.

> EDWARD CARSON (1854–1935). In Ian Colvin, *The Life of Lord Carson*,
> 3.23, 1936

Don't talk to me about naval tradition. It's nothing but rum,
sodomy and the lash.

> WINSTON CHURCHILL (1874–1965). Remark, 1911. In Sir Peter Gretton,
> *Former Naval Person: Winston Churchill and the Royal Navy*, 1, 1968

Damn the torpedoes? Four bells! Captain Drayton, go ahead.
Jouett, full speed.

> DAVID FARRAGUT (1801–1870). During the Battle of Mobile Bay
> (Alabama), 5 August 1864. In Alfred Thayer Mahan, *Great
> Commanders: Admiral Farragut*, 10, 1892 (Popular version: Damn the
> torpedoes! Full speed ahead!)

Tell the men to fire faster and not give up the ship. Fight her till
she sinks!

> JAMES LAWRENCE (1781–1813). Naval captain. While fatally wounded
> aboard the frigate *Chesapeake* in a battle against the British frigate
> *Shannon* off the coast of Boston, 1 June 1813. The popular version of
> Capt. Lawrence's words—"Don't give up the ship!"—are also attributed
> to Capt. James Mugford who died on his schooner *Franklin* during a
> British attack in Boston harbor, 19 May 1776.

The master of the sea must be master of the empire.

> THEMISTOCLES (523?–458 B.C.). As paraphrased by Cicero (106–43
> B.C.), *Ad Atticum*, 10.8, tr. E. O. Winstedt, 1913

To an active external commerce, the protection of a naval force is
indispensable.

> GEORGE WASHINGTON (1732–1799). Message to Congress, 7 December
> 1796

❦

Join the navy and see the world.

> SLOGAN (AMERICAN)

NECESSITY

See also • Chance ○ Destiny ○ Fate ○ Fortune ○ Luck ○
Machiavellianism: Napoleon (6)

Necessity has no law.

> ST. AUGUSTINE (A.D. 354–430). *Soliloquies*, 2

"Necessity iz the mother ov invenshun," and *Pattent Wright* iz the
father.

> JOSH BILLINGS (1818–1885). "Slips of the Pen," *His Works, Complete*,
> 1881

Invention is not infrequently the mother of necessity.

> SAMUEL BUTLER (1835–1902). *Further Extracts from the Note-Books of
> Samuel Butler*, 2, ed. A. T. Bartholomew, 1934

Necessity . . . even makes cowards brave.

> CATILINE (108–62 B.C.). Roman political leader

Necessity makes an honest man a knave.

> DANIEL DEFOE (1660–1731). *Serious Reflections during the Life and
> Surprising Adventures of Robinson Crusoe*, 2, 1720

All things happen by virtue of necessity.

> DEMOCRITUS (460–370 B.C.). As paraphrased by Diogenes Laertius
> (A.D. 3rd cent.), *Lives of Eminent Philosophers*, 9.7, tr. R. D. Hicks, 1925

Necessity dispenseth with Decorum.

> THOMAS FULLER (1654–1734). Comp., *Gnomologia: Adages and
> Proverbs*, 3515, 1732

Necessity never made [a] good bargain.

> JAMES HOWELL (1593–1666). Comp., "Divers Centuries of New Sayings,"
> (p. 6), *Paroimiographia: Proverbs, or Old Sayed Sawes & Adages in
> English . . . Italian, French and Spanish*, 1659

Wisdom: A term Pride uses when talking of Necessity.

> ELBERT HUBBARD (1856–1915). *The Roycroft Dictionary Concocted by
> Ali Baba and the Bunch on Rainy Days*, p. 165, 1914

Whatever is universally necessary has been granted to mankind
on easy terms.

SAMUEL JOHNSON (1709–1784). In *The Idler* (English journal), 57, 19 May 1759

When everything becomes unbearable . . . Then necessity makes the law, or changes it.

JOSEPH JOUBERT (1754–1824). 1815, *Pensées*, 1838, tr. Paul Auster, 1983

In early life I was inclined to believe in what I understand is called the "Doctrine of Necessity"—that is, that the human mind is impelled to action, or held in rest by some power, over which the mind itself has no control.

ABRAHAM LINCOLN (1809–1865). Replying to charges of religious infidelity, handbill addressed to the voters of the Seventh Congressional District (Illinois), 31 July 1846

Prudent men make the best of circumstances in their actions, and, although constrained by necessity to a certain course, make it appear as if done from their own liberality.

MACHIAVELLI (1469–1527). *The Discourses*, 1.51, 1517, tr. Christian E. Detmold, 1940

So spake the Fiend, and with necessity,
The Tyrant's plea, excus'd his devilish deeds.

JOHN MILTON (1608–1674). *Paradise Lost*, 4.393, 1667

Don't talk to me of goodness, of abstract justice, of natural law. Necessity is the highest law.

NAPOLEON (1769–1821). Remark, April 1815, *The Mind of Napoleon: A Selection from His Written and Spoken Words*, 202, ed. J. Christopher Herold, 1955

Over the course of history, men learn that iron necessity is neither iron nor necessary.

FRIEDRICH NIETZSCHE (1844–1900). *Human, All Too Human*, 514, 1878, tr. Marion Faber, 1984

Necessity is the plea for every infringement of human freedom. It is the argument of tyrants; it is the creed of slaves.

WILLIAM PITT THE YOUNGER (1759–1806). One month before becoming prime minister, House of Commons speech, 18 November 1783

Even God is said not to be able to fight against necessity.

PLATO (427?–347 B.C.). *Laws*, 5.741, tr. Benjamin Jowett, 1894

The true creator is necessity, which is the mother of our invention.

PLATO (427?–347 B.C.). *The Republic*, 2.369, tr. Benjamin Jowett, 1894 (Popular version: Necessity is the mother of invention.)

See Accident: Anonymous (American) ○ Invention: Gerald Brenan

Necessity is a law that justifies itself.

PUBLIUS SYRUS (85–43 B.C.). *Moral Sayings*, 325, tr. Darius Lyman, Jr., 1862

You cannot escape necessities, but you can overcome them.

SENECA THE YOUNGER (5? B.C.–A.D. 65). "On Allegiance to Virtue," *Moral Letters to Lucilius*, 37.3, tr. Richard M. Gummere, 1918

Gaunt: There is no virtue like necessity.

SHAKESPEARE (1564–1616). *Richard II*, 1.3.278, 1595

I find no hint throughout the universe
Of good or ill, of blessing or of curse;
I find alone Necessity Supreme.

JAMES THOMSON (1834–1882). "The City of Dreadful Night," 1874

Necessity is the mother of freedom.

ALVIN TOFFLER (1928–). *Powershift: Knowledge, Wealth, and Violence at the Edge of the 21st Century*, 28, 1990

☙

Necessity makes lawful what would otherwise be unlawful.

SAYING (LATIN)

Where necessity pinches, boldness is prudence.

SAYING

NEGOTIATION

See also • Alliances ○ Appeasement ○ Argument ○ Diplomacy ○ International Relations ○ Persuasion ○ Quarrels ○ Reason ○ Tact ○ Treaties

Negotiation from strength.

DEAN ACHESON (1893–1971). A favorite saying. In Richard J. Barnet, *Roots of War*, 3.3, 1971

Bluff is the essence of the bargainer's art.

RICHARD J. BARNET (1929–). *Roots of War*, 3.3, 1971

The secret of negotiation is to harmonize the real interests of the parties concerned.

FRANÇOIS de CALLIÈRES (1645–1717). *De la manière de négocier avec les souverains*, 1716

Unless both sides win, no agreement can be permanent.

JIMMY CARTER (1924–). Charlie Rose television interview, PBS, 17 January 1995

The necessary talents for negotiation are: the great art of pleasing and engaging the affection and confidence, not only of those with whom you are to cooperate, but even of those whom you are to oppose; to conceal your own thoughts and views, and to discover other people's; to gain the absolute command over your temper and your countenance, that no heat may provoke you to say, nor no change of countenance to betray, what should be a secret. Please all who are worth pleasing; offend none. Counterwork your rivals with diligence and dexterity, but at the same time with the utmost personal civility to them; and be firm without heat.

LORD CHESTERFIELD (1694–1773). Slightly modified. Letter to his son, 26 September 1752

To jaw-jaw is always better than to war-war.

WINSTON CHURCHILL (1874–1965). White House luncheon speech, Washington, 26 June 1954

Firmness in support of fundamentals, with flexibility in tactics and methods, is the key to any hope of progress in negotiation.

DWIGHT D. EISENHOWER (1890–1969). Television broadcast (before talks with Soviet Premier Nikita Khrushchev at Camp David), 10 September 1959

Now one of you is to divide it and the other to get first choice.

> IDA STOVER EISENHOWER (1862–1946). Mother of Dwight D. Eisenhower. When two of her sons would squabble over desert portions. In James David Barber, *The Presidential Character: Predicting Performance in the White House,* 5, 1972

Negotiations without weapons are like music without instruments.

> FREDERICK II (1712–1786). In Heinrich von Treitschke, *The Life of Frederick the Great,* p. 138, ed. Douglas Sladen, 1915

In negotiating with Persons, observe their Temper and (as far as Prudence will give leave) comply with their Humor: Suffer them to speak their Pleasure freely; seem to be pleased, if not with their Opinion and Party, yet with the Elocution and Ability; this may probably draw them on to let fall something that may be for thy Advantage.

> THOMAS FULLER (1654–1734). Comp. *Introductio ad Prudentiam,* 1452, 1731

Many things are lost for want of asking.

> GEORGE HERBERT (1593–1633). Comp. *Outlandish Proverbs,* 968, 1640

It's a well-known proposition that you know who's going to win a negotiation: it's he who pauses the longest.

> ROBERT HOLMES à COURT (1937–1990). In *Sydney Morning Herald,* 24 May 1986

Let us never negotiate out of fear, but let us never fear to negotiate.

> JOHN F. KENNEDY (1917–1963). *Inaugural Address,* 20 January 1961

A good definition of an equitable settlement is one that will make both sides unhappy.

> HENRY A. KISSINGER (1923–). *White House Years,* 10, 1979

The optimum moment for negotiations is when things appear to be going well. To yield to pressures is to invite them; to acquire the reputation for short staying power is to give the other side a powerful incentive for protracting negotiations. When a concession is made voluntarily, it provides the greatest incentive for reciprocity.

> HENRY A. KISSINGER (1923–). *White House Years,* 12, 1979

It is generally unwise . . . to raise an issue when one is not prepared to accept the likely response.

> HENRY A. KISSINGER (1923–). *White House Years,* 14, 1979

I tended to share Metternich's view that the perfectly straightforward person was the most difficult to deal with.

> HENRY A. KISSINGER (1923–). In Walter Isaacson, *Kissinger: A Biography,* 24, 1992

It is easy to know when a government wishes for peace by observing the character of the person sent to negotiate for it.

> NAPOLEON (1769–1821). Slightly modified. *In the Words of Napoleon,* p. 65, tr. Daniel Savage Gray, 1977

When people inflict great wrongs upon one another, you are likely to hear it said afterward, "If only they had talked it over first."

> JOHANN HEINRICH PESTALOZZI (1746–1827). *The Education of Man: Aphorisms,* 5, tr. Heinz and Ruth Norden, 1951

Who makes a timid request invites denial.

> SENECA THE YOUNGER (5? B.C.–A.D. 65). *Hippolytus,* l. 590, tr. Frank Justus Miller, 1917

Negotiating with men's vanity gives one the best bargain, for one often receives the most substantial advantages in return for very little of substance.

> ALEXIS de TOCQUEVILLE (1805–1859). *Recollections,* 3.3, 1893, tr. George Lawrence, 1964

Guns are left to do what words
Might have done earlier, rightly used.

> JOHN WALLER (1917–)

NEUROSIS

See also • Mental Illness ○ Neurosis & Psychosis ○ Psychoanalysis: [especially] Anonymous ○ Psychotherapy

All neurotic symptoms have as their object the task of safeguarding the patient's self-esteem.

> ALFRED ADLER (1870–1937). *The Individual Psychology of Alfred Adler: A Systematic Presentation in Selections from His Writings,* 10.A.1 (1913), ed. Heinz L. Ansbacher and Rowena R. Ansbacher, 1956

To some degree or other, every neurotic restricts his sphere of action, his contacts with the whole situation. He tries to keep at a distance the real confronting problems of life and confines himself to circumstances in which he feels able to dominate. In this way he builds for himself a narrow stable, closes the door, and spends his life away from the wind, the sunlight, and the fresh air.

> ALFRED ADLER (1870–1937). *The Individual Psychology of Alfred Adler: A Systematic Presentation in Selections from His Writings,* 10.C.3 (1931), ed. Heinz L. Ansbacher and Rowena R. Ansbacher, 1956
>
> See Inferiority: Adler

A neurosis [is] nothing but a failure in the process of domestication.

> FRANZ G. ALEXANDER (1891–1964). *Our Age of Unreason: A Study of the Irrational Forces in Social Life,* 1942

In "neurosis" one lends false primacy to the reactions of others.

> DAVID COOPER (1931?–). "The Other Shore of Therapy," *The Death of the Family,* 1970

[Neurotic] symptoms are created in order to avoid the *danger situation* of which anxiety sounds the alarm.

> SIGMUND FREUD (1856–1939). *The Problem of Anxiety,* 7, 1926, tr. Henry Alden Bunker, 1936

Early trauma—defense—latency—outbreak of the neurosis—partial return of the repressed material: this was the formula we drew up for the development of a neurosis. Now I will invite the reader to take a step forward and assume that in the history of the human species something happened similar to the events in the life of the individual.

> SIGMUND FREUD (1856–1939). *Moses and Monotheism,* 3.1.4, 1939, tr. Katherine Jones, 1955

Every neurosis is the result of a conflict between man's inherent powers and those forces which block their development.

> ERICH FROMM (1900–1980). *Man for Himself: An Inquiry into the Psychology of Ethics,* 4.5.A, 1947

Whatever complaints the neurotic patient may have, whatever symptoms he may present are rooted in his inability to love, if we mean by love a capacity for the experience of concern, responsibility, respect, and understanding of another person and the intense desire for that other person's growth.

> ERICH FROMM (1900–1980). *Psychoanalysis and Religion*, 4, 1950

Neurotic symptoms are not isolated phenomena which can be dealt with independently from moral problems.

> ERICH FROMM (1900–1980). *Psychoanalysis and Religion*, 4, 1950

The moment of the outbreak of neurosis is not just a matter of chance; as a rule it is most critical. It is usually *the moment when a new psychological adjustment, that is, a new adaptation, is demanded.*

> CARL G. JUNG (1875–1961). "Psychoanalysis and Neurosis," 1916, *Freud and Psychoanalysis*, 1966

Neurosis is an inner cleavage—the state of being at war with oneself. . . . What drives people to war with themselves is the intuition or the knowledge that they consist of two persons in opposition to one another.

> CARL G. JUNG (1875–1961). *Modern Man in Search of a Soul*, 11, tr. W. S. Dell and Cary F. Baynes, 1933
>
> See Soul: Goethe

In [the Middle Ages] they spoke of the devil, today we call it a neurosis.

> CARL G. JUNG (1875–1961). "The Meaning of Psychology for Modern Man," 1933, *Civilization in Transition*, tr. R. F. C. Hull, 1964

The majority of my patients consisted not of believers but of those who had lost their faith. The ones who came to me were the lost sheep.

> CARL G. JUNG (1875–1961). *Memories, Dreams, Reflections*, 4, ed. Aniela Jaffé, 1962

"Neurosis" is just a medical euphemism, for a "state of sin" and social alienation.

> O. HOBART MOWRER (1907–1982). *The Crisis in Psychiatry and Religion*, 9.1, 1961

[Neurosis] is the disease of a bad conscience.

> WILHELM STEKEL (1868–1940). In Cyril Connolly, "Te Palinure Petens," *The Unquiet Grave: A Word Cycle by Palinurus*, 1945

According to [Carl G.] Jung, neurosis followed if either extroversion or introversion became exaggerated. Extreme extroversion led to the individual losing his own identity in the press of people and events. Extreme introversion threatened the subjectively preoccupied individual with loss of contact with external reality.

> ANTHONY STORR (1920–). *Solitude: A Return to the Self*, 6, 1988

The surest way to destroy a neurosis is to induce a sense of creative purpose, of meaning.

> COLIN WILSON (1931–). *Beyond the Outsider: A Philosophy of the Future*, 5, 1965

NEUROSIS & PSYCHOSIS

See also • Mental Illness ○ Neurosis

Traditionally, neurotic patients, however severely handicapped by their symptoms, are not classified as psychotic because they are aware that their mental functioning is disturbed.

> AMERICAN PSYCHIATRIC ASSOCIATION. *Diagnostic and Statistical Manual of Mental Disorders II*, p. 39, 1968

"Neurotic" means he's not as sensible as I am, and "psychotic" means he's even worse than my brother-in-law.

> KARL MENNINGER (1893–1990). Recalled on his death, 18 July 1990

Doubt is to certainty as neurosis is to psychosis. The neurotic is in doubt and has fears about persons and things; the psychotic has convictions and makes claims about them. In short, the neurotic has problems, the psychotic has solutions.

> THOMAS S. SZASZ (1920–). "Mental Illness," *The Second Sin*, 1973

Those who suffer from and complain of their own behavior are usually classified as "neurotic"; those whose behavior makes others suffer, and about whom others complain, are usually classified as "psychotic."

> THOMAS S. SZASZ (1920–). "Summary" (4), *The Myth of Mental Illness: Foundations of a Theory of Personal Conduct*, rev. ed., 1974 (1961)

The neurotic builds castles in the air, the psychotic lives in them, and the psychiatrist collects the rent.

> ANONYMOUS. In Thomas S. Szasz, "Psychiatry," *The Untamed Tongue: A Dissenting Dictionary*, 1990

Everybody's neurotic. Only psychotics aren't neurotic.

> ANONYMOUS. Psychoanalyst. Remark to Joseph Heller. In Jerry Carroll, "A Lucky Man: Joseph Heller's Leisurely Memoir Exposes Roots of 'Catch-22,'" *San Francisco Chronicle*, 18 February 1998

NEUTRALITY

See also • Alliances ○ International Relations ○ Treaties

He that is neither one thing nor the other has no friends.

> AESOP (6th cent. B.C.). "The Bat, the Birds and the Beasts," *Fables*, tr. Joseph Jacobs, 1894

We know what happens to people who stay in the middle of the road: they get run over.

> ANEURIN BEVAN (1897–1960). House of Commons speech, 2 April 1946

A leader who ceases to take sides simply abdicates his role and hands authority over to his strongest competitors.

> ALAN BRINKLEY (1949–). "The Vital Center Will Not Hold," *New York Times Magazine*, 19 January 1997

The consequence is, being of no party,
    I shall offend all parties.

> LORD BYRON (1788–1824). *Don Juan*, 9.26, 1819–1824

The hottest places in hell are reserved for those who in a time of great moral crisis maintain their neutrality.

> DANTE (A.D. 1265–1321). As loosely paraphrased by John F. Kennedy in his remarks at the signing of the charter that established the German Peace Corps, Bonn (West Germany), 24 June 1963

To be neutral when others are at war is a wise course for the strong, who need not fear the victor.

> FRANCESCO GUICCIARDINI (1483–1540). *Remembrances,* C.68, 1530, tr. Mario Domandi, 1965

A prince is further esteemed when he is a true friend or a true enemy, when, that is, he declares himself without reserve in favor of some one or against another. This policy is always more useful than remaining neutral.

> MACHIAVELLI (1469–1527). *The Prince,* 21, 1513, tr. Luigi Ricci, 1903

In the world from now on, neutrality is only a word for deceiving people.

> MAO TSE-TUNG (1893–1976). In Henry A. Kissinger, "Reflections on American Diplomacy" (3), *Foreign Affairs,* October 1956

He who walks in the middle of the road gets hit from both sides.

> GEORGE P. SHULTZ (1920–). In Richard M. Nixon, "The Presidency: 1969–1972" ("1969: President and Congress"), *The Memoirs of Richard Nixon,* 1978

NEWS

See also • Communications ○ Gossip ○ Journalism ○ Journalists ○ Media ○ Newspapers ○ The Press ○ Propaganda ○ Publicity ○ Rumor ○ Television

When a dog bites a man, that is not news because it happens so often. But if a man bites a dog, that is news.

> JOHN B. BOGART (1848–1921). *New York Sun* city editor. 1880s? In F. M. O'Brien, *The Story of the Sun,* 10, 1918

What's wan man's news is another man's throubles.

> FINLEY PETER DUNNE (1867–1936). "The News of a Week," *Observations by Mr. Dooley,* 1902

Nowadays Truth is the greatest News.

> THOMAS FULLER (1654–1734). Comp., *Gnomologia: Adages and Proverbs,* 3689, 1732

In an Ocean of News, scarce a drop of Truth.

> JAMES HOWELL (1593–1666). Comp., "Divers Centuries of New Sayings," (p. 5), *Paroimiographia: Proverbs, or Old Sayed Sawes & Adages in English . . . Italian, French and Spanish,* 1659

Who brings good news may knock boldly.

> JAMES HOWELL (1593–1666). Comp., "French" (p. 8), *Paroimiographia: Proverbs, or Old Sayed Sawes & Adages in English . . . Italian, French and Spanish,* 1659

That's the news from Lake Wobegon, where all the women are strong, the men are good-looking, and all the children are above average.

> GARRISON KEILLOR (1942–). His signature line, *A Prairie Home Companion,* radio entertainment-program series, 1974–1987

People everywhere confuse what they read in newspapers with news.

> A. J. LIEBLING (1904–1963). "A Talkative Something-or-Other," *New Yorker,* 7 April 1956

I do not like to get the news because there has never been an era when so many things were going so right for so many of the wrong persons.

> OGDEN NASH (1902–1971). "Everybody Tells Me Everything," *The Face Is Familiar,* 1940

If You Don't Like the News, Go Out and Make Some of Your Own.

> WES "SCOOP" NISKER. Book title, 1994

News is a business, but it is also a public trust.

> DAN RATHER (1931–). "From Murrow to Mediocrity?" *New York Times,* 10 March 1987

Nobody likes the bringer of bad news.

> SOPHOCLES (496–406 B.C.). *Antigone,* l.270, tr. Elizabeth Wyckoff, 1954

You don't tell us how to stage the news, we won't tell you how to cover it.

> LARRY SPEAKES (1939–). Presidential assistant to Ronald Reagan. Sign on the press secretary's desk in his White House office. In Mark Hertsgaard, "How Reagan Seduced Us: Inside the President's Propaganda Factory," *Village Voice* (New York City), 25 September 1984

A democracy is badly served when newspapers and television focus so intensely on the personal joys and tragedies of famous people. This kind of "news" crowds out more serious issues, and there is an important difference—as the Constitution's framers well knew, and as many people today appear to have forgotten— between the public interest and what interests the public.

> CASS R. SUNSTEIN. "Reinforce the Walls of Privacy," *New York Times,* 6 September 1997

🍃

Bad news is more readily believed than good news.

> SAYING

NEWSPAPERS

See also • Freedom of the Press: Thomas Jefferson (2) ○ Journalism ○ Journalists ○ Media ○ News ○ The Press

Lady Middleton . . . exerted herself to ask Mr. Palmer if there was any news in the paper.
    "No, none at all," he replied, and read on.

> JANE AUSTEN (1775–1817). *Sense and Sensibility,* 1.19, 1811

I am unable to understand how a man of honor can take a newspaper in his hands without a shudder of disgust.

> CHARLES BAUDELAIRE (1821–1867). In Russell Baker, "Besides the Pencil Box," *New York Times,* 4 September 1993

The advertisements in a newspaper are more full of knowledge in respect to what is going on in a state or community than the editorial columns are.

> HENRY WARD BEECHER (1813–1887). "The Press," *Proverbs from Plymouth Pulpit,* ed. William Drysdale, 1887

Newspapers . . . help you forget the previous day.

> ELIAS CANETTI (1905–1994). 1978, *The Secret Heart of the Clock: Notes, Aphorisms, Fragments: 1973-1985,* tr. Joel Agee, 1989

I'm glad I'm not me!

> BOB DYLAN (1941–). While reading a newspaper account about himself. In *Don't Look Back* (documentary film), 1965

I hate to be defended in a newspaper. As long as all that is said is said *against* me, I feel a certain sublime assurance of success but as soon as [honeyed] words of praise are spoken for me, I feel as one that lies unprotected before his enemies.

> RALPH WALDO EMERSON (1803–1882). Journal, 29 September 1838

Headlines twice the size of events.

> JOHN GALSWORTHY (1867–1933). *Over the River,* 27, 1933

The power is to set the agenda. What we print and what we don't print matter a lot.

> KATHARINE GRAHAM (1917–). *Washington Post* publisher. In Donald L. Barlett, "All the Publisher's Presidents," *New York Times Book Review,* 28 February 1993

Nothing can now be believed which is seen in a newspaper. Truth itself becomes suspicious by being put into that polluted vehicle.

> THOMAS JEFFERSON (1743–1826). Letter to John Norvell, 14 June 1807

I really look with commiseration over the great body of my fellow citizens, who, reading newspapers, live and die in the belief that they have known something of what has been passing in the world in their time.

> THOMAS JEFFERSON (1743–1826). Letter to John Norvell, 14 June 1807

Everything you read in the newspapers is absolutely true except for that rare story of which you happen to have firsthand knowledge.

> ERWIN KNOLL (1931–1994). *Progressive* editor. "Knoll's Law of Media Accuracy." In Paul Dickson, comp., *The Official Rules,* p. 138, 1978

A good newspaper, I suppose, is a nation talking to itself.

> ARTHUR MILLER (1915–1944). In *Observer* (British newspaper), 26 November 1961

Newspapers should be limited to advertising.

> NAPOLEON (1769–1821). *In the Words of Napoleon,* p. 9, tr. Daniel Savage Gray, 1977

It will be my earnest aim that *The New York Times* give the news, all the news, in concise and attractive form, in language that is parliamentary in good society, and give it as early, if not earlier, than it can be learned through any other reliable medium; to give the news impartially, without fear or favor, regardless of party, sect or interests involved; to make of the columns of *The New York Times* a forum for the consideration of all questions of public importance, and to that end to invite intelligent discussion from all shades of opinion.

> ADOLPH S. OCHS (1858–1935). On becoming publisher and general manager. "Business Announcement," *New York Times,* 19 August 1896

All the News That's Fit to Print.

> ADOLPH S. OCHS (1858–1935). *New York Times* motto. Adopted in 1896

Whenever I was upset by something in the papers, [Jack] always told me to be more tolerant, like a horse flicking away flies in the summer.

> JACQUELINE KENNEDY ONASSIS (1929–1994). In Ralph G. Martin, *A Hero for Our Time,* 11, 1983

Violence. Sex. . . . Money. Kids. Animals.

> MIKE PEARL. *New York Post* editor. On what makes a tabloid a tabloid. In "Perspectives," *Newsweek,* 29 June 1987

Of all things that Lindbergh's great feat demonstrated, the greatest was to show us that a person could still get the entire front pages without murdering anybody.

> WILL ROGERS (1879–1935). After the first solo-flight across the Atlantic by Charles A. Lindbergh, 22 May 1927, *The Autobiography of Will Rogers,* ed. Donald Day, 1949

Give light and the people will find their own way.

> SCRIPPS-HOWARD NEWSPAPERS. Motto

It is a newspaper's duty to print the news and raise hell.

> WILBUR F. STOREY (1818–1884). *Chicago Times* editor. Stating the newspaper's credo, 1861

I buy newspapers to make money to buy more newspapers to make more money. As for editorial content, that's the stuff you separate the ads with.

> ROY HERBERT THOMSON (1894–1976). Canadian-born British publisher. In Tom Wicker, *On Press,* 9, 1978

The newspapers are the ruling power. What Congress does is an afterclap.

> HENRY DAVID THOREAU (1817–1862). Journal, 17 November 1850

Nothing but a newspaper can drop the same thought into a thousand minds at the same moment.

> ALEXIS de TOCQUEVILLE (1805–1859). *Democracy in America,* 2.2.6, 1840, tr. Henry Reeve and Francis Bowen, 1862

If the Government and the Officers of it are to be the constant theme for Newspaper abuse, and this too without condescending to investigate the motives or the facts, it will be impossible, I conceive, for any man living to manage the helm or to keep the machine together.

> GEORGE WASHINGTON (1732–1799). Letter (marked "private") to Attorney General Edmund Randolph, 26 August 1792

They kill good trees to put out bad newspapers.

> JAMES G. WATT (1938–). Secretary of the interior. In "James Watt on the Griddle," *Newsweek,* 8 March 1982

A newspaper inevitably reflects the character of its community.

> TOM WICKER (1926–). His "First Law of Journalism," *On Press,* 2, 1978

🍂

If you want to know what is really going on in the world, read the business section. The rest is just so much gossip.

> ANONYMOUS (AMERICAN). In M. Hunter Larsen (Petaluma, California), letter to *San Francisco Chronicle,* 20 December 1997

Never pick a fight with anyone who buys ink by the barrel and paper by the ton.

> ANONYMOUS (AMERICAN)

A newspaper [is] a device incapable of distinguishing between a bicycle accident and the collapse of civilization.

> ANONYMOUS. Early 20th cent. In George F. Will, "A Week of Sheer Fakery," *Newsweek,* 15 September 1997

The duty of a newspaper is to comfort the afflicted and afflict the comfortable.

> ANONYMOUS
>
> See Poets: Walt Whitman (2)

To get the truth from a newspaper you have to read between the lies.

> ANONYMOUS

NEWSPEAK

See also • Indoctrination ○ Language ○ Language, Political ○ Media ○ Newspeak: Examples ○ Propaganda ○ Words

The whole aim of Newspeak is to narrow the range of thought. In the end we shall make *thought-crime* literally impossible because there will be no words in which to express it. . . . Every year fewer and fewer words, and the range of consciousness always a little smaller.

> GEORGE ORWELL (1903–1950). *Nineteen Eighty-Four,* 1.5, 1949

Crimestop means the faculty of stopping short, as though by instinct, at the threshold of any dangerous thought. It includes the power of not grasping analogies, of failing to perceive logical errors, of misunderstanding the simplest arguments if they are inimical to Ingsoc [i.e., the Party's ideology], and of being bored or repelled by any train of thought which is capable of leading in a heretical direction. *Crimestop,* in short, means protective stupidity.

> GEORGE ORWELL (1903–1950). *Nineteen Eighty-Four,* 2.9, 1949

Doublethink means the power of holding two contradictory beliefs in one's mind simultaneously, and accepting both of them. The Party intellectual knows in which direction his memories must be altered; he therefore knows that he is playing tricks with reality; but by the exercise of *doublethink* he also satisfies himself that reality is not violated.

> GEORGE ORWELL (1903–1950). *Nineteen Eighty-Four,* 2.9, 1949
>
> See Imperialism: J. A. Hobson (2)

To tell deliberate lies while genuinely believing in them, to forget any fact that has become inconvenient, and then, when it become necessary again, to draw it back from oblivion for just so long as it is needed.

> GEORGE ORWELL (1903–1950). On doublethink. *Nineteen Eighty-Four,* 2.9, 1949

The purpose of Newspeak was not only to provide a medium of expression of the world-view and mental habits proper to the devotees of Ingsoc, but to make all other modes of thought impossible.

> GEORGE ORWELL (1903–1950). Appendix to *Nineteen Eighty-Four,* 1949

NEWSPEAK: EXAMPLES

See also • Empire: Cicero ○ Empire: Galgacus ○ Language, Political ○ Newspeak ○ Nuclear Energy: Jack Herbein ○ Propaganda ○ Vietnam War: Anonymous (American) (1) ○ War: Mao Tse-tung (3) ○ Welfare: Russell Baker

We found the term "killing" too broad and have substituted the more precise, if more verbose, "unlawful or arbitrary deprivation of life."

> ELLIOTT ABRAMS (1948–). Assistant secretary of state for inter-American affairs during the Reagan Administration. Referring to State Department reports on human rights violations in 163 countries. In "Rights Survey Stops Using Word 'Killing'," *New York Times,* 11 February 1984

There must be war for the sake of peace.

> ARISTOTLE (384–322 B.C.). *Politics,* 7.14, tr. Benjamin Jowett, 1885

Vertically challenged = *short*
Chronologically gifted = *old*
Terminally inconvenienced = *dead*
Involuntarily leisured = *unemployed*
Incompletely successful individual = *a failure*
Sobriety deprived = *drunk*
Not necessarily unconstitutional = *clearly wrong, but not illegal.*

> HENRY BEARD and CHRIS CERF (1941–). Format adapted. *The Official Politically Correct Dictionary and Handbook,* 1992. In Heidi Benson, "Translation, Please," *San Francisco Focus,* May 1992

We see [slavery] now in its true light, and regard it as the most safe and stable basis for free institutions in the world.

> JOHN C. CALHOUN (1782–1850). "On Slavery," 1838
>
> See Racist Statements: Calhoun

The Party line is that there is no Party line.

> MILOVAN DJILAS (1911–1995). In Fitzroy Maclean, Disputed Barricade, 15. 1957

[Chloracne, a skin condition caused by exposure to dioxin, is] usually not disabling but may be fatal.

> DOW CHEMICAL CORP. In Erwin Knoll, ed., "Good to the Last Drop," *No Comment,* 1984

We are in an armed conflict; that is the phrase I have used. There has been no declaration of war.

> ANTHONY EDEN (1897–1977). British prime minister. While Egypt was under attack by British, French, and Israeli forces during the Suez Crisis, House of Commons speech, 1 November 1956

That's not a lie; it's a terminological inexactitude.

> ALEXANDER HAIG (1924–). Secretary of state. Television interview, 1983. Winton Churchill used the phrase "terminological inexactitude" during a British election campaign in 1905.

Capital punishment is our society's recognition of the sanctity of human life.

> ORRIN G. HATCH (1934–). Utah senator. In "Overheard," *Newsweek,* 6 June 1988

We call Japanese soldiers fanatics when they die rather than surrender, whereas American soldiers who do the same thing are heroes.

> ROBERT M. HUTCHINS (1899–1977). Lecture, University of Chicago, June 1945

Phrases like "war of attrition" protect the mind from contact with the particular realities of mangled flesh and putrefying corpses.

> ALDOUS HUXLEY (1894–1963). "Abstraction," *Texts and Pretexts: An Anthology of Poetry with Commentaries,* 1933

The *Wall Street Journal,* reporting on the failure of two (out of two) operational flight tests of the cruise missile: "The Air Force doesn't call the tests 'failures,' preferring to call them 'partial successes' because the missiles worked 'flawlessly' until they went off course."

> ERWIN KNOLL (1931–1994). "Look for the Silver Lining," *No Comment,* 1984

They're political bombings. . . . I don't think they kill anybody.

> WALTER LIPPMANN (1889–1974). On B-52 bombing raids of North Vietnam, interview, February 1965. In Eric Alterman, *Sound and Fury: The Washington Punditocracy and the Collapse of American Politics,* 3, 1992

The right to vote belongs only to the people, not to the reactionaries. The combination of these two aspects, democracy for the people and dictatorship over the reactionaries, is the people's democratic dictatorship.

> MAO TSE-TUNG (1893–1976). "On the People's Democratic Dictatorship," 1948, *The Political Thought of Mao Tse-tung,* 3.L, ed. Stuart R. Schram, 1963

To have peace we should be willing . . . to pay any price, even the price of instituting a war to compel cooperation for peace. . . . This peace-seeking policy, though it cast us in a character new to a true democracy—an initiator of a war of aggression—would earn for us a proud and popular title—we would become the first aggressors for peace.

> FRANCIS P. MATTHEWS (1887–1952). Secretary of the navy. Speech, Boston, 25 August 1950

The quick-firing gun is the greatest life-saving instrument ever invented.

> HUDSON MAXIM (1853–1927). Inventor and brother of the Briton who invented the machine gun. 1915. In Eric Korn, "A Gas Masque," *Times Literary Supplement* (London), 16 October 1992

The object of the Republic in prosecuting the war is to bring about a peace.

> NAPOLEON (1769–1821). 21 December 1799, *The Corsican,* ed. R. M. Johnston, 1911

"The New Science of War. High-Tech Warfare—How Many Lives Can It Save?"

> *NEWSWEEK.* Cover story title, 18 February 1991

You always write it's bombing, bombing, bombing. It's air support.

> DAVID H. E. OPFER. Air-force colonel and U.S. Embassy air attaché in Phnom Penh. Complaining to reporters about their coverage of the invasion of Cambodia, 1973. In Morton Mintz and Jerry S. Cohen, *Power, Inc.,* 25, 1976

It had been found necessary to make a readjustment of rations (Squealer always spoke of it as a "readjustment," never as a "reduction").

> GEORGE ORWELL (1903–1950). *Animal Farm: A Fairy Story,* 9, 1945

WAR IS PEACE
FREEDOM IS SLAVERY
IGNORANCE IS STRENGTH

> GEORGE ORWELL (1903–1950). The Party's slogans inscribed on the Ministry of Truth building, *Nineteen Eighty-Four,* 1.1, 1949

The Ministry of Peace concerns itself with war, the Ministry of Truth with lies, the Ministry of Love with torture, and the Ministry of Plenty with starvation.

> GEORGE ORWELL (1903–1950). *Nineteen Eighty-Four,* 2.9, 1949

Goodsex—that is to say, normal intercourse between man and wife, for the sole purpose of begetting children, and without physical pleasure on the part of the woman; all else was *sexcrime.*

> GEORGE ORWELL (1903–1950). Appendix to *Nineteen Eighty-Four,* 1949

It would be insensitive to say Dennis Brown and Ted Washington were fat when they reported to [football training] camp. Let's just say they were over-served.

> SCOTT OSTLER. "All Omens Indicating a 49ers Slide," *San Francisco Chronicle,* 11 August 1993

The war will continue to be prosecuted with vigor, as the best means of securing peace.

> JAMES K. POLK (1797–1849). President. On his administration's policy regarding the Mexican War, annual message to Congress, 8 December 1846
>
> See Mexican War: Polk

If virtue be the spring of a popular government in times of peace, the spring of that government during a revolution is virtue combined with terror: virtue, without which terror is destructive; terror, without which virtue is impotent. Terror is only justice prompt, severe and inflexible; it is then an emanation of virtue; it is less a distinct principle than a natural consequence of the general principle of democracy, applied to the most pressing wants of the country.

> ROBESPIERRE (1758–1794). *Report upon the Principles of Political Morality* (delivered to the Convention in the name of the Committee of Public Safety), 5 February 1794

Most important [for the patient] is a voluntary compliance with the tasks demanded by the therapist.

> HOWARD P. ROME (1910–). Psychiatrist. "On Facing One's Self," *Psychiatric Annals,* December 1982

The game of the Nazis and their collaborators was to blur ideas. The Pétain regime called itself a revolution, and things reached such a point of absurdity that one day the following headline appeared in the *Gerbe:* "The motto of the National Revolution is—*hold fast.*"

> JEAN-PAUL SARTRE (1905–1980). *Literary and Philosophical Essays,* 13.2, 1946, tr. Annette Michelson, 1955

Three Witches: Fair is foul, and foul is fair.

> SHAKESPEARE (1564–1616). *Macbeth,* 1.1.11, 1605

Gentlemen. We are not retreating. We are merely advancing in another direction.

> O. P. SMITH (1893–1977). On the retreat of U.S. forces in North Korea after China's entry into the Korean War, news conference, 4 December 1950

I play to people's fantasies. People may not always think big themselves, but they can still get very excited by those who do. That's why a little hyperbole never hurts. People want to believe that something is the biggest and the greatest and the most spectacular.

I call it truthful hyperbole. It's an innocent form of exaggeration—and a very effective form of promotion.

> DONALD J. TRUMP (1946–) (with TONY SCHWARTZ). *Trump: The Art of the Deal,* 2, 1987

Watt: My credibility was used to get a result.
Rep. Ted Weiss: Wasn't that influence peddling?
Watt: If I were a Democrat, I'd say Jim Watt engaged in influence peddling.
Weiss: And if you were an objective Republican?
Watt: I would say, "There's a skilled, talented man who used his credibility for accomplishing an objective."

> JAMES G. WATT (1938–) Secretary of the interior. Testifying before a Congressional committee on his being paid a $420,000 "consulting fee" for helping a client obtain from the Department of Housing and Urban Development a multi-million dollar loan on a low-income housing project (Watt's services consisted of eight phone calls and a half-hour meeting with HUD Secretary Samuel R. Pierce, Jr.). In *Philadelphia Inquirer,* 10 June 1989
>
> See Lobbies: Harry S. Truman (1)

[Pres. Richard M. Nixon's latest statement] is the Operative White House Position . . . and all previous statements are inoperative.

> RONALD L. ZIEGLER (1939–). Presidential press secretary. After being reminded of earlier statements by the President disavowing involvement in the Watergate breakin. In *Boston Globe,* 18 April 1973

NEW YORK CITY

See also • Cities

You're in New York City now, buddy—wipe that silly grin off your face.

> BALOO. Police officer admonishing a grinning tourist against a background of skyscrapers. Cartoon caption, *National Review,* 16 April 1990

New York, New York—a helluva town,
The Bronx is up, but the Battery's down,
And people ride in a hole in the ground:
New York, New York—it's a helluva town.

> BETTY COMDEN (1915–) and ADOLPH GREEN (1915–). "New York, New York" (song), 1945

Broadway is Trade and Vanity made flesh.

> RALPH WALDO EMERSON (1803–1882). Journal, 31 October 1831

New York is a sucked orange.

> RALPH WALDO EMERSON (1803–1882). "Culture," *The Conduct of Life,* 1860

I like New York in June,
How about you?

> RALPH FREED. "How About You" (song), 1941

Living in New York is like being at some terrible late-night party. You're tired, you've had a headache since you arrived, but you can't leave because then you'd miss the party.

> SIMON HOGGART (1946–). *America: A User's Guide,* 1, 1990

New York, thy name is irreverence and hyperbole. And grandeur.

> ADA LOUISE HUXTABLE. Closing sentences, "A Delightful Walk Downtown," *New York Times,* 20 July 1975

No other place can so convincingly claim to be the capital of capitalism, the capital of the 20th century and the capital of the world.

> KENNETH T. JACKSON. Columbia University professor of history. On New York City, "100 Years of Being Really Big," *New York Times,* 28 December 1997

New York now leads the world's great cities in the number of people around whom you shouldn't make a sudden move.

> DAVID LETTERMAN (1947–). Television entertainment-program host. *Late Night with David Letterman,* NBC, 9 February 1984

The Bronx?
No thonx!

> OGDEN NASH (1902–1971). "Geographical Reflection," *Hard Lines,* 1931

A Tree Grows in Brooklyn.

> BETTY SMITH (1896–1972). Book title, 1943

It is an ugly city, a dirty city. Its climate is a scandal. Its politics are used to frighten children. Its traffic is madness. Its competition is murderous. But there is one thing about it—once you have lived in New York and it has become your home, no other place is good enough.

> JOHN STEINBECK (1902–1968). In Kenneth T. Jackson, "100 Years of Being Really Big," *New York Times,* 28 December 1997

Were all America like this fair city, and all, no, only a small proportion of its population like the friends we left there, I should say, that the land was the fairest in the world.

> FRANCES TROLLOPE (1780–1863). English writer. On New York City, *Domestic Manners of the Americans,* 34, 1832

Manhattan crowds, with their turbulent musical chorus!
Manhattan faces and eyes forever for me.

> WALT WHITMAN (1819–1892). "Give Me the Splendid Silent Sun" (2), 1865, *Leaves of Grass,* 1855–1892

NOBILITY

See also • Aristocracy ○ Class ○ Leaders: Mencius

Nobility of birth commonly abateth industry.

> FRANCIS BACON (1561–1626). "Of Nobility," *Essays,* 1625

Nobility is a graceful ornament to the civil order.

> EDMUND BURKE (1729–1797). *Reflections on the Revolution in France,* p. 245, 1790, Pelican Books edition, 1968
>
> See Aristocracy: Burke

Here all were noble, save Nobility!

> LORD BYRON (1788–1824). *Childe Harold's Pilgrimage,* 1.85, 1812–1818

All nobility in its beginnings was somebody's natural superiority.

> RALPH WALDO EMERSON (1803–1882). "Aristocracy," *English Traits,* 1856

Noblesse oblige [literally, nobility has its obligations] or, superior advantages bind you to larger generosity.

> RALPH WALDO EMERSON (1803–1882). "Progress of Culture," *Letters and Social Aims,* 1876

The nobility, to save a portion of their power, were forced to yield a share of it to the people.

> MACHIAVELLI (1469–1527). *The Discourses,* 1.2, 1517, tr. Christian E. Detmold, 1940

It is the nature of the nobility to desire to dominate.

> MACHIAVELLI (1469–1527). *The Discourses,* 1.40, 1517, tr. Christian E. Detmold, 1940

The privileges of nobility are not in their origin concessions or favors; on the contrary, they are conquests. And their maintenance supposes, in principle, that the privileged individual is capable of reconquering them, at any moment, if it were necessary, and anyone were to dispute them.

> JOSÉ ORTEGA y GASSET (1883–1955). *The Revolt of the Masses,* 7, 1930, tr. anon., 1932

NONCONFORMITY

See also • Conformity ○ Creativity ○ Defiance ○ Dissent ○ Eccentricity ○ Freedom ○ Genius ○ Heresy ○ Independence ○ The Individual ○ Individualism ○ Individuality ○ Martyrdom ○ Minorities ○ Nonconformity, Anti- ○ Nonconformity & Conformity ○ Prejudice ○ Resistance ○ Self-Realization (Becoming) ○ Self-Realization (Being) ○ Self-Reliance ○ Solitude (Being Alone) ○ Solitude (Living Alone) ○ Standing Alone ○ Tolerance

"They Were All Out of Step but Jim"

> IRVING BERLIN (1888–1989). Song title, 1918

Where the way is hardest, there go thou; and what the world casteth away, that take thou up. What the world doth, that do thou not; but in all things walk thou contrary to the world. So thou comest the nearest way to that which thou art seeking.

> JACOB BOEHME (1575–1624). German mystic. In Whitall N. Perry, comp., *A Treasury of Traditional Wisdom,* p. 489, 1986

There can be no assumption that today's majority is "right" and the Amish and others like them are "wrong." A way of life that is odd or even erratic but interferes with no rights or interests of others is not to be condemned because it is different.

> WARREN E. BURGER (1907–1995). In a Supreme Court majority opinion that freed members of religious sects from compulsory school attendance, *Wisconsin v. Yoder,* 15 May 1972

A black swan, a white raven.

> JOHN CLARKE (1596–1658). Comp., *Proverbs: English and Latine,* p. 272, 1639

Where the way is hardest, there go thou:
Follow your own path, and let people talk.

> DANTE (A.D. 1265–1321). "Purgatory" (5.13), *The Divine Comedy,* 1321

What I must do is all that concerns me, not what people think.

> RALPH WALDO EMERSON (1803–1882). "Self-Reliance," *Essays: First Series,* 1841

Whoso would be a man, must be a nonconformist.

> RALPH WALDO EMERSON (1803–1882). "Self-Reliance," *Essays: First Series,* 1841

I shall be telling this with a sigh
Somewhere ages and ages hence:
Two roads diverged in a wood, and I—
I took the one less traveled by,
And that has made all the difference.

> ROBERT FROST (1874–1963). Closing lines, "The Road Not Taken," *Mountain Interval,* 1916

When we lose the right to be different, we lose the right to be free.

> CHARLES EVANS HUGHES (1862–1948). Address commemorating the 150th anniversary of the Battle of Bunker Hill, Faneuil Hall, Boston, 17 June 1925

Freedom to differ is not limited to things that do not matter much. That would be a mere shadow of freedom. The test of its substance is the right to differ as to things that touch the heart of the existing order.

> ROBERT H. JACKSON (1892–1954). *West Virginia State Board v. Barnette,* 1943

[Sir Isaac Newton] stood alone merely because he had left the rest of mankind behind him, not because he deviated from the beaten track.

> SAMUEL JOHNSON (1709–1784). In *The Adventurer* (English journal), 131, 5 February 1754

To the man in the street it has always seemed miraculous that anyone should turn aside from the beaten track with its known destinations, and strike out on the steep and narrow path leading into the unknown. Hence it was always believed that such a man, if not actually, crazy, was possessed by a demon or a god; for the miracle of a man being able to act otherwise than as humanity has always acted could only be explained by the gift of demonic power or divine spirit.

> CARL G. JUNG (1875–1961). Title essay, 1934, *The Development of Personality,* tr. R. F. C. Hull, 1954

In this age, the mere example of nonconformity, the mere refusal to bend the knee to custom, is itself a service.

> JOHN STUART MILL (1806–1873). *On Liberty,* 3, 1859

To be out of harmony with one's surroundings is of course a misfortune, but it is not always a misfortune to be avoided at all costs. Where the environment is stupid or prejudiced or cruel, it is a sign of merit to be out of harmony with it.

> BERTRAND RUSSELL (1872–1970). *The Conquest of Happiness,* 9, 1930

All change in history, all advance, comes from the nonconformists. If there had been no troublemakers, no Dissenters, we should still be living in caves.

> A. J. P. TAYLOR (1906–1990). *The Trouble Makers: Dissent over Foreign Policy, 1792–1939,* 1, 1958

Why should we be in such desperate haste to succeed, and in such desperate enterprises? If a man does not keep pace with his companions, perhaps it is because he hears a different drummer. Let him step to the music that he hears, however measured or far away.

> HENRY DAVID THOREAU (1817–1862). "Conclusion," *Walden; or Life in the Woods,* 1854

NONCONFORMITY, ANTI-

See also • Conformity ○ Independence ○ Individuality ○ Martyrdom ○ Nonconformity ○ Nonconformity & Conformity ○ Prejudice ○ Self-Reliance ○ Tolerance

[God's] bolts fall ever on the highest houses and the tallest trees.
> ARTABANUS (5th cent. B.C.). Persian minister. In Herodotus (484?–420? B.C.), *The Persian Wars*, 7.10, tr. George Rawlinson, 1942

Abnormal, *adj.* Not conforming to standard. In matters of thought and conduct, to be independent is to be abnormal, to be abnormal is to be detested.
> AMBROSE BIERCE (1842–1914). *The Devil's Dictionary*, p. 7, 1911, Dover edition, 1958

Throughout history the mass of mankind has been afraid of traits or ideas that seemed likely to break the sense of communion with others and has found its selfhood a hard burden to bear. Hence it is unnecessary to be surprised at the number of techniques devised by various social groups to break down the individuality of their members or the willingness with which these have generally been accepted.
> J. A. C. BROWN (1911–1964). *Techniques of Persuasion: From Propaganda to Brainwashing*, 10, 1963

Strive not against the stream.
> JOHN CLARKE (1596–1658). Comp., *Proverbs: English and Latine*, p. 53, 1639
> See Conformity: Anonymous (English) ○ Resistance: Fénelon

To be nobody-but-myself—in a world which is doing its best, night and day, to make you like everybody else—means to fight the hardest battle which any human being can fight, and never stop fighting.
> E. E. CUMMINGS (1894–1962). Letter to a high-school editor, 1955. In R. Buckminster Fuller, foreword to *Critical Path*, 1981

Society everywhere is in conspiracy against the manhood of every one of its members. Society is a joint-stock company, in which the members agree, for the better securing of his bread to each shareholder, to surrender the liberty and culture of the eater. The virtue in most request is conformity. Self-reliance is its aversion. It loves not realities and creators, but names and customs.
> RALPH WALDO EMERSON (1803–1882). "Self-Reliance," *Essays: First Series*, 1841

For nonconformity the world whips you with its displeasure. And therefore a man must know how to estimate a sour face.
> RALPH WALDO EMERSON (1803–1882). "Self-Reliance," *Essays: First Series*, 1841

We are sheep with no straight
and narrow;
We are sheep with no meadow.
We are sheep who take the
dangerous pathway thru
the mountain range
to get to the other side of
our soul.
We are the black sheep of
the family
Called Black Sheep folk.
> KAREN FINLEY (1956–). "The Black Sheep," *We Keep Our Victims Ready* (one-woman show), New York City, 1990

There are always two kinds of people in the world—those who pioneer and those who plod. The plodders always attack the pioneers. They say that the pioneers have gobbled up all the opportunity, when, as a plain matter of fact, the plodders would have nowhere to plod had not the pioneers first cleared the way.
> HENRY FORD (1863–1947) (with SAMUEL CROWTHER). *Today and Tomorrow*, 1, 1926

The so-called nonconformists travel in groups and woe unto him who doesn't conform.
> ERIC HOFFER (1902–1983). In Jack Flincher, "Docker of Philosophy," *Life*, 24 March 1967

Society is always trying in some way or other to grind us down to a single flat surface.
> OLIVER WENDELL HOLMES, SR. (1809–1894). *The Professor at the Break-fast Table*, 2, 1860

Oh who is that young sinner with the handcuffs on his wrists?
And what has he been after that they groan and shake their fists?
And wherefore is he wearing such a conscience-stricken air?
Oh they're taking him to prison for the color of his hair.
> A. E. HOUSMAN (1859–1936). "Additional Poems" (18), 1937, *The Collected Poems of A. E. Housman*, 1959

The pride of men will not patiently endure to see one, whose understanding or attainments are but level with their own, break the rules by which they have consented to be bound, or forsake the direction which they submissively follow. All violation of established practice implies in its own nature a rejection of the common opinion . . . : who differs from others without apparent advantage, ought not to be angry if his arrogance is punished with ridicule.
> SAMUEL JOHNSON (1709–1784). In *The Adventurer* (English journal), 131, 5 February 1754

The mass resents the rare spirit who crashes through the gray wall and emerges into the light of disparateness. It therefore has to see to his suppression by punishing him for his uniqueness and, in this manner, holding the rebellious inclinations of its members in check.
> ROBERT LINDNER (1914–1956). *Prescription for Rebellion*, 8, 1952

Nonconformity has become the major if not the only sin we know today.
> ROBERT LINDNER (1914–1956). "Homosexuality and the Contemporary Scene" (2), *Must You Conform?* 1956

The first officer of the Queen Mary has been fired by the Walt Disney Co. after refusing to shave the mustache he has worn for 42 years. . . .
[John Magness, 65,] wore his mustache during an 11-year Navy career in World War II and the Korean War, followed by 15 years as a private yacht captain before signing on with the Queen Mary [8 years ago].

Disney, which operates the Queen Mary . . . , twice suspended Magness during the past month because his thin, gray mustache violates the policy that was set down 35 years ago by Walt Disney, who wore a mustache himself.

> LOS ANGELES DAILY NEWS. "Disney Fires Man for Keeping His
> 42-Year-Old Mustache," San Francisco Chronicle, 4 January 1990

What is no good for the hive is no good for the bee.

> MARCUS AURELIUS (A.D. 121–180). Meditations, 6.54, tr. Maxwell
> Staniforth, 1964

The whole drift of our law is toward the absolute prohibition of all ideas that diverge in the slightest from the accepted platitudes, and behind that drift of law there is a far more potent force of growing custom, and under that custom there is a national philosophy which erects conformity into the noblest of virtues and the free functioning of personality into a capital crime against society.

> H. L. MENCKEN (1880–1956). "The National Letters: The Cultural
> Background," Prejudices: Second Series, 1920

The higher we soar, the smaller we seem to those who cannot fly.

> FRIEDRICH NIETZSCHE (1844–1900). Daybreak, 574, 1881,
> tr. R. J. Hollingdale, 1982

With whom does the greatest danger for the whole human future lie? Is it not with the good and just?—with those who say and feel in their hearts: "We already know what is good and just, we possess it too; woe to those who are still searching for it!"

> FRIEDRICH NIETZSCHE (1844–1900). "Of Old and New Law-Tables"
> (26), Thus Spoke Zarathustra, 1892, tr. R. J. Hollingdale, 1961

The mass crushes beneath it everything that is different, everything that is excellent, individual, qualified and select. Anybody who is not like everybody, who does not think like everybody, runs the risk of being eliminated.

> JOSÉ ORTEGA y GASSET (1883–1955). The Revolt of the Masses,
> 1, 1930, tr. anon., 1932

To do anything that suggested a taste for solitude, even to go for a walk by yourself, was always slightly dangerous. There was a word for it in Newspeak: ownlife, it was called, meaning individualism and eccentricity.

> GEORGE ORWELL (1903–1950). Nineteen Eighty-Four, 1.8, 1949

From childhood upwards, everything is done to make the minds of men and women conventional and sterile. And if, by misadventure, some spark of imagination remains, its unfortunate possessor is considered unsound and dangerous, worthy only of contempt in time of peace and of prison or a traitor's death in time of war.

> BERTRAND RUSSELL (1872–1970). "Individual Liberty and Public
> Control" (2), Atlantic, July 1917

Conventional people are roused to fury by departure from convention, largely because they regard such departures as a criticism of themselves. They will pardon much unconventionality in a man who has enough jollity and friendliness to make it clear, even to the stupidest, that he is not engaged in criticizing them.

> BERTRAND RUSSELL (1872–1970). The Conquest of Happiness, 9, 1930

More cranks take up unfashionable errors than unfashionable truths.

> BERTRAND RUSSELL (1872–1970). "An Outline of Intellectual Rubbish,"
> Unpopular Essays, 1950

Every group stigmatizes anyone who fails in zeal, labor, and sacrifices for group interests.

> WILLIAM GRAHAM SUMNER (1840–1910). Folkways: A Study of the
> Sociological Importance of Usages, Manners, Customs, Mores, and
> Morals, 19, 1907

All the community may scream because one man is born who will not do as it does, who will not conform because conformity to him is death. . . . In the course of generations, however, men will excuse you for not doing as they do, if you will bring enough to pass in your own way.

> HENRY DAVID THOREAU (1817–1862). Journal, 27 December 1858

Our wretched species is so made that those who walk [on] the beaten path always throw stones at those who teach a new path.

> VOLTAIRE (1694–1778). "Literature and Writers," Philosophical
> Dictionary, 1764, tr. Theodore Besterman, 1971

Nonconformity is an empty goal, and rebellion against prevailing opinion merely because it is prevailing should no more be praised than acquiescence to it. Indeed, it is often a mask for cowardice, and few are more pathetic than those who flaunt outer differences to expiate their inner surrender.

> WILLIAM H. WHYTE, JR. (1917–). The Organization Man, 1, 1956

✿

The nail that sticks up gets hammered down.

> SAYING (JAPANESE)

NONCONFORMITY & CONFORMITY

See also • Conformity ○ Independence ○ Individuality ○ Minorities ○ Nonconformity ○ Nonconformity, Anti- ○ Self-Reliance

Allow me to furnish the interior of my head as I please, and I shall put up with a hat like everybody else's.

> HENRI BERGSON (1859–1941). "Final Remarks," The Two Sources of
> Morality and Religion, 1932, tr. R. Ashley Audra and Cloudesley
> Brereton, 1935

I like the sayers of No better than the sayers of Yes.

> RALPH WALDO EMERSON (1803–1882). Journal, 1833

The objection to conforming to usages that have become dead to you is that it scatters your force: loses your time, blears the impression of your character. . . . Do your thing and I shall know you.

> RALPH WALDO EMERSON (1803–1882). Journal, 7 July 1839

A man who is "ill-adjusted to the world" is always on the point of finding himself. One who is adjusted to the world never finds himself, but gets to be a cabinet minister.

> HERMANN HESSE (1877–1962). Reflections, 149, ed. Volker Michels,
> 1974

No man can go too far in independence or in adaptation with impunity.

> HERMANN HESSE (1877–1962). *Reflections,* 245, ed. Volker Michels, 1974

Freedom lies beyond conformity or rebellion.

> SAM KEEN (1931–). *To a Dancing God,* 2, 1970

All the people like us are We,
And every one else is They.

> RUDYARD KIPLING (1865–1936). "We and They" (l.3), *Debits and Credits,* 1919–1926

To revolt or to adapt oneself; there is no other choice in life.

> GUSTAVE LE BON (1841–1931). *Aphorisms of Present Times,* 3.4, 1913, tr. Alice Widener, 1979

Every society honors its live conformists, and its dead trouble-makers.

> MIGNON McLAUGHLIN (1915–). *The Neurotic's Notebook,* 7, 1963

Nonconformity, Holy Disobedience, becomes a virtue and indeed a necessary and indispensable measure of spiritual self-preservation, in a day when the impulse to conform, to acquiesce, to go along, is the instrument which is used to subject men to totalitarian rule and involve them in permanent war.

> A. J. MUSTE (1885–1967). *Of Holy Disobedience* (pamphlet), 1952

"Adjustment or Autonomy?"

> DAVID RIESMAN (1909–) (with NATHAN GLAZER and REUEL DENNEY. Chapter title, *The Lonely Crowd: A Study of the Changing American Character,* 12, 1950, abr., 1953

And remember: conformity means death. Only protest gives a hope of life.

> BERTRAND RUSSELL (1872–1970). Leaflet published during the Cuban Missile Crisis, 24 October 1962, *Unarmed Victory,* 2, 1963

Uniformity brings death, variety brings life.

> HERBERT SPENCER (1820–1903). Letter to T. Buzzard, 15 March 1892. In David Duncan, *Life and Letters of Herbert Spencer,* 2.21, 1908

As to conforming outwardly and living your own life inwardly, I do not think much of that.

> HENRY DAVID THOREAU (1817–1862). Letter to Harrison Blake, 9 August 1850

NONVIOLENCE

See also • Blunders: Mohandas K. Gandhi ○ Democracy: Karl R. Popper ○ Heaven: Micah ○ History ○ Peace ○ Progress ○ Reform ○ Resistance ○ Revolution: John F. Kennedy, Robert F. Kennedy, George Washington ○ Revolution ○ Violence ○ War ○ War & Peace

The only thing that's been a worse flop than the organization of nonviolence has been the organization of violence.

> JOAN BAEZ (1941–). "What Would You Do If?" *Daybreak,* 1970

"Why of the sheep do you not learn peace?"
"Because I don't want you to shear my fleece."

> WILLIAM BLAKE (1757–1827). "Poems and Fragments from the Note-Book" ("An answer to the parson"), 50, 1793?, *The Complete Writings of William Blake,* ed. Geoffrey Keynes, 1966

If there is no other way of preventing the evil destroying the good, I trust I shall use force and give myself up into God's hands.

> MARTIN BUBER (1878–1965). Responding to Mohandas K. Gandhi's article advising Europe's Jews to adopt the practice of nonviolence against Nazi persecution. "The Land and Its Possessors: An Answer to Gandhi," *The Bond* (Jerusalem), 1939.

Nonviolent revolution does not seek the liberation simply of a class or race or nation. It seeks the liberation of mankind. It is our experience that violence shifts the burden of suffering and injustice from one group to another. . . . It destroys one authoritarian structure but creates another.

> COUNCIL OF THE WAR RESISTERS' INTERNATIONAL. "On Wars of Liberation" (a working document prepared at the Council's meeting in Vienna), 17 August 1968

If a nonviolent movement is to cope with deep-seated fears and privileges, its strategy must flow from a sense of the underlying unity of all human beings.

> DAVID DELLINGER (1915–). "The Future of Nonviolence" (1), *Studies on the Left,* Winter 1965

Nonviolent defense requires not only willingness to risk one's life (as any good soldier, rich or poor, will do). It requires renunciation of all claims to special privileges and power at the expense of other people.

> DAVID DELLINGER (1915–). "The Future of Nonviolence" (2), *Studies on the Left,* Winter 1965

A liberation movement that is nonviolent sets the oppressor free as well as the oppressed.

> BARBARA DEMING (1917–). In Jeanne Larson and Madge Micheels-Cyrus, comps., *Seeds of Peace,* p. 172, 1986

Father Zossima: At some thoughts one stands perplexed, especially at the sight of men's sin, and wonders whether one should use force or humble love. Always decide to use humble love! If you resolve on that once and for all, you may subdue the whole world. Loving humility is marvelously strong, the strongest of all things; there is nothing else like it.

> FYODOR DOSTOYEVSKY (1821–1881). *The Brothers Karamazov,* 6.2(f), 1880, tr. Constance Garnett, 1912

The first things to be disrupted by our commitment to nonviolence will be not the system but our own lives.

> JAMES W. DOUGLASS (1939–?). In *Peace Times* (newsletter of the Center for Teaching Peace, Washington), April-May 1992

If a nation of men is exalted to that height of morals as to refuse to fight and choose rather to suffer loss of goods and loss of life than to use violence, they must be not helpless but most effective and great men; they would overawe their invader, and make him ridiculous; they would communicate the contagion of their virtue and inoculate all mankind.

> RALPH WALDO EMERSON (1803–1882). Journal, 21 September 1837

My friend Mr. Thoreau has gone to jail rather than pay his tax. On him they could not calculate. The abolitionists denounce the war and give much time to it, but they pay the tax.

RALPH WALDO EMERSON (1803–1882). Soon after the U.S. declaration of war against Mexico (which Northern abolitionists saw as an attempt to extend the slave-holding area into the Southwest), journal, 1846, undated

With Gandhi nonviolence was a creed, with Congress [the Indian political party] it "was always a policy." Congress adopted nonviolence for the expected gains. Gandhi wanted nonviolence irrespective of the fruits.

LOUIS FISCHER (1896–1970). *The Life of Mahatma Gandhi,* 37, 1950

If a father does an injustice, it is the duty of his children to leave the parental roof. If the headmaster of a school conducts his institution on an immoral basis, the pupils must leave the school. If the chairman of a corporation is corrupt, the members thereof must wash their hands clean of his corruption by withdrawing from it; even so, if a Government does a grave injustice, the subjects must withdraw cooperation wholly or partially, sufficiently to wean the ruler from his wickedness.

MOHANDAS K. GANDHI (1869–1948). In *Young India,* 16 June 1920

Ahimsa . . . is not merely a negative state of harmlessness, but it is a positive state of love, of doing good even to the evildoer.

MOHANDAS K. GANDHI (1869–1948). In *Young India,* 25 August 1920

[He] alone is truly nonviolent who remains nonviolent even though he has the ability to strike.

MOHANDAS K. GANDHI (1869–1948). In *Young India,* 7 May 1925

The acquisition of the spirit of nonresistance is a matter of long training in self-denial and appreciation of the hidden forces within ourselves. It changes one's outlook upon life. It puts different values upon things and upsets previous calculations, and when once it is intensive enough can overtake the whole universe. It is the greatest force because it is the highest expression of the soul.

MOHANDAS K. GANDHI (1869–1948). In *Young India,* 23 September 1926

If we are to be nonviolent, we must then not wish for anything on this earth which . . . the lowest of human beings cannot have.

MOHANDAS K. GANDHI (1869–1948). In Mahadev Desai, *With Gandhiji in Ceylon,* p. 132, 1928

Individuals or nations, who would practice nonviolence, must be prepared to sacrifice [everything] except honor.

MOHANDAS K. GANDHI (1869–1948). In *Harijan,* 5 September 1936

Nonviolence is a power which can be wielded equally by all—children, young men and women or grown-up people—provided they have a living faith in the God of Love and have, therefore, equal love for all mankind.

MOHANDAS K. GANDHI (1869–1948). In *Harijan,* 5 September 1936

The principle of nonviolence necessitates complete abstention from exploitation in any form.

MOHANDAS K. GANDHI (1869–1948). In *Harijan,* 12 November 1938

We are constantly being astonished these days at the amazing discoveries in the field of violence. But I maintain that far more undreamt of and seemingly impossible discoveries will be made in the field of nonviolence.

MOHANDAS K. GANDHI (1869–1948). In *Harijan,* 25 August 1940

Nothing should be done secretly. This is an open rebellion. A free man would not engage in a secret movement.

MOHANDAS K. GANDHI (1869–1948). Speech, 8 August 1942

A nonviolent revolution is not a program of "seizure of power." It is a program of transformation of relationships ending in a peaceful transfer of power.

MOHANDAS K. GANDHI (1869–1948). In *Harijan,* 17 February 1946

The history of mankind is crowded with evidences proving that physical coercion is not adapted to moral regeneration; that the sinful dispositions of men can be subdued only by love; that evil can be exterminated from the earth only by goodness; . . . that there is great security in being gentle, harmless, long-suffering, and abundant in mercy; that it is only the meek who shall inherit the earth, for the violent, who resort to the sword, are destined to perish with the sword. Hence, as a measure of sound policy—of safety to property, life, and liberty—of public quietude and private enjoyment—as well as on the ground of allegiance to HIM who is King of kings, and Lord of lords, we cordially adopt *the nonresistance principle*; being confident that it provides for all possible consequences, will ensure all things needful to us, is armed with omnipotent power, and must ultimately triumph over every assailing force. [Italics added.]

WILLIAM LLOYD GARRISON (1805–1879). Declaration of Sentiments (adopted by the Peace Convention), Boston, 18–20 September 1838. In Wendell Phillips Garrison and Francis Jackson Garrison, *William Lloyd Garrison, 1805–1879: The Story of His Life by His Children,* 2.4, 1884

Nonviolence within a violent society cannot provide a program of action; it is, indeed, a form of complicity with it.

FELIX GREENE (1909–1985). *The Enemy: What Every American Should Know About Imperialism,* 4.3, 1970

Soft is stronger than hard, water than rock, love than violence.

HERMANN HESSE (1877–1962). *Reflections,* 363, ed. Volker Michels, 1974

If things are ever to move upward, someone must be ready to take the first step, and assume the risk of it. No one who is not willing to try charity, to try nonresistance as the saint is always willing, can tell whether these methods will or will not succeed. When they do succeed, they are far more powerfully successful than force or worldly prudence. Force destroys enemies; and the best that can be said of prudence is that it keeps what we already have in safety. But nonresistance, when successful, turns enemies into friends; and charity regenerates its objects.

WILLIAM JAMES (1842–1910). *The Varieties of Religious Experience: A Study in Human Nature,* 14 and 15, 1902

You have heard that it was said, "An eye for an eye and a tooth for a tooth." But I say to you, Do not resist one who is evil. But if any one strikes you on the right cheek, turn to him the other also; and if any one would sue you and take your coat, let him have your cloak as well; and if any one forces you to go one mile, go with him two miles. Give to him who begs from you, and do not refuse him who would borrow from you.

JESUS (A.D. 1st cent.). *Matthew* 5:38–42

See Evil: Saying (Latin) ○ Punishment, Capital: Moses (2)

Put your sword back into its place; for all who take the sword will perish by the sword.

> JESUS (A.D. 1st cent.). *Matthew* 26:52

Christ furnished the spirit and motivation [of nonviolence], while Gandhi furnished the method.

> MARTIN LUTHER KING, JR. (1929–1968). *Stride Toward Freedom*, 5, 1958

To accept passively an unjust system is to cooperate with that system; thereby the oppressed become as evil as the oppressor. Noncooperation with evil is as much a moral obligation as is cooperation with good.

> MARTIN LUTHER KING, JR. (1929–1968). *Stride Toward Freedom*, 11, 1958

The nonviolent approach does not immediately change the heart of the oppressor. It first does something to the hearts and souls of those committed to it. It gives them new self-respect; it calls up resources of strength and courage that they did not know they had. Finally it reaches the opponent and so stirs his conscience that reconciliation becomes a reality.

> MARTIN LUTHER KING, JR. (1929–1968). *Stride Toward Freedom*, 11, 1958

Today the choice is no longer between violence and nonviolence. It is either nonviolence or nonexistence.

> MARTIN LUTHER KING, JR. (1929–1968). *Stride Toward Freedom*, 11, 1958

In any nonviolent campaign there are four basic steps: (1) collection of the facts to determine whether injustices are alive, (2) negotiation, (3) self-purification, and (4) direct action.

> MARTIN LUTHER KING, JR. (1929–1968). "Letter from Birmingham City Jail," 16 April 1963

An individual who breaks a law that conscience tells him is unjust, and willingly accepts the penalty by staying in jail to arouse the conscience of the community over its injustice, is in reality expressing the very highest respect for law.

> MARTIN LUTHER KING, JR. (1929–1968). "Letter from Birmingham City Jail," 16 April 1963
>
> See Law: St. Augustine

I refuse to accept the cynical notion that nation after nation must spiral down a militaristic stairway into the hell of thermonuclear destruction. I believe that unarmed truth and unconditional love will have the final word in reality. This is why right temporarily defeated is stronger than evil triumphant.

> MARTIN LUTHER KING, JR. (1929–1968). Nobel Peace Prize acceptance address, Oslo, 11 December 1964

If in order to win [a revolution], it were necessary to erect a gallows in the public square, then I would prefer to lose.

> ENRICO MALATESTA (1853–1932). Italian anarchist. In *Pensiero e Volonta*, 1 October 1924

And weaponless himself,
Made Arms ridiculous.

> JOHN MILTON (1608–1674). *Samson Agonistes*, l. 130, 1671

Perhaps the great day will come when a people, distinguished by wars and victories and by the highest development of a military order and intelligence, and accustomed to make the heaviest sacrifice for these things, will exclaim of its own free will, "we break the sword," and will smash its military establishment down to its lowest foundations. *Rendering oneself unarmed when one has been the best armed,* out of a height of feeling—that is the means to real peace, which must always rest on a peace of mind.

> FRIEDRICH NIETZSCHE (1844–1900). *The Wanderer and His Shadow*, 1880. In J. Glenn Gray, "Conclusion," *The Warriors*, 1959

I think that if the heart in man could be held down by threats— any kind of threat, whether of jail or of retribution after death— then the highest emblem of humanity would be the lion tamer in the circus with his whip, not the prophet who sacrificed himself. But don't you see, this is just the point—what has for centuries raised man above the beast is not the cudgel but an inward music: the irresistible power of unarmed truth, the powerful attraction of its example.

> BORIS PASTERNAK (1890–1960). *Doctor Zhivago*, 2.10, 1957, tr. Max Hayward and Manya Harari, 1958

Nonviolence, pacifism, that's the greatest thing that I think the human species has to aspire to, because otherwise it's not going to be around.

> MARTIN SCORSESE (1942–). Charlie Rose television interview, PBS, 16 January 1998

Freedom achieved by the sword is uniformly lost again, but . . . it is lasting when gained by peaceful agitation.

> HERBERT SPENCER (1820–1903). *Social Statics*, 3.20.11, 1851

When a rebel army took over a Korean town, all fled the Zen temple except the abbot. The rebel general burst into the temple, and was incensed to find that the master refused to greet him, let alone receive him as a conqueror.

"Don't you know," shouted the general, "that you are looking at one who can run you through without batting an eye?"

"And you," said the abbot, "are looking at one who can be run through without batting an eye."

The general's scowl turned into a smile. He bowed low and left the temple.

> LUCIEN STRYK, TAKASHI IKEMOTO, and TAIGAN TAKAYAMA, *Zen Poems of China and Japan: The Crane's Bill*, 1973

By appealing to conscience and standing on the moral nature of human existence, nonviolence nurtures the atmosphere in which reconciliation and justice become actual possibilities.

> STUDENT NONVIOLENT COORDINATING COMMITTEE (SNCC). "Statement of Purpose," 29 April 1962

Under a government which imprisons any unjustly, the true place for a just man is also a prison. . . . the only house in a slave state in which a free man can abide with honor.

> HENRY DAVID THOREAU (1817–1862). "Civil Disobedience," 1849

If a thousand men were not to pay their tax-bills this year, that would not be a violent and bloody measure, as it would be to pay them, and enable the state to commit violence and shed innocent blood. This is, in fact, the definition of a peaceable revolution.

> HENRY DAVID THOREAU (1817–1862). "Civil Disobedience," 1849

If [the government] is of such a nature that it requires you to be the agent of injustice to another, then I say, break the law. Let your life be a counter friction to stop the machine. What I have to do is to see, at any rate, that I do not lend myself to the wrong I condemn.

HENRY DAVID THOREAU (1817–1862). "Civil Disobedience," 1849

The improvement of life was only accomplished to the extent to which it was based on a change of consciousness, that is, to the extent to which the law of violence was replaced in men's consciousness by the law of love.

LEO TOLSTOY (1828–1910). Appendix ("A Variation of Chapter VIII") to *The Kingdom of God Is Within You*, 1893, tr. Aylmer Maude, 1936

If a protracted politics of nonviolent radical change is beyond the bounds of rational hope, let no one delude oneself that humans are long for this world.

ROBERT C. TUCKER (1918–). "Personality and Political Leadership," *Political Science Quarterly*, Fall 1977

Resolved, That the practice of nonresistance to physical aggression is not only consistent with reason, but the surest method of obtaining a speedy triumph of the principles of universal peace.

WILLIAM WHIPPER (19th cent.). Lumber merchant and political leader. In *The Colored American*, September 1837. Quoted in Louis C. Jones, "A Leader Ahead of His Times," *American Heritage*, June 1963

❧

Nonviolence is love in action. That's God's way of changing things.

ANONYMOUS

NORMALITY

See also • Adjustment ∘ Conformity ∘ Mediocrity

There is nothing so evil, savage, and cruel in nature as the normal man.

HERMANN HESSE (1877–1962). *Reflections*, 114, ed. Volker Michels, 1974

The more a man's life is shaped by the collective norm, the greater is his individual immorality.

CARL G. JUNG (1875–1961). *Psychological Types*, 11.29, 1921, tr. H. G. Baynes and R. F. C. Hull, 1971

There was once a community of scoundrels, that is to say, they were not scoundrels, but ordinary people.

FRANZ KAFKA (1883–1924). 25 October 1917, "The Eight Octavo Notebooks," *Dearest Father: Stories and Other Writings*, tr. Ernst Kaiser and Eithne Wilkins, 1954

The condition of alienation, or being asleep, of being unconscious, of being out of one's mind, is the condition of the normal man.

Society highly values its normal man. It educates children to lose themselves and to become absurd, and thus to be normal.

Normal men have killed perhaps 100,000,000 of their fellow normal men in the last fifty years.

R. D. LAING (1927–1989). *The Politics of Experience*, 1, 1967

See Alienation: Laing

He's a real Nowhere Man,
Sitting in his Nowhere Land,
Making all his nowhere plans
for nobody.
Doesn't have a point of view,
Knows not where he's going to,
Isn't he a bit like you and me?

JOHN LENNON (1940–1980) and PAUL McCARTNEY (1942–). "Nowhere Man" (song), 1965

A divinely average man.

WALT WHITMAN (1819–1892). On himself. In Louis L. Snyder, ed., introduction to "Burroughs on Whitman," *A Treasury of Intimate Biographies*, 1951

NOTEBOOKS

See also • Bible: Ralph Waldo Emerson (2) ∘ Diaries ∘ Journals ∘ Quotations: Theodore C. Sorensen ∘ Thoughts: Joseph Joubert (2), Arthur Schopenhauer ∘ Writing

[Thomas Hobbes] walked much and contemplated, and he had in the head of his Staff a pen and inkhorn, carried always a Notebook in his pocket, and as soon as a notion darted, he presently entered it into his Book, or else he should perhaps have lost it.

JOHN AUBREY (1626–1697). "Thomas Hobbes," *Brief Lives*, ed. Oliver Lawson Dick, 1950

A man would do well to carry a pencil in his pocket and write down the thoughts of the moment. Those that come unsought are commonly the most valuable and should be secured because they seldom return.

FRANCIS BACON (1561–1626). In *Wisdom*, vol. 38, 1962

[John F. Kennedy] relishes notable writing, and has ever since he started collecting examples of good prose and putting them in a bound book, which he was still doing when he started running for president.

BENJAMIN C. BRADLEE (1921–). 12 September 1963, *Conversations with Kennedy*, 1975

[Chess] has this advantage that when it is done it is dead and buried; it is not like writing these stupid notes.

SAMUEL BUTLER (1835–1902). *Further Extracts from the Note-Books of Samuel Butler*, 5, ed. A. T. Bartholomew, 1934

Keep a useful and short commonplace book of what you read, to help your memory only, and not for pedantic quotations.

LORD CHESTERFIELD (1694–1773). Letter to his son, 5 February 1750

My first notebook was a Big Five tablet, given to me [at age five] by my mother with the sensible suggestion that I stop whining and learn to amuse myself by writing down my thoughts.

JOAN DIDION (1934–). "On Keeping a Notebook," 1966, *Slouching Towards Bethlehem*, 1969

We are well advised to keep on nodding terms with the people we used to be, whether we find them attractive company or not. Otherwise they turn up unannounced and surprise us, come hammering on the mind's door at 4 a.m. of a bad night and demand to know who deserted them, who betrayed them, who is going to make amends. We forget all too soon the things we thought we could never forget. We forget the loves and the betrayals alike, forget what we whispered and what we screamed, forget who we were. . . .

It is a good idea, then, to keep in touch, and I suppose that keeping in touch is what notebooks are all about. And we are all on our own when it comes to keeping those lines open to ourselves: your notebook will never help me, nor mine you.

> JOAN DIDION (1934–). "On Keeping a Notebook," 1966, *Slouching Towards Bethlehem*, 1969

Make not Memory thy only Storekeeper, but commit all things that thou wouldest remember to Writing. I approve not so much of loose Papers, which may easily be confused or lost, as of bound Books. . . . Each of these Books ought to be distinct, and of differing Subjects.

One may be of References, which will stand as an Index to all thy Readings. . . .

Another, of Sentences and wise Sayings and Advice; those in Prose by themselves, and the Verse by themselves. . . .

Another, of pleasant little Stories, Adages, Proverbs, Jests, witty Repartees, acute Expressions. . . .

Another of Memorandums; Heads for Enquiry, Doubts, Opinions, Judgments, Problems, Questions, and their Answers and Solutions. . . .

Another, of thy own Observations and Judgments, which thou makest of Men and Things: For a thinking Man is always [discovering] something new.

> THOMAS FULLER (1654–1734). Comp., *Introductio ad Prudentiam*, 1742–1747, 1731

If in his reading [Abraham Lincoln] came across anything that pleased his fancy, he entered it down in a copybook—a sort of repository, in which he was wont to store everything worthy of preservation. "Frequently," related his stepmother [Nancy Hanks Lincoln], "he had no paper to write his pieces down on. Then he would put them with chalk on a board or plank, sometimes only making a few signs of what he intended to write. When he got paper he would copy them, always bringing them to me and reading them. He would ask my opinion of what he had read, and often explained things to me in his plain and simple language."

> WILLIAM H. HERNDON (1818–1891) and JESSE W. WEIK (1857–1930). *Herndon's Lincoln: The True Story of a Great Life*, 2, 1889, Premier Books edition, 1961

A notebook I carry around with me wherever I go. When it is full, I review it. Any quotation or thought worth preserving is copied out.

> ERIC HOFFER (1902–1983). Referring to his "daybook," 4 October 1958 (footnote), *Working and Thinking on the Waterfront: A Journal*, 1969

If only we had [Sir Isaac] Newton's notebooks! If I had a son, I should see to it that all the paper he wrote on was bound up in a book. . . . What pleasure it would give me now to be able to look through all my notebooks! One's own natural history!

> GEORG CHRISTOPH LICHTENBERG (1742–1799). Notebooks, 1764–1799. In J. P. Stern, *Lichtenberg: A Doctrine of Scattered Occasions*, 1959

When [Jonathan] Swift and I were once in the country for some time together, I happened one day to be saying, "That if a man was to take notice of the reflections that came into his mind on a sudden as he was walking in the fields, or sauntering in his study, there might be several of them perhaps as good as his most deliberate thoughts." On this hint, we both agreed to write down all the volunteer reflections that should thus come into our heads, all the time we stayed there. We did so: [afterwards the maxims were] published in our miscellanies. Those at the end of one volume are mine; and those in the other Dr. Swift's.

> ALEXANDER POPE (1688–1744). On the origins of a collection of maxims and aphorisms titled "Thoughts on Various Subjects" in *Miscellanies in Prose and Verse* he and Swift published in 1727. In Joseph Spence, *Observations, Anecdotes, and Characters, of Books and Men Collected from the Conversation of Mr. Pope, and Other Eminent Persons of His Time*, 2nd ed., 4 (1734–1736), 1858

I have a commonplace book for facts, and another for poetry.

> HENRY DAVID THOREAU (1817–1862). In Bronson Alcott, 8 June 1869, *Concord Days*, 1872

My little [note]books were beginnings—they were the ground into which I dropped the seed. . . . I would work in this way when I was out in the crowds, then put the stuff together at home.

> WALT WHITMAN (1819–1892). Remark to the author, 14 August 1888. In Horace Traubel, *Walt Whitman's Camden Conversations*, ed. Walter Teller, 1973

NOVELS

See also • Creativity: First Person: Robert Louis Stevenson, William Makepeace Thackeray ○ Fiction ○ Writing

The artist deals with what cannot be said in words. . . .
The novelist says in words what cannot be said in words.

> BARBARA KINGSOLVER (1955–). "Jabberwocky," 1993, *High Tide in Tucson: Essays from Now or Never*, 1996

Write a nonfiction book, and be prepared for the legion of readers who are going to doubt your fact. But write a novel, and get ready for the world to assume every word is true.

> BARBARA KINGSOLVER (1955–). "The Not-So-Deadly Sin," 1995, *High Tide in Tucson: Essays from Now or Never*, 1996

Characters make their own plot. The dimensions of the characters determine the action of the novel.

> HARPER LEE (1926–). Interview with the author, March 1964. In Roy Newquist, *Counterpoint*, 1964

Readers of novels are a strange folk, upon whose probable or even possible tastes no wise bookmaker would even venture to bet.

> E. V. LUCAS (1868–1938). *Reading, Writing, and Remembering*, 14, 1932

NUCLEAR ENERGY

See also • Environment ○ Misjudgments: Albert Einstein, Lord Ernest Rutherford, David Sarnoff ○ Nuclear Weapons ○ Pollution

The worst is finally over for us. Or has it just begun? As "down-winders," born and raised downwind of the Hanford Nuclear Reservation in Washington [State], we learned several years ago that the Government decided—with cold deliberation—to use us as guinea pigs by releasing radioactivity into our food, water, milk and air without our consent.

Now, we've learned that we can expect continuing cancer cases from our exposure in their "experiment." Is this what it feels like to be raped?

> TOM BAILIE. "Growing Up as a Nuclear Guinea Pig," *New York Times,* 22 July 1990

Many Soviet-built nuclear reactors are as dangerous as the one that exploded at Chernobyl in 1986, and terrorist threats inside Russia have already been made against them. Programs to modernize and safeguard those reactors, already established with Russian support but so far of little consequence, must be hastened and properly funded.

> STEPHEN F. COHEN (1938–). "American Policy & Russia's Future," *Nation,* 12 April 1993

On the blustery shore of Lake Ontario, in Canada's most heavily populated region, four aging nuclear reactors bedeviled by leaks, failures and operators who sometimes drank beer or smoked marijuana on the job are being shut down because they cannot be safely run by one of the largest utility companies in North America.

At the same time, workers are busy excavating a huge site in China, about 60 miles south of Shanghai, where two Canadian reactors similar to the troubled ones in Canada are being built under Canadian supervision.

> ANTHONY DePALMA. Opening paragraphs, "Canadians Export a Type of Reactor They Closed Down," *New York Times,* 3 December 1997

Our nuclear weapons production system has become nothing less than an environmental time bomb. And it will do us little good to protect ourselves from our adversaries if we poison our own people in the process.

> JOHN H. GLENN (1921–). Ohio senator. Referring to the U.S. Government-run nuclear weapons plant at Fernald (16 miles from Cincinnati) where "vast quantities of radioactive and toxic wastes are contaminating offsite drinking water supplies," "The Mini-Hiroshima Near Cincinnati," *New York Times,* 24 January 1989

A normal aberration.

> JACK HERBEIN. Metropolitan Edison vice president. Following the accident at his company's Three Mile Island nuclear power plant in Pennsylvania, 28 March 1979. In "A Nuclear Nightmare," *Time,* 9 April 1979

Nuclear powered vacuum cleaners will probably be a reality within 10 years.

> ALEX LEWYT. Vacuum cleaner manufacturer. 1955. In Christopher Cerf and Victor Navasky, comps., *The Experts Speak: The Definitive Compendium of Authoritative Misinformation,* p. 216, 1984

The Nuclear Regulatory Commission today granted a full-power operating license to the Shoreham nuclear power plant, the $5.5-billion reactor that New York State is ready to scrap.

> CLIFFORD D. MAY. "Nuclear Plan Gains Full U.S. License, Despite Plan to Scrap It," *New York Times,* 21 April 1989. In response to intense public opposition earlier in the year, New York State had announced its intention to dismantle the Long Island plant on grounds that it could not be safely operated.

A nuclear reactor is not a macaroni factory. You can't let it slide into disrepair and then ignore it.

> ALEXANDER NOVITSKAS. Russian mechanic at the nuclear power plant in Smolensk. On the shortage of funds to purchase replacement parts which has led Maxim Katayev, an engineer at the Smolensk plant to warn, "We don't want to have a second Chernobyl. But it could happen, and it gets more likely with every day." In David Filipov, "Nuclear Workers Fear Cash Woes Could Lead to Russian Chernobyl," *San Francisco Chronicle* (originally published in the *Boston* Globe), 19 July 1997

A nuclear power plant is infinitely safer than eating because 300 people choke to death on food every year.

> DIXY LEE RAY (1914–1994). Washington governor and Atomic Energy Commission chairwoman. 1977. In Christopher Cerf and Victor Navasky, comps., *The Experts Speak: The Definitive Compendium of Authoritative Misinformation,* p. 216, 1984

All the waste in a year from a nuclear power plant can be stored under a desk.

> RONALD REAGAN (1911–). In *Burlington Free Press* (Vermont), 15 February 1980

[Nuclear power is] the cleanest, the most efficient and the most economical [energy source], with no environmental problems.

> RONALD REAGAN (1911–). In Frances Gendlin and David Gancher, "Ronald Reagan: A Case of Misunderstanding?" *Sierra,* September-October 1980

Ukrainians have suffered almost four times more radiation-related diseases since the Chernobyl nuclear disaster in 1986, the Health Ministry said today.

The ministry said children were the greatest sufferers, with illnesses from radiation five times the level recorded before the explosion.

"Chernobyl will be with us forever." The Health Minister, Andriy Serdyuk, said at a new conference in Kiev.

> REUTERS. British news service. Opening paragraphs, "Ukraine Tallies Sharp Rise in Illnesses Near Chernobyl," *New York Times,* 23 April 1998

I'm deeply convinced nuclear energy should be developed, but it must be made absolutely safe. My proposal is to put nuclear reactors underground.

> ANDREI D. SAKHAROV (1921–1989). Russian nuclear physicist. In Elisa Tinsley interview, "'It's a Rare Quality' That Sets USA Apart," *USA Today,* 8 November 1988

The nuclear peril is usually seen in isolation from the threats to other forms of life and their ecosystems, but in fact it should be seen as the very center of the ecological crisis—as the cloud-covered Everest of which the more immediate, visible kinds of harm to the environment are the mere foothills.

> JONATHAN SCHELL (1943–). *The Fate of the Earth,* 2, 1982

No degree of prosperity could justify the accumulation of large highly toxic substances which nobody knows how to make "safe" and which remain an incalculable danger to the whole of creation for historical or even geological ages. To do such a thing is a transgression against life itself, a transgression infinitely more serious than any crime ever perpetrated by man.

> E. F. SCHUMACHER (1911–1977). On the radioactive wastes from nuclear reactors in a chapter titled, "Nuclear Energy—Salvation or Damnation?" *Small Is Beautiful: Economics as if People Mattered,* 2.4, 1973

Our children will enjoy in their homes electrical energy too cheap to meter.

> LEWIS L. STRAUSS (1896–1974). Atomic Energy Commission chairman. Referring to electrical power derived from nuclear sources. Speech before the National Association of Science Writers, New York City, 16 September 1954

Up to 40 potential Chernobyls are waiting to happen in the former Soviet Union and Central Europe.

By the time this nuclear nightmare catches the world's attention, it may be too late to prevent a catastrophe that could do irreparable human, economic and environmental damage. Without an international rescue operation, the risks can only escalate.

> MAURICE STRONG (1929–). Secretary General of the United Nations Conference [Brazil] on Environment and Development. "40 Chernobyls Waiting to Happen," *New York Times,* 22 March 1992

The development of atomic power for peaceful progress is desirable and is indeed indispensable.

> ARNOLD J. TOYNBEE (1889–1975). *The Toynbee-Ikeda Dialogue: Man Himself Must Choose,* 7, 1976

Twelve Soviet soldiers were executed for refusing to expose themselves to radioactivity by fighting fires at the Chernobyl reactor, a [German] newspaper reported yesterday.

> UNITED PRESS INTERNATIONAL. "12 Reported Executed in Chernobyl Case," *San Francisco Chronicle,* 15 December 1986

Because nuclear plants don't burn anything to make electricity, nuclear plants don't pollute the air. . . .

To help our economy grow, this country needs a secure, growing supply of electricity. More nuclear plants will give us just that—without sacrificing the quality of our environment.

> U.S. COUNCIL FOR ENERGY AWARENESS. "Nuclear Energy Means Cleaner Air," ad copy. In *Atlantic,* June 1992

⚜

We all live downwind.

> SAYING (AMERICAN)
> See Pollution: Saying (American)

NUCLEAR WEAPONS

See also • Cold War ○ Conversion: James W. Douglass ○ Cuban Missile Crisis ○ Korean War: Douglas MacArthur (3), Harry S Truman (3) ○ Nonviolence: Martin Luther King, Jr. (7) ○ Nuclear Energy ○ Vietnam War: Barry M. Goldwater, Richard M. Nixon ○ Violence ○ War

[While meeting with Pres. Harry S. Truman at the White House] J. Robert Oppenheimer, the ambivalent father of the atomic bomb . . . blurted out, "There's blood on my hands," Truman took aside Secretary of State [Dean] Acheson, who had accompanied [Oppenheimer], and said, "Don't ever bring that man in here again."

> RICHARD J. BARNET (1929–). *Roots of War,* 5.4, 1971

I'd do it again. I still feel that use of the weapon was justified. We were fighting a declared war started by the enemy. We had to make a total commitment to win. [After the attack we] went to the club and had a few snorts. Then I realized it was my birthday. I had really celebrated with a big bang.

> KERMIT BEAHAN. Nagasaki atom-bomb navigator. In "Hue and Cry," *San Francisco Sunday Examiner & Chronicle,* 19 August 1973

We have grasped the mystery of the atom and rejected the Sermon on the Mount. . . . The world has achieved brilliance without wisdom, power without conscience. Ours is a world of nuclear giants and ethical infants. We know more about war than we know about peace, more about killing than we know about living.

> OMAR N. BRADLEY (1893–1981). Army general and Joint Chiefs of Staff chairman. Armistice Day address before the Boston Chamber of Commerce, 10 November 1948

People are still dying, mysteriously and horribly—people who were uninjured in the cataclysm—from an unknown something which I can only describe as the atomic plague. . . .

A peculiar odor . . . given off by the poisonous gas still issues from the earth soaked with radioactivity; against this the inhabitants all wear gauze masks over their mouths and noses; many thousands of people have simply vanished—the atomic heat was so great that they burned instantly to ashes—except that there were no ashes—they were vaporized.

> PETER BURCHETT. In *Daily Express* (British newspaper), 5 September 1945. Quoted in John G. Stoessinger, *Why Nations Go to War,* 3rd ed., 8, 1982 (1974)

A thousand years scarce serve to form a state;
An hour may lay it in the dust.

> LORD BYRON (1788–1824). *Childe Harold's Pilgrimage,* 2:84, 1812–1818

What was gunpowder? Trivial. What was electricity? Meaningless. This Atomic Bomb is the Second Coming in Wrath.

> WINSTON CHURCHILL (1874–1965). Soon after hearing about the first atom bomb test at Alamagordo (New Mexico) on 16 July 1945. Remark to U.S. Secretary of War Henry L. Stimson, July 1945. In John Keegan, *A History of Warfare,* 5, 1994

In the course of a few bewildering years we have found ourselves the master, or indeed the servants, of gigantic powers which confront us with problems never known before. It may be that our perils may prove our salvation. If so, this will depend upon a new elevation of the mind of man which will render him worthy of the secrets he has wrested from nature.

> WINSTON CHURCHILL (1874–1965). Banquet speech at the Royal Academy of Arts, London, 28 April 1954

I think it's a bloody miracle that one of these eggs has not gotten loose in the last 40 years. The subject of control over nuclear weapons is so awful a problem that there aren't any real solutions to them, and you can't relax about it at all.

> WILLIAM E. COLBY (1920–1996). Central Intelligence Agency director. In Patrick E. Tyler, "Troubling Question of Coup: Whose Finger Was on Soviet Nuclear Trigger," *New York Times,* 24 August 1991

Local defense must be reinforced by the further deterrent of massive retaliatory power.

> JOHN FOSTER DULLES (1888–1959). Secretary of state. On nuclear weapons, speech before the Council on Foreign Relations, 12 January 1954. "Massive retaliation" was a major component of American foreign policy during the Cold War.

There will one day spring from the brain of science a machine or force so fearful in its potentialities, so absolutely terrifying, that even man, the fighter, who will dare torture and death in order to inflict torture and death, will be appalled, and so will abandon war forever.

> THOMAS ALVA EDISON (1847–1931). 1922, *The Diary and Sundry Observations of Thomas Alva Edison,* 2.3.10, ed. Dagobert D. Runes, 1948

Some recent work by E[nrico] Fermi and L[eo] Szilard, which has been communicated to me in manuscript, leads me to expect that the element uranium may be turned into a new and important source of energy in the immediate future. Certain aspects of the situation which has arisen seem to call for watchfulness and, if necessary, quick action on the part of Administration. . . .

It may be possible to set up a nuclear chain reaction in a large mass of uranium, by which vast amounts of power and large quantities of new radium-like elements would be generated. . . .

This new phenomenon would also lead to the construction of bombs, and it is conceivable—though much less certain—that extremely powerful bombs of a new type may thus be constructed. A single bomb of this type, carried by boat and exploded in a port, might very well destroy the whole port together with some of the surrounding territory.

> ALBERT EINSTEIN (1879–1955). Letter to Pres. Franklin D. Roosevelt, 2 August 1939 (4 weeks before the start of World War II and 6 years before the atom bomb was dropped on Hiroshima)

For the present [atomic energy] is a menace. Perhaps it is as well that it should be. It may intimidate the human race to bring order into its international affairs, which, without the pressure of fear, it undoubtedly would not do.

> ALBERT EINSTEIN (1879–1955). Closing words, Raymond Swing interview, "Einstein on the Atomic Bomb," *Atlantic,* November 1945

The unleashed power of the atom has changed everything save our modes of thinking, and we thus drift toward unparalleled catastrophe.

> ALBERT EINSTEIN (1879–1955). 24 May 1946. In Ralph E. Lapp, "The Einstein Letter That Started It All," *New York Times Magazine,* 2 August 1964
>
> See Progress: John Stuart Mill

Science has brought forth this danger, but the real problem is in the minds and hearts of men. We will not change the hearts of other men by mechanisms, but by changing *our* hearts and speaking bravely. . . .

When we are clear in heart and mind—only then shall we find courage to surmount the fear which haunts the world.

> ALBERT EINSTEIN (1879–1955). On nuclear weapons, "'The Real Problem Is in the Hearts of Men,'" *New York Times Magazine,* 23 June 1946

When we get to the point, as some day we will, that both sides know that in any outbreak of general hostilities, regardless of the element of surprise, destruction will be both reciprocal and complete, possibly we will have sense enough to meet at the conference table with the understanding that the era of armaments has ended and the human race must conform its actions to this truth or die.

> DWIGHT D. EISENHOWER (1890–1969). Letter to Richard L. Simon, 14 April 1956. In Fred I. Greenstein, *The Hidden-Hand Presidency: Eisenhower as Leader,* 2 (note 67), 1982

The Japanese were ready to surrender and it wasn't necessary to hit them with that awful thing. . . . I hated to see our country be the first to use such a weapon.

> DWIGHT D. EISENHOWER (1890–1969). 1963. In Barton J. Bernstein, "Hiroshima, Rewritten," *New York Times,* 31 January 1995

Following a nuclear attack on the United States, the U.S. Postal Service plans to distribute Emergency Change of Address Cards.

> FEDERAL EMERGENCY MANAGEMENT AGENCY. Executive Order #11490, 1969

I was involved in the original sin, and I have spent a large part of the rest of my life atoning.

> BERNARD T. FELD (1919–1993). Nuclear physicist. In Clifford J. Levy, "Bernard Feld, Who Led Scientists in Fighting Arms Race, Dies at 73," *New York Times,* 20 February 1993

Just as the military power must have a plausible enemy, so also it must have a plausible design for countering the public threat. This is what arms-control negotiations principally accomplish. Rather than limit or even reduce the chance of nuclear destruction, negotiations serve to contain and quiet the public fear of nuclear destruction.

> JOHN KENNETH GALBRAITH (1908–). "The Military Power: Tension as a Servant; Arms Control as an Illusion," speech before the International Physicians for the Prevention of Nuclear War, Cologne (West Germany), 1986. Excerpted in *Harper's,* November 1986

The present insanity of the global arms race, if continued, will lead inevitably to a conflagration so great that Auschwitz will seem like a minor rehearsal.

> BILLY GRAHAM (1918–). Sermon, Auschwitz (Poland), 1978. Quoted by Wes Michaelson and Jim Wallis in their interview with him, *Sojourners,* August 1979

At any given time, the United States has on alert more than 2,300 warheads, delivering a combined explosive power of about 550 megatons (550 million tons of TNT)—the equivalent, to use a popular measure, of 44,000 Hiroshimas.

> BRIAN HALL. "Overkill Is Not Dead: U.S. Nuclear Forces Are Improving—Almost as Fast as Russia's Are Deteriorating. That Increases Instability, Yet Arms Control Remains Perversely Paralyzed," *New York Times Magazine,* 15 March 1998

If there are enough shovels to go around, everybody's going to make it. . . .

You've got to be in a hole. . . . The dirt [covering the hole] really is the thing that protects you from the blast as well as the radiation, if there's radiation. It protects you from the heat. You know, dirt is just great stuff.

THOMAS K. JONES. Deputy Undersecretary of Defense for Research
and Engineering, Strategic and Theater Nuclear Forces. On surviving
a nuclear attack, interview with the author, fall 1981. In Robert Scheer,
With Enough Shovels: Reagan, Bush and Nuclear War, 2, 1982

The development of nuclear weapons [is] the logical culmination of
the technological trend in the Western way of warfare and the ultimate denial of the proposition that war was, or might be, a continuation of politics by other means.

JOHN KEEGAN. Conclusion to *A History of Warfare,* 1994
See War: Karl von Clausewitz (3)

Today every inhabitant of this planet must contemplate the day
when this planet may no longer be habitable. Every man, woman
and child lives under a nuclear sword of Damocles, hanging by the
slenderest of threads, capable of being cut at any moment by accident or miscalculation or madness. . . . Mankind must put an end
to war or war will put an end to mankind.

JOHN F. KENNEDY (1917–1963). United Nations address, New York City,
25 September 1961

The survivors would envy the dead.

NIKITA KHRUSHCHEV (1894–1971). Soviet premier. Referring to nuclear
war, 1962

*Dr. Strangelove; or, How I Learned to Stop Worrying and Love the
Bomb.*

STANLEY KUBRICK (1928–). Film title, 1963

That is the biggest fool thing we have ever done. The bomb will
never go off, and I speak as an expert in explosives.

WILLIAM D. LEAHY (1875–1959). Admiral and chief military adviser to
Presidents Franklin D. Roosevelt and Harry S. Truman. After hearing,
with Truman, a scientific report about the soon-to-be-tested atom bomb,
remarks to the author, 1945. In Harry S. Truman, *Memoirs, Year of
Decisions,* 2, 1955

As the bomb fell over Hiroshima and exploded, we saw an entire
city disappear. I wrote in my log the words: "My God, what have
we done?"

ROBERT LEWIS. Air force captain and *Enola Gay* copilot. Remarks on the
10th anniversary of the atom bomb, 19 May 1955

Delusions of adequacy might propel us into a major debacle, some
"Desert One" on a large scale, and then the shock of defeat and the
fear of its results might tempt us to redeem failure by resorting to
nuclear weapons.

EDWARD N. LUTTWAK (1942–). *The Pentagon and the Art of War: The
Question of Military Reform,* 11, 1985. Desert One was the code name
for the U.S. military operation that in 1980 unsuccessfully attempted to
rescue American hostages being held in Iran.

The utter destructiveness of war now blots out [war as a method for
settling international disputes]. We have had our last chance. If we
will not devise some greater and more equitable system,
Armageddon will be at the door. The problem basically is theological and involves a spiritual recrudescence and improvement of
human character that will synchronize with our almost matchless
advances in science, art, literature, and all material and cultural
developments of the past 2,000 years. It must be of the spirit if we
are to save the flesh.

DOUGLAS MacARTHUR (1880–1964). Speech aboard the battleship
Missouri at the formal surrender of Japan ending World War II,
2 September 1945

In war, as it is waged now, with the enormous losses on both
sides, both sides will lose. It is a form of mutual suicide; and I
believe that the entire effort of modern society should be concentrated on an endeavor to outlaw war as a method of the solution of problems between nations.

DOUGLAS MacARTHUR (1880–1964). Testimony before the Senate
Committee on Armed Services and the Committee on Foreign
Relations, 4 May 1951

The atom bomb is a paper tiger which the U.S. reactionaries use
to scare people. It looks terrible, but in fact it isn't. Of course, the
atom bomb is a weapon of mass slaughter, but the outcome of a
war is decided by the people, not by one or two new types of
weapon.

All reactionaries are paper tigers. In appearance, the reactionaries are terrifying, but in reality they are not so powerful.
From a long-term point of view, it is not the reactionaries but the
people who are really powerful.

MAO TSE-TUNG (1893–1976). Anna Louise Strong interview, August
1946, *Selected Works of Mao Tse-tung,* Foreign Languages Press edition, vol. 4, 1961

When the bomb is detonated in the middle of a city, it is as
though a small piece of the sun has been instantly created.

PHILIP MORRISON. Testimony before Senate Special Committee on
Atomic Energy, 6 December 1945

If the Third World War is fought with nuclear weapons, the fourth
will be fought with bows and arrows.

LORD LOUIS MOUNTBATTEN (1900–1979). In *Maclean's* (Canadian
magazine), 9 November 1975

Nuclear weapons ended World War II and have been the major
factor in preventing World War III. The existence of nuclear
weapons makes even conventional war too risky for aggressors
who might contemplate it. Eliminating nuclear weapons would
simply make the world safe for conventional war.

RICHARD M. NIXON (1913–1994). *In the Arena: A Memoir of Victory,
Defeat and Renewal,* 39, 1990

Our policies of deterrence and of maintaining the balance of
power should enable us to prevent a war in the twenty-first century that would produce hell on earth.

RICHARD M. NIXON (1913–1994). *In the Arena: A Memoir of Victory,
Defeat and Renewal,* 39, 1990

We waited until the blast had passed, walked out of the shelter
and then it was extremely solemn. We knew the world would not
be the same. A few people laughed, a few people cried. Most
people were silent. I remembered the line from the Hindu scripture, the *Bhagavad Gita:* Vishnu is trying to persuade the Prince
that he should do his duty . . . and says, "Now I am become death,
destroyer of worlds." I suppose we all thought that one way or
another. There was a great deal of solemn talk that this was the
end of the great wars of the century.

J. ROBERT OPPENHEIMER (1904–1967). Nuclear physicist and director of the atomic-energy project at Los Alamos (New Mexico), where the atom bomb was developed. Recalling the explosion of the first atom bomb (nicknamed "Fat Man") near Alamogordo Air Base, 5:30 A.M. (zero hour at "Trinity"), 16 July 1945. In Len Giovanitti and Fred Freed, *The Decision to Drop the Bomb,* 12, 1965

The problem is not evil designs on either side but our complacency in hostility, our willingness to go on as we are, our reliance on threats of annihilation to save us from annihilation.

THOMAS POWERS (1940–). On U.S.-Soviet relations, "What Is It About?" *Atlantic,* January 1984

[Pres. Harry S. Truman] ordered a halt to the atomic bombing on August 10 [1945], four days before the Japanese Emperor surrendered [and one day after Nagasaki was atom-bombed], and the reason, according to a Cabinet member present at the meeting, was that "he didn't like the idea of killing . . . 'all those kids.'" [Ellipsis points in original.]

THOMAS POWERS (1940–). "Was It Right?" *Atlantic,* July 1995

My fellow Americans. I am pleased to tell you I just signed legislation which outlaws Russia forever. The bombing begins in five minutes.

RONALD REAGAN (1911–). Off-the-cuff "joke" made while testing the microphone prior to a radio broadcast, 11 August 1984. In John B. Oakes, "Mr. Reagan Bombs," *New York Times,* 18 August 1984

[A] shield that missiles could not penetrate—a shield that could protect us from nuclear missiles just as a roof protects a family from rain.

RONALD REAGAN (1911–). On the protection afforded by the Strategic Defense Initiative ("Star Wars") program, speech before the graduating class of Glassboro High School (New Jersey), 19 June 1986

I think that if the atomic bomb did nothing more, it scared the people to the point where they realized that either they must do something about preventing war or there is a chance that there might be a morning when we would not wake up.

ELEANOR ROOSEVELT (1884–1962). United Nations ambassador. News conference, 3 January 1946

If we have to start over again with another Adam and Eve, then I want them to be Americans and not Russians—and I want them on this continent and not in Europe.

RICHARD RUSSELL (1897–1971). Georgia senator. In a closed Senate session later published in the *Congressional Record,* 1 November 1968. Quoted in "Russell Urges Antimissile Force So Nation Can Rebuild in Event of 'Nuclear Exchange' with Soviet Union," *New York Times,* 24 November 1968

A nuclear holocaust, widely regarded as "unthinkable" but never as undoable, appears to confront us with an action that we can perform but cannot quite conceive.

JONATHAN SCHELL (1943–). *The Fate of the Earth,* 1, 1982

It is of the essence of the human condition that we are born, live for a while, and then die. Through mishaps of all kinds, we may also suffer untimely death, and in extinction by nuclear arms the number of untimely deaths would reach the limit for any one catastrophe: everyone in the world would die. But although the untimely death of everyone in the world would in itself constitute an unimaginably huge loss, it would bring with it a separate, distinct loss that would be in a sense even huger—the cancellation of all future generations of human beings.

JONATHAN SCHELL (1943–). *The Fate of the Earth,* 2, 1982

As long as politics fails to take up the nuclear issue in a determined way, it lives closer than any other activity to the lie that we have all come to live—the pretense that life lived on a nuclear stockpile can last. Meanwhile, we are encouraged not to tackle our predicament but to inure ourselves to it: to develop a special, enfeebled vision, which is capable of overlooking the hugely obvious; a special, sluggish nervous system, which is conditioned not to react even to the most extreme and urgent peril; and a special, constricted mode of political thinking, which is permitted to creep around the edges of the mortal crisis in the life of our species but never to meet it head on.

JONATHAN SCHELL (1943–). *The Fate of the Earth,* 2, 1982

The nuclear powers do not, as the statesmen so often proclaim, possess nuclear weapons with the sole aim of preventing their use and so keeping the peace; they possess them also to defend national interests and aspirations—indeed, to perpetuate the whole system of sovereign states.

JONATHAN SCHELL (1943–). *The Fate of the Earth,* 3, 1982

In our day, when the challenge is not just to apprehend the nuclear peril but to seize a God-given opportunity to dispel it once and for all [through nuclear disarmament], we seem to need, in addition, some other picture to counterpoise against ruined Nagasaki—one showing not what we would lose through our failure but what we would gain by our success. What might that picture be, though? How do you show the opposite of the end of the world?

JONATHAN SCHELL (1943–). Epilogue to "The Gift of Time," *Nation,* 2 February 1998. Earlier in the epilogue, Schell had described Yosuke Yamahata's photographs taken in Nagasaki on 10 August 1945, one day after the city had been atom-bombed.

There will be a moment of supreme decision at the brink of some future world war when our leaders, their fingers dangling above the nuclear button, ponder what to do. As [H. G.] Wells knew, we set our course by the ways in which we think—or decline to think—about war in the weeks and months and years prior to the moment of supreme crisis, and by the little decisions we make in preparation for it.

MICHAEL SHERRY (1945–). "The Slide to Total Air War," *New Republic,* 16 December 1981

It has become almost banal to say that the atomic age has fundamentally altered the nature of war. No nuclear power can tell another: "Do as I say or I shall kill you," but is reduced to saying: "Do as I say or I shall kill us both," which is an entirely different matter.

JOHN G. STOESSINGER (1927–). *Why Nations Go to War,* 3rd ed., 8, 1982 (1974)

[A] world without nuclear weapons would be less stable and more dangerous for all of us.

MARGARET THATCHER (1925–). Remark to Mikhail S. Gorbachev. In George J. Church, "Now, Super-Zero?" *Time,* 27 April 1987

Canadian television interviewer: Ever regret all the people you killed?

Tibbets: No, I've never lost a night's sleep over it, and I never will. . . . I got nothing to be ashamed of. That's how it was.

> PAUL W. TIBBETS, JR.. Air force colonel. Format adapted. Referring to his role as pilot of the *Enola Gay,* the B-29 that dropped the atom bomb on Hiroshima on 6 August 1945. Interviewed at age 79. In Eugene L. Meyer, "Target: Smithsonian," *Washington Post,* 30 January 1995

In an age in which mankind's collective power has suddenly been increased, for good or evil, a thousand-fold through the tapping of atomic energy, the standard of conduct demanded from ordinary human beings can be no lower than the standard attained in times past by rare saints.

> ARNOLD J. TOYNBEE (1889–1975). *A Study of History,* 12.535, 1961

If mankind cannot now bring itself at last to live as one family, the penalty, in our new situation, must be genocide sooner or later.

> ARNOLD J. TOYNBEE (1889–1975). *A Study of History,* 12.620, 1961

This is a great day in the history of the world.

> HARRY S. TRUMAN (1884–1972). Upon learning about the atomic bombing of Hiroshima, 6 August 1945. In John Morrill, "How Wars End," *History Today,* April 1985

Sixteen hours ago an American airplane dropped one bomb on Hiroshima, an important Japanese Army base. That bomb had more power than 20,000 tons of TNT. It had more than 2,000 times the blast power of the British "Grand Slam," which is the largest bomb ever yet used in the history of warfare. . . . It is an atomic bomb. It is a harnessing of the basic power of the universe. The force from which the sun draws its powers has been loosed against those who brought war to the Far East.

> HARRY S. TRUMAN (1884–1972). Radio broadcast, 6 August 1945

The atom bomb was no "great decision." It was used in the war, and, and for your information, there were more people killed in Tokyo than dropping the bomb accounted for. It was merely another powerful weapon in the arsenal of righteousness. The dropping of the bombs stopped the war, saved millions of lives. It is just the same as artillery on our side.

> HARRY S. TRUMAN (1884–1972). Responding to a student's question, seminar on "statescraft," Columbia University (New York City), 28 April 1959, *Truman Speaks,* 1960

I remember in school they showed a film called "A is for Atom, B is for Bomb." I think most of us who grew up in that period, we've all in our own minds added "C is for Cancer, D is for Death."

> PRESTON JAY TRUMAN. Recalling a childhood experience in the 1950s, a time during which he regularly witnessed nuclear blasts at the testing site in Nevada and later the bomb-caused radioactive fallout clouds that passed over his home. Quoted by Carole Gallagher, *American Ground Zero: The Secret Nuclear War.* In Gallagher, "Ground Zero," *New York Times,* 26 March 1993

These [tactical nuclear bombs], if employed once or twice on the right targets, at the right time, would in my judgment, stop *current* aggression, and stop *future* subversion and limited wars before they start.

> NATHAN TWINING (1897–1982). Air force general and Joint Chiefs of Staff chairman. Referring to the Third World, *Neither Liberty Nor Safety: A Hard Look at U.S. Military Policy and Strategy,* 15, 1966

When [an atom bomb] went off, you felt you were in a vapor, like a vacuum, everything still as death—and then this real bright light, so bright I had my hands over my eyes closed and I could see all these bones just like you were looking at an X-ray. The fireball was right straight up over our heads. We had to be in the stem of it. We were only 300 yards from ground zero. The sand had melted into a glaze, like a brown glass. Then we got a sunburn, and the guys all started throwing up in the truck going back, sick as dogs, all of them.

> REASON WAREHIME. Pseudonym. Describing a nuclear explosion (four times bigger than the one at Hiroshima) he witnessed as a Marine at the Nevada test site during the early 1950s. (At the time of the interview he was, at 67, a cancer victim.) Quoted by Carole Gallagher, *American Ground Zero: The Secret Nuclear War,* 1993. In Gallagher, "Ground Zero," *New York Times,* 26 March 1993

A recent historical writer has described the world at that time as one that "believed in established words and was invincibly blind to the obvious in things." Nothing could have been more obvious to the people of the early twentieth century than the rapidity with which war was becoming impossible. And as certainly they did not see it. They did not see it until the atomic bombs burst in their fumbling hands.

> H. G. WELLS (1866–1946). *The World Set Free: A Story of Mankind,* 2.5, 1914

We are heading towards catastrophe. I think the world is going to pieces. I am very pessimistic. Why? Because the world hasn't been punished yet, and the only punishment that could be adequate is the nuclear destruction of the world.

> ELI WIESEL (1928–). John S. Friedman interview, 1978. In George Plimpton, ed., *Writers at Work: Eighth Series,* 1988

Little Boy.

> ANONYMOUS (AMERICAN). Name given to the atom bomb dropped on Hiroshima, 6 August 1945

I secluded myself at home and spent hours before the mirror looking at my own face. What I saw was ugly hunks of flesh, like lava oozing from a crater well, covering the left half of my face, with the eyebrows burned off and my eye and lips pulled out of shape.

> ANONYMOUS (JAPANESE). 14-year-old hibakusha (i.e., an atom-bomb survivor; literally, an "explosion-effected person"). In *Hiroshima and Nagasaki: The Physical, Medical and Social Effects of the Atomic Bombings.* Quoted in John Toland, "The Legacy of Atomic Attack," *San Francisco Sunday Examiner & Chronicle,* 16 August 1981

The only winnable nuclear war is the one we prevent.

> ANONYMOUS

NUMBERS

See also • Facts ○ Figures ○ Mathematics ○ Statistics

When you have mastered the numbers, you will in fact no longer be reading numbers, any more than you read words when reading a book. You will be reading meanings.

> HAROLD GENEEN (1910–1997) (with ALVIN MOSCOW). *Managing,* 9, 1984
>
> See Speaking: Saying

Round numbers are always false.

> SAMUEL JOHNSON (1709–1784). 30 March 1778 (footnote 4). In James Boswell, *The Life of Samuel Johnson,* 1791

Falstaff: Good luck lies in odd numbers. . . . They say there is divinity in odd numbers, either in nativity, chance, or death.

> SHAKESPEARE (1564–1616). *The Merry Wives of Windsor,* 5.1.3, 1600

❧

OBSTACLES

See also • Difficulty

We combat obstacles in order to get repose, and, when got, the repose is insupportable.

> HENRY ADAMS (1838–1918). *The Education of Henry Adams,* 29, 1907

If there are obstacles, the shortest line between two points may be the crooked line.

> BERTOLT BRECHT (1898–1956). *Galileo,* 13, 1939, tr. Charles Laughton, 1961

Man is most uniquely human when he turns obstacles into opportunities.

> ERIC HOFFER (1902–1983). *Reflections on the Human Condition,* 27, 1973

Every *path* hath a puddle.

> JOHN RAY (1628–1705). Comp., *A Collection of English Proverbs,* p. 21, 1678

OBSTINACY

See also • Change & Changelessness ○ Consistency ○ Persistence ○ Resolution

Obstinacy in a bad cause is but constancy in a good.

> SIR THOMAS BROWNE (1605–1682). *Religio Medici,* 1.25, 1642, ed. John Addington Symonds, 1886

THE OBSTINATE MAN does not hold Opinions, but they hold him; for when he is once possessed with an Error, 'tis like the Devil, not to be cast out but with great Difficulty.

> SAMUEL BUTLER (1612–1680). "The Obstinate Man," *The Genuine Remains in Verse and Prose of Mr. Samuel Butler, Author of Hudibras,* vol. 2, 1759

I regret many follies which sprang from my obstinacy; but without that trait I would not have reached my goal.

> CARL G. JUNG (1875–1961). "Retrospect," *Memories, Dreams, Reflections,* ed. Aniela Jaffé, 1962

Obstinacy and heat of opinion is the surest proof of stupidity. Is there anything so certain, resolute, disdainful, contemplative, grave, and serious as an ass.

> MONTAIGNE (1533–1592). "Of the Art of Discussion," *Essays,* 1588, tr. Donald M. Frame, 1958

When will crowds out knowledge, we call the result *obstinacy.*

> ARTHUR SCHOPENHAUER (1788–1860). "On Psychology" (10), 1851, *Essays and Aphorisms,* tr. R. J. Hollingdale, 1970

Stubbornness and stupidity are twins.

> SOPHOCLES (496–406 B.C.). *Antigone,* l.1020, tr. Elizabeth Wyckoff, 1954

Time has a way of demonstrating
the most stubborn are the most intelligent.

> YEVGENY YEVTUSHENKO (1933–). "A Career," *The New Russian Poets: 1953–1966,* tr. George Reavey, 1966

OPINION

See also • Belief ○ Change & Changelessness ○ Consistency ○ Fact ○ Faith ○ Freedom of Thought ○ Ideas ○ Public Opinion ○ Thoughts ○ Words

Everyone Is Entitled to My Opinion.

> DAVID BRINKLEY (1920–). Book title, 1996

I could never divide myself from any man upon the difference of an opinion, or be angry with his judgment for not agreeing with me in that from which, perhaps, within a few days, I should dissent myself.

> SIR THOMAS BROWNE (1605–1682). *Religio Medici,* 1.6, 1642, ed. John Addington Symonds, 1886

For dull, unreflective, merely instinctive as the ordinary man may seem, he has nevertheless, as a quite indispensable appendage, a head that in some degree considers and computes; a lamp or rushlight of understanding has been given him, which, through whatever dim, besmoked, and strangely diffractive media it may shine, is the ultimate guiding light of his whole path: and here, as well as there, now as at all times in man's history, Opinion rules the world.

> THOMAS CARLYLE (1795–1881). "Voltaire," 1829, *Critical and Miscellaneous Essays,* Carey & Hart edition, 1849

Every new opinion, at its starting, is precisely in *a minority of one.* In one man's head alone, there it dwells as yet. One man alone of the whole world believes it; there is one man against all men.

> THOMAS CARLYLE (1795–1881). "The Hero as Prophet," *On Heroes, Hero-Worship, and the Heroic in History,* 1841

The only sin which people never forgive in each other is difference of opinion.

> LYDIAN EMERSON. Ralph Waldo Emerson's wife. In Emerson, journal, July 1841

It is only when proofs are lacking that people try to impose their opinions.

> ANDRÉ GIDE (1869–1951). *More Fruits of the Earth*, 4.1, 1935

What is the foundation of our opinion? numberless things, sometimes reason.

> FULKE GREVILLE (1554–1628). *Maxims, Characters, and Reflections*, p. 167, 1756

Every difference of opinion is not a difference of principle.

> THOMAS JEFFERSON (1743–1826). *First Inaugural Address*, 4 March 1801

Opinion is power.

> THOMAS JEFFERSON (1743–1826). Letter to John Adams, 11 January 1816
>
> See Knowledge: Francis Bacon (1)

The greatest part of mankind have no other reason for their opinions than that they are in fashion.

> SAMUEL JOHNSON (1709–1784). "Macbeth," *The Plays of William Shakespeare*, 1765

Unless they share our opinions, we seldom find people sensible.

> LA ROCHEFOUCAULD (1613–1680). *Maxims*, 347, 1665, tr. Louis Kronenberger, 1959

Nothing can contribute more to peace of soul than the lack of any opinion whatever.

> GEORG CHRISTOPH LICHTENBERG (1742–1799). *Aphorisms*, E.11, 1806, tr. R. J. Hollingdale, 1990

We accumulate our opinions at an age when our understanding is at its weakest.

> GEORG CHRISTOPH LICHTENBERG (1742–1799). *Aphorisms*, H.4, 1806, tr. R. J. Hollingdale, 1990

New opinions are always suspected, and usually opposed, without any other reason, but because they are not already common.

> JOHN LOCKE (1632–1704). "The Epistle Dedicatory," *An Essay Concerning Human Understanding*, 1690, ed. Alexander Campbell Fraser, 1894

People feel sure not so much that their opinions are true as that they should not know what to do without them.

> JOHN STUART MILL (1806–1873). *On Liberty*, 2, 1859

Where there is much desire to learn, there of necessity will be much arguing, much writing, many opinions; for opinion in good men is but knowledge in the making.

> JOHN MILTON (1608–1674). *Areopagitica* (A Speech for the Liberty of Unlicenc'd Printing), 1644

I do not judge opinions by their years.

> MONTAIGNE (1533–1592). "Of Cripples," *Essays*, 1588, tr. Donald M. Frame, 1958

Deeper than men's opinions are the sentiment and circumstances by which opinion is predetermined.

> JOHN MORLEY (1838–1923). *Notes on Politics and History: A University Address*, 3, 1913

Some praise at Morning what they blame at Night;
But always think the last Opinion right.

> ALEXANDER POPE (1688–1744). *An Essay on Criticism*, l.430, 1711

We never are satisfied with our opinions, whatever we may pretend, till they are ratified and confirmed by the suffrages of the rest of mankind.

> SIR JOSHUA REYNOLDS (1723–1792). "Discourse Seven," 10 December 1776, *Discourses on Art*, 1769–1790

Be very wary of opinions that flatter your self-esteem.

> BERTRAND RUSSELL (1872–1970). "An Outline of Intellectual Rubbish," *Unpopular Essays*, 1950

When we pass in review the opinions of former times which are now recognized as absurd, it will be found that nine times out of ten they were such as to justify the infliction of suffering.

> BERTRAND RUSSELL (1872–1970). "Ideas That Have Harmed Mankind," *Unpopular Essays*, 1951

Opinion is ultimately determined by the feelings, and not by the intellect.

> HERBERT SPENCER (1820–1903). *Social Statics*, 4.30.8, 1851
>
> See Feelings: Thomas Carlyle

If there is an opinion, facts will be found to support it.

> JUDY SPROLES. Fallbrook, California. In Scot Morris, "You Make the Laws," *Omni*, May 1979

It were not best that we should all think alike; it is difference of opinion that makes horse races.

> MARK TWAIN (1835–1910). *The Tragedy of Pudd'nhead Wilson*, 19 (epigraph), 1894

❦

Three Spaniards, four opinions.

> SAYING (SPANISH)

OPPORTUNITY

See also • Chance ○ Circumstances ○ Danger ○ Delay ○ Destiny ○ Events ○ Fate ○ Fortune ○ History ○ Luck ○ Misfortune ○ Preparedness: Saying ○ Prudence: Rules ○ Regret ○ Speed ○ Success ○ Temptation ○ Timing ○ World: Ralph Waldo Emerson (5)

A wise man will make more opportunities than he finds.

> FRANCIS BACON (1561–1626). "Of Ceremonies and Respects," *Essays*, 1625

This could but have happened once,
    And we missed it, lost it forever.

> ROBERT BROWNING (1812–1889). Last verse, "Youth and Art," *Dramatis Personae*, 1864

Now the enemy is busy in Russia is the time to "Make hell while the sun shines."

> WINSTON CHURCHILL (1874–1965). Memorandum to Gen. Hastings Lionel Ismay, 23 June 1941 (the day after Germany invaded the Soviet Union). Appendix to *The Second World War: The Grand Alliance*, 1950

Make hay while the sun shineth.

> JOHN CLARKE (1596–1658). Comp., *Proverbs: English and Latine*, p. 233, 1639

That policy that can strike only while the iron is hot will be overcome by that perseverance, which, like Cromwell's, can make the *iron hot by striking*; and he that can only rule the storm must yield to him who can both *raise* and *rule* it.

> C. C. COLTON (1780–1832). *Lacon: or, Many Things in Few Words; Addressed to Those Who Think*, 1.68, 1823

Thou strong seducer, Opportunity!

> JOHN DRYDEN (1631–1700). *The Conquest of Granada*, 2.4.3, 1672

Opportunity always knocks at the least opportune moment.

> DUCHARME'S PRECEPT. In Arthur Bloch, comp., "Advanced Murphology," *Murphy's Law: Book Two*, 1980

We cannot afford to miss any advantage. Never was any man too strong for his proper work.

> RALPH WALDO EMERSON (1803–1882). "Perpetual Forces," *Lectures and Biographical Sketches*, 1883

As the Wind blows, you must set your Sail.

> THOMAS FULLER (1654–1734). Comp., *Gnomologia: Adages and Proverbs*, 738, 1732
>
> See Grace: Swami Prabhavananda

If you have many Irons in the Fire, some will burn.

> THOMAS FULLER (1654–1734). Comp., *Gnomologia: Adages and Proverbs*, 2758, 1732

Gather ye rosebuds while ye may.
Old Time is still a-flying:
And this same flower that smiles today
Tomorrow will be dying.

> ROBERT HERRICK (1591–1674). "To the Virgins, to Make Much of Time," *Hesperides: or Works Both Humane and Divine*, 1648

Unlimited opportunities can be as potent a cause of frustration as a paucity or lack of opportunities.

> ERIC HOFFER (1902–1983). *The True Believer: Thoughts on the Nature of Mass Movements*, 39, 1951

The consequences of a lost chance rarely close the doors to future choice. But they narrow them to alternatives that are all relatively unfavorable in comparison with earlier possibilities.

> SIDNEY HOOK (1902–1989). *The Hero in History*, 8, 1943

Strike while the iron is hot.

> JAMES HOWELL (1593–1666). Comp., "English" (p. 15), *Paroimiographia: Proverbs, or Old Sayed Sawes & Adages in English . . . Italian, French and Spanish*, 1659

You got to get it while you can.

> JANIS JOPLIN (1943–1970). "Get It While You Can" (song), 1967?

Many Irons in the Fire, some must cool.

> JAMES KELLY (18th cent.). Comp., *A Complete Collection of Scottish Proverbs Explained and Made Intelligible to the English Reader*, M.93, 1721

The iron stands hot for the striking.

> SIR A. CLARK KERR. Message to the author, 2 October 1944. In Winston Churchill, *The Second World War: Triumph and Tragedy*, 1.14, 1953

Timid men are more likely to be moved to trepidation than daring in the face of great opportunities.

> HENRY A. KISSINGER (1923–). *A World Restored: Metternich, Castlereagh and the Problems of Peace 1812–1822*, 1.2, 1957

In affairs of importance a man should concentrate not so much on making opportunities as on taking advantage of those that arise.

> LA ROCHEFOUCAULD (1613–1680). *Maxims*, 453, 1665, tr. Leonard Tancock, 1959

While we stop to think, we often miss our opportunity.

> PUBLIUS SYRUS (85–43 B.C.). *Moral Sayings*, 185, tr. Darius Lyman, Jr., 1862

Look to the main chance.

> JOHN RAY (1628–1705). Comp., *A Collection of English Proverbs*, p. 174, 1678

When it's raining porridge, you'll find John's dish right side up.

> LUCY ROCKEFELLER (19th cent.). On her brother John D. Rockefeller. In Joseph Epstein, *Ambition: The Secret Passion*, 2, 1980

Brutus: There is a tide in the affairs of men,
Which, taken at the flood, leads on to fortune;
Omitted, all the voyage of their life
Is bound in shallows and in miseries.
On such a full sea are we now afloat;
And we must take the current when it serves,
Or lose our ventures.

> SHAKESPEARE (1564–1616). *Julius Caesar*, 4.3.218, 1599

❧

Cometh the hour, cometh the man.

> SAYING (ENGLISH)

A missed opportunity is worse than a defeat.

> ANONYMOUS

Winnow while the wind is blowing.

> SAYING (JAPANESE)

OPPOSITES

See also • Compensation ○ Dreams: William Wycherley ○ Ideas: Jean-Paul Sartre ○ Paradoxes ○ Truth: Niels Bohr, John Stuart Mill (2)

Without Contraries is no progression. Attraction and Repulsion, Reason and Energy, Love and Hate, are necessary to Human existence.

> WILLIAM BLAKE (1757–1827). *The Marriage of Heaven and Hell*, 3, 1790–1793?

They that endeavor to abolish vice, destroy also virtue; for contraries, though they destroy one another, are yet the life of one another.

> SIR THOMAS BROWNE (1605–1682). *Religio Medici,* 2.4, 1642, ed. John Addington Symonds, 1886

The energy behind the elemental pair of opposites, fire and water, is one and the same.

> JOSEPH CAMPBELL (1904–1987). *The Hero with a Thousand Faces,* 1.2.4, 1949

Reality is a perpetual process of evolution, propelled by the fertile impact of antagonisms which are resolved each time into a superior synthesis which, itself, creates its opposite and again causes history to advance.

> ALBERT CAMUS (1913–1960). On dialectical materialism, "Historical Rebellion: State Terrorism and Rational Terror," *The Rebel: An Essay on Man in Revolt,* 1951, tr. Anthony Bower, 1956

Real and ideal, reason and instinct, mind and matter, male and female—all should be merged into each other (as the Taoists merged their Yin and Yang into the Tao) and should be regarded as two aspects of the same idea.

> CYRIL CONNOLLY (1903–1974). "La Cle Des Chants," *The Unquiet Grave: A Word Cycle by Palinurus,* 1945

Blessed is the day when the youth discovers that Within and Above are synonyms.

> RALPH WALDO EMERSON (1803–1882). Journal, 21 December 1834

The whole world is a series of balanced antagonisms.

> RALPH WALDO EMERSON (1803–1882). Journal, May 1851

Things go by pairs.
Thoughts go by pairs.

> RALPH WALDO EMERSON (1803–1882). Journal, 1860, undated

On the outside of things seek for differences; on the inside, for likenesses.

> J. C. HARE (1795–1855) and A. W. HARE (1792–1834). *Guesses at Truth: Second Series,* p. 296, 1848, Macmillan edition, 1867

All things come into being by conflict of opposites.

> HERACLITUS (540?–480? B.C.). In Diogenes Laertius (A.D. 3rd cent.), *Lives of Eminent Philosophers,* 9.1, tr. R. D. Hicks, 1925

The non-opposite "is" as little as the opposite. Neither exists for itself, each exists through the other.

> EUGEN HERRIGEL (1885–1955). "Higher Stages of Meditation," *The Method of Zen,* 1960, ed. Hermann Tausend and tr. R. F. C. Hull, 1964

Contraries [are] poles of a unity.

> HERMANN HESSE (1877–1962). *Reflections,* 240, ed. Volker Michels, 1974

There is apparently no surer way of turning a thing into its opposite than by exaggerating it.

> ERIC HOFFER (1902–1983). *The Ordeal of Change,* 4, 1964

The interdependence of the contradictory aspects in all things and the struggle between these aspects determine the life of all things and push their development forward. There is nothing that does not contain contradiction; without contradiction nothing would exist.

> MAO TSE-TUNG (1893–1976). "On Contradiction" (2), August 1937, *Selected Works of Mao Tse-tung,* Foreign Languages Press edition, vol. 1, 1965

The basic opposites at work in the human being are the claims of consciousness and the claims of the unconscious. . . . "Visible and invisible, two worlds meet in man"; and in some way these two worlds must come together and be reconciled.

> P. W. MARTIN (1893–?). *Experiment in Depth: A Study of the Work of Jung, Eliot and Toynbee,* 7, 1955

Often you get the best insights by considering extremes—by thinking of the opposite of that with which you are directly concerned.

> C. WRIGHT MILLS (1916–1962). Appendix (4) to *The Sociological Imagination,* 1959

After a calm, comes the storm; the winds blow by turns; day succeeds night; some of the heavenly bodies rise, and some set. Eternity consists of opposites.

> SENECA THE YOUNGER (5? B.C.–A.D. 65). "On Obedience to the Universal Will," *Moral Letters to Lucilius,* 107.8, tr. Richard M. Gummere, 1918

Things that oppose each other also complement each other.

> SAYING (CHINESE). In Mao Tse-tung, "On Contradiction" (5), August 1937, *Selected Works of Mao Tse-tung,* Foreign Languages Press edition, vol. 1, 1965

Opposites attract.

> SAYING

OPPRESSION

See also • African Americans: Alexis de Tocqueville ○ Child Abuse: [especially] Maria Montessori ○ Class ○ Exploitation ○ Imperialism ○ Inequality ○ Injustice ○ Machiavellianism ○ Manipulation ○ Nations: Lenin ○ Persecution ○ Slavery ○ Tyranny

As long as you keep a person down, some part of you has to be down there to hold him down, so it means you cannot soar as you otherwise might.

> MARIAN ANDERSON (1902–1993). Television interview, CBS, 30 December 1957

It's not the world that was my oppressor, because what the world does to you, if the world does it to you long enough and effectively enough, you begin to do to yourself.

> JAMES BALDWIN (1924–1987). Nikki Giovanni conversation, 4 November 1971, *A Dialogue,* 1973

One of the benefits that oppression confers upon the oppressors is that the most humble among them is made to *feel* superior; thus, a poor white in the South can console himself with the thought that he is not a "dirty nigger"—and the more prosperous whites cleverly exploit this pride.

Similarly, the most mediocre of males feels himself a demigod as compared with women.

> SIMONE de BEAUVOIR (1908–1986). Introduction to *The Second Sex,* 1950, tr. H. M. Parshley, 1952

The most potent weapon in the hands of the oppressor is the mind of the oppressed.

> STEVE BIKO (1946–1977). South African human rights leader. Speech before the Cape Town Conference on Inter-Racial Studies, 1971

He who allows oppression shares the crime.

> ERASMUS DARWIN (1731–1802). *The Botanic Garden: A Poem in Two Parts,* 2.3.456, 1791

In their unrestrained eagerness to possess, the oppressors develop the conviction that it is possible for them to transform everything into objects of their purchasing power; hence their strictly materialistic concept of existence. Money is the measure of all things, and profit the primary goal. . . .

To the oppressor consciousness, the humanization of the "others," of the people, appears not as the pursuit of full humanity, but as subversion.

> PAULO FREIRE (1921–1997). *Pedagogy of the Oppressed,* 1, tr. Myra Bergman Ramos, 1968

All domination involves invasion—at times physical and overt, at times camouflaged, with the invader assuming the role of a helping friend.

> PAULO FREIRE (1921–1997). *Pedagogy of the Oppressed,* 4, tr. Myra Bergman Ramos, 1968

The most odious of all oppressions are those which mask as justice.

> ROBERT H. JACKSON (1892–1854). *Krulewitch v. United States,* 1949

Men, in attempting to avoid fear themselves, give others cause to fear; and the injuries which they ward off from themselves they inflict on others, as though there was a necessity either to oppress or be oppressed.

> LIVY (59 B.C.–A.D. 17). In Machiavelli, *The Discourses,* 1.46, 1517, tr. Luigi Ricci, 1903

You shall not oppress your neighbor or rob him.

> MOSES (14th cent. B.C.). *Leviticus* 19:13

It is not under the burdens of nature that society groans, but the work of caprice, of ostentation, of contemptible vanity, of luxury which is never satisfied, these oppress the world.

> THEODORE PARKER (1810–1860). "Thoughts on Labor," *The Dial* (New England journal), April 1841

The oppressor must have the cooperation of the oppressed, of those he must feel better than. The oppressed and the damned are placed in an inferior position by force of arms, physical strength, and later, by threats of such force. But the long-time maintenance of power over others is secured by psychological manipulation and seduction.

> PATRICIA ROBINSON. *Poor Black Women,* 1968. In Betty Roszak and Theodore Roszak, eds., *Masculine/Feminine: Readings in Sexual Mythology and the Liberation of Women,* 1969

Oppression leaves [slaves] no choice other than resignation or revolution.

> JEAN-PAUL SARTRE (1905–1980). *Literary and Philosophical Essays,* 13.2, 1946, tr. Annette Michelson, 1955

The fundamental conflicts in human life are not between competing ideas—one of which is true and the other false, but rather, between those that hold power and use it to oppress others, and those who are oppressed by power and seek to free themselves of it.

> THOMAS S. SZASZ (1920–). In Phyllis Chesler, *Women & Madness,* 3, 1972

Be neither a hammer nor a nail.

> SAYING

OPTIMISM

See also • Hope ○ Optimism: Examples ○ Optimism & Pessimism ○ Pessimism

Perpetual optimism is annoying.

It is a sign that you are not paying attention.

> MAUREEN DOWD (1952–). Closing words, "Colin Powell Rules!" *New York Times,* 17 September 1995

The ultimate in optimism: Confidence that there is no next world.

> MALCOLM S. FORBES (1919–1990). "Reaching High," *The Sayings of Chairman Malcolm: The Capitalist's Handbook,* 1978

Optimism is a kind of heart stimulant—the digitalis of failure.

> ELBERT HUBBARD (1856–1915). *A Thousand and One Epigrams,* p. 80, 1911

Bein' optimistic after you've got ever'thing you want don't count.

> KIN HUBBARD (1868–1930). *Abe Martin: Hoss Sense and Nonsense,* p. 32, 1926

An optimist is a fellow who believes what's going to be will be postponed.

> KIN HUBBARD (1868–1930)

Optimism is the opium of the people.

> MILAN KUNDERA (1929–). Czech writer. *The Joke,* 3.3, 1967
> See Religion, Anti-: Karl Marx

an optimist is a guy
that has never had
much experience.

> DON MARQUIS (1878–1937). "certain maxims of archy," *archy and mehitabel,* 1927

Perpetual optimism is a force multiplier.

> COLIN L. POWELL (1937–). Saying kept under desk glass, 17 September 1995

Stick with the optimists. It's going to be tough enough even if they're right.

> JAMES RESTON (1909–1995). Advise to his grandson. In *New York Times,* February 1980. Quoted in R. W. Apple, Jr., closing words, "James Reston, a Journalist Nonpareil, Dies at 86," *New York Times,* 8 December 1995

Optimist: One who believes things are so bad they're bound to get better.

> JERRY TUCKER (1941–). *The Experience of Politics: You and American Government,* 2.3, 1974

Cacambo: What is optimism?
Candide: Alas! It is the mania of maintaining that everything is well when we are wretched.

> VOLTAIRE (1694–1778). Format adapted. *Candide,* 19, 1759, tr. Richard Aldington, 1929

❦

Optimist, *n.* Hope-fiend.

> ANONYMOUS

OPTIMISM: EXAMPLES

See also • Hope ○ Optimism ○ Pessimism: Examples ○ Religion: Alfred North Whitehead (1)

What's the use of worrying?
It never was worthwhile,
So, pack up your troubles in your kit-bag
And smile, smile, smile.

> GEORGE ASAF (1880–1951). "Pack Up Your Troubles in Your Old Kit-bag" (song), 1915

You always find something in the last place you look for it.

> JIM BANKS. "Bank's Law of Misplaced Objects." In Paul Dickson, comp., *The New Official Rules,* p. 25, 1989

It ain't over till it's over.

> YOGI BERRA (1925–). On the 1973 National League pennant race

Look not thou down but up!

> ROBERT BROWNING (1812–1889). "Rabbi Ben Ezra" (30), *Dramatis Personae,* 1864

There'll be bluebirds over the white cliffs of Dover,
Tomorrow, just you wait and see.

> NAT BURTON. "The White Cliffs of Dover" (song), 1941

There must be another way, if only because there has to be.

> HERB CAEN (1916–1997). On the prospects for peace, column, *San Francisco Chronicle,* 24 May 1981

Thou hast seen nothing yet.

> CERVANTES (1547–1616). *Don Quixote,* 1.3.11, 1615, tr. Peter Anthony Motteux and John Ozell, 1743

The opera ain't over till the fat lady sings.

> DAN COOK. San Antonio sports broadcaster and writer. Television news broadcast, April 1978

Every day, in every way, I'm getting better and better.

> ÉMILE COUÉ (1857–1926). Faith-cure formula inscribed in his sanitarium, Nancy (France)

Something will turn up.

> BENJAMIN DISARELI (1804–1881). *Popanilla,* 7, 1827. This was the favorite saying of the Micawber character in Charles Dickens's *David Copperfield* (1850).

You ain't seen nothin' yet.

> JIMMY DURANTE (1893–1980). Entertainer. His signature line

Grab your coat, and get your hat,
Leave your worry on the doorstep,

Just direct your feet
To the sunny side of the street.

> DOROTHY FIELDS. "On the Sunny Side of the Street" (song), 1930

Take one thing with another, and the world is a pretty good sort of a world, and it is our duty to make the best of it, and be thankful.

> BENJAMIN FRANKLIN (1706–1790). Letter to Mrs. Jane Mecom, 1 March 1766

It is always darkest just before the day dawneth.

> THOMAS FULLER (1608–1661). *A Pisgah-Sight of Palestine,* 2.2, 1650 (Popular version: It's always darkest just before the dawn.)
>
> See Pessimism—Examples: Alex Clark

Impossible things are simply those which so far have never been done.

> ELBERT HUBBARD (1856–1915). In Alice Hubbard, comp., *An American Bible,* p. 173, 1946

You ain't heard nothin' yet.

> AL JOLSON (1886–1950). His signature line. In *The Jazz Singer* (the first talking film), 1927. Jolson may have used the line as early as 1906.

I've got to admit it's getting better
It's a little better all the time.

> JOHN LENNON (1940–1980) and PAUL McCARTNEY (1942–). "Getting Better" (song), 1967

The nearer the dawn the darker the night,
And by going wrong all things come right;
Things have been mended that were worse,
And the worse, the nearer they are to mend.

> HENRY WADSWORTH LONGFELLOW (1807–1882). "The Baron of St. Castine" (l.265), *Tales of a Wayside Inn,* 1863

Tomorrow, I'll think of some way to get him back. After all, tomorrow is another day.

> MARGARET MITCHELL (1900–1949). Closing words, *Gone with the Wind,* 1936

Throughout the world, there is a faint glow of color on the topmost twigs, the glow of the swelling buds that announce, despite the frosts and storms to come, the approach of spring: signs of life, signs of integration, signs of a deeper faith for living and of an approaching general renewal of humanity.

> LEWIS MUMFORD (1895–1990). *The Conduct of Life,* 9.10, 1951

There's a good time coming.

> SIR WALTER SCOTT (1771–1832). *Rob Roy,* 32, 1817

"Everything's Coming Up Roses."

> STEPHEN SONDHEIM (1930–). Song title. In the musical *Gypsy,* 1959

The road before us is shorter than the road behind.

> LUCY STONE (1818–1893). In Susan B. Anthony and Ida Husted Harper, *History of Woman Suffrage,* 4.13, 1902

Sometimes things can go right only by first going very wrong.

> EDWARD TENNER. *Why Things Bite Back: Technology and the Revenge of Unintended Consequences,* 1996. In George F. Will, "A New Level of Worrying," *Newsweek,* 22 July 1996

The lights begin to twinkle from the rocks;
The long day wanes; the slow moon climbs; the deep
Moans round with many voices. Come, my friends.
'Tis not too late to seek a newer world.

> ALFRED, LORD TENNYSON (1809–1892). "Ulysses," l. 54, 1842

I look . . . not into the night, but to a dawn for which no man ever rose early enough.

> HENRY DAVID THOREAU (1817–1862). January 1853. In Ralph Waldo Emerson, journal, 1862, undated

The difficult we do immediately. The impossible takes a little longer.

> U.S. ARMY CORPS OF ENGINEERS. Motto, World War I

Dr. Pangloss: All events are linked up in this the best of all possible worlds.

> VOLTAIRE (1694–1778). *Candide,* 30, 1759, tr. Richard Aldington, 1929

The strongest and sweetest songs yet remain to be sung.

> WALT WHITMAN (1819–1892). Closing line (of the last revision), *Leaves of Grass,* 1855–1892

So always look for the silver lining
And try to find the sunny side of life.

> P. G. WODEHOUSE (1881–1975). "Look for the Silver Lining," *Sally,* 1929

Happy days are here again,
The skies above are clear again.
Let us sing a song of cheer again,
Happy days are here again!

> JACK YELLEN. "Happy Days Are Here Again" (song). In the musical *Chasing Rainbows,* 1929

❧

After sorrow comes joy.

> SAYING (ARAB)

After darkness comes light.

> SAYING
> See Rain: James Howell

The best is yet to come.

> SAYING

OPTIMISM & PESSIMISM

See also • Despair ○ History: Anonymous ○ Hope ○ Optimism ○ Pessimism ○ Tradition: Lewis Mumford

The pessimist is the man who believes things couldn't possibly be worse, to which the optimist replies, "Oh yes they could."

> VLADIMIR BUKOVSKY. In *Manchester Guardian Weekly* (British newspaper), 10 July 1977

The optimist proclaims we live in the best of all possible worlds; and the pessimist fears this is true.

> JAMES BRANCH CABELL (1879–1958). *The Silver Stallion,* 4.26, 1926

The optimist sees the rose and not its thorns, the pessimist stares at the thorns, oblivious of the rose.

> KAHLIL GIBRAN (1883–1931). "Sayings," *Spiritual Sayings of Kahlil Gibran,* tr. Anthony R. Ferris, 1962

I am neither an optimist nor pessimist, but a possibilist.

> MAX LERNER (1902–1992). Entry, *Who's Who in America,* 1992

I'm a pessimist about probabilities; I'm an optimist about possibilities.

> LEWIS MUMFORD (1895–1990). In Carey Winfrey, "Lewis Mumford Remembers," *New York Times,* 6 July 1977

Optimism assumes, or attempts to prove, that the universe exists to please us, and pessimism that it exists to displease us. Scientifically, there is no evidence that it is concerned with us either one way or the other. The belief in either pessimism or optimism is a matter of temperament, not of reason.

> BERTRAND RUSSELL (1872–1970). *A History of Western Philosophy,* 3.2.24, 1946

My knowledge is pessimistic, but my willing and hoping are optimistic.

> ALBERT SCHWEITZER (1875–1965). *Out of My Life and Thought: An Autobiography,* 21, tr. C. T. Campion, 1933

There is no sadder sight than a young pessimist, except an old optimist.

> MARK TWAIN (1835–1910). 22 December 1903, *Mark Twain's Notebook,* ed. Albert Bigelow Paine, 1935

The pessimist complains about the wind; the optimist expects it to change; the realist adjust the sails.

> WILLIAM ARTHUR WARD (1921–). In "Quotable Quotes," *Reader's Digest,* June 1989

❧

An optimist sees an opportunity in every calamity; a pessimist sees a calamity in every opportunity.

> ANONYMOUS

A pessimist thinks there's nothing so bad it can't get worse; and optimist thinks there's nothing so good it can't get better.

> ANONYMOUS

A stumbling block to the pessimist is a stepping stone to the optimist.

> ANONYMOUS

The optimist's cup is half full; the pessimist's cup is half empty.

> SAYING (OREGON)

ORATORY

See also • Disability: Plutarch ○ Eloquence ○ Public Speaking ○ Speaking ○ Talking

Love, knavery, and necessity make men good orators.

> HENRY G. BOHN (1796–1884)

Read aloud, though alone, and read articulately and distinctly, as if you were reading in public and on the most important occasion.

. . . Never speak quick[ly], till you have first learned to speak well.

> LORD CHESTERFIELD (1694–1773). On developing one's oratorical skills, letter to his son, 9 July 1750

I am not an orator. An orator is spontaneous. The written word—ah, that's different.

> WINSTON CHURCHILL (1874–1965). Remark to the diarist, 9 July 1953. In Lord Moran, *Churchill: Taken from the Diaries of Lord Moran,* 40, 1966

He is the best orator who . . . teaches and delights, and moves the minds of his hearers.

> CICERO (106–43 B.C.). "Treatise on the Best Style of Orators," 1, tr. C. D. Yonge, 1903

The orator masters us by being our tongue.

> RALPH WALDO EMERSON (1803–1882). "Genius," lecture, Masonic Temple, Boston, 9 January 1839

What is said is the least part of the oration.

> RALPH WALDO EMERSON (1803–1882). "Eloquence," *Letters and Social Aims,* 1876

Here comes the Orator! with his Flood of Words, and his Drop of Reason.

> BENJAMIN FRANKLIN (1706–1790). *Poor Richard's Almanack,* October 1735
>
> See Talking: La Rochefoucauld

The orator gives back to his audience in rain what he gets from them in mist.

> WILLIAM EWART GLADSTONE (1809–1898). Attributed. In Eugene C. Gerhart, *America's Advocate: Robert H. Jackson,* 24, 1958

To make the great little, and the little great was the orator's part.

> ISOCRATES (436–338 B.C.). In Ralph Waldo Emerson, journal, 1845, undated

Oratory is the power of beating down your adversary's arguments, and putting better in their place.

> SAMUEL JOHNSON (1709–1784). 8 May 1781. In James Boswell, *The Life of Samuel Johnson,* 1791

All his [oratorical] efforts were made for practical effect. He never spoke merely to be heard.

> ABRAHAM LINCOLN (1809–1865). Henry Clay eulogy, Springfield (Illinois), 6 July 1852

The object of oratory alone is not truth, but persuasion.

> THOMAS BABINGTON MACAULAY (1800–1859). "The Athenian Orators," *Knight's Quarterly Magazine,* August 1824

What orators lack in depth they make up in length.

> MONTESQUIEU (1689–1755). *Lettres persanes.* 1721

Where Judgment has Wit to express it, there's the best Orator.

> WILLIAM PENN (1644–1718). *Some Fruits of Solitude,* 173, 1693

[Polyeuctus] was wont to say that Demosthenes was the greatest orator, but Phocion [Athenian orator, 402?–318 B.C.] the ablest, as he expressed the most sense in the fewest words. And, indeed, it is related that Demosthenes himself, as often as Phocion stood up to plead against him, would say to his acquaintance, "Here comes the knife to my speech."

> PLUTARCH (A.D. 46?–119?). "Demosthenes" (384–322 B.C.), *Parallel Lives,* Dryden edition, 1693
>
> See Talking: La Rochefoucauld

Considering oratory to be, not the creator of persuasion but certainly its co-worker, we should correct Menander's line, "The speaker's nature, not his speech, persuades," for both his nature and his speech do.

> PLUTARCH (A.D. 46?–119?). "Precepts of Statecraft" (5), *Moralia,* vol. 10, tr. W. C. Helmbold, 1936

An orator's life is more convincing than his eloquence.

> PUBLIUS SYRUS (85–43 B.C.). *Moral Sayings,* 507, tr. Darius Lyman, Jr., 1862

All that is produced when imagination is not guided by judgment . . . may be characterized as affected, a fault which is the worst of all faults in oratory.

> QUINTILIAN (A.D. 35?–100?). *Institutio oratoria,* 8.3.56, tr. John Selby Watson, 1856

Antony: I come not, friends, to steal away your hearts:
I am no orator, as Brutus is;
But, as you know me all, a plain blunt man,
That love my friend. . . .
For I have neither wit, nor words, nor worth,
Action, nor utterance, nor the power of speech,
To stir men's blood: I only speak right on;
I tell you that which you yourselves do know.

> SHAKESPEARE (1564–1616). *Julius Caesar,* 3.2.220, 1599

The settled lecturers are as tame as the settled ministers. The audiences do not want to hear any prophets. . . . They ask for orators that will entertain them and leave them where they found them.

> HENRY DAVID THOREAU (1817–1862). Journal, 16 November 1858

❧

The best orator is one who can make men see with their ears.

> SAYING (ARAB)

ORGANIZATIONS

See also • Bureaucracy ○ Business (Commerce) ○ Committees ○ Corporations ○ Experts ○ Government ○ Institutions ○ Leaders ○ Managers ○ Meetings

Failing organizations are usually over-managed and under-led.

> WARREN BENNIS (1925–). Talk, University of Maryland symposium, 21 January 1988

All organizations depend on the existence of shared meanings and interpretations of reality, which facilitate coordinated action.

> WARREN BENNIS (1925–) and BURT NANUS (1936–). "Leading Others, Managing Yourself," *Leaders: The Strategies for Taking Charge,* 1985

Organization is a means of multiplying the strength of an individual.

> PETER F. DRUCKER (1909–). *The Effective Executive,* 1.3.3, 1967

The test of organization is not genius. It is its capacity to make common people achieve uncommon performance.

PETER F. DRUCKER (1909–). *The Effective Executive,* 4.1.1, 1967

In every area of effectiveness within an organization, one feeds the opportunities and starves the problems.

PETER F. DRUCKER (1909–). *The Effective Executive,* 4.3, 1967

Decentralization [should] balance local autonomy in operations with central control of direction and policy.

PETER F. DRUCKER (1909–). *The Effective Executive,* 6.1, 1967

A basic rule of organization is to build the fewest *possible* management levels and forge the shortest possible chain of command.

PETER F. DRUCKER (1909–). *Management: Tasks, Responsibilities, Practices,* 34, 1974, abr., 1977

The counterpart of specialization is always organization—organization is what brings specialists, who as individuals are technically incomplete and largely useless, into a working relationship with other specialists for a complete and useful result.

JOHN KENNETH GALBRAITH (1908–). *Economics and the Public Purpose,* 9.1, 1973

In any great organization it is far, far safer to be wrong with the majority than to be right alone.

JOHN KENNETH GALBRAITH (1908–). In *Guardian* (British newspaper), 28 July 1989

The culture of organization runs strongly to the shifting of problems to others—to an escape from personal mental effort and responsibility. This, in turn, becomes the larger public attitude. It is for others to do the worrying, take the action. In the world of the great organization, problems are not solved but passed on.

And there is a further effect. The delegation process just cited adds ineluctably to the layers of command and to the prestige associated with command. That prestige is regularly measured by the number of the individual's subordinates.

JOHN KENNETH GALBRAITH (1908–). *The Culture of Contentment,* 6, 1992

There is probably no substitute for creating a culture—a set of attitudes, customs and habits throughout the organization—that favors easy two-way communication, in and out of channels, among all layers of the organization. Two key messages should be implicit in such a culture: (1) "You will know what's going on," and (2) "Your voice will be heard."

JOHN W. GARDNER (1912–). *On Leadership,* 8, 1990

Our admiration for great organizations dwindles when once we become aware of the other side of the wonder: the tremendous piling up and accentuation of all that is primitive in man, and the unavoidable destruction of his individuality in the interests of the monstrosity that every great organization in fact is. The man of today, who resembles more or less the collective ideal, has made his heart into a den of murderers . . . even though he himself is not in the least disturbed by it.

CARL G. JUNG (1875–1961). "The Relations between the Ego and the Unconscious" (1.2), 1928, *Two Essays on Analytical Psychology,* R. F. C. Hull, 1953

In the hierarchy each is dependent upon a superior and is in turn superior to some class of his dependents. What holds the machine together is a system of privileges. These may vary according to the opportunities and tastes of those who seek them, from nepotism and patronage in all their aspects to clannishness, hero-worship or a fixed idea.

WALTER LIPPMANN (1889–1974). *Public Opinion,* 14.3, 1922

In general, the more sophisticated the organization, the greater is its efficiency—but also it vulnerability.

EDWARD N. LUTTWAK (1942–). *Coup d'État: A Practical Handbook,* 3, 1968

Organization implies the tendency to oligarchy. . . . As a result of organization, every party or professional union becomes divided into a minority of directors and a majority of directed.

ROBERT MICHELS (1876–1936). "The Iron Law of Oligarchy," *Political Parties,* 1925, tr. Eden and Cedar Paul, 1962. Elsewhere in the same book, Michels wrote pithily, "Who says organization, says oligarchy."

Most people bring three kinds of needs to their organizational existence: a need to be rewarded [tangibly] for what they achieve, a need to be accepted as a unique person, and a need to be appreciated not only for the function performed but also as a human being.

RICHARD TANNER PASCALE (1938–). "Zen and the Art of Management." In *Classic Advice on Handling the Manager's Job (Harvard Business Review on Human Relations,* vol. 3), 1986

An organization is a set of people who are combined [by] virtue of activities directed to common ends.

BERTRAND RUSSELL (1872–1970). *Power: A New Social Analysis,* 11, 1938

Competition for power is of two sorts: between organizations, and between individuals for leadership within an organization.

BERTRAND RUSSELL (1872–1970). *Power: A New Social Analysis,* 11, 1938

Every organization will, in the absence of any counteracting force, tend to grow both in size and in density of power.

BERTRAND RUSSELL (1872–1970). *Power: A New Social Analysis,* 11, 1938

Organizations are of two kinds: those which aim at getting something done and those which aim at preventing something from being done.

BERTRAND RUSSELL (1872–1970). *The Impact of Science on Society,* 2, 1951

Any organization has to strive continuously for the orderliness of *order* and the disorderliness of creative *freedom.* And the specific danger inherent in large-scale organization is that its natural bias and tendency favor order, at the expense of creative freedom.

E. F. SCHUMACHER (1911–1977). *Small Is Beautiful: Economics as if People Mattered,* 4.2, 1973

[Organization] is a tool that permits groups of human beings to aim at and . . . achieve goals that would be far beyond the reach of their powers as individuals.

HERBERT A. SIMON (1916–). "Recent Advances in Organization Theory," in *Research Frontiers in Politics and Government* (Brookings Lectures), 1955

Organizations that continue to depend on a one-size-fits-all approach to personnel, whether in sports or business, tend to lose their top performers to competitors with a more individualistic outlook.

> BILL WALSH (1931–). Football coach. "How to Manage Superstars," *Forbes ASAP,* 7 June 1993

This book is about the organization man. . . . They are not the workers, nor are they the white-collar people in the usual, clerk sense of the word. These people only work for The Organization. The ones I am talking about belong to it as well. They are the ones of our middle class who have left home, spiritually as well as physically, to take the vows of organization life, and it is they who are the mind and soul of our great self-perpetuating institutions.

> WILLIAM H. WHYTE, JR. (1917–). Opening words, *The Organization Man,* 1956

❧

Organization is policy.

> ANONYMOUS. In Emmet John Hughes, *The Living Presidency: The Resources and Dilemmas of the American Presidential Office,* 5.3, 1972
>
> See Presidents & Staff: Becky Norton Dunlop

ORIGINALITY

See also • Creativity ○ Crisis Leaders: Jacob Burckhardt ○ Discovery ○ Ideas ○ Imagination ○ Imitation ○ Inspiration ○ Intuition ○ Invention ○ Plagiarism ○ Revelation ○ Spirituality ○ Writers: Chateaubriand

The will to originality is not the will to be peculiar and unlike anybody else; it means the desire to derive one's consciousness from its primary source.

> NICOLAS BERDYAEV (1874–1948). *The Destiny of Man,* 2.4.2, 1931, tr. Natalie Duddington, 1955

Originality is something that is easily exaggerated, especially by authors contemplating their own work.

> JOHN KENNETH GALBRAITH (1908–). *The Affluent Society,* 1.3, 1958

Originality usually amounts only to plagiarizing something unfamiliar.

> KATHERINE FULLERTON GEROULD (1879–1944). *Modes and Morals,* 7, 1920

People are always talking about originality; but what do they mean? As soon as we are born, the world begins to work upon us, and this goes on to the end. What can we call our own except energy, strength, and will? If I could give an account of all that I owe to great predecessors and contemporaries, there would be but a small balance in my favor.

> GOETHE (1749–1832). 12 May 1825. In Peter Eckermann, *Conversations with Goethe,* 1836–1848, tr. John Oxenford, 1850

In exploring new and doubtful tracts of speculation, the mind strikes out true and original views; as a drop of water hesitates at first what direction it will take, but afterwards follows its own course.

> WILLIAM HAZLITT (1788–1830). "On Novelty and Familiarity," *Table Talk,* 1822

The original insight is most likely to come when elements stored in different compartments of the mind drift into the open, jostle one another, and now and then form new combinations. . . . [Of course] the working out of ideas and insights requires persistent hard thinking.

> ERIC HOFFER (1902–1983). *The Ordeal of Change,* 14, 1964

What is originality? Undetected plagiarism.

> DEAN WILLIAM RALPH INGE (1860–1954).

Originality is the one thing which unoriginal minds cannot feel the use of. . . . They are more in need of originality, the less they are conscious of the want.

> JOHN STUART MILL (1806–1873). *On Liberty,* 3, 1859

Originality is the fine art of remembering what you hear but forgetting where you heard it.

> LAURENCE J. PETER (1919–1990). 15 September, *Peter's Almanac,* 1982

We should imitate the great classics. We would miss, and that miss would be our originality.

> RAYMOND RADIGUET (1903–1923). French poet. Quoted by Jean Cocteau, William Fifield interview. In George Plimpton, ed., *Writers at Work: Third Series,* 1967

Originality consists not only in doing things differently, but also in "doing things better."

> EDWARD C. STEDMAN (1833–1908). *Victorian Poets,* 9, 1875

Originality implies being bold enough to go beyond accepted norms.

> ANTHONY STORR (1920–). *Solitude: A Return to the Self,* 6, 1988

ORTHODOXY

See also • Creed ○ Doctrine ○ Dogma ○ Ideas ○ Ideology ○ System ○ Theories

The difference between Orthodoxy or My-doxy and Heterodoxy or Thy-doxy.

> THOMAS CARLYLE (1795–1881). *The French Revolution,* 2.4.2, 1837

Orthodoxy: A corpse that does not know it is dead.

> ELBERT HUBBARD (1856–1915). *The Roycroft Dictionary Concocted by Ali Baba and the Bunch on Rainy Days,* p. 109, 1914

Orthodoxy means not thinking—not needing to think. Orthodoxy is unconsciousness.

> GEORGE ORWELL (1903–1950). *Nineteen Eighty-Four,* 1.5, 1949

Orthodoxy is my doxy; heterodoxy is another man's doxy.

> WILLIAM WARBURTON (1698–1779). English prelate

Indifference and hypocrisy between them keep orthodoxy alive.

> ISRAEL ZANGWILL (1864–1926). *Children of the Ghetto,* 1892

❧

PACIFISM

See also • Nonviolence ○ Peace ○ War & Peace

I'm not a pacifist. I'm not that brave.

> PHIL DONAHUE (1935–). Television interview, 31 May 1988

A pacifism which can see the cruelties only of occasional military warfare and is blind to the continuous cruelties of our social system is worthless.

> MOHANDAS K. GANDHI (1869–1948). In *Young India,* 18 November 1926

Pacifism is simply undisguised cowardice.

> ADOLF HITLER (1889–1945). Speech, Nuremberg (Germany), 21 August 1926

True pacifism is not nonresistance to evil, but nonviolent resistance to evil.

> MARTIN LUTHER KING, JR. (1929–1968). *Stride Toward Freedom,* 6, 1958

A truly pacifist people would quickly disappear from history.

> GUSTAVE LE BON (1841–1931). *Aphorisms of Present Times,* 4.4, 1913, tr. Alice Widener, 1979

A pacifist is as surely a traitor to his country and to humanity as is the most brutal wrongdoer.

> THEODORE ROOSEVELT (1858–1919). Speech, Pittsburgh, 27 July 1917

Pacifism means letting the nonpacifists have control.

> OSWALD SPENGLER (1880–1936). *Aphorisms,* 367, tr. Gisela Koch-Weser O'Brien, 1967

PAIN

See also • Burdens ○ Compassion ○ Despair ○ Desperation ○ Difficulty ○ Grief ○ Martyrdom ○ Misery ○ Struggle ○ Suffering ○ Unhappiness ○ Wounds ○ Wretchedness

Pain was not given thee merely to be miserable under; learn from it, turn it to account.

> THOMAS CARLYLE (1795–1881). Journal, 8 September 1834. In James Anthony Froude, *Thomas Carlyle: A History of the First Forty Years, 1795–1835,* 2.18, 1882

Pain is part of the body's magic. It is the way the body transmits a sign to the brain that something is wrong.

> NORMAN COUSINS (1912–1990). 1977. "Editor's Odyssey: Gleanings from Articles and Editorials by N.C.," ed. Susan Schiefelbein, *Saturday Review,* 15 April 1978

No gains without pains.

> BENJAMIN FRANKLIN (1706–1790). *Poor Richard's Almanack,* April 1745

I will say nothing against the course of my existence. But at bottom it has been nothing but pain and burden, and I can affirm that during the whole of my 75 years, I have not had four weeks of genuine well-being. It is but the perpetual rolling of a rock that must be raised up again forever.

> GOETHE (1749–1832). 1824. In William James, *The Varieties of Religious Experience: A Study in Human Nature,* 6 and 7, 1902

In the face of pain there are no heroes.

> GEORGE ORWELL (1903–1950). *Nineteen Eighty-Four,* 3.1, 1949
> See Suffering: Victor Hugo

No pain, no balm; no thorns, no throne; no gall, no glory; no cross, no crown.

> WILLIAM PENN (1644–1718). *No Cross, No Crown* (pamphlet), 1669

Pain will force even the truthful to speak falsely.

> PUBLIUS SYRUS (85–43 B.C.). *Moral Sayings,* 232, tr. Darius Lyman, Jr., 1862

The Fellowship of those who bear the Mark of Pain. Who are the members of the Fellowship? Those who have learned by experience what physical pain and bodily anguish mean belong together the world over; they are united by a secret bond.

> ALBERT SCHWEITZER (1875–1965). *On the Edge of the Primeval Forest: The Experiences and Observations of a Doctor in Equatorial Africa,* 11, 1922, tr. C. T. Campion, 1928

He who has been delivered from pain must not think he is now free again, and at liberty to take life up just as it was before, entirely forgetful of the past. He is now a "man whose eyes are open" with regard to pain and anguish, and he must help to overcome those two enemies (so far as human power can overcome them) and to bring the others the deliverance which he has himself enjoyed.

> ALBERT SCHWEITZER (1875–1965). *On the Edge of the Primeval Forest: The Experiences and Observations of a Doctor in Equatorial Africa,* 11, 1922, tr. C. T. Campion, 1928

We should all take our share of the burden of pain which lies upon the world.

> ALBERT SCHWEITZER (1875–1965). *Out of My Life and Thought: An Autobiography,* 21, tr. C. T. Campion, 1933

To a person with a toothache, even if the world is tottering, there is nothing more important than a visit to a dentist.

> GEORGE BERNARD SHAW (1856–1950). Remark to the author, 1940s. In Stephen Winsten, *Days with Bernard Shaw,* 17, 1949

If you are visited by pain, examine your conduct.

> TALMUD (A.D. 1st–6th cent.). Rabbinical writings

Pain is forgetting my purpose.

> MATHIAS YROGOYIN. Personal communication, 1971

PAINTING

See also • Art ○ Creativity: First Person: Paul Klee, Henri Matisse

Every artist dips his brush in his own soul and paints his own nature into his pictures.

> HENRY WARD BEECHER (1813–1887). "Miscellaneous," *Proverbs from Plymouth Pulpit,* ed. William Drysdale, 1887

A great portrait is always more a portrait of the painter than of the painted.

> SAMUEL BUTLER (1835–1902). *The Note-Books of Samuel Butler,* 7, ed. Henry Festing Jones, 1907

If an [art] student is to do any good, his development will epitomize the history of painting.

> SAMUEL BUTLER (1835–1902). *Further Extracts from the Note-Books of Samuel Butler*, 1, ed. A. T. Bartholomew, 1934

The best picture makes us say, I am a painter also.

> RALPH WALDO EMERSON (1803–1882). "Education," lecture, Masonic Temple, Boston, 5 February 1840

The painters of old painted the idea and not merely the shape.

> HSIEH HO (A.D. 5th cent.). In Ananda K. Coomaraswamy, *The Transformation of Nature in Art*, p. 15, 1934

The painter will produce pictures of little merit if he takes the works of others as his standard.

> LEONARDO da VINCI (1452–1519). *Note-books*, 3, tr. Edward McCurdy, 1908

I presume, sir, in painting your beautiful portrait, you took your idea of me from my principles, and not from my person.

> ABRAHAM LINCOLN (1809–1865). Remark ("in a merry voice") to an unnamed artist who apparently had painted his portrait from a photograph, White House, 1864. In F. B. Carpenter, *Six Months at the White House with Abraham Lincoln*, 51, 1866

I have always tried to hide my efforts and wished my works to have the light joyousness of springtime which never lets anyone suspect the labors it has cost.

> HENRI MATISSE (1869–1954). In Theodore F. Wolff, "The Drawings of Henri Matisse," *Christian Science Monitor*, 25 March 1985

When art seems to be empty of meaning, as no doubt some of the abstract painting of our own day actually does seem, what the painting says, indeed what the artist is shrieking at the top of his voice, is that life has become empty of all rational content and coherence. and that, in times like these, is far from a meaningless statement.

> LEWIS MUMFORD (1895–1990). "Art and the Symbol," *Art and Technics*, 1952

I paint things as I think of them, not as I see them.

> PABLO PICASSO (1881–1973). "Picasso Speaks," *Arts Magazine*, May 1923

The people no longer seek consolation in art. But the refined people, the rich, the idlers seek the new, the extraordinary, the extravagant, the scandalous. I have contented these people with all the many bizarre things that come into my head. And the less they understand, the more they admire it. By amusing myself with all these games, all this nonsense, all these picture puzzles, I became famous. . . . I am only a public entertainer who has understood his time. [Ellipsis points in original.]

> PABLO PICASSO (1881–1973). In a Paris quarterly. Quoted in "Personality Parade," *Parade Magazine*, 3 January 1965

Some painters transform the sun into a yellow spot, others transform a yellow spot into the sun.

> PABLO PICASSO (1881–1973). In Roger von Oech, "The Artist," *A Kick in the Seat of the Pants*, 1986

I cannot convince myself that a painting is good unless it is popular. If the public dislikes one of my [*Saturday Evening*] *Post* covers, I can't help disliking it myself.

> NORMAN ROCKWELL (1894–1978). Illustrator. In Arthur C. Danto, "Freckles for the Ages," *New York Times*, 28 September 1986

Painting is silent poetry, and poetry painting that speaks.

> SIMONIDES (556–468 B.C.). In Plutarch (A.D. 46?–119?). *De Gloria Atheniensium*, 3.346

Imagination without skill gives us modern art.

> TOM STOPPARD (1937–). *Artist Descending a Staircase*, 1972

If you want to know all about Andy Warhol, just look at the surface: of my paintings and films and me, and there I am. There's nothing behind it.

> ANDY WARHOL (1927–1987). 1967, "Warhol in His Own Words," ed. Neil Printz. In Kynaston McShine, *Andy Warhol: A Retrospective*, 1986

PARADOXES

See also • Beginnings & Endings: T. S. Eliot (all) ○ Change & Changelessness: Benjamin Disraeli, Heraclitus ○ Compensation ○ Courage: G. K. Chesterton ○ Dreams: Erich Fromm, J. A. Hadfield ○ Environment: Norbert Wiener ○ Ethics: Nicolas Berdyaev (2) ○ Freedom: Anonymous (4) ○ Haste: Francis Bacon ○ Idleness: Saying ○ Knowledge: *Upanishads* ○ Loneliness: Alvin Toffler ○ Love, Romantic: Erich Fromm ○ Nature: Ralph Waldo Emerson (4), Goethe (2) ○ Opposites ○ Price: C. C. Colton ○ Speed: Elbert Hubbard ○ Spirit: Carl G. Jung ○ Spirituality ○ Truth: Henry David Thoreau (1), Anonymous (3) ○ Universe: Dionysius the Areopagite ○ Will, Free: Carl G. Jung, Isaac Bashevis Singer, Howard Zinn ○ Wisdom: Alexander Pope (2)

To speak of the impotence of power is no longer a witty paradox.

> HANNAH ARENDT (1906–1975). *On Violence*, 3, 1970

There is nothing that fails like success.

> G. K. CHESTERTON (1874–1936). *Heretics*, 1, 1905
> See Success: Alexandre Dumas ○ Success: Benjamin Franklin

Heaven and earth do nothing
Yet there is nothing they do not do.

> CHUANG-TZU (369–286 B.C.). As interpreted by Thomas Merton, "Perfect Joy," *The Way of Chuang Tzu*, 1965

[The British Government goes] on in strange paradox, decided only to be undecided, resolved to be irresolute, adamant for drift, solid for fluidity, all-powerful to be impotent.

> WINSTON CHURCHILL (1874–1965). In *Hansard* (British Government publication), 12 November 1936

To be absolutely nothing is to be everything.

> JAMES W. DOUGLASS (1937–). "The Yin-Yang of Resistance and Contemplation," *Resistance and Contemplation: The Way of Liberation*, 1972

You can sink so fast that you think you're flying.

> MARIE von EBNER-ESCHENBACH (1830–1916). *Aphorisms*, p. 31, 1880–1905, tr. David Scrase and Wolfgang Mieder, 1994

At the still point of the turning world. Neither flesh nor
fleshless;
Neither from nor towards; at the still point, there the dance is,
But neither arrest nor movement.

> T. S. ELIOT (1888–1965). "Burnt Norton" (2), *Four Quartets*, 1943

All cases are unique, and very similar to others.

> T. S. ELIOT (1888–1965). *The Cocktail Party*, 2, 1950

God hides things by putting them near us.

> RALPH WALDO EMERSON (1803–1882). "Encyclopedia," p. 138,
> 1824–1836

The current of inward life . . . increases as it is spent.

> RALPH WALDO EMERSON (1803–1882). "The Method of Nature," address,
> Waterville College (Maine), 11 August 1841

Extremes meet: there is no straight line.

> RALPH WALDO EMERSON (1803–1882). Journal, 18 May 1843

We are made of contradictions—our *freedom* is *necessary*.

> RALPH WALDO EMERSON (1803–1882). Journal, 1845, undated

We sink to rise.

> RALPH WALDO EMERSON (1803–1882). "Poetry and Imagination," *Letters
> and Social Aims*, 1876

I'm so busy I don't have time to do anything.

> JOHN FRIEDBERG (1942–). Personal communication, 17 March 1997

Almost anything you do will be insignificant, but it is very important that you do it.

> MOHANDAS K. GANDHI (1869–1948). Attributed? 13 December. In Esther
> Armstrong and Dale Stitt, comps., *Thoughts for the Journey*, 1996

Deep down, I'm pretty superficial.

> AVA GARDNER (1922–1990). In Roland Flamini, *Ava: A Biography*, 8, 1983

It was complete impoverishment that I coveted as the truest possession.

> ANDRÉ GIDE (1869–1951). Journal, 1923 (detached page), tr. Justin
> O'Brien, 1948

All that is outside also is inside.

> GOETHE (1749–1832). In Carl G. Jung, "Psychological Aspects of the
> Mother Archetype," 5, 1938, *The Archetypes and the Collective
> Unconscious*, tr. R. F. C. Hull, 1959

The method of no-method.

> EUGEN HERRIGEL (1885–1955). "Higher Stages of Meditation," *The
> Method of Zen*, 1960, ed. Hermann Tausend and tr. R. F. C. Hull, 1964

My lowliness is my loftiness, my loftiness my lowliness.

> HILLEL (1st cent. B.C.). In *Talmud* (A.D. 1st–6th cent.). Rabbinical
> writings

The furthest way about is the nearest way home.

> JAMES HOWELL (1593–1666). Comp., "English" (p. 18), *Paroimiographia:
> Proverbs, or Old Sayed Sawes & Adages in English . . . Italian, French
> and Spanish*, 1659

We are confronted by the great paradox of human life. It is our
conditioning which develops our consciousness; but in order to
make full use of this developed consciousness, we must start by
getting rid of the conditioning which developed it.

> ALDOUS HUXLEY (1894–1963). "Knowledge and Understanding,"
> *Tomorrow and Tomorrow and Tomorrow and Other Essays*, 1956

There is a Law of Reversed Effort. The harder we try with the conscious will to do something, the less we shall succeed. Proficiency
and the results of proficiency come only to those who have
learned the paradoxical art of doing and not doing, or combining
relaxation with activity, of letting go as a person in order that the
immanent and transcendent Unknown Quantity may take hold.
We cannot make ourselves understand; the most we can do is to
foster a state of mind, in which understanding may come to us.

> ALDOUS HUXLEY (1894–1963). "Knowledge and Understanding,"
> *Tomorrow and Tomorrow and Tomorrow and Other Essays*, 1956

His delight shall be in the fear of the Lord.

> ISAIAH (8th cent. B.C.). *Isaiah* 11:3

A shortcut is the longest distance between two points.

> CHARLES ISSAWI. "Issawi's Laws of Social Motion," *Columbia Forum*,
> Summer 1970

He who finds his life will lose it, and he who loses his life for my
sake will find it.

> JESUS (A.D. 1st cent.). *Matthew* 10:39

My power is made perfect in weakness.

> JESUS (A.D. 1st cent.). In Paul, *2 Corinthians* 12:9

The inner voice is at once our greatest danger and an indispensable help.

> CARL G. JUNG (1875–1961). Title essay, 1934. *The Development of
> Personality*, tr. R. F. C. Hull, 1954

No judgment can be considered to be final in which its reversibil-
ity has not been taken into account.

> CARL G. JUNG (1875–1961). "Approaching the Unconscious:
> The Problem of Types." In Jung, ed., *Man and His Symbols*, 1964

The softest of stuff in the world
Penetrates quickly the hardest;
Insubstantial, it enters
Where no room is.

> LAO-TZU (6th cent. B.C.). *The Way of Life*, 43, tr. R. B. Blakney, 1955

There seems no plan because it is all plan;
there seems no center because it is all center.

> C. S. LEWIS (1898–1963)

Captain Peleg: He's a queer man, Captain Ahab—so some think—
but a good one. Oh, thou'lt like him well enough; no fear, no fear.
He's a grand, ungodly, god-like man.

> HERMAN MELVILLE (1819–1891). *Moby-Dick; or, The Whale*, 16, 1851,
> ed. Harold Beaver, 1972

Dark with excessive bright.

> JOHN MILTON (1608–1674). *Paradise Lost*, 3.380, 1667

Anyone who isn't confused doesn't really understand the situation.

> EDWARD R. MURROW (1908–1965). On the Vietnam War. In Walter
> Bryan, *The Improbable Irish*, 1, 1969

We are treated as impostors, and yet are true; as unknown, and yet well known; as dying, and behold we live; as punished, and yet not killed; as sorrowful, yet always rejoicing; as poor, yet making many rich; as having nothing, yet possessing everything.

> PAUL (A.D. 1st cent.). *2 Corinthians* 6:8–10

How can all things be one, and yet everything have a distinct being of its own?

> PROCLUS (A.D. 412?–485). In Ralph Cudworth, *The True Intellectual System of the Universe,* 1678

Everything is foreknown, but man is free.

> *TALMUD* (A.D. 1st–6th cent.). Rabbinical writings. In Louis I. Newman, comp., *The Talmudic Anthology,* 97, 1945

As the truest society approaches always nearer to solitude, so the most excellent speech finally falls into silence.

> HENRY DAVID THOREAU (1817–1862). Journal, December 1838
> See Silence & Speech: Ralph Waldo Emerson

He will get to the goal first who stands stillest.

> HENRY DAVID THOREAU (1817–1862). Journal, 26 June 1840

It is most remarkable that those flowers which are most emblematical of purity should grow in the mud.

> HENRY DAVID THOREAU (1817–1862). Journal, 20 June 1853

It is the greatest of all advantages to enjoy no advantage at all. I found it invariably true, the poorer I am, the richer I am.

> HENRY DAVID THOREAU (1817–1862). Journal, 5 December 1856

We're all in this together—by ourselves.

> LILY TOMLIN (1939–). In Michèle Brown and Ann O'Connor, comps., "Life," *Hammer and Tongues: The Best of Women's Wit and Humor,* 1986

When I came home I expected a surprise and there was no surprise for me, so, of course, I was surprised.

> LUDWIG WITTGENSTEIN (1889–1951). 1944?, *Culture and Value,* 1977, tr. Peter Winch, 1980

❧

Only those who can see the invisible can do the impossible.

> ANONYMOUS. In Amaro Bhikkhu, *Tudong: The Long Road North,* 2, 1984

Beyond is within.

> ANONYMOUS

We are all free to do as we must.

> ANONYMOUS

Every descent shall have an ascent.

> SAYING (PERSIAN)

PARANOIA

See also • Christianity: William Hirsch ○ Criticism: Ralph Waldo Emerson ○ Delusion ○ Distrust ○ Egomania: First Person ○ Fear ○ Mental Illness ○ Suspicion

I think you're the opposite of a paranoid. I think you go around with the insane delusion that people like you.

> WOODY ALLEN (1935–). *Deconstructing Harry* (film), 1997

A paranoid is a man who knows a little of what's going on.

> WILLIAM S. BURROUGHS (1914–1997). In *Friends* (magazine), 1970

When people get it into their heads that they are being specially favored by the Almighty, they had better as a general rule mind their p's and q's.

> SAMUEL BUTLER (1835–1902). *The Way of All Flesh,* 71, 1903

Paranoia is an illness of power.

> ELIAS CANETTI (1905–1994). "The Case of Schreber, I," *Crowds and Power,* tr. Carol Stewart, 1962

The paranoiac is the exact image of the ruler. The only difference between them lies is their position in the world. . . . One might even think the paranoiac the more impressive of the two because he is sufficient unto himself and cannot be shaken by failure. The opinion of the world is nothing to him. It is his delusion set against the whole world.

> ELIAS CANETTI (1905–1994). "The Case of Schreber, II," *Crowds and Power,* tr. Carol Stewart, 1962

Opposition may become sweet to a man, when he has christened it persecution.

> GEORGE ELIOT (1819–1880). *Janet's Repentance,* 8, 1857

The [paranoid] patient who has a primary tendency to believe himself persecuted draws from this the conclusion that he must necessarily be a very important person and therefore develops a delusion of grandeur.

> SIGMUND FREUD (1856–1939). *A General Introduction to Psychoanalysis,* 26, 1917, tr. Joan Riviere, 1952

I cannot stand the parricidal look in his eye.

> SIGMUND FREUD (1856–1939). Referring to one of his followers. In Helen Walker Puner, *Freud: His Life and His Mind,* 10, 1947

Paranoid, projective and fanatical political thinking are all truly pathological forms of thought processes, different from pathology in the conventional sense only by the fact that political thoughts are shared by a larger group of people and not restricted to one or two individuals.

> ERICH FROMM (1900–1980). *May Man Prevail? An Inquiry into the Facts and Fictions of Foreign Policy,* 1.3, 1961

I always find the fiction that I am being done in by malign influences strangely agreeable.

> JOHN KENNETH GALBRAITH (1908–). Tongue-in-cheek comment, 15 March 1961, *Ambassador's Journal: A Personal Account of the Kennedy Years,* 3, 1969

Only the Paranoid Survive: How to Exploit the Crisis Points That Challenge Every Company and Career.

> ANDREW S. GROVE (1936–). Intel Corp. chairman. Book title, 1996

There is a vital difference between the paranoid spokesman in politics and the clinical paranoiac: although they both tend to be overheated, oversuspicious, overagressive, grandiose, and apocalyptic in expression, the clinical paranoid sees the hostile and conspiratorial world in which he feels himself to be living as directed specifically *against him;* whereas the spokesman of the paranoid style finds it directed against a nation, a culture, a way of life whose fate affects not himself alone but millions of others.

RICHARD HOFSTADTER (1916–1970). Title essay (1), 1963, *The Paranoid Style in American Politics and Other Essays,* 1967

[The paranoid] plays a part so wholeheartedly that he comes to believe that he *is* the character he is impersonating.

ALDOUS HUXLEY (1896–1963). "Writers and Readers," *The Olive Tree and Other Essays,* 1936

Being slightly paranoid is like being slightly pregnant—it tends to get worse.

MOLLY IVINS (1936–). Referring to Ross Perot, Larry King radio interview, 7 October 1993

Even a paranoid can have enemies.

HENRY A. KISSINGER (1923–). In Jerrold Schecter, "His Legacy: Realism and Allure," *Time,* 24 January 1977

Nixon's favor depended on the readiness to fall in with the paranoid cult of the tough guy. The conspiracy of the press, hostility of the Establishment, the flatulence of the Georgetown set, were permanent features of Nixon's conversation, which one challenged only at the cost of exclusion from the inner circle.

HENRY A. KISSINGER (1923–). In Walter Isaacson, *Kissinger: A Biography,* 8, 1992

There are successful and unsuccessful inventors. The unsuccessful ones are called paranoiacs.

ERNST KRETSCHMER (1888–1964). *The Psychology of Men of Genius,* 2.8, tr. R. B. Cattell, 1931
See Genius: Alfred Hock

It seems very strange to me that we have this word [paranoia] which means, in effect, that someone feels that he is being persecuted when the people who are persecuting him don't think that he is. But we haven't got a word for the condition in which you are persecuting someone without realizing it, which I would have thought is as serious a condition as the other, and certainly no less common.

R. D. LAING (1927–1989). *The Facts of Life,* 11, 1976

Refusal to cooperate with the [hospital] psychiatrist, rather than being within his rights under the Fifth Amendment, may be construed as evidence of a "paranoid illness" for which [the patient] requires further psychiatric hospitalization.

RONALD LEIFER (1932–). *In the Name of Mental Health: The Social Functions of Psychiatry,* 5, 1969

It is always easier to locate an external enemy than grapple with an internal condition.

C. WRIGHT MILLS (1916–1962). 1944, *Power, Politics and People: The Collected Essays of C. Wright Mills,* 3.3.6, ed. Irving Louis Horowitz, 1963

My enemies employ more ingenuity in persecuting me than would be required for governing Europe.

ROUSSEAU (1712–1778). In J. F. Nisbet, *The Insanity of Genius,* 4, 1893

The megalomaniac differs from the narcissist by the fact that he wishes to be powerful rather than charming, and seeks to be feared rather than loved. To this type belong many lunatics and most of the great men in history.

BERTRAND RUSSELL (1872–1970). *The Conquest of Happiness,* 1, 1930

Men who allow their love of power to give them a distorted view of the world are to be found in every asylum: one man will think he is the Governor of the Bank of England, another will think he is the King, and yet another will think he is God. Highly similar delusions, if expressed by educated men in obscure language, lead to professorships of philosophy; and if expressed by emotional men in eloquent language, lead to dictatorships.

BERTRAND RUSSELL (1872–1970). *Power: A New Social Analysis,* 16, 1938

On one occasion a man came to ask me to recommend some of my books, as he was interested in philosophy. I did so, but he returned next day saying that he had been reading one of them, and had found only one statement he could understand, and that one seemed to him false. I asked him what it was, and he said it was the statement that Julius Caesar is dead. When I asked him why he did not agree, he drew himself up and said: "Because I am Julius Caesar."

BERTRAND RUSSELL (1872–1970). "An Outline of Intellectual Rubbish," *Unpopular Essays,* 1950

I envy paranoids; they actually feel people are paying attention to them.

SUSAN SONTAG (1933–). In *Time Out* (British magazine), 19 August 1992

Paranoia is a state of heightened awareness. Most people are persecuted beyond their wildest delusions.

CLAUDE STEINER (1935–). "Radical Psychiatry Manifesto." In The Radical Therapist Collective, ed., *The Radical Therapist,* 1971

There's something happening here,
What it is ain't exactly clear.
There's a man with a gun over there,
tellin' me I got to beware.
I think it's time we stop, children,
what's that sound?
Everybody look what's goin' down.
Paranoia strikes deep,
into your life it will creep.
It starts when you're always afraid,
Step out of line, the men come and take you away.
You better stop, hey, what's that sound?
Everybody look what's goin' down.

STEPHEN STILLS (1945–). "For What It's Worth" (song), 1966

What the psychiatrist calls a "delusion of persecution" is one of the most dramatic human defenses against the feeling of personal insignificance and worthlessness. In fact, no one cares a hoot about Jones. He is an extra on the stage of life. But he wants to be a star.

THOMAS S. SZASZ (1920–). "Mental Illness," *The Untamed Tongue: A Dissenting Dictionary,* 1990

I am persecuted by everything in the world, and even by things which are not!

> VOLTAIRE (1694–1778). *Zadig*, 4, 1747, tr. H. I. Woolf, 1949

Ridding oneself of this feeling that the universe has a personal grudge against one is the first and most difficult task in growing to adulthood.

> COLIN WILSON (1931–). Appendix (1) to *Beyond the Outsider: A Philosophy of the Future*, 1965

✱

If people didn't pick on me, I wouldn't be paranoid.

> ANONYMOUS (AMERICAN). Graffito, 1960s

Just because you're paranoid doesn't mean they're not after you.

> ANONYMOUS (AMERICAN). 1960s

[Jesus said:] "Why do you seek to kill me?" The people answered, "You have a demon! Who is seeking to kill you?"

> ANONYMOUS (*BIBLE*). *John* 7:19–20

I'm vigilant; you're suspicious; he's paranoid.

> ANONYMOUS

PARENTS

See also • Abortion ○ Adolescence ○ Age & Youth ○ Babies ○ Birth Control ○ Child Abuse ○ Children ○ Children's Learning ○ Divorce: Fred Rogers ○ Education ○ Family ○ Fathers ○ Grandparents ○ Home ○ Mothers ○ Teachers ○ Youth

The inner and unconscious ideal which guides [the parents'] lives is precisely what touches the child; their words, their remonstrances, their punishments, their bursts of feeling even, are for him merely thunder and comedy; what they worship, this it is which his instinct divines and reflects.

> HENRI AMIEL (1821–1881). Journal, 6 January 1853, tr. Mrs. Humphrey Ward, 1887

It's frightening to think that you mark your children merely by being yourself.

> SIMONE de BEAUVOIR (1908–1986). *Les Belles Images*, 3, 1966, tr. Patrick O'Brian, 1968

Tew bring up a child in the wa he should go—travel that wa yourself.

> JOSH BILLINGS (1818–1885). *His Sayings*, 78, 1867

I'm starting to wonder what my folks were up to at my age that makes them so doggoned suspicious of me all the time!

> MARGARET BLAIR

Fathers and mothers have lost the idea that the highest aspiration they might have for their children is for them to be wise—as priests, prophets or philosophers are wise. Specialized competence and success are all that they can imagine.

> ALLAN BLOOM (1930–1992). "The Clean Slate," *The Closing of the American Mind: How Higher Education Has Failed Democracy and Impoverished the Souls of Today's Students*, 1987

There are times when parenthood seems like nothing but feeding the mouth that bites you.

> PETER DE VRIES (1910–1993). *The Tunnel of Love*, 5, 1954

The values inculcated by status-insecure parents are such that their children learn to put personal success and the acquisition of power above all else. They are taught to judge people for their usefulness rather than their likableness. Their friends, and even future marriage partners, are selected and used in the service of personal advancement; love and affection take second place to knowing the right people. They are taught to eschew weakness and passivity, to respect authority, and to despise those who have not made the socio-economic grade. Success is equated with social esteem and material advantage, rather than with more spiritual values.

> NORMAN F. DIXON (1922–). *On the Psychology of Military Incompetence*, 22, 1976

Come mothers and fathers
Throughout the land
And don't criticize
What you can't understand
Your sons and your daughters
Are beyond your command
Your old road is
Rapidly agin'.
Please get out of the new one
If you can't lend your hand
For the times they are a-changin'.

> BOB DYLAN (1941–). "The Times They Are A-Changin'" (song), 1963

Parents forgive their children least readily for the faults they themselves instilled in them.

> MARIE von EBNER-ESCHENBACH (1830–1916). *Aphorisms*, p. 31, 1880–1905, tr. David Scrase and Wolfgang Mieder, 1994

The thing that impresses me most about America is the way parents obey their children.

> EDWARD VIII (DUKE OF WINDSOR) (1894–1972). In "What Are They Saying," *Look*, 5 March 1957

A low self-love in the parent desires that his child should repeat his character and fortune. . . . I suffer whenever I see that common sight of a parent or senior imposing his opinion and way of thinking and being on a young soul to which they are totally unfit. Cannot we let people be themselves, and enjoy life in their own way? You are trying to make another *you*. One's enough.

> RALPH WALDO EMERSON (1803–1882). "Education," *Lectures and Biographical Sketches*, 1883

Respect the child. Be not too much his parent. Trespass not on his solitude.

> RALPH WALDO EMERSON (1802–1882). "Education," *Lectures and Biographical Sketches*, 1883
>
> See Youth: Confucius

How true Daddy's words were when he said: "All children must look after their own upbringing." Parents can only give good advice or put them on the right paths, but the final forming of a person's character lies in their own hands.

> ANNE FRANK (1929–1945). 15 July 1944, *Anne Frank: The Diary of a Young Girl*, tr. B. M. Mooyaart-Doubleday, 1952

It may be that we were all destined to direct our first sexual impulses toward our mothers, and our first impulses of hatred and violence toward our fathers; our dreams convince us that we were. King Oedipus, who slew his father Laius and wedded his mother Jocasta, is nothing more or less than a wish-fulfillment—the fulfillment of the wish of our childhood.

> SIGMUND FREUD (1856–1939). *The Interpretation of Dreams,* 5.D.b, 1900, tr. A. A. Brill, 1938
> See Dreams: Examples: Sophocles

When our kids are young, many of us rush out to buy a cute little baby book to record the meaningful events of our young child's life. . . . But I've often thought there should be a second book, one with room to record the moral milestones of our child's lives. There might be space to record dates she first shared or showed compassion or befriended a new student or thought of sending Grandma a get-well card or told the truth despite its cost.

> FRED G. GOSMAN. *How to Be a Happy Parent . . . In Spite of Your Children,* 11, 1995

[The parents of prodigies] convey enthusiasm without conveying expectation. They reward their children more for trying than winning.

> EMILY GREENSPAN (1953–). *Little Winners,* 1983. In Jan Krakauer, "What Kind of Breakfast Are They Feeding These Young Champions?" *Washington Post National Weekly Edition,* 15 February 1988

Our children give us the opportunity to become the parents we always wished we'd had.

> LOUISE HART. *The Winning Family: Increasing Self-Esteem in Your Children and Yourself,* 1 (epigraph), 1987

Virtue and a Trade are the best portion for Children.

> GEORGE HERBERT (1593–1633). Comp., *Outlandish Proverbs,* 107, 1640

Where parents do too much for their children, the children will not do much for themselves.

> ELBERT HUBBARD (1856–1915). *The Note Book of Elbert Hubbard,* p. 193, comp. Elbert Hubbard II, 1927

I have come to set a man against his father, and a daughter against her mother, and a daughter-in-law against her mother-in-law; and a man's foes will be those of his own household.

> JESUS (A.D. 1st cent.). *Matthew* 10:35–36

This is a moment that I deeply wish my parents could have lived to share. My father would have enjoyed what you have so generously said of me—and my mother would have believed it.

> LYNDON B. JOHNSON (1908–1973). Responding to introductory remarks, commencement address at Baylor University, Waco (Texas), 28 May 1965

Nothing exerts a stronger psychic effect upon the environment, and especially upon children, than the [unlived] life [of] the parents.

> CARL G. JUNG (1875–1961). "Paracelsus," 1929, *The Spirit in Man, Art, and Literature,* tr. R. F. C. Hull, 1966

If there is anything that we wish to change in our children, we should first examine it and see whether it is not something that could better be changed in ourselves.

> CARL G. JUNG (1875–1961). Title essay, 1934, *The Development of Personality,* tr. R. F. C. Hull, 1954

TWO THINGS I ALWAYS KNEW ABOUT YOU ONE THAT YOU ARE SMART TWO THAT YOU ARE A SWELL GUY LOVE DAD.

> JOSEPH P. KENNEDY (1888–1969). Cable from England to his son John after hearing that he had won scholastic honors at Harvard University, 1940. In James MacGregor Burns, *John Kennedy: A Political Profile,* 3, 1959

The most assiduous task of parenting is to divine the difference between boundaries and bondage.

> BARBARA KINGSOLVER (1955–). "Civil Disobedience at Breakfast," *High Tide in Tucson: Essays from Now or Never,* 1996

It is . . . sometimes easier to head an institute for the study of child guidance than it is to turn one brat into a decent human being.

> JOSEPH WOOD KRUTCH (1893–1970). "Whom Do We Picket Tonight?" *If You Don't Mind My Saying So,* 1964

The sins of children rise up in judgment against their parents.

> CAROLINE LAMB (1785–1828). *Glenarvon,* 1.20, 1816

They fuck you up, your mum and dad.
  They may not mean to, but they do.
They fill you with the faults they had
  And add some extra, just for you.

But they were fucked up in their turn
  By fools in old-style hats and coats,
Who half the time were soppy-stern
  And half at one another's throats.

> PHILIP LARKIN (1922–1985). "This Be the Verse," 1971, *High Windows,* 1974

It is my pleasure that my children are free and happy, and unrestrained by parental tyranny. Love is the chain whereby to bind a child to its parents.

> ABRAHAM LINCOLN (1809–1865). A frequent remark to his wife, Mary. In William H. Herndon (and Jesse W. Weik), *Herndon's Lincoln: The True Story of a Great Life,* 17, 1889, Premier Books edition, 1961

Supported by the authority of all institutions, parenthood has come to amount to little more than a campaign against individuality. Every father and every mother trembles lest an offspring, in act or thought, should be different from his fellows; and the smallest display of uniqueness in a child becomes the signal for the application of drastic measures aimed at stamping out that small fire of noncompliance by which personal distinctness is expressed. In an atmosphere of anxiety, in a climate of apprehension, the parental conspiracy against children is planned.

> ROBERT LINDNER (1914–1956). *Prescription for Rebellion,* 3, 1952

Because children see parents as authority figures and gods, they think that the way you treat them is the way they deserve to be treated: "What you say about me is what I am" is a literal truth to your child. Consequently, when children are treated with respect, they conclude that they deserve respect and hence develop *self*-respect.

> STEPHANIE MARSTON. Psychotherapist. *The Magic of Encouragement: Nurturing Your Child's Self-Esteem,* 1, 1990

The son treats the father with contempt, the daughter rises up against her mother, the daughter-in-law against her mother-in-law; a man's enemies are the men of his own house,

MICAH (8th cent. B.C.). *Micah* 7:6

The free expression of resentment against one's parents represents a great opportunity. It provides access to one's true self, reactivates numbed feelings, opens the way for mourning and—with luck—reconciliation.

ALICE MILLER (1923–). "Unintentional Cruelty Hurts, Too," *For Your Own Good: Hidden Cruelty in Child-Rearing and the Roots of Violence,* tr. Hildegarde and Hunter Hannum, 1983

Honor your father and your mother.

MOSES (14th cent. B.C.). The Fifth Commandment, *Exodus* 20:12

[Show] kindness to parents.

MUHAMMAD (A.D. 570?–632). *Quran,* 17.23, A.D. 670?, tr. Mohammed Marmaduke Pickthall, 1953

The last step in parental love involves the release of the beloved; the willing cutting of the cord that would otherwise keep the child in a state of emotional dependence.

LEWIS MUMFORD (1895–1990). *The Conduct of Life,* 9.8, 1951

There are families in which the father will say to his child, "You'll get a thick ear if you do that again," while the mother, her eyes brimming over with tears, will take the child in her arms and murmur lovingly, "Now, darling, *is* it kind to Mummy to do that?" And who would maintain that the second method is less tyrannous than the first?

GEORGE ORWELL (1903–1950). "Lear, Tolstoy and the Fool," March 1947, *The Collected Essays, Journalism and Letters of George Orwell,* vol. 4, ed. Sonia Orwell and Ian Angus, 1968

Parents . . . are sometimes a bit of a disappointment to their children. They don't fulfill the promise of their early years.

ANTHONY POWELL (1905–). *A Buyer's Market,* 2, 1952

The greatest gifts my parents gave to me . . . were their unconditional love and a set of values. Values that they lived and didn't just lecture about. Values that included an understanding of the simple difference between right and wrong, a belief in God, the importance of hard work and education, self-respect and a belief in America.

COLIN POWELL (1937–). "Will You Help?" *Parade Magazine,* 27 April 1997

Children suck the mother when they are young, and the father when they are old.

JOHN RAY (1628–1705). *A Collection of English Proverbs,* 6, 1983

Call them rules or call them limits, good ones, I believe, have this in common: they serve reasonable purposes; they are practical and within a child's capability; they are consistent; and they are an expression of loving concern.

FRED ROGERS (1928–). *Mister Rogers Talks with Parents,* 6, 1983

The revolution declares war on Original Sin, the dictatorship of parents over their kids.

JERRY RUBIN (1938–1994). *Do It! Scenarios of the Revolution,* 20, 1970

Edgar: Obey thy parents.

SHAKESPEARE (1564–1616). *Othello,* 3.4.82, 1604

Not by authority is your sway to be obtained; neither by reasoning, but by inducement. Show in all your conduct that you are thoroughly your child's friend, and there is nothing that you may not lead him to. The faintest sign of your approval or dissent will be his law.

HERBERT SPENCER (1820–1903). *Social Statics,* 2.17.5, 1851

To parental misconduct is traceable a great part of the domestic disorder commonly ascribed to the perversity of children.

HERBERT SPENCER (1820–1903). *Education: Intellectual, Moral, and Physical,* 3, 1860

The defects of the children mirror the defects of their parents.

HERBERT SPENCER (1820–1903). *Education: Intellectual, Moral, and Physical,* 3, 1860

It is the function of parents to see that their children habitually experience the true consequences of their conduct.

HERBERT SPENCER (1820–1903). *Education: Intellectual, Moral, and Physical,* 3, 1860

TRUST YOURSELF

1. You know more than you think you do.

BENJAMIN SPOCK (1903–1998). Addressing parents, "Preparing for the Baby," *The Common Sense Book of Baby and Child Care,* 1946

[Growing up] is especially difficult to achieve for a child whose parents do not take him seriously; that is, who do not expect proper behavior from him, do not discipline him, and finally, do not respect him enough to tell him the truth.

THOMAS S. SZASZ (1920–). "Tragic Failures," *National Review,* 26 May 1972

My parents were both, in their way, very loving and indulgent. Just the fact that I had the presumption to become an artist is rather ridiculous, isn't it, with no qualifications except that I felt treasured as a child.

JOHN UPDIKE (1932–). Interview with the author. In Naim Attallah, *Singular Encounters,* 1990

[In our current] free, permissive atmosphere, the idea that the individual should be regarded as personally accountable for the way he behaves is, of course, old hat. . . . "If your young son sticks his tongue out at you and calls you a nasty old stinkpot," an article in *American Magazine* good-humoredly, but approvingly, counsels, "just ignore the insult and rejoice secretly that you have such a fine normal child. He is simply channeling his aggressive, aggrieved feelings harmlessly by verbal projection."

WILLIAM H. WHYTE, JR. (1917–). "Groupthink," *Fortune,* March 1952

Children begin by loving their parents; as they grow older they judge them; sometimes they forgive them.

OSCAR WILDE (1854–1900). *The Picture of Dorian Gray,* 5, 1891

Honor your father and mother, even as you honor God, for all three were partners in your creation.

ZOHAR (A.D. 13th cent.). Jewish mystical writings

❦

Children thrive when parents set before them increasingly difficult, but always meetable, challenges.
ANONYMOUS

When you see a problem child, look for a problem parent.
ANONYMOUS

A wise son makes a glad father,
   but a foolish son is a sorrow to his mother.
SAYING (*BIBLE*). *Proverbs* 10:1

Train up a child in the way he should go,
   and when he is old he will not depart from it.
SAYING (*BIBLE*). *Proverbs* 22:6

Spare the rod and spoil the child.
SAYING (ENGLISH)

An apple doesn't usually fall far from the tree.
SAYING (GERMAN)

Those who love their children don't think of the rod.
SAYING (GREEK)

Many a fair flower springs out of a dunghill.
SAYING (NEW ENGLAND)

Clever father, clever daughter; clever mother, clever son.
SAYING (RUSSIAN)

Little children disturb your sleep; big ones, your life.
SAYING (YIDDISH). In Susan Ginsberg, comp., *Family Wisdom: The 2,000 Most Important Things Ever Said About Parenting, Children, and Family Life,* p. 152, 1996

PARIS

See also • Cities ○ France

The last time I saw Paris,
   her heart was warm and gay,
I heard the laughter of her heart
   in ev'ry street café.
OSCAR HAMMERSTEIN II (1895–1960). "The Last Time I Saw Paris" (song). In the musical *Lady Be Good,* 1941

If you are lucky enough to have lived in Paris as a young man, then wherever you go for the rest of your life, it stays with you, for Paris is a moveable feast.
ERNEST HEMINGWAY (1899–1961). *A Moveable Feast,* epigraph, 1964

"How you Gonna Keep 'Em Down on the Farm After They've Seen Paree?"
SAM M. LEWIS (1885–1959) and JOE YOUNG (1889–1939). Referring to American soldiers in France during World War I, song title, 1919

Why, this isn't like a city, it's more like a landscape.
BORIS PASTERNAK (1890–1960). On seeing Paris for the first time. In Ilya Ehrenburg, "1918–1921" (7), *People and Life, 1891–1921,* tr. Anna Bostock

I love Paris in the springtime.
COLE PORTER (1892–1964). "I Love Paris" (song). In the musical *Can-Can,* 1953

Farewell Paris, far-famed Paris, with all your noise and smoke and dirt, where the women have ceased to believe in honor and the men in virtue. We are in search of love, happiness, innocence; the further we go from Paris the better.
ROUSSEAU (1712–1778). *Emile; or, Treatise on Education,* 4, 1762, tr. Barbara Foxley, 1911

Paris is the capital of the world.
LEO TOLSTOY (1828–1910). *War and Peace,* 3.3.29, 1863–1869, tr. Rosemary Edmonds, 1957

PASSION

See also • Abstinence ○ Body ○ Desire ○ Emotion ○ Energy ○ Enthusiasm ○ Excess ○ Fanatics ○ Life: Oliver Wendell Holmes, Jr. (1,2) ○ Lust ○ Moderation ○ Motives ○ Passion, Ruling ○ Pleasure ○ Reason ○ Reason & Passion ○ Self-Discipline ○ Sex ○ Soul & Body ○ Temptation ○ Women & Men ○ Zeal

Without passion man is a mere latent force and possibility, like the flint which awaits the shock of the iron before it can give forth its spark.
HENRI AMIEL (1821–1881). Journal, 17 December 1856, tr. Mrs. Humphrey Ward, 1887

Passion will have all things now.
JOHN BUNYAN (1628–1688). In John Morley, *Notes on Politics and History: A University Address,* 1, 1913

I am ashes where once I was fire.
   And the bard in my bosom is dead;
What I loved I now merely admire,
   And my heart is as gray as my head.
LORD BYRON (1788–1824). At age 35 (a year before his death), "To the Countess of Blessington," 3, 1823

One heat, all know, doth drive out another,
One passion doth expel another still.
GEORGE CHAPMAN (1559?–1634). *Monsieur d'Olive,* 5.1, 1606

Bridle passions, and be yourself a free man.
JOHN CLARKE (1596–1658). Comp., *Proverbs: English and Latine,* p. 284, 1639

The preservation of the species was a point of such necessity that Nature has secured it at all hazards by immensely overloading the passion, at the risk of perpetual crime and disorder.
RALPH WALDO EMERSON (1803–1882). "Culture," *The Conduct of Life,* 1860

If the fire rages uncontrolled in a house, we call it a disastrous conflagration; if it burns in a smelting furnace, we call it a useful industrial force. In other words, our drives and impulses as they live within us are neither good nor bad, right nor wrong.
SIGMUND FREUD (1856–1939). In Helen Walker Puner, *Freud: His Life and His Mind,* 10, 1947

Act nothing in furious Passion; it's putting to Sea in a Storm.

> THOMAS FULLER (1654–1734). Comp., *Introductio ad Prudentiam,* 365, 1731

It is in the way in which we gratify physical needs that the seed of holiness is planted.

> ABRAHAM JOSHUA HESCHEL (1907–1972). *Man Is Not Alone: A Philosophy of Religion,* 25, 1951

Passion often makes fools of the wisest men and gives [to] the silliest wisdom.

> LA ROCHEFOUCAULD (1613–1680). *Maxims,* 6, 1665, tr. Leonard Tancock, 1959

When we resist our passions, it is more on account of their weakness than our strength.

> LA ROCHEFOUCAULD (1613–1680). *Maxims,* 122, 1665, tr. Leonard Tancock, 1959

Absence lessens moderate passions and intensifies great ones, as the wind blows out a candle but fans up a fire.

> LA ROCHEFOUCAULD (1613–1680). *Maxims,* 276, 1665, tr. Leonard Tancock, 1959

A wise man rules his passions, a fool obeys them.

> PUBLIUS SYRUS (85–43 B.C.). *Moral Sayings,* 49, tr. Darius Lyman, Jr., 1862

If our passions are aroused, we are apt to see things in an exaggerated way, or imagine what does not exist.

> ARTHUR SCHOPENHAUER (1788–1860). "Studies in Pessimism: On Women," *Essays of Arthur Schopenhauer,* tr. T. Bailey Saunders, 1851

Hamlet: Give me that man
That is not passion's slave, and I will wear him
In my heart's core, ay, in my heart of heart.

> SHAKESPEARE (1564–1616). *Hamlet,* 3.2.76, 1600

Our moral sense! And is that not a passion? . . . It is the birth of that passion that turns a child into a man.

> GEORGE BERNARD SHAW (1856–1950). *Man and Superman,* 1, 1903

A fiery passion consumes all evidences opposed to its gratification and, fusing together those that serve its purpose, casts them into weapons by which to achieve its end.

> HERBERT SPENCER (1820–1903). *Social Statics,* 2.16.3, 1851

The happiness of a man in this life does not consist in the absence but in the mastery of his passions.

> ALFRED, LORD TENNYSON (1809–1892). In Elbert Hubbard, comp., *Elbert Hubbard's Scrap Book,* p. 83, 1923

[The passions] are the winds that fill the ship's sails. Sometimes they submerge the ship, but without them the ship could not sail.

> VOLTAIRE (1694–1778). *Zadig,* 20, 1747, tr. H. I. Woolf, 1949

There are certain propensities and passions inherent in our nature which will have vent in one shape or another, despite all the combined legislative wisdom of communities.

> WALT WHITMAN (1819–1892). Quoted by Paul Lauter, "Walt Whitman: Love and Comrade." In Norman Kiell, ed., *Psychological Studies of Famous Americans: The Civil War Era,* 1964

The passions are like fire and water, good servants but bad masters.

> SAYING (ENGLISH)
>
> See Money: Saying (French) ○ The Press: James Fenimore Cooper

Rule your passions or they will rule you.

> SAYING (GREEK)

PASSION, RULING

See also • Motives ○ Passion ○ Reason & Passion: Alexander Pope

Two appetites of the creatures; viz., 1. That of self-preservation and defense; and 2. That of multiplying and propagating.

> FRANCIS BACON (1561–1626). *Advancement of Learning,* 7.2, 1605, Willey Book edition, 1944

We must not suppose that, because a man . . . has such [and] such a predominant passion, that he will act invariably and consequentially in the pursuit of it. No. We are complicated machines: and though we have one mainspring that gives motion to the whole, we have an infinity of little wheels, which, in their turns, retard, precipitate, and sometimes stop that motion.

> LORD CHESTERFIELD (1694–1773). Letter to his son, 19 December 1749

It is a cursed evil to any man to become as absorbed in any subject as I am in mine.

> CHARLES DARWIN (1809–1882).

There are two passions which have a powerful influence on the affairs of men. These are ambition and avarice.

> BENJAMIN FRANKLIN (1706–1790). In Bernard A. Weisberger, "The Wrongdoers," *American Heritage,* December 1989

A man like me cannot live without a hobbyhorse, without a consuming passion, without—in Schiller's words—a tyrant. I have found one. In its service I know no limits. It is psychology.

> SIGMUND FREUD (1856–1939). Letter to Wilhelm Fliess, 25 May 1895, tr. Jeffrey Moussaieff Masson, 1985

When you find out a man's ruling passion, beware of crossing him in it.

> WILLIAM HAZLITT (1778–1830). *Characteristics in the Manner of Rochefoucault's Maxims,* 116, 1823

The hot place in a man's consciousness, the group of ideas to which he devotes himself and from which he works, call it *the habitual center of his personal energy.*

> WILLIAM JAMES (1842–1910). *The Varieties of Religious Experience: A Study in Human Nature,* 9, 1902

[The typical Yankee] is eternally torn between a passion for righteousness and a desire to get on in the world.

> SAMUEL ELIOT MORISON (1887–1976). *The Maritime History of Massachusetts,* 2, 1921

The natural man has only two primal passions, to get and to beget.

> SIR WILLIAM OSLER (1849–1919). *Science and Immortality,* 2, 1904

Three passions, simple but overwhelmingly strong, have governed my life: the longing for love, the search for knowledge, and unbearable pity for the suffering of mankind.

> BERTRAND RUSSELL (1872–1970). Opening words, prologue to *The Autobiography of Bertrand Russell: 1872–1914*, 1967

I have only one passion, the love of liberty and human dignity.

> ALEXIS de TOCQUEVILLE (1805–1859). Letter to Henry Reeve, 22 March 1837. In Robert O. Paxton, "The Divided Liberal," *New York Review of Books*, 2 March 1989

PAST

See also • Custom ○ Future ○ History ○ Paradoxes: John Osborne ○ Present ○ Time ○ Tradition

Nothing is more responsible for the good old days than a bad memory.

> FRANKLIN P. ADAMS (1881–1960)

Once upon a time, many years ago, when I was living happily ever after . . . [Ellipsis points in original.]

> MARGARET ANDERSON (1893–1973). Opening paragraph, *The Fiery Fountains: The Autobiography; Continuation and Crisis to 1950*, 1951

The past is a kind of screen upon which we project our vision of the future; and it is indeed a moving picture, borrowing much of its form and color from our fears and aspirations.

> CARL L. BECKER. "What Are Historical Facts?" *Western Political Quarterly*, September 1955

We can only pay our debt to the past by putting the future in debt to ourselves.

> JOHN BUCHAN (1875–1940). Speech to the people of Canada on the Coronation of King George VI, 12 May 1937

Is it not natural that the old should extol the days of their youth; the weak, the era of their strength; the sick, the season of their vigor; and the disappointed, the spring tide of their hopes? Alas, it is not the times that have changed, but themselves.

> C. C. COLTON (1780–1832). *Lacon: or, Many Things in Few Words; Addressed to Those Who Think*, 2.101, 1824

To look back is to relax one's vigil.

> BETTE DAVIS (1908–1989). *The Lonely Life: An Autobiography*, 1, 1962

Be not the slave of your own past.

> RALPH WALDO EMERSON (1803–1882). Journal, 19 June 1838

The Moving Finger writes; and, having writ,
Moves on: nor all your Piety nor Wit
Shall lure it back to cancel half a Line,
Nor all your Tears wash out a Word of it.

> EDWARD FITZGERALD (1809–1883). *The Rubáiyát of Omar Khayyám*, 4th ed., 71, 1871 (1859)

"The Past Is What Catches Up With Us."

> THOMAS FLEMING (1929–). Article title, *New York Times Book Review*, 12 January 1992

The past is not simply the past, but a prism through which the subject filters his own changing self-image.

> DORIS KEARNS GOODWIN (1943–). "Angles of Vision." In Marc Patcher, ed., *Telling Lives: The Art and Craft of American Biography*, 1979

The illusion that times that were are better than those that are, has probably pervaded all ages.

> HORACE GREELEY (1811–1872). *The American Conflict*, 1866

Continuity with the past is not a duty, only a necessity.

> OLIVER WENDELL HOLMES, JR. (1841–1935). Quoted by John Gardner, "The Individual and Society." In *On the Meaning of the University*, ed. Sterling M. McMurrin, 1976

There is no time like the old time when you and I were young.

> OLIVER WENDELL HOLMES, SR. (1809–1894). "No Time Like the Old Time"

Yesterday, all my troubles
seemed so far away.
Now it seems
they're here to stay.
Oh, I believe in yesterday.

> JOHN LENNON (1940–1980) and PAUL McCARTNEY (1942–). "Yesterday" (song), 1965

Let the past as nothing be.

> ABRAHAM LINCOLN (1809–1865). Letter to William H. Herndon, 11 July 1848

Let the dead Past bury its dead.

> HENRY WADSWORTH LONGFELLOW (1807–1882). "A Psalm of Life" (6), *Voices of the Night*, 1839
>
> See The Dead: Jesus

But past who can recall, or done undo?
Not God Omnipotent, Nor Fate.

> JOHN MILTON (1608–1674). *Paradise Lost*, 9.926, 1667

One thing about the past,
It is likely to last.
Some of it is horrid and some sublime,
And there is more of it all the time.

> OGDEN NASH (1902–1971). "Ho, Varlet! My Two Cents' Worth of Penny Postcard!" *You Can't Get There from Here*, 1957

The knowledge of the past is desired only for the service of the future and the present.

> FRIEDRICH NIETZSCHE (1844–1900). *The Use and Abuse of History*, 4, 1874, tr. Adrian Collins, 1949

Before the war, and especially before the Boer War, it was summer all the year round.

> GEORGE ORWELL (1903–1950). Referring to World War I (1914–1918) and the Boar War (1899–1902), *Coming up for Air*, 2.1, 1939

They spend their time mostly looking forward to the past.

> JOHN OSBORNE (1929–1994). *Look Back in Anger*, 2.1, 1956

Your whole past was but a birth and a becoming.

> ANTOINE de SAINT-EXUPÉRY (1900–1944). *The Wisdom of the Sands*, 50, 1948, tr. Stuart Gilbert, 1950

I tell you the past is a bucket of ashes.
I tell you yesterday is a wind gone down,
  a sun dropped in the west.
I tell you there is nothing in the world
  only an ocean of tomorrows,
  a sky of tomorrows.
> CARL SANDBURG (1878–1967). "Prairie," *Cornhuskers*, 1918

Those who cannot remember the past are condemned to repeat it.
> GEORGE SANTAYANA (1863–1952). *The Life of Reason or The Phases of Human Progress*, 1.12, 1905–1906
> See History: Georg Hegel (1), Laurence J. Peter

Antonio: What's past is prologue.
> SHAKESPEARE (1564–1616). *The Tempest*, 2.1.253, 1611

People who are always praising the past
And especially the times of faith as best
Ought to go and live in the Middle Ages
And be burnt at the stake as witches and sages.
> FLORENCE MARGARET "STEVIE" SMITH (1902–1971). "The Past," 1957

We ought not to look back, unless it is to derive useful lessons from past errors and for the purpose of profiting by dear bought experience.
> GEORGE WASHINGTON (1732–1799). Letter to Maj. Gen. John Armstrong, 26 March 1781

Faithfulness to the past can be a kind of death above ground.
> JESSAMYN WEST (1907–1984). *The Life I Really Lived: A Novel*, 15, 1979

The past—the infinite greatness of the past!
For what is the present after all but a growth out of the past.
> WALT WHITMAN (1819–1892). "Passage to India" (1), 1871, *Leaves of Grass*, 1855–1892

Hindsight is always twenty-twenty.
> BILLY WILDER (1906–)

The past suggests what can be, not what must be. It shows not all of what is necessary, but some of what is possible.
> HOWARD ZINN (1922–). *The Politics of History*, 17, 1970

⚑

Things ain't what they used to be—in fact, they never was.
> ANONYMOUS. Ascribed to "a rural philosopher." In Irving Babbitt, *Democracy and Leadership*, 7 (footnote), 1924
> See Past: Anonymous (1)

Nostalgia isn't what it used to be.
> ANONYMOUS. Graffito
> See Future: Paul Valèry

The past is a prison for those who live in it.
> ANONYMOUS

Dwell on the past and you'll lose an eye. Forget the past and you'll lose both eyes.
> SAYING (RUSSIAN). In Aleksandr Solzhenitsyn, preface to *The Gulag Archipelago 1918–1956: An Experiment in Literary Investigation*, tr. Thomas P. Whitney, 1973

PATIENCE

See also • Action ○ Delay ○ Hope ○ Persistence ○ Procrastination ○ Time ○ Waiting

Because of impatience we were driven out of Paradise, because of impatience we cannot return.
> W. H. AUDEN (1907–1973). "The I Without a Self," *The Dyer's Hand and Other Essays*, 1962

There . . . is a limit at which forbearance ceases to be a virtue.
> EDMUND BURKE (1729–1797). *Observations on a Late State of the Nation*, 4th ed., 1769

Patient, *adj.* Lacking sufficient fortitude to demand satisfaction.
> VICTOR L. CAHN (1948–). *The Disrespectful Dictionary*, unpaged, 1974

Patience is the greatest of all virtues.
> DIONYSIUS CATO (A.D. 4th cent.). *Disticha de moribus ad filium*, 1.38

Beware the fury of a patient man.
> JOHN DRYDEN (1631–1700). *Absalom and Achitophel*, 1.1005, 1681

A Temper to bear much, will have much to bear.
> BENJAMIN FRANKLIN (1706–1790). *Poor Richard's Almanack*, July 1752

Bear with Patience what thou canst not remedy with Prudence.
> THOMAS FULLER (1654–1734). Comp., *Introductio ad Prudentiam*, 356, 1731

Patience, that blending of moral courage with physical timidity.
> THOMAS HARDY (1840–1928). *Tess of the D'Urbervilles*, 43, 1891

Patience, time and money accommodate all things.
> JAMES HOWELL (1593–1666). Comp., "Italian" (p. 13), *Paroimiographia: Proverbs, or Old Sayed Sawes & Adages in English . . . Italian, French and Spanish*, 1659

Lack o' pep is often mistaken fer patience.
> KIN HUBBARD (1868–1930). *Abe Martin: Hoss Sense and Nonsense*, p. 19, 1926

Ye have heard of the patience of Job.
> JAMES (A.D. 1st cent.). *James* 5:11 (King James Version)

Patience is necessary, and one cannot reap immediately where one has sown.
> SÖREN KIERKEGAARD (1813–1855). Journal, 1 August 1835, tr. Alexander Dru, 1938

You have to have a lot of patience to learn patience.
> STANISLAW J. LEC (1909–1966). *Unkempt Thoughts*, p. 110, tr. Jacek Galazka, 1962

Patience, the beggar's virtue.
> PHILIP MASSINGER (1583–1640). *A New Way to Pay Old Debts*, 5.1, 1632

Nothing comes of so many things, if you have patience.
> JOYCE CAROL OATES (1938–). "Master Race," *Partisan Review* (50th Anniversary issue), 1984

Patience and Diligence, like Faith, move Mountains.
> WILLIAM PENN (1644–1718). *Some Fruits of Solitude*, 234, 1693

All's well in the end, if you've only the patience to wait.
> RABELAIS (1483?–1553). *Gargantua and Pantagruel,* 4.48, 1532–1552,
> tr. J. M. Cohen, 1955

Duchess of Gloucester: That which in mean men we entitle
patience
Is pale cold cowardice in noble breasts.
> SHAKESPEARE (1564–1616). *Richard II,* 1.2.33, 1595

It is very strange . . . that the years teach us patience; that the
shorter our time, the greater our capacity for waiting.
> ELIZABETH TAYLOR (1912–1975). *A Wreath of Roses,* 10, 1949

Be patient, my soul; await the fulfillment of God's promise, and
you shall enjoy the abundance of His goodness in Heaven.
> THOMAS à KEMPIS (1380–1471). *The Imitation of Christ,* 3.16,
> tr. Leo Sherley-Price, 1952

Patience doesn't always help, but impatience never does.
> SAYING (RUSSIAN)

PATRIOTISM

See also • Country ○ Internationalism ○ Nationalism ○ Nations

Patriotism is in political life what faith is in religion.
> LORD ACTON (1834–1902). "Nationality," 1862, *The History of Freedom
> and Other Essays,* ed. J. N. Figgis and R. V. Laurence, 1907

Patriotism is a lively sense of collective responsibility. Nationalism
is a silly cock crowing on its own dunghill.
> RICHARD ALDINGTON (1892–1962). *The Colonel's Daughter,* 1.6, 1931
> See Nationalism: Albert Schweitzer

In Dr. Johnson's famous dictionary patriotism is defined as the last
resort [*sic*] of a scoundrel. With all due respect to an enlightened
but inferior lexicographer I beg to submit that it is the first.
> AMBROSE BIERCE (1842–1914). *The Devil's Dictionary,* p. 98, 1911,
> Dover edition, 1958

No matter that patriotism is too often the refuge of scoundrels.
Dissent, rebellion, and all-around hell-rousing remain the true
duty of patriots.
> BARBARA EHRENREICH (1941–). Closing paragraph, "Introduction:
> Family Values," 1988, *The Worst Years of Our Lives: Irreverent Notes
> from a Decade of Greed,* 1990

Patriotism . . . applies to true love of one's country and a code of
conduct that echoes such love.
> HOWARD FAST (1914–). In "What Is Patriotism?" *Nation,* 15 July 1991

One of the greatest attractions of patriotism—it fulfills our worst
wishes. In the person of our nation we are able, vicariously, to
bully and cheat. Bully and cheat, what's more, with a feeling that
we are profoundly virtuous.
> ALDOUS HUXLEY (1894–1963). *Eyeless in Gaza,* 17, 1936

Patriotism is the last refuge of a scoundrel.
> SAMUEL JOHNSON (1709–1784). 7 April 1775, in James Boswell, *The
> Life of Samuel Johnson,* 1791

> See Ambition: Oscar Wilde ○ Consistency: Oscar Wilde ○ Cynicism:
> Anonymous (1) ○ Intellectuals: Anthony Lewis ○ Journalism: Walter
> Lippmann (2) ○ Mediocrity: Boris Pasternak ○ Politicians: Boies Penrose
> ○ Reform: Theodore Roosevelt ○ Sex: Quentin Crisp ○ Violence: Isaac
> Asimov ○ War & Economics: Nicholas Rowe

To deride patriotism marks impoverished blood, but to extol it as
an ideal or an impulse above truth and justice, at the cost of the
general interests of humanity, is far worse.
> JOHN MORLEY (1838–1923). *Notes on Politics and History: A University
> Address,* 5, 1913

The noble kind of patriotism . . . aims at ends that are worthy of
the whole of mankind.
> ALBERT SCHWEITZER (1875–1965). *The Philosophy of Civilization: The
> Decay and Restoration of Civilization,* 4, 1923, tr. C. T. Campion, 1923
> See Country: Theodore Roosevelt

Patriotism is sometimes stimulated by religious enthusiasm, and
then it is capable of making prodigious efforts. It is in itself a kind
of religion: it does not reason, but it acts from the impulse of faith
and sentiment.
> ALEXIS de TOCQUEVILLE (1805–1859). *Democracy in America,* 1.14,
> 1835, tr. Henry Reeve and Francis Bowen, 1862

The modern patriotism, the true patriotism, the only rational patriotism is loyalty to the *nation* all the time, loyalty to the government when it deserves it.
> MARK TWAIN (1835–1910). "The Czar's Soliloquy," *North American
> Review,* March 1905

Guard against the impostures of pretended patriotism.
> GEORGE WASHINGTON (1732–1799). *Farewell Address,* 17 September
> 1796

PAY

See also • Money ○ Wages ○ Wealth ○ Work

Work in every hour; paid or unpaid, see only that thou work; and
thou canst not escape the reward.
> RALPH WALDO EMERSON (1803–1882). Journal, 3 August 1842

A good Paymaster never wants Workmen.
> THOMAS FULLER (1654–1734). Comp., *Gnomologia: Adages and
> Proverbs,* 168, 1732

In the business world, everyone is paid in two coins: cash and
experience. Take the experience first; the cash will come later.
> HAROLD GENEEN (1910–1997) (with ALVIN MOSCOW). *Managing,*
> 3 (epigraph), 1984

We're overpaying him, but he's worth it.
> SAMUEL GOLDWYN (1882–1974). In Laurence J. Peter, *The Peter
> Prescription: How to Make Things Go Right,* 12, 1972

Who payeth before hand hath his work ill done.

> JAMES HOWELL (1593–1666). Comp., "Italian" (p. 6), *Paroimiographia: Proverbs, or Old Sayed Sawes & Adages in English . . . Italian, French and Spanish,* 1659

Be content with your pay.

> JOHN THE BAPTIST (A.D. 1st cent.). *Luke* 3:14

Ishmael: Being paid—what will compare with it? The urbane activity with which a man receives money is really marvelous, considering that we so earnestly believe money to be the root of all earthly ills, and on no account can a monied man enter heaven. Ah! how cheerfully we consign ourselves to perdition!

> HERMAN MELVILLE (1819–1891). *Moby-Dick; or, The Whale,* 1, 1851, ed. Harold Beaver, 1972

The really exhausting and the really repulsive labors, instead of being better paid than others, are almost invariably paid the worst of all. . . . The hardships and the earnings, instead of being directly proportional, as in any just arrangements of society they would be, are generally in an inverse ratio to one another.

> JOHN STUART MILL (1806–1873). *Principles of Political Economy with Some of Their Applications to Social Philosophy,* 3rd ed., 2.14.1, 1852

Portia: He is well paid that is well satisfied.

> SHAKESPEARE (1564–1616). *The Merchant of Venice,* 4.1.415, 1596

Whether in the United States or in the international economy, it's a rule with few exceptions: Work is valued by the social value of the worker. A category of work is paid least when women do it, somewhat more when almost any variety of men do it, and much more when men of the "right" race or class do it.

> GLORIA STEINEM (1934–). "Revaluing Economics," *Moving Beyond Words,* 1994

Today's family needs at least two paychecks just to maintain yesterday's standard of living.

> JOHN J. SWEENEY (1934–). Service Employees International Union president. Testimony before the House Committee on Education and Labor, 25 February 1987

Do not hire a man who does your work for money, but him who does it for love, and pay him well.

> HENRY DAVID THOREAU (1817–1862). Journal, 15 June 1852

❦

Who pays the piper calls the tune.

> SAYING (ENGLISH)

Who pays well is well served.

> SAYING (FRENCH)

PEACE

See also • Heaven ○ International Relations ○ Nonviolence ○ Pacifism ○ Peace of Mind ○ Politics ○ Spirituality: Aldous Huxley (1) ○ Victory: Ralph Waldo Emerson ○ War ○ War & Peace ○ War & Psychology

An ounce of peace is worth more than a pound of victory.

> ST. ROBERT BELLARMINE (1542–1621). In Pope John XXIII, appendix 3 (33) to *Journal of a Soul,* 1964, tr. Dorothy White, 1965

Peace, *n.* In international affairs, a period of cheating between two periods of fighting.

> AMBROSE BIERCE (1842–1914). *The Devil's Dictionary,* p. 98, 1911, Dover edition, 1958

Mother Courage: Don't tell me peace has broken out—I've gone and brought all these supplies!

> BERTOLT BRECHT (1898–1956). *Mother Courage,* 8, 1939, tr. Eric Bentley, 1955

Peace is the aim of all the world and . . . justice is the way to attain it.

> MARTIN BUBER (1878–1965). Letter to Mohandas K. Gandhi, 1939. In Allen and Linda Kirschner, eds., *Blessed Are the Peacemakers,* 2, 1971

Peace implies reconciliation.

> EDMUND BURKE (1729–1797). "Conciliation with America," House of Commons speech, 22 March 1775

Peace is made by the biggest battalions!

> GEORGES CLEMENCEAU (1841–1929). Interview with the author. In George Sylvester Viereck, "The Tiger Looks at the Post-War World," *Glimpses of the Great,* 1930

Dreifus: In closing, I read somewhere that you are predicting that the twenty-first century, unlike the twentieth, is to be a century of peace and justice. Why?
Dalai Lama: Because I believe that in the twentieth century, humanity has learned from many, many experiences. Some positive, and many negative. What misery, what destruction! The greatest number of human beings were killed in the two world wars of this century. But human nature is such that when we face a tremendous critical situation, the human mind can wake up and find some other alternative. That is a human capacity.

> DALAI LAMA (1935–). In Claudia Dreifus, "The Dalai Lama of Tibet," *Interview,* 1997

Lord Salisbury and myself have brought you back peace—but a peace, I hope, with honor.

> BENJAMIN DISRAELI (1804–1881). British prime minister. Speech after returning from the Congress of Berlin, London, 16 July 1878
> See World War II: Neville Chamberlain (2)

Peace is more the product of our day-to-day living than of a spectacular program, intermittently executed.

> DWIGHT D. EISENHOWER (1890–1969). Speech, Columbia University, New York City, 23 march 1950

Peace and justice are two sides of the same coin.

> DWIGHT D. EISENHOWER (1890–1969). News conference, Washington, 6 February 1957

I think that people want peace so much that one of these days governments had better get out of the way and let them have it.

> DWIGHT D. EISENHOWER (1890–1969). Television broadcast, 31 August 1959

The god of Victory is said to be one-handed, but Peace gives victory to both sides.

> RALPH WALDO EMERSON (1803–1882). *Journal,* September 1867

Real disarmament cannot come unless the nations of the world cease to exploit one another.

> MOHANDAS K. GANDHI (1869–1948). In *Young India,* 18 November 1926

"Peace upon earth!" was said. We sing it,
And pay a million priests to bring it.
After two thousand years of mass
We've got as far as poison gas.

> THOMAS HARDY (1840–1928). "Christmas: 1924," *Winter Words in Various Moods and Metres,* 1928

Sublime is the moment
When the world is at peace
And the limitless deep
Lies bathed in the morning sun.

> HIROHITO (1901–1989). Untitled poem. In Robert Trumball, "A Leader Who Took Japan to War, to Surrender, and Finally to Peace," *New York Times,* 7 January 1989

Blessed are the peacemakers: for they shall be called the children of God.

> JESUS (A.D. 1st cent.). *Matthew* 5:9 (King James Version)
>
> See America: Richard M. Nixon (1)

The true and solid peace of nations consists not in equality of arms but in mutual trust alone.

> POPE JOHN XXIII (1881–1963). *Pacem in Terris (On Establishing Universal Peace in Truth, Justice, Charity and Liberty),* 113, 11 April 1963

Let us not accept violence as the way of peace. Let us instead begin by respecting true freedom: the resulting peace will be able to satisfy the world's expectations, for it will be a peace built on justice, a peace founded on the incomparable dignity of the free human being.

> POPE JOHN PAUL II (1920–). Message for the Fourteenth World Day of Peace, 1 January 1981

Mutual cowardice keeps us in peace.

> SAMUEL JOHNSON (1709–1784). 28 April 1778, in James Boswell, *The Life of Samuel Johnson,* 1791

It is in the nature of political bodies always to see the evil in the opposite group, just as the individual has an ineradicable tendency to get rid of everything he does not know and does not want to know about himself by foisting it off on somebody else.

Nothing has a more divisive and alienating effect upon society than this moral complacency and lack of responsibility, and nothing promotes understanding and *rapprochement* more than the mutual withdrawal of projections.

> CARL G. JUNG (1875–1961). *The Undiscovered Self,* 6, tr. R. F. C. Hull, 1957
>
> See Enemies: Jung

Never have the nations of the world had so much to lose, or so much to gain. Together we shall save our planet, or together we shall perish in its flames. Save it we can—and save it we must—and then we shall earn the eternal thanks of mankind and, as peacemakers, the eternal blessings of God.

> JOHN F. KENNEDY (1917–1963). United Nations address, New York City, 25 September 1961

Peace is a daily, a weekly, a monthly process, gradually changing opinions, slowly eroding old barriers, quietly building new structures.

> JOHN F. KENNEDY (1917–1963). United Nations address, New York City, 20 September 1963

True peace is not merely the absence of tension; it is the presence of justice.

> MARTIN LUTHER KING, JR. (1929–1968). *Stride Toward Freedom,* 2, 1958

We must come to see that peace is not merely a distant goal we seek, but it is a means by which we arrive at that goal. We must pursue peaceful ends through peaceful means.

> MARTIN LUTHER KING, JR. (1929–1968). "A Christmas Sermon on Peace," radio broadcast, CBC (Canada), 24 December 1967

Two centuries ago, the philosopher Kant predicted that perpetual peace would come about eventually—either as the creation of man's moral aspirations or as the consequence of physical necessity. What seemed utopian then looms as tomorrow's reality; soon there will be no alternative.

> HENRY A. KISSINGER (1923–). United Nations address, New York City, 24 September 1973

Peace depends ultimately not on political arrangements but on the conscience of mankind.

> HENRY A. KISSINGER (1923–). "Golda Meir: An Appreciation," 13 November 1977, *For the Record: Selected Statements, 1977–1980,* 1981

When nations are able to inflict tens of millions of casualties in a matter of hours, peace has become a moral imperative.

> HENRY A. KISSINGER (1923–). *White House Years,* 3, 1979

All we are saying is give peace a chance.

> JOHN LENNON (1940–1980) and PAUL McCARTNEY (1942–). "Give Peace a Chance" (song), 1969

If you wish for peace, understand war.

> B. H. LIDDELL HART (1895–1970). May 1932, *Thoughts on War,* 1.2, 1944
>
> See War & Preparedness: Saying (Latin)

By the time we got to Woodstock
We were half a million strong,
And everywhere was song and celebration,
And I dreamed I saw the bombers
Riding shotgun in the sky,
Turning into butterflies
Above our nation.

> JONI MITCHELL (1943–). "Woodstock" (song), 1969

Universal service is the price of peace.

> LEWIS MUMFORD (1895–1990). *The Conduct of Life,* 9.7, 1951

"Needed: A Department of Peace."

> KARL E. MUNDT (1900–1974). Title of Senate speech, 1945

There is no way to peace. Peace is the way.

> A. J. MUSTE (1885–1967). In "Debasing Dissent" (editorial), *New York Times*, 16 November 1967

Let us then pursue what makes for peace and for mutual up-building.

> PAUL (A.D. 1st cent.). *Romans* 14:19

They pass peaceful lives who ignore *mine* and *thine*.

> PUBLIUS SYRUS (85–43 B.C.). *Moral Sayings*, 790, tr. Darius Lyman, Jr., 1862
>
> See Possessions: Cervantes

We are destined to live together on the same soil in the same land. We, the soldiers who have returned from the battle stained with blood . . . we who have fought against you, the Palestinians—we say to you today in a loud and a clear voice: Enough of blood and tears! Enough!

> YITZHAK RABIN (1922–1995). Israeli prime minister. Speech at the signing of the Palestinian-Israeli peace agreement, White House, 13 September 1993

It isn't enough to talk about peace; one must believe in it. And it isn't enough to believe in it; one must work at it.

> ELEANOR ROOSEVELT (1884–1962). Voice of America radio broadcast, 11 November 1951

Peace, like charity, begins at home.

> FRANKLIN D. ROOSEVELT (1882–1945). Speech, Chatauqua (New York), 14 August 1936
>
> See Charity: Terence o Liberty: James B. Conant

Peace: Time out.

> LEO ROSTEN (1908–1997). "Political Lexicon," *New Republic*, 3 July 1935

Peace will never be entirely secure until men everywhere have learned to conquer poverty without sacrificing liberty or security.

> NORMAN THOMAS (1884–1968). Attributed

All men desire peace but few indeed desire those things which make for peace.

> THOMAS à KEMPIS (1380–1471). *The Imitation of Christ*, quoted by Aldous Huxley, "Seven Meditations." In Christopher Isherwood, ed., *Vedanta for the Western World*, 1945

Only through a harmonization of human wills, in a compact freely entered into in the light of divine necessity, can peace prevail among men.

> ARNOLD J. TOYNBEE (1889–1975). *A Study of History*, 12.535, 1961

Our goal must be not peace in our time but peace for all time.

> HARRY S. TRUMAN (1884–1972). Informal remarks, Galesberg (Illinois), 8 May 1950

1. Open covenants of peace, openly arrived at.

> WOODROW WILSON (1856–1924). "Fourteen Points," Congress speech, 8 January 1918

❦

When The
Power Of Love
Overcomes The
Love of Power
The World Will
Know Peace

> ANONYMOUS (AMERICAN). Inscribed on a soldier's cigarette lighter. In a photograph accompanying Malcolm W. Browne, "Vietnam: Memorabilia of a War Best Forgotten," *New York Times*, 24 April 1994

Peace is people talking together with a heart between them.

> ANONYMOUS (AMERICAN). Eight-year-old child. In Jeanne Larson and Madge Micheels-Cyrus, comps., *Seeds of Peace*, p. 258, 1986

Seek peace, and pursue it.

> ANONYMOUS (*BIBLE*). *Psalms* 34:14

Swords will be beaten into plowshares only after hearts of stone are changed into hearts of flesh.

> ANONYMOUS

Those who prefer victory to peace will have neither.

> ANONYMOUS

Though peace be made, yet it's interest that keeps peace.

> SAYING. In Oliver Cromwell, referring to it as "a maxim not to be despised," Parliament speech, 4 September 1654

If you wish for peace, prepare for peace.

> SAYING
>
> See War & Preparedness: Saying (Latin)

Peace through justice.

> SAYING

PEACE OF MIND

See also • Conscience o Faith: Thomas Merton o Peace o Work: Robert M. Pirsig

Inner peace is beyond victory or defeat.

> *BHAGAVAD GITA* (6th cent. B.C.). 18.26, tr. Juan Mascaró, 1962

That peace which the world cannot give.

> THE BOOK OF COMMON PRAYER. "Evening Prayer," 1662

Looking for peace is like looking for a turtle with a mustache: You won't be able to find it. But when your heart is ready, peace will come looking for you.

> AJAHN CHAH (1918–1992). *Reflections*, 107, 1994

Nothing can bring you peace but yourself. Nothing can bring you peace but the triumph of principles.

> RALPH WALDO EMERSON (1803–1882). Closing words, "Self-Reliance," *Essays: First Series*, 1841

Do everything so as to have thine own Approbation: This is the only Firm Foundation of inward Peace.

> THOMAS FULLER (1654–1734). Comp., *Introductio ad Prudentiam*, 642, 1731

There is no such thing as perpetual Tranquility of mind while we live here; because Life itself is but Motion and can never be without Desire, nor without Fear, no more than without Sense.

THOMAS HOBBES (1588–1679). *Leviathan,* 6, 1651

I do not want the peace which passeth understanding. I want the understanding which bringeth peace.

HELEN KELLER (1880–1968)

Peace does not rest in charters and covenants alone. It lies in the hearts and minds of the people.

JOHN F. KENNEDY (1917–1963). United Nations address, New York City, 20 September 1963

There is no such thing as inner peace. There is only nervousness or death.

FRAN LEBOWITZ (1951–). "Manners," *Metropolitan Life,* 1978

Ishmael: Oh, grassy glades! oh, ever vernal endless landscapes in the soul; in ye—though long parched by the dead drought of the earthy life—in ye, men yet may roll, like young horses in new morning clover; and for some few fleeting moments, feel the cool dew of the life immortal on them. Would to God these blessed calms would last. But the mingled, mingling threads of life are woven by warp and woof: calms crossed by storms, a storm for every calm.

HERMAN MELVILLE (1819–1891). *Moby-Dick; or, The Whale,* 114, 1851, ed. Harold Beaver, 1972

I feel fortunate to have come to that time in life when I can finally enjoy what my Quaker grandmother would have called "peace at the center."

RICHARD M. NIXON (1913–1994). Closing words. *In the Arena: A Memoir of Victory, Defeat and Renewal,* 1990

Lovely, lasting peace of mind,
Sweet delight of human kind.

THOMAS PARNELL (1679–1718). "Hymn to Contentment," 1721

The peace of God which passes all understanding.

PAUL (A.D. 1st cent.). *Philippians* 4:7

PEOPLE

See also • Crowds ○ Man ○ Mankind ○ The Masses ○ The People ○ The Public ○ Society

When dealing with people, let us remember we are not dealing with creatures of logic. We are dealing with creatures of emotion, creatures bristling with prejudices and motivated by pride and vanity.

DALE CARNEGIE (1888–1955). *How to Win Friends and Influence People,* rev. ed., 1.1, 1981 (1936)

The less you mess around with people, the better off people are.

CLINT EASTWOOD (1930–). In Maureen Dowd, "Go Ahead, Make Him Cry," *New York Times,* 26 March 1995

In spite of everything I still believe that people are really good at heart.

ANNE FRANK (1929–1945). 15 July 1944, *Anne Frank: The Diary of a Young Girl,* tr. B. M. Mooyart-Doubleday, 1952
See Ideals: Frank

I was part of that strange race of people aptly described as spending their lives doing things they detest to make money they don't want to buy things they don't need to impress people they dislike.

EMILE HENRY GAUVREAU

If we take people only as they are, we make them worse; if we treat them as though they were what they ought to be, we steer them in the right direction.

GOETHE (1749–1832). *Wilhelm Meister's Apprenticeship,* 7.8, 1796, tr. Hermann J. Weigand, 1949

If people are informed, they will do the right thing. It's when they are not informed that they become hostages to prejudice.

CHARLAYNE HUNTER-GAULT (1942–). In Brian Lanker, "Charlayne Hunter-Gault," *I Dream a World: Portraits of Black Women Who Changed America,* 1989

No one in this world, so far as I know—and I have researched the records for years, and employed agents to help me—has ever lost money by underestimating the intelligence of the great masses of plain people. Nor has anyone ever lost public office thereby.

H. L. MENCKEN (1880–1956). In *Chicago Tribune,* 19 September 1926 (Popular version: Nobody ever went broke underestimating the intelligence of the American public.)
See Leaders & People: Lord Chesterfield

All being said, I like only those people who are useful to me, and only so long as they are useful.

NAPOLEON (1769–1821). Remark to Gen. Gaspard Gourgaud, 1818, *The Mind of Napoleon: A Selection from His Written and Spoken Words,* 15, ed. J. Christopher Herold, 1955

People can be divided into three groups: those who make things happen, those who watch things happen, and those who wonder what happened.

JOHN NEWBERN. "John Newbern's Law," in John Peers, comp., *1,001 Logical Laws,* p. 117, 1979

In all people I see myself; none more and not one a barley-corn less,
And the good or bad I say of myself I say of them.

WALT WHITMAN (1819–1892). "Song of Myself" (20), 1855, *Leaves of Grass,* 1855–1892
See Faces: Whitman

❧

There are four kinds of people: Those who don't have it and know they don't have it; those who don't have it and think they have it; those who have it and don't think they have it; and those who have it and know they have it.

ANONYMOUS

THE PEOPLE

See also • America: Walt Whitman (1) ○ Democracy ○ Man ○ Mankind ○ The Masses ○ People ○ The Public ○ Society

The people are to be taken in very small doses.

> RALPH WALDO EMERSON (1803–1882). Journal, April 1847

The people are a very fickle baby that must have new toys every day.

> EMMA GOLDMAN (1869–1940). "The Traffic in Women," *Anarchism and Other Essays*, 3rd rev. ed., 1917 (1910)

None of us know all the potentialities that slumber in the spirit of the [people], or all the ways in which [people] can surprise us when there is the right interplay of events.

> VÁCLAV HAVEL (1936–). Czech president. *Disturbing the Peace*, 3, 1986, tr. Paul Wilson, 1990

The people long for only two things: bread and circuses.

> JUVENAL (A.D. 60?–127?). *Satires*, 10.79

Why should there not be a patient confidence in the ultimate justice of the people? Is there any better, or equal hope.

> ABRAHAM LINCOLN (1809–1865). *First Inaugural Address*, 4 March 1861

The people are the very substance, the living and free substance, of the body politic. The people are above the State, the people are not for the State, the State is for the people.

> JACQUES MARITAIN (1882–1973). *Man and the State*, 1.6, 1951

The question is: are the people to be *awakened* or to be *used?*

> JACQUES MARITAIN (1882–1973). *Man and the State*, 5.5, 1951

As to the people, they have no understanding, and only repeat what their rulers are pleased to tell them.

> PLATO (427?–347 B.C.). *Protagoras*, 317, tr. Benjamin Jowett, 1894

I am the people—the mob—the crowd—the mass.
Do you know that all the great work of the world is done through me?
I am the workingman, the inventor, the maker of the world's food and clothes.
I am the audience that witnesses history. The Napoleons come from me and the Lincolns. They die. And then I send forth more Napoleons and Lincolns.
I am the seed ground.

> CARL SANDBURG (1878–1967). Opening lines, "I Am the People, the Mob," *Chicago Poems*, 1916

In the darkness with a great bundle of grief
the people march.
In the night, and overhead a shovel of stars for
keeps, the people march:
                    "Where to? what next?"

> CARL SANDBURG (1878–1967). Closing lines, *The People, Yes*, 1936

Pa Joad: We sure are takin' abeatin'.
Ma Joad: I know. That's what make us tough. Rich fellas come up an' th' die an' their kids ain't no good, and they die out, but we keep acomin'. We're the people that live. They can't wipe us out. They can't lick us. We'll go on forever, pa, 'cause we're the people.

> JOHN STEINBECK (1902–1968) (NUNNALLY JOHNSON, scriptwriter). *The Grapes of Wrath* (film), 1940

Anonymous: There used to be a thing or a commodity we put great store by. It was called the People. Find out where the People have gone. I don't mean the square-eyed toothpaste-and-hair-dye people or the new-car-or-bust people, or the success-and-coronary people. Maybe they never existed, but if there ever were the People, that's the commodity the Declaration was talking about, and Mr. Lincoln. . . .
Steinbeck: Maybe the People are always those who used to live the generation before last.

> JOHN STEINBECK (1902–1968). *Travels with Charley: In Search of America*, 3, 1962

The human animal cannot be trusted for anything *good* except en masse. The combined thought and action of the whole people of any race, creed or nationality, will always point in the right direction.

> HARRY S. TRUMAN (1884–1972). Diary, 22 May 1945. In William Hillman, *Mr. President*, 3.2, 1952

In the People was my trust,
And in the virtues which mine eyes had seen.

> WILLIAM WORDSWORTH (1770–1850). *The Prelude; or, Growth of a Poet's Mind; An Autobiographical Poem*, 11.11, 1850

PERCEPTION

See also • Eyes ○ Reality ○ Seeing

If the doors of perception were cleansed, everything would appear as it is, infinite.

> WILLIAM BLAKE (1757–1827). *The Marriage of Heaven and Hell*, 14, 1790–1793?

As a rule we perceive what we expect to perceive. . . . The unexpected is usually not received at all. It is not seen or heard, but ignored. Or it is misunderstood.

> PETER F. DRUCKER (1909–). *Management: Tasks, Responsibilities, Practices*, 30, 1974, abr., 1977

Every new perception attended with a thrill of pleasure.

> RALPH WALDO EMERSON (1803–1882). Journal, 1858, undated

What we perceive and understand depends upon what we are.

> ALDOUS HUXLEY (1894–1963). "Beliefs," *Ends and Means: An Inquiry into the Nature of Ideals and into the Methods Employed for Their Realization*, 1937
>
> See Seeing: William Blake (2)

"VanLandingham: Perception Is Reality."

> TIM KEOWN (1964–). Article headline, *San Francisco Chronicle*, 9 June 1995. The headline was based on San Francisco Giants baseball player William VanLandingham's response to a question about his improved pitching and the possibility that he had changed: "I'm the same guy, with the same personality. It's just perception."

The act of drawing sharpens the perceptions of the draftsman.

> JOHN RUSKIN (1819–1900). Paraphrased by Anthony Storr, *Solitude: A Return to the Self*, 6, 1988

The outer sense alone perceives visible things and the eye of the heart alone sees the invisible.

> RICHARD OF SAINT-VICTOR (A.D. ?–1173). In E. F. Schumacher, *A Guide for the Perplexed*, 4, 1977
>
> See Seeing: Antoine de Saint-Exupéry

PERFECTION

See also • Children's Learning: E. M. Standing (1) ○ Earth: Walt Whitman ○ Egotism: First Person: Ted Turner ○ Evolution: Charles Darwin (3) ○ Excellence: [especially] H. Jackson Brown, Jr. ○ Faults: Benjamin Franklin (2) ○ Last Words: The Buddha ○ Moon: Rabindranath Tagore ○ Purpose: William James, Oscar Wilde ○ Unity: Anthony Storr

It breeds great perfection if the practice be harder than the use.

> FRANCIS BACON (1561–1626). "Of Nature in Men," *Essays,* 1625

Aim at perfection in everything, though in most things it is unattainable; however, they who aim at it, and persevere, will come much nearer it than those whose laziness and despondency make them give it up as unattainable.

> LORD CHESTERFIELD (1694–1773). Letter to his son, 24 May 1750

Ring the bells that still can ring,
Forget your perfect offering.
There's a hole in everything,
That's how the light comes thru.

> LEONARD COHEN (1934–). "Ring the Bells That Still Can Ring" (song), 1992

Everything, by an impulse of its own nature, tends towards its perfection.

> DANTE (A.D. 1265–1321). *Il convito,* 1.1.1, tr. Katharine Hillard, 1889

The closest to perfection a person ever comes is when he fills out a job application form.

> EVAN ESAR (1899–1995)

The very pink of perfection.

> OLIVER GOLDSMITH (1728–1774). *She Stoops to Conquer: Or, the Mistakes of Night,* 1, 1773

Perfection in the art of swordsmanship is reached, according to Takuan, when the heart is troubled by no more thought of I and You, of the opponent and his sword, of one's own sword and how to wield it—no more thought even of life and death. "All is emptiness: your own self, the flashing sword, and the arms that wield it. Even the thought of emptiness is no longer there." From the absolute emptiness, states Takuan, "comes the most wondrous unfoldment of doing."

> EUGEN HERRIGEL (1885–1955). *Zen in the Art of Archery,* p. 104, 1953, tr. R. F. C. Hull, 1964

Mastery in ink-painting is only attained when the hand, exercising perfect control over technique, executes what hovers before the mind's eye at the same moment when the mind begins to form it, without there being a hair's breadth between.

> EUGEN HERRIGEL (1885–1955). *Zen in the Art of Archery,* p. 104, 1953, tr. R. F. C. Hull, 1964

False notes [at a piano concert] are human. Why does everything have to be perfect? You know, perfection itself is imperfection.

> VLADIMIR HOROWITZ (1904–1989). In "Return of the Thunderer," *Newsweek,* 17 May 1965

You must be perfect—just as your Father in heaven is perfect.

> JESUS (A.D. 1st cent.). *Matthew* 5:48

A work is perfectly finished only when nothing can be added to it and nothing taken away.

> JOSEPH JOUBERT (1754–1824). 1809, *Pensées,* 1838, tr. Paul Auster, 1983

The essence of being human is that one does not seek perfection.

> GEORGE ORWELL (1903–1950). "Reflections on Gandhi," January 1949, *The Collected Essays, Journalism and Letters of George Orwell,* vol. 4, ed. Sonia Orwell and Ian Angus, 1968

No perfection is so absolute
That some impurity doth not pollute.

> SHAKESPEARE (1564–1616). *The Rape of Lucrece,* l. 853, 1594

The co-existence of a perfect man and an imperfect society is impossible.

> HERBERT SPENCER (1820–1903). *The Data of Ethics,* 15, 1879

What we do best or most perfectly is what we have most thoroughly learned by the longest practice, and at length it falls from us without our notice, as a leaf from a tree. It is the *last* time we shall do it—our unconscious leavings.

> HENRY DAVID THOREAU (1817–1862). Journal, 11 March 1859

Perfection consists in one thing only: doing the Will of God.

> ST. VINCENT de PAUL (1581–1660). In "Perfection" (6), *Spiritual Diary: Selected Sayings and Examples of Saints,* 1775, St. Paul Editions, 1962

In this broad earth of ours,
Amid the measureless grossness and the slag,
Enclosed and safe within its central heart,
Nestles the seed perfection.

> WALT WHITMAN (1819–1892). "Song of the Universal" (1), 1874, *Leaves of Grass,* 1855–1892

The true perfection of man lies, not in what man has, but in what man is.

> OSCAR WILDE (1854–1900). "The Soul of Man Under Socialism," *Fortnightly Review* (British journal), February 1891

Charity, dear Miss Prism, charity! None of us are [*sic*] perfect. I myself am peculiarly susceptible to draughts.

> OSCAR WILDE (1854–1900). *The Importance of Being Earnest,* 2, 1895

He who does not become perfect in small things will never be so in the great things.

> ST. FRANCIS XAVIER (1506–1552). In "Diligence" (17), *Spiritual Diary: Selected Sayings and Examples of Saints,* 1775, St. Paul Editions, 1962

The intellect of man is forced to choose
Perfection of the life, or of the work.

> WILLIAM BUTLER YEATS (1865–1939). In Catharine R. Stimpson, "Lives of the Geniuses," *New York Times Book Review,* 3 October 1993

❧

Practice makes perfect.

> SAYING (ENGLISH)

PERSECUTION

See also • Conversion: Anonymous (*Bible*) ○ Criticism: Ralph Waldo Emerson ○ Dissent: William Graham Sumner ○ Fanatics: Anonymous ○ Ideas: Aldous Huxley ○ Oppression ○ Prejudice

If you can impress any man with an absorbing conviction of the supreme importance of some moral or religious doctrine; if you can make him believe that those who reject that doctrine are doomed to eternal perdition; if you then give that man power, and by means of his ignorance blind him to the ulterior consequences of his own act—he will infallibly persecute those who deny his doctrine; and the extent of his persecution will be regulated by the extent of his sincerity.

> HENRY THOMAS BUCKLE (1821–1862). *History of Civilization in England,* 1.4, 1858

Religious persecution may shield itself under the guise of a mistaken and over-zealous piety.

> EDMUND BURKE (1729–1797). Speech at the impeachment trial of Warren Hastings, 17 February 1788

Albeit quite unwittingly, an authoritarian upbringing kills three birds with a single stone. It produces submission to the authority of the in-group. It arouses aggression, which is displaced onto a carefully defined out-group. By these means the status-seekers achieve their underlying goal, for the relativity of status depends upon the existence of an underprivileged out-group, and how better to ensure this state of underprivilege than by aggressive persecution.

> NORMAN F. DIXON (1922–). *On the Psychology of Military Incompetence,* 22, 1976

Of all the tyrannies on humankind,
The worst is that which persecutes the mind.

> JOHN DRYDEN (1631–1700). *The Hind and the Panther,* 1.240, 1687

We are more apt to persecute the unfortunates than the scoundrels; the scoundrels may retaliate.

> PAUL ELDRIDGE (1888–1982)

It is very difficult for people to believe the simple fact that every persecutor was once a victim. Yet it should be very obvious that someone who was allowed to feel free and strong from childhood does not have the need to humiliate another person.

> ALICE MILLER (1923–). German psychoanalyst. "Unintentional Cruelty Hurts, Too," *For Your Own Good: Hidden Cruelty in Child-Rearing and the Roots of Violence,* tr. Hildegarde and Hunter Hannum, 1983

PERSEVERANCE

See also • Courage: Euripides ○ Persistence ○ Resolution

Perseverance . . . is the very hinge of all virtues.

> THOMAS CARLYLE (1795–1881). Letter to his brother John, 15 March 1822. In James Anthony Froude, *Thomas Carlyle: A History of the First Forty Years, 1795–1835,* 1.9, 1882

There is a point beyond which perseverance can only be termed desperate folly.

> KARL von CLAUSEWITZ (1780–1831). *On War,* 4.9, 1832, tr. J. J. Graham, 1873

'Tis Perseverance that prevails.

> THOMAS FULLER (1654–1734). Comp., *Gnomologia: Adages and Proverbs,* 5110, 1732

Perseverance is the hard work you do after you get tired of doing the hard work you already did.

> NEWT GINGRICH (1943–). In Christopher Buckley, "Newtie's Greatest Hits," *New York Times Book Review,* 12 March 1995

Though difficulties may still lie ahead, whoever perseveres [with] love will someday find that everything has turned out for the best.

> FRANZ JÄGERSTÄTTER (1907–1943). Austrian farmer. In Gordon Zahn, *In Solitary Witness: The Life and Death of Franz Jägerstätter,* 4, 1964

Great works are performed not by strength but by perseverance.

> SAMUEL JOHNSON (1709–1784). *Rasselas: The Prince of Abyssinia,* 13, 1759

Perseverance is more prevailing than violence, and . . . many things which cannot be overcome when they are together, yield themselves up when taken little by little.

> SERTORIUS (123–72 B.C.). In Plutarch (A.D. 46?–119?), "Sertorius," *Parallel Lives,* Dryden edition, 1693

'Tis known by the name of perseverance in a good cause—and of obstinacy in a bad one.

> LAURENCE STERNE (1713–1768). *Tristram Shandy,* 1.17, 1759-1767
> See Obstinacy: Sir Thomas Browne

PERSISTENCE

See also • Effort ○ Failure: Michael Larsen ○ Industry ○ Obstinacy ○ Patience ○ Perseverance ○ Resolution ○ Success: B. H. Liddell Hart

Little by little does the trick.

> AESOP (6th cent. B.C.). "The Crow and the Pitcher," *Fables,* tr. Joseph Jacobs, 1894

Whoever knocks persistently, ends by entering.

> 'ALI (A.D. 600?–661). *Maxims of 'Ali,* tr. Maulana Akbar, undated

Many strokes fell tall Oaks.

> JOHN CLARKE (1596–1658). Comp., *Proverbs: English and Latine,* p. 36, 1639

Rome was not built in a day.

> JOHN CLARKE (1596–1658). Comp. *Proverbs: English and Latine,* p. 305, 1639
> See Wit: Examples: Jack Kerouac

A diamond is a piece of coal that stuck to the job.

> MICHAEL LARSEN (1941–). *Literary Agents: What They Do, How They Do It, and How to Find and Work with the Right One for You,* rev. ed., 15.7, 1996

Dripping water hollows a stone.

> LUCRETIUS (99–55 B.C.). *On the Nature of Things,* 1.313, tr. R. E. Latham, 1951

Drop upon drop collected will make a river. Rivers upon rivers collected will make a sea.

> SA'DI (A.D. 1213?–1292). *The Gulistan, or Rose Garden,* 8 (Maxim 42), A.D. 1258, tr. Edward Rehatsek, 1964

Ever'thing we do—seems to me is aimed right at goin' on. Seems that way to me. Even gettin' hungry—even bein' sick; some die, but the rest is tougher.

> JOHN STEINBECK (1902–1968). *The Grapes of Wrath,* 28, 1939

The universal line of distinction between the strong and the weak is that one persists; the other hesitates, falters, trifles, and at last collapses or "caves in."

> EDWIN PERCY WHIPPLE (1819–1886). "Character," 1857, *Character and Characteristic Men,* 1884

◈

When asked whether it was far to the next town, the sage replied, "Walk on!"

> ANONYMOUS. In Leo Tolstoy, *The Kingdom of God Is Within You,* 11, 1893

Keep on truckin', mama
Truckin' my blues away.

> ANONYMOUS. "Truckin'" (song), 1930

Step by step.

> SAYING (CHINESE)

Dogged does it.

> SAYING (GREEK)

Step by step one ascends the stairs.

> SAYING (PERSIAN)

Always at it wins the day.

> SAYING

Keep on keepin' on.

> SAYING

PERSONALITY

See also • Character: [especially] Anonymous (3) ○ Children's Learning: Maria Montessori (4) ○ Civilization: Ellen Key ○ Civilization, Modern: Arnold J. Toynbee (2) ○ Dehumanization ○ Evolution: Lewis Mumford ○ Purpose: Erich Fromm ○ Service: Albert Schweitzer ○ Temperament: Arnold J. Toynbee

The existence of personality presupposes the existence of God.

> NICOLAS BERDYAEV (1874–1948). *The Destiny of Man,* 1.3.2, 1931, tr. Natalie Duddington, 1955

Personality has unconditional value. . . . No abstract idea of the good can be put above personality.

> NICOLAS BERDYAEV (1874–1948). *The Destiny of Man,* 2.2.1, 1931, tr. Natalie Duddington, 1955

Learning from experience, learning from people, learning from successes and failures, learning from leaders and followers: personality is formed in these reactions to stimuli in social environments.

> JAMES MacGREGOR BURNS (1918–). *Leadership,* 3, 1978

The well-developed, well-integrated personality is the highest product of evolution, the fullest realization we know of in the universe.

> JULIAN HUXLEY (1887–1975). "Transhumanism," *New Bottles for New Wine,* 1957

Personality can never develop unless the individual chooses his own way, consciously and with moral deliberation.

> CARL G. JUNG (1875–1961). Title essay, 1934, *The Development of Personality,* tr. R. F. C. Hull, 1954

Without necessity nothing budges, the human personality least of all. It is tremendously conservative, not to say torpid. Only acute necessity is able to rouse it. The developing personality obeys no caprice, no command, no insight, only brute necessity.

> CARL G. JUNG (1875–1961). Title essay, 1934, *The Development of Personality,* tr. R. F. C. Hull, 1954

Real increase of personality means consciousness of an enlargement that flows from inner sources.

> CARL G. JUNG (1875–1961). "Concerning Rebirth" (2.2.b), 1950, *The Archetypes and the Collective Unconscious,* tr. R. F. C. Hull, 1959

Personality is still a growing factor in the universe, and is merely in its infancy. Its history is marked by the thousands of years, whereas that of organic nature is marked by the millions. Personality is as yet an inchoate activity of the whole, but nevertheless its character is already distinct and marked; and its future evolution is the largest ray of hope in human, if not terrestrial, destiny.

> JAN CHRISTIAN SMUTS (1870–1950). *Holism and Evolution,* 11, 1926

Personalities are inconceivable except as agents of spiritual activity.

> ARNOLD J. TOYNBEE (1889–1975). "Christianity and Civilization," 1947, *Civilization on Trial,* 1948

Personality change follows change in behavior. Since we are what we do, if we want to change what we are we must begin by changing what we do, must undertake a new mode of action.

> ALLEN WHEELIS (1915–). *How People Change,* 8, 1973
> See Deeds: George Eliot ○ Thinking: Mohandas K. Gandhi

I hope that is the keystone of the arch of my teachings—allowing a place for every man's personality, idiosyncrasy.

> WALT WHITMAN (1819–1892). Remark to the author, 16 June 1889. In Horace Traubel, *Walt Whitman's Camden Conversations,* ed. Walter Teller, 1973

It will be a marvelous thing—the true personality of man—when we see it. It will grow naturally and simply, flowerlike, or as a tree grows. It will not be at discord. It will never argue or dispute. It will not prove things. It will know everything. And yet it will not busy itself about knowledge. It will have wisdom. It's value will not be measured by material things. It will have nothing. And yet it will have everything, and whatever one takes from it, it will still have, so rich will it be. It will not be always meddling with others, or asking them to be like itself. It will love them because they will be different. And yet while it will not meddle with others, it will help all, as a beautiful thing helps us, by being what it is.

> OSCAR WILDE (1854–1900). "The Soul of Man Under Socialism," *Fortnightly Review* (British journal), February 1891

PERSUASION

See also • Advertising ○ Argument ○ Conversion ○ Evangelism ○ Logic ○ Motives ○ Negotiation ○ Propaganda ○ Reason ○ Words

We must approach them on their noble side.
> HENRI AMIEL (1821–1881). *Journal,* 22 April 1878, tr. Mrs. Humphrey Ward, 1887

The most effective way to influence opinion is by the selection and arrangement of the appropriate facts.
> EDWARD HALLETT CARR (1892–1982). *What Is History?* 1, 1961

To please people is a great step toward persuading them.
> LORD CHESTERFIELD (1694–1773). Letter to his son, 1 November 1739

Give your opinion modestly and coolly, which is the only way to convince.
> LORD CHESTERFIELD (1694–1773). Letter to his son, 16 October 1747

Some people are to be reasoned, some flattered, some intimidated, and some teased into a thing; but, in general, all are to be brought into it at last, if skillfully applied to, properly managed, and indefatigably attacked in their several weak places.
> LORD CHESTERFIELD (1694–1773). Letter to his son, 22 May 1749

There is no better way to convince others than first to convince oneself.
> CICERO (106–43 B.C.). In Martin Luther (1483–1546), *Table Talk,* 1566, tr. Preserved Smith and Herbert P. Gallinger, 1915

He who wants to persuade should put his trust not in the right argument, but in the right word. The power of sound has always been greater than the power of sense. . . . Don't talk to me of your Archimedes' lever. He was an absent-minded person with a mathematical imagination. Mathematics commands all my respect, but I have not use for engines. Give me the right word and the right accent, and I will move the world.
> JOSEPH CONRAD (1857–1924). "A Familiar Preface," *A Personal Record,* 1923
>
> See Power: Archimedes

Would you persuade, speak of Interest, not of Reason.
> BENJAMIN FRANKLIN (1706–1790). *Poor Richard's Almanack,* June 1734

To work a Man to thy Bent: 1. Know his Inclinations. 2. Observe his Ends. 3. Search out his Weakness. And so thou mayst either draw or drive him.
> THOMAS FULLER (1654–1734). Comp., *Introductio ad Prudentiam,* 1067, 1731

We are susceptible only to those suggestions with which we are already secretly in accord.
> CARL G. JUNG (1875–1961). *Modern Man in Search of a Soul,* 3, tr. W. S. Dell and Cary F. Baynes, 1933

By persuading others, we convince ourselves.
> JUNIUS (18th cent.). In *The Public Advertiser* (London), 35, 19 December 1769

The passions are the only orators who always convince.
> LA ROCHEFOUCAULD (1613–1680)

The art of persuasion has five chapters: affirmation, repetition, prestige, suggestion, and contagion.
> GUSTAVE LE BON (1841–1931). *Aphorisms of Present Times,* 1.7, 1913, tr. Alice Widener, 1979

If you would win a man to your cause, first convince him that you are his sincere friend.
> ABRAHAM LINCOLN (1809–1865). Address before the Washington Temperance Society, Springfield (Illinois), 22 February 1842

You've got to ac-cent-tchu-ate the positive
Elim-my-nate the negative
Latch on to the affirmative
Don't mess with Mister In-between.
> JOHNNY MERCER (1909–1976). "Ac-cent-tchu-ate the Positive" (song), 1943
>
> See Propaganda: Cyril Falls

Persuasion deals in the coin of self-interest.
> RICHARD E. NEUSTADT (1919–). *Presidential Power: The Politics of Leadership,* 3.3, 1960

Everyone is prejudiced in favor of his own powers of discernment, and will always find an argument most convincing if it leads to the conclusion he has reached for himself; everyone must then be given something he can grasp and recognize as his own idea.
> PLINY THE YOUNGER (A.D. 62?–113?). *Letters,* 1.20, tr. Betty Radice, 1963

One of the best ways to persuade others is with your ears—by listening to them.
> DEAN RUSK (1909–1994)

We address ourselves, not to their humanity but to their self-love, and never talk to them of our necessities but of their advantages.
> ADAM SMITH (1723–1790). *The Wealth of Nations,* 1.2, 1776

The shepherd always tries to persuade the sheep that their interests and his are the same.
> STENDHAL (1783–1842)

I and mine do not convince by arguments, similes, rhymes,
We convince by our presence.
> WALT WHITMAN (1819–1892). "Song of the Open Road" (10), 1856, *Leaves of Grass,* 1855–1892

PESSIMISM

See also • Cynicism ○ Despair ○ Optimism ○ Optimism & Pessimism ○ Pessimism: Examples

All the pessimists in world history together are nothing against reality.
> ELIAS CANETTI (1905–1994). 1971, *The Human Province,* tr. Joachim Neugroschel, 1978

Pessimism about man serves to maintain the status quo. It is a luxury for the affluent, a sop to the guilt of the politically inactive, a comfort to those who continue to enjoy the amenities of privilege.
> LEON EISENBERG (1922–). "The Human Nature of Human Nature," *Science,* 14 April 1972

Pessimism . . . is in brief, playing the sure game. You cannot lose at it; you may gain. It is the only view of life in which you can never be disappointed.

> THOMAS HARDY (1840–1928). In Florence Emily Hardy, *The Later Years of Thomas Hardy,* 7, 1930

A pessimist is usually a feller that haint got th' goods.

> KIN HUBBARD (1868–1930). *Abe Martin's Primer,* unpaged, 1914

A pessimist is a man who looks both ways before crossing a one-way street.

> LAURENCE J. PETER (1919–1990)

A pessimist is a person who has not had enough experience to be a cynic.

> MARY PETTIBONE POOLE. "No Axe to Grind," *A Glass Eye at a Keyhole,* 1938

[A pessimist is] a man who thinks everybody as nasty as himself, and hates them for it.

> GEORGE BERNARD SHAW (1856–1950). *An Unsocial Socialist,* 5, 1887

❧

A pessimist is just a well-informed optimist.

> ANONYMOUS

A pessimist wears both belt and suspenders.

> ANONYMOUS

PESSIMISM: EXAMPLES

See also • Despair ○ Optimism: Examples ○ Pessimism

Just when I finally figure out where it's at, somebody moves it.

> CHATAUQUA BOULEVARD LAW. Window sign, Pacific Palisades (California). In Paul Dickson, comp., *The Official Rules,* p. 47, 1978

Any time things appear to be going better, you have overlooked something.

> CHISHOLM'S LAW OF INEVITABILITY. In Laurence J. Peter, *Peter's People,* 8, 1979

It's always darkest just before the lights go out.

> ALEX CLARK. "Clark's Law." In Paul Dickson, comp., *The Official Rules,* p. 51, 1978
>
> See Optimism: Examples: Thomas Fuller

If you can see the light at the end of the tunnel, you are looking the wrong way.

> BARRY COMMONER (1917–)
>
> See Vietnam War: Henri-Eugene Navarre

We all know the rule of umbrellas—if you take your umbrella, it will not rain; if you leave it, it will.

> RALPH WALDO EMERSON (1803–1882). Journal, 1873, undated

The Other Line moves faster.

> BARBARA ETTORE. "Ettore's Law," in Laurence J. Peter, *Peter's People,* 8, 1979

No matter which way you ride, it's uphill and against the wind.

> FIRST LAW OF BICYCLING. In Paul Dickson, comp., *The Official Rules,* p. 34, 1978

The fairest Silk is the soonest stained.

> THOMAS FULLER (1654–1734). Comp., *Gnomologia: Adages and Proverbs,* 4516, 1732

An object in motion will always be headed in the wrong direction. An object at rest will always be in the wrong place.

> DAVID GERROLD. "Gerrold's Laws of Infernal Dynamics." In Paul Dickson, comp., *The Official Rules,* p. 102, 1978

The probability of anything happening is in inverse ratio to its desirability.

> JOHN W. HAZARD (1912–). "Gumperson's Law," in *Changing Times,* November 1957

A bad fittin' suit never wears out.

> KIN HUBBARD (1868–1930). "August," *Abe Martin's Almanack,* 1908

Never count on anything turnin' up but your toes.

> KIN HUBBARD (1868–1930)

In the fight between you and the world, back the world.

> FRANZ KAFKA (1883–1924). "Reflections on Sin, Pain, Hope, and the True Way" (50), 1917–1920, *The Great Wall of China,* 1931, tr. Willa and Edwin Muir, 1946

If several things that could have gone wrong have not gone wrong, it would have been ultimately beneficial for them to have gone wrong.

> THE LAST LAW. In Arthur Bloch, comp., preface to *Murphy's Law: Book Two,* 1980

If we see light at the end of the tunnel,
It's the light of the oncoming train.

> ROBERT LOWELL (1917–1977). "Since 1939," *Day by Day,* 1977
>
> See Vietnam War: Henri-Eugene Navarre

Things are never so bad that they can't get worse. But they're sometimes so bad they can't get better.

> MIGNON McLAUGHLIN (1915–). *The Second Neurotic's Notebook,* 5, 1966

1. Nothing is as easy as it looks.
2. Everything takes longer than you think.
3. If there is a possibility of several things going wrong, the one that will cause the most damage will be the one to go wrong.

> MURPHY'S LAW: COROLLARIES. In Arthur Bloch, comp., "Murphology," *Murphy's Law: And Other Reasons Why Things Go gnorW,* 1979]

If anything can go wrong, it will.

> GEORGE NICHOLS. Northrop Corp. manager. The original Murphy's Law, attributed, 1949. In John A. Simpson, ed., *The Concise Oxford Dictionary of Proverbs,* p. 4, 1982

If there is a wrong thing to do, it will be done, infallibly.

> GEORGE ORWELL (1903–1950). "War-time Diary," 18 May 1941, *The Collected Essays, Journalism and Letters of George Orwell,* vol. 2, ed. Sonia Orwell and Ian Angus, 1968

Negative predictions yield negative results; positive predictions yield negative results.

> LAURENCE J. PETER (1919–1990). "Peter's Nonreciprocal Law of Predictions," *Peter's People,* 8, 1979

The red light is always longer than the green light.
> LAURENCE J. PETER (1919–1990). "Peter's Theory of Relativity," *Peter's People*, 8, 1979

The person who snores the loudest will fall asleep first.
> PICKETT'S POSTULATE. In John Peers, comp., *1,001 Logical Laws*, p. 171, 1979

Chipped dishes never break.
> POPE'S LAW. In Arthur Bloch, comp., "Household Murphology," *Murphy's Law: Book Three*, 1982

The longer you wait in line, the greater the likelihood that you are standing in the wrong line.
> THE QUEUE PRINCIPLE. In Arthur Bloch, comp., "Situational Murphology," *Murphy's Law: Book Two*, 1980

There are two kinds of adhesive tape: that which won't stay and that which won't come off.
> TELESCO'S LAW OF NURSING. In Arthur Bloch, comp., "Medical Murphology," *Murphy's Law: Book Two*, 1980

A farmer was asked what sort of year he had just had. "Medium," came the reply. "What do you mean by 'medium?'" "Worse than last year but better than next."
> PETER WALKER (1932–). Speech before Royal Horticultural Society, 21 May 1979

There is no way out or round or through. . . . It is the end.
> H. G. WELLS (1866–1946). On his outlook for humanity, in Herbert J. Muller, *The Uses of the Past: Profiles of Former Societies*, 11.1, 1952

Things are never as bad as they turn out to be.
> RICHARD N. WHITE. Cornell University educator. "White's Law." In Paul Dickson, comp., *The Official Explanations*, p. 233, 1980

❦

It if works, it's obsolete.
> ANONYMOUS. In Marshall McLuhan, *Understanding Media: The Extensions of Man*, 1, 1964

Nothing bad ever goes away; nothing good ever stays.
> ANONYMOUS

The lost item is always to be found at the next place you would have looked had you not stopped looking.
> ANONYMOUS

The real descent begins only after hitting bottom.
> ANONYMOUS

Where you are is never where's it's at.
> ANONYMOUS

If I were a hatter, men would come into the world without heads.
> SAYING (GERMAN)

If I dealt in candles, the sun would never set.
> SAYING (YIDDISH)

PHILOSOPHERS

See also • Deception: Anonymous ○ Experts ○ Intellectuals ○ Philosophy ○ Professionals ○ Scholars ○ Teachers ○ Thinkers

Plato is dear to me, but dearer still is truth.
> ARISTOTLE (384–322 B.C.).

A philosopher ought to be someone for whom people remain as important as ideas.
> ELIAS CANETTI (1905–1994). 1967, *The Human Province*, tr. Joachim Neugroschel, 1978

Nothing is so absurd as not to have found an advocate in one of the philosophers.
> CICERO (106–43 B.C.). *De divinatione*, 2.58, tr. C. D. Yonge, 1902

You are a philosopher, Dr. Johnson. I have tried too in my time to be a philosopher; but, I don't know how, cheerfulness was always breaking in.
> OLIVER EDWARDS (1711–1791). 17 April 1778. In James Boswell, *The Life of Samuel Johnson*, 1791

It is only known to Plato that we can do without Plato.
> RALPH WALDO EMERSON (1803–1882). Journal, 10 July 1841

Which was the best age of philosophy? That in which there were yet no philosophers.
> RALPH WALDO EMERSON (1803–1882). Journal, 1852?–1853?, undated

What is the first business of him who philosophizes? To throw away self-conceit. For it is impossible for a man to begin to learn that which he thinks he knows.
> EPICTETUS (A.D. 55?–135?). *Discourses*, 2.17, tr. George Long, 1890?

You philosophers are sages in your maxims, and fools in your conduct.
> BENJAMIN FRANKLIN (1706–1790). "Dialogue Between Franklin and the Gout," 22 October 1780

If I wished to punish a province, I would have it governed by philosophers.
> FREDERICK II (1712–1786)

Many talk like Philosophers and live like Fools.
> THOMAS FULLER (1654–1734). Comp., *Gnomologia: Adages and Proverbs*, 3358, 1732

Philosophers
must ultimately find
their true perfection
in knowing all
the follies of mankind
- by introspection.
> PIET HEIN (1905–). "The Ultimate Wisdom," *Grooks II*, 1968

Philosophers are men hired by the well-to-do to prove that everything is all right.
> OLIVER WENDELL HOLMES, JR. (1841–1935). In J. A. C. Brown, *Techniques of Persuasion: From Propaganda to Brainwashing*, 1, 1963

Aristotle, the Philosopher's Pope.
> JAMES HOWELL (1593–1666). Comp., "Divers Centuries of New Sayings" (p. 5), *Paroimiographia: Proverbs, or Old Sayed Sawes & Adages in English . . . Italian, French and Spanish*, 1659

Speaking of Plato, I will add, that no writer, ancient or modern, has bewildered the world with more *ignes fatui* [i.e., inflamed folly] than this renowned philosopher in Ethics, in Politics and Physics.

> THOMAS JEFFERSON (1743–1826). Letter to William Short, 4 August 1820

That kings should philosophize or philosophers become kings is not to be expected. Nor is it to be wished, since the possession of power inevitably corrupts the untrammeled judgment of reason.

> IMMANUEL KANT (1724–1804). Second supplement to "Perpetual Peace," 1795, *On History,* ed. Lewis White Beck, 1963

In the information age, you don't teach philosophy as they did after feudalism. You perform it. If Aristotle were alive today, he'd have a talk show.

> TIMOTHY LEARY (1920–1996). In *Evening Standard* (British newspaper), 8 February 1989

When philosophers try to be politicians, they generally cease to be philosophers.

> WALTER LIPPMANN (1889–1974). *A Preface to Politics,* 3, 1914

The philosophers have only *interpreted* the world in various ways; the point, however, is to *change* it.

> KARL MARX (1818–1883). *Theses on Feuerbach,* Thesis 11, 1845, *The Marx-Engels Reader,* ed. Robert C. Tucker, 1972

To make light of philosophy is to be a true philosopher.

> BLAISE PASCAL (1623–1662). *Pensées,* 4, 1670, tr. William F. Trotter, 1931

Until philosophers are kings, or the kings and princes of this world have the spirit and power of philosophy, and political greatness and wisdom meet in one, and those commoner natures who pursue either to the exclusion of the other are compelled to stand aside, cities will never have rest from their evils—no, nor the human race—and then only will this our State have a possibility of life and behold the light of day.

> PLATO (427?–347 B.C.). *The Republic,* 5.473, tr. Benjamin Jowett, 1894

He said: Who then are the true philosophers?
Those, I said, who are lovers of the vision of truth.

> PLATO (427?–347 B.C.). *The Republic,* 5.475, tr. Benjamin Jowett, 1894

[In the cave allegory] those whose who are destitute of philosophy may be compared to prisoners in a cave, who are only able to look in one direction because they are bound, and who have a fire behind them and a wall in front. Between them and the wall there is nothing; all that they see are shadows of themselves, and of objects behind them, cast on the wall by the light of the fire. Inevitably they regard these shadows as real, and have no notion of the objects to which they are due. At last some man succeeds in escaping from the cave to the light of the sun; for the first time he sees real things, and becomes aware that he had hitherto been deceived by shadows. If he is the sort of philosopher who is fit to become a guardian, he will feel it is his duty to those who were formerly his fellow prisoners to go down again into the cave, instruct them as to the truth, and show them the way up. But he will have difficulty in persuading them, because, coming out of

the sunlight, he will see shadows less clearly then they do, and will seem to them stupider than before his escape.

> PLATO (427?–347 B.C.). *The Republic,* 7.514, as summarized by Bertrand Russell, *A History of Western Philosophy,* 15, 1946
>
> See Buddhism: *The Book of the Golden Precepts* (6) ○ Heroism: Arnold J. Toynbee

Plato . . . could boast a total of at least nine tyrants among his one-time pupils and associates.

> KARL R. POPPER (1902–1994). *The Open Society and Its Enemies,* 1.7.5, 1945

In our own day the name of philosopher has too often been the mask for the worst vices.

> QUINTILIAN (A.D. 35?–100?). *Institutio oratoria,* 1 (preface), tr. H. E. Butler, 1920

Aristotle could have avoided the mistake of thinking that women have fewer teeth than men by the simple device of asking Mrs. Aristotle to keep her mouth open while he counted.

> BERTRAND RUSSELL (1872–1970). "An Outline of Intellectual Rubbish," *Unpopular Essays,* 1950

[Georg Hegel] set [his philosophy] out with so much obscurity that people thought it must be profound.

> BERTRAND RUSSELL (1872–1970). "Philosophy and Politics," *Unpopular Essays,* 1950

There are some philosophers who exist to uphold the status quo, and others who exist to upset it. . . . For my part, I should reject both those as not being the true business of a philosopher, and I should say the business of a philosopher is not to change the world but to understand it, which is the exact opposite to what Marx said.

> BERTRAND RUSSELL (1872–1970). Woodrow Wyatt television interview, BBC, London, 1959, *Bertrand Russell Speaks His Mind,* 1, 1960

Should you ever intend to dull the wits of a young man and to incapacitate his brains for any kind of thought whatever, then you cannot do better than give him Hegel to read.

> ARTHUR SCHOPENHAUER (1788–1860). In Karl R. Popper, *The Open Society and Its Enemies,* 2.12.5(f), 1945

Leonato: There was never yet philosopher
That could endure the toothache patiently.

> SHAKESPEARE (1564–1616). *Much Ado About Nothing,* 5.1.35, 1598

There are nowadays professors of philosophy but not philosophers. . . . To be a philosopher is not merely to have subtle thoughts, nor even to found a school, but so to love wisdom as to live according to its dictates, a life of simplicity, independence, magnanimity, and trust. It is to solve some of the problems of life, not only theoretically, but practically.

> HENRY DAVID THOREAU (1817–1862). "Economy," *Walden; or Life in the Woods,* 1854

Slavery was contrary to all the moral principles advocated by Plato and Aristotle, yet neither of them saw this because to renounce slavery would have meant the collapse of the life they were living.

> LEO TOLSTOY (1828–1910). *The Kingdom of God Is Within You,* 6, 1893, tr. Aylmer Maude, 1936

A philosopher of imposing stature doesn't think in a vacuum. Even his most abstract ideas are, to some extent, conditioned by what is or what is not known in the time when he lives.

ALFRED NORTH WHITEHEAD (1861–1947). 10 June 1943, *Dialogues of Alfred North Whitehead*, rec. Lucien Price, 1954

❦

Vain is the word of a philosopher which does not heal any suffering of man.

ANONYMOUS. In W. Somerset Maugham, 1944, *A Writer's Notebook*, 1949

PHILOSOPHY

See also • Ideas ○ Ideology ○ Knowledge ○ Logic ○ Mind ○ Philosophers ○ Principles, Moral ○ Principles, Theoretical ○ Reason ○ Religion: [especially] Louis Kossuth ○ Science: [especially] Bertrand Russell (2) ○ Superstition ○ Theories ○ Thinking ○ Truth ○ Wisdom

Philosophy directs us first to seek the goods of the mind, and the rest will either be supplied, or are not much wanted.

FRANCIS BACON (1561–1626). *Advancement of Learning*, 8.2, 1605, Willey Book edition, 1944

A little philosophy inclineth Man's mind to atheism, but depth in philosophy bringeth men's minds about to religion.

FRANCIS BACON (1561–1626). "Of Atheism," *Essays*, 1625

The essence of philosophy is the abandonment of all authority in favor of individual human reason.

ALLAN BLOOM (1930–1992). "From Socrates' *Apology* to Heidegger's *Rektoratsrede*," *The Closing of the American Mind: How Higher Education Has Failed Democracy and Impoverished the Souls of Today's Students*, 1987

I think that philosophy is still rude and elementary. It will one day be taught by poets.

RALPH WALDO EMERSON (1803–1882). Title essay, *Natural History of Intellect and Other Papers*, 1893

Philosophy's work is finding the shortest path between two points.

KAHLIL GIBRAN (1883–1931). "Sayings," *Spiritual Sayings of Kahlil Gibran*, tr. Anthony R. Ferris, 1962

The great difficulty in philosophy is to come to every question with a mind fresh and unshackled by former theories, though strengthened by exercise and information.

WILLIAM HAZLITT (1778–1830). "On Novelty and Familiarity," *Table Talk*, 1822

Philosophy is nothing else than striving . . . to attain to knowledge of God.

HERMETIC BOOKS (2nd?–1st? cent. B.C.). Egyptian metaphysical writings. In Whitall N. Perry, comp., *A Treasury of Traditional Wisdom*, p. 746, 1986

Philosophy, to be relevant, must offer us a wisdom to live by.

ABRAHAM JOSHUA HESCHEL (1907–1972). *Who Is Man?* 1, 1965

Philosophy means thinking things out for oneself. Ultimately, there can be only one true philosophy, since reason is one and we all live in the same world.

DEAN WILLIAM RALPH INGE (1860–1954). "Confessio Fidei," *Outspoken Essays: Second Series*, 1922

All schools of philosophy, and almost all authors, are rather to be frequented for exercise than for weight.

WALTER SAVAGE LANDOR (1775–1864). "Epicurus, Leontion, and Ternissa," *Imaginary Conversations*, 1824–1853

Philosophy easily triumphs over past ills and ills to come, but present ills triumph over philosophy.

LA ROCHEFOUCAULD (1613–1680). *Maxims*, 22, 1665, tr. Leonard Tancock, 1959

The object of [philosophy's] lessons is to form the soul.

THOMAS BABINGTON MACAULAY (1800–1859). "Lord Bacon," *The Edinburgh Review* (Scotland), July 1837

Philosophy, the noblest pursuit of all.

PLATO (427?–347 B.C.). *The Republic*, 6.489, tr. Benjamin Jowett, 1894

Philosophy has had from its earliest days two different objects which were believed to be closely interrelated. On the one hand, it aimed at a theoretical understanding of the structure of the world; on the other hand, it tried to discover and inculcate the best possible way of life.

BERTRAND RUSSELL (1872–1970). "Philosophy for Laymen," *Unpopular Essays*, 1950

Governments make of philosophy a means of serving their state interests, and scholars make of it a trade.

ARTHUR SCHOPENHAUER (1788–1860). In Karl R. Popper, *The Open Society and Its Enemies*, 2.12.1, 1945

Hamlet: There are more things in heaven and earth, Horatio, Than are dreamt of in your philosophy.

SHAKESPEARE (1564–1616). *Hamlet*, 1.5.166, 1600
See Prayer: Alfred, Lord Tennyson

Philosophy begins in wonder.

SOCRATES (470?–399 B.C.). In Plato (427?–347 B.C.), *Theaetetus*, 21, tr. Benjamin Jowett, 1894

The philosophic mind is that which habitually sees the general in the particular, and finds food for the deepest thought in the simplest objects.

LESLIE STEPHEN (1832–1904). "Wordsworth's Ethics," *Cornhill Magazine* (England), August 1876

The broadest philosophy is narrower than the worst poetry.

HENRY DAVID THOREAU (1817–1862). In Ralph Waldo Emerson, journal, September 1845

It is easier to write ten volumes of philosophy than to put one principle into practice.

LEO TOLSTOY (1828–1910). In Stefan Zweig, "Tolstoy: Struggle for Realization," *Master Builders: A Typology of the Spirit*, tr. Eden and Cedar Paul, 1939

There are more truths in twenty-four hours of a man's life than in all the philosophies.

> RAOUL VANEIGEM (1934–). *The Revolution of Everyday Life*, 1.1, 1967

How shallow, puny, and imperfect are efforts to sound the depths in the nature of things. In philosophical discussion, the merest hint of dogmatic certainty as to finality of statement is an exhibition of folly.

> ALFRED NORTH WHITEHEAD (1861–1947). Preface to *Process and Reality: An Essay in Cosmology*, 1929

Philosophy is the endeavor to frame a coherent, logical, necessary system of general ideas in terms of which every element of our experience can be interpreted.

> ALFRED NORTH WHITEHEAD (1861–1947). *Process and Reality: An Essay in Cosmology*, 1.1.1, 1929

The safest general characterization of the European philosophical tradition is that it consists of a series of footnotes to Plato.

> ALFRED NORTH WHITEHEAD (1861–1947). *Process and Reality: An Essay in Cosmology*, 2.1.1, 1929

Philosophy begins in wonder. And, at the end, when philosophic thought has done its best, the wonder remains.

> ALFRED NORTH WHITEHEAD (1861–1947). *Modes of Thought*, 3.8, 1938

PHOTOGRAPHY

See also • Art ○ Media

One picture is worth a thousand words.

> FRED R. BARNARD. Advertising executive. 1921. In Wolfgang Mieder, *Proverbs Are Never Out of Season: Popular Wisdom in the Modern Age*, 6, 1993
>
> See Action & Talk: Tom Warson ○ Quotations: Diogenes ○ Sayings: Saying

I saw you hiding from a flock of paparazzi.
You were hoping, you were hoping that the ground would swallow you.

> PAUL McCARTNEY (1942–). "The World Tonight" (song), 1995

To photograph is to confer importance.

> SUSAN SONTAG (1933–). *On Photography*, 2, 1977

So successful has been the camera's role in beautifying the world that photographs rather than the world, have become the standard of the beautiful.

> SUSAN SONTAG (1933–). *On Photography*, 4, 1977

I am the President of the most powerful nation in the world. I take orders from nobody, except photographers.

> HARRY S. TRUMAN (1884–1972). Remark to foreign dignitaries. In David Binder, "George Tames, Photographer, Dies at 75," *New York Times*, 24 February 1994

Admiring friend: My, that's a beautiful baby you have there!
Mother: Oh, that's nothing—you should see his photograph!

> ANONYMOUS. In Daniel J. Boorstin, *The Image: A Guide to Pseudo-Events in America*, 1 (epigraph), 1961

PHYSICIANS

See also • Disease ○ Doctors ○ Drugs, Medical ○ Food: James Howell ○ Healing ○ Health ○ Professionals ○ Psychiatry ○ Psychiatrists ○ Surgeons

The principal objective of the medical profession is to render service to humanity. . . . In the practice of medicine a physician should limit the source of his professional income to medical services actually rendered by him, or under his supervision to his patients.

> AMERICAN MEDICAL ASSOCIATION. "Principles of Medical Ethics," 1957. In Arnold S. Relman, "What Market Values Are Doing to Medicine," *Atlantic*, March 1992

Our reliance on the physician is a kind of despair of ourselves.

> RALPH WALDO EMERSON (1803–1882). "Beauty," *The Conduct of Life*, 1860

Every physician almost hath his favorite disease.

> HENRY FIELDING (1707–1754). *The History of Tom Jones, A Foundling*, 2.9, 1749

He's the best physician that knows the worthlessness of the most medicines.

> BENJAMIN FRANKLIN (1706–1790). *Poor Richard's Almanack*, September 1733

As to diseases, make a habit of two things: to help, or at least, do no harm.

> HIPPOCRATES (460–377 B.C.). Greek physician. Stating the fundamental principle of what has become known as the Hippocratic (or Physicians') Oath, *Epidemics*, 1.11

If the physician presumes to take into consideration in his work whether a life has value or not, the consequences are boundless and the physician becomes the most dangerous man in the state.

> CHRISTOPH HUFELAND (1762–1836). German physician. In Fredric Wertham, *A Sign for Cain: An Exploration of Human Violence*, 9 (epigraph), 1966

I would prefer to trust a physician who has himself suffered from the malady he would treat.

> MONTAIGNE (1533–1592). *The Autobiography of Michel de Montaigne*, ed. Marvin Lowenthal, 26, 1935

You are a physician, doctor. You would promise life to a corpse if he could swallow pills.

> NAPOLEON (1769–1821). Remark to Dr. Francesco Antommarchi, 1820, *The Mind of Napoleon: A Selection from His Written and Spoken Words*, 168, ed. J. Christopher Herold, 1955

One of the first duties of the physician is to educate the masses not to take medicine.

> SIR WILLIAM OSLER (1849–1919). *Sir William Osler: Aphorisms from His Bedside Teachings and Writings*, ed. William B. Bean, 1950
>
> See Drugs, Medical: Osler

Medicine is not merely a science but an art. The character of the physician may act more powerfully upon the patient than the drugs employed.

> PARACELSUS (1693–1541). *Archidoxies*, 1525?

No physician, in so far as he is a physician, considers his own good in what he prescribes, but the good of his patient; for the true physician is also a ruler having the human body as a subject, and is not a mere moneymaker.

> PLATO (427?–347 B.C.). *The Republic*, 1.342, tr. Benjamin Jowett, 1894

Every man is either a fool or a Physician after thirty years of age.

> JOHN RAY (1628–1705). Comp., *A Collection of English Proverbs*, p. 35, 1678

Pay homage to the physician before you need him.

> *TALMUD* (A.D. 1st–6th cent.). Rabbinical writings. In Louis I. Newman, comp., *The Talmudic Anthology*, 248, 1945

Labor and abstinence are two of the best physicians in the world.

> THOMAS TRYON (17th cent.). *The Country-Man's Companion*, 1684

Men who are occupied in the restoration of health to other men, by the joint exertion of skill and humanity, are above all the great of the earth. They even partake of divinity, since to preserve and renew is almost as noble as to create.

> VOLTAIRE (1694–1778). "Physicians," *Philosophical Dictionary*, 1764, tr. William F. Fleming, 1901

Nothing is more estimable than a physician who, having studied nature from his youth, knows the properties of the human body, the diseases which assail it, the means which will benefit it, exercises his art with caution, and pays equal attention to the rich and the poor.

> VOLTAIRE (1694–1778). "Physicians," *Philosophical Dictionary*, 1764, tr. William F. Fleming, 1901

Physicians are like kings—
They brook no contradiction.

> JOHN WEBSTER (1580?–1625?). *The Duchess of Malfi*, 5.2, 1623

Only the wounded physician heals.

> SAYING (ASIAN). In Carl G. Jung (1875–1961), *Memories, Dreams, Reflections*, 4, ed. Aniela Jaffé, 1962

Physician, heal yourself.

> SAYING (*BIBLE*). Quoted by Jesus, *Luke* 4:23
> See Doctors: Euripides ○ Healing: Saying

Who is the skilled physician? He who can prevent sickness.

> SAYING (HASIDIC)

PITY

See also • Compassion ○ Indifference ○ Kindness ○ Sympathy

He pitieth not the Poor, who relieveth them not, when he well may.

> THOMAS FULLER (1654–1734). Comp., *Gnomologia: Adages and Proverbs*, 2004, 1732

He best can pity who has felt the woe.

> JOHN GAY (1685–1732). *Dione: A Pastoral Tragedy*, 1770

An expression of pity, devoid of genuine sympathy, leads to a new form of paternalism which no self-respecting person can accept.

> MARTIN LUTHER KING, JR. (1929–1968). *Strength to Love*, 3.3, 1963

Pity is feeling sorry for someone; empathy is feeling sorry with someone.

> MARTIN LUTHER KING, JR. (1929–1968). *Where Do We Go from Here: Chaos or Community?* 3.4, 1967

To pity distress is but human: to relieve it is Godlike.

> HORACE MANN (1796–1859). "Lectures on Education," 1837–1840
> See Errors: Alexander Pope (1)

How much to be pitied is he who has no pity!

> PUBLIUS SYRUS (85–43 B.C.). *Moral Sayings*, 263, tr. Darius Lyman, Jr., 1862

A foolish pity quickly overthrows
In war an army, and in peace a state.

> GEORGE WITHER (1588–1667). *Abuses Stript and Whipt*, 1.13, 1613

A little help is worth a lot of pity.

> SAYING (ENGLISH)

PLAGIARISM

See also • Creativity ○ Imitation ○ Originality: Katherine Fullerton Gerould, Dean William Ralph Inge ○ Originality ○ Quotations ○ Writing

Authors hide their big thefts by putting small ones between quotation marks.

> PAUL ELDRIDGE (1888–1982). *Maxims for a Modern Man*, 326, 1965

Immature poets imitate; mature poets steal.

> T. S. ELIOT (1888–1965). "Philip Massinger," *The Sacred Wood*, 1920

It is certain that I cannot always distinguish my own thoughts from those I read, because what I read becomes the very substance and text of my mind.

> HELEN KELLER (1880–1968). When accused of plagiarism. In James R. Kincaid, "Purloined Letters," *New Yorker*, 20 January 1997

Today an original thinker is the person who is the first to steal an idea.

> KARL KRAUS (1874–1936). 1912. In Thomas S. Szasz, *Karl Kraus and the Soul-Doctors: A Pioneer Critic and His Criticism of Psychiatry and Psychoanalysis*, 8, 1976

Though old the thought and oft exprest,
'Tis his at last who says it best.

> JAMES RUSSELL LOWELL (1819–1891). "For an Autograph," *Under the Willows and Other Poems*, 1868

I pounce on what is mine, wherever I find it.

> MARMONTEL (1723–1799). In Ralph Waldo Emerson, "Quotation and Originality," *Letters and Social Aims*, 1876

Borrowing, if it be not bettered by the borrower, is accounted plagiary.

> JOHN MILTON (1608–1674). *Eikonoklastes* (pamphlet), 23, 1659

If you steal from one author, it's plagiarism; if you steal from many, it's research.

> WILSON MIZNER (1876–1933). In Alva Johnston, *The Legendary Mizners*, 4, 1953

The only "ism" she believes in is plagiarism.

> DOROTHY PARKER (1893–1967). On a well-known author. In "Obituary Notes," *Publisher's Weekly,* 19 June 1967

[Computer] technology is changing traditional notions of authorship. The ability we have to rapidly access many different ideas on a subject with ever more refined searches increases the chance that an author is using someone else's ideas, or rather blending original and borrowed thoughts.

> JOHN SEABROOK. "The Big Sellout," *New Yorker,* 20 October 1997

The best ideas are common property.

> SENECA THE YOUNGER (5? B.C.–A.D. 65). "On Old Age," *Moral Letters to Lucilius,* 12.11, tr. Richard M. Gummere, 1918

Whatever is well said by anyone is mine.

> SENECA THE YOUNGER (5? B.C.–A.D. 65). "On Philosophy, the Guide of Life," *Moral Letters to Lucilius,* 16.7, tr. Richard M. Gummere, 1918

If I find in a book anything I can make use of, I take it gratefully. My plays are full of pillage of this kind.

> GEORGE BERNARD SHAW (1856–1950). In Michael Holroyd, *Bernard Shaw: The Pursuit of Power, 1898–1918,* 6.2, 1989

When you start stealing from your own work, you're in bad trouble.

> HUNTER S. THOMPSON (1939–). "June," *Fear and Loathing: On the Campaign Trail, '72,* 1973

Perhaps no poet is a conscious plagiarist, but there seems to be warrant for suspecting that there is no poet who is not at one time or another an unconscious one.

> MARK TWAIN (1835–1910). *Following the Equator: A Journey Around the World,* 8, 1897

Oscar Wilde (after hearing Whistler make a witty remark): I wish that I had said that.
Whistler: You will, Oscar, you will.

> JAMES ABBOTT McNEILL WHISTLER (1834–1903). Format adapted. 1885? In G. H. Fleming, *James Abbott McNeill Whistler: A Life,* 39, 1991

PLANNING

See also • Commanders ○ Decision-Making ○ Details ○ Intelligence, Military ○ Paradoxes: C. S. Lewis ○ Policy ○ Preparedness ○ Strategy, Military

The infirmity of human nature renders all plans precarious in the execution in proportion as they are extensive in the design.

> JEREMY BENTHAM (1748–1832). Preface to *An Introduction to the Principles of Morals and Legislation,* 1789–1823

The best laid schemes o' mice an' men
Gang aft a-gley.

> ROBERT BURNS (1759–1796). "To a Mouse," 1786 (Popular version: The best laid plans of mice and men often go astray.)

What makes a plan capable of producing results is the commitment of key people to work on specific tasks.

> PETER F. DRUCKER (1909–). *Management: Tasks, Responsibilities, Practices,* 8, 1974, abr., 1977

Before thou engagest, ask thyself, What if my Design miscarr[ies]?

> THOMAS FULLER (1654–1734). Comp., *Introductio ad Prudentiam,* 519, 1731

Never commit the Execution of a Design to him that had been unwilling to approve of it.

> THOMAS FULLER (1654–1734). Comp., *Introductio ad Prudentiam,* 614, 1731

An individual who is observed to be inconstant to his plans, or perhaps to carry on his affairs without any plan at all, is marked at once, by all prudent people, as a speedy victim to his own unsteadiness and folly.

> ALEXANDER HAMILTON (1757–1804) or JAMES MADISON (1751–1836). In *The Federalist Papers* (essay series), 62, February? 1788

Any damned fool can write a plan. It's the execution that gets you all screwed up.

> JAMES F. HOLLINGSWORTH. In Harry G. Summers, Jr., *On Strategy: A Critical Analysis of the Vietnam War,* 4, 1982

Many things difficult to design prove easy to performance.

> SAMUEL JOHNSON (1709–1784). *Rasselas: The Prince of Abyssinia,* 13, 1759

It is well to designate a general for a task and let him plan it himself. . . . No plan originated by another will be as sympathetically handled as one's own plan.

> CONRAD H. LANZA (1878–?). Annotator. *Napoleon and Modern War,* 79, 1943

Ensure that both plan and dispositions are flexible—adaptable to circumstances. Your plan should foresee and provide for a next step in case of success or failure.

> B. H. LIDDELL HART (1895–1970). *Strategy,* 20, 1954

[The commander] must always think and plan two battles ahead— the one he is prepared to fight *and* the next one—so that success gained in one battle can be used as a springboard for the next.

> BERNARD LAW MONTGOMERY (1887–1976). *The Memoirs of Field-Marshal Montgomery,* 6, 1958

Strategic planning is worthless—unless there is first a strategic vision.

> JOHN NAISBITT (1929–). *Megatrends: Ten New Directions Transforming Our Lives,* 4, 1984

There is no man more pusillanimous than I when I am planning a campaign. I purposely exaggerate all the dangers . . . that the circumstances make possible. I am in a thoroughly painful state of agitation. This does not keep me from looking quite serene in front of my entourage. . . . Once I have made up my mind, everything is forgotten except what leads to success.

> NAPOLEON (1769–1821). Remark to Pierre Roederer, 1799, *The Mind of Napoleon: A Selection from His Written and Spoken Words,* 305, ed. J. Christopher Herold, 1955

Plans must be simple and flexible. . . . They should be made by the people who are going to execute them.

> GEORGE S. PATTON, JR. (1885–1945). "Letter of Instruction Number 1," 6 March 1944, appendix (D) to *War As I Knew It,* 1947

The final test of a plan is its execution.

> UNITED STATES ARMY. *FM 100-5: Field Service Regulations—Operations,* 98, 1949

❧

The best plan is to profit by the folly of others.

> SAYING (LATIN). In Pliny the Elder (A.D. 23–79), *Natural History*

PLANTS

See also • Nature

What is a weed? A plant whose virtues have not yet been discovered.

> RALPH WALDO EMERSON (1803–1882). "The Fortune of the Republic," lecture, Old South Church, Boston, 30 March 1878

Dandelions and blue flowers are still growing in sunny places. Saw in a barn a prodigious treasure of onions in their silvery coats, exhaling a penetrating perfume.

> NATHANIEL HAWTHORNE (1804–1864). 7 October 1837, *The American Notebooks,* ed. Claude M. Simpson, 1932

Does music make plants grow, or are there among the plants some that are musical?

> GEORG CHRISTOPH LICHTENBERG (1742–1799). *Aphorisms,* 7.244, 1806, tr. R. J. Hollingdale, 1990

PLEASING OTHERS

See also • Conversation: Fulke Greville ◦ Failure: Herbert Bayard Swope ◦ Manners ◦ Persuasion: Lord Chesterfield (1) ◦ Popularity ◦ Respectability

Please all, and you will please none.

> AESOP (6th cent. B.C.). "The Man, the Boy, and the Donkey," *Fables,* tr. Joseph Jacobs, 1894

The only wa tu pleze evra boddy, is tu make evry boddy think yu ar a bigger fule than tha ar.

> JOSH BILLINGS (1818–1885). *His Sayings,* 45, 1867

He makes people pleased with him by making them first pleased with themselves.

> LORD CHESTERFIELD (1694–1773). Letter to his son, 18 January 1750

What pleases you in others will in general please them in you.

> LORD CHESTERFIELD (1694–1773). Letter to his son, 9 July 1750

If you mean to profit, learn to please.

> CHARLES CHURCHILL (1731–1764). *Gotham,* 2.1.8, 1764

He that can please nobody is not so much to be pitied as he that nobody can please.

> C. C. COLTON (1780–1832). *Lacon: or, Many Things in Few Words; Addressed to Those Who Think,* 1.231, 1823

I wish the man to please himself, then he will please me.

> RALPH WALDO EMERSON (1803–1882). Journal, 1861, undated

To serve the Public faithfully, and at the same time please it entirely, is impracticable.

> BENJAMIN FRANKLIN (1706–1790). *Poor Richard's Almanack,* October 1758

The art of pleasing consists in being pleased. To be amiable is to be satisfied with one's self and others.

> WILLIAM HAZLITT (1778–1830). "On Manner," *The Round Table,* 1817

When we are pleased with ourselves, we are pleased with others.

> ELBERT HUBBARD (1856–1915). *The Philosophy of Elbert Hubbard,* p. 156, comp. Elbert Hubbard II, 1930

The fellow that's pleased with everything either don't cut any ice or has something up his sleeve.

> KIN HUBBARD (1868–1930).

No man is much pleased with a companion who does not increase, in some respect, his fondness of himself.

> SAMUEL JOHNSON (1709–1784). In *The Rambler* (English journal), 104, March 1751

Though a man often pleases by inferiority, there are few who desire to give such pleasure.

> SAMUEL JOHNSON (1709–1784). In *The Adventurer* (English journal), 131, 5 February 1754

He that is pleased with himself easily imagines that he shall please others.

> SAMUEL JOHNSON (1709–1784). "Pope," *Lives of the English Poets,* 1781

We have not fully pleased anybody and that's a good sign.

> SOLOMON LISS. Maryland Critical Areas Commission chairman. In Robert Barnes, "Bay Foundation Scores Md. Critical Areas Law," *Washington Post,* 25 June 1988

The man who makes it his business to please the multitude is never done.

> MONTAIGNE (1533–1592). *The Autobiography of Michel de Montaigne,* ed. Marvin Lowenthal, 34, 1935

Don't consider how many you can please, but whom.

> PUBLIUS SYRUS (85–43 B.C.). *Moral Sayings,* 599, tr. Darius Lyman, Jr., 1862

Let your life be pleasing to the multitude, and it cannot be so to yourself.

> PUBLIUS SYRUS (85–43 B.C.). *Moral Sayings,* 1075, tr. Darius Lyman, Jr., 1862

If you try to please everybody, somebody is not going to like it.

> DONALD RUMSFELD (1932–). "Rumsfeld's Rules" (collected while serving at the White House and Pentagon), *Washingtonian,* February 1977

❧

Who would please everybody must rise early.

> SAYING (FRENCH).

PLEASURE

See also • Abstinence ◦ Body: Lewis Mumford ◦ Death: Saying (*Bible*) ◦ Happiness ◦ Joy ◦ Morality: Chamfort ◦ Motives: Jeremy Bentham ◦ Pain ◦ Passion ◦ Puritanism ◦ Self-Discipline ◦ Sex

The master of pleasure is not he who abstains from it, but he who uses it without being carried away by it.

> ARISTIPPUS (435?–366 B.C.)

The love of pleasure is one of the great elementary instincts of human nature.

> ARISTOTLE (384–322 B.C.). *Nicomachean Ethics,* 10.1, tr. J. A. K. Thomson, 1953

People seem to enjoy things more when they know a lot of other people have been left out of the pleasure.

> RUSSELL BAKER (1925–). "The Sport of Counting Each Other Out," *New York Times,* 2 November 1967

Variety is the soul of pleasure.

> APHRA BEHN (1640–1689). *The Rover,* pt. 2, act 1, 1681

Let us have wine and women, mirth and laughter
Sermons and soda water the day after.

> LORD BYRON (1788–1824). *Don Juan,* 2.178, 1819–1824

Business and pleasure, rightly understood, mutually assist each other, instead of being enemies, as silly or dull people often think them. No man tastes pleasures truly who does not earn them by previous business; and few people do business well who do nothing else.

> LORD CHESTERFIELD (1694–1773). Letter to his son, 7 August 1749

Pleasure is a *thief* to business.

> DANIEL DEFOE (1660–1731). *The Complete English Tradesman,* 1.9, 1726

The honest Man takes Pains, and then enjoys Pleasures;
    the Knave takes Pleasure, and then suffers Pains.

> BENJAMIN FRANKLIN (1706–1790). *Poor Richard's Almanack,* May 1755
>
> See Morality: Samuel Butler (1)

Pleasure tasteth well after Service.

> THOMAS FULLER (1654–1734). Comp., *Gnomologia: Adages and Proverbs,* 3887, 1732
>
> See Desire: Saying (English)

It is the pleasure of the bee to gather honey of the flower,
    But it is also the pleasure of the flower to yield its honey to the bee. . . .
    And to both, bee and flower, the giving and the receiving of pleasure is a need and an ecstasy.

> KAHLIL GIBRAN (1883–1931). "On Pleasure," *The Prophet,* 1923

Mankind is safer when men seek pleasure than when they seek the power and the glory.

> GEOFFREY GORER (1939–). British anthropologist. "Man Has No 'Killer' Instinct," *New York Times Magazine,* 27 November 1966

The essence of pleasure is spontaneity.

> GERMAINE GREER (1939–). "Revolution," *The Female Eunuch,* 1970

They that seldom take pleasure seldom give pleasure.

> FULKE GREVILLE (1554–1628). *Maxims, Characters, and Reflections,* p. 192, 1756

The last pleasure in life is the sense of discharging our duty.

WILLIAM HAZLITT (1778–1830). "On Novelty and Familiarity," *Table Talk,* 1822

One cannot have pleasure without giving it.

> HERMANN HESSE (1877–1962). *Siddhartha,* 2 ("Amongst the People"), 1922, tr. Hilda Rosner, 1951

Follow pleasure, and then will pleasure flee;
Flee pleasure, and pleasure will follow thee.

> JOHN HEYWOOD (1497–1580). Comp. *A Dialogue Containing the Number of the Effectual Proverbs in the English Tongue,* 1.11, 1562

No state can be more destitute than that of him who, when the delights of sense forsake him, has no pleasures of the mind.

> SAMUEL JOHNSON (1709–1784). "Cymbeline," *The Plays of William Shakespeare,* 1765

What will you think of pleasures when you no longer enjoy them?

> JOSEPH JOUBERT (1754–1824). 1802, *Pensées,* 1838, tr. Paul Auster, 1983

A pleasure deferred is a pleasure intensified.

> ADAIR LARA (1952–). "Something to Look Forward to," *San Francisco Chronicle,* 11 April 1996

The pursuit of pleasure disguises a struggle for power. . . . Activities ostensibly undertaken purely for enjoyment often have the real object of doing others in.

> CHRISTOPHER LASCH (1932–1994). *The Culture of Narcissism: American Life in an Age of Diminishing Expectations,* 3, 1979

A man should neither pursue nor flee ["natural pleasures"]: he should receive them.

> MONTAIGNE (1533–1592). *The Autobiography of Michel de Montaigne,* ed. Marvin Lowenthal, 15, 1935

Most men that do thrive in the world do forget to take pleasure during the time that they are getting their estate, but reserve that till they have got one and then it is too late for them to enjoy it.

> SAMUEL PEPYS (1633–1703). Diary, 10 March 1666

The sweetest pleasure arises from difficulties overcome.

> PUBLIUS SYRUS (85–43 B.C.). *Moral Sayings,* 989, tr. Darius Lyman, Jr., 1862

Now the Powers of Beauty, Song, and Wine,
Which are most men's delights, are also mine.

> SOLON (630?–560? B.C.). One of the Seven Sages of Greece. In Plutarch (A.D. 46?–119?), "Solon," *Parallel Lives,* Dryden edition, 1693

Who does not love wine, women, and song
Remains a fool his whole life long
Says Doctor Martin Luther.

> JOHANN HEINRICH VOSS (1751–1826). German poet.

Pleasure is Nature's test, her sign of approval.

> OSCAR WILDE (1854–1900). *The Picture of Dorian Gray,* 6, 1891

All the things I really like to do are either immoral, illegal, or fattening.

> ALEXANDER WOOLLCOTT (1887–1943). In Robert E. Drennan, ed., "Alexander Woollcott," *The Algonquin Wits,* 1968

✿

Drugs, sex, and rock 'n roll.
  SAYING (AMERICAN), 1960s

Business before pleasure.
  SAYING (ENGLISH)

POETRY

See also • Art ○ Creativity: [especially] Ralph Waldo Emerson (1)
○ Creativity: First Person ○ Love, Romantic: Muriel Spark ○
Philosophy: Henry David Thoreau ○ Poets ○ Trees: Joyce Kilmer
○ Vision ○ Words ○ Writing

Poetry is that art which selects and arranges the symbols of
thought in such a manner as to excite the imagination the most
powerfully and delightfully.
  WILLIAM CULLEN BRYANT (1794–1878). "The Nature of Poetry," lecture,
    April 1825

Dr. [Samuel] Johnson hearing that Adam Smith, whom he had
once met, relished rhyme, said, "If I had known that, I should
have hugged him."
  RALPH WALDO EMERSON (1803–1882). Speech at the opening of the
    Concord Free Public Library (Massachusetts), autumn 1873

Poetry begins . . . when we look from the center outward.
  RALPH WALDO EMERSON (1803–1882). "Poetry and the Imagination,"
    Letters and Social Aims, 1876

Poetry's a mere drug, Sir.
  GEORGE FARQUHAR (1678–1707). Love and a Bottle, 3.2, 1699

Poetry the common carrier
for the transportation of the public
to higher places
than other wheels can carry it.
  LAWRENCE FERLINGHETTI (1919–). "Populist Manifesto (For Poets, With
    Love)," 1975, The Populist Manifestos, 1981

Poetry is music written for the human voice.
  MRS. FLOWERS. Quoted by Maya Angelou. In Bill Moyers interview,
    Creativity, television documentary series, PBS, 24 February 1992

I'd just as soon play tennis with the net down.
  ROBERT FROST (1874–1963). On writing free verse, lecture, Milton
    Academy (Massachusetts), 17 May 1935

[A poem] begins in delight and ends in wisdom.
  ROBERT FROST (1874–1963). "The Figure a Poem Makes," Collected
    Poems of Robert Frost, 1939

I have a new method of poetry. All you got to do is look over
your notebooks . . . or lay down on a couch, and think of anything that comes into your head, especially the miseries. . . . Then
arrange in lines of two, three or four words each, don't bother
about sentences, in sections of two, three or four lines each.
  ALLEN GINSBERG (1926–1997). Letter to Jack Kerouac and
    Neal Cassady, 1952. In Barry Miles, Ginsberg: A Biography,
    5, 1989

Poetry's role is to provide spontaneous individual candor as distinct from manipulators and brainwash.
  ALLEN GINSBERG (1926–1997). In "Allen Ginsberg Has Terminal
    Cancer," San Francisco Chronicle, 4 April 1997

Science sees signs; Poetry, the thing signified.
  J. C. HARE (1795–1855) and A. W. HARE (1792–1834). Guesses at Truth:
    Second Series, p. 354, 1848, Macmillan edition, 1867

Poetry is to be found nowhere unless we carry it within us.
  JOSEPH JOUBERT (1754–1824). Pensées, 297, 1838, tr. Henry Attwell,
    1877

Poetry has no utility save for the soul's delight.
  JOSEPH JOUBERT (1754–1824). Pensées, 1838, tr. H. P. Collins, 1928

Poetry should surprise by a fine excess, and not by Singularity—
it should strike the Reader as a wording of his own highest
thoughts, and appear almost a Remembrance.
  JOHN KEATS (1795–1821). Letter to John Taylor, 27 February 1818

If poetry comes not as naturally as the Leaves to a tree, it had better not come at all.
  JOHN KEATS (1795–1821). Letter to John Taylor, 27 February 1818

Poetry today is easier to write but harder to remember.
  STANLEY KUNITZ (1905–). In Peter Davison, "Time, Please" (epigraph),
    Atlantic, September 1988

As to the pure mind all things are pure, so to the poetic mind all
things are poetical.
  HENRY WADSWORTH LONGFELLOW (1807–1882). "Twice-Told Tales,"
    Driftwood, 1857

A poem should be wordless
As the flight of birds.
  ARCHIBALD MacLEISH (1892–1982). "Ars Poetica," Streets in the Moon,
    1926

A poem should not mean
But be.
  ARCHIBALD MacLEISH (1892–1982). "Ars Poetica," Streets in the Moon,
    1926

Publishing a volume of poetry today is like dropping a rose petal
down the Grand Canyon and waiting for the echo.
  DON MARQUIS (1878–1937). In Edward Anthony, O Rare Don Marquis,
    6, 1962

Poetry is above all a concentration of the power of language,
which is the power of our ultimate relationship to everything in
the universe.
  ADRIENNE RICH (1929–). Introductory essay to Judy Grahn, The Work
    of a Common Woman, 1978

Our poems will have failed if our readers are not brought by them
beyond the poems.
  MURIEL RUKEYSER (1913–1980). The Life of Poetry, 5, 1949

Poetry is the achievement of the synthesis of hyacinths and bis-
cuits.
  CARL SANDBURG (1878–1967). "Tentative (First Model) Definitions of
    Poetry" (36), Good Morning, America, 1928

My poems are hymns of praise to the glory of life.

> EDITH SITWELL (1887–1964). "Some Notes on My Poetry," *Collected Poems*, 1954

A little *space* encloses a huge void. There, those great whorls, the stars hang. Who can get outside the universe? But the poem was born elsewhere, and need not stay. Like the wild geese of the Arctic it heads home, far above the borders, where most things cannot cross.

> GARY SNYDER (1930–). "On 'As for Poets,'" *Turtle Island*, 1974

Mad Verse, Sad Verse, Glad Verse and Bad Verse.

> JOHN TAYLOR (1580–1653). Book title, 1644

The world is never the same once a good poem has been added to it.

> DYLAN THOMAS (1914–1953). "On Poetry," *Quite Early One Morning*, 1960

The best craftsmanship always leaves holes and gaps . . . so that something that is *not* in the poem can creep, crawl, flash, or thunder in.

> DYLAN THOMAS (1914–1953). "Poetic Manifesto," *Texas Quarterly*, 4, 1961

A true poem is distinguished not so much by a felicitous expression, or any thought it suggests, as by the atmosphere which surrounds it.

> HENRY DAVID THOREAU (1817–1862). "Friday," *A Week on the Concord and Merrimack Rivers*, 1849

A poem is never finished, only abandoned.

> PAUL VALÉRY (1871–1945). In W. H. Auden, "Writing," *A Certain World: A Commonplace Book*, 1971

Poetry is to prose as dancing is to walking.

> JOHN WAIN (1925–1994). Radio broadcast, BBC, London, 13 January 1976

I will not make a poem nor the least part of a poem but has
   reference to the soul,
Because having look'd at the objects of the universe, I find
   there is no one nor any particle of one but has reference to
   the soul.

> WALT WHITMAN (1819–1892). "Starting from Paumanok" (12), 1860, *Leaves of Grass*, 1855–1892

The best prose is that which is most full of poetry.

> VIRGINIA WOOLF (1882–1941). "Montaigne," *The Common Reader* (First Series), 1925

All good poetry is the spontaneous overflow of powerful feelings: it takes its origin from emotion recollected in tranquility.

> WILLIAM WORDSWORTH (1770–1850). Preface to *Lyrical Ballads*, 2nd ed., 1805

What can be explained is not poetry.

> WILLIAM BUTLER YEATS (1865–1939). Recalling his father's words. In Carl Sandburg, "Notes for a Preface," *Complete Poems*, 1950

Poetry is like a bird, it ignores all frontiers.

> YEVGENY YEVTUSHENKO (1933–). Russian poet. 2 July 1967

POETS

See also • Artists ○ Contemplation: Thomas Merton (2) ○ Creativity: [especially] William Pounstone ○ Creativity: First Person: [especially] William Blake (1,2) ○ Dreams: Ralph Waldo Emerson (3) ○ Philosphy: Ralph Waldo Emerson ○ Poetry ○ Writers

The poet's function is to describe, not the thing that has happened, but a kind of thing that might happen. . . . Poetry is something more philosophic and of graver import than history, since its statements are of the nature rather of universals, whereas those of history are singulars.

> ARISTOTLE (384–322 B.C.). *Poetics*, 9, tr. Ingram Bywater, 1954
> See Historians: Alan Bullock

It is a great thing, indeed, to make a proper use of the poetical forms, as also of compounds and strange words. But the greatest thing by far is to be a master of metaphor. It is the one thing that cannot be learnt from others; and it is also a sign of genius, since a good metaphor implies an intuitive perception of the similarity in dissimilars.

> ARISTOTLE (384–322 B.C.). *Poetics*, 22, tr. Ingram Bywater, 1954

One Power alone makes a Poet: Imagination, The Divine Vision.

> WILLIAM BLAKE (1757–1827). Annotation to William Wordsworth's "Poems," *The Complete Writings of William Blake*, ed. Geoffrey Keynes, 1966

When the grasshopper gathers its strength to hop, it does not know where it will land. So it often is with poets.

> GERALD BRENAN (1894–1987). "Literature," *Thoughts in a Dry Season: A Miscellany*, 1978

The worst tragedy for a poet is to be admired through being misunderstood.

> JEAN COCTEAU (1889–1963). "Le Coq et l'Arlequin," *Le Rappel à l'ordre*, 1926

No man was ever yet a great poet, without being at the same time a profound philosopher.

> SAMUEL TAYLOR COLERIDGE (1772–1834). *Biographia Literaria*, 15, 1817

There is a pleasure in poetic pains
Which only poets know.

> WILLIAM COWPER (1731–1800). *The Task*, 2.285, 1785

The great poets are judged by the frame of mind they induce.

> RALPH WALDO EMERSON (1803–1882). Preface to "Parnassus," 1874

A religious poet once told me that he valued his poems, not because they were his, but because they were not. He thought the angels brought them to him.

> RALPH WALDO EMERSON (1803–1882). "Inspiration," *Letters and Social Aims*, 1876

The only teller of news is the poet. When he sings, the world listens with the assurance that now a secret of God is to be spoken.

> RALPH WALDO EMERSON (1803–1882). "Poetry and the Imagination," *Letters and Social Aims*, 1876

The finer the sense of justice, the better poet.

> RALPH WALDO EMERSON (1803–1882). "The Sovereignty of Ethics,"
> *Lectures and Biographical Sketches,* 1883

Constantly risking absurdity
   and death
whenever he performs
   above the heads
      of his audience
the poet like an acrobat
   climbs on rime
      to a high wire of his own making.

> LAWRENCE FERLINGHETTI (1919–). Title poem (15), *A Coney Island of
> the Mind,* 1958

Where are Whitman's wild children,
where the great voices speaking out
with a sense of sweetness and sublimity,
where the great new vision,
the great world-view,
the high prophetic song
of the immense earth
and all that sings in it
And our relation to it—
Poets, descend
to the street of the world once more
And open your minds & eyes
with the old visual delight,
Clear your throat and speak up,
Poetry is dead, long live poetry
with terrible eyes and buffalo strength.
Don't wait for the Revolution
or it'll happen without you.

> LAWRENCE FERLINGHETTI (1919–). "Populist Manifesto (For Poets, With
> Love)," 1975, *The Populist Manifestos,* 1981

No tears in the writer, no tears in the reader. No surprise for the writer, no surprise for the reader. For me the initial delight is in the surprise of remembering something I didn't know I knew.

> ROBERT FROST (1874–1963). "The Figure a Poem Makes," *Collected
> Poems of Robert Frost,* 1939

Modern poets add a lot of water to their ink.

> GOETHE (1749–1832)

Seven cities warr'd for Homer, being dead;
Who, living, had no roof to shroud his head.

> THOMAS HEYWOOD (1574?–1641). *The Hierarchie of the Blesed
> Angells,* 1635

Barefaced poverty drove me to writing verses.

> HORACE (65–8 B.C.)

Many heroes lived before Agamemnon; but all, unwept and unknown, are lost in eternal night because they lacked a sacred poet to sing their glory.

> HORACE (65–8 B.C.)

Poet: A person born with [an] instinct [for] poverty.

> ELBERT HUBBARD (1856–1915). *The Roycroft Dictionary Concocted by
> Ali Baba and the Bunch on Rainy Days,* p. 114, 1914

[The poet] must write as the interpreter of nature, and the legislator of mankind, and consider himself as presiding over the thoughts and manners of future generations; as a being superior to time and place.

> SAMUEL JOHNSON (1709–1784). *Rasselas: The Prince of Abyssinia,*
> 10, 1759

Knowledge of the subject is to the poet what durable materials are to the architect.

> SAMUEL JOHNSON (1709–1784). "Dryden," *Lives of the English Poets,*
> 1781

A rhymer and a poet are two things.

> BEN JONSON (1572–1637). "The Art of Poetry," *Timber: Or, Discoveries,*
> 1640, ed. Ralph S. Walker, 1953

A poet should not walk across a space which he can clear at a bound.

> JOSEPH JOUBERT (1754–1824). *Pensées,* 1838, tr. H. P. Collins, 1928

The true poet dreams being awake.

> CHARLES LAMB (1775–1834). "Sanity of True Genius," *The Last Essays of
> Elia,* 1833

If he [has] a poetic Vein, 'tis to me the strangest thing in the World that the Father should desire or suffer it to be cherished or improved. Methinks the Parents should labor to have it stifled and suppressed as much as may be; and I know not what Reason a Father can have to wish his Son a Poet, who does not desire to have him bid Defiance to all other Callings and Business.

> JOHN LOCKE (1632–1704). *Some Thoughts Concerning Education,* 174,
> 1693

Glorious indeed is the world of God around us, but more glorious the world of God within us. There lies the Land of Song; there lies the poet's native land.

> HENRY WADSWORTH LONGFELLOW (1807–1882). *Hyperion:
> A Romance,* 1.8, 1839

The virtue of such great poets as Shakespeare does not lie in the content of their poetry, but in its music.

> H. L. MENCKEN (1880–1956). "The Poet and His Art" (4), *Prejudices:
> Third Series,* 1922

If the poet can no longer speak for society, but only for himself, then we are at the last ditch.

> HENRY MILLER (1891–1980). *The Time of the Assassins: A Study of
> Rimbaud,* 1, 1946

The poet is a reporter interviewing his own heart.

> CHRISTOPHER MORLEY (1890–1957). *Inward Ho!* 2, 1923

The best of us . . . delight in giving way to sympathy, and are in raptures at the excellence of the poet who stirs our feelings most.

> PLATO (427?–347 B.C.). *The Republic,* 605, tr. Benjamin Jowett, 1894

Poets utter great and wise things which they do not themselves understand.

> PLATO (427?–347 B.C.). In Ralph Waldo Emerson, "History," *Essays: First
> Series,* 1841

Sir, I admit your gen'ral Rule
That every Poet is a Fool:
But you yourself may serve to show it,
That every Fool is not a Poet.

> ALEXANDER POPE (1688–1744). "Epigram from the French," 1732

[The poet] is endowed to speak for those who do not have the gift of language, or to see for those who—for whatever reasons—are less conscious of what they are living through. It is as though the risks of the poet's existence can be put to some use beyond her own survival.

> ADRIENNE RICH (1929–). "Vesuvius at Home: The Power of Emily Dickinson," 1975, *On Lies, Secrets, and Silence: Selected Prose 1966–1978,* 1979

Each man carries within him the soul of a poet who died young.

> CHARLES-AUGUSTIN SAINTE-BEUVE (1804–1869). *Critiques et portraits littéraires,* 1836–1839

When will the efficiency engineers and the poets
   get together on a program?

> CARL SANDBURG (1878–1967). *The People, Yes,* 83, 1936

One thing is certain, that the poet is the only true *man,* and the best of philosophers is a mere caricature in comparison with him.

> FRIEDRICH von SCHILLER (1759–1805). Letter to Goethe, 17 January 1795. In Jacob Burckhardt, *Force and Freedom: An Interpretation of History,* 5 (note 2), ed. James H. Nichols, 1943

Poets are the unacknowledged legislators of the world.

> PERCY BYSSHE SHELLEY (1792–1822). Closing words. *A Defence of Poetry,* 1821, ed. Albert S. Cook, 1890

The poets are only the interpreters of the Gods.

> SOCRATES (470?–399 B.C.). In Plato (427?–347? B.C.), *Ion,* 534, tr. Benjamin Jowett, 1894

My life has been the poem I would have writ,
But I could not both live and utter it.

> HENRY DAVID THOREAU (1817–1862). "Friday," *A Week on the Concord and Merrimack Rivers,* 1849

The works of the great poets have never yet been read by mankind, for only great poets can read them.

> HENRY DAVID THOREAU (1817–1862). "Reading," *Walden; or Life in the Woods,* 1854

I hate the whole race. . . . there is no believing a word they say—your professional poets. I mean—there never existed a more worthless set than Byron and his friends, for example.

> DUKE OF WELLINGTON (1769–1852). In Lady Salisbury, diary, 26 October 1833

I sound my barbaric yawp over the roofs of the world.

> WALT WHITMAN (1819–1892). "Song of Myself" (52), 1855, *Leaves of Grass,* 1855–1892

For the great Idea, the idea of perfect and free individuals,
For that, the bard walks in advance, leader of leaders,
The attitude of him cheers up slaves and horrifies foreign
   despots.

WALT WHITMAN (1819–1892). "By Blue Ontario's Shore" (10), 1856, *Leaves of Grass,* 1855–1892

> See Newspapers: Anonymous (2)

To have great poets, there must be great audiences, too.

> WALT WHITMAN (1819–1892). Closing paragraph, "Ventures, on an Old Theme," *Specimen Days and Collect,* 1882

The poet is individual—he is complete in himself: the others are as good as he; only he sees it, and they do not.

> WALT WHITMAN (1819–1892). In Robert Louis Stevenson, "Walt Whitman" (1), *Familiar Studies of Men and Books,* 1882

The great poet is always a seer, seeing less with the eyes of the body than he does with the eyes of the mind.

> OSCAR WILDE (1854–1900). "The Critic as Artist" (1), *Intentions,* 1891

[I] would prefer being the author of that poem to the glory of beating the French tomorrow.

> JAMES WOLFE (1727–1759). English general. Remark after reciting Thomas Gray's "Elegy Written in a Country Churchyard" on the eve of the Battle of Quebec, during which he was mortally wounded, 12 September 1759. In an account by John Robison (a midshipman eyewitness), 1815
>
> See Excellence: Alexander

Anonymous: How are you?
Yeats: Not very well. I can only write prose today.

> WILLIAM BUTLER YEATS (1865–1939)

POLICE

See also • Crime ○ Justice ○ Law

Gentlemen, get the thing straight for once and for all. The policeman isn't there to create disorder; the policeman is there to preserve disorder.

> RICHARD M. DALEY (1902–1976). Chicago mayor. News conference during the Democratic National Convention, Chicago, July 1968.

Major Strasser has been shot. Round up the usual suspects.

> JULIUS J. EPSTEIN (1909–), PHILIP G. EPSTEIN, and HOWARD KOCH. *Casablanca* (film), 1942, spoken by Claude Rains (in the role of the French police chief)

When the constabulary duty's to be done,
The policeman's lot is not a happy one.

> W. S. GILBERT (1836–1911). *The Pirates of Penzance* (opera), 2, 1879

For the middle class, the police protect property, give directions, and help old ladies. For the urban poor, the police are those who arrest you.

> MICHAEL HARRINGTON (1928–1989). *The Other America: Poverty in the United States,* 1.2, 1962

Last March, four officers were arrested by Internal Affairs agents for stealing cars from city residents and selling them to friends. Nine months later, the accused officers, who have pleaded not guilty, are still on active duty, and the Internal Affairs commanders who uncovered the case have been transferred out of the unit.

> DAVID KOCIENIEWSKI and JOHN SULLIVAN. "Newark Police Troubles: Out of Control at the Top," *New York Times,* 23 December 1995

The art of the police consists in punishing rarely and severely.

> NAPOLEON (1769–1821). Letter to his police minister Joseph Fouché, 20 June 1805, *The Mind of Napoleon: A Selection from His Written and Spoken Words*, 223, ed. J. Christopher Herold, 1955

[The police] invent more than they discover.

> NAPOLEON (1769–1821). Remark to an officer, Elba, 1814? In Louis de Bourrienne, *Memoirs of Napoleon Bonaparte*, 1.31, ed. R. W. Phipps, 1892

A policeman's lot is not so hot.

> CLAYTON RAWSON. *No Coffin for the Corpse*, p. 163, 1942

Policeman are soldiers who act alone; soldiers are policemen who act in unison.

> HERBERT SPENCER (1820–1903). *Social Statics*, 3.21.8, 1851

A total of 1,514 American police officers were killed feloniously or died in the line of duty in the 1980s.

> *WASHINGTON SPECTATOR.* "Violence and Law," 15 June 1991

Bryan Farrell, a Dallas police officer who shot and killed three people in seven months, was dismissed from the force when investigators found notches carved into his service pistol.

> ANONYMOUS. In "No Comment," *Progressive*, July 1989

POLICY

See also • Decision-Making ○ Planning ○ Politics

Newspapers want to know your grand design. Grand design? I make policy as I speak.

> WILLIE BROWN. San Francisco mayor. In John King, "Inside Look at Mayor's Power and Personality," *San Francisco Chronicle*, 23 December 1996

The worst policy is one made in secrecy by the experts.

> JOHN KENNETH GALBRAITH (1908–). Quoted by Michael Leapman. In *Times* (London), 17 June 1971

The New Deal will never be understood by anyone who looks for a single thread of policy, a far-reaching, far-seeing plan. It was a series of improvisations, many adopted very suddenly, many contradictory.

> RICHARD HOFSTADTER (1916–1970). *The American Political Tradition: And the Men Who Made It*, 12.4, 1948

The first Principle of Policy is for a State to preserve itself.

> JAMES HOWELL (1593–1666). Comp., "Divers Centuries of New Sayings" (p. 6), *Paroimiographia: Proverbs, or Old Sayed Sawes & Adages in English . . . Italian, French and Spanish*, 1659

Policy should be tested out on those who will be affected by it, and the details worked out by those who will have to implement it.

> ANTONY JAY (1930–). *Management and Machiavelli: An Inquiry into the Politics of Corporate Life*, 28, 1967

Policy exists in time as well as in space, . . . a measure is correct only if it can be carried out at the proper moment.

> HENRY A. KISSINGER (1923–). "Reflections on American Diplomacy" (2), *Foreign Affairs*, October 1956

Administration is concerned with execution. Policy-making must address itself also to developing a sense of direction.

> HENRY A. KISSINGER (1923–). *The Necessity for Choice: Prospects of American Foreign Policy*, 8.1, 1961

Effective policy depends not only on the skill of individual moves, but even more importantly on their relationship to each other.

> HENRY A. KISSINGER (1923–). *The Necessity for Choice: Prospects of American Foreign Policy*, 8.1, 1961

In a rapidly changing world, once successful patterns of action can become obstacles to effective policy.

> HENRY A. KISSINGER (1923–). *The Necessity for Choice: Prospects of American Foreign Policy*, 8.3, 1961

My policy is to have no policy.

> ABRAHAM LINCOLN (1809–1865). 1861. In Donald Herbert David, *Lincoln Reconsidered: Essays on the Civil War Era*, 7.2, 1956

It was a time when a man with a policy would have been fatal to the country. I have never had a policy; I have simply tried to do what seemed best each day as each day came.

> ABRAHAM LINCOLN (1809–1865). Remark to John M. Palmer. In Emanuel Hertz, ed., "Father Abraham," *Lincoln Talks: A Biography in Anecdote*, 1939
>
> See Events: Georges Clemenceau

In an age that is so full of dangers for the very foundations and safeguards of social order, the only good policy is to pursue no policy.

> METTERNICH (1773–1859). Austrian statesman. Letter to Count d'Apponyi, 27 January 1826

The policy which is not moral must glorify morality.

> NAPOLEON (1769–1821). *Napoleon in His Own Words*, 4, comp. Jules Bertaut, 1916

State policy is merely common sense applied to great things.

> NAPOLEON (1769–1821). Attributed. *The Mind of Napoleon: A Selection from His Written and Spoken Words*, 200, ed. J. Christopher Herold, 1955

The art of policy is knowing when to act, how to act, through whom to act, with what tools to act, and for what purposes to act.

> DEAN RUSK (1909–1994). *As I Saw It*, 33, 1990

The really basic thing in government is policy. Bad administration . . . can destroy good policy, but good administration can never save bad policy.

> ADLAI E. STEVENSON (1900–1965). Speech before the Los Angeles Town Club, 11 September 1952

POLITICAL PARTIES

See also • Assassination: Ronald Reagan (1) ○ Conservatives & Liberals/Radicals ○ Politics

All political parties die at last of swallowing their own lies.

> JOHN ARBUTHNOT (1667–1735). In Richard Garnett, *Life of Ralph Waldo Emerson*, 7, 1888

He's a Democrat, whatever that means, besides brain-dead.

> RUSSELL BAKER (1925–). On Pres. Bill Clinton, "Snouts in the Slops," *New York Times,* 21 October 1995

The greatest difference between the two parties lies in the fact that they back different people, not different ideas, for office.

> WILLIAM F. BUCKLEY, JR. (1925–). On the Democratic and Republican Parties, "The Week," *National Review,* 1 September 1956

In these days, more emphatically than ever, "to live signifies to unite with a party, or to make one."

> THOMAS CARLYLE (1795–1881). "Signs of the Times," 1829, *Critical and Miscellaneous Essays,* Carey & Hart edition, 1849

Ever since the Republican landslide on Nov. 8th, it's been getting dark outside a little earlier every day. You notice that?

> MARIO M. CUOMO (1932–). New York governor. Soon after his failed campaign for a third term, speech before the National Press Club, Washington, 16 December 1994. In Melinda Henneberger, "Cuomo Delivers His Last Speech as Public Official, in a Hurry," *New York Times,* 17 December 1994

Parties like only men who wear blinders and have committed a section of their conscience to their chief.

> ARSÈNE DARMESTETER (1846–1888). "Ernest Renan," 1893

If you will refrain from telling any lies about the Republican party, I'll promise not to tell the truth about the Democrats.

> CHAUNCEY DEPEW (1834–1928). New York senator

The Democratic Party is like a mule. It has neither pride of ancestry nor hope of posterity.

> IGNATIUS DONNELLY (1831–1901). Minnesota legislature speech, 13 September 1860

There's no left wing and no right wing, only up wing and down wing.

> BOB DYLAN (1941–). In Ralph J. Gleason, "Like a Rolling Stone," *American Scholar,* Autumn 1967

There are always two parties, the party of the Past and the party of the Future; the Establishment and the Movement.

> RALPH WALDO EMERSON (1803–1882). "Life and Letters in New England," *Lectures and Biographical Sketches,* 1883

Our two great political parties have really nothing more to propose than the keeping or the taking of the offices from the other party.

> HENRY GEORGE (1839–1897). *Social Problems,* 2, 1883

I always voted at my party's call,
And I never thought of thinking for myself at all.

> W. S. GILBERT (1836–1911). *H.M.S. Pinafore* (opera), 1, 1878

The best Party is but a kind of a conspiracy against the rest of the nation.

> MARQUIS OF HALIFAX (1633–1695). "Of Parties," *Political, Moral and Miscellaneous Reflections,* 1750

Ignorance maketh most men go into a Party, and shame keepeth them from getting out of it.

> MARQUIS OF HALIFAX (1633–1695). "Of Parties," *Political, Moral and Miscellaneous Reflections,* 1750

Some people say we need a third party in this country. I think we could use a second one.

> JIM HIGHTOWER (1943–). In Larry Engelmann, ed., "In Other Words . . . ," *San Francisco Sunday Examiner & Chronicle,* 1 January 1995

If I could not go to heaven but with a party, I would not go there at all.

> THOMAS JEFFERSON (1743–1826). Letter to Francis Hopkinson, 13 March 1789

Men by their constitutions are naturally divided into two parties: 1. Those who fear and distrust the people, and wish to draw all powers from them into the hands of the higher classes. 2. Those who identify themselves with the people, have confidence in them, cherish and consider them as the most honest and safe, although not the most wise depository of the public interests. . . . Call them . . . Whigs and Tories, Republicans and Federalists, Aristocrats and Democrats, or by whatever name you please, they are the same parties still, and pursue the same object.

> THOMAS JEFFERSON (1743–1826). Letter to Henry Lee, 10 August 1824

I don't believe the Democrats or Republicans are lying to us. I think that every dirty, rotten, lowdown thing they say about each other is true!

> A. RAY LAMBSON. Letter to *Los Angeles Times,* 26 October 1994

The Republican and Democratic wings of the Republocratic party.

> HAROLD D. LASSWELL (1902–1978). *Politics: Who Gets What, When, How,* 7, 1936

Whenever a Republican leaves one side of the aisle and goes to the other, it raises the intelligence quotient of both parties.

> CLARE BOOTH LUCE (1903–1987)

A party of order or stability and a party of progress or reform are both necessary elements of a healthy state of political life.

> JOHN STUART MILL (1806–1873). *On Liberty,* 2, 1859

Republicans . . . take care of the big money, for big money takes care of them.

> WILL ROGERS (1879–1935). Weekly column, 14 December 1924, *The Will Rogers Book,* 2.47, comp. Paula McSpadden Love, 1961

The more you read about this Politics thing, you got to admit that each party is worse than the other. The one that's out always looks the best.

> WILL ROGERS (1879–1935). "Breaking into the Writing Game," *The Illiterate Digest,* 1924

I am not a member of any organized party—I'm a Democrat.

> WILL ROGERS (1879–1935). In P. J. O'Brien, *Will Rogers, Ambassador of Good Will, Prince of Wit and Wisdom,* 9, 1935

A conservative Republican is one who doesn't believe anything new should be tried for the first time. A liberal Republican is one who does believe something should be tried for the first time—but not now.

> MORT SAHL (1927–)

I have been thinking that I would make a proposition to my Republican friends. . . . That if they will stop telling lies about the Democrats, we will stop telling the truth about them.

ADLAI E. STEVENSON (1900–1965). A favorite quip, speech, Fresno (California), 10 September 1952

Let me . . . warn you in the most solemn manner against the baneful effects of the spirit of party.

GEORGE WASHINGTON (1732–1799). *Farewell Address,* 17 September 1796

POLITICIANS

See also • Bureaucracy ○ Decision-Making ○ Diplomats ○ Epitaphs: Will Rogers (2) ○ Farming: Jonathan Swift ○ Idealism: Aldous Huxley ○ Leaders ○ Politicians, Corrupt ○ Politics ○ Presidents ○ Professionals ○ Statesmen ○ Statesmen & Politicians ○ Tyrants

No man should be in politics unless he would honestly rather not be there.

HENRY ADAMS (1838–1918). Letter to Henry Cabot Lodge, 15 November 1881

Mark, the great trouble with you is that you refuse to be a demagogue. You will not submerge your principles in order to get yourself elected. You must learn that there are times when a man in public life is compelled to rise above his principles.

HENRY ASHURST (1874–1962). Arizona senator. Attributed. Remark to his colleague Mark Smith during the 1920 campaign. In John F. Kennedy, *Profiles in Courage,* 1, 1956

Dominance and obsession combine to make a potent political personality.

C. S. BLUEMEL (1884–?). *War, Politics, and Insanity,* 8, 1948

The essence of the political animal is the pursuit of power.

DAVID BRINKLEY (1920–). Brian Lamb television interview, C-SPAN, 10 December 1995

I always wanted to get into politics, but I was never light enough to make the team.

ART BUCHWALD (1925–). The *Washington Post's* portly syndicated columnist. In Hunter S. Thompson, "December 1971," *Fear and Loathing: On the Campaign Trail '72,* 1973

The politician . . . is the philosopher in action.

EDMUND BURKE (1729–1797). *Thoughts on the Cause of the Present Discontents* (pamphlet), 23 April 1770

There is no qualification for government but virtue and wisdom.

EDMUND BURKE (1729–1797). *Reflections on the Revolution in France,* p. 139, 1790, Pelican Books edition, 1968

An absolute command of your temper, so as not to be provoked to passion, upon any account; patience, to hear frivolous, impertinent, and unreasonable applications; with address enough to refuse, without offending, or, by your manner of granting, to double the obligation; dexterity enough to conceal a truth without telling a lie; sagacity enough to read other people's countenances; and serenity enough not to let them discover anything by yours; a seeming frankness with a real reserve. There are the rudiments of a politician.

LORD CHESTERFIELD (1694–1773). Letter to his son, 15 January 1748

American journalist: What are the desirable qualifications for any young man who wishes to become a politician?
Churchill: It is the ability to foretell what is going to happen tomorrow, next week, next month, and next year. And to have the ability afterwards to explain why it didn't happen.

WINSTON CHURCHILL (1874–1965). In Norman McGowan, "His Wit and Wisdom," *My Years with Churchill,* 1958

The wise man loves not to thrust himself of his own accord into the administration of public affairs, but . . . , if circumstances oblige him to it, then he does not refuse the office.

CICERO (106–43 B.C.). *On the Commonwealth,* 1.9, tr. C. D. Yonge, 1902

Government is a trust, and the officers of the government are trustees; and both the trust and trustees are created for the benefit of the public.

HENRY CLAY (1777–1852). Speech, Lexington (Kentucky), 16 May 1829

See Empire: John Dryden ○ Power: Edmund Burke (3) ○ Riches: Ralph Waldo Emerson (1)

When called to office, to undertake its duties; when not so called, to lie retired.

CONFUCIUS (551–479 B.C.). *Confucian Analects,* 7.10, tr. James Legge, 1930

Cowardly politicians, members of Congress, and misrepresentatives of the masses.

EUGENE V. DEBS (1855–1926). Speech, Canton (Ohio), 16 June 1918

Politics are too serious a matter to be left to the politicians.

CHARLES de GAULLE (1890–1970). Letter to the author. In Clement Attlee, *A Prime Minister Remembers,* 4, 1961

See Commanders: Georges Clemenceau ○ Environment: Helmut Sihler ○ Priests: Anonymous

Politicians neither love nor hate.

JOHN DRYDEN (1631–1700). *Absalom and Achitophel,* 1.223, 1681

It is our experience that political leaders do not always mean the opposite of what they say.

ABBA EBAN (1915–). In *Observer* (British newspaper), 5 December 1971

A man plunges into politics to make his fortune, and only cares that the world should last his days.

RALPH WALDO EMERSON (1803–1882). Letter to Thomas Carlyle, 7 October 1835

Our senator was of that stuff that our best hope lay in his drunkenness, as that sometimes incapacitated him from doing mischief.

RALPH WALDO EMERSON (1803–1882). Journal, 1854, undated

Wife: The election is over. Why are you still watching Larry King?"
Husband (sitting in front of a television set): I've decided I want my news unfiltered. I don't want some reporter to be a middleman. This way, the politician lies to me directly.

BOB ENGLEBART. Referring to the *Larry King Live* interview-phone-in programs that provided a platform for candidates during the 1992 presidential campaign, cartoon caption, *Hartford Courant.* In Larry King, *On the Line: The New Road to the White House,* 2, 1993

I have heard of some great man, whose rule it was, with regard to offices, *never to ask for them, and never to refuse them;* to which I have always added, in my own practice, *never to resign them.*

> BENJAMIN FRANKLIN (1706–1790). Letter to Mrs. Jane Mecom, 1 March 1766

Despite the absence of any clear foreign policy mandate, the Republicans (and many Democrats) have simply assumed that the public wants to shrink America's role in the world, along with shrinking the Federal Government. They are wrong. The American people are not nearly as isolationist as the moronic politicians who speak in their name.

> THOMAS L. FRIEDMAN (1953–). "Global Mandate," *New York Times,* 5 March 1995

If you want to succeed in politics, you must keep your conscience well under control.

> WILLIAM EWART GLADSTONE (1809–1898). British prime minister

That's the kind of thing Earl's good at—knowing every local politician in the state, and remembering where he itches. Then Earl knows where to scratch him.

> LEWIS GOTTLEIB. On Louisiana Gov. Earl Long. In A. J. Liebling, "The Great State: II Blam—Blam—Blam," *New Yorker,* 4 June 1960

Anonymous: Do you pray for the senators, Dr. Hale?
Hale: No, I look at the senators and pray for the country.

> EDWARD EVERETT HALE (1822–1909). Senate chaplain. Format adapted. In Leon A. Harris, *The Fine Art of Political Wit,* 10, 1964

I have seen in the Halls of Congress more idealism, more humaneness, more compassion, more profiles of courage than in any other institution that I have ever known.

> HUBERT H. HUMPHREY (1911–1978). Speech, Syracuse University (New York), 6 June 1965

With politicians, artful evasion is always preferable to the outright lie.

> MOLLY IVINS (1936–). Adapted. "[Ross] Perot Finds Out the Game Is Hardball," *San Francisco Chronicle,* 17 July 1992

Whenever a man has cast a longing eye on [offices], a rottenness begins in his conduct.

> THOMAS JEFFERSON (1743–1826). Letter to Tench Coxe, 21 May 1799

If the present Congress errs in too much talking, how can it be otherwise in a body to which the people send 150 lawyers, whose trade it is to question everything, yield nothing, and talk by the hour? That 150 lawyers should do business together ought not to be expected.

> THOMAS JEFFERSON (1743–1826). 7 February 1821, *Autobiography,* ed. Thomas Jefferson Randolph, 1829

I seldom think of politics more than 18 hours a day.

> LYNDON B. JOHNSON (1908–1973). Speech in Texas, 1958. In Henry A. Zeiger, *Lyndon B. Johnson,* p. 65, 1965

If you can't come into a roomful of people and tell right away who is for you and who is against you, you have no business in politics.

> SAM JOHNSON (1877–1937). Remark to his son Lyndon. In James David Barber, *The Presidential Character: Predicting Performance in the White House,* 4, 1972

To be successful, a politician had to appear hugely concerned with bettering the lives of ordinary citizens but had to be careful to avoid acting on those concerns so aggressively that they threatened the interests of the business elite.

> MICHAEL KELLY (1951–). Expressing what he believed was a lesson Bill Clinton learned from his first term as Arkansas governor during the late 1970s, "The President's Past," *New York Times Magazine,* 31 July 1994

A "gaffe" occurs not when a politician lies, but when he tells the truth.

> MICHAEL KINSLEY (1951–). "A Gaffe Is When a Politician Tells the Truth," *New Republic,* 18 June 1984

Ninety percent of the politicians give the other ten percent a bad reputation.

> HENRY A. KISSINGER (1923–). Quoted by Richard M. Nixon, Barbara Walters interview, 8 May 1985

All things follow in the train of political connection, and a man lives not by his works but by his office and his friends, by his talent for "staying in the loop," by an air of knowingness rather than a command of knowledge. . . . A man's star rises or falls not so much by reason of what he does or fails to do as by the courtliness of his manner and his refusal to give or take offense.

> LEWIS H. LAPHAM (1935–). *The Wish for Kings: Democracy at Bay,* 3, 1993

The principle trait of the politician, in general, is intense craving for deference; but this motive must be joined with appropriate skills and with propitious circumstances if success is to come.

> HAROLD D. LASSWELL (1902–1978). *Politics: Who Gets What, When, How,* 10, 1936

After you have once ridden behind a motorcycle escort, you are never the same again.

> HERBERT H. LEHMAN (1878–1963). When asked why he was runnning for a second term as senator after previously serving four terms as governor. In Barbara Tuchman, "An Inquiry into the Persistence of Unwisdom in Government," *Esquire,* 1980

If ever this free people—if this Government itself is ever utterly demoralized, it will come from this human wriggle and struggle for office—a way to live without work; from which nature I am not free myself.

> ABRAHAM LINCOLN (1809–1865). Quoted by William H. Herndon, address, Springfield (Illinois), 12 December 1865. In F. B. Carpenter, *Six Months at the White House with Abraham Lincoln,* 79, 1866

Every time I fill a vacant office I make a hundred malcontents and one ingrate.

> LOUIS XIV (1638–1715). French king. In Voltaire, *The Century of Louis XIV,* 26, 1751

did you ever
notice that when
a politician
does get an idea
he usually
gets it all wrong.

DON MARQUIS (1878–1937). "archygrams," *archy s life of mehitabel,* 1933

The opponent in one fight is often the valued ally in the next. The astute politician always keeps the lines of communication humming.

CHRISTOPHER MATTHEWS (1945–). *Hardball: How Politics Is Played— Told by One Who Knows the Game,* 5, 1988

Being in politics is like being a football coach. You have to be smart enough to understand the game and dumb enough to think it's important.

EUGENE McCARTHY (1916–). 1968

Politicians who vote huge expenditures to alleviate problems get reelected; those who propose structural changes to prevent problems get early retirement.

JOHN McCLAUGHRY. "McClaughry's Law of Public Policy." In Paul Dickson, comp., *The Official Rules,* p. 154, 1978

A good politician, under democracy, is quite as unthinkable as an honest burglar.

H. L. MENCKEN (1880–1956). "The Politician," *Prejudices: Fourth Series,* 1924

Anything is moral that furthers the main concern of [the politician's] soul, which is to keep a place at the public trough.

H. L. MENCKEN (1880–1956). *Notes on Democracy,* 2.4, 1926

The occasional mavericks, thrown in by miracle, last a session, and then disappear. The old Congressman, the veteran of genuine influence and power, is either one who is so stupid that the ideas of the mob are his own ideas, or one so far gone in charlatanry that he is unconscious of his shame.

H. L. MENCKEN (1880–1956). On the House of Representatives, *Notes on Democracy,* 2.5, 1926

The typical politician is not only a rascal but also a jackass, so he greatly values the puerile notoriety and adulation that sensible men try to avoid.

H. L. MENCKEN (1880–1956). "The Constitution," *Baltimore Evening Sun,* 19 August 1935

Ultimately, the considerations of a politician are not based upon truth or fact; they are based upon what the public will conceive to be truth or fact.

RAYMOND MOLEY (1886–1975). "History's Bone of Contention: Franklin D. Roosevelt," 1949. In William E. Leuchtenburg, ed., *Franklin D. Roosevelt: A Profile,* 1967

I do not think that I would make a good politician. War is a pretty rough and dirty game. But politics!

BERNARD LAW MONTGOMERY (1887–1976). *The Memoirs of Field-Marshal Montgomery,* 33, 1958

The politician is . . . trained in the art of inexactitude. His words tend to be blunt or rounded because if they have a cutting edge, they may later return to wound him.

EDWARD R. MURROW (1908–1965). Speech, London, 19 October 1959

A true master of politics is able to calculate, down to the smallest fraction, the advantages to which he may put his very faults.

NAPOLEON (1769–1821). A repeated remark, *The Mind of Napoleon: A Selection from His Written and Spoken Words,* 205, ed. J. Christopher Herold, 1955

Public office . . . is the last refuge of the incompetent.

BOIES PENROSE (1860–1921). Pennsylvania senator. In Walter Davenport and Robert B. Vale, "Power and Glory," *Collier's Weekly,* 14 February 1931

See Patriotism: Samuel Johnson

The political life is a life of struggle in which a man is surrounded by enemies who will take advantage of any show of vulnerability.

GEORGE E. REEDY (1917–). *The Twilight of the Presidency,* 7, 1970

I think it is a rule followed by most politicians that you never antagonize any group, no matter how small, if you can avoid it. If you have to choose between two groups, you always choose to antagonize the one that is less vindictive and organized than the others.

JAMES RESTON (1909–1995). Letter to John Howe, 29 September 1954

Men who enter the service of the State should make it their chief study to set out in the world with some notable act which may strike the imagination of the people, and cause themselves to be discussed.

CARDINAL de RETZ (1613–1679). *Memoirs of Cardinal de Retz,* 2, Grolier Society edition, undated

With Congress—every time they make a joke it's a law. And every time they make a law it's a joke.

WILL ROGERS (1879–1935). In P. J. O'Brien, *Will Rogers, Ambassador of Good Will, Prince of Wit and Wisdom,* 9, 1935

Congress is going to start tinkering with the Ten Commandments just as soon as they can find someone in Washington who has read them.

WILL ROGERS (1879–1935). In *Rediscovering Will Rogers,* television documentary, PBS, 30 November 1994

The most successful politician is he who says what everybody is thinking most often and in the loudest voice.

THEODORE ROOSEVELT (1858–1919)

The special skill of the politician consists in knowing what passions can be most easily aroused, and how to prevent them, when aroused, from being harmful to himself and his associates. There is a Gresham's law in politics as in currency; a man who aims at nobler ends than these will be driven out, except in those rare moments (chiefly revolutions) when idealism finds itself in alliance with some powerful movement of selfish passion.

BERTRAND RUSSELL (1872–1970). *Sceptical Essays,* 11, 1928

See Money: Sir Thomas Gresham

An honest politician will not be tolerated by a democracy unless he is very stupid.

BERTRAND RUSSELL (1872–1970). *Sceptical Essays,* 11, 1928

A politician should have three hats: one for throwing in the ring, one for talking through, and one for pulling rabbits out of if elected.

CARL SANDBURG (1878–1967). In Ferdinand Lundberg, comp., *Politicians and Other Scoundrels,* p. 91, 1968

The effectiveness of a politician varies [inversely] to his commitment to principle.

> SAM SHAFFER. "Shaffer's Law," in Paul Dickson, comp., *The Official
> Rules*, p. 219, 1978

Hamlet: The insolence of office.

> SHAKESPEARE (1564–1616). *Hamlet*, 3.1.73, 1600
> See Wealth: Samuel Johnson

Hamlet: A politician . . . one that would circumvent God.

> SHAKESPEARE (1564–1616). *Hamlet*, 5.1.86, 1600

He knows nothing, and he thinks he knows everything. That
points clearly to a political career.

> GEORGE BERNARD SHAW (1856–1950). *Major Barbara*, 3, 1905

A politician will always be there when he needs you.

> RICHARD C. SMOLIK. "Smolik's Law." In Paul Dickson, comp., *The New
> Official Rules*, p. 197, 1989

The old Marxist idea—that the state is nothing more than the
"executive committee" of the ruling corporate power—ignores
what we all know: that politicians more often act on their own
behalf than on the behalf of others.

> ALVIN TOFFLER (1928–). *Powershift: Knowledge, Wealth, and Violence
> at the Edge of the 21st Century*, 4, 1990

A good politician has had to be 75 percent ability and 25 percent
actor, but I can well see the day when the reverse could be true.

> HARRY S. TRUMAN (1884–1972). In Francis X. Clines, "Images:
> Roosevelt to Reagan," *New York Times*, 14 October 1984

What was latent in the public mind was the most important thing
of all for a politician to be able to divine. If he had the talent for
this, a good deal of the rest would be added unto him. And what
he lacked would very likely be forgiven.

> REXFORD G. TUGWELL (1891–1979). Stating Pres. Franklin D.
> Roosevelt's "theory of leadership," *The Democratic Roosevelt:
> A Biography of Franklin D. Roosevelt*, 8, 1957

I'm not a politician and my other habits air [*sic*] good.

> ARTEMUS WARD (1834–1867). "Fourth of July Oration," Weathersfield
> (Connecticut), 1859, *The Complete Works of Artemus Ward*, 1898

The decisive psychological quality of the politician [is] his ability
to let realities work upon him with inner concentration and calmness.

> MAX WEBER (1864–1920). "Politics as a Vocation," 1919, *From Max
> Weber: Essays in Sociology*, tr. H. H. Gerth and C. Wright Mills, 1958

A politician's words reveal less about what he thinks about his
subject than what he thinks about his audience.

> GEORGE F. WILL (1941–). In Richard Reeves, *A Ford, Not a Lincoln*,
> 1, 1975

Politics demands a great capacity for self-deception, which rescues the politician from hypocrisy.

> GARRY WILLS (1934–). *Confessions of a Conservative*, 15, 1979

❧

A politician is a person who approaches every subject with an
open mouth.

ANONYMOUS (AMERICAN). Attributed, in modified form, to
Adlai E. Stevenson. In Leon A. Harris, *The Fine Art of Political Wit*,
11, 1964

POLITICIANS, CORRUPT

Includes • Government Corruption

See also • Campaigns: Hedrick Smith (1) ○ Crime: Anonymous
(American) ○ Corruption ○ Government ○ Lobbies ○
Machiavellianism ○ Politicians ○ Politics ○ Theft ○ Victory:
William L. Marcy

An honest politician is one who when he is bought will stay
bought.

> SIMON CAMERON (1799–1889). Pennsylvania senator

No one should give or receive a present either during a candida-
cy or during or after a term of office.

> CICERO (106–43 B.C.). A proposed law regarding high office holders,
> *De legibus*, 3.4, tr. Clinton Walker Keyes, 1928

An upright [government] minister asks, *what* recommends a man;
a corrupt minister, *who*.

> C. C. COLTON (1780–1832). *Lacon: or, Many Things in Few Words;
> Addressed to Those Who Think*, 1.9, 1823

I acknowledge that my raising these contributions and tax-
deductible donations at the time I did reflected poor judgment.

> ALAN CRANSTON (1914–). California senator. Responding to media
> inquiries about his accepting payments of more than $1,000,000 from
> Charles Keating of the Lincoln Savings & Loan Association in return for
> his support in matters relating to the defunct bank's relations with the
> federal government. In Larry Liebert, "Cranston and Ethics Panel Spar
> Over His Judgment," *San Francisco Chronicle*, 25 July 1991

Society possesses the right to demand from every public servant
an account of his administration.

> THE DECLARATION OF THE RIGHTS OF MAN AND THE CITIZEN.
> France, Article 15, 26 August 1789

This career of plundering and blundering.

> BENJAMIN DISRAELI (1804–1881). Letter to Grey de Wilton, October
> 1873

Money buys access; access buys influence.

> ELIZABETH DREW (1935–). On campaign contributions, Michael Krasny
> radio interview, KQED, San Francisco, 15 May 1997

In a virtuous community men of sense and of principle will always
be placed at the head of affairs. In a declining state of public
morals men will be so blinded to their true interests as to put the
incapable and unworthy at the helm. It is therefore vain to complain of the follies or crimes of a government. We must lay our
hands on our own hearts and say, Here is the sin that makes the
public sin.

> RALPH WALDO EMERSON (1803–1882). "The Individual and State," ser-
> mon, Second Church of Boston, 8 April 1830

It is as bad as going to Congress; none comes back innocent.

> RALPH WALDO EMERSON (1803–1882). Journal, 1851, undated

In 1941 [Sen. Harry S.] Truman had put [his wife] Bess on the payroll at an annual salary that soon became $4,500, a considerable salary for that time and the highest among his office staff. . . . In 1943 he put [his sister] Mary Jane on the payroll at $1,800 a year, and she lived in Grandview [Missouri].

ROBERT H. FERRELL (1921–). *Harry S. Truman: A Life*, 8.2, 1994

They'd do the right thing, if they thought they could get away with it.

A. ERNEST FITZGERALD (1925–). Pentagon official and whistle-blower. Commenting of some of his associates, television interview, June 1988

They that buy an Office must sell something.

THOMAS FULLER (1654–1734). Comp., *Gnomologia: Adages and Proverbs*, 4975, 1732

How shall we try to prevent political corruption by framing new checks and setting one official to watch another official, when the fear of want stimulates the lust for wealth, and the rich thief is honored while honest poverty is despised?

HENRY GEORGE (1839–1897). *Social Problems*, 9, 1883

On 106 occasions, bribes were offered or discussed. On 105 of those occasions, the public official involved accepted the bribe. And on the other occasion he turned it down because he didn't think the amount was enough.

RUDOLPH W. GIULIANI (1944–). U.S. attorney for the Southern District of New York. Reporting the results of a state-wide sting operation involving an FBI agent who posed as a steel-products salesman. In Ralph Blumenthal, "F.B.I. Says Public Officials Accepted 105 of 106 Bribes Offered in 2-Year Operation," *New York Times*, 12 August 1987

Even former Senate colleagues choked on the sudden riches [John] Tower collected from major defense contractors after he left public office. It seemed reasonable to ask whether this $750,000 in consulting fees represented deferred payment for Tower's faithful service to the military-industrial complex or a down payment on future generosity once he headed the Pentagon.

WILLIAM GREIDER (1936–). "Jim Baker's Conflict-of-Interest Problems," *Rolling Stone*, 20 April 1989

No public man can be just a little crooked.

HERBERT HOOVER (1874–1964). 1951, "Herbert Hoover in His Own Words," comp. Louis P. Lochner, *New York Times Magazine*, 9 August 1964

You can't adopt politics as a profession and remain honest.

LOUIS HOWE (1871–1936). Presidential assistant to Franklin D. Roosevelt. Speech, Columbia University, New York City, 17 January 1933

Now an' then an innocent man is sent t' th' legislature.

KIN HUBBARD (1868–1930)

Where the private interests of a member [of Congress] are concerned in a bill of question, he is to withdraw.

THOMAS JEFFERSON (1743–1826). 1801. In Ferdinand Lundberg, *The Rich and the Super-Rich: A Study in the Power of Money Today*, 12, 1968

I refuse to become
An accomplice in theft—which means that no governor
Will accept me on his staff.

JUVENAL (A.D. 60?–127?). *Satires*, 3.49, tr. Peter Green, 1967

One question, among the many others raised in recent weeks, had to do with whether my financial support in any way influenced several political figures to take up my cause. I want to say in the most forceful way that I can: I certainly hope so.

CHARLES KEATING (1923–). Lincoln Savings & Loan Association chairman. In Margaret Carlson, "Keating Takes the Fifth," *Time*, 4 December 1989

Daniel Webster was not as great as he looked. The flaw in the granite was the failure of his moral senses to develop as acutely as his other faculties. He could see nothing improper in writing to the President of the Bank of the United States—at the very time when the Senate was engaged in debate over a renewal of the Bank's charter—noting that "my retainer has not been received or refreshed as usual."

JOHN F. KENNEDY (1917–1963). Referring to the Massachusetts senator (1782–1852), *Profiles in Courage*, 3, 1956

Members of Parliament are allowed to work for private companies, including those with business before Parliament, without specifying the assignment or the pay. But private sexual behavior among consenting adults is considered front-page news if it involves public figures.

STEPHEN KINZER (1951–). On British political morality. "High Crimes and Peccadilloes: Europe's Year of the Scandal," *New York Times*, 3 December 1995

Reasons why members of Congress deserve a pay rise: many big corporations are cutting back on bribes; nearly half the members have never been indicted.

DAVID LETTERMAN (1947–). Slightly modified. In Leah Garchik, "Personals," *San Francisco Chronicle*, 17 November 1989

Politicians [are] a set of men who have interests aside from the interests of the people, and who, to say the most of them, are, taken as a mass, at least one long step removed from honest men. I say this with the greater freedom because, being a politician myself, none can regard it as personal.

ABRAHAM LINCOLN (1809–1865). Illinois legislature speech, 11 January 1837

I say, in the main, the use of money is wrong; but for certain objects, in a political contest, the use of some, is both right, and indispensable. With me, as with yourself, this long struggle has been one of great pecuniary loss. I now distinctly say this. If you shall be appointed a delegate to Chicago, I will furnish one hundred dollars to bear the expenses of the trip.

ABRAHAM LINCOLN (1809–1865). Several months before being nominated for the presidency at the Republican convention, letter to Mark W. Delahay, 16 March 1860

Jim Wright may be a crook, but he's our crook, and we're proud of him.

CHARLIE MILLER. Texas Dairy Queen worker. Commenting on the speaker of the House of Representatives who was known for his ability to channel federal funds to his district and state (he had just announced his decision to resign from Congress while being investigated on corruption charges). In United Press International, "Wright's Town Bemoans Loss of 'Our Crook,'" *San Francisco Chronicle*, 1 June 1989

Everybody is talkin' these days about Tammany men growin' rich on graft, but nobody thinks of drawin' the distinction between honest graft and dishonest graft. There's all the difference in the world between the two. Yes, many of our men have grown rich in politics. I have myself. I've made a big fortune out of the game, and I'm gettin' richer every day, but I've not gone in for dishonest graft—blackmailin' gamblers, saloonkeepers, disorderly people, etc. . . .

There's an honest graft, and I'm an example of how it works. . . . Just let me explain by examples. My party's in power in the city, and it's goin' to undertake a lot of public improvements. Well, I'm tipped off, say, that they're going to lay out a new park at a certain place.

I see my opportunity and I take it. I go to that place and I buy up all the land I can in the neighborhood. Then the board of this or that makes its plan public, and there is a rush to get my land, which nobody cared for before.

Ain't it perfectly honest to charge a good price and make a profit on my investment and foresight? Of course, it is. Well, that's honest graft.

If my worst enemy was given the job of writin' my epitaph when I'm gone, he couldn't do more than write:

"George W. Plunkitt. He Seen His Opportunities, and He Took 'Em."

> GEORGE WASHINGTON PLUNKITT (1842–1924). New York Tammany Hall leader. 1905. In "Plain Words from Truthful George," *American Heritage*, June 1963

[After Solon, the Greek lawgiver (630?–560? B.C.), told his friends of his intention to cancel all debts] they secretly borrowed a great deal of money before the law was published, and a little later, after its publication, they were found to have bought splendid houses and much land with the money they had borrowed, and Solon, who was wronged, was accused of sharing in their wrongdoing.

> PLUTARCH (A.D. 46?–119?). "Precepts of Statecraft" (13), *Moralia*, vol. 10, tr. W. C. Helmbold, 1936

People in Kansas, like most Americans, have a word for a politician who won't sell his soul to gain and hold power.

Loser.

> GEORGE B. PYLE. Closing paragraphs, "In Kansas, We Call It Politics as Usual," *New York Times*, 8 March 1997

What do you suppose [they] are in Congress for, if it ain't to split up the swag?

> WILL ROGERS (1879–1935). 1 January 1928, *The Autobiography of Will Rogers*, ed. Donald Day, 1949

But shucks, we got the best politicians in this country that money can buy.

> WILL ROGERS (1879–1935). *In Will Rogers U.S.A.*, CBS-TV, 9 March 1972

No people is wholly civilized where a distinction is drawn between stealing an office and stealing a purse.

> THEODORE ROOSEVELT (1858–1919). Speech, Chicago, 22 June 1912

You don't cash in on your public service—till you get out.

> WILLIAM SAFIRE (1929–). Referring to Newt Gingrich, who, soon after becoming speaker of the House of Representatives, accepted a $4 million book advance, speech, Washington, 3 February 1995

Vote for Smith! Not Corrupt! Just Ethically Challenged!

> HARLEY SCHWADRON (1942–). Message on a politician's campaign sign, cartoon, *Washington Post National Weekly Edition*, 21 August 1995

I was really too honest a man to be a politician and live.

> SOCRATES (470?–399 B.C.). In Plato (427?–347 B.C.), *Apology*, 36, tr. Benjamin Jowett, 1894

So corrupted . . . and debased was that age by sycophancy that not only the foremost citizens who were forced to save their grandeur by servility, but every ex-consul, most of the ex-praetors and a host of inferior senators would rise in eager rivalry to propose shameful and preposterous motions. Tradition says that Tiberius as often as he left the Senate House used to exclaim in Greek, "How ready these men are to be slaves."

> TACITUS (A.D. 56?–120?). *The Annals*, 3.65, tr. Alfred J. Church and William J. Brodribb, 1942

I went to the store the other day to buy a bolt for our front door, for, as I told the storekeeper, the Governor was coming here. "Aye," said he, "and the Legislature too." "Then I will take two bolts," said I. He said that there had been a steady demand for bolts and locks of late, for our protectors were coming.

> HENRY DAVID THOREAU (1817–1862). Journal, 8 September 1859

There would be no corruption [in public life] if it were not for the corrupters. . . .

We must find a way to make the corrupter as guilty legally as the one who is corrupted.

> HARRY S. TRUMAN (1884–1972). Remark to the author. In William Hillman, *Mr. President*, 1.6, 1952

It could probably be shown by facts and figures that there is no distinctly native American criminal class except Congress.

> MARK TWAIN (1835–1910). *Following the Equator: A Journey Around the World*, 8 (epigraph), 1897

Suppose I am a crook, and suppose I am a congressman, but I repeat myself.

> MARK TWAIN (1835–1910). In George F. Will, introduction to *Restoration: Congress, Term Limits and the Recovery of Deliberative Democracy*, 1992

When I want to buy up any politicians, I always find the anti-monopolists the most purchasable. They don't come so high.

> WILLIAM HENRY VANDERBILT (1821–1885). Financier. In *Chicago Daily News*, 9 October 1882

It used to be that influence-peddling was hidden because people thought it was unacceptable. Now it's a formal part of the system.

> FRED WERTHEIMER (1939–). On Washington's "legalized, institutionalized corruption." In E. J. Dionne, Jr., "History's Sliding Scale of Ethics in the Capital," *New York Times*, 21 April 1989

The Washington style of apology is to say there were appearances of impropriety.

> GEORGE F. WILL (1941–). On corrupt politicians who get caught, commentator, *This Week with David Brinkley*, television news program, ABC, 23 June 1991

❦

Politicians have stopped passing the buck—now it stays with them.

ANONYMOUS

Came to do good and stayed to do well.

SAYING (AMERICAN). Referring to Washington's "brilliant young lawyers." In Russell Baker, "Could Be a Long Season," *New York Times,* 24 April 1993

POLITICS

See also • Anarchism ○ Assassination ○ Bureaucracy ○ Campaigns ○ Class ○ Competition ○ Crime: Anonymous (American) ○ Crises ○ Crowds ○ Democracy ○ Diplomacy: [especially] James A. Baker, Anonymous ○ Elections ○ Government ○ History ○ Imperialism ○ Indoctrination ○ International Relations ○ Leaders ○ Lobbies ○ Machiavellianism ○ Mass Movements ○ Nations ○ Neutrality ○ Nonviolence ○ Peace ○ Policy ○ Political Parties ○ Politicians ○ Politicians, Corrupt ○ Power ○ Presidents ○ Propaganda ○ Prudence: Rules ○ Public Opinion ○ Public Opinion Polls ○ Revolution ○ Self-Interest ○ Tyranny ○ Voting ○ War ○ Washington ○ Watergate

Politics, as a practice, whatever its professions, has always been the systematic organization of hatreds.

HENRY ADAMS (1838–1918). *The Education of Henry Adams,* 1, 1907

Politics is war by other means these days.

ERIC ALTERMAN (1960–). Chris Welch radio interview, KPFA, Berkeley (California), 24 January 1995

See War: Karl von Clausewitz (3)

Politics, *n.* A strife of interests masquerading as a contest of principles. The conduct of public affairs for private advantage.

AMBROSE BIERCE (1841–1914). *The Devil's Dictionary,* p. 101, 1911, Dover edition, 1958

Politics is the art of the possible, the attainable . . . the art of the next best.

OTTO von BISMARCK (1815–1898). German chancellor. Remark to Prince Meyer von Waldeck, 11 August 1867, *Bismarck-Worte,* p. 19, ed. H. Amelung, 1918

As long as I've known anything about politics, I've been skeptical. And it has evolved. The more I saw, the more skeptical I became.

DAVID BRINKLEY (1920–). In Warren Berger, "The Master Skeptic Steps Aside," *New York Times,* 3 November 1996

Magnanimity in politics is not seldom the truest wisdom, and a great empire and little minds go ill together.

EDMUND BURKE (1729–1797). "Conciliation with America," House of Commons speech, 22 March 1775

Vain hope to make people happy by politics!

THOMAS CARLYLE (1795–1881). Journal, 10 October 1831

Politics is not the art of the possible; it is the art of making possible what is necessary.

JACQUES CHIRAC (1932–). French president. Campaign slogan. In Thomas Sancton, "Is This a Crossroads—Or the Edge of a Cliff?" *Time,* 11 December 1995

Power politics is the diplomatic name for the law of the jungle.

ELY CULBERTSON (1891–1955). *Must We Fight Russia?* 2, 1946

The essence of politics is power, the struggle to obtain and to maintain it, and the use made of it.

MICHAEL CURTIS (1923–). Ed., introduction to *The Nature of Politics,* 1962

The big thing in politics is to know when it is time to leave.

CHARLES de GAULLE (1890–1970). "Some General Comments, *Entre Nous* . . . " *Time,* 8 December 1967

Our only safe rule in politics . . . was always to believe that the worst would be done. Then we were not deceived.

RALPH WALDO EMERSON (1803–1882). Journal, 1862, undated

Since it has been agreed among men that to cheat or deceive one's fellow creatures is a mean and criminal action, there has been sought for, and invented, a term that might soften the appellation of the thing, and the word, which undoubtedly has been chosen for the purpose, is *Politics.*

FREDERICK II (1712–1786). "Morning the Fourth," *The Confessions of Frederick the Great,* ed. Douglas Sladen, 1915

Politics and villainy are almost synonymous terms.

FREDERICK II (1712–1786). "Morning the Fifth," *The Confessions of Frederick the Great,* ed. Douglas Sladen, 1915

All politics is global.

THOMAS L. FRIEDMAN (1953–). "Get a Job," *New York Times,* 17 March 1998

Politics is not the art of the possible. It consists in choosing between the disastrous and the unpalatable.

JOHN KENNETH GALBRAITH (1908–). Letter to John F. Kennedy, 2 March 1962, *Ambassador's Journal: A Personal Account of the Kennedy Years,* 15, 1969

If I seem to take part in politics, it is only because politics today encircle us like the coils of a snake from which one cannot get out, no matter how much one tries. I wish to wrestle with the snake.

MOHANDAS K. GANDHI (1869–1948). In *Young India,* 12 May 1920

The best politics is right action.

MOHANDAS K. GANDHI (1869–1948). In American Friends Service Committee, *Speak Truth to Power: A Quaker Search for an Alternative to Violence,* 6 (epigraph), 1955

One of the most underestimated of all political resources is personal attention.

DORIS KEARNS GOODWIN (1943–). *Lyndon Johnson and the American Dream,* 8, 1976

That most basic rule in politics: always stay in with the outs.

DAVID HALBERSTAM (1934–). *The Best and the Brightest,* 18, 1972

Politics is history in the making.

ADOLF HITLER (1889–1945). *Mein Kampf,* 2.2, 1924, tr. Ralph Manheim, 1943

I recognize no moral law in politics. Politics is a game, in which every sort of trick is permissible, and in which the rules are constantly being changed by the players to suit themselves.

> ADOLF HITLER (1889–1945). Remark to the author, 1932–1934. In Hermann Rauschning, *The Voice of Destruction,* 19, 1940

Politics is, among other things, the art of anticipating consequences.

> IRVING HOWE (1920–1993). "The Agony of the Campus," *Dissent,* September-October 1969
>
> See Wisdom: Norman Cousins

Politics are now nothing more than [the] means of rising in the world.

> SAMUEL JOHNSON (1709–1784). 18 April 1775. In James Boswell, *The Life of Samuel Johnson,* 1791

Politics is not about objective reality, but virtual reality. What happens in the political world is divorced from the real world. It exists for only the fleeting historical moment, in a magical movie of sorts, a never-ending and infinitely revisable docudrama. Strangely, the faithful understand that the movie is not true—yet also maintain that it is the only truth that really matters.

> MICHAEL KELLY (1957–). "David Gergen, Master of the Game: How Image Became the Sacred Faith of Washington, and How This Insider's Insider Became Its High Priest," *New York Times Magazine,* 31 October 1993

In politics you have no friends, only allies.

> JOHN F. KENNEDY (1917–1963). In John Henry Cutler, *Honey Fitz: Three Steps to the White House; The Life and Times of John F. (Honey Fitz) Fitzgerald,* 22, 1962

Politics is like football. If you see daylight, go through the hole.

> JOHN F. KENNEDY (1917–1963). In Joseph Alsop, *New York Herald Tribune,* 3 April 1964

The political problem of mankind is to combine three things: Economic Efficiency, Social Justice, and Individual Liberty.

> JOHN MAYNARD KEYNES (1883–1946). "Liberalism and Labour," 1926, *Essays in Persuasion,* 1931

It's a sin in politics to land a soft punch.

> ALF LANDON (1887–1987). In David S. Broder, "Alf Landon: 'It's a Sin to Land a Soft Punch,'" *Washington Post,* 14 December 1977
>
> See Competition: Theodore Roosevelt

Political forms have always been a mask behind which an owning class has sought to protect from invasion the authority which ownership confers; and, when the political forms have endangered the rights of ownership, the class in possession has always sought to adjust them to its needs.

> HAROLD D. LASSWELL (1902–1978). *World Politics and Personal Insecurity,* p. 293, 1935

Politics: Who Gets What, When, How.

> HAROLD D. LASSWELL (1902–1978). Book title, 1936

The economic system is the foundation on which the political superstructure is erected.

> LENIN (1870–1924). "The Three Sources and Three Component Parts of Marxism" (2), March 1913, *Selected Works,* International Publishers edition, 1971

There is no morality in politics; there is only expediency.

> LENIN (1870–1924). Speech, September 1915

Who? Whom? (Who masters whom?) [Kto kovo?]

> LENIN (1870–1924). Defining politics. In Alan Bullock, *Hitler and Stalin: Parallel Lives,* 3.2, 1991

Politics is civil war carried on by other means.

> ALISDAIR C. MACINTYRE (1929–). *After Virtue: A Study in Moral Theory,* 17, 1981
>
> See War: Karl von Clausewitz (3)

The whole aim of practical politics is to keep the populace alarmed (and hence clamorous to be led to safety) by an endless series of hobgoblins, most of them imaginary.

> H. L. MENCKEN (1880–1956). *In Defense of Women,* 13, 1922

Politics, as hopeful men practice it in the world, consists mainly of the delusion that a change in form is a change in substance.

> H. L. MENCKEN (1880–1956). "On Government" (2), *Prejudices: Fourth Series,* 1924

To eschew political motives is a first rule of politics.

> RAYMOND MOLEY (1886–1975). "History's Bone of Contention: Franklin D. Roosevelt," 1949. In William E. Leuchtenburg, ed., *Franklin D. Roosevelt: A Profile,* 1967

There is no substitute for the effective use of political skills to advance the cause of a great idea. Ideas are great arrows, but there has to be a bow. And politics is the bow of idealism.

> BILL MOYERS (1934–). In "L.B.J.'s Young Man 'In Charge of Everything,'" *Time,* 29 October 1965

In politics, an absurdity is not an obstacle.

> NAPOLEON (1769–1821). *In the Words of Napoleon,* p. 73, tr. Daniel Savage Gray, 1977

Politics, very often, is simply economics pursued by other means.

> EDWARD J. NELL. "Value and Capital in Marxian Economics." In David Bell and Irving Kristol, eds., *The Crisis in Economic Theory,* 1981
>
> See War: Karl von Clausewitz (3)

The whole art of politics consists in directing rationally the irrationalities of men.

> REINHOLD NIEBUHR (1892–1971). In Alden Whitman, "Reinhold Niebuhr Is Dead; Protestant Theologian, 78," *New York Times,* 2 June 1971

I played by the rules of politics as I found them.

> RICHARD M. NIXON (1913–1994). In *Times* (London), 26 March 1990
>
> See Leadership: Abraham Lincoln (2)

The worst sin in politics is being boring.

> RICHARD M. NIXON (1913–1994). In Michael Kramer, "The Danger of Dullness," *Time,* 11 March 1996

With all the temptations and degradations that beset it, politics is still the noblest career any man can choose.

> ANDREW OLIVER (1706–1774). Boston political leader. In Adlai E. Stevenson, speech before the Los Angeles Town Club, 11 September 1952

All Politics Is Local.

> THOMAS P. "TIP" O'NEILL, JR. (1912–1994). Book title, 1994, and his signature saying
>
> See Economics: Peggy Noonan

In our age there is no such thing as "keeping out of politics." All issues are political issues, and politics itself is a mass of lies, evasions, folly, hatred and schizophrenia.

> GEORGE ORWELL (1903–1950). "Politics and the English Language," April 1946, *The Collected Essays, Journalism and Letters of George Orwell,* vol. 4, ed. Sonia Orwell and Ian Angus, 1968

Politics is but the common pulse-beat, of which revolution is the fever-spasm.

> WENDELL PHILLIPS (1811–1884). "The Philosophy of the Abolition Movement," speech before the Massachusetts Anti-Slavery Society, Boston, 27 January 1853

What we need . . . is to moralize politics, and not to politicize morals.

> KARL R. POPPER (1902–1994). *The Open Society and Its Enemies,* 1.6.6, 1945

Serial seduction, that's what politics is.

> RICHARD REEVES. Charlie Rose television interview, PBS, 19 October 1993

I am not a believer in the conventional wisdom that character is all in politics. Politics are what count in politics, the reflexes and judgments of political men and women in crisis.

> RICHARD REEVES. "Clouds Over the White House," *San Francisco Chronicle,* 23 December 1993

In matters of state it is necessary to profit from everything possible; whatever is useful is never to be despised.

> CARDINAL RICHELIEU (1585–1642). *Political Testament,* 2.6, tr. Henry Bertram Hill, 1961

Politics in the United States consists of the struggle between those whose change has been arrested by success or failure, on one side, and those who are still engaged in changing themselves, on the other. Agitators of arrested metamorphosis versus agitators of continued metamorphosis.

> HAROLD ROSENBERG (1906–1978). *Discovering the Present: Three Decades of Art, Culture, and Politics,* 24.4, 1973

Politics is only a game, and a shabby game at that, if it is not directed to larger and nobler ends.

> CLINTON ROSSITER (1917–1970). *The American Presidency,* 5, 1956

Those who desire to treat politics and morals apart from one another will never understand either.

> ROUSSEAU (1712–1778). *Emile; or, Treatise on Education,* 4, 1762, tr. Barbara Foxley, 1911

Politics is how you live your life, not whom you vote for.

> JERRY RUBIN (1938–1994). *Do It! Scenarios of the Revolution,* 42, 1970

Nine times out of ten a man's politics can be predicted from the way in which he makes his living.

> BERTRAND RUSSELL (1872–1970). *Sceptical Essays,* 4, 1928

The drama of politics . . . [is] only the people running around trying to change one gang of bandits for another gang of bandits.

> CARL SANDBURG (1878–1967). *The People, Yes,* 68, 1936

Renunciation of world politics offers no protection from its consequences.

> OSWALD SPENGLER (1880–1936). *Aphorisms,* 363, tr. Gisela O'Brien, 1967

What is politics? I'll tell you what politics is. Politics is men who kiss ass for money and women who fuck for it.

> MATTHEW TROY. New York political leader. Remark made outside the courtroom where he had just been sentenced to three years in jail for taking bribes, mid-1970s. In Lewis H. Lapham, *Money and Class in America: Notes and Observations on the Civil Religion,* 5.3, 1988

Money is the mother's milk of politics.

> JESSE UNRUH (1922–1983). California speaker of the Assembly. His signature saying
>
> See Gossip: Herb Caen

Politics is the art of preventing people from taking part in affairs which properly concern them.

> PAUL VALÉRY (1871–1945). "Rhumbs," *Tel Quel,* vol. 2, 1943

The art of politics is ostentatious giving and surreptitious taking.

> ROGER J. VAUGHAN. Economist. In Stephen Labaton, "Presidential Candidates Ignore Banking Problem," *New York Times,* 7 October 1992

The politics we most need right now is the "politics of community." In that birthing process, a prophetic spiritual network—across the lines of race, class, gender, and region—can act as the midwife of new possibilities.

> JIM WALLIS (1948–). *The Soul of Politics: A Practical and Prophetic Vision for Change,* 3, 1994

I have abstrained from having any sentimunts or principles. My pollertics, like my religion, bein of a exceedin accomodatin character.

> ARTEMUS WARD (1834–1867). "The Crisis," 1850s?, *The Complete Works of Artemus Ward,* 1898

Politics makes strange bedfellows.

> CHARLES DUDLEY WARNER (1829–1900). "Fifteenth Week," *My Summer in a Garden,* 1871
>
> See Adversity: Saying (English) o Misery: Shakespeare

One great secret of the art of politics all over the world is never to push evil or beneficial measures to that point where resistance commences on the part of the governed.

> EDWIN PERCY WHIPPLE (1819–1886). "Character," 1857, *Character and Characteristic Men,* 1884

The aim of politics is not "the forc't and outward union of cold and neutrall and inwardly divided minds." Rather, it is a warm citizenship, approximating friendship, based on a sense of shared values and a shared fate.

> GEORGE F. WILL (1941–). Quoting from John Milton's *Areopagitica* (1644), *Statecraft as Soulcraft: What Government Does,* 7, 1983

A week is a long time in politics.

> HAROLD WILSON (1916–1995). British prime minister. Reportedly said during the 1964 sterling crisis.

POLLUTION

See also • Cities: John Steinbeck ○ Environment ○ Nature ○ Nuclear Energy ○ Rivers: John Drinkwater

There was once a town in the heart of America where all life seemed to live in harmony with its surroundings. . . .

Then a strange blight crept over the area and everything began to change. Some evil spell had settled on the community: mysterious maladies swept the flocks of chickens; the cattle and sheep sickened and died. Everywhere was a shadow of death. The farmer spoke of much illness among their families. . . . There had been several sudden and unexplained deaths, not only among adults but even among children, who would be stricken suddenly while at play and die within a few hours.

There was a strange stillness. The birds, for example—where had they gone? . . . It was a spring without voices. . . .

No witchcraft, no enemy action had silenced the rebirth of new life in this stricken world. The people had done it themselves.

> RACHEL CARSON (1907–1964). On the effect of chemical pesticides and fertilizers, and radiation, *Silent Spring*, 1 ("A Fable for Tomorrow"), 1962

This is an era of specialists, each of whom sees his own problem and is unaware of or intolerant of the larger frame into which it fits. It is also an era dominated by industry, in which the right to make a dollar at whatever cost is seldom challenged. When the public protests, confronted with some obvious evidence of damaging results of pesticide applications, it is fed little tranquilizing pills of half truth. . . . The public must decide whether it wishes to continue on the present road, and it can do so only when in full possession of the facts. In the words of Jean Rostand, "The obligation to endure gives us the right to know."

> RACHEL CARSON (1907–1964). *Silent Spring*, 2, 1962

Lulled by the soft sell and the hidden persuader, the average citizen is seldom aware of the deadly materials with which he is surrounding himself; indeed, he may not realize he is using them at all.

> RACHEL CARSON (1907–1964). *Silent Spring*, 11, 1962

For mankind as a whole, a possession infinitely more valuable than individual life is our genetic heritage, our link with past and future. Shaped through long eons of evolution, our genes not only make us what we are, but hold in their minute beings the future—be it one of promise or threat. Yet genetic deterioration through manmade [chemical and radioactive] agents is the menace of our time, "the last and greatest danger to our civilization."

> RACHEL CARSON (1907–1964). *Silent Spring*, 13, 1962

One of the few natural resources China has in abundance, coal accounts for three quarters of total energy consumption. The country's power stations and manufacturing plants are fueled overwhelmingly by coal. Factor in coal's dominant role in keeping people warm, along with the primitive technologies often employed, and it's no surprise that Chinese cities, especially in the industrial, frigid north, have some of the filthiest air on the planet.

> MARK HERTSGAARD (1956–). "Our Real China Problem," *Atlantic*, November 1997

Acid rain was first brought to world attention in 1972. . . .

Half of [the Adirondack Mountain lakes 2000 feet above sea level] that had fish a generation ago no longer do.

> GLADWIN HILL. Citing a 1974 ecological study, "Acid Rain—No One Really Knows Yet How Bad It Really Is," *New York Times*, 12 August 1979

The free market should not include the right to pollute our environment.

> GEORGE S. McGOVERN (1922–). Appearing on *Firing Line*, television interview series, PBS, 13 September 1989

One person's trash basket is another's living space.

> NATIONAL ACADEMY OF SCIENCES. On pollution, "Waste Management and Control," 1965

Heavy pollution may kill you in a hundred days, but without enough heat and food you die in three.

> CHEN QI. Chinese environmental official. Explaining the dilemma in Liaoning, a region of bitter winter cold and 30 percent unemployment. In Mark Hertsgaard, "Our Real China Problem," *Atlantic*, November 1997

Approximately 80 percent of air pollution stems from hydrocarbons released by vegetation, so let's not go overboard in setting and enforcing tough emission standards from man-made sources.

> RONALD REAGAN (1911–). In Carl Pope, "The Candidates and the Issues," *Sierra* (magazine), September-October 1980

Casca: I durst not laugh for fear of opening my lips and receiving the bad air.

> SHAKESPEARE (1564–1616). *Julius Caesar*, 1.2.251, 1599

The difference between man's soot and nature's grime is that nature knows how to clean up after herself.

> STANFORD RESEARCH INSTITUTE. In R. Buckminster Fuller, *I Seem To Be a Verb*, p. 32, 1970

Throw a few chairmen of the board in jail for polluting the air and water, and you'll see pollution disappear quite rapidly. . . . You would also probably see some pretty drastic prison reforms.

> FORTNEY H. STARK, JR. (1931–) California banker and congressman. In "Tumult & Shouting," *San Francisco Sunday Examiner & Chronicle*, 2 January 1972

Everyone lives downstream from someone else.

> SAYING (AMERICAN)
> See Nuclear Energy: Saying (American)

PONDS

See also • Nature

I see where Walden Pond has been drained
to make an amusement park.

> LAWRENCE FERLINGHETTI (1919–). "Autobiography," *A Coney Island of the Mind*, 1958

Drifting in a sultry day on the sluggish waters of the pond, I almost cease to live and begin to be.

> HENRY DAVID THOREAU (1817–1862). Journal, 4 April 1839

POPULARITY

See also • Applause ○ Charm ○ Conformity ○ Fame ○ Likability ○ Manners ○ Praise ○ Pleasing Others ○ Prestige ○ Reputation ○ Respect ○ Respectability ○ Status

If you want to win mankind, you must make them think you love them, and the best way to make them think you love them, is to love them in reality.

> JEREMY BENTHAM (1748–1832). In John Morley, *Notes on Politics and History: A University Address*, 3, 1913

Where one would gain people, remember that nothing is little.

> LORD CHESTERFIELD (1694–1773). Letter to his son, 23 June 1752

The chief way to gain good will is by good deeds.

> CICERO (106–43 B.C.). *De officiis*, 2.9, tr. Harry G. Edinger, 1974

Anonymous: Are you not proud that so many came to see the chosen of the Lord enter in triumph?
Cromwell: Three times as many would have come to see me hanged.

> OLIVER CROMWELL (1599–1658). Format adapted. An exchange recounted by Sigmund Freud in reference to his own popularity. In Hanns Sachs, *Freud: Master and Friend*, 7, 1944

Popularity is a crime from the moment it is sought; it is only a virtue where men have it whether they will or no.

> MARQUIS OF HALIFAX (1633–1695). "Of Ambition," *Political, Moral and Miscellaneous Reflections*, 1750

Popularity? It is glory's small change.

> VICTOR HUGO (1802–1885). *Ruy Blas*, 3.5, 1838

Woe to you, when all men speak well of you, for so their fathers did to the false prophets.

> JESUS (A.D. 1st cent.). *Luke 6:26*

Among the cheerful robots of the mass society, not human virtue but human shortcomings, attractively packaged, lead to popularity and success.

> C. WRIGHT MILLS (1916–1962). *The Causes of World War Three*, 23.1, 1958

Especially in an age as corrupt and ignorant as this, the good opinion of the people is a dishonor.

> MONTAIGNE (1533–1592). "Of Repentance," *Essays*, 1588, tr. Donald M. Frame, 1958

And what is this smile of the world, to win which we are bidden to sacrifice our moral manhood; this frown of the world, whose terrors are more awful than the withering up of truth and the slow going out of light within the souls of us?

> JOHN MORLEY (1838–1923). *On Compromise*, 4, 1877

Do what you think is right and to hell with your popularity.

> BRIAN MULRONEY (1939–). Canadian prime minister. Remark to Pres. Bill Clinton. In *Washington Post*, quoted in Leah Garchik, "Personals," *San Francisco Chronicle*, 4 June 1993

One self-approving hour whole years outweighs
Of stupid starers, and of loud huzzas;
And more true joy Marcellus exil'd feels,
Than Caesar with a senate at his heels.

> ALEXANDER POPE (1688–1744). *An Essay on Man*, 4.255, 1734
> See Self-Respect: Thomas Fuller, Anwar el-Sadat

I am not a college freshman . . . and therefore I am not concerned about my "popularity" save in exactly so far as it is an instrument which will help me to achieve my purposes.

> THEODORE ROOSEVELT (1858–1919). Letter. In James MacGregor Burns, *Presidential Government*, 2, 1965
> See Fame: Booker T. Washington ○ Glory: Plutarch

The love of popularity seems little else than the love of being beloved; and is only blamable when a person aims at the affections of a people by means in appearance honest, but in the end pernicious and destructive.

> WILLIAM SHENSTONE (1714–1764). "On Politics," *Men & Manners*, ed. Havelock Ellis, 1927

Good humor and generosity carry the day with the popular heart all the world over.

> ALEXANDER SMITH (1830–1867). *Dreamthorp*, 12, 1863

Do not be grieved if you do not enjoy popular favor; grieve rather that you do not live as well and carefully as befits a servant of God.

> THOMAS à KEMPIS (1380–1471). *The Imitation of Christ*, 1.21, tr. Leo Sherley-Price, 1952

A brilliant achievement may win for you the favor of a people at one stroke; but to earn the love and respect of the population that surrounds you, a long succession of little services rendered and of obscure good deeds, a constant habit of kindness and an established reputation for disinterestedness will be required.

> ALEXIS de TOCQUEVILLE (1805–1859). *Democracy in America*, 2.2.4, 1840, tr. Henry Reeve and Francis Bowen, 1862
> See Likability: Lord Chesterfield (1)

Everybody's private motto: it's better to be popular than right.

> MARK TWAIN (1835–1910). *Everyone's Mark Twain*, p. 394, comp. Caroline Thomas Harnsberger, 1948

Though I prize, as I ought, the good opinion of my fellow citizens; yet, if I know myself, I would not seek or retain popularity at the expense of one social duty or moral virtue.

> GEORGE WASHINGTON (1732–1799). Letter to Henry "Light-Horse Harry" Lee, 22 September 1788

POPULATION

See also • Man ○ Mankind ○ Society

There is no exception to the rule that every organic being naturally increases at so high a rate, that if not destroyed, the earth would soon be covered by the progeny of a single pair.

> CHARLES DARWIN (1809–1882). *On the Origin of Species by Means of Natural Selection, or the Preservation of Favoured Races in the Struggle for Life*, 3, 1859, ed. J. W. Burrow, 1968

The Population Bomb.

> PAUL EHRLICH (1854–1915). Book title, 1968

The power of population is infinitely greater than the power in the earth to produce subsistence for man.

Population, when unchecked, increases in a geometrical ratio. Subsistence only increases in an arithmetical ratio. A slight acquaintance with numbers will show the immensity of the first power in comparison of the second.

> THOMAS ROBERT MALTHUS (1766–1834). *An Essay on the Principle of Population, as It Affects the Future Improvement of Society,* 1.1, 1798

The power of population is so superior to the power in the earth to produce subsistence for men, that premature death must in some shape or other visit the human race.

> THOMAS ROBERT MALTHUS (1766–1834). *An Essay on the Principle of Population, as It Affects the Future Improvement of Society,* 1.7, 1798

If Nature can and does increase fertility to prevent the extinction of a species by excessive mortality, need we doubt that she can and will decrease it to prevent its extinction by overcrowding? It is certain that she does, in a mysterious way, respond to our necessities, or rather to her own.

> GEORGE BERNARD SHAW (1856–1950). *The Intelligent Woman's Guide to Socialism, Capitalism, Sovietism and Fascism,* 25, 1928

It is obvious that the best qualities in man must atrophy in a standing-room-only environment.

> STEWART L. UDALL (1920–). *The Quiet Crisis,* 13, 1963

PORNOGRAPHY

See also • Sex ○ War: John Rae

Pornography is the undiluted essence of anti-female propaganda.

> SUSAN BROWNMILLER (1935–). *Against Our Will: Men, Women and Rape,* 12, 1975

You can't do *anything* with anybody's body to make it dirty to me. Six people, eight people, one person—you can do only one thing to make it dirty: kill it. Hiroshima was dirty.

> LENNY BRUCE (1925–1966). "The Good-Good Culture," *The Essential Lenny Bruce,* ed., John Cohen, 1967

Pornography is the attempt to insult sex, to do dirt on it.

> D. H. LAWRENCE (1885–1930). "Pornography and Obscenity," 1929, *Phoenix: The Posthumous Papers of D. H. Lawrence,* ed. Edward D. McDonald, 1936

A dirty book worth reading.

> EZRA POUND (1885–1972). On Henry Miller's *Tropic of Cancer* (1934)

Pornography is about dominance. . . . Erotica is about mutuality.

> GLORIA STEINEM (1934–). "Erotica vs. Pornography," *Dangerous Acts and Everyday Rebellions,* 1983

I shall not today attempt further to define the kinds of material . . . embraced within that shorthand description [of obscenity]; and perhaps I could never succeed in intelligibly doing so. But I know it when I see it, and the motion picture involved in this case is not that.

> POTTER STEWART (1915–1985). Supreme Court associate justice. *Jacobellis v. Ohio,* 1964

POSSESSIONS

See also • Desire: Samuel Johnson ○ Equality: Aristotle ○ Excess: Albert Camus ○ Gifts: *Bhagavad Gita* ○ Last Words: Elizabeth I ○ Luxury ○ Materialism ○ Money ○ Property ○ Wealth

It is not what he has, nor even what he does, which directly expresses the worth of a man, but what he is.

> HENRI AMIEL (1821–1881). 15 December 1859, tr. Mrs. Humphrey Ward, 1887
>
> See Esteem: Ralph Waldo Emerson ○ Knaves: Samuel Butler (2)

A good life requires a supply of external goods, in a less degree when men are in a good state, in a greater degree when they are in a lower state.

> ARISTOTLE (384–322 B.C.). *Politics,* 7.13, tr. Benjamin Jowett, 1885

We go on multiplying our conveniences only to multiply our cares. We increase our possessions only to the enlargement of our anxieties.

> ANNA C. BRACKETT (1836–1911). *The Technique of Rest,* 2, 1892
>
> See Wealth: Hillel

Have, *v.* To no longer desire.

> VICTOR L. CAHN (1948–). *The Disrespectful Dictionary,* unpaged, 1974

Those two fatal words, mine and thine.

> CERVANTES (1547–1616). *Don Quixote,* 1.2.3, 1615, tr. Peter Anthony Motteux and John Ozell, 1743
>
> See Peace: Publius Syrus

Possessions possess.

> PAUL ELDRIDGE (1888–1982). *Maxims for a Modern Man,* 2781, 1965

People who get through life dependent on other people's possessions are always the first to lecture you on how little possessions count.

> BEN ELTON. "Strategic Decision," *Stark,* 1989

Things are in the saddle,
And ride mankind.

> RALPH WALDO EMERSON (1803–1882). "Ode, Inscribed to W. H. Channing" (l. 50), *Poems,* 1847

For each artificial want that can be invented and added to the ponderous expense, there is new clapping of hands of newspaper editors, and the donkey public. To put one more rock to be lifted betwixt a man and his true ends.

> RALPH WALDO EMERSON (1803–1882). Journal, August 1853

The difference between men and boys
is the price of their toys.

> MALCOLM S. FORBES (1919–1990). "Simple Truths," *The Sayings of Chairman Malcolm: The Capitalist's Handbook,* 1978
>
> See Benjamin Franklin in Age & Youth

Bishop: It seems to me that it is very hard and difficult to possess nothing in the world.

St. Francis: My Lord, if we had any possessions, we should also be forced to have arms to protect them, since possessions are a cause of disputes and strife, and, in many ways, we should be hindered from loving God and our neighbor. Therefore, in this life, we wish to have no temporal possessions.

> ST. FRANCIS (A.D. 1181?–1226). Format adapted. In *The Legend of the Three Companions.* Quoted in *Catholic Worker,* October-November 1997

Now I've a sheep and a cow, everybody bids me good morrow.

> BENJAMIN FRANKLIN (1706–1790). *Poor Richard's Almanack,* June 1736

Prospect is often better than Possession.

> THOMAS FULLER (1654–1734). Comp., *Gnomologia: Adages and Proverbs,* 3958, 1732

Naked I came from my mother's womb, and naked shall I return.

> JOB. *Job* 1:21

The young man said to him, "All these [commandments] I have observed; what do I still lack?" Jesus said to him, "If you would be perfect, go, sell what you possess and give to the poor, and you will have treasure in heaven; and come, follow me." When the young man heard this he went away sorrowful; for he had great possessions.

> MATTHEW (A.D. 1st cent.). *Matthew* 19:20–22

Dependence upon material possessions inevitably results in the destruction of human character.

> AGNES E. E. MEYER (1887–1970). *Out of These Roots: The Autobiography of an American Woman,* 1, 1953

It is an embarrassment to the possessor to have more than he needs.

> PUBLIUS SYRUS (85–43 B.C.). *Moral Sayings,* 1063, tr. Darius Lyman, Jr., 1862

The first of possessions, self-possession.

> JOHN RUSKIN (1819–1900)

It is preoccupation with possession, more than anything else, that prevents men from living freely and nobly.

> BERTRAND RUSSELL (1872–1970). *Principles of Social Reconstruction,* 8, 1916

There is no greater calamity than worldly goods.
Both their possession and their want are griefs.

> SA'DI (A.D. 1213?–1292). *The Gulistan, or Rose Garden,* 2 (Story 28), A.D. 1258, tr. Edward Rehatsek, 1964

Many possessions, if they do not make a man better, are at least expected to make his children happier; and this pathetic hope is behind many exertions.

> GEORGE SANTAYANA (1863–1952). *The Life of Reason or The Phases of Human Progress,* 2.3, 1905–1906

Nothing shall seem to me so truly my possessions as the gifts I have wisely bestowed.

> SENECA THE YOUNGER (5? B.C.–A.D. 65). "On the Happy Life" (20.4), *Moral Essays,* tr. John W. Basore, 1932

No man can swim ashore and take his baggage with him.

> SENECA THE YOUNGER (5? B.C.–A.D. 65). "On the Futility of Halfway Measures," *Moral Letters to Lucilius,* 22.12, tr. Richard M. Gummere, 1918

Ownership is an extension of the personality. . . . He who has no instinct for possession lacks personality.

> OSWALD SPENGLER (1880–1936). *Aphorisms,* 306, tr. Gisela Koch-Weser O'Brien, 1967

That is mine which none can steal from me.

> HENRY DAVID THOREAU (1817–1862). In Bronson Alcott, 5 April 1869, *Concord Days,* 1872

Fortune bids me to follow philosophy with fewer encumbrances.

> ZENO (335?–263? B.C.). When informed that all his possessions had been lost in a shipwreck. In Seneca the Younger (5? B.C.–A.D. 65). "On Tranquillity of Mind" (14.3), *Moral Essays,* tr. John W. Basore, 1932

POVERTY

See also • Adversity ○ Class ○ Economics ○ Exploitation: [especially] Isaiah, Arthur Schopenhauer ○ Homelessness ○ Hunger ○ Money ○ Oppression ○ Rich & Poor ○ Simple Living ○ Unemployment ○ Wages ○ Wealth ○ Wealth & Poverty ○ Welfare

The poor man's conscience is clear; yet he is ashamed. . . . He feels himself out of the sight of others, groping in the dark. Mankind takes no notice of him: he rambles and wanders unheeded. In the midst of a crowd, at church, in the market . . . he is in as much obscurity as he would be in a garret or a cellar. He is not disapproved, censured or reproached: *he is only not seen.* . . . To be wholly overlooked, and to know it, are intolerable.

> JOHN ADAMS (1735–1826). *Discourses on Davila,* 5, 1790

Poverty is the parent of revolution and crime.

> ARISTOTLE (384–322 B.C.). *Politics,* 2.6, tr. Benjamin Jowett, 1885

Poverty is not wholly a personal failure. It also represents the failure of an economic system. And the remedy is not wholly one of charity, but of political and economic action. Poverty is a reflection also on those who are not poor.

> BROOKS ATKINSON (1894–1984). 24 August, *Once Around the Sun,* 1951

Anyone who has ever struggled with poverty knows how extremely expensive it is to be poor.

> JAMES BALDWIN (1924–1987). *Nobody Knows My Name: More Notes of a Native Son,* 3, 1961

Poor fowk are soon pish'd on.

> HENRY G. BOHN (1796–1884). Comp., *A Hand-Book of Proverbs,* p. 475, 1860

We will turn parasites and slaves, prostitute ourselves, swear and lie, damn our bodies and souls, forsake God, abjure religion, steal, rob, murder, rather than endure this unsufferable yoke of poverty, which doth so tyrannize, crucify, and generally depress us.

> ROBERT BURTON (1577–1640). *The Anatomy of Melancholia,* 1.2.4.6, 1621–1651

The sternest but most efficient of all schools—poverty.

> ANDREW CARNEGIE (1835–1919). In Dixon Wecter, *The Hero in America: A Chronicle of Hero-Worship*, 12.1, 1941

Poverty . . . [is] the way to heaven.

> ST. JOHN CHRYSOSTOM (A.D. 347–407). In Robert Burton, *The Anatomy of Melancholia*, 1.2.4.6, 1621–1651

As for tramps and wastrels there ought to be proper Labor Colonies where they could be sent for considerable periods and made to realize their duty to the State.

> WINSTON CHURCHILL (1874–1965). Letter to King George V, 10 February 1911

Thousands upon thousands are yearly brought into a state of real poverty by their great anxiety not to be thought poor.

> WILLIAM COBBETT (1763–1835). *Advice to Young Men and (incidentally) to Young Women*, 58, 1980 (1830)

"Nobody Knows You When You're Down and Out."

> JIMMIE COX. Song title, 1923

To live in poverty is to live with constant uncertainty, to accept galling indignities, and to expect harassment by the police, welfare officials, and employers, as well as by others who are poor and desperate.

> BARBARA EHRENREICH (1941–). *Fear of Falling: The Inner Life of the Middle Class*, 1, 1990

Poverty demoralizes.

> RALPH WALDO EMERSON (1803–1882). "Wealth," *The Conduct of Life*, 1860

God said, I am tired of kings,
I suffer them no more;
Up to my ear the morning brings
The outrage of the poor.

> RALPH WALDO EMERSON (1803–1882). "Boston Hymn" (2), *May-Day and Other Pieces*, 1867

Genius and virtue, like diamonds, are best plain set—set in lead, set in poverty. The greatest man in history was the poorest.

> RALPH WALDO EMERSON (1803–1882). "Domestic Life," *Society and Solitude*, 1870

Poverty makes Men ridiculous.

> THOMAS FULLER (1654–1734). Comp., *Gnomologia: Adages and Proverbs*, 3911, 1732

The poor Man's Shilling is but a Penny.

> THOMAS FULLER (1654–1734). Comp., *Gnomologia: Adages and Proverbs*, 4716, 1732

To be poor . . . is the only thing now-a-days men are ashamed of.

> JOHN GAY (1685–1732). *Polly*, 1.11, 1729

The other America, the America of poverty, is hidden today in a way that it never was before. Its millions are socially invisible to the rest of us. . . .

    The poor are increasingly slipping out of the very experience and consciousness of the nation.

> MICHAEL HARRINGTON (1928–1989). *The Other America: Poverty in the United States*, 1.1, 1962

Poverty should be defined psychologically in terms of those whose place in the society is such that they are internal exiles who, almost inevitably, develop attitudes of defeat and pessimism and who are therefore excluded from taking advantage of new opportunities.

> MICHAEL HARRINGTON (1928–1989). Appendix (1) to *The Other America: Poverty in the United States*, 1962

Literally and truly, one cannot get on well in the world without money. To be in want of it, is to pass through life with little credit or pleasure; it is to live out of the world, or to be despised if you come into it . . . ; it is to be scrutinized by strangers, and neglected by friends; it is to a thrall to circumstances, an exile in one's own country.

> WILLIAM HAZLITT (1778–1830). "On the Want of Money," *Table Talk*, 1822

Three possibilities were . . . open to such of the poor as found themselves in the path of bourgeois society [following the French and Industrial Revolutions]. . . . They could strive to become bourgeois; they could allow themselves to be ground down; or they could rebel.

> E. J. HOBSBAWM (1917–). *The Age of Revolution: 1789–1848*, 11.1, 1962

When you're poor, you grow up fast.

> BILLIE HOLIDAY (1915–1959) (with WILLIAM DUFTY). *Lady Sings the Blues*, 1, 1956

Poor men have no souls.

> JAMES HOWELL (1593–1666). Comp. "English" (p. 7), *Paroimiographia: Proverbs, or Old Sayed Sawes & Adages in English . . . Italian, French and Spanish*, 1659

Poverty parteth friends.

> JAMES HOWELL (1593–1666)

We have grown literally afraid to be poor. We despise anyone who elects to be poor in order to simplify and save his inner life. If he does not join the general scramble and pant with the money-making street, we deem him spiritless and lacking in ambition. We have lost the power even of imagining what the ancient idealization of poverty could have meant: the liberation from material attachments, the unbribed soul.

> WILLIAM JAMES (1842–1910). *The Varieties of Religious Experience: A Study in Human Nature*, 14 and 15, 1902

A poor man is despised the whole world over.

> JEROME K. JEROME (1859–1927). "On Being Hard Up," *The Idle Thoughts of an Idle Fellow; A Book for an Idle Holiday*, 1892

You always have the poor with you.

> JESUS (A.D. 1st cent.). *Matthew* 26:11
>
> See Stupidity: Henry David Thoreau

Blessed are you poor, for yours is the kingdom of God.

> JESUS (A.D. 1st cent.). *Luke* 6:20

This administration today, here and now, declares unconditional war on poverty.

> LYNDON B. JOHNSON (1908–1973). Annual message to Congress, 8 January 1964

All crimes are safe, but hated poverty.
This, only this, the rigid law pursues.

SAMUEL JOHNSON (1709–1784). "London: A Poem," l. 159, 1738

Poverty is a great enemy to human happiness; it certainly destroys liberty, and it makes some virtues impracticable and others extremely difficult.

SAMUEL JOHNSON (1709–1784). 7 December 1782. In James Boswell, *The Life of Samuel Johnson,* 1791

The poorest people in our country today, on the whole, are working every day. But they are earning wages so low that they cannot begin to function in the mainstream of the economic life of our nation. . . . We have thousands and thousands of people working on full-time jobs, with part-time incomes.

MARTIN LUTHER KING, JR. (1929–1968). "Why We Must Go to Washington," 15 January 1968

There is nothing new about poverty. What is new is that we now have the techniques and the resources to get rid of poverty. The real question is whether we have the will.

MARTIN LUTHER KING, JR. (1929–1968). Passion Sunday sermon at the National Cathedral, Washington, 31 March 1968

The trouble with being poor is that it takes up all your time.

WILLEM de KOONING (1904–1997). Attributed

Few, save the poor, feel for the poor.

LETITIA ELIZABETH LANDON (1802–1838). "The Poor," *The Poetical Works of Miss Landon,* 1839

It is not only poverty that has caused crime. In a very real sense it is crime that has caused poverty, and is the most powerful cause of poverty today.

JOHN LEWIS (1880–1969). Georgia congressman. "Crime as a Cause of Poverty," *Atlantic,* July 1995

Hard as it may appear in individual instances, dependent poverty ought to be held disgraceful. Such a stimulus seems to be absolutely necessary to promote the happiness of the great mass of mankind.

THOMAS ROBERT MALTHUS (1766–1834). *An Essay on the Principle of Population or A View of Its Past and Present Effects on Human Happiness,* rev. ed., 3.6, 1803

Even poverty itself, which appears to be the great spur to industry, when it has once passed certain limits, almost ceases to operate.

THOMAS ROBERT MALTHUS (1766–1834). *An Essay on the Principle of Population or A View of Its Past and Present Effects on Human Happiness,* rev. ed., 3.14, 1803

When one has shoes, he won't have a coat. I choke up watching the children walk in the mud. It seems that some new people have arrived in the favela. They are ragged with undernourished faces. They improvised a shack. It hurts me to see so much pain, reserved for the working class. I stared at my new companion in misfortune. She looked at the favela with its mud and sickly children. It was the saddest look I'd ever seen. Perhaps she has no more illusions. She had given her life over to misery.

There will be those who reading what I write will say—this is untrue. But misery is real.

What I revolt against is the greed of men who squeeze other men as if they were squeezing oranges.

CAROLINA MARIA de JESUS. Brazilian street scavenger. 29 May 1958, *Child of the Dark: The Diary of Carolina Maria de Jesus,* tr. David St. Clair, 1962

A poor man though he speak the truth is not believed.

MENANDER (343?–291 B.C.). Fragment, 856, tr. Francis G. Allinson, 1921

The poor will never cease out of the land.

MOSES (14th cent. B.C.). *Deuteronomy,* 15:11

Poverty is not merely the lack of adequate financial resources. It entails a more profound kind of deprivation, a denial of full participation in the economic, social, and political life of society and an inability to influence decisions that affect one's life. It means being powerless in a way that assaults not only one's pocketbook but also one's fundamental human dignity. Therefore, we should seek solutions that enable the poor to help themselves through such means as employment. Paternalistic programs which do too much *for* and too little *with* the poor are to be avoided.

NATIONAL CONFERENCE OF CATHOLIC BISHOPS. *Economic Justice for All: Pastoral Letter on Catholic Social Teaching and the U.S. Economy,* 188, 1986

We expressly prohibit and forbid all persons of either sex, of any locality and of any age, of whatever breeding and birth, and in whatever condition they may be, able-bodied or invalid, sick or convalescent, curable or incurable, to beg in the city and suburbs of Paris . . . under pain of being whipped for the first offense, and for the second condemned to the galleys if men and boys, banished if women and girls.

PARLEMENT OF PARIS. Edict (7), 1657. In Michel Foucault, *Madness and Civilization: A History of Insanity in the Age of Reason,* 2, 1961, tr. Richard Howard, 1965

The real disgrace of poverty [is] not in owning to the fact but in declining the struggle against it.

PERICLES (495?–429 B.C.). Funeral oration, 431 B.C. In Thucydides (460?–400? B.C.), *The Peloponnesian War,* 2.40, tr. Richard Crawley and rev. T. E. Wick, 1982

When *poverty* comes in at the doors, love leaps out at the windows.

JOHN RAY (1628–1705). Comp., *A Collection of English Proverbs,* p. 191, 1678

I see one-third of a nation ill-housed, ill-clad, ill-nourished.

FRANKLIN D. ROOSEVELT (1882–1945). *Second Inaugural Address,* 20 January 1937

I remembered the way out suggested by a great princess when told that the peasants had no bread: "Well, let them eat cake."

ROUSSEAU (1712–1778). *Confessions,* 6 (1737–1741), 1781, tr. J. M. Cohen, 1953

He is aware of the condition of the poor
Who has himself fallen into a state of distress.

SA'DI (A.D. 1213?–1292). *The Gulistan, or Rose Garden,* 8 (Maxim 45), A.D. 1258, tr. Edward Rehatsek, 1964

Have you seen them with savings gone
   furniture and keepsakes pawned
   And the pawn tickets blown away in cold winds?
   by one letdown and another ending
   in what you might call slums—
To be named perhaps in case reports
   and tabulated and classified
   among those who have crossed over
   from the employables into the unemployables?

> CARL SANDBURG (1878–1967). *The People, Yes*, 38, 1936

World poverty is primarily a problem of two million villages, and thus a problem of two [billion] villagers. The solution cannot be found in the cities of the poor countries. Unless life in the hinterland can be made tolerable, the problem of world poverty is insoluble and will inevitably get worse.

> E. F. SCHUMACHER (1911–1977). *Small Is Beautiful: Economics as if People Mattered*, 3.3, 1973

Poverty prevails when people have enough to keep body and soul together but little to spare, whereas in misery they cannot keep body and soul together, and even the soul suffers deprivation.

> E. F. SCHUMACHER (1911–1977). "A Culture of Poverty." In Dom Moraes, ed., *Voices for Life: Reflections on the Human Condition*, 1975

It is not the man who has little, but the man who craves more, that is poor.

> SENECA THE YOUNGER (5? B.C.–A.D. 65). "On Discursiveness in Reading," *Moral Letters to Lucilius*, 2.6, tr. Richard M. Gummere, 1918
>
> See Riches: John Muir

No society can surely be flourishing and happy, of which the far greater part of the members are poor and miserable.

> ADAM SMITH (1723–1790). *The Wealth of Nations*, 1.8, 1776

Poverty is no disgrace to a man, but it is confoundedly inconvenient.

> SYDNEY SMITH (1771–1845). *Sydney Smith: His Wit and Wisdom*, p. 89, ed. J. Potter Briscoe, 1900

There is only one trespass that our civilization does not forgive, and that is being poor.

> ROBERT STRAUSZ-HUPÉ (1903–). In Samuel Hughes, "Robert Strausz-Hupé's Long Walk on the Right Side," *Pennsylvania Gazette*, October 1995

Let the poor be members of thy household.

> *TALMUD* (A.D. 1st–6th cent.). Rabbinical writings. In Louis I. Newman, comp., *The Talmudic Anthology*, 252, 1945

That the greatest of evils is idleness, that the poor are the victims, not of circumstances, but of their own "idle, irregular and wicked courses," that the truest charity is not to enervate them by relief, but so to reform their characters that relief may be unnecessary—such doctrines turned severity from a sin into a duty, and froze the impulse of natural pity with the assurance that, if indulged, it would perpetuate the suffering which it sought to allay.

> R. H. TAWNEY (1880–1962). *Religion and the Rise of Capitalism: A Historical Study*, 4.4, 1926

None can be an impartial or wise observer of human life but from the vantage ground of what *we* should call voluntary poverty.

> HENRY DAVID THOREAU (1817–1862). "Economy," *Walden; or Life in the Woods*, 1854
>
> See Simple Living: Seneca the Younger

Again and again I congratulate myself on my so-called poverty. I was almost disappointed yesterday to find thirty dollars in my desk which I did not know that I possessed, though now I should be sorry to lose it.

> HENRY DAVID THOREAU (1817–1862). Journal, 8 February 1857

I've never been poor, only broke. Being poor is a frame of mind. Being broke is only a temporary situation.

> MIKE TODD (1909–1958). In "Death of a Showman," *Newsweek*, 31 March 1958

Remember the poor—it costs nothing.

> MARK TWAIN (1835–1910). Attributed. *The Wit and Wisdom of Mark Twain*, p. 36, ed. Alex Ayres, 1987

Forgive us for pretending to care for the poor, when we do not like poor people and do not want them in our homes.

> UNITED PRESBYTERIAN CHURCH. *Litany for Holy Communion*, 1968

The poor make themselves poorer as apes of the rich.

> LEW WALLACE (1827–1905). *Ben-Hur: A Tale of the Christ*, 4.11, 1880

When you are down and out, something always turns up—and it's usually the noses of your friends.

> ORSON WELLES (1915–1985)

The real tragedy of the poor is that they can afford nothing but self-denial.

> OSCAR WILDE (1854–1900). *The Picture of Dorian Gray*, 6, 1891

✖

They need a hand; they get the finger.

> ANONYMOUS

He who oppresses a poor man insults his Maker,
   but he who is kind to the needy honors him.

> SAYING (*BIBLE*). Proverbs, 14:31

Poverty is a sort of leprosy.

> SAYING (FRENCH)

Poverty has no kin.

> SAYING (ITALIAN)

Poverty is a sin the rich cannot forgive.

> SAYING (RUSSIAN)

Poverty is the heritage of poverty.

> SAYING (RUSSIAN)

Poverty is slavery.

> SAYING (SOMALI)

Poverty is no disgrace, but it's no great honor either.

> SAYING (YIDDISH)

POWER

See also • Ambition ○ Authority ○ Competition ○ Corruption ○ Cruelty ○ Dehumanization ○ Exploitation ○ Force ○ Freedom: Milton Friedman (1) ○ Happiness: Thomas Jefferson ○ Idolatry: Friedrich Nietzsche ○ International Relations ○ Leaders: Montesquieu ○ Love: Carl G. Jung, Alan Paton, Rabindranath Tagore (1) ○ Machiavellianism ○ Money: [especially] Elbert Hubbard, Larry Makinson, Medici Family, Oscar Wilde ○ Paradoxes: Hannah Arendt: Jesus (2) ○ Politics ○ Prestige ○ Public Opinion: John J. McCoy ○ Purpose: Theodore Roosevelt ○ Self-Interest ○ Status ○ Strength ○ Success ○ Tyranny ○ Violence: [especially] Ralph Waldo Emerson, Mao Tse-tung (2) ○ Virtue: Thomas Babington Macaulay ○ Weakness ○ Wealth: [especially] Henry David Thoreau ○ Will: Proclus

Power tends to corrupt and absolute power corrupts absolutely.

> LORD ACTON (1834–1902). English historian. Letter to Bishop Mandell Creighton, 5 April 1887, *Essays on Freedom and Power*, ed. Gertrude Himmelfarb, 1949
>
> See Publicity: Anthony Price

The lust for power never dies—
  men cannot have enough.

> AESCHYLUS (525–456 B.C.). *Agamemnon*, l. 1355, tr. Robert Fagles, 1975

Give me a lever long enough and a fulcrum strong enough, and single-handedly I will move the world.

> ARCHIMEDES (287?–212 B.C.). In Pappus of Alexandria (4th cent. A.D.), *Synagoge*, 8.10.11
>
> See Persuasion: Joseph Conrad

Power corresponds to the human ability not just to act but to act in concert. Power is never the property of an individual; it belongs to a group and remains in existence only so long as the group keeps together.

> HANNAH ARENDT (1906–1975). *On Violence*, 2, 1970
>
> See Arendt in Strength

The desire [for] power in excess, caused the angels to fall.

> FRANCIS BACON (1561–1626). "Of Goodness, and Goodness of Nature," *Essays*, 1625

It is a strange desire to seek power and to lose liberty, or to seek power over others and to lose power over a man's self.

> FRANCIS BACON (1561–1626). "Of Great Place," *Essays*, 1625

Political power and wealth are inseparable. Those who have power have the means to gain wealth and must center all their efforts upon acquiring it, for without it they will not be able to retain their power. Those who are wealthy must become strong, for, lacking power, they run the risk of being deprived of their wealth.

> MIKHAIL BAKUNIN (1814–1876). *Science and the Urgent Revolutionary Task* (pamphlet), 1870. In *The Political Philosophy of Bakunin: Scientific Anarchism*, 4.2, ed. G. P. Maximoff, 1953

Power abdicates only under stress of counter-power.

> MARTIN BUBER (1878–1965). *Paths in Utopia*, 9, 1946, tr. R. F. C. Hull, 1949

I know of nothing sublime, which is not some modification of power.

> EDMUND BURKE (1729–1797). *A Philosophical Inquiry into the Origin of Our Ideas of the Sublime and the Beautiful*, 2.5, 1756

Unnatural power corrupts both the heart and the understanding.

> EDMUND BURKE (1729–1797). *A Vindication of Natural Society*, p. 42, M. Cooper edition, 1756

As wealth is power, so all power will infallibly draw wealth to itself by some means or other.

> EDMUND BURKE (1729–1797). House of Commons speech, 11 February 1780

All persons possessing any portion of power ought to be strongly and awfully impressed with an idea that they act in trust.

> EDMUND BURKE (1729–1797). *Reflections on the Revolution in France*, p. 190, 1790, Pelican Books edition, 1968
>
> See Empire: John Dryden ○ Politicians: Henry Clay ○ Riches: Ralph Waldo Emerson (1)

There is but one just use of power, and it is to serve people.

> GEORGE BUSH (1924–). *Inaugural Address*, 20 January 1989

[Feeling] entitled to power, . . . when it comes to getting it, is tantamount to being halfway home. Talent, energy and self-discipline and, oh yeah, good luck take one the rest of the way. Still, there's no taking the first step without a sense of self-worth.

> MARY CANTWELL. "The Women in Their Ranks," *New York Times Magazine*, 19 November 1995

Power, for the sake of lording it over fellow creatures or adding to personal pomp, is rightly judged base. But power in a national crisis, when a man believes he knows what orders should be given, is a blessing.

> WINSTON CHURCHILL (1874–1965). *The Second World War: Their Finest Hour*, 1.1, 1949

The arts of power and its minions are the same in all countries and in all ages. It marks its victim; denounces [him]; and excites the public odium and the public hatred, to conceal its own abuses and encroachments.

> HENRY CLAY (1777–1852). Senate speech, 14 March 1837

Power multiplies flatterers, and flatterers multiply our delusions by hiding us from ourselves.

> C. C. COLTON (1780–1832). *Lacon: or, Many Things in Few Words; Addressed to Those Who Think*, 2.25, 1824

The need to exert power, when thwarted in the open fields of life, is the more likely to assert itself in trifles.

> CHARLES HORTON COOLEY (1864–1929). *Human Nature and the Social Order*, rev. ed., 5, 1922 (1902)

Power always has most to [fear] from its own illusions.

> JAMES FENIMORE COOPER (1789–1851). Introduction to *The American Democrat*, 1838

The goddess Nemesis . . . symbolizes retributive justice for those who fail to recognize the limits of power.

> PETER W. DICKSON. *Kissinger and the Meaning of History*, note 38 (ch. 2), 1978

Power concedes nothing without a demand. It never did, and it never will.

> FREDERICK DOUGLASS (1817–1895). Letter to Gerrit Smith, 30 March 1849

Here is the secret:

A man is a very small thing whilst he works by and for himself but an immense and omnipotent worker as soon as he puts himself right with the law of nature. . . .

It is as when you come to a conflagration with your fire engine—no matter how good the machine, you will make but a feeble spray, whilst you draw from your own tub: But once get your hose . . . dipped in the river, or in the harbor, and you can pump as long as the sea holds out.

> RALPH WALDO EMERSON (1803–1882). "Notebook WO Liberty," p. 104, 1855

Practical power. Men admire the man who can organize their wishes and thoughts in stone and wood and steel and brass.

> RALPH WALDO EMERSON (1803–1882). "Courage," *Society and Solitude,* 1870

All spiritual or real power makes its own place.

> RALPH WALDO EMERSON (1803–1882). "Aristocracy," *Lectures and Biographical Sketches,* 1883

The power of a man increases steadily by continuance in one direction.

> RALPH WALDO EMERSON (1803–1882). "Perpetual Forces," *Lectures and Biographical Sketches,* 1883

The lust for power is not rooted in strength but in weakness.

> ERICH FROMM (1900–1980). *Escape from Freedom,* 5.1, 1941

The Arrogance of Power

> J. WILLIAM FULBRIGHT (1905–1995). Book title, 1966

Perhaps the oldest and certainly the wisest strategy for the exercise of power is to deny that it is possessed.

> JOHN KENNETH GALBRAITH (1908–). *Economics and the Public Purpose,* 1.2, 1973

Power that comes from service faithfully rendered ennobles.

> MOHANDAS K. GANDHI (1869–1948). In *Young India,* 11 September 1924

Follower: What would be your first act [immediately after discovering you had the] power to shape the destinies of mankind? *Gandhi* (after a pause): I would pray for the courage instantly to renounce that power.

> MOHANDAS K. GANDHI (1869–1948). Format adapted. In James W. Douglass, *The Non-Violent Cross: A Theology of Revolution and Peace,* 11, 1969

The most dangerous thing about power is to employ it where it is not applicable.

> DAVID HALBERSTAM (1934–). *The Best and the Brightest,* 6, 1972

We, sir, are feverishly in pursuit of power. . . . For us the pursuit of power is not an anemic theory: the will to power is for us literally the whole meaning of this life.

> ADOLF HITLER (1889–1945). Remark to the author, 1932–1934. In Hermann Rauschning, *The Voice of Destruction,* 19, 1940

The price to be paid for distrusting power is always smaller than the price to be paid for worshipping it.

> JIM HOAGLAND (1941–). Closing paragraph. "How the Jones Case Plays in Paris," *Washington Post National Weekly Edition,* 13 April 1998

What quality soever maketh a man beloved or feared of many, or the reputation of such quality, is Power because it is a means to have the assistance and service of many.

> THOMAS HOBBES (1588–1679). *Leviathan,* 10, 1651

Power corrupts the few, while weakness corrupts the many.

> ERIC HOFFER (1902–1983). *The Passionate State of Mind: And Other Aphorisms,* 41, 1954

Every man who strikes blows for power, for influence, for institutions, for the right, must be just as good an anvil as he is a hammer.

> JOSIAH GILBERT HOLLAND (1819–1881). "Anvils and Hammers," *Gold-Foil, Hammered from Popular Proverbs,* 1860

The measure of power is obstacles overcome.

> OLIVER WENDELL HOLMES, JR. (1841–1935). "The Soldier's Faith," Memorial Day address, Harvard University, Cambridge (Massachusetts), 30 May 1895

The only prize much cared for by the powerful is power. The prize of the general is not a bigger tent, but command.

> OLIVER WENDELL HOLMES, JR. (1841–1935). "Law and the Court," speech at a dinner of the Harvard Law School Association of New York, 15 February 1913

Nothing discloses real character like the use of power. It is easy for the weak to be gentle. Most people can bear adversity. But if you wish to know what a man really is, give him power. This is the supreme test. It is the glory of Lincoln that, having almost absolute power, he never abused it, except upon the side of mercy.

> ROBERT G. INGERSOLL (1833–1899). Untitled essay. In Allen T. Rice, ed., *Reminiscences of Abraham Lincoln,* 1885

An honest man can feel no pleasure in the exercise of power over his fellow citizens.

> THOMAS JEFFERSON (1743–1826). Letter to John Melish, 13 January 1813

Power is always gradually stealing away from the many to the few because the few are more vigilant and consistent.

> SAMUEL JOHNSON (1709–1784). In *The Adventurer* (English journal), 45, 10 April 1753

Power is neither angel nor brute, but, like man himself a composite creature, uniting in itself two contradictory natures.

> BERTRAND de JOUVENEL (1903–1987). *On Power: Its Nature and the History of Its Growth,* 6.15, 1945, tr. J. F. Huntington, 1948

One acts now, even though conditions are not perfect, even though later information may change the situation. Power does not tarry or it is not power at all.

EUGENE KENNEDY. "Political Power and American Ambivalence," *New York Times Magazine,* 19 March 1978

[Power] waxes in secrecy and wanes in bright light.

EUGENE KENNEDY. "Political Power and American Ambivalence," *New York Times Magazine,* 19 March 1978

What is needed is a realization that power without love is reckless and abusive and that love without power is sentimental and anemic. Power at its best is love implementing the demands of justice.

MARTIN LUTHER KING, JR. (1929–1968). *Where Do We Go from Here: Chaos or Community?* 2.2, 1967

Enlarged material powers spell enlarged peril if there is not proportionate growth of the soul.

MARTIN LUTHER KING, JR. (1929–1968). *Where Do We Go from Here: Chaos or Community?* 6.1, 1967

Power is the ultimate aphrodisiac.

HENRY A. KISSINGER (1923–). In Ralph Blumenfeld et al., *Henry Kissinger: The Private and Public Story,* 16, 1974

See Fame: Graham Greene

Power should not be concentrated in the hands of so few, and powerlessness in the hands of so many.

MAGGIE KUHN (1905–1995). "How to Forget Age Bias," *Ms.,* June 1975

The vaster the power gained, the vaster the appetite for more.

URSULA K. LE GUIN (1929–). *The Lathe of Heaven,* 9, 1971

We . . . are so dazzled by power and prestige as to forget our essential fragility. Willingly or not, we come to terms with power, forgetting that we are all in the ghetto, that the ghetto is walled in, that outside the ghetto reign the lords of death, and that close by the train is waiting.

PRIMO LEVI (1919–1987). Auschwitz survivor. *The Drowned and the Saved,* 2, 1986, tr. Raymond Rosenthal, 1988

It is easier to develop great power than it is to know how to use it well.

WALTER LIPPMANN (1889–1974). "The Rise of the United States," *New York Herald Tribune,* 11 September 1945

Power consists of being able to require others to accept your reality. The politically strong totally reject what you have to say if it conflicts with the official view of reality. . . . The essence of power for these people is that they control the vision of reality. When you put forward an alternative to that, they get very angry because you are breaking an essential monopoly.

DAVID MacMICHAEL. "Calling the Bluff," *Sojourners,* September, 1984

Power never takes a back step—only in the face of more power.

MALCOLM X (1925–1965). "Prospects for Freedom in 1965," speech, New York City, 7 January 1965, *Malcolm X Speaks,* 12, 1965

That there is . . . in all power a constant tendency to encroach is an incontrovertible truth.

THOMAS ROBERT MALTHUS (1766–1834). *An Essay on the Principle of Population or A View of Its Past and Present Effects on Human Happiness,* rev. ed., 4.6, 1803

Power is the force by means of which you can oblige others to obey you. *Authority* is the *right* to direct and command, to be listened to or obeyed by others. Authority requests Power. Power without authority is tyranny.

JACQUES MARITAIN (1882–1973). *Man and the State,* 5.4, 1951

Today the real test of power is not capacity to make war but capacity to prevent it.

ANNE O'HARE McCORMICK (1882?–1954)

Was there ever any domination which did not appear natural to those who possessed it?

JOHN STUART MILL (1806–1873). *The Subjection of Women,* 1, 1869

Every man invested with power is apt to abuse it. . . .

To prevent this abuse, it is necessary from the very nature of things that power should be a check to power.

MONTESQUIEU (1689–1755). *The Spirit of the Laws,* 11.4, 1748, tr. Thomas Nugent, 1750, Hafner Publishing edition, 1949

My power depends on my glory, and my glory on my victory. My power would fall were I not to support it by new glory and new victories. Conquest has made me what I am, and conquest alone can maintain me.

NAPOLEON (1769–1821). Remark to the author, 1800. In Louis de Bourrienne, *Memoirs of Napoleon Bonaparte,* 1.28, ed. R. W. Phipps, 1892

Power is my mistress. I have worked too hard at her conquest to allow anyone to take her away from me or even covet her. Although you say that power came to me of its own accord, I know what it has cost me—the sufferings, the sleepless nights, the scheming. Two weeks ago, I would not have dreamed of treating him unjustly. Now I am unforgiving. I shall smile at him with my lips— but he has slept with my mistress.

NAPOLEON (1769–1821). On hearing that his brother Joseph Bonaparte's ambition was to be designated his heir apparent, remark to Pierre Roederer, 1804, *The Mind of Napoleon: A Selection from His Written and Spoken Words,* 325, ed. J. Christopher Herold, 1955

[Women] belong to the highest bidder. Power is what they like— it is the greatest of all aphrodisiacs.

NAPOLEON (1769–1821). Attributed. In Constant Louis Wairy (his valet), *Mémoirs de Constant, premier valet de l'empereur,* 1831.

See Fame: Graham Greene

Every group, as every individual, has expansive desires which are rooted in the instinct of survival and soon extend beyond it. The will-to-live becomes the will-to-power. Only rarely does nature provide armors of the defense which cannot be transmuted into instruments of aggression.

REINHOLD NIEBUHR (1892–1971). *Moral Man and Immoral Society: A Study in Ethics and Politics,* 1, 1932

The concept of power, whether of a god or of a man, always includes both the ability to help and the ability to harm.

FRIEDRICH NIETZSCHE (1844–1900). *The Will to Power* (notebooks, 1883–1888), 352, 1911, tr. Walter Kaufmann and R. J. Hollingdale, 1967

Where I found a living creature, there I found the will to power; and even in the will of the servant I found the will to be master.

FRIEDRICH NIETZSCHE (1844–1900). "Of Self-Overcoming," *Thus Spoke Zarathustra,* 1892, tr. R. J. Hollingdale, 1961

See God & Man: Albert Schweitzer

Power-worship blurs political judgment because it leads almost unavoidably, to the belief that present trends will continue. Whoever is winning at the moment will always seem invincible.

> GEORGE ORWELL (1903–1950). "James Burnham and the Managerial Revolution," May 1946, *The Collected Essays, Journalism and Letters of George Orwell,* vol. 4, ed. Sonia Orwell and Ian Angus, 1968
>
> See Idolatry: Orwell

It is not merely that "ower corrupts"; so also do the ways of attaining power.

> GEORGE ORWELL (1903–1950). "Arthur Koestler," 1946, *The Collected Essays, Journalism and Letters of George Orwell,* vol. 3, ed. Sonia Orwell and Ian Angus, 1968

Power is power over human beings. Over the body—but, above all, over the mind.

> GEORGE ORWELL (1903–1950). Referring to his futuristic dystopia, *Nineteen Eighty-Four,* 3.3, 1949

Power is in inflicting pain and humiliation. Power is in tearing human minds to pieces and putting them together again in new shapes of our own choosing.

> GEORGE ORWELL (1903–1950). *Nineteen Eighty-Four,* 3.3, 1949
>
> See Brainwashing: Orwell (2)

Power is wonderful, and absolute power is absolutely wonderful.

> ROSS PEROT (1930–). Charlie Rose television interview, PBS, 18 October 1994

Unlimited power is apt to corrupt the minds of those who possess it.

> WILLIAM PITT THE ELDER (1708–1778). Referring to the case of John Wilkes, House of Lords speech, 9 January 1770

Power creates its own resistance.

> JAMES RESTON (1909–). In Harold Faber, "*Faber's Law:* If There Isn't a Law, There Will Be," *New York Times Magazine,* 17 March 1968

Anonymous: What really drives people like congressmen and senators?
Sen. Ribicoff: It's not fame, at least not in the sense of publicity. They see their names and faces in the paper so often they take it for granted. It's not money. There may be some congressmen with deals going, but most lose money while in office because of the cost of campaigning and entertaining. It's not even the exercise of power, at least not in the sense of putting a bill through or having a part in policy decisions. For most of them it is something else. It's more . . . *seeing people jump.* It's a feeling . . . knowing that anywhere they go, people will move for them, give way, run errands, gather around . . . and *jump.*

> ABRAHAM RIBICOFF (1910–?). Format adapted. Talk to a group of students at the American Studies Club, 1953? In Tom Wolfe, "The Ultimate Power: Seeing 'Em Jump," *New York,* 23 December 1968

Power must be linked with responsibility and obliged to defend and justify itself within the framework of the general good.

> FRANKLIN D. ROOSEVELT (1882–1945). January 1945. In Richard Hofstadter, *The American Political Tradition: And the Men Who Made It,* 12.5, 1948

A good many of you are probably acquainted with the old proverb: "Speak softly and carry a big stick—you will go far." If a man continually blusters, if he lacks civility, a big stick will not save him from trouble; and neither will speaking softly avail, if back of the softness there does not lie strength, power.

> THEODORE ROOSEVELT (1858–1919). "National Duties," 2 September 1901, *The Strenuous Life: Essays and Addresses,* 1905
>
> See Competition: Roosevelt

Power always brings with it responsibility. You cannot have power to work well without having so much power as to be able to work ill.

> THEODORE ROOSEVELT (1858–1919). Speech, Milwaukee, 7 September 1910

The fundamental concept in social science is Power, in the same sense in which Energy is the fundamental concept in physics.

> BERTRAND RUSSELL (1872–1970). *Power: A New Social Analysis,* 1, 1938

Power may be defined as the production of intended effects.

> BERTRAND RUSSELL (1872–1970). *Power: A New Social Analysis,* 3, 1938

Direct power over the body. This is the power of armies and police forces. Then there is the power of reward and punishment, which is called the economic power. And then finally there is propaganda power, a power to persuade. I think these are the three main kinds of power.

> BERTRAND RUSSELL (1872–1970). Woodrow Wyatt television interview, BBC, London, 1959, *Bertrand Russell Speaks His Mind,* 6, 1960

Without exercise, the sinews of power atrophy.

> WILLIAM SAFIRE (1929–). *Before the Fall: An Inside View of the Pre-Watergate White House,* 3.5, 1975

All power is of God.

> JOHN SELDEN (1584–1654). "Power: State" (4), *Table Talk,* 1689, ed. Frederick Pollock, 1927

He is most powerful who has power over himself.

> SENECA THE YOUNGER (5? B.C.–A.D. 65). "On the Part Played by Philosophy in the Progress of Man," *Moral Letters to Lucilius,* 90.34, tr. Richard M. Gummere, 1918

You cannot have power for good without having power for evil too.

> GEORGE BERNARD SHAW (1856–1950). *Major Barbara,* 3, 1905

Power does not corrupt men; fools, however, if they get into a position of power, corrupt power.

> GEORGE BERNARD SHAW (1856–1950). Remark to the author, 1940s. In Stephen Winsten, *Days with Bernard Shaw,* 25, 1949

People do things for the powerful; they do not wait to be asked.

> EARL SHORRIS. "Reflections on Power: A Dissenting View," 4.3, *Harper's,* May 1985

Power usually gravitates to officials with operational responsibility at the expense of long-term planners.

> HEDRICK SMITH (1933–). "The Making of a Chief of Staff, 1981," *New York Times,* 8 February 1982

You only have power over people so long as you don't take *everything* away from them. But when you've robbed a man of *everything* he's no longer in your power—he's free again.

> ALEKSANDR SOLZHENITSYN (1918–). *The First Circle,* 17, 1964, tr. Michael Guybon, 1968

Power corrupts, but lack of power corrupts absolutely.

> ADLAI E. STEVENSON (1900–1965). In *Observer* (British newspaper), January 1963

Power takes as ingratitude the writhings of its victims.

> RABINDRANATH TAGORE (1861–1941). *Stray Birds,* 158, 1914

Ultimately, if by slow degrees, power follows the ability to wield it.

> R. H. TAWNEY (1880–1962). *The Acquisitive Society,* 9, 1920

Unlimited power is in itself a bad and dangerous thing. Human beings are not competent to exercise it with discretion. God alone can be omnipotent because his wisdom and his justice are always equal to his power. . . . When I see that the right and the means of absolute command are conferred on any power whatever, be it called a people or a king, an aristocracy or a democracy, a monarchy or a republic, I say there is the germ of tyranny, and I seek to live elsewhere, under other laws.

> ALEXIS de TOCQUEVILLE (1805–1859). *Democracy in America,* 1.15, 1835, tr. Henry Reeve and Francis Bowen, 1862

The real cause, the effective one, that makes men lose power is that they have become unworthy to exercise it.

> ALEXIS de TOCQUEVILLE (1805–1859). Chamber of Deputies speech, Paris, 29 January 1848, *Recollections,* 1.1, 1893, tr. George Lawrence, 1964

Power is defined [as] the ability to make certain things happen, or to prevent certain things from happening.

> ALVIN TOFFLER (1928–). *The Third Wave,* 27, 1980

Knowledge, violence, and wealth, and the relationships among them, define power in society.

> ALVIN TOFFLER (1928–). *Powershift: Knowledge, Wealth, and Violence at the Edge of the 21st Century,* 2, 1990
>
> See Knowledge: Toffler

If you wish to be powerful, pretend to be powerful.

> HORNE TOOKE (1736–1812). In Samuel Taylor Coleridge, 1 May 1832, *Table Talk,* 1835
>
> See Success: La Rochefoucauld

Material power that is not counterbalanced by adequate spiritual power, that is, by love and wisdom, is a curse.

> ARNOLD J. TOYNBEE (1889–1975). *Surviving the Future,* 4, 1971

We have, I fear, confused power with greatness.

> STEWART L. UDALL (1920–). Commencement address at Dartmouth College, Hanover (New Hampshire), 13 June 1965

Men with power have an extraordinary capacity to convince themselves that what they want to do coincides with what society needs done for its [own] good.

> RAYMOND VERNON. "The Multinational Enterprise: Power Versus Sovereignty," *Foreign Affairs,* July 1971

The balance of power.

> SIR ROBERT WALPOLE (1676–1745). House of Commons speech, 13 February 1741

Extensive powers not exercised as far as was necessary have, I believe, scarcely ever failed to ruin the possessor.

> GEORGE WASHINGTON (1732–1799). Letter to Joseph Reed, 4 July 1780

Love of power and proneness to abuse it . . . [predominate] in the human heart.

> GEORGE WASHINGTON (1732–1799). *Farewell Address,* 17 September 1796

Power . . . is a means at its purest. For that very reason it is the supreme end for all those who have not understood.

> SIMONE WEIL (1909–1943). *The Simone Weil Reader,* 4 ("Metaxu"), ed. George A. Panichas, 1977

Power is getting others to do one's will.

> GARRY WILLS (1934–). Epilogue to *The Kennedy Imprisonment: A Meditation on Power,* 1981

The wondrous influence of power gently used.

> WILLIAM WORDSWORTH (1770–1850). *The Prelude; or, Growth of a Poet's Mind: An Autobiographical Poem,* 12.15, 1850

❧

Power tends to corrupt; the *illusion* of power corrupts absolutely.

> ANONYMOUS. In John W. Gardner, *On Leadership,* 6, 1990

Power tends to consolidate as internal and external opportunities and risks increase.

> ANONYMOUS

Right reigns, might rules.

> ANONYMOUS

Might makes right.

> SAYING
>
> See Right: Saying

Let might serve right.

> SAYING

PRAISE

See also • Applause ○ Censure ○ Criticism ○ Deception: Molière ○ Flattery ○ Insult ○ Judging Others ○ Popularity: Jesus ○ Popularity ○ Praise: Examples

One who praises you for qualities you lack, will next be found blaming you for faults not yours.

> 'ALI (A.D. 600?–661). *Maxims of 'Ali,* tr. Maulana Akbar, undated. In Whitall N. Perry, comp., *A Treasury of Traditional Wisdom,* p. 127, 1986

When you do well, do not praise yourself but the gods.

> BIAS (6th cent. B.C.). One of the Seven Sages of Greece

Accepting praize that iz not our due iz not mutch better than tew be a receiver of stolen goods.

JOSH BILLINGS (1818–1885). "Stray Children," *Everybody's Friend, or; Josh Billing's Encyclopedia and Proverbial Philosophy of Wit and Humor,* 1874

I have cum tew the konklusion that what every boddy praizes wants cluss watching.

JOSH BILLINGS (1818–1885). "Remnants," *His Works, Complete,* 1881

Praise out of season, or tactlessly bestowed, can freeze the heart as much as blame.

PEARL S. BUCK (1892–1973). "First Meeting," *To My Daughters, With Love,* 1967

Watch how a man takes praise, and there you have the measure of him.

THOMAS BURKE (1886–1945). In *T.P.'s Weekly,* 8 June 1928

The advantage of doing one's praising for oneself is that one can lay it on so thick and exactly in the right places.

SAMUEL BUTLER (1835–1902). *The Way of All Flesh,* 34, 1903

Praise, when it is not deserved, is the severest satire and abuse.

LORD CHESTERFIELD (1694–1773). Letter to his son, 15 July 1739

Expect not praise without envy until you are dead.

C. C. COLTON (1780–1832). *Lacon: or, Many Things in Few Words; Addressed to Those Who Think,* 1.245, 1823

The house praises the carpenter.

RALPH WALDO EMERSON (1803–1882). Journal, 28 September 1836

A little praise
Goes a great ways.

RALPH WALDO EMERSON (1803–1882). "Encyclopedia," p. 138, 1824-1836

Praise little, but dispraise less.

THOMAS FULLER (1654–1734). Comp., *Introductio ad Prudentiam,* 148, 1731

Neither praise, not dispraise thyself; thy Actions will do it enough.

THOMAS FULLER (1654–1734). Comp., *Introductio ad Prudentiam,* 338, 1731

If evil Men speak good, or good Men evil of thee; examine thy Actions, and suspect thyself.

THOMAS FULLER (1654–1734). Comp., *Introductio ad Prudentiam,* 1252, 1731

The paying of compliments is a middle-class convention, for this class needs the assurance compliments provide. In the upper class there's never any doubt of one's value, and it all goes without saying.

PAUL FUSSELL (1924–). *Class,* 2, 1983

My soul preached to me and said, "Do not be delighted because of praise, and do not be distressed because of blame.

KAHLIL GIBRAN (1883–1931). *Secrets of the Heart,* 2, ed. Stanley Hendricks, 1968

See Self-Realization (Being): *Bhagavad Gita* ○ Wisdom: Lao-tzu (2)

To speak highly of one with whom we are intimate is a species of egotism.

WILLIAM HAZLITT (1778–1830). *Characteristics in the Manner of Rochefoucault's Maxims,* 3, 1823

How little it requires to disconcert or soothe the mind that is greedy for praise.

HORACE (65–8 B.C.). *Epistles.* In Arthur Schopenhauer, "The Wisdom of Life" (4.1), *Essays of Arthur Schopenhauer,* tr. T. Bailey Saunders, 1851

Praise, like gold and diamonds, owes its value only to its scarcity.

SAMUEL JOHNSON (1709–1784). In *The Rambler* (English journal), 127, 6 June 1751

As he succeeds,
He takes no credit
And just because he does not take it,
Credit never leaves him.

LAO-TZU (6th cent. B.C.). *The Way of Life,* 2, tr. R. B. Blakney, 1955

There are reproaches that compliment, and compliments that disparage.

LA ROCHEFOUCAULD (1613–1680). *Maxims,* 148, 1665, tr. Louis Kronenberger, 1959

I do the very best I know how—the very best I can; and I mean to keep doing so until the end. If the end brings me out all right, what is said against me won't amount to anything. If the end brings me out wrong, ten angels swearing I was right would make no difference.

ABRAHAM LINCOLN (1809–1865). In F. B. Carpenter, *Six Months at the White House with Abraham Lincoln,* 68, 1866

There's no praise to beat the sort you can put in your pocket.

MOLIÈRE (1622–1673). *Le Bourgeois gentilhomme,* 1, 1670, tr. John Wood, 1959

Your self-condemnation is always accredited, your self-praise discredited.

MONTAIGNE (1533–1592). "Of the Art of Discussion," *Essays,* 1588, tr. Donald M. Frame, 1958

So long as you are praised, think only that you are not yet on your own path but on that of another.

FRIEDRICH NIETZSCHE (1844–1900). *Assorted Opinions and Maxims,* 340, 1879, tr. R. J. Hollingdale, 1977

Men can endure to hear others praised only so long as they can . . . persuade themselves of their own ability to equal the actions recounted: when this point is passed, envy comes in and with it incredulity.

PERICLES (495?–429 B.C.). Funeral oration, 431 B.C. In Thucydides (460?–400? B.C.), *The Peloponnesian War,* 2.35, tr. Richard Crawley and rev. T. E. Wick, 1982

Damn with faint praise.

ALEXANDER POPE (1688–1744). *An Epistle to Dr. Arbuthnot,* l. 201, 1735

Speak well of your friend in public, admonish in secret.

PUBLIUS SYRUS (85–43 B.C.). *Moral Sayings,* 870, tr. Darius Lyman, Jr., 1862

Do you want to injure someone's reputation? Don't speak ill of him, speak too well.

ANDRÉ SIEGFRIED. *Quelques maximes,* 1943

The love of praise is the desire of obtaining the favorable sentiments of our brethren. The love of praiseworthiness is the desire of rendering ourselves the proper objects of those sentiments.

ADAM SMITH (1723–1790). *The Theory of Moral Sentiments*, 3.2, 1759

The acknowledgment of effort has to be tailor-made. People pick up on canned compliments, especially if they hear the same things being said to other people. Nothing is more effective than sincere, accurate praise, and nothing is more lame than a cookie-cutter compliment.

BILL WALSH (1931–). "The Case for Kudos," *Forbes ASAP,* 10 October 1994

✺

Praise from your own mouth stinks.

SAYING (GERMAN)

The work praises the worker.

SAYING (GERMAN)

Praise loudly, blame softly.

SAYING (RUSSIAN)

Too much or too little praise is dispraise.

SAYING

Better merit without praise than praise without merit.

SAYING

Honest criticism is the highest praise.

SAYING

PRAISE: EXAMPLES

See also • Criticism: Examples ○ Critics: Examples ○ Misjudgments ○ Praise

Success did not inflate him nor misfortune depress him.

CLAUDE AUCHINLECK (1884–1981). British general. On Gen. William Slim (1891–1970). In Norman F. Dixon, *On The Psychology of Military Incompetence,* 27, 1976

For one who lived among enemies so long:
if often he was wrong and, at times, absurd,
to us he is no more a person
now but a whole climate of opinion.

W. H. AUDEN (1907–1973). "In Memory of Sigmund Freud" (17), 1939, *Collected Poems,* ed. Edward Mendelson, 1976

No dancer can watch Fred Astaire and not know that we all should have been in another business.

MIKHAIL BARYSHNIKOV (1948–). In Jack Kroll, "Never Gonna Dance Again," *Newsweek,* 6 July 1987

He opened us—
who was a key,
who was a man.

GWENDOLYN BROOKS (1917–). "Malcolm X," 1967. In Angelo Carli and Theodore Kilman, eds., *The Now Voices: The Poetry of the Present,* p. 111, 1971

Long shall we seek his likeness, long in vain,
And turn to all of him which may remain,
Sighing that nature form'd but one such man,
And broke the die—in molding Sheridan!

LORD BYRON (1788–1824). On the Irish playwright Richard Sheridan, closing lines, "Monody on the Death of the Right Hon. R. B. Sheridan," 1816

The largest soul that was in all England.

THOMAS CARLYLE (1795–1881). On Samuel Johnson, "The Hero as Man of Letters," *On Heroes, Hero-Worship, and the Heroic in History,* 1841

If anything happened to that man, I couldn't stand it. He is the truest friend; he has the farthest vision; he is the greatest man I have ever known.

WINSTON CHURCHILL (1874–1965). On Franklin D. Roosevelt, soon after the Casablanca Conference in November 1943. In Doris Kearns Goodwin, *No Ordinary Time: Franklin and Eleanor Roosevelt: The Home Front in World War II,* 16, 1994

Shakespeare . . . is of no age—nor of any religion, or party or profession. The body and substance of his works came out of the unfathomable depths of his own oceanic mind.

SAMUEL TAYLOR COLERIDGE (1772–1834). 15 March 1834, *Table Talk,* 1835

Newton, childlike sage!
Sagacious reader of the works of God.

WILLIAM COWPER (1731–1800). *The Task,* 3.252, 1785

A great singer is born in every generation, but why did Frank Sinatra have to be born in mine?

BING CROSBY (1904–1977). As recalled by Herb Caen in a column celebrating Sinatra's 80th birthday, *San Francisco Chronicle,* 11 December 1995

Lenny Bruce was dead.
He was the brother you never had.

BOB DYLAN (1941–). "Lenny Bruce" (song), 1981

Generations to come, it may be, will scarce believe that such a one as this ever in flesh and blood walked upon the earth.

ALBERT EINSTEIN (1879–1955). On the occasion of Mohandas K. Gandhi's 75th birthday, 2 October 1944, *Out of My Later Years,* rev. ed., 45, 1956 (1950)

Tacitus, the wisest of historians.

RALPH WALDO EMERSON (1803–1882). "Books," *Society and Solitude,* 1870

Lenin was the steel that bends.

LOUIS FISCHER (1896–1970). *The Life of Lenin,* 37, 1964

From an old man who greets in the Ruler the Hero of Culture.

SIGMUND FREUD (1856–1939). Inscription in his book sent as a gift to Benito Mussolini, 1933. In Ernest Jones, *The Life and Work of Sigmund Freud,* 3.4, 1953–1957

At his best when things were at their worst.

J. F. C. FULLER (1878–1966). On Winston Churchill, *The Conduct of War: 1789–1961,* 13.2, 1961

Knowledge is power. But knowledge without character and wisdom is nothing, or worse. These the President also had in rich measure. But I come back to the grasp of issues, the breadth of information and the power of concentration. Perhaps these come naturally. I suspect, in fact, that few men in history have ever combined natural ability with such powers of mental self-discipline.

> JOHN KENNETH GALBRAITH (1908–). On John F. Kennedy.
> In *Washington Post,* 25 November 1963, appendix (3) to *Ambassador's Journal: A Personal Account of the Kennedy Years,* 1969
>
> See Criticism: Examples: Thomas C. Reeves

A humankindly man.

> MAXIM GORKY (1868–1936). On Leo Tolstoy. In Stefan Zweig, "Tolstoy: Envoy," *Master Builders: A Typology of the Spirit,* tr. Eden and Cedar Paul, 1939

Lincoln, with all his foibles, is the greatest character since Christ.

> JOHN HAY (1838–1905). Lincoln's private secretary during the Civil War and later secretary of state. Closing words, letter to William H. Herndon, 5 September 1866. In Emanuel Hertz, ed., *The Hidden Lincoln: From the Letters and Papers of William H. Herndon,* 2.1, 1940

[Mark Twain] was sole, incomparable, the Lincoln of our literature.

> WILLIAM DEAN HOWELLS (1837–1920). *My Mark Twain: Reminiscences and Criticisms,* 1.26, 1910

Lincoln was not a type. He stands alone—no ancestors, no fellows, and no successors.

> ROBERT G. INGERSOLL (1833–1899). Untitled essay. In Allen T. Rice, ed., *Reminiscences of Abraham Lincoln,* 1885

His character was, in its mass, perfect, in nothing bad, in few points indifferent; and it may truly be said that never did nature and fortune combine more perfectly to make a man great.

> THOMAS JEFFERSON (1743–1826). On George Washington, letter to Dr. Walter Jones, 2 January 1814

If I were to lose Boswell, it would be a limb amputated.

> SAMUEL JOHNSON (1709–1784). 1 April 1781 (note). In James Boswell, *The Life of Samuel Johnson,* 1791

You could not stand five minutes with that man beneath a shed while it rained, but you must be convinced you had been standing with the greatest man you had ever yet seen.

> SAMUEL JOHNSON (1709–1784). On Edmund Burke. In Hester Lynch Piozzi, *Anecdotes of the Late Samuel Johnson, LL.D.,* p. 135, 1786, ed. S. C. Roberts, 1932

He was not of an age, but for all time!

> BEN JONSON (1572–1637). "To the Memory of My Beloved, the Author, Mr. William Shakespeare," 1623

I think this is the most extraordinary collection of talent, of human knowledge, that has ever been gathered together at the White House—with the possible exception of when Thomas Jefferson dined alone.

> JOHN F. KENNEDY (1917–1963). After-dinner speech before a group of American Nobel laureates, 29 April 1962

Sadat was more than the sum of his parts. By one of the miracles of creation the peasant's son, the originally underestimated politi-

cian, had the wisdom and courage of the statesman and occasionally the insight of the prophet.

> HENRY A. KISSINGER (1923–). On Egyptian Pres. Anwar el-Sadat, *Years of Upheaval,* 13, 1982

A citizen, first in war, first in peace, and first in the hearts of his countrymen.

> HENRY "LIGHT-HORSE HARRY" LEE (1756–1818). Eulogy for George Washington, House of Representatives, 26 December 1799

[Winston] Churchill's eloquence is the man himself, and the secret of his fascination is his magnanimity.

> WALTER LIPPMANN (1889–1974). "The Fascination of Greatness," *New York Herald Tribune,* 7 September 1943

That nation has not lived in vain which has given the world Washington and Lincoln, the best great men and the greatest good men whom history can show.

> HENRY CABOT LODGE (1902–1985). Massachusetts legislature speech, 12 February 1909

There must be something essentially noble in an elective ruler who can descend to the level of confidential ease without forfeiting respect. . . . No higher compliment was ever paid to a nation than the simple confidence, the fireside plainness, with which Mr. Lincoln always addresses himself to the reason of the American people.

> JAMES RUSSELL LOWELL (1819–1891). "Abraham Lincoln," 1964, *My Study Windows,* 1871

Homely, dispassionate, showing all the rough-edged process of his thought as it goes along, yet arriving at his conclusions with an honest kind of everyday logic, he is so eminently our representative man, that, when he speaks, it seems as if the people were listening to their own thinking aloud.

> JAMES RUSSELL LOWELL (1819–1891). "Abraham Lincoln," 1864, *My Study Windows,* 1871

Joseph Vissarionovich Stalin, the greatest genius of the present age, the great teacher of the world communist movement, the comrade-in-arms of the immortal Lenin, has departed from the world.

> MAO TSE-TUNG (1893–1976). "The Greatest Friendship," March 1953, *The Political Thought of Mao Tse-tung,* 10.H, ed. Stuart R. Schram, 1963

[Dwight D. Eisenhower] merely has to smile at you, and you trust him at once. He is the very incarnation of sincerity.

> BERNARD LAW MONTGOMERY (1887–1976). *The Memoirs of Field-Marshal Montgomery,* 33, 1958

[Emily] Dickinson, our supreme poet of inwardness.

> JOYCE CAROL OATES (1938–). "The One Unforgivable Sin," *New York Times Book Review,* 25 July 1993

Here was a great woman; a magnificent, generous, gallant, reckless, fated fool of a woman. There was never a place for her in the ranks of the terrible, slow army of the cautious. She ran ahead, where there were no paths.

> DOROTHY PARKER (1893–1967). On Isadora Duncan (1878–1927, dancer), "Poor, Immortal Isadora," *New Yorker,* 14 January 1928

His soul was no different from any other man's, only greater.

> HESTER LYNCH PIOZZI (1741–1821). On Samuel Johnson. In David Kahn, letter to *New York Times Magazine,* 25 January 1998

You were the best. Don't tell the others.

> MIKE ROYKO (1933–1997). *Chicago Tribune* columnist. Identical inscription in a book given each of his research assistants. In Don Terry, "Mike Royko, the Voice of the Working Class, Dies at 64," *New York Times,* 30 April 1997

Beneath the imitation-oak-grained formica veneer is solid oak, beneath that phony image of character *is* character: a confidence in his vision, a love of his country, a desire to be remembered as somebody who mattered because he rediscovered our faith in ourselves—and was not afraid to affirm it at a time when affirmation seemed out of date.

> WILLIAM SAFIRE (1929–). On Richard M. Nixon. Epilogue to *Before the Fall: An Inside View of the Pre-Watergate White House,* 1975

Not often in the story of mankind does a man arrive on earth who is both steel and velvet, who is as hard as rock and soft as drifting fog, who holds in his heart and mind the paradox of terrible storm and peace unspeakable and perfect. Here and there across the centuries come reports of men who have these contrasts. And the incomparable Abraham Lincoln, born 150 years ago this day, is an approach if not a perfect realization of this character.

> CARL SANDBURG (1878–1967). Commemorating the 150th anniversary of Abraham Lincoln's birth, Congress address, 12 February 1959

I wrote numerous articles about Freud and was one of the first to recognize the greatness of this genius . . . I was the apostle of Freud who was my Christ!

> WILHELM STEKEL (1868–1940). *The Autobiography of Wilhelm Stekel: The Life Story of a Pioneer Psychoanalyst,* 4, ed. Emil A. Gutheil, 1950

I sleep each night a little better, a little more confidently because Lyndon Johnson is President.

> JACK VALENTI (1921–). Presidential assistant. Advertising Federation of America Convention speech, Boston, 28 June 1965, *A Very Human President,* 2 ("The White House Staff"), 1976

I see the President [Abraham Lincoln] often. I think better of him than many do. He has conscience and homely shrewdness—conceals an enormous tenacity under his mild, gawky western manner. The difficulties of his situation have been unprecedented in the history of statesmanship. That he has conserved the government so far is a miracle itself.

> WALT WHITMAN (1819–1892). Letter to James P. Kirkwood, 27? April 1864

The indomitable heart and arm—proofs of the never-broken line,
Courage, alertness, patience, faith, the same—e'en in defeat defeated not, the same.

> WALT WHITMAN (1819–1892). On George Washington, "Washington's Monument, February, 1885," 1885, *Leaves of Grass,* 1855–1892

PRAYER

See also • Confession ∘ God ∘ Justice, Saying (Islamic) ∘ Prayers ∘ Religion ∘ Repentance ∘ Revelation ∘ Sea: George Herbert ∘ Silence ∘ Spirituality

"Why Should We Not Pray to Our Mother Who Art in Heaven, As Well As to Our Father?"

> SUSAN B. ANTHONY (1820–1906). Headline. In *Revolution* (feminist newspaper), 18 March 1869

In the religion which we shall call dynamic, prayer is independent of its verbal expression; it is an elevation of the soul that can dispense with speech.

> HENRI BERGSON (1859–1941). "Static Religion," *The Two Sources of Morality and Religion,* 1932, tr. R. Ashley Audra and Cloudesley Brereton, 1935

Pray, *v.* To ask that the laws of the universe be annulled in behalf of a single petitioner confessedly unworthy.

> AMBROSE BIERCE (1842–1914). *The Devil's Dictionary,* p. 102, 1911, Dover edition, 1958

Before prayer, give to charity.

> THE BRATZLAVER (1770–1811). In Louis I. Newman, comp., *The Hasidic Anthology,* 132.23.B.15, 1934

Do not pray for tasks equal to your powers. Pray for powers equal to your tasks.

> PHILLIPS BROOKS (1835–1893). "Going Up to Jerusalem," *Selected Sermons,* ed. William Scarlett, 1949

We call prayer . . . that speech of man to God which, whatever else is asked, ultimately asks for the manifestation of the divine Presence.

> MARTIN BUBER (1878–1965). *Eclipse of God: Studies in the Relation between Religion and Philosophy,* 8, tr. Maurice S. Friedman, 1952

God answers all our prayers. Sometimes the answer is yes. Sometimes the answer is no. Sometimes the answer is, you've to got to be kidding!

> JIMMY CARTER (1924–). Larry King television interview, CNN, 18 November 1997

When you abandon yourself to cowardice and baseness, it is vain to call upon the gods; they are offended and hostile.

> CATO THE YOUNGER (95–46 B.C.). Speech before the Roman Senate. In Sallust (86?–34? B.C.), *The War with Catiline,* 52.29, tr. J. C. Rolfe, 1921

He prayeth well, who loveth well
Both man and bird and beast.
He prayeth best, who loveth best
All things both great and small;
For the dear God who loveth us,
He made and loveth all.

> SAMUEL TAYLOR COLERIDGE (1772–1834). *The Rime of the Ancient Mariner,* 7, 1798

Then I turned my face to the Lord God, seeking him by prayer and supplications with fasting.

> DANIEL (8th cent. B.C.). *Daniel* 9:3

When I pray for something, I do not pray; when I pray for nothing, I really pray. . . . To pray for anything except God might be called idolatry.

> MEISTER ECKHART (A.D. 1260?–1328?). "Fragments" (34), *Meister Eckhart: A Modern Translation,* tr. R. B. Blakney, 1941

I have never wished there was a God to call on—I have often wished there was a God to thank.

> F. SCOTT FITZGERALD (1896–1940). "The Note-Books" (N), *The Crack-Up,* ed. Edmund Wilson, 1945

Work as if you were to live 100 years,
Pray as if you were to die Tomorrow.

> BENJAMIN FRANKLIN (1706–1790). *Poor Richard's Almanack,* May 1757

Prayer is an impossibility without a living faith in the presence of God within.

> MOHANDAS K. GANDHI (1869–1948). In *Young India,* 20 December 1928

You pray in your distress and in your need; would that you might pray also in the fullness of your joy and in your days of abundance.

> KAHLIL GIBRAN (1883–1931). "On Prayer," *The Prophet,* 1923

Prayer is an invitation to God to intervene in our lives.

> ABRAHAM JOSHUA HESCHEL (1907–1972). *Man's Quest for God: Studies in Prayer and Symbolism,* 1, 1954

Certain thoughts are prayers. There are moments when, whatever be the attitude of the body, the soul is on its knees.

> VICTOR HUGO (1802–1885). "Saint Denis" (5.4), *Les Misérables,* tr. Charles E. Wilbour, 1862

Seek the Lord while he may be found,
  call upon him while he is near.

> ISAIAH (8th cent. B.C.) *Isaiah* 55:6

When you pray, you must not be like the hypocrites; for they love to stand and pray in the synagogues and at the street corners, that they may be seen by men. Truly, I say to you, they have their reward. But when you pray, go into your room and shut the door and pray to your Father who is in secret; and your Father who sees in secret will reward you.

> JESUS (A.D. 1st cent.). *Matthew* 6:5–6

Prayer is a marvelous and necessary supplement of our feeble efforts, but it is a dangerous substitute.

> MARTIN LUTHER KING, JR. (1929–1968). *Strength to Love,* 15.2, 1963

God seems to have left the receiver off the hook, and time is running out.

> ARTHUR KOESTLER (1905–1983). *The Ghost in the Machine,* 18, 1967

A single grateful thought towards heaven is the most complete prayer.

> GOTTHOLD EPHRAIM LESSING (1729–1781). *Minna von Barnhelm,* 2.7, 1767

The value of persistent prayer is not that he will hear us . . . but that we will finally hear him.

> WILLIAM McGILL. "Prayer Unceasing," *Living Church,* 28 September 1986

To spend more time in learning is better than spending more time in praying.

> MUHAMMAD (A.D. 570?–632). *The Sayings of Muhammad,* 277, tr. Abdullah Al-Suhrawardy, 1941

The harvest comes home not for praying but for tilling.

> PLOTINUS (A.D. 205–270). *The Enneads,* 3.2.8, tr. Stephen MacKenna and B. S. Page, 1952

In the presence of God we speak too much; we do not listen enough.

> JOSEPH ROUX (1834–1886). *Meditations of a Parish Priest,* 10.20, tr. Isabel F. Hapgood, 1886

An act of goodness surpasses a thousand prayers.

> SA'DI (A.D. 1213?–1292). *The Maxims of Sa'di,* 1, tr. Mehdi Nakosteen, 1977

We take care what we speak to men, but to God we may say anything.

> JOHN SELDEN (1584–1654). "Prayer" (7), *Table Talk,* 1689, ed. Frederick Pollock, 1927

When you pray, know before Whom you stand.

> TALMUD (A.D. 1st–6th cent.). Rabbinical writings. In Louis I. Newman, comp., *The Talmudic Anthology,* 60, 1945

More things are wrought by prayer
Than this world dreams of.

> ALFRED LORD TENNYSON (1809–1892). "The Passing of Arthur" (l. 415), *The Idylls of the King,* 1859–1885
>
> See Philosophy: Shakespeare

He listens equally to the prayers of the believer and the unbeliever.

> HENRY DAVID THOREAU (1817–1862). Journal, 7 January 1842

When prayer—the communion between human person and divine person—has been raised to its highest degree of spiritual intensity, it is transmuted into another kind of experience. At this higher spiritual level, personality is transcended, and, with it, the separateness that is personality's limitation. At this supra-personal spiritual height, the experience is unitive. At this height, God and man do not commune with each other because, at this height, they are identical.

> ARNOLD J. TOYNBEE (1889–1975). *Experiences,* 1.9 (Annex 4), 1969

You can't pray a lie.

> MARK TWAIN (1835–1910). *The Adventures of Huckleberry Finn,* 31, 1884

I have never made but one prayer to God, a very short one: "O Lord, make my enemies ridiculous." And God granted it.

> VOLTAIRE (1694–1778). Letter to M. Damilaville, 16 May 1767

When the gods wish to punish us, they answer our prayers.

> OSCAR WILDE (1854–1900). *An Ideal Husband,* 2, 1895

To pray is to think about the meaning of life.

> LUDWIG WITTGENSTEIN (1889–1951). 11 June 1916, *Notebooks, 1914–1916,* ed. G. E. M. Anscombe, 1961

The heart's cry to God is the highest form of prayer.

> ZOHAR (A.D. 13th cent.). Jewish mystical writings. In Louis I. Newman, comp., *The Talmudic Anthology,* 257, 1945

❧

Better one honest tear than a hundred earnest prayers; better one kind deed than a hundred honest tears.

> ANONYMOUS

The fewer the words, the better the prayer.

> SAYING (GERMAN)

Prayer without study is like a soul without a body.

SAYING (JEWISH)

A good deed is the best prayer.

SAYING (MEXICAN)

Pray as if everything depends on God; act as if everything depends on you.

SAYING

PRAYERS

See also • God ○ God & Man: First Person ○ Prayer ○ Revelations ○ Suffering: Levi Yitzhak ○ Values: Anonymous

Hold back, O my God, these torrents which overwhelm me, or else enlarge my capacity for their reception.

MARGARET MARY ALACOQUE (19th cent.). In William James, *The Varieties of Religious Experience: A Study in Human Nature,* 14 and 15, 1902

I come to ask Thee to give me Thyself.

ANSARI OF HERAT. In Aldous Huxley, *The Perennial Philosophy,* 5, 1946

You made us for yourself, and our hearts find no peace until they rest in you.

ST. AUGUSTINE (A.D. 354–430). *Confessions,* 1.1, A.D. 400?, tr. R. S. Pine-Coffin, 1961

I went round the streets and squares of the city of this world seeking thee, and I found thee not, because in vain I sought without for him who was within myself.

ST. AUGUSTINE (A.D. 354–430.). Quoted by Swami Prabhavananda, "Sri Ramakrishna, Modern Spirit, and Religion." In Christopher Isherwood, ed., *Vedanta for the Western World,* 1945

Who am I? This or the other?
Am I one person today, and tomorrow another?
Am I both at once? A hypocrite before others,
and before myself a contemptibly woebegone weakling?
Or is something within me still like a beaten army,
fleeing in disorder from victory already achieved?

Who am I? They mock em, these lonely questions of mine.
Whoever I am, thou knowest, O God, I am thine.

DIETRICH BONHOEFFER (1906–1945). July 1944, *Letters and Papers from Prison,* ed. Eberhard Bethge, 3, 1970

Depart from me for you are a sinful God, O Lord!

SAMUEL BUTLER (1835–1902). *Further Extracts from the Note-Books of Samuel Butler,* 4, ed. A. T. Bartholomew, 1934

Holy is your name, holy is your work, holy are the days that return to you. Holy are the years that you uncover. Holy are the hands that are raised to you, and the weeping that is wept to you. Holy is the fire between your will and ours, in which we are refined. Holy is that which is unredeemed, covered with your patience. Holy are the souls in your unnaming. Holy, and shining with a great light, is every living thing, established in the world and covered with time, until your name is praised.

LEONARD COHEN (1934–). *The Book of Mercy,* 43, 1984

'Twas my one Glory—
Let it be
Remembered
I was owned of Thee—

EMILY DICKINSON (1830–1886). "'Twas my one Glory" (complete poem), 1865?

Lord, make me an instrument of Your peace!
Where there is hatred, let me sow love;
Where there is injury, pardon;
Where there is doubt, faith;
Where there is despair, hope;
Where there is darkness, light;
Where there is sadness, joy.

O divine Master, grant that I may not so much seek
To be consoled as to console;
To be understood as to understand;
To be loved as to love.
For it is in giving that we receive;
It is in pardoning that we are pardoned;
And it is in dying that we are born to eternal life.

ST. FRANCIS OF ASSISI (A.D. 1181?–1226). Attributed. "The Prayer of St. Francis," tr. Leo Sherley-Price

Forgive, O Lord, my little jokes on Thee
And I'll forgive Thy great big one on me.

ROBERT FROST (1874–1963). "Cluster of Faith," *In the Clearing,* 1962

I have sought Thy nearness;
With all my heart have I called Thee,
And going out to meet Thee
I found Thee coming toward me.

JUDAH HALEVI (A.D. 1085–1140). *Selected Poems,* tr. Nina Salamon, 1924

For the sin we have committed by ignoring the poor. . . .
And for the sin we have committed by not respecting God's image in every human being. . . .
And for the sin we have committed by not allowing others to become what they could be. . . .
And for the sin we have committed by keeping silent in the face of evil. . . .
For all these sins, O God of forgiveness, forgive us, pardon us, and grant us atonement.

ROBERT HAMMER, JACK RIEMER, and JULES HARLOW. "Confession of Sins." In Jules Harlow, ed., *Yearnings: Prayer and Meditation for the Days of Awe,* 1968

Our Father who art in heaven,
Hallowed be thy name.
Thy kingdom come,
Thy will be done,
  On earth as it is in heaven.
Give us this day our daily bread;
And forgive us our debts,
  As we also have forgiven our debtors;
And lead us not into temptation,
  But deliver us from evil.

JESUS (A.D. 1st cent.). *Matthew* 6:9–13

Oh God, in accepting one another wholeheartedly, fully, completely, we accept You, and we thank You, and we adore You, and we love You with our whole being because our being is in Your being, our spirit is rooted in Your spirit.

    THOMAS MERTON (1915—1968). "Special Closing Prayer," offered at the First Spiritual Summit Conference, Calcutta, 1968 (shortly before his death), *A Thomas Merton Reader,* ed. Thomas P. McDonnell, 1974

Thou O Spirit, that dost prefer
Before all Temples th' upright heart and pure.

    JOHN MILTON (1608–1674). *Paradise Lost,* 1.17, 1667

The things, Good Lord, that I pray for, give me thy grace to labor for.

    SIR THOMAS MORE (1478–1535). "For Grace," 1534–1535, *Conscience Decides: Letters and Prayers from Prison,* ed. Dame Bede Foord, 1971

If now I have found favor in thy sight, O Lord, let the Lord, I pray thee, go in the midst of us, although it is a stiff-necked people; and pardon our iniquity and our sin, and take us for thy inheritance.

    MOSES (14th cent. B.C.). *Exodus* 34:9

Grant that I may do the deeds that win Your love.

    MUHAMMAD (A.D. 570?–632). *The Sayings of Muhammad,* 328, tr. Abdullah Al-Suhrawardy, 1941

Lead, kindly Light, amid the encircling gloom,
  Lead Thou me on;
The night is dark, and I am far from home;
  Lead Thou me on!
Keep Thou my feet; I do not ask to see
  The distant scene; one step enough for me.

    CARDINAL JOHN HENRY NEWMAN (1801–1890). "Lead Kindly Light," *The Pillar of Cloud,* 1832

God, give us grace to accept with serenity the things which cannot be changed, courage to change the things which should be changed, and the wisdom to distinguish the one from the other.

    REINHOLD NIEBUHR (1892–1971). "The Serenity Prayer," 1934. Niebuhr's authorship is questionable. In 1950 he said, "It may have been spooking around for years, even centuries, but I don't think so. I do honestly believe that I wrote it myself." Beginning in 1962 he accepted copyright fees for the prayer from Hallmark Cards, however, he reportedly said on more than one occasion that he was not the prayer's author. (In "Niebuhr's Serenity," *The "Quote . . . Unquote" Newsletter* [London], "Special Edition", 1998)

Beloved Pan, and all ye other gods who haunt this place, give me beauty in the inward soul; and may the outward and inward man be at one.

    PLATO (427?–347 B.C.). *Phaedrus,* 279, tr. Benjamin Jowett, 1894

Teach me to feel another's Woe;
To hide the Fault I see;
That Mercy I to others show,
That Mercy show to me.

    ALEXANDER POPE (1688–1744). "The Universal Prayer," 9, 1738

O, heavenly Father, protect and bless all things that have breath; guard them from all evil, and let them sleep in peace.

    ALBERT SCHWEITZER (1875–1965). Recalling a prayer he composed as a young child, *Memoirs of Childhood and Youth,* 2, 1925, tr. C. T. Campion, 1949

O make in me these civil wars to cease.

    SIR PHILIP SIDNEY (1554–1586). In E. Stanley Jones, *Conversion,* 1, 1959

Lead me in the center of thy silence to fill my heart with songs.

    RABINDRANATH TAGORE (1861–1941). *Stray Birds,* 286, 1914

Let this be my last word, that I trust in thy love.

    RABINDRANATH TAGORE (1861–1941). Closing words, *Stray Birds,* 1914

Most loving father, what may I say? I am in dire straits. Save me from this hour. Yet it is for Your glory that I have been brought to this hour, and that I may learn that You alone can deliver me from the depths of my humiliation.

    THOMAS à KEMPIS (1380–1471). *The Imitation of Christ,* 3.29, tr. Leo Sherley-Price, 1952

I thank you, God. I do not deserve anything, I am unworthy of the least regard; and yet I am made to rejoice. I am impure and worthless, and yet the world is gilded for my delight and holidays are prepared for me, and my path is strewn with flowers.

    HENRY DAVID THOREAU (1817–1862). Journal, 17 August 1851

Thou dost show me the path of life;
  in thy presence there is fullness of joy,

    ANONYMOUS (*BIBLE*). *Psalms* 16:11

My God, my God, why hast thou forsaken me?

    ANONYMOUS (*BIBLE*). *Psalms* 22:1

The Lord is my shepherd, I shall not want;
  he makes me lie down in green pastures.
He leads me beside still waters;
  he restores my soul.
He leads me in paths of righteousness
  for his name's sake.
Even though I walk through the valley of the shadow of death,
  I fear no evil;
for thou art with me;
  thy rod and thy staff,
  they comfort me.

    ANONYMOUS (*BIBLE*). *Psalms* 23:1–4

As a hart longs for flowing streams,
  so longs my soul for thee, O God.
My soul thirsts for God,
  for the living God.
When shall I come and behold the face of God?
My tears have been my food day and night,
while men say to me continually,
  "Where is your God?"

    ANONYMOUS (*BIBLE*). *Psalms* 42:1–3

Rouse thyself! Why sleepest thou, O Lord?
  Awake! Do not cast us off forever!

    ANONYMOUS (*BIBLE*). *Psalms* 44:23

Create in me a clean heart, O God,
   and put a new and right spirit within me.
Cast me not away from thy presence,
   and take not thy holy Spirit from me.
Restore to me the joy of thy salvation,
   and uphold me with a willing spirit.

> ANONYMOUS (*BIBLE*). *Psalms* 51:10–12

Thou art my Father,
   my God, and the Rock of my salvation.

> ANONYMOUS (*BIBLE*). *Psalms* 89:26

How long, O Lord? Wilt thou hide thyself forever?

> ANONYMOUS (*BIBLE*). *Psalms* 89:46

Now I lay me down to sleep;
I pray the Lord my soul to keep.
If I should die before I wake,
I pray the Lord my soul to take.

> ANONYMOUS (ENGLISH). Variants of this prayer have been traced back to A.D. 12th cent.; the now-popular version first appeared in *The New England Primer* in the early 1780s.

Oh, Lord of the Universe
I will sing Thee a song.
Where canst Thou be found,
And where canst Thou not be found?
Where I pass—there art Thou.
Where I remain—there, too, Thou art.
Thou, Thou, and only Thou.
   Doth it go well—'tis thanks to Thee.
Doth it go ill—ah, 'tis also thanks to Thee
   Thou art, Thou hast been, and Thou wilt be.
Thou didst reign, Thou reignest, and Thou wilt reign.
   Thine is Heaven, Thine is Earth.
Thou fillest the high regions,
And Thou fillest the low regions.
Wheresoever I turn, Thou, oh Thou, art there.

> ANONYMOUS (JEWISH). From an east-European ghetto. Quoted by Leon Stein, "Hasidic Music," *Chicago Jewish Forum,* Fall 1943. In Joseph Campbell, *The Hero with a Thousand Faces,* 1.2.4, 1949

PREACHERS

See also • Christianity ○ Church: Ralph Waldo Emerson (1) ○ Clergy ○ Priests ○ Rabbis

Be what you wish others to become. Let yourself and not your words preach for you.

> HENRI AMIEL (1821–1881). Journal, 7 April 1851, tr. Mrs. Humphrey Ward, 1887

He preaches well that lives well, quoth Sancho; that's all the Divinity I understand.

> CERVANTES (1547–1616). *Don Quixote,* 2.3.20, 1615, tr. Peter Anthony Motteux and John Ozell, 1743

His preaching much, but more his practice wrought;
(A living sermon of the truths he taught).

> JOHN DRYDEN (1631–1700). "The Character of a Good Parson" (l.77), *Fables,* 1700

The test of the worth of a preacher is when his congregation [goes] away saying, not "What a beautiful sermon! but "I will do something."

> ST. FRANCIS de SALES (1567–1622)

None preaches better than the ant, and she says nothing.

> BENJAMIN FRANKLIN (1706–1790). *Poor Richard's Almanack,* July 1736

An ounce of performance is worth more than a pound of preachment.

> ELBERT HUBBARD (1856–1915)

Father Mapple: Jonah did the Almighty's bidding. And what was that, shipmates? To preach the Truth to the face of Falsehood! That was it!

> HERMAN MELVILLE (1819–1891). *Moby-Dick; or, The Whale,* 9, 1851, ed. Harold Beaver, 1972

Preachers say, Do as I say, not as I do. But if a physician had the same disease upon him that I have, and he should bid me do one thing and himself do quite another, could I believe him?

> JOHN SELDEN (1584–1654). "Preaching" (13), *Table Talk,* 1689, ed. Frederick Pollock, 1927

He was a preacher . . . and never charged nothing for his preaching, and it was worth it, too.

> MARK TWAIN (1835–1910). *The Adventures of Huckleberry Finn,* 33, 1884

PREDICTION

See also • Dreams: [especially] Ralph Waldo Emerson (6) ○ Future ○ History: Page Smith ○ Misjudgments ○ Prophets

He is not the best prophet who guesses well, and he is not the wisest man whose guess turns out well in the event, but he who, whatever the event be, takes reason and probability for his guide.

> EURIPIDES (485?–406 B.C.). In Ralph Waldo Emerson, "Demonology," *Lectures and Biographical Sketches,* 1883

There are two classes of people who tell what is going to happen in the future: Those who don't know, and those who don't know they don't know.

> JOHN KENNETH GALBRAITH (1908–). In Steve Coll, closing paragraph, "The Long Shadow of Black Monday" *Washington Post,* 28 February 1988

Persistent prophecy is a familiar way of assuring the event.

> GEORGE GISSING (1857–1903)

The best qualification of a prophet is to have a good memory.

> MARQUIS OF HALIFAX (1633–1695). "Experience," *Political, Moral and Miscellaneous Reflections,* 1750

I know of no way of judging the future but by the past.

> PATRICK HENRY (1736–1799). Virginia House of Burgesses speech, Richmond, 23 March 1775

> See Future: Frederic Harrison, Edward Weyer, Jr.,

The only way to predict the future is to have power to shape the future.

> ERIC HOFFER (1902–1983). *The Passionate State of Mind: And Other Aphorisms*, 78, 1954

Forecast: To observe that which has passed, and guess it will happen again.

> ELBERT HUBBARD (1856–1915). *The Roycroft Dictionary Concocted by Ali Baba and the Bunch on Rainy Days*, p. 56, 1914

Such . . . is the uncertainty of all human affairs, that security and despair are equal follies; and as it is presumption and arrogance to anticipate triumphs, it is weakness and cowardice to prognosticate miscarriages.

> SAMUEL JOHNSON (1709–1784). In *The Rambler* (English journal), 43, 14 August 1750

My gran'ther's rule was safer'n 'tis to crow:
Don't never prophesy—unless ye know.

> JAMES RUSSELL LOWELL (1819–1891). *The Bigelow Papers: Second Series*, 2, 1967

The most reliable way to anticipate the future is by understanding the present.

> JOHN NAISBITT (1929–). Introduction to *Megatrends: Ten New Directions Transforming Our Lives*, 1984

Futurism isn't prediction anymore. It's state-of-the-art propaganda. It's future creation. [Futurists] put their clients in a state of fear and then explain that they hold the secret knowledge that can save them.

> DOUGLAS RUSHKOFF. Futurist. In Michael Krantz, "Cashing in on Tomorrow," *Time*, 15 July 1996

He robs present ills of their power who has perceived their coming beforehand.

> SENECA THE YOUNGER (5? B.C.–A.D. 65). "On Consolation to Marcius" (9.5), *Moral Essays*, tr. John W. Basore, 1932

The future is endowed with *essential unpredictability,* and this is the only prediction we can make.

> PAUL VALÉRY (1871–1945). *The Outlook for Intelligence*, 4, tr. Denise Folliot and Jackson Mathews, 1963

The wisest prophets make sure of the event first.

> HORACE WALPOLE (1717–1797). Letter to Thomas Walpole, 19 February 1785

❦

To prophesy is extremely difficult—especially with respect to the future.

> SAYING (CHINESE)

PREJUDICE

See also • African Americans ○ Anti-Semitic Statements ○ Anti-Semitism ○ Bigotry ○ Cruelty: Meir Kahane ○ Dehumanization ○ Fanatics ○ Hate ○ Holocaust ○ Ideals: Paul Eldridge ○ Martyrdom ○ Misogynous Statements ○ Native Americans ○ Nonconformity ○ Nonconformity, Anti- ○ People: Charlayne Hunter-Gault ○ Racism: [especially] Pearl S. Buck ○ Racist Statements ○ Sexism ○ Sexist Statements ○ Thinking: William James ○ Tolerance ○ Witchcraft

The truth is, like the ancient Greeks and Romans, [Samuel Johnson] allowed himself to look upon all nations but his own as barbarians. . . . If he was particularly prejudiced against the Scots, it was because they were more in his way.

> JAMES BOSWELL (1740–1795). Introduction to *The Journal of a Tour to the Hebrides, with Samuel Johnson, L.L.D.,* 1786

The enemy is brownness and whiteness, maleness and femaleness. The enemy is our urgent need to stereotype and close off people, places, and events into isolated categories. Hatred, distrust, irresponsibility, unloving, classism, sexism, and racism, in their myriad forms, cloud our vision and isolate us. . . . We close off avenues of communication and vision so that individual and communal trust, responsibility, loving, and knowing are impossible.

> ANDREA CANAAN. "Brownness." In Cherríe Moraga and Gloria Anzaldúa, eds., *This Bridge Called My Back: Writings by Radical Women of Color,* 1981

I am free of all prejudice. I hate everyone equally.

> W. C. FIELDS (1879–1946). Comedian. In Jerome Beatty, Jr., "Trade Winds," *Saturday Review,* 28 January 1967

You've got to be taught to be afraid
Of people whose eyes are oddly made,
Of people whose skin is a different shade.
You've got to be carefully taught.

You've got to be taught before it's too late,
Before you are six or seven or eight,
To hate all the people your relatives hate.
You've got to be carefully taught.

> OSCAR HAMMERSTEIN II (1895–1960). "You've Got to Be Carefully Taught" (song). In the musical *South Pacific,* 1949

Prejudice is the child of ignorance.

> WILLIAM HAZLITT (1778–1830). "On Prejudice," *Sketches and Essays,* 1839

Religion, patriotism, race, and sex are the favorite red herrings of foul political method—they are the most successful because they explode so easily and flood the mind with those unconscious prejudices which make critical thinking difficult.

> WALTER LIPPMANN (1889–1974). *A Preface to Politics,* 8, 1914

No man is prejudiced in favor of a thing knowing it to be wrong. He is attached to it on the belief of its being right, and when he sees it is not so, the prejudice will be gone.

> THOMAS PAINE (1737–1809). *The Rights of Man,* 2 ("Preface"), 1792

Prejudice will fall in a combat with interest.

> THOMAS PAINE (1737–1809). *The Rights of Man,* 2 ("Introduction"), 1792

We can discover the fact that we had a prejudice only after having got rid of it.

> KARL R. POPPER (1902–1994). *The Open Society and Its Enemies,* 2.23, 1945

[Our prejudices are] so deeply rooted that we never think of them as prejudices but call them common sense.

> GEORGE BERNARD SHAW (1856–1950). *The Intelligent Woman's Guide to Socialism, Capitalism, Sovietism and Fascism,* 81, 1928

We all decry prejudice, yet are all prejudiced.

> HERBERT SPENCER (1820–1903). *Social Statics,* 2.17.2, 1851

The first problem for all of us, men and women, is not to learn, but to unlearn. We are filled with the popular wisdom of several centuries just past, and we are terrified to give it up. Patriotism means obedience, age means wisdom, woman means submission, black means inferior: these are preconceptions imbedded so deeply in our thinking that we honestly may not know that they are there.

> GLORIA STEINEM (1934–). "'The First Problem for All of Us, Men and Women, Is to Unlearn,'" *New York Times,* 26 August 1971

The scapegoat is necessary as a symbol of evil which it is convenient to cast out of the social order and, which, through its very being, confirms the remaining members of the community as good.

> THOMAS S. SZASZ (1920–). *The Manufacture of Madness: A Comparative Study of the Inquisition and the Mental Health Movement,* 14, 1970

It is never too late to give up your prejudices.

> HENRY DAVID THOREAU (1817–1862). "Economy," *Walden; or Life in the Woods,* 1854

I am quite sure . . . I have no race prejudice, and I think I have no color prejudices, nor caste prejudices. Indeed, I know it. I can stand any society. All I care to know is that a man is a human being—that is enough for me; he can't be any worse.

> MARK TWAIN (1835–1910). "Concerning the Jews," *Harper's,* September 1899

PREPAREDNESS

See also • Planning ○ Prudence: Rules ○ Safety ○ Success ○ War & Preparedness

The scouts' motto is founded on my initials, it is: BE PREPARED which means, you are always to be in a state of readiness in mind and body to do your DUTY.

> ROBERT BADEN-POWELL (1857–1941). English general and founder of the Boy Scouts. *Scouting for Boys,* pt. 1, 1908

Forewarned forearmed.

> CERVANTES (1547–1616). *Don Quixote,* 2.3.10, 1615, tr. Peter Anthony Motteux and John Ozell, 1743
>
> See Danger: Thomas Fuller (1)

Nor must we forget King Ubu who won a victory *because* he had taken no preliminary steps of any kind.

> CHARLES de GAULLE (1890–1970). "The Conduct of War" (1), *The Edge of the Sword,* 1934, tr. Gerald Hopkins, 1960

You'll find us rough, Sir, but you'll find us ready.

> CHARLES DICKENS (1812–1870). *David Copperfield,* 3, 1850

Tito was experiencing that inexorable law of human souls that we prepare ourselves for sudden deeds by the reiterated choice of good or evil that gradually determines character.

> GEORGE ELIOT (1819–1880). *Romola,* 2.3, 1863

The right performance of this hour's duties will be the best preparation for the hours or ages that follow it.

> RALPH WALDO EMERSON (1803–1882). "Immortality," *Letters and Social Aims,* 1876

Those who prepared for all the emergencies of life beforehand may equip themselves at the expense of joy.

> E. M. FORSTER (1879–1970). *Howard's End,* 7, 1910

Make thy Model before thou buildest; and go not too far in it without due Preparation.

> THOMAS FULLER (1654–1734). Comp., *Introductio ad Prudentiam,* 1197, 1731

In fair Weather prepare for foul.

> THOMAS FULLER (1654–1734). Comp., *Gnomologia: Adages and Proverbs,* 2818, 1732

Get thy spindle and distaff ready, and God will send thee Flax.

> JAMES HOWELL (1593–1666). Comp., "Divers Centuries of New Sayings" (p. 8), *Paroimiographia: Proverbs, or Old Sayed Sawes & Adages in English . . . Italian, French and Spanish,* 1659

Provide for the worst, the best will save itself.

> JAMES HOWELL (1593–1666). Comp., "English" (p. 17), *Paroimiographia: Proverbs, or Old Sayed Sawes & Adages in English . . . Italian, French and Spanish,* 1659

Responsibility comes to one who is prepared for it as certainly as harvest follows seed time.

> ROBERT H. JACKSON (1892–1954). Supreme Court associate justice. Dedicating the Jamestown High School building (New York), 1935. In Eugene C. Gerhart, *America's Advocate: Robert H. Jackson,* 24, 1958

I think the necessity of being *ready* increases. Look to it.

> ABRAHAM LINCOLN (1809–1865). Entire letter to Pennsylvania Gov. Andrew G. Curtin, 8 April 1861 (four days before the firing on Fort Sumter that began the Civil War)

You prepare the ground so that a lucky accident can happen.

> SIDNEY LUMET (1924–). Film maker. Charlie Rose television interview, PBS, 14 April 1995

The ability to be cool, confident, and decisive in crisis is not an inherited characteristic but is the direct result of how well the individual has prepared himself for the battle.

> RICHARD M. NIXON (1913–1994). *Six Crises,* 1 (epigraph), 1962

We cannot make it rain, but we can see to it that the rain falls on prepared soil.

> HENRI J. M. NOUWEN (1932–1996). "Do Not Worry, All Things Will Be Given," *Catholic Agitator,* September 1980

Where observation is concerned, chance favors only the prepared mind.

> LOUIS PASTEUR (1822–1895). Address given at the inauguration of the science faculty, University of Lille, Douai (France), 7 December 1854
>
> See Luck: Elmer G. Leterman

Preparation prevents piss-poor performance.

> NOLAN RICHARDSON. Basketball coach. Charlie Rose television interview, PBS, 1 April 1994

Hamlet: If it be now, 'tis not to come; if it be not to come, it will be now; if it be not now, yet it will come: the readiness is all.
SHAKESPEARE (1564–1616). *Hamlet,* 5.2.230, 1600

They who are ready to go are already invited.
HENRY DAVID THOREAU (1817–1862). Journal, 2 July 1840

Timely disbursements to prepare for danger frequently prevent much greater disbursements to repel it.
GEORGE WASHINGTON (1732–1799). *Farewell Address,* 17 September 1796

❧

Hope for the best and prepare for the worst.
SAYING (ENGLISH)

Preparedness heralds opportunity.
SAYING

PRESENT

See also • Days ○ Future ○ Past ○ Time

Real generosity toward the future lies in giving all to the present.
ALBERT CAMUS (1913–1960). "Thought at the Meridian: Beyond Nihilism," *The Rebel: An Essay on Man in Revolt,* 1951, tr. Anthony Bower, 1956

We cannot overstate our debt to the Past, but the moment has the supreme claim.
RALPH WALDO EMERSON (1803–1882). "Quotation and Originality," *Letters and Social Aims,* 1876

No mind is much employed upon the present: recollection and anticipation fill up almost all our moments.
SAMUEL JOHNSON (1709–1784). *Rasselas: The Prince of Abyssinia,* 30, 1759

The present may be as much determined by the future as by the past.
LEWIS MUMFORD (1895–1990). *The Conduct of Life,* 5.3, 1951

Let others worship the past; I much prefer the present,
Am delighted to be alive today.
OVID (43 B.C.–A.D. 17?). *The Art of Love,* 3.121, tr. Peter Green, 1982

The present is the future of the past.
KARL R. POPPER (1902–1994). *The Open Society and Its Enemies,* 2.22, 1945

The present is a fulcrum on which the future and the past lie balanced.
JONATHAN SCHELL (1943–). *The Fate of the Earth,* 2, 1982

I've always had two or more tracks running in my head. The pleasurable one was thinking forward to some future scene. imagining what should be, planning on the edge of fantasy. The other played underneath with all too realistic fragments of what I should have done. There it was in perfect microcosm, the past and future coming together to squeeze out the present—which is the only time in which we can be fully alive. . . . These past and future tracks have gradually dimmed until they are rarely heard. More and more, there is only the full, glorious, alive-in-the-moment, don't-give-a-damn yet caring-for-everything sense of the right now.
GLORIA STEINEM (1934–). "Doing Sixty," *Moving Beyond Words,* 1994

The meeting of two eternities, the past and future . . . is precisely the present moment.
HENRY DAVID THOREAU (1817–1862). "Economy," *Walden; or Life in the Woods,* 1854

Now or never! You must live in the present, launch yourself on every wave, find your eternity in each moment.
HENRY DAVID THOREAU (1817–1862). Journal, 24 April 1859

❧

The present is the past's student and the future's teacher.
ANONYMOUS

There's no time like the present.
SAYING (ENGLISH)

PRESIDENTS

See also • Campaigns ○ Campaign Slogans ○ Commanders ○ Criticism: Examples ○ Cuban Missile Crisis: John F. Kennedy (1,2) ○ Decision-Making ○ Democracy ○ Details ○ Elections ○ International Relations ○ Kings ○ Leaders ○ Politicians ○ Politics ○ Praise: Examples ○ Presidents & People ○ Presidents & Staff ○ Prime Ministers ○ Statesmen ○ Vice Presidents ○ Watergate

[The President] resembles the commander of a ship at sea. He must have a helm to grasp, a course to steer, a port to seek.
HENRY ADAMS (1838–1918). In Arthur M. Schlesinger, Jr., "The Ultimate Approval Rating," *New York Times Magazine,* 15 December 1996

I can tell you this: no man who ever held the office of President would congratulate a friend on obtaining it. Make no mistake about it, the four most miserable years of my life were my four years in the Presidency.
JOHN QUINCY ADAMS (1767–1848). In A. E. Hotchner, comp., "Grouse Under Pressure: The White House Was No Picnic," *New York Times,* 8 October 1995

He should be a master politician who is above politics.
JAMES DAVID BARBER (1939–). "Man, Mood, and the Presidency." In Rexford G. Tugwell and Thomas E. Cronin, eds., *The Presidency Reappraised,* 1974

Anybody that wants the presidency so much that he'll spend two years organizing and campaigning for it is not to be trusted with the office.
DAVID S. BRODER (1929–). "The Qualities We Want in a President," *Washington Post,* 18 July 1973

The distinctive personality characteristics of a particular president, informed by his prior experience, contribute significantly to the targets he selects for special concern.
JOSEPH A. CALIFANO, JR. (1931–). Presidential assistant to Lyndon B. Johnson and secretary of health, education, and welfare. *A Presidential Nation,* 11, 1975

A President [must sometimes] feel as though he is leading a heavy wagon down a steep hill—not so much pulling as hurrying to keep from being run over.

DOUGLASS CATER (1923–1995). Presidential assistant to Lyndon B. Johnson. *Power in Washington: A Critical Look at Today's Struggle to Govern in the Nation's Capital,* 5, 1964

As for me, I would rather be right than be President.

HENRY CLAY (1777–1852). Responding to a Senate colleague who had told him that his Compromise of 1850 proposals for preserving the Union would hurt his chances for the Presidency by alienating anti-slavery Northerners. Senate speech, 1850

See Repartee—Examples: Thomas Brackett Reed

The character of a President colors his entire administration.

CLARK M. CLIFFORD (1906–). Presidential assistant to Harry S Truman and secretary of defense. "The Presidency As I Have Seen It" (A Special Section). In Emmet John Hughes, *The Living Presidency: The Resources and Dilemmas of the American Presidential Office,* 1972

Don't let [the White House] fool you. It's the crown jewel of the federal prison system.

BILL CLINTON (1946–). Remark to his political advisers while touring the White House a few days after his inauguration. In Sidney Blumenthal, "The Education of a President," *New Yorker,* 24 January 1994

[The President] shall take care that the laws be faithfully executed.

CONSTITUTION OF THE UNITED STATES. Article 2, Section 3, 17 September 1789

I think the American public wants a solemn ass as a President. And I think I'll go along with them.

CALVIN COOLIDGE (1872–1933). Remark to Ethel Barrymore. In "People," *Time,* 16 May 1955

[The presidential office] remains a great mystery. . . . Like the glory of a morning sunrise, it can only be experienced—it cannot be told.

CALVIN COOLIDGE (1872–1933). In Arthur M. Schlesinger, Jr., "The Ultimate Approval Rating," *New York Times Magazine,* 15 December 1996

Beware the insecure, driven candidate. Drive is needed, but carefully distinguish *drive* from *drivenness.* The former is a necessity, the latter may be fatal.

THOMAS E. CRONIN (1940–). *The State of the Presidency,* 2nd ed., 4, 1980

The exact dimensions of executive power at any given moment [are] largely the consequence of the incumbent's character and energy combined with the overarching needs of the day, the challenges to system survival and regeneration.

THOMAS E. CRONIN (1940–). *The State of the Presidency,* 2nd ed., 4, 1980

Oh, that lovely title, ex-President.

DWIGHT D. EISENHOWER (1890–1969). In *New York Post,* 26 October 1959

I probably long ago used up my time; but you know, there is one thing about being the President, it is hard to tell him to sit down.

DWIGHT D. EISENHOWER (1890–1969). During a speech. In "'If it wasn't for the honor of the thing . . . ,'" *American Heritage,* August 1964

Most presidents are merely clerks of some real power which stands erect at their side and does its will by them.

RALPH WALDO EMERSON (1803–1882). Sermon (1829–1832), *Young Emerson Speaks: Unpublished Discourses on Many Subjects,* p. 229, ed. Arthur Cushman McGiffert, Jr., 1938

American democracy has revived the oldest political institution of the race, the elective kingship.

HENRY JONES FORD (1851–1925). *The Rise and Growth of American Politics,* 22, 1898

I don't know what to do or where to turn on this taxation matter. Somewhere there must be a book that tells all about it, where I could go to straighten it out in my mind. But I don't know where the book is, and maybe I couldn't read it if I found it! My God, this is a hell of a place for a man like me to be!

WARREN G. HARDING (1865–1923). In David Wallechinsky and Irving Wallace, *The People's Almanac #2,* p. 188, 1978

A successful President must want personal power and enjoy its use.

ERWIN C. HARGROVE (1930–). *The Power of the Modern Presidency,* 1, 1974

The American President probably may make a public display of almost any mood or emotion, from rage to grief, with no harm to his leadership so grave as a show of hesitation.

EMMET JOHN HUGHES (1920–). Presidential assistant to Dwight D. Eisenhower. *The Living Presidency: The Resources and Dilemmas of the American Presidential Office,* 4.4, 1972

I can say with truth mine is a situation of dignified slavery.

ANDREW JACKSON (1767–1845). During the second year of his eight-year Presidency, letter to T. R. J. Chester, 30 November 1829

To be effective, a President must find a style of media use which is consistent with his personal capacity.

DOROTHY BUCKTON JAMES. *The Contemporary Presidency,* 2, 1969

[The Presidency] is but a splendid misery.

THOMAS JEFFERSON (1743–1826). Letter to Elbridge Gerry, 13 May 1797

All I have I would have given gladly not to be standing here today.

LYNDON B. JOHNSON (1908–1973). Five days after the assassination of John F. Kennedy, Congress speech, 27 November 1963

It is true that a house divided against itself is a house that cannot stand. There is a division in the American house now and believing this as I do, I have concluded that I should not permit the Presidency to become involved in the partisan divisions that are developing in this political year. Accordingly, I shall not seek, and I will not accept, the nomination of my party for another term as your President.

LYNDON B. JOHNSON (1908–1973). Television broadcast, 31 March 1968

I had given [the Presidency] everything that was in me.

> LYNDON B. JOHNSON (1908–1973). Closing words. *The Vantage Point: Perspectives of the Presidency, 1963–1969,* 1971

Anonymous: What is it like being President?
Johnson: When you run, they are always snapping at your ass. When you stop, they f___ you to death.

> LYNDON B. JOHNSON (1908–1973). Format adapted. In Hugh Sidey, "H. Ross Clinton?" *Time,* 23 May 1994

The Presidency has made every man who occupied it, no matter how small, bigger than he was; and no matter how big, not big enough for its demands.

> LYNDON B. JOHNSON (1908–1973). In Jess Brallier and Sally Chabert, comps., "Lyndon B. Johnson," *Presidential Wit and Wisdom,* 1996

A President certainly must have . . . character, judgment, vigor, intellectual curiosity, a sense of history, and a strong sense of the future.

> JOHN F. KENNEDY (1917–1963). Henry Brandon interview, *Sunday Times* (London), 3 July 1960. In Christopher Silvester, ed., *The Norton Book of Interviews: An Anthology from 1859 to the Present Day,* 1996

A President has a "conflict budget"—he must be selective; he cannot dissipate his limited political resources by engaging in too many fights at once.

> LOUIS W. KOENIG (1916–). *The Chief Executive,* 15, 1964

Friend: Now, Mr. Lincoln, I want you to be honest with me and tell me how you like being President of the United States?
Lincoln: You have heard the story, haven't you, about the man who was tarred and feathered and carried out of town on a rail? A man in the crowd asked him how he liked it. His reply was that if it was not for the honor of the thing, he would much rather walk.

> ABRAHAM LINCOLN (1809–1865). Format adapted. 1861? In Emanuel Hertz, ed., "Party Leader," *Lincoln Talks: A Biography in Anecdote,* 1939

You have little idea of the terrible weight of care and sense of responsibility of this office of mine. Schenck, if to be at the head of Hell is as hard as what I have to undergo here, I could find it in my heart to pity Satan himself.

> ABRAHAM LINCOLN (1809–1865). Remark to Gen. Robert E. Schenck. In Allen T. Rich, ed., introduction to *Reminiscences of Abraham Lincoln,* 1885

I hope you will perfectly easy about having nominated me; don't be troubled about it; *I forgive you.*

> ABRAHAM LINCOLN (1809–1865). His parting words to an editor who claimed he was the first to suggest his name for the Presidency. In Francis Fisher Browne, *The Every-Day Life of Abraham Lincoln,* 3.4, 1887

The presidency is not an office to be either solicited or declined.

> WILLIAM LOUNDES (1782–1822). South Carolina congressman. After his state legislature nominated him for the Presidency, December 1821

You can't have one kind of man and another kind of President.

> LYNN MARTIN (1939–). Republican National Convention speech, Houston, 18 August 1992

Washington ensured the survival of the world's first modern democracy. He was the Commander-in-Chief that the Revolutionaries had expected him to be but, more than that, he was the man who would not be king.

> WILLIAM MARTIN. *George Washington: The Man Who Wouldn't Be King,* television documentary, PBS, 1992

In the Presidency it is character that counts above all.

> DAVID McCULLOUGH (1933–). "A Touch of Harry in the Night," *New York Times,* 2 December 1994

You can only judge a president by the consequences of his decisions.

> BILL MOYERS (1934–). In Terrence O'Flaherty, "A Southern Newsman on a 'Creetivity' Kick," *San Francisco Chronicle,* 10 January 1982

He teaches less by telling than by doing (or not doing).

> RICHARD E. NEUSTADT (1919–). Political scientist and presidential assistant to Harry S. Truman. *Presidential Power: The Politics of Leadership,* 5.3, 1960

[The President is] a decision-machine.

> RICHARD E. NEUSTADT (1919–). In Arthur M. Schlesinger, Jr., *A Thousand Days: John F. Kennedy in the White House,* 25.3, 1965

On this occasion, three years after we came here, we have to think in terms of what has happened that would not have happened if we had not been here.

> RICHARD M. NIXON (1913–1994). Impromptu speech to the Cabinet at a private dinner, 20 January 1972. In William Safire, *Before the Fall: An Inside View of the Pre-Watergate White House,* 7.6, 1975

Let me just say this. And I want to say this to the television audience. I made my mistakes, but in all of my years of public life I have never profited, never profited from public service. I've earned every cent.

And in all my years of public life I have never obstructed justice. And I think, too, that I can say that in my years of public life that I welcome this kind of examination because people have got to know whether or not their President is a crook. Well I'm not a crook. I've earned everything I've got.

> RICHARD M. NIXON (1913–1994). Responding to a question about his tax returns, news conference with the Associated Press Managing Editors Association, Disney World, Orlando (Florida), 17 November 1973

When the President does it, that means that it's not illegal.

> RICHARD M. NIXON (1913–1994). David Frost television interview, 20 May 1977

> See Kings: William Blackstone ○ Kings: Louis XIV

With me it is emphatically true that the Presidency is "no bed of roses."

> JAMES K. POLK (1797–1849). 4 September 1847, *Polk: The Diary of a President, 1845–1849,* ed. Allan Nevins, 1929

[John F. Kennedy] had no use for process, with its note making, minute taking, little boxes on charts showing the Planning Board and the Operations Coordinating Board. He did not think of himself as being on top of a chart; rather, he wanted to be in the center, the center of all the action.

> RICHARD REEVES. *President Kennedy: Profile of Power,* 1, 1993

The Presidency is not merely an administrative office. That's the least of it. It is more than an engineering job, efficient or inefficient. It is preeminently a place of moral leadership. All our great Presidents were leaders of thought at times when certain historic ideas in the life of the nation had to be clarified. . . .

Isn't that what the office is—a superb opportunity for reapplying, applying in new conditions, the simple rules of human conduct we always go back to?

> FRANKLIN D. ROOSEVELT (1882–1945). In Anne O'Hare McCormick, "Roosevelt's View of the Big Job," *New York Times Magazine*, 11 September 1932

[Abraham Lincoln] was a sad man because he couldn't get it all at once. And nobody can.

> FRANKLIN D. ROOSEVELT (1882–1945). In Arthur M. Schlesinger, Jr., *The Age of Roosevelt: The Coming of the New Deal*, 32.9, 1959

One thing is sure. We have to do something. We have to do the best we know how at the moment. . . . If it doesn't turn out right, we can modify it as we go along.

> FRANKLIN D. ROOSEVELT (1882–1945). In James David Barber, *The Presidential Character: Predicting Performance in the White House*, 7, 1972

I have enjoyed every moment of this so-called arduous and exacting task.

> THEODORE ROOSEVELT (1958–1919). Remark to William Jennings Bryan, 1908

The White House is a bully pulpit!

> THEODORE ROOSEVELT (1958–1919). In Hamilton Basso, *Mainstream*, 8.5, 1943

[The President is almost] a king and prime minister rolled into one.

> THEODORE ROOSEVELT (1858–1919). In Douglass Cater, *Power in Washington: A Critical Look at Today's Struggle to Govern in the Nation's Capital*, 4, 1964

Most Presidents would like to satisfy the historians and offer "creative leadership," but history of provides very few opportunities for this sort of work. What it provides, most of the time, is trouble to be avoided. Commanding the ship of state is largely a matter of seeing to it that it stays afloat and clear of the reefs.

> RICHARD H. ROVERE (1915–1979). "The Loneliest Place in the World," *American Heritage*, August 1964

The president [may be rightly seen] not as the ultimate decision-maker but as the preeminent "national highlighter," whose most important task is not to settle all issues, but to identify a handful of issues of truly national importance and focus on them the attention, visibility, and support that only a president can provide.

> LESTER M. SALAMON (1943–). "Conclusion: Beyond the Presidential Illusion—Toward a Constitutional Presidency." In Hugh Heclo and Salamon, *The Illusion of Presidential Government*, 1981

It was not any technical wizardry as a politician but rather [Franklin D. Roosevelt's] brilliant dramatization of politics as the medium for education and leadership which accounted for his success.

> ARTHUR M. SCHLESINGER JR. (1917–). Historian and presidential assistant to John F. Kennedy. *The Age of Roosevelt: The Coming of the New Deal*, 34.9, 1959

I will not accept if nominated and will not serve if elected.

> WILLIAM TECUMSEH SHERMAN (1820–1891). Telegram to Gen. Henderson at the Republican National Convention, Chicago, 5 June 1884, *Memoirs of Gen. W. T. Sherman*, 4th ed., 27, 1891 (1875)

A President's authority is not as great as his responsibility.

> THEODORE C. SORENSEN (1928–). Presidential assistant to John F. Kennedy. *Decision-Making in the White House: The Olive Branch or the Arrows*, 3, 1963

Charlie Rose: What have you learned the most, what lessons? *Stephanopoulos:* I think the hardest thing to know is when to fight [on a particular issue] and when to make a deal.

> GEORGE STEPHANOPOULOS (1961–). Presidential assistant to Bill Clinton. Rose television interview, PBS, 18 November 1993

[Abraham Lincoln] never wasted anything, and would always give more to his enemies than he would to his friends; and the reason was, because he never had anything to spare, and in the close calculation of attaching the factions to him, he counted upon the abstract affection of his friends as an element to be offset against some gift with which he must appease his enemies. . . .

Adhesion was what he wanted; if he got it gratuitously, he never wasted his substance paying for it.

> LEONARD SWETT (1825–1889). Letter to the author, 17 January 1866. In William H. Herndon and Jesse W. Weik, *Herndon's Lincoln: The True Story of a Great Life*, 18, 1889, Premier Books edition, 1961

Boys, if you ever pray, pray for me now. I don't know if you fellows ever had a load of hay fall on you, but when they told me yesterday what had happened, I felt like the moon, the stars and all the planets had fallen on me. I've got the most terrible job a man ever had.

> HARRY S. TRUMAN (1884–1972). Remark to reporters on succeeding to the Presidency following the death of Franklin D. Roosevelt, 13 April 1945. In Robert J. Donovan, *Conflict and Crisis: The Presidency of Harry S. Truman, 1945–1948*, 2, 1977

I have tried my best to give the nation everything I had in me. There are probably a million people who could have done the job better than I did it, but I had the job and I had to do it, and I always quote an epitaph on a tombstone in Tombstone, Ariz. *Here lies Jack Williams. He done his damndest.*

> HARRY S. TRUMAN (1884–1972). In "The Presidency: The Answer Man," *Time*, 28 April 1952

Within the first few months I discovered that being a President is like riding a tiger. A man has to keep on riding or be swallowed. The fantastically crowded nine months of 1945 taught me that a President either is constantly on top of events or, if he hesitates, events will soon be on top of him. I never felt I could let up for a single moment.

> HARRY S. TRUMAN (1884–1972). Opening words, *Memoirs: Years of Trial and Hope*, 1956
>
> See Events: Henry A. Kissinger (2) o International Relations: Napoleon

It was part of [Franklin D. Roosevelt's] conception of his role that he should never show exhaustion, boredom, or irritation.

> REXFORD G. TUGWELL (1891–1979). Economist and undersecretary of agriculture. In Arthur M. Schlesinger, Jr., *The Age of Roosevelt: The Coming of the New Deal*, 35.2, 1959
>
> See Commanders: George S. Patton, Jr.,

An extrovert, exuberant and cordial, [Franklin D. Roosevelt] maintained an impenetrable reserve. The warmth and geniality of his manner masked an inner detachment.

> SIDNEY WARREN (1916–). *The President as World Leader,* 11, 1964

The President must have not only the courage of his convictions but also the courage to change his convictions.

> SIDNEY WARREN (1916–). *The President as World Leader,* 23, 1964

My movements to the chair of Government will be accompanied by feelings not unlike those of a culprit, who is going to the place of his execution: so unwilling am I, in the evening of a life nearly consumed in public cares, to quit a peaceful abode for an Ocean of difficulties, without that competency of political skill, abilities, and inclination, which is necessary to manage the helm.

> GEORGE WASHINGTON (1732–1799). On the eve of assuming the Presidency, letter to Acting Secretary of War Henry Knox, 1 April 1789

The President is there in the White House for you, it is not you who are here for him.

> WALT WHITMAN (1819–1892). "A Song for Occupations" (4), 1855, *Leaves of Grass,* 1855–1892

The President is at liberty, both in law and in conscience, to be as big a man as he can. His capacity will set the limit.

> WOODROW WILSON (1856–1924). *Constitutional Government in the United States,* 3, 1908

The office of President requires the constitution of an athlete, the patience of a mother, and the endurance of an early Christian.

> WOODROW WILSON (1856–1924). In A. E. Hotchner, comp., "Grouse Under Pressure: The White House Was No Picnic," *New York Times,* 8 October 1995

PRESIDENTS & PEOPLE

See also • Commanders & Soldiers ○ Leaders & People ○ Lobbies: Harry S. Truman ○ Presidents

A President should not go around telling the world he is in charge of his administration. If he has to do that, he will only reinforce doubts on that score.

> LAURENCE I. BARRETT (1935–). *Gambling with History: Reagan in the White House,* 21, 1983

[Franklin D.] Roosevelt . . . was an eminently "practical" man. He had no over-all plans to remake America but a host of projects to improve this or that situation. He was a creative thinker in a "gadget" sense: immediate steps to solve specific day-to-day problems. . . . What excited Roosevelt was not grand economic or political theory but concrete achievements that people could touch and see and use.

> JAMES MacGREGOR BURNS (1918–). *Roosevelt: The Lion and the Fox,* 12, 1956

Being president is like running a cemetery; you've got a lot of people under you and nobody's listening.

> BILL CLINTON (1946–). Speech, Galesburg (Illinois). In "Viewpoint," *U.S. News & World Report,* 23 January 1995

The presidency is always too strong when we dislike the incumbent. Its limitations are bemoaned, however, when we believe the incumbent is striving valiantly to serve the public interest as we define it.

> THOMAS E. CRONIN (1940–). *The State of the Presidency,* 2nd ed., 1, 1980

He must summon his people to be with him—yet stand above, not squat beside them. He must question his own wisdom and judgment—but not too severely. He must hear the opinions and heed the powers of others—but not too abjectly. He must appease the doubts of the critic and assuage the hurts of the adversary—sometimes. He must ignore their views and achieve their defeat—sometimes. . . . He must respect action—without unharnessing it from reason. He must respect words—without becoming intoxicated with his own. He must have a sense of purpose inspiring him to magnify the trivial event to serve his distant aim—and to grasp the thorniest crisis as if it were the merest nettle. He must be pragmatic, calculating, and earthbound—and still know when to spurn the arithmetic of expediency for the act of brave imagination, the sublime gamble with no hope other than the boldness of his vision.

> EMMET JOHN HUGHES (1920–). Presidential assistant to Dwight D. Eisenhower. *The Living Presidency: The Resources and Dilemmas of the American Presidential Office,* 3.3, 1972

I'm the only President you've got.

> LYNDON B. JOHNSON (1908–1973). News conference, Washington, 27 April 1964

Each President is the President not only of all who live, but, in a very real sense, of all those who have yet to live.

> JOHN F. KENNEDY (1917–1963). In Theodore C. Sorensen, *Kennedy,* 15, 1965

I am, as you know, only the servant of the people.

> ABRAHAM LINCOLN (1809–1865). Letter to James Gilmore, 13 March 1861

Sen. Horace Maynard: Beware, Mr. President, and do not go too fast. There is danger ahead.
Lincoln (good-naturedly): I know that, but I shall go just so fast and only so fast as I think I'm right and the people are ready for the step.

> ABRAHAM LINCOLN (1809–1865). Format adapted. 1861. In William H. Herndon (and Jesse W. Weik), *Herndon's Lincoln: The True Story of a Great Life,* 17, 1889, Premier Books edition, 1961

Anonymous Senator: You say you are the people's attorney. Now, you will admit that this course would be most popular.
Lincoln: But I am not going to let my client manage the case against my judgment. As long as I am attorney for the people I shall manage the case to the best of my ability. They will have a chance to put me out, by and by, if my management is not satisfactory.

> ABRAHAM LINCOLN (1809–1865). Format adapted. In Francis Fisher Browne, *The Every-Day Life of Abraham Lincoln,* 3.8, 1887

If the economy is good, the President could be having sex with a horse [and nobody would care].

> BILL MAHER. Jay Leno television interview, *The Tonight Show,* NBC, 23 May 1997

The moving factor in [presidential] prestige is what men . . . see happening to *themselves.*

> RICHARD E. NEUSTADT (1919–). Political scientist and presidential assistant to Harry S. Truman. *Presidential Power: The Politics of Leadership,* 5.2, 1960

A President's success is measured by his domestic and international achievements, not by his popularity in the polls.

> RICHARD M. NIXON (1913–1994). *In the Arena: A Memoir of Victory, Defeat and Renewal,* 31, 1990

The presidential burden . . . does not lie in the workload. It stems from the crushing responsibility of political decisions, with life and death literally hanging in the balance for hundreds of millions of people.

> GEORGE E. REEDY (1917–). Presidential assistant to Lyndon B. Johnson. *The Twilight of the Presidency,* 2, 1970

The president's ability to place his views before the public is important primarily because he can usually set the terms of the national debate—and anyone who can set the terms of a debate can win it.

> GEORGE E. REEDY (1917–). *The Twilight of the Presidency,* 3, 1970

The whole country is with [Franklin D. Roosevelt] just so he does something.

> WILL ROGERS (1879–1835). On the day after the President's inauguration in the midst of an economic crisis that threatened to shut down the entire country, 5 March 1933. In James David Barber, *The Presidential Character: Predicting Performance in the White House,* 7, 1972

What higher obligation does a President have than to explain his intentions to the people and persuade them that the direction he wishes to go is right? Politics in a democracy, is at the end, an educational process.

> ARTHUR M. SCHLESINGER JR. (1917–). "A Clinton Card, So Far," *New York Times,* 11 April 1993

PRESIDENTS & STAFF

Includes • Presidents & Cabinet ○ Presidents & Government

See also • Bureaucracy ○ Commanders & Staff ○ Decision-Making ○ Details ○ Leaders & Staff ○ Presidents

In the relationship between the president and the secretary of state, it is imperative that both understand at all times which one is president.

> DEAN ACHESON (1893–1971). In Dean Rusk, *As I Saw It,* 32, 1990

Staff members tend to become courtiers. This is true everywhere, but nowhere more so than in the White House. And the result is deepening presidential isolation and unrealism as the White House becomes, in Senator Charles Mathias' words, a presidential "house of mirrors" in which all views and ideas tend to reflect and reinforce [the President's].

> GRAHAM ALLISON and PETER SZANTON. "Organizing for the Decade Ahead." In Henry Owen and Charles L. Schultze, eds., *Setting National Priorities: The Next Ten Years,* 1976

Why do we expect our Presidents to control destiny when they cannot even control the House of Representatives?

> RUSSELL BAKER (1925–). 6 August, *Poor Russell's Almanac,* 1972

Don't lose face, because loss of face betokens loss of will, and loss of will tempts enemies to go for your jugular.

> RUSSELL BAKER (1925–). Advice a President is likely to hear from the "professional national-security bureaucracy," "Make It Bill and Lyndon," *New York Times,* 9 October 1993

[A President's advisers] exercise their power chiefly by filtering the information that reaches the President and by interpreting the outside world for him. They structure his choices.

> RICHARD J. BARNET (1929–). *Roots of War,* 4.1, 1971

Because he is so dependent upon his principal assistants, the President in effect makes policy when he selects them. Indeed, he probably exerts his greatest influence over future policy when he recruits his leading advisers.

> RICHARD J. BARNET (1929–). *Roots of War,* 4.1, 1971

[Franklin D.] Roosevelt's test of a man was not his basic philosophy, or lack of one, but the sweep of his information, his ability to communicate, and his willingness to share ideas.

> JAMES MacGREGOR BURNS (1918–). *Roosevelt: The Lion and the Fox,* 8, 1956

The test of a great President is not whether he can delegate neat packets of power to subordinates, conduct an orderly administration, and follow the prescribed channels of the organization chart on the wall, but whether he can recruit the ablest men, inspire them to their best performance behind great ideas, and make those ideas politically viable.

> JAMES MacGREGOR BURNS (1918–). "Test of a President," *New York Times Magazine,* 1 May 1960

Presidents tend to equate loyalty to integrity.

> JOSEPH A. CALIFANO, JR. (1931–). Presidential assistant to Lyndon B. Johnson and secretary of health, education and welfare. *A Presidential Nation,* 9, 1975
>
> See Disloyalty: Califano

A president needs men around him who bleed when he is cut.

> JOSEPH A. CALIFANO, JR. (1931–). Adapted. *A Presidential Nation,* 9, 1975
>
> See Disloyalty: Califano

Where presidents fail to recognize that an enemy on one issue can be an ally on another, they serve the people badly.

> JOSEPH A. CALIFANO, JR. (1931–). *A Presidential Nation,* 10, 1975

The Eisenhower [staff] could be compared to a football team—elaborate planning, great attention to coordinating everybody, and interminable time spent in the huddles. The Kennedy team was more along the lines of basketball: everybody was on the move all the time. Nobody had a very clearly defined position. The President had a habit of throwing the ball in any direction and he expected it to be kept bouncing.

> DOUGLASS CATER (1923–1995). Presidential assistant to Lyndon B. Johnson. *Power in Washington: A Critical Look at Today's Struggle to Govern in the Nation's Capital,* 5, 1964

One rule of action more important than all others consists in never doing anything that some one else can do for you.

> CALVIN COOLIDGE (1872–1933). In James D. Barber, *The Presidential Character: Predicting Performance in the White House*, 5, 1972

Personnel is policy.

> BECKY NORTON DUNLOP. Opening words, "The Role of the White House Office of Presidential Personnel." In Robert Rector and Michael Sanera, eds., *Steering the Elephant: How Washington Works*, 1987
>
> See Organizations: Anonymous

[Franklin D. Roosevelt] would give you a job to do and leave you free to do it by yourself. He never told you how to do it.

> PHILIP FLEMING. General. In Arthur M. Schlesinger, Jr., *The Age of Roosevelt: The Coming of the New Deal*, 33.5, 1959

Access to the President is the coin of the realm.

> DORIS KEARNS GOODWIN (1943–). Slightly modified. *Lyndon Johnson and the American Dream*, 11, 1976

The Kennedy people spoke in shorthand, almost a code, the fewer words the better, for tartness and brevity showed that you understood the code, were on the inside.

> DAVID HALBERSTAM (1934–). On John F. Kennedy's staff. *The Best and the Brightest*, 2, 1972

Every President needs his son of a bitch, and I'm Nixon's.

> H. R. HALDEMAN (1926–1993). Presidential assistant. In news reports, 30 August 1973

No President can be a prisoner of his staff unless he chooses to be. [Dwight D.] Eisenhower was not a prisoner. He simply wanted his staff to handle a good many things that held no interest for him. . . . He wanted to be free for the big decisions.

> ERWIN C. HARGROVE (1930–). *Presidential Leadership: Personality and Political Style*, 6, 1966

The main basis for [Franklin D.] Roosevelt's influence over those who worked for him was his capacity to inspire them. "After an hour with the President I could eat nails for lunch," one associate commented.

> ERWIN C. HARGROVE (1930–). *The Power of the Modern Presidency*, 9, 1974

Wanting to leave is a source of great power in government. . . . If they move in on you, go after your turf, you just say, "Be my guest. I want out. Take all of it, not just a little." And then they look at you and think, "Uh-oh, there's something dangerous about this one." And they leave you entirely alone.

> BRYCE HARLOW (1916–). Presidential assistant to Dwight D. Eisenhower. Lynne Cheney interview, "A Quality of Judgment," *Washingtonian*, April 1985

However much Cabinet members profess loyalty to the President, they quickly become enmeshed in a network of institutional relationships, each of which commands a certain degree of allegiance from the Cabinet member if he is to operate successfully within it.

> JOHN HART. "The President and His Staff." In Malcolm Shaw, ed., *The Modern Presidency: From Roosevelt to Reagan*, 1987

[Staff members] do the President's bidding as though the President were doing it himself. . . . Ultimately, the President himself is answerable for the activities of his staff.

> JOHN HART. "The President and His Staff." In Malcolm Shaw, ed., *The Modern Presidency: From Roosevelt to Reagan*, 1987

The Tycoon is in fine whack. I have rarely seen him more serene and busy. He is managing this war, the draft, foreign relations, and planning a reconstruction of the Union, all at once. I never knew with what tyrannous authority he rules the Cabinet till now. The most important things he decides and there is no cavil.

> JOHN HAY (1838–1905). Presidential assistant to Abraham Lincoln and secretary of state. Letter to John Nicolay, 7 August 1863

[Harry S.] Truman always gave everybody the feeling that the minor functionary was a vital cog in the machine.

> KEN HECHLER. *Working with Truman: A Personal Memoir of the White House Years*, 1, 1982

[The internal management problem of the president] is to use those who serve him without becoming dependent on them.

> HUGH HECLO (1943–). "The Changing Presidential Office." In James P. Pfiffner, ed., *The Managerial Presidency*, 1991

[Franklin D.] Roosevelt constructed a circle with himself at the hub. Eisenhower designed a pyramid with himself at the apex.

> STEPHEN HESS (1933–). Presidential assistant to Dwight D. Eisenhower and Richard M. Nixon. Introduction to *Organizing the Presidency*, 1976

Bottlenecks develop as too many agencies are funneled through too few presidential assistants.

> STEPHEN HESS (1933–). *Organizing the Presidency*, 1, 1976

A Cabinet-centered government in domestic affairs and a White House-centered government in foreign affairs.

> STEPHEN HESS (1933–). On Richard M. Nixon's concept of the Presidency, *Organizing the Presidency*, 7, 1976

When a President receives his major advice from those most responsible for its effectuation, there is a higher probability of achieving results than when policy is imposed by presidential representatives, usually the White House staff.

> STEPHEN HESS (1933–). *Organizing the Presidency*, 8, 1976

There is much to recommend having potential presidential aides step down [from top positions in education, law, business and government], rather than up, to White House service.

> STEPHEN HESS (1933–). *Organizing the Presidency*, 9, 1976

Well, it's probably better to have [J. Edgar Hoover] inside the tent pissing out, then [*sic*] outside pissing in.

> LYNDON B. JOHNSON (1908–1973). On his 1964 decision to retain the aging Federal Bureau of Investigation director. In David Halberstam, *The Best and the Brightest*, 20, 1972

Frank, the next time you want a dam in Idaho, you just go to Walter Lippmann for it.

> LYNDON B. JOHNSON (1908–1973). Intimidating remark to Idaho Sen. Frank Church at a White House meeting, March 1965 (earlier Church became one of the first senators to oppose the Vietnam War, citing Lippmann as an authority who urged a negotiated settlement). In Ronald Steel, *Walter Lippmann and the American Century*, 43, 1980

Deference invited excesses.

> RICHARD TANNER JOHNSON (1927–). On Harry S. Truman's relation-
> ship with certain key members of his Cabinet. *Managing the White
> House: An Intimate Study of the Presidency,* 3, 1974

Loyalty is enhanced by selecting unknown men whose only reason for being is by the president's grace alone.

> RICHARD TANNER JOHNSON (1927–). *Managing the White House:
> An Intimate Study of the Presidency,* 7, 1974

[Richard M. Nixon's] staff prepared a "script" about each visitor to
the Oval Office that told who he was and the nature of his business. It even provided suggested subjects for small talk and indicated how long the audience was to last.

> RICHARD TANNER JOHNSON (1927–). *Managing the White House:
> An Intimate Study of the Presidency,* 7, 1974

Tell the President that the way to solve his problem is to find that
one man who would turn out to be . . . possessed of high competence, great physical vigor, and *a passion for anonymity.*

> TOM JONES. Private secretary to British Prime Minister Stanley Baldwin.
> Remark to Louis Brownlow, 1936

Why the hell didn't I know about this before.

> JOHN F. KENNEDY (1917–1963). A repeated remark to staff members,
> quoted by Richard Reeves. In Charlie Rose television interview, PBS,
> 19 October 1993

[Lyndon B. Johnson] never picked on me because I would have
just walked out.

> ROBERT KINTNER (1928–). Presidential assistant. In Merle Miller, *Lyndon:
> An Oral Biography,* 6 ("Flaws in the Ointment"), 1980

One does not really think in this job. One reacts on the basis of
thinking already done.

> HENRY A. KISSINGER (1923–). Presidential assistant to Richard M.
> Nixon. Anticipating the time pressures of his new job, December 1968.
> In Ralph Blumenfeld et al., *Henry Kissinger: The Private and Public
> Story,* 21, 1974

We are the President's men, and we must behave accordingly.

> HENRY A. KISSINGER (1923–). Suggesting that the White House's for-
> eign policy staff was just carrying out Pres. Richard M. Nixon's orders
> regarding the Cambodian invasion, May 1970. In Marvin Kalb and
> Bernard Kalb, *Kissinger,* 7, 1974. Carl Bernstein and Bob Woodward
> titled their 1974 book on the Watergate investigation *All the President's
> Men.*

The influence of a Presidential Assistant derives almost exclusively from the confidence of the President, not from administrative
arrangements.

> HENRY A. KISSINGER (1923–). *White House Years,* 2, 1979

[Presidential] advisers without a clear-cut area of responsibility
eventually are pushed to the periphery by day-to-day operators.

> HENRY A. KISSINGER (1923–). *Years of Upheaval,* 4, 1982

[Richard M.] Nixon . . . was convinced that my special talents
would flourish best under conditions of personal insecurity; . . .
he periodically saw to it that I developed some doubts about his
purposes or priorities or about my standing with him.

> HENRY A. KISSINGER (1923–). *Years of Upheaval,* 4, 1982

Propinquity to the President's office is one of the better ways of
judging the relative importance of White House aides.

> HENRY A. KISSINGER (1923–). *Years of Upheaval,* 5, 1982

It may be true that the President [Franklin D. Roosevelt] formally
overruled them on very few occasions but this was only because
informal discussions of the President with Leahy, Marshall, King
and Arnold [the country's top military leaders during World War II]
usually led them to know in advance the President's views.

> T. B. KITTREDGE. Military officer, Historical Section, Joint Chiefs of Staff.
> In Robert E. Sherwood, *Roosevelt and Hopkins: An Intimate History,*
> no. 446 (notes to ch. 20), 1948

Every delegation of power is . . . a risk to be taken, and this makes
his judgment of men a matter of supreme importance. He must
know that the men he uses will see things through his eyes.

> HAROLD LASKI (1893–1950). In Sidney Warren, *The President as World
> Leader,* 23, 1964

Your dispatch saying "I cant get those regts. off [to Washington]
because I cant get quick work out of the U.S. disbursing officer &
the Paymaster" is received.

Please say to these gentlemen that if they do not work quickly I
will make quick work with them. . . .

> ABRAHAM LINCOLN (1809–1965). Following defeats of Union forces in
> Virginia, and at a time when Washington was under threat of attack,
> telegram to Massachusetts Gov. John A. Andrew, 12 August 1862

I have got you together to hear what I have written down. I do not
wish your advice about the main matter—for that I have determined for myself.

> ABRAHAM LINCOLN (1809–1965). In announcing at a Cabinet meeting his
> decision to issue the Emancipation Proclamation, June 1863. In Salmon
> P. Chase (secretary of treasury), diary. Quoted in Emmet John Hughes,
> *The Living Presidency: The Resources and Dilemmas of the American
> Presidential Office,* 5.3, 1972

Schenck and Piatt are good fellows. . . . But they run their machine
on too high a level for me. They never could understand that I was
the boss.

> ABRAHAM LINCOLN (1809–1865). On his refusal to promote the author
> because he had exceeded his authority in carrying out an earlier assign-
> ment. In Donn Piatt, "Abraham Lincoln," *Memories of the Men Who
> Saved the Union,* 1887

Presidents . . . become hermits only at their peril. Running the executive branch is now a team sport. It is operated best by politicians
who thrive on command, possess a fine and sure touch for the
levers of power and enjoy the company of those who serve them.

> CHRISTOPHER MATTHEWS (1945–). "All the Presidents' Cliques," *New
> York Times Book Review,* 13 November 1988

Good Presidents make good staffs, not vice versa.

> BILL MOYERS (1934–). Presidential assistant to Lyndon B. Johnson.
> In Charles Roberts, *LBJ's Inner Circle,* 2, 1965

Any aide who demonstrates to others that he has the President's
consistent confidence and a consistent part in presidential business
will acquire so much business on his own account that he becomes
in some sense independent of his chief.

> RICHARD E. NEUSTADT (1919–). Political scientist and presidential assis-
> tant to Harry S. Truman. *Presidential Power: The Politics of Leadership,*
> 3.2, 1960

[The President should] induce as much uncertainty as possible about the consequences of ignoring what he wants. If he cannot make men think him bound to win, his need is to keep them from thinking they can cross him without risk, or that they can be sure what risks they run. At the same time (no mean feat) he needs to keep them from fearing lest he leave them in the lurch if they support him.

> RICHARD E. NEUSTADT (1919–). *Presidential Power: The Politics of Leadership,* 4.2, 1960

[Franklin D. Roosevelt] changed his [unofficial] sources [of information] as his interests changed, but no one who had ever interested him was quite forgotten or immune to sudden use.

> RICHARD E. NEUSTADT (1919–). *Presidential Power: The Politics of Leadership,* 7.1, 1960

•

The President's chief function is to lead, not to administer; it is not to oversee every detail, but to put the right people in charge, to provide them with basic guidance and direction and to let them do the job.

> RICHARD M. NIXON (1913–1994). Television broadcast, 19 September 1968

I want the whole staff in the strongest possible terms to be informed that unless they can say something positive about my operations and that of the White House staff they should say nothing.

> RICHARD M. NIXON (1913–1994). Memorandum to H. R. Haldeman and John Ehrlichman, 16 June 1969. In Bruce Oudes, ed., *From: The President,* 1989

If [a leader] cannot be a good butcher himself, he needs someone who can be. . . . In my own administration Bob Haldeman got a reputation for ruthlessness. One reason was that he performed for me a lot of the butcher's tasks that I could not bring myself to perform directly.

> RICHARD M. NIXON (1913–1994). *Leaders,* 9, 1982
> See Prime Ministers: William Ewart Gladstone

Three qualities should be considered in evaluating applicants for [staff] positions—head, heart, and guts.

> RICHARD M. NIXON (1913–1994). *In the Arena: A Memoir of Victory, Defeat and Renewal,* 30, 1990

As if to compensate for the dearth of substantive presidential dialogue, the White House communications staff machinery has become even more elaborate.

> BRADLEY H. PATTERSON, JR. (*1921*–). Presidential assistant to Dwight D. Eisenhower. Referring to the Reagan Administration, *The Ring of Power: The White House Staff and Its Expanding Role in Government,* 12, 1988

A chief of staff cannot afford to let *any* people or information go past him [to the president] without review. The hotter the enthusiast who marches toward the Oval Office, the colder must be the scrutiny.

> BRADLEY H. PATTERSON, JR. (1913–1994). *The Ring of Power: The White House Staff and Its Expanding Role in Government,* 23, 1988

The *appearance* of impropriety is itself the impropriety. . . . The "appearance" rule is not in any law; it is tougher than law. It is the unrelenting standard for men and women who serve near the presidency.

> BRADLEY H. PATTERSON, JR. (1913–1994). *The Ring of Power: The White House Staff and Its Expanding Role in Government,* pt. 4, 1988

I prefer to supervise the whole operations of the government myself than entrust the public business to subordinates, and this makes my duties very great.

> JAMES K. POLK (1797–1849). 29 December 1848 (6 months before his death at age 54), *Polk: The Diary of a President, 1845–1849,* ed. Allan Nevins, 1929
> See Details: Franklin D. Roosevelt

Eventually a good staff man becomes so finely attuned to the President's thinking that communication is almost subliminal.

> CHARLES ROBERTS. *LBJ's Inner Circle,* 3, 1965

Wendell Willkie (Republican presidential nominee, 1940): Why do you keep Hopkins so close to you? You surely must realize that people distrust him, and they resent his influence.
Roosevelt: . . . Someday you may well be sitting here where I am now as President of the United States. And when you are, you'll be looking at that door over there and knowing that practically everybody who walks through it wants something out of you. You'll learn what a lonely job this is, and you'll discover the need for somebody like Harry Hopkins who asks for nothing except to serve you.

> FRANKLIN D. ROOSEVELT (1882–1945). Format adapted. 19 January 1941. In Robert E. Sherwood, *The White House Papers of Harry L. Hopkins,* 1, 1949

The great majority of the instruments with which I work have each some big flaw. I have to endeavor to bear down as lightly as possible on the flaw and get the best results I can in spite of it; and when the instrument finally breaks, grin and pick up another one, probably no better and work as long as I can with it in its turn.

> THEODORE ROOSEVELT (1858–1919). Letter to his son Kermit, 1907

I determined on the move without consulting the Cabinet, precisely as I took Panama without consulting the Cabinet. A council of war never fights, and in a crisis, the duty of a leader is to lead and not to take refuge behind the generally timid wisdom of a multitude of councilors.

> THEODORE ROOSEVELT (1858–1919). On his decision to send an American "battle fleet" on a voyage around the world in 1907. *Autobiography,* 15, 1913

Know when you have a bias, pro or con, on people or issues, and make the President aware of it so that he can take it into account.

> DONALD RUMSFELD (1932–). "Rumsfeld's Rules" (collected while serving at the White House and Pentagon), *Washingtonian,* February 1977

[H. R.] *Haldeman organized the execution of the President's orders. . . .*
Haldeman also had *the responsibility not to carry out orders* he felt were ill-conceived or badly put.

> WILLIAM SAFIRE (1929–). Presidential assistant to Richard M. Nixon and journalist. *Before the Fall: An Inside View of the Pre-Watergate White House,* 4.6, 1975

[Franklin D. Roosevelt] deliberately organized—or disorganized—his system of command to insure that important decisions were passed on to the top. His favorite technique was to keep grants of authority incomplete, jurisdictions uncertain, charters overlapping.

ARTHUR M. SCHLESINGER JR. (1917–). Historian and presidential assistant to John F. Kennedy. *The Age of Roosevelt: The Coming of the New Deal,* 32.9, 1959

See Leaders & Staff: Thomas Fuller

Students of public administration have never taken sufficient account of the capacity of lower levels of government to sabotage or defy even a masterful President.

ARTHUR M. SCHLESINGER JR. (1917–). *The Age of Roosevelt: The Coming of the New Deal,* 33.3, 1959

[Franklin D. Roosevelt] had a genius for being indirect with people. Nearly all around him had the chilling fear, generally shoved to the back of their minds, that he regarded them as expendable.

ARTHUR M. SCHLESINGER JR. (1917–). *The Age of Roosevelt: The Coming of the New Deal,* 33.3, 1959

If the manipulation of insecurity was part of Roosevelt's method, the provision of charm and consolation was an equally indispensable part. . . . As William Phillips put it, "He had a rare capacity for healing the wounded feelings which he had inadvertently caused." Roosevelt called this process "hand-holding."

ARTHUR M. SCHLESINGER JR. (1917–). *The Age of Roosevelt: The Coming of the New Deal,* 33.4, 1959

[Franklin D. Roosevelt] gave his appointees wide discretion—even to the point of overlooking their disregard of presidential directives—so long as they seemed on top of their responsibilities.

ARTHUR M. SCHLESINGER, JR. (1917–). *The Age of Roosevelt: The Coming of the New Deal,* 33.5, 1959

Every important mistake has been the consequence of excessive deference to the permanent government.

ARTHUR M. SCHLESINGER, JR. (1917–). *A Thousand Days: John F. Kennedy in the White House,* 25.3, 1965

Reliance on official channels has never proven to be wise. For there will always be subordinates who are willing to tell a President only what they want him to hear, or, what is even worse, only what they think he wants to hear.

THEODORE C. SORENSEN (1928–). Presidential assistant to John F. Kennedy. *Decision-Making in the White House: The Olive Branch or the Arrows,* 3, 1963

As national problems become more complex and interrelated, requiring continuous, firsthand knowledge of confidential data and expert analysis, very few outsiders are sufficiently well informed.

THEODORE C. SORENSEN (1928–). *Decision-Making in the White House: The Olive Branch or the Arrows,* 5, 1963

The most articulate, authoritative man may only be making bad advice sound good, while driving into silence less aggressive or more cautious advisers.

THEODORE C. SORENSEN (1928–). *Decision-Making in the White House: The Olive Branch or the Arrows,* 5, 1963

A President does not have to be a great creative or innovative thinker, as helpful as that may be. For an almost endless flow of new ideas will almost certainly come to him and his real task is to discriminate and choose among them. Similarly, he does not personally have to be a great administrator, but he has to choose and guide those who are. He has to be as discriminating in his judgment of men as of ideas.

THEODORE C. SORENSEN (1928–). "The Presidency As I Have Seen It" (A Special Section). In Emmet John Hughes, *The Living Presidency: The Resources and Dilemmas of the American Presidential Office,* 1972

All the President is, is a glorified public relations man who spends his time flattering, kissing, and kicking people to get them to do what they are supposed to do anyway.

HARRY S. TRUMAN (1884–1972). Letter to his sister Mary Jane Truman, 14 November 1947

He'll sit right here and he'll say, "Do this! Do that!" *And nothing will happen.* Poor Ike—it won't be a bit like the army. He'll find it very frustrating.

HARRY S. TRUMAN (1884–1972). On presidential candidate Dwight D. Eisenhower, summer 1952. In Richard E. Neustadt, *Presidential Power: The Politics of Leadership,* 2.1, 1960

Franklin D. Roosevelt won the Second World War with a smaller staff than the First Lady has today.

GEORGE F. WILL (1941–). Slightly modified. Brian Lamb television panel conversation, C-SPAN, 31 July 1994. Abraham Lincoln won the Civil War with a staff consisting of two secretaries.

Issues are nearly always cross-cutting and impossible to assign to a single department or agency, and the consequent problems of coordination and communication are difficult to resolve.

ROBERT WILLIAMS. "The Presidency and the Executive Branch." In Malcolm Shaw, ed., *The Modern Presidency: From Roosevelt to Reagan,* 1987

Don't cross the Boss.

GARRY WILLS (1934–). Referring to the presidency, "Backstairs at Court," *New York Review of Books,* 15 May 1975

A friend of mine says that every man who takes office in Washington either grows or swells; and when I give a man an office, I watch him carefully to see whether he is swelling or growing.

WOODROW WILSON (1856–1924). Speech before the National Press Club, Washington, 15 May 1916

If you want your memoranda read, put it on one page.

WOODROW WILSON (1856–1924). Remark to Assistant Secretary of the Navy Franklin D. Roosevelt. In Arthur M. Schlesinger, Jr., *The Age of Roosevelt: The Coming of the New Deal,* 32.7, 1959

❧

[John Ehrlichman] leaves no more blood on the floor than he has to.

ANONYMOUS (AMERICAN). White House staffer. On one of Richard M. Nixon's top assistants. In J. Anthony Lukas, "The Story So Far," *New York Times Magazine,* 22 July 1973

Don't do anything you're not prepared to see in the papers the next morning.

ANONYMOUS (AMERICAN). On "the first law of life in the White House." In Peter Goldman, "Rx for Trouble," *Newsweek,* 31 July 1978

THE PRESS

See also • Censorship ○ Freedom of the Press ○ Journalism ○ Media ○ News ○ Newspapers

The press is the hired agent of a monied system, and set up for no other purpose than to tell lies where their interests are involved. One can trust nobody and nothing.

> HENRY ADAMS (1838–1918). *The Letters of Henry Adams,* ed. Worthington Chauncey Ford, 1930–1938

[The Washington press] spends too much time talking to the movers and shakers and not enough time talking to those who are moved and shaken.

> BEN H. BAGDIKIAN (1920–). In "Political Warming—Republican Discord Is Shaping Next Year's Presidential Weather," *Washington Spectator,* 1 November 1995

An honest, fearless press is the public's first protection against gangsterism, local or international.

> RICHARD BROOKS (1944–). *Deadline U.S.A.* (film), 1952, spoken by Humphrey Bogart

The press, like fire, is an excellent servant, but a terrible master.

> JAMES FENIMORE COOPER (1789–1851). "On the Press," *The American Democrat,* 1838
>
> See Money: Saying (French) ○ Passion: Saying (English)

The press rules the people, and capital rules the press.

> HENRY GEORGE (1839–1897). *Social Problems,* 7, 1883

The press has its own version of Gresham's Law: the tendency, in the competition for readers, to let the scandalous and sensational drive out serious news.

> ANTHONY LEWIS (1927–). "Freedom of the Press," *New York Times,* 24 December 1993
>
> See Money: Sir Thomas Gresham

[The press] is seldom intelligent, save in the arts of the mob-master. It is never courageously honest. Held harshly to a rigid correctness of opinion by the plutocracy that controls it with less and less attempt at disguise, and menaced on all sides by censorships that it dare not flout, it sinks rapidly into formalism and feebleness. Its yellow section is perhaps its most respectable section for there the only vestige of the old free journalist survives.

> H. L. MENCKEN (1880–1956). "The National Letters: The Cultural Background," *Prejudices: Second Series,* 1920

In dealing with the press, do yourself a favor. Stick with one of three responses: (a) I know and I can tell you, (b) I know and I can't tell you, or (3) I don't know.

> DAN RATHER (1931–). "The Rather Rule," in Donald Rumsfeld, "Rumsfeld's Rules" (collected while serving at the White House and Pentagon), *Washingtonian,* February 1977

The Press today is an army with carefully organized arms and branches, with journalists as officers, and readers as soldiers. But here, as in every army, the soldier obeys blindly, and war aims and operation plans change without his knowledge. The reader neither knows, nor is allowed to know, the purposes for which he is used, nor even the role that he is to play. A more appalling caricature of freedom of thought cannot be imagined. Formerly a man did not dare to think freely. Now he dares, but cannot; his will to think is only a willingness to think to order, and this is what he feels as *his* liberty.

> OSWALD SPENGLER (1880–19936). "Philosophy of Politics," *The Decline of the West,* 1918–1922, tr. Charles Francis Atkinson, 1962
>
> See Truth: Spengler

The Press is the Arkermejian leaver which moves the world.

> ARTEMUS WARD (1834–1867). "Celebration at Baldinsville in Honor of the Atlantic Cable," *The Complete Works of Artemus Ward,* 1898

The press in our free country is reliable and useful not because of its good character but because of its great diversity. As long as there are many owners, each pursuing his own brand of truth, we the people have the opportunity to arrive at the truth and to dwell in the light. The multiplicity of ownership is crucial. It's only when there are few owners, or, as in a government-controlled press, one owner, that the truth becomes elusive and the light fails.

> E. B. WHITE (1899–1985). Letter to W. B. Jones, 30 January 1976, *Letters of E. B. White,* ed. Dorothy Lobrano Guth, 1976

In old days men had the rack. Now they have the Press.

> OSCAR WILDE (1854–1900). "The Soul of Man Under Socialism," *Fortnightly Review* (British journal), February 1891

While the press can't tell people what to think, it certainly can tell them what to think about.

> ANONYMOUS

PRESTIGE

See also • Authority: [especially] Harold D. Lasswell and Abraham Kaplan ○ Fame ○ Popularity ○ Power ○ Reputation ○ Respect ○ Respectability ○ Status

There can be no prestige without mystery, for familiarity breeds contempt.

> CHARLES de GAULLE (1890–1970). "Of Prestige" (2), *The Edge of the Sword,* 1934, tr. Gerald Hopkins, 1960
>
> See Familiarity: Aesop

Since society as a whole needs the magically effective figure, it uses the needful will to power in the individual, and the will to submit in the mass, as a vehicle, and thus brings about the creation of personal prestige.

> CARL G. JUNG (1875–1961). "The Relations between the Ego and the Unconscious" (1.2), 1928, *Two Essays on Analytical Psychology,* tr. R. F. C. Hull, 1953

Prestige is the mainspring of all authority. Neither gods, kings, nor women have ever reigned without it.

> GUSTAVE LE BON (1841–1931). *The Crowd: A Study of the Popular Mind,* 2.3.3, 1895, Viking Press edition, 1960

Ill-treat men as you will, massacre them by millions, be the cause of invasion upon invasion, all is permitted you if you possess prestige in a sufficient degree and the talent necessary to uphold it.

> GUSTAVE LE BON (1841–1931). *The Crowd: A Study of the Popular Mind,* 2.3.3, 1895, Viking Press edition, 1960

From the moment prestige is called in question it ceases to be prestige.

> GUSTAVE LE BON (1841–1931). *The Crowd: A Study of the Popular Mind,* 2.3.3, 1895, Viking Press edition, 1960

Force can command obedience, but prestige removes even the idea of disobedience.

> GUSTAVE LE BON (1841–1931). *Aphorisms of Present Times,* 1.8, 1913, tr. Alice Widener, 1979

Prestige involves at least two persons: one to claim it and another to honor the claim. . . . In the status system of a society these claims are organized as rules and expectations which regulate who successfully claims prestige, from whom, in what ways, and on what basis. The level of self-esteem enjoyed by given individual is more or less set by this status system.

> C. WRIGHT MILLS (1916–1962). *White Collar: The American Middle Classes,* 11 (introduction), 1951

Prestige is the shadow of money and power. Where these are, there it is.

> C. WRIGHT MILLS (1916–1962). *The Power Elite,* 4.3, 1956

Prestige buttresses power, turning it into authority, and protecting it from social challenge.

> C. WRIGHT MILLS (1916–1962). *The Power Elite,* 4.4, 1956

PRICE

See also • Business (Commerce) ◦ Economics ◦ Merchants & Customers ◦ Money ◦ Profit & Loss ◦ Trade (Commerce) ◦ Value

What this country needs is a good five-cent nickel.

> FRANKLIN P. ADAMS (1881–1960). In Robert E. Drennan, ed., "Franklin P. Adams," *The Algonquin Wits,* 1968

You may not get what you paid for, but you will pay for what you get.

> MAYA ANGELOU (1928–). In Merla Zellerbach, "The Best Quips of 1982," *San Francisco Chronicle,* 22 December 1982

Price, *n.* Value, plus a reasonable sum for the wear and tear of conscience in demanding it.

> AMBROSE BIERCE (1842–1914). *The Devil's Dictionary,* p. 104, 1911, Dover edition, 1958

"The Best Things in Life Are Free."

> LEW BROWN (1893–1958) and BUDDY DE SILVA. Song title. In the musical *Good News,* 1927

Price is what you pay. Value is what you get.

> WARREN BUFFETT (1930–). "About Investing: Know the Difference Between Price and Value," *Warren Buffett Speaks: Wit and Wisdom from the World's Greatest Investor,* comp. Janet Lowe, 1997

That which cost[s] little is less valued.

> CERVANTES (1547–1616). *Don Quixote,* 1.4.7, 1615, tr. Peter Anthony Motteux and John Ozell, 1743

Anything worth having has its price.

> JOAN DIDION (1934–). "On Self-Respect," 1961, *Slouching Towards Bethlehem,* 1969

There's No Such Thing as a Free Lunch.

> MILTON FRIEDMAN (1912–). Book title, 1975
> See Compensation: Epictetus

Better be cheated in the price than in the quality of [the] goods.

> BALTASAR GRACIÁN (1601–1658). *The Art of Worldly Wisdom,* 157, 1647, tr. Joseph Jacobs, 1943

It is only a sentimental half-truth that the best things in life are free; while they may be, it is equally true that we need the money to buy the time to enjoy them.

> SYDNEY J. HARRIS (1917–1986). *Pieces of Eight,* 4, 1982

Ill ware is never cheap.

> GEORGE HERBERT (1593–1633). Comp., *Outlandish Proverbs,* 61, 1640 (Popular version: Poor quality is never cheap.)

O God! that bread should be so dear,
And flesh and blood so cheap!

> THOMAS HOOD (1799–1845). "The Song of the Shirt," 5, 1843

Never buy what you do not want, because it is cheap; it will be dear to you.

> THOMAS JEFFERSON (1743–1826). "A Decalogue of Canons for Observation in Practical Life," #4, letter to Thomas Jefferson Smith, 21 February 1825

The more necessary a thing is for living beings, the more easily it is found and the cheaper it is; the less necessary it is, the rarer and dearer it is.

> MOSES MAIMONIDES (A.D. 1135–1204). *The Guide for the Perplexed,* 3.12, A.D. 1190, tr. M. Friedländer, 1904

What this country needs is a really good five-cent cigar.

> THOMAS R. MARSHALL (1854–1925). Vice president. Remark to John Crockett, chief clerk of the Senate, during a tedious debate, 1917, quoted in *New York Tribune,* 4 January 1920

Those things are dearest to us that have cost us most.

> MONTAIGNE (1533–1592). "Of the Affection of Fathers for Their Children," *Essays,* 1588, tr. Donald M. Frame, 1958

If you have to ask the price, you can't afford it.

> J. P. MORGAN (1837–1913). In Bennett Cerf, *Laughing Stock,* 1945
> See Riches: J. Paul Getty

All that has a price is of little value.

> FRIEDRICH NIETZSCHE (1844–1900). "Of Old and New Law-Tables" (12), *Thus Spoke Zarathustra,* 1892, tr. R. J. Hollingdale, 1961

Our country has plenty of five-cent cigars; but the trouble is, they charge 15 cents for 'em.

> WILL ROGERS (1879–1935). In *Will Rogers U.S.A.,* CBS-TV, 9 March 1972

The real price of every thing . . . is the toil and trouble of acquiring it.

> ADAM SMITH (1723–1790). *The Wealth of Nations,* 1.5, 1776

The cost of a thing . . . is the amount of life it requires to be exchanged for it, immediately or in the long run.

> HENRY DAVID THOREAU (1817–1862). Journal, 1845, undated

The superior gratification derived from the use and contemplation of costly and supposedly beautiful products is, commonly, in great measure a gratification of our sense of costliness masquerading under the name of beauty.

> THORSTEIN VEBLEN (1857–1929). *The Theory of the Leisure Class: An Economic Study of Institutions,* 6, 1899

I had to pay much for what I got, but what I got made what I paid for it, much as it was, seem cheap.

> WALT WHITMAN (1819–1892). Remark to the author, 20 January 1889. In Horace Traubel, *Walt Whitman's Camden Conversations,* ed. Walter Teller, 1973

Nowadays people know the price of everything and the value of nothing.

> OSCAR WILDE (1854–1900). *The Picture of Dorian Gray,* 4, 1891

🌿

Free lunches aren't.

> SAYING

PRIDE

See also • Confidence ○ Dignity ○ Egotism ○ Envy ○ Humility ○ Self-Love ○ Self-Respect ○ Vanity: [especially] Jane Austen

There is no man so unsafe as he that is . . . too Proud to be told Truth, or have his Errors taken Notice of.

> SAMUEL BUTLER (1612–1680). "Unclassified Prose Observations from the Butler's Manuscript," *Prose Observations,* ed. Hugh de Quehen, 1979

There is a paradox in pride—it makes some men ridiculous, but prevents others from becoming so.

> C. C. COLTON (1780–1832). *Lacon: or, Many Things in Few Words; Addressed to Those Who Think,* 1.207, 1823

Puff'd with pride.

> JOHN DRYDEN (1631–1700). *Absalom and Achitophel,* 1.479, 1681

The proud hate Pride—in others.

> BENJAMIN FRANKLIN (1706–1790). *Poor Richard's Almanack,* December 1751

Pride may lurk under a threadbare Cloak.

> THOMAS FULLER (1654–1734). Comp., *Gnomologia: Adages and Proverbs,* 3947, 1732

'Tis Pride, and not Nature, that craves much.

> THOMAS FULLER (1654–1734). Comp., *Gnomologia: Adages and Proverbs,* 5112, 1732

When a proud Man hears another praised, he thinks himself injured.

> THOMAS FULLER (1654–1734). Comp., *Gnomologia: Adages and Proverbs,* 5541, 1732

The haughty looks of man shall be brought low,
   and the pride of men shall be humbled;
and the Lord alone will be exalted in that day.

> ISAIAH (8th cent. B.C.). *Isaiah* 2:11

Pride is a vice, which pride itself inclines every man to find in others, and to overlook in himself.

> SAMUEL JOHNSON (1709–1784). "Browne," *Lives of the English Poets,* 1781

"Oh, Why Should the Spirit of Mortal Be Proud?"

> WILLIAM KNOX (1789–1825). Poem title, 1824

All men have an equal share of pride; the only difference is in their ways and means of showing it.

> LA ROCHEFOUCAULD (1613–1680). *Maxims,* 35, 1665, tr. Leonard Tancock, 1959

Nature . . . endowed us with pride to spare us the pain of knowing our imperfections.

> LA ROCHEFOUCAULD (1613–1680). *Maxims,* 36, 1665, tr. Louis Kronenberger, 1959

Pride . . . is never so well disguised and able to take people in as when masquerading as humility.

> LA ROCHEFOUCAULD (1613–1680). *Maxims,* 254, 1665, tr. Leonard Tancock, 1959

"I have done that," says my memory. "I cannot have done that," says my pride, and remains inexorable. Eventually—memory yields.

> FRIEDRICH NIETZSCHE (1844–1900). *Beyond Good and Evil,* 68, 1886, tr. Walter Kaufmann, 1966

Would the boy you were be proud of the man you are?

> LAURENCE J. PETER (1919–1990)

Pride is prosperity's common vice.

> PUBLIUS SYRUS (85–43 B.C.). *Moral Sayings,* 987, tr. Darius Lyman, Jr., 1862

Agamemnon: He that is proud eats up himself.

> SHAKESPEARE (1564–1616). *Troilus and Cressida,* 2.3.164, 1601

PRIESTS

See also • Christianity ○ Clergy ○ Preachers ○ Rabbis

As a priest
A piece of mere church furniture at best.

> WILLIAM COWPER (1731–1800). "Tirocinium: Or, a Review of Schools," l. 424, 1785

It is the office of the priest . . . to see the creation with a new eye.

> RALPH WALDO EMERSON (1803–1882). Journal, 21 July 1829

Once we had wooden chalices and golden priests, now we have golden chalices and wooden priests.

> RALPH WALDO EMERSON (1803–1882). "The Preacher," *Lectures and Biographical Sketches,* 1883

Like people, like priest.

> HOSEA (8th cent. B.C.). *Hosea* 4:9

In all ages of the world, priests have been enemies [of] liberty.

> DAVID HUME (1711–1776). "Of the Parties of Great Britain," *Essays, Moral and Political,* vol. 1, 1741

In every country and in every age the priest has been hostile to liberty. He is always in alliance with the despot, abetting his abuses in return for protection to his own.

> THOMAS JEFFERSON (1743–1826). Letter to Horatio Gates Spafford, 17 March 1814

Priests and rituals are only crutches for the crippled life of the soul.

> FRANZ KAFKA (1883–1924). In Gustav Janouch, *Conversations with Kafka*, p. 93, tr. Goronwy Rees, 1953

Usually, the state will know how to win the priests over because it needs their most private, secret education of souls and knows how to appreciate servants who seem outwardly to represent a quite different interest. Without the help of priests, no power can become "legitimate."

> FRIEDRICH NIETZSCHE (1844–1900). *Human, All Too Human*, 472, 1878, tr. Marion Faber, 1984

There will shortly be no priests, I say their work is done.

> WALT WHITMAN (1819–1892). "By Blue Ontario's Shore" (13), 1856, *Leaves of Grass*, 1855–1892

❧

Everybody his own priest.

> ANONYMOUS. During the Reformation (16th cent.). In Friedrich Nietzsche, *The Will to Power* (notebooks, 1883-1888), 93, 1911, tr. Walter Kaufmann and R. J. Hollingdale, 1967

Religion is too serious a matter to be left to the priests.

> ANONYMOUS
>
> See Commanders: Georges Clemenceau o Environment: Helmut Sihler o Politicians: Charles de Gaulle

God's friend, the priest's foe.

> SAYING (GERMAN)

PRIME MINISTERS

See also • Confidence—First Person: Winston Churchill, Margaret Thatcher o Leaders o Presidents

It was a nation and race dwelling all round the globe that had the lion heart. I had the luck to be called upon to give the roar. I also hope that I sometimes suggested to the lion the right place to use his claws.

> WINSTON CHURCHILL (1874–1965). On his role as prime minister during World War II, address marking his 80th birthday, Westminster Hall, London, 30 November 1954

Yes, I have climbed to the top of the greasy pole.

> BENJAMIN DISRAELI (1804–1881). After being appointed British prime minister, remark, February 1868

I never deny; I never contradict; I sometimes forget.

> BENJAMIN DISRAELI (1804–1881). British prime minister. On his relations with Queen Victoria. Remark to Lord Esher. In Elizabeth Longford, *Victoria R I*, 27, 1964
>
> See Complaint: Disraeli

The first essential for a prime minister is to be a good butcher.

> WILLIAM EWART GLADSTONE (1809–1898). British prime minister. In Winston Churchill, "Herbert Henry Asquith," *Great Contemporaries*, 1937
>
> See Presidents & Staff: Richard M. Nixon (3)

I don't care what damned lie we must tell, but not a man of you shall leave this room until we have all agreed to tell the same damned lie.

> LORD MELBOURNE (1779–1848). British prime minister. Remark at a cabinet meeting. In George Bernard Shaw, *Everybody's Political What's What*, 33, 1944

I don't mind how much my Ministers talk, as long as they do what I say.

> MARGARET THATCHER (1925–). British prime minister. In *Observer* (British newspaper), 27 January 1980

Being prime minister is a lonely job. . . . You cannot lead from the crowd.

> MARGARET THATCHER (1925–). *The Downing Street Years*, 1, 1993

PRINCES

See also • Kings o Leaders o Machiavellianism o Religion, Anti-: Arthur Schopenhauer o Rulers o Tyrants

Let princes and States choose such ministers as are more sensible of duty than of rising.

> FRANCIS BACON (1561–1626). "Of Ambition," *Essays*, 1625

It is of singular use to princes if they take the opinions of their council both separately and together, for private opinion is more free, but opinion before others is more reverend.

> FRANCIS BACON (1561–1626). "Of Counsel," *Essays*, 1625

What is called a great minister is one who serves his prince according to what is right; and when he finds he cannot do so, retires.

> CONFUCIUS (551–479 B.C.). *Confucian Analects*, 11.23, tr. James Legge, 1930
>
> See Commanders: Napoleon (2)

When a prince's personal conduct is correct, his government is effective without the issuing of orders. If his personal conduct is not correct, he may issue orders, but they will not be followed.

> CONFUCIUS (551–479 B.C.). *Confucian Analects*, 13.6, tr. James Legge, 1930

The world is like a game in which there are both honest and dishonest players, so that a prince who plays in this game must learn how to cheat, not in order to do it, but in order not to be the dupe of others.

> FREDERICK II (1712–1786). *Anti-Machiavel*, 18, 1740, tr. Paul Sonnino, 1981
>
> See William Cowper in Prudence: Rules

The true religion of a prince is his interest and his glory.

> FREDERICK II (1712–1786). "Morning the Second," *The Confessions of Frederick the Great*, ed. Douglas Sladen, 1915

It was held to be the duty of a prince to impose on his subjects the dictates of his own conscience.

> EDWARD GIBBON (1737–1794). *The Decline and Fall of the Roman Empire*, 49, 1776-1788

If princes would reflect how much they are in the power of their ministers, they would be more circumspect in the choice of them.

> MARQUIS OF HALIFAX (1633–1695). "Maxims of State" (21), *Miscellanies*, 1700

Privacy of thought is the true mark of a great prince. No one knows for sure what he is or what he is up to, but all feel the tremendous pressure of his expansive personality bearing down upon them. A great prince is never really known as such, and if he is known as a prince he is something less than a perfect specimen.

> EUGENE E. JENNINGS (1926–). *An Anatomy of Leadership: Princes, Heroes, and Superman*, 4, 1960

The clemency of princes is often nothing but policy to gain popular affection.

> LA ROCHEFOUCAULD (1613–1680). *Maxims*, 15, 1665, tr. Leonard Tancock, 1959

A wise prince will seek means by which his subjects will always and in every possible condition of things have need of his government, and then they will always be faithful to him.

> MACHIAVELLI (1469–1527). *The Prince*, 9, 1513, tr. Luigi Ricci, 1903

When princes think more of luxury than of arms, they lose their state.

> MACHIAVELLI (1469–1527). *The Prince*, 14, 1513, tr. Luigi Ricci, 1903

A man who wishes to make a profession of goodness in everything must necessarily come to grief among so many who are not good. Therefore it is necessary for a prince, who wishes to maintain himself, to learn how not to be good, and to use this knowledge and not use it, according to the necessity of the case.

> MACHIAVELLI (1469–1527). *The Prince*, 15, 1513, tr. Luigi Ricci, 1903

Above all [the prince] must abstain from taking people's property, for men forget more easily the death of their father than the loss of their patrimony.

> MACHIAVELLI (1469–1527). *The Prince*, 17, 1513, tr. Luigi Ricci, 1903

A prince . . . must imitate the fox and the lion, for the lion cannot protect himself from traps, and the fox cannot defend himself from wolves. One must therefore be a fox to recognize traps, and a lion to frighten wolves.

> MACHIAVELLI (1469–1527). *The Prince*, 18, 1513, tr. Luigi Ricci, 1903
> See Leaders: Napoleon (1)

A prince need trouble little about conspiracies when the people are well disposed, but when they are hostile and hold him in hatred, then he must fear everything and everybody.

> MACHIAVELLI (1469–1527). *The Prince*, 19, 1513, tr. Luigi Ricci, 1903

Even though the prince has no originality, if he can recognize the bad and good works of his ministers and correct the one and encourage the other, then his ministers, knowing they cannot hope to deceive him, will remain good.

> MACHIAVELLI (1469–1527). Adapted. *The Prince*, 22, 1513, tr. Luigi Ricci, 1903

There is no other way of guarding one's self against flattery than by letting men understand that they will not offend you by speaking the truth; but when everyone can tell you the truth, you lose their respect. A prudent prince must therefore take a third course, by choosing for his council wise men, and giving these alone full liberty to speak the truth to him, but only of those things that he asks and of nothing else; but he must ask them about everything and hear their opinion, and afterwards deliberate by himself in his own way.

> MACHIAVELLI (1469–1527). *The Prince*, 23, 1513, tr. Luigi Ricci, 1903

A prince . . . ought to be a great asker and a patient listener of the truth about those things of which he has inquired; indeed, if he finds that anyone has scruples in telling him the truth he should be angry.

> MACHIAVELLI (1469–1527). *The Prince*, 23, 1513, tr. Luigi Ricci, 1903

It is an infallible rule that a prince who is not wise himself cannot be well-advised.

> MACHIAVELLI (1469–1527). *The Prince*, 23, 1513, tr. Luigi Ricci, 1903

A prince who fails to punish [evil-doers] so that they shall not be able to do any more harm will be regarded as either ignorant or cowardly.

> MACHIAVELLI (1469–1527). *The Discourses*, 2.23, 1517, tr. Christian E. Detmold, 1940

A prince . . . who wishes to guard against conspiracies should fear those on whom he has heaped benefits quite as much, and even more, than those whom he has wronged; for the latter lack the convenient opportunities which the former have in abundance. The intention of both is the same for the thirst of dominion is as great as that of revenge, and even greater. A prince, therefore, should never bestow so much authority upon his friends but that there should always be a certain distance between them and himself, and that there should always be something left for them to desire.

> MACHIAVELLI (1469–1527). *The Discourses*, 3.6, 1517, tr. Christian E. Detmold, 1940

The example of the prince is followed by the masses, who keep their eyes always upon their chief.

> LORENZO de MEDICI (1449–1492). In Machiavelli, *The Discourses*, 3.29, 1517, tr. Christian E. Detmold, 1940

A prince should suspect everything.

> NAPOLEON (1769–1821). *Napoleon in His Own Words*, 4, comp. Jules Bertaut, 1916

This maxim so necessary for princes—"always to sacrifice the little affairs to the greater."

> CARDINAL de RETZ (1613–1679). *Memoirs of Cardinal de Retz*, 2, Grolier Society edition, undated

A prince who wishes to achieve great things must learn to deceive.

> XENOPHON (431?–352? B.C.). Greek historian. As paraphrased by Machiavelli. *The Discourses*, 2.13, 1517, tr. Christian E. Detmold, 1940

PRINCIPLES, MORAL

See also • Achievement: Henry A. Kissinger ○ Creed ○ Doctrine ○ Ideals ○ Ideas ○ Killing: Henry Miller ○ Maxims ○ Meaning ○ Morality ○ Peace of Mind: Ralph Waldo Emerson ○ Philosophy ○ Principles, Theoretical ○ Proverbs ○ Purpose ○ Resolution: Thomas Paine ○ Systems ○ Values

It is always easier to fight for one's principles than to live up to them.

> ALFRED ADLER (1870–1937). Remark to a friend. In Phyllis Bottome, *Alfred Adler: A Biography,* 5, 1939
>
> See Martyrdom: William Makepeace Thackeray ○ Religion: Georg Christoph Lichtenberg (1)

Expedients are for the hour, but principles are for the ages.

> HENRY WARD BEECHER (1813–1887). "Morals," *Proverbs from Plymouth Pulpit,* ed. William Drysdale, 1887

There is probably no direct way to get in touch with our inner selves or to seek out satisfaction and happiness. It's best to live by sound principles—honesty, courage, liberty, and love—and then to await what unfolds. When, inevitably, we go astray for a time, we must return, once again, to living by the principles we cherish. The formula isn't all that difficult to understand; applying it is the work of a lifetime.

> PETER R. BREGGIN (1936–). *The Heart of Being Helpful: Empathy and the Creation of a Healing Presence,* 13, 1997

[Abraham Lincoln] stuck to general principles with bullheaded stubbornness, improvising the details as he went along, measuring his success by results alone.

> COURTLANDT CANBY. Ed., introduction to *Lincoln and the Civil War: A Profile and a History,* 1958

A people that values its privileges above its principles soon loses both.

> DWIGHT D. EISENHOWER (1890–1969). *First Inaugural Address,* 20 January 1953

Every principle is a war-note. Whoever attempts to carry out the rule of right and love and freedom must take his life in his hand.

> RALPH WALDO EMERSON (1803–1882). Journal, fall 1859

We may be personally defeated, but our principles never!

> WILLIAM LLOYD GARRISON (1805–1879). Declaration of Sentiments, Philadelphia, 6 December 1833. In Wendell Phillips Garrison and Francis Jackson Garrison, *William Lloyd Garrison, 1805–1879: The Story of His Life by His Children,* 1.12, 1884

To have doubted one's own first principles is the mark of a civilized man.

> OLIVER WENDELL HOLMES, JR. (1841–1935). "Ideals and Doubts," *Illinois Law Review,* May 1915

While we should never give up our principles, we must also realize that we cannot maintain our principles unless we survive.

> HENRY A. KISSINGER (1923–). "Reflections on American Diplomacy" (2), *Foreign Affairs,* October 1956

Important principles may, and must, be inflexible.

> ABRAHAM LINCOLN (1809–1865). Last public address, Washington, 11 April 1865

I *don't* believe in princerple
But O, I *du* in interest.

> JAMES RUSSELL LOWELL (1819–1891). *The Bigelow Papers: First Series,* 6, 1848

A return to first principles in a republic is sometimes caused by the simple virtues of one man. . . . [H]is good example has such an influence that the good men strive to imitate him, and the wicked are ashamed to lead a life so contrary to his example.

> MACHIAVELLI (1469–1527). *The Discourses,* 3.1, 1517, tr. Christian E. Detmold, 1940

The most useful thing about a principle is that it can always be sacrificed to expediency.

> W. SOMERSET MAUGHAM (1874–1965). *The Circle,* 3, 1921

Our differences are policies; our agreements, principles.

> WILLIAM McKINLEY (1843–1901). Speech, Des Moines (Iowa), 1901

The citizen is influenced by principle in direct proportion to his distance from the political situation.

> MILTON RAKOVE. Stating "Rakove's law of principle and politics." In *Virginia Quarterly Review,* vol. 41, 1965

All the great things of humanity have been accomplished in the name of absolute principles.

> ERNEST RENAN (1823–1892). *The Life of Jesus,* 20, 1863, Modern Library edition, 1927

Prosperity is the best protector of principle.

> MARK TWAIN (1835–1910). *Following the Equator: A Journey Around the World,* 38 (epigraph), 1897

PRINCIPLES, THEORETICAL

See also • Circumstances ○ Events ○ Ideas ○ Maxims ○ Philosophy ○ Principles, Moral ○ Proverbs ○ Theories ○ Systems

Exceptions rule.

> ANTHONY'S OBSERVATION. In John Peers, comp., *1,001 Logical Laws,* p. 17, 1979

All generalizations are false, including this one.

> ALEXANDER CHASE. *Perspectives,* 1966

Principles and rules are intended to provide a thinking man with a frame of reference.

> KARL von CLAUSEWITZ (1780–1831). In Harry G. Summers, Jr., *On Strategy: A Critical Analysis of the Vietnam War,* 6, 1982

General principles . . . are to the facts as the root and sap of a tree [are] to its leaves.

> SAMUEL TAYLOR COLERIDGE (1772–1834). *The Statesman's Manual; The Bible the Best Guide to Political Skill and Foresight: A Lay Sermon Addressed to the Higher Classes of Society,* p. 13, 1816

My mind seems to have become a kind of machine for grinding general laws out of large collections of facts.

> CHARLES DARWIN (1809–1882). 1 May 1881, *The Autobiography of Charles Darwin and Selected Letters,* 2, ed. Francis Darwin, 1892

Exceptions are not always the proof of the old rule; they can also be the harbinger of a new one.

> MARIE von EBNER-ESCHENBACH (1830–1916). *Aphorisms*, p. 40, 1880–1905, tr. David Scrase and Wolfgang Mieder, 1994

The value of a principle is the number of things it will explain.

> RALPH WALDO EMERSON (1803–1882). "The Preacher," *Lectures and Biographical Sketches*, 1883

The grasp of principle which makes detail easy can only come when innate capacity has been evoked and molded by high training.

> RICHARD B. HALDANE (1856–1928). "Leaders and Specialists," 1913, *Selected Addresses and Essays*, 1928

Rules and models destroy genius and art.

> WILLIAM HAZLITT (1778–1830). "On Taste," *Sketches and Essays*, 1839

Every science has for its basis a system of principles as fixed and unalterable as those by which the universe is regulated and governed. Man cannot make principles; he can only discover them.

> THOMAS PAINE (1737–1809). *The Age of Reason: Being an Investigation of True and Fabulous Theology*, 1, 1794

A precedent embalms a principle.

> WILLIAM SCOTT (1745–1836). English jurist. In Benjamin Disraeli, House of Commons speech, 22 February 1848

The way is long if one follows precepts, but short . . . if one follows patterns.

> SENECA THE YOUNGER (5? B.C.–A.D. 65). "On Sharing Knowledge," *Moral Letters to Lucilius*, 6.5, tr. Richard M. Gummere, 1918

A principle—as its very name implies—is something which comes first. A principle is a master key which opens a thousand locks; a compass which will guide you, even on an uncharted sea.

> E. M. STANDING (1887–?). Preface to *Maria Montessori: Her Life and Work*, 1957

There are no absolute rules of conduct, either in peace or war. Everything depends on circumstances.

> LEON TROTSKY (1879–1940). *My Life*, 35, 1930, Universal Library edition, 1960

❦

The exception proves the rule.

> SAYING

PRISON

See also • Crime ○ Dehumanization ○ Justice ○ Punishment

Jails and prisons are designed to break human beings, to convert the population into specimens in a zoo—obedient to our keepers, but dangerous to each other.

> ANGELA DAVIS (1944–). "Reflections on the Black Woman's Roles in the Community of Slaves," *Black Scholar*, December 1971

[Felon's] minds should be broken on the rack and wheel, instead of their bodies, and they can only have their obstinate and guilty principles crushed and destroyed by severe treatment.

> F. GRAY (19th cent.). Defending the new social experiment called imprisonment, *Prison Discipline in America*, 1847. In Alan W. Scheflin and Edward M. Opton, Jr., *The Mind Manipulators: A Non-Fiction Account*, 2, 1978

Have not prisons—which kill all will and force of character in man, which enclose within their walls more vices than are met with on any other spot of the globe—always been universities of crime?

> PETER KROPOTKIN (1842–1921). *Anarchism: Its Philosophy and Ideal* (pamphlet), 1896, *Kropotkin's Revolutionary Pamphlets*, ed. Roger N. Baldwin, 1927

A governor of a certain state was visiting the state prison, and stopped to talk with a number of prisoners. They told him their story, and in every instance it was one of wrong suffered by an innocent person. There was one man, however, who admitted his crime and the justice of his sentence. "I must pardon you," said the governor; "I can't have you in here corrupting all these good men."

> ABRAHAM LINCOLN (1809–1865). In Brant House, comp., "1864," *Lincoln's Wit*, 1958

In Totalitaria, jails and concentration camps by the score are built in order to provoke fear and awe among the population. . . . In these centers of fear, nobody is really corrected; he is, as it were, expelled from humanity, wasted, killed—but not too quickly, lest the terrorizing influence be diminished. The truth of the matter is that these jails are built not for real criminals, but rather for their terrorizing effect on the bystanders, the citizens of Totalitaria.

> JOOST A. M. MEERLOO (1903–1976). *The Rape of the Mind: The Psychology of Thought Control, Menticide, and Brainwashing*, 7, 1956

The Kolyma was the greatest and most famous island, the pole of ferocity of that amazing country of *Gulag* which, though scattered in an Archipelago geographically, was, in the psychological sense, fused into a continent—an almost invisible, almost imperceptible country inhabited by the zek people.

And this Archipelago crisscrossed and patterned that other country within which it was located, like a gigantic patchwork, cutting into its cities, hovering over its streets. Yet there were many who did not even guess at its presence and many, many others who had heard something vague. And only those who had been there knew the whole truth.

But, as though stricken dumb on the islands of the Archipelago, they kept their silence.

> ALEKSANDR SOLZHENITSYN (1918–). Preface to *The Gulag Archipelago 1918–1956: An Experiment in Literary Investigation*, tr. Thomas P. Whitney, 1973

Many Alabamans delight in the chain gangs' reappearance. Drivers roll down their windows to taunt the prisoners, barking like dogs. Others look on the predominantly black gangs and feel nostalgia for the South they knew as children. "I love seeing 'em in chains," one elderly white woman said, "They ought to make them pick cotton."

> BRENT STAPLES. "The Chain Gang Show: Humiliating Prisoners, for Political Profit," *New York Times Magazine*, 17 September 1995

What would help in prisons would be educational opportunity for cooperative prisoners in a meditative environment, with job programs and small-business support in the communities on the outside. Instead we pay rich contractors to build enormously expensive kennels, with jobs for guards from the middle class.

Thinking of the poor as human and prison as rehabilitation makes sense if we are really interested in reducing crime. More prisons and longer sentences might be harder on criminals, but they are softer on crime.

> VIVIENNE VERDON-ROE. Bolinas, California. Letter to *New York Times,* 4 November 1994

You felons on trial in courts,
You convicts in prison cells, you sentenced assassins chain'd and
  handcuff'd with iron,
Who am I too that I am not on trial or in prison?
Me ruthless and devilish as any, that my wrists are not chain'd
  with iron, or my ankles with iron?

> WALT WHITMAN (1819–1892). "You Felons on Trial in Courts," 1860, *Leaves of Grass,* 1855–1892

I know not whether Laws be right,
  Or whether Laws be wrong;
All that we know who lie in gaol
  Is that the wall is strong;
And that each day is like a year,
  A year whose days are long.

> OSCAR WILDE (1854–1900). *The Ballad of Reading Gaol,* 5.1, 1898

✹

Remember those who are in prison, as though in prison with them.

> ANONYMOUS (*BIBLE*). *Hebrews* 13:3

PRIVACY

See Right to Privacy

PROBLEMS & SOLUTIONS

See also • Advice: Patanjali ○ Decision-Making ○ Difficulty ○ Questions & Answers ○ Wisdom: Bertrand Russell (2)

I have yet to see any problem, however complicated, which, when you looked at it in the right way, did not become still more complicated.

> PAUL ALDERSON. In William Thorpe, "Reductionism v. Organicism," *New Scientist,* 25 September 1969

There is no such thing as a single problem; . . . all problems are interrelated.

> SAUL D. ALINSKY (1909–1972). *Reveille for Radicals,* 11, 1969

You're either part of the solution or you're part of the problem.

> ELDRIDGE CLEAVER (1935–1998). Speech before the San Francisco Barristers' Club, September 1968. In editor's introduction to *Eldridge Cleaver: Post Prison Writings and Speeches,* ed. Robert Scheer, 1969

Problems that go away by themselves come back by themselves.

> MARCY E. DAVIS. "Davis's Dictum." In Paul Dickson, comp., *The Official Explanations,* p. 46, 1980

The older I get, the more wisdom I find in the ancient rule of taking first things first—a process which often reduces the most complex human problems to manageable proportions.

> DWIGHT D. EISENHOWER (1890–19969). "Let's Be Honest with Ourselves," *Reader's Digest,* December 1963

Len says one steady pull more ought to do it.
He says the best way out is always through.

> ROBERT FROST (1874–1963). "A Servant to Servants," *North of Boston,* 1914

If thy Business be perplexed, divide it, and look upon all its Parts and sides.

> THOMAS FULLER (1654–1734). Comp., *Introductio ad Prudentiam,* 583, 1731

At the bottom of every social problem we will find a social wrong.

> HENRY GEORGE (1839–1897). *Social Problems,* 1, 1883

To see a problem clearly is three parts of the way to solving it.

> J. A. HADFIELD (1882–1967). *Dreams and Nightmares,* 4, 1954

You can only hope to find a lasting solution to a conflict if you have learned to see the other [person] objectively, but, at the same time, to experience his difficulties subjectively.

> DAG HAMMARSKJÖLD (1905–1961). 1955, *Markings,* tr. Leif Sjöberg and W. H. Auden, 1964

Problems worthy
  of attack
prove their worth
  by hitting back.

> PIET HEIN (1905–). "Problems," *Grooks,* 1966

Problems increase in geometric ratio; solutions, in arithmetic ratio.

> CHARLES ISSAWI. "Issawi's Laws of Social Motion," *Columbia Forum,* Summer 1970

There are no problems we cannot solve together, and very few we can solve by ourselves.

> LYNDON B. JOHNSON (1908–1973). News conference, Johnson City (Texas), 28 November 1964

[Life's greatest problems] can never by solved but only outgrown.

> CARL G. JUNG (1875–1961). Introduction (2) to *Commentary* (on *The Secret of the Golden Flower*), 1929, tr. Cary F. Baynes, 1961

To ask the right question is already half the solution of a problem.

> CARL G. JUNG (1875–1961). "Archetypes of the Collective Unconscious," 1934, *The Archetypes and the Collective Unconscious,* tr. R. F. C. Hull, 1959

Problems are only opportunities in work clothes.

> HENRY KAISER (1882–1967)

No problem of human destiny is beyond human beings.

> JOHN F. KENNEDY (1917–1963). Address, American University, Washington, 10 June 1963

The best way to solve any problem is to remove its cause.

> MARTIN LUTHER KING, JR. (1929–1968). *Stride Toward Freedom*, 11, 1958

All too frequently a problem evaded is a crisis invited.

> HENRY A. KISSINGER (1923–). *Years of Upheaval*, 16, 1982

There is at bottom only one problem in the world. . . . How does one break through? How does one get into the open? How does one burst the cocoon and become a butterfly?

> THOMAS MANN (1875–1955). *Doctor Faustus*, 1947. In Robert Lindner, *Prescription for Rebellion*, 10 (epigraph), 1952

Don't fight the problem. Decide it!

> GEORGE C. MARSHALL (1880–1959). A repeated precept. In Dean Acheson, *Present at the Creation: My Years in the State Department*, 76, 1969

May we, God helping us, be part of the answer, not part of the problem.

> PETER MARSHALL (1902–1949). In "Quotable Quotes," *Reader's Digest*, October 1966

Mankind never sets problems for itself which it cannot solve.

> KARL MARX (1818–1883). In Allan Bloom, "Our Ignorance," *The Closing of the American Mind: How Higher Education Has Failed Democracy and Impoverished the Souls of Today's Students*, 1987

There is always an easy solution to every human problem—neat, plausible, and wrong.

> H. L. MENCKEN (1880–1956). "The Divine Afflatus, *Prejudices: Second Series*, 1920

Know that many personal troubles cannot be solved merely as troubles, but must be understood in terms of public issues—and in terms of the problems of history-making. Know that the human meaning of public issues must be revealed by relating them to personal troubles— and to the problems of the individual life.

> C. WRIGHT MILLS (1916–1962). Appendix (4) to *The Sociological Imagination*, 1959

The real problem of our existence lies in the fact that we ought to love one another, but do not.

> REINHOLD NIEBUHR (1892–1971). *Christian Realism and Political Problems*, 8, 1953

The solution to a problem changes the nature of the problem.

> JOHN PEERS. "Peers's Law," introduction to *1,001 Logical Laws*, 1979

The true problems of living—in politics, economics, education, marriage, etc.—are always problems of overcoming or reconciling opposites. They are divergent problems and have no solution in the ordinary sense of the word. They demand of man not merely the employment of his reasoning powers but the commitment of his whole personality.

> E. F. SCHUMACHER (1911–1977). *Small Is Beautiful: Economics as if People Mattered*, 2.1, 1973

Lady Macbeth: Things without all remedy
Should be without regard: what's done is done.

> SHAKESPEARE (1564–1616). *Macbeth*, 3.2.11, 1605

No real problem has a solution.

> SMITH'S LAW. In Arthur Bloch, comp., "Problematics," *Murphy's Law: Book Three*, 1982

Clinging to the past is the problem. Embracing change is the answer.

> GLORIA STEINEM (1934–). "Doing Sixty," *Moving Beyond Words*, 1994

All social and political problems are interwoven—that energy, for example, affects economics, which in turn affects health, which in turn affects education, work, family life, and a thousand other things. The attempt to deal with neatly defined problems in isolation from one another . . . creates only confusion and disaster.

> ALVIN TOFFLER (1928–). *The Third Wave*, 27, 1980

[My teacher] H. J. Haselfoot . . . taught me the sovereign intellectual art of deliberately taking time—even when time is short—to let the mind play round a problem and try to grasp it as a whole before plunging into any attempt to solve it in detail.

> ARNOLD J. TOYNBEE (1889–1975). *A Study of History*, 10.226, 1954

If this stone won't budge at present and is wedged in, move some of the other stones round it first.

> LUDWIG WITTGENSTEIN (1889–1951). 1940, *Culture and Value*, 1977, tr. Peter Winch, 1980

❧

If all you've got is a hammer, nearly everything looks like a nail.

> SAYING

No problema!

> SAYING. In James Cameron and William Wisher, *Terminator II* (film), 1991, spoken (repeatedly) by Arnold Schwarzenegger

Solutions multiply problems.

> SAYING

The easiest solutions are tried last.

> SAYING

PROCRASTINATION

See also • Action ∘ Delay ∘ Idleness ∘ Laziness ∘ Patience ∘ Punctuality ∘ Time

Never do today what you can do as well tomorrow; because something may occur to make you regret your premature action.

> AARON BURR (1756–1836)

Know the true value of time; snatch, seize, and enjoy every moment of it. No idleness, no laziness, no procrastination; never put off till tomorrow what you can do today.

> LORD CHESTERFIELD (1694–1773). Letter to his son, 26 December 1749

Tomorrow, every Fault is to be amended;
but that Tomorrow never comes.

> BENJAMIN FRANKLIN (1706–1790). *Poor Richard's Almanack*, July 1756

What may be done at any Time will be done at no Time.

> THOMAS FULLER (1654–1734). Comp., *Gnomologia: Adages and Proverbs*, 5500, 1732

Postponement: The father of failure.
> ELBERT HUBBARD (1856–1915). *The Roycroft Dictionary Concocted by Ali Baba and the Bunch on Rainy Days,* p. 117, 1914

Never put off till tomorrow the fun you can have today.
> ALDOUS HUXLEY (1894–1963). *Brave New World,* 6.1, 1932

procrastination is the
art of keeping
up with yesterday.
> DON MARQUIS (1878–1937). "certain maxims of archy," *archy and mehitabel,* 1927

Never put off till tomorrow what you can avoid altogether.
> PRESTON'S AXIOM. In John Peers, comp., *1,001 Logical Laws,* p. 64, 1979

I never put off till tomorrow what I can possibly do . . . the day after.
> OSCAR WILDE (1854–1900). In Hesketh Pearson, *Oscar Wilde: His Life and Wit,* 12, 1946

Procrastination is the thief of time.
> EDWARD YOUNG (1683–1765). *The Complaint: or, Night Thoughts on Life, Death, and Immortality,* 1.394, 1742–1745
> See Punctuality: Oscar Wilde

❦

If it weren't for the last minute, nothing would get done.
> ANONYMOUS

One of these days is none of these days.
> SAYING (ENGLISH)

The road of by and by leads to the house of never.
> SAYING (SPANISH)

PROFESSIONALS

See also • Clergy ○ Doctors ○ Economists ○ Executives ○ Experts ○ Intellectuals ○ Lawyers ○ Philosophers ○ Physicians ○ Politicians ○ Surgeons

Incomprehensible jargon is the hallmark of a profession.
> KINGMAN BREWSTER, JR. (1919–). Speech before the British Institute of Management, 13 December 1977

It is hard to say whether the doctors of law or divinity have made the greater advances in the lucrative business of mystery.
> EDMUND BURKE (1729–1797). *A Vindication of Natural Society,* p. 88, M. Cooper edition, 1756

The professions are be definition—or perhaps we should say by aspiration—autonomous, and not beholden to the mighty. Otherwise they would have no legitimacy in the public's eye: Claims to professional objectivity and neutrality cannot be made from an actual position of servility.
> BARBARA EHRENREICH (1941–). *Fear of Falling: The Inner Life of the Middle Class,* 4, 1990

The trail of the serpent reaches into all the lucrative professions and practices of man. Each has its own wrongs. Each finds a ten-der and very intelligent conscience a disqualification for success. Each requires of the practitioner a certain shutting of the eyes, a certain dapperness and compliance, an acceptance of customs, a sequestration from the sentiments of generosity and love, a compromise of private opinion and lofty integrity.
> RALPH WALDO EMERSON (1803–1882). "Man the Reformer," lecture, Masonic Temple, Boston, 25 January 1841

Being a professional is doing all the things you love to do on the days when you don't feel like doing them.
> JULIUS ERVING (1950–). Basketball player. Quoted by David Halberstam, Charlie Rose television interview, PBS, 23 July 1993

It is wonderful, when a calculation is made, how little the mind is actually employed in the discharge of any profession.
> SAMUEL JOHNSON (1709–1784). 6 April 1775. In James Boswell, *The Life of Samuel Johnson,* 1791

The essence of a genuine professional man is that he cannot be bought.
> H. L. MENCKEN (1880–1956). "On Getting a Living," *Baltimore Evening Sun,* 12 May 1924

Professional men, they have no cares;
Whatever happens, they get theirs.
> OGDEN NASH (1902–1971). "I Yield to My Learned Brother, or Is There a Candlestick Maker in the House?" *Many Long Years Ago,* 1945

All professions are conspiracies against the laity.
> GEORGE BERNARD SHAW (1856–1950). *The Doctor's Dilemma,* 1, 1906

❦

Professionals built the *Titanic,* amateurs built the ark.
> ANONYMOUS

The more doctors, the more disease; the more lawyers, the more crime; the more philosophers, the more folly; the more priests, the more sin.
> ANONYMOUS

PROFIT & LOSS

See also • Business (Commerce) ○ Capitalism ○ Defeat ○ Economics ○ Merchants & Customers ○ Money ○ Price ○ Stock Market ○ Trade (Commerce) ○ Victory

When opportunities for profit diminish, opportunities for jobs likewise disappear.
> AMERICAN FEDERATION OF LABOR. Resolution of the Executive Council, 31 January 1940

It seems to be a law in American life that whatever enriches us anywhere except in the wallet inevitably becomes uneconomic.
> RUSSELL BAKER (1925–). "Save the Zephyr," *New York Times,* 24 March 1968

People before Profits.
> LLOYD BENTSEN (1921–). Democratic vice presidential campaign slogan, 1988

Watch the costs and the profits will take care of themselves.

> ANDREW CARNEGIE (1835–1919). A favorite saying. Quoted in
> *The American Experience,* television documentary series, PBS,
> 20 January 1997
> See Thrift: Saying (English) (2)

It is a socialist idea that making profits is a vice; I consider the real vice is making losses.

> WINSTON CHURCHILL (1874–1965)

Profit is the result of risks wisely selected.

> FREDERICK BARNARD HAWLEY. *Enterprise and the Productive Process,*
> 6, 1907

Shun evil profit, for dishonest gain
Is just the same as failure.

> HESIOD (8th cent. B.C.). *Works and Days,* l. 352, tr. Dorothea Wender,
> 1973
> See Money: Horace ○ Victory & Defeat: Saying (Arab)

In the state of nature profit is the measure of right.

> THOMAS HOBBES (1588–1679). *Philosophical Rudiments Concerning
> Government and Society,* 1, 1651

What affects us most is the gain and loss not in substance but in self-esteem.

> ERIC HOFFER (1902–1983). *The Passionate State of Mind: And Other
> Aphorisms,* 229, 1954

The stink of profit is sweet
Whatever its source.

> JUVENAL (A.D. 60–? 127?). *Satires,* 14.202, tr. Peter Green, 1967

The engine which drives Enterprise is not Thrift, but Profit.

> JOHN MAYNARD KEYNES (1883–1946). *A Treatise on Money,* 3, 1930

You think that the only thing that counts is the bottom line! What a presumptuous thing to say. The bottom line is in heaven.

> EDWIN H. LAND (1909–1991). Inventor and founder of Poloroid Corp.
> Responding to a question about the "bottom line" implications of a
> new product (Polavision), shareholders' annual meeting, 26 April 1977

To put pressure upon the destitute for the sake of gain and to make a profit out of the need of another is condemned by all laws, human or divine.

> POPE LEO XIII (1810–1903). *Rerum Novarum (On the Condition of
> Workers),* 15 May 1891

The cause of profit is that labor produces more than is required for its support.

> JOHN STUART MILL (1806–1873). *Principles of Political Economy with
> Some of Their Applications to Social Philosophy,* 1.15.5, 1848

That cold, still statistic of profit and loss is a statement about someone's happiness and someone else's pain.

> CARL OGLESBY (1935–). *Containment and Change: Two Dissenting
> Views of American Foreign Policy,* 4, 1967

There are occasions when it is undoubtedly better to incur loss than to make gain.

> PLAUTUS (254–184 B.C.). *The Captives,* 2.2.77, tr. Henry Thomas Riley,
> 1894 (Popular version: Sometimes the best gain is to lose.)

Profits in trade can be made only by another's loss.

> PUBLIUS SYRUS (85–43 B.C.). *Moral Sayings,* 435, tr. Darius Lyman, Jr.,
> 1862 (Popular version: One's gain is another's loss.)

In [Carthage], no crime that leads to gain is considered shameful.

> POLYBIUS (208?–126? B.C.). *The Histories,* 6.56, tr. Mortimer Chambers,
> 1966

Nothing contributes so much to the prosperity and happiness of a country as high profits.

> DAVID RICARDO (1772–1823). *On Protection to Agriculture,* 5, 1822

One loses, all lose; one gains, all gain.

> SAYING
> See Unity: Mohandas K. Gandhi

PROGRESS

See also • Beginnings & Endings ○ Censorship: George Bernard Shaw ○ Change ○ Civilization ○ Creativity ○ Discontent: Thomas Alva Edison ○ Evolution ○ Friends: Seneca the Younger ○ History ○ Individuality: Mohandas K. Gandhi ○ Invention ○ Life ○ Man ○ Minorities: H. L. Mencken ○ Nonviolence ○ Problems & Solutions ○ Purpose ○ Reform ○ Science ○ Self-Realization (Being) ○ Success ○ Technology ○ World

Frozen food is not progress.

> RUSSELL BAKER (1925–). 29 September, *Poor Russell's Almanac,*
> 1972

In order that progress be realized, perhaps it is necessary that all evil alternatives be exhausted.

> LOUIS BLANC (1811–1882)

Progress is
The law of life—man is not man as yet.

> ROBERT BROWNING (1812–1889). *Paracelsus,* 5.729, 1835

All progress is based upon a universal innate desire on the part of every organism to live beyond its income.

> SAMUEL BUTLER (1835–1902), *The Note-Books of Samuel Butler,* 1, ed.
> Henry Festing Jones, 1907

Progress in history, unlike evolution in nature, rests on the transmission of acquired assets. These assets include both material possessions and the capacity to master, transform, and utilize one's environment. Indeed, the two factors are closely interconnected, and react on one another.

> EDWARD HALLETT CARR (1892–1982). *What Is History?* 5, 1961

Man in this moment of his history has emerged in greater supremacy over the forces of nature than has ever been dreamed of before. He has it in his power to solve quite easily the problems of material existence. He has conquered the wild beasts, and he has even conquered the insect and microbes. There lies before him, as he wishes, a golden age of peace and progress. All is in his hand. He has only to conquer his last and worst enemy—himself. With vision, faith and courage, it may be within our power to win a crowning victory for all.

> WINSTON CHURCHILL (1874–1965). House of Commons speech,
> 28 March 1950

Our moral progress may be measured by the degree in which we sympathize with individual suffering and individual joy.

> GEORGE ELIOT (1819–1880). In John Morley, "The Life of George Eliot," *Critical Miscellanies,* vol. 3, 1886

Not fare well,
But fare forward, voyagers.

> T. S. ELIOT (1888–1965). "The Dry Salvages" (3), *Four Quartets,* 1943
> See Effort: Eliot (1)

As usual, what we call "Progress" is the exchange of one Nuisance for another Nuisance.

> HAVELOCK ELLIS (1859–1939). 31 July 1912, *Fountain of Life: Being the Impressions and Comments of Havelock Ellis,* 1930

Liberty is an accurate index, in men and nations, of general progress.

> RALPH WALDO EMERSON (1803–1882). "The Fugitive Slave Law." Address, The Tabernacle, New York City, 7 March 1854

Change is not always progress. . . . A fever of newness has been everywhere confused with the spirit of progress.

> HENRY FORD (1863–1947). In Daniel J. Boorstin, *Democracy and Its Discontents: Reflections on Everyday America,* 9, 1975

The progress of society rests upon the opposition between succeeding generations.

> SIGMUND FREUD (1856–1939). In Bruce Mazlish, "The Mills: Father and Son," *Horizon,* Summer 1970

All progress is gained through mistakes and their rectification. No good comes fully fashioned, out of God's hand, but has to be carved out through repeated experiments and repeated failures by ourselves. This is the law of individual growth. The same law controls social and political evolution also. The right to err, which means the freedom to try experiments, is the universal condition of all progress.

> MOHANDAS K. GANDHI (1869–1948). *M. K. Gandhi: Speeches and Writings,* p. 245, 1918

Each step upward makes me feel stronger and fit for the next step.

> MOHANDAS K. GANDHI (1869–1948). In *Young India,* 9 April 1925

Progress is our most important product.

> GENERAL ELECTRIC CORP. Motto

So long as all the increased wealth which modern progress brings goes but to build up great fortunes, to increase luxury and make sharper the contrast between the House of Have and the House of Want, progress is not real and cannot be permanent. The reaction must come. The tower leans from its foundation, and every new story but hastens the final catastrophe.

> HENRY GEORGE (1839–1897). "Introductory: The Problem," *Progress and Poverty: An Inquiry into the Cause of Industrial Depressions and of Increase of Want with Increase of Wealth,* 1879

All that is human must retrograde if it [does] not advance.

> EDWARD GIBBON (1737–1794). *The Decline and Fall of the Roman Empire,* 71, 1776–1788

Progress has not followed a straight ascending line, but a spiral with rhythms of progress and regression, of evolution and dissolution.

> GOETHE (1749–1832)

Progress, and at the same time resistance.

> FRANCIS GUIZOT (1787–1874). French historian. In Herbert Spencer, *Social Statics,* 4.31.5, 1851

Human development is a form of chronological unfairness, since late-comers are able to profit by the labors of their predecessors without paying the same price.

> ALEKSANDR HERZEN (1812–1870). In Hannah Arendt, *On Violence,* 1, 1970

We are not going [around] in circles, we are going upwards. The path is a spiral.

> HERMANN HESSE (1877–1962). *Siddhartha,* 1 ("With the Samanas"), 1922, tr. Hilda Rosner, 1951

The control of our being is not unlike the combination of a safe. One turn of the knob rarely unlocks the safe. Each advance and retreat is a step toward one's goal.

> ERIC HOFFER (1902–1983). *The Passionate State of Mind: And Other Aphorisms,* 196, 1954

The impulse to escape an untenable situation often prompts human beings not to shrink back but to plunge ahead.

> ERIC HOFFER (1902–1983). *The Ordeal of Change,* 15.5, 1964

Up to now, whenever a society turned a new leaf, it had the devil at its elbow.

> ERIC HOFFER (1902–1983). *Reflections on the Human Condition,* 38, 1973

I find the great thing in this world is not so much where we stand, as in what direction we are moving: To reach the port of heaven, we must sail sometimes with the wind and sometimes against it— but we must sail, and not drift, nor lie at anchor.

> OLIVER WENDELL HOLMES, SR. (1809–1894). *The Autocrat at the Breakfast-Table,* 4, 1858

Industrialism is the systematic exploitation of wasting assets. In all too many cases, the thing we call progress is merely an acceleration in the rate of that exploitation.

> ALDOUS HUXLEY (1894–1963). "The Double Crisis," *Themes and Variations,* 1950

Every great advance in natural knowledge has involved the absolute rejection of authority, the cherishing of the keenest skepticism, the annihilation of the spirit of blind faith.

> T. H. HUXLEY (1825–1895). "On the Advisableness of Improving Natural Knowledge," 1866, *Lay Sermons, Addresses and Reviews,* 1870

Human progress never rolls in on wheels of inevitability. It comes through the tireless efforts and persistent work of men willing to be co-workers with God, and without this hard work, time itself becomes an ally of the forces of social stagnation.

> MARTIN LUTHER KING, JR. (1929–1968). "Letter from Birmingham City Jail," 16 April 1963

Periods of confused anarchy . . . seem always destined to precede the birth of every new society.

> GUSTAVE LE BON (1841–1931). Introduction to *The Crowd: A Study of the Popular Mind,* 1895, Viking Press edition, 1960

Is it progress if a cannibal uses knife and fork?

    STANISLAW J. LEC (1909–1966). *Unkempt Thoughts*, p. 78, tr. Jacek
    Galazka, 1962

Persevering in one's existence is the particular quality of the
organism; it is not a progress towards achievement, followed by
stasis, which is the machine's mode, but an interactive, rhythmic,
and unstable process, which constitutes an end in itself.

    URSULA K. LE GUIN (1929–). "A Non-Euclidean View of California as a
    Cold Place to Be," 1982, *Dancing at the Edge of the World: Thoughts
    on Words, Women, Places,* 1989

One step forward, two steps back. . . . It happens in the lives of
individuals, and it happens in the history of nations and in the
development of parties.

    LENIN (1870–1924). *One Step Forward, Two Steps Backward* (pam-
    phlet), 1904

The spiritual development of humanity as a whole is like a pyramid, or a mountain peak, where all angles of ascent tend to converge the higher they climb.

    B. H. LIDDELL HART (1895–1970). "The Problem of Religion and World
    Order," *Why Don't We Learn from History?* 1944

For collective action it suffices if the mass can be managed; collective growth is only possible through the freedom and enlargement of individual minds.

    B. H. LIDDELL HART (1895–1970). "Some Conclusions," *Why Don't We
    Learn from History?* 1944

Human affairs [are] in a state of perpetual movement, always
either ascending or declining.

    MACHIAVELLI (1469–1527). *The Discourses.* Introduction to the Second
    Book, 1517, tr. Christian E. Detmold, 1940

No great improvements in the lot of mankind are possible until a
great change takes place in the fundamental constitution of their
modes of thought.

    JOHN STUART MILL (1806–1873). *Autobiography,* 7, 1873

    See Nuclear Weapons: Albert Einstein (3)

Progress . . . depends on the play of forces within the community and external to it. It depends on the room left by the state for
the enterprise, energy, and initiative of the individual. . . . It
depends on no single element in social being, but on the confluence of many tributaries in a great tidal stream of history.

    JOHN MORLEY (1838–1923). *Notes on Politics and History: A University
    Address,* 7, 1913

Faith in the creative process, in the dynamics of emergence, in the
values and purposes that transcend past achievements and past
forms, is the precondition of all further growth.

    LEWIS MUMFORD (1895–1990). *The Conduct of Life,* 8.6, 1951

[Human progress] unites the person and the community; and one
is not less necessary than the other. For without the social process
the individual effort would be lost, and without the individual bid
for freedom society would be curbed and confined, as most historic civilizations have in fact been confined, by its very success.

    LEWIS MUMFORD (1895–1990). *The Transformations of Man,* 4.6, 1956

He has drawn back, only in order to have enough room for his leap.

    FRIEDRICH NIETZSCHE (1844–1900). *Human, All Too Human,* 273, 1878,
    tr. Marion Faber, 1984

It is not sufficient that man should be able to free himself from what
he is already and take on a new form, as the serpent sloughs its skin
and is left with another. Progress demands that this new form
should rise above the old and to this end should preserve it and
turn it to account, that it should take off from the old, climbing on
its shoulders as a high temperature mounts on lower [temperatures].
To progress is to accumulate being, to store up reality.

    JOSÉ ORTEGA y GASSET (1883–1955). *Toward a Philosophy of History,*
    1941. In Hans Meyerhoff, ed., *The Philosophy of History in Our Time,*
    1959

Nature acts by progress. . . . It goes and returns, then advances further, then twice as much backwards, then more forward than ever,
etc.

    BLAISE PASCAL (1623–1662). *Pensées,* 355, 1670, tr. William F. Trotter,
    1931

Every step of progress the world has made has been from scaffold
to scaffold and from stake to stake.

    WENDELL PHILLIPS (1811–1884). Speech for women's rights, Worcester
    (Massachusetts), 15 October 1851

All criticism consists in pointing out some contradictions or dis-
crepancies, and scientific progress consists largely in the elimination
of contradictions wherever we find them.

    KARL R. POPPER (1902–1994). *The Open Society and Its Enemies,* 2.12.2,
    1945

The reason why the race of man moves slowly is because it must
move all together.

    THOMAS BRACKETT REED (1839–1902). Speech, Waterville (Maine),
    30 July 1885

The test of our progress is not whether we add more to the abundance of those who have much; it is whether we provide enough
for those who have too little.

    FRANKLIN D. ROOSEVELT (1882–1945). *Second Inaugural Address,* 20
    January 1937

The free intellect is the chief engine of human progress.

    BERTRAND RUSSELL (1872–1970). *The Practice and Theory of
    Bolshevism,* 2nd ed., 8, 1948

Progress . . . requires the utmost scope for personal initiative that is
compatible with social order.

    BERTRAND RUSSELL (1872–1970). *Authority and the Individual,* 6, 1949

All the important human advances that we know of since historical
times began have been due to individuals of whom the majority
faced virulent public opposition.

    BERTRAND RUSSELL (1872–1970). Woodrow Wyatt television interview,
    BBC, London, 1959, *Bertrand Russell Speaks His Mind,* 10, 1960

We are drawn back in order to be propelled forward like an arrow
from a bow.

    HUGH SCHONFIELD (1901–1988). Introduction to *The Essene Odyssey:
    The Mystery of the True Teacher and the Essene Impact on the
    Shaping of Human Destiny,* 1984

The absolute impossibility of the continuance of the state in its present condition must become the universal conviction before things can become in any way better.

> ALBERT SCHWEITZER (1875–1965). *The Philosophy of Civilization: Civilization and Ethics,* 22, 1923, tr. C. T. Campion and Mrs. Charles E. B. Russell, 1946

Every step of progress means a duty repudiated, and a scripture torn up.

> GEORGE BERNARD SHAW (1856–1950). "The Two Pioneers," *The Quintessence of Ibsenism,* 1891

The period of time covered by history is far too short to allow of any perceptible progress in the popular sense of Evolution of the Human Species. The notion that there has been any such Progress since Caesar's time (less than 20th centuries ago) is too absurd for discussion. All the savagery, barbarism, dark ages and the rest of it of which we have any record as existing in the past exists at the present moment.

> GEORGE BERNARD SHAW (1856–1950). Notes ("Apparent Anachronisms") to *Caesar and Cleopatra,* 1899

The reasonable man adapts himself to the world: the unreasonable one persists in trying to adapt the world to himself. Therefore all progress depends on the unreasonable man.

> GEORGE BERNARD SHAW (1856–1950). "Maxims for Revolutionists: Reason," *Man and Superman,* 1903

All progress has resulted from people who took unpopular positions.

> ADLAI E. STEVENSON (1900–1965). Speech, Princeton University (New Jersey), 22 March 1954

If the arrangement of society is bad (as ours is), and a small number of people have power over the majority and oppress it, every victory over Nature will inevitably serve only to increase that power and that oppression. This is what is actually happening.

> LEO TOLSTOY (1828–1910). 1895? In Aldous Huxley, *Science, Liberty and Peace,* 1, 1946

The regular social process through which a growing society advances from one stage in its growth to another is a compound movement in which a creative individual or minority first withdraws from the common life of the society, then works out, in seclusion, a solution for some problem with which the society as a whole is confronted, and finally re-enters into communion with the rest of the society in order to help it forward on its road by imparting to it the results of the creative work which the temporarily secluded individual or minority has accomplished during the interval between withdrawal and return.

> ARNOLD J. TOYNBEE (1889–1975). *A Study of History,* 8.109, 1954

Man would not have attained the possible unless time and again he had reached out for the impossible.

> MAX WEBER (1864–1920). "Politics as a Vocation," 1919, *From Max Weber: Essays in Sociology,* tr. H. H. Gerth and C. Wright Mills, 1958

It is possible to believe that all the human mind has ever accomplished is but the dream before the awakening.

> H. G. WELLS (1866–1946). "The Discovery of the Future," lecture, Royal Institute, London, 24 January 1902

And step by step, since time began,
I see the steady gain of man.

> JOHN GREENLEAF WHITTIER (1807–1892). "The Chapel of the Hermits," 1851

The direction of progress is inside out.

> ANONYMOUS

PROMISCUITY

See also • Sex

Debauchery is liberating because it creates no obligations. In it you possess only yourself; hence it remains the favorite pastime of the great lovers of their own person.

> ALBERT CAMUS (1913–1960). *The Fall,* p. 103, tr. Justin O'Brien, 1956

Of course, I screwed around when I was younger, but you don't think I'd be crazy enough to do that now?

> JOHN F. KENNEDY (1917–1963). Remark to the author, 1959. In Ralph G. Martin, *A Hero for Our Time,* 22 (epigraph), 1983

Promiscuity is the death of love.

> EDNA O'BRIEN (1932–). In Michael Krasny radio interview, KQED, San Francisco, 16 October 1995

Yes, Juan: we know the libertine's philosophy. Always ignore the consequences to the woman.

> GEORGE BERNARD SHAW (1856–1950). *Man and Superman,* 3, 1903

PROMISES

See also • Honesty ○ Integrity ○ Success: Napoleon ○ Woods: Robert Frost

An honest man's word is as good as his bond.

> CERVANTES (1547–1616). *Don Quixote,* 2.4.34, 1615, tr. Peter Anthony Motteux and John Ozell, 1743 (Popular version: Let your word be your bond.)

Promises are not binding which were extorted by intimidation or which we make when misled by false pretenses.

> CICERO (106–43 B.C.). *De officiis,* 1.10, tr. Walter Miller, 1913

Promise little and do much; so shalt thou have Thanks.

> THOMAS FULLER (1654–1734). Comp., *Introductio ad Prudentiam,* 111, 1731

Promises may get Friends, but 'tis Performances that keep them.

> THOMAS FULLER (1654–1734). Comp., *Gnomologia: Adages and Proverbs,* 3957, 1732

Vows made in Storms are forgot[ten] in Calms.

> THOMAS FULLER (1654–1734). Comp., *Gnomologia: Adages and Proverbs,* 5408, 1732

Don't ever promise more than you can deliver, but always deliver more than you promise.

> LOU HOLTZ (1937–). Football coach. Larry King television interview, CNN, 20 August 1993

Do not swear, either by heaven or by earth or with any other oath, but let your yes be yes and your no be no; that you may not fall under condemnation.

> JAMES (A.D. 1st cent.). *James* 5:12

A Nod of an honest Man is enough.

> JAMES KELLY (18th cent.). Comp., *A Complete Collection of Scottish Proverbs Explained and Made Intelligible to the English Reader,* A.21, 1721

We promise according to our hopes, and perform according to our fears.

> LA ROCHEFOUCAULD (1613–1680). *Maxims,* 38, 1665, tr. Kenneth Pratt, 1931

If you make a bad bargain, *hug* it the tighter.

> ABRAHAM LINCOLN (1809–1865). Recalling his father's dictum, letter to Joshua F. Speed, 25 February 1842

Bad promises are better broken than kept.

> ABRAHAM LINCOLN (1809–1865). Last public speech, Washington, 11 April 1865
>
> See Custom: Thomas Fuller (1)

Governments keep their promises only when they are forced to do so, or when it will be to their advantage.

> NAPOLEON (1769–1821). 1815–1818, *Talks of Napoleon at St. Helena* (with Gen. Gaspard Gourgaud), 4, tr. Elizabeth Wormeley Latimer, 1904

A contract is a mutual promise.

> WILLIAM PALEY (1743–1805). *The Principles of Moral and Political Philosophy,* 3.1.6, 1784

You must not pledge your own *health.*

> JOHN RAY (1628–1705). Comp., *A Collection of English Proverbs,* p. 152, 1678

Contract: an agreement that is binding on the weaker party.

> FREDERICK SAWYER

Promises and pie crust are made to be broken.

> JONATHAN SWIFT (1667–1745). *A Complete Collection of Genteel and Ingenious Conversation,* 1, 1738

The righteous promise little and perform much, the wicked promise much and perform not even a little.

> TALMUD (A.D. 1st–6th cent.). Rabbinical writings

The vow that binds too strictly snaps itself.

> ALFRED, LORD TENNYSON (1809–1892). "The Last Tournament" (l. 652), *The Idylls of the King,* 1859–1885

An ounce of performance is worth pounds of promises.

> MAE WEST (1893–1980). "Misc. West," *The Wit and Wisdom of Mae West,* ed. Joseph Weintraub, 1967

❧

Promises don't fill the belly.

> SAYING (GERMAN)
>
> See Words: Thomas Fuller (3)

PROPAGANDA

See also • Advertising ○ Art ○ Brainwashing ○ Censorship ○ Crowds ○ Deception ○ Dehumanization ○ Education ○ Evangelism ○ Freedom of Speech ○ Freedom of the Press ○ Freedom of Thought ○ Ideas ○ Ideology ○ Indoctrination ○ Language ○ Language, Political ○ Literature ○ Lying ○ Manipulation ○ Mass Movements ○ Machiavellianism ○ Media ○ News ○ Newspeak ○ Newspeak: Examples ○ Publicity ○ Public Opinion ○ Public Relations ○ Public Speaking ○ Radio ○ Rumor ○ Television ○ Truth ○ Tyranny ○ Tyrants: Aldous Huxley ○ War ○ Words ○ Writing

The function of the propagandist is much broader in scope that that of a mere dispenser of information to the press. The United States Government should create a secretary of public relations as member of the president's Cabinet. The function of this official should be correctly to interpret America's aims and ideals throughout the world, and to keep the citizens of this country in touch with governmental activities and the reasons which prompt them. He would, in short, interpret the people to the government and the government to the people.

> EDWARD L. BERNAYS (1891–1995). *Propaganda,* 1, 1928

Most people *want* to feel that issues are simple rather than complex, *want* to have their prejudices confirmed, *want* to feel that they "belong" with the implication that others do not, and *need* to pinpoint an enemy to blame for their frustrations. This being the case, the propagandist is likely to find that his suggestions have fallen on fertile soil so long as he delivers his message with an eye to the existing attitudes and intellectual level of his audience.

> J. A. C. BROWN (1911–1964). *Techniques of Persuasion: From Propaganda to Brainwashing,* 1, 1963

The essence of propaganda is the presentation of one side of the picture only.

> J. A. C. BROWN (1911–1964). *Techniques of Persuasion: From Propaganda to Brainwashing,* 1, 1963

All propaganda messages tend to occur in three stages: the stage of drawing attention and arousing interest, the stage of emotional stimulation, and the stage of showing how the tension thus created can be relieved (i.e., by accepting the speaker's advice).

> J. A. C. BROWN (1911–1964). *Techniques of Persuasion: From Propaganda to Brainwashing,* 3, 1963

A modern dictator with the resources of science at his disposal can easily lead the public on from day to day, destroying all persistency of thought and aim, so that memory is blurred by the multiplicity of daily news and judgment baffled by its perversion.

> WINSTON CHURCHILL (1874–1965). *The Second World War,* 1948–1953. In Douglass Cater, *The Fourth Branch of Government,* 10, epigraph, 1959

All State propaganda exalts comradeship, for it is this gregarious herd-sense and herd-smell which keeps people from thinking and so reconciles them to the destruction of their private lives.

> CYRIL CONNOLLY (1903–1974). "Ecce Gubernator," *The Unquiet Grave: A Word Cycle by Palinurus,* 1945

The best form of newspaper propaganda was not "propaganda" (i.e., editorials and exhortation), but slanted news which appeared to be straight.

> LEONARD W. DOOB (1909–). "Goebbels' Principles of Propaganda," 1950. In Daniel Katz et al., eds., *Public Opinion and Propaganda: A Book of Readings*, 1954

For Goebbels, anxiety was a double-edged sword: too much anxiety could produce panic and demoralization, too little could lead to complacency and inactivity. An attempt was constantly made, therefore, to achieve a balance between the two extremes.

> LEONARD W. DOOB (1909–). "Goebbels' Principles of Propaganda," 1950. In Daniel Katz et al., eds., *Public Opinion and Propaganda: A Book of Readings*, 1954

The danger of total propaganda is not that the propaganda will be believed. The danger is that nothing will be believed. . . . The end result of total propaganda are not fanatics, but cynics.

> PETER F. DRUCKER (1909–). *Management: Tasks, Responsibilities, Practices*, 30, 1974, abr., 1977

Action makes propaganda's effect irreversible. He who acts in obedience to propaganda can never go back. He is now obliged to *believe* in that propaganda because of his past action. He is obliged to receive from it his justification and authority, without which his action will seem to him absurd or unjust, which would be intolerable.

> JACQUES ELLUL (1912–1994). *Propaganda: The Formation of Men's Attitudes*, 1.1, 1962, tr. Konrad Kellen and Jean Learner, 1965

Propaganda by its very nature is an enterprise for perverting the significance of events and of insinuating false intentions. . . . The propagandist must insist on the purity of his own intentions and, at the same time, hurl accusations at his enemy.

> JACQUES ELLUL (1912–1994). *Propaganda: The Formation of Men's Attitudes*, 1.2, 1962, tr. Konrad Kellen and Jean Learner, 1965

Propaganda is the inevitable result of the various components of the technological society, and plays so central a role in the life of that society that no economic or political development can take place without the influence of its great power. . . . [In all social endeavors] the need for psychological influence to spur allegiance and action is everywhere the decisive factor, which progress demands and which the individual seeks in order to be delivered from his own self.

> JACQUES ELLUL (1912–1994). *Propaganda: The Formation of Men's Attitudes*, 3.2, 1962, tr. Konrad Kellen and Jean Learner, 1965

Every new idea will . . . be troublesome to [the individual's] entire being. He will defend himself against it because it threatens to destroy his certainties. He thus actually comes to hate everything opposed to what propaganda has made him acquire. Propaganda has created in him a system of opinions and tendencies which may not be subjected to criticism. . . .

Incidentally, this refusal to listen to new ideas usually takes on an ironic aspect: the man who has been successfully subjected to a vigorous propaganda will declare that *all new ideas are propaganda*.

> JACQUES ELLUL (1912–1994). *Propaganda: The Formation of Men's Attitudes*, 4, 1962, tr. Konrad Kellen and Jean Learner, 1965

[Propaganda aims] in general to make the most of successes and the least of reverses.

> CYRIL FALLS (1888–1971). *Ordeal by Battle*, 1, 1943
> See Persuasion: Johnny Mercer

From one day to another, another nation is made out to be utterly depraved and fiendish, while one's own nation stands for everything that is good and noble. Every action of the enemy is judged by one standard—every action of oneself by another. Even good deeds by the enemy are considered a sign of particular devilishness, meant to deceive us and the world, while our bad deeds are necessary and justified by our noble goals which they serve.

> ERICH FROMM (1900–1980). *The Art of Loving*, 4, 1956

Propaganda has only one object: to conquer the masses. Every means that furthers this aim is good; every means that hinders it is bad.

> JOSEPH GOEBBELS (1897–1945). German minister of propaganda. 1929. In introduction to *The Goebbels Diaries, 1942–1943*, tr. Louis P. Lochner, 1948

That's my trade. Hatred. It takes you a long way further than any other emotion.

> JOSEPH GOEBBELS (1897–1945). Remark to the author. In Rosita Forbes, *These Men I Knew*, 2, 1940

A sharp sword must always stand behind propaganda if it is to be really effective.

> JOSEPH GOEBBELS (1897–1945). 20 September 1943, *The Goebbels Diaries, 1942–1943*, tr. Louis P. Lochner, 1948

Propaganda, as inverted patriotism, draws nourishment from the sins of the enemy. If there are no sins, invent them! The aim is to make the enemy appear so great a monster that he forfeits the rights of a human being.

> SIR IAN HAMILTON (1853–1947). *The Soul and Body of an Army*, 10, 1921

Propaganda, n. Their lies.
Public information, n. Our lies.

> EDWARD S. HERMAN (1925–)

The "societal purpose" of the media is to inculcate and defend the economic, social, and political agenda of privileged groups that dominate the domestic society and the state. The media serve this purpose in many ways: through selection of topics, distribution of concerns, framing of issues, filtering of information, emphasis and tone, and by keeping debate within the bounds of acceptable premises.

> EDWARD S. HERMAN (1925–) and NOAM CHOMSKY (1928–). *Manufacturing Consent: The Political Economy of the Mass Media*, 7, 1988

How a report is framed, which facts it contains and emphasizes and which it ignores, and in what context, are as important to shaping opinion as the bare facts themselves.

> MARK HERTSGAARD (1956–). "How Reagan Seduced Us: Inside the President's Propaganda Factory," *Village Voice* (New York City), 25 September 1984

The most brilliant propagandist technique will yield no success unless one fundamental principle is borne in mind constantly and with unflagging attention. It must confine itself to a few points and repeat them over and over.

> ADOLF HITLER (1889–1945). *Mein Kampf,* 1.6, 1924, tr. Ralph Manheim, 1943

In view of the primitive simplicity of their minds, [the masses] more easily fall a victim to a big lie than to a little one.

> ADOLF HITLER (1889–1945). *Mein Kampf,* 1.10, 1924, tr. Ralph Manheim, 1943

The results at which I have to aim are only to be attained by systematic corruption of the possessing and governing classes. Business advantages, erotic satisfactions, and ambition, that is to say, the will to power, are the three stops in our propaganda organ.

> ADOLF HITLER (1889–1945). Table talk, 1932–1934. In Hermann Rauschning, *The Voice of Destruction,* 19, 1940

By the skillful and sustained use of propaganda, one can make a people see even heaven as hell or an extremely wretched life as paradise.

> ADOLF HITLER (1889–1945). In Cyril Falls, *Ordeal by Battle,* 1, 1943
> See Mind: John Milton

Propaganda . . . serves more to justify ourselves than to convince others; and the more reason we have to feel guilty, the more fervent our propaganda.

> ERIC HOFFER (1902–1983). *The True Believer: Thoughts on the Nature of Mass Movements,* 84, 1951

The real persuaders are our appetites, our fears and above all our vanity. The skillful propagandist stirs and coaches these internal persuaders.

> ERIC HOFFER (1902–1983). *The Passionate State of Mind: And Other Aphorisms,* 218, 1954

Propaganda does not deceive people; it merely helps them to deceive themselves.

> ERIC HOFFER (1902–1983). *The Passionate State of Mind: And Other Aphorisms,* 260, 1954

Propaganda gives force and direction to the successive movements of popular feeling and desire; but it does not do much to create those movements. The propagandist is a man who canalizes an already existing stream. In a land where there is no water, he digs in vain.

> ALDOUS HUXLEY (1894–1963). "Writers and Readers," *The Olive Tree and Other Essays,* 1936

The greatest triumphs of propaganda have been accomplished, not be doing something, but by refraining from doing. Great is truth, but still greater, from a practical point of view, is silence about truth.

> ALDOUS HUXLEY (1894–1963). Foreword (1946) to *Brave New World,* 1932

Certain educators . . . disapproved of the teaching of propaganda analysis on the grounds that it would make adolescents unduly cynical. Nor was it welcomed by the military authorities, who were afraid that recruits might start to analyze the utterances of drill sergeants. And then there were the clergymen and the advertisers. The clergymen were against propaganda analysis as tending to undermine belief and diminish churchgoing; the advertisers objected on the grounds that it might undermine brand loyalty and reduce sales.

> ALDOUS HUXLEY (1894–1963). On the Institute for Propaganda Analysis which was founded in the United States in 1937 and folded in 1941, "Education for Freedom," *Brave New World Revisited,* 1958

By actions which compel general attention, the new idea seeps into people's minds and wins converts. One such act may, in a few days, make more propaganda than thousands of pamphlets.

> PETER KROPOTKIN (1842–1921). "The Spirit of Revolt," 1880, *Kropotkin's Revolutionary Pamphlets,* ed. Roger N. Baldwin, 1927

By using accurate details to imply a misleading picture of the whole, the artful propagandist, it has been said, makes truth the principle form of falsehood.

> CHRISTOPHER LASCH (1932–1994). *The Culture of Narcissism: American Life in an Age of Diminishing Expectations,* 4, 1979

In propaganda as in advertising, the important consideration is not whether information accurately describes an objective situation but whether it sounds true.

> CHRISTOPHER LASCH (1932–1994). *The Culture of Narcissism: American Life in an Age of Diminishing Expectations,* 4, 1979

The art of crisis management, now widely acknowledged to be the essence of statecraft, owes its vogue to the merger of politics and spectacle. Propaganda seeks to create in the public a chronic sense of crisis, which in turn justifies the expansion of executive power and the secrecy surrounding it.

> CHRISTOPHER LASCH (1932–1994). *The Culture of Narcissism: American Life in an Age of Diminishing Expectations,* 4, 1979

The propagandist operates chiefly by means of the *printed* word; the agitator operates with the *living* [i.e., spoken] word.

> LENIN (1870–1924). *What Is To Be Done? Burning Questions of Our Movement,* 3.B, 1902, International Publishers edition, 1929

The educator tries to tell people *how* to think; the propagandist, *what* to think. The educator strives to develop individual responsibility; the propagandist, mass effects. . . . The educator fails unless he achieves an open mind; the propagandist, unless he achieves a closed mind.

> EVERETT DEAN MARTIN (1880–1941). "Our Invisible Masters," *Forum,* vol. 81, 1929

The propagandist can retard or accelerate a trend in public opinion, but he cannot reverse it.

> EDWARD R. MURROW (1908–1965). On television propaganda, as paraphrased by J. A. C. Brown, *Techniques of Persuasion: From Propaganda to Brainwashing,* 3, 1963

Almost all propaganda is designed to create fear. Heads of governments and their officials know that a frightened people is easier to govern, will forfeit rights it would otherwise defend, is less likely to demand a better life, and will agree to millions and millions being spent on "Defense."

> J. B. PRIESTLY (1894–1984). "The Root Is Fear," *Outcries and Asides,* 1974

The four basic criteria of successful propaganda—it must be seen, understood, remembered and acted upon.

TERENCE H. QUALTER (1925–). *Propaganda and Psychological Warfare*, 4, 1962

Propaganda may have some importance in . . . bringing waverers back into the fold, reviving flagging enthusiasms, bringing official views to the notice of the apathetic and the uninterested, announcing changes in the details of basic policy, highlighting certain effects from time to time, but the principal effect is that of confirming people in the "rightness" of their already firmly-held beliefs.

TERENCE H. QUALTER (1925–). *Propaganda and Psychological Warfare*, 6, 1962

Why is propaganda so much more successful when it stirs up hatred than when it tries to stir up friendly feeling?

BERTRAND RUSSELL (1872–1970). *The Conquest of Happiness*, 6, 1930

In each country the propaganda is controlled by the state and is what the state likes. And what the state likes is to have you quite ready to commit murder when you're told to.

BERTRAND RUSSELL (1872–1970). Woodrow Wyatt television interview, BBC, London, 1959, *Bertrand Russell Speaks His Mind*, 8, 1960

Propaganda that aims to induce major changes is certain to take great amounts of time, resources, patience, and indirection, except in times of revolutionary crisis when old beliefs have been shattered and new ones have not yet been provided.

BRUCE LANNES SMITH (1909–). "Propaganda." In Robert McHenry, ed., *The New Encyclopedia Brittanica*, 15th ed., 26.176, 1992

Propaganda: dissemination of ideas, information, or rumor for the purpose of helping or injuring an institution, a cause, or a person.

WEBSTER'S THIRD NEW INTERNATIONAL DICTIONARY OF THE ENG-LISH LANGUAGE UNABRIDGED, ed., Philip Babcock Gove, p. 1817, 1961

Propaganda . . . becomes at last more credible to its disseminators than to its targets.

GARRY WILLS (1934–). *The Kennedy Imprisonment: A Meditation on Power*, 18, 1981

See Lying: Elbert Hubbard

PROPERTY

See also • Class ○ Consumerism ○ Luxury ○ Machines ○ Materialism ○ Money ○ Possessions ○ Real Estate ○ Rights: Theodore Roosevelt ○ Science ○ Sharing ○ Wealth

The power of perpetuating our property in our families is one of the most valuable and interesting circumstances belonging to it, and that which tends the most to the perpetuation of society itself. It makes our weakness subservient to our virtue; it grafts benevolence even upon avarice.

EDMUND BURKE (1729–1797). *Reflections on the Revolution in France*, p. 140, 1790. Pelican Books edition, 1968

Property, gentlemen, is murder!

ALBERT CAMUS (1913–1960). *The Fall*, p. 128, tr. Justin O'Brien, 1956

Upon the sacredness of property civilization itself depends—the right of the laborer to his hundred dollars in the savings bank, and equally the right of the millionaire to his millions.

ANDREW CARNEGIE (1835–1919). "Wealth," *North American Review*, June 1889

I do not . . . find fault with the accumulation of property, provided it hurts nobody, but unjust acquisition of it is always to be avoided.

CICERO (106–43 B.C.). *De officiis*, 1.8, tr. Walter Miller, 1913

Property has its duties as well as its rights.

THOMAS DRUMMOND (1797–1840). Letter to the Earl of Donoughmore, 22 May 1838

The reliance on Property, including the reliance on governments which protect it, is the want of self-reliance.

RALPH WALDO EMERSON (1803–1882). "Self-Reliance," *Essays: First Series*, 1841

Christian tradition has never upheld this right [to private property] as absolute and untouchable. . . .

The right to private property is subordinated to the right to common use, to the fact that goods are meant for everyone.

POPE JOHN PAUL II (1920–). *Laborem Exercens (On Human Work)*, 15 September 1981

Yes, sir. Influence must ever be in proportion to property; and it is right it should.

SAMUEL JOHNSON (1709–1784). 18 August 1773. In James Boswell, *The Journal of a Tour to the Hebrides, with Samuel Johnson, L.L.D.*, 1786

See Class: Alexander Hamilton ○ Wealth: John Jay

Property is desirable, is a positive good in the world.

ABRAHAM LINCOLN (1809–1865). *First Annual Message to Congress*, 3 December 1861

Private property is . . . a system of legal rights and duties. Under changing conditions the system must be kept in accord with the grand ends of civil society.

WALTER LIPPMANN (1889–1974). *The Public Philosophy*, 9.2, 1955

The most common and durable source of factions has been the various and unequal distribution of property. Those who hold and those who are without property have ever formed distinct interests in society.

JAMES MADISON (1751–1836). In *The Federalist Papers* (essay series), 10, 23 November 1787

Property covereth a multitude of woes.

MENANDER (343?–291 B.C.). Fragment, 90, tr. Francis G. Allinson, 1921

Private property, in every defense made of it, is supposed to mean, the guarantee to individuals of the fruits of their own labor and abstinence.

JOHN STUART MILL (1806–1873). *Principles of Political Economy with Some of Their Applications to Social Philosophy*, 2.1.3, 1848

Property is theft.

PIERRE-JOSEPH PROUDHON (1809–1865). *What is Property?* 1, 1840

See Money: Seneca the Younger

In the last analysis the property-owning class is loyal only to its own property.

JOHN REED (1887–1920). In *Liberator* (magazine), 1918–1924

The man who wrongly holds that every human right is secondary to his profit must now give way to the advocate of human welfare, who rightly maintains that every man holds his property subject to the general right of the community to regulate its use to whatever degree the public welfare may require it.

THEODORE ROOSEVELT (1858–1919). "The New Nationalism," speech, Osawatomie (Kansas), 31 August 1910

The property which every man has in his own labor, as it is the original foundation of all other property, so it is the most sacred and inviolable.

ADAM SMITH (1723–1790). *The Wealth of Nations*, 1.10.2, 1776

The greater part of modern property . . . is merely a form of private taxation which the law allows certain persons to levy on the industry of others. . . . Its essential feature [is] that it confers upon its owners income unaccompanied by personal service.

R. H. TAWNEY (1880–1962). *The Acquisitive Society*, 5, 1920

Property set out with being booty held as trophies of the successful raid.

THORSTEIN VEBLEN (1857–1929). *The Theory of the Leisure Class: An Economic Study of Institutions*, 2, 1899

Property not merely has duties, but has so many duties that its possession to any large extent is a bore.

OSCAR WILDE (1854–1900). "The Soul of Man Under Socialism," *Fortnightly Review* (British journal), February 1891

The demon of property has even been at hand to encroach on the sacred rights of men, and to fence round with awful pomp laws that war with justice.

MARY WOLLSTONECRAFT (1759–1797). *A Vindication of the Rights of Men*, p. 8, 1790

PROPHETS

See also • Clergy ○ Dreams: [especially] *Talmud* (2) ○ Mysticism ○ Prediction ○ Religion ○ Revelation ○ Saints ○ Spirituality ○ Vision ○ Wisdom: Euripides

I am no prophet, nor a prophet's son; but I am a herdsman, and a dresser of sycamore trees, and the Lord took me from following the flock, and the Lord said to me, "Go, prophesy to my people Israel."

AMOS (8th cent. B.C.). *Amos* 7:14–15

The prophets mean more than their words.

LEO BAECK (1873–1956). "Prophetic Religion and Community of Faith," *The Essence of Judaism,* 1936, ed. Irving Howe, 1948

Prophecy is malicious deception. . . . Can you imagine anything more disgusting than a prophet?

ELIAS CANETTI (1905–1994). 1980, *The Secret Heart of the Clock: Notes, Aphorisms, Fragments: 1973–1985,* tr. Joel Agee, 1989

Every prophet has to come from civilization, but every prophet has to go into the wilderness. He must have a strong impression of a complex society and all that it has to give, and then he must serve periods of isolation and meditation. This is the process by which psychic dynamite is made.

WINSTON CHURCHILL (1874–1965). In *Sunday Chronicle* (British newspaper), 8 November 1931

An impulse as irresistible as in the acorn to germinate is in the soul of the prophet to speak.

RALPH WALDO EMERSON (1803–1882). Journal, 20 October 1833

What concerns the prophet is the human event as a divine experience. History to us is the record of human experience; to the prophet it is a record of God's experience.

ABRAHAM JOSHUA HESCHEL (1907–1972). *The Prophets,* 9, 1962

The prophet perceives the whole world in terms of justice or injustice.

ABRAHAM JOSHUA HESCHEL (1907–1972). *The Prophets,* 11, 1962

It is not enough for a prophet to be inspired by God; he also must be informed about the world. The world and its fate are very dear to him. There is no hostility to civilization, only to its abuses.

ABRAHAM JOSHUA HESCHEL (1907–1972). *The Prophets,* 21, 1962

What the poets know as poetic inspiration, the prophets call divine revelation.

ABRAHAM JOSHUA HESCHEL (1907–1972). *The Prophets,* 22, 1962

The well-adjusted make poor prophets.

ERIC HOFFER (1902–1983). *The True Believer: Thoughts on the Nature of Mass Movements,* 51, 1951

The prophets . . . were a blend of the reactionary and radical. They preached a return to the ancient faith and also envisaged a new world and a new life.

ERIC HOFFER (1902–1983). *The True Believer: Thoughts on the Nature of Mass Movements,* 52, 1951

And I heard the voice of the Lord saying, "Whom shall I send, and who will go for us?" Then I said, "Here I am! Send me."

ISAIAH (8th cent. B.C.). *Isaiah* 6:8

[The people say] to the prophets,
  "Prophesy not to us what is right;
  speak to us smooth things, prophesy illusions,
leave the way, turn aside from the path,
  let us hear no more of the Holy One of Israel."

ISAIAH (8th cent. B.C.). *Isaiah* 30:10–11

A genuine first-hand religious experience . . . is bound to be a heterodoxy to its witnesses, the prophet appearing as a mere lonely madman. If his doctrine prove contagious enough to spread to any others, it becomes a definite and labeled heresy. But if it then still prove contagious enough to triumph over persecution, it becomes itself an orthodoxy; and when a religion has become an orthodoxy, its day of inwardness is over: the spring is dry; the faithful live at second hand exclusively and stone the prophets in their turn.

WILLIAM JAMES (1842–1910). *The Varieties of Religious Experience: A Study in Human Nature,* 14 and 15, 1902

Beware of false prophets, who come to you in sheep's clothing but inwardly are ravenous wolves. You will know them by their fruits.

> JESUS (A.D. 1st cent.). *Matthew* 7:15–16

A prophet is not without honor except in his own country and in his own house.

> JESUS (A.D. 1st cent.). *Matthew* 13:57

O Jerusalem, Jerusalem, killing the prophets and stoning those who are sent to you!

> JESUS (A.D. 1st cent.). *Matthew* 23:37

Statesmen, even warriors, focus on the world in which they live; to prophets, the "real" world is the one they want to bring into being.

> HENRY A. KISSINGER (1923–). *Diplomacy*, 2, 1994

Ages when custom is unsettled are necessarily ages of prophecy.

> WALTER LIPPMANN (1889–1974). *A Preface to Morals*, 15.1, 1929

God, when he makes the prophet, does not unmake the man.

> JOHN LOCKE (1632–1704). *An Essay Concerning Human Understanding*, 4.19.14, 1690, ed. Alexander Campbell Fraser, 1894

Many unhappy persons affected by ambitious mania, or theomania, are looked upon as prophets, and their delusions taken for revelations.

> CESARE LOMBROSO (1836–1909). *The Man of Genius*, 3.4, 1888, ed. Havelock Ellis, 1896. Earlier in the same chapter, Lombroso noted that the Hebrew word *nabi*, as used in the Bible, means both prophet and madman.

a prophet said i is not
without honor save on his own
planet.

> DON MARQUIS (1878–1937). "archy hears from mars," *archy and mehitabel*, 1927

But Moses said to the Lord, "Oh, my Lord, I am not eloquent, either heretofore or since thou hast spoken to thy servant; but I am slow of speech and of tongue." Then the Lord said to him, "Who has made man's mouth? Who makes him dumb, or deaf, or seeing, or blind?" Is it not I, the Lord? Now therefore go, and I will be with your mouth and teach you what you shall speak. But he said, "Oh, my Lord, send, I pray, some other person."

> MOSES (14th cent. B.C.). *Exodus* 4:10–13

Would that all the Lord's people were prophets, that the Lord would put his spirit upon them!

> MOSES (14th cent. B.C.). *Numbers* 11:29

Hear my words: If there is a prophet among you, I the Lord make myself known to him in a vision, I speak with him in a dream.

> MOSES (14th cent. B.C.), AARON (14th cent. B.C.), and MIRIAM (14th cent. B.C.). *Numbers* 12:6

[The] prophets left society, generally, as they found it; they might mildly rebuke its institutions, but they left them alone. They turned their attention rather to the individual soul, in whose depths they thought the essential work could be done.

> LEWIS MUMFORD (1895–1990). *The Transformations of Man*, 4.4, 1956

The prophet himself stands under the judgment which he preaches. If he does not know that, he is a false prophet.

> REINHOLD NIEBUHR (1892–1971). *Beyond Tragedy: Essays on the Christian Interpretation of History*, 5.5, 1938

To prophesy is to speak of God, not from outward proofs, but from an inward and immediate feeling.

> BLAISE PASCAL (1623–1662). *Pensées*, 732, 1670, tr. William F. Trotter, 1931

He who prophesies speaks to men for their upbuilding and encouragement and consolation.

> PAUL (A.D. 1st cent.). *1 Corinthians* 14:3

The words of the prophets
Are written on the subway walls
And tenement halls
And whispered in the sounds of silence.

> PAUL SIMON (1941–). "The Sound of Silence," song, 1964

There were as many prophetesses as prophets in Israel.

> *TALMUD* (A.D. 1st–6th cent.). Rabbinical writings

Anybody who set up in the present-day world to be a prophet . . . would rightly be treated as a figure of fun.

> ARNOLD J. TOYNBEE (1889–1975). *A Study of History*, 12.4, 1961

The personal call is the decisive element distinguishing the prophet from the priest. The latter lays claim to authority by virtue of his service in a sacred tradition, while the prophet's claim is based on personal revelation and charisma.

> MAX WEBER (1864–1920). "The Prophet," 1922, *On Charisma and Institution Building: Selected Papers*, ed. S. N. Eisenstadt, 1968

One thing I learned, never to be a prophet. . . . Prophecy is a dangerous thing. No prophet has died a natural death.

> ELI WIESEL (1928–). Response to a question from the audience, National Press Club speech, Washington, 20 May 1997

Is it the prophet's thought I speak, or am I raving?

> WALT WHITMAN (1819–1892). "Prayer of Columbus," 1874, *Leaves of Grass*, 1855–1892

PROSPERITY

See also • Adversity ○ Campaign Slogans: Slogan (American) (14) ○ Fortune ○ Prosperity & Adversity ○ Wealth

Prosperity is only an instrument to be used, not a deity to be worshipped.

> CALVIN COOLIDGE (1872–1933). Speech, Boston, 11 June 1928

Prosperity has damn'd more Souls than all the Devils together.

> THOMAS FULLER (1654–1734). Comp., *Gnomologia: Adages and Proverbs*, 3963, 1732

Prosperity is a worthy goal of aspiration and a promised reward for good living.

> ABRAHAM JOSHUA HESCHEL (1907–1972). *Man Is Not Alone: A Philosophy of Religion*, 25, 1951

Prosperity cannot be restored by raids upon the public treasury.

> HERBERT HOOVER (1874–1964). Press statement, 9 December 1930, soon after the start of the Depression

Prosperity is just around the corner.

> HERBERT HOOVER (1874–1964). "Sixty Days Proclamation," March 1931

Armaments, universal debt, and planned obsolescence—those are the three pillars of Western prosperity.

> ALDOUS HUXLEY (1894–1963). *Island*, 9, 1962

Prosperity can only be lasting if it is based on justice.

> THEODORE ROOSEVELT (1858–1919). In Hermann Hagedorn and Sidney Wallach, "Signposts for Americans: The Business of Living," *A Theodore Roosevelt Round-Up*, 1958

The intoxication of prosperity.

> ADAM SMITH (1723–1790). *The Theory of Moral Sentiments*, 6.3, 1759
> See Victory: Arnold J. Toynbee

Few of us can stand prosperity. Another man's I mean.

> MARK TWAIN (1835–1910). *Following the Equator: A Journey Around the World*, 40 (epigraph), 1897
> See Adversity: Twain

❧

To have national prosperity we need to spend, but to have individual prosperity we must save.

> ANONYMOUS

PROSPERITY & ADVERSITY

See also • Adversity ∘ Friends: John Ray (1) ∘ Prosperity ∘ Remorse: Rousseau ∘ Service: Publius Syrus ∘ Wealth & Poverty

Prosperity doth best discover vice, but adversity doth best discover virtue.

> FRANCIS BACON (1561–1626). "Of Adversity," *Essays*, 1625

The virtue of Prosperity is temperance; the virtue of Adversity is fortitude.

> FRANCIS BACON (1561–1626). "Of Adversity," *Essays*, 1625

Adversity is sometimes hard upon a man; but for one man who can stand prosperity, there are a hundred that will stand adversity.

> THOMAS CARLYLE (1795–1881). "The Hero as Man of Letters," *On Heroes, Hero-Worship, and the Heroic in History*, 1841

He that swells in prosperity will shrink in Adversity.

> THOMAS FULLER (1654–1734). Comp., *Gnomologia: Adages and Proverbs*, 2321, 1732

Prosperity proves the fortunate; adversity, the great.

> PLINY THE YOUNGER (A.D. 62?–113?). *Panegyric*, 31

Prosperity makes friends; adversity tries them.

> PUBLIUS SYRUS (85–43 B.C.). *Moral Sayings*, 872, tr. Darius Lyman, Jr., 1862

One must taste adversity in order to relish prosperity.

> SA'DI (A.D. 1213?–1292). *The Maxims of Sa'di*, 3, tr. Mehdi Nakosteen, 1977

Prosperity does not exalt the wise man, nor does adversity cast him down.

> SENECA THE YOUNGER (5? B.C.–A.D. 65). "On Consolation to Helvia" (5.1), *Moral Essays*, tr. John W. Basore, 1932

❧

In prosperity, caution; in adversity, patience.

> SAYING (DUTCH)

PROTEST

See • Silence & Protest

PROSTITUTION

See also • Sex

A House Is Not a Home.

> POLLY ADLER (1900–1962). San Francisco madam. Book title, 1945

Prostitutes don't sell their bodies, they rent their bodies. Housewives sell their bodies when they get married.

> FLORYNCE KENNEDY (1916–). *Color Me Flo: My Hard Life and Good Times*, 1, 1976

The worst part about prostitution is that you're obliged not to sell sex only, but your humanity. That's the worst part of it: that what you're selling is your human dignity. Not really so much in bed, but in accepting the agreement—in becoming a bought person.

> KATE MILLET (1934–). Paraphrasing "J," a prostitute she interviewed for the essay, "Prostitution: A Quartet for Female Voices." In Vivian Gornick, and Barbara K. Moran, eds., *Woman in Sexist Society: Studies in Power and Powerlessness*, 1971

Women are always held responsible for the supposed evilness of sex—it's not just Eve and Pandora. The prostitution laws are a contemporary example. Soliciting is an offense in thirty-four states, whereas customers are subject to legal action in only fourteen states. Moreover, prostitutes are jailed in virtually every state, and customers—not at all.

> GAYLE RUBIN. "Woman as Nigger," *The Argus* (Ann Arbor, Michigan), 1969. In Betty Roszak and Theodore Roszak, eds., *Masculine/Feminine: Readings in Sexual Mythology and the Liberation of Women*, 1969

Into this anonymous pit they climb—a fumbling, frightened, pathetic man and a cold, contemptuous, violated woman—prepared to exchange for twenty dollars no more than ten minutes of animal sex, untouched by a stroke of their common humanity.

> GAIL SHEEHY (1937–). *Hustling: Prostitution in Our Wide-Open Society*, 3, 1973

It is a silly question to ask a prostitute why she does it. . . . These are the highest-paid "professional" women in America.

> GAIL SHEEHY (1937–). *Hustling: Prostitution in Our Wide-Open Society*, 4, 1973

Not till the sun excludes you do I exclude you.

> WALT WHITMAN (1819–1892). "To a Common Prostitute," 1860, *Leaves of Grass*, 1855-1892

PROVERBS

See also • Aphorisms ○ Axioms ○ Epigrams ○ Maxims ○ Principles, Moral ○ Principles, Theoretical ○ Quotations ○ Sayings

Proverb: A popular short saying, with words of advice or warning.
> THE ADVANCED LEARNER'S DICTIONARY OF CURRENT ENGLISH. In Ronald Ridout and Clifford Witting, introduction to *English Proverbs Explained*, 1967

The genius, wit, and spirit of a nation are discovered in its proverbs.
> FRANCIS BACON (1561–1626). In Selwyn Gurney Champion, comp., *Racial Proverbs: A Selection of the World's Proverbs Arranged Linguistically*, p. 4, 1938

Proverbs are *strategies* for dealing with *situations*. In so far as situations are typical and recurrent in a given social structure, people develop names for them and strategies for handling them.
> KENNETH BURKE. "Literature as Equipment for Living" (1), *The Philosophy of Literary Form: Studies in Symbolic Action*, 1941

Do not overlard your common discourse with that glut of proverbs.
> CERVANTES(1547–1616). *Don Quixote*, 2.4.43, 1615, tr. Peter Anthony Motteux and John Ozell, 1743

A proverb is a short sentence based on long experience.
> CERVANTES (1547–1616). In Stefan Kanfer, "Proverbs or Aphorisms?" *Time*, 11 July 1983

Proverbial expressions and trite sayings are the flowers of the rhetoric of a vulgar man. . . . A man of fashion never has recourse to proverbs and vulgar aphorisms.
> LORD CHESTERFIELD (1694–1773). Letter to his son, 27 September 1749

A frequent review of proverbs should enter into our reading.
> ISAAC D'ISRAELI (1766–1848). In Selwyn Gurney Champion, comp., *Racial Proverbs: A Selection of the World's Proverbs Arranged Linguistically*, p. 3, 1938

He repeated to himself an old French proverb that he had made up that morning.
> F. SCOTT FITZGERALD (1896–1940). "The Note-Books" (E), *The Crack-Up*, ed. Edmund Wilson, 1945

Nothing ever becomes real till it is experienced—even a proverb is no Proverb to you till your Life has illustrated it.
> JOHN KEATS (1795–1821). Letter to George and Georgiana Keats, 19 March 1819

Proverbs, the ready money of human experience.
> JAMES RUSSELL LOWELL (1819–1891). "Abraham Lincoln," 1864, *My Study Windows*, 1871

Proverbs have never claimed to be universally true, but they are correct in certain given contexts and situations.
> WOLFGANG MIEDER (1944–). *Introduction to Proverbs Are Never Out of Season: Popular Wisdom in the Modern Age*, 1993

[A proverb is] a concise statement of an apparent truth which has currency.
> WOLFGANG MIEDER (1944–). Paraphrasing his teacher Prof. Stuart A. Gallacher, *Proverbs Are Never Out of Season: Popular Wisdom in the Modern Age*, 2, 1993

Proverbs contain the value system of the time of their origin.
> WOLFGANG MIEDER (1944–). *Proverbs Are Never Out of Season: Popular Wisdom in the Modern Age*, 4, 1993

Proverbs put old heads on young shoulders.
> CHARLES READE (1814–1884). *The Cloister and the Hearth*, 24, 1861

Proverbs were at their height in Shakespeare's time, and it is more than probable that any proverbs attributable to Shakespeare had a previous existence, even if in a less memorable form.
> RONALD RIDOUT and CLIFFORD WITTING. Introduction to *English Proverbs Explained*, 1967

[A proverb is] the wit of one man, the wisdom of many.
> LORD JOHN RUSSELL (1792–1878). In *Quarterly Review* (English journal), September 1850

Most of our pocket wisdom is conceived for the use of mediocre people, to discourage them from ambitious attempts, and generally console them in their mediocrity.
> ROBERT LOUIS STEVENSON (1850–1894). On "the cowardly proverbs," "Crabbed Age and Youth," *Virginibus Puerisque*, 1881

A proverb has been defined as the wit of one and the wisdom of many; it is often the sophistry of a few and the unreason of the multitude.
> ANONYMOUS (AMERICAN). "Influence of Proverbs," *New York Times*, 29 April 1877

Besides being wise, the Preacher also taught the people knowledge, weighing and studying and arranging proverbs with great care.
> ANONYMOUS (*BIBLE*). Ecclesiastes 12:9

Solomon made a book of proverbs, but a book of proverbs never made a Solomon.
> SAYING (ENGLISH)

Proverbs are the wisdom of the ages.
> SAYING (GERMAN)

A proverb is a little gospel.
> SAYING (SPANISH)

PRUDENCE

See also • Boldness: Thomas Fuller, Sayings (2) ○ Courage: Fénelon ○ Prudence, Rules ○ Safety ○ Security ○ Wisdom

First of all virtues, prudence.
> EDMUND BURKE (1729–1797). *Reflections on the Revolution in France*, p. 153, 1790, Pelican Books edition, 1968
>
> See Courage: Winston Churchill ○ Humility: St. Augustine ○ Self-Discipline: Adam Smith (2) ○ Self-Respect: John Herschel

Prudence is very inclined to preserve what one possesses, but courage alone knows how to acquire.
> FREDERICK II (1712–1786). In Heinrich von Treitschke, *The Life of Frederick the Great*, p. 139, ed. Douglas Sladen, 1915

A grain of Prudence is worth a Pound of Craft.

> THOMAS FULLER (1654–1734). Comp., *Gnomologia: Adages and Proverbs*, 187, 1732

Good Nature is a great Misfortune if it want[s] Prudence.

> THOMAS FULLER (1654–1734). Comp., *Gnomologia: Adages and Proverbs*, 1721, 1732

Wise venturing is the most commendable part of human prudence.

> MARQUIS OF HALIFAX (1633–1695). "Boldness," *Political, Moral and Miscellaneous Reflections*, 1750

Prudence and love are not made for each other: as love waxes, prudence wanes.

> LA ROCHEFOUCAULD (1613–1680). *Maxims*, 546, 1665, tr. Leonard Tancock, 1959

Prudence consists in being able to know the nature of the difficulties, and taking the least harmful as good.

> MACHIAVELLI (1469–1527). *The Prince*, 21, 1513, tr. Luigi Ricci, 1903

There may be circumstances in which even prudence directs us to trust entirely to chance.

> CARDINAL de RETZ (1613–1679). "Political Maxims from Cardinal de Retz" (23). In Lord Chesterfield (1694–1773). *Letters, Sentences, and Maxims*, Chesterfield Society edition, undated

Prudence when stretched too far blocks the road of progress.

> SAYING (CHINESE)

PRUDENCE: RULES

See also • Competition ○ Danger ○ Distrust ○ Effort ○ Money ○ Opportunity ○ Preparedness ○ Prudence ○ Safety ○ Self-Interest ○ Speed ○ Success ○ Suspicion ○ Thrift ○ Time ○ Weakness: Saying (Burmese)

Never play cards with a man called Doc. Never eat at a place called Mom's. Never sleep with a woman whose troubles are worse than your own.

> NELSON ALGREN (1909–1981). *A Walk on the Wild Side*, 3, 1956

Seek to make thy course regular that men may know beforehand what they may expect.

> FRANCIS BACON (1561–1626). "Of Great Place," *Essays*, 1625

He that cannot see well, let him go softly.

> FRANCIS BACON (1561–1626). "Ornamenta Rationalia; or, Elegant Sentences," *The Essays; or, Counsels, Civil and Moral*, A. L. Burt edition, 1883

Always bear in mind what the country mother said to her daughter who was coming up to town to be apprenticed to the Bond Street Millinery, "For heaven's sake be good; but if you can't be good, be careful."

> ARTHUR M. BINSTEAD. *Pitcher in Paradise*, 8, 1903

Do not all you can; spend not all you have; believe not all you hear; and tell not all you know.

> HENRY G. BOHN (1796–1884). Comp., *A Hand-Book of Proverbs*, p. 344, 1860

Look twice before you leap.

> CHARLOTTE BRONTË (1816–1855). *Shirley*, 9, 1849

'Tis the part of a wise man to keep himself today for tomorrow, and not venture all his eggs in one basket.

> CERVANTES (1547–1616). *Don Quixote*, 1.3.9, 1615, tr. Peter Anthony Motteux and John Ozell, 1743

A limb may be lost in preference to the whole body.

> CICERO (106–43 B.C.). *Philippics*, 8.5, tr. C. D. Yonge, 1903
>
> See Constitutions: Abraham Lincoln

Cut your coat according to your cloth.

> JOHN CLARKE (1596–1658). Comp., *Proverbs: English and Latine*, p. 128, 1639

Look before you leap.

> JOHN CLARKE (1596–1658). Comp., *Proverbs: English and Latine*, p. 266, 1639

Deliberate with caution, but act with decision; and yield with graciousness, or oppose with firmness.

> C. C. COLTON (1780–1832). *Lacon: or, Many Things in Few Words; Addressed to Those Who Think*, 1.284, 1823
>
> See Action & Thought: Saying (Greek)

That thou may'st injure no man, dove-like be,
And serpent-like, that none may injure thee!

> WILLIAM COWPER (1731–1800). "Epigrams, Translated from the Latin of Owen" ("Prudent Simplicity"), 1803
>
> See Princes: Frederick II (1)

Fight fair but don't f'rget th' other la-ad may not know where th' belt line is.

> FINLEY PETER DUNNE (1867–1936). "Americans Abroad," *Mr. Dooley's Philosophy*, 1900

If it works, don't fix it.

> FIRST RULE OF RURAL MECHANICS. In Paul Dickson, *The Official Rules*, p. 12, 1978

Let all your things have their places; let each part of your business have its time.

> BENJAMIN FRANKLIN (1706–1790). Virtue #3 (Order), 1784, *Autobiography*, 1798

Drive the Nail that will go.

> THOMAS FULLER (1654–1734). Comp., *Gnomologia: Adages and Proverbs*, 1336, 1732

It is a good Blade that bends well.

> THOMAS FULLER (1654–1734). Comp., *Gnomologia: Adages and Proverbs*, 2853, 1732

The Orange that is too hard squeez'd yields a bitter juice.

> THOMAS FULLER (1654–1734). Comp., *Gnomologia: Adages and Proverbs*, 4696, 1732

There is a Time to wink as well as to see.
> THOMAS FULLER (1654–1734). Comp., *Gnomologia: Adages and Proverbs*, 4885, 1732

Want of Care does us more Damage than want of Knowledge.
> THOMAS FULLER (1654–1734). Comp., *Gnomologia: Adages and Proverbs*, 5414, 1732

With Foxes we must play the Fox.
> THOMAS FULLER (1654–1734). Comp., *Gnomologia: Adages and Proverbs*, 5797, 1732

Never contend with a man who has nothing to lose.
> BALTASAR GRACIÁN (1601–1658). *The Art of Worldly Wisdom*, 172, 1647, tr. Joseph Jacobs, 1943

Love your neighbor, yet pull not down your hedge.
> GEORGE HERBERT (1593–1633). Comp., *Outlandish Proverbs*, 141, 1640
> See Trust: Saying (Arab)

He that lies with the dogs, riseth with fleas.
> GEORGE HERBERT (1593–1633). Comp., *Outlandish Proverbs*, 343, 1640

Give losers leave to talk.
> GEORGE HERBERT (1593–1633). Comp., *Outlandish Proverbs*, 602, 1640

Preserve a sense of right proportion, for
Fitness is all-important, in all things.
> HESIOD (8th cent. B.C.). *Work and Days*, l. 698, tr. Dorothea Wender, 1973

Better is half a loaf than no bread.
> JOHN HEYWOOD (1497–1580). Comp., *A Dialogue Containing the Number of the Effectual Proverbs in the English Tongue*, 1.11, 1562

'Tis ill waking of a sleeping dog.
> JAMES HOWELL (1593–1666). Comp., "English" (p. 5), *Paroimiographia: Proverbs, or Old Sayed Sawes & Adages in English . . . Italian, French and Spanish*, 1659 (Popular version: Let sleeping dogs lie.)

Don't cut what you can untie.
> JOSEPH JOUBERT (1754–1824). 1797, *Pensées*, 1838, tr. Paul Auster, 1983

The squeaky wheel doesn't always get greased; it often get replaced.
> KEITH'S OBSERVATION. In John Peers, comp., *1,001 Logical Laws*, p. 156, 1979

In everything, consider the consequences.
> LA FONTAINE (1621–1695). *Fables*, 3.5, 1668–1679

Yield larger things to which you can show no more than equal right; and yield lesser ones, though clearly your own. Better give your path to a dog than be bitten by him in contesting for the right.
> ABRAHAM LINCOLN (1809–1865). Letter to James M. Cutts, Jr., 26 October 1863

We won't jump that ditch until we come to it.
> ABRAHAM LINCOLN (1809–1865). In Donn Piatt, "Abraham Lincoln," *Memories of the Men Who Saved the Union*, 1887

It is not well to threaten before having the power to act.
> MACHIAVELLI (1469–1527). *The Discourses*, 1.44, 1517, tr. Christian E. Detmold, 1940

Maneuvering for petty advantage is short-sighted.
> MAO TSE-TUNG (1893–1976). Expressing a basic principle of Chinese statecraft, paraphrased by Henry A. Kissinger, *Years of Upheaval*, 3, 1982

"Hang a Lantern on Your Problem."
> CHRISTOPHER MATTHEWS (1945–). Chapter title, *Hardball: How Politics Is Played—Told by One Who Knows the Game*, 10, 1988

Be nice to people on your way up because you'll meet 'em on your way down.
> WILSON MIZNER (1876–1933). In Alva Johnston, *The Legendary Mizners*, 4, 1953

Have a Care . . . where there is more Sail than Ballast.
> WILLIAM PENN (1644–1718). *Some Fruits of Solitude*, 260, 1693

To do two things at once is to do neither.
> PUBLIUS SYRUS (85–43 B.C.). *Moral Sayings*, 7, tr. Darius Lyman, Jr., 1862

Divide the fire, and you will sooner put it out.
> PUBLIUS SYRUS (85–43 B.C.). *Moral Sayings*, 201, tr. Darius Lyman, Jr., 1862

Piss not against the wind.
> JOHN RAY (1628–1705). Comp., *A Collection of English Proverbs*, p. 189, 1678

Lead your life so you wouldn't be ashamed to sell the family parrot to the town gossip!
> WILL ROGERS (1879–1935). "New York, Then and Now," comp. Bryan B. Sterling, *New York Times*, 15 August 1985

A barking dog never bites; that is, he never barks while he's biting.
> LOUIS A. SAFIAN. Comp., *The Book of Updated Proverbs*, 1, 1967

Never kick a man when he's down—he may get up.
> LOUIS A. SAFIAN. Comp., *The Book of Updated Proverbs*, 1, 1967

Before you take anything away, you must have something better to put in its place.
> ARTHUR SCHOPENHAUER (1788–1860). "Religion and Other Essays: A Dialogue," *Essays of Arthur Schopenhauer*, tr. T. Bailey Saunders, 1851
> See Computers: Peter H. Lewis

Clarence: A little fire is quickly trodden out,
Which, being suffered, rivers cannot quench.
> SHAKESPEARE (1564–1616). *King Henry VI*, Part III, 4.8.7, 1590

Countess of Rousillon: Love all, trust a few,
Do wrong to none.
> SHAKESPEARE (1564–1616). *All's Well that Ends Well*, 1.1.73, 1602

Fool: Have more than thou showest,
Speak less than thou knowest,
Lend less than thou owest.
> SHAKESPEARE (1564–1616). *King Lear*, 1.4.131, 1605

Lord Chamberlain: Press not a falling man too far!
> SHAKESPEARE (1564–1616). *King Henry VIII,* 3.2.334, 1612

Never, never, never, never outshine the big boss.
> R. G. H. SIU (1917–). *The Craft of Power,* 1.54, 1984

When a dog runs at you, whistle for him.
> HENRY DAVID THOREAU (1817–1862). Journal, 26 June 1840

Let me say to you and to myself in one breath, Cultivate the tree which you have found to bear fruit in your soil.
> HENRY DAVID THOREAU (1817–1862). Journal, 1850, undated

Put all your eggs in the one basket and—*watch that basket.*
> MARK TWAIN (1835–1910). *The Tragedy of Pudd'nhead Wilson,* 15 (epigraph), 1894

Have a place for everything and keep the thing somewhere else. This is not advice, it is merely custom.
> MARK TWAIN (1835–1910). 4 July 1898, *Mark Twain's Notebook,* ed. Albert Bigelow Paine, 1935

If you don't like the heat, get out of the kitchen.
> HARRY VAUGHAN (1893–1981). Quoted by his friend Harry S. Truman to explain his decision not to run for re-election. In "The Presidency" (footnote), *Time,* 28 April 1952

Ride with no one who doesn't want to ride with you.
> GERALD WILSON. *Chato's Land* (film), 1971, spoken by Jack Palance
> See Distrust: Wade Hudson

🌿

Don't bite off more than you can chew.
> SAYING (AMERICAN)

Don't swap horses in midstream.
> SAYING (AMERICAN)

If you can't lick 'em, join 'em.
> SAYING (AMERICAN)

No one tests the depths of a river with both feet.
> SAYING (ASHANTI)

Cross the stream where it is shallowest.
> SAYING (ENGLISH)

Don't cut the bough you're sitting on.
> SAYING (ENGLISH)

The squeaky wheel gets the grease.
> SAYING (ENGLISH)

Better bend than break.
> SAYING (FRENCH)

If you can't bite, don't show your teeth.
> SAYING (FRENCH)

Don't throw the baby out with the dirty bath water.
> SAYING (GERMAN)

There's many a slip between the cup and the lip.
> SAYING (GREEK)

Measure twice and cut once.
> SAYING (ITALIAN)

Never spur a willing horse.
> SAYING (ITALIAN)

Think much, speak little, write less.
> SAYING (ITALIAN)

No call alligator long mouth till you pass him.
> SAYING (JAMAICAN)

Don't stretch yourself longer than your blanket.
> SAYING (ROMANIAN)

If you're afraid of the wolves, don't go into the forest.
> SAYING (RUSSIAN)

Don't mend your neighbor's fence before looking to your own.
> SAYING (TANZANIAN)

Three things it is best to avoid: a strange dog, a flood, and a man who thinks he is wise.
> SAYING (WELSH)

Them that's going, git on the wagon. Them that ain't, git out of the way.
> SAYING. Quoted by Martin Luther King, Jr., during the march from Selma (Mississippi), to Montgomery (Alabama), 1965. In "Mr. Bush, the Wagon's Leaving" (editorial), *New York Times,* 16 May 1990
> See Leaders: Laurence J. Peter

Don't cross a bridge till you come to it.
> SAYING
> See Trouble: Saying (English)

Don't kindle a fire you can't put out.
> SAYING

Don't stitch your seam before you've tacked it.
> SAYING

Good fences make good neighbors.
> SAYING

Good neighbors make good fences.
> SAYING

Let well enough alone.
> SAYING

Never go through what you can go around.
> SAYING

Never swim toward a sinking ship.
> SAYING

PRUDERY

See also • Abstinence ○ Puritanism ○ Sex

The peculiarity of prudery is to multiply sentinels, in proportion as the fortress is less threatened.

> VICTOR HUGO (1802–1885). "Marius" (2.8), *Les Misérables*, tr. Charles E. Wilbour, 1862

To receive a piece of jewelry from a man to whom you were not engaged was a sign of being a fast woman, and the idea that you would permit any man to kiss you before you were engaged to him never even crossed my mind.

> ELEANOR ROOSEVELT (1884–1962). *This Is My Story*, 3, 1937

PSYCHIATRIC TREATMENT

See also • Drugs, Psychiatric ○ Psychiatry ○ Psychosurgery ○ Psychotherapy ○ Shock Treatment

The brain- and mind-disabling hypothesis states that the more potent somatic therapies in psychiatry, that is, the major tranquilizers, lithium, ECT, and psychosurgery, produce brain damage and dysfunction, and that this damage and dysfunction is the primary, clinical or so-called beneficial effect. The individual subjected to the dysfunction becomes less able and more helpless, ultimately becoming . . . more suggestible or easy to influence.

> PETER R. BREGGIN (1936–). "Disabling the Brain with Electroshock." In Maurice Dongier and Eric D. Wittkower, eds., *Divergent Views in Psychiatry*, 1981

[In cases of enuresis, i.e., bedwetting] I apply usually [in the region of the boy's sexual organ] a tolerably strong current for one to two minutes; at the close, a wire electrode is introduced about two centimeters into the urethra—in girls I apply "small" sponge electrode between the labia close to the meatus urethrae—and the faradic current passed for one to two minutes with such a strength that a distinct, somewhat painful sensation is produced.

> WILHELM ERB (1840–1921). *Handbook of Electrotherapy*, 1881. In Thomas S. Szasz, *The Myth of Psychotherapy: Mental Healing as Religion, Rhetoric, and Repression*, 6.1, 1978

Doctor L. Valentin has published some valuable observations concerning the cure of mania by the application of fire. I have many times applied the iron at a red heat to the neck, in mania with fury, and sometimes with success.

> JEAN ESQUIROL (1772–1840). *Mental Maladies: A Treatise on Insanity*, 1.5, 1838, tr. E. K. Hunt, 1845. In Thorne Shipley, ed., *Classics in Psychology*, 1961

A young man with chronic auditory hallucinations was treated according to the principle that increasing external auditory stimulation decreases the likelihood of auditory hallucinations. Listening to a radio through stereo headphones in conditions of low auditory stimulation eliminated the patient's hallucinations.

> ROBERT FEDER. "Auditory Hallucinations Treated by Radio Headphones," *American Journal of Psychiatry*, September 1982

"Deaths Force Mental Health Officials to Find New Ways of Restraining Patients."

> LISA W. FODERARO. Headline of article reporting on the deaths of 18 mental patients in restraints and seclusion in New York State's public mental hospitals between 1988 and 1992, *New York Times*, 1 August 1994

In my department at the Vienna Polyclinic, we use drugs, and use electroconvulsive treatment. I have signed authorization for lobotomies without having cause to regret it. In a few cases, I have even carried out transorbital lobotomy. However, I promise you that the human dignity of our patients is not violated in this way. . . . What matters is not a technique or therapeutic approach as such, be it drug treatment or shock treatment, but the spirit in which it is being carried out.

> VIKTOR E. FRANKL (1905–1997). "'Nothing but—': On Reductionism and Nihilism," *Encounter*, November 1969

I am not sure but that, in this progressive age, it may not in future be deemed political economy to stamp out insanity by removing the ovaries of insane women.

> WILLIAM GOODELL. Physician. 1881. In Andrew Scull and Diane Favreau, "'A Chance to Cut Is a Chance to Cure': Sexual Surgery for Psychosis in Three Nineteenth Century Societies" (note 23), *Research in Law, Deviance and Social Control*, vol. 8, 1986

A special building must be set aside for the physical treatment of the mentally disturbed. This building should have a special bathing section, with all kinds of baths, showers, douches, and immersion vessels. It must also have a special correction and punishment room with all the necessary equipment, including a Cox swing (or, better, rotating machine), Reil's fly-wheel, pulleys, punishment chair, Langermann's cell, etc.

> JOHANN CHRISTIAN HEINROTH (1773–1843). *Textbook of Disturbances of Mental Life or Disturbances of the Soul and Their Treatment*, 502, 1818, tr. J. Schmorak, 1975

Schneider even recommended mustard baths, especially for sly, restless, evasive, brooding or phlegmatic mental patients. Curiously, Cox prescribed baths in thin gruel or in water and milk, and Schneider, baths in gravy for patients who refused their food.

> EMIL KRAEPELIN (1856–1926). German psychiatrist. *One Hundred Years of Psychiatry*, p. 68, 1917, tr. Wade Baskin, 1962

We must give the old alienists credit for having exhibited both sincerity and inventiveness in putting into practice the therapeutic principles which they considered sound. Advice given by Neumann suggests the course of treatment that might have been prescribed for a new patient in a state of agitation: "They bring the patient to the restraining chair, bleed him, put ten or twelve leeches on his head, cover him with cold, wet towels, pour about fifty buckets of cold water over his head and let him eat thin soup, drink water and take glauber salts."

> EMIL KRAEPELIN (1856–1926). *One Hundred Years of Psychiatry*, p. 82, 1917, tr. Wade Baskin, 1962

The same doctor [Horn] named as one of the most innocuous, comfortable and safest devices for calming patients the cruciform stance. The patient was harnessed and tied in a standing position, and with arms outstretched for 8 or 10 hours. This was supposed to mitigate delirious outbursts, encourage fatigue and sleep, render the patient harmless and obedient, and awaken in him a feeling of respect for the doctor.

> EMIL KRAEPELIN (1856–1926). *One Hundred Years of Psychiatry*, p. 86, 1917, tr. Wade Baskin, 1962

I keep no rank, nor station.
Cured, I am frizzled, stale and small.

> ROBERT LOWELL (1917–1977). "Home After Three Months Away," 1959

The blood of maniacs is sometimes so lavishly spilled, and with so little discernment, as to render it doubtful whether the patient or his physician has the best claim to the appellation of a madman. This reflection naturally suggests itself upon seeing many a victim of medical presumption, reduced by the depleting system of treatment to a state of extreme debility or absolute idiotism. At the same time, I do not wish to be understood as altogether proscribing the use of the lancet in this formidable disorder. My intention is solely to deprecate its abuse.

> PHILIPPE PINEL (1745–1826). *A Treatise on Insanity,* 6.108, 1801, tr. D. D. Davis, 1806

How are we to distinguish between the exasperation caused by the chains and the symptoms peculiar to the illness?

> PHILIPPE PINEL (1745–1826). In Anthony M. Graziano, "In the Mental-Health Industry, Illness Is Our Most Important Product," *Psychology Today,* January 1972

I have contrived a chair and introduced it to our Hospital to assist in curing madness. It binds and confines every part of the body. By keeping the trunk erect, it lessens the impetus of blood toward the brain. . . . Its effects have been truly delightful to me. It acts as a sedative to the tongue and temper as well as to the blood vessels. In twenty-four, twelve, six, and in some cases in four hours, the most refractory patients have been composed. I have called it a *Tranquilliser.*

> BENJAMIN RUSH (1745–1813). 10 June 1810. In David Herman and Jim Green, "What Treatment?" *Madness: A Study Guide,* 1991

TERROR acts powerfully upon the body, through the medium of the mind, and should be employed in the cure of madness. . . .
   FEAR, accompanied with PAIN, and a sense of SHAME, has sometimes cured this disease. Bartholin speaks in high terms of what he calls "flagellation" in certain diseases.

> BENJAMIN RUSH (1745–1813). *Medical Inquiries and Observations Upon the Diseases of the Mind,* 2nd ed., 7, 1818

For many centuries [the mad] have been treated like criminals, or shunned like beasts of prey. . . . Happily these times of cruelty to this class of our fellow creatures, and insensibility to their sufferings, are now passing away.

> BENJAMIN RUSH (1745–1813). *Medical Inquiries and Observations Upon the Diseases of the Mind,* 2nd ed., 8, 1818

Macbeth: Canst thou not minister to a mind diseased? . . .
Doctor: Therein the patient
Must minister to himself.

> SHAKESPEARE (1564–1616). *Macbeth,* 5.3.40, 1605

These sundry procedures [i.e., lobotomy and several forms of shock treatment] produce "beneficial" results by reducing the patient's capacity for being human. The philosophy is something to the effect that it is better to be a contented imbecile than a schizophrenic.

> HARRY STACK SULLIVAN (1892–1949). Psychiatrist. Referring to psychiatry's "decortication treatments," "Conceptions of Modern Psychiatry," *Psychiatry,* February 1940

PSYCHIATRISTS

See also • Doctors ○ Physicians ○ Psychiatry

Dr. Gaston Ferdière, head doctor at the Rodez Asylum, told me he was there to reform my poetry.

> ANTONIN ARTAUD (1896–1948). "Van Gogh: The Man Suicided by Society," 1947, *Antonin Artaud Anthology,* ed. Jack Hirschman, 1965

[Psychiatrists] must now decide what is to be the immediate future of the human race. No one else can. And this is the prime responsibility of psychiatry.

> G. BROCK CHISHOLM. Psychiatrist. "The Psychiatry of Enduring Peace and Social Progress," *Psychiatry,* January 1946

Do you know why psychiatrists go into their specialty? It is because they do not feel that they are normal, and they go into this work because it is a means of sublimation for this feeling—a means of assuring themselves that they are really normal. Society puts them in charge of the mentally abnormal, and so they feel reassured.

> SIGMUND FREUD (1856–1939). 27 February 1930. In Smiley Blanton, *Diary of My Analysis with Sigmund Freud,* 1971

Anyone who would go to a psychiatrist ought to have his head examined.

> SAMUEL GOLDWYN (1882–1974)

The physician of the psyche appears to the patient as helper and savior, as father and benefactor, as a sympathetic friend, as friendly teacher, but also as a judge who weighs the evidence, passes judgment, and executes the sentence, and at the same time seems to be the visible God to the patient.

> JOHANN CHRISTIAN HEINROTH (1773–1843). *Textbook of Disturbances of Mental Life or Disturbances of the Soul and Their Treatment,* 369, 1818, tr. J. Schmorak, 1975

[The psychiatrist] is inclined to suspect the mental sanity of anybody who sees more than plain madness in the ravings of a lunatic.

> CARL G. JUNG (1875–1961). "On the Psychogenesis of Schizophrenia," 1939, *The Psychogenesis of Mental Disease,* tr. R. F. C. Hull, 1960

These manufacturers of madness—who cry, "Anything to treat?" is now heard all over the land. . . . Their teaching enlarges irresponsibility and thus diminishes the personality.

> KARL KRAUS (1874–1936). 1910. In Thomas S. Szasz, *Karl Kraus and the Soul-Doctors: A Pioneer Critic and His Criticism of Psychiatry and Psychoanalysis,* 6, 1976

The primitive predecessors of the contemporary psychiatrist were men of considerable social power. The modern psychiatrist differs from the shaman not because he has abandoned social power for medical science, but because he has disguised his power with the rhetoric of medicine and science instead of magic and religion.

> RONALD LEIFER (1932–). *In the Name of Mental Health: The Social Functions of Psychiatry,* 4, 1969

A physician acquires the obedience and affections of his deranged patients by ACTS of KINDNESS. For this purpose, all his directions for discontinuing painful or disagreeable remedies, and all his pleasant prescriptions, should be delivered in the presence of his patients; while [those] of an unpleasant nature, should be delivered only to their keepers.

BENJAMIN RUSH (1745–1813). *Medical Inquiries and Observations Upon the Diseases of the Mind,* 2nd ed., 7, 1818

Psychiatric training is the ritualized indoctrination of the young physician into the theory and practice of psychiatric violence.

THOMAS S. SZASZ (1920–). Hungarian-born American psychiatrist. "Psychiatry," *The Second Sin,* 1973

Doctors control diseases, not persons; psychiatrists control persons, not diseases.

THOMAS S. SZASZ (1920–). "Medicine and Psychiatry," *Heresies,* 1976

☙

Mystification is the psychiatrist's defense against the danger of being found out.

ANONYMOUS

PSYCHIATRY

See also • Doctors ○ Drugs, Psychiatric ○ Healing ○ Mental Hospitals ○ Mental Illness ○ Physicians ○ Psychiatric Treatment ○ Psychiatrists ○ Psychoanalysis ○ Psychosurgery ○ Psychotherapy ○ Shock Treatment

As far as the woman is concerned, psychiatry is an extraordinary confidence trick: the unsuspecting creature seeks aid because she feels unhappy, anxious and confused, and psychology persuades her to seek the cause in *herself.* The person is easier to change than the status quo which represents a higher value in the psychologists' optimistic philosophy. If all else fails, largactil [i.e., Thorazine], shock treatment, hypnosis and other forms of "therapy" will buttress the claim of society.

GERMAIN GREER (1939–). "The Psychological Sell," *The Female Eunuch,* 1970

Psychiatry can so easily be a technique of brainwashing, of inducing behavior that is adjusted, by (preferably) non-injurious torture. In the best places, where straitjackets are abolished, doors are unlocked, leucotomies largely forgone, these can be replaced by more subtle lobotomies and tranquilizers that place the bars of Bedlam and the locked doors *inside* the patient.

R. D. LAING (1927–1989). British psychiatrist. Preface to the Pelican edition (1964), *The Divided Self: An Existential Study of Sanity and Madness,* 1959

To be convincingly respectful of personal liberty, a nation must be governed by laws that are neither harsh nor restrictive, or *it must convey the image of being so governed.* To convey this image, it is useful for a portion of its social control apparatus to be visible and for another portion to be invisible or disguised. The practice of involuntary psychiatric hospitalization is well suited to the task of disguised social control.

RONALD LEIFER (1932–). Psychiatrist. *In the Name of Mental Health: The Social Functions of Psychiatry,* 5, 1969

Of all tyrannies a tyranny sincerely exercised for the good of its victims may be the most oppressive. It may be better to live under robber barons than under omnipotent moral busybodies. The robber baron's cruelty may sometimes sleep, his cupidity may at some point be satiated; but those who torment us for our own good will torment us without end for they do so with the approval of their own conscience. . . . Their very kindness stings with intolerable insult. To be "cured" against one's will and cured of states which we may not regard as disease is to be put on a level with those who have not yet reached the age of reason.

C. S. LEWIS (1898–1963). "The Humanitarian Theory of Punishment," *God in the Dock,* 1970

If Institutional Psychiatry is harmful to the so-called mental patient, this is not because it is liable to abuse, but rather because harming persons categorized as insane is its essential function: Institutional Psychiatry is, as it were, designed to protect and uplift the group (the family, the State), by persecuting and degrading the individual (as insane or ill).

THOMAS S. SZASZ (1920–). Hungarian-born American psychiatrist. Introduction to *The Manufacture of Madness: A Comparative Study of the Inquisition and the Mental Health Movement,* 1970

The fundamental error of psychiatry is that it regards life as a problem to be solved, instead of as a purpose to be fulfilled.

THOMAS S. SZASZ (1920–). "Psychiatry," *Heresies,* 1976

The psychiatric profession's most distinguishing feature . . . [is] the deliberate, systematic dehumanization of man, in the name of mental health.

THOMAS S. SZASZ (1920–). Foreword to Seth Farber, *Madness, Heresy, and the Rumor of Angels: The Revolt Against the Mental Health System,* 1993

☙

Psychiatry is to medicine what astrology is to astronomy.

ANONYMOUS

PSYCHOANALYSIS

See also • Mental Illness ○ Neurosis ○ Psychiatry ○ Psychotherapy ○ The Unconscious

Today I resumed my practice and saw my first batch of nuts again. I must now transmute the nervous energy gained during my holiday into money to fill my depleted purse.

SIGMUND FREUD (1856–1939). Letter to Carl G. Jung, 1 October 1910, tr. Ralph Manheim, 1974

[Psychoanalysis] presupposes the consent of the person who is being analyzed and a situation in which there is a superior and a subordinate.

SIGMUND FREUD (1856–1939). *On the History of the Psychoanalytic Movement,* 3, 1914, tr. Joan Riviere and rev. James Strachey, 1962

See Psychotherapy: Carl G. Jung (4)

[Psychoanalysis] is in essence a cure through love.

SIGMUND FREUD (1856–1939). In Bruno Bettelheim, "Two Views of Freud" (1), 1958, *Freud's Vienna and Other Essays,* 1989

Our psychoanalysis has also had bad luck. No sooner had it begun to interest the world because of the war neuroses than the war comes to an end.

SIGMUND FREUD (1856–1939). Letter to Sandor Ferenczi, 1919. In Thomas S. Szasz, *The Myth of Psychotherapy: Mental Healing as Religion, Rhetoric, and Repression,* 7.7, 1978

The words, "secular pastoral worker," might well serve as a general formula for describing the function which the analyst, whether he is a doctor or a layman, has to perform in his relation to the public.

> SIGMUND FREUD (1856–1939). *Postscript* (1927) to *The Question of Lay Analysis,* 1926, tr. James Strachey, 1950

The whole theory of psychoanalysis is . . . built up on the perception of the resistance offered to us by the patient when we attempt to make his unconscious conscious to him.

> SIGMUND FREUD (1856–1939). *New Introductory Lectures on Psychoanalysis,* 31, 1933, tr. James Strachey, 1965
>
> See The Unconscious (all)

A man of about thirty strikes us as a youthful, somewhat unformed individual, whom we expect to make powerful use of the possibilities for development opened up to him by analysis. A woman of the same age, however, often frightens us by her psychical rigidity and unchangeability. . . . There are no paths open to further development; it is as though the whole process had already run its course and remains thenceforward unsusceptible to influence.

> SIGMUND FREUD (1856–1939). *New Introductory Lectures on Psychoanalysis,* 33, 1933, tr. James Strachey, 1965

The special conditions of analytic work do actually cause the analyst's own defects to interfere with his making a correct assessment of the state of things in his patient and reacting to them in a useful way. It is therefore reasonable to expect of an analyst, . . . a considerable degree of mental normality and correctness. In addition, he must possess some kind of superiority, so that in certain analytic situations he can act as a model for his patient and in others as a teacher. And finally he must not forget that the analytic relationship is based on a love of truth—that is, on a recognition of reality—and that it precludes any kind of sham or deceit.

> SIGMUND FREUD (1856–1939). "Analysis Terminable and Interminable" (7), 1937, tr. James Strachey, 1964

We serve the patient in various functions, as an authority and a substitute for his parents, as a teacher and educator.

> SIGMUND FREUD (1856–1939). *An Outline of Psychoanalysis,* 6, 1940, tr. James Strachey, 1969

Freud's aim was to found a movement for the ethical liberation of man, a new secular and scientific religion for an elite which was to guide mankind.

> ERICH FROMM (1900–1980). On psychoanalysis, *Sigmund Freud's Mission: An Analysis of His Personality and Influence,* 10, 1959

Freud is the father of psychoanalysis. It had no mother.

> GERMAINE GREER (1939–). "The Psychological Self," *The Female Eunuch,* 1970

Psychoanalysis is the disease of which it claims to be the cure.

> KARL KRAUS (1874–1936). 1913. In Thomas S. Szasz, *Karl Kraus and the Soul-Doctors: A Pioneer Critic and His Criticism of Psychiatry and Psychoanalysis,* 2.2, 1976
>
> See Socialism: George F. Will

The practice of psychoanalysis as a therapeutic method is really hardly anything more than re-education.

> EVERETT DEAN MARTIN (1880–1941). *The Behavior of Crowds: A Psychological Study,* 10, 1920

When [Sigmund Freud] discussed with us the psychoanalytic therapy of neurosis he used a picture-postcard of the most ordinary kind for making his point. The picture showed a yokel—we would say a hillbilly—in a hotel bedroom trying to blow out the electric light like a candle. "If you attack the symptom directly, you act in the same way as this man. You must look for the switch."

> HANNS SACHS (1881–1947). *Freud: Master and Friend,* 3, 1944

Psychoanalysis is a religion disguised as a science: As Abraham received the Laws of God from Jehovah to whom he claimed to have had special access, so Freud received the Laws of Psychology from the Unconscious to which he claimed to have had special access.

> THOMAS S. SZASZ (1920–). "Psychoanalysis," *The Untamed Tongue: A Dissenting Dictionary,* 1990

The ideas of Freud were popularized by people who only imperfectly understood them, who were incapable of the great effort required to grasp them in their relationship to larger truths, and who therefore assigned to them a prominence out of all proportion to their true importance.

> ALFRED NORTH WHITEHEAD (1861–1947). 3 June 1943, *Dialogues of Alfred North Whitehead,* rec. Lucien Price, 1954

Psychoanalysis is the opium of the neurotics.

> ANONYMOUS

PSYCHOSURGERY

See also • Dehumanization: Lewis Mumford (2) ∘ Psychiatric Treatment ∘ Psychiatry ∘ Surgeons

A major difficulty was that psychosurgery, which mutilated irrevocably a part of the brain, was final. Not a dispensable part, such as the appendix, is removed, but an area essential to the human being—his personality—is forever destroyed.

> FRANZ G. ALEXANDER (1891–1964) and SHELDON T. SELESNICK. *The History of Psychiatry: An Evaluation of Psychiatric Thought and Practice from Prehistoric Times to the Present,* 18, 1966

Cingulotomy [a psychosurgical technique] has a 30-year history. Over 700 operations have been studied. Despite its efficacy and safety in some of the most incapacitating depression, pain, and anxiety states, it has not been widely accepted. Incorrect association with the frontal lobe ablations in the 1950s has led to erroneous perception of the procedure as personality-altering.

> ANTHONY J. BOUCKOMS. "Stereotactic Cingulotomy Used in Intractable Affective Disorder," *Psychiatric Times,* November 1989

The [lobotomy] technique severs the nerves that deliver emotional power to ideas. Along with a cure comes some loss in the patient's imaginative power. But that's what we want to do. They are sick in their imaginations.

> WALTER FREEMAN (1895–1972). 1948. In William Arnold, *Shadowland,* 45, 1978

Some patients come to operation [lobotomy] at the end of a long and exasperating series of medical treatments, hospital treatments, shock treatments, including endocrines and vitamins mixed with their physiotherapy and psychotherapy. They are still desperate, and will go to any length to get rid of their distress. Other patients can't be dragged into the hospital and have to be held down on a bed in a hotel room until sufficient shock treatment can be given to render them manageable.

> WALTER FREEMAN (1895–1972) and JAMES W. WATTS (1904–1994). *Psychosurgery in the Treatment of Mental Disorders and Intractable Pain,* 2nd ed., 8, 1950

We vividly recall (Case 156) a negress of gigantic proportions who for years was confined to a strong room at St. Elizabeths Hospital. When it came time to transfer her to the Medical Surgical Building for operation [lobotomy], five attendants were required to restrain her while the nurse gave her the hypodermic. The operation was successful in that there were no further outbreaks, but for many months after operation this patient's reputation was such that she was allowed few privileges, and even three years after operation, when she could well have been taken care of at home, her husband refused to try it. He was still scared of the 72 inches and 300 lbs. of ferocious humanity. Yet from the day after operation (and we demonstrated this repeatedly to the timorous ward personnel) we could playfully grab Oretha by the throat, twist her arm, tickle her in the ribs and slap her behind without eliciting anything more than wide grin or a hoarse chuckle. This patient has been earning her living in Denver for the past two years.

> WALTER FREEMAN (1895–1972) and JAMES W. WATTS (1904–1994). *Psychosurgery in the Treatment of Mental Disorders and Intractable Pain,* 2nd ed., 20, 1950

The doctors kept talking to Rosemary [who had been given a local anesthetic], getting her to sing or count. When the patient became sleepy and disoriented, the two doctors could tell the operation was working. As long as she continued to sing out and to add and subtract, the doctors kept cutting away, destroying a larger and larger area of the brain. . . .

Rosemary had been Rose's child, Rose's burden, and her daughter was now [after the operation] like a painting that had been brutally slashed so it was scarcely recognizable.

> LAURENCE LEAMER. On the lobotomy operation performed by Walter Freeman and James W. Watts in 1941 on Rosemary Kennedy, *The Kennedy Women: The Saga of an American Family,* 13, 1994

A Salvation Army worker, a very high-ranking office. She married a clergyman. For years she lay in hospital, constantly complaining that she had committed sins against the Holy Ghost. She complained of it for weeks and months, and her poor husband did his best to distract her, but without success. Then we decided to operate upon her. . . . After the dressing had been taken off, I asked her, "How are you now? What about the Holy Ghost?" Smiling, she answered, "Oh, the Holy Ghost; there is no Holy Ghost."

> GÖSTA RYLANDER (1903–1979). "Personality Analysis before and after Frontal Lobotomy," 1948. In William Sargant, *Battle for the Mind: A Physiology of Conversion and Brain-Washing,* 4, 1956

Genuine religious conversions are also seen after the new modified lobotomy operations. For the mind is freed from its old strait-jacket and new religious beliefs and attitudes can now more easily take the place of the old.

> WILLIAM SARGANT (1907–1988). British psychiatrist. *Battle for the Mind: A Physiology of Conversion and Brain-Washing,* 4, 1956

Conscience can now be eliminated surgically without any impairment of day to day working efficiency.

> WILLIAM SARGANT (1907–1988). British psychiatrist. On psychosurgery, "The Movement in Psychiatry Away from the Philosophical: New Chemical and Physical Methods of Freeing Tormented Minds," *Times* (London), 22 August 1974

Freeman and Watts described the four-year-old [they lobotomized in 1943] as "absolutely incorrigible, destructive, assaultive," with "his face a mass of bruises" from self-inflicted injuries. "Unfortunately the possibility in this case will remain unknown," they wrote, "because after return home, and when things were going well, he contracted meningitis and died three weeks after the operation."

> DAVID SHUTTS. *Lobotomy: Resort to the Knife,* 6, 1982

He's like a log, you could sit on him.

> ANONYMOUS (AMERICAN). Father referring to his lobotomized son. In Robert Lindner, *Prescription for Rebellion,* 2, 1952

I'd rather have a bottle in front of me than a frontal lobotomy.

> ANONYMOUS (AMERICAN)

PSYCHOTHERAPY

See also • Mental Illness ○ Neurosis ○ Psychiatric Treatment ○ Psychiatry ○ Psychoanalysis ○ Religion: Carl G. Jung ○ Self-Realization (Becoming) ○ The Unconscious

I've spent 15 years in therapy. One more year and I'm going to Lourdes.

> WOODY ALLEN (1935–). In Charles Krauthammer, "Under a Thatched Roof, With Warren Christopher," *Weekly Standard,* 6 May 1996

Much [of psychotherapy] sounds like confession without penance.

> TIMOTHY BENEKE. "The Case Against Psychotherapy," *East Bay Express* (Berkeley, California), 7 October 1988

The fact is that psychotherapy is far less dependent upon technique than it is upon the personal relationship between physician and patient.

> ANTON T. BOISEN (1876–1965). Clergyman. *The Exploration of the Inner World: A Study of Mental Disorder and Religious Experience,* 10, 1936

In the treatment of nervous cases, he is the best physician who is the most ingenious inspirer of hope.

> SAMUEL TAYLOR COLERIDGE (1772–1834). 2 January 1833, *Table Talk,* 1835

We've Had a Hundred Years of Psychotherapy—And the World's Getting Worse.

> JAMES HILLMAN and MICHAEL VENTURA. Book title, 1992

The cure works best when the doctor himself believes in his own formulae, otherwise he may be overcome by scientific doubt and so lose the proper convincing tone.

> CARL G. JUNG (1875–1961). Letter to Dr. R. Loÿ, 12 January 1913, "Some Crucial Points in Psychoanalysis," 1914, *Freud and Psychoanalysis,* tr. R. F. C. Hull, 1961

The doctor should not strive to heal at all costs. One has to be exceedingly careful not to impose one's own will and conviction on the patient. . . . Sometimes it is really a question whether you are allowed to rescue a man from the fate he must undergo for the sake of his further development.

> CARL G. JUNG (1875–1961). *Analytical Psychology: Its Theory and Practice* (The Tavistock Lectures), 4, 1935

In psychotherapy, enthusiasm is the secret of success.

> CARL G. JUNG (1875–1961). "On the Psychogenesis of Schizophrenia," 1939, *The Psychogenesis of Mental Disease,* tr. R. F. C. Hull, 1960

The crucial point is that I confront the patient as one human being to another. Analysis is a dialogue demanding two partners. . . . The doctor has something to say, but so has the patient.

> CARL G. JUNG (1875–1961). *Memories, Dreams, Reflections,* 4, ed. Aniela Jaffé, 1962
>
> See Psychoanalysis: Sigmund Freud (2)

Learn your theories well but put them aside when you confront the mystery of the living soul.

> CARL G. JUNG (1875–1961). In Seth Farber, *Madness, Heresy, and the Rumor of Angels: The Revolt Against the Mental Health System,* 8, 1993

Psychotherapy is an educational process, primarily. . . . Its goal is that of transformation: it seeks to transform the negative protest and rebellion of the patient into positive expression of the rebellious urge.

> ROBERT LINDNER (1914–1956). Psychoanalyst. *Prescription for Rebellion,* 4, 1952

There is no better therapy than a job and a paycheck.

> WILLIAM MENNINGER (1900–1966). Psychiatrist. In Steven Rosner, "Treatment in China," *Mental Hygiene,* Summer 1976

In a culture in which interpersonal relationships are generally considered to provide the answer to every form of distress, it is sometimes difficult to persuade well-meaning helpers that solitude can be as therapeutic as emotional support.

> ANTHONY STORR (1920–). British psychiatrist. *Solitude: A Return to the Self,* 3, 1988

If the Other's affliction lies in his soul rather than his body, then our urge to help him cannot be satisfied without our feeling empathy for him, indeed, without our establishing a bond of intimacy with him.

> THOMAS S. SZASZ (1920–). Foreword to Seth Farber, *Madness, Heresy, and the Rumor of Angels: The Revolt Against the Mental Health System,* 1993

THE PUBLIC

See also • Man ○ Mankind ○ The Masses ○ People ○ The People ○ Society

There is not a more mean, stupid, dastardly, pitiful, selfish, spiteful, envious, ungrateful animal than the Public. It is the greatest of cowards, for it is afraid of itself.

> WILLIAM HAZLITT (1778–1830). "On Living to Oneself," *Table Talk,* 1822

The public [has] neither shame nor gratitude.

> WILLIAM HAZLITT (1778–1830). *Characteristics in the Manner of Rochefoucault's Maxims,* 85, 1823

The public is merely a multiplied "me."

> MARK TWAIN (1835–1910)

The public is a ferocious beast; one must either chain it up or flee from it.

> VOLTAIRE (1694–1778). Letter to Mlle. Quinault, 16 August 1738

PUBLICITY

See also • Advertising ○ Celebrity ○ Democracy: Arthur M. Schlesinger, Jr. ○ Fame ○ Gossip ○ Indoctrination ○ Journalism: Paul Fussell ○ Justice: Arnold Bennett ○ News ○ Propaganda ○ Public Relations ○ Rumor

There's no such thing as bad publicity except your own obituary.

> BRENDAN BEHAN (1923–1964). In Dominic Behan, *My Brother Brendan,* 15, 1965

'Tis better never to be named than to be ill spoken of.

> SUSANNA CENTLIVRE (1667?–1723). *The Basset-Table,* 1, 1705

I don't care what you say about me, as long as you say *something* about me, and as long as you spell my name right.

> GEORGE M. COHAN (1878–1942). In John McCabe, *George M. Cohan: The Man Who Owned Broadway,* 13, 1973

I wonder how long it will be before I write something again. Not too long, I hope. A man must get himself talked about.

> SIGMUND FREUD (1856–1939). Letter to his fiancé Martha Bernays, 7 February 1884, tr. Tania and James Stern, 1960

Bad publicity tends to arouse my sympathy for its object.

> ALEXANDER HAIG (1924–). *Caveat: Realism, Reagan and Foreign Policy,* 1984, excerpted in *Time,* 2 April 1984

Puff Graham.

> WILLIAM RANDOLPH HEARST (1863–1951). Telegram sent to the editors of his media empire early in the career of evangelist Billy Graham, 1949. In Nancy Gibbs and Richard N. Ostling, "God's Billy Pulpit," *Time,* 15 November 1993

There is nothing more dreadful to an author than neglect, compared with which reproach, hatred and opposition are names of happiness.

> SAMUEL JOHNSON (1709–1784) In *The Rambler* (English journal), 2, 24 March 1750

I would rather be attacked than unnoticed. For the worst thing you can do to an author is to be silent as to his works. An assault upon a town is a bad thing; but starving it is still worse.

> SAMUEL JOHNSON (1709–1784). 26 March 1779. In James Boswell, *The Life of Samuel Johnson,* 1791
>
> See Critics: Johnson (2)

To have news value is to have a tin can tied to one's tail.

T. E. LAWRENCE (1888–1935). Letter to Sir Evelyn Wrench, March 1935

In every field of human endeavor, he that is first must perpetually live in the white light of publicity.

THEODORE F. MacMANUS. "The Penalty of Leadership," *Saturday Evening Post*, 2 January 1915

Publicity is like power, Major Butler—it's a rare man who isn't corrupted by it.

ANTHONY PRICE (1928–). *Colonel Butler's Wolf*, 2, 1972
See Power: Lord Acton

This is the only country in the world where failing to promote yourself is widely regarded as being arrogant.

GARRY TRUDEAU (1948–). On his reluctance to grant interviews. In "Overheard," *Newsweek*, 6 October 1986

You can't con people, at least not for long. You can create excitement, you can do wonderful promotion and get all kinds of press, and you can throw in a little hyperbole. But if you don't deliver the goods, people will eventually catch on.

DONALD J. TRUMP (1946–) (with TONY SCHWARTZ). *Trump: The Art of the Deal*, 2, 1987

Publicity is like eating peanuts. Once you start you can't stop.

ANDY WARHOL (1927–1987). 1979, "Warhol in His Own Words," ed. Neil Printz. In Kynaston McShine, *Andy Warhol: A Retrospective*, 1986
See Television: Orson Welles

There is only one thing in the world worse than being talked about, and that is not being talked about.

OSCAR WILDE (1854–1900). *The Picture of Dorian Gray*, 1, 1891

❧

Any publicity is good publicity.

SAYING

The only bad publicity is no publicity.

SAYING

PUBLIC OPINION

See also • Conformity ○ Democracy, Anti-: James Fenimore Cooper (2) ○ Ideas ○ Indoctrination ○ Leaders & People: Doris Kearns Goodwin, Henry A. Kissinger (3) ○ Majorities ○ Media ○ Opinion ○ Politics ○ Propaganda ○ Public Opinion Polls ○ Tyranny: John Stuart Mill ○ Words

Public opinion is, with multitudes, a second conscience; with some, the only one.

WILLIAM R. ALGER (1822–1905)

Public opinion is no more than this;
What people think that other people think.

ALFRED AUSTIN (1835–1913). *Prince Lucifer*, 1887. In Daniel J. Boorstin, *Democracy and Its Discontents: Reflections on Everyday America*, 2, 1975

That cruelest of tyrants—PUBLIC OPINION.

ELENA PETROVNA BLAVATSKY (1831–1891). "A Paradoxical World," *Lucifer*, February 1889

Public opinion is the last refuge of a politician without any opinion of his own.

MARK BONHAM-CARTER (1922–1994)

This "superior morality" is properly rather an "inferior criminality," produced not by greater love of Virtue, but by greater perfection of Police; and of that far subtler and stronger Police, called Public Opinion.

THOMAS CARLYLE (1795–1881). "Signs of the Times," 1829, *Critical and Miscellaneous Essays*, Carey & Hart edition, 1849

I never said that the *voice of the people* was of course the *voice of God*. It may be; but it may be, and with equal probability, the *voice of the Devil*. (Vox populi vox diaboli.)

SAMUEL TAYLOR COLERIDGE (1772–1834). Adapted. 29 April 1832, *Table Talk*, 1835

"They say" is the monarch of this country.

JAMES FENIMORE COOPER (1789–1851). "'They Say,'" *The American Democrat*, 1838

If by the people you understand the multitude, the *hoi polloi*, 'tis no matter what they think; they are sometimes in the right, sometimes in the wrong: their judgment is a mere lottery.

JOHN DRYDEN (1631–1700). *Of Dramatick Poesie: An Essay*, 1668

It is said public opinion will not bear it. Really? Public opinion, I am sorry to say, will bear a great deal of nonsense. There is scarce any absurdity so gross whether in religion, politics, science, or manners, which it will not bear.

RALPH WALDO EMERSON (1803–1882). Journal, December 1827

Manufacture of public opinion.

RALPH WALDO EMERSON (1803–1882). "Success," *Society and Solitude*, 1870
See Manipulation: Walter Lippmann

Singularity in right hath ruined many: Happy those who are convinced of the general Opinion.

BENJAMIN FRANKLIN (1706–1790). *Poor Richard's Almanack*, October 1757

What is thought to be the responsible public opinion is, at any given time, a reflection of the needs and interests of the corporate technostructure.

JOHN KENNETH GALBRAITH (1908–). *A Life in Our Times: Memoirs*, 33, 1981
See Aristocracy: John Stuart Mill (2) ○ Class: Karl Marx and Friedrich Engels (1)

It is the absolute right of the state to supervise the formation of public opinion.

JOSEPH GOEBBELS (1897–1945). German minister of propaganda. Speech before journalists, Berlin, October 1933

Nothing makes the multitude angrier than when someone forces them to change their opinion of him.

> HERMANN HESSE (1877–1962). *Reflections,* 100, ed. Volker Michels, 1974

Public opinion, a vulgar, impertinent, anonymous tyrant who deliberately makes life unpleasant for anyone who is not content to be the average man.

> DEAN WILLIAM RALPH INGE (1860–1954). "Our Present Discontents," *Outspoken Essays: First Series,* 1919

It is rare that the public sentiment decides immorally or unwisely, and the individual who differs from it ought to distrust and examine well his own opinion.

> THOMAS JEFFERSON (1743–1826). Letter to William Findley, 24 March 1801

The good opinion of mankind, like the lever of Archimedes, with the given fulcrum, moves the world.

> THOMAS JEFFERSON (1743–1826). Letter to *Correa della Sera,* 27 December 1814

Public opinion is founded to a great extent on a property basis. What lessens the value of property is opposed, what enhances its value is favored.

> ABRAHAM LINCOLN (1809–1865). Speech, Hartford (Connecticut), 5 March 1860

He who captures the symbols by which public feeling is for the moment contained, controls by that much the approaches of public policy.

> WALTER LIPPMANN (1889–1974). *Public Opinion,* 13.3, 1922

World opinion? I don't believe in world opinion. The only thing that matters is power.

> JOHN J. McCLOY (1895–1989). Disarmament coordinator. Remark during a White House conference, September 1961.

In politics it is almost a triviality to say that public opinion now rules the world.

> JOHN STUART MILL (1806–1873). *On Liberty,* 3, 1859

The law of public opinion is the universal law of gravitation in political history.

> JOSÉ ORTEGA y GASSET (1883–1955). *The Revolt of the Masses,* 14.1, 1930, tr. anon., 1932

Public opinion, because of the tremendous urge to conformity in gregarious animals, is less tolerant than any system of law.

> GEORGE ORWELL (1903–1950). "Politics vs. Literature: An Examination of *Gulliver's Travels,*" September-October 1946, *The Collected Essays, Journalism and Letters of George Orwell,* vol. 4, ed. Sonia Orwell and Ian Angus, 1968
>
> See Law: Abraham Lincoln (2)

The People's Voice is odd,
It is, and it is not, the voice of God.

> ALEXANDER POPE (1688–1744). *Imitations of Horace,* 2.1(Epistle).89, 1733–1738

The fact that an opinion has been widely held is no evidence whatever that it is not utterly absurd; indeed in view of the silliness of the majority of mankind, a widespread belief is more likely to be foolish than sensible.

> BERTRAND RUSSELL (1872–1970). *Marriage and Morals,* 5, 1929

There is . . . no point in deliberately flouting public opinion; this is still to be under its domination, though in a topsy-turvy way. But to be genuinely indifferent to it is both a strength and a source of happiness.

> BERTRAND RUSSELL (1872–1970). *The Conquest of Happiness,* 9, 1930

A new public opinion must be created privately and unobtrusively. The existing one is maintained by the Press, by propaganda, by organization, and by financial and other influences which are at its disposal. This unnatural way of spreading ideas must be opposed by the natural one, which goes from man to man and relies solely on the truth of the thoughts and the hearer's receptiveness for new truth.

> ALBERT SCHWEITZER (1875–1965). *The Philosophy of Civilization: The Decay and Restoration of Civilization,* 4, 1923, tr. C. T. Campion, 1923

[Public opinion] rarely considers the needs of the next generation or the history of the last. It is frequently hampered by myths and misinformation, by stereotypes and shibboleths, and by an innate resistance to innovation.

> THEODORE C. SORENSEN (1928–). *Decision-Making in the White House: The Olive Branch or the Arrows,* 4, 1963

By whatever political laws men are governed in the ages of equality, it may be foreseen that faith in public opinion will become for them a species of religion, and the majority its ministering prophet.

> ALEXIS de TOCQUEVILLE (1805–1859). *Democracy in America,* 2.1.2, 1840, tr. Henry Reeve and Francis Bowen, 1862

Great and rapid changes in human opinions have been produced far less by the force of reasoning than by the authority of a name.

> ALEXIS de TOCQUEVILLE (1805–1859). *Democracy in America,* 2.3.21, 1840, tr. Henry Reeve and Francis Bowen, 1862

Public opinion does not need hundreds and thousands of years for its formation and growth for it possesses an infectious quality of acting on people and attracting collective masses with great rapidity.

> LEO TOLSTOY (1828–1910). *The Kingdom of God Is Within You,* 10, 1893, tr. Aylmer Maude, 1936

Public opinion is stronger than the legislature, and nearly as strong as the ten commandments.

> CHARLES DUDLEY WARNER (1829–1900). "Sixteenth Week," *My Summer in a Garden,* 1871

It always has been, and will continue to be, my earnest desire to learn and to comply, as far as is consistent, with the public sentiment; but it is on *great* occasions *only,* and after time has been given for cool and deliberate reflection, that the *real* voice of the people can be known.

> GEORGE WASHINGTON (1732–1799). Letter to Edward Carrington, 1 May 1796

In proportion as the structure of a government gives force to public opinion, it is essential that public opinion should be enlightened.

> GEORGE WASHINGTON (1732–1799). *Farewell Address,* 17 September 1796

✹

The voice of the people is the voice of God. [Vox populi vox dei.]
    SAYING (LATIN)

PUBLIC OPINION POLLS

See also • Campaigns: Zolton Ferency ○ Politics ○ Presidents &
    People: Richard M. Nixon ○ Public Opinion

If Rosa Parks had taken a poll before she sat down in the bus in
Montgomery, she'd still be standing.
    MARY FRANCES BERRY. In Brian Lanker, "Mary Frances Berry,"
        I Dream a World: Portraits of Black Women Who Changed America,
        1989

November saw China enter the [Korean War] with a rush.
MacArthur's armies were driven back almost to Pusan again. Gallup
polls of October had shown 64 percent of the public in favor of taking all Korea, rather than stopping at the prewar line. By January
1951 they showed 66 percent for getting out of Korea altogether.
    GALLUP POLL. As summarized by Richard E. Neustadt and Ernest
        R. May, *Thinking in Time: The Uses of History for Decision-Makers,*
        3, 1986

The worse I do, the more popular I get.
    JOHN F. KENNEDY (1917–1963). On his increased popularity as measured
        in a public opinion poll taken soon after the Bay of Pigs failure, 3 May
        1961. In Arthur M. Schlesinger, Jr., *A Thousand Days: John F. Kennedy
        in the White House,* 11.4, 1965

Public opinion polls are useful if a politician uses them only to learn
approximately what the people are thinking, so that he can talk to
them more intelligently. The politician who sways with the polls is
not worth his pay. And I believe the people eventually catch up
with the man who merely tells them what he thinks they want to
hear.
    RICHARD M. NIXON (1913–1994). *Six Crises,* 3, 1962

Polls are like perfume—nice to smell, dangerous to swallow.
    SHIMON PERES (1923–). In William Safire, "What's With Assad?"
        New York Times, 13 October 1994

I wonder how far Moses would have gone if he had taken a poll
in Egypt? What would Jesus Christ have preached if He had taken
a poll in the land of Israel?
    HARRY S. TRUMAN (1884–1972). Remark to the author. In William
        Hillman, *Mr. President,* 1.1, 1952

✹

Pollster: Which is the greatest problem facing democracy in the
United States today: public ignorance or public apathy?
Anonymous: I don't know and I don't care.
    ANONYMOUS. Late 1970s. Format adapted. In Thomas E. Cronin,
        The State of the Presidency, 2nd ed., 11, 1980

Pollsters don't vote. People do.
    ANONYMOUS

The only poll that counts is taken on Election Day.
    ANONYMOUS

PUBLIC RELATIONS

See also • Advertising ○ Charisma: Raymond K. Price ○ Fame ○
    Indoctrination ○ Propaganda ○ Publicity

From a public relations point of view, the Boston Tea Party [1773]
was an overt act staged to dramatize American resistance to British
authority.
    EDWARD L. BERNAYS (1891–1995). *Public Relations,* 5, 1952

The counsel on public relations not only knows what news value
is, but knowing it, he is in a position to *make news happen.* He is
a creator of events.
    EDWARD L. BERNAYS (1891–1995). In Daniel J. Boorstin, *The Image:
        A Guide to Pseudo-Events in America,* 1.1, 1961

Two centuries ago when a great man appeared, people looked for
God's purpose in him. Today we look for his press agent.
    DANIEL J. BOORSTIN (1914–). *The Image: A Guide to Pseudo-Events in
        America,* 2 (introduction), 1961

By 1920, public relations had become a way of American life and
livelihood; ham-fisted Barnumesque methods had given way to sur-
veys and polls, and a newborn "science" began to call itself "the
engineering of consent." The patina of science was, of course, just
that; in fact, a cynical new game of thought-shaping was born.
    JAMES R. GAINES (1947–). *Wit's End: Days and Nights of the Algonquin
        Round Table,* 2, 1977

✹

[During the 1920s Edward L. Bernays] was instrumental in making
it acceptable for women to smoke in public, sponsoring, on behalf
of the American Tobacco Company's Lucky Strike cigarettes,
demonstrations in which debutantes gathered on street corners to
light up. The cigarettes were even called "torches of freedom."
    ANONYMOUS. In "Edward Bernays, 'Father of Public Relations' and
        Leader in Opinion Making, Dies at 103," *New York Times,* 10 March
        1995. The same obituary also reported, "In his later years, beginning in
        the early 1960s, [Bernays] was a public opponent of smoking and took
        part in anti-smoking campaigns."

The best PR is no PR.
    SAYING (AMERICAN). In "Public Relations Today," *Business Week,* 2 July
        1960

PUBLIC SPEAKING

See also • Argument ○ Eloquence ○ Oratory ○ Speaking ○ Talking ○
    Words

I do not object to people looking at their watches when I am speaking. But I strongly object when they start shaking them to make certain they are still going.
    LORD BIRKETT (1883–1962). British lawyer. In *Observer* (British newspa-
        per), 30 October 1960

He is considered the most graceful speaker who can say nothing in
[the] most words.
    SAMUEL BUTLER (1835–1902). *Further Extracts from the Note-Books of
        Samuel Butler,* 5, ed. A. T. Bartholomew, 1934

I have just got a new theory of eternity.

> ALBERT EINSTEIN (1879–1955). Remark to a table-mate while listening to long-winded speeches at a National Academy of Science dinner honoring him. In Daniel S. Greenberg, "A Statue Without Stature," *Washington Post,* 12 December 1978

Condense some daily experience into a glowing symbol, and an audience is electrified.

> RALPH WALDO EMERSON (1803–1882). "Eloquence," *Letters and Social Aims,* 1876

If you find me this evening speaking without reserve, pray consider that you are only sharing the thoughts of a man who allows himself to think audibly.

> MOHANDAS K. GANDHI (1869–1948). Speech at the opening ceremonies of the Hindu University Central College, Benares (India), 4 February 1916. In Louis Fischer, *The Life of Mahatma Gandhi,* 17, 1950

[Abraham Lincoln] wrote [the "House Divided" speech], that fine effort, an argumentative one, in slips, put those slips in his hat, numbering them, and when he was done with the ideas, he gathered up the scraps, put them in the right order, and wrote out his speech, read it to me before it was delivered, and in the evening delivered it just as written without notes.

> WILLIAM H. HERNDON (1818–1891). Address, 1887. In Emanuel Hertz, ed., "Lincoln the Individual," *The Hidden Lincoln: From the Letters and Papers of William H. Herndon,* 2.3. 1940
>
> See Unity: Abraham Lincoln

Why doesn't the fellow who says, "I'm no speechmaker," let it go at that instead of giving a demonstration.

> KIN HUBBARD (1868–1930)

It was not the object of Demosthenes to make the Athenians cry out "What a splendid speaker!" but to make them say "Let us march against Philip."

> JOHN STUART MILL (1806–1873). "On Education," inaugural address on being installed as rector, University of St. Andrews (Scotland), 1 February 1867

Three things matter in a speech; who says it, how he says it, and what he says—and, of the three, the last matters the least.

> JOHN MORLEY (1838–1923)

A speech is poetry: cadence, rhythm, imagery, sweep! A speech reminds us that words, like children, have the power to make dance the dullest beanbag of a heart.

> PEGGY NOONAN (1950–). *What I Saw at the Revolution: A Political Life in the Reagan Era,* 5, 1990

Promptitude in speaking, which depends on activity of thought, can be retained only by exercise. Such exercise we may best use by speaking daily in the hearing of several persons, especially of those for whose judgment and opinion we have most regard; for it rarely happens that a person is sufficiently severe with himself. Let us, however, rather speak alone than not speak at all. There is also another kind of exercise, that of meditating upon whole subjects and going through them in silent thought (. . . to speak, as it were, within ourselves), an exercise which may be pursued at all times and in all places, when we are not actually engaged in any other occupation.

> QUINTILIAN (A.D. 35?–100?). *Institutio oratoria,* 10.7.24–25, tr. John Selby Watson, 1856

Be sincere; be brief; be seated.

> FRANKLIN D. ROOSEVELT (1882–1945). Advice on speechmaking to his son James. In Bill Adler, comp., *Presidential Wit: From Washington to Johnson,* p. 164, 1966

Antony: Friends, Romans, countrymen, lend me your ears.

> SHAKESPEARE (1564–1616). *Julius Caesar,* 3.2.79, 1599

There is always a single ear in the audience, to which we address ourselves.

> HENRY DAVID THOREAU (1817–1862). Journal, 2 February 1841

The one great rule of composition—and if I were a professor of rhetoric, I should insist on this—is, to *speak the truth.* This first, this second, this third; pebbles in your mouth or not.

> HENRY DAVID THOREAU (1817–1862). "The Last Days of John Brown," eulogy, 4 July 1860

Sometimes men who cannot speak, can . . . have a greater effect, in the right circumstances, than the finest speakers. They bring only one idea, the idea of the moment, engraved in a single phrase, and then somehow they place it on the rostrum like an inscription in big letters which all read and immediately recognize in their own thoughts.

> ALEXIS de TOCQUEVILLE (1805–1859). *Recollections,* 2.9, 1893, tr. George Lawrence, 1964

I . . . never could make a good impromptu speech without several hours to prepare it.

> MARK TWAIN (1835–1910). Impromptu speech at the Thirteenth Regiment Reunion of the Army of Tennessee, Chicago, 12 November 1879

New York, I have emptied entire halls.

> SWAMI VIVEKANANDA (1863–1902). In introduction to Christopher Isherwood, ed., *Vedanta for the Western World,* 1945

Lady Basildon: I don't know how the unfortunate men in the House stand these long debates.
Lady Goring: By never listening.

> OSCAR WILDE (1854–1900). *An Ideal Husband,* 1, 1895

PUBLISHERS

See also • Books ∘ Editors ∘ Freedom of the Press: A. J. Liebling ∘ Journalists ∘ Media ∘ News ∘ Newspapers

At Random House we have a great number of splendid young writers under contract. Their books may be hard to sell now, but I think we're betting on the right horses. Within the next five years we'll be coming out with names that will flash across the literary heavens. . . .

I'm being the eternal optimist, but this is the heart and soul of publishing and the joy of being a publisher.

> BENNETT CERF (1898–1971). Closing paragraphs, interview with the author, July 1963. In Roy Newquist, *Counterpoint,* 1964

The minute you try to talk business with him he takes the attitude that he is a gentleman and a scholar, and the moment you try to approach him on the level of his moral integrity he starts to talk business.

> RAYMOND CHANDLER (1888–1959). On "the publisher," letter to Dale Warren, 2 June 1947, *Selected Letters of Raymond Chandler,* ed. Frank MacShane, 1981

As repressed sadists are supposed to become policemen or butchers so those with an irrational fear of life become publishers.

> CYRIL CONNOLLY (1903–1974). *Enemies of Promise,* 10, 1938

Even though some say that an avant-garde in literature no longer exists, the smaller independent publisher is itself still a true avant-garde, its place still out there, scouting the unknown.

> LAWRENCE FERLINGHETTI (1919–). Introduction to *City Lights Pocket Poets Anthology,* 1995

I estimate (based on some rough numbers from the Library of Congress) that humanity now publishes as many words every week or so as it did in all human history up to 1800.

> JAMES GLEICK. "Bartlett Updated: Renewing the Idea of a Shared Culture," *New York Times Book Review,* 8 August 1993

You may remember that the Dial Press had been asking me for some years for a manuscript, but when I sent the [manuscript] of *AF [Animal Farm]* they returned it, saying shortly that "it was impossible to sell animal stories in the USA."

> GEORGE ORWELL (1903–1950). Letter to Leonard Moore, 23 February 1946, *The Collected Essays, Journalism and Letters of George Orwell,* vol. 4, ed. Sonia Orwell and Ian Angus, 1968

[Publishers] are like Methodists. They love to keep the Sabbath and everything else they can lay their hands on.

> AMANDA ROS. Letter to Lord Ponsonby, 1910

The trouble with the publishing business is that too many people who have half a mind to write a book do so.

> WILLIAM TARG. Editor. In William Rossa Cole, "'No Author Is a Man of Genius to His Publisher'" [Heinrich Heine's observation], *New York Times Book Review,* 3 September 1989

How often we recall, with regret, that Napoleon once shot at a magazine editor and missed him and killed a publisher. But we remember, with charity, that his intentions were good.

> MARK TWAIN (1835–1910). Letter to Henry Alden, 11 November 1906

Publish and be damned.

> DUKE OF WELLINGTON (1769–1852). Attributed. Rejecting a publisher's request for a bribe to exclude certain defamatory passages from a courtesan's memoirs. In Roy Jenkins, "The Iron Duke," *New York Times Book Review,* 2 November 1997

❦

First you have the writer who can write but can't spell. Then you have the editor who can spell but can't write. Finally you have the publisher who can neither spell nor write, and he makes all the money.

> ANONYMOUS. In Michael Larsen, *Literary Agents: What They Do, How They Do It, and How to Find and Work with the Right One for You,* rev. ed., 13.3, 1996

PUNCTUALITY

See also • Procrastination ○ Time

Punctuality is the soul of business.

> THOMAS CHANDLER HALIBURTON (1796–1865). *Sam Slick's Wise Saws,* 3, 1853

To let people wait is to commit an injustice.

> LA BRUYÈRE (1645–1696). "Of Opinions," 81, *The Characters,* 1688, tr. Henri van Laun, 1929

Punctuality is the politeness of kings.

> LOUIS XVIII (1755–1824). French king

I owe all my success in life to having been always a quarter of an hour beforehand.

> HORATIO NELSON (1758–1805). In Elbert Hubbard, comp., *Elbert Hubbard's Scrap Book,* p. 133, 1923

Ford: Better three hours too soon than a minute too late.

> SHAKESPEARE (1564–1616). *The Merry Wives of Windsor,* 2.2.327, 1600

Keeping another person waiting is a basic tactic for defining him as inferior and oneself as superior.

> THOMAS S. SZASZ (1920–). "Social Relations," *The Second Sin,* 1973

Punctuality is the virtue of the bored.

> EVELYN WAUGH (1903–1966). Diary, 26 March 1962

He was always late on principle, his principle being that punctuality is the thief of time.

> OSCAR WILDE (1854–1900). *The Picture of Dorian Gray,* 4, 1891
>
> See Procrastination: Edward Young

❦

People count up the faults of those who keep them waiting.

> SAYING (FRENCH)

Better early than late; better late than never.

> SAYING

PUNISHMENT

See also • Brainwashing ○ Crime ○ Guilt ○ Justice ○ Law ○ Morality ○ Punishment, Capital ○ Torture ○ Trials ○ Violence

The punishment shall fit the offense.

> CICERO (106–43 B.C.). *De legibus,* 3.20, tr. Clinton Walker Keyes, 1928

I hear much of People's calling out to punish the Guilty, but very few are concern'd to clear the Innocent.

> DANIEL DEFOE (1660–1731). *An Appeal to Honour and Justice, Tho' it be of His Worst Enemies,* 1715

The great Thieves punish the little ones.

> THOMAS FULLER (1654–1734). Comp., *Gnomologia: Adages and Proverbs,* 4565, 1732

What . . . can be more shameless than for society to make an example of those whom she has goaded to the breach of order, instead of amending her own institutions which, by straining order into tyranny, produced the mischief?

> WILLIAM GODWIN (1756–1836). English philosopher. On the penal laws, *An Enquiry Concerning the Principles of Political Justice*, 7.3, 1793

Wherever a knave is not punished, an honest man is laughed at.

> MARQUIS OF HALIFAX (1633–1695). "Of Punishment," *Political, Moral and Miscellaneous Reflections*, 1750

Punishment: The justice that the guilty deal out to those who are caught.

> ELBERT HUBBARD (1856–1915). *The Roycroft Dictionary Concocted by Ali Baba and the Bunch on Rainy Days*, p. 121, 1914

Someone must have slandered Joseph K. because one morning, without his having done anything wrong, he was arrested.

> FRANZ KAFKA (1883–1924). Opening words, *The Trial*, 1925, tr. Willa and Edwin Muir, 1930

Corporal punishment is as humiliating for him who gives it as for him who receives it; it is ineffective besides. Neither shame nor physical pain have any other effect than a hardening one.

> ELLEN KEY (1849–1926). *The Century of the Child*, 8, 1909

Beulah Easton of Bloomington, Illinois, was sentenced to pay a $50 fine for criminal trespass after distributing copies of the Declaration of Independence at a shopping center.

> ERWIN KNOLL (1931–). Editor. "Spirit of '84," *No Comment*, 1984

Penalties serve to deter those who are not inclined to commit any crimes.

> KARL KRAUS (1876–1936). "Lord, Forgive Them . . . ," *Half-Truths & One-and-a-Half Truths: Selected Aphorisms*, ed. Harry Zohn, 1976

A Chicago high school punished truants by making them listen to Frank Sinatra records.

> BILL MANDEL. "The Year 1992: Calling It Like It Was," *San Francisco Sunday Examiner and Chronicle*, 20 December 1992

Mistrust all in whom the urge to punish is strong!

> FRIEDRICH NIETZSCHE (1844–1900). "Of the Tarantulas," *Thus Spoke Zarathustra*, 1892, tr. R. J. Hollingdale, 1961

To spare the guilty is to injure the innocent.

> PUBLIUS SYRUS (85–43 B.C.). *Moral Sayings*, 113, tr. Darius Lyman, Jr., 1862

Leniency gives rise to the ultimately necessary exercise of a degree of cruelty which could have been avoided by the employment of an efficacious punishment at an earlier time.

> CARDINAL RICHELIEU (1585–1642). *Political Testament*, 2.5, tr. Henry Bertram Hill, 1961

The reformative effect of punishment is a belief that dies hard, chiefly I think, because it is so satisfying to our sadistic impulses.

> BERTRAND RUSSELL (1872–1970). "Ideas That Have Harmed Mankind," *Unpopular Essays*, 1951

⚓

No crime without punishment, no punishment without crime.

> SAYING

PUNISHMENT, CAPITAL

See also • Assassination: George Bernard Shaw (2) ○ Crime ○ Golden Rule: Moses ○ Justice ○ Murder ○ Newspeak—Examples: Orrin G. Hatch ○ Punishment ○ Torture ○ Violence

Capital punishment is murder pure and simple. . . . It is the most striking instance of the state overstepping its legitimate boundaries, for human life belongs to God and not to man.

> NICOLAS BERDYAEV (1874–1948). *The Destiny of Man*, 2.4.6, 1931, tr. Natalie Duddington, 1955

There, but for the grace of God, goes John Bradford.

> JOHN BRADFORD (1510?–1555). English Protestant martyr. While observing several criminals being taken to execution, *The Writings of John Bradford*, 1853. (Popular version: There, but for the grace of God, go I.) Shortly thereafter, Bradford was charged with sedition and heresy, and burned at the stake.
>
> See Wickedness: Billy Graham

Of course the death penalty is cruel and unusual. That's what people like about it.

> DANZIGER. Cartoon balloon. In *Christian Science Monitor*, 1990

One of the oldest Russian proverbs remains as inexorably true in modern America: "No one is hanged who has money in his pocket." Or, one might say, capital punishment is only for those without capital.

> SYDNEY J. HARRIS (1917–1986). Syndicated column, *Chicago Daily News*, April 1971

Who hangs one corrects a thousand.

> JAMES HOWELL (1593–1666). Comp., "Divers Centuries of New Sayings" (p. 8), *Paroimiographia: Proverbs, or Old Sayed Sawes & Adages in English . . . Italian, French and Spanish*, 1659

Depend upon it, Sir, when a man knows he is to be hanged in a fortnight, it concentrates his mind wonderfully.

> SAMUEL JOHNSON (1709–1784). 19 September 1777. In James Boswell, *The Life of Samuel Johnson*, 1791

There is no man so good that if he placed all his actions and thoughts under the scrutiny of the laws, he would not deserve hanging ten times in his life.

> MONTAIGNE (1533–1592). "Of Vanity," *Essays*, 1588, tr. Donald M. Frame, 1958

You shall not permit a sorcerer to live.
    Whoever lies with a beast shall be put to death.
    Whoever sacrifices to any god, save the Lord only, shall be utterly destroyed.

> MOSES (14th cent. B.C.). *Exodus* 22:18–20

Your eye shall not pity; it shall be life for life, eye for eye, tooth for tooth, hand for hand, foot for foot.

> MOSES (14th cent. B.C.). *Deuteronomy* 19:21
>
> See Nonviolence: Jesus (1)

Must we kill to prevent there being any wicked? This is to make both parties wicked instead of one.

> BLAISE PASCAL (1623–1662). *Pensées*, 911, 1670, tr. William F. Trotter, 1931

It is the deed that teaches, not the name we give it. Murder and capital punishment are not opposites that cancel one another, but similars that breed their kind.

> GEORGE BERNARD SHAW (1856–1950). "Maxims for Revolutionists: Crime and Punishment," *Man and Superman,* 1903

Since executions [in the United States] were resumed in 1977:
- Someone who kills a white is ten times more likely to be executed than someone who kills a black.
- A black who kills a white is about five times more likely to be executed than a white who kills a white.
- A black who kills a white is about sixty times more likely to be executed than a black who kills a black.
- And the most telling fact of all: Though there have been well over 2,500 white on black homicides nationally since 1977 [through 1987], not a single state has yet put to death a white who killed a black.

> CARL SICILIANO and MEG HYRE. "Racism, Silence, and the Subversion of Justice," *Catholic Worker,* December 1988

The punishment of criminals should be useful. A hanged man is good for nothing and a man condemned to public labor still serves the fatherland and is a living lesson.

> VOLTAIRE (1694–1778). "Civil and Ecclesiastical Laws," *Philosophical Dictionary,* 1764, tr. Theodore Besterman, 1971

[Capital punishment] is inhuman because its deterrent effects are now recognized as a myth. It is unjust because it leaves no remedy for a mistake. It is unequal because it is exacted almost exclusively of the poor and the ignorant. It is, in short, a relic of the barbarous days when our law demanded an eye for an eye.

> EDWARD BENNETT WILLIAMS. *One Man's Freedom,* 14, 1962

Jailer: To you, Socrates, whom I know to be the noblest and gentlest and best of all who ever came to this place, I will not impute the angry feelings of other men, who rage and swear at me, when in obedience to the authorities, I bid them drink the poison—indeed, I am sure that you will not be angry with me; for others, as you are aware, and not I, are to blame. And so fare you well, and try to bear lightly what must needs be—you know my errand. Then bursting into tears he turned away and went out.

> ANONYMOUS (GREEK). In Plato (427?–347 B.C.), *Phaedo,* 116, tr. Benjamin Jowett, 1894

PURITANISM

See also • Abstinence ○ Hypocrisy ○ Moral Indignation ○ Pleasure ○ Prudery ○ Self-Righteousness ○ Sex

Puritans should wear fig leaves on their eyes.

> STANISLAW J. LEC (1909–1966). *Unkempt Thoughts,* p. 137, tr. Jacek Galazka, 1962

The Puritans tried to choke the craving for pleasure in early New England. They had no theaters, no dances, no festivals. They burned witches instead.

> WALTER LIPPMANN (1889–1974). *A Preface to Politics,* 2, 1914

The Puritan hated bear-baiting, not because it gave pain to the bear, but because it gave pleasure to the spectators.

> THOMAS BABINGTON MACAULAY (1800–1859). *The History of England,* 1.2, 1849–1861

The objection to Puritans is not that they try to make us think as they do, but that they try to make us do as they think.

> H. L. MENCKEN (1880–1956). *A Little Book in C Major,* 5.22, 1916

It is not actually a sign of spiritual eminence to be moral in the Puritan sense: it is simply a sign of docility, of lack of enterprise and originality, of cowardice.

> H. L. MENCKEN (1880–1956). *Notes on Democracy,* 3.2, 1926

Puritanism—The haunting fear that someone, somewhere, may be happy.

> H. L. MENCKEN (1880–1956). *A Mencken Chrestomathy,* 30 ("Arcana Coelestia"), 1949`

The Puritan's idea of Hell is a place where everybody has to mind his own business.

> WENDELL PHILLIPS (1811–1884). Attributed

Next to enjoying ourselves, the next greatest pleasure consists in preventing others from enjoying themselves, or, more generally, in the acquisition of power. Consequently those who live under the dominion of Puritanism become exceedingly desirous of power.

> BERTRAND RUSSELL (1872–1970). *Sceptical Essays,* 10, 1928
> See Abstinence: Russell

What [the Puritans] took away from sex they added to gluttony.

> BERTRAND RUSSELL (1872–1970). *Marriage and Morals,* 20, 1929

I believe we are descendid from the Puritins, who nobly fled from a land of despitism to a land of freedim, where they could not only enjoy their own religion, but prevent everybody else from enjoyin his.

> ARTEMUS WARD (1834–1867). "Is Introduced at the Club," *The Complete Works of Artemus Ward,* 1898

PURPOSE

See also • Civilization ○ Goals ○ God ○ God & History ○ Happiness: Helen Keller (1) ○ History ○ Ideals ○ Life ○ Man ○ Meaning ○ Means & Ends ○ Motives ○ Pain: Mathias Yrogoyin ○ Principles, Moral ○ Progress ○ Resolution ○ Self-Realization (Being) ○ Success ○ Unity: Walt Whitman ○ Values

Not only to see and find the Divine in oneself, but to see and find the Divine in all, not only to seek one's own individual liberation and perfection, but to seek the liberation and perfection of others is the complete law of the spiritual being.

> SRI AUROBINDO (1872–1950). "Conditions for the Coming of the Spiritual Age," *The Essential Aurobindo,* ed. Robert A. McDermott, 1973

Let your aim be the good of all.

> *BHAGAVAD GITA* (6th cent. B.C.). 3.20, tr. Juan Mascaró, 1962
> See Action: Marcus Aurelius

Caesar, when embarking in a storm, said that it was not necessary he should live, but that is was absolutely necessary he should get to the place to which he was going.

> LORD CHESTERFIELD (1731–1800). Letter to his son, 24 November 1749
> See Duty: Frederick II

Men deal with life as children with their play,
Who first misuse, then cast their toys away;
Live to no sober purpose, and contend
That their Creator had no serious end.

> WILLIAM COWPER (1731–1800). "Hope," l. 127, 1782

Grand Inquisitor: The secret of man's being is not only to live but to have something to live for.

> FYODOR DOSTOYEVSKY (1821–1881). *The Brothers Karamazov,* 5.5, 1880, tr. Constance Garnett, 1912

Time past and time future
What might have been and what has been
Point to one end, which is always present.

> T. S. ELIOT (1888–1965). "Burnt Norton" (1), *Four Quartets,* 1943

The human soul, the world, the universe are laboring on to their magnificent consummation. We are not fashioned . . . marvelously for nought.

> RALPH WALDO EMERSON (1803–1882). Journal, 5 December 1820

The purpose of life on earth is that the soul should grow—
    So grow! By doing what is right.

> ZELDA FITZGERALD (1900–1948). Letter to her husband F. Scott Fitzgerald, 1944. In Nancy Milford, *Zelda,* 21, 1970

Man's main task is to give birth to himself, to become what he potentially is. The most important product of his effort is his own personality.

> ERICH FROMM (1900–1980). *Man for Himself: An Inquiry into the Psychology of Ethics,* 4.5.C, 1947

Make it thy chief Design and thy great Business, not to be Rich and Great: but so to live in this World as that thou mayest reasonably believe thou hast God for thy Friend.

> THOMAS FULLER (1654–1734). Comp., *Introductio ad Prudentiam,* 939, 1731

A good Cause makes a stout Heart and a strong Arm.

> THOMAS FULLER (1654–1734). Comp., *Gnomologia: Adages and Proverbs,* 140, 1732

A small body of determined spirits fired by an unquenchable faith in their mission can alter the course of history.

> MOHANDAS K. GANDHI (1869–1948). In *Harijan,* 19 November 1938

The purpose of life is undoubtedly to know oneself. We cannot do it unless we learn to identify ourselves with all that lives. The sum total of that life is God. Hence the necessity of realizing God living within every one of us. . . .
    The instrument of this knowledge is boundless, selfless service.

> MOHANDAS K. GANDHI (1869–1948). In Mahadev Desai, *The Diary of Mahadev Desai,* 1953

A straight path never leads anywhere except to the objective.

> ANDRÉ GIDE (1869–1951). Journal, 28 October 1922, tr. Justin O'Brien, 1948

Higher aims are in themselves more valuable, even if unfulfilled, than lower ones quite attained.

> GOETHE (1749–1832). *The Maxims and Reflections of Goethe,* 500, tr. T. Bailey Saunders, 1892

As surely as we are driven to live, we are driven to serve spiritual ends that surpass our own interests. . . . We are not only in need of God but also in need of serving His ends, and these ends are in need of us.

> ABRAHAM JOSHUA HESCHEL (1907–1972). *God in Search of Man: A Philosophy of Judaism,* 28, 1955
> See God & History: Heschel

Man's only legitimate end in life is to finish God's work—to bring to full growth the capacities and talents implanted in us.

> ERIC HOFFER (1902–1983). *The Ordeal of Change,* 11, 1964

There must be in this world a task with an appeal so strong that were we to have a taste of it we would hold on and be rid for good of our restlessness. . . .
    The pioneer task of making the desert flower would certainly fill the bill.

> ERIC HOFFER (1902–1983). *The Ordeal of Change,* 16, 1964

God is. That is the primordial fact. It is in order that we may discover this fact for ourselves, by direct experience, that we exist. The final end and purpose of every human being is the unitive knowledge of God's being.

> ALDOUS HUXLEY (1894–1963). "Seven Meditations." In Christopher Isherwood, ed., *Vedanta for the Western World,* 1945

Man's perfection would be the fulfillment of his end; and his end would be union with his Maker.

> WILLIAM JAMES (1842–1910). *The Varieties of Religious Experience: A Study in Human Nature,* 14 and 15, 1902

Everything living strives for wholeness.

> CARL G. JUNG (1875–1961). "On the Nature of Dreams," 1945, *The Structure and Dynamics of the Psyche,* tr. R. F. C. Hull, 1960

As far we can discern, the sole purpose of human existence is to kindle a light in the darkness of mere being.

> CARL G. JUNG (1875–1961). *Memories, Dreams, Reflections,* 11, ed. Aniela Jaffé, 1962

I still believe that standing up for the truth of God is the greatest thing in the world. This is the end of life. The end of life is not to be happy. The end of life is not to achieve pleasure and avoid pain. The end of life is to do the will of God, come what may.

> MARTIN LUTHER KING, JR. (1929–1968). "The Most Durable Power," sermon, Montgomery (Alabama), 6 November 1956

The Almighty has His own purposes.

> ABRAHAM LINCOLN (1809–1865). *Second Inaugural Address,* 4 March 1865

It is a man's proper business to seek happiness and avoid misery.

> JOHN LOCKE (1632–1704). "Thus I Think." In Lord King, *The Life of John Locke*, 2.120, 1830

Not enjoyment, and not sorrow,
  Is our destined end or way;
But to act, that each tomorrow
  Find us farther than today.

> HENRY WADSWORTH LONGFELLOW (1807–1882). "A Psalm of Life," 3, *Voices of the Night*, 1839

The highest aim of man: the knowledge of God.

> MOSES MAIMONIDES (A.D. 1135–1204). *The Guide for the Perplexed*, 3.54, A.D. 1190, tr. M. Friedländer, 1904

Be ashamed to die until you have won some victory for humanity.

> HORACE MANN (1796–1859). Antioch College president. Closing words of his last public address, Yellow Springs (Ohio), 1859

All of us are working together for the same end; some of us knowingly and purposefully, others unconsciously. . . . To one man falls this share of the task, to another that; indeed, no small part is performed by that very malcontent who does all he can to hinder and undo the course of events.

> MARCUS AURELIUS (A.D. 121–180). *Meditations*, 6.42, tr. Maxwell Staniforth, 1964

Ours is a world where people don't know what they want and are willing to go through hell to get it.

> DON MARQUIS (1878–1937). In "Thoughts on the Business of Life," *Forbes*, 8 June 1992

Captain Ahab: The path to my fixed purpose is laid with iron rails, whereon my soul is grooved to run.

> HERMAN MELVILLE (1819–1891). *Moby-Dick; or, The Whale*, 37, 1851, ed. Harold Beaver, 1972

Until he has been part of a cause larger than himself, no man is truly whole.

> RICHARD M. NIXON (1913–1994). *First Inaugural Address*, 20 January 1969

The end to aim at is assimilation to God.

> PLATO (427?–347 B.C.). In Diogenes Laertius (A.D. 3rd cent.), *Lives of Eminent Philosophers*, 3.78, tr. R. D. Hicks, 1925

Figuring out who you are is the whole point of the human experience.

> ANNA QUINDLEN (1953–). "One View Fits All," *New York Times*, 6 September 1992

Power undirected by high purpose spells calamity; and high purpose by itself is utterly useless if the power to put it into effect is lacking.

> THEODORE ROOSEVELT (1858–1919). 1911, "Words for Today—by Theodore Roosevelt," ed. Hermann Hagedorn, *New York Times Magazine*, 27 October 1957

If life is to be fully human it must serve some end which seems, in some sense, outside human life, some end which is impersonal and above mankind, such as God or truth or beauty. Those who best promote life do not have life for their purpose. They aim rather at what seems like a gradual incarnation, a bringing into our human existence of something eternal, something that appears to imagination to live in a heaven remote from strife and failure and the devouring jaws of Time.

> BERTRAND RUSSELL (1872–1970). *Principles of Social Reconstruction*, 8, 1916

Our plans miscarry because they have no aim. When a man does not know what harbor he is making for, no wind is the right wind.

> SENECA THE YOUNGER (5? B.C.–A.D. 65). "On the Supreme Good," *Moral Letters to Lucilius*, 71.3, tr. Richard M. Gummere, 1918

This is the true joy in life, the being used for a purpose recognized by yourself as a mighty one; the being thoroughly worn out before you are thrown on the scrapheap; the being a force of Nature instead of a feverish, selfish, little clod of ailments and grievances complaining that the world will not devote itself to making you happy.

> GEORGE BERNARD SHAW (1856–1950). Dedicatory epistle to *Man and Superman*, 1903

I tell you that as long as I can conceive something better than myself I cannot be easy unless I am striving to bring it into existence or clearing the way for it. That is the law of my life. That is the working within me of Life's incessant aspiration to higher organization, wider, deeper, intenser self-consciousness, and clearer self-understanding.

> GEORGE BERNARD SHAW (1856–1950). *Man and Superman*, 3, 1903

There are two things to aim at in life: first, to get what you want; and, after that, to enjoy it. Only the wisest of mankind achieve the second.

> LOGAN PEARSALL SMITH (1865–1946). *Afterthoughts*, 1, 1931

The knowledge and love of God is the ultimate aim to which all our actions should be directed.

> BARUCH SPINOZA (1632–1677). *Tractatus Theologico-Politicus*, 4, 1670, tr. R. H. M. Elwes, 1895

Ma Joad: Ever'thing we do—seems to me is aimed right at goin' on. Seems that way to me. Even gettin' hungry—even bein' sick; some die, but the rest is tougher. Jus' try to live the day, jus' the day. . . .
  Just' live the day. Don't worry yaself.

> JOHN STEINBECK (1902–1968). *The Grapes of Wrath*, 28, 1939

We may not arrive at our port within a calculable period, but we would preserve the true course.

> HENRY DAVID THOREAU (1817–1862). "Economy," *Walden; or Life in the Woods*, 1854

Every nail driven should be as another rivet in the machine of the universe, you carrying on the work.

> HENRY DAVID THOREAU (1817–1862). "Conclusion," *Walden; or Life in the Woods*, 1854

Pursue some path, however narrow and crooked, in which you can walk with love and reverence.

> HENRY DAVID THOREAU (1817–1862). Journal, 18 October 1855

A new and fair division of the goods and rights of this world should be the main object of those who conduct human affairs.

> ALEXIS de TOCQUEVILLE (1805–1859). In Henry George, *Progress and Poverty: An Inquiry into the Cause of Industrial Depressions and of Increase of Want with Increase of Wealth,* 6.1 (epigraph), 1879

Man lives consciously for himself but unconsciously he serves as an instrument for the accomplishment of historical and social ends.

> LEO TOLSTOY (1835–1910). *War and Peace,* 3.1.1, 1863–1869, tr. Rosemary Edmonds, 1957

It is a man's task to execute, within the time that God allots to him on Earth, a human mission to do God's will by working for the coming of God's Kingdom in Earth as it is in Heaven.

> ARNOLD J. TOYNBEE (1889–1975). *A Study of History,* 10.39, 1954

What is the chief end of man? To glorify God and to enjoy Him forever.

> *WESTMINSTER SHORTER CATECHISM OF THE PRESBYTERIAN CHURCH.* In Dean Rusk, As I Saw It, 13, 1990

Apart from some transcendent aim the civilized life either wallows in pleasure or relapses slowly into a barren repetition with waning intensities of feeling.

> ALFRED NORTH WHITEHEAD (1861–1947). *Adventures of Ideas,* 5.7, 1933

The aim of life is self-development. To realize one's nature perfectly—that is what each of us is here for.

> OSCAR WILDE (1854–1900). *The Picture of Dorian Gray,* 2, 1891

It is the preservation of the species, not of individuals, which appears to be the design of Deity throughout the whole of nature.

> MARY WOLLSTONECRAFT (1759–1797). Letter, 1796

Happy are those whose purpose has found them.

> ANONYMOUS

QUALITY

See also • Excellence ○ Quantity ○ Value

All things . . . are best to those who know no better.

> SAMUEL BUTLER (1612–1680). "Ignorance," *Prose Observations,* ed. Hugh de Quehen, 1979

The proof of the pudding is in the eating.

> CERVANTES (1547–1616). *Don Quixote,* 1.4.10, 1615, tr. Peter Anthony Motteux and John Ozell, 1743

From want of skill to convey quality, we hope to move admiration by quantity.

> RALPH WALDO EMERSON (1803–1882). "The Superlative," *Lectures and Biographical Sketches,* 1883

Good is not good, where better is expected.

> THOMAS FULLER (1608–1661). *The Church-History of Britain,* 1655

You may know by a Handful the whole Sack.

> THOMAS FULLER (1654–1734). Comp., *Gnomologia: Adages and Proverbs,* 5949, 1732

The tree is known by its fruit.

> JESUS (A.D. 1st cent.). *Matthew* 12:33

It is quality rather than quantity that matters.

> SENECA THE YOUNGER (5? B.C.–A.D. 65). "On Sophistical Argumentation," *Moral Letters to Lucilius,* 34.1, tr. Richard M. Gummere, 1918

"Quality" is best measured by those who "use" a product rather than by those who make it.

> HUNTER S. THOMPSON (1939–). Letter to Lt. Col. Frank Campbell, 6 January 1958, *The Proud Highway: Saga of a Desperate Southern Gentleman, 1955-1967,* ed. Douglas Brinkley, 1997

Ask the dweller, not the builder.

> SAYING (GREEK)
> See Doctors: Saying (1)

QUANTITY

See also • Quality ○ Value

Less is more.

> ROBERT BROWNING (1812–1889). "Andrea del Sarto" (l. 78), *Men and Women,* 1855

A few honest men are better than numbers.

> OLIVER CROMWELL (1599–1658). Letter to Sir William Spring, September 1643

To be satisfied with little is hard, to be satisfied with a lot is impossible.

> MARIE von EBNER-ESCHENBACH (1830–1916). *Aphorisms,* p. 28, 1880–1905, tr. David Scrase and Wolfgang Mieder, 1994

The bigger they come, the harder they fall.

> BOB FITZSIMMONS (1863–1917). British boxer. When asked by a newspaper reporter if he could defeat the much heavier James J. Jeffries (Fitzsimmons lost the fight), 9 June 1899
>
> See Defiance: Jimmy Clift

An Inch in a Man's Nose is much.

> THOMAS FULLER (1654–1734). Comp., *Gnomologia: Adages and Proverbs*, 634, 1732

Trust not a great Weight to a slender Thread.

> THOMAS FULLER (1654–1734). Comp., *Gnomologia: Adages and Proverbs*, 5289, 1732

Little and good is twice good.

> BALTASAR GRACIÁN (1601–1658). *The Art of Worldly Wisdom*, 299, 1647, tr. Joseph Jacobs, 1943

The idea of growth for its own sake is precisely the philosophy of the cancer cell.

> SYDNEY J. HARRIS (1917–1986). *Pieces of Eight*, 2, 1982

A little yeast leavens the whole lump.

> PAUL (A.D. 1st cent.). *Galatians* 5:9

The bigger they come, the harder they hit.

> PERKINS' POSTULATE. In L. M. Boyd, "Grab Bag," *San Francisco Chronicle*, 16 June 1990

A *little* body doth often harbor a great soul.

> JOHN RAY (1628–1705). Comp., *A Collection of English Proverbs*, p. 16, 1678

Little boats must keep near shore.
Larger ships may venture more.

> JOHN RAY (1628–1705). Comp., *A Collection of English Proverbs*, p. 112, 1678

Better one's *house* too little one day than too big all the year after.

> JOHN RAY (1628–1705). Comp., *A Collection of English Proverbs*, p. 158, 1678

Great *weights* hang on small wires.

> JOHN RAY (1628–1705). Comp., *A Collection of English Proverbs*, p. 216, 1678

A swarm of gnats will overpower an elephant.

> SA'DI (A.D. 1213?–1292). *The Gulistan, or Rose Garden*, 3 (Story 28), A.D. 1258, tr. Edward Rehatsek, 1964

Small Is Beautiful.

> E. F. SCHUMACHER (1911–1977). Book title, 1973

What I wish to emphasize is the *duality* of the human requirement when it comes to the question of size: there is no *single* answer.

For his different purposes man needs different structures, both small ones and large ones, some exclusive and some comprehensive. . . . For constructive work, the principal task is always the restoration of some kind of balance. Today, we suffer from an almost universal idolatry of giantism. It is therefore necessary to insist on the virtues of smallness—where this applies. (If there were a prevailing idolatry of smallness, irrespective of subject or purpose, one would have to try and exercise influence in the opposite direction.)

> E. F. SCHUMACHER (1911–1977). *Small Is Beautiff: Economics as if People Mattered*, 1.5, 1973

We are beginning to realize that neither big nor small is beautiful, but that appropriate scale, and that the intelligent meshing of big and small is most beautiful of all.

> ALVIN TOFFLER (1928–). *The Third Wave*, 19, 1980

✥

Good things come in small packages.

> SAYING (FRENCH)

Little and often makes a lot in time.

> SAYING (GERMAN)

Better long little than soon nothing.

> SAYING (SCOTTISH)

Bigger is better.

> SAYING

Smaller is better.

> SAYING

Less more, more less!

> SAYING

QUARRELS

See also • Argument ○ Negotiation ○ Reason

It ain't bekauze lovers are so sensitiff that they quarrel so often, it iz bekauze thare iz so mutch phun in making up.

> JOSH BILLINGS (1818–1885). "Plum Pits," *Everybody's Friend, or; Josh Billing's Encyclopedia and Proverbial Philosophy of Wit and Humor*, 1874

Those who in quarrels interpose,
Must often wipe a bloody nose.

> JOHN GAY (1685–1732). *Fables*, 1.34, 1727–1738

If they have a bad master, they keep quarreling with him; if they have a good master, they keep quarreling with one another.

> OLIVER GOLDSMITH (1728–1774). *The Good-Natur'd Man*, 1, 1768

Adjusting Quarrels proves Good Will;
Preventing them is nobler still.

> ARTHUR GUITERMAN (1871–1943). "Of Quarrels," *A Poet's Proverbs: Being Mirthful, Sober, and Fanciful Epigrams on the Universe, With Certain Old Irish Proverbs, All in Rhymed Couplets*, 1924

We are never so much disposed to quarrel with others as when we are dissatisfied with ourselves.

> WILLIAM HAZLITT (1778–1830). *Characteristics in the Manner of Rochefoucault's Maxims*, 163, 1823

Quarrels would not last long if the fault were on one side only.

> LA ROCHEFOUCAULD (1613–1680). *Maxims*, 496, 1665, tr. Leonard Tancock, 1959

The advice of a father to his son "Beware of entrance to a quarrel, but being in, bear it that the opposed may beware of thee" [Shakespeare, *Hamlet*, 1.3.65, 1600], is good, and yet not the best. Quarrel not at all. No man resolved to make the most of himself, can spare time for personal contention.
> ABRAHAM LINCOLN (1809–1865). Letter to James M. Cutts, Jr., 26 October 1863

It is easier to refrain than to retreat from a [quarrel].
> SENECA THE YOUNGER (5? B.C.–A.D. 65). "On Anger" (3.8.8), *Moral Essays*, tr. John W. Basore, 1928

King Henry: Thrice is he arm'd that hath his quarrel just.
> SHAKESPEARE (1564–1616). *Henry VI*, Part II, 3.2.233, 1590

For souls in growth, great quarrels are great emancipations.
> LOGAN PEARSALL SMITH (1865–1946). *Afterthoughts*, 1, 1931

It takes two to make a quarrel.
> SOCRATES (470?–399 B.C.). Adapted. In Diogenes Laertius (A.D. 3rd cent.), *Lives of Eminent Philosophers*, 2.5, tr. R. D. Hicks, 1925

There is no such test of a man's superiority of character as in the well-conducting of an unavoidable quarrel; and to be engaged in no quarrels but those that are unavoidable.
> HENRY TAYLOR (1800–1886). *The Statesman*, 15, 1836

Thrice is he arm'd that hath his quarrel just. And four times he who gets his fist in fust.
> ARTEMUS WARD (1834–1867). Humorist. Attributed

❧

He who meddles in a quarrel not his own
  is like one who takes a passing dog by the ears.
> SAYING (*BIBLE*). Proverbs 26:17

When one will not, two cannot quarrel.
> SAYING (SPANISH)

Great quarrels often arise from small occasions but never from small causes.
> SAYING. In Winston Churchill, *My Early Life: A Roving Commission*, 18, 1930

QUESTIONS & ANSWERS

See also • Last Words: Gertrude Stein ○ Problems & Solutions ○ Science: [especially] Jacob Bronowski, Erwin Chargaff

If you don't like the question that's asked, answer some other question.
> HOWARD BAKER (1925–). Newsweek National Security Forum (panel discussion), Washington, 18 September 1995

Gentlemen, I am ready for the questions to my answers.
> CHARLES de GAULLE (1890–1970). Addressing reporters at the beginning of a news conference. In Michael Wines, "In Scripts for Bush, Questions on Images," *New York Times*, 28 November 1991

How many roads must a man walk down
Before you call him a man? . . .

The answer, my friend, is blowin' in the wind,
The answer is blowin' in the wind.
> BOB DYLAN (1941–). "Blowin' in the Wind," (song), 1962

When we have arrived at the question, the answer is already near.
> RALPH WALDO EMERSON (1803–1882). Journal, April 1852

The noblest question in the world is,
  What Good may I do in it?
> BENJAMIN FRANKLIN (1706–1790). *Poor Richard's Almanack,* December 1737

Ask me no questions, and I'll tell you no fibs.
> OLIVER GOLDSMITH (1728–1774). *She Stoops to Conquer: Or, the Mistakes of Night,* 2, 1773

The shortest answer is doing.
> GEORGE HERBERT (1593–1633). Comp., *Outlandish Proverbs,* 552, 1640

It is not enough for me to ask questions; I want to know how to answer the one question that seems to encompass everything I face: What am I here for?
> ABRAHAM JOSHUA HESCHEL (1907–1972). *Who Is Man?* 4, 1965

The question of a wise man is half the answer.
> SOLOMON IBN GABIROL (A.D. 1021?–1069?). *Choice of Pearls,* 3, tr. A. Cohen, 1925

What of the answers
I must find questions for?
> BOB KAUFMAN (1925–1986). "Jail Poems" (7), 1959, *Solitudes Crowded with Loneliness,* 1965

The way a question is put can often predetermine an answer.
> HENRY A. KISSINGER (1923–). In Harry G. Summers, Jr., *On Strategy: A Critical Analysis of the Vietnam War,* 4, 1982

Many people today don't want honest answers insofar as honest means unpleasant or disturbing. They want a soft answer that turneth away anxiety. They want answers that are, in effect, escapes.
> LOUIS KRONENBERGER (1904–1980). "Unbrave New World," *The Cart and the Horse,* 1964

We ask a thousand minute questions about the mechanisms and the institutions that surround us: the one question we do not dare to ask is: What is our true nature?
> LEWIS MUMFORD (1895–1990). *The Conduct of Life,* 9.2, 1951

It is not every question that deserves an answer.
> PUBLIUS SYRUS (85–43 B.C.). *Moral Sayings,* 581, tr. Darius Lyman, Jr., 1862

Before I refuse to take your questions, I have an opening statement.
> RONALD REAGAN (1911–). Speech. In Lou Cannon, "Thanks for the Reaganisms," *Washington Post,* 2 January 1989

There aren't any embarrassing questions—just embarrassing answers.
> CARL T. ROWAN, JR. (1925–). Referring to press-conference questions. In "The Talk of the Town," *New Yorker,* 7 December 1963

The Serpent: You see things; and you say, "Why?" But I dream things that never were; and I say, "Why not?"

GEORGE BERNARD SHAW (1856–1950). *Back to Methuselah: A Metabiological Pentateuch,* 1.1, 1921

A question not to be asked is a question not to be answered.

ROBERT SOUTHEY (1774–1843). *The Doctor,* 3, 1812

The day after never, we will have an explanation.

HENRY DAVID THOREAU (1817–1862). Journal, 8 November 1857

The "silly" question is the first intimation of some totally new development.

ALFRED NORTH WHITEHEAD (1861–1947)

You are also asking me questions and I hear you,
I answer that I cannot answer, you must find out for yourself.

WALT WHITMAN (1819–1892). "Song of Myself" (46), 1855, *Leaves of Grass,* 1855–1892

See Self-Realization: Whitman (2)

❧

Those who have the answer have misunderstood the question.

ANONYMOUS

Ask a silly question and you'll get a silly answer.

SAYING (AMERICAN)

No answer is also an answer.

SAYING (DANISH)

There's no good answer to a stupid question.

SAYING (RUSSIAN). In James Reston, "Some Russian Proverbs," *New York Times,* 2 February 1983

Never answer a question before it's asked.

SAYING

QUOTATIONS

See also • Aphorisms ○ Axioms ○ Epigrams ○ Maxims ○ Plagiarism ○ Proverbs ○ Sayings

Books of quotations are an elemental model of how culture is perpetuated, the wisdom of the tribe passed on to posterity, to be added to, edited, and modified by subsequent generations.

ROBERT ANDREWS

Shakespeare was a dramatist of note
Who lived by writing things to quote.

H. C. BUNNER (1855–1896)

It is a good thing for an uneducated man to read books of quotations. Bartlett's *Familiar Quotations* is an admirable work, and I studied it intently. The quotations when engraved upon the memory give you good thoughts. They also make you anxious to read the authors and look for more.

WINSTON CHURCHILL (1874–1965). *My Early Life: A Roving Commission,* 9, 1930

Beware of thinkers whose minds function only when they are fueled by a quotation.

E. M. CIORAN (1911–1995). *Anathemas and Admirations,* 9, 1986, tr. Richard Howard, 1991

When found, make a note of.

CHARLES DICKENS (1812–1870). On quotations, *Dombey and Son,* 15, 1848

One original thought is worth a thousand mindless quotings.

DIOGENES (4th cent. B.C.). In William Safire, "Worth a Thousand Words," *New York Times Magazine,* 7 April 1996

See Action & Talk: Tom Warson ○ Photography: Fred R. Barnard ○ Sayings: Saying

Immortality. I notice that as soon as writers broach this question they begin to quote. I hate quotations. Tell me what you know.

RALPH WALDO EMERSON (1803–1882). Journal, May 1849

By necessity, by proclivity and by delight, we all quote.

RALPH WALDO EMERSON (1803–1882). "Quotation and Originality," *Letters and Social Aims,* 1876

Next to the originator of a good sentence is the first quoter of it.

RALPH WALDO EMERSON (1803–1882). "Quotation and Originality," *Letters and Social Aims,* 1876

Quotation confesses inferiority.

RALPH WALDO EMERSON (1803–1882). "Quotation and Originality," *Letters and Social Aims,* 1876

We are as much informed of a writer's genius by what he selects as by what he originates.

RALPH WALDO EMERSON (1803–1882). "Quotation and Originality," *Letters and Social Aims,* 1876

Search not Authors to say what thou canst as well say thyself.

THOMAS FULLER (1654–1734). Comp., *Introductio ad Prudentiam,* 362, 1731

Few things are more tempting to a writer than to repeat, admiringly, what he has said before.

JOHN KENNETH GALBRAITH (1908–). Foreword (3) to *Economics and the Public Purpose,* 1973

He that tries to recommend [Shakespeare] by select quotations, will succeed like the pedant in *Hierocles,* who, when he offered his house to sale, carried a brick in his pocket as a specimen.

SAMUEL JOHNSON (1709–1784). Preface to *The Plays of William Shakespeare,* 1765

The ultimate stroke for a Washington wordsmith isn't getting the right quotation for your client out of Bartlett's. It's getting something your client says into Bartlett's.

CLARK JUDGE. Speech writer and presidential assistant to Ronald Reagan. As paragraphed by Victor Gold, "Who Said That?" *Denver Post Magazine,* 3 July 1994

As a general rule, *Misquotations drive out real quotes.* This is The Immutable Law of Misquotation. Misquotation takes three basic forms: (1) putting the wrong words in the right mouth; (2) putting the right words in the wrong mouth; and (3) putting the wrong words in the wrong mouth.

RALPH KEYES (1945–). *"Nice Guys Finish Seventh": False Phrases, Spurious Sayings, and Familiar Misquotations,* 1, 1992

This is the Achilles heel of quotation collections: An initial error in one will be repeated so often by others that over time it gains authority through repetition alone.

> RALPH KEYES (1945–). *"Nice Guys Finish Seventh": False Phrases, Spurious Sayings, and Familiar Misquotations*, 13, 1992

I do not speak the minds of others except to speak my own mind better.

> MONTAIGNE (1533–1592). "Of the Education of Children," *Essays*, 1588, tr. Donald M. Frame, 1958

A fine quotation is a diamond on the finger of a man of wit, and a pebble in the hand of a fool.

> JOSEPH ROUX (1834–1886). *Meditations of a Parish Priest*, 1.74, tr. Isabel F. Hapgood, 1886

I shall never be ashamed to quote a bad author if what he says is good.

> SENECA THE YOUNGER (5? B.C.–A.D. 65). "On Tranquillity of Mind," (11.8), *Moral Essays*, tr. John W. Basore, 1932

"This is what Zeno said." But what have you yourself said? "This is the opinion of Cleanthes." But what is your own opinion? How long shall you march under another man's orders? Take command, and utter some word which posterity will remember. Put forth something from your own stock.

> SENECA THE YOUNGER (5? B.C.–A.D. 65). "On the Futility of Learning Maxims," *Moral Letters to Lucilius*, 33.7, tr. Richard M. Gummere, 1918

I often quote myself; it adds spice to my conversation.

> GEORGE BERNARD SHAW (1854–1950). In Kenneth L. Calkins, "As Someone Famous Probably Once Said . . . ," *Wall Street Journal*, 7 January 1988

[Pres. John F. Kennedy] was not reluctant . . . to pack his speeches with statistics and quotations—frequently too many for audiences unaccustomed to his rapid-fire delivery. While I learned to keep a *Bartlett's* and similar works handy, the senator was the chief source of his own best quotations. Some were in the black notebooks he had kept since college—some were in favorite reference books on his desk, such as Agar's *The Price of Union*—most were in his head.

> THEODORE C. SORENSEN (1928–). *Kennedy*, 2, 1965

It seems to be full of quotations.

> ANONYMOUS (AMERICAN). Remark by a theater-goer after seeing a performance of Shakespeare's *Hamlet*. In Alfred Kazin, "Where Would Emerson Find His Scholar Now?" *American Heritage*, December 1987

RABBIS

See also • Clergy ○ Judaism ○ Preachers ○ Priests

Blessed is He who has not made me a rabbi.

> JACOB EMDEN (1697–1776). Scholar

The rabbis . . . stand . . . as the legitimate successors and continuators of the prophets.

> ROBERT TRAVERS HERFORD. *Pharisaism*, p. 66, 1912

The scribes and the Pharisees sit on Moses' seat; so practice and observe whatever they tell you, but not what they do; for they preach, but do not practice. They bind heavy burdens, hard to bear, and lay them on men's shoulders; but they themselves will not move them with their finger. They do all their deeds to be seen by men; for they make their phylacteries broad and their fringes long, and they love the place of honor at feasts and the best seats in the synagogues, and salutations in the market places, and being called rabbi by men.

> JESUS (A.D. 1st cent.). *Matthew* 23:2–4

Woe to you, scribes and Pharisees, hypocrites! because you shut the kingdom of heaven against men; for you neither enter yourselves nor allow those who would enter to go in.

> JESUS (A.D. 1st cent.). *Matthew* 23:13

"Rabbi" means "my teacher." The rabbi is not a priest or minister, in the Christian sense. He is not an intermediary between God and man; nor is he a spiritual arbiter; nor does he exercise any formal religious authority over others; nor does he enjoy hierarchical status. . . . A rabbi's influence rests on his learning, his character, his personal qualities.

> LEO ROSTEN (1908–1997). Comp., *Leo Rosten's Treasury of Jewish Quotations*, p. 375, 1972

RACE

See also • Racism

Skins may differ, but affection
Dwells in white and black the same.

> WILLIAM COWPER (1731–1800). "The Negro's Complaint," l. 15, 1793

RACISM

See also • African Americans ○ Anti-Semitic Statements ○ Anti-Semitism ○ Hate ○ Native Americans ○ Prejudice ○ Punishment, Capital: Carl Siciliano and Meg Hyre ○ Race ○ Racist Statements

Racism is the dogma that one ethnic group is condemned by nature to congenital inferiority and another group is destined to congenital superiority.

> RUTH BENEDICT (1887–1948). *Race: Science and Politics*, 7, 1940

Racism remains in the eyes of history . . . merely another instance of the persecution of minorities for the advantage of those in power.

> RUTH BENEDICT (1887–1948). *Race: Science and Politics*, 8, 1940

The basic tenet of black consciousness is that the black man must reject all value systems that seek to make him a foreigner in the country of his birth and reduce his basic human dignity.

> STEVE BIKO (1946–1977). South African human rights leader. In *Boston Globe,* 25 October 1977

Race prejudice is not only a shadow over the colored—it is a shadow over all of us, and the shadow is darkest over those who feel it least and allow its evil effects to go on.

> PEARL S. BUCK (1892–1973). *What America Means to Me,* 1, 1943

We first crush people to the earth, and then claim the right of trampling on them forever, because they are prostrate.

> LYDIA MARIA CHILD (1802–1880). "An Appeal on Behalf of That Class of Americans Called Africans," 1833

Racism keeps people who are being managed from finding out the truth through contact with each other.

> SHIRLEY CHISHOLM (1924–). *Unbought and Unbossed,* 13, 1970

We have to be honest, we have to be truthful and speak to the one dirty secret in American life, and that is racism.

> HENRY CISNEROS (1947–). Secretary of housing and Urban Development. In Steven V. Roberts, "Lift Every Voice and Sing—A New Song," *U.S. News & World Report,* 19 April 1993

To be a Negro is to participate in a culture of poverty and fear that goes far deeper than any law for or against discrimination. . . . After the racist statutes are all struck down, after legal equality has been achieved in the schools and in the courts, there remains the profound institutionalized and abiding wrong that white America has worked on the Negro for so long.

> MICHAEL HARRINGTON (1928–1989). *The Other America: Poverty in the United States,* 4 (introduction), 1962

Racism . . . made me less than I might have been.

> GEORGE JACKSON (1941–1971). In Eve Pell, "George Jackson, Remembered," *San Francisco Sunday Examiner & Chronicle,* 17 August 1975

Be assured that no person living wishes more sincerely than I do, to see a complete refutation of the doubts I have myself entertained and expressed on the grade of understanding allotted to [Negroes] by nature, and to find that in this respect they are on a par with ourselves. My doubts were the result of personal observation on the limited sphere of my own State, where the opportunities for the development of their genius were not favorable, and those of exercising it still less so. I expressed them therefore with great hesitation; but whatever be their degree of talent it is no measure of their rights. Because Sir Isaac Newton was superior to others in understanding, he was not therefore lord of the person or property of others.

> THOMAS JEFFERSON (1743–1826). Letter to Henri Gregoire, 25 February 1809
>
> See Racist Statements: Jefferson (all)

If you can convince the lowest white man he's better than the best colored man, he won't notice you're picking his pocket. Hell, give him somebody to look down on, and he'll empty his pockets for you.

> LYNDON B. JOHNSON (1908–1973). Remark to the writer, 1960. In Bill Moyers, "What a Real President Was Like," *Washington Post,* 13 November 1988

We have talked long enough in this country about equal rights. We have talked for one hundred years or more. It is time now to write the next chapter, and to write it in the books of law.

> LYNDON B. JOHNSON (1908–1973). Address to Congress 27 November 1963

One hundred years of delay have passed since President Lincoln freed the slaves, yet their heirs, their grandsons, are not fully free. They are not yet freed from the bonds of injustice. They are not yet freed from social and economic oppression. And this nation, for all its hopes and all its boasts, will not be fully free until all its citizens are free.

> JOHN F. KENNEDY (1917–1963). Television broadcast, 11 June 1963

No one has been barred on account of his race from fighting or dying for America—there are no "white" or "colored" signs on the foxholes or graveyards of battle.

> JOHN F. KENNEDY (1917–1963). Calling for civil rights legislation, Message to Congress, 19 June 1963

Our nation is moving toward two societies, one black, one white—separate and unequal.

> OTTO KERNER, JR. (1908–1976). *Report of the National Advisory Commission on Civil Disorders* (better known as the Kerner Commission Report), p. 1, 1968

The inseparable twin of racial injustice is economic injustice.

> MARTIN LUTHER KING, JR. (1929–1968). *Strength to Love,* 17.1, 1963

When a white man in Africa by accident looks into the eyes of a native and sees the human being (which it is his chief preoccupation to avoid), his sense of guilt, which he denies, fumes up in resentment and he brings down the whip.

> DORIS LESSING (1919–). *The Grass Is Singing,* 8, 1950

Racism is not the black community's only problem. Slavery and segregation are not the only explanation for the scourge of premature pregnancy and premature death. In the next stage of the civil-rights struggle, the true heroes will be those who focus inward as well as outward, who don't just make demands on the government but who demand discipline and responsibility from themselves and their children. Continuing to foster self-reliance and self-regard is just as important in combating racism in others.

> STEVEN V. ROBERTS (1943–). "Lift Every Voice and Sing—A New Song," *U.S. News & World Report,* 19 April 1993

It was my good fortune at Santiago to serve beside colored troops. A man who is good enough to shed his blood for the country is good enough to be given a square deal afterward. More than that no man is entitled to, and less than that no man shall have.

> THEODORE ROOSEVELT (1858–1919). Speech, Springfield (Illinois), 4 June 1903
>
> See Racist Statements: Roosevelt (2)

Who can describe the injustice and the cruelties that in the course of centuries [the colored peoples of the world] have suffered at the hands of Europeans? . . .

We and our civilization are burdened, really, with a great dept. We are not free to confer benefits on these men, or not, as we please; it is our duty. Anything we give them is not benevolence but atonement.

ALBERT SCHWEITZER (1875–1965). *On the Edge of the Primeval Forest: The Experiences and Observations of a Doctor in Equatorial Africa,* 11, 1922, tr. C. T. Campion, 1928

We don't want apartheid liberalized. We want it dismantled. You can't improve something that is intrinsically evil.

BISHOP DESMOND TUTU (1931–). In *Observer* (British newspaper), 10 March 1985

Racism originates in domination and provides the social rationale and philosophical justification for debasing, degrading, and doing violence to people on the basis of color.

JIM WALLIS (1948–). *The Soul of Politics: A Practical and Prophetic Vision for Change,* 5, 1994

❧

ERACISM.

SLOGAN (AMERICAN). Bumper sticker, 1990s

RACIST STATEMENTS

See also • African Americans ○ Anti-Semitic Statements ○ Anti-Semitism ○ Madness: Samuel A. Cartwright ○ Native Americans ○ Prejudice ○ Racism

Democracy inevitably takes the tone of the lower portions of society, and, if there are great diversities, degrades the higher. Slavery is the only protection that has ever been known against this tendency, and it is so far true that slavery is essential to democracy. For where there are great incongruities in the constitution of society, if the American were to admit the Indians, the Chinese, the Negroes, to the rights to which they are justly jealous of admitting European emigrants, the country would be thrown into disorder, and if not, would be degraded to the level of the barbarous races. . . . This is a good argument. . . , in the interest of all parties, against the emancipation of the blacks.

LORD ACTON (1834–1902). English historian. "Political Causes of the American Revolution," 1861, *Essays on Freedom and Power,* ed. Gertrude Himmelfarb, 1949

The result of my researches is that Negroes are intellectually children; physically one of the lowest races; inclining with the other blacks, especially the South Sea Negroes, most of all to the monkey type, though with a tendency, even in the extremes, towards the real human form. This opinion I have repeatedly expressed, without drawing from it any objectionable consequence, unless, perhaps, that no colored race, least of all the Negroes, can have a common origin with ourselves.

LOUIS AGASSIZ (1807–1873). Swiss-born American naturalist. In Lord Acton, "Political Causes of the American Revolution," 1861, *Essays on Freedom and Power,* ed. Gertrude Himmelfarb, 1949

God has not been preparing the English-speaking and Teutonic peoples for a thousand years for nothing but vain and idle self-administration. No. He made us master organizers of the world to establish system where chaos reigned. He has given us the spirit of progress to overwhelm the forces of reaction throughout the earth. He has made us adept in government that we may administer government among savage and senile peoples. Were it not for such a force as this the world would relapse into barbarism and night. And of all our race He has marked the American people as His chosen nation to finally lead in the redemption of the world.

ALBERT J. BEVERIDGE (1862–1927). Senate speech, 9 January 1900

The black race . . . came among us in a low, degraded, and savage condition, and in the course of a few generations it has grown up under the fostering care of our institutions, reviled as they have been, to its present comparatively civilized condition.

JOHN C. CALHOUN (1782–1850). South Carolina senator and U.S. vice president. "The Reception of Abolition Petitions," speech, 6 February 1837

See Newspeak—Examples: Calhoun

No, I don't believe it's prejudice. I truly believe [African Americans] may not have some of the necessities to be, let's say, a field manager or perhaps a general manager.

AL CAMPANIS (1917–1998). Los Angeles Dodgers executive. When asked why baseball had no black managers, general managers or owners, suggesting that the answer was prejudice, Ted Koppel television interview, ABC, 6 April 1987

[The Arawaks of the Bahama Islands] brought us parrots and balls of cotton and spears and many other things, which they exchanged for the glass beads and hawks' bells. They willingly traded everything they owned. . . . They were well-built, with good bodies and handsome features. . . . They do not bear arms and do not know them, for [when] I showed them a sword, they took it by the edge and cut themselves out of ignorance. They have no iron. Their spears are made of cane. . . . They would make fine servants. . . . With fifty men we could subjugate them all and make them do whatever we want.

CHRISTOPHER COLUMBUS (1451–1506). On his initial impressions soon after coming ashore in the "new world." Ship's log, 1492. In Howard Zinn, *A People's History of the United States,* 1, 1980

All these niggers in L.A. city government . . . all of 'em should be lined up against a wall and fucking shot.

MARK FUHRMAN (1952–). Los Angeles police detective. Taped remark to screenwriter Laura Hart McKinny revealed during the O. J. Simpson trial. In Charles Lane, "Juiced" (epigraph), *New Republic,* 11 September 1995

Blood mixture and the resultant drop in the racial level is the sole cause of the dying out of old cultures; for men do not perish as a result of lost wars, but by the loss of that force of resistance which is contained only in pure blood.

All who are not of good race in this world are chaff.

ADOLF HITLER (1889–1945). *Mein Kampf,* 1.11, 1924, tr. Ralph Manheim, 1943

This is probably the first time and this is the first country in which people are being taught to realize that, of all the tasks which we have to face, the noblest and most sacred for mankind is that each racial species must preserve the purity of the blood which God has given it.

ADOLF HITLER (1889–1945). Reichtag speech, Berlin, 30 January 1937

Everything about the behavior of American society reveals that it's half Judaized, and the other half negrified. How can one expect a State like that to hold together?

ADOLF HITLER (1889–1945). 7 January 1942, *Hitler's Secret Conversations, 1941–1944,* tr. Norman Cameron and R. H. Stevens, 1953

There is no doubt that the Negro's brain bears a great resemblance to a European female or child's brain and thus approaches the ape far more than the European, while the Negress approaches the ape still nearer.

JAMES HUNT (19th cent.). London Anthropological Society president. 1863. In Gloria Steinem, *Revolution from Within: A Book of Self-Esteem,* 3.3, 1992

They are more ardent after their female: but love seems with them to be more an eager desire, than a tender delicate mixture of sentiment and sensation. Their griefs are transient. Those numberless afflictions, which render it doubtful whether heaven has given life to us in mercy or in wrath, are less felt, and sooner forgotten with them. In general, their existence appears to participate more of sensation than reflection. To this must be ascribed their disposition to sleep when abstracted from their diversions, and unemployed in labor.

THOMAS JEFFERSON (1743–1826). *Notes on the State of Virginia,* 14, 1785

See Racism: Jefferson

Comparing them by their faculties of memory, reason, and imagination, it appears to me, that in memory they are equal to the whites; in reason much inferior, as I think one could scarcely be found capable of tracing and comprehending the investigations of Euclid; and that in imagination they are dull, tasteless, and anomalous.

THOMAS JEFFERSON (1743–1826). *Notes on the State of Virginia,* 14, 1785

Never yet could I find that a black had uttered a thought above the level of plain narration; never see even an elementary trait of painting or sculpture. . . . Misery is often the parent of the most affecting touches in poetry—Among the blacks is misery enough, God knows, but no poetry.

THOMAS JEFFERSON (1743–1826). *Notes on the State of Virginia,* 14, 1785

The mental inferiority of the negro to the white or yellow races is a fact. . . .

The mental constitution of the negro is very similar to that of a child, normally good-natured and cheerful, but subject to sudden fits of emotion and passion during which he is capable of performing acts of singular atrocity; impressionable, but often exhibiting in the capacity of servant a doglike fidelity which has stood the supreme test.

THOMAS ATHOL JOYCE. Honorable Secretary of the Anthropological Society. "Negro." In *The Encyclopedia Brittanica,* 11th ed., 19.344–345, 1911

Ron Wakabayashi (National Director, Japanese American Citizens League), Letter to editor: The article "How to Gyp the Japs" (TRB column, September 2) is catchy. I had to wonder whether any of those involved gave any thought that it was at the same time ugly and offensive. . . .
Kinsley (TRB), reply: Don't be so stuffy. "Japs" is not an ethnic slur, like "niggers" or "kikes" (or "slants"). It is a national nickname, like "Yanks" or "Brits" (or, at worst, "Frogs"): mocking, perhaps, but surely not beyond the pale, especially in the title of an article ridiculing anti-Japanese sentiment.

MICHAEL KINSLEY (1951–). Format adapted. Letters section, *New Republic,* 18 November 1985

Take up the White Man's burden—
    Send forth the best ye breed—
Go bind your sons to exile
    To serve your captives' need;
To wait in heavy harness
    On fluttered folk and wild—
Your new-caught, sullen peoples,
    Half devil and half child.

RUDYARD KIPLING (1865–1936). Opening stanza, "The White Man's Burden," 1899

I am not nor ever have been in favor of bringing about in any way the social and political equality of the white and black races—that I am not nor ever have been in favor of making voters or jurors of negroes, nor of qualifying them to hold office, nor to intermarry with white people; and I will say in addition to this that there is a physical difference between the white and black races which I believe will forever forbid the two races living together on terms of social and political equality. And inasmuch as they cannot so live, while they do remain together there must be the position of superior and inferior, and I, as much as any other man, am in favor of having the superior position assigned to the white race.

ABRAHAM LINCOLN (1809–1865). Lincoln-Douglas debate, Charleston (Illinois), 18 September 1858

If you stay here much longer, you'll all be slitty-eyed.

PRINCE PHILIP (1921–). Duke of Edinburgh. Remark to British students in Peking (China), 16 October 1986. In *Times* (London), 17 October 1986

God proclaims as a first principle to the rulers, and above all else, that there is nothing which they should so anxiously guard, or of which they are to be such good guardians, as of the purity of the race.

PLATO (427?–347 B.C.). *The Republic,* 3.415, tr. Benjamin Jowett, 1894

I suppose I should be ashamed to say that I take the Western view of the Indian. I don't go so far as to think that the only good Indians are the dead Indians, but I believe nine out of every ten are, and I shouldn't like to inquire too closely into the case of the tenth. The most vicious cowboy has more moral principle than the average Indian.

THEODORE ROOSEVELT (1858–1919). Speech, New York City, January 1886. In Hermann Hagedorn, *Roosevelt in the Bad Lands,* 21, 1921

Now as to the Negroes! I entirely agree with you that as a race and in the main they are altogether inferior to the whites.

THEODORE ROOSEVELT (1858–1919). Letter to Owen Wister, 27 April 1906

See Racism: Roosevelt

All the claims of superiority of the whites over the blacks on account of their color are founded alike in ignorance and inhumanity. If the color of the negroes be the effect of a disease, instead of inviting us to tyrannize over them, it should entitle them to a double portion of our humanity, for disease all over the world has always been the signal for immediate and universal compassion.

The facts and principles which have been delivered should teach white people the necessity of keeping up that prejudice against such connections with them as would tend to infect posterity with any portion of their disorder. . . .

Is the color of the negroes a disease? Then let science and humanity combine their efforts, and endeavor to discover a remedy for it. Nature has lately unfurled a banner upon this subject. She has begun spontaneous cures of this disease in several black people in this country.

> BENJAMIN RUSH (1745–1813). "Observations intended to favour a supposition that the Black Color (as it is called) of the Negroes is derived from the Leprosy." In Daniel J. Boorstin, *The Lost World of Thomas Jefferson*, 3, 1948

The day is not far distant when the whole hemisphere will be ours in fact as, by virtue of our superiority of race, it already is ours morally.

> WILLIAM HOWARD TAFT (1857–1930). President. Referring to the Western Hemisphere, 1912. In Jenny Pearce, *Under the Eagle: U.S. Intervention in Central America and the Caribbean*, 1, 1981

I draw the line in the dust and toss the gauntlet before the feet of tyranny, and I say segregation now, segregation tomorrow, segregation forever!

> GEORGE C. WALLACE (1919–1998). Gubernatorial inaugural address, Montgomery (Alabama), 19 January 1963

When we are dealing with the Caucasian race [in America], we have methods that will test . . . loyalty. But when we deal with the Japanese, we are in an entirely different field.

> EARL WARREN (1891–1974). California attorney general and U.S. Supreme Court chief justice. On the decision to send Japanese Americans to relocation camps soon after the start of World War II, 1942.

I believe in white supremacy until the blacks are educated to a point of responsibility. I don't believe in giving authority and positions of leadership and judgment to irresponsible people.

> JOHN WAYNE (1907–1979). Richard Warren Lewis interview, *Playboy*, May 1971

The Oriental doesn't put the same high price on life as does a westerner. Life is plentiful, life is cheap in the Orient. And as their philosophy of life expresses it, life is not important.

> WILLIAM C. WESTMORELAND (1914–). In *Radio Times* (British magazine), 1976

Segregation is not humiliating but a benefit, and ought to be so regarded by you gentlemen.

> WOODROW WILSON (1856–1924). Speech before a group of Negro leaders, Washington, November 1913

RADIO

See also • Media ○ Propaganda ○ Television

There, I guess that will hold the little bastards for another night.

> "UNCLE DON" CARNEY. After finishing the live broadcast of a popular children's program, assuming the microphone was turned off, 1930s.

Radio lets people see things with their own ears.

> NEW YORK TIMES. "With Our Own Eyes" (editorial), 30 January 1986

TV gives everyone an image, but radio gives birth to a million images in a million brains.

> PEGGY NOONAN (1950–). *What I Saw at the Revolution: A Political Life in the Reagan Era*, 2, 1990

RAIN

See also • Months: John Clarke ○ Nature ○ Pollution: Gladwin Hill ○ Weather

Though April showers may come your way,
They bring the flowers that bloom in May,
So if it's raining, have no regrets,
Because it isn't raining rain you know,
It's raining violets.

> B. G. DeSYLVA. "April Showers" (song). In the musical *Bomba*, 1921
>
> See John Clarke in Months

"A Hard Rain's A Gonna Fall."

> BOB DYLAN (1941–). Song title, 1965

Rain, rain. The good rain, like a bad preacher, does not know when to leave off.

> RALPH WALDO EMERSON (1803–1882). Journal, 23 April 1834

After rain comes fair weather.

> JAMES HOWELL (1593–1666). Comp., "English" (p. 2), *Paroimiographia: Proverbs, or Old Sayed Sawes & Adages in English . . . Italian, French and Spanish*, 1659
>
> See Optimism: Examples: Saying (1)

The rain in Spain stays mainly in the plain.

> ALAN JAY LERNER (1918–1986). "The Rain in Spain" (song). In the musical *My Fair Lady*, 1956

The next time it begins to rain, try to forget everything your mother taught you about "catching your death of cold," lie down on your belly, nestle your chin into the grass, and get a frog's-eye view of how raindrops fall. You'll see how the raindrops hit the individual blades of grass, causing them to bend down. This bending absorbs the energy of the raindrop, and the raindrop slides gently off the blade of grass, which immediately springs up again, waiting to catch another raindrop. Perhaps it's just my own sense of humor, but the sight of hundreds of blades of grass bowing down and popping back up like piano keys strikes me as one of the merriest sights in the world, and I've spent embarrassing amounts of time crawling through wet meadows in the rain, witnessing the wonderful antics of the blades of grass.

> MALCOLM MARGOLIN (1940–). *The Earth Manual: How to Work on Wild Land Without Taming It*, rev. ed., 5, 1985

Good luck and good work for the happy mountain raindrops, each one of them a high waterfall in itself, descending from the cliffs and hollows of the clouds to the cliffs and hollows of the rocks, out of the sky-thunder into the thunder of the falling rivers. Some, falling on meadows and bogs, creep silently out of sight to the grass roots, hiding softly as in a nest, slipping, oozing hither, thither, seeking and finding their appointed work. Some, descending through the spires of the woods, sift spray through the shining needles, whispering peace and good cheer to each one of them.

> JOHN MUIR (1838–1914). 19 July 1869, "The Yosemite," *My First Summer in the Sierra,* 5 1911

Sir John will go, though he were sure it would rain cats and dogs.

> JONATHAN SWIFT (1667–1745). *A Complete Collection of Genteel and Ingenious Conversation,* 2, 1738

For many years I was self-appointed inspector of snowstorms and rainstorms, and did my duty faithfully, though I never received one cent for it.

> HENRY DAVID THOREAU (1817–1862). Journal, 22 February (year unknown), 1845–1847

❦

And rain fell upon the earth forty days and forty nights. On the very same day Noah and his sons, Shem and Ham and Japheth, and Noah's wife and the three wives of his sons with them entered the ark, they and every beast according to its kind.

> ANONYMOUS (*BIBLE*). *Genesis* 6:12-14

If the rain can git [*sic*] in the way of a crop, it'll rain.

> SAYING (CALIFORNIA). In John Steinbeck, *The Grapes of Wrath,* 28, 1939

It never rains but it pours.

> SAYING (ENGLISH)

The sharper the storm, the sooner it's over.

> SAYING (ENGLISH)

A sunshiny shower won't last half an hour.

> SAYING (NEW ENGLAND)

RAINBOWS

See also • Nature

Somewhere over the rainbow
Way up high,
There's a land that I heard of
Once in a lullaby.

> E. Y. "YIP" HARBURG (1898–1981). "Over the Rainbow" (song). In the musical film, *The Wizard of Oz,* 1939

My heart leaps up when I behold
A rainbow in the sky.

> WILLIAM WORDSWORTH (1770–1850). Opening lines, "My Heart Leaps Up When I Behold," 1807

RAPE

See also • Child Abuse: [especially] Maya Angelou ∘ Crime ∘ Sex ∘ Violence

It is little wonder that rape is one of the least-reported crimes. Perhaps it is the only crime in which the victim becomes the accused and, in reality, it is she who must prove her good reputation, her mental soundness, and her impeccable propriety.

> FREDA ADLER (1934–). *Sisters in Crime: The Rise of the New Female Criminal,* 9, 1975

Man's discovery that his genitalia could serve as a weapon to generate fear must rank as one of the most important discoveries of prehistoric times, along with the use of fire and the first crude stone axe. From prehistoric times to the present, I believe, rape has played a critical function. It is nothing more or less than a conscious process of intimidation by which all men keep all women in a state of fear.

> SUSAN BROWNMILLER (1935–). *Against Our Will: Men, Women and Rape,* 1, 1975

A sexual invasion of the body by force, an incursion into the private, personal inner space without consent—in short, an internal assault from one of several avenues and by one of several methods—constitutes a deliberate violation of emotional, physical and rational integrity and is a hostile, degrading act of violence that deserves the name of rape.

> SUSAN BROWNMILLER (1935–). *Against Our Will: Men, Women and Rape,* 12, 1975

Fighting back. On a multiplicity of levels, that is the activity we must engage in, together, if we—women—are to redress the imbalance and rid ourselves and men of the ideology of rape.

Rape can be eradicated, not merely controlled or avoided on an individual basis, but the approach must be long-range and cooperative, and must have the understanding and good will of many men as well as women.

My purpose in this book has been to give rape its history. Now we must deny it a future.

> SUSAN BROWNMILLER (1935–). Closing paragraphs, *Against Our Will: Men, Women and Rape,* 12, 1975

Rape is a form of violence involving the personal humiliation of the victim.

> RUTH HERSCHBERGER. "Is Rape a Myth?" 1948. In Betty Roszak and Theodore Roszak, eds., *Masculine/Feminine: Readings in Sexual Mythology and the Liberation of Women,* 1969

Woman was and is condemned to a system under which the lawful rapes exceed the unlawful ones a million to one.

> MARGARET SANGER (1883–1966). *Woman and the New Race,* 14, 1920

It's like the weather. If it's inevitable, just relax and enjoy it.

> CLAYTON WILLIAMS. Texas gubernatorial candidate. When asked by reporters for his views on rape, April 1990

READING

See also • Books ∘ Children's Learning ∘ Education: [especially] Holbrook Jackson ∘ Knowledge ∘ Libraries ∘ Writing

Reading is to the mind what exercise is to the body.

> JOSEPH ADDISON (1672–1719) and RICHARD STEELE (1672–1729). In *The Tatler* (English essay series), 147, 18 March 1710

I took a speed-reading course where you run your finger down the middle of the page and was able to read War and Peace in twenty minutes. It's about Russia.

> WOODY ALLEN (1935–). In Phyllis Mindell, letter to *New York Times,* 3 September 1995

Read, mark, learn, and inwardly digest.

THE BOOK OF COMMON PRAYER. 1662

All you learn and all you can read will be of little use if you do not think and reason upon it yourself. One reads to know other people's thoughts; but if we take them upon trust, without examining and comparing them with our own, it is really living upon other people's scraps or retailing other people's goods. To know the thoughts of others is of use because it suggests thoughts to oneself and helps one to form a judgment, but to repeat other people's thoughts without considering whether they are right or wrong is the talent only of a parrot or at most a player.

LORD CHESTERFIELD (1694–1773). Letter to his son, "Thursday," 1740?, undated

My deafness deprives me of the only rational pleasure that I can have at my age, which is society; so that I read my eyes out every day, that I may not hang myself.

LORD CHESTERFIELD (1694–1773). At age 74, letter to his son, 12 March 1768

Some read to think, these are rare; some to write, these are common; and some read to talk, and these form the great majority.

C. C. COLTON (1780–1832). Lacon: or, Many Things in Few Words; Addressed to Those Who Think, 1.554, 1823

The best of all ways to make one's reading valuable is to write about it, and so I hope my Cousin Elizabeth has a blank book where she keeps some record of her thoughts.

RALPH WALDO EMERSON (1803–1882). Letter to Elizabeth Tucker, 1 February 1832

One must be an inventor to read well. . . . There is then creative reading as well as creative writing.

RALPH WALDO EMERSON (1803–1882). "The American Scholar," address, Harvard University, Cambridge (Massachusetts), 31 August 1837

The art of reading is to skip judiciously.

PHILIP G. HAMERTON (1834–1894). The Intellectual Life, 4.4, 1873

We read to train the mind, to fill the mind, to rest the mind, to recreate the mind, or to escape the mind.

HOLBROOK JACKSON (1874–1948). Maxims of Books and Reading, 2, 1934

A man ought to read just as inclination leads him; for what he reads as a task will do him little good. A young man should read five hours in a day, and so may acquire a great deal of knowledge.

SAMUEL JOHNSON (1709–1784). 14 July 1763. In James Boswell, The Life of Samuel Johnson, 1791

He has left off reading altogether, to the great improvement of his originality.

CHARLES LAMB (1775–1834). "Detached Thoughts on Books and Reading," The Last Essays of Elia, 1833

There are very many people who read simply to prevent themselves from thinking.

GEORG CHRISTOPH LICHTENBERG (1742–1799). Aphorisms, G.29, 1806, tr. R. J. Hollingdale, 1990

When I read aloud two senses catch the idea: first I see what I read; second, I hear it, and therefore I can remember it better.

ABRAHAM LINCOLN (1809–1865). In William H. Herndon and Jesse W. Weik, Herndon's Lincoln: The True Story of a Great Life, 11, 1889, Premier Books edition, 1961. Herndon, who for many years was Lincoln's law partner, reported that "Lincoln never read any other way but aloud."

Reading furnishes our mind only with materials of knowledge; it is thinking [that] makes what we read ours.

JOHN LOCKE (1632–1704). The Conduct of the Understanding, 20, 1706

Reading does not make a man wise; it only makes him learned.

W. SOMERSET MAUGHAM (1874–1965). 1892. A Writer's Notebook, 1949

"We Are What We Read."

MARK CRISPIN MILLER. Article headline, New York Times Book Review, 18 September 1988

See Food: Anthelme Brillat-Savarin ○ Writing: Michael Wood

Reading not only enlarges and challenges the mind; it also engages and exercises the brain. Today's youth who sits mesmerized by a television screen is not going to be tomorrow's leader. Television watching is passive. Reading is active.

RICHARD M. NIXON (1913–1994). Leaders, 9, 1982

I divide all readers into two classes; those who read to remember and those who read to forget.

WILLIAM L. PHELPS (1865–1943)

In reading, the mind is, in fact, only the playground of another's thoughts. So it comes about that if anyone spends almost the whole day in reading, and by way of relaxation devotes the intervals to some thoughtless pastime, he gradually loses the capacity for thinking; just as the man who always rides, at last forgets how to walk. This is the case with many learned persons; they have read themselves stupid.

ARTHUR SCHOPENHAUER (1788–1860). "Religion and Other Essays: On Books and Reading," Essays of Arthur Schopenhauer, tr. T. Bailey Saunders, 1851

You can never read bad literature too little, nor good literature too much.

ARTHUR SCHOPENHAUER (1788–1860). "Religion and Other Essays: On Books and Reading," Essays of Arthur Schopenhauer, tr. T. Bailey Saunders, 1851

A man should read only when his own thoughts stagnate at their source, which will happen often enough even with the best of minds. On the other hand, to take up a book for the purpose of scaring away one's own original thoughts is sin against the Holy Spirit. It is like running away from nature to look at a museum of dried plants or gaze at a landscape in copperplate.

ARTHUR SCHOPENHAUER (1788–1860). "The Art of Literature: On Thinking for One's Self," Essays of Arthur Schopenhauer, tr. T. Bailey Saunders, 1851

People say that life is the thing, but I prefer reading.

LOGAN PEARSALL SMITH (1865–1946). Afterthoughts, 6, 1931

See Books: Oliver Wendell Holmes, Sr.

❧

Caveat lector. [Let the reader beware.]
SAYING (LATIN)
See Merchants & Customers: Saying (Latin)

REAL ESTATE

See also • Property ∘ Stock Market

Year after year they voted cent. per cent.,
Blood, sweat, and tear-wrung millions—why? for rent!
LORD BYRON (1788–1824). *The Age of Bronze,* 14, 1823
See World War II: Winston Churchill (1)

A man complained that [on] his way home to dinner he had every day to pass through that long field of his neighbor's. I advised him to buy it, and it would never seem long again.
RALPH WALDO EMERSON (1803–1882). Journal, April 1847

Before I built a wall I'd ask to know
What I was walling in or walling out,
And to whom I was like to give offense.
Something there is that doesn't love a wall,
That wants it down.
ROBERT FROST (1874–1963). "Mending Wall," *North of Boston,* 1914

The best investment on earth is earth.
LOUIS GLICKMAN. Real estate investor. In *New York Post,* 3 September 1957

What we call real estate—the solid ground to build a house on—is the broad foundation on which nearly all the guilt of this world rests.
NATHANIEL HAWTHORNE (1804–1864). *The House of the Seven Gables,* 17, 1851

Woe to those who join house to house,
who add field to field,
until there is no more room,
and you are made to dwell alone
in the midst of the land.
ISAIAH (8th cent. B.C.). *Isaiah* 5:8

An acre in Middlesex is better than a principality in Utopia.
THOMAS BABINGTON MACAULAY (1800–1859). "Lord Bacon," *The Edinburgh Review* (Scotland), July 1837

I am amused to see from my window here how busily man has divided and staked off his domain. God must smile at [the] puny fences running hither and thither everywhere over the land.
HENRY DAVID THOREAU (1817–1862). Journal, 20 February 1842

❧

He that has lands has quarrels.
SAYING (ENGLISH)

REALITY

See also • Appearances ∘ Facts ∘ Illusion ∘ Imagination: Rousseau ∘ Knowledge ∘ Perception: [especially] Tim Keown ∘ Truth ∘ Unity: Hakuin, Martin Luther King, Jr.

Reality Isn't What It Used to Be.
WALTER TRUETT ANDERSON (1923–). Book title, 1990

Reality is that which, when you stop believing in it, doesn't go away.
PHILIP K. DICK (1928–1982). 1972, introduction to *I Hope I Shall Arrive Soon: How to Build a Universe That Doesn't Fall Apart Two Days Later,* ed. Mark Hurst and Paul Williams, 1985

To see reality in our time is to see the world as crucifixion.
JAMES W. DOUGLASS (1937–). Opening words, *The Non-Violent Cross: A Theology of Revolution and Peace,* 1969

Human kind
Cannot bear very much reality.
T. S. ELIOT (1888–1965). "Burnt Norton" (1), *Four Quartets,* 1943

Reality is the ultimate illusion.
MAL HANCOCK. Cartoon balloon. *Mal, San Francisco Sunday Examiner & Chronicle,* 25 February 1990

Reality cannot be ignored except at a price; and the longer the ignorance is persisted in, the higher and the more terrible becomes the price that must be paid.
ALDOUS HUXLEY (1894–1963). "Religion and Time." In Christopher Isherwood, ed., *Vedanta for the Western World,* 1945

Reality leaves a lot to the imagination.
JOHN LENNON (1940–1980). Appearing on *The Way It Is,* television program, CBS, June 1969

Without our knowing it, we see reality through glasses colored by the subconscious memory of previous experiences.
THOMAS MERTON (1915–1968). *No Man Is an Island,* 3.8, 1955

Reality is for people who can't face drugs.
LAURENCE J. PETER (1919–1990). "Peter's Stoned Principle," *Peter's People,* 8, 1979

Each time that we approach the study of human reality from a new point of view we rediscover that indissoluble dyad, Being and Nothingness.
JEAN-PAUL SARTRE (1905–1980). *Being and Nothingness: A Phenomenological Essay on Ontology,* 2.2.1.B, 1943, tr. Hazel E. Barnes, 1956

Reality is not about facts, but about the relationship of facts to one another.
RONALD STEEL (1931–). "Living with Walter Lippmann." In William Zinsser, ed., *Extraordinary Lives: The Art and Craft of American Biography,* 1988

Reality, no matter how widened and heightened our perceptions, never ceases to be anything but the effect on us of an infinite mystery.
LAURENS van der POST (1906–1996). "The Man and the Place," *Jung and the Story of Our Time,* 1975

What is reality anyway! It's nothing but a collective hunch.
JANE WAGNER (1935–). *The Search for Signs of Intelligent Life in the Universe* (comedy show), 1985, performed by Lily Tomlin

❦

Do not adjust you mind—the fault is in reality.
> ANONYMOUS (ENGLISH). Graffito, Oxford University, 1972

REASON

See also • Argument ○ Cause & Effect ○ Common Sense ○ Conscience ○ Creativity ○ Faith ○ Faith & Reason ○ Feeling: James E. Miller, Jr. ○ Ideas ○ Idolatry: Mohandas K. Gandhi ○ Imagination: [especially] Percy Bysshe Shelley, Arnold J. Toynbee ○ Judgment ○ Logic ○ Memory ○ Mind ○ Negotiation ○ Passion ○ Persuasion ○ Philosophy ○ Quarrels ○ Reason & Passion ○ Religion: George Washington ○ Tact ○ Thinking ○ Understanding: William Hazlitt

Rational, that is to say, conforms to the necessities of things.
> ISAIAH BERLIN (1909–1997). *Two Concepts of Liberty*, 4, 1958

We are indebted for all our Miseries to our Distrust of that Guide which Providence thought sufficient for our Condition, our own Natural Reason, which rejecting both in Human and Divine things, we have given our Necks to the Yoke of Political and Theological Slavery.
> EDMUND BURKE (1729–1797). *A Vindication of Natural Society*, p. 103, M. Cooper edition, 1756

There is hardly any error into which men may not easily be led if they base their conduct upon reason only.
> SAMUEL BUTLER (1835–1902). *Erewhon, Or: Over the Range*, 21, 1872

Reason is itself a matter of faith. It is an act of faith to assert that our thoughts have any relation to reality at all.
> G. K. CHESTERTON (1874–1936). *Orthodoxy*, 32, 1909

We should never allow ourselves to be persuaded excepting by the evidence of our Reason, of our Reason and not of our imagination nor of our senses.
> DESCARTES (1596–1650). In E. F. Schumacher, *A Guide for the Perplexed*, 1.2, 1977

He who will not reason is a bigot; he who cannot is a fool; and he who dares not is a slave.
> SIR WILLIAM DRUMMOND (1585–1649)

When Reason preaches, if you won't hear her, she'll box your Ears.
> BENJAMIN FRANKLIN (1706–1790). *Poor Richard's Almanack*, March 1753

So convenient a thing it is to be a *reasonable creature*, since it enables one to find or make a reason for everything one has a mind to do.
> BENJAMIN FRANKLIN (1706–1790). 1771, *Autobiography*, 1798

A scientific or a rationally valid statement means that the power of reason is applied to all the available data of observation without any of them being suppressed or falsified for the sake of a desired result.
> ERICH FROMM (1900–1980). *Man for Himself: An Inquiry into the Psychology of Ethics*, 4.6, 1947

Let Reason, not impulse, be your guide.
> KAHLIL GIBRAN (1883–1931). *Secrets of the Heart*, 5, ed. Stanley Hendricks, 1968
>
> See Conscience: Saying

The greatest deceiver in the world is human reason.
> FULKE GREVILLE (1554–1628). *Maxims, Characters, and Reflections*, p. 113, 1756

In an unreasonable age, a man's reason let loose would undo him.
> MARQUIS OF HALIFAX (1633–1695). "Of Caution and Suspicion," *Political, Moral and Miscellaneous Reflections*, 1750

Nothing hath an uglier look to us than reason, when it is not [on] our side.
> MARQUIS OF HALIFAX (1633–1695). "Reason and Passion," *Political, Moral and Miscellaneous Reflections*, 1750

In what we really understand, we reason but little.
> WILLIAM HAZLITT (1788–1830). "On the Conduct of Life," *Literary Remains*, 1836

Extreme rationalism may be defined as the failure of reason to understand itself.
> ABRAHAM JOSHUA HESCHEL (1907–1972). *God in Search of Man: A Philosophy of Judaism*, 1, 1955

Nobuddy ever listened t' reason on a' empty stomach.
> KIN HUBBARD (1868–1930). *Abe Martin: Hoss Sense and Nonsense*, p. 22, 1926

Come now, let us reason together, says the Lord.
> ISAIAH (8th cent. B.C.). *Isaiah* 1:18

Neither believe nor reject anything because any other persons or description of persons have rejected or believed it. Your own reason is the only oracle given you by heaven.
> THOMAS JEFFERSON (1743–1826). Letter to his nephew Peter Carr, 10 August 1787

Reason must be our last judge and guide in everything.
> JOHN LOCKE (1632–1704). An *Essay Concerning Human Understanding*, 4.19.14, 1690, ed. Alexander Campbell Fraser, 1894

God has not created anything better than Reason. . . . Understanding is by it, and God's wrath is caused by disregard of it.
> MUHAMMAD (A.D. 570?–632). *The Sayings of Muhammad*, 372, tr. Abdullah Al-Suhrawardy, 1941

Trust in reason—why not mistrust?
> FRIEDRICH NIETZSCHE (1844–1900). *The Will to Power* (notebooks, 1883–1888), 578, 1911, tr. Walter Kaufmann and R. J. Hollingdale, 1967

The last proceeding of reason is to recognize that there is an infinity of things which are beyond it.
> BLAISE PASCAL (1623–1662). *Pensées*, 267, 1670, tr. William F. Trotter, 1931

The object of reasoning is to find out, from the consideration of what we already know, something else which we do not know.
> CHARLES SANDERS PEIRCE (1839–1914). "The Fixation of Belief," *Popular Science Monthly*, November 1877

Rational thought is not non-intuitive; it is, rather, intuition *submitted to tests and checks* (as opposed to intuition run wild).

> KARL R. POPPER (1902–1994). *The Open Society and Its Enemies,* 2.24.5 (note 58), 1945

The God whom I adore is not the God of darkness. He has not given me understanding in order to forbid me to use it; to tell me to [surrender] my reason is to insult the giver of reason.

> ROUSSEAU (1712–1778). *Emile; or, Treatise on Education,* 4 ("The Creed of a Savoyard Priest"), 1762, tr. Barbara Foxley, 1911

It is by virtue of his reasoning faculty that man does not live in the present only, like the brute, but looks about him and considers the past and the future.

> ARTHUR SCHOPENHAUER (1788–1860). "Studies in Pessimism: On Women," *Essays of Arthur Schopenhauer,* tr. T. Bailey Saunders, 1851

At our birth nature . . . gave us reason, not perfect, but capable of being perfected.

> SENECA THE YOUNGER (5? B.C.–A.D. 65). "On the Shortness of Life," *Moral Letters to Lucilius,* 49.12, tr. Richard M. Gummere, 1918

The supreme triumph of reason, the analytical—that is, the destructive and dissolvent—faculty, is to cast doubt upon its own validity.

> MIGUEL de UNAMUNO (1864–1936). *Tragic Sense of Life,* 5, 1913, tr. J. E. Crawford Flitch, 1921

Reason only discovers the shortest way: it does not discover the destination.

> GEORGE BERNARD SHAW (1856–1950). *The Intelligent Woman's Guide to Socialism, Capitalism, Sovietism and Fascism,* 74, 1928

Men who are governed by reason . . . desire for themselves nothing which they do not also desire for the rest of mankind, and, consequently, are just, faithful, and honorable in their conduct.

> BARUCH SPINOZA (1632–1677). "Piety and Selfishness," *Ethics,* 1677, tr. Dagobert D. Runes, 1957

Reason consists of always seeing things as they are.

> VOLTAIRE (1694–1778). "Enthusiasm," *Philosophical Dictionary,* 1764, tr. Theodore Besterman, 1971

Faith in reason is the trust that the ultimate natures of things lie together in a harmony which excludes mere arbitrariness. . . . To experience this faith is to know that in being ourselves we are more than ourselves: to know that our experience, dim and fragmentary as it is, yet sounds the utmost depths of reality: to know that detached details merely in order to be themselves demand that they should find themselves in a system of things.

> ALFRED NORTH WHITEHEAD (1861–1947). *Science and the Modern World,* 1, 1925

REASON & PASSION

See also • Emotion ○ Passion ○ Reason

Man in the present state of society appears to me to be more corrupted by his reason than by his passions.

> CHAMFORT (1741–1794). *Maxims and Thoughts,* 1, 1796, tr. W. S. Merwin, 1984

Where passion rules, how weak does reason prove!

> JOHN DRYDEN (1631–1700). *The Rival Ladies,* 2.1, 1664

If *Passion* drives, let *Reason* hold the Reins.

> BENJAMIN FRANKLIN (1706–1790). *Poor Richard's Almanack,* May 1749

Your reason and your passion are the rudder and the sails of your seafaring soul.

If either your sails or your rudder be broken, you can but toss and drift, or else be held at a standstill in mid-seas.

> KAHLIL GIBRAN (1883–1931). "On Reason and Passion," *The Prophet,* 1923

I would have you consider your judgment and your appetite even as you would two loved guests in your house.

Surely, you would not honor one guest above the other; for he who is more mindful of one loses the love and the faith of both.

> KAHLIL GIBRAN (1883–1931). "On Reason and Passion," *The Prophet,* 1923

Passion and Reason, Self-division cause.

> FULKE GREVILLE (1554–1628). "Choras of Priests," *Mustapha,* 1609

Reason is, and ought only to be, the slave of the passions, and can never pretend to any other office than to serve and obey them.

> DAVID HUME (1711–1776). *A Treatise of Human Nature,* 1739–1740. In Anthony Storr, *Churchill's Black Dog, Kafka's Mice, and Other Phenomena of the Human Mind,* 3, 1988

My great religion is a belief in the blood, the flesh, as being wiser than the intellect. We can go wrong in our minds. But what our blood feels and believes and says is always true. The intellect is only a bit and a bridle.

> D. H. LAWRENCE (1885–1930). Letter to Ernest Collings, 17 January 1913

No clear thinking is possible in a passion—any more than it is possible to see clearly through glasses that are covered with steam.

> B. H. LIDDELL HART (1895–1970). "The Illusion of Treaties," *Why Don't We Learn from History?* 1944

Desire sways me one way, reason another. I see which is the better course, and I approve it; but still I follow the worse.

> OVID (43 B.C.–A.D. 17?). *Metamorphoses,* 7.23, tr. Mary M. Innes, 1955
> See Humility: First Person: Paul ○ Mankind: Ralph Waldo Emerson

The ruling Passion, be it what it will,
The ruling Passion conquers Reason still.

> ALEXANDER POPE (1688–1744). *Moral Essays,* 3.153, 1731–1735

Men are not rational beings, as commonly supposed. A man is a bundle of instincts, feelings, sentiments, which severally seek their gratification, and those which are in power get hold of the reason and use it to their own ends, and exclude all other sentiments and feelings from power.

> HERBERT SPENCER (1820–1903). Letter to J. A. Skilton, 10 January 1895. In David Duncan, *Life and Letters of Herbert Spencer,* 2.23, 1908

Passion and prejudice govern the world; only under the name of reason.

> JOHN WESLEY (1703–1791). Letter to Joseph Benson, 5 October 1770

RECONCILIATION

See also • Appeasement: Anonymous (1) ○ Christianity: Paul (2) ○ Forgiveness: Anton T. Boisen ○ Friends & Enemies ○ Nonviolence: Martin Luther King, Jr. (3) ○ Peace: Edmund Burke

In the world as it is "reconciliation" means that one side has the power and the other side gets reconciled to it.

> SAUL D. ALINSKY (1909–1972). Afterword to *Reveille for Radicals*, 1969

How often could things be remedied by a word. How often is it left unspoken.

> NORMAN DOUGLAS (1868–1952). 21 November, *An Almanac*, 1945

'Tis much safer for thee to reconcile an Enemy than conquer him.

> THOMAS FULLER (1654–1734). Comp., *Introductio ad Prudentiam*, 782, 1731

If you are offering your gift at the altar, and there remember that your brother has something against you, leave your gift there before the altar and go; first be reconciled to your brother, and then come, and offer your gift.

> JESUS (A.D. 1st cent.). *Matthew* 5:23–24

A stable social structure thrives not on triumphs but on reconciliations.

> HENRY A. KISSINGER (1923–). *A World Restored: Metternich, Castlereagh and the Problems of Peace 1812–1822*, 11.1, 1957

A reconciliation without an explanation that error lay on both sides is not a true reconciliation.

> *MIDRASH* (4th cent. B.C.–A.D. 12th cent.). Rabbinical writings. In Louis I. Newman, comp., The Talmudic Anthology, 245, 1945

Reconciliation with our social enemies [is] a precondition to reconciliation with God.

> CHED MYERS. "The Cross and the Cold War: The Ephesian Gospel of Peace," *Sojourners*, November 1986

REDEMPTION

See also • Confession ○ Conversion ○ Day of Judgment ○ Evangelism ○ Forgiveness ○ God & Man ○ Grace ○ Heaven ○ Religion ○ Repentance ○ Revelations ○ Salvation ○ Self-Realization (Becoming)

Oblivion is at the root of exile the way memory is at the root of [redemption].

> THE BAAL SHEM TOV (1690?–1760). In Eli Wiesel, "The School of Pshiskhe," *Souls on Fire*, tr. Marion Wiesel, 1972. (Alternative translation: In remembrance resides the secret of redemption.)

The lapse of superconsciousness into the state of unconsciousness is precisely the meaning of the Biblical image of the Fall. . . . Redemption consists in the return to superconsciousness.

> JOSEPH CAMPBELL (1904–1987). *The Hero with a Thousand Faces*, 2.1.1, 1949

No human being is so bad as to be beyond redemption.

> MOHANDAS K. GANDHI (1869–1948). In *Young India*, 26 March 1931
> See Salvation: William James (1)

We must . . . redeem our minds before we redeem our bodies.

> JUDAH LEIB GORDON (19th cent.). Letter to S. Bernfeld, 31 January 1888

God is waiting for us to redeem the world. We should not spend our life hunting for trivial satisfactions while God is waiting constantly and keenly for our effort and devotion.

> ABRAHAM JOSHUA HESCHEL (1907–1972). *Man's Quest for God: Studies in Prayer and Symbolism*, 6, 1954

Their redemption began when they ceased to tolerate their slavery.

> ABRAHAM JOSHUA HESCHEL (1907–1972). On the Hebrew slaves in Egypt, *A Passion for Truth*, 9, 1973

The process is one of redemption, not of mere reversion to natural health, and the sufferer, when saved, is saved by what seems to him a second birth, a deeper kind of conscious being than he could enjoy before.

> WILLIAM JAMES (1842–1910). *The Varieties of Religious Experience: A Study in Human Nature*, 6 and 7, 1902

The dreams of redemption, whereby God descends into the human realm and man mounts up to the realm of divinity.

> CARL G. JUNG (1875–1961). "A Psychological Approach to the Dogma of the Trinity" (4.3), 1942, *Psychology and Religion: West and East*, tr. R. F. C. Hull, 1958

The most severe birth pains occur just before delivery. Likewise, the gravest tribulations will immediately precede the Redemption.

> THE KORETZER (1726–1791). In Louis I. Newman, comp., *The Hasidic Anthology*, 43.14, 1934

Not sackcloth and fasting avail, but repentance and good deeds.

> *TALMUD* (A.D. 1st–6th cent.). Rabbinical writings

The very idea of redemption implies a spiritual necessity.

> SIMONE WEIL (1909–1943). *The Simone Weil Reader*, 5 ("The Things of the World"), ed. George A. Panichas, 1977

No redemption without repentance, restitution and reconciliation.

> ANONYMOUS

REFLECTION

See also • Books: Chamfort ○ Contemplation ○ Experience: Rousseau, Arthur Schopenhauer ○ Ideas: Jean-Paul Sartre ○ Thinking ○ Wisdom: Baltasar Gracián (1) ○ Wretchedness: Publius Syrus (1)

To reflect is to look back over what has been done so as to extract the net meanings which are the capital stock for intelligent dealing with further experiences.

> JOHN DEWEY (1859–1952). *Experience and Education*, 7, 1938

To reflect is to receive truth immediately from God without any medium. That is living faith. To take on trust certain facts is a dead faith—inoperative. . . . You are as one who has a private door that leads him to the King's chamber. You have learned nothing rightly that you have not learned so.

> RALPH WALDO EMERSON (1803–1882). Journal, 29 July 1831

Whatever good results I find in my reflections come to me when I am walking.

> GOETHE (1749–1832). In Alfred Hock, *Reason and Genius: Studies in Their Origin,* 2.1.3, 1960

Reflection makes men cowards.

> WILLIAM HAZLITT (1778–1830). *Characteristics in the Manner of Rochefoucault's Maxims,* 228, 1823

The truth about Mr. Lincoln is that he read less and thought more than any man in his sphere in America. . . . He was concentrated in his thoughts and had great continuity of reflection.

> WILLIAM H. HERNDON (1818–1891) and JESSE W. WEIK (1857–1930). *Herndon's Lincoln: The True Story of a Great Life,* 20, 1889, Premier Books edition, 1961

It is not a guiding spirit that reveals to me secretly in a flash what I must say or do, but thought and reflection.

> NAPOLEON (1769–1821). In Charles Bugnet, "Results" (Development of a Leader), *Foch Speaks,* tr. Russell Green, 1929

To doubt everything and to believe everything are two equally convenient solutions; both free us from the necessity of reflection.

> HENRI POINCARÉ (1854–1912). Introduction to *Science and Hypothesis,* 1903

Reflection is the beginning of reform.

> MARK TWAIN (1835–1910). "Theoretical and Practical Morals," speech before the New Vagabonds Club of London, 8 July 1899

REFORM

See also • Change ○ Democracy: Karl R. Popper ○ History ○ Minorities: Margaret Mead ○ Nonviolence ○ Reformers ○ Remorse: William Cowper ○ Revolution: [especially] Edward George Bulwer-Lytton ○ Self-Realization (Becoming)

Every reform carries the seed of its own abuse.

> WILLIAM COHEN (1940–). Appearing on *Meet the Press,* television news program, NBC, 9 March 1997

Attempts at reform, when they fail, strengthen despotism; as he that struggles tightens those cords he does not succeed in breaking.

> C. C. COLTON (1780–1832). *Lacon: or, Many Things in Few Words; Addressed to Those Who Think,* 1.440, 1823

There are two schools of social reform. One bases itself upon the notion of a morality which springs from an inner freedom, something mysteriously cooped up within personality. It asserts that the only way to change institutions is for men to purify their own hearts, and that when this has been accomplished, change of institutions will follow of itself. The other school denies the existence of any such inner power. . . . It says that men are made what they are by the forces of the environment, that human nature is purely malleable, and that till institutions are changed, nothing can be done. . . . There is an alternative to being penned in between these two theories. We can recognize that all conduct is interaction between elements of human nature and the environment, natural and social.

> JOHN DEWEY (1859–1952). Introduction to *Human Nature and Conduct: An Introduction to Social Psychology,* 1922

A healthy man'll never rayform while he has the strength.

> FINLEY PETER DUNNE (1876–1936). "Reform Administration," *Observations by Mr. Dooley,* 1902

Middle-class-led reform movements, from the Progressive Era to the War on Poverty, have been marred by an elitist distance from the would-be beneficiaries of reform.

> BARBARA EHRENREICH (1941–). *Fear of Falling: The Inner Life of the Middle Class,* 6, 1990

All reform aims, in some one particular, to let the soul have its way through us.

> RALPH WALDO EMERSON (1803–1882). "The Over-Soul," *Essays: First Series,* 1841

Reform must come from within, not from without. You cannot legislate for virtue.

> CARDINAL JAMES GIBBONS (1834–1921). Address, Baltimore, 13 September 1909

It is not so much the system as man himself that must be reformed.

> ANDRÉ GIDE (1869–1951). Journal (detached page), 1918, tr. Justin O'Brien, 1948

If the Russian word "perestroika" has easily entered the international lexicon, this is due to more than just interest in what is going on in the Soviet Union. Now the whole world needs restructuring, i.e., progressive development, a fundamental change.

> MIKHAIL S. GORBACHEV (1931–). *Perestroika: New Thinking for Our Country and the World,* 7 (Conclusion), 1987

Individual reformation [is] a necessary prerequisite and condition of social reformation.

> ALDOUS HUXLEY (1894–1963). "Idolatry." In Christopher Isherwood, ed., *Vedanta for the Western World,* 1945
>
> See Revolutionaries: Ho Chi Minh (1)

Why, Sir, most schemes of political improvement are very laughable things.

> SAMUEL JOHNSON (1709–1784). 26 October 1769. In James Boswell, *The Life of Samuel Johnson,* 1791

It is difficult to reform a household gradually; it may be better done by a system totally new.

> SAMUEL JOHNSON (1709–1784). Letter to the author, 3 July 1778. In James Boswell, *The Life of Samuel Johnson,* 1791

The art of holding onto power . . . is to make reform seem so tantalizingly close as to dull the edge of militancy and force the purest revolutionaries into the peripheries of political action.

> ANDREW KOPKIND (1935–1994). "Are We in the Middle of a Revolution?" *New York Times Magazine,* 10 November 1968

Social reform is the desperate decision to remove corns from a person suffering from cancer.

> KARL KRAUS (1874–1936). "Lord, Forgive Them . . .," *Half-truths & One-and-a-Half Truths: Selected Aphroisms,* ed. Harry Zorn, 1976

Turn where we may, within, around, the voice of great events is proclaiming to us, "Reform, that you may preserve."

> THOMAS BABINGTON MACAULAY (1800–1859). On parliamentary reform, House of Commons speech, 2 March 1831
>
> See Change & Changelessness: Edmund Burke

[States are ruined] because they do not modify their institutions to suit the changes of the times.

> MACHIAVELLI (1469–1527). *The Discourses,* 3.9, 1517, tr. Christian E. Detmold, 1940

A small and temporary improvement may really be the worst enemy of a great and permanent improvement, unless the first is made on the lines and in the direction of the second.

> JOHN MORLEY (1838–1923). *On Compromise,* 5, 1877

As to reformation, whenever it comes, it must be from the Nation, and not from the Government.

> THOMAS PAINE (1737–1809). *The Rights of Man,* 2.5, 1792

To give up the task of reforming society is to give up one's responsibility as a free man.

> ALAN PATON (1903–1988). "The Challenge of Fear," *Saturday Review,* 9 September 1967

The place to improve the world is first in one's own heart and head and hands, and then work outward from there.

> ROBERT M. PIRSIG (1928–). *Zen and the Art of Motorcycle Maintenance: An Inquiry into Values,* 25, 1974

There is no question in my mind that it is time for the country to become fairly radical for a generation. History shows that where this occurs occasionally, nations are saved from revolution.

> FRANKLIN D. ROOSEVELT (1882–1945). Letter to John A. Kingsbury, May 1930

A caustic observer once remarked that when Dr. Johnson spoke of patriotism as the last refuge of a scoundrel, "he was ignorant of the infinite possibility contained in the word 'reform.'"

> THEODORE ROOSEVELT (1858–1919). "Latitude and Longitude Among Reformers," June 1900, *The Strenuous Life: Essays and Addresses,* 1905
> See Patriotism: Samuel Johnson

The standard reaction to pressure for radical change is to buy it off. Across America, a strategy of campus containment is emerging, which reads: grant with relative grace the minor changes and options that don't endanger or change the system itself.

> MICHAEL ROSSMAN. "The Sound of Marching, Charging Feet," *Rolling Stone,* 5 April 1969

The impetus to reform or revolution springs in every age from the realization of the contrast between the external order of society and the moral standards recognized as valid by the conscience or reason of the individual.

> R. H. TAWNEY (1880–1962). *Religion and the Rise of Capitalism: A Historical Study,* 2.3, 1926

Moral reform is an effort to throw off sleep.

> HENRY DAVID THOREAU (1817–1862). "Where I Lived, and What I Lived For," *Walden; or Life in the Woods,* 1854

When property becomes so fluctuating and the love of property so restless and so ardent, I cannot but fear that men may arrive at such a state as to regard every new theory as a peril, every innovation as an irksome toil, every social improvement as a stepping stone to revolution, and so refuse to move altogether for fear of being moved too far. I dread . . . lest they should at last so entirely give way to a cowardly love of present enjoyment as to lose sight of the interests of their future selves and those of their descendants and prefer to glide along the easy current of life rather than to make, when it is necessary, a strong and sudden effort to a higher purpose.

> ALEXIS de TOCQUEVILLE (1805–1859). *Democracy in America,* 2.3.21, 1840, tr. Henry Reeve and Francis Bowen, 1862

Individual enlightenment is the indispensable means of social reform.

> ARNOLD J. TOYNBEE (1889–1975). *The Toynbee-Ikeda Dialogue: Man Himself Must Choose,* 12, 1976
> See Revolutionaries: Ho Chi Minh (1)

Nothing so needs reforming as other people's habits.

> MARK TWAIN (1835–1910). *The Tragedy of Pudd'nhead Wilson,* 15 (epigraph), 1894

Beginning reform is beginning revolution.

> DUKE OF WELLINGTON (1769–1852). Letter to Mrs. Arbuthnott, 7 November 1830. In John Keegan, *The Mask of Command,* 2, 1987

✻

In some states, reform means turning out the fat hogs and bringing in the lean ones.

> ANONYMOUS (AMERICAN)

Any reform that does not result in the exact opposite of what it was intended to do must be considered a success.

> ANONYMOUS

REFORMERS

See also • Conservatives ○ Leaders ○ Liberals ○ Reform ○ Revolutionaries

The successful change agent makes sure that the old guard isn't frightened at the prospect of change.

> WARREN BENNIS (1925–). *Why Leaders Can't Lead: The Unconscious Conspiracy Continues,* 22, 1989

Before yu undertaik tew change a man's politiks or religion, be sure yu hav got a better one to offer him.

> JOSH BILLINGS (1818–1885). "Chicken Feed," *Everybody's Friend, or, Josh Billing's Encyclopedia and Proverbial Philosophy of Wit and Humor,* 1874

The best reformers the world haz ever seen are thoze who commense on themselves.

> JOSH BILLINGS (1818–1885). "Nosegays," *Everybody's Friend, or, Josh Billing's Encyclopedia and Proverbial Philosophy of Wit and Humor,* 1874

Reforms and discoveries are like offenses; they must needs come, but woe unto that man through whom they come.

> SAMUEL BUTLER (1835–1902). *Further Extracts from the Note-Books of Samuel Butler,* 1, ed. A. T. Bartholomew, 1934

Vain hope to make mankind happy by politics! You cannot drill a regiment of knaves into a regiment of honest men, enregiment and organize them as cunningly as you will. Give us the honest men, and the well-ordered regiment comes of itself. Reform one man—reform thy own inner man; it is more than scheming out reforms for a nation.

THOMAS CARLYLE (1795–1881). Journal, 10 October 1831. In James Anthony Froude, *Thomas Carlyle: A History of the First Forty Years, 1795–1835*, 2.9, 1882

A man that'd expict to thrain lobsters to fly in a year is called a loonytic; but a man that thinks men can be tur-rned into angels be an iliction is called a rayformer an' remains at large.

FINLEY PETER DUNNE (1867–1936). "Casual Observations," *Mr. Dooley's Philosophy*, 1900

[The rayformer] don't undherstand that people wud rather be wrong an' comfortable thin right in jail.

FINLEY PETER DUNNE (1867–1936). "Reform Administration," *Observations by Mr. Dooley*, 1902

It is better sometimes not to follow great reformers of abuses beyond the threshold of their homes.

GEORGE ELIOT (1819–1880). *Adam Bede*, 5, 1859

One man appears whose nature is to all men's eyes conserving and constructive; his presence supposes a well-ordered society, agriculture, trade, large institutions, and empire. . . . Men rightly go for him, and reject the reformer, so long as he comes only with ax and crowbar.

RALPH WALDO EMERSON (1803–1882). "Montaigne; or, The Skeptic," *Representative Men*, 1850

No sagacious man will long retain his sagacity if he lives exclusively among reformers and progressive people, without periodically returning into the settled system of things, to correct himself by a new observation from that old standpoint.

NATHANIEL HAWTHORNE (1804–1864). In John Morley, "Emerson" (3), *Critical Miscellanies*, vol. 1, 1886

Eager souls, mystics and revolutionaries, may propose to refashion the world in accordance with their dreams; but evil remains, and so long as it lurks in the secret places of the heart, utopia is only the shadow of a dream.

NATHANIEL HAWTHORNE (1804–1864). In Carol Muske Dukes, "When 'The System' Worked," *New York Times*, 30 May 1995

There is a moment in the career of almost every faultfinding man of words when a deferential or conciliatory gesture from those in power may win over to their side. At a certain stage, most men of words are ready to become timeservers and courtiers. Jesus Himself might not have preached a new Gospel had the dominant Pharisees taken Him into the fold, called Him Rabbi, and listened to Him with deference.

ERIC HOFFER (1902–1983). *The True Believer: Thoughts on the Nature of Mass Movements*, 105, 1951

The Reformer is a savior or a rebel, . . . depending largely upon whether he succeeds or fails.

ELBERT HUBBARD (1856–1915). *The Note Book of Elbert Hubbard*, p. 201, comp. Elbert Hubbard II, 1927

See Revolutionaries: Erich Fromm, Artemus Ward

Let's all join th' good roads movement an' mend our own ways.

KIN HUBBARD (1868–1930). *Abe Martin's Primer*, unpaged, 1914

The reformer must attack simultaneously on all the fronts, from the metaphysical to the economic; if he does not, he cannot hope to achieve more than a partial success.

ALDOUS HUXLEY (1894–1963). "Justifications," *The Olive Tree and Other Essays*, 1936

The office of reformer of the superstitions of a nation is ever dangerous.

THOMAS JEFFERSON (1743–1826). Letter to William Short, 4 August 1820

He that attempts to change the course of his own life very often labors in vain: and how shall we do that for others, which we are seldom able to do for ourselves?

SAMUEL JOHNSON (1709–1784). *Rasselas: The Prince of Abyssinia*, 29, 1759

The reformer operates on parts where the revolutionist operates on wholes.

HORACE M. KALLEN. In James MacGregor Burns, *Leadership*, 7, 1978

Lighthouses don't go running all over an island looking for boats to save; they just stand there shining.

ANNE LAMOTT (1954–). *Bird by Bird: Some Instructions on Writing and Life*, 5, 1995

Unless the reformer can invent something which substitutes attractive virtues for attractive vices, he will fail.

WALTER LIPPMANN (1889–1974). *A Preface to Politics*, 2, 1914

There is nothing more difficult to carry out, nor more doubtful of success, nor more dangerous to handle, than to initiate a new order of things. For the reformer has enemies in all those who profit by the old order, and only lukewarm defenders in all those who would profit by the new order, this lukewarmness arising partly from fear of their adversaries, who have the laws in their favor; and partly from the incredulity of mankind, who do not truly believe in anything new until they have actual experience of it. . . . Thus it comes about that all the armed prophets have conquered and unarmed ones failed.

MACHIAVELLI (1469–1527). *The Prince*, 6, 1513, tr. Luigi Ricci, 1903

Toward the end of the book (the time is 1914) Demian says to his friend Sinclair: ". . . . The new is beginning and for those who cling to the old the new will be horrible. What will you do?"

The right answer would be: "Assist the new without sacrificing the old."

THOMAS MANN (1875–1955). Introduction (1947) to Hermann Hesse, *Demian: The Story of Emil Sinclair's Youth*, 1919, tr. Michael Roloff and Michael Lebeck, 1965

A man should bend to the prevailing mood;
And it's assuredly a signal folly
To try to reform and cure society.

MOLIÈRE (1622–1673). *Le Misanthrope*, 1, 1666, tr. Morris Bishop, 1957

Mankind . . . are always ripe enough to understand their true interest, provided it be presented clearly to their understanding, and that in a manner not to create suspicion by anything like self-design, nor offend by assuming too much. Where we would wish to reform we must not reproach.

THOMAS PAINE (1737–1809). Letter to Marquis de Lafayette, 9 February 1792, *The Rights of Man*, 2 ("Dedication"), 1792

If we would amend the World, we should mend Ourselves and teach our Children to be not what we are but what they should be.

WILLIAM PENN (1644–1718). *Some Fruits of Solitude*, 214, 1693

[The reformer] wants his conscience to be your guide.

LAURENCE J. PETER (1919–1990). Comp., *Peter's Quotations: Ideas for Our Time*, p. 447, 1977

Among the wise and high-minded people who in self-respecting and genuine fashion strive earnestly for peace, there are the foolish fanatics always to be found in such a movement and always discrediting it—the men who form the lunatic fringe in all reform movements.

THEODORE ROOSEVELT (1858–1919). *An Autobiography*, 7, 1913

Hamlet: The time is out of joint: O cursed spite,
That ever I was born to set it right!

SHAKESPEARE (1564–1616). *Hamlet*, 1.5.189, 1600

If you rebel against high-heeled shoes, take care to do it in a very smart hat.

GEORGE BERNARD SHAW (1856–1950). *The Intelligent Woman's Guide to Socialism, Capitalism, Sovietism and Fascism*, 79, 1928

"We Must Reform Society before We Can Reform Ourselves."

GEORGE BERNARD SHAW (1856–1950). Section heading, *Parents and Children*, 1914

All Reformers, however strict their social conscience, live in houses just as big as they can pay for.

LOGAN PEARSALL SMITH (1865–1946). *Afterthoughts*, 3, 1931

There is an idea abroad among moral people that they should make their neighbors good. One person I have to make good: myself.

ROBERT LOUIS STEVENSON (1850–1894)

Everyone of us is a child of his age and cannot get out of it. He is in the stream and is swept along with it. All his sciences and philosophy come to him out of it. Therefore the tide will not be changed by us. . . . It is the greatest folly of which a man can be capable, to sit down with a slate and pencil to plan out a new social world.

WILLIAM GRAHAM SUMNER (1840–1910). Closing words, "The Absurd Effort to Make the World Over," 1894, *War and Other Essays*, 1911

We go about mending the times, when we should be building the eternity.

HENRY DAVID THOREAU (1817–1862). Journal, 11 February 1841

If anything ail a man, so that he does not perform his functions, if he have a pain in his bowels even—for that is the seat of sympathy—he forthwith sets about reforming the world.

HENRY DAVID THOREAU (1817–1862). "Economy," *Walden; or Life in the Woods*, 1854

I believe that what so saddens the reformer is not his sympathy with his fellows in distress, but, though he be the holiest son of God, is his private ail. Let this be righted, let the spring come to him, the morning rise over his couch, and he will forsake his generous companions without apology.

HENRY DAVID THOREAU (1817–1862). "Economy," *Walden; or Life in the Woods*, 1854

The self-styled reformers, the greatest bores of all.

HENRY DAVID THOREAU (1817–1862). "Visitors," *Walden; or Life in the Woods*, 1854

No man can struggle with advantage against the spirit of his age and country.

ALEXIS de TOCQUEVILLE (1805–1859). *Democracy in America*, 2.3.21, 1840, tr. Henry Reeve and Francis Bowen, 1862

The reform leader . . . espouses the political community's sustaining myth, its professed ideal culture patterns, and defines the deviation of certain practices from those patterns as a wrong situation that can and should be corrected by changing the practices. Revolutionary leadership, on the other hand, sees and defines the collective situation as so irremediably wrong that the only possible solution is a fundamental reconstitution of society.

ROBERT C. TUCKER (1918–). *Politics as Leadership*, rev. ed., 3, 1995 (1981)

The greater the reform needed, the greater the Personality you need to accomplish it.

WALT WHITMAN (1819–1892). "To a Pupil," 1860, *Leaves of Grass*, 1855–1892

The eager and often inconsiderate appeals of reformers and revolutionists are indispensable, to counterbalance the inertness and fossilism making so large a part of human institutions.

WALT WHITMAN (1819–1892). *Democratic Vistas*, 1871, *Walt Whitman: Complete Poetry and Collected Prose*, ed. Justin Kaplan, p. 950, 1982

❦

Oh, you're the son of a bitch who's trying to change our system.

ANONYMOUS (AMERICAN). A Pittsburgh slum dweller's remark to Norman Thomas, who had introduced himself, while campaigning as the Socialist Party's presidential candidate in 1948. In Lance Morrow, "A Cry for Leadership," *Time*, 6 August 1979

REGRET

See also • Age: Scott Nearing ○ Complaint ○ Guilt ○ Opportunity ○ Remorse ○ Wisdom: Henry David Thoreau (3)

His one regret in life is that he is not someone else.

WOODY ALLEN (1935–). Writing in the third person, "About the Author," *Getting Even*, 1971

One man says he can regret nothing. A god? A stone?

ELIAS CANETTI (1905–1994). 1959, *The Human Province*, tr. Joachim Neugroschel, 1978

I regret nothing, says arrogance; I will regret nothing, says inexperience.

MARIE von EBNER-ESCHENBACH (1830–1916). *Aphorisms*, p. 47, 1880–1905, tr. David Scrase and Wolfgang Mieder, 1994

Like the greedy merchants of bazaars, if we get out of life what we ask for, we are unhappy for not having asked for more.

> PAUL ELDRIDGE (1888–1982). *Maxims for a Modern Man,* 1195, 1965

Footfalls echo in the memory
Down the passage which we did not take
Towards the door we never opened
Into the rose-garden.

> T. S. ELIOT (1888–1965). "Burnt Norton," 1, *Four Quartets,* 1943

I think I don't regret a single "excess" of my responsive youth—I only regret, in my chilled age, certain occasions and possibilities I didn't embrace.

> HENRY JAMES (1843–1916). Letter to Hugh Walpole, 21 August 1913

It is a mortifying reflection for any man to consider what he has done compared with what he might have done.

> SAMUEL JOHNSON (1709–1784). Slightly modified. Quoted by Rev. Dr. Maxwell, 1770. In James Boswell, *The Life of Samuel Johnson,* 1791

It is not what you are; it's what you don't become that hurts.

> OSCAR LEVANT (1906–1972). *Humoresque* (film), 1946, an ad-libbed line spoken by himself

Repeated polls over the years have found people's biggest lifetime regret is not getting enough education or not taking it seriously enough.

> MALCOLM RITTER. "What We Come to Regret," *San Francisco Chronicle,* 25 October 1993

A hundred years of regret
Pay not a farthing of debt.

> CHARLES HADDON SPURGEON (1834–1892). *John Ploughman's Talks,* 12, 1869

The greater part of what my neighbors call good I believe in my soul to be bad, and if I regret anything it is very likely to be my good behavior. What demon possessed me that I behaved so well?

> HENRY DAVID THOREAU (1817–1862). "Economy," *Walden; or Life in the Woods,* 1854

Never, never waste a minute on regret. It's a waste of time.

> HARRY S. TRUMAN (1884–1972). In Janet Landman, *Regret: The Persistence of the Possible,* 1993

Of all sad words of tongue or pen,
The saddest are these: "It might have been!"

> JOHN GREENLEAF WHITTIER (1807–1892). "Maud Muller," l. 105, 1854

Things said or done long years ago,
Or things I did not do or say
But thought that I might say or do,
Weigh me down, and not a day
But something is recalled,
My conscience or my vanity appalled.

> WILLIAM BUTLER YEATS (1865–1939). "Vacillation" (5), *The Winding Stair and Other Poems,* 1933

❦

Woulda, coulda, shoulda.

> SAYING (AMERICAN)

There's no use crying over spilt milk.

> SAYING (ENGLISH)

What's done is done and can't be undone.

> SAYING (ENGLISH)

RELIGION

See also • Belief ○ Bible: [especially] Walt Whitman ○ Buddhism ○ Christianity ○ Church ○ Civilization ○ Clergy ○ Confession ○ Conversion ○ Cults ○ Dreams: Emil A. Gutheil (2) ○ Faith ○ Forgiveness ○ Freedom of Religion ○ God ○ Good & Evil ○ Grace ○ Guilt ○ History ○ Immortality ○ Innocence ○ Judaism ○ Meditation ○ Miracles ○ Morality ○ Mysticism ○ Myths ○ Prayer ○ Prophets ○ Redemption ○ Religion, Anti- ○ Religion & Science ○ Repentance ○ Revelation ○ Saints ○ Salvation ○ Scripture ○ Self-Realization (Becoming) ○ Self-Realization (Being) ○ Soul ○ Spirituality: [especially] Richard M. Gross ○ Spirituality: First Person ○ Superstition ○ Witchcraft ○ Yoga ○ Zen

Religion is . . . mystical in its root and practical in its fruits, a communion with God, a calm and deep enthusiasm, a love which radiates, a force which acts, a happiness which overflows.

> HENRI AMIEL (1821–1881). Journal, 28 April 1866, tr. Mrs. Humphrey Ward, 1887

Since Luther's time there has been a conviction, more or less rooted, that a man may by an intellectual process think out a religion for himself, and that, as the highest of all duties, he ought to do so.

> WALTER BAGEHOT (1826–1877). *Physics and Politics, or Thoughts on the Application of the Principles of "Natural Selection" and "Inheritance" to Political Society,* 5.1, 1872

Morality must always precede and accompany religion, and yet religion is much more than morality.

> HENRY WARD BEECHER (1813–1887). *Life Thoughts,* p. 295, rec. Edna Dean Proctor, 1858

Religion [is] the crystallization, brought about by a scientific process of cooling, of what mysticism had poured, while hot, into the soul of man. Through religion all men get a little of what a few privileged souls possessed in full.

> HENRI BERGSON (1859–1941). "Dynamic Religion," *The Two Sources of Morality and Religion,* 1932, tr. R. Ashley Audra and Cloudesley Brereton, 1935

The end of all religion is not states of feeling but the transformation of the personality.

> ANTON T. BOISEN (1876–1965). *The Exploration of the Inner World: A Study of Mental Disorder and Religious Experience,* 7, 1936

Religion is born when we accept the ultimate frustration of mere human effort, and at the same time realize the strength which comes from union with superhuman reality.

> JOHN BUCHAN (1875–1940). "The Other Side of the Hill" (4), *Pilgrim's Way: An Essay in Recollection,* 1940

Show me an absurdity in Religion, [and] I will undertake to show you an hundred in Political Laws and Institutions.

> EDMUND BURKE (1729–1797). *A Vindication of Natural Society,* p. 103, M. Cooper edition, 1756

I think people can never have *enough* of religion, if they are to have any.

> LORD BYRON (1788–1824). Letter to Thomas Moore, 4 March 1822

A man's religion is the chief fact with regard to him.

> THOMAS CARLYLE (1795–1881). "The Hero as Divinity," *On Heroes, Hero-Worship, and the Heroic in History,* 1841

The faith that stands on authority is not faith. The reliance on authority measures the decline of religion, the withdrawal of the soul.

> RALPH WALDO EMERSON (1803–1882). "The Over-Soul," *Essays: First Series,* 1841

You say, there is no religion now. "Tis like saying, in rainy weather, there is no sun.

> RALPH WALDO EMERSON (1803–1882). Journal, 1850, undated

When believers and unbelievers live in the same manner—I distrust the religion.

> RALPH WALDO EMERSON (1803–1882). Journal, 1864, undated

We are born too late for the old and too early for the new faith.

> RALPH WALDO EMERSON (1803–1882). "The Preacher," *Lectures and Biographical Sketches,* 1883

All the religion we have is the ethics of one or another holy person; as soon as character appears, be sure love will, and veneration, and anecdotes, and fables about him, and delight of good men and women in him.

> RALPH WALDO EMERSON (1803–1882). "The Sovereignty of Ethics," *Lectures and Biographical Sketches,* 1883

Religion [is] any system of thought and action shared by a group which gives the individual a frame of orientation and an object of devotion.

> ERICH FROMM (1900–1980). *Psychoanalysis and Religion,* 3, 1950

A good Life is the only Religion.

> THOMAS FULLER (1654–1734). Comp., *Gnomologia: Adages and Proverbs,* 158, 1732

I have been experimenting with myself and my friends by introducing religion into politics. Let me explain what I mean by religion. . . . It is the permanent element in human nature which counts no cost too great in order to find full expression and which leaves the soul utterly restless until it has found itself, known its Maker and appreciated the true correspondence between the Maker and itself.

> MOHANDAS K. GANDHI (1869–1948). In *Young India,* 12 May 1920

You should be pioneers in presenting a living faith to the world, and not the dry bones of a traditional faith which the world will not grasp.

> MOHANDAS K. GANDHI (1709–1784). In Mahadev Desai, *With Gandhiji in Ceylon,* p. 112, 1928

The essence of true religious teaching is that one should serve and befriend all. . . . It is easy enough to be friendly to one's friends. But to befriend the one who regards himself as your enemy is the quintessence of true religion. The other is mere business.

> MOHANDAS K. GANDHI (1709–1784). In *Harijan,* 11 May 1947
> See Love: Sigmund Freud (2), Jesus, Saying (2) ○ Self-Love: Moses

The grand premise of religion is that *man is able to surpass himself;* that man who is part of this world may enter into a relationship with Him who is greater than the world.

> ABRAHAM JOSHUA HESCHEL (1907–1972). *God in Search of Man: A Philosophy of Judaism,* 3, 1955

Religion begins with a consciousness that something is asked of us.

> ABRAHAM JOSHUA HESCHEL (1907–1972). *God in Search of Man: A Philosophy of Judaism,* 16, 1955

The purpose of religion is not to satisfy the needs we feel but to create in us the need of serving ends, of which we otherwise remain oblivious.

> ABRAHAM JOSHUA HESCHEL (1907–1972). *God in Search of Man: A Philosophy of Judaism,* 34, 1955

It is conceivable for states to get together and have a United Nations, but it is still inconceivable to have a United Religions.

> ABRAHAM JOSHUA HESCHEL (1907–1972). "Choose Life!" *Jubilee,* January 1966

We are for religion against the religions.

> VICTOR HUGO (1802–1885). "Cosette" (7.8), *Les Misérables,* tr. Charles E. Wilbour, 1862

Vedanta Philosophy consists of three propositions. First, that Man's real nature is divine. Second, that the aim of human life is to realize this divine nature. Third, that all religions are essentially in agreement.

> CHRISTOPHER ISHERWOOD (1904–1986). Introduction to *Vedanta for the Western World,* 1945

It is in our lives, and not from our words, that our religion must be read.

> THOMAS JEFFERSON (1743–1826). Letter to Mrs. Samuel H. Smith, 6 August 1816

1. That there is one only God, and he all perfect.
2. That there is a future state of rewards and punishments.
3. That to love God with all thy heart and thy neighbor as thyself is the sum of religion.

> THOMAS JEFFERSON (1743–1826). Specifying the "doctrines of Jesus." Letter to Dr. Benjamin Waterhouse, 26 June 1822

All religions are therapies for the sorrows and disorders of the soul.

> CARL G. JUNG (1875–1961). "The Detachment of Consciousness from the Object," *Commentary* (on *The Secret of the Golden Flower*), 1929, tr. Cary F. Baynes, 1961
> See Religion, Anti-: Sigmund Freud (1)

Religion, the philosophy of the heart . . . and philosophy, the religion of the mind.

> LOUIS KOSSUTH (1802–1894). Exiled Hungarian statesman. Speech, Lexington (Massachusetts), May 1852

Is it not strange that men are so keen to *fight* for religion and so unkeen to *live* according to its precepts?

GEORG CHRISTOPH LICHTENBERG (1742–1799). *Aphorisms*, L.85, 1806, tr. R. J. Hollingdale, 1990

See Martyrdom: William Makepeace Thackeray o Principles, Moral: Alfred Adler

How infinitely much there is in these words: "Commune with your own heart upon your bed, and be still. Offer the sacrifices of righteousness, and put your trust in the Lord." A whole religion?

GEORG CHRISTOPH LICHTENBERG (1742–1799). Quoting *Psalms* 4:5–6

The only religion is conscience in action.

HENRY DEMAREST LLOYD (1847–1903). Journalist

To insure a long existence to religious sects or republics, it is necessary frequently to bring them back to their original principles.

MACHIAVELLI (1469–1527). *The Discourses,* 3.1, 1517, tr. Christian E. Detmold, 1950

The only true world solution today is governments guided by true religion—of the spirit.

MALCOLM X (1925–1965) (with ALEX HALEY). *The Autobiography of Malcolm X,* 19, 1965

Spiritual rebirth is the key to the aspirations of all the higher religions.

THOMAS MERTON (1915–1968). "Rebirth and the New Man in Christianity," *Love and Living,* ed. Naomi Burton Stone and Brother Patrick Hart, 1985

For Modes of Faith, let graceless zealots fight;
His can't be wrong whose life is in the right.

ALEXANDER POPE (1688–1744). *An Essay on Man,* 3.305, 1734

Religion is the endeavor of divided and incomplete human personality to attain unity and completion.

CHARLES FRANCIS POTTER (1885–1962). Introduction to *The Great Religious Leaders,* 1962

Every great religion is some noble soul's conflict written large.

CHARLES FRANCIS POTTER (1885–1962). *The Great Religious Leaders,* 3, 1962

Religion must not be either egocentric or altruistic, but theocentric. We have to center our whole thought and mind upon God, and then extend our arms to everyone, embracing them all in the love of God.

SWAMI PRABHAVANAND (1893–1976). "The Sermon on the Mount—V." In Christopher Isherwood, ed., *Vedanta for the Western World,* 1945

Fanatical religion driven to a certain point is almost as bad as none at all, but not quite.

WILL ROGERS (1879–1935). *There's Not a Bathing Suit in Russia,* 8, 1927

You take religion backed up by Commerce and it's awful hard for a heathen to overcome.

WILL ROGERS (1879–1935). "A Rogers Thesaurus," ed. Cleveland Amory, *Saturday Review,* 25 August 1962

The lovers of God have no religion but God alone.

RUMI (A.D. 1207?–1273). Persian Sufi poet. In Dag Hammarskjöld, 1955, *Markings,* tr. Leif Sjöberg and W. H. Auden, 1964

Religious doctrines which are founded merely on authority, miracles and revelations, are only suited to the childhood of humanity.

ARTHUR SCHOPENHAUER (1788–1860). "Religion and Other Essays: A Dialogue," *Essays of Arthur Schopenhauer,* tr. T. Bailey Saunders, 1851

Your religion was written on tablets of stone, by the iron finger of your God, lest you forget it. The red men could never remember it or comprehend it. Our religion is the traditions of our ancestors, the dreams of our old men, given them by the Great Spirit, and the visions of our [chiefs], and is written in the hearts of our people.

SEATTLE (1786?–1866). Native American chief. Speech. In Louis Thomas Jones, *Aboriginal American Oratory,* 1965

There is only one religion, though there are a hundred versions of it.

GEORGE BERNARD SHAW (1856–1950). Preface to *Plays Pleasant and Unpleasant,* vol. 2, 1898

Religion is a deeply personal thing in which man and God go it alone together, without the witch doctor in the middle.

FRANK SINATRA (1915–1998). Interview, *Playboy,* February 1963

We have just enough religion to make us hate, but not enough to make us love one another.

JONATHAN SWIFT (1667–1745). "Thoughts on Various Subjects" (expanded from a version published in 1711), *Miscellanies in Prose and Verse* (published with Alexander Pope), vol. 1, 1727

Religion has been converted from the keystone which holds together the social edifice into one department within it, and the idea of a rule of right is replaced by economic expediency as the arbiter of policy and the criterion of conduct.

R. H. TAWNEY (1880–1962). *Religion and the Rise of Capitalism: A Historical Study,* 5, 1926

The first step toward the nonreligion of the Western world was made by religion itself. When it defended its great symbols, not as symbols but as literal stories, it had already lost the battle.

PAUL TILLICH (1886–1965). "The Lost Dimension in Religion," *Saturday Evening Post,* 14 June 1958

Religion, after all, is the serious business of the human race.

ARNOLD J. TOYNBEE (1889–1975). Closing words, "The Unification of the World and the Change in Historical Perspective," 1947, *Civilization on Trial,* 1948

True religion [is] right belief and right feeling taking effect in right action. Without right action, right feeling and right belief have no virtue in them.

ARNOLD J. TOYNBEE (1889–1975). "Ten Basic Questions—and Answers," *New York Times Magazine,* 20 February 1955

Religion consists in the simple feeling of a relationship of dependence upon something above us and a desire to establish relations with this mysterious power.

MIGUEL de UNAMUNO (1864–1936). *Tragic Sense of Life,* 10, 1913, tr. J. E. Crawford Flitch, 1921

[The religions] are all so many paths leading to the same goal.

SWAMI VIVEKANANDA (1863–1902). "An Unpublished Lecture." In Christopher Isherwood, ed., *Vedanta for the Western World,* 1945

The end of all religions is the realizing of God in the soul. That is the universal religion.

> SWAMI VIVEKANANDA (1863–1902). *What Religion Is*, 1.1, ed. Swami Vidyatmananda, 1963

At the core of prophetic religion is transformation—a change of heart, a revolution of the spirit, a conversion of the soul that issues forth in new personal and social behavior.

> JIM WALLIS (1948–). *The Soul of Politics: A Practical and Prophetic Vision for Change*, 3, 1994

Religion is as necessary to reason as reason is to religion. The one cannot exist without the other.

> GEORGE WASHINGTON (1732–1799). In James K. Paulding, *The Life of Washington*, 22, 1848

[Religion] is the one element in human experience which persistently shows an upward trend. It fades and then recurs. But when it renews its force, it recurs with an added richness and purity of content. The fact of the religious vision, and its history of persistent expansion, is our one ground for optimism. Apart from it, human life is a flash of occasional enjoyments lighting up a mass of pain and misery, a bagatelle of transient experience.

> ALFRED NORTH WHITEHEAD (1861–1947). *Science and the Modern World*, 12, 1925

Religion is what the individual does with his own solitariness. It runs through three stages, if it evolves to its final satisfaction. It is the transition from God the void to God the enemy, and from God the enemy to God the companion.

> ALFRED NORTH WHITEHEAD (1861–1947). *Religion in the Making*, 1.1, 1926

There is no false Religion—Each one is divine. Each one means exactly the state of development of the people—they have arrived at that—by-and-by they will pass on farther.

> WALT WHITMAN (1819–1892). "Notes for Lectures on Religion," *Walt Whitman's Workshop: A Collection of Unpublished Manuscripts*, ed. Clifton Joseph Furness, 1964

Religion is . . . the calm bottom of the sea at its deepest point, which remains calm however high the waves on the surface may be.

> LUDWIG WITTGENSTEIN (1889–1951). 1946, *Culture and Value*, 1977, tr. Peter Winch, 1980

❧

Politics and science beat the path religion walks on.

> ANONYMOUS

Yesterday's religion is today's mythology: today's mysticism is tomorrow's religion.

> ANONYMOUS

RELIGION, ANTI-

See also • Atheism ○ Church ○ Cults ○ Religion ○ Religion & Science

All religions are founded on blood, for all . . . rest essentially on the idea of sacrifice—that is, on the perpetual immolation of humanity to the insatiable vengeance of divinity.

> MIKHAIL BAKUNIN (1814–1876). *Federalism, Socialism, and Anti-Theologism*. In *The Political Philosophy of Bakunin: Scientific Anarchism*, 1.11, ed. G. P. Maximoff, 1953

Religion, *n*. A daughter of Hope and Fear, explaining to Ignorance the nature of the Unknowable.

> AMBROSE BIERCE (1842–1914). *The Devil's Dictionary*, p. 109, 1911, Dover edition, 1958

The religion of one seems madness unto another.

> SIR THOMAS BROWNE (1605–1682). *Hydriotaphia: Urn Burial*, 4, 1658, ed. John Addington Symonds, 1886

Religion makes the free by nature slaves!

> WILLIAM COWPER (1731–1800). "Tirocinium: Or, a Review of Schools," l. 184, 1785

Of all plagues with which mankind are curst,
Ecclesiastic tyranny's the worst.

> DANIEL DEFOE (1660–1731). *The True-Born Englishman*, 2.299, 1701

Unbelief, skepticism, and thoroughgoing atheism not only abet but are practically synonymous with mental health; . . . devout belief, dogmatism, and religiosity distinctly contribute to and in some ways are equal to mental or emotional disturbance.

> ALBERT ELLIS (1869–1951). "The Case Against Religiosity," published by the Institute of Rational Emotive Therapy, 1983

The religion of one age is the literary entertainment of the next.

> RALPH WALDO EMERSON (1803–1882). "Character," *Lectures and Biographical Sketches*, 1883

Thus religion would be the universal obsessional neurosis of humanity. . . .

   If on the one hand religion brings with it obsessional limitation, which can only be compared to an individual obsessional neurosis, it comprises on the other hand a system of wish-illusions, incompatible with reality, such as we find in an isolated form only in Meynert's amentia, a state of blissful hallucinatory confusion.

> SIGMUND FREUD (1856–1939). *The Future of an Illusion*, 8, 1927, tr. W. D. Robson-Scott, 1953
>
> See Religion: Carl G. Jung

The effect of the consolations of religion may be compared to that of a narcotic.

> SIGMUND FREUD (1856–1939). *The Future of an Illusion*, 9, 1927, tr. W. D. Robson-Scott, 1953

The various modes of worship, which prevailed in the Roman world, were all considered by the people as equally true; by the philosopher as equally false; and by the magistrate as equally useful.

> EDWARD GIBBON (1737–1794). *The Decline and Fall of the Roman Empire*, 2, 1776–1788
>
> See Study: Francis Bacon (3)

Most men's anger about religion is as if two men should quarrel for a lady they neither of them care for.

> MARQUIS OF HALIFAX (1633–1695). "Religion," *Political, Moral and Miscellaneous Reflections*, 1750

What is ordinarily called "religion" is a substitute. . . . The substitute has the obvious purpose of replacing *immediate [religious]*

experience by a choice of suitable symbols supported by an organized dogma and ritual.

> CARL G. JUNG (1875–1961). "Psychology and Religion" (2), 1938,
> *Psychology and Religion: West and East,* tr. R. F. C. Hull, 1958

There is no formal religion that does not insist, as its first requirement, on a confession of conformity. Nor is there, any longer, a
religion that offers a path to Heaven other than the autobahn of
submission. One and all, they have conspired, in the name of the
Spirit, against the spirit of man: one and all, they have sold him
into slavery. Under threat of damnation, hell-fire, . . . they have
ordered him to renounce protest, to forego revolt, to be passive,
to surrender.

> ROBERT LINDNER (1914–1956). Title essay (3), *Must You Conform?*
> 1956

Religion is poison.

> MAO TSE-TUNG (1893–1976). Remark to Dalai Lama. Quoted by Martin
> Scorsese, Charlie Rose television interview, PBS, 16 January 1998

Religion is the sigh of the oppressed creature, the sentiment of a
heartless world, and the soul of soulless conditions. It is the
opium of the people.

> KARL MARX (1818–1883). Introduction to *Contribution to the Critique of
> Hegel's* Philosophy of Right, 1844, *The Marx-Engels Reader,* 2nd ed.,
> ed. Robert C. Tucker, 1978

> See Art: W. Somerset Maugham ○ Communism: Clare Boothe Luce ○
> Cults: Berkeley Rice ○ Custom: Ralph Waldo Emerson ○ Drugs,
> Psychiatric: Aldous Huxley ○ Films: Aldous Huxley ○ Fools: Abraham
> Joshua Heschel ○ Gossip: Erica Jong (2) ○ Inflation: Henry Hazlitt ○
> Optimism: Milan Kundera ○ Sports: Russell Baker ○ Television: Edward
> R. Murrow ○ Words: Rudyard Kipling

To sum up:
1. The cosmos is a gigantic flywheel making 10,000 revolutions a
   minute.
2. Man is a sick fly taking a dizzy ride on it.
3. Religion is the theory that the wheel was designed and set
   spinning to give him the ride.

> H. L. MENCKEN (1880–1956). Closing words, "Ad Imaginem Dei Creavit
> Illum: Coda," *Prejudices: Third Series,* 1922

All religions die of one disease, that of being found out.

> JOHN MORLEY (1838–1923)

Religion is a species of mental disease. It has always had a pathological reaction on mankind.

> BENITO MUSSOLINI (1883–1945). Speech, Lausanne (Switzerland), July
> 1904

Wherever the religious neurosis has appeared on the earth so far,
we find it connected with three dangerous prescriptions as to regimen: solitude, fasting, and sexual abstinence.

> FRIEDRICH NIETZSCHE (1844–1900). *Beyond Good and Evil,* 47, 1886,
> tr. Helen Zimmern, 1909

I am myself a dissenter from all known religions, and I hope that
every kind of religious belief will die out. I do not believe that, on
. . . balance, religious belief has been a force for good. Although
I am prepared to admit that in certain times and places it has had
some good effects, I regard it as belonging to the infancy of

human reason, and to a stage of development which we are now
outgrowing.

> BERTRAND RUSSELL (1872–1970). *Sceptical Essays,* 12, 1928

The utility of religion [is] as a prop of thrones . . . ; every wise
prince who loves his throne and his family will appear at the head
of his people as an exemplar of true religion.

> ARTHUR SCHOPENHAUER (1788–1860). "Religion and Other Essays:
> A Dialogue," *Essays of Arthur Schopenhauer,* tr. T. Bailey Saunders,
> 1851

You may go over the world and you will find that every form of
religion which has breathed upon this earth has degraded women.
There is not one which has not made her subject to man.

> ELIZABETH CADY STANTON (1815–1902). Speech before the 17th
> Annual Convention of the National Woman Suffrage Association,
> Washington, 20? January 1885

You are perfectly right, Sire. A wise and courageous prince, with
money, troops, and laws, can perfectly well govern men without
the aid of religion, which was made only to deceive them; but the
stupid people would soon make one for themselves, and as long
as there are fools and rascals there will be religions.

> VOLTAIRE (1694–1778). Letter to Frederick II, 5 January 1767

RELIGION & SCIENCE

See also • Communications: Arnold J. Toynbee ○ Religion ○
Religion, Anti- ○ Science ○ Superstition: Theodore Roosevelt ○
Technology

The more we learn of science, the more we see that its wonderful mysteries are all explained by a few simple laws so connected together and so dependent upon each other, that we see the
same mind animating them all.

> OLYMPIA BROWN (1835–1900). First ordained American woman.
> Sermon, January 1895, Mukwonago (Wisconsin), *Olympia Brown,
> An Autobiography,* ed. Gwendolen B. Willis, 1960

Science and religion . . . are two sides of the same glass, through
which we see darkly until these two, focusing together, reveal the
truth.

> PEARL S. BUCK (1892–1973). *A Bridge for Passing,* 3, 1962

The cosmic religious experience is the strongest force and the
noblest driving force behind scientific research.

> ALBERT EINSTEIN (1879–1955). "Religion and Science," *New York
> Times Magazine,* 9 November 1930

Science without religion is lame; religion without science is blind.

> ALBERT EINSTEIN (1879–1955). "Science and Religion," 1941, *Out of My
> Later Years,* rev. ed., 8.2, 1956 (1950)

True science and true religion are twin sisters, and the separation
of either from the other is sure to prove the death of both. Science
prospers exactly in proportion as it is religious; and religion flourishes in exact proportion to the scientific depth and firmness of its
basis.

> T. H. HUXLEY (1825–1895). In Herbert Spencer, *Education: Intellectual,
> Moral, and Physical,* 1, 1860

Today there is a wide measure of agreement, which on the physical side of science approaches almost to unanimity, that the stream of knowledge is heading toward a nonmechanical reality; the universe begins to look more like a great thought than like a great machine. Mind no longer appears as an accidental intruder into the realm of matter; we are beginning to suspect that we ought rather to hail it as the creator and governor of the realm of matter.

> SIR JAMES HOPWOOD JEANS (1877–1946). English physicist. Quoted by Joyce Carol Oates, "New Heaven and Earth," 1972. In Caroline Shrodes et al., eds., *The Common Reader*, 3rd ed., 1985

Science deals mainly with facts; religion deals mainly with values. The two are not rivals. They are complementary.

> MARTIN LUTHER KING, JR. (1929–1968). *Strength to Love*, 1.1, 1963

The means by which we live have outdistanced the ends for which we live. Our scientific power has outrun our spiritual power. We have guided missiles and misguided men.

> MARTIN LUTHER KING, JR. (1929–1968). *Strength to Love*, 7.3, 1963

I have seen the science I worshipped, and the aircraft I loved, destroying the civilization I expected them to serve. . . . To progress, even to survive, we must learn to apply the truths of God to the direction of our science.

> CHARLES A. LINDBERGH (1902–1974). In "Lindbergh: The Way of a Hero," *Time*, 26 May 1967

[The] flight from and hatred of technology is self-defeating. The Buddha, the Godhead, resides quite as comfortably in the circuits of a digital computer or the gears of a cycle transmission as he does at the top of a mountain or in the petals of a flower. To think otherwise is to demeans the Buddha—which is to demean oneself.

> ROBERT M. PIRSIG (1928–). *Zen and the Art of Motorcycle Maintenance: An Inquiry into Values*, 1, 1974

Science is not only compatible with spirituality; it is a profound source of spirituality.

> CARL SAGAN (1934–1996). *The Demon-Haunted World: Science as a Candle in the Dark*, 2, 1995

Every genuine scientist must be finally a metaphysician.

> GEORGE BERNARD SHAW (1856–1950). Preface ("The Homeopathic Reaction Against Darwinism") to *Back to Methuselah: A Metabiological Pentateuch*, 1921

Mystics always hope that science will some day overtake them.

> BOOTH TARKINGTON (1869–1946). "Stars in the Dust-Heap," *Looking Forward to the Great Adventure*, 1926

The most miraculous thing is happening. . . . The physicists are getting down to the nitty-gritty, they've really just about pared things down to the ultimate details, and the last thing they ever expected to happen is happening. God is showing through. They hate it, but they can't do anything about it. Facts are facts.

> JOHN UPDIKE (1932–). *Roger's Version*, 1, 1986

We would be a lot better off if the Government would take its money out of science and put it into astrology and the reading of palms. I used to think that science would save us. I beg you to believe in the most ridiculous of all superstitions: that humanity is at the center of the universe, the fulfiller or the frustrator of the grandest dreams of God Almighty. If you can believe that and make others believe it, human beings might stop treating each other like garbage.

> KURT VONNEGUT, JR. (1922–). Commencement address at Bennington College (Vermont). In "American Notes," *Time*, 29 June 1970

When the anthropologists arrive, the gods depart.

> SAYING (HAITIAN)

REMORSE

See also • Alcohol: George Ade ◦ Greatness: Shakespeare (1) ◦ Guilt ◦ Hate: Albert Einstein ◦ Regret ◦ Repentance

Remorse is the poison of life.

> EMILY BRONTË (1818–1948). *Jane Eyre*, 14, 1847

Remorse begets reform.

> WILLIAM COWPER (1731–1800). *The Task*, 5.618, 1785

Remorse drives the weak to despair and the strong to sainthood.

> MARIE von EBNER-ESCHENBACH (1830–1916). *Aphorisms*, p. 69, 1880–1905, tr. David Scrase and Wolfgang Mieder, 1994

Chronic remorse, as all the moralists are agreed, is a most undesirable sentiment. If you have behaved badly, repent, make what amends you can and address yourself to the task of behaving better next time. On no account brood over your wrongdoing. Rolling in the muck is not the best way of getting clean.

> ALDOUS HUXLEY (1894–1963). Opening paragraph, foreword (1946) to *Brave New World*, 1932

Remorse: regret that one waited so long to do it.

> H. L. MENCKEN (1880–1956). *A Little Book in C Major*, 5.7, 1916

Farewell Remorse: all Good to me is lost;
Evil be thou my Good.

> JOHN MILTON (1608–1674). *Paradise Lost*, 4.109, 1667

Remorse sleeps while fate is kind but grows sharp in adversity.

> ROUSSEAU (1712–1778). *Confessions*, 2 (1728–1731), 1781, tr. J. M. Cohen, 1953

REPARTEE

See also • Conversation ◦ Insult ◦ Repartee: Examples ◦ Wit

Repartee is what you wish you'd said.

> HEYWOOD BROUN (1888–1939). In Robert E. Drennan, ed., "Heywood Broun," *The Algonquin Wits*, 1968

Silence is the unbearable repartee.

> G. K. CHESTERTON (1874–1936)

A majority is always the best repartee.

> BENJAMIN DISRAELI (1804–1881). *Tancred: Or, The New Crusade*, 2.14, 1847

Better never than late.

FIRST RULE OF REPARTEE. In Paul Dickson, comp., *The Official Explanations*, p. 189, 1980

REPARTEE: EXAMPLES

See also • Criticism: Examples ○ Insult ○ Repartee ○ Wit: Examples

Woman (on a very hot day): Good afternoon, Mr. Berra. My, you look mighty cool today.
Berra: Thank you, ma'am. You don't look so hot yourself.

YOGI BERRA (1925–). In Phil Pepe, *The Wit and Wisdom of Yogi Berra*, 11, 1965

Richard Porson: Yes, Mr. Southey is indeed a wonderful poet. He will be read when Homer and Virgil are forgotten.
Byron: But not till then.

LORD BYRON (1788–1824). Format adapted. In John Berryman, "The Other Cambridge," *Love and Fame*, 1970

Nancy Astor: Winston, if I were married to you, I'd put poison in your coffee.
Churchill: If I were your husband, I'd drink it.

WINSTON CHURCHILL (1874–1965). Format adapted. 1912. In Consuelo Vanderbilt Balsan, *The Glitter and the Gold*, 7, 1952

George Bernard Shaw (telegram): Am reserving two tickets for you for my premiere, come and bring a friend—if you have one.
Churchill (telegram): Impossible to be present for the first performance. Will attend the second—if there is one.

WINSTON CHURCHILL (1874–1965). Format adapted. In William Manchester, *Winston Spencer Churchill: The Last Lion; Visions of Glory, 1874–1932*, 3, 1983

Photographer: I hope, sir, that I will shoot your picture on your hundredth birthday.
Churchill (after pausing briefly to look him over): I don't see why not, young man. You look reasonably fit and healthy.

WINSTON CHURCHILL (1874–1965). On his 75th birthday, London, 30 November 1949. In Norman McGowan, "At Hyde Park Gate," *My Years with Churchill*, 1958

Alexander Smyth (a windbag congressmember): You, sir, speak for the present generation; but I speak for posterity.
Clay: Yes, and you seem resolved to speak until the arrival of *your* audience.

HENRY CLAY (1777–1852). Kentucky senator. Format adapted. In Epes Sargent, *The Life and Public Services of Henry Clay, Down to 1848*, 8, 1852

Woman: You must talk to me, Mr. Coolidge. I made a bet today that I could get more than two words out of you.
Coolidge (who was noted for his taciturnity): You lose.

CALVIN COOLIDGE (1872–1933). Format adapted. In Ishbel Ross, *Grace Coolidge and Her Era: The Story of a President's Wife*, 3, 1962

Mrs. Grace Coolidge: What was the sermon about?
Coolidge: Sin.
Mrs. Coolidge: Well, what did the preacher say about sin?
Coolidge: He was against it.

CALVIN COOLIDGE (1872–1933). Format adapted. Attributed. When told of the account, Coolidge reportedly laughed and said that it "would be even funnier if it were true."

Peter Lorre: You despise me, don't you?
Humphrey Bogart: Well, if I gave it any thought, I would.

JULIUS J. EPSTEIN (1909–), PHILIP G. EPSTEIN, and HOWARD KOCH. *Casablanca* (film), 1942

Claude Rains: And what in heaven's name brought you to Casablanca?
Humphrey Bogart: My health. I came to Casablanca for the waters.
Rains: What waters? We're in the desert.
Bogart: I was misinformed.

JULIUS J. EPSTEIN (1909–), PHILIP G. EPSTEIN, and HOWARD KOCH. *Casablanca* (film), 1942

Someone: Have a nice day!
Another: Thank you, but I have other plans.

PAUL FUSSELL (1924–). Format adapted

Man: President [Franklin D. Roosevelt] is his own worst enemy.
George: Not as long as I'm alive, he's not.

WALTER GEORGE (1878–1957). Georgia senator, Format adapted, 1938. In Cokie Roberts, "Divided Government Is the Best Revenge," *New York Times*, 27 August 1992

Comte de Vergennes: You replace Mr. [Benjamin] Franklin [as minister to France]?
Jefferson: I succeed him: no one could replace him.

THOMAS JEFFERSON (1743–1826). Format adapted, 1785

Lady (expecting an elaborate defense): How did you come to define in your Dictionary *pastern* as the *knee* of a horse?
Johnson: Ignorance, Madam, pure ignorance.

SAMUEL JOHNSON (1709–1784). Format adapted, 1755. In James Boswell, *The Life of Samuel Johnson*, 1791

Kennedy: How did you like the article about you in the *New York Times* this morning?
John Kenneth Galbraith: I object to the *Times* describing me as arrogant.
Kennedy: I don't see why. Everybody else does.

JOHN F. KENNEDY (1917–1963). Format adapted. 30 March 1961. In Galbraith, *Ambassador's Journal: A Personal Account of the Kennedy Years*, 3, 1969

Member of the Washington press corps: Do you prefer to be called Mr. Secretary or Dr. Secretary?
Kissinger: I do not stand on protocol. If you just call me Excellency, it will be okay.

HENRY A. KISSINGER (1923–). Format adapted. Soon after being appointed secretary of state, September 1973. In Walter Isaacson, *Kissinger: A Biography*, 22, 1992

Woman: Oh, Dr. Kissinger, thank you for saving the world.
Kissinger: You're welcome.

HENRY A. KISSINGER (1923–). Format adapted, 1973. In Helen Thomas, *Chronicle* staff interview, "Uncovering the White House," *San Francisco Sunday Examiner & Chronicle*, 29 January 1995

Elderly German man (peering at him): You know, you look a lot like Herr Kissinger.
Kissinger: A lot of people tell me that.

> HENRY A. KISSINGER (1923–). Format adapted. In Ralph Blumenfeld et al., *Henry Kissinger: The Private and Public Story,* 16, 1974

Young girl (on a long line of well-wishers at a White House reception): Mr. Lincoln, I wish you would say something to me that I will always remember.
Lincoln: I think you are the prettiest girl I have seen this evening.

> ABRAHAM LINCOLN (1809–1965). Format adapted. Following his *Second Inaugural Address,* 4 March 1865. In Colin Bingham, comp., *Men and Affairs: A Modern Miscellany,* p. 437, 1968

Congressman (after running his hand over Longworth's bald head): It feels just like my wife's behind.
Longworth: Why, so it does.

> NICHOLAS LONGWORTH (1869–1931). Ohio speaker of the House of Representatives. Format adapted

William McK. Springer (quoting Henry Clay in a speech): As for me, I would rather be right than be President.
Reed: Well, the gentleman will never be either.

> THOMAS BRACKETT REED (1839–1902). Maine speaker of the House of Representatives. Format adapted. In Samuel W. McCall, *The Life of Thomas Brackett Reed,* 21, 1914
>
> See Presidents: Henry Clay

Roosevelt: I'd like to see 16 lions turned loose on the Congress.
Man: Might not the lions make a mistake?
Roosevelt: Not if they stayed there long enough.

> FRANKLIN D. ROOSEVELT (1885–1945). Adapted. At a time when relations between himself and Capitol Hill were particularly bad. In Herman Finer, *The Presidency: Crisis and Regeneration,* 2, 1960

Prince Henry: I never thought to hear you speak again.
King Henry: Thy wish was father, Harry, to that thought.

> SHAKESPEARE (1564–1616). *Henry IV,* Part II, 4.5.92, 1597

Woman (letter): You have the greatest brain in the world, and I have the most beautiful body; so we ought to produce the most perfect child.
Shaw (letter): What if the child inherits my body and your brains?

> GEORGE BERNARD SHAW (1856–1950). Format adapted. In Hesketh Pearson, "En Pantoufles," *George Bernard Shaw: His Life and Personality,* 1963

Shaw (to a woman seated next to him at a dinner party): Madam, if I gave you a million pounds, would you have sexual intercourse with me?
Woman (after some thought): I think I would.
Shaw: Would you do it for a fiver?
Woman: Sir, what kind of woman do you think I am?
Shaw: I thought we had established that, and were merely haggling over the price?

> GEORGE BERNARD SHAW (1856–1950). Format adapted

Heckler (from the crowd): Tell 'em what's on your mind, Al. It won't take long.
Smith (grinning and pointing at the man): Stand up, pardner, and I'll tell 'em what's on both our minds. It won't take any longer.

> AL SMITH (1873–1944). New York governor. Format adapted. In "Lyndon's Fables," *Time,* 8 May 1964

Man (to his friend): I think it a shame that you have not spoken to your wife. How do you explain it? How do you justify it?
Friend: I didn't want to interrupt her.

> MARK TWAIN (1835–1910). Format adapted. "Chapters from My Autobiography," *North American Review,* 15 March 1907

Hatcheck girl: Goodness, what beautiful diamonds!
West: Goodness had nothing to do with it, dearie.

> MAE WEST (1893–1980). In *Night after Night* (film), 1932

Customs inspector (New York City): Have you anything to declare?
Wilde: Nothing, nothing but my genius!

> OSCAR WILDE (1854–1900). Format adapted, 2 January 1882. In H. Montgomery Hyde, *Oscar Wilde: The Aftermath,* 2.3, 1963

Earl of Sandwich: 'Pon my honor, Wilkes, I don't know whether you'll die on the gallows or of the pox.
Wilkes: That must depend, my lord, upon whether I first embrace your lordship's principles or your lordship's mistresses.

> JOHN WILKES (1725–1797). English political leader. Format adapted. In Sir Charles Petrie, *The Four Georges: A Revaluation of the Period from 1714–1830,* 4, 1935

✿

Bus driver (on being handed a transfer): Madam, this transfer is three days old.
Elderly passenger (with a stern look): That's how long I've been waiting.

> ANONYMOUS (AMERICAN). Format adapted. The driver laughed and waved her on. In Jack Rosenbaum's, column, *San Francisco Progress,* 1989

Q: Why does a Jew always answer a question with a question?
A: And why should a Jew *not* answer a question with a question?

> ANONYMOUS (JEWISH). In Erica Jong, *Fear of Flying,* 1, 1973

REPENTANCE

See also • Confession ○ Evil ○ Forgiveness: [especially] Abraham Lincoln ○ God ○ Guilt ○ Innocence ○ Morality ○ Nations: Aleksandr Solzhenitsyn ○ Prayer ○ Redemption ○ Religion ○ Remorse: [especially] Aldous Huxley ○ Salvation ○ Sin

Pardon cannot precede repentance, and repentance only begins with humility.

> HENRI AMIEL (1821–1881). Journal, 9 April 1856, tr. Mrs. Humphrey Ward, 1887

The best way I kno ov tew repent ov enny thing iz tew do better next time.

> JOSH BILLINGS (1818–1885). "Hooks & Eyes," *Everybody's Friend, or; Josh Billing's Encyclopedia and Proverbial Philosophy of Wit and Humor,* 1874

In repenting ov sins, men are apt tew repent ov thoze they haint got, and overlook thoze they hav.

> JOSH BILLINGS (1818–1885). "Ink Lings," *Everybody's Friend, or; Josh Billing's Encyclopedia and Proverbial Philosophy of Wit and Humor,* 1874

Repentanse should be the effekt ov love—not fear.

> JOSH BILLINGS (1818–1885). "Ink Lings," *Everybody's Friend, or; Josh Billing's Encyclopedia and Proverbial Philosophy of Wit and Humor,* 1874

There is no sin that will not be forgiven by sincere repentance.

> THE BRATZLAVER (1770–1811). In Louis I. Newman, comp., *The Hasidic Anthology,* 146.10.A.18, 1934

Your past sins shall be forgiven if you begin now to do right, for that is repentance.

> JAMES FREEMAN CLARKE (1810–1888). *Self-Culture: Physical, Intellectual, Moral, and Spiritual,* 21, 1880

Repentance is but want of pow'r to sin.

> JOHN DRYDEN (1631–1700). "Palamon and Arcite" (3.813), *Fables: Ancient and Modern,* 1700

The more grievous a man's sins seem to him, the readier God is to forgive them. . . . They are annihilated as if they had never happened, if only the repentance be whole.

> MEISTER ECKHART (A.D. 1260?–1328?). "The Talks of Instruction" (13), *Meister Eckhart: A Modern Translation,* tr. R. B. Blakney, 1941

Repentance is a respite between two sins.

> PAUL ELDRIDGE (1888–1982). *Maxims for a Modern Man,* 1926, 1965

Amendment is Repentance.

> THOMAS FULLER (1654–1734). Comp., *Introductio ad Prudentiam,* 665, 1731

Repentance means to change your way of living. It means to change your mind. You are going in one direction in your life, but then you turn and go in another direction.

> BILLY GRAHAM (1918–). "We Have Hope!" *Decision,* January 1993

The greatest need in America at the moment is for a moral and spiritual renewal. This comes, I believe, only as we turn in repentance and faith to the living God, who stands ready to forgive and renew us from within.

> BILLY GRAHAM (1918–). Closing paragraph, "The Moral Weight of Leadership," *New York Times,* 17 March 1998

We as often repent the good we have done as the ill.

> WILLIAM HAZLITT (1778–1830). *Characteristics in the Manner of Rochefoucault's Maxims,* 127, 1823

There is always a way that leads out of guilt: repentance or turning to God.

> ABRAHAM JOSHUA HESCHEL (1907–1972). *The Insecurity of Freedom: Essays on Human Existence,* 10, 1967

There will be more joy in heaven over one sinner who repents than over ninety-nine righteous persons who need no repentance.

> JESUS (A.D. 1st cent.). *Luke* 15:7

The gates of repentance are always open.

> MIDRASH (4th cent. B.C.– A.D. 12th cent.). Rabbinical writings. In Louis I. Newman, comp., *The Talmudic Anthology,* 282, 1945

Repentance makes man a new creature.

> MIDRASH (4th cent. B.C.– A.D. 12th cent.). Rabbinical writings. In Louis I. Newman, comp., *The Talmudic Anthology,* 282, 1945

A sincere repenter of faults is like him who has committed none.

> MUHAMMAD (A.D. 570?–632). *The Sayings of Muhammad,* 381, tr. Abdullah Al-Suhrawardy, 1941

Refer not to a penitent's evil deed, not even in jest.

> ORHOT TZADDIKIM (15th cent.). In Joseph L. Baron, Comp., *A Treasury of Jewish Quotations,* p. 407, 1956

It's never too *late* to repent.

> JOHN RAY (1628–1705). Comp., *A Collection of English Proverbs,* p. 165, 1678
>
> See Age: Saying (English) (4)

The gate of repentance will not be locked against worshippers till the sun rises in its setting place.

> SA'DI (A.D. 1213?–1292). *The Gulistan, or Rose Garden,* 5 (Story 20), A.D. 1258, tr. Edward Rehatsek, 1964

The best way to repent for a wrong is by not repeating it.

> THOMAS S. SZASZ (1920–). *Psychiatric Slavery,* 5, 1977

If a man repents of his evil deeds, and then returns to the same deeds, he has not truly repented.

> TALMUD (A.D. 1st–6th cent.). Rabbinical writings. In Louis I. Newman, comp., *The Talmudic Anthology,* 282, 1945

Repentance is connected with spiritual growth, just as the breaking of the shell is connected with the hatching of the birdling.

> LEO TOLSTOY (1828–1910). *Thoughts and Aphorisms,* 1.8, 1886–1893, tr. Leo Wiener, 1905

Repentance must be something more than mere remorse for sins; it comprehends a change of nature befitting heaven.

> LEW WALLACE (1827–1905). *Ben-Hur: A Tale of the Christ,* 6.2, 1880

What consoles one nowadays is not repentance, but pleasure. Repentance is quite out of date.

> OSCAR WILDE (1854–1900). *Lady Windermere's Fan,* 4, 1892

The moment of repentance is the moment of initiation.

> OSCAR WILDE (1854–1900). *De Profundis,* 1905

✹

A prodigal's repentance is a priceless treasure.

> SAYING (CHINESE)

Repentant tears wash out the stain of guilt.

> SAYING (LATIN)

REPUTATION

See also • Names ○ Popularity ○ Prestige ○ Respectability ○ Status

Reputation is the road to power.

> JEREMY BENTHAM (1748–1832). *An Introduction to the Principles of Morals and Legislation,* 10.23, 1789–1823

It aint often that a man's reputashun outlasts his munny.

> JOSH BILLINGS (1818–1885). *His Sayings,* 39, 1867

Tew enjoy a good reputashun, giv publickly, and steal privately.

> JOSH BILLINGS (1818–1885). "Lightning Bugs," *Everybody's Friend, or; Josh Billing's Encyclopedia and Proverbial Philosophy of Wit and Humor,* 1874

Were it not so useful, a good reputation would not be worth lifting a finger to obtain.

> CHRYSIPPUS (280?–206 B.C.). Adapted. In Arthur Schopenhauer, "The Wisdom of Life" (4.4), *Essays of Arthur Schopenhauer,* tr. T. Bailey Saunders, 1851

He that hath an ill name is half hang'd.

> JOHN CLARKE (1596–1658). Comp., *Proverbs: English and Latine,* p. 164, 1639

There are two modes of establishing our reputation: to be praised by honest men, and to be abused by rogues.

> C. C. COLTON (1780–1832). *Lacon: or, Many Things in Few Words; Addressed to Those Who Think,* 1.218, 1823

Some of the fascination of a name
Surrender judgment, hood-wink'd.

> WILLIAM COWPER (1731–1800). *The Task,* 6.101, 1785

The reputations of the nineteenth century will one day be quoted to prove its barbarism.

> RALPH WALDO EMERSON (1803–1882). "Uses of Great Men," *Representative Men,* 1850

You can't build a reputation on what you are going to do.

> HENRY FORD (1863–1947). In David St. Leger, comp., *A Treasury of Wisdom and Inspiration,* p. 111, 1954

Reputation is commonly measur'd by the Acre.

> THOMAS FULLER (1654–1734). Comp., *Gnomologia: Adages and Proverbs,* 4023, 1732

On the choice of friends
Our good or evil name depends.

> JOHN GAY (1685–1732). *Fables,* 1.23, 1727–1738

What is said behind your back is the community's estimate of you.

> E. W. HOWE (1853–1937). *Country Town Sayings: A Collection of Paragraphs from The Atchison Globe,* p. 256, 1911

Worldly wisdom teaches us that it is better for the reputation that one should fail conventionally than to succeed unconventionally.

> JOHN MAYNARD KEYNES (1883–1946). *The General Theory of Employment, Interest and Money,* 4.12, 1935

The most valuable of all human possessions, next to a superior and disdainful air, is the reputation of being well-to-do.

> H. L. MENCKEN (1880–1956). "Advice to Young Men: To Him that Hath," *Prejudices: Third Series,* 1922

Until you've lost your reputation, you never realize what a burden it was or what freedom really is.

> MARGARET MITCHELL (1900–1949). *Gone with the Wind,* 9, 1936

Many consult their reputation; but few their conscience.

> PUBLIUS SYRUS (85–43 B.C.). *Moral Sayings,* 254, tr. Darius Lyman, Jr., 1862

To be good and to be ill spoken of by the people
Is better than to be bad and considered good by them.

> SA'DI (A.D. 1213?–1292). *The Gulistan, or Rose Garden,* 2 (Story 23), A.D. 1258, tr. Edward Rehatsek, 1964

Reputation . . . must not guide but follow our actions.

> SENECA THE YOUNGER (5? B.C.–A.D. 65). "On Benefits" (6.43.3), *Moral Essays,* tr. John W. Basore, 1935

Iago: Reputation is . . . oft got without merit, and lost without deserving.

> SHAKESPEARE (1564–1616). *Othello,* 2.3.268, 1604

Iago: Who steals my purse steals trash; 'tis something, nothing;
'Twas mine, 'tis his, and has been slave to thousands;
But he that filches from me my good name
Robs me of that which not enriches him
And makes me poor indeed.

> SHAKESPEARE (1564–1616). *Othello,* 3.3.156, 1604

Unhappy is the man whose reputation is greater than his work.

> SILVANUS (A.D. ?–414)

Of all things human the most precarious and transitory is a reputation for power which has no strong support of its own.

> TACITUS (A.D. 56?–120?). *The Annals,* 13.19, tr. Alfred J. Church and William J. Brodribb, 1942

I would rather make my name than inherit it.

> WILLIAM MAKEPEACE THACKERAY (1811–1863). *The Virginians,* 26, 1859

Conspicuous waste and conspicuous leisure are reputable because they are evidence of pecuniary strength; pecuniary strength is reputable or honorific because, in the last analysis, it argues success and superior force.

> THORSTEIN VEBLEN (1857–1929). *The Theory of the Leisure Class: An Economic Study of Institutions,* 7, 1899

I wrote the story myself. It's about a girl who lost her reputation and never missed it.

> MAE WEST (1893?–1980). "A Way with Words," ed. Jim Koch, *New York Times,* 15 August 1993

One can survive everything nowadays, except death, and live down anything except a good reputation.

> OSCAR WILDE (1854–1900). *A Woman of No Importance,* 1, 1894

❦

A good name is to be chosen rather than great riches.

> SAYING (*BIBLE*). Proverbs 22:1

RESISTANCE

There are circumstances which have to do with simple human honor. No matter the risk. To resist and not surrender.

> ANTONIN ARTAUD (1896–1948)

When you've written to your president, to your congressman, to your senator and nothing, nothing has come of it, you take to the streets.

> ERICA BOUZA. Human rights activist. In Studs Terkel, *The Great Divide: Second Thoughts on the American Dream,* 1 ("The Public Eye"), 1988

The guard dies but does not surrender.

> PIERRE CAMBRONNE (1770–1842). French general. Attributed (he denied having said it). Responding to a surrender demand at the Battle of Waterloo (Belgium) where he commanded a division of the Imperial Guard, June 1815

The purse is any Highwayman's who might meet me with a loaded pistol: but the Self is mine and God my Maker's; it is not yours; and I will resist you to the death.

> THOMAS CARLYLE (1795–1881). "The Hero as King," *On Heroes, Hero-Worship, and the Heroic in History,* 1841

Everything that lives, resists; that which does not resist allows itself to be cut up piecemeal.

> GEORGES CLEMENCEAU (1841–1929). In Harold D. Lasswell and Abraham Kaplan, *Power and Society: A Framework for Political Inquiry,* 1915, 10.3, 1950

I resist, therefore I am.

> JAMES W. DOUGLASS (1937–). "Revolution through Solitude," *Resistance and Contemplation: The Way of Liberation,* 1972
>
> See Consumerism: Anonymous (American) ○ Thinking: Descartes

Don't let them tame you!

> ISADORA DUNCAN (1877–1927). Curtain speech, Symphony Hall, Boston, 1922

I will surrender to the Divine—to nothing less.

> RALPH WALDO EMERSON (1803–1882). Journal, 18 June 1839

While we go with the stream, we are unconscious of its rapid course; but when we begin to stem it ever so little, it makes itself felt.

> FÉNELON (1651–1715). In Aldous Huxley, *The Perennial Philosophy,* 9, 1946
>
> See Nonconformity, Anti-:John Clarke

"They didn't succeed in turning us into them," Cacho El Kadri wrote to me.
   It was in the last days of the military dictatorship in Uruguay. We had eaten fear for breakfast, fear for lunch and for dinner, fear. But they had not succeeded in turning us into them.

> EDUARDO GALEANO (1940–). "The Challenge" (complete entry). *The Book of Embraces,* 1989, tr. Cedric Belfrage with Mark Schafer, 1991

The spirit of resistance to government is so valuable on certain occasions that I wish it to be always kept alive. It will often be exercised when wrong, but better so than not to be exercised at all.

> THOMAS JEFFERSON (1743–1826). Letter to Abigail Adams, 2 February 1787

I will be conquered; I will not capitulate.

> SAMUEL JOHNSON (1709–1784). Remark during his last days, November 1784. In James Boswell, *The Life of Samuel Johnson,* 1791

Sometimes I'm in Washington, then in Pennsylvania, Arizona, Texas, Alabama, Colorado, Minnesota. My address is like my shoes. It travels with me. I abide where there is a fight against wrong.

> MARY "MOTHER" JONES (1830–1930). Irish-born American labor leader. Testimony at a Congressional hearing. In Elizabeth Gurley Flynn, *I Speak My Own Piece: Autobiography of "The Rebel Girl,"* 1955

Heaven should bend, the earth should crumble, and man should refuse to capitulate.

> THE KOTZKER (1787–1859). In Abraham Joshua Heschel, *A Passion for Truth,* 9, 1973

Unlike other creatures of earth, man cannot submit, cannot surrender his birthright of protest, for rebellion is one of his essential dimensions. He cannot deny it and remain man. In order to live he must rebel. Only total annihilation of humanity as a species can eliminate this in-built necessity.

> ROBERT LINDNER (1914–1956). Title essay (4), *Must You Conform?* 1956

He don't take shovin'.

> JERRY PARSONS. In his Alabama idiom, on Pres. Dwight D. Eisenhower. In Sherman Adams, *Firsthand Report: The Story of the Eisenhower Administration,* 2, 1961

Choosing to die resisting, rather than to live submitting, they fled only from dishonor, but met danger face to face.

> PERICLES (495?–429 B.C.). Funeral oration, 431 B.C. In Thucydides (460?–400? B.C.), *The Peloponnesian War,* 2.42, tr. Richard Crawley and rev. T. E. Wick, 1982

There is a time when the operation of the machine becomes so odious, makes you so sick at heart that you can't take part; you can't even tacitly take part, and you've got to put your bodies upon the levers, upon all the apparatus, and you've got to make it stop. And you've got to indicate to the people who run it, to the people who own it, that unless you're free the machine will be prevented from working at all.

> MARIO SAVIO (1942–1996). Free speech movement leader. University of California, Berkeley, 1964

Sly: I'll not budge an inch.

> SHAKESPEARE (1564–1616). Induction (1.13) to *The Taming of the Shrew,* 1593

Hamlet: To be, or not to be: that is the question:
Whether 'tis nobler in the mind to suffer
The slings and arrows or outrageous fortune,
Or to take arms against a sea of troubles.

> SHAKESPEARE (1564–1616). *Hamlet,* 3.1.56, 1600

O men of Athens . . . either acquit me or not; but whichever you do, understand that I shall never alter my ways, not even if I have to die many times.

> SOCRATES (470?–399 B.C.). In Plato (427?–347 B.C.), *Apology,* 29, tr. Benjamin Jowett, 1894

That which we are, we are—
One equal temper of heroic hearts,
Made weak by time and fate, but strong in will
To strive, to see, to find, and not to yield.

> ALFRED, LORD TENNYSON (1809–1892). Closing lines, "Ulysses," 1842

It is better to die on your feet than to live on your knees!

> EMILIANO ZAPATA (1877?–1919). Attributed. During the Spanish Civil War, Dolores Ibárruri (better known as La Pasionaria) popularized the slogan (on the Republican side) in a radio broadcast from Paris to the women of Spain, 3 September 1936.

RESOLUTION

See also • Courage ○ Decisiveness ○ Defeat: Helen Keller ○ Difficulty: Saying (Chinese) ○ Effort ○ Force: Henry A. Kissinger ○ Industry ○ Irresolution ○ Obstinacy ○ Perseverance ○ Persistence ○ Purpose ○ Resistance ○ Will ○ Winning: Saying (American) (3)

I am hurt but I am not slain! I will lie me down and bleed awhile—then I'll rise and fight again.

> ST. BARTON'S ODE. In Bob Woodward, "Nixon Past, Present and Past Again," Washington Post National Weekly Edition, 23 April 1990

A man in earnest finds means, or, if he cannot find, creates them. A vigorous purpose makes much out of little, breathes power into weak instruments, disarms difficulties, and even turns them into assistances. Every condition has means of progress, if we have spirit enough to use them.

> WILLIAM ELLERY CHANNING (1780–1842). "Self-Culture." Address, Boston, September 1838

The superior man is correctly firm and not firm merely.

> CONFUCIUS (551–479 B.C.). Confucian Analects, 15.36, tr. James Legge, 1930

Resolve to perform what you ought; perform without fail what you resolve.

> BENJAMIN FRANKLIN (1706–1790). Virtue #4 ("Resolution"), 1784, Autobiography, 1798

I purpose [sic] to fight it out on this line if it takes all summer.

> ULYSSES S. GRANT (1822–1855). On his upcoming campaign in Virginia, dispatch from his field headquarters to Gen. Henry W. Halleck in Washington, 11 May 1864

If you see the President, tell him that whatever happens there will be no turning back.

> ULYSSES S. GRANT (1822–1855). Before the Battle of Cold Harbor (Virginia), May 1864

I'm gonna do better than learn to walk, I'm gonna learn to run.

> ALEX HALEY (1921–1992). Words of the slave Kunta Kinte after his foot was cut off as punishment for trying to escape, Roots (television adaptation), 1976

When the morning's freshness has been replaced by the weariness of midday, when the leg muscles quiver under the strain, the climb seems endless, and, suddenly, nothing will go quite as you wish—it is then that you must not hesitate.

> DAG HAMMARSKJÖLD (1905–1961). 1956, Markings, tr. Leif Sjöberg and W. H. Auden, 1964

These [Persian messengers] will not be hindered from accomplishing at their best speed the distance which they have to go, either by snow, or rain, or heat, or by the darkness of night.

> HERODOTUS (484?–420? B.C.). The Persian Wars, 8.98, tr. George Rawlinson, 1942. The U.S. Post Office has adopted a variant of this observation for its motto. The inscription on the Post Office Building in New York City reads: "Neither snow, nor rain, nor heat, nor gloom of night stays these couriers from the swift completion of their appointed rounds."

Let every nation know, whether it wishes us well or ill, that we shall pay any price, bear any burden, meet any hardship, support any friend, oppose any foe to assure the survival and the success of freedom.

> JOHN F. KENNEDY (1917–1963). Inaugural Address, 20 January 1961

Always bear in mind that your own resolution to succeed is more important than any other one thing.

> ABRAHAM LINCOLN (1809–1865). Letter to Isham Reavis, 5 November 1855

I must save this government if possible. What I cannot do, of course I will not do; but it may as well be understood, once for all, that I shall not surrender this game leaving any available card unplayed.

> ABRAHAM LINCOLN (1809–1865). Letter to Reverdy Johnson, 26 July 1862

Resolve, and thou art free.

> HENRY WADSWORTH LONGFELLOW (1807–1882). The Masque of Pandora, 6, 1875

There comes a time in a man's life when to get where he has to go—if there are no doors or windows—he walks through a wall.

> BERNARD MALAMUD (1914–1946). "Man in the Drawer," Rembrandt's Hat, 1973

O uncle! I swear that if they put the sun on my right hand and the moon on my left, I will not renounce the career I have entered upon until God give me success, or I perish.

> MUHAMMAD (A.D. 570?–632). When urged to abandon his unpopular cause

I love the man that can smile in trouble, that can gather strength from distress, and grow brave by reflection. 'Tis the business of little minds to shrink; but he whose heart is firm, and whose conscience approves his conduct, will pursue his principles unto death.

> THOMAS PAINE (1737–1809). The Crisis (pamphlet), 1, 23 December 1776

Alexander was not easily to be diverted from anything he was bent upon. For fortune having hitherto seconded him in his designs, made him resolute and firm in his opinions.

> PLUTARCH (A.D. 46?–119?). "Alexander," Parallel Lives, Dryden edition, 1693

I shall not hesitate . . . to ask help wherever
Help may be found. If the gods above are no use to me, then I'll
Move all hell.

> VIRGIL (70–19 B.C.). Aeneid, 7.111, tr. C. Day Lewis, 1952

Dear camerado! I confess I have urged you onward with me, and
still urge you, without the least idea what is our destination,
Or whether we shall be victorious, or utterly quell'd and
defeated.

> WALT WHITMAN (1819–1892). "As I Lay with My Head in Your Lap
> Camerado," 1865, *Leaves of Grass,* 1855–1892

If we've got the stuff in us, if we're dead in earnest about it, it'll
find its own way of getting out.

> WALT WHITMAN (1819–1892). Remark to the author, 31 May 1888.
> In Horace Traubel, *Walt Whitman's Camden Conversations,* ed. Walter
> Teller, 1973

Paths clear before those who know where they're going and are
determined to get there.

> ANONYMOUS

Resolution in a bad cause is called stubbornness; stubbornness in
a good cause is called resolution.

> ANONYMOUS

RESPECT

See also • Dignity ○ Esteem ○ Modesty: Anonymous ○ Popularity
○ Prestige ○ Respectability ○ Self-Esteem ○ Self-Respect ○ Status

He who demands respekt almost allways deserves it.

> JOSH BILLINGS (1818–1885). "Glass Dimonds," *Everybody's Friend, or;
> Josh Billing's Encyclopedia and Proverbial Philosophy of Wit and
> Humor,* 1874

You must be respectable, if you will be respected.

> LORD CHESTERFIELD (1694–1773). Letter to his son, 8 January 1750

I can't get no respect.

> RODNEY DANGERFIELD (1921–). Comedian. His signature line

Everyone should be respected as an individual, but no one idol-
ized.

> ALBERT EINSTEIN (1879–1955). "My Credo," *Wisdom,* January 1956

In civilized society, external advantages make us more respected.
A man with a good coat upon his back meets with a better reception than he who has a bad one.

> SAMUEL JOHNSON (1709–1784). 20 July 1763. In James Boswell, *The
> Life of Samuel Johnson,* 1791

When once the means of living have been obtained, the far
greater part of the remaining labor and effort which takes place
on the earth has for its object to acquire the respect or the favorable regard of mankind, to be looked up to, or at all events not
to be looked down upon by them.

> JOHN STUART MILL (1806–1873). "Utility of Religion," *Three Essays on
> Religion,* 1874

To win confidence in advance of success is the most difficult political accomplishment.

> NAPOLEON (1769–1821). *Napoleon in His Own Words,* 4, comp. Jules
> Bertaut, 1916

What starts the process, really, are laughs and slights and snubs.
But if you are reasonably intelligent and if your anger is deep and
strong enough, you learn you can change those attitudes by excellence, personal gut performance, while those who have everything are sitting on their fat butts.

> RICHARD M. NIXON (1913–1994). Remark to Ken Clawson. In Tom
> Morganthau, "The Rise and Fall and Rise and Fall and Rise of Nixon,"
> *Newsweek,* 2 May 1994

That wealth and greatness are often regarded with the respect and
admiration which are due only to wisdom and virtue; and that the
contempt, of which vice and folly are the only proper objects, is
often most unjustly bestowed upon poverty and weakness, has
been the complaint of moralists in all ages.

> ADAM SMITH (1723–1790). *The Theory of Moral Sentiments,* 1.3.3, 1759

RESPECTABILITY

See also • Conformity ○ Pleasing Others ○ Popularity ○
Reputation ○ Respect ○ Rich & Poor: Thomas Love Peacock ○
Status

By respectable people (in the fashionable cant of the day) are
meant those who have not a particle of regard for anyone but
themselves, who have feathered their own nests, and only want
to lie snug and warm in them.

> WILLIAM HAZLITT (1778–1830). "On Respectable People," *Table Talk,*
> 1822

They would not get a scratch with a pin to save the universe. They
are more affected by the overturning of a plate of turtle soup than
by the starving of a whole country.

> WILLIAM HAZLITT (1778–1830). "On Respectable People," *Table Talk,*
> 1822

With them, all is well if they are well off.

> WILLIAM HAZLITT (1778–1830). "On Respectable People," *Table Talk,*
> 1822

Respectability: The dickey on the bosom of civilization.

> ELBERT HUBBARD (1856–1915). *The Roycroft Dictionary Concocted by
> Ali Baba and the Bunch on Rainy Days,* p. 129, 1914

I don't know what the soul of a scoundrel is like, but I think I
know what the soul of a respectable man is like, and it's enough
to make one shudder.

> JOSEPH-MARIE de MAISTRE (1753–1821). In Albert Camus, 27 May
> 1950, *Notebooks: 1942–1951,* tr. Justin O'Brien, 1966

The secret of respectability is to ignore what you don't understand.

> CHRISTOPHER MORLEY (1890–1957). *Where the Blue Begins,* 2, 1922

My life has been one long descent in to respectability.

> MANDY RICE-DAVIES. On reports that the former call girl was on social
> terms with Sir Denis Thatcher, the former British prime minister's hus-
> band. In Lynn Barber, *Sunday Independent* (British newspaper),
> 31 March 1991

The more things a man is ashamed of, the more respectable he is.

> GEORGE BERNARD SHAW (1856–1950). *Man and Superman,* 1, 1903

Well, dearie, men have to do some awfully mean things to keep up their respectability.

> GEORGE BERNARD SHAW (1856–1950). *Fanny's First Play*, 3, 1911

Virtue has never been as respectable as money.

> MARK TWAIN (1835–1910)

Respectability, *n.* The social status of people whose sins haven't quite caught up with them.

> EDMUND H. VOLKART (1919–). *The Angel's Dictionary: A Modern Tribute to Ambrose Bierce*, p. 165, 1986

I have been gradooly growin respectabler and respectabler ev'ry year. I luv my children, and never mistake another man's wife for my own.

> ARTEMUS WARD (1834–1867). "Artemus Ward's Autobiography," *The Complete Works of Artemus Ward*, 1898

Respectability has no use for me: I suppose the distaste is mutual.

> WALT WHITMAN (1819–1892). Remark to the author, 10 September 1888. In Horace Traubel, *Walt Whitman's Camden Conversations*, ed. Walter Teller, 1973

❧

Respectable, *adj.* Tamed, mediocre, bought.

> ANONYMOUS

RESPONSIBILITY

See also • Burdens ○ Character ○ Difficulty ○ Dignity ○ Duty ○ Freedom: [especially] Anonymous (5) ○ God & the World: Carl G. Jung ○ Guilt ○ History: Franz Kafka ○ Honesty ○ Indifference ○ Integrity ○ Morality: [especially] F. A. Hayek ○ Self-Discipline ○ Self-Realization (Becoming): [especially] P. W. Martin (1), Thomas S. Szasz ○ Self-Reliance ○ Silence & Protest ○ Struggle ○ World War II: Dwight D. Eisenhower (1)

Responsible persons are mature people who have taken charge of themselves and their conduct, who *own* their actions and *own up* to them—who *answer* for them.

> WILLIAM J. BENNETT (1943–). *The Book of Virtues: A Treasury of Great Moral Stories*, 3 (introduction), 1993

Am I my brother's keeper?

> CAIN. *Genesis* 4:9 (King James Version)

Today more than ever before life must be characterized by a sense of Universal responsibility, not only nation to nation and human to human, but also human to other forms of life.

> DALAI LAMA (1935–). In World Wildlife Fund Thailand, *A Cry from the Forest*, 1987

Let every man shovel out his own snow and the whole city will be passable.

> RALPH WALDO EMERSON (1803–1882). Journal, summer 1840

It will not do to diminish personal responsibility: do not give money and teach the man to expect it. Do not give him a Bible, or a genius, to think for him.

> RALPH WALDO EMERSON (1803–1882). Journal, 1846, undated

The weight of the Universe is pressed down on the shoulders of each moral agent to hold him to his task. The only path of escape known in all the worlds of God is performance. You must do your work, before you shall be released.

> RALPH WALDO EMERSON (1803–1882). "Worship," *The Conduct of Life*, 1860

Do not be so wary of making enemies or of displeasing others that you neglect your obligations.

> FRANCESCO GUICCIARDINI (1483–1540). *Remembrances*, C.217, 1530, tr. Mario Domandi, 1965

In a free society, all are involved in what some are doing. Some are guilty, all are responsible.

> ABRAHAM JOSHUA HESCHEL (1907–1972). Address, Town Hall, New York City, 1966

Responsibility is the price of freedom.

> ELBERT HUBBARD (1856–1915). In Alice Hubbard, comp., *An American Bible*, p. 219, 1946

Every one to whom much is given, of him will much be required.

> JESUS (A.D. 1st cent.). *Luke* 12:48

Each individual in fact has moral responsibility for the acts which he personally performs; no one can be exempted from this responsibility, and on the basis of it everyone will be judged by God Himself.

> POPE JOHN PAUL II (1920–). Closing words, "Evangelium Vitae" (encyclical letter), 30 March 1995

Moral responsibility is not just a matter of avoiding harm to others; it also means helping people in need.

> MICHAEL NEDELSKY. South Dakota educator. Personal communication, 19 October 1987

I've always wanted responsibility because I want the power responsibility brings.

> SAM RAYBURN (1882–1961). Texas speaker of the House of Representatives. In Robert A. Caro, *The Path to Power: The Years of Lyndon Johnson*, 18, 1982

The first requisite of a good citizen in this republic of ours is that he shall be able and willing to pull his weight.

> THEODORE ROOSEVELT (1858–1919). Speech, New York City, 11 November 1902

A man may not be responsible for his actions in an hour of tribulation and pain.

> TALMUD (A.D. 1st–6th cent.). Rabbinical writings

❧

As you make your bed, so you must lie on it.

> SAYING (ENGLISH)

REVELATION

See also • Creativity ○ Dreams ○ God ○ God & Man ○ Grace ○ Ideas: William James (1) ○ Imagination ○ Inspiration ○ Intuition ○ Invention ○ Mysticism ○ Prayer ○ Prophets ○ Revelations ○ Silence ○ Solitude ○ Spirituality ○ Vision

All revelation is summons and sending.

> MARTIN BUBER (1878–1965). *I and Thou*, 3, 1923, tr. Ronald Gregor Smith, 1958

Men have come to speak of the revelation as somewhat long ago given and done, as if God were dead.

> RALPH WALDO EMERSON (1803–1882). "The Divinity School Address," Cambridge (Massachusetts), 15 July 1838
>
> See Atheism: Friedrich Nietzsche (1)

If he would know what the great God speaketh, he must "go into his closet and shut the door," as Jesus said [*Matthew* 6:6]. God will not make himself manifest to cowards. He must greatly listen to himself, withdrawing himself from all the accents of other men's devotion. Even their prayers are hurtful to him, until he ha[s] made his own.

> RALPH WALDO EMERSON (1803–1882). "The Over-Soul," *Essays: First Series*, 1841

We distinguish the announcements of the soul, its manifestations of its own nature, by the term *Revelation*. . . . This communication is an influx of the Divine mind into our mind.

> RALPH WALDO EMERSON (1803–1882). "The Over-Soul," *Essays: First Series*, 1841

The poor Jews of the wilderness cried: "Let not the Lord speak to us; let Moses speak to us." But the simple and sincere soul makes the contrary prayer: "Let no intruder come between thee and me; deal Thou with me; let me know it is thy will, and I ask no more." The excellence of Jesus, and of every true teacher, is, that he affirms the Divinity in him and in us—not thrusts himself between it and us.

> RALPH WALDO EMERSON (1803–1882). "Character," *Lectures and Biographical Sketches*, 1883

He reveals Himself daily to every human being but we shut our ears to "the still small voice."

> MOHANDAS K. GANDHI (1869–1948). In *Young India*, 25 May 1921

The Lord whose oracle is at Delphi neither reveals nor conceals, but he indicates his meaning through hints.

> HERACLITUS (540?–480? B.C.). In Karl R. Popper, *The Open Society and Its Enemies*, 1.2, 1945

To the Biblical man, the miracle of revelation was not only in the fact of God speaking but also in the fact of man being able to endure it.

> ABRAHAM JOSHUA HESCHEL (1907–1972). *God in Search of Man: A Philosophy of Judaism*, 20, 1955

Revelation is a moment in which God succeeded in reaching man; an event to God and an event to man. To receive a revelation is to witness how God is turning toward man.

> ABRAHAM JOSHUA HESCHEL (1907–1972). *God in Search of Man: A Philosophy of Judaism*, 21, 1955

Revelation is but a beginning, our deeds must continue, our lives must complete it.

> ABRAHAM JOSHUA HESCHEL (1907–1972). *God in Search of Man: A Philosophy of Judaism*, 23, 1955

Revelation can be either doubted or affirmed but neither denied nor proved.

> ABRAHAM JOSHUA HESCHEL (1907–1972). *God in Search of Man: A Philosophy of Judaism*, 24, 1955

Morning by morning he wakens,
  he wakens my ear
to hear as those who are taught.
The Lord God has opened my ear,
  and I was not rebellious,
I turned not backward.

> ISAIAH (8th cent. B.C.). *Isaiah* 50:4–5

This commandment which I command you this day is not too hard for you, neither is it far off. It is not in heaven, that you should say, "Who will go up for us to heaven, and bring it to us, that we may hear it and do it?" . . . But the word is very near you; it is in your mouth and in your heart, so that you can do it.

> MOSES (14 cent. B.C.). *Deuteronomy* 30:11–14

Joan: I hear voices telling me what to do. They come from God.
Robert: They come from your imagination.
Joan: Of course. That is how the messages of God come to us.

> GEORGE BERNARD SHAW (1856–1950). *Saint Joan*, 1, 1923

If God has spoken, why is the universe not convinced?

> PERCY BYSSHE SHELLEY (1792–1822). "Notes" (7.92), *Queen Mab: A Philosophical Poem: With Notes*, 1813

This sign, which is a kind of voice, first began to come to me when I was a child; it always forbids but never commands me to do anything which I am going to do.

> SOCRATES (470?–399 B.C.). In Plato (427?–347 B.C.), *Apology*, 31, tr. Benjamin Jowett, 1894

To shut the ears to the immediate voice of God, and prefer to know him by report will be the only sin.

> HENRY DAVID THOREAU (1817–1862). Letter to Isaiah Williams, 8 September 1841

The One True God had taken this opportunity of the opening of men's minds through the collision and collapse of their old local traditions; He had taken advantage of this excruciating experience, in order to illuminate these momentarily open minds with a fuller and truer vision of His nature and purpose than they had been capable of receiving before.

> ARNOLD J. TOYNBEE (1889–1975). "Encounters Between Civilizations" (2), 1947, *Civilization on Trial*, 1948

✺

Thus the Lord used to speak to Moses face to face, as a man speaks to his friend.

> ANONYMOUS (*BIBLE*). *Exodus* 33:11

They shut their ears and say they cannot hear Thee.

> ANONYMOUS (CHRISTIAN). 1500?

Every revelation rightly understood and acted upon clears the way for a higher one.

> ANONYMOUS

REVELATIONS

See also • Christianity ○ Conversion: Anonymous (*Bible*) ○ Creativity: First Person ○ Dreams: Examples ○ God & Man: First Person ○ Heaven ○ Judaism ○ Prayers ○ Redemption ○ Revelation ○ Salvation ○ Spirituality: First Person

I hate, I despise your feasts,
   and I take no delight in your
     solemn assemblies. . . .
Take away from me the noise of
   your songs;
   to the melody of your harps I
     will not listen.
But let justice roll down like waters,
   and righteousness like an ever-
     flowing stream.

> AMOS (8th cent. B.C.). *Amos* 5:21–24

"Behold, the days are coming,"
   says the Lord God,
  "when I will send a famine on
    the land;
not a famine of bread, nor a thirst
   for water,
  but of hearing the words of the
    Lord."

> AMOS (8th cent. B.C.). *Amos* 8:11

In every age I come back
To deliver the holy,
To destroy the sin of the sinner,
To establish righteousness.

> *BHAGAVAD GITA* (6th cent. B.C.). 4, tr. Swami Prabhavananda and Christopher Isherwood, 1954

I am desire when this is pure, when this desire is not against righteousness.

> *BHAGAVAD GITA* (6th cent. B.C.). 7.11, tr. Juan Mascaró, 1962

Though a man be soiled
With the sins of a lifetime,
Let him but love me,
Rightly resolved,
In utter devotion:
I see no sinner,
That man is holy.

> *BHAGAVAD GITA* (6th cent. B.C.). 9, tr. Swami Prabhavananda and Christopher Isherwood, 1954

Know that with one single fraction of my Being I pervade and support the Universe, and know that I AM.

> *BHAGAVAD GITA* (6th cent. B.C.). 10.42, tr. Juan Mascaró, 1962

Who have all the powers of their soul in harmony, and the same loving mind for all; who find joy in the good of all beings—they reach in truth my very self.

> *BHAGAVAD GITA* (6th cent. B.C.). 12.4, tr. Juan Mascaró, 1962

Value life, and preserve life for My sake!

> ROBERT BROWNING (1812–1889). "The Pope," *The Ring and the Book,* 1869

If a wicked man turns away from all his sins which he has committed and keeps all my statutes and does what is lawful and right, he shall surely live; he shall not die. None of the transgressions which he has committed shall be remembered against him; for the righteousness which he has done he shall live. Have I any pleasure in the death of the wicked, says the Lord God, and not rather that he should turn from his way and live?

> EZEKIEL (6th cent. B.C.). *Ezekiel* 18:21–23

A new heart I will give you, and a new spirit I will put within you; and I will take out of your flesh the heart of stone and give you a heart of flesh. And I will put my spirit within you, and cause you to walk in my statutes and be careful to observe my ordinances.

> EZEKIEL (6th cent. B.C.). *Ezekiel* 36:26–27
> See Heaven: Abraham Joshua Heschel (2)

If in the twilight of memory we should meet once more, we shall speak again together and you shall sing to me a deeper song.

> KAHLIL GIBRAN (1883–1931). "The Farewell," *The Prophet,* 1923

I am thou, and thou art I; and wheresoever thou mayest be I am there. In all am I scattered, and whensoever thou willest, thou gatherest Me; and gathering Me, thou gatherest Thyself.

> *GOSPEL OF EVE.* Quoted by St. Epiphanius (A.D. 315?–403), *Haeresses.* In Joseph Campbell, prologue (3) to *The Hero with a Thousand Faces,* 1949

If goodness lead him not, yet weariness
may toss him to My breast.

> GEORGE HERBERT (1593–1633). "The Pulley." In Arnold J. Toynbee, *A Study of History,* 12.569, 1961

I will heal their faithlessness;
   I will love them freely,
    for my anger has turned from them.

> HOSEA (8th cent. B.C.). *Hosea* 14:5

When you spread forth your hands,
   I will hide my eyes from you;
even though you make many prayers,
   I will not listen;
    your hands are full of blood.
Wash yourselves; make yourselves clean;
   remove the evil of your doings
    from before my eyes;
cease to do evil,
   learn to do good;
seek justice
   correct oppression;
defend the fatherless,
   plead for the widow.

> ISAIAH (8th cent. B.C.). *Isaiah* 1:15–17

I, I am the Lord,
   and besides me there is no savior.

> ISAIAH (8th cent. B.C.). *Isaiah* 43:11
> See Idolatry: Moses

I form light and create darkness,
    I make weal and create woe,
    I am the Lord, who do all these things.

> ISAIAH (8th cent. B.C.). *Isaiah* 45:7

But Zion said, "the Lord has forsaken me,
    my Lord has forgotten me."
Can a woman forget her sucking child,
        that she should have no compassion
        on the son of her womb.
Even these may forget,
    yet I will not forget you.

> ISAIAH (8th cent. B.C.). *Isaiah* 49:14–15

For a brief moment I forsook you,
    but with great compassion
        I will gather you.
In overflowing wrath for a moment
    I hid my face from you,
but with everlasting love
    I will have compassion on you,
    says the Lord, your Redeemer.

> ISAIAH (8th cent. B.C.). *Isaiah* 54:7–8

My house shall be called a house of prayer
    for all peoples.

> ISAIAH (8th cent. B.C.). *Isaiah* 56:7

I the Lord love justice,
    I hate robbery and wrong.

> ISAIAH (8th cent. B.C.). *Isaiah* 61:8

"Who art thou?"
I am thyself.

> *JAIMINÎYA UPANISAD BRÂHMANA.* Hindu Vedic commentary. 3.1.6. In
> Whitall N. Perry, comp., *A Treasury of Traditional Wisdom*, p. 891, 1986

Let not the wise man glory in his wisdom, let not the mighty man glory in his might, let not the rich man glory in his riches; but let him who glories glory in this, that he understands and knows me, that I am the Lord who practices kindness, justice, and righteousness in the earth; for in these things I delight.

> JEREMIAH (7th cent. B.C.). *Jeremiah* 9:23–24

I will turn their mourning into joy.
    I will comfort them, and give them
        gladness for sorrow.

> JEREMIAH (7th cent. B.C.). *Jeremiah* 31:13

I will put my law within them, and I will write it upon their hearts and I will be their God, and they shall be my people. And no longer shall each man teach his neighbor and each his brother, saying, "Know the Lord," for they shall all know me, from the least of them to the greatest, says the Lord; for I will forgive their iniquity, and I will remember their sin no more.

> JEREMIAH (7th cent. B.C.). *Jeremiah* 31:33–34

Then I saw a new heaven and a new earth; for the first heaven and the first earth had passed away, and the sea was no more. And I saw the holy city, new Jerusalem, coming down out of heaven from God, prepared as a bride adorned for her husband; and I heard a great voice from the throne saying, "Behold, the dwelling of God is with men. He will dwell with them, and they shall be his people, and God himself will be with them; he will wipe away every tear from their eyes, and death shall be no more, neither shall there be mourning nor crying nor pain any more, for the former things have passed away."

And he who sat upon the throne said, "Behold, I make all things new."

> JOHN (A.D. 1st cent.). *Revelation* 21:1–5. The word "revelation" derives
> from "apocalypse" in Greek.
> See Self-Realization (Becoming): P. W. Martin (2)

Have I not commanded you? Be strong and of good courage; be not frightened, neither be dismayed; for the Lord your God is with you wherever you go.

> JOSHUA (14th cent. B.C.). *Joshua* 1:9

At that moment I experienced the presence of the Divine as I had never before experienced him. It seemed as though I could hear the quiet assurance of an inner voice, saying, "Stand up for righteousness, stand up for truth. God will be at your side forever." Almost at once my fears began to pass from me. My uncertainty disappeared. I was ready to face anything. The outer situation remained the same, but God had given me inner calm.

> MARTIN LUTHER KING, JR. (1929–1968). Describing his late-night experi-
> ence at the kitchen table in his home on 27 January 1956 during the
> Montgomery (Alabama) bus boycott. Daily death threats to him and his
> family had brought him to the point of giving up the struggle, *Strength
> to Love*, 13.3, 1963

Return to me, and I will return to you, says the Lord of hosts.

> MALACHI. *Malachi* 3:7

Then Moses said to God, "If I come to the people of Israel and say to them, 'The God of your fathers has sent me to you,' and they ask me, 'What is his name?' what shall I say to them?" God said to Moses, "I am who I am."

> MOSES (14th cent. B.C.). *Exodus* 3:13–14

The Lord passed before him, and proclaimed, "The Lord, the Lord, a God merciful and gracious, slow to anger, and abounding in steadfast love and faithfulness, keeping steadfast love for thousands, forgiving iniquity and transgression and sin, but who will by no means clear the guilty, visiting the iniquity of the fathers upon the children and the children's children, to the third and the fourth generation."

> MOSES (14th cent. B.C.). *Exodus* 34:6–7

You shall be holy; because I, the Lord your God, am holy.

> MOSES (14th cent. B.C.). *Leviticus* 19:2

Remember Me, I will remember you.

> MUHAMMAD (A.D. 570?–632). *Quran*, 2.152, A.D. 670?, tr. Mohammed
> Marmaduke Pickthall, 1953

O Muhammad, hadst thou not been, I would not have created the sky.

> MUHAMMAD (A.D. 570?–632). In Joseph Campbell, epilogue (2) to
> *The Hero with a Thousand Faces*, 1949

I was a hidden treasure; I wished to be known; therefore I created the world.

> MUHAMMAD (A.D. 570?–632). In Titus Burckhardt, *Introduction aux
> doctrines ésotériques de l'Islam*, 1955

Compare not thyself with others, but with Me.

> BLAISE PASCAL (1623–1662). *Pensées*, 555, 1670, tr. William F. Trotter, 1931

Late on the third day, at the very moment when, at sunset, we were making our way [by boat] through a herd of hippopotamuses, there flashed upon my mind, unforeseen and unsought, the phrase, "Reverence for Life." The iron door had yielded: the path in the thicket had become visible. Now I had found my way to the idea in which affirmation of the world and ethics are contained side by side! Now I knew that the ethical acceptance of the world and of life, together with the ideals of civilization contained in this concept, has a foundation in thought.

> ALBERT SCHWEITZER (1875–1965). *Out of My Life and Thought: An Autobiography*, 13, tr. C. T. Campion, 1933

Strike out courageously! Do not ask where your efforts will take you on the infinite ocean! It is my will that you should swim.

> ALBERT SCHWEITZER (1875–1965). *Christianity and the Religions of the World*, 1939

Truly do I exist in all beings, but I am most manifest in man. The human heart is my favorite dwelling place.

> *SRIMAD BHAGAVATAM* (5th? cent. B.C.). Hindu scriptures, 11.2. In *The Wisdom of God*, tr. Swami Prabhavananda, 1943

All duties, if accompanied by devotion to me, lead to the supreme good and to eternal liberation.

> *SRIMAD BHAGAVATAM* (5th? cent. B.C.). Hindu scriptures, 11.11. In *The Wisdom of God*, tr. Swami Prabhavananda, 1943

When the Egyptians were drowning, the angels wished to sing. But God said, "My children are dying, and you would sing?"

> *TALMUD* (A.D. 1st–6th cent.). Rabbinical writings. Referring to the legend of Moses' parting of the Red Sea. In Louis I. Newman, comp., *The Talmudic Anthology*, 103, 1945

Whatever you offer to Me besides yourself, I account as nothing; I seek not your gift, but yourself.

> THOMAS à KEMPIS (1379–1471). *The Imitation of Christ*, 4.8, tr. Leo Sherley-Price, 1952
>
> See Giving: Walt Whitman (1)

Not by might, nor by power, but by my Spirit, says the Lord of hosts.

> ZECHARIAH (6th cent. B.C.). *Zechariah* 4:6

Thus says the Lord of hosts, Render true judgments, show kindness and mercy each to his brother, do not oppress the widow, the fatherless, the sojourner, or the poor; and let none of you devise evil against his brother in your heart.

> ZECHARIAH (6th cent. B.C.). *Zechariah* 7:9–10

❦

Be still, and know that I am God.

> ANONYMOUS (*BIBLE*). *Psalms* 46:10

I love those who love me,
    and those who seek me diligently
        find me.

> ANONYMOUS (*BIBLE*). *Proverbs* 8:17

REVENGE

See also • Crime ○ Forgiveness ○ Hate ○ Justice ○ Madness: Herman Melville (1) ○ Malice ○ Mercy

Revenge and punishment are different things. Punishment is inflicted for the sake of the person punished; revenge for that of the punisher, to satisfy his feelings.

> ARISTOTLE (384–322 B.C.). *Rhetoric*, 1.10, tr. W. Rhys Roberts, 1954

A man that studieth revenge keeps his own wounds green, which otherwise would heal.

> FRANCIS BACON (1561–1626). "Of Revenge," *Essays*, 1625

Men are more prone to revenge Injuries than to requite Kindnesses.

> THOMAS FULLER (1654–1734). Comp., *Gnomologia: Adages and Proverbs*, 3389, 1732

Revenge is profitable, gratitude is expensive.

> EDWARD GIBBON (1737–1794). *The Decline and Fall of the Roman Empire*, 11, 1776-1788

Living well is the best revenge.

> GEORGE HERBERT (1593–1633). Comp., *Outlandish Proverbs*, 524, 1640

O revenge, how sweet thou art!

> BEN JONSON (1572–1637). *Epicoene: Or, The Silent Woman*, 4.5, 1620

O vengeance is good, . . . sweeter than life itself—
That's how the ignorant talk.

> JUVENAL (A.D. 60?–127?). *Satires*, 13.80, tr. Peter Green, 1967

Revenge, at first though sweet,
Bitter ere long back on itself recoils.

> JOHN MILTON (1608–1674). *Paradise Lost*, 9.171, 1667

❦

Revenge does not long remain unrevenged.

> SAYING (GERMAN)

Blood doesn't wash away blood.

> SAYING (PERSIAN)

No revenge is more honorable than the one not taken.

> SAYING (SPANISH)

REVOLUTION

See also • Class ○ Conservatives ○ Crises ○ Crowds ○ Evolution ○ History ○ Imperialism ○ International Relations ○ Liberals ○ Mass Movements ○ Mobs ○ Nonviolence: [especially] Mohandas K. Gandhi (11) ○ Politics: [especially] Wendell Phillips ○ Reform ○ Revolutionaries ○ Revolutionary War: John Adams ○ Tyranny ○ Violence: [especially] Thomas Jefferson ○ War ○ War & Revolution

Everywhere inequality is a cause of revolution.

> ARISTOTLE (384–322 B.C.). *Politics*, 5.1, tr. Benjamin Jowett, 1885

To die for the revolution is a one-shot deal; to live for the revolution means taking on the more difficult commitment of changing our day-to-day life patterns.

FRANCES M. BEAL. "Double Jeopardy: To Be Black and Female."
In Robin Morgan, ed., *Sisterhood Is Powerful: An Anthology of
Writings from the Women's Liberation Movement,* 1970

Revolution, *n.* In politics, an abrupt change in the form of misgovernment.

AMBROSE BIERCE (1842–1914). *The Devil's Dictionary,* p. 113, 1911,
Dover edition, 1958

Revolutions are born of hope.

CRANE BRINTON (1898–1968). *The Anatomy of Revolution,* 9.2, 1952

A reform is a correction of abuses; a revolution is a transfer of
power.

EDWARD GEORGE BULWER-LYTTON (1803–1873). On the Reform Bill,
House of Commons speech, 1866

The most important of all revolutions, . . . a revolution in sentiments, manners and moral opinions.

EDMUND BURKE (1729–1797). *Reflections on the Revolution in France,*
p. 175, 1790, Pelican Books edition, 1968

A revolution [is] . . . an act of violence whereby one class shatters
the authority of another.

JAMES MacGREGOR BURNS (1918–). *Leadership,* 8, 1978

All modern revolutions have ended in a reinforcement of the
power of the State.

ALBERT CAMUS (1913–1960). "Historical Rebellion: State Terrorism and
Irrational Terror," *The Rebel: An Essay on Man in Revolt,* 1951,
tr. Anthony Bower, 1956

Do you think that revolutions are made with rose water?

CHAMFORT (1741–1794). Remark to Marmontel who was denouncing
the excesses of the French Revolution. In Samuel Arthur Bent, comp.,
Familiar Short Sayings of Great Men, 5th ed. rev., p. 111, 1887

The thing worse than rebellion is the thing that causes rebellion.

FREDERICK DOUGLASS (1817–1895). "Reconstruction," *Atlantic,*
December 1866

Revolutions go not backward.

RALPH WALDO EMERSON (1803–1882). "War," lecture, American Peace
Society, Boston, 12 March 1838

Let our affection flow out to our fellows; it would operate in a day
the greatest of all revolutions. It is better to work on institutions
by the sun than by the wind. . . . Let the amelioration in our laws
of property proceed from the concession of the rich, not from the
grasping of the poor.

RALPH WALDO EMERSON (1803–1882). "Man the Reformer," lecture,
Masonic Temple, Boston, 25 January 1841

People here [in England] expect a revolution. There will be no
revolution, none that deserves to be called so. There may be a
scramble for money. But as the people we see want the things we
now have, and not better things, it is very certain that they will,
under whatever change of forms, keep the old system.
When I see changed men, I shall look for a changed world.

RALPH WALDO EMERSON (1803–1882). Journal, London, April 1848

It is absolutely essential that the oppressed participate in the revolutionary process with an increasingly critical awareness of their
role as Subjects of the transformation.

PAULO FREIRE (1921–1997). *Pedagogy of the Oppressed,* 3, tr. Myra
Bergman Ramos, 1968

All successful revolutions are the kicking in of a rotten door.

JOHN KENNETH GALBRAITH (1908–). *The Age of Uncertainty,* 3, 1977

The revolution is not an apple that falls when it is ripe. You have
to make it fall.

ERNESTO "CHE" GUEVARA (1928–1967). Boualam Rouissi interview,
14 March 1965, *Che Guevara Speaks,* ed. George Lavan, 1967

Waste no time with revolutions that do not remove the causes of
your complaints but simply change the faces of those in charge.

FRANCESCO GUICCIARDINI (1483–1540). *Remembrances,* C.50, 1530,
tr. Mario Domandi, 1965

Treason doth never prosper, what's the reason?
For if it prosper, none dare call it Treason.

SIR JOHN HARINGTON (1561–1612). *Epigrams,* 4.5, 1618

Utopianism is probably a necessary social device for generating the
superhuman efforts without which no major revolution is achieved.

E. J. HOBSBAWM (1917–). *Primitive Rebels: Studies in Archaic Forms of
Social Movement in the 19th and 20th Centuries,* 4, 1959

It is not actual suffering but the taste of better things which excites
people to revolt.

ERIC HOFFER (1902–1983). *The True Believer: Thoughts on the Nature of
Mass Movements,* 22, 1951

It is not the wickedness of the old regime [the masses] rise against
but its weakness.

ERIC HOFFER (1902–1983). *The True Believer: Thoughts on the Nature of
Mass Movements,* 109, 1951

If we glance at the most important revolutions in history, we see at
once that the greatest number of these originated in the periodical
revolutions of the human mind.

WILHELM von HUMBOLDT (1767–1835). *The Limits of State Action,* 16,
1854, ed. J. W. Burrow, 1969

Prudence, indeed, will dictate that governments long established
should not be changed for light and transient causes; and accordingly all experience hath shown that mankind are more disposed to
suffer, while evils are sufferable, than to right themselves by abol-
ishing the forms to which they are accustomed. But when a long
train of abuses and usurpations, pursuing invariably the same
object, evinces a design to reduce them under absolute despotism,
it is their right, it is their duty, to throw off such government, and
to provide new guards for their future security.

THOMAS JEFFERSON (1743–1826). Declaration of Independence, 4 July
1776

See Government: George Mason

Those who make peaceful revolution impossible will make violent revolution inevitable.

JOHN F. KENNEDY (1917–1963). Speech before Latin-American diplomats on the first anniversary of the Alliance for Progress, White House,
12 March 1962

A revolution is coming—a revolution which will be peaceful if we are wise enough; compassionate if we care enough; successful if we are fortunate enough—but a revolution which is coming whether we will it or not. We can affect its character, we cannot alter its inevitability.

ROBERT F. KENNEDY (1925–1968). Senate speech, May 1966

An acceptable [revolutionary] ideology is usually one ambiguous enough to satisfy a wide variety of people, but what this really means is that those adopting an ideology for their own must be able to read into it what they would like to see.

CARL LEIDEN and KARL M. SCHMITT. *The Politics of Violence: Revolution in the Modern World,* 6, 1968

Without a revolutionary theory there cannot be a revolutionary movement.

LENIN (1870–1924). *What Is To Be Done? Burning Questions of Our Movement,* 1.D, 1902, International Publishers edition, 1929

A revolution is impossible without a revolutionary situation; furthermore, not every revolutionary situation leads to revolution.

LENIN (1870–1924). "The Collapse of the Second International," June 1905, *The Lenin Reader,* 8, ed. Stefan T. Possony, 1966

The government is tottering. We must deal it the death blow at any cost. To delay action is the same as death.

LENIN (1870–1924). Closing words, letter to the Central Executive Committee, 6 November 1917

Revolution is impossible without a nationwide crisis affecting both the exploited and the exploiters.

LENIN (1870–1924) *"Left-Wing" Communism—An Infantile Disorder,* 9, 1920, International Publishers edition, 1971

The more violence, the less revolution.

BARTHELEMY de LIGT. In Aldous Huxley, "Social Reform and Violence," *Ends and Means: An Inquiry into the Nature of Ideals and into the Methods Employed for Their Realization,* 1937

Any people anywhere, being inclined and having the power, have the right to *rise* up, and shake off the existing government, and form a new one that suits them better. This is a most valuable—a most sacred right—a right, which we hope and believe, is to liberate the world.

ABRAHAM LINCOLN (1809–1865). "On the War with Mexico," House of Representatives speech, 12 January 1848

The responsibility for insurrections rests in the last analysis upon the unimaginative greed and endless stupidity of the dominant classes. . . . Confronted with the deep insurgency of labor what do capitalists and their spokesmen do? They resist every demand, submit only after a struggle, and prepare a condition of war to the death.

WALTER LIPPMANN (1889–1974). *A Preface to Politics,* 9, 1914

A revolution is not a dinner party, or writing an essay, or painting a picture, or doing embroidery.

MAO TSE-TUNG (1893–1976). "Report on an Investigation of the Peasant Movement in Hunan," February 1927, *Selected Works of Mao Tse-tung,* Foreign Languages Press edition, vol. 1, 1965

Revolutions are the locomotives of history.

KARL MARX (1818–1883). In Lenin, *Two Tactics of Social Democracy in the Democratic Revolution,* 13, July 1905, International Publishers edition, 1971

A revolution is not necessarily *progressive.* It may very well be regressive, in deliberate reaction to progressive movements of the time or to reforms enacted by the government.

JAMES H. MEISEL. *Counter-Revolution: How Revolutions Die,* 1, 1966

Political revolutions . . . do not often accomplish anything of genuine value; their one undoubted effect is simply to throw out one gang of thieves and put in another. After a revolution, of course, the successful revolutionists always try to convince doubters that they have achieved great things, and usually they hang any man who denies it.

H. L. MENCKEN (1880–1956). "Matters of State: Le Contrat Social," *Prejudices: Third Series,* 1922

All political revolutions, not affected by foreign conquest, originate in moral revolutions. The subversion of established institutions is merely one consequence of the previous subversion of established opinions.

JOHN STUART MILL (1806–1873). "A Few Observations on the French Revolution," 1833, *Dissertations and Discussions,* vol. 1, 1859–1875

Every revolution has its counterrevolution—that is a sign the revolution is for real.

C. WRIGHT MILLS (1916–1962). *Listen, Yankee: The Revolution in Cuba,* 3 (introduction), 1960

A revolution can be neither made nor stopped. The only thing that can be done is for one or several of its children to give it a direction by dint of victories.

NAPOLEON (1769–1821). Remark to Gen. Charles Montholon, 1816, *The Mind of Napoleon: A Selection from His Written and Spoken Words,* 86, ed. J. Christopher Herold, 1955

A revolution is an idea which has found its bayonets.

NAPOLEON (1769–1821). In Edouard Guillon, *Napoléon et la Suisse, 1803–1815,* 1910

Vanity made the [French] Revolution; liberty was only a pretext.

NAPOLEON (1769–1821). In Eric Hoffer, *The True Believer: Thoughts on the Nature of Mass Movements,* 105, 1951

Any revolution has to start with the transformation of the individual, otherwise individuals are corrupted by the power they get if their revolution succeeds.

WES "SCOOP" NISKER. Broadcast journalist. In Derk Richardson, "Zen and Now," *East Bay Express,* Berkeley (California), 6 August 1993

Two viewpoints [on revolution] are always tenable. The one, how can you improve human nature until you have changed the system? The other, what is the use of changing the system before you have improved human nature? They appeal to different individuals, and they probably show a tendency to alternate in point of time. The moralist and the revolutionary are constantly undermining one another.

GEORGE ORWELL (1903–1950). "Charles Dickens" (1), 1940, *The Collected Essays, Journalism and Letters of George Orwell,* vol. 1, ed. Sonia Orwell and Ian Angus, 1968

Until they become conscious they will never rebel, and until after they have rebelled they cannot become conscious.

GEORGE ORWELL (1903–1950). *Nineteen Eighty-Four,* 1.7, 1949

The Social Revolution will be moral, or it will not be.

CHARLES PÉGUY (1873–1914). "The Modern World: Socialism and the Modern World," *Basic Verities: Prose and Poetry,* tr. Ann and Julian Green, 1943

Revolutions are not made: they come. A revolution is as natural a growth as an oak. It comes out of the past. Its foundations are laid far back.

WENDELL PHILLIPS (1811–1884). Speech before the Massachusetts Anti-Slavery Society, Boston, 28 January 1852

If a revolution destroys a systematic government, but the systematic patterns of thought that produced that government are left intact, then those patterns will repeat themselves in the succeeding government.

ROBERT M. PIRSIG (1928–). *Zen and the Art of Motorcycle Maintenance: An Inquiry into Values,* 8, 1974

There is a revolution coming. It will not be like revolutions of the past. It will originate with the individual and with culture, and it will change the political structure only as its final act. It will not require violence to succeed, and it cannot be successfully resisted by violence.

CHARLES A. REICH (1928–). *The Greening of America: The Youth Revolution Is Trying to Make American Livable,* 1, 1970

In the face of so much violence, fear and polarization in our land, we call for a moral revolution, which begins with a fundamental respect for human life, which recovers a sense of right and wrong.

BISHOP JOHN H. RICARD (1940–). U.S. Catholic Bishops' Domestic Policy Committee chairman. In "Notable and Quotable," *San Diego Union-Tribune,* 20 November 1995

All revolutionary changes are unthinkable until they happen—and then they are understood to be inevitable.

THEODORE ROSZAK (1933–). *The Making of the Counter Culture: Reflections on the Technocratic Society and Its Youthful Opposition,* 2, 1969

The history of the French Revolution is analogous to that of the Commonwealth of England: fanaticism, victory, despotism, collapse, and reaction.

BERTRAND RUSSELL (1872–1970). *Power: A New Social Analysis,* 10, 1938

While revolutions at first may devour their children, in the end the children sometimes devour their revolution. . . . A successful revolution begins to develop a stake in the *status quo.*

ARTHUR M. SCHLESINGER, JR. (1917–). *The Bitter Heritage: Vietnam and American Democracy,* 1941–1966, 7, 1967

The revolution will not be televised,
The revolution will be no re-run, brothers,
The revolution will be live.

GIL SCOTT-HERON (1949–). "The Revolution Will Not Be Televised" (song), 1974

Revolutions have never lightened the burden of tyranny; they have only shifted it to another shoulder.

GEORGE BERNARD SHAW (1856–1950). "Preface to the Revolutionist's Handbook," *Man and Superman,* 1903

The victor in a revolution is never a single class . . . , but an idea that carries *everyone* forward.

OSWALD SPENGLER (1880–1936). *Aphorisms,* 349, tr. Gisela Koch-Weser O'Brien, 1967

The difference between reactionary repression and revolutionary repression is the difference between cat shit and dog shit.

LEO TOLSTOY (1828–1910). Adapted. In Theodore Roszak, appendix to *The Making of the Counter Culture: Reflections on the Technocratic Society and Its Youthful Opposition,* 1969

Insurrection, like war, is a continuation of politics with other instruments.

LEON TROTSKY (1879–1940). *The History of the Russian Revolution,* 3.6, tr. Max Eastman, 1932

See War: Karl von Clausewitz (3)

The fundamental premise of a revolution is that the existing social structure has become incapable of solving the urgent problems of development of the nation.

LEON TROTSKY (1879–1940). *The History of the Russian Revolution,* 3.6, tr. Max Eastman, 1932

The revolution, like Saturn, devours its children.

PIERRE VERGNIAUD (1753–1793). A moderate who was himself "devoured" (i.e., guillotined). In Crane Brinton, *The Anatomy of Revolution,* 5.1, 1952

The happiness of nations can be accomplished by pacific revolutions in their political system without the destructive intervention of the sword.

GEORGE WASHINGTON (1732–1799). Reply to the Legislature of Pennsylvania, 5 September 1789

Bliss was it in that dawn to be alive,
But to be young was very Heaven!

WILLIAM WORDSWORTH (1770–1850). On the French Revolution, *The Prelude; or, Growth of a Poet's Mind; An Autobiographical Poem,* 11.108, 1850

Each [revolutionary] movement relying on violence contains a potential seed of future counter-revolution in those of its own ranks and file who emerge from the struggle dissatisfied and who are conditioned to use violence as a means for solving their problems.

J. K. ZAWODNY. "Guerrilla and Sabotage: Organization, Operations, Motivations, Escalation," *Annals of the American Academy of Political and Social Science,* May 1962

Rebellion to tyrants is obedience to God.

ANONYMOUS (ENGLISH). Inscription on the cannon near the grave of John Bradshaw on the island of Jamaica. In 1649, Bradshaw presided at the trial of the "tyrant, traitor, and murderer" Charles I and sentenced him to death.

[The Samnites] had revolted against the Romans because peace is more burdensome for men who are enslaved than war is for men who are free.

> ANONYMOUS. Slightly modified. In Machiavelli, *The Discourses*, 3.44, 1517, tr. Christian E. Detmold, 1940

The Revolution is a *praxis* which forges its ideas in action.

> ANONYMOUS. In Jean-Paul Sartre, "Ideology and Revolution," *Studies on the Left*, vol. 1, no. 3, 1960

Humanity must choose between revolution without bloodshed and bloodshed without revolution.

> ANONYMOUS

The revolution devours everyone who fails to keep pace with it.

> ANONYMOUS

Liberty, Equality, Fraternity. [Liberté, Egalité, Fraternité.]

> SLOGAN (FRENCH). French Revolution, 1789

Peace, bread and land.

> SLOGAN (RUSSIAN). Bolshevik Party, Russian Revolution, 1917

We shall overcome. [Vencéramos.]

> SLOGAN (SPANISH). Republican Party, Spanish Civil War, 1936

REVOLUTIONARIES

See also • Conservatives ○ Conservatives & Liberals/Radicals ○ Crisis Leaders ○ Ethics: Mikhail Bakunin ○ Leaders ○ Liberals ○ Reformers ○ Revolution ○ Tyrants

There is no other man who is absorbed by the revolution 24 hours a day, who has no other thoughts but the thought of the revolution, and who, even when he sleeps, dreams of nothing but the revolution.

> P. AXELROD. On Lenin (1870–1924). In Herbert J. Muller, *The Uses of the Past: Profiles of Former Societies*, 9.3, 1952

Take the most radical revolutionist and place him upon the all-Russian throne or give him dictatorial power, of which so many of our green revolutionists daydream, and within a year he will have become worse than the Emperor himself.

> MIKHAIL BAKUNIN (1814–1876). *Science and the Urgent Revolutionary Task* (pamphlet), 1870. In *The Political Philosophy of Bakunin: Scientific Anarchism*, 4.2, ed. G. P. Maximoff, 1953
>
> See Anarchism: Bakunin (2)

This ideal world of our revolutionaries . . . is a flaming sense of the immediacy of the ideal, a feeling that there is something in all men better than their present fate, and a conviction that what is, not only ought not, but need not, be.

> CRANE BRINTON (1898–1968). *The Anatomy of Revolution*, 2.3, 1952

Successful revolutionists . . . endeavor to create a myth of their own revolution, which becomes the last one necessary.

> CRANE BRINTON (1898–1968). *The Anatomy of Revolution*, 3.3, 1952

No good revolutionary leader would ever bunt.

> CRANE BRINTON (1898–1968). *The Anatomy of Revolution*, 7.4, 1952

Every revolutionary ends by becoming either an oppressor or a heretic.

> ALBERT CAMUS (1913–1960). "Historical Rebellion: Rebellion and Revolution," *The Rebel: An Essay on Man in Revolt*, 1951, tr. Anthony Bower, 1956

I began revolution with eighty-two men. If I had to do it again, I do it with ten or fifteen men and absolute faith. It does not matter how small you are if you have faith and plan of action.

> FIDEL CASTRO (1926–). In Philip Benjamin, "Castro Gets a Noisy Reception Here," *New York Times*, 22 April 1959

Those who cry most loudly that we must smash and destroy are later found among the administrators of some new system of repression.

> NOAM CHOMSKY (1928–). Introduction to *American Power and the New Mandarins*, 1969

I wonder if today's radicals will not be as reactionary as I am when they are as old as I am. You soon wear out your foolishness, it's just the measles of your intellectual growth.

> WILL DURANT (1885–1981). In "Tumult & Shouting," *San Francisco Sunday Examiner & Chronicle*, 5 January 1969

Abuse is a proof that you are felt. If they praise you, you will work no revolution.

> RALPH WALDO EMERSON (1803–1882). Journal, 1850, undated

The revolution is made neither by the leaders for the people, nor by the people for the leaders, but by both acting together in unshakable solidarity.

> PAULO FREIRE (1921–1997). *Pedagogy of the Oppressed*, 3, tr. Myra Bergman Ramos, 1968

The successful revolutionary is a statesman, the unsuccessful one is a criminal.

> ERICH FROMM (1900–1980). *Escape from Freedom*, 7.2, 1941
>
> See Reformers: Elbert Hubbard

Revolutions attract men who have an eye for the main chance.

> JOHN KENNETH GALBRAITH (1908–). *The Age of Uncertainty*, 3, 1977

In a revolution one wins or dies.

> ERNESTO "CHE" GUEVARA (1928–1967). "Farewell Letter to Fidel," 1965, *Che Guevara Speaks*, ed. George Lavan, 1967

At the risk of seeming ridiculous, let me say that the true revolutionary is guided by a great feeling of love. . . .

We must strive every day so that this love of living humanity will be transformed into actual deeds, into acts that serve as examples, as a moving force.

> ERNESTO "CHE" GUEVARA (1928–1967). "Notes on Man and Socialism in Cuba," 1965, *Che Guevara Speaks*, ed. George Lavan, 1967

Hatred as an element of the struggle, relentless hatred of the enemy that impels us over and beyond the natural limitations of man, and transforms us into effective, violent, selected and cold killing machines.

> ERNESTO "CHE" GUEVARA (1928–1967). Quoted by Stokely Carmichael (Kwame Ture), "Black Power." In David Cooper, ed., *The Dialectics of Liberation*, 1968

Most revolutions soon become either corrupt or repressive because the qualities that make men successful revolutionaries drive them to other excesses after they have achieved power.

SYDNEY J. HARRIS (1917–1986). *Pieces of Eight,* 3, 1982

The test of greatness in revolutionaries has always been their capacity to discover the new and unexpected characteristics of revolutionary situations and to adapt their tactics to them. Like the surfer, the revolutionary does not create the waves on which he rides, but balances on them.

E. J. HOBSBAWM (1917–). *Revolutionaries: Contemporary Essays,* 9, 1973

We carry out the revolution with a view to transforming the world and society. To transform the world and society, we must first and foremost transform ourselves.

HO CHI MINH (1892–1969). Speech, 7 September 1957, *Ho Chi Minh on Revolution,* ed. Bernard B. Fall, 1967

See Reform: Aldous Huxley, Arnold J. Toynbee

The revolution is the work of the masses, not that of a few heroic individuals.

HO CHI MINH (1892–1969). Speech, 7 September 1957, *Ho Chi Minh on Revolution,* Bernard B. Fall, 1967

From first to last it was Lenin. Without him there would have been no October Revolution.

SIDNEY HOOK (1902–1989). *The Hero in History: A Study in Limitation and Possibility,* 11.2 & 3, 1943

Nothing stands between the people's miserable present and its glorious future, except a minority, perhaps a majority, of perverse or merely ignorant individuals. All that is necessary is to liquidate a few thousands, or it may be a few millions, of these living obstacles to progress, and then to coerce and propagandize the rest into acquiescence. When these unpleasant but necessary preliminaries are over, the golden age will begin. Such is the theory of that secular apocalypticism, which is the religion of revolutionaries. But in practice, it is hardly necessary to say, the means employed positively guarantee that the end actually reached shall be profoundly different from that which the prophetic theorists envisaged.

ALDOUS HUXLEY (1894–1963). "Religion and Time." In Christopher Isherwood, ed., *Vedanta for the Western World,* 1945

Unswerving dedication to the final aim must be combined with extreme flexibility in the choice of means.

JOHN KEEP. "Lenin as Tactician." In Leonard Schapiro and Peter Reddaway, eds., *Lenin, the Man, the Theorist, the Leader,* 1967

Revolutionaries always start from a position of inferior physical strength; their victories are primarily triumphs of conception or of will.

HENRY A. KISSINGER (1923–). "The White Revolutionary: Reflections on Bismarck," *Daedalus,* Summer 1968

To be a revolutionary is to love your life enough to change it, to choose struggle instead of exile, to risk everything with only the glimmering hope of a world to win.

ANDREW KOPKIND (1935–1994). "Are We in the Middle of a Revolution?" *New York Times Magazine,* 10 November 1968

Revolutionary leaders are usually men of early middle age, that is, men of considerable maturity, but not yet old enough to have been co-opted into the ruling elite. Most often they are middle class in origin, because the upper classes are on the whole satisfied with society and the lower classes too lacking in skills to create a revolutionary movement.

CARL LEIDEN and KARL M. SCHMITT. *The Politics of Violence: Revolution in the Modern World,* 5, 1968

During the lifetime of great revolutionaries, the oppressing classes constantly hounded them, received their theories with the most savage malice, the most furious hatred and the most unscrupulous campaigns of lies and slander. After their death, attempts are made to convert them into harmless icons, to canonize them, . . . and to hallow their *names* to a certain extent for the "consolation" of the oppressed classes and with the object of duping the latter, while at the same time robbing the revolutionary theory of its *substance,* blunting its revolutionary edge and vulgarizing it.

LENIN (1870–1924). *The State and Revolution,* 1.1, 1917, International Publishers edition, 1971

If you are not able to adapt yourself, if you are not inclined to crawl in the mud, you are not a revolutionary but a chatterbox.

LENIN (1870–1924). In C. L. Sulzberger, "Khrushchev's Lenin: II—The Parrot's New Word," *New York Times,* 13 June 1956

Rebel Without a Cause.

ROBERT LINDNER (1914–1956). Book title, 1944, and film title (an unrelated project featuring James Dean), 1955

We will not reply in words. Our reply shall be couched in terms of lead. We are in power. Nobody will deny it. By virtue of that power we shall remain in power. . . . This, then, is our answer. We have no words to waste on you. When you reach out your vaunted strong hands for our palaces and purpled ease, we will show you what strength is. In roar of shell and shrapnel and in whine of machine guns will our answer be couched. We will grind you revolutionists down under our heel, and we shall walk upon your faces. [Ellipsis points in original.]

JACK LONDON (1876–1916). *The Iron Heel,* 1907. In Bernard Crick, *George Orwell: A Life,* 4, 1980

See Cruelty: George Orwell

Anyone who can be proved to be a seditious person is an outlaw before God and the emperor; and whoever is the first to put him to death does right and well. . . . Therefore let everyone who can, smite, slay, and stab, secretly or openly, remembering that nothing can be more poisonous, hurtful, or devilish than a rebel. It is just as when one must kill a mad dog; if you do not strike him, he will strike you, and a whole land with you.

MARTIN LUTHER (1483–1546). During the Peasants' Revolt in Germany, *Against the Robbing and Murdering Hordes of Peasants* (pamphlet), May 1525

They tell me the Huks [a Philippine guerrilla group] are socialistic, that they are revolutionaries, but I haven't got the heart to go after them. If I worked in those sugar fields, I'd probably be a Huk myself.

DOUGLAS MacARTHUR (1880–1964). Remark to his staff, 1945. In William Manchester, *American Caesar: Douglas MacArthur: 1880–1964,* 7, 1978

See Revolutionary War: William Pitt the Elder

Insurrection is an art quite as much as war . . . and subject to certain rules of procedure, which, when neglected, will produce the ruin of the party neglecting them . . . Firstly, never play with insurrection unless you are fully prepared to face the consequences of your play. . . . Secondly, the insurrection career once entered upon, act with the greatest determination, and on the offensive. The defensive is the death of every armed uprising.

> KARL MARX (1818–1883). In Lenin, "Can the Bolsheviks Retain State Power? Postscript," 14 October 1917, *The Lenin Reader,* 8, ed. Stefan T. Possony, 1966

In the struggles for political emancipation, everybody knows how often its champions are bought off by bribes or daunted by terrors.

> JOHN STUART MILL (1806–1873). *The Subjection of Women,* 1, 1869

To win and hold the revolution [the modern revolutionary] must seize and control the key positions of political society—the ministries of Interior, Defense and Popular Information.

> SIGMUND NEUMANN. "The International Civil War," *World Politics,* April 1949

The main fact about the revolutionary is that he demands total change.

> CARL OGLESBY (1935–). *Containment and Change: Two Dissenting Views of American Foreign Policy,* 6, 1967

Men do not imperil their own and others' lives for unimpressive reasons. They are sharp accountants on the subject of staying alive. When they do something dangerous, they have been convinced that not to do it was more dangerous.

> CARL OGLESBY (1935–). *Containment and Change: Two Dissenting Views of American Foreign Policy,* 6, 1967

Revolutionary consciousness exists for the first time when the victim elaborates his experience of injustice into an inclusive definition of the society in which he lives.

> CARL OGLESBY (1935–). *Containment and Change: Two Dissenting Views of American Foreign Policy,* 6, 1967

I used to be very revolutionary, but now I think that nothing can be gained by brute force. People must be drawn to good by goodness.

> BORIS PASTERNAK (1890–1960). *Doctor Zhivago,* 8.5, 1957, tr. Max Hayward and Manya Harari, 1958

Revolutions are made by fanatical men of action with one-track minds, geniuses in their ability to confine themselves to a limited field.

> BORIS PASTERNAK (1890–1960). *Doctor Zhivago,* 14.14, 1957, tr. Max Hayward and Manya Harari, 1958

When it was told [Caesar] that Antony and Dolabella were in a plot against him, he said he did not fear such fat, luxurious men, but rather the pale, lean fellows, meaning Cassius and Brutus.

> PLUTARCH (A.D. 46?–119?). "Caesar" (100–44 B.C.), *Plutarch's Lives,* Dryden edition, 1693

Caesar: Let me have men about me that are fat;
Sleek-headed men and such as sleep o' nights:
Yond Cassius has a lean and hungry look;
He thinks too much: such men are dangerous.

> SHAKESPEARE (1564–1616). *Julius Caesar,* 1.2.192, 1599

The best revolutionaries are those who are free . . . in the sense that their self-identity and personal stability does not depend on their political role.

> RICHARD SHAULL (1919–). *Containment and Change: Two Dissenting Views of American Foreign Policy,* 11, 1967

I am, and have always been, and shall now always be, a revolutionary writer, because our laws make law impossible; our liberties destroy all freedom; our property is organized robbery; our morality is an impudent hypocrisy; our wisdom is administered by inexperienced or mal-experienced dupes, our power wielded by cowards and weaklings and our honor false in all its points. I am an enemy of the existing order for good reasons.

> GEORGE BERNARD SHAW (1856–1950). Preface ("Sane Conclusions") to *Major Barbara,* 1905

The moment a revolution becomes a government it necessarily sets to work to exterminate revolutionists. . . . For when the revolution triumphs, revolution becomes counter-revolution.

> GEORGE BERNARD SHAW (1856–1950). In Michael Holroyd, *Bernard Shaw: The Lure of Fantasy, 1918–1950,* 4.1, 1991

[Karl] Marx was a frustrated bourgeois—hence his hatred of the bourgeoisie.

> OSWALD SPENGLER (1880–1936). *Aphorisms,* 287. tr. Gisela Koch-Weser O'Brien, 1967

The revolutionary activist must stand on solid moral ground, if he is to be more than a political bandit.

> ROBERT TABER (1917–?). *War of the Flea: A Study of Guerrilla Warfare Theory and Practice,* 10, 1965

Rebels and dissidents challenge the complacent belief in a just world, and, as the theory would predict, they are usually denigrated for their efforts. While they are alive, they may be called "cantankerous," "crazy," "hysterical," "uppity," or "duped." Dead, some of them become saints and heroes, the sterling characters of history. It's a matter of proportion. One angry rebel is crazy, three is a conspiracy, 50 is a movement.

> CAROL TAVRIS. "Anger in an Unjust World," *Anger: The Misunderstood Emotion,* 1982

[The makers of the French Revolution] had that arrogant self-confidence which often points the way to disaster yet, lacking which, a nation can but relapse into a servile state. In short, they had a fanatical faith in their vocation—that of transforming the social system, root and branch, and regenerating the whole human race. Of this passionate idealism was born what was in a fact a new religion, giving rise to some of those vast changes in human conduct that religion has produced in other ages. It weaned them away from self-regarding emotions, stimulated them to heroic deeds and altruistic sacrifices, and often made them indifferent to all those petty ammenities of life which mean so much to us today.

> ALEXIS de TOCQUEVILLE (1805–1859). *The Old Regime and the French Revolution,* 3.2, 1856, tr. Stuart Gilbert, 1955

Traters, I will here remark, are a onfortnit class of peple. If they wasn't, they wouldn't be traters. They conspire to bust up a country—they fail, and they're traters. They bust her, and they become statesmen and heroes.

ARTEMUS WARD (1834–1867). "The Tower of London," *The Complete Works of Artemus Ward,* 1898

See Reformers: Elbert Hubbard

✹

There are two things about a revolution to remember: first, we're gonna get our asses kicked and second, we're gonna win.

ANONYMOUS (AMERICAN). Poster, 1970s

Revolutionaries and tyrants breed each other.

ANONYMOUS

REVOLUTIONARY WAR

See also • America ○ Country: Nathan Hale ○ International Relations ○ Navy: John Paul Jones ○ Revolution ○ Rights: Thomas Jefferson ○ War

The Revolution was affected before the war commenced. The Revolution was in the minds and hearts of the people. . . .

This radical change in the principles, opinions, sentiments, and affections of the people was the real American Revolution.

JOHN ADAMS (1735–1826). Letter to Hezekiah Niles, 13 February 1818

We most solemnly, before God and the world, declare, that, exerting the utmost energy of those powers, which our beneficent Creator hath graciously bestowed upon us, the arms we have been compelled by our enemies to assume, we will, in defiance of every hazard, with unabating firmness and perseverance, employ for the preservation of our liberties; being with one mind resolved to die freemen rather than to live slaves.

JOHN DICKINSON (1732–1808) and THOMAS JEFFERSON (1743–1826). Writing on behalf of a seven-member committee appointed by the Continental Congress, *Declaration of the Causes and Necessity of Taking Up Arms,* 6 July 1776

By the rude bridge that arched the flood,
  Their flag to April's breeze unfurled,
Here once the embattled farmer stood,
  And fired the shot heard round the world.

RALPH WALDO EMERSON (1803–1882). "Concord Hymn" (1), *Poems,* 1847. Emerson introduced his poem on 19 April 1836 at the unveiling ceremony for the Battle Monument in Concord (Massachusetts), where the Revolutionary War began on the same day in 1775.

"Rules by Which a Great Empire May Be Reduced to a Small One."

BENJAMIN FRANKLIN (1706–1790). Essay title. On British colonial policies pertaining to America before the outbreak of the Revolutionary War, 1773

It is the common observation here that our cause is the cause of all mankind, and that we are fighting for their liberty in defending our own.

BENJAMIN FRANKLIN (1706–1790). Describing the attitude in Paris toward the American Revolution, letter to Samuel Cooper, 1777

Our hopes are not placed in any particular city or spot of ground, but in preserving a good army, furnished with proper necessaries, to take advantage of favorable opportunities, and waste and defeat the enemy by piecemeal.

ALEXANDER HAMILTON (1757–1804). On American strategy during the Revolutionary War, letter to Hugh Knox. In Nathan Schachner, *Alexander Hamilton,* 6.3, 1946

Is life so dear or peace so sweet, as to be purchased at the price of chains and slavery? Forbid it, Almighty God! I know not what course others may take, but as for me, give me liberty or give me death!

PATRICK HENRY (1736–1799). Speech before the Virginia House of Burgesses, St. John's Episcopal Church, Richmond, 23 March 1775. These famous words, of doubtful authenticity, were not recorded at the time. They were reconstructed from accounts of two of Henry's contemporaries and were first published in William Wirt's *Sketches of the Life and Times of Patrick Henry,* 1817.

I have not yet begun to fight.

JOHN PAUL JONES (1747–1792). Naval captain. Attributed. Responding to a British ultimatum that he surrender his sinking ship, the *Bon Homme Richard,* in a battle he eventually won, 23 September 1779

It was not the mere matter of the separation of the colonies from the motherland; but something in the Declaration [of Independence] giving liberty, not alone to the people of this country, but hope to the world for all future time. It was that which gave promise that in due time the weights should be lifted from the shoulders of all men, and that *all* should have an equal chance. This is the sentiment embodied in that Declaration of Independence.

ABRAHAM LINCOLN (1809–1865). Speech, Independence Hall, Philadelphia, 22 February 1861

See Rights: Thomas Jefferson

We have it in our power to begin the world over again. A situation, similar to the present, hath not happened since the days of Noah until now. The birthday of a new world is at hand.

THOMAS PAINE (1737–1809). Appendix to *Common Sense,* 1776

These are the times that try men's souls. The summer soldier and the sunshine patriot will, in this crisis, shrink from the service of his country; but he that stands it *now,* deserves the love and thanks of man and woman.

THOMAS PAINE (1737–1809). Opening words, *The Crisis* (pamphlet), 1, 23 December 1776

Stand your ground. Don't fire unless fired upon. But if they mean to have a war let it begin here!

JONAS PARKER (18th cent.). Captain. Before the Battle of Lexington (Massachusetts), 19 April 1775

If I were an American, as I am an Englishman, while a foreign troop was landed in my country I never would lay down my arms—never, never, never!

WILLIAM PITT THE ELDER (1708–1778). House of Lords speech, 18 November 1777

See Revolutionaries: Douglas MacArthur

Don't one of you fire 'til you see the whites of their eyes.

WILLIAM PRESCOTT (1726–1795). Colonel. Before the Battle of Bunker Hill (Massachusetts), 17 June 1775

See Soldiers: Frederick II (1)

The time is now near at hand which must probably determine whether Americans are to be Freemen or Slaves. . . . The fate of unborn Millions will now depend, under God, on the Courage and Conduct of this army. Our cruel and unrelenting Enemy leaves us no choice but a brave resistance, or the most abject submission; this is all we can expect. We have, therefore, to resolve to conquer or die.

> GEORGE WASHINGTON (1732–1799). General orders to his army, 2 July 1776

On our Side, the War should be defensive. It has even been called a War of Posts. That we should on all Occasions avoid a general Action, or put anything to the Risk, unless compelled by a necessity, into which we ought never to be drawn.

> GEORGE WASHINGTON (1732–1799). Referring to his army's defensive posture during the Revolutionary War, letter to the John Hancock, President of the Continental Congress, 8 September 1776

Victory or Death.

> GEORGE WASHINGTON (1732–1799). 24? December 1776. In Benjamin Rush, *The Autobiography of Benjamin Rush,* 5, ed. George W. Corner, 1948. Rush set the context for Washington's words: "I visited Genl. Washington in company with Col. Jos. Reed at the General's quarters [near the Delaware River across from Trenton, New Jersey]. . . . He appeared much depressed, and lamented the ragged and dissolving state of his army in affecting terms. I gave him assurance of the disposition of Congress to support him, under his present difficulties and distresses. While I was talking to him, I observed him to play with his pen and ink upon several small pieces of paper. One of them by accident fell upon the floor near my feet. I was struck with the inscription upon it. It was 'Victory or Death.'" On 25 December, Washington led his army across the ice-clogged Delaware River and the next day, in a surprise attack, captured 918 Hessian troops in the Battle of Trenton.

Our cause is noble; it is the cause of Mankind!

> GEORGE WASHINGTON (1732–1799). Referring to the Revolutionary War, letter to James Warren, 31 March 1779

❧

Don't tread on me!

> SLOGAN (AMERICAN). Motto on the first American flag, raised by John Paul Jones on the flagship *Alfred,* 3 December 1775

RICH & POOR

See also • Poverty ○ Riches ○ Speaking: Michael Caine ○ Strength & Weakness ○ Success & Failure ○ Victory & Defeat ○ Wealth ○ Wealth & Poverty

The whole Business of the Poor is to administer to the Idleness, Folly, and Luxury of the Rich; and that of the Rich, in return, to find the best Methods of confirming the Slavery and increasing the Burdens of the Poor.

> EDMUND BURKE (1729–1797). *A Vindication of Natural Society,* p. 90, M. Cooper edition, 1756

When a country is well governed, poverty and a mean condition are things to be ashamed of. When a country is ill governed, riches and honor are things to be ashamed of.

> CONFUCIUS (551–479 B.C.). *Confucian Analects,* 8.13, tr. James Legge, 1930

If you live according to nature, you will never be poor; if you live according to [public] opinion, you will never be rich.

> EPICURUS (341–270 B.C.). In Seneca the Younger (5? B.C.–A.D. 65), "On Philosophy, the Guide of Life," *Moral Letters to Lucilius,* 16.7, tr. Richard M. Gummere, 1918

The Pleasures of the Rich are bought with the Tears of the Poor.

> THOMAS FULLER (1654–1734). Comp., *Gnomologia: Adages and Proverbs,* 4707, 1732

Riches are Honorable, for they are Power. Poverty, Dishonorable.

> THOMAS HOBBES (1588–1679). *Leviathan,* 10, 1651

When poor, [the Romans] robbed others, and when rich, themselves.

> SAMUEL JOHNSON (1709–1784). In C. C. Colton, *Lacon: or, Many Things in Few Words; Addressed to Those Who Think,* 2.134, 1824

If a free society cannot help the many who are poor, it cannot save the few who are rich.

> JOHN F. KENNEDY (1917–1963). *Inaugural Address,* 20 January 1961

A man is rich whose income is larger than his expenses, and he is poor if his expenses are greater than his income.

> LA BRUYÈRE (1645–1696). "Of the Gifts of Fortune" (49), *The Characters,* 1688, tr. Henri van Laun, 1929

Being poor is like being a child. Being rich is like being an adult: you get to do whatever you want. Everyone is nice when they have to be; rich people are nice when they feel like it.

> FRAN LEBOWITZ (1951–). James Atlas interview, "What They Look Like to the Rest of Us," *New York Times Magazine,* 19 November 1995

Money . . . buys privacy, silence. The less money you have, the noisier it is; the thinner your walls, the closer your neighbors. . . . The first thing you notice when you step into the house or apartment of a rich person is how quiet it is.

> FRAN LEBOWITZ (1951–). James Atlas interview, "What They Look Like to the Rest of Us," *New York Times Magazine,* 19 November 1995

Respectable means rich, and decent means poor. I should die if I heard my family called decent.

> THOMAS LOVE PEACOCK (1785–1866). *Crotchet Castle,* 3, 1831

Philip the Bastard: Well, whiles I am a beggar, I will rail
And say there is no sin but to be rich;
And being rich, my virtue then shall be
To say there is no vice, but beggary.

> SHAKESPEARE (1564–1616). *King John,* 2.1.593, 1596

Wherever there is great property, there is great inequality. For one very rich man there must be at least five hundred poor, and the affluence of the few supposes the indigence of the many. The affluence of the rich excites the indignation of the poor, who are often both driven by want, and prompted by envy, to invade his possessions. It is only under the shelter of the civil magistrate that the owner of that valuable property, which is acquired by the labor of many years, or perhaps of many successive generations, can sleep a single night in security.

> ADAM SMITH (1723–1790). *The Wealth of Nations,* 5.1.2, 1776

The desire of acquiring the comforts of the world haunts the imagination of the poor, and the dread of losing them that of the rich.

> ALEXIS de TOCQUEVILLE (1805–1859). *Democracy in America,* 2.2.10, 1840, tr. Henry Reeve and Francis Bowen, 1862

The advantages of the rich over the poor could not and cannot be maintained by anything but violence.

> LEO TOLSTOY (1828–1910). *The Kingdom of God Is Within You,* 12.1, 1893, tr. Aylmer Maude, 1936

I've been poor and I've been rich. And believe me, rich is best.

> SOPHIE TUCKER (1884–1966). In "Business: Advertising," *Time,* 16 November 1953

The poor have more children, but the rich have more relatives.

> ANONYMOUS

The rich are satisfied with what they have, no matter how little; the poor are dissatisfied with what they have, no matter how much.

> ANONYMOUS

The rich are hated; the poor are despised.

> SAYING (ASHANTI)

The rich and the poor meet together;
the Lord is the maker of them all.

> SAYING (*BIBLE*). *Proverbs* 22:2

Better is a poor man who walks in his integrity
than a rich man who is perverse in his ways.

> SAYING (*BIBLE*). *Proverbs* 28:6

Rich in rubles, rich in sorrows; poor in rubles, richer in sorrows.

> SAYING (RUSSIAN)

If the rich could hire others to die for them, the poor could make a nice living.

> SAYING (YIDDISH)

RICHES

See also • Heaven: Jesus (6) ○ Money ○ Rich & Poor ○ Wealth

Strive to be rich not in possessions, but in courage and merit.

> AGESILAUS II (444–360 B.C.). In Plutarch (A.D. 46?–119?), "Sayings of the Spartans: Agesilaus" (31), *Plutarch on Sparta,* tr. Richard J. A. Talbert, 1988

The ways to enrich are many, and most of them foul.

> FRANCIS BACON (1561–1626). "Of Riches," *Essays,* 1625

Riches [mean] . . . freedom from niggling details.

> JAMES DAVID BARBER (1939–). *The Presidential Character: Predicting Performance in the White House,* 9, 1972

Rize arly, work hard, and late, live on what yu kant sell, giv nothing awa, and if yu don't die ritch, and go tu the devil, yu ma sue me for damages.

> JOSH BILLINGS (1818–1885). *His Sayings,* 71, 1867

The man who dies . . . rich dies disgraced.

> ANDREW CARNEGIE (1835–1919). "Wealth," *North American Review,* June 1889

You will hear everlastingly, in all discussions about newspapers, companies, aristocracies, or party politics, this argument that the rich man cannot be bribed. The fact is, of course, that the rich man is bribed; he has been bribed already. That is why he is a rich man.

> G. K. CHESTERTON (1874–1936). In Garry Wills, *The Kennedy Imprisonment: A Meditation on Power,* pt. 2 (epigraph), 1981

The rich man is not one who is in possession of much, but one who gives much.

> ST. JOHN CHRYSOSTOM (A.D. 347?–407). *Homilies,* A.D. 388?

Ernest Hemingway: I'm getting to know the rich.
Colum: The only difference between the rich and other people is that the rich have more money.

> MARY COLUM. Critic. Format adapted. At lunch during the early 1930s. In Matthew J. Bruccoli, *Some Sort of Epic Grandeur: The Life of F. Scott Fitzgerald,* 51, 1981. Hemingway popularized Colum's quip, without attribution, in his short story, "The Snows of Kilimanjaro" (*Esquire,* August 1936).

Riches are a trust. . . .
  Power is a trust. . . .
  Talents are a *trust* too; that is the condition of their increase. They must be put out to use, or they will ruin the steward.

> RALPH WALDO EMERSON (1803–1882). Journal, 21 July 1831
>
> See Empire: John Dryden ○ Politicians: Henry Clay ○ Power: Edmund Burke (3)

The art of getting rich consists not in industry, much less in saving, but in a better order, a timeliness, in being at the right spot.

> RALPH WALDO EMERSON (1803–1882). "Wealth," *The Conduct of Life,* 1860

Everyone asks if a man is rich, no one if he is good.

> EURIPIDES (485?–406 B.C.). In Robert Burton, *The Anatomy of Melancholia,* 1.2.4.6, 1621-1651

He is not genteel, handsome, witty, brave, good-humored, but he is rich, rich, rich, rich, rich—that one word contradicts everything you can say against him.

> HENRY FIELDING (1707–1754). *The Miser,* 3.7, 1733

Let me tell you about the very rich. They are different from you and me. They possess and enjoy early, and it does something to them, makes them soft where we are hard, and cynical where we are trustful, in a way that, unless you were born rich, it is very difficult to understand. They think, deep in their hearts, that they are better than we are because we had to discover the compensations and refuges of life for ourselves.

> F. SCOTT FITZGERALD (1896–1940). "The Rich Boy" (1), *All the Sad Young Men,* 1926

Never trust a country where the rich live behind high walls and tinted windows. That is a place that is not prospering as one country. That is a place where the rich not only say, "I don't want you to see how I live," but "I don't want to see how you live."

> THOMAS L. FRIEDMAN (1953–). *"Tinted Windows," New York Times,* 23 June 1997

Riches are [gotten] with Pain, kept with Care, and lost with Grief.

> THOMAS FULLER (1654–1734). Comp., *Gnomologia: Adages and Proverbs,* 4043, 1732

Riches rather enlarge than satisfy Appetites.

> THOMAS FULLER (1654–1734). Comp., *Gnomologia: Adages and Proverbs,* 4048, 1732

Riches well got and well used are a great Blessing.

> THOMAS FULLER (1654–1734). Comp., *Gnomologia: Adages and Proverbs,* 4049, 1732

If you can actually count your money, then you are not a really rich man.

> J. PAUL GETTY (1892–1976). Industrialist and founder of Getty Oil Co. In Bernard Levin, *The Pendulum Years: Britain and the Sixties,* 1, 1970
> See Price: J. P. Morgan

I am indeed rich, since my income is superior to my expense, and my expense is equal to my wishes.

> EDWARD GIBBON (1737–1794). *Memoirs of My Life and Writings,* p. 111, 1796, Alex. Murray edition, 1869

The Rich knows not who is his friend.

> GEORGE HERBERT (1593–1633). Comp., *Outlandish Proverbs,* 865, 1640

It must be great to be rich and let the other fellow keep up appearances.

> KIN HUBBARD (1868–1930). In Charles McCabe, "The Fearless Spectator," *San Francisco Chronicle,* 23 September 1971

Having given all he had,
He then is very rich indeed.

> LAO-TZU (6th cent. B.C.). *The Way of Life,* 81, tr. R. B. Blakney, 1955

The rich man's identity is less diversified than ever before: he is distinguished only by his commercial acumen as measured by his net worth.

> MICHAEL LEWIS. "The Rich: How They're Different . . . Than They Used to Be," *New York Times Magazine,* 19 November 1995

I don't believe in a law to prevent a man from getting rich; it would do more harm than good.

> ABRAHAM LINCOLN (1809–1865). Speech, New Haven (Connecticut), 6 March 1860

If a man would guide his life by true philosophy, he will find ample riches in a modest livelihood enjoyed with a tranquil mind.

> LUCRETIUS (99–55 B.C.). *On the Nature of Things,* 5.1115, tr. R. E. Latham, 1951

When a man tells you that he got rich through hard work, ask him: "Whose?"

> DON MARQUIS (1878–1937). In Edward Anthony, *O Rare Don Marquis,* 11, 1962

We simply must believe that the American rich are happy, else our confidence in the whole endeavor might be shaken. For of all the possible values of human society, one and one only is [the] truly sovereign, truly universal, truly sound, truly and completely acceptable goal of man in America. That goal is money, and let there be no sour grapes about it from the losers.

> C. WRIGHT MILLS (1916–1962). *The Power Elite,* 7.4, 1956

I am richer than Harriman. I have all the money I want and he hasn't.

> JOHN MUIR (1838–1914). Referring to financier A. E. Harriman. In introduction to *The Wilderness World of John Muir,* comp. Edwin Way Teale, 1954
> See Poverty: Seneca the Younger

You can never be too skinny or too rich.

> BARBARA "BABE" PALEY (1915–1978). Socialite. Attributed

Very rich and very good at the same time he cannot be.

> PLATO (427?–347 B.C.). *Laws,* 5.742, tr. Benjamin Jowett, 1894
> See Money: Henry David Thoreau (1)

When riches and virtue are placed together in the scales of the balance, the one always rises as the other falls.

> PLATO (427?–347 B.C.). *The Republic,* 8.550, tr. Benjamin Jowett, 1894

We may see the small value God has for riches by the people he gives them to.

> ALEXANDER POPE (1688–1744). "Thoughts on Various Subjects," *Miscellanies in Prose and Verse* (published with Jonathan Swift), vol. 2, 1727. The initials "D. A." following this maxim in the text has led some scholars to believe that the author was Pope's friend Dr. (John) Arbuthnot.

The art of becoming "rich" . . . is not absolutely nor finally the art of accumulating much money for ourselves, but also of contriving that our neighbors shall have less. In accurate terms, it is "the art of establishing the maximum inequality in our own favor."

> JOHN RUSKIN (1819–1900). *Unto This Last,* 2, 1860

What is really desired, under the name of riches, is, essentially, power over men; in its simplest sense, the power of obtaining for our own advantage the labor of servant, tradesman, and artist; in wider sense, authority of directing large masses of the nation to various ends (good, trivial, or hurtful, according to the mind of the rich person).

> JOHN RUSKIN (1819–1900). *Unto This Last,* 2, 1860
> See Money: Oscar Wilde (3)

That country is the richest which nourishes the greatest number of noble and happy human beings; that man is richest who, having perfected the functions of his own life to the utmost, has also the widest helpful influence, both personal and by means of his possessions, over the lives of others.

> JOHN RUSKIN (1819–1900). *Unto This Last,* 4, 1860

The wise man does not deem himself undeserving of any of the gifts of Fortune. He does not love riches, but he would rather have them; he does not admit them to his heart, but to his house, and he does not reject the riches he has, but he keeps them and wishes them to supply ampler material for exercising his virtue.

SENECA THE YOUNGER (5? B.C.–A.D. 65). "On the Happy Life" (21.4), *Moral Essays,* tr. John W. Basore, 1932

In my eyes riches have a certain place, in yours they have the highest; in fine, I own my riches, yours own you.

SENECA THE YOUNGER (5? B.C.–A.D. 65). "On the Happy Life" (22.5), *Moral Essays,* tr. John W. Basore, 1932

See Wealth: Bion

The shortest cut to riches is to despise riches.

SENECA THE YOUNGER (5? B.C.–A.D. 65). "On Good Company," *Moral Letters to Lucilius,* 62.3, tr. Richard M. Gummere, 1918

With the greater part of rich people, the chief enjoyment of riches consists in the parade of riches, which in their eye is never so complete as when they appear to possess those decisive marks of opulence which nobody can possess but themselves.

ADAM SMITH (1723–1790). *The Wealth of Nations,* 1.11.2, 1776

It is the wretchedness of being rich that you have to live with rich people.

LOGAN PEARSALL SMITH (1865–1946). *Afterthoughts,* 4, 1931

A society is rich when material goods, including capital, are cheap, and human beings dear: indeed the word "riches" has no other meaning. The interest of those who own the property used in industry . . . is that their capital should be dear and human beings cheap.

R. H. TAWNEY (1880–1962). *The Acquisitive Society,* 7, 1920

The rich man . . . is always sold to the institution which makes him rich.

HENRY DAVID THOREAU (1817–1862). "Civil Disobedience," 1849

A man is rich in proportion to the number of things which he can afford to let alone.

HENRY DAVID THOREAU (1817–1862). "Where I Lived, and What I Lived For," *Walden; or Life in the Woods,* 1854

What's the subject of life—to get rich? All of those fellows out there getting rich could be dancing around the real subject of life.

PAUL A. VOLCKER (1927–). Federal Reserve Board chairman. In Eric Gelman et al., "America's Money Master," *Newsweek,* 24 February 1986

❦

He who trusts in his riches will wither,
  but the righteous will flourish like a green leaf.

SAYING (*BIBLE*). *Proverbs* 11:28

Riches are often abused but seldom refused.

SAYING (DANISH)

Much industry and little conscience make a man rich.

SAYING (ENGLISH)

Deceive, but do not insult, the rich and powerful.

SAYING (JAPANESE)

RIDICULE

See also • Criticism ○ Heroism: Miguel de Unamuno ○ Insult ○ Slander ○ Wit

Acquaintance: They deride thee, O Diogenes!
Diogenes: But I am not derided.

DIOGENES (410?–320? B.C.). Greek philosopher. Format adapted. In Ralph Waldo Emerson, journal, 1870, undated

See Self-Respect: Ralph Waldo Emerson

Of all the griefs that harass the distress'd,
Sure the most bitter is a scornful jest.

SAMUEL JOHNSON (1709–1784). "London: A Poem," l. 166, 1738

I have endured a great deal of ridicule without much malice; and have received a great deal of kindness, not quite free from ridicule.

ABRAHAM LINCOLN (1809–1865). Letter to James H. Hackett, 2 November 1863

No one becomes a laughingstock who laughs at himself.

SENECA THE YOUNGER (5? B.C.–A.D. 65). "On the Firmness of the Wise Man" (17.3), *Moral Essays,* tr. John W. Basore, 1928

You are not yet blessed, if the multitude does not laugh at you.

SENECA THE YOUNGER (5? B.C.–A.D. 65). *De moribus.* In Whitall N. Perry, comp., *A Treasury of Traditional Wisdom,* p. 127, 1986

Ridicule is the best test of truth.

LORD SHAFTESBURY (1621–1683). In Lord Chesterfield, letter to his son, 6 February 1752

Joan: Thou art a rare noodle, Master. Do what was done last time is thy rule, eh?
Courcelles (rising in anger): Noodle indeed! dost thou dare call me noodle?

GEORGE BERNARD SHAW (1856–1950). *Saint Joan,* 6, 1923

When a man is unable to understand a thing, he ridicules it.

LEO TOLSTOY (1828–1910). *Thoughts and Aphorisms,* 13.5, 1886–1893, tr. Leo Wiener, 1905

RIGHT

See also • Good ○ Religion: R. H. Tawney ○ Right & Wrong ○ Wrong

You cannot make yourself feel something you do not feel, but you can make yourself do right in spite of your feelings.

PEARL S. BUCK (1892–1973). "My Neighbor's Son," *To My Daughters, With Love,* 1967

There are many things which in and of themselves seem morally right, but which under certain circumstances prove to be not morally right.

CICERO (106–43 B.C.). *De officiis,* 3.25, tr. Walter Miller, 1913

It is never too late to do right.

RALPH WALDO EMERSON (1803–1882). Letter to his cousin Elizabeth Tucker, 1 February 1832

It is by no means necessary that I should live, but it is by all means necessary that I should act rightly.

RALPH WALDO EMERSON (1803–1882). Journal, 1854, undated

See Right & Wrong: Socrates

My principle is to do whatever is right, and leave consequences to Him who has the disposal of them.

THOMAS JEFFERSON (1743–1826). Letter, 20 September 1813

The time is always right to do right.

MARTIN LUTHER KING, JR. (1929–1968). "Letter from Birmingham City Jail," 16 April 1963

I think it better to do right, even if we suffer in so doing, than to incur the reproach of our consciences and posterity.

ROBERT E. LEE (1807–1870). Letter to James Alexander Seddon, 6 March 1864. In J. F. C. Fuller, *Grant and Lee: A Study in Personality and Generalship*, 3, 1957

Whatever is, is right.

ALEXANDER POPE (1688–1744). *An Essay on Man*, 1.294, 1734

Questions of right have no bearing on human existence.

AYN RAND (1905–1982). *Atlas Shrugged*, 2.4, 1957

"Right" conduct is conduct which promotes the general good.

BERTRAND RUSSELL (1872–1970). *Human Society in Ethics and Politics*, 1.4, 1962

The odd thing is that we are so used to the triumph of evil, of might over right, that the very consciousness of being right makes us feel doomed and we capitulate in advance.

VALERIY TARSIS (1906–). *Ward 7: An Autobiographical Novel*, 6, 1965, tr. Katya Brown, 1966

I shall continue to do what I think is right whether anybody likes it or not.

HARRY S. TRUMAN (1884–1972). 1950. In William Hillman, *Mr. President*, 5.5, 1952

Always do right. This will gratify some people, and astonish the rest.

MARK TWAIN (1835–1910). Note to the Young People's Society, Greenpoint Presbyterian Church, Brooklyn, 16 February 1901

Do right, and you will be conspicuous.

MARK TWAIN (1835–1910). In Albert Bigelow Paine, *Mark Twain: A Biography*, 3.1134, 1912

❧

Right wrongs no one.

SAYING (SCOTTISH)

Right makes might.

SAYING

See Faith: Abraham Lincoln ∘ Power: Saying

RIGHT & WRONG

See also • Good ∘ Good & Evil ∘ Right ∘ Wrong

When we've had lunch, your preaching can begin. . . .
You may proclaim, good sirs, your fine philosophy
But till you feed us, right and wrong can wait!

BERTOLT BRECHT (1898–1956). *The Threepenny Opera*, 2.3, 1928, tr. Eric Bentley, 1964 (Popular version [last sentence]: Food first, then ethics.)

It may make a difference to all eternity whether we do right or wrong today.

JAMES FREEMAN CLARKE (1810–1888). In Elbert Hubbard, comp., *Elbert Hubbard's Scrap Book*, p. 95, 1923

The only right is what is after my constitution; the only wrong what is against it.

RALPH WALDO EMERSON (1803–1882). "Self-Reliance," *Essays: First Series*, 1841

There is no right and wrong; only power and weakness.

PAUL ELDRIDGE (1888–1982). *Maxims for a Modern Man*, 1577, 1965

If a man has acted right, he has done well, though alone; if wrong, the sanction of all mankind will not justify him.

HENRY FIELDING (1707–1754)

Right is whatever profits a nation, wrong is whatever harms it.

HANS FRANK (1900–19456). Shortly after being appointed governor-general of Nazi-occupied Poland. Address before the Academy of German Law, 3 December 1939

The creed which accepts, as the foundation of morals, Utility, or the Greatest-happiness Principle, holds that actions are right in proportion as they tend to promote happiness, wrong as they tend to produce the reverse of happiness.

JOHN STUART MILL (1806–1873). *Utilitarianism*, 2, 1863

See Good & Evil: Francis Hutcheson ∘ Government: George Washington ∘ Happiness: Jeremy Bentham ∘ States: Plato (2)

A man who is good for anything ought not to calculate the chance of living or dying; he ought only to consider whether in doing anything he is doing right or wrong—acting the part of a good man or of a bad.

SOCRATES (470?–399 B.C.). In Plato (427?–347 B.C.). *Apology*, 28, tr. Benjamin Jowett, 1894

See Right: Ralph Waldo Emerson (2)

Everybody I see about me seems bent on teaching his contemporaries, by precept and example, that what is useful is never wrong. Will nobody undertake to make them understand how what is right may be useful?

ALEXIS de TOCQUEVILLE (1805–1859). *Democracy in America*, 2.2.8, 1840, tr. Henry Reeve and Francis Bowen, 1862

RIGHTS

See also • Children's Learning: Maria Montessori (4) ∘ Equality ∘ Freedom ∘ Freedom of Conscience ∘ Freedom of Religion ∘ Freedom of Speech ∘ Freedom of the Press ∘ Freedom of Thought ∘ Justice ∘ Liberty: [especially] Johann Heinrich Pestalozzi, Theodore Roosevelt ∘ Right to Privacy ∘ Right to Silence ∘ Tyranny: Anonymous (3)

There are no rights whatever without corresponding duties.

> Samuel Taylor Coleridge (1772–1834). 20 November 1831, *Table Talk,* 1835

In respect of their rights men are born and remain free and equal.

> THE DECLARATION OF THE RIGHTS OF MAN AND THE CITIZEN. France, Article 1, 26 August 1789

The final end of every political institution is the preservation of the natural and imprescriptible rights of man. These rights are those of liberty, property, security and resistance to oppression.

> THE DECLARATION OF THE RIGHTS OF MAN AND THE CITIZEN. France, Article 2, 26 August 1789

Freedom is the right to be wrong, not the right to do wrong.

> JOHN G. DIEFENBAKER (1895–1979). Canadian prime minister. In "Quotable Quotes," *Reader's Digest,* September 1979

No private rights can prevail over the inalienable right of society to save itself.

> JULES DUFAURE (1798–1881). French political leader. 1849. In Alexis de Tocqueville, *Recollections,* 9, 1893, tr. George Lawrence, 1964

Don't ask f'r rights. Take thim. An' don't let anny wan give thim to ye. A right that is handed to ye f'r nawthin' has somethin' th' matter with it.

> PETER FINLEY DUNNE (1867–1936). "On Woman Suffrage," *American Magazine,* 1906

I hold it to be the inalienable right of anybody to go to hell in his own way.

> ROBERT FROST (1874–1963). Address, Berkeley (California), 1935

Rights that do not flow directly from duty well performed are not worth having.

> MOHANDAS K. GANDHI (1869–1948). In *Harijan,* 6 July 1947

Human beings have an inalienable right to invent themselves; when that right is pre-empted, it is called brainwashing.

> GERMAINE GREER (1939–). "Real lives, or readers' digest," *Times* (London), 1 February 1986

The sacred rights of mankind are not to be rummaged for among old parchments or musty records. They are written, as with a sunbeam, in the whole volume of human nature, by the hand of the divinity itself, and can never be erased or obscured by mortal power.

> ALEXANDER HAMILTON (1757–1804). Written at age 19, *The Farmer Refuted* (pamphlet), 5 February 1775

There are inalienable obligations as well as inalienable rights.

> ABRAHAM JOSHUA HESCHEL (1907–1972). *Who Is Man?* 6, 1965

Close by the rights of Man, side by side with them, at least, are the rights of the Soul.

> VICTOR HUGO (1802–1885). "Cosette" (7.5), *Les Misérables,* tr. Charles E. Wilbour, 1862

We hold these truths to be self-evident; that all men are created equal; that they are endowed by their Creator with certain unalienable rights; that among these are life, liberty, and the pursuit of happiness.

> THOMAS JEFFERSON (1743–1826). Declaration of Independence, 4 July 1776
>
> See Feminism: Elizabeth Cady Stanton ○ Government: John Locke ○ Revolutionary War: Abraham Lincoln

I believe each individual is naturally entitled to do as he pleases with himself and the fruit of his labor, so far as it in no [way] interferes with any other man's rights.

> ABRAHAM LINCOLN (1809–1865). Speech, Chicago, 10 July 1858

The rights and interests of every or any person are only secure from being disregarded when the person interested is himself able and habitually disposed to stand up for them.

> JOHN STUART MILL (1806–1873). *Considerations on Representative Government,* 3, 1861

My belief has always been . . . that wherever in this land any individual's Constitutional rights are being unjustly denied, it is the obligation of the federal government—at point of bayonet if necessary—to restore that individual's Constitutional rights.

> RONALD REAGAN (1911–). News conference, Washington, 17 May 1983

Where there are no rights, there are no duties.

> HENRI BENJAMIN de REBECQUE (1767–1830). "On Political Reactions," France, 6.1, 1797

I believe in property rights; I believe that normally the rights of property and humanity coincide; but sometimes they conflict, and when this is so, I put human rights above property rights.

> THEODORE ROOSEVELT (1858–1919). In *Outlook,* 15 November 1913

Everyone has the right to a standard of living adequate for the health and well-being of himself and of his family, including food, clothing, housing and medical care and necessary social services, and the right to security in the event of unemployment, sickness, disability, widowhood, old age or other lack of livelihood in circumstances beyond his control.

> UNIVERSAL DECLARATION OF HUMAN RIGHTS. United Nations, Article 25.1, 10 December 1948

The greatest right in the world is the right to be wrong.

> HARRY WEINBERGER (1888–?). "The First Casualties in War," letter to *New York Evening Post,* 10 April 1917

The American idea is that government exists to protect, not to give, the most fundamental rights which, as Jefferson wrote 220 July Fourths ago, are "inalienable" because they exist independent of, and prior to, government.

> GEORGE F. WILL (1941–). "Speaking of Free Speech . . . ," *Newsweek,* 8 July 1996

🌿

The right to wave your fist ends where your neighbor's nose begins.

> SAYING (AMERICAN)
>
> See Tobacco: Anonymous (American)

RIGHT TO PRIVACY

Includes • Privacy

See also • Computers: Alan W. Scheflin and Edward M. Opton, Jr. ○ Freedom ○ Freedom of Thought ○ Rights ○ Right to Silence ○ Secrets ○ Solitude (Being Alone) ○ Solitude (Living Alone)

What is surprising is that so many ordinary American citizens tolerate without protest the most shameless invasion of their privacy. . . .

A man's sex life, political views and childhood relationship with his mother are his own business, and nobody else's. The proper response about such matters is a loud, positive: "IT'S NONE OF YOUR LOUSY BUSINESS."

> STEWART ALSOP (1914–1974). "'It's None of Your Lousy Business,'" *Saturday Evening Post,* 13 June 1964

To surrender what is most profound and mysterious in one's being and personality at any price less than that of absolute reciprocity is profanation.

> HENRI AMIEL (1821–1881). Journal, 26 December 1852, tr. Mrs. Humphrey Ward, 1887

The makers of our Constitution undertook to secure conditions favorable to the pursuit of happiness. They recognized the significance of man's spiritual nature, of his feelings and of his intellect. They knew that only a part of the pain, pleasure and satisfactions of life are to be found in material things. They sought to protect Americans in their beliefs, their thoughts, their emotions and their sensations. They conferred, as against the Government, the right to be let alone—the most comprehensive of rights and the right most valued by civilized men.

> LOUIS D. BRANDEIS (1856–1941). *Olmstead v. United States,* 1928

A man always is to be himself the judge how much of his mind he will show to other men; even to those he would have work along with him. There are impertinent inquiries made: your rule is, to leave the inquirer *un*informed on that matter; not, if you can help it, misinformed; but precisely as dark as he was!

> THOMAS CARLYLE (1795–1881). "The Hero as King," *On Heroes, Hero-Worship, and the Heroic in History,* 1841

"If everybody minded their own business," the Duchess said, in a hoarse growl, "the world would go round a deal faster than it does."

> LEWIS CARROLL (1832–1898). *Alice's Adventures in Wonderland,* 6, 1865

Let every man mind his own business.

> CERVANTES (1547–1616). *Don Quixote,* 1.3.8, 1615, tr. Peter Anthony Motteux and John Ozell, 1743

I never thrust my nose into other men's porridge.

> CERVANTES (1547–1616). *Don Quixote,* 1.3.11, 1615, tr. Peter Anthony Motteux and John Ozell, 1743

The right of the people to be secure in their persons, houses, papers, and effects, against unreasonable searches and seizures, shall not be violated, and no warrants shall issue but upon probable cause, supported by oath or affirmation, and particularly describing the place to be searched, and the persons or things to be seized.

> CONSTITUTION OF THE UNITED STATES. Bill of Rights, Fourth Amendment, 15 December 1791

No rights can be dearer . . . than exemptions from unseasonable invasions on [one's] time by the course-minded and ignorant.

> JAMES FENIMORE COOPER (1789–1851). "An Aristocrat and a Democrat," *The American Democrat,* 1838

It's enough for a man to understand his own business, and not to interfere with other people's.

> CHARLES DICKENS (1812–1870). *A Christmas Carol,* 1, 1843

The American government is premised on the theory that if the mind of man is to be free, his ideas, his beliefs, his ideology, his philosophy must be placed beyond the reach of government.

> WILLIAM O. DOUGLAS (1898–1980). "The Bill of Rights," *Freedom of the Mind,* 1962

Don't you meddle with me, and I won't meddle with you.

> GEORGE ELIOT (1819–1880). *Adam Bede,* 53, 1859

He that puts on a public Gown must put off a private Person.

> THOMAS FULLER (1654–1734). Comp., *Gnomologia: Adages and Proverbs,* 2257, 1732

Silence and anonymity are no longer safeguards. All asylums of the spirit have been destroyed. The counsel of prudent withdrawal and disinterested curiosity from afar . . . would today almost certainly arouse the suspicions of the secret police.

> SIDNEY HOOK (1902–1989). *The Hero in History: A Study in Limitation and Possibility,* 1, 1943

The closer and more confidential our relationship with someone, the less we are entitled to ask about what we are not voluntarily told.

> LOUIS KRONENBERGER (1904–1980). "Aphorisms," *Vogue,* 1 March 1964

To extend the bounds of what may be called moral police until it encroaches on the most unquestionably legitimate liberty of the individual is one of the most universal of all human propensities.

> JOHN STUART MILL (1806–1873). *On Liberty,* 4, 1859

In their vigorous advocacy of the public's right to know, the media frequently violate a right that has a higher standing—the individual's right to privacy.

> RICHARD M. NIXON (1913–1994). *In the Arena: A Memoir of Victory, Defeat and Renewal,* 24, 1990

Big Brother Is Watching You.

> GEORGE ORWELL (1903–1950). The caption under the ubiquitous poster of a glaring Big Brother, *Nineteen Eigthy-Four,* 1.1, 1949

A man has a right to pass through this world, if he wills, without having his picture published, his business enterprises discussed, his successful experiments written up for the benefit of others, or his eccentricities commented upon, whether in handbills, circulars, catalogues, newspapers or periodicals.

> ALTON B. PARKER (1852–1926). *Roberson v. Rochester Folding Box Co.,* 1901

The poorest man may in his cottage bid defiance to all the forces of the Crown. It may be frail—its roof may shake—the wind may blow through it—the storm may enter—the rain may enter—but the King of England cannot enter!—all his forces dare not cross the threshold of the ruined tenement!

> WILLIAM PITT THE ELDER (1708–1778). House of Commons speech, March 1763

The pretension of man to explore the conscience of others, the forcible rape of secrecy, are a diabolical parody of the all-seeing-ness of God.

> JEAN ROLIN (1900–?). *Police Drugs*, 7.2, tr. Laurence J. Bendit, 1956

No one should compel himself to show to others more of his inner life than he feels it natural to show.

> ALBERT SCHWEITZER (1875–1965). *Memoirs of Childhood and Youth*, 5, 1925, tr. C. T. Campion, 1949

Putting trust in people will produce trustworthy people. That is the foremost of the many reasons against the widespread and routine use of lie detector tests. Management through fear and intimidation is not the way to promote honesty and protect security.

> GEORGE P. SHULTZ (1920–). Secretary of state. Speech, Washington, 9 January 1989

The Fourth Amendment and the personal rights which it secures have a long history. At the very core stands the right of a man to retreat into his own home and there be free from unreasonable governmental intrusion.

> POTTER STEWART (1915–1985). On electronic eavesdropping, *Silverman v. United States*, 1961

RIGHT TO SILENCE

See also • Freedom ○ Freedom of Speech ○ Freedom of Thought ○ Rights ○ Right to Privacy ○ Torture ○ Trials

The American system of criminal prosecution is accusatorial, not inquisitional, and the Fifth Amendment is its essential mainstay.

> WILLIAM J. BRENNAN, JR. (1906–1997). *Mallow v. Hogan*, 1964

Personal freedom consists largely in having a defense against questions. The most blatant tyranny is the one which asks the most blatant questions.

> ELIAS CANETTI (1905–1994). "Elements of Power: Question and Answer," *Crowds and Power*, tr. Carol Stewart, 1962

No person shall be . . . compelled in any criminal case to be a witness against himself.

> CONSTITUTION OF THE UNITED STATES. Bill of Rights, Fifth Amendment, 15 December 1791

The Fifth Amendment is an old friend, and a good one. It is one of the great landmarks in man's struggle to be free of tyranny, to be decent and civilized. It is our way to escape torture. It protects man against any form of Inquisition. It is part of our respect for the dignity of man.

> WILLIAM O. DOUGLAS (1898–1980). February 15, *An Almanac of Liberty*, 1954

See Witchcraft: Heinrich Kramer and James Sprenger (3)

The right to free speech is easily vitiated in the absence of an enforceable right to remain silent.

> JOHN V. LINDSAY (1921–). New York mayor. "Our Precious Right to Be Unheard," *Life*, 6 October 1967

The Miranda decision is wrong. We managed very well in this country for 175 years without it. It's practical effect is to prevent the police from talking to the person who knows the most about the crime—namely, the perpetrator.

> EDWIN MEESE III (1931–). Attorney general. On the Supreme Court decision in *Miranda v. Arizona* (1966) requiring police to inform criminal suspects of their right to remain silent, interview, "Reagan Seeks Judges with 'Traditional Approach,'" *U.S. News & World Report*, 14 October 1985

In law, the right to keep silent is a logical corollary to the general principle of presumed innocence.

> JEAN ROLIN (1900–?). *Police Drugs*, 7.1, tr. Laurence J. Bendit, 1956

A man may not accuse himself of a crime.

> TALMUD (A.D. 1st–6th cent.). Rabbinical writings. In Louis I. Newman, comp., *The Talmudic Anthology*, 189, 1945

Silence is equivalent to confession.

> TALMUD (1st–6th cent. A.D.). Rabbinical writings. In Louis I. Newman, comp., *The Talmudic Anthology*, 189, 1945

The right to silence is more than the mere right to refuse to answer incriminating questions. It is the respect which society pays to the inviolability of each man's soul in an era when hypnotism, narco-analysis, truth serums, lie detectors and other scientific devices are being used to force the revelation of truths by persons who desire to keep them secret . . . It is a last bastion against an ever more omnipotent government. It is the final shield against invasion of the soul. Protection from this kind of assault is the *sine qua non* of the essential dignity of man.

> EDWARD BENNETT WILLIAMS (1920–1988). *One Man's Freedom*, 8, 1962

RIVERS

See also • Despair: Henry David Thoreau ○ Nature

It fills me full of joie de viver
To look across the Hudson River.

> FRANKLIN P. ADAMS (1881–1960). Diary, 24 March 1924

I hate all dams, large and small. . . .
  If you are against a dam, you are for a river.

> DAVID R. BROWER (1912–). In John McPhee, *Encounters with the Archdruid*, 3, 1971

"River, Stay 'Way from My Door."

> MORT DIXON. Song title, 1931

When you defile the pleasant streams
And the wild bird's aboding place,
You massacre a million dreams
And cast your spittle in God's face.

> JOHN DRINKWATER (1882–1937). English poet and playwright

Then the good river-god [took] the form of my valiant Henry Thoreau here and introduced me to the riches of his shadowy, star-lit, moonlit stream, a lovely new world lying as close and yet as unknown to this vulgar trite one of streets and shops as death to life, or poetry to prose. Through one field only we went to the boat and then left all time, all science, all history, behind us and entered into Nature with one stroke of a paddle. Take care, good friend! I said, as I looked west into the sunset overhead and underneath, and he with his face toward me rowed towards it—take care; you know not what you do, dipping your wooden oar into this enchanted liquid, painted with all reds and purples and yellows which glows under and behind you. Presently this glory faded and the stars came and said "Here we are," and began to cast such private and ineffable beams as to stop all conversation.

> RALPH WALDO EMERSON (1803–1882). Journal, 6 June 1841

The stream can never rise above the springhead.

> THOMAS FULLER (1654–1734). Comp., *Gnomologia: Adages and Proverbs,* 4771, 1732 (Popular version: A stream cannot rise above its source.)

Ol' man river, dat ol' man river,
He must know sumpin', but don't say nothin',
He jus' keeps rollin',
He jus' keeps rollin' along.

> OSCAR HAMMERSTEIN (1895–1960). "Ol' Man River" (song). In the musical *Showboat,* 1927

Free the rivers.

> JOHN MUIR (1838–1914). Statement opposing the building of dams

Rivers are roads which move, and which carry us whither we desire to go.

> BLAISE PASCAL (1623–1662). *Pensées,* 17, 1670, tr. William F. Trotter, 1931

ROGUES

See also • Fools: George Bernard Shaw (2) ○ Knaves ○ Law: Josiah Gilbert Holland ○ Scoundrels

E'ry inch that is not fool is rogue.

> JOHN DRYDEN (1631–1700). *Absalom and Achitophel,* 2.463, 1681

Little Rogues easily become great Ones.

> BENJAMIN FRANKLIN (1706–1790). *Poor Richard's Almanack,* September 1754

Nobody calls himself Rogue.

> THOMAS FULLER (1654–1734). Comp., *Gnomologia: Adages and Proverbs,* 3545, 1732

No Rogue like . . . the godly Rogue.

> THOMAS FULLER (1654–1734). Comp., *Gnomologia: Adages and Proverbs,* 3624, 1732

Many a man would have turned rogue if he had known how.

> WILLIAM HAZLITT (1778–1830). "On Knowledge of the World," *Sketches and Essays,* 1839

When a rogue kisses you, count your teeth.

> SAYING (JEWISH)

ROME

See also • Cities ○ Italy

Rome was not built in a day.

> JOHN CLARKE (1596–1658). Comp., *Proverbs: English and Latine,* p. 305, 1639
>
> See Wit: Examples: Jack Kerouac

The smoke, the wealth, the noise of Rome.

> HORACE (65–8 B.C.). *Odes,* 3.29, *The Complete Works of Horace,* ed. Casper J. Kraemer, Jr., 1936

All roads lead to Rome.

> VOLTAIRE (1694–1778). Letter to Madame de Fontaine, 23 September 1750

Not every road leads to Rome.

> SAYING (SLOVENIAN)

RULERS

See also • Despots: B. H. Liddell Hart ○ Kings ○ Leaders ○ Machiavellianism ○ Princes ○ Tyrants

They should rule who are able to rule best.

> ARISTOTLE (384–322 B.C.). *Politics,* 2.11, tr. Benjamin Jowett, 1885

Those who rule us are like you and me. It is a frightening situation.

> BROOKS ATKINSON (1894–1984). 27 January, *Once Around the Sun,* 1951

Grand Inquisitor: Who can rule men if not he who holds their conscience and their bread in his hands.

> FYODOR DOSTOYEVSKY (1821–1881). *The Brothers Karamazov,* 5.5, 1880, tr. Constance Garnett, 1912

The art of governing is a great *métier,* requiring the whole man, and . . . it is therefore not well for a ruler to have too strong tendencies for other affairs.

> GOETHE? (1749–1832). 18 February 1831. In Peter Eckermann, *Conversations with Goethe,* 1836-1848, tr. John Oxenford, 1850

To rule is easy; to govern, difficult.

> GOETHE (1749–1832). In Laurence J. Peter, *Peter's People,* 8, 1979

To overlook forms a large part of the work of ruling.

> BALTASAR GRACIÁN (1601–1658). *The Art of Worldly Wisdom,* 88, 1647, tr. Joseph Jacobs, 1943

To earn his keep a good and wise ruler shares the work of tilling the land with his people. He rules while cooking his own meals.

> HSÜ HSING. In Mencius (371?–289? B.C.). *Mencius,* 3.A.4, tr. D. C. Lau, 1970

A prudent ruler ought not to keep faith when by doing so would be against his interest, and when the reasons which made him bind himself no longer exist. If men were all good, this precept would not be a good one; but as they are bad, and would not [keep] faith with you, so you are not bound to keep faith with them.

> MACHIAVELLI (1469–1527). *The Prince,* 18, 1513, tr. Luigi Ricci, 1903

The first impression that one gets of a ruler and of his brains is from seeing the men that he has about him.

> MACHIAVELLI (1469–1527). *The Prince*, 22, 1513, tr. Luigi Ricci, 1903

All rulers remember never to esteem a man so lightly as to believe that, having heaped injuries and insults upon him, he will not seek to revenge himself, even at the risk of his own life.

> MACHIAVELLI (1469–1527). *The Discourses*, 2.28, 1517, tr. Christian E. Detmold, 1940

Bad rulers . . . are in constant fear lest others are conspiring to inflict upon them the punishment which they are conscious of deserving.

> MACHIAVELLI (1469–1527). *The Discourses*, 3.6, 1517, tr. Christian E. Detmold, 1940

In the last analysis, in order to rule one must be a soldier: without spurs and boots, no government.

> NAPOLEON (1769–1821). Remark to Emmanuel Las Cases, 5 July 1816, *The Mind of Napoleon: A Selection from His Written and Spoken Words*, 104, ed. J. Christopher Herold, 1955

One rules men better by their vices than by their virtues.

> NAPOLEON (1769–1821). *In the Words of Napoleon*, p. 84, tr. Daniel Savage Gray, 1977

The secret of rulership is to combine a belief in one's infallibility with the power to learn from past mistakes.

> GEORGE ORWELL (1903–1950). *Nineteen Eighty-Four*, 2.9, 1949

The stronger shall rule, and the weaker be ruled.

> PLATO (427?–347 B.C.). *Laws*, 3.690, tr. Benjamin Jowett, 1894

The ruler who is good for anything ought not to beg his subjects to be ruled by him.

> PLATO (427?–347 B.C.). *The Republic*, 6.489, tr. Benjamin Jowett, 1894

The State in which the rulers are most reluctant to govern is always the best and most quietly governed, and the state in which they are most eager, the worst.

> PLATO (427?–347 B.C.). *The Republic*, 7.520, tr. Benjamin Jowett, 1894

A cheerful obedience is universal when the worthy bear rule.

> PUBLIUS SYRUS (85–43 B.C.). *Moral Sayings*, 632, tr. Darius Lyman, Jr., 1862

Not the least of the qualities that go into the making of a great ruler is the ability of letting others serve him.

> CARDINAL RICHELIEU (1585–1642). *Political Testament*, 1.4

A people always minds its rulers best
When it is neither humored nor oppressed.

> SOLON (630?–560? B.C.). One of the Seven Sages of Greece. In Plutarch (A.D. 46?–119?). "Poplicola and Colon Compared," *Parallel Lives*, Dryden edition, 1693

The aggressiveness of the ruling power inside a society increases with its aggressiveness outside the society.

> HERBERT SPENCER (1820–1903). "The Sins of Legislators," *The Man versus the State*, 1884

It is much safer to obey than to rule.

> THOMAS à KEMPIS (1380–1471). *The Imitation of Christ*, 1.9, tr. Leo Sherley-Price, 1952

Rulers who destroy men's freedom commonly begin by trying to retain its forms. . . . They cherish the illusion that they can combine the prerogatives of absolute power with the moral authority that comes from popular assent.

> ALEXIS de TOCQUEVILLE (1805–1859). *The Old Regime and the French Revolution*, 2.3, 1856, tr. Stuart Gilbert, 1955

Ruling means using force, and using force means doing what the man subjected to violence does not wish done, and to which the perpetrator would certainly object if the violence were applied to himself. Therefore, to rule means to do to others what we would not have done to ourselves—that is, doing wrong.

> LEO TOLSTOY (1828–1910). *The Kingdom of God Is Within You*, 10, 1893, tr. Aylmer Maude, 1936

Rulers always try to draw as many citizens as possible into as much participation as possible in the crimes they commit.

> LEO TOLSTOY (1828–1910). *The Kingdom of God Is Within You*, 12.3, 1893, tr. Aylmer Maude, 1936

Rulers who have adopted the religion favored by the most numerous, or at any rate the most vigorous, section of their subjects have generally prospered, whether actuated by religious sincerity or by political cynicism.

> ARNOLD J. TOYNBEE (1889–1975). *A Study of History*, 1934–1939, abr. D. C. Somervell, 1.562, 1965

The virtue of its ruler is a far greater safeguard to a state than a frontier of inaccessible cliffs.

> WU-TZU. In appendix to Sun-tzu (4th cent. B.C.), *The Art of War*, tr. Samuel B. Griffith, 1963

🌿

If you would rule the world quietly, you must keep it amused.

> ANONYMOUS. In Ralph Waldo Emerson, "the maxim of the tyrant," "New England Reformers," *Essays: Second Series*, 1844

There are those who use their minds and there are those who use their muscles. The former rule; the latter are ruled. Those who rule are supported by those who are ruled.

> SAYING (CHINESE). In Mencius (371?–289? B.C.), *Mencius*, 3.A.4, tr. D. C. Lau, 1970

No ruler sins as long as he is ruler.

> SAYING (GREEK)

No ruler but God.

> SLOGAN (HEBREW). Among followers of Judas of Galilee, A.D. 1st cent. In Hugh Schonfield, *The Essene Odyssey: The Mystery of the True Teacher and the Essene Impact on the Shaping of Human Destiny*, 1.14, 1984

RUMOR

See also • Gossip ○ News ○ Propaganda ○ Publicity

A rumor will travel fastest to the place where it will cause the greatest harm.

> GUSTAVO N. AGRAIT. "Agrait's Law." In Paul Dickson, comp., *The Official Explanations*, p. 2, 1980

The noise of Rumor's thousand tongues.

> THOMAS CARLYLE (1795–1881). "On History," 1830, *Critical and
> Miscellaneous Essays,* Carey & Hart edition, 1849

Every whisper of infamy is industriously circulated, every hint of suspicion eagerly improved, and every failure of conduct joyfully published by those whose interest it is that the eye and voice of the public should be employed on any rather than on themselves.

> SAMUEL JOHNSON (1709–1784). In *The Rambler* (English journal), 76,
> 8 December 1750

Rumor: Rumor is a pipe
Blown by surmises, jealousies, conjectures.

> SHAKESPEARE (1564–1616). Induction (l. 15) to *Henry IV,* Part II, 1597

Doctor: Foul whisperings are abroad.

> SHAKESPEARE (1564–1616). *Macbeth,* 5.1.79, 1605

Be not hasty to believe flying Reports to the Disparagement of any.

> GEORGE WASHINGTON (1732–1799). Copybook, 1748 (at age 16). *Rules
> of Civility & Decent Behaviour in Company and Conversation,* #50. The
> rules were an amended version of Francis Hawkins's 1640 translation of
> *Decency of Conversation Among Men* (French Jesuit writing, 1595).

RUSSIA (SOVIET UNION)

See also • Assassination: Anonymous (Russian) ○ Nations ○
World War II

The whole of Russia is our orchard.

> ANTON CHEKHOV (1860–1904). *The Cherry Orchard,* 2, 1904,
> tr. David Magarshack, 1950

I cannot forecast to you the action of Russia. It is a riddle wrapped in a mystery inside an enigma; but perhaps there is a key. That key is Russian national interest.

> WINSTON CHURCHILL (1874–1965). Radio broadcast, BBC, London,
> 1 October 1939

The Soviet people want full-blooded and unconditional democracy.

> MIKHAIL S. GORBACHEV (1931–). Speech, July 1988

The evolution of the Soviet system itself, or rather the lack of it; the realization, as communications improved, that they could not hope to compete with the West in the post-industrial age; the *embourgeoisement* of the Soviet people.

> MICHAEL HOWARD (1941–). Presenting three of the reasons for the
> Soviet Union's breakup, "Winning the Peace," *Times Literary
> Supplement* (London), 8 January 1993

Russia is a country which it is easy to get into, but very difficult to get out of.

> HENRI de JOMINI (1779–1869). On Napoleon's invasion in 1812.
> In F. W. von Mellenthin, *Panzer Battles,* 10, 1956

The paradox of Russian history lies in the continuing ambivalence between messianic drive and a pervasive sense of insecurity.

> HENRY A. KISSINGER (1923–). *Diplomacy,* 6, 1994

Rule 1, on page 1 of the book of war, is: "Do not march on Moscow!"

> BERNARD LAW MONTGOMERY (1887–1976). In *Hansard* (British
> Government publication), 20 May 1962

Since 1930 I had seen little evidence that the USSR was progressing towards anything that one could truly call Socialism. On the contrary, I was struck by clear signs of its transformation into a hierarchical society, in which the rulers have no more reason to give up their power than any other ruling class.

> GEORGE ORWELL (1903–1950). "Author's Preface to the Ukrainian
> Edition of *Animal Farm,*" March 1947, *The Collected Essays,
> Journalism and Letters of George Orwell,* vol. 3, ed. Sonia Orwell
> and Ian Angus, 1968

In your discussions of the nuclear freeze proposals, I urge you to beware the temptation of pride . . . and the aggressive impulses of an evil empire.

> RONALD REAGAN (1911–). On the Soviet Union, speech before the
> National Association of Evangelicals, Orlando (Florida), 8 March
> 1983. George Lucas popularized the term *evil empire* in his 1977 film,
> *Star Wars.*

Russians watched with fury and envy as a small percentage of people grew rich in an environment of almost general chaos and criminality. Capitalism in Russia had produced far more Al Capones than Henry Fords. . . . In fact, the economy hardly merited the name of capitalism at all, since it operated largely outside the framework of law.

> DAVID REMNICK (1958–). *Resurrection: The Struggle for a New Russia,*
> 3, 1997

This universal, obligatory force-feeding with lies is now the most agonizing aspect of existence in our country—worse than all our material miseries, worse than any lack of civil liberties.

> ALEKSANDR SOLZHENITSYN (1918–). *Letter to the Soviet Leaders,*
> 5, tr. Hilary Sternberg, 1974

Nothing is impossible in Russia but reform.

> OSCAR WILDE (1854–1900). *Vera, or The Nihilists,*
> 1, 1883

SAFETY

See also • Danger ○ Liberty: Benjamin Franklin ○ Mistakes ○
Moderation: Ovid ○ Preparedness ○ Prudence ○ Prudence: Rules
○ Security ○ Speed

Our insignificance is often the cause of our safety.

> AESOP (6th cent. B.C.). "The Great and the Little Fishes," *Fables,*
> tr. Thomas James, 1848

Early and provident fear is the mother of safety.

EDMUND BURKE (1729–1797). House of Commons speech, 11 May 1792

There is always safety in valor.

RALPH WALDO EMERSON (1803–1882). "The Times," *English Traits*, 1856

Fasten your seat belts. It's going to be a bumpy night.

JOSEPH L. MANKIEWICZ (1903–1993). *All About Eve* (film), 1950, spoken by Bette Davis

Be prepared for Truth at all hours and in the most fantastic disguises. This is the only safety.

CHRISTOPHER MORLEY (1890–1957). *Inward Ho!* 1, 1923

If the highest aim of a captain were to preserve his ship, he would keep it in port forever.

ST. THOMAS AQUINAS (A.D. 1225–1274). In Richard M. Nixon, *1999: Victory Without War*, 10, 1988

That cannot be safe which is not honorable.

ANONYMOUS (ROMAN). In Tacitus (A.D. 56?–120?). *The History*, 1.33, tr. Alfred J. Church and William J. Brodribb, 1942

Better safe than sorry.

SAYING (ENGLISH)

Safety first.

SAYING (ENGLISH)

There's safety in numbers.

SAYING

SAINTS

See also • Angels ○ Clergy ○ Mysticism ○ Nonviolence: William James ○ Prophets ○ Religion ○ Spirituality ○ Temptation: Jean Anouilh

The true saint goes in and out amongst the people and eats and sleeps with them and buys and sells in the market and marries and takes part in social intercourse, and never forgets God for a single moment.

ABÛ SA'ÎD IBN ABI 'l-KHAYR (A.D. 967–1049). In Reynold A. Nicholson, *Studies in Islamic Mysticism*, p. 55, 1921

Saint, *n.* A dead sinner revised and edited.

AMBROSE BIERCE (1842–1914). *The Devil's Dictionary*, p. 119, 1911, Dover edition, 1958

Thus say the common people that know him: "A saint abroad, and a devil at home."

JOHN BUNYAN (1628–1688). *The Pilgrim's Progress*, 1.5, 1678–1684

When I feed the hungry, they call me a saint. When I ask why they have no food, they call me a Communist.

ARCHBISHOP HELDER CAMARA (1909–). On his serving the poor in Brazil. In Archbishop John R. Quinn, letter to *New York Times*, 31 March 1991

Jean Tarrou: It comes to this: what interests me is learning how to become a saint.
Bernard Rieux: But you don't believe in God.
Tarrou: Exactly! Can one be a saint without God?—that's the problem, in fact the only problem, I'm up against today.

ALBERT CAMUS (1913–1960). Format adapted. *The Plague*, 4, 1947, tr. Stuart Gilbert, 1948

When they call you a saint, it means basically that you are not to be taken seriously.

DOROTHY DAY (1897–1980). In Peter Steinfels, "Beliefs," *New York Times*, 15 November 1997

The virtues of society are the vices of the saint.

RALPH WALDO EMERSON (1803–1882). "Circles," *Essays: First Series*, 1841

They are not all Saints who use Holy Water.

THOMAS FULLER (1654–1734). Comp., *Gnomologia: Adages and Proverbs*, 4956, 1732

The way of the world is to praise dead saints and to persecute living ones.

NATHANIEL HOWE. Sermon, 1810?

As far as this world goes, anyone who makes an out-and-out saint of himself does so at his peril.

WILLIAM JAMES (1842–1910). *The Varieties of Religious Experience: A Study in Human Nature*, 14 and 15, 1902

Innumerable times [the saints] have proved themselves prophetic. Treating those whom they met, in spite of the past, in spite of all appearances, as worthy, they have stimulated them to *be* worthy, miraculously transformed them by their radiant example and by the challenge of their expectation.

WILLIAM JAMES (1842–1910). *The Varieties of Religious Experience: A Study in Human Nature*, 14 and 15, 1902

No possible degree of holiness or heroism which has ever been recorded of the greatest saints is beyond what [God] is determined to produce in every one of us in the end.

C. S. LEWIS (1898–1963). *Mere Christianity*, rev. ed., 4.9, 1952

A man becomes a saint not by conviction that he is better than sinners but by the realization that he is one of them, and that all together need the mercy of God!

THOMAS MERTON (1915–1968). *New Seeds of Contemplation*, 8, 1961

Be careful in dealing with a man who cares nothing for sensual pleasures, nothing for comfort or praise or promotion, but is simply determined to do what he believes to be right. He is a dangerous and uncomfortable enemy because his body which you can always conquer gives you so little purchase over his soul.

GILBERT MURRAY (1866–1957). Australian-born British scholar. In Louis Fischer, *The Life of Mahatma Gandhi*, 15, 1950

Living with a saint is more grueling than being one.

ROBERT NEVILLE

Saints and poets are hills touched with the dawn while the valley is in darkness.

AUSTIN O'MALLEY (1858–1932)

Many people genuinely do not wish to be saints, and it is probable that some who achieve or aspire to sainthood have never felt much temptation to be human beings.

> GEORGE ORWELL (1903–1950). "Reflections on Gandhi," January 1949, *The Collected Essays, Journalism and Letters of George Orwell*, vol. 4, ed. Sonia Orwell and Ian Angus, 1968

Saints should always be judged guilty until they are proved innocent.

> GEORGE ORWELL (1903–1950). "Reflections on Gandhi," January 1949, *The Collected Essays, Journalism and Letters of George Orwell*, vol. 4, ed. Sonia Orwell and Ian Angus, 1968

It is easier to make a saint out of a libertine than out of a prig.

> GEORGE SANTAYANA (1863–1952). *The Life of Reason or The Phases of Human Progress*, 3.11, 1905–1906

The only difference between the saint and the sinner is that every saint has a past, and every sinner has a future.

> OSCAR WILDE (1854–1900). *A Woman of No Importance*, 3, 1894

[The saintly] leader is the least accommodating to followers. The ancient prophet must deliver the message God gives him, whether it has any effect or not. There is no absolutism like that of the saints. They must please their God, not their followers—but, paradoxically, that is what draws followers.

> GARRY WILLS (1934–). *Certain Trumpets: The Call of Leaders*, 16, 1994

❦

Oh when the saints go marching in.
When the saints go marching in.
Oh Lord, I want to be in their number,
When the saints go marching in.

> ANONYMOUS (BAHAMIAN?). "When the Saints Go Marching In" (spiritual), 19th cent.

The greater the sinner, the greater the saint.

> SAYING (ENGLISH)

Young devil, old saint.

> SAYING (ENGLISH)

Young saint, old devil.

> SAYING (ENGLISH)

Even a saint sins seven times a day.

> SAYING (POLISH)

Many a saint is but a failed sinner.

> SAYING

SALVATION

See also • Church: St. Augustine ∘ Confession ∘ Conversion ∘ Day of Judgment ∘ Evangelism ∘ Forgiveness ∘ God ∘ God & Man ∘ Heaven ∘ Nations: Mohandas K. Gandhi ∘ Redemption ∘ Religion ∘ Repentance ∘ Revelations ∘ Self-Realization (Becoming)

To peoples as to individuals, righteousness is the way of salvation.

> MATTHEW ARNOLD (1822–1888). *Literature and Dogma: An Essay Towards a Better Apprehension of the Bible*, 1873

My salvation is not only bound up with that of other men but also with that of animals, plants, minerals, of every blade of grass—all must be transfigured and brought into the Kingdom of God.

> NICOLAS BERDYAEV (1874–1948). Slightly modified. *The Destiny of Man*, 3.3, 1931, tr. Natalie Duddington, 1955

Grace is necessary to salvation, free will equally so—but grace in order to give salvation, free will in order to receive it.

> ST. BERNARD (A.D. 1090–1153)

All salvation is through Christ.

> SIR THOMAS BROWNE (1605–1682). *Religio Medici*, 1.54, 1642, ed. John Addington Symonds, 1886

There is no personal salvation; there is no national salvation, except through science.

> LUTHER BURBANK (1849–1926). Horticulturist
> See Science: Robert G. Ingersoll (2)

More and more often he catches himself thinking that there is no way to save humanity.
      Is that an attempt to rid himself of responsibility?

> ELIAS CANETTI (1905–1994). 1975, *The Secret Heart of the Clock: Notes, Aphorisms, Fragments: 1973–1985*, tr. Joel Agee, 1989

Salvation is attained not by subscription to metaphysical dogmas, but solely by love of God that fulfills itself in action.

> CHASDAI CRESCAS (1340?–1412). Jewish philosopher. In Victor Gollancz, comp., *Man and God: Passages Chosen and Arranged to Express a Mood About the Human and Divine*, 4.3.1, 1951

Father Zossima: There is only one means of salvation. Make yourself responsible for all men's sins.

> FYODOR DOSTOYEVSKY (1821–1881). *The Brothers Karamazov*, 6.2(f), 1880, tr. Constance Garnett, 1912

Even in the most wretched being there is a tiny hook on which a thread of salvation could be fastened.

> MARIE von EBNER-ESCHENBACH (1830–1916). *Aphorisms*, p. 85, 1880–1905, tr. David Scrase and Wolfgang Mieder, 1994

There is a divine Providence in the world, which will not save us but through our own cooperation.

> RALPH WALDO EMERSON (1803–1882). Closing words, "The Fugitive Slave Law," address, The Tabernacle, New York City, 7 March 1854

The knowledge of sin is the beginning of salvation.

> EPICURUS (341–270 B.C.). In Seneca the Younger (5? B.C.–A.D. 65). "On Travel as a Cure for Discontent," *Moral Letters to Lucilius*, 28.9, tr. Richard M. Gummere, 1918

Good Works will never save you, but you can never be saved without them.

> THOMAS FULLER (1654–1734). Comp., *Gnomologia: Adages and Proverbs*, 1738, 1732

The fabled godly Elephant King . . . was saved only when he thought he was at his last gasp.

> MOHANDAS K. GANDHI (1869–1948). In *Young India*, 4 June 1925

Who e'er aspiring, struggles on,
For him there is salvation.

GOETHE (1749–1832). *Faust,* 5.5 ("Mountain Gorges"), 1808–1832, tr. George Madison Priest, 1959

We never can be sure in advance of any man that his salvation by the way of love is hopeless.

WILLIAM JAMES (1842–1910). *The Varieties of Religious Experience: A Study in Human Nature,* 14 and 15, 1902

See Redemption: Mohandas K. Gandhi

There is a certain uniform deliverance in which religions all appear to meet. It consists of two parts:
1. An uneasiness; and
2. Its solution.
1. The uneasiness, reduced to its simplest terms, is a sense that there is *something wrong about us* as we naturally stand.
2. The solution is a sense that *we are saved from the wrongness* by making proper connection with the higher powers.

WILLIAM JAMES (1842–1910). *The Varieties of Religious Experience: A Study in Human Nature,* 20, 1902

See Self-Realization (Becoming): P. W. Martin (3)

No man has the right to abandon the care of his salvation to another.

THOMAS JEFFERSON (1743–1826). "Notes on Locke and Shaftesbury," 1776

He who endures to the end will be saved.

JESUS (A.D. 1st cent.). *Matthew* 24:13

See Evangelism: Jesus

It is our first duty to serve society, and, after we have done that, we may attend wholly to the salvation of our own souls.

SAMUEL JOHNSON (1709–1784). 15 February 1766. In James Boswell, *The Life of Samuel Johnson,* 1791

Salvation is of the Lord.

JONAH. *Jonah* 2:9 (King James Version)

If left to himself, [man] can naturally bring about his own salvation. Who has produced Christ? Who has produced Buddha?

CARL G. JUNG (1875–1961). 1931. Quoted by Margaret Gildea, "Jung: As Seen by an Editor, a Student and a Disciple." In Ferne Jensen, ed., *C. G. Jung, Emma Jung and Toni Wolff: A Collection of Remembrances,* 1982

Human salvation lies in the hands of the creatively maladjusted.

MARTIN LUTHER KING, JR. (1929–1968). *Strength to Love,* 2.3, 1963

God works by contraries so that a man feels himself to be lost in the very moment when he is on the point of being saved.

MARTIN LUTHER (1483–1546). *Ninety-Five Theses,* 31 October 1517

What [Marx and Lenin] say is that slaves should arise and struggle for truth. There never has been any supreme savior, nor can we rely on gods or emperors. We rely entirely on ourselves for our salvation. Who has created the world of men? We the laboring masses.

MAO TSE-TUNG (1893–1976). "Summary of Chairman Mao's Talk with Responsible Comrades at Various Places during His Provincial Tour," mid-August to September 1971, *Chairman Mao Talks to the People: Talks and Letters: 1956–1971,* tr. John Chinnery and Tieyun and ed. Stuart Schram, 1974

God has willed that we should all depend on one another for our salvation, and all strive together for our own mutual good and our own common salvation.

THOMAS MERTON (1915–N1968). *The Seven Storey Mountain,* 2.1.2, 1948

To ensure moral salvation, it is primarily necessary to *depend* on oneself because in the moment of peril we are *alone.*

MARIA MONTESSORI (1870–1952). *Spontaneous Activity in Education,* 7, tr. Florence Simmonds, 1917

For its effective salvation mankind will need to undergo something like a spontaneous religious conversion: one that will replace the mechanical world picture with an organic world picture, and give to the human personality, as the highest known manifestation of life, the precedence it now gives to its machines and computers. This order of change is as hard for most people to conceive as was the change from the classic power complex of Imperial Rome to that of Christianity, or, later, from supernatural medieval Christianity to the machine-modeled ideology of the seventeenth century. But such changes have repeatedly occurred all through history; and under catastrophic pressure they may occur again. Of only one thing we may be confident. If mankind is to escape its programmed self-extinction the God who saves us will not descend from the machine: he will rise up again in the human soul.

LEWIS MUMFORD (1895–1990). *The Pentagon of Power: The Myth of the Machine,* 14.6, 1970

Nothing can save us but divine intervention.

CHRISTABEL PANKHURST (1880–1958). Speech, California, 1930

Work out your own salvation with fear and trembling; for God is at work in you, both to will and to work for his good pleasure.

PAUL (A.D. 1st cent.). *Philippians* 2:12–13

Salvation and justice are not to be found in revolution, but in evolution through concord.

POPE PIUS XII (1876–1958). In Pope John XXIII, *Pacem in Terris (On Establishing Universal Peace in Truth, Justice, Charity and Liberty),* 162, 11 April 1963

To me the sole hope of human salvation lies in teaching Man to regard himself as an experiment in the realization of God, to regard his hands as God's hands, his brain as God's brain, his purpose as God's purpose. He must regard God as a helpless Longing, which *longed* him into existence by its desperate need for an executive organ.

GEORGE BERNARD SHAW (1856–1950). Letter to Lady Gregory, 19 August 1909

When one sees this universe as ephemeral, one gains true discrimination and turns away from worldliness. The Self becomes the Savior of self.

SRIMAD BHAGAVATAM (5th? cent. B.C.). Hindu scriptures. 11.3, in *The Wisdom of God,* tr. Swami Prabhavananda, 1943

If mankind does respond to the challenge of its present self-imposed ordeal by saving itself from self-inflicted genocide, this will have been the reward of a common effort to transcend all the traditional divisions and to live as one family for the first time since mankind made its . . . appearance on this planet.

ARNOLD J. TOYNBEE (1889–1975). *A Study of History,* 12.143, 1961

Anything We Love Can Be Saved.
> ALICE WALKER (1944–). Book title, 1997

❦

Whoever calls upon the name of the Lord shall be saved.
> ANONYMOUS (*BIBLE*). *Acts* 2:21 (echoing Joel 2:32)

SAN FRANCISCO

See also • Cities ○ California

Isn't it nice that people who prefer Los Angeles to San Francisco live there?
> HERB CAEN (1916–1997)

I regret that I have but one life to live in San Francisco.
> HERB CAEN (1916–). Column marking his "day" and the dedication of Herb Caen Way in San Francisco, where his newspaper column had appeared regularly since 5 July 1938, *San Francisco Chronicle,* 14 June 1996
>
> See Country: Nathan Hale

One day if I do go to heaven, I'm going to do what every San Franciscan does who goes to heaven: he looks around and says, "It ain't bad, but it ain't San Francisco."
> HERB CAEN (1916–). Remarks at the celebration of his "day," Embarcadero, San Francisco, 14 June 1996

I left my heart in San Francisco
High on a hill it calls to me.
To be where little cable cars
Climb halfway to the stars,
The morning fog may chill the air—
I don't care.
> DOUGLAS CROSS and GEORGE CORY. "I Left My Heart in San Francisco" (song), 1954

I went to San Francisco.
I saw the bridges high,
Spun across the water
Like cobwebs in the sky.
> LANGSTON HUGHES (1902–1967). "Trip: San Francisco" (complete poem), 1958, *The Collected Poems of Langston Hughes,* ed. Arnold Rampersad and David Roessel, 1994

San Francisco has only one drawback. 'Tis hard to leave.
> RUDYARD KIPLING (1865–1936). Following a visit

[San Francisco is] a two-day city unless Joe DiMaggio is out of town—then it's one-day.
> LEONARD LYONS (1906–1976). *New York Post* journalist. In Herb Caen, column, *San Francisco Chronicle,* 20 May 1993

While walking on lower Octavia [a street in San Francisco] something kept bothering me. Why would people build such nice Victorians under a freeway?
> STRANGE de JIM. In Herb Caen, column, *San Francisco Chronicle,* 10 February 1974

The coldest winter I ever spent was a summer in San Francisco.
> MARK TWAIN (1835–1910). Attributed

It is an odd thing, but everyone who disappears is said to be seen at San Francisco. It must be a delightful city, and possess all the attractions of the next world.
> OSCAR WILDE (1854–1900). *The Picture of Dorian Gray,* 19, 1891

❦

[After the plane landed, the flight] attendant said, "Ladies and gentlemen, we would like to be the first to welcome you to San Francisco. Unfortunately, this is Las Vegas."
> ANONYMOUS. As reported by Dwayne Chestnut. In Herb Caen, column, *San Francisco Chronicle,* 11 August 1993

SATIRE

See also • Crowds: William Graham Sumner ○ Humor ○ Praise: Lord Chesterfield ○ Ridicule ○ Wit

The difference between a satirist and a humorist is that the satirist shoots to kill while the humorist brings his prey back alive.
> PETER DE VRIES (1910–1993). Interview with the author, March 1964. In Roy Newquist, *Counterpoint,* 1964

Satire is exaggeration and distortion to make a point.
> OLIVER STONE (1946–). Charlie Rose television interview, PBS, 16 August 1994

Satire is a sort of glass, wherein beholders do generally discover everybody's face but their own.
> JONATHAN SWIFT (1667–1745). Preface to *The Battle of the Books,* 1704

In modern America, anyone who attempts to write satirically about the events of the day finds it difficult to concoct a situation so bizarre that it may not actually come to pass while his article is still on the presses.
> CALVIN TRILLIN (1935–). Introduction to *Uncivil Liberties,* 1982

Criticizing a political satirist for being unfair is like criticizing a nose guard for being physical.
> GARRY TRUDEAU (1948–). In Jonathan Alter, "Real Life with Garry Trudeau," *Newsweek,* 15 October 1990

SAYINGS

See also • Aphorisms ○ Axioms ○ Epigrams ○ Maxims ○ Proverbs ○ Quotations

Most collectors of verses and sayings proceed as though they were eating cherries or oysters, choosing the best first, and ending by eating them all.
> CHAMFORT (1741–1794). *Maxims and Thoughts,* 1, 1796, tr. W. S. Merwin, 1984

A transmitter and not a maker.
> CONFUCIUS (551–479 B.C.). Referring to himself and his sayings, *Confucian Analects,* 7.1, tr. James Legge, 1930

Not a tenth Part of this Wisdom was my own . . . , but rather the *Gleanings* I had made of the Sense of all Ages and Nations.

> BENJAMIN FRANKLIN (1706–1790). On the sayings and maxims in his *Poor Richard's Almanack,* "The Way to Wealth," 7 July 1757. Between 1733 and 1758, Franklin published 1044 sayings in his *Almanacks.* He drew them mostly from several popular collections of sayings published in England during the previous 100 years. While modifying and polishing many, he himself, according to Wolgang Mieder (editor of *A Dictionary of American Proverbs,* 1991), coined no more than 20 of the sayings.

Almost every wise saying has an opposite one, no less wise, to balance it.

> GEORGE SANTAYANA (1863–1952)

❦

One saying is worth a thousand words.

> SAYING
>
> See Action & Talk: Tom Warson ○ Photography: Fred R. Barnard ○ Quotations: Diogenes

SCHIZOPHRENIA

See also • Freedom of Speech: Thomas S. Szasz ○ Mental Illness ○ Paranoia ○ Suspicion

Once precipitated into psychosis, the patient has a course to run. He is, as it were, embarked upon a voyage of discovery which is only completed by his return to the normal world, to which he comes back with insights different from those of the inhabitants who never embarked on such a voyage. Once begun, a schizophrenic episode would appear to have as definite a course as an initiation ceremony—a death and rebirth—into which the novice may have been precipitated by his family life or by adventitious circumstance, but which in its course is largely steered by [an internal] process.

> GREGORY BATESON (1904–1980). *Introduction to Perceval's Narrative: A Patient's Account of His Psychosis, 1830–1832,* 1961

Our schizophrenic patient is actually experiencing inadvertently that same beatific ocean deep which the yogi and saint are ever striving to enjoy: except that, whereas they are swimming in it, he is drowning.

> JOSEPH CAMPBELL (1904–1987). "Schizophrenia—the Inward Journey," 1970, *Myths to Live By,* 1972

Schizophrenic symptoms are virtually whatever makes the family unbearably anxious about the tentatively independent behavior of one of its offspring.

> DAVID COOPER (1931–?). *Psychiatry and Anti-Psychiatry,* 1, 1967

Paraphrenics [i.e., schizophrenics] display two fundamental characteristics: megalomania and diversion of their interest from the external world—from people and things. In consequence of the latter change, they become inaccessible to the influence of psychoanalysis and cannot be cured by our efforts.

> SIGMUND FREUD (1856–1939). *On Narcissism: An Introduction,* 1914, tr. James Strachey, 1955

We had a [schizophrenic] patient with whom it was impossible to carry on a sane conversation; he produced only a crazy mixture of delusional ideas and queer words. This man once went down with a serious physical illness, and I expected it would be very difficult to treat him. But not at all. He was entirely changed; he became friendly and obliging, and carried out all the doctor's orders with patience and gratitude. His eyes lost their evil darting looks, and shone quietly and with understanding. One morning I came to his room with the usual greeting: "Good morning, how are you?" But the patient forestalled me with his well-known refrain: "Here comes another of the dog and monkey troupe wanting to play the Savior." Then I knew his physical trouble was over. From that moment the whole of his reason was as if blown away again.

> CARL G. JUNG (1875–1961). "The Content of the Psychoses," 1908, *The Psychogenesis of Mental Disease,* tr. R. F. C. Hull, 1960

Our second patient today, a girl of twenty-nine, also shows marked excitement. When brought into the room, she lets herself slide on the ground, throws herself about, kicks with her legs, claps her hands, plucks at her hair, and makes it untidy, pulls out a whole bunch of it, makes faces, hides her face, and spits round about her. She does not generally react at all when spoken to or pricked with a needle, but resists violently if you try to take her hand or to pour water on her. She obeys no kind of orders.

> EMIL KRAEPELIN (1856–1926). Describing (in her presence) a patient with "katatonic excitement" to a class of medical students, *Lectures on Clinical Psychiatry,* 9, 1904?, 3rd English edition, rev. and ed. Thomas Johnstone, 1913

Clinical Biography of a Schizophrenic. . . .
1. The patient was a *good,* normal, healthy child; until she gradually began
2. To be *bad,* to do or say things that caused great distress, and which were on the whole "put down" to naughtiness or bad ness, until
3. This went beyond all tolerable limits so that she could only be regarded as completely *mad.*

> R. D. LAING (1927–1989). *The Divided Self: An Existential Study of Sanity and Madness,* 11, 1960

Without exception the experience and behavior that gets labeled schizophrenic is *a special strategy a person invents in order to live in an unlivable situation.* In his life situation the person has come to feel he is in an untenable position. He cannot make a move, or make no move, without being beset by contradictory and paradoxical pressures and demands, pushes and pulls, both internally from himself, and externally from those around him. He is, as it were, in a position of checkmate.

> R. D. LAING (1927–1989). *The Politics of Experience,* 5, 1967

Research into the origins of schizophrenia is hunting a hare whose tracks are in the mind of the hunters.

> R. D. LAING (1927–1989). "The Study of Family and Social Contexts," 1967, *The Politics of the Family and Other Essays,* 1969

The attribution to the other of an incapacity to form a human relationship was and is *the* basis for the diagnosis of schizophrenia.

> R. D. LAING (1927–1989). *Wisdom, Madness & Folly: The Making of a Psychiatrist,* 1, 1985

I avoid using words like schizophrenia just as I avoid using words like "wop" and "nigger."

> KARL MENNINGER (1893–1990). Psychiatrist. "Psychiatrists Use
> Dangerous Words," *Saturday Evening Post,* 25 April 1964

One modern theory of schizophrenia suggests that sufferers lack some aspect of selective discrimination. Overwhelmed by stimuli which they can neither order nor disregard, they are compelled to withdraw as far as possible from the impact of the world.

> ANTHONY STORR (1920–). *Churchill's Black Dog, Kafka's Mice, and
> Other Phenomena of the Human Mind,* 7, 1988

"Schizophrenia" is a strategic label, like "Jew" was in Nazi Germany. If you want to exclude people from the social order you must justify this to others but especially to yourself. So you invent a justificatory rhetoric. That's what the really nasty psychiatric words are all about: they are justificatory rhetoric, legitimizing the removal of the people so labeled from society. It's like labeling a package "garbage"; it means, "take it away," "get it out of my sight," etc. That's what the word "Jew" meant in Nazi Germany; it did not mean a person with a certain kind of religious belief. It meant "vermin," "gas him!" I am afraid that "schizophrenia" and "sociopathic personality" and many other psychiatric diagnostic terms mean exactly the same thing.

> THOMAS S. SZASZ (1920–). Jon Ecker interview, *New Physician,* June
> 1969

If you talk to God, you are praying; if God talks to you, you have schizophrenia.

> THOMAS S. SZASZ (1920–). "Schizophrenia," *The Second Sin,* 1973

The symbol that most specifically characterizes psychiatrists as members of a distinct group of doctors is the concept of schizophrenia; and the ritual that does so most clearly is their diagnosing this disease in persons who do not want to be their patients.

> THOMAS S. SZASZ (1920–). Preface to *Schizophrenia: The Sacred
> Symbol of Psychiatry,* 1976

The claim that some people have a disease called schizophrenia (and that some, presumably, do not) was based not on any medical discovery but on medical authority, that it was, in other words, the result not of empirical or scientific work, but of ethical and political decision making.

> THOMAS S. SZASZ (1920–). *Schizophrenia: The Sacred Symbol of
> Psychiatry,* 1, 1976

The old philosophy was that parents, especially mothers, caused their kids to become schizophrenic. Now we see that when a kid is this crazy, he'll make the family begin to seem crazy.

> JOHN TALBOTT (1935–). Psychiatrist. In Erik Eckholm, "Schizophrenia's
> Victims Include Strained Families, *New York Times,* 17 March 1986

It is now known that schizophrenia and manic-depressive illness are brain diseases, with structural and functional brain changes, just as multiple sclerosis, Parkinson's disease, and Alzheimer's disease are. As with these other diseases we do not yet know the precise neurochemical, neuropathological, and genetic sequence of causal events, but it *is* clear that these events are biological in nature.

> E. FULLER TORREY (1937–). Psychiatrist. "The Mental-Health Mess,"
> *National Review,* 28 December 1992

❦

Schizophrenia is caused by the fact that young people no longer obey their parents.

> ANONYMOUS. In *Journal of Mental Science,* 1904. Quoted in David
> Cooper, *Psychiatry and Anti-Psychiatry,* 3 (epigraph), 1967

Schizophrenia is a term psychiatrists hang on people who won't knuckle under to their authority.

> ANONYMOUS

SCHOLARS

See also • Education ○ Intellectuals ○ Knowledge ○ Learning (Process) ○ Philosophers ○ Reading: Arthur Schopenhauer (1) ○ Study ○ Teachers ○ Thinkers ○ Wisdom: Montaigne

It is the way of scholars to show all they know and oppose further information.

> FRANCIS BACON (1561–1626). *Advancement of Learning,* 6.3 (Learning),
> 1605, Willey Book edition, 1944

A mechanic is driven by his work all day, but it ends at night; it has an end. But the scholar's work has none.

> RALPH WALDO EMERSON (1803–1882). Journal, 1845, undated

A Scholar is a man with this inconvenience, that when you ask him his opinion of any matter, he must go home and look up his manuscripts to know.

> RALPH WALDO EMERSON (1803–1882). Journal, July 1855

A learned blockhead is a greater blockhead than an ignorant one.

> BENJAMIN FRANKLIN (1706–1790). *Poor Richard's Almanack,* November
> 1734
>
> See Books: Alexander Pope

Tim was so learned that he could name a Horse in nine Languages: So ignorant, that he bought a Cow to ride on.

> BENJAMIN FRANKLIN (1706–1790). *Poor Richard's Almanack,* November
> 1750

I begin by taking. I shall find scholars afterwards to demonstrate my perfect right.

> FREDERICK II (1712–1786). Remark to his ministers, 1756

It is the vice of scholars to suppose that there is no knowledge in the world but that of books.

> WILLIAM HAZLITT (1778–1830). "On the Conduct of Life," *Literary
> Remains,* 1836

He that lives well is learned enough.

> GEORGE HERBERT (1593–1633). Comp., *Outlandish Proverbs,*
> 86, 1640

To talk in public, to think in solitude, to read and to hear, to inquire and answer inquiries, is the business of a scholar. He wanders about the world without pomp or terror, and is neither known nor valued but by men like himself.

> SAMUEL JOHNSON (1709–1784). *Rasselas: The Prince of Abyssinia,*
> 8, 1759

Who are the learned? [Those] who practice what they know.

> MUHAMMAD (A.D. 570?–632). *The Sayings of Muhammad,* 294, tr. Abdullah Al-Suhrawardy, 1941

Learned men are the cisterns of knowledge, not the fountainheads.

> JAMES NORTHCOTE (1746–1831). In William Hazlitt, "Conversation the Fourth," *Conversations of James Northcote, Esq., R.A.,* 1830

The joy of the pedant who has found out some useless fact.

> GEORGE ORWELL (1903–1950). *Nineteen Eighty-Four,* 3.1., 1949

A scholar without practice is a tree without fruit.

> SA'DI (A.D. 1213?–1292). *The Gulistan, or Rose Garden,* 8 (Maxim 50), A.D. 1258, tr. Edward Rehatsek, 1964

The scholars learn, not for the sake of knowledge and insight, but to be able to chatter and give themselves airs.

> ARTHUR SCHOPENHAUER (1788–1860). "The Art of Literature: On Men of Learning," *Essays of Arthur Schopenhauer,* tr. T. Bailey Saunders, 1851

A learned man is an idler who kills time with study.

> GEORGE BERNARD SHAW (1856–1950). "Maxims for Revolutionists: Education," *Man and Superman,* 1903

Scholars are wont to sell their birthright for a mess of learning.

> HENRY DAVID THOREAU (1817–1862). "Sunday," *A Week on the Concord and Merrimack Rivers,* 1849

The scholar may be sure that he writes the tougher truth for the calluses on his palms.

> HENRY DAVID THOREAU (1817–1862). "Sunday," *A Week on the Concord and Merrimack Rivers,* 1849

❦

Scholars should not study so much that they have no time to think.

> ANONYMOUS (JEWISH)

Not every sage is a scholar; nor is every scholar a sage.

> ANONYMOUS

A mere scholar, a mere ass.

> SAYING (ENGLISH)

SCHOOL

See also • College ○ Education ○ Learning (Process) ○ Teachers ○ University

When a youngster like Lincoln sought to educate himself, the immediately available obvious things for him to learn were the Bible, Shakespeare and Euclid. Was he really worse off than those who try to find their way through the technical smorgasbord of the current school system, with its utter inability to distinguish between important and unimportant in any way other than by the demands of the market?

> ALLAN BLOOM (1930–1992). "The Clean Slate," *The Closing of the American Mind: How Higher Education Has Failed Democracy and Impoverished the Souls of Today's Students,* 1987

"Reeling and Writhing, of course, to begin with," the Mock Turtle replied [to the question of what was taught in school], "and then the different branches of Arithmetic—Ambition, Distraction, Uglification, and Derision."

> LEWIS CARROLL (1832–1898). *Alice's Adventures in Wonderland,* 9, 1865

The sheltering of upper income children in private schools not only accelerates the deterioration of public education, it hides its consequences from precisely those people who could do something about it.

> HODDING CARTER (1935–). "In Public Schools, Class Will Tell," *New York Times,* 13 June 1990

To be in the weakest camp is to be in the strongest school.

> G. K. CHESTERTON (1874–1936). *Heretics,* 5, 1905

The school's major function is to teach all the children their "place" in the status ordering of the community. Its input is all the children. Its output is youths who know their place. . . .

No school that is too successful in teaching children not to be prejudiced can continue to be supported by the power order of the society.

> DAN W. DODSON. "An Urgent Concern," *Saturday Review,* 15 May 1965

Twenty years of schoolin'
And they put you on the day shift.

> BOB DYLAN (1941–). "Subterranean Homesick Blues" (song), 1965

[Public school graduates] go forth . . . into a world of whose richness and subtlety they have no conception. They go forth into it with well-developed bodies, fairly developed minds, and undeveloped hearts.

> E. M. FORSTER (1879–1970). "Notes on the English Character," *Abinger Harvest: A Miscellany,* 1927. "Public school" is the British term for private, boarding school.

At a good Table we may go to School.

> THOMAS FULLER (1654–1734). Comp., *Gnomologia: Adages and Proverbs,* 823, 1732

The long schooling is a way of keeping the young on ice.

> PAUL GOODMAN (1911–1972). "The Empty Society," *Commentary,* October 1966

Cuis servire est regnare is Groton's motto. "To serve is to rule." The overt teaching was that the finest life is service to God, your family and your state, but the covert teaching, far more subtle and insidious, was somewhat different: ultimately, strength is more important; there is a ruling clique; there is a thing called privilege. . . . That is the real world and it is going to remain that way, so you might as well get used to it.

> DAVID HALBERSTAM (1934–). On the prestigious prep school in Massachusetts attended by some of the leading members of the Washington elite during the 1960s, *The Best and the Brightest,* 4, 1972

School is an institution built on the axiom that learning is the result of teaching. And institutional wisdom continues to accept this axiom, despite overwhelming evidence to the contrary.

> IVAN ILLICH (1926–). *Deschooling Society,* 2.2, 1970

Everywhere the hidden curriculum of schooling initiates the citizens to the myth that bureaucracies guided by scientific knowledge are efficient and benevolent. Everywhere this same curriculum instills in the pupil the myth that increased production will provide a better life.

> IVAN ILLICH (1926–). *Deschooling Society,* 6, 1970

School is about two parts ABCs to fifty parts Where Do I Stand in the Great Pecking Order of Humankind.

> BARBARA KINGSOLVER (1955–). "Life Without Go-Go Boots," 1990, *High Tide in Tucson: Essays from Now or Never,* 1996

You must adjust. . . . This is the legend imprinted in every schoolbook, the invisible message on every blackboard. Our schools have become vast factories for the manufacture of robots.

> ROBERT LINDNER (1914–1956). Title essay (3), *Must You Conform?* 1956

The school system, custodian of print culture, has no place for the rugged individual. It is, indeed, the homogenizing hopper into which we toss our integral tots for processing.

> MARSHALL McLUHAN (1911–1980). "Cervantes confronted typographic man in the figure of Don Quixote," *The Gutenberg Galaxy: The Making of Typographic Man,* 1962
>
> See Individualism: Herbert Hoover

My grandmother wanted me to have an education, so she kept me out of school.

> MARGARET MEAD (1901–1978). In Barb Lundgren, comp., *MINDFULL Quotations,* unpaged, 1997

[Most of our schools] are a real jail of captive youth.

> MONTAIGNE (1533–1592). "Of the Education of Children," *Essays,* 1588, tr. Donald M. Frame, 1958

[A school should be] a prepared environment in which the child, set free from undue adult intervention, can live its life according to the laws of its development.

> MARIA MONTESSORI (1870–1952). In E. M. Standing, *Maria Montessori: Her Life and Work,* 7, 1957

Show me a man who has enjoyed his schooldays, and I'll show you a bully and a bore.

> ROBERT MORLEY (1908–1992). British actor

One of the marks of the new school and the new university will be the provision of hours of withdrawal, not spent in classroom study or in sport, in the midst of its regular work day: a period of concentration and reflection, in which the work of active selection and spiritual assimilation can go on.

> LEWIS MUMFORD (1895–1990). *The Conduct of Life,* 9.4, 1951

Virtue consisted in winning: it consisted in being bigger, stronger, handsomer, richer, more popular, more elegant, more unscrupulous than other people—in dominating them, bullying them, making them suffer pain, making them look foolish, getting the better of them in every way. Life was hierarchical and whatever happened was right. There were the strong, who deserved to win and always did win, and there were the weak, who deserved to lose and always did lose, everlastingly.

> GEORGE ORWELL (1903–1950). Describing with bitterness the values of St. Cyprian's, the Scottish boarding school he attended on a scholarship between his eighth and twelfth years, "Such, Such Were the Joys" (5), September-October 1952 (written in 1947), *The Collected Essays, Journalism and Letters of George Orwell,* vol. 4, ed. Sonia Orwell and Ian Angus, 1968

School is an invaluable adjunct to the home, but it is a wretched substitute for it.

> THEODORE ROOSEVELT (1858–1919). In Hermann Hagedorn and Sidney Wallach, "Signposts for Americans: Character and Conduct," *A Theodore Roosevelt Round-Up,* 1958

Ask not what your school can do for you, but what you can do for your school.

> GEORGE ST. JOHN. Choate School headmaster. A favorite saying.
> Pres. Kennedy attended Choate during St. John's tenure. In G. William Domhoff, *Who Rules America Now?: A View for the '80's,* 2, 1983
> See Country: John F. Kennedy

My schooling did me a great deal of harm and no good whatever; it was simply dragging a child's soul through the dirt.

> GEORGE BERNARD SHAW (1856–1950). "School," *Parents and Children,* 1914

My schooling not only failed to teach me what it professed to be teaching, but prevented me from being educated to an extent which infuriates me when I think of all I might have learned at home by myself.

> GEORGE BERNARD SHAW (1856–1950). *Everybody's Political What's What?* 22, 1944

The schools teach only one side of their subjects; and until their graduates know both sides they had better know nothing.

> GEORGE BERNARD SHAW (1856–1950). *Everybody's Political What's What?* 24, 1944

I have never let my schooling interfere with my education.

> MARK TWAIN (1835–1910). Attributed. *Everyone's Mark Twain,* p. 553, ed. Caroline Thomas Harnsberger, 1948

In the field of public education, the doctrine of "separate but equal" has no place. Separate educational facilities are inherently unequal.

> EARL WARREN (1891–1974). *Brown v. Board of Education of Topeka, Kansas,* 1954

Schools, as they are now regulated, are the hotbeds of vice and folly, and the knowledge of human nature, supposed to be attained there, merely cunning selfishness.

> MARY WOLLSTONECRAFT (1759–1797). *A Vindication of the Rights of Woman,* 12, 1792

The first gold star a child gets in school for the mere performance of a needful task is its first lesson in graft.

> PHILIP WYLIE (1902–1971). *Generation of Vipers,* 7, 1942

SCIENCE

See also • Civilization ○ Communications ○ Computers ○ Creativity ○ Creativity: First Person ○ Discovery ○ Experts ○ Intellectuals ○ Inventions ○ Machines ○ Philosophy ○ Principles, Theoretical: Thomas Paine ○ Progress ○ Religion & Science ○ Space ○ Superstition ○ Technology

I firmly believe that before many centuries more, science will be the master of man. The engines he will have invented will be beyond his strength to control. Some day science may have the existence of mankind in its power, and the human race commit suicide by blowing up the world.

> HENRY ADAMS (1838–1918). Letter to his brother George, 11 April 1862. In Leo Marx, *The Machine in the Garden: Technology and the Pastoral Ideal in America,* 5.5, 1964

When I am in the company of scientists, I feel like a shabby curate who has strayed by mistake into a drawing room full of dukes.

> W. H. AUDEN (1907–1973). "The Poet and the City," *The Dyer's Hand and Other Essays,* 1962

Experimentation must always be devised in view of a preconceived idea, no matter if the idea be not very clear nor very well-defined. As for noting the results of the experiment, . . . we must here, as always, observe without a preconceived idea.

> CLAUDE BERNARD (1813–1878). *An Introduction to the Study of Experimental Medicine,* 1.1.6, 1865, tr. Henry Copley Greene, 1927

The revolution which the experimental method has affected in the sciences is this: It has put a scientific criterion in the place of personal authority.

> CLAUDE BERNARD (1813–1878). *An Introduction to the Study of Experimental Medicine,* 1.2.4, 1865, tr. Henry Copley Greene, 1927

That is the essence of science: ask an impertinent question, and you are on the way to a pertinent answer.

> JACOB BRONOWSKI (1908–1974). *The Ascent of Man,* 4, 1973

Science is wonderfully equipped to answer the question "how?" but it gets terribly confused when you ask the question "why?"

> ERWIN CHARGAFF (1905–). In *Columbia Forum,* Summer 1969

$E=mc^2$.

> ALBERT EINSTEIN (1879–1955). The equation for his theory of relativity (energy equals mass times the speed of light squared), "Ist die Traeit einer Korpers von seinem Energiegehalt Abhängig?" *Annalen der Physik,* 1905.

The grand aim of all science is to cover the greatest number of empirical facts by logical deduction from the smallest number of hypotheses or axioms.

> ALBERT EINSTEIN (1879–1955). In Lincoln Barnett, "The Meaning of Einstein's New Theory," *Life,* 9 January 1950

If I would be a young man again and had to decide how to make my living, I would not try to become a scientist or scholar or teacher. I would rather choose to be a plumber or a peddler in the hope to find that modest degree of independence still available under present circumstances.

> ALBERT EINSTEIN (1879–1955). Letter to *Reporter,* 18 November 1954 (Popular version: If only I had known, I would have become a watchmaker.)

When a man sits with a pretty girl for an hour, it seems like a minute. But let him sit on a hot stove for a minute—and it's longer than any hour. That's relativity.

> ALBERT EINSTEIN (1879–1955). Explaining tongue-in-cheek his theory of relativity, recalled on his death, 18 April 1955

Science is no illusion. But it would be an illusion to suppose that we could get anywhere else what it cannot give us.

> SIGMUND FREUD (1856–1939). Closing words, *The Future of an Illusion,* 1927, tr. W. D. Robson-Scott, 1953
>
> See Knowledge: Freud

The reason for so much bad science is not that talent is rare, not at all; what is rare is character.

> SIGMUND FREUD (1856–1939). 3 January 1935. In Joseph Wortis, *Fragments of an Analysis with Freud,* 1954

Science has radically changed the conditions of human life on earth. It has expanded our knowledge and our power but not our capacity to use them with wisdom.

> J. WILLIAM FULBRIGHT (1905–1995). *Old Men and New Realities,* 5, 1964

[Science] has challenged the super-eminence of religion; it has turned all philosophy out of doors except that which clings to its skirts; it has thrown contempt on all learning that does not depend on it; and it has bribed the skeptics by giving us immense material comforts.

> KATHERINE FULLERTON GEROULD (1879–1944). *Modes and Morals,* 4, 1920

Science is the knowledge of Consequences, and dependence of one fact upon another.

> THOMAS HOBBES (1588–1679). *Leviathan,* 5, 1651

Science . . . takes no cognizance of the things that make life worth living, for the simple reason that beauty, love, and so on, are not measurable quantities, and science deals only with what can be measured.

> ALDOUS HUXLEY (1894–1963). "Pascal" (23), *Do What You Will: Twelve Essays,* 1929

The man of science has learned to believe in justification, not by faith, but by verification.

> T. H. HUXLEY (1825–1895). "On the Advisableness of Improving Natural Knowledge," 1866, *Lay Sermons, Addresses and Reviews,* 1870

The great tragedy of Science—the slaying of a beautiful hypothesis by an ugly fact.

> T. H. HUXLEY (1825–1895). "Biogenesis and Abiogenesis," 1870, *Critiques and Addresses,* 1873

Reason, Observation, and Experience—the Holy Trinity of Science.

> ROBERT G. INGERSOLL (1833–1899). "Science," *The Philosophy of Ingersoll,* ed. Vere Goldthwaite, 1906

Science has founded the only true religion. Science is the only redemption of this world.

> ROBERT G. INGERSOLL (1833–1899). "Science," *The Philosophy of Ingersoll,* ed. Vere Goldthwaite, 1906
>
> See Salvation: Luther Burbank

Science is not . . . a perfect instrument, but it is a superb and invaluable tool that works harm only when taken as an end in itself.

> CARL G. JUNG (1875–1961). Introduction (1) to *Commentary* (on *The Secret of the Golden Flower*), 1929, tr. Cary F. Baynes, 1961

I am sorry to say that there is too much point to the wisecrack that life is extinct on other planets because their scientists were more advanced than ours.

> JOHN F. KENNEDY (1917–1963). Speech, Washington, 11 December 1959

We have genuflected before the god of science only to find that it has given us the atomic bomb, producing fears and anxieties that science can never mitigate.

> MARTIN LUTHER KING, JR. (1929–1968). Strength to Love, 13.3, 1963

If a scientist uncovers a publishable fact, it will become central to his theory.

> MANN'S LAW. In Albert Bloch, comp., "Advanced Researchmanship," Murphy's Law, Book Two, 1980

To study any subject scientifically one needs a detached attitude, which is obviously harder when one's own interests or emotions are involved.

> GEORGE ORWELL (1903–1950). "Antisemitism in Britain," February 1945, The Collected Essays, Journalism and Letters of George Orwell, vol. 3, ed. Sonia Orwell and Ian Angus, 1968

Science is built up of facts, as a house is built of stones; but an accumulation of facts is no more a science than a heap of stones is a house.

> HENRI POINCARÉ (1854–1912). Science and Hypothesis, 9, 1905

It is his intuition, his mystical insight into the nature of things, rather than his reasoning which makes a great scientist.

> KARL R. POPPER (1902–1994). The Open Society and Its Enemies, 2.24.1, 1945

The work of science is to substitute facts for appearances, and demonstrations for impressions.

> JOHN RUSKIN (1819–1900). The Stones of Venice, 3.2.8, 1851–1853

The sciences have developed in an order the reverse of what might have been expected. What was most remote from ourselves was first brought under the domain of law, and then, gradually, what was nearer: first the heavens, next the earth, then animal and vegetable life, then the human body, and last of all (as yet very imperfectly) the human mind.

> BERTRAND RUSSELL (1872–1970). Religion and Science, 3, 1935

Science is what we know, and philosophy is what we don't know.

> BERTRAND RUSSELL (1872–1970). "Philosophy for Laymen," Unpopular Essays, 1950

If you have a good scientific imagination, you can think of all sorts of things that might be true, and that's the essence of science. You first think of something that might be true—then you look to see if it is, and generally it isn't.

> BERTRAND RUSSELL (1872–1970). Woodrow Wyatt television interview, BBC, London, 1959, Bertrand Russell Speaks His Mind, 1, 1960

The test of science is predictability.

> ARTHUR M. SCHLESINGER, JR. (1917–). "The Historian as Artist," Atlantic, July, 1963

Science is organized knowledge.

> HERBERT SPENCER (1820–1903). Education: Intellectual, Moral, and Physical, 2, 1860

There should be no articles of faith in science, unless it be the faith that no discovery, no law, is so absolute that it cannot be superseded.

> ANTHONY STORR (1920–). Feet of Clay: Saints, Sinners, and Madmen: A Study of Gurus, 10, 1996

Everywhere order reigns, so that when some circumstances have been noted we can foresee that others will be present. The progress of science consists in observing these interconnections and in showing with a patient ingenuity that the events of this ever-shifting world are but examples of a few general connections or relations called laws. To see what is general in what is particular and what is permanent in what is transitory is the aim of scientific thought.

> ALFRED NORTH WHITEHEAD (1861–1947). An Introduction to Mathematics, 1, 1911

A science which hesitates to forget its founders is lost.

> ALFRED NORTH WHITEHEAD (1861–1947)

I like the scientific spirit—the holding off, the being sure but not too sure, the willingness to surrender ideas when the evidence is against them: this is ultimately fine—it always keeps the way beyond open.

> WALT WHITMAN (1819–1892). Remark to the author, 4 May 1888. In Horace Traubel, Walt Whitman's Camden Conversations, ed. Walter Teller, 1973

I have great faith in science—real science: The science that is the science of the soul as well as the science of the body (you know many men of half sciences seem to forget the soul).

> WALT WHITMAN (1819–1892). Remark to the author, 4 August 1888. In Horace Traubel, Walt Whitman's Camden Conversations, ed. Walter Teller, 1973

Man has to awaken to wonder—and so perhaps do peoples. Science is a way of sending him to sleep again.

> LUDWIG WITTGENSTEIN (1889–1951). 1930. Culture and Value, 1977, tr. Peter Winch, 1980

"Scientism"—authority set above free inquiry.

> PHILIP WYLIE (1902–1971). Generation of Vipers, 10, 1942

SCOTLAND

See also • Nations ○ Prejudice: James Boswell

The grandest moral attribute of a Scotsman, Maggie, that he'll do nothing which might damage his career.

> J. M. BARRIE (1860–1937). What Every Woman Knows, 1908

Treacherous Scotland, to no interest true.

> JOHN DRYDEN (1631–1700). "Death of Oliver Cromwell," 17, 1658

To make a Scotchman valiant, let him be back'd by an Englishman.

> JAMES HOWELL (1593–1666). Comp., "Divers Centuries of New Sayings" (p. 6), Paroimiographia: Proverbs, or Old Sayed Sawes & Adages in English . . . Italian, French and Spanish, 1659

OATS—A grain which in England is generally given to horses, but in Scotland supports the people.

> SAMUEL JOHNSON (1709–1784). Preface to A Dictionary of the English Language, 1755

The noblest prospect which a Scotchman ever sees is the high road that leads him to England!

> SAMUEL JOHNSON (1709–1784). 6 July 1763. In James Boswell, *The Life of Samuel Johnson*, 1791

Much may be made of a Scotchman, if he be *caught* young.

> SAMUEL JOHNSON (1709–1784). Spring 1772. In James Boswell, *The Life of Samuel Johnson*, 1791

SCOUNDRELS

See also • Knaves ○ Middle Age: George Bernard Shaw ○ Normality: Franz Kafka ○ Patriotism: Samuel Johnson ○ Persecution: Paul Eldridge ○ Rogues

If we had done for ourselves what we have done for Italy, what scoundrels we would have been.

> CONTE CAMILLO BENSO di CAVOUR (1810–1861). Italian statesman. In Edward J. Conry, "The Indivisibility of Ethics," *New York Times*, 3 March 1991

As long as a scoundrel is illustrious he can count on the support of most men.

> FREDERICK II (1712–1786). *Anti-Machiavel*, 6, 1740, tr. Paul Sonnino, 1981

It is possible to be a great scoundrel without ever doing anything that is forbidden.

> HERMANN HESSE (1877–1962). *Reflections*, 105, ed. Volker Michels, 1974

A scoundrel is a person who pursues his or her own personal gratification without regard to the feelings and interests of others.

> GEORGE BERNARD SHAW (1856–1950). *Everybody's Political What's What?* 38, 1944

SCRIPTURE

See also • Bible ○ Dreams: D. Simpson ○ Religion

When thy mind leaves behind its dark forest of delusion, thou shalt go beyond the scriptures of times past.

> *BHAGAVAD GITA* (6th cent. B.C.). 2.52, tr. Juan Mascaró, 1962

You rule the Scripture, not the Scripture you.

> JOHN DRYDEN (1631–1700). *The Hind and the Panther*, 2.769, 1687

I think that in the discussion of natural problems we ought to begin not with the Scriptures, but with experiments and demonstrations.

> GALILEO (1564–1642). *The Authority of Scripture in Philosophical Controversies*

Search the scriptures.

> JESUS (A.D. 1st cent.). *John* 5:39

All Scripture is inspired by God and profitable for teaching, for reproof, for correction, and for training in righteousness, that the man of God may be complete, equipped for every good work.

> PAUL (A.D. 1st cent.). *2 Timothy* 3:16

There is something nearer to us than Scriptures, to wit, the Word in the heart from which all Scriptures come.

WILLIAM PENN (1644–1718). In Aldous Huxley, *The Perennial Philosophy*, 1, 1946

There is one Lord revealed in many scriptures.

> SARAHA. Buddhist saint. "Saraha's Treasury of Songs." In Edward Conze, ed., *Buddhist Texts Through the Ages*, p. 79, 1954

Antonio: The devil can cite Scripture for his purpose.

> SHAKESPEARE (1564–1616). *The Merchant of Venice*, 1.3.99, 1596

Obey the Scriptures until you are strong enough to do without them.

> SWAMI VIVEKANANDA (1863–1902). In Christopher Isherwood, ed., introduction to *Vedanta for the Western World*, 1945

SCULPTURE

See also • Art ○ Creativity

When Michelangelo in the traditional story explained that he carved his statue of David simply by taking away the superfluous marble, he meant that his peculiar vision dwelt somehow in that particular block of stone.

> DANIEL J. BOORSTIN (1914–). *The Image: A Guide to Pseudo-Events in America*, 5 (introduction), 1961

A sculptor wields
The chisel, and the stricken marble grows
To beauty.

> WILLIAM CULLEN BRYANT (1794–1878). *The Flood of Years*, l. 42, 1878

I've seen much finer women, ripe and real,
Than all the nonsense of their stone ideal.

> LORD BYRON (1788–1824). *Don Juan*, 2.118, 1819–1824

The value of statuary is owing to its difficulty. You would not value the finest head cut upon a carrot.

> SAMUEL JOHNSON (1709–1784). 19 March 1776. In James Boswell, *The Life of Samuel Johnson*, 1791

It is only well with me when I have a chisel in my hand.

> MICHELANGELO (1475–1564)

One who loves a statue loves not the clay, not the plaster or the bronze, but the achievement of the sculptor's mind.

> ANTOINE de SAINT-EXUPÉRY (1900–1944). *The Wisdom of the Sands*, 4, 1948, tr. Stuart Gilbert, 1950

Dr. Josiah Bartlett handed me a paper today, desiring me to subscribe for a statue to Horace Mann. I declined, and said that I thought a man ought not any more to take up room in the world after he was dead.

> HENRY DAVID THOREAU (1817–1862). Journal, 18 September 1859

From my pillow, looking forth by light
Of moon or favoring stars, I could behold
The antechapel where the statue stood
Of Newton with his prism and silent face,
The marble index of a mind for ever
Voyaging through strange seas of Thought, alone.

> WILLIAM WORDSWORTH (1770–1850). *The Prelude; or, Growth of a Poet's Mind: An Autobiographical Poem*, 3.58, 1850

❧

The better the sculptor, the fewer the chips.
SAYING

SEA

See also • Nature ○ Navy ○ Ships

Water, water, everywhere,
And all the boards did shrink;
Water, water, everywhere,
Nor any drop to drink.
SAMUEL TAYLOR COLERIDGE (1772–1834). *The Rime of the Ancient Mariner*, 2, 1798 (Popular version: Water, water everywhere but not a drop to drink.)

The ocean is a large drop; the drop, a small ocean.
RALPH WALDO EMERSON (1803–1882). Journal, 24 June 1836

A drop of water has the properties of the sea, but cannot exhibit a storm.
RALPH WALDO EMERSON (1803–1882). "Swedenborg; or The Mystic," *Representative Men*, 1850

I discovered the secret of the sea in meditation upon the dewdrop.
KAHLIL GIBRAN (1883–1931). "Sayings," *Spiritual Sayings of Kahlil Gibran*, tr. Anthony R. Ferris, 1962

The Old Man and the Sea.
ERNEST HEMMINGWAY (1899–1961). Book title, 1952

He that will learn to pray let him go to Sea.
GEORGE HERBERT (1593–1633). Comp., *Outlandish Proverbs*, 84, 1640

"Would'st thou"—so the helmsman answered,
   "Learn the secret of the sea?
Only those who brave its dangers
   Comprehend its mystery!"
HENRY WADSWORTH LONGFELLOW (1807–1882). "The Secret of the Sea" (8), *The Seaside and the Fireside*, 1850

Ishmael: Whenever I find myself growing grim about the mouth; whenever it is a damp, drizzly November in my soul; whenever I find myself involuntarily pausing before coffin warehouses, and bringing up the rear of every funeral I meet; and especially whenever my hypos get such an upper hand of me, that it requires a strong moral principle to prevent me from deliberately stepping into the street, and methodically knocking people's hat off—then, I account it high time to get to sea as soon as I can.
HERMAN MELVILLE (1819–1891). *Moby-Dick; or, The Whale*, 1, 1851, ed. Harold Beaver, 1972

Ishmael: There is, one knows not what sweet mystery about this sea, whose gently awful stirrings seem to speak of some hidden soul beneath.
HERMAN MELVILLE (1819–1891). *Moby-Dick; or, The Whale*, 111, 1851, ed. Harold Beaver, 1972

"A man who is not afraid of the sea will soon be drowned," he said, "for he will be going out on a day he shouldn't. But we do be afraid of the sea, and we do only be drownded now and again."
J. M. SYNGE (1871–1909). *The Aran Islands*, pt. 2, 1907

O hear us when we cry to thee,
For those in peril on the sea.
WILLIAM WHITING (19th cent.). "Eternal Father, Strong to Save" (hymn), 1869

❧

Rough seas make good sailors.
SAYING

SEASONS

See also • Days ○ Months ○ Nature ○ Time ○ Weather

One swallow does not make a spring; neither does one fine day.
ARISTOTLE (384–322 B.C.). *Nichomachean Ethics*, 1.7, tr. J. A. K. Thomson, 1953

The English winter—ending in July,
   To recommence in August.
LORD BYRON (1788–1824). *Don Juan*, 13.42, 1819–1824

Over increasingly large areas of the United States, spring now comes unheralded by the return of the birds, and the early mornings are strangely silent where once they were filled with the beauty of bird song.
RACHEL CARSON (1907–1964). *Silent Spring*, 8, 1962

In this country there are only two seasons winter and winter.
SHELAGH DELANEY (1939–). Referring to England, *A Taste of Honey*, 1.2, 1958

Inebriate of Air—am I—
And Debauchee of Dew—
Reeling—thro endless summer days—
From inns of Molten Blue—
EMILY DICKINSON (1830–1886). "I taste a liquor never brewed," 1860?

There came a Day at Summer's full,
Entirely for me—
I thought that such were for the Saints,
Where Resurrections—be—
EMILY DICKINSON (1830–1886). "There came a Day at Summer's full," 1861?

Spring is the Period
Express from God.
EMILY DICKINSON (1830–1886). "Spring is the Period," 1864?

In Maine they have not a summer but a thaw.
RALPH WALDO EMERSON (1803–1882). Journal, 1844?–1845?, undated

Spring still makes spring in the mind
   When sixty years are told:
Love wakes anew this throbbing heart,
   And we are never old.
Over the winter glaciers
   I see the summer glow,
And through the wild-piled snowdrift
   The warm rosebuds below.
RALPH WALDO EMERSON (1803–1882). Closing stanza, "The World-Soul," *May-Day and Other Pieces*, 1867

Summertime
An' the livin' is easy.
> IRA GERSHWIN (1896–1983). "Summertime" (song), in the musical *Porgy and Bess*, 1935

Every mile is two in winter.
> GEORGE HERBERT (1593–1633). Comp., *Outlandish Proverbs*, 949, 1640

Summer afternoon—summer afternoon . . . the two most beautiful words in the English language.
> HENRY JAMES (1843–1916). In Edith Wharton, *A Backward Glance*, 10, 1934

There seems to be so much more winter than we need this year.
> KATHLEEN NORRIS (1880–1966). *Bread and Roses*, 14, 1936

The Long Hot Summer.
> IRVING RAVETCH and HARRIET FRANK. Film title, 1958 (based on William Faulkner's short story, "The Long Summer," 1940)

The trumpet of a prophecy! O Wind,
If Winter comes, can Spring be far behind?
> PERCY BYSSHE SHELLEY (1792–1822). *Ode to the West Wind*, 5, 1819

See Desperation: Albert Camus ∘ Misfortune: Ho Chi Minh

The world's favorite season is the spring. All things seem possible in May.
> EDWIN WAY TEALE (1899–1980). *North with the Spring*, 3, 1951

In the spring a young man's fancy
lightly turns to thoughts of love.
> ALFRED, LORD TENNYSON (1809–1892). "Locksley Hall," l. 20, 1842

If the race had never lived through a winter, what would they think was coming?
> HENRY DAVID THOREAU (1817–1862). Journal, 8 November 1850

Live in each season as it passes; breathe the air, drink the drink, taste the fruit, and resign yourself to the influences of each. . . . Some men think that they are not well in spring, or summer, or autumn, or winter; it is only because they are not *well in* them.
> HENRY DAVID THOREAU (1817–1862). Journal, 23 August 1853

To shorten the winter, borrow some money due in the spring.
> W. J. VOGEL. In Paul Dickson, comp., *The Official Explanations*, p. 229, 1980

❦

We have two seasons: winter and Fourth of July.
> SAYING (NEW ENGLAND)

Snowy winter, plentiful harvest.
> SAYING (VERMONT)

Vermont has nine months of winter and three months of damned poor sledding.
> SAYING (VERMONT)

SECRETS

See also • Deception ∘ Intelligence, Military ∘ Nonviolence: Mohandas K. Gandhi (10) ∘ Right to Privacy

First to watch, and then to speed. For . . . [what] maketh the politic man go invisible is secrecy in the council and celerity in the execution. For when things are once come to the execution, there is no secrecy comparable to celerity—like the motion of a bullet in the air, which flieth so swift as it outruns the eye.
> FRANCIS BACON (1561–1626). "Of Delays," *Essays*, 1625

Secrecy necessarily breeds suspicion.
> LOUIS D. BRANDEIS (1856–1941). Letter to Cyrus Adler, 10 August 1915

Make a clean breast! Recount! A secret's safe
'Twixt you, me, and the gatepost!
> ROBERT BROWNING (1812–1889). *The Inn Album*, 2, 1875

There are some occasions when a man must tell half his secret in order to conceal the rest. . . . Great skill is necessary to know how far to go and where to stop.
> LORD CHESTERFIELD (1694–1773). Among "maxims" enclosed with a letter to his son, 15 January 1753

Concealment impossible
In will out.
> RALPH WALDO EMERSON (1803–1882). "Notebook F No. 1," p. 23, 1836–1840

Three may keep a Secret if two of them are dead.
> BENJAMIN FRANKLIN (1706–1790). *Poor Richard's Almanack*, July 1735

If you would keep your Secret from an enemy,
tell it not to a friend.
> BENJAMIN FRANKLIN (1706–1790). *Poor Richard's Almanack*, August 1741

We dance round in a ring and suppose,
But the Secret sits in the middle and knows.
> ROBERT FROST (1874–1963). "The Secret Sits," *A Witness Tree*, 1942

The experience of the world inculcates a discrete reserve on the subject of our person and estate, and we soon learn that a free disclosure of our riches or poverty would provoke the malice of envy, or encourage the insolence of contempt.
> EDWARD GIBBON (1737–1794). *Memoirs of My Life and Writings*, p. 50, 1796, Alex. Murray edition, 1869

Neither tell secrets nor listen to them.
> BALTASAR GRACIÁN (1601–1658). *The Art of Worldly Wisdom*, 238, 1647, tr. Joseph Jacobs, 1943

Love, Cough, and Itch cannot be conceal'd.
> JAMES HOWELL (1594?–1666). Comp., "French" (p. 2), *Paroimiographia: Proverbs, or Old Sayed Sawes & Adages in English . . . Italian, French and Spanish*, 1659

How can we expect somebody else to keep our secret if we cannot keep it ourselves?
> LA ROCHEFOUCAULD (1613–1680). *Maxims*, 584, 1665, tr. Leonard Tancock, 1959

The art of secrecy lies in being so open about most things that the few things that matter are not even suspected to exist.

> B. H. LIDDELL HART (1895–1970). *Strategy,* 15, 1954

If you wish to keep your private affairs secret, keep your servants well paid.

> NAPOLEON (1769–1821). *In the Words of Napoleon,* p. 88, tr. Daniel Savage Gray, 1977

The first rule in keeping secrets is nothing on paper.

> THOMAS POWERS (1940–). *The Man Who Kept the Secrets: Richard Helms and the CIA,* 9, 1981

A secret may be sometimes best kept by keeping the secret of its being a secret.

> HENRY TAYLOR (1800–1886). *The Statesman,* 18, 1836

There must be some narrowness in the soul that compels one to have secrets.

> HENRY DAVID THOREAU (1817–1862). Journal, 21 February 1842

Everyone is a moon, and has a dark side which he never shows to anybody.

> MARK TWAIN (1835–1910). *Following the Equator: A Journey Around the World,* 66 (epigraph), 1897

They are so pleased to find out other people's secrets. It distracts public attention from their own.

> OSCAR WILDE (1854–1900). *An Ideal Husband,* 2, 1895

❧

A secret's a secret's till it's told.

> SAYING (AMERICAN)

SECURITY

See also • Prudence ○ Safety

There is no happiness without security—I mean the prospect of being able to rely on the permanence of a state into which one has settled oneself. This assurance is to be found either in the mastering of things, or in the mastering of self which makes one independent of things.

> HENRI BERGSON (1859–1941). "Final Remarks," *The Two Sources of Morality and Religion,* 1932, tr. R. Ashley Audra and Cloudesley Brereton, 1935

Distrust and caution are the parents of security.

> BENJAMIN FRANKLIN (1706–1790). *Poor Richard's Almanack,* July 1733

He that is too secure is not safe.

> THOMAS FULLER (1654–1734). Comp., *Gnomologia: Adages and Proverbs,* 2195, 1732

Security is when everything is settled, when nothing can happen to you; security is the denial of life.

> GERMAINE GREER (1939–). "Security," *The Female Eunuch,* 1970

Fear of oppression disposeth a man to . . . seek aid by society, for there is no other way by which a man can secure his life and liberty.

> THOMAS HOBBES (1588–1679). *Leviathan,* 11, 1651

Liberty is in fact only a secondary need; the primary need is security.

> BERTRAND de JOUVENEL (1903–1987). *On Power: Its Nature and the History of Its Growth,* 18.1, 1945, tr. J. F. Huntington, 1948

Most people want security in this world, not liberty.

> H. L. MENCKEN (1880–1956). *Minority Report: H. L. Mencken's Notebooks,* 170, 1956

SEEING

See also • Eyes ○ Imagination: Ralph Waldo Emerson (1) ○ Perception ○ Understanding: Paul ○ Vision

We are like dwarfs on the shoulders of giants, so that we can see more than [the ancients] and things at a greater distance.

> BERNARD OF CHARTES (A.D. ?–1130?). In John of Salisbury, *The Metalogicon,* 3.4, A.D. 1159

To See a World in a Grain of Sand
And a Heaven in a Wild Flower,
Hold Infinity in the palm of your hand
And Eternity in an hour.

> WILLIAM BLAKE (1757–1827). Opening lines, "Auguries of Innocence," 1789

As a man is, so he sees.

> WILLIAM BLAKE (1757–1827). Letter to Rev. D. Trusler, 23 August 1799
>
> See Perception: Aldous Huxley

The true seeing is within.

> GEORGE ELIOT (1819–1880). *Middlemarch,* 19, 1871–1872

If we live truly, we shall see truly.

> RALPH WALDO EMERSON (1803–1882). Journal, 13 November 1838

Men who are out of humor with themselves often see their own condition reflected in the world outside them, and everything seems amiss because it is not well with themselves.

> JAMES ANTHONY FROUDE (1818–1894). *Thomas Carlyle: A History of the First Forty Years, 1795–1835,* 1.5, 1882

The same objects appear pleasing or displeasing, as the circumstances in which we see them are comfortable or uncomfortable.

> FULKE GREVILLE (1554–1628). *Maxims, Characters, and Reflections,* p. 110, 1756

Set your sights beyond what you can see. There is true majesty in the concept of an unseen power which can neither be measured nor weighed.

> TED KOPPEL (1940–). Commencement address at Duke University, Durham (North Carolina), 1987. In Arianna Huffington, "OK, Commence—But No Politics, Poseurs, Puppets," *San Francisco Sunday Examiner & Chronicle,* 26 May 1996

We love to see through others, but we dislike being seen through.

> LA ROCHEFOUCAULD (1613–1680). *Maxims,* 632, 1665, tr. Louis Kronenberger, 1959

We evolve into the images we carry in our minds. We become what we see.

> JERRY MANDER (1936–). *Four Arguments for the Elimination of Television,* 11, 1977

If I have seen further (than you and Descartes), it is by standing upon the shoulders of Giants.

> SIR ISAAC NEWTON (1642–1727). Letter to Robert Hooke, 5 February 1675

All that we see or seem
Is but a dream within a dream.

> EDGAR ALLAN POE (1809–1849). "A Dream Within a Dream," *Tamerlane and Other Poems,* 1827

Hundreds of people can talk for one who can think, but thousands can think for one who can see. To see clearly is poetry, prophecy, and religion—all in one.

> JOHN RUSKIN (1819–1900). *Modern Painters,* 3.4.16.28, 1843–1860, ed. Ernest Rhys, 1906

It is only with the heart that one can see rightly; what is essential is invisible to the eye.

> ANTOINE de SAINT-EXUPÉRY (1900–1944). *The Little Prince,* 21, tr. Katherine Woods, 1943
>
> See Perception: Richard of Saint-Victor

Our task is to look at the world and see it whole.

> E. F. SCHUMACHER (1911–1977). *A Guide for the Perplexed,* 2, 1977

We see things as we are not as they are.

> JENNIFER STONE. Radio commentary, KPFA, Berkeley (California), 7 August 1997

He sees himself in all he sees.

> ALFRED, LORD TENNYSON (1809–1892). *In Memoriam A. H. H.,* 97, 1850

How hard I find it to see what is *right in front of my eyes!*

> LUDWIG WITTGENSTEIN (1889–1951). 1940, *Culture and Value,* 1977, tr. Peter Winch, 1980

❧

How easy it is to see in others what we dare not see in ourselves.

> ANONYMOUS

SELF

See also • Conscience ○ Consciousness: [especially] William Wordsworth ○ Heart ○ Meditation ○ Mind ○ Mysticism ○ Self-Control ○ Self-Deception ○ Self-Denial ○ Self-Discipline ○ Self-Interest ○ Self-Knowledge ○ Self-Love ○ Self-Realization (Becoming) ○ Self-Realization (Being) ○ Self-Reliance ○ Self-Respect ○ Self-Righteousness ○ Self-Sacrifice ○ Self-Trust ○ Soul ○ Spirit ○ Spirituality ○ The Unconscious

The center of the universe is still the self.

> HENRI AMIEL (1821–1881). Journal, 1 February 1852, tr. Mrs. Humphrey Ward, 1887

My inner self was a house divided against itself.

> ST. AUGUSTINE (A.D. 354–430). *Confessions,* 8.8, A.D. 400?, tr. R. S. Pine-Coffin, 1961

Thy Self is the master of thyself, and thy Self is thy refuge.

> THE DHAMMAPADA: THE PATH OF PERFECTION (1st cent. B.C.). 380, tr. Juan Mascaró, 1973

A man finds out that there is somewhat in him that knows more than he does.

Then he comes presently to the curious question, who's who? which of these two is really me? the one that knows more, or the one that knows less? the little fellow or the big fellow?

> RALPH WALDO EMERSON (1803–1882). Journal, 1859, undated

There seemed to be two pleading in me.

> GEORGE FOX (1624–1691). 1647, *The Journal of George Fox,* 1694, rev. Norman Penney, 1924

The self is as strong as it is active.

> ERICH FROMM (1900–1980). *Escape from Freedom,* 7.2, 1941

If better were within, better would come out.

> THOMAS FULLER (1654–1734). Comp., *Gnomologia: Adages and Proverbs,* 2672, 1732

Everything in me calls out to be revised, amended, reeducated.

> ANDRÉ GIDE (1869–1951). Journal, 19 January 1916, tr. Justin O'Brien, 1948

One does not get to know that one exists until one rediscovers oneself in others.

> GOETHE (1749–1832). Letter to Auguste Stolberg, 13 February 1775, *Wisdom and Experience,* tr. Hermann J. Weigand, 1949

Nothing in the world is more distasteful to a man than to take the path that leads to himself.

> HERMANN HESSE (1877–1962). *Demian: The Story of Emil Sinclair's Youth,* 2, 1919, tr. Michael Roloff and Michael Lebeck, 1965
>
> See Soul: Carl G. Jung

There is a "me" in the infinite above, as there is a "me" in the infinite below. The "me" below is the soul; the "me" above is God.

> VICTOR HUGO (1802–1885). "Cosette" (7.5), *Les Misérables,* tr. Charles E. Wilbour, 1862

The Self, the immanent Godhead, the Kingdom of Heaven within us.

> ALDOUS HUXLEY (1894–1963). "Distractions—II." In Christopher Isherwood, ed., *Vedanta for the Western World,* 1945

Half myself mocks the other half.

> JOSEPH JOUBERT (1754–1824). 1813, *Pensées,* 1838, tr. Paul Auster, 1983

Conscious and unconscious are not necessarily in opposition to one another, but complement one another to form a totality, which is the *self.*

> CARL G. JUNG (1875–1961). "The Relations between the Ego and the Unconscious" (2.1), 1928, *Two Essays on Analytical Psychology,* tr. R. F. C. Hull, 1953
>
> See Consciousness: Jung (1)

As a whole, we are . . . so estranged from the inner world that many are arguing that it does not exist; and that even if it does exist, it does not matter.

> R. D. LAING (1927–1989). *The Politics of Experience,* 2, 1967

The living self has one purpose only: to come into its own fullness of being.

> D. H. LAWRENCE (1885–1930). "Democracy" (4), 1936?, *Selected Essays,* ed. Richard Aldington, 1950

Part of me suspects that I'm a loser, and the other part of me thinks I'm God Almighty.

> JOHN LENNON (1940–1980). David Sheff interview with Lennon and Yoko Ono, *Playboy*, January 1981

There is a deep disorder in our society which comes not from the machinations of our enemies and from the adversities of the human condition but from within ourselves.

> WALTER LIPPMANN (1889–1974). *The Public Philosophy*, 1.1, 1955

There is as much difference between us and ourselves as between us and others.

> MONTAIGNE (1533–1592). "Of the Inconsistency of Our Actions," *Essays*, 1588, tr. Donald M. Frame, 1958

The self holds both a hell and a heaven that rationalism, too confident of the powers of reason alone, never penetrates.

> LEWIS MUMFORD (1895–1990). *The Conduct of Life*, 9.1, 1951

To the possession of the self the way is inward.

> PLOTINUS (A.D. 205–270). *The Enneads*, 6.6.1, tr. Stephen MacKenna and B. S. Page, 1952

In my head there is a permanent opposition party; and whenever I take any step or come to any decision—though I may have given the matter mature consideration—it afterward attacks what I have done, without, however, being each time necessarily in the right.

> ARTHUR SCHOPENHAUER (1788–1860). "Studies in Pessimism: Further Psychological Observations," *Essays of Arthur Schopenhauer*, tr. T. Bailey Saunders, 1851

Every day I plead my cause before the bar of self. When the light has been removed from sight, and my wife, long aware of my habit, has become silent, I scan the whole of my day and retrace all my deeds and words. I conceal nothing from myself, I omit nothing. For why should I shrink from any of my mistakes, when I may commune thus with myself.

> SENECA THE YOUNGER (5? B.C.–A.D. 65). "On Anger" (3.36.2), *Moral Essays*, tr. John W. Basore, 1928

This demigod within the breast appears, like the demigods of the poets, thought partly of immortal, yet partly too of mortal extraction.

> ADAM SMITH (1723–1790). *The Theory of Moral Sentiments*, 3.2, 1759

Inner space is the real frontier.

> GLORIA STEINEM (1934–). In Michael Larsen, *Literary Agents: What They Do, How They Do It, and How to Find and Work with the Right One for You*, rev. ed., 16.3, 1996
>
> See Space: Gene Roddenberry

I found in myself, and still find, an instinct toward a higher or, if it is named, spiritual life, as do most men, and another toward a primitive rank and savage one, and I reverence them both.

> HENRY DAVID THOREAU (1817–1862). "Higher Laws," *Walden; or Life in the Woods*, 1854

Be a Columbus to whole new continents and worlds within you, opening new channels, not of trade, but of thought. Every man is the lord of a realm beside which the earthly empire of the Czar is but a petty state.

> HENRY DAVID THOREAU (1817–1862). "Conclusion," *Walden; or Life in the Woods*, 1854

Introspection has two possible alternative objectives. It may be a retreat into one's self from contact with other people and with the universe, or it may be a search, in the subconscious depths of the psyche, for contact with the ultimate spiritual reality. Introspection with the first of these objectives is isolationist; introspection with the second objective is unitive. The first is negative; the second is positive.

> ARNOLD J. TOYNBEE (1889–1975). *The Toynbee-Ikeda Dialogue: Man Himself Must Choose*, 3, 1976
>
> See Self-Knowledge: Walter Lippmann

Seek . . . thyself!

> MIGUEL de UNAMUNO (1864–1936). *Tragic Sense of Life*, 10, 1913, tr. J. E. Crawford Flitch, 1921

We feel safe, huddled within human institutions—churches, banks, madrigal groups—but these concoctions melt away at the basic moment. The self's responsibility, then, is to achieve rapport if not rapture with the giant, cosmic other: to appreciate, let's say, the walk back from the mailbox.

> JOHN UPDIKE (1932–). Closing words, *Self-Consciousness: Memoirs*, 1989

I celebrate myself, and sing myself.
And what I assume you shall assume,
For every atom belonging to me as good belongs to you.

> WALT WHITMAN (1819–1892). Opening lines, "Song of Myself," 1855, *Leaves of Grass*, 1855–1892

There is that in me—I do not know what it is—but I know it is in me.

> WALT WHITMAN (1819–1892). "Song of Myself" (50), 1855, *Leaves of Grass*, 1855–1892

SELF-CONTROL

See also • Abstinence ○ Self ○ Self-Denial ○ Self-Discipline ○ Self-Esteem: Thomas S. Szasz

Men are qualified for civil liberty in exact proportion to their disposition to put moral chains upon their own appetites. . . . Society cannot exist unless a controlling power upon will and appetite be placed somewhere; and the less of it there is within, the more there must be without.

> EDMUND BURKE (1729–1797). Letter to a member of the French National Assembly, 1791

Everything that frees our spirit without giving us control of ourselves is ruinous.

> GOETHE (1749–1832). *The Maxims and Reflections of Goethe*, 33, tr. T. Bailey Saunders, 1892

The greatest strength and wealth is self-control.

> PYTHAGORAS (6th cent. B.C.)

A little self-control at the right moment may prevent much subsequent compulsion at the hands of others.

> ARTHUR SCHOPENHAUER (1788–1860). "Counsels and Maxims" (2.15), *Essays of Arthur Schopenhauer*, tr. T. Bailey Saunders, 1851

❧

A man without self-control is like a city broken into and left without walls.

SAYING (*BIBLE*). *Proverbs* 25:28

SELF-DECEPTION

See also • Deception ○ Delusion ○ Illusion ○ Lying: Lord Byron (1), Aldous Huxley ○ Self

We begin by fooling others and end up fooling ourselves.

ERIC ALTERMAN (1960–). Introduction to *Sound and Fury: The Washington Punditocracy and the Collapse of American Politics*, 1992

Self-deception once yielded to, *all* other deceptions follow naturally more and more.

THOMAS CARLYLE (1795–1881). "The Hero as King," *On Heroes, Hero-Worship, and the Heroic in History*, 1841

Self-deceit—the refuge of the weak.

LOUIS de CAULAINCOURT (1773–1827). *With Napoleon in Russia*, 12, ed. George Libaire, 1935

Nothing is as easy as deceiving yourself, for what you wish you readily believe.

DEMOSTHENES (384–322 B.C.). *Olynthiaca*, 3.19

A man [cannot] dupe others long, who has not duped himself first.

RALPH WALDO EMERSON (1803–1882). Journal, 1852, undated

Who has deceiv'd thee so oft as thy self?

BENJAMIN FRANKLIN (1706–1790). *Poor Richard's Almanack*, January 1738

There are many who have grave scruples about deceiving others but think it as nothing to deceive themselves.

ERIC HOFFER (1902–1983). *The Passionate State of Mind: And Other Aphorisms*, 71, 1954

Self-deception, credulity and charlatanism are somehow linked together.

ERIC HOFFER (1902–1983). *The Passionate State of Mind: And Other Aphorisms*, 83, 1954

The great deceivers of the world begin by deceiving themselves. They have to, or they wouldn't be so good at it.

MOLIÈRE (1622–1673). *Le Malade imaginaire*, 3, 1673, tr. Miles Malleson, 1960

It is amazing how people deceive themselves and others when it is to their interest to do so.

JAWAHARLAL NEHRU (1889–1964). 27 September 1932, *Glimpses of World History*, rev. ed., 98, 1939

The worst of all deceptions is self-deception.

SOCRATES (470?–399 B.C.). In Plato (427?–327 B.C.), *Cratylus*, 428

SELF-DENIAL

See also • Abstinence ○ Asceticism ○ Self ○ Self-Control ○ Self-Discipline

Self-denial, the parent of all virtue.

THOMAS CARLYLE (1795–1881). "Signs of the Times," 1829, *Critical and Miscellaneous Essays*, Carey & Hart edition, 1849

Our self-denial must first of all be humble. Otherwise it is a contradiction in terms. If we deny ourselves in order to think ourselves better than other men, our self-denial is only self-gratification.

THOMAS MERTON (1915–1968). *No Man Is an Island*, 6.7, 1955

Self-denial is not a virtue: it is only the effect of prudence on rascality.

GEORGE BERNARD SHAW (1856–1950). "Maxims for Revolutionists: Virtues and Vices," *Man and Superman*, 1903

SELF-DISCIPLINE

See also • Abstinence ○ Asceticism ○ Character ○ Children's Learning: Robert Lindner ○ Empire: Publius Syrus ○ Excess ○ Freedom: Marie von Ebner-Eschenbach ○ Moderation ○ Passion ○ Pleasure ○ Responsibility ○ Self ○ Self-Control ○ Self-Denial ○ Self-Realization (Becoming) ○ Self-Respect: Abraham Joshua Heschel ○ Temptation ○ Victory

What it lies in our power to do, it lies in our power not to do.

ARISTOTLE (384–322 B.C.). *Nicomachean Ethics*, 3.5, tr. J. A. K. Thomson, 1953

How ridiculous is Caesar and Bonaparte wandering from one extreme of civilization to the other to conquer men—himself, the while, unconquered, unexplored, almost wholly unsuspected to himself.

RALPH WALDO EMERSON (1803–1882). "Trust Yourself," sermon, Second Church of Boston, 3 December 1830

Discipline should not be practiced like a rule imposed on oneself from the outside, but that it becomes an expression of one's own will; that it is felt as pleasant, and that one slowly accustoms oneself to a kind of behavior which one would eventually miss, if one stopped practicing it.

ERICH FROMM (1900–1980). *The Art of Loving*, 4, 1956

What can there be higher than that which is its own master?

PLOTINUS (A.D. 205–270). *The Enneads*, 6.8.12, tr. Stephen MacKenna and B. S. Page, 1952

Right discipline consists, not in external compulsion, but in habits of mind which lead spontaneously to desirable rather than undesirable activities.

BERTRAND RUSSELL (1872–1970). *On Education: Especially in Early Childhood*, 1, 1926

If the people cannot govern themselves, they must be governed by somebody.

GEORGE BERNARD SHAW (1856–1950). *Annajanska*, 1919, *The Complete Plays of Bernard Shaw*, p. 854, 1965

Self-command, by which we are enabled to abstain from present pleasure or to endure present pain, in order to obtain a greater pleasure or to avoid a greater pain in some future time.

ADAM SMITH (1723–1790). *The Theory of Moral Sentiments*, 4.2, 1759

Self-command is not only itself a great virtue, but from it all the other virtues seem to derive their principle luster.

> ADAM SMITH (1723–1790). *The Theory of Moral Sentiments,* 6.3, 1759
>
> See Courage: Winston Churchill ○ Humility: St. Augustine ○ Prudence: Edmund Burke ○ Self-Respect: John Herschel

If you can win complete mastery over self, you will easily master all else. To triumph over self is the perfect victory.

> THOMAS à KEMPIS (1379–1471). *The Imitation of Christ,* 3.53, tr. Leo Sherley-Price, 1952

Discipline yourself only to yield to love.

> HENRY DAVID THOREAU (1817–1862). Journal, 30 January 1852

Make it a point to do something every day that you don't want to do. This is the golden rule for acquiring the habit of doing your duty without pain.

> MARK TWAIN (1835–1910). *Following the Equator: A Journey Around the World,* 58 (epigraph), 1897

He who rules his spirit [is better] than he who takes a city.

> SAYING (*BIBLE*). Proverbs 16:32
>
> See Victory: *The Dhammapada*

SELF-ESTEEM

See also • Esteem ○ Neurosis: Alfred Adler ○ Profit & Loss: Eric Hoffer ○ Respect ○ Self-Respect ○ Truth: Thomas Merton (3)

Self-esteem, *n.* An erroneous appraisement.

> AMBROSE BIERCE (1842–1914). *The Devil's Dictionary,* p. 123, 1911, Dover edition, 1958

He who sets a very high value upon himself has the less need to be esteemed by others.

> SAMUEL BUTLER (1612–1680). "Unclassified Prose Observations from the Butler's Manuscript," *Prose Observations,* ed. Hugh de Quehen, 1979

Deliver me from . . . him who acquires self-esteem by finding fault with others.

> KAHLIL GIBRAN (1883–1931). "Sayings," *Spiritual Sayings of Kahlil Gibran,* tr. Anthony R. Ferris, 1962

By suppressing desire we try to rebuild and bolster self-esteem.

> ERIC HOFFER (1902–1983). *The Passionate State of Mind: And Other Aphorisms,* 5, 1954

Tackling a job that seems worth doing, and doing it in a competent manner, is . . . the best way for a person to gain self-esteem.

> JOHN HOLT (1923–1985). Pat Stone interview, *Mother Earth News,* July-August 1980

$$\text{Self-esteem} = \frac{\text{Success}}{\text{Pretensions}}$$

> WILLIAM JAMES (1842–1910). *The Principles of Psychology,* 10, 1890

Learning to deal with setbacks, and maintaining the persistence and optimism necessary for childhood's long road to mastery are the real foundations of lasting self-esteem.

> LILIAN G. KATZ. "Reading, Writing, Narcissism," *New York Times,* 15 July 1993

Oft times nothing profits more
Than self-esteem, grounded on just and right
Well manag'd.

> JOHN MILTON (1608–1674). *Paradise Lost,* 8.571, 1667

Self-esteem isn't everything; it's just that there's nothing without it.

> GLORIA STEINEM (1934–). *Revolution from Within: A Book of Self-Esteem,* 1.1, 1992

Self-control and self-esteem vary directly: The more self-esteem a person has, the greater, as a rule, is his desire, and his ability, to control himself.

The desire to control others and self-esteem vary inversely: the less self-esteem a person has, the greater, as a rule, is his desire, and his ability, to control others.

> THOMAS S. SZASZ (1920–). "Control and Self-Control," *Heresies,* 1976
>
> See Self-Respect: Abraham Joshua Heschel

Only individuals with an aberrant temperament can in the long run retain self-esteem in the face of the disesteem of their fellows.

> THORSTEIN VEBLEN (1857–1929). *The Theory of the Leisure Class: An Economic Study of Institutions,* 2, 1899

SELF-INTEREST

See also • Action & Talk: Walter Savage Landor ○ Ambition ○ Competition ○ Cooperation ○ Egoism ○ Exploitation ○ Giving ○ Greed ○ International Relations ○ Machiavellianism ○ Motives ○ Politics ○ Power ○ Prudence: Rules ○ Self ○ Selfishness ○ Self-Love ○ Self-Sacrifice ○ Service: [especially] Elbert Hubbard ○ Success ○ Tyranny

An enlightened self-interest.

> EDMUND BURKE (1729–1797). *Reflections on the Revolution in France,* p. 256, 1790, Pelican Books edition, 1968

The passion of self-aggrandizement is persistent but plastic; it will never disappear from a vigorous mind, but may become morally higher by attaching itself to a larger conception of what constitutes the self.

> CHARLES HORTON COOLEY (1864–1929). *Human Nature and the Social Order,* rev. ed., 6, 1922 (1902)

Few Men will be better than their Interest bids them.

> THOMAS FULLER (1654–1734). Comp., *Gnomologia: Adages and Proverbs,* 1527, 1732

We are all practical in our own interest and idealists when it concerns others.

> KAHLIL GIBRAN (1883–1931). "Sayings," *Spiritual Sayings of Kahlil Gibran,* tr. Anthony R. Ferris, 1962

In proportion as men are made to understand their true interests, they will conduct themselves wisely.

> WILLIAM GODWIN (1756–1836). *Enquiry Concerning Political Justice and Its Influence on Morals and Happiness,* 4.2.3, 1793, ed. and abr. Raymond A. Preston, 1926

In history an additional result is commonly produced by human actions beyond that which they aim at and obtain, that which they immediately recognize and desire. They gratify their own interest;

but something further is thereby accomplished, latent in the actions in question, though not present to their consciousness, and not included in their design.

> GEORG HEGEL (1770–1831). Introduction (3.2.2) to *Philosophy of History*, 1832, tr. John Sibree, 1900

If I am not for myself, who is for me? And when I am for myself only, what am I? And if not now, when?

> HILLEL (1st cent. B.C.). In *Talmud* (A.D. 1st–6th cent.). Rabbinical writings

Work for yourself by working for the good of all.

> ELBERT HUBBARD (1856–1915). In Alice Hubbard, comp., *An American Bible*, p. 231, 1946

Interest is the ruling motive of mankind.

> SAMUEL JOHNSON (1709–1784). In *The Adventurer* (English journal), 137, 26 February 1754

A Man is a Lion in his own Cause.

> JAMES KELLY (18th cent.). Comp., *A Complete Collection of Scottish Proverbs Explained and Made Intelligible to the English Reader*, A.30, 1721

Furthering the common good does not require that we forego self-interest, but rather that we are able to see our own interests linked to those of others. It requires a society that enables citizens to express the very human need to act on our deepest values as well as on our private interests.

> FRANCES MOORE LAPPÉ (1944–). *Rediscovering America's Values*, 6 ("Summing Up the Dialogue"), 1989

Self-interest blinds some, but enlightens others.

> LA ROCHEFOUCAULD (1613–1680). *Maxims*, 40, 1665, tr. Leonard Tancock, 1959

Self-interest sets in motion virtues and vices of all kinds.

> LA ROCHEFOUCAULD (1613–1680). *Maxims*, 253, 1665, tr. Leonard Tancock, 1959

Let each of you look not only to his own interests, but also to the interests of others.

> PAUL (A.D. 1st cent.). *Philippians* 2:4

Looking Out for Number One.

> ROBERT J. RINGER (1938–). Book title, 1977

Men alter their demeanor and sentiments just as fast as their interest changes.

> ARTHUR SCHOPENHAUER (1788–1860). "Counsels and Maxims" (3.29), *Essays of Arthur Schopenhauer*, tr. T. Bailey Saunders, 1851

A man's interest in the world is only the overflow from his interest in himself.

> GEORGE BERNARD SHAW (1856–1950). *Heartbreak House: A Fantasia in the Russian Manner on English Themes*, 2, 1919

It is not from the benevolence of the butcher, the brewer, or the baker, that we expect our dinner, but from their regard to their own interest. We address ourselves, not to their humanity but to their self-love, and never talk to them of our own necessities but of their advantages. Nobody but a beggar chooses to depend chiefly upon the benevolence of his fellow-citizens. Even a beggar does not depend upon it entirely.

> ADAM SMITH (1723–1790). *The Wealth of Nations*, 1.2, 1776

Every individual necessarily labors to render the annual revenue of the society as great as he can. He generally, indeed, neither intends to promote the public interest, nor knows how much he is promoting it. . . . He is in this, as in many other cases, led by an invisible hand to promote an end which was no part of his intention. Nor is it always the worse for the society that it was no part of it. By pursuing his own interest he frequently promotes that of the society more effectually than when he really intends to promote it. I have never known much good done by those who affected to trade for the public good.

> ADAM SMITH (1723–1790). *The Wealth of Nations*, 4.2, 1776

✹

Nations and classes are governed by no law but that of self-interest.

> ANONYMOUS

Look after Number One.

> SAYING. Quoted by Rabelais, letter, 15 February 1536

SELFISHNESS

See also • Egoism ∘ Greed ∘ Self-Interest ∘ Service

Selfishness is that detestable vice which no one will forgive in others, and no one is without in himself.

> HENRY WARD BEECHER (1813–1887). *Life Thoughts*, p. 140, rec. Edna Dean Proctor, 1858

There is a benevolence in all wise selfishness.

> HENRY WARD BEECHER (1813–1887). "Business," *Proverbs from Plymouth Pulpit*, ed. William Drysdale, 1887

We are all selfish and I no more trust myself than others with a good motive.

> LORD BYRON (1788–1824). Letter to Lady Melbourne, 28 September 1813

Selfish persons are incapable of loving others, but they are not capable of loving themselves either.

> ERICH FROMM (1900–1980). *The Art of Loving*, 2.3.d, 1956

The essence of man, his uniqueness, is in his power to surpass the self, to rise above his needs and selfish motives.

> ABRAHAM JOSHUA HESCHEL (1907–1972). *God in Search of Man: A Philosophy of Judaism*, 39, 1955

The deep-rooted selfishness, which forms the general character of the existing state of society, is *so* deeply rooted only because the whole course of existing institutions tends to foster it.

> JOHN STUART MILL (1806–1873). *Autobiography*, 7, 1873

SELF-KNOWLEDGE

See also • Crime: Henry Miller ∘ Knowledge ∘ Self ∘ Self-Trust ∘ Virtue: Jean Paul Friedrich Richter

Let me know myself, Lord, and I shall know Thee.
> ST. AUGUSTINE (A.D. 354–430). *Soliloquies*, 2

Self-Knowledge is of loving deeds the child.
> *THE BOOK OF THE GOLDEN PRECEPTS.* Ancient Buddhist writing. 2, tr. Helena Petrovna Blavatsky, 1889

How little do we know that which we are!
How less what we may be!
> LORD BYRON (1788–1824). *Don Juan,* 15.99, 1819–1824

Study the heart and the mind of man, and begin with your own. Meditation and reflection must lay the foundation of that knowledge, but experience and practice must, and alone can, complete it.
> LORD CHESTERFIELD (1694–1773). Letter to his son, 6 June 1751

Know thyself: to what depths of vain, egocentric brooding has that dictum led!
> NORMAN DOUGLAS (1868–1952). 13 March, *An Almanac,* 1945

Observe all men; thy self most.
> BENJAMIN FRANKLIN (1706–1790). *Poor Richard's Almanack,* August 1740

No Man is the worse for knowing the worst of himself.
> THOMAS FULLER (1654–1734). Comp., *Gnomologia: Adages and Proverbs,* 3601, 1732

The purpose of life is undoubtedly to know oneself. We cannot do it unless we learn to identify ourselves with all that lives. The sum total of that life is God. . . . The instrument of this knowledge is boundless, selfless service.
> MOHANDAS K. GANDHI (1869–1948). Letter to Muriel Lester, 21 June 1932

Self-knowledge is the beginning of self-improvement.
> BALTASAR GRACIÁN (1601–1658). *The Art of Worldly Wisdom,* 69, 1647, tr. Joseph Jacobs, 1943

Surely people must know themselves. So few ever think about anything else.
> J. C. HARE (1795–1855) and A. W. HARE (1792–1834). *Guesses at Truth: Second Series,* p. 531, 1848, Macmillan edition, 1867

All men have the capacity of knowing themselves and acting with moderation.
> HERACLITUS (540?–480? B.C.). In Kathleen Freeman, tr., *Ancilla to Pre-Socratic Philosophers: A Complete Translation of the Fragments in Diels,* Fragmente der Vorsokratiker, 22.116, 1983 (1948)

"Know thy God" [*1 Chronicles* 28:9] rather than "Know Thyself" is the categorical imperative of the biblical man. There is no self-understanding without God-understanding.
> ABRAHAM JOSHUA HESCHEL (1907–1972). Closing words, *The Prophets,* 1962

If most of us remain ignorant of ourselves, it is because self-knowledge is painful and we prefer the pleasures of illusion.
> ALDOUS HUXLEY (1894–1963). *The Perennial Philosophy,* 9, 1946

It is wisdom to know others;
It is enlightenment to know one's self.
> LAO-TZU (6th cent. B.C.). *The Way of Life,* 33, tr. R. B. Blakney, 1955

Our greatest instrument for understanding the world—introspection. . . . The best way of knowing the inwardness of our neighbors is to know ourselves.
> WALTER LIPPMANN (1889–1974). *A Preface to Politics,* 4, 1914
> See Self: Arnold J. Toynbee

He who knows his own self knows God.
> MUHAMMAD (A.D. 570?–632). *The Sayings of Muhammad,* 282, tr. Abdullah Al-Suhrawardy, 1941;

I must first know myself, as the Delphian inscription says; to be curious about that which is not my concern, while I am still in ignorance of my own self would be ridiculous.
> PLATO (427?–347 B.C.). *Phaedrus,* 229–230, tr. Benjamin Jowett, 1894

Know then thyself, presume not God to scan,
The proper study of Mankind is Man.
> ALEXANDER POPE (1688–1744). *An Essay on Man,* 2.1, 1734

As he who does not know himself does not know others, so it may be said with equal truth, that he who does not know others knows himself but very imperfectly.
> SIR JOSHUA REYNOLDS (1723–1792). "Discourse Seven," 10 December 1776, *Discourses on Art,* 1769–1790

The high peak of knowledge is perfect self-knowledge.
> RICHARD OF SAINT-VICTOR (A.D. ?–1173). *Richard of Saint-Victor,* tr. Clare Kirchberger, 1957

Ophelia: We know what we are, but know not what we may be.
> SHAKESPEARE (1564–1616). *Hamlet,* 4.5.42, 1600

What is really important in Man is the part of him that we do not yet understand.
> GEORGE BERNARD SHAW (1856–1950). "The Revolutionist's Handbook" (2), *Man and Superman,* 1903

I was a poor young colored man but I had the strength of a man who comes to know himself.
> NATE SHAW. *All God's Dangers: The Life of Nate Shaw,* ed. Theodore Rosengarten, 1974. In Wendell Berry, "A Remarkable Man" (3), 1975, *What Are People For?: Essays,* 1990

This is . . . self-knowledge—for a man to know what he knows, and what he does not know.
> SOCRATES (470?–399 B.C.). In Plato (427?–347 B.C.), *Charmides,* 167, tr. Benjamin Jowett, 1894

Know the enemy and know yourself, and you can fight a hundred battles with no danger of defeat.
> SUN-TZU (4th cent. B.C.). In Mao Tse-tung, "Problems of Strategy in China's Revolutionary War" (1.4), December 1936, *Selected Works of Mao Tse-tung,* Foreign Languages Press edition, vol. 1, 1965

Anonymous: What is difficult?
Thales: To know thyself.
> THALES (625?–547? B.C.). One of the Seven Sages of Greece. Format adapted. In Diogenes Laertius (A.D. 3rd cent.), *Lives of Eminent Philosophers,* 1.1, tr. R. D. Hicks, 1925

Unless we can bear self-mortification, we shall not be able to carry self-examination to the necessary painful lengths. Without humility there can be no illuminating self-knowledge.

> ARNOLD J. TOYNBEE (1889–1975). *A Study of History,* 12.60, 1961

If the axiom of the ancient Greeks was "know thyself," that of Americans is more likely to be "know thy stuff."

> DIXON WECTER (1906–1950). *The Hero in America: A Chronicle of Hero-Worship,* 16.1, 1941

"Know thyself" was written over the portal of the antique world. Over the portal of the new world, "Be thyself" shall be written.

> OSCAR WILDE (1854–1900). "The Soul of Man Under Socialism," *Fortnightly Review* (British journal), February 1891

No self-knowledge without self-confrontation; no self-realization without self-knowledge.

> ANONYMOUS

SELF-LOVE

See also • Dignity ○ Egoism ○ Egotism ○ Love ○ Pride ○ Self ○ Self-Interest ○ Self-Respect ○ Self-Trust ○ Vanity

All the affectionate feelings of a man for others are an extension of his feelings for himself.

> ARISTOTLE (384–322 B.C.). *Nichomachean Ethics,* 9.8, tr. J. A. K. Thomson, 1953

He who don't luv himself vents hiz spleen bi hating everyboddy else.

> JOSH BILLINGS (1818–1885). "Bred and Butter," *Everybody's Friend, or; Josh Billing's Encyclopedia and Proverbial Philosophy of Wit and Humor,* 1874

Remove self-love from love, and not much would be left.

> CHAMFORT (1741–1794). *Maxims and Thoughts,* 6, 1796, tr. W. S. Merwin, 1984

If it is a virtue to love my neighbor as a human being, it must be a virtue—and not a vice—to love myself, since I am a human being too.

> ERICH FROMM (1900–1980). *The Art of Loving,* 2.3.d, 1956

If you love yourself too much, nobody else will love you at all.

> THOMAS FULLER (1654–1734). Comp., *Gnomologia: Adages and Proverbs,* 2768, 1732

It is not love of self but hatred of self which is at the root of the troubles that afflict our world.

> ERIC HOFFER (1902–1983). *The Passionate State of Mind: And Other Aphorisms,* 100, 1954

The correlative to loving our neighbors as ourselves is hating ourselves as we hate our neighbors.

> OLIVER WENDELL HOLMES, SR. (1809–1894). *The Professor at the Breakfast-Table,* 11, 1860

To love one's self in the right way and to love one's neighbor are absolutely analogous concepts, are at bottom one and the same.

> SÓREN KIERKEGAARD (1813–1855). *Works of Love,* 1847, tr. David F. Swenson, 1946

[The Lord said,] You shall not take vengeance or bear any grudge against the sons of your own people, but you shall love your neighbor as yourself.

> MOSES (14th cent. B.C.). *Leviticus* 19:18
> See Love: Freud (2), Jesus, Saying (2) ○ Religion: Mohandas K. Gandhi (3)

Not Man alone, but all that roam the wood,
Or wing the sky, or roll along the flood,
Each loves itself, but not itself alone.

> ALEXANDER POPE (1688–1744). *An Essay on Man,* 3.119, 1734

Two consistent motions act the Soul;
And one regards Itself, and one the Whole.
   Thus God and Nature link'd the gen'ral frame,
And bade Self-love and Social be the same.

> ALEXANDER POPE (1688–1744). *An Essay on Man,* 3.315, 1734
> See Motives: Pope

Self-love seems so often unrequited.

> ANTHONY POWELL (1905–). *The Acceptance World: A Novel,* 1, 1955

Dauphin: Self-love, my liege, is not so vile a sin
As self-neglecting.

> SHAKESPEARE (1564–1616). *Henry V,* 2.4.74, 1598

This self-love is the instrument of our conservation; it resembles the instrument that perpetuates the species: It is necessary, it is dear to us, it gives us pleasure, and it must be hidden.

> VOLTAIRE (1694–1778). "Self-Love," *Philosophical Dictionary,* 1764, tr. Theodore Besterman, 1971

Would you hurt a man keenest, strike at his self-love.

> LEW WALLACE (1827–1905). *Ben-Hur: A Tale of the Christ,* 6.2, 1880

Whate'er th' Almighty's subsequent command,
His first command is this—"Man, love thyself."

> EDWARD YOUNG (1683–1765). *The Complaint: or, Night Thoughts on Life, Death, and Immortality,* 7.168, 1742–1745

Who loves himself need fear no rivals.

> SAYING (LATIN)

SELF-REALIZATION (BECOMING)

See also • Beginnings & Endings: T. S. Eliot (3) ○ Buddhism: The Buddha ○ Change ○ Children's Learning ○ Conversion ○ Crises ○ Despair ○ Desperation ○ Education ○ Enlightenment ○ Evolution ○ Faith ○ God ○ Integrity ○ Learning (Process) ○ Morality ○ Mysticism ○ Nonconformity ○ Psychotherapy ○ Redemption ○ Reform ○ Responsibility ○ Salvation ○ Self ○ Self-Discipline ○ Self-Knowledge: Anonymous ○ Self-Realization (Being) ○ Self-Reliance ○ Solitude (Being Alone) ○ Spirituality ○ Struggle ○ Transformation ○ The Unconscious ○ Virtue

Be always displeased at what thou art, if thou desirest to attain to what thou art not.

> ST. AUGUSTINE (A.D. 354–430). In Francis Quarles, *Emblems*, 4.3, 1635

Thou canst not travel on the Path before thou hast become that Path itself.

> *THE BOOK OF THE GOLDEN PRECEPTS.* Ancient Buddhist writing. 1, tr. Helena Petrovna Blavatsky, 1889

Have patience, Candidate, as one who fears no failure, courts no success. Fix thy Soul's gaze upon the star whose ray thou art.

> *THE BOOK OF THE GOLDEN PRECEPTS.* Ancient Buddhist writing. 2, tr. Helena Petrovna Blavatsky, 1889

Our discontent begins by finding false villains whom we can accuse of deceiving us. Next we find false heroes whom we expect to liberate us. The hardest, most discomfiting discovery is that each of us must emancipate himself.

> DANIEL J. BOORSTIN (1914–). *The Image: A Guide to Pseudo-Events in America*, 6.5, 1961

Everything has to be rethought.

> ELIAS CANETTI (1905–1994). 1959, *The Human Province*, tr. Joachim Neugroschel, 1978

> See Civilization, Modern: George F. Will ○ Values: Friedrich Nietzsche

The important thing is this: to be able at any moment to sacrifice what we are for what we could become.

> CHARLES DU BOS (1882–1939). *Approximations*, 3, 1922–1937

He not busy being born
Is busy dying.

> BOB DYLAN (1941–). "It's Alright, Ma (I'm Only Bleeding)" (song), 1965

The difficulties increase the closer we approach the goal.

> GOETHE (1749–1832). "From Ottilie's Journal," 2.5, *Elective Affinities*, 1809, tr. R. J. Hollingdale, 1971

If a way to the Better there be, it exacts a full look at the Worst.

> THOMAS HARDY (1840–1928). "In Tenebris II," *Poems of the Past and Present*, 1901

Be what you are. This is the first step toward becoming better than you are.

> J. C. HARE (1795–1855) and A. W. HARE (1792–1834). *Guesses at Truth: Second Series*, p. 502, 1848, Macmillan edition, 1867

[The mind] is no longer directed to a set question but to something asked unspoken, to some ultimate question that cannot be put into words. It is a question, now, not of illumination through vision, but of illumination through at-one-ment.

> EUGEN HERRIGEL (1885–1955). "Higher Stages of Meditation," *The Method of Zen*, 1960, ed. Hermann Tausend and tr. R. F. C. Hull, 1964

We must become so alone, so utterly alone, that we withdraw into our innermost self. It is a way of bitter suffering. But then our solitude is overcome, we are no longer alone, for we find that our innermost self is the spirit, that it is God, the indivisible. And suddenly we find ourselves in the midst of the world, yet undisturbed by its multiplicity, for in our innermost soul we know ourselves to be one with all being.

> HERMANN HESSE (1877–1962). *Reflections*, 195, ed. Volker Michels, 1974

One finds that one can *wait* for everything patiently, and that is one of life's great arts. One finds also that each thing comes duly, one thing after the other, so that one gains time to make one's footing sure before advancing farther. And then everything occurs to us at the right moment, just what we ought to do, etc., and often in a very striking way, just as if a third person were keeping watch over those things which we are in easy danger of forgetting. . . .

The highest resources of worldly wisdom are unable to attain that which, under divine leading, comes to us of its own accord.

> CARL HILTY (1833–1909). *Happiness: Essays on the Meaning of Life*, tr. Francis Greenwood Peabody. In William James, *The Varieties of Religious Experience: A Study in Human Nature*, 19, 1902

The true end of Man . . . is the highest and most harmonious development of his powers to a complete and consistent whole. Freedom is the first and indispensable condition which the possibility of such a development presupposes; but there is besides another essential—intimately connected with freedom, it is true—a variety of situations. Even the most free and self-reliant of men is hindered in his development, when set in a monotonous situation.

> WILHELM von HUMBOLDT (1767–1835). *The Limits of State Action*, 2, 1854, ed. J. W. Burrow, 1969

To be clearly and constantly aware of the divine guidance is given only to those who are already far advanced in the life of the spirit. In its earlier stages we have to work, not by the direct perception of God's successive graces, but by faith in their existence. We have to accept as a working hypothesis that the events of our lives are not merely fortuitous, but deliberate tests of intelligence and character, specially devised occasions (if properly used) for spiritual advance. Acting upon this working hypothesis, we shall treat no occurrence as intrinsically unimportant. We shall never make a response that is inconsiderate, or a mere automatic expression of our self-will, but always give ourselves time, before acting or speaking, to consider what course of behavior would seem to be most in accord with the will of God, most charitable, most conducive to the achievement of our final end.

> ALDOUS HUXLEY (1894–1963). "Seven Meditations." In Christopher Isherwood, ed., *Vedanta for the Western World*, 1945

You have to trust your inner knowing. If you have a clear mind and an open heart, you won't have to search for direction. Direction will come to you.

> PHIL JACKSON (1945–) (with HUGH DELEHANTY). *Sacred Hoops: Spiritual Lessons of a Hardwood Warrior*, 7, 1995

The descent into the depths always seems to precede the ascent.

> CARL G. JUNG (1875–1961). "Archetypes of the Collective Unconscious," 1934, *The Archetypes and the Collective Unconscious*, tr. R. F. C. Hull, 1959

Whoever looks into the mirror of the water will see first of all his own face. Whoever goes to himself risks a confrontation with himself. The mirror does not flatter, it faithfully shows whatever looks into it. . . . The mirror lies behind the mask and shows the true face.

This confrontation is the first test of courage on the inner way, a test sufficient to frighten off most people.

CARL G. JUNG (1875–1961). "Archetypes of the Collective
Unconscious," 1934, *The Archetypes and the Collective Unconscious*,
tr. R. F. C. Hull, 1959

There is no recrossing the Rubicon.

CARL G. JUNG (1875–1961). "Individual Dream Symbolism in Relation
to Alchemy" (3.2.14), 1935, *Psychology and Alchemy*, tr. R. F. C. Hull,
1968

Sometimes snakes can't slough. They can't burst their old skin.
Then they go sick and die inside the old skin, and nobody ever
sees the new pattern.

It needs a real desperate recklessness to burst your old skin at
last. You simply don't care what happens to you, if you rip yourself in two, so long as you do get out.

It also needs a real belief in the new skin. Otherwise you are
likely never to make that effort. Then you gradually sicken and
go rotten and die in the old skin.

D. H. LAWRENCE (1885–1930). *Studies in Classic American Literature*,
5, 1923

The turning point in the process of growing up is when you discover the core of strength within you that survives all hurt.

MAX LERNER (1902–1992). "Faubus and Little Rock," *The Unfinished
Country*, 1959

Very often the only way to get a quality in reality is to start behaving as if you had it already.

C. S. LEWIS (1898–1963). *Mere Christianity*, rev. ed., 4.7, 1952

The central danger of the constructive technique is failure to be
responsible. Instead of making one's own decisions, the forces of
the unconscious are accepted as oracular. . . . Instead of making
the experiment oneself, some charismatic person is transformed
into the God-man who will do the great deed. Instead of the living acceptance of the experience, an intellectual formula is
sought. As methods, these are spurious. Responsibility is the
touchstone of the constructive technique.

P. W. MARTIN (1893–?). *Experiment in Depth: A Study of the Work of
Jung, Eliot and Toynbee*, 10, 1955

The good news is not primarily of hardship and of suffering, but
of creative experience, an immense enlargement and enrichment
of life. No aspect of the experiment in depth is more characteristic than this perceiving of everything, the inward world and the
outward world alike, with eyes that, for the first time, see. That
the way is hard is certain. But no less certain is its wonder.
"Behold, I make all things new [*Revelation* 21:5]."

P. W. MARTIN (1893–?). *Experiment in Depth: A Study of the Work of
Jung, Eliot and Toynbee*, 10, 1955

See Revelations: John

As William James points out, the first stage in the process [of indi-
viduation] is the realization that "there is *something wrong about
us* as we naturally stand." Without this realization, nothing happens.

P. W. MARTIN (1893–?). *Experiment in Depth: A Study of the Work of
Jung, Eliot and Toynbee*, 11, 1955

See Salvation: William James (2)

It is only by the breaking up of the established pattern that the
process of individuation becomes possible. On the other hand,
individuation is not likely to come of itself. From the very outset
anyone undertaking the experiment in depth is well advised to do
everything in his power to bring into operation two great integrative factors: the fellowship of a working group; and the contact
with the deep center.

P. W. MARTIN (1893–?). *Experiment in Depth: A Study of the Work of
Jung, Eliot and Toynbee*, 11, 1955

[Conditions required for individuation:] First, that consciousness
must not seek to use the Self for its own power or prestige. If it
does, the creative contact is lost. Second, that consciousness must
never relinquish its right and duty to [make] its own decisions in
all matters where consciousness is directly involved. If it does, the
Self may collapse or become ambivalent. Consciousness plays its
part in the forming and firming of the whole spirit not by abdi-
cating but by using its faculties to the full. Third, that without love
the Self cannot hold together. . . . There can be knowledge, intellect, genius even: but without love there is not integration.

P. W. MARTIN (1893–?). *Experiment in Depth: A Study of the Work of
Jung, Eliot and Toynbee*, 11, 1955

What matters in the end . . . is not the methods but the attitude
behind them. If that is right, the methods work. If the attitude is
wrong, methods are meaningless. The search is for the living God,
the creative ground of all we are and can become. Only "in spirit and in truth," the whole-hearted devotion fundamental both to
religion and to science, can it be undertaken.

P. W. MARTIN (1893–?). *Experiment in Depth: A Study of the Work of
Jung, Eliot and Toynbee*, 12, 1955

Every step in personal growth needs isolation, needs inner conversation and deliberation and a reviewing with the self.

JOOST A. M. MEERLOO (1903–1976). *The Rape of the Mind: The
Psychology of Thought Control, Menticide, and Brainwashing*, 12, 1956

Before we can realize who we really are, we must become conscious of the fact that the person we think we are, here and now,
is at best an impostor and a stranger.

THOMAS MERTON (1915–1968). *The New Man*, 74, 1961

Voyages are accomplished inwardly, and the most hazardous
ones, needless to say, are made without moving from the spot.

HENRY MILLER (1891–1980). *The Colossus of Maroussi*, 1, 1941

All has been given, as the mystics say. We have only to open our
eyes and hearts to become one with that which is.

HENRY MILLER (1891–1980). Epilogue to *The Smile at the Foot of the
Ladder*, 1948

The development of the individual can be described as a succession of new births at consecutively higher levels.

MARIA MONTESSORI (1870–1952). As paraphrased by E. M. Standing,
preface to *Maria Montessori: Her Life and Work*, 1957

The sense of community is indispensable . . . to full self-realization.

HERBERT J. MULLER (1905–1982). *The Uses of the Past: Profiles of
Former Societies*, 11.2, 1952

We must first say No to the dominant claims of our time, before we shall be able to say Yes to those we shall create to replace them. Perhaps the chief curse of our condition, at first, will be the realization of how far we shall have to go before we become self-acting, self-directed, self-confident persons once more: how far the events that have victimized the last two generations, the series of wars, revolutions, economic catastrophes, and more wars, culminating in the prospect of even more meaningless forms of random slaughter, are the result of our own continued self-abdication.

LEWIS MUMFORD (1895–1990). *The Conduct of Life*, 9.4, 1951

Withdrawal, detachment, simplification, reflection, liberation from automatism—these are all but preliminary steps in the rebuilding of the self and the renewal of the society of which we a part. These initial acts may, and in fact must, be taken by each of us alone: but the purpose of our withdrawal, of our fasting and purgation, is to reawaken our appetite for life, to make us keen to discriminate between food and poison and ready to exercise choice. Once we have taken the preparatory steps, we must return to the group and reunite ourselves with those who have been undergoing a like regeneration and are thereby capable of assuming responsibility and taking action. In relatively short order this fellowship may enfold men and women in every country, of every religious faith, of every cultural pattern.

LEWIS MUMFORD (1895–1990). *The Conduct of Life*, 9.7, 1951

To a crisis of the spirit, we need an answer of the spirit. And to find that answer, we need only look within ourselves. We listen to the better angels of our natures, we find that they celebrate the simple things, the basic things—such as goodness, decency, love, kindness.

RICHARD M. NIXON (1913–1994). *First Inaugural Address*, 20 January 1969

The search is what anyone would undertake if he were not sunk in the everydayness of his own life. This morning, for example, I felt as if I had come to myself on a strange island. And what does such a castaway do? Why, he pokes around the neighborhood and he doesn't miss a trick.

To become aware of the possibility of the search is to be onto something. Not to be onto something is to be in despair.

WALKER PERCY (1916–1990). *The Moviegoer*, 1.1, 1961

Withdraw into yourself and look. And if you do not find yourself beautiful yet, act as does the creator of a statue that is to be made beautiful: he cuts away here, he smoothes there, he makes this line lighter, this other purer, until a lovely face has grown upon his work. So do you also: cut away all that is excessive, straighten all that is crooked, bring light to all that is overcast, labor to make all one glow of beauty and never cease chiseling your statue, until there shall shine out on you from it the godlike splendor of virtue, until you shall see the perfect goodness surely established in the stainless shrine.

PLOTINUS (A.D. 205–270). *The Enneads*, 1.6.9, tr. Stephen MacKenna and B. S. Page, 1952

Steep and craggy is the path of the gods.

PORPHYRY (A.D. 233–304). In Ralph Waldo Emerson, "Culture," *The Conduct of Life*, 1860

The way upward from inertia to illumination passes through the sphere of action.

SWAMI PRABHAVANANDA (1893–1976). "The Sermon on the Mount—IV." In Christopher Isherwood, ed., *Vedanta for the Western World*, 1945

See Action: Dag Hammarskjöld

God is preparing you to receive the nectar of Ananda. If you get it without the proper preparation to stand it, your mind and body will be shattered to pieces. So He is gradually preparing you and when He knows that you are ready to receive Him, then He comes to you in all His glory.

SWAMI RAMDAS (1886–1963). In Whitall N. Perry, comp., *A Treasury of Traditional Wisdom*, p. 296, 1986

There is no growth except in the fulfillment of obligations.

ANTOINE de SAINT-EXUPÉRY (1900–1944). *Flight to Arras*, 20, tr. Lewis Galantière, 1942

Manhood and sagacity ripen of themselves; it suffices not to repress or distort them.

GEORGE SANTAYANA (1863–1952). *Character and Opinion in the United States*, 2, 1920

We only become what we are by the radical and deep-seated refusal of that which others have made of us.

JEAN-PAUL SARTRE (1905–1980). Preface to Frantz Fanon, *The Wretched of the Earth*, 1961, tr. Constance Farrington, 1963

He who would arrive at the appointed goal must follow a single road and not wander through many ways.

SENECA THE YOUNGER (5? B.C.–A.D. 65). "On Sophistical Argumentation," *Moral Letters to Lucilius*, 45.1, tr. Richard M. Gummere, 1918

One grows or dies. There is no third possibility.

OSWALD SPENGLER (1880–1936). *Aphorisms*, 147, tr. Gisela Koch-Weser O'Brien, 1967

Simplicity and truth of character are not produced by the constraint of laws, nor by the authority of the state; no one the whole world over can be forced or legislated into a state of blessedness; the means required for such a consummation are faithful and brotherly admonition, sound education, and, above all, free use of the individual judgment.

BARUCH SPINOZA (1632–1677). *Tractatus Theologico-Politicus*, 7, 1670, tr. R. H. M. Elwes, 1895

An individual is the end product of the *decisions* he has made. He who fails to make decisions, for the consequences of which he is responsible, is not a person. The ego, the self, the personality—call it what you will—comes into being and grows through the process of making responsible decisions.

THOMAS S. SZASZ (1920–). Epilogue to *Law, Liberty, and Psychiatry: An Inquiry into the Social Uses of Mental Health Practices*, 1963

See Mankind: Meryl Streep

Self-reverence, self-knowledge, self-control,
These three alone lead life to sovereign power.

ALFRED, LORD TENNYSON (1809–1892). "Oenone," l. 142, 1842

Men may rise on steppingstones
Of their dead selves to higher things.

ALFRED, LORD TENNYSON (1809–1892). *In Memoriam A. H. H.*, 1, 1850

And ah for a man to arise in me,
That the man I am may cease to be!

> ALFRED, LORD TENNYSON (1809–1892). *Maud,* 1.2.6, 1855

Our molting season, like that of the fouls, must be a crisis in our lives.

> HENRY DAVID THOREAU (1817–1862). "Economy," *Walden; or Life in the Woods,* 1854

If one advances confidently in the direction of his dreams, and endeavors to live the life which he has imagined, he will meet with a success unexpected in common hours. . . . In proportion as he simplifies his life, the laws of the universe will appear less complex, and solitude will not be solitude, nor poverty poverty, nor weakness weakness. If you have built castles in the air, your work need not be lost; that is where they should be. Now put the foundations under them.

> HENRY DAVID THOREAU (1817–1862). "Conclusion," *Walden; or Life in the Woods,* 1854
>
> See Simple Living: Thoreau (2)

It is a spiral path within the pilgrim's soul.

> HENRY DAVID THOREAU (1817–1862). Journal, 29 October 1857

Each time we make a [life-]style choice, a super-decision, each time we link up with some particular subcultural group or groups, we make some change in our self-image. We become, in some sense, a different person, and we perceive ourselves as different. Our old friends, those who knew us in some previous incarnation, raise their eyebrows. They have a harder and harder time recognizing us, and, in fact, we experience increasing difficulty in identifying with, or even sympathizing with, our own past selves.

> ALVIN TOFFLER (1928–). *Future Shock,* 14, 1970

The journey is there and every single one of us has got to go through it, and you can't dodge it, and the purpose of everything and the whole of existence is to equip you to take another step, and another step, and another step, and so on.

> JESSE WATKINS. In R. D. Laing, *The Politics of Experience,* 7, 1967

No one achieves a house by blueprints alone, no matter how accurate or detailed. A time comes when one must take up hammer and nails. In building a house the making of blueprints may be delegated to an architect, the construction to a carpenter. In building the house of one's life or in its remodeling, one may delegate nothing; for the task can be done, if at all, only in the workshop of one's own mind and heart, in the most intimate rooms of thinking and feeling where none but one's self has freedom of movement or competence or authority.

> ALLEN WHEELIS (1915–). *How People Change,* 8, 1973

We create ourselves. The sequence is suffering, insight, will, action, change.

> ALLEN WHEELIS (1915–). *How People Change,* 8, 1973

Love the earth and sun and the animals, despise riches, . . . devote your income and labor to others, hate tyrants, argue not concerning God, have patience and indulgence toward the people, take off your hat to nothing known or unknown, . . . re-examine all you have been told at school or church or in any book, dismiss whatever insults your own soul, and your very flesh shall be a great poem.

> WALT WHITMAN (1819–1892). Preface (1855) to *Leaves of Grass,* 1855–1892

Not I, nor anyone else can travel that road for you,
You must travel it for yourself.

It is not far, it is within reach,
Perhaps you have been on it since you were born and did not know,
Perhaps it is everywhere on water and on land.

> WALT WHITMAN (1819–1892). "Song of Myself" (46), 1855, *Leaves of Grass,* 1855–1892
>
> See Questions & Answers: Whitman

Sail forth—steer for the deep waters only,
Reckless O soul, exploring, I with thee, and thou with me,
For we are bound where mariner has not yet dared to go,
And we will risk the ship, ourselves and all.

> WALT WHITMAN (1819–1892). "Passage to India" (9), 1871, *Leaves of Grass,* 1855–1892

❦

Nought is given 'neath the sun,
Nought is had that is not won.

> ANONYMOUS (SWEDISH). Hymn. In Dag Hammarskjöld, 1955, *Markings,* tr. Leif Sjöberg and W. H. Auden, 1964

Begin within.

> ANONYMOUS

The inner journey begins the moment we realize that there's more to reality than meets the eye, and that we are capable of knowing and doing everything needed to reach our destination.

> ANONYMOUS

The light is reached not by turning back from the darkness, but by going through it.

> ANONYMOUS

The way in is the way out.

> ANONYMOUS

When your cart reaches the foot of the mountain, a path will appear.

> SAYING (CHINESE)

Traveler, there is no path; paths are made by walking.

> SAYING (SPANISH). In Henry A. Kissinger, *Years of Upheaval,* 1, 1982

SELF-REALIZATION (BEING)

See also • Action ○ Character ○ Dignity ○ Evolution ○ Freedom ○ God ○ Happiness ○ Heaven ○ Man ○ Nonconformity ○ Progress ○ Purpose ○ Self ○ Self-Realization (Becoming) ○ Soul ○ Spirituality ○ Success ○ The Unconscious

His attitude is the same toward friend and foe. He is indifferent to honor and insult, heat and cold, pleasure and pain. He is free from attachment. He values praise and blame equally. He can control his speech. He is content with whatever he gets. His home is everywhere and nowhere.

> BHAGAVAD GITA (6th cent. B.C.). 12, tr. Swami Prabhavananda and Christopher Isherwood, 1954
>
> See Praise: Kahlil Gibran o Wisdom: Lao-tzu (2)

One who practices the Truth, one who lives according to the Way, is one who embodies wisdom and compassion.

> AMARO BHIKKHU (1956–). Buddhist monk. "Wisdom," Silent Rain: Talks & Travels, 1996. In Tibetan, according to Bhikkhu, the word "lama" (as in Dalai Lama) is derived from "la" (wisdom) and "ma" (compassion).

To feel thyself abiding in all things, all things in Self.

> THE BOOK OF THE GOLDEN PRECEPTS. Ancient Buddhist writing. 3, tr. Helena Petrovna Blavatsky, 1889

The ultimate aim of the quest . . . must be neither release nor ecstasy for oneself, but wisdom and power to serve others.

> JOSEPH CAMPBELL (1904–1987). "Schizophrenia—the Inward Journey," 1970, Myths to Live By, 1972

The followers of Buddha Gotama are awake . . . , and ever by night and by day they find joy in love for all beings.

> THE DHAMMAPADA: THE PATH OF PERFECTION (1st cent. B.C.). 300, tr. Juan Mascaró, 1973

Every man takes care that his neighbor shall not cheat him. But a day comes when he begins to care that he [does] not cheat his neighbor. Then all goes well. He has changed his market cart for a chariot of the sun.

> RALPH WALDO EMERSON (1803–1882). "Worship," The Conduct of Life, 1860

Who is wise? He that learns from everyone.
Who is powerful? He that governs his Passions.
Who is rich? He that is content.
Who is that? Nobody.

> BENJAMIN FRANKLIN (1706–1790). Poor Richard's Almanack, July 1755

He who at every moment is all he is capable of being.

> DAG HAMMARSKJÖLD (1905–1961). 1954, Markings, tr. Leif Sjöberg and W. H. Auden, 1964

Most people are like a falling leaf that drifts and turns in the air, flutters, and falls to the ground. But a few others are like stars which travel one defined path: no wind reaches them, they have within themselves their guide and path.

> HERMANN HESSE (1877–1962). Siddhartha, 2 ("Amongst the People"), 1922, tr. Hilda Rosner, 1951

The real "haves" are they who can acquire freedom, self-confidence and even riches without depriving others of them.

> ERIC HOFFER (1902–1983). The Passionate State of Mind: And Other Aphorisms, 115, 1954

To grow mature is to separate more distinctly, to connect more closely.

> HUGO von HOFMANNSTHAL (1874–1929). The Book of Friends, 1922

The man who escapes from egotism into super-personality has transcended his old idolatrous loyalty, not only to himself, but also to the local divinities—nation, party, class, deified boss.

> ALDOUS HUXLEY (1894–1963). "Decentralization and Self-Government," Ends and Means: An Inquiry into the Nature of Ideals and into the Methods Employed for Their Realization, 1937
>
> See Crowds: Huxley

He can engage in actions and experience enjoyments without fear of corruption or enslavement.

> WILLIAM JAMES (1842–1910). The Varieties of Religious Experience: A Study in Human Nature, 14 and 15, 1902

Individuation does not shut one out from the world, but gathers the world to oneself.

> CARL G. JUNG (1875–1961). "On the Nature of the Psyche" (8), 1947, The Structure and Dynamics of the Psyche, tr. R. F. C. Hull, 1960

The word "sein" signifies in German both things: to be, and to belong to Him.

> FRANZ KAFKA (1883–1924). "Reflections on Sin, Pain, Hope, and the True Way" (44), 1917–1920, The Great Wall of China, 1931, tr. Willa and Edwin Muir, 1936

One ought to be mixed up with the world and to be able to wash one's hands of it—to be part of the world and also outside it. One [has] to be both involved and detached at the same time.

> THE KOTZKER (1787–1859). In Abraham Joshua Heschel, A Passion for Truth, 4, 1973
>
> See Enlightenment: Huang-Po

One whose chief regard is for his own mind, and for the divinity within him and the service of its goodness, will strike no poses, utter no complaints, and crave neither for solitude nor yet for a crowd.

> MARCUS AURELIUS (A.D. 121–180). Meditations, 3.7, tr. Maxwell Staniforth, 1964

The superior man is never in anyone's way.

> NAPOLEON (1769–1821). Napoleon in His Own Words, 1, comp. Jules Bertaut, 1916

A man's maturity consists in having found again the seriousness one had as a child, at play.

> FRIEDRICH NIETZSCHE (1844–1900). Beyond Good and Evil, 94, 1886, tr. Walter Kaufmann, 1966

Now I am nimble, now I fly, now I see myself under myself, now a god dances within me.

> FRIEDRICH NIETZSCHE (1844–1900). "Of Reading and Writing," Thus Spoke Zarathustra, 1892, tr. R. J. Hollingdale, 1961

When I was a child, I spoke like a child, I thought like a child, I reasoned like a child; when I became a man, I gave up childish ways.

> PAUL (A.D. 1st cent.). 1 Corinthians 13:11

Spiritual living is a fulfillment from moment to moment, in which the outer person is in a state of living rapport with the inner being and becomes an extension thereof.

> N. SRI RAM (1889–?). Thoughts for Aspirants, 19, 1972

Integration means the creation of an inner unity, a center of strength and freedom, so that the being ceases to be a mere object, acted upon by outside forces, and becomes a subject, acting from its own "inner space" into the space outside itself.

> E. F. SCHUMACHER (1911–1977). *A Guide for the Perplexed,* 3.3, 1977

King Henry: Presume not that I am the thing I was;
For God doth know, so shall the world perceive,
That I have turn'd away my former self.

> SHAKESPEARE (1564–1616). *Henry IV,* Part II, 5.5.60, 1597

Hamlet: A man that fortune's buffets and rewards
Hast ta'en with equal thanks.

> SHAKESPEARE (1564–1616). *Hamlet,* 3.2.72, 1600
>
> See Victory & Defeat: Rudyard Kipling ○ Victory & Defeat: Henry Wadsworth Longfellow

I had become a new person; and those who knew the old person laughed at me. The only man who behaved sensibly was my tailor: he took my measure anew every time he saw me, whilst all the rest went in with their old measurements and expected me to fit them.

> GEORGE BERNARD SHAW (1856–1950). *Man and Superman,* 1, 1903

The She-Ancient: You use a glass mirror to see your face: You use works of art to see your soul. But we who are older use neither glass mirrors nor works of art. We have a direct sense of life. When you gain that you will put aside your mirrors and statues, your toys and your dolls.

> GEORGE BERNARD SHAW (1856–1950). *Back to Methuselah: A Metabiological Pentateuch,* 5, 1921

The ultimate man will be one whose private requirements coincide with public ones. He will be that manner of man who, in spontaneously fulfilling his own nature, incidentally performs the functions of a social unit, and yet is only enabled so to fulfill his own nature by all others doing the like.

> HERBERT SPENCER (1820–1903). *Social Statics,* 4.30.13, 1851

In all the relations of life, [Helvidius Priscus] was ever the same, despising wealth, steadily tenacious of right, and undaunted by danger.

> TACITUS (A.D. 56?–120?). *The History,* 4.5, tr. Alfred J. Church and William J. Brodribb, 1942

I am a human being, so there is nothing human that I do not feel to be my concern.

> TERENCE (190?–159 B.C.). *Heauton timoroumenos,* l. 77. In Arnold J. Toynbee, *Experiences,* 1.6.2 (footnote), 1969 (Popular version: I am a human being; nothing human is alien to me.)

The Master is his own path.

> TUAN-MU TZ'U (5th cent. B.C.). In Confucius, *The Sayings of Confucius,* 14.28, tr. James R. Ware, 1955

To live with fear and not be afraid is the final test of maturity.

> EDWARD WEEKS. "A Quarter Century: Its Retreats," *Look,* 18 July 1961

One of the signs of passing youth is the birth of a sense of fellowship with other human beings as we take our place among them.

> VIRGINIA WOOLF (1882–1941). "Hours in a Library," *Times Literary Supplement* (London), 30 November 1916

This man is freed from servile bands,
    Of hope to rise, or fear to fall:
Lord of himself, though not of lands;
    And, having nothing, yet hath all.

> SIR HENRY WOTTON (1568–1639). "The Character of a Happy Life," 1651

Men can starve from a lack of self-realization as much as they can from a lack of bread.

> RICHARD WRIGHT (1908–1960). *Native Son,* 3, 1940

SELF-RELIANCE

See also • Character ○ Conformity ○ Dignity ○ Freedom ○ Helping Others ○ Independence ○ Individuality ○ Nature: Ralph Waldo Emerson (5) ○ Nonconformity ○ Nonconformity, Anti- ○ Nonconformity & Conformity ○ Responsibility ○ Self ○ Self-Realization (Becoming) ○ Self-Trust ○ Service ○ Standing Alone

The gods help them that help themselves.

> AESOP (6th cent. B.C.). "Hercules and the Wagoner," *Fables,* tr. Joseph Jacobs, 1894

Self-sufficiency . . . has three meanings. The first is that one should not depend upon others for one's daily bread. The second is that one should have developed the power to acquire knowledge for oneself. The third is that a man should be able to rule himself, to control his senses and his thoughts.

> VINOBA BHAVE (1895?–1982). *Thoughts on Education,* 6, tr. Marjorie Sykes, 1964

Self-made men are most alwus apt tew to be a leetle too proud ov the job.

> JOSH BILLINGS (1818–1885). "Koarse Shot," *Everybody's Friend, or; Josh Billing's Encyclopedia and Proverbial Philosophy of Wit and Humor,* 1874

No bird soars too high, if he soars with his own wings.

> WILLIAM BLAKE (1757–1827). "Proverbs of Hell," *The Marriage of Heaven and Hell,* 7.15, 1790–1793?

[Horace] Greeley knew he was a self-made man, and was always glorifying his maker.

> HENRY CLAPP. In Ralph Waldo Emerson, journal, 1868, undated

Need co-author for a book on self-reliance.

> CURRENT COMEDY. Newspaper classified ad. In "Laughter, The Best Medicine," *Reader's Digest,* April 1994

"I learned," said the melancholy Pestalozzi, "that no man in God's wide earth is either willing or able to help any other man." Help must come from the bosom alone.

> RALPH WALDO EMERSON (1803–1882). "The American Scholar," address, Harvard University, Cambridge (Massachusetts), 31 August 1837

The new individual must work out the whole problem of science, letters and theology for himself; can owe his fathers nothing.

> RALPH WALDO EMERSON (1803–1882). Journal, 28 May 1839

Welcome evermore to gods and men is the self-helping man. For him all doors are flung wide: him all tongues greet, all honors crown, all eyes follow with desire. Our love goes out to him and embraces him because he did not need it.

> RALPH WALDO EMERSON (1803–1882). "Self-Reliance," *Essays: First Series,* 1841

Self-help the law of nature.

> RALPH WALDO EMERSON (1803–1882). Journal, 1846, undated

If you would have a faithful Servant, and one that you like, serve yourself.

> BENJAMIN FRANKLIN (1706–1790). "The Way to Wealth," 7 July 1757

If you would have your Business done, go; If not, send.

> BENJAMIN FRANKLIN (1706–1790). "The Way of Wealth," 7 July 1757

Where self-reliance is the order of the day . . . , there are no leaders and no followers . . . [:] all are leaders and all are followers.

> MOHANDAS K. GANDHI (1869–1948). *Satyagraha in South Africa,* p. 288, 1928

Pack your own parachute.

> T. L. HAKALA. "Hakala's Rule of Survival." In Paul Dickson, comp., *The Official Explanations,* p. 79, 1980

A man is to go about his own business as if he had not a friend in the world to help him in it.

> MARQUIS OF HALIFAX (1633–1695). "Of Caution and Suspicion," *Political, Moral and Miscellaneous Reflections,* 1750

He that relieth upon himself will be oppressed by others with offers of their services.

> MARQUIS OF HALIFAX (1633–1695). "Of Caution and Suspicion," *Political, Moral and Miscellaneous Reflections,* 1750

Independence of mind or strength of character is rarely found among those who cannot be confident that they will make their way by their own effort.

> F. A. HAYEK (1899–1992). *The Road to Serfdom,* 9, 1944

He was a self-made man who owed his lack of success to nobody.

> JOSEPH HELLER (1923–). *Catch-22,* 3, 1961

He that will be served must be patient.

> GEORGE HERBERT (15931–633). Comp., *Outlandish Proverbs,* 354, 1640

Let every tub stand upon [its] own bottom.

> JAMES HOWELL (1593–1666). Comp., "English" (p. 17), *Paroimiographia: Proverbs, or Old Sayed Sawes & Adages in English . . . Italian, French and Spanish,* 1659

Do not lean on anyone, and let no one lean on you.

> ELBERT HUBBARD (1856–1915). In Alice Hubbard, comp., *An American Bible,* p. 235, 1946

Every human being should be taught that his first duty is to take care of himself, and that to be self-respecting he must be self-supporting. To live on the labor of others, either by force which enslaves, or by cunning which robs, or by borrowing or begging, is wholly dishonorable.

> ROBERT G. INGERSOLL (1833–1899). "Education," *The Philosophy of Ingersoll,* ed. Vere Goldthwaite, 1906

Never trouble another for what you can do yourself.

> THOMAS JEFFERSON (1743–1826). "A Decalogue of Canons for Observation in Practical Life," #2, letter to Thomas Jefferson Smith, 21 February 1825

It's all right to tell a man to lift himself by his own bootstraps, but it is a cruel jest to say to a bootless man that he ought to lift himself by his own bootstraps.

> MARTIN LUTHER KING, JR. (1929–1968). Passion Sunday sermon at the National Cathedral, Washington, 31 March 1968
> See Thrift: Oscar Wilde

The spirit of self-help is the root of all genuine growth in the individual.

> SAMUEL SMILES (1812–1904). *Self-Help,* 1, 1859

There is some of the same fitness in a man's building his own house that there is in a bird's building its own nest. Who knows but if men constructed their dwellings with their own hands, and provided food for themselves and families simply and honestly enough, the poetic faculty would be universally developed, as birds universally sing when they are so engaged?

> HENRY DAVID THOREAU (1817–1862). "Economy," *Walden; or Life in the Woods,* 1854

How can a rational being be ennobled by anything that is not obtained by its *own* exertions?

> MARY WOLLSTONECRAFT (1759–1797). *A Vindication of the Rights of Woman,* 3, 1792

⚘

Abraham Lincoln was born in a log cabin which he built with his own hands.

> ANONYMOUS (AMERICAN). University of Wisconsin student, "the epitome of self-help." As reported by Professor Helen White to Dixon Wecter, *The Hero in America: A Chronicle of Hero-Worship,* 10.1, 1941

God helps those who help themselves. God help those who don't.

> ANONYMOUS

Hoe your own row.

> SAYING (AMERICAN)

Paddle your own canoe.

> SAYING (AMERICAN)

If you want a thing done well, do it yourself.

> SAYING (ENGLISH)

God helps the sailor, but he must row.

> SAYING (GERMAN)

SELF-RESPECT

See also • Confidence ○ Criticism: Kahlil Gibran ○ Dignity ○ Esteem ○ Honor ○ Inferiority ○ Parents: Stephanie Marston ○ Pride ○ Respect ○ Self ○ Self-Esteem ○ Self-Love ○ Self-Trust

To free us from the expectations of others, to give us back to ourselves—there lies the great, singular power of self-respect.

> JOAN DIDION (1934–). "On Self-Respect," 1961, *Slouching Towards Bethlehem,* 1969

Nothing dies harder than the desire to think well of oneself.

> T. S. ELIOT (1888–1965). "Shakespeare and the Stoicism of Seneca," 1927

Gurowski asked "Where is this bog? I wish to earn some money: I wish to dig peat."—"O no, indeed, sir, you cannot do this kind of degrading work."—"I cannot be degraded. I am Gurowski."

> RALPH WALDO EMERSON (1803–1882). Journal, 1861, undated
>
> See Ridicule: Diogenes

Regard not so much what the World thinks of thee, as what thou thinkest of thyself.

> THOMAS FULLER (1654–1734). Comp., *Introductio ad Prudentiam*, 1552, 1731
>
> See Popularity: Alexander Pope

Respect yourself if you would have others respect you.

> BALTASAR GRACIÁN (1601–1658). *The Art of Worldly Wisdom*, 284, 1647, tr. Joseph Jacobs, 1943
>
> See Confidence: Goethe (1) ○ Friends: Thomas Fuller (3)

Self-respect—that cornerstone of all virtue.

> JOHN HERSCHEL (1792–1871). Address, London, 29 January 1833
>
> See Courage: Winston Churchill ○ Humility: St. Augustine ○ Prudence: Edmund Burke ○ Self-Discipline: Adam Smith (2)

Self-respect is the fruit of discipline; the sense of dignity grows with the ability to say No to oneself.

> ABRAHAM JOSHUA HESCHEL (1907–1972). *The Insecurity of Freedom: Essays on Human Existence*, 3, 1967
>
> See Self-Esteem: Thomas S. Szasz

Self-respect. The secure feeling that no one, as yet, is suspicious.

> H. L. MENCKEN (1880–1956). *A Book of Burlesques*, 11, 1920

I was brought up to believe that how I saw myself was more important than how others saw me.

> ANWAR el-SADAT (1918–1981). *In Search of Identity: An Autobiography*, 3:4, 1978
>
> See Popularity: Alexander Pope

What reason is there to admire ourselves because we are not as bad as the worst?

> SENECA THE YOUNGER (5? B.C.–A.D. 65). Preface (1.5) to *Natural Questions*, tr. Thomas A. Corcoran, 1921

Self-respect is to the soul as oxygen is to the body. Deprive a person of oxygen, and you kill his body; deprive him of self-respect, and you kill his spirit.

> THOMAS S. SZASZ (1920–). "Social Relations," *The Second Sin*, 1973

The calm existence that is mine when I
Am worthy of myself.

> WILLIAM WORDSWORTH (1770–1850). *The Prelude; or, Growth of a Poet's Mind: An Autobiographical Poem*, 1.349, 1850

✹

Most of all, reverence thyself.

> SAYING (LATIN)

SELF-RIGHTEOUSNESS

See also • Anger ○ Envy ○ Hypocrisy ○ Moral Indignation ○ Puritanism

The greatest menace to our civilization today is the conflict between giant organized systems of self-righteousness—each system only too delighted to find that the other is wicked—each only too glad that the sins give it the pretext for still deeper hatred and animosity. The effect of the whole situation is barbarizing.

> SIR HERBERT BUTTERFIELD (1900–1979). *Christianity, Diplomacy and War*, 4, 1953

Self-righteousness is a loud din raised to drown the voice of guilt within us.

> ERIC HOFFER (1902–1983). *The True Believer: Thoughts on the Nature of Mass Movements*, 69, 1951

Self-righteousness is a manifestation of self-contempt.

> ERIC HOFFER (1902–1983). *The Ordeal of Change*, 11, 1964

Our faults and sins seem all the bigger when they are seen by the world against the excessively self-righteous picture that is our official version of ourselves.

> WALTER LIPPMANN (1889–1974). "The Grace of Humility," *New York Herald Tribune*, 24 September 1957

Righteousness cannot be born until self-righteousness is dead.

> BERTRAND RUSSELL (1872–1970). *Justice in War-Time*, 1916

A self-righteous country soon forgets its righteousness and remembers only the self.

> GEORGE BERNARD SHAW (1856–1950). Remark to the author, 1940s. In Stephen Winsten, *Days with Bernard Shaw*, 23, 1949

SELF-SACRIFICE

See also • Giving ○ Hypocrisy ○ Martyrdom ○ Self ○ Self-Interest

If [Sydney Carton] had given any utterances to his [last thoughts], . . . they would have been these: . . .
   "It is a far, far better thing that I do, than I have ever done; it is a far, far better rest that I go to than I have ever known.

> CHARLES DICKENS (1812–1870). Closing words, *A Tale of Two Cities*, 1859. Carton, the novel's hero, was guillotined after arranging to take the place of the condemned Charles Darnay during the French Revolution.

No sacrifice is worth the name unless it is a joy. Sacrifice and a long face go ill together.

> MOHANDAS K. GANDHI (1869–1948). In *Young India*, 25 June 1925

How much easier is self-sacrifice than self-realization!

> ERIC HOFFER (1902–1983). *Reflections on the Human Condition*, 107, 1973

Sacrifice is a form of bargaining.

> HOLBROOK JACKSON (1874–1948)

Greater love has no man than this, that a man lay down his life for his friends.

> JESUS (A.D. 1st cent.). *John* 15:13

A sensible human once said . . . "She's the sort of woman who lives for others—you can always tell the others by their hunted expression."

> C. S. LEWIS (1898–1963). *The Screwtape Letters,* rev. ed., 26, 1982 (1942)

Men are more ready to sacrifice their lives than their livelihood: and to sacrifice their own importance often comes hardest of all.

> B. H. LIDDELL HART (1895–1970). November 1935, *Thoughts on War,* 10, 1944

Man is not a sacrificial animal, that he has the right to exist for his own sake, neither sacrificing himself to others, nor others to himself.

> AYN RAND (1905–1982). Alvin Toffler interview, *Playboy,* March 1964

Self-sacrifice enables us to sacrifice others without blushing.

> GEORGE BERNARD SHAW (1856–1950). "Maxims for Revolutionists: Self-Sacrifice," *Man and Superman,* 1903

I have alreddy given two cousins to the war, & I stand reddy to sacrifiss my wife's brother ruther'n not see the rebelyin krusht. And if wuss cums to wuss I'll shed ev'ry drop of blud my able-bodied relations has got to prosekoot the war.

> ARTEMUS WARD (1834–1867). "Artemus Ward to the Prince of Wales," *The Complete Works of Artemus Ward,* 1898

It takes a thoroughly selfish age, like our own, to deify self-sacrifice.

> OSCAR WILDE (1854–1900). "The Critic as Artist" (2), *Intentions,* 1891

I wish there were some great orator who could go about and make men drunk with this spirit of self-sacrifice.

> WOODROW WILSON (1856–1924). In Garry Wills, *Nixon Agonistes: The Crisis of the Self-Made Man,* 4.4 (epigraph), 1969

Too long a sacrifice
Can make a stone of the heart.

> WILLIAM BUTLER YEATS (1865–1939). "Easter 1916" (4), *Michael Robartes and the Dancer,* 1921

SELF-TRUST

See also • Self ○ Self-Knowledge ○ Self-Love ○ Self-Reliance ○ Self-Respect ○ Trust

Trust to that prompting within you.

> RALPH WALDO EMERSON (1803–1882). Journal, 3 April 1831

With the exercise of self-trust new powers shall appear.

> RALPH WALDO EMERSON (1803–1882). Journal, 27 May 1839
> See Success: Emerson

Trust thyself: every heart vibrates to that iron string.

> RALPH WALDO EMERSON (1803–1882). "Self-Reliance," *Essays: First Series,* 1841

A self-trust . . . is a trust in God himself.

> RALPH WALDO EMERSON (1803–1882). "Aristocracy," *Lectures and Biographical Sketches,* 1883

If you can trust yourself when all men doubt you,
    But make allowance for their doubting too. . . .

> RUDYARD KIPLING (1865–1936). "If," *Rewards and Fairies,* 1910

Trust thyself, and another shall not betray thee.

> WILLIAM PENN (1644–1718). *Some Fruits of Solitude,* 147, 1693

Trust no one but yourself.

> VEGETIUS (A.D. 4th cent.). *De Re Militari,* A.D. 378. In Thomas R. Phillips, ed., *Roots of Strategy,* p. 174, 1940

◢

Self-trust is the wellspring of courage.

> ANONYMOUS

Trust everybody but yourself most.

> SAYING (DANISH)

SENTIMENTALITY

See also • Compassion ○ Deception ○ Hypocrisy ○ Indifference

Sentimentality, the ostentatious parading of excessive and spurious emotion, is the mark of dishonesty, the inability to feel.

> JAMES BALDWIN (1924–1987). "Everybody's Protest Novel," 1949, *Notes of a Native Son,* 1955

Like many men who are compulsively cruel to their womenfolk, he also shed tears at the cinema, and showed a disproportinate concern for insects.

> SHIRLEY HAZZARD (1931–). *The Bay of Noon: A Novel,* 7, 1970

Sentimentality is the superstructure erected upon brutality.

> CARL G. JUNG (1875–1961). "'Ulysses': A Monologue," 1932, *The Spirit in Man, Art, and Literature,* tr. R. F. C. Hull, 1966

Sentimentality is the emotional promiscuity of those who have no sentiment.

> NORMAN MAILER (1923–). *Cannibals and Christians,* 2, 1966

Sentimentality is only sentiment that rubs you up the wrong way.

> W. SOMERSET MAUGHAM (1874–1965). 1941, *A Writer's Notebook,* 1949

Sentimentality—the indulgence of feeling without commitments in thought and action.

> HERBERT J. MULLER (1905–1982). *The Uses of the Past: Profiles of Former Societies,* 11.2, 1952

The tears that are shed for fictitious sorrow are admirably adapted to make us proud of all the virtues which we do not possess.

> ROUSSEAU (1712–1778). In Mary Wollstonecraft, *A Vindication of the Rights of Men,* p. 27, 1790

Donalbain: To show an unfelt sorrow is an office
Which the false man does easy.

> SHAKESPEARE (1564–1616). *Macbeth,* 2.3.141, 1605

The sentimentalist is always a cynic at heart. Indeed sentimentality is merely the Bank-holiday of cynicism.

> OSCAR WILDE (1854–1900). In Hesketh Pearson, *Oscar Wilde: His Life and Wit,* 12, 1946

SERVICE

See also • Action ○ Compassion ○ Cooperation ○ Giving ○ Good ○ Greatness: Martin Luther King, Jr. ○ Helping Others ○ Joy: Marcus Aurelius ○ Life: Lewis Mumford (2) ○ Morality ○ Peace: Lewis Mumford ○ Pleasure: Thomas Fuller ○ Selfishness ○ Self-Interest ○ Self-Reliance ○ Self-Knowledge: Mohandas K. Gandhi ○ Soul: Erica Jong ○ Success: Marianne Williamson ○ Virtue

To serve is beautiful, but only if it is done with joy and a whole heart and a free mind.

> PEARL S. BUCK (1892–1973). "Men and Women," *To My Daughters, With Love,* 1967

Service is the rent that you pay for room on this earth.

> SHIRLEY CHISHOLM (1924–). In Brian Lanker, "Shirley Chisholm," *I Dream a World: Portraits of Black Women Who Changed America,* 1989

What is sometimes called a benevolent interest in others may be but an unwitting mask for an attempt to dictate to them what their good shall be, instead of an endeavor to free them so that they may seek and find the good of their own choice.

> JOHN DEWEY (1859–1952). *Democracy and Education: An Introduction to the Philosophy of Education,* 9.2.2, 1916

There is no greater satisfaction for a just and well-meaning person than the knowledge that he has devoted his best energies to the service of the good cause.

> ALBERT EINSTEIN (1879–1955). Closing words, "The Negro Question," *Pageant,* January 1946

Serve self you serve society
Serve society serve yourself.

> RALPH WALDO EMERSON (1803–1882). "Notebook F No. 1," p. 28, 1836–1840

Recall the face of the poorest and the most helpless man whom you may have seen and ask yourself, if the step you contemplate is going to be of any use to *him.* Will he be able to gain anything by it? Will it restore him to a control over his own life and destiny?

> MOHANDAS K. GANDHI (1869–1948). *The Selected Works of Mahatma Gandhi,* 6.535, ed. Shriman Narayan, 1968

The best servant does his work unseen.

> OLIVER WENDELL HOLMES, SR. (1809–1894). *The Poet at the Breakfast-Table,* 5, 1872

Human service is the highest form of self-interest.

> ELBERT HUBBARD (1856–1915). *The Note Book of Elbert Hubbard,* p. 29, comp. Elbert Hubbard II, 1927

While over Alabama earth
These words are gently spoken
Serve—and hate will die unborn
Love—and chains are broken.

> LANGSTON HUGHES (1902–1967). "Alabama Earth" (At Booker Washington's grave), 1928, *The Collected Poems of Langston Hughes,* ed. Arnold Rampersad and David Roessel, 1994

He rises by lifting others.

> ROBERT G. INGERSOLL (1833–1899). "Liberty"

Thinks any human ills outside his concern? It's this
That sets us apart from dumb brutes, it's why we alone
Have a soul that's worthy of reverence, why we're imbued
With a divine potential. . . .
When the world was still new, our common Creator granted
The breath of life alone, but on us he further bestowed
Sovereign reason, the impulse to aid one another.

> JUVENAL (A.D. 60?–127?). *Satires,* 15.140, tr. Peter Green, 1967

A large part of altruism, even when it is perfectly honest, is grounded upon the fact that it is uncomfortable to have unhappy people about one.

> H. L. MENCKEN (1880–1956). "On the Nature of Man: The Altruist," *Prejudices: Fourth Series,* 1924

If you have a suffering friend, be a resting-place for his suffering, but a resting-place like a hard bed, a camp-bed: thus you will serve him best.

> FRIEDRICH NIETZSCHE (1844–1900). "Of the Compassionate," *Thus Spoke Zarathustra,* 1892, tr. R. J. Hollingdale, 1961

To be of true service I must know two things: his need, my capacity.

> NIKITA NIKOLAYEVICH PANIN (1855–?)

For mortal to aid mortal—this is god; and this is the road to eternal glory.

> PLINY THE ELDER (A.D. 23–79). *Natural History,* 2.5, tr. H. Rackham, 1938

He finds assistance in adversity who renders services in prosperity.

> PUBLIUS SYRUS (85–43 B.C.). *Moral Sayings,* 1016, tr. Darius Lyman, Jr., 1862

Only those who respect the personality of others can be of real use to them.

> ALBERT SCHWEITZER (1875–1965). *Memoirs of Childhood and Youth,* 5, 1925, tr. C. T. Campion, 1949

Like a bridge over troubled water
I will lay me down.

> PAUL SIMON (1941–). "Bridge over Troubled Water" (song), 1969

The man who is himself at ease can best attend to the distress of others.

> ADAM SMITH (1723–1790). *The Theory of Moral Sentiments,* 3.3, 1759

The proverb warns that, "You should not bite the hand that feeds you." But maybe you should, if it prevents you from feeding yourself.

> THOMAS S. SZASZ (1920–). "Control and Self-Control," *The Second Sin,* 1973

To be of most service to my brother I must meet him on the most equal and even ground.

> HENRY DAVID THOREAU (1817–1862). Journal, 8 February 1841

Men attend to the interests of the public, first by necessity, afterwards by choice; what was intentional becomes an instinct, and by dint of working for the good of one's fellow citizens, the habit and the taste for serving them are at length acquired.

> ALEXIS de TOCQUEVILLE (1805–1859). *Democracy in America,* 2.2.4, 1840, tr. Henry Reeve and Francis Bowen, 1862

People who serve you without love get even behind your back.

> WALT WHITMAN (1819–1892). Remark to the author, 18 May 1888. In Horace Traubel, *Walt Whitman's Camden Conversations,* ed. Walter Teller, 1973

SEX

See also • Abortion ○ Abstinence ○ Adultery ○ AIDS ○ Asceticism ○ Birth Control ○ Body ○ Brain: Woody Allen, Carl G. Jung ○ Chastity ○ Child Abuse ○ Desire ○ Feminism ○ Homosexuality ○ Impotence ○ Kissing ○ Literature: David Lodge ○ Love, Romantic: [especially] Peter R. Breggin ○ Lust ○ Marriage ○ Masturbation ○ Men ○ Misogynous Statements ○ Money: James Baldwin ○ Passion ○ Pornography ○ Promiscuity ○ Prostitution ○ Prudery ○ Puritanism ○ Rape ○ Sex Education ○ Sexist Statements ○ Sexual Dissatisfaction ○ Sexual Harassment ○ Sexual Repression ○ Sexual Revolution ○ Soul & Body ○ Sports: Piet Hein ○ Sterilization ○ Women ○ Women & Men ○ Worry: J. P. Donleavy

Is sex dirty? Only if it's done right.

> WOODY ALLEN (1935–). *Everything You Always Wanted to Know about Sex* (film), 1972

That was the most fun I've had without laughing.

> WOODY ALLEN (1935–) and MARSHALL BRICKMAN (1941–). *Annie Hall* (film), 1977, spoken by Allen to Diane Keaton

Eros, builder of cities.

> W. H. AUDEN (1907–1973). "In Memory of Sigmund Freud" (28), 1939, *Collected Poems,* ed. Edward Mendelson, 1976

I'm as pure as the driven slush.

> TALLULAH BANKHEAD (1903–1968). Actress. In *Observer* (British newspaper), 24 February 1957

The highest level of sexual excitement is in a monogamous relationship.

> WARREN BEATTY (1937–). In *Observer* (British newspaper), 27 October 1991

Sex pleasure in woman . . . is a kind of magic spell; it demands complete abandon; if words or movements oppose the magic of caresses, the spell is broken.

> SIMONE de BEAUVOIR (1908–1986). *The Second Sex,* 14, 1950, tr. H. M. Parshley, 1952

Spontaneity [in love-making] is everything. . . . Sexual converse ought to proceed like verbal converse with mutual give and take.

> GERALD BRENAN (1894–1987). "Love," *Thoughts in a Dry Season: A Miscellany,* 1978

The Joy of Sex.

> ALEX COMFORT (1920–). Book title, 1972

Sex is the last refuge of the miserable.

> QUENTIN CRISP (1908–). *The Naked Civil Servant,* 8, 1968
>
> See Patriotism: Samuel Johnson

Ignorance of the necessity for sexual intercourse to the health and virtue of both man and woman is the most fundamental error in medical and moral philosophy.

> GEORGE DRYSDALE. *The Elements of Social Science,* 1854

While it is perfectly true that sexual energy may be in large degree arrested, and transformed into intellectual and moral forms, yet it is also true that pleasure itself, and above all, sexual pleasure, wisely used and not abused, may prove the stimulus and liberator of our finest and most exalted activities.

> HAVELOCK ELLIS (1859–1939). "The Objects of Marriage," *Little Essays on Love and Virtue,* 1922

No act can be quite so intimate as the sexual embrace. In its accomplishment, for all who have reached a reasonably human degree of development, the communion of bodies becomes the communion of souls.

> HAVELOCK ELLIS (1859–1939). "The Objects of Marriage," *Little Essays on Love and Virtue,* 1922

I'll have what she's having.

> NORA EPHRON (1941–). *When Harry Met Sally . . .* (film), 1989. Woman diner to waiter after observing Meg Ryan, at another table, acting out an orgasm

Rarely use venery [i.e., sexual intercourse] but for health or offspring, never to dullness, weakness, or the injury of your own or another's peace or reputation.

> BENJAMIN FRANKLIN (1706–1790). Virtue #12 ("Chastity"), 1784, *Autobiography,* 1798

I know nothing about sex, because I was always married.

> ZSA ZSA GABOR (1920–). In Michèle Brown and Ann O'Connor, comps., "Sex," *Hammer and Tongues: The Best of Women's Wit and Humor,* 1986

The sexuo-economic relationship . . . sexualizes our industrial relationship and commercializes our sex-relation.

> CHARLOTTE PERKINS GILMAN (1860–1935). *Women and Economics: The Economic Factor Between Men and Women as a Factor in Social Revolution,* 6, 1899

I think our young people are getting it all together. Not that I think you should be making love all the time—who can do it all the time? Though I *do* try.

> CARY GRANT (1904–1986). In Guy Flatley, "Cary—From Mae to September," *New York Times,* 22 July 1973

If I were asked for a one-line answer to the question, "What makes a woman good in bed?" I would say, "A man who is good in bed."

> BOB GUCCIONE (1930–). Interview. In Wendy Leigh, *Speaking Frankly: What Makes a Woman Good in Bed,* 1978

But did thee feel the earth move?

> ERNEST HEMINGWAY (1899–1961). *For Whom the Bell Tolls,* 13, 1940

The sexual embrace, worthily understood, can only be compared with music and with prayer.

> JAMES HILTON (1900–1954). As paraphrased by Havelock Ellis, "The Objects of Marriage," *Little Essays of Love and Virtue,* 1922

First it was passion, then it became duty, and finally an intolerable burden.

> CARL G. JUNG (1875–1961). "Marriage as a Psychological Relationship," 1925, *The Development of Personality,* tr. R. F. C. Hull, 1954

These two
Imparadis'd in one another's arms.

> JOHN MILTON (1608–1674). *Paradise Lost,* 4.505, 1667

C'mon, baby, light my fire
Try to set the night on fire.

> JIM MORRISON (1943–1971) and ROBBY KRIEGER. "Light My Fire"
> (song), 1967

Sex is the ersatz, or substitute, religion of the 20th century.

> MALCOLM MUGGERIDGE (1903–1990). "The Titans: United States of
> America," television broadcast, BBC, London, 16 January 1962

When a man is in union with his wife in a spirit of holiness and
purity, the Divine Presence is with them.

> NAHMANIDES (A.D. 1194?–1270). In Ben Zion Bokser, *From the World
> of Cabalah,* 1954

Electric flesh-arrows . . . traversing the body. A rainbow of color
strikes the eyelids. A foam of music falls over the ears. It is the
gong of the orgasm.

> ANAÏS NIN (1903–1977). October 1937, *The Diary of Anaïs Nin,* 1966

What [D. H.] Lawrence is trying to do, I think, is to portray the sex
relation as something sacred. . . . I think Lawrence tried to portray this relation as in a real sense an act of holy communion. For
him flesh was sacramental of the spirit.

> JOHN ROBINSON (1919–1983). Bishop of Woolwich. Spoken as a
> defense witness in a case brought against Penguin Books for publish-
> ing *Lady Chatterly's Lover,* 27 October 1960

Making love? It's a communion with a woman. The bed is the holy
table. There I find passion—and purification.

> OMAR SHARIF (1932–). In *City Limits* (London), 18 December 1986

Traditionally, men used power to gain sex, and women used sex
to gain power.

> THOMAS S. SZASZ (1920–). "Men and Women," *Heresies,* 1976

Sex without love is as hollow and ridiculous as love without sex.

> HUNTER S. THOMPSON (1939–). Letter to Ann Frick, 4 June 1958, *The
> Proud Highway: Saga of a Desperate Southern Gentleman, 1955–1967,*
> ed. Douglas Brinkley, 1997

Sex is like money; only too much is enough.

> JOHN UPDIKE (1932–). *Couples,* 5, 1968

If God created the world, He created sex, and one way to con-
strue our inexhaustible sexual interest is as a form of the praise of
creation. Says the *Song of Solomon,* "The joints of thy thighs *are*
like jewels, the work of the hands of a cunning workman." [7:1,
King James Version]

> JOHN UPDIKE (1932–). "Even the Bible Is Soft on Sex," *New York
> Times Book Review,* 20 June 1993

Sex is a conversation carried out by other means.

> PETER USTINOV (1921–). Interview. In Wendy Leigh, *Speaking Frankly:
> What Makes a Woman Good in Bed,* 1978

It's not the men in my life that counts—it's the life in my men.

> MAE WEST (1893–1980). "Misc. West," *The Wit and Wisdom of Mae
> West,* ed. Joseph Weintraub, 1967

I like a man [who] takes his time.

> MAE WEST (1893–1980). "Misc. West," *The Wit and Wisdom of Mae
> West,* ed. Joseph Weintraub, 1967

Men like women with a past—because they hope history will
repeat itself.

> MAE WEST (1893–1980). "A Way with Words," ed. Jim Koch, *New York
> Times,* 15 August 1993

You know how Americans are when it comes to sex: the men
can't keep from lying, and the women can't keep from telling the
truth.

> ROBIN ZANDER. Musician in the band Cheap Trick. On being voted
> 1977's sexiest man by a New Jersey women's club

❦

Sex[ual] intercourse is the great sacrament of life.

> ANONYMOUS. In Havelock Ellis, "The Objects of Marriage," *Little Essays
> on Love and Virtue,* 1922

Each is pleasured in the act of pleasuring the other.

> ANONYMOUS

Bed is the poor man's opera.

> SAYING (ITALIAN)

SEX EDUCATION

See also • Sex

I don't think kids should be told about sex until they're old
enough to keep it under control.

> R. COBB. Ridiculing the taboo against sex education in the schools, car-
> toon balloon, 1960s

*Everything You Always Wanted to Know about Sex, But Were
Afraid to Ask.*

> DAVID R. REUBEN (1933–). Psychiatrist. Book title, 1970

SEXISM

See also • Feminism ∘ Men ∘ Misogynous Statements ∘ Prejudice
∘ Religion, Anti-: Elizabeth Cady Stanton ∘ Sexist Statements ∘
Women

The fact is, women are in chains, and their servitude is all the
more debasing because they do not realize it.

> SUSAN B. ANTHONY (1820–1906). In Lynn Sherr and Jurate Kazickas,
> eds., *The Liberated Woman's Appointment Calendar,* 1975

Let me state here and now that the black woman in America can
justly be described as a "slave of a slave."

> FRANCES M. BEAL. "Double Jeopardy: To Be Black and Female," 1969.
> In Robin Morgan, ed., *Sisterhood Is Powerful: An Anthology of
> Writings from the Women's Liberation Movement,* 1970

[Sexism] can never be seen in isolation. It has to be placed in the
context of its interconnections with racism, and especially with
class exploitation.

> ANGELA DAVIS (1944–). "Women, Race, and Class: An Activist
> Perspective," *Women's Studies Quarterly,* Winter 1982

When a man gives his opinion, he's a man. When a woman gives her opinion, she's a bitch.

> BETTE DAVIS (1908–1989). Attributed

From the first dawn of life unto the grave,
Poor womankind's in every state a slave.

> SARAH EGERTON (1670–1723). "The Emulation," 1703

The big lie perpetrated on Western society is the idea of women's inferiority, a lie so deeply ingrained in our social behavior that merely to recognize it is to risk unraveling the entire fabric of civilization.

> MOLLY HASKELL (1940–). Opening sentence, *From Reverence to Rape: The Treatment of Women in the Movies,* 2nd ed., 1987 (1974)

[Sexism is] behavior, policy, language, or other action of men or women which expresses the institutionalized, systematic, comprehensive, or consistent view that women are inferior.

> CHERIS KRAMARAE (1938–) and PAULA A. TREICHLER. Comps., *A Feminist Dictionary: In Our Own Words,* p. 411, 1985

The term girl not only serves to avoid certain anxiety-arousing connotations inherent in the word woman regarding aggression, sexuality, and reproduction, it also serves to impart a tone of frivolousness and lack of seriousness to ambitious, intellectual, and competitive strivings that women may pursue.

> HARRIET E. LERNER. "Girls, Ladies, or Women? the Unconscious Dynamics of Language Choice," *Comprehensive Psychiatry,* March-April 1976

Nobody objects to a woman being a good writer or sculptor or geneticist as long as she manages also to be a good wife, mother, good-looking, good-tempered, well-dressed, well-groomed, unaggressive.

> MARYA MANNES (1907–1990). "New Bites by a Girl Gadfly," *Life,* 12 June 1964

Men do not want solely the obedience of women, they want their sentiments . . . not a forced slave but a willing one. . . . They have therefore put everything in practice to enslave their minds. . . . All women are brought up from the very earliest years in the belief that their ideal of character is the very opposite to that of men; not self-will and government by self-control, but submission and yielding to the control of others.

> JOHN STUART MILL (1806–1873). *The Subjection of Women,* 1, 1869

What is now called the nature of women is an eminently artificial thing—the result of forced repression in some directions, unnatural stimulation in others.

> JOHN STUART MILL (1806–1873). *The Subjection of Women,* 1, 1869

The rationale which accompanies that imposition of male authority euphemistically referred to as "the battle of the sexes" bears a certain resemblance to the formulas of nations at war, where any heinousness is justified on the grounds that the enemy is either an inferior [part of the] species or really not human at all.

> KATE MILLET (1934–). *Sexual Politics,* 2.6, 1969

The personal is political. . . . What seem to be "personal" problems of women have their roots in the political system which oppresses women.

> ROSARIO MORALES. "Stop Leaving Women Out of the Proletariat," *Guardian,* 15 August 1973

Our smiles and glances,
the ways we walk, sit, laugh, the games we must play
with men and even oh my Ancient Mother God the games
we must play among ourselves—these are the ways we pass
unnoticed, by the Conquerors.
They're always watching,
invisibly electroded in our brains,
to be certain we implode our rage against each other
and not explode it against them.

> ROBIN MORGAN (1941–). Ed., introduction ("Letter To A Sister Underground"), *Sisterhood Is Powerful: An Anthology of Writings from the Women's Liberation Movement,* 1970

Woman is the nigger of the world.

> YOKO ONO (1933–). Interview, *Nova* (magazine), 1968

Woman's degradation is in man's idea of his sexual rights. Our religion, laws, customs, are all founded on the belief that woman was made for man.

> ELIZABETH CADY STANTON (1815–1902). Letter to Susan B. Anthony, 14 June 1860

To think that all in me of which my father would have felt a proper pride had I been a man, is deeply mortifying to him because I am a woman.

> ELIZABETH CADY STANTON (1815–1902). *Elizabeth Cady Stanton,* ed. Theodore Stanton and Harriot Stanton Blatch, 1922

The average woman [in the United States] earned only 53 cents for every dollar paid to a man.

> UNITED STATES CENSUS. 1990. As paraphrased by Dennis J. Opatrny, "Men Make a Buck, Women Earn 60¢ [in California]," *San Francisco Sunday Examiner & Chronicle,* 28 March 1993

The ownership of women begins in the lower barbarian stages of culture, apparently with the seizure of female captives. The original reason for the seizure and appropriation of women seems to have been their usefulness as trophies.

> THORSTEIN VEBLEN (1857–1929). *The Theory of the Leisure Class: An Economic Study of Institutions,* 2, 1899

The real issue between men and women is not sex, but the inequality of power. . . . The name of the pattern is patriarchy—the subordination of women to men. It is a structure of domination. And like the division of the world between rich and poor and the institutional character of white racism, sexism is also systematic, with clear social purposes.

> JIM WALLIS (1948–). *The Soul of Politics: A Practical and Prophetic Vision for Change,* 6, 1994

A rule of men over women remained an established feature of highly civilized societies. It survived as a hangover from barbarism.

> ALFRED NORTH WHITEHEAD (1861–1947). *Adventures of Ideas,* 5.6, 1933

Women are told from their infancy, and taught by the example of their mothers, that a little knowledge of human weakness, justly termed cunning, softness of temper, *outward* obedience, and a scrupulous attention to a puerile kind of propriety, will obtain for them the protection of men; and should they be beautiful, everything else is needless, for at least twenty years of their lives.

> MARY WOLLSTONECRAFT (1759–1797). *A Vindication of the Rights of Woman*, 2, 1792

The condition of women affords in all countries the best criterion by which to judge the character of men.

> FRANCES WRIGHT (1795–1852). March 1820, *Views of Society and Manners in America*, 1821

SEXIST STATEMENTS

See also • Feminism ○ Marriage: William Blackstone, *The Book of Common Prayer* ○ Men ○ Misogynous Statements ○ Prejudice ○ Psychoanalysis: Sigmund Freud (5) ○ Sex ○ Sexism ○ Witchcraft ○ Women ○ Women & Men

The male is by nature superior, and the female inferior; and the one rules, and the other is ruled; this principle, of necessity, extends to all mankind.

> ARISTOTLE (384–322 B.C.). *Politics*, 1.5, tr. Benjamin Jowett, 1885

Less equipped psychologically to "stay the course" in the brawling arenas of business, commerce, industry, and the professions, women are physically unequipped to compete in the worlds of athletics and arms.

> PATRICK J. BUCHANAN (19938–). Syndicated column, 1989. In Steven A. Holmes, "White House Hopes to Trip Buchanan on His Paper Trail," *New York Times*, 1 March 1992

They ought to mind home—and be well fed and clothed—but not mixed in society. Well educated, too, in religion—but to read neither poetry nor politics—nothing but books of piety and cookery. Music—drawing—dancing—also a little gardening and plowing now and then. I have seen them mending the roads in Epirus with good success. Why not, as well hay-making and milking?

> LORD BYRON (1788–1824). Quoted with approval by the author. In Arthur Schopenhauer, "Studies in Pessimism: On Women," *Essays of Arthur Schopenhauer*, tr. T. Bailey Saunders, 1851

Women . . . are only children of a larger growth.

> LORD CHESTERFIELD (1694–1773). Letter to his son, 5 September 1748

Nothing would induce me to vote for giving women the franchise. I am not going to be henpecked into a question of such importance.

> WINSTON CHURCHILL (1874–1965). 1910? In Robert Lewis Taylor, *Winston Churchill: An Informal Study of Greatness*, 1952

We all know how much further women go than men in their social rivalries and jealousies. Woman suffrage would give to the wives and daughters of the poor a new opportunity to gratify their envy and mistrust of the rich. Meantime these new voters would become the purchased or cajoled victims of plausible political manipulators, or the intimidated or helpless voting vassals of imperious employers.

> GROVER CLEVELAND (1837–1908). "Would Woman Suffrage Be Unwise?" *Ladies' Home Journal*, October 1905

Man is more courageous, pugnacious, and energetic than woman, and has a more inventive genius.

> CHARLES DARWIN (1809–1882). *The Descent of Man and Selection in Relation to Sex*, 2nd ed., 19, 1874

Housekeeping and the care and education of children claim the whole person and practically rule out any profession. . . .

It seems a completely unrealistic notion to send women into the struggle for existence in the same way as men. Am I to think of my delicate, sweet girl as a competitor?

> SIGMUND FREUD (1856–1939). Letter to his fiancé Martha Bernays, 15 November 1883, tr. Tania and James Stern, 1960

The effect of penis-envy has a share . . . in the physical vanity of women, since they are bound to value their charms more highly as a late compensation for their original sexual inferiority. Shame, which is considered to be a feminine characteristic *par excellence* but is far more a matter of convention than might be supposed, has as its purpose, we believe, concealment of genital deficiency.

> SIGMUND FREUD (1856–1939). *New Introductory Lectures on Psychoanalysis*, 33, 1933, tr. James Strachey, 1965

Her world is her husband, her family, her children and her home. We do not find it right when the woman presses into the world of the man.

> ADOLF HITLER (1889–1945). In Lucy Komisar, *The New Feminism*, 10, 1971

A man of straw is worth a woman of gold.

> JAMES HOWELL (1593–1666). Comp., "Italian" (p. 5), *Paroimiographia: Proverbs, or Old Sayed Sawes & Adages in English . . . Italian, French and Spanish*, 1659

Words are women, deeds are men.

> JAMES HOWELL (1593–1666). Comp. "Italian" (p. 7), *Paroimiographia: Proverbs, or Old Sayed Sawes & Adages in English . . . Italian, French and Spanish*, 1659
>
> See Women & Men: Margaret Thatcher

A man's foremost interest should be his work. But [for] a woman—man *is* her work and her business. Yes, I know it sounds like a convenient philosophy of the selfish male when I say that. But marriage means a home. And home is like a nest—not enough room for both birds at once. One sits inside, the other perches on the edge and looks about and attends to all outside business.

> CARL G. JUNG (1875–1961). "Men, Women, and God," 25–29 April 1955, *C. G. Jung Speaking: Interviews and Encounters*, ed. William McGuire and R. F. C. Hull, 1977

Men have broad and large chests, and small narrow hips, and more understanding than women, who have but small and narrow breasts, and broad hips, to the end they should remain at home, sit still, keep house, and bear and bring up children.

> MARTIN LUTHER (1483–1546). *Table Talk*, 725, 1566, tr. William Hazlitt, 1857

Should Woman Learn the Alphabet?

> SILVAIN MARECHAL. French writer. Book title, 1801 (the book proposed a law that denied the alphabet to women). In Cheris Kramarae and Paula A. Treichler, eds., "Words on a Feminist Dictionary," *A Feminist Dictionary: In Our Own Words,* 1985

Equality for women? That is madness. Women are our property; we are not theirs. They give us children . . . and belong to us as the fruit-bearing tree belongs to the gardener.

> NAPOLEON (1769–1821). *In the Words of Napoleon,* p. 104, tr. Daniel Savage Gray, 1977

If civilization had been left in female hands, we would still be living in grass huts.

> CAMILLE PAGLIA (1947–). Introduction to *Sex, Art, and American Culture: Essays,* 1992

As the church is subject to Christ, so let wives also be subject in everything to their husbands.

> PAUL (A.D. 1st cent.). *Ephesians* 5:24
> See Unity: Paul

You husbands, live considerately with your wives, bestowing honor on the woman as the weaker sex.

> PETER (A.D. 1st cent.). *1 Peter* 3:7

All the pursuits of men are the pursuits of women also, but in all of them a woman is inferior to a man.

> PLATO (427?–347 B.C.). *The Republic,* 5.455, tr. Benjamin Jowett, 1894

A woman's thoughts, beyond the range of her immediate duties, should be directed to the study of men, or the acquirement of that agreeable learning whose sole end is the formation of taste; for the works of genius are beyond her reach, and she has neither the accuracy nor the attention for success in the exact sciences.

> ROUSSEAU (1712–1778). *Emile; or, Treatise on Education,* 5, 1762, tr. Barbara Foxley, 1911

The man should be strong and active; the woman should be weak and passive; the one must have both the power and the will; it is enough that the other should offer little resistance.

> ROUSSEAU (1712–1778). *Emile; or, Treatise on Education,* 5, 1762, tr. Barbara Foxley, 1911

The claim that American women are downtrodden and unfairly treated is the fraud of the century.

> PHYLLIS SCHLAFLY (1924–). In Lisa Cronin Wohl, "Phyllis Schlafly: 'The Sweetheart of the Silent Majority,'" *Ms.,* March 1974

The weakness of their reasoning faculty also explains why it is that women show more sympathy for the unfortunate than men do, and so treat them with more kindness and interest.

> ARTHUR SCHOPENHAUER (1788–1860). "Studies in Pessimism: On Women," *Essays of Arthur Schopenhauer,* tr. T. Bailey Saunders, 1851

They form the *sexus sequior*—the second sex, inferior in every respect to the first; their infirmities should be treated with consideration; but to show them great reverence is extremely ridiculous, and lowers us in their eyes.

> ARTHUR SCHOPENHAUER (1788–1860). "Studies in Pessimism: On Women," *Essays of Arthur Schopenhauer,* tr. T. Bailey Saunders, 1851

This Number Two of the human race.

> ARTHUR SCHOPENHAUER (1788–1860). "Studies in Pessimism: On Women," *Essays of Arthur Schopenhauer,* tr. T. Bailey Saunders, 1851

Hamlet: Frailty, thy name is woman!

> SHAKESPEARE (1564–1616). *Hamlet,* 1.2.146, 1600

Biologically and temperamentally, I believe, women were made to be concerned first and foremost with child care, husband care and home care.

> BENJAMIN SPOCK (1903–1998). In Barbara Sinclair Deckard, *The Women's Movement: Political, Socioeconomic, and Psychological Issues,* 2nd ed., 1, 1979

The Queen is most anxious to enlist everyone who can speak or write to join in checking this mad, wicked folly of "Woman's Rights" with all its attendant horrors on which her poor, feeble sex is bent, forgetting every sense of womanly feeling and propriety. It is a subject which makes the Queen so furious that she cannot contain herself. God created men and women different—then let them remain each in their own position.

> VICTORIA (1819–1901). British queen. Referring to herself in the third person. Memorandum on women's suffrage, 29 May 1870.

✿

To the woman [the Lord God] said,
"I will greatly multiply your pain in childbearing;
   in pain you shall bring forth children,
yet your desire shall be for your husband,
   and he shall rule over you."

> ANONYMOUS (*BIBLE*). *Genesis* 3:16

A girl is worth only a tenth of a boy.

> SAYING (CHINESE)

One boy is better than three girls.

> SAYING (GERMAN)

A woman's place is in the home.

> SAYING
> See Feminism: Saying (American)

SEXUAL DISSATISFACTION

See also • Impotence ○ Sex

Whenever they were in bed together and he failed to come up to scratch she felt as badly let down as when her car refused to start. Resentment, followed by indignation.

> GERALD BRENAN (1894–1987). "Love," *Thoughts in a Dry Season: A Miscellany,* 1978

I am happy now that Charles calls on my bedchamber less frequently than of old. As it is, I now endure but two calls a week, and when I hear his steps outside my door I lie down on my bed, close my eyes, open my legs and think of England.

> LADY ALICE HILLINGDON (1857–1959). Referring to her husband

Another condition for the zipless fuck was brevity.

> ERICA JONG (1942–). *Fear of Flying,* 1, 1973

Women complain about sex more often than men. Their gripes fall into two major categories: (1) Not enough, (2) Too much.

> ANN LANDERS (1918–). *Ann Landers Says Truth Is Stranger . . .* , 2, 1968

It's all this cold-hearted fucking that is death and idiocy.

> D. H. LAWRENCE (1885–1930). *Lady Chatterly's Lover,* 14, 1928

You mustn't force sex to do the work of love or love to do the work of sex.

> MARY McCARTHY (1912–1989). *The Group,* 2, 1963

What a let-down! I was ready for a tour round his Eiffel Tower, but all I got was a limp excuse and not-tonight-Josephine. Next time it had better be the real French stick, François, not a soggy brioche.

> RUTH MORGAN (1920–1978). *Jeu d'Esprit,* 9, 1968

When sex is good, it's 10 percent of the relationship. When it's bad, it's 90 percent.

> CHARLES MUIR. Hawaiian yoga teacher. In Katy Butler, "In the New Age, Sex Is a Soul-Mate," *San Francisco Chronicle,* 7 March 1994

Morality in sexual situations, when it is free from superstition, consists essentially of respect for the other person, and unwillingness to use that person solely as a means of personal gratification, without regard to his or her desires.

> BERTRAND RUSSELL (1872–1970). *Marriage and Morals,* 11, 1929

Holden Caulfield: Sex is something I really don't understand too hot. You never know *where* the hell you are. I keep making up these sex rules for myself, and then I break them right away.

> J. D. SALINGER (1919–). *The Catcher in the Rye,* 9, 1951

A mutual and satisfied sexual act is of great benefit to the average woman, the magnetism of it is health giving. When it is not desired on the part of the woman and she gives no response, it should not take place. The submission of her body without love or desire is degrading to the woman's finer sensibility, all the marriage certificates on earth to the contrary notwithstanding.

> MARGARET SANGER (1883–1966). "Coitus Interruptus," *Family Limitations,* 1914

SEXUAL HARASSMENT

See also • Sex

[Sexual] harassment can be different things to different people. . . . It's harassment when something starts bothering somebody.

> GEORGE PALMER. Du Pont & Co. spokesman. In Joseph Pereira, "Women Allege Atmosphere in Offices Constitutes Harassment," *Wall Street Journal,* 10 February 1988

SEXUAL REPRESSION

See also • Newspeak—Examples: George Orwell (4) ○ Sex ○ Tyranny

There is no doubt that the practice [of female genital mutilation] is a means of suppressing and controlling the sexual behavior of women. Female circumcision is a physiological chastity belt.

> SUE ARMSTRONG. South African journalist. "Female Circumcision: Fighting a Cruel Tradition," *New Scientist,* 2 February 1991

I know I felt the need [for] a girl when I was 12 or 13—I think every boy does. Yet our society sets out to divorce boys and girls. They even have bucket seats in cars now, so you can't neck in a drive-in.

> CARY GRANT (1904–1986). In Guy Flatley, "Cary—From Mae to September," *New York Times,* 22 July 1973

Sexuality poorly repressed unsettles some families; well repressed, it unsettles the whole world.

> KARL KRAUS (1874–1936). 1911. In Thomas S. Szasz, *Karl Kraus and the Soul-Doctors: A Pioneer Critic and His Criticism of Psychiatry and Psychoanalysis,* 8, 1976

[Julia] had grasped the inner meaning of the Party's sexual puritanism. It was not merely that the sex instinct created a world of its own which was outside the Party's control and which therefore had to be destroyed if possible. What was more important was that sexual privation induced hysteria, which was desirable because it could be transformed into war fever and leader worship.

> GEORGE ORWELL (1903–1950). *Nineteen Eighty-Four,* 2.3, 1949

When you make love, you're using up energy; and afterwards you feel happy and don't give a damn for anything. [The Party] can't bear you to feel like that. They want you to be bursting with energy all the time. All this marching up and down and cheering and waving flags is simply sex gone sour. If you're happy inside yourself, why should you get excited about Big Brother and the Three-Year Plans and the Two Minutes Hate and all the rest of their bloody rot?

> GEORGE ORWELL (1903–1950). *Nineteen Eighty-Four,* 2.3., 1949

It is illegal in England to state in print that a wife can and should derive sexual pleasure from intercourse.

> BERTRAND RUSSELL (1872–1970). *Marriage and Morals,* 8, 1929

SEXUAL REVOLUTION

See also • Feminism ○ Sex

I wouldn't be surprised [if my daughter had an affair]. I think she's a perfectly normal human being like all young girls. If she wanted to continue, I would certainly counsel and advise her on the subject. And I'd want to know pretty much about the young man . . . whether it was a worthwhile encounter. . . . She's pretty young to start affairs, [but] she's a big girl.

> BETTY FORD (1918–). Appearing on *60 Minutes,* television magazine program, CBS, 10 August 1975

For most Americans, the sexual revolution was not a vast national orgy of swingers. There was never widespread approval of adultery or promiscuity. The revolution—evolution is a better word— appeared rather as a massive questioning of the double standard and the sexual constraints we grew up with.

> ELLEN GOODMAN (1941–). ". . . And the New Fear of Sex," *Washington Post,* 28 October 1986

As political and economic freedom diminishes, sexual freedom tends compensatingly to increase. . . . In conjunction with the freedom to daydream under the influence of dope and movies and the radio, it will help to reconcile [the dictator's] subjects to servitude which is their fate.

ALDOUS HUXLEY (1894–1963). Foreword (1946) to *Brave New World,* 1932

Whenever an instinct has been underrated, an abnormal overvaluation is bound to follow. . . . Before Freud nothing was allowed to be sexual, now everything is nothing but sexual.

CARL G. JUNG (1875–1961). "Analytical Psychology and Education" (2), 1924, *The Development of Personality,* tr. R. F. C. Hull, 1954

Woman: I thought you were a modern couple.
Man: Yes, she's very modern, and I'm very couple.

DIANE KURYS and OLIVER SCHATZKY. *A Man in Love* (film), 1987

Women [today] make sexual demands and offer sexual potentialities that their mothers would never have dreamed of, or would only have dreamed of. By the same token, they make demands for understanding and companionship. Men . . . do not always welcome the "cooperation" and companionship from the opposite sex that the dropping of an older tariff permits and in a way requires.

DAVID RIESMAN (1909–) (with NATHAN GLAZER and REUEL DENNEY). *The Lonely Crowd: A Study of the Changing American Character,* 14.2, 1950, abr., 1953

There is [sexual] permissiveness in the technocratic society; but it is only for the swingers and the big spenders. It is the reward that goes to reliable, politically safe henchmen of the status quo.

THEODORE ROSZAK (1933–). *The Making of the Counter Culture: Reflections on the Technocratic Society and Its Youthful Opposition,* 1, 1969

❧

In my state [Texas] they really raise hell about the new [more open sexual] morality. This one old geezer said he was against it for three reasons. "First, it's against the law of nature. Second, it's destructive of family living. And third, I ain't getting none of it."

ANONYMOUS (AMERICAN). In James A. Michener, "The Revolution in Middle-Class Values," *New York Times Magazine,* 18 August 1968

SHAME

See also • Glory ○ Guilt: [especially] Edmund H. Volkart, Anonymous (1) ○ Honor

Whilst Shame keeps its watch, Virtue is not wholly extinguished in the heart.

EDMUND BURKE (1729–1797). *Reflections on the Revolution in France,* p. 218, 1790, Pelican Books edition, 1968

Corruption, bribes or cronyism have come to infect virtually every economic interaction in this country—whether it's building a bridge or getting a job. The tone is set from the top. President Suharto's family owns a slice of virtually every major Indonesian industry—including airlines, television stations, power plants, toll roads, telephones, even a national auto production project protected by special tariffs. No wonder a local joke has it that the Suhartos have everything—except a sense of shame.

THOMAS L. FRIEDMAN (1953–). "From the Top," *New York Times,* 17 July 1997

We should be ashamed of resting or having a square meal so long as there is one able-bodied man or woman without work or food.

MOHANDAS K. GANDHI (1869–1948). In *Young India,* 6 October 1921

Shame is a disease of the last age; this seemeth to be cured of it.

MARQUIS OF HALIFAX (1633–1695). "Shame," *Political, Moral and Miscellaneous Reflections,* 1750

There is a good reason the words "shameful" and "shameless" define the same conduct. You know you've behaved shamefully if you have exposed other people to needless annoyance or embarrassment. You don't know you've behaved shamelessly if you don't get this point.

CHRISTOPHER HITCHENS (1949–). "The Death of Shame," *Vanity Fair,* March 1996

One of the misfortunes of our time is that in getting rid of false shame we have killed off so much real shame as well.

LOUIS KRONENBERGER (1904–1980). *Company Manners: A Cultural Inquiry into American Life,* 2.1, 1954

If one is ashamed, there is no better remedy than to practice benevolence.

MENCIUS (371?–289? B.C.). *Mencius,* 2.A.7, tr. D. C. Lau, 1970

Shame is like everything else; live with it for long enough and it becomes part of the furniture.

SALMAN RUSHDIE (1947–). *Shame,* 1.2, 1983

Are you not ashamed of heaping up the greatest amount of money and honor and reputation, and caring so little about wisdom and truth and the greatest improvement of the soul?

SOCRATES (470?–399 B.C.). In Plato (427?–347 B.C.), *Apology,* 29, tr. Benjamin Jowett, 1894

I never wonder to see men wicked, but I often wonder to see them not ashamed.

JONATHAN SWIFT (1667–1745). "Thoughts on Various Subjects" (expanded from a version published in 1711), *Miscellanies in Prose and Verse* (published with Alexander Pope), vol. 1, 1727

❧

Past shame, past grace.

SAYING

SHARING

See also • Cooperation ○ Friends: Abraham Joshua Heschel ○ Giving ○ Happiness: Thomas Merton (1) ○ Luck: Saying (Irish) ○ Property

I do detest everything which is not perfectly mutual.

LORD BYRON (1788–1824). Letter to Lady Melbourne, 21 October 1813

I hate privilege and monopoly. Whatever cannot be shared with the masses is taboo to me.

MOHANDAS K. GANDHI (1869–1948). In *Harijan,* 2 November 1934
See Democracy: Walt Whitman (1)

A decent man at table the other day, taking the only remaining potato out of the dish on the end of his knife, offered his friend half of it!

> NATHANIEL HAWTHORNE (1804–1864). 23 August 1838, *The American Notebooks*, ed. Claude M. Simpson, 1932

He who has two coats, let him share with him who has none; and he who has food, let him do likewise.

> JOHN THE BAPTIST (A.D. 1st cent.). *Luke* 3:11

Imagine no possessions
I wonder if you can
No need for greed and hunger
A brotherhood of man
Imagine all the people
Sharing all the world.

> JOHN LENNON (1940–1980). "Imagine" (song), 1971

The more we share, the more we have.

> LEONARD NIMOY (1931–). In "Quotable Quotes," *Reader's Digest*, August 1992

Friends share all things.

> PYTHAGORAS (580?–500? B.C.). In Diogenes Laertius (A.D. 3rd cent.), *Lives of Eminent Philosophers*, 8.10, tr. R. D. Hicks, 1925

No good thing is pleasant to possess without friends to share it.

> SENECA THE YOUNGER (5? B.C.–A.D. 65). "On Sharing Knowledge," *Moral Letters to Lucilius*, 6.4, tr. Richard M. Gummere, 1918

Let us possess things in common; for birth is ours in common. Our relations with one another are like a stone arch, which would collapse if the stones did not mutually support each other.

> SENECA THE YOUNGER (5? B.C.–A.D. 65). "On the Usefulness of Basic Principles," *Moral Letters to Lucilius*, 95.53, tr. Richard M. Gummere, 1918

Now the company of those who believed were of one heart and soul, and no one said that any of the things which he possessed was his own, but they had everything in common. . . . There was not a needy person among them, for as many as were possessors of lands or houses sold them, and brought the proceeds of what was sold and laid it at the apostles' feet; and distribution was made to each as any had need.

> ANONYMOUS (*BIBLE*). *Acts* 4:32–35
> See Work: Louis Blanc, Karl Marx

Neither aim for nor accept anything that cannot be shared with everyone.

> ANONYMOUS

Shared joys are doubled; shared sorrows are halved.

> SAYING (ENGLISH)
> See Friends: Francis Bacon

Share and share alike.

> SAYING

SHIPS

See also • Misjudgments: Anonymous ○ Navy: [especially] James Lawrence ○ Sea

No man will be a sailor, who has contrivance enough to get himself into a jail; for being in a ship is being in a jail, with the chance of being drowned.

> SAMUEL JOHNSON (1709–1784). 31 August 1773. In James Boswell, *The Journal of a Tour to the Hebrides, with Samuel Johnson, L.L.D.*, 1786

A ship is always referred to as "she" because it costs so much to keep one in paint and powder.

> CHESTER W. NIMITZ (1885–1966). Speech before the Society of Sponsors of the United States Navy, 13 February 1940

Some went down to the sea in ships,
  doing business on the great waters

> ANONYMOUS (*BIBLE*). *Psalms* 107:23

Titanic passenger: Is this ship really unsinkable?
Deckhand: God himself could not sink this ship.

> ANONYMOUS. Format adapted. Southampton (England), 10 April 1912. In Christopher Cerf and Victor Navasky, comps., *The Experts Speak: The Definitive Compendium of Authoritative Misinformation*, p. 233, 1984. Four nights later, after hitting an iceberg in the North Atlantic south of Newfoundland, the *Titanic* sank with a loss of more than 1,500 lives.

SHOCK TREATMENT

See also • Psychiatric Treatment ○ Psychiatry ○ War & Psychology: Adrienne Rich ○ Witchcraft: Jan Ehrenwald

An extensive American Psychiatric Association membership survey reports that 41% of the respondents agreed with the statement, "It is likely that ECT produces slight or subtle brain damage"; 26% disagreed.

> AMERICAN PSYCHIATRIC ASSOCIATION TASK FORCE ON ELECTRO-CONVULSIVE THERAPY. Adapted. *Electroconvulsive Therapy* (Task Force Report 14), 1, 1978

In light of the available evidence, "brain damage" need not be included [in the informed-consent form for electroconvulsive treatment] as a potential risk.

> AMERICAN PSYCHIATRIC ASSOCIATION TASK FORCE ON ELECTRO-CONVULSIVE THERAPY. *The Practice of Electroconvulsive Therapy: Recommendations for Treatment, Training, and Privileging*, 3.5, 1990

Recent memory loss [produced by ECT] could be compared to erasing a tape recording.

> ROBERT E. ARNOT (1916–). "Observations on the Effects of Electric Convulsive Treatment in Man—Psychological," *Diseases of the Nervous System*, September 1975

Anyone who has gone through the electric shock . . . never again rises out of its darkness and his life has been lowered a notch.

> ANTONIN ARTAUD (1896–1948). "Insanity and Black Magic," 1946, *Antonin Artaud: Selected Writings*, ed. Susan Sontag, 1973

[In April 1950, a "mute and autistic" 34½-month-old boy was administered 20 ECTs after being referred to the children's ward of New York's Bellevue Hospital. A month later he was discharged.] The discharge note indicated "moderate improvement, since he was eating and sleeping better, was more friendly with the other children, and he was toilet trained."

> LAURETTA BENDER (1897–1987). "The Development of a Schizophrenic Child Treated with Electric Convulsions at Three Years of Age." In Gerald Caplan, ed., *Emotional Problems of Early Childhood,* 1955

Within hours of arriving at the hospital, I was very carefully treated with electric-shock therapy. ECT is horribly misunderstood. People have this ghastly image of someone standing in a tub of water and putting his finger in a socket. I knew better. I had done some shows about it. The hospital requires a release for ECT. I was so disoriented I couldn't figure out what they were asking me to sign, but I signed anyway. In my case, ECT was miraculous. My wife was dubious, but when she came into my room afterward, I sat up and said, "Look who's back among the living." It was like a magic wand. ECT is used as a jump starter to get you back. From that point on—six weeks I was in the hospital and to this day—I've been treated with medication.

> DICK CAVETT (1936–). Television talk-program host. Describing his experience with ECT during his "biggest depressive episode" in 1980, "Goodbye, Darkness," *People,* 3 August 1992

Dr. Max Fink of the State University of New York at Stony Brook, a leading proponent, believes ECT should be given to "all patients whose condition is severe enough to require hospitalization."

> EDWARD EDELSON. "ECT Elicits Controversy—And Results," *Houston Chronicle,* 28 December 1988

The principal complications of EST [i.e., ECT] are death, brain damage, memory impairment, and spontaneous seizures. These complications are similar to those seen after head trauma, with which EST has been compared.

> MAX FINK (1923–). "Efficacy and Safety of Induced Seizures (EST) in Man," *Comprehensive Psychiatry,* January-February 1978

I can't prove there's no brain damage [from ECT]. I can't prove there are no other sentient beings in the universe, either. But scientists have been trying for thirty years to find both, and so far they haven't come up with a thing.

> MAX FINK (1923–). In Russ Rymer, "Electroshock," *Hippocrates,* March-April 1989

ECT is one of God's gifts to mankind.

> MAX FINK (1923–). In Sandra G. Boodman, "Shock Therapy: It's Back," *Washington Post,* 24 September 1996

[After the shock treatment] I rise disembodied from the dark to grasp and attach myself like a homeless parasite to the shape of my identity and its position in space and time. At first I cannot find my way, I cannot find myself where I left myself, someone has removed all trace of me. I am crying.

> JANET FRAME (1924–). *Faces in the Water,* 1.1, 1961

What these shock doctors don't know is about writers and such things as remorse and contrition and what they do to them. They should make all psychiatrists take a course in creative writing so they'd know about writers. . . .

Well, what is the sense of ruining my head and erasing my memory, which is my capital, and putting me out of business? It was a brilliant cure but we lost the patient. It's a bum turn, Hotch, terrible.

> ERNEST HEMINGWAY (1899–1961). Remarks to the author who was visiting him at the Mayo Clinic where Hemingway was undergoing electroshock, June 1961. In A. E. Hotchner, *Papa Hemingway: A Personal Memoir,* 14, 1966. On 2 July 1961, a few days after being released from the Mayo Clinic following a second ECT series Hemingway killed himself with a shotgun.
>
> See Suicide: Hemingway (2)

Perhaps we are doing the right thing but in a very crude way just as if one were trying to right a watch with a hammer.

> HAROLD E. HIMWICH. "Electroshock: A Round Table Discussion," *American Journal of Psychiatry,* November 1943

This brings us for a moment to a discussion of the brain damage produced by electroshock. . . . Is a certain amount of brain damage not necessary in this type of treatment? Frontal lobotomy indicates that improvement takes place by a definite damage of certain parts of the brain.

> PAUL H. HOCH (1902–1964). "Discussion and Concluding Remarks," *Journal of Personality,* 1948

All patients who remain unimproved after ECT are inclined to complain bitterly of their memory difficulties.

> LOTHAR B. KALINOWSKY (1899–1992) and PAUL H. HOCH (1902–1964). *Shock Treatments, Psychosurgery and Other Somatic Treatments in Psychiatry,* 3.B.13, 1952

It's more dangerous to drive to the hospital than to have the treatment. The unfair stigma against [ECT] is denying a remarkably effective medical treatment to patients who need it.

> CHARLES KELLNER. *Convulsive Therapy* editor. In Dennis Cauchon, "Shock Therapy," *USA Today,* 6 December 1995

We started by inducing two to four grand mal convulsions daily until the desired degree of regression was reached. . . . We considered a patient had regressed sufficiently when he wet and soiled, or acted and talked like a child of four. . . .

Sometimes the confusion passes rapidly and patients act as if they had awakened from dreaming; their minds seem like clean slates upon which we can write.

> CYRIL J. C. KENNEDY and DAVID ANCHEL. "Regressive Electric-Shock in Schizophrenics Refractory to Other Shock Therapies." *Psychiatric Quarterly,* 2, 1948

The Shock Shop, Mr. McMurphy, is jargon for the EST machine, the Electro Shock Therapy. A device that might be said to do the work of the sleeping pill, the electric chair, *and* the torture rack.

> KEN KESEY (1935–). *One Flew Over the Cuckoo's Nest,* 1, 1962

What I think it did was to act like a Roto-Rooter on the depression. It just reamed me clear and the depression was gone.

> ROLAND KOHLOFF. New York Philharmonic timpanist. In Lisa W. Foderaro, "With Reforms in Treatment, Shock Therapy Loses Shock," *New York Times,* 19 July 1993

The disturbance in memory [caused by ECT] is probably an integral part of the recovery process. I think it may be true that these people have for the time being at any rate more intelligence than they can handle and that the reduction of intelligence is an important factor in the curative process.

> ABRAHAM MYERSON (1881–1948). In discussion of Franklin G. Ebaugh et al., "Fatalities Following Electric Convulsive Therapy: A Report of 2 Cases with Autopsy Findings," *Transactions of the American Neurological Association,* June 1942

I do not know any formal use of [shock treatment] in brain washing [*sic*] but it seems possible it could be so used. One can conjure up an image of large groups of dissidents in a police state being kept in a contented state of apathy by shock treatment.

> ROBERT PECK. Psychiatrist. *The Miracle of Shock Treatment,* 8, 1974

A vast medical literature provides strong evidence that electroconvulsive therapy causes permanent brain damage, including loss of memory and catastrophic deterioration of personality. . . . During my 20 years as a community psychiatrist I have treated many patients who have been subjected to shock therapy. My experience as a clinician corroborates the many empirical studies that conclude that electroconvulsive therapy is abusive and inhumane, and causes irreversible physical and emotional damage.

> HUGH L. POLK. Letter to *New York Times,* 1 August 1993

Interviewer: You say you'd rather have a lobotomy than electroconvulsive shock? Do you have some pretty solid ideas about what electroconvulsive shock does?
Pribram: No—I just know what the brain looks like after a series of shocks—and it's not very pleasant to look at.

> KARL PRIBRAM (1919–). Neurosurgeon. "From Lobotomy to Physics to Freud . . . an Interview with Karl Pribram," *APA Monitor* (American Psychological Association), September-October 1974

The most persistent impression obtained is that the shock patients show a picture resembling the post-lobotomy syndrome.

> LEON SALZMAN (1915–). "An Evaluation of Shock Therapy," *American Journal of Psychiatry,* March 1947

Electroconvulsive therapy in effect may be defined as a controlled type of brain damage produced by electrical means. . . .
   In all cases the ECT "response" is due to the concussion-type, or more serious, effect of ECT. The patient "forgets" his symptoms because the brain damage destroys memory traces in the brain, and the patient has to pay for this by a reduction in mental capacity of varying degree.

> SIDNEY SAMENT. Neurologist. Letter to *Clinical Psychiatry News,* March 1983

SILENCE

See also • Meditation ○ Prayer ○ Revelation ○ Silence & Protest ○ Silence & Speech ○ Solitude (Being Alone) ○ Spirituality

Thought works in silence, so does virtue. One might erect statues to Silence.

> THOMAS CARLYLE (1795–1881). Journal, 28? September 1830. In James Anthony Froude, *Thomas Carlyle: A History of the First Forty Years, 1795–1835,* 2.4, 1882

Silence is the mother of truth.

> BENJAMIN DISRAELI (1804–1881). *Tancred: Or, The New Crusade,* 4.4, 1847

Let us be silent—so we may hear the whisper of the gods.

> RALPH WALDO EMERSON (1803–1882). "Friendship," *Essays: First Series,* 1841

Quietness is indeed a sign of strength. But quietness may also help one to achieve strength.

> FRANZ KAFKA (1883–1924). In Gustav Janouch, *Conversations with Kafka,* p. 106, tr. Goronwy Rees, 1953

Whom the heart of man shuts out,
Sometimes the heart of God takes in,
And fences them all round about
With silence mid the world's loud din.

> JAMES RUSSELL LOWELL (1891–1891). "The Forlorn," 1842

Claudio: Silence is the perfectest herald of joy.

> SHAKESPEARE (1564–1616). *Much Ado About Nothing,* 2.1.317, 1598

Silence is the language of God.

> SWAMI SIVANANDA (1887–1963). 1945. In Whitall N. Perry, comp., *A Treasury of Traditional Wisdom,* p. 993, 1986

First the silence. Then the voice of the silence.

> E. M. STANDING (1887–?). *Maria Montessori: Her Life and Work,* 13, 1957

[Silence] is when we hear inwardly; sound, when we hear outwardly.

> HENRY DAVID THOREAU (1817–1862). "Friday," *A Week on the Concord and Merrimack Rivers,* 1849

Silence is the universal refuge, . . . our inviolable asylum, where no indignity can assail.

> HENRY DAVID THOREAU (1817–1862). "Friday," *A Week on the Concord and Merrimack Rivers,* 1849

It [would be] vain for me to endeavor to interpret the Silence. She cannot be done into English.

> HENRY DAVID THOREAU (1817–1862). "Friday," *A Week on the Concord and Merrimack Rivers,* 1849

SILENCE & PROTEST

See also • Compassion ○ Defiance ○ Duty: *Talmud* ○ Evil ○ Guilt ○ Indifference ○ Morality ○ Resistance ○ Responsibility ○ Silence ○ Silence & Speech

We live in an age when silence is not only criminal but suicidal. If they take you in the morning, they will be coming for us that night.

> JAMES BALDWIN (1924–1987). "Open Letter to My Sister, Miss Angela Davis," *New York Review of Books,* 7 January 1971

What kind of an age is it
When to talk of trees
Is almost a crime
Because of the crimes
It leaves unsaid!

> BERTOLT BRECHT (1898–1956). "To Those Born Later" (1), 1936–1938. In *Body Politic,* p. 11, July-August 1970

An event has happened, upon which it is difficult to speak, and impossible to be silent.

> EDMUND BURKE (1729–1797). Speech at the impeachment trial of Warren Hastings, 5 May 1789

A time comes when silence is betrayal.

> CLERGY AND LAYMEN CONCERNED ABOUT VIETNAM. Executive Committee statement. In Martin Luther King, Jr., "Declaration of Independence from the War in Vietnam," sermon, Riverside Church, New York City, 4 April 1967

Since then, at an uncertain hour,
    That agony returns;
And till my ghastly tale is told,
    This heart within me burns.

> SAMUEL TAYLOR COLERIDGE (1772–1834). *The Rime of the Ancient Mariner*, 7, 1798
>
> See Sylvia Writers: Plath

I have begun several times many things, and I have often succeeded at last. I will sit down, but the time will come when you will hear me.

> BENJAMIN DISRAELI (1804–1881). His first House of Commons speech, 7 December 1837

I stir in it for the sad reason that no other mortal will move, and if I do not, why, it is left undone.
    The amount of it, be sure, is merely a Scream; but sometimes a scream is better than a thesis.

> RALPH WALDO EMERSON (1803–1882). On his efforts to stop the U.S. Government's forced expulsion of the Cherokee Nation from its land, journal, 23 April 1838

As we must account for every idle Word, so must we likewise for every idle Silence.

> THOMAS FULLER (1654–1734). Comp., *Introductio ad Prudentiam*, 575, 1731

Silence becomes cowardice when occasion demands speaking out the whole truth and acting accordingly.

> MOHANDAS K. GANDHI (1869–1948). In *Harijan*, 7 April 1946

I am aware that many object to the severity of my language [on the issue of slavery], but is there not cause for severity? I will be as harsh as truth, and as uncompromising as justice. On this subject, I do not wish to think, or speak, or write with moderation. No! No! Tell a man whose house is on fire, to give a moderate alarm; tell him to moderately rescue his wife from the hands of the ravisher; tell the mother to gradually extricate her babe from the fire into which it has fallen—but urge me not to use moderation in a cause like the present. I am in earnest—I will not equivocate—I will not excuse—I will not retreat a single inch; and I will be heard.

> WILLIAM LLOYD GARRISON (1805–1879). In *The Liberator* (inaugural issue), 1 January 1831

I may be arrested, I may be tried and thrown into jail, but I never will be silent.

> EMMA GOLDMAN (1869–1940). "Address to the Jury," *Mother Earth*, July 1917

If I say, "I will not mention him,
    or speak any more in his name,"
there is in my heart as it were
    a burning fire
    shut up in my bones,
and I am weary with holding it in,
    and I cannot.

> JEREMIAH (7th cent. B.C.). *Jeremiah* 20:9
>
> See Writers: Sylvia Plath

I hate a fellow whom pride, or cowardice, or laziness drives into a corner, and who does nothing when he is there but sit and *growl*; let him come out as I do, and *bark*.

> SAMUEL JOHNSON (1709–1784). In Hester Lynch Piozzi, *Anecdotes of the Late Samuel Johnson, LL.D.*, p. 161, 1786, ed. S. C. Roberts, 1932

We shall have to repent in this generation not merely for the vitriolic words and actions of the bad people, but for the appalling silence of the good people.

> MARTIN LUTHER KING, JR. (1929–1968). "Letter from Birmingham City Jail," 16 April 1963,
>
> See Truth & Untruth: Anonymous (2)

The day we see the truth and cease to speak is the day we begin to die.

> MARTIN LUTHER KING, JR. (1929–1968). In Joycelyn Elders, "Someone Had to Speak Up," *New York Times*, 20 December 1994

The true crime, the collective, general crime of almost all Germans of that time [i.e., the Nazi period] was that of lacking the courage to speak.

> PRIMO LEVI (1919–1987). *The Drowned and the Saved*, 8, 1986, tr. Raymond Rosenthal, 1988

It is impossible to remain silent in the face of tyranny without, by this very act of silence, becoming an agent of that tyranny.

> JEFFREY MOUSSAIEFF MASSON (1941–). Conclusion to *Against Therapy: Emotional Tyranny and the Myth of Psychological Healing*, 1988

Silence is the first thing within the power of the enslaved to shatter. From that shattering, everything else spills forth.

> ROBIN MORGAN (1941–). *The Demon Lover: On the Sexuality of Terrorism*, 10, 1989

In Germany they came first for the Communists, and I didn't speak up because I wasn't a Communist. Then they came for the Jews, and I didn't speak up because I wasn't a Jew. Then they came for the trade unionists, and I didn't speak up because I wasn't a trade unionist. Then they came for the Catholics, and I didn't speak up because I was a Protestant. Then they came for me, and by that time no one was left to speak up.

> MARTIN NIEMOELLER (1892–1984). German theologian imprisoned throughout World War II. Attributed

He who does not bellow the truth when he knows the truth makes himself the accomplice of liars and forgers.

> CHARLES PÉGUY (1873–1914). "Basic Verities: The Honest People," *Basic Verities: Prose and Poetry*, tr. Ann and Julian Green, 1943

Among the minor tragedies in Washington in the last generation has been the triumph of good manners over honest convictions. . . .

The polite conspiracy of silence that has tended to prevail in the last quarter century in Washington.

JAMES RESTON (1909–1995). "The Nixon-Hickel Affair," *New York Times*, 27 November 1970

We who have a voice must speak for the voiceless.

ARCHBISHOP OSCAR ROMERO (1917–1980). In Roy Bougeois, "Personal Witness," *In These Times*, 29 April 1992

Men of Athens, I honor and love you; but I shall obey God rather than you, and while I have life and strength I shall never cease from the practice and teaching of philosophy, exhorting anyone whom I meet and saying to him after my manner: You, my friend—a citizen of the great and mighty and wise city of Athens—are you not ashamed of heaping up the greatest amount of money and honor and reputation, and caring so little about wisdom and truth and the greatest improvement of the soul, which you never regard or heed at all!

SOCRATES (470?–399 B.C.). In Plato (427?–347 B.C.), *Apology*, 29, tr. Benjamin Jowett, 1894

Whoever lives through a trial, or takes part in an event that weighs on man's destiny or frees him, is duty-bound to transmit what he has seen, felt and feared. . . . To live an experience or create a vision, and not transform it into link and promise, is to turn it into a gift of death.

ELI WIESEL (1928–). "To a Young Jew of Today," *One Generation After*, tr. Lily Edelman and the author, 1965

There may be times when we are powerless to prevent injustice, but there must never be a time when we fail to protest.

ELI WIESEL (1928–). "Hope, Despair, and Memory," Nobel Peace Prize acceptance address, Oslo, 11 December 1986

❧

No one was angry enough to speak out.

ANONYMOUS (EGYPTIAN). Inscription on a pyramid, quoted by Robert F. Kennedy (1925–1968)

Silence is the voice of complicity.

SAYING (AMERICAN). 1980s

Open your mouth, judge righteously,
    maintain the rights of the poor and needy.

SAYING (*BIBLE*). Proverbs 31:9

SILENCE & SPEECH

See also • Right to Silence ○ Silence ○ Silence & Protest ○ Speaking ○ Talking

Silence is deep as eternity; speech is shallow as time.

THOMAS CARLYLE (1795–1881). "Memoirs of the Life of Scott," 1838, *Critical and Miscellaneous Essays*, Carey & Hart edition, 1849

I will begin to speak, when I have that to say which had not better be unsaid.

CATO THE YOUNGER (95–46 B.C.). Replying to criticism for being silent. In Plutarch (A.D. 46?–119?). "Cato the Younger," *Parallel Lives*, Dryden edition, 1693

M.—— who was asked to talk on various public or private abuses replied coldly, "No day goes by that I do not add to the list of things about which I shall never speak. The longest list belongs to the greatest philosopher."

CHAMFORT (1741–1794). In Albert Camus, "Chamfort," *Sewanee Review*, Winter 1948

Speak to th' purpose or hold your peace.

JOHN CLARKE (1596–1658). Comp., *Proverbs: English and Latine*, p. 11, 1639

When you have nothing to say, say nothing.

C. C. COLTON (1780–1832). *Lacon: or, Many Things in Few Words; Addressed to Those Who Think*, 1.183, 1823

If you don't say anything, you won't be asked to repeat yourself.

CALVIN COOLIDGE (1872–1933)

Nothing more enhances authority than silence. It is the crowning virtue of the strong, the refuge of the weak, the modesty of the proud, the pride of the humble, the prudence of the wise, and the sense of fools.

CHARLES de GAULLE (1890–1970). "Of Prestige" (2), *The Edge of the Sword*, 1934, tr. Gerald Hopkins, 1960

Blessed is the man who, having nothing to say, abstains from giving us wordy evidence of the fact.

GEORGE ELIOT (1819–1880). *Impressions of Theophrastus Such*, 4, 1879

With all progress this happens, that speech becomes less, and finally ceases in a nobler silence.

RALPH WALDO EMERSON (1803–1882). Journal, September 1842

See Paradoxes: Henry David Thoreau (1)

Silence is sometimes
Better than speech, and speech sometimes than silence.

EURIPIDES (485?–406 B.C.). *Orestes*, l. 630, tr. A. S. Way, 1956

Silence is not always a Sign of Wisdom,
    but Babbling is ever a Mark of Folly.

BENJAMIN FRANKLIN (1706–1790). *Poor Richard's Almanack*, April 1758

He cannot speak well that cannot hold his tongue.

THOMAS FULLER (1654–1734). Comp., *Gnomologia: Adages and Proverbs*, 1820, 1732

Silence is subversive—the womb of yet unborn cries of rebellion.

ERIC HOFFER (1902–1983). *The Temper of Our Time*, 4, 1967

Sometimes it seems that people hear best what we do not say.

ERIC HOFFER (1902–1983). *Reflections on the Human Condition*, 132, 1973

He who does not understand your silence will probably not understand your words.

ELBERT HUBBARD (1856–1915). *A Thousand and One Epigrams*, p. 60, 1911

If everybuddy thought before they spoke ther' wouldn' be enough noise in this world t' scare a jaybird.

> KIN HUBBARD (1868–1930). "January," *Abe Martin's Almanack,* 1908

Whereas speaking distracts, silence and work collect thoughts and strengthen the spirit.

> ST. JOHN OF THE CROSS (1542–1591). In Aldous Huxley, *The Perennial Philosophy,* 15, 1946

There's something still better than silence, 'tis this—to speak the truth.

> JOSEPH KIMCHI (A.D. 1105–1170). *Shekel Hakodesh,* tr. Hermann Gollancz, 1919

Those who know do not talk
And talkers do not know.

> LAO-TZU (6th cent. B.C.). *The Way of Life,* 56, tr. R. B. Blakney, 1955

Sometimes you have to be silent to be heard.

> STANISLAW J. LEC (1909–1966). *Unkempt Thoughts,* p. 87, tr. Jacek Galazka, 1962

I am very little inclined on any occasion to say anything unless I hope to produce some good by it.

> ABRAHAM LINCOLN (1809–1865). Speech to Union Meeting, Washington, 6 August 1862

It is difficult to keep quiet if you have nothing to say.

> MALCOLM MARGOLIN (1940–). Personal communication, 2 July 1992

"Only Talk When It Improves the Silence."

> CHRISTOPHER MATTHEWS (1945–). Chapter title, *Hardball: How Politics Is Played—Told by One Who Knows the Game,* 8, 1988

It was said of Abbot Agatho that for three years he carried a stone in his mouth until he learned to be silent.

> THOMAS MERTON (1915–1968). Tr., "Some Sayings of the Desert Fathers" (15), *The Wisdom of the Desert,* 1960

Silence is Wisdom where Speaking is Folly.

> WILLIAM PENN (1644–1718). *Some Fruits of Solitude,* 129, 1693

The deepest rivers flow with the least sound.

> QUINTUS CURTIUS RUFUS (A.D. 2nd cent.). *Alexander the Great,* 7.4
> See Talking: Saying (English) (2)

[Thomas Babington Macaulay] has occasional flashes of silence, that make his conversation perfectly delightful.

> SYDNEY SMITH (1771–1845). In Lady Holland, *A Memoir of the Reverend Sydney Smith,* 1.11, 1855

The camps had taught him that people who kept silent bore something within themselves.

> ALEKSANDR SOLZHENITSYN (1918–). *Cancer Ward,* 31, tr. Rebecca Frank, 1968

Silence alone is worthy to be heard.

> HENRY DAVID THOREAU (1817–1865). Journal, 21 January 1853

The right word may be effective, but no word was ever as effective as a rightly timed pause.

> MARK TWAIN (1835–1910). Introduction to *Mark Twain's Speeches,* ed. Albert Bigelow Paine, 1923

It's better to keep your mouth shut and appear stupid than to open it and remove all doubt.

> MARK TWAIN (1835–1910). Attributed. *The Wit and Wisdom of Mark Twain,* p. 5, ed. Alex Ayres, 1987

❦

There are silences that speak louder than words.

> ANONYMOUS

If speech is silver, silence is gold.

> SAYING (ARAB)

Even a fool who keeps silent is considered wise.

> SAYING (*BIBLE*). *Proverbs* 17:28

Silence is golden.

> SAYING (ENGLISH)
> See Tact: Samuel Butler

There should be a reason for speech but not for silence.

> SAYING (FRENCH)

Speaking comes by nature; silence, by understanding.

> SAYING (GERMAN)

God gave us teeth to hold back our tongue.

> SAYING (GREEK)

Silence is a fence for wisdom, but it is not wisdom.

> SAYING (JEWISH)

Some folks speak from experience; others, from experience, don't speak.

> SAYING (WISCONSIN)

SIMPLE LIVING

See also • Life ○ Poverty ○ Simplicity

If by renouncing the luxuries of life we can lighten the burdens of others . . . surely the simplification of our wants is a thing greatly to be desired!

> MOHANDAS K. GANDHI (1869–1948). In *Indian Opinion,* 26 August 1905

A visible simplicity of life,
Embracing unpretentious ways,
And small self-interest
And poverty of coveting.

> LAO-TZU (6th cent. B.C.). *The Way of Life,* 19, tr. R. B. Blakney, 1955

Frugal living in terms of ephemeral goods means a dogged adherence to simplicity, a conscious avoidance of any unnecessary elaborations, and a magnanimous rejection of luxury—puritanism, if you like, on the ephemeral side. This makes it possible to enjoy a high standard of living on the eternal side, as a compensation and reward.

> E. F. SCHUMACHER (1911–1977). "A Culture of Poverty." In Dom Moraes, ed., *Voices for Life: Reflections on the Human Condition,* 1975]

Living simply is voluntary poverty.

> SENECA THE YOUNGER (5? B.C.–A.D. 65). "On Philosophy and Riches," *Moral Letters to Lucilius,* 17.5, tr. Richard M. Gummere, 1918
>
> See Poverty: Henry David Thoreau (1)

How many things I can do without.

> SOCRATES (470?–399 B.C.). While visiting a market glutted with wares. In Diogenes Laertius (A.D. 3rd cent.), *Lives of Eminent Philosophers,* 2.5, tr. R. D. Hicks, 1925

I am nearest to the gods in that I have the fewest wants.

> SOCRATES (470?–399 B.C.). Adapted. In Diogenes Laertius (A.D. 3rd cent.), *Lives of Eminent Philosophers,* 2.5, tr. R. D. Hicks, 1925

Reduce the complexity of life by eliminating the needless wants of life, and the labors of life reduce themselves.

> EDWIN WAY TEALE (1899–1980). "February 4," *Circle of the Seasons,* 1953

I am convinced, both by faith and experience, that to maintain one's self on this earth is not a hardship but a pastime, if we will live simply and wisely.

> HENRY DAVID THOREAU (1817–1862). "Economy," *Walden; or Life in the Woods,* 1854

Our life is frittered away by detail. . . . Simplify, simplify, simplify! . . . Simplicity of life and elevation of purpose.

> HENRY DAVID THOREAU (1817–1862). "Where I Lived, and What I Lived For," *Walden; or Life in the Woods,* 1854
>
> See Self-Realization (Becoming): Thoreau (2)

The wealthiest man among us is the best:
No grandeur now in nature or in book
Delights us. Rapine, avarice, expense,
This is idolatry; and these we adore:
Plain living and high thinking are no more.

> WILLIAM WORDSWORTH (1770–1850). "Written in London, September, 1802," l. 7, 1807

❧

Live simply so others may simply live.

> SLOGAN (AMERICAN). 1970s

SIMPLICITY

See also • Art ○ Simple Living ○ Style

It may be that the whole is simple, and that we are looking at it from the wrong point of view.

> HENRI BERGSON (1859–1941). "Dynamic Religion," *The Two Sources of Morality and Religion,* 1932, tr. R. Ashley Audra and Cloudesley Brereton, 1935

Everything should be made as simple as possible, but not simpler.

> ALBERT EINSTEIN (1879–1955). In "Quotable Quotes," *Reader's Digest,* July 1977

It is very hard to be simple enough to be good.

> RALPH WALDO EMERSON (1803–1882). Journal, 23 October 1837

Everything is simpler than you think and at the same time more complex than you imagine.

> GOETHE (1749–1832)

He was one of the greatest scientists the world has ever known, yet if I had to convey the essence of Albert Einstein in a single word, I would choose *simplicity*.

> BANESH HOFFMANN. Opening words, "My Friend, Albert Einstein," *Reader's Digest,* January 1968

There is nothing so simple that it cannot be made difficult.

> MERLE P. MARTIN. "The Instant Analyst," *Journal of Systems Management,* 1975

The important things are always simple: the simple things are always hard.

> MURPHY'S LAWS FOR GRUNTS. One of 20 anonymously created laws widely distributed among military personnel during the Gulf War (1990–1991). In Paul Dixon, "Getting a Handle on Life's Slippery Truths," *San Francisco Chronicle,* 24 December 1992

It's just that simple.

> ROSS PEROT (1930–). His signature line, popularized during the 1992 presidential campaign

One always begins with the simple, then comes the complex, and by superior enlightenment one often reverts in the end to the simple. Such is the course of human intelligence.

> VOLTAIRE (1694–1778). "Religion," *Philosophical Dictionary,* 1764, tr. Theodore Besterman, 1971

Seek simplicity and distrust it.

> ALFRED NORTH WHITEHEAD (1861–1947). *The Concept of Nature,* 7 (closing words), 1926

The art of art, the glory of expression and the sunshine of the light of letters, is simplicity.

> WALT WHITMAN (1819–1892). Preface (1855) to *Leaves of Grass,* 1855–1892

SIN

See also • Despair: C. S. Lewis ○ Dissatisfaction: Nikos Kazantzakis ○ Evil ○ Forgiveness ○ Innocence ○ Judging Others: Jesus (2) ○ Morality ○ Nonconformity, Anti-: Robert Lindner (2) ○ Repentance ○ Revelation: Henry David Thoreau ○ Salvation: Epicurus ○ Success: Ambrose Bierce, William Napier ○ Technology: Aldous Huxley (1) ○ Temptation ○ Vice

Sin begins as a spider's web and becomes as a ship's rope.

> AKIBA (A.D. 40?–135?). In *Midrash* (4th cent. B.C.– A.D. 12th cent.). Rabbinical writings

Inaction in a deed of mercy becomes an action in a deadly sin.

> THE BOOK OF THE GOLDEN PRECEPTS. Ancient Buddhist writing. 2.17, tr. Helena Petrovna Blavatsky, 1889

Pride, covetousness, lust, anger, gluttony, envy and sloth are the seven capital sins.

> *A CATECHISM OF CHRISTIAN DOCTRINE FOR GENERAL USE.* 1866
>
> See Virtue: Oscar Wilde

'Tis sin to misemploy an hour.

> JOHN DRYDEN (1631–1700). *Absalom and Achitophel,* 1.613, 1681

That which we call sin in others, is experiment for us.

> RALPH WALDO EMERSON (1803–1882). "Experience," *Essays: Second Series,* 1844
>
> See Mistakes: Anonymous (1)

Whoever sins least, he is the best man; for no man is innocent, no one free from blame.

> EPICHARMUS (530?–440? B.C.). In Kathleen Freeman, tr., *Ancilla to Pre-Socratic Philosophers: A Complete Translation of the Fragments in Diels,* Fragmente der Vorsokratiker, 23.46, 1983 (1948)

It's natural
that we should sin, being human.

> EURIPIDES (485?–406 B.C.). *Hippolytus,* l. 610, tr. David Grene, 1942

The supreme sin is not to be able to forgive yourself.

> WALDO FRANK (1889–1967). In introduction (Lewis Mumford) to *Memoirs of Waldo Frank,* ed. Alan Trachtenberg, 1973

It is sinful to buy and use articles made by sweated labor.

> MOHANDAS K. GANDHI (1869–1948). In *Young India,* 13 October 1921

Hate the sin and not the sinner.

> MOHANDAS K. GANDHI (1869–1948). *An Autobiography: The Story of My Experiments with Truth,* 4.9, 1929, tr. Mahadev Desai, 1940

The seven social sins: . . . politics without principle, wealth without work, commerce without morality, pleasure without conscience, education without character, science without humanity, and worship without sacrifice.

> MOHANDAS K. GANDHI (1869–1948). Quoted by his grandson Arun Gandhi. In Jim Wallis, introduction to *The Soul of Politics: A Practical and Prophetic Vision for Change,* 1994

The most unpardonable sin in society is independence of thought.

> EMMA GOLDMAN (1869–1940). "Minorities Versus Majorities," *Anarchism and Other Essays,* 3rd rev. ed., 1917 (1910)

Indifference to the sublime wonder of living is the root of sin.

> ABRAHAM JOSHUA HESCHEL (1907–1972). *God in Search of Man: A Philosophy of Judaism,* 4, 1955

The greatest sin of man is to forget that he is a prince.

> ABRAHAM JOSHUA HESCHEL (1907–1972). *God in Search of Man: A Philosophy of Judaism,* 42, 1955

Sin has many tools, but a lie is the handle which fits them all.

> OLIVER WENDELL HOLMES, SR. (1809–1894). *The Autocrat of the Breakfast-Table,* 6, 1858

We are not punished for our sins, but by them.

> ELBERT HUBBARD (1856–1915). *A Thousand and One Epigrams,* p. 68, 1911

The only sin is to be unkind.

> ELBERT HUBBARD (1856–1915). *A Thousand and One Epigrams,* p. 99, 1911

No sin is so light that it may be overlooked; no sin is so heavy that it may not be repented of.

> MOSES IBN EZRA (A.D. 1070?–1138?)

Your iniquities have made a separation
  between you and your God.
And your sins have hid his face from you
  so that he does not hear.

> ISAIAH (8th cent. B.C.). *Isaiah* 59:2

Whoever knows what is right to do and fails to do it, for him it is sin.

> JAMES (A.D. 1st cent.). *James* 4:17
>
> See Inaction: *The Book of the Golden Precepts*

If we say we have no sin, we deceive ourselves, and the truth is not in us.

> JOHN (A.D. 1st cent.). *1 John* 1:8

Nature is not at all lenient with sinners who are unconscious of their sins. She punishes them just as severely as if they had committed a conscious offense.

> CARL G. JUNG (1875–1961). "Psychology and Religion" (3), 1938, *Psychology and Religion: West and East,* tr. R. F. C. Hull, 1958

We are sinful not merely because we have eaten of the Tree of Knowledge, but also because we have not yet eaten of the Tree of Life.

> FRANZ KAFKA (1883–1924). "Reflections on Sin, Pain, Hope, and the True Way" (79), 1917–1920, *The Great Wall of China,* 1931, tr. Willa and Edwin Muir, 1946

The biggest sin is sitting on your ass.

> FLORYNCE R. KENNEDY (1916–). In Gloria Steinem, "The Verbal Karate of Florynce R. Kennedy, Esq.," *Ms.,* March 1973

The sin ye do by two and two ye must pay for one by one!

> RUDYARD KIPLING (1865–1936). "Tomlinson," 1891, *Barrack-Room Ballads,* 1893

[Sin] isn't the breaking of divine commandments. It is the breaking of one's own integrity.

> D. H. LAWRENCE (1885–1930). *Studies in Classic American Literature,* 8, 1923

A man does not sin by commission only, but often by omission.

> MARCUS AURELIUS (A.D. 121–180). *Meditations,* 9.5, tr. Maxwell Staniforth, 1964

There is no sin but ignorance.

> CHRISTOPHER MARLOW (1564–1593). Prologue to *The Jew of Malta,* 1633

People are no longer sinful, they are only immature or underprivileged or frightened or, more particularly, sick.

> PHYLLIS McGINLEY (1905–1978). "In Defense of Sin," *The Province of the Heart,* 1959

Many are saved from sin by being so inept at it.

> MIGNON McLAUGHLIN (1915–). *The Neurotic's Notebook,* 8, 1963

All sin is rooted in the failure of love.

> THOMAS MERTON (1915–1968). *No Man Is an Island,* 2.5, 1955

The mercy of God does not suspend the laws of cause and effect. When God forgives me a sin, He destroys the guilt of sin but the effects and the punishment of sin remain.

> THOMAS MERTON (1915–1968). *No Man Is an Island,* 11.11, 1955

One of the brethren had sinned, and the priest told him to leave the community. So then Abbot Bessarion got up and walked out with him, saying: I too am a sinner!

> THOMAS MERTON (1915–1968). Tr., "Some Sayings of the Desert Fathers" (40), *The Wisdom of the Desert,* 1960

Never despair because of your sins. Counterbalance them now with many good deeds.

> MIDRASH (4th cent. B.C.– A.D. 12th cent.). Rabbinical writings

If there be a God, *since* there is a God, the human race is implicated in some terrible aboriginal calamity. It is out of joint with the purposes of its Creator. This is a fact, a fact as true as the fact of its existence; and thus the doctrine of what is theologically called original sin becomes to me almost as certain as that the world exists, and as the existence of God.

> CARDINAL JOHN HENRY NEWMAN (1801–1890). *Apologia pro Vita Sua: Being a History of His Religious Opinions,* 5, 1864, ed. Martin J. Svaglic, 1967

The desire of one man to live on the fruits of another's labor is the original sin of the world.

> JAMES O'BRIEN (1805–1864). Attributed

If thou knewest thy sins, thou wouldst lose heart.

> BLAISE PASCAL (1623–1662). *Pensées,* 553, 1670, tr. William F. Trotter, 1931

All have sinned and fall short of the glory of God.

> PAUL (A.D. 1st cent.). *Romans* 3:23
> See Guilt: Muhammad o Judging Others: Shakespeare

The wages of sin is death.

> PAUL (A.D. 1st. cent.). *Romans* 6:23

How many are there who do not sin from lack of desire or lack of occasion?

> JOSEPH ROUX (1834–1886). *Meditations of a Parish Priest,* 4.83, tr. Isabel F. Hapgood, 1886

The whole conception of "Sin" is one which I find very puzzling, doubtless owing to my sinful nature.

> BERTRAND RUSSELL (1872–1970). "An Outline of Intellectual Rubbish," *Unpopular Essays,* 1950

You don't make up for your sins in church; you do it in the street, you do it at home. The rest is bullshit and you know it.

> MARTIN SCORSESE (1942–) and MARDIK MARTIN. *Mean Streets* (film), 1973

It is not the sins but with the sinners that most men are angry.

> SENECA THE YOUNGER (5? B.C.–A.D. 65). "On Anger" (2.28.8), *Moral Essays,* tr. John W. Basore, 1928

Who, when he may, forbids not sin, commands it.

> SENECA THE YOUNGER (5? B.C.–A.D. 65). *Troades,* l. 290, tr. Frank Justus Miller, 1917

King Henry: "Forbear to judge, for we are sinners all.

> SHAKESPEARE (1564–1616). *Henry VI,* Part II, 3.3.31, 1590

Lear: I am a man
More sinn'd against than sinning.

> SHAKESPEARE (1564–1616). *King Lear,* 3.2.58, 1605

The seven deadly sins. . . . Yes, the deadly seven. Food, clothing, firing, rent, taxes, respectability and children.

> GEORGE BERNARD SHAW (1856–1950). *Major Barbara,* 3, 1905

There is no record of Christ's having ever said to any man: "Go and sin as much as you like: you can put it all on me." He said, "Sin no more."

> GEORGE BERNARD SHAW (1856–1950). Preface ("The Confusion of Christendom") to *Androcles and the Lion,* 1912

There is no man who does not sin.

> SOLOMON (10th cent. B.C.). *I Kings* 8:46
> See Guilt: Muhammad o Judging Others: Shakespeare

I would rather be called a fool all my days than sin for a single moment before God.

> TALMUD (A.D. 1st–6th cent.). Rabbinical writings. In Louis I. Newman, comp., *The Talmudic Anthology,* 326, 1945

We cannot well do without our sins; they are the highway of our virtue.

> HENRY DAVID THOREAU (1817–1862). Journal, 22 March 1842

Sin is a Reflection upon God.

> BENJAMIN WHICHCOTE (1609–1683). *Moral and Religious Aphorisms,* 1101, 1753

There is no sin except stupidity.

> OSCAR WILDE (1854–1900). "The Critic as Artist" (2), *Intentions,* 1891

❦

Sin is the root of suffering.

> SAYING

SINCERITY

See also • Fanatics: Oscar Wilde o Hypocrisy o Truth: Rousseau o Truthfulness

Sincerity . . . is the first characteristic of all men in any way heroic.

> THOMAS CARLYLE (1795–1881). "The Hero as Prophet," *On Heroes, Hero-Worship, and the Heroic in History,* 1841

Perfect sincerity offers
No guarantee.

> CHUANG-TZU (369–286 B.C.). As interpreted by Thomas Merton, "Apologies," *The Way of Chuang Tzu,* 1965

Individuals are considered sincere when there is little or no discrepancy between the goals they seek and those they claim to be seeking.

> LEONARD W. DOOB (1909–). *Public Opinion and Propaganda,* 12, 1948

Bolsheviks are sincere. Fascists are sincere. Lunatics are sincere. People who believe the earth is flat are sincere. They can't all be right. Better make certain first you've got something to be sincere about and with.

> TOM DRIBERG (1905–1976). In *Daily Express* (British newspaper), 1937

Deal so plainly with man and woman, as to constrain the utmost sincerity, and destroy all hope of trifling with you. [Sincerity] is the highest compliment you pay.

> RALPH WALDO EMERSON (1803–1882). "The Over-Soul," *Essays: First Series,* 1841
>
> See Truthfulness: George Bush

Use no hurtful deceit; think innocently and justly and, if you speak, speak accordingly.

> BENJAMIN FRANKLIN (1706–1790). Virtue #7 ("Sincerity"), 1784, *Autobiography,* 1798

Learn to be sincere. Even if you have to fake it.

> DAVID GERROLD. In Paul Dickson, comp., *The Official Rules,* p. 220, 1978

(a) Never mean what you say.
(b) Never say what you mean.
(c) Be sincere.

> DEBBI GOGLIO. Coming-of-age advice for girls (in their relationships with boys) to the author. In Sally Belfrage, *Un-American Activities,* 1994. Quoted in Carol Brightman, "Undercover," *Nation,* 11 July 1994

Sincerity: A mental attitude acquired after long practice by man, in order to conceal his ulterior motives. . . . (A sincere man is one who bluffs only a part of the time.)

> ELBERT HUBBARD (1856–1915). *The Roycroft Dictionary Concocted by Ali Baba and the Bunch on Rainy Days,* p. 135, 1914

Weak people cannot be sincere.

> LA ROCHEFOUCAULD (1613–1680). *Maxims,* 316, 1665, tr. Louis Kronenberger, 1959

Sincerity consists in a certain tranquil courage by which we dare to enter existence, as we are.

> LOUIS LAVELLE (1883–1951). French philosopher

Let us speak, though we show all our faults and weaknesses—for it is a sign of strength to be weak, to know it, and out with it—not in a set way and ostentatiously, though, but incidentally and without premeditation.

> HERMAN MELVILLE (1819–1891). Letter to Nathaniel Hawthorne, 29 June 1851

We are in the presence of the contradiction of a style of living which cultivates sincerity and is at the same time a fraud.

> JOSÉ ORTEGA y GASSET (1883–1955). *The Revolt of the Masses,* 9, 1930, tr. anon., 1932

Sincerity is the foundation of the spiritual life.

> ALBERT SCHWEITZER (1875–1965). *Out of My Life and Thought: An Autobiography,* 21, tr. C. T. Campion, 1933

Albany: The weight of this sad time we must obey;
Speak what we feel, not what we ought to say.

> SHAKESPEARE (1564–1616). *King Lear,* 5.3.323, 1605

It is dangerous to be sincere unless you are also stupid.

> GEORGE BERNARD SHAW (1856–1950). "Maxims for Revolutionists: Stray Sayings," *Man and Superman,* 1903

When an individual takes a sincere step, then all the gods attend, and his single deed is sweet.

> HENRY DAVID THOREAU (1817–1862). Journal, 9 April 1841

A little sincerity is a dangerous thing, and a great deal of it is absolutely fatal.

> OSCAR WILDE (1854–1900). "The Critic as Artist" (2), *Intentions,* 1891
>
> See Advice: Wilde

SINGLEHOOD

Includes • Bachelorhood

See also • Celibacy ∘ Marriage

Failure to marry in either sex is the consequence of the fear of it. There is increasing recognition that bachelorhood is symptomatic of psychopathology.

> IRVING BIEBER (1908–). Psychiatrist. In "The Pleasures & Pain of the Single Life" (essay), *Time,* 15 September 1967

A Man without a Wife is but half a Man.

> BENJAMIN FRANKLIN (1706–1790). *Poor Richard's Almanack,* January 1755

The most threatened group in human societies, as in animal societies, is the unmated male: the unmated male is more likely to wind up in prison or in an asylum or dead than his mated counterpart. He is less likely to be promoted at work, and he is considered a poor credit risk.

> GERMAINE GREER (1939–). *Sex and Destiny: The Politics of Human Fertility,* 2, 1984

Marriage is the best state for man in general; and every man is a worse man, in proportion as he is unfit for the married state.

> SAMUEL JOHNSON (1709–1784). 22 March 1776. In James Boswell, *The Life of Samuel Johnson,* 1791

I've always held that a bachelor is a fellow who never makes the same mistake once.

> ALAN LeMAY, JESSE LASKY, JR., and C. GARDNER SULLIVAN. *Northwest Mounted Police* (film), 1940, spoken by Gary Cooper to Madeleine Carroll

He marries best who puts it off until it is too late.

> H. L. MENCKEN (1880–1956). *A Little Book in C Major,* 7.25, 1916

I have more than enough of a wife in my art.

> MICHELANGELO (1564–1664). In Cesare Lombroso, *The Man of Genius,* 1.2, 1888, ed. Havelock Ellis, 1896

A woman without a man is like a fish without a bicycle.

> GLORIA STEINEM (1934–). Attributed

Anonymous: When should a man marry?
Thales: A young man not yet, an elder man not at all.

> THALES (625?–547? B.C.). Format adapted. In Francis Bacon, "Of Marriage and Single Life," *Essays,* 1625

Nowadays all the married men live like bachelors, and all the bachelors like married men.

> OSCAR WILDE (1854–1900). *The Picture of Dorian Gray,* 15, 1891

Bigamy is having one husband too many. Monogamy is the same.

> ANONYMOUS. In Erica Jong, *Fear of Flying,* 1 (epigraph), 1973

For years I searched for the perfect woman. Finally I found her . . . but she had only one fault. She was searching for the perfect man.

> ANONYMOUS

A bachelor is but half a pair of scissors.

> SAYING (AMERICAN)

Woman without man is like a field without seed.

> SAYING (ETHIOPIAN)

One stone does not grind the meal.

> SAYING (WEST AFRICAN)

SKEPTICISM

See also • Belief ○ Certainty ○ Conviction ○ Cynicism ○ Doubt ○ Faith ○ Ideas

To be constantly skeptical is to believe in doubt, which is after all a form of faith.

> CRANE BRINTON (1898–1968). *The Anatomy of Revolution,* 1.2, 1952

I am driven to express my faith by a series of skepticisms.

> RALPH WALDO EMERSON (1803–1882). Journal, 1845, undated

Value of the Skeptic is the resistance to premature conclusions.

> RALPH WALDO EMERSON (1803–1882). Journal, 1845, undated

A just thinker will allow full swing to his skepticism.

> RALPH WALDO EMERSON (1803–1882). "Worship," *The Conduct of Life,* 1860

I am too much of a skeptic to deny the possibility of anything.

> T. H. HUXLEY (1825–1895). Letter to Herbert Spencer, 22 March 1886

We must be skeptical even of our skepticism.

> BERTRAND RUSSELL (1872–1970). *Sceptical Essays,* 11, 1928

[My grandmother] believed in nothing. Her skepticism alone kept her from being an atheist.

> JEAN-PAUL SARTRE (1905–1980). *The Words,* 1, 1964, tr. Bernard Frechtman, 1981

The thorough skeptic is a dogmatist. He enjoys the delusion of complete futility.

> ALFRED NORTH WHITEHEAD (1861–1947). "Mathematics and the Good," *The Philosophy of Alfred North Whitehead,* ed. Paul A. Schilpp, 1941

Skepticism is the beginning of Faith.

> OSCAR WILDE (1854–1900). *The Picture of Dorian Gray,* 17, 1891

SKILL

See also • Ability ○ Talent

Skill to do comes of doing.

> RALPH WALDO EMERSON (1803–1882). "Old Age," *Society and Solitude,* 1870

All skill ought to be exerted for universal good; every man has owed much to others, and ought to repay the kindness that he has received.

> SAMUEL JOHNSON (1709–1784). *Rasselas: The Prince of Abyssinia,* 6, 1759

A carpenter or a carriage maker can pass on to another the rules of his craft, but he cannot make him skillful.

> MENCIUS (371?–289? B.C.). *Mencius,* 7.B.5, tr. D. C. Lau, 1970

Do you see a man skillful in his work?
  he will stand before kings.

> SAYING (*BIBLE*). Proverbs 22:29

SKY

See also • Clouds ○ Nature

Blue skies
Smiling at me
Nothing but blue skies
Do I see.

> IRVING BERLIN (1888–1989). "Blue Skies" (song), 1926

The Sky is the daily bread of the eyes.

> RALPH WALDO EMERSON (1803–1882). Journal, 25 May 1843

Thank God, men cannot as yet fly, and lay waste the sky as well as the earth!

> HENRY DAVID THOREAU (1817–1862). Journal, 3 January 1861

SLANDER

See also • Calumny ○ Criticism ○ Gossip ○ Insult ○ Ridicule ○ Wit

He that flings Dirt at another dirtieth himself most.

> THOMAS FULLER (1654–1734). Comp., *Gnomologia: Adages and Proverbs,* 2107, 1732

Slander would not stick if it had not always something to lay hold.

> MARQUIS OF HALIFAX (1633–1695). "Slander," *Political, Moral and Miscellaneous Reflections,* 1750
>
> See Criticism: Thomas Fuller

Abuse is an indirect species of homage.

> WILLIAM HAZLITT (1778–1830). "Common Places" (22), *Literary Examiner* (English journal), September-December 1823

Truth is generally the best vindication against slander.

> ABRAHAM LINCOLN (1809–1865). Letter to Edwin M. Stanton, 14 July 1864
>
> See Calumny: George Washington

Just deeds are the best answer to injurious words.

> JOHN MILTON (1608–1674). *Observations upon the Articles of Peace with the Irish Rebels,* 1649

No matter: I will live so that none shall believe him.

> PLATO (427?–347 B.C.). When told that someone had spoken ill of him. In Bronson Alcott, 3 August 1869, *Concord Days,* 1872

I complained before a learned man that someone had accused me of corruption. He said, "Put him to shame by your good conduct."

> SA'DI (A.D. 1213?–1292). *The Maxims of Sa'di,* 7, tr. Mehdi Nakosteen, 1977

Slander injures three persons: the slanderer, the recipient of the slander, and the person slandered.

> TALMUD (A.D. 1st–6th cent.). Rabbinical writings. In Louis I. Newman, comp., *The Talmudic Anthology,* 344, 1945

To speak no slander, no, nor listen to it.

> ALFRED, LORD TENNYSON (1809–1892). "Guinevere" (l. 469), *The Idylls of the King,* 1859–1885

He slandered the world in revenge for his complete lack of success in it.

> VOLTAIRE (1694–1778). *Zadig,* 4, 1747, tr. H. I. Woolf, 1949

Denials never quite catch up with charges.

> TOM WICKER (1926–). In Janet Malcolm, "The Morality of Journalism," *New York Review of Books,* 1 March 1990

❦

If you throw enough dirt, some will stick.

> SAYING (LATIN)

SLANG

See also • Language

Dialect tempered with slang is an admirable medium of communication between persons who have nothing to say and persons who would not care for anything properly said.

> THOMAS BAILEY ALDRICH (1836–1907). "Leaves from a Notebook," *Ponkapog Papers,* 1903

The function of any slang is to give secrecy to the users; to prevent their being understood by outsiders.

> BERGEN EVANS (1904–1978). In "The Teen-Agers: Rites, Styles, Passwords," *Newsweek,"* 21 March 1966

Slang is the vengeance of the anonymous masses for the linguistic thralldom imposed on them by the educated classes.

> MARIO PEI (1901–1978). Linguist

Slang is a language that rolls up its sleeves, spits on its hands and goes to work.

> CARL SANDBURG (1878–1967). In "Minstrel of America: Carl Sandburg," *New York Times,* 13 February 1959

SLAVERY

See also • African Americans ○ Civil War: Abraham Lincoln (3) ○ Cruelty ○ Debt: Saying (*Bible*) ○ Defiance ○ Dehumanization ○ Exploitation ○ Freedom ○ Holocaust ○ Newspeak—Examples: John C. Calhoun ○ Oppression ○ Philosophers: Leo Tolstoy ○ Progress ○ Race ○ Racism ○ Responsibility ○ Revolution: Anonymous (1) ○ Silence & Protest: William Lloyd Garrison ○ Tyranny ○ Unity: Abraham Lincoln ○ War: Vauvenargues

Is there anyone . . . intended by nature to be a slave, and for whom such a condition is expedient and right, or rather is not all slavery a violation of nature?

There is no difficulty in answering this question, on grounds both of reason and of fact. For that some should rule and others be ruled is a thing not only necessary, but expedient; for from the hour of their birth, some are marked out for subjection, others for rule.

> ARISTOTLE (384–322 B.C.). *Politics,* 1.5, tr. Benjamin Jowett, 1885
>
> See Inequality: Martin Luther ○ Leaders & People: Sigmund Freud

Slavery is so intolerable a condition that the slave can hardly escape deluding himself into thinking that he is choosing to obey his master's commands when, in fact, he is obliged to.

> W. H. AUDEN (1907–1973). "Writing," *The Dyer's Hand and Other Essays,* 1962

The chains ov slavery are none the less gauling for being made ov gold.

> JOSH BILLINGS (1818–1885). "Embers on the Harth," *Everybody's Friend, or; Josh Billing's Encyclopedia and Proverbial Philosophy of Wit and Humor,* 1874
>
> See Gold: Thomas Fuller (2)

The tyrant grinds down his slaves and they don't turn against him, they crush those beneath them.

> EMILY BRONTË (1818–1948). *Wuthering Heights,* 11, 1847

The real slavery in Egypt was this: that the Israelites learned to endure it.

> SIMCHA BUNAM (1765–1827)

Heredity bondsmen! know ye not
Who would be free themselves must strike the blow?

> LORD BYRON (1788–1824). *Childe Harold's Pilgrimage,* 2.76, 1812–1818

The slave begins by demanding justice and ends by wanting to wear a crown. He must dominate in his turn.

> ALBERT CAMUS (1913–1960). "Metaphysical Rebellion," *The Rebel: An Essay on Man in Revolt,* 1951, tr. Anthony Bower, 1956

Slavery is no more sinful, by the Christian code, than it is sinful to wear a whole coat, while another is in tatters, to eat a better meal than a neighbor, or otherwise to enjoy ease and plenty, while our fellow creatures are suffering and in want.

> JAMES FENIMORE COOPER (1789–1851). "On Slavery," *The American Democrat,* 1838

[Captain Fitz-Roy, of the *Beagle,* and I] had several quarrels; for instance, early in the voyage at Bahia, in Brazil, he defended and praised slavery, which I abominated, and told me that he had just visited a great slave owner, who had called up many of his slaves and asked them whether they were happy, and whether they wished to be free, and all answered "No." I then asked him, perhaps with a sneer, whether he thought that the answer of slaves in the presence of their master was worth anything?"

CHARLES DARWIN (1809–1882). 1831, *The Autobiography of Charles Darwin and Selected Letters,* 2, ed. Francis Darwin, 1892

It would astonish one, unaccustomed to a slaveholding life, to see with what wonderful ease a slaveholder can find things of which to make occasion to whip a slave. A mere look, word, or motion—a mistake, accident, or want of power—are all matters for which a slave may be whipped at any time. Does a slave look dissatisfied? It is said, he has the devil in him, and it must be whipped out. . . . Does he forget to pull off his hat at the approach of a white person? Then he is wanting in reverence, and should be whipped for it. Does he ever venture to vindicate his conduct, when censured for it? Then he is guilty of impudence—one of the greatest crimes of which a slave can be guilty.

FREDERICK DOUGLASS (1817–1895). *Narrative of the Life of Frederick Douglass, an American Slave, Written by Himself,* 10, 1845

I have found that to make a contented slave, it is necessary to make a thoughtless one. It is necessary to darken his moral and mental vision, and, as far as possible, to annihilate the power of reason. He must be able to detect no inconsistencies in slavery; he must be made to feel that slavery is right; and he can be brought to that only when he ceases to be a man.

FREDERICK DOUGLASS (1817–1895). *Narrative of the Life of Frederick Douglass, an American Slave, Written by Himself,* 10, 1845

Slaves are generally expected to sing as well as to work.

FREDERICK DOUGLASS (1817–1895). *Narrative of the Life of Frederick Douglass an American Slave, Written by Himself,* 1845

Every one of us should be ashamed to be free while his brother is a slave.

FREDERICK DOUGLASS (1817–1895). In Lerone Bennett, Jr., *Pioneers in Protest,* 1968

Happy slaves are the bitterest enemies of freedom.

MARIE von EBNER-ESCHENBACH (1830–1916). *Aphorisms,* p. 77, 1880–1905, tr. David Scrase and Wolfgang Mieder, 1994

He who does his own work frees a slave. He who does not his own work is a slaveholder.

RALPH WALDO EMERSON (1803–1882). Journal, 1844, undated

To make good the cause of Freedom against Slavery you must be . . . Declarations of Independence walking.

RALPH WALDO EMERSON (1803–1882). "Notebook WO Liberty," p. 199, 1855

You [would] avoid slavery? Take care that others are not your slaves.

EPICTETUS (A.D. 55?–135?). Fragment, 42, tr. George Long, 1890?
See Democracy: Abraham Lincoln (2)

Formerly, men were made slaves under physical compulsion, now they are enslaved by the temptation of money and of the luxuries that money can buy.

MOHANDAS K. GANDHI (1869–1948). *Hind Swaraj or Indian Home Rule,* 4, 1938

Enslave but a single human being, and the liberty of the world is put in peril.

WILLIAM LLOYD GARRISON (1805–1879). 1835. In Wendell Phillips Garrison and Francis Jackson Garrison, *William Lloyd Garrison, 1805–1879: The Story of His Life by His Children,* 1.14, 1884

The man who gives me employment, which I must have or suffer, that man is my master, let me call him what I will.

HENRY GEORGE (1839–1897). *Social Problems,* 5, 1883

No one is more a slave than he who thinks he is free without being so.

GOETHE (1749–1832). "From Ottilie's Journal," *Elective Affinities,* 2.5, 1809, tr. R. J. Hollingdale, 1971

If a slave says to his master, "You are not my master," the master shall cut off his ear.

HAMMURABI CODE (21st cent. B.C.). Babylonia

The whole commerce between master and slave is a perpetual exercise of the most boisterous passions, the most unremitting despotism on the one part, and degrading submissions on the others.

THOMAS JEFFERSON (1743–1826). *Notes on the State of Virginia,* 18, 1785

I had him severely flogged in the presence of his old companions.

THOMAS JEFFERSON (1743–1826). Referring to Jame Hubbard, an escaped slave who had been captured and returned to Jefferson's plantation in September 1805. In William Cohen, "Thomas Jefferson and the Problem of Slavery," 1969. Quoted in Conor Cruise O'Brien, "Thomas Jefferson: Radical and Racist," *Atlantic,* October 1996

We make ourselves slaves to our pleasures, and we serve fame and ambition, which is an equal slavery.

BEN JONSON (1572–1637). "Of Worthless Aims," *Timber: Or, Discoveries,* 1640, ed. Ralph S. Walker, 1953

If men and women are in chains anywhere in the world, then freedom is endangered everywhere.

JOHN F. KENNEDY (1917–1963). Campaign statement, Washington, 2 October 1960
See Injustice: Martin Luther King, Jr.

In this enlightened age there are few, I believe, but what will acknowledge that slavery as an institution is a moral and political evil in any country. . . . I think it, however, a greater evil to the white than to the black race, and while my feelings are strongly enlisted in behalf of the latter, my sympathies are more strong for the former.

ROBERT E. LEE (1807–1870). Letter to his wife Mary Anne, 6 December 1856

Are we so accustomed to our chains that we are no longer conscious of them?

> B. H. LIDDELL HART (1895–1970). "The Perpetuation of Compulsion?" *Why Don't We Learn from History?* 1944

By God, boys, if I ever get a chance to hit that thing, I'll hit it and hit it hard.

> ABRAHAM LINCOLN (1809–1865). Attributed by his friend John Hanks, at a slave auction in New Orleans, 1828. In Dixon Wecter, *The Hero in America: A Chronicle of Hero-Worship,* 10.1, 1941. This quotation has little credibility because Hanks accompanied Lincoln on their flatboat trip down the Mississippi River only as far as St. Louis.

Although volume upon volume is written to prove slavery a very good thing, we never hear of the man who wishes to take the good of it, *by being a slave himself.*

> ABRAHAM LINCOLN (1809–1865). "Fragments on Government," 1854?, *Abraham Lincoln: Speeches and Writings, 1832–1858,* Library of America edition, 1989

This is a world of compensations; and he who would *be* no slave must consent to *have* no slave. Those who deny freedom to others, deserve it not for themselves; and, under a just God, cannot long retain it.

> ABRAHAM LINCOLN (1809–1865). Letter to Henry L. Pierce et al., 6 April 1859
>
> See Democracy: Lincoln (2)

I am naturally anti-slavery. If slavery is not wrong, nothing is wrong.

> ABRAHAM LINCOLN (1809–1865). Letter to Albert G. Hodges, 4 April 1864

Many politicians of our time are in the habit of laying it down as a self-evident proposition, that no people ought to be free till they are fit to use their freedom. The maxim is worthy of the fool in the old story, who resolved not to go into the water till he had learned to swim. If men are to wait for liberty till they become wise and good in slavery, they may indeed wait forever.

> THOMAS BABINGTON MACAULAY (1800–1859). "John Milton," *The Edinburgh Review* (Scotland), August 1825

It is as difficult to make a people free that is resolved to live in servitude as it is to subject a people to servitude that is determined to remain free.

> MACHIAVELLI (1469–1527). *The Discourses,* 3.8, 1517, tr. Christian E. Detmold, 1940

Slaves, be obedient to those who are your earthly masters, with fear and trembling, in singleness of heart, as to Christ.

> PAUL (A.D. 1st cent. A.D.). *Ephesians* 6:5

A slave is one who waits for someone else to free him.

> EZRA POUND (1885–1972). "Gists," *Impact: Essays on Ignorance and the Decline of American Civilization,* ed. Noel Stock, 1960

Would you deliver people into bondage? Persuade them to despise one another, destroy their mutual respect.

> PIERRE-JOSEPH PROUDHON (1809–1865). *De la justice dans la révolution et dans l'église,* 1858

There is no subjection so complete as that which preserves the forms of freedom; it is thus that the will itself is taken captive.

> ROUSSEAU (1712–1778). *Emile; or, Treatise on Education,* 2, 1762, tr. Barbara Foxley, 1911

Man was born free; and everywhere he is in chains. One thinks himself the master of others, and still remains a greater slave than they.

> ROUSSEAU (1712–1778). *The Social Contract,* 1.1, 1762, tr. G. D. H. Cole, 1950

Slaves lose everything in their chains, even the desire of escaping them: they love their servitude.

> ROUSSEAU (1712–1778). *The Social Contract,* 1.2, 1762, tr. G. D. H. Cole, 1950

I know that I am a slave, and you are my lord. The law of this country has made you my master. You can bind my body, tie my hands, govern my actions: you are the strongest, and society adds to your power; but with my will, sir, you can do nothing.

> GEORGE SAND (1804–1876). Preface to *Indiana,* 1832

Man, having enslaved the elements, remains himself a slave.

> PERCY BYSSHE SHELLEY (1792–1822). *A Defence of Poetry,* p. 37, 1821, ed. Albert S. Cook, 1890

Those who enslave other peoples enslave themselves.

> HERBERT SPENCER (1820–1903). Letter to Sir Robert Giffin, 17 May 1901. In David Duncan, *Life and Letters of Herbert Spencer,* 2.27, 1908

All Government without the Consent of the Governed is the very Definition of Slavery.

> JONATHAN SWIFT (1667–1745). "A Letter to the Whole People of Ireland," 13 October 1724, *The Drapier's Letters to the People of Ireland against recovering Wood's Halfpence,* 1724, ed. Herbert Davis, 1935
>
> See Democracy: Abraham Lincoln (1) ○ Government: Thomas Jefferson (1)

Talk about slavery! It is not the peculiar institution of the South. It exists wherever men are bought and sold, wherever a man allows himself to be made a mere thing or a tool, and surrenders his inalienable rights of reason and conscience. Indeed, this slavery is more complete than that which enslaves the body alone.

> HENRY DAVID THOREAU (1817–1862). Journal, 4 December 1860

The essence of all slavery consists in taking the produce of another's labor by force. It is immaterial whether the force be founded upon ownership of the slave or ownership of the money that he must get to live.

> LEO TOLSTOY (1828–1910). *What Then Must We Do?* 1886

Slavery degrades men so much that they become enamored of it.

> VAUVENARGUES (1715–1747). *Reflections and Maxims,* 22, 1746, tr. F. G. Stevens, 1940

In nothing was slavery so savage and relentless as in its attempted destruction of the family instincts of the Negro race in America. Individuals, not families; shelters, not homes; herding, not marriage, were the cardinal sins of that system of horrors.

> FANNIE BARRIER WILLIAMS (1855–1944). Human rights activist. In Bert James Loewenberg and Ruth Bogin, *Black Women in Nineteenth-Century American Life,* 3, 1976

❧

Oh, freedom! Oh, freedom
Oh, freedom over me!
Before I'd be a slave,
I'd be buried in my grave,
And go home to my Lord
And be free!

> ANONYMOUS (AFRICAN-AMERICAN). "Oh, Freedom!" hymn

George Francis Train (speech in New York City): Slavery is a divine institution.
Elderly man (in the audience): So is hell.

> ANONYMOUS (AMERICAN). Format adapted. In Ralph Waldo Emerson, journal, 1862, undated

We used to own our slaves; now we rent them.

> ANONYMOUS (AMERICAN). Farmer. Appearing on Edward R. Murrow, *Harvest of Shame,* television documentary, CBS, Thanksgiving Day, 1960

We will have a good master when every person is his own.

> ANONYMOUS (FRENCH). Graffito, student revolt, 1968

A slave is a human being who is legally not a person but a thing.

> ANONYMOUS. In Abraham Lincoln, "lost speech," (unrecorded at the time), Bloomington (Illinois), 29 May 1856

The heaviest chains are inside.

> ANONYMOUS

The most pitiful slaves think they are free.

> ANONYMOUS

SLEEP

See also • Fatigue ○ Laziness

Early to bed and early to rise makes a man healthy, wealthy and wise.

> JOHN CLARKE (1596–1658). Comp., *Proverbs: English and Latine,* p. 91, 1639
> See Maxims: Mark Twain (2)

There will be enough sleeping in the Grave.

> BENJAMIN FRANKLIN (1706–1790). "The Way of Wealth," 7 July 1757

One hour's sleep before midnight is worth three after.

> GEORGE HERBERT (1593–1633). Comp., *Outlandish Proverbs,* 882, 1640

Sleep and his twin brother Death.

> HOMER (8th? cent. B.C.). *The Iliad,* 9.310, tr. E. V. Rieu, 1950

Where sleep is concerned, too much is a bad thing.

> HOMER (8th? cent. B.C.). *The Odyssey,* 15.392, tr. E. V. Rieu, 1946

I never take a nap after dinner but when I have had a bad night, and then the nap takes me.

> SAMUEL JOHNSON (1709–1784). Quoted by Dr. Burney, 1776. In James Boswell, *The Life of Samuel Johnson,* 1791

Now I lay me down to sleep,
I pray the Lord my soul to keep;
If I should die before I wake,
I pray the Lord my soul to take.

> *THE NEW ENGLAND PRIMER.* 14, Boston, 1784 (1691)

O Sleep, in whom all things find rest, most peaceful of the gods, you who calm the mind, put cares to flight, soothe limbs wearied by harsh tasks and refresh them for their toil.

> OVID (43 B.C.–A.D. 17?). *Metamorphoses,* 11.620, tr. Mary M. Innes, 1955

Pisanio: I have not slept one wink.

> SHAKESPEARE (1564–1616). *Cymbeline,* 3.4.104, 1609

Thou sleepest, Brutus, and yet Rome is in chains.

> VOLTAIRE (1694–1778). *The Death of Caesar,* 2.2, 1731

❧

Sweet is the sleep of the laborer.

> ANONYMOUS (*BIBLE*). *Ecclesiastes* 5:12

If you can't get to sleep, try lying on the end of the bed—you might drop off.

> ANONYMOUS

Eat little, sleep sound.

> SAYING (IRANIAN)

The more you sleep, the less you live.

> SAYING (POLISH)

SLOWNESS

See also • Delay ○ Haste ○ Safety ○ Speed

Slow and sure.

> JOHN CLARKE (1596–1658). Comp., *Proverbs: English and Latine,* p. 304, 1639

Leave to the diamond its ages to grow, nor expect to accelerate the births of the eternal.

> RALPH WALDO EMERSON (1803–1882). "Friendship," *Essays: First Series,* 1841

Ride softly, that you may get home the sooner.

> THOMAS FULLER (1654–1734). Comp., *Gnomologia: Adages and Proverbs,* 4050, 1732

We must creep before we can go.

> JAMES HOWELL (1593–1666). Comp., "English" (p. 4), *Paroimiographia: Proverbs, or Old Sayed Sawes & Adages in English . . . Italian, French and Spanish,* 1659

There is a slowness in affairs which ripens them, and a slowness which rots them.

> JOSEPH ROUX (1834–1886). *Meditations of a Parish Priest,* 4.93, tr. Isabel F. Hapgood, 1886

The nobler and more perfect a thing is, the later and slower it is in arriving at maturity.

> ARTHUR SCHOPENHAUER (1788–1860). "Studies in Pessimism: On Women," *Essays of Arthur Schopenhauer,* tr. T. Bailey Saunders, 1851

Friar Laurence: Wisely and slow; they stumble that run fast.

> SHAKESPEARE (1564–1616). *Romeo and Juliet,* 2.3.94, 1594

🐌

Slow and steady wins the race.

> SAYING (GREEK)

Walkers outdistance runners.

> ANONYMOUS

SLUMS

See also • Cities ○ Ghettos ○ Poverty

To some extent, if you've seen one city slum, you've seen them all.

> SPIRO T. AGNEW (1918–1996). Speech, Detroit, 18 October 1968

I classify São Paulo this way: The Governor's Palace is the living room. The mayor's office is the dining room and the city is the garden. And the favela is the back yard where they throw the garbage.

> CAROLINA MARIA de JESUS. Brazilian street scavenger. 15 May 1958, *Child of the Dark: The Diary of Carolina Maria de Jesus,* tr. David St. Clair, 1962

The slum is the measure of civilization.

> JACOB RIIS (1849–1914)

SMILES

See also • Charm: Seymour St. John ○ Laughter: [especially] Lord Chesterfield

So, pack up your troubles in your old kit-bag
And smile, smile, smile.

> GEORGE ASAF (1880–1951). "Pack Up Your Troubles in Your Old Kit-bag" (song), 1915

The smiler with the knife beneath his cloak.

> GEOFFREY CHAUCER (1343–1400). "The Knight's Tale" (3), *The Canterbury Tales,* 1390?, tr. NevillCoghill, 1951

Start each day with a smile—and get it over with.

> W. C. FIELDS (1880–1946). In L. M. Boyd, "Hurts So Good," *San Francisco Sunday Examiner & Chronicle,* 12 March 1995

If you do not smile, you are judged lacking in a "pleasing personality"—and you need to have a pleasing personality if you want to sell your services, whether as a waitress, a salesman, or a physician. Only those at the bottom of the social pyramid, who sell nothing but their physical labor, and those at the very top do not need to be particularly "pleasant." Friendliness, cheerfulness, and everything that a smile is supposed to express, become automatic responses which one turns on and off like an electric switch.

> ERICH FROMM (1900–1980). *Escape from Freedom,* 7.1, 1941

Some by their continual grinning and showing their Teeth make Men doubt whether they honor them, or laugh at them.

> THOMAS FULLER (1654–1734). Comp., *Introductio ad Prudentiam,* 1395, 1731

Little F. H—— used to look into E——'s mouth to see where her smiles came from.

> NATHANIEL HAWTHORNE (1804–1864). Referring to two young children not further identified, 1840, *The American Notebooks,* ed. Claude M. Simpson, 1932

Man, false man, smiling, destructive man.

> NATHANIEL LEE (1653–1692). *Theodosius,* 3.2, 1680

Hamlet: One may smile, and smile, and be a villain.

> SHAKESPEARE (1564–1616). *Hamlet,* 1.5.108, 1600

In the sunshine of your smile.

> FRANCIS EDWARD SMEDLEY (1818–1864). *Frank Fairleigh,* 45, 1850

When you call me that, *smile!*

> OWEN WISTER (1860–1938). *The Virginian,* 2, 1902

Everyone smiles in the same language.

> SAYING
>
> See Eyes: George Herbert

SNAKES

See also • Animals

Four snakes gliding up and down a hollow for no purpose that I could see—not to eat, not for love, but only gliding.

> RALPH WALDO EMERSON (1803–1882). Journal, 11 April 1834

SOCIALISM

See also • Capitalism ○ Class ○ Communism ○ Economics ○ Fascism ○ Freedom ○ Reformers: Anonymous (American) ○ Tyranny

With cake for none until all had bread.

> CLEMENT ATTLEE (1883–1967). British prime minister. On socialism. In Charles L. Mee, Jr., *Meeting at Potsdam,* 2, 1975

Freedom without Socialism is privilege and injustice. . . . Socialism without freedom is slavery and brutality.

> MIKHAIL BAKUNIN (1814–1876). *Federalism, Socialism, Anti-Theologism.* In *The Political Philosophy of Bakunin: Scientific Anarchism,* 3.1, ed. G. P. Maximoff, 1953

Are we never to learn that Socialism has its roots in envy and in nothing else?

> NORMAN DOUGLAS (1868–1952). 13 May, *An Almanac,* 1945

In the service of the people, we followed such a policy that socialism would not lose its human face.

> ALEXANDER DUBCEK (1921–1992). Czech Communist Party first secretary. In *Rudé Právo,* 19 July 1968

The fundamental point that democratic socialists have always made remains as true today and as relevant as ever: That human needs must come first; that people are more important than profits; and that some things—health, housing, food, education—which are essential to human survival and dignity must be guaranteed as human rights.

> BARBARA EHRENREICH (1941–). "Whose Socialism?" *Z Magazine*, January 1990

Because of its progress, modern civilization creates an ever-increasing mass of unadapted people always ready to struggle against it. They form the majority of socialists.

> GUSTAVE LE BON (1841–1931). *Aphorisms of Present Times*, 4.3, 1913, tr. Alice Widener, 1979

He is no socialist who will not sacrifice his fatherland for the triumph of the social revolution.

> LENIN (1870–1924). Quoted by Edward Mead Earle, "Lenin, Trotsky, Stalin: Soviet Concepts of War." In Earle, ed., *Makers of Modern Strategy*, 1943

What the collectivist age wants, allows, and approves is the perpetual holiday from the self.

> THOMAS MANN (1875–1955). "Europe, Beware," *The Thomas Mann Reader*, ed. Joseph W. Angell, 1950

When [socialism's] rough voice chimes in with the battle cry *"As much state as possible,"* it will at first make the cry noisier than ever; but soon the opposite cry will be heard with the greater: *"As little state as possible."*

> FRIEDRICH NIETZSCHE (1844–1900). *Human, All Too Human*, 473, 1878, tr. Marion Faber, 1984

By bringing the whole of life under the control of the State, Socialism necessarily gives power to an inner ring of bureaucrats, who in almost every case will be men who want power for its own sake and will stick at nothing in order to retain it.

> GEORGE ORWELL (1903–1950). Reviewing *The Road to Serfdom* by F. A. Hayek, 9 April 1944. *The Collected Essays, Journalism and Letters of George Orwell*, vol. 3, ed. Sonia Orwell and Ian Angus, 1968

No one can be, at the same time, a sincere Catholic and a true Socialist.

> POPE PIUS XI (1857–1939). *Quadragesimo Anno (On Reconstructing the Social Order)*, 15 May 1931

Socialism . . . is too ready to suppose that better economic conditions will of themselves make men happy. It is not only more material goods that men need, but more freedom, more self-direction, more outlet for creativeness, more opportunity for the joy of life, more voluntary cooperation and less involuntary subservience to purposes not their own.

> BERTRAND RUSSELL (1872–1970). *Principles of Social Reconstruction*, 1, 1916

There is only one sort of genuine socialism, the democratic sort, by which I mean the organization of society for the benefit of the whole people.

> GEORGE BERNARD SHAW (1856–1950). In Sheila Graham, "Shaw Views Fate of Beaten Hitler," *New York Times*, 25 July 1941

All socialism is slavery. . . . That which fundamentally distinguishes the slave is that he labors under coercion to satisfy another's desires.

> HERBERT SPENCER (1820–1903). "The Coming Slavery," *The Contemporary Review*, April 1884

Democracy and socialism have nothing in common but one word: equality. But notice the difference: while democracy seeks equality in liberty, socialism seeks equality in restraint and servitude.

> ALEXIS de TOCQUEVILLE (1805–1859). Constituent Assembly speech, Paris, 12 September 1848

In a country where the sole employer is the State, opposition means death by slow starvation. The old principle: who does not work shall not eat, has been replaced by a new one: who does not obey shall not eat.

> LEON TROTSKY (1879–1940). In F. A. Hayek, *The Road to Serfdom*, 9 (epigraph), 1944

Socialism is an expression of the disease for which it purports to be the cure.

> GEORGE F. WILL (1941–). *Statecraft as Soulcraft: What Government Does*, 5, 1983
>
> See Psychoanalysis: Karl Kraus

SOCIETY

See also • Civilization ∘ Crowds ∘ Majorities ∘ Man ∘ Mankind ∘ The Masses ∘ Men ∘ People ∘ The People ∘ Population ∘ The Public

Society is indeed a contract. . . . It is a partnership in all science; a partnership in all art; a partnership in every virtue, and in all perfection. As the ends of such a partnership cannot be obtained except in many generations, it becomes a partnership not only between those who are living, but between those who are living, those who are dead, and those who are to be born.

> EDMUND BURKE (1729–1797). *Reflections on the Revolution in France*, p. 194, 1790, Pelican Books edition, 1968

The state of society is one in which the members have suffered amputation from the trunk, and strut about so many walking monsters—a good finger, a neck, a stomach, an elbow, but never a man.

> RALPH WALDO EMERSON (1803–1882). "The American Scholar," address, Harvard University, Cambridge (Massachusetts), 31 August 1837

The virtue of society is really the basis of its stability.

> RALPH WALDO EMERSON (1803–1882). Journal, 2 October 1837

Did you ever see a pail of swill given to a pen of hungry hogs? That is human society as it is.

> HENRY GEORGE (1839–1897). *Social Problems*, 8, 1883

I believe that the present organization of society, as bad as it is, is better than any other that has ever been proposed.

> H. L. MENCKEN (1880–1956). "The Dismal Science," *Prejudices: Third Series*, 1922

A society [such] as ours eventually ties itself up into knots by its inability to put first things first.

> LEWIS MUMFORD (1895–1990). *The Conduct of Life,* 9.6, 1951

The existing social order is a swindle and its cherished beliefs mostly delusions.

> GEORGE ORWELL (1903–1950). "Mark Twain—The Licensed Jester,"
> 26 November 1943, *The Collected Essays, Journalism and Letters of
> George Orwell,* vol. 2, ed. Sonia Orwell and Ian Angus, 1968

Though the world contains many things which are thoroughly bad, the worst thing in it is society.

> ARTHUR SCHOPENHAUER (1788–1860). "Counsels and Maxims" (2.9),
> *Essays of Arthur Schopenhauer,* tr. T. Bailey Saunders, 1851

The final decision as to what the future of a society shall be depends not on how near its organization is to perfection, but on the degrees of worthiness in its individual members.

> ALBERT SCHWEITZER (1875–1965). *The Philosophy of Civilization: The
> Decay and Restoration of Civilization,* 4, 1923, tr. C. T. Campion, 1923

A society can be no better than the men and women who compose it.

> ADLAI E. STEVENSON (1900–1965). Speech, Kasson (Minnesota),
> 6 September 1952

Societies, like individuals, have their crises and their spiritual revolutions.

> R. H. TAWNEY (1880–1962). *Religion and the Rise of Capitalism:
> A Historical Study,* 5, 1926

Human society is a network of relations—spiritual, animate, physical—between human beings, alive, dead, and still unborn.

> ARNOLD J. TOYNBEE (1889–1975). Appendix ("Groping in the Dark,"
> 1), *An Historian's Approach to Religion,* 2nd ed., 1979 (1956)

How society waits unform'd, and is for a while between things ended and things begun.

> WALT WHITMAN (1819–1892). "Thoughts" (1), 1860, *Leaves of Grass,*
> 1855–1892

Society is a hall of distorting mirrors.

> COLIN WILSON (1931–). *The Outsider,* 9, 1956

The death throes of the old society are the birth pangs of the new one.

> ANONYMOUS

SOLDIERS

See also • Army ○ Assassination: Archbishop Oscar Romero ○ Civil War: Alva Griest ○ Commanders ○ Commanders & Soldiers ○ Bravery: Napoleon ○ Strategy, Military ○ Vietnam War: Ron Kovic and Oliver Stone, John Langone, Joe MacDonald, Michael Norman, Anonymous (2–4) ○ War ○ World War I: Edgar Lee Masters, John McCrea, James H. Meisel, Anonymous (French) ○ World War II: Irving Berlin, Dwight D. Eisenhower (2), Paul Fussell, Audie Murphy, George Taylor, Anonymous (British) (2)

Onward! Christian soldiers,
Marching as to war,
With the Cross of Jesus
Going on before.

> SABINE BARING-GOULD (1834–1924). "Onward! Christian Soldiers"
> (song), 1870?

The young soldier is taught as his first duty to obey his superior without consulting his conscience.

> WILLIAM ELLERY CHANNING (1780–1842). "Remarks on the Life and
> Character of Napoleon Bonaparte," 1, 1827–1828

Boys are the cash of war. Whoever said
we're not free-spenders doesn't know our likes.

> JOHN CIARDI (1916–). "New Year's Eve," *This Strangest Everything,*
> 1966

War is the province of danger, and therefore courage above all things is the first quality of a warrior.

> KARL von CLAUSEWITZ (1780–1831). *On War,* 1.3, 1832, tr. J. J. Graham,
> 1873

The master class has always declared the wars; the subject class has always fought the battles. The master class has had all to gain and nothing to lose, while the subject class has had nothing to gain and all to lose—especially their lives. They have always taught you that it is your patriotic duty to go to war and slaughter yourselves at their command.

> EUGENE V. DEBS (1855–1926). Speech, Canton (Ohio), 16 June 1918
> See Unity: Debs

The soldier must always adapt himself to circumstances and exploit them.

> CHARLES de GAULLE (1890–1970). "Of Doctrine" (1), *The Edge of the
> Sword,* 1934, tr. Gerald Hopkins, 1960

[Military codes of honor] are designed to ensure that threatening situations are met by fight rather than flight. They do this by making the social consequences of flight rather more unpleasant than the physical consequences of fight. Whereas the latter might lead to physical pain, mutilation and death, the former eventuates with far greater certainty in personal guilt and public shame.

> NORMAN F. DIXON (1922–). *On the Psychology of Military Incompetence,*
> 18, 1976

By push of bayonets, no firing till you see the whites of their eyes.

> FREDERICK II (1712–1786). Before the Battle of Prague, 6 May 1757
> See Revolutionary War: William Prescott

Rascals, would you live forever?

> FREDERICK II (1712–1786). Attributed. To his Guards during the Battle
> of Kolin (Westphalia), 18 June 1757
> See World War I: Dan Daly

In war it is not just the weak soldiers, or the sensitive ones, or the highly imaginative or cowardly ones, who will break down. Inevitably, all will break down if in combat long enough.

> PAUL FUSSELL (1924–). *Wartime: Understanding and Behavior in the
> Second World War,* 18, 1989

It is essential to persuade the soldier that those he is being urged to massacre are bandits who do not deserve to live; before killing other good, decent fellows like himself, his gun would fall from his hands.

ANDRÉ GIDE (1869–1951). Journal, 10 February 1943, tr. Justin O'Brien, 1951

Cannon is expensive; cannon fodder cheap.

JOHN GUNTHER (1901–1970). *Inside Europe,* rev. ed., 9, 1937 (1936)

They wrote in the old days that it is sweet and fitting to die for one's country. But in modern war there is nothing sweet nor fitting in your dying. You will die like a dog for no good reason.

ERNEST HEMINGWAY (1899–1961). "Notes on the Next War," *Esquire,* September 1935

Older men declare war. But it is youth that must fight and die.

HERBERT HOOVER (1874–1964). Republican National Convention speech, Chicago, 27 June 1944

Old men declare wars because they have failed to solve complex political and economic problems. They then send young men to go fight them. Of course, the old men have to make up patriotic and emotional rationales to justify their stupidity.

ARTHUR HOPPE (1925–). "A Cause to Die for," *San Francisco Chronicle,* 22 August 1990

Here dead lie we because we did not choose
    To live and shame the land from which we sprung.
Life, to be sure, is nothing much to lose;
    But young men think it is, and we were young.

A. E. HOUSMAN (1859–1936). *More Poems,* 36 (complete poem), 1936, *The Collected Poems of A. E. Housman,* 1959

For it's Tommy this, an' Tommy that, an' "Chuck him out,
    the brute!"
But it's "Savior of 'is country" when the guns begin to
    shoot.

RUDYARD KIPLING (1865–1936). "Tommy," *Barrack-Room Ballads,* 1893

If any question why we died,
Tell them, because our fathers lied.

RUDYARD KIPLING (1865–1936). "Common Form," *The Years Between,* 1919

I don't think old men ought to promote wars for young men to fight. I don't like warlike old men.

WALTER LIPPMANN (1889–1974). Television interview, May 1961. In Ronald Steel, *Walter Lippmann and the American Century,* 40, 1980

I still remember the refrain of one of the most popular barrack ballads of that day [around the turn of the century] which proclaimed most proudly that "Old soldiers never die, they just fade away." And like the old soldier of that ballad, I now close my military career and just fade away—an old soldier who tried to do his duty as God gave him the light to see that duty. Goodbye.

DOUGLAS MacARTHUR (1880–1964). Announcing his retirement after Pres. Harry S. Truman dismissed him from command of UN forces in Korea, Congress address, 19 April 1951

See Immortality: MacArthur

However horrible the incidents of war may be, the soldier who is called upon to offer and to give his life for his country is the noblest development of mankind.

DOUGLAS MacARTHUR (1880–1964). Speech, United States Military Academy, West Point (New York), 12 May 1962

Look at an infantryman's eyes and you can tell how much war he has seen.

BILL MAULDIN (1921–). *Up Front,* p. 42, 1945

Friendly fire—isn't.
Never forget that your weapon was made by the lowest bidder.
If your attack is going really well, it's an ambush.
The enemy diversion you are ignoring is the main attack.

MURPHY'S LAWS FOR GRUNTS. Format adapted. Four of 20 laws widely distributed among military personnel during the Gulf War (1990–1991). In Paul Dixon, "Getting a Handle on Life's Slippery Truths," *San Francisco Chronicle,* 24 December 1992

See Stupidity: Murphy's Laws for Grunts

When the drum has beaten the charge, when you must march straight upon the foe, bayonets fixed, your gloomy silence pledging victory—soldiers, remember to be worthy of yourselves!

NAPOLEON (1769–1821). Proclamation to his army before the Battle of Arcola (Italy), 11 November 1796, *The Mind of Napoleon: A Selection from His Written and Spoken Words,* 280, ed. J. Christopher Herold, 1955

Soldiers are made on purpose to be killed.

NAPOLEON (1769–1821). 1815–1818, *Talks of Napoleon at St. Helena* (with Gen. Gaspard Gourgaud), 13, tr. Elizabeth Wormeley Latimer, 1904

The first quality of a soldier is the ability to support fatigue and privations; valor is only secondary.

NAPOLEON (1769–1821). *Maximes de Guerre,* 58, 1830–1874. In Conrad H. Lanza, annotator, *Napoleon and Modern War,* 1943

Do not place military cemeteries where they can be seen by replacements marching to the front.

GEORGE S. PATTON, JR. (1885–1945). "Battle tricks" for officers, *War As I Knew It,* 3.1.3, 1947

The little girl saw her first troop parade and asked,
    "What are those?"
"Soldiers."
"What are soldiers?"
"They are for war. They fight and each tries
    to kill as many of the other side as he can."
The girl held still and studied,
"Do you know . . . I know something?"
"Yes, what is it you know?"
"Sometime they'll give a war
    and nobody will come." [Ellipsis points in original.]

CARL SANDBURG (1878–1967). *The People, Yes,* 23, 1936

As every combat veteran knows, war is primarily sheer boredom punctuated by moments of stark terror.

HARRY G. SUMMERS, JR. (1932–). Infantry colonel. *On Strategy: A Critical Analysis of the Vietnam War,* 14, 1982

"Forward, the Light Brigade!"
Was there a man dismay'd?
Not tho' the soldier knew
    Some one had blunder'd.
Theirs not to make reply,
Theirs not to reason why,
Theirs but to do and die.
Into the valley of Death
    Rode the six hundred.

> ALFRED, LORD TENNYSON (1809–1892). "The Charge of the Light
> Brigade," 2, *Maude, and Other Poems,* 1855

The first step in making a soldier has always been to stamp the individuality out of him.

> PHILIP WYLIE (1902–1971). *Generation of Vipers,* 16, 1942

SOLITUDE (BEING ALONE)

See also • Creativity: Abraham Joshua Heschel ○ Creativity—
First Person: Ralph Waldo Emerson, Goethe (2), Richard Wagner
(2) ○ Greatness: Arthur Schopenhauer ○ Loneliness ○ Mind:
Saying (2) ○ Nonconformity ○ Nonconformity, Anti-: George
Orwell ○ Right to Privacy ○ Self-Realization (Becoming): [espe-
cially] Hermann Hesse ○ Silence ○ Solitude (Living Alone) ○
Spirituality

Alone, *adj.* In bad company.

> AMBROSE BIERCE (1842–1914). *The Devil's Dictionary,* p. 11, 1911,
> Dover edition, 1958

Solitude—A good place tew visit, but a poor place tew stay.

> JOSH BILLINGS (1818–1885). "Billings Lexicon," *Everybody's Friend, or;
> Josh Billing's Encyclopedia and Proverbial Philosophy of Wit and
> Humor,* 1874

A wize man never enjoys himself so mutch, nor a phool so little,
az when alone.

> JOSH BILLINGS (1818–1885). "Koarse Shot," *Everybody's Friend, or; Josh
> Billing's Encyclopedia and Proverbial Philosophy of Wit and Humor,*
> 1874

Solitude is the place of purification.

> MARTIN BUBER (1878–1965). *I and Thou,* 3, 1923, tr. Ronald Gregor
> Smith, 1958

I only go out to get me a fresh appetite for being alone.

> LORD BYRON (1788–1824). Journal, 12 December 1813

Better be alone than in bad company.

> JOHN CLARKE (1596–1658). Comp., *Proverbs: English and Latine,*
> p. 291, 1639

The secret of solitude is that there is no solitude.

> JOSEPH COOK. "Conscience," *Monday Lectures,* 1880

Oh, solitude! where are the charms
That sages have seen in thy face?

> WILLIAM COWPER (1731–1800). "Verses Supposed to Be Written by
> Alexander Selkirk," l. 5, 1782

I live in that solitude which is painful in youth, but delicious in the
years of maturity.

> ALBERT EINSTEIN (1879–1955)

To go into solitude, a man needs to retire as much from his chamber as from society. I am not solitary whilst I read and write, though
nobody is with me. But if a man would be alone, let him look at
the stars.

> RALPH WALDO EMERSON (1803–1882). Title essay, *Nature,* 1836

Solitude is naught and society is naught. Alternate them and the
good of each is seen.

> RALPH WALDO EMERSON (1803–1882). Journal, 12 June 1838

Expect me not to show cause why I seek or why I exclude company.

> RALPH WALDO EMERSON (1803–1882). "Self-Reliance," *Essays: First
> Series,* 1841

Great decisions in the realm of thought and momentous discoveries and solutions of problems are only possible to an individual
working in solitude.

> SIGMUND FREUD (1856–1939). *Group Psychology and the Analysis of the
> Ego,* 3, 1921, tr. James Strachey, 1922

The fear of being alone with ourselves is . . . a feeling of embarrassment, bordering sometimes on terror at seeing a person at once
so well known and so strange; we are afraid and run away. We thus
miss the chance of listening to ourselves, and we continue to ignore
our conscience.

> ERICH FROMM (1900–1980). *Man for Himself: An Inquiry into the
> Psychology of Ethics,* 4.2.B, 1947

Endeavor to make thy own Company pleasant to thee.

> THOMAS FULLER (1654–1734). Comp., *Introductio ad Prudentiam,* 99, 1731

I never said, "I want to be alone." I only said, "I want to be *let*
alone!" There is all the difference.

> GRETA GARBO (1905–1990). In John Bainbridge, "'The Braveness to Be
> Herself,'" *Life,* 24 January 1955

I was never less alone than when by myself.

> EDWARD GIBBON (1737–1794). *Memoirs of My Life and Writings,* p. 53,
> 1796, Alex. Murray edition, 1869

Solitude either develops the mental power, or renders men dull and
vicious.

> VICTOR HUGO (1802–1885). *The Toilers of the Sea,* 1.1.6, 1866

It may be laid down as a position which will seldom deceive, that
when a man cannot bear his own company, there is something
wrong.

> SAMUEL JOHNSON (1709–1784). In *The Rambler* (English journal), 5,
> 3 April 1750

Solitude is un-American.

> ERICA JONG (1942–). Expressing a popular view, *Fear of Flying,* 1, 1973

I find it hard to leave Paris because I must part from my friends;
and the country, because I must part from myself.

> JOSEPH JOUBERT (1754–1824). *Pensées,* 1838, tr. Katherine Lyttelton,
> 1898

A solitude is the audience chamber of God.

> WALTER SAVAGE LANDOR (1775–1864). "Lord Brooke and Sir Philip Sidney," *Imaginary Conversations*, 1824-1853

What a commentary on our civilization, when being alone is considered suspect; when one has to apologize for it, make excuses, hide the fact that one practices it—like some secret vice!

> ANNE MORROW LINDBERGH (1906–). "Moon Shell," *Gift from the Sea*, 1955
>
> See Thinking: Ralph Waldo Emerson (1)

Solitude is as needful to the imagination as society is wholesome for the character.

> JAMES RUSSELL LOWELL (1819–1891). "Dryden," *Among My Books*, 1870

There is no free society without silence, without the internal and external spaces of solitude in which individual freedom can develop.

> HERBERT MARCUSE (1898–1979). Jean-Louis Ferrier, et al. interview, "Marcuse Defines His New Left Line," *New York Times Magazine*, 27 October 1968

Then Jesus was led up by the Spirit into the wilderness to be tempted by the devil. And he fasted forty days and forty nights, and afterward he was hungry.

> MATTHEW (A.D. 1st cent.). *Matthew* 4:1–2

There is no true intimacy between souls who do not know how to respect one another's solitude.

> THOMAS MERTON (1915–1968). *No Man Is an Island*, 9.3, 1955

Solitude sometimes is best society,
And short retirement urges sweet return.

> JOHN MILTON (1608–1674). *Paradise Lost*, 9.249, 1667

Nature has made us a present of a broad capacity for entertaining ourselves apart, and often calls us to do so, to teach us that we owe ourselves in part to society, but in the best part to ourselves.

> MONTAIGNE (1533–1592). "Of Giving the Lie," *Essays*, 1588, tr. Donald M. Frame, 1958

No one can help us to achieve the intimate isolation by which we find our secret worlds, so mysterious, rich and full. If others intervene, it is destroyed. This degree of thought, which we attain by freeing ourselves from the external world, must be fed by the inner spirit, and our surroundings cannot influence us in any way other than to leave us in peace.

> MARIA MONTESSORI (1870–1952). *The Child in the Family*, 6, 1956, tr. Nancy Rockmore Cirillo, 1970

Always alone in the midst of men, I come to my room to dream by myself, to abandon myself to my melancholy in all its sharpness.

> NAPOLEON (1769–1821). Manuscript, 1786 (at age 17), *The Mind of Napoleon: A Selection from His Written and Spoken Words*, 49, ed. J. Christopher Herold, 1955

One man runs to his neighbor because he is looking for himself, and another because he wants to lose himself. Your bad love of yourselves makes solitude a prison to you.

> FRIEDRICH NIETZSCHE (1844–1900). "Of Love of One's Neighbor," *Thus Spoke Zarathustra*, 1892, tr. R. J. Hollingdale, 1961

All the unhappiness of men arises from one single fact, that they cannot stay quietly in their own chamber.

> BLAISE PASCAL (1623–1662). *Pensées*, 139, 1670, tr. William F. Trotter, 1931

Flight of the alone to the Alone.

> PLOTINUS (A.D. 205–270). *The Enneads*, 6.9. In Arnold J. Toynbee, *A Study of History*, 12.533, 1961

Solitude vivifies; isolation kills.

> JOSEPH ROUX (1834–1886). *Meditations of a Parish Priest*, 5.60, tr. Isabel F. Hapgood, 1886

The young should early be trained to bear being left alone; for it is a source of happiness and peace of mind.

> ARTHUR SCHOPENHAUER (1788–1860). "Counsels and Maxims" (2.9), *Essays of Arthur Schopenhauer*, tr. T. Bailey Saunders, 1851

They are never alone that are accompanied [by] noble thoughts.

> SIR PHILIP SIDNEY (1554–1586). *The Arcadia*, bk. 1, 1590–1593

I find it wholesome to be alone the greater part of the time. . . . I love to be alone. I never found the companion that was so companionable as solitude. We are for the most part more lonely when we go abroad among men than when we stay in our chambers. A man thinking or working is always alone, let him be where he will.

> HENRY DAVID THOREAU (1817–1862). "Solitude," *Walden; or Life in the Woods*, 1854
>
> See Loneliness: Thoreau

Our language has wisely sensed the two sides of man's being alone. It has created the word "loneliness" to express the pain of being alone. And it has created the word "solitude" to express the glory of being alone.

> PAUL TILLICH (1886–1965). "Loneliness and Solitude" (2), *The Eternal Now: Sermons*, 1933

That inward eye
Which is the bliss of solitude.

> WILLIAM WORDSWORTH (1770–1850). "I Wandered Lonely as a Cloud," l. 21, 1807
>
> See Flowers: Wordsworth (1)

❦

If you don't like being in your own company, what makes you think others will?

> ANONYMOUS

SOLITUDE (LIVING ALONE)

See also • Loneliness ○ Nonconformity ○ Right to Privacy ○ Solitude (Being Alone)

Who knows the world lives alone.

> 'ALI (A.D. 600?–661). *Maxims of 'Ali*, tr. Maulana Akbar, undated. In Whitall N. Perry, comp., *A Treasury of Traditional Wisdom*, p. 525, 1986

The proof that the state is a creation of nature and prior to the individual is that the individual, when isolated, is not self-sufficing; and therefore he is like a part in relation to the whole. But he who is unable to live in society, or who has no need [for society] because he is sufficient for himself, must be either a beast or a god.

> ARISTOTLE (384–322 B.C.). *Politics,* 1.2, tr. Benjamin Jowett, 1885

Those who retire from the world on akount ov its sin and peskyness must not forgit that they hav got tew keep kompany with a person who wants just as much watching as ennyboddy else.

> JOSH BILLINGS (1818–1885). *On Ice: and Other Things,* 60, 1868

The departure from the world is regarded not as a fault, but as the first step into that noble path at the remotest turn of which illumination is to be won.

> JOSEPH CAMPBELL (1904–1987). *The Hero with a Thousand Faces,* 1.2.5, 1949

Secret and self-contained, and solitary as an oyster.

> CHARLES DICKENS (1812–1870). On Ebenezer Scrooge, *A Christmas Carol: A Ghost Story of Christmas,* 1, 1843

I lived in solitude in the country and noticed how the monotony of a quiet life stimulates the creative mind.

> ALBERT EINSTEIN (1879–1955). Speech, Albert Hall, London, October 1933, *Out of My Later Years,* rev. ed., 24, 1956 (1950)

My dear Henry,
    A frog was made to live in a swamp, but a man was not made to live in a swamp. Yours ever,
        R.

> RALPH WALDO EMERSON (1803–1882). Referring to his friend Henry David Thoreau who would occasionally live alone in the swamps and woods, journal, 11 May 1858

Man seems to be made neither to live alone nor with others.

> FULKE GREVILLE (1554–1628). *Maxims, Characters, and Reflections,* p. 143, 1756

The genuine solitaries of life fear intimacy more than loneliness.

> CAROLYN HEILBRUN (1926–). "Marriage Is the Message," *Ms.,* August 1974

Separate not yourself from the community.

> HILLEL (1st cent. B.C.). In *Talmud* (A.D. 1st–6th cent.). Rabbinical writings

Those who have most loudly advertised their passion for seclusion and their intimacy with nature, from Petrarch down, have been mostly sentimentalists, unreal men, misanthropes on the spindle side, solacing an uneasy suspicion of themselves by professing contempt for their kind.

> JAMES RUSSELL LOWELL (1819–1891). "Thoreau," *My Study Windows,* 1871

"He who seeks may easily get lost himself. It is a crime to go apart and be alone"—Thus speaks the herd.

> FRIEDRICH NIETZSCHE (1844–1900). "Of the Way of the Creator," *Thus Spoke Zarathustra,* 1892, tr. R. J. Hollingdale, 1961

No one man is capable, without the aid of society, of supplying his own wants; and those wants, acting upon every individual, impel the whole of them into society, as naturally as gravitation acts to a center.

> THOMAS PAINE (1737–1809). *The Rights of Man,* 2.1, 1792

The retreat to the desert . . . became the condition and the prelude of higher destinies.

> ERNEST RENAN (1823–1892). *The Life of Jesus,* 6, 1863, Modern Library edition, 1927

Something of the hermit's temper is an essential element in many forms of excellence, since it enables men to resist the lure of popularity, to pursue important work in spite of general indifference or hostility, and arrive at opinions which are opposed to prevalent errors.

> BERTRAND RUSSELL (1872–1970). *Power: A New Social Analysis,* 2, 1938

If we are to survive, we must have ideas, vision, courage. These things are rarely produced by committees. Everything that matters in our intellectual and moral life begins with an individual confronting his own mind and conscience in a room by himself.

> ARTHUR M. SCHLESINGER, JR. (1917–). "The Decline of Greatness," *Saturday Evening Post,* 1 November 1958

I went to the woods because I wished to live life deliberately, to front only the essential facts of life, and see if I could not learn what it had to teach, and not, when I came to die, discover that I had not lived.

> HENRY DAVID THOREAU (1817–1862). "Where I Lived, and What I Lived For," *Walden; or Life in the Woods,* 1854

I left the woods for as good a reason as I went there. Perhaps it seemed to me that I had several more lives to live, and could not spare any more time for that one.

> HENRY DAVID THOREAU (1817–1862). "Conclusion," *Walden; or Life in the Woods,* 1854

No human being—not even a hermit in the desert—can contract out of being a social creature; sociality is a built-in feature of human nature.

> ARNOLD J. TOYNBEE (1889–1975). *Experiences,* 1.9 (Annex 2), 1969

There comes a moment in everybody's life when he must decide whether he'll live among human beings or not—a fool among fools or a fool alone.

> THORNTON WILDER (1897–1975). *The Matchmaker,* 4, 1954

We're all of us sentenced to solitary confinement inside our own skins, for life!

> TENNESSEE WILLIAMS (1911–1983). *Orpheus Descending,* 2.1, 1957

We do not yet know when being alone will lead to creative "social, artistic, philosophic or characterological performances" and when mental illness will be the outcome.

> GREGORY ZILBOORG (1890–1959). Psychiatrist. As paraphrased by Frieda Fromm-Reichmann, *Psychoanalysis and Psychotherapy: Selected Papers of Frieda Fromm-Reichmann,* 23, ed. Dexter M. Bullard, 1959

❧

Then the Lord God said, "It is not good that the man should be alone; I will make him a helper fit for him."

    ANONYMOUS (*BIBLE*). *Genesis* 2:18

Recluse *n.* someone for whom one's company and two's a crowd.

    ANONYMOUS

SOLUTIONS

See • Problems & Solutions

SORROW

See also • Grief ○ Heaven: Ho Chi Minh ○ Optimism—Examples: Saying (Arab) ○ Unhappiness

The busy bee has no time for sorrow.

    WILLIAM BLAKE (1757–1827). "Proverbs of Hell," *The Marriage of Heaven and Hell*, 7.11, 1790–1793?

Sorrow makes us all children again, destroys all difference of intellect. The wisest knows nothing.

    RALPH WALDO EMERSON (1803–1882). Written a few days after the death of his son Waldo, journal, 30 January 1842

Who never ate his bread in sorrow,
Who never spent the darksome hours
Weeping and watching for the morrow
He know ye not, ye heavenly powers.

    GOETHE (1749–1832). *Wilhelm Meister's Apprenticeship*, 2.13, 1796, tr. Thomas Carlyle, 1824

Believe me, every heart has its secret sorrow which the world knows not; and oftentimes we call a man cold, when he is only sad.

    HENRY WADSWORTH LONGFELLOW (1807–1882). *Hyperion: A Romance*, 3.4, 1839

Sorrow, the great idealizer.

    JAMES RUSSELL LOWELL (1819–1891). "Spenser," *Among My Books*, 1870

Patience is a remedy for every sorrow.

    PUBLIUS SYRUS (85–43 B.C.). *Moral Sayings*, 170, tr. Darius Lyman, Jr., 1862

Sorrow comes unsent for.

    JOHN RAY (1628–1705). Comp., *A Collection of English Proverbs*, p. 204, 1678

Romeo: Parting is such sweet sorrow.

    SHAKESPEARE (1564–1616). *Romeo and Juliet*, 2.2.186, 1594

King Claudius: When sorrows come, they come not single spies, But in battalions.

    SHAKESPEARE (1564–1616). *Hamlet*, 4.5.78, 1600
    See Misfortune: Josh Billings

Malcolm: Give sorrow words: the grief that does not speak Whispers the o'er-fraught heart and bids it break.

    SHAKESPEARE (1564–1616). *Macbeth*, 4.3.9, 1605

Where there is sorrow there is holy ground.

    OSCAR WILDE (1854–1900). *De Profundis*, 1905

❧

Small sorrows speak; great ones are silent.

    SAYING (LATIN)

SOUL

See also • Body ○ Conscience ○ Dehumanization: George Orwell (1) ○ Heart ○ Meditation ○ Mind: [especially] Anonymous (4) ○ Mind & Body ○ Mysticism ○ Self ○ Self-Realization (Becoming): Walt Whitman (3) ○ Self-Realization (Being) ○ Soul & Body ○ Spirit ○ Spirituality ○ Truth: Eric Hoffer ○ The Unconscious ○ Unity: Alexander Pope (1) ○ Virtue: Alexander Pope ○ World: Ralph Waldo Emerson (2,3)

Every act of admiration, prayer, praise, worship, desire, hope implies and predicts the future apotheosis of the soul.

    BRONSON ALCOTT (1799–1888). "Orphic Sayings" (10), *The Dial* (New England journal), July 1840

My soul is a witness for my Lord.

    JAMES BALDWIN (1924–1987). Closing words, "Malcolm and Martin," *Esquire,* April 1972

Thy soul can be thy friend, and thy soul can be thy enemy.

    BHAGAVAD GITA (6th cent. B.C.). 6.5, tr. Juan Mascaró, 1962
    See Spirit: Carl G. Jung

[The] soul is a lamp whose light is steady, for it burns in a place where no winds come.

    BHAGAVAD GITA (6th cent. B.C.). 6.19, tr. Juan Mascaró, 1962

Everywhere the human soul stands between a hemisphere of light and another of darkness; on the confines of two everlasting hostile empires, Necessity and Free Will.

    THOMAS CARLYLE (1795–1881). "Goethe's Works," 1832, *Critical and Miscellaneous Essays,* Carey & Hart edition, 1849

If there is a soul, what is it, and where did it come from, and where does it go? Can anyone who is guided by his reason possibly imagine a soul independent of a body, or the place of its residence, or the character of it, or anything concerning it? If man is justified in any belief or disbelief on any subject, he is warranted in the disbelief in a soul. Not one scrap of evidence exists to prove any such impossible thing.

    CLARENCE DARROW (1857–1938). "Why I Am an Agnostic." In Arthur and Lila Weinberg, eds., *Verdicts Out of Court,* 1963

The Soul unto itself
Is an imperial friend—
Or the most agonizing Spy—
An Enemy—could send—

    EMILY DICKINSON (1830–1886). "The Soul unto itself," 1862?
    See Spirit: Carl G. Jung

The soul! That unhappy word has been the refuge of empty minds ever since the world began.

> NORMAN DOUGLAS (1868–1952). 22 December, *An Almanac,* 1945

The soul is not like God: she is identical with Him.

> MEISTER ECKHART (A.D. 1260?–1328?). In Franz Pfeiffer, *Meister Eckhart,* 1.128, 1857, tr. C. de B. Evans, 1924

Excite the soul, and the weather and the town and your condition in the world all disappear; the world itself loses its solidity, nothing remains but the soul and the Divine Presence in which it lives.

> RALPH WALDO EMERSON (1803–1882). Journal, 29 December 1834

That shudder of awe and delight with which the individual soul always mingles with the universal soul.

> RALPH WALDO EMERSON (1803–1882). "The Over-Soul," *Essays: First Series,* 1841

The soul knows only the soul; the web of events is the flowing robe in which she is clothed.

> RALPH WALDO EMERSON (1803–1882). "The Over-Soul," *Essays: First Series,* 1841

The powers of the soul are commensurate with its needs.

> RALPH WALDO EMERSON (1803–1882). In Michael Dirda, "Journey Into the Self," *Washington Post National Weekly Edition,* 24 April 1995

The soul unfolds itself like a lotus of countless petals.

> KAHLIL GIBRAN (1883–1931). "On Self-Knowledge," *The Prophet,* 1923

Two souls, alas, are housed within my breast,
And each will wrestle for the mastery there.

> GOETHE (1749–1832). *Faust,* 1 ("Outside the City Gate"), 1808–1832, tr. Philip Wayne, 1959
>
> See Neurosis: Carl G. Jung (2)

UniverSoul.

> FRANKLIN GREENWALD (1945–). Personal communication, 8 October 1996

Out of the night that covers me,
    Black as the Pit from pole to pole,
I thank whatever gods may be
    For my unconquerable soul.
In the fell clutch of circumstance
    I have not winced nor cried aloud.
Under the bludgeonings of chance
    My head is bloody, but unbowed. . . .
It matters not how strait the gate,
    How charged with punishments the scroll,
I am the master of my fate:
    I am the captain of my soul.

> W. E. HENLEY (1849–1903). *Echoes,* 4 (To R.T.H.B.), 1872–1889, *Poems,* 1898

Souls are made of dawn-stuff and starshine.

> ELBERT HUBBARD (1856–1915). *The Note Book of Elbert Hubbard,* p. 159, comp. Elbert Hubbard II, 1927

What shall it profit a man, if he shall gain the whole world, and lose his own soul?

> JESUS (A.D. 1st cent.). *Mark* 8:36 (King James Version)

The soul is awakened through service.

> ERICA JONG (1942–). *Fear of Fifty: A Midlife Memoir,* 10, 1994

People will do anything, no matter how absurd, in order to avoid facing their own souls.

> CARL G. JUNG (1875–1961). *Psychology and Alchemy,* 2.3.1, 1944, tr. R. F. C. Hull, 1968
>
> See Self: Hermann Hesse

Now I don't know what the soul is, but whatever it is, I know that it can humble itself.

> ABRAHAM LINCOLN (1809–1865). In Richard Hofstadter, *The American Political Tradition: And the Men Who Made It,* 5.7, 1948

The soul . . . is audible, not visible.

> HENRY WADSWORTH LONGFELLOW (1807–1887). In Elbert Hubbard, comp., *Elbert Hubbard's Scrap Book,* p. 228, 1923

The laws of the civil magistrate's government extend no further than over the body or goods, and to that which is external: for over the soul God will not suffer any man to rule; only he himself will rule there.

> MARTIN LUTHER (1483–1546). In Roger Williams, "Scriptures and Reasons," *The Bloudy Tenent of Persecution for Cause of Conscience Discussed,* 1644, ed. Edward Bean Underhill, 1848

All religion, all life, all art, all expression come down to this: to the effort of the human soul to break through its barrier of loneliness, of intolerable loneliness, and make some contact with another seeking soul, or with what all souls seek, which is (by any name) God.

> DON MARQUIS (1878–1937). *Chapters for the Orthodox,* 11, 1934

This twofold nature of man is so evident that some have thought that we have two souls.

> BLAISE PASCAL (1623–1662). *Pensées,* 417, 1670, tr. William F. Trotter, 1931

Self-motion is the very idea and essence of the soul.

> PLATO (427?–347 B.C.). *Phaedrus,* 245, tr. Benjamin Jowett, 1894
>
> See Spirit: Georg Hegel

The soul of man is immortal and imperishable.

> PLATO (427?–347 B.C.). *The Republic,* 10.608, tr. Benjamin Jowett, 1894

The soul of man . . . is a portion or a copy of the soul of the Universe and is joined together on principles and in proportions corresponding to those which govern the Universe.

> PLUTARCH (A.D. 46?–119?). "On Moral Virtue" (3), *Moralia,* vol. 6, tr. W. C. Helmbold, 1939

The growth of the soul may be compared to the growth of a plant. In both cases, no new properties are imparted by the operation of external causes, but only the inward tendencies are called into action and clothed with strength.

> GEORGE RIPLEY (1802–1880). "Discourses on the Philosophy of Religion," 1836. In George Hochfield, ed., *Selected Writings of The American Transcendentalists,* 1966

Hamlet: O my prophetic soul!

> SHAKESPEARE (1564–1616). *Hamlet,* 1.5.40, 1600

Let a man be of good cheer about his soul, who having cast away the pleasures and ornaments of the body as alien to him and working harm rather than good, has sought after the pleasures of knowledge; and has arrayed the soul, not in some foreign attire, but in her own proper jewels: temperance, and justice, and courage, and nobility, and truth—in these adorned she is ready to go on her journey to the world below, when her hour comes.

> SOCRATES (470?–399 B.C.). In Plato (427?–347 B.C.), *Phaedo*, 114–115, tr. Benjamin Jowett, 1894

A fella ain't got a soul of his own, but on'y a piece of a big one.

> JOHN STEINBECK (1902–1968). *The Grapes of Wrath*, 28, 1939

Methinks my own soul must be a bright invisible green.

> HENRY DAVID THOREAU (1817–1862). "Wednesday," *A Week on the Concord and Merrimack Rivers*, 1849

Human souls have an absolute value in the sight of God.

> ARNOLD J. TOYNBEE (1889–1975). "Ten Basic Questions—and Answers," *New York Times Magazine*, 20 February 1955

As my soul moves my body, even so is God the mover of my soul. Soul within soul.

> SWAMI VIVEKANANDA (1863–1902). *What Religion Is*, 7.2, ed. Swami Vidyatmananda, 1963

I loafe and invite my soul,
I lean and loafe at my ease observing a spear of summer grass.

> WALT WHITMAN (1819–1892). "Song of Myself" (1), 1855, *Leaves of Grass*, 1855–1892

Only the soul is of itself.

> WALT WHITMAN (1819–1892). Preface (1855) to *Leaves of Grass*, 1855–1992

What do you suppose will satisfy the soul, except to walk free and own no superior.

> WALT WHITMAN (1819–1892). "Laws for Creations," 1860, *Leaves of Grass*, 1855–1892

This is thy hour O Soul, thy free flight into the wordless,
Away from books, away from art, the day erased, the lesson done,
Thee fully forth emerging, silent, gazing, pondering the themes thou lovest best,
Night, sleep, death and the stars.

> WALT WHITMAN (1819–1892). "A Clear Midnight" (complete poem), 1881. *Leaves of Grass*, 1855–1892

This soul, or life within us, by no means agrees with the life outside us. If one has the courage to ask her what she thinks, she is always saying the very opposite to what other people say.

> VIRGINIA WOOLF (1882–1941). "Montaigne," *The Common Reader* (First Series), 1925

Each soul and spirit, prior to its entering into this world, consists of a male and female united into one being.

> *ZOHAR* (A.D. 13th cent.). Jewish mystical writings. In Joseph Campbell, *The Hero with a Thousand Faces*, 2.1.4, 1949

⚜

My soul waits for the Lord
    more than watchmen for the morning,
    more than watchmen for the morning.

> ANONYMOUS (*BIBLE*). *Psalms* 130.6

Let the immortal depth of your Soul lead you.

> ANONYMOUS. In Ralph Waldo Emerson, journal, 7 June 1841

What shall it profit a man, if he shall gain his soul, and lose the world?

> ANONYMOUS

SOUL & BODY

See also • Blessings: Anonymous ○ Body ○ Happiness: Voltaire ○ Mind ○ Mind & Body ○ Passion ○ Sex ○ Soul ○ Spirit ○ Work: Henry David Thoreau (1) ○ Wounds: Saying (Arab)

The body is the implement of the soul; and the soul, of God.

> ANACHARSIS (6th? cent. B.C.)

Your body is the harp of your soul,
    And it is yours to bring forth sweet music from it or confused sounds.

> KAHLIL GIBRAN (1883–1931). "On Pleasure," *The Prophet*, 1923

All of us . . . have mortal bodies, composed of perishable matter, but the soul lives forever: it is a portion of the Deity housed in our bodies.

> JOSEPHUS (A.D. 37?–100?). *The Jewish War*, 3.8.5, tr. H. St. John Thackeray, 1926

The soul has a taste for goodness, just as the body has an appetite for pleasure.

> JOSEPH JOUBERT (1754–1824). *Pensées*, 1838, tr. H. P. Collins, 1928

There are . . . no entirely *separate* souls. . . . God alone is wholly without body.

> GOTTFRIED LEIBNITZ (1649–1716). *The Monadology*, 72, 1714, *The Philosophic Works of Leibnitz*, ed. George Martin Duncan, 1908

The well-being of the soul can only be obtained after that of the body has been secured.

> MOSES MAIMONIDES (A.D. 1135–1204). *The Guide for the Perplexed*, 3.27, A.D. 1190, tr. M. Friedländer, 1904

If . . . one has a fine body and a poor soul, he has a fine boat and a poor pilot.

> MENANDER (343?–291 B.C.). Fragment, 1100, tr. Francis G. Allinson, 1921

We must believe the legislator when he tells us that the soul is in all respects superior to the body, and that even in life what makes each one of us to be what we are is only the soul.

> PLATO (427?–347 B.C.). *Laws*, 12.959, tr. Benjamin Jowett, 1894

Conscience is the voice of the soul; the passions are the voice of the body.

> ROUSSEAU (1712–1778). *Emile; or, Treatise on Education*, 4 ("The Creed of a Savoyard Priest"), 1762, tr. Barbara Foxley, 1911

The soul is the voice of the body's interests.

> GEORGE SANTAYANA (1863–1952). *The Life of Reason or The Phases of Human Progress,* 1.9, 1905–1906

The soul is not disfigured by the ugliness of the body, but rather the opposite, that the body is beautified by the comeliness of the soul.

> SENECA THE YOUNGER (5? B.C.–A.D. 65). "On Various Aspects of Virtue," *Moral Letters to Lucilius,* 75.11, tr. Richard M. Gummere, 1918

Lord Illingworth: The soul is born old and grows young. That is the comedy of life.
Mrs. Allonby: And the body is born young and grows old. That is life's tragedy.

> OSCAR WILDE (1854–1900). *A Woman of No Importance,* 1, 1894

Meditation and prayer are to the soul what reflection, study, and conversation are to the mind and what exercise, physical work, and sports are to the body.

> ANONYMOUS

The body is either the temple of the soul or its prison.

> ANONYMOUS

SOVIET UNION

See • Russia (Soviet Union)

SPACE

See also • Brotherhood: Archibald MacLeish ◦ Misjudgments: Lee De Forest ◦ Science ◦ Taxes: Wernher von Braun ◦ Technology

Houston, Tranquility Base here. The Eagle has landed.

> NEIL A. ARMSTRONG (1930–). Radio message from the spacecraft *Apollo XI* announcing the first landing on the moon, 20 July 1969

That's one small step for man, one giant leap for mankind.

> NEIL A. ARMSTRONG (1930–). On becoming the first human to set foot on the moon, 20 July 1969

So there he is at last. Man on the moon. The poor magnificent bungler!
  He can't even get to the office without undergoing the agonies of the damned, but give him a little metal, a few chemicals, some wire and twenty or thirty billion dollars and, vroom!, there he is, up on a rock a quarter of a million miles up in the sky.

> RUSSELL BAKER (1925–). "Why on Earth Are We There? Because It's Impossible," *New York Times,* 21 July 1969

Our goal is nothing less than to establish the United States as the preeminent spacefaring nation.

> GEORGE BUSH (1924–). Speech commemorating the 20th anniversary of the first moon landing, National Air and Space Museum, Washington, 20 July 1989

I believe this nation should commit itself to achieving the goal, before this decade is out, of landing a man on the moon and returning him safely to earth.

> JOHN F. KENNEDY (1917–1963). Supplementary State of the Union Message, 25 May 1961

What can we gain by sailing to the moon if we are not able to cross the abyss that separates us from ourselves?

> THOMAS MERTON (1915–1968). *The Wisdom of the Desert,* p. 11, 1960

Astronauts . . . submit to the severest bodily ordeals in order to satisfy the ritual demands for space travel to distant parts of the solar system. To a certain degree, vicarious participation in these rites by the earthbound inhabitants of the planet, made possible through film, television and radio, restores the waning sense of high adventure; and the ever present possibility of death in a cosmic setting augments, as in motor racing, the daily doses of untrammeled gladiatorial violence faithfully provided by the mass media.

> LEWIS MUMFORD (1895–1990). *The Pentagon of Power: The Myth of the Machine,* 13.1, 1970

Obviously, a major malfunction.

> STEPHEN A. NESBITT. National Aeronautic Space and Administrations public affairs officer. While covering the takeoff of space shuttle *Challenger,* which exploded moments after liftoff, killing its seven crew members, Cape Canaveral, Florida, 28 January 1986

This is the greatest week in the history of the world since the Creation, because as a result of what happened in this week, the world is bigger, infinitely.

> RICHARD M. NIXON (1913–1994). Welcoming astronauts returning from the moon, aboard aircraft carrier *Hornet,* 24 July 1969. In Stephen E. Ambrose, *Nixon: The Triumph of a Politician,* 13, 1989

All systems go. Everything is A-OK!

> JOHN A. POWERS. A repeated remark during the launching of American spacecraft, 1959–1964

Robinson: I think we could regard the solar system as an achievable goal for humanity. . . .
Jim Lehrer (interrupting): But for what purpose?
Robinson: These are places that could become second homes or vacation homes. Mars in particular is very well-suited for the process of terra-forming, of giving it an earthlike environment.

> KIM STANLEY ROBINSON (1952–). Science fiction writer. Several days after the first spaceship landing on Mars. On *NewsHour with Jim Lehrer,* television news program, PBS, 14 July 1997

Space—the final frontier.

> GENE RODDENBERRY (1921–1991). *Star Trek* (television series), 1966–1969
>
> See Self: Gloria Steinem

The space program is morally indefensible, not in itself, but because it has been given priority over the feeding and clothing and housing of the poor majority of the human race.

> ARNOLD J. TOYNBEE (1889–1975). *Surviving the Future,* 6, 1971

The Right Stuff.

> TOM WOLFE (1931–). Referring to the original astronauts, book title, 1979

✺

Here men from the planet Earth first set foot on the moon, July 1969 A.D. We came in peace for all mankind.

> ANONYMOUS (AMERICAN). Plaque marking the spot on the moon where the historic event took place.

SPEAKING

See also • Action & Talk ○ Conversation ○ Eloquence ○ Freedom of Speech ○ Oratory ○ Public Speaking ○ Silence & Speech ○ Talking ○ Words ○ Writing

Always be ready to speak your mind, and a base man will avoid you.

> WILLIAM BLAKE (1757–1827). "Proverbs of Hell," *The Marriage of Heaven and Hell*, 8.17, 1790–1793?

The poor speak very fast, with quick movements, to attract attention. The [rich] move slowly and they speak slowly; they don't need to get your attention because they've already got it.

> MICHAEL CAINE (1933–). In Joan Barthel, "Michael Caine: Versatile & Very Smart," *Cosmopolitan*, June 1986

To speak as though it were the last sentence allowed you.

> ELIAS CANETTI (1905–1994). 1957, *The Human Province*, tr. Joachim Neugroschel, 1978

Think before thou speakest.

> CERVANTES (1547–1616). *Don Quixote*, 1.4.3, 1615, tr. Peter Anthony Motteux and John Ozell, 1743

A word spoken is past recalling.

> JOHN CLARKE (1596–1658). Comp., *Proverbs: English and Latine*, p. 49, 1639

Speech is power: speech is to persuade, to convert, to compel.

> RALPH WALDO EMERSON (1803–1882). "Social Aims," *Letters and Social Aims*, 1876

Think before you speak is criticism's motto; speak before you think, creation's.

> E. M. FORSTER (1879–1970). "The Raison d'Être of Criticism in the Arts," *Two Cheers for Democracy*, 1951

Speak not but what may benefit others or yourself; avoid trifling conversation.

> BENJAMIN FRANKLIN (1706–1790). Virtue #2 ("Silence"), 1784, *Autobiography*, 1798

Consider not so much who speaks, as what is spoken.

> THOMAS FULLER (1654–1734). Comp., *Introductio ad Prudentiam*, 109, 1731

The End of Speech is first to be understood, and then to be believed.

> THOMAS FULLER (1654–1734). Comp., *Introductio ad Prudentiam*, 1314, 1731

If no thought
your mind does visit,
make your speech
not too explicit.

> PIET HEIN (1905–). "The Case for Obscurity (On thoughts and words)," *Grooks*, 1966

He speaks reserv'dly, but he speaks with force,
Nor can one word be changed but for a worse.

> HOMER (8th? cent. B.C.). *The Odyssey*, 8.191, tr. Alexander Pope, 1726

Lucidity of speech is unquestionably one of the surest tests of mental precision. . . . In my experience a confused talker is never a clear thinker.

> DAVID LLOYD GEORGE (1863–1945). Quoted by John Terraine, "Field-Marshal The Earl Haig." In Michael Carver, ed., *The War Lords*, 1976

A man's character is revealed by his speech.

> MENANDER (343?–291 B.C.). Fragment, 72, tr. Francis G. Allinson, 1921

Any man may speak truly; but to speak with order, wisely, and competently, of that, few men are capable.

> MONTAIGNE (1533–1592). "Of the Art of Discussion," *Essays*, 1588, tr. Donald M. Frame, 1958

They find themselves judged not by how they speak but by what they say. . . . Frequently the glibbest talker turns out to be the shallowest thinker.

> RICHARD M. NIXON (1913–1994). *Leaders*, 9, 1982

Speak properly, and in as few Words as you can, but always plainly; for the End of Speech is not Ostentation, but to be understood.

> WILLIAM PENN (1644–1718). *More Fruits of Solitude*, 122, 1693

Speech is a mirror of the soul; as a man speaks, so is he.

> PUBLIUS SYRUS (85–43 B.C.). *Moral Sayings*, 1873, tr. Darius Lyman, Jr., 1862

Prepare to speak only when
Thy words are likely to have effect.

> SA'DI (A.D. 1213?–1292). *The Gulistan, or Rose Garden*, 8 (Caution), A.D. 1258, tr. Edward Rehatsek, 1964

Think nothing, Thekla!
Speak what thou *feelest*.

> FRIEDRICH von SCHILLER (1759–1805). *The Death of Wallenstein*, 3.21, 1799, tr. Samuel T. Coleridge, 1800

Let us say what we feel, and feel what we say; let speech harmonize with life.

> SENECA THE YOUNGER (5? B.C.–A.D. 65). "On the Diseases of the Soul," *Moral Letters to Lucilius*, 75.4, tr. Richard M. Gummere, 1918

Do not be hasty to praise or blame; speak always as though you were giving testimony before the judgment seat of the gods.

> SENECA THE YOUNGER (5? B.C.–A.D.65). "De moribus," 76

Queen Gertrude: O Hamlet, speak no more:
Thou turn'st mine eyes into my very soul.

> SHAKESPEARE (1564–1616). *Hamlet*, 3.4.88, 1600

Hurried speech is a form of deference.

> EARL SHORRIS. "Reflections on Power: A Dissenting View" (4.9), *Harper's*, May 1985

Men use thought only to justify their wrongdoings and speech only to conceal their thoughts.

> VOLTAIRE (1694–1778). *Le Chapon et la Poularde,* 14, 1766
>
> See Words: Thomas Fuller (1)

Think before you Speak, pronounce not imperfectly, nor bring out your Words too hastily but orderly and distinctly.

> GEORGE WASHINGTON (1732–1799). Copybook, 1748 (at age 16), *Rules of Civility & Decent Behaviour in Company and Conversation,* #73. The rules were an amended version of Francis Hawkins's 1640 translation of *Decency of Conversation Among Men* (French Jesuit writing, 1595).

We speak words, we hear meanings.

> SAYING
>
> See Numbers: Harold Geneen

SPECIALISTS

See also • Experts

The specialist learns more and more about less and less until, finally, he knows everything about nothing; whereas the generalist learns less and less about more and more until, finally, he knows nothing about everything.

> DONSEN'S LAW. In Paul Dickson, comp., *The Official Rules,* p. 65, 1978

Specialized meaninglessness has come to be regarded, in certain circles, as a kind of hallmark of true science.

> ALDOUS HUXLEY (1894–1963). "Beliefs," *Ends and Means: An Inquiry into the Nature of Ideals and into the Methods Employed for Their Realization,* 1937

[The specialist] is an invaluable servant and an impossible master.

> HAROLD LASKI (1893–1950). In Theodore C. Sorensen, *Decision-Making in the White House: The Olive Branch or the Arrows,* 5, 1963

Wherever learning breeds specialists, the sum of human culture is enhanced thereby. That is the illusion and consolation of specialists.

> ANTONIO MACHADO (1875–1939). *Juan de Mairena,* 1943

More and more, our life has been governed by specialists, who know too little of what lies outside their province to be able to know enough about what takes place within it.

> LEWIS MUMFORD (1895–1990). *The Conduct of Life,* 7.2, 1951

SPEED

See also • Action ○ Danger ○ Decisiveness ○ Delay ○ Indecision ○ Opportunity ○ Prudence: Rules ○ Safety ○ Slowness ○ Success

Well done is quickly done.

> CAESAR AUGUSTUS (63 B.C.–A.D. 14). In Suetonius (A.D. 69?–122). *The Twelve Caesars,* 2.25, tr. Robert Graves and rev. Michael Grant, 1979

"Well, in *our* country," said Alice, still panting a little, "you'd generally get to somewhere else—if you ran very fast for a long time as we've been doing."

"A slow sort of country!" Said the Queen. "Now, *here,* it takes all the running *you* can do, to keep in the same place. If you want to get somewhere else, you must run at least twice as fast as that!"

> LEWIS CARROLL (1832–1898). *Through the Looking-Glass and What Alice Found There,* 2, 1872

Whoever is in a hurry shows that the thing he is about is too big for him.

> LORD CHESTERFIELD (1694–1773). Letter to his son, 20 August 1749

Soon ripe, soon rotten.

> JOHN CLARKE (1596–1658). Comp., *Proverbs: English and Latine,* p. 84, 1639

In skating over thin ice, our safety is in our speed.

> RALPH WALDO EMERSON (1803–1882). "Prudence," *Essays: First Series,* 1841

Good and quickly seldom meet.

> GEORGE HERBERT (1593–1633). Comp., *Outlandish Proverbs,* 580, 1640

To go fast, go slow.

> ELBERT HUBBARD (1856–1915). *A Thousand and One Epigrams,* p. 89, 1911

Every man rushes elsewhere and into the future because no man has arrived at himself.

> MONTAIGNE (1533–1592). "Of Physiognomy," *Essays,* 1588, tr. Donald M. Frame, 1958

Order is . . . the true key to rapidity of reaction.

> MARIA MONTESSORI (1870–1952). *Spontaneous Activity in Education,* 8, tr. Florence Simmonds, 1917

There are some as goes rootling and tearing about. But, Lor' bless you, sir, I get to Saturday night as soon as any of 'em.

> ANONYMOUS (ENGLISH). Woodsman's remark to the author's father in the 1870s. In Alfred North Whitehead, "Memories," *Atlantic,* June 1936
>
> See Haste: Saying (Arab)

Quickly done, quickly undone.

> SAYING (LATIN)

The quickest way to do many things is to do one thing at a time.

> SAYING (NEW ENGLAND)

SPIRIT

See also • Conscience ○ Self ○ Self-Realization (Becoming): Richard M. Nixon ○ Soul ○ Soul & Body ○ Spirituality ○ World: Laurens van der Post

Spirit is the real and eternal; matter is the unreal and temporal.

> MARY BAKER EDDY (1821–1910). *Science and Health with Key to the Scriptures,* p. 468, 1875

Spirit is matter reduced to an extreme thinness: O *so* thin!

> RALPH WALDO EMERSON (1803–1882). "Experience," *Essays: Second Series,* 1844

Spirit is essentially the result of its own activity.

GEORG HEGEL (1770–1831). Introduction (3.2.3) to *Philosophy of History,* 1832, tr. John Sibree, 1900

See Soul: Plato (1)

The body without the spirit is a corpse; the spirit with the body is a ghost.

ABRAHAM JOSHUA HESCHEL (1907–1972). *God in Search of Man: A Philosophy of Judaism,* 33, 1955

The spirit is willing, but the flesh is weak.

JESUS (A.D. 1st cent.). *Matthew* 26:41

See Will: Ovid

The spirit . . . is two-faced and paradoxical: a great help and an equally great danger.

CARL G. JUNG (1875–1961). "On the Nature of the Psyche" (8), 1947, *The Structure and Dynamics of the Psyche,* tr. R. F. C. Hull, 1960

See Soul: Bhagavad Gita (1) ◦ Soul: Emily Dickinson

I am certain that after the dust of centuries have passed over our cities, we, too, will be remembered not for victories or defeats in battle or politics, but for our contribution to the human spirit.

JOHN F. KENNEDY (1917–1963). Television broadcast (closed-circuit), 29 November 1962

Our national strength matters, but the spirit which informs and contols our strength matters just as much.

JOHN F. KENNEDY (1917–1963). Address, Amherst College (Massachusetts), 26 October 1963

Terrible things are happening to me. The "Spirit" or "Real I" is showing an alarming tendency to become much more personal and is taking the offensive, and behaving just like God. You'd better come on Monday at the latest or I may have entered a monastery.

C. S. LEWIS (1898–1963). Letter to Owen Barfield, 3? February 1930, *Letters of C. S. Lewis,* ed. W. H. Lewis and Walter Hooper, 1993. Lewis converted to Christianity the following year.

Either we learn to understand the tremendous forces operating in the human sprit, or these forces are well calculated to destroy us.

P. W. MARTIN (1893–?). *Experiment in Depth: A Study of the Work of Jung, Eliot and Toynbee,* 9, 1955

Do you not know that your body is a temple of the Holy Spirit within you, which you have from God?

PAUL (A.D. 1st cent.). *1 Corinthians* 6:19

If you are led by the Spirit, you are not under the law.

PAUL (A.D. 1st cent.). *Galatians* 5:18

The fruit of the Spirit is love, joy, peace, patience, kindness, goodness, faithfulness, gentleness, self-control.

PAUL (A.D. 1st cent.). *Galatians* 5:22–23

The life of the spirit demands readiness for renunciation when the occasion arises, but is in its essence as positive and as capable of enriching individual existence as mind and instinct are. It brings with it the joy of vision, of the mystery and profundity of the world, of the contemplation of life, and above all the joy of universal love.

BERTRAND RUSSELL (1872–1970). *Principles of Social Reconstruction,* 7, 1916

I know the untamable spirit of the man; bent it cannot be—but it can be broken.

SENECA THE YOUNGER (5? B.C.–A.D. 65). *Thyestes,* l. 190, tr. Frank Justus Miller, 1917

See Defeat: Ernest Hemingway

The deepest of all the patterns in the human spirit is one of departure and return and the journey implicit in between.

LAURENS van der POST (1906–1996). "Point of Total Return," *Jung and the Story of Our Time,* 1975

SPIRITUALITY

See also • Contemplation ◦ Courage: Mohandas K. Gandhi ◦ Creativity ◦ Discovery ◦ Dreams ◦ God ◦ God & Man: First Person ◦ Grace ◦ Ideas ◦ Imagination ◦ Inspiration ◦ Intuition ◦ Invention ◦ Meditation ◦ Mysticism ◦ Originality ◦ Paradoxes ◦ Prayer ◦ Prophets ◦ Religion ◦ Revelation ◦ Saints ◦ Self ◦ Self-Realization (Becoming) ◦ Self-Realization (Being) ◦ Silence ◦ Solitude ◦ Soul ◦ Spirituality: First Person ◦ The Unconscious ◦ Yoga ◦ Zen

Spiritual life always implies something higher than itself towards which it is ascending.

NICOLAS BERDYAEV (1874–1948). *The Destiny of Man,* 1.1, 1931, tr. Natalie Duddington, 1955

The definition of *spiritual* should be, *that which is its own evidence.*

RALPH WALDO EMERSON (1803–1882). "Experience," *Essays: Second Series,* 1844

The spiritual quest begins, for most people, as a search for meaning.

MARILYN FERGUSON. *The Aquarian Conspiracy: Personal and Social Transformation in the 1980s,* 11, 1980

Spirituality is to religion as justice is to law.

RICHARD M. GROSS (1944–). Personal communication, 2 May 1998

Emotion is inseparable from being filled with the spirit, which is above all a state of being moved.

ABRAHAM JOSHUA HESCHEL (1907–1972). *The Prophets,* 18, 1962

Peace is a necessary condition of spirituality, no less than an inevitable result of it.

ALDOUS HUXLEY (1894–1963). "Seven Meditations." In Christopher Isherwood, ed., *Vedanta for the Western World,* 1945

The path of spirituality is a knife-edge between abysses.

ALDOUS HUXLEY (1894–1963). *The Perennial Philosophy,* 4, 1946

The religious experience . . . is that which lives itself out within the private breast. First-hand individual experience of this kind has always appeared as a heretical sort of innovation to those who witnessed its birth. Naked comes it into the world and lonely; and it has always, for a time at least, driven him who had it into the wilderness.

WILLIAM JAMES (1842–1910). *The Varieties of Religious Experience: A Study in Human Nature,* 14 and 15, 1902

Any attempt to create a spiritual attitude by splitting off and suppressing the instincts is a falsification. Nothing is more repulsive than a furtively prurient spirituality; it is just as unsavory as gross sensuality. . . . Both [spirituality and sensuality] must live, each drawing life from the other.

> CARL G. JUNG (1875–1961). "Marriage as a Psychological Relationship,"
> 1925, *The Development of Personality,* tr. R. F. C. Hull, 1954

No matter what the world thinks about religious experience, the one who has it possesses a great treasure, a thing that has become for him a source of life, meaning, and beauty, and that has given a new splendor to the world and to mankind. . . . Where is the criterion by which you could say that such a life is not legitimate, that such an experience is not valid?

> CARL G. JUNG (1875–1961). "Psychology and Religion" (3), 1938,
> *Psychology and Religion: West and East,* tr. R. F. C. Hull, 1958

Religious experience is absolute; it cannot be disputed. You can only say that you have never had such an experience, whereupon your opponent will reply: "Sorry, I have." And there the discussion will end.

> CARL G. JUNG (1875–1961). "Psychology and Religion" (3), 1938,
> *Psychology and Religion: West and East,* tr. R. F. C. Hull, 1958

We cannot be filled unless we are first emptied, to make room for what is to come.

> THOMAS MERTON (1915–1968). *The Seven Storey Mountain* (from the
> unpublished, original manuscript, 1948), *A Thomas Merton Reader,* 5.1,
> ed. Thomas P. McDonnell, 1974

Religion is a set of social and political institutions and *spirituality* is a private pursuit which may or may not take place in a church setting.

> D. PATRICK MILLER. Journalist. In Eric Utne, "Editor's Note," *Utne Reader,*
> January-February 1991

The spiritual life does not remove us from the world but leads us deeper into it.

> HENRI J. M. NOUWEN (1932–1996). "Do Not Worry, All Things Will Be
> Given," *Catholic Agitator,* September 1980

I don't view medicine, psychology, and spirituality as different camps. When I use the word *spirituality,* I don't necessarily mean religion; I mean whatever it is that helps you feel connected to something that is larger than yourself.

> DEAN ORNISH (1953–). San Francisco cardiologist. Speech before the
> Commonwealth Club of California, San Rafael, 21 January 1994

Communion with the transcendent powers . . . is not a feat that can be achieved by anyone; it is a mystery peculiar to the one elected, and is therefore through and through personal in character.

> THEODORE ROSZAK (1933–). *The Making of the Counter Culture:
> Reflections on the Technocratic Society and Its Youthful Opposition,*
> 8, 1969

Ethical existence [is] the highest manifestation of spirituality.

> ALBERT SCHWEITZER (1875–1965). *The Mysticism of Paul the Apostle,*
> 12, 1929, tr. William Montgomery, 1931

Glendower: I can call spirits from the vasty deep.
Hotspur: Why, so can I, or so can any man;
But will they come when you do call for them?

> SHAKESPEARE (1564–1616). *Henry IV,* Part I, 3.1.53, 1597
> See Leaders & People: Ronald Lewin

Patient and regular practice is the whole secret of spiritual realization. Do not be in a hurry in spiritual life. Do your utmost, and leave the rest to God.

> SWAMI SHIVANANDA (1887–1963). "Spiritual Maxims." In Christopher
> Isherwood, ed., *Vedanta for the Western World,* 1945

By curious indirections only can there be any statement of the spiritual world.

> WALT WHITMAN (1819–1892). "Notes for Lectures on Religion," *Walt
> Whitman's Workshop: A Collection of Unpublished Manuscripts,* ed.
> Clifton Joseph Furness, 1964

SPIRITUALITY: FIRST PERSON

See also • Creativity: First Person ○ Dreams: Examples ○ God & Man: First Person ○ Mysticism ○ Prayers ○ Revelations ○ Spirituality

I was in a state of quiet, almost passive enjoyment, not actually thinking, but letting ideas, images, and emotions flow of themselves, as it were, through my mind. All at once, without warning of any kind, I found myself wrapped in a flame-colored cloud. For an instant I thought of fire, an immense conflagration somewhere close by in that great city; the next, I knew that the fire was within myself. Directly afterward there came upon me a sense of exultation, of immense joyousness accompanied or immediately followed by an intellectual illumination impossible to describe. Among other things, I did not merely come to believe, but I saw that the universe is not composed of dead matter, but is, on the contrary, a living Presence. I became conscious in myself of eternal life.

> R. M. BUCKE. Canadian psychiatrist. 1901, recalling an experience he
> had had 25 years before. In William James, *The Varieties of Religious
> Experience: A Study in Human Nature,* 16 and 17, 1902

Recognizing the poverty of philosophical opinions, not adhering to any of them, seeking the truth, *I saw.*

> THE BUDDHA (6th cent. B.C.). *Suttanipata,* 4.9.3. In E. F. Schumacher,
> *A Guide for the Perplexed,* 4, 1977

And I, who neared the goal of all my nature,
    felt my soul, at the climax of its yearning,
    suddenly, as it ought, grow calm with rapture.

> DANTE (A.D. 1265–1321). "Paradise" (33.46), *The Divine Comedy,* 1321,
> tr. John Ciardi, 1954

Here my powers rest from their high fantasy,
    but already I could feel my being turned—
    instinct and intellect balanced equally.
as in a wheel whose motion nothing jars—
by the Love that moves the Sun and the other stars.

> DANTE (A.D. 1265–1321). Closing lines, "Paradise," *The Divine Comedy,*
> 1321, tr. John Ciardi, 1954

I accuse myself of sloth and unprofitableness day by day but when these waves of God flow into me, I no longer reckon lost time.

> RALPH WALDO EMERSON (1803–1882). Journal, 10 May 1840

The peculiar quality of the voice was something unforgettable because it was like God had a human voice, with all the infinite tenderness and anciency and mortal gravity of a living Creator speaking to his son. . . .

My first thought was this was what I was born for, and second thought, never forget—never forget, never renege, never deny. Never deny the voice—no never *forget* it, don't get lost mentally wandering in other spirit worlds or American or job worlds or advertising worlds or war worlds or earth worlds. But the spirit of the universe was what I was born to realize. . . . God was in front of my eyes—existence itself was God. Well, the formulations are like that—I didn't formulate it in exactly those terms; what I was seeing was a visionary thing, it was a lightness in my body, my body suddenly felt *light,* and a sense of cosmic consciousness, vibrations, understanding, awe, and wonder and surprise. And it was a sudden awakening into a totally deeper real universe than I'd been existing in.

> ALLEN GINSBERG (1926–1997). Referring to an experience he had in 1948 at age 22, Thomas Clarke interview, 1965. In George Plimpton, ed., *Writers at Work: Third Series,* 1967

A longing pure and not to be described
drove me to wander over woods and fields,
and in a mist of hot abundant tears
I felt a world arise and live for me.

> GOETHE (1749–1832). *Faust,* 1808–1832. In Colin Wilson, *Religion and the Rebel,* 1.2, 1957

Those inner states were so fantastically beautiful that by comparison this world appeared downright ridiculous. . . .

It is impossible to convey the beauty and intensity of emotion during those visions. They were the most tremendous things I have ever experienced.

> CARL G. JUNG (1875–1961). *Memories, Dreams, Reflections,* 10, ed. Aniela Jaffé, 1962

I was alone upon the seashore as all these thoughts flowed over me, liberating and reconciling. . . . Earth, heaven, and sea resounded as in one vast world-encircling harmony. It was as if the chorus of all the great who had ever lived were about me. I felt myself one with them, and it appeared as if I heard their greeting: "Thou too belongest to the company of those who overcome."

> MALWIDA von MEYSENBUG. 1900. In William James, *The Varieties of Religious Experience: A Study in Human Nature,* 16 and 17, 1902

Something profoundly convulsive and disturbing suddenly becomes visible and audible with indescribable definiteness and exactness. One hears—one does not seek; one takes—one does not ask who gives: a thought flashes out like lightning, inevitably without hesitation—I have never had any choice about it. There is an ecstasy whose terrific tension is sometimes released by a flood of tears, during which one's progress varies from involuntary impetuosity to involuntary slowness. There is the feeling that one is utterly out of hand, with the most distinct consciousness of an infinitude of shuddering thrills that pass through one from head to foot.

> FRIEDRICH NIETZSCHE (1844–1900). "Thus Spake Zarathustra: A Book for All and None" (3), *Ecce Homo,* 1908, tr. Clifton Fadiman, 1927

I have never had any revelations through anesthetics, but a kind of waking trance . . . I have frequently had, quite up from boyhood, when I have been all alone. This has come upon me through repeating my own name to myself silently, till all at once, as it were out of the intensity of the consciousness of individuality, individuality itself seemed to dissolve and fade away into boundless being, and this not a confused state but the clearest, the surest of the surest, utterly beyond words—where death was an almost laughable impossibility—the loss of personality (if so it were) seeming no extinction, but the only true life.

> ALFRED, LORD TENNYSON (1809–1892). Letter to B. P. Blood. In William James, *The Varieties of Religious Experience: A Study in Human Nature,* 16 and 17, 1902

My desire for knowledge is intermittent; but my desire to commune with the spirit of the universe, to be intoxicated with the fumes, call it, of that divine nectar, to bear my head through atmospheres and over heights unknown to my feet, is perennial and constant.

> HENRY DAVID THOREAU (1817–1862). Journal, 9 February 1851

There comes into my mind such an indescribable, infinite, all-absorbing, divine, heavenly pleasure, a sense of elevation and expansion, and [I] have nought to do with it. I perceive that I am dealt with by superior powers. This is a pleasure, a joy, an existence which I have not procured myself. I speak as a witness on the stand, and tell what I have perceived.

> HENRY DAVID THOREAU (1817–1862). On his boyhood "ecstasies," journal, 16 July 1851

In London in the southern section of the Buckingham Palace Road, walking southward along the pavement skirting the west wall of Victoria Station, the writer, once, one afternoon not long after the end of the First World War—he had failed to record the exact date—had found himself in communion, not just with this or that episode in History, but with all that had been, and was, and was to come. In that instant he was directly aware of the passage of History gently flowing through him in a mighty current, and of his own life welling like a wave in the flow of this vast tide.

> ARNOLD J. TOYNBEE (1889–1975). Referring to himself in the third person, *A Study of History,* 10.139, 1954

❧

Something in myself made me feel myself a part of something bigger than I, that was controlling. I felt myself one with the grass, the trees, birds, insects, everything in Nature. I exulted in the mere fact of existence, of being a part of it all—the drizzling rain, the shadows of the clouds, the tree-trunks, and so on.

> ANONYMOUS (AMERICAN). Quoted by Edwin Diller Starbuck, *The Psychology of Religion: An Empirical Study of the Growth of Religious Consciousness,* 1899. In William James, *The Varieties of Religious Experience: A Study in Human Nature,* 16 and 17, 1902

SPORTS

See also • Baseball ○ Basketball ○ Boxing ○ Competition ○ Defeat ○ Exercise ○ Football ○ Golf ○ Leaders ○ Mountain Climbing ○ Track & Field ○ Victory

In America, it is sport that is the opiate of the masses.

> RUSSELL BAKER (1925–). "The Muscular Opiate," *New York Times,*
> 3 October 1967
>
> See Religion, Anti-: Karl Marx

There is no business like show business—except sports business.

> WILLIAM J. BAKER. *Sports in the Western World,* 19, 1982
> {no subtitle}

Sports do not build character. They reveal it.

> HEYWOOD HALE BROUN (1888–1939). In James A. Michener, *Sports in
> America,* 1, 1976

The human spirit sublimates
the impulses it thwarts;
a healthy sex life mitigates
the lust for other sports.

> PIET HEIN (1905–). "Hint and Suggestion (Admonitory grook addressed
> to youth)," *Grooks,* 1966

What disqualifies war from being a true game is probably what also disqualifies the stock market and business—the rules are not fully known nor accepted by all the players.

> MARSHALL McLUHAN (1911–1980). *Understanding Media: The
> Extensions of Man,* 24, 1964

Sport in the sense of a mass-spectacle, with death to add to the underlying excitement, comes into existence when a population has been drilled and regimented and depressed to such an extent that it needs at least a vicarious participation in difficult feats of strength or skill or heroism in order to sustain its waning life-sense.

> LEWIS MUMFORD (1895–1990). *Technics and Civilization,* 6.11, 1934

The one nice thing about sports is that they prove men do have emotions and are not afraid to show them.

> JANE O'REILLY. *The Girl I Left Behind,* 5, 1980

Serious sport has nothing to do with fair play. It is bound up with hatred, jealously, boastfulness, disregard of all rules and sadistic pleasure in witnessing violence: in other words it is war minus the shooting.

> GEORGE ORWELL (1903–1950). "The Sporting Spirit," 1945,
> *The Collected Essays, Journalism and Letters of George Orwell,*
> vol. 4, ed. Sonia Orwell and Ian Angus, 1968

For the most part the spectator's stake in the proceedings is the gratification that comes from identifying with success. Whoever can provide such vicarious joy needs no other justification as a human being. The capacity of one man's actions to buttress the self-esteem of another is demonstrably a potent force—a force that has been exploited whenever possible by the entrepreneurs of sports events.

> MICHAEL ROBERTS. "The Vicarious Heroism of the Sports Spectator,"
> *New Republic,* 23 November 1974

A white kid tries to become President of the United States, and all the skills and knowledge he picks up on the way can be used in a thousand different jobs. A black kid tries to become Willie Mays, and all the tools he picks up on the way are useless to him if he doesn't become Willie Mays.

> MELVIN ROGERS. Basketball coach. Remark to the author. In Jack Olsen,
> *The Black Athlete: A Shameful Story,* 1, 1968

Most sorts of diversion in men, children, and other animals, are an imitation of fighting.

> JONATHAN SWIFT (1667–1745). "Thoughts on Various Subjects"
> (expanded from a version published in 1711), *Miscellanies in Prose
> and Verse* (published with Alexander Pope), vol. 1, 1727

The Battle of Waterloo was won on the playing fields of Eton.

> DUKE OF WELLINGTON (1769–1852). Attributed

STANDING ALONE

See also • Defiance ○ Democracy: R. H. Tawney ○ Dissent ○ Heresy ○ Independence ○ Individuality ○ Leaders: Henry A. Kissinger (1) ○ Minorities ○ Nonconformity ○ Resistance ○ Self-Reliance

I may stand alone,
But would not change my free thoughts for a throne.

> LORD BYRON (1788–1824). *Don Juan,* 11.90, 1819–1824

The heroes, the saints, and sages—they are those who face the world alone.

> NORMAN DOUGLAS (1868–1952). *South Wind,* 11, 1917

Whoso goes to walk alone, accuses the whole world; he declareth all to be unfit to be his companions; it is very uncivil, nay, insulting; Society will retaliate.

> RALPH WALDO EMERSON (1803–1882). "The Transcendentalist," lecture,
> Masonic Temple, Boston, December 1840

It is only as a man puts off all foreign support, and stands alone, that I see him to be strong and to prevail. He is weaker by every recruit to his banner.

> RALPH WALDO EMERSON (1803–1882). "Self-Reliance," *Essays: First
> Series,* 1841

The man that stands by himself, the universe stands by him also.

> RALPH WALDO EMERSON (1803–1882). "Behavior," *The Conduct of Life,*
> 1860

Strength of numbers is the delight of the timid. The valiant in spirit glory in fighting alone.

> MOHANDAS K. GANDHI (1869–1948). In *Young India,* 17 June 1926

Facing the world together is a tactic of politics, but facing it alone seems to be the characteristic creative stance.

> RICHARD HOFSTADTER (1916–1970). *Anti-Intellectualism in American
> Life,* 10.7, 1962

The test we must set for ourselves [is] not to march alone but to march in such a way that others will wish to join us.

> HUBERT H. HUMPHREY (1911–1978). Speech, Buffalo (New York),
> 7 January 1967

Dr. Stockmann: The strongest man in the world is the one who stands most alone.

> HENRIK IBSEN (1828–1906). *An Enemy of the People,* 5, 1882,
> tr. Rolf Fjelde, 1965

Oh, cursed be that arrogant satisfaction in standing alone.

> SÓREN KIERKEGAARD (1813–1855). Journal, 8 May 1838, tr. Alexander Dru, 1938

Kissinger: I've always acted alone. Americans like that immensely. Americans like the cowboy who leads the wagon train by riding ahead alone on his horse, the cowboy who rides all alone into the town, the village, with his horse and nothing else. Maybe even without a pistol, since he doesn't shoot. He acts, that's all, by being in the right place at the right time. In short, a Western.
Fallaci: I see. You see yourself as a kind of Henry Fonda, unarmed and ready to fight with his fists for honest ideals. Alone, courageous.
Kissinger: Not necessarily courageous. In fact, this cowboy doesn't have to be courageous. All he needs is to be alone, to show others that he rides into the town and does everything by himself. This amazing, romantic character suits me precisely because to be alone has been part of my style or, if you like, my technique.

> HENRY A. KISSINGER (1923–). 2 November 1972. In Oriana Fallaci, *Interview with History,* tr. John Shepley, 1976. Dr. Kissinger later commented on this exchange in *White House Years,* 33, 1979: "I do not believe that I said this in that context or that it was about myself. I am convinced that I may have been the subject of some skillful editing; and Ms. Fallaci has consistently refused to make the tapes available to other journalists."

I stand alone. All else is swamped by Pharisaism.
To live life to the end is not a childish task.

> BORIS PASTERNAK (1890–1960). "The Poems of Yurii Zhivago" ("Hamlet"), *Doctor Zhivago,* 1957, tr. Bernard Guilbert Guerney, 1958

The strongest man is strongest when alone.

> FRIEDRICH von SCHILLER (1759–1805). *William Tell,* 1.3, 1804, tr. Theodore Martin, 1894

In this long struggle [for women's suffrage] I have never felt that we stood alone, for as the representatives of a living truth we are ever linked with the great and grand of all ages, in every latitude and clime, with those able and willing to live or die for a principle.

> ELIZABETH CADY STANTON (1815–1902). Closing words, address before the convention of the International Council of Women, March 1888

If no one responds to your call, Walk alone, Walk alone.

> RABINDRANATH TAGORE (1861–1941). In Louis Fischer, *The Life of Mahatma Gandhi,* 49, 1950

STARDOM

See also • Celebrity ○ Fame ○ Heroism: Henry A. Kissinger (2)

If you become a star, *you* don't change, everyone else does.

> KIRK DOUGLAS (1916–)

Stardom can be a gilded slavery.

> HELEN HAYES (1900–1993). *On Reflection: An Autobiography,* 14, 1968

The real superstar is a man or a woman raising six kids on $150 a week.

> SPENCER HAYWOOD (1949). Basketball player. In Bob Green, "How Never to Be at a Loss for Words," *San Francisco Sunday Examiner & Chronicle,* 8 July 1979

I love being a star more than life itself.

> JANIS JOPLIN (1943–1970). Rock singer

When you're on the screen, no matter who you're with or what you're doing, the audience is looking at you. That's star quality.

> CHARLES SCHNEE. *The Bad and the Beautiful* (film), 1952, spoken by Kirk Douglas

STARS

See also • Nature

The Pistol Star (so called because of the shape of a gaseous nebula surrounding it) burns with the brightness of 10 million Suns and is so large that it would fill the entire space inside Earth's orbit.

> GEORGE JOHNSON. "Casting an Eye on Sights Unseen," *New York Times,* 12 October 1997

Th' evening star
Love's harbinger.

> JOHN MILTON (1608–1674). *Paradise Lost,* 11.588, 1667

Solemn loveliness of the night. Vast star-garden of the Universe.

> JOHN MUIR (1838–1914). Journal, 16? July 1890. In *John of the Mountains: The Unpublished Journals of John Muir,* ed. Linnie Marsh Wolfe, 1938

Twinkle, twinkle, little star.
How I wonder what you are!
Up above the world so high,
Like a diamond in the sky.

> ANN TAYLOR (1782–1866) and JANE TAYLOR (1783–1824). "The Star," *Rhymes for the Nursery,* 1806

The stars are God's dreams, thoughts remembered in the silence of the night.

> HENRY DAVID THOREAU (1817–1862). Journal, 25 March 1842

Behold how the evening now steals over the fields, the shadows of the trees creeping farther and farther into the meadow, and erelong the stars will come to bathe in these retired waters.

> HENRY DAVID THOREAU (1817–1862). "Thursday," *A Week on the Concord and Merrimack Rivers,* 1849

STATES

See also • Country ○ Honesty: George Washington (1) ○ Nations

'Tis a great age when the state is nothing and Man is all.

> BRONSON ALCOTT (1799–1888). Journal, 10 November 1851, ed. Odell Shepard, 1938

The state, according to Hitler, [is] only a "means" for the conservation of the race, as the state, according to Bolshevik propaganda, is only an instrument in the struggle of classes.

> HANNAH ARENDT (1906–1975). *The Origins of Totalitarianism,* 11.1, 1973

In the youth of a state arms do flourish; in the middle age of a state, learning; and then both of them together for a time; in the declining age of a state, mechanical arts and merchandise.

> FRANCIS BACON (1561–1626). "Of Vicissitude of Things," *Essays,* 1625

Alongside all swindlers the state now stands . . . as swindler-in-chief.

> JACOB BURCKHARDT (1818–1897). *Judgments on History and Historians,* 84, tr. Harry Zohn, 1958

The state is a system, including private institutions that set conditions for public policy, which are relatively stable, changing slowly if at all. . . . The government consists of whatever groups happen to control the political system, one component of the state system, at a particular moment.

> NOAM CHOMSKY (1928–). *Turning the Tide: U.S. Intervention in Central America and the Struggle for Peace,* 5.1.4, 1985

The honor of the state must be regarded as sacred.

> KARL von CLAUSEWITZ (1780–1831). 1805. In Peter Paret, *Clausewitz and the State,* 5, 1976

A state worthy of the name has no friends—only interests.

> CHARLES de GAULLE (1890–1970). "The Thoughts of Charles de Gaulle," ed. Jack Monet, *New York Times,* 12 May 1968
>
> See International Relations: Lord Palmerston

The state is made for man, not man for the State.

> ALBERT EINSTEIN (1879–1955). "The Disarmament Conference of 1932," *The World As I See It,* tr. Alan Harris, 1934

The state is nothing but a machine for the oppression of one class by another, and indeed in the democratic republic no less than in the monarchy.

> FREDERICK ENGELS (1820–1895). Introduction (1891) to Karl Marx, *The Civil War in France,* 1871

The state has forbidden to the individual the practice of wrongdoing, not because it desires to abolish it, but because it desires to monopolize it.

> SIGMUND FREUD (1856–1939). "Thoughts for the Times on War and Death" (1), 1915, tr. James Strachey, 1957

The nation-state . . . has proven too large to offer a sense of community and belonging to its citizens, yet too small to cope with the globalization of finance and communication or ecological risk.

> NATHAN GARDELS. "Doing As the Romans Do," *Washington Post National Weekly Edition,* 18 April 1994

The march of God in the world, that is what the state is. The basis of the state is the power of reason actualizing itself as will.

> GEORG HEGEL (1770–1831). "Additions" (152), *Philosophy of Right,* 1821, tr. T. M. Knox, 1942

Only in the state does man have a rational existence. . . . Man owes his entire existence to the state, and has his being within it alone. Whatever worth and spiritual reality he possesses are his solely by virtue of the state.

> GEORG HEGEL (1770–1831). Introduction to *Philosophy of History,* 1832, tr. H. B. Nisbet, 1975

The state is the servant of the citizen, and not his master.

> JOHN F. KENNEDY (1917–1963). State of the Union Message, 11 January 1962

The state is force.

> MACHIAVELLI (1469–1527). In John Morley, *Notes on Politics and History: A University Address,* 8, 1913

Every state tends to become a police state.

> LEWIS MUMFORD (1895–1990). *The Conduct of Life,* 6.4, 1951

In proportion as you give the State power to do things *for* you, you give it power to do things *to* you.

> ALBERT JAY NOCK (1870–1945). *Memoirs of a Superfluous Man,* 10, 1943

The first and highest form of the state and of the government and of the law is that in which there prevails most widely the ancient saying, that "Friends have all things in common."

> PLATO (427?–347 B.C.). *Laws,* 5.739, tr. Benjamin Jowett, 1894

Our aim in founding the State was not the disproportionate happiness of any one class, but the greatest happiness of the whole.

> PLATO (427?–347 B.C.). *The Republic,* 4.420, tr. Benjamin Jowett, 1894
>
> See Good & Evil: Francis Hutcheson ∘ Government: George Washington ∘ Happiness: Jeremy Bentham ∘ Right & Wrong: John Stuart Mill

The principal source of the harm done by the State is the fact that power is its chief end.

> BERTRAND RUSSELL (1872–1970). *Principles of Social Reconstruction,* 2, 1916

The state is primarily an organization for killing foreigners.

> BERTRAND RUSSELL (1872–1970). Woodrow Wyatt television interview, BBC, London, 1959, *Bertrand Russell Speaks His Mind,* 8, 1960

The State is constantly forcing the consciences of men by violence and cruelty. Not content with exacting money from us for the maintenance of its soldiers and policemen, its gaolers and executioners, it forces us to take an active personal part in its proceedings on pain of becoming ourselves the victims of its violence.

> GEORGE BERNARD SHAW (1856–1950). Preface ("Christianity and Anarchism") to *Major Barbara,* 1905

A state is regulated by two things: reward and punishment.

> SOLON (630?–560? B.C.). In Cicero (106–43 B.C.), *Ad Brutum,* 1.15.3

Anonymous: What is the ideal state?
Solon: That in which injury done to the least of its citizens is an injury done to all.

> SOLON (630?–560? B.C.)

Beyond maintaining justice, the state cannot do anything else without transgressing justice.

> HERBERT SPENCER (1820–1904). In Henry Thomas and Dana Lee Thomas, "Herbert Spencer," 5, *Living Biographies of Great Philosophers,* 1941

The state is an instrument in the hands of the ruling class for suppressing the resistance of its class enemies. *In this respect* the dictatorship of the proletariat in no way differs, in essence, from the dictatorship of any other class, for the proletarian state is an instrument for the suppression of the bourgeoisie.

JOSEPH STALIN (1879–1953). *Foundations of Leninism*, 4.2, 1924, International Publishers edition, 1934

The State always has the sole purpose to limit, tame, subordinate the individual.

MAX STIRNER (1806–1856). *The Ego and His Own*, 5.B (The State), 1845, tr. Stephen T. Byington, 1907, and ed. John Carroll, 1971

There will never be a free and enlightened State until the State comes to recognize the individual as a higher and independent power, from which all its own power and authority are derived, and treats him accordingly.

HENRY DAVID THOREAU (1817–1862). "Civil Disobedience," 1849

A state may be defined as a nonvoluntary system of impersonal relations that is maintained partly by force exercised by a governing minority and partly by the consent, or at least the acquiescence, of this governing minority's subjects.

ARNOLD J. TOYNBEE (1889–1975). *A Study of History*, 12.308, 1961

The responsibility of the great states is to serve and not to dominate the world.

HARRY S. TRUMAN (1884–1972). Message to Congress, 16 April 1945, four days after succeeding Franklin D. Roosevelt as President

STATESMEN

See also • Ambassadors ○ Cuban Missile Crisis ○ Decision-Making ○ Diplomacy ○ Diplomats ○ Events: Henry A. Kissinger (2) ○ History: B. H. Liddell Hart (3) ○ International Relations ○ Leaders ○ Machiavellianism: Charles de Gaulle ○ Politicians ○ Presidents ○ Statesmen & Politicians ○ Treaties: Johannes Haller ○ War: Winston Churchill

A constitutional statesman is in general a man of common opinions and uncommon abilities.

WALTER BAGEHOT (1826–1877). "Sir Robert Peel," *Biographical Studies*, 1880

In a sense, international politics has always been treated by diplomats as something of a game. Winners get to be called statesmen.

RICHARD J. BARNET (1929–). *Roots of War*, 5.1, 1971

An elder statesman is somebody old enough to know his own mind and to keep quiet about it.

BERNARD M. BARUCH (1870–1965)

If the people knew what sort of men statesmen were, they would rise and hang the whole lot of them.

JOHN BRIGHT (1811–1889). English reformer. 1880, remark to the writer. In Mandell Creighton, letter to Lord Acton, 9 April 1887, *Essays on Freedom and Power*, ed. Gertrude Himmelfarb, 1949

A disposition to preserve and an ability to improve, taken together, would be my standard of a statesman.

EDMUND BURKE (1729–1797). *Reflections on the Revolution in France*, p. 267, 1790, Pelican Books edition, 1968

Everything which falls under the heading of unselfishness is inappropriate to the action of a state. No one has a right to be unselfish with other people's interests.

HUGH CECIL (1869–1956). British political leader. In Reinhold Niebuhr, *Moral Man and Immoral Society*, 10, 1932

No lover ever studied every whim of his mistress as I did those of President [Franklin D.] Roosevelt.

WINSTON CHURCHILL (1874–1965). On his World War II ally. In John Colville (Churchill's secretary), 2 May 1948. *The Fringes of Power: 10 Downing Street Diaries, 1939–1955*, 35, 1985

I had to deal in the Peace Conference with two men, one of whom thought he was Napoleon and the other Jesus Christ.

GEORGES CLEMENCEAU (1841–1929). French premier. On David Lloyd George and Woodrow Wilson, respectively, his British and American counterparts during the Versailles Treaty negotiations, 1919

A basic truth of statecraft—get the fashionable intellectuals on your side and you can get away with murder!

JOHN R. ELTING (1911–). *The Superstrategists: Great Captains, Theorists and Fighting Men Who Have Shaped the History of Warfare*, 5, 1985

For a statesman—any schoolchild knows that hot air rises to the top.

F. SCOTT FITZGERALD (1896–1940). "The Note-Books" (E), *The Crack-Up*, ed. Edmund Wilson, 1945

A statesman, we are told, should follow public opinion. Doubtless . . . as a coachman follows his horses, having firm hold on the reins, and guiding them. [Ellipsis points in original.]

J. C. HARE (1795–1855) and A. W. HARE (1792–1834). *Guesses at Truth: First Series*, p. 236, 1827, Macmillan edition, 1867

The test of a statesman . . . is his ability to recognize the real relationship of forces and to make this knowledge serve his ends.

HENRY A. KISSINGER (1923–). *A World Restored: Metternich, Castlereagh and the Problems of Peace 1812–1822*, 17.3, 1957

The statesman is . . . like one of the heroes in classical drama who has had a vision of the future but cannot transmit it directly to his fellow-men and who cannot validate its "truth." Nations learn only by experience; they "know" only when it is too late to act. But statesmen must act *as if* their intuition were already experience, as if their inspiration were truth. It is for this reason that statesmen often share the fate of prophets, that they are without honor in their own country, that they always have a difficult task in legitimizing their programs domestically, and that their greatness is usually apparent only in retrospect when their intuition has become experience. The statesman must therefore be an educator; he must bridge the gap between a people's experience and his vision, between a nation's tradition and its future. . . . A statesman who limits his policy to the experience of his people will doom himself to sterility.

HENRY A. KISSINGER (1923–). *A World Restored: Metternich, Castlereagh and the Problems of Peace 1812–1822*, 17.3, 1957

Any statesman must strike a balance between capability and intention.

HENRY A. KISSINGER (1923–). Walter Laqueur interview, "The Lessons of the Past," *Washington Quarterly*, January 1978

There is a margin between necessity and accident, in which the statesman by perseverance and intuition must choose and thereby shape the destiny of his people. To ignore objective conditions is perilous; to hide behind historical inevitability is tantamount to moral abdication; it is to neglect the elements of strength and hope and inspiration which through the centuries have sustained mankind.

> HENRY A. KISSINGER (1923–). *White House Years,* 3, 1979

A statesman's final test . . . is whether he has made a contribution to the well-being of mankind.

> HENRY A. KISSINGER (1923–). *Years of Upheaval,* 8, 1982

Keep strong, if possible. In any case, keep cool. Have unlimited patience. Never corner an opponent, and always assist him to save his face. Put yourself in his shoes—so as to see things through his eyes. Avoid self-righteousness like the devil—nothing is so self-blinding.

> B. H. LIDDELL HART (1895–1970). Advice to statesmen, *Deterrent or Defense: A Fresh Look at the West's Military Position in 1960,* 1960. In John F. Kennedy, "Books in the News," *Saturday Review,* 3 September 1960

Honest statesmanship is the wise employment of individual meannesses for the public good.

> ABRAHAM LINCOLN (1809–1865). In J. F. C. Fuller, *Grant and Lee: A Study in Personality and Generalship,* 2, 1957

[The] capacity to act upon the hidden realities of a situation in spite of appearances is the essence of statesmanship. It consists in giving the people not what they want but what they will learn to want. It requires due courage which is possible only in a mind that is detached from the agitations of the moment. It requires the insight which comes only from an objective and discerning knowledge of the facts, and a high and imperturbable disinterestedness.

> WALTER LIPPMANN (1889–1974). *A Preface to Morals,* 13.6, 1929

The ideal of a practical statesman [is] to aim at the best, and to take the next best, if he is lucky enough to get even that.

> JAMES RUSSELL LOWELL (1819–1891). "Abraham Lincoln," 1864, *My Study Windows,* 1871

Undoubtedly the highest function of statesmanship is by degrees to accommodate the conduct of communities to ethical laws, and to subordinate the conflicting self-interests of the day to higher and more permanent concerns.

> JAMES RUSSELL LOWELL (1819–1891). "Abraham Lincoln," 1864, *My Study Windows,* 1871

A ginooine statesman should be on his guard,
Ef he *must* hev beliefs, nut to b'lieve 'em tu hard.

> JAMES RUSSELL LOWELL (1819–1891). *The Bigelow Papers: Second Series,* 5, 1867

In our country and in our times no man is worthy of the honored name of statesman, who does not include the highest practicable education of the people in all his plans of administration.

> HORACE MANN (1796–1859). "Necessity of Education in a Republican Government," 1838, *Lectures in Education,* 1845

Is a statesman made for sensibility? Is he not a completely eccentric being—always alone on the one side, with the world on the other?

> NAPOLEON (1769–1821). Remark, 1800s, *The Mind of Napoleon: A Selection from His Written and Spoken Words,* 204, ed. J. Christopher Herold, 1955

Metternich comes close to being a statesman: he lies very well.

> NAPOLEON (1769–1821). Remark, 1800s, *The Mind of Napoleon: A Selection from His Written and Spoken Words,* 234, ed. J. Christopher Herold, 1955

A man who in terms of his personal style is very strong and very tough where necessary—steely but who is subtle and appears almost gentle. The tougher his position, usually, the lower his voice.

> RICHARD M. NIXON (1913–1994). Number 8 of 9 "character characteristics" he had in common with Chinese Premier Chou En-lai with whom he was scheduled to meet in July 1972. Memorandum to Henry A. Kissinger, 19 July 1971. In Bruce Oudes, ed., *The President, Richard Nixon's Secret Files,* 1988

You can always get the truth from an American statesman after he has turned seventy, or given up all hope of the presidency.

> WENDELL PHILLIPS (1811–1884). Speech, 7 November 1860

[The statesman] must not lead so far in advance as to be lost sight of, nor lead too directly in the direction of which the popular mind may not approve.

> DONN PIATT (19th cent.). "William H. Seward," *Memories of the Men Who Saved the Union,* 1887

The statesman who is surest that he can divine the future most urgently invites his own retribution.

> ARTHUR M. SCHLESINGER, JR. (1917–). *The Bitter Heritage: Vietnam and American Democracy,* 1941–1966, 7, 1967

Saints can be pure but statesmen must be responsible. As trustees for others, they must defend interests and compromise principles. In politics, practical and prudential judgment must have priority over moral verdicts.

> ARTHUR M. SCHLESINGER, JR. (1917–). "The Necessary Amorality of Foreign Affairs," *Harper's,* August 1971

The born statesman stands beyond true and false. He does not confuse the logic of events with the logic of systems. He has convictions, certainly, that are dear to him, but he has them as a private person; no real politician ever felt himself tied to them when in action. "The doer is always conscienceless; no one has a conscience except the spectator," said Goethe.

> OSWALD SPENGLER (1880–1936). "Philosophy of Politics," *The Decline of the West,* 1918–1922, tr. Charles Francis Atkinson, 1962

The ruling minority [is] the instrument wherewith [the statesman] can carry his purposes into effect.

> OSWALD SPENGLER (1880–1936). "What Statesmen Must Know." In Edwin Franden Dakin, ed., *Today and Destiny: Vital Excerpts from The Decline of the West of Oswald Spengler,* 1940

The expansion of his own class or nation at the expense of others.

> OSWALD SPENGLER (1880–1936). On the statesman's goal, *Aphorisms,* 187. tr. Gisela Koch-Weser O'Brien, 1967

By then [1990] I had learned that I had to defer to [Pres. George Bush] in conversation and not to stint the praise. If that was what was necessary to secure Britain's interests and influence, I had no hesitation in eating a little humble pie.

> MARGARET THATCHER (1925–). British prime minister. *The Downing Street Years,* 1993. In Martin Walker, "Queen Maggie and Her Court," *Washington Post National Weekly Edition,* 8 November 1993

In statesmanship get the formalities right, never mind about the moralities.

> MARK TWAIN (1835–1910). *Following the Equator: A Journey Around the World,* 65 (epigraph), 1897

STATESMEN & POLITICIANS

See also • Politicians ∘ Statesmen

A politician thinks of the next election; a statesman thinks of the next generation.

> JAMES FREEMAN CLARKE (1810–1888). Attributed

A statesman makes the occasion, but the occasion makes the politician.

> GEORGE S. HILLARD (1808–1879). Eulogy for Daniel Webster, Faneuil Hall, Boston, 30 November 1852

The politician regards public opinion as a given fact and submits to it, whereas the statesman creates public opinion, seeing through the talk of the day to the hidden will, which he awakens.

> KARL JASPERS (1883–1969). *The Future of Mankind,* 14, 1958, tr. E. B. Ashton, 1961

A politician was a person with whose politics you did not agree. When you did agree, he was a statesman.

> DAVID LLOYD GEORGE (1863–1945). Speech, Central Hall, Westminster (England), 2 July 1935

People are so much nicer to you in other countries than they are at home. At home, you always have to be a politician; when you're abroad, you almost feel yourself a statesman.

> HAROLD MACMILLAN (1894–1986). British prime minister. Returning from a trip abroad. In "What They Are Saying," *Look,* 15 April 1958

To find the means of accomplishing what *borné* politicians pronounce impracticable is the test of statesmanship.

> JOHN STUART MILL (1806–1873). "Reorganization of the Reform Party," *The London and Westminster Review* (English journal), April 1839

Anyone who would be a statesman has to be a successful politician first.

> RICHARD M. NIXON (1913–1994). *Leaders,* 9, 1982

The statesman shears the sheep, the politician skins them.

> AUSTIN O'MALLEY (1858–1932)

A statesman is a successful politician who is dead.

> THOMAS BRACKETT REED (1839–1902). In Henry Cabot Lodge, *The Democracy of the Constitution,* 7, 1915

I'm proud that I'm a politician. A politician is a man who understands government, and it takes a politician to run a government. A statesman is a politician who's been dead 10 or 15 years.

> HARRY S. TRUMAN (1884–1972). Speech before the Reciprocity Club, Washington, 11 April 1958

STATISTICS

See also • Facts ∘ Figures ∘ Lying: Benjamin Disraeli ∘ Mathematics ∘ Numbers

Statistics are like alienists [i.e., psychiatrists]—they will testify for either side.

> FIORELLO LA GUARDIA (1882–1947). "The Banking Investigations," *Liberty,* 13 May 1933

He uses statistics as a drunken man uses lampposts—for support rather than illumination.

> ANDREW LANG (1844–1912). Scottish writer

The statistical method is of use only to those who have found it out.

> WALTER LIPPMANN (1889–1974). *A Preface to Politics,* 4, 1914

A single death is a tragedy; a million deaths is a statistic.

> JOSEPH STALIN (1879–1953). In Anne Freemantle, opening words, "Unwritten Pages at the End of a Diary," *New York Times Book Review,* 28 September 1958
>
> See Murder: Beilby Porteus

There are two kinds of statistics: the kind you look up and the kind you make up.

> REX STOUT (1886–1975). *Death of a Doxy: A Nero Wolfe Novel,* 9, 1966

STATUS

See also • Authority ∘ Fame ∘ Parents: Norman F. Dixon ∘ Popularity ∘ Power ∘ Prestige: [especially] C. Wright Mills (1) ∘ Reputation ∘ Respect ∘ Success ∘ Wealth

The actions of those who hold great power, and pass their lives in a lofty station, are known to all the world. So it comes to pass that in the highest position there is the least freedom of action.

> JULIUS CAESAR (100–44 B.C.). Roman Senate speech. In Sallust (86?–34? B.C.), *The War with Catiline,* 51.12, tr. J. C. Rolfe, 1921

Rank without merit earns deference without respect.

> CHAMFORT (1741–1794). *Maxims and Thoughts,* 1, 1796, tr. W. S. Merwin, 1984

By virtue of position, certain individuals in our society are accorded the privilege of stating as fact what, in the nature of things, is unknowable. The tycoon and college president have well-recognized rights along these lines.

> JOHN KENNETH GALBRAITH (1908–). *The Affluent Society,* 14.4, 1958

It is stepping very low to get very high.

> MARQUIS OF HALIFAX (1633–1695). "Of Ambition," *Political, Moral and Miscellaneous Reflections,* 1750

Identification with one's office or one's title is very attractive. . . . In vain would one look for a personality behind the husk. Underneath all the padding one would find a very pitiable little creature. That is why the office—or whatever this outer husk may be—is so attractive: it offers easy compensation for personal deficiencies.

> CARL G. JUNG (1875–1961). "The Relations between the Ego and the Unconscious" (1.2), 1928, *Two Essays on Analytical Psychology*, tr. R. F. C. Hull, 1953

It is not titles that honor men, but men honor the titles.

> MACHIAVELLI (1469–1527). *The Discourses*, 3.38, 1517, tr. Christian E. Detmold, 1940

Status refers to the amounts of deference received.

> C. WRIGHT MILLS (1916–1962). Appendix (3) to *The Sociological Imagination*, 1959

The status seekers . . . are people who are continually straining to surround themselves with visible evidence of the superior rank they are claiming.

> VANCE PACKARD (1914–). *The Status Seekers: An Exploration of Class Behavior in America and the Hidden Barriers that Affect You, Your Community, Your Future. A "View of Contemporary Pride and Prejudice,"* 1, 1959

Physical closeness to the center of power is considered evidence of status, and nobody wants to be put out "in left field."

> VANCE PACKARD (1914–). *The Status Seekers: An Exploration of Class Behavior in America and the Hidden Barriers that Affect You, Your Community, Your Future. A "View of Contemporary Pride and Prejudice,"* 8, 1959

Place, that great object which divides the wives of aldermen, is the end of half the labors of human life; and is the cause of all the tumult and bustle, all the rapine and injustice, which avarice and ambition have introduced into this world.

> ADAM SMITH (1723–1790). *The Theory of Moral Sentiments*, 1.3.2, 1759

In Boston they ask, How much does he know? In New York, How much is he worth? In Philadelphia, Who were his parents?

> MARK TWAIN (1835–1910). "What Paul Bourget Thinks of Us," *North American Review*, January 1895

One does not "make much of a showing" in the eyes of the large majority of the people whom one meets with except by unremitting demonstration of ability to pay.

> THORSTEIN VEBLEN (1857–1929). In C. Wright Mills, *White Collar: The American Middle Classes*, 11.4.2, 1951

STERILIZATION

See also • Birth Control ○ Euthanasia ○ Sex ○ Violence

In Californian mental hospitals . . . sterilization is not performed if strong objections are offered to it, though, by a wise precaution, the inmates of mental homes are not allowed out, even for a short period, without sterilization. Yet, in spite of the operation being, at all events by law, compulsory, there is no reason to believe that the sterilized persons often resent it.

> HAVELOCK ELLIS (1859–1939). "Eugenics and the Future" (1), *More Essays of Love and Virtue*, 1931

Those who are physically and mentally unhealthy and un-worthy must not perpetuate their suffering in the body of their children. . . .

A prevention of the faculty and opportunity to procreate on the part of the physically degenerate and mentally sick, over a period of only six hundred years, would not only free humanity from an immeasurable misfortune, but would lead to a recovery which today seems scarcely conceivable.

> ADOLF HITLER (1889–1945). *Mein Kampf*, 2.2, 1924, tr. Ralph Manheim, 1943

It is better for all the world, if instead of waiting to execute degenerate offspring for crime, or let them starve for their imbecility, society can prevent those who are manifestly unfit from continuing their kind. The principle that sustains compulsory vaccination is broad enough to cover cutting the Fallopian tubes. . . . Three generations of imbeciles are enough.

> OLIVER WENDELL HOLMES, JR. (1841–1935). Writing the majority Supreme Court opinion upholding the right of the state of Virginia to sterilize Carrie Buck who was deemed "feeble-minded," *Buck v. Bell*, 1927

The upper economic classes are presumably slightly better endowed with ability—at least with ability to succeed in our social system—and yet are not reproducing fast enough to replace themselves, either absolutely or as a percentage of the total population. We may, therefore, try to remedy this state of affairs, by pious exhortation and appeals to patriotism, or by the more tangible methods of family allowances, cheaper education, or income-tax rebates for children. The lowest strata, allegedly less well-endowed genetically, are reproducing relatively too fast. Therefore birth-control methods must be taught them; they must not have too easy access to relief or hospital treatment lest the removal of the last check on natural selection should make it too easy for children to be produced or to survive; long unemployment should be a ground for sterilization, or at least relief should be contingent upon no further children being brought into the world; and so on. That is to say, much of our eugenic program will be curative and remedial merely, instead of preventive and constructive.

> JULIAN HUXLEY (1887–1975). "Eugenics and Society," *Man Stands Alone*, 1941

Persons with a definite transmissible taint ought not to be allowed to procreate. Many high-minded men and women already accept this duty and act upon it; the reckless must be restrained by the State. For it is obvious that when the State takes upon itself the burden of providing for all the defectives that are born, it is entirely within its rights in insisting that the number of these worse than useless mouths shall not be wantonly increased.

> DEAN WILLIAM RALPH INGE (1860–1954). "Eugenics," *Outspoken Essays: Second Series*, 1922

Measures of sterilization should, in my opinion, be very definitely confined to persons who are *mentally* defective. I cannot favor laws such as that of Idaho, which allows sterilization of "mental defectives, epileptics, habitual criminals, moral degenerates, and sex perverts." The last two categories here are very vague, and will be determined differently in different communities. The law of Idaho would have justified the sterilization of Socrates, Plato, Julius Caesar, and St. Paul.

> BERTRAND RUSSELL (1872–1970). *Marriage and Morals*, 18, 1929

STOCK MARKET

Includes • Wall Street

See also • Business (Commerce) ○ Capitalism ○ Clothes: Oscar Wilde ○ Corporations ○ Gambling ○ Misjudgments: Herbert Hoover, Thomas W. Lamont ○ Money ○ Profit & Loss ○ Real Estate

It is a curious fact that capital is generally most fearful when prices of commodities and securities are low and safe, and boldest at the heights when there is danger.

> BERNARD M. BARUCH (1870–1965). In "Baruch Epigrams Widely Repeated," *New York Times,* 21 June 1965

I . . . tried to buy good businesses at fair prices rather than fair businesses at good prices.

> WARREN BUFFETT (1930–). In "Thoughts on the Business of Life," *Forbes,* 13 January 1997

Rule No. 1: Never lose money. Rule No. 2: Never forget Rule No. 1.

> WARREN BUFFETT (1930–). "About Investing: Have a Philosophy," *Warren Buffett Speaks: Wit and Wisdom from the World's Greatest Investor,* ed. Janet Lowe, 1997

Investment must be rational. If you can't understand it, don't do it.

> WARREN BUFFETT (1930–). "About Investing: Only Buy Securities That You Understand," *Warren Buffett Speaks: Wit and Wisdom from the World's Greatest Investor,* ed. Janet Lowe, 1997

I used to think that if there was reincarnation, I wanted to come back as the President or the Pope or as a .400 baseball hitter. But now I would like to come back as the bond market. You can intimidate everybody.

> JAMES CARVILLE (1944–). Political consultant. In Louis Uchitelle, "Why America Won't Boom," *New York Times,* 12 June 1994

Wall Street, where enough is never enough.

> ALISON LEIGH COWAN. "Divorce, Wall Street Style," *New York Times,* 22 January 1989

What will ultimately frighten the market? It could be the upcoming recession. Maybe the Washington scandals. Or maybe something as simple as someone important saying, "Boo!"

> JOHN CRUDELE. "Dow a False Harbinger of Market Health?" *San Francisco Sunday Examiner & Chronicle,* 25 February 1996

'Tis sweet to know that stocks will stand
When we with Daisies lie—
That Commerce will continue—
And Trades as briskly fly—

> EMILY DICKINSON (1830–1886). "If I should die," 1858?

There are old traders around and bold traders around, but there are no old, bold traders around.

> BOB DINDA

I took such pains not to keep my money in the house, but to put it out of the reach of burglars by buying stock, and had no guess that I was putting it into the hands of these very burglars now grown wiser and standing dressed as Railway Directors.

> RALPH WALDO EMERSON (1803–1882). Journal, 1857, undated

Wisdom says: you can make 1,000 percent on your investment, but lose only 100 percent.

> GERSHON EVAN. Complete letter to the Editor, *Newsweek,* 1 December 1997

The best investment opportunities [arise] when you are broke.

> FIRESTONE'S PRINCIPLE OF INVESTMENT TIMING. In John Peers, comp., *1,001 Logical Laws,* p. 90, 1979

[Financier] George Soros likes to say, "I am the most highly paid theater critic in the world." The leaders put on the show, the money managers write the reviews and the countries suffer (or enjoy) the consequences.

> THOMAS L. FRIEDMAN (1953–). "The Global Casino," *New York Times,* 1 March 1995

Financial genius consists almost entirely of avarice and a rising market.

> JOHN KENNETH GALBRAITH (1908–). "Financial Genius Is Before the Fall," *Harper's,* November 1969

How do we know when irrational exuberance has unduly escalated [stock market] values, which then become subject to unexpected and prolonged contractions as they have in Japan over the last decade?

> ALAN GREENSPAN (1926–). Speech at an American Enterprise Institute dinner, Washington, 5 December 1996. In Floyd Norris, "Greenspan Asks a Question and Global Markets Wobble," *New York Times,* 7 December 1996

The [stock] market seems to have a way of finding news appropriate to its frame of mind.

> ALBERT HAAS, JR. San Francisco investment analyst. In "The Worries of Wall Street," *Newsweek,* 28 June 1965

As depicted by James Stewart [in his book *Den of Thieves*], Wall Street was a world unto itself greased by the exchange of favors. Money, power and sex defined status. Providing for one's family was the ostensible excuse for any behavior, and only suckers played without an edge.

> MAX HOLLAND. "Greed Is All Right," *Nation,* 16 December 1991

In this game if you want a friend, you get a dog.

> CARL C. ICAHN (1936–). Financier. Appearing in *Pinnacle,* television documentary, CNN, 21 January 1989
>
> See Washington: Harry S. Truman

[Widespread] speculation for profit leads away from normal, rational behavior to what have been described as "manias" or "bubbles." The word "mania" emphasizes the irrationality; "bubble" foreshadows the bursting.

> CHARLES P. KINDLEBERGER (1910–). *Manias, Panics, and Crashes: A History of Financial Crises,* 2, 1978

The panic feeds on itself, as did the speculation, until one or more of three things happen: (1) prices fall so low that people are again tempted to move back into less liquid assets; (2) trade is cut off by setting limits on price declines, shutting down exchanges, or otherwise closing trading; or (3) a lender of last resort succeeds in convincing the market that money will be made available in sufficient volume to meet the demand for cash. Confidence may be restored even if a large volume of money is not issued against other assets; the mere knowledge that one can get money is frequently sufficient to eliminate the desire.

CHARLES P. KINDLEBERGER (1910–). *Manias, Panics, and Crashes: A History of Financial Crises*, 2, 1978

As the boom mounts to a crescendo, it must be slowed down without precipitating a panic. After a crash has occurred, it is important to wait long enough for the insolvent firms to fail, but not so long as to let the crisis spread to solvent firms needing liquidity.

CHARLES P. KINDLEBERGER (1910–). On the intervention of lenders of last resort during financial crises, *Manias, Panics, and Crashes: A History of Financial Crises*, 9, 1978

More people get killed chasing after a higher yield than looking down the barrel of a gun.

WILLIAM LeFEVRE. Investment analyst. In Herb Greenberg, "Taking the Bull by the Horns," *San Francisco Chronicle*, 14 February 1992

The longer a stock or an index trades in a very narrow range, when it does break out, either way, the ultimate move is intensified.

WILLIAM LeFEVRE. In Chet Currier (Associated Press), "Market's Calm Seas May Roil Again Soon," *San Francisco Chronicle*, 1 August 1994

Never buy at the bottom, and always sell too soon.

JESSE L. LIVERMORE. In "Thoughts on the Business of Life," *Forbes*, 30 October 1989

Every time you think you've got the key to the market, some SOB changes the lock.

G. M. LOEB (1899–). Quoted by Louis Rukeyser, television moderator, *Wall Street Week*, PBS, 9 May 1996

I like to buy a company any fool can manage because eventually one will.

PETER LYNCH (1944–). Fidelity Magellan Fund manager. In "News/Trends," *Fortune*, 28 December 1992

Television newscaster: Jitters on Wall Street today over rumors that Alan Greenspan said, "A rich man can as soon enter Heaven as a camel fit through the eye of a needle."

ROBERT MANKOFF. Cartoon caption, *New Yorker*, 6 January 1997

Anonymous: What should I do about my stocks? I can't sleep nights.
Morgan: I'd sell down to the sleeping point.

J. P. MORGAN (1837–1913). Format adapted. In Paul A. Samuelson, "Science and Stocks," *Newsweek*, 19 September 1966

The market always will do whatever it has to do to embarrass the maximum number of people.

MICHAEL MURPHY. Stock market newsletter publisher. In Herb Greenberg, "Business Insider," *San Francisco Chronicle*, 21 May 1991

It's just as I have been constantly telling you, "Don't gamble"; take all your savings and buy some good stock and hold it till it goes up, then sell it.

If it don't go up, don't buy it.

WILL ROGERS (1879–1935). 31 October 1929 (two days after the stock-market crash), *The Autobiography of Will Rogers*, ed. Donald Day, 1949

Here's a rule for stock pickers. If the company bilks investors and fools the analysts, it's a sell. If it bilks and fools Uncle Sam, it's a hold or a buy.

JOHN ROTHCHILD. "Crime and Not Much Punishment: When Uncle Sam Gets Bilked by Favored Corporations, He Tends to Forgive and Forget," *San Francisco Sunday Examiner & Chronicle*, 28 February 1993

If an abnormal return is promised, there must be an abnormal risk.

HOBART ROWEN (1918–1995). "The first rule of investing," "Unheeded Warnings on the Peso," *Washington Post National Weekly Edition*, 13 February 1995

Wall Street indexes predicted nine out of the last five recessions!

PAUL A. SAMUELSON (1915–). "Science and Stocks," *Newsweek*, 19 September 1966

The sophisticates never feel comfortable unless they can be reassured that relatively uninformed investors are going the other way with some conviction. It all has to do with Accumulation and Distribution. When the sophisticates are Accumulating, they have to be Accumulating from someone, and when they are Distributing, somebody has to be there to buy.

ADAM SMITH (pen name of GEORGE J. W. GOODMAN). *The Money Game*, 14, 1967

Insider information is the coin of the realm.

JAMES STEWART. Journalist. Appearing on *Inside Opinion*, CNBC, 9 March 1994

When countries have had a string of boom years, megalomania sets in and their governments and large investors come to feel that ordinary economic rules that apply to others do no apply to them.

LESTER C. THUROW (1938–). *The Future of Capitalism*, 1995. In "Asia: The Collapse and the Cure," *New York Review of Books*, 5 February 1998

The question is not whether an [economic] earthquake will occur. It will. The only question is when, and whether it occurs as one big shock or as a series of smaller shocks that do less damage. But when conditions have existed for a long period of time and nothing happens, humans, being human, begin to believe that it is possible to defy economic gravity forever. . . . But let no one doubt that this earthquake will happen. . . . The forces on each side of the fault are enormous.

LESTER THUROW (1938–). *The Future of Capitalism*, 1995. In "Asia: The Collapse and the Cure," *New York Review of Books*, 5 February 1998

October. This is one of the peculiarly dangerous months to speculate in stocks. The others are, July, January, September, April, November, May, March, June, December, August, and February.

> MARK TWAIN (1835–1910). *The Tragedy of Pudd'nhead Wilson,* 13 (epigraph), 1894

"Wall Street Lays an Egg."

> VARIETY. Headline, 30 October 1929, the day after the stock-market crash

A melt-up.

> LARRY WACHTEL. Investment analyst. The day after a day 92.49 point jump in the Dow Jones Industrial Average (22 February). In "Notebook," *Time,* 4 March 1996

"Stocks Steady After Decline."

> WALL STREET JOURNAL. Headline, 30 October 1929, the day after the stock-market crash

Over the last decade and a half, as the Dow [Jones Average] has ascended from 800 to 8,000, luring tens of millions of middle-class Americans into the market, we have developed a mass culture of investing, the first to exist anywhere in the world. American democratic capitalism has brought about the *democratization* of capitalism.

> JACOB WEISBERG. "United Shareholders of America," *New York Times Magazine,* 25 January 1998

The stock-market boom expresses the health of our economy. For millions of people, the rising Dow means an unanticipated degree of prosperity and bodes well for an earlier and more secure retirement. . . .

That said, it is nonetheless worth pausing to fret over the distortions that the rising market brings to our political and cultural life. A soaring Dow does not necessarily mean a healthy society. Even as a rising market makes many of us richer, it exacerbates inequality. By setting up speculative riches as an aspiration, it belittles the traditional virtues of industry and thrift.

> JACOB WEISBERG. "United Shareholders of America," *New York Times Magazine,* 25 January 1998

One trade away from humility.

> STANLEY WEISER (1946–) and OLIVER STONE (1946–). *Wall Street* (film), 1987

With an evening coat and a white tie . . . anybody, even a stockbroker, can gain a reputation for being civilized.

> OSCAR WILDE (1854–1900). *The Picture of Dorian Gray,* 1, 1891

On Wall Street he and a few others—how many?—three hundred, four hundred, five hundred?—had become precisely that . . . Masters of the Universe. There was . . . no limit whatsoever! [Ellipsis points in original.]

> TOM WOLFE (1931–). On fictional bond dealer Sherman McCoy, *The Bonfire of the Vanities,* 1, 1987

If you just keep your eyes open, you can identify [stock-buying manias] at the time, but you never can be certain just how far they'll run.

> MARTIN ZWEIG. Investment analyst. In Chet Currier, "Record Year for IPOs on Wall Street: Initial-Public Offering Mania May Be Good for Economy, but Bad for Investors," *San Francisco Chronicle,* 27 December 1993

The suckers haven't permanently deserted the stock market. They are merely waiting until the prices get too high again.

> ANONYMOUS (AMERICAN)

The stock market is the numbers game of the rich.

> ANONYMOUS (AMERICAN)

If it sounds too good to be true, it probably is.

> SAYING (AMERICAN). Quoted as "a sound investment principle" by Arthur Levitt (Securities and Exchange Commission chairman), speech, "Town Hall on the Air," KOIT, San Francisco, 15 January 1995

Bulls and bears can make money, but hogs can't.

> SAYING (WALL STREET)

Buy low; sell high.

> SAYING (WALL STREET)

Buy on the canons; sell on the trumpets.

> SAYING (WALL STREET)

Buy on the rumor; sell on the news.

> SAYING (WALL STREET)

Don't fight the tape.

> SAYING (WALL STREET)

Let profits run; cut losses.

> SAYING (WALL STREET)

No one was ever ruined by taking a profit.

> SAYING (WALL STREET)

Stock prices fall faster than they rise.

> SAYING (WALL STREET)

The trend is your friend.

> SAYING (WALL STREET)

STRANGERS

See also • Alienation

With what ease I become a stranger to myself.

> HENRI AMIEL (1821–1881). Journal, July 1864, tr. Mrs. Humphrey Ward, 1887

The man you see is an unfortunate wanderer who has strayed here, and now commands our care, since all strangers and beggars come under the protection of Zeus.

> HOMER (8th? cent. B.C.). *The Odyssey,* 6.205, tr. E. V. Rieu, 1946

The gods do disguise themselves as strangers from abroad, and wander round our towns in every kind of shape to see whether people are behaving themselves or getting out of hand.

> HOMER (8th? cent. B.C.). *The Odyssey,* 17.285, tr. E. V. Rieu, 1946

And how am I to face the odds
Of man's bedevilment and God's?
I, a stranger and afraid
In a world I never made.

> A. E. HOUSMAN (1859–1936). *Last Poems,* 12, 1922, *The Collected Poems of A. E. Housman,* 1959

As you receive the stranger, so you receive your God.

> JOHN CASPAR LAVATER (1741–1801). *Aphorisms on Man,* 340, 1788

When one is a stranger to oneself then one is estranged from others too.

> ANNE MORROW LINDBERGH (1906–). "Moon Shell," *Gift from the Sea,* 1955

I have been a stranger in a strange land.

> MOSES (14th cent. B.C.). *Exodus* 2:22 (King James Version)

The American people believe that a stranger is a friend they have yet to meet.

> RONALD REAGAN (1911–). Speech at welcoming ceremonies for Premier Mikhail S. Gorbachev, White House, 8 December 1987

Blanche DuBois: I have always depended on the kindness of strangers.

> TENNESSEE WILLIAMS (1911–1983). *A Streetcar Named Desire,* 11, 1947

Do not neglect to show hospitality to strangers, for thereby some have entertained angels unawares.

> ANONYMOUS (*BIBLE*). *Hebrews* 13:2

STRATEGY, MILITARY

See also • Army ○ Commanders ○ Deception ○ Decision-Making ○ Defeat ○ Guerrilla Warfare ○ Intelligence, Military ○ Navy ○ Planning ○ Principles, Theoretical ○ Prudence—Rules: Saying ○ Revolutionary War: George Washington (2) ○ Soldiers ○ Timing ○ Victory ○ War

Never go the same way twice!

> CHARLES C. ARNDT (1919–1965). Marine sergeant. Battle of Guadalcanal, 1942

Rommel in attack never worried about his own flanks: a punch protects itself.

> CORRELLI BARNETT (1927–). Referring to German Field Marshal Erwin Rommel (1891–1944), *The Desert Generals,* 4.3, 1960

The distinction between politics and strategy diminishes as the point of view is raised. At the summit true politics and strategy are one.

> WINSTON CHURCHILL (1874–1865). *The World Crisis,* 1923–1931. In Algis Valiunas, "A Ground War for All Time: Churchill's Forgotten Masterpiece," *American Spectator,* April 1991

The best Strategy is *always to be very strong,* first generally, then at the decisive point.

> KARL von CLAUSEWITZ (1780–1831). *On War,* 3.11, 1832, tr. J. J. Graham, 1873

Seize, keep, and exploit the initiative.

> JOHN R. ELTING (1911–). Appendix to *The Superstrategists: Great Captains, Theorists and Fighting Men Who Have Shaped the History of Warfare,* 1985

The first object is to strike; the second, to guard against the return blow.

> CYRIL FALLS (1888–1971). *Ordeal by Battle,* 2, 1943

I always make it a rule to get there first with the most men.

> NATHAN BEDFORD FORREST (1821–1877). Confederate general (Popular version: I git thar fustest with the mostest men.)

It is absolutely necessary to change your methods often and imagine new decoys. If you always act in the same manner, you soon will be interpreted.

> FREDERICK II (1712–1786). *The Instruction of Frederick the Great for His Generals,* 1747. In Thomas R. Phillips, ed., *Roots of Strategy,* p. 348, 1940;

The fighting power of an army lies in its organization, which can be destroyed either by wearing it down or by rendering it inoperative. The first comprises killing, wounding, and capturing the enemy's soldiers—body warfare; the second, in rendering inoperative his power of command—brain warfare.

> J. F. C. FULLER (1878–1966). British general and military writer. Summarizing his "Plan 1919" (May 1918), *The Conduct of War: 1789–1961,* 12.5, 1961

The method of attack is in theory always simple—namely, the establishment of a protective fulcrum upon which to move an offensive lever. In other words, a self-protective base of action from which offensive power can be launched.

> J. F. C. FULLER (1878–1966). *Armored Warfare,* 7, 1943

Neither the defensive nor the offensive is inherently stronger or weaker; they are complementary operations, and which is the more suitable to an occasion depends on the circumstances which surround it.

> J. F. C. FULLER (1878–1966). *The Conduct of War: 1789–1961,* 4.7, 1961
> See Guerrilla Warfare: Mao Tse-tung (6)

Find out where your enemy is, get at him as soon as you can and strike him as hard as you can, and keep moving on.

> ULYSSES S. GRANT (1822–1885). In Bruce Catton, *This Hallowed Ground,* 11.2, 1956

Hit hard, hit fast, hit often!

> WILLIAM F. "BULL" HALSEY (1882–1959). Signal to the Third Fleet, 1944

Always mystify, mislead, and surprise the enemy.

> THOMAS JONATHAN "STONEWALL" JACKSON (1820–1863). In G. F. R. Henderson, *The Science of War,* 2, ed. Neill Malcolm, 1905

To move swiftly, strike vigorously, and secure all the fruits of victory is the secret of successful war.

> THOMAS JONATHAN "STONEWALL" JACKSON (1820–1863). In G. F. R. Henderson, *The Science of War,* 2, ed. Neill Malcolm, 1905

If the enemy divides his forces on an extended front, the best direction of the maneuver line will be upon his center; but in every other case . . . the best direction will be upon one of the flanks, and then upon [his] rear.

HENRI de JOMINI (1779–1869). *Summary of the Art of War*, 3, 1807, ed. J. D. Hittle, 1947

Reading Lenin or Mao or Stalin, one is struck by the emphasis on the relationship between political, military, psychological and economic factors . . . and on the need for dominating a situation by flexible tactics and inflexible purpose.

HENRY A. KISSINGER (1923–). "Reflections on American Diplomacy" (5), *Foreign Affairs*, October 1956

I was too weak to defend, so I attacked.

ROBERT E. LEE (1807–1870). Summing up his successful strategy during the Battle of Chancellorsville (Virginia). In Eric Larrabee, epilogue to *Commander in Chief: Franklin Delano Roosevelt, His Lieutenants, and Their War*, 1987

See World War I: Ferdinand Foch

If you strike steel, pull back; if you strike mush, keep going.

LENIN (1870–1924). In Theodore C. Sorensen, *Kennedy*, 24, 1965

The "expanding torrent" method [involved] . . . dispersion in probing, concentration in striking, and renewed expansion in exploiting the penetration. I . . . likened the method to "the play of lightning flashes," where the strike comes before the flash is seen and thus allows no time to counteract it.

B. H. LIDDELL HART (1895–1970). British captain. On the method he developed in 1920, *The Liddell Hart Memoirs, 1895–1938*, 7, 1965

A decisive result through *surprise* may come by striking at an unexpected moment, or from an unexpected direction, or owing to the unexpected strength put into the blow. It will normally be a compound of all three methods.

B. H. LIDDELL HART (1895–1970). October 1922, *Thoughts on War*, 9.5, 1944

In war the power to use two fists is an inestimable asset. To feint with one fist and strike with the other yields an advantage, but a still greater advantage lies in being able to interchange them— to convert the feint into the real blow if the opponent uncovers himself.

B. H. LIDDELL HART (1895–1970). November 1929, *Thoughts on War*, 1.3, 1944

The most effective indirect approach is one that lures or startles the opponent into a false move—so that, as in jujitsu, his own effort is turned into the lever of his overthrow.

B. H. LIDDELL HART (1895–1970). *Strategy*, 10, 1954

A strategist should think in terms of paralyzing, not of killing. Even on the lower plane of warfare, a man killed is merely one man less, whereas as a man unnerved is a highly infectious carrier of fear, capable of spreading an epidemic of panic. . . . The sword drops from a paralyzed hand.

B. H. LIDDELL HART (1895–1970). *Strategy*, 15, 1954

For success, two major problems must be solved—*dislocation* and *exploitation*. One precedes and one follows the actual blow. . . . You cannot hit the enemy with effect unless you have first created the opportunity; you cannot make that effect decisive unless you exploit the second opportunity that comes before he can recover.

B. H. LIDDELL HART (1895–1970). *Strategy*, 20, 1954

Because its essence is the clash of antagonistic and outmaneuvering wills, strategy usually proceeds by paradox rather than conventional "linear" logic.

EDWARD N. LUTTWAK (1942–). *The Pentagon and the Art of War: The Question of Military Reform*, 11, 1985

The object of strategic retreat is to conserve military strength and prepare for the counteroffensive.

MAO TSE-TUNG (1893–1976). "Problems of Strategy in China's Revolutionary War" (5.3), December 1936, *Selected Works of Mao Tse-tung*, Foreign Languages Press edition, vol. 1, 1965

You will usually find that the enemy has three courses open to him, and of these he will adopt the fourth.

HELMUTH von MOLTKE (1800–1891). Prussian general. In John Connell, *Wavell: Scholar and Soldier*, 5, 1964

Strategy is the art of making use of time and space. I am less chary of the latter than the former. Space we can recover, lost time never.

NAPOLEON (1769–1821). Letter to Baron von Stein, 14 January 1814. In J. F. C. Fuller, *The Conduct of War*, 3.3, 1961

The great art of winning a battle consists in changing one's line of operations in the middle of the action.

NAPOLEON (1769–1821). Remark to Gen. Gaspard Gourgaud, 1818, *The Mind of Napoleon: A Selection from His Written and Spoken Words*, 294, ed. J. Christopher Herold, 1955

Never attack in front a position which can be taken by turning!

NAPOLEON (1769–1821). *Maximes de Guerre*, 16, 1830–1874. In Conrad H. Lanza, annotator, *Napoleon and Modern War*, 1943

Grab the enemy by the nose and kick him in the pants.

GEORGE S. PATTON, JR. (1885–1945). "Training Memoranda to His Regiment," *Cavalry Journal*, 1940. In Martin Blumenson, *The Patton Papers, 1885–1940*, 47, 1972

There is only one tactical principle which is not subject to change. It is: "To so use the means at hand to inflict the maximum amount of wounds, death, and destruction on the enemy in the minimum time."

GEORGE S. PATTON, JR. (1885–1945). "Letter of Instruction Number 2," 3 April 1944, appendix (D) to *War As I Knew It*, 1947

In military operations what is done openly and by force is much less than what is done by stratagem and the use of opportunity.

POLYBIUS (208?–126? B.C.). *The Histories*, 9.12, tr. W. R. Paton, 1925

See Success: Machiavelli (1) ○ Tyrants: Aristotle (1) ○ War: Thomas Hobbes (1)

Our strategy to go after this army is very, very simple. First, we're going to cut it off, and then we're going to kill it.

COLIN L. POWELL (1937–). Referring to the Iraqi Army during the Gulf War, Pentagon press briefing, 23 January 1991

Coil yourself omnidirectionally!

R. G. H. SIU (1917–). *The Craft of Power*, 1.55, 1984

When capable, feign incapacity; when active, inactivity.

SUN-TZU (4th cent. B.C.). "Estimates" (18), *The Art of War*, tr. Samuel B. Griffith, 1963

To win one hundred victories in one hundred battles is not the acme of skill. To subdue the enemy without fighting is the acme of skill.

> SUN-TZU (4th cent. B.C.). "Offensive Strategy" (3), *The Art of War,* tr. Samuel B. Griffith, 1963

If I am able to determine the enemy's dispositions while at the same time I conceal my own, then I can concentrate and he must divide. And if I concentrate while he divides, I can use my entire strength to attack a fraction of his.

> SUN-TZU (4th cent. B.C.). "Weaknesses and Strengths" (13), *The Art of War,* tr. Samuel B. Griffith, 1963

An army avoids strength and strikes weakness.

> SUN-TZU (4th cent. B.C.). "Weaknesses and Strengths" (27), *The Art of War,* tr. Samuel B. Griffith, 1963

March by an indirect route and divert the enemy by enticing him with a bait. . . . One able to do this understands the strategy of the direct and the indirect.

> SUN-TZU (4th cent. B.C.). "Maneuver" (3), *The Art of War,* tr. Samuel B. Griffith, 1963

In mobile warfare, the tactics are not the main thing. The decisive factor is the organization of one's resources—to maintain the momentum.

> RITTER von THOMA (1891–1948). In B. H. Liddell Hart, *The German Generals Talk,* 12, 1948

Part of the victory consists in throwing the enemy into disorder before you engage them.

> VEGETIUS (A.D. 4th cent.). *De Re Militari,* A.D. 378. In Thomas R. Phillips, ed., *Roots of Strategy,* p. 158, 1940

To distress the enemy more by famine than the sword is a mark of consummate skill.

> VEGETIUS (A.D. 4th cent.). *De Re Militari,* A.D. 378. In Thomas R. Phillips, ed., *Roots of Strategy,* p. 174, 1940

❦

At the end of the most grandiose plans and strategies is a soldier walking point.

> ANONYMOUS (AMERICAN). Caption of a poster at the War Plans Directorate in the Pentagon. In Harry G. Summers, Jr., "U.S.—Stung in Vietnam—Is Determined to Complete the Equation of War in Gulf," *Los Angeles Times,* 13 February 1991

Surround, splinter, and smash in detail!

> SAYING (SOVIET). Red Army
>
> See Machiavellianism: Saying (Latin)

Operate upon the enemy's communications as much as possible without exposing your own.

> SAYING. In Abraham Lincoln, letter to Gen. George B. McClellan, 13 October 1862

Threaten broadly, strike narrowly.

> SAYING

STRENGTH

See also • Power ∘ Strength & Weakness ∘ Weakness

Strength unequivocally designates something in the singular, an individual entity; it is the property inherent in an object or person and belongs to its character, which may prove itself in relation to other things or persons, but is essentially independent of them.

> HANNAH ARENDT (1906–1975). *On Violence,* 2, 1970
>
> See Power: Arendt

Everything nourishes what is strong already.

> JANE AUSTEN (1775–1817). *Pride and Prejudice,* 9, 1813

The strength of a man consists in finding out the way in which God is going, and going in that way too.

> HENRY WARD BEECHER (18113–1887). *Life Thoughts,* p. 54, rec. Edna Dean Proctor, 1858

He who has the most friends and the fewest enemies is the strongest.

> LORD CHESTERFIELD (1694–1773). Letter to his son, 11 November 1752

We acquire the strength we have overcome.

> RALPH WALDO EMERSON (1803–1882). "Considerations by the Way," *The Conduct of Life,* 1860

Concentration is the secret of strength in politics, in war, in trade, in short, in all management of human affairs.

> RALPH WALDO EMERSON (1803–1882). "Power," *The Conduct of Life,* 1860. This is Emerson's paraphrase of an observation from the *Times* (London) which he had copied into his journal in October 1849.

If you're strong enough, there *are* no precedents.

> F. SCOTT FITZGERALD (1896–1940). "The Note-Books" (O), *The Crack-Up,* ed. Edmund Wilson, 1945
>
> See Greatness: Richard M. Nixon

Strength does not come from physical capacity. It comes from an indomitable will.

> MOHANDAS K. GANDHI (1869–1948). In *Young India,* 11 August 1920

God, the Lord, is my strength.

> HABAKKUK (7th cent. B.C.). *Habakkuk* 3:19

The world breaks everyone, and afterwards many are strong at the broken places.

> ERNEST HEMINGWAY (1899–1961). *A Farewell to Arms,* 34, 1929
>
> See Disaster: Henry Wadsworth Longfellow

Brute strength bereft of reason falls of its own weight.

> HORACE (65–8 B.C.). *Odes,* 3.4

He knows not his own strength that hath not met adversity.

> BEN JONSON (1572–1637). "Explorata," *Timber: Or, Discoveries,* 1640, ed. Ralph S. Walker, 1953

You have overcome a meeting with death. That gives one strength.

> FRANZ KAFKA (1883–1924). In Gustav Janouch, *Conversations with Kafka,* p. 61, tr. Goronwy Rees, 1953

The strength of the Pack is the Wolf, and the strength of the Wolf is the Pack.

> RUDYARD KIPLING (1865–1936). "The Law of the Jungle," *The Second Jungle Book,* 1895

Draw your strength from who you are.

> RUSSELL MEANS (1939–). "Fighting Words on the Future of the Earth," *Mother Jones,* December 1980

When we are strong, we are always much greater than the things that happen to us.

> THOMAS MERTON (1915–1968). *No Man Is an Island,* 7.7, 1955

True strength lies in submission which permits one to dedicate his life, through devotion, to something beyond himself.

> HENRY MILLER (1891–1980). *The Time of the Assassins: A Study of Rimbaud,* 2, 1946

What does not kill me makes me stronger.

> FRIEDRICH NIETZSCHE (1844–1900). "Maxims and Arrows" (8), *Twilight of the Idols,* 1889, tr. R. J. Hollingdale, 1968
>
> See Disaster: Henry Wadsworth Longfellow

I'm as strong as a bull moose, and you can use me to the limit.

> THEODORE ROOSEVELT (1858–1919). Letter to Mark Hanna, 27 June 1900

Who is strong? He who subdues his impulses.

> TALMUD (A.D. 1st–6th cent.). Rabbinical writings. In Louis I. Newman, comp., *The Talmudic Anthology,* 127, 1945

My strength is as the strength of ten,
  Because my heart is pure.

> ALFRED, LORD TENNYSON (1809–1892). "Sir Galahad," l. 3, 1842

Man's greatest strength is shown in standing still.

> EDWARD YOUNG (1683–1765). *The Complaint: or, Night Thoughts on Life, Death, and Immortality,* 8.912, 1742–1745

❦

A chain is no stronger than its weakest link.

> SAYING (ENGLISH)
>
> See Weakness: George Herbert

Gentle in manner, strong in deed.

> SAYING (LATIN). Wooden-block sign on the desk of Pres. Dwight D. Eisenhower. In Sherman Adams, *Firsthand Report: The Story of the Eisenhower Administration,* 4, 1961

Three things give hardy strength: sleeping on hairy mattresses, breathing cold air, and eating dry food.

> SAYING (WELSH)

STRENGTH & WEAKNESS

See also • Adversity: Anonymous (2) ∘ Paradoxes: Jesus (2) ∘ Power: [especially] Eric Hoffer, Adlai E. Stevenson ∘ Rich & Poor ∘ Strategy, Military: Sun-tzu ∘ Strength ∘ Success & Failure ∘ Tyranny: Anonymous (4) ∘ Victory & Defeat ∘ Weakness ∘ Wealth & Poverty

The weak have one weapon: the errors of those who think they are strong.

> GEORGES BIDAULT (1899–1983). French resistance leader during World War II and prime minister. In *Observer* (British newspaper), 15 July 1962

The weak are the most treacherous of us all. They come to the strong and drain them. . . . They are everyone's concern and like vampires they suck our life's blood.

> BETTE DAVIS (1908–1989). *The Lonely Life: An Autobiography,* 20, 1962

Men are strong so long as they represent a strong idea; they become powerless when they oppose it.

> SIGMUND FREUD (1856–1939). *On the History of the Psychoanalytic Movement,* 3, 1914, tr. Joan Riviere and rev. James Strachey, 1962

The authoritarian character feels the more aroused the more helpless his object has become.

> ERICH FROMM (1900–1980). *Escape from Freedom,* 5.1, 1941

We are not weak if we make a proper use of those means which the God Nature has placed in our power. . . . The battle, sir, is not to the strong alone; it is to the vigilant, the active, the brave.

> PATRICK HENRY (1736–1799). Speech before the Virginia House of Burgesses, St. John's Episcopal Church, Richmond, 23 March 1775

The strong must flourish by force, and the weak subsist by stratagem.

> SAMUEL JOHNSON (1709–1784). "Talisker in Sky," *A Journey to the Western Islands,* 1775

When the weak act with restraint, it encourages further pressures and brings home to their opponents the strength of their position.

> HENRY A. KISSINGER (1923–). *White House Years,* 21, 1979

Weakness is wretchedness! To be strong
Is to be happy!

> HENRY WADSWORTH LONGFELLOW (1807–1882). "The Golden Legend" (2), 1851, *Christus: A Mystery,* 1872

The strong are good; only the weak are wicked.

> NAPOLEON (1769–1821). Manuscript, 1791, *The Mind of Napoleon: A Selection from His Written and Spoken Words,* 206, ed. J. Christopher Herold, 1955

The moral dilemma that is presented to the weak in a world governed by the strong: Break the rules or perish.

> GEORGE ORWELL (1903–1950). "Such, Such Were the Joys" (5), September-October 1952 (written in 1947). *The Collected Essays, Journalism and Letters of George Orwell,* vol. 4, ed. Sonia Orwell and Ian Angus, 1968

In a just cause the weak will beat the strong.

> SOPHOCLES (496?–406 B.C.). *Oedipus at Colonus,* l. 880, tr. Robert Fitzgerald, 1941

To the tune of the strong, the weak must dance.

> NAHMAN SYRKIN. "Natzionale Freiheit," 1917

The strong do what they can, and the weak suffer what they must.

> THUCYDIDES (460?–400? B.C.). *The Peloponnesian War,* 5.89, tr. Richard Crawley and rev. T. E. Wick, 1982

❦

Whether the knife falls on the melon, or the melon on the knife, the melon suffers.

> SAYING (HINDU)

STRUGGLE

See also • Adversity ○ Burdens ○ Civil War: Abraham Lincoln (2) ○ Competition ○ Defiance ○ Difficulty ○ Effort ○ Genius: Anonymous (3) ○ Grief ○ Martyrdom ○ Misfortune ○ Pain ○ Problems & Solutions ○ Progress ○ Prosperity & Adversity ○ Resistance ○ Responsibility ○ Salvation: Goethe ○ Self-Realization (Becoming) ○ Success ○ Trouble ○ Unhappiness ○ Work

The great function of conflict is that it arouses *consciousness.*

> JAMES MacGREGOR BURNS (1918–). Doris Kearns Goodwin interview, "True Leadership," *Psychology Today,* October 1978

If it was a worthwhile fight, it didn't matter who won; some good was sure to come of it.

> RICHARD BROOKS (1944–). *Deadline U.S.A.* (film), 1952, spoken by Ethyl Barrymore

It is in strife that life lies, and were there no opposing forces there would be neither moral nor immoral, neither victory nor defeat.

> SAMUEL BUTLER (1835–1902). *The Note-Books of Samuel Butler,* 2, ed. Henry Festing Jones, 1907

"Every wall is a door," Emerson correctly said. Let us not look for the door, and the way out, anywhere but in the wall against which we are living. Instead, let us seek respite where it is—in the very thick of the battle.

> ALBERT CAMUS (1913–1960). "Create Dangerously" (3), 1957, *Resistance, Rebellion, and Death,* tr. Justin O'Brien, 1961

Conflict is the gadfly of thought. It stirs us to observation and memory. It instigates to invention. It shocks us out of sheep-like passivity.

> JOHN DEWEY (1859–1952). *Human Nature and Conduct: An Introduction to Social Psychology,* 4.2, 1922

The struggle which is not joyous is the wrong struggle. The joy of the struggle is not hedonism and hilarity, but the sense of purpose, achievement and dignity.

> GERMAINE GREER (1939–). Introduction to *The Female Eunuch,* 1970

Out of opposition, a new birth.

> CARL G. JUNG (1875–1961). *Psychology of the Transference,* 9 (closing words), 1946, tr. R. F. C. Hull, 1954

Every talent must unfold itself in fighting.

> FRIEDRICH NIETZSCHE (1844–1900). In Max Lerner, "America Agonistes" (5), *Foreign Affairs,* January 1974. Lerner commented, "If one substituted 'meaningful struggle' for 'fighting,' then it would express a crucial continuing element in the American character."

We are not contending against flesh and blood, but against the principalities, against the powers, against the world rulers of this present darkness.

> PAUL (A.D. 1st cent.). *Ephesians* 6:12
> See Authority: Paul

I wish to preach, not the doctrine of ignoble ease, but the doctrine of the strenuous life, the life of toil and effort, of labor and strife; to preach that the highest form of success which comes, not to the man who desires mere easy peace, but to the man who does not shrink from danger, from hardship, or from bitter toil, and who out of these wins the splendid ultimate triumph.

A life of slothful ease, a life of that peace which springs merely from lack either of desire or of power to strive after great things, is as little worthy of a nation as of an individual.

> THEODORE ROOSEVELT (1858–1919). Title essay, 10 April 1899, *The Strenuous Life: Essays and Addresses,* 1905

We take no delight in existence except when we are struggling for something.

> ARTHUR SCHOPENHAUER (1788–1860). "Studies in Pessimism: The Vanity of Existence," *Essays of Arthur Schopenhauer,* tr. T. Bailey Saunders, 1851

Who has a fiercer struggle than he who strives to conquer himself?

> THOMAS à KEMPIS (1380–1471). *The Imitation of Christ,* 1.3, tr. Leo Sherley-Price, 1952

The vehement struggle so fierce for unity in one's-self.

> WALT WHITMAN (1819–1892). "Thoughts," 1, 1860, *Leaves of Grass,* 1855–1892

Nothing, I am sure, calls forth the faculties so much as the being obliged to struggle with the world.

> MARY WOLLSTONECRAFT (1759–1797). "Matrimony," *Thoughts on the Education of Daughters,* 1787

STUDY

See also • Books: Anonymous (*Bible*) ○ Knowledge ○ Learning (Process) ○ Scholars

To spend too much time in studies, is sloth; to use them too much for ornament, is affectation; to make judgment wholly by their rules is the humor of a scholar.

> FRANCIS BACON (1561–1626). "Of Studies," *Essays,* 1625

Studies . . . give forth directions too much at large, except they be bounded in by experience.

> FRANCIS BACON (1561–1626). "Of Studies," *Essays,* 1625

Crafty men condemn studies; simple men admire them; and wise men use them.

> FRANCIS BACON (1561–1626). "Of Studies," *Essays,* 1625
> See Religion, Anti-: Edward Gibbon

No matter how occupied a man may be, he must snatch at least one hour for study daily.

> THE BRATZLAVER (1770–1811). In Louis I. Newman, comp., *The Hasidic Anthology,* 174.24.A.26, 1934

The elevation of the mind ought to be the principal end of all our studies.

> EDMUND BURKE (1729–1797). *A Philosophical Inquiry into the Origin of Our Ideas of the Sublime and the Beautiful,* 1.19, 1756

Let the great book of the world be your principal study.

> LORD CHESTERFIELD (1694–1773). Letter to his son, 7 April 1751

Study the teachings of the Great Sages of all sects impartially.

> GAMPOPA (A.D. 12th cent.). Tibetan religious leader. In Whitall N. Perry, comp., *A Treasury of Traditional Wisdom,* p. 798, 1986

The love of study, a passion which derives fresh vigor from enjoyment, supplies each day, each hour, with a perpetual source of independent and rational pleasure.

> EDWARD GIBBON (1737–1794). *Memoirs of My Life and Writings,* p. 110, 1796, Alex. Murray edition, 1869

[Alexander] Pope, finding little advantage from external help, resolved thenceforward to direct himself, and at twelve formed a plan of study which he completed with little other incitement than the desire of excellence.

> SAMUEL JOHNSON (1709–1784). "Pope," *Lives of the English Poets,* 1781

Just as eating contrary to the inclination is injurious to the health, so study without desire spoils the memory, and it retains nothing that it takes in.

> LEONARDO da VINCI (1452–1519). *Note-books,* 1, tr. Edward McCurdy, 1908

Shun those studies in which the work that results dies with the worker.

> LEONARDO da VINCI (1452–1519). *Note-books,* 1, tr. Edward McCurdy, 1908

Study in joy and good cheer, in accordance with your intelligence and heart's dictates.

> RASHI (A.D. 1040–1105)

The great business of study is to form a *mind* adapted and adequate to all times and all occasions; to which all nature is then laid open, and which may be said to possess the key of her inexhaustible riches.

> SIR JOSHUA REYNOLDS (1723–1792). "Discourse Eleven," 10 December 1782, *Discourses on Art,* 1769–1790

Every great study is not only an end [in] itself, but also a means of creating and sustaining a lofty habit of mind.

> BERTRAND RUSSELL (1872–1970). "The Study of Mathematics," *Mysticism and Logic,* 1918

My own course [of study]—not intentionally pursued, but spontaneously pursued—may be characterized as little reading and much thinking, and thinking about facts learned at first hand.

> HERBERT SPENCER (1820–1903). Letter to Leslie Stephen, 2 July 1899. In David Duncan, *Life and Letters of Herbert Spencer,* 2.23, 1908

STUPIDITY

See also • Fools ○ Ignorance ○ Illusion ○ Intelligence ○ Sin: Oscar Wilde

Stupidity . . . is nature's favorite resource for preserving steadiness of conduct and consistency of opinion.

> WALTER BAGEHOT (1826–1877). Letter to *London Inquirer* (British newspaper), 1851

With Stupidity and sound Digestion man may front much.

> THOMAS CARLYLE (1795–1881). *Sartor Resartus: The Life and Opinions of Herr Teufelsdröckh,* 2.7, 1835

If you leap into a Well, Providence is not bound to fetch you out.

> THOMAS FULLER (1654–1734). Comp., *Gnomologia: Adages and Proverbs,* 2795, 1732

Anonymous: Are you stupid or something?
Forrest Gump: My mamma always said, "Stupid is as stupid does."

> WINSTON GROOM (ERIC ROTH, scriptwriter). *Forrest Gump* (film), 1994, spoken by Tom Hanks

Stupidity often saves a man from going mad.

> OLIVER WENDELL HOLMES, SR. (1809–1894). *The Autocrat of the Breakfast-Table,* 2, 1858

It is so pleasant to come across people more stupid than ourselves. We love them at once for being so.

> JEROME K. JEROME (1859–1927). "On Cats and Dogs," *The Idle Thoughts of an Idle Fellow; A Book for an Idle Holiday,* 1892

The probability of someone watching you is proportional to the stupidity of your action.

> A. KINDSVATER (Zurich). "MIST's Law (Man in the Street). In Scot Morris, "You Make the Laws," *Omni,* May 1979

Kid, life's hard. But it's a lot harder if you're stupid.

> ROBERT MITCHUM (1917–1997). In Tom Tico, letter to *San Francisco Chronicle,* 29 July 1997

If it's stupid but works, it ain't stupid.

> MURPHY'S LAWS FOR GRUNTS. One of 20 laws widely distributed among military personnel during the Gulf War (1990–1991). In Paul Dixon, "Getting a Handle on Life's Slippery Truths," *San Francisco Chronicle,* 24 December 1992
>
> See Soldiers: Murphy's Laws for Grunts

Nobody is so stupid as not to be good for something.

> NAPOLEON (1769–1821). Remark to Pierre Roederer, 1800s, *The Mind of Napoleon: A Selection from His Written and Spoken Words,* 8, ed. J. Christopher Herold, 1955

Whoever was stupid was beneath worry or thought; you did not have to figure them out. This eliminated hundreds of people. In this life you had time only for a certain amount of thinking, and there was no need to waste any of it on people who were not threatening.

> JOYCE CAROL OATES (1938–). *A Garden of Earthly Delights,* 3.7, 1967

The American people are a very generous people and will forgive almost any weakness, with the possible exception of stupidity.

> WILL ROGERS (1879–1935). "Another Hot Confession in the Oil Scandal," *The Illiterate Digest,* 1924

There is nothing as stupid as an educated man if you get him off the thing he was educated in.

> WILL ROGERS (1879–1935). Weekly column, 5 July 1931, *The Will Rogers Book,* 6.7, comp. Paula McSpadden Love, 1961

The worst thing about stupidity is its insistency.

> SAM'S DESPAIR. In John Peers, comp., *1,001 Logical Laws,* p. 137, 1979

Against stupidity the gods
Themselves contend in vain.

> FRIEDRICH von SCHILLER (1759–1805). *The Maid of Orleans,* 3.6, 1801, tr. Anna Swanwick, 1854

When a stupid man is doing something he is ashamed of, he always declares that it is his duty.

> GEORGE BERNARD SHAW (1856–1950). *Caesar and Cleopatra,* 3, 1899

Like many men of genius he could not understand why things obvious to him should not be so at once to other people, and found it easier to believe that they were corrupt than that they could be so stupid.

> GEORGE BERNARD SHAW (1856–1950). Preface to *The Apple Cart,* 1928

The stupid you have always with you.

> HENRY DAVID THOREAU (1817–1862). Journal, 13 February 1860
>
> See Poverty: Jesus (1)

Wooden-headedness consists of assessing a situation in terms of preconceived, fixed notions while ignoring or rejecting any contrary signs. It is acting according to wish while not allowing oneself to be confused by the facts.

> BARBARA W. TUCHMAN (1912–1989). "An Inquiry into the Persistence of Unwisdom in Government," *Esquire,* 1980

Whenever a man does a thoroughly stupid thing, it is always from the noblest motives.

> OSCAR WILDE (1854–1900). *The Picture of Dorian Gray,* 6, 1891

In public affairs, stupidity is more dangerous than knavery.

> WOODROW WILSON (1856–1924). *The New Freedom: A Call for the Emancipation of the Generous Energies of a People,* 3, 1913

STYLE

See also • Art ○ Fashion ○ Simplicity ○ Writers ○ Writing

Style to be good must be clear. . . . Clearness is secured by using the words that are current and ordinary.

> ARISTOTLE (384–322 B.C.). *Rhetoric,* 3.2, tr. W. Rhys Roberts, 1954

If the thought or substance is fully mastered, the style will take care of itself. Good style in writing is like happiness in living—something that comes to you, if it comes at all, only if you are preoccupied with something else: if you deliberately go after it, you will probably not get it.

> CARL L. BECKER (1873–1945). "The Art of Writing," *Detachment and the Writing of History: Essays and Letters of Carl L. Becker,* ed. Phil L. Snyder, 1958

The style is the man himself.

> GEORGES-LOUIS de BUFFON (1707–1788). Address on being admitted to the French Academy, 25 August 1753

A man's style in any art should be like his dress—it should attract as little attention as possible.

> SAMUEL BUTLER (1835–1902). *The Note-Books of Samuel Butler,* 7, ed. Henry Festing Jones, 1907
>
> See Words: Samuel Taylor Coleridge ○ Writing: Leon Trotsky

A good style. Nothing can be added to it, neither can anything be taken from it.

> RALPH WALDO EMERSON (1803–1882). Journal, 17 August 1837

To me style is just the outside of content, and content the inside of style, like the outside and inside of the human body—both go together, they can't be separated.

> JEAN-LUC GODARD (1930–). In Richard Roud, introduction to *Godard on Godard: Critical Writings,* ed. Jean Narboni and Tom Milne, 1972

The style of a writer is a faithful representative of his mind; therefore, if any man would write in a clear style, let him first be clear in his thoughts; and if any man would write in a noble style, let him first possess a noble soul.

> GOETHE (1749–1832). 14 April 1824. In Peter Eckermann, *Conversations with Goethe,* 1836–1848, tr. John Oxenford, 1850

The florid style is the reverse of the familiar. The last is employed as an unvarnished medium to convey ideas; the first is resorted to as a spangled veil to conceal the want of them.

> WILLIAM HAZLITT (1778–1830). "On Familiar Style," *Table Talk,* 1822

Style has to do with the way in which ideas are believed and advocated rather than with the truth or falsity of their content.

> RICHARD HOFSTADTER (1916–1970). Title essay (1), 1963, *The Paranoid Style in American Politics and Other Essays,* 1967

Style in writing or speaking is formed very early in life, while the imagination is warm, and impressions are permanent.

> THOMAS JEFFERSON (1743–1826). Letter to J. Bannister, Jr., 15 October 1785

Not very graceful, but I am growing old enough not to care much for the manner of doing things.

> ABRAHAM LINCOLN (1809–1873). Referring to a brief speech he had just given from a window in the White House to serenaders, remark to the author. In John Hay, diary, 23 August 1864, *Lincoln and the Civil War in the Diaries and Letters of John Hay,* ed. Tyler Dennett, 1939

Style is the cutting edge of content.

> NORMAN MAILER (1921–)

A good style should show no signs of effort. What is written should seem a happy accident.

> W. SOMERSET MAUGHAM (1874–1965). *The Summing Up,* 13, 1938

The essence of a sound style is that it cannot be reduced to rules—that it is a living and breathing thing, with something of the devilish in it—that it fits its proprietor tightly and ever so loosely, as his skin fits him.

> H. L. MENCKEN (1880–1956). "The Fringes of Lovely Letters: Literature and the Schoolma'm," *Prejudices: Fifth Series,* 1926

[Henry David] Thoreau's peculiar triumph as a stylist is to transform reality itself by way of his perception of it—to transmute it into *his* language.

> JOYCE CAROL OATES (1938–). "The Mysterious Mr. Thoreau," *New York Times Book Review,* 1 May 1988

By the time you have perfected any style of writing, you have always outgrown it.

> GEORGE ORWELL (1903–1950). "Why I Write," summer 1946, *The Collected Essays, Journalism and Letters of George Orwell,* vol. 1, ed. Sonia Orwell and Ian Angus, 1968

When we see a natural style, we are astonished and delighted; for we expected to see an author, and we find a man.

> BLAISE PASCAL (1623–1662). *Pensées,* 29, 1670, tr. William F. Trotter, 1931

Style. Thick, heavy syllables that deafen the reader and prevent the sentence from being heard.

> JULES RENARD (1864–1910). Journal, June 1908, tr. Louise Bogan and Elizabeth Roget, 1964

Style in writing is not just elegance in phrasing; it should marshal argument and prose to move or persuade.

> WILLIAM SAFIRE (1929–). "Stylish Books and Koobs," *New York Times Magazine,* 20 August 1995

Style is nothing but the mere silhouette of thought; and an obscure or bad style means a dull or confused brain.

> ARTHUR SCHOPENHAUER (1788–1860). "The Art of Literature: On Style," *Essays of Arthur Schopenhauer,* tr. T. Bailey Saunders, 1851

The first rule . . . for a good style is that the author should have something to say; nay, this is in itself almost all that is necessary.

> ARTHUR SCHOPENHAUER (1788–1860). "The Art of Literature: On Style," *Essays of Arthur Schopenhauer,* tr. T. Bailey Saunders, 1851

Style is the garb of thought.

> SENECA THE YOUNGER (5? B.C.–A.D. 65). "On the Superficial Blessings," *Moral Letters to Lucilius,* 95.2, tr. Richard M. Gummere, 1918 (Popular version: Style is the dress of thought.)
>
> See Language: Samuel Johnson

Octavius Caesar: I do not much dislike the matter, but
The manner of his speech.

> SHAKESPEARE (1564–1616). *Antony and Cleopatra,* 2.2.113, 1606

[Samuel] Butler had no style at all, which is the supreme sort of style.

> GEORGE BERNARD SHAW (1856–1950). Remark to the author, 1940s. In Stephen Winsten, *Days with Bernard Shaw,* 14, 1949

In composing, as a general rule, run your pen through every other word you have written; you have no idea what vigor it will give your style.

> SYDNEY SMITH (1771–1845). In Lady Holland (his daughter), *A Memoir of the Reverend Sydney Smith,* 1.11, 1855

Proper words in proper places make the true definition of a style.

> JONATHAN SWIFT (1667–1745). Letter to a young clergyman, 9 January 1720

A style in which the matter is all in all, and the manner nothing at all.

> HENRY DAVID THOREAU (1817–1862). Journal, 1 November 1851

All styles are good, except the tiresome kind.

> VOLTAIRE (1694–1778). Preface to *L'Enfant prodigue,* 1736

If you are attacked on your style, never answer; your work alone should reply.

> VOLTAIRE (1694–1778). "Authors," *Philosophical Dictionary,* 1764, tr. Wade Baskin, 1961

Style takes its final shape more from attitudes of mind than from principles of composition.

> E. B. WHITE (1899–1985). In William Strunk, Jr., *The Elements of Style,* 5, 1959

He most honors my style who learns under it to destroy the teacher.

> WALT WHITMAN (1819–1892). "Song of Myself" (47), 1855, *Leaves of Grass,* 1855–1892

The point is, not to prove your possession of a style, but to move the people along the line of their nobler impulses. The style will readily enough accommodate itself.

> WALT WHITMAN (1819–1892). Remark to the author, 20 July 1888. In Horace Traubel, *Walt Whitman's Camden Conversations,* ed. Walter Teller, 1973

SUCCESS

See also • Achievement ∘ Ambition ∘ Competition ∘ Cooperation ∘ Defeat ∘ Details ∘ Effort ∘ Executives ∘ Failure ∘ Fame ∘ Genius: Anonymous (1) ∘ Happiness: [especially] Anonymous ∘ Industry ∘ Machiavellianism ∘ Opportunity ∘ Power ∘ Preparedness ∘ Progress ∘ Prudence: Rules ∘ Purpose ∘ Resolution: Abraham Lincoln (1) ∘ Self-Interest ∘ Self-Realization (Being) ∘ Speed ∘ Status ∘ Struggle ∘ Success & Failure ∘ Timing: Anonymous ∘ Trifles ∘ Victory ∘ Wealth ∘ Work

'Tis not in mortals to command success,
But we'll do more, Sempronius; we'll deserve it.

> JOSEPH ADDISON (1672–1719). *Cato,* 1.2, 1713
>
> See Honor: Saying (Portuguese)

Eighty percent of success is showing up.

> WOODY ALLEN (1935–). In Thomas J. Peters and Robert H. Waterman, Jr., *In Search of Excellence: Lessons from America's Best-Run Companies,* 5 (epigraph), 1982

The penalty of success is to be bored by people who used to snub you.

> NANCY ASTOR (1879–1964). In *Daily Express* (British newspaper), 12 January 1956

If you are mediocre and you grovel, you shall succeed.

> BEAUMARCHAIS (1732–1799). *The Marriage of Figaro,* 3.3, 1784

Success, *n.* The one unpardonable sin against one's fellows.

> AMBROSE BIERCE (1842–1914). *The Devil's Dictionary,* p. 128, 1911, Dover edition, 1958

Success . . . is not often gained by direct effort as by careful, systematic, thorough preparation for duty.

> GEORGE S. BOUTWELL (1818–1905). Untitled essay. In Allen T. Rice, ed., *Reminiscences of Abraham Lincoln,* 1885

Did [Eleanor Roosevelt] succeed because of or in spite of the unhappiness and insecurity of her early life?

> JAMES MacGREGOR BURNS (1918–). *Leadership,* 3, 1978

It took me twenty years to become an overnight success.

> EDDIE CANTOR (1892–1964). Entertainer. Attributed

Ever since his boyhood in Johnson City, Lyndon Johnson had displayed a remarkable talent for making a favorable impression on older men who possessed power—and for making it with startling rapidly.

> ROBERT A. CARO (1935–). *The Path to Power: The Years of Lyndon Johnson,* 23, 1982

You have still a surer way than this of rising, and which is wholly in your own power. Make yourself necessary.

> LORD CHESTERFIELD (1694–1773). Letter to his son, 9 February 1748

There are only two ways . . . of succeeding. One is by doing very good work, the other is by cheating.

> G. K. CHESTERTON (1874–1936). "The Fallacy of Success," *All Things Considered,* 1908

Go back a little to leap further.

> JOHN CLARKE (1596–1658). Comp., *Proverbs: English and Latine,* p. 56, 1639

Success seems to be that which forms the distinction between confidence and conceit.

> C. C. COLTON (1780–1832). *Lacon: or, Many Things in Few Words; Addressed to Those Who Think,* 1.75, 1823

Success is counted sweetest
By those who ne'er succeed.

> EMILY DICKINSON (1830–1886). "Success is counted sweetest," 1859?

The secret of success is constancy of purpose.

> BENJAMIN DISRAELI (1804–1881). Banquet speech before the National Union of Conservative and Constitutional Associations, Crystal Palace, London, 24 June 1872

There is a vast difference between success at twenty-five and success at sixty. At sixty, nobody envies you. Instead, everybody rejoices generously, sincerely, in your good fortune.

> MARIE DRESSLER (1869–1934). *My Own Story,* 17, 1934

Presence of mind and courage in distress
Are more than armies to procure success.

> JOHN DRYDEN (1631–1700). *Aureng-Zebe,* 2, 1675

Nothing succeeds like success.

> ALEXANDRE DUMAS (1824–1895). *Ange Pitou,* 1.7, 1853
> See Excess: Oscar Wilde ○ Paradoxes: G. K. Chesterton

Sucksess.

> BOB DYLAN (1941–). One-word placard used as a song prop. In *Don't Look Back* (documentary film), 1967

If *A* is a success in life, then *A* equals *x* plus *y* plus *z*. Work is *x*; *y* is play; and *z* is keeping your mouth shut.

> ALBERT EINSTEIN (1879–1955). In *Observer* (British newspaper), 15 January 1950

It's them as take advantage that get advantage i' this world, *I* think: folks have to wait long enough afore it's brought to 'em.

> GEORGE ELIOT (1819–1880). *Adam Bede,* 32, 1859

Success is relative:
It is what we can make of the mess we have made of things.

> T. S. ELIOT (1888–1965). *The Family Reunion,* 2.3, 1939

Self-trust is the first secret of success.

> RALPH WALDO EMERSON (1803–1882). "Success," *Society and Solitude,* 1870
> See Self-Trust: Emerson (2)

Although it is difficult to arrange, one reasonably certain way to attain success is to have a strong-willed and intelligent mother who is disappointed in her husband and thus channels all her emotional energy and ambition into you, her son.

> JOSEPH EPSTEIN (1937–). *Ambition: The Secret Passion,* 2, 1980

If at first you don't succeed, try, try again. Then quit. No use being a damn fool about it.

> W. C. FIELDS (1880–1946). *Drat! being the encapsulated view of life by W. C. Fields in his own words,* p. 106, comp. Richard J. Anobile, 1975

Success . . . is a result, not a goal.

> GUSTAVE FLAUBERT (1821–1880). Letter to Maxime du Camp, 26 June 1852

By the time
    we make it.
    we've had it.

> MALCOLM S. FORBES (1919–1990). "Arrived," *The Sayings of Chairman Malcolm: The Capitalist Handbook,* 1978

The whole secret of a successful life is to find out what it is one's destiny to do, and then do it.

> HENRY FORD (1863–1947). "Success," *Forum,* October 1928

Success has ruined many a man.

> BENJAMIN FRANKLIN (1706–1790). *Poor Richard's Almanack,* December 1752
> See Paradoxes: G. K. Chesterton

Success is never blamed.

> THOMAS FULLER (1654–1734). Comp., *Gnomologia: Adages and Proverbs,* 4273, 1732
> See Victory: Baltasar Gracián

Success can only be measured in terms of distance traveled.

> MAVIS GALLANT (1922–). *Green Water, Green Sky,* 1, 1959

If you work hard and play by the rules in this great country, you can get ahead.

> RICHARD A. GEPHARDT (1941–). Missouri senator. Speech at the Communications Workers of America Conference, Washington, 3 April 1995

It is not always by plugging away at a difficulty and sticking at it that one overcomes it; but, rather, often by working on the one next to it. Certain people and certain things require they be approached on an angle.

> ANDRÉ GIDE (1869–1951). Journal, 26 October 1924, tr. Justin O'Brien, 1951

Success means only doing what you do well [and] letting someone else do the rest.

> GOLDSTEIN'S TRUISM. In John Peers, comp., *1,001 Logical Laws,* p. 15, 1979

Knowing what you want is the first step in getting it.

> LOUISE HART. Psychologist. *The Winning Family: Increasing Self-Esteem in Your Children and Yourself,* 9, 1987

In love, in war, in conversation, in business, confidence and resolution are the principal things.

> WILLIAM HAZLITT (1788–1830). "On the Qualifications Necessary to Success in Life," *Table Talk,* 1822

It happens that the outer goal, the disk of paper, is hit without the archer's taking aim, and that the hits are only outward confirmations of inner events.

> EUGEN HERRIGEL (1885–1955). *Zen in the Art of Archery,* p. 82, 1953, tr. R. F. C. Hull, 1964

Success, as in the Calvinist scheme, is taken as the outward sign of an inward state of grace.

> RICHARD HOFSTADTER (1916–1970). "Cuba, the Philippines, and Manifest Destiny" (5), 1952, *The Paranoid Style in American Politics and Other Essays,* 1967

Young man, the secret of my success is that at an early age I discovered I was not God.

> OLIVER WENDELL HOLMES, JR. (1841–1935). Replying to a reporter's question on his 90th birthday, 8 March 1931

I've always been in the right place at the right time. Of course, I steered myself there.

> BOB HOPE (1903–). In Merla Zellerbach "Revealing Secrets of Their Success," *San Francisco Chronicle,* 11 July 1979

One overmuch elated with success
A change of fortune plunges in distress.

> HORACE (65–8 B.C.). *Epistles,* 1.10, *The Complete Works of Horace,* ed. Casper J. Kraemer, Jr., 1936

There is no such thing as success in a bad business.

> ELBERT HUBBARD (1856–1915). *The Note Book of Elbert Hubbard,* p. 21, comp. Elbert Hubbard II, 1927

Success in life consists in convincing yourself that you are the whole cheese, and then getting the world to accept your view.

> ELBERT HUBBARD (1856–1915). *The Note Book of Elbert Hubbard,* p. 44, comp. Elbert Hubbard II, 1927

Do your work with your whole heart and you will succeed—there is so little competition!

> ELBERT HUBBARD (1856–1915). *The Note Book of Elbert Hubbard,* p. 84, comp. Elbert Hubbard II, 1927

Pray that success will not come any faster than you are able to endure it.

> ELBERT HUBBARD (1856–1915). *The Note Book of Elbert Hubbard,* p. 140, comp. Elbert Hubbard II, 1927

Live so as to get the approbation of your Other Self, and success is yours.

> ELBERT HUBBARD (1856–1915). In Alice Hubbard, comp., *An American Bible,* p. 177, 1946

Success is ten percent opportunity and ninety percent intelligent hustle.

> ELBERT HUBBARD (1856–1915). In Alice Hubbard, comp., *An American Bible,* p. 251, 1946
> See Genius: Thomas Alva Edison

He has achieved success who has lived well, laughed often and loved much.

> ELBERT HUBBARD (1856–1915). "Epigrams," *The Elbert Hubbard Notebook,* comp., Orlando R. Petrocelli, 1980

For most people, the fantasy is driving around in a big car, having all the chicks you want and being able to pay for it. It always has been, still is, and always will be. And anyone who says it isn't is talking bullshit.

> MICK JAGGER (1943–)

The moral flabbiness born of the exclusive worship of the bitch-goddess *success.* That—with the squalid cash interpretation put on the word success—is our national disease.

> WILLIAM JAMES (1842–1910). Letter to H. G. Wells, 11 September 1906

Think of all the really successful men and women you know. Do you know a single one who didn't learn very young the trick of calling attention to himself in the right quarters?

> STORM JAMESON (1891–1986). *A Cup of Tea for Mr. Thorgill,* 7, 1957

When the press talks about my successes as Senate majority leader, they always emphasize my capacity to persuade, to wheel and deal. Hardly anyone ever mentions that I usually had more and better information than my colleagues.

> LYNDON B. JOHNSON (1908–1973). In John W. Gardner, *On Leadership,* 6, 1990

The way to rise is to obey and please.

> BEN JONSON (1572–1637). *Sejanus His Fall,* 3.3, 1603

Success hath made me wanton. I could skip
Out of my skin now, like a subtle snake,
I am so limber.

> BEN JONSON (1572–1637). *Volpone or The Foxe,* 3.1, 1607

Perhaps we need, for worldly success, virtues which make us loved and vices which make us feared.

> JOSEPH JOUBERT (1754–1824). *Pensées,* 1838, tr. H. P. Collins, 1928

Find a need and fill it.

> HENRY J. KAISER (1882–1967). Industrialist. His motto

The measure of a man's success in life is not the money he's made. It's the kind of family he has raised. In that I've been mighty lucky.

> JOSEPH P. KENNEDY (1888–1969). In Joseph Epstein, *Ambition: The Secret Passion,* 5, 1980

Life is a succession of moments
To live each one is to succeed.

> CORITA KENT (1918–). In Mary Bruno, "Portrait of an Artist," *Newsweek,* 17 December 1984

Creativity is constantly in danger of being destroyed by success. The more effectively the environment is mastered, the greater is the temptation to rest on one's oars.

> HENRY A. KISSINGER (1923–). *The Necessity for Choice: Prospects of American Foreign Policy,* 8.3, 1961

The more people you yourself can put and keep on hold, the more successful you will seem.

MICHAEL KORDA (1933–). Using the telephone as a metaphor. In Joseph Epstein, *Ambition: The Secret Passion,* 7, 1980

There are but two ways of rising in the world: either by your own industry or by the folly of others.

LA BRUYÈRE (1645–1696). "Of the Gifts of Fortune" (52), *The Characters,* 1688, tr. Henri van Laun, 1929

If you wish to be out front,
Then act as if you were behind.

LAO-TZU (6th cent. B.C.). *The Way of Life,* 66, tr. R. B. Blakney, 1955

In order to succeed in the world people do their utmost to appear successful.

LA ROCHEFOUCAULD (1613–1680). *Maxims,* 56, 1665, tr. Leonard Tancock, 1959

See Power: Horne Tooke

Sweet Smell of Success.

ERNEST LEHMAN (1920–). Book and film title, 1957

Success is as much a matter of luck as of ability, but perhaps even more, of persistence in "sticking it" until the luck turns.

B. H. LIDDELL HART (1895–1970). *The Liddell Hart Memoirs, 1895–1938,* 3, 1965

The way for a young man to rise is to improve himself every way he can, never suspecting that anybody wishes to hinder him.

ABRAHAM LINCOLN (1809–1865). Letter to William H. Herndon, 10 July 1848

Success is that old ABC—ability, breaks, and courage.

CHARLES LUCKMAN (1909–?). In *New York Mirror,* 19 September 1955

The successful organization man can hear orders that are never uttered. In order to move up in the managerial ranks one must be "smart enough" to "catch on" without being told everything.

FERDINAND LUNDBERG (1902–1995). *The Rich and the Super-Rich: A Study in the Power of Money Today,* 8, 1968

Men [seldom] rise from low condition to high rank without employing either force or fraud, unless that rank should be attained either by gift or inheritance.

MACHIAVELLI (1469–1527). *The Discourses,* 2.13, 1517, tr. Christian E. Detmold, 1940

See Strategy: Polybius ○ Tyrants: Aristotle (1) ○ War: Thomas Hobbes (1)

Whoever desires constant success must change his conduct with the times.

MACHIAVELLI (1469–1527). *The Discourses,* 3.9, 1517, tr. Christian E. Detmold, 1940

The successful people are the ones who can think up things for the rest of the world to keep busy at.

DON MARQUIS (1878–1937)

How to Succeed in Business Without Really Trying.

SHEPHERD MEAD (1914–). Book title, 1952

Willy Loman: The man who makes an appearance, the man who creates personal interest, is the man who gets ahead. Be liked and you will never want.

ARTHUR MILLER (1915–). *Death of a Salesman,* 1, 1949

There is only one success . . .—to be able to spend your life in your own way, and not to give others absurd maddening claims upon it.

CHRISTOPHER MORLEY (1890–1957). *Where the Blue Begins,* 8, 1922

Success in war, like charity in religion, covers a multitude of sins.

WILLIAM NAPIER (1785–1860)

See Blunders: George Bernard Shaw

To promise and not to keep your promise is the way to get on in the world.

NAPOLEON (1769–1821). 1815–1818, *Talks of Napoleon at St. Helena* (with Gen. Gaspard Gourgaud), 16, tr. Elizabeth Wormeley Latimer, 1904

If at first you don't succeed, try, try again.

T. H. PALMER. *Teacher's Manual,* p. 223, 1840

The problem with success is that its formula is the same as the one for ulcers.

LAURENCE J. PETER (1919–1990). 28 August, *Peter's Almanac,* 1982

In looking at the world *as it is,* we shall find it folly to deny that, to worldly success, a surer path is Villainy than Virtue.

EDGAR ALLAN POE (1809–1849). June 1849, *Marginalia,* University Press of Virginia edition, 1981

Don't try to go too fast. Learn your job. Don't ever talk until you know what you're talking about. . . . If you want to get along, go along.

SAM RAYBURN (1882–1961). Texas speaker of the House of Representatives. In Neil MacNeil, *Forge of Democracy: the House of Representatives,* 6, 1963

W. Dennis Thomas: Would you explain the secret of your success as head of Merrill Lynch?
Regan: That's not a big conversation. It's one word—anticipation.

DONALD T. REGAN (1918–). Format adapted. In Gerald M. Boyd, "'General Contractor' of the White House Staff," *New York Times,* 4 March 1986

The danger of success is that it makes us forget the world's dreadful injustice.

JULES RENARD (1864–1910). Journal, January 1908, tr. Louise Bogan and Elizabeth Roget, 1964

In the choice of your profession or your business employment, let your first thought be: Where can I fit in so that I may be most effective in the work of the world? Where can I lend a hand in a way most effective to advance the general interests? Enter life in such a spirit, choose your vocation in that way, and you have taken the first step on the highest road to a large success.

JOHN D. ROCKEFELLER (1839–1937). In Upton Sinclair, ed., *The Cry for Justice: An Anthology of the Literature of Social Protest,* 14, 1915

To accomplish almost anything worthwhile, it is necessary to compromise between the ideal and the practical.

FRANKLIN D. ROOSEVELT (1882–1945). In Drew Pearson and Robert S. Allen, "How the President Works," *Harper's,* June 1936

There can be no falser standard [of success] than that set by the deification of material well-being in and for itself.

> THEODORE ROOSEVELT (1858–1919). Speech, Sorbonne (Paris), 23 April 1910

The great secret of success is to go through life as a man who never gets used up. That is possible for him who never argues and strives with men and facts, but in all experience retires upon himself, and looks for the ultimate cause of things in himself.

> ALBERT SCHWEITZER (1875–1965). *Memoirs of Childhood and Youth*, 5, 1925, tr. C.T. Campion, 1949

Success is what people settle for when they can't think of something noble enough to be worth failing at.

> LAURENCE SHAMES (1951–). 12 April 1986

The first requisite to success in life is to be a good animal. The best brain is found of little service, if there be not enough vital energy to work it.

> HERBERT SPENCER (1820–1903). *Education: Intellectual, Moral, and Physical*, 2, 1860

The main factor in practical success is not the rational analysis of facts and situations, but the instantaneous perception of the possibilities and applicable measures inherent in the situation.

> OSWALD SPENGLER (1880–1936). *Aphorisms*, 241, tr. Gisela Koch-Weser O'Brien, 1967

All great successes are the result of cool consideration, long silence and waiting, strict self-control, and above all renunciation of intoxication and exhibitionism.

> OSWALD SPENGLER (1880–1936). *Aphorisms*, 243, tr. Gisela Koch-Weser O'Brien, 1967

Success to me is having ten honeydew melons and eating only the top half of each one.

> BARBRA STREISAND (1942–). In "Success Is a Baked Potato," *Life*, 20 September 1963

[Abraham] Lincoln's whole life was a calculation of the law of forces and ultimate results. The world to him was a question of cause and effect. He believed the results to which certain causes tended would surely follow. He did not believe that these results could be materially hastened or impeded. . . . He believed from the first, I think, that the agitation of slavery would produce its overthrow, and he acted upon the result as though it was present from the beginning. His tactics were to get himself in the right place and remain there still until events would find him in that place.

> LEONARD SWETT (1825–1889). Letter to William H. Herndon, 17 July 1866. In Emanuel Hertz, ed., *The Hidden Lincoln: From the Letters and Papers of William H. Herndon*, 2.1, 1940

The arts of rising . . . have commonly some mixture of baseness—more or less according as the aid from natural endowments is less or more.

> HENRY TAYLOR (1800–1886). *The Statesman*, 14, 1836

You wish to rise: make enemies.

> TALLEYRAND (1754–1838). Advice to Louis-Adolphe Thiers

What is success? I think it is a mixture of having a flair for the thing that you are doing; knowing that it is not enough, that you have got to have hard work and a certain sense of purpose.

> MARGARET THATCHER (1925–). In *Parade*, 13 July 1986

I have not succeeded if I have an antagonist who fails. It must be humanity's success.

> HENRY DAVID THOREAU (1817–1862). Journal, 22 March 1842

If the day and the night are such that you greet them with joy, and life emits a fragrance like flowers and sweet-scented herbs, is more elastic, more starry, more immortal—that is your success.

> HENRY DAVID THOREAU (1817–1862). "Higher Laws," *Walden; or Life in the Woods*, 1854

We must walk consciously only part way toward our goal, and then leap in the dark to our success.

> HENRY DAVID THOREAU (1817–1862). Journal, 11 March 1859

All you need in this life is ignorance and confidence, then success is sure.

> MARK TWAIN (1835–1910). Letter to Mary Hallock Foote, 2 December 1887. In Benjamin DeCasseres, *When Huck Finn Went Highbrow*, p. 7, 1934

Don't be irreplaceable. If you can't be replaced, you can't be promoted.

> UPWARD-MOBILITY RULE. In Paul Dickson, comp., *The Official Explanations*, p. 227, 1980

I have learned that success is to be measured not so much by the position that one has reached in life as by the obstacles which he has overcome while trying to succeed.

> BOOKER T. WASHINGTON (1856–1915). *Up from Slavery*, 2, 1901

The best career advice to give the young is "Find out what you like doing best and get someone to pay you for doing it."

> KATHERINE WHITEHORN (1928–). In *Observer* (British newspaper), 1975

The measure of success is not how much money you have in the bank, but rather how much money the bank will lend you.

> JACK W. WHITEMAN. "Whiteman's Finding: Measure of Success." In Paul Dickson, comp., *The Official Explanations*, p. 233, 1980

Have the past struggles succeeded?
What has succeeded? yourself? your nation? Nature?
Now understand me well—it is provided in the essence of things
   that from any fruition of success, no matter what, shall come
   forth something to make a greater struggle necessary.

> WALT WHITMAN (1819–1892). "Song of the Open Road" (14), 1856, *Leaves of Grass*, 1855–1892

Success means we go to sleep at night knowing that our talents and abilities were used in a way that served others.

> MARIANNE WILLIAMSON (1953–). "Work," *A Return to Love: Reflections on the Principles of a Course in Miracles*, 1992

Success is just a matter of luck. Ask any failure!

> EARL WILSON (1907–1987). In "Quotable Quotes," *Reader's Digest*, September 1966

Success in life depends on two things: luck and pluck, luck in finding someone to pluck.

> ED WYNN (1885–1965). 1952

Success for the most part attends those who act boldly, not those who weigh everything, and are [slow] to venture.

> XERXES (519?–465 B.C.). Persian king. In Herodotus (484?–420? B.C.), *The Persian Wars*, 7.50, tr. George Rawlinson, 1942

Don't believe all the baloney people tell you when they're describing what they're going to do for you someday soon. Nem di gelt. [Get the money.]

> HENNY YOUNGMAN (1906–1998). When asked the secret of his lasting success in show business. In Mervyn Rothstein, "Henny Youngman, King of One-Liners, Is Dead at 91 after 6 Decades in Comedy," *New York Times*, 25 February 1998

Success is going straight—around the circle.

> ANONYMOUS (CHINESE). Quoted by Richard Tanner Pascale, "Zen and the Art of Management." In *Classic Advice on Handling the Manager's Job* (*Harvard Business Review on Human Relations*, vol. 3), 1986

Some people reach the top of the ladder only to find it is leaning against the wrong wall.

> ANONYMOUS

All goes well for those who keep their eye on the ball, their ear to the ground, and their shoulder to the wheel.

> ANONYMOUS

Effort measures success better than outcome.

> ANONYMOUS

What gains success is push and pull; the more there is of one, the less need there is of the other.

> ANONYMOUS

Come early, stay late.

> SAYING (AMERICAN)

The dictionary is the only place where success comes before work.

> ANONYMOUS (AMERICAN)

SUCCESS & FAILURE

See also • Failure ○ Rich & Poor ○ Strength & Weakness ○ Success ○ Victory & Defeat ○ Wealth & Poverty

Success contains within it the germs of failure, and the reverse is also true.

> CHARLES de GAULLE (1890–1970). Remark to the writer. In C. L. Sulzberger, "Foreign Affairs: The Last Giant," *New York Times*, 30 April 1969

Success makes us intolerant of failure, and failure makes us intolerant of success.

> WILLIAM FEATHER (1889–1981)

I have always been more afraid of failing than hopeful of success.

> SAMUEL JOHNSON (1709–1784). On courting the "favor of the great," 22 September 1777. In James Boswell, *The Life of Samuel Johnson*, 1791

A reputation for success tends to be self-fulfilling. Equally, failure feeds on itself.

> HENRY A. KISSINGER (1923–). *Years of Upheaval*, 18, 1982

Banality in the mouth of a failed businessman or an unpublished novelist sounds banal; in the mouth of David Rockefeller or Philip Roth the same words acquire the weight of oracle.

> LEWIS H. LAPHAM (1935–). *Money and Class in America: Notes and Observations on the Civil Religion*, 2, 1988

The chief factor in any man's success or failure must be his own character.

> THEODORE ROOSEVELT (1858–1919). "National Duties," 2 September 1901, *The Strenuous Life: Essays and Addresses*, 1905

When we watch a child trying to walk, we see its countless failures; its successes are but few. If we had to limit our observation within a narrow space of time, the sight would be cruel.

> RABINDRANATH TAGORE (1861–1941)

Success invites envy; failure, contempt.

> ANONYMOUS

Success, *n*. More achievement than expectation.
Failure, *n*. More expectation than achievement.

> ANONYMOUS

The cost of success is exceeded only by the cost of failure.

> ANONYMOUS

SUCKERS

See also • Fools ○ Stock Market: Max Holland ○ Stock Market: Anonymous (American) (1)

Never give a sucker an even break.

> EDWARD FRANCIS ALBEE (1857–1930)

There's a sucker born every minute.

> JOSEPH "PAPER COLLAR JOE" BESSIMER. Con man. 1880s. Quoted by A. H. Saxon, *P. T. Barnum: The Legend and the Man*, 1889. In Linda Altshuler, letter to *New York Times*, 15 July 1996

It is morally wrong to allow suckers to keep their money.

> "CANADA BILL" JONES

There is no crime in the cynical American calendar more humiliating than to be a sucker.

> MAX LERNER (1902–1992). *Actions and Passions: Notes on the Multiple Revolution of Our Time*, 1949

Show me a guy who has feelings, and I'll show you a sucker.

> RICHARD SALE. *Suddenly* (film), 1954, spoken by Frank Sinatra (in the role of Johnny Baron, a paid assassin)

A sucker is a fool that bites at any bait.

> BURTON STEVENSON

❧

A sucker is born every minute, and two to take him.

> SAYING (AMERICAN)

SUFFERING

See also • Joy ○ Pain ○ Wounds

To suffer through one's own fault is a torment worthy of the lost.

> HENRI AMIEL (1821–1881). Journal, 8 November 1852, tr. Mrs. Humphrey Ward, 1887

[Job] does not ask, "Why does God *permit* me to suffer these things?" but "Why does God *make* me suffer these things?"

> MARTIN BUBER (1878–1965). The Prophetic Faith, 8.B, 1949

Deep, unspeakable suffering may well be called a baptism, a regeneration, the initiation into a new state.

> GEORGE ELIOT (1819–1880). Adam Bede, 42, 1859

It is only the strong who are strengthened by suffering; the weak are made weaker.

> LION FEUCHTWANGER (1884–1958). In Paris Gazette, 1940

If Afflictions refine some, they consume others.

> THOMAS FULLER (1654–1734). Comp., Gnomologia: Adages and Proverbs, 2666, 1732

Suffering cleanses only when it is free of resentment.

> ERIC HOFFER (1902–1983). The Passionate State of Mind: And Other Aphorisms, 263, 1954

Complete success alienates a man from his fellows, but suffering makes kinsmen of us all.

> ELBERT HUBBARD (1856–1915). In Alice Hubbard, comp., An American Bible, p. 157, 1946

When the limit of suffering is overpassed, the most imperturbable virtue is disconcerted.

> VICTOR HUGO (1802–1885). "Saint Denis" (15.1), Les Misérables, tr. Charles E. Wilbour, 1862

See Pain: George Orwell

Oh, if there is a man out of hell that suffers more than I do, I pity him!

> ABRAHAM LINCOLN (1809–1865). Remark to a visitor following the Army of the Potomac's defeat at Fredericksburg in 1862. In Emanuel Hertz, ed., "Father Abraham," Lincoln Talks: A Biography in Anecdote, 1939

It is not true that suffering ennobles the character; happiness does that sometimes, but suffering, for the most part, makes men petty and vindictive.

> W. SOMERSET MAUGHAM (1874–1965). The Moon and Sixpence, 17, 1919

Captain Ahab: This lovely light, it lights not me; all loveliness is anguish to me, since I can ne'er enjoy. Gifted with the high perception, I lack the low, enjoying power; damned, most subtly and most malignantly! damned in the midst of Paradise!

> HERMAN MELVILLE (1819–1891). Moby-Dick; or, The Whale, 37, 1851, ed. Harold Beaver, 1972

It is not so much the suffering as the senselessness of it that is unendurable.

> FRIEDRICH NIETZSCHE (1844–1900). As paraphrased by Nicolas Berdyaev, The Destiny of Man, 2.2.5, 1931, tr. Natalie Duddington, 1955

The sufferings of this present time are not worth comparing with the glory that is to be revealed to us. . . . The creation itself will be set free from its bondage to decay and will obtain the glorious liberty of the children of God. We know that the whole creation has been groaning in travail together until now.

> PAUL (A.D. 1st cent.). Romans 8:18–22

Perhaps the worst thing about suffering is that it finally hardens the hearts of those around it.

> GLORIA STEINEM (1934–). "Ruth's Song," Outrageous Acts and Everyday Rebellions, 1983

It is not why I suffer, that I wish to know, but only whether I suffer for your sake.

> LEVI YITZHAK (?–1809). In Martin Buber, "Levi Yitzhak of Berditchev," Tales of the Hasidim: The Early Masters, tr. Olga Marx, 1947

SUICIDE

See also • Death ○ Depression ○ Despair ○ Desperation ○ Faith ○ Hope ○ Killing ○ Misery: Abraham Lincoln ○ Murder ○ Unhappiness ○ Violence

To kill oneself as a means of escape from poverty or disappointed love or bodily or mental anguish is the deed of a coward rather than a brave man.

> ARISTOTLE (384–322 B.C.). Nichomachean Ethics, 3.7, tr. J. A. K. Thomson, 1953

A poor fellow went to hang himself, but finding by chance a hidden pot containing money, flung away the rope, and went merrily home, but he that had hidden the money, when he found it had been removed by someone, hanged himself with the rope the other man had left behind.

> AUSONIUS (A.D. 310?–395?). Latin poet. In J. R. Whitwell, Analecta Psychiatrica, D.24, 1976

What a humiliation for me when someone standing next to me heard a flute in the distance and *I heard nothing*, or someone heard a *shepherd singing* and again I heard nothing. Such incidents drove me almost to despair; a little more of that and I would have ended my life—it was only *my art* that held me back.

> LUDWIG van BEETHOVEN (1770–1827). In Anthony Storr, Solitude: A Return to the Self, 4, 1988

For those who took the initiative in killing themselves, the SS issued (in Dachau in 1933) a special order: prisoners who attempted suicide but did not succeed were to receive twenty-five lashes and prolonged solitary confinement. Supposedly this was to punish them for their failure to do away with themselves; but I am convinced it was much more to punish them for the act of self-determination.

> BRUNO BETTELHEIM (1903–1990). In W. H. Auden, "Camps, Concentration," A Certain World: A Commonplace Book, 1971

I am leaving at last a world where the heart must either break or turn to bronze.

> CHAMFORT (1741–1794). Suicide note

When I was young, for two or three years the light faded out of the picture. I did my work. I sat in the House of Commons, but black depression settled on me. It helped me to talk to Clemmie about it. I don't like standing near the edge of a platform when an express train is passing through. I like to stand right back and if possible to get a pillar between me and the train. I don't like to stand by the side of a ship and look down into the water. A second's action would end everything. A few drops of desperation.

> WINSTON CHURCHILL (1874–1965). Remark to the diarist (his personal doctor), 14 August 1944. In Lord Moran, *Churchill: Taken from the Diaries of Lord Moran*, 19, 1966
>
> See Depression: Churchill

There are many who dare not kill themselves for fear of what the neighbors will say.

> CYRIL CONNOLLY (1903–1974). "Te Palinure Petens," *The Unquiet Grave: A Word Cycle by Palinurus*, 1945

Nine men in ten are suicides.

> BENJAMIN FRANKLIN (1706–1790). In *Poor Richard's Almanack*, October 1749

No neurotic harbors thoughts of suicide which are not murderous impulses against others redirected upon himself.

> SIGMUND FREUD (1856–1939). In Cyril Connolly, "Te Palinure Petens," *The Unquiet Grave: A Word Cycle by Palinurus*, 1945

One reason I was in a great deal of trouble was that I had been extremely accommodating in my willingness to believe what the other fellow asked me to believe.

> R. BUCKMINSTER FULLER (1895–1983). On his being near suicide as a young man. In Walter Truett Anderson, "Bucky Fuller: Technological Guru," *New Realities*, June 1979. Eventually, Fuller made a conscious decision to take responsibility for his life: "number one . . . I was going to have to do some of my own thinking."

The real reason for not committing suicide is because you always know how swell life gets again after the hell is over.

> ERNEST HEMINGWAY (1899–1961). Letter, 1926. In Frederick Busch, "Reading Hemingway Without Guilt," *New York Times Book Review*, 12 January 1992

What does a man care about? Staying healthy. Working good. Eating and drinking with his friends. Enjoying himself in bed. I haven't any of them.

> ERNEST HEMINGWAY (1899–1961). Remarks to the author a few weeks before committing suicide, June 1961. In A. E. Hotchner, *Papa Hemingway: A Personal Memoir*, 14, 1966
>
> See Shock Treatment: Hemingway

This morning, for the first time in a long time, the joy again of imagining a knife twisted in my heart.

> FRANZ KAFKA (1883–1924). 2 November 1911, *The Diaries of Franz Kafka, 1910–1913*, tr. Joseph Kresh, 1948

Suicide is what the death certificate says when one dies of depression.

> PETER D. KRAMER. Psychiatrist. "What Ivanov Needs in the 90's Is an Anti-Depressant," *New York Times*, 21 December 1997

He blew his mind out in a car
He didn't notice that the lights had changed.

> JOHN LENNON (1940–1980) and PAUL McCARTNEY (1942–). "A Day in the Life" (song), 1967

I have for these last ten days been so troubled by the many disappointments I have had that I think if it were possible to vex me so for a fortnight longer it would make an end of me. In short, I am weary of my life.

> DUKE OF MARLBOROUGH (1650–1722). In Anthony Storr, *Churchill's Black Dog, Kafka's Mice, and Other Phenomena of the Human Mind*, 1, 1988

Is it hard for the reader to believe that suicides are sometimes committed to forestall the committing of murder? There is no doubt of it. Nor is there any doubt that murder is sometimes committed to avert suicide.

> KARL MENNINGER (1893–1990). *The Crime of Punishment*, 7, 1968

Life is a slavery if the freedom to die is wanting.

> MONTAIGNE (1533–1592). "A Custom of the Island of Cea," *Essays*, 1588, tr. Donald M. Frame, 1958

Lucius Arruntius killed himself, he said, to escape both the future and the past.

> MONTAIGNE (1533–1592). "A Custom of the Island of Cea," *Essays*, 1588, tr. Donald M. Frame, 1958

One commits suicide to escape disgrace, not to escape misfortune.

> NAPOLEON (1769–1821). *In the Words of Napoleon*, p. 93, tr. Daniel Savage Gray, 1977

The relatives of a suicide resent him for not having stayed alive out of consideration for their reputation.

> FRIEDRICH NIETZSCHE (1844–1900). *Human, All Too Human*, 322, 1878, tr. Marion Faber, 1984

Razors pain you;
Rivers are damp;
Acids stain you;
And drugs cause cramp.
Guns aren't lawful;
Nooses give;
Gas smells awful;
You might as well live.

> DOROTHY PARKER (1893–1967). "Résumé," *Enough Rope*, 1926

[Suicide] is a privilege of man, which the diety does not possess.

> PLINY THE ELDER (A.D. 23–79). In J. R. Whitwell, *Analecta Psychiatrica*, D.30, 1976

The news has just come that Silius Italicus has starved himself to death in his house near Naples. Ill health was the reason.

> PLINY THE YOUNGER (A.D. 62?–113?). *Letters*, 3.7, tr. Betty Radice, 1963

Suicide is madness.

> BENJAMIN RUSH (1745–1813). 5 November 1810, "Notes for Lectures," *The Autobiography of Benjamin Rush: His "Travels Through Life" together with his "Commonplace Book for 1789–1813,"* ed. George W. Corner, 1948

Dear World,
   I am leaving you because I am bored. I am leaving you with your worries. Good luck.

> GEORGE SANDERS (1906–1972). English-born American actor. Suicide note, 25 April 1972
>
> See Boredom: C. C. Colton

Hamlet: O, that this too too sullied flesh would melt,
Thaw and resolve itself into a dew!
O that the Everlasting had not fix'd
His canon 'gainst self-slaughter!

> SHAKESPEARE (1564–1616). *Hamlet,* 1.2.129, 1600

We must allow men to do themselves great injuries in order to avoid a greater evil—slavery.

> VAUVENARGUES (1715–1747). *Reflections and Maxims,* 162, 1746, tr. F. G. Stevens, 1940

The man who, in a fit of melancholy, kills himself today may have wished to live had he waited a week.

> VOLTAIRE (1694–1778). "Cato," *Philosophical Dictionary,* 1764

SUN

See also • Nature

The sun—my almighty physician.

> THOMAS JEFFERSON (1743–1826). Letter to James Monroe, 1785

He makes his sun rise on the evil and on the good.

> JESUS (A.D. 1st cent.). *Matthew* 5:45

The Sun does not move.

> LEONARDO da VINCI (1452–1519)

A large red drop of sun lingered on the horizon and then dripped over and was gone.

> JOHN STEINBECK (1902–1968). *The Grapes of Wrath,* 6, 1939

The sun is but a morning star.

> HENRY DAVID THOREAU (1817–1862). Closing words, *Walden; or Life in the Woods,* 1854

Give me the splendid silent sun with all his beams full-dazzling.

> WALT WHITMAN (1819–1892). "Give Me the Splendid Silent Sun" (1), 1865, *Leaves of Grass,* 1855–1892

❧

The sun also ariseth, and the sun goeth down, and hasteth to his place where he arose.

> ANONYMOUS (*BIBLE*). *Ecclesiastes* 1:5 (King James Version). Ernest Hemingway titled his 1926 novel *The Sun Also Rises.*

SUPERSTITION

See also • Belief ○ Philosophy ○ Reformers: Thomas Jefferson ○ Religion ○ Science ○ Wisdom: Henry David Thoreau (2) ○ Witchcraft

Sickness and sorrows come and go, but a superstitious soul hath no rest.

> ROBERT BURTON (1577–1640). *The Anatomy of Melancholy,* 3.4.1.3, 1621–1651

Nothing is useless. A superstition is a hamper or a basket to carry useful lessons in.

> RALPH WALDO EMERSON (1803–1882). Journal 25 November 1836

Men run out of one superstition into an opposite superstition.

> RALPH WALDO EMERSON (1803–1882). "The Scholar," *Lectures and Biographical Sketches,* 1883

The superstition in which we grew up,
Though we may recognize it, does not lose
Its power over us—Not all are free
Who make mock of their chains.

> GOTTHOLD EPHRAIM LESSING (1729–1781). *Nathan the Wise,* 1779, tr. Bayard Quincy Morgan, 1955

There is superstition in science quite as much as there is superstition in theology, and it is all the more dangerous because those suffering from it are profoundly convinced that they are freeing themselves from all superstition.

> THEODORE ROOSEVELT (1858–1919). In Hermann Hagedorn and Sidney Wallach, "Signposts for Americans: Random Thoughts," *A Theodore Roosevelt Round-Up,* 1958

Superstition . . . is engendered, preserved, and fostered by fear.

> BARUCH SPINOZA (1632–1677). Preface to *Tractatus Theologico-Politicus,* 1670, tr. R. H. M. Elwes, 1895

Let me make the superstitions of a nation, and I care not who makes its laws or its songs either.

> MARK TWAIN (1835–1910). *Following the Equator: A Journey Around the World,* 51 (epigraph), 1897
>
> See Economists: Paul A. Samuelson ○ Music: Andrew Fletcher of Saltoun

The most superstitious times have always been those of the most horrible crimes.

> VOLTAIRE (1694–1778). "Superstition" (1), *Philosophical Dictionary,* 1764, tr. Theodore Besterman, 1971

The superstitious man is to the rascal what the slave is to the tyrant.

> VOLTAIRE (1694–1778). "Superstition" (2), *Philosophical Dictionary,* 1764, tr. Theodore Besterman, 1971

Superstition . . . is the *Counterfeit* of Religion.

> BENJAMIN WHICHCOTE (1609–1683). *Moral and Religious Aphorisms,* 929, 1753

SURGEONS

See also • Doctors ○ Healing ○ Physicians ○ Professionals ○ Psychosurgery

There is a substantial and enlarging body of medical information and opinion to the effect that these deformities [small breasts] are really a disease.

AMERICAN SOCIETY OF PLASTIC SURGEONS. A lobbying group for 4,500 doctors. Memo to Food and Drug Administration (FDA) during a "practice enhancement" campaign on behalf of breast implant operations in the early 1980s. In Nicholas Regush, "Toxic Breasts," *Mother Jones,* January-February 1992

I got the bill for my surgery. Now I know what those doctors were wearing masks for.

JAMES H. BOREN (1925–)

Surgeons must be very careful
When they take the knife!
Underneath their fine incisions
Stirs the Culprit—*Life!*

EMILY DICKINSON (1830–1886). "Surgeons must be very careful," 1859?

Surgery is the cry of defeat in medicine.

MARTIN H. FISCHER (1879–?)

The best Surgeon is he that has been well hack'd himself.

THOMAS FULLER (1654–1734). Comp., *Gnomologia: Adages and Proverbs,* 4419, 1732

Americans spend $17 billion a year on bypass operations.

BETTY FUSSELL. "A Mystery on Every Plate," *New York Times,* 23 December 1993

Retired California policeman Steven Radford has spent $20,000 on seven cosmetic surgery procedures to make him look like Tom Arnold.

NEW REPUBLIC. "Notebook," 18 September 1995

The surgeon is quiet, he does not speak.
He has seen too much of death, his hands are full of it.

SYLVIA PLATH (1932–1963). "The Courage of Shutting-Up," *Winter Trees,* 1971

Cultural influence is such in this city [Houston] that for a woman to feel attractive usually includes a Mercedes, a gold Rolex, and three or four operations—nose, breasts, liposuctions.

FRANKLIN ROSE. Plastic surgeon. In Nicholas Regush, "Toxic Breasts," *Mother Jones,* January-February 1992

There is a fashion in operations, as there is in sleeves and skirts.

GEORGE BERNARD SHAW (1856–1950). Preface ("The Craze for Operations") to *The Doctor's Dilemma,* 1906

A good surgeon must have an eagle's eye, a lion's heart, and a lady's hand.

SAYING (ENGLISH)

Diet cures more than the lancet.

SAYING (SPANISH)

Big surgeon, big incision.

SAYING

SUSPICION

See also • Danger ○ Deception: George Herbert (1) ○ Distrust ○ Fear ○ Paranoia ○ Prudence: Rules

Whosoever is found variable and changeth manifestly without manifest cause giveth suspicion of corruption.

FRANCIS BACON (1561–1626). "Of Great Place," *Essays,* 1625

Every boddy in this world wants watching, but none more than ourselves.

JOSH BILLINGS (1818–1885). "Fust Impreshuns," *Everybody's Friend, or; Josh Billing's Encyclopedia and Proverbial Philosophy of Wit and Humor,* 1874

A weak man wants az mutch watching as a bad one.

JOSH BILLINGS (1818–1885). "Koarse Shot," *Everybody's Friend, or; Josh Billing's Encyclopedia and Proverbial Philosophy of Wit and Humor,* 1874

Always sensitive to any change in the east, Hitler's suspicions of the Russians mounted in proportion to the treachery of his own intentions.

ALAN BULLOCK (1914–). On Hitler's thinking in June 1940 while the Battle of France was being fought, *Hitler: A Study in Tyranny,* rev. ed., 10.6, 1960 (1953)

I wished my wife to be not so much as suspected.

JULIUS CAESAR (100–44 B.C.). Justifying his divorce from Pompeia, who had become innocently involved in a scandal. In Plutarch (A.D. 46?–119?), "Caesar," *Parallel Lives,* Dryden edition, 1693

I begin to smell a rat.

CERVANTES (1547–1616). *Don Quixote,* 1.4.10, 1615, tr. Peter Anthony Motteux and John Ozell, 1743

It was a maxim with Foxey—our revered father, gentlemen—"Always suspect everybody."

CHARLES DICKENS (1812–1870). *The Old Curiosity Shop,* 66, 1841

Suspicion may be no Fault, but showing it may be a great one.

THOMAS FULLER (1654–1734). Comp., *Gnomologia: Adages and Proverbs,* 4295, 1732

A wise man will keep his suspicions muzzled, but he will keep them awake.

MARQUIS OF HALIFAX (1633–1695). "Of Caution and Suspicion," *Political, Moral and Miscellaneous Reflections,* 1750

He that is never suspected is either very much esteemed or very much despised.

MARQUIS OF HALIFAX (1633–1695). "Of Caution and Suspicion," *Political, Moral and Miscellaneous Reflections,* 1750

A man prone to suspect evil is most looking in his neighbor for what he sees in himself.

J. C. HARE (1795–1855) and A. W. HARE (1792–1834). *Guesses at Truth: First Series,* p. 206, 1827, Macmillan edition, 1867

Suspicion often creates what it suspects.

C. S. LEWIS (1898–1963). "Screwtape Proposes a Toast," *The World's Last Night and Other Essays,* 1959

There are two kinds of fools: those who suspect nothing and those who suspect everything.

CHARLES-JOSEPH de LIGNE (1735–1814). *Mes Ecarts*

The noble mind suspecteth no guile without cause.

> JOHN LYLY (1554?–1606). "Euphues," *Euphues: The Anatomy of Wit,*
> 1579

Suspicion is the companion of mean souls, and the bane of all good society.

> THOMAS PAINE (1737–1809). "Of the Present Ability of America,"
> *Common Sense,* 1776

Suspicion begets suspicion.

> PUBLIUS SYRUS (85–43 B.C.). *Moral Sayings,* 928, tr. Darius Lyman, Jr.,
> 1862

Gloucester: Suspicion always haunts the guilty mind;
The thief doth fear each bush an officer.

> SHAKESPEARE (1564–1616). *Henry VI,* Part III, 5.6.11, 1590

🌿

Where there's smoke there's fire.

> SAYING

SWITZERLAND

See also • Nations

They say that if the Swiss had designed these mountains [the Alps], they'd be rather flatter.

> PAUL THEROUX (1941–). *The Great Railway Bazaar: By Train Through
> Asia,* 2, 1975

[The Swiss] had brotherly love, they had five hundred years of democracy and peace, and what did that produce? The cuckoo clock.

> ORSON WELLES (1915–1985). Written during the shooting of *The Third
> Man* (film), 1949. Spoken by Welles (in the role of Harry Lime). After
> the film came out, Welles was informed that Switzerland never made
> cuckoo clocks; the "credit" belonged to Bavaria.

SYMPATHY

See also • Compassion ○ Indifference ○ Kindness ○ Pity

The pleasure and pain of others is his own pleasure and pain.

> BHAGAVAD GITA (6th cent. B.C.). 6.32, tr. Juan Mascaró, 1962
> See Good: Percy Bysshe Shelley

The more we feel sorry for ourselves, the less sorry others will feel for us. People don't waste their small store of sympathy on those who can provide it so richly for themselves.

> GERALD BRENAN (1894–1987). "Life," *Thoughts in a Dry Season:
> A Miscellany,* 1978

Our sympathy is cold to the relation of distant misery.

> EDWARD GIBBON (1737–1794). *The Decline and Fall of the Roman
> Empire,* 49, 1776-1788

Sympathy . . . is not an end in itself. . . . Not mere feeling, but action, will mitigate the world's misery, society's injustice or the people's alienation from God.

> ABRAHAM JOSHUA HESCHEL (1902–1972). *The Prophets,* 18, 1962

There is much noise made about [sympathy for the distress of others], but it is greatly exaggerated. No, Sir, we have a certain degree of feeling to prompt us to do good: more than that, Providence does not intend. It would be misery to no purpose.

> SAMUEL JOHNSON (1709–1784). 19 October 1769. In James Boswell,
> *The Life of Samuel Johnson,* 1791

None can usurp this height . . .
But those to whom the miseries of the world
Are misery, and will not let them rest.

> JOHN KEATS (1795–1821). "The Fall of Hyperion: A Dream," 1.147, 1856

True sympathy is the personal concern which demands the giving of one's soul.

> MARTIN LUTHER KING, JR. (1929–1968). *Strength to Love,* 3.3, 1963

The more you are drawn to put yourself in the place of the other person, the more you feel the pain inflicted upon him, the insult offered him, the injustice of which he is a victim, the more will you be urged to act so that you may prevent the pain, insult, or injustice.

> PETER KROPOTKIN (1842–1921). *Anarchist Morality* (pamphlet, 5), 1909,
> *Kropotkin's Revolutionary Pamphlets,* ed. Roger N. Baldwin, 1927

Health and wealth prevent men from experiencing misfortunes, and thus make them callous to their suffering fellow-creatures; whilst they who already are burdened by their own miseries feel most tenderly those of others.

> LA BRUYÈRE (1645–1696). "Of Mankind" (79), *The Characters,* 1688,
> tr. Henri van Laun, 1929

To understand another person [is] *to imitate his feelings in ourselves.*

> FRIEDRICH NIETZSCHE (1844–1900). *Daybreak,* 142, 1881,
> tr. R. J. Hollingdale, 1982

Sympathy is two hearts tugging at *one* load.

> CHARLES H. PARKHURST (1842–1933). "The Good Samaritan," sermon

Rejoice with those who rejoice, weep with those who weep.

> PAUL (A.D. 1st cent.). *Romans* 12:15

Anyone can sympathize with another's sorrow, but to sympathize with another's joy is the attribute of an angel.

> ARTHUR SCHOPENHAUER (1788–1860). In William James, letter to Mrs.
> Francis J. Child, 27 March 1885

It is by changing places in fancy with the sufferer that we come either to conceive or to be affected by what he feels.

> ADAM SMITH (1723–1790). *The Theory of Moral Sentiments,* 1.1.1, 1759

A stranger to human nature, who saw the indifference of men about the misery of their inferiors, and the regret and indignation which they feel for the misfortunes and sufferings of those above them, would be apt to imagine that pain must be more agonizing, and the convulsions of death more terrible, to persons of higher rank than to those of meaner stations.

> ADAM SMITH (1723–1790). *The Theory of Moral Sentiments,* 1.3.2. 1759

They had souls large enough to feel the wrongs of others.

> ELIZABETH CADY STANTON (1815–1902). "Seneca Falls Convention."
> In E. C. Stanton et al., *A History of Woman Suffrage,* 1881

The more you join with people in their joys and their sorrows, the more nearer and dearer they come to be to you.

> MARK TWAIN (1835–1910). *Tom Sawyer Abroad,* 11, 1894

A generous heart suffers for the misfortunes of others as much as though it had caused them.

> VAUVENARGUES (1715–1747). *Reflections and Maxims,* 173, 1746, tr. F. G. Stevens, 1940

I do not ask the wounded person how he feels,
I myself become the wounded person.

> WALT WHITMAN (1819–1892). In Fredric Wertham, *A Sign for Cain: An Exploration of Human Violence,* 10, 1966

SYSTEMS

See also • Creed ○ Doctrine ○ Dogma ○ Ideas ○ Ideology ○ Orthodoxy ○ Principles, Moral ○ Principles, Theoretical ○ Theories ○ Writing: Georg Christoph Lichtenberg

The test of every religious, political, or educational system is the man which it forms.

> HENRI AMIEL (1821–1881). Journal, 17 June 1852, tr. Mrs. Humphrey Ward, 1887

The more ridiculous a belief system, the higher the probability of its success.

> WAYNE R. BARTZ. "Keys to Success," *Human Behavior,* May 1975

Thought once awakened does not again slumber; unfolds itself into a System of Thought; grows, in man after man, generation after generation—till its full stature is reached, and *such* System of Thought can grow no farther, but must give place to another.

> THOMAS CARLYLE (1795–1881). "The Hero as Divinity," *On Heroes, Hero-Worship, and the Heroic in History,* 1841

My "system" is not for promulgation first of all; it is for serving myself to live by. That is the great purpose of it to me.

> THOMAS CARLYLE (1795–1881). "The Hero as King," *On Heroes, Hero-Worship, and the Heroic in History,* 1841

Somebody has to sit in the British Museum again like Marx and figure out a new system; a new blueprint. Another century has gone, technology has changed everything completely, so it's time for a new utopian system.

> ALLEN GINSBERG (1926–1997). Thomas Clarke interview, 1965. In George Plimpton, ed., *Writers at Work: Third Series,* 1967

Any fool [can] devise a more consistent system than exists, but even a despot rarely can institute one.

> A. L. KROEBER (1876–1960). *The Nature of Culture,* 14, 1952

The envious nature of men, so prompt to blame and so slow to praise, makes the discovery and introduction of any new principles and systems as dangerous almost as the exploration of unknown seas and continents.

> MACHIAVELLI (1469–1527). Introduction to the First Book, *The Discourses,* 1517, tr. Christian E. Detmold, 1940

The jealousy with which new systems of theory are watched and the readiness with which they are banned . . . indicate the force which is really attributed to them by authority.

> CHARLES E. MERRIAM (1876–1953). *Political Power,* 9, 1934

It is equally deadly for a mind to have a system or to have none. Therefore it will have to decide to combine both.

> FRIEDRICH von SCHLEGEL (1772–1829). "Selected Aphorisms from *The Athenaeum*" (53), *Dialogue on Poetry and Literary Aphorisms,* 1797–1800, tr. Ernst Behler and Roman Struc, 1968

Idiosyncratic belief systems which are shared by only a few adherents are likely to be regarded as delusional. Belief systems which may be just as irrational but which are shared by millions are called world religions.

> ANTHONY STORR (1920–). *Feet of Clay: Saints, Sinners, and Madmen: A Study of Gurus,* 10, 1996

❦

TACT

See also • Charm ○ Diplomacy ○ Manners ○ Negotiation ○ Persuasion ○ Talking ○ Words

Sir Roger heard them both . . . and after having paused some time told them, with the air of a man who would not give his judgment rashly, that much might be said on both sides.

> JOSEPH ADDISON (1672–1719). In *The Spectator* (English essay series), 122, 20 July 1711

It is tact that is golden, not silence.

> SAMUEL BUTLER (1835–1902). *The Note-Books of Samuel Butler,* 14, ed. Henry Festing Jones, 1907

See Silence & Speech: Saying (English)

Tact teaches you when to be silent.

> BENJAMIN DISRAELI (1804–1881). *Endymion,* 61, 1880

To be agreeable while disagreeing—that's an art.

> MALCOLM S. FORBES (1919–1990). "Arrived," *The Sayings of Chairman Malcolm: The Capitalist's Handbook,* 1978

Some men's No is thought more of than the Yes of others. . . . Your refusal need not be pointblank: let the disappointment come by degrees.

> BALTASAR GRACIÁN (1601–1658). *The Art of Worldly Wisdom,* 70, 1647, tr. Joseph Jacobs, 1943

Tact is . . . a kind of mind-reading.

> SARAH ORNE JEWETT (1849–1909). *The Country of the Pointed Firs,* 10, 1896

Tact [is the] ability to tell a man he's open-minded when he has a hole in his head.

> F. G. KERNAN

The sharpness of a refusal or the edge of a rebuke may be blunted by an appropriate story so as to save wounded feelings and yet serve the purpose.

> ABRAHAM LINCOLN (1809–1865). On a lawyer colleague. In Anthony Gross, ed., *Lincoln's Own Stories*, 6, 1912

Tact is the art of putting your foot down without stepping on anyone's toes.

> LAURENCE J. PETER (1919–1990). 26 July, *Peter's Almanac*, 1982

Base and absurd requests he should reject, not harshly but gently, informing the askers by way of consolation that the requests are not in accord with their own excellence and reputation.

> PLUTARCH (A.D. 46?–119?). "Precepts of Statecraft" (13), *Moralia*, vol. 10, tr. W. C. Helmbold, 1936

Tact is the ability to describe others as they see themselves.

> MARY PETTIBONE POOLE. "Made in Manhattan," *A Glass Eye at a Keyhole*, 1938

[Tact] is a number of qualities working together: insight into [human nature], sympathy, self control, a knack of inducing self-control in others, avoidance of human blundering, readiness to give the immediate situation an understanding mind and a second thought. Tact is not only kindness, but kindness skillfully extended.

> J. G. RANDALL. *Mr. Lincoln*, ed. Richard N. Current, 7.2, 1957

Don't say "Hang this up for me" to one from a family where there was a hanging.

> TALMUD (A.D. 1st–6th cent.). Rabbinical writings

Talk to every woman as if you loved her, and to every man as if he bored you, and at the end of your first season you will have the reputation of possessing the most perfect social tact.

> OSCAR WILDE (1854–1900). *A Woman of No Importance*, 3, 1894

Tact is the art of making a point without making an enemy.

> SAYING (MISSISSIPPI)

TALENT

See also • Ability ○ Genius & Talent ○ Skill

If divorced from rectitude, [talent] will prove more of a demon than a god.

> WILLIAM ELLERY CHANNING (1780–1842). "Self-Culture," address, Boston, September 1838

Talent for talent's sake is a bauble and a show. Talent working with joy in the cause of universal truth lifts the possessor to new power as a benefactor.

> RALPH WALDO EMERSON (1803–1882). "Progress of Culture," *Letters and Social Aims*, 1876

A true talent delights the possessor first.

> RALPH WALDO EMERSON (1803–1882). "The Scholar," *Lectures and Biographical Sketches*, 1883

Hide not your Talents, they for Use were made.
What's a Sun-Dial in the Shade!

> BENJAMIN FRANKLIN (1706–1790). *Poor Richard's Almanack*, October 1750

There is no substitute for talent. Industry and all the virtues are of no avail.

> ALDOUS HUXLEY (1894–1963). *Point Counter Point*, 13, 1928

Everyone has talent. What is rare is the courage to follow the talent to the dark place where it leads.

> ERICA JONG (1942–). "The Artist as Housewife." In Francine Kragbrun, ed., *The First Ms. Reader*, 1972

TALKING

See also • Action & Talk ○ Conversation ○ Eloquence ○ Freedom of Speech ○ Ideas: Voltaire ○ Oratory ○ Public Speaking ○ Silence & Speech ○ Speaking ○ Tact ○ Wisdom: Anonymous (2) ○ The Wise & the Foolish: Plato ○ Words ○ Writing

The less said the better.

> JANE AUSTEN (1775–1817). *Sense and Sensibility*, 2.5, 1811

I don't kare how mutch a man talks, if he will only say it in a few wurds.

> JOSH BILLINGS (1818–1885). *On Ice: and Other Things*, 66, 1868

It requires more good judgment to kno when tew talk, than what tew say.

> JOSH BILLINGS (1818–1885). "Kindling Wood," *Everybody's Friend, or; Josh Billing's Encyclopedia and Proverbial Philosophy of Wit and Humor*, 1874

He said
Little, but to the purpose.

> LORD BYRON (1788–1824). *Don Juan*, 9:83, 1819–1824

Take care of the sense, and the sounds will take care of themselves.

> LEWIS CARROLL (1832–1898). *Alice's Adventures in Wonderland*, 9, 1865
> See Thrift: Saying (English) (2)

Mind not only what people say, but how they say it; and if you have any sagacity, you may discover more truth by your eyes than by your ears. People can say what they will, but they cannot look just as they will; and their looks frequently [reveal] what their words are calculated to conceal.

> LORD CHESTERFIELD (1694–1773). Letter to his son, 10 March 1746
> See Words: Henry David Thoreau

He does not say a word more than necessary.

> CHARLES de GAULLE (1890–1970). "Of Prestige" (2), *The Edge of the Sword*, 1934, tr. Gerald Hopkins, 1960

Far more numerous was the herd of such,
Who think too little, and who talk too much.

> JOHN DRYDEN (1631–1700). *Absalom and Achitophel*, 1.533, 1681

The unsaid part is the best of every discourse.

> RALPH WALDO EMERSON (1803–1882). Journal, 20 June 1835

Do not *say* things. What you *are* stands over you the while and thunders so that I cannot hear what you say to the contrary.

> RALPH WALDO EMERSON (1803–1882). Journal, 9 August 1840

When the eyes say one thing, and the tongue another, a practiced man relies on the language of the first.

> RALPH WALDO EMERSON (1803–1882). "Behavior," *The Conduct of Life,* 1860
>
> See Words: Henry David Thoreau

A man cannot utter two or three sentences without disclosing to intelligent ears precisely where he stands in life and thought.

> RALPH WALDO EMERSON (1803–1882). "Worship," *The Conduct of Life,* 1860

An ear which hears not what men say, but hears what they do not say.

> RALPH WALDO EMERSON (1803–1882). "Worship," *The Conduct of Life,* 1860

A soft Tongue may strike hard.

> BENJAMIN FRANKLIN (1706–1790). *Poor Richard's Almanack,* October 1744

Half the world is composed of people who have something to say and can't, and the other half who have nothing to say and keep on saying it.

> ROBERT FROST (1875–1963)

Every Ass loves to hear himself bray.

> THOMAS FULLER (1654–1734). Comp., *Gnomologia: Adages and Proverbs,* 1404, 1732

Every man hears only what he understands.

> GOETHE (1749–1832). *The Maxims and Reflections of Goethe,* 383, tr. T. Bailey Saunders, 1892

Small talk drives out meaningful talk.

> DOUG "LEO" HANBURY. "Leo's Law," in Paul Dickson, comp., *The Official Explanations,* p. 124, 1980
>
> See Money: Sir Thomas Gresham

A person who talks with equal vivacity on every subject, excites no interest in any.

> WILLIAM HAZLITT (1778–1830). *Characteristics in the Manner of Rochefoucault's Maxims,* 179, 1823

The tongue is not steel, yet it cuts.

> GEORGE HERBERT (1593–1633). Comp., *Outlandish Proverbs,* 838, 1640
>
> See Words: Saying (Bible) (1)

A sharp tongue is the only edged tool that grows keener with constant use.

> WASHINGTON IRVING (1783–1859). "Rip Van Winkle," *The Sketch Book,* 1820

We seldom regret talking too little, but very often talking too much. This is a well-known maxim which everybody knows and nobody practices.

> LA BRUYÈRE (1645–1696). "Of Mankind" (149), *The Characters,* 1688, tr. Henri van Laun, 1929

As the stamp of great minds is to suggest much in few words, so, contrariwise, little minds have the gift of talking a great deal and saying nothing.

> LA ROCHEFOUCAULD (1613–1680). *Maxims,* 142, 1665, tr. Leonard Tancock, 1959
>
> See Oratory: Benjamin Franklin, Plutarch (1)

In times like the present, men should utter nothing for which they would not willingly be responsible through time and in eternity.

> ABRAHAM LINCOLN (1809–1865). *Second Annual Message to Congress,* 1 December 1862

Most people have a furious itch to talk about themselves and are restrained only by the disinclination of others to listen. Reserve is an artificial quality that is developed in most of us but as the result of innumerable rebuffs.

> W. SOMERSET MAUGHAM (1874–1965). *The Summing Up,* 19, 1938

Talking much about oneself can also be a means to conceal oneself.

> FRIEDRICH NIETZSCHE (1844–1900). *Beyond Good and Evil,* 169, 1886, tr. Walter Kaufmann, 1966

Take your choice: talk about others and be a gossip or talk about yourself and be a bore.

> LAURENCE J. PETER (1919–1990). 27 July, *Peter's Almanac,* 1982

They talk most who have the least to say.

> MATTHEW PRIOR (1664–1721). *Alma,* 2, 1718

Listen to me . . . as you would if I were talking to myself. I am admitting you to my inmost thoughts, and am having it out with myself, merely making use of you as my pretext.

> SENECA THE YOUNGER (5? B.C.–A.D. 65). "On the Good Which Abides," *Moral Letters to Lucilius,* 27.1, tr. Richard M. Gummere, 1918

Boy: The saying is true, "The empty vessel makes the greatest sound."

> SHAKESPEARE (1564–1616). *Henry V,* 4.4.72, 1598

Polonius: Give every man thy ear, but few thy voice. Take each man's censure, but reserve thy judgment.

> SHAKESPEARE (1564–1616). *Hamlet,* 1.3.68, 1600

That's as well said as if I had said it myself.

> JONATHAN SWIFT (1667–1745). *A Complete Collection of Genteel and Ingenious Conversation,* 2, 1738

Lesson to the Indiscreet. They who say all they think, and tell all they know, put others on their guard and prevent themselves from being told anything of consequence.

> HORACE WALPOLE (1717–1797). 1781, *A Note Book of Horace Walpole,* 1927

The chief effect of talk on any subject is to strengthen one's own opinion.

> CHARLES DUDLEY WARNER (1829–1900). "Sixth Study," 3, *Backlog Studies,* 1873

I love talking about nothing, father. It is the only thing I know anything about.

> OSCAR WILDE (1854–1900). *An Ideal Husband,* 1, 1895

❧

Excessive talk suggests ulterior motives or dishonesty.

> ANONYMOUS

Those who talk to themselves are seldom interrupted.

> ANONYMOUS

Talk doesn't cook rice.

> SAYING (CHINESE and JAPANESE)
> See Words: Thomas Fuller (3)

Talk is cheap.

> SAYING (ENGLISH)

The noisiest streams are the shallowest.

> SAYING (ENGLISH)
> See Silence & Speech: Quintus Curtius Rufus

Great talker, great liar.

> SAYING (FRENCH)

Utter not a word by which anyone could be wounded.

> SAYING (HINDU). In C. S. Lewis, appendix (1) to *The Abolition of Man,*
> 1947

Talk less, say more.

> SAYING

Think more than you talk, and talk less than you listen.

> SAYING

Well understood is well said.

> SAYING

TAXES

See also • Economics ○ Government ○ Inflation: Milton Friedman and Rose Friedman (3) ○ Wealth

The power to tax is the power to rule.

> BROOKS ATKINSON (1894–1984). 1 March, *Once Around the Sun,* 1951

There is just one thing I can promise you about the outer space program: Your tax dollar will go farther.

> WERNHER von BRAUN (1912–1977). German-born American engineer.
> In Jeffery L. Yablon, comp., *Tax Notes,* 14 November 1994

To tax and to please, no more than to love and be wise, is not given to men.

> EDMUND BURKE (1729–1797). "American Taxation," House of
> Commons speech, 19 April 1774

My opponent won't rule out raising taxes, but I will. The Congress will push me to raise taxes, and I'll say no, and they'll push, and I'll say no, and they'll push again, and I'll say to them, "Read my lips: No new taxes."

> GEORGE BUSH (1924–). Presidential nomination acceptance speech,
> New Orleans, 18 August 1988. On 26 June 1990, Pres. Bush called for
> tax increases, and the *New York Post* front-paged the story with his
> photograph and the headline, "Read My Lips . . . I Lied."

The Income Tax: The Root of All Evil.

> FRANK CHODOROV. Book title, 1954

The collection of any taxes which are not absolutely required, which do not . . . contribute to the public welfare, is only a species of legalized larceny.

> CALVIN COOLIDGE (1872–1933). *Inaugural Address,* 4 March 1925

[Suggested simplified tax form:] How much money did you make last year? Mail it in.

> STANTON DELAPLANE (1907–1988). Journalist. In Jeffery L. Yablon,
> comp., "As Certain as Death—Quotations about Taxes," *Tax Notes,* 14
> November 1994

The more heavily a man is supposed to be taxed, the more power he has to escape being taxed.

> DIOGENES'S FIRST DICTUM. In Paul Dickson, comp., *The Official
> Rules,* p. 63, 1978

To tax the community for the advantage of a class is not protection: it is plunder.

> BENJAMIN DISRAELI (1804–1881). House of Commons speech,
> 14 March 1850

Myth number one: [Pres. Ronald] Reagan presided over vast giveaways to the rich.

In fact, during the 1980s, the affluent paid more in federal taxes than ever before. Even though the top marginal tax rate declined from 70% to 28%, the proportion of taxes collected from the top 1% of income-earners went from 18% of all revenues in 1981 to 28% in 1988. The top 5% of earners bore 35% of the tax burden in 1981. In 1988, Reagan's last year in office, they paid 46%. Meanwhile the tax share of middle- and lower-income Americans declined.

> DINESH D'SOUZA (1961–). "How Reagan Reelected Clinton, *Forbes,*
> 3 November 1997

Of all debts, men are least willing to pay the taxes. What a satire is this on government!

> RALPH WALDO EMERSON (1803–1882). "Politics," *Essays: Second Series,*
> 1844

We are taxed twice as much by our *Idleness,* three times as much by our *Pride,* and four times as much by our *Folly,* and from these Taxes the Commissioners cannot ease or deliver us by allowing an Abatement.

> BENJAMIN FRANKLIN (1706–1790). "The Way to Wealth," 7 July 1757

[A] society which turns so many of its best and brightest into tax lawyers may be doing something wrong.

> HOFFMAN F. FULLER. In Jeffery L. Yablon, comp., "As Certain as
> Death—Quotations about Taxes," *Tax Notes,* 14 November 1994

The only effective design for diminishing the income inequality inherent in capitalism is the progressive income tax.

> JOHN KENNETH GALBRAITH (1908–). *The Culture of Contentment,*
> 15, 1992

To abolish all taxation save that upon land values.

> HENRY GEORGE (1839–1897). On his single-tax theory, *Progress and Poverty: An Inquiry into the Cause of Industrial Depressions and of Increase of Want with Increase of Wealth*, 8.2, 1879

When Mazarin was shown some satirical songs on a new tax, "Let them sing," said he, "as long as they pay."

> GOETHE (1749–1832). *The Maxims and Reflections of Goethe*, 375, tr. T. Bailey Saunders, 1892

Reverse Robin Hood—take from the needy and give to the greedy.

> WILLIAM H. GRAY III (1941–). Pennsylvania congressman. Describing a proposed capital-gains tax cut, television interview, CNN, 15 September 1990

Can taxation without representation have been any worse than it is with it?

> SYDNEY J. HARRIS (1917–1986). *Pieces of Eight*, 4, 1982

Only the little people pay taxes.

> LEONA HELMSLEY (1920–). Attributed to her by a discharged housekeeper in testimony at Helmsley's trial for tax evasion. In Mark Shields, "Anger About Privilege," *Washington Post*, 30 July 1989

Taxes are what we pay for civilized society.

> OLIVER WENDELL HOLMES, JR. (1841–1935). *Compania General de Tabacos de Filipinas v. Collector of Internal Revenue*, 1927

The story is always the same [in Congress]: Higher rates are imposed and at the same time loopholes are carefully framed which permit the wealthy to get out from under the higher taxes.

> HUBERT H. HUMPHREY (1911–1978). In Ferdinand Lundberg, *The Rich and the Super-Rich: A Study in the Power of Money Today*, 12, 1968

High interest rates are the cruelest taxes of all.

> LEE IACOCCA (1924–). Chrysler Corp. chairman. "Forget Commissions, Fix the Budget!" *Washington Post*, 12 March 1989

Render to Caesar the things that are Caesar's, and to God the things that are God's.

> JESUS (A.D. 1st cent.). On the payment of taxes, *Mark* 12:17

The king employs a considerable part of the tribute in grants of largesse, bestowed by way of banquets or presents, to those whose support consolidates his authority, whereas their defection would endanger it. Do we not see modern governments as well using the public funds to endow social groups or classes, whose votes they are anxious to secure? Today the name is different, and it is called the redistribution of incomes by taxation.

> BERTRAND de JOUVENEL (1903–1987). *On Power: Its Nature and the History of Its Growth*, 6.16, 1945, tr. J. F. Huntington, 1948

The Internal Revenue Service sent a registered letter to Lloyd Rummer advising him that his company, Empire Auto Parts, Colville, Washington, owed the government one cent.

> ERWIN KNOLL (1931–1994). "A Penny Saved," *No Comment*, 1984

A taxpayer is someone who doesn't have to take a civil service examination to work for the government.

> KRUEGER'S LAW. In John Peers, comp., *1,001 Logical Laws*, p. 100, 1979

[A tax loophole is] something that benefits the other guy. If it benefits you, it is tax reform.

> RUSSELL B. LONG (1918–). Louisiana senator. In Richard Stengel, "Farewell to a Quartet of Kings of the Hill," *Time*, 10 November 1986

The power to tax involves the power to destroy.

> JOHN MARSHALL (1755–1835). *McCulloch v. Maryland*, 1819

The average American of today works more than a full day in every week to support his government. It already costs him more than his pleasures and almost as much as his vices, and in another half century, no doubt, it will begin to cost as much as his necessities.

> H. L. MENCKEN (1880–1956). "On Government" (1), *Prejudices: Fourth Series*, 1924

The less chance you have of successfully defending your income tax return, the greater the chance it will be randomly selected for audit.

> MOISE'S MAXIM. Slightly modified. In John Peers, comp., *1,001 Logical Laws*, p. 181, 1979

Avoid falsehoods like the plague except in matters of taxation, which do not count, since here you are not lying to take someone else's goods, but to prevent your own from being unjustly seized.

> GIOVANNI MORELLI (1816–1891). In "Thoughts on the Business of Life," *Forbes*, 15 April 1991

Anybody has a right to evade taxes if he can get away with it. No citizen has a moral obligation to assist in maintaining the government. If Congress insists on making stupid mistakes and passing foolish tax laws, millionaires should not be condemned if they take advantage of them.

> J. P. MORGAN (1837–1913). In Jeffery L. Yablon, comp., "As Certain as Death—Quotations about Taxes," *Tax Notes*, 14 November 1994

When people ask, "Why should the rich pay a larger percent of their income than middle-income people?"—my answer is not an answer most people get: It's because their power developed from laws that enriched them.

> RALPH NADER (1934–). Debra J. Saunders interview, "Public Citizen Number One," *San Francisco Sunday Examiner & Chronicle*, 13 October 1996

The more you earn, the less you keep,
And now I lay me down to sleep.
I pray the Lord my soul to take,
If the tax collector hasn't got it before I wake.

> OGDEN NASH (1902–1971). Closing lines, "One from One Leaves Two," *The Primrose Path*, 1935

Taxation without representation is tyranny.

> JAMES OTIS (1725–1783). Attributed. Supposedly used in a Boston court as an argument against British search warrants, February 1761.

What at first was plunder assumed the softer name of revenue.

> THOMAS PAINE (1737–1809). *The Rights of Man*, 2.2, 1792

The taxing power of government must be used to provide revenues for legitimate government purposes. It must not be used to regulate the economy or bring about social change. We've tried that, and surely we must be able to see it doesn't work.

> RONALD REAGAN (1911–). State of the Union Message, 18 February 1981

The Income Tax has made more Liars out of the American people than Golf has.

> WILL ROGERS (1879–1935). "Helping the Girls with Their Income Taxes," *The Illiterate Digest*, 1924

The subjects of every state ought to contribute towards the support of the government, as nearly as possible, in proportion to their respective abilities; that is, in proportion to the revenue which they respectively enjoy under the protection of the state.

> ADAM SMITH (1723–1790). *The Wealth of Nations*, 5.2.2, 1776

In the fourteenth century the principle of "No taxation without the people's consent" seemed as well established in France as in England herself.

> ALEXIS de TOCQUEVILLE (1805–1859). *The Old Regime and the French Revolution*, 2.10, 1856, tr. Stuart Gilbert, 1955

What is the difference between a taxidermist and a tax collector? The taxidermist takes only your skin.

> MARK TWAIN (1835–1910). 30 December 1902, *Mark Twain's Notebook*, ed. Albert Bigelow Paine, 1935

The thing generally raised on city land is taxes.

> CHARLES DUDLEY WARNER (1829–1900). "Sixteenth Week," *My Summer in a Garden*, 1871

No taxes can be devised which are not more or less inconvenient and unpleasant.

> GEORGE WASHINGTON (1732–1799). *Farewell Address*, 17 September 1796

Government expands to absorb revenue and then some.

> TOM WICKER (1926–). In Harold Faber, "*Faber's Law*: If There Isn't a Law, There Will Be," *New York Times Magazine*, 17 March 1968

❦

I believe we should all pay our tax bill with a smile. I tried—but they wanted cash.

> ANONYMOUS

Taxes on wealth is capital punishment.

> ANONYMOUS

The Eiffel Tower
is the Empire State
Building after taxes.

> ANONYMOUS. In "Thoughts on the Business of Life, *Forbes*, 29 December 1997

I've taken a tax deduction, you've found a tax loophole, he's evading his taxes.

> ANONYMOUS

The only thing worse than having to pay an income tax is having no income to tax.

> ANONYMOUS

No taxation without representation.

> SLOGAN (AMERICAN). 1770s

TEACHERS

See also • Children ○ Children's Learning ○ Education ○ Gurus ○ Learning (Process) ○ Parents ○ Scholars ○ School ○ University

A teacher affects eternity; he can never tell where his influence stops.

> HENRY ADAMS (1838–1918). *The Education of Henry Adams*, 20, 1907

The province of the instructor should be . . . awakening, invigorating, directing, rather than the forcing of the child's faculties upon prescribed and exclusive courses of thought. He should look to the child to see what is to be done, rather than to his book or his system. The Child is the Book. The operations of his mind are the true system.

> BRONSON ALCOTT (1799–1888). Letter, 1828. In George Hochfield, ed., introduction (5) to *Selected Writings of The American Transcendentalists*, 1966

To know how to suggest is the great art of teaching.

> HENRI AMIEL (1821–1881). Journal, 16 November 1864, tr. Mrs. Humphrey Ward, 1887

[The best that the] great teachers can do for us is to help us to discover what is already present in ourselves.

> IRVING BABBITT (1865–1933). *Democracy and Leadership*, 7, 1924

To receive a particular conclusion upon . . . the accepted authority of an admired instructor is obviously not so vivifying to the argumentative and questioning intellect as to argue out conclusions for yourself.

> WALTER BAGEHOT (1826–1877). *Physics and Politics, or Thoughts on the Application of the Principles of "Natural Selection" and "Inheritance" to Political Society*, 5.1, 1872

A teacher's major contribution may pop out anonymously in the life of some ex-student's grandchild.

> WENDELL BERRY (1934–). "Wallace Stegner and the Great Community," *What Are People For?: Essays*, 1990

The true teacher does not teach, yet one may educate oneself at his side; in just the same way the wise man does not create folk culture, but it takes form naturally in his presence.

> VINOBA BHAVE (1895–1982). *Thoughts on Education*, 1, tr. Marjorie Sykes, 1964

Let the teacher go into a village and take part in the crafts which are being practiced there, along with his pupils.

> VINOBA BHAVE (1895–1982). *Thoughts on Education*, 55, tr. Marjorie Sykes, 1964

Much advanced teaching today takes the form of a brief lecture followed by a period of discussion during which the audience identifies itself with the information, voices its criticisms, and discovers the knowledge for itself.

> J. A. C. BROWN (1911–1964). *Techniques of Persuasion: From Propaganda to Brainwashing*, 3, 1963

Teachers provide a social and intellectual environment in which students can learn.

> JAMES MacGREGOR BURNS (1918–). *Leadership*, 17, 1978

"Teachers" . . . treat students neither coercively nor instrumental-ly but as joint seekers of truth and of mutual actualization. They help students define moral values not by imposing their own moralities on them but by positing situations that pose hard moral choices and then encouraging conflict and debate. They seek to help students rise to higher stages of *moral reasoning* and hence to higher levels of *principled judgment*.

> JAMES MacGREGOR BURNS (1918–). *Leadership*, 17, 1978

The authority of those who teach is often an obstacle to those who want to learn.

> CICERO (106–43 B.C.). In Montaigne, "Of the Education of Children," *Essays*, 1588, tr. Donald M. Frame, 1958

I do not open up the truth to one who is not eager to get knowl-edge. . . . When I have presented one corner of a subject to any-one, and he cannot from it learn the other three, I do not repeat my lesson.

> CONFUCIUS (551–479 B.C.). *Confucian Analects*, 7.8, tr. James Legge, 1930

[Heraclitus] was nobody's pupil, but he declared that he "inquired of himself," and learned everything from himself.

> DIOGENES LAERTIUS (A.D. 3rd cent.). *Lives of Eminent Philosophers*, 9.1, tr. R. D. Hicks, 1925

It is the supreme art of the teacher to awaken joy in creative expression and knowledge.

> ALBERT EINSTEIN (1879–1955)

There is no teaching until the pupil is brought into the same state or principle in which you are; a transfusion takes place; he is you, and you are he.

> RALPH WALDO EMERSON (1803–1882). "Spiritual Laws," *Essays: First Series*, 1841

The cardinal virtue of a teacher [is] to protect the pupil from his own influence.

> RALPH WALDO EMERSON (1803–1882). "Notebook Platoniana," p. 11, 1845–1848

Have the self-command you wish to inspire. Your teaching and discipline must have the reserve and taciturnity of Nature. Teach them to hold their tongues by holding your own. Say little; do not snarl; do not chide; but govern by the eye. See what they need, and that the right thing is done.

> RALPH WALDO EMERSON (1803–1882). "Education," *Lectures and Biographical Sketches*, 1883

Of course you will insist on modesty in the children, and respect to their teachers, but if the boy stops you in your speech, cries out that you are wrong and sets you right, hug him!

> RALPH WALDO EMERSON (1803–1882). "Education," *Lectures and Biographical Sketches*, 1883

Charming women can true converts make,
We love the precepts for the teacher's sake.

> GEORGE FARQUHAR (1678–1707). *The Constant Couple, or a Trip to the Jubilee*, 5.3, 1699

He that teaches himself,
   hath a fool for a master.

> BENJAMIN FRANKLIN (1706–1790). *Poor Richard's Almanack*, January 1741
>
> See Doctors: Saying (2)

The teacher is no longer merely the-one-who-teaches, but one who is himself taught in dialogue with the students, who in turn while being taught also teach.

> PAULO FREIRE (1921–1997). On "problem-posing education," *Pedagogy of the Oppressed*, 2, tr. Myra Bergman Ramos, 1968

When the National Science Foundation asked the "breakthrough" scientists what they felt was the most favorable factor in their education, the answer was almost uniformly, "intimate associa-tion with a great, inspiring teacher."

> R. BUCKMINSTER FULLER (1895–1983). *I Seem To Be a Verb*, p. 82, 1970

No man can reveal to you aught but that which already lies half asleep in the dawning of your knowledge.
   The teacher who walks in the shadow of the temple, among his followers, gives not of his wisdom but rather of his faith and his lovingness.
   If he is indeed wise he does not bid you enter the house of his wisdom, but rather leads you to the threshold of your own mind.

> KAHLIL GIBRAN (1883–1931). "On Teaching," *The Prophet*, 1923

Good teaching is one-fourth preparation and three-fourths the-ater.

> GAIL GODWIN (1937–). *The Odd Woman*, 3, 1974

Those who are incapable of teaching young minds to reason, pre-tend that it is impossible. The truth is, they are fonder of making their pupils talk well than think well; and much the greater num-ber are better qualified to give praise to a ready memory than a sound judgment.

> OLIVER GOLDSMITH (1728–1774). Introduction to *The History of England: In a Series of Letters from a Nobleman to His Son*, 1764

Make your friends your teachers and mingle the pleasures of con-versation with the advantages of instruction.

> BALTASAR GRACIÁN (1601–1658). *The Art of Worldly Wisdom*, 11, 1647, tr. Joseph Jacobs, 1943

The vanity of teaching often tempteth a man to forget he is a blockhead.

> MARQUIS OF HALIFAX (1633–1695). "Of Vanity," *Political, Moral and Miscellaneous Reflections*, 1750

One father is more than a hundred Schoolmasters.

> GEORGE HERBERT (1593–1633). Comp., *Outlandish Proverbs*, 686, 1640

Knowledge—like the sky—is never private property. No teacher has a right to withhold it from anyone who asks for it. Teaching is the art of sharing.

> ABRAHAM JOSHUA HESCHEL (1907–1972). *A Passion for Truth*, 3, 1973

He does not educate children but rejoices in their happiness.

> HERMANN HESSE (1877–1962). *Reflections*, 324, ed. Volker Michels, 1974

I had no teacher but myself.

> HOMER (8th? cent. B.C.). *The Odyssey*, 22.342, tr. E. V. Rieu, 1946

We learn by teaching.

> JAMES HOWELL (1593–1666). Comp., "Italian" (p. 7), *Paroimiographia: Proverbs, or Old Sayed Sawes & Adages in English . . . Italian, French and Spanish*, 1659

Ask the beasts, and they will teach you;
   The birds of the air, and they will tell you.

> JOB. *Job* 12:7

There is no method of teaching that of which anyone is ignorant but by means of something already known.

> SAMUEL JOHNSON (1709–1784). In *The Idler* (English journal), 34, 9 December 1758

An understanding heart is everything in a teacher. . . . One looks back with appreciation to the brilliant teachers, but with gratitude to those who touched our human feelings. The curriculum is so much necessary raw material, but warmth is the vital element for the growing plant and for the soul of the child.

> CARL G. JUNG (1875–1961). "The Gifted Child," 1942, *The Development of Personality*, tr. R. F. C. Hull, 1954

Don't put your faith in anyone, you have it all inside you. You're always asking the masters, why don't you ask yourselves? Forget the masters.

> KRISHNAMURTI (1895–1986). In Henry Miller, "The Spirit: Spiritual Life," *Nothing But the Marvelous: Wisdoms of Henry Miller*, ed. Blair Fielding, 1991

He teaches not by speech
But by accomplishment.

> LAO-TZU (6th cent. B.C.). *The Way of Life*, 2, tr. R. B. Blakney, 1955

[A pupil] will better comprehend the Foundations and Measures of Decency and Justice, and have livelier, and more lasting Impressions of what he ought to do, by giving his Opinion on Cases propos'd, and reasoning with his Tutor on fit Instances than by giving a silent, negligent, sleepy Audience to his Tutor's Lectures.

> JOHN LOCKE (1632–1704). *Some Thoughts Concerning Education*, 98, 1693

The role of the teacher [is] one of directing activity rather than actually teaching.

> TERRY MALLOY. *Montessori and Your Child: A Primer for Parents*, 4, 1974

The teacher who is attempting to teach without inspiring the pupil with a desire to learn is hammering on cold iron.

> HORACE MANN (1796–1859)

There is nothing which spreads more contagiously from teacher to pupil than elevation of sentiment: Often and often have students caught from the living influence of a professor a contempt for mean and selfish objects, and a noble ambition to leave the world better than they found it; which they have carried with them throughout life.

> JOHN STUART MILL (1806–1873). "On Education," inaugural address on being installed as rector, University of St. Andrews (Scotland), 1 February 1867

On completion of a task or exercise, the children demonstrate with joyous effusion the higher process which is beginning within them. "All the children," says Miss George, "show that pride we ourselves experience when we have really produced something worthwhile. They skip round me, and throw their arms about my neck, when they have learned to do some simple thing, saying: 'I did it all alone,' 'You didn't think I could do that,' or 'I did it better today than yesterday.'"

> MARIA MONTESSORI (1870–1952). Slightly modified, *Spontaneous Activity in Education*, 3, tr. Florence Simmonds, 1917

The greatest sign of success for a teacher . . . is to be able to say, "The children are now working as if I did not exist."

> MARIA MONTESSORI (1870–1952). *The Absorbent Mind*, 27, 1949, tr. Claude A. Claremont, 1969

The essential part of the activity is initiated by the child. As soon as the child has reached the age when he is capable of meaningful action, he is in a position to continue his education on his own, repeating voluntarily those physical exercises that engage the reasoning process. He accomplishes in this fashion a work that is perfectly independent, in which he involves himself and in which the teacher does not interfere. Her job is limited to offering the materials and suffices if she demonstrates their use; after that, she leaves the child with his work.

> MARIA MONTESSORI (1870–1952). Arguing against passive imitation, *The Child in the Family*, 10, 1956, tr. Nancy Rockmore Cirillo, 1970

Always in our presentation we must give something which does not exceed the child's powers, and yet at the same time calls forth effort.

> MARIA MONTESSORI (1870–1952). In E. M. Standing, *Maria Montessori: Her Life and Work*, 18, 1957

All new knowledge gladdens [the teacher] only to the extent that he can teach it.

> FRIEDRICH NIETZSCHE (1844–1900). *Human, All Too Human*, 200, 1878, tr. Marion Faber, 1984

I bid you lose me and find yourselves.

> FRIEDRICH NIETZSCHE (1844–1900). "Of the Bestowing Virtue" (3), *Thus Spoke Zarathustra*, 1892, tr. R. J. Hollingdale, 1961

These teachers of submission! Wherever there is anything small and sick and scabby, there they crawl like lice; and only my disgust stops me from cracking them.

> FRIEDRICH NIETZSCHE (1844–1900). "Of the Virtue That Makes Small" (3), *Thus Spoke Zarathustra*, 1892, tr. R. J. Hollingdale, 1961

He who wishes to teach us a truth should not tell it to us, but simply suggest it with a brief gesture, a gesture which starts an ideal trajectory in the air along which we glide until we find ourselves at the feet of the new truth.

> JOSÉ ORTEGA y GASSET (1883–1955). "Preliminary Meditation," *Meditations on Quixote*, 1914

If a man understands something and does not practice it, how can he teach it to his neighbor?

POEMEN THE SHEPHERD (A.D. ?–450?). In "Pi: Poeman" (197), *The Sayings of the Desert Fathers: The Alphabetical Collection,* tr. Benedicta Ward, 1975

Men must be taught as if you taught them not;
And Things unknown propos'd as Things forgot.

ALEXANDER POPE (1688–1744). *An Essay on Criticism,* l. 574, 1711

The man who really knows can tell all that is transmissible in a very few words. The economic problem of the teacher (of violin or of language or of anything else) is how to string it out so as to be paid for more lessons.

EZRA POUND (1885–1972). *ABC of Reading,* 1.8, 1934

Let his austerity not be stern, nor his affability too easy, lest dislike arise from the one, or contempt from the other.

QUINTILIAN (A.D. 35?–100?). *Institutio oratoria,* 2.2.5, tr. John Selby Watson, 1856

[Pupils] more willingly attend to one who gives directions than to one who finds faults.

QUINTILIAN (A.D. 35?–100?). *Institutio oratoria,* 2.6.3, tr. John Selby Watson, 1856

The Master is, above all, an embodiment of Truth, and to follow the Master is to follow that Truth which is equally in ourselves.

N. SRI RAM (1889–?). *Thoughts for Aspirants,* 22, 1972

Few have been taught to any purpose who have not been their own teachers. We prefer those instructions which we have given ourselves, from our affection [for] the instructor.

SIR JOSHUA REYNOLDS (1723–1792). "Discourse Two," 11 December 1769, *Discourses on Art,* 1769-1790

Teach your scholar to observe the phenomena of nature; you will soon rouse his curiosity, but if you would have it grow, do not be in too great a hurry to satisfy this curiosity. Put the problems before him and let him solve them himself. Let him know nothing because you have told him, but because he has learned it for himself. Let him not be taught science, let him discover it. If ever you substitute authority for reason, he will cease to reason; he will be a mere plaything of other people's thoughts.

ROUSSEAU (1712–1778). *Emile; or, Treatise on Education,* 3, 1762, tr. Barbara Foxley, 1911

Teach by doing whenever you can, and only fall back upon words when doing it is out of the question.

ROUSSEAU (1712–1778). *Emile; or, Treatise on Education,* 3, 1762, tr. Barbara Foxley, 1911

See Learning (Process): Aristotle

As soon as he begins to reason let there be no comparison with other children, no rivalry, no competition, not even in running races. I would far rather he did not learn anything than have him learn it through jealousy or self-conceit. Year by year I shall just note the progress he had made, I shall compare the results with those of the [previous] year, I shall say, "You have grown so much; that is the ditch you jumped, the weight you carried . . . etc.; let us see what you can do now."

ROUSSEAU (1712–1778). *Emile; or, Treatise on Education,* 3, 1762, tr. Barbara Foxley, 1911

The teacher's art consists in this: To turn the child's attention from trivial details and to guide his thoughts continually towards relations of importance which he will one day need to know, that he may judge rightly of good and evil in society.

ROUSSEAU (1712–1778). *Emile; or, Treatise on Education,* 3, 1762, tr. Barbara Foxley, 1911

Keep your pupil busy with the good deeds that are within his power, let the cause of the poor be his own, let him help them not merely with his money, but with his service; let him work for them, protect them, let his person and his time be at their disposal; let him be their agent; he will never all his life long have a more honorable office. How many of the oppressed, who have never got a hearing, will obtain justice when he demands it for them with that courage and firmness which the practice of virtue inspires.

ROUSSEAU (1712–1778). *Emile; or, Treatise on Education,* 4, 1762, tr. Barbara Foxley, 1911

We will not attach him to any sect, but we will give him the means to choose for himself according to the right use of his own reason.

ROUSSEAU (1712–1778). *Emile; or, Treatise on Education,* 4, 1762, tr. Barbara Foxley, 1911

It should be quite unnecessary to [reveal] the moral; the right telling of the story should be sufficient. Do not moralize, but let the facts produce their own moral in the child's mind.

BERTRAND RUSSELL (1872–1970). *Education and the Good Life,* 11, 1926

More important than the curriculum is the question of the methods of teaching and the spirit in which the teaching is given.

BERTRAND RUSSELL (1872–1970). *Education and the Good Life,* 16, 1926

Sit at the feet of the master long enough, and they'll start to smell.

JOHN SAUGET. "Sauget's Law of Education." In Paul Dickson, comp., *The New Official Rules,* p. 187, 1989

The educator is like a good gardener, whose function is to make available healthy, fertile soil in which a young plant can grow strong roots; through these it will extract the nutrients it requires. The young plant will develop in accordance with its own laws of being, which are far more subtle than any human can fathom, and will develop best when it has the greatest possible freedom to choose exactly the nutrients it needs.

E. F. SCHUMACHER (1911–1977). *A Guide for the Perplexed,* 9.2, 1977

Choose as a guide one who you will admire more when you see him act than when you hear him speak.

SENECA THE YOUNGER (5? B.C.–A.D. 65). "On Choosing Our Teachers," *Moral Letters to Lucilius,* 50.2, tr. Richard M. Gummere, 1918

Desdemona: Those that do teach young babes
Do it with gentle means and easy tasks.

SHAKESPEARE (1564–1616). *Othello,* 4.2.111, 1604

He who can, does. He who cannot, teaches.

> GEORGE BERNARD SHAW (1856–1950). "Maxims for Revolutionists: Education," *Man and Superman,* 1903

The Bishop: I'm not a teacher: only a fellow-traveler of whom you asked the way. I pointed ahead—ahead of myself as well as you.

> GEORGE BERNARD SHAW (1856–1950). *Getting Married* (one-act play), 1908

Young men of the richer classes, who have not much to do, come about me of their own accord; they like to hear the pretenders examined, and they often imitate me, and proceed to examine others; there are plenty of persons, as they quickly discover, who think that they know something, but really know little or nothing; and then those who are examined by them instead of being angry with themselves are angry with me: this confounded Socrates, they say; this villainous misleader of youth!

> SOCRATES (470?–399 B.C.). In Plato (427?–347 B.C.), *Apology,* 23, tr. Benjamin Jowett, 1894

I educate, not by lessons, but by going about my business.

> SOCRATES (470?–399 B.C.). In Ralph Waldo Emerson. "Plato; or, The Philosopher," *Representative Men,* 1850

Within the tablets of thy mind write this
That I have said to thee.

> SOPHOCLES (496?–406 B.C.). "Fragments" (535), *Sophocles: Tragedies and Fragments,* 1, tr. E. H. Plumptre, 1865

The influence of a genuine educator lies in what he is rather than in what he says.

> OSWALD SPENGLER (1880–1936). *Aphorisms,* 329, tr. Gisela Koch-Weser O'Brien, 1967

Whenever the child is not concentrated on some creative activity, the teacher need have no scruples about breaking into his life, and presenting him with some of the exercises of practical life or any other lesson, always remembering, however, to obtain the child's consent.

> E. M. STANDING (1887–?). *Maria Montessori: Her Life and Work,* 13, 1957

As the base rhetorician uses language to increase his own power, to produce converts to his own cause, and to create loyal followers of his own person—so the noble rhetorician uses language to wean men away from their inclination to depend on authority, to encourage them to think and speak clearly, and to teach them to be their own masters.

> THOMAS S SZASZ (1920–). *Karl Kraus and the Soul-Doctors: A Pioneer Critic and His Criticism of Psychiatry and Psychoanalysis,* 3, 1976

The art of teaching is the art of assisting discovery.

> MARK VAN DOREN (1894–1972). In "Quotable Quotes," *Reader's Digest,* March 1965

The mediocre teacher tells. The good teacher explains. The superior teacher demonstrates. The great teacher inspires.

> WILLIAM ARTHUR WARD (1921–)

Schoolmasters and parents exist to be grown out of.

> JOHN WOLFENDEN (1906–1985). In *Sunday Times* (London), 13 June 1958

Dionysius the Renegade: Why am I the only pupil you do not correct?
Zeno: Because I mistrust you.

> ZENO (335?–263? B.C.). In Diogenes Laertius (A.D. 3rd cent.), *Lives of Eminent Philosophers,* 7.1, tr. R. D. Hicks, 1925

❧

One is prohibited from teaching others unless specifically requested to do so.

> ANONYMOUS (BUDDHIST). In Amaro Bhikkhu, introduction to *Tudong: The Long Road North,* 1984

We shall all have a good teacher when each of us is his own.

> ANONYMOUS (FRENCH). Graffito, student revolt, 1968

I make honorable things pleasant to children.

> ANONYMOUS (GREEK). Spartan teacher when asked about his method. In Plutarch (A.D. 46?–119?). "Can Virtue Be Taught?" (1), *Moralia,* vol. 6, tr. W. C. Helmbold, 1939

I watched him tie his shoelaces.

> ANONYMOUS (HASIDIC). An Hasid responding to the question of what he had done while spending a year of study with his "rebbi" (i.e., rabbi). In Perle S. Epstein, *Pilgrimage: Adventures of a Wandering Jew,* 1979

Become the lesson you would teach; be what you would have others become.

> ANONYMOUS

Follow the Way, not the teacher of the Way.

> ANONYMOUS

Successful teachers are surpassed by their pupils.

> ANONYMOUS

They teach well who build on what their students already know.

> ANONYMOUS

When the student is ready, the teacher arrives; when the teacher is ready, the student arrives.

> ANONYMOUS

Teachers open the door, but you must enter by yourself.

> SAYING (CHINESE). In David Schiller, *The Little Zen Companion,* p. 102, 1994

The Master says it once.

> SAYING (CHINESE). In Carl G. Jung, *Analytical Psychology: Its Theory and Practice* (The Tavistock Lectures), 4, 1935

One mother can achieve more than a hundred teachers.

> SAYING (JEWISH)

TEARS

Tears are Summer showers to the soul.

> ALFRED AUSTIN (1835–1913). *Savonarola*, 4, 1881

I'm just as blue as the sky,
Since love is gone,
Can't pull myself together.
Guess I'll hang my tears out to dry.

> SAMMY CAHN (1913–1993). "Guess I'll Hand My Tears Out to Dry"
> (song), 1944

'Tis in vain to do or mollify
It with thy tears, or sweat, or blood.

> JOHN DONNE (1572–1631). *An Anatomy of the World*, l. 430, 1611, ed.
> Roger E. Bennett, 1942
>
> See World War II: Winston Churchill (1)

Father Zossima: Water the earth with the tears of your joy and love
those tears. Don't be ashamed of that ecstasy, prize it, for it is a
gift of God.

> FYODOR DOSTOYEVSKY (1821–1881). *The Brothers Karamazov*, 6.2(h),
> 1880, tr. Constance Garnett, 1912

A tear is deeper than the sea.

> SAMUEL JACOB IMBER (1889–1942)

When Nature
Gave tears to mankind, she proclaimed that tenderness was
   endemic
In the human heart: of all our impulses, this
Is the highest and best.

> JUVENAL (A.D. 60?–127?). *Satires*, 15.131, tr. Peter Green, 1967

What happens to all the tears we do not shed?

> JULES RENARD (1864–1910). Journal, November 1906, tr. Louise Bogan
> and Elizabeth Roget, 1964

Lofty mountains are full of springs; great hearts are full of tears.

> JOSEPH ROUX (1834–1886). *Meditations of a Parish Priest*, 5.56,
> tr. Isabel F. Hapgood, 1886

With a smile on her lips, and a tear in her eye.

> SIR WALTER SCOTT (1771–1832). *Marmion*, 6.14, 1808

Antony: If you have tears, prepare to shed them now.

> SHAKESPEARE (1564–1616). *Julius Caesar*, 3.2.173, 1599

My heart today smiles at its past night of tears
like a wet tree glistening in the sun
after the rain is over.

> RABINDRANATH TAGORE (1861–1941). *Fireflies*, p. 52, 1928

Tears break through the gates . . . of heaven.

> TALMUD (A.D. 1st–6th cent.). Rabbinical writings. In Louis I. Newman,
> comp., *The Talmudic Anthology*, 259, 1945
>
> See Heaven: *Zohar*

Tears, idle tears, I know not what they mean,
Tears from the depths of some divine despair.

> ALFRED, LORD TENNYSON (1809–1892). "Song" (2), *The Princess*,
> 1847

TECHNOLOGY

See also • Communications ○ Computers ○ Creativity ○ Experts
   ○ Inventions ○ Machines ○ Progress ○ Religion & Science:
   [especially] Robert M. Pirsig ○ Science ○ Space ○ Tools

If the human race wants to go to hell in a basket, technology can
help it get there by jet. It won't change the desire or the direction,
but it can greatly speed the passage.

> CHARLES M. ALLEN. "Unity in a University," speech, Wake Forest
> University, Winston-Salem (North Carolina), 25 April 1967

In guessing the direction of technology, it is wise to ask who is in
the best position to profit most.

> BEN H. BAGDIKIAN (1920–)

The environmental crisis is somber evidence of an insidious fraud
hidden in the vaunted productivity and wealth of modern, tech-
nology-based society.

> BARRY COMMONER (1917–). *The Closing Circle: Nature, Man, and
> Technology*, 1972

America's technology has turned in upon itself; its corporate form
makes it the servant of profits, not the servant of human needs.

> ALICE EMBREE. "Media Images 1: Madison Avenue Brainwashing—
> The Facts." In Robin Morgan, ed., *Sisterhood Is Powerful:
> An Anthology of Writings from the Women's Liberation Movement*,
> 1970

Technology . . . the knack of so arranging the world that we need
not experience it.

> MAX FRISCH (1911–1991). Swiss writer. *Homo Faber*, 2, 1957

If there is technological advance without social advance, there is,
almost automatically, an increase in human misery, in impoverishment.

> MICHAEL HARRINGTON (1928–1989). Appendix (1) to *The Other
> America: Poverty in the United States*, 1962

In an age of advanced technology, inefficiency is the sin against
the Holy Ghost.

> ALDOUS HUXLEY (1894–1963). Foreword (1946) to *Brave New World*,
> 1932

Modern technology has led to the concentration of economic and
political power, and to the development of a society controlled
(ruthlessly in the totalitarian states, politely and inconspicuously in
the democracies) by Big Business and Big Government.

> ALDOUS HUXLEY (1894–1963). "Over-Organization," *Brave New World
> Revisited*, 1958

A world technology means either a world government or world
suicide.

> MAX LERNER (1902–1992). "The Imagination of H. G. Wells," *Actions
> and Passions: Notes on the Multiple Revolution of Our Time*, 1949

Our technology, wiser than we, has given us the unforeseen and
unforeseeable means of worldwide understanding at the moment
when worldwide understanding is the only possible means to lasting peace.

> ARCHIBALD MacLEISH (1892–1982). In J. A. C. Brown, *Techniques of
> Persuasion: From Propaganda to Brainwashing*, 12, 1963

The very success of mechanization has put the products of high technology under the control of routineers, lovers of compulsion and conformity, whose chief concern is to keep the wheels running smoothly. Even when they do not win complete control, the process itself becomes automatized—which means that it becomes, from a human standpoint, boring and finally meaningless. Instead of finding the rewards in the day's work, the majority of workers, high and low, look for their rewards outside it: in sport, excitement, luxury.

LEWIS MUMFORD (1895–1990). *The Transformations of Man*, 6.4, 1956

The nihilism of technology lies not only in the fact that it is the most perfect expression of the will to power . . . but also in the fact that it lacks meaning.

OCTAVIO PAZ (1914–). "The Channel and the Signs," *Alternating Current*, 1967

The technocratic imperative: "What can be done must be done."

THEODORE ROSZAK (1933–). Appendix to *The Making of the Counter Culture: Reflections on the Technocratic Society and Its Youthful Opposition*, 1969

We are too prone to make technological instruments the scapegoats for the sins of those who wield them. The products of modern science are not in themselves good or bad; it is the way they are used that determines their value.

DAVID SARNOFF (1891–1971). In Marshall McLuhan, *Understanding Media: The Extensions of Man*, 1, 1964

The primary task of technology, it would seem, is to lighten the burden of work man has to carry in order to stay alive and develop his potential.

E. F. SCHUMACHER (1911–1977). *Small Is Beautiful: Economics as if People Mattered*, 2.5, 1973

Technology . . . is a queer thing. It brings you great gifts with one hand, and it stabs you in the back with the other.

C. P. SNOW (1905–1980). In Anthony Lewis, "Dear Scoop Jackson," *New York Times*, 15 March 1971

The law of unintended consequences governs all technological revolutions.

JOEL L. SWERDLOW. "Information Revolution," *National Geographic*, October 1995

Technological innovation consists of three stages, linked together into a self-reinforcing cycle. First, there is the creative, feasible idea. Second, its practical application. Third, its diffusion through society.

The process is completed, the loop closed, when the diffusion of technology embodying the new idea, in turn, helps generate new creative ideas.

ALVIN TOFFLER (1928–). *Future Shock*, 2, 1970

Man cannot live by technology alone.

ARNOLD J. TOYNBEE (1889–1975). "The Unification of the World and the Change in Historical Perspective," 1947, *Civilization on Trial*, 1948
See Food: Moses

Technology: the invention, manufacture, and use of tools.

ARNOLD J. TOYNBEE (1889–1975). *A Study of History*, 12.658, 1961

TELEPHONE

See also • Communications

In Hell all the messages you ever left on answering machines will be played back to you.

JUDY HORACEK. Australian cartoonist. *Life on the Edge*, 1992

When you dial a wrong number, you never get a busy signal.

KOVAC'S CONUNDRUM. In Arthur Bloch, comp., "Household Murphology," *Murphy's Law: Book Two*, 1980

Well, if I called the wrong number, why did you answer the phone?

JAMES THURBER (1894–1961). Cartoon caption, *New Yorker*, 5 June 1937

If the phone doesn't ring, you'll know it's me.

ANONYMOUS

TELEVISION

See also • Art ○ Creativity ○ Culture: Andrei Sakharov ○ Films ○ Journalism: John Birt ○ Journalists ○ Media ○ Misjudgments: Darryl F. Zanuck ○ News ○ Propaganda ○ Radio ○ Reading: Richard M. Nixon

All television is children's television.

RICHARD P. ADLER. In Jonathan Rowe, "Modern Advertising: The Hidden Persuasion," *Christian Science Monitor*, 29 January 1987

The minds that control [television] are so small that you could put them in the navel of a flea and still have room for a network vice president's heart.

FRED ALLEN (1894–1956)

Imitation is the sincerest form of television.

FRED ALLEN (1894–1956)
See Imitation: Saying (English)

Television is the first truly democratic culture—the first culture available to everyone and entirely governed by what the people want. The most terrifying thing is what people do want.

CLIVE BARNES (1927–). In "Arts in the 60's: Coming to Terms with Society and Its Woes" (a round-table discussion), *New York Times*, 30 December 1969

Nothing is really real unless it "happens" on television. . . .

Television has brought an inversion of our consciousness. When we take our eyes off the tube, we see things that are not quite authentic—or, rather, which gain authenticity only by their resemblance to how things happen on television.

DANIEL J. BOORSTIN (1914–). "The Great Electronic Dictator," *New York Times Book Review*, 19 February 1978

Television is an amusement park. . . . We're in the boredom-killing business.

PADDY CHAYEFSKY (1923–1981). *Network* (film), 1976, spoken by Peter Finch (in the role of Howard Beal)

Television is the source from which most people now receive their news. It is also usually rated the most believable of their sources for following public events. The younger and less educated people are, the more they watch television and depend on it for interpreting political developments.

> THOMAS E. CRONIN (1940–). *The State of the Presidency,* 2nd ed., 3, 1980

I might have had trouble saving France in 1946—I didn't have television then.

> CHARLES de GAULLE (1890–1970). In "Small Screen, Super Weapon" (epigraph), *Newsweek,* 19 August 1963

The worst thing to be known as is intelligent. If that happens, we're doomed. Please do not call me *intelligent*. Call me *outrageous*. I'd rather be called *sleazy* than identified as *intelligent*.

> PHIL DONAHUE (1935–). On what it takes to succeed on daytime television. In "No Comment," *Progressive,* February 1989

There is no reason to confuse television news with journalism.

> NORA EPHRON (1941–). *Scribble Scribble: Notes on the Media,* 5, 1978

Life is not made up of dramatic incidents—not even the life of a nation. It is made up of slowly evolving events and processes, which newspapers, by a score of different forms of emphasis, can reasonably attempt to explore from day to day.

But television news jerks from incident to incident. For the real world of patient and familiar arrangements, it substitutes an unreal world of constant activity, and the effect is already apparent in the way in which the world behaves. It is almost impossible, these days, to consider any problem or any event except as a crisis; and, by this very way of looking at it, it in fact becomes a crisis.

> HENRY FAIRLIE (1924–1990). "Can You Believe Your Eyes?" *Horizon,* Spring 1967

Television makes so much [money] at its worst that it can't afford to do its best.

> FRED W. FRIENDLY (1915–1998). Editors interview, "The 'Television Fiasco,'" *U.S. News & World Report,* 12 June 1967

A new dictum of post-modern politics: Power no longer comes from the barrel of the gun or even the tireless effort of party apparatchiks in the precincts or at the convention. Power comes from the angle of the camera.

> NATHAN GARDELS. Referring to television. "Doing As the Romans Do," *Washington Post National Weekly Edition,* 18 April 1994

The commercial is the purpose, the essence; the program is the package.

> TODD GITLIN (1943–). "Sixteen Notes on Television and the Movement." In George Abbott White and Charles Hamilton Newman, eds., *Literature in Revolution,* 1972

Why should people go out and pay to see bad movies when they can stay at home and see bad television for nothing?

> SAM GOLDWYN (1882–1974). In *Observer* (British newspaper), 9 September 1956

Journalism as theater [is what] TV news is.

> THOMAS GRIFFITH (1915–). "Excluded from the Big Moment," *Time,* 9 February 1981

More and more, what doesn't show up on the screen doesn't exist, and what shows up badly is doomed.

> STANLEY HOFFMAN (1928–). "Semidetached Politics" (3), *New York Review of Books,* 8 November 1984

All television is educational television. The only question is, what is it teaching?

> NICHOLAS JOHNSON. Federal Communications Commission chairman. In Joan Barthel, "Notes in a Viewer's Album," *Life,* 10 September 1971

The conversation of politics now is carried on in the vernacular of advertising. The big sell, the television sell, appears to be the only way to sell. Increasingly, and especially in Washington, how well one does on television has come to determine how well one does in life.

> MICHAEL KELLY (1957–). "David Gergen, Master of the Game: How Image Became the Sacred Faith of Washington, and How This Insider's Insider Became Its High Priest," *New York Times Magazine,* 31 October 1993

It is not that what is purveyed to [children] is always directly hurtful, intentionally or otherwise. Some of it even tries to be helpful. The evil lies rather in the forfeiture of what the child might otherwise be doing if he or she were not watching television.

> GEORGE F. KENNAN (1904–). *Around the Cragged Hill: A Personal and Political Philosophy,* 8, 1993

[The viewer] watches me and he chooses to believe that I believe what he believes.

> TED KOPPEL (1940–). On his "fill-in-the-blank quality" (Marchand) as a broadcast journalist. In Philip Marchand, "Designing a Video Mask of Many Faces," *New York Times,* 13 August 1989

Isn't it odd that networks accept billions of dollars from advertisers to *teach* people to use products and then proclaim that children aren't *learning* about violence from their steady diet of it on television!

> TONI LIEBMAN. "A Call to Action," *NYSAEYC Reporter,* Fall 1993

Television seems to be addictive. Because of the way the visual signal is processed in the mind, it inhibits cognitive processes. Television qualifies more as an instrument of brainwashing, sleep induction and/or hypnosis than anything that stimulates conscious learning processes.

Television is a form of sense deprivation, causing disorientation and confusion. It leaves viewers less able to tell the real from the not-real, the internal from the external, the personally experienced from the externally implanted. It disorients a sense of time, place, history and nature.

Television is an instrument of transmutation, turning people into their TV images.

> JERRY MANDER (1936–). *Four Arguments for the Elimination of Television,* 11, 1977

I find television very educational. Every time someone switches it on, I go into another room and read a good book.

> GROUCHO MARX (1895–1977).

The success of any TV performer depends on his achieving a low-pressure style of presentation.

> MARSHALL McLUHAN (1911–1980). In Joe McGinniss, *The Selling of the President 1968*, 2, 1969

I invite you to sit down in front of your television set when your station goes on the air . . . and keep your eyes glued to that set until the station signs off. I can assure you that you will observe a vast wasteland.

> NEWTON MINOW (1926–). Federal Communications Commission chairman. Speech before the National Association of Broadcasters, Washington, 9 May 1961

This instrument can teach. It can illuminate. Yes, and it can even inspire. But it can do so only to the extent that humans are determined to use it to those ends. Otherwise, it is merely wires and lights in a box.

> EDWARD R. MURROW (1908–1965). Speech before the Radio and Television News Directors Association, Chicago, 15 October 1958

If television and radio are to be used for the entertainment of all of the people all of the time, we have come perilously close to discovering the real opiate of the people.

> EDWARD R. MURROW (1908–1965). Speech (after receiving the Albert Einstein Award), Brandeis University, Waltham (Massachusetts), 1958. In Alexander Kendrick, *Prime Time: The Life of Edward R. Murrow*, 10, 1969
>
> See Religion, Anti-: Karl Marx

If we were to do the Second Coming of Christ in color for a full hour, there would be a considerable number of stations which would decline to carry it on the grounds that a Western or a quiz show would be more profitable.

> EDWARD R. MURROW (1908–1965). Letter to a minister, 1958. In Alexander Kendrick, *Prime Time: The Life of Edward R. Murrow*, 10, 1969
>
> See Communications: Lewis Mumford

Children are inclined to learn from television [because] . . . it is never too busy to talk to them, and it never has to brush them aside while it does household chores. Unlike their preoccupied parents, television seems to want their attention at any time, and goes to considerable lengths to attract it.

> NATIONAL COMMISSION ON THE CAUSES AND PREVENTION OF VIOLENCE. In "Excerpts from National Panel's Statement on Violence in TV Entertainment," *New York Times*, 25 September 1969

Image is, I think, all-important in television. That's why, frankly, you should be more concerned about your makeup artist than your researcher, the one that blows your hair dry than what's between your ears. That's television.

> RICHARD M. NIXON (1913–1994). Morton Kondrake television interview, PBS, 4 May 1990

A show can "appeal" to a child . . . without necessarily offering the child amusement or pleasure. It appeals if it helps him express his inner tensions and fantasies in a manageable way. It appeals if it gets him a little scared or mad or befuddled and then offers him a way to get rid of his fear, anger, or befuddlement.

> VANCE PACKARD (1914–). Summarizing a finding from a television motivational research study titled "Now, for the Kiddies . . . ," *The Hidden Persuaders*, 15, 1957

The price of admission is candid conversation.

> MIKE WALLACE (1918–). On being a *60 Minutes* guest (the popular television magazine program was celebrating its 25th anniversary at the time), John Chancellor interview, CNN, 11 November 1993

I hate television. I hate it as much as peanuts. But I can't stop eating peanuts.

> ORSON WELLES (1915–1985). In *New York Herald Tribune*, 12 October 1956
>
> See Publicity: Andy Warhol

The Plug-In Drug.

> MARIE WINN. On television, book title, 1977

What programs like *60 Minutes*—and their equivalents in the printed press—are after is not social or political justice, but grist for the mill, and the easiest, most lurid way to provide it is to chase after individuals rather than institutions.

> JONATHAN YARDLEY (1939–). On "the conversion of journalism into entertainment," "The Truly Corrupt Vs. the Merely Sleazy," *Washington Post National Weekly Edition*, 7 October 1991

Some television programs are so much chewing gum for the eyes.

> ANONYMOUS (AMERICAN). James Mason Brown quoting his very young son's friend

Daddy, Daddy, there's the man who lives in our TV.

> ANONYMOUS (AMERICAN). Child who spotted a much-televised political leader at a campaign rally, in *Boston Globe*, 21 November 1986

Television changes events merely by covering them.

> ANONYMOUS

The worst television programs are the ones not quite bad enough to switch off.

> ANONYMOUS

If it bleeds, it leads.

> SAYING (AMERICAN). On television news

TEMPERAMENT

See also • Emotion ○ Fate: Novalis ○ Feeling ○ Happiness: La Rochefoucauld ○ Optimism & Pessimism: Bertrand Russell

The four temperaments are: 1. the melancholic or earthy; 2. the phlegmatic or aqueous; 3. the choleric or fiery; 4. the sanguine or ethereal.

> JACOB BOEHME (1575–1624). *Von der Geburt und Bezeichnung aller Wesen*, 1620

The conduct of men depends upon the temperament, not upon a bunch of musty maxims.

> BENJAMIN DISRAELI (1804–1881)

Temperament is the iron wire on which the beads are strung.

> RALPH WALDO EMERSON (1803–1882). "Experience," *Essays: Second Series*, 1844

Our temperaments differ in capacity of heat, or, we boil at different degrees.

> RALPH WALDO EMERSON (1803–1882). "Eloquence," *Society and Solitude,* 1870

The sanguine always hope, the gloomy always despond, from temperament and not from forethought.

> WILLIAM HAZLITT (1778–1830). "Belief, whether Voluntary," *Winterslow: Essays and Characters,* 1850

A second-class intellect, but a first-class temperament.

> OLIVER WENDELL HOLMES, JR. (1841–1935). On Pres. Franklin D. Roosevelt. Remark to a friend, 1933. In James MacGregor Burns, *Roosevelt: The Lion and the Fox,* 8, 1956

One's actual temperament . . . is the foundation of one's personality.

> ARNOLD J. TOYNBEE (1889–1975). *A Study of History,* 12.62, 1961

A first-class intellect, but a second-class temperament.

> TOM WICKER. Slightly modified. On Pres. Richard M. Nixon, Brian Lamb television interview, C-SPAN, 29 April 1994

The most valuable thing I inherited was a temperament that does not revolt against Necessity and that is constantly renewed in Hope.

> THORNTON WILDER (1897–1975). Richard H. Goldstone interview, 1956. In Malcolm Cowley, ed., *Writers at Work: First Series,* 1958

❦

Temperament is destiny.

> ANONYMOUS
>
> See Body: Napoleon ○ Character: Heraclitus

TEMPTATION

See also • Marriage: George Bernard Shaw (2) ○ Opportunity ○ Passion ○ Self-Discipline ○ Sin ○ Virtue: George Bernard Shaw

Saintliness is also a temptation.

> JEAN ANOUILH (1910–1987). *Becket,* 3, 1959

It is good to be without vices, but it is not good to be without temptations.

> WALTER BAGEHOT (1826–1877). "Sir George Cornewall Lewis," *Biographical Studies,* 1880

There are some temptations which are so strong that they must be virtues.

> CHARLES BAUDELAIRE (1821–1867). In Albert Camus, April 1939, *Notebooks: 1935–1942,* tr. Philip Thody, 1963

The Woman tempted me—and tempts me still!
Lord god, I pray You that she ever will!

> EDMUND VANCE COOKE (1866–1932). "Adam"

The amount of temptation required differentiates the honest from the dishonest.

> PAUL ELDRIDGE (1888–1982). *Maxims for a Modern Man,* 1095, 1965

The last temptation is the greatest treason:
To do the right deed for the wrong reason.

> T. S. ELIOT (1888–1965). *Murder in the Cathedral,* 1, 1935

We gain the strength of the temptation we resist.

> RALPH WALDO EMERSON (1803–1882). "Compensation," *Essays: First Series,* 1841

If today I repent, it is not for having yielded to some [temptations], but for having resisted so many others.

> ANDRÉ GIDE (1869–1951). *More Fruits of the Earth,* 3.3, 1935

The older you get, the easier it is to resist temptation, but the harder it is to find.

> JOSEPH H. HUMPERT. "Humpert Unhappy Homily." In Paul Dickson, comp., *The New Official Rules,* p. 102, 1989

Temptation is an irresistible force at work on a movable body.

> H. L. MENCKEN (1890–1957). *A Mencken Chrestomathy,* 30 ("The Mind of Man"), 1949

Blessed is he who has never been tempted, for he knows not the frailty of his rectitude.

> CHRISTOPHER MORLEY (1890–1957). *Inward Ho!* 1, 1923

'Tis no Sin to be tempted, but to be overcome.

> WILLIAM PENN (1644–1718). *Some Fruits of Solitude,* 450, 1693

I never resist temptation because I have found that things that are bad for me do not tempt me.

> GEORGE BERNARD SHAW (1856–1950). "An Interlude," *The Apple Cart,* 1928

Do not try to find a place free from temptations and troubles. Rather, seek a peace that endures even when you are beset by various temptations and tried by much adversity.

> THOMAS à KEMPIS (1379–1471). *The Imitation of Christ,* 3.12, tr. Leo Sherley-Price, 1952

There are several good protections against temptations, but the surest is cowardice.

> MARK TWAIN (1835–1910). *Following the Equator: A Journey Around the World,* 36 (epigraph), 1897

The only way to get rid of temptation is to yield to it.

> OSCAR WILDE (1854–1900). *The Picture of Dorian Gray,* 2, 1891

I can resist everything except temptation.

> OSCAR WILDE (1854–1900). *Lady Windermere's Fan,* 1, 1892

Do you really think, Arthur, that it is weakness that yields to temptation? I tell you that there are terrible temptations that it requires strength, strength and courage, to yield to.

> OSCAR WILDE (1854–1900). *The Ideal Husband,* 2, 1895

Even more pure,
As tempted more.

> WILLIAM WORDSWORTH (1770–1850). "Character of the Happy Warrior," l. 23, 1807

TERRORISM

See also • Cruelty ○ Dehumanization ○ Holocaust ○ Machiavellianism ○ Torture ○ Tyranny ○ Violence ○ War

The climax of terror is reached when the police state begins to devour its own children, when yesterday's executioner becomes today's victim.
> HANNAH ARENDT (1906–1975). *On Violence,* 3, 1970

The terrorist and the policeman both come from the same basket.
> JOSEPH CONRAD (1857–1924). *The Secret Agent,* 4, 1907

Terrorism and deception are weapons not of the strong but of the weak.
> MOHANDAS K. GANDHI (1869–1948). In *Young India,* 22 September 1920

Terrorism set up by reformers may be just as bad as Government terrorism, and it is often worse because it draws a certain amount of false sympathy.
> MOHANDAS K. GANDHI (1869–1948). In *Young India,* 18 December 1924

"Terrorism" is what we call the violence of the weak, and we condemn it; "war" is what we call the violence of the strong, and we glorify it.
> SYDNEY J. HARRIS (1917–1986). "Nations Should Submit to the Rule of Law," *Clearing the Ground,* 1986

Terror is the most effective political instrument. I shall not permit myself to be robbed of it simply because a lot of stupid, *bourgeois* mollycoddles choose to be offended by it.
> ADOLF HITLER (1889–1945). Table talk, 1933. In Hermann Rauschning, *The Voice of Destruction,* 6, 1940

The most horrible warfare is the kindest. I shall spread terror by the surprise employment of all my measures. The important thing is the sudden shock of an overwhelming fear of death. Why should I use different measures against my internal political opponents? These so-called atrocities spare me a hundred thousand individual actions against disobedience and discontent. People will think twice before opposing us when they hear what to expect in the camps.
> ADOLF HITLER (1889–1945). Table talk, 1933. In Hermann Rauschning, *The Voice of Destruction,* 6, 1940

The practice of terror serves the true believer not only to cow and crush his opponents but also to invigorate and intensify his own faith.
> ERIC HOFFER (1902–1983). *The True Believer: Thoughts on the Nature of Mass Movements,* 85, 1951

Argentina today is governed by terrorists in military uniforms. They have unleashed a reign of savagery unmatched in the modern history of the western hemisphere, dwarfing in scope and intensity even the post-coup repression in Pinochet's Chile and the terror of Duvalier's Haiti. Since the military takeover on May 24, 1976, in the name of freedom and with the stated ultimate goal of returning the nation to democracy, between 10,000 and 15,000 people have been killed after being kidnapped by police from their homes or offices. Their mutilated bodies have been dumped in the River Plate or cremated late at night at the Chacarita cemetery in Buenos Aires.
> STEPHEN KINZER (1951–). "Argentina in Agony," *New Republic,* 23 and 30 December 1978

Good and decent people must be protected and persuaded by gentle means, but the rabble must be led by terror.
> NAPOLEON (1769–1821). Letter to Charles Lebrun, 19 May 1811, *The Mind of Napoleon: A Selection from His Written and Spoken Words,* 128, ed. J. Christopher Herold, 1955

Murders instill terror. Terror is the means whereby the armed forces maintain their authority.
> ARYEH NEIER (1937–). Americas Watch director. Referring to El Salvador, testimony before the Subcommittee on the Western Hemisphere, 2 February 1984. In Noam Chomsky, *Turning the Tide: U.S. Intervention in Central America and the Struggle for Peace,* 1.3.2, 1985

One leads the people by reason, the enemies of the people by terror.
> ROBESPIERRE (1758–1794). French revolutionary leader. In David P. Jordan, *The Revolutionary Career of Maximilien Robespierre,* 11, 1985

There were two "Reigns of Terror" . . . one wrought murder in hot passion, the other in heartless cold blood. . . . What is the horror of swift death by the ax compared with lifelong death from hunger, cold, insult, cruelty, and heartbreak?
> MARK TWAIN (1835–1910). *A Connecticut Yankee in King Arthur's Court,* 13, 1889

❧

It is no great matter whether they that die on account of religion be guilty or innocent, provided we terrify the people by such examples.
> ANONYMOUS (SPANISH). Inquisitor. In Herbert J. Muller, *Freedom in the Western World: From the Dark Ages to the Rise of Democracy,* 5.4, 1963

THEATER

See also • Acting ○ Actors ○ Art ○ Creativity ○ Critics: Examples ○ Films ○ Media ○ Tragedy

The lights go down and the pulse goes up.
> JUDITH ANDERSON (1898–1992). Recalled on her death, 3 January 1992

We need above all a theater that wakes us up: nerves and heart.
> ANTONIN ARTAUD (1896–1948). Quoted by Oliver Stone. In Glenn Collins, "For Oliver Stone, It's Time to Move on from Vietnam," *New York Times,* 2 January 1990

Your audience gives you everything you need. They tell you. There is no director who can direct you like an audience.
> FANNY BRICE (1891–1951). In Norman Katkov, *The Fabulous Fanny,* 6, 1952

Give My Regards to Broadway,
    Remember me to Herald Square,
Tell all the gang at Forty-second Street
    That I will soon be there.
> GEORGE M. COHAN (1878–1942). "Give My Regards to Broadway" (song), 1904

Wave after wave of love flooded the stage and washed over me. This was the beginning of the one great durable romance of my life.

> BETTE DAVIS (1908–1989). Recalling her first solo curtain call. In Leroy Arrows, "Hollywood Gives Bette Davis a Top Award—Now What She Wants Is a Really Good Role," *People,* 21 March 1977

The audience wants to be reminded of their own humanity.

> OLYMPIA DUKAKIS (1931–). Graduation address at the American Conservatory Theater, San Francisco, 10 May 1997

We do not go [to the theater], like our ancestors, to escape from the pressure of reality, so much as to confirm our experience of it.

> CHARLES LAMB (1775–1834). "On the Artificial Comedy of the Last Century," *The Essays of Elia,* 1823

The audience is a not the least important actor in the play and if it will not do its allotted share the play falls to pieces.

> W. SOMERSET MAUGHAM (1874–1965). *The Summing Up,* 36, 1938

The structure of a play is always the story of how the birds came home to roost.

> ARTHUR MILLER (1915–). "Shadows of the Gods," *Harper's,* August 1958

In the popular theater, a hero is one who believes that all women are ladies; a villain, one who believes that all ladies are women.

> GEORGE JEAN NATHAN (1882–1958). "Theatre" (47), *American Mercury,* September 1929

If I walk on the stage with a certain attitude, people will understand immediately.

> GERALDINE PAGE (1924–1987). In Eric Maisel, comp., *Artists Speak: A Sketchbook,* unpaged, 1993

"I know why I lost my crowd tonight," said a flame of an actor. "I never can do anything with them unless I love them."

> CARL SANDBURG (1878–1967). *The People, Yes,* 84, 1936

The stage is not merely the meeting place of all the arts, but is also the return of art to life.

> OSCAR WILDE (1854–1900). "The Truth of Masks," *Intentions,* 1891

A dramatist is one who believes that the pure event, an action involving human beings, is more arresting than any comment that can be made upon it.

> THORNTON WILDER (1897–1975). Richard H. Goldstone interview, 1956. In Malcolm Cowley, ed., *Writers at Work: First Series,* 1958

Every now and then when you're on the stage, you hear the best sound that a player can hear. It is a sound you can't get in movies or in television. It is the sound of a wonderful, deep silence that means you've hit them where they live.

> SHELLEY WINTERS (1922–). "That Wonderful, Deep Silence," *Theatre Arts,* June 1956

❧

The show must go on.

> SAYING (AMERICAN)

Those in the free seats are the first to hiss.

> SAYING (CHINESE)

THEFT

See also • Cheating ○ Corruption ○ Crime ○ Hunger: Pearl S. Buck ○ Judges: Shakespeare ○ Lying: John Clarke ○ Politicians, Corrupt ○ Punishment: Thomas Fuller ○ Suspicion: Shakespeare ○ Time: Anonymous

He who withholds but a pennyworth of worldly goods from his neighbor, knowing him to be in need of it, is a robber in the sight of God.

> MEISTER ECKHART (A.D. 1260?–1328?)

The thief steals from himself. The swindler swindles himself.

> RALPH WALDO EMERSON (1803–1882). "Compensation," *Essays: First Series,* 1841

All stealing is comparative. If you come to absolutes, pray who does not steal?

> RALPH WALDO EMERSON (1803–1882). "Experience," *Essays: Second Series,* 1844

Always set a thief to catch a thief.

> THOMAS FULLER (1608–1661). *The Church-History of Britain,* 4.3, 1655

The Receiver
Is as bad as the Thiever.

> THOMAS FULLER (1654–1734). Comp., *Gnomologia: Adages and Proverbs,* 6162, 1732

Some men rob you with a six-gun,
Some with a fountain pen.

> WOODY GUTHRIE (1912–1967). "Pretty Boy Floyd the Outlaw" (song), 1961

Where there be no receivers, there be no thieves.

> JOHN HEYWOOD (1497–1580). Comp., *A Dialogue Containing the Number of the Effectual Proverbs in the English Tongue,* 1.12, 1562

A thief believes everybody steals.

> E. W. HOWE (1853–1937). *Country Town Sayings: A Collection of Paragraphs from The Atchison Globe,* p. 48, 1911

Many a man is saved from being a thief by finding everything locked up.

> E. W. HOWE (1853–1937). *Ventures in Common Sense,* 4.29, 1919

Do not defraud.

> JESUS (A.D. 1st cent.). *Mark* 10:19

I asked a man in prison once how he happened to be there and he said he had stolen a pair of shoes. I told him if he had stolen a railroad he would be a United States Senator.

> MARY "MOTHER" JONES (1830–1930). Speech, 1903, *The Autobiography of Mother Jones,* 10, 1925

You shall not steal.

> MOSES (14th cent. B.C.). The 8th Commandment, *Exodus* 20:15

For de little stealin' dey gits you in jail soon or late. For de big stealin' dey makes you Emperor and puts you in de Hall o' Fame when you croaks.

> EUGENE O'NEILL (1888–1953). *The Emperor Jones,* 1, 1921

Let the thief no longer steal, but rather let him labor, doing honest work with his hands, so that he may be able to give to those in need.

>   PAUL (A.D. 1st cent.). *Ephesians* 4:28

[The] "robbing of the poor because he is poor," is especially the mercantile form of theft, consisting in taking advantage of a man's necessities in order to obtain his labor or property at a reduced price. The ordinary highwayman's opposite form of robbery—of the rich, because he is rich—does not appear to occur so often to the old merchant's mind; probably because, being less profitable and more dangerous than the robbery of the poor, it is rarely practiced by persons of discretion.

>   JOHN RUSKIN (1819–1900). *Unto This Last*, 3, 1860

The faults of the burglar are the qualities of the financier.

>   GEORGE BERNARD SHAW (1856–1950). Preface ("The Weaknesses of the Salvation Army") to *Major Barbara*, 1905

A clever theft was praiseworthy among the Spartans; and it is equally so among Christians, provided it be on a sufficiently large scale.

>   HERBERT SPENCER (1820–1903). *Social Statics*, 2.16.3, 1851

The rich rob the poor, and the poor rob each other.

>   SOJOURNER TRUTH (1797–1883)

❦

Old thieves never die, they just steal away.

>   ANONYMOUS

The difference between a pickpocket and a robber baron is mostly a matter of opportunity.

>   ANONYMOUS

He who holds the ladder is as guilty as the thief.

>   SAYING (GERMAN)

Steal money, you're sent to prison; steal a country, you're made a king.

>   SAYING (JAPANESE)

Call one a thief, and he will steal.

>   SAYING. In Thomas Carlyle, *Sartor Resartus: The Life and Opinions of Herr Teufelsdröckh*, 2.1, 1835

There's no honor among thieves.

>   SAYING

The thief is the first to cry thief.

>   SAYING

THEORIES

See also • Creed ○ Doctrine ○ Dogma: [especially] John Dewey ○ Ideas ○ Ideology ○ Orthodoxy ○ Philosophy ○ Principles, Theoretical ○ Science: Mann's Law ○ Systems

I have steadily endeavored to keep my mind free so as to give up any hypothesis, however much beloved (and I cannot resist forming one on every subject), as soon as facts are shown to be opposed to it.

>   CHARLES DARWIN (1809–1882). 1 May 1881, *The Autobiography of Charles Darwin and Selected Letters*, 2, ed. Francis Darwin, 1892
>   See Creativity: William James

It is a capital mistake to theorize before one has data.

>   SIR ARTHUR CONAN DOYLE (1859–1930). "Scandal in Bohemia," *The Adventures of Sherlock Holmes*, 1891

A theory is the more impressive the greater the simplicity of its premises is, the more different kinds of things it relates, and the more extended is its area of applicability.

>   ALBERT EINSTEIN (1879–1955). "Notes for an Autobiography," *Saturday Review*, 26 November 1949

An ounce of action is worth a ton of theory.

>   FRIEDRICH ENGELS (1820–1895). In Reg Groves, *The Strange Case of Victor Grayson*, 2, 1975
>   See Action & Thought: Booker T. Washington

All theory, my friend, is gray,
But green is life's glad golden tree.

>   GOETHE (1749–1832). *Faust*, 1 ("Faust's Study," 3), 1808–1832, tr. Philip Wayne, 1959

To a very large extent we will have to rely on mathematical beauty and consistency to find the ultimate Theory of Everything. Nevertheless, I am confident we will discover it by the end of the 21st century and probably much sooner. I would take a bet at 50–50 odds that it will be within 20 years starting now.

>   STEPHEN HAWKING (1942–). British astrophysicist. Addressing a White House cultural gathering hosted by Hillary Rodham Clinton, 19 March 1998. In David Perlman, "A Dazzling Night in D.C. with a Brilliant Thinker," *San Francisco Chronicle*, 20 March 1998

We study theory in order to apply it, not for its own sake.

>   HO CHI MINH (1892–1969). Speech, 7 September 1957, *Ho Chi Minh on Revolution*, ed. Bernard B. Fall, 1967

Every theory enables us to husband our strength. It puts in the place of innumerable experiences a general judgment as a symbol and, by offering a precise, ordered collection of experiences, it saves us a lot of separate observations, descriptions, and controls.

>   ALFRED HOCK (1869–?). *Reason and Genius: Studies in Their Origin*, 2.4.1, 1960

Most theories of the state are merely intellectual devices invented by philosophers for the purpose of proving that the people who actually wield power are precisely the people who ought to wield it.

>   ALDOUS HUXLEY (1894–1963). "Nature of the Modern State," *Ends and Means: An Inquiry into the Nature of Ideals and into the Methods Employed for Their Realization*, 1937

The moment a person forms a theory, his imagination sees in every object only the traits which favor that theory.

>   THOMAS JEFFERSON (1743–1826). Letter to Charles Thompson, 20 September 1787

One can easily throw dust into one's own eyes with theories.

>   CARL G. JUNG (1875–1961). "Analytical Psychology and Education" (3), 1924, *The Development of Personality*, tr. R. F. C. Hull, 1954

The ultimate, most holy form of theory is action. . . . Theory has worth as preparation only; the critical struggle lies in the Act.

> NIKOS KAZANTZAKIS (1883–1957). Letter to his wife, Galatea, April 1923. In introduction to *The Saviors of God: Spiritual Exercises*, 1927, tr. Kimon Friar, 1960

Practice proves more than theory.

> ABRAHAM LINCOLN (1809–1865). *Second Annual Message to Congress*, 1 December 1862

That is the true test of a brilliant theory. What first is thought to be wrong is later shown to be obvious.

> ASSAR LINDBECK (1930–). Swedish economist. In Steve Lohr, "A Professor at M.I.T. Wins Nobel; Studied Market Shifts and Saving," *New York Times*, 16 October 1985

Our theory is not a dogma, but a *guide to action*.

> KARL MARX (1818–1883) and FRIEDRICH ENGELS (1820–1895). In Lenin, *"Left-Wing" Communism—An Infantile Disorder*, 8, 1920, International Publishers edition, 1971

There is something unsatisfactory in tracing an historical change to an individual theorist because a theory does not gain ground unless material conditions favor it.

> GEORGE ORWELL (1903–1950). Reviewing *The British Way in Warfare* by B. H. Liddell Hart, 21 November 1942, *The Collected Essays, Journalism and Letters of George Orwell*, vol. 2, ed. Sonia Orwell and Ian Angus, 1968

One can sometimes extract a valuable suggestion even from an absurd philosophical theory.

> KARL R. POPPER (1902–1994). *The Open Society and Its Enemies*, 2.14, 1945

With their minds fixed on complicated theories, people lost the ability to come to terms with reality.

> ERWIN ROMMEL (1891–1944). 1942 *The Rommel Papers*, 9, ed. B. H. Liddell Hart, 1953

Very dangerous things, theories.

> DOROTHY L. SAYERS (1893–1957). *The Unpleasantness at the Bellona*, 4, 1928

It is amazing how much theory we can do without when work actually begins.

> E. F. SCHUMACHER (1911–1971). British economist. "Schumacher's Conclusion." In Paul Dickson, comp., *The New Official Rules*, p. 189, 1989

The stupidity of a theory has never impeded its influence.

> OSWALD SPENGLER (1880–1936). *Aphorisms*, 332, tr. Gisela Koch-Weser O'Brien, 1967

How empty is theory in presence of fact!

> MARK TWAIN (1835–1910). *A Connecticut Yankee in King Arthur's Court*, 43, 1890

THINKERS

See also • Genius ○ Intellectuals ○ Philosophers ○ Scholars ○ Speaking: David Lloyd George, Richard M. Nixon

In every epoch of the world, the great event, parent of all others, is it not the arrival of a Thinker in the world!

> THOMAS CARLYLE (1795–1881). "The Hero as Divinity," *On Heroes, Hero-Worship, and the Heroic in History*, 1841

The profound thinker always suspects that he is superficial.

> BENJAMIN DISRAELI (1804–1881). *Contarini Fleming: A Psychological Autobiography*, 4.5, 1832

Beware when the great God lets loose a thinker on this planet. Then all things are at risk. . . . The very hopes of man, the thoughts of his heart, the religion of nations, the manners and morals of mankind, are all at the mercy of a new generalization.

> RALPH WALDO EMERSON (1803–1882). "Circles," *Essays: First Series*, 1841

To the men of practical power . . . the man of ideas appears out of his reason. They alone have reason.

> RALPH WALDO EMERSON (1803–1882). "Montaigne; or, The Skeptic," *Representative Men*, 1850

There is indeed this vice about men of thought, that you cannot quite trust them . . . because they have a hankering to play Providence and make a distinction in favor of themselves from the rules they apply to the human race.

> RALPH WALDO EMERSON (1803–1882). Title essay, *Natural History of Intellect and Other Papers*, 1893

In periods of "cultural lag" (where ideas have failed to keep pace with physical progress), the maladjustment between ideology and human reality spurs the search for "new" insights. The thinkers are the sensitive antennae of society, the first to sense keenly the attitudes of an emerging age and be able to express them in a period when a changing society finds the hitherto predominant sentiments, formerly satisfactory, becoming less convincing.

> CARL G. GUSTAVSON (1915–). *A Preface to History*, 12, 1955

An avant-garde thinker is someone who is ready to repudiate his own ideas as soon as a sufficient number of the public begin to accept them.

> SYDNEY J. HARRIS (1917–1986). *Pieces of Eight*, 4, 1982

No one can be a great thinker who does not recognize that as a thinker it is his first duty to follow his intellect to whatever conclusions it may lead.

> JOHN STUART MILL (1806–1873). *On Liberty*, 2, 1859

The thinker stands in the same relation to the ordinary book-philosopher as an eyewitness does to the historian; [the thinker] speaks from direct knowledge of his own.

> ARTHUR SCHOPENHAUER (1788–1860). "The Art of Literature: On Thinking for One's Self," *Essays of Arthur Schopenhauer*, tr. T. Bailey Saunders, 1851

The difference between the shallowest routineer and the deepest thinker appears, to the latter, trifling; to the former, infinite.

> GEORGE BERNARD SHAW (1856–1950). "Maxims for Revolutionists: Greatness," *Man and Superman*, 1903

The great thinkers from whom we derive inspiration enjoyed insights beyond their own systems. They made statements hard to reconcile with the neat little ways of thought which we pin on to their names.

> ALFRED NORTH WHITEHEAD (1861–1947). *Modes of Thought*, 2.4, 1938

THINKING

See also • Action & Thought ○ Books: Elbert Hubbard (2) ○ Contemplation ○ Creativity ○ Freedom of Thought ○ Ideas ○ Judgment ○ Machines: Howard Mumford Jones ○ Mind ○ Philosophy ○ Reading: Lord Chesterfield (1), John Locke ○ Reason ○ Reflection ○ Sin: Emma Goldman ○ Thoughts ○ Truth: Arthur Schopenhauer

The good man is glad to hold converse with himself, for he has pleasant memories of the past and fair hopes for the future, on which he can dwell with satisfaction; nor has he any lack of topics upon which to exercise the speculative powers of his mind.

> ARISTOTLE (384–322 B.C.). *Nicomachean Ethics*, 9.4, tr. J. A. K. Thomson, 1953

If thought is life
And strength and breath,
And the want
Of thought is death.

> WILLIAM BLAKE (1757–1827). "The Fly," *Songs of Experience*, 1794

All thinking is . . . a state of unrest tending towards equilibrium.

> SAMUEL BUTLER (1835–1902). *The Note-Books of Samuel Butler*, 5, ed. Henry Festing Jones, 1907

Some people have not time [for what Lord Shaftesbury has called self-conversation], and fewer have inclination to enter into that conversation; nay, very many dread it and fly to the most trifling dissipations in order to avoid it; but, if a man would allot half an hour every night for this self-conversation and recapitulate with himself whatever he has done, right or wrong, in the course of the day, he would be both the better and the wiser for it.

> LORD CHESTERFIELD (1694–1773). Letter to his son, 30 September 1763

This morning I *thought,* hence lost my bearings, for a good quarter of an hour.

> E. M. CIORAN (1911–1995). *Anathemas and Admirations*, 7, 1986, tr. Richard Howard, 1991

The impulse to communicate is not so much a result of thought as it is an inseparable part of it. They are like root and branch, two phases of a common growth.

> CHARLES HORTON COOLEY (1864–1929). *Human Nature and the Social Order*, rev. ed., 3, 1922 (1902)

I think, therefore I am.

> DESCARTES (1596–1650). *Discourse on Method*, 4, 1637, tr. Laurence J. Lafleur, 1964
>
> See Consumerism: Anonymous (American) ○ Resistance: James W. Douglass

Thought runs ahead and foresees outcomes, and thereby avoids having to await the instruction of actual failure and disaster.

> JOHN DEWEY (1859–1952). *Human Nature and Conduct: An Introduction to Social Psychology*, 3.3, 1922

There is no expedient to which a man will not go to avoid the real labor of thinking.

> THOMAS ALVA EDISON (1847–1931). Motto (posted throughout his laboratories)

In this world, if a man sits down to think, he is immediately asked if he has the headache.

> RALPH WALDO EMERSON (1803–1882). Journal, 16 September 1833
>
> See Solitude: Anne Morrow Lindbergh

What is the hardest task in the world? To think.

> RALPH WALDO EMERSON (1803–1882). "Intellect," *Essays: First Series*, 1841

Thought is like the weather, or birth, or death: we must take it as it comes.

> RALPH WALDO EMERSON (1803–1882). Journal, August 1847

I like not the man who is thinking how to be good, but the man thinking how to accomplish his work.

> RALPH WALDO EMERSON (1803–1882). Journal, 1865, undated

Think of three Things: whence you came, where you are going, and to whom you must account.

> BENJAMIN FRANKLIN (1706–1790). *Poor Richard's Almanack*, May 1755

All thought is a feat of association: having what's in front of you bring up something in your mind that you almost didn't know you knew. Putting this and that together. That click.

> ROBERT FROST (1874–1963). Richard Poirier interview. In George Plimpton, ed., *Writers at Work: Second Series*, 1963

It is for want of thinking that most Men are undone.

> THOMAS FULLER (1654–1734). Comp., *Gnomologia: Adages and Proverbs*, 2934, 1732

A man is but the product of his thoughts; what he thinks, he becomes.

> MOHANDAS K. GANDHI (1869–1948). *Ethical Religion*, p. 60, 1930
>
> See Deeds: George Eliot ○ Personality: Allen Wheelis

The greatest part of the business of the world is the effect of not thinking.

> MARQUIS OF HALIFAX (1633–1695). "Quiet," *Political, Moral and Miscellaneous Reflections*, 1750

Right living is a way to right thinking.

> ABRAHAM JOSHUA HESCHEL (1907–1972). *God in Search of Man: A Philosophy of Judaism*, 28, 1955

Much of man's thinking is propaganda of his appetites.

> ERIC HOFFER (1902–1983). *The Passionate State of Mind: And Other Aphorisms*, 261, 1954

Thinking is a brain exercise—and no faculty grows save as it is exercised.

> ELBERT HUBBARD (1856–1915). *The Note Book of Elbert Hubbard*, p. 64, comp. Elbert Hubbard II, 1927

Most of one's life is one prolonged effort to prevent oneself thinking.

> ALDOUS HUXLEY (1894–1963). "Wordsworth in the Tropics," *Do What You Will*, 1929

My existence does not depend on the fact that I am thinking; it depends on the fact that, whether I know it or not, I am being thought—being thought by a mind much greater than the consciousness which I ordinarily identify with myself.

> ALDOUS HUXLEY (1894–1963). "The Education of an Amphibian," *Tomorrow and Tomorrow and Tomorrow and Other Essays*, 1956

A great many people think they are thinking when they are merely rearranging their prejudices.

> WILLIAM JAMES (1842–1910). Attributed

Thinking
Chattering to myself
Avoiding silence.

> SAM KEEN (1931–). *Beginnings Without End*, 1, 1975

If you make people think they're thinking, they'll love you; but if you really make them think, they'll hate you.

> DON MARQUIS (1878–1937). "The Sun Dial" (column), *New York Sun*

Ishmael: All deep, earnest thinking is but the intrepid effort of the soul to keep the open independence of her sea; while the wildest winds of heaven and earth conspire to cast her on the treacherous, slavish shore.

> HERMAN MELVILLE (1819–1891). *Moby-Dick; or, The Whale*, 23, 1851, ed. Harold Beaver, 1972

The clarity of my ideas and my ability to prolong my occupations indefinitely without experiencing fatigue is explained by my keeping each object and each business filed in my head as in a chest of drawers. When I wish to interrupt one occupation, I shut its drawer and open another. They do not mix, and when I am busy with one I am not importuned or tired by the other. . . . When I want to sleep, I shut all the drawers, and I am fast asleep.

> NAPOLEON (1769–1821). 1815–1816. Adapted. In Emmanuel Las Cases, *Mémorial de Sainte Hélène*, 1840

The Power of Positive Thinking.

> NORMAN VINCENT PEALE (1898–1993). Book title, 1952

To think is to search for clearings in a wood.

> JULES RENARD (1864–1910). Journal, March 1894, tr. Louise Bogan and Elizabeth Roget, 1964

Men fear thought as they fear nothing else on earth—more than ruin, more even than death. Thought is subversive and revolutionary, destructive and terrible; thought is merciless to privilege, established institutions, and comfortable habits; thought is anarchic and lawless, indifferent to authority, careless to the well-tried wisdom of the ages.

> BERTRAND RUSSELL (1872–1970). *Principles of Social Reconstruction*, 5, 1916

Mere experience can as little as reading supply the place of thought. [Experience] stands to thinking in the same relation in which eating stands to digestion and assimilation.

ARTHUR SCHOPENHAUER (1788–1860). "The Art of Literature: On Thinking for One's Self," *Essays of Arthur Schopenhauer*, tr. T. Bailey Saunders, 1851

Renunciation of thinking is a declaration of spiritual bankruptcy.

> ALBERT SCHWEITZER (1875–1965). *Out of My Life and Thought: An Autobiography*, 21, tr. C. T. Campion, 1933

Few people think more than two or three times a year; I have made an international reputation for myself by thinking once or twice a week.

> GEORGE BERNARD SHAW (1856–1950)

I catch myself philosophizing most eloquently when first returning to consciousness in the night or morning. I make the truest observations and distinctions then when the will is yet wholly asleep, and mind works like a machine without friction. . . . There is a moment in the dawn when the darkness of the night is dissipated, and before the exhalations of the day begin to rise, when we see all things more truly than at any other time.

> HENRY DAVID THOREAU (1817–1862). Journal. In Bronson Alcott, 22 July 1869, *Concord Days*, 1872

Thought and feeling take counsel together and supplement one another in turn.

> VAUVENARGUES (1715–1747). *Reflections and Maxims*, 150, 1746, tr. F. G. Stevens, 1940

THOUGHTS

See also • Action & Thought ○ Books: Ralph Waldo Emerson (5) ○ Creativity ○ Freedom of Thought ○ Greatness: Ralph Waldo Emerson (6) ○ Ideas ○ Opinion ○ Thinking ○ Words

Our very best thoughts often cum tew us sudden, but seldum perfekt. They require polishing up tew make them komplete.

> JOSH BILLINGS (1818–1885). "Fust Impreshuns," *Everybody's Friend, or; Josh Billing's Encyclopedia and Proverbial Philosophy of Wit and Humor*, 1874

One thought fills immensity.

> WILLIAM BLAKE (1757–1827). "Proverbs of Hell," *The Marriage of Heaven and Hell*, 8.16, 1790–1793?

The more profound the thought, the more burdensome. What is in will out.

> RALPH WALDO EMERSON (1803–1882). Journal, 15 October 1836

Like the New England soil, my talent is good only whilst I work it. If I cease to task myself, I have no thoughts.

> RALPH WALDO EMERSON (1803–1882). Journal, 1849?–1850?, undated

Music first before thought.

> RALPH WALDO EMERSON (1803–1882). "Notebook Phi," p. 90, 1838–1851?

My best thought came from others. I heard in their words my own meaning, but a deeper sense than they put on them. And could well and best express myself in other people's phrases, but to finer purpose than they knew.

> RALPH WALDO EMERSON (1803–1882). Journal, 1855, undated

For provocation of thought, we use ourselves and use each other. Some perceptions—I think the best—are granted to the single soul; they come from the depth and go to the depth and are the permanent and controlling ones. Others it takes two to find. We must be warmed by the fire of sympathy, to be brought into the right conditions and angles of vision.

RALPH WALDO EMERSON (1803–1882). "Inspiration," *Letters and Social Aims*, 1876

In the effort to unfold our thought to a friend we make it clearer to ourselves.

RALPH WALDO EMERSON (1803–1882). "Social Aims," *Letters and Social Aims*, 1876

Nature provided for the communication of thought, by planting with it in the receiving mind a fury to impart it. . . . One burns to tell the new fact, the other burns to hear it.

RALPH WALDO EMERSON (1803–1882). "Education," *Lectures and Biographical Sketches*, 1883

As certainly as water falls in rain on the tops of mountains and runs down into valleys, plains and pits, so does thought fall first on the best minds, and runs down, from class to class, until it reaches the masses, and works revolutions.

RALPH WALDO EMERSON (1803–1882). "The Man of Letters," *Lectures and Biographical Sketches*, 1883

There was never anything that did not proceed from a thought.

RALPH WALDO EMERSON (1803–1882). "The Scholar," *Lectures and Biographical Sketches*, 1883

The history of thought is the history of an ever-increasing approximation to the truth.

ERICH FROMM (1900–1980). *Man for Himself: An Inquiry into the Psychology of Ethics*, 4.6, 1947

A man may dwell so long upon a thought that it may take him prisoner.

MARQUIS OF HALIFAX (1633–1695). "Faculties of the Mind," *Political, Moral and Miscellaneous Reflections*, 1750

It is a nice mean between letting the thought languish for want of exercise, and tiring it by giving it too much.

MARQUIS OF HALIFAX (1633–1695). "Faculties of the Mind," *Political, Moral and Miscellaneous Reflections*, 1750

The very minute a thought is threatened with publicity it seems to shrink towards mediocrity.

OLIVER WENDELL HOLMES, SR. (1809–1894). *The Poet at the Breakfast-Table*, 12, 1872

Thought forms in the soul in the same way clouds form in the air.

JOSEPH JOUBERT (1754–1824). 1786, *Pensées*, 1838, tr. Paul Auster, 1983

These thoughts form not only the foundation of my work, but of my life.

JOSEPH JOUBERT (1754–1824). On the thoughts in his notebooks, 1804, *Pensées*, 1838, tr. Paul Auster, 1983

O for a Life of Sensations rather than of Thoughts!

JOHN KEATS (1795–1821). Letter to Benjamin Bailey, 22 November 1817

First thought, best thought.

JACK KEROUAC (1922–1969). In Allen Ginsberg, motto, "Social Study," *Vanity Fair*, March 1994

The thoughts that come often unsought, and, as it were, drop into the mind, are commonly the most valuable of any we have.

JOHN LOCKE (1632–1704). Letter to Samuel Bold, 16 May 1699

Thoughts that come on doves' feet guide the world.

FRIEDRICH NIETZSCHE (1844–1900). "The Stillest Hours," *Thus Spoke Zarathustra*, 1892, tr. R. J. Hollingdale, 1961

The greatest thoughts are grasped last. . . . The light of the most distant star reaches man last and before it has arrived every person denies that there is such a star.

FRIEDRICH NIETZSCHE (1844–1900). In Alfred Hock, *Reason and Genius: Studies in Their Origin*, 1.2, 1960

There are two distinct classes of what are called thoughts: Those that we produce in ourselves by reflection and the act of thinking, and those that bolt into the mind of their own accord.

THOMAS PAINE (1737–1809). *The Age of Reason: Being an Investigation of True and Fabulous Theology*, 1, 1794

How very commonly we hear it remarked that such and such thoughts are beyond the compass of words! I do not believe that any thought, properly so called, is out of the reach of language.

EDGAR ALLAN POE (1809–1849). March 1846, *Marginalia*, University Press of Virginia edition, 1981

The finest thought runs the risk of being irrevocably forgotten if we do not write it down.

ARTHUR SCHOPENHAUER (1788–1860). "The Art of Literature: On Thinking for One's Self," *Essays of Arthur Schopenhauer*, tr. T. Bailey Saunders, 1851

Nothing was ever so unfamiliar and startling to me as my own thoughts.

HENRY DAVID THOREAU (1817–1862). Journal, 10 July 1840

Do not seek expressions, seek thoughts to be expressed.

HENRY DAVID THOREAU (1817–1862). Journal, 25 December 1851

If I were confined to a corner of a garret all my days, like a spider, the world would be just as large to me while I had my thoughts about me.

HENRY DAVID THOREAU (1817–1862). "Conclusion," *Walden; or Life in the Woods*, 1854

When a thought is not robust enough to stand expression in simple terms, it is a sign that it should be rejected.

VAUVENARGUES (1715–1747). *Reflections and Maxims*, 3, 1746, tr. F. G. Stevens, 1940

Great thoughts spring from the heart.

VAUVENARGUES (1715–1747). *Reflections and Maxims*, 127, 1746, tr. F. G. Stevens, 1940

It belongs to the self-respect of intellect to pursue every tangle of thought to its final unravelment.

ALFRED NORTH WHITEHEAD (1861–1947). *Science and the Modern World*, 12, 1925

THRIFT

See also • Economics ○ Excess ○ Greed ○ Misers: [especially]
Chamfort ○ Moderation ○ Money ○ Prudence: Rules ○ Wealth

Penny wise, pound foolish.

> ROBERT BURTON (1577–1640). "Democritus to the Reader,"
> *The Anatomy of Melancholy,* 1621–1651

How large an income is thrift!

> CICERO (106–43 B.C.). *Paradoxa stoicorum,* 6, tr. H. Rackham, 1942

Everybody is always in favor of general economy and particular
expenditure.

> ANTHONY EDEN (1897–1977). British prime minister. In *Observer*
> (British newspaper), 17 June 1956

A man often pays dear for a small frugality.

> RALPH WALDO EMERSON (1803–1882). "Compensation," *Essays: First
> Series,* 1841

The true thrift is always to spend on the higher plane.

> RALPH WALDO EMERSON (1803–1882). "Wealth," *The Conduct of Life,*
> 1860

For Age and Want, save while you may;
No Morning Sun lasts a whole Day.

> BENJAMIN FRANKLIN (1706–1790). "The Way of Wealth," 7 July 1757

Make no expense but to do good to others or yourself; i.e., waste
nothing.

> BENJAMIN FRANKLIN (1706–1790). Virtue #5 ("Frugality"), 1784,
> *Autobiography,* 1798

Spare no expense to make everything as economic as possible.

> SAMUEL GOLDWYN (1884–1974)

Better spare at brim than at bottom.

> JOHN HEYWOOD (1497–1580). Comp., *A Dialogue Containing
> the Number of the Effectual Proverbs in the English Tongue,*
> 2.5, 1562

Little and oft fill the purse.

> JAMES HOWELL (1593–1666). Comp., "Italian" (p. 8), *Paroimiographia:
> Proverbs, or Old Sayed Sawes & Adages in English . . . Italian, French
> and Spanish,* 1659

A feller is often called thrifty when he's really broke.

> KIN HUBBARD (1868–1930). "April," *Abe Martin's Almanack,*
> 1908

Economy does not lie in sparing money but in spending it wisely.

> T. H. HUXLEY (1825–1895). *Aphorisms and Reflections,* 349, 1907

Without frugality none can be rich, and with it very few would be
poor.

> SAMUEL JOHNSON (1709–1784). In *The Rambler* (English journal), 57,
> 2 October 1750

Better long little than soon nothing.

> JAMES KELLY (18th cent.). Comp., *A Complete Collection of Scottish
> Proverbs Explained and Made Intelligible to the English Reader,*
> B.58, 1721

Spend not where you may save; spare not where you must spend.

> JOHN RAY (1628–1705). Comp., *A Collection of English Proverbs,*
> p. 348, 1678

Economy is the art of making the most of life.

> GEORGE BERNARD SHAW (1856–1950). "Maxims for Revolutionists:
> Virtues and Vices," *Man and Superman,* 1903

The love of economy is the root of all virtue.

> GEORGE BERNARD SHAW (1856–1950). "Maxims for Revolutionists:
> Virtues and Vices," *Man and Superman,* 1903
> See Greed: Paul

It was said of old Sarah, Duchess of Marlborough, that she never
put dots over her i's, to save ink.

> HORACE WALPOLE (1717–1797). Letter to Sir Horace Mann, 4 October
> 1785

To recommend thrift to the poor is both grotesque and insulting.
It is like advising a man who is starving to eat less.

> OSCAR WILDE (1854–1900). "The Soul of Man Under Socialism,"
> *Fortnightly Review* (British journal), February 1891
> See Self-Reliance: Martin Luther King, Jr.,

Going from thrift to extravagance is easy; going from extravagance
to thrift is hard.

> SAYING (CHINESE)

A penny saved is a penny earned.

> SAYING (ENGLISH)

Take care of the pence, for the pounds will take care of themselves.

> SAYING (ENGLISH). In Lord Chesterfield, letter to his son, 6 November
> 1747
> See Means & Ends: Mohandas K. Gandhi (2) ○ Profit & Loss: Andrew
> Carnegie ○ Talking: Lewis Carroll ○ Time: Chesterfield (1)

Waste not, want not.

> SAYING (ENGLISH)

If a few sen do not go, many sen will not come.

> SAYING (JAPANESE)

Save today, safe tomorrow.

> SAYING (OKLAHOMA)

Use it up, wear it out, make it do or do without.

> SAYING (VERMONT)

Those who save, have; those who have get.

> SAYING

TIME

See also • Action ○ Days ○ Delay ○ Doctors: Seneca the Younger
○ Drugs, Medical: Saying ○ Eternity ○ Future ○ Idleness ○
Laziness ○ Months ○ Nature ○ Past ○ Patience ○ Present ○
Procrastination ○ Prudence: Rules ○ Punctuality ○ Seasons ○
Timing

Oh! do not attack me with your watch. A watch is always too fast or too slow. I cannot be dictated to by a watch.

> JANE AUSTEN (1775–1817). *Mansfield Park,* 9, 1814

Time iz like money, the less we hav ov it teu spare the further we make it go.

> JOSH BILLINGS (1818–1885). "Petter Pods." *Everybody's Friend, or; Josh Billing's Encyclopedia and Proverbial Philosophy of Wit and Humor,* 1874

Query: How contrive not to waste one's time?
Answer: By being fully aware of it all the while.

> ALBERT CAMUS (1913–1960). *The Plague,* 1, 1947, tr. Stuart Gilbert, 1948

And what if you were told: One more hour?

> ELIAS CANETTI (1905–1994). 1985, *The Secret Heart of the Clock: Notes, Aphorisms, Fragments: 1973–1985,* tr. Joel Agee, 1989

Time wounds all heels.

> FRANK CASE. *Tales of a Wayward Inn,* 11, 1938

Take care of the minutes, for the hours will take care of themselves.

> LORD CHESTERFIELD (1694–1773). Letter to his son, 6 November 1747
> See Thrift: Saying (English) (2)

No indolence, no laziness; but employ every minute in your life in active pleasures or useful employments.

> LORD CHESTERFIELD (1694–1773). Letter to his son, 5 March 1752

Time and Tide tarry [for] no man.

> JOHN CLARKE (1596–1658). Comp., *Proverbs: English and Latine,* p. 308, 1639

Time trieth all things.

> JOHN CLARKE (1596–1658). Comp., *Proverbs: English and Latine,* p. 308, 1639

Time, consoler of affliction and softener of anger.

> CHARLES DICKENS (1812–1870). *Doombey and Son,* 47, 1848

Time goes, you say? Ah no!
Alas, Time stays, *we* go.

> AUSTIN DOBSON (1840–1921). "The Paradox of Time," *Proverbs in Porcelain,* 1877

Dost thou love Life? then do not squander Time;
    for that's the Stuff Life is made of.

> BENJAMIN FRANKLIN (1706–1790). *Poor Richard's Almanack,* June 1746

Time is Money.

> BENJAMIN FRANKLIN (1706–1790). "Advice to a Young Tradesman," 1748

There are years when nothing happens and years in which centuries happen.

> CARLOS FUENTES (1928–). "The New World Disorder," *San Francisco Sunday Examiner & Chronicle,* 4 July 1993

Those that make the best Use of their Time have none to spare.

> THOMAS FULLER (1654–1734). Comp., *Gnomologia: Adages and Proverbs,* 5029, 1732

No person will have occasion to complain of the want of time who never loses any. It is wonderful how much may be done if we are always doing.

> THOMAS JEFFERSON (1743–1826). Letter to his daughter Martha, 5 May 1787

I'm forty six. . . . I grew up in a gentler, slower time. When Ike was president, Christmases were years apart, and now it's about five months from one to the next.

> GARRISON KEILLOR (1942–). Introduction to *We Are Still Married: Stories & Letters,* 1989

Those who make the worst use of their time are the first to complain of its brevity.

> LA BRUYÈRE (1645–1696). "Of Opinions" (101), *The Characters,* 1688, tr. Henri van Laun, 1929

You can ask me for anything you like, except time.

> NAPOLEON (1769–1821). Remark to one of his officers, 11 March 1803, *The Corsican: A Diary of Napoleon's Life in His Own Words,* ed. R. M. Johnston, 1911

A Murid: What am I to do? I am troubled by the people, many of whom pay me visits. By their coming and going they encroach upon my precious time.
His Pur: Lend something to every one of them who is poor and ask something from every one who is rich and they will come round thee no more.

> SA'DI (A.D. 1213?–1292). Format adapted. *The Gulistan, or Rose Garden,* 2 (Story 38), 1258 A.D., tr. Edward Rehatsek, 1964

The years pass more quickly as we become older.

> ARTHUR SCHOPENHAUER (1788–1860). "Counsels and Maxims" (2.9), *Essays of Arthur Schopenhauer,* tr. T. Bailey Saunders, 1851

Ah! the clock is always slow;
It is later than you think.

> ROBERT W. SERVICE (1874–1958). "It Is Later Than You Think," *Ballads of a Bohemian,* 1921

King Richard: I wasted time, and now doth time waste me.

> SHAKESPEARE (1564–1616). *Richard II,* 5.5.49, 1595

Gaining time is gaining everything in love, trade, and war.

> JOHN SHEBBEARE (1709–1788). *The Marriage Act,* 1, 1754

There has been so great a revolution in our time-scale that, if I were to try to plot out to scale, on one of these pages, a chart of the history of this planet since its birth, I should not be able to make so short a period as eleven hundred years visible to the naked eye.

> ARNOLD J. TOYNBEE (1889–1975). "Encounters Between Civilizations" (1), 1947, *Civilization on Trial,* 1948

❦

A thousand years in thy sight
    are but as yesterday when it is past,
    or as a watch in the night.

> ANONYMOUS (*BIBLE*). *Psalms* 90:4

The thief to be most wary of is the one who steals your time.

> ANONYMOUS

A stitch in time saves nine.
SAYING (ENGLISH)

Who waits for time, loses time.
SAYING (ITALIAN)

What time would it be if all the clocks were stopped?
SAYING (ZEN). In John Kane, ed., *Moving Forward, Keeping Still: The Gateway to Eastern Wisdom,* p. 113, 1997

Method makes time.
SAYING

Time enough is little enough.
SAYING

Time flies.
SAYING

Time heals all wounds.
SAYING

Time will tell.
SAYING

TIMING

See also • Opportunity ○ Right: Martin Luther King, Jr. ○ Time

Thare iz a time for all things, thare is a time tew pray, and thare iz a time to say *amen,* rool up yare sleeves and pitch in.
JOSH BILLINGS (1818–1885). "Stray Children," *Everybody's Friend, or; Josh Billing's Encyclopedia and Proverbial Philosophy of Wit and Humor,* 1874

There is in everything a maturity that must be waited for. He is a fortunate man who arrives at the same moment that it does.
CHAMFORT (1741–1794). *Maxims and Thoughts,* 8, 1796, tr. W. S. Merwin, 1984

Set not your Loaf in, till the Oven's hot.
THOMAS FULLER (1654–1734). Comp., *Gnomologia: Adages and Proverbs,* 4110, 1732

There is a critical Minute for all Things.
THOMAS FULLER (1654–1734). Comp., *Gnomologia: Adages and Proverbs,* 4873, 1732

It is very important to be born or to live in a time that prizes highly the virtues and qualities in which you excel.
FRANCESCO GUICCIARDINI (1483–1540). *Remembrances,* C.31, 1530, tr. Mario Domandi, 1965

Come the right moment, a pawn can bring you victory.
HO CHI MINH (1892–1969). "Learning to Play Chess" (poem), *Ho Chi Minh on Revolution,* ed. Bernard B. Fall, 1967

Without ["the sense of timing"], great intelligence can be ineffective. Coupled with strong will, it can carry a mediocre mind to the heights.
SIDNEY HOOK (1902–1989). *The Hero in History: A Study in Limitation and Possibility,* 11.2 & 3, 1943

The right time comes when one is ready.
CARL G. JUNG (1875–1961). Quoted by Suzanne Percheron, "Memory of C. G. Jung," 1935–1961. In Ferne Jensen, ed., *C. G. Jung, Emma Jung and Toni Wolff: A Collection of Remembrances,* 1982

Death and taxes and childbirth! There's never any convenient time for any of them.
MARGARET MITCHELL (1900–1949). *Gone with the Wind,* 38, 1936

Books, doctrines, ideas have been compared to the flowers in a garden. 'Tis not always the best argument that prevails, and the gardener wins the prize who chooses his season right.
JOHN MORLEY (1838–1923). *Notes on Politics and History: A University Address,* 3, 1913

There is a moment in every battle at which the least maneuver is decisive and gives superiority, as one drop of water causes overflow.
NAPOLEON (1769–1821). Dictation, 1820?, *The Mind of Napoleon: A Selection from His Written and Spoken Words,* 295, ed. J. Christopher Herold, 1955

At times it is folly to hasten; at other times, to delay. The wise do everything in its proper time.
OVID (43 B.C.–A.D. 17?)

The main thing is to know and seize the critical moment.
CARDINAL de RETZ (1613–1679). *Memoirs of Cardinal de Retz,* 1, Grolier Society edition, undated

Edgar: Ripeness is all.
SHAKESPEARE (1564–1616). *King Lear,* 5.2.11, 1605

There is a time for departure even when there's no certain place to go.
TENNESSEE WILLIAMS (1911–1983). *Camino Real,* 8, 1953

For everything there is a season, and a time for every matter under heaven:
a time to be born, and a time to die;
a time to plant, and a time to pluck up what is planted.
ANONYMOUS (*BIBLE*). *Ecclesiastes,* 3:1–2

In love, sport, trade, and war, timing is a necessary but insufficient condition for success.
ANONYMOUS

Half the trouble in this world comes from saying "yes" too quick, and "no" not soon enough.
SAYING (AMERICAN)

The ripe melon falls of itself.
SAYING (CHINESE)

The value of an act is judged by its timing.
SAYING (TAOIST)

Everything in its time.
SAYING

Too much too soon; too little too late.
SAYING

TOBACCO

See also • Addiction ○ Advertising Copy & Slogans ○ Alcohol ○ Coffee ○ Drugs, Illegal ○ Public Relations: Anonymous

My neighbor stopped smoking yesterday. He is survived by a wife and child.
HARRY C. BAUER. In Herb Caen, column, *San Francisco Chronicle*, 23 April 1978

Smoking tobacco [is] a pacifier for adults.
A. A. BRILL (1874–1928). Psychoanalyst. As cited by Vance Packard, *The Hidden Persuaders*, 9, 1957

Tobacco, divine, rare, superexcellent tobacco, which goes far beyond all the panaceas, potable gold and philosopher's stones, a sovereign remedy to all diseases. A good vomit, I confess, a virtuous herb, if it be well qualified, opportunely taken, and medicinally used, but as it is commonly abused by most men, which take it as tinkers do ale, 'tis a plague, a mischief, a violent purger of goods, lands, health; hellish, devilish and damned tobacco, the ruin and overthrow of body and soul.
ROBERT BURTON (1577–1640). *The Anatomy of Melancholy*, 2.4.2.1, 1621-1651

The tobacco industry, the tobacco farmers, the federal government, all citizens ought to have an accurate and enlightened education program and research program to make the smoking of tobacco even more safe than it is today.
JIMMY CARTER (1924–). Speech at a "noisy tobacco country rally," Wilson (North Carolina), 5 August 1978. In Examiner News Services, "Carter Vow to Growers of Tobacco," *San Francisco Sunday Examiner & Chronicle*, 6 August 1978

Washington's capacity for justifying the unjustifiable is boundless. Another "good guy," former Johnson White House Adviser Harry McPherson, explains that he and his partners Ms. [Ann] Richards [former Texas governor] and Mr. [George] Mitchell [former Senate majority leader] took on their tobacco clients to advance the country's public health because the multibillion settlement will provide funds for programs aimed at cutting teen-age smoking and helping smokers quit their habit. In the Orwellianism of the season, he explained to The [New York] Times's Jill Abramson: "this is a chance to work on an issue that if it is completely successful would make a very large contribution to the public health of the country."
  The McPherson-Richards-Mitchell law firm has already earned more than $5 million this year from the five largest tobacco companies.
MAUREEN DOWD (1952–). "Integrity Clearance Sale," *New York Times*, 20 December 1997. In June 1997 tobacco lawyers and state attorneys generals agreed on a $368.5 billion settlement protecting the industry against future damage claims by smokers.

Back to Paris, yesterday at noon. Notable improvement, though my throat is still irritated. I ought to give up smoking. And as I write these words I light another cigarette.
ANDRÉ GIDE (1869–1951). Journal, 9 March 1930, tr. Justin O'Brien, 1951

The American Cancer Society, which held its 17th annual Great American Smokeout last week, says 418,000 Americans die from tobacco-related illnesses each year—nearly eight times as many Americans as were killed in all the years of Vietnam.
  In business, of course, it is dollars above all. If you have to step over corpses to collect your cash, so be it. Money excuses everything.
BOB HERBERT (1923–). "'If I Had Known,'" *New York Times*, 21 November 1995

The top executives of the seven largest American tobacco companies testified in Congress today that they did not believe that cigarettes were addictive, but that they would rather their own children did not smoke.
PHILIP J. HILTS. Opening paragraph, referring to hearings before the House Energy and Commerce Subcommittee on Health and the Environment, "Tobacco Chiefs Say Cigarettes Aren't Addictive," *New York Times*, 15 April 1994

When I don't smoke, I scarcely feel as if I'm living. I don't feel as if I'm living unless I'm killing myself.
RUSSELL HOBAN (1925–). *Turtle Diary*, 7, 1975

I am 45 years old, and I had been a smoker for 27 years. Since I began to jog in late November 1977, I haven't touched or wanted a cigarette. The mere thought of inhaling cigarette smoke, now, fills me with revulsion. I suspect that there is some biochemical or physiological connection between jogging (or running) and no desire to smoke.
JUDITH KNAUER. Letter to *Prevention*, September 1978

[Tobacco is] the single most important preventable cause of death, responsible for 1 out of every 6 deaths in the U.S.
C. EVERETT KOOP (1916–). Physician and surgeon general. In Anastasia Toufexis, "A Not-So-Happy Anniversary," *Time*, 23 January 1989

Years from now, I'm afraid that our nation will look back on this application of free trade policy [to the sale of tobacco products overseas] and find it scandalous, as the rest of the world does now. . . . At a time when we are pleading with foreign governments to stop the export of cocaine, it is the height of hypocrisy for the United States to export tobacco.
C. EVERETT KOOP (1916–). Physician and surgeon general. In Alexander Cockburn, "Getting Opium to the Masses: The Political Economy of Addiction," *Nation*, 30 October 1989

Stinking'st of the stinking kind,
Filth of the mouth and fog of the mind
CHARLES LAMB (1775–1834). "A Farewell to Tobacco" (8), *Poems*, 1818

For thy sake, TOBACCO, I
Would do anything but die.
CHARLES LAMB (1775–1834). "A Farewell to Tobacco" (11), *Poems*, 1818

When you think of the relative harm done by tobacco and drugs, it is amazing that tobacco company executives are treated as respectable people. They wear suits, and they have fine lawyers, but they do much more harm than drug peddlers.

The attorney general of Mississippi, Mike Moore, gave that reality blunt expression last weekend on CBS television's "60 Minutes." It was a revised version of the program originally held back for fear of a lawsuit by the Brown & Williamson Tobacco Corporation.

"I'm used to dealing with cocaine dealers and crack dealers," Mr. Moore said. "And I have never seen damage done like the tobacco company has done. There's no comparison."

> ANTHONY LEWIS (1027–). "Prohibition Folly," *New York Times,* 12 February 1996

For the majority of people, the use of tobacco has a beneficial effect, far better for you than taking tranquilizers.

> IAN G. MACDONALD. "A Los Angeles surgeon who smokes but doesn't inhale." In "Smoking and Health: The U.S. Decision," *Newsweek,* 18 November 1963

When [children] become early teenagers, the addictive industries claw at them in such subtle and nonsubtle ways—tobacco, alcohol, drugs. Four-hundred and twenty thousand American died last year from tobacco-related diseases. Most of the smokers are hooked under the age of fifteen. Talk about child molesters!

> RALPH NADER (1934–). Green Party presidential nomination acceptance speech, Los Angeles, 19 August 1996

I have every sympathy with the American who was so horrified by what he had read of the effects of smoking that he gave up reading.

> HENRY G. STRAUSS

The data that we have been able to see has all been statistical data that has not convinced me that smoking causes death.

> ANDREW H. TISCH (1949–). Lorillard, Inc. chairman. Testimony at hearings before the House Energy and Commerce Subcommittee on Health and the Environment, 14 April 1994. In photograph (balloon) accompanying Barry Meier, "Among Cigarette Makers, Old Habits Die Hard," *New York Times,* 7 September 1997

> THE TOBACCO INSTITUTE
> is pleased to announce that
> BONNIE ST. CLAIR PARKER
> formerly
> Staff Director
> and
> Staff Administrator
> Select Committee on Ethics
> United States Senate
> has joined The Institute as
> Senate Liaison
> Federal Government Relations

> THE TOBACCO INSTITUTE. April 1988, "Memo of the Month," *Washington Monthly,* October 1988

To cease smoking is the easiest thing. I ought to know. I've done it a thousand times.

> MARK TWAIN (1835–1910). *The Wit and Wisdom of Mark Twain,* p. 215, ed. Alex Ayres, 1987

Warning: The Surgeon General Has Determined That Cigarette Smoking Is Dangerous to You Health.

> U.S. SURGEON GENERAL. Statement required by federal law on cigarette packages and in cigarette ads, 1970s

In a move that stunned tobacco foes, the [American Cancer Society's] San Francisco unit announced that it would give its humanitarian award to Mayor [Willie] Brown, who has received more tobacco contributions than any other politician in U.S. history. . . .

Public records show that between 1981 and 1995, then-[California] Assembly Speaker Brown received more than $750,000 in campaign donations, gifts and legal fees from tobacco interests, while repeatedly voting with the tobacco lobby on bills directly affecting the cigarette industry's bottom line.

> LANCE WILLIAMS. "Cancer Society Honoring Tobacco Favorite Brown," *San Francisco Sunday Examiner & Chronicle,* 15 September 1996

❦

A person's right to smoke ends where the next person's nose begins.

> ANONYMOUS (AMERICAN)
> See Rights: Saying (American)

Cigarettes, they're killers.

> SLOGAN (AMERICAN). American Cancer Society, 1960s

TOLERANCE

See also • Dissent ○ Hate ○ Intolerance ○ Nonconformity ○ Nonconformity, Anti- ○ Prejudice ○ Reason

Religious tolerance is a kind of infidelity.

> AMBROSE BIERCE (1842–1914)

If there is but one truth, and you have that truth completely, toleration of differences means an encouragement to error, crime, evil, sin.

> CRANE BRINTON (1898–1968). On revolutionary fanaticism, *The Anatomy of Revolution,* 7.3, 1952

More and more people care about religious tolerance as fewer and fewer care about religion.

> ALEXANDER CHASE. *Perspectives,* 1966

Tolerance is the virtue of the man without convictions.

> G. K. CHESTERTON (1874–1936)

We are none of us tolerant in what concerns us deeply and entirely.

> SAMUEL TAYLOR COLERIDGE (1772–1834). *Letters, Conversations, and Recollections of S. T. Coleridge,* ed. Thomas Allsop, 1836

We tolerate when we have lost the power to persecute.

> PAUL ELDRIDGE (1888–1982). *Maxims for a Modern Man,* 863, 1965

We are all tolerant enough of those who do not agree with us, provided only they are sufficiently miserable.

> DAVID GRAYSON (1870–1946). *Adventures in Contentment,* 10, 1907

Tolerance is only another name for indifference.

> W. SOMERSET MAUGHAM (1874–1965). 1896, *A Writer's Notebook,* 1949

Mankind are greater gainers by suffering each other to live as seems good to themselves than by compelling each to live as seems good to the rest.

> JOHN STUART MILL (1806–1873). *On Liberty,* 1, 1859

The degree of tolerance [for individual differences] attainable at any moment depends on the strain under which society is maintaining its cohesion.

> GEORGE BERNARD SHAW (1856–1950). Preface ("Variability of Toleration") to *Saint Joan,* 1923

Nobody asks you of what religion you are, but if you can do the job.

> ALEXIS de TOCQUEVILLE (1805–1859). On the "extreme tolerance" he found in Detroit ("a fine American village"). Notebook, 22 July 1832, *Journey to America,* 4, tr. George Lawrence, 1971

We make allowances only for the faultless.

> VAUVENARGUES (1715–1747). *Reflections and Maxims,* 169, 1746, tr. F. G. Stevens, 1940

What is toleration? It is the prerogative of humanity. We are all steeped in weaknesses and errors: Let us forgive one another's follies, it is the first law of nature.

> VOLTAIRE (1715–1747). "Toleration" (1), *Philosophical Dictionary,* 1764, tr. Theodore Besterman, 1971

TOOLS

See also • Blame: Saying (Swahili) ○ Machines ○ Technology: [especially] Arnold J. Toynbee (2)

Man is a Tool-using Animal. . . . Nowhere do you find him without Tools; without Tools he is nothing, with Tools he is all.

> THOMAS CARLYLE (1795–1881). *Sartor Resartus: The Life and Opinions of Herr Teufelsdröckh,* 1.5, 1835

Have thy tools ready. God will find thee work.

> CHARLES KINGSLEY (1819–1875). English clergyman. Attributed

We become what we behold. We shape our tools and then our tools shape us.

> MARSHALL McLUHAN (1911–1980). In Lewis Lapham, "The Spanish Armadillo," *Harper's,* April 1997

Men have become the tools of their tools.

> HENRY DAVID THOREAU (1817–1862). Journal, 1845, undated

TORTURE

See also • Brainwashing ○ Crime ○ Cruelty ○ Dehumanization ○ Holocaust ○ Prison ○ Punishment ○ Punishment, Capital ○ Right to Silence ○ Terrorism ○ Tyranny ○ Violence ○ Witchcraft: Heinrich Kramer and James Sprenger (3)

Torture is a very humiliating experience. The goal is not to obtain information but to punish and break you so that you won't do anything against the authorities. You are made an example to others so that they will be too terrified to do anything either.

> ISABEL ALLENDE (1942–). Chilean writer. 1990

The human rights issue that dominates all others in the Republic of Guatemala is that people who oppose or are imagined to oppose the government are systematically seized without warrant, tortured, and murdered, and that these tortures and murders are part of a deliberate and long-standing program of the Guatemalan government.

> AMNESTY INTERNATIONAL. "Guatemala: A Government Program of Political Murder." Shortened from AI's report on Guatemala, 8 February 1981, *New York Review of Books,* 19 March 1981

Doctors, attached to the various torture centers [during the Algerian War], intervene after every session in order to put the tortured back into condition for new sessions. Under the circumstances, the important thing is for the prisoner not to give the slip to the team in charge of the questioning: in other words, to remain alive. Everything—heart stimulants, massive doses of vitamins—is used before, during, and after the sessions to keep the Algerian hovering between life and death. Ten times the doctor intervenes, ten times he gives the prisoner back to the pack of torturers.

> FRANTZ FANON (1925–1961). *A Dying Colonialism,* 4, 1959, tr. Haakon Chevalier, 1965

They tortured him—seeking in him their thoughts.

> STANISLAW J. LEC (1909–1966). *More Unkempt Thoughts,* p. 30, tr. Jacek Galazka, 1968

As long as human beings can sit and watch with hands folded while their fellowmen are tortured and butchered, so long will civilization be a hollow mockery, a wordy phantom suspended like a mirage above a swelling sea of murdered carcasses.

> HENRY MILLER (1891–1980). *The Colossus of Maroussi,* 2, 1941

The true inquisitor is a creature of policy, not a man of blood by taste.

> JOHN MORLEY (1838–1923). "Robespierre" (2), *Critical Miscellanies,* vol. 1, 1886

Make the skipper [of the seized fishing boat] speak, and I even give you authority to promise him his pardon if he gives information; and if he should seem to hesitate, you can go so far as to follow the custom as to men suspected of being spies, and squeeze his thumbs in the hammer of a musket.

> NAPOLEON (1769–1821). Letter to Gen. Nicolas Soult, 13 February 1804, *New Letters of Napoleon I,* tr. Lady Mary Loyd, 1898

No democracy is as stalked by terrorism as Israel. Because of that threat, Israeli law allows its security service to use what it calls "a moderate measure of physical pressure" when interrogating Palestinians. These measures, which include violent shaking and hanging shackled prisoners in painful positions, clearly come under the definition of torture in the international conventions that Israel has signed. Israel must vigorously protect its security, but not by the use of torture. . . .

The character of a country is determined in some measure by how it treats its enemies and prisoners.

> *NEW YORK TIMES.* "Using Torture in Israel" (editorial), 9 May 1997

There were times when his nerve so forsook him that he began shouting for mercy even before the beating began, when the mere sight of a fist drawn back for a blow was enough to make him pour forth a confession of real and imaginary crimes.

> GEORGE ORWELL (1903–1950). *Nineteen Eighty-Four*, 3.2., 1949

In Northern Ireland, sensory deprivation was deliberately used as part of the technique employed in the interrogation of suspected terrorists. The procedures were as follows. The heads of the detainees were covered with a thick black hood, except when they were being interrogated. They were subjected to a continuous monotonous noise of such volume that communication with other detainees was impossible. They were required to stand facing a wall with legs apart, leaning on their fingertips. In addition, they were deprived of sleep during the early days of the operation, and given no food or drink other than one round of bread and one pint of water at six-hourly intervals. . . .

   Psychiatric examination of these men after their release revealed persistent symptoms: nightmares, waking tension and anxiety, suicidal thought, depression, and a variety of physical complaints like headaches and peptic ulcers which are commonly considered to be connected with stress. Responsible psychiatric opinion considered that some, at least, of the hooded men would never recover from their experience.

> ANTHONY STORR (1920–). *Solitude: A Return to the Self*, 3, 1988. When the facts about this torture became known in Britain, there were demonstrations and protests. Eventually, in the early 1970s, Prime Minister Edward Heath banned the practice.

"Believe as we do or thou shalt be burned." This is the voice of a victorious party. It is the enforcement of uniformity against dissent. Systematic and legal torture then becomes an engine of uniformity. . . . Like every other system of policy it loses its effect on the imagination by familiarity, and that effect can be regained only by intensifying it. Therefore where torture has been long applied we find that it is developed to grades of incredible horror.

> WILLIAM GRAHAM SUMNER (1840–1910). *Folkways: A Study of the Sociological Importance of Usages, Manners, Customs, Mores, and Morals*, 233, 1907

TRACK & FIELD

See also • Sports

The art of running the mile consists, in essence, of reaching the threshold of unconsciousness at the instant of breasting the tape.

> PAUL O'NEIL. In "An SI Sampler," *Sports Illustrated*, 15 August 1955

TRADE (COMMERCE)

See also • Business (Commerce) ○ Competition ○ Corporations ○ Economics ○ Merchants & Customers ○ Money ○ Price ○ Profit & Loss ○ Self-Interest: Adam Smith (2) ○ Trade (Occupation) ○ Work

Nothing can be more surely established than that a Government which interferes with any trade injures that trade.

> WALTER BAGEHOT (1826–1877). *Lombard Street*, 4, 1873

Trade knows no flag.

> ANDREW CARNEGIE (1835–1919). In Colin Bingham, comp., *Men and Affairs: A Modern Miscellany*, p. 406, 1968

Trade. . . , like blood, should circularly flow.

> JOHN DRYDEN (1631–1700). *Annus Mirabilis*, 2, 1666

We rail at trade, but the historian of the world will see that it was the principle of liberty; that it settled America, and destroyed feudalism, and made peace and keeps peace; that it will abolish slavery.

> RALPH WALDO EMERSON (1803–1882). Journal, 31 December 1844

Trade follows the flag.

> JAMES A. FROUDE (1818–1894). In *Fraser's Magazine* (England), January 1870

The usual Trade and Commerce is cheating all round by Consent.

> THOMAS FULLER (1654–1734). Comp., *Gnomologia: Adages and Proverbs*, 4814, 1732

Trade could not be managed by those who manage it if it had much difficulty.

> SAMUEL JOHNSON (1709–1784). Letter to Hester Lynch Piozzi (Mrs. Thrale), 16 November 1779

Trade curses everything it handles; and though you trade in messages from heaven, the whole curse of trade attaches to the business.

> HENRY DAVID THOREAU (1817–1862). "Economy," *Walden; or Life in the Woods*, 1854

Trade must regulate itself.

> SAYING (AMERICAN)

TRADE (OCCUPATION)

See also • Ability ○ Merchants & Customers ○ Trade (Commerce) ○ Work

He that hath a Trade hath an Estate.

> BENJAMIN FRANKLIN (1706–1790). *Poor Richard's Almanack*, January 1742

Every Man to his Trade.

> THOMAS FULLER (1654–1734). Comp., *Gnomologia: Adages and Proverbs*, 1435, 1732

Jack of all trades and master of none.

> SAYING (ENGLISH)

TRADITION

See also • Custom ○ Law ○ Past

"Tradition" is very often an excuse word for people who don't want to change.

> RED BARBER (1908–1992). Baseball announcer. Radio interview, NPR, 4 August 1988

Tradition means giving votes to the most obscure of all classes, our ancestors. It is the democracy of the dead.

> G. K. CHESTERTON (1874–1936). *Orthodoxy,* 4, 1909

A love for tradition has never weakened a nation, indeed, it has strengthened nations in their hour of peril; but the new view must come, the world must roll forward.

> WINSTON CHURCHILL (1874–1965). House of Commons speech, 29 November 1944

Whatever long time has sanctioned,
that is a law forever;
the law tradition makes
is the law of nature.

> EURIPIDES (485?–406 B.C.). *The Bacchae,* l. 890, tr. William Arrowsmith, 1959

Tradition: A clock that tells what time it was.

> ELBERT HUBBARD (1856–1915). *The Roycroft Dictionary Concocted by Ali Baba and the Bunch on Rainy Days,* p. 154, 1914

Civilization is impossible without traditions, and progress impossible without the destruction of those traditions. The difficulty, and it is an immense difficulty, is to find a proper equilibrium between stability and variability.

> GUSTAVE LE BON (1841–1931). *The Crowd: A Study of the Popular Mind,* 2.1.2, 1895, Viking Press edition, 1960

The tradition of all the dead generations weighs like a nightmare on the brain of the living.

> KARL MARX (1818–1883). *The Eighteenth Brumaire of Louis Napoleon,* 1, 1852, *The Marx-Engels Reader,* 2nd ed., ed. Robert C. Tucker, 1978

Tradition is a guide and not a jailer.

> W. SOMERSET MAUGHAM (1874–1965). *The Summing Up,* 60, 1938

Tradition is living and active, but convention is passive and dead. Tradition does not form us automatically: we have to work to understand it. Convention is accepted passively, as a matter of routine.

> THOMAS MERTON (1915–1968). *No Man Is an Island,* 8.16, 1955

Traditionalists are pessimists about the future and optimists about the past.

> LEWIS MUMFORD (1895–1990). In Laurence J. Peter, *Peter's People,* 8, 1979

❧

To go back to tradition is the first step forward.

> SAYING (AFRICAN)

TRAGEDY

See also • Calamity ○ Comedy: [especially] Mel Brooks ○ Defeat ○ Disaster ○ Misfortune ○ Soul & Body: Oscar Wilde ○ Trouble ○ World: Horace Walpole

The tragedy of a man who has found himself out.

> J. M. BARRIE (1860–1937). *What Every Woman Knows,* 4, 1908

The tragedy of life is not that man loses but that he almost wins.

> HEYWOOD BROUN (1888–1939). "Sport for Art's Sake," *Pieces of Hate, and Other Enthusiasms,* 1922

All tragedies are finish'd by a death,
All comedies are ended by a marriage.

> LORD BYRON (1788–1824). *Don Juan,* 3.9, 1819–1824

A time comes when one can no longer feel the emotion of love. The only thing left is tragedy.

> ALBERT CAMUS (1913–1960). October 1941, *Notebooks: 1935–1942,* tr. Philip Thody, 1963

That there should one Man die ignorant who had capacity for Knowledge, this I call a tragedy.

> THOMAS CARLYLE (1795–1881). *Sartor Resartus: The Life and Opinions of Herr Teufelsdröckh,* 3.4, 1835

An American Tragedy.

> THEODORE DREISER (1871–1945). Book title, 1925

The cheapness of man of every day's tragedy.

> RALPH WALDO EMERSON (1803–1882). "Uses of Great Men," *Representative Men,* 1850

Melodramas are, by definition, black versus white, where the villain takes all the badness on himself and gives all the goodness to the hero; whereas, in tragedy, fault is always shared by the hero.

> ORRIN E. KLAPP (1915–). *Symbolic Leaders: Public Dramas and Public Men,* 3 (footnote #25), 1964

True tragedy may be defined as a dramatic work in which the outward failure of the principal personage is compensated for by the dignity and greatness of his character.

> JOSEPH WOOD KRUTCH (1893–1970). Introduction to Eugene O'Neill, *Nine Plays,* 1932

The great tragedy of life is not that men perish, but that they cease to love.

> W. SOMERSET MAUGHAM (1874–1965). *The Summing Up,* 77, 1938

The tragedy of life doesn't lie in not reaching your goal. The tragedy lies in having no goal to reach.

> BENJAMIN E. MAYS (1894–1984). Morehead College president. In Sara Rimer, "Arms Spending Draws Criticism at Barnard Rite," *New York Times,* 16 May 1985

The tragic feeling is evoked in us when we are in the presence of a character who is ready to lay down his life, if need be, to secure one thing—his sense of personal dignity.

> ARTHUR MILLER (1915–). "Tragedy and the Common Man," *New York Times,* 27 February 1949

Perhaps the real tragedy in the history of man came about . . . when he first realized that it was necessary for him to go outside of his own person to offer worship to a deity.

> FRIEDRICH NIETZSCHE (1844–1900). *My Sister and I,* 3.38, tr. Oscar Levy, 1951

The tragedy of man is what dies inside himself while he still lives.

> ALBERT SCHWEITZER (1875–1965)

The only real tragedy in life is the being used by personally mind-ed men for purposes which you recognize to be base.

> GEORGE BERNARD SHAW (1856–1950). Epistle dedicatory to *Man and Superman*, 1903

There are two tragedies in life. One is to lose your heart's desire. The other is to gain it.

> GEORGE BERNARD SHAW (1856–1950). *Man and Superman*, 4, 1903

Tragedy if it is not noble is not tragedy.

> PAGE SMITH (1917–1995). *The Historian and History*, 10, 1964

Is not the decisive difference between comedy and tragedy that tragedy denies us another chance?

> JOHN UPDIKE (1932–). *Self-Consciousness: Memoirs*, 6, 1989

In this world there are only two tragedies. One is not getting what one wants, and the other is getting it. The last is much the worst; the last is a real tragedy!

> OSCAR WILDE (1854–1900). *Lady Windermere's Fan*, 3, 1892

TRAINS

See also • Machines

There isn't a train I wouldn't take.

> EDNA ST. VINCENT MILLAY (1892–1950). "Travel," l. 11, 1921

The greatest benefit conferred by the railways is that they spare millions of draught-horses their miserable existence.

> ARTHUR SCHOPENHAUER (1788–1860). "On Religion" (3), 1851, *Essays and Aphorisms*, tr. R. J. Hollingdale, 1970

After the first powerful plain manifesto
The black statement of pistons, without more fuss
But gliding like a queen, she leaves the station.

> STEPHEN SPENDER (1909–1995). "The Express," 1933

TRANSFORMATION

See also • Books: Bell Hooks ○ Change ○ Children's Learning: E. M. Standing (1) ○ Civilization, Modern: Lewis Mumford ○ Compassion: Martin Luther King, Jr. ○ Faith: James W. Douglass ○ Goals: Lewis Mumford ○ Human Nature: Billy Graham ○ Internationalism: Lewis Mumford (2) ○ Liberation: Paulo Freire ○ Mysticism: Henri Bergson (6) ○ Religion: Anton T. Boisen, Jim Wallis ○ Revolution: Wes "Scoop" Nisker ○ Revolutionaries: Ho Chi Minh ○ Self-Realization (Becoming) ○ Self-Realization (Being) ○ The Unconscious: Lewis Mumford

[There] is a deliberate, terrific refusal to respond to anything but the deepest, highest, richest answer to the as yet unknown demand of some waiting void within: a kind of total strike, or rejection of the offered terms of life, as a result of which some power of transformation carries the problem to a plane of new magnitudes, where it is suddenly and finally resolved.

> JOSEPH CAMPBELL (1904–1987). *The Hero with a Thousand Faces*, 1.1.2, 1949

The sacred call is transformative. It is an invitation to our souls, a mysterious voice reverberating within, a tug on our hearts that can neither be ignored nor denied. It contains, by definition, the purest message and promise of essential freedom. It touches us at the center of our awareness. When such a call occurs and we hear it—*really* hear it—our shift to higher consciousness is assured. As Maimonides, the twelfth-century rabbinical authority, physician, and philosopher said,

"The sound of the shofar calls to us: Awaken, sleepers, from your sleep, arise, slumberers, from your slumber, and examine your deeds, . . . look after your own souls, and improve your ways."

> DAVID A. COOPER. Closing paragraphs, "Invitation to the Soul," *Parabola*, Spring 1994. The shofar is the ram's horn sounded in synagogue services during the Ten Days of Penitence.

Transformation means replacing old values with new ones in the evolution of conscious life.

> KAZIMIERZ DABROWSKI. Polish psychiatrist. Adapted. *Positive Disintegration*, 3, ed. Jason Aronson, 1964

He must dare to leap into the Origin, so as to live by the Truth and in the Truth, like one who has become one with it. He must become a pupil again, a beginner; conquer the last and steepest stretch of the way, undergo new transformations. If he survives its perils, then is his destiny fulfilled: face to face he beholds the unbroken Truth, the Truth beyond all truths, the formless Origin of origins, the Void which is the All; is absorbed into it and from it emerges reborn.

> EUGEN HERRIGEL (1885–1955). *Zen in the Art of Archery*, p. 109, 1953, tr. R. F. C. Hull, 1964

He must get beyond the opposites in which he is still caught, as a prelude to a transformation that is no longer of his own doing, but is something that "happens" to him.

> EUGEN HERRIGEL (1885–1955). "Zen Priests," *The Method of Zen*, 1960, ed. Hermann Tausend and tr. R. F. C. Hull, 1964

You don't go through a deep personal transformation without some kind of dark night of the soul.

> SAM KEEN (1931–). Jerry Brown radio interview, KPFA, Berkeley (California), 19 October 1995

Any transformation of one person invites accommodating trans-formations in others. But we [i.e., society] have highly developed strategies of exclusion and isolation to forestall such eventualities. It threatens a macrorevolution. These possibilities of revolution are occurring all the time, and the forces of counterrevolution and reaction are very strong. Most of the microsocial revolutions of this order are "nipped in the bud."

> R. D. LAING (1927–1989). "Metanoia: Some Experiences at Kingsley Hall, London," 1968. In Hendrik M. Ruitenbeek, ed., *Going Crazy: The Radical Therapy of R. D. Laing and Others*, 1972

The principal means by which the creative possibilities of the deep unconscious may be reached is the transforming symbol. Anyone wholeheartedly engaging in the experiment in depth will find, as a normal fact of experience, that the unconscious repeat-edly produces shapes, objects, phrases, ideas, which have this peculiar quality: if put to their right use they make possible a re-direction of energy and, by so doing, progressively transform the man who uses them.

> P. W. MARTIN (1893–?). *Experiment in Depth: A Study of the Work of Jung, Eliot and Toynbee*, 6, 1955

Individuation is something which is wrought upon a man, not something he can do for himself. This does not mean that the man's part is simply to sit back and wait. On the contrary, he has to put all he has—and much more than he knows he has—in the work. But the process itself, the "inward transforming experience," is not within his power to command.

> P. W. MARTIN (1893–?). *Experiment in Depth: A Study of the Work of Jung, Eliot and Toynbee,* 8, 1955

Characteristically, it is when a man is at the end of his strength and endurance, but nevertheless holds on, that the transforming symbol floats into consciousness.

> P. W. MARTIN (1893–?). *Experiment in Depth: A Study of the Work of Jung, Eliot and Toynbee,* 11, 1955

An underlying urge to self-transformation possibly lies at the basis of all existence, finding expression in the process of growth, development, renewal, directed change, perfection.

> LEWIS MUMFORD (1895–1990). *The Transformations of Man,* 4.2, 1956

Growth and self-transformation cannot be delegated.

> LEWIS MUMFORD (1895–1990). *The Transformations of Man,* 9.6, 1956

Ripeness is the condition for any organic transformation. . . . Today, neither the technical means nor the relevant social pressures are absent: it is rather the inner readiness that is lacking. Our generation needs faith in the process of life sufficient to bring about a willing surrender to life's new demands.

> LEWIS MUMFORD (1895–1990). *The Transformations of Man,* 9.6, 1956

Do not be conformed to this world but be transformed by the renewal of your mind, that you may prove what is the will of God, what is good and acceptable and perfect.

> PAUL (A.D. 1st cent.). *Romans* 12:2

TRAVEL

See also • Cities ○ Leisure ○ Nations

People say you have to travel to see the world. Sometimes I think that if you just stay in one place and keep your eyes open, you're going to see just about all that you can handle.

> PAUL AUSTER (1947–). *Smoke* (film), 1995, spoken by Harvey Keitel (in the role of Auggie Wren, a Brooklyn cigar store owner)

The traveler was active; he went strenuously in search of people, of adventure, or experience. The tourist is passive; he expects interesting things to happen to him. He goes "sightseeing."

> DANIEL J. BOORSTIN (1914–). *The Image: A Guide to Pseudo-Events in America,* 3.2, 1961

If it is better to travel than to arrive, it is because traveling is a constant arriving, while arrival that precludes further traveling is most easily attained by going to sleep or dying.

> JOHN DEWEY (1859–1952). *Human Nature and Conduct: An Introduction to Social Psychology,* 4.1, 1922

Coningsby: There is nothing I should like so much as to travel.
The Stranger: You are traveling. Every moment is travel, if understood.

> BENJAMIN DISRAELI (1804–1881). Format adapted. *Coningsby: Or, The New Generation,* 3.1, 1844

Traveling is a fool's paradise. We owe to our first travels the discovery that place is nothing. At home I dream that at Naples, at Rome, I can be intoxicated with beauty and lose my sadness. I pack my trunk, embrace my friends, embark on the sea, and at last wake up in Naples and there beside me is the Stern Fact, the Sad Self unrelenting, identical, that I fled from. . . . My Giant goes with me wherever I go.

> RALPH WALDO EMERSON (1803–1882). Journal, 28 May 1839

If an Ass goes a-traveling, he'll not come home a Horse.

> THOMAS FULLER (1654–1734). Comp., *Gnomologia: Adages and Proverbs,* 2668, 1732

The longest journey
Is the journey inwards.

> DAG HAMMARSKJÖLD (1905–1961). 1950, *Markings,* tr. Leif Sjöberg and W. H. Auden, 1964

The soul of a journey is liberty, perfect liberty, to think, feel, do just as one pleases.

> WILLIAM HAZLITT (1778–1830). "On Going a Journey," *Table Talk,* 1822

The world may be known
Without leaving the house.

> LAO-TZU (6th cent. B.C.). *The Way of Life,* 47, tr. R. B. Blakney, 1955

Remember wherever you go, there you are.

> EARL MacRAUCH. *The Adventures of Buckaroo Bonzi Across the Eighth Dimension* (film), 1984

Though they carry nothing forth with them, yet in all their journey they lack nothing. For wheresoever they come, they be at home.

> SIR THOMAS MORE (1478–1535). "Of Their Journeying or Travelling Abroad," *Utopia,* bk. 2, 1516, tr. Ralph Robinson, 1937

A rolling stone gathers no moss.

> PUBLIUS SYRUS (85–43 B.C.). *Moral Sayings,* 524, tr. Darius Lyman, Jr., 1862

A rolling stone gathers momentum.

> VIRGINIA M. SHARPLES. "Sharples's Philosophy." In Paul Dickson, comp., *The Official Explanations,* p. 202, 1980

Why do you wonder that globe-trotting does not help you, seeing that you always take yourself with you? The reason which set you wandering is ever at your heels.

> SOCRATES (470?–399 B.C.). In Seneca the Younger (5? B.C.–A.D. 65). "On Travel as a Cure for Discontent," *Moral Letters to Lucilius,* 28.2, tr. Richard M. Gummere, 1918

To travel hopefully is a better thing than to arrive.

> ROBERT LOUIS STEVENSON (1850–1894). "El Dorado," *Virginibus Puerisque,* 1881

A simple woman down in Tyngsborough, at whose house I once stopped to get a draught of water, when I said, recognizing the bucket, that I had stopped there nine years before for the same purpose, asked if I was not a traveler, supposing that I had been traveling ever since, and had now come round again.

> HENRY DAVID THOREAU (1817–1862). "Thursday," *A Week on the Concord and Merrimack Rivers,* 1849

I have traveled a good deal in Concord.

> HENRY DAVID THOREAU (1817–1862). "Economy," *Walden; or Life in the Woods,* 1854

Only that traveling is good which reveals to me the value of home and enables me to enjoy it better.

> HENRY DAVID THOREAU (1817–1862). Journal, 11 March 1856

My advice to any traveler who is traveling in order to learn would be: "Fight tooth and nail to be permitted to travel in what is technically the least efficient way."

> ARNOLD J. TOYNBEE (1889–1975). *Experiences,* 1.6.2, 1969

I girdled Asia, bore her blows,
Her summer suns, her winter snows,
Trod plain and hill from Rum to Ch'in:
Yet all I learnt I found within.

> ARNOLD J. TOYNBEE (1889–1975). Untitled (complete poem), written in China, December 1929. *Experiences,* 3.6, 1969

Afoot and light-hearted I take to the open road,
Healthy, free, the world before me,
The long brown path before leading wherever I choose.

> WALT WHITMAN (1819–1892). Opening lines, "Song of the Open Road," 1856, *Leaves of Grass,* 1855–1892

Long having wander'd since, round the earth having wander'd,
Now I face home again, very pleas'd and joyous,
(But where is what I started for so long ago?
And why is it yet unfound?)

> WALT WHITMAN (1819–1892). "Facing West from California's Shores," 1860, *Leaves of Grass,* 1855–1892

This ain't the Waldorf; if it was, you wouldn't be here.

> ANONYMOUS (AMERICAN). Notice in country hotels, 1900?

If you lived here, you'd be home now.

> ANONYMOUS. Highway sign. In Arthur Bloch, comp., *Murphy's Law: Book Two,* p. 73, 1980

The heaviest baggage for a traveler is an empty purse.

> SAYING (ENGLISH)

Good company on the road is the shortest cut.

> SAYING (ITALIAN)

Wherever you go, the sky is the same color.

> SAYING (PERSIAN)

TREATIES

See also • Alliances ○ Appeasement ○ Diplomacy ○ International Relations ○ Negotiation ○ Neutrality

Treaties are like roses and young girls. They last while they last.

> CHARLES de GAULLE (1890–1970). On Franco-German treaty talks. In "The Unvisit," *Time,* 12 July 1963

Weak nations sign treaties; strong ones break them.

> PAUL ELDRIDGE (1888–1982). *Maxims for a Modern Man,* 2001, 1965

No state has ever entered a treaty for any other reason than self-interest. A statesman who has any other motive would deserve to be hung.

> JOHANNES HALLER. German writer. *The Aero Buelow,* in Reinhold Niebuhr, *Moral Man and Immoral Society,* 4, 1932

The best negotiated treaties are but the law of the stronger.

> VAUVENARGUES (1715–1747). *Reflections and Maxims,* 309, 1746, tr. F. G. Stevens, 1940

Treaties which are not built upon reciprocal benefits are not likely to be of long duration.

> GEORGE WASHINGTON (1732–1799). Letter to Comte de Moustier, 26 March 1788

TREES

See also • Forests ○ Heaven: Micah ○ Nature ○ Wilderness: [especially] John Muir (3) ○ Woods

Of all man's works of art, a cathedral is greatest. A vast and majestic tree is greater than that.

> HENRY WARD BEECHER (1813–1887). "Nature," *Proverbs from Plymouth Pulpit,* ed. William Drysdale, 1887

Pines a thousand years old. Every year they must go farther for them: they recede, like beavers and Indians, before the white man.

> RALPH WALDO EMERSON (1803–1882). Journal, 1846, undated

On the banks, on both sides of the river, there will grow all kinds of trees for food. Their leaves will not wither nor their fruit fail, but they will bear fresh fruit every month, because the water for them flows from the sanctuary. Their fruit will be for food, and their leaves for healing.

> EZEKIEL (6th cent. B.C.). *Ezekiel* 47:12

He that plants trees loves others beside himself.

> THOMAS FULLER (1654–1734). Comp., *Gnomologia: Adages and Proverbs,* 2248, 1732

The trees reflected in the river—they are unconscious of a spiritual world so near them. So are we.

> NATHANIEL HAWTHORNE (1804–1864). 27 July 1844, *The American Notebooks,* ed. Claude M. Simpson, 1932

I think that I shall never see
A poem lovely as a tree. . . .
Poems are made by fools like me,
But only God can make a tree.

> JOYCE KILMER (1886–1918). Title poem, *Trees and Other Poems,* 1914. Kilmer was killed in action during World War I.

I think that I shall never see
A billboard lovely as a tree.
Indeed, unless the billboards fall
I'll never see a tree at all.

> OGDEN NASH (1902–1971). "Song of the Open Road," *Happy Days,* 1933

Once you've seen one redwood, you've seen them all.

> RONALD REAGAN (1911–). In Ted Morgan, "The Good Life," *New York Times Magazine,* 4 July 1976

A tree drops a leaf on my shoulder and goes back to dreaming.
    JULES RENARD (1864–1910). Journal, October 1904. tr. Louise Bogan
        and Elizabeth Roget, 1964

A man does not plant a tree for himself; he plants it for posterity.
    ALEXANDER SMITH (1830–1867). Dreamthorp, 11, 1863

The redwoods, once seen, leave a mark or create a vision that stays with you always. No one has ever successfully painted or photographed a redwood tree. The feeling they produce is not transferable. From them comes silence and awe. It's not only their unbelievable stature, nor the color which seems to shift and vary under your eyes, no, they are not like any trees we know, they are ambassadors from another time.
    JOHN STEINBECK (1902–1968). Travels with Charley: In Search of
        America, 3, 1962

This poor globe, how it must itch in many places! Will no god be kind enough to spread a salve of birches over its sores?
    HENRY DAVID THOREAU (1817–1862). "Tuesday," A Week on the
        Concord and Merrimack Rivers, 1849

❧

You can always tell a dogwood by its bark.
    ANONYMOUS (AMERICAN)

Out of the ground the Lord God made to grow every tree that is pleasant to the sight and good for food, the tree of life also in the midst of the garden, and the tree of the knowledge of good and evil.
    ANONYMOUS (BIBLE). Referring to "the garden in Eden, the east,"
        Genesis 2:9

A civilization flourishes when people plant trees under whose shade they will never sit.
    SAYING (GREEK). In Maureen Dowd, "Letters From the Edge," New
        York Times, 25 January 1996

TRIALS

See also • Crime ◦ Judges ◦ Juries ◦ Justice ◦ Law ◦ Lawyers ◦ Liberty: Felix Frankfurter ◦ Punishment ◦ Right to Silence ◦ Witnesses

This trial is a travesty; it's a travesty of a mockery of a sham of a mockery of a travesty of two mockeries of a sham. I move for a mistrial.
    WOODY ALLEN (1935–). Bananas (film), 1971, spoken by Allen (in the
        role of Fielding Mellish)

Bring in the guilty bastard. We'll give him a fair trial, and then we'll hang him.
    ROY BEAN (1825?–1903). Jurist

It is better that ten guilty persons escape than one innocent suffer.
    WILLIAM BLACKSTONE (1723–1780). Commentaries on the Laws of
        England, 4.27, 1765–1769

To declare that in the administration of the criminal law the end justifies the means—to declare that the government may commit crimes in order to secure the conviction of a private criminal—would bring terrible retribution.
    LOUIS D. BRANDEIS (1856–1941). Supreme Court associate justice. In
        Edward Bennett Williams, One Man's Freedom, 7, 1962

One of the fundamental tenets of our criminal justice system is that prosecutors must be bound to seek the truth and live by it, whether that leads to convictions or acquittals.
    DICK BURR. Texas Resource Center litigation director. In Sam Howe
        Verhovek, "Texas Cleared to Execute Man in Unusual Case," New York
        Times, 4 January 1995

Justice, though due to the accused, is due to the accuser also.
    BENJAMIN N. CARDOZO (1870–1938). Snyder v. Commonwealth of
        Massachusetts, 1934

"Let the jury consider their verdict," the King said, for about the twentieth time that day.
    "No, no!" said the Queen. "Sentence first—verdict afterwards."
    LEWIS CARROLL (1832–1898). Alice's Adventures in Wonderland, 12, 1865

Lucius Cassius, whom the Roman people considered the wisest and most conscientious of judges, was in the habit of asking repeatedly in trials, "who has profited by it." Such is the way of the world: no man attempts to commit a crime without the hope of profit. (Italics added.)
    CICERO (106–43 B.C.). Pro sexto roscio amerino, 30, tr. John Henry
        Freese, 1930 (Popular version: For whose advantage?)

Agree, for the Law is costly.
    JOHN CLARKE (1596–1658). Comp., Proverbs: English and Latine,
        p. 62, 1639

In all criminal prosecutions, the accused shall enjoy the right to a speedy and public trial, by an impartial jury of the State and district wherein the crime shall have been committed, . . . and to be informed of the nature and cause of the accusation; to be confronted with the witnesses against him; to have compulsory process for obtaining witnesses in his favor, and to have the assistance of counsel for his defense.
    CONSTITUTION OF THE UNITED STATES. Bill of Rights, Sixth
        Amendment, 15 December 1791

I think it a less evil that some criminals should escape than that the Government should play an ignoble part.
    OLIVER WENDELL HOLMES, JR. (1841–1935). Olmstead v. United States,
        1928

It is more dangerous that even a guilty person should be punished without the forms of law than that he should escape.
    THOMAS JEFFERSON (1743–1826). Letter to William Carmichael, 27 May
        1788

To no one will we sell, to no one will we deny or delay right or justice.
    MAGNA CHARTA. English charter of rights. 40, A.D. 1215

He confesses his crime who flees the tribunal.
    PUBLIUS SYRUS (85–43 B.C.). Moral Sayings, 256, tr. Darius Lyman, Jr.,
        1862

Justice, which is quick and which dispenses with the protections of freedom is rarely justice.

> EDWARD BENNETT WILLIAMS (1920–1988). *One Man's Freedom,* 11, 1962

It must be admitted that our present process of adjudication lack[s] both simplicity and promptness, that they are necessarily expensive, and that a rich litigant can almost always tire a poor one out and readily cheat him of his rights by simply leading him through an endless maze of appeals and technical delays.

> WOODROW WILSON (1856–1924). *Constitutional Government in the United States,* 6, 1908

❦

In civil cases money talks; in criminal cases money walks.

> ANONYMOUS

No weight whatever to confessions outside the courtroom!

> ANONYMOUS

An act does not make one guilty unless the mind is guilty.

> SAYING (LATIN)

An act done against your will is not your act.

> SAYING (LATIN)

The burden of proof lies upon him who affirms, not upon him who denies.

> SAYING (LATIN)

Where there is consent, there is no injury.

> SAYING (LATIN)

He that goes to law holds a wolf by the ears.

> SAYING. In Robert Burton, "Democritus to the Reader," *The Anatomy of Melancholy,* 1621–1651

Justice delayed is justice denied.

> SAYING

TRIFLES

See also • Cause & Effect: Georg Christoph Lichtenberg ○ Details ○ Failure ○ Success

The most important events . . . are often determined by very trivial [things].

> CICERO (106–43 B.C.). *Philippics,* 5.10, tr. C. D. Yonge, 1903

Trifles make the sum of life.

> CHARLES DICKENS (1812–1870). *David Copperfield,* 53, 1850

You know my method. It is founded upon the observance of trifles.

> SIR ARTHUR CONAN DOYLE (1859–1930). "The Boscombe Valley Mystery," *The Adventures of Sherlock Holmes,* 1892

He that despiseth small things will perish by little and little.

> RALPH WALDO EMERSON (1803–1882). "Prudence," *Essays: First Series,* 1841

A flake of snow brought the avalanche down.

> RALPH WALDO EMERSON (1803–1882). Journal, 1844?–1845?, undated

Be not disturbed at trifles, or at accidents common or unavoidable.

> BENJAMIN FRANKLIN (1706–1790). Virtue #11 ("Tranquillity"), 1784, *Autobiography,* 1798

A small Leak will sink a great Ship.

> THOMAS FULLER (1654–1734). Comp., *Gnomologia: Adages and Proverbs,* 407, 1732

For want of a nail the shoe is lost, for want of a shoe the horse is lost, for want of a horse the rider is lost.

> GEORGE HERBERT (1593–1633). Comp., *Outlandish Proverbs,* 499, 1640

From a small spark a huge fire.

> JAMES HOWELL (1593–1666). Comp., "Spanish" (p. 11), *Paroimiographia: Proverbs, or Old Sayed Sawes & Adages in English . . . Italian, French and Spanish,* 1659

The human tendency to regard little things as important has produced very many great things.

> GEORG CHRISTOPH LICHTENBERG (1742–1799). *Aphorisms,* G.46, 1806, tr. R. J. Hollingdale, 1990

Avoid trivia.

> GEORGE C. MARSHALL (1880–1959). General and secretary of state. Remark to the author. In George F. Kennan, *Memoirs: 1925–1950,* 14, 1967

Light minds are captivated by trifles.

> OVID (43 B.C.–A.D. 17?). *The Art of Love,* 1.159, tr. Peter Green, 1982

Nature makes a single trivial error sufficient to cause failure in a design, but correctness in every detail barely enough for success.

> POLYBIUS (208?–126? B.C.). *The Histories,* 9.12, tr. W. R. Paton, 1925

I believe that the mind can be permanently profaned by the habit of attending to trivial things, so that all our thoughts shall be tinged with triviality.

> HENRY DAVID THOREAU (1817–1862). "Life Without Principle," *Atlantic,* October 1863

You've got to think about "big things" while you're doing small things, so that all the small things go in the right direction.

> ALVIN TOFFLER (1928–). 1988

A consideration of petty circumstances is the tomb of great things.

> VOLTAIRE (1694–1778). In James Russell Lowell, "Abraham Lincoln," 1864, *My Study Windows,* 1871

A grain of sand in a man's flesh, and empires totter and fall!

> ÉMILE ZOLA (1840–1902). Referring to Napoleon III's gallstone, *The Downfall,* 1892

❦

The last straw broke the camel's back.

> SAYING

TROUBLE

See also • Calamity ○ Defeat ○ Difficulty ○ Disaster ○ Misfortune ○ Struggle ○ Tragedy ○ Unhappiness

The Wicked grow worse, and the good Men better for Trouble.

> THOMAS FULLER (1654–1734). Comp., *Gnomologia: Adages and Proverbs,* 4826, 1732

Trouble creates a capacity to handle it.

> OLIVER WENDELL HOLMES, JR. (1841–1935)

Nobody ever grew despondent lookin' fer trouble.

> KIN HUBBARD (1868–1930). *Abe Martin: Hoss Sense and Nonsense,* p. 67, 1926

Man is born to trouble
as the sparks fly upward.

> JOB. *Job* 5:7

We all have strength enough to endure the troubles of others.

> LA ROCHEFOUCAULD (1613–1680). *Maxims,* 19, 1665, tr. Leonard Tancock, 1959

> See Adversity: Mark Twain ○ Grief: Shakespeare (3) ○ Misfortune: Alexander Pope

If we do not deal with our troubles, they are sure to deal with us.

> ANN MORROW LINDBERGH (1906–). *The Wave of the Future: A Confession of Faith,* p. 34, 1940

there is always
a comforting thought
in time of trouble when
it is not our trouble.

> DON MARQUIS (1878–1937). "comforting thoughts," *archy does his part,* 1935

People could survive their natural trouble all right if it weren't for the trouble they make for themselves.

> OGDEN NASH (1902–1971). "Little Miss Muffet Sat on a Prophet—And Quite Right," *I'm a Stranger Here Myself,* 1938

In a troubled State we must do as in foul weather upon the Thames: not think to cut directly through so the boat may be quickly full of water; but rise and fall as the waves do, give as much as conveniently we can.

> JOHN SELDEN (1584–1654). "Power: State" (10), *Table Talk,* 1689, ed. Frederick Pollock, 1927

Many of our troubles may be explained from the fact that we live according to a pattern, and, instead of arranging our lives according to reason, are led astray by convention.

> SENECA THE YOUNGER (5? B.C.–A.D. 65). "On the Conflict between Pleasure and Virtue," *Moral Letters to Lucilius,* 123.6, tr. Richard M. Gummere, 1918]

Troubles hurt the most
when they prove self-inflicted.

> SOPHOCLES (496?–406 B.C.). *Oedipus Rex,* l. 1231, tr. David Grene, 1942

> See Misfortune: Oscar Wilde

At the least, bear [trouble] bravely if you cannot bear it cheerfully.

> THOMAS à KEMPIS (1380–1471). *The Imitation of Christ,* 3.57, tr. Leo Sherley-Price, 1952

❧

Never trouble trouble till trouble troubles you.

> SAYING (ENGLISH)

> See Prudence: Rules: Saying (2)

TRUST

See also • Belief ○ Distrust ○ Faith ○ God & Man—First Person: Job ○ Loyalty ○ Self-Trust

Trust only those who stand to lose as much as you when things go wrong.

> BRALEK'S RULE FOR SUCCESS. In Arthur Bloch, comp., "Expertsmanship," *Murphy's Law: Book Three,* 1982

Trust, *v.* To lay oneself open to deception.

> VICTOR L. CAHN (1948–). *The Disrespectful Dictionary,* unpaged, 1974

First try and then trust.

> JOHN CLARKE (1596–1658). Comp., *Proverbs: English and Latine,* p. 90, 1639

Put your trust in God, my boys, but mind to keep your powder dry.

> OLIVER CROMWELL (1599–1658). Attributed. Speech to his army at the Battle of Edgehill (England), 23 October 1642

Thrust ivrybody—but cut th' ca-ards.

> FINLEY PETER DUNNE (1867–1936). "Casual Observations," *Mr. Dooley's Philosophy,* 1900

All I have seen teaches me to trust the Creator for all I have not seen.

> RALPH WALDO EMERSON (1803–1882). "Immortality," *Letters and Social Aims,* 1876

It is an equal Failing to trust everybody and to trust nobody.

> THOMAS FULLER (1654–1734). Comp., *Gnomologia: Adages and Proverbs,* 2893, 1732

In the darkest night to be certain of the dawn . . . to go through Hell and to continue to trust in the goodness of God—this is the challenge and the way.

> ABRAHAM JOSHUA HESCHEL (1907–1972). *A Passion for Truth,* 9, 1973

Trust what moves you most deeply.

> SAM KEEN (1931–). *Beginnings Without End,* 7, 1975

And this be our motto, "In God is our trust."

> FRANCIS SCOTT KEY (1779–1843). "The Star-Spangled Banner" (U.S. national anthem), 4, 13–14 September 1814

Trusting in Him who can go with me, and remain with you, and be everywhere for good, let us confidently hope that all will yet be well.

> ABRAHAM LINCOLN (1809–1865). Upon his departure for Washington to assume his duties as President two months before the outbreak of the Civil War, "Farewell Address," Springfield (Illinois), 11 February 1861

It is better to trust virtue than fortune.

> PUBLIUS SYRUS (85–43 B.C.). *Moral Sayings,* 974, tr. Darius Lyman, Jr., 1862

Trust is the coin of the realm.

> GEORGE P. SHULTZ (1920–). Speech, 9 January 1989

O, yet we trust that somehow good
  Will be the final goal of ill. . . .
Behold, we know not anything;
  I can but trust that good shall fall
  At last—far off—at last, to all,
And every winter change to spring.

> ALFRED, LORD TENNYSON (1809–1892). *In Memoriam A. H. H.*, 54, 1850

Trust one who has gone through it.

> VIRGIL (70–19 B.C.). *Aeneid*, 11.283

❦

Trust everyone till you have reason not to.

> ANONYMOUS

Trust in God but tie your camel.

> SAYING (ARAB)
>
> See Prudence: Rules: George Herbert (1)

Trust in the Lord with all you heart,
  and do not rely on your own insight.
In all your ways acknowledge him,
  and he will make straight your paths.

> SAYING (*BIBLE*). *Proverbs* 3:5–6

Trust in God but put your shoulder to the wheel.

> SAYING (POLISH)

Trust, but verify!

> SAYING (RUSSIAN)

Trust in God but look to yourself.

> SAYING (RUSSIAN)

TRUTH

See also • Creativity ○ Deception ○ Discovery ○ Errors ○ Facts ○ Falsehood ○ Honesty ○ Ideas ○ Illusion ○ Intuition: Arthur Koestler ○ Knowledge ○ Lying ○ Philosophy ○ Propaganda ○ Reality ○ Truth & Untruth ○ Truthfulness ○ War: Hiram Johnson ○ Wisdom ○ Words ○ Writers: [especially] Anne Lamott

The truth which makes men free is for the most part the truth which men prefer not to hear.

> HERBERT AGAR (1897–1980). *A Time for Greatness*, 7, 1942

Why does truth engender hatred?

> ST. AUGUSTINE (A.D. 354–430). *Confessions*, 10.23, A.D. 400?, tr. R. S. Pine-Coffin, 1961

What is Truth? said jesting Pilate; and would not stay for an answer.

> FRANCIS BACON (1561–1626). Opening words, "Of Truth," *Essays*, 1625

Pushing any truth out very far, you are met by a counter-truth.

> HENRY WARD BEECHER (1813–1887). "Truth," *Proverbs from Plymouth Pulpit*, ed. William Drysdale, 1887

The truth shall make men free, but they must freely accept it and not be brought to it by force.

> NICOLAS BERDYAEV (1874–1948)

Az a gineral thing, if yu want tew git at the truth ov a perlitikal argyment, hear both sides and beleave neither.

> JOSH BILLINGS (1818–1885). *His Sayings*, 77, 1867

Two sorts of truths[:] profound truths recognized by the fact that the opposite is also a profound truth, in contrast to trivialities where opposites are obviously absurd.

> NIELS BOHR (1885–1962). Danish nuclear physicist. Quoted by Hans Bohr, "My Father." In Stefan Rozental, ed., *Niels Bohr: His Life and Work as Seen by His Friends and Colleagues*, 1967 (1964)

"Truth" has been displaced by "believability" as the test of the statements which dominate our lives.

> DANIEL J. BOORSTIN (1914–). *The Image: A Guide to Pseudo-Events in America*, 5.4, 1961

For the masses, truth originated in authority rather than in the evidence of their own senses or the conclusions arrived at by independent thought.

> J. A. C. BROWN (1911–1964). *Techniques of Persuasion: From Propaganda to Brainwashing*, 1, 1963

Men take so much Delight in lying that Truth is sometime[s] forced to disguise herself in the habit of Falsehood to get [attention].

> SAMUEL BUTLER (1613–1680). "Criticisms upon Books and Authors," *Prose Observations*, ed. Hugh de Quehen, 1979

'Tis strange—but true; for truth is always strange;
  Stranger than fiction: if it could be told.

> LORD BYRON (1788–1824). *Don Juan*, 14.101, 1819–1824

What we call basic truths are simply the ones we discover after all the others.

> ALBERT CAMUS (1913–1960). *The Fall*, p. 84, tr. Justin O'Brien, 1956

There are two kinds of truth: the truth that lights the way and the truth that warms the heart. The first of these is science, and the second is art.

> RAYMOND CHANDLER (1888–1959). "Great Thought," *The Notebooks of Raymond Chandler*, 1976

Truths begin by a conflict with the police and end by calling them in.

> E. M. CIORAN (1911–1995). *A Short History of Decay*, 1 ("Itinerary of Hate"), 1949, tr. Richard Howard, 1975

Truth—is as old as God—
His Twin identity
And will endure as long as He
A Co-Eternity—

> EMILY DICKINSON (1830–1886). "Truth—is as old as God," 1864?

For Truth has such a face and such a mien,
As to be lov'd needs only to be seen.

> JOHN DRYDEN (1631–1700). *The Hind and the Panther*, 1.33, 1687

If God were able to backslide from the truth, I would cling to the truth and let God go.

> MEISTER ECKHART (A.D. 1260?–1328?)

Truth is what stands the test of experience.

> ALBERT EINSTEIN (1879–1955). Closing words, "The Laws of Science and the Laws of Ethics," 1950, *Out of My Later Years,* rev. ed., 16, 1956 (1950)

Wherever the truth is injured, defend it.

> RALPH WALDO EMERSON (1803–1882). Journal, 29 March 1834

Every involuntary repulsion that arises in your mind, give heed unto. It is the surface of a central truth.

> RALPH WALDO EMERSON (1803–1882). Journal, 14 October 1834

The one condition coupled with the gift of truth is its use.

> RALPH WALDO EMERSON (1803–1882). "The Method of Nature." Address, Waterville (later Colby) College (Maine), 11 August 1841

God offers to every mind its choice between truth and repose. Take which you please—you can never have both. Between these, as a pendulum, man oscillates.

> RALPH WALDO EMERSON (1803–1882). "Intellect," *Essays: First Series,* 1841

What is true anywhere is true everywhere.

> RALPH WALDO EMERSON (1803–1882). "Culture," *The Conduct of Life,* 1860

The truth, the hope of any time, must always be sought in the minorities.

> RALPH WALDO EMERSON (1803–1882). "Progress of Culture," *Letters and Social Aims,* 1876

Truth enters the mind so easily that when we hear it for the first time it seems as if we were simply recalling it to memory.

> BERNARD de FONTENELLE (1657–1757). *Histoire de l'Académe royal des sciences,* 1702-1740

Half the Truth is often a great Lie.

> BENJAMIN FRANKLIN (1706–1790). *Poor Richard's Almanack,* July 1758

Truth fears no Trial.

> THOMAS FULLER (1654–1734). Comp., *Gnomologia: Adages and Proverbs,* 5297, 1732

Truth may sometimes come out of the Devil's Mouth.

> THOMAS FULLER (1654–1734). Comp., *Gnomologia: Adages and Proverbs,* 5308, 1732

Faith perceives Truth sooner than Experience can.

> KAHLIL GIBRAN (1883–1931). "Sayings," *Spiritual Sayings of Kahlil Gibran,* tr. Anthony R. Ferris, 1962

It is the property of truth to diffuse itself.

> WILLIAM GODWIN (1756–1836). *Enquiry Concerning Political Justice and Its Influence on Morals and Happiness,* 4.2.3, 1793, ed. and abr. Raymond A. Preston, 1926

Political truth is libel; religious truth, blasphemy.

> WILLIAM HAZLITT (1778–1830). "Common Places" (42), *Literary Examiner* (English journal), September-December 1823

Grasping the truth means neither more nor less than being gripped by it on a plane beyond your own thinking.

> EUGEN HERRIGEL (1885–1955). "Communication with the Whole of Being," *The Method of Zen,* 1960, ed. Hermann Tausend and tr. R. F. C. Hull, 1964

Truth, [which] opposeth no man's profit, nor pleasure, is to all men welcome.

> THOMAS HOBBES (1588–1679). Closing words, *Leviathan,* 1651

The weakness of a soul is proportionate to the number of truths which must be kept from it.

> ERIC HOFFER (1902–1983). *The Passionate State of Mind: And Other Aphorisms,* 61, 1954

The best test of truth is the power of the thought to get itself accepted in the competition of the market.

> OLIVER WENDELL HOLMES, JR. (1841–1935). *Abrams v. United States,* 1919

The easiest rationalization for the refusal to seek the truth is the denial that truth exists.

> SIDNEY HOOK (1902–1989)

When we really live truth, we will cease to talk about it.

> ELBERT HUBBARD (1856–1915). In Alice Hubbard, comp., *An American Bible,* p. 159, 1946

History warns us that it is the customary fate of new truths to begin as heresies and to end as superstitions.

> T. H. HUXLEY (1825–1895). "The Coming of Age of *The Origin of Species,*" *Science and Culture and Other Essays,* 1881

New truth is always a go-between, a smoother-over of transitions. It marries old opinion to new fact so as ever to show a minimum of jolt, a maximum of continuity.

> WILLIAM JAMES (1842–1910). *Pragmatism,* 2, 1907

There is not a truth existing which I fear, or would wish unknown to the whole world.

> THOMAS JEFFERSON (1743–1826). Letter to Henry Lee, 15 May 1826

You will know the truth, and the truth will make you free.

> JESUS (A.D. 1st cent.). *John* 8:32

But it's the truth even if it didn't happen.

> KEN KESEY (1935–). *One Flew Over the Cuckoo's Nest,* 1, 1962
> See Books: Ernest Hemingway

Two half-truths do not a make a truth.

> ARTHUR KOESTLER (1905–1983). Preface to *The Ghost in the Machine,* 1967

We live in a culture that would absolutely fall apart if the truth were told.

> R. D. LAING (1927–1989). Richard Leviton interview, *East West Journal,* September 1987

Truth does not do as much good in the world as the semblance of truth does evil.

> LA ROCHEFOUCAULD (1613–1680). *Maxims,* 67, 1665, tr. Leonard Tancock, 1959

We should not take offense when people hide the truth from us, since so often we hide it from ourselves.

> LA ROCHEFOUCAULD (1613–1680). *Maxims,* 516, 1665, tr. Leonard Tancock, 1959

Uncomfortable truths travel with difficulty.

> PRIMO LEVI (1919–1987). *The Drowned and the Saved,* 7, 1986, tr. Raymond Rosenthal, 1988

Even truth needs to be clad in new garments if it is to appeal to a new age.

> GEORG CHRISTOPH LICHTENBERG (1742–1799). *Aphorisms,* C.33, 1806, tr. R. J. Hollingdale, 1990

The path of truth is paved with critical doubt, and lighted by the spirit of objective inquiry.

> B. H. LIDDELL HART (1895–1970). "The Scientific Approach," *Why Don't We Learn from History?* 1944

It is a duty we owe to God as the fountain and author of all truth, who is truth itself: and it is a duty also we owe our own selves, if we will deal candidly and sincerely with our own souls, to have our minds constantly disposed to entertain and receive truth wheresoever we meet with it, or under whatsoever appearance of plain or ordinary, strange, new, or perhaps displeasing, it may come in our way.

> JOHN LOCKE (1632–1704). "Study." In Lord King, *The Life of John Locke,* 1.187, 1830

Who dares
To say that he alone has found the truth?

> HENRY WADSWORTH LONGFELLOW (1807–1882). "Louis Endicott," *The New England Tragedies,* 1868

Truth will out.

> JOHN LYDGATE (1370?–1450?)
>
> See Love, Romantic: William Congreve o Nature: Aesop

Truth hath the prerogative to speak with plainness and the modesty to bear with patience.

> JOHN LYLY (1554?–1606). "To My Very Good Friends . . . ," *Euphues: The Anatomy of Wit,* 1579

Time advances; facts accumulate; doubts arise. Faint glimpses of truth begin to appear, and shine more and more unto the perfect day. The highest intellects, like the tops of mountains, are the first to catch and reflect the dawn. They are bright, while the level below is still in darkness. But soon the light, which at first illuminated only the loftiest eminences, descends on the plain and penetrates to the deepest valley. First come hints, then fragments of systems, then defective systems, then complete and harmonious systems. The sound opinion, held for a time by one bold speculator, becomes the opinion of a small minority, of a strong minority, of a majority—of mankind.

> THOMAS BABINGTON MACAULAY (1800–1859). "Sir James Mackintosh," *The Edinburgh Review* (Scotland), July 1835

Just because you have heard a thing so often that it bores you is no sign it isn't true.

> DON MARQUIS (1878–1937). *The Almost Perfect State,* 5, 1927

There are no new truths, but only truths that have not been recognized by those who have perceived them without noticing. A truth is something that everyone can be shown to know and to have known, as people say, all along.

> MARY McCARTHY (1912–1989). "Philosophy at Work," *New Yorker,* 18 October 1958

The average man does not get pleasure out of an idea because he thinks it is true; he thinks it is true because he gets pleasure out of it.

> H. L. MENCKEN (1880–1956). *Damn! A Book of Calumny,* 40, 1918

The truth, to the overwhelming majority of mankind, is indistinguishable from a headache.

> H. L. MENCKEN (1880–1956). Lecture before the Institute of Arts and Sciences, Columbia University, New York City, 4 January 1940

We cannot possess the truth fully until it has entered into the very substance of our life by good habits and by a certain perfection of moral activity.

> THOMAS MERTON (1915–1968). *No Man Is an Island,* 8.6, 1955

We are much like Pilate. We are always asking, "What is truth?" and then crucifying the truth that stands before our eyes.

> THOMAS MERTON (1915–1968). *No Man Is an Island,* 10.3, 1955

What we pretend to be defending as the "truth" is really our own self-esteem.

> THOMAS MERTON (1915–1968). *No Man Is an Island,* 10.8, 1955

The real advantage which truth has consists in this, that when an opinion is true, it may be extinguished once, twice, or many times, but in the course of ages there will generally be found persons to rediscover it, until some one of its reappearances falls on a time when from favorable circumstances it escapes persecution until it has made such head as to withstand all subsequent attempts to suppress it.

> JOHN STUART MILL (1806–1873). *On Liberty,* 2, 1859

Truth, in the great practical concerns of life, is [mostly] a question of the reconciling and combining of opposites.

> JOHN STUART MILL (1806–1873). *On Liberty,* 2, 1859

Our truth of nowadays is not what is, but what others can be convinced of.

> MONTAIGNE (1533–1592). "Of Giving the Lie," *Essays,* 1588, tr. Donald M. Frame, 1958

All repressed truths become poisonous.

> FRIEDRICH NIETZSCHE (1844–1900). "Of Self-Overcoming," *Thus Spoke Zarathustra,* 1892, tr. R. J. Hollingdale, 1961

Not even the most devastating truth can be *told;* it must be *evoked.*

> JOYCE CAROL OATES (1938–). "Selections from a Journal: January 1985–January 1988," 1985. In Daniel Halpern, ed., *Antaeus,* Autumn 1988

One has only to think of the sinister possibilities of the radio, state-controlled education and so forth, to realize that "the truth is great and will prevail" is a prayer rather than an axiom.

> GEORGE ORWELL (1903–1950). Reviewing *Power: A New Social Analysis* by Bertrand Russell, January 1939, *The Collected Essays, Journalism and Letters of George Orwell,* vol. 1, ed. Sonia Orwell and Ian Angus, 1968

Such is the irresistible nature of truth that all it asks, and all it wants, is the liberty of appearing.

> THOMAS PAINE (1737–1809). *The Rights of Man,* 2 ("Introduction"), 1792

We know truth, not only by reason, but also by the heart.

> BLAISE PASCAL (1623–1662). *Pensées,* 282, 1670, tr. William F. Trotter, 1931

Jesus: For this I was born, and for this I have come into the world, to bear witness to the truth. Everyone who is of the truth hears my voice.
Pilate: What is truth?

> PILATE (A.D. 1st cent.). Roman procurator of Judea. Format adapted. At the trial of Jesus, *John* 18:37–38

The truth knocks on the door and you say, "Go away, I'm looking for the truth," and so it goes away. Puzzling.

> ROBERT M. PIRSIG (1928–). *Zen and the Art of Motorcycle Maintenance: An Inquiry into Values,* 1, 1974

A man is not to be reverenced more than the truth.

> PLATO (427?–347 B.C.). *The Republic,* 10.595, tr. Benjamin Jowett, 1894

The truth never arrives neatly wrapped.

> THOMAS POWERS (1940–). "The Sins of a President," *New York Times Book Review,* 30 November 1997

It [is] dangerous to follow truth too near, lest she should kick out our teeth.

> SIR WALTER RALEIGH (1554–1618). In C. C. Colton, *Lacon: or, Many Things in Few Words; Addressed to Those Who Think,* 2.108, 1824

That is *true* which all men say.

> JOHN RAY (1628–1705). Comp., *A Collection of English Proverbs,* p. 211, 1678

The simplest schoolboy is now familiar with truths for which Archimedes would have sacrificed his life.

> ERNEST RENAN (1823–1892). *Souvenirs d'enfance et de jeunesse,* 1883

All my assertions are but reasons to doubt me. Seek truth for yourself; for my own part I only promise you sincerity.

> ROUSSEAU (1712–1778). *Emile; or, Treatise on Education,* 4 ("The Creed of a Savoyard Priest"), 1762, tr. Barbara Foxley, 1911

The simplest and most necessary truths are always the last believed.

> JOHN RUSKIN (1819–1900). *Modern Painters,* 3.4.17.34, 1843–1860, ed. Ernest Rhys, 1906

Like all dreamers, I confused disenchantment with truth.

> JEAN-PAUL SARTRE (1905–1980). *The Words,* 2, 1964, tr. Bernard Frechtman, 1981

Truth that has been merely learned is like an artificial limb. . . . It adheres to us only because it is put on. But truth acquired by thinking of our own is like a natural limb; it alone really belongs to us.

> ARTHUR SCHOPENHAUER (1788–1860). "The Art of Literature: On Thinking for One's Self," *Essays of Arthur Schopenhauer,* tr. T. Bailey Saunders, 1851

Truth has no special time of its own. Its hour is now—always, and indeed most truly when it seems most unsuitable to actual circumstances.

> ALBERT SCHWEITZER (1875–1965). *On the Edge of the Primeval Forest: The Experiences and Observations of a Doctor in Equatorial Africa,* 11, 1922, tr. C. T. Campion, 1928

It is the fate of every truth to be a subject for laughter until it is generally recognized.

> ALBERT SCHWEITZER (1875–1965). *The Philosophy of Civilization: Civilization and Ethics,* 21, 1923, tr. C. T. Campion and Mrs. Charles E. B. Russell, 1946

Truth will never be discovered if we rest contented with discoveries already made.

> SENECA THE YOUNGER (5? B.C.–A.D. 65). "On the Futility of Learning Maxims," *Moral Letters to Lucilius,* 33.10, tr. Richard M. Gummere, 1918

A Strange Lady: The truth is the one thing nobody will believe.

> GEORGE BERNARD SHAW (1856–1950). *The Man of Destiny* (one-act play), 1898

If the truth of all things always existed in the soul, then the soul is immortal. Wherefore be of good cheer, and try to recollect what you do not know, or rather what you do not remember.

> SOCRATES (470?–399 B.C.). In Plato (427?–347 B.C.), *Meno,* 86, tr. Benjamin Jowett, 1894

I would ask you to be thinking of the truth and not of Socrates: agree with me, if I seem to you to be speaking the truth; or if not, withstand me might and main, that I may not deceive you as well as myself in my enthusiasm, and like the bee, leave my sting in you before I die.

> SOCRATES (470?–399 B.C.). In Plato (427?–327 B.C.), *Phaedo,* 91, tr. Benjamin Jowett, 1894

When truth is discovered by someone else, it loses something of its attractiveness.

> ALEKSANDR SOLZHENITSYN (1918–). *Candle in the Wind,* 3, 1960, tr. Keith Armes, 1973

Ethical truth is as exact and as peremptory as physical truth.

> HERBERT SPENCER (1820–1903). *Social Statics,* 2.9.6, 1851
> See Morality: Voltaire

What is truth? For the multitude, that which it continually reads and hears. . . . What the Press wills, is true. Its commanders evoke, transform, interchange truths. Three weeks of press-work, and the "truth" is acknowledged by everybody.

> OSWALD SPENGLER (1880–1936). "Philosophy of Politics," *The Decline of the West,* 1918–1922, tr. Charles Francis Atkinson, 1962
> See The Press: Spengler

Truth is not always the best basis for happiness. . . . There are people who perish when their eyes are opened.

> WILHELM STEKEL (1868–1940). *The Autobiography of Wilhelm Stekel: The Life Story of a Pioneer Psychoanalyst,* 7, ed. Emil A. Gutheil, 1950

Truth . . . must be clothed with flesh and blood, or it cannot tell its whole story.

> ROBERT LOUIS STEVENSON (1850–1894). "Henry David Thoreau: His Character and Opinions" (3), *Familiar Studies of Men and Books,* 1882

Truth is always paradoxical.

> HENRY DAVID THOREAU (1817–1862). Journal, 26 June 1840

All perception of truth is the detection of an analogy.

> HENRY DAVID THOREAU (1817–1862). Journal, 5 September 1851

A higher truth, though only dimly hinted at, thrills us more than a lower expressed.

> HENRY DAVID THOREAU (1817–1862). Journal, 1 November 1857

Can the truth of life have been revealed to me only to give my whole life the lie?

> LEO TOLSTOY (1828–1910). *War and Peace,* 4.1.16, 1863–1869, tr. Rosemary Edmonds, 1957

People adopt the truth not only because they come to know it by a prophetic insight, or by experience of life, but also because when the teaching is sufficiently widely diffused men at a lower stage of development accept it all at once, simply through confidence in those who have adopted it by the inward method and are applying it in life.

> LEO TOLSTOY (1828–1910). *The Kingdom of God Is Within You,* 10, 1893, tr. Aylmer Maude, 1936

Truth is stranger than fiction, but it is because Fiction is obliged to stick to possibilities; Truth isn't.

> MARK TWAIN (1835–1910). *Following the Equator: A Journey Around the World,* 15 (epigraph), 1897

Truth is more of a stranger than fiction.

> MARK TWAIN (1835–1910). 4 July 1898, *Mark Twain's Notebook,* ed. Albert Bigelow Paine, 1935

Truth is mighty and will prevail. There is nothing the matter with this, except that it ain't so.

> MARK TWAIN (1835–1910). 4 July 1898, *Mark Twain's Notebook,* ed. Albert Bigelow Paine, 1935

Few people have enough character to endure the truth, and to speak it.

> VAUVENARGUES (1715–1747). *Reflections and Maxims,* 235, 1746, tr. F. G. Stevens, 1940

Truth is one; the sages speak of it by many names.

> VEDAS (10th? cent. B.C.). Hindu scriptures. In Joseph Campbell, preface to *The Hero with a Thousand Faces,* 1949

This is the character of truth: it is of all time, It is for all men, it has only to show itself to be recognized, and one cannot argue against it.

> VOLTAIRE (1694–1778). "Sect," *Philosophical Dictionary,* 1764, tr. Abner Kneeland, 1836

Few dare to announce an unwelcome truth.

> EDWIN PERCY WHIPPLE (1694–1778). *Character and Characteristic Men,* 1, 1884

What plays the devil in human affairs is mistaking a half-truth for a whole truth.

> ALFRED NORTH WHITEHEAD (1861–1947). 13 January 1944, *Dialogues of Alfred North Whitehead,* rec. Lucien Price, 1953

All truths wait in all things,
They neither hasten their own delivery nor resist it.

> WALT WHITMAN (1819–1892). "Song of Myself" (30), 1855, *Leaves of Grass,* 1855–1892

Truths that wake,
  To perish never.

> WILLIAM WORDSWORTH (1770–1850). "Ode: Intimations of Immortality from Recollections of Early Childhood," 9, 1807

❦

Truth angers those whom it does not convince.

> ANONYMOUS

Knowing the truth and living it are two things.

> ANONYMOUS

The truth seekers hear out the heretics as well as the believers.

> ANONYMOUS

The truth is paradoxical and logical by turns.

> ANONYMOUS

The truth may not make us free, but we cannot be free without it.

> ANONYMOUS

The truth hurts, but only when it ought to.

> SAYING (AMERICAN)

Buy truth, and do not sell it.

> SAYING (BIBLE). *Proverbs* 23:23

An ill-timed truth is as bad as a lie.

> SAYING (GERMAN)

The truth is brought by a lame messenger.

> SAYING (GERMAN)

Truth is often eclipsed but never extinguished.

> SAYING (LATIN)

TRUTH & UNTRUTH

See also • Errors ∘ Falsehood ∘ Lying ∘ Truth ∘ Truthfulness

We must ever wade through error in our advance towards truth; and it may even be said that in many cases we exhaust almost every variety of error before we attain the desired goal.

> CHARLES BABBAGE (1792–1871). English mathematician and inventor. *Ninth Bridgewater Treatise,* 27, 1837

It dont take mutch tew prove a truth. It iz only a lie that requires grate argumentatiff ability.

JOSH BILLINGS (1818–1885). "Chicken Feed," *Everybody's Friend, or; Josh Billing's Encyclopedia and Proverbial Philosophy of Wit and Humor,* 1874

The nearer men come to Truth, . . . the more dangerous their mistakes are.

SAMUEL BUTLER (1612–1680). "Unclassified Prose Observations from the Butler's Manuscript," *Prose Observations,* ed. Hugh de Quehen, 1979

I only wish I could discover the truth as easily as I can expose falsehood.

CICERO (106–43 B.C.). *De natura deorum,* 1.91, tr. H. Rackham, 1933

Craft must have Clothes, but Truth loves to go naked.

THOMAS FULLER (1654–1734). Comp., *Gnomologia: Adages and Proverbs,* 1200, 1732

It is in numberless instances happier to have a false opinion which we believe true than a true one of which we doubt.

FULKE GREVILLE (1554–1628). *Maxims, Characters, and Reflections,* p. 173, 1756

Not, "Is it Old or is it New?"
But, "Is it False or is it True?"

ARTHUR GUITERMAN (1871–1943). "Of Truth," *A Poet's Proverbs: Being Mirthful, Sober, and Fanciful Epigrams on the Universe, With Certain Old Irish Proverbs, All in Rhymed Couplets,* 1924

Irrationally held truths may be more harmful than reasoned errors.

T. H. HUXLEY (1825–1895). "The Coming of Age of *The Origin of Species,*" *Science and Culture,* 1881

It is error alone which needs the support of government. Truth can stand by itself.

THOMAS JEFFERSON (1743–1826). *Notes on the State of Virginia,* 17, 1785

We are not afraid to follow truth wherever it may lead, nor to tolerate any error so long as reason is left free to combat it.

THOMAS JEFFERSON (1743–1826). Letter to William Roscoe, 27 December 1820

An error crowned with prestige always will be more powerful than a truth without prestige.

GUSTAVE LE BON (1841–1931). *Aphorisms of Present Times,* 1.8, 1913, tr. Alice Widener, 1979

Speaking the truth is a petty-bourgeois prejudice. A lie, on the other hand, is often justified by the end.

LENIN (1870–1924). "Unpublished notes." *Bulletin of the Institute for the Study of the U.S.S.R.,* May 1962. In Alfreds Berzins, *The Two Faces of Co-Existence,* 1, 1967

The most dangerous untruths are truths slightly distorted.

GEORG CHRISTOPH LICHTENBERG (1742–1799). *Aphorisms,* H.7, 1806, tr. R. J. Hollingdale, 1990

I shall try to correct errors when shown to be errors, and I shall adopt new views so fast as they shall appear to be true views.

ABRAHAM LINCOLN (1809–1865). Letter to Horace Greeley, 22 August 1862

It is one thing to show a man that he is in an error, and another to put him in possession of truth.

JOHN LOCKE (1632–1704). *An Essay Concerning Human Understanding,* 4.7.11, 1690, ed. Alexander Campbell Fraser, 1894

Truth forever on the scaffold, Wrong forever on the throne—
Yet that scaffold sways the future, and behind the dim unknown,
Standeth God within the shadow, keeping watch above his own.

JAMES RUSSELL LOWELL (1819–1891). "The Present Crisis," 8, 1844

Superstition, idolatry, and hypocrisy, have ample wages, but truth goes a-begging.

MARTIN LUTHER (1483–1546). *Table Talk,* 53, 1566, tr. William Hazlitt, 1857

Let [Truth] and Falsehood grapple; who ever knew Truth put to the worse, in a free and open encounter?

JOHN MILTON (1608–1674). *Areopagitica* (A Speech for the Liberty of Unlicenc'd Printing), 1644

The errors of an original mind are often more fruitful than the truths of a more limited one.

LEWIS MUMFORD (1895–1990). Introduction to Waldo Frank, *Memoirs of Waldo Frank,* ed. Alan Trachtenberg, 1973

Truth on this side of the Pyrenees, error on the other side.

BLAISE PASCAL (1623–1662). *Pensées,* 294, 1670, tr. William F. Trotter, 1931

The truth may hurt, but lies can kill.

MORT SAHL (1927–)

A lie travels round the world while Truth is putting on her boots.

CHARLES HADDON SPURGEON (1834–1892)

If you shut your door to all errors, truth will be shut out.

RABINDRANATH TAGORE (1861–1941). *Stray Birds,* 130, 1914

[*The Adventures of Tom Sawyer*] is mostly a true book, with some stretchers.

MARK TWAIN (1835–1910). In opening paragraph, *The Adventures of Huckleberry Finn,* 1884

❦

Truth and Falsehood were bathing; Falsehood came out of the water first and dressed herself in Truth's clothes. Truth, unwilling to put on the garments of Falsehood, went naked.

ANONYMOUS. Fable. In Cheris Kramarae and Paula A. Treichler, comps., *A Feminist Dictionary: In Our Own Words,* p. 290, 1985

Error tends to multiply itself; truth is forever one.

ANONYMOUS

We are responsible not only for the lies we speak but for the truths we fail to speak.

ANONYMOUS

See Silence & Speech: Martin Luther King, Jr. (2)

An old error is always more popular than a new truth.

SAYING (GERMAN)

Truth gives a short answer; lies go roundabout.

SAYING (GERMAN)

TRUTHFULNESS

See also • Deception ○ Honesty ○ Hypocrisy ○ Integrity ○ Lying ○ Public Speaking: Henry David Thoreau (2) ○ Sincerity ○ Truth ○ Truth & Untruth

His style is mistaken for fantastic, drug-crazed exaggeration, but that was to be expected. As always in this country, they only laugh at you when you tell the truth.

> EDWARD ABBEY. On Hunter S. Thompson. In Douglas Brinkley, "Hunter Thompson Raw," *At Random,* Spring-Summer 1997

A truth that's told with bad intent
Beats all the Lies you can invent.

> WILLIAM BLAKE (1757–1827). "Auguries of Innocence," l. 53, 1789

Candor is a compliment.

> GEORGE BUSH (1924–). *Inaugural address,* 20 January 1989
>
> See Sincerity: Ralph Waldo Emerson

But now I'm going to be immoral; now
  I mean to show things really as they are,
Not as they ought to be.

> LORD BYRON (1788–1824). *Don Juan,* 12.40, 1819–1824

Again and again there comes a time in history when the man who dares to say that two and two make four is punished with death.

> ALBERT CAMUS (1913–1960). *The Plague,* 2, 1947, tr. Stuart Gilbert, 1948

Observe the looks and countenances of those who speak, which is often a surer way of discovering the truth than from what they say.

> LORD CHESTERFIELD (1694–1773). Letter to his son, 30 October 1747

Though the whole world grumble, I will speak my mind.

> CICERO (106–43 B.C.). *De oratore,* 1.44, tr. E. W. Sutton and H. Rackham, 1942

Mr. Lely, I desire you would use all your skill to paint my picture truly like me, and not flatter me at all, but remark all these roughnesses, pimples, warts and everything as you see me, otherwise I will not pay a farthing for it.

> OLIVER CROMWELL (1599–1658). Remark to the artist Peter Lely, 1657? In Horace Walpole, *Anecdotes of Painting in England,* 12, 1762–1771 (Popular version: Paint me, warts and all.)

It is the duty of everyone to spread what he believes to be the truth.

> CHARLES DARWIN (1809–1882). Letter to Dr. F. E. Abbott, 16 November 1871, *The Autobiography of Charles Darwin and Selected Letters,* 3, ed. Francis Darwin, 1892

Tell all the Truth but tell it slant—
Success in Circuit lies
Too bright for our infirm Delight
The Truth's superb surprise
As Lightning to the Children eased
With explanation kind
The Truth must dazzle gradually
Or every man be blind—

> EMILY DICKINSON (1830–1886). "Tell all the Truth but tell it slant" (complete poem), 1868?

Speak the truth, and all nature and all spirits help you with unexpected furtherance. Speak the truth, and all things alive or brute are vouchers, and the very roots of the grass underground there do seem to stir and move to bear you witness.

> RALPH WALDO EMERSON (1803–1882). "The Divinity School Address," Cambridge (Massachusetts), 15 July 1838

Whatever games are played with us, we must play no games with ourselves, but deal in our privacy with the last honesty and truth.

> RALPH WALDO EMERSON (1803–1882). "Illusions," *The Conduct of Life,* 1860

Tell not an improbable truth.

> THOMAS FULLER (1654–1734). Comp., *Introductio ad Prudentiam,* 1626, 1731

An honest man speaks truth, *though* it may give offense; a vain man, *in order that it may.*

> WILLIAM HAZLITT (1778–1830). *Characteristics in the Manner of Rochefoucault's Maxims,* 387, 1823

It is always the best policy to speak the truth—unless, of course, you are an exceptionally good liar.

> JEROME K. JEROME (1859–1927). *The Idle Thoughts of an Idle Fellow; A Book for an Idle Holiday,* 1892

Do not throw your pearls before swine lest they trample them underfoot and turn to attack you.

> JESUS (A.D. 1st cent.). *Matthew* 7:6

As a child I was taught that to tell the truth was often painful. As an adult I have learned that not to tell the truth is more painful.

> JUNE JORDAN (1939–). *On Call: Political Essays,* 10, 1985

Truth uncompromisingly told will always have its ragged edges.

> HERMAN MELVILLE (1819–1891). *Billy Budd,* 28, ed. Harrison Hayford and Merton M. Sealts, Jr., 1962

It is hard to believe that a man is telling the truth when you know that you would lie if you were in his place.

> H. L. MENCKEN (1880–1956). *A Little Book in C Major,* 2.15, 1916

We must not always say everything, for that would be folly; but what we say must be what we think.

> MONTAIGNE (1533–1592). "Of Presumption," *Essays,* 1588, tr. Donald M. Frame, 1958

Tell the truth when you can, and when you can't, don't tell a lie.

> BILL MOYERS (1934–). Recalling his father's dictum. In "L.B.J.'s Young Man 'In Charge of Everything,'" *Time,* 29 October 1965

Have I then become your enemy by telling you the truth?

> PAUL (A.D. 1st cent.). *Galatians* 4:16

They deem him their worst enemy who tells them the truth.

> PLATO (427?–347 B.C.). *The Republic,* 4.426, tr. Benjamin Jowett, 1894

Who dares to tell himself the truth?

> SENECA THE YOUNGER (5? B.C.–A.D. 65). "Of Peace of Mind" (1), *Minor Dialogues,* tr. Aubrey Stewart, 1889

Hotspur: O, while you live, tell truth and shame the devil!

> SHAKESPEARE (1564–1616). *Henry IV,* Part I, 3.1.62, 1597

The righteous man takes his life in his hand whenever he utters the truth.

> GEORGE BERNARD SHAW (1856–1950). Letter, *The Wit and Wisdom of Bernard Shaw,* 25, ed. Stephen Winsten, 1949

The most awful thing that one can do is to tell the truth. It's all right in my case because I am not taken seriously.

> GEORGE BERNARD SHAW (1856–1950)
> See Jokes: Shaw (2)

I have a sufficient witness to the truth of what I say—my poverty.

> SOCRATES (470?–399 B.C.). In Plato (427?–347 B.C.), *Apology,* 31, tr. Benjamin Jowett, 1894

There are only two ways of telling the complete truth—anonymously and posthumously.

> THOMAS SOWELL (1930–)

Speaking the truth is a luxury few people can afford.

> THOMAS S. SZASZ (1920–). "Language," *The Second Sin,* 1973

In proportion to our truthfulness and confidence in one another, our lives are divine and miraculous, and answer to our ideal.

> HENRY DAVID THOREAU (1817–1862). "Wednesday," *A Week on the Concord and Merrimack Rivers,* 1849

I never give them hell. I just tell the truth, and they think it is hell.

> HARRY S. TRUMAN (1884–1972). On his campaigning technique. In "What They Are Saying," *Look,* 3 April 1956
> See Campaigns: Truman (2)

If you tell the truth, you don't have to remember anything.

> MARK TWAIN (1835–1910). 2 February 1894, *Mark Twain's Notebook,* ed. Albert Bigelow Paine, 1935
> See Lying: Saying (Latin)

"George," said his father, "do you know who killed that beautiful little cherry tree yonder in the garden?" . . . Looking at his father with the sweet face of youth brightened with the inexpressible charm of all-conquering truth, he bravely cried out, "I can't tell a lie. I did cut it with my hatchet."

> PARSON WEEMS (1759–1825). An apocryphal story, *The Life of George Washington: With Curious Anecdotes, Equally Honorable to Himself and Exemplary to His Young Countrymen,* 2, 1806

I usually say what I really think. A great mistake nowadays. It makes one so liable to be misunderstood.

> OSCAR WILDE (1854–1900). *An Ideal Husband,* 2, 1895

❦

Speak the truth, but have one foot in the stirrup.

> SAYING (TURKISH)

Speak the truth, but ride a fast horse.

> SAYING (WEST TEXAS). Quoted by Jim Hightower, Brian Lamb television interview, C-SPAN, 21 December 1997

Only children, fools, drunkards, and madmen speak the truth.

> SAYING

TYRANNY

See also • Assassination ○ Brainwashing ○ Capitalism ○ Class ○ Communism ○ Competition ○ Crises ○ Crowds ○ Cruelty ○ Deception ○ Dehumanization ○ Democracy ○ Despots ○ Dictators ○ Exploitation ○ Fascism ○ Freedom ○ Government ○ Indoctrination ○ Inequality ○ Injustice ○ Machiavellianism ○ Mass Movements ○ Oppression ○ Persecution: John Dryden ○ Power: [especially] Jacques Maritain, Alexis de Tocqueville (1) ○ Propaganda ○ Revolution ○ Self-Interest ○ Sexual Repression ○ Slavery ○ Socialism ○ Terror ○ Torture ○ Tyrants ○ Violence ○ War

The most successful tyranny is not the one that uses force to assure uniformity but the one that removes the awareness of other possibilities.

> ALLAN BLOOM (1930–1992). "From Socrates' *Apology* to Heidegger's *Rektoratsrede,*" *The Closing of the American Mind: How Higher Education Has Failed Democracy and Impoverished the Souls of Today's Students,* 1987

The moment a man says, "give up your rights, here is money," there is tyranny. It comes masquerading in monks' cowls, and in citizens' coats, comes savagely or comes politely. But it is tyranny.

> RALPH WALDO EMERSON (1803–1882). Journal, 1851, undated

The totalitarian brand of tyranny has perfected an awesome technique for stripping the individual of all material and spiritual resources which might bolster his independence and self-respect. It deprives him of every alternative and refuge—even that of silence or retreat into solitariness.

> ERIC HOFFER (1902–1983). *The Ordeal of Change,* 10, 1964

Tyranny is the exercise of Power beyond Right.

> JOHN LOCKE (1632–1704). *Two Treatises of Government,* 2.199, 1690

Wherever Law ends Tyranny begins.

> JOHN LOCKE (1632–1704). *Two Treatises of Government,* 2.202, 1690

To usurp supreme and absolute authority . . . in a free state and subject it to tyranny, the people must have already become corrupt by gradual steps from generation to generation.

> MACHIAVELLI (1849–1527). *The Discourses,* 3.8, 1517, tr. Christian E. Detmold, 1940

The accumulation of all powers, legislative, executive, and judiciary, in the same hands, whether of one, a few, or many, and whether hereditary, self-appointed, or elective, may justly be pronounced the very definition of tyranny.

> JAMES MADISON (1751–1836). In *The Federalist Papers* (essay series), 47, 1 February 1788

Society . . . practices a social tyranny more formidable than many kinds of political oppression, since, though not usually upheld by such extreme penalties, it leaves fewer means of escape, penetrating much more deeply into the details of life, and enslaving the soul itself. Protection, therefore, against the tyranny of the magistrate is not enough: there needs protection also against the tyranny of the prevailing opinion and feeling; against the tendency of society to impose, by other means than civil penalties, its own ideas and practices as rules of conduct on those who dissent from them.

> JOHN STUART MILL (1806–1873). *On Liberty,* 1, 1859

Tyranny, like hell, is not easily conquered; yet we have this consolation with us, that the harder the conflict, the more glorious the triumph.

> THOMAS PAINE (1737–1809). *The Crisis* (pamphlet), 1, 23 December 1776

Tyranny is always better organized than freedom.

> CHARLES PÉGUY (1873–1914). "War and Peace: War and Peace," *Basic Verities: Prose and Poetry,* tr. Ann and Julian Green, 1943

Of all forms of tyranny the least attractive and the most vulgar is the tyranny of mere wealth, the tyranny of a plutocracy.

> THEODORE ROOSEVELT (1858–1919). *An Autobiography,* 12, 1913

[The] readiness to cringe is accompanied by an equal readiness to tyrannize. . . . The treatment of women by their husbands and children by their parents has been tyrannical in proportion as the servility of subjects to rulers has been extreme.

> HERBERT SPENCER (1820–1903). *Social Statics,* 4.30.6, 1851

Fetters and headsmen were the coarse instruments that tyranny formerly employed; but the civilization of our age has perfected despotism itself. . . . Under the absolute sway of one man the body was attacked in order to subdue the soul; but the soul escaped the blows which were directed against it and rose proudly superior. Such is not the course adopted by tyranny in democratic republics; there the body is left free, and the soul is enslaved. The master no longer says: "You shall think as I do or you shall die"; but he says: "You are free to think differently from me and to retain your life, your property, and all that you possess; but you are henceforth a stranger among your people. . . . Your fellow creatures will shun you like an impure being; and even those who believe in your innocence will abandon you, lest they should be shunned in their turn."

> ALEXIS de TOCQUEVILLE (1805–1859). *Democracy in America,* 1.15, 1835, tr. Henry Reeve and Francis Bowen, 1862

I would detest individual tyranny less than collective tyranny. A despot always has some good moments; a group of despots, never.

> VOLTAIRE (1694–1778). "Tyranny," *Philosophical Dictionary,* 1764, tr. Wade Baskin, 1961

There is a natural and necessary progression from the extreme of anarchy to the extreme of Tyranny; . . . arbitrary power is most easily established on the ruins of Liberty abused to licentiousness.

> GEORGE WASHINGTON (1732–1799). Circular to the states, 8 June 1783

❦

A government is tyrannical to the degree that it uses violence and the threat of violence to maintain itself.

> ANONYMOUS

Propaganda, exploitation, and violence make up tyranny's unholy trinity.

> ANONYMOUS

The worst tyranny is better than the best anarchy; the worst liberty is better than the best tyranny.

> ANONYMOUS

Under a tyranny, the privileges of the strong are rights and the rights of the weak are privileges.

> ANONYMOUS

TYRANTS

See also • Appeasement: Anonymous (2) ∘ Conservatives ∘ Crisis Leaders ∘ Despots ∘ Dictators ∘ Kings: [especially] Robert Herrick ∘ Leaders ∘ Machiavellianism ∘ Princes ∘ Revolutionaries: [especially] Anonymous ∘ Rulers ∘ Tyranny

Anyone who obtains power by force or fraud is at once thought to be a tyrant.

> ARISTOTLE (384–322 B.C.). *Politics,* 5.10, tr. Benjamin Jowett, 1885
>
> See Strategy: Polybius ∘ Success: Machiavelli (1) ∘ War: Thomas Hobbes (1)

A tyrant should also endeavor to know what each of his subjects says or does, and should employ spies . . . for the fear of informers prevents people from speaking their minds, and if they do, they are more easily found out. Another art of the tyrant is to sow quarrels among the citizens.

> ARISTOTLE (384–322 B.C.). *Politics,* 5.11, tr. Benjamin Jowett, 1885

It is characteristic of a tyrant to dislike everyone who has dignity or independence; he wants to be alone in his glory, but anyone who claims a like dignity or asserts his independence encroaches upon his prerogative, and is hated by him as an enemy to his power.

> ARISTOTLE (384–322 B.C.). *Politics,* 5.11, tr. Benjamin Jowett, 1885

Whereas states consist of two classes, of poor men and of rich, the tyrant should lead both to imagine that they are preserved and prevented from harming one another by his rule.

> ARISTOTLE (384–322 B.C.). *Politics,* 5.11, tr. Benjamin Jowett, 1885

The tyrant is proud, and therein resides his doom. He is proud because he thinks of his strength as his own; thus he is in the clown role, as a mistaker of shadow for substance; it is his destiny to be tricked.

> JOSEPH CAMPBELL (1904–1987). *The Hero with a Thousand Faces,* 2.3.3, 1949

The welfare of the people . . . has always been the alibi of tyrants, and it provides the further advantage of giving the servants of tyranny a good conscience. . . . The very ones who make use of such alibis know they are lies; they leave to their intellectuals on duty the chore of believing in them and of proving that religion, patriotism, and justice need for their survival the sacrifice of freedom.

> ALBERT CAMUS (1913–1960). "Homage to an Exile," 1955, *Resistance, Rebellion, and Death,* tr. Justin O'Brien, 1961

The heavier this Napoleon trampled on the world, holding it tyrannously down, the fiercer would the world's recoil against him be one day. Injustice pays itself with frightful compound interest.

> THOMAS CARLYLE (1795–1881). "The Hero as King," *On Heroes, Hero-Worship, and the Heroic in History,* 1841

The worst tyrants are those which establish themselves in our own breasts.

> WILLIAM ELLERY CHANNING (1780–1842). "Spiritual Freedom," sermon, 26 May 1830

Nature has left this tincture in the blood,
That all men would be tyrants if they could.

> DANIEL DEFOE (1660–1731). Addenda to *The History of the Kentish Petition*, 1713

Find out just what people will submit to, and you have found out the exact amount of injustice and wrong which will be imposed upon them. . . . The limits of tyrants are prescribed by the endurance of those whom they suppress.

> FREDERICK DOUGLASS (1817–1895). Letter to Gerrit Smith, 30 March 1849

The mortar that holds together the rule of tyrants is the blood of citizens.

> FRANCESCO GUICCIARDINI (1483–1540). *Remembrances*, B.20, 1530, tr. Mario Domandi, 1965

Tyrants are at all times mad with the lust [for] power.

> WILLIAM HAZLITT (1778–1830). "Common Places" (80), *Literary Examiner* (English journal), September-December 1823

Every tyrant who ever lived has believed in freedom—for himself.

> ELBERT HUBBARD (1856–1915). *A Thousand and One Epigrams*, p. 19, 1911

People may start out with an initial prejudice against tyrants; but when tyrants or would-be tyrants treat them to adrenalin-releasing propaganda about the wickedness of their enemies—particularly of enemies weak enough to be persecuted—they are ready to follow [the tyrants] with enthusiasm.

> ALDOUS HUXLEY (1894–1963). "The Arts of Selling," *Brave New World Revisited*, 1958

If we will not be governed by God, we must be governed by Tyrants.

> WILLIAM PENN (1644–1718). "Essay Towards the Present and Future Peace of Europe," 1693

This and no other is the root from which a tyrant springs: When he first appears, he is a protector.

> PLATO (427?–347 B.C.). *The Republic*, 8.565, tr. Benjamin Jowett, 1894

[The tyrant] is always stirring up some war or other, in order that the people may require a leader.

> PLATO (427?-347 B.C.), *The Republic*, 8.567, tr. Benjamin Jowett, 1894

When such men are only private individuals and before they get power, this is their character: they associate entirely with their own flatterers or ready tools; or if they want anything from anybody, they in their turn are equally ready to bow down before them; they profess every sort of affection for them, but when they have gained their point they know them no more. . . .

They are always either the masters or servants and never the friends of anybody; the tyrant never tastes of true freedom or friendship.

> PLATO (427?–347 B.C.). *The Republic*, 9.575-576, tr. Benjamin Jowett, 1894

The tyrant scorns love; he is content with fear. If he seeks to win the love of his subjects, it is for political reasons; and if he finds a more economical way to enslave them, he adopts it immediately.

> JEAN-PAUL SARTRE (1905–1980). *Being and Nothingness: A Phenomenological Essay on Ontology*, 3.3.1, 1943, tr. Hazel E. Barnes, 1956

Queen Margaret: How can tyrants safely govern home,
Unless abroad they purchase great alliance?

> SHAKESPEARE (1564–1616). *Henry VI*, Part III, 3.3.69, 1590

People will endure their tyrants for years, but they tear their deliverers to pieces if a millennium is not created immediately.

> WOODROW WILSON (1856–1924). In John Dos Passos, *Mr. Wilson's War*, 5.22, 1963

❧

The only morality the tyrant recognizes is obedience to him.

> ANONYMOUS

The tyrant binds his followers to him by making them accomplices in his crimes.

> ANONYMOUS

The tyrant confuses those he can't convince, corrupts those he can't confuse, and crushes those he can't corrupt.

> ANONYMOUS

To promote the illusion of liberality, the tyrant may tolerate some opposition, but only so long as it remains ineffective.

> ANONYMOUS

What finally brings down the tyrant is his relentless sacrifice of principle to expediency.

> ANONYMOUS

❧

THE UNCONSCIOUS

See also • Adolescence: Ralph Waldo Emerson ○ Christianity: Thomas Carlyle (1) ○ Conscience ○ Consciousness ○ Dreams ○ Heart ○ Mind: [especially] Sigmund Freud ○ Mysticism ○ Psychoanalysis ○ Psychotherapy ○ Self ○ Self-Realization (Becoming) ○ Self-Realization (Being) ○ Soul ○ Spirituality ○ Transformation: P. W. Martin (1)

The frog, the serpent, the rejected one, is the representative of that unconscious deep ("so deep that the bottom cannot be seen") wherein are hoarded all of the rejected, unadmitted, unrecognized, unknown, or undeveloped factors, laws, and elements of existence. [Parenthesized material in original.]

> JOSEPH CAMPBELL (1904–1987). *The Hero with a Thousand Faces*, 1.1.1, 1949

Opposite ideas exist side by side in the unconscious without contradicting each other.

> GEOFFREY A. DUDLEY. *How to Understand Your Dreams*, 2, 1963

The poets and philosophers before me discovered the unconscious. What I discovered was the scientific method by which the unconscious can be studied.

> SIGMUND FREUD (1856–1939). Quoted on his 70th birthday, 6 May 1926. In Lionel Trilling, "Freud and Literature" (1), *The Liberal Imagination: Essays on Literature and Society,* 1950
>
> See Dreams: Freud (3)

The governing rules of logic carry no weight in the unconscious; it might be called the Realm of the Illogical.

> SIGMUND FREUD (1856–1939). *An Outline of Psychoanalysis,* 5, 1940, tr. James Strachey, 1969

Man cannot persist long in a conscious state, he must throw himself back into the Unconscious, for his root lives there.

> GOETHE (1749–1832). In Lancelot Law Whyte, *The Unconscious Before Freud,* 6, 1960

The unconscious [at times] produces contents which are valid not only for the person concerned, but for others as well, in fact for a great many people and possible for all.

> CARL G. JUNG (1875–1961). "The Relations between the Ego and the Unconscious" (2.1), 1928, *Two Essays on Analytical Psychology,* tr. R. F. C. Hull, 1953

By understanding the unconscious we free ourselves from its domination.

> CARL G. JUNG (1875–1961). "The Detachment of Consciousness from the Object," *Commentary* (on *The Secret of the Golden Flower*), 1929, tr. Cary F. Baynes, 1961

[The unconscious] is dangerous only when our conscious attitude towards it becomes hopelessly false. And this danger grows in the measure that we practice repressions. But as soon as the patient begins to assimilate the contents that were previously unconscious, the danger from the side of the unconscious diminishes.

> CARL G. JUNG (1875–1961). *Modern Man in Search of a Soul,* 1, tr. W. S. Dell and Cary F. Baynes, 1933

The other side.

> CARL G. JUNG (1875–1961). Referring to the "unconscious," 1933. Quoted by Isabelle Hamilton Rey, "Memory of C. G. Jung." In Ferne Jensen, ed., *C. G. Jung, Emma Jung and Toni Wolff: A Collection of Remembrances,* 1982

A more or less superficial layer of the unconscious is undoubtedly personal. I call it the *personal unconscious.* But this personal unconscious rests upon a deeper layer, which does not derive from personal experience and is not a personal acquisition but is inborn. The deeper layer I call the *collective unconscious.* I have chosen the term "collective" because this part of the unconscious is not individual but universal; in contrast to the personal psyche, it has contents and modes of behavior that are more or less the same everywhere and in all individuals.

> CARL G. JUNG (1875–1961). "Archetypes of the Collective Unconscious," 1934, *The Archetypes and the Collective Unconscious,* tr. R. F. C. Hull, 1959
>
> See Dreams: Jung (3)

Once the exploration of the unconscious has [begun] . . . , the individual is confronted with the abysmal contradictions of human nature, and this confrontation in turn leads to the possibility of a direct experience of light and darkness, of Christ and the devil.

> CARL G. JUNG (1875–1961). *Psychology and Alchemy,* 1, 1944, tr. R. F. C. Hull, 1953
>
> See God & the Devil: Hermann Hesse (2) ○ Mankind: John Lennon

I prefer the term "the unconscious," knowing that I might equally well speak of "God" or "daimon" if I wished to express myself in mythic language.

> CARL G. JUNG (1875–1961). *Memories, Dreams, Reflections,* 12.1, ed. Aniela Jaffé, 1962

The part played by the unconscious in all our acts is immense, and that played by reason very small. The unconscious acts like a force still unknown.

> GUSTAVE LE BON (1841–1931). Introduction to *The Crowd: A Study of the Popular Mind,* 1895, Viking Press edition, 1960

The unconscious is not fundamentally a menace, a source of fear and misgiving. It is the wellspring of life, both for the individual and for the peoples of the world.

> P. W. MARTIN (1893–?). *Experiment in Depth: A Study of the Work of Jung, Eliot and Toynbee,* 10, 1955

It is not just the animal past that lives on in man's unconscious: the emergent future that has not yet taken form is likewise present: all that promises to release man from fixations and regressions and to open up untested modes of being and becoming, of transfiguration and transformation.

> LEWIS MUMFORD (1895–1990). *The Transformations of Man,* 9.2, 1956

Every extension of knowledge arises from making conscious the unconscious.

> FRIEDRICH NIETZSCHE (1844–1900). In Lancelot Law Whyte, *The Unconscious Before Freud,* 8, 1960
>
> See Enlightenment: D. T. Suzuki

The unconsciousness of man is the consciousness of God.

> HENRY DAVID THOREAU (1817–1862). "Thursday," *A Week on the Concord and Merrimack Rivers,* 1849

The nature of man himself is hidden in the deepest and darkest corner of the unconscious, of the elemental, of the sub-soil. Is it not self-evident that the greatest efforts of investigative thought and creative initiative will be in that direction?

> LEON TROTSKY (1879–1940). *Literature and Revolution,* 8, 1925, tr. Rose Strunsky, 1960

UNDERSTANDING

See also • Forgiveness: Walter Lippmann ○ Wisdom ○ Wisdom & Knowledge

We only understand that which is already within us.

> HENRI AMIEL (1821–1881). Journal, 7 April 1866, tr. Mrs. Humphrey Ward, 1887

Those who understand only what can be explained understand very little.

> MARIE von EBNER-ESCHENBACH (1830–1916). *Aphorisms,* p. 19, 1880–1905, tr. David Scrase and Wolfgang Mieder, 1994

Sometimes it proves the highest understanding not to understand.

> BALTASAR GRACIÁN (1601–1658). *The Art of Worldly Wisdom,* 73, 1647, tr. Joseph Jacobs, 1943

In what we really understand, we reason but little.

> WILLIAM HAZLITT (1778–1830). "On the Conduct of Life," *Literary Remains,* 1836

Much learning does not teach understanding.

> HERACLITUS (540?–480? B.C.). In Diogenes Laertius (A.D. 3rd cent.), *Lives of Eminent Philosophers,* 9.1, tr. R. D. Hicks, 1925

You never really understand a person until you consider things from his point of view—until you climb into his skin and walk around in it.

> HARPER LEE (1926–). *To Kill a Mockingbird,* 3, 1960
> See Judging Others: Hillel, Saying (Native American)

Now we see in a mirror dimly, but then face to face. Now I know in part, then I shall understand fully.

> PAUL (A.D. 1st cent.). *1 Corinthians* 13:12

It is difficult to get a man to understand something when his salary depends upon his not understanding it.

> UPTON SINCLAIR (1878–1968)

❧

I hear and I forget;
I see and I remember;
I do and I understand.

> SAYING (CHINESE)
> See Learning (Process): Aristotle

UNEMPLOYMENT

See also • Idleness ○ Poverty ○ Unions ○ Wages ○ Work

This is the golden age of the bottom line. When you're out of work, don't scowl and whine. Unemployment's good for the bottom line.

So smile, be happy, flash the "O.K." sign because you're doing your bit for the bottom line.

> RUSSELL BAKER (1925–). Opening paragraphs, "What a Line," *New York Times,* 6 August 1995

A man willing to work, and unable to find work, is perhaps the saddest sight that Fortune's inequality exhibits under this sun.

> THOMAS CARLYLE (1795–1881). *Chartism,* 4, 1840

In order to mitigate unemployment attending business depression, we urge the enactment of legislation authorizing that construction and repair of public works be initiated in periods of acute unemployment.

> DEMOCRATIC NATIONAL PLATFORM. 1924

Whenever there are in any country uncultivated lands and unemployed poor, it is clear that the laws of property have been so far extended as to violate natural right.

> THOMAS JEFFERSON (1743–1826). Letter to James Madison, 28 October 1785

Men might as well be imprisoned, as excluded from the means of earning their bread.

> JOHN STUART MILL (1806–1873). *On Liberty,* 2, 1859

It's amazing how radical an unemployed conservative can become.

> LAURENCE J. PETER (1919–1990). 28 February, *Peter's Almanac,* 1982

Unemployment is a reproach to a democratic government.

> JOAN ROBINSON (1903–1983). "What Has Become of the Keynesian Revolution?" In Milo Keynes, ed., *Essays on John Maynard Keynes,* 1975

The greatest deprivation anyone can suffer is to have no chance of looking after himself and making a livelihood.

> E. F. SCHUMACHER (1911–1977). *Small Is Beautiful: Economics as if People Mattered,* 3.4, 1973

It's a recession when your neighbor loses his job; it's a depression when you lose your own.

> HARRY S. TRUMAN (1884–1972). Interview, *New York World Telegram,* 12 April 1958

❧

The unemployment rate is 100 percent if it is you who is unemployed.

> ANONYMOUS

If you think the system is working, ask someone who isn't.

> SAYING (AMERICAN)

UNHAPPINESS

See also • Adversity ○ Anxiety ○ Burdens ○ Compassion ○ Complaint ○ Depression ○ Despair ○ Desperation ○ Difficulty ○ Dissatisfaction ○ Grief ○ Happiness ○ Misery ○ Misfortune ○ Pain ○ Sorrow ○ Struggle ○ Suicide ○ Trouble ○ Wretchedness ○ Youth: Beaumarchais

Man's Unhappiness . . . comes of his Greatness; it is because there is an Infinite in him, which with all his cunning he cannot quite bury under the Finite. . . . Try him with half of a Universe, of an Omnipotence, he sets to quarreling with the proprietor of the other half, and declares himself the most maltreated of men. Always there is a black spot in our sunshine: It is even, as I said, the *Shadow of Ourselves.*

> THOMAS CARLYLE (1795–1881). *Sartor Resartus: The Life and Opinions of Herr Teufelsdröckh,* 2.9, 1835

I envy those unhappy from their birth,
For to be bred and seasoned in misfortune
  Is to be iron to it,
But there is something in the pang of change
  More than the heart can bear,
Unhappiness remembering happiness.

> EURIPIDES (485?–406 B.C.). *Iphigenia in Tauris,* l. 1115, tr. Witter Bynner, 1956

Since thou canst not be wholly happy, take it in good part, that thou art not wholly unhappy.

> THOMAS FULLER (1654–1734). Comp., *Introductio ad Prudentiam,* 658, 1731

I cried at first . . . and then, it was such a beautiful day, that I forgot to be unhappy.

> FRANCES NOYES HART. "Green Gardens," *Scribner's Magazine,* July 1921

Unhappiness is not knowing what we want and killing ourselves to get it.

> DON HEROLD (1889–1966)

The world will never be long without some good reason to hate the unhappy; their real faults are immediately detected; and if those are not sufficient to sink them into infamy, an additional weight of calumny will be superadded.

> SAMUEL JOHNSON (1709–1784). In *The Adventurer* (English journal), 99, 16 October 1753

Years ago a person, he was unhappy, didn't know what to do with himself—he'd go to church, start a revolution—*something.* Today you're unhappy? Can't figure it out? What is the salvation? Go shopping.

> ARTHUR MILLER (1915–). *The Price,* 1, 1968

We are more unhappy to see people ahead of us than happy to see people behind us.

> MONTAIGNE (1533–1592). "Of Vanity," *Essays,* 1588, tr. Donald M. Frame, 1958

Unhappy [is] he who cannot do the good he would.

> PUBLIUS SYRUS (85–43 B.C.). *Moral Sayings,* 704, tr. Darius Lyman, Jr., 1862

Since unhappiness excites interest, many, in order to render themselves interesting, feign unhappiness.

> JOSEPH ROUX (1834–1886). *Meditations of a Parish Priest,* 5.24, tr. Isabel F. Hapgood, 1886

The most intelligent young people in Western countries tend to have that kind of unhappiness that comes of finding no adequate employment for their best talents.

> BERTRAND RUSSELL (1872–1970). *The Conquest of Happiness,* 10, 1930

When a man has lost all happiness,
he's not alive. Call him a breathing corpse.

> SOPHOCLES (496?–406 B.C.). *Antigone,* l. 1160, tr. Elizabeth Wyckoff, 1954
>
> See Death: William Cowper

UNIONS

See also • Class ○ Corporations ○ Unemployment ○ Wages ○ Work

Strike while your employer has a big contract.

> AMBROSE BIERCE (1842–1914). "Wise Saws and Modern Instances, or Poor Richard in Reverse," 1911

In 1954, 35.5 percent of all workers [in the United States] belonged to unions; [in 1995], only 15.5 percent.

> ABBOTT COMBES. "Sunday," *New York Times Magazine,* 3 September 1995

There is no right to strike against the public safety by anybody, anywhere, any time.

> CALVIN COOLIDGE (1872–1933). Referring to a strike by the Boston police force, telegram to Samuel Gompers, American Federation of Labor president, 14 September 1919

A scab in labor unions is the same as a traitor to his country.

> EUGENE V. DEBS (1855–1926)

Management and union may be likened to that serpent of the fables who on one body had two heads that fighting each other with poisoned fangs, killed themselves.

> PETER F. DRUCKER (1909–). *The New Society: The Anatomy of the Industrial Order,* 14, 1951

Work and pray, live on hay,
You'll get pie in the sky when you die.

> JOE HILL (1879–1915). Industrial Workers of the World leader. "The Preacher and the Slave" (song), 1911

I will die like a true-blue rebel. Don't waste any time in mourning—organize!

> JOE HILL (1879–1915). Farewell telegram to Bill Haywood, 18 November 1915. The next day Hill, having been convicted of what some believe was the trumped-up charge of killing a Salt Lake City grocer during a robbery, was executed by a firing squad.

No tin hat brigade of goose-stepping vigilantes or Bible-babbling mob of blackguarding and corporation-paid scoundrels will prevent the onward march of labor.

> JOHN L. LEWIS (1880–1969). United Mine Workers Union president. Speech, 5 September 1937

America faces a litany of social problems: illiteracy, crime, drug abuse, homelessness and escalating environmental decay in the central cities; rampant cultural and spiritual barrenness, and growing concentrations of economic and political power.

Why is it that the politicians, academics and religious leaders who can see so clearly the corrosive effects of oppression in socialist countries are virtually blind to the connection between social decay and the continued attacks upon unions and workers' rights at home?

> ERIC MANN. United Automobile Workers member and writer. "We Back Solidarity [the Polish trade union] and Bust Our Unions," *New York Times,* 7 May 1988

It is one of the characteristics of a free and democratic modern nation that it have free and independent labor unions.

> FRANKLIN D. ROOSEVELT (1882–1945). Speech before the Teamsters' Union Convention, Washington, 11 September 1940

It is essential that there should be organizations of labor. This is an era of organization. Capital organizes and therefore labor must organize.

THEODORE ROOSEVELT (1858–1919). Speech, Milwaukee, 14 October 1912

Where the union movement gets weak is where you have all those goddamn paid union staff organizers, who are no longer workers. They build a union bureaucracy which is just as decadent and as inflexible as management bureaucracy.

BENJAMIN S. ROSENTHAL (1923–1983). New York congressman. In Daniel Rapoport, *Inside the House: An Irreverent Guided Tour Through the House of Representatives,* 6, 1975

Eight hours for work,
Eight hours for sleep,
Eight hours for what you will.

SLOGAN (AMERICAN). National Labor Union of the United States, 1866

UNITED STATES

See • America

UNITY

See also • Brotherhood ∘ Buddhism: *The Book of the Golden Precepts* (5) ∘ Class: Gloria Steinem ∘ Community ∘ Equality ∘ Freedom ∘ Good & Evil: Aldous Huxley (1) ∘ Heaven ∘ Internationalism ∘ Knowledge: *Srimad Bhagavatam* ∘ Mankind ∘ Paradoxes: Proclus ∘ Religion & Science: Olympia Brown ∘ Self-Realization (Being): *The Book of the Golden Precepts* ∘ Struggle: Walt Whitman ∘ Universe: [especially] Dionysius the Areopagite, Hakuin, Marcus Aurelius ∘ World: [especially] André Gide

Union gives strength.

AESOP (6th cent. B.C.). "The Bundle of Sticks," *Fables,* tr. Joseph Jacobs, 1894 (Alternative translation: Unity gives strength.)

United we stand, divided we fall.

AESOP (6th cent. B.C.). "The Four Oxen and the Lion," *Fables,* tr. Joseph Jacobs, 1894

We, like parted drops of rain,
Swelling till they meet and run,
Shall be all absorbed again,
Melting, flowing into one.

BRONSON ALCOTT (1799–1888). "Stanzas" (8), *The Dial* (New England journal), July 1840

Then I was standing on the highest mountain of them all. . . . And I saw that the sacred hoop of my people was one of many hoops that made one circle, wide as daylight and as starlight, and in the center grew one mighty flowering tree to shelter all the children of one mother and one father. And I saw that it was holy.

BLACK ELK (1862–1950). In John G. Niehardt (Flaming Arrow), *Black Elk Speaks,* 3, 1961

The life of humanity is one whole, it is only to our frail powers of perception that its fluctuations in time or place are a rise and fall,

fortune and misfortune. The truth is that they are governed by a higher necessity.

JACOB BURCKHARDT (1818–1897). "On Fortune and Misfortune in History," 1871, *Force and Freedom: An Interpretation of History,* ed. James H. Nichols, 1943

Are not the mountains, waves, and skies, a part
Of me and of my soul, as I of them?

LORD BYRON (1788–1824). *Childe Harold's Pilgrimage,* 3.75, 1812–1818

Your Honor, years ago I recognized my kinship with all living beings, and I made up my mind that I was not one bit better than the meanest on earth. I said then, and I say now, that while there is a lower class, I am in it; while there is a criminal element, I am of it; and while there is a soul in prison, I am not free.

EUGENE V. DEBS (1855–1926). Opening words. Pre-sentencing statement to the court, Canton (Ohio), 14 September 1918
See Soldiers: Debs

All for one, and one for all.

ALEXANDRE DUMAS (1824–1895). *The Three Musketeers,* 9, 1844

All religions, arts and sciences are branches of the same tree.

ALBERT EINSTEIN (1879–1955). Opening words, message to the Young Men's Christian Association on its Founder's Day, 11 October 1937, *Out of My Later Years,* rev. ed., 4, 1956 (1950)

The reason why the world lacks unity, and lies broken and in heaps, is because man is disunited with himself.

RALPH WALDO EMERSON (1803–1882). "Prospects," *Nature,* 1836

It is one light which beams out of a thousand stars. It is one soul which animates all men.

RALPH WALDO EMERSON (1803–1882). "The American Scholar," address, Harvard University, Cambridge (Massachusetts), 31 August 1837

We are all boarders on one table—White man, black man, ox and eagle, bee and worm.

RALPH WALDO EMERSON (1803–1882). Journal, 13 July 1840

We must all hang together, or, most assuredly, we shall all hang separately.

BENJAMIN FRANKLIN (1706–1790). Attributed. Remark to John Hancock at the signing of the Declaration of Independence, Philadelphia, 4 July 1776

The whole Ocean is made of single Drops.

THOMAS FULLER (1654–1734). Comp., *Gnomologia: Adages and Proverbs,* 4825, 1732

I believe in the essential unity of man and, for that matter, all that lives. Therefore, I believe that if one man gains spiritually, the whole world gains with him; and, if one man falls, the whole world falls to that extent.

MOHANDAS K. GANDHI (1869–1948). In *Young India,* 4 December 1924
See Death: John Donne (1) ∘ Profit & Loss: Anonymous

The vast man in whom you are all but cells and sinews.

KAHLIL GIBRAN (1883–1931). "The Farewell," *The Prophet,* 1923

Those who are awake have One common world.

> HERACLITUS (540?–480? B.C.). In Karl R. Popper, *The Open Society and Its Enemies*, 1.2, 1945

All things come out of the one, and the one out of all things.

> HERACLITUS (540?–480? B.C.). In Bertrand Russell, *A History of Western Philosophy*, 1.1.4, 1946

What happens to one of us sooner or later happens to all; we have always been inescapably involved in a common destiny.

> GEORGE D. HERRON (1862–1925). In Upton Sinclair, ed., *The Cry for Justice: An Anthology of the Literature of Social Protest*, 16, 1915

In our innermost soul we know ourselves to be one with all being.

> HERMANN HESSE (1877–1962). *Reflections*, 195, ed. Volker Michels, 1974

If a kingdom is divided against itself, that kingdom cannot stand. And if a house is divided against itself, that house will not be able to stand.

> JESUS (A.D. 1st cent.). *Mark* 3:24–25

I am not anything that is anything I am not.

> BOB KAUFMAN (1925–1986). "I, Too, Know What I Am Not," *Solitudes Crowded with Loneliness*, 1965

Whatever affects one directly affects all indirectly. I can never be what I ought to be until you are what you ought to be, and you can never be what you ought to be until I am what I ought to be. This is the interrelated structure of reality.

> MARTIN LUTHER KING, JR. (1929–1968). *Strength to Love*, 7.2, 1963

"A house divided against itself cannot stand."

I believe this government cannot endure, permanently half *slave* and half *free*.

I do not expect the Union to be *dissolved*—I do not expect the house to *fall*—but I *do* expect it will cease to be divided.

It will become *all* one thing, or *all* the other.

> ABRAHAM LINCOLN (1809–1865). "House Divided" speech, Lincoln-Douglas debate, Springfield (Illinois), 16 June 1858
>
> See Public Speaking: William H. Herndon

The prophecy of a world moving toward political unity is the light which guides all that is best, most vigorous, most truly alive in the work of our time. It gives sense to what we are doing. Nothing else does.

> WALTER LIPPMANN (1889–1974). "Reflection After Armistice Day," *New York Herald Tribune*, 12 November 1931

One World or None.

> WALTER LIPPMANN (1889–1974). Book title, 1946

Don't we all have the same father? Didn't the same God create us all?

> MALACHI. *Malachi* 2:10

The world order is a unity made up of multiplicity: God is one, pervading all things; all being is one, all law is one . . . and all truth is one.

> MARCUS AURELIUS (A.D. 121–180). *Meditations*, 7.9, tr. Maxwell Staniforth, 1964

When we try to pick out anything by itself, we find it hitched to everything else in the universe. One fancies a heart like our own must be beating in every crystal and cell.

> JOHN MUIR (1838–1914). 27 July 1869, *My First Summer in the Sierra*, 6 ("Mount Hoffman and Lake Tenaya"), 1911

It is not in numbers but in unity that our great strength lies.

> THOMAS PAINE (1737–1809). "Of the Present Ability of America," *Common Sense*, 1776

There is neither Jew nor Greek, there is neither slave nor free, there is neither male nor female; for you are all one in Christ Jesus.

> PAUL (A.D. 1st cent.). *Galatians* 3:28
>
> See Sexist Statements: Paul

Nothing is foreign: Parts relate to whole;
One all-extending all-preserving Soul
Connects each being, greatest with the least;
Made Beast in aid of Man, and Man of Beast;
All serv'd, all serving! nothing stands alone;
The chain holds on, and where it ends, unknown.

> ALEXANDER POPE (1688–1744). *An Essay on Man*, 3.21, 1734

Just as short of Reason he must fall,
Who thinks all made for one, not one for all.

> ALEXANDER POPE (1688–1744). *An Essay on Man*, 3.47, 1734

The way of unity is love manifested as service.

> N. SRI RAM (1889–?). *Thoughts for Aspirants*, 14, 1972

As soon as [the] multitude is . . . united in one body, it is impossible to offend against one of the members without attacking the body, and still more, to offend against the body without the members resenting it.

> ROUSSEAU (1712–1778). *The Social Contract*, 1.7, 1762, tr. G. D. H. Cole, 1950

Mankind has become so much one family that we cannot insure our own prosperity except by insuring that of everyone else. If you wish to be happy yourself, you must resign yourself to seeing others also happy.

> BERTRAND RUSSELL (1872–1970). "The Science to Save Us from Science," *New York Times Magazine*, 19 March 1950

Isn't everyone a part of everyone else?

> BUDD SCHULBERG (1914–). *On the Waterfront* (film), 1954, spoken by Eva Marie Saint

Only that which is universal in obliging us to concern ourselves with all beings brings us truly into relationship with the Universe and the will which manifests itself in it.

> ALBERT SCHWEITZER (1875–1965). "The Problem of Ethics for Twentieth-Century Man," *Saturday Review*, 13 June 1953

One for all, or all for one.

> SHAKESPEARE (1564–1616). *The Rape of Lucrece*, l. 144, 1594

We are members one of another; so that you cannot injure or help your neighbor without injuring or helping yourself.

> GEORGE BERNARD SHAW (1856–1950). Preface ("The Alternative to Barabbas") to *Androcles and the Lion*, 1912

No one can be perfectly free till all are free; no one can be perfectly moral till all are moral; no one can be perfectly happy till all are happy.

> HERBERT SPENCER (1820–1903). *Social Statics*, 4.30.16, 1851
>
> See Mikhail Bakunin in Freedom

I'll be aroun' in the dark. I'll be ever'where—wherever you look. Wherever they's a fight so hungry people can eat, I'll be there. Wherever they's a cop beatin' up a guy, I'll be there. If Casy knowed, why, I'll be in the way guys yell when they're mad an'— I'll be in the way kids laugh when they're hungry an' they know supper's ready. An' when our folks eat the stuff they raise an' live in the houses they build—why, I'll be there.

> JOHN STEINBECK (1902–1968). Tom Joad's parting words to his mother when corrupt police officials forced him to leave a farm-labor camp in California during the Depression, *The Grapes of Wrath* (novel), 28, 1939

The sense of perfect harmony with the universe, of perfect harmony with another person, and of perfect harmony with the self are intimately connected; indeed, I believe them to be essentially the same phenomena.

> ANTHONY STORR (1920–). *Solitude: A Return to the Self*, 12, 1988

Unity in variety is the plan of the universe.

> SWAMI VIVEKANANDA (1863–1902). *What Religion Is,* 1.4, ed. Swami Vidyatmananda, 1963

We can find common ground only by moving to higher ground.

> JIM WALLIS (1948–). Introduction to *The Soul of Politics: A Practical and Prophetic Vision for Change,* 1994

The things we, as human beings, do not have in common are as nothing to the things that we do have in common.

> ALFRED NORTH WHITEHEAD (1861–1947). 17 June 1941, *Dialogues of Alfred North Whitehead,* rec. Lucien Price, 1954

Lo, soul! seest thou not God's purpose from the first?
The earth to be spann'd, connected by network,
The races, neighbors, to marry and be given in marriage,
The oceans to be cross'd, the distant brought near,
The lands to be welded together.

> WALT WHITMAN (1819–1892). "Passage to India" (2), 1871, *Leaves of Grass,* 1855-1892

One World.

> WENDELL WILLKIE (1892–1944). Book title, 1943

Dust as we are, the immortal spirit grows
Like harmony in music; there is a dark
Inscrutable workmanship that reconciles
Discordant elements, makes them cling together
In one society.

> WILLIAM WORDSWORTH (1770–1850). *The Prelude; or, Growth of a Poet's Mind: An Autobiographical Poem,* 1.339, 1850

All is One.

> XENOPHANES (560?–478? B.C.). In W. Y. Evans-Wentz, *Tibetan Yoga and Secret Doctrines,* p. 163, 1958
>
> See God: Moses (2) ○ God & the World: Anonymous (2)

❦

A rising tide lifts all boats.

> SAYING (AMERICAN). 1960s. Popularized by the Kennedy family.

There is no they, only us.

> SAYING (AMERICAN). Bumper sticker

Unity is in multiplicity and multiplicity is in unity.

> SAYING (SUFI)

Unite or Die.

> SLOGAN (AMERICAN). Caption under the drawing of a snake divided into eight parts (on a flag), 1754

UNIVERSE

See also • God & the World ○ Unity ○ World

Is the universe a great mechanism, a great computation, a great symmetry, a great accident or a great thought?

> JOHN D. BARROW. University of Sussex astronomer. In John Edge, comp., "In an On-Line Salon, Scientists Sit Back and Ponder: What Is the Question You Are Asking Yourself," *New York Times,* 30 December 1997

Gazing up at the stars, for the first time, the first, I laid my heart open to the benign indifference of the universe.

> ALBERT CAMUS (1913–1960). From the closing paragraph, *The Stranger,* 1942, tr. Stuart Gilbert, 1946

The universe . . . is both One and Many.

> DIONYSIUS THE AREOPAGITE (A.D. 1st cent.). Syrian Christian writer. In Whitall N. Perry, comp., *A Treasury of Traditional Wisdom,* p. 775, 1986

The universe is represented in an atom, in a moment of time.

> RALPH WALDO EMERSON (1803–1882). "The Over-Soul," *Essays: First Series,* 1841

All aspects of the universe—the relative and the absolute—are but one in reality.

> HAKUIN (1685–1768). Japanese Zen master. *The Embossed Tea Kettle and Other Works of Hakuin Zenji,* p. 111, tr. R. D. M. Shaw, 1963
>
> See World: André Gide

In my youth I regarded the universe as an open book, printed in the language of physical equations, whereas now it appears to me as a text written in invisible ink, of which in our rare moments of grace we are able to decipher a small fragment.

> ARTHUR KOESTLER (1905–1983). Epilogue to *Bricks to Babel: Selected Writings with Author's Comments,* 1980

Always think of the universe as one living organism, with a single substance and a single soul.

> MARCUS AURELIUS (A.D. 121–180). *Meditations,* 4.40, tr. Maxwell Staniforth, 1964

The universe is a sphere whose center is wherever there is intelligence. The sun is not so central as a man.

> HENRY DAVID THOREAU (1817–1862). "Friday," *A Week on the Concord and Merrimack Rivers,* 1849

The universe becomes intelligible to the extent of our ability to apprehend it as a whole.

> ARNOLD J. TOYNBEE (1889–1975). Preface to *Civilization on Trial,* 1948

Perhaps the immense Milky Way which on clear nights we behold stretching across the heavens, this vast encircling ring in which our planetary system is itself but a molecule, is in turn but a cell in the Universe, in the Body of God.

> MIGUEL de UNAMUNO (1864–1936). *Tragic Sense of Life,* 7, 1913, tr. J. E. Crawford Flitch, 1921

I heard what was said of the universe,
Heard it and heard it of several thousand years;
It is middling well as far as it goes—but is that all?

> WALT WHITMAN (1819–1892). "Song of Myself" (41), 1855, *Leaves of Grass,* 1855–1892

And there is no object so soft but it makes the hub for the
   wheel'd universe.
And I say to any man or woman, Let your soul stand cool and
   composed before a million universes.

> WALT WHITMAN (1819–1892). "Song of Myself" (48), 1855, *Leaves of Grass,* 1855–1892

UNIVERSITY

See also • College ○ Education ○ Learning (Process) ○ Libraries: Thomas Carlyle ○ School ○ Teachers

I was dropped by New York University because of bad marks. I was a film major.

> WOODY ALLEN (1935–). Academy-Award winning film maker. William E. Geist interview, *Rolling Stone,* 9 April 1987

You can always tell a Harvard man, but you can't tell him much.

> JAMES BARNES (1866–1936)

I was a modest, good-humored boy. It is Oxford that has made me insufferable.

> SIR MAX BEERBOHM (1872–1956). "Going Back to School," *More,* 1899

The most important function of the university in an age of reason is to protect reason from itself, by being the model of true openness.

> ALLAN BLOOM (1930–1992). "From Socrates' *Apology* to Heidegger's *Rektoratsrede,*" *The Closing of the American Mind: How Higher Education Has Failed Democracy and Impoverished the Souls of Today's Students,* 1987

They have professors of all the languages of the principal beasts and birds.

> SAMUEL BUTLER (1835–1902). On one feature of his utopian university, *The Note-Books of Samuel Butler,* 18, ed. Henry Festing Jones, 1907

The first duty of a university is to teach wisdom, not a trade; character, not technicalities. We want a lot of engineers in the modern world, but we don't want a world of engineers.

> WINSTON CHURCHILL (1874–1965). Address, University of Copenhagen, 10 October 1950

These kids are smart. But I'd as soon take a python to bed as hire one.

> NED DEWEY. On recent business school graduates. In Bruce Nussbaum and Alex Beam, "Remaking the Harvard B-School," *Business Week,* 24 March 1986

Ye can lade a man up to th' university, but ye can't make him think.

> FINLEY PETER DUNNE (1867–1936). "Mr. Carnegie's Gift," *Mr. Dooley's Opinions,* 1901

A university education should equip one to entertain three things: a friend, an idea and one's self.

> THOMAS EHRLICH (with JULIET FREY). *The Courage to Inquire: Ideals and Realities in Higher Education,* 1, 1995

Universities are, of course, hostile to geniuses, [who], seeing and using ways of their own, discredit the routine.

> RALPH WALDO EMERSON (1803–1882). Journal, 1854, undated

If you feel that you have both feet planted on level ground, then the university has failed you.

> ROBERT F. GOHEEN (1919–). Princeton University president. Speech. In "People," *Time,* 23 June 1961

We Teach Success.

> HOFSTRA UNIVERSITY. Hempstead (New York). Slogan in ad, *New York Times,* 21 April 1993

The modern university confers the privilege of dissent on those who have been tested and classified as potential money-makers or power-holders. . . . Schools select for each successive level those who have, at earlier stages in the game, proved themselves good risks for the established order.

> IVAN ILLICH (1926–). *Deschooling Society,* 3, 1970

Any attempt to reform the university without attending to the system of which it is an integral part is like trying to do urban renewal in New York City from the twelfth story up.

> IVAN ILLICH (1926–). *Deschooling Society,* 3, 1970

I find that the three major administrative problems on a campus are sex for the students, athletics for the alumni, and parking for the faculty.

> CLARK KERR (1911–). University of California president. Address. University of Washington, Seattle, in "View from the Bridge," *Time,* 17 November 1958

The real University is a state of mind. It is that great heritage of rational thought that has been brought down to us through the centuries and which does not exist at any specific location. . . . The real University is nothing less than the continuing body of reason itself.

> ROBERT M. PIRSIG (1928–). *Zen and the Art of Motorcycle Maintenance: An Inquiry into Values,* 13, 1974

It is time that we had uncommon schools, that we did not leave off our education when we begin to be men and women. It is time that villages were universities, and their elder inhabitants the fellows of universities.

> HENRY DAVID THOREAU (1817–1862). "Reading," *Walden; or Life in the Woods,* 1854

Four years was enough of Harvard. I still had a lot to learn but had been given the liberating notion that now I could teach myself.

> JOHN UPDIKE (1932–). In Doris G. Kinney, "Old, Old, Harvard," *Life*, September 1986
>
> See Education: Arnold J. Toynbee (2)

Business success is by common consent, and quite uncritically, taken to be conclusive evidence of wisdom even in matters that have no relation to business affairs. So that it stands as a matter of course that businessmen must be preferred for the guardianship and control of that intellectual enterprise for the pursuit of which the university is established.

> THORSTEIN VEBLEN (1857–1929). *The Higher Learning in America: A Memorandum on the Conduct of the Universities by Business Men*, 5, 1918

The function of a University is to enable you to shed details in favor of principles.

> ALFRED NORTH WHITEHEAD (1861–1947). *The Aims of Education and Other Essays*, 2, 1929

The literary side of a technical education should consist in an effort to make the pupils enjoy literature. It does not matter what they know, but the enjoyment is vital. The great English Universities, under whose direct authority school children are examined in plays of Shakespeare, to the certain destruction of their enjoyment, should be prosecuted for soul murder.

> ALFRED NORTH WHITEHEAD (1861–1947). *The Aims of Education and Other Essays*, 4, 1929

The tragedy of the world is that those who are imaginative have but slight experience, and those who are experienced have feeble imaginations. Fools act on imagination without knowledge; pedants act on knowledge without imagination. The task of a university is to weld together imagination and experience.

> ALFRED NORTH WHITEHEAD (1861–1947). *The Aims of Education and Other Essays*, 7.2, 1929

VALOR

See also • Bravery ○ Courage ○ Courage, Moral

The better part of valor is indiscretion.

> SAMUEL BUTLER (1835–1902). *Further Extracts from the Note-Books of Samuel Butler*, 2, ed. A. T. Bartholomew, 1934

Valor lies just halfway between rashness and cowheartedness.

> CERVANTES (1547–1616). *Don Quixote*, 2.3.4, 1615, tr. Peter Anthony Motteux and John Ozell, 1743
>
> See Courage: Plutarch

Valor consists in the power of self-recovery.

> RALPH WALDO EMERSON (1803–1882). "Circles," *Essays: First Series*, 1841

Valor can do but little without discretion.

> JOHN RAY (1628–1705). Comp., *A Collection of English Proverbs*, p. 21, 1678

Valor is a gift. Those having it never know for sure whether they have it till the test comes. And those having it in one test never know for sure if they will have it when the next test comes.

> CARL SANDBURG (1878–1967). In news reports, 14 December 1954

Falstaff: The better part of valor is discretion.

> SHAKESPEARE (1564–1616). *Henry IV*, Part I, 5.4.120, 1597 (Popular version: Discretion is the better part of valor.)
>
> See Biography: Justin Kaplan

Benedick: In a false quarrel there is no true valor.

> SHAKESPEARE (1564–1616). *Much Ado About Nothing*, 5.1.120, 1598
>
> See Courage: Manfred Rommel

Caesar: Cowards die many times before their deaths;
The valiant never taste of death but once.

> SHAKESPEARE (1564–1616). *Julius Caesar*, 2.1.32, 1599

Valor was there only hope.

> TACITUS (A.D. 56?–120?). *The History*, 2.20, tr. Alfred J. Church and William J. Brodribb, 1942

There is a great difference between valor and a contempt for life.

> SAYING (LATIN)

There can be no true valor in a bad cause.

> SAYING
>
> See Courage: Manfred Rommel

VALUE

See also • Business (Commerce) ○ Economics ○ Merchants & Customers ○ Money ○ Price ○ Quality ○ Quantity ○ Values ○ Wisdom: Lao-tzu (4)

To gain that which is worth having, it may be necessary to lose everything else.

> BERNADETTE DEVLIN (1947–). Preface to *The Price of My Soul*, 1969

The Worth of a thing is best known by the want of it.

> JAMES KELLY (18th cent.). Comp., *A Complete Collection of Scottish Proverbs Explained and Made Intelligible to the English Reader*, T.274, 1721

Labor is the true standard of value.

> ABRAHAM LINCOLN (1809–1865). Speech, Pittsburgh, 15 February 1861

Nothing can have value without being an object of utility.

> KARL MARX (1818–1883). *Capital: A Critique of Political Economy,* 1.1, 1867–1894, tr. Samuel Moore and Edward Aveling, 1906

Everything is worth what its purchaser will pay for it.

> PUBLIUS SYRUS (85–43 B.C.). *Moral Sayings,* 847, tr. Darius Lyman, Jr., 1862 (Popular version: The worth of a thing is what it will bring.)

Value is the life-giving power of anything; cost, the quantity of labor required to produce it; price, the quantity of labor which its possessor will take in exchange for it.

> JOHN RUSKIN (1819–1900). *Munera Pulveris,* 1.12, 1862

A thing is worth precisely what it can do for you; not what you choose to pay for it.

> JOHN RUSKIN (1819–1900). *The Queen of the Air,* 3.125, 1869

How many things we fail to realize are superfluous until they begin to be wanting.

> SENECA THE YOUNGER (5? B.C.–A.D. 65). "On the Conflict between Pleasure and Virtue," *Moral Letters to Lucilius,* 123.6

The word VALUE . . . has two different meanings, and sometimes expresses the utility of some particular object, and sometimes the power of purchasing other goods which the possession of that object conveys. The one may be called "value in use"; the other, "value in exchange."

> ADAM SMITH (1723–1790). *The Wealth of Nations,* 1.4, 1776

Each person is born to one possession which outvalues all his others—his last breath.

> MARK TWAIN (1835–1910). *Following the Equator: A Journey Around the World,* 42 (epigraph), 1897

There is no such thing as absolute value in this world. You can only estimate what a thing is worth to *you.*

> CHARLES DUDLEY WARNER (1829–1900). "Sixteenth Week," *My Summer in a Garden,* 1871

❧

A penny in a pinch is worth a pound.

> SAYING (ENGLISH)

Thirst teaches the value of water.

> SAYING (Russian)

VALUES

See also • Change: John Naisbitt ○ Civilization: George P. Shultz ○ Conformity: William H. Whyte, Jr. (1) ○ Consumerism ○ Conversion: Robert Penn Warren ○ Culture ○ Education: [especially] Dean William Ralph Inge ○ Faith: Dean William Ralph Inge ○ Ideals ○ Materialism ○ Meaning ○ Morality ○ Motives ○ Parents: Norman F. Dixon, Colin Powell ○ Principles, Moral ○ Purpose ○ Transformation: Kazimierz Dabrowski ○ Value ○ World: Abraham Joshua Heschel

The supreme value and the highest good is not life as such, but spiritual life rising up to God—not the quantity, but the quality of life.

> NICOLAS BERDYAEV (1874–1948). *The Destiny of Man,* 1.1, 1931, tr. Natalie Duddington, 1955

Authentic values are those by which a life can be lived, which can form a people that produces great deeds and thoughts.

> ALLAN BLOOM (1930–1992). "Values," *The Closing of the American Mind: How Higher Education Has Failed Democracy and Impoverished the Souls of Today's Students,* 1987

The fundamental value in relations among people is to respect the dignity and the individuality of fellow men, to treat them not as objects to be manipulated for our purposes or in accordance with our values but as persons, with their own rights and their own values—as persons to be persuaded, not coerced, not forced, not bulldozed, not brainwashed.

> MILTON FRIEDMAN (1912–). "Is Capitalism Humane?" (1978), *Bright Promises, Dismal Performance: An Economist's Protest,* ed. William R. Allen, 1983

It is not our affluence, or our plumbing, or our clogged freeways that grip the imagination of others. Rather, it is the values upon which our system is built. These values imply our adherence not only to liberty and individual freedom, but also to international peace, law and order, and constructive social purpose. When we depart from these values, we do so at our peril.

> J. WILLIAM FULBRIGHT (1905–1995). Senate speech, 29 June 1961

If you want a sense of the personal values we should be communicating to children, get the Boy Scout or Girl Scout handbook. Or go and look at *Readers' Digest* and *The Saturday Evening Post* from around 1955. Healthy societies send healthy signals to their children and to those who have become temporarily confused at any age.

> NEWT GINGRICH (1943–). *To Renew America,* 6, 1995

We need spiritual values, we need a revolution of the mind.

> MIKHAIL S. GORBACHEV (1931–). Speech, Rome. In Richard Lacayo, "Turning Visions into Reality," *Time,* 11 December 1989

If one benefits tangibly from the exploitation of others who are weak, is one morally implicated in their predicament? Or are basic rights of human existence confined to the civilized societies that are wealthy enough to afford them? Our values are defined by what we will tolerate when it is done to others.

> WILLIAM GREIDER (1936–). *One World, Ready or Not: The Manic Logic of Global Capitalism,* 1997. Excerpted in Utne Reader, May-June, 1997

Without commonly shared and widely entrenched moral values and obligations, neither the law, nor democratic government, nor even the market economy, will function properly.

> VÁCLAV HAVEL (1936–). "Politics, Morality, and Civility," *Summer Meditations,* 1991, tr. Paul Wilson, 1992

We no longer know how to justify any value except in terms of expediency. Man is willing to define himself as "a seeker after the maximum degree of comfort for the minimum expenditure of energy." He equates value with that which avails. He feels, acts, and thinks as if the sole purpose of the universe were to satisfy his needs.

> ABRAHAM JOSHUA HESCHEL (1907–1972). *The Insecurity of Freedom: Essays on Human Existence,* 3, 1967

A true revolution of values will soon look uneasily on the glaring contrast of poverty and wealth.

MARTIN LUTHER KING, JR. (1929–1968). *Where Do We Go from Here: Chaos or Community?* 6.3, 1967

A genuine revolution of values means in the final analysis that our loyalties must become ecumenical rather than sectional. Every nation must now develop an overriding loyalty to mankind as a whole in order to preserve the best in their individual societies.

MARTIN LUTHER KING, JR. (1929–1968). "Declaration of Independence from the War in Vietnam," sermon, Riverside Church, New York City, 4 April 1967

The abuses of nineteenth-century industrialism which spawned Marxism were due above all to the enthronement of efficiency and productivity as the primary goals. The real evil was that the values of the industrial process achieved primacy over those of human dignity.

HENRY A. KISSINGER (1923–). *The Necessity for Choice: Prospects of American Foreign Policy,* 7.1, 1961

If a nation values anything more than freedom, it will lose its freedom; and the irony of it is that if it is comfort or money that it values more, it will lose that too.

W. SOMERSET MAUGHAM (1874–1965). *Strictly Personal,* 31, 1941

The moral uneasiness of our time—in politics and economics, in family life, educational institutions, and even in our churches—is due to this key fact: the older values and codes of uprightness no longer grip us, nor have they been replaced by new values and codes which would lend moral meaning and sanction to the life-routines we must now follow.

C. WRIGHT MILLS (1916–1962). 1952, *Power, Politics and People: The Collected Essays of C. Wright Mills,* 3.6.2, ed. Irving Louis Horowitz, 1963

Revaluation of all values!

FRIEDRICH NIETZSCHE (1844–1900). Closing words, *The Anti-Christ,* 1895, tr. R. J. Hollingdale, 1968

See Civilization, Modern: George F. Will ○ Self-Realization (Becoming): Elias Canetti

There's a tendency to throw aside old values as belonging to an earlier generation. Don't discard those values that have proven, over the period of time, their value. Just believe in those values that made our nation great and keep them: faith, family, hard work, and, above all, freedom.

RONALD REAGAN (1911–). Speech before junior livestock competition participants at the Illinois State Fair, Springfield, 12 August 1986

As for China's old moral standards, they are not yet lost sight of by the people of China. First come loylty and filial devotion, then kindness and love, then faithfulness and justice, then harmony and peace.

SUN YAT-SEN (1866–1925). Speech, 2 March 1924

I was brought up by a Victorian grandmother. We were taught to work jolly hard. We were taught to prove ourselves; we were taught self-reliance; we were taught to live within our income. . . . You were taught that cleanliness is next to godliness. You were

taught self-respect. You were taught always to give a hand to your neighbor. You were taught tremendous pride in your country. All of these things are Victorian values.

MARGARET THATCHER (1925–). Radio interview, LBC, London, 15 April 1983

❧

Slow me down, Lord, and inspire me to send my roots deep into the soil of life's enduring values that I may grow toward the stars of my greater destiny.

ANONYMOUS

VANITY

See also • Conceit ○ Conscience: Martin Luther King, Jr. ○ Egotism ○ Envy ○ Pride ○ Self-Love

Vanity and pride are different things, though the words are often used synonymously. A person may be proud without being vain. Pride relates more to our opinion of ourselves; vanity, to what we would have others think of us.

JANE AUSTEN (1775–1817). *Pride and Prejudice,* 5, 1813

The good things that men do kan oftner be traced tew their vanity than tew their virtew.

JOSH BILLINGS (1818–1885). "Kindling Wood," *Everybody's Friend, or; Josh Billing's Encyclopedia and Proverbial Philosophy of Wit and Humor,* 1874

Only vain people wage war against the vanity of others.

COUNTESS OF BLESSINGTON (1789–1849). *The Confessions of an Elderly Lady,* p. 163, 1838

Vanity, or to call it by a gentler name, the desire of admiration and applause, is, perhaps, the most universal principle of human actions. . . . Where that desire is wanting, we are apt to be indifferent, listless, indolent, and inert.

LORD CHESTERFIELD (1694–1773). Letter to his son, 16 November 1752

Vanity . . . betokens a weak ego.

NORMAN F. DIXON (1922–). *On the Psychology of Military Incompetence,* 27, 1976

Vain-Glory flowereth, but beareth no Fruit.

BENJAMIN FRANKLIN (1706–1790). *Poor Richard's Almanack,* April 1756

I scarce ever heard or saw the introductory words, *"Without vanity I may say,"* etc., but some vain thing immediately followed.

BENJAMIN FRANKLIN (1706–1790). 1771, *Autobiography,* 1798

The indigent world could be clothed out of the trimmings of the vain.

OLIVER GOLDSMITH (1728–1774). *She Stoops to Conquer: Or, the Mistakes of Night,* 1, 1773

Some men's heads are as easily blown away as their hats.

MARQUIS OF HALIFAX (1633–1695). "Of Vanity," *Political, Moral and Miscellaneous Reflections,* 1750

We probably have a greater love for those we support than those who support us. Our vanity carries more weight than our self-interest.

> ERIC HOFFER (1902–1983). *The Passionate State of Mind: And Other Aphorisms*, 202, 1954

Nothing so soothes our vanity as a display of greater vanity in others; it makes us vain, in fact, of our modesty.

> LOUIS KRONENBERGER (1904–1980). "Aphorisms," *Vogue*, 1 March 1964

What makes the vanity of others intolerable is that it hurts our own.

> LA ROCHEFOUCAULD (1613–1680). *Maxims*, 389, 1665, tr. Leonard Tancock, 1959

The most violent passions sometimes let us relax, but vanity keeps us perpetually on the go.

> LA ROCHEFOUCAULD (1613–1680). *Maxims*, 443, 1665, tr. Leonard Tancock, 1959

There are two parts in . . . vainglory, namely, to esteem ourselves too highly, and not to esteem others highly enough.

> MONTAIGNE (1533–1592). "Of Presumption," *Essays*, 1588, tr. Donald M. Frame, 1958

To be a Man's own Fool is bad enough, but the Vain Man is Everybody's.

> WILLIAM PENN (1644–1718). *More Fruits of Solitude*, 241, 1693

The highest form of vanity is love of fame.

> GEORGE SANTAYANA (1863–1952). *The Life of Reason or The Phases of Human Progress*, 2.6, 1905–1906

You're so vain,
you probably think this song is about you.

> CARLY SIMON (1945–). "You're So Vain" (song), 1973

A man receives the shocks of life on the buffer of his vanity.

> ALEXANDER SMITH (1830–1867). *Dreamthorp*, 8, 1863

"All is vanity," except to love God and serve Him alone.

> THOMAS à KEMPIS (1380–1471). *The Imitation of Christ*, 1.1, tr. Leo Sherley-Price, 1952

There are no grades of vanity, there are only grades of ability in concealing it.

> MARK TWAIN (1835–1910). 26 November 1896. *Mark Twain's Notebook*, ed. Albert Bigelow Paine, 1935

Vanity as an impulse has without a doubt been of far more benefit to civilization than modesty has ever been.

> W. E. WOODWARD (1874–1950). *George Washington: The Image and the Man*, 5.1, 1926

❦

Vanity of vanities, says the Preacher; all is vanity.

> ANONYMOUS (*BIBLE*). *Ecclesiastes*, 12:8

VEGETARIANISM

See also • Food

Much meat, much malady.

> JOHN CLARKE (1596–1658). Comp., *Proverbs: English and Latine*, p. 98, 1639

You have just dined, and however scrupulously the slaughterhouse is concealed in the graceful distance of miles, there is complicity.

> RALPH WALDO EMERSON (1803–1882). "Fate," *The Conduct of Life*, 1860

I have known many meat eaters to be far more nonviolent than vegetarians.

> MOHANDAS K. GANDHI (1869–1948). In *Harijan*, 25 August 1940

Vegetables are interesting but lack a sense of purpose when unaccompanied by a good cut of meat.

> FRAN LEBOWITZ (1951–). "Food for Thought and Vice Versa," *Metropolitan Life*, 1978

I impute a great Part of our Diseases in *England* to our eating too much *Flesh* and too little *Bread*.

> JOHN LOCKE (1632–1704). *Some Thoughts Concerning Education*, 14, 1693

It is nearly 50 years since I was assured by a conclave of doctors that if I did not eat meat, I should die of starvation.

> GEORGE BERNARD SHAW (1856–1950). At age 87. *Everybody's Political What's What?* 21, 1944

I think that everything connected with vegetarianism is of the highest importance because there will never be any peace in the world so long as we eat animals. . . . I had felt guilty and ashamed about the fact that I had eaten the flesh of an animal. I think that animals are as much God's creatures as men are. And we have to respect and love them, not slaughter them.

> ISAAC BESHIVER SINGER (1904–1991). In Rynn Berry, *Famous Vegetarians and Their Favorite Recipes*, 1990

The road to health is paved with vegetables, fruits, beans, rice and grains.

> POLLY STRAND. Letter to *San Francisco Chronicle*, 19 March 1993

It is a part of the destiny of the human race, in its gradual improvement, to leave off eating animals, as surely as the savage tribes have left off eating each other when they came into contact with the more civilized.

> HENRY DAVID THOREAU (1817–1862). "Higher Laws," *Walden; or Life in the Woods*, 1854

Mr. Delamotte and I began to try whether life might not be as well sustained by one sort as by [a] variety of food. We chose to make the experiment with bread, and were never more vigorous and healthy than while we tasted nothing else.

> JOHN WESLEY (1703–1791). Journal, 30 March 1736

On an average day in America, 130,000 cattle, 7,000 calves, 360,000 pigs, and 24 million chickens are killed.

> JOY WILLIAMS. "The Inhumanity of the Animal People," *Harper's*, August 1997

❦

And God said, "Behold, I have given you every plant yielding seed which is upon the face of all the earth, and every tree with seed in its fruit; you shall have them for food."

> ANONYMOUS (*BIBLE*). *Genesis* 1:29

VICE

See also • Evil ∘ Morality ∘ Sin ∘ Virtue ∘ Virtue & Vice

Vices are their own punishment.

> AESOP (6th cent. B.C.). "Avaricious and Envious," *Fables,* tr. Joseph Jacobs, 1894
>
> See Virtue & Vice: Baltazar Gracián

The vices we scoff at in others laugh at us within ourselves.

> SIR THOMAS BROWNE (1605–1682). *Christian Morals,* 3.15, 1716, ed. John Addington Symonds, 1886

Vice is its own reward.

> QUENTIN CRISP (1908–). *The Naked Civil Servant,* 2, 1968

It is by means of my vices that I understand yours.

> RALPH WALDO EMERSON (1803–1882). Journal, 1844?–1845, undated

What maintains one Vice would bring up two Children.

> BENJAMIN FRANKLIN (1706–1790). *Poor Richard's Almanack,* September 1747

The second Vice is Lying; the first is Running in Debt.

> BENJAMIN FRANKLIN (1706–1790). *Poor Richard's Almanack,* August 1748

Vice would be frightful if it did not wear a Mask.

> THOMAS FULLER (1654–1734). Comp., *Gnomologia: Adages and Proverbs,* 5360, 1732

The hour of reformation is always delayed; every delay gives vice another opportunity of fortifying itself by habit.

> SAMUEL JOHNSON (1709–1784). In *The Rambler* (English journal), 155, 10 September 1751

When the vices give us up, we flatter ourselves that we are giving up them.

> LA ROCHEFOUCAULD (1613–1680). *Maxims,* 192, 1665, tr. Leonard Tancock, 1959

Everybody likes to see somebody else get caught for the vices practiced by themselves.

> MARYA MANNES (1904–1990). *More in Anger,* 2.3, 1958

Some, either from being glued to vice by a natural attachment, or from long habit, no longer recognize its ugliness.

> MONTAIGNE (1533–1592). "Of Repentance," *Essays,* 1588, tr. Donald M. Frame, 1958

The vices of others we keep before our eyes, our own behind our back.

> SENECA THE YOUNGER (5? B.C.–A.D. 65). "On Anger" (2.28.8), *Moral Essays,* tr. John W. Basore, 1928

Vice is waste of life. Poverty, obedience and celibacy are the canonical vices.

> GEORGE BERNARD SHAW (1856–1950). "Maxims for Revolutionists: Virtues and Vices," *Man and Superman,* 1903

When we are shocked at vice, we express a lingering sympathy with it. Dry rot, rust, and mildew shock no man, for none is subject to them.

> HENRY DAVID THOREAU (1817–1862). Journal, 22 June 1840

The mercenary sacrifice of the public good to a private interest is the eternal stamp of vice.

> VAUVENARGUES (1715–1747). In Ralph Waldo Emerson, "Character," *Lectures and Biographical Sketches,* 1883

He hasn't a single redeeming vice.

> OSCAR WILDE (1854–1900)

❧

Cultivate vices when you are young, and when you are old they will not forsake you.

> ANONYMOUS

VICE PRESIDENTS

See also • Presidents

The most insignificant office that ever the invention of man contrived or his imagination conceived.

> JOHN ADAMS (1735–1826). First American vice president. On the vice presidency. In Doris Kearns Goodwin, *Lyndon Johnson and the American Dream,* 6, 1976

It only takes one vote to win the Vice Presidential nomination.

> ROBERT J. DOLE (1923–). On a presidential nominee's power to choose his running mate, television appearance, CNN, 15 June 1991

The vice presidency is the sand trap of American politics.

> HOWARD FINEMAN (1948–). "Rx for the Veep," *Newsweek,* 20 May 1991

The vice presidency isn't worth a pitcher of warm piss.

> JOHN NANCE GARNER (1868–1967). Vice president during the Roosevelt Administration, 1937–1941. In O. C. Fisher, *Cactus Jack,* p. 118, 1982 (Popular version: The vice presidency isn't worth a pitcher of warm spit.)

Every time I came into John Kennedy's presence, I felt like a goddamn raven hovering over his shoulder.

> LYNDON B. JOHNSON (1908–1973). Vice president. In Doris Kearns Goodwin, *Lyndon Johnson and the American Dream,* 6, 1976

Once there were two brothers. One ran away to sea, the other was elected vice president, and nothing was ever heard from either of them again.

> THOMAS R. MARSHALL (1845–1925). Vice president during the Wilson Administration, 1913–1921

The Republican vice Presidential candidate—who asks you to place him a heartbeat from the Presidency—has attacked me for saying in a court deposition that the character of Alger Hiss was good.

> ADLAI STEVENSON (1900–1965). Campaign speech, Cleveland Arena, 1952. In William Safire, *Safire's New Political Dictionary: The Definitive Guide to the New Language of Politics,* p. 321, 1993 (1968)

After all, I'm just a—what do they call it?—political eunuch.

> HARRY S. TRUMAN (1884–1972). Referring to his lack of influence as vice president, remark to reporters, 3 March 1945. In Alonzo L. Hamby, *Man of the People: A Life of Harry S. Truman,* 17.5, 1995. Two months later, on the death of Franklin D. Roosevelt, Truman became President.

VICTORY

See also • Competition ○ Defeat ○ Effort: Mohandas K. Gandhi (1) ○ Losing ○ Peace: St. Robert Bellarmine, Ralph Waldo Emerson, Anonymous (2) ○ Profit & Loss ○ Revolutionary War: George Washington (3) ○ Self-Discipline: Thomas à Kempis ○ Sports ○ Strategy, Military ○ Success ○ Victory & Defeat ○ War ○ Winning: [especially] Vince Lombardi (1,2), Henry "Red" Sanders ○ World War II: Winston Churchill (3)

I will not steal a victory.

> ALEXANDER (356–323 B.C.). In Plutarch (A.D. 46?–119?), "Alexander," *Parallel Lives,* Dryden edition, 1693

You know, Hannibal, how to gain a victory, but not how to use it.

> BARCAS (3rd cent. B.C.). Remark to his son, the Carthaginian commander, who had been slow to follow up his victory over the Roman army at the Battle of Cannae (Italy) in 216 B.C. In Plutarch (A.D. 46?–119?), "Fabius," *Parallel Lives,* Dryden edition, 1693

All victories are vain but the last.

> CORRELLI BARNETT (1927–). *The Desert Generals,* 5.3, 1960

In war, victory goes to those armies whose leaders' uniforms are least impressive.

> ROGER A. BEAUMONT and BERNARD J. JAMES. "The Sukhomlinov Effect," *Horizon,* Winter 1971

Victory comes, at times, just when one no longer expects it.

> MARTIN BUBER (1878–1965). "Gandhi, Politics, and Us," 1930, *Pointing the Way,* 1957

The greatest of victories is the victory over oneself.

> THE DHAMMAPADA: THE PATH OF PERFECTION (1st cent. B.C.). 105, tr. Juan Mascaró, 1973
> See Self-Discipline: Saying (*Bible*)

The real and lasting victories are those of peace and not of war.

> RALPH WALDO EMERSON (1803–1882). "Worship," *The Conduct of Life,* 1860
> See War & Peace: Emerson, John Milton, Theodore Roosevelt

The will to conquer is the first condition of victory.

> FERDINAND FOCH (1851–1929). In Charles Bugnet, "Results" (Development of a Leader), *Foch Speaks,* tr. Russell Green, 1929

Do not scorn little victories.

> ANDRÉ GIDE (1869–1951). Journal, January 1912, tr. Justin O'Brien, 1948

The victor need not explain.

> BALTASAR GRACIÁN (1601–1658). *The Art of Worldly Wisdom,* 66, 1647, tr. Joseph Jacobs, 1943
> See Success: Thomas Fuller

It is a great victory that comes without blood.

> GEORGE HERBERT (1593–1633). Comp., *Outlandish Proverbs,* 227, 1640

The victor will not be asked afterwards whether he told the truth or not. In starting and waging war, it is not right that matters, but victory.

> ADOLF HITLER (1889–1945). Speech to German generals on the eve of World War II, 22 August 1939

In war . . . there can be no substitute for victory.

> DOUGLAS MacARTHUR (1880–1964). Congress address, 19 April 1951

[Politicians in the United States] see nothing wrong in the rule, that to the victor belong the spoils of the enemy.

> WILLIAM L. MARCY (1786–1857). New York senator and U.S. secretary of state. Senate speech, 25 January 1832

Nature has doomed me to win none but outward victories!

> NAPOLEON (1769–1821). Letter to Josephine, 1796. In Emil Ludwig, *Napoleon,* 2.4, 1925, tr. Eden and Cedar Paul, 1926

The first step towards victory . . . is to gain courage.

> PLUTARCH (A.D. 46?–119?). "Themistocles," *Parallel Lives,* Dryden edition, 1693

Victory waits upon unity of action.

> PUBLIUS SYRUS (85–43 B.C.). *Moral Sayings,* 336, tr. Darius Lyman, Jr., 1862

Another such victory would utterly undo me.

> PYRRHUS (318?–272 B.C.). Greek general. Slightly modified. On his costly victory over the Romans at the Battle of Asculum (Italy), 279 B.C. In Plutarch (A.D. 46?–119?), "Pyrrhus," *Parallel Lives,* Dryden edition, 1693. The term "Pyrrhic victory" is derived from Pyrrhus's comment.
> See Defeat: Garry Wills

"The Intoxication of Victory."

> ARNOLD J. TOYNBEE (1889–1975). Chapter title, *A Study of History,* 4.505, 1939
> See Prosperity: Adam Smith

⚜

He conquers twice who restrains himself in victory.

> ANONYMOUS. In Francis Bacon, "Ornamenta Rationalia; or, Elegant Sentences," *The Essays; or, Counsels, Civil and Moral,* A. L. Burt edition, 1883

In the moment of victory, tighten your helmet strap.

> SAYING (JAPANESE). In William Manchester, *American Caesar: Douglas MacArthur: 1880–1964,* 9, 1978

VICTORY & DEFEAT

See also • Defeat ○ Rich & Poor ○ Strength & Weakness ○ Success & Failure ○ Victory ○ Wealth & Poverty

As always, victory finds a hundred fathers but defeat is an orphan.

> COUNT CIANO (1903–1944). Italian foreign minister, Benito Mussolini's son-in-law. On Italy's military defeats during World War II, 9 September 1942, *The Ciano Diaries, 1939–1943,* 1946. Pres. John F. Kennedy popularized the saying when, in taking responsibility for the failed Bay of Pigs invasion (Cuba), he remarked at a news conference, "There's an old saying that victory has a hundred fathers and defeat is an orphan." (21 April 1961)

There are many victories worse than a defeat.

> GEORGE ELIOT (1819–1880). "Janet's Repentance" (6), *Scenes of Clerical Life,* 1857

I am *Defeated* all the time; yet to Victory I am born.

> RALPH WALDO EMERSON (1803–1882). Journal, April 1842

The victor will always be the judge, and the vanquished will always be the accused.

> HERMANN GOERING (1893–1946). His defense theme at the Nuremberg Trials, 1946. In Albert Camus, "Historical Rebellion: State Terrorism and Irrational Terror," *The Rebel: An Essay on Man in Revolt*, 1951, tr. Anthony Bower, 1956

If you can meet with Triumph and Disaster
And treat those two impostors just the same. . . .

> RUDYARD KIPLING (1865–1936). "If—," *Reward and Fairies*, 1910
> See Self-Realization (Being): Shakespeare (2)

Not in the clamor of the crowded street,
    Not in the shouts and plaudits of the throng,
    But in ourselves, are triumph and defeat.

> HENRY WADSWORTH LONGFELLOW (1807–1882). Closing lines, "The Poets," *A Book of Sonnets*, 1876
> See Self-Realization (Being): Shakespeare (2)

Previous victories . . . are all canceled by present defeats.

> MACHIAVELLI (1469–1527). *The Discourses*, 1.53, 1517, tr. Christian E. Detmold, 1940

There are defeats more triumphant than victories.

> MONTAIGNE (1533–1592). "Of Cannibals," *Essays*, 1588, tr. Charles Cotton and W. C. Hazlitt, 1877

The Romans do not lose their courage in defeat, nor does victory make them overbearing.

> SCIPIO AFRICANUS (236–183? B.C.). Roman general. In Machiavelli, *The Discourses*, 3.31, 1517, tr. Christian E. Detmold, 1940

A sudden crushing defeat is apt to stimulate the defeated party to set its house in order and prepare to make a victorious response.

> ARNOLD J. TOYNBEE (1889–1975). *A Study of History*, 19341–939, abr. D. C. Somervell, 2.395, 1965

🌿

An ignominious victory is a defeat.

> SAYING (ARAB)
> See Money: Horace ○ Profit & Loss: Hesiod

Defeat teaches better than victory.

> SAYING (JAPANESE)

Better defeat in a good cause than victory in a bad one.

> SAYING

VIETNAM WAR

See also • Guerrilla Warfare ○ International Relations ○ Majorities: Richard M. Nixon ○ War

It is worse than immoral, it's a mistake.

> DEAN ACHESON (1893–1971). Secretary of state. On the U.S. role in Vietnam.
> See Blunders: Joseph Fouché

By 1970, more bombs had been dropped on Vietnam than all targets in the whole of human history.

> STEPHEN E. AMBROSE (1936–). *Rise to Globalism: American Foreign Policy, 1938–1980*, 11, 1971

I predict that you will sink step by step into a bottomless military and political quagmire, however much you spend in men and money.

> CHARLES de GAULLE (1890–1970). On U.S. involvement in Vietnam, remark to Pres. John F. Kennedy, June 1961, "The World," *Memoirs of Hope: Renewal and Endeavor*, tr. Terence Kilmartin, 1971

You have broader considerations that might follow what you might call the "falling domino" principle. You have a row of dominoes set up. You knock over the first one, and what will happen to the last one is that it will go over very quickly. So you have the beginning of a disintegration that would have the most profound influences.

> DWIGHT D. EISENHOWER (1890–1969). On what was later called the "domino theory," with specific reference to the impending defeat of besieged French forces at Dienbienphu, news conference, Washington, 7 April 1954

President Johnson had wanted to end the war; so, too, had President Kennedy. But to end the war and not to lose it: The distinction was crucial, and particularly crucial after all the American lives that had been spent and all the political rhetoric expended.

> FRANCES FITZGERALD. *Fire in the Lake: The Vietnamese and the Americans in Vietnam*, 17, 1972

In the U.S. Army alone, over one thousand officers and NCOs [noncommissioned officers] were killed or wounded by their own men.

> RICHARD A. GABRIEL (1942–). *Military Incompetence: Why the American Military Doesn't Win*, 1, 1985

I'd drop a low-yield atomic bomb on Chinese supply lines in North Vietnam or maybe shell 'em with the Seventh Fleet.

> BARRY M. GOLDWATER (1909–1998). In "GOP's Goldwater: Busting Out All Over," *Newsweek*, 20 May 1963

One way to get out of going to Vietnam was to have your father killed at Anzio and not be born.

> ANNE HERBERT. "I Would Like to Write a Silence," *Co-Evolution*, Winter 1976. American forces suffered severe casualties during the Battle of Anzio (Italy) in January 1944.

The Communists have developed a new kind of aggression in which one country sponsors internal war within another.

> ROGER HILSMAN (1919–). Forward to Vo Nguyen Giap, *People's War, People's Army*, 1962

Shit, man, he's the only boy we got out there.

> LYNDON B. JOHNSON (1908–1973). When asked by Stanley Karnow if he really believed that South Vietnamese Pres. Ngo Dinh Diem was "the Winston Churchill of Southeast Asia," May 1961. In David Halberstam, *The Best and the Brightest*, 8, 1972

Aggression unchallenged is aggression unleashed.

> LYNDON B. JOHNSON (1908–1973). Responding to the Gulf of Tonkin incident, three days after which Congress passed the Gulf of Tonkin Resolution further escalating U.S. involvement in the war, television broadcast, 4 August 1964

I am not going to lose Vietnam. I am not going to be the president who saw Southeast Asia go the way China went.

> LYNDON B. JOHNSON (1908–1973). Remark to Henry Cabot Lodge, the U.S. ambassador to South Vietnam, November 1963. In Louis W. Koenig, *The Chief Executive*, 15, 1964

I didn't just screw Ho Chi Minh; I cut his pecker off.

> LYNDON B. JOHNSON (1908–1973). On U.S. "retaliatory air strikes" against oil installations in Vinh (North Vietnam) shortly after the Gulf of Tonkin incident, August 1964
>
> See Loyalty: Johnson

I feel like a hitchhiker on a Texas highway in the middle of a hailstorm; I can't run, I can't hide, and I can't make it go away.

> LYNDON B. JOHNSON (1908–1973).

Now we have a problem in making our power credible, and Vietnam is the place.

> JOHN F. KENNEDY (1917–1963). Remark to *New York Times* columnist James Reston following the Kennedy-Khrushchev meeting in Vienna, June 1961. In Stanley Karnow, *Vietnam: A History*, 7, 1983

Somehow this madness must cease. I speak as a child of God and brother to the suffering poor of Vietnam and the poor of America who are paying the double price of smashed hopes at home and death and corruption in Vietnam. . . . The great initiative in this war is ours. The initiative to stop it must be ours.

> MARTIN LUTHER KING, JR. (1929–1968). "Declaration of Independence from the War in Vietnam," sermon, Riverside Church, New York City, 4 April 1967

I refuse to believe that a fourth-rate power like North Vietnam does not have a breaking point.

> HENRY A. KISSINGER (1923–). Remark (as Pres. Richard M. Nixon's national security adviser), 1969. In Ralph Blumenfeld et al., *Henry Kissinger: The Private and Public Story*, 1, 1974

The perennial error of our military policy in Vietnam: acting sufficiently strongly to evoke storms of protest but then by hesitation depriving our actions of decisive impact.

> HENRY A. KISSINGER (1923–). *White House Years*, 12, 1979

Sometimes I wish I'd . . . [pause] The first time I got hit I got shot in the foot. I could have laid down. Who gives a crap now if I was a hero or not. I was paralyzed, castrated that day. Why? I was so stupid. I think, Timmy, I'd give everything I believe in, everything I've got, to have my body back again, just to be whole again. I'm not whole, never will be. And that's the way it is, isn't it?

> RON KOVIC (1946–) and OLIVER STONE (1946–). *Born on the Fourth of July* (film based on Vietnam veteran Kovic's 1976 autobiography of the same title), 1989

A 1979 survey concluded that more Vietnam veterans have died by their own hand than in combat (58,022).

> JOHN LANGONE. "The War That Has No Ending," *Discover*, June 1985

Come on, Mothers, throughout the land,
Pack your boys off to Vietnam;
Come on, Fathers, don't hesitate,

Send your sons off before it's too late;
You can be the first one on your block
To have your boy come home in a box.

> "COUNTRY" JOE McDONALD (1942–). "I-Feel-Like-I'm-Fixin'-to-Die Rag" (song), 1965

We of the Kennedy and Johnson Administrations who participated in the decision on Vietnam acted according to what we thought to be the principles and traditions of this nation. Yet we were wrong, terribly wrong.

> ROBERT S. McNAMARA (1916–). Secretary of defense. Opening paragraph, *In Retrospect: The Tragedy and Lessons of Vietnam*, 1995

A year ago none of us could see victory. There wasn't a prayer. Now we can see it clearly—like light at the end of a tunnel.

> HENRI-EUGENE NAVARRE (1898–1983). French general. Eight months before the French defeat at Dienbienphu. In "Battle of Indo-China," *Time*, 28 September 1953. According to *A Supplement to the Oxford English Dictionary* (p. 1015, 1986), the phrase "light at the end of the tunnel" dates back at least to 1922.
>
> See Pessimism—Examples: Barry Commoner, Robert Lowell

These guys kill a lot of our people, and I think Buddha will forgive me.

> NGUYEN LOAN (1931–1998). South Vietnamese police chief. After killing a bound Vietcong prisoner with a bullet through the head fired at close range on a Saigon street, Tet Offensive, 1968. Eddie Adams's photograph of the murder is one of the most famous taken during the war.

Out here in this dreary, difficult war, I think history will record that this may have been one of America's finest hours.

> RICHARD M. NIXON (1913–1994). During a visit to Vietnam. In Garry Wills, *Nixon Agonistes: The Crisis of the Self-Made Man*, 4.4, 1969

I call it the Madman Theory, Bob. I want the North Vietnamese to believe I've reached the point where I might do *anything* to stop the war. We'll just slip the word to them that, "for God's sake, you know Nixon is obsessed about Communists. We can't restrain him when he's angry—and he has his hand on the nuclear button"—and Ho Chi Minh himself will be in Paris in two days begging for peace.

> RICHARD M. NIXON (1913–1994). 1969. Remark to the author. In H. R. Haldeman (with Joseph DiMona), *The Ends of Power*, 3.2, 1978. Pres. Nixon later wrote, "One of [Secretary of State Henry A. Kissinger's] strongest suits [in negotiating with the North Vietnamese] was that I had a reputation for unpredictability." (*In the Arena: A Memoir of Victory, Defeat and Renewal*, 33, 1990)

If when the chips are down, the world's most powerful nation . . . acts like a pitiful, helpless giant, the forces of totalitarianism and anarchy will threaten free nations and free institutions throughout the world.

> RICHARD M. NIXON (1913–1994). Announcing the invasion of Cambodia, televised speech, 30 April 1970

Had there been no Watergate, there's no question that South Vietnam would be a free, independent country today and a very prosperous one, rather than one of the poorest countries in the world under the communist rule.

> RICHARD M. NIXON (1913–1994). Morton Kondrake television interview, *Richard Nixon Reflects*, PBS, 4 May 1990

War makes men like me, hollow men, men weighed down by memory, out of time and out of place, men who spend their lives trying to recover what has been lost, men haunted by the awful mystery that spared them, that left them alone, walking in the empty spaces.

> MICHAEL NORMAN. Closing words. "The Hollow Man: One of the Worst Things about Vietnam Is That It Killed Even Those Who Survived," *New York Times Magazine,* 26 May 1996

We should declare war on North Vietnam. . . . We could pave the whole country and put parking stripes on it, and still be home for Christmas.

> RONALD REAGAN (1911–). Interview, *Fresno Bee,* 10 October 1965

The [Vietnam War Memorial] Wall became a magnet for citizens of every generation, class, race, and relationship to the war perhaps because it is the only great public monument that allows the anesthetized holes in the heart to fill with a truly national grief.

> ADRIENNE RICH (1929–). August 1991, *What Is Found There: Notebooks on Poetry and Politics,* 14, 1993. The black granite wall in Washington, inscribed with the names of the Americans who died in Vietnam, was designed by Maya Lin.

Cambodia is one country where we can say with complete assurance that our hands are clean and our hearts are pure.

> WILLIAM P. ROGERS (1913–). Secretary of state. Asserting that the U.S. was not violating Cambodian neutrality during the Vietnam War, testimony before Senate Foreign Relations Committee in closed session, March 1970, one year after he himself had helped formulate the plan for secretly bombing that country. In Seymour Hersh, "Rogers Said 'Our Hands Are Clean,'" *New York Times,* 25 July 1973

As secretary of state I made two serious mistakes with respect to Vietnam. First, I overestimated the patience of the American people, and second, I underestimated the tenacity of the North Vietnamese.

> DEAN RUSK (1909–1994). *As I Saw It,* 31, 1990

The Vietnam story is a tragedy without villains.

> ARTHUR M. SCHLESINGER, JR. (1917–). In Lewis H. Lapham, *Money and Class in America: Notes and Observations on the Civil Religion,* 5.2, 1988

One of the big lessons [of the Vietnam War] is, if you are going to be in a war, you better be in it to win, and not tie your hands the way we did.

> GEORGE P. SHULTZ (1920–). In Bernard Gwertzman, "The Shultz Method: How the New Secretary of State Is Trying to Stabilize Foreign Policy," *New York Times Magazine,* 2 January 1983

[Bombing North Vietnam is] like a big sporting event to me. I seem to enjoy the competition. . . . The night hops are really spectacular. It's like Disneyland, the Fourth of July and World War movies all rolled into one. [Ellipsis points in original.]

> JEREMY TAYLOR. Lt. commander, Attack Squadron 113 on the carrier *Enterprise.* In "Tumult & Shouting," *San Francisco Sunday Examiner & Chronicle,* 16 July 1967

There was no alternative to "search and destroy" type operations, except, of course, a different name for them.

> WILLIAM C. WESTMORELAND (1914–). In Harry G. Summers, Jr., *On Strategy: A Critical Analysis of the Vietnam War,* 15, 1982

We won the war after we left, in effect. One of our great strategic aims was to stop the Communist advance in Southeast Asia, and when you look at Southeast Asia today, the Communists have made no gains. Today, Vietnam is a basket case run by a bunch of old men and is a threat to no one but itself.

> WILLIAM C. WESTMORELAND (1914–). In Fox Butterfield, "Voices from the Past Sound Out Again," *New York Times,* 25 January 1991

It became necessary to destroy the town to save it.

> ANONYMOUS (AMERICAN). Officer explaining "the decision to bomb and shell the town regardless of civilian casualties to rout the Vietcong" (reporter's words). In Associated Press, "Major Describes Move," *New York Times,* 8 February 1968
> See World War II: Anonymous (American) (2)

A shell came right in this man's trench and what they had to send home would probably fit inside a handkerchief.

> ANONYMOUS (AMERICAN). Marine at Khe Sanh, 1968. In Michael Maclear, *The Ten Thousand Day War: Vietnam, 1945–1975,* 12, 1981

We are the unwilling, led by the unqualified, doing the unnecessary for the ungrateful.

> ANONYMOUS (AMERICAN). 1960s

I do not like to hit a village. You know you are hitting women and children. But you've got to decide that your cause is noble and that the work has to be done.

> ANONYMOUS (AMERICAN). Air force pilot in Vietnam. In *New York Times.* Quoted in Arthur M. Schlesinger, Jr., "The Necessary Amorality of Foreign Affairs," *Harper's,* August 1971

Col. Harry G. Summers: You never defeated us on the battlefield. *Anonymous* (North Vietnamese colonel): That may be so, but it is also irrelevant.

> ANONYMOUS (VIETNAMESE). After the war. In Stanley Karnow, *Vietnam: A History,* 1, 1983

If you've got them by the balls, their hearts and minds will follow.

> SLOGAN (AMERICAN). Probably originated before the 1960s when it became popular. Charles Colson, a presidential assistant to Richard M. Nixon, reported receiving a plaque inscribed with this slogan from a member of the Green Berets. Colson hanged the plaque on the wall of his White House office. Later, the slogan became identified with the Nixon Administration. (In Ralph Keyes, *"Nice Guys Finish Seventh": False Phrases, Spurious Sayings, and Familiar Misquotations,* 6, 1992)

Hell no, we won't go.

> SLOGAN (AMERICAN). Referring to the draft, 1960s

Hey, hey, LBJ, how many kids did you kill today?

> SLOGAN (AMERICAN), 1960s

Make love, not war.

> SLOGAN (AMERICAN), 1960s

VIOLENCE

See also • Assassination ○ Crime ○ Cruelty ○ Dehumanization ○ Euthanasia ○ Force ○ Gun Control ○ History ○ Holocaust ○ Killing ○ Machiavellianism ○ Murder ○ Nonviolence ○ Nuclear Weapons ○ Power ○ Punishment ○ Punishment, Capital ○ Rape ○ Revolution ○ Sterilization ○ Suicide ○ Terrorism: [especially] Sydney J. Harris ○ Torture ○ Tyranny: [especially] Anonymous (1) ○ War

The practice of violence, like all action, changes the world, but the most probable change is to a more violent world.

> HANNAH ARENDT (1906–1975). *On Violence*, 3, 1970

Violence is the last refuge of the incompetent.

> ISAAC ASIMOV (1920–1992). In "Quotable Quotes," *Reader's Digest*, October 1977
>
> See Patriotism: Samuel Johnson

It is desirable and it is necessary that the condition of affairs in Germany and of her constitutional relations should be improved; but this cannot be accomplished by speeches and resolutions of a majority, but only by iron and blood [eisen und blut].

> OTTO von BISMARCK (1815–1898). Testifying before the Budget Commission of the Prussian House of Delegates, 30 September 1862 (Popular version: Not by parliamentary speeches and majority votes are the great questions of the day decided but by iron and blood.)
>
> See War: Quintilian

Violence is as American as the Fourth of July and cherry pie.

> H. RAP BROWN (1943–). "'We Burned Detroit Down and Put America on Notice,'" *Open City* (Los Angeles), 17 August 1967

You can get a lot more done with a kind word and a gun, than with a kind word alone.

> AL CAPONE (1899–1947). Chicago mobster. Attributed. In William Safire, "Wedges and Bounces," *New York Times Magazine*, 20 September 1992

All violence . . . is not power but the absence of power.

> RALPH WALDO EMERSON (1803–1882). "Character," *Lectures and Biographical Sketches*, 1883

At the level of individuals, violence is a cleansing force. It frees the native from his inferiority complex and from his despair and inaction; it makes him fearless and restores his self-respect.

> FRANTZ FANON (1925–1961). "Concerning Violence," *The Wretched of the Earth*, 1961, tr. Constance Farrington, 1963

Where there is only a choice between cowardice and violence, I would advise violence.

> MOHANDAS K. GANDHI (1869–1948). In *Young India*, 11 August 1920

I am an uncompromising opponent of violent methods even to serve the noblest of causes.

> MOHANDAS K. GANDHI (1869–1948). In *Young India*, 11 December 1924

Nothing enduring can be built on violence.

> MOHANDAS K. GANDHI (1869–1948). In *Young India*, 15 November 1928

The tree of liberty must be refreshed from time to time with the blood of patriots and tyrants. It is its natural manure.

> THOMAS JEFFERSON (1743–1826). On Shays's Rebellion which was started by debt-ridden farmers in Massachusetts in August 1786. Letter to Col. William S. Smith, 13 November 1787

Violence is an admission that one's ideas and goals cannot prevail on their own merits.

> EDWARD M. KENNEDY (1932–). 10 June 1970. *A People of Compassion: The Concerns of Edward Kennedy*, ed. Thomas P. Collins and Louis M. Savary, 1972

Almost all significant changes in history have involved violence and upheaval.

> HENRY A. KISSINGER (1923–). *Diplomacy*, 2, 1994

Not a single question pertaining to the class struggle has ever been settled except by violence. Violence when it is committed by the toiling and exploited masses is the kind of violence of which we approve.

> LENIN (1870–1924). Speech before the Third Congress of Soviets, 24 January 1918
>
> See War & Revolution: Mao Tse-tung

No one need think that the world can be ruled without blood. The civil sword shall and must be red and bloody.

> MARTIN LUTHER (1483–1546). In R. H. Tawney, *Religion and the Rise of Capitalism: A Historical Study*, 2.2, 1926

Historical experience is written in iron and blood.

> MAO TSE-TUNG (1893–1976). *Guerrilla Warfare*, 3, 1937, tr. Samuel B. Griffith, 1940

Every Communist must grasp the truth, "Political power grows out of the barrel of a gun."

> MAO TSE-TUNG (1893–1976). "Problems of War and Strategy" (2), 6 November 1938, *Selected Works of Mao Tse-tung*, Foreign Languages Press edition, vol. 2, 1965

Violence in government as in other relations is a confession of failure.

> CHARLES E. MERRIAM (1876–1953). *Political Power*, 7, 1934
>
> See Force: Alfred North Whitehead

Blood alone moves the wheels of history.

> BENITO MUSSOLINI (1883–1945). Speech, Parma (Italy), 13 December 1914

Nothing has ever been established except by the sword.

> NAPOLEON (1769–1821). *Napoleon in His Own Words*, 1, comp. Jules Bertaut, 1916
>
> See Force: Napoleon

If I must choose between a policy of blood and iron and one of milk and water . . . why I am for the policy of blood and iron. It is better not only for the nation but in the long run for the world.

> THEODORE ROOSEVELT (1858–1919). Letter to a friend, December 1914. In Henry A. Kissinger, *Diplomacy*, 2, 1994

Violence does not and cannot exist by itself; it is invariably intertwined with *the lie*.

> ALEKSANDR SOLZHENITSYN (1918–). Nobel Prize (in literature) acceptance address, 1970

To commit violent and unjust acts, it is not enough for a government to have the will or even the power; the habits, ideas, and passions of the time must lend themselves to their committal.

> ALEXIS de TOCQUEVILLE (1805–1859)

Violence is not the problem; it is a consequence of the problem.

> JIM WALLIS (1948–). *The Soul of Politics: A Practical and Prophetic Vision for Change,* 1, 1994

VIRTUE

See also • Character ○ Courage: Samuel Johnson (1), John Locke, Clare Booth Luce ○ Deeds ○ Democracy: Henry Hyde ○ Dignity ○ Good ○ Happiness ○ Honesty ○ Integrity ○ Moderation: Anonymous ○ Money: Henry David Thoreau (1) ○ Morality ○ Self-Realization (Becoming) ○ Service ○ Virtue & Vice ○ Vice ○ Wisdom: David Starr Jordan, Saying (Japanese)

It is the repeated performance of just and temperate actions that produces virtue.

> ARISTOTLE (384–322 B.C.). *Nichomachean Ethics,* 2.4, tr. J. A. K. Thomson, 1953

Virtue is more clearly shown in the performance of fine actions than in the nonperformance of base ones.

> ARISTOTLE (384–322 B.C.). *Nichomachean Ethics,* 4.1, tr. J. A. K. Thomson, 1953

In the virtue of each the virtue of all is involved.

> ARISTOTLE (384–322 B.C.). *Politics,* 7.13, tr. Benjamin Jowett, 1885

Virtue is like precious odors, most fragrant when they are . . . crushed.

> FRANCIS BACON (1561–1626). "Of Adversity," *Essays,* 1625

Virtue is like a rich stone, best plain set.

> FRANCIS BACON (1561–1626). "Of Beauty," *Essays,* 1625

We should make virtue our master, not our servant.

> JOSH BILLINGS (1818–1885). *On Ice: and Other Things,* 43, 1868

If a man was kompletely virtewous, i doubt whether he would be happy here, he would be so lonesum.

> JOSH BILLINGS (1818–1885). "Glass Dimonds," *Everybody's Friend, or; Josh Billing's Encyclopedia and Proverbial Philosophy of Wit and Humor,* 1874
>
> See Loneliness: Mark Twain

Without liberty virtue cannot exist.

> EDMUND BURKE (1729–1797). Slightly modified. *Reflections on the Revolution in France,* p. 203, 1790, Pelican Books edition, 1968

Virtue can be afforded only by the poor, who have nothing to lose.

> ALEXANDER CHASE. *Perspectives,* 1966

The superior man thinks of virtue; the small man thinks of comfort.

> CONFUCIUS (551–479 B.C.). *Confucian Analects,* 4.11, tr. James Legge, 1930

Virtue, thriving most where little seen.

> WILLIAM COWPER (1731–1800). *The Task,* 3.664, 1785

Virtue secures its own success.

> DEMOSTHENES (384–322 B.C.). In Ralph Waldo Emerson, journal, September 1841

One can acquire some virtues by feigning them for a long time.

> MARIE von EBNER-ESCHENBACH (1830–1916). *Aphorisms,* p. 47, 1880–1905, tr. David Scrase and Wolfgang Mieder, 1994

He only acquires [virtue] who endures routine and sweat and postponement of fancy to the achievement of a worthy end.

> RALPH WALDO EMERSON (1803–1882). Journal, 1845, undated

There is no virtue except by god's grace.

> M. ESPRIT. *On the Falseness of Human Virtues.* In Voltaire, "Falseness of Human Virtues," *Philosophical Dictionary,* 1764, tr. Theodore Besterman, 1971

Everyone suspects himself of at least one of the cardinal virtues.

> F. SCOTT FITZGERALD (1896–1940). *The Great Gatsby,* 3, 1925

No longer virtuous no longer free, is a Maxim as true with regard to a private Person as a Commonwealth.

> BENJAMIN FRANKLIN (1706–1790). *Poor Richard's Almanack,* September 1739

Virtue is prais'd by all; but practiced by few.

> THOMAS FULLER (1654–1734). Comp., *Gnomologia: Adages and Proverbs,* 5379, 1732

Virtue's Paths are first rugged, then pleasant.

> THOMAS FULLER (1654–1734). Comp., *Gnomologia: Adages and Proverbs,* 5391, 1732

The virtue of a human being is the application of his capacity to the general good.

> WILLIAM GODWIN (1756–1836). *Enquiry Concerning Political Justice and Its Influence on Morals and Happiness,* 4.6, 1793, ed. and abr. Raymond A. Preston, 1926

Virtue consists in actions, and not in words.

> WILLIAM GODWIN (1756–1836). *Caleb Williams,* 3, 1794

The virtue which requires to be ever guarded is scarce worth the sentinel.

> OLIVER GOLDSMITH (1728–1774). *The Vicar of Wakefield,* 5, 1766

It is of the essence of virtue that the good is not to be done for the sake of a reward.

> ABRAHAM JOSHUA HESCHEL (1907–1972). *God in Search of Man: A Philosophy of Judaism,* 36, 1955

The purpose of all virtue is to lead us to union with God.

> ST. JOHN OF THE CROSS (1542–1591). In "Union" (1), *Spiritual Diary: Selected Sayings and Examples of Saints,* 1775, St. Paul Editions, 1962

When a virtuous man is raised, it brings gladness to his friends, grief to his enemies, and glory to his posterity.

> BEN JONSON (1572–1637). "Of Statecraft," *Timber: Or, Discoveries,* 1640, ed. Ralph S. Walker, 1953

A man of highest virtue
Will not display it as his own.

> LAO-TZU (6th cent. B.C.). *The Way of Life,* 38, tr. R. B. Blakney, 1955

Greater virtues are needed to bear good fortune than bad.

> LA ROCHEFOUCAULD (1613–1680). *Maxims,* 25, 1665, tr. Leonard Tancock, 1959

Virtue would not go nearly so far if vanity did not keep her company.

> LA ROCHEFOUCAULD (1613–1680). *Maxims,* 200, 1665, tr. Louis Kronenberger, 1959

The Principle of all Virtue and Excellency lies in a Power of denying ourselves the Satisfaction of our own Desires, where Reason does not authorize them. This Power is to be got and improv'd by Custom, made easy and familiar by an *early* Practice.

> JOHN LOCKE (1632–1704). *Some Thoughts Concerning Education,* 38, 1693

The highest proof of virtue is to possess boundless power without abusing it.

> THOMAS BABINGTON MACAULAY (1800–1859). "Joseph Addison," *The Edinburgh Review* (Scotland), July 1843

I cannot praise a fugitive and cloistered virtue, unexercised and unbreathed, that never sallies out and seeks her adversary, but slinks out of the race, where that immortal garland is to be run for, not without heat and dust.

> JOHN MILTON (1608–1674). *Areopagitica* (A Speech for the Liberty of Unlicenc'd Printing), 1644

The value and height of true virtue lies in the ease, utility, and pleasure of its practice, which is so far from being difficult that children can master it as well as men, the simple as well as the subtle.

> MONTAIGNE (1533–1592). "Of the Education of Children," *Essays,* 1588, tr. Donald M. Frame, 1958

Virtue is herself her own coveted reward.

> OVID (43 B.C.–A.D. 17?). *Tristia,* 5.14, tr. Arthur Leslie Wheeler, 1924 (Popular version: Virtue is its own reward.)
>
> See Love: John Vanbrugh o Virtue & Vice: Baltazar Gracián

When we are planning for posterity, we ought to remember that virtue is not hereditary.

> THOMAS PAINE (1737–1809). "Of the Present Ability of America," *Common Sense,* 1776

A [noble] spirit will seek the reward of virtue in the consciousness of it, rather than in popular opinion.

> PLINY THE YOUNGER (A.D. 62?–113?). *Letters,* 1.8, tr. Betty Radice, 1963
>
> See Justice: Rousseau (1)

Virtue is victorious over fortune. (Virtus Victris Fortunae.)

> POLY PREP. Motto. Adopted at the Brooklyn school's founding in 1854

What nothing earthly gives, or can destroy,
The soul's calm sunshine, and the heartfelt joy,
Virtue's prize.

> ALEXANDER POPE (1688–1744). *An Essay on Man,* 4.167, 1734

If self-knowledge is the road to virtue, so is virtue still more the road to self-knowledge.

> JEAN PAUL FRIEDRICH RICHTER (1763–1825). *Hesperus,* 12, 1795

One advantage resulting from virtuous actions is that they elevate the mind and dispose it to attempt others more virtuous still.

> ROUSSEAU (1712–1778). *Confessions,* 3 (1731–1732), 1781, tr. J. M. Cohen, 1953

Fortune can snatch away only what she herself has given. But virtue she does not give; therefore she cannot take it away. Virtue is free, inviolable, unmoved, unshaken, so steeled against the blows of chance that she cannot be bent, much less broken.

> SENECA THE YOUNGER (5? B.C.–A.D. 65). "On the Firmness of the Wise Man" (5.4), *Moral Essays,* tr. John W. Basore, 1928

Virtue depends partly upon training and partly upon practice; you must learn first, and then strengthen your learning by action.

> SENECA THE YOUNGER (5? B.C.–A.D. 65). "On the Value of Advice," *Moral Letters to Lucilius,* 94.47, tr. Richard M. Gummere, 1918

Virtue is insufficient temptation.

> GEORGE BERNARD SHAW (1856–1950)

The man
Of virtuous soul commands not, nor obeys.

> PERCY BYSSHE SHELLEY (1792–1822). *Queen Mab: A Philosophical Poem: With Notes,* 3, 1813

Concern for our own happiness recommends to us the virtue of prudence; concern for that of other people, the virtues of justice and beneficence.

> ADAM SMITH (1723–1790). *The Theory of Moral Sentiments,* 6.3, 1759

Virtue comes to the virtuous by the gift of God.

> SOCRATES (470?–399 B.C.). In Plato (427?–347 B.C.), *Meno,* 100, tr. Benjamin Jowett, 1894

Virtue's a thing that none can take away;
But money changes owners all the day.

> SOLON (630?–560? B.C.). One of the Seven Sages of Greece. In Plutarch (A.D. 46?–119?), "Solon," *Parallel Lives,* Dryden edition, 1693

Virtue is nothing else but action in accordance with the laws of one's own nature.

> BARUCH SPINOZA (1632–1677). "Piety and Selfishness," *Ethics,* 1677, tr. Dagobert D. Runes, 1957

Seven virtues minister before the Throne of Glory: Wisdom, Justice, Righteousness, Kindness, Compassion, Truth and Peace.

> TALMUD (A.D. 1st–6th cent.). Rabbinical writings. In Louis I. Newman, comp., *The Talmudic Anthology,* 127, 1945

Virtue is a bravery so hardy that it deals in what it has no experience in. . . . It goes singing to its work. Effort is its relaxation.

> HENRY DAVID THOREAU (1817–1862). Journal, 1 January 1842

What is virtue, my friend? It is to do good. Do it, that is enough. We shall not worry about your motives.

> VOLTAIRE (1694–1778). "Falseness of Human Virtues," *Philosophical Dictionary,* 1764, tr. Theodore Besterman, 1971

I have seen men incapable of learning, I have never seen any incapable of virtue.

> VOLTAIRE (1694–1778). "Philosopher," *Philosophical Dictionary*, 1764, tr. Theodore Besterman, 1971

Nowadays, with our modern mania for morality, everyone has to pose as a paragon of purity, incorruptibility, and all the other seven deadly virtues.

> OSCAR WILDE (1854–1900). *An Ideal Husband*, 1, 1895
>
> See Sin: *A Catechism of Christian Doctrine for General Use*

By virtue I mean nothing arcane or obscure. I mean good citizenship, whose principal components are moderation, social sympathy and willingness to sacrifice private desires for public ends.

> GEORGE F. WILL (1941–). *Statecraft as Soulcraft: What Government Does*, 6, 1983

Society can only be happy and free in proportion as it is virtuous.

> MARY WOLLSTONECRAFT (1759–1797). *A Vindication of the Rights of Woman*, 12, 1792

Virtue is true self-interest pursued.

> EDWARD YOUNG (1683–1765). *The Complaint: or, Night Thoughts on Life, Death, and Immortality*, 7.142, 1742–1745

No happiness without virtue; no virtue without wisdom; no wisdom without love.

> ANONYMOUS

Virtue lends itself to every good cause but sells itself to no cause, however good.

> ANONYMOUS

All virtue is summed up in dealing justly.

> SAYING (GREEK). In Aristotle (384–322 B.C.), *Nichomachean Ethics*, 5.1, tr. J. A. K. Thomson, 1953

Poverty does not destroy virtue, nor wealth bestow it.

> SAYING (SPANISH)

Virtue grows younger every year.

> SAYING (RUSSIAN)

VIRTUE & VICE

See also • Good & Evil ◦ Morality ◦ Vice ◦ Virtue

Virtue is a mean between two vices.

> ARISTOTLE (384–322 B.C.). *Nichomachean Ethics*, 2.6

Every excellency, and every virtue, has its kindred vice or weakness; and if carried beyond certain bounds, sinks into one or the other. Generosity often runs into profusion, economy into avarice, courage into rashness, caution into timidity, and so on.

> LORD CHESTERFIELD (1694–1773). Letter to his son, 22 February 1748

Vice has more martyrs than virtue; and it often happens that men suffer more to be lost than to be saved.

> C. C. COLTON (1780–1832). *Lacon: or, Many Things in Few Words; Addressed to Those Who Think*, 1.170, 1823

This is the tax a man must pay to his virtues—they hold up a torch to his vices, and render those frailties notorious in him which would have passed without observation in another.

> C. C. COLTON (1780–1832). *Lacon: or, Many Things in Few Words; Addressed to Those Who Think*, 1.237, 1823

Vices are sometimes only virtues carried to excess!

> CHARLES DICKENS (1812–1870). *Dombey and Son*, 58, 1848

There is a capacity of virtue in us, and there is a capacity of vice to make your blood creep.

> RALPH WALDO EMERSON (1803–1882). Journal, 25 April 1831

Virtue consists in 1. Prudence. 2. Temperance. 3. Fortitude. 4. Justice.

> To which are opposed, 1. Folly. 2. Desire. 3. Fear. 4. Deceit.
>
> EPICURUS (341–270 B.C.). In Thomas Jefferson, "Syllabus of the Doctrines of Epicurus," letter to William Short, 31 October 1819

Search others for their Virtues, and thyself for thy Vices.

> THOMAS FULLER (1654–1734). Comp., *Introductio ad Prudentiam*, 192, 1731

It is easier to run from Virtue to Vice than from Vice to Virtue.

> THOMAS FULLER (1654–1734). Comp., *Gnomologia: Adages and Proverbs*, 2931, 1732

Just as virtue is its own reward, so is vice its own punishment.

> BALTASAR GRACIÁN (1601–1658). *The Art of Worldly Wisdom*, 90, 1647, tr. Joseph Jacobs, 1943
>
> See Virtue: Aesop in Vice and Ovid

There are amiable vices and obnoxious virtues.

> WILLIAM HAZLITT (1778–1830). *Characteristics in the Manner of Rochefoucault's Maxims*, 46, 1823

We as often dislike others for their virtues as their vices.

> WILLIAM HAZLITT (1778–1830). *Characteristics in the Manner of Rochefoucault's Maxims*, 115, 1823

Vice may be had in abundance without trouble; the way is smooth and her dwelling place is near. But before virtue the gods have set toil.

> HESIOD (8th cent. B.C.). In Plato (427?–347 B.C.), *The Republic*, 2.364, tr. Benjamin Jowett, 1894

If he does really think that there is no distinction between virtue and vice, why, Sir, when he leaves our houses, let us count our spoons.

> SAMUEL JOHNSON (1709–1784). 14 July 1763. In James Boswell, *The Life of Samuel Johnson*, 1791
>
> See Honor: Ralph Waldo Emerson

Every vice is a virtue gone to seed.

> SAM KEEN (1931–). *Beginnings Without End*, 2, 1975

This virtuous man promotes agreement;
The vicious man allots the blame.

> LAO-TZU (6th cent. B.C.). *The Way of Life*, 79, tr. R. B. Blakney, 1955

Father Mapple: Sin that pays its way can travel freely, and with a passport; whereas Virtue, if a pauper, is stopped at all frontiers.

> HERMAN MELVILLE (1819–1891). *Moby-Dick; or, The Whale*, 9, 1851, ed. Harold Beaver, 1972

All fashionable vices pass for virtues.

> MOLIÈRE (1622–1673). *Don Juan*, 5.2, 1665, tr. Donald M. Frame, 1981

I prefer an accommodating vice to an obstinate virtue.

> MOLIÈRE (1622–1673). *Amphitryon*, 1.4, 1666

The four political virtues: wisdom, temperance, courage, and justice.

> PLATO (427?–347 B.C.). Slightly modified. *The Republic*, 4.433, tr. Benjamin Jowett, 1894

Virtuous and vicious ev'ry Man must be,
Few in th' extreme, but all in the degree.

> ALEXANDER POPE (1688–1744). *An Essay on Man*, 2.231, 1734

Sometimes Virtue starves, while Vice is fed.

> ALEXANDER POPE (1688–1744). *An Essay on Man*, 4.149, 1734

Vice, like virtue,
Grows in small steps.

> RACINE (1639–1699). *Phaedra*, 4, 1677, tr. Robert Henderson, 1931

[Virtue] needs a director and guide. Vice can be learned even without a teacher.

> SENECA THE YOUNGER (5? B.C.–A.D. 65). Closing words, *Natural Questions*, tr. Thomas A. Corcoran, 1921

Friar Laurence: Virtue itself turns vice, being misapplied;
And vice sometimes by action dignified.

> SHAKESPEARE (1564–1616). *Romeo and Juliet*, 2.3.21, 1594

Bassanio: There is no vice so simple but assumes
Some mark of virtue on his outward parts.

> SHAKESPEARE (1564–1616). *The Merchant of Venice*, 3.2.81, 1596

Escalus: Some rise by sin, and some by virtue fall.

> SHAKESPEARE (1564–1616). *Measure for Measure*, 2.1.38, 1604

Griffith: Men's evil manners live in brass; their virtues
We write in water.

> SHAKESPEARE (1564–1616). *King Henry VIII*, 4.2.46, 1612

I never was so rapid in my virtue but my vice kept up with me. . . .

    We are double-edged blades, and every time we whet our virtue the return stroke straps our vice.

> HENRY DAVID THOREAU (1817–1862). Journal, 8 February 1841

It is queer how it is always one's virtues and not one's vices that precipitate one into disaster.

> REBECCA WEST (1892–1983). *There Is No Conversation*, 1, 1935

❦

Folks who have not vices have generally very few virtues.

> ANONYMOUS (AMERICAN). Quoted by Abraham Lincoln (1809–1865). In F. B. Carpenter, *Six Months at the White House with Abraham Lincoln*, 24, 1866

The man of God knows no sin, no virtue.

> SAYING (SUFI)

VISION

See also • Creativity ○ Dreams: [especially] Anonymous (*Bible*) (2) ○ Poetry ○ Prophets ○ Revelation ○ Seeing ○ Spirituality ○ Wisdom ○ Wisdom & Knowledge: Anonymous (1)

We are all visionaries, and what we see is our soul in things.

> HENRI AMIEL (1821–1881). Journal, 5 February 1853, tr. Mrs. Humphrey Ward, 1887

Very often [the poetic vision] comes slowly, bit by bit, like a scene set on the stage. At other times, however, it is sudden and fleeting. Something passes before your eyes, and it must be seized quickly or it is lost.

> GUSTAVE FLAUBERT (1821–1880). In J. F. Nisbet, *The Insanity of Genius*, 10, 1893

Medical materialism finished up Saint Paul by calling his vision on the road to Damascus "a discharging lesion of the occipital cortex, he being an epileptic."

> WILLIAM JAMES (1842–1910)

The idea is to seek a vision that gives you purpose in life and then to implement that vision. The vision by itself is one half, one part, of a process. It implies the necessity of living that vision, otherwise the vision will sink back into itself.

> LEWIS P. JOHNSON. "Seeking the Spirit Path," *Parabala*, February 1987

[Visions] are like dreams, only they occur in the waking state.

> CARL G. JUNG (1875–1961). "The Psychological Foundations of Belief in Sprits," 1920, *The Structure and Dynamics of the Psyche*, tr. R. F. C. Hull, 1960
>
> See Dreams: Henry David Thoreau (2)

We ought not to question whence; there is no whence, no coming or going in place; now it is seen and now not seen. We must not run after it, but fit ourselves for the vision and then wait tranquilly for its appearance, as the eye waits on the rising of the sun, which in its own time appears above the horizon—out of the ocean, as the poets say—and gives itself to our sight.

> PLOTINUS (A.D. 205–270). *The Enneads*, 5.5.8, tr. Stephen MacKenna and B. S. Page, 1952

Visionary people are visionary partly because of the very great many things they don't see.

> BERKELEY RICE (1937–). "Skinner Agrees He Is the Most Important Influence in Psychology," *New York Times Magazine*, 17 March 1968

Vision is the art of seeing things invisible.

> JONATHAN SWIFT (1667–1745). "Thoughts on Various Subjects" (expanded from a version published in 1711), *Miscellanies in Prose and Verse* (published with Alexander Pope), vol. 1, 1727

The vision we now require is nothing short of a new covenant. At root, we need to return to our spiritual identity as the children of God.

> JIM WALLIS (1948–). *The Soul of Politics: A Practical and Prophetic Vision for Change*, 3, 1994

The visionary disciplines himself to see the world always as if he had only just seen it for the first time.

COLIN WILSON (1931–). "An Autobiographical Introduction," *Religion and the Rebel,* 1957

Whither is fled the visionary gleam?
Where is it now, the glory and the dream?

WILLIAM WORDSWORTH (1770–1850). "Ode: Intimations of Immortality from Recollections of Early Childhood," 4, 1807

The fool no less than the sage, the sage no more than the knave, all are visionaries once they hit the pillow.

ANONYMOUS

Where there is no vision, the people perish.

SAYING (*BIBLE*). *Proverbs* 29:18 (King James Version)

VOTING

See also • Campaigns ○ Elections ○ Politics

The elector, who gives his vote for one whom he is persuaded on good grounds is dishonest in his motives, abuses the most sacred of his public duties.

JAMES FENIMORE COOPER (1789–1851). "On the Duties of Publick or Political Station," *The American Democrat,* 1838

Hell, I never vote *for* anybody. I always vote *against.*

W. C. FIELDS (1879–1946). In Robert Lewis Taylor, *W. C. Fields: His Follies and Fortunes,* 25, 1949

When people put their ballots in the boxes, they are, by that act, inoculated against the feeling that the government is not theirs. They then accept, in some measure, that its errors are their errors, its aberrations their aberrations, that any revolt will be against themselves. It's a remarkably shrewd and rather conservative arrangement when one thinks of it.

JOHN KENNETH GALBRAITH (1908–). *The Age of Uncertainty,* 12, 1977

In this country, the vote is not the bottom line—the bottom line is.

RICHARD M. GROSS (1944–). "Selected Aphorisms," *Personal Political Perplexing,* 1998

Our democracy is but a name. We vote? What does that mean? It means that we choose between two bodies of real, though not avowed, autocrats. We choose between Tweedledum and Tweedledee.

HELEN KELLER (1880–1968). Letter to an English suffragist, 1911. In Howard Zinn, *The Twentieth Century: A People's History,* 2, 1984

The ballot is stronger than the bullet.

ABRAHAM LINCOLN (1809–1865). "Lost speech" (unrecorded at the time), Bloomington (Illinois), 29 May 1856

Voting is simply a way of determining which side is the stronger without putting it to the test of fighting.

H. L. MENCKEN (1880–1956). *Minority Report: H. L. Mencken's Notebooks,* 312, 1956

Let us hold our noses and do our duty.

H. L. MENCKEN (1880–1956). On voting (when given a poor choice of candidates). In Garry Wills, *Nixon Agonistes: The Crisis of the Self-Made Man,* 4.2, 1969

It's not the voting that's democracy, it's the counting.

TOM STOPPARD (1937–). *Jumpers,* 1, 1972

The fate of the country does not depend on how you vote at the polls—the worst man is as strong as the best at that game; it does not depend on what kind of paper you drop into the ballot box once a year, but on what kind of man you drop from your chamber into the street every morning.

HENRY DAVID THOREAU (1817–1862). "Slavery in Massachusetts," speech, Farmingham, 4 July 1854

Ballot, *n.* In democracies, the means by which the lesser of two or more political evils is transformed into the "people's choice."

EDMUND H. VOLKART (1919–). *The Angel's Dictionary: A Modern Tribute to Ambrose Bierce,* p. 30, 1986

Be shure and vote at least once at all elecshuns.

ARTEMUS WARD (1834–1867). "Fourth of July Oration," Weathersfield (Connecticut), 1859, *The Complete Works of Artemus Ward,* 1898

Act as if the whole election depended on your single vote.

JOHN WESLEY (1703–1791). "A Word to a Freeholder," 1748

❧

When I die I want to be buried in Chicago so I can still be active in politics.

ANONYMOUS (AMERICAN). Referring to the voter registration of the dead by some Chicago politicians. Quoted by Scott Simon, host, radio magazine program, NPR, 7 June 1997

If voting changed anything, it would be illegal.

SAYING (AMERICAN). 1960s

❧

WAGES

See also • Business (Commerce) ○ Class ○ Economics ○ Exploitation ○ Money ○ Pay ○ Unemployment ○ Unions ○ Wealth ○ Work

Wages is a cunning device of the devil, for the benefit of tender consciences who would retain all the advantages of the slave system, without the expense, trouble, and odium of being slaveholders.

ORESTES A. BROWNSON (1803–1876). "The Laboring Classes," *Boston Quarterly Review,* July-October 1840

"A fair day's wages for a fair day's work": it is as just a demand as Governed men ever made of Governing. It is the everlasting right of man.

THOMAS CARLYLE (1795–1881). *Past and Present*, 1.3, 1843. According to Nigel Rees, the slogan was probably spoken for the first time by T. Attwood in a House of Commons speech, 14 June 1839

If you pay not a Servant his Wages, he will pay himself.

THOMAS FULLER (1654–1734). Comp., *Gnomologia: Adages and Proverbs*, 2778, 1732

It is a truism that labor is most productive where its wages are largest. Poorly paid labor is inefficient labor, the world over.

HENRY GEORGE (1839–1897). *Progress and Poverty: An Inquiry into the Cause of Industrial Depressions and of Increase of Want with Increase of Wealth*, 9.2, 1879

Wages are the price of labor.

SIR JOHN RICHARD HICKS (1904–1989). *The Theory of Wages*, 1.1, 1932

Raising the wages of day-laborers is wrong; for it does not make them live better; but only makes them idler, and idleness is a very bad thing for human nature.

SAMUEL JOHNSON (1709–1784). Cited under the date of 30 March 1783. In James Boswell, *The Life of Samuel Johnson*, 1791

Wages are determined by the bitter struggle between capitalist and worker.

KARL MARX (1818–1883). "First Manuscript" (1), 1844, *Early Writings*, tr. T. B. Bottomore, 1963

For many wage earners *work is perceived as a form of punishment* which is the price to be paid for various kinds of satisfactions away from the job.

DOUGLAS McGREGOR (1906–1964). *The Human Side of Enterprise*, 3, 1960

It is known that the bad workmen who form the majority of the operatives in many branches of industry are decidedly of [the] opinion that bad workmen ought to receive the same wages as good, and that no one ought to be allowed, through piecework or otherwise, to earn by superior skill or industry more than others can without it.

JOHN STUART MILL (1806–1873). *On Liberty*, 4, 1859

The wages of a hired servant shall not remain with you all night until the morning.

MOSES (14th cent. B.C.). *Leviticus* 19:13

Give the laborer his wage before his perspiration [dries].

MUHAMMAD (A.D. 570?–632). *The Sayings of Muhammad*, 266, tr. Abdullah Al-Suhrawardy, 1941

He who *serves* well needs not be afraid to ask his wages.

JOHN RAY (1628–1705). Comp., *A Collection of English Proverbs*, p. 23, 1678

Wages should be left to the fair and free competition of the market, and should never be controlled by the interference of the legislature.

DAVID RICARDO (1772–1823). *On the Principles of Political Economy and Taxation*, 4, 1817

No business which depends for existence on paying less than living wages to its workers has any right to continue in this country.

. . . And by living wages I mean more than a bare subsistence level—I mean the wages of decent living.

FRANKLIN D. ROOSEVELT (1882–1945). Public statement, 16 June 1933

Where wages are high . . . we shall always find the workmen more active, diligent, and expeditious, than where they are low.

ADAM SMITH (1723–1790). *The Wealth of Nations*, 1.8, 1776

The true laborer is recompensed by his labor, not by his employer. Industry is its own wages. . . . Our true endeavor cannot be thwarted, nor we be cheated of our earnings unless by not earning them.

HENRY DAVID THOREAU (1817–1862). Journal, 1 July 1840

Most men would feel insulted if it were proposed to employ them in throwing stones over a wall, and then in throwing them back, merely that they might earn their wages. But many are no more worthily employed now.

HENRY DAVID THOREAU (1817–1862). "Life Without Principle," *Atlantic*, October 1863

One man's wage rise is another man's price increase.

SIR HAROLD WILSON (1916–1995). In *Observer* (British newspaper), 11 January 1970

❦

A fair day's wage for a fair day's work; a fair day's work for a fair day's wage.

ANONYMOUS

WAITING

See also • Events: Anonymous (2) ○ Patience ○ Self-Realization (Becoming): Carl Hilty

Estragon: Charming spot. Inspiring prospects. Let's go.
Vladimir: We can't.
Estragon: Why not?
Vladimir: We're waiting for Godot.

SAMUEL BECKETT (1906–1989). *Waiting for Godot*, 1, 1955

Waste not thy gifts
In profitless waiting for the gods' descent.

ROBERT BROWNING (1812–1889). *Paracelsus*, 1835. In Ralph Waldo Emerson, journal, October 1842

Sitting here in limbo waiting for the tide to flow.

JIMMY CLIFF (1948–). "Sitting in Limbo" (song), 1973

We generally learn how to wait when there is nothing more to wait for.

MARIE von EBNER-ESCHENBACH (1830–916). *Aphorisms*, p. 21, 1880–1905, tr. David Scrase and Wolfgang Mieder, 1994

Everything comes to him who hustles while he waits.

THOMAS ALVA EDISON (1847–1931). In *Golden Book*, April 1931

There is a difference between the waiting of the prophet and the standing still of the fool.

RALPH WALDO EMERSON (1803–1882). Journal, 27 August 1836

They who wait for the Lord
    shall renew their strength,
    they shall mount up with wings
        like eagles,
they shall run and not be weary,
    they shall walk and not faint.

> ISAIAH (8th cent. B.C.). *Isaiah* 40:31

Perhaps this quiet yet unquiet waiting is the harbinger of grace, or perhaps it is grace itself.

> FRANZ KAFKA (1883–1924). In Gustav Janouch, *Conversations with Kafka,* p. 93, tr. Goronwy Rees, 1953

A man watches his pear tree day after day, impatient for the ripening of the fruit. Let him attempt to *force* the ripening of the fruit, and he may spoil both fruit and tree. But let him patiently *wait,* and the ripe pear at length falls into his lap!

> ABRAHAM LINCOLN (1809–1865). Remark to George Thompson, 7 April 1864. In F. B. Carpenter, *Six Months at the White House with Abraham Lincoln,* 24, 1866

Let us, then, be up and doing,
    With a heart for any fate;
Still achieving, still pursuing,
    Learn to labor and to wait.

> HENRY WADSWORTH LONGFELLOW (1807–1882). Closing words, "A Psalm of Life," *Voices of the Night,* 1839

Ah, "all things come to those who wait,"
(I say these words to make me glad),
But something answers, soft and sad,
"They come, but often come too late."

> MARY SINGLETON (1843–1905). *Tout vient à quit sait attendre*

All good abides with him who waiteth *wisely*.

> HENRY DAVID THOREAU (1817–1862). "Monday," *A Week on the Concord and Merrimack Rivers,* 1849

WALL STREET

See • Stock Market

WAR

See also • Army ○ Civil War ○ Class ○ Cold War ○ Commanders ○ Competition ○ Crises ○ Crowds ○ Cruelty ○ Cuban Missile Crisis ○ Defeat ○ Dehumanization ○ Guerrilla Warfare ○ Gulf War ○ Hell ○ History ○ Imperialism ○ Intelligence, Military ○ International Relations ○ Korean War ○ Mass Movements ○ Militarism ○ Mobs ○ Navy ○ Nonviolence ○ Nuclear Weapons ○ Peace ○ Politics ○ Propaganda ○ Revolution ○ Revolutionary War ○ Slavery ○ Soldiers ○ Strategy, Military ○ Success: William Napier ○ Tyranny ○ Victory ○ Vietnam War ○ Violence ○ War & Economics ○ War & Peace ○ War & Preparedness ○ War & Psychology ○ War & Revolution ○ World War I ○ World War II

The stakes of war are the existence, the creation or the elimination of States.

> RAYMOND ARON (1905–1983). In Michael Howard, "The Causes of War," 1981, *The Causes of War: And Other Essays,* 2nd ed., 1983

Never, never, never believe any war will be smooth and easy, or that anyone who embarks on the strange voyage can measure the tides and hurricanes he will encounter. The Statesman who yields to war fever must realize that once the signal is given, he is no longer the master of policy but the slave of unforeseeable and uncontrollable events.

> WINSTON CHURCHILL (1874–1965). *My Early Life: A Roving Commission,* 18, 1930

War . . . is an act of violence intended to compel our opponent to fulfill our will.

> KARL von CLAUSEWITZ (1780–1831). *On War,* 1.1.2, 1832, tr. J. J. Graham, 1873

Now, philanthropists may easily imagine there is a skillful method of disarming and overcoming an enemy without causing great bloodshed, and that this is the proper tendency of the Art of War. However plausible this may appear, still it is an error which must be extirpated; for in such dangerous things as War, the errors which proceed from a spirit of benevolence are the worst.

> KARL von CLAUSEWITZ (1780–1831). *On War,* 1.1.3, 1832, tr. J. J. Graham, 1873
>
> See World War I: Wilhelm II (1)

War is not merely a political act, but also a real political instrument, a continuation of political commerce, a carrying out of the same by other means.

> KARL von CLAUSEWITZ (1780–1831). *On War,* 1.1.24, 1832, tr. J. J. Graham, 1873 (Popular version: War is a continuation of politics by other means.)
>
> See Diplomacy: Chou En-Lai, Charles Krauthammer ○ Nuclear Weapons: John Keegan ○ Politics: Eric Alterman, Alisdair C. Macintyre, Edward J. Nell ○ Revolution: Leon Trotsky (1) ○ War & Economics: Anonymous ○ Writing: Philippe Sollers

And blood in torrents pour
In vain—always in vain,
For war breeds war again.

> JOHN DAVIDSON. "War Song," 7, 1899

I hate war as only a soldier who has lived it can, only as one who has seen its brutality, its futility, and its *stupidity*.

> DWIGHT D. EISENHOWER (1890–1969). Speech, Ottawa (Canada), 10 January 1946

Every gun that is fired, every warship launched, every rocket fired signifies, in the final sense, a theft from those who hunger and are not fed, those who are cold and are not clothed. . . . This is not a way of life at all, in any true sense. Under the cloud of threatening war, it is humanity hanging from a cross of iron.

> DWIGHT D. EISENHOWER (1890–1969). "The Chance for Peace," speech before the American Society of Newspaper Editors, Washington, 16 April 1953

War is a respectable term for *goondaism* [hooliganism] practiced on a mass or national scale.

> MOHANDAS K. GANDHI (1869–1948). In *Harijan,* 15 September 1946

War is the admission of defeat in the face of conflicting interests.

> GERMAN GREER (1939–). "Revolution," *The Female Eunuch,* 1970

War is father and king of all.

> HERACLITUS (540?–480? B.C.). In T. V. Smith, ed., "Heraclitus" (44),
> *From Thales to Plato*, 2, 1934 (Popular version: War is the father of all
> things.)

When war begins, then hell openeth.

> GEORGE HERBERT (1593–1633). Comp., *Jacula Prudentum*, 1141, 1651

Force and Fraud are in war the two Cardinal virtues.

> THOMAS HOBBES (1588–1679). *Leviathan*, 13, 1651
> See Strategy: Polybius o Success: Machiavelli (1) o Tyrants: Aristotle (1)

[In time of war] there is no place for Industry, because the fruit thereof is uncertain; and consequently no Culture of the Earth, . . . no Knowledge of the face of the Earth, no account of Time, no Arts, no Letters, no Society, and which is worst of all, continual fear and danger of violent death, and the life of man, solitary, poor, nasty, brutish, and short.

> THOMAS HOBBES (1588–1679). *Leviathan*, 13, 1651

The first casualty, when war comes, is truth.

> HIRAM JOHNSON (1866–1945). California governor and U.S. senator.
> Senate speech, 1918 (Popular version: The first casualty of war is truth.)

The belief that we some day shall be able to prevent war is to me one with the belief in the possibility of making humanity *really* human.

> ELLEN KEY (1849–1926). Preface to *War, Peace, and the Future*, 1916

Everything in war is barbaric. . . . But the worst barbarity of war is that it forces men collectively to commit acts against which individually they would revolt with their whole being.

> ELLEN KEY (1849–1926). *War, Peace, and the Future*, 6, 1916

The most persistent sound which reverberates through man's history is the beating of war drums.

> ARTHUR KOESTLER (1905–1983). "Prologue: The New Calendar," *Janus:
> A Summing Up*, 1978

War is a part of a whole, that whole is politics.

> LENIN (1870–1924). Marginalia in his copy of Clausewitz' *On War*. In
> Raymond L. Garthoff, *How Russia Makes War: Soviet Military Doctrine*,
> 1, 1954

Wars are inevitable so long as society is divided into classes, so long as the exploitation of man by man exists.

> LENIN (1870–1924). In Raymond L. Garthoff, *How Russia Makes War:
> Soviet Military Doctrine*, 3, 1954

I know war as few other men now living know it, and nothing to me is more revolting. I have long advocated its complete abolition, as its very destructiveness on both friend and foe has rendered it useless as a method of settling international disputes.

> DOUGLAS MacARTHUR (1880–1964). Congress address, 19 April 1951

The great question is, can war be outlawed from the world? If so, it would mark the greatest advance in civilization since the Sermon on the Mount. . . . It would not only create new moral and spiritual values, it would produce an economic wave of prosperity that would raise the world's standard of living beyond anything ever dreamed of by man.

> DOUGLAS MacARTHUR (1880–1964). "War Is No Longer a Medium of
> Practical Settlement of International Differences," address at an
> American Legion dinner honoring him, Ambassador Hotel, Los
> Angeles, 26 January 1955

War is waged by men; not by beasts, or by gods. It is a peculiarly human activity. To call it a crime against mankind is to miss at least half its significance; it is also the punishment of a crime.

> FREDERIC MANNING. Recalling World War I, 1929. In Paul Fussell,
> "My War," *The Boy Scout Handbook and Other Observations*,
> 1982

War is the highest form of struggle for resolving contradictions, when they have developed to a certain stage, between classes, nations, states, or political groups.

> MAO TSE-TUNG (1893–1976). "Problems of Strategy in China's
> Revolutionary War," December 1936, *Selected Works of Mao Tse-tung*,
> Foreign Languages Press edition, vol. 1, 1965

Politics is war without bloodshed, while war is politics with bloodshed.

> MAO TSE-TUNG (1893–1976). "On Protracted War" (64), May 1938,
> *Selected Works of Mao Tse-tung*, Foreign Languages Press edition, vol.
> 2, 1965

We are advocates of the abolition of war, we do not want war; but war can only be abolished through war, and in order to get rid of the gun it is necessary to take up the gun.

> MAO TSE-TUNG (1893–1976). "Problems of War and Strategy" (2), 6
> November 1938, *Selected Works of Mao Tse-tung*, Foreign Languages
> Press edition, vol. 2, 1965

War is sacred; it is instituted by God; it is one of the divine laws of the world; it upholds in men all the great and noble sentiments—honor, self-sacrifice, virtue and courage. It is War alone that saves men from falling into the grossest materialism.

> HELMETH von MOLTKE (1800–1891). In Leo Tolstoy, *The Kingdom of
> God Is Within You*, 6, 1893, tr. Aylmer Maude, 1936

War hath no fury like a noncombatant.

> C. E. MONTAGUE (1867–1928). *Disenchantment*, 16.5, 1922
> See War & Psychology: William James

War is both the product of an earlier corruption and a producer of new corruptions.

> LEWIS MUMFORD (1895–1990). *The Conduct of Life*, 1.3, 1951

War alone brings up to its highest tension all human energy and puts the stamp of nobility upon the peoples who have the courage to meet it.

> BENITO MUSSOLINI (1883–1945). In "'Peace an Illusion,' Writes
> Mussolini," *New York Times*, 11 January 1935

The problem after a war is with the victor. He thinks he has just proved that war and violence pay. Who will now teach him a lesson?

> A. J. MUSTE (1885–1967). "Crisis in the World and in the Peace
> Movement," *The Essays of A. J. Muste*, ed. Nat Hentoff, 1967

You say it is the good cause that hallows even war? I tell you: it is the good war that hallows every cause.

> FRIEDRICH NIETZSCHE (1844–1900). "Of War and Warriors," *Thus
> Spoke Zarathustra*, 1892, tr. R. J. Hollingdale, 1961

The hypocrisy . . . of denouncing war while wanting to preserve the kind of society that makes war inevitable.

> GEORGE ORWELL (1903–1950). "As I Please," 12 July 1944, *The Collected Essays, Journalism and Letters of George Orwell,* vol. 3, ed. Sonia Orwell and Ian Angus, 1968

The war is waged by each ruling group against its own subjects, and the object of war is not to make or prevent conquests of territory, but to keep the structure of society intact.

> GEORGE ORWELL (1903–1950). On the function of war in his futuristic dystopia, *Nineteen Eighty-Four,* 2.9, 1949

Warfare seems to signify blood and iron [sanguinem et ferrum].

> QUINTILIAN (A.D. 35?–100?). *Declamationes*
>
> See Violence: Otto von Bismarck

You can no more win a war than you can win an earthquake.

> JEANNETTE RANKIN (1880–1973). Montana congresswoman. Campaign speech, 1943. In Hannah Josephson, *Jeannette Rankin: First Lady in Congress,* 8, 1974

War is death's feast.

> JOHN RAY (1628–1705). Comp., *A Collection of English Proverbs,* p. 27, 1678

War means an ugly mob-madness, crucifying the truth-tellers, choking the artists, sidetracking reforms, revolutions, and the working of social forces.

> JOHN REED (1887–1920). "Whose War?" *The Masses,* April 1917

Rules of War: The laws that make it illegal to hit below the toes.

> LEO ROSTEN (1908–1997). "Political Lexicon," *New Republic,* 3 July 1935

Wherever there is war, there must be injustice on one side or on the other, or on both.

> JOHN RUSKIN (1819–1900). *Modern Painters,* 3.4.18.32, 1843–1860, ed. Ernest Rhys, 1906

Behind all war has been the pressure of population.

> MARGARET SANGER (1883–1966). *Woman and the New Race,* 13, 1920

The statement that war is a continuation of policy by other means has become a catch phrase and is therefore dangerous. We can say with equal truth: War is the bankruptcy of policy.

> HANS VON SEECKT (1866–1936). German general. "The Attainable Object," *Thoughts of a Soldier,* 1929?, tr. Gilbert Waterhouse, 1930

War with its million horrors.

> PERCY BYSSHE SHELLEY (1792–1822). *Queen Mab: A Philosophical Poem: With Notes,* 5, 1813

War is barbarism. . . . It is only those who have neither fired a shot nor heard the shrieks and groans of the wounded who cry aloud for blood, more vengeance, more desolation. War is hell.

> WILLIAM TECUMSEH SHERMAN (1820–1891). Speech before the graduating class of the Michigan Military Academy, 19 June 1879
>
> See Civil War: Sherman (all)

War crushes with bloody heel all justice, all happiness, all that is Godlike in man. In our age there can be no peace that is not honorable; there can be no war that is not dishonorable.

> CHARLES SUMNER (1811–1874). "The True Grandeur of Nations," speech, 4 July 1845

When Vitellius was dead, the war had indeed come to an end, but peace had yet to begin. Sword in hand, throughout the capital, the conquerors hunted down the conquered with merciless hatred. The streets were choked with carnage. . . . But the ferocity, which in the first impulse of hatred could be gratified only by blood, soon passed into the greed of gain.

> TACITUS (A.D. 56?–120?). *The History,* 4.1, tr. Alfred J. Church and William J. Brodribb, 1942

A long war almost always reduces nations to the wretched alternative of being abandoned to ruin by defeat or to despotism by success.

> ALEXIS de TOCQUEVILLE (1805–1859). *Democracy in America,* 1.8, 1835, tr. Henry Reeve and Francis Bowen, 1862

We have to abolish War and Class—and abolish them now—under pain, if we flinch or fail, of seeing them win a victory over man which, this time, would be conclusive and definitive.

> ARNOLD J. TOYNBEE (1889–1975). "The Present Point in History," 1947, *Civilization on Trial,* 1948

O Lord, our God, help us to tear their soldiers to bloody shreds with our shells; help us to cover their smiling fields with the pale forms of their patriot dead; help us to drown the thunder of the guns with the shrieks of their wounded, writhing in pain; help us to lay waste their humble homes with a hurricane of fire; help us to wring the hearts of their unoffending widows with unavailing grief; help us to turn them out roofless with their little children to wander unfriended the wastes of their desolated land in rags and hunger and thirst, sport of the sun-flames of summer and the icy winds of winter, broken in spirit, worn with travail, imploring Thee for the refuge of the grave and denied it—for our sakes who adore Thee, Lord, blast their hopes, blight their lives, protract their bitter pilgrimage, make heavy their steps, water their way with tears, stain the white snow with the blood of their wounded feet! We ask it, in the spirit of love, of Him Who is the Source of Love, and Who is the ever-faithful refuge and friend of all that are sore beset and seek His aid with humble and contrite hearts. Amen.

> MARK TWAIN (1835–1910). "The War-Prayer," 1916 (written in 1904–1905), *A Pen Warmed-up in Hell: Mark Twain in Protest,* ed. Frederick Anderson, 1972. After dictating the "Prayer," Twain decided not to have it published during his lifetime: "I have told the truth in that, and only dead men can tell the truth in this world." (In *The Wit and Wisdom of Mark Twain,* p. 243, ed. Alex Ayres, 1987)

We have war because we are not sufficiently heroic for a life which does not need war.

> BARTOLOMEO VANZETTI (1888–1927). In Fredric Wertham, *A Sign for Cain: An Exploration of Human Violence,* 15 (epigraph), 1966

War is not so heavy a burden as slavery.

> VAUVENARGUES (1715–1747). *Reflections and Maxims,* 21, 1746, tr. F. G. Stevens, 1940

My first wish is to see this plague to mankind banished from off the Earth, and the sons and daughters of this world employed in more pleasing and innocent amusements than in preparing implements and exercising them for the destruction of mankind.

> GEORGE WASHINGTON (1732–1799). On war. Letter to David Humphreys, 25 July 1785

I was in the midst of it all—saw war where war is worst—not on the battlefields, no—in the hospitals: . . . there I mixed with it: and now I say God damn the wars—all wars: God damn every war: God damn 'em! God damn 'em!

> WALT WHITMAN (1819–1892). Remark to the author, 13 December 1888. In Horace Traubel, *Walt Whitman's Camden Conversations*, ed. Walter Teller, 1973. Whitman cared for wounded and sick soldiers as a hospital volunteer in Washington during the Civil War.

❧

War is a continuation of politics by every means.

> ANONYMOUS (GERMAN). In *Signal* (magazine), 1943?

A great war leaves a country with three armies: an army of cripples, an army of mourners, and an army of thieves.

> SAYING (GERMAN)

The last argument of kings. [Ultima ratio regum.]

> SAYING (LATIN). On war. Louis XV (French king) ordered this phrase engraved on his cannon, 1735?

WAR & ECONOMICS

See also • Economics ○ Imperialism ○ Nations: Ernest Hemingway ○ War ○ War & Preparedness

History is replete with examples of empires mounting impressive military campaigns on the cusp of their impending economic collapse.

> ERIC ALTERMAN (1960–). *Sound and Fury: The Washington Punditocracy and the Collapse of American Politics*, 12.2, 1992

Peoples no longer go to war for the sake of wounded pride, prestige or glory. They fight to avoid starvation, so they say—in reality to maintain a certain standard of living, below which they believe that life would not be worthwhile.

> HENRI BERGSON (1859–1941). "Final Remarks," *The Two Sources of Morality and Religion*, 1932, tr. R. Ashley Audra and Cloudesley Brereton, 1935

The Pentagon system has become our system of state intervention in the economy. The state quite naturally turns to this method when it is necessary to "get the country moving again."

> NOAM CHOMSKY (1928–). Referring to "'military Keynesianism': the creation of a state-guaranteed market for high technology rapidly-obsolescing waste production, meaning armaments," *Turning the Tide: U.S. Intervention in Central America and the Struggle for Peace*, 4.5, 1985

Sooner or later every war of trade becomes a war of blood.

> EUGENE V. DEBS (1855–1926). Speech, Canton (Ohio), 16 June 1918

In the councils of government, we must guard against the acquisition of unwarranted influence, whether sought or unsought, by the military-industrial complex. The potential for the disastrous rise of misplaced power exists and will persist. We must never let the weight of this combination endanger our liberties or democratic processes. We should take nothing for granted.

> DWIGHT D. EISENHOWER (1890–1969). Farewell address, 17 January 1961
>
> See Militarism: George Washington

Guns will make us powerful; butter will only make us fat.

> HERMANN GOERING (1893–1946). German political leader. Advocating increased armament expenditures, radio broadcast, summer 1936. The irony of these words was not lost on those who were aware of Goering's weight problems.

There is money in war. There is money in fear of war.

> JOHN GUNTHER (1901–1970). *Inside Europe*, rev. ed., 11, 1937 (1936)

A wonderful time—the War:
when money rolled in
and blood rolled out.
  But blood
  was far away
  from here—
Money was near.

> LANGSTON HUGHES (1902–1967). "Green Memory" (complete poem), 1949, *The Collected Poems of Langston Hughes*, ed. Arnold Rampersad and David Roessel, 1994

In man, as in ants, war in any serious sense is bound up with the existence of accumulations of property to fight about.

> JULIAN HUXLEY (1887–1975). "War as Biological Phenomenon," *On Living in a Revolution*, 1944

The wonder of this month's military-procurement scandal is that it can still scandalize us. The practices that are being exposed—the revolving door between government and industry, the mutual backscratching between the military and the companies that build its weapons—aren't abuses of the system. They *are* the system.

> DAVID IGNATIUS (1950–). "Our Weird Weapons Bazaar," *Washington Post*, 26 June 1988

A nation that continues year after year to spend more money on military defense than on programs of social uplift is approaching spiritual death.

> MARTIN LUTHER KING, JR. (1929–1968). "Declaration of Independence from the War in Vietnam," sermon, Riverside Church, New York City, 4 April 1967

It is part of the general pattern of misguided policy that our country is now geared to an arms industry which was bred in an artificially induced psychosis of war hysteria and nurtured upon an incessant propaganda of fear.

> DOUGLAS MacARTHUR (1880–1964). Speech before the Michigan state legislature, Lansing, 15 May 1952

Make wars unprofitable and you make them impossible.

> A. PHILIP RANDOLPH (1889–1979). "The Cause and Remedy of Race Riots," *The Messenger*, 1919

War, the needy bankrupt's last resort.

> NICHOLAS ROWE (1674–1718). *Pharsalia*, 1718 (Popular version: War is the last refuge of the bankrupt.)
>
> See Patriotism: Samuel Johnson

Wars are occasioned by the love of money.

> SOCRATES (470?–399 B.C.). In Plato (427?–347 B.C.), *Phaedo*, 66, tr. Benjamin Jowett, 1894

Why, my fellow citizens, is there any man here or any woman—let me say, is there any child here—who does not know that the seed of war in the modern world is industrial and commercial rivalry?

> WOODROW WILSON (1856–1924). Speech before a gathering of war veterans, St. Louis, 5 September 1919

❧

War is a continuation of business by other means.

> ANONYMOUS
>
> See Diplomacy: Charles Krauthammer ○ War: Karl von Clausewitz (3)

WAR & PEACE

See also • Nonviolence ○ Pacifism ○ Peace ○ War ○ War & Psychology

War compels men to be just and temperate, whereas the enjoyment of good fortune and the leisure which comes with peace tends to make them insolent.

> ARISTOTLE (384–322 B.C.). *Politics,* 7.15, tr. Benjamin Jowett, 1885

No one is so foolish as to prefer to peace war, in which, instead of sons burying their fathers, fathers bury their sons.

> CROESUS (6th cent. B.C.). Lydian king. Remark to King Cyrus. In Herodotus (484?–420? B.C.), *The Persian Wars,* 1.87, tr. George Rawlinson, 1942

The world will never have lasting peace so long as men reserve for war the finest human qualities. Peace, no less than war, requires idealism and self-sacrifice and a righteous and dynamic faith.

> JOHN FOSTER DULLES (1888–1959). 9 March 1955

The manhood that has been in war must be transferred to the cause of peace, before war can lose its charm, and peace be venerable to men.

> RALPH WALDO EMERSON (1803–1882). "War," lecture, American Peace Society, Boston, 12 March 1838
>
> See Victory: Emerson

There never was a good war or a bad peace.

> BENJAMIN FRANKLIN (1706–1790). Letter to Josiah Quincy, 11 September 1783

The problem of war is no ordinary one, to be combated and resolved like other social issues. It demands an emotional reorientation of such a kind that men will thenceforth date their liberation from that day. In Biblical language, this transformation will be apocalyptic in kind, comparable to the ancient command of the Lord: Let there be light! Afterward, men will be unable to comprehend how it was they could have lived in darkness.

> J. GLENN GRAY (1913–1977). "Conclusion," *The Warriors: Reflections on Men in Battle,* 1959

War protects the people from the corruption which an everlasting peace would bring upon it. History shows phases which illustrate how successful wars have checked internal unrest. . . . These Nations, torn by internal strife, win peace at home as a result of war abroad.

> GEORG HEGEL (1770–1831). *Philosophy of Right,* 1821. In Karl R. Popper, *The Open Society and Its Enemies,* 2.12.5(d), 1945

Mankind has grown great in eternal struggles, and only in eternal peace does it perish.

> ADOLF HITLER (1889–1945). *Mein Kampf,* 1.4, 1924, tr. Ralph Manheim, 1943

What we now need to discover in the social realm is the moral equivalent of war: something heroic that will speak to men as universally as war does, and yet will be as compatible with their spiritual selves as war has proven itself to be incompatible.

> WILLIAM JAMES (1842–1910). *The Varieties of Religious Experience: A Study in Human Nature,* 14 and 15, 1902

In times of peace the people look most to their representatives; but in war, to the executive solely.

> THOMAS JEFFERSON (1743–1826). Letter to Caesar A. Rodney, 10 February 1810

Wars are bred by poverty and oppression. Continued peace is possible only in a relatively free and prosperous world.

> GEORGE C. MARSHALL (1880–1959). 1956

Peace hath her victories
No less renown'd than war.

> JOHN MILTON (1608–1674). "Sonnet 16," l. 10, May 1652
>
> See Victory: Ralph Waldo Emerson

I love war and responsibility and excitement. Peace is going to be Hell on me.

> GEORGE S. PATTON, JR. (1885–1945). Letter to his wife Beatrice, 12 April 1945. In Ladislas Farago, *Patton: Ordeal and Triumph,* 41, 1963

No more war, war never again! Peace, it is peace which must guide the destinies of peoples and of all mankind.

> POPE PAUL VI (1897–1978). United Nations address, New York City, 4 October 1965

The motto of war is: "Let the strong survive; let the weak die." The motto of peace is: "Let the strong help the weak to survive."

> FRANKLIN D. ROOSEVELT (1882–1945). Speech before the Congress and Supreme Court of Brazil, Rio de Janeiro, 27 November 1936

All the great masterful races have been fighting races. . . . No triumph of peace is quite so great as the supreme triumph of war.

> THEODORE ROOSEVELT (1858–1919). Address, Naval War College, Newport (Rhode Island), June 1897
>
> See Victory: Ralph Waldo Emerson

We have contingency plans for war, but none for peace.

> THEODORE C. SORENSEN (1928–). Appearing on *The Today Show,* television morning program, NBC, November 1989

Peace hath higher tests of manhood
Than battle ever knew.

> JOHN GREENLEAF WHITTIER (1807–1892). "The Hero," 19, 1853

WAR & PREPAREDNESS

See also • Army ○ Nations: Henry Cabot Lodge ○ Preparedness ○ War ○ War & Economics

Weapons are like money; no one knows the meaning of *enough.*

> MARTIN AMIS (1949–). Introduction to *Einstein's Monsters,* 1987

More and more the arms race is theater, but the evidence is powerful that the audience reaction is perverse; consciously engendered fear in the adversary produces aggressive behavior as well as caution. In any particular situation, it is quite unpredictable which it will be.

> RICHARD J. BARNET (1929–). "Losing Moral Ground," *Sojourners,* March 1985

How many thousand men can he bring (onto) the field?

> FREDERICK II (1712–1786). When told of the disaffection of one of his subjects. In Thomas Babington Macaulay, "Frederic the Great," *The Edinburgh Review* (Scotland), April 1842

One sword keeps another in its sheath.

> GEORGE HERBERT (1593–1633). Comp., *Outlandish Proverbs,* 723, 1640

The intensely sharp competitive *preparation* for war by the nations *is the real war,* permanent, unceasing, and that the battles are only a sort of public verification of the mastery gained during the "peace"-interval.

> WILLIAM JAMES (1842–1910). *The Moral Equivalent of War* (pamphlet), 1910

The constant acceleration of preparation [for war] may well, without specific intent, ultimately produce a spontaneous combustion.

> DOUGLAS MacARTHUR (1880–1964). Speech before the Los Angeles Civic Club, 26 January 1955

Among other evils caused by being disarmed, it renders you contemptible.

> MACHIAVELLI (1469–1527). *The Prince,* 14, 1513, tr. Luigi Ricci, 1903

Nations do not mistrust each other because they are armed; they are armed because they mistrust each other.

> RONALD REAGAN (1911–). United Nations address, New York City, 22 September 1986

Pierre Laval (French foreign minister): Can't you do something to encourage religion and the Catholics in Russia? It would help me so much with the Pope.
Stalin: Oho! The Pope! How many divisions has *he* got?

> JOSEPH STALIN (1879–1953). Format adapted. May 1935. In Winston Churchill, *The Second World War: The Gathering Storm,* 1.8, 1948

The arms race is based on an optimistic view of technology and a pessimistic view of man. It assumes there is no limit to the ingenuity of science and no limit to the deviltry of human beings.

> I. F. STONE (1907–1989). "Nixon and the Arms Race," *New York Review of Books,* 27 March 1969

A wise rule would be to make up your mind soberly what you want, peace or war, and then to get ready for what you want; for what you prepare for is what you shall get.

> WILLIAM GRAHAM SUMNER (1840–1910). Slightly modified. Title essay, *War and Other Essays,* 1911

You can do everything with bayonets, Sire, except sit on them.

> TALLEYRAND (1754–1838). Remark to Napoleon. In José Ortega y Gasset, *The Revolt of the Masses,* 14.1, 1930, tr. anon., 1932

❧

If you wish for peace, prepare for war.

> SAYING (LATIN). In John Keegan, *A History of Warfare,* 5, 1994
> See Peace: B. H. Liddell Hart, Saying (1)

WAR & PSYCHOLOGY

See also • Dehumanization ○ Peace ○ War ○ War & Peace ○ World War I

A general and a bit of shooting makes you forget your troubles. It takes your mind off the cost of living.

> BRENDAN BEHAN (1923–1964). *The Hostage,* 3, 1958

There is nothing like a war for breaking down class and other barriers and creating feelings of friendship and cooperation within a country because all its previously inwardly-directed aggression and resentment comes to be directed against an external enemy.

> J. A. C. BROWN (1911–1964). *Techniques of Persuasion: From Propaganda to Brainwashing,* 4, 1963

I feel very lonely without a war. Do you feel like that?

> WINSTON CHURCHILL (1874–1965). Remark to the diarist, 22 June 1945. In Lord Moran, *Churchill: Taken from the Diaries of Lord Moran,* 25, 1966

The day after tomorrow . . . there will be a great battle, for which the entire Army is longing. I myself look forward to this day with joy as I would to my own wedding day.

> KARL von CLAUSEWITZ (1780–1831). Two days before Napoleon defeated the Prussians in the Battle of Jena (Germany), letter, 12 October 1806

In ev'ry heart
Are sown the sparks of fi'ry war.
Occasion needs but fan them, and they blaze.

> WILLIAM COWPER (1731–1800). *The Task,* 5.205, 1785

Why do you and I and so many other people rebel so violently against war? Why do we not accept it as another of the many painful calamities of life? After all, it seems quite a natural thing, no doubt it has a good biological basis and in practice it is scarcely avoidable.

> SIGMUND FREUD (1856–1939). Letter to Albert Einstein, September 1932, tr. James Strachey, 1963

Man lives *by* habits, indeed, but what he lives *for* is thrills and excitements. The only relief from Habit's tediousness is periodical excitement. From time immemorial wars have been, especially for noncombatants, the supremely thrilling excitement.

> WILLIAM JAMES (1842–1910). Dinner address before the World's Peace Congress, Boston, 7 October 1904
> See War: C. E. Montague

The germs of war lie within ourselves—not in economics, politics or religion as such.

> B. H. LIDDELL HART (1895–1970). "The Germs of War," *Why Don't We Learn from History?* 1944

So strong is this propensity of mankind to fall into mutual animosities, that where no substantial occasion presents itself, the most frivolous and fanciful distinctions have been sufficient to kindle their unfriendly passions and excite their most violent conflicts.

JAMES MADISON (1751–1836). In *The Federalist Papers* (essay series), 10, 23 November 1787

Any terroristic regime compels its victims to repress their reactions of rebellion and anger. The more these reactions are repressed, the more the victims develop tremendous inner rage, which must bide its time and wait until it is permitted some socially sanctioned form of explosion. War is often such a universal panic, a mass discharge of accumulated internal rage.

JOOST A. M. MEERLOO (1903–1976). *The Rape of the Mind: The Psychology of Thought Control, Menticide, and Brainwashing*, 9, 1956

"The Root of War Is Fear."

THOMAS MERTON (1915–1968). Chapter title, *New Seeds of Contemplation*, 16, 1961

Under peaceful conditions a warlike man sets upon himself.

FRIEDRICH NIETZSCHE (1844–1900). *Beyond Good and Evil*, 76, 1886, tr. Walter Kaufmann, 1966

War is, after all, the universal perversion. We are all tainted: if we cannot experience our perversion at first hand we spend our time reading war stories, the pornography of war; or seeing war films, the blue films of war; or titillating our senses with the imagination of great deeds, the masturbation of war.

JOHN RAE (1931–). *The Custard Boys*, 13, 1961

War is bestowed like electroshock on the depressive nation: thousands of volts jolting the system, an artificial galvanizing, one effect of which is loss of memory. War comes at the end of the twentieth century as absolute failure of imagination, scientific and political. That a war can be represented as helping a people to "feel good" about themselves, their country, is a measure of that failure.

ADRIENNE RICH (1929–). January 1991, *What Is Found There: Notebooks on Poetry and Politics*, 3, 1993

Every man who has in him any real power of joy in battle knows that he feels it when the wolf begins to rise in his heart; he does not then shrink from blood or sweat or deem that they mar the fight; he revels in them, in the toil, the pain, and the danger, as but setting off the triumph.

THEODORE ROOSEVELT (1858–1919). Essay. In Richard Hofstadter, *The American Political Tradition: And the Men Who Made It*, 9.1, 1948

War . . . seems a mere madness, a collective insanity.

BERTRAND RUSSELL (1872–1970). *Principles of Social Reconstruction*, 1, 1916

A great many people enjoy a war provided it's not in their neighborhood and not too bad.

BERTRAND RUSSELL (1872–1970). Woodrow Wyatt television interview, BBC, London, 1959. *Bertrand Russell Speaks His Mind*, 3, 1960

It's very absurd when a war is imminent. Immense crowds assemble in Trafalgar Square to applaud. They echo the Government's decision to have them killed. It's odd. It's not what you would expect of human nature.

BERTRAND RUSSELL (1872–1970). Woodrow Wyatt television interview, BBC, London, 1959, *Bertrand Russell Speaks His Mind*, 3, 1960

See World War I: Russell, Woodrow Wilson (2)

Men may speculate as they will; they may talk of patriotism; they may draw a few examples from ancient story, of great achievements performed by its influence; but whoever builds upon it as a sufficient Basis for conducting a long and [bloody] War will find themselves deceived in the end. . . . A great and lasting War can never be supported on this principle alone. It must be aided by a prospect of Interest or some reward. For a time, it may of itself push Men to Action, to bear much, to encounter difficulties; but it will not endure unassisted by Interest.

GEORGE WASHINGTON (1732–1799). Letter to John Banister, 21 April 1778

As long as war is regarded as wicked, it will always have its fascination. When it is looked upon as vulgar, it will cease to be popular.

OSCAR WILDE (1854–1900). "The Critic as Artist" (2), *Intentions*, 1891

WAR & REVOLUTION

See also • Revolution ○ War

A civil war . . . is like the heat of a fever, but a foreign war is like the heat of exercise and serveth to keep the body in health.

FRANCIS BACON (1561–1626). "Of the True Greatness of Kingdoms and Estates," *Essays*, 1625

Two States . . . [are] ready to forsake their enmities and their open warfare as soon as the threat of a social revolution appears on the horizon.

MIKHAIL BAKUNIN (1814–1876). *Science and the Urgent Revolutionary Task* (pamphlet), 1870. In *The Political Philosophy of Bakunin: Scientific Anarchism*, 4.2, ed. G. P. Maximoff, 1953

The only way to save our empires from the encroachment of the people is to engage in war, and thus substitute national passions for social aspirations.

CATHERINE II (1729–1796)

War protects the people from the corruption which an everlasting peace would bring upon it. History shows phases which illustrate how successful wars have checked internal unrest. . . . These Nations, torn by internal strife, win peace at home as a result of war abroad.

GEORG HEGEL (1770–1831). *Philosophy of Right*, 1821. In Karl R. Popper, *The Open Society and Its Enemies*, 2.12.5(d), 1945

Internal strife is a thing as much worse than war carried on by a united people, as war itself is worse than peace.

HERODOTUS (484?–420? B.C.). *The Persian Wars*, 8.3, tr. George Rawlinson, 1942

History knows only two kinds of war, just and unjust. We support just wars and oppose unjust wars. All counterrevolutionary wars are unjust, all revolutionary wars are just.

MAO TSE-TUNG (1893–1976). "Problems of Strategy in China's Revolutionary War" (1.3), December 1936, *Selected Works of Mao Tse-tung*, Foreign Languages Press edition, vol. 1, 1965

See Violence:Lenin

Europe is but one province of the world. When we make war, we make civil war.

> NAPOLEON (1769–1821). Remark to Louis de Bourrienne, 1802? *The Mind of Napoleon: A Selection from His Written and Spoken Words,* 313, ed. J. Christopher Herold, 1955

With modern technique most empires are fairly safe except against external attack, and revolution is only to be expected after defeat in war.

> BERTRAND RUSSELL (1872–1970). *Power: A New Social Analysis,* 11, 1938

❧

Revolution is internalized war; war is externalized revolution.

> ANONYMOUS

WASHINGTON

See also • Cities ○ Politics

You will be measured in this town by the enemies you destroy. The bigger they are, the bigger you will be.

> JOHN B. CONNALLY (1917–1993). Texas governor and U.S. secretary of the treasury. On Washington, remark to the author. In Henry A. Kissinger, *White House Years,* 22, 1979

Don't write anything down, but save everything that anyone else writes down.

> MAUREEN DOWD (1952–). A rule for surviving in Washington. In John Leo, "An Aphorism a Day . . . ," *U.S. News & World Report,* 9 January 1995

I was not meant for the job or the spotlight of public life in Washington. Here ruining people is considered sport.

> VINCENT W. FOSTER, JR. (1945–1993). Last paragraph of his suicide note. In R. W. Apple, Jr., "Note from White House Aide: A Mixture of Fury and Despair," *New York Times,* 11 August 1993

If you can't deal every day with having people trying to destroy you, you shouldn't even think of coming down here.

> ALAN GREENSPAN (1926–). To a New Yorker who was considering a top administrative appointment in Washington. In *Washington Post,* 6 June 1994

The gleaming temples of democracy that tourists visit in Washington, the marble shrines to great leaders and great ideals, are no longer an appropriate emblem for the nation's capital. Washington now is more aptly visualized as a grand bazaar—a steamy marketplace of tents, stalls, and noisy peddlers. The din of buying and selling drowns out patriotic music.

> WILLIAM GREIDER (1936–). *Who Will Tell the People: The Betrayal of American Democracy,* 4, 1992

[In Washington, the key question is] who is doing the fucking and who is getting fucked.

> LYNDON B. JOHNSON (1908–1973). In George E. Reedy, *Lyndon B. Johnson: A Memoir,* 7, 1982

Washington is like a Roman arena. Gladiators do battle, and the spectators determine who survives by giving the appropriate signal, just as in the Coliseum.

> HENRY A. KISSINGER (1923–). *Years of Upheaval,* 10, 1982

The District of Columbia is [sometimes] one gigantic ear.

> RONALD REAGAN (1911–). News conference. In Thomas Griffith, "Mr. Optimism Meets the Skeptical Fourth Estate," *Time,* 23 November 1981

Nothing ever gets settled in this town. It's not like running a company or even a university. It's—it's a seething debating society in which the debate never stops, in which people never give up, including me, and that's the atmosphere in which you administer.

> GEORGE P. SHULTZ (1920–). On Washington, testimony before the House Foreign Affairs Committee, 8 December 1986

If you want a friend in Washington, get a dog.

> HARRY S. TRUMAN (1884–1972). In Helen Thomas, speech before the Commonwealth Club of California, San Francisco, 17 February 1995
>
> See Wall Street: Carl C. Icahn

Washington [is] a city of northern charm and southern efficiency.

> ANONYMOUS. In John F. Kennedy, remarks to the Trustees and Advisory Committee of the National Cultural Center, Washington, 14 November 1961

WATERGATE

See also • Newspeak—Examples: Ronald L. Ziegler ○ Politics ○ Presidents ○ The Press: John N. Mitchell ○ Vietnam War: Richard N. Nixon (4)

I began by telling the President that there was a cancer growing on the Presidency.

> JOHN W. DEAN III (1938–). On payoff money for the Watergate burglars. Watergate hearings, 25 June 1975

I think we ought to let him hang there. Let him twist slowly, slowly in the wind.

> JOHN EHRLICHMAN (1925–). On acting FBI Director L. Patrick Gray, telephone remark to John Dean early in the Watergate investigation. In *White House Transcripts,* 7 March 1973. Gray resigned one month later, after it was disclosed that he had destroyed documents Dean had given him.

My fellow Americans, our long national nightmare is over. Our Constitution works. Our great republic is a government of laws, not of men.

> GERALD R. FORD (1913–). Following the resignation of Richard M. Nixon and his own succession to the Presidency, television broadcast, 9 August 1974

I don't give a shit what happens. I want you all to stonewall it, let them plead the Fifth Amendment, cover-up or anything else, if it'll save it—save the plan. That's the whole point.

> RICHARD M. NIXON (1913–1994). Remark to John Dean, John Ehrlichman, H. R. Haldeman, and John N. Mitchell in the President's office at the Executive Office Building, March 1973

We must maintain the integrity of the White House, and that integrity must be real, not transparent. There can be no whitewash at the White House.

> RICHARD M. NIXON (1913–1994). On the Watergate investigation, television broadcast, 30 April 1973

The most personally disturbing myth was that I deliberately lied throughout the Watergate period in my news conferences and in my speeches. While I did some stupid things during the Watergate period, I was not that stupid. . . . I made no statements that I did not think were true at the time I made them.

> RICHARD M. NIXON (1913–1994). *In the Arena: A Memoir of Victory, Defeat and Renewal,* 2, 1990
>
> See Criticism—Examples: Barry M. Goldwater, Harry S. Truman

In retrospect I would say that Watergate was one part wrongdoing, one part blundering, and one part political vendetta [by my enemies].

> RICHARD M. NIXON (1913–1994). *In the Arena: A Memoir of Victory, Defeat and Renewal,* 2, 1990

[A] third-rate burglary attempt.

> RONALD L. ZIEGLER (1939–). Presidential press secretary. On the Watergate break-in when it was first reported, summer 1972. In Henry A. Kissinger, *Years of Upheaval,* 4, 1982

WEAKNESS

See also • Inferiority ○ Power ○ Strength ○ Strength & Weakness ○ Truth: Eric Hoffer ○ Weaknesses

The concessions of the weak are the concessions of fear.

> EDMUND BURKE (1729–1797). "Conciliation with America," House of Commons speech, 22 March 1775

He that makes himself a sheep shall be eaten [by] the wolf.

> JOHN CLARKE (1596–1658). Comp., *Proverbs: English and Latine,* p. 284, 1639

The thread breaks where it is weakest.

> GEORGE HERBERT (1593–1633). Comp., *Outlandish Proverbs,* 596, 1640
>
> See Strength: Saying (English)

In the process of tearing loose from nature it was the weak who took the first steps. Chased out of the forest by the strong, they first essayed to walk erect, and in the intensity of their soul first uttered words, and first grabbed a stick to use as weapon and tool. The weak's singular capacity for evolving substitutes for that which they lack suggest that they played a chief role in the evolvement of technology.

> ERIC HOFFER (1902–1983). *The Ordeal of Change,* 15.5, 1964
>
> See Defeat: Hoffer

Instead of being the leaven of history and the mainspring of the ascending movement of man, the weak [in contemporary society] are likely to be cast aside as a waste product. One is justified in fearing that the elimination of the weak as shaping factors may mean the end of history—the reversion of history to zoology.

> ERIC HOFFER (1902–1983). *The Ordeal of Change,* 15.7, 1964

There are two kinds of weakness, that which breaks and that which bends.

> JAMES RUSSELL LOWELL (1819–1891). "Shakespeare Once More," *Among My Books,* 1870

To be weak is miserable
Doing or Suffering.

> JOHN MILTON (1608–1674). *Paradise Lost,* 1.157, 1667

Gregory: The weakest goes to the wall.

> SHAKESPEARE (1564–1616). *Romeo and Juliet,* 1.1.15, 1594

There is a great difference between doing what one does not approve, and feigning to approve what one does; the one is the weakness of a feeble person, the other befits the temper of a lackey.

> ALEXIS de TOCQUEVILLE (1805–1859). *Democracy in America,* 1.15, 1835, tr. Henry Reeve and Francis Bowen, 1862

❦

When you are weak, humble yourself.

> SAYING (BURMESE)

Toes that are tender will be stepped upon.

> SAYING (VERMONT)

WEAKNESSES

See also • Defects ○ Faults ○ Weakness

Men are much more unwilling to have their weaknesses and their imperfections known than their crimes.

> LORD CHESTERFIELD (1694–1773). Letter to his son, 5 September 1748

People who have no weaknesses are terrible; there is no way of taking advantage of them.

> ANATOLE FRANCE (1844–1924). *The Crime of Sylvestre Bonnard,* 2.4 (June 6), 1881, tr. Lafcadio Hearn, 1890

❦

The greatest weakness of all is the fear of appearing weak.

> SAYING (FRENCH)

WEALTH

See also • Ambition ○ Business (Commerce) ○ Class ○ Consumerism ○ Economics ○ Exploitation ○ Gold ○ Greed ○ Idolatry: Andrew Carnegie ○ Industry ○ Leisure ○ Luxury ○ Materialism ○ Money ○ Pay ○ Possessions ○ Poverty ○ Power: [especially] Mikhail Bakunin, Edmund Burke (3) ○ Property ○ Prosperity ○ Rich & Poor ○ Riches ○ Status ○ Success ○ Taxes: [especially] Dinesh D'Souza ○ Thrift ○ Wages ○ Wealth & Poverty

Wealthy men are insolent and arrogant; their possession of wealth affects their understanding; they feel as if they had every good thing that exists; wealth becomes a sort of standard of value for everything else, and therefore they imagine there is nothing it cannot buy.

> ARISTOTLE (384–322 B.C.). *Rhetoric,* 2.16, tr. W. Rhys Roberts, 1954

He has not acquired a fortune; the fortune has acquired him.

> BION (325?–255? B.C.). On a miser. In Diogenes Laertius (A.D. 3rd cent.), *Lives of Eminent Philosophers,* 4.7, tr. R. D. Hicks, 1925
>
> See Riches: Seneca the Younger (2)

To be clever enough to get all that money, one must be stupid enough to want it.

> G. K. CHESTERTON (1874–1936). "The Paradise of Thieves,"
> *The Wisdom of Father Brown*, 1914

Wealth . . . is a relative thing since he that has little and wants less is richer than he that has much but wants more. . . . A tub was large enough for Diogenes, but a world was too little for Alexander.

> C. C. COLTON (1780–1832). *Lacon: or, Many Things in Few Words;
> Addressed to Those Who Think*, 1.194, 1823

Our wealth is often a snare to ourselves, and always a temptation to others.

> C. C. COLTON (1780–1832). *Lacon: or, Many Things in Few Words;
> Addressed to Those Who Think*, 1.426, 1823

I am absolutely convinced that no wealth in the world can help humanity forward, even in the hands of the most devoted worker in this cause. The example of great and pure characters is the only thing that can produce fine ideas and noble deeds. Money only appeals to selfishness and always tempts its owners irresistibly to abuse it.

Can anyone imagine Moses, Jesus, or Gandhi armed with the moneybags of Carnegie?

> ALBERT EINSTEIN (1879–1955). "Of Wealth," *The World As I See It*,
> 1, tr. Alan Harris, 1934

The Way to Wealth, if you desire it, is as plain as the Way to Market. It depends chiefly on two Words, Industry and Frugality; i.e., Waste neither Time nor Money, but make the best Use of both.

> BENJAMIN FRANKLIN (1706–1790). "Advice to a Young Tradesman,"
> 1748
>
> See Fortune: John Ray ○ Industry: Franklin (4)

Wealth is not without its advantages and the case to the contrary, although it has often been made, has never proved widely persuasive.

> JOHN KENNETH GALBRAITH (1908–). Opening words, *The Affluent
> Society*, 1958

Great wealth always supports the party in power, no matter how corrupt it may be. It never exerts itself for reform, for it instinctively fears change. It never struggles against misgovernment. When threatened by the holders of political power, it does not agitate, nor appeal to the [public]; it buys them off.

> HENRY GEORGE (1839–1897). *Social Problems*, 2, 1883

Millions is craft. Billions is art.

> WILLIAM HAMILTON. One well-dressed man to another at a cocktail
> party, cartoon caption, *New Yorker*, 12 December 1994

The point is to get so much money that money's not the point anymore.

> WILLIAM HAMILTON. One young man to another at a cocktail lounge,
> cartoon caption, *Forbes*, 14 October 1996

Knowledge makes one laugh, but wealth makes one dance.

> GEORGE HERBERT (1593–1633). Comp., *Outlandish Proverbs*, 957, 1640

The more wealth, the more worry.

> HILLEL (1st cent. B.C.)
>
> See Possessions: Anna C. Brackett

The Book of Wealth: In Which It Is Proved from the Bible That It Is the Duty of Every Man to Become Rich.

> THOMAS P. HUNT (19th cent.). Clergyman. Book title, 1836

The people who own the country ought to govern it.

> JOHN JAY (1745–1829). Supreme Court chief justice. One of his favorite
> maxims. In Frank Monaghan, *John Jay: Defender of Liberty Against
> Kings & Peoples*, 15.5, 1935.
>
> See Property: Samuel Johnson

Do not lay up for yourselves treasures on earth, where moth and rust consume and where thieves break in and steal, but lay up for yourselves treasures in heaven, where neither moth nor rust consumes and where thieves do not break in and steal. For where your treasure is, there will your heart be also.

> JESUS (A.D. 1st cent.). *Matthew* 6:19–21

Sir, the insolence of wealth will creep out.

> SAMUEL JOHNSON (1709–1784). 18 April 1778. In James Boswell,
> *The Life of Samuel Johnson*, 1791
>
> See Politicians: Shakespeare (1)

A man who knows how to make good bargains or finds his money increase in his coffers thinks presently that he has a good deal of brains and is almost fit to be a statesman.

> LA BRUYÈRE (1645–1696). "Of the Gifts of Fortune" (37),
> *The Characters*, 1688, tr. Henri van Laun, 1929

The shortest and best way of making your fortune is to let people clearly see that it is [in] their interest to promote yours.

> LA BRUYÈRE (1645–1696). "Of the Gifts of Fortune" (45),
> *The Characters*, 1688, tr. Henri van Laun, 1929

It is wealth to be content.

> LAO-TZU (6th cent. B.C.). *The Way of Life*, 33, tr. R. B. Blakney,
> 1955

Wealth may be an excellent thing, for it means power, it means leisure, it means liberty.

> JAMES RUSSELL LOWELL (1819–1891). Harvard University anniversary
> address, Cambridge (Massachusetts), 8 November 1886
>
> See Money: Horace Walpole

Nelson Rockefeller is reported to have said to Diego Rivera, who objected to making changes in the mural he was painting in the Rockefeller Center, "It's my wall."

> EUGENE McCARTHY (1916–). "Corporations," *Progressive Populist*,
> September 1996

Wealth is so much the greatest good that Fortune has to bestow, that in the Latin and English languages it has usurped her name.

> LORD MELBOURNE (1779–1848). British prime minister. In Lord David
> Cecil, *Melbourne*, 9, 1954

Wealth, properly employed, is a blessing; and a man may lawfully endeavor to increase it by honest means.

> MUHAMMAD (A.D. 570?–632 A.D.). *The Sayings of Muhammad*, 386,
> tr. Abdullah Al-Suhrawardy, 1941

I believe the power to make money is a gift from God—just as the instincts for art, music, literature, the doctor's talent, the nurse's, yours—to be developed and used to the best of our ability for the good of mankind. Having been endowed with the gift I possess, I believe it is my duty to make money and still more money; and to use the money I make for the good of my fellow man according to the dictates of my conscience.

> JOHN D. ROCKEFELLER, SR. (1839–1937). In John Thomas Flynn, *God's Gold: The Story of Rockefeller and His Times,* 8.8.4, 1932

Probably the greatest harm done by vast wealth is the harm that we of moderate means do ourselves when we let the vices of envy and hatred enter deep into our own natures.

> THEODORE ROOSEVELT (1858–1919). Speech, Providence, 23 August 1902

Malefactors of great wealth.

> THEODORE ROOSEVELT (1858–1919). Speech, Provincetown (Massachusetts), 20 August 1907

Undefended wealth invites aggression.

> THEODORE ROOSEVELT (1858–1919). Message to Congress, 14 April 1908

There is no Wealth but Life.

> JOHN RUSKIN (1819–1900). *Unto This Last,* 4, 1860

The energetic men who make great fortunes seldom desire the actual money: they desire the sense of power through a contest, and the joy of successful activity.

> BERTRAND RUSSELL (1872–1970). *Principles of Social Reconstruction,* 3, 1916
> See Money: Donald J. Trump

A great fortune is a great slavery.

> SENECA THE YOUNGER (5? B.C.–A.D. 65). "On Consolation to Polybius" (6.5), *Moral Essays,* tr. John W. Basore, 1932

Under existing circumstances wealth cannot be enjoyed without dishonor or forgone without misery.

> GEORGE BERNARD SHAW (1856–1950). "The Fabian Election Manifesto," 1892

I am a Millionaire. That is my religion.

> GEORGE BERNARD SHAW (1856–1950). *Major Barbara,* 2, 1905

Wealth is a power usurped by the few to compel the many to labor for their benefit.

> PERCY BYSSHE SHELLEY (1792–1822). "Notes" (5.63), *Queen Mab: A Philosophical Poem: With Notes,* 1813

Millionaires are a product of natural selection, acting on the whole body of men to pick out those who can meet the requirements of certain work to be done. . . . It is because they are thus selected that wealth—both their own and that entrusted to them—aggregates under their hands. . . . They get high wages and live in luxury, but the bargain is a good one for society. There is the intensest competition for their place and occupation. This assures us that all who are competent for this function will be employed in it, so that the cost of it will be reduced to the lowest terms.

> WILLIAM GRAHAM SUMNER (1840–1910). Sociologist. In Kevin Phillips, *The Politics of Rich and Poor: Wealth and the American Electorate in the Reagan Aftermath,* 3, 1991

Societies may be called Acquisitive Societies [when] their whole tendency and interest and preoccupation is to promote the acquisition of wealth.

> R. H. TAWNEY (1880–1962). *The Acquisitive Society,* 3, 1920

Wealth, no less than knowledge, is power.

> HENRY DAVID THOREAU (1817–1862). Journal, 25 January 1841
> See Knowledge: Francis Bacon (1)

The share of total net worth of the top one-half of 1 percent of the population rose from 26 to 31 percent in just six years, between 1983 and 1989. By the early 1990s the share of wealth (more than 40 percent) held by the top 1 percent of the population was essentially double what it had been in the mid-1970s.

> LESTER C. THUROW (1938–). "Why Their World Might Crumble," *New York Times Magazine,* 19 November 1995

Energy makes more fortunes than prudence.

> VAUVENARGUES (1715–1747). *Reflections and Maxims,* 181, 1746, tr. F. G. Stevens, 1940

Not even a collapsing world looks dark to a man who is about to make his fortune.

> E. B. WHITE (1899–1985). "Intimations," *One Man's Meat,* 1944

❦

How little we need measures our wealth better than how much we have.

> ANONYMOUS

A good wife and health is a man's best wealth.

> SAYING (ENGLISH)

Wealth in men's eyes is honored most of all,
And of all things on earth hath chiefest power.

> SAYING (GREEK). In Euripides (485?–406 B.C.). *The Phoenician Maidens,* l. 430, tr. A. S. Way, 1956

Wealth is measured not by what you have but by what you've given away.

> SAYING (NATIVE AMERICAN)

WEALTH & POVERTY

See also • Class ○ Classes, Two ○ Exploitation ○ Inequality: Mohandas K. Gandhi ○ Poverty ○ Prosperity & Adversity ○ Rich & Poor ○ Strength & Weakness ○ Success & Failure ○ Values: Martin Luther King, Jr. (1) ○ Victory & Defeat ○ Virtue: Saying (Spanish) ○ Wealth

We have extravagance and greed, public poverty and private opulence.

> CATO THE YOUNGER (96–46 B.C.). Roman Senate speech. In Sallust (86?–34? B.C.), *The War with Catiline,* 52.22, tr. J. C. Rolfe, 1921

Ill fares the land, to hastening ills a prey,
Where wealth accumulates, and men decay.
Princes and lords may flourish, or may fade;
A breath can make them, as a breath has made;
But a bold peasantry, their country's pride,
When once destroy'd, can never be supplied.

> OLIVER GOLDSMITH (1728–1774). *The Deserted Village,* l. 51, 1770

Wherever wealth abounds, and the poor continue to suffer, we must confront God's judgment.

> MARK O. HATFIELD (1922–). Oregon senator. "Crisis in American Leadership," *Liberty,* September-October 1973

The desire to gain wealth and the fear to lose it are our chief breeders of cowardice and propagators of corruption. . . . Think of the strength which personal indifference to poverty would give us if we were devoted to unpopular causes. We need no longer hold our tongues or fear to vote the revolutionary or reformatory ticket. Our stocks might fall, our hopes of promotion vanish, our salaries stop, our club doors close in our faces; yet, while we lived, we would imperturbably bear witness to the spirit, and our example would help to set free our generation.

> WILLIAM JAMES (1842–1910). *The Varieties of Religious Experience: A Study in Human Nature,* 14 and 15, 1902

All the arguments which are brought to represent poverty as no evil, show it to be evidently a great evil. You never find people laboring to convince you that you may live very happily upon a plentiful fortune.

> SAMUEL JOHNSON (1709–1784). 20 July 1763. In James Boswell, *The Life of Samuel Johnson,* 1791

There is inherited wealth in this country and also inherited poverty.

> JOHN F. KENNEDY (1917–1963). Address, Amherst College (Massachusetts), 26 October 1963

a louse i
used to know
told me that
millionaires and
bums tasted
about alike
to him.

> DON MARQUIS (1878–1937). "random thoughts by archy," *archy s life of mehitabel,* 1933

Accumulation of wealth at one pole is . . . at the same time accumulation of misery, agony of toil, slavery, ignorance, brutality, mental degradation, at the other pole.

> KARL MARX (1818–1883). *Capital: A Critique of Political Economy,* 25.4, 1867–1894, tr. Samuel Moore and Edward Aveling, 1906

It is a Reproach to Religion and Government to suffer so much Poverty and Excess.

> WILLIAM PENN (1644–1718). *Some Fruits of Solitude,* 52, 1693

"Ah, what can I do?" say a powerless few
With a lump in your throat
   and a tear in your eye,
Can't you see that their poverty's
   profiting you?

> BUFFY SAINTE MARIE (1941–). "My Country 'Tis of Thy People You're Dying" (song), 1966

King Lear: Through tatter'd clothes small vices do appear;
Robes and furr'd gowns hide all. Plate sin with gold,
And the strong lance of justice hurtless breaks,
Arm it in rags, a pigmy's straw does pierce it.

> SHAKESPEARE (1564–1616). *King Lear,* 4.6.168, 1605

Money is the way we keep score. This feeling has been a long time in the making. It goes away sometimes in depressions, when wealth briefly becomes suspect and poverty is not dishonorable. The rest of the time, poverty is very close to criminal. The worst crimes a man can commit, other than the crimes of violence which for one with property would have to be considered irrational, are crimes against capital. A man can break most of the Commandments with impunity, but please, let him not go bust, that will get him ostracized faster than lying, fudging on his income taxes, cheating, adultery, and coveting all the oxes and asses there are.

> ADAM SMITH. (Pen name of GEORGE J. W. GOODMAN). *The Money Game,* 21, 1968

Wealth corrupts, poverty kills.

> ANONYMOUS

From poverty to wealth is a hard journey, but the way back is easy.

> SAYING (JAPANESE)
>
> See Misfortune: Saying (Yiddish)

Wealth may be concealed but not poverty.

> SAYING (PHILIPPINE)

WEATHER

See also • Fog ○ Months ○ Misjudgments: Anonymous (American) (1) ○ Nature ○ Rain ○ Seasons

Every day we have some weather, and yesterday was no exception.

> JOHN CARR. Journalist. In Russell Baker, "The Prattle Deluge," *New York Times,* 11 April 1995

Some are weatherwise, some are otherwise.

> BENJAMIN FRANKLIN (1706–1790). *Poor Richard's Almanack,* December 1735
>
> See Wisdom: James Howell

Change of Weather is the Discourse of Fools.

> THOMAS FULLER (1654–1734). Comp., *Gnomologia: Adages and Proverbs,* 1082, 1732

A well-known American writer said once that, while everybody talked about the weather, nobody seemed to do anything about it.

> HARTFORD COURANT. Editorial, 24 August 1897. Often attributed to Mark Twain, who lived in Hartford and was a friend of Charles Dudley Warner (the *Courant* editorial writer). (In "Ever the Twain," *The "Quote . . . Unquote" Newsletter* [London], "Special Edition," 1998) (Popular version: Everybody talks about the weather but nobody does anything about it.)

Those that are weatherwise are rarely otherwise.

> RICHARD INWARDS (19th cent.). *Weather Lore,* p. 1, 1893

It could be rain
It could be snow
Weathermen never know.

> WILLARD SCOTT (1934–). Weather forecaster. *The Today Show,* television morning program, NBC, 27 November 1995

Whenever people talk to me about the weather, I always feel quite certain that they mean something else.

> OSCAR WILDE (1854–1900). *The Importance of Being Earnest*, 1, 1895

❧

If you don't like the weather in New England, just wait a minute and it will change.

> SAYING (NEW ENGLAND)

WEEPING

See also • Sorrow: Goethe ○ Tears

I did not weep; I had turned [to] stone inside.

> DANTE (1265–1321). "Inferno," (33.49), *The Divine Comedy*, 1321, tr. John Ciardi, 1954

To weep for joy is a kind of Manna.

> GEORGE HERBERT (1593–1633). Comp., *Outlandish Proverbs*, 462, 1640

Jesus wept.

> JOHN (A.D. 1st cent.). *John* 11:35 (the *Bible's* shortest verse). Jesus was "deeply moved" when he saw Mary and "the Jews who came with her" weeping over the death of her brother Lazarus.

Lost cash breeds honest weeping.

> JUVENAL (A.D. 60?–127?). *Satires*, 13.134, tr. Peter Green, 1967

Sometimes, when the wind is blowing in my hair,
I cry, because its coolness is too beautiful.

> BOB KAUFMAN (1925–1986). "Image of Wind," *Solitudes Crowded with Loneliness*, 1965

Why can I not weep?

> NAPOLEON (1769–1821). On hearing of Gen. Desaix's death during the Battle of Marengo (Italy), May 1800. In Albert Carr, *Napoleon Speaks*, 8, 1941

When I heard these words [concerning the plight of Jerusalem] I sat down and wept, and mourned for days; and I continued fasting and praying before the God of heaven.

> NEHEMIAH (5th cent. B.C.). *Nehemiah* 1:4
> See Depression: Mohandas K. Gandhi

I often want to cry. That is the only advantage women have over men—at least they can.

> JEAN RHYS (1890?–1979). *Good Morning, Midnight*, 2, 1939

King Richard: I weep for joy.

> SHAKESPEARE (1564–1616). *Richard II*, 3.1.4, 1595

❧

Weeping may tarry for the night
   but joy comes with the morning.

> ANONYMOUS (*BIBLE*). *Psalms* 30:5

WELFARE

See also • Charity ○ Government ○ Nations: Albert Jay Nock ○ Poverty ○ Unemployment

How come it's a subsidy when Pan American Airlines asks the Government for a hundred million dollars to keep flying, but when people ask for considerably less to keep going it is a Federal handout?

> RUSSELL BAKER (1925–). "Who Is Who on First," *New York Times*, 31 August 1974

The lessons of paternalism ought to be unlearned and the better lesson taught that, while the people should patriotically and cheerfully support their government, its functions do not include the support of the people.

> GROVER CLEVELAND (1837–1908). *Second Inaugural Address*, 4 March 1893

The welfare approach is a temporary expedient. It is a crutch. As such it may be very effective, may indeed be crucial to survival. But if taken for permanent and seen as the final answer, it will eventually cripple management and workers, company, economy and society.

> PETER F. DRUCKER (1909–). *Management: Tasks, Responsibilities, Practices*, 18, 1974, abr., 1977

To his eternal dishonor, in 1996 [Pres. Bill] Clinton signed a welfare bill that ends the federal responsibility to children in poverty and, as an added insult, provides funds to enroll their mothers in what the right styles as "chastity training."

> BARBARA EHRENREICH (1941–). "Sex Happens," *Progressive*, March 1998

[Direct welfare] is a bad program, not because it gives money to the poor, but because it produces poor people, because it encourages people to be on welfare instead of being on wages. I don't blame them. If you and I are fools enough to make it to their advantage to subsist on welfare rather than work, they would be foolish not to take advantage of it.

> MILTON FRIEDMAN (1912–). "Economic Myths and Public Opinion," January 1976, *Bright Promises, Dismal Performance: An Economist's Protest*, ed. William R. Allen, 1983

The impersonal hand of government can never replace the helping hand of a neighbor.

> HUBERT H. HUMPHREY (1911–1978). Speech, 10 February 1965

Welfare is a contemporary example of the [charity] system as it corrodes generation after generation of the poor, presupposing a benevolent master and grateful serf mentality, leaving its victims on the short rations of charity and cultivating an enervating dependence which only further dependence can satisfy. This is, of course, not really welfare, but neo-feudalism.

> KATE MILLET (1934–). *Sexual Politics*, 3 ("Political" [footnote]), 1969

Cato the Younger, seeing that the people were being greatly stirred up by his enemy Caesar . . . and were dangerously inclined towards a revolution, persuaded the senate to vote a dole to the poor, and the giving of this halted the disturbance and ended the uprising.

> PLUTARCH (A.D. 46?–119?). Slightly modified. "Precepts of Statecraft" (24), *Moralia*, vol. 10, tr. W. C. Helmbold, 1936

Government has a final responsibility for the welfare of its citizens. If private cooperative effort fails to provide work for willing hands and relief for the unfortunate, those suffering hardship through no fault of their own have a right to call upon the government for aid. And a government worthy of the name must make a fitting response.

> FRANKLIN D. ROOSEVELT (1882–1945). Annual message to Congress, 3 January 1938

‿

Welfare should be a safety net not a hammock.

> ANONYMOUS (AMERICAN)

WICKED

See also • Evil ○ Wrong

I have seen men in the depth of wickedness, and I have thought to myself, "There I go, except by the grace of God."

> BILLY GRAHAM (1918–). "The Moral Weight of Leadership," *New York Times,* 17 March 1998
>
> See Punishment, Capital: John Bradford

"There is no peace," says the Lord, "for the wicked."

> ISAIAH (8th cent. B.C.). *Isaiah* 48:22

Wickedness is always easier than virtue, for it takes the shortcut to everything.

> SAMUEL JOHNSON (1709–1784). 17 September 1773. In James Boswell, *The Journal of a Tour to the Hebrides, with Samuel Johnson, L.L.D.,* 1786

Most men are not wicked. . . . They are sleepwalkers, not evildoers.

> FRANZ KAFKA (1883–1924). In Gustav Janouch, *Conversations with Kafka,* pp. 58–59, tr. Goronwy Rees, 1953

All wickedness is weakness.

> JOHN MILTON (1608–1674). *Samson Agonistes,* l. 834, 1671

I would rather be called a fool all my days than to be wicked before the Lord for a single moment.

> *TALMUD* (A.D. 1st–6th cent.). Rabbinical writings. In Louis I. Newman, comp., *The Talmudic Anthology,* 77, 1945

‿

The more wicked a man is, the less fault he finds with himself.

> SAYING (WELSH)

WILDERNESS

See also • Camping ○ Environment ○ Forests ○ God & Nature: John Muir (all) ○ Mountains ○ Nature ○ Trees ○ Woods

A Wilderness Bill of Rights.

> WILLIAM O. DOUGLAS (1898–1980). Book title, 1965

The Call of the Wild.

> JACK LONDON (1876–1916). Book title, 1903

All the wilderness seems to be full of tricks and plans to drive and draw us up into God's light.

> JOHN MUIR (1838–1914). While working as a sheepherder, 1869, *My First Summer in the Sierra,* 1911

In this silent, serene wilderness the weary can gain a heart-bath in perfect peace.

> JOHN MUIR (1838–1914). Journal, 16? July 1890. In *John of the Mountains: The Unpublished Journals of John Muir,* ed. Linnie Marsh Wolfe, 1938

The clearest way into the Universe is through a forest wilderness.

> JOHN MUIR (1838–1914). Journal, 11-19 July 1890. In *John of the Mountains: The Unpublished Journals of John Muir,* ed. Linnie Marsh Wolfe, 1938

Away, away, from men and town,
To the wild wood and the downs—
To the silent wilderness
Where the soul need not repress
Its music.

> PERCY BYSSHE SHELLEY (1792–1822). "To Jane: The Invitation," l. 21, 1822

For one that comes [into the wilderness] with a pencil to sketch or sing, a thousand come with an ax or rifle.

> HENRY DAVID THOREAU (1817–1862). "Chesuncook," *The Main Woods,* 1864

WILL

See also • Irresolution ○ Resistance: Alfred, Lord Tennyson ○ Resolution ○ Slavery: George Sand ○ Strength: Mohandas K. Gandhi ○ Will, Free

Where there's a will, there's a won't.

> AMBROSE BIERCE (1842–1914). "Wise Saws and Modern Instances, or Poor Richard in Reverse," 1911

The good of man is in the will, and the evil too.

> EPICTETUS (A.D. 55?–135?). *Discourses,* 1.25, tr. George Long, 1890?

Nothing is impossible to a willing heart.

> JOHN HEYWOOD (1497–1580). Comp., *A Dialogue Containing the Number of the Effectual Proverbs in the English Tongue,* 1.4, 1562

It is not faith, but will, that is the mover of mountains.

> GUSTAVE LE BON (1841–1931). *The Psychology of the Great War,* 1.2.3, tr. E. Andrews, 1916

Will springs from the two elements of moral sense and self-interest.

> ABRAHAM LINCOLN (1809–1865). Speech, Springfield (Illinois), 26 June 1857

Though the strength is lacking, yet the willingness is praiseworthy.

> OVID (43 B.C.–A.D. 17?). *The Pontic Epistles,* 3.4
>
> See Spirit: Jesus

Will is the measure of Power.

> PROCLUS (A.D. 410?–485). Greek philosopher. In Ralph Waldo Emerson, journal, 1843, undated

No arsenal or no weapon in the arsenals of the world is so formidable as the will and moral courage of free men and women.

> RONALD REAGAN (1911–). *First Inaugural Address,* 20 January 1981

"Where there is a will, there is a way," says the proverb. Not entirely true; but it is true that where there is no will, there is no way.

> THOMAS S. SZASZ (1920–). "Personal Conduct," *The Second Sin,* 1973

WILL, FREE

See also • Destiny ○ Fate ○ Fortune: Machiavelli (1) ○ Freedom ○ Paradoxes: *Talmud,* Anonymous (2) ○ Soul: Thomas Carlyle ○ Will

Everything is determined, the beginning as well as the end, by forces over which we have no control. It is determined for the insect as well as for the star. Human beings, vegetables or cosmic dust, we all dance to a mysterious tune, intoned in the distance by an invisible player.

> ALBERT EINSTEIN (1879–1955). Interview with the author. In George Sylvester Viereck, closing words, "What Life Means to Einstein," *Glimpses of the Great,* 1930

To deny the freedom of the will is to make morality impossible.

> JAMES ANTHONY FROUDE (1818–1894). "Calvinism," *Short Studies on Great Subjects,* 1867-1883

There is a measure of free will within a system of predestination.

> ALDOUS HUXLEY (1894–1963). "Religion and Temperament." In Christopher Isherwood, ed., *Vedanta for the Western World,* 1945

Sir, we *know* will is free, and *there's* an end on't.

> SAMUEL JOHNSON (1709–1784). 10 October 1769. In James Boswell, *The Life of Samuel Johnson,* 1791

Free will is doing gladly and freely that which one must do.

> CARL G. JUNG (1875–1961). Quoted in "Contributions from the Analytical Psychology Club of San Francisco" (Mary S. Howells). In Ferne Jensen, ed., *C. G. Jung, Emma Jung and Toni Wolff: A Collection of Remembrances,* 1982

A free will and a will [subject to] moral laws are identical.

> IMMANUEL KANT (1724–1804). *Foundations of the Metaphysics of Morals,* 3, 1797, tr. Lewis White Beck, 1969

We are responsible human beings, not blind automatons; persons, not puppets. By endowing us with freedom, God relinquished a measure of his own sovereignty and imposed certain limitations upon himself. If his children are free, they must do his will by a voluntary choice.

> MARTIN LUTHER KING, JR. (1929–1968). *Strength to Love,* 8.3, 1963

God will not do everything, in order not to deprive us of free will and the portion of the glory that falls to our lot.

> MACHIAVELLI (1469–1527). *The Prince,* 26, 1513, tr. Luigi Ricci, 1903

Human beings can control their own acts, but not the consequences of their acts either to themselves or to others.

> JOHN STUART MILL (1806–1873). *Principles of Political Economy with Some of Their Applications to Social Philosophy,* 2.1.1, 1848

We must believe in free will. We have no choice.

> ISAAC BASHEVIS SINGER (1904–1991). In Stefan Kanfer, "The Last Teller of Tales," *Time,* 5 August 1991

Freedom is the content. Necessity is the form. . . .

Only by uniting them do we get a clear conception of the life of man.

> LEO TOLSTOY (1828–1910). "Epilogue" (2.10), *War and Peace,* 1863–1869, tr. Rosemary Edmonds, 1957

Acting as if we are free is a way of resolving the paradox of determinism and freedom.

> HOWARD ZINN (1922–). *The Politics of History,* 17, 1970

Free will and determinism are like a game of cards. The hand that is dealt you represents determinism. The way you play your hand represents free will.

> ANONYMOUS (INDIAN). Quoted by Norman Cousins, "A Game of Cards." In Edward P. Morgan, ed., *This I Believe,* 1952

WINNING

See also • Defeat ○ Losing ○ Victory

Every time you win, you're reborn; when you lose, you die a little.

> GEORGE ALLEN (1922–). Football coach. In James A. Michener, *Sports in America,* 13, 1976. Fred Barnes has quoted Allen phrasing the same idea more pithily, "Victory is life: losing is death." (In "Washington Diarist," *New Republic,* 30 November 1992)

A winner [is] somebody you mess with only if you don't mind getting your block knocked off.

> RUSSELL BAKER (1925–). "Could Be a Long Season," *New York Times,* 24 April 1993

You have deeply ventured;
But all must do so who would greatly win.

> LORD BYRON (1788–1824). *Marino Faliero, Doge of Venice,* 1.2, 1821

The Winner-Take-All Society: How More and More Americans Compete for Ever Fewer and Bigger Prizes, Encouraging Economic Waste, Income Inequality, and an Impoverished Cultural Life,

> ROBERT H. FRANK and PHILIP J. COOK. Economists. Book title, 1995

I'd rather be a poor winner than any kind of loser.

> GEORGE S. KAUFMAN (1889–1961). Remark during a poker game. In James R. Gaines, *Wit's End: Days and Nights of the Algonquin Round Table,* 4, 1977

There's nothing like a couple of wins to put a spring in your step.

> CHARLES KRAUTHAMMER (1950–). Commentator. *Inside Washington,* television news program, PBS, 20 June 1993

The world is won by those who let it go!
But when you try and try,
The world is then beyond the winning.

> LAO-TZU (6th cent. B.C.). *The Way of Life,* 48, tr. R. B. Blakney, 1955

Winning isn't everything, but wanting to win is.

> VINCE LOMBARDI (1913–1970). In Robert Riger, "Pro Football's Bright New Breed," *Esquire*, November 1962

Winning isn't everything. It's the only thing.

> VINCE LOMBARDI (1913–1970). Football coach. In Jerry Kramer, 25 July 1967, *Instant Replay: The Green Bay Diary of Jerry Kramer*, 1968. Shortly before his death in 1970 Lombardi told Jerry Izenberg, "I wish to hell I'd never said the damned thing. I meant the effort . . . I meant having a goal . . . I sure as hell didn't mean for people to crush human values and morality." (Ellipsis points in original.) (In James A. Michener, *Sports in America*, 13, 1976)

Since one has to take sides, one might as well join the side which is winning. . . . It is better to eat than be eaten.

> NAPOLEON (1769–1821). *In the Words of Napoleon*, p. 72, tr. Daniel Savage Gray, 1977

The Theory & Practice of Gamesmanship; or, The Art of Winning Games Without Actually Cheating.

> STEPHEN POTTER (1900–1969). Book title, 1947

Winning Through Intimidation.

> ROBERT J. RINGER (1938–). Book title, 1973

Sure, winning isn't everything. It's the only thing.

> HENRY "RED" SANDERS. Football coach. In Joel Sayre, "He Flies on One Wing," *Sports Illustrated*, 26 December 1955

King Henry: Nothing can seem foul to those that win.

> SHAKESPEARE (1564–1616). *Henry IV*, Part 1, 5.1.9, 1597

Remember, nobody wins unless everybody wins.

> BRUCE SPRINGSTEEN (1949–). In Dave Marsh, *Glory Days: Bruce Springsteen in the 1980s*, 12, 1987

Next to a battle lost, the greatest misery is a battle won.

> DUKE OF WELLINGTON (1769–1852). Letter to Lady Frances Shelley after defeating Napoleon in the Battle of Waterloo (Belgium), 19 June 1815

❦

He who dies with the most toys wins.

> SAYING (AMERICAN). 1980s. In Barbara Ehrenreich, *Fear of Falling: The Inner Life of the Middle Class*, 5, 1990

All the world loves a winner.

> SAYING (AMERICAN)
>
> See Love: Ralph Waldo Emerson (2)

Winners never quit; quitters never win.

> SAYING (AMERICAN)

You can't win 'em all.

> SAYING (AMERICAN)

WISDOM

See also • Advice ○ Common Sense ○ Creativity ○ Doubt: C. C. Colton ○ Fools ○ Judgment ○ Knowledge ○ Philosophy ○ Prudence ○ Truth ○ Understanding ○ Vision ○ Wisdom & Knowledge ○ The Wise & the Foolish

Wisdom
comes alone through suffering.

> AESCHYLUS (525–456 B.C.). *Agamemnon*, l. 177, tr. Richmond Lattimore, 1953

Wisdom that don't make us happier aint worth plowing for.

> JOSH BILLINGS (1818–1885). *On Ice: and Other Things*, 66, 1868

The soundest wisdum cums from experience, but thare iz a nearer road to it allmost az sure—reading and reflekshun.

> JOSH BILLINGS (1818–1885). "Nosegays," *Everybody's Friend, or; Josh Billing's Encyclopedia and Proverbial Philosophy of Wit and Humor*, 1874

The road of excess leads to the palace of Wisdom.

> WILLIAM BLAKE (1757–1827). "Proverbs of Hell," *The Marriage of Heaven and Hell*, 7.3, 1790–1793?
>
> See Excess: Wilhelm von Humboldt ○ The Wise & the Foolish: Ralph Waldo Emerson

Wisdom consists . . . in proportioning means to ends.

> LORD BOLINGBROKE (1678–1751). *The Idea of a Patriot King*, p. 15, 1749, ed. Sydney W. Jackman, 1965

The only infallible criterion of wisdom to vulgar minds—success.

> EDMUND BURKE (1729–1797). Letter to a member of the French National Assembly, 1791

I love wisdom more than she loves me.

> LORD BYRON (1788–1824). *Don Juan*, 6.63, 1819–1824

Wisdom consists of the anticipation of consequences.

> NORMAN COUSINS (1912–1990). 1975, "Editor's Odyssey: Gleanings from Articles and Editorials by N.C.," ed. Susan Schiefelbein, *Saturday Review*, 15 April 1978
>
> See Politics: Irving Howe

Wisdom and goodness are twin-born, one heart
Must hold both sisters, never seen apart.

> WILLIAM COWPER (1731–1800). "Expostulations," l. 634, 1782

The wisdom of Love . . . the highest wisdom ever known upon this earth.

> CHARLES DICKENS (1812–1870). *The Mystery of Edwin Drood*, 10, 1870

What is all wisdom save a collection of platitudes?

> NORMAN DOUGLAS (1868–1952). 3 April, *An Almanac*, 1945

History teaches us that men and nations behave wisely once they have exhausted all other alternatives.

> ABBA EBAN (1915–). Speech, London, 16 December 1970

The fear of man is the beginning of wisdom.

> PAUL ELDRIDGE (1888–1982). *Maxims for a Modern Man*, 1293, 1965

The invariable mark of wisdom is to see the miraculous in the common.

> RALPH WALDO EMERSON (1803–1882). "Prospects," *Nature*, 1836

We are wiser . . . than we know.

> RALPH WALDO EMERSON (1803–1882). Journal, 29 October 1838

To finish the moment, to find the journey's end in every step of the road, to live the greatest number of good hours, is wisdom.

> RALPH WALDO EMERSON (1803–1882). "Experience," *Essays: Second Series*, 1844

Wisdom has its root in goodness and not goodness its root in wisdom.

> RALPH WALDO EMERSON (1803–1882). Journal, 1857, undated

Now that is the wisdom of a man, in every instance of his labor, to hitch his wagon to a star, and see his chore done by the gods themselves.

> RALPH WALDO EMERSON (1803–1882). "Civilization," *Society and Solitude*, 1870

He is a wise man who does not grieve for the things which he has not, but rejoices for those which he has.

> EPICTETUS (A.D. 55?–135?). Fragment, 129, tr. George Long, 1890?

An ounce of Wisdom is worth a Pound of Wit.

> THOMAS FULLER (1654–1734). Comp., *Gnomologia: Adages and Proverbs*, 658, 1732

He is not Wise who is not wise for himself.

> THOMAS FULLER (1654–1734). Comp., *Gnomologia: Adages and Proverbs*, 1939, 1732

The hallmark of the conventional wisdom is acceptability. It has the approval of those to whom it is addressed.

> JOHN KENNETH GALBRAITH (1908–). *The Affluent Society*, 2.3, 1958

The conventional wisdom protects the continuity in social thought and action. . . . But there are also grave drawbacks and even dangers in a system of thought which by its very nature and design avoids accommodation to circumstances until change is dramatically forced upon it.

> JOHN KENNETH GALBRAITH (1908–). *The Affluent Society*, 2.6, 1958

True wisdom consists in tracing effects to their causes.

> OLIVER GOLDSMITH (1728–1774). Introduction to *The History of England*, 1764

Self-reflection is the school of wisdom.

> BALTASAR GRACIÁN (1601–1658). *The Art of Worldly Wisdom*, 69, 1647, tr. Joseph Jacobs, 1943

An ounce of wisdom is worth more than tons of cleverness.

> BALTASAR GRACIÁN (1601–1658). *The Art of Worldly Wisdom*, 92, 1647, tr. Joseph Jacobs, 1943

Being wise doth either make men our friends or discourage them from being our enemies.

> MARQUIS OF HALIFAX (1633–1695). "Wisdom," *Political, Moral and Miscellaneous Reflections*, 1750

The awe of God is wisdom.

> ABRAHAM JOSHUA HESCHEL (1907–1972). *God in Search of Man: A Philosophy of Judaism*, 7, 1955

Wisdom is the ability to look at all things from the point of view of God.

> ABRAHAM JOSHUA HESCHEL (1907–1972). *God in Search of Man: A Philosophy of Judaism*, 7, 1955

Wisdom at times is found in folly.

> HORACE (65–8 B.C.). *Odes*, 4.12 (closing line), *The Complete Works of Horace*, ed. Casper J. Kraemer, Jr., 1936

Some are wise, and some are otherwise.

> JAMES HOWELL (1593–1666). Comp., "English" (p. 1), *Paroimiographia: Proverbs, or Old Sayed Sawes & Adages in English . . . Italian, French and Spanish*, 1659
> See Weather: Benjamin Franklin

The wise hold all earthly ties lightly—they are stripping for eternity.

> ELBERT HUBBARD (1856–1915). In Alice Hubbard, comp., *An American Bible*, p. 198, 1946

Wisdom denotes the pursuing of the best ends by the best means.

> FRANCIS HUTCHESON (1694–1746). Scottish philosopher. *Inquiry into the Original of Our Ideas of Beauty and Virtue*, 1.5.16, 1725

The first step in the acquisition of wisdom is silence, the second listening, the third memory, the fourth practice, the fifth teaching others.

> SOLOMON IBN GABIROL (A.D. 1021?–1069?). *Choice of Pearls*, 39, tr. A. Cohen, 1925

Woe to those who are wise in their own eyes.

> ISAIAH (8th cent. B.C.). *Isaiah* 5:21

The art of being wise is the art of knowing what to overlook.

> WILLIAM JAMES (1842–1910). *The Principles of Psychology*, 22, 1890

Wisdom is knowing what to do next; virtue is doing it.

> DAVID STARR JORDAN (1851–1931). *The Philosophy of Hope*, 2nd ed. (1st ed. title: *The Philosophy of Despair*), p. 39, 1907 (1902)

Common sense suits itself to the ways of the world. Wisdom tries to conform to the ways of Heaven.

> JOSEPH JOUBERT (1754–1824). *Pensées*, 1838, tr. Katherine Lyttelton, 1898

Wise men hear and see
As little children do.

> LAO-TZU (6th cent. B.C.). *The Way of Life*, 49, tr. R. B. Blakney, 1955

The Wise Man is moved
Neither by affection
Nor yet by estrangement
Or profit or loss
Or honor or shame.

> LAO-TZU (6th cent. B.C.). *The Way of Life*, 56, tr. R. B. Blakney, 1955
> See Praise: Kahlil Gibran ◦ Self-Realization (Being): Bhagavad Gita

[The Wise Man] grabs at nothing and so never misses.

> LAO-TZU (6th cent. B.C.). *The Way of Life*, 64, tr. R. B. Blakney, 1955

The Wise Man wants the unwanted;
he sets no high value on anything
because it is hard to get.

> LAO-TZU (6th cent. B.C.). *The Way of Life*, 64, tr. R. B. Blakney, 1955

It is easier to be wise for others than for oneself.

> LA ROCHEFOUCAULD (1613–1680). *Maxims*, 132, 1665, tr. Leonard Tancock, 1959

Only by unlearning Wisdom comes.

> JAMES RUSSELL LOWELL (1819–1891). "The Parting of the Ways,"
> 8, 1849
>
> See Learning (Knowledge): Henry David Thoreau

To do justly is the only wisdom.

> MARCUS AURELIUS (A.D 121–180). *Meditations,* 4.37, tr. Maxwell
> Staniforth, 1964

If you have wisdom, what do you lack? If you lack wisdom, what do you have?

> *MIDRASH* (4th cent. B.C.–12th cent. A.D.). Rabbinical writings

In the experience I have of myself I find enough to make me wise, if I were a good scholar.

> MONTAIGNE (1533–1592). "Of Experience," *Essays,* 1588, tr. Donald M.
> Frame, 1958

To accomplish his purpose, a wise man will even carry his enemy on his back.

> *PANCHATANTRA* (A.D. 6th cent.). Sanskrit animal fables

Wisdom lies neither in fixity nor in change, but in the dialectic between the two.

> OCTAVIO PAZ (1914–). In *Times* (London), 8 June 1989

What is it to be wise?
'Tis but to know how little can be known;
To see all others' faults, and feel our own.

> ALEXANDER POPE (1688–1744). *An Essay on Man,* 4.260, 1734

That Man divine whom Wisdom calls her own,
Great without Title, without Fortune bless'd,
Rich ev'n when plunder'd, honor'd while oppress'd,
Lov'd without youth, and follow'd without power
At home tho' exil'd, free, tho' in the Tower.

> ALEXANDER POPE (1688–1744). *Imitations of Horace,* 1.1(Epistle).
> 180, 1733–1738

Wisdom is acquired by meditation.

> PUBLIUS SYRUS (85–43 B.C.). *Moral Sayings,* 184, tr. Darius Lyman, Jr.,
> 1862

Wisdom enters not into the malicious heart.

> RABELAIS (1494–1553). *Gargantua and Pantagruel,* 2.8, 1532–1552,
> tr. J. M. Cohen, 1955

There is no wisdom without love.

> N. SRI RAM (1889–?). *Thoughts for Aspirants,* 4, 1972

To be conscious of one's ignorance is the beginning of wisdom.

> N. SRI RAM (1889–?). *Thoughts for Aspirants,* 4, 1972
>
> See Ignorance: Benjamin Disraeli

He is wise that can make a friend of a foe.

> JOHN RAY (1628–1705). Comp., *A Collection of English Proverbs,*
> p. 369, 1678

We are wise by other people's experience.

> SAMUEL RICHARDSON (1689–1761). *Clarissa: or The History of a Young
> Lady,* 1, 1748

Nine-tenths of wisdom is being wise in time.

> THEODORE ROOSEVELT (1858–1919). Speech, Lincoln (Nebraska),
> 14 June 1917

Wisdom is equanimity in the presence of intolerable or threatening ideas.

> LEO ROSTEN (1908–1997). Interview with the author, September 1963.
> In Roy Newquist, *Counterpoint,* 1964

To conquer fear is the beginning of wisdom.

> BERTRAND RUSSELL (1872–1970). "An Outline of Intellectual Rubbish,"
> *Unpopular Essays,* 1950

Of the several factors that contribute to wisdom, I should put first a sense of proportion: the capacity to take account of all the important factors in a problem and to attach to each its due weight.

> BERTRAND RUSSELL (1872–1970). Slightly modified. "Knowledge
> and Wisdom," *Portraits from Memory, and Other Essays,* 1956

Many men would have arrived at wisdom had they not believed themselves to have arrived there already.

> SENECA THE YOUNGER (5? B.C.–A.D. 65). "Of Peace of Mind" (1),
> *Minor Dialogues,* tr. Aubrey Stewart, 1889

The Wise Man can receive neither Injury nor Insult.

> SENECA THE YOUNGER (5? B.C.–A.D. 65). "On the Firmness of the Wise
> Man" (epigraph), *Moral Essays,* tr. John W. Basore, 1928

The highest duty and the highest proof of wisdom—that deed and word should be in accord.

> SENECA THE YOUNGER (5? B.C.–A.D. 65). "On Practicing What You
> Preach," *Moral Letters to Lucilius,* 14.2, tr. Richard M. Gummere, 1
> 918

Wisdom knows the proper limits of things.

> SENECA THE YOUNGER (5? B.C.–A.D. 65). "On the Value of Advice,"
> *Moral Letters to Lucilius,* 94.16, tr. Richard M. Gummere, 1918

A man may be thought wise; but the Athenians, I suspect, do not much trouble themselves about him unless he begins to impart his wisdom to others.

> SOCRATES (470?–399 B.C.). After being charged with corrupting Athens'
> youth through his teachings. In Plato (427?–347 B.C.), *Euthyphro,* 3,
> tr. Benjamin Jowett, 1894

The highest wisdom consist[s] in distinguishing between good and evil.

> SOCRATES (470?–399 B.C.). As paraphrased by Seneca the Younger
> (5? B.C.–A.D. 65), "On the Supreme Good," *Moral Letters to Lucilius,*
> 71.7, tr. Richard M. Gummere, 1918

The true wisdom is to be always seasonable, and to change with a good grace in changing circumstances.

> ROBERT LOUIS STEVENSON (1850–1894). "Crabbed Age and Youth,"
> *Virginibus Puerisque,* 1881

The highest wisdom is kindness.

> *TALMUD* (1st–6th cent. A.D.). Rabbinical writings. In Lewis Browne, ed.,
> *The Wisdom of Israel,* rev. ed., p. 157, 1955 (1948)

All this worldly wisdom might be regarded as the once unamiable heresy of some wise man.

> HENRY DAVID THOREAU (1817–1862). "Monday," *A Week on the
> Concord and Merrimack Rivers,* 1849

A man is wise with the wisdom of his time only, and ignorant with its ignorance. Observe how the greatest minds yield in some degree to the superstitions of their age.

> HENRY DAVID THOREAU (1817–1862). Journal, 31 January 1853

I have always been regretting that I was not as wise as the day I was born.

> HENRY DAVID THOREAU (1817–1862). "Where I Lived, and What I Lived For," *Walden; or Life in the Woods,* 1854

Is there any such thing as wisdom not applied to life?

> HENRY DAVID THOREAU (1817–1862). "Life Without Principle," *Atlantic,* October 1863

Wisdom—meaning judgment acting on experience, common sense, available knowledge, and a decent appreciation of probability.

> BARBARA W. TUCHMAN (1912–1989). "An Inquiry into the Persistence of Unwisdom in Government," *Esquire,* 1980

Wisdom cannot be pass'd from one having it to another not having it,
Wisdom is of the soul, is not susceptible of proof, is its own proof.

> WALT WHITMAN (1819–1892). "Song of the Open Road" (6), 1856, *Leaves of Grass,* 1855–1892

❦

Wisdom is divided into two parts: (a) having a great deal to say, and (b) not saying it.

> ANONYMOUS

Conventional wisdom is to wisdom what junk food is to food.

> ANONYMOUS

The Lord gives wisdom;
  from his mouth come knowledge and understanding.

> SAYING (*BIBLE*). Proverbs 2:6

The fear of the Lord is the beginning of wisdom.

> SAYING (*BIBLE*). Proverbs 9:10

Wisdom is better than strength.

> SAYING (*BIBLE*). Ecclesiastes 9:16 (King James Version)

The beginning of wisdom is to call things by their right names.

> SAYING (CHINESE)
> See Names: Henry David Thoreau

Wisdom hears one thing and understands three things.

> SAYING (CHINESE)
> See Words: Terence

The wise are only once betrayed.

> SAYING (GERMAN)
> See Deception: Saying (American)

Wisdom and virtue are like the two wheels of a cart.

> SAYING (JAPANESE)

Wise late, old soon; wise soon, old late.

> SAYING

Wisdom takes counsel of itself.

> SAYING

WISDOM & KNOWLEDGE

See also • Genius & Talent ○ Knowledge ○ Understanding ○ Wisdom

When learning and wisdum hitch up together, they are a bully team.

> JOSH BILLINGS (1818–1885). Slightly modified. *On Ice: and Other Things,* 76, 1868

Wisdom iz ov the natur ov genius, while learning iz ov the natur of tallent.

> JOSH BILLINGS (1818–1885). *On Ice: and Other Things,* 76, 1868

It is better to have wisdom without learning than learning without wisdom.

> C. C. COLTON (1780–1832). *Lacon: or, Many Things in Few Words; Addressed to Those Who Think,* 2.26, 1824

Knowledge and wisdom, far from being one,
Have oft-times no connection. Knowledge dwells
In heads replete with thoughts of other men;
Wisdom, in minds attentive to their own.
Knowledge, a rude unprofitable mass,
The mere materials with which wisdom builds,
Till smooth'd and squar'd and fitted to it place,
Does but encumber whom it seems t'enrich.
Knowledge is proud that he has learn'd so much;
Wisdom is humble that he knows no more.

> WILLIAM COWPER (1731–1800). *The Task,* 6.88, 1785

Where is the wisdom we have lost in knowledge?
Where is the knowledge we have lost in information?

> T. S. ELIOT (1888–1965). *The Rock,* 1, 1934

'Tis not knowing much, but what is useful, that makes a wise Man.

> THOMAS FULLER (1654–1734). Comp., *Gnomologia: Adages and Proverbs,* 5097, 1732

The seat of knowledge is in the head; of wisdom in the heart.

> WILLIAM HAZLITT (1778–1830). *Characteristics in the Manner of Rochefoucault's Maxims,* 380, 1823

Much learning does not teach understanding.

> HERACLITUS (540?–480? B.C.). In Diogenes Laertius (A.D. 3rd cent.), *Lives of Eminent Philosophers,* 9.1, tr. R. D. Hicks, 1925

Knowledge is fostered by curiosity; wisdom is fostered by awe.

> ABRAHAM JOSHUA HESCHEL (1907–1972). *Who Is Man?* 5, 1965

Knowledge can be communicated, but not wisdom.

> HERMANN HESSE (1877–1962). *Siddhartha,* 2 ("Govinda"), 1922, tr. Hilda Rosner, 1951

Ours is a world in which knowledge accumulates and wisdom decays.

> ALDOUS HUXLEY (1894–1963). "Censorship and Spoken Literature," *Tomorrow and Tomorrow and Tomorrow and Other Essays,* 1956

Knowledge is acquired when we succeed in fitting a new experience into the system of concepts based upon our old experiences. Understanding comes when we liberate ourselves from the old and so make possible a direct, unmediated contact with the new, the mystery, moment by moment, of our existence.

> ALDOUS HUXLEY (1894–1963). "Knowledge and Understanding," *Tomorrow and Tomorrow and Tomorrow and Other Essays,* 1956

Knowledge comes by taking things apart. But wisdom comes by putting things together.

> JOHN A. MORRISON

There is a great deal I do *not* want to know. Wisdom sets bounds even to knowledge.

> FRIEDRICH NIETZSCHE (1844–1900). "Maxims and Arrows" (5), *Twilight of the Idols,* 1889, tr. R. J. Hollingdale, 1968

What we call sense or wisdom is knowledge, ready for use, made effective, and bears the same relation to knowledge itself that bread does to wheat. The full knowledge of the parts of a steam engine and the theory of its action may be possessed by a man who could not be trusted to pull the lever to its throttle.

> SIR WILLIAM OSLER (1849–1919). "The Student Life" (2), valedictory address, McGill University, Montreal, 14 April 1905, *A Way of Life and Selected Writings of Sir William Osler,* 1951

Wisdom is not knowledge, but lies in the use we make of knowledge.

> N. SRI RAM (1889–?). *Thoughts for Aspirants,* 4, 1972

Sciences may be learned by rote, but wisdom not.

> LAURENCE STERNE (1713–1768). *Tristam Shandy,* 5, 1759–1767

First learn much, and then seek to understand it profoundly.

> TALMUD (A.D. 1st–6th cent.). Rabbinical writings. In Louis I. Newman, comp., *The Talmudic Anthology,* 387, 1945

Wisdom is supple; folly keeps a groove.

> THEOGNIS (6th cent. B.C.). Greek poet. In Lewis Mumford, *The Conduct of Life,* 5.6, 1951

In a sense, knowledge shrinks as wisdom grows: for details are swallowed up in principles. . . . The habit of the active utilization of well-understood principles is the final possession of wisdom.

> ALFRED NORTH WHITEHEAD (1861–1947). *The Aims of Education and Other Essays,* 3, 1929

You cannot be wise without some basis of knowledge, but you may easily acquire knowledge and remain bare of wisdom.

> ALFRED NORTH WHITEHEAD (1861–1947). *The Aims of Education and Other Essays,* 3, 1929

❦

Better an ounce of wisdom than a pound of knowledge; better an ounce of vision than a pound of wisdom.

> ANONYMOUS

Knowledge is organized and accessible information; wisdom is knowledge used effectively in the service of worthy ends.

> ANONYMOUS

Not even a great library could contain the whole of human knowledge, but the wisdom of the ages could fit easily into a small pamphlet.

> ANONYMOUS

Knowledge without wisdom is a load of books on an ass's back.

> SAYING (JAPANESE)

Knowledge from books; wisdom from life.

> SAYING (JEWISH)

Less knowledge, more wisdom!

> SAYING

THE WISE & THE FOOLISH

See also • Fools ○ Wisdom

The wise man is happy when he gains his own approbation and the fool when he recommends himself to the applause of those about him.

> JOSEPH ADDISON (1672–1719). In *The Spectator* (English essay series), 73, 24 May 1711

God save the phools! and don't let them run out, for if it want for them, wise men couldn't get a livin.

> JOSH BILLINGS (1818–1885). *His Sayings,* 32, 1867

A fool sees not the same tree that a wise man sees.

> WILLIAM BLAKE (1757–1827). "Proverbs of Hell," *The Marriage of Heaven and Hell,* 7.8, 1790–1793?

There are more fools than wise men, and even in the wise there is more folly than wisdom.

> CHAMFORT (1741–1794). *Maxims and Thoughts,* 2, 1796, tr. W. S. Merwin, 1984

Design'd by nature wise, but self-made fools.

> WILLIAM COWPER (1731–1800). "Tirocinium" l. 837, 1785

The wise through excess of wisdom is made a fool.

> RALPH WALDO EMERSON (1803–1882). "Experience," *Essays: Second Series,* 1844
>
> See William Blake in Wisdom

The wisest men follow their own direction
And listen to no prophet guiding them.
None but the fools believe in oracles,
Forsaking their own judgment.

> EURIPIDES (485?–406 B.C.). *Iphigenia in Tauris,* l. 570, tr. Witter Bynner, 1956

A fool's Paradise is a wise man's hell.

> THOMAS FULLER (1608–1661). *The Holy State and the Profane State,* 4.20, 1642

The wise Man, even when he holds his Tongue, says more than the Fool when he speaks.

> THOMAS FULLER (1654–1734). Comp., *Gnomologia: Adages and Proverbs,* 4834, 1732

Fools and wise folk are alike harmless. It is the half-wise and the half-foolish, who are the most dangerous.

> GOETHE (1749–1832). *The Maxims and Reflections of Goethe,* 276, tr. T. Bailey Saunders, 1892

A wise man gets more use from his enemies than a fool from his friends.

> BALTASAR GRACIÁN (1601–1658). *The Art of Worldly Wisdom,* 84, 1647, Joseph Jacobs, 1943

The wise does at once what the fool does at last.

> BALTASAR GRACIÁN (1601–1658). *The Art of Worldly Wisdom,* 268, 1647, tr. Joseph Jacobs, 1943

A fool will admire or like nothing that he understands, a man of sense nothing but what he understands.

> MARQUIS OF HALIFAX (1633–1695). "Of Folly and Fools," *Political, Moral and Miscellaneous Reflections,* 1750

Little is needed to make a wise man happy, but nothing can content a fool.

> LA ROCHEFOUCAULD (1613–1680). *Maxims,* 538, 1665, tr. Leonard Tancock, 1959

Let no one deceive himself. If any one among you thinks that he is wise in this age, let him become a fool that he may become wise. For the wisdom of this world is folly with God.

> PAUL (A.D. 1st cent.). *1 Corinthians* 3:18–19
> See Insanity: Herman Melville

Wise men talk because they have something to say: fools because they have to say something.

> PLATO (427?–347 B.C.)

The wise man takes pleasure in what is honorable, but the fool is not vexed by shamefulness.

> PLUTARCH (A.D. 46?–119?). "On Moral Virtue" (6), *Moralia,* 6, tr. W. C. Helmbold, 1939

A hundred fools together will not make one wise man.

> ARTHUR SCHOPENHAUER (1788–1860). "The Wisdom of Life" (2), *Essays of Arthur Schopenhauer,* tr. T. Bailey Saunders, 1851

Wisdom and folly, if pushed far enough, kick into each other.

> ANONYMOUS

The wise seek wisdom; the fool has found it.

> SAYING (ILLINOIS)

Wisdom is born: folly is learned.

> SAYING (RUSSIAN)

The wise grow wiser with age; the foolish, more foolish.

> SAYING (JEWISH)

The wise learn from the mistakes of others; the foolish, not even from their own.

> SAYING

WIT

See also • Comedy ○ Humor ○ Insult ○ Laughter ○ Repartee ○ Ridicule ○ Satire ○ Slander ○ Wit: Examples ○ Words

Wit [is] well-bred insolence.

> ARISTOTLE (384–322 B.C.). *Rhetoric,* 2.12, tr. W. Rhys Roberts, 1954

Wit makes yu think, humor makes you laff.

> JOSH BILLINGS (1818–1885). "Stray Children," *Everybody's Friend, or; Josh Billing's Encyclopedia and Proverbial Philosophy of Wit and Humor,* 1874

Wit makes its own welcome and levels all distinctions. No dignity, no learning, no force of character, can make any stand against good wit.

> RALPH WALDO EMERSON (1803–1882). "The Comic," *Letters and Social Aims,* 1876

Wit is the salt of conversation, not the food.

> WILLIAM HAZLITT (1778–1830). "On Wit and Humour," *Lectures on the English Comic Writers,* 1819
> See Conversation: Josh Billings

All the wit in the world is lost upon him who has none.

> LA BRUYÈRE (1645–1696). In Arthur Schopenhauer, "The Art of Literature: On Genius," *Essays of Arthur Schopenhauer,* tr. T. Bailey Saunders, 1851

Impropriety is the soul of wit.

> W. SOMERSET MAUGHAM (1874–1965). *The Moon and Sixpence,* 4, 1919

There's a hell of a distance between wisecracking and wit. Wit has truth in it; wisecracking is simply calisthenics with words.

> DOROTHY PARKER (1893–1967). Marion Capron interview, 1956. In Malcolm Cowley, ed., *Writers at Work: First Series,* 1958

Wit is a happy and striking way of expressing a Thought.

> WILLIAM PENN (1644–1718). *Some Fruits of Solitude,* 168, 1693

Less Judgment than Wit is more Sail than Ballast.

> WILLIAM PENN (1644–1718). *Some Fruits of Solitude,* 171, 1693

True Wit is Nature to Advantage drest,
What oft was Thought, but ne'er so well Exprest.

> ALEXANDER POPE (1688–1744). *An Essay on Criticism,* l. 297, 1711

The wit which is allied to moral grandeur is that which fools forgive the least.

> ERNEST RENAN (1823–1892). *The Life of Jesus,* 21, 1863, Modern Library edition, 1927

Falstaff: I am not only witty in myself, but the cause that wit is in other men.

> SHAKESPEARE (1564–1616). *Henry IV,* Part II, 1.2.10, 1597
> See Bores: Samuel Foote

Falstaff: A good wit will make use of anything.

> SHAKESPEARE (1564–1616). *Henry IV,* Part II, 1.2.275, 1597

Polonius: Brevity is the soul of wit.

> SHAKESPEARE (1564–1616). *Hamlet,* 2.2.90, 1600

Hamlet: They have a plentiful lack of wit.

> SHAKESPEARE (1564–1616). *Hamlet,* 2.2.201, 1600

Wit consists in knowing the resemblance of things that differ, and the differences of things that are alike.

> MADAME de STAËL (1766–1817). *De l'Allemagne,* 1810

Other people's wit does not entertain us for long.

> VAUVENARGUES (1715–1747). *Reflections and Maxims,* 114, 1746, tr. F. G. Stevens, 1940

❦

Wit is the sudden marriage of ideas which before their union were not perceived to have any relation.

> ANONYMOUS. In Mark Twain, 6 August 1885, *Mark Twain's Notebook,* ed. Albert Bigelow Paine, 1935

WIT: EXAMPLES

See also • Criticism: Examples ○ Critics: Examples ○ Repartee: Examples ○ Wit

I do most of my work sitting down. That's where I shine.

> ROBERT BENCHLEY (1889–1945). In Robert E. Drennan, ed., "Robert Benchley," *The Algonquin Wits,* 1968

Nobody goes there any more because it's overcrowded.

> YOGI BERRA (1925–). On a popular restaurant. In Robert Lipsyte, "The Man and the Myth," *New York Times,* 25 October 1963

If Casey Stengel were alive today, he'd be turning over in his grave.

> YOGI BERRA (1925–). Attributed. In Thomas K. McCraw, "Deficit Lessons: Hamilton the Hero . . . ," *New York Times,* 2 May 1993

It's déjà vu all over again.

> YOGI BERRA (1925–). Attributed (he denied having said it)

When you come to a fork in the road, take it.

> YOGI BERRA (1925–). Attributed

If God thought that nudity was OK, we would have been born naked.

> ELLIS' ELOQUENCE. In John Peers, comp., *1,001 Logical Laws,* p. 24, 1979

Games
What reason to think Charles I consented to his execution?
They axed him whether he would or no. . . .
How could the Children of Israel sustain themselves for forty days in the desert?
Because of the sand-which-is there.

> RALPH WALDO EMERSON (1803–1882). Journal, November 1850

A verbal contract isn't worth the paper it is written on.

> SAM GOLDWYN (1882–1974). In Alva Johnston, *The Great Goldwyn,* 1, 1937

Gentlemen, include me out.

> SAM GOLDWYN (1882–1974). Informing associates that he was quitting their organization. In Alva Johnston, *The Great Goldwyn,* 1, 1937

I can answer you in two words: "Im possible."

> SAM GOLDWYN (1882–1974). Attributed. In Alva Johnston, *The Great Goldwyn,* 1, 1937

I read part of it all the way through.

> SAM GOLDWYN (1882–1974). In Alva Johnston, *The Great Goldwyn,* 1, 1937

Th' weddin' over at th' Tilford Moots farm went off without a hitch Saturday night. Th' bridegroom didn' show up.

> KIN HUBBARD (1868–1930). "May," *Abe Martin's Almanack,* 1908

Walking on water wasn't built in a day.

> JACK KEROUAC (1922–1969). Quoted by Allen Ginsberg. In *The Life and Times of Allen Ginsberg* (film), 1993
> See Rome: John Clarke

About as big as the small end of nothing whittled to a point.

> KEN KESEY (1935–). *One Flew Over the Cuckoo's Nest,* 2, 1962

He was now without means and out of business, but was anxious to remain with his friends who had treated him with so much generosity, especially as he had nothing elsewhere to go to.

> ABRAHAM LINCOLN (1809–1865). After being defeated as a candidate for the Illinois legislature in 1832. Third-person autobiographical sketch written for John L. Scripps, June? 1860

Send two dozen roses to Room 424 and put "Emily, I love you" on the back of the bill.

> GROUCHO MARX (1895–1977). In *A Day at the Races* (film), 1937

Please accept my resignation. I don't want to belong to any club that will accept me as a member.

> GROUCHO MARX (1895–1977). Telegram to the Delaney Club, *Groucho and Me,* 26, 1959
> See Humility: First Person: Abraham Lincoln (2)

Good work, Mary. We all knew you had it in you.

> DOROTHY PARKER (1893–1967). Wiring collect to a friend who had just given birth. In Alexander Woollcott, "Our Mrs. Parker," *While Rome Burns,* 1934

Tell him I've been too fucking busy—or vice versa.

> DOROTHY PARKER (1893–1967). Attributed. Explaining her failure to meet a deadline. In John Keats, *You Might as Well Live,* 5, 1970

[Thomas] Crapper invented the modern flush toilet.

> LAURENCE J. PETER (1919–1990). *Peter's People,* 7, 1979

An archaeologist is a person whose career lies in ruins.

> LAURENCE J. PETER (1919–1990). 3 December, *Peter's Almanac,* 1982

You have made a very good start in life, and your friends have great hope for you when you grow up.

> ELIHU ROOT (1845–1937). Secretary of war. Tongue-in-cheek congratulatory note to Pres. Theodore Roosevelt on his 46th birthday, 17 October 1904. In Erwin Knoll, "Big as All Outdoors," *New York Times Book Review,* 28 February 1993

There's a time in every man's life and I've had plenty of them.

> CASEY STENGEL (1890?–1975). Quoted in *Baseball,* television documentary series, PBS, September 1994

There is a solid bottom everywhere. We read that the traveler asked the boy if the swamp before him had a hard bottom. The boy replied that it had. But presently the traveler's horse sank in up to the girths, and he observed to the boy. "I thought you said that this bog had a hard bottom." "So it has," answered the latter, "but you have not got half way to it yet."

> HENRY DAVID THOREAU (1817–1862). "Conclusion," *Walden; or Life in the Woods,* 1854

Englishmen! You want to kill me because I am a Frenchman! Am I not punished enough, in not being an Englishman?

> VOLTAIRE (1694–1778). Facing an angry Francophobic London crowd which was shouting for his death (they cheered his words and escorted him to safety), 1727. In *Great Lives, Great Deeds,* publ. Reader's Digest Association, p. 473, 1964

I now bid you a welcome adoo.

> ARTEMUS WARD (1834–1867). "The Shakers," *The Complete Works of Artemus Ward,* 1898

By a sudden and adroit movement I placed my left eye against his fist.

> ARTEMUS WARD (1834–1867)

One must have a heart of stone to read the death of Little Nell without laughing.

> OSCAR WILDE (1854–1900). On the heroine of Charles Dickens' *The Old Curiosity Shop.* In *The Wit and Humor of Oscar Wilde,* 6, ed. Alvin Redman, 1959

❦

Don't look at me, sir, with—ah—in that tone of voice.

> ANONYMOUS. In *Punch* (British humor magazine), vol. 87, p. 38, 1884

WITCHCRAFT

See also • Heresy ○ Misogynous Statements ○ Prejudice ○ Religion ○ Sexist Statements ○ Superstition ○ Terrorism: Anonymous (Spanish)

Witchcraft was hung, in History,
But History and I
Find all the Witchcraft that we need
Around us, every Day—

> EMILY DICKINSON (1830–1886). "Witchcraft was hung, in History," 1883?

Far from recognizing their plight for what it was, the witch hunters and exorcists fought the witches' delusions on the level of the deluded, and whenever the patient failed to respond to exorcism by persuasion, prayer or the sacraments, they saw no choice but to resort to their own brand of shock treatment: burning at the stake.

> JAN EHRENWALD (1900–1988). Psychiatrist. *From Medicine Man to Freud: An Anthology,* 7, 1956

The rich, the powerful, the well-connected and those well situated within a large group of kin, could and probably would retaliate if they were accused of witchcraft. Such accusations would have been pushed only in unusual circumstances. But against those who were more or less incapable of retaliation, the old, the poor and especially women, and those who had already alienated the communi-

ty by their lewd, immoral or quarrelsome behavior, accusations could be brought with relative impunity.

> LELAND L. ESTES. "The Medical Origins of the European Witch Craze: A Hypothesis," *Journal of Social History,* vol. 17, 1984

The stereotype of the witch did not precede the hunts, but was the result of the hunts themselves. Put another way, it was the witch craze that produced the witch and not, as has been traditionally argued, the figure of the witch that stimulated hunting.

> LELAND L. ESTES. "The Medical Origins of the European Witch Craze: A Hypothesis," *Journal of Social History,* vol. 17, 1984

In England, during the first eighty years of the seventeenth century . . . about forty-two thousand witches were burnt in the presence of a delighted audience numbering thousands of people.

In the blindness and stubbornness of belief in witchcraft, the wisest and highest in the land were as ecstatically bigoted as the masses of the people.

> THEO. B. HYSLOP (1863–1933). *The Great Abnormals,* 4, 1925

In most instances the crime of witchcraft was merely the pretext through which the Roman Church prosecuted those who would not embrace their faith. In this they were urged on by men in power who wished to rid themselves of their enemies.

> THEO. B. HYSLOP (1863–1933). *The Great Abnormals,* 4, 1925

All witchcraft comes from carnal lust, which is in women insatiable. . . . Wherefore for the sake of fulfilling their lusts they consort even with devils. More such reasons could be brought forward, but to the understanding it is sufficiently clear that it is no matter for wonder that there are more women than men found infected with the heresy of witchcraft.

> HEINRICH KRAMER (15th cent.) and JAMES SPRENGER (15th cent.). *Malleus Maleficarum,* 1.6, 1486, tr. Montague Summers, 1928

Although far more women are witches than men . . . yet men are more often bewitched than women.

> HEINRICH KRAMER (15th cent.) and JAMES SPRENGER (15th cent.). *Malleus Maleficarum,* 2.2.2, 1486, tr. Montague Summers, 1928

Common justice demands that a witch should not be condemned to death unless she is convicted by her own confession.

> HEINRICH KRAMER (15th cent.) and JAMES SPRENGER (15th cent.). *Malleus Maleficarum,* 3.13, 1486, tr. Montague Summers, 1928. Here and elsewhere in this inquisitorial tract, torture was authorized to extort confessions from witches in part "because of the great trouble caused by [their] stubborn silence."
>
> See Right to Silence: William O. Douglas

I should have no compassion on these witches; I would burn all of them.

> MARTIN LUTHER (1483–1546). *Table Talk,* 581, 1566, tr. William Hazlitt, 1857

Thou shalt not suffer a witch to live.

> MOSES (14th cent. B.C.). *Exodus* 22:18 (King James Version)

❦

To disbelieve in witchcraft is the greatest of heresies.

> SAYING. In Heinrich Kramer and James Sprenger, *Malleus Maleficarum,* title page (epigraph), 1486. Quoted in H. R. Trevor-Roper, "Witches and Witchcraft: An Historical Essay (1)," *Encounter,* May 1967

WITNESSES

See also • Falsehood: Moses ○ Justice ○ Trials: [especially] Constitution of the United States

If a fact is fully proved by two witnesses, it is as good as if proved by a hundred.

> J. BULLER. *Calliand v. Vaughan,* 1798

Eyes are more exact witnesses than ears.

> HERACLITUS (540?–480? B.C.). In T. V. Smith, ed., "Heraclitus" (15), *From Thales to Plato,* 2, 1934

Witnesses should know that they stand before God Who will call them to account.

> TALMUD (A.D. 1st–6th cent.). Rabbinical writings. In Louis I. Newman, comp., *The Talmudic Anthology,* 175, 1945

Without confrontation and cross examination, a man brought before a hearing board is subject to trial by inquisition.

> EDWARD BENNETT WILLIAMS (1920–1988). *One Man's Freedom,* 11, 1962

❦

False in one thing, false in everything.

> SAYING (LATIN)

One eye witness is worth more than ten ear witnesses.

> SAYING (LATIN)

One witness is no witness.

> SAYING (LATIN)

Witnesses are weighed not counted.

> SAYING (LATIN)

WOMEN

See also • America: Alexis de Tocqueville (4) ○ Feminism ○ Man ○ Mankind ○ Men ○ Misogynous Statements ○ Sexism ○ Sexist Statements ○ Women & Men

"If God made anything better than a girl," Dover thought, "He sure kept it to Himself."

> NELSON ALGREN (1909–1981). *A Walk on the Wild Side,* 3, 1956

One is not born, but rather becomes a woman.

> SIMONE de BEAUVOIR (1908–1986). *The Second Sex,* 12, 1950, tr. H. M. Parshley, 1952
> See Genius: de Beauvoir

Her, gracious, graceful, graceless Grace.

> LORD BYRON (1788–1824). *Don Juan,* 16.49, 1819–1824

Heav'n has no Rage like Love to Hatred turn'd,
Nor Hell a Fury, like a Woman scorn'd.

> WILLIAM CONGREVE (1670–1729). *The Mourning Bride,* 3.8, 1697
> (Popular version:

She takes just like a woman, yes, she does
She makes love just like a woman, yes, she does
And she aches just like a woman
But she breaks just like a little girl.

> BOB DYLAN (1941–). "Just Like a Woman" (song), 1966

Our greatest debt to woman is of a musical character, and not describable.

> RALPH WALDO EMERSON (1803–1882). Journal, 1847-1848, undated

The great question that has never been answered and which I have not been able to answer, despite my thirty years of research into the feminine soul, is "What does a woman want?"

> SIGMUND FREUD (1856–1939). Remark to Marie Bonaparte. In Ernest Jones, *The Life and Work of Sigmund Freud,* 25, 1953–1957, abr., 1961

"There Is Nothin' Like a Dame."

> OSCAR HAMMERSTEIN II (1895–1960). Song title. In the musical *South Pacific,* 1949

There is in every true woman's heart a spark of heavenly fire, which lies dormant in the broad daylight of prosperity, but which kindles up and beams and blazes in the dark hour of adversity.

> WASHINGTON IRVING (1783–1859). "The Wife," *The Sketch Book,* 1820

it s cheerio
my deario that
pulls a lady through.

> DON MARQUIS (1878–1937). "cheerio, my deario," *archy and mehitabel,* 1927

Grace was in all her steps, Heav'n in her Eye,
In every gesture dignity and love.

> JOHN MILTON (1608–1674). *Paradise Lost,* 8.488, 1667

O fairest of Creation, last and best
Of all God's works, Creature in whom excell'd
Whatever can to sight or thought be form'd,
Holy, divine, good, amiable, or sweet!

> JOHN MILTON (1608–1674). *Paradise Lost,* 9.896, 1667

If I have to, I can do anything.
I am strong, I am invincible, I am woman.

> HELEN REDDY (1941–). "I Am Woman" (song), 1972

Across the curve of the earth, there are women getting up before dawn, in the blackness before the point of light, in the twilight before sunrise; there are women rising earlier than men and children to break the ice, to start the stove, to put up the pap, the coffee, the rice, to iron the pants, to braid the hair, to pull the day's water up from the well, to boil water for tea, to wash the children for school, to pull the vegetables and start the walk to market, to run to catch the bus for the work that is paid. I don't know when most women sleep.

> ADRIENNE RICH (1929–). "Notes Toward a Politics of Location," 1984, *Blood, Bread, and Poetry: Selected Prose 1979–1985,* 1986

Shall I compare thee to a summer's day?

> SHAKESPEARE (1564–1616). *Sonnets,* 18.1, 1609

There was a Woman, beautiful as morning.

> PERCY BYSSHE SHELLEY (1792–1822). *The Revolt of Islam,* 16, 1817

Women have gone through a real revolution in this country. They have started trusting one another.

> MARLO THOMAS (1943–). In "Currents," *U.S. News & World Report,* 12 October 1987

The female woman is one of the greatest institooshuns of which this land can boste.

> ARTEMUS WARD (1834–1867). "Woman's Rights," *The Complete Works of Artemus Ward*, 1898

As a woman, I have no country. As a woman, I want no country. As a woman, my country is the whole world.

> VIRGINIA WOOLF (1882–1941). *Three Guineas*, 3, 1938
>
> See Internationalism: Thomas Paine

WOMEN & MEN

See also • Feminism ∘ Love, Romantic ∘ Man ∘ Marriage ∘ Misogynous Statements ∘ Passion ∘ Sex ∘ Sexist Statements ∘ Weeping: Jean Rhys ∘ Women

These impossible women! How they do get around us!
The poet was right: can't live with them, or without them!

> ARISTOPHANES (450?–388? B.C.). *Lysistrata*, l. 1038, tr. Dudley Fitts, 1954
>
> See Marriage: Socrates

No man naturally can imagine any more compelling business for a woman than being interested in him.

> MARY AUSTIN (1868–1934). *A Woman of Genius*, 4.6, 1912

Let men say whate'er they will,
Woman, woman, rules them still.

> ISAAC BICKERSTAFF (1733–1808?). *The Sultan*, 2.1, 1775

That's the nature of women . . . not to love when we love them, and to love when we love them not.

> CERVANTES (1547–1616). *Don Quixote*, 1.3.6, 1615, tr. Peter Anthony Motteux and John Ozell, 1743

The relations between men and women are like those between Europe and the Indies: at once commerce and a war.

> CHAMFORT (1741–1794). *Maxims and Thoughts*, 6, 1796, tr. W. S. Merwin, 1984

I'm not denyin' the women are foolish: God Almighty made 'em to match the men.

> GEORGE ELIOT (1819–1880). *Adam Bede*, 53, 1859

Male and female represent the two sides of the great radical dualism. But, in fact, they are perpetually passing into one another. Fluid hardens to solid, solid rushes to fluid. There is no wholly masculine man, no purely feminine woman.

> MARGARET FULLER (1810–1850). "The Great Lawsuit. Man versus Men. Woman verses Women," *The Dial* (New England journal), July 1843

I think older women with younger men threaten all the right people.

> WILLIAM HAMILTON. One woman to another at a cocktail party. Cartoon caption, *New Yorker*, 16 December 1996

I am little other than a cloud at such seasons [of gloom]; but she contrives to make me a sunny one; for she gets into the remotest recesses of my heart, and shines all through me.

> NATHANIEL HAWTHORNE (1804–1864). Referring to his wife Sophia, 28 August 1842. *The American Notebooks*, ed. Claude M. Simpson, 1932

You know you don't have to act with me, Steve. You don't have to say anything, and you don't have to do anything. Not a thing. Oh, maybe just whistle. You know how to whistle, don't you, Steve? You just put your lips together and blow.

> ERNEST HEMINGWAY (1899–1961) (JULES FURTHMAN and WILLIAM FAULKNER, scriptwriters). *To Have and Have Not* (film), 1944, spoken by Lauren Bacall to Humphrey Bogart as she was leaving his hotel room (Popular version: If you want anything, just whistle.)

Man has his will—but woman has her way!

> OLIVER WENDELL HOLMES, SR. (1809–1894). *The Autocrat of the Breakfast-Table*, 2 ("This Is It" [poem]), 1858

Woman and Man are like Lodestone and Iron.

> JAMES HOWELL (1593–1666). Comp., "Divers Centuries of New Sayings" (p. 5), *Paroimiographia: Proverbs, or Old Sayed Sawes & Adages in English . . . Italian, French and Spanish*, 1659

There was never a Jack but there was a Jill.

> JAMES KELLY (18th cent.). Comp., *A Complete Collection of Scottish Proverbs Explained and Made Intelligible to the English Reader*, T.111, 1721

The silliest woman can manage a clever man; but it needs a very clever woman to manage a fool.

> RUDYARD KIPLING (1865–1936). "Three and—an Extra," *Plain Tales from the Hills*, 1888

As unto the bow the cord is,
So unto the man is woman;
Though she bends him, she obeys him,
Though she draws him, yet she follows;
Useless each without the other!

> HENRY WADSWORTH LONGFELLOW (1807–1882). *The Song of Hiawatha*, 10, 1855

I generally had to give in.

> NAPOLEON (1769–1821). On his relationship with Josephine, 19 May 1816

Woman, as they grow older, rely more and more on cosmetics. Men, as they grow older, rely more and more on a sense of humor.

> GEORGE JEAN NATHAN (1882–1958). "Cosmetics vs. Humor," *American Mercury*, July 1925

Only he who is sufficiently a man will *redeem the woman* in woman.

> FRIEDRICH NIETZSCHE (1844–1900). "Of the Virtue that Makes Small" (2), *Thus Spoke Zarathustra*, 1892, tr. R. J. Hollingdale, 1961

Woman was God's *second* mistake.

> FRIEDRICH NIETZSCHE (1844–1900). *The Anti-Christ*, 48, 1895, tr. R. J. Hollingdale, 1968

The first great step is to like yourself enough to pick someone who likes you, too.

> JANE O'REILLY. "View from the Bed," *Ms.*, April 1973

Guys and Dolls.

> DAMON RUNYON (1884–1946). Book title, 1931; musical title, 1950; and film title, 1950

Orinthia (to Magnus): All men are fools and moral cowards when you come to know them. But you are less of a fool and less of a moral coward than any I have ever known. You have almost the making of a first-rate woman in you.

> GEORGE BERNARD SHAW (1856–1950). "An Interlude," *The Apple Cart,* 1928

Think what cowards men would be if they had to bear children. Women are an altogether superior species.

> GEORGE BERNARD SHAW (1856–1950). Remark to the author, 1940s. In Stephen Winsten, *Days with Bernard Shaw,* 17, 1949

In politics, if you want anything said, ask a man. If you want anything *done,* ask a woman.

> MARGARET THATCHER (1925–). In "The Tough Top Tory in Britain Wants To Be 'Madame P.M.,'" *People,* 15 September 1975
>
> See Sexist Statements: James Howell (2)

[Male and female are] two halves of a split pea.

> *UPANISHADS* (10th?–6th? cent. B.C.). Hindu scriptures. In Joseph Campbell, *The Hero with a Thousand Faces,* 1.2.5, 1949

Whatever women do, they must do twice as well as men to be thought of half as good. Luckily, this is not difficult.

> CHARLOTTE WHITTON (1896–1975). After being elected mayor of Ottawa. In *Canada Month,* June 1963

Women have many faults
Men have only two:
Everything they say
And everything they do.

> ANONYMOUS

Men and women are kneaded from the same dough.

> SAYING (RUSSIAN)

Men make houses, women make homes.

> SAYING

WONDER

See also • Awe ○ Curiosity ○ Human Nature: Alfred North Whitehead ○ Knowledge: Abraham Joshua Heschel, Charles Morgan ○ Miracles ○ Mystery

We carry within us the wonders we seek [outside] us.

> SIR THOMAS BROWNE (1605–1682). *Religio Medici,* 1.15, 1642, ed. John Addington Symonds, 1886

The world will never starve for wonders; but only for want of wonder.

> G. K. CHESTERTON (1874–1936). Inscription on the General Motors Building, A Century of Progress Exposition, Chicago

Men love to wonder, and that is the seed of our science.

> RALPH WALDO EMERSON (1803–1882). "Works and Days," *Society and Solitude,* 1860

I am perpetually awaiting
a rebirth of wonder.

> LAWRENCE FERLINGHETTI (1919–). "I Am Waiting," *A Coney Island of the Mind,* 1958

Wonder is a state of mind in which . . . nothing is taken for granted. . . . Each thing is a surprise, *being is unbelievable.* We are amazed at seeing anything at all; amazed not only at particular values and things but *at the unexpectedness of being as such,* at the fact that there is being at all.

> ABRAHAM JOSHUA HESCHEL (1907–1972). *Man Is Not Alone: A Philosophy of Religion,* 2, 1951

I think us here to wonder, myself. To wonder. To ast. And that in wondering bout the big things and asting bout the big things, you learn about the little ones, almost by accident. But you never know nothing more about the big things than you start out with. The more I wonder, he say, the more I love.

And people start to love you back, I bet, I say.

They do, he say, surprise.

> ALICE WALKER (1944–). *The Color Purple,* p. 247, 1982, Washington Square Press edition, 1983

WOODS

See also • Forests ○ Nature ○ Trees ○ Wilderness

In the woods too, a man casts off his years, as the snake his slough, and at what period soever of life, is always a child. In the woods is a perpetual youth. . . . In the woods, we return to reason and faith. There I feel that nothing can befall me in life—no disgrace, no calamity, . . . which nature cannot repair. Standing on the bare ground—my head bathed by the blithe air, and uplifted into infinite space—all mean egotism vanishes. I become a transparent eyeball; I am nothing; I see all; the currents of the Universal Being circulate through me; I am part or particle of God.

> RALPH WALDO EMERSON (1803–1882). Title essay, *Nature,* 1836

A walk in the woods is only an exalted dream.

> RALPH WALDO EMERSON (1803–1882). Journal, 29 September 1839

Being in the woods is being in church. On my knees, digging down through the pale layers of fallen leaves for leeks, I can see how life works to bring itself into existence and to proliferate in its forms. A vast community of microorganisms, numberless companions to the trees in their centuries-long endeavor of niche-building and niche-filling, is making leaves into soil, black, rich, clean, and alive. The vitality of this climax community is insistent. Three weeks after the snowmelt, there are thousands of maple seedlings bursting towards a spot of sun; citron-colored leaves unfold from bronze sheaths at the tips of frail-seeming beech whips.

> STEPHANIE MILLS (1948–). "Fate and Faith," *Whatever Happened to Ecology?* 1989

He who cuts down woods beyond a certain limit exterminates birds.

> HENRY DAVID THOREAU (1817–1862). Journal, 17 May 1853

If a man walk in the woods for love of them half of each day, he is in danger of being regarded as a loafer; but if he spends his whole day as a speculator, shearing off those woods and making earth bald before her time, he is esteemed an industrious and enterprising citizen. As if a town had no interest in its forests but to cut them down!

HENRY DAVID THOREAU (1817–1862). "Life Without Principle," *Atlantic,* October 1863

One impulse from a vernal wood
May teach you more of man,
Of moral evil and of good,
Than all the sages can.

WILLIAM WORDSWORTH (1770–1850). "The Tables Turned," l. 21, 1798

WORDS

See also • Argument ○ Books ○ Creativity ○ Creativity—First Person: Arthur Miller ○ Eloquence ○ Ideas ○ Knowledge: Kahlil Gibran ○ Language ○ Literature ○ Names ○ Newspeak ○ Opinion ○ Persuasion ○ Poetry ○ Propaganda ○ Public Opinion ○ Public Speaking ○ Silence & Speech ○ Speaking ○ Tact ○ Talking: [especially] Saying (Hindu) ○ Thoughts ○ Truth ○ Wit ○ Wounds: Saying (Arab) ○ Writers ○ Writing

Words may be deeds.

AESOP (6th cent. B.C.). "The Trumpeter Taken Prisoner," *Fables,* tr. Joseph Jacobs, 1894

See Action & Talk: Socrates

All words are pegs to hang ideas on.

HENRY WARD BEECHER (1813–1887). "The Human Mind," *Proverbs from Plymouth Pulpit,* ed. William Drysdale, 1887

Be not the slave of Words.

THOMAS CARLYLE (1795–1881). *Sartor Resartus: The Life and Opinions of Herr Teufelsdröckh,* 1.8, 1835

"When *I* use a word," Humpty Dumpty said, in rather a scornful tone, "it means just what I choose it to mean—neither more nor less."

"The question is," said Alice, "whether you *can* make words mean so many different things."

"The question is," said Humpty Dumpty, "which is to be master—that's all."

LEWIS CARROLL (1832–1898). *Through the Looking-Glass and What Alice Found There,* 6, 1872

Broadly speaking, short words are best, and the old words, when short, are the best of all.

WINSTON CHURCHILL (1874–1965). "Riches of English Language," speech, 1947, *Winston Churchill: His Complete Speeches 1897–1963,* vol. 7, ed. Robert R. James, 1974

The words in prose ought to express the intended meaning, and no more; if they attract attention to themselves, it is, in general, a fault.

SAMUEL TAYLOR COLERIDGE (1772–1834). 3 July 1833, *Table Talk,* 1835

See Style: Samuel Butler ○ Writing: Leon Trotsky

A word is dead
When it is said,
Some say.
I say it just
Begins to live
That day.

EMILY DICKINSON (1830–1886). "A word is dead," 1872?

With words we govern men.

BENJAMIN DISRAELI (1804–1881). *Contarini Fleming: A Psychological Autobiography,* 1.21, 1832

Where shall the word be found, where will the word
Resound? Not here, there is not enough silence.

T. S. ELIOT (1888–1965). *Ash Wednesday,* 5, 1930

The more perfect the understanding between men, the less need of words.

RALPH WALDO EMERSON (1803–1882). Journal, 11 October 1838

You can stroke people with words.

F. SCOTT FITZGERALD (1896–1940). "Note-Books" (O), *The Crack-Up,* ed. Edmund Wilson, 1945

Anyone who wishes to become a good writer should endeavor, before he allows himself to be tempted by the more showy qualities, to be direct, simple, brief, vigorous, and lucid.

This general principle may be translated into practical rules in the domain of vocabulary as follows:
Prefer the familiar word to the far-fetched.
Prefer the concrete word to the abstract.
Prefer the single word to the circumlocution.
Prefer the simple word to the long.
Prefer the Saxon word to the Romance.

H. W. FOWLER (1858–1933) and F. G. FOWLER. Opening paragraphs, *The King's English,* 3rd ed., 1930

Sticks and stones may break our bones, but words will break our hearts.

ROBERT FULGHUM (1937–). *All I Really Need to Know I Learned in Kindergarten: Uncommon Thoughts on Common Things,* p. 20, 1988

Words which were invented to express our Thoughts seem now to be applied only to the concealing them with a good Grace.

THOMAS FULLER (1654–1734). Comp., *Introductio ad Prudentiam,* 1679, 1731

See Speaking: Voltaire

A Deluge of Words and a Drop of Sense.

THOMAS FULLER (1654–1734). Comp., *Gnomologia: Adages and Proverbs,* 72, 1732

Fair Words fill not the Belly.

THOMAS FULLER (1654–1734). Comp., *Gnomologia: Adages and Proverbs,* 1491, 1732

See Promises: Saying (German) ○ Talking (3): Saying (Chinese and Japanese)

Words—so innocent and powerless as they are, as standing in a dictionary, how potent for good and evil they become, in the hands of one who knows how to combine them!

NATHANIEL HAWTHORNE (1804–1864). 17 November 1847. *The American Notebooks,* ed. Claude M. Simpson, 1932

I hate anything that occupies more space than it is worth. . . . I hate to see a parcel of big words without anything in them.

WILLIAM HAZLITT (1778–1830). "On Familiar Style," *Table Talk,* 1822

All our words from loose using have lost their edge.

ERNEST HEMINGWAY (1899–1961). *Death in the Afternoon,* 7, 1932

Fine words dress ill deeds.

> GEORGE HERBERT (1593–1633). Comp., *Outlandish Proverbs,* 479, 1640

A word t' th' wise is unnecessary.

> KIN HUBBARD (1868–1930). "September," *Abe Martin's Almanack,* 1908

In the beginning was the Word, and the Word was with God, and the Word was God.

> JOHN (A.D. 1st cent.). *John* 1:1
>
> See Deeds: Goethe

Before employing a fine word, make a place for it.

> JOSEPH JOUBERT (1754–1824). *Pensées,* 302, 1838, tr. Henry Attwell, 1877

The true word leads; the untrue misleads.

> FRANZ KAFKA (1883–1924). In Gustav Janouch, *Conversations with Kafka,* p. 97, tr. Goronwy Rees, 1953

Words ought to be a little wild for they are the assault of thoughts on the unthinking.

> JOHN MAYNARD KEYNES (1883–1946). "National Self-Sufficiency," *New Statesman* (British magazine), 15 July 1933

Words are . . . the most powerful drug used by mankind.

> RUDYARD KIPLING (1865–1936). Speech, London, 14 February 1923
>
> See Karl Marx in Religion, Anti-

As honest words may not sound fine,
Fine words may not be honest ones.

> LAO-TZU (6th cent. B.C.). *The Way of Life,* 81, tr. R. B. Blakney, 1955

He can compress the most words into the smallest ideas of any man I ever met.

> ABRAHAM LINCOLN (1809–1865). On a lawyer colleague. In Anthony Gross, ed., *Lincoln's Own Stories,* 2, 1912

Words make another place, a place to escape to with your spirit alone.

> ROBERT MacNEIL (1931–). *Wordstruck: A Memoir,* 1, 1989

It has not been for nothing that the word has remained man's principal toy and tool: without the meanings and values it sustains, all man's other tools would be worthless.

> LEWIS MUMFORD (1895–1990). *The Transformations of Man,* 1.3, 1956

A mass of Latin words falls upon the facts like soft snow, blurring the outlines and covering up all the details. The great enemy of clear language is insincerity. When there is a gap between one's real and one's declared aims, one turns, as it were instinctively to long words and exhausted idioms, like a cuttlefish squirting out ink.

> GEORGE ORWELL (1903–1950). "Politics and the English Language," April 1946, *The Collected Essays, Journalism and Letters of George Orwell,* vol. 4, ed. Sonia Orwell and Ian Angus, 1968

Probably it is better to put off using words as long as possible and get one's meaning as clear as one can through pictures or sensations.

> GEORGE ORWELL (1903–1950). "Politics and the English Language," April 1946, *The Collected Essays, Journalism and Letters of George Orwell,* vol. 4, ed. Sonia Orwell and Ian Angus, 1968

One can often be in doubt about the effect of a word or a phrase, and one needs rules that one can rely on when instinct fails. I think the following rules will cover most cases:

i. Never use a metaphor, simile or other figure of speech which you are used to seeing in print.
ii. Never use a long word where a short one will do.
iii. If it is possible to cut a word out, always cut it out.
iv. Never use the passive where you can use the active.
v. Never use a foreign phrase, a scientific word or a jargon word it you can think of any everyday English equivalent.
vi. Break any of these rules sooner than say anything outright barbarous.

> GEORGE ORWELL (1903–1950). "Politics and the English Language," April 1946, *The Collected Essays, Journalism and Letters of George Orwell,* vol. 4, ed. Sonia Orwell and Ian Angus, 1968

Uncommon things must be said in common words, if you would have them to be received in less than a century.

> COVENTRY PATMORE (1823–1996). Letter to H. S. Sutton, 25 March 1847

He that uses many words for explaining any subject, does, like the cuttlefish, hide himself for the most part in his own ink.

> JOHN RAY (1628–1705). *The Wisdom of God Manifested in the Works of the Creation,* 2nd ed., 1692

To use many words to communicate few thoughts is everywhere the unmistakable sign of mediocrity. To gather much thought into few words stamps the man of genius.

> ARTHUR SCHOPENHAUER (1788–1860). "The Art of Literature: On Style," *Essays of Arthur Schopenhauer,* tr. T. Bailey Saunders, 1851

Our words should aim not to please, but to help.

> SENECA THE YOUNGER (5? B.C.–A.D. 65). "On the Diseases of the Soul," *Moral Letters to Lucilius,* 75.5, tr. Richard M. Gummere, 1918

Clown: Words are grown so false, I am loath to prove reason with them.

> SHAKESPEARE (1564–1616). *Twelfth Night,* 3.1.27, 1599

Polonius: What do you read, my lord?
Hamlet: Words, words, words.

> SHAKESPEARE (1564–1616). *Hamlet,* 2.2.191, 1600

Pandarus: Words pay no debts.

> SHAKESPEARE (1564–1616). *Troilus and Cressida,* 3.2.58, 1601

Man does not live by words alone, despite the fact that sometimes he has to eat them.

> ADLAI E. STEVENSON (1900–1965). Speech, Colorado Volunteers for Stevenson dinner, Denver, 5 September 1952
>
> See Food: Moses

Man is a creature who lives not upon bread alone, but principally by catchwords.

> ROBERT LOUIS STEVENSON (1850–1894). Title essay (2), *Virginibus Puerisque,* 1881
>
> See Food: Moses

There are not words enough in all Shakespeare to express the merest fraction of a man's experience in an hour.

> ROBERT LOUIS STEVENSON (1850–1894). "Walt Whitman" (1), *Familiar Studies of Men and Books,* 1882

A word to the wise is enough.

> TERENCE (190?–159 B.C.). *Phormio*, 3.545
>
> See Wisdom: Saying (Chinese) (2)

You know about a person who deeply interests you more than you can be told. A look, a gesture, an act, which to everybody else is insignificant tells you more about that one than words can.

> HENRY DAVID THOREAU (1817–1862). Journal, 20 February 1859
>
> See Talking: Lord Chesterfield, Ralph Waldo Emerson (3)

The difference between the *almost right* word and the *right* word is really a large matter—'tis the difference between the lightning bug and the lightning.

> MARK TWAIN (1835–1910). "The Art of Composition," 1890, *Life As I Find It,* ed. Charles Neider, 1961

A limited vocabulary, but one with which you can make numerous combinations, is better than thirty thousand words that only hamper the action of the mind.

> PAUL VALÉRY (1871–1945). *The Outlook for Intelligence,* 8, tr. Denise Folliot and Jackson Mathews, 1963

On the spoken word, all the gods depend, all beasts and men; in the word live all creatures . . . the Word is the navel of the divine world.

> *VEDAS* (10th? cent. B.C.). Hindu scriptures. In Norman Mailer, "'The Writer's Imagination and the Imagination of the State': Two Views," *New York Review of Books,* 13 February 1986

❧

Thy word is a lamp to my feet
  and a light to my path.

> ANONYMOUS (*BIBLE*). *Psalms* 119:105

There is one whose rash words are like sword thrusts,
  but the tongue of the wise brings healing.

> SAYING (*BIBLE*). *Proverbs* 12:18
>
> See Talking: George Herbert ○ Writing: Edward George Bulwer-Lytton

To make an apt answer is a joy to a man,
  and a word in season, how good it is!

> SAYING (*BIBLE*). *Proverbs* 15:23

Sticks and stones may break my bones, but words can never harm me.

> SAYING (ENGLISH)

A word out of season may mar a whole life.

> SAYING (GREEK)

One kind word can warm three winter months.

> SAYING (JAPANESE)

Better one word too few than one too many.

> SAYING (MALTESE)

Better one word before than two after.

> SAYING (WELSH)

Words should be weighed and not counted.

> SAYING (YIDDISH)

The more words, the less wisdom.

> SAYING

WORK

See also • Business (Commerce) ○ Business (Occupation) ○ Class ○ Economics: [especially] National Conference of Catholic Bishops ○ Effort ○ Farming ○ Gardening ○ Idleness ○ Industry ○ Laziness ○ Leisure ○ Money ○ Pay ○ Struggle ○ Success ○ Trade (Commerce) ○ Trade (Occupation) ○ Unemployment ○ Unions ○ Wages ○ Wealth ○ Worry: Robert Frost

It is not real work unless you would rather be doing something else.

> J. M. BARRIE (1860–1937). Rectorial address, St. Andrew's University, Scotland, 3 May 1922

Work is effort applied toward some end. The most satisfying work involves directing our efforts towards achieving ends that we ourselves endorse as worthy expressions of our talent and character.

> WILLIAM J. BENNETT (1943–). *The Book of Virtues: A Treasury of Great Moral Stories,* 5 (introduction), 1993

Let each produce according to his aptitudes and his force; let each consume according to his need.

> LOUIS BLANC (1811–1882). French Socialist writer. *Organisation du travail,* 1840
>
> See Sharing: Anonymous (*Bible*)

In a State of Nature, it is an invariable Law that a Man's Acquisitions are in proportion to his Labors. In a State of Artificial Society, it is a Law as constant and as invariable that those who labor most enjoy the fewest things; and that those who labor not at all have the greatest Number of Enjoyments. A Condition of things this, strange and ridiculous beyond Expression.

> EDMUND BURKE (1729–1797). *A Vindication of Natural Society,* p. 90, M. Cooper edition, 1756

The dignity of every occupation wholly depends upon the quantity and the kind of virtue that may be exerted in it.

> EDMUND BURKE (1729–1797). *Reflections on the Revolution in France,* p. 351, 1790, Pelican Books edition, 1968

Most people work just hard enough not to get fired and get paid just enough money not to quit.

> GEORGE CARLIN (1937–). *Brain Droppings,* p. 206, 1997

Work smarter, not harder.

> RON CARSWELL. "Carswell Law of Productivity." In Paul Dickson, comp., *The Official Explanations,* p. 33, 1980

Sweet is the fruit of labor.

> JOHN CLARKE (1596–1658). Comp., *Proverbs: English and Latine,* p. 163, 1639

Work is an extension of personality. It is achievement. It is one of the ways in which a person defines himself, measures his worth, and his humanity.

> PETER F. DRUCKER (1909–). *Management: Tasks, Responsibilities, Practices,* 14, 1974, abr., 1977

All play and no work makes Jack a mere toy.

> MARIA EDGEWORTH (1768–1849). *Harry and Lucy*, 1801

The Carpenter's cord, if you hold your ear close enough, is musical in the breeze.

> RALPH WALDO EMERSON (1803–1882). Journal, 22 April 1842

To every reproach, I know now but one answer, namely, to go again to my own work.

"But you neglect your relations." Yes, too true, then I will work the harder.

"But you have no genius." Yes, then I will work the harder.

"But you have no virtues." Yes, then I will work the harder.

> RALPH WALDO EMERSON (1803–1882). Journal, October 1851

Every man is a consumer, and ought to be a producer. He fails to make his place good in the world unless he not only pays his debt but also adds something to the common wealth.

> RALPH WALDO EMERSON (1803–1882). "Wealth," *The Conduct of Life*, 1860

The mechanic at his bench carries a quiet heart and assured manners, and deals on even terms with men of any condition.

> RALPH WALDO EMERSON (1803–1882). "Wealth," *The Conduct of Life*, 1860

It has been computed by some political arithmetician that, if every man and woman would work for four hours each day on something useful, that labor would produce sufficient to procure all the necessaries and comforts of life, want and misery would be banished out of the world, and the rest of the twenty-four hours might be leisure and pleasure.

> BENJAMIN FRANKLIN (1706–1790). Letter to Benjamin Vaughan, 26 July 1784

By working faithfully eight hours a day, you may eventually get to be a boss and work twelve hours a day.

> ROBERT FROST (1874–1963)

Men for the sake of getting a living forget to live.

> MARGARET FULLER (1810–1850). *Summer on the Lakes*, 7, 1844

Let him that earns the Bread eat it.

> THOMAS FULLER (1654–1734). Comp., *Gnomologia: Adages and Proverbs*, 3183, 1732

For some, and probably a majority, [work] remains a stint to be performed. It may be preferable, especially in the context of social attitudes toward production, to doing nothing. Nevertheless it is fatiguing or monotonous or, at a minimum, a source of no particular pleasure. The reward rests not in the task but in the pay.

For others work . . . is an entirely different matter. it is taken for granted that it will be enjoyable. If it is not, this is a source of deep dissatisfaction or frustration.

> JOHN KENNETH GALBRAITH (1908–). *The Affluent Society*, 24.4, 1958

After it has discharged its task, the soul moves with greater ease and enjoys life. There is nothing more wretched than well-being without work. This is enough to make the finest of nature's gifts turn sour.

> GOETHE (1749–1832). Diary, 13 January 1779, tr. Hermann J. Weigand, 1949

When work is a pleasure, life is a joy. When work is a duty, life is slavery.

> MAXIM GORKY (1868–1936). *The Lower Depths*, 1, 1903, tr. Alexander Bakshy, 1945

Work is the means of living, but it is not living.

> JOSIAH GILBERT HOLLAND (1819–1881). "High Life and Low Life," *Plain Talks on Familiar Subjects*, 1866

Work was made for man, and not man for work. Work is man's servant, both in its results to the worker and the world. Man is not work's servant, save as an almost universal perversion has made him such.

> JOSIAH GILBERT HOLLAND (1819–1881). "Work and Play," *Plain Talks on Familiar Subjects*, 1866

All work and no play makes Jack a dull boy.

> JAMES HOWELL (1593–1666). Comp., "English" (p. 12), *Paroimiographia: Proverbs, or Old Sayed Sawes & Adages in English . . . Italian, French and Spanish*, 1659

We work to become, not to acquire.

> ELBERT HUBBARD (1856–1915). *A Thousand and One Epigrams*, p. 30, 1911

Human labor cannot be treated merely as a resource necessary for production—the so-called "work force." Man cannot be regarded as a tool of production. Man is the creator of work and its craftsman. Everything must be done to ensure that work does not lose its proper dignity. The purpose of work—of all work—is man himself. By means of his work he should be able to perfect and deepen his own personality.

> POPE JOHN II (1920–). Homily, Poland, 2 June 1997. In "On the Question of Human Work," *Catholic Worker*, December 1997

It's been a hard day's night,
And I've been working like a dog.

> JOHN LENNON (1940–1980) and PAUL McCARTHY (1942–). "A Hard Day's Night" (song), 1964

The lady—bearer of this—says she has two sons who want to work. Set them at it, if possible. Wanting to work is so rare a merit that it should be encouraged.

> ABRAHAM LINCOLN (1809–1865). Letter to Maj. George D. Ramsay, 17 October 1861

His brow is wet with honest sweat,
He earns whate'er he can,
And looks the whole world in the face,
For he owes not any man.

> HENRY WADSWORTH LONGFELLOW (1807–1882). "The Village Blacksmith," 2, 1839

In any given group, the most will do the least and the least the most.

> MERLE P. MARTIN. "The Instant Analyst," *Journal of Systems Management*, 1975

From each according to his ability, to each according to his needs.

> KARL MARX (1818–1883). *Critique of the Gotha Programme*, 1.3, May 1875, *The Marx-Engels Reader*, 2nd ed., ed. Robert C. Tucker, 1978
>
> See Sharing: Anonymous (*Bible*)

There is nothing laudable in work for work's sake.

> JOHN STUART MILL (1806–1873). "The Negro Question," *Frazer's Magazine* (England), January 1850

It is no light thing to have secured a livelihood on condition of going through life masked and gagged.

> JOHN MORLEY (1838–1923). *On Compromise,* 3, 1877

America has entered the age of the contingent or temporary worker, of the consultant and subcontractor, of the just-in-time work force—fluid, flexible, disposable. This is the future. Its message is this: You are on your own. For good (sometimes) and ill (often), the workers of the future will constantly have to sell their skills, invent new relationships with employers who must, themselves, change and adapt constantly in order to survive in a ruthless global market.

This is the new metaphysics of work. Companies are portable, workers are throwaway.

> LANCE MORROW (1939–). "The Temping of America," *Time,* 29 March 1993

Work expands so as to fill the time available for its completion.

> C. NORTHCOTE PARKINSON (1909–1993). "Parkinson's Law," *Parkinson's Law and Other Studies in Administration,* 1, 1957

The thing to do when working on a motorcycle, as in any other task, is to cultivate the peace of mind, which does not separate one's self from one's surroundings. When that is done successfully, then everything else follows naturally. Peace of mind produces right values, right values produce right thoughts. Right thoughts produce right actions and right actions produce work which will be a material reflection for others to see of the serenity at the center of it all.

> ROBERT M. PIRSIG (1928–). *Zen and the Art of Motorcycle Maintenance: An Inquiry into Values,* 25, 1974
>
> See Motorcycles: Pirsig

Working is so satisfying that if we didn't have to work to eat, we'd have to invent some other reason for doing it.

> ANDREW S. ROONEY (1919–). "When Tennis Balls Once Were White," *San Francisco Sunday Examiner & Chronicle,* 25 May 1987

In order that people may be happy in their work, these three things are needed: they must be fit for it; they must not do too much of it; and they must have a sense of success in it—not a doubtful sense, such as needs some testimony of other people for its confirmation, but a sure sense, or rather knowledge, that so much work has been done well, and fruitfully done, whatever the world may say or think about it.

> JOHN RUSKIN (1819–1900). *Pre-Raphaelitism* (pamphlet), 1851

If wars are eliminated and production is organized scientifically, it is probable that four hours' work a day will suffice to keep everybody in comfort.

> BERTRAND RUSSELL (1872–1970). *Sceptical Essays,* 17.4, 1928

Work . . . is desirable, first and foremost, as a preventive of boredom. . . . It [also] makes holidays much more delicious when they come.

> BERTRAND RUSSELL (1872–1970). *The Conquest of Happiness,* 14, 1930

Work is of two kinds: first, altering the position of matter at or near the earth's surface relatively to other such matter; second, telling other people to do so. The first kind is unpleasant and ill paid; the second is pleasant and highly paid.

> BERTRAND RUSSELL (1872–1970). Title essay, 1932, *In Praise of Idleness and Other Essays,* 1986

It's not work, if you love what you're doing.

> STEVE SEARS (1941–1996). Personal communication, 8 October 1988

Labor is required for physical, and leisure for moral improvement. . . . A state which should combine the advantages of both would be subjected to the evils of neither.

> PERCY BYSSHE SHELLEY (1792–1822). "Notes" (5.63), *Queen Mab: A Philosophical Poem: With Notes,* 1813

The man whose whole life is spent in performing a few simple operations, of which the effects too are, perhaps, always the same, or very nearly the same, has no occasion to exert his understanding or to exercise his invention in finding out expedients for removing difficulties which never occur. He naturally loses, therefore, the habit of such exertion, and generally becomes as stupid and ignorant as it is possible for a human creature to become.

> ADAM SMITH (1723–1790). *The Wealth of Nations,* 5.1.3.2, 1776

Good for the body is the work of the body, good for the soul the work of the soul, and good for either the work of the other.

> HENRY DAVID THOREAU (1817–1862). Journal, 23 January 1841

For more than five years I maintained myself . . . solely by the labor of my hands, and I found, that by working about six weeks in a year, I could meet all the expenses of living.

> HENRY DAVID THOREAU (1817–1862). "Economy," *Walden; or Life in the Woods,* 1854

In proportion as the principle of the division of labor is more extensively applied, the workman becomes more weak, more narrow-minded, and more dependent. The art advances, the artisan recedes.

> ALEXIS DE TOCQUEVILLE (1805–1859). *Democracy in America,* 2.2.20, 1840, tr. Henry Reeve and Francis Bowen, 1862

Physical labor not only does not exclude the possibility of mental activity, but improves and stimulates it.

> LEO TOLSTOY (1828–1910). *What Then Must We Do?* 38, 1886

It ought to be made possible for everyone to earn his living by doing work that is of intrinsic value and that is felt to be such by the worker himself. At present, most people do their work in order to earn the maximum remuneration and not for the sake of the value of the work itself. The profit motive ought no longer to be given top priority. But this most desirable change of motivation can be brought about only by a change of heart.

> ARNOLD J. TOYNBEE (1889–1975). *The Toynbee-Ikeda Dialogue: Man Himself Must Choose,* 5, 1976

Work keeps at bay three great evils: boredom, vice, and need.

> VOLTAIRE (1694–1778). *Candide,* 30, 1759, tr. Richard Aldington, 1929

Article XXIX: Every adult who needs it shall be given meaningful work to do, at a living wage.

> KURT VONNEGUT (1922–). A proposed Constitutional amendment, *Timequake,* 45, 1997

There is as much dignity in tilling a field as in writing a poem.

> BOOKER T. WASHINGTON (1856–1915). Atlanta Exposition address, 18 September 1895, *Up from Slavery: An Autobiography,* 14, 1901

My observation on every employment in life is that wherever and whenever one person is found adequate to the discharge of a duty by close application thereto, it is worse executed by two persons, and scarcely done at all if three or more are employed therein.

> GEORGE WASHINGTON (1732–1799). Letter to Secretary of War Henry Knox, 24 September 1792

Eight people will do ten people's work better than twelve people.

> JACK W. WHITEMAN. "Whiteman's Finding: First Corollary to Parkinson's Law." In Paul Dickson, comp., *The Official Explanations,* p. 233, 1980

❧

Much of the world's work is done by men who do not feel quite well.

> ANONYMOUS. In John Kenneth Galbraith, *The Age of Uncertainty,* 3, 1977

Work is the price you pay for money.

> ANONYMOUS

Commit your work to the Lord,
  and your plans will be established.

> SAYING (*BIBLE*). Proverbs 16:3

Work makes free. [Arbeit macht frei.]

> SAYING (GERMAN). Inscription on the main gate at Auschwitz, 1940s

WORLD

See also • Earth ○ Epitaphs: Robert Frost ○ Evolution ○ God & History ○ God & the World ○ Heaven ○ History ○ Internationalism ○ Man ○ Nature ○ Optimist—Examples: Benjamin Franklin ○ Progress ○ Unity ○ Universe

A miscalculation? The world?

> ELIAS CANETTI (1905–1994). 1985, *The Secret Heart of the Clock: Notes, Aphorisms, Fragments: 1973–1985,* tr. Joel Agee, 1989

This world, after all our science and sciences, is still a miracle; wonderful, inscrutable, *magical* and more, to whosoever will *think* of it.

> THOMAS CARLYLE (1795–1881). "The Hero as Divinity," *On Heroes, Hero-Worship, and the Heroic in History,* 1841

The world may turn topsy-turvy in an hour.

> JOHN CLARKE (1596–1658). Comp., *Proverbs: English and Latine,* p. 124, 1639

This world is not Conclusion.
A Species stands beyond—
Invisible, as Music—
But positive, as Sound—
It beckons, and it baffles—
Philosophy—don't know—
And through a Riddle, at the last—
Sagacity, must go—
To guess it, puzzles scholars—
To gain it, Men have borne
Contempt of Generations
And Crucifixion, shown.

> EMILY DICKINSON (1830–1886). "This world is not Conclusion," 1862?

This is the way the world ends
Not with a bang but a whimper.

> T. S. ELIOT (1888–1965). Closing lines, *The Hollow Men,* 1925

He that succeeds in the world loves it. He that fails in it hates it.

> RALPH WALDO EMERSON (1803–1882). Journal, 17 January 1831

This world—this shadow of the soul, or *other me*—lies wide around. Its attractions are the keys which unlock my thought and make me acquainted with myself.

> RALPH WALDO EMERSON (1803–1882). "The American Scholar," address, Harvard University, Cambridge (Massachusetts), 31 August 1837

The world [is] the mirror of the soul.

> RALPH WALDO EMERSON (1803–1882). "The Divinity School Address," Cambridge (Massachusetts), 15 July 1838

The world globes itself in a drop of dew.

> RALPH WALDO EMERSON (1803–1882). "Compensation," *Essays: First Series,* 1841

The world is all gates, all opportunities, strings of tension waiting to be struck.

> RALPH WALDO EMERSON (1803–1882). "Resources," *Letters and Social Aims,* 1876

What's wrong with this world is, it's not finished yet. It is not completed to that point where man can put his final signature to the job and say, "It is finished. We made it, and it works."

Because only man can complete it. Not God, but man. It is man's high destiny and proof of his immortality too, that his is the choice between ending the world, effacing it from the long annals of time and space, and completing it.

> WILLIAM FAULKNER (1897–1962). Opening words, "Faith or Fear," *Atlantic,* August 1953

The world is a beautiful place
  to be born into
if you don't mind some people dying
  all the time
or maybe only starving
  some of the time
which isn't half so bad
  if it isn't you.

> LAWRENCE FERLINGHETTI (1919–). "Pictures of the Gone World" (11), 1955, *A Coney Island of the Mind,* 1958

I believe that there are not two separate worlds, the spiritual and the material. . . . They are two aspects of one and the same universe.

> ANDRÉ GIDE (1869–1951). Journal, 15 May 1949, tr. Justin O'Brien, 1951
> See Universe: Hakuin

The world as you have known it never existed.

> MAL HANCOCK. Cartoon caption, Mal, San Francisco Sunday Examiner & Chronicle, 25 October 1922

Robert Jordan: I have fought for what I believed in for a year now. If we win here, we will win everywhere. The world is a fine place and worth fighting for, and I hate very much to leave it.

> ERNEST HEMINGWAY (1899–1961). *For Whom the Bell Tolls,* 43, 1940. Jordan, the novel's hero, had joined the Republican army during the Spanish Civil War. Facing imminent death, he had this thought as he lay wounded and alone covering his comrades' retreat.

In moments of sensing the ineffable, we are as certain of the value of the world as we are of its existence. There must be a value which was worth the world's coming into being.

> ABRAHAM JOSHUA HESCHEL (1907–1972). *Man Is Not Alone: A Philosophy of Religion,* 3, 1951

Mankind's common instinct for reality . . . has always held the world to be essentially a theater for heroism.

> WILLIAM JAMES (1842–1910). *The Varieties of Religious Experience: A Study in Human Nature,* 14 and 15, 1902

The world hangs on a thin thread, and that thread is the psyche of man.

> CARL G. JUNG (1875–1961). Quoted by Tom Dozier, *Houston Post,* 16 September 1957. In Richard I. Evans, prologue to *Conversations with Carl Jung, and Reactions from Ernest Jones,* 1964

Call the world, if you Please, "The vale of Soul-making."

> JOHN KEATS (1795–1821). Letter to George and Georgiana Keats, 21 April 1819

This great machine of the world.

> JOHN LOCKE (1632–1704). "Study." In Lord King, *The Life of John Locke,* 1.198, 1830

The world is fleeting; all things pass away;
Or is it we that pass and they that stay.

> LUCIAN (A.D. 120?–180?). Greek satirist

The world's an orphan's home.

> MARIANNE MOORE (1887–1972). In Anne Lamott, *Bird by Bird: Some Instructions on Writing and Life,* 4 ("Giving"), 1995

This world is a prison for the Faithful, but a Paradise for unbelievers.

> MUHAMMAD (A.D. 570?–632). *The Sayings of Muhammad,* 434, tr. Abdullah Al-Suhrawardy, 1941

The world [is] a work of art that gives birth to itself.

> FRIEDRICH NIETZSCHE (1844–1900). *The Will to Power* (notebooks, 1883–1888), 796, 1911, tr. Walter Kaufmann and R. J. Hollingdale, 1967

O what a crocodilian world is this!

> FRANCIS QUARLES (1592–1644). *Emblems,* 1.4, 1635

The world is a perpetual caricature of itself; at every moment it is the mockery and the contradiction of what it is pretending to be.

> GEORGE SANTAYANA (1863–1952). "Dickens," *Soliloquies in England and Later Soliloquies,* 1922

The world is a ghastly drama of will-to-live divided against itself.

> ALBERT SCHWEITZER (1975–1965). *The Philosophy of Civilization: Civilization and Ethics,* 21, 1923, tr. C. T. Campion and Mrs. Charles E. B. Russell, 1946

Jaques: All the world's a stage,
And all the men and women merely players.

> SHAKESPEARE (1564–1616). *As You Like It,* 2.7.139, 1599

Miranda: How beauteous mankind is! O brave new world,
That has such people in't!

> SHAKESPEARE (1564–1616). *The Tempest,* 5.1.184, 1611

We read the world wrong and say that it deceives us.

> RABINDRANATH TAGORE (1861–1941). *Stray Birds,* 75, 1914

This world is thy inn; the World-to-Come is thy home.

> TALMUD (A.D. 1st–6th cent.). Rabbinical writings. In Louis I. Newman, comp., *The Talmudic Anthology,* 354, 1945

The world is like a ladder—some ascend and some descend.

> TALMUD (A.D. 1st–6th cent.). Rabbinical writings. In Louis I. Newman, comp., *The Talmudic Anthology,* 408, 1945

So many worlds, so much to do,
So little done, such things to be.

> ALFRED, LORD TENNYSON (1809–1892). *In Memoriam A. H. H.,* 73, 1850

The world is a looking glass, and gives back to every man the reflection of his own face. Frown at it, and it will in turn look sourly upon you; laugh at it and with it, and it is a jolly kind companion.

> WILLIAM MAKEPEACE THACKERAY (1811–1863). *Vanity Fair: A Novel Without a Hero,* 2, 1847-1848

This world is but canvas to our imaginations.

> HENRY DAVID THOREAU (1817–1862). "Wednesday," *A Week on the Concord and Merrimack Rivers,* 1849

We are ever dying to one world and being born into another.

> HENRY DAVID THOREAU (1817–1862). Journal, 1850, undated

The physical world is spirit seen from without, and the spirit is world viewed from within.

> LAURENS van der POST (1906–1996). "The Man and the Place," *Jung and the Story of Our Time,* 1975

This world is a comedy to those that think, a tragedy to those that feel.

> HORACE WALPOLE (1717–1797). Letter to Anne, the Countess of Upper Ossory, 16 August 1776

I see trees of green, red roses too,
I see them bloom for me and you.
And I think to myself,
What a wonderful world.

> GEORGE DAVID WEISS (1940–) and BOB THIELE. "What a
> Wonderful World" (song), 1967, popularized by Louis "Satchmo"
> Armstrong

The world is a stage, but the play is badly cast.

> OSCAR WILDE (1854–1900). "Lord Arthur Savile's Crime," 1887,
> *Lord Arthur Savile's Crime and Other Stories*, 1891

In the very world, which is the world
Of all of us—the place where, in the end
We find our happiness, or not at all!

> WILLIAM WORDSWORTH (1770–1850). *The Prelude; or, Growth of a
> Poet's Mind; An Autobiographical Poem*, 11.142, 1850

The world's a prophecy of worlds to come.

> EDWARD YOUNG (1683–1765). *The Complaint: or, Night Thoughts
> on Life, Death, and Immortality*, 7.16, 1742-1745

❧

That this world, under God, shall have a new birth of freedom.

> ANONYMOUS (AMERICAN). Inscription on the Liberty Bell in West
> Berlin's Schöneberg City Hall, 1950. The bell was a gift from the
> American people soon after the Soviet Union lifted its 15-month block-
> ade of the city.
>
> See Civil War: Abraham Lincoln (5)

To know the world, first know yourself. To change the world, first change yourself.

> ANONYMOUS

WORLD WAR I

See also • Germany: Sir Eric Geddes ○ International Relations ○ War

We were confronting the alternatives of a domestic crash and a foreign war, when we entered the war.

> CHARLES A. BEARD (1874–1948). Historian. On World War I. In George
> Seldes, *One Thousand Americans*, 7, 1947

Over there, over there,
Send the word, send the word, over there,
That the Yanks are coming, the Yanks are coming . . .
And we won't be back till it's over, over there.

> GEORGE M. COHAN (1878–1942). "Over There" (song), 1917

Come on, you sons of bitches! Do you want to live forever?

> DAN DALY. Marine sergeant. To his platoon during the Battle of Belleau
> Wood (France), June 1918. In Robert T. Cochran, "Smedly Butler:
> A Pint-Size Marine for All Seasons," *Smithsonian*, June 1984
>
> See Soldiers: Frederick II (2)

Between [the invading Germans] and me there is now a bloody iron curtain which has descended forever!

> ELIZABETH (1903–?). Bavarian-born Belgian queen. Following the out-
> break of World War I, 1914
>
> See Cold War: Winston Churchill

My center is giving way, my right falling back; the situation excellent. I shall attack.

> FERDINAND FOCH (1851–1929). French general. Message during the
> First Battle of the Marne (France), 6–9 September 1914. In Raymond
> Recouly, *Foch: The Winner of the War*, 5, 1919, tr. Mary Cadwalader
> Jones, 1920
>
> See Strategy, Military: Robert E. Lee

The lamps are going out all over Europe: we shall not see them lit again in our lifetime.

> SIR EDWARD GREY (1862–1933). British foreign secretary. 3? August
> 1914

To me those hours seemed like a release from the painful feelings of my youth. Even today I am not ashamed to say that, overpowered by stormy enthusiasm, I fell down on my knees and thanked Heaven from an overflowing heart for granting me the good fortune of being permitted to live at this time.

> ADOLF HITLER (1889–1945). Recalling his reaction to the news that
> World War I had started (he enlisted soon afterwards), *Mein Kampf*,
> 1.5, 1924, tr. Ralph Manheim, 1943

The trenches were the concentration camps of the First World War.

> ROBERT KEE (1919–). In John Keegan, *The Face of Battle*,
> 4 ("The View from Across No-man's-land"), 1976

The war of 1914–1918 was imperialist (that is, an annexationist, predatory, war of plunder) on the part of both sides; it was a war for the division of the world, for the partition and repartition of colonies and spheres of influence of finance capital, etc.

> LENIN (1870–1924). Preface (6 July 1920) to *Imperialism: The Highest
> Stage of Capitalism*, 1917, International Publishers edition, 1971

This war, like the next war, is a war to end war.

> DAVID LLOYD GEORGE (1863–1945). British prime minister. Attributed.
> 1918?

Stranger! Tell the people of Spoon River two things:
First that we lie here, obeying their words;
And next that had we known what was back of their words
We should not be lying here!

> EDGAR LEE MASTERS (1869–1950). "Unknown Soldiers" (complete
> poem), *The New Spoon River*, 1924

We are the Dead. Short days ago
We lived, felt dawn, saw sunset glow,
Loved and were loved, and now we lie
In Flanders fields.

> JOHN McCREA (1872–1918). Canadian medical officer. "In Flanders
> Fields," April 1915. McCrea, who was fatally wounded in 1918, wrote
> the poem soon after the Second Battle of Ypres (France); it was pub-
> lished anonymously in *Punch*, 8 December 1915.

All over Europe, young men went to war just as they would go on an unexpected holiday, delighted to escape the daily boredom of their clerking. It was the upheaval of the masses against the bastilles of technological society. Ironically, that revolt was masterminded by the very lords of the bastilles.

> JAMES H. MEISEL (1966–). Referring to World War I, "Conclusions:
> A Surfeit of Answers," *Counter-Revolution: How Revolutions Die*, 1966

They shall not pass!

> ROBERT-GEORGES NIVELLE (1857–1924). French general. Battle of Verdun (France), February 1916

I was in the library in 1915, studying a Latin poet, and all of a sudden I thought: "War can't be this bad." So I walked out and enlisted.

> LESTER B. PEARSON (1897–1972). Canadian prime minister. In John Robinson Beal, *The Pearson Phenomenon*, 2, 1964

All Quiet on the Western Front.

> ERICH MARIA REMARQUE (1898–1970). Book title, 1929

Germany has reduced savagery to a science, and this great war for the victorious peace of justice must go on until the German cancer is cut clean out of the world body.

> THEODORE ROOSEVELT (1858–1919). Speech, Johnstown (Pennsylvania), 30 September 1917

I spent the evening of August 4 [1914] walking round the streets, especially in the neighborhood of Trafalgar Square, noticing cheering crowds, and making myself sensitive to the emotions of passersby. During this and the following days I discovered to my amazement that average men and women were delighted at the prospect of war. I had fondly imagined, what most Pacifists contended, that wars were forced upon a reluctant population by despotic and Machiavellian governments.

> BERTRAND RUSSELL (1872–1970). "Experiences of a Pacifist in the First World War," *Portraits from Memory, and Other Essays*, 1956
>
> See War & Psychology: Russell (3)

In 1914, in my fifty-ninth year, I was astonished and scandalized to find traces of war excitement still stirring in me.

> GEORGE BERNARD SHAW (1856–1950). *Everybody's Political What's What?* 1944

When at last it was over, the war had many diverse results and one dominant one transcending all others: disillusion.

> BARBARA TUCHMAN (1912–1989). On World War I, "Afterword," *The Guns of August*, 1962

In the first five months [of World War I], one out of every 10 British soldiers died; cats nested in corpses; German prisoners carrying bayonets with serrated edges could expect no quarter; and Field Marshal [Douglas] Haig, preparing for the Somme, wrote, "I feel that every step in my plan has been taken with Divine help."

> PETER VANSITTART. "Discipline by Firing Squad," *New York Times Book Review*, 15 July 1984

The War That Will End War.

> H. G. WELLS (1866–1946). Book title, 1914

My soul is torn asunder, but everything must be put to fire and blood. The throats of men and women, children and the aged must be cut and not a tree nor a house left standing. With such methods of terror, which alone can impress so degenerate a people as the French, the war will finish before two months, while if I use humanitarian methods, it may endure for years. Despite all my repugnance, I have had to choose the first system.

WILHELM II (1859–1941). German kaiser. Letter to his ally Franz Josef, the Austrian emperor, soon after the outbreak of World War I, August 1914

> See War: Karl von Clausewitz (2)

You will be home before the leaves have fallen from the trees.

> WILHELM II (1859–1941). German kaiser. Speech to troops leaving for the front at the beginning of World War I (1914–1918), August 1914. In Barbara Tuchman, *The Guns of August*, 9, 1962
>
> See Korean War: Douglas MacArthur (2)

The world must be made safe for democracy. Its peace must be planted upon the tested foundations of political liberty. We have no selfish ends to serve. We desire no conquest, no dominion. We seek no indemnities for ourselves, no material compensation for the sacrifices we shall freely make.

> WOODROW WILSON (1856–1924). Message to Congress asking for a declaration of war against Germany, 2 April 1917

Think what it was they were applauding! My message today was a message of death to our young men.

> WOODROW WILSON (1856–1924). Remark to Joseph Tumulty on Pres. Wilson's message to Congress asking for a declaration of war against Germany, 2 April 1917
>
> See War & Psychology: Bertrand Russell (3)

This is the culminating and final war for human liberty.

> WOODROW WILSON (1856–1924). Referring to World War I, message to Congress, 8 January 1918

❦

Every man becomes civilized between the ages of eighteen and twenty-five. If he does not go through a civilizing experience at that time in his life, he will not go not be a civilized man. And the men who went to war at eighteen missed the period of civilizing, and they could never be civilized. They were a lost generation. Naturally if they are at war, they do not have the influences of women, of parents, and of preparation.

> ANONYMOUS (FRENCH). A hotel keeper (Hotel Pernollet). Referring to World War I veterans. In Gertrude Stein, *Everybody's Autobiography*, 2, 1937

Your King and Country need you.

> SLOGAN (ENGLISH). Recruiting poster, 1914

WORLD WAR II

See also • Commanders ○ Defeat: Winston Churchill ○ England: Winston Churchill ○ Freedom: Franklin D. Roosevelt (2) ○ Holocaust ○ Intelligence, Military: Roberta Wohlstetter (1,2) ○ International Relations ○ Nuclear Weapons ○ War

They've got us surrounded again, the poor bastards!

> CREIGHTON ABRAMS (1914–1974). Colonel and later commander of U.S. forces in Vietnam. While leading a tank breakthru to beleaguered American forces in Bastogne (France) during the Battle of the Bulge, December 1944

This is the army, Mr. Jones,
No private baths or telephones.

> IRVING BERLIN (1888–1989). "This Is the Army" (song), 1942

Stalin's hostility toward the Anglo-American bloc derived, in part, from his conviction that the western powers had deliberately contrived to let Russia and German fight each other into exhaustion and thereby establish world hegemony for capitalism; the war had been won, so it was said, with "British brains, American brawn and Russian blood."

> ANTHONY CAVE BROWN (1930–). Epilogue to *Bodyguard of Lies,* 1975

How horrible, fantastic, incredible it is that we should be digging trenches and trying on gas masks here because of a quarrel in a far away country [Czechoslovakia] between people of whom we know nothing.

> NEVILLE CHAMBERLAIN (1869–1940). British prime minister. Shortly before signing the Munich Pact which in effect ceded Czechoslovakia to Germany, radio broadcast, BBC, London, 27 September 1938

My good friends, this is the second time in our history that there has come back from Germany to Downing Street peace with honor. I believe it is peace for our time. I thank you from the bottom of our hearts. And now I recommend you to go home and sleep quietly in your beds.

> NEVILLE CHAMBERLAIN (1869–1940). British prime minister. Speech at 10 Downing Street before a jubilant London crowd after returning from the Munich Conference with Adolf Hitler and Édouard Daladier, 30 September 1938
>
> See Peace: Benjamin Disraeli

I have nothing to offer but blood, toil, tears, and sweat.

> WINSTON CHURCHILL (1874–1965). House of Commons speech (his first after becoming prime minister), 13 May 1940 (Popular version: I have nothing to offer but blood, sweat, and tears.) Earlier Churchill had written of Russia's soldiers during World War I, "Their sweat, their tears, their blood bedewed the endless plain." (*The Unknown War,* 1, 1931)
>
> See Real Estate: Lord Byron ○ Tears: John Donne

You ask, what is our aim? I can answer in one word: Victory—victory at all costs, victory in spite of all terror, victory however long and hard the road may be; for without victory there is no survival.

> WINSTON CHURCHILL (1874–1965). House of Commons speech, 13 May 1940

We must be very careful not to assign to this deliverance attributes of a victory. Wars are not won by evacuations.

> WINSTON CHURCHILL (1874–1965). Referring to the successful evacuation of 300,000 Allied soldiers from Dunkirk during the Battle of France, House of Commons speech, 4 June 1940

We shall defend our island, whatever the cost may be. We shall fight on the beaches, we shall fight on the landing grounds, we shall fight in the fields and in the streets, we shall fight in the hills; we shall never surrender.

> WINSTON CHURCHILL (1874–1965). At Britain's darkest moment in the war (after the evacuation at Dunkirk), House of Commons speech, 4 June 1940

The gratitude of every home in our Island, in our Empire, and indeed throughout the world, except in the abodes of the guilty, goes out to the British airmen who, undaunted by odds, unwearied in their constant challenge and mortal danger, are turning the tide of the World War by their prowess and devotion. Never in the field of human conflict was so much owed by so many to so few.

> WINSTON CHURCHILL (1874–1965). Referring to Royal Air Force pilots during the Battle of Britain, House of Commons speech, 20 August 1940
>
> See Manipulation: Aldous Huxley (1)

[In 1940] when I warned [the Vichy government in France] that Britain would fight on alone whatever they did, their generals told their Prime Minister and his divided Cabinet, "In three weeks England will have her neck wrung like a chicken." Some chicken! Some neck!

> WINSTON CHURCHILL (1874–1965). Canadian Parliament speech, Ottawa, 30 December 1941

In War: Resolution
In Defeat: Defiance
In Victory: Magnanimity
In Peace: Good Will

> WINSTON CHURCHILL (1874–1965). "Moral of the Work," epigraph, *The Second World War: The Gathering Storm,* 1948. Responding to a request, Churchill had proposed the same words for an inscription on a World War I monument in France but was turned down. (In Churchill, *My Early Life: A Roving Commission,* 26, 1930)

The few Japanese they found were diseased and crippled wretches by the trail-side and were bayoneted by Marines, furnishing a grim line for Puller's later report on the action: "The pig-sticking was fine."

> BURKE DAVIS. Describing a patrol in New Guinea, February 1943, *Marine! The Life of Lt. Gen. Lewis B. (Chesty) Puller, USMC (Ret.),* 12, 1962

Our landings . . . have failed to gain a satisfactory foothold and I have withdrawn the troops. . . . If any blame or fault attaches to the attempt, it is mine alone.

> DWIGHT D. EISENHOWER (1890–1969). From a statement he, as Supreme Allied Commander, planned to issue if the D-Day invasion scheduled for the next day had failed (penciled onto a notebook page), 5 June 1944. In Paul Fussell, "How the Leaders Led," *Newsweek,* 23 May 1994

The battlefield at Falaise [France] was unquestionably one of the greatest "killing grounds" of any of the war areas. . . . Forty-eight hours after the closing of the gap I was conducted through it on foot, to encounter scenes that could be described only by Dante. It was literally possible to walk for hundreds of yards at a time, stepping on nothing but dead and decaying flesh.

> DWIGHT D. EISENHOWER (1890–1969). August 1944, *Crusade in Europe,* 15, 1949

A Japanese attack on Pearl Harbor is a strategic impossibility.

> GEORGE FIELDING ELIOT (1894–1971). "The Impossible War with Japan," *American Mercury,* September 1938

Before that day was over I was sprayed with the contents of a soldier's torso when I was lying behind him and he knelt to fire at a machine gun holding us up: he was struck in the heart, and out of the holes in the back of his field jacket flew little clouds of tissue, blood, and powdered cloth.

> PAUL FUSSELL (1924–). While serving as a platoon leader in the 103rd Infantry Division in France near the German border, 15 March 1945, "My War," *The Boy Scout Handbook and Other Observations,* 1982

No enemy bomber can reach the Ruhr. If one reaches the Ruhr, my name is not Goering. You can call me Meyer.

> HERMANN GOERING (1893–1946). German air minister. Remark, 1938

The Third Fleet's sunken and damaged ships have been salvaged and are retiring at high speed toward the enemy.

> WILLIAM F. "BULL" HALSEY, JR. (1882–1959). Admiral. After hearing claims during the Battle of Leyte Gulf (Philippines) that the Japanese had virtually annihilated his fleet, report to headquarters, 14 October 1944. In E. B. Potter, *Bull Halsey,* 17, 1985

We have only to kick in the door, and the whole rotten structure will come crashing down.

> ADOLF HITLER (1889–1945). After deciding to invade the Soviet Union, remark to Gen. Alfred Jodl, April 1941. In Alan Bullock, *Hitler: A Study in Tyranny,* rev. ed., 12.1, 1960 (1953)

The last great decisive battle of this year will mean the annihilation of [the Soviet Union]. . . . The enemy is already beaten and will never be in a position to rise again.

> ADOLF HITLER (1889–1945). Four months after invading the Soviet Union and two months before the German defeat at the Battle of Moscow, radio broadcast, 3 October 1941

I've always detested snow. Bormann, you know, I've always hated it. Now I know why. It was a presentiment.

> ADOLF HITLER (1889–1945). Following his army's defeat at the gates of Moscow by Soviet forces (and the Russian winter), remark to Martin Bormann, one of his top aides, 19 February 1942, *Hitler's Secret Conversations, 1941–1944,* tr. Norman Cameron and R. H. Stevens, 1953

I came through and I shall return.

> DOUGLAS MacARTHUR (1880–1964). On arriving in Australia from Corregidor Island in the Philippines, 17 March 1942, *Reminiscences,* 5, 1964. After landing on Leyte Island, 20 October 1944, Gen. MacArthur said in a radio broadcast, "People of the Philippines: I have returned. By the grace of Almighty God, our forces stand again on Philippine soil—soil consecrated in the blood of our two peoples. . . . The hour of your redemption is here." (In *Reminiscences,* 6)

I feel like a fugitive from th' law of averages.

> BILL MAULDIN (1921–). One front-line soldier to another during a bombardment, cartoon caption, *Up Front: Text and Pictures,* p. 38, 1945

Nuts!

> ANTHONY McAULIFFE (1898–1975). Responding to a surrender demand after his unit was surrounded by German forces at Bastogne (France) during the Battle of the Bulge, 22 December 1944. Gen. McAuliffe recounted the incident in a BBC broadcast on 3 January 1945: "When we got the [surrender demand], we thought it was the funniest thing we ever heard. I just laughed and said, 'Nuts,' but the German major who brought it wanted a formal answer. So I decided well, I'd just say 'Nuts.' So I had it written out, 'Quote, to the German commander: Nuts. Signed, the American commander, unquote.'"

Bill Moyers: What happened to a man who was hit by one of those shells or who was near one of those shells?
Morgan: Completely disintegrated if he was hit within a few yards of him [*sic*]. These are what missing-in-action means, means there's not enough to find to bury you really.

> LOREN MORGAN. Army surgeon. In *From D-Day to the Rhine with Bill Moyers,* television documentary, PBS, 1 March 1990

War is like a giant pack rat. It takes something from you, and it leaves something behind in its stead. It burned me out in some ways, so that now I feel like an old man, but still sometimes act like a dumb kid. It made me grow up too fast.

> AUDIE MURPHY (1924–1971). America's most decorated World War II hero. In *New York Journal-American,* 30 August 1955

Among the men who fought on Iwo Jima, uncommon valor was a common virtue.

> CHESTER W. NIMITZ (1885–1966). Pacific Fleet commander. Communiqué, March 1945

Now, I want you to remember that no son of a bitch ever won a war by dying for his country. He won it by making the other poor son of a bitch die for his country.

> GEORGE S. PATTON, JR. (1885–1945). 1943. In James M. Gavin, "Two Fighting Generals: Patton and MacArthur," *Atlantic,* June 1965

A clear cold Christmas, lovely weather for killing Germans, which seems a bit queer, seeing Whose birthday it is.

> GEORGE S. PATTON, JR. (1885–1945). During the Battle of the Bulge (France), diary, 25 December 1944. In Martin Blumenson, *The Patton Papers, 1940–1945,* 33, 1974

And while I am talking to you mothers and fathers, I give you one more assurance. I have said this before, but I shall say it again and again and again: Your boys are not going to be sent into any foreign wars.

> FRANKLIN D. ROOSEVELT (1882–1945). Campaign speech, Boston, 30 October 1940

Yesterday, December 7, 1941—a date which will live in infamy—the United States of America was suddenly and deliberately attacked by naval and air forces of the Empire of Japan.

> FRANKLIN D. ROOSEVELT (1882–1945). Referring to Pearl Harbor, war message to Congress, 8 December 1941

I can handle that old buzzard.

> FRANKLIN D. ROOSEVELT (1882–1945). Referring to Joseph Stalin before their first meeting at the Teheran Conference (Iran), 28 November 1943. In Thomas A. Bailey, *Presidential Greatness: The Image and the Man from George Washington to the Present,* 12, 1966

The question was how we should maneuver [the Japanese] into the position of firing the first shot without allowing too much danger to ourselves.

> HENRY L. STIMSON (1867–1930). Secretary of war. Diary, 25 November 1941

Two kinds of people are staying on this beach, the dead and those who are going to die.

> GEORGE TAYLOR. Army colonel. Urging and leading his troops forward from the midst of the carnage on Omaha Beach in Normandy (France) during the D-Day invasion, 6 June 1944. In Paul Fussell, "How the Leaders Led," *Newsweek,* 23 May 1994

An American staggered and crumpled to the road. A guard kept kicking him in the ribs. The American tried painfully to rise and extended a pleading hand to the Japanese. The guard deliberately placed the tip of his bayonet on the prisoner's neck and drove it home. He yanked it free and plunged it again into the American's body. . . .

Between 7,000 and 10,000 [Filipino and American soldiers] died on the march from malaria, starvation, beatings or execution. Of these, approximately 2,330 were Americans.

> JOHN TOLAND (1912–). Referring to the 60-mile "Bataan Death March" following the Japanese conquest of the Philippines Islands, April 1942, *The Rising Sun: The Decline and Fall of the Japanese Empire,* 11.4, 1970

If we see that Germany is winning, we ought to help Russia; and if Russia is winning, we ought to help Germany; and that way let them kill as many as possible, although I don't want to see Hitler victorious under any circumstances.

> HARRY S. TRUMAN (1884–1972). Soon after Germany's invasion of the Soviet Union in World War II, Senate speech, July 1941. In James MacGregor Burns, *Roosevelt: The Soldier of Freedom,* 3, 1970

[Ultra, code name for intelligence derived by the British Secret Service from decrypted German wireless traffic, provided] top allied commanders . . . the unique experience of knowing not only the precise composition, strength and location of the enemy's forces, but also, with few exceptions, of knowing beforehand exactly what he intended to do in the many operations and battles of World War II.

> W. WINTERBOTHAM. *The Ultra Secret,* 1, 1974. Magic, Ultra's American counterpart, played an equally important role in the Pacific war, most notably in May 1942 at the Battle of Midway, where foreknowledge of enemy plans enabled an American naval force to decisively defeat a much stronger Japanese fleet.

I fear we have only awakened a sleeping giant, and his reaction will be terrible.

> ISOROKU YAMAMOTO (1884–1943). Japanese admiral. Referring to the Pearl Harbor attack which he had helped plan, December 1941. In A. J. P. Taylor, *Listener* (British magazine), 9 September 1976

❧

And when he goes to heaven
To Saint Peter he will tell,
Another Marine reporting, sir;
I've served my time in hell.

> ANONYMOUS (AMERICAN). Epitaph on the grave marking of Marine Private First Class Cameron, Guadalcanal, 1942

We sure liberated the hell out of this place.

> ANONYMOUS (AMERICAN). Soldier in the ruins of a Normandy village (France), 1944. In Max Miller, *The Far Shore: With Official U.S. Navy and Coast Guard Photographs,* 1945
>
> See Vietnam War: Anonymous (American) (1)

They're overpaid, overfed, oversexed and over here.

> ANONYMOUS (BRITISH). On American GIs stationed in England during World War II

[Two British soldiers carrying a wounded comrade on a stretcher were returning to their lines in Burma] when they heard a rustling

in the bushes and the click of a rifle-bolt. Out into their path stepped a 6-ft. Japanese with his rifle at the ready. He looked at [them] and then without a word or gesture dropped the muzzle of his rifle and stepped back into the jungle.

> ANONYMOUS (BRITISH). In *Leicester Evening Mail,* 19 May 1944. Quoted in Victor Gollancz, comp., *Man and God: Passages Chosen and Arranged to Express a Mood About the Human and Divine,* 3.10, 1951

These endured all and gave all that justice among nations might prevail and that mankind might enjoy freedom and inherit peace.

> ANONYMOUS. Normandy Chapel inscription, France. In American Battle Monuments Commission, *Normandy American Cemetery and Memorial,* p. 16, 1975

WORRY

See also • Anxiety ○ Fear ○ Optimism—Examples: George Asaf, Dorothy Field

It helps to write down half a dozen things which are worrying me. Two of them, say, disappear; about two nothing can be done, so it's no use worrying; and two perhaps can be settled.

> WINSTON CHURCHILL (1874–1965). Remark to the diarist, 14 August 1944. In Lord Moran, *Churchill: Taken from the Diaries of Lord Moran,* 19, 1966

But Jesus, when you don't have any money, the problem is food. When you have money, it's sex. When you have both, it's health you worry about, getting ruptured or something. If everything is simply jake, then you're frightened of death.

> J. P. DONLEAVY (1926–). *The Ginger Man,* 5, 1955

The reason why worry kills more people than work is that more people worry than work.

> ROBERT FROST (1874–1963)

Worry is interest paid on trouble before it falls due.

> DEAN WILLIAM RALPH INGE (1860–1954). In *Observer* (British newspaper), 14 February 1932

How much pain have cost us the evils which have never happened.

> THOMAS JEFFERSON (1743–1826). "A Decalogue of Canons for Observation in Practical Life," #8, letter to Thomas Jefferson Smith, 21 February 1825

Sorrow is soon enough when it comes.

> JAMES KELLY (18th cent.). Comp., *A Complete Collection of Scottish Proverbs Explained and Made Intelligible to the English Reader,* S.48, 1721

It is not work that kills, but "worry."

> DINAH MARIE MULOCK. *Young Mrs. Jardine,* 3.9, 1879

He suffers more than is necessary, who suffers before it is necessary.

> SENECA THE YOUNGER (5? B.C.–A.D. 65). "On the Fickleness of Fortune," *Moral Letters to Lucilius,* 98.8, tr. Richard M. Gummere, 1918

Jus' live the day. Don' worry yaself.

> JOHN STEINBECK (1902–1968). *The Grapes of Wrath,* 28, 1939

We are, perhaps, uniquely among the earth's creatures, the worrying animal. We worry away our lives, fearing the future, discontent with the present, unable to take in the idea of dying, unable to sit still.

> LEWIS THOMAS (1913–). "The Youngest and Brightest Thing Around," *The Medusa and the Snail: More Notes of a Biology Watcher,* 1979

☙

What? Me worry?

> ANONYMOUS (AMERICAN). The catch phrase of the goofy-looking cartoon character Alfred E. Neuman in *Mad* (magazine), 1955, adapted from an early 20th century advertising slogan

WOUNDS

See also • Misfortune: Ralph Waldo Emerson ○ Pain ○ Revenge: Francis Bacon ○ Suffering ○ Sympathy: Walt Whitman ○ Time: Saying (3)

A wound, a red badge of courage.

> STEPHEN CRANE (1871–1900). *The Red Badge of Courage,* 9, 1895

The fact remains that while slaying the giant, the wounded have to be cared for.

> DOROTHY DAY (1897–1980). In *Catholic Worker,* December 1969

A *Wounded* Deer—leaps highest.

> EMILY DICKINSON (1830–1886). "A *Wounded* Deer—leaps highest," 1860?

A voice said, Look me in the stars
And tell me truly, men of earth,
If all the soul-and-body scars
Were not too much to pay for birth.

> ROBERT FROST (1874–1963). "A Question" (complete poem), *A Witness Tree,* 1942

The wound that bleedeth inwardly is most dangerous.

> JOHN LYLY (1554?–1606). "Euphues," *Euphues: The Anatomy of Wit,* 1579

It is the insult and not the injury that makes the deeper wounds.

> H. L. MENCKEN (1880–1956). "The Politician," *Prejudices: Fourth Series,* 1924

Romeo: He jests at scars that never felt a wound.

> SHAKESPEARE (1564–1616). *Romeo and Juliet,* 2.2.1, 1594
>
> See Love, Romantic: John Caspar Lavater

Iago: What wound did ever heal but by degrees?

> SHAKESPEARE (1564–1616). *Othello,* 2.3.376, 1604

Within her breast the silent wound lives on.

> VIRGIL (70–19 B.C.). *Aeneid,* 4.67, tr. Allen Mandelbaum, 1961

If one asks him, "What are these wounds on your back?" He will say, "The wounds I received in the house of my friends."

> ZECHARIAH (6th cent. B.C.). *Zechariah* 13:6

☙

The sword wounds the body, but words wound the soul.

> SAYING (Arab)

WRETCHEDNESS

See also • Misery ○ Pain ○ Salvation: Marie von Ebner-Eschenbach ○ Unhappiness

I seemed to have nothing given me but eyes, whereby to discern my own wretchedness.

> THOMAS CARLYLE (1795–1881). *Sartor Resartus: The Life and Opinions of Herr Teufelsdröckh,* 2.7, 1835

A man must be in sympathy with society about him, or else, not wish to be in sympathy with it. If neither of these two, he must be wretched.

> RALPH WALDO EMERSON (1803–1882). Journal, 14 March 1848

None are completely wretched but those who are without hope.

> WILLIAM HAZLITT (1778–1830). *Characteristics in the Manner of Rochefoucault's Maxims,* 34, 1823

None are wretched but by their own fault.

> SAMUEL JOHNSON (1709–1784). *Rasselas: The Prince of Abyssinia,* 22, 1759

It is a kind of death to live in wretchedness.

> OVID (43 B.C.–A.D. 17?). *The Pontic Epistles,* 3.4, tr. Henry T. Riley, 1903

The wretched reflect either too much or too little.

> PUBLIUS SYRUS (85–43 B.C.). *Moral Sayings,* 225, tr. Darius Lyman, Jr., 1862

It is a consolation to the wretched to have companions in misery.

> PUBLIUS SYRUS (85–43 B.C.). *Moral Sayings,* 995, tr. Darius Lyman, Jr., 1862
>
> See Misery: Saying (English)

WRITERS

See also • Artists ○ Books ○ Creativity ○ Creativity—First Person: [especially] Stephen King ○ Critics: Examples ○ Editors ○ Historians ○ Journalists ○ Poets ○ Publishers ○ Style: [especially] Goethe, H. L. Mencken, Arthur Schopenhauer (2), George Bernard Shaw ○ Words: [especially] H. W. Fowler and F. G. Fowler ○ Writing

One writes to teach, to move or to delight.

> RODOLPHUS AGRICOLA (1444?–1485). In Ezra Pound, *ABC of Reading,* 1.8, 1934

Writers, like teeth, are divided into incisors and grinders.

> WALTER BAGEHOT (1826–1877). "The First Edinburgh Reviewers," *Estimates of Some Englishmen and Scotchmen,* 1858

The reason why so few good books are written is that so few people who can write know anything.

> WALTER BAGEHOT (1826–1877). "Shakespeare," *Literary Studies,* 1879

One writes out of one thing only—one's own experience. Everything depends on how relentlessly one forces from this experience the last drop, sweet or bitter, it can possibly give.

> JAMES BALDWIN (1924–1987). "Autobiographical Notes," 1955, *Notes of a Native Son,* 1955

When I am dead, I hope it may be said:
"His sins were scarlet, but his books were read."

> HILAIRE BELLOC (1870–1953). "On His Books," *Sonnets and Verses*, 1923

It took me fifteen years to discover that I had no talent for writing, but I couldn't give it up because by that time I was too famous.

> ROBERT BENCHLEY (1889–1945). In Nathaniel Benchley, *Robert Benchley: A Biography*, 1, 1955

Scribbler, *n.* A professional writer whose views are antagonistic to one's own.

> AMBROSE BIERCE (1842–1914). *The Devil's Dictionary*, p. 122, 1911, Dover edition, 1958

It is by sitting down to write every morning that one becomes a writer.

> GERALD BRENAN (1894–1987). "Writing," *Thoughts in a Dry Season: A Miscellany*, 1978

I never make [my books]: they grow; they come to me and insist on being written.

> SAMUEL BUTLER (1835–1902). *The Note-Books of Samuel Butler*, 7, ed. Henry Festing Jones, 1907

I have written so much about myself because I am the subject on which I am the best informed.

> SAMUEL BUTLER (1835–1902). *Further Extracts from the Note-Books of Samuel Butler*, 1, ed. A. T. Bartholomew, 1934

I do think . . . the mighty stir made about scribbling and scribes, by themselves and others—a sign of effeminacy, degeneracy, and weakness. Who would write, who had anything better to do?

> LORD BYRON (1788–1824). Journal, 24 November 1813

To withdraw *myself* from *myself* (oh that cursed selfishness) has ever been my sole, my entire, my sincere motive in scribbling at all; . . . by the action it affords to the mind, which else recoils upon itself.

> LORD BYRON (1788–1824). Journal, 27 November 1813

The nobility of our calling will always be rooted in two commitments difficult to observe: refusal to lie about what we know, and resistance to oppression.

> ALBERT CAMUS (1913–1960). Nobel Prize (in literature) acceptance address, Stockholm, 10 December 1957

We [writers] must know that we can never escape the common misery and that our only justification, if indeed there is a justification, is to speak up, insofar as we can, for those who cannot do so. But we must do so for all those who are suffering at this moment, whatever may be the glories, past or future, of the States and parties oppressing them: for the artist there are no privileged torturers.

> ALBERT CAMUS (1913–1960). "Create Dangerously" (3), 1957, *Resistance, Rebellion, and Death*, tr. Justin O'Brien, 1961

At the wishes of many people, he decided to write the same thing yet again.

> ELIAS CANETTI (1905–1994). 1968, *The Human Province*, tr. Joachim Neugroschel, 1978

There is a great discovery still to be made in literature, that of paying literary men by the quantity they *do not* write.

> THOMAS CARLYLE (1795–1881). "Memoirs of the Life of Scott," 1838, *Critical and Miscellaneous Essays*, Carey & Hart edition, 1849

The original writer is not one who imitates nobody, but one whom nobody can imitate.

> CHATEAUBRIAND (1768–1848). *Le Génie du Christianisme*, 2.1.3, 1802

That writer does the most, who gives his reader the most knowledge, and takes from him the least time.

> C. C. COLTON (1780–1832). Preface to *Lacon: or, Many Things in Few Words; Addressed to Those Who Think*, vol. 1, 1823

Better to write for yourself and have no public than to write for the public and have no self.

> CYRIL CONNOLLY (1903–1974). In "Miscellany: Last Words," *New Statesman* (British magazine), 25 February 1933

First we eat, then we beget; first we read, then we write.

> RALPH WALDO EMERSON (1803–1882). Journal, December? 1842

Happy is he who . . . writes from the love of imparting certain thoughts and not from the necessity of sale—who writes always to *the unknown friend*.

> RALPH WALDO EMERSON (1803–1882). Journal, April 1848

The good writer seems to be writing about himself, but has his eye always on that thread of the Universe which runs through himself and all things.

> RALPH WALDO EMERSON (1803–1882). Journal, 1867?, undated

The writer is an explorer. Every step is an advance into new land.

> RALPH WALDO EMERSON (1803–1882). Journal, 2 October 1870

The writer's only responsibility is to his art. He will be completely ruthless if he is a good one. He has a dream. It anguishes him so much he must get rid of it. He has no peace until then. Everything goes by the board: honor, pride, decency, security, happiness, all, to get the book written. If a writer has to rob his mother, he will not hesitate; the "Ode on a Grecian Urn" is worth any number of old ladies.

> WILLIAM FAULKNER (1897–1962). Jean Stein vanden Heuvel interview, 1956. In Malcolm Cowley, ed., *Writers at Work: First Series*, 1958

One of my greatest pleasures in writing has come from the thought that perhaps my work might annoy someone of comfortably pretentious position. Then comes the saddening realization that such people rarely read.

> JOHN KENNETH GALBRAITH (1908–). *A Life in Our Times: Memoirs*, 2, 1981

I aim to give to those who read me strength, joy, courage, defiance, and perspicacity—but I take care above all not to give them directions, for I feel that they can and must find them by themselves. I was about to say: in themselves.

> ANDRÉ GIDE (1869–1951). "Portraits and Aphorisms: Characters," 1931, *Pretexts: Reflections on Literature and Morality*, ed. Justin O'Brien, 1959

My writings oft displease you: what's the matter?
You love not to hear truth, nor I to flatter.

> SIR JOHN HARINGTON (1561–1612). *Epigrams*, 1.59, 1618

Forget your personal tragedy. We are all bitched from the start, and you especially have to be hurt like hell before you can write seriously. But when you get the damned hurt, use it—don't cheat with it.

> ERNEST HEMINGWAY (1899–1961). Letter to F. Scott Fitzgerald, 28 May 1934

Suffer like a bastard when don't write, or just before, and feel empty and fucked out afterwards. But never feel as good as while writing.

> ERNEST HEMINGWAY (1899–1961). Letter to Malcolm Cowley, 14 November 1945

The most essential gift for a good writer is a built-in, shock-proof, shit detector. This is the writer's radar and all great writers have had it.

> ERNEST HEMINGWAY (1899–1961). George Plimpton interview, 1958? In Plimpton, ed., *Writers at Work: Second Series,* 1963

In today's [book] market, writers can't just be writers. They have to be performers and publicists as well. The image of the lonely writer honing his or her art is fast becoming outdated. What's demanded instead is something else: a hook, a smile and a shoeshine.

> JOSHUA HENKIN. Closing paragraph, "Writer with a Roadshow," *New York Times,* 5 July 1997

The chief glory of every people arises from its authors.

> SAMUEL JOHNSON (1709–1784). Preface to *A Dictionary of the English Language,* 1756

No man but a blockhead every wrote, except for money.

> SAMUEL JOHNSON (1709–1784). 5 April 1776. In James Boswell, *The Life of Samuel Johnson* 1791

The two most engaging powers of an author: new things are made familiar, and familiar things are made new.

> SAMUEL JOHNSON (1709–1784). "Pope," *Lives of the English Poets,* 1781

The gift of expression is not the same as that of conception: the first makes great writers; the second, great minds.

> JOSEPH JOUBERT (1754–1824). *Pensées,* 311, 1838, tr. Henry Attwell, 1877

I want to escape the unrest, to shut out the voices around me and within me, and so I write.

> FRANZ KAFKA (1883–1924). In Gustav Janouch, *Conversations with Kafka,* p. 105, tr. Goronwy Rees, 1953

My entire soul is a cry, and all my work the commentary on that cry.

> NIKOS KAZANTZAKIS (1885–1957). Greek writer. Author's introduction to *Report to Greco,* 1961, tr. P. A. Bien, 1965

Write straight into the emotional center of things. Write toward vulnerability. Don't worry about appearing sentimental. Worry about being unavailable; worry about being absent or fraudulent. Risk being unliked. Tell the truth as you understand it. If you're a writer, you have a moral obligation to do this. And it is a revolutionary act—truth is always subversive.

> ANNE LAMOTT (1954–). *Bird by Bird: Some Instructions on Writing and Life,* 5, 1995

If the wisdom of the rich consists in what the rich want to hear and think about themselves, it is not surprising that the rich nation confers its richest rewards on those writers who can preserve the illusions of innocence.

> LEWIS H. LAPHAM (1935–). *Money and Class in America: Notes and Observations on the Civil Religion,* 5.3, 1988

If you're a writer, you want to get your soul out there, where people can look at it.

> JEREMY LARNER. Radio interview, KQED, San Francisco, 15 October 1988

Writers have to get used to launching something beautiful and watching it crash and burn. They also have to learn when to let go control, when the work takes off on its own and flies, farther than they ever planned or imagined, to places they didn't know they knew. All makers must leave room for the acts of the spirit. But they have to work hard and carefully, and wait patiently, to deserve them.

> URSULA K. LE GUIN (1929–). Closing words, "'Where Do You Get Your Ideas From,'" 1987, *Dancing at the Edge of the World: Thoughts on Words, Women, Places,* 1989

A good rule for writers: do not explain overmuch.

> W. SOMERSET MAUGHAM (1874–1965). 1941, *A Writer's Notebook,* 1949

Consciously or unconsciously, all writers employ the dream. . . . The waking mind, you see, is the least serviceable in the arts. In the process of writing one is struggling to bring out what is unknown to himself. To put down merely what one is conscious of means nothing.

> HENRY MILLER (1891–1980). George Wickes interview, 1961. In George Plimpton, ed., *Writers at Work: Second Series,* 1963

I'm always looking for the author who can lift me out of myself.

> HENRY MILLER (1891–1980). George Wickes interview, 1961. In George Plimpton, ed., *Writers at Work: Second Series,* 1963

Putting aside the need to earn a living, I think there are four great motives for writing, at any rate for writing prose.
1. Sheer egoism. Desire to seem clever, to be talked about, to be remembered after death, to get your own back on grownups who snubbed you in childhood, etc., etc.
2. Aesthetic enthusiasm. Perception of beauty in the external world, or, on the other hand, in words and their right arrangement.
3. Historical impulse. Desire to see things as they are, to find out true facts and store them up for the use of posterity.
4. Political purpose. Desire to push the world in a certain direction, to alter other people's idea of the kind of society that they should strive after.

> GEORGE ORWELL (1903–1950). Abridged. "Why I Write," summer 1946, *The Collected Essays, Journalism and Letters of George Orwell,* vol. 1, ed. Sonia Orwell and Ian Angus, 1968

A word is not the same with one writer as with another. One tears it from his guts. The other pulls it out of his overcoat pocket.

> CHARLES PÉGUY (1873–1914). "Basic Verities: The Honest People," *Basic Verities: Prose and Poetry,* tr. Ann and Julian Green, 1943

You ask me why I spend my life writing?
Do I find entertainment?
Is it worthwhile?
Above all, does it pay?
If not, then, is there a reason? . . .
I write only because
There is a voice within me
That will not be still. [Ellipsis points in original.]

> SYLVIA PLATH (1932–1963). Untitled, 1948. In introduction to *Letters Home: Correspondence 1950–1963,* ed. Amelia Schober Plath, 1975
>
> See Silence & Protest: Samuel Taylor Coleridge, Jeremiah

What task in life could I have performed nobler than this, to write what is of great service to mankind and to bring the nature of things into the light for all to see?

> PLATO (427?–347 B.C.). *Epistles,* 7.341.d, tr. John Harward, 1932

Next to the doing of things that deserve to be written, there is nothing that gets a man more credit, or gives him more pleasure, than to write things that deserve to be read.

> PLINY THE YOUNGER (A.D. 62?–113?). As paraphrased by Lord Chesterfield, letter to his son, "Saturday," 1739?, undated

More writers fail from lack of character than from lack of intelligence.

> EZRA POUND (1885–1972). *ABC of Reading,* 2 ("Whitman"), 1934

A writer should never be brief at the expense of being clear.

> ARTHUR SCHOPENHAUER (1788–1860). "The Art of Literature: On Style," *Essays of Arthur Schopenhauer,* tr. T. Bailey Saunders, 1851

He who writes carelessly confesses . . . that he does not attach much importance to his own thoughts.

> ARTHUR SCHOPENHAUER (1788–1860). "The Art of Literature: On Style," *Essays of Arthur Schopenhauer,* tr. T. Bailey Saunders, 1851

Writers should use common words to say uncommon things.

> ARTHUR SCHOPENHAUER (1788–1860). "The Art of Literature: On Style," *Essays of Arthur Schopenhauer,* tr. T. Bailey Saunders, 1851

I have withdrawn not only from men, but from affairs, especially from my own affairs; I am working for later generations, writing down some ideas that may be of assistance to them.

> SENECA THE YOUNGER (5? B.C.–A.D. 65). "On the Philosopher's Seclusion," *Moral Letters to Lucilius,* 8.2, tr. Richard M. Gummere, 1918

You may well ask me why . . . I took the trouble to write [books]. I can only reply that I do not know. There was no why about it: I had to: that was all. [Ellipsis points in original.]

> GEORGE BERNARD SHAW (1856–1950). In Hesketh Pearson, "Grand Old Boy," *George Bernard Shaw: His Life and Personality,* 1963 (1942)

What I like in a good author is not what he says, but what he whispers.

> LOGAN PEARSALL SMITH (1865–1946). *Afterthoughts,* 6, 1931

For a country to have a great writer . . . is like having another government. No regime has ever loved great writers, only minor ones.

> ALEKSANDR SOLZHENITSYN (1918–). *The First Circle,* 57, 1964, tr. Michael Guybon, 1968

I have often thought that this might be my last book. I don't really mean that because I will be writing books until I die. But I want to write this one *as though* it were my last book.

> JOHN STEINBECK (1902–1968). Excerpts selected by George Plimpton and Frank Crowther. In Plimpton, ed., *Writers at Work: Fourth Series,* 1976

[Writing is] the only thing that, when I'm doing it, I don't feel I should really be doing something else.

> GLORIA STEINEM (1934–). Mirium Berkley interview, *Publishers Weekly,* 12 August 1983

I am now trying an experiment very frequent among modern authors; which is to write upon nothing; when the subject is utterly exhausted, to let the pen still move on; by some called the ghost of wit, delighting to walk after the death of its body.

> JONATHAN SWIFT (1667–1745). "The Conclusion," *A Tale of a Tub,* 1704

The most important thing a writer can have [is] the ability to live with constant loneliness and a strong sense of revulsion for the banalities of everyday socializing.

> HUNTER S. THOMPSON (1939–). Letter to Larry Callen, 4 July 1958, *The Proud Highway: Saga of a Desperate Southern Gentleman, 1955–1967,* ed. Douglas Brinkley, 1997

The author's character is read from title page to end.

> HENRY DAVID THOREAU (1817–1862). Journal, 28 February 1841

Hard and steady and engrossing labor with the hands, especially out of doors, is invaluable to the literary man and serves him directly.

> HENRY DAVID THOREAU (1817–1862). Journal, 20 November 1851

Began another boy's book—more to be at work than anything else. I have written 400 pages on it—therefore it is very nearly half done. It is Huck Finn's Autobiography. I like it only tolerably well, as far as I have got, and may possibly pigeonhole or burn the MS when it is done.

> MARK TWAIN (1835–1910). Letter to William Dean Howells, 9 August 1876. Twain was referring to *The Adventures of Huckleberry Finn,* which was published in 1884.

I hope, reader, . . . we shall meet again. And we shall recognize one another. And forgive me if I have troubled you more than was needful and inevitable, more than I intended to do when I took up my pen to distract you for a while from your distractions. And may God deny you peace, but give you glory!

> MIGUEL de UNAMUNO (1864–1936). Closing words, *Tragic Sense of Life,* 1913, tr. J. E. Crawford Flitch, 1921

The moment when the finished book or, better yet, a tightly packed carton of finished books arrives on my doorstep is the moment of truth, of culmination; its bliss lasts as much as five minutes, until the first typographical error or production flaw is noticed.

> JOHN UPDIKE (1932–). "Me and My Books: How Did They Assume a Life of Their Own?" *New Yorker,* 3 February 1997

If one is to write, one must believe—in the truth and worth of the scrawl, in the ability of the reader to receive and decode the message. No one can write decently who is distrustful of the reader's intelligence, or whose attitude is patronizing.

E. B. WHITE (1899–1985). In William Strunk, Jr., *The Elements of Style*, 5, 1959

The whole duty of a writer is to please and satisfy himself, and the true writer always plays to an audience of one. Let him start sniffing the air, or glancing, at the Trend Machine, and he is as good as dead, although he may make a nice living.

E. B. WHITE (1899–1985). In William Strunk, Jr., *The Elements of Style*, 5, 1959

A writer can do nothing for men more necessary, satisfying, than just simply to reveal to them the infinite possibilities of their own souls.

WALT WHITMAN (1819–1892). Remark to the author, 21 November 1888. In Horace Traubel, *Walt Whitman's Camden Conversations,* ed. Walter Teller, 1973

Everybody is writing, writing, writing—worst of all, writing poetry. It'd be better if the whole tribe of the scribblers—every damned one of us—were sent off somewhere with tool chests to do some honest work.

WALT WHITMAN (1819–1892). Remark to the author, 23 January 1889. In Horace Traubel, *Walt Whitman's Camden Conversations,* ed. Walter Teller, 1973

I have had people say to me: "Walt, you write as if it was no effort whatever for you to do so." That may be how it looks but that's not how it is.

WALT WHITMAN (1819–1892). Remark to the author, 4 May 1889. In Horace Traubel, *Walt Whitman's Camden Conversations,* ed. Walter Teller, 1973

See Excellence: Michelangelo

The meaning . . . of a writer will be found not just in what he intends to say, or what he does literally say, but in the effect of his writing on living beings.

HOWARD ZINN (1922–). *The Politics of History,* 17, 1970

❦

The best writers make the fewest words go the longest way.

ANONYMOUS

WRITING

See also • Art ○ Autobiography ○ Biography ○ Books ○ Creativity ○ Creativity: First Person ○ Fiction ○ Journals ○ Language ○ Literature ○ Memoirs ○ Novels ○ Plagiarism ○ Poetry ○ Propaganda ○ Reading ○ Speaking ○ Style: [especially] Carl L. Becker, W. Somerset Maugham, George Orwell, William Safire, Sydney Smith, Jonathan Swift, E. B. White ○ Talking ○ Words ○ Writers

The grate art in writing well, iz tew kno when tew stop.

JOSH BILLINGS (1818–1885). *His Sayings,* 22, 1867

Often when I write I am trying to make words do the work of line and color. I have the painter's sensitivity to light. Much . . . of my writing is verbal painting.

ELIZABETH BOWEN (1899–1973). British writer. In Victoria Glendinning, *Elizabeth Bowen,* 3, 1978

The pen is mightier than the sword.

EDWARD GEORGE BULWER-LYTTON (1803–1873). *Richelieu,* 2.2, 1839

See Words: Saying (*Bible*) (1)

Good writing is rewriting.

TRUMAN CAPOTE (1924–1984). Remark to Judy Green. In Julie Baumgold, "Unanswered Prayers. Part II: The Magical Drape," *New York,* 26 November 1984

Writing a book is an adventure. To begin with, it is a toy and an amusement; then it becomes a mistress, and then it becomes a master, and then a tyrant. The last phase is that just as you are about to be reconciled to your servitude, you kill the monster, and fling him out to the public.

WINSTON CHURCHILL (1874–1965). In William Safire, "Gifts of Gab for '95," *New York Times Magazine,* 18 December 1994

The philosophy of transition and connection; or the art by which one step in an evolution of thought is made to arise out of another: all fluent and effective composition depends on the connections.

THOMAS DE QUINCEY (1785–1859). The first of "two capital secrets in the art of prose composition," *Sketches of Life and Manners,* 1835

All writing comes by the grace of God.

RALPH WALDO EMERSON (1803–1882). "Experience," *Essays: Second Series,* 1844

Writing should be the settlement of dew on the leaf.

RALPH WALDO EMERSON (1803–1882). Journal, 1845, undated

Let the reader find that he cannot afford to omit any line of your writing because you have omitted every word that he can spare.

RALPH WALDO EMERSON (1803–1882). Journal, 1862, undated

For me, writing is foremost a mode of thinking and, when it works well, an act of discovery.

JOSEPH EPSTEIN (1937–). "Postscript on Process." In X. J. Kennedy and Dorothy M. Kennedy, eds., *The Bedford Reader,* 2nd ed., 1985

Writing is easy. All you do is stare at a blank sheet of paper until drops of blood form on your forehead.

GENE FOWLER (1890–1960)

About this time [around age 15] I met with an odd volume of the *Spectator.* . . . I bought it, read it over and over, and was much delighted with it. I thought the writing excellent, and wished, if possible, to imitate it. With this view I took some of the papers, and, making short hints of the sentiment in each sentence, laid them by a few days, and then, without looking at the book, tried to complete the papers again, by expressing each hinted sentiment at length, and as fully as it had been expressed before, in any suitable words that should come to hand. Then I compared my *Spectator* with the original, discovered some of my faults, and corrected them.

BENJAMIN FRANKLIN (1706–1790). 1771, *Autobiography,* 1798

The Six Golden Rules of Writing: Read, read, read, and write, write, write.

ERNEST GAINES. In Michael Larsen, *Literary Agents: What They Do, How They Do It, and How to Find and Work with the Right One for You,* rev. ed., 14 (introduction), 1996

It has always been my practice to cast a long paragraph in a single mold, to try it by my ear, to deposit it in my memory, but to suspend the action of the pen till I had given the last polish to my work.

> EDWARD GIBBON (1737–1794). *Memoirs of My Life and Writings,* p. 93, 1796, Alex. Murray edition, 1869

For a long time now I have tried simply to write the best I can. Sometimes I have good luck and write better than I can.

> ERNEST HEMINGWAY (1899–1961). George Plimpton interview, 1958? In Plimpton, ed., *Writers at Work: Second Series,* 1963

I have taken as my ruling idea the determination never to write a false line.

> ERNEST HEMINGWAY (1899–1961). "Ernest Hemingway," *Wisdom* (magazine), vol. 38, 1962

I never wrote a "good" line, but the moment after it was written it seemed a hundred years old.

> OLIVER WENDELL HOLMES, SR. (1809–1894). *The Autocrat of the Breakfast-Table,* 2, 1858

Read over your compositions, and wherever you meet with a passage which you think is particularly fine, strike it out.

> SAMUEL JOHNSON (1709–1784). Recalling a college tutor's dictum, 30 April 1773. In James Boswell, *The Life of Samuel Johnson,* 1791

The method of [Alexander] Pope . . . was to write his first thoughts in his first words, and gradually to amplify, decorate, rectify, and refine them.

> SAMUEL JOHNSON (1709–1784). "Pope," *Lives of the English Poets,* 1781

Tormented by the cursed ambition always to put a whole book in a page, a whole page in a sentence, and this sentence in a word. I am speaking of myself.

> JOSEPH JOUBERT (1754–1824). 1815, *Pensées,* 1838, tr. Paul Auster, 1983

Writing [is] a form of prayer.

> FRANZ KAFKA (1883–N1924). "Fragments from Notebooks and Loose Pages," *Dearest Father: Stories and Other Writings,* tr. Ernst Kaiser and Eithne Wilkins, 1954

It is the glory and the merit of some men to write well, and of others not to write at all.

> LA BRUYÈRE (1645–1696). "Of Works of the Mind" (59), *The Characters,* 1688, tr. Henri van Laun, 1929

You should write, first of all, to please yourself. You shouldn't care a damn about anybody else at all. But writing can't be a way of life; the important part of writing is living. You have to live in such a way that your writing emerges from it.

> DORIS LESSING (1919–). Interview with the author, October 1963. In Roy Newquist, *Counterpoint,* 1964

Writing is an excellent means of awakening in every man the system slumbering within him.

> GEORG CHRISTOPH LICHTENBERG (1742–1799). *Aphorisms,* J.2, 1806, tr. R. J. Hollingdale, 1990

Writing—the art of communicating thoughts to the mind, through the eye—is the great invention of the world. . . . Great, very great in enabling us to converse with the dead, the absent, and the

unborn, at all distances of time and space; and great not only in its direct benefits, but greatest help, to all other inventions.

> ABRAHAM LINCOLN (1809–1865). "Lecture on Discoveries and Inventions," Jacksonville (Illinois), 11 February 1859

The secret of good writing is telling the truth.

> GORDON LISH. Dick Cavett television interview, CNBC, 25 August 1991

The essence of writing is to know your subject.

> DAVID McCULLOUGH (1933–). "The Unexpected Harry Truman." In William Zinsser, ed., *Extraordinary Lives: The Art and Craft of American Biography,* 1988

What I offer here [in my writings] is not my teaching, but my study; not a lesson for others, but for myself.

> MONTAIGNE (1533–1592). *The Autobiography of Michel de Montaigne,* ed. Marvin Lowenthal, 13, 1935

The problem is to teach ourselves to think, and the writing will take care of itself.

> CHRISTOPHER MORLEY (1890–1957). *Inward Ho!* 6, 1923

My ambition is to say in ten sentences what everyone else says in a book—what everyone else *does not* say in a book.

> FRIEDRICH NIETZSCHE (1844–1900). "Expeditions of an Untimely Man" (51), *Twilight of the Idols,* 1889, tr. R. J. Hollingdale, 1968

As it is my design to make those that can scarcely read understand, I shall therefore avoid every literary ornament and put it in language as plain as the alphabet.

> THOMAS PAINE (1737–1809). In Gordon S. Wood, "Disturbing the Peace," *New York Review of Books,* 8 June 1995

I have made this letter longer than usual because I lack the time to make it short.

> BLAISE PASCAL (1623–1662). *Lettres provinciales,* 16, 1657

No writing is good that does not tend to better mankind some way or other.

> ALEXANDER POPE (1688–1744). In Joseph Spence, *Observations, Anecdotes, and Characters, of Books and Men Collected from the Conversation of Mr. Pope, and Other Eminent Persons of His Time,* 2nd ed., 5 (1737–1739), 1858

Every word that contributes neither to the sense nor the embellishment of what we write may be called vicious.

> QUINTILIAN (A.D. 35?–100?). *Institutio oratoria,* 8.3.55, tr. John Selby Watson, 1856

By writing quickly we are not brought to write well, but by writing well we are brought to write quickly.

> QUINTILIAN (A.D. 35?–100?). *Institutio oratoria,* 10.3.10, tr. John Selby Watson, 1856

[Writing and speaking, when carefully performed, may be] reciprocally beneficial, as it appears that by writing we speak with great accuracy, and by speaking we write with great ease.

> QUINTILIAN (A.D. 35?–100?). *Institutio oratoria,* 10.7.29, tr. John Selby Watson, 1856

Why use a modifier to set straight a not-quite-right noun when the right noun is available?

> WILLIAM SAFIRE (1929–). Giving as an example "failed coup" instead of "putsch," "When Putsch Comes to Coup," *New York Times Magazine*, 22 September 1991

"Fool!" said my Muse to me, "look in thy heart, and write."

> SIR PHILIP SIDNEY (1554–1586). English poet. *Astrophel and Stella*, 1, 1595

Writing is the continuation of politics by other means.

> PHILIPPE SOLLERS (1936–). "Ecriture et Révolution," *Tel Quel: Théorie d'Ensemble*, 1968
> See War: Karl von Clausewitz (3)

You will write if you will write without thinking of the result in terms of a result, but think of the writing in terms of discovery, which is to say the creation must take place between the pen and the paper, not before in a thought or afterwards in a recasting. Yes, before in a thought, but not in careful thinking. It will come if it is there and if you will let it come.

> GERTRUDE STEIN (1874–1946). John Hyde Preston interview (2), *Atlantic*, August 1935. In Christopher Silvester, ed., *The Norton Book of Interviews: An Anthology from 1859 to the Present Day*, 1996

The surest way to arouse and hold the attention of the reader is by being specific, definite, and concrete. The greatest writers—Homer, Dante, Shakespeare—are effective largely because they deal in particulars and report the details that matter. Their words call up pictures.

> WILLIAM STRUNK, JR. (1869–1946). *The Elements of Style*, 2.11, 1918, rev. E. B. White, 1959

Vigorous writing is concise. A sentence should contain no unnecessary words, a paragraph no unnecessary sentences, for the same reason that a drawing should have no unnecessary lines and a machine no unnecessary parts. This requires not that the writer make all his sentences short, or that he avoid all detail and treat his subjects only in outline, but that every word tell.

> WILLIAM STRUNK, JR. (1869–1946). *The Elements of Style*, 2.13, 1918, rev. E. B. White, 1959

How vain it is to sit down to write when you have not stood up to live!

> HENRY DAVID THOREAU (1817–1862). Journal, 19 August 1851

Sentences which suggest far more than they say, which have an atmosphere about them, which do not merely report an old, but make a new, impression . . . : to frame these, that is the *art* of writing.

> HENRY DAVID THOREAU (1817–1862). Journal, 22 August 1851

Write while the heat is in you.

> HENRY DAVID THOREAU (1817–1862). Journal, 10 February 1852

Write regularly, day in and day out, at whatever times of day you find that you write best. Don't wait till you feel that you are in the mood. Write, whether you are feeling inclined to write or not.

> ARNOLD J. TOYNBEE (1889–1975). *Experiences*, 1.6.2, 1969

Technique is noticed most markedly in the case of those who have not mastered it.

> LEON TROTSKY (1879–1940). *Literature and Revolution*, 6, 1925, tr. Rose Strunsky, 1960
> See Style: Samuel Butler ○ Words: Samuel Taylor Coleridge

It takes a heap of sense to write good nonsense.

> MARK TWAIN (1835–1910). March 1879, *Mark Twain's Notebook & Journals*, vol. 2, ed. Frederick Anderson et al., 1975

There ain't nothing more to write about, and I am rotten glad of it, because if I'd 'a' knowed what a trouble it was to make a book I wouldn't 'a' tackled it, and ain't a-going to no more.

> MARK TWAIN (1835–1910). *The Adventures of Huckleberry Finn*, 43, 1884

As to the Adjective: when in doubt, strike it out.

> MARK TWAIN (1835–1910). *The Tragedy of Pudd'nhead Wilson*, 11 (epigraph), 1894

You always find things you didn't know you were going to say, and that is the adventure of writing.

> JOHN UPDIKE (1932–). Interview with the author. In Naim Attallah, *Singular Encounters*, 1990

The best writing has no lace on its sleeves.

> WALT WHITMAN (1819–1892). Remark to the author, 23 June 1888. In Horace Traubel, *Walt Whitman's Camden Conversations*, ed. Walter Teller, 1973

The secret of it all, is to write in the gush, the throb, the flood, of the moment—to put things down without deliberation—without worrying about their style—without waiting for a fit time or place. I always worked that way. I took the first scrap of paper, the first doorstep, the first desk, and wrote—wrote, wrote. . . . By writing at the instant the very heartbeat of life is caught.

> WALT WHITMAN (1819–1892). Remark to the author, 22 July 1888. In Horace Traubel, *Walt Whitman's Camden Conversations*, ed. Walter Teller, 1973

My rule has been, so far as I could have any rule (I could have no cast-iron rule)—my rule has been, to write what I have to say the best way I can—then lay it aside—taking it up again after some time and reading it afresh—the mind new to it. If there's no jar in the new reading, well and good—that's sufficient for me.

> WALT WHITMAN (1819–1892). Remark to the author, 16 October 1888. In Horace Traubel, *Walt Whitman's Camden Conversations*, ed. Walter Teller, 1973

I hate commas in the wrong places.

> WALT WHITMAN (1819–1892). Remark to the author, 22 January 1889. In Horace Traubel, *Walt Whitman's Camden Conversations*, ed. Walter Teller, 1973

Watch yourself closely. Make a habit of noting things you see . . . . Fear nothing except to overstep the truth.

> WALT WHITMAN (1819–1892). Remark to the author, 27 January 1889. In Horace Traubel, *Walt Whitman's Camden Conversations*, ed. Walter Teller, 1973

Invariably, it is this for which I write: the joy . . . of an argument firmly made, like a nail straightly driven, its head flush to the plank.

> GEORGE F. WILL (1941–). "Journalism and Friendship," 19 January 1981, *The Pursuit of Virtue and Other Tory Notions*, 1982

Writing came easy—it would only get hard when I got better at it.

GARRY WILLS (1934–). *Confessions of a Conservative,* 4, 1979

"We Are What We Write."

MICHAEL WOOD. Article headline, *New York Times Book Review,* 21 May 1995

See Food: Anthelme Brillat-Savarin ○ Reading: Mark Crispin Miller

Avoid clichés like the plague.

ANONYMOUS

Eschew obfuscation!

ANONYMOUS

WRITTEN HISTORY

See • Historians

WRONG

See also • Evil ○ Right ○ Wicked

In order to be wronged, a man must (1) suffer actual harm, (2) suffer it against his will.

ARISTOTLE (384–322 B.C.). *Rhetoric,* 1.13, tr. W. Rhys Roberts, 1954

For the most part, people are led to wrongdoing in order to secure some personal end; in this vice, avarice is generally the controlling motive.

CICERO (106–43 B.C.). *De officiis,* 1.6, tr. Walter Miller, 1913

Rather suffer wrong than do it.

THOMAS FULLER (1654–1734). Comp., *Introductio ad Prudentiam,* 224, 1731

All wrongs recoil upon the doer.

ELBERT HUBBARD (1856–1915). *A Thousand One Epigrams,* p. 23, 1911

There is an element of real wrongness in this world, which is neither to be ignored nor evaded, but which must be squarely met and overcome by an appeal to the soul's heroic resources.

WILLIAM JAMES (1842–1910). *The Varieties of Religious Experience: A Study in Human Nature,* 14 and 15, 1902

I do not do wrong to serve God!

JOAN OF ARC (1412?–1431). 27 March 1431, at her trial on charges of witchcraft and heresy, *Joan of Arc,* tr. Willard Trask, 1936

Doing wrong damages both aggressor and victim.

POPE JOHN PAUL II (1920–). United Nations address, New York City, 5 October 1995

Those who follow the wrong have generally first taken care to be voluntarily ignorant of the right.

JOHN STUART MILL (1806–1873). "On Education," inaugural address on being installed as rector, University of St. Andrews (Scotland), 1 February 1867

I feel very strongly that if any people are oppressed anywhere, the wrong inevitably reacts in the end on those who oppress them; for it is an immutable law in the spiritual world that no one can wrong others and yet in the end himself escape unhurt.

THEODORE ROOSEVELT (1858–1919). In Hermann Hagedorn and Sidney Wallach, "Signposts for Americans: Random Thoughts," *A Theodore Roosevelt Round-Up,* 1958

Two wrongs don't make a right.

SAYING (ENGLISH)

YOGA

See also • Contemplation ○ Meditation ○ Religion ○ Spirituality ○ Zen

Yoga is the ability to direct the mind exclusively towards an object and sustain that direction without any distractions.

PATANJALI (2nd cent. B.C.). Indian yogi. *Patanjali's Yogasutras: An Introduction,* 1.2, tr. T. K. V. Desikachar, 1987

What is Yoga? According to the greatest of yogi teachers, Patanjali [2nd cent. B.C.], *"Yoga is the control of the ideas in the mind."* Our circumstances are not merely the facts of life as we meet them, but also, and even more, the ideas in our minds. It is impossible to obtain any control over circumstances without first obtaining control over the ideas in one's mind, and the most important—as well as most universal—teaching of all the religions is that . . .

clarity of vision can be attained only by him who succeeds in putting the "thinking function" in its place, so that it maintains silence when ordered to do so and moves into action only when given a definite and specific task.

E. F. SCHUMACHER (1911–1977). *A Guide for the Perplexed,* 6, 1977

YOUTH

See also • Adolescence ○ Age ○ Age & Youth ○ Children ○ Faults: Thomas Fuller (1) ○ Illusions: Napoleon ○ Middle Age ○ Parents ○ Unhappiness: Bertrand Russell

A man that is young in years may be old in hours, if [has] lost no time.

FRANCIS BACON (1561–1626). "Of Youth and Age," *Essays,* 1625

I am not young enough to know everything.

> J. M. BARRIE (1860–1937). *The Admirable Crichton*, 1, 1902

Youth is unhappy because it is faced with this terrible choice: love without peace, or peace without love.

> BEAUMARCHAIS (1732–1799). *The Barber of Seville*, 2, 1775, tr. Albert Bermel, 1975

I shall soon be six-and-twenty. Is there anything in the future that can possibly console us for not being always *twenty-five!*

> LORD BYRON (1788–1824). Journal, 1 December 1813

In my hot youth—when George the Third was King.

> LORD BYRON (1788–1824). *Don Juan*, 1.212, 1819–1824

Young men are as apt to think themselves wise enough, as drunken men are to think themselves sober enough.

> LORD CHESTERFIELD (1694–1773). Letter to his son, 15 January 1753

Twenty to twenty-five! Those are the years!

> WINSTON CHURCHILL (1874–1965). *My Early Life: A Roving Commission*, 4, 1930

A youth is to be regarded with respect.

> CONFUCIUS (551–479 B.C.). *Confucian Analects*, 9.22, tr. James Legge, 1930
>
> See Parents: Ralph Waldo Emerson (2)

I remember my youth and the feeling that will never come back any more—the feeling that I could last forever, outlast the sea, the earth, and all men; the deceitful feeling that lures us on to joys, to perils, to love, to vain effort—to death; the triumphant conviction of strength, the heat of life in the handful of dust, the glow in the heart that with every year grows dim, grows cold, grows small, and expires—and expires, too soon, too soon—before life itself.

> JOSEPH CONRAD (1857–1924). Title story, 1902, *Youth: A Narrative, and Two Other Stories*, 1927

The young always have the same problem—how to rebel and conform at the same time. They have now solved this by defying their elders and copying one another.

> QUENTIN CRISP (1908–). *The Naked Civil Servant*, 19, 1968

The Youth of a Nation are the trustees of Posterity.

> BENJAMIN DISRAELI (1804–1881). *Sybil: Or, The Two Nations*, 6.13, 1845

You remain young as long as you can still learn, can accept new conventions, and can stand contradictions.

> MARIE von EBNER-ESCHENBACH (1830–916). *Aphorisms*, p. 62, 1880–1905, tr. David Scrase and Wolfgang Mieder, 1994

In youth, the day is not long enough.

> RALPH WALDO EMERSON (1803–1882). Journal, April 1861

Had I the wealth of an Asian king,
or a palace crammed with gold,
both would I give for youth,
loveliest in wealth,
in poverty, loveliest.

> EURIPIDES (485?–406? B.C.). *Heracles*, l. 640, tr. William Arrowsmith, 1956

Everyone believes in his youth that the world really began with him, and that all merely exist for his sake.

> GOETHE (1749–1832). On "the arrogance of youth," 6 December 1829. In Peter Eckermann, *Conversations with Goethe*, 1836–1848, tr. John Oxenford, 1850

No young man believes he shall ever die.

> WILLIAM HAZLITT (1778–1830). "On the Feeling of Immortality in Youth," *Table Talk*, 1822

Youth is a thing not to be proud of, but rather a thing to be grateful for.

> E. W. HOWE (1853–1937). *Ventures in Common Sense*, 18.4, 1919

Men grow to the stature to which they are stretched when they are young.

> ANTONY JAY (1930–). *Management and Machiavelli: An Inquiry into the Politics of Corporate Life*, 8, 1967

It is while we are young that the habit of industry is formed. If not then, it never is afterwards. The fortune of our lives, therefore, depends on employing well the short period of youth.

> THOMAS JEFFERSON (1743–1826). Letter to his daughter Martha, 28 March 1787

Towering in the confidence of twenty-one.

> SAMUEL JOHNSON (1709–1784). Letter to Bennet Langton, 9 January 1758. In James Boswell, *The Life of Samuel Johnson*, 1791

Youth is a perpetual intoxication, a fever of the brain.

> LA ROCHEFOUCAULD (1613–1680). *Maxims*, 271, 1665, tr. Louis Kronenberger, 1959

How beautiful is youth! how bright it gleams
With its illusions, aspirations, dreams!

> HENRY WADSWORTH LONGFELLOW (1807–1882). "Morituri Salutamus" (Poem for the Fiftieth Anniversary of the Class of 1825 in Bowdoin College), 1875

If youth be a defect, it is one that we outgrow only too soon.

> JAMES RUSSELL LOWELL (1819–1891). Harvard University anniversary address, Cambridge (Massachusetts), 8 November 1886

Youth is the seed time of good habits, as well in nations as in individuals.

> THOMAS PAINE (1737–1809). "Of the Present Ability of America," *Common Sense*, 1776

Clown: What's to come is still unsure:
In delay there lies no plenty;
Then come kiss me, sweet and twenty,
Youth's a stuff will not endure.

> SHAKESPEARE (1564–1616). *Twelfth Night*, 2.3.50, 1599

Cleopatra: My salad days,
When I was green in judgment.

> SHAKESPEARE (1564–1616). *Antony and Cleopatra*, 1.5.75, 1606

Youth is a wonderful thing. What a crime to waste it on children.

> GEORGE BERNARD SHAW (1856–1950). In "Quotable Quotes," *Reader's Digest*, April 1940

Don't laugh at a youth for his affectations; he is only trying on one face after another to find his own.
> LOGAN PEARSALL SMITH (1865–1946). *Afterthoughts,* 2, 1931

What is more enchanting than the voices of young people, when you can't hear what they say.
> LOGAN PEARSALL SMITH (1865–1946). *Afterthoughts,* 2, 1931

Am I the person who used to wake in the middle of the night and laugh with the joy of living? Who worried about the existence of God, and danced with young ladies till long after daybreak? Who sang "Auld Lang Syne" and howled with sentiment, and more than once gazed at the full moon through a blur of great, romantic tears?
> LOGAN PEARSALL SMITH (1865–1946). "Last Words," *More Trivia,* 1934

I must laugh and dance and sing
Youth is such a lovely thing.
> ALINE THOMAS (1910–). "A Song of Youth"

In America the young are always ready to give to those who are older than themselves the full benefits of their inexperience.
> OSCAR WILDE (1854–1900). "The American Invasion," *Court and Society Review* (England), March 1887

Youth smiles without any reason. It is one of its chiefest charms.
> OSCAR WILDE (1854–1900). *The Picture of Dorian Gray,* 14, 1891

To get back my youth I would do anything in the world, except take exercise, get up early, or be respectable.
> OSCAR WILDE (1854–1900). *The Picture of Dorian Gray,* 19, 1891

Those whom the gods love grow young.
> OSCAR WILDE (1854–1900). "A Few Maxims for the Instruction of the Over-Educated," *Saturday Review* (British journal), 17 November 1894

❧

Youth is not a time of life—it is a state of mind.
> ANONYMOUS. Framed message in Gen. MacArthur's office. In William Manchester, *American Caesar: Douglas MacArthur: 1880–1964,* 9, 1978

ZEAL

See also • Enthusiasm ○ Fanatics ○ Passion

Instead of clearing his own heart, the zealot tries to clear the world.
> JOSEPH CAMPBELL (1904–1987). *The Hero with a Thousand Faces,* 1.2.5, 1949

Too much zeal offends
where indirection works.
> EURIPIDES (485?–406 B.C.). *Orestes,* l. 700, tr. William Arrowsmith, 1958

Zeal is fit only for Wise Men, but is found mostly in Fools.
> THOMAS FULLER (1654–1734). Comp., *Gnomologia: Adages and Proverbs,* 6068, 1732

Zeal without Knowledge is Fire without Light.
> THOMAS FULLER (1654–1734). Comp., *Gnomologia: Adages and Proverbs,* 6069, 1732

It is good to be zealously affected in a good thing.
> PAUL (A.D. 1st cent.). *Galatians* 4:18 (King James Version)

Too much zeal creates suspicion.
> GEORGE WASHINGTON (1732–1799). In P. M. Zall, ed., "Aphorisms on Money and Human Nature," *George Washington Laughing: Humorous Anecdotes by and About Our First President from Original Sources,* 1989
>
> See Diplomats: Talleyrand

Too much zeal spoils everything.
> SAYING (FRENCH)

ZEN

See also • Buddhism ○ Contemplation ○ Enlightenment: D. T. Suzuki, Saying (Zen) ○ Meditation: [especially] Gilbert Highet ○ Nonviolence: Lucien Stryk ○ Religion ○ Spirituality ○ Yoga

Reverence for all life is the formula of Zen Buddhism, and in this is hidden the secret of Zen.
> EUGEN HERRIGEL (1885–1955). "Man's Fall and Fulfillment," *The Method of Zen,* 1960, ed. Hermann Tausend and tr. R.F.C. Hull, 1964
>
> See Ethics: Albert Schweitzer (2-4)

Zen and the Art of Motorcycle Maintenance: An Inquiry into Values.
> ROBERT M. PIRSIG (1928–). Book title, 1974

Zen teaches nothing. Whatever teachings there are in Zen, they come out of one's own mind. We teach ourselves; Zen merely points the way.
> D. T. SUZUKI (1870–1966). *An Introduction to Zen Buddhism,* 2, 1934

The meaning of the proposition "A is A" is realized only when "A is not-A." To be itself is not to be itself—this is the logic of Zen, and satisfies all our aspirations.
> D. T. SUZUKI (1870–1966). *An Introduction to Zen Buddhism,* 4, 1934

Zen wants to live from within. Not to be bound by rules, but to be creating one's own rules—this is the kind of life which Zen is trying to have us live. Hence its illogical, or rather superlogical, statements.
> D. T. SUZUKI (1870–1966). *An Introduction to Zen Buddhism,* 4, 1934

Zen wants absolute freedom, even from God.
> D. T. SUZUKI (1870–1966). *An Introduction to Zen Buddhism,* 7, 1934

The Zen discipline gives birth to the unshakable conviction that there is something going on beyond mere thinking.

> D. T. SUZUKI (1870–1966). Slightly modified. *An Introduction to Zen Buddhism,* 8, 1934

As long as there is any thought of anybody, be he God or devil, knowing of our doings and making recompense, Zen would say, "You are not one of us." Deeds that are the product of such thought leave "traces" and "shadows." . . . No traces of self-conceit or self-glorification are to be left behind even after the doing of good, much less the thought of recompense, even by God.

> D. T. SUZUKI (1870–1966). *An Introduction to Zen Buddhism,* 9, 1934

Especially in Zen is this true; abstract ideas that do not reflect themselves forcibly and efficiently in practical living are regarded as of no value. Conviction must be gained through experience and not through abstraction.

> D. T. SUZUKI (1870–1966). *An Introduction to Zen Buddhism,* 9, 1934

The most difficult thing is always to keep your beginner's mind. There is no need to have a deep understanding of Zen. Even though you read much Zen literature, you must read each sentence with a fresh mind. You should not say, "I know what Zen is," or "I have attained enlightenment." This is also the real secret of the arts: always be a beginner.

> SHUNRYU SUZUKI. "Prologue," *Zen Mind, Beginner's Mind,* ed. Trudy Dixon, 1970

If you try to calm your mind, you will be unable to sit; and if you try not to be disturbed, your effort will not be the right effort. The only effort that will help you is to count your breathing, or to concentrate on your inhaling and exhaling. We say concentration, but to concentrate your mind on something is not the true purpose of Zen. The true purpose is to see things as they are . . . and to let everything go as it goes. This is to put everything under control in its widest sense. Zen practice is to open up our small mind. So concentrating is just an aid to help you realize "big mind," or the mind that is everything. If you want to discover the true meaning of Zen in your everyday life, you have to understand the meaning of keeping your mind on your breathing and your body in the right posture in zazen [meditation in a sitting position].

> SHUNRYU SUZUKI. "Right Practice," *Zen Mind, Beginner's Mind,* ed. Trudy Dixon, 1970

The Zen school is based on our actual nature, on our true mind as expressed and realized in practice. Zen does not depend on a particular teaching nor does it substitute teaching for practice. We practice zazen to express our true nature, not to attain enlightenment.

> SHUNRYU SUZUKI. "Epilogue," *Zen Mind, Beginner's Mind,* ed. Trudy Dixon, 1970

INDEX BY AUTHOR OR SOURCE

INDEX OF SUBJECT CATEGORIES

About the Editor

Leonard Roy Frank, a native of Brooklyn, graduated from the Wharton School of the University of Pennsylvania in 1954. Since 1959, he has resided in San Francisco, where he has managed his own art gallery and has edited two earlier collections of quotations: *Frank Quotes* (1970) and *Influencing Minds: A Reader in Quotations* (1995).